ORDER FORM

FD/95

Prices are for current editions only.
Call 1-800-FILMBKS or 310/471-8066 for more information.

YES! PLEASE SEND THE FOLLOWING BOOKS:

QTY.	ANNUAL DIRECTORIES	PRICE	CA. TAX	TOTAL
___	FILM DISTRIBUTION GUIDE	$125.00	$10.31	$____
___	FILM DIRECTORS—11th Ed.	$65.00	$5.36	$____
___	PRODS/STUDIOS/AGENTS & CASTING DIRECTORS—4th Ed.	45.00	3.71	$____
___	CINEMATOGRAPHERS, PRODUCTIONDESIGNERS COSTUME DESIGNERS & FILM EDITORS—4th Ed.	45.00	3.71	$____
___	FILM WRITERS—5th Ed.	55.00	4.54	$____
___	FILM COMPOSERS—2nd Ed.	45.00	3.71	$____
___	TV WRITERS—3rd Ed.	45.00	3.71	$____
___	TV DIRECTORS—2nd Ed.	40.00	3.30	$____
___	FILM ACTORS GUIDE—2nd Ed.	65.00	5.36	$____
___	SPECIAL EFFECTS & STUNTS—2nd Ed.	39.95	3.30	$____

UPS SHIPPING CHARGES CONT. USA/CANADA		
First Directory	$6.00	$18.00
Add'l. Directory	$3.00	$5.00

SUBTOTAL $_____
ADD IN SHIPPING $_____
TOTAL ORDER $_____

SHIPPING CHARGES (Overseas)	AIRMAIL	SURFACE
Film Directors	$30.00	$10.00
Add'l. Directories	$25.00	$8.00

For Faster Service Call
310/471-8066 or
1/800-FILMBKS

**FAX ORDERS ACCEPTED:
310/471-4969**

PAYMENT IS BY:
Check _____ Money Order_____ Visa_____ MC ___ AMEX_____
Card No._____ Exp. Date_____
Signature_____
(exactly as it appears on your card)

SHIP BOOKS TO:
NAME _____
COMPANY _____ PHONE (very imp't.!) _____
ADDRESS _____
CITY/STATE/ZIP _____

ORDER FORM

S0-CAJ-832   FD/95

Prices are for current editions only.
Call 1-800-FILMBKS or 310/471-8066 for more information.

YES! PLEASE SEND THE FOLLOWING BOOKS:

QTY.	ANNUAL DIRECTORIES	PRICE	CA. TAX	TOTAL
___	FILM DISTRIBUTION GUIDE	$125.00	$10.31	$____
___	FILM DIRECTORS—11th Ed.	$65.00	$5.36	$____
___	PRODS/STUDIOS/AGENTS & CASTING DIRECTORS—4th Ed.	45.00	3.71	$____
___	CINEMATOGRAPHERS, PRODUCTIONDESIGNERS COSTUME DESIGNERS & FILM EDITORS—4th Ed.	45.00	3.71	$____
___	FILM WRITERS—5th Ed.	55.00	4.54	$____
___	FILM COMPOSERS—2nd Ed.	45.00	3.71	$____
___	TV WRITERS—3rd Ed.	45.00	3.71	$____
___	TV DIRECTORS—2nd Ed.	40.00	3.30	$____
___	FILM ACTORS GUIDE—2nd Ed.	65.00	5.36	$____
___	SPECIAL EFFECTS & STUNTS—2nd Ed.	39.95	3.30	$____

UPS SHIPPING CHARGES CONT. USA/CANADA		
First Directory	$6.00	$18.00
Add'l. Directory	$3.00	$5.00

SUBTOTAL $_____
ADD IN SHIPPING $_____
TOTAL ORDER $_____

SHIPPING CHARGES (Overseas)	AIRMAIL	SURFACE
Film Directors	$30.00	$10.00
Add'l. Directories	$25.00	$8.00

For Faster Service Call
310/471-8066 or
1/800-FILMBKS

**FAX ORDERS ACCEPTED:
310/471-4969**

PAYMENT IS BY:
Check _____ Money Order_____ Visa_____ MC ___ AMEX_____
Card No._____ Exp. Date_____
Signature_____
(exactly as it appears on your card)

SHIP BOOKS TO:
NAME _____
COMPANY _____ PHONE (very imp't.!) _____
ADDRESS _____
CITY/STATE/ZIP _____

PLEASE SEND ME INFORMATION ON BEING LISTED OR UPDATING MY ENTRY IN THE FOLLOWING DIRECTORIES:

☐ Michael Singer's FILM DIRECTORS: A Complete Guide (see page 731)

☐ Film Producers, Studios, Agents and Casting Directors Guide

☐ Cinematographers, Production Designers, Costume Designers Film Editors and Set Decorators Guide

☐ Special Effects and Stunts Guide

☐ Film Writers Guide

☐ TV Directors Guide

☐ TV Writers Guide

☐ Film Composers Guide

☐ Film Actors Guide

ALL LISTINGS ARE FREE

If you have any questions call us at 310/471-8066

Name_____
Company_____
Address_____
City/State/Zip_____
Phone/Fax_____ FD/95

READER SURVEY

FD/95

Dear Reader:
In order to serve you better, we would appreciate your taking a few moments to answer these questions and send back this postage-paid postcard. Thank you. —Lone Eagle Publishing

How do you use this directory?
☐ Daily ☐ Weekly ☐ Monthly ☐ Other_____
☐ Hiring ☐ Research ☐ Other_____
How many people in your office use this directory?_____
Do you recommend this directory to your colleagues? ☐ Yes ☐ No
Are you on a standing order? ☐ Yes   ☐ No
Have you bought other editions of this directory in the past? ☐ Yes ☐ No
Do you use other Lone Eagle Directories?
If so, which ones?_____
Suggestions for improvement:
_____
_____
_____

Primary area of responsibilty: (please check all appropriate boxes)
☐ Film Production ☐ TV Production ☐ Distribution (Film/TV)
☐ Broadcast (including Cable) ☐ Music ☐ Theatre ☐ Exhibition
☐ Post-Prod. Facilities/Services to the Industry ☐ Other Allied Industries

Job Description:
☐ Management ☐ Producer ☐ Director ☐ Writer ☐ Production Management ☐ Location Management ☐ Other_____

Personal Information:
Annual Income
☐ Under $25K ☐ $25K-$50K
☐ $50K-$100K ☐ $100k-$200K
☐ $200K+
Education Level
☐ High School Degree
☐ College Degree
☐ Graduate Degree

Computer Information:
What type(s) of computer(s) do you use?
☐ MAC ☐ IBM/Compatible
Do you have a CD-ROM Drive?
☐ MAC ☐ IBM/Compatible
Would you use Lone Eagle Directories on CD-ROM? ☐ Yes ☐ No
Would you access Lone Eagle Directories online? ☐ Yes ☐ No

NO POSTAGE
NECESSARY
IF MAILED IN THE
UNITED STATES

BUSINESS REPLY MAIL
FIRST CLASS MAIL PERMIT NO. 70556 LOS ANGELES, CA 90077

POSTAGE WILL BE PAID BY ADDRESSEE:

LONE EAGLE PUBLISHING COMPANY
2337 ROSCOMARE RD STE# 9
LOS ANGELES CA 90099-1710

NO POSTAGE
NECESSARY
IF MAILED IN THE
UNITED STATES

BUSINESS REPLY MAIL
FIRST CLASS MAIL PERMIT NO. 70556 LOS ANGELES, CA 90077

POSTAGE WILL BE PAID BY ADDRESSEE:

LONE EAGLE PUBLISHING COMPANY
2337 ROSCOMARE RD STE# 9
LOS ANGELES CA 90099-1710

MICHAEL SINGER'S

FILM DIRECTORS: A COMPLETE GUIDE

11th International Edition

COMPILED AND EDITED BY MICHAEL SINGER
ASSOCIATE EDITOR   BETHANN WETZEL

LONE EAGLE PUBLISHING CO.
Los Angeles, California

Michael Singer's FILM DIRECTORS: A Complete Guide
Eleventh International Edition
Copyright © 1995 by Michael Singer

LONE EAGLE PUBLISHING CO.
2337 Roscomare Road, Suite Nine
Los Angeles, CA 90077-1851
310/471-8066

Page 8	BLACK BEAUTY © 1994 Warner Bros., a division of Time Warner Entertainment Company, L.P. All rights reserved.	
Page 12	BLACK BEAUTY © 1994 Warner Bros., a division of Time Warner Entertainment Company, L.P. All rights reserved.	
Page 14	BATMAN FOREVER © 1995 Warner Bros., a division of Time Warner Entertainment Company, L.P. All rights reserved.	
Page 18	BATMAN FOREVER © 1995 Warner Bros., a division of Time Warner Entertainment Company, L.P. All rights reserved.	
Page 26	FREE WILLY © 1993 Warner Bros. Productions LTD. Regency Enterprises V.O.F. Le Studio Canal+ All rights reserved.	
Page 30	FREE WILLY © 1993 Warner Bros. Productions LTD. Regency Enterprises V.O.F. Le Studio Canal+ All rights reserved.	

Printed in the United States of America

Cover design by Heidi Frieder
Logo Art by Liz and Frank Ridenour
Photograph of Harry Hurwitz on page 2 by Joy Sirott Hurwitz
Paintings of Chaplin on pages 4 and 6 by Harry Hurwitz
Photographs of Robert Wise on pages 33 and 36 courtesy of Robert Wise

This book was entirely typeset using an Apple Quadra 950, New Gen Turbo Printer, Microsoft Word and Aldus Pagemaker.

Printed by McNaughton & Gunn, Saline, Michigan 48176
Printed entirely on recycled paper.

ISBN: 0-943728-74-6
ISSN 0740-2872

NOTE: We have made every reasonable effort to ensure that the information contained herein is as accurate as possible. However, errors and omissions are sure to occur and are unintentional. We would appreciate your notifying us of any which you may find.

Lone Eagle Publishing
is a division of Lone Eagle
Productions, Inc.

LONE EAGLE PUBLISHING STAFF
Publishers .... Joan V. Singleton
Ralph S. Singleton
VP - Editorial .... Bethann Wetzel
Customer Service .... Douglas Deacon
Art Director .... Heidi Frieder
Computer Consultant .... Clive McKay

LETTER FROM THE PUBLISHERS

The film industry is under attack from Washington . . . again. It seems whenever we can't explain or take responsibility for any of the things happening in our society which we don't want or like, we blame Hollywood. Such an easy target. And yet, we challenge one person out there who is attacking Hollywood to imagine life without movies or television. Everyone might be able to give up parts, but not all. "I can't live without my sports programs," (what could be more brutal than boxing?); "I need to watch the news every night," (some of the most graphic violence we have seen has been on the news.); "Natural Born Killers was too violent," (But, don't stop those great Stallone, Schwarzenegger, Van Damme movies!) The point we are making here is that it has become much too fashionable to blame everyone and take responsibility for nothing.

Michael Singer, in the formidable Eleventh International Edition of his **Film Directors: A Complete Guide**, is attempting to enlighten us by documenting the incredible range of work that film directors have done. Among these over 41,000 films listed here are works that have touched, moved and inspired audiences all over the world. And not just films from "the good old days." As you browse through **Film Directors: A Complete Guide**, look at the titles and remember the films. Then think what it would be like if someone whose taste and sensibilities were different from yours could prevent some of these films from being made or shown. That, to us, is a scarier thought than too much violence or sex in films.

Michael Singer—one of the most tireless and humble editors we have ever met—doesn't think he has done a remarkable job. We should all aspire to his level of perfection and excellence. This year alone Michael has added over 400 directors and over 7,000 new titles! Less dedicated editors would have been content to add the few hundred films eligible for Academy consideration.

This is unabashedly the best work on film directors available today. We don't say that only as proud publishers, but also as ones who have spent a good portion of last year researching the so-called "competition." We also don't say that alone. We have letters, faxes, (and now e-mail, too) telling us so.

We realize that this work is due in part to Michael's tireless devotion to perfection, and to the fact that our readers give us feedback on what they want. Keep speaking up and telling us (and Washington) what you want.

We, at least, do listen to you.

Look for Lone Eagle on the World Wide Web soon.

Joan Singleton and Ralph Singleton
Publishers

TABLE OF CONTENTS

INTRODUCTION

"As this book enters its second decade..."

Now *there's* a weird concept! But indeed, Film Directors: A Complete Guide *is* entering its second decade, and to celebrate that amazing fact, I felt an ethical urge to actually try and live up to the book's admittedly grandiose title by making it...well...more *complete*. In addition to the usual three or four hundred or so new inclusions in the main listings section, you will find the *Notable Directors of the Past* feature hopefully made all the more notable by the addition of some 100 filmmakers. I must confess that some of the additions reveal the author's eccentric tastes perhaps more than necessary, such as the inclusion of directors famed for their early 1960s Italian spear-and-sandal pseudo-epics (i.e., Vittorio Cottafavi), or those who specialized in 1930s and '40s cliffhanging serials (i.e. Ford Beebe and B. Reeves Eason.) Ridiculous though most of those movies might have been, they influenced successive generations of filmgoers in their youth.

On the other hand, I have to throw up my keyboard-withered hands in submission to the fact that come hell or high water, trying to live up to the book's title is ultimately self-defeating. The fact is that despite gargantuan efforts, there will always be exclusions and inaccuracies in this book. Indeed, the moment the manuscript is delivered (or the floppy disks, as the case may be), it's already slightly dated. If we could bring the world to a halt—like Michael Rennie in Robert Wise's *THE DAY THE EARTH STOOD STILL*—we could spend a few eons or so catching up on the facts. But the earth turns, the sun also rises, the moon makes its nightly visitation, and directors, by gosh, just keep adding credits to their resumes. In fact, it seems that every second movie is directed by a first-time filmmaker. Perhaps the home video market explains this explosion in domestic production, and I'm often incredulous that a good portion of the films listed in the Hollywood trades' production charts under "independents" never seem to make it onto theatre screens, heading directly onto the racks, and perhaps international distribution (what else is there to do in Ulaanbaatar on a Thursday night?)

Thus, like any good Buddhist, I must accept the Nature of Things . . . particularly the non-illusory fact that there are hundreds—perhaps thousands (in India alone, maybe)—of filmmakers across the globe whose names do not appear in this book. To them, I can only mutter a humble apology, as I do to the faithful reader, and pay silent homage to their work and your tolerance. To assuage my guilt, I can only remember what this book was originally intended to be . . . a reference primarily intended for the U.S. film industry and not for the Society for the Preservation of Luxembourgian Cinema. In other words, if this is indeed a scholarly tome, it is purely by happy accident and not by design. Nevertheless, I hope that the number of foreign filmmakers listed in this book, and their voluminous titles, serve to remind the reader that movies ain't all made in Hollywood. In fact, when one despairs of the bland, processed, lifeless, star-heavy, self-serving, high-concept crap that all too often passes for American Cinema these days, I recommend a plunge into the waters of foreign film, where you may well re-discover the reason you fell in love with the movies in the first place (on the other hand, you'll also have an opportunity to experience bland, processed, lifeless, star-heavy, self-serving, high-concept crap...in a foreign language!)

In this eleventh edition, we return to the six interview format of the *From the Directors Chair* section after last year's sole extended conversation with Oliver Stone. As usual, it's a diverse group, which this year includes a top contemporary filmmaker who glories in his profession (Joel Schumacher); a traditionalist from Down Under whose muscular-but-sensitive approach to moviemaking has made him popular with U.S. studios (Simon Wincer); a venerable artist who has made immeasurable contributions to motion pictures throughout his 60-year-long career (Robert Wise); a newcomer to directing who has already made her bones as a topnotch screenwriter (Caroline Thompson); a Texas tyro-on-the-rise not yet in his late 20s (Robert Rodriguez) and a self-described fringe filmmaker (Harry Hurwitz) whose fascinating tale of struggle in the industry probably speaks for more than half of the directors listed in this book.

I'm fortunate to have many friends and colleagues who give me immeasurable assistance from year to year in the completion of these volumes. First and foremost, thanks to my associate editor Bethann Wetzel, who functions not only as a brilliant helper, but also as a damn good friend. Signor Lorenzo Codelli of Trieste, Italy, persists in delivering unto me nearly all information relating to Italian directors, including complete filmographies, addresses and telephone numbers. Considering the fact that Lorenzo is one of Italy's most prominent film writers and personalities, you'd think he would at least demand my first born in compensation. But in fact, Lorenzo's generosity comes without expectation of reward. He is truly a remarkable man. Much gratitude to my friend and (former) neighbor Karen Achenbach for providing me with the complete filmography of John Woo, and thanks to Maestro Woo for providing his filmography to Karen. The Directors Guild of Great Britain kindly provided me with a gratis copy of their 1994 directory, thus sparing me the horror of having to figure out how to convert dollars into British pound sterling for the mail order. Most of all, *domo arigato goziemashta* to Yuko Kikuchi of Kumamoto, Japan, for helping me with the compilation and translation of Japanese directors and titles, introducing me to the great animated films of Hayao Miyazaki and Isao Takahata, and most particularly, for marrying me in the early months of 1994 and bringing Miyako Louisa Kikuchi Singer into the world in the first month of 1995. This book—and just about everything else in my !ife—is dedicated to them both.

Michael Singer
Los Angeles, California

KEY TO ABBREVIATIONS

(TF)   =   TELEFEATURE
Motion pictures made for television with an on-air running
time of 1-1/2 hours to 4-1/2 hours on commercial television;
or 1 hour to 4 hours on non-commercial television.

(CTF)   =   CABLE TELEFEATURE
Motion pictures made for cable television with an on-air
running time of 1 hour to 4 hours.

(HVF)   =   HOME VIDEO FEATURE
Feature length motion picture made especially for the home
video market (1 or more hours).

(MS)   =   MINISERIES
Motion pictures made for television with an on-air running
time of 4-1/2 hours and more on commercial television;
or 4 hours or more on non-commercial television.

(CMS)   =   CABLE MINISERIES
Motion pictures made for cable television with an on-air
running time of 4 hours or more.

(FD)   =   FEATURE DOCUMENTARY
Documentary films made for theatrical distribution or feature
length (1 or more hours).

(TD)   =   TELEVISION DOCUMENTARY
Documentary films made for television of feature length
(1-1/2 hours or more on commercial television, 1 or more
hours on non-commercial television).

(CTD)   =   CABLE TELEVISION DOCUMENTARY
Documentary films made for cable television of feature
length (1 or more hours).

(HVD)   =   HOME VIDEO DOCUMENTARY
Documentary film made especially for the home video
market of feature length (1 or more hours).

(AF)   =   ANIMATED FEATURE
Animated theatrical motion picture of feature length
(1 or more hours).

(S)   =   SERIAL
Theatrical motion picture exhibited in multiple parts or
chapters

(ATF)   =   ANIMATED TELEFEATURE
Animated motion picture made for television of feature
length (1-1/2 or more hours).

(AHVF)   =   ANIMATED HOME VIDEO FEATURE
Animated film made especially for the home video market of
feature length (1 or more hours).

(FCD)   =   FEATURE CONCERT DOCUMENTARY
Full-length motion picture primarily comprised of musical
concert material (1 or more hours).

(TCD) = TELEVISION CONCERT DOCUMENTARY
Documentary made for television primarily comprised of musical concert material (1-1/2 or more hours on commercial television, 1 hour or more on non-commercial television).

(CCD) = CABLE CONCERT DOCUMENTARY
Documentary made especially for cable television primarily comprised of musical concert material (1 or more hours).

(HVCD) = HOME VIDEO CONCERT DOCUMENTARY
Documentary made especially for the home video market primarily comprised of musical concert material (1 or more hours).

(PF) = PERFORMANCE FILM
Motion picture of feature length comprised of non-musical performance material (1 or more hours).

(TPF) = TELEVISION PERFORMANCE FILM
Motion picture made for television comprised of non-musical performance material (1-1/2 or more hours on commercial television, 1 hour or more on non-commercial television).

(CPF) = CABLE TELEVISION PERFORMANCE FILM
Motion picture made for cable television comprised of non-musical performance material (1 or more hours).

(HVPF) = HOME VIDEO PERFORMANCE FILM
Motion picture especially made for the home video market comprised of non-musical performance material (1 or more hours).

KEY TO SYMBOLS

*   after a director's name denotes membership in the Directors Guild of America

†   after a director's names denotes deceased

★   after a film title denotes a directorial Academy Award nomination

★★   after a film title denotes a directorial Academy Award win

☆   after a film title denotes a directorial Emmy Award nomination

☆☆   after a film title denotes a directorial Emmy Award win

HOW TO USE THIS BOOK

The main intention of this book is to provide an easy, practical and comprehensive reference to selected international film directors and their work. We have no desire to editorialize or pontificate on the careers of these filmmakers. Their credits speak for themselves.

Among our features are:

- An alphabetical listing of directors by name and a concise rundown of their credits by year.

- *FROM THE DIRECTOR'S CHAIR*, conversations between the editor and six diverse filmmakers.

- A cross-referenced index to over 41,000 film titles in alphabetical order followed by the names of their directors. This will help those who remember the name of a film, but not its director.

- Academy and Emmy Award nominees and winners among the directors listed in the book.

- *NOTABLE DIRECTORS OF THE PAST*, highlighting the careers of selected filmmakers since the end of the 19th century.

Some words of explanation (the same old story) about the listings:

DIRECTORS: The listings herein are selective by necessity, as the inclusion of every person who ever directed a full-length film would inflate the guide to encyclopedic proportions. Selecting is not an easy task, and we are—as always—open to suggestions and submissions. In fact, a justifiable request for inclusion is always honored. Although the listed directors are primarily active, also included are some retired greats out of sheer respect for their place in film history. Foreign directors included herein represent those whose films have had some distribution and recognition in the United States, or those who have gained the most prominence in their own countries.

The reader should be reminded that because we list only full-length features and telefeatures, a director whose last credit in the book is ten years old could be one of the many who is consistently employed in short-form episodic television. Birthdates, birthplaces and contacts have been provided whenever possible, but it's well known that all three are subject to change without notice. An asterisk following a director's name denotes membership in the Directors Guild of America.

(Note on the alphabetizing of Asian directors' names: In China, Hong Kong, Taiwan, Korea, Japan and other parts of Asia, tradition dictates that when writing one's name, the family name always precedes the given name, i.e., Kurosawa Akira or Lee Jang-Ho rather than Akira Kurosawa or Jang-Ho Lee. However, through the years, the Japanese have followed the western custom of first name first, family name last, when writing or speaking their names for non-Japanese. Therefore, we all know the director of *SEVEN SAMURAI* as Akira Kurosawa. In China, Taiwan and Korea, however, the original tradition remains. Although we would address Xie Jin as "Mr. Xie," it would be confusing by our own standards to list him in the book as Jin Xie. The exceptions to this rule are those Chinese directors who have westernized given names, such as Edward Yang, Ann Hui and Johnny Mak.)

FILMS: For an appropriate apologia for credits not included, please see this edition's Introduction. In any case, while we make every effort to insure that credits are as complete as possible, the now famous "Spanish/Bulgarian Syndrome" (also known as the "Icelandic/Moroccan Syndrome") continues to plague the editor. This refers to the inevitable discovery, usually in the wee hours of the morning whilst staring blankly at a flickering television screen, of an obscure film heretofore not included in a director's *oeuvre*, a Spanish/Bulgarian co-production released theatrically only in Sofia, not in Madrid, and definitely not in the United States. God knows how these films are discovered and aired by the local networks, but they do help us complete our task at hand. Also, there's been a tremendous proliferation of films which bypass theatrical release and head directly for the video racks. Despite this, most of them are not listed herein as (HVF), or features made for home video. In truth, although they may not make it into movie theatres in the U.S., they can often be found entertaining the locals in Jakarta, Oaxaca, Islamabad or Nairobi. Indeed, the definitions are blurring year by year. In 1994, for example, we saw the first case of a mini-series being filmed for home video release first, and television airing later. And *TEXAS* will never be the same. Also, several recent films ostansibly shot for theatrical distribution wind up as "world premieres" on cable TV networks. Are they features or television movies? Only their producers know for sure...

The criteria for listed films, in terms of running times, are as follows:

Features: A running time of 60 minutes or longer. Although it pains us to exclude short subjects of fine quality, including such films would legitimately mean that we should also accept episodic TV programs as well, which usually run from 22 to 45 minutes in length without commercials.

Telefeatures: On commercial television, an air time of 90 minutes to 4-1/2 hours. This is not as eccentric as it might seem—without commercials, a 90 minute television program still runs approximately 72 minutes—the length of a short feature—and a 4-1/2 hour "mini-series" clocks in at about 3 hours and 45 minutes, which is the length of such long features as *GONE WITH THE WIND* and *HEAVEN'S GATE*. On non-commercial television, air times of 60 minutes to 4 hours are acceptable because of the elimination of any commercial interruptions.

Television Mini-Series: On commercial television, an air time of 4-1/2 hours or longer, or 4 hours or more on non-commercial television.

Animated Features: A running time of 60 minutes or longer, whether made theatrically or for television.

Documentaries: A running time of 60 minutes or longer, whether made theatrically or for television.

Concert Documentaries: A running time of 60 minutes or longer, whether made theatrically or for television.

Performance Films: A running time of 60 minutes or longer, whether made theatrically or for television.

Serials: Multiple-episode theatrical film (this art form is now dormant).

Videotaped television dramas—some of which are called "movies" by the networks—are *not* included. Although truly impressive work has been done on video, such as Edward Zwick's *SPECIAL BULLETIN* and Anthony Page's *THE MISSILES OF OCTOBER*, we feel obliged to live up to the *film* in our book's title. (Although here again, definitions are starting to become somewhat muddy. After all, some films have been shot either partially or in their entirety on video or HDTV, and transferred to film afterwards. And in 1994, Oliver Stone's *NATURAL BORN KILLERS* made extensive use of video as an intrinsic part of the film's style and story.)

TITLES: Films are often known by a multiplicity of titles in the course of international distribution. Since this is a U.S.-based book, American release titles are utilized with alternate titles following in *italics*, e.g.,

BUTCHER, BAKER, NIGHTMARE MAKER *NIGHT WARNING/MOMMA'S BOY*
Royal American, 1981

In the case of films from England, Australia or other English-speaking foreign countries, a title in italics usually represents the original title in that country if different from its American release title, e.g.,

THE ROAD WARRIOR *MAD MAX II* Warner Bros., 1982, Australian

For foreign films which were distributed in the United States, the American title is listed first, followed by the original foreign-language title, only if its meaning is substantially different from the English, e.g.,

ALL SCREWED UP *TUTTO A POSTE E NIENTE IN ORDINE* New Line Cinema, 1974, Italian

Films that did not receive American distribution are generally listed under their original foreign-language titles, as are films which were actually released in the U.S. under those original titles, e.g.,

LA BELLA DI ROMA Lux Film, 1955, Italian

or:

LA VIE CONTINUE Triumph/Columbia, 1982, French

However, this method isn't exactly scientific. Original foreign-language titles are primarily provided for films from countries that utilize the Roman alphabet. Transliterations from other alphabets—whether Arabic, Cyrillic, Chinese, Thai, Japanese or Indian— would prove rather more difficult, and rather less accurately rendered, so titles in their English translations are generally listed. The reader should bear in mind that since language is a highly relative matter, these translations are sometimes awkwardly rendered into English, as a phrase in one language can be all but untranslatable in another. For example, one word in Japanese—often a language of poetic nuance rather than nail-on-the-head directness—sometimes necessitates a bizarre concoction of mismatched English words strung together in seemingly haphazard array. This is why the Shochiku company has promoted Kinji Fukasaku's latest film—titled *CHUSHINGURA GAIDEN YOTSUYA KAIDAN*—as simply *CREST OF BETRAYAL* in the U.S. trade papers. Why? Because in English, the Japanese title would have to be translated into something like *THE UNTOLD, INSIDE STORY OF THE LOYAL FORTY-SEVEN MASTERLESS SAMURAI COMBINED WITH THE YOTSUYA GHOST STORY*. All Japanese know the separate, famous and oft-filmed legends of *CHUSHINGURA* and *YOTSUYA KAIDAN* (which the new movie combines), but us *gaijin* wouldn't stand a chance. So here's how this credit appears within:

CREST OF BETRAYAL *CHUSHINGURA GAIDEN YOTSUYA KAIDAN* Shochiku, 1994, Japanese

But I can go one better...Hayao Miyazaki and Isao Takahata's feature-length animated film *HEISEI TANUKI GASSEN POM POKO*—Japan's official 1994 entry for Academy Award consideration in the Best Foreign-Language Film category and one of that country's most successful films of the year—defies even the most eloquent translators. Translated word-for-word from the Japanese, the title in English would resemble the following (or something like it): *CURRENT ERA OF JAPANESE HISTORY* (Heisei) *RACCOON* (Tanuki) *WAR IN THE ANCIENT SAMURAI STYLE* (Gassen) *ONOMATOPOEIAC WORD DESCRIBING SOUND A RACCOON MAKES POUNDING ON HIS DRUM-LIKE BELLY* (Pom Poko). Deeply evocative in the original, it's utterly ridiculous in English. But as you can see, if and when they get around to releasing the film in the United States, a simplified title like THE GREAT RACCOON WAR loses virtually everything in the translation.

DISTRIBUTORS AND PRODUCTION COMPANIES: Original American distributors of feature films are listed whenever possible, although movies often change their distributors through the course of time. For foreign films that received no US distribution, the original distributors or production companies in their respective countries are included whenever possible.

Telefeatures and television mini-series are identified with the names of their production companies rather than the networks on which they aired.

Production companies are also listed for features which have not yet found distributors.

YEAR OF RELEASE: This is often extremely hard to determine. Usually, a foreign film is released to the United States a year or two (sometimes more) after its initial appearance in its own country. Therefore, for the sake of accuracy, the *original* year of release is provided rather than the American release date. Also, there are many U.S. films which are completed in one year and released in another. We generally utilize the year in which a film is reviewed in *Daily Variety* or other trade publications. Needless to say, there are often differences of opinion as to when certain films, domestic *and* foreign, were first exhibited. The dates herein may be at variance with other sources. Also release dates for films not yet distributed are projections.

COUNTRY OF ORIGIN: These are the years of incredibly complex international co-production deals. How does one explain that a film made in England with an American director, French producer and international cast, but registered in Panama for tax purposes is, therefore, a Panamanian film? We have opted for realism based upon the nationalities of production personnel and geographic locations of companies with financial participation.

CONTACT INFORMATION: This is probably the least reliable category of the book, only because home and office addresses and agents routinely change not only from year to year, but often from minute to minute. Please note that agencies and management companies mentioned as contacts in the book several times are telescoped from listing to listing to just agency name, city and telephone number. PLEASE CHECK THE AGENCY LISTINGS IN THE BACK OF THE BOOK FOR COMPLETE ADDRESS INFORMATION. Also, remember that if a filmmaker's name is asterisked, denoting membership in the Directors Guild of America, current contact information can be obtained by calling (213) 851-3671.

FROM THE
DIRECTOR'S CHAIR

HARRY HURWITZ

MOST OF THE OVER 4,500 DIRECTORS WHOSE CREDITS ARE LISTED in this book do not inhabit the same plane of professional existence as Steven Spielberg. In fact, most of them struggle for their art, and worry about where their next job is coming from. Many of these directors are just as talented and intelligent—if not more so—than some of their more famous colleagues. Harry Hurwitz is a man who cheerfully admits that he's still a struggler, and still something of a maverick outsider in the movie business.

Hurwitz has found his greatest success in the art world, where his paintings and other works have wound up in the permanent collections of such mighty institutions as the Metropolitan Museum of Art in New York, the National Gallery of Art in Washington, D.C., the Philadelphia Museum of Art, the New York University Art Collection, and more, including various private collections. Beginning life as a professor of film and drawing, teaching at New York University, Cooper Union and the Parsons School of Design, among others, Hurwitz always wanted to make movies, and always has.

Harry Hurwitz has led several lives as a movie director, beginning with the more personal films he was determined to make. His 1970 cult classic THE PROJECTIONIST was one of that year's most critically acclaimed films, influenced by Hurwitz's own inner life and the films of Charlie Chaplin, a lifelong obsession for the filmmaker. Other Hurwitz films on the subject of films are THE ETERNAL TRAMP, his examination of Chaplin's immortal character, the fictitious THE COMEBACK TRAIL and vastly enjoyable "mockumentary" THAT'S ADEQUATE!, which premiered at the Sundance Film Festival. As a director-for-hire, Hurwitz has specialized in such moderately-budgeted comedies and thrillers as SAFARI 3000, THE ROSEBUD BEACH HOTEL and FLESHTONE. And as his intentionally sleazy *nom-de-cinema* Harry Tampa, Hurwitz shepherded such soft-core romps as FAIRY TALES, AUDITIONS and NOCTURNA. Whatever it took to keep making movies, Hurwitz was there with a knowing wink and a smile.

Meanwhile, Hurwitz has also written several screenplays, including the original draft of what became UNDER THE RAINBOW, and most recently, THE FOURTH RIVER for future production by Paramount. It's been a fascinating road . . . and it ain't over yet, as Hurwitz energetically explains in the following conversation . . .

MICHAEL SINGER: You've described yourself as "a filmmaker who never really made it" in the industry. You won't hear many directors referring to themselves quite so honestly.

HARRY HURWITZ: Well, making movies was always my agenda, not making "it." Making "it" involves a lot of sacrifice and compromise, but I'm a filmmaker and a painter, and that was my life, that was my passion. I always managed to make every painting I ever wanted to make, and I made every movie I ever wanted to make . . . except for the one that I hope to do next. And the point of making it in the industry . . . I made my first five features without even being in the industry. I worked out of New York. I was making my living as a college professor, so I didn't even look to my art for financial sustenance. First of all, we're living in a culture that doesn't even dignify the artist. The artist has to teach, or have another job. I never heard of a proctologist who had to teach all week so he could practice proctology on the weekend. And as a filmmaker, I began with the same spirit that I did as a painter. Then, I got to see that I could make more money by joining

Painting of Chaplin by Harry Hurwitz

the industry than by teaching. In other words, I realized that I'd rather make bad movies than do good teaching. The movies that I do for myself I manage to do once every five years. I write it, I direct it, I cut it, I produce it. And it's not an ego thing. It's just that I wouldn't have anybody come in and paint the red in my painting. It's a complete work, and good or bad, I stand behind it. Whereas to make a living, I am now a writer and director for hire, in which I'm perfectly prepared to compromise. I feel very comfortable joining a system which, by the way, I revere. There's always been a perverse marriage between art and industry, going back to Michelangelo and the Pope. My heroes are Chaplin, Griffith, Welles, Hawks, Kubrick, Hitchcock, Lubitsch, and they all worked within the system.

Now, when you say that you've made every film that you've wanted to make, does that exclude some of the films that you have made?

No! I've made some awful films, but they've been for other people. They're films that I either didn't write or that I didn't write and produce. On every movie that I wanted to make for myself, I went out and raised the

money and made the movie, and had nobody to answer to. There was no question of the final cut anymore than I would have somebody else put the finishing touches on a painting. But on movies that I've done for hire, I'm a good collaborator and good team player.

Yet you had a big influence on some notable students who went on to have good careers.

Well, I didn't say I was a bad teacher. I just felt resentful not being able to make a living in my chosen profession. In other words, I had to work in another field in order to support my family and myself and put a roof over our heads and pay for the rent. And it turned out that I did have an influence on some students who went on make movies, like Joe Dante, Jonathan Kaplan and Jon Davison, and perhaps others I don't know about.

I understand that it was Joe Dante who said that there was a little bit of Harry Hurwitz in every film he's made.

What he told me was, there's a little bit of THE PROJECTIONIST in every movie he's ever made. That film had an impact on him. But you know, I taught painting, drawing, film history and film aesthetics. I never taught anyone how to make a movie.

How did you become a professor at the age of twenty-five?

I already had two one-man shows in New York as a painter and printmaker, and had my work in the permanent collections of the Metropolitan Museum of Art, the National Art Gallery in Washington and the Philadelphia Museum of Fine Art. So I had this very impressive background as a painter, not as a filmmaker, and my first teaching jobs were in drawing, painting and design. Basically, the job was always about how much money I could make in the shortest period of time so I could do my real job, which was making movies and painting pictures.

Were you a film buff as a child?

As a child I was not only a film buff—but films saved my life. I was one of those kids who lived in movie theatres. The safest place in the world was the darkness of that theatre. My teachers and parents couldn't find me because I was in the dark. I could fall into that big screen and literally leave reality. Because there is no reality in film. People talk about "realistic" films, but all art is a lie. All art is an abstraction of reality. "Real" is when you've had your last dream and you open your eyes and wake up. Movies are very much like dreams because you see them in the dark.

What kind of films did you like most?

I loved all kinds of movies. In fact, I think it was Welles who said, "There's no such thing as a bad movie. The fact that they move is miraculous." The only movies I don't like are pretentious movies. And also, anybody who actually makes a movie, to me, is a hero. Everybody talks about making movies, wanting to make movies—they write screenplays, they develop, they talk, they try to raise money, they almost make a movie. But to me, one of the great achievements on this planet is those people who actually went and got a film in the can. I think they should get medals for actually finishing a movie. And that's why my motto has always been "Make that movie." I used to teach my students that. Go out and do it. If you can't raise the money from a studio, raise the money from dentists. If you can't do that, borrow money and use your credit card. If you can't do that, do it on the cuff any way you can. If you can't make it for $10-million, make it for $1-million. If you can't make it for $1-million, shoot it in 16mm and do it for $350,000.

I haven't made my movies the easy way. It's been a hard life, and that's why I've been kind of a maverick, because it was more important to make the movie than to make the money or to "make it." I'm still trying to figure out what "it" is, because it's so fickle, so fleeting and so intangible. And I'm a happy man. At this stage of my life, I feel absolutely fulfilled. I feel rich and famous . . . in my own life. Because my priorities have not only to do with my art, but also my family. I don't let other people identify me, I certainly don't let the industry identify me, and I don't identify myself as a filmmaker or as an artist. I'm trying to be a complete person, and at the end of it all, I think I'll feel pretty good. I'll just say that I did most of the things I wanted to do, and I have three kids that I feel blessed having had, and I'm married to a woman who is so supportive and wonderful that she enriches my life. I'm a happy man.

Your films have taken you around the world, yes? You actually directed two films in Africa.

I just finished a picture in Africa called FLESHTONE, and I got to do a film for hire that I directed for United Artists called SAFARI 3000, which was the worst script I ever read, and had the best time making because I brought my three boys and

> " . . . one of the great achievements on this planet is those people who actually went and got a film in the can. I think they should get medals for actually finishing a movie."
>
> —Harry Hurwitz

my then-fiancee, now wife, to Africa. It's a great thing for a father to be able to say, "Hey kids, I'm pulling you out of school so we can go to Africa to make a movie." I got to go to Beijing for the first American film festival that was mounted by the Museum of Modern Art, and I was honored that my film, THE PROJECTIONIST, was chosen as one of twenty, from BIRTH OF A NATION to the present, to be shown there. And I got to see that film in a theatre filled with 3,000 Chinese who laughed in the right places.

If your filmography could be converted into a charted heartbeat, there would be serious fibrillation.

Oh yeah. And don't forget the stuff I did under another name.

You mean the immortal Harry Tampa?

Harry Tampa's a legend in his own slime. You know, I did those awful disco vampire movies and used another name, but I had a great time. Everyone knew who Harry Tampa really was, but I used the other name because it was my way of saying look, I really know the difference. There's a place for this and a place for that. In life, there are some people that you give your total integrity to, your good friends and your family and your mate. Then there are people that you give a little integrity to, and those are the associates you have. Then there are some people that you don't have any problem lying to, because you don't give a shit. And that's how it is with film. There are movies that I'm uncompromising about, and there are movies when I say let's go play and have a good time and I'll give you what you want.

When you're on set as Harry Tampa, are you actually a different person than when you're Harry Hurwitz?

No. I try to make the best movie and find the little gems and pearls that I can slip into these films. What happens is, I'm constantly betrayed by my conviction as an artist. Basically, on the highest level, you try to achieve excellence. That's what the ascent of man is about, people trying to achieve excellence and enriching the world. But you've got to make a buck. Rembrandt was a scoundrel. He used to sign his students' paintings and sell them. I'm not one of those guys who say that you must be the pure artist only, and I don't think I'm that pure. I know I have skills I can sell, that I'm really good at, that doesn't involve my soul and my heart. And on the other hand, I'm not embarrassed to use the word "art." Film is an art. It's also the film *industry*. Again, that perverse marriage is what always comes together. It's impossible to make any kind of art without dealing with technology. The painter has to buy the paint and the canvas, and once the picture's finished you have to sell it. What are you going to do, put it in your closet? So there's a great schizo thing going on in even the purest of artists. You know, Van Gogh was dying to sell his paintings. He craved acceptance. You don't paint for yourself, and you don't make movies for yourself. You make movies for an imaginary audience that's going to sit there and be moved by what you make. Movies are probably one of the most emotional experiences we have in life outside of the real moments of our lives. When do you ever cry or laugh or tremble in fear or get as sexually or romantically aroused in any other artificial situation other than in a movie theatre, when you just become a blithering idiot? And it's wonderful, it's thrilling. You know, it's not so much fun in real life to have a guy with a chainsaw chase you.

"Charlie's Dream" by Harry Hurwitz (Acrylics)
Courtesy Anne & Arnold Kopelson

I don't know. It could be interesting.
You never know in Los Angeles. This is a great town for . . .

. . . Blithering idiots?
It's a great town for blithering idiots and inspired geniuses. It's a great town for movie stars and serial killers. It's a great town for a lot of things, but it's not a city. That's always been its problem. L.A. thinks it's a city, but it's not. The only important thing about L.A. is Hollywood, which doesn't really exist. Hollywood was probably the great American cultural gift to the 20th century, and it doesn't really exist in physical space because it's in Culver City, it's in the Valley . . . you know, I think Paramount's the only legitimately Hollywood-based studio. And of course, Chaplin was based in Hollywood. L.A. is lucky because it has Hollywood.

THE PROJECTIONIST is your most famous and heralded film, and I think it holds up beautifully. I actually find it to be a rather spooky movie, just as I think silent movies are spooky.

Well, by seeing old movies you're seeing dead people, right?

Yes. You're watching ghosts.
Right. Not only that, you're seeing them in black and white. And in THE PROJECTIONIST, the fantasy episodes were in black and white and the "real-life" episodes were in color. Somebody once said that there were no really great movie stars in color. It sounds like a glib statement, but if you think about it, those were huge, glowing black and white images made out of light and dark, shadows being projected by light being pushed through various densities of emulsion on a piece of acetate and projected onto a screen. Color film has the color of skin, so people in color are more real. They're not gods and goddesses, like the stars we see in black and white.

There's a loss of that dreamlike quality in color.
Yes. The old films are haunting. They're spooky because you're taken back to a time that never really existed. We're not talking about old documentaries, but dramatic films, which were abstractions of reality. It was all fictional and dreamlike and idealized. What amazes me was how cinematically literate the people of the 1930s and '40s were. They really understood the language of the movies. I mean, they could listen to Noel Coward and actually enjoy it. And we're not talking about New York and sophisticated cities, we're talking about all across the country. Today, film viewers are more narcissistic and they just want to see their own culture reflected. They're not interested in sitting through dialogue . . . they want it fast. It's a result, I guess, of McDonalds and MTV. But in the old days, I'm amazed that pictures like TROUBLE IN PARADISE were successful. I'm amazed that Ernst Lubitsch was a successful director. He made very sophisticated, urbane comedies.

Why your lifelong obsession with Charlie Chaplin? I mean, it seems redundant to ask somebody why they love Chaplin. The whole world loves Chaplin.
Well, you said the key word, which is "lifelong." The first movie I ever saw was a little Chaplin short. My

parents took me to Coney Island, where they had a theatre that only showed Chaplin shorts. Then I saw the reissue of THE GOLD RUSH when I was four-and-a-half years old, and all through my life this incredible character of The Tramp kept appearing and impacting on me in a new way during each age. One of my first films was about Chaplin, THE ETERNAL TRAMP, narrated by Gloria Swanson, which was not so much about the man as about the character he made famous. I think that The Tramp is one of the most extraordinary fictional inventions. He's as profound as Hamlet or Don Quixote. Chaplin didn't make comedies. He made these incredible films that dealt with so many things on so many levels.

Chaplin was so easily identifiable by the average person, who understood what it was like to be alienated, to be the outsider, not to get the girl, to be hard up for money. And also, Chaplin was one of the greatest actors of all time. Laurence Olivier said that Chaplin was the greatest actor in movies. Chaplin was a comic and a tragic actor at the same time, because he dealt with that thin line between pathos and humor. And he drew his comedy out of the deprivation of his childhood. His whole screen persona was based on his deprived childhood, when he was always hungry. Food is always an issue in his movies—eating his shoe in THE GOLD RUSH, the Dance of the Rolls, eating the confetti as spaghetti in CITY LIGHTS. Chaplin's body of work was the most autobiographical, I think, of any filmmaker's work. If you look at it it's encoded, always reliving and recreating his childhood and trying to make it come out right through that character. I don't know anything, really, about Chaplin the man, and I'm not really interested. But I believe the character he created was so profound and moved me emotionally all my life. It was a lifelong love affair with this character that I must have identified with through my own sense of alienation, loneliness, rejection. Because I was one of those kids who didn't play ball and got beat up a lot. But I found pleasure sitting in the movie theatres, or at home drawing pictures.

Hence, THE PROJECTIONIST is . . .

. . . Is me. Of course. It's a metaphorical image of myself. And the nature of the film is really about the daily bombardment of ideas and ideologies and feelings and thoughts that we go through, so the whole picture is about fragmentation. Our lives are made up of little serials. You drop one thing, you go to another, you're juggling 40 different parts of your life: the emotional part, the political part, the moral part. We're constantly being tempted, we're constantly being bombarded, so that's why THE PROJECTIONIST is full of commercials, superhero serials. It's this fragmenting of time, which is what our days are like.

One of your more recent films, THAT'S ADEQUATE, was a very funny celebration of well-intentioned schlock.

It's a "mockumentary" about a fictitious studio called Adequate Pictures, the worst studio in Hollywood, celebrating its 60th anniversary. Their motto is, "An idea that's appealing is worth stealing." It's an affectionate satire of the studio system, but I just used this schlock studio because it's so extreme. It's just a crazy look at our preposterous, insane industry.

Let's face it, no matter how much of a business or an industry this is, what it always comes down to is that guy on the set with some idea in his brain that he's trying to turn into "reality." I'm always amazed when I go to production meetings, and whatever is down on that sheet of paper called the script, they're going to make happen by hook or by crook.

Let's put it this way . . . if screenplays were written in stone, then you would go to the theatre, be handed a script, sit down in the dark, the lights would come up and someone would say "Now turn to page one." The screenplay is just a point of departure. You gotta make a movie! An unfilmed screenplay is a dead thing. It's an architect's blueprint. I love improvisation, but I also have a great reverence for directors who literally follow a screenplay, like Hitchcock. But the crafting of a screenplay has to be flexible as well. Even Shakespeare is altered on the stage.

In the end, film is not a literary medium. People think that movies have a close kinship with literature and painting, but no . . . it's with music, because it's an art form that exists in time. It starts now and ends an hour-and-a-half later, like a piece of music. It exists in rhythms so that you can put together little pieces of time strung together. When you have three shots creating a whole new emotion, even though they have nothing to do with each other individually, it's like taking three notes and making a chord out of it. That's why music is the only other art that was ever necessary to film. There never were silent films . . . they were always accompanied by music. The sound film made it seem more real. Color made it seem more real. The more technologically proficient we get, the more we lose that fantasy element. On the other hand, the vicariousness of the experience is now greater than ever. I think it's all wonderful.

I still go to the movies like a 12-year-old. I pay money and give them my brain and say "hold it at the box office, I'll get it on the way out." I go in and I'm willing to believe what anybody tells me . . . unless they're pretentious and they're liars. It's like going to a party. The one you don't want to deal with is the one who's phony and really isn't talking straight. But any kind of movie that makes me feel something is a good movie . . . because that's what it's all about!

★ ★ ★

7

CAROLINE THOMPSON

ONE OF THE FIRST WORDS EVER SPOKEN by Caroline Thompson was "aminal"—close enough to the real thing to indicate her future passion for those creatures of a non-human aspect. And throughout her as yet relatively brief life, Thompson has maintained strong emotional connections not only with "aminals," but also with the child who felt such a powerful empathy for them.

It was only natural that the celebrated writer of such films as EDWARD SCISSORHANDS, THE ADDAMS FAMILY, THE SECRET GARDEN, HOMEWARD BOUND: THE INCREDIBLE JOURNEY and TIM BURTON'S THE NIGHTMARE BEFORE CHRISTMAS should choose BLACK BEAUTY as her first directing effort. The besieged equine hero of Anna Sewell's classic novel certainly fits into the overall framework of Thompson's work. Every one of her scripts has dealt with the sad and sweet alienation that automatically comes with being either a member of the animal or human child kingdoms.

Thompson was born and raised near Washington, D.C., the daughter of a lawyer and teacher. After graduating from Amherst College, she moved to Burbank, California, with a few horses and other household pets. Her first work to be seen by the public was a novel, *First Born*, which Thompson describes as a "dark tale of the ultimate outsider." She then met another ultimate outsider—director Tim Burton—a kindred spirit who helped launch her film career with the acclaimed gothic fairy tale EDWARD SCISSORHANDS. Now Thompson's career has definitely taken on a life and character of its own, demonstrating the writer/director's uniquely . . . animistic . . . approach to life.

MICHAEL SINGER: Was directing something that you had always planned on doing throughout your writing career, or was it a decision that you came to during that process?
CAROLINE THOMPSON? Well, I wish I could say I'd planned to do *anything* I've done in my life, but I can't. So I didn't really plan it so much as . . . as kind of fell toward it. Which is to say that, other than EDWARD SCISSORHANDS, my writing career has been filled with frustration, in terms of the execution of my work. And that's not to say that it hasn't in places been executed brilliantly, but I usually found that I didn't even hear my dialogue on screen the way I heard it in my head. I didn't see the same pictures I saw in my head...and it's a very frustrating feeling. I'm sure every writer feels it. In the execution of EDWARD SCISSORHANDS, that's the one place where the director and I saw the same movie

to a "t", so it was a completely satisfying experience creatively. Short of that, it hasn't been a completely satisfying life. And I would also say, though, that the other thing is that when you're a writer of screenplays, just generically, it's not an end. Finishing a script is not an end of finishing something, you know? If it's going to live, it's going to live on film, and the desire to follow through my own work became really, really strong. Plus, the particulars of this were such that I was asked by Warner Bros. to do BLACK BEAUTY, it hadn't been my idea. And I was really sort of sorry it hadn't been, because it was a great idea to do it. But I couldn't think of a director who I would *want* to do it. And I love this animal so much—I mean, I am a complete horse nut and have been since I was a little kid.

The smell of horses literally surrounds this movie.

I'm really happy to hear that, because that's what I'd hoped. And I just couldn't—I ran through the people in my mind, and there was nobody who I would trust with it. And I don't mean "trust" in a grand way, I mean really in a micro way, because so much of it is about the deliberate and actual details of these animals' presences, and you have to know horses to know what you're going for. I mean, I know enough about their behavior to know how to get what I want, and that made it a very efficient process as opposed to a horrifyingly inefficient process, which a person who didn't know horses could have found themselves stuck in to begin with. And also, again, the particulars of the details of the way they behave to me is endlessly fascinating, and to a person who doesn't love them, I don't see how it could be.

To the uninformed—namely the person who either didn't see HOMEWARD BOUND or had no idea of your long-held love for horses—it might have seemed an offbeat choice for a first directing effort from one who had become known for unconventional scripts.

Well, it was considered a very conventional choice by some people, and I really resent that . . . In fact it's a very unconventional film. To me, that's just the kind of reaction people have when they're looking at the surface of things and not thinking underneath.

Why do you consider BLACK BEAUTY to be an unconventional film?

Well, it's unconventional in that first of all, if you turned off the sound, you'd understand everything that was going on. It's very emotionally powerful. To me, it's exactly the same movie as EDWARD SCISSORHANDS. It just has a different protagonist. And okay, the production design doesn't twist your brain the way it would on EDWARD SCISSORHANDS, but it's not about production design. But emotionally, it's exactly the same movie. I mean, they're all the same movie, but literally, those two are the same movie. It's about coming into a world where you feel completely welcomed at first, and then it turns against you, and yet you keep your sweetness throughout. It's the same character . . . but on the other hand, it always made me laugh for them to see EDWARD SCISSORHANDS as "weird" and "quirky" and "unconventional." I mean, to me, it's just another metaphor for feeling like an outsider . . . you know, you can see any dog in the world and say, "Gosh, the world wasn't made for that dog. How weird would it be to *be* that dog?"

It's been interesting to be asked about where things come from, because then you think about it, right? And I finally realized, because people were always saying, "Boy, you must have had an unhappy childhood", and I didn't, or, "Boy, you must have had a weird life", and I didn't. But what I do carry around is a really, really,

really strong feeling of what it was like to be, say, three or four years old and two-and-a-half feet tall, and try to sit in a chair. . . and your feet don't touch, and you can't reach the table. In other words, I have a really strong sense memory of the disproportion of the world to me, and I think that everything I do comes from that. And, okay, so you're either a character with scissors for hands, or you're a horse . . . you're *still* a creature in a world that isn't made for you. To me, they're the same. I get really angry when people tell me that BLACK BEAUTY is conventional material. I mean, to me, THE SECRET GARDEN's a far more conventional story . . . far more.

Well, considering the fact that it's a multi-character piece—told from the point of view of an animal—that in itself is highly unconventional.

I suppose that's *literally* unconventional, and it hurt me when people couldn't go with that. I loved seeing the world as best I could through the eyes of this creature that, to me, is the most bizarre creature on earth. I mean, think about it . . . they actually want to be part of our lives. Only a dog is the other creature that wants to be part of our lives. And people think they're stupid.

So, you were asked to do the movie by Warner Bros., and you go over to England, and it's the first time you've directed, and you're working with a highly experienced British crew. Was it daunting?

Well, I trust my "bullshit" meter completely, and that's sort of what I hoped would carry me through, and in fact, it did. I knew that I would be far better off if I could afford to hire people who knew what they were doing. And luckily, I'm not insecure enough that I couldn't hire them.

It's not like, "Oh, I can't hire someone as experienced as John Box. Let me hire somebody who . . . "

. . . Who I can tell what to do. No. John Box and I told each other what to do, you know what I mean? John Box, who I must say was the single most enthusiastic of all the production designers I interviewed, brought such devotion to me and the project, that I was astonished. I mean, I was surrounded by Academy Award winners, from Jenny Beavan, the costume designer, to Claire Simpson , our editor, John Box, and Simon Kaye, who did our sound. They were so devoted and so enthusiastic every single day, that I just felt blessed to have them there.

And I'm also not afraid to ask people's opinions. That doesn't mean I'll always do what they suggest, but I'm happy to ask, "What do you think, what do you think, what do you think?" Some people at first took that as a sign of lack of leadership, but they quickly came to realize that it was an honest question, but not an insecure question. You know, not a question of "please tell me what to do. I was just asking, "What do you think?" You know, at first some of them were afraid to answer because they're not used to having their boss say, "What do you think", but it really became a wonderful sort of large partnership with a lot of people. And I'll try to run every set that way.

I have seen directors—and I won't name them—who will tell the sound guy how to do his job. Well, you know what? That sound guy knows his job a lot better than the director knows the sound guy's job. What's the point of hiring the sound guy if you're going to tell him how to do his job? I want to make an atmosphere in which I inspire people to do their jobs the best they can do them. And that was really how I saw the goal, from the horse trainer to the production designer.

So, there was no intimidation or anything like that. I didn't have time to be intimidated either. It's just too much work. And casting, I was really lucky that people like David Thewlis were unknown here. And I tried in each instance to cast slightly against type, slightly against expectation, because I wanted it to be a rich movie. I didn't want it to be a conventional movie. I didn't want it to be a sentimental movie, which was its greatest risk. I wanted it to be filled with sentiment but not "ooky" sentimental.

> "I have seen directors —and I won't name them—who will tell the sound guy how to do his job. Well, you know what? That sound guy knows his job a lot better than the director knows the sound guy's job."
> —Caroline Thompson

Your re-creation of Victorian England was, I thought, visually rich. Much of it reminded me of Hogarth.

Oh, how cool. Thank you. We had Hogarth prints all over the walls in the production office. Actually, our riskiest and most successful choice was using Blenheim Palace for Victorian London. It worked like gangbusters because you really felt the claustrophobia, yet we were in this not so big, very controllable space. And so we got to roll camera all day instead of direct traffic all day, which was essential on a schedule like ours.

Logistically tough movie . . .

Very tough movie. A big movie, and a scope that I've never written before.

Was the writer at war with the director at that point?

Oh, not at war . . . it was just the director was going, "Damn you! Damn you!" Because when you think about it, my movies really haven't been chock full of

action sequences at all. But again, I just sort of . . . put my head down and marched forward and did my best.

So, you make the movie. You get it done. It gets good reviews. It opens, and . . .

It dies.

Why?

Well, it's not a summer movie. And it was released not just in the summer but at the height of summer. It came out the same weekend as THE MASK. It wasn't marketed honestly, in my opinion. I'm being straight. It was sold both too coldly and too fuzzily. It wasn't sold as a story with any balls, or any spirit. And it has both of those things. I felt that it was misrepresented in its advertising. It wasn't sold aggressively. I think the studio was in a quandary having only me to promote, because I'm not exactly well known, and so, you know, given that—I mean, David Thewlis did come for a day of publicity in New York, but he's not exactly a household word here. And, so I think that was a problem for them.

BLACK BEAUTY was brought out the week after LASSIE, and if you look at the two posters, they're identical. The campaigns are identical. There's nothing that distinguishes this film in its campaign to make you think, "Oh, that's different," which it is. And, as I said, to bring it out at the height of summer is just foolhardy. This is a movie that should have been platformed, in my opinion—given a chance to build as opposed to just go wide. And it should have come out in the autumn or at a down time, not at the hottest time of the year. And maybe then, it would have had a chance in the marketplace. You know, I can't say that the audience would have gone for it, I have no idea. But I don't think an audience was given a chance to go for it.

What do you think of the explanation that American kids raised as they are these days can in no way relate to a story that takes place in Victorian England?

Well, THE SECRET GARDEN did a heck of a lot better than this movie. It made $32-million dollars. So, you know, so much for that. I mean, that's not huge numbers, but it's certainly respectable numbers. So, I don't really think that's true. And if it is, well, who knows what any of us is doing? On the other hand, I will always be grateful to Warner Bros., for letting me make the movie I wanted to make. They were absolutely great to me in the sense that they really creatively left me alone to make the best film I could, and not every studio in town will do that. And I will be grateful 'till I die to them for that.

You've had a kind of a special relationship with Warner Bros.
Well, yeah, I've done two films there now. Yeah ... I mean, they've been great to me . . . they've been wonderful. They really have believed in me, and that's been real important.

Caroline Thompson on the set of BLACK BEAUTY.
BLACK BEAUTY © 1994 Warner Bros., a division of Time Warner Entertainment Company, L.P. All rights reserved.

Keith Hamshere

Obviously, you're not discouraged by the . . .
No, I'm saddened, you know? I'm sad. I went from shock to the kind of depression where you sleep 20 hours a day. I did that for a week or so. On the other hand, first of all, I'm not a person easily embittered.

And secondly, so many people whom I respect enormously have really genuinely loved the movie. You know, you can tell when somebody's bullshitting you, and to feel that, okay, I've made something—and I'm not inclined to love my own work, by the way. I actually hate most of the things I've done—and I loved this film. I was very proud of it. But to get the kind of confirmation from people who I really respect has meant tons. So, you know, it's not—it's like you say to yourself, okay, how would I have rather this happened? Well, I would obviously have rather had it done really well at the box office. Okay, well if you had to put yourself in a situation where you had a choice of making a movie you were proud of or having it do well at the box office, which would you rather? Make a movie you're proud of, obviously. And I *got* to do that. And that's not nothing—that's a huge thing.

Your career is a living example that what industry wisdom would never think would work . . . works.

Well, that's true. Tim Burton is the prime example of it, I think. Especially starting with EDWARD SCISSORHANDS. I mean, that never would have gotten made except under very special circumstances. Yeah. And I'm pleased with that, only because it makes me proud of the audience. It makes me proud of the people out there who want to see things that are good and different and strange.

So now, at this point on, are Caroline Thompson the screenwriter and the director two different people. Do you have separate careers?
Well, not really, because I learned so much about screenwriting from directing. I mean, I learned about things that I hadn't really even thought about, like how do you get from one scene to the next—what's the cut? And I learned—you know, there's certain things, certain sort of tricks I'll do in a script to get myself out of trouble that would put the director straight into trouble, you know? And so, the two people in me know exactly what I'm doing now, and when I'm doing it.

So you're not leaving your career as screenwriter separate from directing behind . . .
Well, in terms of just work, when I'm a writer, I lead the best life in the world. Which is to say I write about two thirds of the day and then I horseback ride the other third of the day, and then I go out in the evening and see a movie or something. I mean, it's the best life in the world. And when I'm a director, I'm leading the worst life in the world.

Up at five . . .
Up at five—and you know, I only stopped *dreaming* about the shooting of BLACK BEAUTY about three weeks ago. And so, we're not talking about an 18 hour a day job, we're talking about a 24 hour a day obsession. And not that I don't get obsessed about my screenwriting work—I do—but on the other hand, I always have been able to leave it at the desk. This I couldn't leave at the desk. It totally took me over and ruined parts of my life. And I'm happy to have my life ruined sometimes, but I can't have it ruined all the time. Just for me... I can't do it. And so, for example, I'm doing an adaptation of an E.B. White book, STUART LITTLE, for Columbia right now, for fun. You know, to me that's fun. It's almost relaxing to be able to do something that I'm not going to direct. It was never intended for me to direct it, I don't even want to direct it, but I'm having fun doing the writing on it. It's like a vacation. And then I have scripts that I very much want to direct. So, I'm just trying to find the balance. You know, I cannot become a movie monk. I cannot give my whole life up to working on movies every day, all day. I mean, some people might say that means I'm not the real thing. I say it means I'm a human being. But no, it's true . . . it's like, what kind of devotion do you have?

12

And I say I have a tremendous amount of devotion, and it's a very, very deep devotion, but it's just devotion that is measured by desire to lead a good life as well. So, I'm greedy.

I want to ask one more question, and it's this tremendous empathy you have, not just for animals, but also—and I think, or course, the two are very strongly related—for children.

Yeah, I love kids. First of all, I think they're way smarter than adults. I think they're way more honest than adults. Both as themselves and as an audience. I love them as an audience. They're very pure in their reactions. But I think it goes back to what I was saying about that feeling of disproportion. My strongest feeling in my life is a feeling of disproportion—of the world not being in proportion to me. And kids feel that all the time. I mean, that is the definition of being a child. I don't have any kids myself. Maybe it's because I still feel like one of them and it wouldn't make any sense. But I do find if I'm in a room with adults and children, that I go to hang out with the children. Because to me, their imaginations are much more interesting. It's like they're on acid all the time. And I just love their brains, and I love the way their thoughts work—you know, they are far more witty in their illogic than so-called adults are in their logic. They track things sensationally, and they track things emotionally rather than tracking things logically. And the kind of discoveries that they make about the world every day just by the nature of their minds is paradise to me.

Well, I don't know if you believe the whole Wordsworthian concept—which is also prevalent in Balinese culture—about children coming directly from God, and therefore wiser than adults.

Well, exactly. I think that we get stupider as we get older because out of fear, we try to organize our lives so desperately. And children don't have that fear. Innately, they don't have that fear. The most touching thing that's happened to me lately is I've been asked to be the honoree for an organization that's for child abuse victims. And that's touched me more than anything I've been asked to participate in. I mean, if I have contributed to kids, that's the best compliment I could ever have been paid. I really do think that they have a magical vision of our world.

JOEL SCHUMACHER

W**HAT A LONG, STRANGE, AND WONDERFUL TRIP** it's been for Joel Schumacher, one of the industry's most sought-after "A" list directors. Schumacher's seamless technique, fine work with actors and noticeable lack of pretension have resulted in a number of popular works of first-class Hollywood entertainment, including ST. ELMO'S FIRE, THE LOST BOYS, FLATLINERS, FALLING DOWN and THE CLIENT. Schumacher was then passed the baton of that great hunk of enduring American mythology—the Dark Knight—as the director of the epic-sized BATMAN FOREVER, the record-breaking blockbuster of Summer '95.

Schumacher emerged from the excesses of the fashion world in the overheated '60s—during which time he made a name for himself as a designer and co-owner of a hugely popular New York City store called Paraphernalia—as a costume designer on such films as Frank Perry's PLAY IT AS IT LAYS, Herbert Ross' THE LAST OF SHEILA, Paul Mazursky's BLUME IN LOVE and Woody Allen's SLEEPER and INTERIORS. Schumacher's dogged determination to direct led him to discover his considerable talents as a screenwriter on SPARKLE and CAR WASH, both of which demonstrated his ability to deftly juggle ensemble stories and characters. He got his first directing breaks on the telefilms THE VIRGINIA HILL STORY and the much-acclaimed AMATEUR NIGHT AT THE DIXIE BAR AND GRILL before making his feature debut on THE INCREDIBLE SHRINKING WOMAN. Schumacher's career was truly launched by the raucous D.C. CAB, and then the era-defining ST. ELMO'S FIRE (writing both films, the latter in collaboration with Carl Kurlander).

In the following conversation, which took place during principal photography of BATMAN FOREVER, the remarkably candid Schumacher chronicles his life in the movies . . . which really began at the age of seven in a Queens, New York movie house . . .

MICHAEL SINGER: You're a rare case in the history of film, in that never before has someone who began his career as a costume designer for motion pictures gone on to become a successful director. Did you always want to make movies?
JOEL SCHUMACHER: Since I was seven-years-old. I grew up behind the Sunnyside Theatre in a poor neighborhood in Queens, Long Island City.

I *lived* in that theatre. I was one of those kids who had to be dragged out of the theatre. When I was about nine, I built a marionette theatre, along with the sets, costumes and marionettes themselves. I wrote these little plays and performed them with the puppets. Looking back on them now, I realize that since I had

seen no theatre, I think I was trying to make movies in my own way. So yes, I always wanted to make movies, and I really consider myself extremely fortunate to have realized that dream.

In essence, everything that you achieved before entering the movie business—design school, your boutique in New York, the costume and set designing—were just vehicles toward the goal of directing.
But I didn't know that. You know, we were poor. My father died when I was four. My mother worked in a store selling dresses six days a week and three nights a week to support us. There were no film schools then, no film colony in New York. I needed to make a living,

and I had a dream of supporting my mother, so I went to art school. I had a scholarship to the Parsons School of Design, and I did the windows at Henri Bendel at night to support myself through school. I made a hundred dollars a week.

Everybody said that I had a great eye and a lot of style, and that I should go into the fashion business. I majored in fashion design at art school, graduated in 1965, and opened my store, Paraphernalia, with two other people in September of that year. It became an overnight success, and I went from making a hundred dollars a week to $20,000 a year. But then Charles Revson, who owned Revlon, bought out my contract, and I was suddenly making $65,000 a year. I was only out of school for a few months, and all of my dreams of taking my mother out of her little apartment in Queens and giving her some privilege came true. But she died suddenly right at that moment, in October of '65. It was very traumatic, because I had sort of done all that for her. And it was a strange period for me, because by this time I was smack dab in the middle of the entire beautiful people '60s madness of New York City at that time, and I was rapidly becoming a drug addict. After my mother's death, I just plunged into it. And also, I really didn't like the fashion world. I really wanted to make movies and be part of that world.

So I stayed in and out of the fashion world through the late '60s. I did Halston's first collection with him, when he was designing clothes. I worked for Diana Vreeland at *Vogue*. I always worked with very interesting, exciting people, but I was really one of the casualties of the '60s in the sense that I just became hopelessly immersed in drugs, sex and rock and roll. None of my life made sense. I just kept getting offers in the fashion world, and I didn't want that. I didn't know how to get into the movie world. I didn't know what I was doing. I really crashed and burned. I was down to 130 pounds, I had lost five teeth, I owed $50,000 in debts . . . my brain and my body hadn't been connected for years. I finally got off hard drugs in 1970, and I'm sure you've heard many people describe it as really feeling like you've been born again. I had to piece my life together, start all over again.

I decided that I was going to try and work in the movie business, but I had destroyed my reputation, and people were right to flee from me because like all drug addicts, I was irresponsible, self-consumed and reckless. So my old boss at Bendel's, Geraldine Stutz, gave me a chance again. I went back to my old job, did the windows and rebuilt the store, attracting a lot of attention again. Of course, I was making $10,000 a year and I owed $50,000, $30,000 of which was to the Federal Government. It was a tough year. I went through about a year-and-a-half living on two dollars a day. It was

quite an interesting experience. Then I started getting offers to do art direction and styling in commercials. I really needed the money, and it also gave me a chance to work near the camera for the first time. I worked with some of the great commercial directors: Howard Zieff, Steve Horn, Lear Levin. Then through a friend, I met Dominick Dunne, who's now a world-famous author but was then a producer. I talked him into giving me a two-week trial period as a costume designer on an independent film he was producing called PLAY IT AS IT LAYS.

Which Frank Perry directed.

Frank Perry was kind enough to give me the chance, but it was really Dominick who kind of hounded him into letting me do this. The movie was from a great book of Joan Didion's, and she and John Gregory Dunne wrote the screenplay. So I gave up my apartment, my job at Bendel's, my life in New York. I gave up everything, and came out to Los Angeles the Christmas of 1971.

You obviously survived the two week trial.

I passed the two week trial, and then I did several other movies as costume designer. The fourth film was SLEEPER with Woody Allen, who was not getting along with theproduction designer. Woody was the first director that I had worked with who really encouraged me to step outside my department and make other contributions to the film. So I started working on some of the sets and production design with him. And he also encouraged me to be a director. He's still one of my greatest supporters.

Did he encourage you to write as well?

Yes, and he still encourages me to take bigger and bigger risks. He also gave me a wonderful piece of advice, which I always tell young people who are starting out or are at film schools. When I told Woody I wanted to be a director, and he told me that he thought I would be some day, I said that it seemed so far away. And he said, "Yeah, but take a good look at the business. There's a handful of geniuses touched by the gods. The rest of them . . . if they can do it, you can do it. And you can do it better." I always tell that to people who are starting out, because it's really true. I'm not one of the handful of geniuses touched by the gods. I'm just a hard-working director, and I really worked my way up to this position in the business. It can be done.

Shortly thereafter, you started to write screenplays?

I knew that I was never going to be a director through the costume and production design route, but I saw writers getting the opportunity to direct some of their work. I was living in a $60-a-month apartment in Hollywood, I had a little car, and was paying off my debts. I sat down at the kitchen table and started to write a script . . . and it sold for $9,000 to Barry Diller and a wonderful woman named Deanne Barkley who worked for him. At the time they were doing movies at ABC, before Barry became the head of ABC. It didn't get made, but I sold it. So fueled with this triumph—and you can imagine how much selling something for $9,000 meant to me then—I wrote a feature on spec, SPARKLE. Well, that sold to Robert Stigwood and Warner Bros., and did get made. It's a small movie, but it was my first movie. It was Sam O'Steen's first feature as a director. It also introduced actors Lonette McKee, Irene Cara, Dorian Harewood and Philip Michael Thomas, and Curtis Mayfield did the wonderful score. It's become a cult movie, and I'm proud of it.

It was also the first indication of how in tune you've always been the popular culture that surrounds you.

I'm from the streets of Long Island City. I am a pop culture sponge. When rock and roll happened, it happened to *me*. I remember when I used to sneak a radio under the covers late at night to listen to a program that Alan Freed used to host that played what was then known as "race records." These fantastic black singers were singing music that is now called rhythm and blues. I remember Elvis Presley's first television appearance. I grew up when all the songs were by Tony Bennett, Georgia Gibbs, Teresa Brewer, Patti Page and Doris Day. The music was all big band influenced. And then suddenly this whole other pure American pop culture art form happened. At the same time I was in the movie theatres where this other great pop culture phenomenon—the American movie—was happening to me. Fabulous movies with Marilyn Monroe, James Dean, Montgomery Clift and Marlon Brando were being made then. And at the same time, just by accident, there was a tiny little theatre in our neighborhood called the "Center" that showed foreign films. So I was watching DeSica and Fellini and Renoir and Kurosawa. That's why I always say that I'm a pop culture sponge. It's just what I live and breathe.

So in SPARKLE, your first script to be filmed, you married your fascination with both film and music.

Yes, but not thinking about it. I used to stand outside all night at the Brooklyn Paramount so we could be in at the 9:00 AM rock and roll show. That's what SPARKLE is all about. I just wrote about something I

> "I'm not one of the handful of geniuses touched by the gods. I'm just a hard-working director, and I really worked my way up to this position in the business. It can be done."
>
> —Joel Schumacher

knew. Then I wrote CAR WASH, which was a big hit. So I was able to use my writing to direct television movies. The second one, AMATEUR NIGHT AT THE DIXIE BAR AND GRILL, won a lot of awards. I was hoping to do as much TV work as they would allow me, hoping to build that into some kind of feature career. I got offered features right after I did AMATEUR NIGHT. And I said yes to THE INCREDIBLE SHRINKING WOMAN because I thought with my background in costumes and sets that it would be fun to do. And I had also been a big fan of Lily Tomlin.

I've read of the raw terror that you felt at that time.

Well, I truly did not know what I was doing. And you know, I will always be grateful to Ned Tanen—who was running Universal at that time—for giving me that break. What a courageous man. Because I didn't know what I was doing. It was a strange thing. I wanted to be a director ever since I was a child, I thought that it was my calling. So naturally, I thought that when I did my first feature it would be pure genius. And it wasn't. I was so ignorant and so desperately ungifted that it was a shock to me. I was very confused after SHRINKING WOMAN, even though it was relatively well-received. But I was so astounded by my own lack of talent that I didn't know what to do with the rest of my life. But then, Thom Mount and Bruce Berman—who were then both executives at Universal—called and offered me a small, inexpensive movie called D.C. CAB. I was going to leave the business, but I thought I would try and see if I could do a good job, and if I really enjoyed directing.

And it was a big commercial hit.

Well, D.C. CAB certainly wasn't LAWRENCE OF ARABIA, but it was a step forward. It was received well, and did well at the box office.

Did it give you your confidence back?

Well, I enjoyed the process. It was a modest movie, but better than the first one. Then I started getting offered wacky comedies, and I realized that if I wanted to make a better movie I'd probably have to create it for myself.

So with my assistant at the time, Carl Kurlander, we sat down and wrote ST. ELMO'S FIRE. I had lived in Georgetown for part of the shooting of D.C. CAB, and was fascinated with after-college life, because

17

Georgetown is a small community that seems to be of, by and for 22 year-olds. When we made the movie in 1984, we were in the middle of the '80s yuppie madness. It was a period when young graduates had to have a 25 year-plan. They had to have the right car, the right clothes, the right everything. They had to know who they were marrying and how many children they were going to have. So I decided to make a film about how difficult the personal, social, sexual, political life was for these people, and also how difficult it is to stay with a group of friends. But in casting the movie and writ-

Joel Schumacher lines up a shot on BATMAN FOREVER

ing it I had no idea it would have the impact that it did, because I didn't realize that people would identify with it on such a strong basis.

Your life must have changed radically once again after the success of ST. ELMO'S FIRE.

Well, it did. I started getting offered all the yuppie angst movies, but I felt like I had already covered that area. So Mark Canton, Bruce Berman (who had moved to Warner Bros.) and Dick Donner offered me THE LOST BOYS. I thought I was going to say no, because the characters were all children, and I didn't think I was the right director. I called everybody to tell them I didn't think it was for me, but everybody had gone to lunch. So I went out jogging, and while I was doing that I thought, wouldn't it be great if they were *teenage* vampires, like a band of gypsies, with rock and roll? Everyone liked the idea, so we made the film, and it was a hit. There were a lot of people who didn't think I was a real director until THE LOST BOYS, even with the success of ST. ELMO'S FIRE.

THE LOST BOYS was a very different project from what you had previously done. Obviously, you were trying to demonstrate your range. How did the industry react?

I became the vampire horror director, but I was lucky to get offered COUSINS, a romantic comedy which was 180 degrees away from LOST BOYS. And then I made FLATLINERS, which was a great time. Then I was going off to do THE PHANTOM OF THE OPERA, and it got canceled because Andrew Lloyd Webber was divorcing Sarah Brightman, and it became part of the legal entanglements.

I know that its cancellation was a huge disappointment to you, but have you been able to divert any of your PHANTOM intentions into BATMAN FOREVER?

Oh yes. In a way, BATMAN is a better PHANTOM.

DYING YOUNG followed FLATLINERS, which seems to have been a very risky project from the start.

I'm proud of the movie, and I think Campbell Scott and Julia Roberts did an extraordinary job. But I'm not sure if I was the right director for that movie, and I'm not sure I did it for the right reasons. I had fallen in love with Julia Roberts on FLATLINERS. But you don't do a movie because you're crazy about the movie star . . . you do a movie because you're crazy about the movie. And I don't know if it's the movie I would necessarily have done if Julia hadn't asked me to do it. There's no answer. But then I really got lucky. Warners offered me FALLING DOWN. And then to top that luck, Michael Douglas said yes to playing the lead.

FALLING DOWN was a highly topical and controversial piece that really changed the way people perceived you as a filmmaker. Is that why you did it?

I was pissed off at America. We were in bad shape, and I was angry. Everybody was angry. I think all the credit for FALLING DOWN goes to Ebbe Roe Smith, who wrote it, because it really hit a nerve. It was a tough movie to make. We were on the mean streets of L.A. before, during and after the riots. We were rocking and rolling on those streets.

What about THE CLIENT? It's not only been a great box office hit, but it won you the best personal notices of your career.

It's all thanks to John Grisham. Listen, it wasn't a novel in search of a movie . . . it *was* a movie! From the minute that boy gets dragged into that car until the last goodbye on the airfield, it's a movie. And I got a great cast. I'm a very cast dependent director.

You seem to be a director who actually *likes* actors.

Well, you know, if you're going to be a painter, you'd better love paint. You better love color. I have friends who are directors who tell me they hate actors. I don't know how they go to work every day. It would be so painful. I love actors. I like to see them shine. I want them to be at their best.

How did you feel when Warner Bros. asked you to direct BATMAN FOREVER?

I was down in Memphis and New Orleans getting ready to do THE CLIENT when I was summoned to Burbank for a meeting with Bob Daly and Terry Semel. They were wonderful, and we had a great meeting, and I said that I would really love to do the movie only if Tim Burton wanted me to do it. And thankfully, he did.

What do you bring to the project?

Well, Batman was created in 1939, which is the year I was born. I grew up on Batman comics. I found them to be darker, sexier, more fun and iconoclastic than other comics. The whole legend of Batman has dark elements, but the comics are also done in bold, colorful strokes. I'm trying to capture both of these elements, so that the audience will have a visual ride as well as an engaging story.

Are you concerned about the inevitable comparisons with Tim Burton's two Batman films?

I think Tim did a wonderful job with the other movies, but to copy someone isn't really to flatter them. I think it was incumbent upon us to give our own version of the Batman legend, trying to incorporate some of the great things Tim started, but also to give it a fresh look. Most of all, I want people to enjoy themselves.

You work in a wide range of genres, as if you never want to repeat yourself thematically or even cinematically.

I think that there are a lot of great directors who excel by doing a version of the same movie over and over again. But I think the only way that I can learn is by doing something new that challenges me. I feel if I grow as a man and as a director, then hopefully the audience will get a better movie. Not that I think it's necessary for the audience to know that I made it, because I don't think it's necessary for the audience to know the director's name. I think it's important for the movie to have an effect, that they just have an experience.

You don't seem to separate yourself from the audience. Perhaps you're not all that different now than the kid who spent hours in the Sunnyside Theatre?

I hope not. Sitting there in the dark, I had such great experiences watching those movies. I still do. I still love to go to the movies. It's my favorite thing to do . . . next to making them. I was such a lonely, disconnected kid, and those movies I saw reached out to me. If I can make movies, and they reach out to other people in the darkness, then I don't feel so lonely and disconnected anymore. That's the real thrill. Not fame, not fortune, not any of that. I've been lucky that all my movies have found an audience. Maybe not blockbuster audiences, but large enough for all of the films to have been profitable and known. And it's very exciting to go to Tokyo or Sydney or Rome and meet strangers that know and have been touched by my films in some way. I consider myself a very privileged and lucky man. And my worst days are when I forget how lucky I really am.

ROBERT RODRIGUEZ

T HERE ARE FLAVORS-OF-THE-MONTH . . . and then there is Robert Rodriguez. And very few people doubt that Rodriguez has what it takes to avoid the Hollywood deflavorizing machine and maintain his very own brand of high-octane, low-cost, maverick moviemaking. The 25 year-old Rodriguez shot the wildly acclaimed EL MARIACHI for seven thousand bucks, so ridiculously cheap that it even defies jokey one-liners. Made as a throwaway for the Spanish-language video market, Rodriguez was astonished when Columbia Pictures bought it for remake purposes, and dumbfounded that they actually wanted to release the original version.

The third eldest in an Austin, Texas family of ten, Rodriguez demonstrated an early interest in cartooning and filmmaking. While attending the University of Texas at Austin, he created a daily comic strip entitled "Los Hooligans," which ran for three years in the *Daily Texan* newspaper. Simultaneously—and from childhood—Rodriguez shot nearly 30 short narrative movies, with borrowed video equipment and no money. An award-winning video anthology, AUSTIN STORIES, boosted Rodriguez into film school where he produced his first 16mm short.

This film, BEDHEAD, went on to win a significant number of awards in film festivals across the U.S. High on its success during the summer break of 1991, Rodriguez wrote, shot, sound-recorded, edited and directed EL MARIACHI. He produced with his childhood friend, Carlos Gallardo, starring in the title role as the Hombre Sin Nombre who unwittingly becomes involved in havoc, chaos and mayhem in a Mexican border town.

In-between the first EL MARIACHI and the second—entitled DESPERADO, shot in the same border town of Acuna but with an astronomical budget of five million dollars and Antonio Banderas in the leading role—Rodriguez directed ROAD RACERS, one of the most popular of Showtime's REBEL HIGHWAY series of homages to '50s American International teen sleaze flicks. And after bringing the apocalypse back to Acuna in the second MARIACHI epic, Rodriguez joined Quentin Tarantino, Allison Anders, and Alexandre Rockwell for the omnibus FOUR ROOMS.

MICHAEL SINGER: It's funny. ROAD RACERS was obviously the work of somebody who felt very affectionately toward those old American International teen movies that the Showtime series was based on, but you were too young to actually grow up with them. You must have discovered them all on video or TV runs.

ROBERT RODRIGUEZ: Oh yeah. They sent me the tapes of the movies that we were remaking. In fact, they wouldn't send me ROAD RACERS because it was so terrible. I wanted to live up to the old posters, which said stuff like, "Some have to dance, some have to kill! Then you'd watch the movie and they were lame, you know? So it was like, we're going to do the poster *be-*

yond the poster? Make it as sordid and crazy as they promised, and then some.

ROAD RACERS was great fun, and one of the things that interested me is that I think your background as a cartoonist came out very strongly in the piece.
Did it really? Why's that?

Because there was so much comical material that defied all logic as we know it, which is the cartoonist's hallmark.
What in particular?

The skating rink scene, where our hero is greasing the floor by skating on his head? That's not necessarily the kind of thing one would normally see.
Yeah, I guess you've got to kind of mix it together, because ideas for a strip or a movie can come kind of at the same time. We were just driving along, me and my cowriter, trying to come up with ideas—we had ten days to write the ROAD RACERS script, so we had to do it very quickly. We were taking a road trip from San Antonio to Mexico, and going through San Antonio, we saw an old skating rink and I just said, "Hey, we've got to get a skating rink scene in the movie", which leads to a rumble on roller skates—never thinking it'd actually make it into the movie. But when they give you free reign like that, we actually thought, well, it'd be a challenge to actually just try to pull it off in the time we have, with all the crazy shots we designed. We did, and it was fun.

There's a tradition of cartoonists who became filmmakers, and most of them became really, really good filmmakers.
Really?

David Lynch, Frank Tashlin, Tim Burton . . .
My earliest movies were actually cartoon movies. I would spend all day in school in the back of the class—because I wasn't very good in school—using the margins to do STAR WARS things, like, you know, little stick figures, and then, "Ssshhh", a light saber would come out, so if you flip it, you had a lot of room to have, like? spaceships going, and I'd spend hours doing that. And I'd show it to the students—you know, these paperback dictionaries—and they'd all laugh, and so I'd feel good because my grades were so low, it made me feel good about something about myself. But I never thought it would go anywhere. But then I got a video camera, and I'd make little claymation movies, and then movies with my brothers and sisters. Then I started a daily comic strip in Austin at the University of Texas. I had it for three years. A daily strip, so my drawing got much better, and you know, you're writing, and comic timing develops, I guess, just by practicing. You had to

turn that thing every day or you wouldn't get paid, so those little eight bucks a day that I'd get doing that strip was what kept me practicing and made my drawings improve.

It seems that people who started either in animation or cartoons seem to have a much less limited notions of what they can do on film. Their visual sensibilities seem to be much expanded. Do you feel that you owe anything as a filmmaker to your background as a cartoonist?
Sure, sure. Do I owe it to drawing?

Yeah.
I think just because you don't even think about it, anything you visualize, you can immediately make concrete by drawing it. So, you feel like you can make any vision that you have in your head a reality, either on film or on video, or on paper. I think I get kind of the two mixed together, because there was stuff in ROAD RACERS that people asked, "how are you gonna do this?" . . . Then I'd make a drawing of the actual contraption that I'd need them to build me so we could pull off that head slick, and I don't know, it just kind of goes hand in hand. And they'd see it and go, "oh, okay", and then they'd build it, and there you go. They make it and it works fine. So, you know, I think a lot of the ideas I get visually, just being able to put them down and show somebody else, to reaffirm what you have in your head, just goes a long way.

On the other hand, I don't get the impression from either EL MARIACHI or ROAD RACERS that you do a lot of storyboarding.
[*raises eyebrows*] Why do you think that?

Because your films are very spontaneous.
Everyone else thinks that I do storyboards for all the movies.

Well, I don't. So who's right?
I used to. I used to early on for my short movies, but I didn't draw one frame for EL MARIACHI, because you usually do storyboards to show other people what you have in mind. But since I didn't have a crew on EL MARIACHI, why draw for myself? You see it in your head, and you know a lot of it's going to change on location—you're going to be very spontaneous—and I didn't need to draw it down because I was already watching it in my head. On ROAD RACERS I drew out the roller skating rink scene for the crew, very much stick figures and stuff. We had about 12 hours to shoot 52 setups for that scene, which was . . . impossible. A normal Hollywood movie will get through 15 or 20 setups if they're *fast*. To explain everything I needed to the crew would just take forever, because they would

have told me that there was no way I could have gotten all those shots in one day.

What's your record for a number of setups in one day?

On ROAD RACERS, 78 for a single camera. And it was because they were going to start cutting my scenes out. We had a 13 day shooting schedule, and we could have shot it easily in 13 days, but it would have looked like a cable movie. You know, the camera sitting in the corner. And that's not what I wanted. I wanted it to have some more setups to cut, because I love to edit. ROAD RACERS is a fast cars and rock 'n' roll kind of movie—it's got to look like a really high octane chromium film—and I was so used to getting so many setups on EL MARIACHI, because I was basically doing everything by myself. That's why people thought EL MARIACHI looked more expensive than it was . . . because of the number of setups . . . and people in this town know that setups usually cost more.

To say that it looked more expensive than it was is an understatement, to say the least. It looked like a $2 million picture, if not more.

I didn't know. To me, it looked alright. It was a little slow, but when I was making it, I thought, well, if I just had a little more time. Not necessarily money . . . just a little more time. Our camera got taken away after the 14th day.

So you're shooting schedule on EL MARIACHI was 14 days?

Yeah. And the funny thing is that on ROAD RACERS we only had 13. So see, when I produce, I get more days out of my budget.

Yeah, but we're talking about a budget that was probably lower than most directors' cellular phone bills for a week.

I know, I know. It's talking about two different things. One's making a movie for the sake of making a movie, and another is doing a job. I mean, you're getting paid, and you spend, and it's not your money. That was my money on EL MARIACHI, and you're more careful. You're paying for your own materials and you're just trying to make a film and learn from it. You're not going to turn it into a big production.

> " . . . no matter if you've got 100 people or two people on the crew—when you push the button and start shooting. That moment is what you're getting. The rest is just decoration."
>
> —Robert Rodriguez

So when you finally do a movie that costs $10 million . . .

Maybe I'll shoot it in *nine* days? I'm going to try and produce my next picture so that I can kind of put the money where it belongs. Everyone shoots differently, but for me, a lot of money can get wasted very easily.

But you're sort of at a crossroads now. You're about to do DESPERADO with a much higher budget. Like . . . maybe $3 million?

Five, man.

Five . . . whoa.

Well, you know, because we have some name actors, it goes quick. But it's going to look much more expensive than five. The whole idea is to put the money on the screen, and shoot 35mm and scope, but I want it small so I can run free. Because really, all it comes down to—no matter if you've got 100 people or two people on the crew—is the moment when you push the button and start shooting. That moment is what you're getting. The rest is just decoration. It doesn't need all the frills, because it's not that kind of a movie.

Do you actually worry about inevitably working on films with bigger budgets?

I wouldn't do it right now. I think as time goes on and I start producing more of my own things and move up little by little, I'll be able to do something I never could have done if I hadn't done MARIACHI or ROAD RACERS first.

Is it true that when you made MARIACHI, you never conceived of it getting U.S. distribution?

Oh, not at all. I would have shot it in English if I expected it to get released in the U.S. It was just a very plotted thing for me to do, because my short films had gotten to the point where they started winning festivals. You know, you've got to cultivate your talent. I mean, you can't just go take a class and think you're going to be a filmmaker. So when I saw my little movies starting to win festivals after so many years just shooting on home video, I thought, wow, I can actually make it in this business, even from Texas, it I were just to get more practice telling feature-length stories. So the whole MARIACHI idea was to shoot three low-budget Spanish-language action movies so that if the movies were terrible, no one would ever see them. But

23

I knew that I could shoot on 16mm, but edit on 3/4-inch video at a local public access station. I could have a 3/4-inch master that I could sell to a Spanish distributor for the straight-to-video market. That way, I could keep the cost under $10,000 and make back maybe, you know, a profit of maybe another ten grand. That's why I kept the budget so low, because I could only sell it for so much. I figured I could learn sound, camera, lighting, feature stories and directing, all in one year on three small action movies. I'd have three features under my belt. You can't beat that. It's the best film school, because you make all your money back. So I knew that after that year, I would have a great demo reel . . . I'd just take the best scenes from the three movies. That's why EL MARIACHI ends the way it does. He becomes the Mariachi in the first movie, because then we were going to do something like THE ROAD WARRIOR and MAD MAX BEYOND THUNDER-

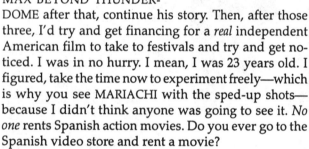

Robert Rodriguez at work on ROAD RACERS

DOME after that, continue his story. Then, after those three, I'd try and get financing for a *real* independent American film to take to festivals and try and get noticed. I was in no hurry. I mean, I was 23 years old. I figured, take the time now to experiment freely—which is why you see MARIACHI with the sped-up shots—because I didn't think anyone was going to see it. *No one* rents Spanish action movies. Do you ever go to the Spanish video store and rent a movie?

Sometimes, actually.
You do, really? They're pretty terrible, aren't they?

They're the worst.
That's why we thought we couldn't lose. That was the whole plan. So when it got bought by Columbia, it was a surprise. But they bought it to remake because they liked the story. But then when the guys upstairs said "We like it the way it is, we want to release it the way it is," then it got funky, and I thought, whoa, that's really outrageous. A Spanish-language movie released in the States by a major studio? We made the *Guinness Book of World Records* for the lowest-budget movie ever released by a studio. So it wasn't anything conceivably planned at all.

Were you freaked out at first?
Yeah, it was a gradual process, you know? First I got the agent off it, which really blew me away because I thought it would take me . . . maybe the third film before I'd get a big agency like that to sign me up. And

then they started sending it around as a sample of my work and I got deal off of it. Just off that same seven thousand dollar tape, you know—pop it in and watch it—and then Columbia bought it, so that freaked me out because I got much more money than I would have just selling to the Spanish video market—and then they wanted to release it, and it won festivals—so it was like, God, the movie wasn't *that* great! It was good, but I could do better if I just knew people were going to actually *watch* it. I would have put so much more work into it. There were so many things that I was just like, eh, it's hot . . . one take . . . let's get out of here.

How many takes do you normally do?
The most takes we did on ROAD RACERS was five.

So when you hear of a director doing more than 30 takes on a scene . . .
I can't relate to that at all. But it if that works for him, you know, that's that kind of just sucks the fun and energy out of what you can make happen. You know, maybe when I'm older, I'll be sitting in my hotel room watching via satellite what they're feeding in from the set. "Come on guys, more setups. You're moving too slow down there." You never know. It could get to that point. They already can sit in a trailer and watch what's going on. They don't even have to talk with anybody. That kind of takes the fun out of it for me. I might go into painting after that, or, you know, aluminum siding.

Come to think of it, because of the budget, you wouldn't have used video assist on either film.
No, it's terrible. I tried it on ROAD RACERS. You just can't tell on that thing. It's all flickery, and black and white, and fuzzy. I just prefer being behind the camera and looking through the lens, and being right there near the actors. It seems like you're making the movie that way. I can see why some directors forget to say "action" or "cut," because you don't feel like you're part of it anymore. You want to feel like you're making your picture, and not like some assembly line's doing it for you.

What I loved about EL MARIACHI was that it was almost as if Sam Peckinpah had taken over a Rene Cardona, Jr. movie. It had a kind of glorious sleaziness about it. Very atmospheric. When you were growing up, did you watch a lot of "B" Mexican movies?

No, not really. I mean, I'd see some of the comedies and some of the pictures from the golden era. But I really got the idea to make EL MARIACHI when I was on the set of LIKE WATER FOR CHOCOLATE.

What town was it shot in?

Acuna, across the border from Del Rio, Texas. There's nothing there, it's like a dust town, but for some reason all these movies are shooting there now. I used to shoot video movies with my friend Carlos Gallardo, who was working in production on LIKE WATER FOR CHOCOLATE, so I was shooting behind-the-scenes video and one of the production managers said, "Hey, why don't you come make one of these cheap Spanish action movies for us? We spent 30 grand on 'em." I said "Wow, 30 grand for those horrible things? Man, we can do much better than that, just me and my friend here." That's how we got the idea to do it, and capture the town and its atmosphere.

We did our homework, and rented some of those movies, and they were all shot in apartments. Really low budget, no atmosphere, and no action, even though they're called action movies. So Acuna turned into a whole backlot to shoot in and capture the energy they weren't capturing in those other low-budget movies. We didn't really see anything we were modeling EL MARIACHI after, except maybe THE ROAD WARRIOR or the Clint Eastwood Italian westerns, in that we would have a character created in the first movie and go on for two more. A complete genre picture. People wonder why my first picture isn't a personal kind of story. Because I was just making an exploitation flick to get some practice. I didn't think it would end up winning prestigious film festivals. That just goes to show that no matter what, don't copy what the last success was. At the time SLACKER was coming out, and I could have gone and made one of those Austin-type movies. And here I was making a Mexican exploitation flick. And *that* ended up being what people wanted next. You never know. Just follow your own thing.

Did EL MARIACHI actually have a theatrical release in Mexico?

Oh yeah. It got a lot of publicity, and did fairly well, but by the time the video came out, people had all heard about it and realized that it wasn't just another one of those Spanish action movies. It was a complete joke, because "Mariachi" means "guitar player." I figured that no one in the U.S. would ever see it, because no one goes and rents movies in the Spanish market. And no one in the Spanish market would see it, because no one would rent an action movie called THE GUITAR PLAYER. So I thought that no one would find it except the poor slob who, when all the other action movies are out, finally says, "Alright, I'll rent this one," and it has more action than the other ones—with titles like RABID DOG and DEATH BY FIRE—put together. That was the whole joke. But now it's gotten quite popular in Mexico on video.

Has that put you into contact with Mexican directors?

Yeah. They're good guys, real nice guys. I'm glad they're doing well, because they've just got their own nice demeanor about them, and yet, wild imaginations. We ought to do something together. Maybe an anthology centered around the Day of the Dead, something like that. It would be fun.

Now you've have your foot on both sides of the border with EL MARIACHI and ROAD RACERS.

It's nice to have two sides, to be able to choose the best from your favorite parts of each culture is really wonderful. I'm a North American director, and a Hispanic director. It's nice to be able to distinguish yourself a little bit.

And you have no problem distinguishing yourself that way?

No, not at all. I figure that's why I was born the way I was. It's great that DESPERADO will be the first decently-budgeted Hollywood movie with a Latin hero in it. I mean, you never see that.

How do you maintain your purity now, being out here in Los Angeles?

I don't live here. I live in Austin, Texas. I'm only out here because we're casting, but we're going to Mexico in a couple of weeks and I won't even be back here until editing time in late November.

How long is your shooting schedule on DESPERADO?

Forty-two shooting days. Can you believe that?

Shooting in Mexico versus shooting in the United States? Any difference for you?

God, like night and day? In the U.S., if you want to shoot, you can't just call the cops and say "Close up the street first. Oh, and by the way, can we borrow your .45?" Down there we could. Or go into the jailhouse and say, "Could you please move all the prisoners into this other cell so we can film in this one? In fact, do you want to play the jail guard in the movie?" You can't do that here.

Have you become a local hero for a lot of tough guys across the border, like Coppola did here after he made THE GODFATHER?

Oh jeez, I don't know. I'm afraid to find out!

SIMON WINCER

ALTHOUGH HE HAD DIRECTED MORE THAN 200 hours of television (winning an Emmy Award in the process) and no fewer than seven feature films, it took a 7,000 pound aquatic mammal named Willy to really put Simon Wincer's name on the map of the very top Hollywood directors hailing from Down Under . . . joining a growing list that already includes George Miller, Bruce Beresford, Phillip Noyce and Fred Schepisi. The huge success of FREE WILLY in 1993 left little doubt that Wincer's ease with actors of various species on rugged outdoors locations marked him as a filmmaker comfortable in surroundings that would make other filmmakers head back to the Winnebago in a flash.

Of course, this came as no surprise to anyone following Wincer's 20 year-long career in long-form filmmaking. Early efforts in Australian television for the Sydney-born Wincer naturally led to a feature career, and he enjoyed his first big home country hit with 1983's period horseracing film PHAR LAP, which also won many fans stateside. Lured to the U.S. in 1985 to direct the science fantasy D.A.R.Y.L. for Paramount, Wincer then stayed to direct two TV movies before returning home for the historical feature THE LIGHTHORSEMEN, which rivaled such epics of old as THE CHARGE OF THE LIGHT BRIGADE and GUNGA DIN in scale.

In 1989, Wincer's cross-Pacific career culminated with his Emmy-winning direction of the mini-series LONESOME DOVE, one of the most acclaimed and honored programs of all television history. Based on Larry McMurtry's bestselling novel, it recreated the American West and its inhabitants with an almost primal power that transcended the genre, particularly for that medium. After the entertaining Aussie western QUIGLEY DOWN UNDER, Wincer took a lighter look at the American frontier in LIGHTNING JACK (fitting in a few well-received episodes of George Lucas' YOUNG INDIANA JONES series inbetween). Most recently, Wincer took off for another suitably exotic location—northern Thailand—for his wartime adventure OPERATION DUMBO DROP, which promises to once again expand his reputation as a director born for the big screen.

MICHAEL SINGER: Hollywood tends to stereotype directors, and at this juncture in your career, you are seen as a "great outdoors" filmmaker, specializing in wide open spaces, animals and action.
SIMON WINCER: I think these days everyone tends to get pigeonholed a bit. Maybe they think I'm the large mammal guy because of FREE WILLY and OPERATION DUMBO DROP, but if my films have a strength, it's a strong emotional line, whether it's got to do with animals or humans or both. And I would like to be thought of, when I've finished my filmmaking career, as a person who has made a whole range of films of all different genres and subject matters. I suppose I made a good western with LONESOME DOVE, so I was perceived as a western guy. Then FREE WILLY, so I'm the animal and kid guy. But my career goes back to 1972 when I started directing for television, and I've done a wide body of

work, some epic, like the YOUNG INDIANA JONES TV episodes and THE LIGHTHORSEMEN, more contemporary melodramas, like the mini-series BLUEGRASS and THE LAST FRONTIER.

You seem to work in a solid tradition of telling the story at hand in a clear, cohesive way on film with few fancy frills.

It's very rare that you go to the movies and you don't see a fine looking film, but what makes a successful film is script, story and character, always. The script is where it starts and finishes, and it doesn't matter how technically fine it is. If you don't have a good script and story, you don't have anything. When you first start directing, you tend to worry a lot more about what the camera's doing than the form and content, which are actually the most important things. The biggest mistake a director can make is to be so busy worrying about moving the camera and getting pretty shots that he or she forgets about more important things like pace. It's very rare to see a film these days that isn't atmospheric . . . but if it's atmospheric and dramatic and moving and the story and character are right, than you've got something really special.

Every thirty second TV spot you see these days is technically gorgeous, so with the talent working behind the camera nowadays, it no longer seems to be such a remarkable accomplishment to make your movie look like a painting.

I think there's a bit too much emphasis on technical filmmaking, and we've all got to keep up with it because every film is competing for its place in the market. Then suddenly you get a film that doesn't rely on technical razzle-dazzle—like FOUR WEDDINGS AND A FUNERAL—and it takes the world by storm because it's *not* high concept. That's what I love to see. Certainly, the projects that I'm developing are more along that vein.

You directed, what, somewhere around 200 hours of television before your first feature?

Oh yeah . . . probably closer to 250. That's great mileage, just in terms of directing experience, working behind the camera, a great learning process. So many great American directors have come up through that school: Steven Spielberg, Sydney Pollack, Richard Donner, Sidney Lumet, John Frankenheimer. When they got in the field of feature films, their technical knowledge was like driving a car, second nature. What they concentrate on is script and story, and this is why those guys keep making successful movies—because they know what makes films work.

But for the last twenty years or so, we've seen a trend toward giving every other successful screenwriter who's never shot a foot of film an opportunity to direct a feature.

Well, there's a universal shortage of good scripts, and sometimes the only way a studio can get it is to offer the writer a chance to direct either that one or another. But there's a danger in this because, if you've never worked on a set before, it's daunting. It's not an easy job. Just through growing up in television, I found it amazingly difficult to achieve the day. It's still challenging. So how anyone who has sat at a computer writing a script can just walk onto a set—even having been through film school—and direct a movie, to me is awesome. You can have a visualization of how a movie should be, but the reality is that filmmaking is about making decisions and compromise and knowing when to say yes and knowing when to say no. That just comes through experience and miles under your belt. I think that's why so many of these inexperienced filmmakers get into trouble . . . they rely on the people around them, and the people around them don't always have the answers because they're used to servicing more experienced directors.

The Australian directors of your generation—Bruce Beresford, George Miller, Phillip Noyce, etc.—have accomplished an extraordinary degree of success in the United States. Why do you think that happened?

I think we all grew up making films and television commercials and television series on very, very limited budgets, and were very disciplined about the amount of film we were able to shoot and the number of set-ups we had to achieve in a day and the number of pages we had to shoot. We learned to do it economically and efficiently—we had to—and when we got a chance to direct pictures in America, we leapt at it and proved that we could do the job without too much drama.

When you were growing up in Australia and getting interested in film, what were the movies and filmmakers that inspired you?

I've loved the movies all my life, but I never knew that I was going to have a career in film until quite late. Television came when I was a young boy at school in 1956, and that was the year of the Olympic games in Melbourne. This whole new world lit up before my eyes, and it seemed like what I wanted to be a part of. I wanted to be a television director, doing variety shows, outside broadcasts and stuff like that. And I achieved that fairly early in my career.

Then I started working part-time in theatre to gain more knowledge of working with actors, and I decided that film was the way to go. But as a kid growing up, there were Saturday matinees at the Rose Bay Winter Garden, a suburban theatre in Sydney, always a great serial with a cliffhanger ending to start things off, then a "B" picture and an "A" picture. I had fairly eclectic tastes, I guess. But the first film that really had an enormous impact on me was LAWRENCE OF ARABIA. I was about 18 years old when I saw it, and absolutely bowled over. It was just so far ahead of anything I'd ever seen before. And to this day, David Lean is the filmmaker I most admire. He made such an extraordinary range of films.

You've made several films in that epic mode, including THE LIGHTHORSE-MEN, your YOUNG INDIANA JONES episodes and LONESOME DOVE, which really brought you great attention in the States.

I knew I was the perfect person for LONESOME DOVE, but I had to prove that. I had just finished THE LIGHTHORSEMEN as a feature, and they needed somebody who could handle a high-powered cast, big landscapes and story, on a TV schedule. It was like a perfect marriage for me, because I was doing a genre that I loved, and I think I do have a good eye for landscapes. Although I grew up in the city, I spent half my life in the Australian bush on horseback.

> "What makes a successful film is script, story and character, always. The script is where it starts and finishes, and it doesn't matter how technically fine it is. If you don't have a good script and story, you don't have anything. "
> —Simon Wincer

You still maintain a ranch in the Australian countryside, which reminds me of some of the great American western filmmakers, who were cowboys themselves.

When John Ford went out to make a western, he would camp out there on location. That's the sort of filmmaking that I love. One of the happiest working experiences of my life was on the YOUNG INDIANA JONES series, when we lived under canvas for seven weeks in Kenya. It was very remote, five hours from the closest major town. It was just wonderful to be there making a movie in the most exotic location, and to eat, breathe and sleep nothing else but making a movie in a great place. You can't help but be influenced by everything that's going on around you.

Your historical films tend to be both very realistic and romantic at the same time.

LONESOME DOVE was a good deal dustier and sweatier than the others. I'm a stickler for detail, but only to the point where it doesn't interfere with the drama. If a hat's too big for an actor and it looks like

it's wearing *him*, then I would rather go with a smaller hat that's not necessarily historically correct.

Let's talk about FREE WILLY for a bit. It was a bonafide sleeper smash that sort of came out of nowhere. But did you know during production what kind of potential it had?

During production, everyone at Warners tended to think of FREE WILLY as the "little" kid and whale movie, and because it was being produced by the Donners and ran very smoothly, they tended to leave us alone. It wasn't until my first cut preview that the studio realized what we had— we scored higher than any previous Warner Bros. movie, including BATMAN and the LETHAL WEAPON films. From the second day of the shoot, Nick Brown, the film's editor, kept nagging me that we really had something special, this kid and this whale. His enthusiasm was boundless. And as I started looking at the cut material early on, I realized that it was indeed very special. I did have confidence, but I never quite thought that it would be as successful as it turned out to be. The first time I saw the rough cut, which was 154 minutes long, we were all absolutely flabbergasted. I looked across at Nick and Basil Poledouris, the film's composer, and we all had tears running down our cheeks. It's always exciting when that happens because the first cut is usually so depressing. It's often the worst moment in a director's life when he sits down to look at the first cut and can only see the problems.

How would you characterize your work with actors? Do you like to give them a lot of room?

I see myself as a conductor, if you will. Usually, a week or two before we start shooting, I just like to sit in a room and talk—first individually and then as a group—so that we're all of a like mind about characterization and the tone of the movie. Then I like to give the actors a lot of freedom in terms of both movement and blocking, so that it's very loose. We sort of workshop the blocking, and obviously with action it has to be more specific, but I'm always open to suggestions. But actors ultimately understand character even more than the director. And as long as they're not running off the rails, I think it's nice to give them as much freedom and flexibility as possible within the overall framework that you have to set for them.

You're not exactly Hitchcockian in that approach.

To me, the director is the audience. And if the actor's doing something that you think the audience isn't going to respond to, then I tend to suggest something here and there. But I tend to arrive at everything through quite a lot of rehearsal, particularly on the set before you shoot the scene. You can rehearse before you start, but it's never the same until people arrive in costume on the set.

Technically, you seem to favor the anamorphic format, which seems to suit not only the subject matter of your films, but your compositional eye as well.

I do like shooting anamorphic. It's great for actors because they've got a lot more freedom within the frame. You can have five actors in a very tight shot in an anamorphic frame, and when you're doing something for television, they're all sort of standing on each other's toes.

Are there any films you would make differently if you shot them today ... and are there some films you wish you hadn't made at all?

Oh no ... they're all part of your life and you love them for one reason or another. I suppose the film that I have the most regrets about is HARLEY DAVIDSON AND THE MARLBORO MAN, yet it keeps popping up as one of those movies that people enjoy as a guilty pleasure.

Simon Wincer directs Lori Petty on the set of FREE WILLY

B y the time this interview appears, you will already have finished shooting a Vietnam-set film—OPERATION DUMBO DROP—in the wilds of Northern Thailand. What attracted you to the project?

First and foremost, it's just a wonderful story about a group of men who keep a promise. It's about two men in particular—one who wants to leave a positive mark behind before he leaves the country—and the other guy who is sent in to replace him. This group doesn't necessarily start out by sharing the same philosophy, but by the end they're all united in their cause, and put their lives on the line to do it. OPERATION DUMBO DROP is a really joyous movie, and if I do it right, it will be a great adventure, fun and very emotional.

It sort of sounds like the perfect Simon Wincer movie.

Yeah, because there's an elephant in it, right? Well, okay. Action, humor, an exotic location,

... and a large mammal.

★ ★ ★

ROBERT WISE

SINCE HIS FIRST DIRECTORIAL EFFORT—Val Lewton's chilling 1944 production of THE CURSE OF THE CAT PEOPLE—the name "Robert Wise" has been synonymous with films that entertain and enlighten, of all genres and sizes. It's been a courageous career, filled not with one landmark, but several. The Indiana native made his way to Hollywood in 1933, winding up in RKO's editing department, working his way up to cutter on such notable films as THE HUNCH-BACK OF NOTRE DAME (1939) and projects of no less import than Orson Welles' CITIZEN KANE and MAGNIFICENT AMBERSONS. Given his first shot at directing by Lewton, Hollywood's resident master of atmospheric terror, Wise proceeded to learn his art by directing eight more features for RKO during the '40s. These included another well-received Lewton production, THE BODY SNATCHER; the *noir* western BLOOD ON THE MOON; and the gritty and powerful THE SET-UP, considered by most boxing film fans to be the best of its kind. Early on, Wise established a strong streak of humanity in his work that informed every genre he attempted—which was virtually every genre invented for the cinema.

Throughout the 1950s, Wise worked for several major studios on war films (THE DESERT RATS; DESTINATION GOBI; RUN SILENT, RUN DEEP), westerns (TWO FLAGS WEST; TRIBUTE TO A BAD MAN), melodramas (THREE SECRETS; THE HOUSE ON TELEGRAPH HILL; THE CAPTIVE CITY; EXECUTIVE SUITE; UNTIL THEY SAIL), science fiction (the undisputed classic THE DAY THE EARTH STOOD STILL), costume spectacle (HELEN OF TROY), boxing biopic (SOMEBODY UP THERE LIKES ME), romantic comedy (SOMETHING FOR THE BIRDS; THIS COULD BE THE NIGHT), suspense (ODDS AGAINST TOMORROW) and topical drama (I WANT TO LIVE!), which brought Wise his first Oscar nomination.

But it was really WEST SIDE STORY that lifted Wise to true directing superstardom at the dawn of the '60s, a rich decade for the filmmaker which was to see him at the helm of several extraordinary films, both large and small. Following the gigantic success of WEST SIDE STORY—for which Wise won Oscars as Best Director and as the Best Picture producer—with the more intimate TWO FOR THE SEESAW and THE HAUNTING, Wise then filmed THE SOUND OF MUSIC, won his third and fourth Academy Awards for directing and Best Picture producer, and created a timeless family classic.

For those who feared that Wise had shucked off the more serious examinations of the human condition for which he was known, THE SAND PEBBLES (1966) was a return to form, albeit on a massive scale. One of the bravest American films of its time, Wise dared to use three hours of a big studio, roadshow picture to tell a relentlessly downbeat story of Jake Holman (Steve McQueen in his best performance), a doomed sailor who becomes an existential victim of foolhardy U.S. military intervention in 1920s China. For contemporary audiences, the parallels to a more recent foolhardy U.S. military intervention in Asia were unmistakable. The film, now available on laserdisc in an uncut, letterboxed format, continues to gain in reputation.

Wise's next film, also on a grand scale, was 1968's STAR!, toplining Julie Andrews as British musical star Gertrude Lawrence. A failure in its day, the film's stature has also been revived due to its recently restored video and laserdisc release. Wise's work since then has included the compelling science "fact" thriller THE ANDROMEDA STRAIN (1971) and the first STAR TREK feature, a huge success in 1979.

At the time of this conversation with Wise, the great filmmaker had just suffered the disappointment of losing financing on what was intended to be his first film in more than five years, because of a budget which was in its entirety less than an American movie star's per-film salary.

It's a sad commentary . . . but Robert Wise has no intentions of hanging up his spikes and retiring his number. After all, he's only directed 39 features, and there are several more good ones yet to be made . . .

MICHAEL SINGER: I read a couple of weeks ago that you've been in some stage of preparation for another film. Is this a project you want to talk about at this point?
ROBERT WISE: Yes, I can talk about it. Like so many of us, we have projects that sometimes take a long time to get off the ground. I've had an option on a book called AND MILES TO GO, which was first published in 1963 or '64, and then republished in the early '80s. I've had an option for about five years, and last fall, I got a French company interested in financing the picture. They read the treatment and liked the idea. I first met with them in Paris in October '93, after I'd been encamped in Belgium at a film festival. Two months later, I flew back to Paris with a screenwriter, Carmen Culver. The story is centered around a very famous Polish Arabian stallion that was born in a stud farm outside of Warsaw just before the start of World War II, and tells his whole story during the entire war. It's a true story about a real horse and the interesting people involved with him.

Anyway, we had a very good meeting and went on to Warsaw for research. The writer went about her work, writing a first and then second draft script, and I returned to Poland and selected a cinematographer,

production designer, costume designer, assistant director. I met with actors in Poland who could work in English, also did some casting here in Los Angeles. Everything was going fine until the latter part of April '94, when we turned in the budget. And then everything stopped. It was about $3 million more than they anticipated, although interestingly enough, all along the line, nobody from the French company had ever asked me how much I thought the film was going to cost. I didn't get myself too concerned about the budget, because they didn't seem to be concerned. So now everything's on hold, and it looks like they're not going to go ahead with it, so we're trying to set up the project someplace else.

It seems that in this day and age, $3 million sounds like a diminutive amount of money to prevent a film from being made.
Yes, this was not a big budget, only $11 million and a half or so. But they're used to $7 or 8 million, I guess. Anyway, we have reasonable hope and it's already in the hands of a German producer who's expressed a lot of interest in the project. And my associate in Paris says that two or three other sources in France may be interested, so it's very possible that we'll get it in turnaround

and get it set up someplace else. But in the meantime, we've obviously had to postpone the start. I was planning on . . . I should be in Poland right now. We'd be just a week ahead of shooting, actually. We were supposed to start on the 16th of August.

This must be a great frustration to you.
It is.

It's rather amazing to consider the difficulties you've had in mounting this project with your incredible background, but these days, the American industry seems to think that film history began with JAWS. Have you been frustrated by this as well?
Well, I suppose I've been frustrated by that to a certain extent, because I haven't been doing any films in recent years. And that would seem to be an indication that the studio executives now—so many of them younger people—really don't know my track record. A lot of them think I've been in the business too long now, and there can't be much juice left. And so, yes, I've been pretty conscious of that, you bet—and a victim of it, in some sense.

Ageism has become a big problem in Hollywood.
Sure. It's all over town, and not just with directors. It's with writers, who have an awful time. I understand that it got so bad with writers, that there seemed to be some kind of onus against any writer over 35 years old, and they set up a special committee at the Writers Guild to look into this whole thing. What they've been able to do about it, I don't know.

It certainly infuriates me, because for ,e your films were seminal experiences that started to teach me what a film director really was, and what they do.
Well, I'm glad that my films brought something to you—made you start thinking about films, how they get made, what goes into getting them up on screen. You know, most people don't realize all the planning, the work, the preparation, above and beyond the script, that goes into making a film, and that's absolutely as it should be . . . it should look like it's just *happening* up there on screen. People shouldn't be thinking about how it got there, how you were able to manage it. It should all be seamless and together, and all the work and sweat and strain and effort that we put into making it should never show. Hopefully, this moving image up there that captures you, gets you involved . . . that's all it should be.

Your work has never had a showboating quality to it, with technique dominating substance. To some degree, we never really emerged from the period when auteurist critics like Andrew Sarris were dumping great craftsmen like yourself, Lewis Milestone

and William Wyler into negative categories. Do you have an opinion on this?
Well, I do have an opinion, and I feel very strongly that those of us who were not necessarily "auteurs" were rather badly treated. And I don't think this was a reflection of the general movie-going public. So, it seems to me that some of those critics were a bit out of step with the vast viewing public who seemed to relate more to the kind of work that we were doing.

When I was young and fell in love with movies, the name "Robert Wise" was more a symbol than something flesh-and-blood. It was an emblem for movies that were larger-than-life, yet entirely human. And all I knew was that I was going to have one hell of a great time at the movies . . . and learn something to boot.

What you've just said that's important to me is "learn something to boot." Because I've been asked many times what the **steps** are to my taking on a given project, and I have to start off by saying that whether it will be based on an original screenplay, book, play or short story . . . how does it grab me as a reader? Does it catch me up? Because I'm the audience as I read it, and it has to be something that involves me with story and plot. That's primary, the initial reaction that gets me involved.

Next, as I think about it, what does it have to say about man and his world? But it must be said in terms of story, plot and character. It must not be said by getting on the soapbox. The message should flow from the story, the characters and the plot. My one prime exception to that, of course, was THE DAY THE EARTH STOOD STILL, in which the conclusion *was* the message.

The next step, of course, is whether the story is cinematic. Is it a story that can be put on the screen? And the last step is that I have to start thinking about what the cost would be, because that's the first thing that's going to be asked by the front office.

One of your strongest films, I think, was THE SAND PEBBLES, which packed a very powerful message within its narrative. It was an expensive roadshow picture which nonetheless was essentially a downbeat story about American military intervention in Asia, and you actually made it during . . .
The Vietnam War. I had always been fascinated by Mainland China, which was the setting of Richard McKenna's book. I had never been there, and couldn't go there even when I did the film. At that time, we weren't even allowed to visit China. I had to do all my research on the story from newsreels, books, pictures and stories. But when I first read the book, I thought to myself that it seemed time for the American public to

be reminded that the phrase, "Yankee, Go Home!" didn't start just in World War II. It had been happening throughout the 20th Century, when we were showing off our military might here and there. And in the case of THE SAND PEBBLES, other countries besides the United States had gunboats patrolling the Yangtze.

At the time I got the project underway, Vietnam was still on the back burner, and my then wife and I decided to take some time off after shooting THE HAUNT-

Robert Wise directs. Photo courtesy Robert Wise

ING in London and take a three-month trip around the world. This was 1963. We went to Saigon—because I knew I was going to do THE SAND PEBBLES and wanted to see if there were any possible locations there. And I'll never forget that when we landed in Saigon, there was just row after row of American Air Force planes at the airport. Saigon was filled with American soldiers, what we then called "advisers"—about 10,000 of them—and we could see the foreshadow of what was to come. By the time THE SAND PEBBLES got made and was released, the war in Vietnam was in full swing and people thought that Vietnam was what we had in mind for the film all along. It wasn't, but it turned out to be quite prophetic in terms of what was happening once again in Asia.

I understand that the shoot was quite a logistical nightmare in Taiwan and Hong Kong.

The places we could shoot were so limited. Even getting the okay to shoot in Taiwan took a long time. We had all kinds of terrible weather problems, winds that would switch all the time. Every day we would have five or six different call sheets, depending on the weather, wind direction and river currents. And several times during the shoot, the weather would change so fast that I'd have to get all my extras—perhaps a thousand of them—changed from summer to winter

clothes because we had to change sequences. It was in every way the most difficult film I've done so far. It was a monster fighting us every minute, and all of us who were on it all the way through thought that it didn't matter if it was successful in theatres or with audiences . . . it was just a real triumph to get it done and up on the screen.

As a matter of fact, when Francis Coppola was over in the Philippines shooting APOCALYPSE NOW, I guess he heard about some of the problems we had on THE SAND PEBBLES, because his office called and asked if we could possibly get a 16mm print over to him in the jungle so he could show it to the crew. I guess he said "Hey guys, let's hang in there and get it done . . . *they* did!"

You mentioned THE HAUNTING just before. To me, it's still the most innovative and frightening horror movie ever made. But I've recently read that someone plans to remake it, which I find even more frightening.

Me too. I've had so many people tell me over the years that THE HAUNTING was the scariest picture they'd ever seen, because it didn't really *show* anything, and they want to know how I did it. Well, it all comes from Val Lewton and the power of suggestion. The greatest fear that people have is fear of the unknown.

Of course, you directed your first two pictures for Val Lewton at RKO in the early 1940s. What about WEST SIDE STORY? That changed film musicals forever.

WEST SIDE STORY was a challenge, of course. It was extraordinary on stage. I don't know of any stage musical that told so much of its story through dance. Not just song, but dance. Jerry Robbins' choreography was revolutionary on the stage, and we had to figure out how to adapt it for the screen, and even improve on it if possible. The two mediums are different . . . that's the challenge. With the stage, you have the proscenium arch, so you're not quite into reality. You're removed from reality, so actors can go out of dialogue into song, or out of dialogue into dance without the audience feeling a little tinge of embarrassment. The screen is a very real medium, and it doesn't take kindly to stylizations unless it's an utter fantasy, like THE WIZARD OF OZ.

The challenges that Robbins and myself and our associates had was how to take all the stylized aspects of WEST SIDE STORY and put them against the most authentic backgrounds. I was the one who insisted that we had to go to New York for all the daytime scenes. We had to shoot them on real city streets. The studio wanted me to see if we could find something in Los Angeles, but I said "No way." Once we're through the daytime scenes, the rest of it's all sunset and night, where we could do effect lighting on stages, that's alright. And I remember Jerry Robbins saying to me,

"Bob, I agree with you about going to New York, but boy, you've given me the biggest challenge in the world . . . to take my most stylized dancing, which is in the prologue, and put against real backgrounds. We knew we had to deliver New York to start with, and I didn't want to do that same opening shot across the river with the bridge and the skyline. So I started thinking, and wondered what New York would look like from *straight down*! And that ended up as the very opening of the film, with a real New York that even New Yorkers hadn't seen, a bit abstract. That was the genesis of that opening in WEST SIDE STORY.

And thereby, you pretty much invented MTV.

[*laughs*] I suppose so. Forgive me.

But immediately after WEST SIDE STORY, which was a giant roadshow film that was a huge hit and won 10 Academy Awards, you made two intimate pictures, TWO FOR THE SEESAW and THE HAUNTING, rather than another epic. Why?

Well, I did WEST SIDE STORY, so I thought, fine, I've done my musical. So I went on about my business making other films. TWO FOR THE SEESAW came to me prepackaged in a sense by The Mirisch Company. They had already signed Bob Mitchum and Shirley MacLaine, and then I liked the script by Isobel Lennart, whom I'd worked with before.

I had my hands on THE HAUNTING for quite awhile. That's one I actually was very instrumental in getting. So many of my films have come to me from producers and studios, sometimes with a first draft script already done. But this one I found. I was at Goldwyn Studios doing post-production work on WEST SIDE STORY and I read a review of Shirley Jackson's novel *The Haunting of Hill House* in *Time Magazine*. I looked it up and found out that it hadn't been picked up by any of the majors, so I read it, loved it, and thought that there was a hell of a picture in it. In a way, making THE HAUNTING was kind of a tribute to Lewton. Finally, we took it to MGM. But they only wanted to put $1 million into the film, and the best budget I could get out of Culver City was one million and four, and they didn't want to go ahead. But I was going over to London about that time for a command performance of WEST SIDE STORY, and someone said, "Hey, you know, MGM has a nice little

studio over in England at Borehamwood . . . maybe they'd be able to get you a better price on this. So I gave the script to them in London, and they came back with a budget of one million and fifty thousand, and the studio went for it. That's how I happened to make THE HAUNTING in England, even though it has a New England backdrop.

Personally, THE HAUNTING is one of my favorites. I've done 39 pictures and I have about a dozen favorites, but THE HAUNTING is always one of them. I think it's one of my very best directorial jobs. I'm very proud of what I got up on the screen.

> "You know, most people don't realize all the planning, the work, the preparation, above and beyond the script, that goes into making a film, and that's absolutely as it should be . . . it should look like it's just *happening* up there on screen."—Robert Wise

You did several historical films, but really only one costume epic—HELEN OF TROY.

Yeah, that was my first and last venture into spectacle. People have asked me many times what my favorite genre is. I don't have a favorite, but I have two unfavorites: westerns and spectacles. I haven't made a western since the mid-'50s, because they were being done to death as both movies and TV series. And I found out that the spectacle wasn't a genre that I enjoyed when I shot HELEN OF TROY all over Italy.

But a lot of people *did* enjoy HELEN OF TROY. I understand that the film had a big impact on Oliver Stone when he saw it as a youngster.

[*laughs*] Yes. He once approached me at a Directors Guild function and told me that. I was quite flattered.

I've also heard that the film is, unfortunately, in a deteriorated condition and in dire need of restoration.

That's true. And even though I didn't exactly enjoy making it, I would be very pleased if HELEN OF TROY could be restored . . . but such an expensive task needs some sponsorship.

Let's talk a little about your background, if we may. You began working at RKO in 1933 as a messenger?

A film carrier, really. I was carrying prints of films to the projection rooms for executive screenings, checking prints, patching leader and stuff like that.

Had you been attracted to editing, or was it something you just fell into?

No. I dropped out of college after one year at Franklin College near Indianapolis. It was the height of the Depression. I couldn't go back the second year. I had an older brother who was working at RKO, in the accounting department, and my family told me to go Los Angeles to join my brother, get a job and earn a decent living. It was just that basic . . . I had to work. Had I been able to go on in college, I wanted to be a journalist.

So in July of '33, my brother David got me an appointment with Tommy Little, head of the property department. And fortunately for me, he didn't need anybody right then. So another week went by, and he got me an appointment with Jimmy Wilkinson, head of the film editing department, and he said he could use another kid—eager, a strong back and willing to work hard—in the shipping room. So that was my break. Then I had to work my way up through all the aspects of editing and finally into directing.

You put in more than a few 24 hour days, I understand.
Yeah, a lot. Particularly in sound effects editing.

I can't let this conversation go by without asking you at least one question about CITIZEN KANE, although by now it's probably the most chronicled film in history.
I would imagine so.

But when you were editing the film, you had to be aware of just how extraordinary it was.
I've been asked many times if those of us working on KANE realized at the time that we were making something that would be thought of 50 years later as perhaps the greatest picture ever made, and I have to say no, none of us did. I don't even think that Orson—who had a pretty good size ego—felt that. But you couldn't look at those dailies coming in every day and not realize you were getting something quite extraordinary. It was just thrilling. We couldn't wait to see the dailies every day. They were so different, so unusual, so strong, so dynamic. Full of marvelous performances, from people we didn't know, because in fact none of those actors had been on the screen except in bit parts. The camerawork, the setups, the angles, the dynamics . . . we knew it was extraordinary, but we didn't anticipate the fame down through the years.

You've worked with a lot of good cinematographers. Did you have a personal favorite to collaborate with?
No. Many directors like to work with the same DP, but I never felt that strongly. I don't think there's any DP that I worked with on more than two films. Bob Surtees did two of mine, and Dick Kline did two, I think. I like to cast my cinematographer for the given project and the cinematic style that I feel is right for it. And although they're all very professionally capable, some are stronger for one kind of film than the other. For instance, Curly (Lionel) Linden did I WANT TO LIVE

for me. I wanted a very documentary, realistic, grainy look in black and white, and I didn't know Curly, but I'd seen some of his work at Paramount. But I would never have used Curly for THE SOUND OF MUSIC because that was not his forte. I wanted somebody to give it a softer, more romantic look, and that was Ted McCord.

Your visual style always adjusted to the material.
Yes.

. . . Rather than the other way around.
I guess that's why esoteric critics have accused me of not having a style. But I've done so many genres, and I've tried to address each project in the cinematic terms that I think are appropriate to each.

Rather than ask another question, I wonder if you have anything to say to the American film industry at this point in time?
Well, the only thing I would say is that I think this industry should—if it can keep the box office coming in—try and do fewer action pieces with gratuitous violence. I would hope that we would tend to have fewer and fewer of those and more adult, mature, dramatic stories that don't rely on effects, but instead rely on human interaction. That would be my hope.

I'd like to point out, though, that you've never shied away from violence on-screen. I think in particular of THE SET-UP and THE SAND PEBBLES. However, your intent was to show the impact of such violence on the human body and spirit.
Right! I think humanity has to come through strongly in all films . . . no matter *what* the genre is.

★ ★ ★

FILM DIRECTORS

INDEX OF FILM DIRECTORS
DGA

Note: This is not an index of every director, only those listed in this directory who are members of the Directors Guild of America. This list is meant as a quick *name-only* reference when searching for a director or director's name. Full credits follow in the Listing Section.

* = denotes Directors Guild of America

A

Paul Aaron*
Robert J. Abel*
Jim Abrahams*
Edward Abroms*
David Acomba*
Catlin Adams*
Anita W. Addison*
Lou Adler*
Alan Alda*
Adell Aldrich*
Jason Alexander*
Corey Allen*
Debbie Allen*
Lewis Allen*
Woody Allen*
Paul Almond*
John A. Alonzo*
Robert Altman*
Joe Alves*
Rod Amateau*
Jon Amiel*
Franco Amurri*
Michael Anderson*
Ken Annakin*
Jean-Jacques Annaud*
David Anspaugh*
Greg Antonacci*
Lou Antonio*
Michael Apted*
Alfonso Arau*
Alan Arkin*
Allan Arkush*
George Armitage*
Gillian Armstrong*
Vic Armstrong*
Gwen Arner*
Frank Arnold *
Newt Arnold*
Karen Arthur*
William Asher*
Christopher Ashley*
David Ashwell*
John Astin*
Richard Attenborough*
Daniel Attias*
Ray Austin*
Hy Averback*
Rick Avery*
John G. Avildsen*
Meiert Avis*
Jon Avnet*

Dan Aykroyd*
Mario Azzopardi*

B

Hector Babenco*
John Badham*
Reza Badiyi*
Max Baer, Jr.*
Fax Bahr*
Chuck Bail*
John Bailey*
Graham Baker*
Kurt Baker*
Ralph Bakshi*
Bob Balaban*
Peter Baldwin*
Carroll Ballard*
Anne Bancroft*
Jack Baran*
Norberto Barba*
Richard L. Bare*
Clive Barker*
Neema Barnette*
Don Barnhart*
Allen Baron*
Bruno Barreto*
Chuck Barris*
Steve Barron*
Paul Bartel*
William S. Bartman*
Hal Barwood*
Fred Barzyk*
Richard Baskin*
Saul Bass*
Kent Bateman*
Craig R. Baxley*
David Beaird*
Robert B. Bean*
Chris Bearde*
Warren Beatty*
Gabrielle Beaumont*
Harold Becker*
Terry Bedford*
Greg Beeman*
Martin Bell*
Earl Bellamy*
Donald Bellisario*
Jerry Belson*
Jack Bender*
Richard Benjamin*
Richard C. Bennett*
Robby Benson*
Robert Benton*

Bruce Beresford*
Rick Berger*
Andrew Bergman*
David Berlatsky*
Adam Bernstein*
Armyan Bernstein*
Walter Bernstein*
John Berry*
Bernardo Bertolucci*
Gill Bettman*
Jonathan Betuel*
Radha Bharadwaj*
Edward Bianchi*
Kathryn Bigelow*
Tony Bill*
Bruce Bilson*
Danny Bilson*
John Binder*
Mike Binder*
Steve Binder*
Mack Bing*
Patricia Birch*
Noel Black*
Michael Blakemore*
Ken Blancato*
William Peter Blatty*
Corey Blechman*
Jeff Bleckner*
Bruce Block*
Jeffrey Bloom*
Jeff Blyth*
Hart Bochner*
Budd Boetticher*
Paul Bogart*
Peter Bogdanovich*
Clifford Bole*
Joseph Bologna*
Craig Bolotin*
Ben Bolt*
Gregory J. Bonann*
Timothy Bond*
Peter Bonerz*
John Boorman*
H. Gordon Boos*
Michael Bortman*
Lisa Bourgoujian*
Serge Bourguignon*
George Bowers*
Chuck Bowman*
Rob Bowman*
Kenneth Bowser*
Gianni Bozzacchi*
Robert (Bob) Bralver*
Marco Brambilla*
Bill Brame*
Kenneth Branagh*

Joshua Brand*
Larry Brand*
Marlon Brando*
Charles Braverman*
Martin Brest*
Marshall Brickman*
Paul Brickman*
Alan Bridges*
Beau Bridges*
Burt Brinckerhoff*
Merrill Brockway*
Kevin Brodie*
Albert Brooks*
Bob Brooks*
James L. Brooks*
Joseph Brooks*
Mel Brooks*
Barry Brown*
Kirk Browning*
Colin Bucksey*
Allan Burns*
Geoff Burrowes*
James Burrows*
Tim Burton*
John A. Bushelman*
Robert Butler*
Zane Buzby*
John Byrum*

C

James Caan*
Michael Caffey*
Christopher Cain*
James Cameron*
Donald Cammell*
Joe Camp*
Roy Campanella Ii*
Michael Campus*
Dyan Cannon*
Lamar Card*
John (Bud) Cardos*
Topper Carew*
Lewis John Carlino*
Charles Robert Carner*
Glenn Gordon Caron*
John Carpenter*
Terry Carr*
David Carradine*
David Carson*
Thomas Carter*
Steve Carver*
Ron Casden*
Nick Castle*

Hoite Caston*
Gilbert Cates*
Joseph Cates*
Michael Caton-Jones*
James Cellan-Jones*
Everett Chambers*
Gregg Champion*
Matthew Chapman*
Michael Chapman*
David Chase*
Jeremiah Chechik*
Douglas Cheek*
Robert Chenault*
John Cherry*
Stanley Z. Cherry*
Lionel Chetwynd*
Colin Chilvers*
Stephen Chiodo*
Marvin J. Chomsky*
Thomas Chong*
Joyce Chopra*
Roger Christian*
Byron Chudnow*
Michael Cimino*
Bob Clark*
James B. Clark*
Matt Clark*
Malcolm Clarke*
William F. Claxton*
Dick Clement*
Graeme Clifford*
Larry Cohen*
Rob Cohen*
Steve Cohen*
John David Coles*
Richard A. Colla*
Robert Collins*
Chris Columbus*
Richard Compton*
William Condon*
Kevin Connor*
Robert Conrad*
James A. Contner*
James L. Conway*
Fielder Cook*
Martha Coolidge*
Hal Cooper*
Jackie Cooper*
Stuart Cooper*
Francis Ford Coppola*
Bill Corcoran*
Nicholas Corea*
John Cornell*
Eugene Corr*
Charles Correll*
Richard Correll*
William H. (Bill) Cosby, Jr.*
Don Coscarelli*
John Cosgrove*
George Pan Cosmatos*
Kevin Costner*
Manny Coto*
Jack Couffer*
Jerome Courtland*
Nell Cox*
William Crain*
Peter Crane*
Wes Craven*

Lol Creme*
Kevin G. Cremin*
Richard Crenna*
Michael Crichton*
Cameron Crowe*
Christopher Crowe*
Billy Crystal*
Alfonso Cuaron*
Robert Culp*
Sean S. Cunningham*
William Curran*
Dan Curtis*

D

Bob Dahlin*
Robert Dalva*
Mel Damski*
Rod Daniel*
Herbert Danska*
Joe Dante*
Philip D'antoni*
Richard Danus*
Frank Darabont*
Joan Darling*
James Darren*
Jules Dassin*
Boaz Davidson*
Gordon Davidson*
Martin Davidson*
Andrew Davis*
Gary Davis*
Ernest Day*
Robert Day*
Lyman Dayton*
William Dear*
Jan De Bont*
Frederick De Cordova*
Frank De Felitta*
Philip Deguere*
Donna Deitch*
Steve Dejarnatt*
Ate De Jong*
Fred Dekker*
Bill D'Elia*
Francis DElia*
Rudy Deluca*
Dom De Luise*
Bob Demchuk*
Johanna Demetrakas*
Jonathan Demme*
Ted Demme*
Robert De Niro*
Brian Dennehy*
Pen Densham*
Brian De Palma*
Frank De Palma*
John Derek*
Caleb Deschanel*
Louis D'Esposito*
Andre De Toth*
Howard Deutch*
Tom Desimone*
Danny Devito*
David Devries*
Maury Dexter*

Ernest R. Dickerson*
Mario Di Leo*
Michael Dinner*
Vincent Dipersio*
Mark Disalle*
Ivan Dixon*
Edward Dmytryk*
Frank Q. Dobbs*
Kevin James Dobson*
Roger Donaldson*
Stanley Donen*
Walter Doniger*
Tom Donnelly*
Clive Donner*
Richard Donner*
Mary Agnes Donoghue*
Martin Donovan*
Tom Donovan*
Robert Dornhelm*
Kirk Douglas*
Peter Douglas*
Robert Downey*
Stan Dragoti*
James R. (Jim) Drake*
Charles S. Dubin*
Jay Dubin*
Roger Duchowny*
Dennis Dugan*
Michael Dugan*
John Duigan*
Bill Duke*
Daryl Duke*
Duwayne Dunham*
Rudy Durand*

E

Clint Eastwood*
Thom Eberhardt*
Uli Edel*
Blake Edwards*
Vincent Edwards*
Jan Egleson*
Rafael Eisenman*
Jan Eliasberg*
Lawrence (Larry) Elikann*
Lang Elliott*
Roland Emmerich*
David Engelbach*
George Englund*
Robert Englund*
Nora Ephron*
John Erman*
Emilio Estevez*
Corey Michael Eubanks*
Bruce A. Evans*
David Mickey Evans*

F

Peter Faiman*
Ferdinand Fairfax*
Harry Falk*
Jamaa Fanaka*

James Fargo*
Mike Farrell*
Linda Feferman*
Dennis Feldman*
Kerry Feltham*
Georg J. Fenady*
Abel Ferrara*
Pablo Ferro*
Mike Figgis*
Kenneth Fink*
Ken Finkleman*
Sam Firstenberg*
Bill Fishman*
Jack Fisk*
Gary Fleder*
Richard Fleischer*
Andrew Fleming*
Theodore J. Flicker*
John Florea*
John Flynn*
James Foley*
Peter Fonda*
Bryan Forbes*
Stephen H. Foreman*
Milos Forman*
Bill Forsyth*
John W. Fortenberry*
Robert Fowler*
William A. Fraker*
David Frankel*
John Frankenheimer*
Carl Franklin*
Howard Franklin*
Jeff Franklin*
Richard Franklin*
James Frawley*
Stephen Frears*
Herb Freed*
Jerrold Freedman*
Robert Freedman*
Joan Freeman*
Michael Fresco*
Rick Friedberg*
Bud Friedgen*
William Friedkin*
Kim Friedman*
Richard Friedman*
Seymour Friedman*
Bill Froelich*
Mark Frost*
E. Max Frye*
Samuel Fuller*
Allen Funt*
Sidney J. Furie*

G

George Gage*
Claude Gagnon*
Timothy Galfas*
George Gallo*
Herb Gardner*
Jack Garfein*
Lila Garrett*
Mick Garris*
Jerome Gary*

Costa-Gavras*
Ben Gazzara*
Fred Gerber*
Brian Gibson*
Mel Gibson*
Brian Gilbert*
Lewis Gilbert*
David Giler*
Stuart Gillard*
Terry Gilliam*
Vern Gillum*
Frank D. Gilroy*
Robert Ginty*
Bob Giraldi*
Paul Michael Glaser*
Lesli Linka Glatter*
John Glen*
Peter Glenville*
Arne Glimcher*
Gary Goddard*
Menahem Golan*
Jack Gold*
Dan Goldberg*
Gary David Goldberg*
Mark Goldblatt*
Allan Goldstein*
Amy Goldstein*
Scott Goldstein*
James Goldstone*
Steve Gomer*
Nick Gomez*
Bert I. Gordon*
Bryan Gordon*
Keith Gordon*
Berry Gordy*
Carl Gottlieb*
Lisa Gottlieb*
Michael Gottlieb*
Heywood Gould*
William A. Graham*
Brian Grant*
Lee Grant*
Alex Grasshoff*
Walter Grauman*
John Gray*
Janet Greek*
Bruce Seth Green*
David Green*
Guy Green*
Walon Green*
Richard Alan Greenberg*
David Greene*
Sparky Greene*
Bud Greenspan*
Robert Greenwald*
David Greenwalt*
Gary Grillo*
Ulu Grosbard*
Larry Gross*
David Grossman*
Robert Guenette*
James William Guercio*
Christopher Guest*
John Guillermin*
Nathaniel Gutman*
Andre Guttfreund*
Claudio Guzman*
Stephen Gyllenhaal*

H

Charles Haas*
Taylor Hackford*
Piers Haggard*
Paul Haggis*
Larry Hagman*
Stuart Hagmann*
Charles Haid*
Randa Haines*
William (Billy) Hale*
Jack Haley, Jr.*
Adrian Hall*
Peter Hall*
Daniel Haller*
Todd Hallowell*
Lasse Hallstrom*
Guy Hamilton*
Strathford Hamilton*
John Hancock*
Curtis Hanson*
Joseph C. Hanwright*
Shawn Hardin*
Joseph Hardy*
Rod Hardy*
Dean Hargrove*
Renny Harlin*
Robert Harmon*
Curtis Harrington*
Damian Harris*
Harry Harris*
James B. Harris*
John Harrison*
Bruce Hart*
David Hartwell*
Anthony Harvey*
Patrick Hasburgh*
Nick Havinga*
Jeffrey Hayden*
Sidney Hayers*
Helaine Head*
Robert Heath*
Amy Heckerling*
Rob Hedden*
David Heeley*
Richard T. Heffron*
Monte Hellman*
Gunnar Hellstrom*
David Hemmings*
Buck Henry*
Brian Henson*
Stephen Herek*
Rowdy Herrington*
Marshall Herskovitz*
John Herzfeld*
Jon Hess*
Gordon Hessler*
Fraser C. Heston*
Peter Hewitt*
Christopher Hibler*
George Roy Hill*
Jack Hill*
Walter Hill*
Arthur Hiller*
William Byron Hillman*
Rupert Hitzig*

Jack B. Hively*
Lyndall Hobbs*
Gregory Hoblit*
Victoria Hochberg*
Mike Hodges*
Gary Hoffman*
Michael Hoffman*
Tamar Simon Hoffs*
Jack Hofsiss*
Rod Holcomb*
Agnieszka Holland*
Savage Steve Holland*
Todd Holland*
Tom Holland*
Allan Holzman*
Harry Hook*
Kevin Hooks*
Lance Hool*
Tobe Hooper*
Stephen Hopkins*
Dennis Hopper*
Jeffrey Hornaday*
Peter Horton*
John Hough*
Ellen Hovde*
Karin Howard*
Ron Howard*
Reginald Hudlin*
Hugh Hudson*
Roy Huggins*
Albert Hughes*
Allen Hughes*
John Hughes*
Terry Hughes*
Peter Hunt*
Peter H. Hunt*
Tim Hunter*
Harry Hurwitz*
Waris Hussein*
Danny Huston*
Brian G. Hutton*
Willard Huyck*
Nessa Hyams*
Peter Hyams*

I

Leon Ichaso*
Eric Idle*
Kevin Inch*
Daniel Irom*
John Irvin*
Robert Iscove*
Neal Israel*
Peter Israelson*
James Ivory*

J

David S. Jackson*
Mick Jackson*
Ron Jacobs*
Just Jaeckin*

Stanley Jaffe*
Steven Charles Jaffe*
Henry Jaglom*
Jerry Jameson*
Annabel Jankel*
Charles Jarrott*
Norman Jewison*
Phil Joanou*
Roland Joffe*
Alan Johnson*
Kenneth Johnson*
Lamont Johnson*
Patrick Read Johnson*
Jim Johnston*
Joe Johnston*
David Jones*
Eugene S. Jones*
L.Q. Jones*
Glenn Jordan*
Neil Jordan*
Nathan Juran*

K

George Kaczender*
Jeremy Paul Kagan*
Jeff Kanew*
Marek Kanievska*
Garson Kanin*
Hal Kanter*
Ed Kaplan*
Jonathan Kaplan*
Michael Karbelnikoff*
Eric Karson*
Lawrence Kasdan*
Elliott Kastner*
Michael Katleman*
Milton Katselas*
Lee H. Katzin*
Jonathan Kaufer*
Philip Kaufman*
Robert Kaylor*
Elia Kazan*
Nicholas Kazan*
James Keach*
Diane Keaton*
David Keith*
Harvey Keith*
Asaad Kelada*
Frederick King Keller*
Barnet Kellman*
Gene Kelly*
Burt Kennedy*
Tom Kennedy*
Irvin Kershner*
Bruce Kessler*
Michael Kidd*
Beeban Kidron*
Fritz Kiersch*
Bruce Kimmel*
Rick King*
Zalman King*
Richard Kinon*
Robert Kirk*
Robert Klane*
Dennis Klein*

I
N
D
E
X

O
F

F
I
L
M

D
I
R
E
C
T
O
R
S

Allan Nicholls*
Mike Nichols*
Jack Nicholson*
Martin Nicholson*
John Nicolella*
Leonard Nimoy*
Nigel Noble*
Aaron Norris*
Bill L. Norton*
Noel Nosseck*
Geoffrey Nottage*
Thierry Notz*
Amram Nowak*
Cyrus Nowrasteh*
Phillip Noyce*
David Nutter*
Christian I. Nyby II*

O

Pat O'Connor*
Peter O'Fallon*
Terrence O'Hara*
Michael O'Herlihy*
Tom O'Horgan*
Joel Oliansky*
Ken Olin*
Edward James Olmos*
Robert Vincent O'Neil*
Stuart Orme*
James Orr*
Kenny Ortega*
Sam O'Steen*
Linda Otto*
Frank Oz*

P

Anthony Page*
Alan J. Pakula*
Rospo Pallenberg*
Conrad E. Palmisano*
Bruce Paltrow*
Norman Panama*
Dean Parisot*
Alan Parker*
Francine Parker*
Gordon Parks*
James D. Parriott*
Robert Parrish*
John Pasquin*
Ivan Passer*
Matthew Patrick*
John Patterson*
Willi Patterson*
David Paulsen*
Richard Pearce*
Stephen J. Peck*
Larry Peerce*
Melissa Jo Peltier*
Arthur Penn*
Leo Penn*
Frank Perry*

Steve Perry*
Bill Persky*
Charlie Peters*
Wolfgang Petersen*
Ann Petrie*
Daniel Petrie*
Daniel Petrie, Jr.*
Donald Petrie*
Joseph Pevney*
John Peyser*
William Phelps*
Win Phelps*
Lee Philips*
Maurice Phillips*
Frank Pierson*
Sam Pillsbury*
Seth Pinsker*
Ernest Pintoff*
Allen Plone*
S. Lee Pogostin*
Sidney Poitier*
Jeff Pollack*
Sydney Pollack*
Abraham Polonsky*
Ted Post*
Gerry Poulson*
John Power*
Michael Preece*
Michael Pressman*
Ruben Preuss*
Barry Primus*
Jonathan Prince*
Alex Proyas*
Richard Pryor*
Luis Puenzo*
Lou Puopolo*
Evelyn Purcell*
Joseph Purcell*
Dorothy Ann Puzo*
Joe Pytka*
Albert Pyun*

Q

James Quinn*
Gene Quintano*
Carlo U. Quinterio*

R

Peter Rader*
Bob Rafelson*
Stewart Raffill*
Alan Rafkin*
Sam Raimi*
Harold Ramis*
I. C. Rapoport*
Irving Rapper*
Steve Rash*
Daniel Raskov*
Harry Rasky*
Tina Rathborne*
Ousama Rawi*

John Rawlins*
Spiro Razatos*
Eric Red*
Robert Redford*
Peyton Reed*
Jerry Rees*
Patrick Regan*
Alastair Reid*
Carl Reiner*
Rob Reiner*
Deborah Reinisch*
Allen Reisner*
Karel Reisz*
Ivan Reitman*
Norman Rene*
Adam Resnick*
Burt Reynolds*
Gene Reynolds*
Kevin Reynolds*
Michael Ray Rhodes*
David Lowell Rich*
John Rich*
Matty Rich*
Dick Richards*
Lloyd Richards*
Ron Richards*
William Richert*
Anthony Richmond*
W.D. Richter*
Tom Rickman*
Michael Ritchie*
Joan Rivers*
Seymour Robbie*
Jerome Robbins*
Matthew Robbins*
Mike Robe*
James Roberson*
Cliff Robertson*
Bruce Robinson*
Phil Alden Robinson*
Franc Roddam*
Robert Rodriguez*
Nicolas Roeg*
Doug Rogers*
Sutton Roley*
George A. Romero*
Darrell James Roodt*
Bethany Rooney*
Tom Ropelewski*
Robert L. Rosen*
Stuart Rosenberg*
Ralph Rosenblum*
Keva Rosenfeld*
Scott Rosenfelt*
Rick Rosenthal*
Mark Rosner*
Herbert Ross*
Bobby Roth*
Joe Roth*
Richard Rothstein*
Joseph Ruben*
Bruce Joel Rubin*
Alan Rudolph*
Louis Rudolph*
Richard Rush*
Ken Russell*
Aaron Russo*
Mark Rydell*

S

William Sachs*
Daniel Sackheim*
James Steven Sadwith*
Gene Saks*
Sidney Salkow*
Mikael Salomon*
Coke Sams*
Ian Sander*
Jay Sandrich*
Arlene Sanford*
Jonathan Sanger*
Jimmy Sangster*
David Saperstein*
Deran Sarafian*
Richard C. Sarafian*
Joseph Sargent*
Marina Sargenti*
Peter Sasdy*
Oley Sassone*
Ron Satlof*
Philip Saville*
Tom Savini*
Joseph L. Scanlan*
Don Scardino*
Steven Schachter*
George Schaefer*
Jerry Schafer*
Don Schain*
Jerry Schatzberg*
Robert Scheerer*
Andrew Scheinman*
Carl Schenkel*
Richard Schenckman*
Fred Schepisi*
Richard Schickel*
Lawrence J. Schiller*
Tom Schiller*
Thomas Schlamme*
George Schlatter*
John Schlesinger*
Volker Schlondorff*
Paul Schneider*
Sascha Schneider*
Paul Schrader*
Myrl A. Schreibman*
Barbet Schroeder*
Carl Schultz*
Michael Schultz*
Joel Schumacher*
Douglas Schwartz*
Arnold Schwarzenegger*
Martin Scorsese*
George C. Scott*
James Scott*
Michael Scott*
Oz Scott*
Ridley Scott*
Tony Scott*
Steven Seagal*
Peter Segal*
Arthur Allan Seidelman*
Susan Seidelman*
Jack M. Sell*
David Seltzer*

I
N
D
E
X

O
F

F
I
L
M

D
I
R
E
C
T
O
R
S

Y

Peter Yates*
Linda Yellen*
Bud Yorkin*
Jeffrey Young*
Robert M. Young*
Roger Young*
James Yukich*
Larry Yust*

Z

Steven Zaillian*
Lili Fini Zanuck*
Kristi Zea*
Franco Zeffirelli*
Robert Zemeckis*
Howard Zieff*
Vernon Zimmerman*
Michael Zinberg*
Fred Zinnemann*
Randall Zisk*
Joseph Zito*
Lee David Zlotoff*
Vilmos Zsigmond*
David Zucker*
Jerry Zucker*
Charlotte Zwerin*
Edward Zwick*
Joel Zwick*

★ ★ ★

INDEX OF FILM DIRECTORS
NON-DGA

Note: This is not an index of every director, only those listed in this directory who are not members of the Directors Guild of America. This list is meant as a quick *name-only* reference when searching for a director or director's name. Full credits follow in the Listing Section.

A

Jefri Aalmuhammed
Veikko Aaltonen
Lewis Abernathy
Sene Absa
Jon Acevski
Jovan Acin
Robert Allan Ackerman
Daniel Adams
Doug Adams
Al Adamson
Percy Adlon
Phil Agland
Carlos Garcia Agraz
Jose Luis Garcia Agraz
Martin L. Aguilar
Charlie Ahearn
Chantal Akerman
Moustapha Akkad
Jordan Alan
John Albo
William (Will) Aldis
Tomas Gutierrez Alea
Mike Alexander
James Algar
Daniel Algrant
Don Allan
A.K. Allen
David Allen
Roger Allers
Michael Almereyda
Pedro Almodovar
Gregory Ryan Alosio
Emmett Alston
Denis Amar
Suzana Amaral
Gianni Amelio
Gideon Amir
Marino Amoruso
Robert Amram
Joseph R. Andaloro
Torgny Anderberg
Allison Anders
Andy Anderson
Kurt Anderson
Laurie Anderson
Paul Anderson
Sarah Pia Anderson
Steve Anderson
Wes Anderson
Mario Andreacchio
Scott Andrews
Yves Angelo

Theo Angelopoulos
Jeff Angelucci
Kenneth Anger
Erik Anjou
Brian Anthony
Eleanor Antin
Michelangelo Antonioni
Daniel Appleby
Norman Apstein
Manuel Gutierrez Aragon
Gregg Araki
Vicente Aranda
Denys Arcand
Alexandre Arcady
Noel Archambault
Francesca Archibugi
Dario Argento
Adolfo Aristarain
Michael Armstrong
Moira Armstrong
Robin B. Armstrong
Lucie Arnaz
Jerry Aronson
Isaac Artenstein
Peter Askin
Samson Aslanian
Olivier Assayas
Dimitri Astrakhan
J.D. Athens
Francisco Athle
David Attwood
Bille August
Paul Auster
Michael Austin
Claude Autant-Lara
Igor Auzins
Roger Avary
Pupi Avati
Howard (Hikmet) Avedis
Carlos Avila
Jac Avila
Tom Avildsen
Gabriel Axel
George Axelrod
Iradj Azimi

B

Beth B
Scott B
Bassek Ba Kobhio
Jean Bach
Randall Badat
Phil Badger

Yong-Kyun Bae
Ted Bafaloukos
Orlando Bagwell
Norma Bailey
Patrick Bailey
Fred Baker
Robert S. Baker
Roy Ward Baker
Ferdinando Baldi
Murray Ball
George Baluzy
Michael Baluzy
John Banas
Albert Band
Charles Band
Tamasaburo Bando
Mirra Bank
Uri Barbash
John Barbour
Joseph Barbera
Eric Barbier
Barry Barclay
Paris Barclay
Georges Bardawil
Juan Antonio Bardem
James H. Barden
Leora Barish
Edward S. Barkin
Anthony Barnao
Michael Barnard
Steve Barnett
Douglas Barr
Lezli-An Barrett
Arthur Barron
Zelda Barron
Ian Barry
Sean Barry
Dick Bartlett
Sean Barton
Jahnu Barua
Paolo Barzman
Giulio Base
Jules Bass
Lawrence Bassoff
Michal Bat-Adam
Bradley Battersby
Roy Battersby
Giacomo Battiato
Noah Baumbach
Lamberto Bava
Jack Baxter
Peter Baxter
Michael Bay
Stephen Bayly
Alan Beattie
Gorman Bechard
Josh Becker

James Becket
Michael Beckham
Andrew Behar
Ridha Behi
Jean-Jacques Beineix
Jean-Pierre Bekolo
Mikhail Belikov
Jeffrey Bell
Marco Bellocchio
Vera Belmont
Remy Belvaux
Maria Luisa Bemberg†
Joel Bender
Terry Benedict
Shyam Benegal
Roberto Benigni
Mark Benjamin
Bill Bennett
Gary Bennett
Rodney Bennett
Jacques W. Benoit
Alan Benson
Obie Benz
Alain Berberian
Luca Bercovici
Pamela Berger
Daniel Bergman
Ingmar Bergman
Robert Bergman
Eleanor Bergstein
Steven Berkoff
Luis Garcia Berlanga
Ted Berman
Chris Bernard
Sam Bernard
Edward Bernds
Claude Berri
Bill Berry
Tom Berry
Attila Bertalan
Giuseppe Bertolucci
Jean-Louis Bertucelli
Michael Berz
James Beshears
Dan Bessie
Luc Besson
Nigol Bezjian
Robert Bierman
Jean-Claude Biette
Charles Biggs
Robert Bilheimer
Kevin Billington
William Bindley
Steve Bing
Antonia Bird
Stewart Bird

Andrew Birkin
Alan Birkinshaw
Shem Bitterman
Loren Bivens
Jon Blair
Les Blair
Lorne Blair
Ronee Blakley
Michel Blanc
Harrod Blank
Jonathan Blank
Les Blank
Bertrand Blier
Doug Block
George Bloomfield
Rex Bloomstein
Chris Blum
Andy Blumenthal
Don Bluth
David Blyth
Sergei Bodrov
Yurek Bogayevicz
Willy Bogner
Ted A. Bohus
Yves Boisset
Jerome Boivin
Mauro Bolognini
James Bond III
Lee Bonner
Rene Bonniere
J.R. Bookwalter
José Luis Borau
John Borden
Lizzie Borden
Robert Boris
Arthur Borman
Walerian Borowczyk
Clay Borris
Dave Borthwick
John Boskovich
Rachid Bouchareb
Patrick Bouchitey
Roy Boulting
David R. Bowen
Jenny Bowen
John R. Bowey
Anthony J. Bowman
Pearl Bowser
Muriel Box
Daniel Boyd
Don Boyd
Danny Boyle
Samuel Bradford
John Bradshaw
Randy Bradshaw
Klaus Maria Brandauer
Richard Brander
Clark Brandon
Charlotte Brandstrom
Patrick Braoude
Tinto Brass
Peter Bratt
Mary Ann Braubach
Michel Brault
Edgar Michael Bravo
Julian Breen
Anja Breien
Catherine Breillat
Valerie Breiman

Tia Brelis
Mario Brenta
Robert Bresson
Joe Brewster
Salome Breziner
Steven Brill
Richard Broadman
Jeff Broadstreet
Deborah Brock
Al Brodax
John C. Broderick
Matthew Broderick
Hugh Brody
Rex Bromfield
Peter Brook
Adam Brooks
Nicholas (Nick) Broomfield
Philip Brophy
Barry Alexander Brown
Bruce Brown
Georg Stanford Brown
Gregory Brown
Jim Brown
Julie Brown
Tony Brown
Kevin Brownlow
James Bruce
James Bryan
Bill Bryden
Tony Buba
Larry Buchanan
Noel Buckner
Jan Bucquoy
Colin Budd
Robin Budd
John Carl Buechler
Richard Bugajski
Penelope Buitenhuis
Jillian Bullock
Alan Bunce
Mark Buntzman
Juan-Luis Buñuel
Alexander Buravsky
Derek Burbidge
George Burdeau
Robert A. Burge
Stuart Burge
Martyn Burke
Tom Burman
Charles Burnett
Edward Burns
Ken Burns
Ric Burns
Jeff Burr
Christine Burrill
Tim Burstall
Geoff Burton
William Bushnell, Jr.
George Butler
Hendel Butoy
David Byrne
John Byrne

C

Ellen Cabot
Sergio Cabrera
Michael Cacoyannis
Gerald Cain
Simon Callow
Julia Cameron
Ken Cameron
Juan Jose Campanella
Doug Campbell
Graeme Campbell
Martin Campbell
Nicholas Campbell
Norman Campbell
Anna Campion
Jane Campion
Mario Camus
Alex Canawati
Danny Cannon
Elliot Caplan
Bernt Capra
Leos Carax
Jack Cardiff
J.S. Cardone
Gilles Carle
Carlo Carlei
Henning Carlsen
Marcel Carne
Marc Caro
Stephen Carpenter
Fabio Carpi
Adrian Carr
Michael Carreras
J. Larry Carroll
Robert Martin Carroll
Willard Carroll
L.M. 'Kit' Carson
Dick Carter
Alexander Cassini
P.J. Castellaneta
Sergio M. Castilla
Alien Castle
Don Cato
Alain Cavalier
Liliana Cavani
Felipe Cazals
Jeff Celentano
Claude Chabrol
Gurinder Chadha
Youssef Chahine
P. Chalong
Georges Chamchoum
Evans Chan
Jackie Chan
Pauline Chan
Tony Chan
Bae Chang-Ho
Robert Chappell
Joe Chappelle
Mehdi Charef
Paul Chart
Etienne Chatiliez
Amin Q. Chaudhri
Shu Lea Cheang
Peter Chelsom

Kaige Chen
Pierre Chenal
Ayoka Chenzira
Patrice Chereau
Wayne Chesler
Scott E. Chester
Jacob C.L. Cheung
Andrew Chiaramonte
Mel Chionglo
Stephan Chodorov
Park Choi-Su
Mohamed Chouikh
Elie Chouraqui
Christine Choy
Nathaniel Christian
Grigori Chukhrai
Ji-Young Chung
Vera Chytilova
Gerard Ciccoritti
Matt Cimber
Souleymane Cissé
Richard Ciupka
Robert Clapsadle
Bruce Clark
Duane Clark
Frank C. Clark
Greydon Clark
Larry Clark
Lawrence Gordon Clark
Richard Clark
Ron Clark
William Clark
Frank Clarke
James Kenelm Clarke
Shirley Clarke
Stanley Bennett Clay
Tom Clegg
William B. Clemens
René Clement
Ron Clements
Peter Clifton
Art Clokey
Robert Clouse
Martin Clunes
Craig Clyde
Lewis Coates
Stacy Cochran
Joel Coen
Annette Cohen
Dan Cohen
David Cohen
Eli Cohen
Howard R. Cohen
Martin Cohen
Neil Cohen
S.E. Cohen
Michael Cohn
Peter Cohn
Isabel Coixet
Harley Cokliss
Carl Colby
Henry Cole
Jack Cole
Kermit Cole
Marcus Cole
William Cole
Robert Collector
Carl-Jan Colpaert

Werner Herzog
Eugene Hess
Charlton Heston
Rod Hewitt
Jochen Hick
George Hickenlooper
Bruce Hickey
Anthony Hickox
James Hickox
Scott Hicks
Howard Himelstein
Gregory Hines
David Hinton
Gregory Hippolyte
Bettina Hirsch
Yim Ho
Jeno Hodi
Peter Hoffman
Gray Hofmeyr
P.J. Hogan
Horant H. Hohlfield
Randy Holland
Alan Holleb
Graham Holloway
Jay Holman
Christopher Holmes
Fred Holmes
Jason Holt
Roger Holzberg
Elliott Hong
James Hong
Claudia Hoover
Margot Hope
Anthony Hopkins
John Hopkins
Richard Horian
Rebecca Horn
Aleks Horvat
Bob Hoskins
Dan Hoskins
Robert Hossein
Hsiao-Hsien Hou
Robert (Bobby) Houston
Adam Coleman Howard
John Howley
Frank Howson
Hou Hsiao-Hsien
Talun Hsu
V.V. Hsu
Ann Hu
King Hu
George Huang
Jianxin Huang
Jean-Loup Hubert
Tom Huckabee
John W. Huckert
Gary Hudson
Rolando Hudson
Carol Hughes
David Hughes
Kenneth (Ken) Hughes
Robert C. Hughes
Ann Hui
Michael Hui
Daniele Huillet
Donald Hulette
Ron Hulme
Edward Hume
Samo Hung

Tran Anh Hung
Jackson Hunsicker
Maurice Hunt
Caroline Huppert
William T. Hurtz
Sam Hurwitz
Jimmy Huston
Nicholas Hytner

I

Kon Ichikawa
Hassan Ildari
Yuri Illienko
Kwon-Taek Im
Shohei Imamura
Samuel (Shmuel) Imberman
Markus Imhoof
Keith Ingham
Otar Ioselliani
Matthew Irmas
Sam Irvin
David Irving
Alberto Isaac
James Isaac
Eva Isaksen
Gerald I. Isenberg
Sogo Ishii
Juzo Itami
Kenchi Iwamoto

J

David Jablin
Del Jack
Donald G. Jackson
Douglas Jackson
George Jackson
Lewis Jackson
Peter Jackson
Philip Jackson
Simcha Jacobovici
Alan Jacobs
Jerry P. Jacobs
Jon Jacobs
Lawrence-Hilton Jacobs
Rick Jacobson
Joseph Jacoby
Gualtiero Jacopetti
Ray Jafelice
Patrick Jamain
Pedr James
Steve James
Miklos Jancso
Lee Jang-Ho
Conrad Janis
Frederic Jardin
Jim Jarmusch
Laurence Jarvik
Vadim Jean
Roland Jefferson
Lionel Jeffries
Michael Jenkins
Alain Jessua

Jean-Pierre Jeunet
Chung Ji-Young
Wen Jiang
He Jianjun
Huang Jianxin
Neal Jimenez
Orlando Jimenez-Leal
Xie Jin
Robert Jiras
Jaromil Jires
Mike Jittlov
Alejandro Jodorowsky
Steve Jodrell
Michael Joens
Arthur Joffe
Mark Joffe
Kristin Johannesdottir
Cindy Lou Johnson
David Johnson
Jed Johnson
Sandy Johnson
Aaron Kim Johnston
Heather Johnston
Scott Johnston
Jyll Johnstone
Oskar Jonasson
Amy Holden Jones
Charles M. (Chuck) Jones
Gary Jones
James Cellan Jones
Mark Jones
Robert Jones
Terry Jones
Tommy Lee Jones
Jon Jost
Paul Joyce
C. Courtney Joyner
Gerard Jugnot
Jon Juhlin
Isaac Julien
Jan Jung
Paul Justman

K

Gaston Kaboré
Karel Kachyna
Haruki Kadokawa
Jeff Kahn
Chen Kaige
Constance Kaiserman
Tom Kalin
Scott Kalvert
Jay Kamen
Stuart Kaminsky
Steven Kampmann
Shusuke Kaneko
Vitali Kanevski
Woo-Suk Kang
Charles T. Kanganis
Alexis Kanner
Betty Kaplan
Mike Kaplan
Nelly Kaplan
Shekhar Kapur
Wong Kar-Wai

Janice Karman
Mathieu Kassovitz
Leonard Kastle
Daphna Kastner
Douglas Katz
Michael Katz
Charles Kaufman
Jim Kaufman
Lloyd Kaufman
Mani Kaul
Aki Kaurismäki
Mika Kaurismäki
Anwar Kawadri
Jerzy Kawalerowicz
Gilbert Lee Kay
Jonathon Kay
Bob Keen
Nietzchka Keene
Don Keeslar
Douglas Keeve
Michael Kehoe
Patrick Keiller
P. James Keitel
Harry Keller
David Kellogg
Diane Kelly
Jude Kelly
Nancy Kelly
Rory Kelly
Nicholas Kendall
Fred Kennamer
Chris Kennedy
Michael Kennedy
Donald Kent
Gary Kent
Larry Kent
Frank Kerr
Alek Keshishian
Michael Keusch
Mustapha Khan
Michel Khleifi
Abbas Kiarostami
Krzysztof Kieslowski
Gerard Kikoine
J. Douglas Kilgore
John Kincade
Tim Kincaid
Allan King
Christopher Lloyd King
Robert Lee King
Stephen King
Alan Kingsberg
Margy Kinmonth
Keisuke Kinoshita
Ephraim Kishon
Takeshi Kitano
R.J. Kizer
Rick Klass
Damian Klaus
Jonathan Klein
William Klein
Walter Klenhard
Elem Klimov
Alexander Kluge
Robert Knights
Masaki Kobayashi
Phillip Koch
Oja Kodar

Scott McGehee
Scott McGinnis
Don McGlynn
Joseph McGrath
Thomas McGuane
Mary McGuckian
Doug McHenry
George McIndoe
Laurie McInnes
Chris McIntyre
Duncan McLachlan
Steve McLean
Don McLennan
Ken McMullen
Mary McMurray
Nick Mead
Nancy Meckler
Leslie Megahey
Francis Megahy
Dariush Mehrjui
Deepa Mehta
Ketan Mehta
Myron Meisel
Adolfas Mekas
Jonas Mekas
Andre Melancon
Bill Melendez
James Melkonian
John Mellencamp
Vladimir Menshov
Jiri Menzel
Ismail Merchant
James Merendino
Jalal Merhi
Joseph Merhi
Elias Merhige
William Mesa
Marta Meszaros
Tim Metcalfe
Radley Metzger
Kevin Meyer
Turi Meyer
Mike Michaels
Roger Michell
Scott Michell
Dave Michener
George Mihalka
Ted V. Mikels
Nikita Mikhalkov
Andrei Mikhalkov-
Konchalovsky
Rentaro Mikuni
Kathy Milani
Christopher Miles
Catherine Millar
Gavin Millar
Claude Miller
David Lee Miller
Jonathan Miller
Neal Miller
Rebecca Miller
Tony Miller
William P. (Bill) Milling
Reginald Mills
Michael Miner
Tsai Ming-Liang
David Mingay
Ho Quang Minh
Trinh T. Minh-Ha

Joseph Minion
Cecilia Miniucchi
Rob Minkoff
Soraya Mire
Dan Mirvish
Bob Misiorowski
Merata Mita
David Mitchell
Sollace Mitchell
Alexander Mitta
Hayao Miyazaki
Moshe Mizrahi
Serge Moati
Ben Model
Moebius
Edouard Molinaro
Rauni Mollberg
Sarah Mondale
Paul Mones
Mario Monicelli
Christopher Monger
Meredith Monk
Philippe Monnier
Giuliano Montaldo
Eduardo Montes
Monty Montgomery
Patrick Montgomery
Charles Phillip Moore
Michael Moore
Ronald W. Moore
Simon Moore
Steve Moore
Jocelyn Moorhouse
Christopher Morahan
Jacobo Morales
Rick Moranis
Gerard Mordillat
Jeanne Moreau
Nanni Moretti
W.T. Morgan
Robert Morin
Yoshimitsu Morita
Jon Moritsugu
Louis Morneau
Bob Morones
Graham Morris
Judy Morris
Bruce Morrison
Paul Morrissey
Jeff Morton
Rocky Morton
Elijah Moshinsky
Roger E. Mosley
Jonathan Mostow
Caroline Ahlfors Mouris
Frank Mouris
Eric Mueller
Kathy Mueller
Robert Mugge
Marilyn Mulford
Ray Muller
Mark Mullin
Ron Mulvihill
Christopher Munch
Richard W. Munchkin
Jag Mundhra
Ian Mune
Jimmy T. Murakami
Ryu Murakami

Fredi M. Murer
John Murlowski
James Muro
Dean Murphy
Don Murphy
Edward Murphy
Maurice Murphy
Tab Murphy
Don Murray
Robin P. Murray
Paul Murton
John Musker

N

Marva Nabili
Amir Naderi
Robert Kent Nagy
Mira Nair
Desmond Nakano
Yoko Narahashi
Leon Narbey
Yousry Nasrallah
Gregory Nava
Thomas L. Neff
Alberto Negrin
Dan Neira
Jessie Nelson
Jan Nemec
Pengau Nengo
Greg Neri
Cathe Neukum
Chris Newby
Anthony Newley
Ted Newsom
Phil Nibbelink
Maurizio Nichetti
Michael Nickles
Ted Nicolaou
Wu Nien-Jen
George T. Nierenberg
Rob Nilsson
Michele Noble
Chris Noonan
Tom Noonan
Leslie Norman
Ron Norman
Zack Norman
Jonathan Nossiter
Rachid Nougmanov
Blaine Novak
Maria Novaro
Simon Nuchtern
Victor Nuñez
William Nunez
Trevor Nunn
Francesco Nuti
Colin Nutley
Bruno Nuytten
Peter Nydrle
Roger Nygard
Sven Nykvist
Ron Nyswaner

O

Vern Oakley
Dan O'Bannon
Rockne S. O'Bannon
Jim O'Brien
John O'Brien
Jeffrey Obrow
Maurice O'Callaghan
Mike Ockrent
Jack O'Connell
Raoul O'Connell
James O'Connolly
David Odell
Keith O'Derek
Takao Ogawara
George Ogilvie
Kohei Oguri
Gerry O'Hara
Kihachi Okamoto
Steven Okazaki
Kazuyoshi Okuyama
Ronan O'leary
Christopher Olgiati
David Oliver
Michael Oliver
Ron Oliver
Ruby L. Oliver
Hector Olivera
Marty Ollstein
Ermanno Olmi
William Olsen
Stellan Olsson
David O'Malley
Emiko Omori
Kazuki Omori
Ron O'Neal
Marcel Ophuls
Peer J. Oppenheimer
Mario Orfini
Dominic Orlando
Peter Ormrod
Emmerich Oross
Dennis O'Rourke
James R. Orr
Nagisa Oshima
Aziz M. Osman
Cliff Osmond
Suzanne Osten
Martin Ostrow
Thaddeus O'Sullivan
Dominique Othenin-Girard
Katsuhiro Otomo
Filippo Ottoni
Idrissa Ouedraogo
Gerard Oury
Horace Ove
Cliff Owen
Don Owen
Jan Oxenberg

S

Randa Chahal Sabbag
Paul Sabella
Alan Sacks
Henri Safran
Yoichi Sai
Junji Sakamoto
David Salle
Walter Salles, Jr.
James Salter
Deepa Mehta Saltzman
Paul Saltzman
Victor Salva
Gabriele Salvatores
Harold (Hal) Salwen
Glen Salzman
Barry Samson
Ake Sandgren
Jerry Sangiuliano
Jorge Sanjines
Cirio H. Santiago
Damon Santostefano
Vic Sarin
Valeria Sarmiento
Michael Sarne
Junya Sato
Shimako Sato
Bradd Saunders
Scott Saunders
Carlos Saura
Claude Sautet
Pierre Sauvage
Nancy Savoca
Geoffrey Sax
John Saxon
Daoud Abdel Sayed
John Sayles
Allen Schaaf
Eric Schaeffer
Francis (Franky) Schaeffer
Danny Schechter
Hans Scheepmaker
Maximilian Schell
Henning Schellerup
Jeffrey Noyes Scher
Paul Schibli
Suzanne Schiffman
Julian Schlossberg
Oliver Schmitz
David Schmoeller
Robert A. Schnitzer
Pierre Schoendoerffer
Renen Schorr
Dale Schott
Leonard Schrader
William Schreiner
Frank C. Schroeder
Michael Schroeder
Werner Schroeter
Stefan Schwartz
Arnold Schwartzman
Ettore Scola
Art Scott
Campbell Scott
Cynthia Scott

George Scribner
Sandra Seacat
John Seale
Mike Sedan
Jakov Sedlar
Paul Seed
Bob Seeley
Michael Seitzman
Henry Selick
Arnaud Selignac
Ian Sellar
Peter Sellars
Charles E. Sellier, Jr.
Arna Selznick
Ousmane Sembene
Mrinal Sen
Dominic Sena
Ron Senkowski
Eva Sereny
Yahoo Serious
Alex Sessa
Philip Setbon
Vernon Sewell
Jeff Seymour
John Sexton
Shabba-Doo
Michael Shackleton
Susan Shadburne
Steven Shainberg
Pete Shaner
Ken Shapiro
Jim Sharman
Don Sharp
Ian Sharp
Peter Shatalow
Chris Shaw
Scott Shaw
Steven Shaw
Robert Shaye
Linda Shayne
Bashar Shbib
Katt Shea
Donald Shebib
Simon S. Sheen
Stanley Sheff
Riki Shelach
Toby Shelton
Richard Shepard
Sam Shepard
Bill Shepherd
John Sheppard
John Shepphird
Adrian Shergold
Jim Sheridan
Frank Shields
Peter Shillingford
Barry Shils
Nelson Shin
Stephen Shin
Kaneto Shindo
Masahiro Shinoda
Talia Shire
John Shorney
Ken Short
Mina Shum
M. Night Shyamalan
Mussef Sibay
Andy Sidaris

Adi Sideman
David Siegel
Slobodan Sijan
Andrew Silver
Diane Silver
Marc Silverman
Lawrence L. Simeone
Anthony Simmons
Adam Simon
Francis Simon
Jane Simpson
Michael A. Simpson
Andrew Sinclair
Gerald Seth Sindell
Bryan Singer
Gail Singer
Bernhard Sinkel
Gary Sinyor
Vilgot Sjoman
Calvin Skaggs
Jerzy Skolimowski
Bob Skotak
Lane Slate
Brian Sloan
Holly Goldberg Sloan
James Slocum
Jon Small
John Smallcombe
Bruce Smith
Clive A. Smith
Howard Smith
John N. Smith
Kevin Smith
Kent Smith
Noella Smith
Peter Smith
Tony Smith
Jonathan Smythe
Roberto Sneider
Sherry Sneller
Michele Soavi
Steven Soderbergh
Rainer Soehnlein
Iaian Softley
Fernando E. Solanas
Abbie C. Solarez
Russell Solberg
Silvio Soldini
Todd Solondz
Ola Solum
Paul Sommer
Cherd Songsri
Susan Sontag
Alberto Sordi
Dror Soref
Carlos Sorin
Jim Sotos
Thierno Faty Sow
Larry G. Spangler
Teresa Sparks
Aaron Speiser
Michael Spence
Brenton Spencer
Jane Spencer
Scott Spiegel
Tony Spiradakis
G. D. Spradlin
Tim Spring

Christopher St. John
Eric Steven Stahl
Terence Stamp
Jeremy Stanford
Richard Stanley
Jeff Stanzler
Ringo Starr
Steven Starr
Ray Dennis Steckler
Jeff Stein
Ken Stein
Michael Steinberg
Ziggy Steinberg
Daniel Steinmann
Martin Stellman
Noah Stern
Tom Stern
Jean-François Stevenin
Art Stevens
David Stevens
Stella Stevens
Rick Stevenson
Alan Stewart
John Stewart
Whit Stillman
John Stix
Jerry Stoeffhaas
Bryan Michael Stoller
Norman Stone
Tad Stones
Tom Stoppard
Esben Storm
Jean-Marie Straub
Joseph Strick
Wesley Strick
John Strickland
John Strysik
Brian Stuart
Charles Sturridge
Eliseo Subiela
Richard Rainer Sudborough
Andrew Sugerman
Daniele J. Suissa
Fred G. Sullivan
Kevin Sullivan
Tim Sullivan
Jeremy Summers
Shirley Sun
Cedric Sundström
Hal Sutherland
Kiefer Sutherland
Seijun Suzuki
Jan Svankmajer
Peter Svatek
Jan Sverak
Stephen Swartz
Charles Swenson
Larry Swerdlove
Saul Swimmer
Brad Swirnoff
Hans-Jurgen Syberberg
Peter Sykes
Istvan Szabo

Sa-Sz

FILM
DIRECTORS
GUIDE

NON-DGA

INDEX OF FILM DIRECTORS

T

Michael Taav
Sylvio Tabet
Juan Carlos Tabio
Jean-Charles Tacchella
Robert Taicher
Renee Tajima
Rea Tajiri
Isao Takahata
Beat Takeshi
Yojiro Takita
Len Talan
C.M. Talkington
Lee Tamahori
Augusto Tamayo
Harry Tampa
Bill Tannebring
Terrel Tannen
Alain Tanner
Daniel Taplitz
Quentin Tarantino
Anna Maria Tato
David Tausik
John Tatoulis
Bertrand Tavernier
Paolo Taviani
Vittorio Taviani
Alex Taylor
Baz Taylor
Robert Taylor
Andre Techine
Julien Temple
Conny Templeman
Kevin S. Tenney
Rinken Teruya
Hiroshi Teshigahara
Peter Tewksbury
Tiana Thi Thanh Nga
Anna Thomas
Antony Thomas
John G. Thomas
Pascal Thomas
Ralph Thomas
Theodore Thomas
Brett Thompson
Ernest Thompson
Harry Thompson
Randy Thompson
Karen Thorsen
Zhuangzhuang Tian
Tiana
Wu Tianming
Antonio Tibaldi
Robert Tiffe
Bruce W. Timm
Douglas Tirola
Stacy Title
Moufida Tlatli
Stephen Tobolowsky
Valeri Todorovski
Susan Todd
Ricky Tognazzi
Sergio Toledo
Stephen Tolkin
Ro Tomono

Stanley Tong
Giuseppe Tornatore
Joe Tornatore
Gabe Torres
Cinzia Th Torrini
Serge Toubiana
Moussa Toure
Bud Townsend
Pat Townsend
Ian Toynton
John Travers
Joey Travolta
Brian Trenchard-Smith
Barbara Trent
Blair Treu
Dale Trevillion
Nadine Trintignant
Rose Troche
Jan Troell
Marc C. Tropia
Tano Tropia
Gary Trousdale
Fernando Trueba
Ming-Liang Tsai
Talan Tsu
Hark Tsui
Shinya Tsukamoto
Slava Tsukerman
Stanley Tucci
Anand Tucker
David Tucker
Montgomery Tully
Sophia Turkiewicz
Rose-Marie Turko
Ann Turner
Clive Turner
Paul Turner
Rob Turner
John Turturro
David N. Twohy
Tracy Tynan

U

Liv Ullmann
Stuart Urban
Jeff Ureles
Jamie Uys
Uzo

V

John Valadez
Mike Valerio
Nick Vallelonga
Jean-Claude Van Damme
Jaco Van Dormael
Melvin Van Peebles
William Vanderkloot
Norman Thaddeus Vane
Gus Van Sant, Jr.
Sterling Vanwagenen
Carlo Vanzina
Agnes Varda

Joseph B. Vasquez
Isela Vega
Adrian Velicescu
Michael Ventura
Geraldo Vera
Ben Verbong
Carlo Verdone
Pat Verducci
Michael Verhoeven
Henri Verneuil
Daniel Vigne
Camilo Vila
Reynaldo Villalobos
Teresa Villaverde
Joseph Vilsmaier
Christian Vincent
Jesse Vint
Will Vinton
Marcela Fernandez Violante
Jon Voight
Paul G. Volk
Gabe Von Dettre
Katja Von Garnier
Rosa Von Praunheim
Daisy Von Scherler Mayer
Max Von Sydow
Lars Von Trier
Margarethe Von Trotta
Frank Von Zerneck, Jr.
Kurt Voss

W

Orin Wachsberg
Daniel Wachsmann
Jane Wagner
Paul Wagner
Andrzej Wajda
Grant Austin Waldman
Giles Walker
Peter Walker
Robert Walker
Stephen Wallace
Anthony Waller
Aisling Walsh
Peter Wang
Steve Wang
Wayne Wang
Daniel Lardner Ward
Nick Ward
Vincent Ward
Regis Wargnier
Paul Warner
Catherine Warnow
Deryn Warren
Jennifer Warren
Don Was
Peter Watkins
John Watson
Paul Watson
Roy Watts
Keoni Waxman
Peter Webb
Stephen Weeks
John Weidner
Samuel Weil

Yossi Wein
Hal Weiner
Regina Weinreich
Sandra Weintraub
Roger Weisberg
Rob Weiss
Ellen Weissbrod
David Wellington
Peter Wells
Simon Wells
Jiang Wen
Wim Wenders
Richard Wenk
Lina Wertmuller
Howard Wexler
George Whaley
Claude Whatham
Jim Wheat
Ken Wheat
David Wheatley
Anne Wheeler
Preston A. Whitmore, II
Stephen Whittaker
Rob Whittlesey
Michael Whyte
David Wickes
Gregory C. Widen
Bo Widerberg
Andrew Wild
Gordon Wiles
Ethan Wiley
Jenny Wilkes
Charles Wilkinson
Paul Williams
Richard Williams
Wade Williams
Fred Williamson
Bruce Wilson
Jim Wilson
Sandra (Sandy) Wilson
Kurt Wimmer
Jonathan Allen Winfrey
Gary Winick
Terence H. Winkless
David Winning
Terry Winsor
Alex Winter
Donovan Winter
Michael Winterbottom
Franz Peter Wirth
Forest Wise
Kirk Wise
Carol Wiseman
Frederick Wiseman
Stephen Withrow
Peter Wittman
Ira Wohl
Annett Wolf
Kirk Wolfinger
Peter Wollen
Dan Wolman
Wallace Wolodarsky
Kar-Wai Wong
Kirk Wong
Kang Woo-Suk
Leslie Woodhead
Dan Woodruff
Mel Woods

Abbe Wool
Jeff Woolnough
Aaron Worth
David Worth
Soenke Wortmann
Casper Wrede
Geoffrey Wright
Patrick Wright
Thomas Lee Wright
Nien-Jen Wu
Tianming Wu
Robert Wuhl
Rudolph (Rudy) Wurlitzer
David Wyles
Jim Wynorski

X

Jin Xie
Zhou Xiaowen

Y

Greg Yaitanes
Boaz Yakin
Yoji Yamada
Takaya Yamazaki
Mitsuo Yanagimachi
Edward Yang
Louis Yansen
Bob Yari
Rebecca Yates
Yevgeny Yevtushenko
Li Yin
Ho Yim
Zhang Yimou
Bae Yong-Kyun
Jeff Yonis
Yaky Yosha
Hiroaki Yoshida
Andrew Young
Freddie Young
John G. Young
Robert William Young
Ronny Yu
Zhang Yuan
Corey Yuen
Robert Yuhas
Prince Chatri Yukol
Paul Yule
Johnny Yune
Peter Yuval
Brian Yuzna

Z

Maurizio Zaccaro
Steve Zacharias
Nancy Zala
Alain Zaloum
Krzysztof Zanussi
John Zaritsky
Alan Zaslove
Yolande Zauberman
Paul Zehrer
Jimmy Zeilinger
Yuri Zeltser
Laurie Zemelman
Yimou Zhang
Xiaowen Zhou
Tian Zhuangzhuang
Claude Zidi
Howard Ziehm
Rafal Zielinski
Paul Ziller
Zoe Zinman
Peter Zinner
Milan Zivkovich
Dick Zondag
Ralph Zondag
Albert Zugsmith
Howard Zuker
Frank Zuniga
Marcos Zurinaga
Terry Zwigoff

★ ★ ★

A

JEFRI AALMUHAMMED
BROTHER MINISTER: THE ASSASSINATION OF MALCOLM X (FD)
co-director with Jack Baxter, X-Ceptional Productions/Illuminati
Entertainment Group/Why Productions, 1994

VEIKKO AALTONEN
Contact: Finnish Film Foundation, Kanavakatu 12, SF-00160
Helsinki, Finland, tel.: 0/17-77-27

THE FINAL ARRANGEMENT 1987, Finnish
THE PRODIGAL SON Villealfa Filmproductions, 1993, Finnish
OUR FATHER... Villealfa Filmproductions, 1994, Finnish

PAUL AARON*
Business: Elsboy Entertainment, 1581 N. Crescent Heights Blvd.,
Los Angeles, CA 90046, 213/656-3800
Agent: CAA - Beverly Hills, 310/288-4545

A DIFFERENT STORY Avco Embassy, 1978
A FORCE OF ONE American Cinema, 1979
THE MIRACLE WORKER (TF) Katz-Gallin Productions/Half-Pint
Productions, 1979
THIN ICE (TF) CBS Entertainment, 1981
MAID IN AMERICA (TF) CBS Entertainment, 1982
DEADLY FORCE Embassy, 1983
WHEN SHE SAYS NO (TF) I&C Productions/Jozak-Decade
Enterprises, 1984
MAXIE Orion, 1985
MORGAN STEWART'S COMING HOME co-director with
Terry Winsor, released under pseudonym of Alan Smithee,
New Century/Vista, 1987
IN LOVE AND WAR (TF) Carol Schreder Productions/Tisch-Avnet
Productions, 1987
UNTAMED LOVE (CTF) Cathy Lee Crosby Productions/Carroll
Newman Productions/Hearst Entertainment, 1994

ROBERT J. ABEL*
b. March 10, 1937 - Cleveland, Ohio
Contact: Directors Guild of America - Los Angeles, 213/851-3671

ELVIS ON TOUR (FCD) co-director with Pierre Adidge,
MGM, 1972
LET THE GOOD TIMES ROLL (FCD) co-director with Sidney Levin,
Columbia, 1973

LEWIS ABERNATHY
HOUSE IV New Line Home Video, 1992

JIM ABRAHAMS*
b. May 10, 1944 - Shorewood, Wisconsin
Agent: UTA - Beverly Hills, 310/273-6700

AIRPLANE! co-director with David Zucker & Jerry Zucker,
Paramount, 1980
TOP SECRET! co-director with David Zucker & Jerry Zucker,
Paramount, 1984
RUTHLESS PEOPLE co-director with David Zucker & Jerry Zucker,
Buena Vista, 1986
BIG BUSINESS Buena Vista, 1988
WELCOME HOME, ROXY CARMICHAEL Paramount, 1990
HOT SHOTS! 20th Century Fox, 1991
HOT SHOTS! PART DEUX 20th Century Fox, 1993

EDWARD ABROMS*
Agent: The Artists Group - Los Angeles, 310/552-1100

SULTAN AND THE ROCK STAR (TF) Walt Disney
Productions, 1978
THE IMPOSTER (TF) Warner Bros. TV, 1985

SENE ABSA
Contact: SIDEC, 12 rue Beranger Ferraud, B P 335, Dakar, Senegal,
tel.: 21-45-76

TWISTE A POPENGUINE Cameras Continentales/France 2, 1994,
Senegalese-French

JON ACEVSKI
Business: Hollywood Road Studios - London, tel.: 71/223-4897
Contact: British Film Commission, 70 Baker Street, London W1M 1DJ,
England, tel.: 171/224-5000

FREDDIE AS F.R.O.7 (AF) Miramax Films, 1992, British
FREDDIE GOES TO WASHINGTON (AF) Hollywood Road Studios,
1993, British

JOVAN ACIN
b. May 23, 1941 - Belgrade, Yugoslavia

THE CONCRETE ROSE 1975, Yugoslavian
HEY BABU RIBA *DANCING ON WATER* Orion Classics,
1986, Yugoslavian

ROBERT ALLAN ACKERMAN
Contact: ICM - Beverly Hills, 310/550-4000

MRS. CAGE (TF) Haft-Nasatir Productions/Dan Lupovitz
Productions, 1992
DAVID'S MOTHER (TF) Morgan Hill Films/Hearst Entertainment
Productions, 1994
SAFE PASSAGE New Line Cinema, 1994

DAVID ACOMBA*
Address: 63 Beaconsfield Avenue, Toronto, Ontario M6J 3J1,
Canada, 416/538-4239
Agent: APA - Los Angeles, 310273-0744

SLIPSTREAM 1973, Canadian
HANK WILLIAMS: THE SHOW HE NEVER GAVE Simcom/Film
Consortium of Canada, 1982, Canadian
NIGHT LIFE Wild Night Productions, 1989

CATLIN ADAMS*
b. October 11, 1950 - Los Angeles, California
Address: 1317 N. Orange Grove Avenue, Los Angeles, CA 90046
Agent: Writers & Artists Agency - Los Angeles, 310/824-6300

STICKY FINGERS Spectrafilm, 1988
STOLEN: ONE HUSBAND (TF) King Phoenix Entertainment, 1990

DANIEL ADAMS
RELIGION, INC. Blossom Pictures, 1989
PRIMARY MOTIVE Blossom Pictures, 1992

DOUG ADAMS
BLACKOUT Magnum Entertainment, 1988

AL ADAMSON
Business: Independent-International Pictures, 223 State Highway 18,
East Brunswick, NJ, 908/249-8982

TWO TICKETS TO TERROR Victor Adamson, 1964
GUN RIDERS *FIVE BLOODY GRAVES/LONELY MAN*
Independent-International, 1969
BLOOD OF DRACULA'S CASTLE Crown International, 1969
SATAN'S SADISTS Independent-International, 1970

HELL'S BLOODY DEVILS *THE FAKERS*
Independent-International, 1970
HORROR OF THE BLOOD MONSTERS *VAMPIRE MEN OF THE
LOST PLANET* Dalia, 1971
THE FEMALE BUNCH Dalia, 1971
LAST OF THE COMANCHEROS Independent-International, 1971
BLOOD OF GHASTLY HORROR *THE FIEND WITH THE
ATOMIC BRAIN* Independent-International, 1972
ANGELS' WILD WOMEN *ROUGH RIDERS* 1972
THE BRAIN OF BLOOD *BRAIN DAMAGE/THE BRAIN*
Hemisphere, 1972
DRACULA VS. FRANKENSTEIN *THE REVENGE OF DRACULA*
Independent-International, 1973
THE DYNAMITE BROTHERS Cinemation, 1974
GIRLS FOR RENT *I SPIT ON YOUR CORPSE*
Independent-International, 1974
THE NAUGHTY STEWARDESSES
Independent- International, 1975
STUD BROWN Cinemation, 1975
BLAZING STEWARDESSES Independent-International, 1975
JESSIE'S GIRL Manson International, 1976
BLACK HEAT Independent-International, 1976
CINDERELLA 2000 Independent-International, 1977
BLACK SUMURAI BLLJ International, 1977
SUNSET COVE Cal-Am Artists, 1978
DEATH DIMENSION *FREEZE BOMB* Movietime, 1978
NURSE SHERRI *HOSPITAL OF TERROR*
Independent-International, 1978
CARNIVAL MAGIC Krypton Corporation, 1982

ANITA W. ADDISON*
Agent: ICM - Beverly Hills, 310/550-4000

THERE ARE NO CHILDREN HERE (TF) Do We Inc./Harpo
Productions/LOMO Productions, 1993

LOU ADLER*
b. Los Angeles, California
Contact: Jerry Rosen, Glass & Rosen, 16530 Ventura Blvd. -
Suite 202, Encino, CA 91436, 818/907-1600

UP IN SMOKE Paramount, 1978
LADIES AND GENTLEMEN...THE FABULOUS STAINS
Paramount, 1982

PERCY ADLON
b. June 1, 1935 - Munich, Germany
Agent: William Morris Agency - Beverly Hills, 310/273-7451

THE GUARDIAN AND HIS POET (TF) 1978, West German
CELESTE New Yorker, 1981, West German
FIVE LAST DAYS 1982, West German
THE SWING 1983, West German
SUGARBABY Kino International, 1985, West German
HERSCHEL AND THE MUSIC OF THE STARS (TF)
Bayerischer Rundfunk, 1985, West German
BAGDAD CAFE *OUT OF ROSENHEIM* Island Pictures, 1987,
West German-U.S.
ROSALIE GOES SHOPPING Four Seasons Entertainment, 1989,
West German-U.S.
SALMONBERRIES Weltvertrieb/Pelemele Film, 1991, German
YOUNGER & YOUNGER Pelemele Film/BR/Duckster/Leora, 1993

PHIL AGLAND
Contact: British Film Commission, 70 Baker Street, London
W1M 1DJ, England, tel.: 171/224-5000

CHINA: BEYOND THE CLOUDS (TD) River Film Productions/
National Geographic Society/Channel 4/Canal Plus, 1994,
British-U.S.-French

CARLOS GARCIA AGRAZ
(See Carlos GARCIA AGRAZ)

JOSE LUIS GARCIA AGRAZ
(See Jose Luis GARCIA AGRAZ)

MARTIN L. AGUILAR
MOONDANCE Ziggurat Film Releasing, 1994

CHARLIE AHEARN
WILD STYLE First Run Features, 1983

CHANTAL AKERMAN
b. June 1950 - Brussels, Belgium
Home: Valkendael 15, 1820 Strombeck-Beuer, Belgium,
tel: 02/267-4049
Contact: National Tourist Office, 61 Rue de Marche Aux Herbes,
B1000 Brussels, Belgium, tel: 02/513-8940

HOTEL MONTEREY 1972, Belgian
LE 15/18 co-director, 1973, Belgian
HANGING OUT - YONKERS 1974
JE, TU, IL, ELLES 1974, Belgian
JEANNE DIELMAN, 23 QUAI DE COMMERCE, 1080 BRUXELLES
1975, Belgian
NEWS FROM HOME 1976, Belgian
LES RENDEZVOUS D'ANNA Gaumont, 1979, French
DIS MOI 1980, Belgian
TOUTE UN NUITE Paradise Films/Avidia Films, 1982, Belgian
LES ANNEES 80S Paradise Films, 1983, Belgian
L'HOMME A LA VALISE 1983, Belgian
PINA BAUSCH (FD) Institut National de la Communication/
Antenne-2/R.M. Arts/RTBF/SSR, 1983, Belgian
WINDOW SHOPPING 1986, French
SEVEN WOMEN, SEVEN SINS co-director, ASA Communications,
1987, West German-French-U.S.-Austrian-Belgian
HISTOIRES D'AMERIQUE Mallia Films/Paradise Films/La Sept/
The Pompidou Center/R.T.D.F./French Ministry of Culture/
Belgian Ministry of French Culture, 1989, French-Belgian
NIGHT AND DAY International Film Circuit, 1991,
French-Belgian-German
CONTRE L'OUBLI co-director, Les Films du Paradoxe/Amnesty
International/PRV, 1992, French
D'EST Paradise Films/Lieurac Productions, 1993,
French-Belgian-Portuguese
A COUCH IN NEW YORK UGC, 1995, German-French

MOUSTAPHA AKKAD
b. Syria
Business: Trancas International Films, Inc., 9229 Sunset Blvd. -
Suite 415, Los Angeles, CA 90069, 310/657-7670

MOHAMMAD, MESSENGER OF GOD *THE MESSAGE*
Tarik, 1977, Lebanese-British
LION OF THE DESERT United Film Distribution,
1981, Libyan-British

JORDAN ALAN
Contact: Shari Cohen, Christensen, White, Miller, Fink & Jacobs -
Los Angeles, 310/282-6260

TERMINAL BLISS Buena Vista, 1990
LOVE & HAPPINESS Terminal Bliss Pictures, 1995

JOHN ALBO
Contact: Writers Guild of America, West - Los Angeles, 310/550-1000
Attorney: James Bird, Esq. - Los Angeles, 310/379-8332

FLEXING WITH MONTY Quarter Moon Films, 1994

ALAN ALDA*
b. January 28, 1936 - New York, New York
Agent: UTA - Beverly Hills, 310/273-6700

THE FOUR SEASONS Universal, 1981
SWEET LIBERTY Universal, 1986
A NEW LIFE Paramount, 1988
BETSY'S WEDDING Buena Vista, 1990

WILLIAM (WILL) ALDIS

Agent: William Morris Agency - Beverly Hills, 310/859-4000

STEALING HOME   co-director with Steven Kampmann,
   Warner Bros., 1988

ADELL ALDRICH*

b. June 11, 1943 - Los Angeles, California
Home: 7453 Mulholland Drive, Los Angeles, CA 90046,
   213/487-4870

DADDY, I DON'T LIKE IT LIKE THIS (TF)   CBS Entertainment, 1978
THE KID FROM LEFT FIELD (TF)   Gary Coleman Productions/
   Deena Silver-Kramer's Movie Company, 1979

TOMAS GUTIERREZ ALEA

(See Tomas GUTIERREZ ALEA)

JASON ALEXANDER*

(Jay Scott Greenspan)
b. September 23, 1959 - Newark, New Jersey
Agent: William Morris Agency - Beverly Hills, 310/859-4000

STRANGER THINGS   Columbia, 1995

MIKE ALEXANDER

Contact: British Film Commission, 70 Baker Street, London
   W1M 1DJ, England, tel.: 171/224-5000

DREAMING (TF)   BBC, 1990, Scottish
AS AN EILEAN *FROM THE ISLAND* (TF)   Comataidh Telebhisein
   Gaidhlig/Channel 4/Grampian TV/Ross & Cromarty District
   Council/Pelicula Films, 1993, Scottish-British
MAIRI MHOR: NA H-ORAIN 'SA BEATHA *MAIRI MHOR:
   HER LIFE AND SONGS*   Freeway Films/BBC Scotland,
   1994, Scottish

JAMES ALGAR

b. June 11, 1912 - Modesto, California

THE LIVING DESERT (FD)   Buena Vista, 1953
THE VANISHING PRAIRIE (FD)   Buena Vista, 1954
THE AFRICAN LION (FD)   Buena Vista, 1955
SECRETS OF LIFE (FD)   Buena Vista, 1956
WHITE WILDERNESS (FD)   Buena Vista, 1958
JUNGLE CAT (FD)   Buena Vista, 1960
THE LEGEND OF LOBO   Buena Vista, 1962
THE BEST OF WALT DISNEY'S TRUE-LIFE ADVENTURES (FD)
   Buena Vista, 1975

DANIEL ALGRANT

Agent: CAA - Beverly Hills, 310/288-4545

NAKED IN NEW YORK   Fine Line Features/
   New Line Cinema, 1993

DON ALLAN

b. 1958 - Toronto, Ontario, Canada
Business: Revolver Film Company, 217 Richmond Street West -
   2nd Floor, Toronto, Ontario M5V 1WZ, Canada, 416/979-9777

JUNGLEGROUND   Norstar Entertainment, 1995, Canadian

A.K. ALLEN

(See Janet GREEK)

COREY ALLEN*

(Alan Cohen)
b. June 29, 1934 - Cleveland, Ohio
Agent: Irv Schechter Company - Beverly Hills, 310/278-8070

PINOCCHIO   EUE, 1971
SEE THE MAN RUN (TF)   Universal TV, 1971
CRY RAPE! (TF)   Leonard Freeman Productions, 1973

YESTERDAY'S CHILD (TF)   co-director with Bob Rosenbaum,
   Paramount TV, 1977
THUNDER AND LIGHTNING   20th Century-Fox, 1978
AVALANCHE   New World, 1979
STONE (TF)   Stephen J. Cannell Productions/Universal TV, 1979
THE MAN IN THE SANTA CLAUS SUIT (TF)   Dick Clark
   Productions, 1979
THE RETURN OF FRANK CANNON (TF)   QM Productions, 1980
MURDER, SHE WROTE: THE MURDER OF SHERLOCK
   HOLMES (TF)   Universal TV, 1984
CODENAME: FIREFOX (TF)   Universal TV, 1985
BRASS (TF)   Carnan Productions/Jaygee Productions/
   Orion TV, 1985
BEVERLY HILLS COWGIRL BLUES (TF)   The Leonard Goldberg
   Company, 1985
I-MAN (TF)   Mark H. Ovitz Productions/Walt Disney
   Productions, 1986
THE LAST FLING (TF)   Leonard Hill Films, 1987
DESTINATION AMERICA (TF)   Stephen J. Cannell
   Productions, 1987
J.J. STARBUCK (TF)   Stephen J. Cannell Productions, 1987
STAR TREK: THE NEXT GENERATION (TF)
   Paramount TV, 1987
THE ANN JILLIAN STORY (TF)   ITC, 1988
MOMENT OF TRUTH: STALKING BACK (TF)   O'Hara-Horowitz
   Productions, 1993

DAVID ALLEN

Business: David Allen Productions, 918 W. Oak Street, Burbank,
   CA 91508, 818/845-9270 or 818/848-0303

THE DUNGEONMASTER   co-director, Empire Pictures, 1985
PUPPET MASTER II   Full Moon Entertainment, 1990
PRIMIEVALS   Full Moon Entertainment, 1994

DEBBIE ALLEN*

b. January 16, 1950 - Houston, Texas
Business Manager: Gail Meredith, Red Bird Productions, Inc.,
   c/o R. Katz Enterprises, 345 N. Maple Drive - Suite 205,
   Beverly Hills, CA 90210
Agent: William Morris Agency - Beverly Hills, 310/859-4000

POLLY (TF)   Echo Cove Productions/Walt Disney TV, 1989
POLLY COMIN' HOME (TF)   Echo Cove Productions/Walt
   Disney TV, 1990
STOMPIN' AT THE SAVOY (TF)   1992
OUT OF SYNC   BET Films, 1995

LEWIS ALLEN*

b. December 25, 1905 - Shropshire, England
Home: 11667 Gorham Avenue - Suite 204, Los Angeles, CA 90049,
   310/820-8277

THE UNINVITED   Paramount, 1944
OUR HEARTS WERE YOUNG AND GAY   Paramount, 1944
THE UNSEEN   Paramount, 1945
THOSE ENDEARING YOUNG CHARMS   RKO Radio, 1945
THE PERFECT MARRIAGE   Paramount, 1947
THE IMPERFECT LADY   Paramount, 1947
DESERT FURY   Paramount, 1947
SO EVIL MY LOVE   Paramount, 1948
SEALED VERDICT   Paramount, 1948
CHICAGO DEADLINE   Paramount, 1949
APPOINTMENT WITH DANGER   Paramount, 1951
VALENTINO   Columbia, 1951
AT SWORD'S POINT   RKO Radio, 1952
SUDDENLY   United Artists, 1954
A BULLET FOR JOEY   United Artists, 1955
ILLEGAL   Warner Bros., 1955
ANOTHER TIME, ANOTHER PLACE   Paramount, 1958
WHIRLPOOL   Continental, 1959, British

F
I
L
M

D
I
R
E
C
T
O
R
S

WOODY ALLEN*

(Allen Stewart Konigsberg)
b. December 1, 1935 - Brooklyn, New York
Personal Manager: Jack Rollins/Charles Joffe, 130 West 57th Street,
   New York, NY, 212/582-1940
Agent: Sam Cohn, ICM - Los Angeles, 212/556-5600

WHAT'S UP, TIGER LILY?   American International, 1966
TAKE THE MONEY AND RUN   Cinerama Releasing
   Corporation, 1969
BANANAS   United Artists, 1971
EVERYTHING YOU ALWAYS WANTED TO KNOW ABOUT SEX*
   (*BUT WERE AFRAID TO ASK)   United Artists, 1972
SLEEPER   United Artists, 1973
LOVE AND DEATH   United Artists, 1975
ANNIE HALL ★★   United Artists, 1977
INTERIORS ★   United Artists, 1978
MANHATTAN   United Artists, 1979
STARDUST MEMORIES   United Artists, 1980
A MIDSUMMER NIGHT'S SEX COMEDY
   Orion/Warner Bros., 1982
ZELIG   Orion/Warner Bros., 1983
BROADWAY DANNY ROSE ★   Orion, 1983
THE PURPLE ROSE OF CAIRO   Orion, 1985
HANNAH AND HER SISTERS ★   Orion, 1986
RADIO DAYS   Orion, 1987
SEPTEMBER   Orion, 1987
ANOTHER WOMAN   Orion, 1988
NEW YORK STORIES   co-director with Francis Ford Coppola &
   Martin Scorsese, Buena Vista, 1989
CRIMES AND MISDEMEANORS ★   Orion, 1989
ALICE   Orion, 1990
SHADOWS AND FOG   Orion, 1992
HUSBANDS AND WIVES   TriStar, 1992
MANHATTAN MURDER MYSTERY   TriStar, 1993
BULLETS OVER BROADWAY ★   Miramax Films, 1994
DON'T DRINK THE WATER (TF)   Magnolia Productions/
   Sweetland Film Corporation/BVI/Jean Doumanian
   Productions, 1994
WOODY ALLEN FALL PROJECT '94   Miramax Films, 1995

ROGER ALLERS

Business: Walt Disney Animation,, 500 S. Buena Vista Street,
   Burbank, CA 91521, 818/560-1000

THE LION KING (AF)   co-director with Rob Minkoff,
   Buena Vista, 1994

RENE ALLIO†

b. 1924 - Marseille, France
d. 1995

THE SHAMELESS OLD LADY   Continental, 1965, French
L'UNE ET L'AUTRE   1967, French
PIERRE ET PAUL   1969, French
LES CAMISARDS   1971, French
RUDE JOURNEE POUR LA REINE   1973, French
MOI PIERRE RIVIERE   1976, French
RETOUR A MARSEILLE   1980, French

MICHAEL ALMEREYDA

Contact: Writers Guild of America, East - New York City,
   212/767-7800

TWISTER   Greycat Films, 1990
ANOTHER GIRL, ANOTHER PLANET   Nabu Prlductions, 1992
NADJA   Kino Link, 1994

PEDRO ALMODOVAR

b. September 25, 1951 - Calzada de Calatrava, La Mancha, Spain
Business: El Deseo S.A., Ruiz Perello 15, Madrid 28028, Spain,
   tel.: 255-0285
Agent: CAA - Beverly Hills, 310/288-4545

PEPI, LUCI, BOM   *PEPI, LUCI, BOM & OTRAS CHICAS*
   Cinevista, 1980, Spanish
LABERINTO DE PASIONES   Musidora, 1982, Spanish
DARK HABITS   Cinevista, 1984, Spanish
WHAT HAVE I DONE TO DESERVE THIS?   Cinevista,
   1985, Spanish
MATADOR   Cinevista, 1986, Spanish
LAW OF DESIRE   Cinevista/Promovision International,
   1987, Spanish
WOMEN ON THE VERGE OF A NERVOUS BREAKDOWN
   Orion Classics, 1988, Spanish
TIE ME UP! TIE ME DOWN!   *ATAME*   Miramax Films,
   1990, Spanish
HIGH HEELS   Miramax Films, 1991, Spanish-French
KIKA   October Films, 1993, Spanish-French
LA FLOR DE MI SECRETO   El Deseo S.A., 1995, Spanish

PAUL ALMOND*

b. April 26, 1931 - Montreal, Quebec, Canada
Home: P.O. Box 954, Malibu, CA 90265, 310/456-3573
Attorney: Eric Weissmann, Weissmann, Wolff, Bergman, Coleman &
   Silverman, 9665 Wilshire Blvd. - Suite 900, Beverly Hills, CA
   90212, 310/858-7888

SEVEN UP GRANADA (TF)   1964, British
BACKFIRE   Anglo Amalgamated, 1962, British
THE DARK DID NOT CONQUER (TF)   CBC, 1963, Canadian
JOURNEY TO THE CENTRE (TF)   CBC, 1963, Canadian
ISABEL   Paramount, 1968, Canadian
ACT OF THE HEART   Universal, 1970, Canadian
JOURNEY   EPOH, 1972, Canadian
FELLOWSHIP (TF)   CBC, 1976, Canadian
EVERY PERSON IS GUILTY (TF)   CBC, 1979, Canadian
FOR THE RECORD (TF)   1980, Canadian
FINAL ASSIGNMENT   Almi Cinema 5, 1980, Canadian
UPS AND DOWNS   *PREP SCHOOL*   CENTURY GROUP LTD.,
   1983, Canadian
CAPTIVE HEARTS   MGM/UA, 1987, Canadian
THE DANCE GOES ON   Quest Film Productions, 1992, Canadian

JOHN A. ALONZO*

b. 1934 - Dallas, Texas
Agent: Harris & Goldberg - Los Angeles, 310/553-5200

FM   Universal, 1978
CHAMPIONS...A LOVE STORY (TF)   Warner Bros. TV, 1979
PORTRAIT OF A STRIPPER (TF)   Moonlight Productions/
   Filmways, 1979
BELLE STARR (TF)   Entheos Unlimited Productions/Hanna-Barbera
   Productions, 1980
BLINDED BY THE LIGHT (TF)   Time-Life Films, 1980

GREGORY RYAN ALOSIO

Business Manager: June Hatch, Hatch Entertainment, Inc., 10880
   Wilshire Blvd. - Suite 911, Los Angeles, CA 90024, 310/441-5110

PRIVATE AFFAIR   Filmpartners Company, 1991

EMMETT ALSTON

NEW YEAR'S EVIL   Cannon, 1981
NINE DEATHS OF THE NINJA   Crown International, 1985
DEMONWARP   Vidmark, 1988
TIGER SHARK   Chappell Productions, 1989, U.S.-Filipino
ACROSS MANILA BAY   Kelday International, 1989, Filipino
LITTLE NINJAS AND THE SACRED TREASURE
   Comet Entertainment, 1992

ROBERT ALTMAN*
b. February 20, 1925 - Kansas City, Missouri
Agent: William Morris Agency - Beverly Hills, 310/859-4000

THE DELINQUENTS   United Artists, 1957
THE JAMES DEAN STORY (FD)   co-director with
   George W. George, Warner Bros., 1957
NIGHTMARE IN CHICAGO (TF)   MCA-TV, 1964
COUNTDOWN   Warner Bros., 1968
THAT COLD DAY IN THE PARK   Commonwealth United,
   1969, Canadian-U.S.
M*A*S*H ★   20th Century-Fox, 1970
BREWSTER McCLOUD   MGM, 1970
McCABE & MRS. MILLER   Warner Bros., 1971
IMAGES   Columbia, 1972, Irish
THE LONG GOODBYE   United Artists, 1973
THIEVES LIKE US   United Artists, 1974
CALIFORNIA SPLIT   Columbia, 1974
NASHVILLE ★   Paramount, 1975
BUFFALO BILL AND THE INDIANS or SITTING BULL'S HISTORY
   LESSON   United Artists, 1976
3 WOMEN   20th Century-Fox, 1977
A WEDDING   20th Century-Fox, 1978
A PERFECT COUPLE   20th Century-Fox, 1979
QUINTET   20th Century-Fox, 1979
HEALTH   20th Century-Fox, 1980
POPEYE   Paramount, 1980
COME BACK TO THE 5 & DIME JIMMY DEAN, JIMMY DEAN
   Cinecom, 1982
STREAMERS   United Artists Classics, 1983
SECRET HONOR   Sandcastle 5, 1984
THE LAUNDROMAT (CTF)   Byck-Lancaster Productions/
   Sandcastle 5 Productions, 1985
FOOL FOR LOVE   Cannon, 1985
BEYOND THERAPY   New World, 1987
O.C. AND STIGGS   MGM/UA, 1987, filmed in 1983
THE DUMB WAITER (TF)   Secret Castle Productions, 1987
ARIA   co-director, Miramax Films, 1987, British
THE ROOM (TF)   Sandcastle 5 Productions/Secret Castle
   Productions, 1987
THE CAINE MUTINY COURT MARTIAL (TF)
   CBS Entertainment, 1988
VINCENT & THEO   Hemdale, 1990, British-French
THE PLAYER ★   Fine Line Features/New Line Cinema, 1992
SHORT CUTS ★   Fine Line Features/New Line Cinema, 1993
READY TO WEAR (PRET-A-PORTER)   Miramax Films, 1994
KANSAS CITY   CIBY 2000, 1995, U.S.-French

JOE ALVES*
b. May 21, 1938 - San Leandro, California
Home: 4176 Rosario Road, Woodland Hills, CA 91364,
   818/346-4624
Agent: The Gersh Agency - Beverly Hills, 310/274-6611

JAWS 3-D   Universal, 1983

DENIS AMAR
Agent: Voyez Mon Agent - Paris, tel.: 1/47-23-55-80
Contact: French Film Office, 745 Fifth Avenue, New York,
   NY 10151, 212/832-8860

ASPHALTE   1981, French
L'ADDITION   THE CAGED HEART   New World, 1985, French
INSTANT JUSTICE   Warner Bros., 1987, Gibralter, uncredited
ENNEMIS INTIMES   Les Films Ariane, 1987, French
WINTER OF '54   HIVER 54, L'ABBE PIERRE   Circle Releasing,
   1990, French
CONTRE L'OUBLI   co-director, Les Films du Paradoxe/Amnesty
   International/PRV, 1992, French

SUZANA AMARAL
b. Brazil
Contact: Concine/National Cinema Council, Rua Mayrink Veiga 28,
   Rio de Janeiro, Brazil, tel.: 2/233-8329

THE HOUR OF THE STAR   Kino International, 1986, Brazilian

ROD AMATEAU*
b. December 20, 1923 - New York, New York
Home: 133-1/2 S. Linden Drive, Beverly Hills, CA 90212,
   310/274-3865
Agent: CAA - Beverly Hills, 310/288-4545

THE BUSHWHACKERS   Realart, 1951
MONSOON   United Artists, 1952
PUSSYCAT, PUSSYCAT, I LOVE YOU   United Artists, 1970, British
THE STATUE   Cinerama Releasing Corporation, 1971, British
WHERE DOES IT HURT?   American International, 1972, British
DRIVE IN   Columbia, 1976
THE SENIORS   Cinema Shares International, 1978
HITLER'S SON   1978, British
UNCOMMON VALOR (TF)   Brademan-Self Productions/
   Sunn Classic, 1983
HIGH SCHOOL U.S.A. (TF)   Hill-Mandelker Films, 1983
LOVELINES   TriStar, 1984
THE GARBAGE PAIL KIDS MOVIE   Atlantic Releasing
   Corporation, 1987

GIANNI AMELIO
b. 1945 - San Pietro Magisano (Catanzaro), Italy
Home: via della Paglia 9, Rome, Italy, tel.: 06/588-1434

LA FINE DEL GIOCO (TF)   RAI, 1970, Italian
LA CITTA' DEL SOLE (TF)   RAI, 1973, Italian
BERTOLUCCI SECONDO IL CINEMA (TD)   RAI, 1976, Italian
LA MORTE AL LAVORO (TF)   RAI, 1978, Italian
EFFETTI SPECIALI (TD)   RAI, 1978, Italian
IL PICCOLO ARCHIMEDE (TF)   RAI, 1979, Italian
COLPIRE AL CUORE   Antea Cinematografica/RAI, 1982, Italian
I VELIERI (TF)   RAI, 1983, Italian
I RAGAZZI DI VIA PANISPERNA (TF)   RAI, 1988, Italian
OPEN DOORS   Orion Classics, 1990, Italian
STOLEN CHILDREN (IL LADRO DI BAMBINI)   The Samuel Goldwyn
   Company, 1992, Italian-French-Swiss
LAMERICA   Cecchi Gori Group Tiger Cinematografica/Arena Films/
   Raiuno/Vega Films/Canal Plus/Centre National de la
   Cinematographie, 1994, Italian-French-Swiss

JON AMIEL*
b. 1948 - London, England
Address: 30 Wolseley Road, London N8 8RP, England,
   tel.: 181/348-9602
Agent: ICM - Beverly Hills, 310/550-4000 or: Judy Daish Associates -
   London, tel.: 171/262-1101

A SUDDEN WRENCH (TF)   BBC, 1983, British
BUSTED (TF)   BBC, 1984, British
GATES OF GOLD (TF)   BBC Belfast, 1984, Northern Irish
TANDOORI NIGHTS (TF)   Channel 4, 1985, British
THE SILENT TWINS (TF)   BBC, 1985, British
THE SINGING DETECTIVE (TF)   BBC/ABC Australia,
   1986, British-Australian
QUEEN OF HEARTS   Cinecom, 1989, British
TUNE IN TOMORROW... AUNT JULIA AND THE SCRIPTWRITER
   Cinecom, 1990
SOMMERSBY   Warner Bros., 1993
COPYCAT   Warner Bros., 1995

GIDEON AMIR
Business: Action Plus Pictures, 999 N. Doheny Drive - Suite 411,
   Los Angeles, CA 90069, 310/271-8596
Contact: Writers Guild of America, West - Los Angeles, 310/550-1000

P.O.W. THE ESCAPE   Cannon, 1986
ACCIDENTS   Trans World Entertainment, 1988, Australian

MARINO AMORUSO
OF MOOSE AND MEN: THE ROCKY AND BULLWINKLE
   STORY (TD)   Georgetown Television Productions, 1991

ROBERT AMRAM
b. June 12, 1930 - Budapest, Hungary
Business: Amram Films, 8741 Shoreham Drive, Los Angeles,
   CA 90069, 213/657-3692

SENTINELS OF SILENCE (FD)   1972
SKY HIGH! (FD)   1975
PACIFIC CHALLENGE (FD)   1975
THE LATE GREAT PLANET EARTH (FD)   1980

FRANCO AMURRI*
b. September 12, 1958 - Rome, Italy
Address: via N. Piccolomini 34, Rome, Italy, tel.: 06/637-5286
Agent: The Gersh Agency - Beverly Hills, 310/274-6611
Attorney: Barry Hirsch, 1888 Century Park East, Los Angeles,
   CA 90067, 310/553-0305

IL RAGAZZO DEL PONY EXPRESS   Numero Uno, 1986, Italian
DA GRANDE   Gruppo BEMA, 1986, Italian
FLASHBACK   Paramount, 1990
MONKEY TROUBLE   New Line Cinema, 1994

JOSEPH R. ANDALORO
ONE GLORIOUS SUMMER   Phase One Productions, 1995

TORGNY ANDERBERG
Contact: Swedish Film Institute, P.O. Box 27126, 102 52 Stockholm,
   Sweden, tel.: 08/665-1100

TRAIN TO HEAVEN   Filmstallet/Exat/Condor Film/Cinemateca
   Ecuador, 1989, Swedish-Ecuadorian

ALLISON ANDERS
Agent: Broder-Kurland-Webb-Uffner Agency - Beverly Hills,
   310/281-3400

BORDER RADIO   co-director with Dean Lent & Kurt Voss,
   International Film Marketing, 1988
GAS FOOD LODGING   I.R.S. Releasing, 1992
MI VIDA LOCA/MY CRAZY LIFE   Sony Pictures Classics, 1993
FOUR ROOMS   co-director with Quentin Tarantino,
   Alexandre Rockwell & Robert Rodriguez, Miramax Films, 1995
GRACE OF MY HEART   Gramercy Pictures, 1995

ANDY ANDERSON
Business: 817/461-1228

POSITIVE I.D.   Universal, 1987

KURT ANDERSON
MARTIAL OUTLAW   Image Organization, 1993
OPEN FIRE   Republic Pictures, 1994
DEAD COLD   Vantana Productions, 1995

LAURIE ANDERSON
Agent: William Morris Agency - Beverly Hills, 310/859-4000

HOME OF THE BRAVE (FCD)   Cinecom, 1986

MICHAEL ANDERSON*
b. January 30, 1920 - London, England
Agent: Paul Burford, 52 Yorkminster Road, North York, Ontario
   M2P 1M3, Canada, 416/886-0333

PRIVATE ANGELO   co-director with Peter Ustinov,
   Associated British Picture Corporation, 1949, British
WATERFRONT WOMEN   *WATERFRONT*   Rank, 1950, British
HELL IS SOLD OUT   Eros, 1951, British
NIGHT WAS OUR FRIEND   Monarch, 1951, British
WILL ANY GENTLEMAN?   Associated British Picture Corporation,
   1953, British
THE HOUSE OF THE ARROW   Associated British Picture
   Corporation, 1953, British
THE DAM BUSTERS   Warner Bros., 1955, British
1984   Columbia, 1956, British

AROUND THE WORLD IN 80 DAYS ★   United Artists, 1956
BATTLE HELL   *YANGTSE INCIDENT*   DCA, 1957, British
CHASE A CROOKED SHADOW   Warner Bros., 1958, British
SHAKE HANDS WITH THE DEVIL   United Artists, 1959, British
THE WRECK OF THE MARY DEARE   MGM, 1959
ALL THE FINE YOUNG CANNIBALS   MGM, 1960
THE NAKED EDGE   United Artists, 1961
FLIGHT FROM ASHIYA   United Artists, 1964
WILD AND WONDERFUL   Universal, 1964
OPERATION CROSSBOW   MGM, 1965, British-Italian
THE QUILLER MEMORANDUM   Paramount, 1966, British
THE SHOES OF THE FISHERMAN   MGM, 1968
POPE JOAN   Columbia, 1972, British
DOC SAVAGE, THE MAN OF BRONZE   Warner Bros., 1975
CONDUCT UNBECOMING   Allied Artists, 1975, British
LOGAN'S RUN   MGM/United Artists, 1975
ORCA   Paramount, 1976
DOMINIQUE   Sword And Sworcery Productions, 1979, British
THE MARTIAN CHRONICLES (TF)   Charles Fries Productions/
   Stonehenge Productions, 1980
MURDER BY PHONE   New World, 1983, Canadian
SECOND TIME LUCKY   United International Pictures, 1984,
   New Zealand-Australian
SEPARATE VACATIONS   RSL Entertainment, 1986, Canadian
SWORD OF GIDEON (CTF)   Alliance Entertainment/Les Films
   Ariane/HBO Premiere Films/CTV/Telefilm Canada/Rogers
   Cablesystems/Radio-Canada, 1986, Canadian-French
THE JEWELLER'S SHOP   PAC/RAI-1/Alliance Entertainment/
   International Movies Productions, 1988, Italian-French-Canadian
MILLENNIUM   20th Century Fox, 1989, Canadian-U.S.
YOUNG CATHERINE (CTF)   Consolidated Entertainment/Primedia/
   Lenfilm, 1991, U.S.-British-Soviet
THE SEA WOLF (CTF)   Bob Banner Associates/Primedia
   Productions/Andrew J. Fenady Productions, 1993
RUGGED GOLD (CTF)   Alliance Communications/The Gibson
   Group/Official Canada-New Zealand/The Family Channel, 1994,
   Canadian-New Zealand-U.S.

PAUL ANDERSON
Agent: UTA - Beverly Hills, 310/273-6700 or
   ICM - London, tel.: 171/636-6565
Manager: Carlyle Management - Los Angeles, 213/469-3086

SHOPPING   Film Four International/Polygram/Kuzui Enterprises/
   WMG/Impact Pictures, 1994, British
MORTAL KOMBAT   New Line Cinema, 1995
SYDNEY   Rysher Entertainment, 1995

SARAH PIA ANDERSON
Home: Flat 2, 32 Woodland Rise, London N10 3UG, England,
   tel.: 181/883-3600
Agent: Ken McReddie - London, tel.: 171/439-1456

DR. FINLAY (MS)   co-director with Patrick Lau, Scottish TV
   Enterprises, 1994, Scottish

STEVE ANDERSON
Agent: The Gersh Agency - Beverly Hills, 310/274-6611

SOUTH CENTRAL   Warner Bros. 1992

WES ANDERSON
Agent: UTA - Beverly Hills, 310/273-6700

BOTTLE ROCKET   Columbia, 1995

MARIO ANDREACCHIO
Contact: Australian Film Commission, 150 William Street,
   Woolloomooloo NSW 2011, Australia, tel.: 2/321-6444

NAPOLEON   The Samuel Goldwyn Company, 1995,
   Australian-Japanese

SCOTT ANDREWS
FRONTLINE: SCHOOL COLORS   *SCHOOL COLORS* (TD)
   WGBH-Boston, 1994

YVES ANGELO
Contact: French Film Office, 745 Fifth Avenue, New York,
NY 10151, 212/832-8860

COLONEL CHABERT   October Films, 1994, French

THEO ANGELOPOULOS
(Theodoros Angelopoulos)
b. April 27, 1935 - Athens, Greece
Address: 7 Charitos Street, Klonaki, Athens 10675, Greece
Contact: Greek Film Centre, 10 Panepistimiou Avenue,
Athens 106 71, Greece, tel.: 01/363-1733 or 01/363-4586

RECONSTRUCTION   1970, Greek
DAYS OF '36   1973, Greek
THE TRAVELLING PLAYERS   1975, Greek
THE HUNTERS   1978, Greek
MEGALEXANDROS   1980, Greek
ATHENS (FD)   1982, Greek
JOURNEY TO CYTHERA   Greek Film Centre, 1984, Greek
O MELISSOKOMOS   Greek Film Centre/Theo Angelopoulos
Productions/Marin Karmitz Productions/ICC/RAI/RAITRE/ERT-1,
1986, Greek-French-Italian
LANDSCAPE IN THE MIST   New Yorker , 1988,
Greek-French-Italian
THE SUSPENDED STEP OF THE STORK   Arena Films/Greek
Film Centre/Theo Angelopoulos Productions/Vega Film/Erre
Produzioni/Canal PlusERT-1/RAI-1/Greek Ministry of Culture &
Communication, 1991, Greek-French-Swiss-Italian
THE BEEKEEPER   1993, Greek
THE GLANCE OF ULYSSES   Theo Angelopoulos/Paradis Films/
Basic Cinematografica/Greek Film Centre, 1995,
Greek-French-Italian

JEFF ANGELUCCI
THE ACTOR   The Blum Group, 1989

KENNETH ANGER
b. 1932 - Santa Monica, California

ESCAPE EPISODE   1944-46
FIREWORKS   1947, French
PUCE MOMENT   1949, French
LA LUNE DES LAPINS, French
LA JEUNE HOMME ET LA MORT   1953, French
EAUX D'ARTIFICE   1953, French
INAUGURATION OF THE PLEASURE DOME   1954-66, French
THELMA ABBEY   1955, French
THE STORY OF O   1958-61, French, incomplete
SCORPIO RISING   1962-64
INVOCATION OF MY DEMON BROTHER   1969
RABBIT'S MOON   1971
LUCIFER RISING   1973, re-released in revised version in 1980

ERIK ANJOU
Agent: The Partos Company - Los Angeles, 213/876-5500

THE COOL SURFACE   Penn/Eden West Pictures, 1993

KEN ANNAKIN*
b. August 10, 1914 - Beverley, East Yorkshire, England
Home: 3510 Sweetwater Mesa Road, Malibu, CA 90265,
310/456-2352
Business Manager: Stephany Hurkos, 12214 Viewcrest Road,
Studio City, CA 91064, 818/763-6601

HOLIDAY CAMP   Universal, 1947, British
MIRANDA   Eagle-Lion, 1948, British
BROKEN JOURNEY   Eagle-Lion, 1948, British
HERE COME THE HUGGETTS   General Film Distributors,
1948, British
QUARTET   co-director with Ralph Smart, Harold French &
Arthur Crabtree, Eagle-Lion, 1948, British
VOTE FOR HUGGETT   General Film Distributors, 1949, British
THE HUGGETTS ABROAD   General Film Distributors, 1949, British
LANDFALL   Associated British Picture Corporation, 1949, British

TRIO   co-director with Harold French, Paramount, 1950, British
HOTEL SAHARA   United Artists, 1951, British
THE STORY OF ROBIN HOOD   co-director with Alex Bryce,
RKO Radio, 1952, U.S.-British
OUTPOST IN MALAYA   *THE PLANTER'S WIFE*   United Artists,
1952, British
THE SWORD AND THE ROSE   RKO Radio, 1953, U.S.-British
DOUBLE CONFESSION   Stratford, 1953, British
YOU KNOW WHAT SAILORS ARE   United Artists, 1954, British
LAND OF FURY   *THE SEEKERS*   Universal, 1955, British
LOSER TAKES ALL   British Lion, 1956, British
VALUE FOR MONEY   Rank, 1957, British
THREE MEN IN A BOAT   DCA, 1958, British
ACROSS THE BRIDGE   Rank, 1958, British
THIRD MAN ON THE MOUNTAIN   Buena Vista, 1959, U.S.-British
ELEPHANT GUN   *NOR THE MOON BY NIGHT*   Lopert,
1959, British
SWISS FAMILY ROBINSON   Buena Vista, 1960
THE HELLIONS   Columbia, 1962, British
A COMING-OUT PARTY   *VERY IMPORTANT PERSON*
Union, 1962, British
THE FAST LADY   Rank, 1962, British
CROOKS ANONYMOUS   Allied Artists, 1962, British
THE LONGEST DAY   co-director with Andrew Marton &
Bernhard Wicki, 20th Century-Fox, 1962
THOSE MAGNIFICENT MEN IN THEIR FLYING MACHINES
20th Century-Fox, 1965, British
BATTLE OF THE BULGE   Warner Bros., 1965
UNDERWORLD INFORMERS   *THE INFORMERS*   Continental,
1966, British
THE LONG DUEL   Paramount, 1967, British
THE BIGGEST BUNDLE OF THEM ALL   MGM, 1968, U.S.-Italian
THOSE DARING YOUNG MEN IN THEIR JAUNTY JALOPIES
Paramount, 1969, British-Italian-French
CALL OF THE WILD   Constantin, 1975, West German-Spanish
PAPER TIGER   Joseph E. Levine Presents, 1976, British
MURDER AT THE MARDI GRAS (TF)   The Jozak Company/
Paramount TV, 1978
HAROLD ROBBINS' THE PIRATE (TF)   Howard W. Koch
Productions/Warner Bros. TV, 1978
THE 5TH MUSKETEER   Columbia, 1979, Austrian
INSTITUTE FOR REVENGE (TF)   Gold-Driskill Productions/
Columbia TV, 1979
CHEAPER TO KEEP HER   American Cinema, 1980
THE PIRATE MOVIE   20th Century-Fox, 1982, Australian
THE NEW ADVENTURES OF PIPPI LONGSTOCKING
Columbia, 1988
JOSEPH AND EMMA   Independent, 1991
GENGHIS KHAN   International Cinema Company/Vision
International, 1993, British-Italian

JEAN-JACQUES ANNAUD*
b. October 1, 1943 - Draveil, France
Home: Le Moulin, Chevry 45210, Ferrieres, France, tel.: 33/38909830
Business: Reperage, 16, rue Saint Vincent, 75018 Paris, France,
tel.: 1/42-51-20-00
Agent: ICM - Beverly Hills, 310/550-4000

BLACK AND WHITE IN COLOR   *LA VICTOIRE EN CHANTANT*
Allied Artists, 1978, French-Ivory Coast-Swiss
COUP DE TETE   *HOTHEAD*   Quartet, 1980, French
QUEST FOR FIRE   20th Century-Fox, 1982, Canadian-French
THE NAME OF THE ROSE   20th Century Fox, 1986,
West German-Italian- French
THE BEAR   TriStar, 1988, French
THE LOVER   MGM, 1992, French

DAVID ANSPAUGH*
b. September 24, 1946 - Decatur, Indiana
Agent: ICM - Beverly Hills, 310/550-4000

HOOSIERS   Orion, 1986
DEADLY CARE (TF)   Universal TV, 1987
FRESH HORSES   Columbia/WEG, 1988
IN THE COMPANY OF DARKNESS (TF)   Windy City Productions/
MCA TV Entertainment, 1993
RUDY   TriStar, 1993
MOONLIGHT AND VALENTINO   Gramercy Pictures, 1995

BRIAN ANTHONY
b. April 4, 1956 - New York, New York
Business: Victor Motion Pictures, 1506 Corinth Avenue - Suite 202,
   Los Angeles, CA 90025, 310/478-1806

VICTOR'S BIG SCORE   Mushikuki Productions, 1992
CAMP STALAG   Victor Motion Pictures, 1993

ELEANOR ANTIN
THE MAN WITHOUT A WORLD   Milestone Films, 1992

GREG ANTONACCI*
Agent: ICM - Beverly Hills, 310/550-4000

SPLASH, TOO (TF)   Mark H. Ovitz Productions/
   Walt Disney TV, 1988

LOU ANTONIO*
b. Oklahoma City, Oklahoma
Agent: ICM - Beverly Hills, 310/550-4000

SOMEONE I TOUCHED (TF)   Charles Fries Productions, 1975
LANIGAN'S RABBI (TF)   Universal TV, 1976
RICH MAN, POOR MAN - BOOK II (TF)   Universal TV, 1976
THE GIRL IN THE EMPTY GRAVE (TF)   NBC-TV, 1977
SOMETHING FOR JOEY (TF) ☆   MTM Productions, 1977
THE CRITICAL LIST (TF)   MTM Productions, 1978
A REAL AMERICAN HERO (TF)   Bing Crosby Productions, 1978
BREAKING UP IS HARD TO DO (TF)   Green-Epstein Productions/
   Columbia TV, 1979
SILENT VICTORY: THE KITTY O'NEILL STORY (TF) ☆
   Channing-Debin-Locke Company, 1979
THE CONTENDER (TF)   co-director with Harry Falk,
   Universal TV, 1980
WE'RE FIGHTING BACK (TF)   Highgate Pictures, 1981
THE STAR MAKER (TF)   Channing-Debin-Locke Company/Carson
   Productions, 1981
SOMETHING SO RIGHT (TF)   List-Estrin Productions/Tisch-Avnet
   Television, 1982
BETWEEN FRIENDS (CTF)   HBO Premiere Films/Marian Rees
   Associates/Robert Cooper Films III/List-Estrin Productions,
   1983, U.S.-Canadian
A GOOD SPORT (TF)   Ralph Waite Productions/
   Warner Bros. TV, 1984
THREESOME (TF)   CBS Entertainment, 1984
REARVIEW MIRROR (TF)   Simon-Asher Entertainment/Sunn
   Classic Pictures, 1984
AGATHA CHRISTIE'S 'THIRTEEN AT DINNER' (TF)
   Warner Bros. TV, 1985
ONE TERRIFIC GUY (TF)   CBS Entertainment, 1986
PALS (TF)   Robert Halmi, Inc., 1987
MAYFLOWER MADAM (TF)   Robert Halmi, Inc., 1987
THE OUTSIDE WOMAN (TF)   Green-Epstein Productions, 1989
DARK HOLIDAY (TF)   Peter Nelson-Lou Antonio Productions/
   The Finnegan-Pinchuk Company/Orion TV, 1989
FACE TO FACE (TF)   Robert Halmi, Inc., 1990
THIS GUN FOR HIRE (CTF)   BBK Productions, 1991
LIES BEFORE KISSES (TF)   Grossbart-Barnett Productions/
   Spectator Films, 1991
THE LAST PROSTITUTE (CTF)   BBK Productions/Carmen Culver
   Films/MCA-TV Entertainment, 1991
THE RAPE OF DR. WILLIS (TF)   Interprod Productions, 1991
A TASTE FOR KILLING (CTF)   Bodega Bay Productions/MCA TV
   Entertainment, 1992
NIGHTMARE IN THE DAYLIGHT (TF)   Smith-Richmond
   Productions/Saban-Scherick Productions, 1992

MICHELANGELO ANTONIONI
b. September 29, 1912 - Ferrara, Italy
Home: via Vincenzo Tiberio 18, Rome, Italy, tel: 06/333-1988

STORY OF A LOVE AFFAIR   New Yorker, 1950, Italian
I VINTI   Film Costellazione, 1953, Italian
LA SIGNORA SENZA CAMELIE   1953, Italian
LOVE IN THE CITY   co-director with Federico Fellini,
   Alberto Lattuada, Carlo Lizzani, Francesco Maselli & Dino Risi,
   Italian Films Export, 1953, Italian

LE AMICHE   Trion Falcine/Titanus, 1955, Italian
IL GRIDO   Astor, 1957, Italian
L'AVVENTURA   Janus, 1961, Italian
LA NOTTE   Lopert, 1961, Italian-French
L'ECLISSE   Times, 1962, Italian-French
RED DESERT   Rizzoli, 1965, Italian-French
I TRE VOLTI   co-director with Mauro Bolognini & Franco Indovina,
   De Laurentiis, 1964, Italian
BLOW-UP ★   Premier, 1966, British-Italian
ZABRISKIE POINT   MGM, 1970
CHUNG KUO (FD)   Golan Productions, 1972, Italian
THE PASSENGER *PROFESSIONE: REPORTER*
   MGM/United Artists, 1975, Italian-French-Spanish-U.S.
THE MYSTERY OF OBERWALD   RAI/Polytel International,
   1980, Italian
IDENTIFICATION OF A WOMAN   Iter Film/Gaumont,
   1982, Italian-French
KUMBHA MELA (FD)   1989, Italian
NOTO-MAVDORLI-VULCANO-STROMBOLI-CARNEVALE (FD)
   1991, Italian
BEYOND THE CLOUDS   co-director with Wim Wenders, Cecchi
   Gori Group/Road Movies/Stephan Tchalgadjeff-Philippe Carcasson,
   1995, Italian-German-French

DANIEL APPLEBY
BOUND & GAGGED, A LOVE STORY   Northern Arts
   Entertainment, 1993

NORMAN APSTEIN
Business: Doublesteen Productions, 8724 Remmet Avenue,
   Canoga Park, CA 91304, 818/882-8547

THE ICE CREAM MAN   Doublesteen Productions, 1994

MICHAEL APTED*
b. February 10, 1941 - Aylesbury, Buckinghamshire, England
Business: Osiris Films, 300 S. Lorimar Plaza - Bldg. 137 Room 1089,
   Burbank, CA 91505, 818/954-7692
Agent: CAA - Beverly Hills, 310/288-4545
Business Manager: Gary Cohen, Michael Apted Film Company,
   1800 Century Park East - Suite 300, Los Angeles, CA 90067,
   310/203-0777

NUMBER 10 (TF)   Granada TV, 1968, British
BIG BREADWINNER HOG (TF)   Granada TV, 1968, British
YOUR NAME'S NOT GOD, IT'S EDGAR (TF)   Granada TV,
   1968, British
IN A COTTAGE HOSPITAL (TF)   Granada TV, 1969, British
DON'T TOUCH HIM, HE MIGHT RESENT IT (TF)   Granada TV,
   1970, British
SLATTERY'S MOUNTED FOOT (TF)   London Weekend TV/
   Kestrel Films, 1970, British
THE DAY THEY BURIED CLEAVER (TF)   Granada TV,
   1970, British
BIG SOFT NELLIE (TF)   Granada TV, 1971, British
THE MOSEDALE HORSESHOE (TF)   Granada TV, 1971, British
ONE THOUSAND POUNDS FOR ROSEBUD (TF)   Granada TV,
   1971, British
ANOTHER SUNDAY AND SWEET F.A. (TF)   Granada TV,
   1972, British
JOY (TF)   BBC, 1972, British
SAID THE PREACHER (TF)   BBC, 1972, British
THE STYLE OF THE COUNTESS (TF)   Granada TV, 1972
THE REPORTERS (TF)   BBC, 1972, British
BUGGINS' ERMINE (TF)   Granada TV, 1972, British
KISSES AT FIFTY (TF)   BBC, 1973, British
HIGH KAMPF (TF)   BBC, 1973, British
JACK POINT (TF)   BBC, 1973, British
THE TRIPLE ECHO   Altura, 1973, British
POOR GIRL (TF)   Granada TV, 1974, British
A GREAT DAY FOR BONZO (TF)   Granada TV, 1974, British
STARDUST   Columbia, 1975, British
WEDNESDAY LOVE (TF)   BBC, 1975, British
THE COLLECTION (TF) ☆☆   Granada TV, 1976, British
STRONGER THAN THE SUN (TF)   BBC, 1977, British
THE SQUEEZE   Warner Bros., 1977, British
AGATHA   Warner Bros., 1979, British

COAL MINER'S DAUGHTER   Universal, 1980
CONTINENTAL DIVIDE   Universal, 1981
KIPPERBANG   *P'TANG YANG, KIPPERBANG*   MGM/UA Classics,
   1983, British
GORKY PARK   Orion, 1983
FIRSTBORN   Paramount, 1984
28 UP (FD)   First Run Features, 1984, British,
   originally filmed for television
BRING ON THE NIGHT (FCD)   The Samuel Goldwyn
   Company, 1985
CRITICAL CONDITION   Paramount, 1987
GORILLAS IN THE MIST   Universal, 1988
THE LONG WAY HOME (TCD)   Yerosha Productions/Granada TV/
   CBS Music Video Enterprises, 1989, British
CLASS ACTION   20th Century Fox, 1991
35 UP (FD)   The Samuel Goldwyn Company, 1991, British,
   originally filmed for television
INCIDENT AT OGLALA (FD)   Miramax Films, 1992
THUNDERHEART   TriStar, 1992
BLINK   New Line Cinema, 1994
MOVING THE MOUNTAIN (FD)   October Films, 1994, British
NELL   20th Century Fox, 1994

MANUEL GUTIERREZ ARAGON
(See Manuel GUTIERREZ ARAGON)

GREGG ARAKI
THREE BEWILDERED PEOPLE IN THE NIGHT
   Desperate Pictures, Ltd.
THE LONG WEEKEND (O' DESPAIR)
   Desperate Pictures, Ltd., 1989
THE LIVING END   October Films, 1992
TOTALLY F****D UP   Strand Releasing, 1993
THE DOOM GENERATION   The Samuel Goldwyn Company, 1995

VICENTE ARANDA
b. 1926 - Barcelona, Spain
Contact: Spanish Film Institute, San Marcos 40, Madrid 28004,
   Spain, tel.: 1/532-5089

BRILLANTE PORVENIR   1964, Spanish
FATA MORGANA   1966, Spanish
LAS CRUELES   1968, Spanish
EL CADAVER EXQUISITO   1970, Spanish
BAILANDO CON PARKER   1971, Spanish
LA NOVIA ENSANGRENTADA   1972, Spanish
CAMBIO DE SEXO   1976, Spanish
LA MUCHACHA DE LAS BRAGAS DE ORO   1979, Spanish
ASESINATO EN EL COMITE CENTRAL   1981, Spanish
FANNY PELOPAJA   1983, Spanish
TIEMPO DE SILENCIO   1985, Spanish
EL LUTE   1987, Spanish
EL LUTE II: MANANA SERE LIBRE   1988, Spanish
SI TE DICEN QUE CAI...   1989, Spanish
LOVERS   Aries Film Releasing, 1991, Spanish
EL AMANTE BILINGUE   Lola Films/Atrium Productions/Cartel/
   Sogepaq/Antena 3 TV/International Dean Film, 1993,
   Spanish-Italian
INTRUSO   Pedro Costa P.C.S.A./Atrium Productions/Promociones
   Audiovisuales Reunidas/Antena 3-TV, 1993, Spanish
LA PASION TURCA   Lolafilms/Cartel/Sogepaq, 1995, Spanish

ALFONSO ARAU*
Agent: CAA - Beverly Hills, 310/288-4545

THE BAREFOOT EAGLE   Televicine International Distribution
   Corporation, 1967, Mexican
CALZONZIN INSPECTOR   Azteca Films, 1974, Mexican
MOJADO POWER   Producciones AA, 1980, Mexican
CHIDO GUAN   General International, 1984, Mexican
LIKE WATER FOR CHOCOLATE (COMO AGUA PARA
   CHOCOLATE)   Miramax Films, 1992, Mexican
A WALK IN THE CLOUDS   20th Century Fox, 1995

DENYS ARCAND
b. June 25, 1941 - Deschambault, Quebec, Canada
Address: 3365 Ridgewood - Suite 1, Montreal, Quebec H3V 1B4,
   Canada, 514/341-6139
Agent: CAA - Beverly Hills, 310/288-4545

ON EST AU COTON (FD)   National Film Board of Canada,
   1970, Canadian
QUEBEC: DUPLESSIS ET APRES... (FD)   National Film Board
   of Canada, 1972, Canadian
LA MAUDITE GALETTE   France Film, 1972, Canadian
REJEANNE PADOVANI   Cinak, 1972, Canadian
GINA   1975, Canadian
LE CONFORT ET L'INDIFFERENCE (FD)   Canadian Empire Inc.,
   1982, Canadian
THE CRIME OF OVIDE PLOUFFE   co-director with Gilles Carle,
   Cine Plouffe II/CBC/National Film Board of Canada,
   1984, Canadian
MURDER IN THE FAMILY (MS)   co-director with Gilles Carles,
   ICC/Filmax/Antenne-21 Films A2, 1985, Canadian-French
THE DECLINE OF THE AMERICAN EMPIRE   Cineplex Odeon,
   1986, Canadian
JESUS OF MONTREAL   Orion Classics, 1990, Canadian
MONTREAL VU PAR...   co-director with Patricia Rozema,
   Jacques Leduc, Michel Brault, Atom Egoyan & Lea Pool,
   Cinema Plud Distribution, 1991, Canadian
LOVE AND HUMAN REMAINS   Sony Pictures Classics,
   1993, Canadian

ALEXANDRE ARCADY
Business: Alexandre Films, 14, rue de Marignan, 75008 Paris,
   France, tel.: 1/45-62-0204
Contact: French Film Office, 745 Fifth Avenue, New York, NY 10151,
   212/832-8860

LE GRAND PARDON   1982, French
FOR SASHA   *POUR SACHA*   MK2 Productions USA, 1991, French
LE GRAND PARDON II   UGC, 1992, French
DIS MOI OUI   Lumiere Pictures, 1995, French

NOEL ARCHAMBAULT
AT THE MAX   *ROLLING STONES AT THE MAX* (FCD)
   co-director with Julien Temple, Roman Kroiter & David Douglas,
   BCL Presentation/IMAX Corporation, 1991, U.S.-Canadian

FRANCESCA ARCHIBUGI
b. 1961 - Rome, Italy
Home: viale Parioli 98, Rome, Italy, tel.: 06/808-8736

MIGNON E' PARTITA   Ellepi Film/RAI, 1987, Italian
VERSO SERA   Ellepi Film/RAI/Paradis Films, 1990, Italian-French
IL GRANDE COCOMERO   Ellepi Film/Chrysalide Films, 1993,
   Italian-French
CON GLI OCCHI CHIUSI   MG/Italian International Film/Paradis
   Films/Cartel/RAI/Canal Plus 1994, Italian-French-Spanish

DARIO ARGENTO
b. September 7, 1940 - Rome, Italy
Contact: A.D.C., via Baiamonti 2, Rome, Italy, tel.: 06/325-2222
Agent: UTA - Beverly Hills, 310/273-6700

THE BIRD WITH THE CRYSTAL PLUMAGE   UMC, 1970,
   Italian-West German
CAT O'NINE TAILS   National General, 1971,
   Italian-West German-French
FOUR FLIES ON GREY VELVET   Paramount, 1972, Italian-French
LE CINQUE GIORNATE   Seda Spettacoli, 1973, Italian
DEEP RED   Howard Mahler Films, 1976, Italian
SUSPIRIA   International Classics, 1977, Italian
INFERNO   20th Century-Fox, 1980, Italian
UNSANE   *TENEBRAE*   Bedford Entertainment/Film Gallery,
   1982, Italian
CREEPERS   *PHENOMENA*   New Line Cinema, 1985, Italian
OPERA   Dacfilm/RAI, 1987, Italian
TWO EVIL EYES   co-director with George A. Romero,
   Taurus Entertainment, 1990, Italian
TRAUMA   ADC, 1993, U.S.-Italian

ADOLFO ARISTARAIN
b. October 19, 1943 - Buenos Aires, Argentina
Agent: APA - Los Angeles, 310/273-0744
Contact: Instituto Nacional de Cinematografia, Lima 319, 1073
   Buenos Aires, Argentina, tel.: 37-9091

LA PARTE DEL LEON   1978, Argentine
LA PLAYA DEL AMOR   Aries Cinematografica, 1979, Argentine
LA DISCOTECA DEL AMOR   Aries Cinematografica,
   1980, Argentine
TIEMPO DE REVANCHA   Aries Cinematografica, 1981, Argentine
ULTIMAS DIAS DE LA VICTIMA   Aries Cinematografica,
   1982, Argentine
AVENTURAS DE PEPE CARVALHO (MS)   1983-85, Spanish
THE STRANGER   Columbia, 1987, Argentine-U.S.
A PLACE IN THE WORLD   First Look Films, 1992,
   Argentine-Spanish

ALAN ARKIN*
b. March 26, 1934 - New York, New York
Agent: William Morris Agency - Beverly Hills, 310/859-4000

LITTLE MURDERS   20th Century-Fox, 1970
FIRE SALE   20th Century-Fox, 1977

ALLAN ARKUSH*
b. April 30, 1948 - New York, New York
Agent: ICM - Beverly Hills, 310/550-4000

HOLLYWOOD BOULEVARD   co-director with Joe Dante,
   New World, 1976
DEATHSPORT   co-director with Henry Suso, New World, 1978
ROCK 'N' ROLL HIGH SCHOOL   New World, 1979
HEARTBEEPS   Universal, 1981
GET CRAZY   Embassy, 1983
CADDYSHACK II   Warner Bros., 1988
XXX'S & OOO'S (TF)   Nightwatch Productions/Moving Target
   Productions/New World Entertainment, 1994
REBEL HIGHWAY: SHAKE, RATTLE AND ROCK   SHAKE, RATTLE
   AND ROCK (CTF)   Drive In Classics Cinema/Showtime, 1994
YOUNG AT HEART (TF)   TSProductions/Warner Bros., TV, 1995

GEORGE ARMITAGE*
Agent: ICM - Beverly Hills, 310/550-4000

PRIVATE DUTY NURSES   New World, 1972
HIT MAN   MGM, 1973
VIGILANTE FORCE   United Artists, 1976
HOT ROD (TF)   ABC Circle Films, 1979
MIAMI BLUES   Orion, 1990

GILLIAN ARMSTRONG*
b. December 18, 1950 - Melbourne, Australia
Agent: CAA - Beverly Hills, 310/288-4545

THE SINGER AND THE DANCER   Gillian Armstrong Productions,
   1976, Australian
MY BRILLIANT CAREER   Analysis, 1980, Australian
STARSTRUCK   Cinecom International, 1982, Australian
MRS. SOFFEL   MGM/UA, 1984
HARD TO HANDLE: BOB DYLAN WITH TOM PETTY AND THE
   HEARTBREAKERS (HVCD)   CBS/Fox Video Music, 1986
HIGH TIDE   TriStar, 1987, Australian
FIRES WITHIN   MGM-Pathe Communications, 1991
THE LAST DAYS OF CHEZ NOUS   Fine Line Features/New Line
   Cinema, 1991, Australian
LITTLE WOMEN   Columbia, 1994

MICHAEL ARMSTRONG
b. July 24, 1944 - Bolton, Lancashire, England
Home: 114 N. Doheny Drive, Los Angeles, CA 90048

HORROR HOUSE   THE HAUNTED HOUSE OF HORROR
   American International, 1970, British-U.S.
MARK OF THE DEVIL   Hallmark Releasing Corporation, 1970,
   West German-British

MOIRA ARMSTRONG
Agent: Peter Murphy, Curtis Brown - London, tel.: 171/734-9633

HOW MANY MILES TO BABYLON (TF)   BBC, 1982, British
ALL FOR LOVE: LETTING THE BIRDS GO FREE (TF)   Granada TV,
   1982, British
THE DUN ROAMIN' RISING (TF)   BBC, 1987, British
THE MOUNTAIN AND THE MOLEHILL (TF)   BBC, 1988, British
A SAFE HOUSE (TF)   BBC, 1990, British
COUNTESS ALICE (TF)   BBC, 1992, British
BODY AND SOUL (MS)   Red Rooster Films/TV Entertainment
   Productions/Carlton TV, 1993, British

ROBIN B. ARMSTRONG
Business: Open Road Productions Ltd., 6101 Morella Avenue,
   North Hollywood, CA 91606, 818/980-1100

PASTIME   ONE CUP OF COFFEE   Miramax Films, 1991

VIC ARMSTRONG*
(Victor M. Armstrong)
Agent: The Gersh Agency - Beverly Hills, 3210/274-6611
Address: 1714 Sunset Plaza Drive, Los Angeles, CA 90069,
   310/652-3007 or: Binfield Grove, Binfield, Berks AG12 5PL,
   England, tel.: 0344/483326

ARMY OF ONE   Vision International, 1993, South African

LUCIE ARNAZ
b. July 17, 1951 - Los Angeles, California
Agent: William Morris Agency - Beverly Hills, 310/859-4000

LUCY AND DESI: A HOME MOVIE (TD)   co-director with
   Laurence Luckinbill, Arluck Entertainment, 1993

GWEN ARNER*
Agent: APA - Los Angeles, 310/273-0744

MY CHAMPION   Shochiku, 1981, Japanese-U.S.
MOTHER'S DAY ON WALTON'S MOUNTAIN (TF)
   Lorimar Productions/Amanda Productions, 1982
A MATTER OF PRINCIPLE (TF)   Rubicon Film Productions, 1984
NECESSARY PARTIES (TF)   The Corelli Co./WonderWorks, 1988
MAJORITY RULE (CTF)   Ultra Entertainment/Citadel Pictures, 1992

FRANK ARNOLD*
b. May 9, 1938 - Sydney, Australia
Agent: Shapiro-Lichtman Talent Agency - Beverly Hills, 310/859-8877

DELTA (MS)   Australian Broadcasting Corporation, 1970, Australian
EVERYONE'S GOT WHEELS (TF)   Australian Broadcasting
   Corporation, 1971, Australian
LINEHAUL (TF)   Australian Broadcasting Corporation,
   1973, Australian
CASTAWAY (MS)   Australian Broadcasting Corporation/
   Portman Productions/Bayerischer Rundfunk, 1973,
   Australian-British-German
LINDSAY'S BOY (TF)   Australian Broadcasting Corporation,
   1974, Australian
RECORD OF INTERVIEW (TF)   Australian Broadcasting
   Corporation, 1975, Australian
BEN HALL (MS)   co-director with Don Chaffey, BBC/Australian
   Broadcasting Corporation/20th Century-Fox, 1975,
   British-Australian
RUSH (MS)   co-director with Rob Stewart & Michael Jenkins,
   Australian Broadcasting Corporation/Scottish & Global/Antenne-2,
   1976, Australian-French
GOING HOME (TF)   Australian Broadcasting Corporation,
   1977, Australian
RIPKIN (TF)   Australian Broadcasting Corporation,
   1978, Australian
PATROL BOAT (MS)   Australian Broadcasting Corporation/Universal
   Television, 1979, Australian
LAY ME DOWN IN LILAC FIELDS (TF)   Australian Broadcasting
   Corporation, 1981, Australian

RUNAWAY ISLAND (TF)   Grundy Motion Pictures/Telecip,
    1983, Australian
FIVE MILE CREEK (MS)   co-director with George Miller,
    Michael Jenkins & Di Drew, Valstar/The Disney Channel,
    1983, U.S.- Australian
BUTTERFLY ISLAND (MS)   Independent Productions/BBC/Family
    Channel, 1984, Australian-British-U.S.
THE HAUNTED SCHOOL (MS)   Australian Broadcasting
    Corporation/Revcom, 1985, Australian
A WALTZ THROUGH THE HILLS (TF)   Barron Films/WonderWorks/
    Primetime, 1988, Australian-U.S.
BUTTERFLY ISLAND 3 (MS)   co-director with Di Drew,
    Mediacast/Otis Pictures, 1992, Australian
JOSH KIRBY: TIME WARRIOR (TF)   (The Human Pets;
    Trapped On Toyworld; Lost World of The Giants)   co-director with
    Ernest Farino & Peter Sasdy, Full Moon Entertainment, 1995
FOR THE LOVE OF MY DAUGHTER (TF)   Robert Greenwald
    Productions, 1995

NEWT ARNOLD*

(Newton Arnold)
Business Manager: Gary Osheroff, Jonevan Productions, Inc.,
    929 East 2nd Street - Suite 201, Los Angeles, CA 90012,
    213/687-3107

BLOODSPORT   Cannon, 1987

JERRY ARONSON

THE LIFE AND TIMES OF ALLEN GINSBERG (FD)
    First Run Features, 1994

ISAAC ARTENSTEIN

b. Mexico
Business: Cinewest Productions, 700 Adella Lane, Coronado,
    CA 92118, 619/437-8764

BREAK OF DAWN   Platform Releasing, 1988

KAREN ARTHUR*

b. August 24, 1941 - Omaha, Nebraska
Agent: Paradigm - Los Angeles, 310/277-4400

LEGACY   Kino International, 1976
THE MAFU CAGE   Clouds Productions, 1979
CHARLESTON (TF)   Robert Stigwood Productions/
    RSO, Inc., 1979
RETURN TO EDEN (MS)   McElroy & McElroy/Hanna-Barbera
    Australia Productions, 1983, Australian
VICTIMS FOR VICTIMS (TF)   Daniel L. Paulson - Loehr Spivey
    Productions/Orion TV, 1984
A BUNNY'S TALE (TF)   Stan Margulies Company/ABC
    Circle Films, 1985
THE RAPE OF RICHARD BECK (TF)   Robert Papazian
    Productions/Henerson-Hirsch Productions, 1985
CROSSINGS (MS)   Aaron Spelling Productions, 1986
LADY BEWARE   Scotti Brothers, 1987
CRACKED UP (TF)   Aaron Spelling Productions, 1987
EVIL IN CLEAR RIVER (TF)   The Steve Tisch Company/Lionel
    Chetwynd Productions/Phoenix Entertainment Group, 1988
BRIDGE TO SILENCE (TF)   Fries Entertainment/Briggle,
    Hennessy, Carrothers & Associates, 1989
BLUE BAYOU (TF)   Fisher Entertainment/Touchstone TV, 1990
FALL FROM GRACE (TF)   NBC Productions, 1990
BUMP IN THE NIGHT (TF)   Craig Anderson Productions/RHI
    Entertainment, 1991
THE JACKSONS: AN AMERICAN DREAM (TF)   Stan Margulies
    Company/de Passe Entertainment/Motown Record Company/
    Polygram Filmed Entertainment, 1992
THE DISAPPEARANCE OF CHRISTINA (CTF)   B.A.L. Productions/
    MCA-TV Entertainment, 1993
AGAINST THEIR WILL: WOMEN IN PRISON (TF)   Their Own
    Productions/Jaffe-Braunstein Films/ABC, 1994
LOVE AND BETRAYAL: THE MIA FARROW STORY (TF)
    Fox Circle Productions, 1995

WILLIAM ASHER*

b. 1919
Business Manager: David Capell, 2121 Avenue of the Stars,
    Los Angeles, CA 90067, 310/553-0310
Agent: The Cooper Agency - Los Angeles, 310/277-8422

LEATHER GLOVES   co-director with Richard Quine,
    Columbia, 1948
THE SHADOW ON THE WINDOW   Columbia, 1956
THE 27TH DAY   Columbia, 1956
BEACH PARTY   American International, 1963
JOHNNY COOL   United Artists, 1963
MUSCLE BEACH PARTY   American International, 1963
BIKINI BEACH   American International, 1964
BEACH BLANKET BINGO   American International, 1965
HOW TO STUFF A WILD BIKINI   American International, 1965
FIREBALL 500   American International, 1966
BUTCHER, BAKER, NIGHTMARE MAKER   *NIGHT WARNING/*
    MOMMA'S BOY   Comworld, 1981
MOVERS & SHAKERS   MGM/UA, 1985
I DREAM OF JEANNIE: 15 YEARS LATER (TF)   Can't Sing Can't
    Dance Productions/Columbia TV, 1985
RETURN TO GREEN ACRES (TF)   JaYgee Productions/
    Orion TV, 1990

CHRISTOPHER ASHLEY*

Contact: Directors Guild of America - Los Angeles, 213/851-3671

JEFFREY   Orion Classics, 1995

DAVID ASHWELL*

Contact: Directors Guild of America - Los Angeles, 213/851-3671

YOU RUINED MY LIFE (TF)   Lantana-Kosberg Productions/
    Mark H. Ovitz Productions/Walt Disney TV, 1987

PETER ASKIN

Agent: ICM - Beverly Hills, 310/550-4000

SPIC-O-RAMA (CTPF)   House of Fun Productions/HBO
    Comedy Hour, 1993

SAMSON ASLANIAN

TORMENT   co-director with John Hopkins, New World, 1986

OLIVIER ASSAYAS

Agent: Artmedia, 10, avenue George V, 75008 Paris, France,
    tel.: 1/47-23-78-60
Contact: French Film Office, 745 Fifth Avenue, New York,
    NY 10151, 212/832-8860

DESORDRE   Forum Distribution, 1986, French
L'ENFANT D'HIVER   Gemini Films/GPFI, 1989, French
PARIS S'EVEILLE   Arena Films/Erre Produzioni, 1991,
    French-Italian
UNE NOUVELLE VIE   Arena Films/La Sept/Lumiere/Vega Film/
    Alia Film/Canal Plus/Cofimage 4/Investimage 4/N.C./Television
    Suisse/D.F.1., 1993, French-Swiss
L'EAU FROIDE   Ima Films/La Sept-Arte/SFP Production/Sony
    Music Entertainment, 1994, French

JOHN ASTIN*

b. March 30, 1930 - Baltimore, Maryland
Business Manager: Ralph Turner, Turner Accountancy, 9200 Sunset
    Blvd. - Suite 701, Los Angeles, CA 90069, 310/273-4260

OPERATION PETTICOAT (TF)   Universal TV, 1977
ROSSETTI AND RYAN: MEN WHO LOVE WOMEN (TF)
    Universal TV, 1977

DIMITRI ASTRAKHAN

Contact: Confederation of Film-Makers Unions, Vasilyevskaya
    Street 13, 123 825 Moscow, Russia, tel.: 095/250-4114

GET THEE OUT!   First Run Features, 1991, Soviet
YOU ARE MY ONE AND ONLY   Lenfilm, 1993, Russian

J.D. ATHENS
(See J.F. LAWTON)

FRANCISCO ATHLE
Contact: IMCINE, Tepic #40, P.B. Colonia Roma Sur, Mexico City,
C.P. 06760, Mexico, tel.: 525/584-7283

LOLO   Centro de Capacitacion Cinematografica/IMCINE/Estudios
Churubusco, 1993, Mexican

RICHARD ATTENBOROUGH*
b. August 29, 1923 - Cambridge, England
Business: Richard Attenborough Productions Ltd., Beaver Lodge,
Richmond Green, Surrey TW9 1NQ, England, tel.: 181/940-7234
Agent: CAA - Beverly Hills, 310/288-4545 or
AIM/John Redway Associates - London, tel.: 171/836-2001

OH! WHAT A LOVELY WAR   Paramount, 1969, British
YOUNG WINSTON   Columbia, 1972, British
A BRIDGE TOO FAR   United Artists, 1977, British
MAGIC   20th Century-Fox, 1978
GANDHI ★★   Columbia, 1982, British-Indian
A CHORUS LINE   Columbia, 1985
CRY FREEDOM   Universal, 1987, British-U.S.
CHARLIE   TriStar, 1992, U.S.-British
SHADOWLANDS   Savoy Pictures, 1993, British-U.S.

DANIEL ATTIAS*
Agent: Broder-Kurland-Webb-Uffner Agency - Beverly Hills,
310/281-3400

SILVER BULLET   Paramount, 1985

DAVID ATTWOOD
Contact: British Film Commission, 70 Baker Street, London
W1M 1DJ, England, tel.: 171/224-5000
Agent: William Morris Agency - Beverly Hills, 310/859-4000

FLOWERS IN THE RAIN (TF)   BBC, 1984, British
WILD WEST   Channel 4/British Screen/Initial Films, 1992, British

BILLE AUGUST
b. 1948 - Denmark
Agent: CAA - Beverly Hills, 310/288-4545

IN MY LIFE   Konsortiet Honningmane, 1978, Danish
ZAPPA   Per Holst Filmpruktion/DR-F1, 1983, Danish
TWIST AND SHOUT   Miramax Films, 1984, Danish
BUSTER'S WORLD   Crone Film Production/DR-TV/Danish Film
Institute, 1984, Danish, originally made for television
PELLE THE CONQUEROR   Miramax Films,
1988, Danish-Swedish
THE BEST INTENTIONS   The Samuel Goldwyn Company, 1992
Swedish-Danish-Finnish-Norwegian-British-German-French
THE HOUSE OF THE SPIRITS   Miramax Films, 1993,
German-Danish-Portuguese-U.S.
JERUSALEM   SVT-1/Svensk Filmindustri/Metronome Film/Marko
Rohr Productions/Schibstedt Film/DR-TV/NRK-TV/RUV-TV,
1995, Swedish-Danish

PAUL AUSTER
Agent: William Morris Agency - Beverly Hills, 310/859-4000

BLUE IN THE FACE   co-director with Wayne Wang,
Miramax Films, 1995

MICHAEL AUSTIN
Agent: UTA - Beverly Hills, 310/273-6700 or:
Peters Fraser & Dunlop - London, tel.: 171/344-1000

PRINCESS CARABOO   TriStar, 1994, British-U.S.

RAY AUSTIN*
(Raymond Austin/Baron DeVere-Austin of Delvin/
Lord of Bradwell)
b. December 5, 1932 - London, England
Agent: Tom Chasin, The Chasin Agency - Los Angeles, 310/278-7505
Business Manager: David Licht, Licht & Licht, 9171 Wilshire Blvd.,
Los Angeles, CA, 310/278-1920

IT'S THE ONLY WAY TO GO   Hallelujah, 1970, British
FUN AND GAMES   1971, British
THE VIRGIN WITCH   Joseph Brenner Associates, 1972, British
HOUSE OF THE LIVING DEAD   1973, British
SWORD OF JUSTICE (TF)   Universal TV, 1978
THE HARDY BOYS (TF)   Universal TV, 1978
TALES OF THE GOLD MONKEY (TF)   Universal TV/Belisarius
Productions, 1982
THE RETURN OF THE MAN FROM U.N.C.L.E. (TF)   Michael Sloan
Productions/Viacom Productions, 1983
THE ZANY ADVENTURES OF ROBIN HOOD (TF)   Bobka
Productions/Charles Fries Entertainment, 1984
LIME STREET (TF)   R.J. Productions/Bloodworth-Thomason-Mozark
Productions/Columbia TV, 1985
RETURN OF THE SIX MILLION DOLLAR MAN AND THE BIONIC
WOMAN (TF)   Michael Sloan Productions/Universal TV, 1987

CLAUDE AUTANT-LARA
b. August 5, 1903 - Luzarches, France
Contact: French Film Office, 745 Fifth Avenue, New York, NY 10151,
212/832-8860

CIBOULETTE   1933, French
THE MYSTERIOUS MR. DAVIS   1936, British
L'AFFAIRE DU COURIER DE LYON   co-director with
Maurice Lehmann, 1937, French
LE RUISSEAU   co-director with Maurice Lehmann, 1938, French
FRIC-FRAC   co-director with Maurice Lehmann, 1939, French
LE MARIAGE DE CHIFFON   1942, French
LETTRES D'AMOUR   1942, French
DOUCE   1943, French
SYLVIE ET LE FANTOME   1946, French
DEVIL IN THE FLESH   A.F.E. Corporation, 1947, French
OCCUPE-TOI D'AMELIE   1949, French
THE RED INN   Arthur Davis Associates, 1951, French
THE SEVEN DEADLY SINS   co-director, Arlan Fictures, 1952,
French-Italian
LE BON DIEU SANS CONFESSION   1953, French
LE ROUGE ET LE NOIR   1954, French
THE GAME OF LOVE   LE BLE EN HERBE   Times Film Corporation,
1954, French
MARGUERITE DE LA NUIT   1956, French
FOUR BAGS FULL   LA TRAVERSEE DE PARIS   Trans-Lux,
1956, French
LOVE IS MY PROFESSION   EN CAS DE MALHEUR   Kingsley
International, 1958, French
LE JOUEUR   1958, French
THE GREEN MARE   Zenith International, 1959, French-Italian
LES REGATES DE SAN FRANCISCO   1960, French
LE BOIS DES AMANTS   1960, French
VIVE HENRI IV...VIVE L'AMOUR!   1961, French
THE STORY OF THE COUNT OF MONTE CRISTO   THE COUNT
OF MONTE CRISTO/LE COMTE DE MONTE CRISTO
Warner Bros., 1961, French-Italian
THOU SHALT NOT KILL   Gala, 1961,
Yugoslavian-French-Italian-Liechtenstein
ENOUGH ROPE   LE MEURTIER   Artixo Productions, 1963,
French-Italian-West German
LE MAGOT DE JOSEFA   1963, French
LE JOURNAL D'UNE FEMME EN BLANC   1965, French
LE NOUVEAU JOURNAL D'UNE FEMME EN BLANC   1966, French
THE OLDEST PROFESSION   LE PLUS VIEUX METIER DU MONDE
co-director with Jean-Luc Godard, Franco Indovina,
Mauro Bolognini, Philippe de Broca & Michael Pfleghar,
Goldstone, 1967, Italian-French-West German
LE FRANCISCAIN DE BOURGES   1968, French
LES PATATES   1969, French
LE ROUGE ET LE BLANC   1971, French
GLORIA   1977, French

IGOR AUZINS

Contact: Australian Film Commission, 150 William Street,
   Woolloomooloo NSW 2011, Australia, tel.: 2/321-6444

ALL AT SEA (TF)   1977, Australian
HIGH ROLLING   Hexagon Productions, 1977, Australian
THE NIGHT NURSE (TF)   Reg Grundy Organization,
   1978, Australian
WATER UNDER THE BRIDGE (TF)   Shotton Productions,
   1980, Australian
TAURUS RISING (MS)   1982, Australian
WE OF THE NEVER NEVER   Triumph/Columbia, 1983, Australian
THE COOLANGATTA GOLD   Film Gallery, 1984, Australian

ROGER AVARY

Agent: William Morris Agency - Beverly Hills, 310/859-4000

KILLING ZOE   October Films, 1994
MR. STITCH   Rysher Entertainment/Mr. Stitch Productions, 1995

PUPI AVATI
(Giuseppe Avati)
b. November 3, 1938 - Bologna, Italy
Home: via del Babuino 135, Rome, Italy, tel.: 06/321-4851

BALSAMUS L'UOMO DI SATANA   Magic Film, 1968, Italian
THOMAS...GLI INDEMONIATI   Cidierre Cinematografica,
   1969, Italian
LA MAZURKA DEL BARONE DELLA SANTA E DEL FICO FIORONE
   Euro International Films, 1974, Italian
BORDELLA   Euro International Films, 1975, Italian
LA CASA DALLE FINESTRE CHE RIDONO   AMA Film,
   1976, Italian
TUTTI DEFUNTI TRANNE I MORTI   AMA Film, 1977, Italian
JAZZ BAND (TF)   AMA Film, 1978, Italian
LE STRELLE NEL FOSSO   AMA Film, 1978, Italian
CINEMA!!! (TF)   AMA Film/RAI, 1979, Italian
AIUTAMI A SOGNARE   AMA Film/RAI, 1981, Italian
DANCING PARADISE (TF)   AMA Film/RAI, 1981, Italian
UNA GITA SCOLASTICA   AMA Film/RAI, 1983, Italian
ZEDER   AMA Film, 1983, Italian
NOI TRE   Istituto Luce/RAI/Due A Film, 1984, Italian
IMPIEGATI   Due A Film/Dania Film/National Cinematografica/Filmes
   International, 1984, Italian
FESTA DI LAUREA   Due A Film/Dania Film/Filmes International/
   National Cinematografica, 1985, Italian
REGALO DI NATALE   Due A Film, 1986, Italian
THE LAST MINUTE   International Film Exchange, 1987, Italian
SPOSI   co-director, Due A Film, 1988, Italian
THE STORY OF BOYS AND GIRLS   Aries Releasing, 1990, Italian
BIX   Due A Film/Union/RAI, 1991, Italian-U.S.
FRATELLI E SORELLE   Due A Film/Filmauro/RAI, 1992, Italian
MAGNIFICAT   Due A Film/Istituto Luce/Italnoleggio Cinematografico/
   Pentafilm/Union P.N., 1993, Italian
L'AMICO D'INFANZIA   Due A Film/Filmauro, 1994, Italian-U.S.
DICHIARAZIONI D'AMORE   Due A Film/Filmauro, 1994, Italian

HOWARD (HIKMET) AVEDIS

Attorney: Jerome E. Weinstein, Weinstein & Hart, 433 N. Camden
   Drive - Suite 600, Beverly Hills, CA 90210, 310/274-7157

THE STEPMOTHER   Crown International, 1973
THE TEACHER   Crown International, 1974
DR. MINX   Dimension, 1975
THE SPECIALIST   Crown International, 1975
SCORCHY   American International, 1976
TEXAS DETOUR   Cinema Shares International, 1978
THE FIFTH FLOOR   Film Ventures International, 1980
SEPARATE WAYS   Crown International, 1981
MORTUARY   Artists Releasing Corporation/Film Ventures
   International, 1983
THEY'RE PLAYING WITH FIRE   New World, 1984
KIDNAPPED   Virgin Vision, 1987

HY AVERBACK*
b. 1925
Agent: CAA - Beverly Hills, 310/288-4545

CHAMBER OF HORRORS   Warner Bros., 1966
WHERE WERE YOU WHEN THE LIGHTS WENT OUT?
   MGM, 1968
I LOVE YOU, ALICE B. TOKLAS   Warner Bros., 1968
THE GREAT BANK ROBBERY   Warner Bros., 1969
SUPPOSE THEY GAVE A WAR AND NOBODY CAME?
   Cinerama Releasing Corporation, 1970
RICHIE BROCKELMAN: MISSING 24 HOURS (TF)
   Universal TV, 1976
THE LOVE BOAT II (TF)   Aaron Spelling Productions, 1977
MAGNIFICENT MAGNET OF SANTA MESA (TF)
   Columbia TV, 1977
THE NEW MAVERICK (TF)   Cherokee Productions/
   Warner Bros. TV, 1978
A GUIDE FOR THE MARRIED WOMAN (TF)
   20th Century-Fox TV, 1978
PEARL (TF)   Silliphant-Konigsberg Productions/
   Warner Bros. TV, 1978
THE NIGHT RIDER (TF)   Stephen J. Cannell Productions/
   Universal TV, 1979
SHE'S IN THE ARMY NOW (TF)   ABC Circle Films, 1981
THE GIRL, THE GOLD WATCH AND DYNAMITE (TF)
   Fellows-Keegan Company/Paramount TV, 1981
WHERE THE BOYS ARE   TriStar, 1984
THE LAST PRECINCT (TF)   Stephen J. Cannell Productions, 1986

RICK AVERY*
Address: 3518 Cahuenga Blvd. West - Suite 300, Hollywood, CA
   90068, 213/874-3174 or: 310/462-2301

THE EXPERT   Axis Films International, 1994
DEADLY TAKEOVER   Nu Image, 1995, U.S.-South African

CARLOS AVILA
LA CARPA   American Playhouse/Film Festival of International
   Cinema Students/National Latino Communications Center/Echo
   Park Filmworks, 1993

JAC AVILA
b. 1952 - Bolivia
Business: Mountain Top Films, 48 East Broadway - Suite 3,
   New York, NY 10002, 212/741-1814

KRIK? KRAK! TALES OF A NIGHTMARE   co-director with
   Vanyoska Gee, Mountain Top Films, 1988,
   Haitian-U.S.-Canadian

JOHN G. AVILDSEN*
b. 1936 - Chicago, Illinois
Agent: UTA - Beverly Hills, 310/273-6700

TURN ON TO LOVE   Haven International, 1969
GUESS WHAT WE LEARNED IN SCHOOL TODAY?
   Cannon, 1970
JOE   Cannon, 1970
CRY UNCLE!   Cambist, 1971
OKAY BILL   Four Star Excelsior, 1971
THE STOOLIE   Jama, 1972
SAVE THE TIGER   Paramount, 1973
FORE PLAY   co-director with Bruce Malmuth & Robert McCarty,
   Cinema National, 1975
W.W. AND THE DIXIE DANCEKINGS   20th Century-Fox, 1975
ROCKY ★★   United Artists, 1976
SLOW DANCING IN THE BIG CITY   United Artists, 1978
THE FORMULA   MGM/United Artists, 1980
NEIGHBORS   Columbia, 1982
A NIGHT IN HEAVEN   20th Century-Fox, 1983
THE KARATE KID   Columbia, 1984
THE KARATE KID PART II   Columbia, 1986
HAPPY NEW YEAR   Columbia, 1987
FOR KEEPS   TriStar, 1988
LEAN ON ME   Warner Bros., 1989

THE KARATE KID PART III   Columbia, 1989
ROCKY V   MGM/UA, 1990
THE POWER OF ONE   Warner Bros., 1992,
    U.S.-German-French-Australian
8 SECONDS   New Line Cinema, 1994

TOM AVILDSEN
Home: 1636 S. Cedar, Spokane, WA 99203, 509/838-8010

THINGS ARE TOUGH ALL OVER   Columbia, 1982

MEIERT AVIS*
Contact: Directors Guild of America - Los Angeles, 213/851-3671

FAR FROM HOME   Vestron, 1989

JON AVNET*
(Jonathan Michael Avnet)
b. November 17, 1947 - Brooklyn, New York
Business: The Avnet-Kerner Company, 3815 Hughes Avenue,
    Culver City, CA 90232, 310/838-2500
Agent: CAA - Beverly Hills, 310/288-4545

BETWEEN TWO WOMEN (TF)   The Jon Avnet Company, 1986
FRIED GREEN TOMATOES   Universal, 1991
THE WAR   Universal, 1994
UP CLOSE AND PERSONAL   Buena Vista, 1995

GABRIEL AXEL
b. 1918 - Paris, France
Address: 48, quai Jemmapes, 75010 Paris, France,
    tel.: 1/42-49-24-27
Contact: French Film Office, 745 Fifth Avenue, New York, NY 10151,
    212/832-8860

GULD OG GRONNE SKOVE   1959, Danish
TRE PIGER I PARIS   1963, Danish
HAGBARD AND SIGNE   *THE RED MANTLE*   Prentoulis Films,
    1967, Danish-Swedish-Icelandic
BELOVED TOY   1968, Danish
AMOUR   1970, Danish
MED KAERLIG HILSEN   1971, Danish
FAMILIEN GYLDENKAAL   1975, Danish
ALT PAA ET BRAET   1976, Danish
THE CRIME OF OUR TIME (TF)   French
THE NIGHT WATCH (TF)   French
THE VICAR OF TOURS (TF)   French
THE COLUMNS OF HEAVEN (MS)   1986, French
BABETTE'S FEAST   Orion Classics, 1987, Danish-French
CHRISTIAN   Chrysalide Films/Victoria Films/Ellepi Film/Dania Film/
    DMV Distribuzione/Reteitalia, 1989, Danish-French-Italian
PRINCE OF JUTLAND   Les Films Ariane/Woodline Films/Kenneth
    Madsen Filmproduktion/Films Roses, 1994,
    French-British-Danish-German

GEORGE AXELROD
b. June 9, 1922 - New York, New York
Personal Manager: Krost/Chapin Management - Los Angeles,
    310/281-3595

LORD LOVE A DUCK   United Artists, 1966
THE SECRET LIFE OF AN AMERICAN WIFE
    20th Century-Fox, 1968

DAN AYKROYD*
(Daniel Edward Aykroyd)
b. July 1, 1952 - Ottawa, Ontario, Canada
Agent: CAA - Beverly Hills, 310/288-4545
Contact: Los Angeles, 310/203-0262

NOTHING BUT TROUBLE   Warner Bros., 1991

IRADJ AZIMI
Contact: French Film Office, 745 Fifth Avenue, New York, NY 10151,
    212/832-8860

LES JOURS GRIS   1975, French
UTOPIA   1978, French
LES ILES   1982, French
LE RADEAU DE LA MEDUSA   Utopia Productions, 1992, French

MARIO AZZOPARDI*
b. 1950 - Malta
Address: 2395 Carrington Place, Oakville, Ontario L6J 5P5, Canada,
    416/844-6645
Agent: APA - Los Angeles, 310/273-0744

DEADLINE   The Horror Film Production Inc./Henry Less &
    Associates, 1980, Canadian
STATE OF SURVIVAL   1986, Canadian
NOWHERE TO HIDE   New Century/Vista, 1987, U.S.-Canadian
DIVIDED LOYALTIES (TF)   History Productions/CTV,
    1991, Canadian

B

BETH B
Business: B Movies, Inc., 45 Crosby Street, New York, NY 10012

THE OFFENDERS   co-director with Scott B, B Movies, 1980
VORTEX   co-director with Scott B, B Movies, 1983
SALVATION!   Circle Films, 1987
SHUT UP AND SUFFER   B Movies, 1991
TWO SMALL BODIES   Castle Hill Productions, 1993, German

SCOTT B
Agent: The Tantleff Office - New York, 212/941-3939

THE OFFENDERS   co-director with Beth B, B Movies, 1980
VORTEX   co-director with Beth B, B Movies, 1983

BASSEK BA KOBHIO
b. 1957 - Cameroon
Contact: FEPACI (Pan-African Federation of Film-Makers),
    01 B.P. 2524, Ouagadougou 01, Burkina Faso, tel.: 226/31-02-58
    or: French Film Office, 745 Fifth Avenue, New York, NY 10151,
    212/832-8860

FESTAC 88 (FD)   1989, Cameroonian
SANGO MALO   Les Films Terre Africaine/Fodic/Cameroon
    Radio and TV/Disproci/French Ministry of Cooperation and
    Development/Channel 4/COE/Hubert Bals Foundation, 1991,
    Cameroonian-Burkina Faso-French-British-Italian-Dutch
LE GRAND BLANC DE LAMBARENE   L.N. Productions,
    1995, French

HECTOR BABENCO*
b. February 7, 1946 - Buenos Aires, Argentina
Agent: ICM - Beverly Hills, 310/550-4000

KING OF THE NIGHT   1975, Brazilian
LUCIO FLAVIO   Unifilm/Embrafilme, 1978, Brazilian
PIXOTE   Unifilm/Embrafilme, 1981, Brazilian
KISS OF THE SPIDER WOMAN ★   Island Alive/FilmDallas,
    1985, Brazilian-U.S.
IRONWEED   TriStar, 1987
AT PLAY IN THE FIELDS OF THE LORD   Universal, 1991

JEAN BACH

A GREAT DAY IN HARLEM (FD)   Castle Hill Productions/Esquire
   Magazine, 1994

RANDALL BADAT

Agent: Paradigm - Los Angeles, 310/277-4400
Contact: Writers Guild of America, West - Los Angeles, 310/550-1000

SURF II   Arista, 1983

PHIL BADGER

THE FORGOTTEN ONE   Spirited Productions, 1990

JOHN BADHAM*

b. August 25, 1939 - Luton, England
Agent: William Morris Agency - Beverly Hills, 310/859-4000

THE IMPATIENT HEART (TF)   Universal TV, 1971
ISN'T IT SHOCKING? (TF)   ABC Circle Films, 1973
THE LAW (TF)   Universal TV, 1974
THE GUN (TF)   Universal TV, 1974
REFLECTIONS OF MURDER (TF)   ABC Circle Films, 1974
THE GODCHILD (TF)   MGM TV, 1974
THE KEEGANS (TF)   Universal TV, 1976
THE BINGO LONG TRAVELING ALL STARS AND MOTOR KINGS
   Universal, 1976
SATURDAY NIGHT FEVER   Paramount, 1977
DRACULA   Universal, 1979
WHOSE LIFE IS IT ANYWAY?   MGM/United Artists, 1981
BLUE THUNDER   Columbia, 1983
WARGAMES   MGM/UA, 1983
AMERICAN FLYERS   Warner Bros., 1985
SHORT CIRCUIT   TriStar, 1986
STAKEOUT   Buena Vista, 1987
BIRD ON A WIRE   Universal, 1990
THE HARD WAY   Universal, 1991
POINT OF NO RETURN   Warner Bros., 1993
ANOTHER STAKEOUT   Buena Vista, 1993
DROP ZONE   Paramount, 1994
NICK OF TIME   Paramount, 1995

REZA BADIYI*

b. April 17, 1936 - Iran
Agent: Irv Schechter Company - Beverly Hills, 310/278-8070
Personal Manager: Leonard Granger, 9903 Kip Drive, Beverly Hills,
   CA 90210, 310/858-1573

DEATH OF A STRANGER   Delta Commerz, 1972,
   West German-Israeli
THE EYES OF CHARLES SAND (TF)   Warner Bros. TV, 1972
TRADER HORN   MGM, 1973
THE BIG BLACK PILL (TF)   Filmways/NBC Entertainment, 1981
OF MICE AND MEN (TF)   Of Mice and Men Productions, 1981
WHITE WATER REBELS (TF)   CBS Entertainment, 1983
MURDER ONE, DANCER 0 (TF)   Mickey Productions, 1983
POLICEWOMAN CENTERFOLD (TF)
   Moonlight Productions, 1983
BLADE IN HONG KONG (TF)   Terry Becker Productions, 1985
IN THE HEAT OF THE NIGHT: A MATTER OF JUSTICE (TF)
   Juanita Bartlett Productions/Metro-Goldwyn-Mayer, 1994
CAGNEY & LACEY: TOGETHER AGAIN (TF)   The Rosenzweig
   Company/CBS, 1995

YONG-KYUN BAE

(See Bae YONG - KYUN)

MAX BAER, JR.*

b. December 4, 1937 - Oakland, California
Business Manager: Roger Camras, 10433 Wilshire Blvd.,
   Los Angeles, CA 90024, 310/470-2808

THE WILD McCULLOCHS   American International, 1975
ODE TO BILLY JOE   Warner Bros., 1976
HOMETOWN, U.S.A.   Film Ventures International, 1979

TED BAFALOUKOS

b. May 18, 1946 - Athens, Greece
Home: P.O. Box 400, Canal Street Station, New York, NY 10013
Contact: Keller & Vandernoth - New York City, 212/741-0202

ROCKERS   New Yorker, 1979

ORLANDO BAGWELL

Contact: Writers Guild of America, East - New York City,
   212/767-7800

MALCOLM X: MAKE IT PLAIN (TD)   Blackside Inc./Roja
   Productions, 1994
FREDERICK DOUGLASS: WHEN THE LION WROTE HISTORY (TD)
   WETA-Washington, D.C./Roja Productions, 1994

FAX BAHR*

Address: 6646 Hollywood Blvd. - Suite 215, Los Angeles, CA 90028,
   213/962-8412
Agent: UTA - Beverly Hills, 310/273-6700

HEARTS OF DARKNESS: A FILMMAKER'S APOCALYPSE (FD)
   co-director with George Hickenlooper, Showtime/ZM Productions/
   Zoetrope, 1991, released theatrically by Triton Pictures

CHUCK BAIL*

Business: Shaman Productions, 9312 Lasaine Avenue, Northridge,
   CA 91325

BLACK SAMSON   Warner Bros., 1974
CLEOPATRA JONES AND THE CASINO OF GOLD
   Warner Bros., 1975
GUMBALL RALLY   Warner Bros., 1976
CHOKE CANYON   United Film Distribution, 1986
STREET CORNER JUSTUS   Steel City Films, 1995

JOHN BAILEY*

b. August 10, 1942 - Moberly, Montana
Agent: UTA - Beverly Hills, 310/273-6700

THE SEARCH FOR SIGNS OF INTELLIGENT LIFE IN THE
   UNIVERSE (PF)   Orion Classics, 1991
CHINA MOON   Orion, 1994, filmed in 1991
MARIETTE IN ECSTASY   Savoy Pictures, 1995

NORMA BAILEY

b. 1949 - Winnipeg, Manitoba, Canada
Business: Flat City Films, 336 Queenston Street, Winnipeg, Manitoba
   R3N OW8, Canada, 204/489-6181

PERFORMER   1979, Canadian
NOSE AND TINA   1980, Canadian
IT'S HARD TO GET IT HERE   1985, Canadian
DAUGHTERS OF THE COUNTRY (TF)   1986, Canadian
MARTHA, RUTH & EDIE   1987, Canadian
BORDERTOWN CAFE   Flat City Films, 1991, Canadian

PATRICK BAILEY

b. April 17, 1947 - Crawfordsville, Indiana
Home: 14401 Villa Woods Place, Pacific Palisades, CA 90272,
   310/454-4713

DOOR TO DOOR   Castle Hill Productions, 1984

FRED BAKER

LENNY BRUCE WITHOUT TEARS (FD)   Video Tape Network, 1972
MURDER SHE SINGS   92 Releasing Organization, 1986
WHITE TRASH   Fred Baker Film & Video Company, 1992

GRAHAM BAKER*

Agent: The Gersh Agency - Beverly Hills, 310/274-6611

THE FINAL CONFLICT   20th Century-Fox, 1981
IMPULSE   20th Century Fox, 1984
ALIEN NATION   20th Century Fox, 1988
BORN TO RIDE   Warner Bros., 1991

KURT BAKER*

Business: Eclectic Concepts Limited - Los Angeles, 310/476-7095,
fax: 310/471-0528

THE IMPORTANCE OF BEING EARNEST   Eclectic Concepts/
Paco Global Inc., 1991

ROBERT S. BAKER

b. 1916 - London, England
Contact: British Film Commission, 70 Baker Street, London
W1M 1DJ, England, tel.: 171/224-5000

BLACKOUT   Lippert, 1950, British
13 EAST STREET   1952, British
THE STEEL KEY   Eros Films, 1953, British
PASSPORT TO TREASON   Astor, 1956, British
JACK THE RIPPER   Embassy, 1959, British
THE SIEGE OF SIDNEY STREET   Columbia, 1960, British
THE HELLFIRE CLUB   Embassy, 1961, British
THE SECRET OF MONTE CRISTO   *THE TREASURE OF MONTE
CRISTO*   MGM, 1961, British

ROY WARD BAKER

b. 1916 - London, England
Agent: Michael Whitehall Ltd. - London, tel.: 171/244-8466

THE OCTOBER MAN   Eagle-Lion, 1947, British
THE WEAKER SEX   Eagle-Lion, 1948, British
PAPER ORCHID   1949, British
OPERATION DISASTER   *MORNING DEPARTURE*   Universal,
1950, British
HIGHLY DANGEROUS   Lippert, 1951, British
I'LL NEVER FORGET YOU   *THE HOUSE IN THE SQUARE*
20th Century-Fox, 1951, British
DON'T BOTHER TO KNOCK   20th Century-Fox, 1952
NIGHT WITHOUT SLEEP   20th Century-Fox, 1952
INFERNO   20th Century-Fox, 1953
PASSAGE HOME   1955, British
JACQUELINE   Rank, 1956, British
TIGER IN SMOKE   1956, British
THE ONE THAT GOT AWAY   Rank, 1958, British
A NIGHT TO REMEMBER   Rank, 1958, British
THE SINGER NOT THE SONG   Warner Bros., 1962, British
FLAME IN THE STREETS   Atlantic Pictures, 1962, British
THE VALIANT   co-director with Giorgio Capitani, United Artists,
1962, British-Italian
TWO LEFT FEET   1963, British
FIVE MILLION YEARS TO EARTH   *QUATERMASS AND THE PIT*
20th Century-Fox, 1968, British
THE ANNIVERSARY   20th Century-Fox, 1968, British
THE SPY KILLER (TF)   Halsan Productions, 1969
FOREIGN EXCHANGE (TF)   Halsan Productions, 1970
MOON ZERO TWO   Warner Bros., 1970, British
THE VAMPIRE LOVERS   American International, 1970, British
THE SCARS OF DRACULA   American Continental,
1971, British
DR. JEKYLL AND SISTER HYDE   American International,
1972, British
ASYLUM   Cinerama Releasing Corporation, 1972, British
THE VAULT OF HORROR   Cinerama Releasing Corporation,
1973, British
AND NOW THE SCREAMING STARTS   Cinerama Releasing
Corporation, 1973, British
THE 7 BROTHERS MEET DRACULA   *THE LEGEND OF THE
SEVEN GOLDEN VAMPIRES*   Dynamite Entertainment,
1979, British
MINDER (TF)   1979, British
THE FLAME TREES OF THIKA (MS)   London Films Ltd./
Consolidated Productions Ltd., 1980, British
THE MONSTER CLUB   ITC, 1981, British
THE MASKS OF DEATH (TF)   Tyburn Productions, 1984, British
FAIRLY SECRET ARMY II (MS)   Video Arts Television/Channel 4,
1985, British
THE IRISH R.M. II (MS)   Channel 4, 1985, British

MINDER VI (MS)   co-director with Francis Megahy, Terry Green &
Bill Brayne, Euston Films, 1988, British
THE GOOD GUYS (MS)   co-director with Simon Langton &
Stuart Urban, Havahall Pictures/London Weekend TV,
1991, British
THE GOOD GUYS SERIES II (MS)   Havahall Pictures/LWT,
1992, British

RALPH BAKSHI*

b. October 26, 1938 - Haifa, Palestine
Agent: ICM - Beverly Hills, 310/550-4000
Business: Ralph Bakshi Productions, 8125 Lankershim Blvd.,
North Hollywood, CA 91605, 818/985-4463

FRITZ THE CAT (AF)   American International, 1972
HEAVY TRAFFIC (AF)   American International, 1973
COONSKIN (AF)   Bryanston, 1974
WIZARDS (AF)   20th Century-Fox, 1977
THE LORD OF THE RINGS (AF)   United Artists, 1978
AMERICAN POP (AF)   Paramount, 1981
HEY GOOD LOOKIN' (AF)   Warner Bros., 1982
FIRE AND ICE (AF)   20th Century-Fox, 1983
IMAGINING AMERICA (TF)   co-director with Matt Mahurin,
Mustapha Khan & Ed Lachman, Vanguard Films, 1989
COOL WORLD   Paramount, 1992
REBEL HIGHWAY: COOL AND THE CRAZY   *COOL AND THE
CRAZY* (CTF)   Drive-In Classics Cinema/Showtime, 1994

BOB BALABAN*

b. August 16, 1945 - Chicago, Illinois
Agent: ICM - Beverly Hills, 310/550-4000
Business Manager: Gelfand, Rennert & Feldman - New York,
212/682-0234

PARENTS   Vestron, 1989
MY BOYFRIEND'S BACK   Buena Vista, 1993
THE LAST GOOD TIME   The Samuel Goldwyn Company, 1994

FERDINANDO BALDI

Home: via Arrigo Boito 71, Rome, Italy, tel.: 06/86202405

THE TARTARS   co-director with Richard Thorpe, MGM,
1960, Italian
DAVID AND GOLIATH   co-director with Richard Pottier,
Allied Artists, 1960, Italian
DUEL OF CHAMPIONS   co-director with Terence Young,
Medallion, 1961, Italian-Spanish
IL PISTOLERO DELL'AVE MARIA   BRCSRL,
1970, Italian-Spanish
BLINDMAN   20th Century-Fox, 1972, Italian
CARAMBOLA   B.R.C./Aetoscin, 1974, Italian
GET MEAN   Cee Note, 1976, Italian
NOVE OSPITI PER UN DELITTO   Overseas, 1976, Italian
MY NAME IS TRINITY   1976, Italian
THE SICILIAN CONNECTION   Joseph Green Pictures,
1977, Italian
L'INQUILINA DEL PIANO DI SOPRA   Fair Film, 1977, Italian
LA SELVAGGIA   *GEOMETRA PRINETTI SEL
VAGGIAMENTEOSVALDO*   Interfilm, 1978, Italian
LA RAGAZZA DEL VAGONE LETTO   1979, Italian
COMIN' AT YA   Filmways, 1981, U.S.-Spanish
TREASURE OF THE FOUR CROWNS   Cannon,
1983, U.S.-Spanish

PETER BALDWIN*

Agent: Irv Schechter Company - Beverly Hills, 310/278-8070

THE HARLEM GLOBETROTTERS ON GILLIGAN'S ISLAND (TF)
Sherwood Schwartz Productions, 1981
THE BRADY GIRLS GET MARRIED (TF)   Sherwood Schwartz
Productions, 1981
LOTS OF LUCK (CTF)   Tomorrow Entertainment, 1985
A VERY BRADY CHRISTMAS (TF)   Sherwood Schwartz
Productions/Paramount TV, 1988

MURRAY BALL

Contact: New Zealand Film Commission, P.O. Box 11-546,
Wellington, New Zealand, tel.: 4/385-9754

FOOTROT FLATS (AF)   Magpie Productions, 1986, New Zealand

CARROLL BALLARD*

b. October 14, 1937 - Los Angeles, California
Agent: CAA - Beverly Hills, 310/288-4545

THE BLACK STALLION   United Artists, 1979
NEVER CRY WOLF   Buena Vista, 1983
NUTCRACKER: THE MOTION PICTURE   Atlantic Releasing
    Corporation, 1986
WIND   TriStar, 1992, U.S.-Japanese

GEORGE BALUZY

NATURAL BORN CRAZIES   co-director with Michael Baluzy,
    Amazing Movies, 1994

MICHAEL BALUZY

NATURAL BORN CRAZIES   co-director with George Baluzy,
    Amazing Movies, 1994

JOHN BANAS

EMMA, QUEEN OF THE SOUTH SEAS (TF)   Anro Productions,
    1988, Australian

ANNE BANCROFT*

(Anna Maria Louisa Itallano)
b. September 17, 1931 - Bronx, New York
Agent: ICM - Los Angeles, 310/550-4000
Business: Brooksfilms Limited, 20th Century Fox, P.O. Box 900,
    Beverly Hills, CA 90213, 310/203-1375
Business Manager: Bernstein, Fox & Goldberg - 310/277-3373

FATSO   20th Century-Fox, 1980

ALBERT BAND

(Alfredo Antonini)
b. May 7, 1924 - Paris, France
Business: Full Moon Entertainment, 3030 Andrita Street,
    Los Angeles, CA 90065, 213/341-5959

THE YOUNG GUNS   Allied Artists, 1956
I BURY THE LIVING   United Artists, 1958
FACE OF FIRE   Allied Artists, 1959
THE AVENGER   Medallion, 1962, Italian-French
MASSACRO AL GRANDE CANYON   Metra Film,
    1965, Italian
THE TRAMPLERS   Embassy, 1966, Italian
DRACULA'S DOG   Crown International, 1978
SHE CAME TO THE VALLEY   RGV Pictures, 1979
GHOULIES II   Empire Pictures, 1988
JOEY TAKES A CAB   BandCompany, 1991
PREHYSTERIA!   co-director with Charles Band,
    Trimark Pictures, 1993
DOCTOR MORDRID   co-director with Charles Band,
    Full Moon Entertainment, 1994

CHARLES BAND

b. 1952 - Los Angeles, California
Business: Full Moon Entertainment, 3030 Andrita Street,
    Los Angeles, CA 90065, 213/341-5959

CRASH   Group 1, 1977
PARASITE   Embassy, 1982
METALSTORM: THE DESTRUCTION OF JARED-SYN
    Universal, 1983
THE DUNGEONMASTER   co-director, Empire Pictures, 1985
FUTURE COP   Empire Pictures, 1985
PULSEPOUNDERS   Empire Pictures, 1988
MERIDIAN   JGM Enterprises, 1990
CRASH AND BURN   Full Moon Entertainment, 1990

TRANCERS II   Full Moon Entertainment, 1991
DOLLMAN VS. DEMONIC TOYS   Full Moon Entertainment, 1993
PREHYSTERIA!   co-director with Albert Band,
    Trimark Pictures, 1993
DOCTOR MORDRID   co-director with Albert Band,
    Full Moon Entertainment, 1994

TAMASABURO BANDO

b. Japan
Contact: Nihon Eiga Kantoku Kyokai (Japan Film Directors
    Association), La Fontenu Building -4th Floor, 23-2 Maruyama-cho,
    Shibuya-ku, Tokyo, Japan, tel.: 3/3461-4411

OPERATION ROOM   TV Asahi/Shochiku, 1991, Japanese
WOMEN OF THE DREAM   *YEARNING*   Shochiku/Asahi
    Newspaper Company/Daio Seishi/TV Asahi/Komai Associates/
    Akaike Sangyo, 1993, Japanese

MIRRA BANK

ENORMOUS CHANGES AT THE LAST MINUTE   co-director with
    Ellen Hovde, TC Films International, 1985
NOBODY'S GIRLS: FIVE WOMEN OF THE WEST (FD)   1994
NOBODY'S GIRLS (TF)   Maryland Public Television, 1995

JACK BARAN*

Home: 1059 S. Alfred Street, Los Angeles, CA 90035,
    213/653-4749
Agent: Daniel Ostroff, The Daniel Ostroff Agency - Los Angeles,
    310/278-2020

DESTINY TURNS ON THE RADIO   Savoy Pictures, 1995

NORBERTO BARBA*

Agent: Premiere Artists Agency - Los Angeles, 310/271-1414

BLUE TIGER   First Look Pictures, 1994

URI BARBASH

b. Israel
Contact: Israel Film Centre, Ministry of Industry & Trade,
    30 Agron Street, P.O. Box 299, Jerusalem 94190, Israel,
    tel.: 972/210433 or 210297

STIGMA   1983, Israeli
BEYOND THE WALLS   Warner Bros., 1984, Israeli
UNSETTLED LAND   *ONCE WE WERE DREAMERS*   Hemdale,
    1987, U.S.-Israeli
ONE OF US   Nachshon Films, 1989, Israeli
WHERE EAGLES FLY   Nachshon Films, 1990, Israeli
REAL TIME   Sunrise Films, 1991, Israeli
BEYOND THE WALLS 2   Sunrise Films, 1992, Israeli
THE GOLDEN BRIDGE   Noah Film Ltd., 1992, Israeli
LICK THE BERRY   1993, Israeli

JOHN BARBOUR

Contact: Writers Guild of America, West - Los Angeles, 310/550-1000

THE JFK ASSASSINATION: THE JIM GARRISON TAPES (FD)
    Blue Ridge/Filmtrust, 1992

JOSEPH BARBERA

b. 1911 - New York, New York
Business: Hanna-Barbera Productions, 3400 Cahuenga Blvd. West,
    Hollywood, CA 90068, 213/851-5000

HEY THERE, IT'S YOGI BEAR (AF)   co-director with William Hanna,
    Columbia, 1964
A MAN CALLED FLINTSTONE (AF)   co-director with William Hanna,
    Columbia, 1966
ESCAPE FROM GRUMBLE GULTCH (AF)   co-director with
    William Hanna, Hanna-Barbera Productions, 1983
JETSONS: THE MOVIE (AF)   co-director with William Hanna,
    Universal, 1990

ERIC BARBIER

Agent: Artmedia, 10, avenue George V, 75008 Paris, France,
tel.: 1/47-23-78-60
Contact: French Film Office, 745 Fifth Avenue, New York,
NY 10151, 212/832-8860

LE BRASIER   Warner Bros., 1990, French

BARRY BARCLAY

b. 1944 - Wairarapa, New Zealand
Business: Pacific Film Productions Ltd., P.O. Box 2040, Wellington,
New Zealand, tel.: 4/872-191

THE TOWN THAT LOST A MIRACLE (FD)   Pacific Film Productions,
1972, New Zealand
TANGATA WHENUA (MS)   Pacific Film Productions,
1974, New Zealand
ASHES (FD)   Pacific Film Productions, 1975, New Zealand
AUTUMN FIRES (FD)   Pacific Film Productions,
1977, New Zealand
THE NEGLECTED MIRACLE (FD)   Pacific Film Productions,
1984, New Zealand
NGATI   Pacific Film Productions/New Zealand Film Commission,
1987, New Zealand
TE RUA   Pacific Film Productions/New Zealand Film Commission/
Berlin Senate & Film Commission/Avalon, 1991, New Zealand

PARIS BARCLAY

Agent: William Morris Agency - Beverly Hills, 310/859-4000
Personal Manager: Lovett Management - Santa Monica,
310/451-2536

DON'T BE A MENACE TO SOUTH CENTRAL WHILE DRINKING
JUICE IN THE HOOD   Island Pictures, 1994

GEORGES BARDAWIL

Contact: French Film Office, 745 Fifth Avenue, New York,
NY 10151, 212/832-8860

SECRETS SHARED WITH A STRANGER   Flach Film,
1995, French

JUAN ANTONIO BARDEM

b. July 2, 1922 - Madrid, Spain
Contact: Spanish Film Institute, San Marcos 40, Madrid 28004,
Spain, tel.: 1/532-5089

ESA PAREJA FELIZ   co-director with Luis Garcia Berlanga,
1951, Spanish
NOVIO A LA VISTA   co-director with Luis Garcia Berlanga,
1953, Spanish
COMICOS   1953, Spanish
FELICES PASCUAS   1954, Spanish
AGE OF INFIDELITY *MUERTE DI UN CICLISTA*   Janus, 1955,
Spanish-Italian
THE LOVEMAKER *CALLE MAYOR*   Trans-Lux, 1958,
Spanish-French
LA VENGANZA   1958, Spanish
SONATAS   1959, Spanish
A LAS CINCO DE LA TARDE   1960, Spanish
LOS INOCENTES   1962, Spanish
NUNCA PASA NADA   1962, Spanish
THE UNINHIBITED *LOS PIANOS MECANICOS*
Peppercorn-Wormser, 1965, Spanish-Italian-French
EL ULTIMO DIA DE LA GUERRA   1969, Spanish-Italian-U.S.
VARIETES   1971, Spanish
LA CORRUPCION DE CHRIS MILLER   1973, Spanish
THE MYSTERIOUS ISLAND OF CAPTAIN NEMO
L'ILE MYSTERIEUSE   co-director with Henri Colpi,
1973, French-Spanish
BEHIND THE SHUTTERS   1973, Spanish
EL PODOR DEL DESEO   1976, Spanish
FOUL PLAY   1976, Spanish
THE DOG   1977, Spanish
EL PUENTE   1977, Spanish
SIETE DIAS DE ENERO   1979, Spanish
THE WARNING   1982, Bulgarian-Soviet-East German
LORCA, LA MUERTE DE UN POETA   1987, Spanish

JAMES H. BARDEN

THE JUDAS PROJECT   RS Entertainment, 1990

RICHARD L. BARE*

Home: 700 Harbor Island Drive, Newport Beach, CA 92660,
714/675-6269

SMART GIRLS DON'T TALK   Warner Bros., 1948
FLAXY MARTIN   Warner Bros., 1949
THE HOUSE ACROSS THE STREET   Warner Bros., 1949
THIS SIDE OF THE LAW   Warner Bros., 1950
RETURN OF THE FRONTIERSMAN   Warner Bros., 1950
PRISONERS OF THE CASBAH   Columbia, 1953
THE OUTLANDERS   Warner Bros., 1956
THE STORM RIDERS   Warner Bros., 1956
BORDER SHOWDOWN   Warner Bros., 1956
THE TRAVELLERS   Warner Bros., 1957
SHOOT-OUT AT MEDICINE BEND   Warner Bros., 1957
GIRL ON THE RUN   Warner Bros., 1958
THIS REBEL BREED   Warner Bros., 1960
WICKED, WICKED   MGM, 1973

LEORA BARISH

Agent: CAA - Beverly Hills, 310/288-4545

VENUS RISING   I.R.S. Releasing, 1995

CLIVE BARKER*

b. 1952 - Liverpool, England
Agent: CAA - Beverly Hills, 310/288-4545

HELLRAISER   New World, 1987, British
TRANSMUTATIONS   Empire Pictures, 1988, British
NIGHTBREED   20th Century Fox, 1990
LORD OF ILLUSION   MGM-UA, 1995

EDWARD S. BARKIN

Agent: APA - Los Angeles, 310/273-0744

RIFT   Off-Screen Productions, 1993
MURDERS & ACQUISITIONS   Curb Organization, 1994

ANTHONY BARNAO

ANNIE'S GARDEN   Leibert-Summers Productions, 1994

MICHAEL BARNARD

Business: Michael R. Barnard Productions, 2219 W. Olive Avenue -
Suite 100, Burbank, CA 91506, 818/386-5857

SHOPPING MALL   The Gustafson Group/D.H.B. Films, 1985
NIGHTS IN WHITE SATIN   Mediacom Productions, 1987

STEVE BARNETT

Agent: Writers & Artists Agency - Los Angeles, 310/824-6300

HOLLYWOOD BOULEVARD II   Concorde, 1991
MIND WARP   Fangoria Films, 1992
MISSION OF JUSTICE   Image Organization/Westwind
Productions, 1992
SCANNER COP 2   Republic Pictures, 1994

NEEMA BARNETTE*

Business: Harlem Lite Inc., 4219 Olive Street - Suite 119, Burbank,
CA 91505, 213/669-1050
Agent: CAA - Beverly Hills, 310/288-4545
Personal Manager: Carlyle Productions and Management,
639 N. Larchmont - Suite 207, Los Angeles, CA 90004,
213/469-3086

BETTER OFF DEAD (TF)   Heller-Steinem Productions/Viacom
Productions, 1993
SCATTERED DREAMS: THE KATHRYN MESSENGER STORY (TF)
Robert Greenwald Productions, 1993
SIN AND REDEMPTION (TF)   The Stonehenge Company/
Viacom, 1994
SPIRIT LOST   BET Films, 1995

DON BARNHART*
Home: 4434 Moorpark Way "A", Toluca Lake, CA 91602,
818/769-8455
Agent: Shapiro-Lichtman Talent Agency - Los Angeles, 310/859-8877

SAVED BY THE BELL - HAWAIIAN STYLE (TF)   Peter Engel
Productions/NBC, 1992

ALLEN BARON*
b. 1935 - New York, New York
Home: 407 S. Spalding Drive, Beverly Hills, CA 90212, 310/553-4050
Agent: Paul Leserman, 3700 Wilshire Blvd. - Suite 575,
Los Angeles, CA 90010, 213/738-1264

BLAST OF SILENCE   Universal, 1961
PIE IN THE SKY   Allied Artists, 1964
RED, WHITE AND BLUE   George Edwards Productions, 1970
FOX FIRE LIGHT   Ramblin International, 1981

DOUGLAS BARR
Agent: Broder-Kurland-Webb-Uffner Agency - Beverly Hills,
310/281-3427
Business Manager: Jamner, Pariser, Meschures - Los Angeles,
310/652-0222

DEAD BADGE   Dead Badge Productions, 1995

BRUNO BARRETO*
b. 1955 - Brazil
Business: Producoes Cinematograficas L.C. Barreto Ltda., Rua
Visconde De Caravelas, 28-Botafogos, Rio de Janeiro, Brazil, tel.:
021/286-7186
Address: 3000 Olympic Blvd. - Suite 2325, Santa Monica,
CA 90404, 310/449-4030
Agent: CAA - Beverly Hills, 310/288-4545

A ESTRELA SOBE   1974, Brazilian
DONA FLOR AND HER TWO HUSBANDS   New Yorker,
1977, Brazilian
AMADA AMANTE   1979, Brazilian
AMOR BANDIDO   Analysis Releasing Corporation, 1982, Brazilian
GABRIELA   MGM/UA Classics, 1983, Brazilian-Italian
ALEM DA PAIXAO   1985, Brazilian
HAPPILY EVER AFTER   European Classics, 1985, Brazilian
ROMANCE DA EMPREGADA   Embrafilme, 1988, Brazilian
A SHOW OF FORCE   Paramount, 1990
THE HEART OF JUSTICE (CTF)   Amblin Entertainment/Turner
Network TV/Michael Brandman Productions, 1993
ACTS OF LOVE   CineTel Films, 1995

LEZLI-AN BARRETT
Agent: Casarotto Ramsay - London, 171/287-4450
Address: 28 Combermere Road, London SW9 9RE, England,
tel.: 171/737-3370

BUSINESS AS USUAL   Cannon, 1987, British

CHUCK BARRIS*
b. June 3 - Philadelphia, Pennsylvania
Contact: Directors Guild of America - Los Angeles, 213/851-3671

THE GONG SHOW MOVIE   Universal, 1980

ARTHUR BARRON
Contact: Writers Guild of America, West - Los Angeles, 310/550-1000
Contact: Bloom, Dekom, Hergott & Cook - Los Angeles,
310/278-8622

THE WRIGHT BROTHERS (TF)   PBS-TV, 1971
JEREMY   United Artists, 1973
BROTHERS   Warner Bros., 1977
CRIMES OF VIOLENCE (TD)   Arnold Shapiro Productions/
KTLA-TV, 1988

STEVE BARRON*
b. May 4, 1956 - Dublin, Ireland
Business: Limelight Films, 6806 Lexington Avenue, Los Angeles, CA
90038, 213/464-5808 or: Limelight Films, 3 Bromley Place, London
W1P 5HB, England, tel.: 171/255-3939
Agent: ICM - London, tel.: 171/636-6565

ELECTRIC DREAMS   MGM/UA, 1984, British
TEENAGE MUTANT NINJA TURTLES   New Line Cinema, 1990
CONEHEADS   Paramount, 1993

ZELDA BARRON
b. England
Business: Limelight Films, 6806 Lexington Avenue, Los Angeles,
CA 90038, 213/464-5808 or:
Limelight Films, 3 Bromley Place, London W1P 5HB, England,
tel.: 171/255-3939
Agent: The Artists Agency - Los Angeles, 310/277-7779
Contact: British Film Commission, 70 Baker Street, London
W1M 1DJ, England, tel.: 171/224-5000

SECRET PLACES   TLC Films/20th Century-Fox, 1984, British
SHAG   Hemdale, 1988
FORBIDDEN SUN   Filmscreen/Marlborough Films, 1989, British

IAN BARRY
Contact: Australian Film Commission, 150 William Street,
Woolloomooloo NSW 2011, Australia, tel.: 2/321-6444

CRIME BROKER   Toei Video/Portman Entertainment, 1993,
Japanese-Australian
THE SEVENTH FLOOR   Rutherford Films Holdings,
1994, Australian
BLACKWATER TRAIL   Rutherford Film Holdings, 1995, Australian

SEAN BARRY
(Sean Barry Weske)
b. March 2, 1940 - London, England
Address: P.O. Box 2504, Redondo Beach, CA 90278, 310/370-1539

THE UGLY BATTLE   Sean Barry Productions, 1967, Italian
THE FORGOTTEN WAR   *GROSSKRIEG*   Sean Barry Productions,
1968, West German-Italian
THE DOLPHIN'S QUEST   Sean Barry Productions, 1968, Italian
THE STUDIO KIDS (TF)   co-director with George McIndoe, BMPC,
1973, British
LAZY DAYS (TF)   co-director with George McIndoe, Sean Barry
Productions, 1973, British

PAUL BARTEL*
b. August 6, 1938 - Brooklyn, New York
Agent: APA - Los Angeles, 310/273-0744

PRIVATE PARTS   MGM, 1972
DEATH RACE 2000   New World, 1975
CANNONBALL   New World, 1976
EATING RAOUL   20th Century Fox International Classics, 1982
NOT FOR PUBLICATION   The Samuel Goldwyn Company, 1984
LUST IN THE DUST   New World, 1985
THE LONGSHOT   Orion, 1986
SCENES FROM THE CLASS STRUGGLE IN BEVERLY HILLS
Cinecom, 1989
SHELF LIFE   Northern Arts Entertainment, 1994

DICK BARTLETT
OLLIE HOPNOODLE'S HAVEN OF BLISS (CTF)   The Disney
Channel/Creative Television Associates/Pholly Inc., 1988

WILLIAM S. BARTMAN*
Home: 6607 Colgate Avenue, Los Angeles, CA 90048, 818/907-9661
Agent: Tom Klassen, 73 Market Street, Venice, CA 90291,
   310/396-5937

O'HARA'S WIFE   Davis-Panzer Productions, 1982

SEAN BARTON
CURSE III: BLOOD SACRIFICE   Blue Rock Films Ltd./
   Screen Media Ltd., 1991

JAHNU BARUA
b. October 17, 1952 - India
Address: 9 Dutt Kudir, Plot 20/12, Wadala, Bombay 400 031, India
Contact: Films Division, Ministry of Information & Broadcasting,
   24 Dr G Beshmukh Marg, Bombay 40026, India, tel: 36-1461

APAROOPA   1982, Indian
APEKSHA   1984, Indian
PAPORI   1986, Indian
HALODHIA CHORAYE BAODHAN KHAI   1988, Indian
BANANI   Purbanchal Film Cooperative Society, 1990, Indian
PHIRINGOTI   Patkai Pictures, 1991, Indian
KUSHAR KONWAR   Government of West Bengal, 1994, Indian

HAL BARWOOD*
b. Hanover, New Hampshire
Agent: ICM - Beverly Hills, 310/550-4000

WARNING SIGN   20th Century Fox, 1985

PAOLO BARZMAN
Address: Place de la Danse, 30700 Saint-Siffret, France,
   tel.: 16/66-22-79-34
Contact: French Film Office, 745 Fifth Avenue, New York,
   NY 10151, 212/832-8860

R.S.V.P.   The Movie Group, 1992, U.S.-French
TIME IS MONEY   Les Acacias Cineaudience, 1994, French

FRED BARZYK*
Business: Creative Television Association, 90 Windom Street,
   Boston, MA 02134, 617/783-2103

BETWEEN TIME & TIMBUKTU (TF)   PBS, 1974
THE PHANTOM OF THE OPEN HEARTH (TF)   co-director with
   David R. Loxton, WNET-13 Television Laboratory/WGBH New
   Television Workshop, 1976
CHARLIE SMITH AND THE FRITTER TREE (TF)   co-director with
   David R. Loxton, WNET-13 Television Laboratory/WGBH New
   Television Workshop, 1978
THE LATHE OF HEAVEN (TF)   co-director with David R. Loxton,
   WNET-13 Television Laboratory/Taurus Film, 1980
COUNTDOWN TO LOOKING GLASS (CTF)   L & B Productions/
   Primedia Productions, 1984
THE STAR-CROSSED ROMANCE OF JOSEPHINE
   COSNOWSKI (TF)   WGBH New TV Workshop/Creative
   TV Associates, 1985
JENNY'S SONG (TF)   Westinghouse Broadcasting, 1988
THE MAD HOUSERS (TF)   WBZ-TV/Group W, 1990
THE LAST FERRY HOME (TF)   WCVB-Boston, 1992

GIULIO BASE
b. December 6, 1964 - Turin, Italy
Home: via San Liberio 20, Rome, Italy, tel.: 06/684-7512

CRACK   Numero Uno International/Raitre, 1991, Italian
LEST   Claudio Bonivento Production, 1993, Italian
POLIZIOTTI   Cecchi Gori Group, 1995, Italian

RICHARD BASKIN*
Agent: CAA - Beverly Hills, 310/288-4545

SING   TriStar, 1989

JULES BASS
Business: Rankin-Bass Productions, Inc., 24 West 55th Street,
   New York, NY 10019, 212/582-4017

MAD MONSTER PARTY (AF)   Embassy, 1967
THE WACKY WORLD OF MOTHER GOOSE (AF)   1968
THE HOBBIT (ATF)   co-director with Arthur Rankin, Jr.,
   Rankin-Bass Productions, 1977
RUDOLPH AND FROSTY (ATF)   co-director with Arthur Rankin, Jr.,
   Rankin-Bass Productions, 1979
THE RETURN OF THE KING (ATF)   co-director with
   Arthur Rankin, Jr., Rankin-Bass Productions, 1979
THE LAST UNICORN (AF)   co-director with Arthur Rankin, Jr.,
   Jensen Farley Pictures, 1982
THE FLIGHT OF DRAGONS (ATF)   co-director with
   Arthur Rankin, Jr., Rankin-Bass Productions, 1986
THE WIND IN THE WILLOWS (ATF)   co-director with
   Arthur Rankin, Jr., Rankin-Bass Productions, 1987, filmed in 1985

SAUL BASS*
b. May 8, 1920 - New York, New York
Business: Saul Bass/Herb Yager & Associates, 7039 Sunset Blvd.,
   Los Angeles, CA 90028, 213/466-9701

PHASE IV   Paramount, 1974

LAWRENCE BASSOFF
Business: Dauntless Director, 228 Main Street - Suite D, Venice, CA
   90291, 310/553-5380

WEEKEND PASS   Crown International, 1984
HUNK   Crown International, 1987

MICHAL BAT-ADAM
Contact: Israel Film Centre, Ministry of Industry & Trade,
   30 Agron Street, P.O. Box 299, Jerusalem 94190, Israel,
   tel.: 972/210433 or 219297

EACH OTHER   MOMENTS   Franklin Media, 1979, Israeli-French
THE THIN LINE   New Yorker, 1980, Israeli
YOUNG LOVE   GUY Film Productions Ltd., 1983, Israeli
THE LOVER   Cannon, 1986, Israeli
A THOUSAND WIVES   THE THOUSAND WIVES OF NAFTALI
   Angelika Films, 1989, Israeli
LA FEMME DU DESERTEUR   Mimar Films/Mod Films/Solyfic/
   Investimage 3, 1993, French-Israeli
AN IMAGINED AUTOBIOGRAPHY   Transfax Film, 1994, Israeli

KENT BATEMAN*
Telephone: 801/649-8887

SNOWMAN   International Picture Show, 1973

BRADLEY BATTERSBY
Agent: Paradigm - Los Angeles, 310/277-4400

BLUE DESERT   Neo Films/First Look Films, 1991

ROY BATTERSBY
Agent: Peters Fraser & Dunlop - London, tel.: 171/344-1000

THE BODY   MGM, 1970, British
ROLL ON FOUR O'CLOCK (TF)   Granada TV, 1971, British
LEEDS UNITED (TF)   BBC, 1973, British
THE PALESTINIAN (TD)   1978, British
WINTER FLIGHT   Cinecom, 1984, British,
   originally made for television
MR. LOVE (TF)   Enigma/Goldcrest Films & TV, 1986, British
EUROCOPS: FIRING THE BULLETS (TF)   Picture Palace
   Productions/Channel 4/European Co-Production Associates,
   1988, British
INSPECTOR MORSE: FAT CHANCE (TF)   Central TV,
   1991, British
BETWEEN THE LINES (TF)   BBC, 1993, British
A TOUCH OF FROST (TF)   Yorkshire TV, 1994, British

GIACOMO BATTIATO
b. 1943 - Verona, Italy
Agent: Carol Levi, via G. Carducci 10, Rome, Italy, tel.: 06/486961

IL MARSIGLIESE (TF)   RAI, 1975, Italian
UN DELITTO PERBENE (TF)   RAI, 1976, Italian
IL GIORNO DEI CRISTALLI (TF)   RAI, 1977, Italian
MARTIN EDEN (TF)   RAI, 1979, Italian
COLOMBA (TF)   RAI, 1981, Italian
I PALADINI   Vides Produzione, 1983, Italian
BLOOD TIES   IL CUGINO AMERICANO (CTF)   RAI/Racing
   Pictures/Showtime, 1986, Italian-U.S.
STRADIVARIUS   Titanus, 1988, Italian
UNA VITA SCELLERATA   RAI/Cinemax/Taurus Film, 1990,
   Italian-West German-French
CRONACA DI UN AMORE VIOLATO   Sacis, 1995, Italian

NOAH BAUMBACH
KICKING AND SCREAMING   Trimark Pictures, 1995

LAMBERTO BAVA
(John Old, Jr.)
b. 1944 - Rome, Italy
Home: Piazzate Clodio 22, Rome, Italy, tel.: 06/372-2203

LA VENERE D'ILLE (TF)   co-director with Mario Bava, RAI,
   1978, Italian
MACABRO   A.M.A. Film/Medusa Distribuzione, 1980, Italian
LA CASA CON LA SCALA NEL BUIO   National Cinematografica/
   Nuova Dania Cinematografica, 1983, Italian
BLASTFIGHTER   National Cinematografica/Nuova Dania
   Cinematografica, 1984, Italian
MONSTER SHARK   *SHARK ROSSO NELL'OCEANO*
   Cinema Shares International, 1984, Italian
DEMONI   Dac Film, 1985, Italian
DEMONI 2   Dac Film, 1986, Italian
MORIRAI A MEZZANOTTE   Dania Film/Reteitalia, 1986, Italian
LE FOTO DI GIOIA   Devon Film/Dania Film/Medusa Distribuzione/
   Filmes International, 1987, Italian
L'UOMO CHE NON VOLEVA MORIRE   1989, Italian
IL MAESTRO DEL TERRORE (TF)   1989, Italian
IL GIOCO (TF)   ANFRI/Reteitalia/Hamster Productions, 1989, Italian
SABBAH, LA MASCHERA DEL DEMONIO   Anfri/Reteitalia,
   1990, Italian
THE CAVE OF THE GOLDEN ROSE (MS)   Reteitalia/TV3 Televisio
   de Catalunya/NDR International, 1991, Italian-Spanish
BODY PUZZLE   *MISTERIA*   PAC Produzioni, 1992, Italian

CRAIG R. BAXLEY*
Agent: Favored Artists Agency - Los Angeles, 213/247-1040

ACTION JACKSON   Lorimar, 1988
I COME IN PEACE   Triumph Releasing Corporation, 1991
STONE COLD   Columbia, 1991
RAVEN (TF)   Invader Productions/Columbia TV, 1992
REVENGE ON THE HIGHWAY (TF)   Arvin Kaufman Productions/
   Saban Entertainment, 1992
A FAMILY TORN APART (TF)   River City Productions/
   Robert Halmi Inc., 1993
DEEP RED (CTF)   Dave Bell Associates/MCA TV, 1994
DECONSTRUCTING SARAH (CTF)   Best Shot Productions/Carla
   Singer Productions/MCA TV/USA Network, 1994
THE AVENGING ANGEL (CTF)   Turner Pictures/Esparza-Katz
   Productions/Curtis-Lowe Productions/First Corps Endeavors, 1995

JACK BAXTER
BROTHER MINISTER: THE ASSASSINATION OF MALCOLM X (FD)
   co-director with Jefri Aalmuhammed, X-Ceptional Productions/
   Illuminati Entertainment Group/Why Productions, 1994

PETER BAXTER
REASON TO BELIEVE   Organic Artists Productions, 1993

MICHAEL BAY
Agent: CAA - Beverly Hills, 310/288-4545

BAD BOYS   Columbia, 1995

STEPHEN BAYLY
b. July 7, 1942 - Baltimore, Maryland
Business: Red Rooster Films, 29 Floral Street, London WC2E 9DP,
   England, tel.: 171/379-7727
Agent: Peters Fraser & Dunlop - London, tel.: 171/344-1000
Contact: British Film Commission, 70 Baker Street, London
   W1M 1DJ, England, tel.: 171/224-5000

JONI JONES (MS)   1982, British
AND PIGS MIGHT FLY (TF)   1983, British
THE DREAM FACTORY (TD)   1984, British
THE WORKS (TF)   S4C, 1984, Welsh
COMING UP ROSES   Skouras Pictures, 1986, Welsh
DIAMOND'S EDGE   *JUST ASK FOR DIAMOND*   Kings Road/JGM
   Enterprises, 1988, British

DAVID BEAIRD*
b. Shreveport, Louisiana
Agent: William Morris Agency - Beverly Hills, 310/859-4000

OCTAVIA   International Film Marketing, 1984
THE PARTY ANIMAL   International Film Marketing, 1984
MY CHAUFFEUR   Crown International, 1985
PASS THE AMMO   New Century/Vista, 1988
IT TAKES TWO   MGM/UA, 1988
SCORCHERS   Goldcrest Films/Nova Entertainment, 1991

ROBERT B. BEAN*
Home: 8 Hilltop Road, Norwalk, CT 06854, 203/853-1352

MADE FOR EACH OTHER   20th Century-Fox, 1971

CHRIS BEARDE*
Address: 29169 Heathercliff Road - Suite 216-496, Malibu, CA
   90265, 310/478-8494

HYSTERICAL   Embassy, 1983

ALAN BEATTIE
DELUSION   New Line Cinema, 1981
THE HOUSE WHERE DEATH LIVES   New American, 1984
STAND ALONE   New World, 1985

WARREN BEATTY*
(Henry Warren Beatty)
b. March 30, 1937 - Richmond, Virginia
Agent: CAA - Beverly Hills, 310/288-4545
Business Manager: Traubner & Flynn - Los Angeles, 310/277-3000

HEAVEN CAN WAIT ★   co-director with Buck Henry,
   Paramount, 1978
REDS ★★   Paramount, 1981
DICK TRACY   Buena Vista, 1990

GABRIELLE BEAUMONT*
Business Manager: Rick Shepherd, Shepherd Associates,
   9200 Sunset Blvd. - Suite PH22, Los Angeles, CA 90069,
   310/858-2200

VELVET HOUSE   Cannon, 1969, British
THE JOHNSTOWN MONSTER   Sebastian Films, Ltd., 1971, British
THE GODSEND   Cannon, 1980, British
DEATH OF A CENTERFOLD: THE DOROTHY STRATTEN
   STORY (TF)   Wilcox Productions/MGM TV, 1981
SECRETS OF A MOTHER AND DAUGHTER (TF)   The Shpetner
   Company, 1983
GONE ARE THE DAYES (CTF)   Walt Disney Productions, 1984
THE CORVINI INHERITANCE (TF)   Fox-Hammer, 1984
HE'S MY GIRL   Scotti Brothers, 1987
CARMILLA (CTF)   Think Entertainment, 1989
ONE LAST CHANCE (TF)   BBC, 1990, British
FATAL INHERITANCE   Smart Egg Pictures, 1991
MOMENT OF TRUTH: CRADLE OF CONSPIRACY (TF)
   O'Hara-Horowitz Productions/NBC Productions, 1994

F
I
L
M

D
I
R
E
C
T
O
R
S

GORMAN BECHARD
b. March 15, 1959 - Waterbury, Connecticut
Business: Generic Films, Inc., P.O. Box 2715, Waterbury, CT 06723,
   203/756-3017

DISCONNECTED   Generic Films/Reel Movies International, 1984
AND THEN?   Generic Films, 1985
PSYCHOS IN LOVE   Generic Films, 1986
PANDEVIL   Empire Pictures, 1988
TWENTY QUESTIONS   Generic Films, 1988
TEENAGE SLASHER SLUTS   Empire Pictures, 1988
GALACTIC GIGOLO   Urban Classics, 1988
PSYCHOS ON PARADE   Generic Films, 1989
CEMETERY HIGH   Titan Productions/Generic Films, 1989

HAROLD BECKER*
b. New York, New York
Agent: CAA - Beverly Hills, 310/288-4545

THE RAGMAN'S DAUGHTER   Penelope Films, 1972, British
THE ONION FIELD   Avco Embassy, 1979
THE BLACK MARBLE   Avco Embassy, 1980
TAPS   20th Century-Fox, 1981
VISION QUEST   Warner Bros., 1985
THE BOOST   Hemdale, 1988
SEA OF LOVE   Universal, 1989
MALICE   Columbia, 1993
CITY HALL   Columbia, 1995

JOSH BECKER
LUNATICS: A LOVE STORY   Renaissance Pictures, 1991
HERCULES IN THE MAZE OF THE MINOTAUR (TF)   Renaissance
   Pictures/Universal TV, 1994

JAMES BECKET
Home: 823 N. Sweetzer Ave., Los Angeles, CA 90069, 213/655-6869
Agent: Robert O. Kaplan, 1999 Avenue of the Stars,
   Los Angeles, CA, 310/552-0808

SANCTUARY (TF)   1986
ULTERIOR MOTIVES   Den Pictures, 1990
BIG BOYS DON'T CRY (TF)   Churchill Entertainment, 1992
NATURAL CAUSES   Pacific Rim Productions, 1994, U.S.-Thai
THE BEST REVENGE   Redeeming Features, 1995
FAST FORWARD (TF)   Wild Films, 1995

MICHAEL BECKHAM
Contact: British Film Commission, 70 Baker Street, London
   W1M 1DJ, England, tel.: 171/224-5000

TINY REVOLUTIONS (TF)   Granada TV, 1981, British

TERRY BEDFORD*
(Terence L. Bedford)
b. 1943 - London, England
Business: Terry Bedford Productions, Inc., c/o Paneth, Haber &
   Zimmerman, 600 Third Avenue - 8th Floor, New York, NY 10016,
   212/503-8822
Agent: ICM - Beverly Hills, 310/550-4000

FREEDOM OF THE DIG (TF)   BBC, 1976, British
SLAYGROUND   Universal/AFD, 1983, British

GREG BEEMAN*
Agent: ICM - Beverly Hills, 310/550-4000
Personal Manager: 3 Arts Entertainment - Beverly Hills, 310/888-3200

THE RICHEST CAT IN THE WORLD (TF)   Les Alexander
   Productions/Walt Disney, TV, 1986
LITTLE SPIES (TF)   Walt Disney TV, 1986
LICENSE TO DRIVE   20th Century Fox, 1988
MOM & DAD SAVE THE WORLD   Warner Bros., 1992
TENDERFOOTS   20th Century Fox, 1995
PROBLEM CHILD 3: JUNIOR IN LOVE (TF)   Telvan Productions/
   Robert Simonds Company, 1995

ANDREW BEHAR
TIE-DYED: ROCK 'N ROLL'S MOST DEADICATED FANS (FD)
   Padded Cell Pictures/Arrowood, 1995

RIDHA BEHI
Contact: French Film Office, 745 Fifth Avenue, New York,
   NY 10151, 212/832-8860

LES HIRONDELLES NE MEURENT PAS A JERUSALEM
   Baba Films/Alya Films, 1994, French-Tunisian

JEAN-JACQUES BEINEIX
b. 1946 - Paris, France
Business: Cargo Film, 2 rue Biot, 75017 Paris, France,
   tel.: 1/43-87-33-38
Contact: French Film Office, 745 Fifth Avenue, New York,
   NY 10151, 212/832-8860

DIVA   United Artists Classics, 1982, French
THE MOON IN THE GUTTER   Triumph/Columbia,
   1983, French-Italian
BETTY BLUE   *37.2 DEGREES LE MATIN*   Alive Films,
   1986, French
ROSELYNE AND THE LIONS   Four Seasons Entertainment,
   1989, French
IP5: L'ILE AUX PACHYDERMES   Gaumont, 1992, French
OTAKU (FD)   Cargo Films/France 2/Television Suisse Romande,
   1994, French-Swiss

JEAN-PIERRE BEKOLO
Contact: FEPACI (Pan-African Federation of Film-Makers,
   01 B.P. 2524, Ouagadougou, Burkina Faso, tel.: 226/31-02-58

QUARTIER MOZART   Ministere de la Cooperation et du
   Developpement de Kola Case/Centre National de la
   Cinematographie/l'Agence de Cooperation Culturelle/Technique,
   d'Ecran du Sud/Cameroon Radio Television/Ministere de la
   Culture (Cameroun), 1992, French-Cameroonian

MIKHAIL BELIKOV
Contact: Confederation of Film-Makers Unions, Vasilyevskaya
   Street 13, 123 825 Moscow, Russia, tel.: 095/250-4114

RASPAD   MK2 Productions USA, 1991, Soviet

JEFFREY BELL
Agent: Jim Preminger Agency - Los Angeles, 310/475-9491

RADIO INSIDE (CTF)   MGM-UA Communications/Showtime
   Entertainment. 1994

MARTIN BELL*
Address: 134 Spring Street, New York, NY 10012, 212/925-2770

STREETWISE (FD)   Angelika Films, 1984
A MATTER OF TRUST: BILLY JOEL IN THE U.S.S.R. (CTCD)
   Rick London Productions/Martin Bell Productions/Robert
   Dalrymple Films, 1988
AMERICAN HEART   Trimark Pictures, 1993

EARL BELLAMY*
b. March 11, 1917 - Minneapolis, Minnesota
Home: 6763 Chama River Court, Rio Rancho, NM 87124,
   505/867-3735

SEMINOLE UPRISING   Columbia, 1955
BLACKJACK KETCHUM, DESPERADO   Columbia, 1956
TOUGHEST GUN IN TOMBSTONE   United Artists, 1958
STAGECOACH TO DANCERS' ROCK   Universal, 1962
FLUFFY   Universal, 1965
INCIDENT AT PHANTOM HILL   Universal, 1966
GUNPOINT   Universal, 1966
MUNSTER, GO HOME   Universal, 1966
THREE GUNS FOR TEXAS   co-director with David Lowell Rich &
   Paul Stanley, Universal, 1968
BACKTRACK   Universal, 1969
THE PIGEON (TF)   Thomas-Spelling Productions, 1969

DESPERATE MISSION (TF)   20th Century-Fox TV, 1971
THE TRACKERS (TF)   Aaron Spelling Productions, 1971
SEVEN ALONE   Doty-Dayton, 1975
SIDECAR RACERS   Universal, 1975, Australian
PART 2 WALKING TALL   American International, 1975
AGAINST A CROOKED SKY   Doty-Dayton, 1975
FLOOD! (TF)   Irwin Allen Productions/20th Century-Fox TV, 1976
FIRE! (TF)   Irwin Allen Productions/20th Century-Fox TV, 1977
SIDEWINDER ONE   Avco Embassy, 1977
SPEEDTRAP   First Artists, 1978
DESPERATE WOMEN (TF)   Lorimar Productions, 1978
THE CASTAWAYS OF GILLIGAN'S ISLAND (TF)
   Sherwood Schwartz Productions, 1979
VALENTINE MAGIC ON LOVE ISLAND (TF)   Dick Clark
   Productions/PKO/Osmond Television, 1980
MAGNUM THRUST   Shenandoah Films, 1981

DONALD BELLISARIO*
Business: Belisarius Productions, 100 Universal City Plaza -
   Building 426C, Universal City, CA 91608, 818/777-3381
Agent: Norman Kurland, Broder-Kurland-Webb-Uffner Agency -
   Beverly Hills, 310/281-3400
Business Manager: Zane J. Lubin, Zane Lubin & Associates,
   12700 Ventura Blvd. - Suite 140, Studio City, CA 91604

AIRWOLF (TF)   Belisarius Productions/Universal TV, 1984
THREE ON A MATCH (TF)   Belisarius Productions/TriStar TV, 1987
LAST RITES   MGM-UA, 1988

MARCO BELLOCCHIO
b. November 9, 1939 - Piacenza, Italy
Home: Viale Angelico 36/B, Rome, Italy

FIST IN HIS POCKET   Peppercorn-Wormser, 1965, Italian
CHINA IS NEAR   Royal Films International, 1967, Italian
AMORE E RABBIA   co-director, 1969, Italian
NEL NOME DEL PADRE   1972, Italian
SBATTI IL MOSTRO IN PRIMA PAGINA   1972, Italian
MATTA DA SLEGARE (FD)   11 Marzo Cinematografica,
   1975, Italian
VICTORY MARCH   Summit Features, 1976, Italian-French
LES YEUX FERTILES   1977, French-Italian
IL GABBIANO (TF)   RAI, 1977, Italian
LA MACCHINA CINEMA (TD)   RAI, 1978, Italian
LEAP INTO THE VOID   Summit Features, 1979, Italian
THE EYES, THE MOUTH   Triumph/Columbia, 1983, Italian-French
HENRY IV   Orion Classics, 1984, Italian
DEVIL IN THE FLESH   Istituto Luce/Italnoleggio,
   1986, Italian-French
LA VISIONE DEL SABBA   Bema/Reteitalia, 1987, Italian
LA CONDANNA   Cineeuropa 92 SRL/Italnoleggio Cinematografica/
   RAI/Banfilm/Cactus Film, 1991, Italian-French-Swiss
IL SOGNO DELLA FARFALLA   Filmalbatros/Waka Films/Pierre
   Grise Productions/RAI-2/SSR/TSI Televisione Svizzera/Federal
   Office of Culture (Switzerland)/Istituto Luce/Happy Valley Films,
   1994, Italian-Swiss-German-French

VERA BELMONT
Contact: French Film Office, 745 Fifth Avenue, New York,
   NY 10151, 212/832-8860

ROUGE BAISER   Circle Releasing, 1985, French
MILENA   Shapiro Glickenhaus Entertainment, 1991,
   French-Canadian-German

JERRY BELSON*
Agent: ICM - Beverly Hills, 310/550-4000
Contact: Directors Guild of America - Los Angeles, 213/851-3671

JEKYLL AND HYDE...TOGETHER AGAIN   Paramount, 1982
SURRENDER   Warner Bros., 1987

REMY BELVAUX
Contact: National Tourist Office, 61 Rue de Marche Aux Herbes,
   B1000 Brussels, Belgium, tel.: 02/513-8940

MAN BITES DOG   co-director with Andre Bonzel &
   Benoit Poelvoorde, Roxie Releasing, 1992, Belgian

MARIA LUISA BEMBERG†
b. April 14, 1940 - Buenos Aires, Argentina
d. 1995

MOMENTOS   GEA Cinematografica, 1981, Argentine
SENORA DE NADIE   GEA Cinematografica, 1982, Argentine
CAMILA   European Classics, 1984, Argentine-Spanish
MISS MARY   New World, 1986, Argentine
YO, LA PEOR DE TODAS   GEA Producciones SRL,
   1990, Argentine
I DON'T WANT TO TALK ABOUT IT   Sony Pictures Classics,
   1993, Argentine-Italian

JACK BENDER*
Agent: Richland/Wunsch/Hohman Agency - Los Angeles,
   310/278-1955

IN LOVE WITH AN OLDER WOMAN (TF)   Pound Ridge Productions/
   Charles Fries Productions, 1982
TWO KINDS OF LOVE (TF)   CBS Entertainment, 1983
SHATTERED VOWS (TF)   Bertinelli-Pequod Productions, 1984
DEADLY MESSAGES (TF)   Columbia TV, 1985
LETTING GO (TF)   Adam Productions/ITC Productions, 1985
THE MIDNIGHT HOUR (TF)   ABC Circle Films, 1985
THE BLACKBOARD JUNGLE (TF)   MGM-UA TV, 1987
SIDE BY SIDE (TF)   Avnet-Kerner Productions, 1988
TRICKS OF THE TRADE (TF)   Leonard Hill Films, 1988
MY BROTHER'S WIFE (TF)   Robert Greenwald Productions/Adam
   Productions, 1989
THE DREAMER OF OZ (TF)   Bedrock Productions/Adam
   Productions/Spelling Entertainment, 1990
THE PERFECT TRIBUTE (TF)   Dorothea Petrie Productions/
   Proctor & Gamble Productions/World International Network, 1991
CHILD'S PLAY 3   Universal, 1991
LOVE CAN BE MURDER (TF)   Konigsberg-Sanitsky
   Productions, 1992
NED BLESSING: THE STORY OF MY LIFE AND TIMES (TF)
   Wittliff-Pangaen Productions/Hearst Entertainment/CBS
   Entertainment, 1993
ARMED AND INNOCENT (TF)   Gillian Productions/Republic
   Pictures, 1994
DANIELLE STEEL'S FAMILY ALBUM   FAMILY ALBUM (TF)
   The Cramer Company/NBC Productions, 1994
GAMBLER V: PLAYING FOR KEEPS (TF)   Kenny Rogers
   Productions/World International Network/RHI Entertainment, 1994

JOEL BENDER
THE IMMORTALIZER   RCA/Columbia Home Video/Film West, 1990
RICH GIRL   Studio Three Film Corporation, 1991
IN THE MIDNIGHT HOUR   In the Midnight Hour Productions, 1992

TERRY BENEDICT
HALF A DOG'S LIFE   Sound Shore Productions, 1995

SHYAM BENEGAL
b. 1934 - Hyderabad, India
Contact: National Film Development Corporation of India,
   Discovery of India Building, Nehru Centre, Dr Annie Besant
   Road, Worli, Bombay 400018, India, tel.: 4949856

THE SEEDLING   1973, Indian
CHARANDAS, THE THIEF   1975, Indian
NIGHT'S END   1975, Indian
THE CHURNING   1976, Indian
THE ROLE   1977, Indian
THE BOON   1978, Indian
THE OBSESSION   1978, Indian
THE MACHINE AGE   1981, Indian
ASCENDING SCALE   1982, Indian
MARKET PLACE   1983, Indian
SATYAJIT RAY (FD)   National Film Development Corporation
   of India, 1985, Indian
SEVENTH HORSE OF THE SUN'S CHARIOT   National Film
   Development Corporation of India, 1991, Indian
ANTARNAAD   1992, Indian

SEVENTH HORSE OF THE SUN   National Film Development
   Corporation of India, 1993, Indian
MAMMO   National Film Development Corporation of India,
   1994, Indian
MAKING OF THE MAHATMA   Echo Productions/South African
   Broadcasting Corporation/Government of India, 1995,
   Indian-South African

ROBERTO BENIGNI
b. 1952 - Florence, Italy
Home: via Icilio 9, Rome, Italy, tel.: 06/575-8856
Contact: via Traversa dio Vergaio, 44, Prato, Florence, Italy

TU MI TURBI   Best International Films, 1982, Italian
NON CI RESTA CHE PIANGERE   co-director with Massimo Troisi,
   Yarno Cinematografica/Best International Films, 1984, Italian
IL PICCOLO DIAVOLO   Warner Bros. Italia, 1988, Italian
JOHNNY STECCHINO   New Line Cinema, 1991, Italian
IL MOSTRO   UGC Image/Melampro/Iris Film/Canal Plus/La Sept
   Cinema/Sofinergie, 1994, Italian-French

MARK BENJAMIN
THE LAST PARTY (FD)   co-director with Marc Levin,
   Triton Pictures, 1993

RICHARD BENJAMIN*
b. May 22, 1938 - New York, New York
Agent: The Gersh Agency - Beverly Hills, 310/274-6611

MY FAVORITE YEAR   MGM/UA, 1982
RACING WITH THE MOON   Paramount, 1984
CITY HEAT   Warner Bros., 1984
THE MONEY PIT   Universal, 1986
LITTLE NIKITA   Columbia, 1988
MY STEPMOTHER IS AN ALIEN   Columbia/WEG, 1988
DOWNTOWN   20th Century Fox, 1990
MERMAIDS   Orion, 1990
MADE IN AMERICA   Warner Bros., 1993
MILK MONEY   Paramount, 1994
MRS. WINTERBOURNE   TriStar, 1995, U.S.-Canadian

BILL BENNETT
Contact: Australian Film Commission, 150 William Street,
   Woolloomooloo NSW 2011, Australia, tel.: 2/321-6444

A STREET TO DIE   Mermaid Beach Productions, 1986, Australian
BACKLASH   The Samuel Goldwyn Company, 1986, Australian
DEAR CARDHOLDER   Mermaid Beach Productions/Multifilms,
   1987, Australian
JILTED   J.C. Williamson/Mermaid Beach Productions,
   1987, Australian
MALPRACTICE   Film Australia, 1989, Australian
MORTGAGE   Film Australia, 1990, Australian
SPIDER & ROSE   Dendy Films/Australian Film Finance Corporation,
· 1994, Australian
TWO IF BY SEA   Warner Bros., 1995

GARY BENNETT
RAIN WITHOUT THUNDER   Orion Classics, 1992

RICHARD C. BENNETT*
Home: 17136 Index Street, Granada Hills, CA 91344, 818/363-3381
Business Manager: Melvyn Shiaman, 5850 Canoga Avenue -
   Suite 120, Woodland Hills, CA 91367, 818/884-2500

HARPER VALLEY PTA   April Fools, 1978
THE ESCAPE OF A ONE-TON PET (TF)
   Tomorrow Entertainment, 1978
A STATE OF EMERGENCY   Esstar Productions, 1986

RODNEY BENNETT
Contact: British Film Commission, 70 Baker Street,
   London W1M 1DJ, England, tel.: 171/224-5000

EDWIN (TF)   Anglia TV, 1983, British
LOVE SONG (TF)   Anglia TV, 1984, British

MONSIGNOR QUIXOTE (TF)   Euston Films, 1985, British
DARLING BUDS OF MAY (TF)   Yorkshire TV, 1990, British
SOLDIER SOLDIER (TF)   Central Films, 1993

JACQUES W. BENOIT
b. 1948
Address: 4139 Avenue Old Orchard, Montreal, Quebec H4A 3B3,
   Canada, 514/484-3952

LE DIABLE A QUATRE   National Film Board of Canada/Societe
   Radio-Quebec, 1988, Canadian
HOW TO MAKE LOVE TO A NEGRO WITHOUT GETTING TIRED
   Angelika Films, 1989, Canadian-French

ALAN BENSON
Contact: British Film Commission, 70 Baker Street, London
   W1M 1DJ, England, tel.: 171/224-5000

THE MAKING OF SGT. PEPPER (TD)   Really Useful Group/Isis/
   London Weekend TV, 1992, British

ROBBY BENSON*
(Robert Segal)
b. January 21, 1956 - Dallas, Texas
Home: 19732 Henshaw Stret, Woodland Hills, CA 91364,
   818/705-5542
Agent: The Rothman Agency - Beverly Hills, 310/247-9898
Business Manager: Doug Chapin, Krost/Chapin Management, Inc.,
   9130 Wilshire Blvd. - Suite 205, Beverly Hills, CA 90212,
   310/281-3585

WHITE HOT   *CRACK IN THE MIRROR*   Triax Entertainment
   Group, 1988
MODERN LOVE   Triumph Releasing Corporat;ion, 1990

ROBERT BENTON*
b. September 29, 1932 - Waxahachie, Texas
Business: 110 West 57th Street - 5th Floor, New York, NY 10019,
   212/247-5652
Agent: Sam Cohn, ICM - New York City, 212/556-5600 or
   Beverly Hills, 310/550-4000

BAD COMPANY   Paramount, 1972
THE LATE SHOW   Warner Bros., 1976
KRAMER VS. KRAMER ★★   Columbia, 1979
STILL OF THE NIGHT   MGM/UA, 1982
PLACES IN THE HEART ★   TriStar, 1984
NADINE   TriStar, 1987
BILLY BATHGATE   Buena Vista, 1991
NOBODY'S FOOL   Paramount, 1994

OBIE BENZ
HEAVY PETTING (FD)   Skouras Pictures, 1989
THE HISTORY OF ROCK 'N' ROLL (TD)   co-director, Andrew Solt
   Productions/QDE/Telepictures Productions/Time-Life Video &
   Television/Warner Bros. TV Distribution Prime Time
   Entertainment Network, 1995

ALAIN BERBERIAN
Contact: French Film Office, 745 Fifth Avenue, New York,
   NY 10151, 212/832-8860

LA CITE DE LA PEUR: UNE COMEDIE FAMILIALE   Telema/Canal
   Plus/France 3 Cinema/M6 Films, 1994, French

LUCA BERCOVICI
Business Manager: David Arntzen, The Business Management Office,
   4605 Lankershim Blvd. - Suite 325, North Hollywood, CA 91602,
   818/509-1811

GHOULIES   Empire Pictures, 1985
ROCKULA   Cannon, 1990
DARK TIDE   Tapestry Films, 1993

BRUCE BERESFORD*

b. August 16, 1940 - Sydney, Australia
Agent: William Morris Agency - Beverly Hills, 310/859-4000

THE ADVENTURES OF BARRY McKENZIE   Longford Productions,
   1972, Australian
BARRY McKENZIE HOLDS HIS OWN   Satori, 1974, Australian
SIDE BY SIDE   GTO, 1975, British
DON'S PARTY   Satori, 1976, Australian
THE GETTING OF WISDOM   Atlantic Releasing Corporation,
   1977, Australian
MONEY MOVERS   South Australian Film Corporation,
   1978, Australian
BREAKER MORANT   New World/Quartet, 1980, Australian
THE CLUB   South Australian Film Corporation, 1981, Australian
PUBERTY BLUES   Universal Classics, 1982, Australian
TENDER MERCIES ★   Universal/AFD, 1983
KING DAVID   Paramount, 1985, U.S.-British
THE FRINGE DWELLERS   Atlantic Releasing Corporation,
   1986, Australian
CRIMES OF THE HEART   DEG, 1986
ARIA   co-director, Miramax Films, 1987, British
HER ALIBI   Warner Bros., 1989
DRIVING MISS DAISY   Warner Bros., 1989
MISTER JOHNSON   Avenue Pictures, 1991
BLACK ROBE   The Samuel Goldwyn Company,
   1991, Canadian-Australian
RICH IN LOVE   MGM, 1992
A GOOD MAN IN AFRICA   Gramercy Pictures, 1994, British
SILENT FALL   Warner Bros., 1994
LAST DANCE   Buena Vista, 1995

PAMELA BERGER

THE IMPORTED BRIDEGROOM   Lara Classics, 1989
KILIAN'S CHRONICLE   Lara Classics, 1994

RICK BERGER*

Agent: Paul Kohner, Inc. - Los Angeles, 310/550-1060

THE SITTER (TF)   FNM Films, 1991

ANDREW BERGMAN*

b. February 20, 1945 - Queens, New York
Business: Lobell-Bergman Productions, 9336 W. Washington Blvd.,
   Culver City, CA 90230, 310/202-3362
Agent: CAA - Beverly Hills, 310/288-4545

SO FINE   Warner Bros., 1981
THE FRESHMAN   TriStar, 1990
HONEYMOON IN VEGAS   Columbia, 1992
IT COULD HAPPEN TO YOU   TriStar, 1994

DANIEL BERGMAN

Contact: Swedish Film Institute, P.O. Box 27-126, S-102-52
   Stockholm, Sweden, tel.: 08/665-1100

SUNDAY'S CHILDREN   First Run Features, 1992,
   Swedish-Danish-Norwegian-Finnish-Icelandic

INGMAR BERGMAN

(Ernst Ingmar Bergman)
b. July 14, 1918 - Uppsala, Sweden
Contact: Swedish Film Institute, P.O. Box 27-126, S-102-52
   Stockholm, Sweden, tel.: 8/665-1100
Agent: Paul Kohner, Inc. - Beverly Hills, 310/550-1060

CRISIS   Svensk Filmindustri, 1945, Swedish
IT RAINS ON OUR LOVE   Sveriges Folkbiografer, 1946, Swedish
THE LAND OF DESIRE   Sveriges Folkbiografer, 1947, Swedish
NIGHT IS MY FUTURE   Terrafilm, 1948, Swedish
PORT OF CALL   Janus, 1948, Swedish
THE DEVIL'S WANTON   Terrafilm, 1949, Swedish
THREE STRANGE LOVES   *THIRST*   Janus, 1949, Swedish
TO JOY   Janus, 1950, Swedish
THIS CAN'T HAPPEN HERE   Svensk Filmindustri, 1951, Swedish
ILLICIT INTERLUDE   *SOMMARLEK*   Janus, 1951, Swedish

SECRETS OF WOMEN   Janus, 1952, Swedish
MONIKA   Janus, 1953, Swedish
SAWDUST AND TINSEL   *THE NAKED NIGHT*   Janus,
   1953, Swedish
A LESSON IN LOVE   Janus, 1954, Swedish
DREAMS   Janus, 1955, Swedish
SMILES OF A SUMMER NIGHT   Janus, 1955, Swedish
THE SEVENTH SEAL   Janus, 1957, Swedish
WILD STRAWBERRIES   Janus, 1957, Swedish
SO CLOSE TO LIFE   Janus, 1958, Swedish
THE MAGICIAN   Janus, 1958, Swedish
THE VIRGIN SPRING   Janus, 1960, Swedish
THE DEVIL'S EYE   Janus, 1960, Swedish
THROUGH A GLASS DARKLY   Janus, 1961, Swedish
WINTER LIGHT   Janus, 1962, Swedish
THE SILENCE   Janus, 1963, Swedish
ALL THESE WOMEN   Janus, 1964, Swedish
PERSONA   United Artists, 1966, Swedish
HOUR OF THE WOLF   United Artists, 1968, Swedish
SHAME   United Artists, 1968, Swedish
FARO DOCUMENT (TD)   1969, Swedish
THE RITUAL   Janus, 1969, Swedish, originally made for television
THE PASSION OF ANNA   United Artists, 1969, Swedish
THE TOUCH   Cinerama Releasing Corporation, 1971, Swedish,
   originally made for television
CRIES AND WHISPERS ★   New World, 1972, Swedish
SCENES FROM A MARRIAGE   Cinema 5, 1973, Swedish,
   originally made for television
THE MAGIC FLUTE   Surrogate, 1975, Swedish,
   originally made for television
FACE TO FACE ★   Paramount, 1976, Swedish
THE SERPENT'S EGG   Paramount, 1978, West German
AUTUMN SONATA   New World, 1978, West German
FROM THE LIFE OF THE MARIONETTES   Universal/AFD,
   1980, West German
FARO DOCUMENT 1979 (TD)   Cinematograph, 1979, Swedish
FANNY AND ALEXANDER ★   Embassy, 1983,
   Swedish-French-West German
AFTER THE REHEARSAL   Triumph/Columbia, 1983,
   Swedish-West German, originally made for television
DOCUMENT FANNY AND ALEXANDER (FD)   Swedish Film
   Institute, 1986, Swedish
THE BLESSED ONES (TF)   STV2, 1986, Swedish
FINAL CRY   *SISTA SKRIGET* (TF)   SVT-1, 1994, Swedish

ROBERT BERGMAN

Agent: Susan Grant, The Artists Group - Los Angeles,
   310/552-1100

SKULL: A NIGHT OF TERROR   1988
A WHISPER TO A SCREAM   1989
HURT PENGUINS   co-director with Myra Fried, 1992, Canadian

ELEANOR BERGSTEIN

Agent: CAA - Beverly Hills, 310/288-4545
Contact: Writers Guild of America, East - New York City,
   212/767-7800

LET IT BE ME   Savoy Pictures, 1995

STEVEN BERKOFF

b. 1937 - London, England
Contact: British Film Commission, 70 Baker Street, London
   W1M 1DJ, England, tel.: 171/224-5000

DECADENCE   Delux Productions/Vendetta Films/Schlammer
   Productions/Filmstiftung Nordrhein-Westfalen, 1994,
   British-German

LUIS GARCIA BERLANGA
(See Luis GARCIA BERLANGA)

DAVID BERLATSKY*
Address: 123 California Street - Suite 112, Santa Monica, CA 90403, 310/395-1435
Business Manager: Jerome S. Klein, Jerome S. Klein Company, 18401 Burbank Blvd. - Suite 211, Tarzana, CA 91356, 818/343-0333

THE FARMER   Columbia, 1977

TED BERMAN
Contact: 818/956-2612

THE FOX AND THE HOUND (AF)   co-director with Art Stevens & Richard Rich, Buena Vista, 1981
THE BLACK CAULDRON (AF)   co-director with Richard Rich, Buena Vista, 1985

CHRIS BERNARD
Contact: British Film Commission, 70 Baker Street, London W1M 1DJ, England, tel.: 171/224-5000

LETTER TO BREZHNEV   Circle Releasing, 1985, British
CONSPIRACY   Target International, 1990, British
A LITTLE BIT OF LIPPY (TF)   BBC, 1992, British

SAM BERNARD
PAYBACK   Trimark Pictures, 1994

EDWARD BERNDS
b. 1911
Contact: Writers Guild of America, West - Los Angeles, 310/550-1000

BLONDIE'S SECRET   Columbia, 1948
BLONDIE'S BIG DEAL   Columbia, 1949
BLONDIE HITS THE JACKPOT   Columbia, 1949
FEUDIN' RHYTHM   Columbia, 1949
BEWARE OF BLONDIE   Columbia, 1950
BLONDIE'S HERO   Columbia, 1950
GASOLINE ALLEY   Columbia, 1951
CORKY OF GASOLINE ALLEY   Columbia, 1951
GOLD RAIDERS   United Artists, 1951
HAREM GIRL   Columbia, 1952
ACE LUCKY   Columbia, 1952
WHITE LIGHTNING   Allied Artists, 1953
PRIVATE EYES   Allied Artists, 1953
LOOSE IN LONDON   Allied Artists, 1953
HOT NEWS   Allied Artists, 1953
THE BOWERY BOYS MEET THE MONSTERS   Allied Artists, 1954
JUNGLE GENTS   Allied Artists, 1954
BOWERY TO BAGDAD   Allied Artists, 1955
SPY CHASERS   Allied Artists, 1955
WORLD WITHOUT END   Allied Artists, 1956
NAVY WIFE   Allied Artists, 1956
DIG THAT URANIUM   Allied Artists, 1956
CALLING HOMICIDE   Allied Artists, 1956
THE STORM RIDER   20th Century-Fox, 1957
REFORM SCHOOL GIRL   American International, 1957
ESCAPE FROM RED ROCK   20th Century-Fox, 1958
QUANTRILL'S RAIDERS   20th Century-Fox, 1958
SPACE MASTER X-7   20th Century-Fox, 1958
QUEEN OF OUTER SPACE   Allied Artists, 1958
JOY RIDE   Allied Artists, 1958
ALASKA PASSAGE   20th Century-Fox, 1959
THE RETURN OF THE FLY   20th Century-Fox, 1959
VALLEY OF THE DRAGONS   Columbia, 1961
THE THREE STOOGES MEET HERCULES   Columbia, 1962
THE THREE STOOGES IN ORBIT   Columbia, 1962
PREHISTORIC VALLEY   ZRB Productions, 1966

ADAM BERNSTEIN*
Contact: Directors Guild of America - Los Angeles, 213/851-3671

IT'S PAT   Buena Vista, 1994

ARMYAN BERNSTEIN*
Business: Beacon Pictures, 1041 N. Formosa Avenue, Los Angeles, CA 90046, 213/850-2651
Agent: CAA - Beverly Hills, 310/288-4545

WINDY CITY   Warner Bros., 1984
CROSS MY HEART   Universal, 1987

WALTER BERNSTEIN*
b. August 29, 1929 - Chicago, Illinois
Home: 320 Central Park West, New York, NY 10025, 212/724-1821
Agent: Sam Cohn, ICM - New York City, 212/556-5600

LITTLE MISS MARKER   Universal, 1980
WOMEN & MEN 2: IN LOVE THERE ARE NO RULES (CTF)   co-director with Mike Figgis & Kristi Zea, David Brown Productions/HBO Showcase, 1991

CLAUDE BERRI
(Claude Langmann)
b. July 1, 1934 - Paris, France
Business: Renn Productions, 10 rue Lincoln, 75008 Paris, France, tel.: 1/256-2590
Agent: ICM France - Paris, tel.: 1/723-7860

LE BAISERS   co-director, 1964, French
LE CHANCE ET L'AMOUR   co-director, 1964, French
THE TWO OF US   *LE VIEL HOMME ET L'ENFANT*   Cinema 5, 1968, French
MARRY ME! MARRY ME!   *MAZEL TOV OU LE MARIAGE*   Allied Artists, 1969, French
THE MAN WITH CONNECTIONS   *LE PISTONNE*   Columbia, 1970, French
LE CINEMA DU PAPA   Columbia, 1971, French
LE SEX SHOP   Peppercorn-Wormser, 1973, French
MALE OF THE CENTURY   Joseph Green Pictures, 1975, French
THE FIRST TIME   EDP, 1976, French
ONE WILD MOMENT   Quartet/Films Incorporated, 1978, French
A NOUS DEUX   AMLF, 1979, French
JE VOUS AIME   Renn Films/FR3/Cinevog, 1980, French
LE MAITRE D'ECOLE   AMLF, 1981, French
TCHAO PANTIN   European Classics, 1983, French
JEAN DE FLORETTE   Orion Classics, 1987, French
MANON OF THE SPRING   Orion Classics, 1987, French
URANUS   Prestige, 1991, French
GERMINAL   Sony Pictures Classics, 1993, French-Belgian-Italian

BILL BERRY
Contact: Writers Guild of America, West - Los Angeles, 310/550-1000

OFF THE MARK   Fries Entertainment, 1987

JOHN BERRY*
b. 1917 - New York, New York
Address: 8 rue Levert, 75020 Paris, France, tel.: 1/43-49-09-61
Agent: Shapiro-Lichtman Talent Agency - Los Angeles, 310/859-8877

MISS SUSIE SLAGLE'S   Paramount, 1945
FROM THIS DAY FORWARD   RKO Radio, 1946
CROSS MY HEART   Paramount, 1946
CASBAH   Universal, 1948
TENSION   MGM, 1949
HE RAN ALL THE WAY   United Artists, 1951
C'EST ARRIVE A PARIS   1952, French
CA VA BARDER   1954, French
JE SUIS UN SENTIMENTAL   1955, French
PANTALOONS   *DON JUAN*   United Motion Picture Organizations, 1956, French-Spanish
OH, QUE MAMBO   1958, French
TAMANGO   Valiant, 1959, French
MAYA   MGM, 1966
A TOUT CASSER   1967, French
CLAUDINE   20th Century-Fox, 1974
THIEVES   Paramount, 1977
SPARROW (TF)   1978

THE BAD NEWS BEARS GO TO JAPAN   Paramount, 1978
ANGEL ON MY SHOULDER (TF)   Mace Neufeld Productions/
   Barney Rosenzweig Productions/Beowulf Productions, 1980
SISTER, SISTER (TF)   20th Century-Fox TV, 1982
HONEYBOY (TF)   Fan Fares Inc. Productions/Estrada
   Productions, 1982
LE VOYAGE A PAIMPOL   Jomy Productions/FR3/AFC,
   1985, French
MALDONNE   Cannon France, 1987, French-Belgian
A CAPTIVE IN THE LAND   Gloria Productions/Gorky Film Studios/
   Soviet American Films, 1991, U.S.-Soviet

TOM BERRY

Business: Allegro Films Inc., 2187 rue Lariviere, Montreal, Quebec
   H2K 2A3, Canada, 514/288-9408

BLIND FEAR   Malofilm Group, 1989, Canadian
THE AMITYVILLE CURSE   Vidmark, 1990
TWIN SISTERS   Allegro Films/Eurogroup Films/Image Organization,
   1991, Canadian-French

ATTILA BERTALAN

Contact: Directors Guild of Canada, 225 Richmond Street, Toronto
   M5V 1W2, Canada, 416/351-8200

A BULLET IN THE HEAD   Creon Productions, 1991, Canadian

BERNARDO BERTOLUCCI*

b. March 16, 1940 - Parma, Italy
Home: via della Lungara 3, Rome, Italy 00165, tel.: 06/580-5335
Business: Recorded Picture Company, 8-12 Broadwick Street,
   London W1V 1FH, England, tel.: 171/439-0607
Agent: ICM - Beverly Hills, 310/550-4000

LA COMMARE SECCA   1962, Italian
BEFORE THE REVOLUTION   New Yorker, 1964, Italian
PARTNER   New Yorker, 1968, Italian
AMORE E RABBIA   co-director, 1969, Italian
THE SPIDER'S STRATAGEM   New Yorker, 1970, Italian
THE CONFORMIST   Paramount, 1971,
   Italian-French-West German
LAST TANGO IN PARIS ★   United Artists, 1973, Italian-French
1900   Paramount, 1977, Italian
LUNA   20th Century-Fox, 1979, Italian-U.S.
TRAGEDY OF A RIDICULOUS MAN   The Ladd Company/
   Warner Bros., 1982, Italian
THE LAST EMPEROR ★★   Columbia, 1987, British-Chinese
THE SHELTERING SKY   Warner Bros., 1990, British
LITTLE BUDDHA   Miramax Films, 1993, British-French

GIUSEPPE BERTOLUCCI

b. February 16, 1947 - Parma, Italy
Home: via Bassini 9, Rome, Italy, tel.: 06/531-3365

ANDARE E VENIRE (TF)   RAI, 1972, Italian
AB CINEMA (FD)   Ovidio Assonitis, 1975, Italian
SE NON E' ANCORA LA FELICITA (TD)   Raiuno, 1976, Italian
BERLINGUER TI VOGLIO BENE   AMA Film, 1977, Italian
OGGETTI SMARRITI   Fiction Cinematografica, 1980, Italian
PANNI SPORCHI (TF)   Unitelefilm, 1980, Italian
EFFETTI PERSONALI (TF)   RAI Bologna, 1983, Italian
SEGRETI SEGRETI   AMA Film/Istituto Luce, 1985, Italian
TUTTOBENIGNI (PF)   Best International Film, 1986, Italian
IL PERCHE' E IL PERCOME (TD)   Raitre, 1987, Italian
STRANA LA VITA   AMA Film/Dania Film/Medusa/Reteitalia,
   1987, Italian
I CAMMELLI   Colorado Film/Dania Film/Medusa Distribuzione/
   National Cinematografica/Reteitalia, 1988, Italian
AMORI IN CORSO   Mito Film/Raidue, 1989, Italian
LA DOMENICA SPECIALMENTE   co-director, Basic
   Cinematografica, 1991, Italian
TROPPO SOLE   La Banda Magnetica/Navert Film/Reteitalia,
   1994, Italian

JEAN-LOUIS BERTUCELLI

b. June 1942 - Paris, France
Address: 9, rue Bernard, 75014 Paris, France, tel.: 1/45-42-11-92
Contact: French Film Office, 745 Fifth Avenue, New York, NY 10151,
   212/832-8860

RAMPARTS OF CLAY   Cinema 5, 1970, French
PAULINA 1880   1972, French
ON S'EST TROMPE D'HISTOIRE AMOUR   1974, French
DOCTEUR FRANCOISE GAILLAND   1976, French
L'IMPRECATEUR   1977, French
LA CHANCE D'AVOIR UN FILS COMME CA (TF)   1979, French
INTERDIT AUX MOINS DE 13 ANS   1982, French
STRESS   1985, French
AUJOURD'HUI PEUT-ETRE   Agepro Cinema/M.F. Productions,
   1991, French
LECLANDESTIN (TF)   Alya Productions, 1994, French

MICHAEL BERZ

SNOW WHITE   Cannon, 1987, U.S.-Israeli

JAMES BESHEARS

HOMEWORK   Jensen-Farley Pictures, 1982

DAN BESSIE

HARD TRAVELING   New World, 1986
TURNABOUT: THE STORY OF THE YALE PUPPETEERS (FD)
   Shire Films, 1993

LUC BESSON

b. March 18, 1959 - Paris, France
Business: Les Films du Dolphin, 70 rue Ponthieu, 75008 Paris, France
Agent: CAA - Beverly Hills, 310/288-4545

LE DERNIER COMBAT   Gaumont/Les Films du Loup/Constantin
   Alexandrof Productions, 1983, French
SUBWAY   Island Pictures, 1985, French
KAMIKAZE   co-director with Didier Grousset, Gaumont,
   1987, French
THE BIG BLUE   Columbia/WEG, 1988, French
LA FEMME NIKITA NIKITA   The Samuel Goldwyn Company,
   1990, French
ATLANTIS   Gaumont/Cecchi Gori Group Tiger Cinematografica,
   1991, French-Italian
THE PROFESSIONAL LEON   Columbia, 1994, U.S.-French

GILL BETTMAN*

Home: 10521 Selkirk Lane, Los Angeles, CA 90077, 310/475-3906
Agent: Stephanie Rogers & Associates - Los Angeles, 213/851-5155
Business Manager: Alan L. Grodin, Cooper, Epstein & Hurewitz,
   345 N. Maple Drive - Suite 200, Beverly Hills, CA 90210,
   310/205-8305

CRYSTAL HEART   Izaro Films/Eagle Films Corporation, 1985
NEVER TOO YOUNG TO DIE   Paul Releasing, 1986

JONATHAN BETUEL*

Agent: William Morris Agency - Beverly Hills, 310/859-4000

MY SCIENCE PROJECT   Buena Vista, 1985
T. REX   New Line Cinema, 1995

NIGOL BEZJIAN

CHICKPEAS   Independent, 1994

RADHA BHARADWAJ*

Contact: Bill Skryzniarz, Rosenfeld, Meyer and Susman,
   9601 Wilshire Blvd., Beverly Hills, CA 90212, 310/858-7700

CLOSET LAND   Universal, 1991

**F
I
L
M**

**D
I
R
E
C
T
O
R
S**

EDWARD BIANCHI*
b. April 24, 1942
Business: Stella Pictures, 36 Gramercy Park East, New York,
   NY 10010, 212/228-3668
Agent: Scott Yoselow, The Gersh Agency - New York City,
   212/997-1818

THE FAN   Paramount, 1981
OFF AND RUNNING   Rank Organisation/Aaron Russo
   Entertainment, 1992

ROBERT BIERMAN
Address: 8 Berners Mew, London W1P 3DG, England,
   tel.: 71/636-4226
Agent: ICM - Beverly Hills, 310/550-4000 or:
   The Casarotto Company - London, tel.: 71/287-4450

APOLOGY (CTF)   Roger Gimbel Productions/Peregrine
   Entertainment/ASAP Productions/HBO, 1986, U.S.-Canadian
VAMPIRE'S KISS   Hemdale, 1988
A CURIOUS SUICIDE (TF)   HTV/Crossbow, British
FRANKENSTEIN'S BABY (TF)   BBC, British
CLARISSA (TF)   BBC, 1991, British
BETWEEN THE LINES (TF)   BBC, 1993
MURDER IN MIND (TF)   BBC, 1994

JEAN-CLAUDE BIETTE
Contact: French Film Office, 745 Fifth Avenue, New York,
   NY 10151, 212/832-8860

LE THEATRE DES MATIERES   1978, French
LOIN DE MANHATTAN   1981, French
LES CHAMPIGNON DES CARPATHES   Films du Losange,
   1990, French
CHAISSE GARDE   Les Films du Dauphin/CACEA/ROC,
   1993, French

KATHRYN BIGELOW*
b. 1952
Business: First Light Productions, 10201 W. Pico Blvd. -
   Bungalow 218, Los Angeles, CA 90035, 310/203-2112
Agent: CAA - Beverly Hills, 310/288-4545

THE LOVELESS   co-director with Monty Montgomery,
   Atlantic Releasing Corporation, 1981
NEAR DARK   DEG, 1987
BLUE STEEL   MGM/UA, 1990
POINT BREAK   20th Century Fox, 1991
WILD PALMS (MS)   co-director with Peter Hewitt, Keith Gordon &
   Phil Joanou, Ixtlan Corporation/Greengrass Productions, 1993
STRANGE DAYS   20th Century Fox, 1995

CHARLES BIGGS
RIDERS IN THE STORM   Coldstone Pictures International, 1994
SLAUGHTER'S GOLD   Sparrow Movie Company, 1995

ROBERT BILHEIMER
ENDGAME   San Quentin Drama Workshop, 1994

TONY BILL*
b. August 23, 1940 - San Diego, California
Business: Barnstorm Films, 73 Market Street, Venice, CA 90291,
   310/396-5937
Agent: ICM - Los Angeles, 213/550-4000

MY BODYGUARD   20th Century-Fox, 1980
SIX WEEKS   Universal, 1982
LOVE THY NEIGHBOR (TF)   Patricia Nardo Productions/
   20th Century Fox TV, 1984
FIVE CORNERS   Cineplex Odeon, 1987
CRAZY PEOPLE   Paramount, 1990
CAPTIVE HEART   MGM, 1993
A HOME OF OUR OWN   Gramercy Pictures, 1993
NEXT DOOR (CTF)   Nederlander Television & Film Productions/
   Tudor Entertainment/TriStar TV, 1994
ONE CHRISTMAS (TF)   Davis Entertainment, 1994

KEVIN BILLINGTON
b. 1933 - England
Agent: Judy Daish Associates - London, tel.: 171/262-1101

INTERLUDE   Columbia, 1968, British
THE RISE AND RISE OF MICHAEL RIMMER   Warner Bros.,
   1970, British
THE LIGHT AT THE EDGE OF THE WORLD   National General,
   1971, U.S.-Spanish
VOICES   Hemdale, 1973, British
AND NO ONE COULD SAVE HER (TF)   Associated London Films,
   1973, British
ECHOES OF THE SIXTIES (TD)   ALA Productions, 1979
THE GOOD SOLDIER (TF)   Granada TV, 1981, British
THE OUTSIDE EDGE (TF)   London Weekend TV, 1982, British
REFLECTIONS (TF)   Court House Films/Film Four International,
   1984, British
FACE OF THE EARTH (TF)   BBC Wales, 1988, Welsh
HEARTLAND (TF)   BBC, 1989, British
A TIME TO DANCE (TF)   BBC Scotland, 1991, Scottish

BRUCE BILSON*
b. May 19, 1928 - Brooklyn, New York
Business: Downwind Enterprises, Inc., 12505 Sarah Street,
   Studio City, CA 91604, 818/985-5121
Agent: Ronald Leif, Contemporary Artists - Santa Monica,
   310/395-1800

THE GIRL WHO CAME GIFT-WRAPPED (TF)   Spelling-Goldberg
   Productions, 1974
DEAD MAN ON THE RUN (TF)   Sweeney-Finnegan
   Productions, 1975
THE NEW DAUGHTERS OF JOSHUA CABE (TF)
   Spelling-Goldberg Productions, 1976
BJ & THE BEAR (TF)   Universal TV, 1978
THE NORTH AVENUE IRREGULARS   Buena Vista, 1979
DALLAS COWBOYS CHEERLEADERS (TF)   Aubrey-Hammer
   Productions, 1979
PLEASURE COVE (TF)   Lou Shaw Productions/David Gerber
   Company/Columbia TV, 1979
THE GHOSTS OF BUXLEY HALL (TF)   Walt Disney
   Productions, 1980
CHATTANOOGA CHOO CHOO   April Fools, 1984
FINDER OF LOST LOVES (TF)   Aaron Spelling Productions, 1984
GIDGET'S SUMMER REUNION (TF)   Ackerman-Riskin Productions/
   Columbia TV, 1985
THE BRADYS (TF)   Brady Productions/Paramount TV, 1990

DANNY BILSON*
Home: 5009 Biloxi Avenue, North Hollywood, CA 91601,
   818/980-4876
Agent: CAA - Beverly Hills, 310/288-4545

ZONE TROOPERS   Empire Pictures, 1986
THE WRONG GUYS   New World, 1988
HUMAN TARGET (TF)   director of additional sequences, Pet Fly
   Productions/Warner Bros. TV, 1992
VIPER (TF)   Pet Fly Productions/Paramount Network TV, 1993

JOHN BINDER*
Agent: APA - Los Angeles, 310/273-0744

UFORIA   Universal, 1984

MIKE BINDER*
Agent: UTA - Beverly Hills, 310/273-6700
Business: Mike Binder Productions, Columbia Pictures -
   Los Angeles, 310/280-6752

CROSSING THE BRIDGE   Buena Vista, 1992
INDIAN SUMMER   Buena Vista, 1993
BLANKMAN   Columbia, 1994

STEVE BINDER*

Office: 310/207-4427
Attorney: Jared Levine, Gruber, Wender & Levine, 315 South Beverly Drive - Suite 400, Beverly Hills, CA 90212, 310/553-6900

MELISSA   Shetler-Le Mos Productions, 1995

WILLIAM BINDLEY

Agent: William Morris Agency - Beverly Hills, 310/859-4000

THE HOMEROOM NEWS   Creative Edge Films, 1989
JUDICIAL CONSENT (CTF)   Rysher Entertainment/Prelude Pictures, 1995, originally filmed for theatrical distribution

MACK BING*

Home: 26, Quinta do Belomonte, Alafarrobieras, 8500 Portimao, Portugal, tel.: 351-82-25450
Business Manager: Howard Brown, 1801 Avenue of the Stars - Suite 703, Los Angeles, CA 90067, 213/556-0733

ALL THE LOVING COUPLES   U-M, 1969
THE CLASS OF '74   co-director with Arthur Marks, Crest, 1972
GABRIELLA   1974

STEVE BING

Agent: UTA - Beverly Hills, 310/273-6700

EVERY BREATH   Trimark Pictures, 1993

PATRICIA BIRCH*

Attorney: Marsha Brooks, Colton/Hartwick/Yamin/Sheresky, 79 Madison Avenue, New York, NY 10016, 212/532-5100

GREASE 2   Paramount, 1982

ANTONIA BIRD

Address: 17 Virginia Road, London E2 7NF, England
Agent: ICM - London, tel.: 171/636-6565

THIN AIR (MS)   BBC, 1989, British
SOUTH OF THE BORDER (MS)   BBC, 1990, British
THE MEN'S ROOM (MS)   BBC, 1991, British
A MASCULINE ENDING (TF)   BBC, 1992, British
FULL STRETCH (MS)   Meridian/ITV, 1993, British
PRIEST (TF)   BBC, 1994, British
MAD LOVE   Buena Vista, 1995

STEWART BIRD

Contact: Writers Guild of America, East - New York City, 212/767-7800

HOME FREE ALL   Almi Classics, 1984

ANDREW BIRKIN

Agent: ICM - London, tel.: 171/636-6565

BURNING SECRET   Vestron, 1988, U.S.-British-West German
SALT ON OUR SKIN   *DESIRE*   Neue Constantin/Torii Productions/Telescene Film Group/RTL/Canal Plus, 1993, German-French-Canadian
THE CEMENT GARDEN   October Films, 1993, German-British-French

ALAN BIRKINSHAW

Contact: British Film Commission, 70 Baker Street, London W1M 1DJ, England, tel.: 171/224-5000

GREED   1981, British
BUT I HAVE PROMISES TO KEEP   Doordarshan, 1987, Indian
SWEETER THAN WINE   1988, British
TEN LITTLE INDIANS   Cannon, 1989, British

THE HOUSE OF USHER   21st Century Distribution, 1990, British-South African
THE MASQUE OF THE RED DEATH   21st Century Distribution, 1990, British

SHEM BITTERMAN

PEEPHOLE   Solomonness Productions, 1992

LOREN BIVENS

Contact: Texas Film Commission, P.O. Box 12728, 201 East 5th Street - Suite B-6, Austin, TX 78711, 512/469-9111

TRESPASSES   co-director with Adam Roarke, Shapiro Entertainment, 1987

NOEL BLACK*

b. 1937 - Chicago, Illinois
Home: 218 East 12th Street, New York, NY 10003, 212/529-2766
Agent: Tom Chasin, The Chasin Agency - Los Angeles, 310/278-7505

TRILOGY: THE AMERICAN BOY (TF)   ABC Stage 67, 1968
PRETTY POISON   20th Century-Fox, 1968
COVER ME BABE   20th Century-Fox, 1970
JENNIFER ON MY MIND   United Artists, 1971
MULLIGAN'S STEW (TF)   Paramount TV, 1977
MIRRORS   First American, 1978
A MAN, A WOMAN AND A BANK   Avco Embassy, 1979, Canadian
THE GOLDEN HONEYMOON (TF)   Learning in Focus, 1980
THE OTHER VICTIM (TF)   Shpetner Company, 1981
PRIME SUSPECT (TV)   Tisch-Avnet Television, 1982
THE ELECTRIC GRANDMOTHER (TF)   Highgate Pictures, 1982
HAPPY ENDINGS (TF)   Motown Productions, 1983
PRIVATE SCHOOL   Universal, 1983
QUARTERBACK PRINCESS (TF)   CBS Entertainment, 1983
DEADLY INTENTIONS (TF)   Green-Epstein Productions, 1985
PROMISES TO KEEP (TF)   Sandra Harmon Productions/ Green-Epstein Productions/Telepictures, 1985
A TIME TO TRIUMPH (TF)   Billos-Kauffman Productions/Phoenix Entertainment Group, 1986
MY TWO LOVES (TF)   Alvin Cooperman Productions/Taft Entertainment TV, 1986
CONSPIRACY OF LOVE (TF)   New World TV, 1987
DOCTORS WILDE (TF)   Columbia TV, 1987
THE TOWN BULLY (TF)   Dick Clark Productions, 1988
THE EYES OF THE PANTHER (CTF)   Think Entertainment, 1989
THE HOLLOW BOY (TF)   Learning in Focus, 1991

JON BLAIR

Contact: British Film Commission, 70 Baker Street, London W1M 1DJ, England, tel.: 171/224-5000

SCHINDLER (TD)   Thames TV, 1983, British

LES BLAIR

b. October 23, 1941 - Manchester, England
Agent: Elaine Steel - London, tel.: 171/346-6950

BLOOMING YOUTH (TF)   BBC, 1971, British
LAW AND ORDER (TF)   BBC, 1978, British
BEYOND THE PALE (TF)   BBC, 1980, British
THE NATION'S HEALTH (TF)   Euston Films/Channel 4, 1983, British
NUMBER ONE   Mark Forstater Productions/Stageforum Productions, 1984, British
HONEST, DECENT AND TRUE (TF)   BBC, 1985, British
LONDON'S BURNING (TF)   London Weekend TV, 1986, British
LEAVE TO REMAIN   Spellbound Productions/Film Four International, 1988, British
FILIPINA DREAM GIRLS (TF)   BBC, 1991, British
BAD BEHAVIOUR   October Films, 1993, British

F I L M   D I R E C T O R S

LORNE BLAIR
Address: Pengosekan, Bali, Indonesia

RING OF FIRE (TD)   Blair Brothers Productions/
   WGBH-Boston, 1987

MICHAEL BLAKEMORE*
b. June 18, 1928 - Sydney, Australia
Agent: The Lantz Office - New York City, 212/586-0200 or:
   Bernard Hunter - London, tel.: 181/878-6308

A PERSONAL HISTORY OF THE AUSTRALIAN SURF (FD)
   Adams-Parker Films, 1982, Australian
PRIVATES ON PARADE   Orion Classics, 1983, British
TALES FROM THE HOLLYWOOD HILLS: THE OLD RELIABLE (TF)
   WNET-NY/Zenith Productions, 1988
COUNTRY LIFE   Miramax Films, 1994, Australian

RONEE BLAKLEY
b. 1946 - Caldwell, Idaho
Contact: Screen Actors Guild - Los Angeles, 213/954-1600

I PLAYED IT FOR YOU (FD)   Ronee Blakley Productions, 1985

MICHEL BLANC
Agent: Voyez Mon Agent - Paris, tel.: 1/47-23-55-80
Contact: French Film Office, 745 Fifth Avenue, New York,
   NY 10151, 212/832-8860

GROSSE FATIGUE   Gaumont/TF1 Films, 1994, French

KEN BLANCATO*
Address: 178 S. Victory Blvd. - Suite 208, Burbank, CA 91502,
   818/841-0596
Agent: ICM - Beverly Hills, 310/550-4000
Business Manager: Peter Grossman, Weissman, Wolff,
   9665 Wilshire Blvd. - Suite 900, Beverly Hills, CA 90212,
   310/858-7888

STEWARDESS SCHOOL   Columbia, 1986

HARROD BLANK
Business: Flower Films, 10341 San Pablo Avenue, El Cerrito,
   CA 94530, 415/525-0942

WILD WHEELS (FD)   Tara Releasing, 1992

JONATHAN BLANK
SEX, DRUGS AND DEMOCRACY (FD)
   Red Hot Productions, 1994

LES BLANK
b. November 27, 1935 - Tampa, Florida
Business: Flower Films, 10341 San Pablo Avenue, El Cerrito,
   CA 94530, 415/525-0942

DRY WOOD AND HOT PEPPER (FD)   Flower Films, 1973
A POEM IS A NAKED PERSON (FD)   Skyhill Films/
   Flower Films, 1974
CHULAS FRONTERAS (FD)   Brazos Films, 1976
ALWAYS FOR PLEASURE (FD)   Flower Films, 1978
GARLIC IS AS GOOD AS 10 MOTHERS (FD)   Flower Films, 1980
BURDEN OF DREAMS (FD)   Flower Films, 1982
IN HEAVEN THERE IS NO BEER? (FD)   Flower Films, 1984
ZIVELI: MEDICINE FOR THE HEART (FD)   Flower Films, 1987
J'AI ETE AU BAL (I WENT TO THE DANCE)   co-director with
   Chris Strachwitz, Brazos Films/Flower Films, 1989
PUAMANA (FD)   Flower Films, 1991
INNOCENTS ABROAD   *THE GRAND TOUR* (FD)
   Flower Films/BBC/Centre de l'Audio-Visuel a Bruxelles/
   La Sept/WNET-13/WDR/Miel Van Hoogenbemt, 1992,
   U.S.-British-Belgian-French-German
THE MAESTRO: KING OF THE COWBOY ARTISTS (FD)
   Flower Films, 1995

WILLIAM PETER BLATTY*
b. 1928 - New York, New York
Agent: The Artists Agency - Los Angeles, 310/277-7779

THE NINTH CONFIGURATION   Warner Bros., 1979,
   re-released under title TWINKLE, TWINKLE 'KILLER' KANE
   by United Film Distribution in 1980
THE EXORCIST III   20th Century Fox, 1990

COREY BLECHMAN*
Agent: ICM - Beverly Hills, 310/550-4000

THE THREE WISHES OF BILLY GRIER (TF)
   I & C Productions, 1984

JEFF BLECKNER*
b. August 12, 1943 - Brooklyn, New York
Home: 4701 Natoma Avenue, Woodland Hills, CA 91364
Agent: CAA - Beverly Hills, 310/288-4545

RYAN'S FOUR (TF)   Fair Dinkum Inc./Groverton Productions/
   Paramount TV, 1983
WHEN YOUR LOVER LEAVES (TF)   Major H Productions, 1983
CONCEALED ENEMIES (TF) ☆☆   WGBH-Boston/Goldcrest Films
   and Television/Comworld Productions, 1984, U.S.-British
DO YOU REMEMBER LOVE (TF) ☆   Dave Bell Productions, 1985
BROTHERLY LOVE (TF)   CBS Entertainment, 1985
FRESNO (MS)   MTM Productions, 1986
WHITE WATER SUMMER   Columbia, 1987
TERRORIST ON TRIAL: THE UNITED STATES VS.
   SALIM AJAMI (TF)   George Englund Productions/Robert
   Papazian Productions, 1988
MY FATHER, MY SON (TF)   Fred Weintraub Productions/
   John J. McMahon Productions, 1988
FAVORITE SON (MS)   NBC Productions, 1988
LAST WISH (TF)   Grossbart-Barnett Productions, 1992
IN SICKNESS AND IN HEALTH (TF)   Konigsberg-Sanitsky
   Productions, 1992
THE ROUND TABLE (TF)   Spelling TV, 1992
IN THE BEST OF FAMILIES: MARRIAGE, PRIDE AND
   MADNESS (TF)   AMBROCO Media Group/Dan Wigutow
   Productions, 1994
A FATHER FOR CHARLIE (TF)   Jacobs-Gardner Productions/
   LoGo Entertainment/Finnegan-Pinchuk Productions, 1995
SERVING IN SILENCE: THE MARGARETHE CAMMERMEYER
   STORY (TF)   Barwood Films/Storyline Prods./Trillium Prods./
   TriStar TV, 1995

BERTRAND BLIER
b. March 14, 1939 - Paris, France
Agent: ICM France - Paris, tel.: 1/723-7860
Contact: French Film Office, 745 Fifth Avenue, New York, NY 10151,
   212/832-8860

HITLER? CONNAIS PAS!   Chaumiane, 1963, French
SI J'ETAIS UN ESPION (OU BREAKDOWN)   Pathe/Sirius/UGC/
   CFDC, 1967, French
GOING PLACES   *LES VALSEUSES*   Cinema 5, 1974, French
FEMMES FATALES   *CALMOS*   New Line Cinema, 1976, French
GET OUT YOUR HANDKERCHIEFS   New Line Cinema,
   1978, French
BUFFET FROID   Parafrance, 1979, French
BEAU PERE   New Line Cinema, 1981, French
MY BEST FRIEND'S GIRL   European International, 1983, French
SEPARATE ROOMS   *NOTRE HISTOIRE*   Spectrafilm,
   1984, French
MENAGE   *TENUE DE SOIREE*   Cinecom, 1986, French
TOO BEAUTIFUL FOR YOU   Orion Classics, 1989, French
MERCI LA VIE   Cine Valse/Film Par Film/Orly Film/D.D. Production/
   SEDIF/Films A2, 1991, French
UN, DEUX, TROIS: SOLEIL   Gaumont, 1993, French
MON HOMME   Canal Plus, 1995, French

BRUCE BLOCK*
Contact: Directors Guild of America - Los Angeles, 213/851-3671

PRINCESS ACADEMY   Empire Pictures, 1987, Yugoslavian-French

DOUG BLOCK

Business: Blockbusters, 150 West 26th Street - Room 302, New York, NY 10001, 212/727-8319

THE HECK WITH HOLLYWOOD! (FD)   Original Cinema, 1991

JEFFREY BLOOM*

Business Manager: Steven Katz, Silverberg, Katz, Thompson & Braun, 11766 Wilshire Blvd. - Suite 700, Los Angeles, CA 90025, 310/445-5888

DOGPOUND SHUFFLE   Paramount, 1974, Canadian
THE STICK UP   Trident-Barber, 1978, British
BLOOD BEACH   Jerry Gross Organization, 1981
JEALOUSY (TF)   Charles Fries Productions/Alan Sacks Productions, 1983
STARCROSSED (TF)   Fries Entertainment, 1985
THE RIGHT OF THE PEOPLE (TF)   Big Name Films/Fries Entertainment, 1986
FLOWERS IN THE ATTIC   New World, 1987

GEORGE BLOOMFIELD

b. 1930 - Montreal, Quebec, Canada
Home: 50 Admiral Road, Toronto, Ontario M5R 2LF, Canada, 416/967-0826

JENNY   Cinerama Releasing Corporation, 1970
TO KILL A CLOWN   20th Century-Fox, 1972
CHILD UNDER A LEAF   Cinema National, 1974, Canadian
LOVE ON THE NOSE (TF)   CBC, 1974, Canadian
NELLIE McCLUNG (TF)   CBC, 1978, Canadian
RIEL   CBC/Green River Productions, 1979, Canadian
NOTHING PERSONAL   American International, 1980, Canadian
DOUBLE NEGATIVE   Best Film and Video, 1981, Canadian
THE CAMPBELLS (MS)   John Delmage/CTV/Settler Film Productions/Scottish TV/Fremantle International/Telefilm Canada, 1986, Canadian-Scottish
AFRICAN JOURNEY (TF)   The Film Works, 1990, Canadian

REX BLOOMSTEIN

Business: Nucleus Productions, 25 Willow Road, London NW3 1TL

STRANGEWAYS (TD)   BBC, 1981, British
AUSCHWITZ AND THE ALLIES (TD)   BBC, 1983, British
MARTIN LUTHER KING - THE LEGACY (TD)   Thames TV, 1987, British
JEWISH HUMOUR - AMERICAN STYLE (TD)   Zenith Productions, 1989, British
THE LONGEST HATRED (TD)   Nucleus Productions/Thames TV/WGBH-Boston, 1991, British-U.S.
PRISONERS OF CONSCIENCE (TD)   BBC, 1991, British
THE THAMES TORSO MURDERS (TD)   Channel 4, 1992, British
HUMAN RIGHTS - HUMAN WRONGS (TD)   BBC, 1992, British
THE SOUTH BANK SHOW: CLIFF RICHARD (TD)   ITV, 1993, British
NIGHTMARE'S END: THE LIBERATION OF THE CAMPS (CTD)   Nucleus ZProductions/Channel 4/The Discovery Channel, 1995, British-U.S.

CHRIS BLUM

BIG TIME (FCD)   Island Pictures, 1988

ANDY BLUMENTHAL

BLOODFIST II   Concorde, 1991

DON BLUTH

b. September 13, 1938 - El Paso, Texas
Business: Fox Animation Studios, Inc., 2747 E. Camelback Road, Phoenix, AZ 85016

THE SECRET OF NIMH (AF)   MGM/UA, 1982
AN AMERICAN TAIL (AF)   Universal, 1986
THE LAND BEFORE TIME (AF)   Universal, 1988
ALL DOGS GO TO HEAVEN (AF)   MGM/UA, 1989
ROCK-A-DOODLE (AF)   The Samuel Goldwyn Company, 1992

HANS CHRISTIAN ANDERSEN'S THUMBELINA   *THUMBELINA* (AF)   co-director with Gary Goldman, Warner Bros., 1994
A TROLL IN CENTRAL PARK (AF)   co-director with Gary Goldman, Warner Bros., 1994
THE PEBBLE AND THE PENGUIN (AF)   co-director with Gary Goldman, MGM-UA, 1995

DAVID BLYTH

b. 1956 - Auckland, New Zealand
Agent: Susan Grant, The Artists Group - Los Angeles, 310/552-1100

ANGELMINE   1978, New Zealand
A WOMAN OF GOOD CHARACTER (TF)   Rosenzweig Entertainment, 1982, New Zealand
DEATH WARMED UP   Tucker Production Company/New Zealand Film Commission, 1984, New Zealand
RED BLOODED AMERICAN GIRL   SC Entertainment, 1990, Canadian
MOONRISE   *MY GRANDFATHER'S A VAMPIRE*   Republic Pictures, 1991, New Zealand
KAHU AND MAIA (TF)   He Taonga Films, 1993, New Zealand

JEFF BLYTH*

Home: 802 Foxkirk, Glendale, CA 91206, 818/244-9202

CHEETAH   Buena Vista, 1989

HART BOCHNER*

b. December 3, 1956 - Toronto, Ontario, Canada
Agent: UTA - Beverly Hills, 310/273-6700

PCU   20th Century Fox, 1994

SERGEI BODROV

Contact: Confederation of Film-Makers Unions, Vasilyevskaya Street 13, 123 825 Moscow, Russia, tel.: 095/250-4114

THE NON-PROFESSIONALS   1986, Soviet
FREEDOM IS PARADISE   1989, Soviet
THE RUSSIANS   1992, Russian
I WANTED TO SEE ANGELS   Screen Angel Productions/12-A Studio, 1992, Russian
ROI BLANC DAME ROUGE   Lumiere/Alhena Films/Mosfilm/Metropolis Filmproduktion/Studio Courier/Canal Plus/Eurimages/Cofimage/l'Est de la Confederation Suisse, 1993, French-Swiss-Russian-German

BUDD BOETTICHER*
(Oscar Boetticher, Jr.)
b. July 29, 1916 - Chicago, Illinois
Address: P.O. Box 1137, Ramona, CA 92065

ONE MYSTERIOUS NIGHT   Columbia, 1944
THE MISSING JUROR   Columbia, 1944
A GUY, A GAL AND A PAL   Columbia, 1945
ESCAPE IN THE FOG   Columbia, 1945
YOUTH ON TRIAL   Columbia, 1945
THE FLEET THAT CAME TO STAY   Paramount, 1946
ASSIGNED TO DANGER   Eagle-Lion, 1948
BEHIND LOCKED DOORS   Eagle-Lion, 1948
THE WOLF HUNTERS   Monogram, 1949
BLACK MIDNIGHT   Monogram, 1949
KILLER SHARK   Monogram, 1950
THE BULLFIGHTER AND THE LADY   Republic, 1951
THE SWORD OF D'ARTAGNAN   Universal, 1951
THE CIMARRON KID   Universal, 1951
RED BALL EXPRESS   Universal, 1952
BRONCO BUSTER   Universal, 1952
HORIZONS WEST   Universal, 1952
CITY BENEATH THE SEA   Universal, 1953
SEMINOLE   Universal, 1953
THE MAN FROM THE ALAMO   Universal, 1953
EAST OF SUMATRA   Universal, 1953
WINGS OF THE HAWK   Universal, 1953
THE MAGNIFICENT MATADOR   20th Century-Fox, 1955
THE KILLER IS LOOSE   United Artists, 1956

SEVEN MEN FROM NOW   Warner Bros., 1956
THE TALL T   Columbia, 1957
DECISION AT SUNDOWN   Columbia, 1958
BUCHANAN RIDES ALONE   Columbia, 1958
RIDE LONESOME   Columbia, 1959
WESTBOUND   Warner Bros., 1959
COMANCHE STATION   Columbia, 1960
THE RISE AND FALL OF LEGS DIAMOND   Warner Bros., 1960
A TIME FOR DYING   Etoile, 1971
ARRUZA (FD)   Avco Embassy, 1972
MY KINGDOM FOR... (FD)   Lusitano Productions, 1985

PAUL BOGART*
b. November 21, 1919 - New York, New York
Business: Tiber Productions, Inc., 760 N. La Cienega Blvd.,
   Los Angeles, CA 90069, 213/652-0222
Agent: William Morris Agency - Beverly Hills, 310/859-4000

A MEMORY OF TWO MONDAYS (TF)   WNET, 1969
MARLOWE   MGM, 1969
HALLS OF ANGER   United Artists, 1970
SKIN GAME   Warner Bros., 1971
IN SEARCH OF AMERICA (TF)   Four Star Productions, 1971
CANCEL MY RESERVATION   Warner Bros., 1972
CLASS OF '44   Warner Bros., 1973
TELL ME WHERE IT HURTS (TF)   Tomorrow Entertainment, 1974
MR. RICCO   MGM, 1975
WINNER TAKE ALL (TF)   The Jozak Company, 1975
THE THREE SISTERS   NTA, 1977
FUN AND GAMES (TF)   released under pseudonym of Alan Smithee,
   Kanin-Gallo Productions/Warner Bros. TV, 1980
OH, GOD! YOU DEVIL   Warner Bros., 1984
THE CANTERVILLE GHOST (TF)   Pound Ridge Productions/
   Inter-Hemisphere Productions/HTV/Columbia TV,
   1986, U.S.-British
NUTCRACKER: MONEY, MADNESS AND MURDER (MS)
   Green Arrow Productions/Warner Bros. TV, 1987
TALES FROM THE HOLLYWOOD HILLS: NATICA JACKSON (TF)
   WNET/Zenith Productions/KCET, 1987
TORCH SONG TRILOGY   New Line Cinema, 1988
NEIL SIMON'S BROADWAY BOUND   *BROADWAY BOUND* (TF) ☆
   ABC Productions, 1992
THE GIFT OF LOVE (TF)   Marian Rees Associates/Family
   Productions, 1994
THE HEIDI CHRONICLES (CTF)   Michael Brandman Productions/
   Turner Pictures, 1995

YUREK BOGAYEVICZ
b. Poland
Agent: The Gersh Agency - Beverly Hills, 310/274-6611

ANNA   Vestron, 1987
THREE OF HEARTS   New Line Cinema, 1993

PETER BOGDANOVICH*
b. July 30, 1939 - Kingston, New York
Agent: CAA - Beverly Hills, 310/288-4545

TARGETS   Paramount, 1968
DIRECTED BY JOHN FORD (FD)   American Film Institute, 1971
THE LAST PICTURE SHOW ★   Columbia, 1971
WHAT'S UP, DOC?   Warner Bros., 1972
PAPER MOON   Paramount, 1973
DAISY MILLER   Paramount, 1974
AT LONG LAST LOVE   20th Century-Fox, 1975
NICKELODEON   Columbia, 1976
SAINT JACK   New World, 1979
THEY ALL LAUGHED   United Artists Classics, 1982
MASK   Universal, 1985
ILLEGALLY YOURS   MGM/UA, 1988
TEXASVILLE   Columbia, 1990
NOISES OFF   Buena Vista, 1992
THE THING CALLED LOVE   Paramount, 1993

WILLY BOGNER
FIRE AND ICE   Concorde, 1987

TED A. BOHUS
VAMPIRE VIXENS FROM VENUS   Filmline Communications, 1994

YVES BOISSET
b. March 14, 1939 - Paris, France
Agent: ICM France - Paris, tel.: 1/723-7860
Contact: French Film Office, 745 Fifth Avenue, New York,
   NY 10151, 212/832-8860

COPLAN SAUVE SA PEAU   1968, French
THE COP   Audubon, 1970, French
LE SAUT DE L'ANGE   1971, French
THE FRENCH CONSPIRACY   *L'ATTENTAT*   1972, French
R.A.S.   1973, French
UNE FOLLE A TUER   1975, French
DUPONT LA JOIE   1975, French
LE JUGE FAYARD DIT LE SHERIFF   1977, French
UN TAXI MAUVE   1977, French
LA CLE SUR LA PORTE   1978, French
LA FEMME FLIC   1980, French
ALLOMS Z'ENFANATS   1981, French
ESPION LEVE-TOI   1982, French
LE PRIX DU DANGER   1983, French
CANICULE   1986, French
BLEU COMME L'ENFER   1986, French
RADIO CORBEAU   1989, French
LA TRAVESTIE   1989, French
DOUBLE IDENTITY   1991, French
LA TRIBU   1991, French

JEROME BOIVIN
b. 1954
Agent: Voyez Mon Agent - Paris, tel.: 1/47-23-78-60
Contact: French Film Office, 745 Fifth Avenue, New York,
   NY 10151, 212/832-8860

CAFE PRONGEOIR   1982, French
BAXTER   Backstreet Films, 1989, French
CONFESSIONS D'UN BARJO   PCC Productions/Aliceleo/FR3/
   Centre Europeen Cinematographique Rhone-Alpes/Sofinergie 2/
   Investimage 3/CNC/Canal Plus, 1993, French

CLIFFORD BOLE*
Agent: Shapiro-Lichtman Talent Agency - Los Angeles, 310/859-8877

T.J. HOOKER (TF)   Spelling-Goldberg Productions, 1982
PARADISE (TF)   co-director with Michael Lange, CBS, 1989

JOSEPH BOLOGNA*
b. December 30, 1936 - Brooklyn, New York
Business: Taylor/Bologna Productions, Inc., 613 N. Arden Drive,
   Beverly Hills, CA 90210, 310/274-8965
Agent: Metropolitan Talent Agency - Los Angeles, 213/857-4500
Business Manager: Larry Kantor, Zipperstein and Kantor, 16830
   Ventura Blvd. - Suite 326, Encino, CA 91436, 818/986-4640

IT HAD TO BE YOU   co-director with Renee Taylor,
   Limelite Studios, 1989
OH NO, NOT HER!   co-director with Renee Taylor,
   Cinema Seven Productions, 1995

MAURO BOLOGNINI
b. June 28, 1922 - Pistoia, Italy
Home: Piazza di Spagna 6, Rome, Italy, tel.: 06/679-8369

CI TROVIAMO IN GALLERIA   Athena Cinematografica,
   1953, Italian
I CAVALIERI DELLA REGINA   Thetis Film, 1954, Italian
LA VENA D'ORO   Athena Cinematografica, 1955, Italian
GLI INNAMORATI   Jacovoni, 1955, Italian
GUARDIA, GUARDIA SCELTA, BRIGADIERE E MARESCALLO
   Imperial Film, 1956, Italian
MARISA LA CIVETTA   Ponti/Balcazar, 1957, Italian-Spanish

GIOVANI MARITI   Nepi Film, 1957, Italian
ARRANGIATEVI   Cineriz, 1959, Italian
LA NOTTE BRAVA   *ON ANY STREET/BAD GIRLS DON'T CRY*
Ajace Film/Franco London Film, 1959, Italian-French
IL BELL'ANTONIO   Cino Del Duca/Arco Film/Lyre
Cinematographique, 1960, Italian-French
FROM A ROMAN BALCONY   *LA GIORNATA BALORDA/*
LOVE IS A DAY'S WORK/PICKUP IN ROME   Continental,
1960, Italian-French
LA VIACCIA   Embassy, 1960, Italian
SENILITA'   Zebra Film/Aera Film, 1961, Italian-French
AGOSTINO   Baltea Film, 1962, Italian
LA CORRUZIONE   Arco Film/SOPAC/Burgundia Films,
1963, Italian-French
LA DONNA E' UNA COSA MERAVIGLIOSA   Zebra Film/Aera Film,
1964, Italian-French
LA MIA SIGNORA   co-director with Tinto Brass & Luigi Comencini,
De Laurentiis, 1964, Italian
BAMBOLE!   *LE BAMBOLE*   co-director with Dino Risi,
Luigi Comencini & Franco Rossi, Royal Films International,
1964, Italian-French
I TRE VOLTI   co-director with Michelangelo Antonioni &
Franco Indovina, De Laurentiis, 1964, Italian
MADEMOISELLE DE MAUPIN   Jolly Film/Consortium Pathe/
Tecisa, 1965, Italian-French-Spanish
THE QUEENS   co-director with Luciano Salce, Mario Monicelli &
Antonio Pietrangeli, Royal Films International,
1966, Italian-French
THE WITCHES   co-director with Luchino Visconti,
Pier Paolo Pasolini, Franco Rossi & Vittorio De Sica,
Lopert, 1967, Italian-French
ARABELLA   Cram Film, 1967, Italian
THE OLDEST PROFESSION   *LE PLUX VIEUX METIER*
DU MONDE   co-director with Franco Indovina,
hilippe De Broca, Claude Autant-Lara, Jean-Luc Godard &
Michael Pfleghar, Goldstone, 1968,
French-Italian-West German
·THAT SPLENDID NOVEMBER   *UN BELLISSIMO NOVEMBRE*
United Artists, 1968, Italian
CAPRICCIO ALL'ITALIANA   co-director with Pier Paolo Pasolini,
Mario Monicelli & Steno, De Laurentiis, 1968, Italian
L'ASSOLUTO NATURALE   Tirrenia Studios, 1969, Italian
METELLO   Documento Film, 1969, Italian
BUBU'   BRC, 1970, Italian
IMP ZIONE DI OMICIDIO PER UNO STUDENTE
Documento Film, 1971, Italian
LIBERA AMORE MIO   Roberto Loyolo Cinematografica,
1973, Italian
FATTI DI GENTE PER BENE   Filmarpa/Lira Film, 1974, Italian
DOWN THE ANCIENT STAIRS   20th Century-Fox, 1976,
Italian-French
L'EREDITA' FERRAMONTI   Flag Production, 1976, Italian
GRAN BOLLITO   Triangolo Film, 1977, Italian
DOVE VAI IN VACANZA?   co-director with Luciano Salce &
Alberto Sordi, Rizzoli, 1978, Italian
LA VERA STORIA DELLA SIGNORA DELLE CAMELIE
Opera Film Produzione/Les Films du L'osange,
1980, Italian-French
LA CERTOSA DI PARMA (TF)   RAI, 1984, Italian
LA VENEXIANA   Lux International, 1985, Italian
MOSCA ADDIO   Istituto Luce/Italnoleggio, 1987, Italian
A TIME OF INDIFFERENCE (MS)   Consorzio Europeo/Titanus,
1988, Italian
HUSBANDS AND LOVERS   *LA VILLA DEL VENERDI '*
Metro Film/PAC, 1992, Italian

CRAIG BOLOTIN*
Agent: CAA - Beverly Hills, 310/288-4545

THAT NIGHT   Warner Bros., 1993

BEN BOLT*
(Benedict L. Bolt)
b. May 9, 1952 - England
Agent: The Marion Rosenberg Office - Los Angeles, 213/653-7383 or:
Peters Fraser & Dunlop - London, tel.: 171/344-1000

RAINY DAY WOMEN (TF)   BBC, 1986, British
THE BIG TOWN   Columbia, 1987
NEVER COME BACK (TF)   BBC, 1990, British
NATURAL LIES (TF)   Lawson Productions/London Films/BBC,
1992, British
SCARLET AND BLACK   Miramax Films, 1993, British,
originally filmed for television

GREGORY J. BONANN*
Address: P.O. Box 1404, Pacific Palisades, CA 90272, 310/456-3660

BAYWATCH: NIGHTMARE BAY (TF)   Baywatch Production
Company/All American Television/Tower 12/LBS
Communications, 1991

JAMES BOND III
Agent: Broder-Kurland-Webb-Uffner - Beverly Hillls, 310/281-3400

DEF BY TEMPTATION   Troma, 1990

TIMOTHY BOND*
b. 1942 - Ottawa, Ontario, Canada
Agent: Scott Yoselow, The Gersh Agency - New York City,
212/997-1818

DEADLY HARVEST (TF)   Ambassador Film Distributors,
1976, Canadian
TILL DEATH DO US PART (TF)   CTV, 1982, Canadian
ONE NIGHT ONLY (TF)   RSL Films, 1983, Canadian
OAKMOUNT HIGH (TF)   1985, Canadian
THE LOST WORLD (TF)   Harmony Gold/Silvio Berlusconi
Communications, 1992, Canadian-Italian
RETURN TO THE LOST WORLD (TF)   Harmony Gold/Silvio
Berlusconi Communications, 1992, Canadian-Italian

PETER BONERZ*
b. August 6, 1938 - Portsmouth, New Hampshire
Agent: CAA - Beverly Hills, 310/288-4545
Personal Manager: Shapiro-West, 141 El Camino Drive, Beverly Hills,
CA 90212, 310/278-8896

NOBODY'S PERFEKT   Columbia, 1981
SHARING RICHARD (TF)   Houston Motion Picture Entertainment/
CBS Entertainment, 1988
POLICE ACADEMY 6: CITY UNDER SIEGE   Warner Bros., 1989

LEE BONNER
ADVENTURE OF THE ACTION HUNTERS   Troma, 1987

RENE BONNIERE
Contact: Directors Guild of Canada, 225 Richmond Street, Toronto,
Ontario M5V 1W2, Canada, 416/351-8200

DREAM MAN   Republic Pictures, 1994, Canadian

J.R. BOOKWALTER
Contact: The Suburban Tempe Company, P.O. Box 6573, Akron,
OH 44312, 216/628-9638 or 216/628-1950

THE DEAD NEXT DOOR   Electro Video, 1989
ROBOT NINJA   Cinema Home Video, 1989
ZOMBIE COP   Cinema Home Video, 1991
KINGDOM OF THE VAMPIRE   Cinema Home Video, 1991
MAXIMUM IMPACT   Cinema Home Video, 1992
HUMANOIDS FROM ATLANTIS   Cinema Home Video, 1992

JOHN BOORMAN*

b. January 18, 1933 - Shepperton, Middlesex, England
Business: Merlin Films International, 16 Pembroke Street, Dublin 2,
   Ireland, tel.: 353/1-676-4460
Agent: ICM - London, tel.: 171/636-6565 or Beverly Hills,
   310/550-4000

HAVING A WILD WEEKEND *CATCH US IF YOU CAN*
   Warner Bros., 1965, British
POINT BLANK MGM, 1967
HELL IN THE PACIFIC Cinerama Releasing Corporation, 1968
LEO THE LAST United Artists, 1970, British
DELIVERANCE ★ Warner Bros., 1972
ZARDOZ 20th Century Fox, 1974, British
THE HERETIC: EXORCIST II Warner Bros., 1977
EXCALIBUR Orion/Warner Bros., 1981, British-Irish
THE EMERALD FOREST Embassy, 1985, British
HOPE AND GLORY ★ Columbia, 1987, British
WHERE THE HEART IS Buena Vista, 1990
BEYOND RANGOON Columbia, 1995

H. GORDON BOOS*

Address: 2478 Gower Street, Los Angeles, CA 90068, 213/466-0729

RED SURF Arrowhead Entertainment, 1990
THE GRAVITY OF STARS Arrowhead Entertainment, 1991

JOSÉ LUIS BORAU

b. August 8, 1929 - Zaragoza, Spain
Home: 3491 Shernoll Place, Sherman Oaks, CA 91403,
   818/788-3291
Business: El Iman S.A., Alberto Alcocer 42, Madrid 16, Spain,
   tel.: 250-5534

BRANDY, EL SHERIFF DE LOSATUMBA 1963, Spanish
CRIMEN DE DOBLE FILO 1964, Spanish
HAY QUE MATAR A B 1974, Spanish
FURTIVOS El Iman, 1975, Spanish
LA SABINA El Iman/Svensk Filminstitut, 1979, Spanish-Swedish
ON THE LINE Miramax, 1984, Spanish
TATA´MIA Profilmar/El Iman, 1986, Spanish

JOHN BORDEN

THE NATIVE AMERICANS (CTD) co-director with Phil Lucas &
   George Burdeau, Turner Broadcasting, 1994

LIZZIE BORDEN

(Linda Elizabeth Borden)
b. February 3, 1954 - Detroit, Michigan
Agent: Writers & Artists Agency - Los Angeles, 310/824-6300
Attorney: Weissmann, Wolff, Bergman, Coleman & Silverman,
   9665 Wilshire Blvd. - Suite 900, Beverly Hills, CA 90212,
   310/858-7888

BORN IN FLAMES First Run Features, 1982
WORKING GIRLS Miramax Films, 1986
LOVE CRIMES Millimeter Films, 1992
EROTIQUE co-director with Monika Treut & Clara Law,
   Group 1/Trigon/Tedpoly Films, 1994, U.S.-German-Hong Kong

ROBERT BORIS

b. October 12, 1945 - New York, New York
Agent: Innovative Artists - Los Angeles, 310/553-5200

OXFORD BLUES MGM/UA, 1984, British
STEELE JUSTICE Atlantic Releasing Corporation, 1987
BUY AND CELL Trans World Entertainment, 1989
FRANK AND JESSE (CTF) Trimark Pictures, 1995,
   originally filmed for theatrical release

ARTHUR BORMAN

Agent: UTA - Beverly Hills, 310/273-6700

...AND GOD SPOKE *THE MAKING OF ...AND GOD SPOKE*
   LIVE Entertainment, 1994

WALERIAN BOROWCZYK

b. October 21, 1923 - Kwilcz, Poland
Business: Allegro Productions, 70, rue de Ponthieu, 75008 Paris,
   France, tel.: 1/43-59-84-13
Contact: French Film Office, 745 Fifth Avenue, New York,
   NY 10151, 212/832-8860

MAZEPA 1968, French
GOTO, L'ILE D'AMOUR 1969, French
BLANCHE 1971, French
CONTES IMMORAUX 1974, French
LA BETE 1975, French
DZIELJE GRZECHU 1976, French
LA MARGE 1976, French
L'INTERNO DI UN CONVENTO 1978, French
COLLECTIONS PRIVEES co-director, 1979, French
LES HEROINES DU MAL 1979, French
LULU 1980, French
DOCTEUR JEKYLL ET LES FEMMES 1981, French
L'ART D'AIMER 1983, French
EMMANUELLE 5 1986, French
CEREMONIE D'AMOUR 1988, French

CLAY BORRIS

b. 1950 - New Brunswick, Canada
Home: 14 Wembley Drive, Toronto, Ontario M4L 3E1, Canada,
   416/465-8388
Agent: Ralph Zimmerman, Great North Artists Management, 350
   Dupont Street, Toronto, Ontario M5R 1V9, Canada, 416/925-2051

ROSE'S HOUSE 1977, Canadian
ALLIGATOR SHOES New Cinema, 1981, Canadian
QUIET COOL New Line Cinema, 1986
THE GUNFIGHTERS (TF) Grosso-Jacobson Productions/Alliance
   Entertainment/Tribune Entertainment, 1987, U.S.-Canadian
PROM NIGHT 4: DELIVER US FROM EVIL Norstar Entertainment,
   1991, Canadian
UNDER THE GUN UG Productions, 1994, Canadian
SOMEONE TO DIE FOR ED Productions, 1995, Canadian

DAVE BORTHWICK

Contact: British Film Commission, 70 Baker Street, London
   W1M 1DJ, England, tel.: 171/224-5000

THE SECRET ADVENTURES OF TOM THUMB Tara Releasing,
   1994, British

MICHAEL BORTMAN*

Home: 6369 Ivarene Street, Los Angeles, CA 90068, 213/465-3525
Agent: UTA - Los Angeles, 310/273-6700

CROOKED HEARTS MGM-Pathe Communications, 1991

JOHN BOSKOVICH

Agent: ICM - Beverly Hills, 310/550-4000

WITHOUT YOU I'M NOTHING MCEG, 1990

RACHID BOUCHAREB

b. Algeria
Contact: French Film Office, 745 Fifth Avenue, New York,
   NY 10151, 212/832-8860

BATON ROUGE 1985, French-Algerian
CHEB 1991, French-Algerian
POUSIERRES DE VIE Swift/3B Productions/Hamster Productions/
   La Sept Films/IVP/Tele-Munchen/Paradise Film/Salon Films, 1994,
   French-Algerian-German-Hong Kong

PATRICK BOUCHITEY

Contact: French Film Office, 745 Fifth Avenue, New York, NY 10151,
   212/832-8860

LUNE FROIDE Gaumont, 1991, French

ROY BOULTING
b. November 21, 1913 - Bray, Buckinghamshire, England
Business: Charter Film Productions, Twickenham Studios,
    Twickenham, Middlesex TW1 2AW, England, tel.: 181/892-4477
Agent: AIM & John Redway - London, tel.: 171/836-2001

TRUNK CRIME   Angelo, 1939, British
INQUEST   Grand National, 1939, British
PASTOR HALL   United Artists, 1940, British
THUNDER ROCK   English Films, 1942, British
DESERT VICTORY (FD)   Army Film Unit, 1943, British
TUNISIAN VICTORY (FD)   co-director with Frank Capra,
    Army Film Unit, 1943, British
BURMA VICTORY (FD)   Army Film Unit, 1945, British
THE OUTSIDER   *THE GUINEA PIG*   Pathe, 1948, British
FAME IS THE SPUR   Two Cities, 1949, British
HIGH TREASON   Rank, 1951, British
SAILOR OF THE KING   *SINGLE-HANDED*   20th Century-Fox,
    1953, British
CREST OF THE WAVE   *SEAGULLS OVER SORRENTO*
    co-director with John Boulting, MGM, 1954
JOSEPHINE AND MEN   1955, British
RUN FOR THE SUN   United Artists, 1956, British
BROTHERS IN LAW   British Lion, 1957, British
HAPPY IS THE BRIDE   Kassler, 1959, British
MAN IN A COCKED HAT   *CARLTON-BROWNE OF THE F.O.*
    co-director with Jeffrey Dell, Show Corporation, 1960, British
A FRENCH MISTRESS   Films Around the World, 1960, British
THE RISK   *SUSPECT*   co-director with John Boulting,
    Kingsley International, 1961, British
THE FAMILY WAY   Warner Bros., 1967, British
TWISTED NERVE   National General, 1969, British
THERE'S A GIRL IN MY SOUP   Columbia, 1970, British
UNDERCOVERS HERO   *SOFT BEDS AND HARD BATTLES*
    United Artists, 1975, British
THE LAST WORD   The Samuel Goldwyn Company, 1979
THE MOVING FINGER (TF)   BBC, 1984, British

LISA BOURGOUJIAN*
Contact: Directors Guild of America - Los Angeles, 213/851-3671

THE AMERICAN REVOLUTION (CTD)   Greystone
    Communications/A&E Network, 1994

SERGE BOURGUIGNON*
b. 1928 - France
Home: 18 rue du General Malleterre, 75016 Paris, France,
    tel.: 1/42-24-43-52

SUNDAYS AND CYBELE   *LES DIMANCHES DE VILLE D'AVRAY*
    Davis-Royal, 1962, French
THE REWARD   20th Century-Fox, 1965
TWO WEEKS IN SEPTEMBER   *A COEUR JOIE*   Paramount,
    1967, French
THE PICASSO SUMMER   Warner Bros., 1969
MY KINGDOM FOR A HORSE (FD)   Cheval Magazine,
    1986, French
THE FASCINATION   Samurai Productions, 1987, Japanese
PACIFIC 2000 (TF)   FR3, 1989, French

DAVID R. BOWEN
JEFFREY DAHMER - THE SECRET LIFE   Flourish
    Productions, 1992

JENNY BOWEN
b. San Francisco, California
Agent: Major Clients Agency - Los Angeles, 310/284-6400

STREET MUSIC   Specialty, 1982
THE WIZARD OF LONELINESS   Skouras Pictures, 1988

GEORGE BOWERS*
Home: 6417 Maryland Drive, Los Angeles, CA 90048, 310/931-2363
Business Manager: J. Gunnar Erickson, Armstrong, Hirsch & Levine,
    1888 Century Park East - Suite 1888, Los Angeles, CA 90067,
    310/553-0305

THE HEARSE   Crown International, 1980
BODY AND SOUL   Cannon, 1982
MY TUTOR   Crown International, 1983
PRIVATE RESORT   TriStar, 1985

JOHN R. BOWEY
b. January 4, 1958 - Sussex, England
Contact: A Cut Above Productions, Inc., 11816 Chandler Blvd. -
    Suite 8, North Hollywood, CA 91606, 818/985-2105

MUTATOR   A Cut Above Productions, 1991, filmed in 1989

ANTHONY J. BOWMAN
Agent: Susan Grant, The Artists Group - Los Angeles, 310/552-1100

RELATIVES   Archer Films, 1985, Australian
A DESPERATE FORTUNE   A-Z Communications, 1988, Australian
CAPPUCCINO   Archer Films, 1989, Australian

CHUCK BOWMAN*
Agent: UTA - Beverly Hills, 310/273-6700
Home: 5204 LaForest Drive, La Canada, CA 91011, 818/957-7715

MOMENT OF TRUTH: WHY MY DAUGHTER? (TF)
    O'Hara-Horowitz Productions, 1993
MOMENT OF TRUTH: CAUGHT IN THE CROSSFIRE (TF)
    O'Hara-Horowitz Productions, 1994
MOMENT OF TRUTH: A MOTHER'S DECEPTION (TF)
    O'Hara-Horowitz Productions, 1994

ROB BOWMAN*
Agent: ICM - Beverly Hills, 310/550-4000
Business Manager: Edmund Buccellato, Solomon Ross & Company,
    21300 Victory Blvd. - Suite 1250, Woodland Hills, CA 91367,
    818/999-6071

THE HAT SQUAD (TF)   Stephen J. Cannell Productions, 1992
AIRBORNE   Warner Bros., 1993

KENNETH BOWSER*
Address: 274 Mott Street, New York, NY 10012, 212/431-8155
Agent: Lucy Kroll, Lucy Kroll Agency, 2211 Broadway, New York,
    NY 10024, 212/877-0556

IN A SHALLOW GRAVE   Skouras Pictures, 1988
PRESTON STURGES: THE RISE AND FALL OF AN AMERICAN
    DREAMER (TD)   Barking Dog Productions/American
    Masters, 1990

PEARL BOWSER
THE AMERICAN EXPERIENCE: MIDNIGHT RAMBLE
    MIDNIGHT RAMBLE (TD)   co-director with Bestor Cram,
    Northern Lights, 1994

MURIEL BOX
(Muriel Baker)
b. 1905 - Tolworth, England
Contact: British Film Commission, 70 Baker Street, London
    W1M 1DJ, England, tel.: 171/224-5000

MR. LORD SAYS NO   *THE HAPPY FAMILY*   London Films,
    1952, British
BOTH SIDES OF THE LAW   *STREET CORNER*   Universal,
    1953, British
CASH ON DELIVERY   *TO DOROTHY A SON*   RKO Radio,
    1954, British
THE BEACHCOMBER   United Artists, 1954, British
SIMON AND LAURA   Universal, 1955, British
EYEWITNESS   1956, British

A NOVEL AFFAIR *THE PASSIONATE STRANGER* Continental, 1957, British
THE TRUTH ABOUT WOMEN Continental, 1958, British
SUBWAY IN THE SKY United Artists, 1959, British
THIS OTHER EDEN 1959, British-Irish
TOO YOUNG TO LOVE Rank, 1960, British
THE PIPER'S TUNE 1962, British
RATTLE OF A SIMPLE MAN Continental, 1964, British

DANIEL BOYD
b. September 14, 1956 - Martinsburg, West Virginia
Home: Big Pictures, Inc., 1115 Hollyberry Lane, South Charleston,
    West Virginia 25309, 304/340-1492
Attorney: Benjamin L. Bailey, Bowles, Rice, McDavid, Graff & Love,
    P.O. Box 1386, Charleston, West Virginia 25325, 304/347-1178

CHILLERS Troma, 1988
INVASION OF THE SPACE PREACHERS Troma, 1990
PARADISE PARK Big Pictures, 1991

DON BOYD
Home: Flat 12, 85 Cadagan Gardens, London SW3, England
Agent: ICM - London, tel.: 171/636-6565
Contact: British Film Commission, 70 Baker Street, London
    W1M 1DJ, England, tel.: 171/224-5000

INTIMATE REFLECTIONS 1974, British
EAST OF ELEPHANT ROCK 1977, British-Sri Lankan
THE FOUR SEASON 1977, British
GOLDENEYE (TF) 1989, British
TWENTY-ONE Triton Pictures, 1991, British
MAN, GOD AND AFRICA (TF) 1992, British
KLEPTOMANIA Kleptomania Productions, 1993

DANNY BOYLE
Agent: ICM - London, tel.: 171/636-6565
Contact: British Film Commission, 70 Baker Street, London
    W1M 1DJ, England, tel.: 171/224-5000

SHALLOW GRAVE Gramercy Pictures, 1994, British-Scottish

GIANNI BOZZACCHI*
Telephone: 414/481-2810

I LOVE N.Y. released under pseudonym of Alan Smithee,
    Manhattan Films, 1988
THE IRISH WAY MEI Productions, 1993

SAMUEL BRADFORD
TEEN VAMP New World, 1989

JOHN BRADSHAW
b. 1952 - Stratford, Ontario, Canada
Home: 134 Balmoral Avenue, Toronto, Ontario M4V 1J4, Canada,
    416/922-3801
Agent: Charles Northcote, The Core Group, 489 College Street -
    Suite 501, Toronto, Ontario M6G 1A5, Canada, 416/944-0193

THE BIG SLICE C/FP, 1991, Canadian

RANDY BRADSHAW
Agent: The Barry Perelman Agency - Los Angeles, 310/274-5999

LAST TRAIN HOME (CTF) Atlantis Films Ltd./Great North
    Productions/CBC, 1990, Canadian

ROBERT (BOB) BRALVER*
Home: 17589 Camino De Yatasto, Pacific Palisades, CA 90272,
    310/462-2301
Agent: Ronald Leif, Contemporary Artists - Santa Monica,
    310/395-1800

RUSH WEEK Noble Entertainment/Alpine Releasing Group, 1988
MIDNIGHT RIDE Cannon, 1990

MARCO BRAMBILLA*
Business: RSA USA Inc., 634 N. Lapeer, West Hollywood,
    CA 90069, 310/659-1577
Agent: CAA - Beverly Hills, 310/288-4545
Personal Manager: Carlyle Productions and Management,
    639 N. Larchmont - Suite 207, Los Angeles, CA 90004,
    213/469-3086

DEMOLITION MAN Warner Bros., 1993

BILL BRAME*
b. June 28, 1928
Home: P.O. Box 2228, Pasadena, CA 91102, 818/795-5872

CYCLE SAVAGES Trans American, 1970
JIVE TURKEY Goldstone, 1976

KENNETH BRANAGH*
b. December 10, 1960 - Belfast, Northern Ireland
Agent: CAA - Beverly Hills, 310/288-4545
Business Manager: Larry Berkin, Berkin Accountancy,
    3205 Ocean Park Blvd. - Suite 117, Santa Monica, CA 90405,
    310/450-1040

HENRY V ★ The Samuel Goldwyn Company, 1989, British
DEAD AGAIN Paramount, 1991
PETER'S FRIENDS The Samuel Goldwyn Company,
    1992, British
MUCH ADO ABOUT NOTHING The Samuel Goldwyn Company,
    1993, British-U.S.
MARY SHELLEY'S FRANKENSTEIN *FRANKENSTEIN* TriStar,
    1994, U.S.-British

JOSHUA BRAND*
Business: Brand-Falsey, 3000 Olympic Blvd. - Suite 2575,
    Santa Monica, CA 90404, 310/315-4833
Agent: CAA - Beverly Hills, 310/288-4545

I'LL FLY AWAY (TF) ☆ Falahey-Austin Street Productions/
    Lorimar TV, 1991
A PYROMANIAC'S LOVE STORY Buena Vista, 1995

LARRY BRAND*
Agent: Preferred Artists - Encino, 818/990-0305

THE DRIFTER Concorde, 1988
THE MASQUE OF THE RED DEATH Concorde, 1989
OVEREXPOSED Concorde, 1990
TILL THE END OF THE NIGHT Motion Picture Corporation of
    America, 1994

KLAUS MARIA BRANDAUER
b. June 22, 1944 - Bad Aussee, Austria
Agent: Paul Kohner, Inc. - Los Angeles, 310/550-1060

SEVEN MINUTES *GEORG ELSER: EINER AUS DEUTSCHLAND*
    Hemdale, 1990, West German-U.S.
MARIO UND DER ZAUBERER Senator, 1994, German

RICHARD BRANDER
SIZZLE BEACH, U.S.A. Troma, 1986

MARLON BRANDO*
b. April 3, 1924 - Omaha, Nebraska
Agent: ICM - Beverly Hills, 310/550-4000

ONE-EYED JACKS Paramount, 1961

CLARK BRANDON
SKEETERS New Line Cinema, 1992

CHARLOTTE BRANDSTROM
b. May 30, 1959 - Paris, France
Agent: ICM - Beverly Hills, 310/550-4000

UN ETE D'ORAGES   AAA, 1989, French
SWEET REVENGE (CTF)   Turner Pictures/Chrysalide Films/Canal/
   The Movie Group, 1990, U.S.-French
ROAD TO RUIN   Chrysalide Films/The Movie Group,
   1992, U.S.-French
A BUSINESS AFFAIR   Skouras Pictures, 1993,
   French-British-German-Spanish

PATRICK BRAOUDE
Contact: French Film Office, 745 Fifth Avenue, New York,
   NY 10151, 212/832-8860

NEUF MOIS   AFMD, 1994, French

TINTO BRASS
(Giovanni Tinto Brass)
b. March 26, 1933 - Milan, Italy
Home: Casale Tronconi, via Ferraioli, Isola Farnese, Rome,
   Italy, tel.: 06/379-1224

CHI LAVORA E' PERDUTO   *IN CAPO AL MONDO*
   Zebra Film/Franco London Film, 1963, Italian-French
LA MIA SIGNORA   co-director with Luigi Comencini &
   Mauro Bolognini, De Laurentiis, 1964, Italian
IL DISCO VOLANTE   De Laurentiis, 1964, Italian
CA IRA, IL FIUME DELLA RIVOLTA   Zebra Film, 1965, Italian
YANKEE   Tigielle, 1966, Italian
COL CUORE IN GOLA   Panda/Les Films Corona,
   1967, Italian-French
NEROSUBIANCO   Lion Film, 1969, Italian
DROPOUT   Medusa/Lion Film, 1972, Italian
LA VACANZA   Lion Film, 1972, Italian
L'URLO   Lion Film, 1972, Italian
SALON KITTY   American International, 1976, Italian
CALIGULA   Analysis Film Releasing, 1977, Italian-U.S.
ACTION   Attori Registri Solidali, 1979, Italian
LA CHIAVE   San Francisco Film, 1985, Italian
MIRANDA   San Francisco Film, 1985, Italian
REMEMBERING CAPRI   *CAPRICCIO*   DEG, 1987, Italian
SNACK BAR BUDAPEST   Medusa, 1988, Italian
PAPRIKA   Scena Group, 1991, Italian
COSI FAN TUTTE   Faso Film/San Francisco Film, 1992, Italian
L'UOMO CHE GUARDA   Rodeo Drive/Erre Cinematografica,
   1994, Italian
FERMO POSTA TINTO BRASS   Sacis, 1995, Italian

PETER BRATT
FOLLOW ME HOME   Follow Me Home Productions, 1995

MARY ANN BRAUBACH
b. San Antonio, Texas
Attorney: Frank Gruber, 9601 Wilshire Blvd., Beverly Hills,
   CA 90210, 310/274-5638

A GREAT BUNCH OF GIRLS (FD)   co-director with Tracy Tynan,
   Cowgirl Productions, 1978

MICHEL BRAULT
b. 1928 - Montreal, Quebec, Canada
Home: 1168 Richelieu, Beloeil, Quebec J3G 4R3, Canada,
   514/467-0317
Business: Nanouk Films, Ltee., 1600 avenue de Lorimier, Montreal,
   Quebec H2K 3W5, Canada, 514/521-1984

LES RAQUETTEURS   1958, Canadian
POUR LA SUITE DU MONDE   co-director, 1962, Canadian
ENTRE LA MER ET L'EAU DOUCE   1967, Canadian
LES ENFANTS DU NEANT   1968, Canadian
L'ACADIE L'ACADIE?!?   co-director, 1971, Canadian
LES ORDRES   1973, Canadian
LE SON DES FRANÇAIS EN AMERIQUE (TF)   1974-80, Canadian

A FREEDOM TO MOVE   1985, Canadian
L'EMPRISE (TF)   1988, Canadian
A PAPER WEDDING   Capitol Entertainment, 1989, Canadian
MONTREAL VU PAR...   co-director with Patricia Rozema,
   Jacques Leduc, Atom Egoyan & Lea Pool, Cinema Plus
   Distribution, 1991, Canadian
SHABBAT SHALOM   Les Productions du Verseau/SRC,
   1993, Canadian
MON AMIE MAX   Les Productions du Verseav/Les Productions
   Lazennec/National Film Board of Canada/Telefilm Canada/Sogic/
   Ministere de la Culture et de la Francophonie/Centre National de la
   Cinematographie, 1994, Canadian-French

CHARLES BRAVERMAN*
b. March 3, 1944 - Los Angeles, California
Business: Braverman Productions, 3000 Olympic Blvd.,
   Santa Monica, CA 90404, 310/315-4710
Agent: Premiere Artists Agency - Los Angeles, 310/271-1414

HIT AND RUN   REVENGE SQUAD   Comworld, 1982
PRINCE OF BEL AIR (TF)   Leonard Hill Films, 1986
BROTHERHOOD OF JUSTICE (TF)   Guber-Peters Productions/
   Phoenix Entertainment Group, 1986
FINAL SHOT: THE HANK GATHERS STORY (TF)   McGillen
   Entertainment/Alexander-Enright & Associates/Tribune
   Entertainment, 1992

EDGAR MICHAEL BRAVO
I'LL LOVE YOU FOREVER...TONIGHT   Headliner Releasing, 1993

JULIAN BREEN
(See David DeCOTEAU))

ANJA BREIEN
b. 1940 - Norway
Home: Mellbydalen 8, 0287 Oslo, Norway, tel.: 02/437163

VOLDTEKT   *RAPE*   1971, Norwegian
HUSTRUER   *WIVES*   1975, Norwegian
DEN ALVARSAMMA LEKEN   *GAMES OF LOVE AND LONELINESS*
   1977, Swedish-Norwegian
ARVEN   *NEXT OF KIN*   1979, Norwegian
FORFOLGELSEN   *WITCH HUNT*   1981, Norwegian-Swedish
PAPIRFUGLEN   *PAPER BIRD*   1984, Norwegian
HUSTRUER 10 AR ETTER   *WIVES 10 YEARS AFTER*
   1985, Norwegian
SMYKKETYVEN   *TWICE UPON A TIME*   Norsk Film/Swedish
   Film Institute/Danish Film Institute/Nordic Film & TV, 1990,
   Norwegian-Danish-Swedish

CATHERINE BREILLAT
b. July 13, 1948 - Bressuire, France
Agent: Agents Associes - Paris, tel.: 1/42-56-21-22
Contact: French Film Office, 745 Fifth Avenue, New York,
   NY 10151, 212/832-8860

UNE VRAIE JEUNE FILLE   1976, French, unfinished
TAPAGE NOCTURNE   1979, French
36 FILLETTE   Circle Releasing, 1988, French
SALE COMME UN ANGE   French Production, 1991, French

VALERIE BREIMAN
Agent: The Coppage Company - North Hollywood, 818/980-1106

THE UNSINKABLE SHECKY MOSKOWITZ   TTI, 1990
BIKINI SQUAD   Moonstone Entertainment, 1994
BABES AHOY   Silver Lake International Pictures, 1994

TIA BRELIS
Agent: The Gersh Agency - Beverly Hills, 310/274-6611

TRADING MOM   Trimark Pictures, 1994

MARIO BRENTA
b. April 17, 1942 - Venice, Italy
Business: Ipotesi Cinema, Bassano del Grappa, Italy,
    tel.: 0424/502139

VERMISAT   Eucapia Film/RAI, 1974, Italian
EFFETTO OLMI (TD)   RAI, 1980, Italian
MAICOL   Ipotesi Cinema/Raiuno, 1989, Italian
BARNABO DELLE MONTAGNE   Nautilus Film/Raiuno/Istituto
    Luce/Les Films Number One/Flach Film/T&C AG. Film,
    1994, Italian-French-Swiss

ROBERT BRESSON
b. September 25, 1907 - Bromont-Lamothe, Puy-de-Dome, France
Address: 49, quai Bourbon, 75004 Paris, France, tel.: 1/43-54-37-06
Contact: French Film Office, 745 Fifth Avenue, New York,
    NY 10151, 212/832-8860

LES AFFAIRES PUBLIQUE   Arc Films, 1934, French
LES ANGES DU PECHE   Synops/Roland Tual, 1943, French
THE LADIES OF THE PARK   Brandon, 1945, French
DIARY OF A COUNTRY PRIEST   Brandon, 1950, French
A MAN ESCAPED   Continental, 1956, French
PICKPOCKET   New Yorker, 1959, French
THE TRIAL OF JOAN OF ARC   Pathe Contemporary,
    1962, French
AU HASARD, BALTHAZAR   Cinema Ventures, 1966, French
MOUCHETTE   1967, French
UNE FEMME DOUCE   New Yorker, 1969, French
FOUR NIGHTS OF A DREAMER   New Yorker, 1972, French
LANCELOT OF THE LAKE   New Yorker, 1975, French-Italian
LE DIABLE PROBABLEMENT   Gaumont, 1977, French
L'ARGENT (MONEY)   Cinecom, 1983, French-Swiss

MARTIN BREST*
b. 1951 - Bronx, New York
Business: City Light Films, 2110 Main Street - Suite 200,
    Santa Monica, CA 90405, 310/314-3500
Agent: CAA - Beverly Hills, 310/288-4545

HOT TOMORROWS   American Film Institute, 1977
GOING IN STYLE   Warner Bros., 1979
BEVERLY HILLS COP   Paramount, 1984
MIDNIGHT RUN   Universal, 1988
SCENT OF A WOMAN ★   Universal, 1992

JOE BREWSTER
THE KEEPER   Rada Films, 1994

SALOME BREZINER
Agent: The Gersh Agency -Beverly Hills, 310/274-6611

TOLLBOOTH   Roadkill Films/Sneak Preview Productions, 1994
FAST SOFA   Roadkill Films, 1995

MARSHALL BRICKMAN*
b. August 25, 1941 - Rio de Janeiro, Brazil
Agent: ICM - Beverly Hills, 310/550-4000
Business Manager: Starr & Co., 350 Park Avenue, New York, NY
    10022, 212/759-6556

SIMON   Orion/Warner Bros., 1980
LOVESICK   The Ladd Company/Warner Bros., 1983
THE MANHATTAN PROJECT   20th Century Fox, 1986

PAUL BRICKMAN*
b. Chicago, Illinois
Agent: CAA - Beverly Hills, 310/288-4545

RISKY BUSINESS   The Geffen Company/Warner Bros., 1983
MEN DON'T LEAVE   The Geffen Company/Warner Bros., 1990

ALAN BRIDGES*
b. September 28, 1928 - Liverpool, England
Contact: British Film Commission, 70 Baker Street, London
    W1M 1DJ, England, tel.: 171/224-5000

ACT OF MURDER   Warner-Pathe/Anglo-Amalgamated,
    1964, British
INVASION   Warner-Pathe/Anglo-Amalgamated, 1966, British
THE LIE   BBC, 1970, British
THE HIRELING   Columbia, 1973, British
BRIEF ENCOUNTER (TF)   Carlo Ponti Productions/Cecil Clarke
    Productions, 1974, British
OUT OF SEASON   Athenaeum, 1975, British
SATURDAY, SUNDAY, MONDAY (TF)   Granada TV, 1977, British
AGE OF INNOCENCE   Rank, 1977, British-Canadian
LA PETITE FILLE EN VELOURS BLEU   Warner-Columbia,
    1978, French
RAIN ON THE ROOF (TF)   London Weekend TV, 1980, British
VERY LIKE A WHALE   Black Lion, 1981, British
THE RETURN OF THE SOLDIER   European Classics,
    1982, British
PUDDN'HEAD WILSON (TF)   The Great Amwell Company/
    Nebraska ETY Network/Taurus Film, 1984, U.S.-West German
THE SHOOTING PARTY   European Classics, 1984, British
DISPLACED PERSON (TF)   1985
LITTLE PIG ROBINSON (TF)   1990, British

BEAU BRIDGES*
(Lloyd Vernet Bridges III)
b. December 9, 1941 - Los Angeles, California
Contact: E.B.M., 1800 Avenue of the Stars - Suite 430, Los Angeles,
    CA 90067, 310/843-4868
Agent: CAA - Beverly Hills, 310/288-4545

THE KID FROM NOWHERE (TF)   Cates-Bridges Company, 1982
THE THANKSGIVING PROMISE (TF)   Mark H. Ovitz Productions/
    Walt Disney TV, 1986
THE WILD PAIR   Trans World Entertainment, 1987
SEVEN HOURS TO JUDGMENT   Trans World Entertainment, 1988
SECRET SINS OF THE FATHER (TF)   UltraEnt/Dick Clark
    Film Group, 1994

STEVEN BRILL
Agent: CAA - Beverly Hills, 310/288-4545

HEAVYWEIGHTS   Buena Vista, 1995

BURT BRINCKERHOFF*
b. October 25, 1936
Agent: Shapiro-Lichtman Talent Agency - Los Angeles,
    310/859-8877

TWO BROTHERS (TF)   KCET-TV, 1976
DOGS   R.C. Riddell, 1977
ACAPULCO GOLD   R.C. Riddell, 1978
THE CRACKER FACTORY (TF)   Roger Gimbel Productions/
    EMI TV, 1979
CAN YOU HEAR THE LAUGHTER? THE STORY OF FREDDIE
    PRINZE (TF)   Roger Gimbel Productions/EMI TV, 1979
MOTHER AND DAUGHTER - THE LOVING WAR (TF)
    Edgar J. Scherick Associates, 1980
BRAVE NEW WORLD (TF)   Universal TV, 1980
THE DAY THE WOMEN GOT EVEN (TF)   Otto Salaman
    Productions/PKO, 1980
BORN TO BE SOLD (TF)   Ron Samuels Productions, 1981
A GIRL OF THE LIMBERLOST (TF)   Sascha Schneider
    Productions, 1990
CLARA (CTF)   Nederlander Television & Film Productions, 1991
JAILBIRDS (TF)   Spelling Entertainment, 1991

RICHARD BROADMAN
PRESENT MEMORY (FD)   Full Moon Productions/Cine Research
    Associates, 1989

JEFF BROADSTREET
b. November 7, 1954 - Greencastle, Indiana
Agent: The Artists Group - Los Angeles, 310/552-1100

SEXBOMB   Transcontinental Pictures, 1989
ROCK 'N' ROLL DETECTIVE   Film Barn Productions, 1992

DEBORAH BROCK
Agent: The Gersh Agency - Beverly Hills, 310/274-6611
Business: Fiat Lucre Productions, 11850 Wilshire Blvd., Suite 200,
   Los Angeles, CA 90025

SLUMBER PARTY MASSACRE II   Concorde, 1987
ANDY COLBY'S INCREDIBLE ADVENTURE   Concorde, 1988
ROCK 'N' ROLL HIGH SCHOOL FOREVER   Four Seasons
   Entertainment, 1991

MERRILL BROCKWAY*
Address: 484 West 43rd Street - Apt. 45B, New York, NY 10036,
   212/864-6510
Business Manager: Arthur Greene, 101 Park Avenue, New York,
   NY 10178, 212/661-8200

TENNESSEE WILLIAMS: ORPHEUS OF THE AMERICAN
   STAGE (TD)   PBS, 1994

AL BRODAX
Contact: Writers Guild of America, East - New York City,
   212/767-7800

STRAWBERRY FIELDS (AF)   ITC Productions, 1993

JOHN C. BRODERICK
Home: 20522 Pacific Coast Highway, Malibu, CA 90265,
   213/461-1879
Business: Bop Motion Pictures Ltd., 6 Woodland Way, Petts Wood,
   Kent BR5 1ND, England, tel.: 0689/871535 or 871519

SIX-PACK ANNIE   released under pseudonym of
   Graydon F. David, 1975
BAD GEORGIA ROAD   Dimension, 1976
SAM'S SONG   THE SWAP/LINE OF FIRE   co-director with
   John Shade, released under pseudonym of
   Jordan Leondopoulos, Cannon, 1969
THE WARRIOR AND THE SORCERESS   New Horizons, 1984

MATTHEW BRODERICK
b. August 21, 1962 - New York, New York
Agent: CAA - Beverly Hills, 310/288-4545

INFINITY   Neo Motion Pictures/First Look Pictures, 1995

KEVIN BRODIE*
Business: Farren Entertainment, Inc., 4292 Elmer Avenue,
   Studio City, CA 91602, 818/766-2722

MUGSY'S GIRLS   Shapiro Entertainment/Spectrum Cinema/
   ICE Corporation, 1984
TREACHEROUS   Ulysse Entertainment, 1994

HUGH BRODY
Contact: British Film Commission, 70 Baker Street, London
   W1M 1DJ, England, tel.: 171/224-5000

1919   Spectrafilm, 1985, British
AS LONG AS THE RIVERS FLOW (TD)   co-director, National Film
   Board of Canada, 1992, Canadian

REX BROMFIELD
Home: 1034 Princess Avenue, Victoria, British Columbia V8T 1L1,
   Canada, 604/383-9583
Business: Brom Films Productions 1988 Inc., 6395 Chatham Street,
   West Vancouver, British Columbia V7W 2E1, Canada,
   604/921-9394

LOVE AT FIRST SIGHT   Movietown, 1977, Canadian
TULIPS   co-director with Mark Warren & Al Waxman, released under
   pseudonym of Stan Ferris, Avco Embassy, 1981, Canadian
MELANIE   Jensen Farley Pictures, 1983, Canadian
HOME IS WHERE THE HART IS   Atlantic Releasing Corporation,
   1987, Canadian
CAFE ROMEO   First Cafe Productions, 1991, Canadian

PETER BROOK
b. March 21, 1925 - London, England
Address: c/o C.C.T., 56 rue de Universite, 75007 Paris, France,
   tel.: 331/42-22-93-93

THE BEGGAR'S OPERA   Warner Bros., 1953, British
MODERATO CANTABILE   Royal International,
   1963, French-Italian
LORD OF THE FLIES   Continental, 1963, British
THE PERSECUTION AND ASSASINATION OF JEAN-PAUL
   MARAT AS PERFORMED BY THE INMATES OF THE ASYLUM
   OF CHARENTON UNDER THE DIRECTION OF THE MARQUIS
   DE SADE   MARAT/SADE   United Artists, 1967, British
TELL ME LIES   Continental, 1968, British
KING LEAR   Altura, 1971, British-Danish
MEETINGS WITH REMARKABLE MEN   Libra, 1979, British
LA TRAGEDIE DE CARMEN   MK2/Alby Films/Antenne-2,
   1983, French
THE MAHABHARATA   MK2 USA, 1989, French-British-U.S.

ADAM BROOKS
b. September 3, 1956 - Toronto, Ontario, Canada
Home: 144 Franklin Street, New York, NY 10013, 212/925-8064
Agent: UTA - Beverly Hills, 310/273-6700

ALMOST YOU   TLC Films/20th Century Fox, 1984
RED RIDING HOOD   Cannon, 1987, U.S.-Israeli

ALBERT BROOKS*
(Albert Einstein)
b. July 22, 1947 - Los Angeles, California
Agent: ICM - Beverly Hills, 310/550-4000

REAL LIFE   Paramount, 1979
MODERN ROMANCE   Columbia, 1981
LOST IN AMERICA   The Geffen Company/Warner Bros., 1985
DEFENDING YOUR LIFE   The Geffen Company/
   Warner Bros., 1991

BOB BROOKS*
b. 1927 - Philadelphia, Pennsylvania
Address: Apt. 1107/08, Casablanca, 17 Blvd. du Larvotto,
   Monte Carlo, 98000 Monaco, tel.: 93-5052-98

THE KNOWLEDGE (TF)   1979, British
TATTOO   20th Century-Fox, 1981

JAMES L. BROOKS*
b. May 9, 1940 - North Bergen, New Jersey
Business: Gracie Films, 10202 W. Washington Blvd. - Poitier Building,
   Culver City, CA 90232, 310/280-4222
Agent: ICM - Beverly Hills, 310/550-4000

TERMS OF ENDEARMENT ★★   Paramount, 1983
BROADCAST NEWS   20th Century Fox, 1987
I'LL DO ANYTHING   Columbia, 1994

JOSEPH BROOKS*

Business: Chancery Lane Films, Inc., 41-A East 74th Street,
New York, NY 10021, 212/759-8720

YOU LIGHT UP MY LIFE Columbia, 1977
IF EVER I SEE YOU AGAIN Columbia, 1978
HEADIN' FOR BROADWAY 20th Century-Fox, 1980
INVITATION TO THE WEDDING Chancery Lane Films,
1984, British

MEL BROOKS*

(Melvin Kaminsky)
b. June 28, 1926 - Brooklyn, New York
Business: Brooksfilms Limited, 20th Century Fox, P.O. Box 900,
Beverly Hills, CA 90213, 310/203-1375

THE PRODUCERS Avco Embassy, 1968
THE TWELVE CHAIRS UMC, 1970
BLAZING SADDLES Warner Bros., 1973
YOUNG FRANKENSTEIN 20th Century-Fox, 1974
SILENT MOVIE 20th Century-Fox, 1976
HIGH ANXIETY 20th Century-Fox, 1977
HISTORY OF THE WORLD, PART I 20th Century-Fox, 1981
SPACEBALLS MGM/UA, 1987
LIFE STINKS MGM-Pathe Communications, 1991
ROBIN HOOD: MEN IN TIGHTS 20th Century Fox, 1993
DRACULA: DEAD AND LOVING IT Columbia, 1995

NICHOLAS (NICK) BROOMFIELD

Agent: UTA - Beverly Hills, 310/273-6700 or:
The Casarotto Company - London, tel.: 171/287-4450

DRIVING ME CRAZY First Run Features, 1988, British
DARK SECRETS *DIAMOND SKULLS* Circle Releasing,
1989, British
SPALDING GRAY'S MONSTER IN A BOX
MONSTER IN A BOX (PF) Fine Line Features/New Line
Cinema, 1991, British
AILEEN WUORNOS: THE SELLING OF A SERIAL KILLER (FD)
Strand Releasing, 1992, British
TRACKING DOWN MAGGIE: THE UNAUTHORIZED BIOGRAPHY
OF MARGARET THATCHER (FD) Lafayette Film/Channel 4,
1994, British

PHILIP BROPHY

Contact: Australian Film Commission, 150 William Street,
Woolloomooloo, NSW 2011, Australia, tel.: 2/321-6444

BODY MELT Dumb Films/Body Melt Productions/Australian Film
Commission/Film Victoria, 1993, Australian

BARRY BROWN*

Home: 770 Amalfi Drive, Pacific Palisades, CA 90272,
310/459-4455

THE WAY WE LIVE NOW United Artists, 1970
CLOUD DANCER Blossom, 1980

BARRY ALEXANDER BROWN

Agent: Broder-Kurland-Webb-Uffner Agency - Beverly Hills,
310/281-3400

LONELY IN AMERICA Arista Films, 1990
THE WHO'S TOMMY: THE AMAZING JOURNEY (CTD)
Elegant Films, 1994

BRUCE BROWN

THE ENDLESS SUMMER (FD) Cinema 5, 1966
ON ANY SUNDAY (FD) Cinema 5, 1971
THE ENDLESS SUMMER II (FD) New Line Cinema, 1994

GEORG STANFORD BROWN

b. June 24 - Havana, Cuba
Business: Nexus Productions, Inc., 4049C Radford Avenue,
Studio City, CA 91604, 818/760-4651

ROOTS: THE NEXT GENERATIONS (MS) co-director with
John Erman, Charles Dubin & Lloyd Richards,
Wolper Productions, 1979
GRAMBLING'S WHITE TIGER (TF) Jenner-Wallach Productions/
Inter Planetary Productions, 1981
MIRACLE OF THE HEART: A BOYS TOWN STORY (TF)
Larry White Productions/Columbia TV, 1986
VIETNAM WAR STORY (CTF) co-director with Ray Danton &
Kevin Hooks, Nexus Productions, 1987
KIDS LIKE THESE (TF) Taft Entertainment TV/Nexus
Productions, 1987
ALONE IN THE NEON JUNGLE (TF) Robert Halmi, Inc., 1988
STUCK WITH EACH OTHER (TF) Nexus Productions, 1989
THE LAST P.O.W? THE BOBBY GARWOOD STORY (TF)
Fries Entertainment/Emr Productions/Nexus Productions, 1993
FATHER AND SON: DANGEROUS RELATIONS (TF)
Kushner-Locke Company/Logo Productions/Gregory-Kahn
Productions, 1993

GREGORY BROWN

DEAD MAN WALKING Metropolis Productions/Hit Films, 1988
STREET ASYLUM Metropolis Productions, 1989
CARNAL CRIMES Magnum Entertainment, 1991
STRANGER BY NIGHT Axis Films International, 1994

JIM BROWN

WASN'T THAT A TIME! (FD) United Artists Classics, 1982
HARD TRAVELIN' (TD) Ginger Group/Harold Leventhal
Management, 1984
MUSICAL PASSAGE (FD) Films Inc., 1984
WE SHALL OVERCOME (TD) PBS, 1988
A TRIBUTE TO WOODY GUTHRIE AND LEADBELLY (CTPF)
Showtime, 1988
SONGS OF THE CIVIL WAR (TD) American Documentaries Inc./
Ginger Group, 1991

JULIE BROWN

Agent: ICM - Beverly Hills, 310/550-4000

NATIONAL LAMPOON'S ATTACK OF THE 5 FT. 2 WOMEN (CTF)
co-director with Richard Wenk, Showtime/National Lampoon/
Imagination Productions, 1994

TONY BROWN

Business: Tony Brown Productions, Inc., 1501 Broadway -
Suite 2014, New York, NY 10036, 212/575-0876

THE WHITE GIRL Tony Brown Productions, 1988

KIRK BROWNING*

b. May 28, 1921 - New York, New York
Home: 80 Central Park West, New York, NY 10023, 212/595-6474

BIG BLONDE (TF) PBS-TV, 1980

KEVIN BROWNLOW

b. June 2, 1938 - Crowborough, England
Contact: British Film Commission, 70 Baker Street, London
W1M 1DJ, England, tel.: 171/224-5000

IT HAPPENED HERE co-director with Andrew Mollo, Lopert,
1966, British
WINSTANLEY co-director with Andrew Mollo, 1975, British
HOLLYWOOD (TD) co-director with David Gill, 1980, British
UNKNOWN CHAPLIN (TD) 1983, British
BUSTER KEATON: A HARD ACT TO FOLLOW (TD) British

JAMES BRUCE
THE SUICIDE CLUB   Angelika Films, 1988
DIRTY MONEY   Northern Arts Entertainment, 1994
HEADLESS BODY IN TOPLESS BAR   Green Tea
   Productions, 1995

JAMES BRYAN
DON'T GO IN THE WOODS   Seymour Borde & Associates, 1983
THE EXECUTIONER PART II   21st Century Distribution, 1984
HELL RIDERS   21st Century Distribution, 1985

BILL BRYDEN
b. April 12, 1942 - Greenock, Scotland
Agent: ICM - London, tel.: 171/636-6565

ILL FARES THE LAND   Channel 4, 1982, British
THE HOLY CITY (TF)   BBC, 1986
ARIA   co-director, Miramax Films, 1987, British

TONY BUBA
Business: Tony Buba Productions, 219 Fifth Street, Braddock,
   PA 15104

LIGHTNING OVER BRADDOCK: A RUST BOWL FANTASY (FD)
   Zeitgeist Films, 1989
NO PETS (FD)   Braddock Films, 1994

LARRY BUCHANAN
Home: 4154 B. Via Andorra, Santa Barbara, CA 93105
Business: Larry Buchanan Presents, 610 Anacapa Street,
   Santa Barbara, CA 93001, 805/966-5446

FREE, WHITE AND 21   American International, 1963
UNDER AGE   Falcon International, 1964
THE TRIAL OF LEE HARVEY OSWALD
   Falcon International, 1964
ZONTAR - THE THING FROM VENUS   American
   International, 1966
CREATURE OF DESTRUCTION   American International, 1967
HELL RAIDERS   American International, 1968
MARS NEEDS WOMEN   American International, 1968
STRAWBERRIES NEED RAIN   1970
A BULLET FOR PRETTY BOY   American International, 1970
GOODBYE, NORMA JEAN   Stirling Gold, 1976
HUGHES AND HARLOW: ANGELS IN HELL
   Pro International, 1978
THE LOCH NESS HORROR   Omni-Leisure International, 1982
GOODNIGHT, SWEET MARILYN   Studio Entertainment, 1989
BEYOND THE DOORS   Omni-Leisure International,
   1989, filmed in 1983

NOEL BUCKNER
APOLLO 13: TO THE EDGE AND BACK (TD)   WGBH-Boston/TV
   Asahi/Central TV, 1994, U.S.-Japanese-British

COLIN BUCKSEY*
Agent: ICM - London, tel.: 171/636-6565
Personal Manager: Creative Alliance Management - Los Angeles,
   213/962-6090

BLUE MONEY (TF)   London Weekend TV, 1984, British
THE McGUFFIN (TF)   BBC, 1985, British
CALL ME MISTER (TF)   BBC/Australian Broadcasting Corporation,
   1987, British-Australian
DEALERS   Skouras Pictures, 1989, British
CURIOSITY KILLS (CTF)   Dutch Productions, 1990
NOTORIOUS (CTF)   Berger Queen Productions/Hamster
   Productions/ABC Productions/Capital Cities-ABC Video
   Enterprises, 1992, U.S.-French
TERROR IN THE NIGHT (TF)   The Landsburg Company/
   Cinematigue/CBS Entertainment Productions, 1994

ANNA LEE: HEADCASE (TF)   London Weekend TV, 1994, British
SEPTEMBER (MS)   Hannibal/Portman Productions/Wolfhound Films/
   RHI Entertainment, 1995, British

JAN BUCQUOY
Contact: National Tourist Office, 61 Rue de Marche Aux Herbes,
   B1000 Brussels, Belgium, tel.: 01/513-8940

LA VIE SEXUELLE DES BELGES   Transatlantic Films,
   1994, Belgian

COLIN BUDD
Contact: Australian Film Commission, 150 William Street,
   Woolloomooloo NSW 2011, Australia, tel.: 2/321-6444

HURRICANE SMITH   Warner Bros., 1991, Australian

ROBIN BUDD
Contact: Australian Film Commission, 150 William Street,
   Woolloomooloo NSW 2011, Australia, tel.: 2/321-6444

THE THIEF OF ALWAYS (AF)   Paramount, 1995, U.S.-Australian

JOHN CARL BUECHLER
Business: Imageries Entertainment, Inc., 12031 Vose - Suites 19-21,
   North Hollywood, CA 91605, 818/765-6150
Agent: Stone Manners Agency - Los Angeles, 213/654-7575

THE DUNGEONMASTER   co-director, Empire Pictures, 1985
TROLL   Empire Pictures, 1986
CELLAR DWELLAR   Empire Pictures, 1988
FRIDAY THE 13TH PART VII - THE NEW BLOOD
   Paramount, 1988
GHOULIES GO TO COLLEGE   Taurus Entertainment, 1991

RICHARD BUGAJSKI
b. 1943 - Warsaw, Poland
Home: 41 Lavinia Avenue, Toronto, Ontario M6S 3H9, Canada,
   416/763-4560
Agent: Lynn Kinney Credentials, 387 Bloor Street East, Toronto,
   Ontario M4W 2H7, Canada, 416/926-1507 or: ICM - Beverly Hills,
   310/550-4000

THE OTHER SIDE OF THE FLAME (TF)   1976, Polish
DON CARLOS (TF)   1977, Polish
TRISMUS (TF)   1978, Polish
SPANISH BLOOD (TF)   1978, Polish
CLASSES (TF)   1979, Polish
A WOMAN AND A WOMAN   co-director, 1980, Polish
THE INTERROGATION   1990, Polish, filmed in 1982
CLEARCUT   Northern Arts Entertainment, 1991, Canadian

PENELOPE BUITENHUIS
Contact: Directors Guild of Canada, 225 Richmond Street, Toronto,
   Ontario M5V 1W2, Canada, 416/351-8200

BOULEVARD   Norstar Entertainment, 1994, Canadian

JILLIAN BULLOCK
TRIUMPH OF THE HEART   J. Monique Productions, 1993

ALAN BUNCE
BABAR: THE MOVIE (AF)   New Line Cinema, 1989,
   Canadian-French

MARK BUNTZMAN
Business: Movie Development Corporation, 7979 Willow Glen Road,
   Los Angeles, CA 90046, 213/650-6042

EXTERMINATOR 2   Cannon, 1984

JUAN-LUIS BUÑUEL
b. November 9, 1934 - Paris, France
Address: 107, rue des Artistes, 75014 Paris, France
Agent: Anne Alvarez Correa, 18, Rue Troyon, Paris 75017,
France, tel.: 755 80 85

AU RENDEZ-VOUS DE LA MORT JOYEUSE   United Artists,
1972, French
LA FEMME AUX BOTTES ROUGES   UGC/CFDC,
1974, French-Spanish
LEONOR   CIC, 1975, French-Italian-Spanish
THE ISLAND OF PASSION   1984, French
LA REBELION DE LOS COLGADOS
Sociedad Cooperativa Rio Mixcoac, 1987,
West German-Italian-French-British-Austrian-Mexican

ALEXANDER BURAVSKY
Contact: Confederation of Film-Makers Unions, Vasilyevskaya
Street 13, 123 825 Moscow, Russia, tel.: 095/250-4114

SACRED CARGO   Go Pictures, 1995, U.S.-Russian

DEREK BURBIDGE
Agent: Zoetrope Ltd., Zoetrope House, 93 Union Road, London
SW4 6JD, England, tel.: 171/720-8513

URGH! A MUSIC WAR (FCD)   Filmway, 1982
MEN WITHOUT WOMEN (FCD)   1983
GOIN' HOME: TEN YEARS AFTER (HVCD)   Jem Music Video,
1986, British

GEORGE BURDEAU
THE NATIVE AMERICANS (CTD)   co-director with John Borden &
Phil Lucas, Turner Broadcasting, 1994

ROBERT A. BURGE
VASECTOMY, A DELICATE MATTER   Seymour Borde &
Associates, 1986
KEATON'S COP   Cannon, 1990
THE HOUSE ON TODVILLE ROAD   Third Coast
Entertainment, 1994
DARK DANCER   Third Coast Entertainment, 1994

STUART BURGE
b. January 15, 1918 - Brentwood, England
Agent: Harriet Cruickshank, Cruickschank Cazenove Ltd. - London,
tel.: 171/735-2933

THERE WAS A CROOKED MAN   United Artists, 1962, British
UNCLE VANYA   Arthur Cantor, 1963, British
OTHELLO   Warner Bros., 1967, British
THE MIKADO   Warner Bros., 1967, British
JULIUS CAESAR   American International, 1971, British
SONS AND LOVERS (TF)   BBC, 1979, British
BREAKING UP (TF)   BBC, 1986, British
NAMING THE NAMES (TF)   BBC, 1987, British
THE RAINBOW (TF)   BBC, 1989, British
ALAN BENNETT'S TALKING HEADS (TF)   BBC, 1990, British
CIRCLES OF DECEIT (TF)   BBC, 1990, British
THE HOUSE OF BERNALDA ALBA (TF)   co-director with
Nuria Espert, Holmes Productions/Channel 4/WNET-13,
1991, British-U.S.
AFTER THE DANCE (TF)   BBC, 1992, British

MARTYN BURKE
b. Canada
Agent: ICM - Beverly Hills, 310/550-4000

THE CLOWN MURDERS   1975, Canadian
IDI AMIN: MY PEOPLE LOVE ME (TD)   1975, Canadian
CONNECTIONS: AN INVESTIGATION INTO ORGANIZED
CRIME IN CANADA (TD)   1977-79, Canadian
POWER PLAY   Magnum International Pictures/Cowry Film
Productions, 1978, Canadian-British
THE KGB CONNECTIONS (TD)   1981, Canadian

THE LAST CHASE   Crown International, 1981, Canadian
CINQ DEFIS POUR LE PRESIDENT (TD)   1989, Canadian-French
WITNESSES: WHAT REALLY HAPPENED IN AFGHANISTAN (FD)
Stornoway Productions, 1990, Canadian

TOM BURMAN
MEET THE HOLLOWHEADS   Moviestore Entertainment, 1989

CHARLES BURNETT
b. 1944 - Vicksburg, Mississippi
Agent: Broder-Kurland-Webb-Uffner Agency - Beverly Hills,
310/281-3400

KILLER OF SHEEP   Third World Newsreel, 1973
MY BROTHER'S WEDDING   1983
TO SLEEP WITH ANGER   The Samuel Goldwyn Company, 1990
THE GLASS SHIELD   Miramax Films, 1994, U.S.-French

ALLAN BURNS*
b. Baltimore, Maryland
Agent: CAA - Beverly Hills, 310/288-4545

JUST BETWEEN FRIENDS   Orion, 1986

EDWARD BURNS
Agent: ICM - Beverly Hills, 310/550-4000

THE BROTHERS McMULLEN   Fox Searchlight Pictures, 1995

KEN BURNS
(Kenneth Lauren Burns)
b. 1953 - Brooklyn, New York

BROOKLYN BRIDGE (FD)   1981
THE SHAKERS: HANDS TO WORK, HEARTS TO GOD (FD)   1984
HUEY LONG (FD)   1985
THE STATUE OF LIBERTY (FD)   1985
THOMAS HART BENTON (FD)   1988
THE CONGRESS (FD)   1989
THE CIVIL WAR (TD)   Florentine Films/WETA-Washington, 1990
EMPIRE OF THE AIR: THE MEN WHO MADE RADIO (TD)
Florentine Films/WETA-Washington, 1992
BASEBALL (TD)   Florentine Films/WETA-Washington, 1994

RIC BURNS
Agent: William Morris Agency - Beverly Hills, 310/859-4000

CONEY ISLAND (TD)   Steeplechase Films, 1991
THE DONNER PARTY (TD)   Steeplechase Films/WGBH-Boston/
WNET-13, 1992
THE WAY WEST (TD)   Steeplechase Films/Channel 4/
WGBH-Boston, 1995

JEFF BURR
Agent: Paradigm - Los Angeles, 310/277-4400

DIVIDED WE FALL   co-director, Conquest Entertainment/Pegasus
Productions, 1982
THE OFFSPRING   *FROM A WHISPER TO A SCREAM*
TMS Pictures, 1987
THE VAULT   Empire Pictures, 1988
STEPFATHER II   Millimeter Films, 1989
LEATHERFACE: THE TEXAS CHAINSAW MASSACRE III
New Line Cinema, 1990
EDDIE PRESLEY   Laika Films/Eddie Productions/Fauve
Cinema, 1993
PUPPETMASTER 4   Full Moon Entertainment, 1993
PUMPKINHEAD II   Motion Picture Corporation of America, 1994
NIGHT OF THE SCARECROW   Republic Pictures, 1995

CHRISTINE BURRILL
Agent: Stu Robinson, Paradigm - Los Angeles, 310/277-4400

MARICELA (TF)   KCET/Richard Soto Productions, 1986

GEOFF BURROWES*

Attorney: Myman, Abell, Fineman & Greenspan, 11777 San Vicente
  Blvd. - Suite 600, Los Angeles, CA 90049, 310/281-3434

RETURN TO SNOWY RIVER   Buena Vista, 1988, Australian
RUN   Buena Vista, 1991

JAMES BURROWS*

b. December 30, 1940 - Los Angeles, California
Agent: Bob Broder, Broder-Kurland-Webb-Uffner Agency -
  Beverly Hills, 310/281-3400

MORE THAN FRIENDS (TF)   Reiner-Mishkin Productions/
  Columbia TV, 1978
PARTNERS   Paramount, 1982

TIM BURSTALL

b. April 20, 1929 - Stockton-on-Tees, England
Home: 148 Nichols Street, Fitzroy, Victoria 3065, Australia
Agent: ICM - Beverly Hills, 310/550-4000

TWO THOUSAND WEEKS   Eltham Film Productions/Senior Film
  Productions, 1968, Australian
STORK   Tim Burstall & Associates/Bilcock & Copping Film
  Productions, 1971
LIBIDO   co-director with John B. Murray, Fred Schepisi &
  David Baker, Producers and Directors Guild of Australia,
  1973, Australian
ALVIN PURPLE   Hexagon Productions, 1974, Australian
PETERSEN   Hexagon Productions, 1974, Australian
END PLAY   Hexagon Productions, 1975, Australian
ELIZA FRASER   Hexagon Productions, 1976, Australian
THE LAST OF THE KNUCKLEMEN   1978, Australian
ATTACK FORCE Z   John McCallum Productions/Central Motion
  Picture Corporation, 1980, Australian-Taiwanese
DUET FOR FOUR   Greater Union, 1981, Australian
A DESCANT FOR GOSSIPS (MS)   1983, Australian
THE NAKED COUNTRY   Naked Country Productions,
  1984, Australian
KANGAROO   Cineplex Odeon, 1986, Australian
GREAT EXPECTATIONS - THE UNTOLD STORY   Hemdale,
  1987, Australian
NIGHTMARE AT BITTER CREEK (TF)   Swanton Films/
  Guber-Peters Entertainment Company/Phoenix
  Entertainment Group, 1988

GEOFF BURTON

Contact: Australian Film Commission, 150 William Street,
  Woolloomooloo, NSW 2011, Australia, tel.: 2/321-6444

THE SUM OF US   co-director with Kevin Dowling, The Samuel
  Goldwyn Company, 1994, Australian

TIM BURTON*

b. 1960 - Burbank, California
Agent: CAA - Beverly Hills, 310/288-4545

PEE-WEE'S BIG ADVENTURE   Warner Bros., 1985
BEETLEJUICE   The Geffen Company/Warner Bros., 1988
BATMAN   Warner Bros., 1989
EDWARD SCISSORHANDS   20th Century Fox, 1990
BATMAN RETURNS   Warner Bros., 1992
ED WOOD   Buena Vista, 1994

JOHN A. BUSHELMAN*

Home: 11972 Sunshine Terrace, Studio City, CA 91604,
  818/760-7575

SNIPERS RIDGE   20th Century-Fox, 1961
THE SILENT CALL   20th Century-Fox, 1961
BROKEN LAND   20th Century-Fox, 1962
DAY OF THE NITEMARE   Governor, 1965
CRUISIN' HIGH   Gamma III, 1975
HIGH SEAS HIJACK   Toho/Pine-Thomas Productions,
  1976, Japanese-U.S.

WILLIAM BUSHNELL, JR.

Home: 2751 Pelham Place, Los Angeles, CA 90068,
  213/469-1517
Personal Manager: Harvey Shotz, The Shotz Group - Los Angeles,
  213/659-4030

PRISONERS   1973
THE FOUR DEUCES   Avco Embassy, 1974

GEORGE BUTLER

Business: White Mountain Films, 165 East 80th Street,
  New York, NY 10021

PUMPING IRON (FD)   co-director with Robert Fiore,
  Cinema 5, 1977
PUMPING IRON II: THE WOMEN (FD)   Cinecom, 1985
IN THE BLOOD (FD)   White Mountain Films, 1989

ROBERT BUTLER*

b. November 17, 1927 - Los Angeles, California
Agent: William Morris Agency - Beverly Hills, 310/859-4000

THE COMPUTER WORE TENNIS SHOES   Buena Vista, 1970
THE BAREFOOT EXECUTIVE   Buena Vista, 1971
SCANDALOUS JOHN   Buena Vista, 1971
DEATH TAKES A HOLIDAY (TF)   Universal TV, 1971
NOW YOU SEE HIM, NOW YOU DON'T   Buena Vista, 1972
THE BLUE KNIGHT (TF) ☆   Lorimar Productions, 1973
THE ULTIMATE THRILL   General Cinema, 1974
STRANGE NEW WORLD (TF)   Warner Brothers TV, 1975
DARK VICTORY (TF)   Universal TV, 1976
JAMES DEAN (TF)   The Jozak Company, 1976
MAYDAY AT 40,000 FEET (TF)   Andrew J. Fenady Associates/
  Warner Brothers TV, 1976
IN THE GLITTER PALACE (TF)   The Writer's Company/
  Columbia TV, 1977
HOT LEAD AND COLD FEET   Buena Vista, 1978
A QUESTION OF GUILT (TF)   Lorimar Productions, 1978
LACY AND THE MISSISSIPPI QUEEN (TF)   Lawrence Gordon
  Productions/Paramount TV, 1978
NIGHT OF THE JUGGLER   Columbia, 1980
UNDERGROUND ACES   Filmways, 1981
UP THE CREEK   Orion, 1983
CONCRETE BEAT (TF)   Picturemaker Productions/
  Viacom, 1984
MOONLIGHTING (TF)   Picturemaker Productions/ABC Circle
  Films, 1985
OUR FAMILY HONOR (TF)   Lawrence Gordon-Charles Gordon
  Productions/Lorimar Productions, 1985
LONG TIME GONE (TF)   Picturemaker Productions/ABC Circle
  Films, 1986
OUT ON A LIMB (MS)   Stan Margulies Company/ABC Circle
  Films, 1987
OUT OF TIME (TF)   Columbia TV, 1988
LOIS & CLARK: THE NEW ADVENTURES OF SUPERMAN (TF) ☆
  Roundelay Productions/Warner Bros. TV, 1993
WHITE MILE (CTF)   HBO Pictures/Stonehenge
  Productions, 1994

HENDEL BUTOY

Business: Walt Disney Animation, 500 S. Buena Vista Street,
  Burbank, CA 91521, 818/560-1000

THE RESCUERS DOWN UNDER (AF)   co-director with
  Michael Gabriel, Buena Vista, 1990
FANTASIA CONTINUED (AF)   co-director with George Scribner &
  Scott Johnston, Buena Vista, 1997

ZANE BUZBY*

Agent: UTA - Beverly Hills, 310/273-6700
Manager: Conan Berkeley, Honeyland Productions, 3446 Troy Drive,
  Los Angeles, CA 90068, 213/876-5566

LAST RESORT   Concorde/Cinema Group, 1986

DAVID BYRNE
b. May 14, 1952 - Dumbarton, Scotland
Contact: Gary Kurfirst Management - New York, 212/957-0900

TRUE STORIES   Warner Bros., 1986
BETWEEN THE TEETH (PF)   co-director with David Wild,
   Playdate/Theatre, 1994

JOHN BYRNE
Agent: Harriet Cruickshank, Cruikshank Cazenove Ltd. - London,
   tel.: 171/735-2933
Contact: British Film Commission, 70 Baker Street, London
   W1M 1DJ, England, tel.: 171/224-5000

BOSWELL & JOHNSON - A TOUR OF THE WESTERN ISLES (TF)
   Paravision/BBC, 1993, British

JOHN BYRUM*
b. March 14, 1947 - Evanston, Illinois
Agent: CAA - Beverly Hills, 310/288-4545

INSERTS   United Artists, 1976, British
HEART BEAT   Orion/Warner Bros, 1980
THE RAZOR'S EDGE   Columbia, 1984
THE WHOOPEE BOYS   Paramount, 1986
MURDER IN HIGH PLACES (TF)   Stan Rogow Productions/NBC
   Productions, 1991

C

JAMES CAAN*
b. March 26, 1939 - New York, New York
Business Manager: Marty Licker, Nugit and Licker,
   11999 San Vicente Blvd. - Suite 460, Los Angeles, CA 90049,
   310/472-8900

HIDE IN PLAIN SIGHT   MGM/United Artists, 1980

ELLEN CABOT
(See David DeCOTEAU)

SERGIO CABRERA
Contact: Fundacion Patrimonio Colombiano, Carrera 13 No. 13-24,
   piso 9, Bogota, Colombia, tel.: 57-1/281-5241 or 57-1/283-6495

DUELING TECHNIQUES   1988, Colombian
EL ESTRATEGIA DEL CARACOL   FOCINE/Crear TV/Producciones
   Fotograma, 1992, Colombian
AGUILAS NO CAZAN MOSCOS   Caracol TV/Producciones
   Fotograma/Emme, 1994, Colombian-Italian

MICHAEL CACOYANNIS
(Mikhalis Kakogiannis)
b. June 11, 1922 - Limassol, Cyprus
Address: 15 Mousson Street, Koukaki, Athens 115 24, Greece
Contact: Greek Film Centre, 10 Panepistimiou Avenue,
   Athens 106 71, Greece, tel.: 01/363-1733 or 01/363-4586

WINDFALL IN ATHENS   Audio Brandon, 1953, Greek
STELLA   Milas Films, 1955, Greek
THE FINAL LIE   Finos Films, 1958, Greek
OUR LAST SPRING   Cacoyannis, 1959, Greek
A GIRL IN BLACK   Kingsley International, 1959, Greek
THE WASTREL   Lux/Tiberia, 1960, Italian
ELECTRA   Lopert, 1962, Greek
ZORBA THE GREEK ★   International Classics, 1964, Greek

THE DAY THE FISH CAME OUT   20th Century-Fox,
   1967, British-Greek
THE TROJAN WOMEN   Cinerama Releasing Corporation,
   1971, U.S.-Greek
THE STORY OF JACOB AND JOSEPH (TF)   Screen Gems/
   Columbia TV, 1974
ATTILA '74 (FD)   1975, Greek
IPHIGENIA   Cinema 5, 1977, Greek
SWEET COUNTRY   Cinema Group, 1987, Greek
UP, DOWN AND SIDEWAYS   Michael Cacoyannis Films,
   1993, Greek

MICHAEL CAFFEY*
Agent: Shapiro-Lichtman Talent Agency - Los Angeles, 310/859-8877

SEVEN IN DARKNESS (TF)   Paramount TV, 1969
THE SILENT GUN (TF)   Paramount TV, 1969
THE DEVIL AND MISS SARAH (TF)   Universal TV, 1971
THE HANGED MAN (TF)   Fenady Associates/Bing Crosby
   Productions, 1974
MacGYVER: LEGEND OF THE HOLY ROSE (TF)   co-director with
   Charles Correll, Henry Winkler-John Rich Productions/
   Paramount TV, 1989

CHRISTOPHER CAIN*
b. October 29, 1943 - Sioux Falls, South Dakota
Agent: ICM - Beverly Hills, 310/550-4000

BROTHER, MY SONG   Eagle International, 1976
GRAND JURY   CCF, 1976
THE BUZZARD   CCF, 1976
SIXTH AND MAIN   National Cinema, 1977
THE STONE BOY   TLC Films/20th Century Fox, 1984
THAT WAS THEN...THIS IS NOW   Paramount, 1985
WHERE THE RIVER RUNS BLACK   MGM/UA, 1986
THE PRINCIPAL   TriStar, 1987
YOUNG GUNS   20th Century Fox, 1988
WHEELS OF TERROR (CTF)   Once Upon A Time Productions/
   Wilshire Court Productions, 1990
LAKOTA MOON (TF)   FBC, 1992
PURE COUNTRY   Warner Bros., 1992
THE NEXT KARATE KID   Columbia, 1994
THE AMAZING PANDA ADVENTURE   Warner Bros.,
   1995, Canadian-Chinese

GERALD CAIN
DUST TO DUST   Water Hole Gang, 1994

SIMON CALLOW
Address: c/o Pamela Brooke, Brebner Allen Trapp, 180 Wardour
   Street, London W1V 3AA, England, tel.: 171/413-0869
Agent: Harriet Cruickshank - London, tel.: 171/735-2933

THE BALLAD OF THE SAD CAFE   Angelika Films,
   1991, U.S.-British

JAMES CAMERON*
b. August 16, 1954 - Kapuskasing, Ontario, Canada
Contact: Bert Fields, Greenberg, Glusker, Fields, Claman &
   Machtinger - Los Angeles, 310/553-3610
Business: Lightstorm Entertainment, 919 Santa Monica Blvd.,
   Santa Monica, CA 90401, 310/587-2500

PIRANHA II - THE SPAWNING   Saturn International,
   1983, Italian-U.S.
THE TERMINATOR   Orion, 1984
ALIENS   20th Century Fox, 1986
THE ABYSS   20th Century Fox, 1989
TERMINATOR 2: JUDGMENT DAY   TriStar, 1991
TRUE LIES   20th Century Fox, 1994

JULIA CAMERON
GOD'S WILL   Power and Light Productions, 1989

KEN CAMERON

Agent: Becsey/Wisdom/Kalajian - Los Angeles, 310/550-0535 or:
ICM - London, tel.: 171/636-6565
Business: Pavilion Films, 117 Blues Point Road, McMahons Point,
NSW Australia 2060, tel.: 02/92-8358

MONKEY GRIP   Cinecom, 1982, Australian
CRIME OF THE DECADE (TF)   1984, Australian
FAST TALKING   Cinecom, 1985, Australian
THE GOOD WIFE   Atlantic Releasing Corporation, 1986, Australian
STRINGER (TF)   co-director with Chris Thomson & Kathy Mueller,
Australian Broadcasting Corporation/Televenture Film Productions,
1988, Australian-British
THE CLEAN MACHINE (TF)   Kennedy Miller Productions,
1988, Australian
BANGKOK HILTON (MS)   Kennedy Miller Productions,
1989, Australian
BRIDES OF CHRIST (MS)   Roadshow, Coote & Carroll/Australian
Broadcasting Corporation/Radio Telefis Eireann/Channel 4,
1991, Australian-Irish-British
OLDEST LIVING CONFEDERATE WIDOW TELLS ALL (TF)
RHI Entertainment/Konigsberg-Sanitsky Company, 1994

DONALD CAMMELL*

Home: 9 Rue Delambre, Paris 14, France
Agent: William Morris Agency - Beverly Hills, 310/859-4000

PERFORMANCE   co-director with Nicolas Roeg, Warner Bros.,
1970, British
DEMON SEED   MGM/United Artists, 1977
WHITE OF THE EYE   Palisades Entertainment, 1987, British
THE WILD SIDE   Langley Productions, 1995

JOE CAMP*

b. April 20, 1939 - St. Louis, Missouri
Business: Mulberry Square Productions, Inc., 516B Courthouse
Road, Gulfport, MS 39507, 601/897-2777

BENJI   Mulberry Square, 1974
HAWMPS   Mulberry Square, 1976
FOR THE LOVE OF BENJI   Mulberry Square, 1978
THE DOUBLE McGUFFIN   Mulberry Square, 1979
OH HEAVENLY DOG   20th Century-Fox, 1980
BENJI THE HUNTED   Buena Vista, 1987

JUAN JOSE CAMPANELLA

b. Argentina
Business: Pilgrims 3 Corporation, 173 East 64th Street,
New York, NY 10021, 212/861-0696
Agent: William Morris Agency - Beverly Hills, 310/859-4000

THE BOY WHO CRIED BITCH   Pilgrims 3 Corporation, 1991
MORE THAN FRIENDS: THE COMING OUT OF
HEIDI LEITER (CTF)   Turtleback Productions/
Entertainment Group, 1994

ROY CAMPANELLA II*

Address: 256 S. Robertson Blvd., Beverly Hills, CA 90211,
310/652-6452
Agent: William Morris Agency - Beverly Hills, 310/859-4000

PASSION AND MEMORY (TD)   Morningstar Productions, 1986
BODY OF EVIDENCE (TF)   CBS Entertainment, 1988
QUIET VICTORY: THE CHARLIE WEDEMEYER STORY (TF)
The Landsburg Company, 1988
BROTHER FUTURE (TF)   Laneuville-Morris Entertainment, 1991

DOUG CAMPBELL

Agent: Carl Belfor Entertainment Management Company -
Sherman Oaks, 818/994-8095

SEASON OF FEAR   MGM/UA, 1989
ZAPPED AGAIN   ITC Entertainment Group, 1990
OUT OF THE DARKNESS   Cedar Creek Productions, 1995

GRAEME CAMPBELL

b. 1954 - Montreal, Quebec, Canada
Home: 155-1/2 Euclid Avenue, Toronto, Ontario M6J 2J8, Canada,
416/368-2627
Agent: Stone Manners Agency - Los Angeles, 213/654-7575

INTO THE FIRE   Moviestore Entertainment, 1987, Canadian
MURDER ONE   Miramax Films, 1988, Canadian
BLOOD RELATIONS   Miramax Films, 1988, Canadian
STILL LIFE   SC Entertainment, 1989, U.S.-Canadian
DEADLY BETRAYAL: THE BRUCE CURTIS STORY (TF)
Atlantis Films Ltd./Citadel Films, 1990, Canadian
MAN IN THE ATTIC (TF)   Donald March Productions,
1994, U.S.-Canadian
THE DISAPPEARANCE OF VONNIE (TF)   Morrow-Heus
Productions/TriStar TV, 1994
MAN IN THE ATTIC (CTF)   Atlantis Films/Donald March
Productions/CBS Entertainment/Showtime,
1995, Canadian-U.S.
DEADLOCKED: ESCAPE FROM ZONE 14 (TF)   Pacific Motion
Pictures/Spectator Films/Jaffe-Braunstein Films/Signboard Hill
Productions, 1995, U.S.-Canadian

MARTIN CAMPBELL

b. New Zealand
Agent: ICM - Beverly Hills, 310/550-4000

MUCK & BRASS (TF)   Central TV, 1979
REILLY - ACE OF SPIES (MS)   co-director with Jim Goddard,
Euston Films Ltd., 1981, British
CHARLIE (MS)   Central TV, 1983, British
EDGE OF DARKNESS (MS)   BBC/Lionheart Television International,
1985, British
FRANKIE & JOHNNY (TF)   BBC, 1985, British
CRIMINAL LAW   Hemdale, 1988
DEFENSELESS   Seven Arts/New Line Cinema, 1991
CAST A DEADLY SPELL (CTF)   HBO Pictures/Pacific Western
Productions, 1991
NO ESCAPE   Savoy Pictures, 1994, U.S.-Australian
GOLDENEYE   MGM-UA, 1995, British-U.S.

NICHOLAS CAMPBELL

Contact: Directors Guild of Canada, 225 Richmond Street, Toronto,
Ontario M5V 1W2, Canada, 416/351-8200

STEPPING RAZOR - RED X (FD)   SC Entertainment,
1992, Canadian

NORMAN CAMPBELL

b. 1924 - Los Angeles, California
Address: 20 George Henry Blvd., Willowdale, Ontario M2J 1E2,
Canada, 416/494-8576
Business: CBC, Box 500, Station A, Toronto, Ontario M5W 1E6,
Canada, 416/975-6877

THE MAGIC SHOW   Producers Distributing Company,
1983, Canadian

ANNA CAMPION

Contact: New Zealand Film Commission, P.O. Box 11-546,
Wellington, New Zealand, tel.: 4/385-9754

LOADED   Miramax Films, 1994, British-New Zealand

JANE CAMPION

b. April 30, 1954 - Wellington, New Zealand
Agent: CAA - Beverly Hills, 310/288-4545

TWO FRIENDS (TF)   Australian Broadcasting Corporation,
1986, Australian
SWEETIE   Avenue Pictures, 1989, Australian
AN ANGEL AT MY TABLE   Fine Line Cinema/New Line Cinema,
1990, New Zealand, originally filmed for television
THE PIANO ★   Miramax Films, 1993, New Zealand-French

MICHAEL CAMPUS*
Contact: Directors Guild of America - Los Angeles, 213/851-3671

Z.P.G.   Paramount, 1972
THE MACK   Cinerama Releasing Corporation, 1973
THE EDUCATION OF SONNY CARSON   Paramount, 1974
THE PASSOVER PLOT   Atlas, 1977, U.S.-Israeli

MARIO CAMUS
Contact: Spanish Film Institute, San Marcos 40, Madrid 28004,
   Spain, tel.: 1/532-5089

CON EL VIENTO SOLANO   1965, Spanish
LOS PAJAROS DE BADEN-BADEN   1974, Spanish
LA COLMENA   Agata Films, 1982, Spanish
GUERILLA - LOS DESASTRES DE LA GUERRA   1983, Spanish
THE HOLY INNOCENTS   The Samuel Goldwyn Company,
   1986, Spanish
LA CASA DE BERNALOA ALBA   1987, Spanish
LA RUSA   Pedro Maso Productions, 1988, Spanish
LA FORJA DE UN REBELDE (MS)   RTVE/Beta Film,
   1990, Spanish-West German
DESPUES DEL SUENO   Sogetel/Altea Films/Anola Films,
   1992, Spanish
SOMBRAS EN UNA BATALLA   Cayo Largo Films,
   1993, Spanish
AMOR PROPRIO   Sogetel, 1994, Spanish

ALEX CANAWATI
INEVITABLE GRACE   SilverStar Pictures, 1994

DANNY CANNON
Agent: William Morris Agency - Beverly Hills, 310/859-4000

THE YOUNG AMERICANS   Gramercy Pictures, 1993, British
JUDGE DREDD   Buena Vista, 1995, U.S.-British

DYAN CANNON*
(Samille Diane Friesen)
b. January 4, 1937 - Tacoma, Washington
Agent: ICM - Beverly Hills, 310/550-4000

THE END OF INNOCENCE   Skouras Pictures, 1990

ELLIOT CAPLAN
CAGE/CUNNINGHAM (FD)   October Films, 1992

BERNT CAPRA
Home: 3712 Rodeo Grounds, Malibu, CA 90265, 310/456-6112

MINDWALK   Triton Pictures, 1990

LEOS CARAX
(Alexandre Dupont)
b. 1960 - Suresnes, France
Agent: ICM - Beverly Hills, 310/550-4000

BOY MEETS GIRL   Cinecom/M&R, 1984, French
MAUVAIS SANG   AAA, 1986, French
LES AMANTS DU PONT NEUF   Gaumont, 1991, French

LAMAR CARD*
b. September 8, 1942 - Lookout Mountain, Tennessee
Business: Blue Ridge/Filmtrust, 10490 Santa Monica Blvd.,
   Los Angeles, CA 90025, 310/474-6688

THE CLONES   Premiere International, 1977
SUPERVAN   New World, 1980
DISCO FEVER   Group 1, 1982
TECHNO-FEAR   SGE Entertainment, 1994

JACK CARDIFF
b. September 18, 1914 - Yarmouth, Norfolk, England
Home: 32 Woodland Rise, London N10, England
Agent: Eric L'Epine Smith - London, tel: 171/724-0739

WEB OF EVIDENCE   *BEYOND THIS PLACE*   Allied Artists,
   1959, British
INTENT TO KILL   20th Century-Fox, 1959, British
HOLIDAY IN SPAIN   1960, British
SCENT OF MYSTERY   Todd, 1960, British
SONS AND LOVERS ★   20th Century-Fox, 1960, British
MY GEISHA   Paramount, 1962
THE LION   20th Century-Fox, 1962, British
THE LONG SHIPS   Columbia, 1964, British-Yugoslavian
YOUNG CASSIDY   MGM, 1965, British
THE LIQUIDATOR   MGM, 1966, British
DARK OF THE SUN   *THE MERCENARIES*   MGM, 1968, British
THE GIRL ON A MOTORCYCLE   *NAKED UNDER LEATHER*
   Claridge, 1968, British-French
PENNY GOLD   Scotia-Barber, 1973, British
THE MUTATIONS   Columbia, 1974, British

J.S. CARDONE
(Joseph S. Cardone)
Agent: Circle Talent Associates - Beverly Hills, 310/285-1585

THE SLAYER   21st Century Distribution, 1982
THUNDER ALLEY   Cannon, 1985
SHADOWZONE   JGM Enterprises, 1990
A ROW OF CROWS   Propaganda Films, 1991
ROPE OF SAND   Republic Pictures, 1992
SHADOWHUNTER (CTF)   Republic Pictures/Sandstorm Films, 1993

JOHN (BUD) CARDOS*
Agent: Gerald K. Smith Associates, P.O. Box 7430, Burbank,
   CA 91510, 818/849-5388

SOUL SOLDIER   *THE RED, WHITE AND BLACK*   Fanfare, 1972
DRAG RACER   Robert Glenn Productions, 1974
KINGDOM OF THE SPIDERS   Dimension, 1977
THE DARK   Film Ventures International, 1979
THE DAY TIME ENDED   Compass International, 1979
OTHER REALMS   CKE International, 1983
NIGHT SHADOWS   *MUTANT*   Artists Releasing Corporation/
   Film Ventures International, 1984
SKELETON COAST   Silvertree Pictures/Walanar Group/Breton
   Film Productions, 1988, British
OUTLAW OF GOR   Cannon, 1989, U.S.-British
ACT OF PIRACY   Blossom Pictures, 1990, U.S.-South African

TOPPER CAREW*
(Colin Anthony Carew)
b. July 16, 1943 - Boston, Massachusetts
Address: 211 S. Valley Street, Toluca Lake, CA 91602

BREAKIN' & ENTERIN'   Rainbow TV Works, 1985
TALKIN' DIRTY AFTER DARK   New Line Cinema, 1991

GILLES CARLE
b. 1929 - Maniwaki, Quebec, Canada
Business: Films Gilles Carle Inc., 318 Carre St.-Louis, Montreal,
   Quebec H2X 1A5, Canada, 514/282-1326

LA VIE HEUREUSE DE LEOPOLD Z   NFB, 1965, Canadian
PLACE A OLIVIER GUIMOND   Onyx Films, 1966, Canadian
PLACE AUX JEROLAS   Onyx Films, 1967, Canadian
LE VIOL D'UNE JEUNE FILLE DOUCE   Onyx-Fournier,
   1968, Canadian
RED   Onyx Films/SMA, 1970, Canadian
LES MALES   Onyx Films/France Films, 1970, Canadian
LES CHEVALIERS   COFCI/ORTF, 1972, Canadian
LE VRAIE NATURE DE BERNADETTE   Les Productions
   Carle-Lamy, 1972, Canadian
LES CORPS CELESTES   Les Productions Carle-Lamy,
   1973, Canadian
LA MORT D'UN BUCHERON   Les Productions Carle-Lamy,
   1973, Canadian

LA TETE DE NORMANDE ST. ONGE   Les Productions
    Carle-Lamy, 1975, Canadian
THE ANGEL AND THE WOMAN   RSL Productions,
    1977, Canadian
NORMANDE   Fred Baker Films, 1979, Canadian
FANTASTICA   Les Productions du Verseau/El Productions,
    1980, Canadian-French
THE PLOUFFE FAMILY   ICC/Cine-London Productions,
    1981, Canadian
THE GREAT CHESS MOVIE (FD)   co-director with Camille Coudari,
    1982, Canadian
MARIA CHAPDELAINE   The Movie Store,
    1983, Canadian-French
THE CRIME OF OVIDE PLOUFFE   co-director with Denys Arcand,
    ICC/Filmax/Antenne-2/Films A2, 1985, Canadian-French
MURDER IN THE FAMILY (MS)   co-director with Denys Arcand,
    ICC/Filmax/Antenne-2/Films A2, 1985, Canadian-French
O PICASSO (TD)   Films Transit, 1985, Canadian
SCALP   Via Le Monde Gilles Carle, 1985, Canadian
LA GUEPE   Via Le Monde Francois Floquet, 1986, Canadian
QUEBEC, UN VILLE (FD)   Les Productions Dix-Huit/Films
    Francois Brault, 1988, Canadian
LE DIABLE D'AMERIQUE (FD)   Productions D'Amerique Francaise/
    National Film Board of Canada/P.A.F., 1990, Canadian
LA POSTIERE   Aska Film International/Telefilm Canada/La Societe
    Generale des Industries Culturelles - Quebec/Super Ecran,
    1992, Canadian
MISS MOSCOU (TF)   Cineroux/TV Suisse Romande,
    1992, Canadian-Swiss
BLOOD OF THE HUNTER   Trimark Pictures, 1994, Canadian

CARLO CARLEI

Agent: ICM - Beverly Hills, 310/550-4000

THE FLIGHT OF THE INNOCENT   Rocket Pictures, 1991, Italian
FLUKE   MGM-UA, 1995

LEWIS JOHN CARLINO*
b. January 1, 1932 - New York, New York
Agent: CAA - Beverly Hills, 310/288-4545

THE SAILOR WHO FELL FROM GRACE WITH THE SEA
    Avco Embassy, 1976, British
THE GREAT SANTINI   THE ACE   Orion/Warner Bros., 1980
CLASS   Orion, 1983

HENNING CARLSEN
b. June 4, 1927 - Aalborg, Jutland, Denmark
Contact: Danish Film Institute, Store Soendervoldstraede 4,
    DK-1419 Copenhagen K, Denmark, tel.: 31-57-65-00

DILEMMA   A WORLD OF STRANGERS   Minerva Film/Bent
    Christensen Filmproduktion, 1962, Danish
EPILOGUE   Bent Christensen Filmproduktion/Constantin Films,
    1963, Danish
THE CATS   National Showmanship, 1964, Swedish
HUNGER   Sigma III, 1966, Danish-Norwegian-Swedish
PEOPLE MEET AND SWEET MUSIC FILLS THE HEART
    Trans-Lux, 1967, Danish-Swedish
WE ARE ALL DEMONS   Nordisk Film/Sandrews/Teamfilm/
    Henning Carlsen Film, 1969, Danish-Swedish-Norwegian
ARE YOU AFRAID?   Henning Carlsen Film, 1971, Danish
OH, TO BE ON THE BANDWAGON!   Henning Carlsen Film/
    Nordisk, 1972, Danish
A HAPPY DIVORCE   CFDC, 1975, French-Danish
WHEN SVANTE DISAPPEARED   Dagmar Filmproduktion,
    1976, Danish
DID SOMEBODY LAUGH?   Dagmar Filmproduktion/Sam-Film,
    1978, Danish
YOUR MONEY OR YOUR LIFE   Dagmar Filmproduktion,
    1982, Danish
THE WOLF AT THE DOOR   OVIRI   International Film Marketing,
    1986, Danish-French
TWO GREEN FEATHERS   Northern Light Productions/Zentropa
    Entertainment/Dagmar Film/Multimedia, 1995,
    Norwegian-Danish-German

MARCEL CARNE
b. August 18, 1909 - Paris, France
Agent: Cineart, 16, rue de Marignan, 75008 Paris, France,
    tel.: 1/42-56-35-74
Contact: French Film Office, 745 Fifth Avenue, New York,
    NY 10151, 212/832-8860

NOGENT - ELDORADO DU DIMANCHE (FD)   co-director with
    Michel Sanvoisin, 1929, French
JENNY   1936, French
BIZARRE BIZARRE   DROLE DE DRAME   1937, French
PORT OF SHADOWS   Film Alliance, 1938, French
HOTEL DU NORD   1938, French
DAYBREAK   LE JOUR SE LEVE   Vog, 1939, French
THE DEVIL'S ENVOYS   LES VISITEURS DU SOIR   1942, French
CHILDREN OF PARADISE   Tricolore, 1945, French,
    re-released in 1991 by Films Inc./Entertainment
LES PORTES DE LA NUIT   1946, French
LA MARIE DU PORT   1950, French
JULIETTE OU LA CLE DES SONGES   1951, French
THE ADULTRESS   THERESE RAQUIN   Times Film Corporation,
    1953, French
L'AIR DE PARIS   1954, French
LE PAYS D'OU JE VIENS   1956, French
THE CHEATERS   Continental, 1958, French-Italian
TERRAIN VAGUE   1960, French
DU MOURON POUR LES PETITS OISEAUX   1963, French
TROIS CHAMBRES A MANHATTAN   1965, French
LES JEUNES LOUPS   1968, French
LES ASSASSINS DE L'ORDRE   1971, French
LA MARVEILLEUSE VISITE   1974, French
LA BIBLE (FD)   1976, French
MOUCHE   Alert Film/v. Vietinghoff Film/Erato Film/Italfrance
    Films/S.A.R.L./Filmalpha/Filmstiftung Nordrhein-Westfalen,
    1993, Italian-French-German

CHARLES ROBERT CARNER*
Address: 1855 Westridge Road, Los Angeles, CA 90049,
    310/471-2758
Agent: CAA - Beverly Hills, 310/288-4545

A KILLER AMONG FRIENDS (TF)   Bonnie Raskin Productions/
    Green-Epstein Productions/Lorimar TV, 1992
ONE WOMAN'S COURAGE (TF)   Bonnie Raskin Productions/NBC
    Productions, 1994

MARC CARO
Contact: French Film Office, 745 Fifth Avenue, New York, NY 10151,
    212/832-8860

DELICATESSEN   co-director with Jean-Pierre Jeunet, Miramax
    Films, 1991, French
THE CITY OF LOST CHILDREN   co-director with Jean-Pierre Jeunet,
    Sony Pictures Classics, 1995, French

GLENN GORDON CARON*
Agent: CAA - Beverly Hills, 310/288-4545

CLEAN AND SOBER   Warner Bros., 1988
WILDER NAPALM   TriStar, 1993
LOVE AFFAIR   Warner Bros., 1994

JOHN CARPENTER*
b. January 16, 1948 - Carthage, New York
Agent: ICM - Beverly Hills, 310/550-4000

DARK STAR   Jack H. Harris Enterprises, 1974
ASSAULT ON PRECINCT 13   Turtle Releasing Corporation, 1976
HALLOWEEN   Compass International, 1978
SOMEONE IS WATCHING ME (TF)   Warner Bros. TV, 1978
ELVIS (TF)   Dick Clark Productions, 1979
THE FOG   Avco Embassy, 1981
ESCAPE FROM NEW YORK   Avco Embassy, 1981
THE THING   Universal, 1982
CHRISTINE   Columbia, 1983
STARMAN   Columbia, 1984
BIG TROUBLE IN LITTLE CHINA   20th Century Fox, 1986

PRINCE OF DARKNESS   Universal, 1987
THEY LIVE   Universal, 1988
MEMOIRS OF AN INVISIBLE MAN   Warner Bros., 1992
IN THE MOUTH OF MADNESS   New Line Cinema, 1995
VILLAGE OF THE DAMNED   Universal, 1995

STEPHEN CARPENTER
Contact: Linda Lichter, Lichter, Grossman & Nichols - Los Angeles,
310/205-6999

THE DORM THAT DRIPPED BLOOD *PRANKS* co-director with
Jeffrey Obrow, Artists Releasing Corporation/Film Ventures
International, 1982
THE POWER   co-director with Jeffrey Obrow, Artists Releasing
Corporation/Film Ventures International, 1983
THE KINDRED   co-director with Jeffrey Obrow,
FM Entertainment, 1987

FABIO CARPI
b. January 19, 1925
Home: via di Propaganda 27, Rome, Italy, tel.: 06/678-9710

CORPO D'AMORE   R.T.R./Capricorno Film/Julia Cinematografica,
1972, Italian
QUARTETTO BASILEUS   C.E.P./RAI, 1982, Italian
LE AMBIZIONI SBAGLIATE (TF)   RAI, 1982, Italian
I CANI DI GERUSALEMME (TF)   RAI, 1984, Italian
CESARE MUSATTI, MATEMATICO VENEZIANO (FD)   1985, Italian
BARBABLU' BARBABLU'   Point Royal Film/RAI, 1987, Italian
L'AMORE NECESSARIO   Eidoscope International/Cinemax,
1991, Italian-French
LA PROSSIMA VOLTA IL FUOCO   Gam Film/Ministero del
Turismo e dello Spettacolo/Istituto Luce/Erato Film/Frama Film,
1993, Italian-French-Swiss

ADRIAN CARR
THUNDERFOOT   Journey Group Productions/Northwest
Entertainment Group, 1993

TERRY CARR*
Contact: Marty Weiss, 12100 Wilshire Blvd. - Suite 200, Los Angeles,
CA 90025, 310/820-8872

WELCOME TO 18   American Distribution Group, 1986

DAVID CARRADINE*
b. December 8, 1936 - Hollywood, California
Contact: Directors Guild of America - Los Angeles, 213/851-3671

YOU AND ME   Filmmakers International, 1975
AMERICANA   Crown International, 1983

MICHAEL CARRERAS
b. 1927 - London, England
Contact: British Film Commission, 70 Baker Street, London
W1M 1DJ, England, tel.: 171/224-5000

THE STEEL BAYONET   United Artists, 1958, British
PASSPORT TO CHINA *VISA TO CANTON*   Columbia,
1961, British
THE SAVAGE GUNS   MGM, 1962, Spanish-U.S.
MANIAC   Columbia, 1963, British
WHAT A CRAZY WORLD   Warner-Pathe, 1963, British
THE CURSE OF THE MUMMY'S TOMB   Columbia, 1965, British
PREHISTORIC WOMEN *SLAVE GIRLS*   20th Century-Fox,
1967, British
THE LOST CONTINENT   20th Century-Fox, 1968, British
CALL HIM MR. SHATTER   Avco Embassy, 1975,
British-Hong Kong

J. LARRY CARROLL
b. October 7, 1946
Agent: Shapiro-Lichtman Talent Agency - Los Angeles, 310/859-8877

GHOST WARRIOR *SWORDKILL*   Empire Pictures, 1986

ROBERT MARTIN CARROLL
SONNY BOY   Triumph Releasing Corporation, 1990

WILLARD CARROLL
Business: Hyperion Entertainment, 837 Tracton Avenue - Suite 402,
Los Angeles, CA 90013, 213/625-2921
Agent: William Morris Agency - Beverly Hills, 310/859-4000

THE RUNESTONE   Hyperion Pictures/Signature
Communications, 1992

DAVID CARSON*
Business: Mistral Ltd., 10474 Santa Monica Blvd., Los Angeles,
CA 90025, 310/475-0060
Agent: William Morris Agency - Beverly Hills, 310/859-4000

STAR TREK: DEEP SPACE NINE (TF)   Paramount TV, 1992
SHAMEFUL SECRETS (TF)   Steve White Films/ABC, 1993
SOUTH BEACH (TF)   Wolf Films/Universal TV, 1993
STAR TREK GENERATIONS   Paramount, 1994

L.M. 'KIT' CARSON
b. Dallas, Texas
Personal Manager: Hillard Elkins - Los Angeles, 310/285-0700

THE AMERICAN DREAMER   1971

DICK CARTER
DORIS DAY: A SENTIMENTAL JOURNEY (TD)   WTTW/Arwin, 1991

THOMAS CARTER*
Agent: CAA - Beverly Hills, 310/288-4545

TRAUMA CENTER (TF)   Glen A. Larson Productions/Jeremac
Productions/20th Century-Fox TV, 1983
CALL TO GLORY (TF)   Tisch-Avnet Productions/
Paramount TV, 1984
MIAMI VICE (TF)   The Michael Mann Company/Universal TV, 1984
HEART OF THE CITY (TF)   American Flyer TV Ltd./
20th Century Fox TV, 1986
UNDER THE INFLUENCE (TF)   CBS Entertainment, 1986
A YEAR IN THE LIFE (MS)   Universal TV, 1986
EQUAL JUSTICE (TF)   The Thomas Carter Company/
Orion TV, 1990
SWING KIDS   Buena Vista, 1993

STEVE CARVER*
b. April 5, 1945 - Brooklyn, New York
Home: 29 Lighthouse Street - Apt. 2, Marina del Rey, CA 90292,
310/822-9600

THE ARENA   New World, 1974
BIG BAD MAMA   New World, 1974
CAPONE   20th Century-Fox, 1975
DRUM   United Artists, 1976
FAST CHARLIE...THE MOONBEAM RIDER   Universal, 1979
STEEL   LOOK DOWN AND DIE   World Northal, 1980
AN EYE FOR AN EYE   Avco Embassy, 1981
LONE WOLF McQUADE   Orion, 1983
OCEANS OF FIRE (TF)   Catalina Production Group, 1986
JOCKS   Crown International, 1987
BULLETPROOF   CineTel Films, 1987
RIVER OF DEATH   Cannon, 1989, British
CRAZY JOE   21st Century Distribution, 1992
THE WOLVES   Europex, 1993

RON CASDEN*
Home: P.O. Box 2207, Malibu, CA 90265, 213/457-4215
Agent: The Agency - Los Angeles, 310/551-3000

CAMPUS MAN   Paramount, 1987

ALEXANDER CASSINI
STAR TIME   Northern Arts Entertainment, 1993

P. J. CASTELLANETA
TOGETHER ALONE   Frameline, 1992

SERGIO M. CASTILLA
THE GIRL IN THE WATERMELON   Mommy & Daddy
   Productions, 1994

ALIEN CASTLE
DESIRE AND HELL AT SUNSET MOTEL   Two Moon
   Releasing, 1992
STREETWISE   Trimark Pictures, 1993

NICK CASTLE*
b. September 21, 1947 - Los Angeles, California
Address: 760 N. La Cienega Blvd., Los Angeles, CA 90069,
   213/652-0222
Agent: CAA - Beverly Hills, 310/288-4545

TAG   New World, 1982
THE LAST STARFIGHTER   Universal, 1984
THE BOY WHO COULD FLY   20th Century Fox, 1986
TAP   TriStar, 1989
DENNIS THE MENACE   Warner Bros., 1993
MAJOR PAYNE   Universal, 1995

HOITE CASTON*
Home: 3589 Multiview Drive, Los Angeles, CA 90068,
   213/851-0606
Agent: Steve Lewis, The Directors Network, 12401 Ventura Blvd. -
   Suite C, Studio City, CA 91604, 818/506-3696

THE DIRT BIKE KID   Concorde/Cinema Group, 1986

GILBERT CATES*
b. June 6, 1934 - New York, New York
Business: Gilbert Cates Productions, 10920 Wilshire Blvd. -
   Suite 620, Los Angeles, CA 90024, 310/208-2134
Attorney: Harold Brown, Gang, Tyre, Ramer & Brown,
   6400 Sunset Blvd., Los Angeles, CA 90064, 213/463-4863

RINGS AROUND THE WORLD (FD)   Columbia, 1967
I NEVER SANG FOR MY FATHER   Columbia, 1970
TO ALL MY FRIENDS ON SHORE (TF)   Jemmin & Jamel
   Productions, 1972
SUMMER WISHES, WINTER DREAMS   Columbia, 1973
THE AFFAIR (TF)   Spelling-Goldberg Productions, 1973
ONE SUMMER LOVE   DRAGONFLY   American
   International, 1976
JOHNNY, WE HARDLY KNEW YE (TF)   Talent Associates/Jamel
   Productions, 1977
THE PROMISE   Universal, 1979
THE LAST MARRIED COUPLE IN AMERICA   Universal, 1980
OH, GOD! BOOK II   Warner Bros., 1980
COUNTRY GOLD (TF)   CBS Entertainment, 1982
HOBSON'S CHOICE (TF)   CBS Entertainment, 1983
BURNING RAGE (TF)   Gilbert Cates Productions, 1984
CONSENTING ADULT (TF) ☆   Starger Company/David
   Lawrence and Ray Aghayan Productions, 1985
CHILD'S CRY (TF)   Shoot the Moon Enterprises/Phoenix
   Entertainment Group, 1986
BACKFIRE   New Century/Vista, 1987
FATAL JUDGMENT (TF)   Jack Farren Productions/Group W
   Productions, 1988
MY FIRST LOVE (TF)   The Avnet-Kerner Company, 1988
DO YOU KNOW THE MUFFIN MAN? (TF) ☆   The Avnet-Kerner
   Company, 1989
CALL ME ANNA (TF)   Gilbert Cates Productions/Mianna Pearce
   Productions/Finnegan-PinchukProductions, 1990
ABSOLUTE STRANGERS (TF) ☆   Absolute Strangers Co./Gilbert
   Cates Productions, 1991
CONFESSIONS: TWO FACES OF EVIL (TF)   Cates-Doty
   Productions, 1994

JOSEPH CATES*
b. 1924
Business: 136 East 57th Street, New York, NY 10022, 212/644-8700

GIRL OF THE NIGHT   Warner Bros., 1960
WHO KILLED TEDDY BEAR?   Magna, 1965
FAT SPY   Magna, 1966

DON CATO
DIXIE LANES   SC Entertainment, 1987

MICHAEL CATON-JONES*
b. 1958 - Broxburn, Scotland
Agent: CAA - Beverly Hills, 310/288-4545 or:
   Peters Fraser & Dunlop - London, tel.: 71/344-1000

SCANDAL   Miramax Films, 1989, British
MEMPHIS BELLE   Warner Bros., 1990, U.S.-British
DOC HOLLYWOOD   Warner Bros., 1991
THIS BOY'S LIFE   Warner Bros., 1993
ROB ROY   MGM-UA, 1995, British-U.S.

ALAIN CAVALIER
(Alain Fraisse)
b. September 14, 1931 - Vendome, France
Agent: ICM France - Paris, tel.: 1/723-7860
Contact: French Film Office, 745 Fifth Avenue, New York,
   NY 10151, 212/832-8860

LE COMBAT DANS L'ILE   1962, French
L'INSOUMIS   1964, French
MISE A SAC   1967, French
LA CHAMADE   1968, French
LE PLEIN DE SUPER   1976, French
MARTIN ET LEA   1978, French
CE REPONDEUR NE PREND PAS DE MASSAGES   1979, French
THERESE   1986, French
PORTRAITS D'ALAIN CAVALIER   1988, French
LIBERA ME   UGC, 1993, French

LILIANA CAVANI
b. January 12, 1937 - Carpi, Italy
Home: via Filangeri, 4, Rome, Italy, tel: 06/360-1832

FRANCESCO D'ASSISI (TF)   1966, Italian
GALILEO   Fenice Cinematografica/Rizzoli Film/Kinozenter,
   1968, Italian-Bulgarian
THE YEAR OF THE CANNIBALS   I CANNIBALI   American
   International, 1969, Italian
L'OSPITE   1971, Italian
THE NIGHT PORTER   Avco Embassy, 1974, Italian
MILAREPA   Lotar Film, 1974, Italian
BEYOND GOOD AND EVIL   International Showcase, 1977,
   Italian-French-West German
LA PELLE   Triumph/Columbia, 1981, Italian-French
THE SECRET BEYOND THE DOOR   Gaumont, 1982, Italian
THE BERLIN AFFAIR   Cannon, 1985, Italian-West German
FRANCESCO   Karol Film/RAI/Royal Film, 1989,
   Italian-West German
DOVE SIETE? IO SONO QUI   Italian International Film,
   1993, Italian

FELIPE CAZALS
b. 1937 - Mexico City, Mexico
Address: Hera 31, Depto. 401, Colonia Florida, Mexico D.F.
Contact: IMCINE, Tepic #40, P.B. Colonia Roma Sur, Mexico City,
   C.P. 06760, Mexico, tel.: 525/584-7283

LA MANZANA DE LA DISCORDIA   Azteca Films, 1968, Mexican
FAMILIARIDADES   Azteca Films, 1969, Mexican
EMILIANO ZAPATA   Azteca Films, 1970, Mexican
EL JARDIN DE LA TIA ISABEL   Azteca Films, 1971, Mexican
AQUELLOS ANOS   Azteca Films, 1972, Mexican
LOS QUE VIVEN DONDE SOPLA EL VIENTO SUAVE
   Azteca Films, 1973, Mexican

CANOA   Azteca Films, 1975, Mexican
EL APANDO   Azteca Films, 1975, Mexican
LAS POQUIANCHIS   Azteca Films, 1976, Mexican
LA GUERA RODRIGUEZ   Azteca Films, 1977, Mexican
EL ANO DE LA PESTE   Azteca Films, 1978, Mexican
BAJO LA METRALLA   Azteca Films, 1983, Mexican
LOS MOTIVOS DE LUZ   Producciones Chimalistac, 1985, Mexican
CUENTOS DE LA MADRUGATA   Producciones Chimalistac,
   1985, Mexican
EL TRES DE COPAS   Casablanca Films/Conacine, 1987, Mexican
LO DEL CESAR   Casablanca Films/Television Espanola,
   1987, Mexican
KINO   Cineclipse/RTC/IMCINE/Fomento de la Calidad
   Cinematografica/TV Munchen, 1993, Mexican-German

JEFF CELENTANO

Agent: ICM - Beverly Hills, 310/550-4000
Contact: Jersey Born Pictures, 7920 Sunset Blvd., 4th Floor,
   Los Angeles, CA 90046, 213/850-0919

DICK WARD (Short)   1993
UNDER THE HULA MOON   Jersey Born Pictures, 1995

JAMES CELLAN-JONES*

b. July 13, 1931 - Swansea, Wales
Home: 19 Cumberland Road, Surrey TW 9 3HJ, England,
   tel.: 171/940-8742
Agent: Jane Annakin, William Morris Agency - London,
   tel.: 171/434-2191

THE NELSON AFFAIR   *A BEQUEST TO THE NATION*   Universal,
   1973, British
CAESAR AND CLEOPATRA (TF)   NBC-TV, 1976, U.S.-British
SCHOOL PLAY (TF)   BBC, 1979, British
THE DAY CHRIST DIED (TF)   Martin Manulis Productions/20th
   Century-Fox TV, 1980
THE KINGFISHER (TF)   1982, British
A FINE ROMANCE (TF)   1982, British
SLEEPS SIX (TF)   BBC, 1984, British
OXBRIDGE BLUES (TF)   BBC, 1985, British
SLIP-UP (TF)   BBC/Polymuse, 1986, British
FORTUNES OF WAR (MS)   BBC/WGBH-TV/Primetime TV,
   1987, British-U.S.
THE GRAVY TRAIN GOES EAST (TF)   1991, British
MAIGRET (TF)   co-director with John Glenister, Granada TV,
   1991, British
A PERFECT HERO (MS)   Havahall Pictures/London Weekend TV/
   ITV, 1992, British
HARNESSING PEACOCKS (TF)   Meridian Productions,
   1993, British
A CLASS ACT (TF)   1993, British

CLAUDE CHABROL

b. June 24, 1930 - Paris, France
Agent: Voyez Mon Agent - Paris, tel.: 1/47-23-55-80
Contact: French Film Office, 745 Fifth Avenue, New York,
   NY 10151, 212/832-8860

LE BEAU SERGE   United Motion Picture Organization,
   1958, French
THE COUSINS   Films Around the World, 1959, French
LEDA   *WEB OF PASSION/A DOUBLE TOUR*   Times,
   1959, French
LES BONNES FEMMES   Robert Hakim, 1960, French-Italian
LES GODELUREAUX   Cocinor-Marceau, 1961, French-Italian
SEVEN CAPITAL SINS   co-director with Jean-Luc Godard,
   Roger Vadim, Sylvaine Dhomme, Edouard Molinaro,
   Philippe De Broca, Jacques Demy, Marie-Jose Nat,
   Dominique Paturel, Jean-Marc Tennberg & Perrette Pradier,
   Embassy, 1962, French-Italian
L'OEIL DU MALIN   Lux Film, 1962, French-Italian
OPHELIA   New Line Cinema, 1962, French-Italian
LANDRU   Embassy, 1963, French-Italian
LES PLUS BELLES ESCROQUERIES DU MONDE
   co-director, 1964, French-Italian-Japanese
LE TIGRE AIME LA CHAIR FRAICHE   Gaumont,
   1964, French-Italian

PARIS VU PAR...   co-director, 1965, French
MARIE-CHANTAL CONTRE LE DOCTEUR KHA   SNC,
   1965, French-Italian-Moroccan
LE TIGRE SE PARFUME À LA DYNAMITE   Gaumont, 1965,
   French-Spanish-Italian
LA LIGNE DE DEMARCATION   CCFC, 1966, French
THE CHAMPAGNE MURDERS   *LE SCANDALE*   Universal,
   1967, French
LA ROUTE DE CORINTHE   CCFC, 1967,
   French-Italian-West German
LES BICHES   VGC, 1968, French-Italian
LA FEMME INFIDELE   Allied Artists, 1968, French-Italian
THIS MAN MUST DIE   Allied Artists, 1969, French-Italian
LE BOUCHER   Cinerama Releasing Corporation,
   1969, French-Italian
LA RUPTURE   New Line Cinema, 1970, French-Italian-Belgian
JUST BEFORE NIGHTFALL   Libra, 1971, French-Italian
TEN DAYS' WONDER   Levitt-Pickman, 1971, French
HIGH HEELS   *DOCTEUR POPAUL*   Les Films La Boetie,
   1972, French-Italian
WEDDING IN BLOOD   New Line Cinema, 1973, French-Italian
DE GREY - LE BANC DE DESOLATION (TF)   1973, French
THE NADA GANG   *NADA*   New Line Cinema, 1974, French-Italian
UNE PARTIE DE PLAISIR   Joseph Green Pictures, 1975, French
DIRTY HANDS   *LES INNOCENTS AUX MAIN SALES*
   New Line Cinema, 1975, French-Italian-West German
LES MAGICIENS   1975, French
FOLIES BOURGEOISES   FFCM, 1976,
   French-Italian-West German
ALICE OU LA DERNIERE FUGUE   Filmel-PHPG, 1977, French
LES LIENS DE SANG   Filmcorp, 1978, Canadian-French
VIOLETTE   *VIOLETTE NOZIERE*   New Yorker, 1978, French
FANTOMAS (TF)   1979, French
LE CHEVAL D'ORGEUIL   Planfilm, 1980, French
MADAME LE JUGE (TF)   1980, French
LE SYSTEME DU DOCTEUR GOUDRON ET DU PROFESSEUR
   PLUME (TF)   FR3/Films du Triangle/TCV, 1981, French-Mexican
LES AFFINITES ELECTIVES (TF)   FR3/Telecip/Galaxy Film
   Produktion, 1982, French-West German
LA DANSE DE MORT (TF)   FR3/Technisonor/SFP, 1982, French
LES FANTOMES DU CHAPELIER   Gaumont, 1982, French
THE BLOOD OF OTHERS (CMS)   HBO Premiere Films/ICC/
   Filmax Productions, 1984, Canadian-French
POULET AU VINAIGRE   MK2 Difussion, 1985, French
INSPECTEUR LAVARDIN   MK Difussion, 1986, French
MASQUES   MK2/Films A2, 1987, French
THE CRY OF THE OWL   RS/58, 1988, French-Italian
STORY OF WOMEN   MK2 Productions USA/New Yorker,
   1988, French
QUIET DAYS IN CLICHY   AZ Films Produzione/Italfrance/Direkt
   Films, 1990, Italian-French-West German
CLUB EXTINCTION   *DR. M*   NEF Filmproduktion/Ellepi Film/Clea
   Productions/Deutsches Fersehen/La Sept/Telefilm GmbH., 1990,
   West German-Italian-French
MADAME BOVARY   The Samuel Goldwyn Company, 1991, French
BETTY   MK2, 1992, French
L'OEIL DE VICHY (FD)   Bac Films, 1993, French
L'ENFER   MK2 Difussion/CED Productions/France 3 Cinema/
   Cinemanuel/Canal Plus/Procirep/Conseil Regional Midi Pyrenees,
   1994, French

GURINDER CHADHA

b. Kenya
Agent: ICM - London, tel.: 171/636-6565

BHAJI ON THE BEACH   First Look Pictures, 1993, British

YOUSSEF CHAHINE
(Yussef Shahin)

b. January 25, 1926 - Alexandria, Egypt
Business: Misr International, 35 Champolion Street, Cairo, Egypt
Contact: National Film Centre, City of Arts, Al Ahram Avenue, Giza,
   Cairo, Egypt, tel.: 854807

FATHER AMIN   1950   1950
SON OF THE NILE   1951, Egyptian
THE GREAT CLOWN   1951, Egyptian
LADY ON THE TRAIN   1952, Egyptian

WOMEN WITHOUT MEN 1952, Egyptian
STRUGGLE IN THE VALLEY 1953, Egyptian
DEVIL OF THE SAHARA 1954, Egyptian
STRUGGLE ON THE PIER 1955, Egyptian
YOU ARE MY LOVE 1956, Egyptian
FAREWELL TO YOUR LOVE 1957, Egyptian
CAIRO STATION 1958, Egyptian
JAMILA THE ALGERIAN 1958, Egyptian
FOREVER YOURS 1959, Egyptian
IN YOUR HANDS 1960, Egyptian
A LOVER'S CALL 1961, Egyptian
A MAN IN MY LIFE 1961, Egyptian
AN-NASR SALAH AD-DIN 1963, Egyptian
DAWN OF A NEW DAY 1964, Egyptian
THE RING SELLER 1965, Egyptian
SAND OF GOLD 1966, Egyptian
THE LAND 1969, Egyptian
THE CHOICE 1970, Egyptian
PEOPLE OF THE NILE 1972, Egyptian, filmed in 1967
THE SPARROW 1973, Egyptian
THE RETURN OF THE PRODIGAL SON 1975, Egyptian
ALEXANDRIA...WHY? Misr International Films, 1978, Egyptian
AN EGYPTIAN STORY Misr International Films, 1982, Egyptian
AL WEDAA YA BONAPARTE Misr International Films,
    1985, Egyptian
LE SIXTIEME JOUR Misr International Films, 1986, Egyptian
SARIKAT SAYFEYA 1988, Egyptian
ALEXANDRIA AGAIN AND FOREVER Misr International Films/
    Classics Productions/La Sept, 1990, Egyptian-French
CAIRO AS TOLD BY YOUSSEF CHAHINE (FD) Miroir Productions/
    Misr International Films, 1991, French-Egyptian
AL-MOHAGER THE EMIGRANT Misr Interational Films/Ognon
    Pictures/FR3/La Sept-Arte, 1994, Egyptian-French

P. CHALONG
(See Chalong PAKDEEVICHIT)

EVERETT CHAMBERS*
b. August 19, 1926 - Montrose, California
Contact: Directors Guild of America - Los Angeles, 213/851-3671

RUN ACROSS THE RIVER Omat Corporation, 1959
THE LOLLIPOP COVER Continental, 1964

GEORGES CHAMCHOUM
b. July 16, 1946 - Niger
Home: 811 Linda Flora Drive, Bel Air, CA 90049, 310/472-1792

INSIDE-OUT SPLEEN Miziara Films, 1969, Lebanese-French
SALAM...AFTER DEATH Miziara Films, 1972, Lebanese
LEBANON...WHY? Camera 9 Productions,
    1978-80, British-Lebanese
TELL ME LEBANON co-director with Pierre Unia, Unia Films,
    1990, French

GREGG CHAMPION*
Agent: ICM - Beverly Hills, 310/550-4000

SHORT TIME 20th Century Fox, 1990
THE COWBOY WAY Universal, 1994

EVANS CHAN
CROSSINGS Riverdrive Productions, 1994, U.S.-Hong Kong

JACKIE CHAN
(Chen Yuan-Long)
b. 1954 - Hong Kong
Business: c/o Golden Harvest (HK) Ltd., 8 Hammer Hill Road,
    Ngau Chi Wan, Kowloon, Hong Kong, tel.: 352-8222
Contact: Hong Kong Film Liaison, 10940 Wilshire Blvd. - Suite 1220,
    Los Angeles, CA 90024, 310/208-2678

THE FEARLESS HYENA 1979, Hong Kong
YOUNG MASTER Golden Harvest, 1980, Hong Kong
DRAGON LORD Golden Harvest, 1982, Hong Kong

PROJECT A Golden Harvest, 1983, Hong Kong
POLICE STORY Golden Harvest, 1985, Hong Kong
THE ARMOUR OF GOD Golden Harvest, 1986, Hong Kong
PROJECT A (PART II) Golden Harvest/Golden Way Productions,
    1987, Hong Kong
THE BROTHERS Golden Way Productions, 1987, Hong Kong
POLICE STORY - PART II Golden Harvest, 1988, Hong Kong
MR. CANTON AND LADY ROSE Golden Harvest,
    1989, Hong Kong
THE MIRACLE Golden Harvest, 1990, Hong Kong
ARMOUR OF GOD II: OPERATION CONDOR Golden Harvest,
    1991, Hong Kong

PAULINE CHAN
b. Vietnam
Contact: Australian Film Commission, 150 William Street,
    Woolloomooloo NSW 2011, Australia, tel.: 2/321-6444

TRAPS Ronin Films, 1994, Australian

TONY CHAN
Agent: APA - Los Angeles, 310/273-0744

COMBINATION PLATTER Arrow Releasing, 1993

BAE CHANG-HO
b. May 10, 1953 - Taegu, Korea
Contact: Korean Motion Pictures Promotion Corporation, 34-5,
    3KA Namsan-Dong, Chung-Ku, Seoul, South Korea,
    tel.: 755-9291

PEOPLE IN SLUM AREA 1982, South Korean
THE IRON MEN 1982, South Korean
TROPICAL FLOWER 1983, South Korean
WHALE HUNTER 1984, South Korean
WARM IT WAS THAT WINTER Sekyong Enterprise,
    1984, South Korean
DEEP BLUE NIGHT 1984, South Korean
WHALE HUNTER II 1985, South Korean
HWANG JIN-I 1986, South Korean
OUR SWEET DAYS OF YOUTH 1987, South Korean

ROBERT CHAPPELL
OUTRAGE FUGITIVE Rapi Films, 1994, Indonesian

JOE CHAPPELLE
THIEVES QUARTET Headliner Productions, 1994
HALLOWEEN VI Miramax Films, 1995

MATTHEW CHAPMAN*
b. September 2, 1950
Agent: UTA - Los Angeles, 310/373-6700

HUSSY Watchgrove Ltd., 1980, British
STRANGERS KISS Orion Classics, 1984
SLOW BURN (CTF) Joel Schumacher Productions/Universal
    Pay TV, 1986
HEART OF MIDNIGHT Virgin Vision, 1988

MICHAEL CHAPMAN*
b. November 21, 1935 - New York, New York
Agent: David Gersh, The Gersh Agency - Beverly Hills,
    310/274-6611

ALL THE RIGHT MOVES 20th Century-Fox, 1983
THE CLAN OF THE CAVE BEAR Warner Bros., 1986
THE ANNIHILATOR (TF) Universal TV, 1986
ICELANDIC SAGAS New Line Cinema, 1995

MEHDI CHAREF

b. 1952 - Algeria
Address: c/o Ag. M. Lenoir, 99, boulevard Malesherbes, 75008 Paris,
   tel.: 1/45-63-59/20
Contact: French Film Office, 745 Fifth Avenue, New York,
   NY 10151, 212/832-8860

TEA IN THE HAREM   *LE THE AU HAREM D'ARCHIMEDE*
   M&R Films/Cinecom, 1985, French
MISS MONA   AAA, 1987, French
CAMOMILLE   K.G. Productions, 1988, French
AU PAYS DES JULIET   Erato Films/CEC Rhone Alpes/FR3/
   Investimage 3/CNC/Canal Plus/Region Rhone Alpes,
   1992, French

PAUL CHART

AMERICAN PERFEKT   Type A Films, 1995

DAVID CHASE*

Agent: UTA - Beverly Hills, 310/273-6700
Business Manager: Jess Morgan & Co., 5750 Wilshire Blvd. -
   Suite 590, Los Angeles, CA 90036, 213/937-1552

ALMOST GROWN (TF)   Universal TV/Atlantis Films, 1988

ETIENNE CHATILIEZ

Contact: French Film Office, 745 Fifth Avenue, New York,
   NY 10151, 212/832-8860

LIFE IS A LONG QUIET RIVER   MK2 Productions USA,
   1989, French
TATIE DANIELLE   Prestige, 1990, French
LE BONHEUR EST DANS LE PRE   Canal Plus, 1995, French

AMIN Q. CHAUDHRI

Business: Continental Film Group, Park Street, Sharon, PA 16146,
   412/981-3456

ONCE AGAIN   Continental Film Group, 1986
TIGER WARSAW   Sony Pictures, 1988
AN UNREMARKABLE LIFE   SVS Films, 1989
FINNEGAN'S WAKE   Continental Film Group, 1993

SHU LEA CHEANG

FRESH KILL   The Airwaves Project/ITVS/Channel 4/Woo Art
   International, 1994

JEREMIAH CHECHIK*

b. Montreal, Quebec, Canada
Agent: ICM - Beverly Hills, 310/550-4000
Personal Manager: Carlyle Productions and Management,
   639 N. Larchmont - Suite 207, Los Angeles, CA 90004,
   213/469-3086

NATIONAL LAMPOON'S CHRISTMAS VACATION
   Warner Bros., 1989
BENNY & JOON   MGM, 1993
TALL TALE: THE UNBELIEVABLE ADVENTURES OF PECOS BILL
   Buena Vista, 1995

DOUGLAS CHEEK*

Home: 454 West 25th Street, New York, NY 10001, 213/989-6257

C.H.U.D.   New World, 1984

PETER CHELSOM

b. 1956 - Lancashire, England
Agent: William Morris Agency - Beverly Hills, 310/859-4000

HEAR MY SONG   Miramax Films, 1991, British-Irish
FUNNY BONES   Buena Vista, 1995, British-U.S.

KAIGE CHEN

(See Chen KAIGE)

PIERRE CHENAL

(Pierre Cohen
b. 1903 - Paris, France
Contact: French Film Office, 745 Fifth Avenue, New York, NY 10151,
   212/832-8860

LE MARTYRE DE L'OBESE   1933, French
LA RUE SANS NOM   1933, French
CRIME ET CHATIMENT   1935, French
LES MUTINES DE L'ELSENEUR   1936, French
L'HOMME DE NULLE PART   1937, French-Italian
L'ALIBI   1937, French
L'AFFAIRE LAFARGE   1938, French
LA MAISON DU MALTAIS   1938, French
LE DERNIER TOURNANT   *THE POSTMAN ALWAYS RINGS TWICE*
   1939, French
TODO UN HOMBRE   1943, Argentine
EL MUEROTO FALTA A LA CITA   1944, Argentine
SE ABRE EL ABISMO   1945, Argentine
EL VIAJE SIN REGRESO   1946, Argentine
LA FOIRE AUX CHIMERES   1946, French
CLOCHEMERLE   1948, French
EL IDOLO   1949, Chilean
CONFESIONAL AMANECER   1951, Chilean
NATIVE SON   Classic Pictures, 1951, Argentine
SECTION DES DISPARUS   1956, French
LE FLEUVE D'ARGENT   1956, French
SINNERS OF PARIS   *RAFLES SUR LA VILLE*   Ellis Films,
   1957, French
DANGEROUS GAMES   Warner Bros., 1958, French
LA BETE A L'AFFUT   1959, French
THE NIGHT THEY KILLED RASPUTIN   *LES NUITS DE
   RASPOUTINE*   Brigadier Film Associates, 1960, French-Italian
L'ASSASSIN CONNAIT LA MUSIQUE   1963, French

ROBERT CHENAULT*

Address: 61 Laredo Lane, Palm Desert, CA 92260, 619/341-5999

DECEPTIONS (TF)   co-director with Melville Shavelson,
   Louis Rudolph Productions/Consolidated Productions/
   Columbia TV, 1985, U.S.-British
JENNY'S WAR (TF)   1991

AYOKA CHENZIRA

Contact: Writers Guild of America, East - New York City,
   212/767-7800
Business: Crossgrain Pictures, 300 West 55th Street, New York,
   NY 10019, 212/757-6945

ALMA'S RAINBOW   Paradise Plum/Crossgrain Pictures/Rhinoceros
   Productions/Channel 4, 1994
MOTV (MY OWN TV) (TF)   Red Carnelian Productions/Independent
   Television Service/PBS, 1994

PATRICE CHEREAU

Agent: A. A. G. Beaume-G. Bonnet - Paris, tel.: 1/42-56-22-33
Contact: French Film Office, 745 Fifth Avenue, New York, NY 10151,
   212/832-8860

QUEEN MARGOT   Miramax Films, 1994, French-German-Italian

JOHN CHERRY*

(John R. Cherry III)
Contact: Directors Guild of America - Los Angeles, 213/851-3671

DR. OTTO AND THE RIDDLE OF THE GLOOM BEAM   1985
ERNEST GOES TO CAMP   Buena Vista, 1987
ERNEST SAVES CHRISTMAS   Buena Vista, 1988
ERNEST GOES TO JAIL   Buena Vista, 1990
ERNEST SCARED STUPID   Buena Vista, 1991
ERNEST RIDES AGAIN   Ernest Partners Ltd., 1993

STANLEY Z. CHERRY*

Business: Cherryhill, Inc., 11222 Ventura Blvd., Studio City, CA
91604, 818/760-2804
Agent: Shapiro-Lichtman Talent Agency - Los Angeles, 310/859-8877
Business Manager: Steven Kattleman, Cooper, Epstein, Hurewitz,
345 N. Maple Drive, Beverly Hills, CA 90210, 310/278-1111

BRING ME THE HEAD OF DOBIE GILLIS (TF)
20th Century Fox TV, 1988

WAYNE CHESLER

THE HOTEL MANOR INN   Manor Films, 1994

SCOTT E. CHESTER

TWO ELEVEN   211 Productions, 1995

LIONEL CHETWYND*

b. 1940 - London, England
Agent: Metropolitan Talent Agency - Los Angeles, 213/857-4500
Business Manager: Gang, Tyre, Ramer & Brown, 6400 Sunset Blvd.,
Los Angeles, CA 90028, 213/463-4863

MORNING COMES   1975, Canadian
TWO SOLITUDES   New World-Mutual, 1978, Canadian
THE HANOI HILTON   Cannon, 1987
SO PROUDLY WE HAIL (TF)   Lionel Chetwynd Productions/CBS
Entertainment, 1990

JACOB C.L. CHEUNG

b. September 6, 1959 - Hong Kong
Contact: Hong Kong Film Liaison, 10940 Wilshire Blvd. - Suite 1220,
Los Angeles, CA 90024, 310/208-2678

CHINA'S LAST EUNUCH   1988, Hong Kong, filmed in 1986
BEYOND THE SUNSET   SIL-Metropole Organization, 1988,
Hong Kong
GOOD-BVE HERO   1990, Hong Kong
CAGEMAN   Filmagica Productions, 1993, Hong Kong
ALWAYS ON MY MIND   United Filmmakers Organization/Hui's Film
Production Company/Topping Time Films, 1994, Hong Kong

ANDREW CHIARAMONTE

Contact: Weissmann, Wolff, Bergman, Coleman & Silverman -
Beverly Hills, 310/858-7888

TWOGETHER   Dream Catcher Entertainment Group/Borde Film
Releasing, 1994
DEATH AMONG STRANGERS   1996

COLIN CHILVERS*

b. 1945 - England
Home: P.O. Box 135, Ridgeway, Ontario L0S 1NO, Canada,
416/894-2963 or: 925 S. Ledoux Road - Apt. 4, Los Angeles,
CA 90035, 310/657-8179
Office: 310/659-4848
Agent: London Management - London, tel.: 171/287-9000

WAR OF THE WORLDS (TF)   Triumph Entertainment Corporation
of Canada/Ten-Four Productions/Paramount TV,
1988, Canadian-U.S.
MOONWALKER (FCD)   co-director with Jerry Kramer,
Warner Bros., 1988

STEPHEN CHIODO*

Business: Chiodo Brothers Productions, 425 S. Flower Street,
Burbank, CA 91502, 818/842-5656
Agent: William Morris Agency - Beverly Hills, 310/859-4000

KILLER KLOWNS FROM OUTER SPACE   Trans World
Entertainment, 1988

MEL CHIONGLO

Contact: Film Commission, National Commission for Culture and Arts,
Intramuros, Manila, Philippines

MIDNIGHT DANCERS   Tangent Films, 1994, Filipino

STEPHAN CHODOROV

Contact: Writers Guild of America, East - New York City,
212/767-7800

REDISCOVERING WILL ROGERS (TD)   Oklahoma Educational TV
Authority/WNET-13, 1994

PARK CHOI-SU

b. November 20, 1947 - Chongdo, Kyongsangbukdo, Korea
Contact: Korean Motion Pictures Promotion Corporation, 34-5,
3KA Namsan-Dong, Chung-Ku, Seoul, South Korea,
tel.: 755-9291

THE RAIN ONLY WHEN AT NIGHT   1979, South Korean
THE PAINFUL MATURITY   1980, South Korean
THE WILD DOG   1982, South Korean
THE BELL OF NIRVANA   1983, South Korean
MOTHER   1985, South Korean
THE PILLAR OF MIST   1986, South Korean

MARVIN J. CHOMSKY*

b. May 23, 1929 - New York, New York
Agent: David B. Cohen, David B. Cohen Talent Agency,
131 Spinnaker Court, Marina del Rey, CA 90262, 310/301-0205

ASSAULT ON THE WAYNE (TF)   Paramount TV, 1971
MONGO'S BACK IN TOWN (TF)   Bob Banner Associates, 1971
EVEL KNIEVEL   Fanfare, 1972
FIREBALL FORWARD (TF)   20th Century-Fox TV, 1972
FAMILY FLIGHT (TF)   Universal TV, 1973
FEMALE ARTILLERY (TF)   Universal TV, 1973
THE MAGICIAN (TF)   Paramount TV, 1973
MRS. SUNDANCE (TF)   20th Century-Fox TV, 1974
THE FBI STORY: THE FBI VERSUS ALVIN KARPIS, PUBLIC
ENEMY NUMBER ONE (TF)   QM Productions/Warner
Bros. TV, 1974
ATTACK ON TERROR: THE FBI VS. THE KU KLUX KLAN (TF)
QM Productions, 1975
MACKINTOSH AND T.J.   Penland, 1975
LIVE A LITTLE, STEAL A LOT   MURPH THE SURF
American International, 1975
KATE McSHANE (TF)   Paramount TV, 1975
BRINK'S: THE GREAT ROBBERY (TF)   QM Productions/
Warner Bros. TV, 1976
A MATTER OF WIFE...AND DEATH (TF)   Columbia TV, 1976
LAW AND ORDER (TF)   Paramount TV, 1976
ROOTS (MS) ☆   co-director with David Greene, John Erman &
Gilbert Moses, Wolper Productions, 1977
LITTLE LADIES OF THE NIGHT (TF)   Spelling-Goldberg
Productions, 1977
DANGER IN PARADISE (TF)   Filmways, 1977
HOLOCAUST (MS) ☆☆   Titus Productions, 1978
GOOD LUCK, MISS WYCKOFF   Bel Air/Gradison, 1979
HOLLOW IMAGE (TF)   Titus Productions, 1979
DOCTOR FRANKEN (TF)   co-director with Jeff Lieberman,
Titus Productions/Janus Productions, 1980
ATTICA (TF) ☆☆   ABC Circle Films, 1980
KING CRAB (TF)   Titus Productions, 1980
EVITA PERON (TF)   Hartwest Productions/Zephyr
Productions, 1981
MY BODY, MY CHILD (TF)   Titus Productions, 1982
INSIDE THE THIRD REICH (TF) ☆☆   ABC Circle Films, 1982
I WAS A MAIL ORDER BRIDE (TF)   Jaffe Productions/Tuxedo
Limited Productions/MGM TV, 1982
TANK   Universal, 1984
NAIROBI AFFAIR (TF)   Robert Halmi, Inc., 1984
ROBERT KENNEDY AND HIS TIMES (MS)   Chris-Rose
Productions/Columbia TV, 1985
PETER THE GREAT (MS)   co-director with Lawrence Schiller,
PTG Productions/NBC Productions, 1986
THE DELIBERATE STRANGER (TF)   Stuart Phoenix Productions/
Lorimar-Telepictures, 1986
ANASTASIA: THE MYSTERY OF ANNA (TF)   Telecom
Entertainment/Consolidated Productions/Reteitalia,
1986, U.S.-Italian
ANGEL IN GREEN (TF)   Aligre Productions/Taft Hardy Group,
1987, U.S.-New Zealand

BILLIONAIRE BOYS CLUB (TF) ☆ Donald March/Gross-Weston
Productions/ITC Productions, 1987
BROTHERHOOD OF THE ROSE (TF) NBC Productions, 1989
STRAUSS DYNASTY (MS) MR TV-Film/ORF/ECA, 1990,
Austrian-West German
TELLING SECRETS (TF) Patchett Kaufman Entertainment/World
International Network, 1993
CATHERINE THE GREAT (TF) UFA/Patrola, 1995, German-U.S.

THOMAS CHONG*

b. May 24, 1938 - Edmonton, Canada
Home: 1625 Casale Road, Pacific Palisades, CA 90272,
310/454-3262
Agent: Irvin Arthur Associates - Beverly Hills, 310/278-5934

THE NEXT CHEECH & CHONG MOVIE Universal, 1980
CHEECH & CHONG'S NICE DREAMS Columbia, 1981
CHEECH & CHONG: STILL SMOKIN Paramount, 1983
CHEECH & CHONG'S THE CORSICAN BROTHERS Orion, 1984
FAR OUT MAN New Line Cinema, 1990

JOYCE CHOPRA*

b. 1938
Personal Manager: Creative Alliance Management - Los Angeles,
213/962-6090

SMOOTH TALK Spectrafilm, 1985
THE LEMON SISTERS Miramax Films, 1989
THE WIDOW CLAIRE Lee Caplin Productions, 1991
MURDER IN NEW HAMPSHIRE: THE PAMELA SMART
STORY (TF) New Hampshire Productions, 1991
BABY SNATCHER (TF) Morgan Hill Films/Hearst
Entertainment, 1992
THE DANGER OF LOVE (TF) Lois Luger Productions/Citadel
Pictures, 1992
THE DISAPPEARANCE OF NORA (TF) Citadel Pictures, 1993
THE CORPSE HAD A FAMILIAR FACE (TF) von Zerneck-Sertner
Films/Touchstone TV, 1994
DEADLINE FOR MURDER: FROM THE FILES OF
EDNA BUCHANAN (TF) von-Zerneck-Sertner Films/
Touchstone TV, 1995

MOHAMED CHOUIKH

b. Algeria

RUPTURE 1982, Algerian
EL KALAA CAAIC, 1988, Algerian
YOUCEF, OU LA LEGENDE SU SEPTIEME DORMAND
CAAIC/K Films, 1993, Algerian-French

ELIE CHOURAQUI

b. 1950 - Paris, France
Business: 7 Films Cinema, 4, avenue Jules Janin, 75016 Paris,
tel.: 1/45-03-32-18
Contact: French Film Office, 745 Fifth Avenue, New York,
NY 10151, 212/832-8860

MON PREMIER AMOUR 1978, French
QU'EST-CE QUI FAIT COURIR DAVID? 1982, French
LOVE SONGS PAROLES ET MUSIQUE Spectrafilm, 1984,
Canadian-French
MAN ON FIRE TriStar, 1987, Italian-French
MISS MISSOURI AAA, 1990, French
LES MARMOTTES President Films/7 Films Cinema/TF1 Films/
Canal Plus, 1993, French

CHRISTINE CHOY

b. New York, New York

FROM SPIKES TO SPINDLES (FD) 1976
TO LOVE, HONOR AND OBEY (FD) 1980
BITTER SWEET SURVIVAL (FD) 1981
MISSISSIPPI TRIANGLE (FD) 1983
WHO KILLED VINCENT CHIN? (FD) co-director with
Renee Tajima, 1988
THE BEST HOTEL ON SKID ROW (FD) co-director with
Renee Tajima, 1990

NATHANIEL CHRISTIAN

CALIFORNIA CASANOVA Academy Entertainment, 1991
CLUB FED Prism Entertainment, 1991

ROGER CHRISTIAN*

b. February 25, 1944 - London, England
Business: Christian Emes Rose, Green Garden House,
St. Christopher's Place, London W1, England, tel.: 171/935-1233
Agent: ICM - Beverly Hills, 310/550-4000

THE SENDER Paramount, 1982, U.S.-British
STARSHIP LORCA AND THE OUTLAWS Cinema Group,
1985, British-Australian
NOSTRADAMUS Orion Classics, 1994, British

BYRON CHUDNOW*

Address: 13757 Victory Blvd., Van Nuys, CA 91401,
310/820-1066

THE DOBERMAN GANG Dimension, 1973
THE DARING DOBERMANS Dimension, 1973
THE AMAZING DOBERMANS Golden, 1976

GRIGORI CHUKHRAI

b. May 23, 1921 - Melitopol, Ukraine, U.S.S.R.
Contact: Confederation of Film-Makers Unions, Vasilyevskaya
Street 13, 123 825 Moscow, Russia, tel.: 095/250-4114

NAZAR STODOLYA co-director with K. Ivchenko, 1955, Soviet
THE FORTY-FIRST 1956, Soviet
BALLAD OF A SOLDIER Artkino, 1959, Soviet
CLEAR SKIES 1961, Soviet
THERE WAS AN OLD COUPLE 1965, Soviet
PEOPLE! 1966, Soviet
BATTLE OF STALINGRAD (FD) 1970, Soviet
UNTYPICAL STORY 1977, Soviet

JI-YOUNG CHUNG

Contact: Korean Motion Picture Promotion Corporation, 34-5 3KA
Namsan-Dong, Chung-Ku, Seoul, South Korea, tel.: 755-9291

WHITE BADGE Morning Calm Cinema, 1994, South Korean

VERA CHYTILOVA

b. February 2, 1929 - Ostava, Czechoslovakia
Contact: Czech Film Institute, Narodni tr. 40, 110 00 Prague 1,
Czech Republic, tel.: 422/26-00-87

ANOTHER WAY OF LIFE 1963, Czechoslovakian
PEARLS AT THE BOTTOM co-director,
1965, Czechoslovakian
DAISIES 1966, Czechoslovakian
THE APPLE GAME 1976, Czechoslovakian
PANEL STORY 1979, Czechoslovakian
CALAMITY 1980, Czechoslovakian
CHYTILOVA VERSUS FORMAN (FD) 1981, Czechoslovakian
THE VERY LATE AFTERNOON OF A FAUN
1984, Czechoslovakian
WOLF'S LAIR 1986, Czechoslovakian
THE JESTER AND THE QUEEN Barrandov Film Studio,
1988, Czechoslovakian
SNOWBALL REACTION Barrandov Film Studio,
1989, Czechoslovakian
THE RETURN OF MOZART KF Ltd. Studio,
1991, Czechoslovakian
THE INHERITANCE, OR FUCKOFFGUYSGOODBYE
1993, Czech

GERARD CICCORITTI

b. August 5, 1956 - Toronto, Ontario, Canada
Business: Lightshow Communications, Inc., 77 Mowat Street - Suite 406, Toronto, Ontario M6K 3E3, Canada, 416/538-6815
Agent: Premiere Artists Agency - Los Angeles, 310/271-1414

PSYCHO GIRLS   Cannon, 1985, Canadian
GRAVEYARD SHIFT   Shapiro/Virgin, 1986, Canadian
LOVE AND DIE   Cinema Ventures, 1988, Canadian
GRAVEYARD SHIFT II   Virgin Vision, 1989, Canadian
A WHISPER TO A SCREAM   Distant Horizon/Lighthouse Communications, 1989, Canadian-U.S.
PARIS, FRANCE   Alliance Communications/Lightshow Communications, 1993, Canadian

MATT CIMBER
(Matteo Ottaviano)

SINGLE ROOM FURNISHED   Crown International, 1968
MAN AND WIFE   1970
CALLIOPE   Moonstone, 1971
THE BLACK SIX   Cinemation, 1974
THE CANDY TANGERINE MAN   Moonstone, 1975
GEMINI AFFAIR   Moonstone, 1975
LADY COCOA   Dimension, 1975
THE WITCH WHO CAME FROM THE SEA   Moonstone, 1976
BUTTERFLY   Analysis, 1981
FAKE OUT   Analysis, 1983
A TIME TO DIE   Almi Films, 1983
HUNDRA   Film Ventures International, 1984, Spanish
YELLOW HAIR AND THE FORTRESS OF GOLD
   Crown International, 1984, Spanish
G.L.O.W.   Film Ventures International, 1987
HUNT TO KILL   KP. International, 1991

MICHAEL CIMINO*

b. 1943 - New York, New York
Agent: CAA - Beverly Hills, 310/288-4545

THUNDERBOLT AND LIGHTFOOT   United Artists, 1974
THE DEER HUNTER ★★   Universal, 1978
HEAVEN'S GATE   United Artists, 1980
YEAR OF THE DRAGON   MGM/UA, 1985
THE SICILIAN   20th Century Fox, 1987
DESPERATE HOURS   MGM/UA, 1990

SOULEYMANE CISSÉ

b. April 21, 1940 - Bamako, Mali

CINQ JOURS D'UNE VIE   1972, Malian
DEN MUSO   1975, Malian
BAARA   1979, Malian
FINYE   1982, Malian
BRIGHTNESS   YEELEN   Island Pictures, 1987, Malian

RICHARD CIUPKA

b. 1950 - Liege, Belgium
Address: 71 Cornwall Street, Montreal, Quebec H3P 1M6, Canada, 514/738-9996

CURTAINS   released under pseudonym of Jonathan Stryker, Jensen Farley Pictures, 1983, Canadian
COYOTE   Films Stock International/Molecule/Telefilm Canada/ Societe General des Industries Culturelles/Premier Choix/ TVEC Inc./Canal Plus, 1993, Canadian-French

ROBERT CLAPSADLE

THE RIDE TO WOUNDED KNEE (FD)
   Panorama Entertainment, 1995

BOB CLARK*
(Benjamin Clark)

b. August 5, 1941 - New Orleans, Louisiana
Home: 17352 Sunset Blvd. - Apt. D-604, Pacific Palisades, CA 90272, 310/573-9114
Agent: The Gersh Agency - Beverly Hills, 310/274-6611

DEATHDREAM   1972, Canadian
CHILDREN SHOULDN'T PLAY WITH DEAD THINGS   Gemini Film, 1972, Canadian
DEATH OF NIGHT   Europix International, 1974, Canadian
BLACK CHRISTMAS   SILENT NIGHT, EVIL NIGHT/STRANGER IN THE HOUSE   Warner Bros., 1975, Canadian
BREAKING POINT   20th Century-Fox, 1976, Canadian
MURDER BY DECREE   Avco Embassy, 1979, Canadian-British
TRIBUTE   20th Century-Fox, 1980, U.S.-Canadian
PORKY'S   20th Century-Fox, 1982, U.S.-Canadian
PORKY'S II: THE NEXT DAY   20th Century-Fox, 1983, U.S.-Canadian
A CHRISTMAS STORY   MGM/UA, 1983, Canadian
RHINESTONE   20th Century Fox, 1984
TURK 182   20th Century Fox, 1985
FROM THE HIP   DEG, 1987
LOOSE CANNONS   TriStar, 1990
THE AMERICAN CLOCK (CTF)   TNT Screenworks, 1993
IT RUNS IN THE FAMILY   MGM-UA, 1994

BRUCE CLARK

Contact: Writers Guild of America, West - Los Angeles, 310/550-1000

NAKED ANGELS   Favorite, 1969
THE SKI BUM   Avco Embassy, 1971
HAMMER   United Artists, 1972
GALAXY OF TERROR   New World, 1981

DUANE CLARK

Agent: Shapiro-Lichtman Talent Agency - Los Angeles, 310/859-8877

SHAKING THE TREE   Castle Hill Productions, 1992
BITTER HARVEST   Prism Pictures, 1993

FRANK C. CLARK

BEYOND THE REEF   Universal, 1981

GREYDON CLARK

TOM   Four Star International, 1973
BLACK SHAMPOO   Dimension, 1976
THE BAD BUNCH   Dimension, 1976
SATAN'S CHEERLEADERS   World Amusement, 1977
HI-RIDERS   Dimension, 1978
ANGELS BRIGADE   Arista, 1980
WITHOUT WARNING   Filmways, 1980
THE RETURN   1981
JOYSTICKS   Jensen Farley Pictures, 1982
WACKO   Jensen Farley Pictures, 1983
FINAL JUSTICE   Arista, 1985
UNINVITED   Amazing Movies, 1988
SKINHEADS   Amazing Movies, 1989
OUT OF SIGHT, OUT OF MIND   Spectrum Entertainment, 1990
THE FORBIDDEN DANCE   Columbia, 1990
TERROR OF MANHATTAN   21st Century Distribution, 1992
MAD DOG COLL   co-director with Ken Stein, 21st Century Distribution, 1992, U.S.-Russian
RUSSIAN HOLIDAY   Amazing Movies, 1994
DARK FUTURE   Showcase Entertainment, 1994

JAMES B. CLARK*

Home: 10051-5 Valley Circle Blvd., Chatsworth, CA 91311, 818/998-0962

UNDER FIRE   20th Century-Fox, 1957
SIERRA BARON   20th Century-Fox, 1958
VILLA!!   20th Century-Fox, 1958
THE SAD HORSE   20th Century-Fox, 1959
A DOG OF FLANDERS   20th Century-Fox, 1960
ONE FOOT IN HELL   20th Century-Fox, 1960

THE BIG SHOW   20th Century-Fox, 1961, U.S.-West German
MISTY   20th Century-Fox, 1961
FLIPPER   MGM, 1963
DRUMS OF AFRICA   MGM, 1963
ISLAND OF THE BLUE DOLPHINS   20th Century-Fox, 1964
AND NOW MIGUEL   Paramount, 1966
MY SIDE OF THE MOUNTAIN   Paramount, 1969
THE LITTLE ARK   National General, 1972

LARRY CLARK
KIDS   Miramax Films, 1995

LAWRENCE GORDON CLARK
Contact: British Film Commission, 70 Baker Street, London
   W1M 1DJ, England, tel.: 171/224-5000

ROMANCE ON THE ORIENT EXPRESS (TF)   Frank von Zerneck
   Productions/Yorkshire TV, 1985, U.S.-British
JAMAICA INN (TF)   HTV/Metromedia Producers Corporation/
   United Media, Ltd./Jamaica Inn Productions,
   1985, British-U.S.
MURDER BY THE BOOK (TF)   TVS Ltd./Benton Evans
   Productions, 1986, British
CAPTAIN JAMES COOK (MS)   Australian Broadcasting
   Corporation/Revcom, 1987, Australian
ACT OF BETRAYAL (TF)   Griffin Productions/TVS/Australian
   Broadcasting Corporation/RTE/Strongbow,
   1988, British-Australian
MAGIC MOMENTS (TF)   Arena Films/Yorkshire TV/Atlantic
   Videoventures, 1988, British
JUST ANOTHER SECRET (CTF)   F.F.S. Productions/Taurusfilm/
   Blair Communications/USA Network, 1989, U.S.-British
MURDER BY THE BOOK (CTF)   TVS Productions/Benbow
   Evans Productions, 1990, British-U.S.

MATT CLARK*
Agent: Paul Kohner, Inc. - Los Angeles, 310/550-1060

DA   FilmDallas, 1988

RICHARD CLARK
DR. HACKENSTEIN   Vista Street Productions, 1988

RON CLARK
b. 1933 - Montreal, Quebec, Canada
Home: 325 N. Barrington Avenue, Los Angeles, CA 90049,
   310/827-1717
Business: Augustus Productions, 315 S. Beverly Drive - Suite 412,
   Beverly Hills, CA 90212, 310/553-0171
Agent: David Shapira & Associates - Sherman Oaks, 818/906-0322

THE FUNNY FARM   New World, 1983, Canadian

WILLIAM CLARK
THE GOODBYE BIRD   Leucadia Film Corporation, 1993
WINDRUNNER   Leucadia Film Corporation, 1994

FRANK CLARKE
Agent: ICM - Beverly Hills, 310/550-4000
Contact: British Film Commission, 70 Baker Street, London
   W1M 1DJ, England, tel.: 171/224-5000

BLONDE FIST   Glinwood Films/Film Four International/
   Blue Dolphin Pictures, 1991, British

JAMES KENELM CLARKE
b. 1941 - Gloucestershire, England
Personal Manager: Hamish Gibson, Norfolk International Pictures,
   2706 La Cuesta Drive, Los Angeles, CA 90046, 213/876-4953

GOT IT MADE   Target International, 1973, British
EXPOSE   Target International, 1975, British
LET'S GET LAID   1977, British
FUNNY MONEY   Cannon, 1982, British
LOVE TRAP   1982, British

GOING UNDERCOVER   Miramax Films, 1985
THE HOUSE ON STRAW HILL   Norfolk International, 1988
INTIMATE DETAILS   Axelia International Pictures, 1991

MALCOLM CLARKE*
Agent: ICM - Beverly Hills, 310/550-4000

VOICES FROM A LOCKED ROOM   Columbia, 1995,
   British-Canadian

SHIRLEY CLARKE
(Shirley Brimberg)
b. 1925 - New York, New York
Home: 1301 N. Harper Avenue, Los Angeles, CA 90046

THE CONNECTION   Films Around the World, 1962
THE COOL WORLD   Cinema 5, 1964
ROBERT FROST: A LOVER'S QUARREL WITH
   THE WORLD (FD)   1963
PORTRAIT OF JASON (FD)   Film-Makers, 1967
ORNETTE: MADE IN AMERICA (FD)   Caravan of Dreams
   Productions, 1985

STANLEY BENNETT CLAY
RITUAL   Gotham Entertainment, 1995

WILLIAM F. CLAXTON*
b. October 22, 1914 - California
Home: 1065 Napoli Drive, Pacific Palisades, CA 90272,
   310/454-3246
Agent: Ronald Leif, Contemporary Artists - Santa Monica,
   310/395-1800

HALF PAST MIDNIGHT   20th Century-Fox, 1948
TUCSON   20th Century-Fox, 1949
ALL THAT I HAVE   Family Films, 1951
STAGECOACH TO FURY   20th Century-Fox, 1956
THE QUIET GUN   20th Century-Fox, 1957
YOUNG AND DANGEROUS   20th Century-Fox, 1957
ROCKABILLY BABY   20th Century-Fox, 1957
GOD IS MY PARTNER   20th Century-Fox, 1957
DESIRE IN THE DUST   20th Century-Fox, 1960
YOUNG JESSE JAMES   20th Century-Fox, 1960
LAW OF THE LAWLESS   Paramount, 1963
STAGE TO THUNDER ROCK   Paramount, 1964
NIGHT OF THE LEPUS   MGM, 1972
BONANZA: THE NEXT GENERATION (TF)   Gaylord Production
   Company/LBS Communications/Bonanza Ventures, 1988

TOM CLEGG
Agent: Peters Fraser & Dunlop - London, tel.: 171/344-1000

LOVE IS A SPLENDID ILLUSION   Schulman, 1970, British
SWEENEY 2   EMI, 1978, British
McVICAR   Crown International, 1981, British
G'OLE! (FD)   Warner Bros., 1983, British
THE INSIDE MAN   Producers Enterprises/Nordisk Tonefilm/Terra
   Film International, 1984, British-Swedish
LORD MOUNTBATTEN - THE LAST VICEROY (MS)   George Walker
   TV Productions/Mobil Corporation, 1986, British
ANY MAN'S DEATH   International Entertainment Corporation,
   1990, British
A CASUALTY OF WAR (CTF)   F.F.S. Productions/Taurusfilm/Blair
   Communications, 1990, British
STROKE OF MIDNIGHT   Chrysalide Films/Canal Plus/The Movie
   Group, 1991, French-U.S.
SHARPE'S RIFLES (TF)   Celtic/Picture Palace, 1993, British
SHARPE'S ENEMY (TF)   Celtic/Picture Palace, 1993, British
SHARPE'S COMPANY (TF)   Celtic/Picture Palace, 1993, British
SHARPE'S HONOUR (TF)   Celtic/Picture Palace, 1993, British
SHARPE II (MS)   Celtic/Picture Palace/Central TV, 1995, British

WILLIAM B. CLEMENS
b. September 10, 1905 - Saginaw, Michigan

MAN HUNT   Warner Bros., 1936
THE LAW IN HER HANDS   Warner Bros., 1936

THE CASE OF THE VELVET CLAWS   Warner Bros., 1936
DOWN THE STRETCH   Warner Bros., 1936
HERE COMES CARTER   Warner Bros., 1936
ONCE A DOCTOR   Warner Bros., 1937
THE CASE OF THE STUTTERING BISHOP
   Warner Bros., 1937
TALENT SCOUT   Warner Bros., 1937
FOOTLOOSE HEIRESS   Warner Bros., 1937
MISSING WITNESS   Warner Bros., 1937
TORCHY BLANE IN PANAMA   Warner Bros., 1937
ACCIDENTS WILL HAPPEN   Warner Bros., 1938
MR. CHUMP   Warner Bros., 1938
NANCY DREW, DETECTIVE   Warner Bros., 1938
NANCY DREW, REPORTER   Warner Bros., 1939
NANCY DREW, TROUBLE SHOOTER   Warner Bros., 1939
NANCY DREW AND THE HIDDEN STAIRCASE
   Warner Bros., 1939
THE DEAD END KIDS ON DRESS PARADE
   Warner Bros., 1939
CALLING PHILO VANCE   Warner Bros., 1940
KING OF THE LUMBERJACKS   Warner Bros., 1940
DEVIL'S ISLAND   Warner Bros., 1940
SHE COULDN'T SAY NO   Warner Bros., 1941
KNOCKOUT   Warner Bros., 1941
THE NIGHT OF JANUARY 16TH   Paramount, 1941
A NIGHT IN NEW ORLEANS   Paramount, 1942
SWEATER GIRL   Paramount, 1942
LADY BODYGUARD   Paramount, 1943
THE FALCON IN DANGER   RKO Radio, 1943
THE FALCON AND THE CO-EDS   RKO Radio, 1943
THE FALCON OUT WEST   RKO Radio, 1944
CRIME BY NIGHT   Warner Bros., 1944
THE 13TH HOUR   Columbia, 1947

DICK CLEMENT*
b. September 5, 1937 - West Cliff-on-Sea, England
Agent: Elliot Webb, Broder-Kurland-Webb-Uffner Agency -
   Beverly Hills, 310/281-3400

OTLEY   Columbia, 1969, British
A SEVERED HEAD   Columbia, 1971, British
CATCH ME A SPY   Rank, 1971, British
PORRIDGE   ITC, 1979, British
BULLSHOT!   Island Alive, 1983, British
WATER   Atlantic Releasing Corporation, 1984, British

RENÉ CLEMENT
b. March 18, 1913 - Bordeaux, France
Contact: French Film Office, 745 Fifth Avenue, New York,
   NY 10151, 212/832-8860

LA BATAILLE DU RAIL   1946, French
LE PERE TRANQUILLE   1946, French
LES MAUDITS   1947, French
THE WALLS OF MALAPAGA   Films International of America,
   1949, Italian-French
LE CHATEAU DE VERRE   1950, French-Italian
FORBIDDEN GAMES   Times, 1952, French
LOVERS, HAPPY LOVERS!   MONSIEUR RIPOIS/KNAVE
   OF HEARTS   20th Century-Fox, 1954, French-British
GERVAISE   Continental, 1956, French
THIS ANGRY AGE   Columbia, 1958, Italian-French
PURPLE NOON   TImes, 1960, French-Italian
QUELLE JOIE DE VIVRE   1961, French-Italian
THE DAY AND THE HOUR   MGM, 1962, French-Italian
JOY HOUSE   LES FELINS   MGM, 1964, French
IS PARIS BURNING?   Paramount, 1966, French-U.S.
RIDER ON THE RAIN   Avco Embassy, 1970, French-Italian
THE DEADLY TRAP   LA MAISON SOUS LES ARBRES
   National General, 1971, French-Italian
...AND HOPE TO DIE   LA COURSE DU LIEVRE A TRAVERS
   LES CHAMPS   20th Century-Fox, 1972, French
LA BABY-SITTER   Titanus, 1975, Italian-French-Monacan

RON CLEMENTS
Business: Walt Disney Animation, 500 S. Buena Vista Street,
   Burbank, CA 91521, 818/560-1000

THE GREAT MOUSE DETECTIVE (AF)   co-director with
   John Musker, Dave Michener & Burny Mattinson,
   Buena Vista, 1986
THE LITTLE MERMAID (AF)   co-director with John Musker,
   Buena Vista, 1989
ALADDIN (AF)   co-director with John Musker, Buena Vista, 1992

GRAEME CLIFFORD*
b. Australia
Agent: UTA - Beverly Hills, 310/273-6700

FRANCES   Universal/AFD, 1982
BURKE AND WILLS   Hemdale, 1985, Australian
GLEAMING THE CUBE   20th Century Fox, 1989
THE TURN OF THE SCREW (CTF)   Think Entertainment, 1989
DECEPTION   RUBY CAIRO   Miramax Films, 1993, U.S.-Japanese
PAST TENSE (CTF)   Polygram Filmed Entertainment/Viacom/Arnold
   Kopelson Productions/Showtime Entertainment, 1994

PETER CLIFTON
Contact: British Film Commission, 70 Baker Street, London
   W1M 1DJ, England, tel.: 171/224-5000

POPCORN (FCD)   Sherpix, 1969, U.S.-Australian
SUPERSTARS IN FILM CONCERT (FCD)   National Cinema,
   1971, British
THE SONG REMAINS THE SAME (FCD)   co-director with
   Joe Massot, Warner Bros., 1976, British
SWEET SOUL MUSIC (FCD)   1977, British
THE LONDON ROCK & ROLL SHOW (FCD)   1978, British
ROCK CITY   SOUND OF THE CITY   LONDON 1964-73 (FCD)
   Columbia, 1981, British

ART CLOKEY
THE GUMBY MOVIE (AF)   Premavision/Mars Production
   Group, 1995

ROBERT CLOUSE
Agent: ICM - Beverly Hills, 310/550-4000
Home: 70 Water Street, Ashland, OR 97520, 503/488-0131

DARKER THAN AMBER   National General, 1970
DREAMS OF GLASS   Universal, 1970
ENTER THE DRAGON   Warner Bros., 1973, U.S.-Hong Kong
BLACK BELT JONES   Warner Bros., 1974
GOLDEN NEEDLES   American International, 1974
THE ULTIMATE WARRIOR   Warner Bros., 1976
THE AMSTERDAM KILL   Columbia, 1978, U.S.-Hong Kong
THE PACK   Warner Bros., 1978
GAME OF DEATH   Columbia, 1979, U.S.-Hong Kong
THE OMEGA CONNECTION (TF)   NBC-TV, 1979
THE KIDS WHO KNEW TOO MUCH (TF)   Walt Disney
   Productions, 1980
THE BIG BRAWL   Warner Bros., 1980
FORCE: FIVE   American Cinema, 1981
NIGHT EYES   THE RATS   Warner Bros., 1983, Canadian
DARK WARRIOR   Arista, 1984
GYMKATA   MGM/UA, 1985
CHINA O'BRIEN   Golden Harvest, 1991, U.S.-Hong Kong,
   filmed in 1988
IRON HEART   MCE Group, 1991, U.S.-Hong Kong
CHINA O'BRIEN II   Golden Harvest, 1992, U.S.-Hong Kong,
   filmed in 1989

MARTIN CLUNES
Contact: British Film Commission, 70 Baker Street, London
   W1M 1DJ, England, tel.: 171/224-5000

STAGGERED   Entertainment Film Distributors, 1994, British

CRAIG CLYDE
LITTLE HEROES   Majestic Entertainment, 1991
THE LEGEND OF WOLF MOUNTAIN   Coyote Releasing/
   Hemdale, 1992
WIND DANCER   Majestic/Sunset Hill Productions, 1993
HEAVEN SENT   Majestic/Sunset Hill Partners, 1994

LEWIS COATES
(Luigi Cozzi)
Home: via Cassia 834, pal.F, Rome, Italy, tel: 06/366-8116

LA PORTIERA NUDA   CIA Cinematografica, 1975, Italian
L'ASSASSINO E COSTRETTO AD UCCIDERE ANCORA
   Albione Cinematografica/GIT International, 1976, Italian
DEDICATO A UNA STELLA   Euro, 1978, Italian
STARCRASH   New World, 1979, Italian
ALIEN CONTAMINATION   Cannon, 1980, Italian-West German
HERCULES   MGM/UA/Cannon, 1983, Italian
HERCULES II   Cannon, 1983, Italian
WITCHCRAFT   Film Mirage, 1988, Italian
PAGANINI HORROR   Fulvia Film, 1989, Italian
THE BLACK CAT   21st Century Film Corporation, 1989, Italian
DARIO ARGENTO: MASTER OF HORROR (FD)   S.A.M.A. Film,
   1991, Italian

STACY COCHRAN
Agent: CAA - Beverly Hills, 310/288-4545

MY NEW GUN   I.R.S. Releasing, 1992
BOYS   Buena Vista, 1995

JOEL COEN
b. 1955 - St. Louis Park, Minnesota
Agent: UTA - Beverly Hills, 310/273-6700

BLOOD SIMPLE   Circle Releasing Corporation, 1984
RAISING ARIZONA   20th Century Fox, 1987
MILLER'S CROSSING   20th Century Fox, 1990
BARTON FINK   20th Century Fox, 1991
THE HUDSUCKER PROXY   Warner Bros., 1994
FARGO   Working Title/Polygram Filmed Entertainment,
   1995, U.S.-British

ANNETTE COHEN
Address: 25 Imperial Street, Toronto, Ontario M5P 1C1, Canada,
   416/483-8018

LOVE   co-director with Nancy Dowd, Liv Ullmann & Mai Zetterling,
   Velvet Films, 1982, Canadian

DAN COHEN
THE WHOLE TRUTH   co-director with Jonathan Smythe,
   Cinevista, 1993

DAVID COHEN
b. 1946 - Haifa, Israel
Contact: British Film Commission, 70 Baker Street, London
   W1M 1DJ, England, tel.: 171/224-5000

THE PLEASURE PRINCIPLE   Palace Pictures, 1991, British
PIRATES (TD)   Psychology News/S4C/Gaelic TV Committee/
   The Discovery Channel, 1994, British-Welsh

ELI COHEN
Contact: Israel Film Centre, Ministry of Industry and Trade,
   30 Agron Street, P.O. Box 299, 94190 Jerusalem, Israel,
   tel.: 972/210433 or 290297

RICOCHETS   Marathon Pictures, 1986, Israeli
AVIA'S SUMMER   Shapira Films, 1988, Israeli
THE QUARREL   Atlantis Films/Apple & Honey Productions,
   1991, Canadian
THE WORDMAKER   1994, Israeli
THE SOFT KILL   Dream Entertainment, 1994

HOWARD R. COHEN
Agent: Epstein-Wyckoff-Lamanna & Associates - Beverly Hills,
   310/278-7222

SATURDAY THE 14TH   New World, 1981
SPACE RAIDERS   New World, 1983
SATURDAY THE 14TH STRIKES BACK   Concorde, 1988
TIME TRACKERS   Concorde, 1989
SPACE CASE   Lunar Bynne Limited Productions, 1990
DEATHSTALKER IV   Concorde, 1990

LARRY COHEN*
b. July 15, 1941 - New York, New York
Home: 2111 Coldwater Canyon Blvd., Beverly Hills, CA 90210,
   310/550-7942
Business Manager: David Tiger - 818/999-4420

ONE SHOCKING MOMENT   1965
BONE   Jack H. Harris Enterprises, 1972
BLACK CAESAR   American International, 1973
HELL UP IN HARLEM   American International, 1973
IT'S ALIVE   Warner Bros., 1974
DEMON   GOD TOLD ME TO   New World, 1977
IT LIVES AGAIN   Warner Bros., 1978
THE PRIVATE FILES OF J. EDGAR HOOVER
   American International, 1978
SEE CHINA AND DIE (TF)   CBS, 1981
FULL MOON HIGH   Filmways, 1981
Q   United Film Distribution, 1982
SPECIAL EFFECTS   New Line Cinema, 1985
PERFECT STRANGERS   New Line Cinema, 1985
THE STUFF   New World, 1985
IT'S ALIVE III: ISLAND OF THE ALIVE   Warner Bros., 1987
RETURN TO SALEM'S LOT   Warner Bros., 1987
DEADLY ILLUSION   co-director with William Tannen,
   CineTel Films, 1987
WICKED STEPMOTHER   MGM/UA, 1989
THE AMBULANCE   Triumph Releasing Corporation, 1991

MARTIN COHEN
Business: Amblin Entertainment, 100 Universal City Plaza -
   Bungalow 477, Universal City, CA 91608, 818/777-4600

ONCE IN A BLUE MOON   Lunelife Productions, 1992

NEIL COHEN
Agent: William Morris Agency - Beverly Hills, 310/274-7451

RICH BOYS   *CHIEF ZABU*   co-director with Howard Zuker
   (Zack Norman), International Film Marketing, 1988

ROB COHEN*
b. April 12, 1949 - Cornwall-on-Hudson, New York
Agent: UTA - Beverly Hills, 310/273-6700

A SMALL CIRCLE OF FRIENDS   United Artists, 1980
SCANDALOUS   Orion, 1984
THE ANTAGONISTS (TF)   Universal TV, 1991
DRAGON: THE BRUCE LEE STORY   Universal, 1993
DRAGONHEART   Universal, 1995

S.E. COHEN
MARTIAL LAW   Westwind Productions, 1991

STEVE COHEN*
Address: 6448 1/2 W. Olympic Blvd., Los Angeles, 90048,
   213/653-9077
Agent: Shapiro-Lichtman Talent Agency - Los Angeles, 310/859-8877

TOUGH AND DEADLY   SGE Entertainment, 1994

MICHAEL COHN
INTERCEPTOR   Trimark Pictures, 1992
WHEN THE BOUGH BREAKS   Prism Pictures, 1993

PETER COHN
DRUNKS   Drunks Productions, 1995

ISABEL COIXET
THINGS I NEVER TOLD YOU   Carbo Films, 1995

HARLEY COKLISS
b. February 11, 1945 - San Diego, California
Agent: ICM - London, tel.: 171/636-6565

THAT SUMMER   Columbia, 1979, British
BATTLETRUCK   WARLORDS OF THE 21ST CENTURY
   New World, 1982, U.S.-New Zealand
BLACK MOON RISING   New World, 1986
MALONE   Orion, 1987
DREAM DEMON   Spectrafilm, 1988, British
HERCULES AND THE LOST KINGDOM (TF)   Renaissance
   Pictures/Universal TV, 1994

CARL COLBY
LEGENDS IN LIGHT (CTD)   Highland Productions/Aspect
   Films/Canon, 1995

HENRY COLE
Contact: British Film Commission, 70 Baker Street, London
   W1M 1DJ, England, tel.: 171/224-5000

MAD DOGS & ENGLISHMEN   Moor Street Films, 1995, British

JACK COLE
PROUDHEART (CTF)   Eight Forty Productions, 1993

KERMIT COLE
b. March 18, 1964 - Boston, Massachusetts
Business: 560 West 43rd Street - Apt. 96, New York, NY 10036,
   212/947-3327
Attorney: Wilder, Knight, Cashman, Sherman & Flynn,
   410 Park Avenue, New York, NY 10022, 212/326-0822

LIVING PROOF: HIV & THE PURSUIT OF HAPPINESS (FD)
   First Run Features, 1994

MARCUS COLE
Address: 11 Balmoral Road, Leura, New South Wales 2780,
   Australia, tel.: 47/842253
Agent: Susan Grant, The Artists Group - Los Angeles, 310/552-1100

A FORTUNATE LIFE (MS)   PBL, Australian
THE GREAT BOOKIE ROBBERY (MS)   PBL, 1986, Australian
SPIT McPHEE (MS)   Revcom, Australian
THE GREAT AIR RACE   HALF A WORLD AWAY (MS)
   London Films/Dimsey-Grigsby/Australian Broadcasting
   Corporation, 1992, British-Australian
TRACKS OF GLORY (MS)   Barron Films, 1992,
   Australian-Canadian
SNOWY RIVER - THE McGREGOR SAGA (CMS)   Pro Films,
   1994, Australian
A SEASON OF HOPE (TF)   Getting Out Productions/Signboard Hill
   Productions/Hallmark Entertainment, 1995

WILLIAM COLE
Agent: Premiere Artists Agency - Los Angeles, 310/271-1414

UNVEILED   Olivar Productions, 1993

JOHN DAVID COLES*
Address: 789 West End Avenue, New York, NY 10025,
   212/749-2900
Agent: ICM - Los Angeles, 213/550-4000

SIGNS OF LIFE   Avenue Pictures, 1989
RISING SON (CTF)   Turner Network TV/Sarabande
   Productions, 1990
DARROW (TF)   KCET-TV/Heus-Stept Productions, 1991

THE GOOD FIGHT (CTF)   Freyda Rothstein Productions/Hearst
   Entertainment Productions, 1992
AGAINST HER WILL: THE CARRIE BUCK STORY (TF)
   Janet Faust Krusi Productions/Viacom, 1994
FRIENDS AT LAST (TF)   Procter & Gamble/TeleVest/Atlantis Films
   Ltd./Stewart Pictures/Columbia TriStar TV, 1995, U.S.-Canadian

RICHARD A. COLLA*
Agent: ICM - Beverly Hills, 310/550-4000

THE WORLD IS WATCHING (TF)   Universal TV, 1969
ZIGZAG   MGM, 1970
McCLOUD: WHO KILLED MISS U.S.A.? (TF)   Universal TV, 1970
THE OTHER MAN (TF)   Universal TV, 1970
SARGE: THE BADGE OR THE CROSS (TF)   Universal TV, 1971
THE PRIEST KILLER (TF)   Universal TV, 1971
FUZZ   United Artists, 1972
TENAFLY (TF)   Universal TV, 1973
THE QUESTOR TAPES (TF)   Universal TV, 1974
LIVE AGAIN, DIE AGAIN (TF)   Universal TV, 1974
THE TRIBE (TF)   Universal TV, 1974
THE UFO INCIDENT (TF)   Universal TV, 1975
OLLY OLLY OXEN FREE   Sanrio, 1978
BATTLESTAR GALACTICA   Universal, 1979
DON'T LOOK BACK (TF)   TBA Productions/Satie
   Productions/TRISEME, 1981
STINGRAY (TF)   Stephen J. Cannell Productions, 1985
THAT SECRET SUNDAY (TF)   CBS Entertainment, 1986
SOMETHING IS OUT THERE (TF)   Columbia TV, 1988
NAKED LIE (TF)   Shadowplay Films/Phoenix Entertainment
   Group, 1989
ROXANNE: THE PRIZE PULITZER (TF)
   Qintex Entertainment, 1989
SPARKS: THE PRICE OF PASSION (TF)   Shadowplay Films/Victoria
   Principal Productions/King Phoenix Entertainment, 1990
STORM AND SORROW (CTF)   Accent Entertainment Corporation/
   Hearst Entertainment Productions, 1990
DEADLY MEDICINE (TF)   Steve Krantz Productions, 1991
DESPERATE RESCUE: THE CATHY MAHONE STORY (TF)
   Gimbel-Adelson Productions/Multimedia TV Productions/World
   International Network, 1993
WEB OF DECEPTION (TF)   Morgan Hill Films/Hearst
   Entertainment, 1994
ROSEANNE AND TOM: BEHIND THE SCENES (TF)
   Brian Pike Productions/.NBC Productions, 1994

ROBERT COLLECTOR
Business: Lookout Productions, 10201 W. Pico Blvd.,
   Los Angeles, CA 90035, 310/203-1422
Agent: William Morris Agency - Beverly Hills, 310/859-4000

RED HEAT   TAT Filmproductions/Aida United GMBH/
   International Screen, 1984, West German-U.S.
NIGHTFLYERS   released under pseudonym of T.C. Blake,
   New Century/Vista, 1987

ROBERT COLLINS*
Home: 3998 Sunswept Drive, Studio City, CA 91604, 818/980-6246
Agent: The Agency - Los Angeles, 310/551-3000

SERPICO: THE DEADLY GAME (TF)   Dino De Laurentiis
   Productions/Paramount TV, 1976
THE LIFE AND ASSASSINATION OF THE KINGFISH (TF)
   Tomorrow Entertainment, 1977
WALK PROUD   Universal, 1979
GIDEON'S TRUMPET (TF)   Gideon Productions, 1980
SAVAGE HARVEST   20th Century-Fox, 1981
OUR FAMILY BUSINESS (TF)   Lorimar Productions, 1981
MONEY ON THE SIDE (TF)   Green-Epstein Productions/Hal
   Landers Productions/Columbia TV, 1982
MAFIA PRINCESS (TF)   Jack Farren Productions/Group W
   Productions, 1985
J. EDGAR HOOVER (CTF)   RLC Productions/The Finnegan
   Company/Showtime, 1987
THE HIJACKING OF THE ACHILLE LAURO (TF)   Spectator
   Films/Tamara Asseyev Productions/New World TV, 1989
PRIME TARGET (TF)   RLC Productions/The Finnegan-Pinchuk
   Company/MGM-UA TV, 1989

JOHNNY RYAN (TF)   Dan Curtis TV Productions/MGM-UA TV/NBC Productions, 1990
IN THE ARMS OF A KILLER (TF)   RLC Productions/Monarch Pictures Corporation, 1992

CARL-JAN COLPAERT
b. Belgium
Business: Cineville, 225 Santa Monica Blvd. - Seventh Floor, Santa Monica, CA 90401, 310/394-4699

DELUSION   I.R.S. Releasing, 1991
THE CREW   Cineville, 1994

CHRIS COLUMBUS*
b. 1959 - Spangler, Pennsylvania
Business: 1492 Films, 10201 W. Pico Blvd. - Building 86, Los Angeles, CA 90035, 310/203-3482
Agent: CAA - Beverly Hills, 310/288-4545

ADVENTURES IN BABYSITTING   Buena Vista, 1987
HEARTBREAK HOTEL   Buena Vista, 1988
HOME ALONE   20th Century Fox, 1990
ONLY THE LONELY   20th Century Fox, 1991
HOME ALONE 2: LOST IN NEW YORK   20th Century Fox, 1992
MRS. DOUBTFIRE   20th Century Fox, 1993
NINE MONTHS   20th Century Fox, 1995

LUIGI COMENCINI
b. June 8, 1916 - Salo, Brescia, Italy
Home: via Savoia 82, Rome, Italy, tel: 06/855-5851

PROIBITO RUBARE   Lux Film, 1948, Italian
L'IMPERATORE DI CAPRI   Lux Film, 1949, Italian
PERSIANE CHIUSE   Rovere Film, 1951, Italian
HEIDI   United Artists, 1952, Swiss
LA TRATTA DELLA BIANCHE   Excelsa/Ponti/Dino De Laurentiis Cinematografica, 1952, Italian
BREAD, LOVE AND DREAMS   Italian Film Export, 1953, Italian
LA VALIGIA DEI SOGNI   Mambretti, 1954, Italian
FRISKY   PANE, AMORE E GELOSIA   DCA, 1954, Italian
LA BELLA DI ROMA   Lux Film, 1955, Italian
LA FINESTRA SUL LUNA PARK   Noria Film, 1957, Italian
MARITI IN CITTA   Oscar Film/Morino Film, 1957, Italian
MOGLI PERICOLOSE   Morino/Tempo Film, 1958, Italian
UND DAS AM MONTAGMORGEN   1959, West German
LE SORPRESE DELL'AMORE   Morino/Tempo Film, 1959, Italian
EVERYBODY GO HOME!   Royal Films International, 1960, Italian-French
A CAVALLO DELLA TIGRE   Alfredo Bini, 1961, Italian
IL COMMISSARIO   Dino De Laurentiis Cinematografica, 1962, Italian
BEBO'S GIRL   Continental, 1963, Italian-French
TRE NOTTI D'AMORE   co-director with Renato Costellani & Franco Rossi, Jolly Film/Cormoran Film, 1964, Italian-French
LA MIA SIGNORA   co-director with Mauro Bolognini & Tinto Brass, Dino De Laurentiis Cinematografica, 1964, Italian
BAMBOLE!   co-director with Dino Risi, Franco Rossi & Mauro Bolognini, Royal Films International, 1965, Italian
IL COMPAGNO DON CAMILLO   Rizzoli Film/Francoriz/Omnia Film, 1965, Italian-West German
LA BUGIARDA   Ultra Film/Consortium Pathe/Tecisa, 1965, Italian-French-Spanish
INCOMPRESO   1966, Italian
ITALIAN SECRET SERVICE   1968, Italian
INFANZIA, VOCAZIONE E PRIME ESPERIENZE DI GIACOMO CASANOVA - VENEZIANO   1969, Italian
SENZA SAPERE NULLA DI LEI   Rizzoli Film, 1969, Italian
LO SCOPONE SCIENTIFICO   De Laurentiis, 1972, Italian
LE AVVENTURE DI PINOCCHIO   RAI/ORTF/Bavaria Film, 1972, Italian-French-West German
DELITTO D'AMORE   Documento Film, 1974, Italian
MIO DIO COME SONO CADUTA IN BASSO   Dean Film, 1974, Italian
LA DONNA DELLA DOMENICA   Prinex Italiana/Fox-Lira, 1975, Italian
SUNDAY WOMAN   20th Century-Fox, 1976, Italian-French
BASTA CHE NON SI SAPPIA IN GIRO   co-director with Nanni Loy & Luigi Magni, Medusa, 1976, Italian

SIGNORE E SIGNORI BUONANOTTE   co-director, Titanus, 1976, Italian
QUELLE STRANE OCCASIONI   co-director, Cineriz, 1977, Italian
TILL MARRIAGE US DO PART   Franklin Media, 1977, Italian
L'AMORE IN ITALIA (TF)   1978, Italian
IL GATTO   United Artists, 1978, Italian
TRAFFIC JAM   L'INGORGO   New Image, 1979, Italian-French-Spanish
THEY ALL LOVED HIM   Medusa, 1980, Italian
VOLTATI EUGENIO   Gaumont, 1981, Italian-French
CERCASI GESU   Intercontinental/Nouvelle Cinevog, 1982, Italian-French
IL MATRIMONIO DI CATERINA (TF)   1982, Italian
CUORE (MS)   RAI/Difilm/Antenne-2, 1984, Italian-French
LA STORIA (MS)   RAI/Antenne-2/Ypsilon Cinematografica/Maran Film/TVE, 1986, Italian-French
THE BOY FROM CALABRIA   International Film Exchange, 1987, Italian-French
LA BOHEME   New Yorker, 1988, French
BUON NATALE, BUON ANNO   AFMD, 1990, Italian-French
MARCELLINO PANE E VINO   Production Group/UGC/Video Mercury Film, 1993, Italian-French-Spanish
LES FRANCAIS VUS PAR...   co-director with Werner Herzog, David Lynch & Andrzej Wajda, Erato Films/Socpresse/Figaro Magazine/Antenne-2/Centre National de la Cinematographie, 1993, French

JOE COMERFORD
Contact: Irish Film Institute, 6 Eustace Street, Dublin 2, Ireland, tel.: 679-5744

REEFER AND THE MODEL   1988, Irish
HIGH BOOT BENNY   Sandy Films/ZDF/Radio Teilifis Eireann/La Sept-Arte/Televiso de Catalunya/Channel 4, 1994, Irish-German-French-Spanish-British

RICHARD COMPTON*
Agent: Paradigm - Los Angeles, 310/277-4400

ANGELS DIE HARD   New World, 1970
WELCOME HOME, SOLDIER BOYS   20th Century-Fox, 1972
MACON COUNTY LINE   American International, 1974
RETURN TO MACON COUNTY   American International, 1975
MANIAC   New World, 1977
DEADMAN'S CURVE (TF)   Roger Gimbel Productions/EMi TV, 1978
RAVAGES   Columbia, 1979
WILD TIMES (TF)   Metromedia Producers Corporation/Rattlesnake Productions, 1980
DESPERADO: AVALANCHE AT DEVIL'S RIDGE (TF)   Walter Mirisch Productions/Charles E. Sellier, Jr. Productions/Universal TV, 1988
BAYWATCH: PANIC AT MALIBU PIER (TF)   GTG Entertainment, 1989
BABYLON 5 (TF)   Rattlesnake Productions/Synthetic Worlds Ltd./Warner Bros. TV, 1993

WILLIAM CONDON*
Agent: CAA - Beverly Hills, 310/288-4545

SISTER, SISTER   New World, 1987
MURDER 101 (CTF)   Alan Barnette Productions/MCA-TV Entertainment, 1991
WHITE LIE (CTF)   Alan Barnette Productions/MCA-TV Entertainment, 1991
DEAD IN THE WATER (CTF)   Kevin Bright Productions/MTE Entertainment, 1991
DEADLY RELATIONS (TF)   O.T.M.L. Productions/Wilshire Court Productions, 1993
CANDYMAN: FAREWELL TO THE FLESH   Gramercy Pictures, 1995

NICOLE CONN
Agent: Renaissance-H.N. Swanson - Los Angeles, 310/246-6000

CLAIRE OF THE MOON   Strand Releasing/Demi-Monde Productions, 1992

KEVIN CONNOR*
b. July 14, 1940 - London, England
Home: 7954 Woodrow Wilson Drive, Los Angeles, CA 90046,
213/650-4033
Agent: Becsey/Wisdom/Kalajian - Los Angeles, 310/550-0535 or:
AIM/John Redway Associates - London, tel.: 171/836-2001

FROM BEYOND THE GRAVE   Howard Mahler Films, 1975, British
THE LAND THAT TIME FORGOT   American International,
1975, British
AT THE EARTH'S CORE   American International, 1976, British
DIRTY KNIGHT'S WORK   A CHOICE OF WEAPONS   Gamma III,
1976, British
THE PEOPLE THAT TIME FORGOT   American International,
1977, British
WARLORDS OF ATLANTIS   Columbia, 1978, British
ARABIAN ADVENTURE   AFD, 1979, British
MOTEL HELL   United Artists, 1980
GOLIATH AWAITS (TF)   Larry White Productions/Hugh Benson
Productions/Columbia TV, 1981
THE HOUSE WHERE EVIL DWELLS   MGM/UA,
1982, U.S.-Japanese
MASTER OF THE GAME (MS)   co-director with Harvey Hart,
Rosemont Productions, 1984
MISTRAL'S DAUGHTER (MS)   co-director with Douglas Hickox,
Steve Krantz Productions/R.T.L. Productions/Antenne-2,
1984, U.S.-French
NORTH AND SOUTH, BOOK II (MS)   Wolper Productions/
Robert A. Papazian Productions/Warner Bros. TV, 1986
THE RETURN OF SHERLOCK HOLMES (TF)   CBS Entertainment,
1987, British
THE LION OF AFRICA (CTF)   HBO Pictures/Lois Luger
Productions, 1987
WHAT PRICE VICTORY (TF)   Wolper Productions/Warner
Bros. TV, 1988
DIRTY DOZEN: DANKO'S DOZEN (TF)   MGM-UA TV/Jadran
Films/TV Espanola, 1988, U.S.-Yugoslavian
GREAT EXPECTATIONS (CTF)   The Disney Channel/Primetime
TV/HTV/Tesauro TV, 1989, U.S.-British-Spanish
THE HOLLYWOOD DETECTIVE (CTF)   Casiano-Riggs
Productions/MCA TV/USA Network, 1989
THE MYSTERIES OF THE DARK JUNGLE (MS)   RCS-TV/RAI/
Beta Film/ZDF/ORF/TF1/TVE, 1990, Italian-West German-French
IRAN: DAYS OF CRISIS (CTF)   Gerald Rafshoon-Consolidated
Productions/Atlantique Productions, 1991, U.S.-French
SUNSET GRILL   New Line Cinema, 1993, British-U.S.
LETHAL EXPOSURE (TF)   Allan R. Schwartz Productions/
Papazian-Hirsch Entertainment/Ellipse Programme
Productions, 1993
DIANA: HER TRUE STORY (TF)   Martin Poll Productions,
1993, U.S.-British
JACK REED: BADGE OF HONOR (TF)   Steve Krantz
Productions/Multimedia Productions, 1993
SHADOW OF OBSESSION (TF)   Saban Entertainment, 1994
THE OLD CURIOSITY SHOP (TF)   Curiousity Productions/RHI
Entertainment/Elstree Productions/The Disney Channel,
1995, British-U.S.

ROBERT CONRAD*
(Conrad Robert Falk)
b. March 1, 1935 - Chicago, Illinois
Business: A. Shane Company, 21355 Pacific Coast Highway -
Suite 200, Malibu, CA 90265, 310/456-5655
Agent: David Shapira & Associates - Sherman Oaks, 818/906-0322

HIGH MOUNTAIN RANGERS (TF)   A. Shane Company, 1987
GLORY DAYS (TF)   A. Shane Company/Sibling Rivalries, 1988
JESSE HAWKES (TF)   A. Shane Company, 1989

JAMES A. CONTNER*
Address: 4325 Vantage Avenue, Studio City, CA 91604,
818/506-8728
Agent: Paradigm - Los Angeles, 310/277-4400

HITLER'S DAUGHTER (CTF)   Wilshire Court Productions, 1990
THE 10 MILLION DOLLAR GETAWAY (CTF)   Alan Cooperman
Productions/Wilshire Court Productions, 1991

PALACE GUARD (TF)   Stephen J. Cannell Productions, 1991
THE RETURN OF ELIOT NESS (TF)   Michael Filerman
Productions, 1991
THE COVER GIRL MURDERS (TF)   River Enterprises/Wilshire
Court Productions, 1993

JAMES L. CONWAY*
b. October 27, 1950 - New York, New York
Agent: CAA - Beverly Hills, 310/288-4545

IN SEARCH OF NOAH'S ARK   Sunn Classic, 1976
THE LINCOLN CONSPIRACY   Sunn Classic, 1977
THE INCREDIBLE ROCKY MOUNTAIN RACE (TF)   Sunn Classic
Productions, 1977
THE LAST OF THE MOHICANS (TF)   Sunn Classic
Productions, 1977
BEYOND AND BACK   Sunn Classic, 1978
DONNER PASS: THE ROAD TO SURVIVAL (TF)   Sunn Classic
Productions, 1978
GREATEST HEROES OF THE BIBLE (MS)   Sunn Classic
Productions, 1978
THE FALL OF THE HOUSE OF USHER   Sunn Classic, 1979
HANGAR 18   Sunn Classic, 1980
THE LEGEND OF SLEEPY HOLLOW (TF)   Sunn Classic, 1980
EARTHBOUND   Taft International, 1981
NASHVILLE GRAB (TF)   Taft International, 1981
THE BOOGENS   Jensen Farley Pictures, 1981
THE PRESIDENT MUST DIE   Jensen Farley Pictures, 1981

KEVIN CONWAY
b. May 29, 1942 - New York, New York
Agent: Badgley/Connor - Los Angeles, 310/278-9313

THE SUN AND THE MOON   THE VIOLINS CAME WITH
THE AMERICANS   Double Helix, 1987

RIF COOGAN
(See Adam RIFKIN)

BRUCE COOK
THE CENSUS TAKER   Argentum Productions, 1984
LINE OF FIRE   Shapiro Glickenhaus Entertainment, 1988
NIGHTWISH   Vidmark, 1988
A PARTY CALLED EARTH   Western L.A. Filmproductions, 1991
HUSBANDS, WIVES, MONEY AND MURDER   Cinetrust
Entertainment, 1994

FIELDER COOK*
b. March 9, 1923 - Atlanta, Georgia
Contact: Mort Leavy, Leavy, Rosenswig & Haggman, 11 East 49th
Street, New York, NY 10017, 212/983-0400

PATTERNS   United Artists, 1956
HOME IS THE HERO   Showcorporation, 1961, Irish
A BIG HAND FOR THE LITTLE LADY   Warner Bros., 1966
HOW TO SAVE A MARRIAGE AND RUIN YOUR LIFE
Columbia, 1968
PRUDENCE AND THE PILL   20th Century-Fox, 1968, British
TEACHER, TEACHER (TF) ☆   NBC, 1969
SAM HILL: WHO KILLED THE MYSTERIOUS MR. FOSTER? (TF)
Universal TV, 1971
GOODBYE, RAGGEDY ANN (TF)   Metromedia Producers
Corporation, 1971
THE HOMECOMING (TF) ☆   Lorimar Productions, 1971
THE HANDS OF CORMAC JOYCE (TF)   Crawford Productions/
Foote, Cone & Belding, 1972
EAGLE IN A CAGE   National General, 1972, British-Yugoslavian
MIRACLE ON 34TH STREET (TF)   20th Century-Fox TV, 1973
FROM THE MIXED-UP FILES OF MRS. BASIL E. FRANKWEILER
THE HIDEAWAYS   Cinema 5, 1973
THAT WAS THE WEST THAT WAS (TF)   Universal TV, 1974
MILES TO GO BEFORE I SLEEP (TF)   Tomorrow
Entertainment, 1975
THE RIVALRY (TF)   NBC-TV, 1975
VALLEY FORGE (TF)   Clarion Productions/Columbia TV, 1975
BEAUTY AND THE BEAST (TF)   Palms Films Ltd., 1976, British

JUDGE HORTON AND THE SCOTTSBORO BOYS (TF) ☆
   Tomorrow Entertainment, 1976
A LOVE AFFAIR: THE ELEANOR AND LOU GEHRIG STORY (TF)
   Charles Fries Productions/Stonehenge Productions, 1977
TOO FAR TO GO (TF)   Sea Cliff Productions, 1979
I KNOW WHY THE CAGED BIRD SINGS (TF)   Tomorrow
   Entertainment, 1979
GAUGUIN THE SAVAGE (TF)   Nephi Productions, 1980
FAMILY REUNION (TF)   Creative Projects Inc./Columbia TV, 1981
WILL THERE REALLY BE A MORNING? (TF)   Jaffe-Blakely
   Films/Sama Productions/Orion TV, 1983
WHY ME? (TF)   Lorimar Productions, 1984
EVERGREEN (MS)   Edgar J. Scherick Associates/Metromedia
   Producers Corporation, 1985
SEIZE THE DAY (TF)   Learning in Focus, 1986
A SPECIAL FRIENDSHIP (TF)   Entertainment Partners, 1987

PHILIP J. COOK
INVADER   21st Century Distribution, 1991

TROY COOK
PHOENIX   Triad Studios, 1995

TONY COOKSON
b. New York, New York
Agent: Susan Grant, The Artists Group - Los Angeles, 310/552-1100

AND YOU THOUGHT YOUR PARENTS WERE WEIRD
   Trimark Pictures, 1991

MARTHA COOLIDGE*
b. August 17, 1946 - New Haven, Connecticut
Agent: CAA - Beverly Hills, 310/288-4545

NOT A PRETTY PICTURE   Films Inc., 1976
VALLEY GIRL   Atlantic Releasing Corporation, 1983
JOY OF SEX   Paramount, 1984
THE CITY GIRL   Moon Pictures, 1984
REAL GENIUS   TriStar, 1985
PLAIN CLOTHES   Paramount, 1988
TRENCHCOAT IN PARADISE (TF)   Ogiens-Kate Company
   Productions/The Finnegan-Pinchuk Company, 1989
BARE ESSENTIALS (TF)   Republic Pictures, 1991
RAMBLING ROSE   Seven Arts/New Line Cinema, 1991
CRAZY IN LOVE (CTF)   Ohlmeyer Communications/Karen
   Danaher-Dorr Productions, 1992
LOST IN YONKERS   Columbia, 1993
ANGIE   Buena Vista, 1994
THREE WISHES   Savoy Pictures, 1995

HAL COOPER*
b. February 23, 1923 - New York, New York
Home: 2651 Hutton Drive, Beverly Hills, CA 90210, 310/271-8602
Agent: Metropolitan Talent Agency - Los Angeles, 213/857-4500

MILLION DOLLAR INFIELD (TF)   CBS Entertainment, 1982

JACKIE COOPER*
b. September 15, 1922 - Los Angeles, California
Agent: Ronald Leif, Contemporary Artists - Santa Monica,
   310/395-1800

STAND UP AND BE COUNTED   Columbia, 1971
HAVING BABIES III (TF)   The Jozak Company/Paramount TV, 1978
PERFECT GENTLEMEN (TF)   Paramount TV, 1978
RAINBOW (TF)   Ten-Four Productions, 1978
SEX AND THE SINGLE PARENT (TF)   Time-Life Productions, 1979
MARATHON (TF)   Alan Landsburg Productions, 1980
WHITE MAMA (TF)   Tomorrow Entertainment, 1980
RODEO GIRL (TF)   Steckler Productions/Marble Arch
   Productions, 1980
LEAVE 'EM LAUGHING (TF)   Julian Fowles Productions/Charles
   Fries Productions, 1981
ROSIE: THE ROSEMARY CLOONEY STORY (TF)   Charles Fries
   Productions/Alan Sacks Productions, 1982
MOONLIGHT (TF)   co-director with Rod Holcomb, released under
   pseudonym of Alan Smithee, Universal TV, 1982

GO FOR THE GOLD   Go for the Gold Productions, 1984
GLITTER (TF)   Aaron Spelling Productions, 1984
THE NIGHT THEY SAVED CHRISTMAS (TF)
   Robert Halmi Inc., 1984
IZZY AND MOE (TF)   Robert Halmi Inc., 1985
THE LADIES (TF)   NBC, 1987, filmed in 1983

PETER H. COOPER
Business: Moir Productions, 220 East 23rd Street, New York, NY,
212/213-9797

ORDINARY HEROES   Crow Productions/Ira Barmak
   Productions, 1986

STUART COOPER*
b. 1942 - Hoboken, New Jersey
Agent: Paradigm - Los Angeles, 310/277-4400 or:
   ICM - London, tel.: 171/636-6565

LITTLE MALCOLM AND HIS STRUGGLE AGAINST THE EUNUCHS
   Multicetera Investments, 1974, British
OVERLORD   1975, British
THE DISAPPEARANCE   Levitt-Pickman, 1977, Canadian
A.D. - ANNO DOMINI (MS)   Procter & Gamble Productions/
   International Film Productions, 1985, U.S.-Italian
THE LONG HOT SUMMER (TF)   Leonard Hill Productions, 1985
CHRISTMAS EVE (TF)   NBC Productions, 1986
MARIO PUZO'S THE FORTUNATE PILGRIM   THE FORTUNATE
   PILGRIM (MS)   NBC Productions, 1988
PAYOFF (CTF)   Viacom Pictures/Aurora Productions, 1991
ONE SPECIAL VICTORY (TF)   Port Street Films/NBC
   Productions, 1991
RUBDOWN (CTF)   Wilshire Court Productions/Fast
   Track Films, 1993
DANCING WITH DANGER (CTF)   Fast Track Films/Wilshire Court
   Productions/USA Network, 1994
BITTER VENGEANCE (CTF)   Fast Track Films/Wilshire Court
   Productions/USA Network, 1994
OUT OF ANNIE'S PAST (CTF)   Karen Moore Productions/Point of
   View Productions/MTE, 1995

CHRISTOPHER COPPOLA
Agent: ICM - Beverly Hills, 310/550-4000

DRACULA'S WIDOW   DEG, 1988
GUNFIGHT AT RED DOG CORRAL   Picture Entertainment
   Corporation, 1992
DEADFALL   Trimark Pictures, 1993
LOVELAND   Cineplay International, 1994

FRANCIS FORD COPPOLA*
b. April 7, 1939 - Detroit, Michigan
Business: American Zoetrope, Sentinel Building, 916 Kearny Street,
   San Francisco, CA 94133, 415/788-7500
Agent: CAA - Beverly Hills, 310/288-4545

TONIGHT FOR SURE   Premier Pictures, 1961
DEMENTIA 13   American International, 1963
YOU'RE A BIG BOY NOW   7 Arts, 1966
FINIAN'S RAINBOW   Warner Bros., 1968
THE RAIN PEOPLE   Warner Bros., 1969
THE GODFATHER ★   Paramount, 1972
THE CONVERSATION   Paramount, 1974
THE GODFATHER, PART II ★★   Paramount, 1974
APOCALYPSE NOW ★   United Artists, 1979
ONE FROM THE HEART   Columbia, 1982
THE OUTSIDERS   Warner Bros., 1983
RUMBLE FISH   Universal, 1983
THE COTTON CLUB   Orion, 1984
PEGGY SUE GOT MARRIED   TriStar, 1986
GARDENS OF STONE   TriStar, 1987
TUCKER: THE MAN AND HIS DREAM   Paramount, 1988
NEW YORK STORIES   co-director with Woody Allen &
   Martin Scorsese, Buena Vista, 1989
THE GODFATHER, PART III ★   Paramount, 1990
BRAM STOKER'S DRACULA   DRACULA   Columbia, 1992

FRANK CORACI

MURDERED INNOCENCE   The Rayfield Company III, 1994

GERARD CORBIAU

b. September 19, 1941 - Etterbeck, Brussels, Belgium
Address: rue Hippolyte Boulanger 17, B-1180, Brussels, Belgium,
   tel.: 2/374-4124
Agent: ICM - Beverly Hills, 310/550-4000

THE MUSIC TEACHER   Orion Classics, 1988, Belgian
L'ANNEE DE L'EVEIL   Capricorn/FR3 Films/France K2/RTBF
   Belgium/Sofica Creation/Investimage 2&3/CNC/Canal Plus/
   S.A. Investico/ASLK-CGER Bank/Belgian French Community
   Executive, 1991, French-Belgian
FARINELLI   *FARINELLI IL CASTRATO*   Sony Pictures Classics,
   1994, French-Italian-Belgian

BILL CORCORAN*

(William Joseph Corcoran)
Home: 238 S. Moreno Drive, Beverly Hills, CA, 310/282-8078
Agent: Shapiro-Lichtman Talent Agency - Los Angeles, 310/859-8877

E.A.R.T.H. FORCE (TF)   Paramount Network TV, 1990
STREET JUSTICE: LEGACY (TF)   Stephen J. Cannell
   Productions, 1991
SURVIVE THE NIGHT (CTF)   Heartstar Productions/Once Upon
   A Time/USA Network/RAI/Spectator Films, 1993
SHATTERED TRUST: THE SHARI KARNEY STORY (TF)
   Heartstar Productions/Spectator Films/Michael Jaffe Films, 1993
I KNOW MY SON IS ALIVE (TF)   Alexander-Enright &
   Associates/World Information Network, 1994
TRUST IN ME (TF)   Atlantis Films/Keatley Film/Telefilm Canada/
   BC Film/Rogers Telefund, 1995, Canadian

NICHOLAS COREA*

b. April 7, 1943 - St. Louis, Missouri
Home: 11349 Canton Drive, Studio City, CA 91604, 818/760-7830
Agent: David Shapira & Associates - Sherman Oaks, 818/906-0322

THE ARCHER: FUGITIVE FROM THE EMPIRE (TF)   Mad-Dog
   Productions/Universal TV, 1981

RAFAEL CORKIDI

b. 1930 - Puebla, Mexico
Contact: IMCINE, Tepic #40, P.B. Colonia Roma Sur, Mexico City,
   C.P. 06760, Mexico, tel.: 525/584-7283

ANGELES & QUERUBINES   Azteca Films, 1971, Mexican
AUANDAR ANAPU   Azteca Films, 1974, Mexican
PAFNUCIO SANTO   Azteca Films, 1976, Mexican
DESEOS   Azteca Films, 1977

ROGER CORMAN

b. April 5, 1926 - Los Angeles, California
Business: Concorde Pictures, 11600 San Vicente Blvd.,
   Los Angeles, CA 90049, 310/826-0978 or 310/820-6733

FIVE GUNS WEST   American International, 1955
THE APACHE WOMAN   American International, 1955
THE DAY THE WORLD ENDED   American International, 1956
SWAMP WOMAN   Woolner Brothers, 1956
THE OKLAHOMA WOMAN   American International, 1956
THE GUNSLINGER   ARC, 1956
IT CONQUERED THE WORLD   American International, 1956
NOT OF THIS EARTH   Allied Artists, 1957
THE UNDEAD   American International, 1957
NAKED PARADISE   American International, 1957
ATTACK OF THE CRAB MONSTERS   Allied Artists, 1957
ROCK ALL NIGHT   American International, 1957
TEENAGE DOLL   Allied Artists, 1957
CARNIVAL ROCK   Howco, 1957
SORORITY GIRL   American International, 1957
THE VIKING WOMEN AND THE SEA SERPENT
   American International, 1957
WAR OF THE SATELLITES   Allied Artists, 1958
THE SHE GODS OF SHARK REEF   American International, 1958

MACHINE GUN KELLY   American International, 1958
TEENAGE CAVEMAN   American International, 1958
I, MOBSTER   20th Century-Fox, 1959
A BUCKET OF BLOOD   American International, 1959
THE WASP WOMAN   American International, 1959
SKI TROOP ATTACK   Filmgroup, 1960
THE HOUSE OF USHER   American International, 1960
THE LITTLE SHOP OF HORRORS   Filmgroup, 1960
THE LAST WOMAN ON EARTH   Filmgroup, 1960
CREATURE FROM THE HAUNTED SEA   Filmgroup, 1961
ATLAS   Filmgroup, 1961
THE PIT AND THE PENDULUM   American International, 1961
THE INTRUDER   *I HATE YOUR GUTS*   Pathe American, 1962
THE PREMATURE BURIAL   American International, 1962
TALES OF TERROR   American International, 1962
TOWER OF LONDON   American International, 1962
THE RAVEN   American International, 1963
THE TERROR   American International, 1963
"X" - THE MAN WITH THE X-RAY EYES   American
   International, 1963
THE HAUNTED PALACE   American International, 1963
THE YOUNG RACERS   American International, 1963
THE SECRET INVASION   United Artists, 1964
THE MASQUE OF THE RED DEATH   American International,
   1964, British-U.S.
THE TOMB OF LIGEIA   American International, 1965
THE WILD ANGELS   American International, 1966
THE ST. VALENTINE'S DAY MASSACRE   20th Century-Fox, 1967
THE TRIP   American International, 1967
TARGET: HARRY   released under pseudonym of Harry Neill,
   ABC Pictures International, 1968
BLOODY MAMA   American International, 1970
GAS-S-S-S!...OR IT BECAME NECESSARY TO DESTROY THE
   WORLD IN ORDER TO SAVE IT!   American International, 1970
VON RICHTOFEN AND BROWN   United Artists, 1971
ROGER CORMAN'S FRANKENSTEIN UNBOUND
   FRANKENSTEIN UNBOUND   20th Century Fox, 1990

ALAIN CORNEAU

b. 1943 - Meung-sur-Loire, France
Agent: ICM France - Paris, tel.: 1/723-7860
Contact: French Film Office, 745 Fifth Avenue, New York,
   NY 10151, 212/832-8860

FRANCE SOCIETE ANONYME   1974, French
POLICE PYTHON 357   1976, French
LE MENACE   1977, French
SERE NOIRE   1979, French
LE CHOIS DES ARMES   1981, French
FORT SAGANNE   1984, French
NOCTURNE INDIEN   1989, French
TOUS LES MATINS DU MONDE (ALL THE MORNINGS OF
   THE WORLD)   October Films, 1992, French
CONTRE L'OUBLI   co-director, Les Films du Paradoxe/Amnesty
   International/PRV, 1992, French
LE NOUVEAU MONDE   Bac Films, 1995, French

JOHN CORNELL*

b. 1941 - Kalgoorlie, Australia
Contact: Directors Guild of America - Los Angeles, 213/851-3671

"CROCODILE" DUNDEE II   Paramount, 1988, Australian
ALMOST AN ANGEL   Paramount, 1990, Australian-U.S.

HUBERT CORNFIELD

b. February 9, 1929 - Istanbul, Turkey
Telephone: 310/837-9017
Contact: 310/837-9017

SUDDEN DANGER   United Artists, 1955
LURE OF THE SWAMP   20th Century-Fox, 1957
PLUNDER ROAD   20th Century-Fox, 1957
THE THIRD VOICE   20th Century-Fox, 1959
ANGEL BABY   co-director with Paul Wendkos, Allied Artists, 1961
PRESSURE POINT   United Artists, 1962
THE NIGHT OF THE FOLLOWING DAY   Universal, 1969
LES GRAND MOYENS   Fox, 1976, French

STEPHEN CORNWELL
Agent: The Agency - Los Angeles, 310/551-3000

THE KILLING STREETS   21st Century Distribution, 1991, U.S.-Israeli
THE PHILADELPHIA EXPERIMENT 2   Trimark Pictures, 1993

EUGENE CORR*
Agent: Innovative Artists - Los Angeles, 310/553-5200

OVER-UNDER, SIDEWAYS-DOWN   co-director with Steve Wax &
   Peter Gessner, Steve Wax/Cine-Manifest Productions, 1977
DESERT BLOOM   Columbia, 1986
WALDO SALT: A SCREENWRITER'S JOURNEY (TD)
   co-director with Robert Hillmann, Waldo Productions/
   WNET-New York/The Sundance Institute, 1990

CHARLES CORRELL*
Agent: Metropolitan Talent Agency - Los Angeles, 213/857-4500

MacGYVER: LEGEND OF THE HOLY ROSE (TF)   co-director with
   Michael Caffey, Henry Winkler-John Rich Productions/
   Paramount TV, 1989
GUNSMOKE: THE LAST APACHE (TF)   CBS Entertainment/
   Galatea Productions, 1990
DEADLY DESIRE (CTF)   Wilshire Court Productions, 1991
CRY IN THE WILD: THE TAKING OF PEGGY ANN (TF)
   Ron Gilbert Associates/Leonard Hill Films, 1991
WRITER'S BLOCK (CTF)   Talent Court Productions/Wilshire Court
   Productions, 1991
SHE SAYS SHE'S INNOCENT (TF)   Robert Greenwald
   Productions, 1991
IN THE DEEP WOODS (TF)   Frederic Golchan Productions/Leonard
   Hill Films, 1992
DEAD BEFORE DAWN (TF)   Joel Fields Productions/Leonard
   Hill Films, 1993
MOTHER OF THE BRIDE (TF)   Baby Productions/Leonard
   Hill Films, 1993
MODELS INC. (TF)   Spelling TV, 1994
MacGYVER: TRAIL TO DOOMSDAY (TF)   Gekko Film
   Corporation/Henry Winkler-John Rich Productions/
   Paramount Network TV, 1994
LEGEND (TF)   Gekko Film Corporation/Mike & Bill Productions/
   United Paramount Network, 1995

RICHARD CORRELL*
Agent: CAA - Beverly Hills, 310/288-4545

SKI PATROL   Triumph Releasing Corporation, 1990

MICHAEL CORRENTE
FEDERAL HILL   Trimark Pictures, 1994
AMERICAN BUFFALO   The Samuel Goldwyn Company, 1995

ROBERT CORSINI
STRAIGHT FROM THE STREETS (FD)   co-director with
   Keith O'Derek, Upfront Productions, 1994

IAN CORSON
Contact: Directors Guild of Canada, 225 Richmond Street,
   Toronto M5V 1W2, Canada, 416/351-8200

MALICIOUS   Republic Pictures, 1995, Canadian

BUD CORT
(Walter Edward Cox)
Agent: Judy Schoen & Associates - Los Angeles, 213/962-1950

TED & VENUS   Double Helix Films, 1991

WILLIAM H. (BILL) COSBY, JR.*
b. July 12, 1937 - Philadelphia, Pennsylvania
Business: SHA Enterprises, 5555 Melrose Avenue, Dressing Room
   Building - Suite 109, Hollywood, CA 90038, 213/956-8225
Agent: William Morris Agency - Beverly Hills, 310/274-7451

BILL COSBY, HIMSELF (PF)   20th Century-Fox
   International Classics, 1983

DON COSCARELLI*
b. February 17, 1954 - Tripoli, Libya
Business: Starway International, 2100 Century Park West,
   Los Angeles, CA 90067, 310/556-1448
Agent: APA - Los Angeles, 310/273-0744

JIM - THE WORLD'S GREATEST   Universal, 1976
KENNY AND COMPANY   20th Century-Fox, 1976
PHANTASM   Avco Embassy, 1979
THE BEASTMASTER   MGM/UA, 1982
PHANTASM II   Universal, 1988
SURVIVAL QUEST   MGM/UA, 1989
PHANTASM III: LORD OF THE DEAD (HVF)   MCA-Universal
   Home Video, 1994

JOHN COSGROVE*
Business: Cosgrove-Meurer Productions, 4303 W. Verdugo Avenue,
   Burbank, CA 91505, 818/843-5600

VICTIM OF LOVE: THE SHARON MOHR STORY (TF)
   Cosgrove-Meurer Productions, 1993

GEORGE PAN COSMATOS*
(Yorgo Pan Cosmatos)
b. January 4, 1941 - Greece
Agent: ICM - Beverly Hills, 310/550-4000

MASSACRE IN ROME   *RAPPRESAGLIA*   National General,
   1973, Italian-French
THE CASSANDRA CROSSING   Avco Embassy, 1977,
   British-Italian-West German
RESTLESS   Joseph Brenner Associates, 1978
ESCAPE TO ATHENA   AFD, 1979, British
OF UNKNOWN ORIGIN   Warner Bros., 1983, Canadian
RAMBO: FIRST BLOOD PART II   TriStar, 1985
COBRA   Warner Bros., 1986
LEVIATHAN   MGM/UA, 1989, U.S.-Italian
TOMBSTONE   Buena Vista, 1993
THE SHADOW CONSPIRACY   Buena Vista, 1995

THOMAS COST
PRIME SUSPECT   Premier Pictures/Silver-Regan Productions, 1989
BARDO   Giroscopio Productions, 1991

COSTA-GAVRAS
(See Costa GAVRAS)

KEVIN COSTNER*
b. January 18, 1955 - Los Angeles, California
Business: Tig Productions, 4000 Warner Blvd. - Producers Building 5,
   Burbank, CA 91523, 818/954-4500
Agent: CAA - Beverly Hills, 310/288-4545

DANCES WITH WOLVES ★★   Orion, 1990

MANNY COTO*
Agent: UTA - Beverly Hills, 310/273-6700

PLAYROOM   1990
COVER-UP   TriStar, 1991
DR. GIGGLES   Universal, 1992

VITTORIO COTTAFAVI
b. January 30, 1914 - Modena, Italy
Home: via Monti Parioli 49/A, Rome, Italy, tel.: 6/321-8855

I NOSTRI SOGNI   Iris Film, 1943, Italian
LA FIAMME CHE NON SI SPEGNE   Orsa Film, 1949, Italian
UNA DONNA HA UCCISO   Novissima Film, 1951, Italian
IL BOIA DI LILLA   Venturini Produzioni/Nino Martegani/Atlantis,
   1952, Italian-French
I PIOMBI DI VENEZIA   Venturini Produzione, 1952, Italian
IL CAVALIERE DI MAISON ROUGE   Venturini Produzione,
   1953, Italian
TRAVIATA '53   Venturini Produzione, 1953, Italian
IN AMORE SI PECCA IN DUE   Romana Film, 1953, Italian

UNNA DONNA LIBERA 1954, Italian
AVANZI DI GALERA Venturini Produzione, 1954, Italian
NEL GORGO DEL PECCATO Itala Film, 1954, Italian
FIESTA BRAVA (FD) Phoenix Film/Itala Film, 1956, Spanish-Italian
THE WARRIOR AND THE SLAVE GIRL LA RIVOLTA DEL GLADIATORI Columbia, 1958, Italian
LEGIONS OF THE NILE LE LEGIONI DI CLEOPATRA 20th Century-Fox, 1959, Italian-French-Spanish
MESSALINA American International, 1959, Italian
GOLIATH AND THE DRAGON LA VENDETTA DI ERCOLE American International, 1960, Italian-French
HERCULES AND THE CAPTIVE WOMEN ERCOLE ALLA CONQUISTA DI ATLANTIDE Woolner Brothers, 1961, Italian-French
I CENTO CAVALIERI Domiziana/Productores Cinematograficos Unidos/International Germania Film, 1964, Italian-Spanish-West German

JACK COUFFER*

Contact: Directors Guild of America - Los Angeles, 213/851-3671

NIKKI, WILD DOG OF THE NORTH co-director with Don Haldane, Buena Vista, 1961, U.S.-Canadian
RING OF BRIGHT WATER Cinerama Releasing Corporation, 1969, British
LIVING FREE Columbia, 1972, British
THE DARWIN ADVENTURE 20th Century-Fox, 1972, British
THE LAST GIRAFFE (TF) Westfall Productions, 1979

JEROME COURTLAND*

b. December 27, 1926 - Knoxville, Tennessee
Agent: The Kaplan-Stahler Agency - Beverly Hills, 310/653-4483

RUN, COUGAR, RUN Buena Vista, 1972
DIAMONDS ON WHEELS Buena Vista, 1972, U.S.-British
THE SKY TRAP (TF) Walt Disney Productions, 1979
KNOTS LANDING: JUST LIKE OLD TIMES (TF) Roundelay-MF Productions/Lorimar TV, 1993

JACQUES-YVES COUSTEAU

b. June 11, 1910 - Saint-Andre, France
Address: 25, avenue de Wagram, 75017 Paris, France, tel.: 1/47-66-02-46
Contact: French Film Office, 745 Fifth Avenue, New York, NY 10151, 212/832-8860

THE SILENT WORLD (FD) Columbia, 1956, French
WORLD WITHOUT SUN (FD) Columbia, 1964, French
LE VOYAGE AU BOUT DU MONDE (FD) co-director with Philippe Cousteau, 1976, French

RAOUL COUTARD

b. September 16, 1924 - Paris, France
Home: 34, rue Salvador Allende, 92000 Nanterre, France, tel.: 47-21-53-40
Contact: French Film Office, 745 Fifth Avenue, New York, NY 10151, 212/832-8860

HOA-BINH Transvue, 1971, French
LA LEGION SAUTE SUR KOLWEZI Bela Productions/FR3, 1980, French
S.A.S. A SAN SALVADOR UGC, 1982, French-West German

BILL COUTURIE

Agent: CAA - Beverly Hills, 310/288-4545

DEAR AMERICA: LETTERS HOME FROM VIETNAM (FD) Taurus Entertainment, 1987
EARTH AND THE AMERICAN DREAM (TD) HBO/Couturie Company/BBC, 1993, U.S.-British
STAGES: THE LIFE OF BILL GRAHAM (FD) Couturie Company, 1995
ED Universal, 1995

MICHAEL COVERT

FROM THE EDGE Canned Pictures, 1995

ADRIAN COWELL

Contact: British Film Commission, 70 Baker Street, London W1M 1DJ, England, tel.: 171/224-5000

MURDER IN THE AMAZON (TD) Central Independent TV/Universidade Catolica de Goias, 1989, British-Brazilian
THE DECADE OF DESTRUCTION (TD) PBS/Central Independent TV/KCTS/WGBH/WNET/WPBT/WTVS, 1990, U.S.-British

ALEX COX

b. December 15, 1954 - Liverpool, England
Home: P.O. Box 1002, Venice, CA 90291
Business: Together Brothers Productions Inc., 9505 W. Washington Blvd., Culver City, CA 90230, 310/841-2301
Agent: Stephanie Mann & Associates - Los Angeles, 213/653-7130

REPO MAN Universal, 1984
SID AND NANCY The Samuel Goldwyn Company, 1986, British
STRAIGHT TO HELL Island Films, 1987, British-Spanish
WALKER Universal, 1987, U.S.-Nicaraguan
HIGHWAY PATROLMAN EL PATRULLERO First Look Pictures, 1992, Mexican-Japanese-U.S.
DEATH AND THE COMPASS (TF) BBC, 1992, British
RICHARD III First Look Pictures, 1995, British

NELL COX*

Home: 9015 Burroughs Road, Los Angeles, CA 90046, 213/654-9543

LIZA'S PIONEER DIARY (TF) Nell Cox Films, 1976
THE ROOMMATE Rubicon Film Productions, 1985
KONRAD (TF) Sunn Classics Pictures, 1985
TRAITOR IN MY HOUSE (TF) Educational Film Center/American Film Works Inc./WonderWorks, 1990

PAUL COX
(Paulus Henriqus Benedictus Cox)
b. April 16, 1940 - Venlo, Netherlands
Agent: Becsey/Wisdom/Kalajian - Los Angeles, 310/550-0535

ILLUMINATIONS Illumination Film Productions, 1976, Australian
INSIDE LOOKING OUT Illumination Film Productions, 1977, Australian
KOSTAS Illumination Film Productions, 1979, Australian
LONELY HEARTS The Samuel Goldwyn Company, 1982, Australian
MAN OF FLOWERS Spectrafilm, 1983, Australian
MY FIRST WIFE Spectrafilm, 1984, Australian
CACTUS Spectrafilm, 1986, Australian
HANDLE WITH CARE (TF) Alsof Productions, 1986, Australian
VINCENT - THE LIFE AND DEATH OF VINCENT VAN GOGH Roxie Releasing, 1987, Australian-Dutch
THE PAPER BOY (TF) Australian Children's Television Foundation/ITC, 1987, Australian
ISLAND Roxie Releasing, 1989, Australian
GOLDEN BRAID Cabriolet Films, 1990, Australian
A WOMAN'S TALE Orion Classics, 1991, Australian
THE NUN AND THE BANDIT Greater Union Distributors, 1992, Australian
EXILE Illumination Films, 1994, Australian
EROTIC TALES co-director with Bob Rafelson, Susan Seidelman, Ken Russell, Melvin Van Peebles & Mani Kaul, Regina Ziegler Filmproduktion/Tele-Munchen/Westdeutscher Rundfunk, 1994, German

LUIGI COZZI
(See Lewis COATES)

WILLIAM CRAIN*

b. June 20, 1949
Business: Raindance Entertainment Company, P.O. Box 744, Beverly Hills, CA 90213, 310/874-8978
Agent: Ronald Leif, Contemporary Artists - Santa Monica, 310/395-1800

BLACULA American International, 1972
DR. BLACK, MR. HYDE Dimension, 1976

THE WATTS MONSTER   Dimension, 1979
THE KID FROM NOT-SO-BIG   1982
STANDING IN THE SHADOWS OF LOVE   Brandenberg-Crain
   Productions, 1984

BESTOR CRAM
THE AMERICAN EXPERIENCE: MIDNIGHT RAMBLE
   MIDNIGHT RAMBLE (TD)   co-director with Pearl Bowser,
   Northern Lights, 1994

PETER CRANE*
Business: Alpha Centauri, Ltd., 6061 Galahad Drive, Malibu, CA
   90265, 310/457-4821
Agent: ICM - Beverly Hills, 310/550-4000

HUNTED   Warner/Columbia, 1972, British
ASSASSIN   Warner/Columbia, 1973, British
MOMENTS   Warner/Columbia, 1974, British
COVER UP (TF)   Glen A. Larson Productions/20th Century
   Fox TV, 1984
THE LAW AND HARRY McGRAW: DEAD MEN DON'T MAKE
   PHONE CALLS (TF)   Universal TV, 1987
COOPERSMITH: SWEET SCENT OF MURDER (TF)
   Forbrooke Enterprises/Universal TV, 1992

JAY CRAVEN
WHERE THE RIVERS FLOW NORTH   Caledonia Pictures/Kingdom
   County Productions, 1993

WES CRAVEN*
b. August 2, 1949 - Cleveland, Ohio
Agent: ICM - Beverly Hills, 310/550-4000

LAST HOUSE ON THE LEFT   Hallmark Releasing
   Corporation, 1973
THE HILLS HAVE EYES   Vanguard, 1977
STRANGER IN OUR HOUSE (TF)   Inter Planetary Pictures/
   Finnegan Associates, 1978
DEADLY BLESSING   United Artists, 1981
SWAMP THING   Avco Embassy, 1982
INVITATION TO HELL (TF)   Moonlight Productions II, 1984
A NIGHTMARE ON ELM STREET   New Line Cinema, 1984
CHILLER (TF)   Polar Film Corporation/J.D. Feigleson
   Productions, 1985
THE HILLS HAVE EYES PART II   Castle Hill Productions, 1986
DEADLY FRIEND   Warner Bros., 1986
THE SERPENT AND THE RAINBOW   Universal, 1988
SHOCKER   Universal, 1989
NIGHT VISIONS (TF)   Wes Craven Films/MGM-UA TV, 1990
THE PEOPLE UNDER THE STAIRS   Universal, 1991
WES CRAVEN'S NEW NIGHTMARE   New Line Cinema, 1994
VAMPIRE IN BROOKLYN   Paramount, 1995

WAYNE CRAWFORD
Business: Gibraltar Entertainment, Inc., 14101 Valleyheart Drive -
   Suite 205, Sherman Oaks, CA 91423, 818/501-2076
Agent: Paul Kohner, Inc. - Los Angeles, 310/550-1060

CRIME LORDS   Gibraltar Releasing/Heatherwood Film
   Productions, 1991

LOL CREME*
Business: Medialab, Chelsea Wharf, 15 Lots Road, London
   SW10 0QH, England, tel.: 171/351-5814
Agent: The Marion Rosenberg Office - Los Angeles, 213/653-7383
Contact: British Film Commission, 70 Baker Street, London
   W1M 1DJ, England, tel.: 171/224-5000

THE LUNATIC   Triton Pictures, 1991, Jamaican-British

KEVIN G. CREMIN*
Home: 6550 West Juniper Crest, Agua Dulce, CA 91350,
   805/269-5409

SIRINGO   Rysher Entertainment, 1994

RICHARD CRENNA*
b. November 30, 1926 - Los Angeles, California
Contact: Directors Guild of America - Los Angeles, 213/851-3671

BETTER LATE THAN NEVER (TF)   Ten-Four Productions, 1979

CHARLES CRICHTON
b. August 6, 1910 - Wallasey, Cheshire, England
Agent: MLR Representation Ltd. - London, tel.: 171/351-5442

FOR THOSE IN PERIL   1944, British
PAINTED BOATS   1945, British
DEAD OF NIGHT   co-director with Alberto Cavalcanti,
   Basil Dearden & Robert Hamer, Universal, 1945, British
HUE AND CRY   Fine Arts, 1947, British
AGAINST THE WIND   Eagle Lion, 1948, British
ANOTHER SHORE   Rank, 1948, British
TRAIN OF EVENTS   co-director with Basil Dearden & Sidney Cole,
   Rank, 1949, British
DANCE HALL   Rank, 1950, British
THE LAVENDER HILL MOB   Universal, 1951, British
THE STRANGER IN BETWEEN   *HUNTED*   Universal, 1952, British
THE TITFIELD THUNDERBOLT   Universal, 1953, British
THE LOVER LOTTERY   Continental, 1953, British
THE DIVIDED HEART   Republic, 1954, British
DECISION AGAINST TIME   *THE MAN IN THE SKY*
   MGM, 1956, British
LAW AND DISORDER   co-director with Henry Cornelius,
   Continental, 1958, British
FLOODS OF FEAR   Universal, 1958, British
THE BATTLE OF THE SEXES   Continental, 1959, British
THE BOY WHO STOLE A MILLION   Paramount, 1960, British
THE THIRD SECRET   20th Century-Fox, 1964, British
HE WHO RIDES A TIGER   Sigma III, 1966, British
A FISH CALLED WANDA ★   MGM/UA, 1988, British

MICHAEL CRICHTON*
(John Michael Crichton)
b. October 23, 1942 - Chicago, Illinois
Address: 1750 14th Street - Suite C, Santa Monica, CA 90404,
   310/452-6200
Agent: CAA - Beverly Hills, 310/288-4545

PURSUIT (TF)   ABC Circle Films, 1972
WESTWORLD   MGM, 1973
COMA   MGM/United Artists, 1978
THE GREAT TRAIN ROBBERY   United Artists, 1979, British
LOOKER   The Ladd Company/Warner Bros., 1981
RUNAWAY   TriStar, 1984
PHYSICAL EVIDENCE   Columbia, 1989

DONALD CROMBIE
b. Australia
Agent: ICM - London, tel.: 171/636-6565

WHO KILLED JENNY LANGBY? (TF)   1974, Australian
DO I HAVE TO KILL MY CHILD? (TF)   1976, Australian
CADDIE   Atlantic Releasing Corporation, 1976, Australian
THE IRISHMAN   Forest Home Films, 1978, Australian
CATHY'S CHILD   CB Productions, 1979, Australian
THE KILLING OF ANGEL STREET   Forest Home Films,
   1981, Australian
KITTY AND THE BAGMAN   Quartet/Films Incorporated,
   1982, Australian
ROBBERY UNDER ARMS   co-director with Ken Hannam,
   ITC Productions, 1985, Australian
PLAYING BEATIE BOW   CEL, 1986, Australian
CYCLONE TRACY (MS)   co-director with Kathy Mueller,
   PBL Productions, 1986, Australian
THE ALIEN YEARS (MS)   Resulution/Australian Broadcasting
   Corporation/Revcom TV, 1988, Australian
THE HEROES (TF)   TVS/Network Ten, 1988, British-Australian
THE SAINT IN AUSTRALIA (TF)   Templar Productions/Taffner
   Ramsay Productions, 1989, U.S.-Australian

HEROES II - THE RETURN (TF)   TVS Films/Anthony Buckley
   Productions/Australian Film Finance Corporation,
   1991, British-Australian
ROUGH DIAMONDS   Beyond Films, 1994, Australian

DAVID CRONENBERG
b. March 15, 1943 - Toronto, Ontario, Canada
Business: David Cronenberg Productions, 217 Avenue Road,
   Toronto, Ontario M5R 2J3, Canada, 416/961-3432
Agent: William Morris Agency - Beverly Hills, 310/859-4000

STEREO   Emergent Films, 1969, Canadian
CRIMES OF THE FUTURE   Emergent Films, 1970, Canadian
THEY CAME FROM WITHIN *SHIVERS*   Trans-America,
   1976, Canadian
RABID   New World, 1977, Canadian
THE BROOD   New World, 1979, Canadian
FAST COMPANY   Topar, 1979, Canadian
SCANNERS   Avco Embassy, 1981, Canadian
VIDEODROME   Universal, 1983, Canadian
THE DEAD ZONE   Paramount, 1983, Canadian
THE FLY   20th Century Fox, 1986, U.S-Canadian
DEAD RINGERS   20th Century Fox, 1988, Canadian
NAKED LUNCH   20th Century Fox, 1991, Canadian-British
M. BUTTERFLY   Warner Bros., 1993

HARVEY CROSSLAND
b. 1950 - Ottawa, Ontario, Canada
Home: 3908 W. 51 Avenue, Vancouver, British Columbia V6N 5W1,
   Canada, 604/263-2256
Business: Siren Films Inc., 827 W. Pender Street, Vancouver,
   British Columbia V6C 3G8, Canada, 604/662-8337

FLIERS: PIONEERING CANADIAN AVIATION (TD)
   1980, Canadian
SOMEWHERE BETWEEN   1983, Canadian
ART OF THE INUIT (FD)   1985, Canadian
A LIFE OF INDEPENDENCE (TF)   1986, Canadian
WALKING IN PAIN   1988, Canadian
A DIFFERENT DANCE (TF)   1988, Canadian
THE BURNING SEASON   Siren Films/Primedia Pictures,
   1993, Canadian

AVERY CROUNSE
Business: Elysian Pictures, 650 N. Bronson Avenue - Suite 215,
   Los Angeles, CA 90004, 213/871-8689

EYES OF FIRE   Aquarius/Clark Films, 1984
THE INVISIBLE KID   Taurus Entertainment, 1988
SISTER ISLAND   Elysian Pictures, 1994

CAMERON CROWE*
b. July 13, 1957 - Palm Springs, California
Agent: CAA - Beverly Hills, 310/288-4545

SAY ANYTHING   20th Century-Fox, 1989
SINGLES   Warner Bros., 1992

CHRISTOPHER CROWE*
Agent: UTA - Beverly Hills, 310/273-6700
Business Manager: Edmond Buccellato, Solomon Ross & Company,
   21300 Victory Blvd. - Suite 1250, Woodland Hills, CA 91367,
   818/999-6071

STREETS OF JUSTICE (TF)   Universal TV, 1985
OFF LIMITS   20th Century Fox, 1988
WHISPERS IN THE DARK   Paramount, 1992

DICK CROY
b. January 30, 1943 - Greensberg, Pennsylvania
Agent: Heacock Literary Agency, 1523 Sixth Street, Santa Monica,
   CA 90405, 310/393-6227

THE UNKNOWN FORCE (TF)   International Television Films, 1977

BILLY CRYSTAL*
b. March 14, 1948 - Long Beach, New York
Agent: CAA - Beverly Hills, 310/288-4545

MR. SATURDAY NIGHT   Columbia, 1992
FORGET PARIS   Columbia, 1995

ALFONSO CUARON*
Contact: Directors Guild of America - Los Angeles, 213/851-3671

LOVE IN THE TIME OF HYSTERIA   IMCINE, 1992, Mexican
SOLO CON TU PAREJA   IMCINE, 1993, Mexican
A LITTLE PRINCESS   Warner Bros., 1995

ROBERT CULP*
b. August 16, 1930 - Berkeley, California
Personal Manager: Hillard Elkins, 8306 Wilshire Blvd. - Suite 438,
   Beverly Hills, CA 90211, 310/285-0700

HICKEY AND BOGGS   United Artists, 1972

HOWARD CUMMINGS
STORY OF A MARRIAGE - EPISODE ONE: COURTSHIP (MS)
   Indian Falls Corporation/American Playhouse/
   WGBH-Boston, 1987
BIG TIME (TF)   co-director with Jan Egleson, Advocated
   Productions/WGBH-Boston, 1989

JAMES CUMMINS
Agent: Suan Smith & Associates - Beverly Hills, 213/852-4777

THE BONEYARD   Prism Entertainment, 1991
STALKER   Proto Entertainment, 1992

RUSTY CUNDIEFF
Agent: ICM - Beverly Hills, 310/550-4000

FEAR OF A BLACK HAT   The Samuel Goldwyn Company, 1993
TALES FROM THE HOOD   Savoy Pictures, 1995

SEAN S. CUNNINGHAM*
b. December 31, 1941 - New York, New York
Agent: ICM - Beverly Hills, 310/550-4000

TOGETHER   Hallmark Releasing Corporation, 1971
CASE OF THE FULL MOON MURDERS   *CASE OF THE SMILING
   STIFFS/SEX ON THE GROOVE TUBE*   co-director with
   Brad Talbot, Seaberg, 1974
HERE COME THE TIGERS   American International, 1978
MANNY'S ORPHANS   United Artists, 1979
FRIDAY THE 13TH   Paramount, 1980
A STRANGER IS WATCHING   MGM/United Artists, 1982
SPRING BREAK   Columbia, 1983
THE NEW KIDS   Columbia, 1985
DEEPSTAR SIX   TriStar, 1989

WILLIAM CURRAN*
(William G. Curran)
Home: 242 Bay Street, Santa Monica, CA 90405, 310/392-1035
Agent: Renaissance-H.N. Swanson - Los Angeles, 310/246-6000

LOVE, CHEAT AND STEAL (CTF)   Motion Picture Corporation of
   America, 1993

TERENCE CURREN
Home: 4144 N. Lankershim Blvd. - Suite 220, North Hollywood, CA
   91602, 818/508-3040

INTERVIEW WITH TERROR   Biotone Productions, 1988

D

DAN CURTIS*
b. August 12, 1928 - Bridgeport, Connecticut
Business: Dan Curtis Productions, 10000 W. Washington Blvd. -
 Suite 3014, Culver City, CA 90232, 310/280-6567
Agent: ICM - Beverly Hills, 310/550-4000

HOUSE OF DARK SHADOWS MGM, 1970
NIGHT OF DARK SHADOWS MGM, 1971
THE NIGHT STRANGLER (TF) ABC Circle Films, 1973
THE NORLISS TAPES (TF) Metromedia Producers
 Corporation, 1973
SCREAM OF THE WOLF (TF) Metromedia Producers
 Corporation, 1974
DRACULA (TF) Universal TV/Dan Curtis Productions, 1974
MELVIN PURVIS: G-MAN (TF) American International TV, 1974
THE GREAT ICE RIP-OFF (TF) ABC Circle Films, 1974
TRILOGY OF TERROR (TF) ABC Circle Films, 1975
THE KANSAS CITY MASSACRE (TF) ABC Circle Films, 1975
BURNT OFFERINGS United Artists, 1976
CURSE OF THE BLACK WIDOW (TF) Dan Curtis Productions/
 ABC Circle Films, 1977
WHEN EVERY DAY WAS THE FOURTH OF JULY (TF)
 Dan Curtis Productions, 1978
THE LAST RIDE OF THE DALTON GANG (TF)
 NBC Productions/Dan Curtis Productions, 1979
MRS. R'S DAUGHTER (TF) NBC Productions/Dan Curtis
 Productions, 1979
THE LONG DAYS OF SUMMER (TF) Dan Curtis
 Productions, 1980
THE WINDS OF WAR (MS) ☆ Paramount TV/Dan Curtis
 Productions, 1983
WAR AND REMEMBRANCE (MS) ☆ Dan Curtis Productions/
 ABC Circle Films, 1988-89
DARK SHADOWS (TF) Dan Curtis Productions/
 MGM-UA TV, 1991
INTRUDERS (TF) Osiris Films/Dan Curtis Productions/CBS
 Entertainment, 1992
ME AND THE KID Orion, 1993

DOUGLAS CURTIS
THE SLEEPING CAR Triax Entertainment, 1990

SIMON CURTIS
Contact: British Film Commission, 70 Baker Street, London
 W1M 1DJ, England, tel.: 171/224-5000

THE MOTHER (TF) BBC/Great Performances/WNET-13,
 1994, U.S.-British

JULIE CYPHER
TERESA'S TATTOO CineTel Films/Yankee Entertainment
 Group, 1994

RENEE DAALDER
b. Netherlands

DE BLANKE SLAVIN 1969, Dutch
MASSACRE AT CENTRAL HIGH Brian Distributing, 1976
POPULATION: ONE American Scenes, 1986
HABITAT Matrans Productions, 1995, Canadian

CETIN (SEZEREL) DAGLER
b. February 4, 1949 - Istanbul, Turkey
Address: Varlik Mahallesi, Pirireis Cad 20, Antalya, Turkey,
 Fax: 242/243-1334

BIZIM MAHALLE 1994, Turkish

JOHN DAHL
Agent: UTA - Beverly Hills, 310/273-6700

KILL ME AGAIN MGM-UA, 1989
RED ROCK WEST Roxie Releasing, 1993
THE LAST SEDUCTION October Films, 1994
UNFORGETTABLE MGM-UA, 1995

BOB DAHLIN*
Home: 819 26th Street, Santa Monica, CA 90403, 310/450-6206

MONSTER IN THE CLOSET Troma, 1987

HEINRICH DAHMS
b. October 18, 1954 - South Africa
Business: Desert Pictures, P.O. Box 1002, Parklands 2121,
 South Africa, tel.: 011 2711/646-2606

CITY WOLF Atlas International, 1987, South African
DUNE SURFER I.N Entertainment Group, 1988, South African
AU PAIR Trans Atlantic Entertainment/Gel Productions/Moviworld,
 1991, South African

RENO DAKOTA
AMERICAN FABULOUS First Run Features, 1992

ALESSANDRO D'ALATRI
b.Rome, Italy
Home: Piazza dei Caracci 1, Rome, Italy, tel.: 06/3923215

AMERICANO ROSSO Videa/Raitre, 1991, Italian
SENZA PELLE Rodeo Drive/Istituto Luce/Raidue, 1994, Italian

ZALE DALEN
b. 1947 - Iloilo, Philippines
Address: Site 1, Comp. 23, R.R. #1, 546 Marine Drive, Gibsons,
 British Columbia V0N 1V0, Canada, 604/886-8029
Agent: Natalie Edwards, 11 Dunbar Road, Toronto, Ontario
 M4W 2X5, Canada, 416/922-4437

SKIP TRACER Highlight Productions Ltd., 1977, Canadian
THE HOUNDS OF NOTRE DAME Pan-Canadian Film Distributors,
 1980, Canadian
HOLLYWOOD NORTH Independent Pictures, 1987, Canadian
ANYTHING TO SURVIVE (TF) ATL Productions/B.C. Films,
 1990, U.S.-Canadian
TERMINAL CITY RICOCHET Festival Films, 1990, Canadian
ON THIN ICE: THE TAI BABILONIA STORY (TF) Bernard Rothman
 Productions/Janet Faust Krusi Films/Spectator Films, 1990
EXPECT NO MERCY Le Monde Entertainment/Film One,
 1994, Canadian

TOM DALEY

b. December 28, 1947 - Newark, New Jersey
Business: Pegasus Pictures, 821 Cooke Street, Honolulu, Hawaii
96813, 808/533-1805

THE OUTING *THE LAMP* TMS Pictures, 1987

ROBERT DALVA*

b. April 14, 1942 - New York, New York
Home: 33 Walnut Avenue, Larkspur, CA 94939, 415/924-0164

THE BLACK STALLION RETURNS MGM/UA, 1983

DAMIANO DAMIANI

b. July 23, 1922 - Pasiano, Italy
Home: via delle Terme Deciane 2, Rome, Italy, tel.: 06/575-6356

IL ROSSETTO Europa Cinematografica/Explorer Film/EFPC,
1960, Italian-French
IL SICARIO Europa Cinematografica/Galatea, 1961, Italian
ARTURO'S ISLAND MGM, 1962, Italian
LA RIMPATRIATA Galatea/22 Dicembre/Coronet,
1963, Italian-French
THE EMPTY CANVAS Embassy, 1964, Italian
LA STREGA IN AMORE Arco Film, 1966, Italian
MAFIA *IL GIORNO DELLA CIVETTA* American International,
1968, Italian
A BULLET FOR THE GENERAL *QUIEN SABE?* Avco Embassy,
1968, Italian-Spanish
UNA RAGAZZA PIUTTOSTO COMPLICATA Produzioni Filmena/
Fono Roma, 1969, Italian
CONFESSIONS OF A POLICE CAPTAIN *CONFESSIONE DI
UN COMMISSARIO* 1970, Italian
LA MOGLIE PIU BELLA Explorer '58, 1970, Italian
L'ISTRUTTORIA E CHIUSA DIMENTICHI Fair Film, 1971, Italian
IL SORRISO DEL GRANDE TENTATORE Euro, 1972, Italian
GIROLIMONI - IL MOSTRO DI ROMA Dino De Laurentiis
Cinematografica, 1972, Italian
THE DEVIL IS A WOMAN 20th Century-Fox, 1975, British-Italian
UN GENIO, DUE COMPARI, UN POLLO Rafran Cinematografica,
1975, Italian
I AM AFRAID Auro Cinematografica, 1977, Italian
GOODBYE AND AMEN Cineriz, 1978, Italian-French
UN UOMO IN GINOCCHIO Cineriz, 1979, Italian
TIME OF THE JACKALS Capital, 1980, Italian
AMITYVILLE II: THE POSSESSION Orion, 1982
LA PIOVRA (MS) SACIS, 1984, Italian
ATTACCO ALLA PIOVRA Columbia, 1985, Italian
PIZZA CONNECTION C.G. Silver/Alexandre, 1985, Italian
L'INCHIESTA Italian International, 1987, Italian
IL TRENO DI LENIN (TF) RAI/Beta Taurus/TF1, 1988,
Italian-West German-French
GIOCO AL MASSACRO Sacis, 1989, Italian
IL SOLE BUIO Cecchi Gori/Tiger/Reteitalia, 1990, Italian
L'ANGELO CON LA PISTOLA Officina Cinematografica/Cecchi
Gori Group Tiger Cinematografica, 1992, Italian

MEL DAMSKI*

b. July 21, 1946 - New York, New York
Agent: William Morris Agency - Beverly Hills, 310/859-4000

LONG JOURNEY BACK (TF) Lorimar Productions, 1978
THE CHILD STEALER (TF) The Production Company/
Columbia TV, 1979
A PERFECT MATCH (TF) Lorimar Productions, 1980
WORD OF HONOR (TF) Georgia Bay Productions, 1981
AMERICAN DREAM (TF) Mace Neufeld Productions/Viacom, 1981
FOR LADIES ONLY (TF) The Catalina Production Group/
Viacom, 1981
THE LEGEND OF WALKS FAR WOMAN (TF) Roger Gimbel
Productions/EMI TV/Raquel Welch Productions/Lee Levinson
Productions, 1982
AN INVASION OF PRIVACY (TF) Dick Berg-Stonehenge
Productions/Embassy TV, 1983
YELLOWBEARD Orion, 1983, British
ATTACK ON FEAR (TF) Tomorrow Entertainment, 1984
MISCHIEF 20th Century Fox, 1985

BADGE OF THE ASSASSIN (TF) Blatt-Singer Productions/
Columbia TV, 1985
A WINNER NEVER QUITS (TF) Blatt-Singer Productions/
Columbia TV, 1986
HERO IN THE FAMILY (TF) Barry & Enright Productions/Alexander
Productions/Walt Disney Productions, 1986
MURDER BY THE BOOK Nelson Productions/Orion TV, 1987
THE THREE KINGS (TF) Aaron Spelling Productions, 1987
EVERYBODY'S BABY: THE RESCUE OF JESSICA McCLURE (TF)
Dick Berg-Stonehenge Productions/The Campbell Soup Company/
Interscope Productions, 1989
A CONNECTICUT YANKEE IN KING ARTHUR'S COURT (TF)
Schaefer-Karpf Productions/Consolidated Productions, 1989
THE GIRL WHO CAME BETWEEN THEM (TF) Saban-Scherick
Productions, 1990
HAPPY TOGETHER Borde Releasing Corporation, 1990
BLOOD RIVER (TF) CBS Entertainment/Little Apple
Productions, 1991
SHOOT FIRST: A COP'S VENGEANCE (TF) Harvey Kahn
Productions/Interscope Productions, 1991
WIFE, MOTHER, MURDERER (TF) Wilshire Court
Productions, 1991
BACK TO THE STREETS OF SAN FRANCISCO (TF)
Aaron Spelling Productions, 1992
WILD CARD (CTF) Davis Entertainment/MCA TV, 1992

LAWRENCE DANE

b. 1937 - Masson, Quebec, Canada
Address: P.O. Box 310, Station F, Toronto MHY 2L7, Canada,
416/923-6000

HEAVENLY BODIES MGM/UA, 1985, Canadian

CLAUDE D'ANNA

b. March 31, 1945
Contact: French Film Office, 745 Fifth Avenue, New York, NY 10151,
212/832-8860

LA MORT TROUBLE 1969, French
LA PENT DOUCE 1971, French
TROMP L'OEIL 1974, French
L'ORDRE ET LA SECURITE DU MONDE 1977, French
LE CERCLE DES PASSIONS 1982, French
PARTENAIRES Dedalus/FR3, 1985, French
SALOME Cannon, 1986, Italian-French
MACBETH Dedalus/Unitel/SFPC/Atlantic Consolidated Enterprises,
1987, French-West German-U.S.
EQUIPE DE NUIT Capital Cinema, 1988, French
DAISY ET MONA A.K. Productions/France 2 Cinema, 1994, French

ROD DANIEL*

Agent: Broder-Kurland-Webb-Uffner Agency - Beverly Hills,
310/281-3400

TEEN WOLF Atlantic Releasing Corporation, 1985
STRANDED (TF) Tim Flack Productions/Columbia TV, 1986
LIKE FATHER LIKE SON TriStar, 1987
K-9 Universal, 1989
THE SUPER 20th Century Fox, 1991
BEETHOVEN'S 2ND Universal, 1993

HERBERT DANSKA*

Contact: Directors Guild of America - Los Angeles, 213/851-3671

SWEET LOVE, BITTER *IT WON'T RUB OFF, BABY*
Peppercorn-Wormser, 1967
RIGHT ON! Leacock-Pennebaker, 1970

JOE DANTE*

b. Morristown, New Jersey
Agent: ICM - Beverly Hills, 310/550-4000

HOLLYWOOD BOULEVARD co-director with Allan Arkush,
New World, 1976
PIRANHA New World, 1978
THE HOWLING Avco Embassy, 1980

TWILIGHT ZONE - THE MOVIE   co-director with John Landis,
   Steven Spielberg & George Miller, Warner Bros., 1983
GREMLINS   Warner Bros., 1984
EXPLORERS   Paramount, 1985
AMAZON WOMEN ON THE MOON   co-director with John Landis,
   Carl Gottlieb, Robert K. Weiss & Peter Horton, Universal, 1987
INNERSPACE   Warner Bros., 1987
THE 'BURBS   Universal, 1989
GREMLINS 2 THE NEW BATCH   Warner Bros., 1990
MATINEE   Universal, 1993
REBEL HIGHWAY: RUNAWAY DAUGHTERS
   RUNAWAY DAUGHTERS (CTF)   Drive-In Classics
   Cinema/Showtime, 1994
CAT AND MOUSE   TriStar, 1995

PHILIP D'ANTONI*
b. February 19, 1929 - New York, New York
Business: D'Antoni Productions Group, 1515 Broadway - 40th Floor,
   New York, NY 10036, 212/258-7190

THE SEVEN UPS   20th Century-Fox, 1973

RICHARD DANUS*
Agent: The Wallerstein Company - Los Angeles, 213/782-0225

NO PLACE TO HIDE   Cannon, 1991

FRANK DARABONT*
Agent: UTA - Beverly Hills, 310/273-6700

TILL DEATH DO US PART (CTF)   Niki Marvin Productions/
   USA Network, 1990
BURIED ALIVE (CTF)   Niki Marvin Productions/MCA
   Entertainment, 1990
THE SHAWSHANK REDEMPTION ★   Columbia, 1994

JONATHAN DARBY
THE ENEMY WITHIN (CTF)   HBO Pictures/Vincent Pictures, 1994

JACK DARCUS
b. 1941 - Vancouver, British Columbia, Canada
Home: 8679 Cartier Street, Vancouver, British Columbia VP6 3G3,
   Canada, 604/266-3634
Business: Exile Productions Ltd., 1219 Richards Street, Vancouver,
   British Columbia V6B 3G3, Canada, 604/669-9060

PROXYHAWKS   1970, Canadian
GREAT COUPS OF HISTORY   1970, Canadian
WOLFPEN PRINCIPLE   1973, Canadian
DESERTERS   1982, Canadian
OVERNIGHT   1985, Canadian
KINGSGATE   1989, Canadian
THE PORTRAIT   Raincoast Releasing, 1992, Canadian

JOAN DARLING*
b. April 14, 1935 - Boston, Massachusetts
Home: P.O. Box 6700, Tesuque, NM 87574, 505/983-1690
Agent: William Morris Agency - Beverly Hills, 310/859-4000

FIRST LOVE   Paramount, 1977
WILLA (TF)   co-director with Claudio Guzman, GJL Productions/
   Dove, Inc., 1979
THE CHECK IS IN THE MAIL   Ascot Entertainment Group, 1984
HIROSHIMA MAIDEN (TF)   Arnold Shapiro Productions, 1988

DAVID DARLOW
TAILSPIN: BEHIND THE KOREAN AIRLINE TRAGEDY (CTF)
   Darlow Smithson Productions/HBO Showcase/Granada TV,
   1989, U.S.-British

JAMES DARREN*
b. June 8, 1936 - Philadelphia, Pennsylvania
Agent: The Maggie Field Agency - Studio City, 818/980-2001

POLICE STORY: GLADIATOR SCHOOL (TF)   Columbia TV, 1988

JULIE DASH
Business: Geechee Girls Productions, P.O. Box 13938, Atlanta,
   GA 30324, 404/266-0526
Agent: ICM - Beverly Hills, 310/550-4000

DAUGHTERS OF THE DUST   Kino International, 1991

SEAN DASH
Contact: Century Film Partners

ICE   PM Entertainment Group, 1993
BREAKAWAY   Breakaway Films, 1995

JULES DASSIN*
b. December 12, 1911 - Middletown, Connecticut
Home: Athinaeon Efivon 8, Athens 11521, Greece, tel.: 721-1616

NAZI AGENT   MGM, 1942
THE AFFAIRS OF MARTHA   MGM, 1942
REUNION IN FRANCE   MGM, 1942
YOUNG IDEAS   MGM, 1943
THE CANTERVILLE GHOST   MGM, 1944
A LETTER FOR EVIE   MGM, 1945
TWO SMART PEOPLE   MGM, 1946
BRUTE FORCE   Warner Bros., 1947
THE NAKED CITY   Universal, 1948
THIEVES' HIGHWAY   RKO Radio, 1949
NIGHT AND THE CITY   20th Century-Fox, 1950, British
RIFIFI   Pathe, 1954, French
WHERE THE HOT WIND BLOWS   *LA LOI*   MGM,
   1960, French-Italian
NEVER ON SUNDAY ★   Lopert, 1960, Greek
PHAEDRA   Lopert, 1962, Greek-U.S.-French
TOPKAPI   United Artists, 1964
10:30 P.M. SUMMER   Lopert, 1966, U.S.-Spanish
SURVIVAL '67 (FD)   United, 1968, U.S.-Israeli
UP TIGHT   Paramount, 1968
PROMISE AT DAWN   Avco Embassy, 1970, French-U.S.
A DREAM OF PASSION   Avco Embassy, 1978, Greek-U.S.
CIRCLE OF TWO   World Northal, 1981, Canadian

GEORGE DAUGHERTY
Agent: William Morris Agency - Beverly Hills, 310/859-4000

THE MAGICAL WORLD OF CHUCK JONES (AF)
   Warner Bros., 1992

PIERRE DAVID
b. Montreal, Quebec, Canada
Business: Image Organization, Inc., 9000 Sunset Blvd. - Suite 915,
   Los Angeles, CA 90069, 310/278-8751

SCANNER COP   Republic Pictures, 1993
INFERNO   Republic Pictures, 1995

BOAZ DAVIDSON*
b. August 11, 1943 - Tel Aviv, Palestine
Address: 321 S. Lorraine Blvd., Los Angeles, CA 90020,
   213/937-7567
Business: Nu Image, 110 N. Doheny Drive, Beverly Hills, CA 90211,
   310/246-0240

AZIT THE PARATROOPER DOG   Liran Corporation,
   1972, Israeli
CHARLIE AND A HALF   Filmonde, 1973, Israeli
LUPO GOES TO NEW YORK   Noah Films, 1977, Israeli
THE TZANANI FAMILY   Noah Films, 1978, Israeli
LEMON POPSICLE   Noah Films, 1981, Israeli
GOING STEADY (LEMON POPSICLE II)   Noah Film,
   1981, Israeli
SEED OF INNOCENCE   *TEEN MOTHERS*   Cannon, 1981
X-RAY   *HOSPITAL MASSACRE*   Cannon, 1981
HOT BUBBLEGUM (LEMON POPSICLE III)   Noah Films,
   1981, Israeli
THE LAST AMERICAN VIRGIN   Cannon, 1982

PRIVATE POPSICLE (LEMON POPSICLE IV)   Noah Films, 1982,
   Israeli-West German
ALEX FALLS IN LOVE   Berkey Pathe, 1986, Israeli
DUTCH TREAT   Cannon, 1986
GOING BANANAS   Cannon, 1987
SALSA   Cannon, 1988
AMERICAN CYBORG: STEEL WARRIOR   Cannon,
   1994, U.S.-Israeli
BLOOD RUNNER   Nu Image, 1994
LUNAR COP   Nu Image, 1994

GORDON DAVIDSON*

b. May 7, 1933 - New York, New York
Business: Center Theatre Group, 135 N. Grand Avenue,
   Los Angeles, CA 90012, 213/972-7388
Agent: William Morris Agency - Beverly Hills, 310/859-4000

WHO'S HAPPY NOW? (TF)   WNET-TV, 1968
THE TRIAL OF THE CATONSVILLE NINE   Cinema 5, 1972
IT'S THE WILLINGNESS (TF)   PBS, 1979

MARTIN DAVIDSON*

b. November 7, 1939 - New York, New York
Agent: Innovative Artists - Los Angeles, 310/553-5200

THE LORDS OF FLATBUSH   co-director with Stephen Verona,
   Columbia, 1974
ALMOST SUMMER   Universal, 1978
HERO AT LARGE   MGM/United Artists, 1980
EDDIE AND THE CRUISERS   Embassy, 1983
LONG GONE (CTF)   HBO Pictures/The Landsburg
   Company, 1987
HEART OF DIXIE   Orion, 1989
HARD PROMISES   Columbia, 1992
A MURDEROUS AFFAIR: THE CAROLYN WARMUS STORY (TF)
   Steve White Films/Spectator Films, 1992
FOLLOW THE RIVER (TF)   Signboard Hill Productions, 1995

HOWARD DAVIES

Agent: The Lantz Office - New York City, 212/586-0200 or:
   Peters Fraser & Dunlop - London, tel.: 171/344-1000

THE SECRET RAPTURE   Castle Hill Productions, 1993, British

JOHN DAVIES

b. August 20, 1934 - Birmingham, England
Agent: Peter Murphy, Curtis Brown - London, tel.: 171/437-9700

KIM (TF)   London Films, 1984, British
MISS MARPLE (TF)   BBC, 1986, British
THE CARE OF TIME (TF)   Anglia TV, 1989, British
UNNATURAL CAUSES (TF)   Anglia TV, 1992, British

JOHN T. DAVIES

Business: Frontroom Films Ltd., 101 Upper Tollington Park,
   London N4 4ND, England, tel.: 171/263-5771
Agent: Elizabeth Dench, Seifert Dench Associates - London,
   tel.: 171/437-4551

MY FAVOURITE FROM THE SOUTH   1978, British
CITY FARM   1979, British
MAEVE   1981, British
ACCEPTABLE LEVELS (TF)   Frontroom Productions/Channel 4,
   1983, British
URSULA & GLENYS (TF)   Frontroom Productions, 1985, British

RAY DAVIES

Contact: British Film Commission, 70 Baker Street, London
   W1M 1DJ, England, tel.: 171/224-5000

RETURN TO WATERLOO   New Line Cinema, 1985, British

TERENCE DAVIES

Contact: Three Rivers Ltd., 46 Old Compton Street, London
   W1V 5PB, England, tel.: 171/287-2567, fax: 171/287-3072

DISTANT VOICES, STILL LIVES   Alive Films, 1988, British
THE LONG DAY CLOSES   Sony Pictures Classics, 1992, British
VILE BODIES   Zenith Productions/BAC Films, 1994
THE NEON BIBLE   Miramax Films, 1995, U.S.-British

ANDREW DAVIS*

b. Chicago, Illinois
Agent: CAA - Beverly Hills, 310/288-4545
Attorney: Peter Dekom, Bloom, Dekom & Hergott, 150 S. Rodeo
   Drive - Third Floor, Beverly Hills, CA 90212, 310/859-6800

STONY ISLAND   World Northal, 1980
THE FINAL TERROR   Comworld, 1983
CODE OF SILENCE   Orion, 1985
ABOVE THE LAW   Warner Bros., 1988
THE PACKAGE   Orion, 1989
UNDER SIEGE   Warner Bros., 1992
THE FUGITIVE   Warner Bros., 1993
STEAL BIG, STEAL LITTLE   Savoy Pictures, 1995

BJ DAVIS

Business: B.J. Davis Productions, 2210 Wilshire Blvd. - Suite 645,
   Santa Monica, CA 90403, 213/462-2301

WHITE GHOST   Trans World Entertainment, 1987
QUIET THUNDER   Gibraltar Releasing, 1987
LASER MISSION   Bavarian Films, 1988
CLEANSWEEP   Eagle Entertainment, 1989
THE HOLLYWOOD STUNTMAN (TF)   Crawford Lane
   Productions, 1991
STICKFIGHTER   International Dynamic Pictures, 1994

CHARLES DAVIS

DIE WATCHING   Triboro Entertainment, 1994

DESMOND DAVIS

b. 1928 - London, England
Business: Lancer Film Productions Ltd. - London, tel.: 171/485-1505

THE GIRL WITH GREEN EYES   United Artists, 1964, British
TIME LOST AND TIME REMEMBERED   *I WAS HAPPY HERE*
   Continental, 1966, British
THE UNCLE   Lennart, 1966, British
SMASHING TIME   Paramount, 1967, British
A NICE GIRL LIKE ME   Avco Embassy, 1969, British
CLASH OF THE TITANS   MGM/United Artists, 1981, British
THE SIGN OF FOUR   Mapleton Films Ltd., 1983, British
THE COUNTRY GIRLS   London Films Ltd./Channel 4,
   1983, British
ORDEAL BY INNOCENCE   Cannon, 1984, British
CAMILLE (TF)   Rosemont Productions, 1984, U.S.-British
FREEDOM FIGHTER (TF)   HTV/Columbia TV/Embassy TV,
   1988, U.S.-British
THE MAN WHO LIVED AT THE RITZ (TF)   Harmony Gold, 1988
THE CHIEF (TF)   1990, British

GARY DAVIS*

Home: 6043 Lubao Avenue, Woodland Hills, CA 91367,
   818/462-2301
Agent: William Morris Agency - Beverly Hills, 310/859-4000

CONFLICT OF INTEREST   Frazier Films, 1993

OSSIE DAVIS

b. December 18, 1917 - Cogdell, Georgia
Agent: The Artists Group - Los Angeles, 310/552-1100

COTTON COMES TO HARLEM   United Artists, 1970
BLACK GIRL   Cinerama Releasing Corporation, 1972
KONGI'S HARVEST   Tan Communications, 1973
GORDON'S WAR   20th Century-Fox, 1973
COUNTDOWN AT KUSINI   Columbia, 1976, U.S.-Nigerian

PETER DAVIS

Agent: ICM - Beverly Hills, 310/550-4000

HEARTS AND MINDS (FD)   Warner Bros., 1975
THE RISE AND FALL OF THE BORSCHT BELT (FD)   1986
WINNIE/NELSON (FD)   1986
IN DARKEST HOLLYWOOD: CINEMA & APARTHEID (FD)
   co-director with Daniel Riesenfeld, Nightingale Productions/
   McKinnon Associates, 1994, U.S.-Canadian

TAMRA DAVIS

Agent: UTA - Beverly Hills, 310/273-6700

GUNCRAZY   Academy Entertainment, 1992
CB4   Universal, 1993
BILLY MADISON   Universal, 1995

ANTHONY M. DAWSON
(Antonio Margheriti)

b. September 19, 1930 - Rome, Italy
Home: via Appia Antica 184, Rome Italy, tel.: 06/782-2367

SPACE-MEN   ASSIGNMENT OUTER SPACE   Ultra Film/Titanus,
   1960, Italian
THE OUTSIDER   Ultra Film/Lux Film, 1961, Italian
THE GOLDEN ARROW   MGM, 1962, Italian-U.S.
IL CROLLO DI ROMA   Atlantica Film, 1963, Italian
DANZA MACABRA   Addessi, 1963, Italian
ANTHAR L'INVINCIBILE   Antares Cinematografica, 1964, Italian
I LINGHI CAPELLI DELLA MORTE   Cinegay, 1964, Italian
LA VERGINE DI NORIMBERGA   Atlantica Cinematografica,
   1964, Italian
I GIGANTI DI ROMA   Devon/Radius, 1964, Italian-French
URSUS IL TERRORE DEI KIRGHISI   Adelphia, 1964, Italian
IL PELO NEL MONDO   co-director with Marco Vicario, Atlantica
   Cinematografica, 1964, Italian
LIGHTNING BOLT   OPERAZIONE GOLDMAN   Woolner Brothers,
   1965, Italian-Spanish
WILD, WILD PLANET   I CRIMINALI DELLA GELASSIA
   MGM, 1966, Italian
WAR BETWEEN THE PLANETS   MISSIONE PIANETA ERRANTE
   Fanfare, 1966, Italian
PLANET ON THE PROWL   Mercury, 1966, Italian
SNOW MAN   Mercury, 1966, Italian
A 077 SFIDA AI KILLERS   Aenit/Flora/Regina, 1967, Italian
JOE L'IMPLACABILE   Seven/Hispamer, 1967, Italian-Spanish
NUDE...SI MUORE   Super International Pictures, 1968, Italian
JOKO INVOCA DIO...E MUORI!   Super International Pictures,
   1968, Italian
IO TI AMO   Genesio, 1968, Italian
THE YOUNG, THE EVIL AND THE SAVAGE   SETTE VERGINI
   PER IL DIAVOLO   American International, 1968, Italian
THE INNATURALS   SIP/EDO/CCC, 1969, Italian-West German
...E DIO DISSE A CAINO   DC7, 1970, Italian
L'INAFFERABILE INVINCIBILE   MR. INVISIBILE   EDO/Carsten,
   1970, Italian-West German
NELLA STRETTA MORSA DEL RAGNO   DC7/Terra Filmkunst/
   Paris-Cannes Productions, 1971, Italian-West German-French
NOVELE GALEOTTE D'AMORE   Seven Film, 1972, Italian
FINALMENTE...LE MILLE E UNA NOTTE   Pink Medusa,
   1972, Italian
LA MORTE NEGLI OCCHI DEL GATTO   Starkis/Falcon/Roxy/
   Capitol, 1973, Italian-West German-French
MING, RAGAZZI!   Champion, 1973, Italian
DECAMERON 3   Starkis, 1973, Italian
MANONE IL LADRONE   Laser Film, 1974, Italian

WHISKY E FANTASMI   Champion/Cipi, 1974, Italian-Spanish
LES DIABLESSES   Planfilm, 1974, French-Italian-West German
BLOOD MONEY   Champion/Midega, 1974, Italian-Spanish
TAKE A HARD RIDE   20th Century-Fox, 1974
DEATH RAGE   CON LA RABBIA AGLI OCCHI   S.J. International,
   1977, Italian
THE STRANGER AND THE GUNFIGHTER   Columbia, 1976,
   Italian-Hong Kong
THE SQUEEZE   THE RIP-OFF   Maverick International,
   1976, Italian-U.S.
HOUSE OF 1,000 PLEASURES   Group 1, 1977, Italian
KILLER FISH   Associated Film Distribution, 1978,
   British-Brazilian-French
CANNIBALS IN THE STREETS   Almi Cinema 5, 1980,
   Italian-Spanish
THE LAST HUNTER   HUNTER OF THE APOCALYPSE
   World Northal, 1980, Italian
CAR CRASH   Cleminternational Cinematografica, 1981, Italian
FUGA DALL'ARCIPELAGO MALEDETTO   Flora/Gico
   Cinematografica, 1982, Italian
THE HUNTERS OF THE GOLDEN COBRA   THE RAIDERS OF
   THE GOLDEN COBRA   World Northal, 1982, Italian
YOR, THE HUNTER FROM THE FUTURE   Columbia, 1983,
   Italian-Turkish-U.S.
TORNADO   Gico Cinematografica, 1983, Italian
ARK OF THE SUN GOD   Trans World Entertainment, 1984,
   Italian-Turkish
I SOPRAVVISSUTI DELLA CITTA' MORTA   Flora Film,
   1984, Italian
CODENAME: WILDGEESE   New World, 1984,
   Italian-West German
LA LEGGENDA DEL RUBINO MALESE   L'Immagine, 1985, Italian
COMMANDO LEOPARD   Ascot Distribution, 1985,
   West German-Italian
L'ISOLA DEL TESORO (MS)   RAI/TFI/Bavaria Film, 1987,
   Italian-French-West German
THE COMMANDER   Prestige Film/Ascot Film, 1988,
   Italian-West German
INDIO   Filmauro/RPA/Reteitalia, 1990, Italian
ALIEN DEGLI ABISSI   Gico Cinematografico/Dania Film/National
   Cinematografica, 1990, Italian
INDIO 2: LA RIVOLTA   Filiberto Bandini/RPA International, 1990,
   Italian

ERNEST DAY*

Home: 9 The Ridings, Cobham, Surrey KT11 2PT, England,
   tel.: 37/284-3276
Agent: Smith-Gosnell-Nicholson & Associates - Pacific Palisades,
   310/459-0307

GREEN ICE   Universal/AFD, 1981, British
WALTZ ACROSS TEXAS   Atlantic Releasing Corporation, 1983

JOHN DAY

Contact: New Zealand Film Commission, P.O. Box 11-546,
   Wellington, New Zealand, tel.: 4/385-9754

THE RETURNING   Echo Pictures Limited/New Zealand Film
   Commission, 1991, New Zealand

ROBERT DAY*

b. September 11, 1922 - Sheen, England
Agent: CAA - Beverly Hills, 310/288-4545

THE GREEN MAN   DCA, 1957, British
STRANGERS' MEETING   Rank, 1957, British
THE HAUNTED STRANGLER   GRIP OF THE STRANGLER
   MGM, 1958, British
CORRIDORS OF BLOOD   MGM, 1958, British
FIRST MAN INTO SPACE   MGM, 1959, British
LIFE IN EMERGENCY WARD 10   Eros, 1959, British
BOBBIKINS   20th Century-Fox, 1960, British
TWO-WAY STRETCH   Showcorporation, 1960, British
TARZAN THE MAGNIFICENT   Paramount, 1960, British
CALL ME GENIUS   THE REBEL   Continental, 1961, British
OPERATION SNATCH   Continental, 1962, British
TARZAN'S THREE CHALLENGES   MGM, 1963, British

SHE   MGM, 1965, British
TARZAN AND THE VALLEY OF GOLD   American International,
  1966, U.S.-Swiss
TARZAN AND THE GREAT RIVER   Paramount, 1967
I THINK WE'RE BEING FOLLOWED   1967, British
THE HOUSE ON GREENAPPLE ROAD (TF)   QM Productions, 1970
RITUAL OF EVIL (TF)   Universal TV, 1970
BANYON (TF)   Warner Bros. TV, 1971
IN BROAD DAYLIGHT (TF)   Aaron Spelling Productions, 1971
MR. AND MRS. BO JO JONES (TF)   20th Century-Fox TV, 1971
THE RELUCTANT HEROES (TF)   Aaron Spelling Productions, 1971
THE GREAT AMERICAN BEAUTY CONTEST (TF)
  ABC Circle Films, 1973
DEATH STALK (TF)   Wolper Productions, 1975
THE TRIAL OF CHAPLAIN JENSEN (TF)
  20th Century-Fox TV, 1975
SWITCH (TF)   Universal TV, 1975
A HOME OF OUR OWN (TF)   QM Productions, 1975
TWIN DETECTIVES (TF)   Charles Fries Productions, 1976
KINGSTON: THE POWER PLAY (TF)   Universal TV, 1976
HAVING BABIES (TF)   The Jozak Company, 1976
BLACK MARKET BABY (TF)   Brut Productions, 1977
LOGAN'S RUN (TF)   Goff-Roberts-Steiner Productions/
  MGM TV, 1977
THE INITIATION OF SARAH (TF)   Charles Fries Productions, 1978
THE GRASS IS ALWAYS GREENER OVER THE
  SEPTIC TANK (TF)   Joe Hamilton Productions, 1978
MURDER BY NATURAL CAUSES (TF)   Richard Levinson-William
  Link Productions, 1979
WALKING THROUGH THE FIRE (TF)   Time-Life Films, 1979
THE MAN WITH BOGART'S FACE   *SAM MARLOW, PRIVATE EYE*
  20th Century-Fox, 1980
PETER AND PAUL (TF)   Universal TV, 1981
SCRUPLES (TF)   Lou-Step Productions/Warner Brothers TV, 1981
MARIAN ROSE WHITE (TF)   Gerald Abrams Productions/Cypress
  Point Productions, 1982
RUNNING OUT (TF)   CBS Entertainment, 1983
YOUR PLACE OR MINE (TF)   Poolhouse Productions/Finnegan
  Associates, 1983
CHINA ROSE (TF)   Robert Halmi, Inc., 1983
COOK & PEARY: THE RACE TO THE POLE (TF)
  Robert Halmi, Inc., 1983
HOLLYWOOD WIVES (MS)   Aaron Spelling Productions, 1985
THE LADY FROM YESTERDAY (TF)   Barry Weitz Films/
  Comworld Productions, 1985
LOVE, MARY (TF)   CBS Entertainment, 1985
DIARY OF A PERFECT MURDER (TF)   Viacom Productions, 1986
THE QUICK AND THE DEAD (CTF)   HBO Pictures/Joseph
  Cates Company, 1987
CELEBRATION FAMILY (TF)   Frank von Zerneck Films, 1987
HIGHER GROUND (TF)   Green-Epstein Productions/
  Columbia TV, 1988
FIRE! TRAPPED ON THE 37TH FLOOR (TF)   Papazian-Hirsch
  Productions/Republic Pictures, 1991

JOSEE DAYAN

Home: 41, avenue Rapp, 75007 Paris, France, tel.: 1/45-52-02-87
Contact: French Film Office, 745 Fifth Avenue, New York,
  NY 10151, 212/832-8860

CHOCOLATE   Chrysalide Films/The Movie Group,
  1992, U.S.-French
POLICE SECRETS (MS)   co-director with Michele Ferrand &
  Yves Lafaye, Falcon Productions/FR3/HR/KirchGroup,
  1992, French-German

NISSIM DAYAN

b. 1946 - Tel Aviv, Palestine
Contact: Israel Film Centre, Ministry of Industry & Trade,
  30 Agron Street, P.O. Box 299, 94190 Jerusalem, Israel,
  tel.: 972/210433 or 210297

LIGHT FROM DARKNESS   1972, Israeli
THE END OF MILTON LEVY   1980, Israeli
CHILDREN OF VILLA EMMA (FD)   1983, Israeli
MICHAEL EZRA SAFRA AND SONS (MS)   1983, Israeli
ON A NARROW BRIDGE   Gesher Productions, 1985, Israeli

LYMAN DAYTON*

Contact: Directors Guild of America - Los Angeles, 213/851-3671

BAKER'S HAWK   Doty-Dayton, 1976
RIVALS   World Entertainment, 1979
THE STRANGER AT JEFFERSON HIGH (TF)   Lyman Dayton
  Productions, 1981
THE AVENGING   Comworld, 1981
SOLO   Dayton-Stewart Organization, 1984
THE RED FURY   Dayton-Stewart Organization, 1985
THE DREAM MACHINE   International Creative Exchange, 1991

WILLIAM DEAR*

Agent: UTA - Beverly Hills, 310/273-6700

TIMERIDER   Jensen Farley Pictures1983
HARRY AND THE HENDERSONS   Universal, 1987
IF LOOKS COULD KILL   Warner Bros., 1991
JOURNEY TO THE CENTER OF THE EARTH (TF)
  High Productions, 1993
ANGELS IN THE OUTFIELD   Buena Vista, 1994

JAMES DEARDEN

b. September 14, 1949 - London, England
Agent: ICM - Beverly Hills, 310/550-4000

THE COLD ROOM (TF)   Jethro Films/Mark Forstater Productions,
  1984, British
PASCALI'S ISLAND   Avenue Pictures, 1988, British-U.S.
A KISS BEFORE DYING   Universal, 1991

FRANK DEASY

Agent: Peters Fraser & Dunlop - London, tel.: 171/344-1000

THE COURIER   co-director with Joe Lee, Vestron,
  1988, Irish-British

JOHN DE BELLO

ATTACK OF THE KILLER TOMATOES   1980
HAPPY HOUR   Moviestore Entertainment, 1987
RETURN OF THE KILLER TOMATOES   New World, 1988
KILLER TOMATOES STRIKE BACK! (HVF)   Fox Video, 1991
KILLER TOMATOES EAT FRANCE   Four Square
  Productions, 1992

JAN DE BONT*

b. October 22, 1943 - The Netherlands
Business: Blue Tulip Productions, 10201 W. Pico Blvd., Building 15 -
  Suite 1, Los Angeles, CA 90035, 310/203-2054
Agent: David Gersh, The Gersh Agency - Beverly Hills, 310/274-6611

SPEED   20th Century Fox, 1994
TWISTER   Warner Bros., 1995

GIANFRANCO DE BOSIO

b. September 16, 1924 - Verona, Italy
Home: Corso Magenta 22, Milan, Italy, tel.: 02/805-3638

IL TERRORISTA   22 Dicembre/Galatea, 1964, Italian
LA BETIA   Titanus, 1972, Italian-Yugoslavian
MOSES THE LAWGIVER (MS)   ATV, Ltd./ITC/RAI, 1975,
  British-Italian
MOSES   Avco Embassy, 1976, British-Italian,
  feature film version of MOSES THE LAWGIVER

PHILIPPE DE BROCA

b. March 15, 1933 - Paris, France
Agent: ICM France - Paris, tel.: 41723-7860
Contact: French Film Office, 745 Fifth Avenue, New York,
  NY 10151, 212/832-8860

LES JEUX DE L'AMOUR   1960, French
THE JOKER   Lopert, 1961, French
THE FIVE DAY LOVER   Kinglsey International,
  1961, French-Italian

SEVEN CAPITAL SINS   co-director with Jean-Luc Godard,
   Roger Vadim, Sylvaine Dhomme, Edouard Molinaro,
   Claude Chabrol, Jacques Demy, Marie-Jose Nat,
   Dominique Paturel, Jean-Marc Tennberg & Perrette Pradier,
   Embassy, 1962, French-Italian
CARTOUCHE   Embassy, 1962, French-Italian
LES VEINARDS   co-director, 1962, French
THAT MAN FROM RIO   Lopert, 1964, French-Italian
MALE COMPANION   International Classics,
   1966, French-Italian
UP TO HIS EARS   *LES TRIBULATIONS D'UN CHINOIS
   EN CHINE* Lopert, 1966, French-Italian
THE KING OF HEARTS   Lopert, 1967, French-Italian
THE OLDEST PROFESSION   *LES PLUX VIEUX METIER
   DU MONDE*   co-director with Franco Indovina, Mauro Bolognini,
   Michael Pfleghar, Claude Autant-Lara & Jean-Luc Godard,
   Goldstone, 1968, French-Italian-West German
THE DEVIL BY THE TAIL   Lopert, 1969, French-Italian
GIVE HER THE MOON *LES CAPRICES DE MARIE*
   United Artists, 1970, French-Italian
TOUCH AND GO   *LA ROUTE AU SOLEIL*   Libra, 1971, French
LA POUDRE D'ESCAMPETTE   Columbia,
   1971, French-Italian
CHERE LOUISE   Warner-Columbia, 1972, French-Italian
LE MAGNIFIQUE   Cine III, 1973, French
INCORRIGIBLE   EDP, 1975, French
JULIE-POT-DE-COLLE   Prodis, 1977, French
DEAR DETECTIVE *DEAR INSPECTOR* Cinema 5,
   1978, French
LE CAVALEUR   CCFC, 1979, French
PRACTICE MAKES PERFECT   Quartet/Films Incorporation,
   1980, French
JUPITER'S THIGH *ON A VOLE LA CRUISSE DE JUPITER*
   Quartet/Films Inc., 1980, French
PSY   Ariane Films/Antenne-2, 1981, French
L'AFRICAIN   Renn Productions, 1982, French
LOUISIANA (CTF)   ICC/Antenne-2/Superchannel/CTV/Societe de
   Development de L'Industrie Cinematographique Canadienne,
   1983, Canadian-French
PIRANHA D'AMOUR   AAA, 1985, French
LE CROCODILE   AMLF, 1985, French
LA GITANE   AMLF, 1986, French
CHOUANS   UGC, 1988, French
LES 1,001 NUITS   UGC, 1990, French-Italian
LES CLES DU PARADIS   Messine Productions, 1991, French
LES JARDIN DES PLANTES (TF)   Son Et Lumiere/TF1/Canal
   Plus/Ma Film/Maecenas Film/Magyar Televizio,
   1995, French-Hungarian

CHRISTIAN DE CHALONGE

Address: 16, rue Demarquay, 75010 Paris, France,
   tel.: 1/40-35-52-39
Contact: French Film Office, 745 Fifth Avenue, New York,
   NY 10151, 212/832-8860

DR. PETIOT   Aries Film Releasing, 1991, French

DIMITRI DE CLERCQ

Contact: French Film Office, 745 Fifth Avenue, New York,
   NY 10151, 212/832-8860

UN BRUIT QUI FEND ROU   co-director with Alain Robbe-Grillet,
   Nomad FilmsEuripide Productions/La Sept Cinema/CAB
   Productions/RTBF/Canal Plus/Investimage 4/CNC, 1995,
   French-Swiss-Belgian

FREDERICK DE CORDOVA*

b. October 27, 1910 - New York, New York
Contact: Directors Guild of America - Los Angeles, 213/851-3671

TOO YOUNG TO KNOW   Warner Bros., 1945
HER KIND OF MAN   Warner Bros., 1946
THAT WAY WITH WOMEN   Warner Bros., 1947
LOVE AND LEARN   Warner Bros., 1947
ALWAYS TOGETHER   Warner Bros., 1947
WALLFLOWER   Warner Bros., 1948

FOR THE LOVE OF MARY   Universal, 1948
THE COUNTESS OF MONTE CRISTO   Universal, 1948
ILLEGAL ENTRY   Universal, 1949
THE GAL WHO TOOK THE WEST   Universal, 1949
BUCCANEER'S GIRL   Universal, 1950
PEGGY   Universal, 1950
THE DESERT HAWK   Universal, 1950
BEDTIME FOR BONZO   Universal, 1951
KATIE DID IT   Universal, 1951
LITTLE EGYPT   Universal, 1951
FINDERS KEEPERS   Universal, 1951
HERE COME THE NELSONS   Universal, 1952
BONZO GOES TO COLLEGE   Universal, 1952
YANKEE BUCCANEER   Universal, 1952
COLUMN SOUTH   Universal, 1953
I'LL TAKE SWEDEN   United Artists, 1965
FRANKIE AND JOHNNY   United Artists, 1966

DAVID DeCOTEAU
(Ellen Cabot/Julian Breen)
Telephone: 310/871-0334

DREAMANIAC   Empire Pictures 1987
CREEPOZOIDS   Urban Classics, 1987
SORORITY BABES IN THE SLIMEBALL BOWL-A-RAMA
   Urban Classics, 1988
LADY AVENGER   Southgate Entertainment, 1989
DR. ALIEN   Paramount Home Video, 1989
AMERICAN RAMPAGE   Amazing Movies, 1989
DEADLY EMBRACE   directed under pseudonym of Ellen Cabot,
   Prism Pictures, 1989
MURDER WEAPON   directed under pseudonym of Ellen Cabot,
   Cinema Home Video, 1990
THE GIRL I WANT (CTF)   USA Network
PUPPET MASTER III: TOULON'S REVENGE   Full Moon
   Entertainment, 1991
NAKED INSTINCT   Trident Releasing, 1992
TEST TUBE TEENS FROM THE YEAR 2000   directed under
   pseudonym of Ellen Cabot, Paramount Home Video, 1992
BEACH BABES FROM BEYOND   directed under pseudonym of
   Ellen Cabot, Torchlight Entertainment, 1993
PREHYSTERIA 3   directed under pseudonym of Julian Breen,
   Moonbeam, 1994
BLONDE HEAVEN   directed under pseudonym of Ellen Cabot,
   Torchlight Entertainment, 1994
BEACH BABES II: CAVE GIRL INLAND   directed under pseudonym
   of Ellen Cabot, Torchlight Entertainment, 1994
CASTLE QUEEN   Torchlight Entertainment, 1995
DENIM AND LACE 2000   Torchlight Entertainment, 1995

FRANK DE FELITTA*

b. August 3, 1921 - New York, New York
Agent: Bernard Donnenfeld, 11377 W. Olympic Blvd., Los Angeles,
   CA 90064, 310/312-3153

TRAPPED (TF)   Universal TV, 1973
THE TWO WORLDS OF JENNY LOGAN (TF)   Joe Wizan TV
   Productions/Charles Fries Productions, 1979
DARK NIGHT OF THE SCARECROW (TF)   Joe Wizan TV
   Productions, 1981
KILLER IN THE MIRROR (TF)   Litke-Grossbart Productions/
   Warner Bros. TV, 1986
SCISSORS   DDM Film Corporation, 1991

RAYMOND DeFELITTA

Agent: CAA - Beverly Hills, 310/288-4545
Contact: New York, 212/226-2686

BRONX CHEERS (Short)   1990
CAFE SOCIETY   Cineville/Skyline Entertainment, 1995

ALESSANDRO DE GAETANO

METALBEAST   Blue Ridge Entertainment, 1994

PHILIP DeGUERE*
Telephone: 800/729-7445
Agent: William Morris Agency - Beverly Hills, 310/859-4000

DR. STRANGE (TF)   Universal TV, 1978

ROLF DE HEER
Agent: The Partos Company - Los Angeles, 213/876-5500

TAIL OF A TIGER   Producers Circle, 1986, Australian
INCIDENT AT RAVEN'S GATE   *ENCOUNTER AT RAVEN'S GATE*
   Hemdale, 1988, Australian
DINGO   Greycat Films, 1991, Australian-French
BAD BOY BUBBY   Bubby PL/Fandango/Australian Film Finance
   Corporation/South Australia Film Corporation, 1993,
   Australian-Italian

JAMIL DEHLAVI
b. Pakistan
Contact: British Film Commission, 70 Baker Street, London
   W1M 1DJ, England, tel.: 171/224-5000

THE BLOOD OF HUSSAIN   1980, Pakistani
IMMACULATE CONCEPTION   Film Four International/Dehlavi
   Films, 1992, British

MARK DEIMEL
Agent: The Agency - Los Angeles, 310/551-3000
Personal Manager: Creative Alliance Management - Los Angeles,
   213/962-6090

PERFECT MATCH   Airtight Productions, 1987
DEUCE COUPE   Airtight Filmworks, 1992

DONNA DEITCH*
b. June 8, 1945 - San Francisco, California
Business: Desert Heart Productions, 685 Venice Blvd., Venice,
   CA 90291, 310/827-1515
Agent: Paradigm - Los Angeles, 310/277-4400

DESERT HEARTS   The Samuel Goldwyn Company, 1985
THE WOMEN OF BREWSTER PLACE (TF)   Harpo Productions/
   Phoenix Entertainment Group, 1989
SEXUAL ADVANCES (TF)   Carol Polakoff Productions/
   Spelling TV, 1992
ANGEL OF DESIRE   Trimark Pictures, 1994

STEVE DeJARNATT*
Agent: UTA - Beverly Hills, 310/273-6700

TARZANA (Short)   1979
ALFRED HITCHCOCK PRESENTS (TF)   co-director with
   Randa Haines, Joel Oliansky & Fred Walton,
   Universal TV, 1985
CHERRY 2000   Orion, 1986
MIRACLE MILE   Hemdale, 1988

ATE DE JONG*
Agent: APA - Los Angeles, 310/273-0744
Personal Manager: Carlyle Productions and Management,
   639 N. Larchmont - Suite 207, Los Angeles, CA 90004,
   213/469-3086

BLIND SPOT   Dutch
THE INHERITANCE   Dutch
KNOWN FACES, MIXED FEELINGS   Dutch
A FLIGHT OF RAINBIRDS   Dutch
BURNING LOVE   Dutch
SHADOW OF VICTORY   Dutch
DROP DEAD FRED   New Line Cinema, 1991, U.S.-British
HIGHWAY TO HELL   Hemdale, 1992, filmed in 1989
ALL MEN ARE MORTAL   Novo Films/Rio Film/Sigma
   Filmproductions, 1995, British-French-Dutch

FRED DEKKER*
b. April 9, 1959 - San Francisco, California
Agent: ICM - Beverly Hills, 310/550-4000

NIGHT OF THE CREEPS   TriStar, 1986
THE MONSTER SQUAD   TriStar, 1987
ROBOCOP 3   Orion, 1993

ALEX DE LA IGLESIA
Contact: Spanish Film Institute, San Marcos 40, Madrid 28004,
   Spain, tel.: 1/532-5089

ACCION MUTANTE   El Deseo/CIBY 2000/TVE/Warner Espanola,
   1993, Spanish-French
EL DIA DE LA BESTIA   Sogepaq, 1995, Spanish

JEAN DELANNOY
b. January 12, 1908 - Noisy-le-Sec, France
Home: 86, rue de la Federation, 75015 Paris, France,
   tel.: 1/47-34-37-81
Contact: French Film Office, 745 Fifth Avenue, New York,
   NY 10151, 212/832-8860

PARIS - DEAUVILLE   1935, French
LA VENUS DE L'OR   1938, French
LE DIAMANT NOIR   1940, French
MACAO L'ENFER DE JEU   1940, French
FIEVRES   1941, French
L'ASSASSIN A PEUR LA NUIT   1942, French
PONTACARRAL COLONEL D'EMPIRE   1942, French
L'ETERNEL RETOUR   1943, French
LE BOSSU   1944, French
LA PART DE L'OMBRE   1945, French
LA SYMPHONIE PASTORALE   1946, French
LES JEUX SONT FAITS   1947, French
AUX YEUX DU SOUVENIR   1949, French
LE SECRET DE MAYERLING   1949, French
DIEUX A BESOIN DES HOMMES   1950, French
LE GARCON SAUVAGE   1951, French
THE MOMENT OF TRUTH   Arlan Pictures, 1952, French
DAUGHTERS OF DESTINY   *DESTINEES*   co-director with
   Marcel Pagliero, Arlan Pictures, 1953, French-Italian
THE BED   *SECRETS D'ALCOVE*   co-director, Getz-Kingsley,
   1953, French-Italian
LA ROUTE NAPOLEON   1953, French
OBSESSION   Gibe Films, 1954, French-Italian
CHIENS PERDUS SANS COLLIER   1955, French
MARIE ANTOINETTE   Rizzoli, 1956, French-Italian
THE HUNCHBACK OF NOTRE DAME   *NOTRE DAME DE PARIS*
   RKO Radio, 1956, French
INSPECTOR MAIGRET   *MAIGRET TEND UN PIEGE*   Lopert,
   1958, French-Italian
GUINGUETTE   1959, French
MAIGRET ET L'AFFAIRE SAINT-FIACRE   1959, French
LE BARON DE L'ECLUSE   1960, French
LOVE AND THE FRENCHWOMAN   co-director with Michel Boisrond,
   Rene Clair, Christian-Jaque & Jean-Paul Lechannois,
   Kingsley International, 1960, French
LA PRINCESSE DE CLEVES   1961, French
LE RENDEZ-VOUS   1961, French
VENUS IMPERIALE   1962, French
THIS SPECIAL FRIENDSHIP   *LES AMITIES PARTICULIERES*
   Pathe Contemporary, 1964, French
LE LIT A DEUX PLACES   1965, French
LE MAJORDOME   1965, French
LES SULTANS   1966, French
THE ACTION MAN   *LE SOLEIL DES VOYOUS*
   H.K. Film Distribution, 1967, French
LE PEAU DE TORPEDO   1970, French
PAS FOLLE LA GUEPE   1972, French
THE PASSION OF BERNADETTE   Rachel Productions,
   1990, French
MARIE DE NAZARETH   Azur Films, 1995, French

MARCUS DeLEON
Business: Together Brothers Productions Inc., 9505 W. Washington
Blvd., Culver City, CA 90230, 310/841-2301
Agent: Innovative Artists - Los Angeles, 310/553-5200

KISS ME A KILLER Califilm, 1991
BAKERSFIELD 1995

MIKE de LEON
b. 1947 - Manila, Philippines
Contact: National Commission for Culture and Arts, Intramuros,
Manila, Philippines

THE RITES OF MAY 1976, Filipino
MOMENTS IN STOLEN DREAM 1977, Filipino
WILL YOUR HEART BEAT FASTER? 1980, Filipino
KISAPMATA 1981, Filipino
BATCH '81 1982, Filipino
SISTER STELLA L Regal Films, 1984, Filipino
HEAVEN CAN NEVER BE DIVIDED 1985, Filipino
SOUTHERN WINDS co-director with Shoji Kogami,
Slamet Rahardjo Djarot & Cherd Songsri, NHK Enterprises,
1993, Japanese-Filipino-Thai-Indonesian

BILL D'ELIA*
Home: 5173 Earl Drive, La Canada, CA 91011
Agent: Writers & Artists Agency - Los Angeles, 310/824-6300

THE FEUD Castle Hill Productions, 1990
BIG DREAMS & BROKEN HEARTS: THE DOTTIE
WEST STORY (TF) Ken Kragen Productions/Michele
Lee Productions/CBS, 1995

FRANCIS DELIA*
Home: 14929 Marlin Place, Van Nuys, CA 91405
Agent: Stevens & Associates - Beverly Hills, 310/275-7541

FREEWAY New World, 1988

JEFFREY S. DELMAN
Contact: 1918 Canal Street, # 2, Venice, CA 90291, 310/306-3325
Personal Manager: Matt Kenner, Kenner Organization, 3435 Ocean
Park Blvd., Santa Monica, CA 90405, 310/450-9497

DEAD TIME STORIES Cinema Group, 1986

PETER DEL MONTE
b. 1943 - San Francisco, California
Home: via Poerio 59/D, Rome, Italy, tel: 06/585451

FUORI CAMPO Centro Sperimentale di Cinematografia,
1969, Italian
LA PAROLE A VENIRE RAI, 1970, Italian
IRENE IRENE Cooperative Artea, 1975, Italian
L'ALTRA DONNA RAI/ITF/Polytel International Film, 1980, Italian
PISO PISELLO RAI/Clesi Cinematografica, 1981, Italian
INVITATION AU VOYAGE Mel Difussion/Filmalpha,
1982, French-Italian
PICCOLI FUOCHI Intersound, 1985, Italian
JULIA AND JULIA Cinecom, 1987, Italian
ETOILE Gruppo BEMA/Reteitalia, 1989, Italian
TRACCE DI VITA AMOROSA Aura Film/RAI, 1990, Italian

NATHALIE DELON
Contact: French Film Office, 745 Fifth Avenue, New York,
NY 10151, 212/832-8860

SWEET LIES Island Pictures, 1989, French-U.S.

DEBORAH DEL PRETE
SIMPLE JUSTICE Panorama Entertainment, 1989

GUILLERMO DEL TORO
Agent: The Gersh Agency - Beverly Hills, 310/274-6611

CRONOS October Films, 1993, Mexican

RUDY DeLUCA*
Agent: The Gersh Agency - Beverly Hills, 310/274-6611

TRANSYLVANIA 6-5000 New World, 1985

DOM DE LUISE*
b. August 1, 1933 - Brooklyn, New York
Home: 1186 Corsica Drive, Pacific Palisades, CA 90272,
310/459-2911
Business Manager: Executive Business Management, 132 S. Rodeo
Drive, Beverly Hills, CA 90212, 310/858-2000

HOT STUFF Columbia, 1979

RICHARD DEMBO
b. 1948 - France
Home: 6, rue Bourbon-Chateau, 75006 Paris, France,
tel.: 1/43-29-20-59
Contact: French Film Office, 745 Fifth Avenue, New York,
NY 10151, 212/832-8860

DANGEROUS MOVES Arthur Cohn Productions, 1984, Swiss

BOB DEMCHUK*
Business: Scene East Productions, Ltd., 229 West 97th Street -
Apt. 3B, New York, NY 10025, 212/749-2399

WHATEVER IT TAKES Aquarius, 1986

JOHANNA DEMETRAKAS*
Telephone: 213/224-8061
Agent: The Gersh Agency - Beverly Hills, 310/274-6611

CELEBRATION AT BIG SUR (PF) 20th Century-Fox, 1971

EAMES DEMETRIOS
THE GIVING Northern Arts Entertainment, 1992

JONATHAN DEMME*
b. February 22, 1944 - Baldwin, New York
Business: Clinica Estetico, 127 West 24th Street - 7th Floor,
New York, NY 10011, 212/807-6800
Agent: CAA - Beverly Hills, 310/288-4545

CAGED HEAT New World, 1974
CRAZY MAMA New World, 1975
FIGHTING MAD 20th Century-Fox, 1976
CITIZENS BAND *HANDLE WITH CARE* Paramount, 1977
LAST EMBRACE United Artists, 1979
MELVIN AND HOWARD Universal, 1980
WHO AM I THIS TIME? (TF) Rubicon Film Productions, 1982
SWING SHIFT Warner Bros., 1983
STOP MAKING SENSE (FCD) Cinecom International/
Island Alive, 1984
SOMETHING WILD Orion, 1986
SWIMMING TO CAMBODIA (PF) Cinecom, 1987
MARRIED TO THE MOB Orion, 1988
THE SILENCE OF THE LAMBS ★★ Orion, 1991
COUSIN BOBBY (FD) Cinevista, 1992, U.S.-Spanish
PHILADELPHIA TriStar, 1993

TED DEMME*
Agent: CAA - Beverly Hills, 310/288-4545

DENIS LEARY: NO CURE FOR CANCER (CPF) Full Circle Films/
Showtime, 1993
WHO'S THE MAN New Line Cinema, 1993
THE REF Buena Vista, 1994
BEAUTIFUL GIRLS Mramax Films, 1995

PIERRE DE MORO

b. Corsica
Home: 16816 Charmel Lane, Pacific Palisades, CA 90272,
   310/454-0558 or 310/459-4197

DEVIL'S IVY   1973
CHRISTMAS MOUNTAIN   Christmas Mountain Productions, 1980
SAVANNAH SMILES   Embassy, 1983
HELL HOLE   Arkoff International Pictures, 1985
MICHELANGELO AND ME   Grand Marquee Films/Polivideo,
   1990, U.S.-Swiss

ROBERT DE NIRO*

b. August 17, 1943 - New York, New York
Business: Tribeca, 375 Greenwich Street, New York, NY 10013,
   212/941-4040
Agent: CAA - Beverly Hills, 310/288-4545

A BRONX TALE   Savoy Pictures, 1993

CLAIRE DENIS

Home: 65, rue N.-D. des Champs, 75006 Paris, France
Agent: ICM France - Paris, tel.: 1/723-7860
Contact: French Film Office, 745 Fifth Avenue, New York,
   NY 10151, 212/832-8860

CHOCOLAT   Orion Classics, 1988, French
S'EN FOUT LA MORT   Cinea/Pyramide/Les Films De Mindif/Camera
   One/NEF Production/La Sept, 1990, French
CONTRE L'OUBLI   co-director, Les Films du Paradoxe/Amnesty
   International/PRV, 1992, French
J'AI PAS SOMMEIL   Arena Films/Orsans Productions/Pyramide/
   Les Films de Mindif/France 3 Cinema/MG Films/Agora Film/
   Vega Film, 1994, French

JEAN-PIERRE DENIS

Address: "La Picade," 24110 Saint-Leon-sur-l'Ile, France,
   tel.: 16/53-80-6728
Contact: French Film Office, 745 Fifth Avenue, New York,
   NY 10151, 212/832-8860

FIELD OF HONOR (CHAMP D'HONNEUR)   Orion Classics,
   1987, French

BRIAN DENNEHY*

b. July 9, 1939 - Bridgeport, Connecticut
Contact: Directors Guild of America - Los Angeles, 213/851-3671
Agent: Susan Smith & Associates - Beverly Hills, 213/852-4777

JACK REED: A SEARCH FOR JUSTICE (TF)   Kushner-Locke
   Company/Steve Krantz Productions, 1994

PEN DENSHAM*

b. 1947 - England
Business: Trilogy Entertainment Group, 2401 Colorado Blvd. -
   Suite 100, Santa Monica, CA 90404, 310/449-3095
Agent: ICM - Beverly Hills, 310/550-4000

THE ZOO GANG   co-director with John Watson, New World, 1985
THE KISS   TriStar, 1988, U.S.-Canadian
MOLL FLANDERS   MGM-UA, 1995

RUGGERO DEODATO

(Roger Rockefeller)
Home: via Caroncini 52, Rome, Italy, tel: 06/808-6413

DONNE...BOTTE E BERSAGLIERI   Fida, 1968, Italian
FENOMENAL E IL TESORI DI TUTANKAMEN   Ikar, 1968, Italian
GUNGALA LA PANTERA NUDA   Summa Cinematografica,
   1968, Italian
VACANZE SULLA COSTA SMERALDA   Fida, 1969, Italian
I QUATTRO DEL PATER NOSTER   S.P.E.D. Film, 1969, Italian
ZENABEL   Italiana Cinematografica Artisti Riuniti, 1969, Italian
UNA ONDATA DI PIACERE   Tdl Cinematografica, 1975, Italian
UOMINI SI NASCE POLIZIOTTI SI MUORE   C.P.C. Citta di
   Milano/Tdl Cinematografica, 1976, Italian

ULTIMO MONDO CANNIBALE   Erre Cinematografica, 1977, Italian
L'ULTIMO SAPORE DELL'ARIA   Tritone Cinematografica,
   1978, Italian
CONCORDE AFFAIRE '79   Dania Film/National Cinematografica,
   1979, Italian
CANNIBAL HOLOCAUST   F.D. Cinematografica, 1980, Italian
LA CASA SPERDUTA NEL PARCO   F.D. Cinematografica,
   1980, Italian
I PREDATORI DI ATLANTIDE   Regency Productions, 1983, Italian
INFERNO IN DIRETTA   Racing Pictures, 1985, Italian
THE BARBARIANS   Cannon, 1987, Italian
THE LONE RUNNER   Trans World Entertainment, 1988, Italian
UN DELITTO POCO COMUNE   1988, Italian
CASABLANCA EXPRESS   1988, Italian
PHANTOM OF DEATH   Globe Films/Tandem Cinematografica/
   Reteitalia, 1988, Italian
DIAL: HELP   Metro Film/San Francisco Film, 1989, Italian
OCEANO   San Francisco Film/Cristaldi Film/Cinecitta/Socaem,
   1991, Italian
MOM I CAN DO IT   San Francisco Film, 1992, Italian
JOIN THE GANG 2 (MS)   co-director with Lodovico Gasperini,
   Sacis, 1993, Italian

MANOEL DE OLIVEIRA

b. December 10, 1908 - Oporto, Portugal
Contact: Instituto Portugues de Cinema, Rua San Pedrode
   Alcantara 45, 1200 Lisbon, Portugal, tel.: 3511/346-7395

ESTATUAS DE LISBOA   1931, Portuguese
FAMILICAO   1940, Portuguese
ANIKI-BOBO   1942, Portuguese
ACTO DA PRIMAVERA   1963, Portuguese
O PASSADO E O PRESENTE   1972, Portuguese
BENILDE OU A VIRGEM   1975, Portuguese
AMOR DE PERDICAO   1978, Portuguese
FRANCISCA   1981, Portuguese
MEMORIAS E CONFISSOES   1982, Portuguese
LISBOA CULTURAL (TF)   1983, Portuguese
A PROPOS DE VIGO (TD)   1984, French
THE SATIN SLIPPER   Cannon, 1985, French
MON CAS   Les Films du Passage/La Sept/Filmargen, 1986,
   French-Portuguese
OS CANIBAIS   Filmargem/Gemini Films/AB Cinema/Light Night/
   Pandora Films/Portugese Film Institute/Portuguese Radio and
   Television Company/Calouste Gulbenkian Foundation, 1988,
   Portuguese-French-Italian-Swiss-West German
NON OU A VA GLORIA DE MANDAR   Madragoa Filmes/Tornasol
   Filmes/Gemini Films/SGGC/RTP/Secretaria de Estado Da Cultura/
   Instituto Portugues de Cinema/Camara Municipal de Lisboa/
   Fundacao Calouste Gulbenkian/Fundacao Do Oriente/RTVE/
   Ministerio de la Cultura/CNC/Ministere de la Culture/Eurimages,
   1990, Portuguese-Spanish-French
A DIVINA COMEDIA   Madragoa Filmes/Gemini Films, 1991,
   Portuguese-French
O DIA DO DESESPERO   Madragoa Filmes/Gemini Films, 1992,
   Portuguese-French
VALE ABRAO   Madragoa Filmes/Gemini Films/Light Night
   Productions/IPC/FC Gulbenkian/SEC/CNC/Canal Plus/Office
   Federal de la Culture/TSR/Eurimages, 1993,
   Portuguese-French-Swiss
A CAIXA   Madragoa Filmes/Gemini Films/La Sept Cinema, 1994,
   Portuguese-French
THE CONVENT   1995, French-Portuguese

BRIAN DE PALMA*

b. September 11, 1940 - Newark, New Jersey
Agent: CAA - Beverly Hills, 310/288-4545
Business Manager: Julie Thomson, 5555 Melrose Avenue -
   Lubitsch Annex #119, Hollywood, CA 90038, 213/956-4270

MURDER A LA MOD   Aries, 1968
GREETINGS   Sigma III, 1968
THE WEDDING PARTY   co-director with Wilford Leach &
   Cynthia Munroe, Powell Productions Plus/Ondine, 1969
DIONYSUS IN '69   co-director with Robert Fiore & Bruce Rubin,
   Sigma III, 1970
HI, MOM!   Sigma III, 1970
GET TO KNOW YOUR RABBIT   Warner Bros., 1972

SISTERS   American International, 1973
PHANTOM OF THE PARADISE   20th Century-Fox, 1974
OBSESSION   Columbia, 1976
CARRIE   United Artists, 1976
THE FURY   20th Century-Fox, 1978
HOME MOVIES   United Artists Classics, 1980
DRESSED TO KILL   Filmways, 1980
BLOW OUT   Filmways, 1981
SCARFACE   Universal, 1983
BODY DOUBLE   Columbia, 1984
WISE GUYS   MGM/UA, 1986
THE UNTOUCHABLES   Paramount, 1987
CASUALTIES OF WAR   Columbia, 1989
THE BONFIRE OF THE VANITIES   Warner Bros., 1990
RAISING CAIN   Universal, 1992
CARLITO'S WAY   Universal, 1993
MISSION IMPOSSIBLE   Paramount, 1995

FRANK DE PALMA*

b. May 3, 1957 - Compton, California
Personal Manager: Jon Brown, The Brown Group - Beverly Hills,
   310/247-2755
Attorney: Stephen Breimer, Bloom, Dekom, Hergott & Cook,
   150 S. Rodeo Drive - 3rd Floor, Beverly Hills, CA 90212,
   310/859-6800

ATONEMENT (Short)   1978
THE HIBAKUSHA GALLERY (Short)   1981
FUTURE TENSE (CTF)   Walt Disney Productions, 1983
PRIVATE WAR   Smart Egg Releasing, 1989
MIDNIGHT RUN-AROUND (TF)   Toto Productions/
   Universal TV, 1994

JACQUES DERAY
(Jacques Deray Desrayaud)

b. February 19, 1929 - Lyons, France
Agent: ICM France - Paris, tel.: 1/723-7860
Contact: French Film Office, 745 Fifth Avenue, New York,
   NY 10151, 212/832-8860

LE GIGOLO   1960, French
RIFIFI IN TOKYO   MGM, 1961, French-Italian
PAR UN BEAU MATIN D'ETE   1964, French
SYMPHONY FOR A MASSACRE   7 Arts, 1965, French-Italian
THAT MAN GEORGE!   L'HOMME DE MARRAKECH
   Allied Artists, 1966, French-Italian-Spanish
AVEC LA PEAU AUTRES   1967, French
THE SWIMMING POOL   Avco Embassy, 1970, French-Italian
BORSALINO   Paramount, 1970, French-Italian
DOUCEMENT LES BASSES!   CIC, 1971, French
UN PEU DE SOLEIL DANS L'EAU FROIDE   SNC, 1971, French
THE OUTSIDE MAN   UN HOMME EST MORT   United Artists,
   1973, French-Italian
BORSALINO AND CO.   Medusa, 1974, French-Italian
FLIC STORY   Adel Productions/Lira Films/Mondial, 1975, French
LE GANG   Warner-Columbia, 1977, French
UN PAPILLON SUR L'EPAULE   Action Films, 1978, French
TROIS HOMMES A ABBATRE   Adel Production/Films A2,
   1980, French
LE MARGINAL   Gaumont/Cerito Rene Chateau, 1983, French
ON NE MEURT QUE DEUX FOIS   UGC, 1985, French
REGLEMENTS DE COMPTES   AMLF, 1986, French
MALADIE D'AMOUR   AMLF, 1987, French
LE SOLITAIRE   AMLF/Cerito, 1987, French
LES BOIS NOIRS   BAC Films, 1989, French
NETCHAIEV EST DE RETOUR   BAC Films, 1990, French
CONTRE L'OUBLI   co-director, Les Films du Paradoxe/Amnesty
   International/PRV, 1992, French
UN CRIME   AMLF, 1993, French
L'ORSO DI PELUCHE   Master Movie Distribution/Les Films Alain
   Sarde, 1994, Italian-French
3000 SCENARIOS CONTRE UN VIRUS   co-director, CRIPS/
   Medecine du Monde/APS/AESSA/Blue Films/Bernard Verley
   Films/Frouma Films International/Les Productions de 3eme
   Etage/CNC/Procirep/AFLS/TF1/France 2/France 3/Canal
   Plus/Arte/M6/Agfa, 1994, French

JOHN DEREK*
(Derek Harris)

b. August 12, 1926 - Hollywood, California
Contact: Directors Guild of America - Los Angeles, 213/851-3671

ONCE BEFORE I DIE   7 Arts, 1967, U.S.-Filipino
A BOY...A GIRL   Jack Hanson, 1968
CHILDISH THINGS   Filmworld, 1969
AND ONCE UPON A TIME   FANTASIES   Joseph Brenner
   Associates, 1973
LOVE YOU   1978
TARZAN, THE APE MAN   MGM/United Artists, 1981
BOLERO   Cannon, 1984
GHOSTS CAN'T DO IT   Triumph Releasing Corporation, 1990

DOMINIQUE DERUDDERE

b. 1957 - Turnhout, Belgium
Address: Antoine Dansaertstraat 95, B-1000 Brussels, Belgium
Agent: Voyez Mon Agent - Paris, tel.: 1/47-23-55-80

LOVE IS A DOG FROM HELL   CRAZY LOVE   1987, Belgian
WAIT UNTIL SPRING, BANDINI   Orion Classics, 1989,
   Belgian-French-Italian-U.S.
SUITE 16   Corsan Productions/Theorema Films, 1995,
   Belgian-Dutch-British

GIUSEPPE DE SANTIS

b. February 11, 1917 - Fondi, Italy
Home: Piazza del Commercio 1, Fiano Romano (Rome), Italy,
   tel.: 0765/389220

GIORNI DI GLORIA (FD)   co-director with Mario Serandrei,
   Luchino Visconti & Marcello Pagliero, Ministero Italia Occupata/
   Comando Divisioni Garibaldine Zona Valsesia/PWB Film Division/
   Cineac, 1945, Italian-U.S.-Swiss
CACCIA TRAGICA   ANPI Film, 1946, Italian
BITTER RICE   Lux Film America, 1949, Italian
NON C'E' PACE TRA GLI ULIVI   Lux Film, 1950, Italian
ROME 11 O'CLOCK   Times Film Corporation, 1952, Italian-French
AN MARITO PER ANNA ZACCHEO   Domenico Forges Davanzati,
   1953, Italian
GIORNI D'AMORE   Excelsa Film, 1954, Italian
MEN AND WOLVES   Columbia, 1956, Italian-French
CESTA DUGA GODINU DANA   Jadran Film, 1957, Yugoslavian
LA GARCONNIERE   Roberto Amoroso, 1960, Italian-French
ITALIANO BRAVA GENTE   ITALIANI BRAVA GENTE   Embassy,
   1963, Italian-Soviet
UN APPREZZATO PROFESSIONISTA DI SICURO AVVENIRE
   Filnuova, 1972, Italian

CALEB DESCHANEL*

b. September 21, 1944 - Philadelphia, Pennsylvania
Business: 7000 Romaine Street, Hollywood, CA 90038,
   213/465-6802
Agent: The Gersh Agency - Beverly Hills, 3210/274-6611

THE ESCAPE ARTIST   Orion/Warner Bros., 1982
CRUSOE   Island Pictures, 1988, U.S.-British

TOM DeSIMONE*

Home: 6105 Westpark Drive, North Hollywood, CA 91606,
   818/761-7161
Agent: APA - Los Angeles, 310/273-0744

CHATTER-BOX   American International, 1977
HELL NIGHT   Compass International, 1981
THE CONCRETE JUNGLE   Pentagon, 1982
REFORM SCHOOL GIRLS   New World, 1986
ANGEL III: THE FINAL CHAPTER   New World, 1988

STEVEN E. de SOUZA*

Agent: UTA - Beverly Hills, 310/273-6700

STREET FIGHTER   Universal, 1994, U.S.-Japanese

LOUIS D'ESPOSITO*

Address: 8716 Sunset Plaza Terrace, Los Angeles, CA 90069,
310/659-4891

OPPOSITE CORNERS   Opposite Corners Productions, 1995

ANDRE DE TOTH*

(Sasvrai Farkasfawi Tothfalusi Toth Endre Antai Mihaly)
b. 1910 - Mako, Hungary
Contact: Directors Guild of America - Los Angeles, 213/851-3671

TOPRINI NASZ *BALALAIKA* 1939, Hungarian
OT ORA 40 *5:40 P.M.* 1939, Hungarian
KET LANY AZ UTCAN *THE GIRLS ON THE STREET*
    1939, Hungarian
SEMMELWEIS 1939, Hungarian
HAT HET BOLDOGSAG *SIX WEEKS OF HAPPINESS*
    1939, Hungarian
PASSPORT TO SUEZ   Columbia, 1943
NONE SHALL ESCAPE   Columbia, 1944
DARK WATERS   United Artists, 1944
RAMROD   United Artists, 1947
THE OTHER LOVER   United Artists, 1947
PITFALL   United Artists, 1948
SLATTERY'S HURRICANE   20th Century-Fox, 1949
MAN IN THE SADDLE   Columbia, 1951
CARSON CITY   Warner Bros., 1952
SPRINGFIELD RIFLE   Warner Bros., 1952
LAST OF THE COMANCHES   Columbia, 1952
HOUSE OF WAX   Warner Bros., 1953
THE STRANGER WORE A GUN   Columbia, 1953
THUNDER OVER THE PLAINS   Warner Bros., 1953
RIDING SHOTGUN   Warner Bros., 1954
THE CITY IS DARK   Warner Bros., 1954
THE BOUNTY HUNTER   Warner Bros., 1954
TANGANYIKA   Universal, 1954
THE INDIAN FIGHTER   United Artists, 1955
MONKEY ON MY BACK   United Artists, 1957
HIDDEN FEAR   United Artists, 1957
THE TWO-HEADED SPY   Columbia, 1959
DAY OF THE OUTLAW   United Artists, 1959
MAN ON A STRING   Columbia, 1960
MORGAN THE PIRATE   MGM, 1960, British
THE MONGOLS   co-director with Leopoldo Savina, Colorama,
    1960, Italian
GOLD FOR THE CAESARS   co-director with Sabatino Ciuffini,
    Colorama, 1962, Italian-French
PLAY DIRTY   United Artists, 1968, British

HOWARD DEUTCH*

b. New York, New York
Agent: ICM - Beverly Hills, 310/550-4000

PRETTY IN PINK   Paramount, 1986
SOME KIND OF WONDERFUL   Paramount, 1987
THE GREAT OUTDOORS   Universal, 1988
ARTICLE 99   Orion, 1992
MELROSE PLACE (TF)   Darren Star Productions/Spelling
    Productions, 1992
GETTING EVEN WITH DAD   MGM-UA, 1994

ROSS DEVENISH

b. South Africa
Address: 65 Arlington Road, London NW1 7ES, England,
    tel.: 171/387-1654
Agent: The Artists Agency - Los Angeles, 310/277-7779 or:
    Lemon, Unna & Durridge - London, tel.: 171/727-1346

GOAL!   1966, British
NOW THAT THE BUFFALO'S GONE (FD)   1971, British
BOESMAN AND LENA   Bluewater, 1974, South African
THE GUEST AT STEENKAMPSKRAAL   Guest Productions,
    1977, South African
MARIGOLDS IN AUGUST   Southern Serpent Productions/RM
    Productions, 1980, South African
CHIP OF GLASS RUBY (TF)   Channel 4, 1983, British

BLEAK HOUSE (MS)   BBC, 1985, British
THE HAPPY VALLEY (TF)   BBC, 1986, British
ASINAMALI (TF)   Porterhouse Productions/BBC, 1986, British
DEATH OF A SON (TF)   Centre Films/BBC, 1988, British
AGATHA CHRISTIE'S POIROT (MS)   co-director with
    Andrew Grieve & Stephen Whittaker, London Weekend TV,
    1989, British
MYSTERIOUS AFFAIR AT STYLES (TF)   ITV, 1990, British
CALLING THE SHOTS (TF)   BBC, 1992, British
ONE, TWO BUCKLE MY SHOES (TF)   Carnival/London
    Weekend TV, 1993, British

MICHEL DEVILLE

b. April 13, 1931 - Boulogne-sur-Seine, France
Home: 36, rue Reinhardt, 92100 Boulogne, France, tel.: 46-05-06-64
Contact: French Film Office, 745 Fifth Avenue, New York, NY 10151,
    212/832-8860

UNE BALLE DANS LE CANON   co-director with
    Charles Gerard, 1958
CE SOIR OU JAMAIS   1960, French
ADORABLE MENTEUSE   1961, French
A CAUSE A CAUSE D'UNE FEMME   1962, French
L'APPARTEMENT DES VOLE LA JACONDE   1965, French
MARTIN SOLDAT   1966, French
TENDRE REQUINS   1967, French
BENJAMIN   *BENJAMIN OU LES MEMOIRES D'UN PUCEAU*
    Paramount, 1968, French
BYE BYE BARBARA   1969, French
THE BEAR AND THE DOLL   Paramount, 1970, French
RAPHAEL OU LE DEBAUCHE   Columbia, 1971, French
LA FEMME EN BLEU   Les Films La Boetie, 1973, French-Italian
THE FRENCH WAY   *LE MOUTON ENRAGE*   Peppercorn-Wormser,
    1974, French
L'APPRENTI SALAUD   Prodis, 1977, French
LE DOSSIER 51   1978, French
VOYAGE EN DOUCE   1980, French
EAUX PROFONDES   1982, French
LA PETITE BANDE   1983, French
PERIL   *PERIL EN LA DEMEURE*   Triumph/Columbia, 1985, French
DEATH IN A FRENCH GARDEN   1986, French
LE PALTOQUET   AAA, 1986, French
LA LECTRICE (THE READER)   Orion Classics, 1988, French
NUIT D'ETE EN VILLE   AAA, 1990, French
TOUTES PEINES CONFONDUES   AMLF, 1992, French
CONTRE L'OUBLI   co-director, Les Films du Paradoxe/Amnesty
    International/PRV, 1992, French
AUX PETITS BONHEURS   AMLF, 1993, French

DANNY DeVITO*

b. November 17, 1944 - Asbury Park, New Jersey
Business: Jersey Films, 10202 W. Washington Blvd., Frank Capra
    Building - Suite 112, Culver City, CA 90232, 310/280-4400
Agent: CAA - Beverly Hills, 310/288-4545

THE RATINGS GAME (CTF)   Imagination-New Street
    Productions, 1984
THROW MOMMA FROM THE TRAIN   Orion, 1987
THE WAR OF THE ROSES   20th Century Fox, 1989
HOFFA   20th Century Fox, 1992
MATILDA   Columbia, 1995

BARRY DEVLIN

Agent: Peters Fraser & Dunlop - London, tel.: 171/344-1000

ALL THINGS BRIGHT AND BEAUTIFUL   BBC Enterprises,
    1994, British-Irish

DAVID DeVRIES*

Business: David deVries Films, 100 Riverside Drive, New York,
    NY 10024, 212/580-2888
Address: 607 Grinnel Drive, Burbank, CA 91501, 818/567-2227

HOME AT LAST (TF)   deVries Films, 1988

PATRICK DEWOLF
Agent: ICM France - Paris, tel.: 1/723-7860
Contact: French Film Office, 745 Fifth Avenue, New York,
   NY 10151, 212/832-8860

HALCYON DAYS   Polygram Filmed Entertainment,
   1994, British-French

MAURY DEXTER*
b. 1927
Business Manager: Hank Tani, 12643 Misty Grove Street, Moorpark,
   CA 93021, 805/529-8917

THE HIGH POWERED RIFLE   20th Century-Fox, 1960
WALK TALL   20th Century-Fox, 1960
THE PURPLE HILLS   20th Century-Fox, 1961
WOMAN HUNT   20th Century-Fox, 1961
THE FIREBRAND   20th Century-Fox, 1962
AIR PATROL   20th Century-Fox, 1962
THE DAY MARS INVADED EARTH   20th Century-Fox, 1962
HOUSE OF THE DAMNED   20th Century-Fox, 1962
HARBOR LIGHTS   20th Century-Fox, 1963, U.S.-Puerto Rican
THE YOUNG SWINGERS   20th Century-Fox, 1963
POLICE NURSE   20th Century-Fox, 1963
YOUNG GUNS OF TEXAS   20th Century-Fox, 1963
SURF PARTY   20th Century-Fox, 1963
RAIDERS FROM BENEATH THE SEA   20th Century-Fox, 1964
WILD ON THE BEACH   20th Century-Fox, 1965
THE NAKED BRIGADE   Universal, 1965
MARYJANE   American International, 1968
THE MINI-SKIRT MOB   American International, 1968
BORN WILD   American International, 1968
HELL'S BELLES   American International, 1969

TOM DiCILLO
b. 1953 - North Carolina
Agent: William Morris Agency - Beverly Hills, 310/859-4000

JOHNNY SUEDE   Miramax Films, 1991
LIVING IN OBLIVION   JDI/Lemon Sky Productions, 1995

NIGEL DICK
Agent: Paul Kohner, Inc. - Los Angeles, 213/550-1060

PRIVATE INVESTIGATIONS   MGM/UA, 1987
DEADLY INTENT   Fries Entertainment, 1988
FINAL COMBINATION   Propaganda Films, 1993

ERNEST R. DICKERSON*
b. 1952 - Newark, New Jersey
Agent: UTA - Los Angeles, 310/273-6700

JUICE   Paramount, 1992
SURVIVING THE GAME   New Line Cinema, 1994
TALES FROM THE CRYPT PRESENTS DEMON KNIGHT
   DEMON KNIGHT   Universal, 1995

MARIO DI FIORE
b. June 14, 1968 - Wollongong, Australia
Business: Global International Pictures, 91 Walang Avenue,
   Elstree Heights, 2525 NSW, Australia, tel.: 1/42-765009

AUSTRALIAN NINJA   Transworld Entertainment, 1988, Australian
CLAWS OF DEATH   Transworld Entertainment, 1988, Australian
KARATE COP   Transworld Entertainment, 1988, Australian
REPRISAL   Transworld Entertainment, 1989, Australian
FORTRESS   Transglobal Motion Pictures, 1989, Australian
DANGEROUS GAMES   Transglobal Motion Pictures,
   1990, Australian
BREAKING LOOSE   Screentexts Productions, 1990, Australian
BAD ATTITUDE   Global Motion Pictures Entertainment,
   1991, Australian
OUTBACK BEVERLY HILLS   Global Motion Pictures Entertainment,
   1991, Australian
DEATH OF YESTERDAY   Global Motion Pictures Entertainment,
   1991, Australian

DAUGHTER OF THE STREET   Noduki Films, 1991, Australian
BLUE DAHLIA   Noduki Films, 1992, Australian
STRONG FOREVER   Noduki Films, 1992, Australian
RUN TO PARADISE   Adam Ramos Productions, 1992, Australian
SAY A LITTLE PRAYER   Adam Ramos Productions,
   1993, Australian
CRIME BROKER   Transworld International, 1993, Australian
REICH TRACE   Transworld International, 1993, Australian
AUSTRALIAN NINJA 2   Transworld International, 1993, Australian
HAMMER AND SICKLE   Global International, 1993, Australian
LONG WALK HOME   Global International, 1994, Australian
NO BRIDGE FOR FRANCE   Global International, 1994, Australian
MEN WANTED   Global International, 1994, Australian

CARLOS DIEGUES
b. 1940 - Maceio, Alagoas, Brazil
Business: CDK - Producoes Cinematograficas Ltda., Rua Miguel
   Pereira 62, 2261 Rio de Janeiro, Brazil, tel.: 021/266-7995

GANGA ZUMBA   1963, Brazilian
O GRANDE CIDADE   1966, Brazilian
OS HERDEIROS   1969, Brazilian
QUANDO O CARNAVAL CHEGAR   1972, Brazilian
JOANA FRANCESCA   1973, Brazilian
XICA   *XICA DA SILVA*   New Yorker, 1976, Brazilian
CHUVAS DE VERAO   1978, Brazilian
BYE BYE BRAZIL   Carnaval/Unifilm, 1980, Brazilian
QUILOMBO   New Yorker, 1984, Brazilian
SUBWAY TO THE STARS   FilmDallas, 1987, Brazilian-French
DIAS MELHORES VIRAO   Cinevest/Multiplic/CDK, 1991, Brazilian
VEJA ESSA CANCAO   1994, Brazilian

ALAN DIENSTAG
THE MONEY TREE   Black Sheep Films, 1992

HELMUT DIETL
Agent: ICM - Beverly Hills, 310/550-4000

SCHTONK!   Bavaria Film, 1992, German

ERIN DIGNAM
DENIAL   *LOON*   Filmstar, 1990

MARIO DI LEO*
Business: Di Leo Enterprises, 2100 N. Topanga Canyon Blvd.,
   Topanga, CA 90290, 310/455-1323
Agent: Vincent Panettiere, Panettiere & Co., 1841 N. Fuller Avenue,
   Los Angeles, CA 90046, 213/876-5984

THE FINAL ALLIANCE   International Media Exchange, 1990

STEVE DiMARCO
Contact: Directors Guild of Canada, 225 Richmond Street, Toronto
   M5V 1W2, Canada, 416/351-8200

THICK AS THIEVES   Alliance Communications, 1992, Canadian
BACK IN ACTION   co-director with Paul Ziller, SGE Entertainmnent,
   1994, Canadian
SPIKE OF LOVE   Screaming Slave Sinema/Lightshow
   Communications/Ontario Film Development Corporation,
   1995, Canadian

DENNIS DIMSTER-DENK
MIKEY   Imperial Entertainment, 1992

MARK DINDAL
CATS DON'T DANCE (AF)   Turner Pictures, 1996

JOHN DINGWALL
Contact: Australian Film Commission, 150 William Street,
   Woolloomooloo NSW 2011, Australia, tel.: 2/321-6444

PHOBIA   1988, Australian
THE CUSTODIAN   Beyond Films, 1993, Australian

MICHAEL DINNER*

Agent: ICM - Beverly Hills, 310/550-4000
Personal Manager: 3 Arts Entertainment - Beverly Hills,
   310/888-3200
Business Manager: Victor Meschures, Jamner, Pariser &
   Meschures, 760 N. La Cienega Blvd., Los Angeles,
   CA 90069, 213/652-0222

MISS LONELYHEARTS   H. Jay Holman Productions/American
   Film Institute, 1983
HEAVEN HELP US   TriStar, 1985
OFF BEAT   Buena Vista, 1986
HOT TO TROT   Warner Bros., 1988
RISE & WALK: THE DENNIS BYRD STORY (TF)
   Fox West Pictures, 1994
THICKER THAN BLOOD: THE LARRY McLINDEN STORY (TF)
   Alexander-Enright & Associates, 1994

VINCENT DiPERSIO*

Personal Manager: Creative Alliance Management - Los Angeles,
   213/962-6090

FLYING BLIND (TF)   NBC Productions, 1990,
   originally filmed for theatrical release
AMERICA UNDERCOVER: DEATH ON THE JOB (CTD)
   co-director with William Guttentag, Half-Court Pictures, 1991

JOHN DIRLAM

TO KILL FOR   Moviestore Entertainment, 1991

MARK DISALLE*

Home: P.O. Box 15185, Beverly Hills, CA 90210, 310/273-5874
Agent: The Gersh Agency - Beverly Hills, 310/274-6611
Business Manager: Tom Hansen, Hansen, Jacobsen & Teller,
   335 N. Maple Drive - Suite 270, Beverly Hills, CA 90210,
   310/271-8777

KICKBOXER   co-director with David Worth, Cannon, 1989
THE PERFECT WEAPON   Paramount, 1991

IVAN DIXON*

b. April 6, 1931 - New York, New York
Home: 10 Wailea Ekolu Place - Suite 407, Kihei, HI 96753,
   808/874-0503

TROUBLE MAN   20th Century-Fox, 1972
THE SPOOK WHO SAT BY THE DOOR   United Artists, 1973
LOVE IS NOT ENOUGH (TF)   Universal TV, 1978
MERCY & THUNDER (CTF)   Amblin TV/Brandman
   Productions, 1993

KEN DIXON

SLAVE GIRLS FROM BEYOND INFINITY   Urban Classics, 1987

WHEELER DIXON

b. March 12, 1950 - New Brunswick, New Jersey
Attorney: Mark Brown, Muffly, Oglesby & Brown, 414 S. 11th Street,
   Lincoln, NE 68508, 402/479-3397

THE GAMMA CHRONICLES (MS)   Gold Key Entertainment, 1980
THE GALAXY COLLECTION (TF)   Deliniator Films, 1985

EROS DJAROT

b. 1950 - Indonesia
Contact: Directorate for Film and Video Development,
   Ministry of Information, Jalan Merdeka Barat 9, Jakarta,
   Indonesia, tel: 377408

WOMAN OF COURAGE   TJOET NJA' DHIEN   Ekapraya Films,
   1988, Indonesian
THE SONG OF DEDICATION   co-director with Slamet Rahardjo &
   Gotot Prakosa, Ekapraya Films, 1993, Indonesian

SLAMET RAHARDJO DJAROT

b. Indonesia
Contact: Directorate for Film and Video Development, Ministry of
   Information, Jalan Merdeka Barat 9, Jakarta, Indonesia, tel.: 377408

REMBULAN DAN MATAHARI   1980, Indonesian
SEPUTIH HATINYA SEMERAH BIBIRNYA   1982, Indonesian
PONIRAH TERPIDANA   1983, Indonesian
KEMBANG KERTOS   1984, Indonesian
KODRAT   1986, Indonesian
KASMARAN   1987, Indonesian
MY SKY, MY HOME   Ekapraya Film, 1989, Indonesian
THE SONG OF DEDICATION   co-director with Eros Djarot &
   Gotot Prakosa, Ekapraya Films, 1993, Indonesian
THE LOST CHILD (TF)   1993, Indonesian
SOUTHERN WINDS   co-director with Shoji Kogami, Mike De Leon &
   Cherd Songsri, NHK Enterprises, 1993,
   Japanese-Filipino-Thai-Indonesian

EDWARD DMYTRYK*

b. September 4, 1908 - Grand Forks, Canada
Contact: Directors Guild of America - Los Angeles, 213/851-3671

THE HAWK   Herman Wohl, 1935
TELEVISION SPY   Paramount, 1939
EMERGENCY SQUAD   Paramount, 1940
MYSTERY SEA RAIDERS   Paramount, 1940
GOLDEN GLOVES   Paramount, 1940
HER FIRST ROMANCE   Monogram, 1940
THE DEVIL COMMANDS   Columbia, 1941
UNDER AGE   Columbia, 1941
SWEETHEART OF THE CAMPUS   Columbia, 1941
THE BLONDE FROM SINGAPORE   Columbia, 1941
CONFESSIONS OF BOSTON BLACKIE   Columbia, 1941
SECRETS OF THE LONE WOLF   Columbia, 1941
COUNTER ESPIONAGE   Columbia, 1942
SEVEN MILES FROM ALCATRAZ   RKO Radio, 1942
THE FALCON STRIKES BACK   RKO Radio, 1943
HITLER'S CHILDREN   RKO Radio, 1943
CAPTIVE WILD WOMAN   Universal, 1943
BEHIND THE RISING SUN   RKO Radio, 1943
TENDER COMRADE   RKO Radio, 1943
MURDER MY SWEET   RKO Radio, 1945
BACK TO BATAAN   RKO Radio, 1945
TILL THE END OF TIME   RKO Radio, 1945
CROSSFIRE ★   RKO Radio, 1947
SO WELL REMEMBERED   RKO Radio, 1947
THE HIDDEN ROOM   OBSESSION   British Lion, 1949, British
GIVE US THIS DAY   SALT TO THE DEVIL   Eagle Lion,
   1949, British
MUTINY   Universal, 1952
THE SNIPER   Columbia, 1952
EIGHT IRON MEN   Columbia, 1952
THE JUGGLER   Columbia, 1953
THE CAINE MUTINY   Columbia, 1954
BROKEN LANCE   20th Century-Fox, 1954
THE END OF THE AFFAIR   Columbia, 1954
SOLDIER OF FORTUNE   20th Century-Fox, 1955
THE LEFT HAND OF GOD   20th Century-Fox, 1955
THE MOUNTAIN   Paramount, 1956
RAINTREE COUNTY   MGM, 1957
THE YOUNG LIONS   20th Century-Fox, 1958
WARLOCK   20th Century-Fox, 1959
THE BLUE ANGEL   20th Century-Fox, 1959
WALK ON THE WILD SIDE   Columbia, 1962
THE RELUCTANT SAINT   Davis-Royal, 1962, Italian-U.S.
THE CARPETBAGGERS   Paramount, 1963
WHERE LOVE HAS GONE   Paramount, 1964
MIRAGE   Universal, 1965
ALVAREZ KELLY   Columbia, 1966
ANZIO   Columbia, 1968, Italian
SHALAKO!   Cinerama Releasing Corporation, 1968, British
BLUEBEARD   Cinerama Releasing Corporation, 1972,
   Italian-French-West German
THE HUMAN FACTOR   Bryanston, 1974, British-U.S.
HE IS MY BROTHER   Atlantic Releasing Corporation, 1976

LOC DO
b. October 20, 1968 - Vientane, Laos
Business: Saigon '95 Productions, 612 N. Rural Drive,
   Monterey Park, CA 91754, 818/571-8328

BASTARDS   Descendents of War Productions, 1995

FRANK Q. DOBBS*
Home: P.O. Box 570477, Houston, TX 77157, 713/524-1363

UPHILL ALL THE WAY   New World, 1985

KEVIN JAMES DOBSON*
Agent: The Brandt Company - Sherman Oaks, 818/783-7747
Business Manager: Steven R. Pines, 1180 So. Beverly Drive -
   Suite 320, Los Angeles, CA 90035, 310/203-0320

THE MANGO TREE   1977, Australian
SQUIZZY TAYLOR   Australian
THE DEAN CASE (TF)   Australian
FIVE MILE CREEK (TF)   Australian
THIRD GENERATION (TF)   Australian
GONE TO GROUND (TF)   Australian
THE LES DARCY STORY (TF)   Australian
YOUNG RAMSAY (MS)   Australian
THE LAST OUTLAW (MS)   Australian
I CAN JUMP PUDDLES (MS)   Australian
TANAMERA: LION OF SINGAPORE (MS)   co-director with
   John Power, Reg Grundy Productions/Central Independent
   Television, 1989, Australian-British
CASEY'S GIFT: FOR LOVE OF A CHILD (TF)   American First
   Run Studios, 1990
SHADES OF GRAY (TF)   Republic Pictures, 1991
MIRACLE IN THE WILDERNESS (CTF)   Ruddy & Morgan
   Productions, 1991
SURVIVE THE SAVAGE SEA (TF)   von Zerneck-Sertner Films,
   1992, U.S.-Australian
WHAT SHE DOESN'T KNOW (TF)   Two Short Productions/
   Republic Pictures, 1992
GOLD DIGGERS   Universal, 1995

JAMES DODSON
DEADLY RIVALS   Greenwich Films, 1992
QUEST OF THE DELTA KNIGHTS   Ramsway Ltd./Metro
   Pictures, 1993
LOST STOREHOUSE   Metro Films/Ramsway, 1994

JACQUES DOILLON
b. March 15, 1944 - Paris, France
Business: Lola Films, 60, rue Laugier, 75017 Paris, France,
   tel.: 1/40-54-06-06
Contact: French Film Office, 745 Fifth Avenue, New York,
   NY 10151, 212/832-8860

L'AN 01   1972, French
LES DOIGS DANS LA TETE   1974, French
UN SAC DE BILLES   1975, French
LA FEMME QUI PLEURE   1978, French
LA DROLESSE   1979, French
LA FILLE PRODIGUE   1981, French
LA PIRATE   1984, French
LA VIE DE FAMILLE   1985, French
LA TENTATION D'ISABELLE   1985, French
LA FILLE DE QUINZE ANS   1989, French
LA VENGEANCE D'UNE FEMME   1990, French
LA JEUNE WERTHER   Pan Europeene, 1993, French
DU FOND DU COEUR: GERMAINE ET BENJAMIN
   GMT Productions/La Sept-Arte/SFP/Home Made Movies/
   Club D'Investissement Media/Babelsberg Studio,
   1994, French-German
PONETTE   Canal Plus, 1995, French

JERZY DOMARADZKI
Contact: Film Polski, ul. Mazowiecka 6/8, 00-048 Warsaw,
   Poland, tel.: 48-22/26-84-55 or 48-22/26-09-49

THE BIG RACE   Film Unit X/Poltel/Perspektyva Unit, 1981, Polish
THE TAILOR'S PLANET   Film Unit X, 1983, Polish
WHITE DRAGON   Legend Productions/Perspektyva Unit,
   1986, U.S.-Polish
CUPID'S BOW   Perspektyva Unit, 1987, Polish
RIDERS ON THE STORM   Beyond International, 1990, Australian
LILLIAN'S STORY   CML Films, 1995, Australian

ROGER DONALDSON*
b. November 15, 1945 - Ballarat, Australia
Agent: CAA - Beverly Hills, 310/288-4545 or:
   The Cameron Creswell Agency - Sydney, tel.: 2/356-4677

SLEEPING DOGS   Aardvark Films, 1977, New Zealand
SMASH PALACE   Atlantic Releasing Corporation,
   1981, New Zealand
THE BOUNTY   Orion, 1984, British
MARIE   MGM/UA, 1985
NO WAY OUT   Orion, 1987
COCKTAIL   Buena Vista, 1988
CADILLAC MAN   Orion, 1990
WHITE SANDS   Warner Bros., 1992
THE GETAWAY   Universal, 1994
SPECIES   MGM-UA, 1995

STANLEY DONEN*
b. April 13, 1924 - Columbia, South Carolina
Contact: c/o Wayne Rogers, The La Grange Group, 11828 La Grange
   Avenue, Los Angeles, CA 90025, 310/473-0514

ON THE TOWN   co-director with Gene Kelly, MGM, 1949
ROYAL WEDDING   MGM, 1951
SINGIN' IN THE RAIN   co-director with Gene Kelly, MGM, 1952
LOVE IS BETTER THAN NONE   MGM, 1952
FEARLESS FAGAN   MGM, 1952
GIVE A GIRL A BREAK   MGM, 1953
SEVEN BRIDES FOR SEVEN BROTHERS   MGM, 1954
DEEP IN MY HEART   MGM, 1954
IT'S ALWAYS FAIR WEATHER   co-director with Gene Kelly,
   MGM, 1955
FUNNY FACE   Paramount, 1957
THE PAJAMA GAME   co-director with George Abbott,
   Warner Bros., 1957
KISS THEM FOR ME   20th Century-Fox, 1957
INDISCREET   Warner Bros., 1958, British
DAMN YANKEES   co-director with George Abbott, Warner Bros., 1958
ONCE MORE, WITH FEELING   Columbia, 1960
SURPRISE PACKAGE   Columbia, 1960
THE GRASS IS GREENER   Universal, 1961
CHARADE   Universal, 1964
ARABESQUE   Universal, 1966, British-U.S.
TWO FOR THE ROAD   20th Century-Fox, 1967, British-U.S.
BEDAZZLED   20th Century-Fox, 1967, British
STAIRCASE   20th Century-Fox, 1969, British
THE LITTLE PRINCE   Paramount, 1974, British
LUCKY LADY   20th Century-Fox, 1975
MOVIE MOVIE   Warner Bros., 1978
SATURN 3   AFD, 1980
BLAME IT ON RIO   20th Century Fox, 1984

ARTHUR DONG
FORBIDDEN CITY, U.S.A. (FD)   1989
COMING OUT UNDER FIRE (FD)   Zeitgeist Films, 1994

WALTER DONIGER*
b. July 1, 1917 - New York, New York
Business: Bettina Productions Ltd., 624 So. June Street,
   Los Angeles, CA 90005, 213/937-2101
Agent: Shelly Wile, Wile Enterprises, 2730 Santa Monica Blvd. -
   Suite 500, Santa Monica, CA 90403, 310/828-9768

DUFFY OF SAN QUENTIN   Warner Bros., 1953
THE STEEL CAGE   United Artists, 1954

THE STEEL JUNGLE   Warner Bros., 1955
UNWED MOTHER   Allied Artists, 1958
HOUSE OF WOMEN   Warner Bros., 1960
SAFE AT HOME!   Columbia, 1962
MAD BULL   co-director with Len Steckler, Steckler Productions/
   Filmways, 1977
KENTUCKY WOMAN   Walter Doniger Productions/
   20th Century-Fox TV, 1983

T O M   D O N N E L L Y *
Contact: Directors Guild of America - Los Angeles, 213/851-3671
Agent: The Artists Agency - Los Angeles, 310/277-7779

QUICKSILVER   Columbia, 1986
BLINDSIDED (CTF)   MTE Productions/Alan Barnette
   Productions, 1993

C L I V E   D O N N E R *
b. January 21, 1926 - London, England
Agent: Nigel Britten Management - London, tel.: 171/379-0801

THE SECRET PLACE   Rank, 1957, British
HEART OF A CHILD   Rank, 1958, British
MARRIAGE OF CONVENIENCE   Allied Artists, 1961, British
THE SINISTER MAN   Allied Artists, 1961, British
SOME PEOPLE   American International, 1962, British
THE GUEST   THE CARETAKER   Janus, 1963, British
NOTHING BUT THE BEST   Royal Films International, 1964, British
WHAT'S NEW PUSSYCAT?   United Artists, 1965, British
LUV   Columbia, 1967
HERE WE GO ROUND THE MULBERRY BUSH   Lopert,
   1968, British
ALFRED THE GREAT   MGM, 1969, British
OLD DRACULA   VAMPIRA   American International, 1975, British
ROGUE MALE (TF)   BBC, 1976, British
SPECTRE (TF)   20th Century-Fox TV, 1977
THE THIEF OF BAGHDAD (TF)   Palm Films Ltd., 1979, British
THE NUDE BOMB   Universal, 1980
CHARLIE CHAN AND THE CURSE OF THE DRAGON QUEEN
   American Cinema, 1980
OLIVER TWIST (TF)   Claridge Group Ltd./Grafton Films,
   1982, British
THE SCARLET PIMPERNEL (TF)   London Films Ltd., 1982, British
TO CATCH A KING (CTF)   HBO Premiere Films/Entertainment
   Partners/Gaylord Productions, 1984
A CHRISTMAS CAROL (TF)   Entertainment Partners Ltd.,
   1984, U.S.-British
ARTHUR THE KING (TF)   Martin Poll Productions/Comworld
   Productions/Jadran Film, 1985, U.S.-Yugoslavian
AGATHA CHRISTIE'S 'DEAD MAN'S FOLLY' (TF)
   Warner Bros. TV, 1986, U.S.-British
BABES IN TOYLAND (TF)   Orion TV/Finnegan Associates/
   Bavaria Atelier, 1986
STEALING HEAVEN   Scotti Bros., 1988, U.S.-Yugoslavian
NOT A PENNY MORE, NOT A PENNY LESS (TF)
   BBC/Paramount TV/Revcom, 1990, British-U.S.

J Ö R N   D O N N E R
b. February 5, 1933 - Helsinki, Finland
Business: Jörn Donner Productions, Pohjoisranta 12, SF-00170
   Helsinki, Finland, tel.: 0/1256060

A SUNDAY IN SEPTEMBER   1963, Swedish
TO LOVE   1964, Swedish
ADVENTURE STARTS HERE   1965, Swedish
STIMULANTIA   co-director, 1967, Swedish
ROOFTREE   1967, Swedish
BLACK ON WHITE   1968, Finnish
SIXTYNINE   1969, Finnish
PORTRAITS OF WOMEN   1970, Finnish
ANNA   1970, Finnish
FUCK OFF! IMAGES OF FINLAND (FD)   1971, Finnish
TENDERNESS   1972, Finnish
THE WORLD OF INGMAR BERGMAN (FD)   1975, Swedish
MAN CANNOT BE RAPED   1978, Finnish
9 WAYS TO APPROACH HELSINKI (TD)   1982, Finnish
DIRTY STORY   Jorn Donner Productions, 1984, Finnish

R I C H A R D   D O N N E R *
b. 1939 - New York, New York
Business: Richard Donner Productions, 4000 Warner Blvd. -
   Building 102, Burbank, CA 91522, 818/954-3284
Agent: CAA - Beverly Hills, 310/288-4545

X-15   United Artists, 1961
SALT AND PEPPER   United Artists, 1968, British
LOLA   TWINKY   American International, 1970, British-Italian
LUCAS TANNER (TF)   Universal TV, 1974
SENIOR YEAR (TF)   Universal TV, 1974
A SHADOW IN THE STREETS (TF)   Playboy Productions, 1975
SARAH T. - PORTRAIT OF A TEENAGE ALCOHOLIC (TF)
   Universal TV, 1975
THE OMEN   20th Century-Fox, 1976
SUPERMAN   Warner Bros., 1978, U.S.-British
INSIDE MOVES   AFD, 1980
THE TOY   Columbia, 1982
LADYHAWKE   Warner Bros., 1985
THE GOONIES   Warner Bros., 1985
LETHAL WEAPON   Warner Bros., 1987
SCROOGED   Paramount, 1988
LETHAL WEAPON 2   Warner Bros., 1989
RADIO FLYER   Columbia, 1992
LETHAL WEAPON 3   Warner Bros., 1992
MAVERICK   Warner Bros., 1994
ASSASSINS   Warner Bros., 1995

M A R Y   A G N E S   D O N O G H U E *
b. Queens, New York
Agent: ICM - Beverly Hills, 310/550-4000

PARADISE   Buena Vista, 1991

M A R T I N   D O N O V A N *
(Carlos Enrique Varela y Peralta-Ramos)
b. Argentina
Agent: UTA - Beverly Hills, 310/273-6700

APARTMENT ZERO   Skouras Pictures, 1988, British-Argentine
JAVA NARCISSUS   Propanda Productions, 1990
SEEDS OF TRAGEDY (TF)   Sanford-Pillsbury Productions/
   FNM Films, 1991
DEATH DREAMS (CTF)   Ultra Entertainment/Dick Clark Film Group/
   Roni Weisberg Productions, 1991
MAD AT THE MOON   Michael Jaffe Films Ltd./Spectator Films/
   Cassian Elwes-Kastenbaum Films, 1992
THE SUBSTITUTE (CTF)   Pacific Motion Pictures/Wilshire Court
   Productions, 1993

P A U L   D O N O V A N
b. 1954 - Canada
Address: P.O. Box 2261, Station M, Halifax, Nova Scotia B3J 3L8,
   Canada, 902/420-1577

TORPEDOED   SOUTH PACIFIC 1942   Surfacing Film Productions,
   1980, Canadian
SELF DEFENSE   SIEGE   co-director with Maura O'Connell,
   New Line Cinema, 1983, Canadian
DEF-CON 4   New World, 1985, Canadian
CARIBE   Shapiro Entertainment, 1987, Canadian
THE SQUAMISH FIVE   CBC, 1988, Canadian
NORMAN'S AWESOME EXPERIENCE   Norstar Entertainment,
   1989, Canadian, filmed in 1987
GEORGE'S ISLAND   New Line Cinema, 1991, Canadian
BURIED ON SUNDAY   Alliance Communications/Salter Street
   Films, 1992, Canadian
TOM   Saban Entertainment/Den Productions/Entertainment
   Securities, 1993
LIFE WITH BILLY   Salter Street Films/The Film Works/CBC,
   1993, Canadian
PAINT CANS   Libra Films, 1994, Canadian

TOM DONOVAN*
Address: 650 Park Avenue, New York, NY 10021, 212/737-6910

THE LAST BRIDE OF SALEM (TF)   20th Century-Fox TV, 1974
TRISTAN AND ISOLT   *LOVESPELL*   Clar Productions,
  1981, British

LEE DOO-YONG
b. December 24, 1942 - Seoul, Korea
Contact: Korean Motion Pictures Promotion Corporation, 34-5,
  3KA Namsan-Dong, Chung-Ku, South Korea, tel.: 755-9291

LOST WEDDING VEIL   1970, South Korean
YOUR DADDY LIKE THIS?   1971, South Korean
THE GENERAL IN RED ROBE   1973, South Korean
CHOBUN   1977, South Korean
POLICE STORY   1978, South Korean
MULDORI VILLAGE   1979, South Korean
PIMAK   1980, South Korean
SPINNING WHEEL   1983, South Korean
FIRST SON   1984, South Korean
PONG   1985, South Korean
EUNUCH   1986, South Korean
THE WAY TO CHEONGSONG   Doo Sung Cinema Corporation,
  1991, South Korean

JACQUES DORFMANN
Contact: Directors Guild of Canada, 225 Richmond Street, Toronto,
  Ontario M5V 1W2, Canada, 416/351-8200

SHADOW OF THE WOLF   Triumph Releasing Corporation,
  1993, Canadian-French

ROBERT DORNHELM*
b. Romania
Agent: Tom Chasin, The Chasin Agency - Los Angeles,
  310/278-7505

THE CHILDREN OF THEATRE STREET (FD)
  Peppercorn-Wormser, 1977
SHE DANCES ALONE   Continental, 1982, U.S.-Austrian
DIGITAL DREAMS   Ripple Productions Ltd., 1983
ECHO PARK   Atlantic Releasing Corporation,
  1985, U.S.-Austrian
COLD FEET   Avenue Pictures, 1989
REQUIEM FOR DOMINIC   Hemdale, 1990, Austrian
FATAL DECEPTION: MRS. LEE HARVEY OSWALD (TF)
  David L. Wolper Productions/Bernard Sofronski Productions/
  Warner Bros. TV, 1993

JOHN DORR
LUCK, TRUST & KETCHUP: ROBERT ALTMAN IN CARVER
  COUNTRY (TD)   co-director with Mike Kaplan,
  EZTV/Circle Associates, 1994

DORIS DÖRRIE
(Doris Doerrie)
b. 1955 - Hanover, West Germany
Address: Tengstrasse 16, 8000 Munich 40, Germany
Agent: ICM - New York City, 212/556-5600
Contact: Federal Union of Film and Television Directors in Germany,
  Adelheidstrasse 7, 8000 Munich 40, Germany, tel.: 089/271-6380

DAZWISCHEN   1981, West German
STRAIGHT THROUGH THE HEART   1983, West German
IN THE BELLY OF THE WHALE   1984, West German
MEN...   New Yorker, 1985, West German
PARADIES   Delta Film/H.J. Seybusch/WDR, 1986, West German
ME AND HIM   Columbia, 1988, West German-U.S.
GELD   Olga Film/ZDF, 1990, West German
HAPPY BIRTHDAY, TURKE!   Senator Film, 1991, German
KEINER LIEBT MICH   Cobra Film, 1994, German

NELSON PEREIRA DOS SANTOS
b. October 26, 1928 - Sao Paulo, Brazil
Business: Regina Films, Rua Jornalista Orlando Dantas 1, Botafogo,
  Rio de Janeiro, Brazil, tel.: 021/552-3648

RIO, 40 GRAUS   1954, Brazilian
RIO, ZONE NORTE   1957, Brazilian
VIDAS SECAS   1963, Brazilian
O ALIENISTA   1970, Brazilian
COMO ERA GOSTOSO O MEU FRANCES   1971, Brazilian
QUEM E BETA?   1973, Brazilian
AMULET OF OGUM   New Yorker, 1975, Brazilian
TENDA DA MILAGRES   1975, Brazilian
MEMORIAS DO CARCERE   1984, Brazilian
JUBIABA   1985, Brazilian
A TERCEIRA MARGEM DO RIO   Regina Filmes/Centre of
  Cultural and Educational Production/Institute of Brazilian Art and
  Culture/Ministry of Culture (Cinema), 1994, Brazilian

ALAN DOSSOR
Address: 23 Boscombe Road, London W12 9HS, England,
  tel.: 181/743-2670
Agent: Tim Corrie, Peters Fraser & Dunlop - London,
  tel.: 171/376-7676

ICE DANCE (TF)   BBC, 1989, British
FIRST AND LAST (TF)   BBC, 1990, British
BROKE (TF)   BBC, 1991, British
FLEA BITES (TF)   BBC, 1991, British
FAIR GAME (TF)   BBC, 1993, British
THE GOVERNOR   co-director with Robert Knights & Bob Mahoney,
  La Plante Productions/Samson Films, 1995, British

SHIMON DOTAN
b. December 23, 1949 - Ajud, Romania
Agent: Shapiro-Lichtman Talent Agency - Los Angeles, 310/859-8877

REPEAT DIVE   Original Cinema, 1982, Israeli
83 (FD)   co-director, Tzavta, 1983
THE SMILE OF THE LAMB   Original Cinema, 1986, Israeli
THE FINEST HOUR   21st Century Distribution, 1991, U.S.-Israeli
WARRIORS   Nu Image, 1994, U.S.-Israeli

DAVID DOUGLAS
AT THE MAX   *ROLLING STONES AT THE MAX* (FCD)
  co-director with Julien Temple, Roman Kroiter & Noel Archambault,
  BCL Presentation/IMAX Corporation, 1991, U.S.-Canadian

KIRK DOUGLAS*
(Issur Danielovitch/Isidore Demsky)
b. December 9, 1916 - Amsterdam, New York
Business: The Bryna Company, 141 El Camino Drive, Beverly Hills,
  CA 90212, 310/274-5294

SCALAWAG   Paramount, 1973, U.S.-Italian
POSSE   Paramount, 1975

PETER DOUGLAS*
Agent: CAA - Beverly Hills, 310/288-4545

A TIGER'S TALE   Atlantic Releasing Corporation, 1987

LORENZO DOUMANI
THE LAST PAESAN   LDC Motion Pictures, 1993
STORYBOOK   PM Entertainment Group Group, 1994

NANCY DOWD
b. Framingham, Massachusetts
Agent: ICM - Beverly Hills, 310/550-4000

LOVE   co-director with Annette Cohen, Liv Ullmann & Mai Zetterling,
  Velvet Films, 1982, Canadian

KATHLEEN DOWDEY
b. November 13, 1949 - Washington, D.C.
Business: Five Point Films, Inc., 915 Highland View N.E. - Suite B,
    Atlanta, GA 30306, 404/875-6076
Attorney: Peter Nichols, 9601 Wilshire Blvd. - Suite 825,
    Beverly Hills, CA 90210, 310/858-7888

A CELTIC TRILOGY (FD)   First Run Features, 1979
BLUE HEAVEN   Vestron/Shapiro Entertainment, 1984
DAWN'S EARLY LIGHT: RALPH McGILL AND THE SEGREGATED
    SOUTH (TD)   South Carolina Educational TV Network, 1989

KEVIN DOWLING
Agent: APA Los Angeles, 310/273-0744

THE SUM OF US   co-director with Geoff Burton,
    The Samuel Goldwyn Company, 1994, Australian

ROBERT DOWNEY*
b. June 1936
Home: 1350 1/2 N. Harper Avenue, Los Angeles, CA 90046,
    213/654-5662
Agent: ICM - Beverly Hills, 310/550-4000

BABO 73   1963
CHAFED ELBOWS   Grove Press, 1965
NO MORE EXCUSES   Rogosin, 1968
PUTNEY SWOPE   Cinema 5, 1969
POUND   United Artists, 1970
GREASER'S PALACE   Greaser's Palace, 1972
MAD MAGAZINE PRESENTS UP THE ACADEMY
    Warner Bros., 1980
AMERICA   ASA Communications, 1986
RENTED LIPS   Cineworld, 1988
TOO MUCH SUN   New Line Cinema, 1991

BERT L. DRAGIN
Agent: Solomon Weingarten & Associates - Los Angeles,
    310/394-8866

SUMMER CAMP NIGHTMARE   Concorde, 1986
TWICE DEAD   Concorde, 1988

STAN DRAGOTI*
b. October 4, 1932 - New York, New York
Address: 755 Stradella Road, Los Angeles, CA 90077,
    310/476-6282
Agent: APA - Los Angeles, 310/273-0744
Business Manager: Executive Business Management,
    132 S. Rodeo Drive, Beverly Hills, CA 90212, 310/858-2000

DIRTY LITTLE BILLY   Columbia, 1972
LOVE AT FIRST BITE   American International, 1979
MR. MOM   20th Century-Fox, 1983
THE MAN WITH ONE RED SHOE   20th Century Fox, 1985
SHE'S OUT OF CONTROL   WEG/Columbia, 1989
NECESSARY ROUGHNESS   Paramount, 1991

JAMES R. (JIM) DRAKE*
Business: Brijim Productions, Inc., 5145 Calvin Drive, Tarzana, CA
    91356, 818/344-6548
Agent: ICM - Beverly Hills, 310/550-4000

THIS WIFE FOR HIRE (TF)   The Belle Company/Guillaume-Margo
    Productions/Comworld Productions, 1985
POLICE ACADEMY 4: CITIZENS ON PATROL
    Warner Bros., 1987
GODDESS OF LOVE (TF)   Phil Margo Enterprises/New
    World TV/Phoenix Entertainment Group, 1988
SPEED ZONE   Orion, 1989, U.S.-Canadian
BASED ON AN UNTRUE STORY (TF)
    Westgate Productions, 1993

ANTHONY DRAZAN
Agent: UTA - Beverly Hills, 310/273-6700

ZEBRAHEAD   Triumph Releasing Corporation, 1992
IMAGINARY CRIMES   Warner Bros., 1994

FRED H. DRESCH
MY SAMURAI   Starmax Film Partnership, 1992

DI DREW
b. November 12, 1948
Contact: Australian Film Commission, 150 William Street,
    Woolloomooloo NSW 2011, Australia, tel.: 2/321-6444

FILE MILE CREEK (MS)   co-director with Frank Arnold,
    George Miller & Michael Jenkins, Valstar/The Disney Channel,
    1983, U.S.-Australian
THE RIGHT HAND MAN   FilmDallas, 1987, Australian
TROUBLE IN PARADISE (TF)   Qintex Entertainment,
    1989, U.S.-Australian
BUTTERFLY ISLAND 3 (MS)   co-director with Frank Arnold,
    Mediacast/Otis Pictures, 1992, Australian

SARA DRIVER
b. 1956 - New York, New York

SLEEPWALK   Ottoskop Filmproduktion/Driver Films, 1986,
    West German-U.S.
WHEN PIGS FLY   Allarts/NDF Sumitomo/Pandora Film/Sultan Driver,
    1993, Dutch-Japanese-German-U.S.

DAVID DRURY
Agent: UTA - Beverly Hills, 310/273-6700 or
    ICM - London, tel.: 171/636-6565

CITY (TF)   Granada TV, 1981, British
MINTER (TF)   Granada TV, 1981, British
CITIZEN BULL (TF)   Granada TV, 1982, British
FOREVER YOUNG   Cinecom, 1984, British,
    originally made for television
HOME AND AWAY (TF)   Granada TV, 1984, British
DEFENSE OF THE REALM   Hemdale, 1985, British
TERRA ROXA   Filmefekt, 1986, British
SPLIT DECISIONS   New Century/Vista, 1988
INTRIGUE (TF)   Crew Neck Productions/Linnea Productions/
    Columbia TV, 1988
THE SECRET AGENT (TF)   BBC/WGBH-Boston, 1992, British-U.S.
PRIME SUSPECT 3 (TF)   Granada TV/ITV, 1994, British

LEE DRYSDALE
LEATHER JACKETS   Epic Productions, 1992, filmed in 1990

ADAM DUBIN
DROP DEAD ROCK   Spazz-O Productions, 1995

CHARLES S. DUBIN*
b. February 1, 1919 - New York, New York
Home: 651 Lorna Lane, Los Angeles, CA 90049
Agent: Ronald Leif, Contemporary Artists - Santa Monica,
    310/395-1800

MISTER ROCK & ROLL   Paramount, 1957
TO DIE IN PARIS (TF)   co-director with Allen Reisner,
    Universal TV, 1968
MURDER ONCE REMOVED (TF)   Metromedia Productions, 1971
MURDOCK'S GANG (TF)   Don Fedderson Productions, 1973
MOVING VIOLATION   20th Century-Fox, 1976
THE TENTH LEVEL (TF)   CBS, Inc., 1976
THE DEADLY TRIANGLE (TF)   Columbia TV, 1977
TOPPER (TF)   Cosmo Productions/Robert A. Papazian
    Productions, 1979
ROOTS: THE NEXT GENERATIONS (MS)   co-director with
    John Erman, Lloyd Richards & Georg Stanford Brown,
    Wolper Productions, 1979
THE GATHERING, PART II (TF)   Hanna-Barbera
    Productions, 1979

THE MANIONS OF AMERICA (MS)   co-director with
  Joseph Sargent, Roger Gimbel Productions/EMI TV/
  Argonaut Films Ltd., 1981
MY PALIKARI (TF)   Center for TV in the Humanities, 1982
INTERNATIONAL AIRPORT (TF)   co-director with Don Chaffey,
  Aaron Spelling Productions, 1985
A MASTERPIECE OF MURDER (TF)   20th Century Fox TV, 1986
DROP-OUT MOTHER (TF)   Fries Entertainment/Comco
  Productions, 1988

JAY DUBIN*
Agent: ICM - Beverly Hills, 310/550-4000

DICE RULES (PF)   Seven Arts/New Line Cinema, 1991

ADAM DUBOV
Agent: William Morris Agency - Beverly Hills, 310/859-4000

DEAD BEAT   Distant Horizon, 1994

DANIELE DUBROUX
Contact: French Film Office, 745 Fifth Avenue, New York,
  NY 10151, 212/832-8860

LES AMANTS TERRIBLES   Citevox, 1984, French
LA PETITE ALLUMEUSE   Cannon France, 1987, French
BORDER LINE   Amorces Diffusion, 1992, French-Swiss

REMY DUCHEMIN
Contact: French Film Office, 745 Fifth Avenue, New York,
  NY 10151, 212/832-8860

A LA MODE (IN FASHION) *FAUSTO* Miramax Films,
  1993, French

ROGER DUCHOWNY*
Business: Riverview Films, 100 Universal City Plaza - M.T. 6,
  Universal City, CA 91608, 818/777-2108

MURDER CAN HURT YOU!   Aaron Spelling Productions, 1970

PETER JOHN DUFFELL
Agent: Richard Hatton Ltd. - London, tel.: 181/876-6699

PARTNERS IN CRIME   Allied Artists, 1961, British
THE HOUSE THAT DRIPPED BLOOD   Cinerama Releasing
  Corporation, 1971, British
ENGLAND MADE ME   Cine Globe, 1973, British
INSIDE OUT   Warner Bros., 1976, British
THE RACING GAME (TF)   Yorkshire TV, 1978, British
DAISY (TF)   BBC, 1979, British
MURDER TAP (TF)   BBC, 1979, British
CAUGHT ON A TRAIN (TF)   BBC, 1980
THE WATERFALL (TF)   BBC, 1980, British
BRIGHT EYES (TF)   BBC, 1981, British
EXPERIENCE PREFERRED, BUT NOT ESSENTIAL
  The Samuel Goldwyn Company, 1983, British
THE FAR PAVILIONS (CMS)   Geoff Reeve & Associates/
  Goldcrest, 1984, British
LETTERS TO AN UNKNOWN LOVER (TF)   Portman Productions/
  Channel 4/Antenne-2, 1985, British-French
INSPECTOR MORSE   Zenith Productions, 1988, British
KING OF THE WIND   Davis-Panzer Productions/HTV International,
  1989, British

DENNIS DUGAN*
Agent: CAA - Beverly Hills, 310/288-4545

PROBLEM CHILD   Universal, 1990
BRAIN DONORS   Paramount, 1992
COLUMBO: BUTTERFLY IN SHADES OF GREY (TF)
  Universal TV, 1993
THE SHAGGY DOG (TF)   ZM Productions/Walt Disney TV, 1994

MICHAEL DUGAN*
Home: 77765 California Drive, Palm Desert, CA 92260,
  619/345-9625

MAUSOLEUM   MPM, 1983

CHRISTIAN DUGUAY
Agent: CAA - Beverly Hills, 310/288-4545
Personal Manager: Lovett Management - Santa Monica,
  310/451-2536

SCANNERS II: THE NEW ORDER   Triton Pictures,
  1991, Canadian
LIVE WIRE   Pentamerica Pictures, 1992
SCANNERS III: THE TAKEOVER   Republic Pictures,
  1992, Canadian
MODEL BY DAY (TF)   Fox West Pictures/Lewis H. Chesler-Empath
  Films/Alliance Communications, 1993, U.S.-Canadian
SNOWBOUND: THE JIM AND JENNIFER STOLPA STORY (TF)
  Pacific Motion Pictures (Stolpa) Productions/Jaffe-Braunstein
  Films, 1994, U.S.-Canadian
MILLION DOLLAR BABIES (TF)   Bernard Zukerman Productions/
  Cinar/Canadian Broadcasting Corporation/CBS Entertainment/
  Telefilm Canada/Ontario Film Development Corporation, 1994,
  Canadian-U.S.
SCREAMERS   Allegro Films, 1995, Canadian

JOHN DUIGAN*
b. Australia
Home: 54A Tite Street, London SW3 4JA, England
Agent: CAA - Beverly Hills, 310/288-4545

THE FIRM MAN   John Duigan Productions, 1975, Australian
THE TRESPASSERS   Vega Film Productions, 1976, Australian
MOUTH TO MOUTH   Vega Film Productions, 1978, Australian
DIMBOOLA   Ko-An Productions, 1979, Australian
WINTER OF OUR DREAMS   Satori, 1981, Australian
FAR EAST   Filmco Australia, 1983, Australian
ONE NIGHT STAND   Astra Film Productions/Hoyts-Edgely,
  1984, Australian
STOP WATCH (TF)   ACTF Productions, 1985, Australian
VIETNAM (MS)   co-director with Chris Noonan, Kennedy Miller
  Productions, 1987, Australian
ROOM TO MOVE (TF)   Australian Children's Television Foundation/
  ITC Entertainment, 1987, Australian
THE YEAR MY VOICE BROKE   Avenue Pictures,
  1987, Australian
ROMERO   Four Seasons Entertainment, 1989
FLIRTING   The Samuel Goldwyn Company, 1990, Australian
WIDE SARGASSO SEA   Fine Line Features/New Line Cinema,
  1993, Australian
SIRENS   Miramax Films, 1994, Australian-British
THE JOURNEY OF AUGUST KING   Miramax Films, 1995

BILL DUKE*
b. February 26, 1943 - Poughkeepsie, New York
Home: 2200 Broadview Terrace, Los Angeles, CA 90068,
  213/851-3904
Agent: CAA - Beverly Hills, 310/288-4545

THE KILLING FLOOR (TF)   Public Forum Productions/
  KERA-Dallas-Ft. Worth, 1984
JOHNNIE MAE GIBSON: FBI (TF)   Fool's Cap
  Productions, 1986
A RAGE IN HARLEM   Miramax Films, 1991, U.S.-British
DEEP COVER   New Line Cinema 1992
THE CEMETERY CLUB   Buena Vista, 1993
SISTER ACT 2: BACK IN THE HABIT   Buena Vista, 1993

DARYL DUKE*

b. Vancouver, Canada
Agent: ICM - Beverly Hills, 310/550-4000

THE SASKATCHEWAN (TF)   CBC, 1965, Canadian
THE PSYCHIATRIST: GOD BLESS THE CHILDREN (TF)
   Universal TV, 1970
PAYDAY   Cinerama Releasing Corporation, 1972
HAPPINESS IS A WARM CLUE (TF)   Universal TV, 1973
THE PRESIDENT'S PLANE IS MISSING (TF)
   ABC Circle Films, 1973
I HEARD THE OWL CALL MY NAME (TF)   Tomorrow
   Entertainment, 1973
A CRY FOR HELP (TF)   Universal TV, 1975
THEY ONLY COME OUT AT NIGHT (TF)   MGM TV, 1975
GRIFFIN AND PHOENIX (TF)   ABC Circle Films, 1976
THE SILENT PARTNER   EMC Film/Aurora, 1979, Canadian
THE THORN BIRDS (MS)   David L. Wolper-Stan Margulies
   Productions/Edward Lewis Productions/Warner Bros. TV, 1983
FLORENCE NIGHTINGALE (TF)   Cypress Point Productions, 1985
TAI-PAN   DEG, 1986
WHEN WE WERE YOUNG (TF)   Richard & Esther Shapiro
   Entertainment, 1989
HANG TOUGH   Moviestore Entertainment, 1990, Canadian,
   filmed in 1980
CAUTION: MURDER CAN BE HAZAROUS TO YOUR HEALTH (TF)
   Universal TV, 1991
FATAL MEMORIES (TF)   Green's Point Productions/WIC/
   MGM-UA TV, 1992, U.S.-Canadian

PATRICK SHEANE DUNCAN

Agent: Preferred Artists Agency - Encino, 818/990-0305

84 CHARLIE MOPIC   New Century/Vista, 1989
LIVE! FROM DEATH ROW (TF)   D.R. Productions/Charlie MoPic
   Company, 1992
THE PORNOGRAPHER   Charlie MoPic Company, 1994

DUWAYNE DUNHAM*

Agent: William Morris Agency - Beverly Hills, 310/859-4000

HOMEWARD BOUND: THE INCREDIBLE JOURNEY
   Buena Vista, 1993
LITTLE GIANTS   Warner Bros., 1994

GEOFF DUNLOP

Contact: British Film Commission, 70 Baker Street, London
   W1M 1DJ, England, tel.: 171/224-5000

DANCING (TD)   WNET-13/RM Arts/BBC, 1993, U.S.-British

FRANCOIS DUPEYRON

Contact: French Film Office, 745 Fifth Avenue, New York,
   NY 10151, 211/832-8860

LA MACHINE   Hachette Premiere/DD Productions/Prima/
   M6 Films/France 2 Cinema/Studio Babelsberg/Polygram
   Filmed Entertainment/Studio Images/Canal Plus/CNC/French
   Ministry of Culture/Filmfoerderung Berlin/Filmfoerderungsanstalt,
   1994, French-German

PAUL DURAN

THE SHARK   Downtown Films, 1991
FLESH SUITCASE   Valiant Films, 1995

RUDY DURAND*

Business: Koala Productions, Ltd., 9606 Santa Monica Blvd.,
   Beverly Hills, CA 90210, 310/476-1949
Business Manager: Gary Dohner, Financial Management
   International, 9200 Sunset Blvd., Los Angeles, CA 90069,
   310/859-0655

TILT   Warner Bros., 1979

MARGUERITE DURAS

(Marguerite Donnadieu)

b. April 4, 1914 - Giadinh, French Indochina (Vietnam)
Address: 5, rue Saint-Benoit, 75006 Paris, France
Contact: French Film Office, 745 Fifth Avenue, New York,
   NY 10151, 212/832-8860

LA MUSICA   co-director, 1966, French
DESTROY, SHE SAID   1969, French
JAUNE DE SOLEIL   1971, French
NATHALIE GRANGER   Films Moliere, 1973, French
LA FEMMES DU GANGES   Sunchild Productions, 1974, French
INDIA SONG   Sunchild Productions/Films Armorial, 1975, French
DES JOURNEES ENTIERES DANS LES ARBRES
   Theatre D'Orsay-Duras Films, 1976, French
SON NOM DE VENISE DANS CALCUTTA DESERT (FD)
   Cinema 9, 1976, French
BAXTER, VERA BAXTER   Sunchild Productions, 1977, French
LE CAMION   Films Moliere, 1977, French
LE NAVIRE NIGHT   MK2/Gaumont/Les Films du Losange,
   1979, French
AURELIA STEINER   Hors Champ Diffusion, 1979, French
AGATHA ET LES LECTURES ILLIMITEES   Hors Champ Diffusion,
   1981, French
IL DIALOGO DI ROMA (FD)   RAI/Lunga Cooperative, 1983, Italian
LES ENFANTS   co-director with Jean-Marc Turine & Jean Mascolo,
   French Ministry of Culture/Les Productions Berthemont,
   1985, French

TODD DURHAM

Business: Straightjacket Productions, P.O. Box 1804, Beverly Hills,
   CA 90213, 213/650-2142

VISIONS OF SUGAR-PLUMS   Regency Entertainment, 1984
HYPERSPACE   Regency Entertainment, 1986

ROBERT DUVALL

b. January 5, 1931 - San Diego, California
Business: Butcher's Run Productions, 10202 W. Washington Blvd.,
   Capra Building - Room 207, Culver City, CA 90232, 310/280-5735
Agent: William Morris Agency - Beverly Hills, 310/859-4000

WE'RE NOT THE JET SET (FD)   1975
ANGELO, MY LOVE   Cinecom, 1983

JOHN DWYER

Business: Epic Productions, 1203 West 44th Street, Austin, TX
   78756, 512/452-9461
Attorney: Frank Arnold, Arnold & Booker, 300 West 15th Street,
   Austin, TX 78701, 512/320-5200

CONFESSIONS OF A SERIAL KILLER   Concorde, 1990

H. KAYE DYAL

MEMORY OF US   Cinema Financial of America, 1974
PROJECT ELIMINATOR   South Gate Entertainment, 1991

ROBERT DYKE

MOONTRAP   Shapiro Glickenhaus Entertainment, 1989

BOB DYLAN

(Robert Zimmerman)

b. May 24, 1941 - Hibbing, Minnesota
Agent: William Morris Agency - Beverly Hills, 310/859-4000

RENALDO AND CLARA   Circuit, 1978

E

ALLAN EASTMAN
b. 1950 - Manitoba, Canada
Business: Labyrinth Film & Videoworks, 159 Westminster Avenue,
  Toronto, Ontario M6R 1N8, Canada, 416/537-7455

DEUX EX MACHINA (TF)   1974, Canadian-British
FOREIGNERS (TF)   1975, Canadian-British-French
SNAP SHOT *A SWEETER SONG* Epoh, 1976, Canadian
THE WAR BOY   Norstar Releasing, 1984, Canadian
CRAZY MOON   Miramax, 1985, Canadian
RACE FOR THE BOMB (MS)   1986, Canadian-French
FORD: THE MAN AND THE MACHINE (TF)   Lantana Productions/
  Filmline International Productions/Robert Halmi, Inc.,
  1987, Canadian-U.S.
CHAMPAGNE CHARLIE (TF)   Action Media Group/Telefilm
  Canada/CTV/FR3/La Sept, 1989, Canadian-French
DANGER ZONE   Nu Image, 1995, U.S.-South African

CHARLES EASTMAN
Home: 113B 27th Street, Manhattan Beach, CA 90266,
  310/543-4212

THE ALL-AMERICAN BOY   Warner Bros., 1973

CLINT EASTWOOD*
b. May 31, 1930 - San Francisco, California
Business: Malpaso Productions, 4000 Warner Blvd. - Building 81,
  Burbank, CA 91522, 818/954-3367
Agent: William Morris Agency - Beverly Hills, 310/859-4000

PLAY MISTY FOR ME   Universal, 1971
HIGH PLAINS DRIFTER   Universal, 1972
BREEZY   Universal, 1973
THE EIGER SANCTION   Universal, 1974
THE OUTLAW JOSEY WALES   Warner Bros., 1976
THE GAUNTLET   Warner Bros., 1977
BRONCO BILLY   Warner Bros., 1980
FIREFOX   Warner Bros., 1982
HONKYTONK MAN   Warner Bros., 1982
SUDDEN IMPACT   Warner Bros., 1983
PALE RIDER   Warner Bros., 1985
HEARTBREAK RIDGE   Warner Bros., 1986
BIRD   Warner Bros., 1988
WHITE HUNTER, BLACK HEART   Warner Bros., 1990
THE ROOKIE   Warner Bros., 1990
UNFORGIVEN ★★   Warner Bros., 1992
A PERFECT WORLD   Warner Bros., 1993
THE BRIDGES OF MADISON COUNTY   Warner Bros., 1995

ANDREW EATON
Contact: British Film Commission, 70 Baker Street, London
  W1M 1DJ, England, tel.: 171/224-5000

BIOGRAPHY: JOHN FORD (TD)   BBC/Arts & Entertainment
  Network, 1993, British-U.S.

THOM EBERHARDT*
b. Los Angeles, California
Agent: Daniel Ostroff, The Daniel Ostroff Agency - Los Angeles,
  310/278-2020

SOLE SURVIVOR   International Film Marketing, 1984
NIGHT OF THE COMET   Atlantic Releasing Corporation, 1984
THE NIGHT BEFORE   Kings Road Productions, 1987
WITHOUT A CLUE   Orion, 1988
GROSS ANATOMY   Buena Vista, 1989
PARKER LEWIS CAN'T LOSE (TF)   Fox Broadcasting, 1990
CAPTAIN RON   Buena Vista, 1992

DESIRE ECARÉ
b. April 15, 1939 - Treicheville, Ivory Coast
Contact: Ministry of Information, BP 138, Abidjan, Ivory Coast,
  tel.: 442585

FACES OF WOMEN   New Yorker, 1985, Ivory Coast

NICOLAS ECHEVARRIA
Agent: William Morris Agency - Beverly Hills, 310/859-4000

JUDEA   1989, Mexican
CABEZA DE VACA   Concorde, 1990, Mexican

STEPHEN ECKELBERRY
BREAKING UP WITH PAUL   J.O.E. Productions, 1991
MOVIES MONEY MURDER   Independent, 1992

ULI EDEL*
(Ulrich Edel)
b. April 11, 1947 - Neuberg, West Germany
Contact: Directors Guild of America - Los Angeles, 213/851-3671

THE LITTLE SOLDIER   1970, West German
TOMMI KEHRT ZURUCK   1972, West German
POSTHALTER   1975, West German
CHRISTIANE F. *CHRISTIANE F.: WIR KINDER VOM
  BANNHOF ZOO* 1981, West German
LAST EXIT TO BROOKLYN   Cinecom, 1989, West German-U.S.
BODY OF EVIDENCE   MGM-UA, 1993
REBEL HIGHWAY: CONFESSIONS OF A SORORITY GIRL (CTF)
  CONFESSIONS OF A SORORITY GIRL   Drive-In Classics
  Cinema/Showtime, 1994
TYSON (CTF)   HBO Pictures, 1995

DON EDMONDS
ILSA, SHE DEVIL OF THE OIL SHEIK HAREMS   Canadian-U.S.
BARE KNUCKLES   Intercontinental, 1978
TERROR ON TOUR   World Distributing/Four Features
  Partners, 1983
TOMCAT ANGELS   Troma, 1995

BLAKE EDWARDS*
(William Blake McEdwards)
b. July 26, 1922 - Tulsa, Oklahoma
Agent: William Morris Agency - Beverly Hills, 310/859-4000
Business: Blake Edwards Entertainment, 9336 W. Washington Blvd.,
  Culver City, CA 90230, 310/202-3375

BRING YOUR SMILE ALONG   Columbia, 1955
HE LAUGHED LAST   Columbia, 1956
MISTER CORY   MGM, 1957
THIS HAPPY FEELING   Universal, 1958
THE PERFECT FURLOUGH   Universal, 1959
OPERATION PETTICOAT   Universal, 1959
HIGH TIME   20th Century-Fox, 1960
BREAKFAST AT TIFFANY'S   Paramount, 1961
EXPERIMENT IN TERROR   Warner Bros., 1962
DAYS OF WINE AND ROSES   Warner Bros., 1962
THE PINK PANTHER   United Artists, 1964
A SHOT IN THE DARK   United Artists, 1964
THE GREAT RACE   Warner Bros., 1965
WHAT DID YOU DO IN THE WAR, DADDY?   United Artists, 1966
GUNN   Warner Bros., 1967
THE PARTY   United Artists, 1968
DARLING LILI   Paramount, 1970
WILD ROVERS   MGM, 1971
THE CAREY TREATMENT   MGM, 1972
THE TAMARIND SEED   Avco Embassy, 1974
RETURN OF THE PINK PANTHER   United Artists, 1975, British
THE PINK PANTHER STRIKES AGAIN   United Artists, 1976, British
REVENGE OF THE PINK PANTHER   United Artists, 1978, British
10   Orion/Warner Bros., 1979
S.O.B.   Paramount, 1981
VICTOR/VICTORIA   MGM/United Artists, 1982
TRAIL OF THE PINK PANTHER   MGM/UA, 1982
CURSE OF THE PINK PANTHER   MGM/UA, 1983

THE MAN WHO LOVED WOMEN   Columbia, 1983
MICKI & MAUDE   Columbia, 1984
A FINE MESS   Columbia, 1986
THAT'S LIFE!   Columbia, 1986
BLIND DATE   TriStar, 1987
SUNSET   TriStar, 1988
JUSTIN CASE (TF)   The Blake Edwards Company/
   Walt Disney TV, 1988
SKIN DEEP   20th Century Fox, 1989
PETER GUNN (TF)   The Blake Edwards Company/
   New World TV, 1990
SWITCH   Warner Bros., 1991
SON OF THE PINK PANTHER   MGM-UA, 1993

PETER EDWARDS
GUNS OF HONOR   Vidmark Entertainment, 1994, South African

VINCENT EDWARDS*
(Vincent Edward Zolmo)
b. July 9, 1928 - New York, New York
Contact: Directors Guild of America - Los Angeles, 213/851-3671

MANEATER   Universal TV, 1973

CHRISTINE EDZARD
b. 1945 - Paris, France
Address: Sands Films Ltd., Grices Wharf, 119 Rotherhithe Street,
   London SE16 4NF, England, tel.: 171/231-2209

STORIES FROM A FLYING TRUNK   EMI, 1979, British
BIDDY   Sands Films, Ltd., 1983, British
LITTLE DORRIT, PART I: NOBODY'S FAULT
   Cannon, 1987, British
LITTLE DORRIT, PART II: LITTLE DORRIT'S STORY
   Cannon, 1987, British
THE FOOL   Sands Films, Ltd./Film Four International/British
   Screen/John Tyler, 1990, British
AS YOU LIKE IT   Sands Films Ltd., 1992, British

ARTHUR BJORN EGELI
UNCONDITIONAL LOVE   Prodigy Productions, 1994

JAN EGLESON*
Home: 139 Larch Road, Cambridge, MA 02138, 617/492-2521
Agent: ICM - Beverly Hills, 310/550-4000

BILLY IN THE LOWLANDS   Theatre Company of Boston, 1979
THE DARK END OF THE STREET   First Run Features, 1981
THE LITTLE SISTER (TF)   Shefida Features/American Playhouse/
   Christina Associates, 1986
ROANOAK (TF)   South Carolina ETV Network/First Contact Films/
   National Video Corporation, 1986
LEMON SKY   American Playhouse Theatrical Films, 1988
BIG TIME (TF)   co-director with Howard Cummings,
   Advocated Productions/WGBH-Boston, 1989
A SHOCK TO THE SYSTEM   Corsair Pictures, 1990
AGAINST THE LAW (TF)   Sarabande Productions/
   MGM-UA TV, 1990
JAMES TAYLOR: GOING HOME (CMD)   Lemon Sky Productions/
   Sony Music Video Enterprises, 1992
THE LAST HIT (CTF)   Garson Studios/MTE, 1993
JUSTICE IN A SMALL TOWN (TF)   Hills-Fields Productions, 1994

ATOM EGOYAN
b. 1960 - Cairo, Egypt
Business: Ego Film Arts, 80 Niagara Street, Toronto, Ontario
   M5B 1C5, Canada, 416/369-9093

NEXT OF KIN   Ego Film Arts, 1985, Canadian
FAMILY VIEWING   Ego Film Arts, 1987, Canadian
SPEAKING PARTS   Channel 4/Academy Pictures/Telefilm
   Canada/Ontario Film Development, 1989,
   Canadian-British-Italian
THE ADJUSTER   Orion Classics, 1991, Canadian

MONTREAL VU PAR...   co-director with Patricia Rozema,
   Jacques Leduc, Michel Brault & Lea Pool, Cinema Plus
   Distribution, 1991, Canadian
SPINNER SPENCER (TF)   CBC, 1992, Canadian
CALENDAR   Alliance International, 1993,
   Canadian-German-Armenian
EXOTICA   Miramax Films, 1994, Canadian

RAFAEL EISENMAN*
Telephone: 818/700-7300

LAKE CONSEQUENCE (CTF)   10 db Inc., 1993

GEORGE ELANJIAN, JR.
LIFE'S LITTLE HORRORS   Jaell Productions, 1995

DAVID ELFICK
Contact: Australian Film Commission, 150 William Street,
   Woolloomooloo NSW 2011, Australia, tel.: 2/321-6444

NO WORRIES   Palm Beach Pictures/Initial Films,
   1993, Australian-British

RICHARD ELFMAN
THE FORBIDDEN ZONE   1980
SHRUNKEN HEADS   Full Moon Entertainment, 1994

ROBERT ELFSTROM
THE NASHVILLE SOUND (FD)   co-director with
   David Hoffman, 1970
JOHNNY CASH! THE MAN, HIS WORLD, HIS MUSIC (FD)
   Continental, 1970
PETE SEEGER...A SONG AND A STONE (FD)
   Theatre Exchange, 1972
THE GOSPEL ROAD   20th Century-Fox, 1973
MYSTERIES OF THE SEA (FD)   co-director with Al Giddings,
   Polygram Pictures/Ocean Films Ltd., 1980
MOSES PENDLETON PRESENTS MOSES PENDLETON (FD)
   ABC Video Enterprises, 1982

MICHAEL ELIAS
Agent: CAA - Beverly Hills, 310/288-4545

LUSH LIFE (CTF)   Chanticleer Films, 1994

JAN ELIASBERG*
Agent: William Morris Agency - Beverly Hills, 310/859-4000
Attorney: Alan Wertheimer, Armstrong & Hirsch, 1888 Century
   Park East - Suite 1888, Los Angeles, CA 90067, 310/553-0305

PAST MIDNIGHT   CineTel Films, 1992

LAWRENCE (LARRY) ELIKANN*
b. July 4, 1923 - New York, New York
Agent: William Morris Agency - Beverly Hills, 310/859-4000

JOEY AND REDHAWK (TF)   Daniel Wilson Productions, 1978
THE GREAT WALLENDAS (TF)   Daniel Wilson Productions, 1978
CHARLIE AND THE GREAT BALLOON CHASE (TF)   Daniel Wilson
   Productions, 1981
SPRAGGUE (TF)   MF Productions/Lorimar Productions, 1984
POISON IVY (TF)   NBC Productions, 1985
BERRENGER'S (TF)   co-director with Nicholas Sgarro,
   Roundelay Productions/Lorimar Productions, 1985
PEYTON PLACE: THE NEXT GENERATION (TF)   Michael Filerman
   Productions/20th Century Fox TV, 1985
A LETTER TO THREE WIVES (TF)   20th Century Fox TV, 1985
DALLAS: THE EARLY YEARS (TF)   Roundelay Productions/
   Lorimar-Telepictures, 1986
STRANGER IN MY BED (TF)   Taft Entertainment TV/
   Edgar J. Scherick Productions, 1986
THE HIGH PRICE OF PASSION (TF)   Edgar J. Scherick
   Productions, 1986
HANDS OF A STRANGER (TF)   Taft Entertainment TV, 1987

DANGEROUS AFFECTION (TF) Freyda Rothstein Productions/
Litke-Grossbart Productions/New World TV, 1987
GOD BLESS THE CHILD (TF) Indieprod Company/Phoenix
Entertainment Group, 1988
DISASTER AT SILO 7 (TF) Mark Carliner Productions, 1988
A STONING IN FULHAM COUNTY (TF) The Landsburg
Company, 1988
I KNOW MY FIRST NAME IS STEVEN (TF) ☆ Andrew Adelson
Company/Lorimar TV, 1989
TURN BACK THE CLOCK (TF) Michael Filerman Productions/
Republic Pictures Corporation/NBC Productions, 1989
LAST FLIGHT OUT The Mannheim Company/Co-Star
Entertainment/NBC Productions, 1990
THE BIG ONE: THE LOS ANGELES EARTHQUAKE (TF)
von Zerneck-Sertner Productions, 1990
AN INCONVENIENT WOMAN (TF) ABC Productions, 1991
FEVER (CTF) Saban-Scherick Productions, 1991
ONE AGAINST THE WIND (TF) Karen Mack Productions/
Republic Pictures, 1991
THE STORY LADY (TF) Michael Filerman Productions/NBC
Productions, 1991
BONDS OF LOVE (TF) Hearst Entertainment Productions, 1993
KISS OF A KILLER (TF) Andrew Adelson Company/John Conboy
Productions/ABC Productions, 1993
WHEN LOVE KILLS: THE SEDUCTION OF JOHN HEARN (TF)
Harvey Kahn Productions/Alexander-Enright & Associates/
McGillen Entertainment, 1993
OUT OF DARKNESS (TF) Andrew Adelson Company/Anaid Film
Productions/ABC Productions, 1994
MENENDEZ: A KILLING IN BEVERLY HILLS (TF) Zev Braun
Pictures/TriStar TV, 1994

HARRISON ELLENSHAW

Business: Rutland House Productions, 13155 Magnolia Blvd.,
Sherman Oaks, CA 91423, 818/560-6778
Attorney: Edward Blau, 10100 Santa Monica Blvd., Los Angeles,
CA 90067, 310/556-8468

DEAD SILENCE *STARDUMB* Curb/Esquire Films, 1990

LANG ELLIOTT*

b. 1950 - Los Angeles, California
Address: P.O. Box 7419, Thousand Oaks, CA 91359, 818/501-1821
Attorney: Edward Ezor, 201 S. Lake Avenue - Suite 505,
Pasadena, CA 91101, 818/568-8098

THE PRIVATE EYES New World, 1980
CAGE New Century/Vista, 1989
CAGE II Rocket Pictures International, 1994

STEPHAN ELLIOTT

Agent: William Morris Agency - Beverly Hills, 310/859-4000

FRAUDS J&M Entertainment/Latent Image Productions,
1992, Australian
THE ADVENTURES OF PRISCILLA, QUEEN OF THE DESERT
Gramercy Pictures, 1994, Australian

ARTHUR ELLIS

Address: 41 Bendon Way, Rainham, Kent ME8 0EN, England,
tel.: 0634/376981

DON'T GET ME STARTED *PSYCHOTHERAPY* British Film
Institute/TiMe Medienvertreibs./Skyline Productions/Frankfurter
Filmproduktion/Channel 4/Filmstiftung NRW/Martest Film,
1993, British-German

BOB ELLIS

Agent: The Cameron Creswell Agency - Sydney, tel.: 2/356-4677

UNFINISHED BUSINESS 1985, Australian
WARM NIGHTS ON A SLOW MOVING TRAIN 1986, Australian
GOODBYE PARLIAMENT HOUSE 1987, Australian
DREAMING OF LORDS CML, 1988, Australian
THE NOSTRADAMUS KID 1992, Australian

JOSEPH ELLISON

Agent: Solomon Weingarten & Associates - Los Angeles,
310/394-8866

DON'T GO IN THE HOUSE Film Ventures International, 1980
JOEY Satori Entertainment, 1985

IAN EMES

b. December 17, 1949 - Birmingham, England
Address: R.S.A., 42-44 Beak Street, London W1, England,
tel.: 171/437-7426

THE BEARD (TF) 1980, British
GOODIE-TWO-SHOES (TF) 1984, British
KNIGHTS AND EMERALDS Warner Bros., 1986, British
THE YOB (TF) Comic Strip Productions/Channel 4, 1988, British
THE WALL (TF) 1990, British
KERSPLAT (TF) 1991, British

ROLAND EMMERICH*

Agent: CAA - Beverly Hills, 310/288-4545

THE NOAH'S ARK PRINCIPLE MGM/UA Classics,
1984, West German
MAKING CONTACT *JOEY* New World, 1985, West German
HOLLYWOOD MONSTER Centropolis Film Production/Futura
Filmverlag, 1987, West German
MOON 44 *INTRUDER* Centropolis Film Production,
1989, West German
UNIVERSAL SOLDIER TriStar, 1992
STARGATE MGM-UA, 1994, U.S.-French-German

ROBERT ENDERS

Contact: Writers Guild of America, West - Los Angeles, 310/550-1000
Agent: Peter Crouch & Associates - London, 171/734-2167

STEVIE First Artists, 1978, British

CY ENDFIELD†

b. November, 1914 - Scranton, Pennsylvania
d. 1995

GENTLEMAN JOE PALOOKA Monogram, 1946
STORK BITES MAN United Artists, 1947, British
THE ARGYLE SECRETS Film Classics, 1948, British
JOE PALOOKA IN THE BIG FIGHT Monogram, 1949
THE UNDERWORLD STORY United Artists, 1950
THE SOUND OF FURY United Artists, 1951
TARZAN'S SAVAGE FURY RKO Radio, 1952
COLONEL MARCH INVESTIGATES Criterion, 1953, British
THE MASTER PLAN released under pseudonym of Hugh Raker,
Astor, 1954, British
THE SECRET Eros, 1955, British
CHILD IN THE HOUSE Eros, 1956, British
HELL DRIVERS Rank, 1957, British
SEA FURY Lopert, 1958, British
JET STORM United Producers Organization, 1959, British
MYSTERIOUS ISLAND Columbia, 1861, British
HIDE AND SEEK Universal, 1954, British
ZULU Embassy, 1964, British
SANDS OF THE KALAHARI Paramount, 1965, British
DE SADE American International, 1969, U.S.-West German
UNIVERSAL SOLDIER Hemdale, 1971, British

ANDI ENGEL

b. West Germany
Business: Artificial Eye Film Co., 211 Camden High Street, London
NW1, England, tel.: 171/267-6036

MELANCHOLIA British Film Institute/Lichtblick Filmproduktion/
Channel 4/NDR/Film Fonds Hamburg/Hamburger Filmbuero,
1989, British-West German

JANICE ENGEL

JACKSON BROWNE: GOING HOME (CTCD)   Mojo Productions/
    The Disney Channel, 1994

DAVID ENGELBACH*

b. September 20, 1946 - Philadelphia, Pennsylvania
Agent: Writers & Artists Agency - Los Angeles, 310/824-6300

AMERICA 3000   Cannon, 1986

GEORGE ENGLUND*

b. June 22, 1926 - Washington, D.C.
Agent: CAA - Beverly Hills, 310/288-4545

THE UGLY AMERICAN   Universal, 1963
SIGNPOST TO MURDER   MGM, 1965
ZACHARIAH   Cinerama Releasing Corporation, 1970
SNOW JOB   Warner Bros., 1972
A CHRISTMAS TO REMEMBER (TF)   George Englund
    Productions, 1978
DIXIE: CHANGING HABITS (TF)   George Englund
    Productions, 1983
THE VEGAS STRIP WAR (TF)   George Englund Productions, 1984

ROBERT ENGLUND*

Agent: Abrams Artists & Associates - Los Angeles, 310/859-0625

976-EVIL   New Line Cinema, 1988

ROBERT ENRICO

b. April 13, 1931 - Lievin, France
Agent: ICM France - Paris, tel.: 1/723-7860
Contact: French Film Office, 745 Fifth Avenue, New York,
    NY 10151, 212/832-8860

AU COEUR DE LA VIE   1962, French
LA BELLE VIE   1963, French
THE WISE GUYS   Universal, 1965, French
THE LAST ADVENTURE   I TRE AVVENTURIERI   Universal,
    1969, Italian-French
ZITA   Regional, 1968, French
HO!   1968, French
UN PEU, BEAUCOUP, PASSIONEMENT   CFDC, 1971, French
BOULEVARD DU RHUM   Gaumont, 1971,
    French-Italian-West German
LES CAIDS   Parafrance, 1972, French
LE COMPAGNON INDESIRABLE   1973, French
LE SECRET   Cinema National, 1974, French
THE OLD GUN   Surrogate, 1976, French-West German
COUP DE FOUDRE   1978, French
UN NEVEU SILENCIEUX   MK2, 1979, French
L'EMPREINTE DES GEANTS   Filmel/SNC/FR3/Rialto Film,
    1979, French-West German
HEADS OR TAILS   Castle Hill, 1980, French
FOR THOSE I LOVED   20th Century-Fox, 1983, Canadian-French
ZONE ROUGE   AAA/Revcom Films, 1986, French
DE GUERRE LASSE   Sara Films/TF1, 1987, French
LA REVOLUTION FRANCAISE: LES ANNEES LUMIERE   Ariane
    Films/Films A2/Laura Films/Antea/Les Productions Alliance/Alcor
    Films, 1989, French-West German-Italian-Canadian
VENT D'EST   MC4/Duckstra Productions/SGGC/Prodeve/TF-1/
    Canal Plus/Slav/Cofimage/CNC/Compagnie Lyonnaise de
    Cinema/Television Suisse Romande, 1993, French-Swiss

ILDIKO ENYEDI

Contact: Hungarian Film Institute, Budakeszi u 51 B, 1012
    Budapest, Hungary, tel.: 176-1018 or 176-1322

MY TWENTIETH CENTURY   Aries Film, 1990, Hungarian
MAGIC HUNTER   Accent-Gargantua Motion Pictures/Budapest
    Filmstudio/UGC Images/Vega Film/Studio Babelsberg/WDR
    Fernsehen/La Sept/Schweizer Fernsehen DRS/Isolar Enterprises/
    Motion Picture Foundation of Hungary/Ministere de la Culture
    et de la Francophonie (Centre National de la Cinematographie)/
    Eidgenossiches Department des Innern/Credit Europeen/Canal
    Plus/Eurimages, 1994, Hungarian-Canadian-French-German

NORA EPHRON*

b. May 19, 1941 - New York, New York
Agent: Sam Cohn, ICM - New York City, 212/556-5600

THIS IS MY LIFE   20th Century Fox, 1992
SLEEPLESS IN SEATTLE   TriStar, 1993
MIXED NUTS   TriStar, 1994

MARCELO EPSTEIN

BODY ROCK   New World, 1984

ROB EPSTEIN

(Robert P. Epstein)
b. April 6, 1955 - New Jersey
Business: Telling Pictures, 347 Dolores Street - Suite 307,
    San Francisco, CA 94110, 415/864-6714
Attorney: John Sloss, Morrison & Foerster, 1290 Avenue of the
    Americas, New York, NY 10104, 212/468-8049

WORD IS OUT (FD)   New Yorker, 1977
THE TIMES OF HARVEY MILK (FD)   Cinecom, 1984
COMMON THREADS: STORIES FROM THE QUILT (CTD)
    co-director with Jeffrey Friedman,   Telling Pictures/The
    Couturie Company, 1989
WHERE ARE WE?: OUR TRIP THROUGH AMERICA (FD)
    co-director with Jeffrey Friedman,   Roxie Releasing, 1992
THE CELLULOID CLOSET (CTD)   co-director with Jeffrey Friedman,
    HBO, 1995

VICTOR ERICE

(Victor Erice Aras)
b. 1940 - Carranza, Spain
Contact: Spanish Film Institute, San Marcos 40, Madrid 28004,
    Spain, tel.: 1/532-5089

LOS DESAFIOS   co-director with Claudio Guerin Hill &
    Jose Luis Egea, 1968, Spanish
THE SPIRIT OF THE BEEHIVE   Janus, 1973, Spanish
EL SUR   New Yorker, 1983, Spanish-French
EL SOL DEL MEMBRILLO   Maria Moreno/Igeldo Zine Produkzioak/
    Euskal Media, 1992, Spanish

GORDON ERIKSEN

Home: 116 Prospect Place - Apt. 3, Brooklyn, NY 11217
Contact: Susan Bodine, Esq. - New York, 212/888-1777

THE BIG DIS   co-director with John O'Brien,   First Run
    Features, 1989
SCENES FROM THE NEW WORLD   co-director with
    Heather Johnston, RKGM, 1994

JOHN ERMAN*

b. Chicago, Illinois
Agent: CAA - Beverly Hills, 310/288-4545

MAKING IT   20th Century-Fox, 1971
ACE ELI AND RODGER OF THE SKIES   released under
    pseudonym of Bill Sampson, 20th Century-Fox, 1973
LETTERS FROM THREE LOVERS (TF)   Spelling-Goldberg
    Productions, 1973
GREEN EYES (TF)   ABC, 1977
ROOTS (MS) ☆   co-director with David Greene,
    Marvin J. Chomsky & Gilbert Moses, Wolper Productions, 1977
ALEXANDER: THE OTHER SIDE OF DAWN (TF)   Douglas Cramer
    Productions, 1977
JUST ME & YOU (TF)   Roger Gimbel Productions/EMI, 1978
ROOTS: THE NEXT GENERATIONS (MS)   co-director with
    Charles S. Dubin, Lloyd Richards & Georg Stanford Brown,
    Wolper Productions, 1979
MY OLD MAN (TF)   Zeitman-McNichol-Halmi Productions, 1979
MOVIOLA (MS) ☆   David L. Wolper-Stan Margulies Productions/
    Warner Bros. TV, 1980
THE LETTER (TF)   Hajeno Productions/Warner Bros. TV, 1982
ELEANOR, FIRST LADY OF THE WORLD (TF)
    Murbill Productions/Embassy TV, 1982
ANOTHER WOMAN'S CHILD (TF)   CBS Entertainment, 1983

WHO WILL LOVE MY CHILDREN? (TF) ☆☆
   ABC Circle Films, 1983
A STREETCAR NAMED DESIRE (TF) ☆
   Keith Barish Productions, 1984
THE ATLANTA CHILD MURDERS (TF)   Mann-Rafshoon
   Productions/Finnegan Associates, 1985
RIGHT TO KILL? (TF)   Wrye-Konigsberg Productions/Taper Media
   Enterprises/Telepictures Productions, 1985
AN EARLY FROST (TF) ☆   NBC Productions, 1985
THE TWO MRS. GRENVILLES (TF)   Lorimar-Telepictures, 1987
WHEN THE TIME COMES (TF)   Jaffe-Lansing Productions/
   Republic Pictures, 1987
THE ATTIC: THE HIDING OF ANNE FRANK (TF) ☆   Telecom
   Entertainment/Yorkshire TV, 1988, U.S.-British
DAVID (TF)   Tough Boys Inc./Donald March Productions/ITC
   Entertainment Group, 1988
STELLA   Buena Vista, 1990
THE LAST BEST YEAR (TF)   David W. Rintels Productions/World
   International Network, 1990
THE LAST TO GO (TF)   Freyda Rothstein Productions/Interscope
   Productions, 1991
OUR SONS (TF)   Robert Greenwald Productions, 1991
CAROLINA SKELETONS (TF)   Kushner-Locke Company, 1991
QUEEN (MS)   The Wolper Organization/Bernard Sofronski
   Productions, 1993
BREATHING LESSONS (TF)   Signboard Hill Productions, 1994
SCARLETT (MS)   RHI Entertainment/CBS Entertainment/BetaFilm/
   Silvio Berlusconi Communications/TF1/SAT-1/ORF/Antena-3/
   BSkyB, 1994, U.S.-German-Italian-French-German
THE SUNSHINE BOYS (T)   Metropolitan Productions, 1995

JACK ERSGARD
INVISIBLE: THE CHRONICLE OF BENJAMIN KNIGHT
   Full Moon Entertainment, 1993

NURIA ESPERT
Contact: British Film Commission, 70 Baker Street, London
   W1M 1DJ, England, tel.: 171/224-5000

THE HOUSE OF BERNALDA ALBA (TF)   co-director with
   Stuart Burge, Holmes Productions/Channel 4/WNET-13,
   1991, British-U.S.

JOE ESPOSITO
VOLLEYBALL: THE MOVIE   Future Films/Moviemakers/Summers
   Productions, 1995

EMILIO ESTEVEZ*
b. May 12, 1962 - New York, New York
Agent: UTA - Beverly Hills, 310/273-6700

WISDOM   20th Century Fox, 1987
MEN AT WORK   Triumph Releasing Corporation, 1990
THE WAR AT HOME   Buena Vista, 1995

LUIS ESTRADA
Contact: IMCINE, Tepic #40, P.B. Colonia Roma Sur, Mexico City,
   C.P. 06760, Mexico, tel.: 525/584-7283

BANDIDOS   IMCINE, 1991, Mexican
AMBAR   IMCINE/Bandidos Films, 1994, Mexican

COREY MICHAEL EUBANKS*
Business: Eu-McCoy Film Group, Inc., P.O. Box 16670, Encino,
   CA 91416, 818/344-8574
Address: P.O. Box 427, Santa Ynez, CA 93460, 805/686-4124

BIGFOOT: THE UNFORGETTABLE ENCOUNTER
   PM Entertainment Group Group Group, 1994

BRUCE A. EVANS*
Business: Evans-Gideon Inc., 100 Universal City Plaza - Building 507,
   Suite 4B, Universal City, CA 91608, 818/777-3121
Agent: CAA - Beverly Hills, 310/288-4545

KUFFS   Universal, 1992

DAVID MICKEY EVANS*
Business: Evans/de la Torre Productions, 10201 W. Pico Blvd. -
   Building 78, Los Angeles, CA 90035, 310/203-2683
Agent: UTA - Beverly Hills, 310/273-6700

THE SANDLOT   20th Century Fox, 1993

JOSH EVANS
(Joshua Evans)
b. 1971 - New York, New York
Contact: Screen Actors Guild - Los Angeles, 213/954-1600

INSIDE THE GOLDMINE   Cineville, 1995

MARC EVANS
Contact: British Film Commission, 70 Baker Street, London
   W1M 1DJ, England, tel.: 171/224-5000

THICKER THAN WATER (TF)   BBC Wales/BBC/BBC Enterprises/
   Arts & Entertainment Network, 194, British-Welsh-U.S.

TIM EVERITT
FATALLY YOURS   Quantum Quests/Mid Metro, 1994

MARIANNE EYDE
Contact: Asociacion de Cineastas del Peru, Chiclayo 446,
   Miraflores, Lima, Peru, tel.: 51-14/45-0920

LA VIDA ES UNA SOLA   Kusi Films, 1993, Peruvian

RICHARD EYRE
Agent: Peter Murphy, Curtis Brown - London, tel.: 171/872-0331

THE PLOUGHMAN'S LUNCH   The Samuel Goldwyn Company,
   1983, British
LOOSE CONNECTIONS   Orion Classics, 1983, British
LAUGHTER HOUSE (TF)   Film Four International, 1984, British
PAST CARING (TF)   BBC, 1985, British
THE INSURANCE MAN (TF)   BBC, 1985, British
SINGLETON'S PLUCK (TF)   Greenpoint Films, 1987, British
TUMBLEDOWN (TF)   BBC, 1988, British
SUDDENLY LAST SUMMER (TF)   BBC/WNET-13,
   1993, British-U.S.

JOHN EYRES
Business: EGM Film International, 309 Santa Monica Blvd. -
   Suite 304, Santa Monica, CA 90401, 310/260-9234

PROJECT SHADOWCHASER   EGM Film International, 1991
MONOLITH   EGM Film International, 1993
PROJECT SHADOWCHASER II   Nu Image, 1994
SHADOWCHASER 3   Nu Image, 1994

MARK EZRA
Contact: British Film Commission, 70 Baker Street, London
   W1M 1DJ, England, tel.: 171/224-5000

SAVAGE HEARTS   August Entertainment, 1994, British

F

OTTAVIO FABBRI

Home: via Col di Lana 28, Rome, Italy, tel.: 06/317736

MOVIE RUSH - LA FEBBRE DEL CINEMA   Vides, 1976, Italian
FORMULA 1: LA FEBBRE DELLA VELOCITA'   Racing Pictures, 1978, Italian
BANANA REPUBLIC   Emifilm, 1979, Italian
JOURNEY OF LOVE   Centaur Releasing, 1990, Italian

CHRISTIAN FABER

BAIL JUMPER   Angelika Films, 1990

ROBERTO FAENZA

Home: via Urbana 12/c, Rome, Italy, tel.: 06/474-5539

ESCALATION   Giuseppe Zaccariello, 1968, Italian
H2S   Documento Mars, 1969, Italian
FORZA ITALIA! (FD)   Cooperativa Jean Vigo, 1977, Italian
SI SALVI CHI VUOLE   Cooperativa Jean Vigo, 1980, Italian
COPKILLER   Cooperativa Jean Vigo/RAI, 1982, Italian
THE BACHELOR   *MIO CARO DOTTOR GRASLER*   Greycat Films, 1991, Italian-Hungarian
JONA CHE VISSE NELLA BALENA   Cooperativa Jean Vigo/ French Productions/Gocus Film/RAI, 1993, Italian-French
SOSTIENE PEREIRA   Jean Vigo International/KG Productions/ Mikado Film, 1995, Italian-French

PETER FAIMAN*

Agent: CAA - Beverly Hills, 310/288-4545

"CROCODILE" DUNDEE   Paramount, 1986, Australian
DUTCH   20th Century Fox, 1991

FERDINAND FAIRFAX*

b. August 1, 1944 - London, England
Address: 6 Clapham Common Northside, London SW4 0QW, England, tel.: 171/627-5702
Agent: ICM - London, tel.: 171/636-6565

THE SPEED KING (TF)   BBC, British
DANGER UXB (MS)   Thames TV, 1979, British
WINSTON CHURCHILL - THE WILDERNESS YEARS (MS) Southern Pictures Productions, 1983, British
NATE AND HAYES   *SAVAGE ISLANDS*   Paramount, 1983, New Zealand
THE LAST PLACE ON EARTH (MS)   Central Productions/ Renegade Films, 1985, British
A FIGHTING CHOICE (TF)   Walt Disney Productions, 1986
THE RESCUE   Buena Vista, 1988
THE SECRET LIFE OF IAN FLEMING (CTF)   Saban-Scherick Productions, 1990, U.S.-British
ROYAL CELEBRATION (TF)   BBC, 1993, British

HARRY FALK*

Agent: Gold-Marshall Company, 3500 W. Olive Street - Suite 1400, Burbank, CA 91505, 818/972-4300

THREE'S A CROWD (TF)   Screen Gems/Columbia TV, 1969
THE DEATH SQUAD (TF)   Spelling-Goldberg Productions, 1974
MEN OF THE DRAGON (TF)   Wolper Productions, 1974
THE ABDUCTION OF SAINT ANNE (TF)   QM Productions, 1975
MANDRAKE (TF)   Universal TV, 1979
CENTENNIAL (MS)   co-director with Paul Krasny, Bernard McEveety & Virgil Vogel, Universal TV, 1980
THE NIGHT THE CITY SCREAMED (TF)   David Gerber Company, 1980

THE CONTENDER (TF)   co-director with Lou Antonio, Universal TV, 1980
THE SOPHISTICATED GENTS (TF)   Daniel Wilson Productions, 1981
ADVICE TO THE LOVELORN (TF)   Universal TV, 1981
HEAR NO EVIL (TF)   Paul Pompian Productions/MGM TV, 1982
EMERALD POINT, N.A.S. (TF)   Richard and Esther Shapiro Productions/20th Century-Fox TV, 1983
NORTH BEACH & RAWHIDE (TF)   CBS Entertainment, 1985
HIGH DESERT KILL (CTF)   Lehigh Productions/MCA TV, 1989

JAMAA FANAKA*

Agent: Lenhof/Robinson, 1728 S. La Cienega Blvd., Los Angeles, CA 90035, 310/558-4700
Attorney: Jay Kenoff, 1999 Avenue of the Stars - Suite 1250, Los Angeles, CA 90067, 310/552-0808

WELCOME HOME, BROTHER CHARLES Crown International, 1975
EMMA MAE   Pro-International, 1977
PENITENTIARY   Jerry Gross Organization, 1980
PENITENTIARY II   MGM/UA, 1982
PENITENTIARY III   Cannon, 1987
STREET WARS   Jamaa Fanaka Productions, 1993

JACQUES FANSTEN

b. 1946 - Paris, France
Agent: UTA - Beverly Hills, 310/273-6700
Contact: French Film Office, 745 Fifth Avenue, New York, NY 10151, 212/832-8860

JE DORS COMME UN BEBE   1980, French
NOUS TE MARI-E-RONS   1981, French
APRES TOUT CE QU'ON A FAIT POUR TOI   1982, French
DOROTHEE, DANSEUSE DE CORSE   1983, French
LES LENDEMAINS QUI CHANTENT   1985, French
LES BORDS DES LARMES   1987, French
LE MOUCHAOIR DE JOSEPH   1988, French
CROSS MY HEART   MK2 Productions USA, 1990, French
LA FRACTURE DU MYOCARDE   Belbo Films, 1991, French-Dutch
ROULEZ JEUNESSE   AAA, 1993, French

CLAUDE FARALDO

b. 1936 - France
Agent: Ag. M. Lenoir, 99, boulevard Malesherbes, 75008 Paris, France, tel.: 1/45-63-59-20
Contact: French Film Office, 745 Fifth Avenue, New York, NY 10151, 212/832-8860

LA JEUNE MORTE   1970, French
BOF   1972, French
THEMROC   CIC, 1972, French
TABARNAC   M.D. Films, 1975, French
LES FLEURS DU MIEL   Contrechamp, 1976, French
DEUX LIONS AU SOLEIL   Gaumont, 1980, French
A CERTAIN DESIRE   *FLAGRANT DESIR*   Castle Hill Productions, 1986, French-U.S.

JAMES FARGO*

(Louis James Fargo)
August 4, 1938 - Republic, Washington
Contact: Directors Guild of America - Los Angeles, 213/851-3671

THE ENFORCER   Warner Bros., 1976
EVERY WHICH WAY BUT LOOSE   Warner Bros., 1978
CARAVANS   Universal, 1979, U.S.-Iranian
GAME FOR VULTURES   New Line Cinema, 1980, British
FORCED VENGEANCE   MGM/United Artists, 1982
GUS BROWN AND MIDNIGHT BREWSTER (TF) Kaledonia Productions/Scomi, 1985
THE LAST ELECTRIC KNIGHT (TF)   Walt Disney Productions, 1986
VOYAGE OF THE ROCK ALIENS   *WHEN THE RAIN BEGINS TO FALL*   KGA/Inter Planetary Pictures/Curb Communications, 1988, filmed in 1984
BORN TO RACE   MGM/UA, 1988
RIDING THE EDGE   Trans World Entertainment, 1989
MISSION MORAY   Integrity, 1990

F
I
L
M

D
I
R
E
C
T
O
R
S

ERNEST FARINO
STEEL & LACE   Fries Distribution, 1990
JOSH KIRBY: TIME WARRIOR   co-director with Frank Arnold & Peter Sasdy, Full Moon Entertainment, 1994

DONALD FARMER
COMPELLING EVIDENCE   Stratosphere Entertainment, 1995

MIKE FARRELL*
b. February 6, 1939 - St. Paul, Minnesota
Business: 14011 Ventura Blvd. - Suite 401, Sherman Oaks, CA 91423, 818/789-5766

RUN TILL YOU FALL (TF)   CBS Entertainment, 1988

PETER FARRELLY
Agent: CAA - Beverly Hills, 310/288-4545

DUMB AND DUMBER   New Line Cinema, 1994

ANDRE FARWAGI
Business: Cineflor, 22, rue Rennequin, 75017 Paris, France, tel.: 1/40-54-99-34
Contact: French Film Office, 745 Fifth Avenue, New York, NY 10151, 212/832-8860

ALL MY HUSBANDS   Cineflor/Canal Plus/La Cinq/French Ministry of Culture, 1992, French

JOHN FASANO
Agent: ICM - Beverly Hills, 310/550-4000

ROCK 'N ROLL NIGHTMARE   Shapiro Glickenhaus Entertainment, 1987
BLACK ROSES   Shapiro Entertainment, 1988
THE JITTERS   Gaga Communications, 1989

NEILL FEARNLEY
b. 1953 - Liverpool, England
Business: Reel Possibilities Inc., 4475 Keith Road, West Vancouver, British Columbia V7W 2M4, Canada, 604/922-9148
Agent: Shapiro-Lichtman Talent Agency - Los Angeles, 310/859-8877

THE GIRL FROM MARS (CTF)   Atlantis Films/North Star Entertainment Group/The Family Channel/South Pacific Pictures/ CanWest Broadcasting Ltd./Virtue Rekert Productions/TV New Zealand, 1991, Canadian-U.S.-New Zealand
THE FARE   Entertainment Securities Ltd., 1992, Canadian
BLACK ICE (CTF)   Saban Entertainment/Prism Pictures/ Entertainment Securities Ltd., 1993, U.S.-Canadian

CHRISTIAN FECHNER
Contact: French Film Office, 745 Fifth Avenue, New York, NY 10151, 212/832-8860

JUSTINIEN TROUVE, OU LE BATARD DE DIEU   Gaumont Buena Vista International, 1993, French

LINDA FEFERMAN*
Phone: 213/469-2747
Agent: Marcia Wieder, Wieder Enterprises - Washington, D.C., 202/331-7722

SEVEN MINUTES IN HEAVEN   Warner Bros., 1986

STEVE FEKE
Business: Parnassus Productions, 10000 W. Washington Blvd. - Suite 3007, Culver City, CA 90232, 310/280-6538

KEYS TO FREEDOM   RPB Pictures/Queens Cross Productions, 1990, U.S.-Malaysian

DENNIS FELDMAN*
Agent: ICM - Beverly Hills, 310/550-4000

REAL MEN   MGM/UA, 1987

JOHN FELDMAN
ALLIGATOR EYES   Castle Hill Productions, 1990
DEAD FUNNY   Dead Funny Productions, 1994

KERRY FELTHAM*
b. March 20, 1939 - Edmonton, Alberta, Canada
Home: 16131 Sunset Blvd. - Apt. 7, Pacific Palisades, CA 90272, 310/454-6806
Agent: Mary Beal, The Mary Beal Agency, 144 N. Pass Avenue, Burbank, CA 91502, 818/846-7812

THE GREAT CHICAGO CONSPIRACY CIRCUS   New Line Cinema, 1970

GEORG J. FENADY*
b. July 2, 1930 - Toledo, Ohio
Address: 602 N. Cherokee Avenue, Los Angeles, CA 90004, 213/466-5001
Agent: Ronald Leif, Contemporary Artists - Santa Monica, 310/395-1800

ARNOLD   Cinerama Releasing Corporation, 1974
TERROR IN THE WAX MUSEUM   Cinerama Releasing Corporation, 1974
THE NIGHT THE BRIDGE FELL DOWN (TF)   Irwin Allen Productions/Warner Bros. TV, 1983
CAVE-IN! (TF)   Irwin Allen Productions/Warner Bros. TV, 1983

LARRY FERGUSON
Agent: ICM - Beverly Hills, 310/550-4000

BEYOND THE LAW (CTF)   Poplar Entertainment/Capitol Films, 1994, originally filmed for theatrical release

MICHAEL FERGUSON
b. 1937 - Surrey, England
Business: Flickering Images, Ltd., 65 King Edward's Gr., Teddington, Middlesex TW11 9LZ, England, tel.: 181/943-3290

THE SANDBAGGERS (TF)   Yorkshire TV, 1978, British
AIRLINE (TF)   Yorkshire TV, 1980, British
EDMUND KEAN (TF)   Yorkshire TV, 1981, British
PRIDE OF OUR ALLEY (TF)   Yorkshire TV, 1982, British
KILLER WAITING (TF)   Yorkshire TV, 1983, British
THE GLORY BOYS (TF)   Yorkshire TV/Alan Landsburg Productions, 1984, British-U.S.
LYTTON'S DIARY (TF)   Thames TV, 1985, British
THE BILL (TF)   Thames TV, 1987, British

GUY FERLAND
b. February 18, 1966 - Massachusetts
Agent: William Morris Agency - Beverly Hills, 310/859-4000

THE BABYSITTER   Spelling Films International, 1995

MARCELA FERNANDEZ VIOLANTE
b. June 9, 1941 - Mexico City, Mexico
Contact: IMCINE, Tepic #40, P.B. Colonia Roma Sur, Mexico City, C.P. 06760, Mexico, tel.: 525/584-7283

DE TODOS MODOS JUAN TE LLAMAS   Azteca Films, 1976, Mexican
CANANEA   Azteca Films, 1979, Mexican
MISTERIO   Azteca Films, 1981, Mexican
EN EL PAIS DE LOS PIES LIGEROS   Azteca Films, 1983, Mexican
NOCTURNO AMOR QUE TE VAS   UNAM/D.A.C., 1987, Mexican
GOLPE DE SUERTE   IMCINE, 1992, Mexican

ABEL FERRARA*

Contact: Directors Guild of America - Los Angeles, 213/851-3671

DRILLER KILLER   Rochelle Films, 1979
MS. 45   *ANGEL OF VENGEANCE*   Rochelle Films, 1981
FEAR CITY   Chevy Chase Distribution, 1985
THE GLADIATOR (TF)   Walker Brothers Productions/
   New World TV, 1986
CRIME STORY (TF)   Michael Mann Company/New
   World TV, 1986
CHINA GIRL   Vestron, 1987
CAT CHASER   Vestron, 1989
KING OF NEW YORK   Seven Arts/New Line Cinema,
   1990, U.S.-Italian
BAD LIEUTENANT   Aries Film Releasing, 1992
BODY SNATCHERS   Warner Bros., 1993
DANGEROUS GAME   MGM, 1993
THE ADDICTION   Fast Films, 1995

GIORGIO FERRARA

b. January 19, 1947 - Rome, Italy
Home: via delle Carozze 60, Rome, Italy, tel.: 06/679-2581

UN CUORE SEMPLICE   FilmCoop, 1977, Italian
THE SIEGE OF VENICE   Excelsior Film TV, 1991, Italian-Soviet

GIUSEPPE FERRARA

b. 1932 - Siena, Italy
Home: via Coppi 46, Rome, Italy, tel.: 06/503-8503

I MISTERI DI ROME   co-director, Spa Cinematografica,
   1963, Italian
IL SASSO IN BOCCA   Cine R.D.S., 1970, Italian
FACCIA DI SPIA   Cine 2000, 1975, Italian
PANAGULIS VIVE - PANAGULIS ZEI   Cine 2000/RAI,
   1980, Italian
100 GIORNI A PALERMO   CLCT-TV/Cine 2000/Ombre et Lumiere,
   1984, Italian-French
IL CASO MORO - I GIORNI DELL' IRA   Yarno Cinematografica,
   1986, Italian
NARCOS   Trio Cinematografica/Surf Film/Asbrell Productions,
   1992, Italian-Spanish
GIOVANNI FALCONE   Clemi Cinematografica, 1994, Italian

BRAN FERREN

Business: Associates and Ferren, Wainscott Northwest Road,
   Wainscott, NY 11975

FUNNY (FD)   Original Cinema, 1989

MEL FERRER

b. August 25, 1917 - Elberon, New Jersey

THE GIRL OF THE LIMBERLOST   Columbia, 1945
VENDETTA   RKO Radio, 1950
THE SECRET FURY   RKO Radio, 1950
GREEN MANSIONS   MGM, 1959
EVERY DAY IS A HOLIDAY   *CABRIOLA*   Columbia,
   1966, Spanish

MARCO FERRERI

b. May 11, 1928 - Milan, Italy
Home: Piazza Mattei 10, Rome, Italy, tel.: 06/686-9631

EL PISITO   1958, Spanish
LOS CHICOS   1959, Spanish
EL COCHECITO   1960, Spanish
LE ITALIANE E L'AMORE   co-director, Magic Film, 1961, Italian
THE CONJUGAL BED   *UNA STORIA MODERNA: L'APE REGINA*
   Embassy, 1963, Italian-French
THE APE WOMAN   Embassy, 1964, Italian
CONTROSESSO   co-director with Franco Rossi, Jacques Romain,
   Gianni Puccini & Mino Guerrini, Adelphia Cinematografica/
   France Cinema Production, 1964, Italian-French

KISS THE OTHER SHEIK   *OGGI, DOMANI E DOPODOMANI*
   co-director with Eduardo de Filippo & Luciano Salce, MGM,
   1965, Italian-French
MARCIA NUNZIALE   Sancro Film/Transinter Film,
   1966, Italian-French
L'HAREM   Sancro Film, 1967, Italian
THE MAN WITH THE BALLOONS   Sigma III, 1968, French-Italian
DILLINGER E' MORTO   Pegaso Film, 1969, Italian
THE SEED OF MAN   SRL, 1970, Italian
L'UDIENZA   Vides, 1971, Italian
LIZA   Horizon, 1972, French-Italian
LA GRANDE BOUFFE   ABKCO, 1973, French-Italian
TOUCHEZ PAS LA FEMME BLANCHE   1974, French-Italian
THE LAST WOMAN   Columbia, 1976, Italian-French
BYE BYE MONKEY   Fida, 1978, Italian
CHIEDO ASILO   Gaumont, 1979, Italian-French-Tahitian
TALES OF ORDINARY MADNESS   Fred Baker Films,
   1983, Italian-French
THE STORY OF PIERA   UGC, 1983, Italian-French-West German
IL FUTURO E' DONNA   Faso Film, 1984, Italian
I LOVE YOU   UGC, 1986, French-Italian
COME SONO BUONI I BIANCHI   23 Giugno/Iberoamericana/Camera
   One-Michel Seydoux/JMS Films, 1987, Italian-Spanish-French
LE BANQUET DE PLATON   FIT Productions/FR3/La Sept/BEMA,
   1989, French-Italian
LA CASA DEL SORRISO   Titanus/Scena International,
   1991, Italian
LA CARNE   MMD, 1991, Italian
DIARIO DI UN VIZIO   Italian International Film, 1993, Italian

ROBERT A. FERRETTI

Agent: CNA & Associates - Los Angeles, 310/556-4343

FEAR   CineTel Films, 1988

PABLO FERRO*

Business: Pablo Ferro & Associates, 23036 Gilmore Street,
   West Hills, CA 91307, 818/887-0485

ME MYSELF AND I   I.R.S. Releasing, 1992

LARRY FESSENDEN

THE FRANKENSTEIN COMPLEX   I.R.S. Releasing, 1992

CONNIE FIELD

FREEDOM ON MY MIND (FD)   co-director with Marilyn Mulford,
   Clarity Film Productions, 1994

MICHAEL FIELDS

NOON WINE (TF)   Noon Wine Company, 1985
BRIGHT ANGEL   Hemdale, 1990

PAUL FIERLINGER

DRAWN FROM MEMORY (AF)   Myrupgard Productions, 1992

MIKE FIGGIS*

b. 1949 - Kenya
Agent: ICM - Beverly Hills, 310/550-4000 or:
   Harriet Cruickshank, Cruickshank Cazenove Ltd - London,
   tel.: 171/735-2933
Business Manager: Steven R. Pines, Licker & Pines, 1180 S. Beverly
   Drive - Suite 320, Beverly Hills, CA 90035, 310/203-0320

STORMY MONDAY   Atlantic Releasing Corporation,
   1988, British
INTERNAL AFFAIRS   Paramount, 1990
LIEBESTRAUM   MGM-Pathe Entertainment, 1991
WOMEN & MEN 2: IN LOVE THERE ARE NO RULES (CTF)
   co-director with Walter Bernstein & Kristi Zea, David Brown
   Productions/HBO Showcase, 1991
MR. JONES   TriStar, 1993
THE BROWNING VERSION   Paramount, 1994, British
LEAVING LAS VEGAS   MGM-UA, 1995, U.S.-French

CHARLES FINCH
Business Manager: Laventhol & Horvath -
Los Angeles, 310/553-1040
Business: Ruddy & Morgan Organization, 9300 Wilshire Blvd.,
Suite 508, Beverly Hills, CA 90212, 310/271-7698

PRICELESS BEAUTY   Gruppo BEMA/Reteitalia, 1989, Italian
WHERE SLEEPING DOGS LIE   August Entertainment, 1992

DAVID FINCHER
Agent: CAA - Los Angeles, 310/288-4545

ALIEN 3   20th Century Fox, 1992, U.S.-British
SEVEN   New Line Cinema, 1995

KENNETH FINK*
Agent: CAA - Beverly Hills, 310/288-4545
Personal Manager: Carthay Circle Pictures and Management -
Beverly Hills, 310/657-5454

THE VERNON JOHNS STORY (TF)   Laurel Entertainment/
Tribune Entertainment, 1994
TALL, DARK AND DEADLY (CTF)   Fast Track Films/Wilshire
Court Productions, 1995

KEN FINKLEMAN*
Agent: CAA - Beverly Hills, 310/288-4545

AIRPLANE II: THE SEQUEL   Paramount, 1983
HEAD OFFICE   TriStar, 1986

ALBERT FINNEY
b. May 9, 1936 - Salford, England
Agent: ICM - Beverly Hills, 310/550-4000

CHARLIE BUBBLES   Regional, 1968, British

SAM FIRSTENBERG*
b. 1950 - Israel
Address: 467 S. Almont Drive, Beverly Hills, CA 90211,
310/275-4258

ONE MORE CHANCE   Cannon, 1981
REVENGE OF THE NINJA   MGM/UA/Cannon, 1983
NINJA III: THE DOMINATION   Cannon, 1984
BREAKIN' 2 ELECTRIC BOOGALOO   TriStar/Cannon, 1984
AMERICAN NINJA   Cannon, 1985
AVENGING FORCE   Cannon, 1986
AMERICAN NINJA 2: THE CONFRONTATION   Cannon, 1987
RIVERBEND   Intercontinental Releasing Corporation, 1990
THE DAY WE MET   Roy Productions Ltd., 1990, Israeli
YOUNG COMMANDOS   Cannon, 1991
CYBORG COP   Nu Image, 1993
BLOOD WARRIORS   Rapi Films, 1993, Indonesian
CYBORG COP II   Nu Image, 1993, South African

MICHAEL FIRTH
b. New Zealand
Business: P.O. Box 37-177, Parnell, Auckland, New Zealand,
tel: 09/399-699

OFF THE EDGE   Pentacle, 1977, New Zealand
HEART OF THE STAG   New World, 1984, New Zealand
SYLVIA   MGM/UA Classics, 1985, New Zealand
THE LEADING EDGE   Southern Light Pictures/Everard Films,
1987, New Zealand

MICHAEL FISCHA
MY MOM'S A WEREWOLF   Crown International, 1989
CRACK HOUSE   Cannon, 1989
DEATH SPA *WITCH BITCH*   MPA Home Video, 1990
DELTA HEAT   The Harkham Group/Karen Films/Sawmill
Entertainment, 1992

MAX FISCHER
b. 1929 - Alexandria, Egypt
Address: 4691 Bonavista Avenue, Montreal, Quebec H3W 2C6,
Canada, 514/482-5827

MEWS EN MEIJN   1965, Dutch
DREAMS   1970, Dutch
THE LUCKY STAR   Pickman Films, 1981, Canadian
KILLING 'EM SOFTLY   Intermarket Pictures Corporation,
1985, Canadian
LE PALANQUIN DES LARMES (MS)   1986, Canadian-French
ENTANGLED   Annabelle Films/Parmentier Productions/Canal Plus,
1992, Canadian-French

BERND FISCHERAUER
Contact: Federal Union of Film and Television Directors in Germany,
Adelheidstrasse 7, 8000 Munich 40, Germany, tel.: 089/271-6380

BLOOD AND HONOR: YOUTH UNDER HITLER (MS)
Daniel Wilson Productions/SWF Baden/Taurus Film,
1982, U.S.-West German
REGINA ON THE LADDER TO SUCCESS (MS)   Beta Film,
1990, West German

DEIRDRE FISHEL
RISK   Seventh Art Releasing, 1994

DAVID FISHELSON
CITY NEWS   co-director with Zoe Zinman, Cinecom, 1983

DAVID FISHER
b. April 21, 1948 - Nashville, Tennessee
Home: 14144 Dickens, Apt. 115, Sherman Oaks, CA 91423,
818/907-1368

LIAR'S MOON   Crown International, 1982
TOY SOLDIERS   New World, 1984

JACK FISHER
TORN APART   Castle Hill Productions, 1990

MARY ANN FISHER
LORDS OF THE DEEP   Concorde, 1989

BILL FISHMAN*
Address: 2701 Airport Avenue, Santa Monica, CA 90405,
310/572-6027
Agent: David Gersh, The Gersh Agency - Beverly Hills, 310/274-6611

TAPEHEADS   Avenue Pictures, 1988
CAR 54, WHERE ARE YOU?   Orion, 1994, filmed in 1991

JACK FISK*
b. December 19, 1945 - Ipava, Illinois
Attorney: Steve Briemer - Los Angeles, 310/859-6820

RAGGEDY MAN   Universal, 1981
VIOLETS ARE BLUE   Columbia, 1986
DADDY'S DYIN'...WHO'S GOT THE WILL?   MGM/UA, 1990
FINAL VERDICT (CTF)   Foxboro Entertainment, 1991

PETER FISK
Agent: The Cameron Creswell Agency - Sydney, tel.: 2/356-4677 or:
ICM - London, tel.: 71/636-6565

FRANKIE'S HOUSE (MS)   Anglia Films, 1993, British-Australian

JON FITZGERALD
b. February 9, 1967 - Los Angeles, California
Business: Crystal Beach Entertainment, 2419 Oak Street - Suite A,
Santa Monica, CA 90405, 310/399-5521

SELF PORTRAIT   Crystal Beach Entertainment, 1994

PAUL FLAHERTY
Agent: William Morris Agency - Beverly Hills, 310/859-4000

18 AGAIN New World, 1988
WHO'S HARRY CRUMB? TriStar, 1989
BILLY CRYSTAL: MIDNIGHT TRAIN TO MOSCOW (CTPF) ☆
  Dalrymple Productions/Jennilind Productions, 1989
CLIFFORD Orion, 1994, filmed in 1992

GARY FLEDER*
Business: ACTW Filmworks, 624 Sunset Avenue - Suite 1, Venice,
  CA 90291, 310/396-8982
Agen t: William Morris Agency - Beverly Hills, 310/859-4000

THINGS TO DO IN DENVER WHEN YOU'RE DEAD
  Miramax Films, 1995

ROBERT C. FLEET
THE FRIENDS OF HARRY Legend Productions, 1993

RICHARD FLEISCHER*
b. December 8, 1916 - Brooklyn, New York
Business: Fleischer Studios, 10160 Cielo Drive, Beverly Hills, CA
  90210, 310/276-7503
Agent: Phil Gersh, The Gersh Agency - Beverly Hills, 310/274-6611

CHILD OF DIVORCE RKO Radio, 1946
BANJO RKO Radio, 1947
DESIGN FOR DEATH RKO Radio, 1948
SO THIS IS NEW YORK United Artists, 1948
BODYGUARD Columbia, 1948
MAKE MINE LAUGHS RKO Radio, 1949
THE CLAY PIGEON RKO Radio, 1949
FOLLOW ME QUIETLY RKO Radio, 1949
TRAPPED Eagle Lion, 1949
ARMORED CAR ROBBERY RKO Radio, 1950
THE NARROW MARGIN RKO Radio, 1952
THE HAPPY TIME Columbia, 1952
ARENA MGM, 1953
20,000 LEAGUES UNDER THE SEA Buena Vista, 1954
VIOLENT SATURDAY 20th Century-Fox, 1955
THE GIRL IN THE RED VELVET SWING 20th Century-Fox, 1955
BANDIDO United Artists, 1956
BETWEEN HEAVEN AND HELL 20th Century-Fox, 1956
THE VIKINGS United Artists, 1958
THESE THOUSAND HILLS 20th Century-Fox, 1959
COMPULSION 20th Century-Fox, 1959
CRACK IN THE MIRROR 20th Century-Fox, 1960
THE BIG GAMBLE 20th Century-Fox, 1961
BARABBAS Columbia, 1962, Italian
FANTASTIC VOYAGE 20th Century-Fox, 1966
DR. DOLITTLE 20th Century-Fox, 1967
THE BOSTON STRANGLER 20th Century-Fox, 1968
CHE! 20th Century-Fox, 1969
TORA! TORA! TORA! co-director with Kinji Fukasaku &
  Toshio Masuda, 20th Century-Fox, 1970, U.S.-Japanese
10 RILLINGTON PLACE Columbia, 1971, British
SEE NO EVIL Columbia, 1971, British
THE LAST RUN MGM, 1971
THE NEW CENTURIONS Columbia, 1972
SOYLENT GREEN MGM, 1972
THE DON IS DEAD Universal, 1973
THE SPIKES GANG United Artists, 1974
MR. MAJESTYK United Artists, 1974
MANDINGO Paramount, 1975
THE INCREDIBLE SARAH Reader's Digest, 1976, British
CROSSED SWORDS *THE PRINCE AND THE PAUPER*
  Warner Bros., 1978, British
ASHANTI Columbia, 1979, Swiss-U.S.
THE JAZZ SINGER AFD, 1980
TOUGH ENOUGH 20th Century-Fox, 1983
AMITYVILLE 3-D Orion, 1983
CONAN THE DESTROYER Universal, 1984
RED SONJA MGM/UA, 1985
MILLION DOLLAR MYSTERY DEG, 1987

PETER FLEISCHMANN
Contact: Federal Union of Film and Television Directors in Germany,
  Adelheidstrasse 7, 8000 Munich 40, Germany, tel.: 089/271-6380

HARD TO BE A GOD Hallelujah Film/Sovinfilm/Dovzhenko Studio/
  Garance/Mediactuel, 1990, West German-Soviet-French-Swiss

ANDREW FLEMING*
Agent: UTA - Beverly Hills, 310/273-6700

BAD DREAMS 20th Century Fox, 1988
THREESOME TriStar, 1993
THE CRAFT Columbia, 1995

GORDON FLEMYNG
b. March 7, 1934 - Glasgow, Scotland
Home: 1 Albert Road, Wilmslow, Cheshire SK9 5HT, England,
  tel.: 0625/524198
Agent: ICM - London, tel.: 171/636-6565

SOLD FOR SPARROW Schoenfield, 1962, British
FIVE TO ONE Allied Artists, 1963, British
JUST FOR FUN Columbia, 1963
DR. WHO AND THE DALEKS Continental, 1966, British
DALEKS - INVASION EARTH 2150 A.D. Continental, 1966, British
THE SPLIT MGM, 1968
GREAT CATHERINE Warner Bros., 1968, British
THE LAST GRENADE Cinerama Releasing Corporation,
  1970, British
A GOOD HUMAN STORY (TF) Granada TV, 1977, British
MIRAGE (TF) Granada TV, 1978, British
THE WEDDING (TF) Tyne Tees, 1983, British
PHILBY, BURGESS & McLEAN (TF) Granada TV, British
NOLAN (TF) Granada TV, British
ONE SUMMER (MS) Yorkshire TV, British
FLIGHT INTO HELL (MS) Australian Broadcasting Corporation/
  WWF/Andre Litik Film Productions, 1985, Australian-West German
CLOUD WALTZER (TF) Yorkshire TV/Atlantic VideoVentures,
  1987, British
CONFESSIONAL (MS) Granada TV, 1988-89, British
TAGGART: DOUBLE EXPOSURE (TF) Scottish TV,
  1991, Scottish

RODMAN FLENDER
Agent: ICM - Beverly Hills, 310/550-4000

THE UNBORN Califilm, 1991
IN THE HEAT OF PASSION Concorde, 1992
LEPRECHAUN 2 Trimark Pictures, 1994

MANDIE FLETCHER
Agent: William Morris Agency - Beverly Hills, 310/859-4000

DEADLY ADVICE Mayfair Entertainment International,
  1994, British

CLIVE FLEURY
Address: 34a Gunterstone Road, West Kensington, London W14,
  England, tel.: 171/603-1960
Agent: Jane Annakin, William Morris Agency - London,
  tel.: 171/434-2191

THE BILL (TF) Thames TV, 1989, British
JUPITER MOON (TF) Primetime TV, 1990, British
CAPITAL CITY (TF) Euston Films, 1990, British

THEODORE J. FLICKER*
b. June 6, 1930 - Freehold, New Jersey
Business Manager: Premiere Management, 13400 Riverside Drive,
  Sherman Oaks, CA 91423, 818/382-3599

THE TROUBLEMAKER Janus, 1964
THE PRESIDENT'S ANALYST Paramount, 1967
UP IN THE CELLAR American International, 1970
PLAYMATES (TF) ABC Circle Films, 1972

GUESS WHO'S SLEEPING IN MY BED? (TF)
 ABC Circle Films, 1973
JUST A LITTLE INCONVENIENCE (TF)   Universal TV, 1977
JACOB TWO-TWO MEETS THE HOODED FANG   Cinema Shares
 International, 1978, Canadian
LAST OF THE GOOD GUYS (TF)   Columbia TV, 1978
WHERE THE LADIES GO (TF)   Universal TV, 1980
SOGGY BOTTOM, U.S.A.   Cinemax Marketing &
 Distribution, 1981

KIM FLITCROFT
Agent: Rochelle Stevens & Co. - London, tel.: 171/359-3900

TALES FROM A HARD CITY (TD)   Channel 4/Yorkshire TV/
 La Sept, 1994, British-French

JOHN FLOREA*
Home: 11730-B Moorpark Street, Studio City, CA 91604,
 818/760-3433

INVISIBLE STRANGLER   Seymour Borde & Associates, 1984
HOT CHILD IN THE CITY   Mediacom Filmworks, 1987

ISAAC FLORENTINE
DESERT HAWK   21st Century Distribution, 1992
SAVATE   Mark Damon Productions, 1994

JOHN FLYNN*
Agent: UTA - Beverly Hills, 310/273-6700

THE SERGEANT   Warner Bros., 1968
THE JERUSALEM FILE   MGM, 1972, U.S.-Israeli
THE OUTFIT   MGM, 1974
ROLLING THUNDER   American International, 1978
DEFIANCE   American International, 1980
MARILYN: THE UNTOLD STORY (TF)   co-director with
 Jack Arnold & Lawrence Schiller, Lawrence Schiller
 Productions, 1980
TOUCHED   Lorimar Productions/Wildwoods Partners, 1983
BEST SELLER   Orion, 1987
LOCK UP   TriStar, 1989
OUT FOR JUSTICE   Warner Bros., 1991
NAILS (CTF)   Viacom Pictures, 1992
SCAM (CTF)   Viacom Pictures, 1993
BRAINSCAN   Triumph Releasing Corporation, 1994

THOMAS FLYNN
Agent: UTA - Beverly Hills, 310/273-6700

WATCH IT   Skouras Pictures, 1993

LAWRENCE D. FOLDES
b. November 4, 1959 - Los Angeles, California
Business: Star Cinema Production Group, Inc., 6253 Hollywood
 Blvd. - Suite 927, Los Angeles, CA 90028, 213/463-2000
Attorney: Ronald G. Gabler, 9606 Santa Monica Blvd., Beverly Hills,
 CA 90210, 310/205-8908

MALIBU HIGH   Crown International, 1979
DON'T GO NEAR THE PARK   Cannon, 1981
THE GREAT SKYCOPTER RESCUE   Cannon, 1982
YOUNG WARRIORS   Cannon, 1983
NIGHTFORCE   Vestron, 1987
SOCIAL SUICIDE   Trident Releasing, 1994, filmed in 1991

PETER FOLDY
DEADLY EXPOSURE   21st Century Distribution, 1992
TRYST   MCEG Sterling Entertainment, 1994
WIDOW'S KISS   Rysher Entertainment, 1995

JAMES FOLEY*
Agent: CAA - Beverly Hills, 310/288-4545
Business Manager: Kaufman & Bernstein, 1900 Avenue of the Stars,
 Los Angeles, CA 90067, 310/277-1900

RECKLESS   MGM/UA, 1984
AT CLOSE RANGE   Orion, 1986
WHO'S THAT GIRL   Warner Bros., 1987
AFTER DARK, MY SWEET   Avenue Pictures, 1990
GLENGARRY GLEN ROSS   New Line Cinema, 1992
TWO BITS   Miramax Films, 1995
NO FEAR   Universal, 1995

PETER FONDA*
b. February 23, 1939 - New York, New York
Home: Indian Hill Ranch, 38 Box 2024, Livingston, MO 59047,
 406/222-3686
Agent: UTA - Los Angeles, 310/273-6700
Business Manager: Nanas, Stern, Biers, Neinstein, 9454 Wilshire
 Blvd. - Suite 405, Beverly Hills, CA 90212, 310/273-2501

THE HIRED HAND   Universal, 1971
IDAHO TRANSFER   Cinemation, 1975
WANDA NEVADA   United Artists, 1979

ALLEN FONG
(Fong Yu-Ping)
b. July 10, 1947 - Hong Kong
Business: Dancing Bull Production Company, Room 3, Second Floor,
 Kwong On Commercial Building, 27 Ngoi Tsin Wai Road,
 Kowloon, Hong Kong
Contact: Hong Kong Film Liaison, 10940 Wilshire Blvd. - Suite 1220,
 Los Angeles, CA 90024, 310/208-2678

FATHER AND SON   1983, Hong Kong
AH YING   Array Films, 1984, Hong Kong
JUST LIKE WEATHER   SIL-Metropole Organization,
 1986, Hong Kong
THE VEGETARIAN   1989, Hong Kong
DANCING BULL   Dancing Bull Production Company,
 1990, Hong Kong

KATHLEEN FONMARTY
b. Paris, France
Agent: William Morris Agency - Beverly Hills, 310/859-4000

JALOUSIE   Bac Films, 1992, French

LLOYD FONVIELLE
Agent: ICM - Beverly Hills, 310/550-4000

GOTHAM (CTF)   Showtime/Phoenix Entertainment Group/Keith
 Addis & Associates, 1988

BRYAN FORBES*
(John Theobald Clarke)
b. July 22, 1926 - Stratford-Atte-Bow, England
Home: Seven Pines, Wentworth, Surrey GU25 4QP, England,
 tel.: 9904-2349
Business: Pinewood Studios, Iver Heath, Bucks, England,
 tel.: 344-84-2349
Agent: The Marion Rosenberg Office - Los Angeles, 213/653-7383 or:
 Noel Gay Artists - London, tel.: 171/836-3941

WHISTLE DOWN THE WIND   Pathe-America, 1962, British
THE L-SHAPED ROOM   Columbia, 1963, British
SEANCE ON A WET AFTERNOON   Artixo, 1964, British
KING RAT   Columbia, 1965, British
THE WRONG BOX   Columbia, 1966, British
THE WHISPERERS   United Artists, 1967, British
DEADFALL   20th Century-Fox, 1968, British
THE MADWOMAN OF CHAILLOT   Warner Bros., 1969, British
LONG AGO TOMORROW   *THE RAGING MOON*   Cinema 5,
 1971, British

THE STEPFORD WIVES   Columbia, 1975
THE SLIPPER AND THE ROSE: THE STORY OF CINDERELLA
   Universal, 1976, British
INTERNATIONAL VELVET   MGM/United Artists, 1978, British
SUNDAY LOVERS   co-director with Edouard Molinaro, Dino Risi &
   Gene Wilder, MGM/United Artists, 1981,
   U.S.-British-Italian-French
PHILIP MARLOWE - PRIVATE EYE   *CHANDLERTOWN* (CMS)
   co-director with Peter Hunt, David Wickes & Sidney Hayers,
   HBO/David Wickes Television Ltd./London Weekend Television,
   1983, British
BETTER LATE THAN NEVER   Warner Bros., 1983, British
THE NAKED FACE   Cannon, 1985
THE ENDLESS GAME (CTF)   TVS Films/Reteitalia/Pixit,
   1990, British-Italian

GREG FORD

DAFFY DUCK'S QUACKBUSTERS (AF)   co-director with
   Terry Lennon, Warner Bros., 1988

STEVE FORD

THE DUNGEONMASTER   co-director, Empire Pictures, 1985

TIMOTHY FORDER

Contact: British Film Commission, 70 Baker Street, London
   W1M 1DJ, England, tel.: 171/224-5000

THE MYSTERY OF EDWIN DROOD   Bevanfield Films/First
   Standard Media, 1993, British

STEPHEN H. FOREMAN*

Agent: ICM - Beverly Hills, 310/550-4000

COUGAR! (TF)   ABC Circle Films, 1984

MILOS FORMAN*

b. February 18, 1932 - Caslav, Czechoslovakia
Agent: The Lantz Office - New York City, 212/586-0200

COMPETITION   Brandon, 1963, Czechoslovakian
BLACK PETER   Billings, 1964, Czechoslovakian
LOVES OF A BLONDE   Prominent, 1966, Czechoslovakian
THE FIREMAN'S BALL   Cinema 5, 1968, Czechoslovakian
TAKING OFF   Universal, 1971
VISIONS OF EIGHT (FD)   co-director with Yuri Ozerov,
   Mai Zetterling, Arthur Penn, Michael Pfleghar, Kon Ichikawa,
   Claude Lelouch & John Schlesinger, Cinema 5, 1973
ONE FLEW OVER THE CUCKOO'S NEST ★★
   United Artists, 1976
HAIR   United Artists, 1979
RAGTIME   Paramount, 1981
AMADEUS ★★   Orion, 1984
VALMONT   Orion, 1989, French-British

ROBERT FORSTER

b. July 13, 1941 - Rochester, New York

HOLLYWOOD HARRY   Shapiro Entertainment, 1985

BILL FORSYTH*

(William David Forsyth)
b. July 29, 1946 - Glasgow, Scotland
Agent: CAA - Beverly Hills, 310/288-4545 or:
   Peters Fraser & Dunlop - London, tel.: 171/344-1000

THAT SINKING FEELING   The Samuel Goldwyn Company,
   1979, Scottish
GREGORY'S GIRL   The Samuel Goldwyn Company,
   1982, Scottish
LOCAL HERO   Warner Bros., 1983, British-Scottish
COMFORT AND JOY   Universal, 1984, British-Scottish
HOUSEKEEPING   Columbia, 1987
BREAKING IN   The Samuel Goldwyn Company, 1989

THE SOUTH BANK SHOW: OSCAR MARZAROLI (TD)
   co-director with Charles Gormley, Scottish TV/London
   Weekend TV, 1991, Scottish-British
BEING HUMAN   Warner Bros., 1994, British, filmed in 1992

JOHN W. FORTENBERRY*

Agent: William Morris Agency - Beverly Hills, 310/859-4000

JURY DUTY   TriStar, 1995

GILES FOSTER

Agent: Peters Fraser & Dunlop - London, tel.: 171/344-1000

LAST SUMMER'S CHILD (TF)   BBC, 1982, British
THE AERODROME (TF)   BBC, 1983, British
DUTCH GIRLS (TF)   London Weekend TV, 1984, British
SILAS MARNER (TF)   BBC, 1985, British
NORTHANGER ABBEY (TF)   BBC/Arts & Entertainment Network,
   1986, British
HOTEL DULAC (TF)   Channel 4, 1986, British
CONSUMING PASSIONS   The Samuel Goldwyn Company,
   1988, British
THE TREE OF HANDS   Greenpoint/Granada/British Screen,
   1989, British
THE LILAC BUS (TF)   HTV/RTE/Littlebird, 1990, British
ADAM BEDE (TF)   BBC/WGBH-Boston, 1991, British-U.S.
THE RECTOR'S WIFE (MS)   Talisman/Channel 4, 1993, British

JODIE FOSTER

(Alicia Christian Foster)
b. November 19, 1962 - Los Angeles, California
Agent: ICM - Beverly Hills, 310/550-4000

LITTLE MAN TATE   Orion, 1991
HOME FOR THE HOLIDAYS   Gramercy Pictures, 1995

ROBERT FOWLER*

Contact: Directors Guild of America - Los Angeles, 213/851-3671
Agent: Harold R. Greene, Inc. - Marina Del Rey, 310/823-5393

BELOW THE BELT   Atlantic Releasing Corporation, 1980

ERICA FOX

DEAD WOMEN IN LINGERIE   Seagate Films, 1991

WILLIAM A. FRAKER*

b. 1923 - Los Angeles, California
Home: 2572 Outpost Drive, Hollywood, CA 90068
Agent: Phil Gersh, The Gersh Agency - Beverly Hills, 310/274-6611

MONTE WALSH   National General, 1970
A REFLECTION OF FEAR   Columbia, 1973, British
THE LEGEND OF THE LONE RANGER   Universal/AFD, 1981
B.L. STRYKER: THE DANCER'S TOUCH (TF)   Blue Period
   Productions/T.W.S. Productions/Universal TV, 1989

FREDDIE FRANCIS

b. 1917 - London, England
Home: 12 Ashley Drive, Jersey Road, Osterley, Middlesex
   7W7 5QA, England
Agent: CCA Management - London, tel.: 171/730-8857

TWO AND TWO MAKE SIX   Union, 1962, British
THE BRAIN   *VENGEANCE*   Garrick, 1962, British-West German
PARANOIAC   Universal, 1964, British
NIGHTMARE   Universal, 1964, British
THE EVIL OF FRANKENSTEIN   Universal, 1964, British
TRAITOR'S GATE   Columbia, 1964, British-West German
DR. TERROR'S HOUSE OF HORRORS   Paramount, 1965, British
HYSTERIA   MGM, 1965, British
THE SKULL   Paramount, 1965, British
THE PSYCHOPATH   Paramount, 1966, British
THE DEADLY BEES   Paramount, 1967, British
THEY CAME FROM BEYOND SPACE   Embassy, 1967, British

TORTURE GARDEN   Columbia, 1968, British
DRACULA HAS RISEN FROM THE GRAVE   Warner Bros.,
   1969, British
MUMSY, NANNY, SONNY & GIRLY   *GIRLY*   Cinerama Releasing
   Corporation, 1970, British
TROG   Warner Bros., 1970, British
THE HAPPENING OF THE VAMPIRE   1971, European
TALES FROM THE CRYPT   Cinerama Releasing Corporation,
   1972, British
TALES THAT WITNESS MADNESS   Paramount, 1973, British
THE CREEPING FLESH   Columbia, 1973, British
SON OF DRACULA   Cinemation, 1974, British
CRAZE   Warner Bros., 1974, British
THE GHOUL   Rank, 1974, British
LEGEND OF THE WEREWOLF   Tyburn, 1975, British
THE DOCTOR AND THE DEVILS   20th Century Fox, 1985, British
DARK TOWER   released under pseudonym of Ken Barnett,
   Spectrafilm, 1989, Canadian

KARL FRANCIS

Contact: British Film Commission, 70 Baker Street, London
   W1M 1DJ, England, tel.: 171/224-5000

THE MOUSE AND THE WOMAN   Facelift, 1981, British
AND NOTHING BUT THE TRUTH   *GIRO CITY*   Castle Hill
   Productions, 1982, British
THE HAPPY ALCOHOLIC   1984, Welsh
BOY SOLDIER (TF)   Cine Cymru Productions/Channel 4,
   1986, Welsh
ANGRY EARTH   Bloom Street Productions, 1989, Welsh
MORPHINE AND DOLLY MIXTURES (TF)   BBC, 1990, British
REBECCA'S DAUGHTERS   The Samuel Goldwyn Company,
   1991, British-Welsh
LIFEBOARD (MS)   co-director, Bloom Street Productions/BBC
   Wales, 1993, Welsh

CAROL FRANK

Contact: Writers Guild of America, West - Los Angeles, 310/550-1000

SORORITY HOUSE MASSACRE   Concorde, 1987

ROBERT FRANK

b. November 9, 1924 - Zurich, Switzerland
Contact: Swiss Film Center, Munstergasse 18, CH-8025 Zurich,
   Switzerland, tel.: 1/261-2860

PULL MY DAISY   co-director with Alfred Leslie,
   G-String Productions, 1959
THE SIN OF JESUS   Off-Broadway Productions, 1961
O.K. END HERE   September 20 Productions, 1963
ME AND MY BROTHER   Two Faces Company, 1965-68
CONVERSATIONS IN VERMONT (FD)   Dilexi Foundation, 1969
LIFE-RAFT EARTH (FD)   Portola Institute, 1969
ABOUT ME: A MUSICAL   1971
COCKSUCKER BLUES   *CS BLUES* (FD)   Rolling Stones
   Productions, 1972
KEEP BUSY   1975
LIFE DANCES ON....   1980
ENERGY AND HOW TO GET IT   1981
THIS SONG FOR JACK   1983
CANDY MOUNTAIN   co-director with Rudy Wurlitzer, International
   Film Exchange, 1987, Swiss-French-Canadian
LAST SUPPER   Vega Film/World Wide International TV/BBC,
   1992, Swiss-U.S.-British

CYRIL FRANKEL

b. 1921 - London, England
Contact: British Film Commission, 70 Baker Street, London
   W1M 1DJ, England, tel.: 171/224-5000

MAN OF AFRICA (FD)   1953, British
DEVIL ON HORSEBACK   British Lion, 1954, British
MAKE ME AN OFFER   Dominant Pictures, 1954, British
IT'S GREAT TO BE YOUNG   Fine Arts, 1956, British
NO TIME FOR TEARS   Associated British-Pathe, 1957, British
SHE DIDN'T SAY NO   1958, British

ALIVE AND KICKING   Associated British-British, 1958, British
NEVER TAKE SWEETS FROM A STRANGER   1960, British
WHY BOTHER TO KNOCK   *DON'T BOTHER TO KNOCK*
   Seven Arts, 1961, British
OPERATION SNAFU   *ON THE FIDDLE*   American International,
   1961, British
THE VERY EDGE   Teleworld, 1963, British
THE DEVIL'S OWN   *THE WITCHES*   20th Century-Fox,
   1966, British
THE TRYGON FACTOR   Warner Bros., 1967, British
PERMISSION TO KILL   Avco Embassy, 1975, British-Austrian

DAVID FRANKEL*

Agent: ICM - Beverly Hills, 310/550-4000

MIAMI RHAPSODY   Buena Vista, 1995

JOHN FRANKENHEIMER*

b. February 19, 1930 - Malba, New York
Agent: ICM - Beverly Hills, 310/550-4000

THE YOUNG STRANGER   Universal, 1957
THE YOUNG SAVAGES   United Artists, 1961
ALL FALL DOWN   MGM, 1962
BIRDMAN OF ALCATRAZ   United Artists, 1962
THE MANCHURIAN CANDIDATE   United Artists, 1962
SEVEN DAYS IN MAY   Paramount, 1964
THE TRAIN   United Artists, 1965, U.S.-French-Italian
SECONDS   Paramount, 1966
GRAND PRIX   MGM, 1966
THE FIXER   MGM, 1968, British
THE EXTRAORDINARY SEAMAN   MGM, 1969
THE GYPSY MOTHS   MGM, 1969
I WALK THE LINE   Columbia, 1970
THE HORSEMEN   Columbia, 1971
THE ICEMAN COMETH   American Film Theatre, 1973
IMPOSSIBLE OBJECT   Valoria, 1973, French-Italian
99 AND 44/100 % DEAD   20th Century-Fox, 1974
FRENCH CONNECTION II   20th Century-Fox, 1975
BLACK SUNDAY   Paramount, 1977
PROPHECY   Paramount, 1979
THE CHALLENGE   Embassy, 1982
THE HOLCROFT COVENANT   Universal, 1985
52 PICK-UP   Cannon, 1986
DEAD-BANG   Warner Bros., 1989
THE FOURTH WAR   New Age Releasing, 1990
YEAR OF THE GUN   Triumph Releasing Corporation, 1991
AGAINST THE WALL (CTF) ★★   Producers Entertainment
   Group, 1994
THE BURNING SEASON (CTF)   HBO Pictures, 1994
ANDERSONVILLE (CTF)   Turner Network TV, 1994

CARL FRANKLIN*

Agent: Broder-Kurland-Webb-Uffner Agency - Beverly Hills,
   310/281-3400

EYE OF THE EAGLE II: INSIDE THE ENEMY   Concorde,
   1989, U.S.-Filipino
FULL FATHOM FIVE   Concorde, 1990
ONE FALSE MOVE   I.R.S. Releasing, 1992
SHELTON AVENUE (CMS)   HBO Independent Productions, 1993
DEVIL IN A BLUE DRESS   TriStar, 1995

HOWARD FRANKLIN*

Agent: CAA - Beverly Hills, 310/288-4545

QUICK CHANGE   co-director with Bill Murray, Warner Bros., 1990
THE PUBLIC EYE   Universal, 1992
NICKEL AND DIME   MGM-UA, 1995

JEFF FRANKLIN*

Agent: ICM - Beverly Hills, 310/550-4000

TO GRANDMOTHER'S HOUSE WE GO (TF)   Green-Epstein
   Productions/Jeff Franklin Productions/Lorimar Productions, 1992

RICHARD FRANKLIN*
b. July 15, 1948 - Melbourne, Australia
Agent: Daniel Ostroff, The Daniel Ostroff Agency - Los Angeles,
    310/278-2020

BELINDA   Aquarius, 1972, Australian
LOVELAND   Illustrated, 1973, Australian
THE TRUE STORY OF ESKIMO NELL   *DICK DOWN UNDER*
    Quest Films/Filmways Australasian Distributors, 1975, Australian
FANTASM   Filmways Australasian, 1977, Australian
PATRICK   Cinema Shares International, 1979, Australian
ROAD GAMES   Avco Embassy, 1981, Australian
PSYCHO II   Universal, 1983
CLOAK & DAGGER   Universal, 1984
LINK   Thorn EMI/Cannon, 1986, U.S.-British
BEAUTY & THE BEAST (TF)   Witt Thomas Productions, 1987
A FINE ROMANCE (TF)   Phoenix Entertainment Group, 1988
F/X 2: THE DEADLY ART OF ILLUSION   Orion, 1991
HOTEL SORRENTO   Castle Hill Productions, 1995, Australian

JAMES FRAWLEY*
Business: Port Orchard Films, Oberman, Tivoli, Miller & Low,
    500 S. Sepulveda Blvd., Los Angeles, CA 90049, 310/471-9300
Agent: William Morris Agency - Beverly Hills, 310/859-4000

THE CHRISTIAN LICORICE STORE   National General, 1971
KID BLUE   20th Century-Fox, 1973
DELANCEY STREET: THE CRISIS WITHIN (TF)
    Paramount TV, 1975
THE BIG BUS   Paramount, 1976
THE MUPPET MOVIE   AFD, 1979, British
THE GREAT AMERICAN TRAFFIC JAM (TF)
    Ten-Four Productions, 1980
THE OUTLAWS (TF)   Limekiln and Templar Productions/
    Universal TV, 1984
FRATERNITY VACATION   New World, 1985
WARM HEARTS, COLD FEET (TF)   Lorimar-Telepictures, 1987
ASSAULT AND MATRIMONY (TF)   Michael Filerman
    Productions/NBC Productions, 1987
COLUMBO: MURDER - A SELF PORTRAIT (TF)
    Universal TV, 1989
THE SECRET LIFE OF ARCHIE'S WIFE (TF)   Interscope
    Productions/Consolidated Productions, 1990
ANOTHER MIDNIGHT RUN (TF)   Toto Productions/
    Universal TV, 1994
CAGNEY & LACEY: THE RETURN (TF)   The Rosenzweig
    Company, 1994
THE SHAMROCK CONSPIRACY (TF)   Crescendo Productions/
    Michael Gleason Productions/Paramount Domestic TV, 1995

STEPHEN FREARS*
b. 1941 - Leicester, England
Address: 93 Talbot Road, London W2, England, tel.: 171/229-1808
Agent: William Morris Agency - Beverly Hills, 310/859-4000 or:
    The Casarotto Company - London, tel.: 171/287-4450

GUMSHOE   Columbia, 1971, British
ABEL'S WILL (TF)   BBC, 1977, British
BLOODY KIDS (TF)   Black Lion Films, 1983, British
SAIGON - YEAR OF THE CAT (TF)   Thames TV, 1983, British
THE HIT   Island Alive, 1984, British
MY BEAUTIFUL LAUNDRETTE (TF)   Orion Classics, 1985, British
LOVING WALTER (TF)   Central TV Productions, 1986, British
PRICK UP YOUR EARS   The Samuel Goldwyn Company,
    1987, British
DECEMBER FLOWER (TF)   Granada TV, 1987, British
SAMMY AND ROSIE GET LAID   Cinecom, 1987, British
DANGEROUS LIAISONS   Warner Bros., 1988
THE GRIFTERS ★   Miramax Films, 1990
HERO   Columbia, 1992
THE SNAPPER   Miramax Films, 1993, British,
    originally filmed for television
MARY REILLY   TriStar, 1995, U.S.-British

RICCARDO FREDA
b. February 24, 1909 - Alexandria, Egypt
Home: via di Vigna Stelluti 212, Rome, Italy, tel.: 6/36307149

DON CESARE DI BAZAN   Elica/Artisti Associati, 1942, Italian
NON CANTO PIU'   Vi-Va, 1943, Italian
TUTTA LA CITTA' CANTA   ICI/SAFIR/Appia, 1943-45, Italian
AQUILA NERA   CDI, 1946, Italian
I MISERABILI   *CACCIA ALL'UOMO/TEMPESTA SU PARIGI*
    Lux Film, 1947, Italian
IL CAVALIERE MISTERIOSO   Lux Film, 1948, Italian
GUARANY   Universalia, 1948, Italian
IL CONTE UGOLINO   API Film/Forum Film, 1949, Italian
O CACOULHA DO BARULHO   Luiz Severiano Ribeiro,
    1949, Brazilian
IL FIGLIO DI D'ARTAGNAN   API Film/Augustus Film, 1949, Italian
IL TRADIMENTO   *PASSATO CHE UCCIDE*   Safa Palatino,
    1951, Italian
LA VENDETTA DI AQUILA NERA   API Film, 1951, Italian
VEDI NAPOLI E POI MUORI   API Film, 1951, Italian
LA LEGGENDA DEL PIAVE   API Film/Colamonici/Tupini,
    1952, Italian
SINS OF ROME   *SPARTACO/SPARTACUS AND THE REBEL
    GLADIATORS*   RKO Radio, 1952, Italian
THEODORA, SLAVE EMPRESS   *THEODORA IMPERATRICE
    DI BISANZIO*   Italian Films Export, 1954, Italian-French
DA QUI ALL'ERIDITA'   API Film/Centauro Film, 1955, Italian
BEATRICE CENCI   Electra/Attilio Riccio, 1956, Italian
I VAMPIRI   Titanus/Athena, 1956, Italian
TRAPPED IN TANGIERS   *AGGUATO A TANGERI*
    20th Century-Fox, 1957, Italian-Spanish
THE WHITE WARRIOR   *AGI MURAD, IL DIAVOLO BIANCO*
    Warner Bros., 1959, Italian-Yugoslavian
CALTIKI - THE IMMORTAL MONSTER   Allied Artists, 1959, Italian
THE GIANTS OF THESSALY   Telewide Systems, 1960, Italian
CACCIA ALL'UOMO   Fair Film, 1961, Italian
SAMSON AND THE SEVEN MIRACLES OF THE WORLD
    MACISTE ALLA CORTE DEL GRAN KHAN
    American International, 1961, Italian-French
THE SEVENTH SWORD   *LE SETTE SPADE DEL VENDICATORE*
    Telewide Systems, 1962, Italian
THE WITCH'S CURSE   *MACISTE ALL'INFERNO*   Medallion,
    1962, Italian
THE HORRIBLE DR. HITCHCOCK   Sigma III, 1962, Italian
THE GHOST   Magna Pictures, 1963, Italian
IL MAGNIFICO AVVENTURIERO   Panda Film/Hispamer/Les Films
    du Centaure, 1963, Italian-Spanish-French
GIULIETTA E ROMEO   Imprecine/Hispamer, 1964, Italian-Spanish
GENOVEFFA DI BRABANTE   Imprecine/Hispamer,
    1964, Italian-Spanish
LES DEUX ORPHELINES   Comptoir Francais du Fijlm/Cine Italia,
    1966, French-Italian
COPLAN F X 18 CASSE TOUT   Comptoir Francais du Film/Camera
    Film/Cinerad, 1966, French-Italian
ROGER LA HONTE   Comptoir Francais du Film/Mancori Chretien,
    1967, French-Italian
COPLAN OUVRE LE FEU A MEXICO   Comptoir Francais du Film/
    Fida/Balcazar, 1967, French-Italian-Spanish
LA MORTE NON CONTA I DOLLARI   Cinedi, 1967, Italian
A DOPPIA FACCIA   Colt/Mega Film/Rialto, 1969, Italian-German
L'IGUANA DALLA LINGUA DI FUOCO   Oceania/Les Films Corona/
    Terra Filmkunst, 1970, Italian-French-German
TAMAR, WIFE OF ER   Film Studios of Israel, 1971, Israeli
MURDER OBSESSION   Dionisyo Cinematografica/Gurvitch,
    1980, Italian-French

HERB FREED*
Agent: Norman G. Rudman, Slaff, Mosk & Rudman,
    9200 Sunset Blvd., Los Angeles, CA 90069, 310/275-5351

AWOL   BFB, 1972
HAUNTS   Intercontinental, 1977
BEYOND EVIL   IFI-Scope III, 1980
GRADUATION DAY   IFI-Scope III, 1981
TOMBOY   Crown International, 1985
SURVIVAL GAME   Trans World Entertainment, 1987
MANCHILD   August Entertainment, 1991
STICKIN TOGETHER   August Entertainment, 1992

GORDON FREEDMAN
MARILYN MONROE: LIFE AFTER DEATH (CTD)   Showtime
   Network/Freedman-Greene Productions, 1994

JERROLD FREEDMAN*
Business Manager: Craig Jacobson, Hanson, Jacobson & Teller,
   335 N. Maple Drive, Beverly Hills, CA 90210, 310/271-8777

KANSAS CITY BOMBER   MGM, 1972
A COLD NIGHT'S DEATH (TF)   ABC Circle Films, 1973
BLOOD SPORT (TF)   Danny Thomas Productions, 1973
THE LAST ANGRY MAN (TF)   Screen Gems/Columbia TV, 1974
SOME KIND OF MIRACLE (TF)   Lorimar Productions, 1979
THIS MAN STANDS ALONE (TF)   Roger Gimbel Productions/
   EMI TV/Abby Mann Productions, 1979
THE STREETS OF L.A. (TF)   George Englund Productions, 1979
THE BOY WHO DRANK TOO MUCH (TF)
   MTM Enterprises, 1980
BORDERLINE   AFD, 1980
THE VICTIMS (TF)   Hajeno Productions/Warner Bros. TV, 1982
LEGS (TF)   The Catalina Production Group/Radio City Music Hall
   Productions/Comworld Productions, 1983
THE SEDUCTION OF GINA (TF)   Bertinelli-Jaffee
   Productions, 1984
BEST KEPT SECRETS (TF)   ABC Circle Films, 1984
SEDUCED (TF)   Catalina Production Group/Comworld
   Productions, 1985
THOMPSON'S LAST RUN (TF)   Cypress Point
   Productions, 1986
NATIVE SON   Cinecom, 1986
UNHOLY MATRIMONY (TF)   Edgar J. Scherick Associates/Taft
   Entertainment TV, 1988
THE COMEBACK (TF)   CBS Entertainment, 1989
NIGHT WALK (TF)   Galatea Productions/CBS
   Entertainment, 1989
GOOD NIGHT, SWEET WIFE: A MURDER IN BOSTON (TF)
   CBS Entertainment/Arnold Shapiro Productions, 1990
THE O.J. SIMPSON STORY (TF)   released under pseudonym of
   Alan Smithee, National Studios, 1995

ROBERT FREEDMAN*
Telephone: 310/276-9383

GOIN' ALL THE WAY   Saturn International, 1982

JOAN FREEMAN*
Agent: William Morris Agency - Beverly Hills, 310/859-4000

STREETWALKIN'   Concorde, 1985
SATISFACTION   20th Century Fox, 1988

MORGAN FREEMAN
b. June 1, 1937 - Memphis, Tennessee
Agent: William Morris Agency - Beverly Hills, 310/859-4000

BOPHA!   Paramount, 1993

MICHAEL FRESCO*
Address: 832 36th Avenue, Seattle, WA 98122, 206/720-0246
Agent: ICM - Beverly Hills, 310/550-4000

DAUGHTERS OF PRIVILEGE (TF)   NBC Productions, 1990

ROB FRESCO
Contact: Los Angeles, 310/470-7571

SMALL KILL   Double Helix Films, 1992

RON FRICKE
BARAKA   The Samuel Goldwyn Company, 1993

FRIDRIK THOR FRIDRIKSSON
Contact: Icelandic Film Fund, Laugavegur 24, 121 Reykjavik,
   Iceland, tel.: 1/623580

WHITE WHALES   1987, Icelandic
ROCK IN REYKJAVIK (FD)   Icelandic
CHILDREN OF NATURE   Northern Arts Entertainment, 1991,
   Icelandic-German-Norwegian
MOVIE DAYS   Icelandic Film Corporation/Peter Rommel
   Filmproduction/Zentropa Entertainment, 1993,
   Icelandic-German-Danish
COLD FEVER   Icelandic Film Corporation/Iciclefilm/Pandora
   Film/Sunrise Inc., 1994, Icelandic

MYRA FRIED
Agent: Susan Grant, The Artists Group - Los Angeles,
   310/552-1100

HURT PENGUINS   co-director with Robert Bergman,
   1992, Canadian

RANDALL FRIED
Agent: The Artists Agency - Los Angeles, 310/277-7779

HEAVEN IS A PLAYGROUND   New Line Cinema, 1991

RICK FRIEDBERG*
Agent: M. Kenneth Suddleson, c/o Kaye, Scholer, Fleman,
   Hayes & Handler, 1999 Avenue of the Stars - Suite 1600,
   Los Angeles, CA 90067, 310/788-1271

PRAY TV *K-GOD*   Filmways, 1980
OFF THE WALL   Jensen Farley Pictures, 1983

RICHARD FRIEDENBERG
Contact: Writers Guild of America, West - Los Angeles,
   310/550-1000
Agent: The Daniel Ostroff Agency - Los Angeles, 213/278-2020

THE LIFE AND TIMES OF GRIZZLY ADAMS   Sunn Classic, 1976
FRONTIER FREMONT   Sunn Classic, 1976
THE DEERSLAYER (TF)   Sunn Classic Productions, 1978
THE BERMUDA TRIANGLE   Sunn Classic, 1979

BUD FRIEDGEN*
Contact: Directors Guild of America - Los Angeles, 213/851-3671

THAT'S ENTERTAINMENT! III (FD)   co-director with
   Michael J. Sheridan, MGM, 1994
THE HISTORY OF ROCK 'N' ROLL (TD)   co-director, Andrew Solt
   Productions/QDE/Telepictures Productions/Time-Life Video &
   Television/Warner Bros. TV Distribution Prime Time Entertainment
   Network, 1995

WILLIAM FRIEDKIN*
b. August 29, 1935 - Chicago, Illinois
Agent: ICM - Beverly Hills, 310/550-4000

GOOD TIMES   Columbia, 1967
THE BIRTHDAY PARTY   Continental, 1968, British
THE NIGHT THEY RAIDED MINSKY'S   United Artists, 1968
THE BOYS IN THE BAND   National General, 1970
THE FRENCH CONNECTION ★★   20th Century-Fox, 1971
THE EXORCIST ★   Warner Bros., 1973
SORCERER   Universal/Paramount, 1977
THE BRINK'S JOB   Universal, 1978
CRUISING   United Artists, 1980
DEAL OF THE CENTURY   Warner Bros., 1983
TO LIVE AND DIE IN L.A.   MGM/UA, 1985
PUTTING IT TOGETHER - THE MAKING OF 'THE BROADWAY
   ALBUM' (CCD)   Barwood Films/CBS Music Video
   Enterprises/HBO, 1986
C.A.T. SQUAD (TF)   NBC Productions, 1986
C.A.T. SQUAD: PYTHON WOLF (TF)   NBC Productions, 1988
THE GUARDIAN   Universal, 1990

RAMPAGE   Miramax Films, 1992, filmed in 1987
BLUE CHIPS   Paramount, 1994
REBEL HIGHWAY: JAILBREAKERS   *JAILBREAKERS* (CTF)
    Drive-In Classics Cinema/Showtime, 1994
JADE   Paramount, 1995

ADAM FRIEDMAN
TO SLEEP WITH A VAMPIRE   Concorde, 1993

JEFFREY FRIEDMAN
b. August 8, 1951 - Los Angeles, California
Business: Telling Pictures, 347 Dolores Street - Suite 307,
    San Francisco, CA 94110, 415/864-6714
Attorney: John Sloss, Morrison & Foerster, 1290 Avenue of
    the Americas, New York, NY 10104, 212/468-8049

COMMON THREADS: STORIES FROM THE QUILT (CTD)
    co-director with Rob Epstein, Telling Pictures/The Couturie
    Company, 1989
WHERE ARE WE?: OUR TRIP THROUGH AMERICA (FD)
    co-director with Rob Epstein, Roxie Releasing, 1992
THE CELLULOID CLOSET (CTD)   co-director with Rob Epstein,
    HBO, 1995

KEN FRIEDMAN
Agent: Sanford-Gross & Associates - Los Angeles, 310/208-2100

DEATH BY INVITATION   1971
MADE IN USA   DEG, 1986

KIM FRIEDMAN*
Agent: David Gersh, The Gersh Agency - Beverly Hills, 310/274-6611

BEFORE AND AFTER (TF)   The Konigsberg Company, 1979

PETER FRIEDMAN
SILVERLAKE LIFE: THE VIEW FROM HERE (FD)   co-director with
    Tom Joslin, Silverlake/Channel 4/J.P. Weiner Inc., 1993

RICHARD FRIEDMAN*
Telephone: 213/876-2377
Agent: Broder-Kurland-Webb-Uffner Agency - Beverly Hills,
    310/281-3400

DOOM ASYLUM
DEATH MASK   1984
SCARED STIFF   International Film Marketing, 1987
PHANTOM OF THE MALL: ERIC'S REVENGE
    Fries Distribution, 1989
SHADOW OF A STRANGER (TF)   Doris Keating Productions/
    NBC Productions, 1992
IN THE SHADOWS, SOMEONE IS WATCHING (TF)
    Arvin Kaufman Productions/Saban Entertainment, 1993

SEYMOUR FRIEDMAN*
b. August 17, 1917 - Detroit, Michigan
Business: 43 N. Camden Drive - Suite 1200, Beverly Hills,
    CA 90210, 310/205-2016

TRAPPED BY BOSTON BLACKIE   Columbia, 1948
CHINATOWN AT MIDNIGHT   Columbia, 1949
BODYHOLD   Columbia, 1949
PRISON WARDEN   Columbia, 1949
THE CRIME DOCTOR'S DIARY   Columbia, 1949
THE DEVIL'S HENCHMAN   Columbia, 1949
CUSTOMS AGENT   Columbia, 1950
SON OF DR. JEKYLL   Columbia, 1951
CRIMINAL LAWYER   Columbia, 1951
LONE SHARK   Columbia, 1952
FLAME OF CALCUTTA   Columbia, 1953
KHYBER PATROL   United Artists, 1954
AFRICAN MANHUNT   Republic, 1955
SECRET OF TREASURE MOUNTAIN   Columbia, 1956

MARTYN FRIEND
Agent: Peters Fraser & Dunlop - London, tel.: 171/344-1000

VOYAGE OF CHARLES DARWIN (MS)   BBC, 1980, British
FAIR STOOD THE WIND FOR FRANCE (MS)   BBC, 1982, British
SHACKLETON (MS)   BBC, 1983, British
SUMMER'S LEASE (MS)   BBC, 1989, British
SURVIVAL OF THE FITTEST (TF)   BBC, 1990, British
TITMUSS REGAINED (TF)   New Penny Productions/Thames TV,
    1991, British
INSPECTOR ALLEYN: FINAL CURTAIN (TF)   BBC, 1992, British
LOVE ON A BRANCH LINE (MS)   Theatre of Comedy/DL Taffner,
    1993, British

BILL FROELICH*
Agent: Paradigm - Los Angeles, 310/277-4400

RETURN TO HORROR HIGH   New World, 1987

DAVID FROST
RING OF STEEL   Shapiro Glickenhaus Entertainment, 1993

HARVEY FROST
b. 1947 - London, England
Address: 162 Westminster Avenue, Toronto, Ontario M6R 1N7,
    Canada, 416/588-1096
Agent: ICM - Beverly Hills, 310/550-4000

TEXAS HEAT   UG Productions, 1995
DEADLY AMBITION   UG Productions/LIVE Entertainment,
    1995, Canadian

MARK FROST*
Agent: CAA - Beverly Hills, 310/288-4545

STORYVILLE   20th Century Fox, 1992

WILLIAM FRUET
b. 1933 - Lethbridge, Alberta, Canada
Business: Jaguar Productions Ltd., 51 Olive Avenue, Toronto,
    Ontario M6G 1T7, Canada, 416/535-3569

WEDDING IN WHITE   Avco Embassy, 1973, Canadian
THE HOUSE BY THE LAKE   *DEATH WEEKEND*   American
    International, 1977, Canadian
SEARCH AND DESTROY   *STRIKING BACK*   Film Ventures
    International, 1979
FUNERAL HOME   *CRIES IN THE NIGHT*   MPM, 1981, Canadian
BAKER COUNTY USA   *TRAPPED*   Jensen Farley Pictures, 1982
SPASMS   Producers Distribution Company, 1983, Canadian
FULL CIRCLE AGAIN (TF)   1984, Canadian
BEDROOM EYES   Film Gallery/Aquarius, 1984, Canadian
KILLER PARTY   MGM-UA, 1986, Canadian
CHASING RAINBOWS (MS)   co-director with Mark Blandford,
    Bruce Pittman & Susan Martin, CBC, 1986, Canadian
BLUE MONKEY   Spectrafilm, 1987, Canadian

ROY FRUMKES
b. July 22, 1944 - New York, New York
Business: Bat Track Productions, 166 West 83rd Street, New York,
    NY 10024, 212/873-6626

DOCUMENT OF THE DEAD (FD)   Roy Frumkes
    Productions, 1980
BURT'S BIKERS (TD)   NBC, 1984

BENJAMIN FRY
Contact: British Film Commission, 70 Baker Street, London
    W1M 1DJ, England, tel.: 171/224-5000

E=MC2   E=MC2 Productions Ltd., 1995, British

E. MAX FRYE*

Agent: ICM - Beverly Hills, 310/550-4000
Business Manager: Tom Hansen, Hansen, Jacobson & Teiler,
335 N. Maple Drive - Suite 270, Beverly Hills, CA 90210

AMOS & ANDREW   Columbia, 1993

ROBERT FUEST

b. 1927 - London, England
Home: Sunnyside Radford, Timsbury, Avon, England,
tel.: 076/171043

JUST LIKE A WOMAN   Monarch, 1966, British
AND SOON THE DARKNESS   Levitt-Pickman, 1970, British
WUTHERING HEIGHTS   American International, 1971, British
THE ABOMINABLE DR. PHIBES   American International,
1971, British
DR. PHIBES RISES AGAIN   American International, 1972, British
THE LAST DAYS OF MAN ON EARTH   *THE FINAL PROGRAMME*
New World, 1974, British
THE DEVIL'S RAIN   Bryanston, 1975, U.S.-Mexican
REVENGE OF THE STEPFORD WIVES (TF)   Edgar J. Scherick
Productions, 1980
APHRODITE   Atlantic Releasing Corporation, 1982, French

ATHOL FUGARD

b. June 11, 1932 - Middleburg, South Africa
Contact Information: Dr. Martin Botha, Human Sciences Research
Council, Group for Social Dynamics, Private Bag x41,
Pretoria 0001, South Africa, tel.: 012/202-2308

THE ROAD TO MECCA   co-director with Peter Goldsmid,
Distant Horizon/Videovision Enterprises, 1991, South African

KINJI FUKASAKU

b. 1930 - Ibaraki Prefecture, Japan
Contact: Nihon Eiga Kantoku Kyokai (Japan Film Directors
Association), La Fontenu Building -4th Floor, 23-2 Maruyama-cho,
Shibuya-ku, Tokyo, Japan, tel.: 3/3461-4411

VAGABOND DETECTIVE: TRAGEDY OF RED VALLEY   Toei,
1961, Japanese
VAGABOND DETECTIVE: BLACK WIND PASSED THROUGH THE
CAPE   Toei, 1961, Japanese
GANG VS. G MEN   Toei, 1962, Japanese
PROUD CHALLENGE   Toei, 1962, Japanese
WOLF, PIG AND HUMAN   Toei, 1964, Japanese
JAKOMAN AND IRON   Toei, 1964, Japanese
EXTORTION   Toei, 1966, Japanese
ROWDY RYU OF THE NORTH SEA   Toei, 1966, Japanese
KAISANSHIKI   Toei, 1967, Japanese
THE GREEN SLIME   *GAMMA 3 - BIG SPACE OPERATION*
MGM, 1968, Japanese
BLACKMAIL IS MY LIFE   Toei, 1968, Japanese
BLACK LIZARD   Cinevista, 1968, Japanese
GANG KAISANSHIKI   Toei, 1968, Japanese
HOUSE OF THE BLACK ROSES   Toei, 1969, Japanese
JAPANESE YAKUZA - THE BOSS   Toei, 1969, Japanese
BLOODY CREST   Toei, 1970, Japanese
TORA! TORA! TORA!   co-director with Richard Fleischer &
Toshio Masuda, 20th Century-Fox, 1970, U.S.-Japanese
FOREIGN YAKUZA FORCE   Toei, 1971, Japanese
UNDER THE FLAG OF THE RISING SUN   Toei, 1972, Japanese
HITOKIRIYOTA: PRESENT YAKUZA   Toei, 1972, Japanese
HITOKORIYOTA: MAD DOG THREE BROTHERS
Toei, 1972, Japanese
FIGHT WITHOUT JUSTICE   Toei, 1973, Japanese
FIGHT WITHOUT JUSTICE: HIROSHIMA DEATH FIGHT
Toei, 1973, Japanese
FIGHT WITHOUT JUSTICE: REPRESENTATIVE WAR
Toei, 1973, Japanese
FIGHT WITHOUT JUSTICE: TOP OPERATION
Toei, 1974, Japanese
FIGHT WITHOUT JUSTICE: FINAL CHAPTER
Toei, 1974, Japanese
NEW FIGHT WITHOUT JUSTICE   Toei, 1974, Japanese
PREFECTURE POLICE VS. YAKUZA   Toei, 1975, Japanese
ROOTS OF A BURGLARY   Toei, 1975, Japanese
NEW FIGHT WITHOUT JUSTICE: HEAD OF THE BOSS
Toei, 1975, Japanese
CEMETARY OF JUSTICE   Toei, 1975, Japanese
NEW FIGHT WITHOUT JUSTICE: THE BOSS' LAST DAY
Toei, 1976, Japanese
CRAZY BUS DUEL   Toei, 1976, Japanese
YAKUZA CEMETERY: KUCHINASHI FLOWER
Toei, 1976, Japanese
DOBERMAN DETECTIVE   Toei, 1977, Japanese
HOKURIKU REPRESENTATIVE WAR   Toei, 1977, Japanese
AKOU CASTLE   Toei, 1978, Japanese
MESSAGE FROM SPACE   United Artists, 1978, Japanese
YAGYU FAMILY CONSPIRACY   *THE SHOGUN'S SAMURAI*
Toei, 1978, Japanese
VIRUS   *DAY-OF THE RESURRECTION*   Haruki Kadokawa
Productions, 1980, Japanese
GATE OF THE YOUTH   Toei, 1981, Japanese
DEVIL RESUCITATION   Toei, 1981, Japanese
KAMATA MARCH   Haruki Kadokawa Productions, 1982, Japanese
DOUTONBORI RIVER   Shochiku, 1982, Japanese
LEGEND OF THE DOGS OF SATOMI   Haruki Kadokawa
Productions, 1983, Japanese
THEATRE OF LIFE   Toei, 1983, Japanese
SHANGHAI VANCE KING   Cine Saison/Asahi TV/Shochiku,
1984, Japanese
HOUSE ON FIRE   Takawa-Sato Productions, 1986, Japanese
SURE DEATH IV   Shochiku, 1987, Japanese
REVOLUTION OF THE FLOWERS   Toei, 1988, Japanese
SOMEDAY INTO THE GLARE   Light Vision/Shochiku,
1992, Japanese
THE TRIPLE CROSS   Shochiku, 1993, Japanese
CREST OF BETRAYAL   *CHUSHINGURA GAIDEN YOTSUYA
KAIDAN*   Shochiku, 1994, Japanese

JUN FUKUDA

b. 1923 - Manchuria
Contact: Nihon Eiga Kantoku Kyokai (Japan Film Directors
Association), La Fontenu Building -4th Floor, 23-2 Maruyama-cho,
Shibuya-ku, Tokyo, Japan, tel.: 3/3461-4411

HUMAN TELEGRAPH   Toho, 1960, Japanese
FANG OF THE GANGLAND   Toho, 1962, Japanese
BEST YOUNG MASTER IN JAPAN   Toho, 1962, Japanese
YOUNG MASTER IN HAWAII   Toho, 1963, Japanese
GODZILLA VS. THE SEA MONSTER   *GODZILLA, EBIRAH,
MOTHRA: BIG BATTLE IN THE SOUTH SEA*   Toho,
1966, Japanese
SON OF GODZILLA   Continental, 1967, Japanese
KANTO 55: BIG SPACE ADVENTURE   Toho, 1969, Japanese
GREAT JAPAN PICKPOCKET GROUP   Toho, 1969, Japanese
FRESHMAN YOUNG MASTER   Toho, 1969, Japanese
YOUNG MASTER IN NEW ZEALAND   Toho, 1969, Japanese
COMEDY: THIS IS THE WAY FOR MEN TO LIVE   Toho,
1970, Japanese
CAPITOL OF THE WILD BEAST   Toho, 1970, Japanese
WEST FRAUD, EAST SWINDLE   Toho, 1971, Japanese
GODZILLA VS. GAIGAN   Toho, 1972, Japanese
GODZILLA VS. MEGALON   Cinema Shares International,
1973, Japanese
ESUPAI   Toho, 1974, Japanese
GODZILLA VS. MECHA-GODZILLA   Toho, 1974, Japanese
WAR OF THE PLANETS   Toho, 1977, Japanese

LUCIO FULCI

b. June 17, 1927 - Rome, Italy
Home: via Taro 25, Rome, Italy, tel.: 06/844-2497

I LADRI   I.C.M. Fenix Film, 1959, Italian
I RAGAZZI DEL JUKE-BOX   Era Cinematografica, 1959, Italian
URLATORI ALLA SBARRA   Era Cinematografica, 1960, Italian
COLPO GOBBO ALL'ITALIANA   Mirafilm/Marcus Produzione
Cinematografica, 1962, Italian
I DUE DELLA LEGIONE   Ultra Film, 1962, Italian
LE MASSAGGIATRICI   Panda/Gallus Film, 1962, Italian-French
UNO STRANO TIPO   Giovanni Addessi, 1963, Italian
GLI IMBROGLIONI   Produzione D.S./Tecisa Film,
1963, Italian-Spanish

I MANIACI   Hesperia Cinematografica, 1964, Italian
I DUE EVASI DI SING SING   Mega/Turris, 1964, Italian
002 AGENTI SEGRETISSIMI   Mega Film, 1964, Italian
I DUE PERICOLI PUBBLICI   Aster Film, 1965, Italian
COME INGUAIAMMO L'ESERCITO   Five Film, 1965, Italian
002 OPERAZIONE LUNA   Ima/Agata, 1966, Italian-Spanish
I DUE PARA'   Ima/Agata, 1966, Italian-Spanish
COME SVALIGIAMMO LA BANCA D'ITALIA   Anteaos,
   1966, Italian
LE COLT CANTARONO LA MORTE E FU TEMPO DI MASSACRO
   R.F. Mega, 1966, Italian
COME RUBAMMO LA BOMBA ATOMICA   Five Film, 1967, Italian
IL LUNGO, IL CORTO, IL GATTO   Five Film/Fono Roma,
   1967, Italian
OPERAZIONE SAN PIETRO   Ultra Film, 1967, Italian
UNA SULL'ALTRA   Empire Film, 1969, Italian
BEATRICE CENCI   Filmena, 1969, Italian
UNA LUCERTOLA CON LA PELLE DI DONNA   Apollo Film,
   1971, Italian
ALL'ONOREVOLE PIACCIONO LE DONNE   New Film Productions,
   1972, Italian
NON SI SEVIZIA UN PAPERINO   Medusa, 1972, Italian
ZANNA BIANCA   Oceania Produzioni, 1973, Italian
IL RITORNO DI ZANNA BIANCA   Coralta Cinematografica,
   1974, Italian
IL CAVALIER COSTANTE NICOSIA DEMONIACO OVVERO
   DRACULA IN BRIANZA   Coralta Cinematografica, 1975, Italian
I QUATTRO DELL'APOCALISSE   Coralta Cinematografica,
   1976, Italian
LA PRETORA   Coralta Cinematografica, 1976, Italian
SETTE NOTE IN NERO   Cinecompany, 1977, Italian
SELLA D'ARGENTO   Rizzoli Film, 1978, Italian
ZOMBI 2   Variety Film, 1979, Italian
PAURA NELLA CITTA' DEI MORTI VIVENTI   Dania Film/Medusa
   Distribuzione/National Cinematografica, 1980, Italian
BLACK CAT   Selenia Cinematografica, 1980, Italian
...E TU VIVRAI NEL TERRORE! L'ALDILA'   Fulvia Film,
   1980, Italian
LUCA IL CONTRABBANDIERE   Primex Italiana/C.M.R.
   Cinematografica, 1980, Italian
QUELLA VILLA ACCANTO AL CIMITERO   Fulvia Film,
   1981, Italian
LO SQUARTATORE DI NEW YORK   Fulvia Film, 1981, Italian
MANHATTAN BABY   Fulvia Film, 1982, Italian
I GUERRIERI DELL'ANNO 2072   Regency Productions,
   1983, Italian
MURDEROCK, UCCIDE A PASSO DI DANZA   Scena Film,
   1984, Italian
DANGEROUS OBSESSION   IL MIELE DEL DIAVOLO
   Celebrity Home Entertainment, 1986, Italian
AENIGMA   A.M. Trading International, 1987, Italian
HOUSE OF DOOM (MS)   co-director with Umberto Lenzi,
   Reteitalia/Dania Film, 1989, Italian
UN GATTO NEL CERVELLO   Executive Cine TV, 1990, Italian
VOICES FROM BEYOND   Scena Group/Exclusive Cine TV,
   1991, Italian
LE PORTE DEL SILENZIO   Filmirage, 1992, Italian

FLEMING B. (TEX) FULLER

STRANDED   New Line Cinema, 1987
PREY OF THE CHAMELEON (CTF)   Saban Entertainment/Prism
   Entertainment, 1992

SAMUEL FULLER*

b. August 12, 1911 - Worcester, Massachusetts
Home: 61 Rue de Reuilly, Paris 75012, France, tel.: 43474163
Attorney: Charles Silverberg, 11766 Wilshire Blvd. - Suite 700,
   Los Angeles, CA 90025, 213/222-4500

I SHOT JESSE JAMES   Screen Guild, 1949
THE BARON OF ARIZONA   Lippert, 1950
THE STEEL HELMET   Lippert, 1951
FIXED BAYONETS!   20th Century-Fox, 1951
PARK ROW   United Artists, 1952
PICKUP ON SOUTH STREET   20th Century-Fox, 1953
HELL AND HIGH WATER   20th Century-Fox, 1954
HOUSE OF BAMBOO   20th Century-Fox, 1955
RUN OF THE ARROW   20th Century-Fox, 1957

FORTY GUNS   20th Century-Fox, 1957
CHINA GATE   20th Century-Fox, 1957
VERBOTEN!   Columbia, 1958
THE CRIMSON KIMONO   Columbia, 1959
UNDERWORLD U.S.A.   Columbia, 1961
MERRILL'S MARAUDERS   Warner Bros., 1962
SHOCK CORRIDOR   Allied Artists, 1963
THE NAKED KISS   Allied Artists, 1964
SHARK!   Heritage, 1970, U.S.-Mexican
DEAD PIGEON ON BEETHOVEN STREET   Emerson,
   1972, West German
THE BIG RED ONE   United Artists, 1980
WHITE DOG   Paramount, 1982
THIEVES AFTER DARK   Parafrance, 1983, French
STREET OF NO RETURN   Thunder Films International/
   Animatografo Producoes/FR3, 1989, French-Portuguese

ALLEN FUNT*

b. 1914 - New York, New York
Contact: Directors Guild of America - New York City, 212/851-3671

WHAT DO YOU SAY TO A NAKED WOMAN?   United Artists, 1970
MONEY TALKS   United Artists, 1971

SIDNEY J. FURIE*

b. February 28, 1933 - Toronto, Canada
Agent: ICM - Beverly Hills, 310/550-4000

A DANGEROUS AGE   Ajay, 1959, Canadian
A COOL SOUND FROM HELL   1959, Canadian
DR. BLOOD'S COFFIN   United Artists, 1960, British
THE SNAKE WOMAN   United Artists, 1960, British
DURING ONE NIGHT   NIGHT OF PASSION   Astor, 1961, British
THREE ON A SPREE   United Artists, 1961, British
WONDERFUL TO BE YOUNG!   THE YOUNG ONES
   Paramount, 1961, British
THE BOYS   Gala, 1962, British
THE LEATHER BOYS   Allied Artists, 1964, British
SWINGER'S PARADISE   Universal, 1965, British
THE IPCRESS FILE   Universal, 1965, British
THE APPALOOSA   Universal, 1966
THE NAKED RUNNER   Warner Bros., 1967, British
THE LAWYER   Paramount, 1970
LITTLE FAUSS AND BIG HALSY   Paramount, 1970
LADY SINGS THE BLUES   Paramount, 1972
HIT!   Paramount, 1973
SHEILA LEVINE IS DEAD AND LIVING IN NEW YORK
   Paramount, 1975
GABLE AND LOMBARD   Universal, 1976
THE BOYS IN COMPANY C   Columbia, 1978
THE ENTITY   20th Century-Fox, 1983
PURPLE HEARTS   The Ladd Company/Warner Bros., 1984
IRON EAGLE   TriStar, 1986
SUPERMAN IV: THE QUEST FOR PEACE   Warner Bros., 1987
IRON EAGLE II   TriStar, 1988, Canadian-Israeli
THE TAKING OF BEVERLY HILLS   Columbia, 1991
LADYBUGS   Paramount, 1992
IRON EAGLE IV   Norstar Entertainment, 1995, Canadian
HOLLOW POINT   Nu Image, 1995, Canadian

STEPHEN FURST

Agent: Stephanie Rogers & Associates - Los Angeles, 213/851-5155

NINJA KID   PM Entertainment Group, 1993
MAGIC KID 2   PM Entertainment Group, 1993

TIM FYWELL

Contact: British Film Commission, 70 Baker Street, London
   W1M 1DJ, England, tel.: 171/224-5000

A DARK ADAPTED EYE (TF)   BBC, 1994, British
CRACKER: TO BE A SOMEBODY (TF)   Granada TV/Arts &
   Entertainment Network, 1994, British

G

MITCHELL GABOURIE
BUYING TIME   MGM/UA, 1989

MICHAEL GABRIEL
Business: Walt Disney Animation, 500 S. Buena Vista Street,
   Burbank, CA 91521, 818/560-1000

THE RESCUERS DOWN UNDER (AF)   Buena Vista, 1990
POCAHONTAS (AF)   co-director with Eric Goldberg,
   Buena Vista, 1995

ALAN GADNEY
b. January 1, 1941 - Dayton, Ohio
Business: Festival Films, P.O. Box 10180, Glendale, CA 91209,
   818/222-8626

WEST TEXAS   American Media Productions/American
   Films Ltd., 1973
MOONCHILD   Filmmakers Ltd./American Films Ltd., 1974

GEORGE GAGE*
Home: P.O. Box 2526, Telluride, CO 81435

SKATEBOARD   Universal, 1978
FLESHBURN   Crown International, 1984

CLAUDE GAGNON*
b. 1949 - St.-Hyacinthe, Quebec, Canada
Home: 824 Des Colibris, Longueuil, Quebec J4G 2C1, Canada,
   514/442-4518
Business: Aska Film International Inc., 1600 De Lorimier Avenue -
   Suite 211, Montreal, Quebec H2K 3W5, Canada, 514/521-7103

ESSAI FILMIQUE SUR MUSIQUE JAPONAISE   1974, Japanese
GEININ   1976, Japanese
YUI TO HI   1977, Japanese
KEIKO   1978, Japanese
LAROSE, PIERROT ET LA LUCE   Cinephile, 1982, Canadian
VISAGE PALE   Yoshimura-Gagnon, 1985, Canadian-Japanese
THE KID BROTHER   Kinema Amerika/Yoshimura-Gagnon/Toho,
   1987, Canadian-Japanese-U.S.
THE PIANIST   Aska Film, 1991, Canadian

RENÉ GAINVILLE
Home: 69, rue de Rennes, 75006 Paris, France, tel.: 1/45-48-32-41
Attorney: Marvin B. Meyer, Rosenfeld, Meyer and Susman,
   9601 Wilshire Blvd., Beverly Hills, CA 90210, 310/272-4536

THE MAN FROM MYKONOS   Comptoir Francais du Film,
   1967, French
LE DEMONIAQUE   CCFC Distribution, 1968, French
THE YOUNG COUPLE   UGC/Transworld Attractions, 1969, French
ALISE AND CHLOÉ   Oceanic, 1970, French
LE COMPLOT   CIC, 1975, French
UN BON SAMARITAIN   FR3, 1976, French
L'ASSOCIÉ   Columbia, 1980, French

JOHN GALE
THE FIRING LINE   AIP, 1991, U.S.-Filipino, filmed in 1988

RICARDO JACQUES GALE
ALIEN INTRUDER   PM Entertainment Group, 1992

TIMOTHY GALFAS*
b. December 31, 1934 - Atlanta, Georgia
Agent: Preferred Artists - Encino, 818/990-0305

BOGARD   L-T Films, 1975
THE BLACK STREETFIGHTER   New Line Cinema, 1976
REVENGE FOR A RAPE (TF)   Albert S. Ruddy Productions, 1976
BLACK FIST   Worldwide, 1977
MANEATERS ARE LOOSE! (TF)   Mona Productions/Finnegan
   Associates, 1978
SUNNYSIDE   American International, 1979

JOHN ANDREW GALLAGHER
b. March 1, 1955 - New York, New York
Business: Lexington Productions, 305 Lexington Avenue - Suite 7B,
   New York, NY 10016, 212/689-0104
Attorney: Benton P. Levy, Levy & Hyman, 501 Madison Avenue,
   New York, NY 10022, 212/751-7555

BEACH HOUSE   New Line Cinema, 1982
THIS IS BARBARA BARONDESS: ONE LIFE IS NOT ENOUGH (FD)
   Theatre Lab Productions, 1985
SECRETS OF PRO WRESTLING (HVD)   Commtron, 1988
SECRETS OF PRO WRESTLING, VOLUME TWO (HVD)
   Diamond Entertainment, 1989
STREET HUNTER   21st Century Distribution, 1990
MEN LIE   Lexington Pictures, 1994

FRED GALLO
Agent: The Cooper Agency - Los Angeles, 310/277-8422

DEAD SPACE   Califilm, 1991
FORCED EXPOSURE   Concorde, 1991
DRACULA RISING   Concorde, 1992
PISTOL BLUES   Concorde, 1995

GEORGE GALLO*
Agent: ICM - Beverly Hills, 310/550-4000

29TH STREET   20th Century Fox, 1991
TRAPPED IN PARADISE   20th Century Fox, 1994

CHRISTOPHE GANS
Contact: Directors Guild of Canada, 225 Richmond Street, Toronto,
   Ontario M5V 1W2, Canada, 416/351-8200

H.P. LOVECRAFT'S NECRONOMICON   co-director with Shusuke
   Kaneko & Brian Yuzna, Necronomicon Productions, 1993,
   U.S.-French-Japanese
CRYING FREEMAN   Freeman Productions of Canada,
   1995, Canadian

GIANNA MARIA GARBELLI
Home: Ripa di Porta Ticinese 33, Milan, Italy, tel.: 02/58100660

PORTAGLI I MIEI SALUTI - AVANZI DI GALERA   M Film Produzioni/
   Ministero Turismo Spettacolo, 1993, Italian

JOSE LUIS GARCI
b. 1944 - Madrid, Spain
Agent: Paul Kohner, Inc. - Los Angeles, 310/550-1060

ASSIGNATURA PENDIENTE   1976, Spanish
SOLOS EN LA MADRUGADA   Jose Luis Tafur Productions,
   1977, Spanish
LAS VERDES PRADERAS   1979, Spanish
EL CRACK   Nickelodeon/Acuarius, 1981, Spanish
TO BEGIN AGAIN (A VOLVER EMPEAZAR)   20th Century-Fox
   International Classics, 1982, Spanish
EL CRACK 2   Lola Films/Nickelodeon, 1983, Spanish-Peruvian
SESION CONTINUA   Nickelodeon, 1984, Spanish
COURSE COMPLETED (ASIGNATURA APROBADA)   Nickelodeon,
   1987, Spanish
HISTORIAS DEL OTRO LADO (MS)   Radio Television Espanola,
   1991, Spanish
CANCION DE CUNA   Nickel Odeon Dos, 1994, Spanish

ANDY GARCIA
b. April 12, 1956 - Havana, Cuba
Agent: Paradigm - Los Angeles, 310/277-4400

CACHAO...COMO SI RITMO NO HAY DOS (FD)   Cineson
   Productions/Atlantico Films, 1993

CARLOS GARCIA AGRAZ
Contact: IMCINE, Tepic #40, P.B. Colonia Roma Sur, Mexico City,
   C.P. 06760, Mexico, tel.: 525/584-7283

MI QUERIDO TOM MIX   IMCINE, 1992, Mexican
AMOROSOS FANTASMAS   Televicine, 1994, Mexican

JOSE LUIS GARCIA AGRAZ
(John Agras / Joseph Louis Agraz)
b. November 1952 - Mexico City, Mexico
Contact: IMCINE, Tepic #40, P.B. Colonia Roma Sur, Mexico City,
   C.P. 06760, Mexico, tel.: 525/584-7283

NOCAUT   Azteca Films, 1984, Mexican
NOCHE DE CALIFAS   American General Films, 1986, Mexican
TREASURE OF THE MOON GODDESS   *DREAMS OF GOLD*
   Ascot Entertainment Group, 1987
DESIERTOS MARES   IMCINE/FFCC/Desiertos Films/
   Resonancia/Efeccine, 1994, Mexican
SALON MEXICO   Televicine Mexico, 1995, Mexican

LUIS GARCIA BERLANGA
b. July 12, 1921 - Valencia, Spain
Contact: Spanish Film Institute, San Marcos 40, Madrid 28004,
   Spain, tel.: 1/532-5089

ESA PAREJA FELIZ   co-director with Juan Antonio Bardem,
   1951, Spanish
BIENVENIDO SR. MARSHALL   1953, Spanish
NOVIO A LA VISTA   co-director with Juan Antonio Bardem,
   1953, Spanish
LAS GANCHEROS   1955, Spanish
CALABUCH   1956, Spanish
LOS JUEVES, MILAGRO   1957, Spanish
PLACIDO   1961, Spanish
LAS CUATRO VERDADES   co-director, 1962, Spanish
EL VERDUGO   1963, Spanish
LA BOUTIQUE   1967, Spanish
VIVAN LOS NOVIOS   1971, Spanish
TAMANO NATURAL   1973, Spanish
ESCOPETA NACIONAL   Jet Films, 1978, Spanish
PATRIMONIO NACIONAL   Jet Films/Incine, 1980, Spanish
NACIONAL III   Kaktus, 1983, Spanish
LA VAQUILLA   1985, Spanish
MOROS Y CRISTIANOS   Estela Films, 1987, Spanish
TODOS A LA CARCEL   Sogetel/Central de Producciones
   Audiovisuales/Antea Films, 1993, Spanish

HERB GARDNER*
Agent: The Lantz Office - New York City, 212/586-0200

THE GOODBYE PEOPLE   Embassy, 1984
I'M NOT RAPPAPORT   Gramercy Pictures, 1995

JACK GARFEIN*
b. July 2, 1930 - Mukacevo, Czechoslovakia
Home: 143 Rue St. Martin, Paris 75004, France, tel.: 331/40299744

THE STRANGE ONE   *END AS A MAN*   Columbia, 1957
SOMETHING WILD   United Artists, 1961

PATRICK GARLAND
b. 1936 - London, England
Contact: British Film Commission, 70 Baker Street, London
   W1M 1DJ, England, tel.: 171/224-5000

THE SNOW GOOSE (TF)   NBC, 1971
A DOLL'S HOUSE   Paramount, 1973, Canadian-U.S.
A ROOM OF ONE'S OWN (TF)   Oyster Ltd./Thames TV,
   1990, British

LINDA GARMON
Contact: Writers Guild of America, East - New York City,
   212/767-7800

NOVA: SECRET OF THE WILD CHILD   *SECRET OF THE
WILD CHILD* (TD)   Nova Productions/WGBH-Boston/BBC/NDR
   International Hamburg/Nederlandse Omroepprogramma Stichting,
   1994, U.S.-British-German-Dutch

TONY GARNETT
b. England
Business: Island World Productions Limited, 12-14 Argyll Street,
   London W1V 1AB, England, tel.: 171/734-3536

PROSTITUTE   Mainline Films, 1979, British
DEEP IN THE HEART   *HANDGUN*   Warner Bros., 1981

LILA GARRETT*
b. November 21, 1925 - New York, New York
Agent: Barry Perelman Agency - Los Angeles, 310/274-5999

TERRACES (TF)   Charles Fries Productions/Worldvision, 1977
WHO GETS THE FRIENDS? (TF)   CBS Entertainment, 1988
BRIDESMAIDS (TF)   Motown Productions/Qintex Entertainment/
   Deaune Productions, 1989

MICK GARRIS*
Agent: CAA - Beverly Hills, 310/288-4545

CRITTERS 2   New Line Cinema, 1988
PSYCHO IV: THE BEGINNING (CTF)   MTE/Showtime, 1990
STEPHEN KING'S SLEEPWALKERS   *SLEEPWALKERS*
   Columbia, 1992
STEPHEN KING'S THE STAND · *THE STAND* (MS)   Laurel
   Entertainment/Greengrass Productions, 1994

JEROME GARY*
Address: 2275 N. Chislehurst, Los Angeles, CA 90027,
   213/668-2362
Agent: William Morris Agency - Beverly Hills, 310/859-4000

STRIPPER (FD)   20th Century Fox, 1985
TRAXX   DEG, 1988

TONY GATLIF
Agent: ICM France - Paris, tel.: 1/723-7860
Contact: French Film Office, 745 Fifth Avenue, New York,
   NY 10151, 212/832-8860

LATCHO DROM (SAFE JOURNEY)   Shadow Distribution,
   1993, French

NILS GAUP
Contact: Norwegian Film Institute, Grev Wedels Plass 1,
   N-0161 Oslo 1, Norway, tel.: 2/42-87-40

PATHFINDER   IFEX Film, 1988, Norwegian
SHIPWRECKED   *HAKON HAKONSEN*   Buena Vista, 1990,
   Norwegian-Swedish-U.S.
HEAD ABOVE WATER   Filmkameratene/Svensk Filmindustri,
   1994, Norwegian-Swedish
THE NORTH STAR   AFCL Productions/Nordic Screen Development/
   Federal Films/Urania/New Regency Films, 1995,
   British-Norwegian-French

ELEANOR GAVER
Personal Manager: Creative Alliance Management - Los Angeles,
   213/962-6090

SLIPPING INTO DARKNESS   MCEG, 1990

VICTOR MANUEL GAVIRIA
b. 1955 - Colombia
Address: Calle 32E No., #83B-120, Medellin, Colombia

NIGHT DWELLERS   1985, Colombian
THE OLD GUARD   1985, Colombian
THE MUSICIANS   1985, Colombian
RODRIGO D. - NO FUTURE   Kino International, 1990, Colombian
DON ISA   Igeldo Zine Produkzioak/Fotoclub 76, 1993,
   Colombian-Spanish

COSTA - GAVRAS*
(Konstantinos Gavras)
Home: 244 Rue St. Jacques, Paris 75005, France
Agent: CAA - Beverly Hills, 310/288-4545

THE SLEEPING CAR MURDERS   7 Arts, 1966, French
SHOCK TROOPS   *UN HOMME DE TROP*   United Artists,
   1968, French-Italian
Z ★   Cinema 5, 1969, French-Algerian
THE CONFESSION   Paramount, 1970, French
STATE OF SIEGE   Cinema 5, 1973, French
SPECIAL SECTION   Universal, 1975, French-Italian-West German
CLAIR DE FEMME   Atlantic Releasing Corporation, 1979,
   French-Italian-West German
MISSING   Universal, 1982
HANNA K.   Universal Classics, 1983, French
CONSEIL DE FAMILLE   European Classics, 1986, French
BETRAYED   MGM/UA, 1988
MUSIC BOX   TriStar, 1989
CONTRE L'OUBLI   co-director, Les Films du Paradoxe/Amnesty
   International/PRV, 1992, French
LA PETITE APOCALYPSE   K.G. Productions/Nickelodeon Films/
   Heritage Films, 1993, French-Italian-Polish

JOE GAYTON
Agent: ICM - Beverly Hills, 310/550-4000

WARM SUMMER RAIN   Cinema Corporation of America, 1989
THE OUTPOST   Outpost Productions, 1995

ARMAND GAZARIAN
BADLANDERS   21st Century Distribution, 1991
VIDEO PIRATES FROM MARS   Brie Ventures, 1991
PORTRAIT OF A FRIEND   Gold West Friends, 1994

GYULA GAZDAG
b. 1947 - Budapest, Hungary
Agent: Paul Kohner, Inc. - Los Angeles, 310/550-1060

THE LONG DISTANCE RUNNER (FD)   Balazs Bela Studio,
   1968, Hungarian
THE WHISTLING COBBLESTONE   Mafilm Studio,
   1971, Hungarian
THE RESOLUTION (FD)   co-director with Judit Ember,
   Bela Balazs Studio, 1972, Hungarian
SINGING ON THE TREADMILL   Mafilm-Hunnia Studio,
   1974, Hungarian
SWAP   Objektiv Studio, 1977, Hungarian
LOST ILLUSIONS   Objektiv Studio, 1982, Hungarian
THE BANQUET (TF)   Hungarian TV/Mafilm-Objektiv Studio,
   1982, Hungarian
PACKAGE TOUR (FD)   New Yorker, 1984, Hungarian
A HUNGARIAN FAIRY TALE   Objektiv Studio, 1988, Hungarian
STAND OFF   Objektiv Studio/Mafilm, 1989, Hungarian
HUNGARIAN CHRONICLES (FD)   La Sept, 1991, French

BEN GAZZARA*
(Biagio Anthony Gazzara)
b. August 28, 1930 - New York, New York
Business Manager: Jay Julien, 1501 Broadway, New York, NY
   10036, 212/221-7575

BEYOND THE OCEAN   Scena International/Reteitalia, 1990, Italian

VANYOSKA GEE
b. 1948
Business: Mountain Top Films, 48 East Broadway - Suite 3,
   New York, NY 10002, 212/741-1814

KRIK? KRAK! TALES OF A NIGHTMARE   co-director with Jac Avila,
   Mountain Top Films, 1988, Haitian-U.S.-Canadian

DAVID GELFAND
DOTTIE (TF)   Dottie Films Inc., 1987

DAN GELLER
FROSH: NINE MONTHS IN A FRESHMAN DORM (FD)
   co-director with Dana Goldfine, Landmark Releasing, 1994

ALEX GELMAN
INFINITY   Alternative Distribution System, 1991

JOZSEF GEMES
Contact: Hungarian Film Institute, Budakeszi u 51 B, 1012 Budapest,
   Hungary, tel.: 176-1018 or 176-1322

HEROIC TIMES (AF)   1983, Hungarian
THE PRINCESS AND THE GOBLIN (AF)   Hemdale, 1994,
   British-Hungarian

JIM GEORGE
ROVER DANGERFIELD (AF)   co-director with Bob Seeley,
   Warner Bros., 1991

SCREAMING MAD GEORGE
(Joji Tani)
b. Osaka, Japan
Business: Screaming Mad George Inc., 11750 Roscoe Blvd.,
   Sun Valley, CA 91532, 818/767-1631

THE GUYVER   co-director with Steve Wang, Imperial Entertainment,
   1991, U.S.-Japanese-Taiwanese-South Korean

ALEX GEORGES
CULTIVATING CHARLIE   GMS Productions, 1994

FRED GERBER*
Contact: Directors Guild of America - Los Angeles, 213/851-3671

DUE SOUTH (TF)   Alliance Communications/CTV TV Network,
   1994, Canadian
RENT-A-KID   Initial Ent. Group, 1995

HAILE GERIMA
Business: Howard University, 2400 Sixth Street NW,
   Washington, D.C. 20059, 202/806-6100

HARVEST: 3000 YEARS   1976
ASHES AND DIAMONDS   1982
SANKOFA   Mypheduh Films, 1993,
   U.S.-German-Ghanian-Burkina Faso-British

CHRIS GEROLMO
Agent: CAA - Beverly Hills, 310/288-4545

CITIZEN X (CTF)   Asylum Films/Citadel Ent./HBO Pictures, 1995

THEODORE GERSHUNY
Agent: Mitch Kaplan, Kaplan-Stahler - Beverly Hills, 213/653-4483

LOVE, DEATH   1973
SILENT NIGHT, BLOODY NIGHT   Cannon, 1974
SUGAR COOKIES   Troma, 1977
DEATHHOUSE   Cannon, 1981

NICOLAS GESSNER
b. August 17, 1931 - Budapest, Hungary
Business: Ypsilon Films S.A., 39 Quai de Grenelle, 75015 Paris, France, tel.: 1/45-77-62-25

DER GEFANGENE DER BOTSCHAFT (TF)   Condor Productions, 1963, West German/Swiss
DIAMONDS ARE BRITTLE   *UN MILLIARD DANS UN BILLARD*   20th Century-Fox, 1965, French
THE PEKING BLONDE   Raymond Danon Productions, 1967, French
TWELVE PLUS ONE   Sagittarius Productions, 1969, French
SOMEONE BEHIND THE DOOR   GSF, 1971, French
SAY GOODNIGHT TO GRANDMA (TF)   WDR, 1975, West German
THE LITTLE GIRL WHO LIVES DOWN THE LANE   American International, 1976, U.S.-Canadian-French
IT RAINED ALL NIGHT THE DAY I LEFT   Caneuram/Israfilm/COFCI, 1979, Canadian-Israeli-French
HERR HERR, THE CHOCOLATE MILLIONS (TF)   NDR/Condor Productions/Telefrance Paris, 1981, West German-Swiss-French
MACHO (TF)   Hamster Productions/FR3/HTV, 1983, French-British
LE TUEUR TRISTE (TF)   FR3/Taurus-Beta, 1985, French-West German
DAS ANDERE LEBEN (TF)   WDR, 1987, West German
QUICKER THAN THE EYE   Condor Productions/Crocodile Productions, 1989, Swiss-French
TENNESSEE NIGHTS   Condor Productions/Allianz Films/Intermedia/WDR, 1989, U.S.-Swiss
VISAGES SUISSES (FD)   co-director, Video Films, 1991, Swiss
TWIST OF FATE   Condor Productions/Nelson Entertainment, 1991

TULSHI GHIMIRAY
b. Nepal

BANSURI   Sai Nath Productions, 1979, Nepalese
JAGWAL   1982, Nepalese
KUSHUME RUMAL   1984, Nepalese
LAHUREY   1989, Nepalese
ANNYAYA   Bishwa Productions, 1990, Nepalese
KOSHELI   Ajambari Productions, 1991, Nepalese

CONSTANTINE GIANNARIS
Contact: British Film Commission, 70 Baker Street, London W1M 1DJ, England, tel.: 171/224-5000

3 STEPS TO HEAVEN   Miramax Films, 1995, British

JOE GIANNONE
MADMAN   Jensen Farley Pictures, 1982

RODNEY GIBBONS
Contact: Directors Guild of Canada, 225 Richmond Street, Toronto, Ontario M5V 1W2, Canada, 416/351-8200

THE NEIGHBOR   Image Organization, 1993, Canadian-U.S.

BRIAN GIBSON*
b. September 22, 1944 - Reading, England
Address: 6950 Oporto Drive, Los Angeles, CA 90068, 213/969-0167
Agent: ICM - Beverly Hills, 310/550-4000

JOEY (TF)   BBC, 1975, British
WHERE ADAM STOOD (TF)   BBC, 1976, British
BILLION DOLLAR BUBBLE (TF)   BBC, 1976, British
DINNER AT THE SPORTING CLUB (TF)   BBC, 1978, British
BLUE REMEMBERED HILLS (TF)   BBC, 1980, British
BREAKING GLASS   Paramount, 1980, British
POLTERGEIST II: THE OTHER SIDE   MGM/UA, 1986
THE MURDERERS AMONG US: THE SIMON WIESENTHAL STORY (CTF)   HBO Pictures/Robert Cooper Productions/TVS Films/Citadel Entertainment/Hungarian TV, 1989, U.S.-British-Hungarian
DRUG WARS: THE CAMARENA STORY (MS)   ZZY Inc. Productions/World International Network, 1990

THE JOSEPHINE BAKER STORY (CTF) ☆☆   HBO Pictures/RHI Entertainment/Anglia TV, 1991, U.S.-British
WHAT'S LOVE GOT TO DO WITH IT   *TINA: WHAT'S LOVE GOT TO DO WITH IT*   Buena Vista, 1993
THE JUROR   Columbia, 1995

MEL GIBSON*
b. January 3, 1956 - Peekskill, New York
Business: Icon Productions, Warner Bros., 4000 Warner Blvd., Building 139 - Suite 17 Burbank, CA 91522, 818/954-2960

THE MAN WITHOUT A FACE   Warner Bros., 1993
BRAVEHEART   Paramount, 1995, U.S.-British

GREGORY GIERAS
THE TIN SOLDIER (CTF)   co-director with Jon Voight, Crystal Sky Communications/Showtime, 1995

MARIA GIESE
Contact: British Film Commission, 70 Baker Street, London W1M 1DJ, England, tel.: 171/224-5000

WHEN SATURDAY COMES   Capitol Films/Daly-Lampert-Teper, 1995, British

JONATHAN GIFT
Contact: 818/985-5231
Agent: Production Values Management - Los Angeles, 213/461-0148

VALHALLA   Nova Plus, 1992

BRIAN GILBERT*
Agent: CAA - Beverly Hills, 310/288-4545 or: Peters Fraser & Dunlop - London, tel.: 171/344-1000

SHARMA AND BEYOND   Cinecom, 1984, British, originally made for television
FRENCH LESSON   *THE FROG PRINCE*   Warner Bros., 1984, British
VICE VERSA   Columbia, 1988
NOT WITHOUT MY DAUGHTER   MGM-Pathe Communications, 1991
TOM & VIV   Miramax Films, 1994, British-U.S.

LEWIS GILBERT*
b. March 6, 1920 - London, England
Attorney: Norman Tyre, Gang, Tyre, Ramer & Brown, 6400 Sunset Blvd., Los Angeles, CA 90028, 213/463-4863

THE LITTLE BALLERINA   General Film Distributors, 1947, British
ONCE A SINNER   Butcher, 1950, British
WALL OF DEATH   *THERE IS ANOTHER SIDE*   Realart, 1951, British
THE SCARLET THREAD   Butcher, 1951, British
HUNDRED HOUR HUNT   *EMERGENCY CALL*   Greshler, 1952, British
TIME GENTLEMEN PLEASE!   Eros, 1952, British
THE SLASHER   *COSH BOY*   Lippert, 1953, British
JOHNNY ON THE RUN   co-director with Vernon Harris, Associated British Film Distributors/Children's Film Foundation, 1953, British
BREAK TO FREEDOM   *ALBERT R.N.*   United Artists, 1953, British
THE GOOD DIE YOUNG   United Artists, 1954, British
THE SEA SHALL NOT HAVE THEM   United Artists, 1954, British
CAST A DARK SHADOW   DCA, 1955, British
REACH FOR THE SKY   Rank, 1956, British
PARADISE LAGOON   *THE ADMIRABLE CRICHTON*   Columbia, 1957, British
CARVE HER NAME WITH PRIDE   Lopert, 1958, British
A CRY FROM THE STREETS   Tudor, 1959, British
FERRY TO HONG KONG   20th Century-Fox, 1959, British
SINK THE BISMARCK!   20th Century-Fox, 1960, British
SKYWATCH   *LIGHT UP THE SKY*   Continental, 1960, British
LOSS OF INNOCENCE   *THE GREENGAGE SUMMER*   Columbia, 1961, British

DAMN THE DEFIANT!   *H.M.S. DEFIANT*   Columbia, 1962, British
THE SEVENTH DAWN   United Artists, 1964, U.S.-British
ALFIE   Paramount, 1966, British
YOU ONLY LIVE TWICE   United Artists, 1967, British
THE ADVENTURERS   Paramount, 1970
FRIENDS   Paramount, 1971, British-French
PAUL AND MICHELLE   Paramount, 1974, British-French
OPERATION DAYBREAK   Warner Bros., 1975, British
SEVEN NIGHTS IN JAPAN   EMI, 1976, British-French
THE SPY WHO LOVED ME   United Artists, 1977, British-U.S.
MOONRAKER   United Artists, 1979, British-French
EDUCATING RITA   Columbia, 1983, British
NOT QUITE PARADISE   *NOT QUITE JERUSALEM*
     New World, 1985, British
SHIRLEY VALENTINE   Paramount, 1989, British
STEPPING OUT   Paramount, 1991, U.S.-British
HAUNTED   Lumiere Pictures, 1995, British

DAVID GILER*
Agent: ICM - Beverly Hills, 310/550-4000

THE BLACK BIRD   Columbia, 1975

STUART GILLARD*
b. 1946 - Coronation, Alberta, Canada
Agent: ICM - Beverly Hills, 310/550-4000 or: Lynn Kinney,
     Credentials, 387 Bloor Street East, Toronto, Ontario,
     Canada, 416/926-1507
Personal Manager: Jon Brown, The Brown Group - Beverly Hills,
     310/247-2755

PARADISE   Avco Embassy, 1982, Canadian
THE RETURN OF THE SHAGGY DOG (TF)
     Walt Disney TV, 1987
A MAN CALLED SARGE   Cannon, 1990
THE PATHFINDERS   HBW Film Productions, 1991, Canadian
TEENAGE MUTANT NINJA TURTLES III   New Line Cinema, 1993
THE OUTER LIMITS: SANDKINGS (CTF)   Trilogy Entertainment
     Group/Atlantis Films, 1995, U.S.-Canadian

TERRY GILLIAM*
b. November 22, 1940 - Minneapolis, Minnesota
Address: 51 South Hill Park, London NW3, England
Business: Prominent Features Ltd., 68A Delancey Street, London
     NW1 7RY, England, tel.: 171/284-0242
Agent: CAA - Beverly Hills, 310/288-4545

MONTY PYTHON AND THE HOLY GRAIL   co-director with
     Terry Jones, Cinema 5, 1974, British
JABBERWOCKY   Cinema 5, 1977, British
TIME BANDITS   Avco Embassy, 1981, British
BRAZIL   Universal, 1985, British
THE ADVENTURES OF BARON MUNCHAUSEN
     Columbia, 1989, British
THE FISHER KING   TriStar, 1991
THE TWELVE MONKEYS   Universal, 1995

VERN GILLUM*
Agent: Premiere Artists Agency - Los Angeles, 310/271-1414

BROTHERHOOD OF THE GUN (TF)   Charles E. Sellier
     Productions/Robert Ward Productions, 1991
THEY'VE TAKEN OUR CHILDREN: THE CHOWCHIILLA
     KIDNAPPING (TF)   Ron Gilbert Associates/Joel Fields
     Productions/Leonard Hill Films, 1993

FRANK D. GILROY*
b. October 13, 1925 - New York, New York
Agent: William Morris Agency - New York City, 212/586-5100

DESPERATE CHARACTERS   ITC, 1971
JOHN O'HARA'S GIBBSVILLE (TF)   Columbia TV, 1975
THE TURNING POINT OF JIM MALLOY (TF)   David Gerber
     Company/Columbia TV, 1975
FROM NOON TILL THREE   United Artists, 1976

ONCE IN PARIS...   Atlantic Releasing Corporation, 1978
REX STOUT'S NERO WOLFE (TF)   Emmett Lavery, Jr.
     Productions/Paramount TV, 1979
THE GIG   Castle Hill Productions, 1985
THE LUCKIEST MAN IN THE WORLD   Co-Star
     Entertainment, 1989

MILTON MOSES GINSBERG
COMING APART   Kaleidoscope, 1969
THE WEREWOLF OF WASHINGTON   Diplomat, 1973

ROBERT GINTY*
b. November 14, 1948 - New York, New York
Agent: ICM - Beverly Hills, 310/550-4000

THE BOUNTY HUNTER   A.I.P., 1989
VIETNAM, TEXAS   Vision/Columbia, 1990
SHOOTFIGHTER   A.N.A. Productions, 1992
WOMAN OF DESIRE   Nu Image, 1993

MARITA GIOVANNI
BAR GIRLS   Orion, 1994

BOB GIRALDI*
Business: Giraldi Suarez Productions, 581 Sixth Avenue, New York,
     NY 10011, 212/691-9200

NATIONAL LAMPOON'S MOVIE MADNESS   co-director with
     Henry Jaglom, United Artists, 1982
CLUB MED (TF)   Lorimar Productions, 1986
HIDING OUT   DEG, 1987

BERNARD GIRARD
b. 1930

THE GREEN-EYED BLONDE   Warner Bros., 1957
RIDE OUT FOR REVENGE   United Artists, 1958
AS YOUNG AS WE ARE   Paramount, 1958
THE PARTY CRASHERS   Paramount, 1958
A PUBLIC AFFAIR   Parade, 1962
DEAD HEAT ON A MERRY-GO-ROUND   Paramount, 1966
MAD ROOM   Columbia, 1969
THE HAPPINESS CAGE   *THE MIND SNATCHERS*
     Cinerama Releasing Corporation, 1972
GONE WITH THE WEST   International Cinefilm, 1975

FRANCOIS GIRARD
b. Quebec, Canada
Agent; Becsey/Wisdom/Kalajian - Los Angeles, 310/550-0535

LE DORTOIR (TPF)   Rhombus/CBC, 1991, Canadian
CARGO   Velvet Camera/Cleo 24, 1992, Canadian-French
THIRTY TWO SHORT FILMS ABOUT GLENN GOULD
     The Samuel Goldwyn Company, 1993,
     Canadian-Portuguese-Swedish

JEAN GIRAUD
(See MOEBIUS)

FRANCIS GIROD
Agent: ICM France - Paris, tel.: 1/723-7860
Contact: French Film Office, 745 Fifth Avenue, New York,
     NY 10151, 212/832-8860

L'ELEGANT CRIMINEL   RKO Pictures Distribution, 1992, French
CONTRE L'OUBLI   co-director, Les Films du Paradoxe/Amnesty
     International/PRV, 1992, French
DELIT MINEUR   Oliane Productions/FR1 Films Productions/Canal
     Plus/Investimage 4/Byimages 2/CNC, 1994, French

AMOS GITAI

b. 1950 - Haifa, Israel
Contact: Israel Film Centre, Ministry of Industry & Trade,
30 Agron Street, P.O. Box 299, 94190 Jerusalem, Israel,
tel.: 972/210433 or 210297 or: French Film Office,
745 Fifth Avenue, New York, NY 10151, 212/832-8860

FIELD DIARY (FD)   1982, Israeli
PINEAPPLE (TD)   1983, French
LABOUR FOR SALE *BANGKOK BAHRAIN* (TD)   Amos Gitai
Production/TF1/Channel 4, 1984, Israeli-French-British
ESTHER   1986, Israeli
BRAND NEW DAY (FD)   1987, Israeli
BERLIN JERUSALEM   Agav Films/Channel 4/La Sept/Nova
Films/RAI-2/Orthel Films/NOS/Transfax/La Maison de Culture
du Havre/Hubert Bals Fund/CNC, 1989, French-Israeli
WADI: 1981-1991   1991, Israeli
GOLEM, L'ESPIRIT DE L'EXIL   Agav Films/Allarts/Nova
Films/Friedlander Film/RAI/Groupe TSF/Channel 4/
Canal Plus/CNC/Eurimages Fund, 1992,
French-Dutch-Italian-German-Italian-British
PETRIFIED GARDEN   Agav Films, 1993, French
DANS LA VALLEE DU WUPPER (FD)   Agav Films/La Sept-Arte/
Channel 4/RAI-3/IPS, 1993, French-British
NEL NOME DEL DUCE (FD)   IPS/Agav Films/Channel 4/
La Sept-Arte/RAI-3/Kershet Broadcasting/CNC, 1994,
Italian-French-Israeli

DAVID GLADWELL

b. April 2, 1935 - Gloucester, England
Address: 8 Caldervale Road, London SW4 9LZ, England,
tel.: 171/622-6843

REQUIEM FOR A VILLAGE · BFI Production Board, 1977, British
MEMOIRS OF A SURVIVOR   EMI, 1982, British
O ALIEN! (TF)   1984, British
EARTHSTARS (TF)   1985, British

PAUL MICHAEL GLASER*

b. Cambridge, Massachusetts
Agent: ICM - Los Angeles, 213/550-4000

AMAZONS (TF)   ABC Circle Films, 1984
BAND OF THE HAND   TriStar, 1986
THE RUNNING MAN   TriStar, 1987
THE CUTTING EDGE   MGM-Pathe Communications, 1992
THE AIR UP THERE   Buena Vista, 1994

ARNOLD GLASSMAN

VISIONS OF LIGHT: THE ART OF CINEMATOGRAPHY (FD)
co-director with Todd McCarthy, Kino International,
1992, U.S.-Japanese

LESLI LINKA GLATTER*

Agent: UTA - Beverly Hills, 310/273-6700
Personal Manager: Addis-Wechsler & Associates - Los Angeles,
213/954-9000

INTO THE HOMELAND (CTF)   HBO Pictures/Capistrano
Pictures, 1987
STATE OF EMERGENCY (CTF)   Chestnut Hill Productions/HBO
Showcase, 1994
THE GASLIGHT ADDITION   New Line Cinema, 1995

RICHARD GLATZER

Agent: UTA - Beverly Hills, 310/273-6700

GRIEF   Strand Releasing, 1993

MICHIE GLEASON

Agent: ICM - Beverly Hills, 310/550-4000

BROKEN ENGLISH   Lorimar, 1981
SUMMER HEAT   Atlantic Releasing Corporation, 1987

JOHN GLEN*

b. May 15, 1932 - Sunbury on Thames, England
Address: 9A Barkston Gardens, London SW5, England
Agent: Spyros Skouras, The Skouras Agency - Santa Monica,
310/395-9550

FOR YOUR EYES ONLY   United Artists, 1981, British
OCTOPUSSY   MGM/UA, 1983, British
A VIEW TO A KILL   MGM/UA, 1985, British
THE LIVING DAYLIGHTS   MGM/UA, 1987, British
LICENCE TO KILL   MGM/UA, 1989, British
ACES: IRON EAGLE III   New Line Cinema, 1992
CHRISTOPHER COLUMBUS: THE DISCOVERY   Warner Bros.,
1992, British-Spanish

JOHN GLENISTER

Agent: Peter Murphy, Curtis Brown - London, tel.: 171/872-0331

ORWELL ON JURA (TF)   BBC, 1983, British
GOOD AS GOLD (TF)   BBC, 1985, British
BLUNT (TF)   BBC, 1986, British
AFTER THE WAR (TF)   Granada TV, 1987, British
SOMETIME IN AUGUST (TF)   BBC Scotland, 1988, Scottish
STAY LUCKY (TF)   Yorkshire TV, 1990, British
MISTERIOSO (TF)   BBC Scotland, 1990, British
MAIGRET SETS A TRAP (TF)   Granada TV/WGBH-Boston,
1992, British-U.S.

PIERRE WILLIAM GLENN

Home: 11, rue Cesar Frank, 9440 Santeny, France,
tel.: 42-21-12-07
Contact: French Film Office, 745 Fifth Avenue, New York,
NY 10151, 212/832-8860

TERMINUS *END OF THE LINE*   Hemdale, 1986,
French-West German
23 HEURES 58   MW Productions, 1993, French

PETER GLENVILLE*

b. October 28, 1913 - London, England
Business Manager: Elliot J. Lefkowitz, 641 Lexington Avenue,
New York, NY 10022, 212/758-0860

THE PRISONER   Columbia, 1955, British
ME AND THE COLONEL   Columbia, 1958
SUMMER AND SMOKE   Paramount, 1961
TERM OF TRIAL   Warner Bros., 1963, British
BECKET ★   Paramount, 1964, British
HOTEL PARADISO   MGM, 1966, British
THE COMEDIANS   MGM, 1967, British

JAMES GLICKENHAUS

b. July 24, 1950 - New York, New York
Business: SGE Entertainment, 12001 Ventura Place - 4th Floor,
Studio City, CA 91604, 818/766-8500 or: 1619 Broadway,
New York, NY 10019, 212/265-1150

THE ASTROLOGER   Interstar, 1977
THE EXTERMINATOR   Avco Embassy, 1980
THE SOLDIER   Embassy, 1982
THE PROTECTOR   Warner Bros., 1985, U.S.-Hong Kong
SHAKEDOWN   Universal, 1988
McBAIN   Shapiro Glickenhaus Entertainment, 1991
SLAUGHTER OF THE INNOCENTS   Shapiro Glickenhaus
Entertainment, 1993
TIMEMASTER   SGE Entertainment, 1994

ARNE GLIMCHER*

(Arnold Glimcher)
Agent: CAA - Beverly Hills, 310/288-4545

THE MAMBO KINGS   Warner Bros., 1992
JUST CAUSE   Warner Bros., 1995

KURT GLOOR

b. November 8, 1942 - Zurich, Switzerland
Business: Filmproduktion AG, Spiegelgasse 27, CH-8001 Zurich,
   Switzerland, tel.: 47-87-66

DIE PLOTZLICHE EINSAMKEIT DES KONRAD STEINER
   Kurt Gloor Filmproduktion, 1975, Swiss
LEHMANNS LETZTER (TF)   Swiss TV, 1977, Swiss
DER CHINESE (TF)   Bavaria Filmproduktion Munich,
   1978, West German
DER ERFINDER   Kurt Gloor Filmproduktion, 1980, Swiss
MANN OHNE GEDACHTNIS   Kurt Gloor Filmproduktion,
   1984, Swiss
VISAGES SUISSES (FD)   co-director, Video Films, 1991, Swiss

VADIM GLOWNA

Contact: Federal Union of Film and Television Directors in Germany,
   Adelheidstrasse 7, 8000 Munich 40, Germany, tel.: 089/271-6380

DESPERADO CITY   New Line Cinema, 1981, West German
DEVIL'S PARADISE   Atossa/ZDF, 1987, West German
DER BROCKEN   Ecco Film/NDR/DFF, 1992, German

JEAN-LUC GODARD

b. December 3, 1930 - Paris, France
Business: J.L.G. Films, 99, avenue du Roule, 92200 Neuilly,
   France, tel.: 1/47-47-10-40
Contact: French Film Office, 745 Fifth Avenue, New York,
   NY 10151, 212/832-8860

BREATHLESS   *A BOUT DE SOUFFLE*   Films Around the World,
   1960, French
A WOMAN IS A WOMAN   Pathe Contemporary, 1961, French
SEVEN CAPITAL SINS   co-director with Roger Vadim,
   Sylvaine Dhomme, Edouard Molinaro, Philippe De Broca,
   Claude Chabrol, Jacques Demy, Marie-Jose Nat,
   Dominique Paturel, Jean-Marc Tennberg & Perrette Pradier,
   Embassy, 1962, French-Italian
MY LIFE TO LIVE   Pathe Contemporary, 1962, French
ROGOPAG   co-director, 1962, French
LE PETIT SOLDAT   West End, 1963, French
LES CARABINIERS   West End, 1963, French
CONTEMPT   *LE MEPRIS*   Embassy, 1964, French-Italian
LES PLUS BELLES ESCROQUERIES DU MONDE   co-director,
   1964, French-Italian-Japanese
BAND OF OUTSIDERS   Royal Films International, 1964, French
THE MARRIED WOMAN   Royal Films International, 1964, French
SIX IN PARIS   New Yorker, co-director, French
ALPHAVILLE   Pathe Contemporary, 1965, French
PIERROT LE FOU   Pathe Contemporary, 1965, French
MASCULINE FEMININE   Royal Films International,
   1966, French-Swedish
MADE IN U.S.A.   Pathe Contemporary, 1966, French
TWO OR THREE THINGS I KNOW ABOUT HER
   New Line Cinema, 1967, French
THE OLDEST PROFESSION   *LES PLUS VIEUX METIER DU
MONDE*   co-director with Franco Indovina, Mauro Bolognini,
   Philippe de Broca, Michael Pfleghar, Claude Autant-Lara,
   Goldstone, 1967, Italian-French-West German
FAR FROM VIETNAM (FD)   co-director with Alain Resnais,
   William Klein, Agnes Varda, Joris Ivens & Claude Lelouch,
   New Yorker, 1967, French
LA CHINOISE   Leacock-Pennebaker, 1967, French
WEEKEND   Grove Press, 1968, French-Italian
UN FILM COMME LES AUTRES   1968, French
AMORE E RABBIA   co-director, 1969, Italian-French
LE GAI SAVOIR   EYR, 1969, French
ONE A.M.   Leacock-Pennebaker, 1969, French
SYMPATHY FOR THE DEVIL   *1 + 1*   New Line Cinema,
   1969, British
BRITISH SOUNDS   *SEE YOU AT MAO* (TF)   Kestrel Productions,
   co-director with Jean-Pierre Gorin, 1969, British
WIND FROM THE EAST   co-director with Jean-Pierre Gorin,
   New Line Cinema, 1969, French-Italian-West German
PRAVDA (FD)   co-director with Jean-Pierre Gorin,
   1969, French-Czech

LOTTE IN ITALIA (FD)   co-director with Jean-Pierre Gorin, RAI,
   1970, Italian
VLADIMIR ET ROSA   co-director with Jean-Pierre Gorin,
   1971, French
TOUT VA BIEN   co-director with Jean-Pierre Gorin, New Yorker,
   1972, French-Italian
LETTER TO JANE: INVESTIGATION OF A STILL   co-director with
   Jean-Pierre Gorin, New Yorker, 1972, French
NUMERO DEUX   Zoetrope, 1975, French
COMMENT ÇA VA   1976, French
ICI ET AILLEURS   MK2 Diffusion, 1976, French
SUR ET SOUS LA COMMUNICATION (TD)   INA, 1977, French
FRANCE/TOUR/DETOUR/DEUX/ENFANTS (TD)   co-director with
   Anne-Marie Mieville, Zoetrope, 1980, Swiss-French
EVERY MAN FOR HIMSELF   *SAUVE QUI PEUT LA VIE*
   New Yorker/Zoetrope, 1980, Swiss-French
PASSION   United Artists Classics, 1983, French-Swiss
FIRST NAME: CARMEN   Spectrafilm, 1983, French-Swiss
HAIL MARY   New Yorker, 1985, French-Swiss
DETECTIVE   Spectrafilm, 1985, French
GRANDEUR ET DECADENCE D'UN PETIT COMMERCE
   DE CINEMA (TF)   Hamster Productions, 1986, French
SOIGNE TA DROITE (KEEP UP YOUR RIGHT!)   Galaxy,
   1987, French-Swiss
KING LEAR   Cannon, 1987, U.S.-Swiss
ARIA   co-director, Miramax Films, 1987, British
NOUVELLE VAGUE   Vega Film, 1990, Swiss
VISAGES SUISSES (FD)   co-director, Video Films, 1991, Swiss
GERMANY YEAR 90 NINE ZERO   Cinema Parallel,
   1991, Swiss-French
CONTRE L'OUBLI   co-director, Les Films du Paradoxe/Amnesty
   International/PRV, 1992, French
HELAS POUR MOI   Les Films Alain Sarde/Vega Films/Vente A
   L'Etranger/Canal Plus/Peripheria, 1993, Swiss-French
JLG BY JLG   *JLG/JLG - AUTOPORTRAIT DE DECEMBRE*
   Drift Releasing, 1994, French-Swiss
LES ENFANTS JOVENT A LA RUSSIE (TD)   Cecco Films/Russian
   State Radio & TV, 1995, Swiss-Russian

GARY GODDARD*

Business: Landmark Entertainment, 5200 Lankershim Blvd. -
   7th Floor, North Hollywood, CA 91601, 818/753-6700

MASTERS OF THE UNIVERSE   Cannon, 1987

JIM GODDARD

b. February 2, 1936 - London, England
Agent: Peters Fraser & Dunlop - London, tel.: 171/344-1000

A TALE OF TWO CITIES (TF)   Norman Rosemont Productions/
   Marble Arch Productions, 1980, U.S.-British
REILLY - ACE OF SPIES (MS)   co-director with Martin Campbell,
   Euston Films Ltd., 1984
KENNEDY (MS)   Central Independent Television Productions/Alan
   Landsburg Productions, 1983, British-U.S.
HITLER'S S.S.: PORTRAIT IN EVIL (TF)   Colason Limited
   Productions/Edgar J. Scherick Associates, 1985, British-U.S.
PARKER   Virgin Films, 1985, British
SHANGHAI SURPRISE   MGM/UA, 1986, British-U.S.
THE IMPOSSIBLE SPY (CTF)   HBO Showcase/BBC/Quartet
   International/IMGC, 1987, British-Israeli
THE FOUR MINUTE MILE (TF)   Oscar-Sullivan Productions/Centre
   Films, 1988, Australian
VAN DER VALK - DANGEROUS GAMES (MS)   Elmsgate
   Productions/Thames TV, 1990, British
LIE DOWN WITH LIONS (MS)   Hannibal Films Ltd./Delux
   Productions/Anabase Productions, 1994, British

JILL GODMILOW

FAR FROM POLAND (FD)   Film Forum, 1984
WAITING FOR THE MOON   Skouras Pictures, 1987,
   U.S.-French-British-West German
ROY COHN/JACK SMITH   Good Machine/Pomodori Foundation/
   Laboratory for Icon & Idiom, 1994

MENAHEM GOLAN*
b. May 31, 1929 - Tiberias, Palestine
Contact: Directors Guild of America - Los Angeles, 213/851-3671

EL DORADO   1963, Israeli
TRUNK TO CAIRO   American International, 1967,
   Israeli-West German
THE GIRL FROM THE DEAD SEA   1967, Israeli
TEVYE AND HIS SEVEN DAUGHTERS   Noah Films, 1968, Israeli
FORTUNA   Trans-American, 1969, Israeli
WHAT'S GOOD FOR THE GOOSE   National Showmanship,
   1969, British
MARGO   Cannon, 1970, Israeli
LUPO!   Cannon, 1970, Israeli
QUEEN OF THE ROAD   Noah Films, 1970, Israeli
KATZ AND KARASSO   Noah Films, 1971, Israeli
THE GREAT TELEPHONE ROBBERY   Noah Films, 1972, Israeli
ESCAPE TO THE SUN   Cinevision, 1972,
   Israeli-West German-French
KAZABLAN   MGM, 1973, Israeli
LEPKE   Warner Bros., 1975
DIAMONDS   Avco Embassy, 1975, U.S.-Israeli-Swiss
THE AMBASSADOR   Noah Films, 1976, Israeli
OPERATION THUNDERBOLT   Cinema Shares International,
   1978, Israeli
THE URANIUM CONSPIRACY   Noah Films, 1978,
   Israeli-West German
THE MAGICIAN OF LUBLIN   Cannon, 1979,
   Israeli-West German-U.S.
THE APPLE   Cannon, 1980, U.S.-West German
ENTER THE NINJA   Cannon, 1981
OVER THE BROOKLYN BRIDGE   MGM/UA/Cannon, 1984
THE DELTA FORCE   Canon, 1986
OVER THE TOP   Cannon, 1987
HANNA'S WAR   Cannon, 1988
MACK THE KNIFE   21st Century Distribution, 1989
SILENT VICTIM   21st Century Distribution, 1993
HIT THE DUTCHMAN!   21st Century Distribution,
   1993, U.S.-Russian
CRIME & PUNISHMENT   21st Century Distribution,
   1993, Canadian-Russian
DEADLY HEROES   Trimark Pictures, 1993, U.S.-Israeli

GREGG GOLD
HOUSE OF THE RISING SUN   Mediacom Productions, 1987

JACK GOLD*
b. June 28, 1930 - London, England
Home: 24 Wood Vale, London N10 3DP, England, tel.: 181/883-3491
Agent: Peters Fraser & Dunlop - London, tel.: 171/344-1000

THE BOFORS GUN   Universal, 1968, British
THE RECKONING   Columbia, 1969, British
CATHOLICS (TF)   Sidney Glazier Productions, 1973, British
WHO?   Allied Artists, 1975, British-West German
MAN FRIDAY   Avco Embassy, 1975, British
ACES HIGH   Cinema Shares International, 1977, British
THE MEDUSA TOUCH   Warner Bros., 1978, British
THE SAILOR'S RETURN   Euston Films, Ltd., 1978
THE NAKED CIVIL SERVANT (TF)   Thames TV, 1978, British
CHARLIE MUFFIN   Euston Films, Ltd., 1980, British
LITTLE LORD FAUNTLEROY (TF)   Norman Rosemont
   Productions, 1980, U.S.- British
PRAYING MANTIS   Portman Productions/Channel 4,
   1982, British
RED MONARCH   Enigma Films/Goldcrest Films & Television, Ltd.,
   1983, British
GOOD AND BAD AT GAMES (TF)   Portman Quintet
   Productions, 1983, British
SAKHAROV (CTF)   HBO Premiere Films/Titus Productions,
   1984, U.S.-British
THE CHAIN   Rank, 1985, British
NOEL COWARD'S 'ME AND THE GIRLS' (TF)   BBC/Quintet Films/
   Arts & Entertainment Network, 1985, British-U.S.
MURROW (CTF)   HBO Premiere Films/Titus Productions/TVS, Ltd.
   Productions, 1986, U.S.-British

ESCAPE FROM SOBIBOR (TF) ☆   Rule-Starger Productions/Zenith
   Productions, 1987, U.S.-British
STONES FOR IBARRA (TF)   Titus Productions, 1988
THE TENTH MAN (TF)   Rosemont Productions/William Self
   Productions, 1988, U.S.-British
BALL TRAP ON THE COTE SAUVAGE (TF)   BBC, 1989, British
THE SHLEMIEL, THE SHLEMAZL AND THE DOPPESS (TF)
   BBC, 1990, British
THE ROSE AND THE JACKAL (CTF)   Steve White Productions/
   PWD Productions, 1990
THE WAR THAT NEVER ENDS (TF)   BBC, 1991, British
SHE STOOD ALONE (TF)   Mighty Fortress Productions/Walt
   Disney TV, 1991
LAST ROMANTICS (TF)   1991, British
THE LUCONA AFFAIR (TF)   Tele-Munchen/ABC/RCS/ZDF/
   Majestic/Vienna Film Financing Fund/European Script Fund,
   1993, German-Austrian
THE RETURN OF THE NATIVE (TF)   Craig Anderson Productions/
   Signboard Hill Productions, 1994, British-U.S.

DAN GOLDBERG*
(Daniel Mitchell Goldberg)
Contact: Directors Guild of America - Los Angeles, 213/851-3671

FEDS   Warner Bros., 1988

ERIC GOLDBERG
Business: Walt Disney Animation, 500 S. Buena Vista Street,
   Burbank, CA 91521, 818/560-1000

POCAHONTAS (AF)   co-director with Michael Gabriel,
   Buena Vista, 1995

GARY DAVID GOLDBERG*
Business: Ubu Productions, 5555 Melrose Avenue, Los Angeles,
   CA 90038, 213/956-5058
Agent: UTA - Beverly Hills, 310/273-6700

DAD   Universal, 1989

MARK GOLDBLATT*
Agent: David Gersh, The Gersh Agency - Beverly Hills, 310/274-6611

DEAD HEAT   New World, 1988
THE PUNISHER   New World, 1989

DAN GOLDEN
NAKED OBSESSION   Concorde, 1991
SATURDAY NIGHT SPECIAL   Concorde, 1994

JOHN GOLDEN
Agent: William Morris Agency - New York City, 212/586-5100

FAT GUY GOES NUTZOID   Troma, 1986
THE BOILER ROOM   Eureka Productions, 1987
THE BIG GIVER   Coho Media/New Street Partners, 1988
MANHATTAN MOONSHINE   Coho Media, 1988

MICHAEL GOLDENBERG
Agent: ICM - Beverly Hills, 310/550-4000

AMELIA AND THE KING OF PLANTS   New Line Cinema, 1995

DANA GOLDFINE
FROSH: NINE MONTHS IN A FRESHMAN DORM (FD)
   co-director with Dan Geller, Landmark Releasing, 1994

PAUL GOLDING
Contact: Writers Guild of America, West - Los Angeles, 310/550-1000

PULSE   Columbia, 1988

GARY GOLDMAN

Business: Fox Animation Studios, Inc., 2747 E. Camelback Road,
Phoenix, AZ 85016
Business Manager: Meyer, Benadon & Shapiro - 818/973-4500

HANS CHRISTIAN ANDERSEN'S THUMBELINA
THUMBELINA (AF) co-director with Don Bluth,
Warner Bros., 1994
A TROLL IN CENTRAL PARK (AF) co-director with Don Bluth,
Warner Bros., 1994
THE PEBBLE AND THE PENGUIN (AF) co-director with Don Bluth,
MGM-UA, 1995

JILL GOLDMAN

Agent: Sanford-Gross & Associates - Los Angeles, 310/208-2100

LOVE IS LIKE THAT Boomerang Pictures, 1992

JOHN GOLDSCHMIDT

Business: Viva Pictures Ltd., 14-18 Ham Yard, London W1V 7PD,
England, tel.: 171/494-0772
Agent: ICM - London, tel.: 171/636-6565

SPEND, SPEND, SPEND (TF) BBC, 1978, British
THE EMPEROR OF ATLANTIS (TF) Opera Clasart/WDR/BBC,
1979, West German-British
LIFE FOR CHRISTINE (TF) Granada TV, 1981, British
THE DEVIL'S LIEUTENANT (TF) Bavaria Atelier/Channel 4/ZDF/
RAI/FR3, 1983, West German-British-French-Italian
SHE'LL BE WEARING PINK PYJAMAS Film Four International,
1984, British
A SONG FOR EUROPE (TF) Film Stern TV/Channel 4//ZDF/ORF/
SRG, 1985, West German-British-Austrian
MASCHENKA (TF) Cinema Clasart Film/Channel 4/ZDF/ORF,
1986, West German-British-Austrian

ALLAN GOLDSTEIN*

b. 1951 - Montreal, Quebec, Canada
Home: 2509 Green Valley Road, Los Angeles, CA 90046,
213/656-9332
Agent: William Morris Agency - Beverly Hills, 310/859-4000

THE HOUSE OF DIES DREAR (TF) Children's Television
Workshop, 1984
THE RETURN OF HICKEY (TF) Bar Harbour Film Inc. Productions/
Siren Pictures Corporation/Global TV Network, 1988
THE OUTSIDE CHANCE OF MAXIMILIAN GLICK South Gate
Entertainment, 1988, Canadian
COLD FRONT Cold Front Productions, 1989, Canadian
THE BEGINNING OF THE FIRM (TF) Ronald J. Kahn Productions/
Scholastic Productions/Bar Harbour Film Inc. Productions/Siren
Pictures Corp./The Global TV Network, 1989, U.S.-Canadian
THE PHONE CALL (TF) 3 Themes/Hamster Productions/Venture
Entertainment Group/Niagara TV Ltd./La Cinq, 1990,
Canadian-French
CHAINDANCE Festival Films, 1991, Canadian
DEATH WISH V: THE FACE OF DEATH Cannon,
1993, U.S.-Canadian

AMY GOLDSTEIN*

Home: 913 Euclid Street - Suite 1, Santa Monica, CA 90403,
310/393-5560
Agent: ICM - Beverly Hills, 310/550-4000
Personal Manager: 3 Arts Entertainment - Beverly Hills,
310/888-3200

THE SILENCER Crown International, 1992

SCOTT GOLDSTEIN*

Business: Spirit, 650 N. Bronson Avenue - Suite B122, Los Angeles,
CA 90004, 213/960-4564
Agent: The Chasin Agency - Los Angeles, 310/278-7505

FLANAGAN *WALLS OF GLASS* United Film Distribution, 1985
AMBITION Miramax Films, 1991

JAMES GOLDSTONE*

b. June 8, 1931 - Los Angeles, California
Agent: Geoff Brandt, The Brandt Company - Sherman Oaks,
818/783-7747

SCALPLOCK (TF) Columbia TV, 1966
CODE NAME: HERACLITUS (TF) Universal TV, 1967
IRONSIDE (TF) Universal TV, 1967
SHADOW OVER ELVERON (TF) Universal TV, 1968
JIGSAW Universal, 1968
A MAN CALLED GANNON Universal, 1969
WINNING Universal, 1969
A CLEAR AND PRESENT DANGER (TF) ☆ Universal TV, 1970
BROTHER JOHN Columbia, 1971
RED SKY AT MORNING Universal, 1971
THE GANG THAT COULDN'T SHOOT STRAIGHT MGM, 1972
THEY ONLY KILL THEIR MASTERS 1973
CRY PANIC (TF) Spelling-Goldberg Productions, 1974
DR. MAX (TF) CBS, Inc., 1974
THINGS IN THEIR SEASON (TF) Tomorrow
Entertainment, 1974
JOURNEY FROM DARKNESS (TF) Bob Banner
Associates, 1975
ERIC (TF) Lorimar Productions, 1975
SWASHBUCKLER Universal, 1976
ROLLERCOASTER Universal, 1977
STUDS LONIGAN (MS) Lorimar Productions, 1979
WHEN TIME RAN OUT Warner Bros., 1980
KENT STATE (TF) ☆☆ Inter Planetary Productions/Osmond
Communications, 1981
CHARLES & DIANA: A ROYAL LOVE STORY (TF)
St. Lorraine Productions, 1982
CALAMITY JANE (TF) CBS Entertainment, 1983
RITA HAYWORTH: THE LOVE GODDESS (TF)
The Susskind Co, 1983
SENTIMENTAL JOURNEY (TF) Lucille Ball Productions/
Smith-Richmond Productions/20th Century Fox TV, 1984
THE SUN ALSO RISES (TF) Furia-Oringer Productions/20th
Century Fox TV, 1984
DREAMS OF GOLD: THE MEL FISHER STORY (TF)
Inter Planetary Productions, 1986
EARTH*STAR VOYAGER (TF) Walt Disney TV/Marstar
Productions, 1988
THE BRIDE IN BLACK (TF) Barry Weitz Films/New
World TV, 1990

BOBCAT GOLDTHWAIT

Personal Manager: Rick Rogers, Green, Epstein, Rogers
Management - 818/752-9070

SHAKES THE CLOWN I.R.S. Releasing, 1991

JACOB GOLDWASSER

Contact: Israel Film Centre, Ministry of Industry & Trade,
30 Agron Street, P.O. Box 299, Jerusalem 94190, Israel,
tel.: 972/210433 or 210297

BIG SHOTS Israeli
THE SKIPPER Israeli
OVER THE OCEAN Marek Rozenbaum-Ron Ackerman
Productions/Israel Broadcasting Authority/The Israeli
Fund for Quality Films, 1991, Israeli
MAX & MORRIS 1994, Israeli

STEVE GOMER*

Agent: Susan Smith & Associates - Beverly Hills, 213/852-4777
Personal Manager: 3 Arts Entertainment - Beverly Hills,
213/852-4777

SWEET LORRAINE Angelika Films, 1987
LOVE & OTHER SORROWS (TF) Learning in Focus/American
Playhouse, 1989
FLY BY NIGHT Lumiere Productions, 1993
SUNSET PARK Jersey Films/Project
Heights Productions, 1995

NICK GOMEZ*

Agent: ICM - Beverly Hills, 310/550-4000
Personal Manager: Addis-Wechsler & Associates - Los Angeles,
213/954-9000

LAWS OF GRAVITY   RKO Pictures Distribution, 1992
NEW JERSEY DRIVE   Gramercy Pictures, 1995

SERVANDO GONZALEZ

b. May 15, 1925 - Mexico City, Mexico
Contact: IMCINE, Tepic #40, P.B. Colonia Roma Sur, Mexico City,
C.P. 06760, Mexico, tel.: 525/584-7283

YANCO   Azteca Films, 1960, Mexican
LOS MEDIOCRES   Azteca Films, 1962, Mexican
THE FOOL KILLER   Allied Artists, 1965
VIENTO NEGRO   1965, Mexican
EL ULTIMO TUNEL   IMC/Conacine/F.F.C.C., 1987, Mexican

BERT I. GORDON*

b. September 24, 1922 - Kenosha, Wisconsin
Business: Bert I. Gordon Films, 9640 Arby Drive, Beverly Hills,
CA 90210, Fax: 310/274-2368
Agent: Ronald Leif, Contemporary Artists - Beverly Hills,
310/395-1800

KING DINOSAUR   Lippert, 1955
BEGINNING OF THE END   Republic, 1957
CYCLOPS   American International, 1957
THE AMAZING COLOSSAL MAN   American International, 1957
ATTACK OF THE PUPPET PEOPLE   American
International, 1958
WAR OF THE COLOSSAL BEAST   American International, 1958
THE SPIDER   American International, 1958
THE BOY AND THE PIRATES   United Artists, 1960
TORMENTED   Allied Artists, 1960
THE MAGIC SWORD   United Artists, 1962
VILLAGE OF THE GIANTS   Embassy, 1965
PICTURE MOMMY DEAD   Embassy, 1966
HOW TO SUCCEED WITH SEX   Medford, 1970
NECROMANCY   American International, 1972
THE MAD BOMBER   Cinemation, 1973
THE POLICE CONNECTION   DETECTIVE GERONIMO   1973
THE FOOD OF THE GODS   American International, 1976
EMPIRE OF THE ANTS   American International, 1977
THE COMING   1981
DOING IT   1984
THE BIG BET   Golden Communications, 1986
SATAN'S PRINCESS   Sun Heat Pictures, 1990

BETTE GORDON

Home: 393 Greenwich Street, New York, NY 10013, 212/226-3408

VARIETY   Horizon Films, 1985
SEVEN WOMEN, SEVEN SINS   co-director, ZDF, 1987,
West German-French- U.S.-Austrian-Belgian

BRYAN GORDON*

Agent: UTA - Beverly Hills, 310/273-6700

CAREER OPPORTUNITIES   Universal, 1991

KEITH GORDON*

b. 1961 - Bronx, New York
Agent: UTA - Beverly Hills, 310/273-6700

THE CHOCOLATE WAR   MCEG, 1988
A MIDNIGHT CLEAR   Interstar Releasing, 1992
WILD PALMS (MS)   co-director with Peter Hewitt, Kathryn Bigelow &
Phil Joanou, Ixtlan Corporation/Greengrass Productions, 1993

ROBERT GORDON

Agent: The Gersh Agency - Beverly Hills, 310/274-6611

REVENGE OF THE RED BARON   Concorde, 1994

STUART GORDON

b. 1946
Agent: UTA - Beverly Hills, 310/273-6700

H.P. LOVECRAFT'S RE-ANIMATOR   RE-ANIMATOR
Empire Pictures, 1985
FROM BEYOND   Empire Pictures, 1986
DOLLS   Empire Pictures, 1987
DAUGHTER OF DARKNESS (TF)   King Phoenix
Entertainment, 1990
ROBOTJOX   Triumph Releasing Corporation, 1990
THE PIT AND THE PENDULUM   Full Moon Entertainment, 1991
FORTRESS   Dimension/Miramax Films, 1993, Australian-U.S.
CASTLE FREAK   Full Moon Entertainment, 1995

BERRY GORDY*

b. November 28, 1929
Business: Motown Records Corporation, 6255 Sunset Blvd.,
Hollywood, CA 90028, 213/468-3500

MAHOGANY   Paramount, 1975

CLAUDE GORETTA

b. June 23, 1929 - Geneva, Switzerland
Contact: Swiss Film Center, Munstergasse 18, 8001 Zurich,
Switzerland, tel.: 01/472860

LE FOU   1970, Swiss
LE JOUR DES NOCES (TF)   1971, Swiss
L'INVITATION   Janus, 1973, Swiss
THE WONDERFUL CROOK   PAS SI MERCHANT QUE CA...
New Yorker, 1975, Swiss-French
THE LACEMAKER   New Yorker, 1977, Swiss-French
LES CHEMINS DE L'EXIT OU LES DERNIERES ANNEES DE
JEAN JACQUES ROUSSEAU (MS)   TFI/SSR/Telecip/BBC/
RTB/SRC/TV60, 1978, French
BONHEUR TOI-MEME   Phenix Films/FR3, 1980, French
THE GIRL FROM LORRAINE   LA PROVINCIALE   New Yorker,
1981, French
THE DEATH OF MARIO RICCI   New Line Showcase,
1983, Swiss-French
ORFEO   Antenne-2/Radio France/Total Foundation for Music/SSR/
Instituto Luce/SRC, 1985, French-Swiss-Italian-Canadian
SI LE SOLEIL NE REVENAIT PAS   JMH Productions/Television
Suisse Romande/Marion's Films/Sara Films/Canal Plus,
1987, Swiss-French
LE RAPPORT DU GENDARME (TF)   Television Suisse Romande,
1987, Swiss
VISAGES SUISSES (FD)   co-director, Video Films, 1991, Swiss
L'OMBRE   Les Productions J.M.H./Odessa Film/Bioskop,
1992, Swiss-French-German
GOUPI MAINS ROUGES (TF)   TSR, 1993, Swiss
THE SORROW OF BELGIUM (MS)   NOS, 1994, Dutch

JEAN-PIERRE GORIN

Contact: French Film Office, 745 Fifth Avenue, New York,
NY 10151, 212/832-8860

BRITISH SOUNDS   SEE YOU AT MAO (TF)   co-director with
Jean-Luc Godard, Kestrel Films, 1969, British
WIND FROM THE EAST   co-director with Jean-Luc Godard,
New Line Cinema, 1969, French-Italian-West German
PRAVDA (FD)   co-director with Jean-Luc Godard,
1969, French-Czech
LOTTE IN ITALIA (FD)   co-director with Jean-Luc Godard,
RAI, 1970, Italian
VLADIMIR ET ROSA   co-director with Jean-Luc Godard,
1971, French
TOUT VA BIEN   co-director with Jean-Luc Godard, New Yorker,
1972, French-Italian
LETTER TO JANE: INVESTIGATION OF A STILL   co-director with
Jean-Luc Godard, New Yorker, 1972, French
POTO AND CABENGO (FD)   1982, French
ORDINARY PLEASURES   1985, French
MY CRASY LIFE   Allan-Marks Productions/BBC/FR3, 1992,
U.S.-British-French

CHARLES GORMLEY
Agent: ICM - London, tel.: 171/636-6565

LIVING APART TOGETHER (TF)   Channel 4, 1982, British
GOSPEL ACCORDING TO VIC   *JUST ANOTHER MIRACLE*
   Skouras Pictures, 1986, British
THE SOUTH BANK SHOW: OSCAR MARZAROLI (TD)
   co-director with Bill Forsyth, Scottish TV/London
   Weekend TV, 1991, Scottish-British

MICHAEL GORNICK
CREEPSHOW II   New World, 1987

ANNE GORSAUD
EMBRACE OF THE VAMPIRE   The Ministry of Film/General
   Media Entertainment, 1995

PETER GOTHAR
b. 1947 - Pecs, Hungary
Contact: Hungarian Film Institute, Budakeszi u 51 B, 1012 Budapest,
   Hungary, tel.: 176-1018 or 176-1322

A PRICELESS DAY   Budapest Studio, 1979, Hungarian
TIME STANDS STILL   Budapest Studio, 1982, Hungarian
TIME   Mafilm, 1986, Hungarian
JUST LIKE AMERICA   Mafilm Hunnia Studio, 1987,
   Hungarian-U.S.
THE OUTPOST   Hunnia Film Studio/MTV Dramai Studioja/Pomino
   Film-Nevropa Ltd., 1995, Hungarian-Rumanian

CARL GOTTLIEB*
b. March 18, 1938
Agent: APA - Los Angeles, 310/273-0744
Business Manager: Edward D. Astrin, 16633 Ventura Blvd. -
   Suite 1450, Encino, CA 91436, 818/501-3022

CAVEMAN   United Artists, 1981
AMAZON WOMEN ON THE MOON   co-director with John Landis,
   Joe Dante, Robert K. Weiss & Peter Horton, Universal, 1987

LISA GOTTLIEB*
Agent: Tim Stone, Stone Manners Agency - Los Angeles,
   213/654-7575

JUST ONE OF THE BOYS   Columbia, 1985
ACROSS THE MOON   Hemdale, 1994

MICHAEL GOTTLIEB*
Agent: APA - Los Angeles, 310/273-0744

MANNEQUIN   20th Century Fox, 1987
MR. NANNY   New Line Cinema, 1993
A KID IN KING ARTHUR'S COURT   Buena Vista, 1995

STEVEN GOUGH
Contact: British Film Commission, 70 Baker Street, London
   W1M 1DJ, England, tel.: 171/224-5000

ELENYA   British Film Institute/Franfurter Film/Ffilmiau Llifon/S4C/
   ZDF, 1992, British-German-French

HEYWOOD GOULD*
Contact: Directors Guild of America - Los Angeles, 213/851-3671

ONE GOOD COP   Buena Vista, 1991
TRIAL BY JURY   Warner Bros., 1994

RICHARD GOVERNOR
GHOST TOWN   Trans World Entertainment, 1988

JOE GRAEFF
ROCKIN' THE JOINT: THE LIFE AND TIMES OF BILL HALEY AND
   THE COMETS   Kent-Graeff Productions, 1993

WILLIAM A. GRAHAM*
Agent: CAA - Beverly Hills, 310/288-4545

THE DOOMSDAY FLIGHT (TF)   Universal TV, 1966
THE OUTSIDER (TF)   Universal TV, 1967
WATERHOLE #3   Paramount, 1967
CHANGE OF HABIT   Universal, 1968
THE LEGEND OF CUSTER (TF)   20th Century-Fox, 1968
SUBMARINE X-1   United Artists, 1969, British
TRIAL RUN (TF)   Universal TV, 1969
THEN CAME BRONSON (TF)   Universal TV, 1969
THE INTRUDERS (TF)   Universal TV, 1970
CONGRATULATIONS, IT'S A BOY! (TF)   Aaron Spelling
   Productions, 1971
THIEF (TF)   Metromedia Productions/Stonehenge Productions, 1971
MARRIAGE: YEAR ONE (TF)   Universal TV, 1971
JIGSAW (TF)   Universal TV, 1972
MAGIC CARPET (TF)   Universal TV, 1972
HONKY   Jack H. Harris Enterprises, 1972
COUNT YOUR BULLETS   *CRY FOR ME, BILLY*
   Brut Productions, 1972
BIRDS OF PREY (TF)   Tomorrow Entertainment, 1973
MR. INSIDE/MR. OUTSIDE (TF)   D'Antoni Productions, 1973
POLICE STORY (TF)   Screen Gems/Columbia TV, 1973
SHIRTS/SKINS (TF)   MGM TV, 1973
WHERE THE LILIES BLOOM   United Artists, 1974
TOGETHER BROTHERS   20th Century-Fox, 1974
GET CHRISTIE LOVE! (TF)   Wolper Productions, 1974
LARRY (TF)   Tomorrow Entertainment, 1974
TRAPPED BENEATH THE SEA (TF)   ABC Circle Films, 1974
BEYOND THE BERMUDA TRIANGLE (TF)
   Playboy Productions, 1975
PERILOUS VOYAGE (TF)   Universal TV, 1976
SHARK KILL (TF)   D'Antoni-Weitz Productions, 1976
21 HOURS AT MUNICH (TF)   Filmways, 1976
PART 2 SOUNDER   Gamma III, 1976
MINSTREL MAN (TF)   Roger Gimbel Productions/EMI TV, 1977
THE AMAZING HOWARD HUGHES (TF)   Roger Gimbel
   Productions/EMI TV, 1977
CONTRACT ON CHERRY STREET (TF)   Columbia TV, 1977
CINDY (TF)   John Charles Walters Productions, 1978
ONE IN A MILLION: THE RON LeFLORE STORY (TF)   Roger
   Gimbel Productions/EMI TV, 1978
AND I ALONE SURVIVED (TF)   Jerry Leider-OJL
   Productions, 1978
TRANSPLANT (TF)   Time-Life Productions, 1979
ORPHAN TRAIN (TF)   Roger Gimbel Productions/EMI TV, 1979
GUYANA TRAGEDY: THE STORY OF JIM JONES (TF) ☆
   The Konigsberg Company, 1980
RAGE (TF)   Diane Silver Productions/Charles Fries
   Productions, 1980
DEADLY ENCOUNTER (TF)   Roger Gimbel Productions/
   EMI TV, 1982
M.A.D.D.: MOTHERS AGAINST DRUNK DRIVERS (TF)
   Universal TV, 1983
THE LAST NINJA (TF)   Paramount TV, 1983
HARRY TRACY   Quartet/Films Inc., 1983, Canadian
WOMEN OF SAN QUENTIN (TF)   David Gerber Company/
   MGM-UA TV, 1983
THE CALENDAR GIRL MURDERS (TF)   Tisch-Avnet
   Productions, 1984
SECRETS OF A MARRIED MAN (TF)   ITC Productions, 1984
MUSSOLINI: THE UNTOLD STORY (MS)
   Trian Productions, 1985
THE LAST DAYS OF FRANK AND JESSE JAMES (TF)
   Joseph Cates Productions, 1986
GEORGE WASHINGTON: THE FORGING OF A NATION (TF)
   David Gerber Company/MGM TV, 1986
POLICE STORY II: THE FREEWAY KILLINGS (TF)   David Gerber
   Productions/MGM-UA TV/Columbia TV, 1987
PROUD MEN (TF)   Cowboy Productions/Agamemnon Films
   Productions/von Zerneck-Samuels Productions, 1987

SUPERCARRIER (TF)   Fries Entertainment/Richard Hayward-Real
   Tinsel Productions, 1988
STREET OF DREAMS (TF)   Bill Stratton-Myrtos Productions/
   Phoenix Entertainment Group, 1988
TRUCK ONE (TF)   Grosso-Jacobson Productions/NBC
   Productions, 1989
GORE VIDAL'S BILLY THE KID *BILLY THE KID* (CTF)
   von Zerneck-Sertner Productions, 1989
TRUE BLUE (TF)   Grosso-Jacobson Productions/NBC
   Productions, 1989
MONTANA (CTF)   HBO Productions/Zoetrope Studios/Roger
   Gimbel Productions, 1990
RETURN TO THE BLUE LAGOON   Columbia, 1991
BED OF LIES (TF)   Elliot Friedgen & Co./David L. Wolper
   Productions, 1992
ELVIS AND THE COLONEL: THE UNTOLD STORY (TF)
   Ultra Entertainment/Dick Clark Film Group, 1993
BEYOND SUSPICION (TF)   Patricia K. Meyer Productions/
   von Zerneck-Sertner Films, 1993
A FRIEND TO DIE FOR (TF)   Steve White Productions, 1994
BETRAYED: A STORY OF THREE WOMEN (TF)
   Freyda Rothstein Productions/Hearst Entertainment, 1995

BRIAN GRANT*

Address: 466 N. Croft Avenue, Los Angeles, CA 90048,
   213/655-1963
Agent: William Morris Agency - Beverly Hills, 310/559-4000
Personal Manager: Carlyle Productions and Management,
   639 N. Larchmont - Suite 207, Los Angeles, CA 90004,
   213/469-3086

THE TELL TALE HEART (TF)   Channel 4, 1989, British
SHE WOLFE OF LONDON (TF)   Universal TV, 1990, British
SWEET POISON (CTF)   Smart Money Productions/MCA-TV
   Entertainment, 1991
LOVE KILLS (CTF)   OTML Productions/The Mark Gordon
   Company/Christopher Meledandri Productions/Wilshire
   Court Productions, 1991
TRUE TALES (TF)   The Michael Mannheim Company, 1992
COMPLEX OF FEAR (TF)   Cosgrove-Meurer Productions/World
   International Network, 1993
SENSATION   Party Crashers Inc./Mark Damon Productions/
   Kushner-Locke Productions, 1995

LEE GRANT*

(Lyova Rosenthal)
b. October 31, 1927 - New York, New York
Business: Joseph Feury Productions, Inc., 120 Riverside Drive -
   Suite 5E, New York, NY 10024, 212/877-7700
Agent: ICM - Beverly Hills, 310/550-4000

TELL ME A RIDDLE   Filmways, 1980
THE WILLMAR 8 (FD)   California Newsreel, 1981
WHEN WOMEN KILL (CTD)   HBO/Joseph Feury
   Productions, 1983
A MATTER OF SEX (CTD)   Willmar 8 Productions/Orion TV, 1984
WHAT SEX AM I? (CTD)   Joseph Feury Productions, 1985
DOWN AND OUT IN AMERICA (CTD)   Joseph Feury
   Productions, 1985
NOBODY'S CHILD (TF)   Joseph Feury Productions/Gaylord
   Production Company, 1986
STAYING TOGETHER   Hemdale, 1989
NO PLACE LIKE HOME (TF)   Feury-Grant Productions/
   Orion TV, 1989
WOMEN ON TRIAL (CTD)   Joseph Feury Productions, 1992
SEASON OF THE HEART (TF)   Joseph Feury Productions/RHI
   Entertainment, 1994
FOLLOWING HER HEART (TF)   Atlantis Films/Roni Weisberg
   Productions/Ann-Margret Productions, 1994, U.S.-Canadian
REUNION (TF)   Hart, Thomas & Berlin Productions/RHI
   Entertainment, 1994

MICHAEL GRANT

b. 1952 - Toronto, Ontario, Canada
Home: 463 Puerto Del Mar, Pacific Palisades, CA 90272,
   310/454-1356

THE BROTHERS KEEPER (TF)   1978, Canadian
FATAL ATTRACTION *HEAD ON* Greentree Productions,
   1980, Canadian
MILLENNIUM (TD)   co-director, Biniman Productions Ltd./Adrian
   Malone Productions Ltd./KCET-TV/BBC/The Global TV Network/
   Rogers Telefund/Telefilm Canada, 1991, Canadian-British

ALEX GRASSHOFF*

b. December 10, 1930 - Boston, Massachusetts
Home: 7845 Torreyson Drive, Los Angeles, CA 90046,
   213/874-5020

THE JAILBREAKERS   American International, 1960
YOUNG AMERICANS (FD)   Columbia, 1967
JOURNEY TO THE OUTER LIMITS (FD)   1974
THE LAST DINOSAUR (TF)   co-director with Tom Kotani,
   1977, U.S.-Japanese
SMOKEY AND THE GOODTIME OUTLAWS
   Howco International, 1978
J.D. & THE SALT FLAT KID   The Samuel Goldwyn
   Company, 1978
WACKY TAXI   1982
A BILLION FOR BORIS   Comworld, 1985

WALTER GRAUMAN*

b. March 17, 1922 - Milwaukee, Wisconsin
Home: 9220 Robin Drive, Los Angeles, CA 90069, 310/278-9823
Agent: Bob Broder, Broder-Kurland-Webb-Uffner Agency -
   Beverly Hills, 310/281-3400

THE DISEMBODIED   Allied Artists, 1957
LADY IN A CAGE   United Artists, 1964
633 SQUADRON   United Artists, 1964, British
A RAGE TO LIVE   United Artists, 1965
I DEAL IN DANGER   20th Century-Fox, 1966
DAUGHTER OF THE MIND (TF)   20th Century-Fox, 1969
THE LAST ESCAPE   United Artists, 1970
THE OLD MAN WHO CRIED WOLF (TF)   Aaron Spelling
   Productions, 1970
CROWHAVEN FARM (TF)   Aaron Spelling Productions, 1970
THE FORGOTTEN MAN (TF)   Walter Grauman Productions, 1971
PAPER MAN (TF)   20th Century-Fox TV, 1971
THEY CALL IT MURDER (TF)   20th Century-Fox TV, 1971
DEAD MEN TELL NO TALES (TF)   20th Century-Fox TV, 1971
THE STREETS OF SAN FRANCISCO (TF)   QM Productions, 1972
MANHUNTER (TF)   QM Productions, 1974
FORCE FIVE (TF)   Universal TV, 1975
MOST WANTED (TF)   QM Productions, 1976
ARE YOU IN THE HOUSE ALONE? (TF)   Charles Fries
   Productions, 1978
CRISIS IN MID-AIR (TF)   CBS Entertainment, 1979
THE GOLDEN GATE MURDERS (TF)   Universal TV, 1979
THE TOP OF THE HILL (TF)   Fellows-Keegan Company/
   Paramount TV, 1980
TO RACE THE WIND (TF)   Walter Grauman Productions, 1980
THE MEMORY OF EVA RYKER (TF)   Irwin Allen Productions, 1980
PLEASURE PALACE (TF)   Norman Rosemont Productions/Marble
   Arch Productions, 1980
JACQUELINE SUSANN'S VALLEY OF THE DOLLS 1981 *VALLEY
   OF THE DOLLS 1981* (MS)   20th Century-Fox TV, 1981
BARE ESSENCE (MS)   Warner Bros. TV, 1982
ILLUSIONS (TF)   CBS Entertainment, 1983
COVENANT (TF)   Michael Filerman Productions/20th
   Century Fox TV, 1985
OUTRAGE! (TF)   Irwin Allen Productions/Columbia TV, 1986
WHO IS JULIA? (TF)   CBS Entertainment, 1986
SHAKEDOWN ON THE SUNSET STRIP (TF)
   CBS Entertainment, 1988
NIGHTMARE ON THE 13TH FLOOR (CTF)   G.C. Group Ltd./
   Wilshire Court Productions, 1990

GARY GRAVER

Business: Grand Am, Ltd., 6649 Odessa Avenue, Van Nuys,
CA 91406, 818/780-9000

THE EMBRACERS   Joseph Brenner Associates, 1967
SANDRA   First Leisure, 1969
THE HARD ROAD   UA Theatres-Four Star, 1970
TEXAS LIGHTNING   Film Ventures International, 1981
TRICK OR TREAT   Lone Star, 1983
PARTY CAMP   Lightning Pictures, 1987
MOON IN SCORPIO   Trans World Entertainment, 1988
CROSSING THE LINE   Home Box Office/RCA-Columbia
Video, 1989
ROOTS OF EVIL   Cannon, 1990
NERDS OF A FEATHER   International Investment
Holdings Ltd., 1990
CROSSING THE LINE   RCA/Columbia Home Video, 1990
EVIL SPIRITS   Prism Entertainment, 1991
ANGEL EYES   American Independent, 1991
WORKING WITH ORSON WELLES (FD)   Grand Am, Ltd., 1994

JAMES GRAY

Agent: UTA - Beverly Hills, 310/273-6700

LITTLE ODESSA   Fine Line Features/New Line Cinema, 1995

JOHN GRAY*

Address: 7400 Hollywood Blvd., Los Angeles, CA 90046,
213/874-0936
Agent: ICM - Beverly Hills, 310/550-4000

BILLY GALVIN   Vestron, 1986
WHEN HE'S NOT A STRANGER (TF)   Ohlmeyer
Communications Co., 1989
THE LOST CAPONE (CTF)   Patchett Kaufman Enterprises/
Turner Network TV, 1990
THE MARLA HANSON STORY (TF)   Citadel Entertainment, 1991
AN AMERICAN STORY (TF)   Signboard Hill Productions/RHI
Entertainment, 1992
A PLACE FOR ANNIE (TF)   Gross-Weston Productions/Signboard
Hill Productions/Cannell Entertainment, 1994
BORN TO BE WILD   Warner Bros., 1995, U.S.-Japanese

MIKE GRAY

Agent: William Morris Agency - Beverly Hills, 310/859-4000

WAVELENGTH   New World, 1983

KJELL GREDE

b. 1936 - Stockholm, Sweden
Contact: Swedish Film Institute, P.O. Box 27126, S-10252
Stockholm, Sweden, tel.: 08/665-1100

HUGO AND JOSEFIN   1967, Swedish
HARRY MUNTER   1969, Swedish
CLAIRE LUST   1972, Swedish
A SIMPLE MELODY   1979, Swedish
HIP, HIP, HURRAH!   Swedish Film Institute/Sandrews Film &
Teater/Palle Fogtdal/Danish Film Institute/Norsk Film, 1987,
Swedish-Danish-Norwegian
GOD AFTON, HERR WALLENBERG   Sandrews Film/Scansat/
TV3/Swedish Film Institute/Filmhuset/Film Teknik/HunniaFilm
Studios, 1990, Swedish-Hungarian

JANET GREEK*

Agent: Shapiro-Lichtman Talent Agency - Los Angeles,
310/859-8877

THE LADIES CLUB   directed under pseudonym of A.K. Allen,
New Line Cinema, 1986
SPELLBINDER   MGM/UA, 1988

BRUCE SETH GREEN*

Home: 1729 Bryn Mawr Avenue, Santa Monica, CA 90405,
310/452-1463
Agent: APA - Los Angeles, 310/273-0744

RAGS TO RICHES (TF)   Leonard Hill Films/New World TV, 1987
IN SELF DEFENSE (TF)   Leonard Hill Films, 1987
PERFECT PEOPLE (TF)   Robert Greenwald Productions, 1988
MANHUNT: SEARCH FOR THE NIGHT STALKER (TF)
Leonard Hill Films, 1989
THE LAKER GIRLS (TF)   Viacom Productions/Finnegan-Pinchuk
Productions/Valente-Hamilton Productions, 1990
RUNNING AGAINST TIME (CTF)   Finnegan-Pinchuk Productions/
MCA-TV Entertainment, 1990

DAVID GREEN*

b. London, England
Business: September Films, Silver House, 35 Beak Street,
London W1R 3ED
Agent: ICM - London, tel.: 71/636-6565

WHICKER'S WORLD, CALIFORNIA (MS)   Yorkshire TV,
1980, British
WILFRED AND EILEEN - A LOVE STORY (TF)   BBC, 1981, British
EAST LYNNE (TF)   BBC, 1983, British
THE GOLDEN LAND (TF)   BBC, 1984, British
CAR TROUBLE   CineTel Films, 1986, British
1914 — ALL OUT (TF)   Yorkshire TV, 1986, British
BUSTER   Hemdale, 1988, British
FIRE BIRDS   Buena Vista, 1990

GUY GREEN*

b. 1913 - Somerset, England
Agent: Phil Gersh, The Gersh Agency - Beverly Hills, 310/274-6611

RIVER BEAT   Lippert, 1954, British
POSTMARK FOR DANGER   *PORTRAIT OF ALISON*   RKO Radio,
1955, British
TEARS FOR SIMON   *LOST*   Republic, 1956, British
TRIPLE DECEPTION   *HOUSE OF SECRETS*   Rank, 1956, British
THE SNORKEL   Columbia, 1958, British
DESERT PATROL   *SEA OF SAND*   Universal, 1958, British
S.O.S. PACIFIC   Universal, 1960, British
THE ANGRY SILENCE   Valiant, 1960, British
THE MARK   Continental, 1961, British
LIGHT IN THE PIAZZA   MGM, 1962
DIAMOND HEAD   Columbia, 1963
A PATCH OF BLUE   MGM, 1965
A MATTER OF INNOCENCE   *PRETTY POLLY*   Universal,
1968, British
THE MAGUS   20th Century-Fox, 1968, British
A WALK IN THE SPRING RAIN   Columbia, 1970
LUTHER   American Film Theatre, 1974
JACQUELINE SUSANN'S ONCE IS NOT ENOUGH   *ONCE IS NOT
ENOUGH*   Paramount, 1975
THE DEVIL'S ADVOCATE   Filmworld Distributors, 1978,
West German
JENNIFER: A WOMAN'S STORY (TF)   Marble Arch
Productions, 1979
THE INCREDIBLE JOURNEY OF DR. MEG LAUREL (TF)
Columbia TV, 1979
JIMMY B. & ANDRE (TF)   Georgia Bay Productions, 1980
INMATES: A LOVE STORY (TF)   Henerson-Hirsch Productions/
Finnegan Associates, 1981
ISABEL'S CHOICE (TF)   Stuart Miller-Pantheon TV, 1981
STRONG MEDICINE (TF)   Telepictures Productions/TVS Ltd.
Productions, 1986, U.S.-British

TERRY GREEN

Contact: British Film Commission, 70 Baker Street, London
W1M 1DJ, England, tel.: 171/224-5000

FATHER JIM   East End Films Ltd., 1991, British

WALON GREEN*
b. December 15, 1936 - Baltimore, Maryland
Home: 3089 Seahorse, Ventura, CA 93001, 805/642-2366
Agent: ICM - Beverly Hills, 310/550-4000

SPREE (FD)   co-director with Mitchell Leisen,
   United Producers, 1967
THE HELLSTROM CHRONICLE (FD)   Cinema 5, 1971
THE SECRET LIFE OF PLANTS (FD)   Paramount, 1978

PETER GREENAWAY
b. April 5, 1942 - Wales
Contact: British Film Commission, 70 Baker Street, London
   W1M 1DJ, England, tel.: 171/224-5000

THE FALLS   British Film Institute, 1980, British
THE DRAUGHTMAN'S CONTRACT   United Artists Classics,
   1983, British
MODERN AMERICAN COMPOSERS 1: CAGE AND MONK (TD)
   Trans Atlantic Films/Channel 4, 1984, British
MODERN AMERICAN COMPOSERS 2: GLASS AND ASHLEY (TD)
   Trans Atlantic Films/Channel 4, 1984, British
A ZED AND TWO NOUGHTS   Skouras Pictures,
   1985, British-Dutch
DROWNING BY NUMBERS   Prestige, 1989, British
THE COOK, THE THIEF, HIS WIFE AND HER LOVER
   Miramax Films, 1989, Dutch-French
PROSPERO'S BOOKS   Miramax Films, 1991, British-French
THE BABY OF MACON   Allarts/UGC/Cine Electra/Channel 4/
   Filmstiftung NRW/La Sept Cinema, 1993,
   Dutch-French-British-German
DARWIN (TF)   Telemax/Les Editions Audiovisuelle,
   1993, French-British
THE PILLOW BOOK   1995, British

BRUCE GREENBERG
DEAD GIRLS DON'T DANCE   Security Industries, 1990

LAWRENCE GREENBERG
CUFFDUNK & ROUNDTREE   Transit City Pictures, 1991

RICHARD ALAN GREENBERG*
Agent: UTA - Beverly Hills, 310/273-6700
Business: R/Greenberg Associates, 350 West 39th Street,
   New York, NY, 10018, 212/239-6767

LITTLE MONSTERS   MGM/UA, 1989

WILLIAM R. GREENBLATT
HITS!   Walron Films Ltd./LLC/Symphony Pictures, 1994

DANFORD B. GREENE
Home: 558 E. Channel Road, Santa Monica, CA 90402,
   310/459-2369

THE SECRET DIARY OF SIGMUND FREUD   TLC Films/20th
   Century Fox, 1984

DAVID GREENE*
b. February 22, 1921 - Manchester, England
Agent: CAA - Beverly Hills, 310/288-4545

THE SHUTTERED ROOM   Warner Bros., 1966, British
SEBASTIAN   Paramount, 1968, British
THE STRANGE AFFAIR   Paramount, 1968, British
I START COUNTING   United Artists, 1969, British
THE PEOPLE NEXT DOOR   Avco Embassy, 1970
MADAME SIN (TF)   ITC, 1971, British
GODSPELL   Columbia, 1973
THE COUNT OF MONTE CRISTO (TF)   Norman Rosemont
   Productions/ITC, 1975, U.S.-British
ELLERY QUEEN (TF)   Universal TV, 1975
RICH MAN, POOR MAN (MS)   co-director with Boris Sagal,
   Universal TV, 1976

ROOTS (MS) ☆☆   co-director with Marvin J. Chomsky,
   John Erman & Gilbert Moses, Wolper Productions, 1977
LUCAN (TF)   MGM TV, 1977
THE TRIAL OF LEE HARVEY OSWALD (TF)   Charles Fries
   Productions, 1977
GRAY LADY DOWN   Universal, 1978
FRIENDLY FIRE (TF) ☆☆   Marble Arch Productions, 1979
A VACATION IN HELL (TF)   David Greene Productions/Finnegan
   Associates, 1980
THE CHOICE (TF)   David Greene Productions/Finnegan
   Associates, 1981
HARD COUNTRY   Universal/AFD, 1981
WORLD WAR III (TF)   Finnegan Associates/David Greene
   Productions, 1982
REHEARSAL FOR MURDER (TF)   Levinson-Link Productions/
   Robert Papazian Productions, 1982
TAKE YOUR BEST SHOT (TF)   Levinson-Link Productions/
   Robert Papazian Productions, 1982
GHOST DANCING (TF)   Herbert Brodkin Productions/The Eugene
   O'Neill Memorial Theatre Center/Titus Productions, 1983
PROTOTYPE (TF)   Levinson-Link Productions/Robert
   Papazian Productions, 1983
THE GUARDIAN (CTF)   HBO Premiere Films/Robert Cooper
   Productions/Stanley Chase Productions, 1984, U.S.-Canadian
SWEET REVENGE (TF)   David Greene Productions/Robert
   Papazian Productions, 1984
FATAL VISION (TF) ☆   NBC Productions, 1984
GUILTY CONSCIENCE (TF)   Levinson-Link Productions/Robert
   Papazian Productions, 1985
MURDER AMONG FRIENDS (TF)   Tisch-Avnet Productions/ABC
   Circle Films, 1985
THIS CHILD IS MINE (TF)   Beth Polson Productions/Finnegan
   Associates/Telepictures Productions, 1985
TRIPLECROSS (TF)   TAP Productions/ABC Circle Films, 1986
VANISHING ACT (TF)   Robert Cooper Productions,
   1986, U.S.-Canadian
MILES TO GO... (TF)   Keating-Shostak Productions,
   1986, U.S.-Canadian
CIRCLE OF VIOLENCE: A FAMILY DRAMA (TF)   Sheldon Pinchuk
   Productions/Rafshoon Communications/Finnegan Associates/
   Telepictures Productions, 1986
THE BETTY FORD STORY (TF)   David L. Wolper Productions/
   Warner Bros. TV, 1987
AFTER THE PROMISE (TF)   Tamara Asseyev Productions/New
   World TV, 1987
INHERIT THE WIND (TF)   Vincent Pictures Productions/David
   Greene-Robert Papazian Productions, 1988
LIBERACE: BEHIND THE MUSIC (TF)   Canadian International
   Studios/Kushner-Locke Productions, 1988, U.S.-Canadian
RED EARTH, WHITE EARTH (TF)   Robert Papazian Productions/
   Alan M. Levin Productions, 1989
THE PENTHOUSE (TF)   Greene-White Productions/Spectator
   Films, 1989
SMALL SACRIFICES (TF)   Louis Rudolph Films/Motown
   Productions/Allarcom Ltd./Fries Entertainment,
   1989, U.S.-Canadian
IN THE BEST INTEREST OF THE CHILD (TF)   Papazian-Hirsch
   Entertainment, 1990
WHAT EVER HAPPENED TO BABY JANE? (TF)   Steve White
   Productions/The Aldrich Group/Spectator Films, 1991
THE NIGHT OF THE HUNTER (TF)   Diana Kerew Productions/
   Konigsberg-Sanitsky Productions, 1991
AND THEN SHE WAS GONE (TF)   Steve White Productions/
   Spectator Films, 1991
HONOR THY MOTHER (TF)   Universal-MCA TV/Point of
   View Productions, 1992
WILLING TO KILL: THE TEXAS CHEERLEADER STORY (TF)
   Stockton Briggle Productions/David Eagle Productions/
   Papazian-Hirsch Entertainment, 1992
BEYOND OBSESSION (TF)   Pacific Motion Pictures/Western
   International Communications/Green-Epstein Productions/
   Warner Bros. TV, 1994
SPOILS OF WAR (TF)   Evolution Entertainment/Signboard Hill
   Productions/RHI Entertainment, 1994
CHILDREN OF THE DUST (TF)   The Konigsberg Company,
   1995, U.S.-Canadian

SPARKY GREENE*
b. November 13, 1948 - Chicago, Illinois
Business: Titan Films, 73 Market Street, Venice, CA 90291,
310/349-9319

A SAVAGE HUNGER *THE OASIS* Shapiro Entertainment, 1984

PAUL GREENGRASS
Contact: British Film Commission, 70 Baker Street, London
W1M 1DJ, England, tel.: 171/224-5000

RESURRECTED Film Four International/British Screen/
St. Pancras, 1989, British

BUD GREENSPAN*
Business: Cappy Productions, 33 East 68th Street, New York,
NY 10021, 212/249-1800

THE GLORY OF THEIR TIMES (TD) Cappy Productions, 1977
WILMA (TF) Cappy Productions, 1977
16 DAYS TO GLORY (FD) Paramount, 1985
SEOUL '88: 16 DAYS OF GLORY (CTD) Cappy Productions/
The Disney Channel, 1989
TIME CAPSULE: THE 1936 BERLIN OLYMPIC GAMES (TD)
Cappy Productions, 1989

MAGGIE GREENWALD
Agent: David Gersh, The Gersh Agency - Beverly Hills, 310/274-6611

HOME REMEDY Kino International, 1988
THE KILL OFF Films Around the World, 1989
THE BALLAD OF LITTLE JO Fine Line Features/New Line
Cinema, 1993

ROBERT GREENWALD*
b. August 28, 1945 - New York, New York
Business: Robert Greenwald Productions, 10510 Culver Blvd.,
Culver City, CA 90232, 310/204-0404
Agent: The Gersh Agency - Beverly Hills, 310/274-6611

SHARON: PORTRAIT OF A MISTRESS (TF) Moonlight
Productions/Paramount TV, 1977
KATIE: PORTRAIT OF A CENTERFOLD (TF) Moonlight
Productions/Warner Bros. TV, 1978
FLATBED ANNIE & SWEETIE PIE: LADY TRUCKERS (TF)
Moonlight Productions/Filmways, 1979
XANADU Universal, 1980
FORTY DAYS FOR DANNY (TF) Moonlight Productions/
Filmways, 1982
IN THE CUSTODY OF STRANGERS (TF) Moonlight Productions/
Filmways, 1982
THE BURNING BED (TF) ☆ Tisch-Avnet Productions, 1984
SHATTERED SPIRITS (TF) Sheen-Greenblatt Productions/
Robert Greenwald Productions, 1986
ON FIRE (TF) Robert Greenwald Productions, 1987
SWEET HEARTS DANCE TriStar, 1988
FORGOTTEN PRISONERS: THE AMNESTY FILE (CTF)
Robert Greenwald Productions, 1990
HEAR NO EVIL 20th Century Fox, 1993
A WOMAN OF INDEPENDENT MEANS (MS) Fogwood Films/
Robert Greenwald Prods., 1995

DAVID GREENWALT*
Home: P.O. Box 530, Topanga, CA 90290
Agent: ICM - Beverly Hills, 310/550-4000

SECRET ADMIRER Orion, 1985
HELP WANTED: KIDS (TF) Stan Rogow Productions, 1986
DOUBLE SWITCH (TF) Walt Disney TV, 1987
RUDE AWAKENING co-director with Aaron Russo, Orion, 1989
EXILE (TF) Walt Disney TV, 1990

COLIN GREGG
b. 1947 - Cheltenham, England
Address: 11 Compton Terrace, London N1 2UN, England,
tel.: 171/704-9398
Agent: Linda Seifert, Seifert Dench Associates - London,
tel.: 171/437-4551

BEGGING THE RING (TF) BBC/Colin Gregg Films, 1978, British
THE TRESPASSER (TF) LWT/Polytel, 1981
REMEMBRANCE (TF) Channel 4/Film on Four, 1982, British
TO THE LIGHTHOUSE (TF) BBC/UMF/Colin Gregg Ltd.,
1983, British
LAMB Limehouse/Flickers/Channel 4, 1985, British
UNFINISHED BUSINESS (TF) BBC, 1986, British
WE THINK THE WORLD OF YOU Cinecom, 1988, British
PIE IN THE SKY (MS) co-director, SelecTV/Witzend Productions/
BBC, 1993, British

EZIO GREGGIO
Contact: SIAE, Sezione Cinema, viale della Letteratura 30, Rome,
Italy, tel.: 06/59901

THE SILENCE OF THE HAMS October Films, 1994, Italian

JOHN GREYSON
ZERO PATIENCE Zero Patience Productions, 1994, Canadian

ANDREW GRIEVE
Business: Nigel Britten Management - London, tel.: 171/379-0344

STORYBOOK INTERNATIONAL (MS) HTV, 1984, British
SUSPICION Hemisphere, 1986, British
ON THE BLACK HILL Roxie Releasing, 1987, British
AGATHA CHRISTIE'S POIROT (MS) co-director with
Stephen Whittaker & Ross Devenish, London Weekend TV,
1989, British
LORNA DOONE (TF) Working Title, 1990, British
THE KIDNAPPED PRIME MINISTER (TF) London Weekend TV,
1991, British
THE BIG BATALLIONS (MS) Carnival Films/Channel 4,
1992, British
ALL OR NOTHING AT ALL (TF) Carnival Films/London
Weekend TV, 1993, British
LETTERS FROM THE EAST Lantern East/Lichtblick Filmproduktion/
Axel Films Productions, 1995, British-German-Finnish-Estonian

CHARLES B. GRIFFITH
FORBIDDEN ISLAND Columbia, 1959
HATSANKANIM 1961, Israeli
EAT MY DUST New World, 1976
UP FROM THE DEPTHS New World, 1979
DR. HECKLE AND MR. HYPE Cannon, 1980
SMOKEY BITES THE DUST New World, 1981
WIZARDS OF THE LOST KINGDOM II Concorde, 1989

MARK GRIFFITHS
Attorney: Shelley Surpin, Surpin, Mayersohn & Edelstone -
Los Angeles, 310/552-1808

RUNNING HOT New Line Cinema, 1984
HARDBODIES Columbia, 1984
HARDBODIES 2 CineTel Films, 1986
HEROES STAND ALONE Concorde, 1989
A CRY IN THE WILD Concorde, 1990
ULTRAVIOLET Concorde, 1991
CHEYENNE WARRIOR Concorde, 1994

GARY GRILLO*
Home: 24025 Highlander Road, West Hills, CA 91307, 818/704-9631
Agent: Barry Perelman Agency - Los Angeles, 310/274-5999

AMERICAN JUSTICE The Movie Store, 1986

AURELIO GRIMALDI
b. 1957 - Modica, Italy
Business: Trio Cinema e Televisione, viale Angelico 38, Rome, Italy,
tel.: 06/372-4584

LA DISCESA DI ACLA' A FLORISTELLA   Coop Cineuropa 92/
   Nova Films/Movie 90, 1992, Italian
LA RIBELLE   Taodue/Banda Magnetica/Reteitalia, 1993, Italian
LE BUTTANE   Trio Cinema e Televisione, 1994, Italian

ALAN GRINT
Agent: ICM - London, tel.: 171/636-6565

SHERLOCK HOLMES (TF)   Granada TV, 1985, British
LOST EMPIRES (TF)   Granada TV, 1986, British
THE SECRET GARDEN (TF)   Rosemont Productions,
   1987, U.S.-British
AGATHA CHRISTIE'S "THE MAN IN THE BROWN SUIT" (TF)
   Alan Shayne Productions/Warner Bros. TV, 1989
THE WORLD OF EDDIE WEARY (TF)   Fingertip Productions/
   Yorkshire TV, 1990, British
SPENDER (MS)   co-director with Ian Knox, BBC, 1992, British
THE RUTH RENDELL MYSTERIES: VANITY DIES HARD (TF)
   Blue Heaven Productions/Meridian Broadcasting, 1993, British

ULU GROSBARD*
b. January 9, 1929 - Antwerp, Belgium
Home: 29 West 10th Street, New York, NY 10011
Agent: Sam Cohn, ICM - New York City, 212/556-5600

THE SUBJECT WAS ROSES   MGM, 1968
WHO IS HARRY KELLERMAN AND WHY IS HE SAYING THOSE
   TERRIBLE THINGS ABOUT ME?   National General, 1971
STRAIGHT TIME   Warner Bros., 1978
TRUE CONFESSIONS   United Artists, 1981
FALLING IN LOVE   Paramount, 1984
GEORGIA   Georgia Film Corporation, 1995

LARRY GROSS*
Home: 201 S. Almont Drive, Beverly Hills, CA 90211, 310/274-5945
Agent: CAA - Beverly Hills, 310/288-4545

3:15   Dakota Entertainment, 1986

YORAM GROSS
Business: Yoram Gross Film Studios Pty Ltd., 62-68 Church Street,
   Camperdown, Sydney 2050, Australia, tel.: 2/519-1366

DOT AND THE KANGAROO (AF)   Yoram Gross Film Studios,
   1977, Australian
THE LITTLE CONVICT (AF)   Yoram Gross Film Studios,
   1979, Australian
AROUND THE WORLD WITH DOT (AF)   Yoram Gross Film
   Studios, 1982, Australian
SARAH (AF)   Yoram Gross Film Studios, 1983, Australian
DOT AND THE BUNNY (AF)   Yoram Gross Film Studios,
   1984, Australian
THE CAMEL BOY (AF)   Yoram Gross Film Studios,
   1984, Australian
EPIC (AF)   Yoram Gross Film Studios, 1984, Australian
DOT AND THE KOALA (AF)   Yoram Gross Film Studios,
   1985, Australian
DOT AND KEETO (AF)   Yoram Gross Film Studios,
   1985, Australian
DOT AND THE WHALE (AF)   Yoram Gross Film Studios,
   1986, Australian
DOT AND THE SMUGGLERS (AF)   Yoram Gross Film Studios,
   1986, Australian
DOT GOES TO HOLLYWOOD (AF)   Yoram Gross Film Studios,
   1987, Australian
THE MAGIC RIDDLE (AF)   Yoram Gross Film Studios,
   1990, Australian
BLINKY BILL (AF)   Yoram Gross Film Studios, 1992, Australian
DOT IN SPACE (AF)   Yoram Gross Film Studios, 1995, Australian

DAVID GROSSMAN*
Home: 11200 Sunshine Terrace, Studio City, CA 91604,
   818/980-6451
Agent: Metropolitan Talent Agency - Los Angeles, 213/857-4500

FROG (TF)   Platypus Productions, 1988
FROG TOO (TF)   WonderWorks, 1991

CHARLES GROSVENOR
ONCE UPON A FOREST (AF)   co-director with Dave Michener,
   20th Century Fox, 1993

GLEN GRUNER
Contact: Box 21, Ballwin, MO 63022, 314/391-9636

THE SKID KID (HVF)   Vertical Productions, 1992

ROBERT GUENETTE*
b. January 12, 1935 - Holyoke, Massachusetts
Business: Robert Guenette Productions, 1551 S. Robertson Blvd. -
   Suite 200, Los Angeles, CA 90035, 310/785-9312

THE TREE   Guenette, 1969
THE MYSTERIOUS MONSTERS   Sunn Classic, 1976
THE AMAZING WORLD OF PSYCHIC PHENOMENA
   Sunn Classic, 1976
THE MAN WHO SAW TOMORROW   Warner Bros., 1981
CRAZY ABOUT THE MOVIES: DENNIS HOPPER (CTD)
   Robert Guenette Productions, 1991

JAMES WILLIAM GUERCIO*
Home: Caribou Ranch, Nederland, Colorado 80466,
   303/258-3215
Agent: ICM - Beverly Hills, 310/550-4000

ELECTRA GLIDE IN BLUE   United Artists, 1973

RUY GUERRA
b. August 23, 1931 - Lourenco Marques, Mozambique
Contact: Concine/National Cinema Council, Rua Mayrink Veiga 28,
   Rio de Janeiro, Brazil, tel.: 2/233-8329

OS CAFAJESTES   1962, Brazilian
OS FUZIS   1964, Brazilian
TENDRE CHASSEURS   1969, French
OS DEUSES E OS MORTOS   1970, Brazilian
A QUIEDA   co-director, 1978, Brazilian
MEUDA, MEMORIA E MASSACRE (FD)   1979, Mozambique
ERENDIRA   MGM/UA, 1983, French-Mexican
OPERA DO MALANDRO   The Samuel Goldwyn Company,
   1986, Brazilian
LA FABULA DE LA BELLA PALOMERA   Network Group/
   Television Espanola/New Latin American Film Foundation,
   1988, Spanish-Brazilian
KUARUP   Grapho Pictures/Guerra Films, 1989, Brazilian
ME ALQUILO PARA SONAR   TVE/ING, 1991, Cuban-Spanish

CHRISTOPHER GUEST*
b. February 5, 1948 - New York, New York
Agent: CAA - Beverly Hills, 310/288-4545

THE BIG PICTURE   Columbia, 1989
ATTACK OF THE 50 FT. WOMAN (CTF)   HBO Pictures/
   Warner Bros. TV, 1993

VAL GUEST
b. 1911 - London, England
Business: Val Guest Productions, Ltd., 1033 Sierra Way,
   Palm Springs, CA 92264, 619/323-4127

MISS LONDON LTD.   General Film Distributors, 1943, British
BEES IN PARADISE   General Film Distributors, 1944, British
GIVE US THE MOON   General Film Distributors, 1944, British
I'LL BE YOUR SWEETHEART   General Film Distributors,
   1945, British

JUST WILLIAM'S LUCK   United Artists, 1947, British
WILLIAM COME TO TOWN   United Artists, 1948, British
MURDER AT THE WINDMILL   Grand National, 1949, British
MISS PILGRIM'S PROGRESS   Grand National, 1950, British
THE BODY SAID NO   Eros, 1950, British
MISTER DRAKE'S DUCK   United Artists, 1951, British
PENNY PRINCESS   Universal, 1952, British
LIFE WITH THE LYONS   Exclusive, 1954, British
THE RUNAWAY BUS   Eros, 1954, British
MEN OF SHERWOOD FOREST   Astor, 1954, British
DANCE LITTLE LADY   Renown, 1954, British
THEY CAN'T HANG ME   Independent Film Distributors,
   1955, British
THE LYONS IN PARIS   Exclusive, 1955, British
BREAK IN THE CIRCLE   20th Century-Fox, 1955, British
THE CREEPING UNKNOWN   *THE QUATERMASS EXPERIMENT*
   United Artists, 1955, British
IT'S A WONDERFUL WORLD   Renown, 1956, British
THE WEAPON   Republic, 1956, British
THE SHIP WAS LOADED   *CARRY ON ADMIRAL*   Renown,
   1957, British
ENEMY FROM SPACE   *QUATERMASS II*   United Artists,
   1957, British
THE ABOMINABLE SNOWMAN OF THE HIMALAYAS
   20th Century-Fox, 1957, British
THE CAMP ON BLOOD ISLAND   Columbia, 1958, British
UP THE CREEK   Dominant, 1958, British
FURTHER UP THE CREEK   Warner Bros., 1958, British
EXPRESSO BONGO   Continental, 1959, British
YESTERDAY'S ENEMY   Columbia, 1959
LIFE IS A CIRCUS   1960, British
HELL IS A CITY   Columbia, 1960, British
STOP ME BEFORE I KILL   *THE FULL TREATMENT*
   Columbia, 1961, British
THE DAY THE EARTH CAUGHT FIRE   Universal, 1962, British
JIGSAW   Beverly, 1962, British
80,000 SUSPECTS   Rank, 1963, British
CONTEST GIRL   *THE BEAUTY JUNGLE*   Continental,
   1964, British
WHERE THE SPIES ARE   MGM, 1965, British
CASINO ROYALE   co-director with Ken Hughes, John Huston,
   Joseph McGrath & Robert Parrish, Columbia, 1967, British
ASSIGNMENT K   Columbia, 1968, British
WHEN DINOSAURS RULED THE EARTH   Warner Bros.,
   1969, British
TOOMORROW   FRD, 1970, British
THE PERSUADERS   1971, British
AU PAIR GIRLS   Cannon, 1972, British
CONFESSIONS OF A WINDOW CLEANER   Columbia,
   1974, British
KILLER FORCE   American International, 1975, British-Swiss
THE SHILLINGBURY BLOWERS   *...AND THE BAND PLAYED ON*
   Inner Circle, 1980, British
DANGEROUS DAVIES - THE LAST DETECTIVE   ITC/Inner
   Circle/Maidenhead Films, 1980, British
THE BOYS IN BLUE   MAM Ltd./Apollo Leisure Group, 1983, British
MARK OF THE DEVIL (TF)   1983, British
IN POSSESSION (TF)   1984, British
CHILD'S PLAY (TF)   1985, British
MISTRESS OF THE SEAS (TF)   1986, British

CHARLES GUGGENHEIM

Contact: Writers Guild of America, East - New York City,
   212/767-7800

THE AMERICAN EXPERIENCE: THE JONESTOWN FLOOD (TD)
   WGBH-Boston, 1992
D-DAY REMEMBERED (FD)   Guggenheim Prods./National D-Day
   Museum, 1995

JOHN GUILLERMIN*

b. November 11, 1925 - London, England
Contact: Directors Guild of America - Los Angeles, 213/851-3671

TORMENT   Adelphi, 1949, British
SMART ALEC   Grand National, 1951, British
TWO ON THE TILES   Grand National, 1951, British
FOUR DAYS   Grand National, 1951, British

BACHELOR IN PARIS   *SONG OF PARIS*   Lippert, 1952, British
MISS ROBIN HOOD   Associated British Film Distributors,
   1952, British
OPERATION DIPLOMAT   Butcher, 1953, British
ADVENTURE IN THE HOPFIELDS   British Lion/Children's
   Film Foundation, 1954, British
THE CROWDED DAY   Adelphi, 1954, British
DUST AND GOLD   1955, British
THUNDERSTORM   Allied Artists, 1955, British
TOWN ON TRIAL   Columbia, 1957, British
THE WHOLE TRUTH   Columbia, 1958, British
I WAS MONTY'S DOUBLE   NTA Pictures, 1958, British
TARZAN'S GREATEST ADVENTURE   Paramount,
   1959, British-U.S.
THE DAY THEY ROBBED THE BANK OF ENGLAND   MGM,
   1960, British
NEVER LET GO   Rank, 1960, British
WALTZ OF THE TOREADORS   Continental, 1962, British
TARZAN GOES TO INDIA   MGM, 1962, British-U.S.-Swiss
GUNS AT BATASI   20th Century-Fox, 1964, British-U.S.
RAPTURE   International Classics, 1965, British-French
THE BLUE MAX   20th Century-Fox, 1966, British, U.S.
P.J.   Universal, 1968
HOUSE OF CARDS   Universal, 1969
THE BRIDGE AT REMAGEN   United Artists, 1969
EL CONDOR   National General, 1970
SKYJACKED   MGM, 1972
SHAFT IN AFRICA   MGM, 1973
THE TOWERING INFERNO   20th Century-Fox, 1974
KING KONG   Paramount, 1976
DEATH ON THE NILE   Paramount, 1978, British
MR. PATMAN   Film Consortium, 1980, Canadian
SHEENA   Columbia, 1984
KING KONG LIVES   DEG, 1986
THE TRACKER (CTF)   HBO Pictures/Lance Hool Productions, 1988

PAUL GUNCZLER

b. December 9, 1957 - Augsburg, West Germany
Business: Bagel Film, Herzog-Johann-Str. 26, 8000
   Munich 60, Germany

GEWALT IM FILM (TD)   co-director with Benjamin Wilchfort,
   1983, West German
DIE NACHT AM SEE   KS-Produktion, 1984, West German
SCHIZOPHRENE BEGEGNUNGEN   ZFI/Bagel Film,
   1988, West German

STURLA GUNNARSSON

b. 1951 - Iceland
Home: 43 Glenwood Avenue, Toronto, Ontario M6P 3C7,
   Canada, 416/769-0254

DIPLOMATIC IMMUNITY   Astral Films, 1991, Canadian-Mexican
REGINA VERSUS STEWART (TF)   CBC, 1992, Canadian

HRAFN GUNNLAUGSSON

b. 1948 - Iceland
Address: Bravallagata 20, 101 Reykjavik, Iceland, tel.: 1/28810
Contact: The Icelandic Film Fund, Laugavegur 24, P.O. Box 320,
   121 Reykjavik, Iceland, tel.: 1/623850

FATHER'S ESTATE   1978, Icelandic
INTER NOS   1980, Icelandic
THE HANGMAN AND THE WHORE (TF)   1986, Swedish
WHEN THE RAVEN FLIES   1987, Icelandic
THE SHADOW OF THE RAVEN   20th Century Fox,
   1988, Icelandic-Swedish
THE WHITE VIKING   Filmeffekt/The Nordic Kabel Fund/DR-TV/NRK/
   SVT/YLE/RUV, 1991, Norwegian-Danish-Swedish-Icelandic
THE SACRED MOUND   F.I.L.M./Viking Film/Icelandic Film Fund/
   Sveriges Television Kanal 1/Svensk Filmindustri/Film Teknik/
   Nordisk Film & TV Fund, 1993, Icelandic-Swedish

CARLO GUSTAFF

INDECENT BEHAVIOR II   Magic Hour Productions, 1994

ERIK GUSTAVSON
b. 1955 - Norway
Agent: The Chasin Agency - Los Angeles, 310/278-7505

BLACKOUT Norsk Film, 1985, Norwegian
HERMAN RKO Pictures Distribution, 1990, Norwegian
TELEGRAFISTEN Nordic Screen Development/Schibsted Film/
   Metronome/Norsk Film, 1993, Norwegian-Danish
CAN YOU HEAR ME? Nordic Screen Development,
   1995, Norwegian

TOMAS GUTIERREZ ALEA
b. December 11, 1928 - Havana, Cuba
Agent: ICM - Beverly Hills, 310/550-4000
Contact: Instituto Cubano del Arte e IndustriaCinematograficas
   (ICAIC), Calle 23, No. 1155, Vedado, Havana, Cuba,
   tel.: 53-7/30-5041

EL MEGANO co-director, 1955, Cuban
ESTA TIERRA NEUSTRA 1959, Cuban
ASEMBLEA GENERAL 1960, Cuban
MUERTE AL INVASOR co-director, 1961, Cuban
HISTORIAS DE LA REVOLUCION 1961, Cuban
LAS DOCE SILLAS 1962, Cuban
CUMBITE 1964, Cuban
LA MUERTE DE AN BUROCRATA 1966, Cuban
MEMORIES OF UNDERDEVELOPMENT Tricontinental,
   1968, Cuban
UNA PELEA CUBANA CONTRA LOS DEMONIOS 1971, Cuban
EL ARTE DEL TOBACO 1974, Cuban
THE LAST SUPPER Tricontinental, 1976, Cuban
LOS SOBREVIVIENTES ICAIC, 1979, Cuban
UP TO A POINT New Yorker, 1984, Cuban
CARTAS DEL PARQUE ICAIC, 1988, Cuban
STRAWBERRY AND CHOCOLATE co-director with
   Juan Carlos Tabio, Miramax Films, 1994,
   Cuban-Mexican-Spanish
GUANTANAMERA co-director with Juan Carlos Tabio,
   Tornasol Films/Alta Films/Prime Films/Television Espanola/
   ICAA/Canal Plus Espana, 1995, Cuban-Spanish

MANUEL GUTIERREZ ARAGON
b. 1942 - Spain
Contact: Spanish Film Institute, San Marcos 40, Madrid 28004,
   Spain, tel.: 1/532-5089

HABLA, MUDITA 1973, Spanish
CAMADA NEGRA 1977, Spanish
SONAMBULOS 1977, Spanish
EL CORAZON DEL BOSQUE 1978, Spanish
MARAVILLAS 1980, Spanish
DEMONIOS EN EL JARDIN 1982, Spanish
FEROZ! 1983, Spanish
LA NOCHE MAS HERMOSA Luis Megino Producciones
   Cinematograficas, 1984, Spanish
HALF OF HEAVEN LA MITAD DEL CIELO Skouras Pictures,
   1986, Spanish
MALAVENTURA CB FILM, 1988, Spanish
EL QUIJOTE (TF) Emiliano Piedra Productions/TVE,
   1991, Spanish
EL REY DEL RIO Sogetel/Lolafilms/Animatografo/Celtic Films,
   1995, Spanish-Portuguese-British

NATHANIEL GUTMAN*
Contact: Maio & Associates, 120 El Camino Drive, Beverly Hills,
   CA 90210, 310/859-2309
Agent: Innovative Artists - Los Angeles, 310/553-5200

DEADLINE Skouras Pictures, 1987, West German-Israeli
TWICE UPON A TIME Creative, 1990, West German
LINDA (CTF) Linda Productions/Wilshire Court Productions, 1993

ANDRE GUTTFREUND*
Agent: Premiere Artists Agency - Los Angeles, 310/271-1414
Personal Manager: Carthay Circle Pictures and Management -
   Beverly Hills, 310/657-5454

BREACH OF CONTRACT Atlantic Releasing Corporation, 1984
FEMME FATALE Gibraltar Entertainment, 1991

CLAUDIO GUZMAN*
Address: 1520 S. Beverly Glen - Suite 301, Los Angeles, CA 90024,
   310/788-9078

ANTONIO Guzman Productions, 1973
LINDA LOVELACE FOR PRESIDENT General Film, 1975
WILLA (TF) co-director with Joan Darling, GJL Productions/
   Dove, Inc., 1979
THE HOSTAGE TOWER (TF) Jerry Leider Productions, 1980
FOR LOVERS ONLY (TF) Henerson-Hirsch Productions/Caesar's
   Palace Productions, 1982

STEPHEN GYLLENHAAL*
b. October 4, 1949 - Cleveland, Ohio
Home: 455 S. Irving Blvd., Los Angeles, CA 90020, 213/938-5211
Agent: CAA - Beverly Hills, 310/288-4545

CERTAIN FURY New World, 1985, Canadian
THE ABDUCTION OF KARI SWENSON (TF)
   NBC Productions, 1987
PROMISED A MIRACLE (TF) Dick Clark Productions/Republic
   Pictures Roni Weisberg Productions, 1988
LEAP OF FAITH (TF) Hart, Thomas & Berlin Productions, 1988
FAMILY OF SPIES (MS) King Phoenix Entertainment, 1990
KILLING IN A SMALL TOWN (TF) ☆ The IndieProd Co./Hearst
   Entertainment Prods., 1990
PARIS TROUT (CTF) Viacom Pictures, 1991
WATERLAND Fine Line Features/New Line Cinema,
   1992, British-U.S.
A DANGEROUS WOMAN Gramercy Pictures, 1993
LOSING ISAIAH Paramount, 1995

CHARLES HAAS*
b. 1913 - Chicago, Illinois
Home: 12626 Hortense Street, Studio City, CA 91604, 818/877-5120
Agent: Harold Greene, 8455 Beverly Blvd. , Los Angeles, CA 90069,
   213/852-4959

STAR IN THE DUST Universal, 1956
SCREAMING EAGLES Allied Artists, 1956
SHOWDOWN AT ABILENE Universal, 1956
SUMMER LOVE Universal, 1958
WILD HERITAGE Universal, 1958
THE BEAT GENERATION MGM, 1959
THE BIG OPERATOR MGM, 1959
GIRLS' TOWN MGM, 1959
PLATINUM HIGH SCHOOL MGM, 1960

PHILIP HAAS
Agent: UTA - Beverly Hills, 310/273-6700

THE MUSIC OF CHANCE I.R.S. Releasing, 1993
MONEY MAN Milestone Film & Video, 1993
ANGELS AND INSECTS The Samuel Goldwyn Company,
   1995, British-U.S.

HERVE HACHUEL
b. Madrid, Spain
Business: Tesauro SA, Jose Abascal 44, Madrid 28003, Spain,
tel.: 1/255-1807

PHILIP BANTER   Tesauro Films, 1985, Spanish
VENGEANCE WITH A KISS   Concorde, 1991, U.S.-Spanish

TAYLOR HACKFORD*
b. December 3, 1944
Agent: CAA - Beverly Hills, 310/288-4545

THE IDOLMAKER   United Artists, 1980
AN OFFICER AND A GENTLEMAN   Paramount, 1982
AGAINST ALL ODDS   Columbia, 1984
WHITE NIGHTS   Columbia, 1985
CHUCK BERRY: HAIL! HAIL! ROCK 'N' ROLL! (FD)
   Universal, 1987
EVERYBODY'S ALL-AMERICAN   Warner Bros., 1988
BOUND BY HONOR   *BLOOD IN BLOOD OUT*
   Buena Vista, 1993
DOLORES CLAIBORNE   Columbia, 1995

ROSS HAGEN
Agent: Barry Perelman Agency - Los Angeles, 310/274-5999

B.O.R.N.   The Movie Outfit, 1989
CLICK: THE CALENDAR GIRL KILLER   co-director with
   John Stewart, Crown International, 1990
STREET BEAT   Grand Am, Ltd., 1994
TIME WARS   Grand Am, Ltd., 1994

RUSSELL HAGG
Contact: Australian Film Commission, 150 William Street,
   Woolloomooloo NSW 2011, Australia, tel.: 2/321-6444

CASH & CO. (MS)   co-director with George Miller, Homestead
   Films/Network Seven, 1975, Australian
TANDARRA (MS)   co-director, Homestead Films/Network Seven,
   1976, Australian
RAW DEAL   Greater Union Film Distributors, 1977, Australian
TAXI (TF)   Network Seven, 1979, Australian

PIERS HAGGARD*
b. 1939 - Scotland
Agent: William Morris Agency - Beverly Hills, 310/859-4000 or:
   The Casarotto Company - London, tel.: 171/287-4450

WEDDING NIGHT   *I CAN'T...I CAN'T*   American International,
   1969, Irish
THE BLOOD ON SATAN'S CLAW   *SATAN'S SKIN*
   Cannon, 1971, British
THE QUATERMASS CONCLUSION   Euston Films Ltd.,
   1979, British
THE FIENDISH PLOT OF DR. FU MANCHU   Orion/Warner Bros.,
   1980, British
MRS. REINHARDT (TF)   BBC/WNET-13, 1981, British-U.S.
VENOM   Paramount, 1982, British
ROLLING HOME (TF)   BBC, 1982, British
MARKS (TF)   BBC, 1982, British
DESERT OF LIES (TF)   BBC, 1983, British
WATERS OF THE MOON (TF)   BBC, 1983, British
KNOCKBACK (TF)   BBC, 1984, British
DISNEY'S RETURN TO TREASURE ISLAND   *RETURN TO
   TREASURE ISLAND* (CMS)   The Disney Channel/Harlech TV,
   1986, U.S.-British
VISITORS (TF)   BBC, 1987, British
A SUMMER STORY (TF)   Atlantic Releasing Corporation,
   1988, British
THE FULFILLMENT OF MARY GRAY (TF)   Mary Gray Inc./Lee
   Caplin Productions/Indian Neck Entertainment, 1989
BACK HOME (CTF)   TVS Films/Veronmead Productions/Citadel
   Entertainment, 1990, British
I'LL TAKE ROMANCE (TF)   New World TV, 1990

FOUR EYES AND SIX-GUNS (CTF)   Firebrand Productions/
   Saban-Scherick Productions, 1992
THE LIFEFORCE EXPERIMENT (CTF)   Filmline International/
   Screen Partners/USA Pictures, 1994, U.S.-Canadian
HEARTSTONES   Blue Heaven Productions, 1994

PAUL HAGGIS*
Contact: Directors Guild of America - Los Angeles, 213/851-3671

RED HOT   Hot Red Motion Pictures, 1992, Canadian

LARRY HAGMAN*
b. September 21, 1931 - Fort Worth, Texas
Business: Hagman Productions Inc., 23730 Malibu Colony, Malibu,
   CA 90265, 310/456-5210

BEWARE! THE BLOB   *SON OF BLOB*   Jack H. Harris
   Enterprises, 1972

STUART HAGMANN*
b. September 2, 1942 - Sturgeon Bay, Wisconsin
Telephone: 818/506-1700
Business Manager: Howard M. Borris, Howard Borris & Company,
   8484 Wilshire Blvd. - Suite 500, Beverly Hills, CA 90211,
   213/665-3991

THE STRAWBERRY STATEMENT   MGM, 1970
BELIEVE IN ME   MGM, 1971
SHE LIVES (TF)   ABC Circle Films, 1973
TARANTULAS: THE DEADLY CARGO (TF)   Alan Landsburg
   Productions, 1977

STEVEN HAHN
STARCHASER: THE LEGEND OF ORIN (AF)   Atlantic Releasing
   Corporation, 1985

ZAFAR HAI
Contact: British Film Commission, 70 Baker Street, London
   W1M 1DJ, England, tel.: 171/224-5000

THE PERFECT MURDER   Merchant Ivory Productions,
   1988, British-Indian

CHARLES HAID*
Agent: William Morris Agency - Beverly Hills, 310/859-4000
Business Manager: Charles Stein, Brittcadia Productions,
   12711 Ventura Blvd. - Suite 240, Studio City, CA 91604,
   818/761-5851

IN THE LINE OF DUTY: SIEGE AT MARION (TF)
   Patchett Kaufman Entertainment, 1992
THE NIGHTMAN (TF)   Avnet-Kerner Productions, 1992
COOPERSTOWN (CTF)   Michael Brandman Productions/Amblin
   Entertainment, 1993
IRON WILL   Buena Vista, 1994

RANDA HAINES*
Business: Randa Haines/Todd Black, 10201 W. Pico Blvd. -
   Building 730, Los Angeles, CA 90035, 310/203-2163
Agent: ICM - Beverly Hills, 310/550-4000

UNDER THIS SKY (TF)   Red Cloud Productions/PBS, 1979
THE JILTING OF GRANNY WEATHERALL (TF)   Learning in
   Focus/American Short Story, 1980
SOMETHING ABOUT AMELIA (TF) ☆   Leonard Goldberg
   Productions, 1984
ALFRED HITCHCOCK PRESENTS (TF)   co-director with
   Steve DeJarnatt, Joel Oliansky & Fred Walton,
   Universal TV, 1985
CHILDREN OF A LESSER GOD   Paramount, 1986
THE DOCTOR   Buena Vista, 1991
WRESTLING ERNEST HEMINGWAY   Warner Bros., 1993

WILLIAM (BILLY) HALE*
Agent: ICM - Beverly Hills, 310/550-4000
Attorney: Richard Thompson, Silverberg, Katz, Thompson & Braun,
   11766 Wilshire Blvd. - Suite 700, Los Angeles, CA 90025,
   310/445-5858

HOW I SPENT MY SUMMER VACATION (TF)   Universal TV, 1967
GUNFIGHT IN ABILENE   Universal, 1967
JOURNEY TO SHILOH   Universal, 1968
NIGHTMARE (TF)   CBS, Inc., 1974
THE GREAT NIAGARA (TF)   Playboy Productions, 1974
CROSSFIRE (TF)   QM Productions, 1975
THE KILLER WHO WOULDN'T DIE (TF)   Paramount TV, 1976
STALK THE WILD CHILD (TF)   Charles Fries Productions, 1976
RED ALERT (TF)   The Jozak Company/Paramount TV, 1977
S.O.S. TITANIC (TF)   Roger Gimbel Productions/EMI TV/Argonaut
   Films Ltd., 1979, U.S.-British
MURDER IN TEXAS (TF)   Dick Clark Productions/Billy Hale
   Films, 1981
ONE SHOE MAKES IT MURDER (TF)   The Fellows-Keegan
   Company/Lorimar Productions, 1982
THE DEMON MURDER CASE (TF)   Dick Clark Productions/Len
   Steckler Productions, 1983
LACE (MS)   Lorimar Productions, 1984
LACE 2 (MS)   Lorimar Productions, 1985
HAREM (TF)   Highgate Pictures, 1986
THE MURDER OF MARY PHAGAN (TF)   George Stevens, Jr.
   Productions/Century Tower Productions, 1988
LIBERACE (TF)   The Liberace Foundation for the Performing and
   Creative Arts/Dick Clark Productions/Republic Pictures, 1988
PEOPLE LIKE US (TF)   ITC, 1990

JACK HALEY, JR.*
b. October 25, 1933 - Los Angeles, California
Business: Jack Haley, Jr. Productions, 8255 Beverly Blvd. -
   Penthouse 20, Los Angeles, CA 90048, 310/655-1106

NORWOOD   Paramount, 1970
THE LOVE MACHINE   Columbia, 1971
THAT'S ENTERTAINMENT! (FD)   MGM/United Artists, 1974
THAT'S ENTERTAINMENT, PART 2 (FD)   co-director with
   Gene Kelly, MGM/United Artists, 1976
THAT'S DANCING! (FD)   MGM/UA, 1985
THAT'S DRIVING (FD)   co-director with Tony Nassour,
   Alexia International Pictures, 1992
100 YEARS OF THE HOLLYWOOD WESTERN (TD)
   Jack Haley, Jr. Productions, 1994

ADRIAN HALL*
Home: Route 4, Box 56, Grand Saline, TX 75140, 214/963-7559

THE HOUSE OF MIRTH (TF)   Cinelit Productions/WNET-13, 1981

ANTHONY MICHAEL HALL
b. April 14, 1968 - Boston, Massachusetts
Contact: Screen Actors Guild - Los Angeles, 213/954-1600

HAIL CAESAR   Trimark Pictures, 1994

KENNETH J. HALL
GHOST WRITER   Rumar Films, 1989

PETER HALL*
b. November 22, 1930 - Bury St. Edmunds, Suffolk, England
Business: The Peter Hall Company, c/o Albery Theatre, St. Martin's
   Lane, London WC2N 4AH, England, tel.: 171/867-1123
Agent: ICM - London, tel.: 171/636-6565

WORK IS A FOUR LETTER WORD   Universal, 1968, British
A MIDSUMMER NIGHT'S DREAM   Eagle, 1968, British
PERFECT FRIDAY   Chevron, 1970, British
THE HOMECOMING   American Film Theatre, 1973, British
AKENFIELD (FD)   Angle Films, 1975, British
SHE'S BEEN AWAY   BBC Films, 1989, British
ORPHEUS DESCENDING (CTF)   Nederlander TV & Film
   Productions/Turnet Network TV, 1990

JACOB: A TNT BIBLE STORY (CTF)   LUBE Productions/Raiuno/
   BSkyBLux Film/France 2/ORF/Turner Pictures, 1994,
   Italian-German-U.S.
NEVER TALK TO STRANGERS   Cinevisions/Creative Edge Films,
   1995, Canadian

GUDNY HALLDORSDOTTIR
Contact: The Icelandic Film Fund, Laugavegur 24, 121 Reykjavik,
   Iceland, tel.: 1/623580

UNDER THE GLACIER   1989, Icelandic
THE MEN'S CHOIR   Umbifilm/Artiel/Filmfotograferna, 1993,
   Icelandic-German-Swedish

DANIEL HALLER*
b. 1926 - Los Angeles, California
Home: 5364 Jed Smith Road, Hidden Hills, CA 91302, 818/888-7936

DIE, MONSTER, DIE!   American International, 1965, U.S.-British
DEVIL'S ANGELS   American International, 1967
THE WILD RACERS   American International, 1968
PADDY   Allied Artists, 1970, Irish
PIECES OF DREAMS   United Artists, 1970
THE DUNWICH HORROR   American International, 1970
THE DESPERATE MILES (TF)   Universal TV, 1975
MY SWEET LADY (TF)   Universal TV, 1976
BLACK BEAUTY (MS)   Universal TV, 1978
LITTLE MO (TF)   Mark VII Ltd./Worldvision, 1978
BUCK ROGERS IN THE 25TH CENTURY   Universal, 1979
HIGH MIDNIGHT (TF)   The Mirisch Corporation/Universal TV, 1979
GEORGIA PEACHES (TF)   New World TV, 1980
FOLLOW THAT CAR   New World, 1981
MICKEY SPILLANE'S MARGIN FOR MURDER (TF)
   Hamner Productions, 1981
KNIGHT RIDER (TF)   Glen A. Larson Productions/
   Universal TV, 1982

TODD HALLOWELL*
Agent: UTA - Beverly Hills, 310/273-6700
Home: 5022 Willowcrest Avenue, North Hollywood, CA 91601,
   818/506-4319

LOVE OR MONEY   Hemdale, 1990

LASSE HALLSTROM*
b. 1946 - Stockholm, Sweden
Agent: ICM - Beverly Hills, 310/550-4000
Business Manager: Wayne Mejia, de Blois, Mejia & Co., 9171 Wilshire
   Blvd. - Suite 541, Beverly Hills, CA 90210, 310/273-7769

A LOVER AND HIS LASS   1975, Swedish
ABBA - THE MOVIE   Warner Bros., 1977, Swedish
FATHER TO BE   1979, Swedish
THE ROOSTER   1981, Swedish
HAPPY WE   1983, Swedish
MY LIFE AS A DOG ★   Skouras Pictures, 1985, Swedish
THE CHILDREN OF BULLERBY VILLAGE   Svensk Filmindustri,
   1986, Swedish
MORE ABOUT THE CHILDREN OF BULLERBY VILLAGE
   Svensk Filmindustri, 1987, Swedish
ONCE AROUND   Universal, 1991
WHAT'S EATING GILBERT GRAPE   Paramount, 1993
GAME OF LOVE   Warner Bros., 1995

DAVID HAMILTON
Contact: French Film Office, 745 Fifth Avenue, New York,
   NY 10151, 212/832-8860

BILITIS   Topar, 1976, French
TENDRE COUSINES   Crown International, 1980, French
LAURA, LES OMBRES DE L'ETE   Les Films de L'Alma/CORA,
   1979, French
PREMIERS DESIRS   AMLF, 1983, French-West German
UN ETE A SAINT TROPEZ (FD)   Fugio & Associates/JVC,
   1983, French-Japanese
TATIANA   UGC, 1984, French

DEAN HAMILTON
Contact: Screen Actors Guild - Los Angeles, 213/954-1600

SAVAGE LAND   Hemdale, 1994
HE AIN'T HEAVY   Republic Pictures, 1995

GUY HAMILTON*
b. September, 1922 - Paris, France
Home: 22 Mont Port, Puerto Andraitx, Mallorca, Palma de Mallorca,
   Spain, tel.: 67-15-43
Agent: AA - Paris, tel.: 1/42-56-21-22

THE RINGER   British Lion, 1952, British
THE INTRUDER   Associated Artists, 1953, British
AN INSPECTOR CALLS   Associated Artists, 1954, British
THE COLDITZ STORY   Republic, 1955, British
CHARLEY MOON   British Lion, 1956, British
STOWAWAY GIRL   MANUELA   Paramount, 1957, British
THE DEVIL'S DISCIPLE   United Artists, 1959, British
A TOUCH OF LARCENY   Paramount, 1960, British
THE BEST OF ENEMIES   I DUE NEMICI   Columbia,
   1962, Italian-British
MAN IN THE MIDDLE   20th Century-Fox, 1964, British-U.S.
GOLDFINGER   United Artists, 1964, British
THE PARTY'S OVER   Allied Artists, 1966, British
FUNERAL IN BERLIN   Paramount, 1966, British
BATTLE OF BRITAIN   United Artists, 1969, British
DIAMONDS ARE FOREVER   United Artists, 1971, British
LIVE AND LET DIE   United Artists, 1973, British
THE MAN WITH THE GOLDEN GUN   United Artists,
   1974, British
FORCE 10 FROM NAVARONE   American International, 1978
THE MIRROR CRACK'D   AFD, 1980, British
EVIL UNDER THE SUN   Universal/AFD, 1982, British
REMO WILLIAMS: THE ADVENTURE BEGINS...   Orion, 1985
TRY THIS ON FOR SIZE   Film Number One, 1989, French

JOHN HAMILTON
Contact: Directors Guild of Canada, 225 Richmond Street, Toronto,
   Ontario M5V 1W2, Canada, 416/351-8200

THE MYTH OF THE MALE ORGASM   Telescene Communications/
   Doodskie Film Corporation, 1993, Canadian

STRATHFORD HAMILTON*
Home: 8280 Grandview Drive, Los Angeles, CA 90046,
   213/656-0888
Agent: The Gersh Agency - Beverly Hills, 310/274-6611

BLUEBERRY HILL   MGM/UA, 1988
DIVING IN   Skouras Pictures, 1990
BETRAYAL OF THE DOVE   Private Productions, 1992
TEMPTATION   Dino De Laurentiis Communications, 1994

BARBARA HAMMER
NITRATE KISSES (FD)   Strand Releasing, 1993

PETER HAMMOND
Agent: Chatto & Linnit - London, tel.: 171/930-6677

KILVERT'S DIARY (TF)   BBC, 1979, British
SEASONG (TF)   Euston Films, 1980, British
HAPPY AUTUMN FIELDS (TF)   BBC, 1983, British
THE COMBINATION (TF)   BBC, 1984, British
THE BLUE DRESS (TF)   BBC, 1985, British
THE DEATH OF THE HEART (TF)   Granada TV, 1986, British
SERVICE OF ALL THE DEAD (TF)   Zenith Productions,
   1987, British
THE CHILDREN OF DYNMOUTH (TF)   BBC, 1987, British
THE SIGN OF FOUR (TF)   Granada TV, 1988, British
THE DARK ANGEL (TF)   BBC/TV New Zealand, 1990,
   British-New Zealand
THE SINS OF THE FATHER (TF)   Zenith Productions,
   1990, British
THE MASTER BLACKMAILER (TF)   Granada TV, 1991, British

THE NOBLE BACHELOR (TF)   Granada TV, 1992, British
THE MEMOIRS OF SHERLOCK HOLMES (MS)   co-director,
   Granada TV, 1993, British

CHRISTOPHER HAMPTON
b. January 26, 1946 - Fayal, Azores
Agent: William Morris Agency - Beverly Hills, 310/859-4000

CARRINGTON   Polygram, 1994, British

JOHN HANCOCK*
b. February 12, 1939 - LaPorte, Indiana
Home: 21531 Deerpath Lane, Malibu, CA 90265, 310/456-3627
Agent: Camden-ITG - Los Angeles, 310/289-2700

LET'S SCARE JESSICA TO DEATH   Paramount, 1971
BANG THE DRUM SLOWLY   Paramount, 1973
BABY BLUE MARINE   Columbia, 1976
CALIFORNIA DREAMING   American International, 1979
WEEDS   DEG, 1987
STEAL THE SKY (CTF)   HBO Pictures/Yoram Ben Ami
   Productions/Paramount TV, 1988
PRANCER   Orion, 1989

SUSUMU HANI
b. October 10, 1928 - Tokyo Prefecture, Japan
Contact: Nihon Eiga Kantoku Kyokai (Japan Film Directors
   Association), La Fontenu Building -4th Floor, 23-2 Maruyama-cho,
   Shibuya-ku, Tokyo, Japan, tel.: 3/3461-4411

BAD BOYS   Iwanami Eiga, 1961, Japanese
SHE AND HE   Brandon, 1963, Japanese
BWANA TOSHI   Tokyo Eiga/Showa Eiga, 1965, Japanese
BRIDE OF THE ANDES   Tokyo Eiga/Hani Productions,
   1966, Japanese
NANAMI: INFERNO OF FIRST LOVE   All Stuff Productions/Teatro
   Productions, 1970, Japanese
TIME SCHEDULE IN THE MORNING   Hani Productions/ATG,
   1972, Japanese
A TALE OF AFRICA   Sanrio Film, 1980, Japanese

WILLIAM HANNA
b. July 14, 1911 - Melrose, New Mexico
Business: Hanna-Barbera Productions, 3400 Cahuenga Blvd. West,
   Hollywood, CA 90068, 213/851-5000

HEY THERE, IT'S YOGI BEAR (AF)   co-director with
   Joseph Barbera, Columbia, 1964
A MAN CALLED FLINTSTONE (AF)   co-director with
   Joseph Barbera, Columbia, 1966
ESCAPE FROM GRUMBLE GULTCH (AF)   co-director with
   Joseph Barbera, Hanna-Barbera Productions, 1983
JETSONS: THE MOVIE (AF)   co-director with Joseph Barbera,
   Universal, 1990
I YABBA-DABBA DO! (ATF)   co-director with Ray Patterson,
   Joanna Romersa & Gordon Hunt, Hanna-Barbera
   Productions, 1993
HOLLYROCK-A-BYE BABY (ATF)   co-director with Gordon Hunt,
   Kris Zimmerman, Paul Schibli, Steven McCallum & Glenn Chaika,
   Hanna Barbera Productions/Wang Film Production Company Ltd.
   Taiwan, 1993, U.S.-Taiwanese

BRIAN HANNANT
Contact: Australian Film Commission, 150 William Street,
   Woolloomooloo NSW 2011, Australia, tel.: 2/321-6444

THREE TO GO   co-director with Peter Weir & Oliver Howes,
   Commonwealth Film Unit, 1971, Australian
FLASHPOINT   Film Australia, 1972, Australian
THE TIME GUARDIAN   Hemdale, 1987, Australian

IZHAK HANOOKA
RED NIGHTS   Trans World Entertainment, 1988

MARION HANSEL

Contact: National Tourist Office, 61 Rue de Marche Aux Herbes,
    B1000 Brussels, Belgium, tel.: 02/513-8940

IL MAESTRO   1989, Belgian-Italian
BETWEEN THE DEVIL AND THE DEEP BLUE SEA
    Man's Films, 1995, Belgian

ERIC HANSEN

DESERT STORM   Patriotic Films, 1992

CURTIS HANSON*

b. Los Angeles, California
Agent: UTA - Beverly Hills, 310/273-6700

THE AROUSERS   SWEET KILL   New World, 1976
THE LITTLE DRAGONS   Aurora, 1980
LOSIN' IT   Embassy, 1983, Canadian-U.S.
THE CHILDREN OF TIMES SQUARE (TF)   Gross-Weston
    Productions/Fries Entertainment, 1986
THE BEDROOM WINDOW   DEG, 1987
BAD INFLUENCE   Triumph Releasing Corporation, 1990
THE HAND THAT ROCKS THE CRADLE   Buena Vista, 1992
THE RIVER WILD   Universal, 1994

JOHN HANSON

b. March 7, 1942 - St. Paul, Minnesota
Business: New Front Films, 125 W. Richmond Avenue, Point
    Richmond, CA 94801, 415/231-0225
Agent: Becsey/Wisdom/Kalajian - Los Angeles, 310/550-0535

NORTHERN LIGHTS   co-director with Rob Nilsson, Cine Manifest/
    New Front Films, 1978
WILDROSE   Troma, 1984
SMART MONEY   Skouras Pictures, 1988
SHIMMER   American Playhouse Theatrical Films/WMG/
    Kinowelt, 1993

JOSEPH C. HANWRIGHT*

Home: P.O. Box 478, Ketchum, ID 83340, 208/726-3594

UNCLE JOE SHANNON   United Artists, 1979

KAZUO HARA

Contact: Nihon Eiga Kantoku Kyokai (Japanese Film Directors
    Association), La Fontenu Building -4th Floor, 23-2 Maruyama-cho,
    Shibuya-ku, Tokyo, Japan, tel.: 3/3461-4411

THE EMPEROR'S NAKED ARMY MARCHES ON (FD)   Shisso Pro,
    1987, Japanese
A DEDICATED LIFE (FD)   Eurospace, 1994, Japanese

MASATO HARADA

b. 1949 - Shizuoka Prefecture, Japan
Contact: Nihon Eiga Kantoku Kyokai (Japanese Film Directors
    Association), La Fontenu Building -4th Floor, 23-2 Maruyama-cho,
    Shibuya-ku, Tokyo, Japan, tel.: 3/3461-4411

INDIAN SUMMER: GOODBYE MY MOVIE FRIEND   Kitty Films,
    1979, Japanese
WINDY   CCJ/Manfred Durniok Productions, 1984,
    Japanese-West German
ONYANKO, THE MOVIE   Fuji TV, 1986, Japanese
PARIS-DAKAR 15,000: CHALLENGE OF SUCCESS (FD)
    Tanaka Promotions, 1986, Japanese
GOODBYE MY LOVE   Shochiku/Burning Productions,
    1987, Japanese
GUNHED   Toho/Sunrise Productions, 1989, Japanese
THE PAINTED DESERT   KSS/Shochiku/Wowow Satellite TV,
    1993, U.S.-Japanese
KAMIKAZE TAXI   1994, Japanese
BENEATH THE FLESH   Filmwest Corporation, 1994

SHAWN HARDIN*

Agent: Stone Manners Agency - Los Angeles, 213/654-7575

120-VOLT MIRACLES   OTV Productions, 1992

JOSEPH HARDY*

b. March 8, 1929 - Carlsbad, New Mexico
Agent: CAA - Beverly Hills, 310/288-4545

GREAT EXPECTATIONS (TF)   Transcontinental Film Productions,
    1974, British
A TREE GROWS IN BROOKLYN (TF)   20th Century-Fox TV, 1974
LAST HOURS BEFORE MORNING (TF)   Charles Fries Productions/
    MGM TV, 1975
THE SILENCE (TF)   Palomar Pictures International, 1975
JAMES AT 15 (TF)   20th Century-Fox TV, 1977
THE USERS (TF)   Aaron Spelling Productions, 1978
LOVE'S SAVAGE FURY (TF)   Aaron Spelling Productions, 1979
THE SEDUCTION OF MISS LEONA (TF)   Edgar J. Scherick
    Associates, 1980
DREAM HOUSE (TF)   Hill-Mandelker Films/Time-Life
    Productions, 1981
THE DAY THE BUBBLE BURST (TF)   Tamara Productions/20th
    Century-Fox TV/The Production Company, 1982
NOT IN FRONT OF THE CHILDREN (TF)   Tamtco Productions/
    The Edward S. Feldman Company, 1982
TWO MARRIAGES (TF)   Lorimar Productions/Raven's Claw
    Productions, 1983

JUSTIN HARDY

Contact: British Film Commission, 70 Baker Street, London
    W1M 1DJ, England, tel.: 71/224-5000

A FEAST AT MIDNIGHT   Kwai River Productions, 1994, British

ROBIN HARDY

b. February 10, 1929 - England
Address: c/o Robert Lasky, 1150 Fifth Avenue, New York, NY 10128
Contact: British Film Commission, 70 Baker Street, London
    W1M 1DJ, England, tel.: 171/224-5000

THE WICKER MAN   Warner Bros., 1975, British
THE FANTASIST   ITC, 1986, Irish

ROD HARDY*

Agent: CAA - Beverly Hills, 310/288-4545

THIRST   FG Pictures, 1980, British
UNDER CAPRICORN (MS)   BBC/South Australian Film Corporation,
    1982, Australian
PUNISHMENT (TF)   Ten Network, 1984, Australian
EUREKA STOCKADE (TF)   Metromedia/Henry Crawford
    Productions, 1984, Australian-U.S.
SHADOWS OF THE HEART (MS)   BBC/South Australian Film
    Corporation, 1990, British-Australian
HALF WAY ACROSS THE GALAXY AND TURN LEFT (TF)
    Crawfords Australia, 1991, Australian
BETWEEN LOVE AND HATE (TF)   Cosgrove-Meurer Productions/
    World International Network 1993
RIO DIABLO (TF)   Kenny Rogers Productions/RHI Inc./World
    International Network, 1993
LIES AND LULLABIES (TF)   Susan Dey Productions/
    Alexander-Enright & Associates/Hearst Entertainment
    Productions, 1993
THE ONLY WAY OUT (TF)   Berger Queen Productions/Adam
    Productions/ABC Productions, 1993
MY NAME IS KATE (TF)   a.k.a. Productions/Queen Productions./
    Donna Mills Productions/ABC Productions, 1994
THE YEARLING (TF)   RHI Entertainment/CBS Entertainment, 1994
BUFFALO GIRLS (MS)   de Passe Entertainment/CBS
    Entertainment, 1995
ROBINSON CRUSOE   co-director with George Trumbull Miller,
    Miramax Films, 1995

DAVID HARE
(David Rippon)
b. June 5, 1947 - Sussex, England
Agent: ICM - Beverly Hills, 310/550-4000

DREAMS OF LEAVING (TF)   1980, British
LICKING HITLER (TF)   1983, British
WETHERBY   MGM/UA Classics, 1985, British
PARIS BY NIGHT   Cineplex Odeon, 1988, British
STRAPLESS   Granada Film Productions/Film Four International,
   1989, British
HEADING HOME   BBC, 1991, British

DEAN HARGROVE*
b. July 27, 1938 - Iola, Kansas
Business: Dean Hargrove Productions, 100 Universal City Plaza -
   Building 507, Suite 3E, Universal City, CA 91608, 818/777-8305
Agent: Norman Kurland, Broder-Kurland-Webb-Uffner Agency -
   Beverly Hills, 310/281-3400

THE MANCHU EAGLE CAPER MYSTERY   United Artists, 1975
THE BIG RIP-OFF (TF)   Universal TV, 1975
THE RETURN OF THE WORLD'S GREATEST DETECTIVE (TF)
   Universal TV, 1976
DEAR DETECTIVE (TF)   CBS, 1979

TSUI HARK
(Xu Ke)
b. January 2, 1951 - Vietnam
Business: Film Workshop Company Ltd., 13 Wiltshire Road,
   Kowloon Tong, Hong Kong, tel.: 852/338-9973
Contact: Hong Kong Film Liaison, 10940 Wilshire Blvd. - Suite 1220,
   Los Angeles, CA 90024, 310/208-2678

DIE BIAN   1979, Hong Kong
THE BUTTERFLY MURDERS   1979, Hong Kong
WE'RE GOING TO EAT YOU   1980, Hong Kong
DANGEROUS ENCOUNTER - FIRST KIND   1980, Hong Kong
ALL THE WRONG CLUES   1981, Hong Kong
ZU: WARRIORS FROM THE MAGIC MOUNTAIN
   1983, Hong Kong
ACES GO PLACES III: OUR MAN FROM BOND STREET
   1984, Hong Kong
SHANGHAI BLUES   Film Workshop Company Ltd.,
   1984, Hong Kong
PEKING OPERA BLUES   Gordon's Films, 1986, Hong Kong
A BETTER TOMORROW III: LOVE & DEATH IN SAIGON
   Golden Princess/Film Workshop, 1989, Hong Kong
SWORDSMAN   co-director with King Hu, Ann Hui, Ching Siu Tung,
   Lee Wai Man & Kam Yeung Wah, Film Workshop Company,
   1990, Hong Kong
THE WONDER CHILD   Film Workshop Company,
   1991, Hong Kong
WONG FEI-HUNG   *ONCE UPON A TIME IN CHINA*
   Golden Harvest/Film Workshop, 1991, Hong Kong
A CHINESE GHOST STORY III   Film Workshop Company,
   1991, Hong Kong
WONG FEI-HUNG II   *ONCE UPON A TIME IN CHINA II*
   Golden Harvest, 1992, Hong Kong
GREEN SNAKE   Film Workshop Company/Seasonal Film
   Corporation, 1993, Hong Kong
BUTTERFLY LOVERS   Golden Communications, 1994, Hong Kong
ONCE UPON A TIME IN CHINA V   Golden Communications,
   1994, Hong Kong

RENNY HARLIN*
b. Riihmaki, Finland
Business: Midnight Sun Pictures, 8800 Sunset Blvd., Los Angeles,
   CA 90069, 310/289-7590
Agent: ICM - Beverly Hills, 310/550-4000

BORN AMERICAN   Concorde/Cinema Group, 1986
PRISON   Empire Pictures, 1988
A NIGHTMARE ON ELM STREET PART 4: THE DREAM MASTER
   New Line Cinema, 1988
THE ADVENTURES OF FORD FAIRLANE   20th Century Fox, 1990

DIE HARD 2   20th Century Fox, 1990
CLIFFHANGER   TriStar, 1993
CUTTHROAT ISLAND   MGM-UA, 1995

PAUL HARMON
Contact: Australian Film Commission, 150 William Street,
   Woolloomooloo NSW 2011, Australia, tel.: 2/321-6444

I START ON FRIDAY   Film Australia, 1989, Australian
SHOTGUN WEDDING   FFC, 1992, Australian

ROBERT HARMON*
Agent: UTA - Beverly Hills, 310/273-6700

THE HITCHER   TriStar, 1986
THE TENDER   Triumph Releasing Corporation, 1992
NOWHERE TO HIDE   Columbia, 1993

CURTIS HARRINGTON*
b. September 17, 1928 - Los Angeles, California
Agent: Barry Perelman Agency - Los Angeles, 310/274-5999

NIGHT TIDE   Universal, 1963
QUEEN OF BLOOD   American International, 1966
GAMES   Universal, 1967
HOW AWFUL ABOUT ALLAN (TF)   Aaron Spelling
   Productions, 1970
WHO SLEW AUNTIE ROO?   American International, 1971, British
WHAT'S THE MATTER WITH HELEN?   United Artists, 1971
THE CAT CREATURE (TF)   Screen Gems/Columbia TV, 1973
KILLER BEES (TF)   RSO Films, 1974
THE KILLING KIND   Media Trend, 1974
THE DEAD DON'T DIE (TF)   Douglas S. Cramer Productions, 1975
RUBY   Dimension, 1977
DEVIL DOG: THE HOUND OF HELL (TF)   Zeitman-Landers-Roberts
   Productions, 1978
MATA HARI   Cannon, 1985

DAMIAN HARRIS*
Agent: CAA - Beverly Hills, 310/288-4545

THE RACHEL PAPERS   MGM/UA, 1989, British
DECEIVED   Buena Vista, 1991
BAD COMPANY   Buena Vista, 1995

DENNY HARRIS
Business: Denny Harris of California, Inc., 12166 W. Olympic Blvd.,
   Los Angeles, CA 90064, 310/826-6565

SILENT SCREAM   American Cinema, 1980

FRANK HARRIS
KILLPOINT   Crown International, 1984
LOW BLOW   Crown International, 1986
THE PATRIOT   Crown International, 1986
AFTERSHOCK   Prism Entertainment, 1990
IF WE KNEW THEN   International Film Marketing, 1991

HARRY HARRIS*
b. September 8, 1922 - Kansas City, Missouri
Agent: Ronald Leif, Contemporary Artists, Beverly Hills, 310/395-1800

THE RUNAWAYS (TF)   Lorimar Productions, 1975
THE SWISS FAMILY ROBINSON (TF)   Irwin Allen Productions/
   20th Century-Fox TV, 1975
RIVKIN: BOUNTY HUNTER (TF)   Chiarascurio Productions/
   Ten-Four Productions, 1981
A DAY FOR THANKS ON WALTON'S MOUNTAIN (TF)   Lorimar
   Productions/Amanda Productions, 1982
ALICE IN WONDERLAND (TF)   Irwin Allen Productions/Procter &
   Gamble Productions/Columbia TV, 1985
EIGHT IS ENOUGH: A FAMILY REUNION (TF)   Lorimar TV, 1987
A WALTON THANKSGIVING REUNION (TF)   Lee Rich Company/
   Amanda Productions/Warner Bros. TV, 1993

JAMES B. HARRIS*
b. August 3, 1928 - New York, New York
Business: James B. Harris Productions, 248-1/2 Lasky Drive,
 Beverly Hills, CA 90212, 310/273-4270

THE BEDFORD INCIDENT   Columbia, 1965
SOME CALL IT LOVING   Cine Globe, 1973
FAST-WALKING   Pickman Films, 1982
COP   Atlantic Releasing Corporation, 1988
BOILING POINT   Warner Bros., 1993, U.S.-French

LESLIE HARRIS
b. Cleveland, Ohio
Agent: UTA - Beverly Hills, 310/273-6700

JUST ANOTHER GIRL ON THE I.R.T.   Miramax Films, 1992

RICHARD HARRIS
b. October 1, 1932 - Limerick, Ireland
Agent: William Morris Agency - Beverly Hills, 310/859-4000

THE HERO   *BLOOMFIELD*   Avco Embassy, 1972, Israeli-British

TRENT HARRIS
Agent: Annette Van Doren - Los Angeles, 213/650-3643

RUBIN & ED   I.R.S. Releasing, 1991, U.S.-British
PLAN 10 FROM OUTER SPACE   Plan 10 Productions, 1994

WENDELL B. HARRIS, JR.
CHAMELEON STREET   Northern Arts Entertainment, 1990
NEGROPOLIS   1995

JOHN HARRISON*
Agent: CAA - Beverly Hills, 310/288-4545

TALES FROM THE DARKSIDE: THE MOVIE   Paramount, 1990

JOHN KENT HARRISON
Agent: William Morris Agency - Beverly Hills, 310/859-4000

BEAUTIFUL DREAMERS   Hemdale, 1990, Canadian
ALEXANDER BELL - THE SOUND AND THE SILENCE (MS)
 Atlantis Films, 1992, Canadian
CREATURE, KID AND MARGARET (TF)   Marian Rees
 Associates, 1993
CITY BOY (TF)   Accent Entertainment/New City Productions/
 B.C. Film, 1993, Canadian
WHOSE CHILD IS THIS? THE WAR FOR BABY JESSICA (TF)
 Sofronski Productions/ABC Productions, 1993
FOR THE LOVE OF AARON (TF)   Patterdale Productions/
 The Storytellers Group/Marian Rees Associates, 1994

KEN HARRISON
b. 1942 - Poetry, Texas
Business: Lyric Films, 3527 Oak Lawn Avenue - Suite 520,
 Dallas, TX 75219, 214/691-4524

1918   Cinecom, 1985
ON VALENTINE'S DAY   Angelika Films, 1986
KATHERINE ANNE PORTER: THE EYE OF MEMORY (TF)
 KERA-Dallas/Fort Worth/Lumiere Productions/American
 Masters, 1986
STORY OF A MARRIAGE (MS)   co-director with
 Howard Cummings, Indian Falls Corporation/
 American Playhouse/WGBH-Boston, 1987
NINTH LIFE   Ninth Life, Ltd./Lyric Films, 1991

BRUCE HART*
b. January 15, 1938 - New York, New York
Home: 200 West 86th Street, New York, NY 10024, 212/724-1948

SOONER OR LATER (TF)   Laughing Willow Company/NBC, 1979

CHRISTOPHER HART
Agent: The Artists Agency - Los Angeles, 310/277-7779

EAT AND RUN   New World, 1986

DEREK HART
Contact: British Film Commission, 70 Baker Street, London
 W1M 1DJ, England, tel.: 171/224-5000

BACKSTAGE AT THE KIROV (FD)   Armand Hammer
 Productions, 1983

JACOBSEN HART
STEEL FRONTIER   co-director with Paul G. Volk, PM Entertainment
 Group, 1994

HAL HARTLEY
Business: True Fiction Pictures, 12 West 27th Street - 10th Floor,
 New York, NY 10001, 212/684-4284

THE UNBELIEVABLE TRUTH   Miramax Films, 1990
TRUST   Fine Line Features/New Line Cinema, 1991, U.S.-British
SIMPLE MEN   Fine Line Features/New Line Cinema, 1992,
 U.S.-British-German-Italian
SURVIVING DESIRE (TF)   KCET-TV/South Carolina ETV/
 WGBH-Boston/WNET-TV, 1992
AMATEUR   Sony Pictures Classics, 1994, U.S.-French-British

PHILIP HARTMAN
Agent: William Morris Agency - Beverly Hills, 310/859-4000

NO PICNIC   Gray City/Great Jones Film Group/Films Charas, 1988

DAVID HARTWELL*
Agent: Sanford-Gross & Associates - Los Angeles, 310/208-2100

LOVE IS A GUN   Trimark Pictures, 1994

ANTHONY HARVEY*
b. June 3, 1931 - London, England
Agent: Susan Smith & Associates - Beverly Hills, 213/852-4777 or:
 AIM/John Redway Associates - London, tel.: 171/836-2001
Business Manager: Arthur Greene, 101 Park Avenue - 43rd Floor,
 New York, NY 10178, 212/661-8200

DUTCHMAN   Continental, 1967, British
THE LION IN WINTER ★   Avco Embassy, 1968, British
THEY MIGHT BE GIANTS   Universal, 1971
THE GLASS MENAGERIE (TF)   Talent Associates, 1973
THE ABDICATION   Warner Bros., 1974, British
THE DISAPPEARANCE OF AIMEE (TF)   Tomorrow
 Entertainment, 1976
PLAYERS   Paramount, 1979
EAGLE'S WING   International Picture Show, 1980, British
RICHARD'S THINGS   New World, 1981, British
THE PATRICIA NEAL STORY (TF)   co-director with Anthony age,
 Lawrence Schiller Productions, 1981
SVENGALI (TF)   Robert Halmi Productions, 1983
THE ULTIMATE SOLUTION OF GRACE QUIGLEY
 GRACE QUIGLEY   Cannon, 1984
THIS CAN'T BE LOVE (TF)   Davis Entertainment/Pacific Motion
 Pictures Corporation/World International Network, 1994

GAIL HARVEY
Contact: Directors Guild of Canada, 225 Richmond Street, Toronto
 M5V 1W2, Canada, 416/351-8200

THE SHOWER   Shower Productions, 1992, Canadian
COLD SWEAT   Norstar Entertainment, 1993, Canadian

RUPERT HARVEY

Business: Sho Films, 2300 Duane Street - Suite 9, Los Angeles,
CA 90039, 213/665-9088

CRITTERS 4: THEY'RE INVADING YOUR SPACE (HVF)
New Line Cinema, 1992

JOHN HARWOOD

LETTER TO DAD   Image, 1992
ROUNDUP   Image, 1993

PATRICK HASBURGH*

Agent: CAA - Beverly Hills, 310/288-4545

ASPEN EXTREME   Buena Vista, 1993

MASAMI HATA

Contact: Japan Film Library Council (Kawakita Memorial Film
Institute), Ginza-Hata Building 4-5, 4-Chome Ginza, Chuo-ku,
Tokyo, Japan, tel.: 3/35616719

LITTLE NEMO: ADVENTURES IN SLUMBERLAND (AF)
co-director with William T. Hurtz, Hemdale, 1992, Japanese

MASANORI HATA

Contact: Nihon Eiga Kantoku Kyokai (Japan Film Directors
Association), La Fontenu Building - 4th Floor, 23-2 Maruyama-cho,
Shibuya-ku, Tokyo, Japan, tel.: 3/3461-4411

THE ADVENTURES OF MILO AND OTIS   *THE ADVENTURES
OF CHATRAN*   Columbia, 1986, Japanese

BOB HATHCOCK

DUCK TALES, THE MOVIE: TREASURES OF THE
LOST LAMP (AF)   Buena Vista, 1991

KAYO HATTA

PICTURE BRIDE   Miramax Films, 1994

MAURICE HATTON

b. England
Business: Mithras Film, 3 Cambridge Gate, Regent's Park, London
NW1, England, tel.: 171/486-1400

PRAISE MARX AND PASS THE AMMUNITION   1968, British
THE BOUNCING BOY (TF)   1872, British
BITTER HARVEST (TF)   1973, British
NELLY'S VERSION (TF)   1983, British
THE REWARDS OF VIRTUE   1983, British
AMERICAN ROULETTE   Film Four International/British Screen/
Mandemar Group, 1988, British

WINGS HAUSER

Contact: Screen Actors Guild - Hollywood, 213/954-1600

COLDFIRE   PM Entertainment Group, 1990
LIVING TO DIE   PM Entertainment Group, 1990
SKINS   Sunset Films International, 1994

MARY HAVERSTICK

SHADES OF BLACK   Headliner Productions, 1994

NICK HAVINGA*

Agent: The Cooper Agency - Los Angeles, 310/277-8422

SINGLE WOMEN, MARRIED MAN (TF)   Michele Lee Productions/
CBS Entertainment, 1989

KAIZO HAYASHI

b. 1957 - Kyoto, Japan
Business: Eizo Tantei Sha Co., 201 Koyama - Bldg. 1, 1-26-5,
Umegaoka, Setagaya-ku, Toyko 154, Japan, tel.: 03/439-2603

TO SLEEP SO AS TO DREAM   New Yorker, 1985, Japanese
CIRCUS BOYS   CBS-Sont, 1989, Japanese
ZIPANG · Toho, 1989, Japanese
THE MOST TERRIBLE TIME IN MY LIFE   Herald Ace, 1994,
Japanese-Taiwanese
STAIRWAY TO THE DISTANT PAST   *HARUKANARU JIDAI NO
KAIDAN O*   For Life Records, 1995, Japanese

JEFFREY HAYDEN*

Business: The Saint/Hayden Co., 11811 W. Olympic Blvd.,
Los Angeles, CA 90064, 310/996-7756
Agent: Phil Gersh, The Gersh Agency - Beverly Hills, 310/274-6611

PRIMARY COLORS: THE STORY OF CORITA (TD)   South Carolina
ETV/The Saint-Hayden Company, 1991

SIDNEY HAYERS*

b. Edinburgh, Scotland
Agent: Irv Schechter Company - Beverly Hills, 310/278-8070 or:
AIM/John Redway Associates - London, tel.: 171/836-2001

VIOLENT MOMENT   Anglo-Amalgamated, 1959, British
THE WHITE TRAP   Anglo-Amalgamated, 1959, British
CIRCUS OF HORRORS   American International, 1960, British
THE MALPAS MYSTERY   Anglo-Amalgamated, 1960, British
ECHO OF BARBARA   Rank, 1961, British
BURN, WITCH, BURN   *NIGHT OF THE EAGLE*   American
International, 1962, British
THIS IS MY STREET   Anglo-Amalgamated, 1963, British
THREE HATS FOR LISA   Anglo-Amalgamated, 1963, British
THE TRAP   Rank, 1966, British
FINDERS KEEPERS   United Artists, 1967, British
THE SOUTHERN STAR   Columbia, 1969, French-British
MISTER JERICO (TF)   ITC, 1970, British
IN THE DEVIL'S GARDEN   *ASSAULT*   Hemisphere, 1971, British
THE FIRECHASERS   Rank, 1971, British
INN OF THE FRIGHTENED PEOPLE   *TERROR FROM UNDER
THE HOUSE/REVENGE*   Hemisphere, 1973, British
DEADLY STRANGERS   Fox-Rank, 1974, British
DIAGNOSIS: MURDER   CIC, 1975, British
WHAT CHANGED CHARLEY FARTHING?   Stirling Gold,
1976, British
ONE WAY   Silhouette Film Productions, 1976
THE SEEKERS (TF)   Universal TV, 1978
THE LAST CONVERTIBLE (MS)   co-director with Jo Swerling, Jr. &
Gus Trikonis, Roy Huggins Productions/Universal TV, 1979
CONDOMINIUM (TF)   Universal TV, 1980
PHILIP MARLOWE - PRIVATE EYE   *CHANDLERTOWN* (CMS)
co-director with Bryan Forbes, Peter Hunt & David Wickes,
HBO/David Wickes Television Ltd./London Weekend Television,
1983, British

DAVID HAYMAN

b. Glasgow, Scotland
Address: 4 Fielding Road, London W14 0LL, England,
tel.: 171/602-7772
Agent: Peters Fraser & Dunlop - London, tel.: 171/344-1000

YOU'VE NEVER SLEPT IN MINE (TF)   BBC, 1984, British
ONE DAY (TF)   BBC, 1986, British
BRIEF ENCOUNTER (TF)   BBC, 1986, British
GOVAN GHOST STORY (TF)   BBC, 1989, British
SILENT SCREAM   British Film Institute/Film Four International,
1990, British
FIRM FRIENDS (MS)   Zenith Productions/Tyne Tees TV,
1992, British
BLACK AND BLUE (TF)   BBC, 1992, British
THE HAWK   Castle Hill Productions, 1993, British
A WOMAN'S GUIDE TO ADULTERY   Hartswood Films,
1993, British

TODD HAYNES
POISON   Zeitgeist Films, 1991
SAFE   Sony Pictures Classics, 1995

JACK HAZAN
Contact: British Film Commission, 70 Baker Street, London
   W1M 1DJ, England, tel.: 171/224-5000

A BIGGER SPLASH (FD)   Lagoon Associates, 1975, British
RUDE BOY   co-director with David Mingay, Atlantic Releasing
   Corporation, 1980, British

STAN HAZE
Contact: Screen Actors Guild - Los Angeles, 213/954-1600

HIGH COUNTRY JUSTICE   J.S. Matt Productions, 1994

PING HE
(See He PING)

JIANJUN HE
(See He JIANJUN)

HELAINE HEAD*
Agent: Gold Marshak Associates - Burbank, 818/972-4300
Peronal Manager: Hillard Elkins Management, 800 N. Roxbury Drive,
   Beverly Hills, CA, 310/285-0700

YOU MUST REMEMBER THIS (TF)   Longridge Enterprises/
   QED West/Limbo Productions, 1992
SIMPLE JUSTICE (TF)   WGBH-Boston/WNET-13/
   KCET-Los Angeles, 1993
A PERRY MASON MYSTERY: THE CASE OF THE LETHAL
   LIFESTYLE (TF)   Dean Hargrove Productions/The Fred
   Silverman Company/Viacom Productions, 1994

JONATHAN HEAP
Personal Manager: Creative Alliance Management - Los Angeles,
   213/962-6090

BENEFIT OF THE DOUBT   Miramax Films, 1993

ROBERT HEATH*
Home: 3713 Goodland Avenue, Studio City, CA 91604,
   818/761-0001

HUGH HEFNER: ONCE UPON A TIME (FD)
   I.R.S. Releasing, 1992

SIMON HEATH
b. Australia
Address: c/o Denny Bond, Management 3, Lazy Creek Ranch,
   4570 Encino Avenue, Encino, CA 91316, 818/783-3713

BULLAMAKANKA   Bullamakanka Film Productions,
   1984, Australian
CHARLY'S WEB   Budei Holdings, 1986, Australian

DAVID HEAVENER
Business: Silver Lake International Pictures, 719 N. Micheltorena
   Street, Los Angeles, CA 90026, 213/662-6095

TWISTED JUSTICE   Seymour Borde & Associates, 1990
PRIME TARGET   Hero Films, 1991
EYE OF THE STRANGER   Silver Lake International Pictures, 1994
FINAL SHOWDOWN   Silver Lake International Pictures, 1994

AMY HECKERLING*
b. May 7, 1954 - Bronx, New York
Agent: CAA - Beverly Hills, 310/288-4545

FAST TIMES AT RIDGEMONT HIGH   Universal, 1982
JOHNNY DANGEROUSLY   20th Century Fox, 1984

NATIONAL LAMPOON'S EUROPEAN VACATION
   Warner Bros., 1985
LOOK WHO'S TALKING   TriStar, 1989
LOOK WHO'S TALKING TOO   TriStar, 1990
CLUELESS   Paramount, 1995

ROB HEDDEN*
Home: 2905 Zell Drive, Laguna Beach, CA 92651, 714/494-6088
Agent: Daniel Ostroff, The Daniel Ostroff Agency - Los Angeles,
   310/278-2020

FRIDAY THE 13TH, PART VIII: JASON TAKES MANHATTAN
   Paramount, 1989

DAVID HEELEY*
Address: 31 West 31st Street, New York, NY 10001, 212/239-6969

KATHARINE HEPBURN: 'ALL ABOUT ME' (CTD)
   Turner Pictures, 1993

RICHARD T. HEFFRON*
b. October 6, 1930 - Chicago, Illinois
Agent: CAA - Beverly Hills, 310/288-4545

DO YOU TAKE THIS STRANGER? (TF)   Universal TV, 1971
FILLMORE (FCD)   20th Century-Fox, 1972
TOMA (TF)   Universal TV, 1973
OUTRAGE! (TF)   ABC Circle Films, 1973
NEWMAN'S LAW   Universal, 1974
THE MORNING AFTER (TF)   Wolper Productions, 1974
THE ROCKFORD FILES (TF)   Universal TV, 1974
THE CALIFORNIA KID (TF)   Universal TV, 1974
LOCUSTS (TF)   Paramount TV, 1974
I WILL FIGHT NO MORE FOREVER (TF)   Wolper Productions, 1975
DEATH SCREAM (TF)   RSO Films, 1975
TRACKDOWN   United Artists, 1976
FUTUREWORLD   American International, 1976
YOUNG JOE, THE FORGOTTEN KENNEDY (TF)
   ABC Circle Films, 1977
OUTLAW BLUES   Warner Bros., 1977
SEE HOW SHE RUNS (TF)   CLN Productions, 1978
TRUE GRIT: A FURTHER ADVENTURE (TF)   Paramount TV, 1978
FOOLIN' AROUND   Columbia, 1978
A RUMOR OF WAR (TF)   Charles Fries Productions, 1980
A WHALE FOR THE KILLING (TF)   Play Productions/Beowulf
   Productions, 1981
I, THE JURY   20th Century-Fox, 1982
A KILLER IN THE FAMILY (TF)   Stan Margulies Productions/Sunn
   Classic Pictures, 1983
THE MYSTIC WARRIOR (MS)   David L. Wolper-Stan Margulies
   Productions/Warner Bros. TV, 1984
V: THE FINAL BATTLE (TF)   Blatt-Singer Productions/Warner
   Bros. TV, 1984
ANATOMY OF AN ILLNESS (TF)   Hamner Productions/CBS
   Entertainment, 1984
NORTH AND SOUTH (MS)   Wolper Productions/Warner
   Bros. TV, 1985
SAMARITAN (TF)   Levine-Robins Productions/Fries
   Entertainment, 1986
GUILTY OF INNOCENCE: THE LENELL GETER STORY (TF)
   Embassy TV, 1986
CONVICTED: A MOTHER'S STORY (TF)   NBC Productions, 1987
NAPOLEON AND JOSEPHINE: A LOVE STORY (TF)
   David L. Wolper Productions/Warner Bros. TV, 1987
BROKEN ANGEL (TF)   The Stan Margulies Company/
   MGM-UA TV, 1988
PANCHO BARNES (TF)   Blue Andre Productions/Orion TV, 1988
LA REVOLUTION FRANCAISE: LES ANNEES TERRIBLES
   Ariane Films/Films A2/Laura Films/Les Productions Alliance/
   Alcor Films, 1989, French-West German-Italian-Canadian
TAGGET (CTF)   Mirisch Films/Tagget Productions, 1991

LYNN HEGARTY
Contact: Australian Film Commission, 150 William Street,
   Woolloomooloo NSW 2011, Australia, tel.: 2/321-6444

HOW WONDERFUL   Film Australia, 1989, Australian

CHRIS HEGEDUS
Business: Pennebaker Associates, 21 West 86th Street, New York,
NY 10024, 212/496-9199

TOWN BLOODY HALL (FD) co-director with D.A. Pennebaker,
Pennebaker Associates, 1980
ROCKABY (TD) co-director with D.A. Pennebaker,
Pennebaker Associates, 1983
DANCE BLACK AMERICA (FD) co-director with D.A. Pennebaker,
Pennebaker Associates, 1985
ROCKY X (FD) co-director with D.A. Pennebaker,
Pennebaker Associates, 1986
DEPECHE MODE 101 (FCD) co-director with D.A. Pennebaker &
David Dawkins, Westwood One Radio, 1989
THE MUSIC TELLS YOU (FD) co-director with D.A. Pennebaker,
Pennebaker Associates, 1992
THE WAR ROOM (FD) co-director with D.A. Pennebaker,
October Films, 1993
WOODSTOCK: THE LOST PERFORMANCES (CTCD) co-director
with D.A. Pennebaker & Erez Laufer, Showtime Entertainment
Group/Gravity Unlimited/Pennebaker Associates, 1994

SARAH HELLINGS
Address: 29 Park Hill, London W5 2JS, England, tel.: 181/998-4189
Agent: Jane Annakin, William Morris Agency - London,
tel.: 171/434-2191

THE ZERO OPTION (TF) Central TV, 1988, British
RUTH RENDELL MYSTERY MOVIE: MEANS OF EVIL (TF)
TVS, 1991, British
TAGGART: GINGERBREAD (TF) STV, 1992, British
THE MEMOIRS OF SHERLOCK HOLMES: THE RED CIRCLE (TF)
Granada TV, 1993, British
THE MEMOIRS OF SHERLOCK HOLMES: THE DYING
DETECTIVE (TF) Granada TV, 1993, British
THE MEMOIRS OF SHERLOCK HOLMES: THE CARDBOARD
BOX (TF) Granada TV, 1993, British

JEROME HELLMAN
b. September 4, 1928 - New York, New York
Address: 1211 Sunset Plaza Drive - Suite 404, Los Angeles,
CA 90069, 310/854-6054

PROMISES IN THE DARK Orion/Warner Bros., 1979

MONTE HELLMAN*
b. July 12, 1932 - New York, New York
Address: 11075 Santa Monica Blvd. - Suite 275, Los Angeles,
CA 90025, 310/479-5581

BEAST FROM HAUNTED CAVE Allied Artists, 1959
BACK DOOR TO HELL 20th Century-Fox, 1964
FLIGHT TO FURY Harold Goldman Associates, 1967, U.S.-Filipino
THE SHOOTING American International, 1966
RIDE IN THE WHIRLWIND American International, 1966
TWO-LANE BLACKTOP Universal, 1971
COCKFIGHTER *BORN TO KILL* New World, 1974
CHINA 9 LIBERTY 37 Titanus, 1978, Italian
IGUANA Enterprise Iguana Film Productions, 1988, Italian
SILENT NIGHT, DEADLY NIGHT III: BETTER WATCH OUT
International Video Enterprises, 1989

GUNNAR HELLSTROM*
Home: 1831 Selby Avenue, Los Angeles, CA 90025, 310/475-4142
Business: Artistfilm, Toro, 14992 Nynashamn, Sweden,
tel.: 46/752-31160

THE NAME OF THE GAME IS KILL (TF) Universal TV, 1968
MARK, I LOVE YOU (TF) The Aubrey Company, 1980
RASKENSTAM Sandrews, 1983, Swedish
ZORN Sandrews/Swedish Television Channel 1 Drama/Nordisk
Film & TV Fund/NRK/FST/YLE/RUV/Nordic Coproduction Fund/
Artistfilm, 1994, Swedish-Danish-Norwegian-Finnish

HENRI HELMAN
Home: 7, rue de l'Ecole de Medecine, 75005 Paris, France,
tel.: 1/43-29-39-43
Agent: Voulez Mon Agent - Paris, tel.: 1/47-23-55-80
Contact: French Film Office, 745 Fifth Avenue, New York,
NY 10151, 212/832-8860

LE COEUR FROID Films Moliere, 1977, French
WHERE IS PARSIFAL? TriStar, 1984, British

DAVID HELPERN, JR.
I'M A STRANGER HERE MYSELF (FD) October Films, 1974
HOLLYWOOD ON TRIAL (FD) Lumiere, 1976
SOMETHING SHORT OF PARADISE American International, 1979

DAVID HEMMINGS*
b. November 18, 1941 - Guildfold, Surrey, England
Agent: Stone Manners Agency - Los Angeles, 213/654-7575
Business Manager: Burton Merrill, Individual Productions, Inc.,
4260 Arcola Avenue, Toluca Lake, CA 91602, 818/763-6903

RUNNING SCARED Paramount, 1972, British
THE 14 MGM-EMI, 1973, British
JUST A GIGOLO United Artists Classics, 1978, West German
THE SURVIVOR Hemdale, 1981, Australian
TREASURE OF THE YANKEE ZEPHYR *RACE TO THE
YANKEE ZEPHYR* Artists Releasing Corporation/Film
Ventures International, 1984, New Zealand-British
THE KEY TO REBECCA (TF) Taft Entertainment TV/Castle Combe
Productions, 1985, U.S.-British
WEREWOLF (TF) Lycanthrope Productions/TriStar TV, 1987
IN THE HEAT OF THE NIGHT (TF) The Fred Silverman Company/
Jadda Productions/MGM-UA TV, 1988
DAVY CROCKETT: RAINBOW IN THE THUNDER (TF)
Echo Cove Productions/Walt Disney TV, 1988
QUANTUM LEAP (TF) Belisarius Productions/Universal TV, 1989
HARDBALL (TF) Columbia TV/NBC Productions, 1989
DARK HORSE Republic Pictures International, 1992
PASSPORT TO MURDER (TF) FTM Productions, 1993

CLARK HENDERSON
b. February 11, 1951 - Palo Alto, California
Address: 6120 Rodgerton Drive, Hollywood, CA 90068,
213/469-4193

SAIGON COMMANDOS Concorde, 1988
HIGHRIDERS Concorde, 1990
PRIMARY TARGET Concorde
CIRCLE OF FEAR Concorde

JOHN HENDERSON
Contact: British Film Commission, 70 Baker Street, London
W1M 1DJ, England, tel.: 171/224-5000

THE BORROWERS (TF) Working Title TV/BBC/Turner Network TV/
BBC's Children International/The Children's Film Foundation/de
Faria Company, 1993, British-U.S.
LOCH NESS Working Title Films, 1995, British

FRANK HENENLOTTER
Business: Smilin' City Productions - New York City, 212/929-7591

BASKET CASE Analysis, 1982
BRAIN DAMAGE Palisades Entertainment, 1988
FRANKENHOOKER Shapiro Glickenhaus Entertainment, 1990
BASKET CASE 2 Shapiro Glickenhaus Entertainment, 1990
BASKET CASE 3: THE PROGENY Shapiro Glickenhaus
Entertainment, 1991

KIM HENKEL
Contact: Writers Guild of America, West - Los Angeles, 310/550-1000
Telephone: 512/749-5701

THE RETURN OF THE TEXAS CHAINSAW MASSACRE
Return Productions, 1995

BUCK HENRY*
b. 1930 - New York, New York
Agent: William Morris Agency - Beverly Hills, 310/859-4000

HEAVEN CAN WAIT ★   co-director with Warren Beatty,
   Paramount, 1978
FIRST FAMILY   Warner Bros., 1980

BRIAN HENSON*
Business: Jim Henson Productions, Raleigh Studios, 5358 Melrose
   Avenue, West Office Building - Suite 300W, Hollywood,
   CA 90038, 213/960-4096

THE MUPPET CHRISTMAS CAROL   Buena Vista, 1992
THE MUPPET TREASURE ISLAND   Buena Vista,
   1995, U.S.-British

PERRY HENZELL
Contact: Jamaica Film and Entertainment Office, 35 Trafalgar
   Road - 3rd Floor, Kingston, 10 Jamaica, tel.: 809/929-9450

THE HARDER THEY COME   New World, 1972, Jamaican
NO PLACE LIKE HOME   1986, Jamaican, incomplete

STEPHEN HEREK*
b. November 10, 1958 - San Antonio, Texas
Agent: ICM - Beverly Hills, 310/550-4000

CRITTERS   New Line Cinema, 1985
BILL & TED'S EXCELLENT ADVENTURE   Orion, 1989
THE GIFTED ONE (TF)   Richard Rothstein Productions/
   NBC Productions, 1989
DON'T TELL MOM THE BABYSITTER'S DEAD   Warner Bros., 1991
THE MIGHTY DUCKS   Buena Vista, 1992
THE THREE MUSKETEERS   Buena Vista, 1993
MR. HOLLAND'S OPUS   Buena Vista, 1995
101 DALMATIONS   Buena Vista, 1996

MARIA HERITIER
HEADING HOME   On Board Production Associates, 1995

MARK HERMAN
Agent: William Morris Agency - Beverly Hills, 310/859-4000

BLAME IT ON THE BELLBOY   Buena Vista, 1992, British

JAIME HUMBERTO HERMOSILLO
b. 1942 - Aguascalientes, Mexico
Home: Ostia 2943-6, Providencia, Guadalajara, Jalisco, Mexico,
   C.P. 44620, tel.: 36/423226
Agent: Rene Fuentes-Chao, Cinevista, Inc., 353 West 39th Street,
   New York, NY 10018, 212/947-4373
Contact: IMCINE, Tepic #40, P.B. Colonia Roma Sur, Mexico City,
   C.P. 06760, Mexico, tel.: 525/584-7283

LA VERDADERA VOCACION DE MAGDALENA   Azteca Films,
   1971, Mexican
EL SENOR DE OSANTO   Azteca Films, 1972, Mexican
EL CUMPLEANOS DEL PERRO   Azteca Films, 1974, Mexican
LA PASION SEGUN BERENICE   Azteca Films, 1977, Mexican
NAUFRAGIO   Azteca Films, 1978, Mexican
MATINEE   Azteca Films, 1978, Mexican
EL AMOR LIBRE   Azteca Films, 1979, Mexican
LAS APARIENCIAS ENGANAN   Azteca Films, 1982, Mexican
MARIA DE MI CORAZON   Azteca Films, 1983, Mexican
CONFIDENCIAS   Azteca Films, 1984, Mexican
DONA HERLINDA AND HER TWO SONS   Cinevista, 1985, Mexican
EL ETERNO ESPLENDOR   Azteca Films, 1987, Mexican
CLANDESTINO DESTINO   Clasa Films Mundiales, 1987, Mexican
EL VERANO DE LA SENORITA FORBES   Television Espanola/
   TVE/ICAIC, 1988, Cuban-Mexican-Spanish
INTIMIDADES EN UN CUARTO DE BANO   Profesionales y
   Sociedad Cooperativa de Producciones/Cinematografica Jose
   Revueltas, 1990, Mexican
LA TAREA   Clasa Films Mundiales, 1990, Mexican
ENCUENTRO INESPERADO   Clasa Films Mundiales,
   1993, Mexican

TIBOR HERNADI
FELIX THE CAT (AHV)   Buena Vista Home Video, 1991

DENIS HEROUX
b. 1940 - Montreal, Quebec, Canada
Address: 28, rue Roskilde, Montreal, Quebec H2V 2N5, Canada,
   514/272-0526
Business: Astral Europa Communications, 2100 Ste-Catherine Ouest,
   Montreal, Quebec H3H 2T3, Canada, 514/939-5000

SEUL OU AVEC D'AUTRES   1963, Canadian
VALERIE   1968, Canadian
L'INITIATION   1969, Canadian
QUELQUES ARPENTS DE NEIGE   1972, Canadian
JACQUES BREL IS ALIVE AND WELL AND LIVING IN PARIS
   American Film Theatre, 1974, Canadian-French

ANTHONY HERRERA
THE WIDE NET (TF)   Wide Net Company/WGBH-Boston, 1987

GERARDO HERRERO
SHORTCUT TO PARADISE   Tornasol Films/Tornacine/Shortcut to
   Paradise/TVE/Canal Plus, 1994, Spanish-Puerto Rican

MARK HERRIER
Contact: Screen Actors Guild - Los Angeles, 213/954-1600

POPCORN   Studio Three Film Corporation, 1991, U.S.-Jamaican

ROWDY HERRINGTON*
Agent: William Morris Agency - Beverly Hills, 310/859-4000

JACK'S BACK   Cinema Group, 1988
ROAD HOUSE   MGM/UA, 1989
GLADIATORS   Columbia, 1992
STRIKING DISTANCE   Columbia, 1993

W. BLAKE HERRON
SKIN ART   ITC Entertainment Group, 1993

JOEL HERSHMAN
Contact: Hershman/Swords Productions, Warner Bros. - Burbank,
   818/954-3288

HOLD ME, THRILL ME, KISS ME   October Films, 1993

MARSHALL HERSKOVITZ*
Agent: CAA - Beverly Hills, 310/288-4545

COMING OF AGE AT JEFFERSON HALL (CTF)   Showtime, 1985
JACK THE BEAR   20th Century Fox, 1993

MICHAEL HERZ
b. May 9, 1949 - New York, New York
Business: Troma, Inc., 733 Ninth Avenue, New York, NY 10019,
   212/757-4555

SQUEEZE PLAY!   co-director with Samuel Weil, Troma, 1980
WAITRESS!   co-director with Samuel Weil, Troma, 1982
STUCK ON YOU!   co-director with Samuel Weil, Troma, 1983
THE FIRST TURN-ON!   co-director with Samuel Weil, Troma, 1984
THE TOXIC AVENGER   co-director with Samuel Weil, Troma, 1984
THE TOXIC AVENGER: PART II   co-director with Samuel Weil,
   Troma, 1988
TROMA'S WAR   co-director with Samuel Weil, Troma, 1988
SGT. KABUKIMAN NYPD   co-director with Lloyd Kaufman,
   Troma, 1991

JOHN HERZFELD*
Agent: William Morris Agency - Beverly Hills, 310/859-4000

TWO OF A KIND   20th Century-Fox, 1983
DADDY (TF)   Robert Greenwald Productions, 1987

A FATHER'S REVENGE (TF)   Shadowplay-Rosco Productions/
    Phoenix Entertainment Group, 1988
THE RYAN WHITE STORY (TF)   The Landsburg Company, 1989
THE PREPPIE MURDER (TF)   Jack Grossbart Productions/
    Spectator Films, 1989
THE FIFTH CORNER (TF)   John Herzfeld Productions/
    Adelson-Baumgarten Productions/TriStar TV, 1992
CASUALTIES OF LOVE: THE 'LONG ISLAND LOLITA' STORY (TF)
    Diane Sokolow Productions/TriStar TV, 1993
BARBARA TAYLOR BRADFORD'S REMEMBER   *REMEMBER* (TF)
    List-Estrin Productions/H.R. Productions/NBC Productions, 1993

WERNER HERZOG
(Werner Stipetic)
b. September 5, 1942 - Sachrang, Germany
Address: Neureutherstrasse 20, D-8000, Munich 13, Germany
Contact: Federal Union of Film and Television Directors in Germany,
    Adelheidstrasse 7, 8000 Munich 40, Germany, tel.: 089/271-6380

DIE FLIEGENDEN ARZTE VON OSTAFRIKA   1968, West German
SIGNS OF LIFE   Werner Herzog Filmproduktion,
    1968, West German
BEHINDERTE ZUKUNFT   1970, West German
EVEN DWARFS STARTED SMALL   New Line Cinema,
    1971, West German
LAND OF SILENCE AND DARKNESS (FD)   New Yorker,
    1972, West German
AGUIRRE, THE WRATH OF GOD   New Yorker, 1973,
    West German- Mexican-Peruvian
THE MYSTERY OF KASPAR HAUSER   *EVERY MAN FOR
    HIMSELF AND GOD AGAINST ALL*   Cinema 5,
    1974, West German
HEART OF GLASS   New Yorker, 1976, West German
STROSZEK   New Yorker, 1977, West German
FATA MORGANA   New Yorker, 1978, West German
WOYZECK   New Yorker, 1979, West German
NOSFERATU THE VAMPYRE   20th Century-Fox, 1979,
    West German-French-U.S.
GOD'S ANGRY MAN (FD)   1980, West German
FITZCARRALDO   New World, 1982, West German
WHERE THE GREEN ANTS DREAM   Orion Classics,
    1984, West German
COBRA VERDE   DEG, 1988, West German
HERDSMEN OF THE SUN (FD)   Interama, 1988, French
A PATRIARCH IN WINTER (FD)   Werner Herzog Filmproduktion,
    1990, West German
ECHOES FROM A SOMBER EMPIRE (FD)   New Yorker 1990,
    German-French
SCHREI AUS STEIN   Sera Film/Molecule/Films A2/Stock
    International, 1991, German-French-Canadian
LESSONS OF DARKNESS (TD)   Premiere Productions/BBC/
    Canal Plus France/Canal Plus Spain/ITEL, 1992,
    British-French-Spanish
LES FRANCAIS VUS PAR...   cp-director with David Lynch,
    Andrzej Wajda & Luigi Comencini, Erato Films/Socpresse/
    Figaro Magazine/Antenne-2/Centre National de la
    Cinematographie, 1993, French

EUGENE HESS
Business: Hess-Lippert Films, 1045 Ocean Avenue, Santa Monica,
    CA 90403, 310/394-1121

DON'T DO IT   Hess-Lippert Films/Julian R. Films, 1994

JON HESS*
Business: Modern World Pictures, 4063 Redwood Avenue,
    Los Angeles, CA 90066, 310/827-7121
Agent: CAA - Beverly Hills, 310/288-4545

THE LAWLESS LAND   Concorde, 1988
WATCHERS   Universal, 1988, Canadian
THE ASSASSINATION   *ASSASSINATION WITH CAUSE*
    L.A. Film Group/Tamaulipas S.A., 1990, U.S.-Mexican
NOT OF THIS WORLD (TF)   Barry & Enright Productions,1991
ALLIGATOR II: THE MUTATION   Group 1, 1991
EXCESSIVE FORCE   New Line Cinema, 1993

GORDON HESSLER*
b. 1930 - Berlin, Germany
Business: Rova, Inc., 7474 Hillside Avenue, Los Angeles, CA 90046,
    213/874-2498
Agent: Shelly Wile Enterprises, 2730 Wilshire Blvd. - Suite 500,
    Santa Monica, CA 90403, 310/829-9768

THE WOMAN WHO WOULDN'T DIE   *CATACOMBS*
    Warner Bros., 1965, British
THE OBLONG BOX   American International, 1969, British
THE LAST SHOT YOU HEAR   20th Century-Fox, 1969, British
SCREAM AND SCREAM AGAIN   American International, .
    1970, British
CRY OF THE BANSHEE   American International, 1970, British
MURDERS IN THE RUE MORGUE   American International,
    1971, British
EMBASSY   Hemdale, 1973, British
SCREAM, PRETTY PEGGY (TF)   Universal TV, 1973
SKYWAY TO DEATH (TF)   Universal TV, 1974
HITCHHIKE! (TF)   Universal TV, 1974
A CRY IN THE WILDERNESS (TF)   Universal TV, 1974
BETRAYAL (TF)   Metromedia Productions, 1974
THE GOLDEN VOYAGE OF SINBAD   Columbia, 1974, British
TRACCO DI VELENO IN UNA COPPA DI CHAMPAGNE
    Arden, 1975, Italian
THE STRANGE POSSESSION OF MRS. OLIVER (TF)
    The Shpetner Company, 1977
PUZZLE (TF)   Australian Broadcasting Commission/Trans-Atlantic
    Enterprises, 1978, Australian
SECRETS OF THREE HUNGRY WIVES (TF)   Penthouse
    Productions, 1978
KISS MEETS THE PHANTOM OF THE PARK (TF)   Hanna-Barbera
    Productions/KISS Productions, 1978
BEGGERMAN, THIEF (TF)   Universal TV, 1980
THE SECRET WAR OF JACKIE'S GIRLS (TF)   Public Arts
    Productions/Penthouse Productions/Universal TV, 1980
ESCAPE FROM EL DIABLO   Cinema Presentations International,
    1983, U.S.- Spanish-British
PRAY FOR DEATH   American Distribution Group, 1985
RAGE OF HONOR   American Distribution Group, 1986
THE MISFIT BRIGADE   *WHEELS OF TERROR*   Trans World
    Entertainment, 1987, U.S.-British
OUT ON BAIL   Trans World Entertainment, 1988,
    U.S.-South African
THE GIRL IN A SWING   Millimeter Films, 1989, British-Danish
JOURNEY OF HONOR   Rocket Films, 1992, U.S.-Japanese

CHARLTON HESTON
(Charles Carter)
b. October 4, 1924 - St. Helen, Michigan
Agent: ICM - Beverly Hills, 310/550-4000

ANTONY AND CLEOPATRA   Rank, 1973, British-Spanish-Swiss
MOTHER LODE   Agamemnon Films, 1982, Canadian
A MAN FOR ALL SEASONS (CTF)   Agamemnon Films/British Lion,
    1988, U.S.-British

FRASER C. HESTON*
Agent: Brad Gross, Sanford-Gross & Associates - Los Angeles,
    213/208-2100

TREASURE ISLAND (CTF)   Agamemnon Films/British Lion,
    1990, British-U.S.
THE CRUCIFER OF BLOOD (CTF)   Turner Pictures/Agamenon
    Films/British Lion, 1991, U.S.-British
NEEDFUL THINGS   Columbia, 1993

PETER HEWITT*
Agent: CAA - Beverly Hills, 310/288-4545

BILL & TED'S BOGUS JOURNEY   Orion, 1991
WILD PALMS (MS)   co-director with Kathryn Bigelow, Keith Gordon &
    Phil Joanou, Ixtlan Corporation/Greengrass Productions, 1993
TOM SAWYER   Painted Fence Productions, 1995

ROD HEWITT

Agent: Barry Perelman Agency - Los Angeles, 310/274-5999

VERNE MILLER   Alive Films, 1987
THE DANGEROUS   West Side Studios, 1994

CHRISTOPHER HIBLER*

Agent: Norman Kurland, Broder-Kurland-Webb-Uffner Agency -
  Beverly Hills, 310/281-3400

FATAL CONFESSION: A FATHER DOWLING MYSTERY (TF)
  The Fred Silverman Company/Strathmore Productions/
  Viacom, 1987
FATHER DOWLING MYSTERIES: THE MISSING BODY
  MYSTERY (TF)   The Fred Silverman Company/Dean
  Hargrove Productions, 1989
MATLOCK: THE WITNESS KILLINGS (TF)   Dean Hargrove
  Productions/The Fred Silverman Company/Viacom, 1991
DIAGNOSIS OF MURDER (TF)   The Fred Silverman Company/
  Dean Hargrove Productions/Viacom Productions, 1992

JOCHEN HICK

Contact: Federal Union of Film and Television Directors in Germany,
  Adelheidstrasse 7, 8000 Munich 40, Germany, tel.: 089/271-6380

VIA APPIA   Strand Releasing, 1991, German
MENMANIACS: THE LEGACY OF LEATHER (FD)   Galeria Alaska,
  1995, German

GEORGE HICKENLOOPER

HEARTS OF DARKNESS: A FILMMAKER'S APOCALYPSE (CTD)
  co-director with Fax Bahr, Showtime/ZM Productions/Zoetrope,
  1991, released theatrically by Triton Pictures
PICTURE THIS - THE TIMES OF PETER BOGDANOVICH IN
  ARCHER CITY, TEXAS (FD)   Kino-Eye American, 1992
THE GREY KNIGHT   Motion Picture Corporation of America, 1993
THE LOW LIFE   Zuckerman-Heminway Productions/Autumn
  Pictures, 1995

BRUCE HICKEY

NECROPOLIS   Empire Pictures, 1986

ANTHONY HICKOX

WAXWORK   Vestron, 1988
SUNDOWN: THE VAMPIRE IN RETREAT   Vestron, 1990
WAXWORK II: LOST IN TIME   LIVE Entertainment/
  Seven Arts, 1992
HELLRAISER III: HELL ON EARTH   Dimension, 1992
WARLOCK: THE ARMAGEDDON   Trimark Pictures, 1993
FULL ECLIPSE (CTF)   HBO Pictures, 1993

JAMES HICKOX

CHILDREN OF THE CORN III: URBAN HARVEST
  Miramax Films, 1994

SCOTT HICKS

Contact: Australian Film Commission, 150 William Street,
  Woolloomooloo NSW 2011, Australia, tel.: 2/321-6444

THE SPACE SHUTTLE (CTD)   Discovery Productions/Beyond
  International, 1994, U.S.-Australian
SHINE   Momentum Films, 1995, Australian

GEORGE ROY HILL*

b. December 20, 1922 - Minneapolis, Minnesota
Agent: CAA - Beverly Hills, 310/288-4545
Business Manager: Edwin S. Brown, 1325 Avenue of the Americas -
  Suite 2977, New York, NY 10019, 212/484-7182

PERIOD OF ADJUSTMENT   MGM, 1962
TOYS IN THE ATTIC   United Artists, 1963
THE WORLD OF HENRY ORIENT   United Artists, 1964
HAWAII   United Artists, 1966
THOROUGHLY MODERN MILLIE   Universal, 1967

BUTCH CASSIDY AND THE SUNDANCE KID ★
  20th Century-Fox, 1969
SLAUGHTERHOUSE-FIVE   Universal, 1971
THE STING ★★   Universal, 1973
THE GREAT WALDO PEPPER   Universal, 1975
SLAP SHOT   Universal, 1977
A LITTLE ROMANCE   Orion/Warner Bros., 1979, U.S.-French
THE WORLD ACCORDING TO GARP   Warner Bros., 1982
THE LITTLE DRUMMER GIRL   Warner Bros., 1984
FUNNY FARM   Warner Bros., 1988

JACK HILL*

b. January 28, 1933 - Los Angeles, California
Home: 16918 Schoolcraft Street, Van Nuys, CA 91406, 818/342-6877

BLOOD BATH   co-director with Stephanie Rothman,
  American International, 1966
SPIDER BABY   *THE LIVER EATERS/CANNIBAL ORGY*   1968
PIT STOP   Distributors International, 1969
THE BIG DOLL HOUSE   New World, 1971
THE BIG BIRD CAGE   New World, 1972
COFFY   American International, 1973
FOXY BROWN   American International, 1974
THE SWINGING CHEERLEADERS   Centaur, 1974
SWITCHBLADE SISTERS   Centaur, 1975

WALTER HILL*

b. January 10, 1942 - Long Beach, California
Agent: William Morris Agency - Beverly Hills, 310/859-4000

HARD TIMES   Columbia, 1975
THE DRIVER   20th Century-Fox, 1978
THE WARRIORS   Paramount, 1979
THE LONG RIDERS   United Artists, 1980
SOUTHERN COMFORT   20th Century-Fox, 1981
48 HRS.   Paramount, 1982
STREETS OF FIRE   Universal, 1984
BREWSTER'S MILLIONS   Universal, 1985
CROSSROADS   Columbia, 1986
EXTREME PREJUDICE   TriStar, 1987
RED HEAT   TriStar, 1988
JOHNNY HANDSOME   TriStar, 1989
ANOTHER 48 HRS.   Paramount, 1990
TRESPASS   Universal, 1992
GERONIMO: AN AMERICAN LEGEND   Columbia, 1993
WILD BILL   MGM-UA, 1995
GUNDOWN   New Line Cinema, 1996

ARTHUR HILLER*

b. November 22, 1923 - Edmonton, Alberta, Canada
Agent: The Gersh Agency - Beverly Hills, 310/274-6611

THE CARELESS YEARS   United Artists, 1957
THE MIRACLE OF THE WHITE STALLIONS   Buena Vista, 1963
THE WHEELER DEALERS   MGM, 1963
THE AMERICANIZATION OF EMILY   MGM, 1964
PROMISE HER ANYTHING   Paramount, 1966
PENELOPE   MGM, 1966
TOBRUK   Universal, 1967
THE TIGER MAKES OUT   Columbia, 1967
POPI   United Artists, 1969
THE OUT-OF-TOWNERS   Paramount, 1970
LOVE STORY ★   Paramount, 1970
PLAZA SUITE   Paramount, 1971
THE HOSPITAL   United Artists, 1971
MAN OF LA MANCHA   United Artists, 1972, Italian-U.S.
THE CRAZY WORLD OF JULIUS VROODER
  20th Century-Fox, 1974
THE MAN IN THE GLASS BOOTH   American Film Theatre, 1975
W.C. FIELDS AND ME   Universal, 1976
SILVER STREAK   20th Century-Fox, 1975
THE IN-LAWS   Columbia, 1979
NIGHTWING   Columbia, 1979
MAKING LOVE   20th Century-Fox, 1982
AUTHOR! AUTHOR!   20th Century-Fox, 1982
ROMANTIC COMEDY   MGM/UA, 1983
THE LONELY GUY   Universal, 1984
TEACHERS   MGM/UA, 1984

**F
I
L
M**

**D
I
R
E
C
T
O
R
S**

OUTRAGEOUS FORTUNE   Buena Vista, 1987
SEE NO EVIL, HEAR NO EVIL   TriStar, 1989
TAKING CARE OF BUSINESS   Buena Vista, 1990
MARRIED TO IT   Orion, 1991
THE BABE   Universal, 1992

WILLIAM BYRON HILLMAN*
b. Evergreen, Illinois
Home: P.O. Box 321, Tarzana, CA 91356, 818/705-3456
Agent: David Shapira & Associates - Sherman Oaks, 818/906-0322

BETTA BETTA   Commonwealth United, 1971
THE TRAIL RIDE   Gulf States, 1973
THE PHOTOGRAPHER   Avco Embassy, 1974
THE MAN FROM CLOVER GROVE   American Cinema, 1977
THETUS   Rachel's Releasing Corporation, 1979
DOUBLE EXPOSURE   Crown International, 1982
THE MASTER   Front Line Releasing, 1984
RAGIN' CAJUN   International Film Completion Corporation/
   Walanar Group/Loner Productions, 1991, filmed in 1987

HOWARD HIMELSTEIN
Agent: Joel Behr, Behr & Robinson - Los Angeles, 310/556-9222

POWER OF ATTORNEY   Cinevu Films, 1995, Canadian

GREGORY HINES
b. February 14, 1946 - New York, New York
Agent: CAA - Beverly Hills, 310/288-4545

BLEEDING HEARTS   City Films, 1995

DAVID HINTON
THE MAKING OF A LEGEND: "GONE WITH THE WIND" (CTD)
   Turner Entertainment/Selznick Properties Ltd., 1988

GREGORY HIPPOLYTE
(Alexander Gregory Hippolyte)
Business: Axis Films International, 9301 Wilshire Blvd. - Suite 208,
   Beverly Hills, CA 90210, 310/278-9981

SECRET GAMES   Axis Films International, 1991
CARNAL CRIMES   Axis Films International, 1991
MIRROR IMAGES   Axis Films International, 1992
SECRET GAMES II: THE ESCORT   Axis Films
   International, 1992
MIRROR IMAGES II   Axis Films International, 1992
ANIMAL INSTINCTS   Axis Films International, 1992
SINS OF THE NIGHT   Axis Films International, 1993
NIGHT RHYTHMS   Axis Films International, 1993
SECRET GAMES 3   Axis Films International, 1993
ANIMAL INSTINCTS 2   Axis Films International, 1994
BODY OF INFLUENCE   Axis Films International, 1994
OBJECT OF OBSESSION   Axis Films International, 1994

BETTINA HIRSCH
Agent: The Gersh Agency - Beverly Hills, 310/274-6611

MUNCHIES   Concorde, 1987

RUPERT HITZIG*
Address: 3760 Grand View Blvd., Los Angeles, CA 90066,
   310/390-9360

NIGHT VISITOR   MGM/UA, 1989
BACKSTREET DREAMS   Trimark Pictures, 1990
THE LEGEND OF O.B. TAGGART   Northern Arts
   Entertainment, 1994

JACK B. HIVELY*
Home: 8265 Mannix Drive, Los Angeles, CA 90046, 213/654-2188

THE ADVENTURES OF HUCKLEBERRY FINN (TF)   Sunn Classic
   Productions, 1981
CALIFORNIA GOLD RUSH (TF)   Sunn Classic Productions, 1981

YIM HO
(Yen Hao)
b. 1952 - Hong Kong
Contact: Hong Kong Film Liaison, 10940 Wilshire Blvd. - Suite 1220,
   Los Angeles, CA 90024, 310/208-2678

THE EXTRAS   1978, Hong Kong
THE HAPPENINGS   1979, Hong Kong
WEDDING BELLS, WEDDING BELLES   1980, Hong Kong
HOMECOMING   Bluebird Movie Enterprises/Target Film Company,
   1984, Hong Kong
BUDDHA'S LOCK   Shenzhen Film Enterprise/Highland Film
   Enterprise, 1987, Chinese-Hong Kong
RED DUST   Tomson Films/Pineast Pictures, 1990, Hong Kong
THE KING OF CHESS   Golden Princess/Film Workshop Company,
   1991, Hong Kong
THE DAY THE SUN TURNED COLD   Kino International,
   1994, Hong Kong

LYNDALL HOBBS*
Home: 3333 Bonnie Hill Drive, Los Angeles, CA 90068,
   213/851-0953
Agent: William Morris Agency - Beverly Hills, 310/859-4000 or:
   The Cameron Creswell Agency - Sydney, tel.: 02/358-6433 or:
   ICM - London, tel.: 171/636-6565
Personal Manager: Addis-Wechsler & Associates - Los Angeles,
   213/954-9000

BACK TO THE BEACH   Paramount, 1987

GREGORY HOBLIT*
Agent: UTA - Beverly Hills, 310/273-6700

L.A. LAW (TF)   20th Century Fox TV, 1986
ROE VS. WADE (TF) ☆   The Manheim Company/NBC
   Productions, 1989
CLASS OF '61 (TF)   Amblin TV/Universal TV, 1993
PRIMAL FEAR   Paramount, 1995

VICTORIA HOCHBERG*
Home: 6825 Alta Loma Terrace, Hollywood, CA 90068,
   213/874-5064
Agent: ICM - Beverly Hills, 310/550-4000

JACOB HAVE I LOVED (TF)   KCET-LA/Victoria Hochberg
   Productions, 1989
SWEET 15 (TF)   Richard Soto Productions, 1990

MIKE HODGES*
b. July 29, 1932 - Bristol, England
Home: Websley Farm, Durweston, Blandford Forum, Dorset
   DT11 0QG, England, tel.: 0258-453188
Agent: Stephen Durbridge, Lemon, Unna & Durbridge - London,
   tel.: 171/727-1346

SUSPECT (TF)   Thames TV, 1968, British
RUMOUR (TF)   Thames TV, 1969, British
THE MANIPULATOR (TF)   London Weekend TV, 1971, British
GET CARTER   MGM, 1971, British
PULP   United Artists, 1972, British
THE TERMINAL MAN   Warner Bros., 1974
FLASH GORDON   Universal, 1980, British
MISSING PIECES (TF)   Entheos Unlimited Productions/TTC, 1983
SQUARING THE CIRCLE (TF)   TVS Ltd./Metromedia Producers
   Corporation/Brittanic Film and TV Ltd., 1984, British-U.S.
MORONS FROM OUTER SPACE   Universal, 1985, British
MIXED DOUBLES (TF)   Telepictures Productions, 1986
FLORIDA STRAITS (CTF)   HBO Premiere Films/Robert Cooper
   Productions, 1986
A PRAYER FOR THE DYING   The Samuel Goldwyn Company,
   1987, British
BLACK RAINBOW   Goldcrest Films, 1989, British-U.S.
DANDELION DEAD (TF)   London Weekend TV, 1994, British

JENO HODI

AMERICAN KICKBOXER II
NO GOODBYES   Sam Yeong Film Company/One Stop
   Entertainment, 1993
STRONG CITY   HedCo Ltd., 1994

GARY HOFFMAN*

Contact: Directors Guild of America - Los Angeles, 213/851-3671

BONNIE AND CLYDE: THE TRUE STORY (TF)   Hoffman-Israel
   Productions/FNM Films, 1992

MICHAEL HOFFMAN*

Agent: ICM - Beverly Hills, 310/550-4000

PRIVILEGED   New Yorker, 1982, British
RESTLESS NATIVES   Orion Classics, 1985, British
PROMISED LAND   Vestron, 1988
SOME GIRLS   MGM/UA, 1988
SOAPDISH   Paramount, 1991
RESTORATION   Miramax Films, 1995, U.S.-British
PRIDE AND PREJUDICE   Warner Bros., 1995, British

PETER HOFFMAN

VALENTINO RETURNS   Vidmark International, 1989

TAMAR SIMON HOFFS*

Address: 2078 Prosser Avenue, Los Angeles, CA 90025,
   310/446-0076

THE ALLNIGHTER   Universal, 1987

GRAY HOFMEYR

Contact Information: Dr. Martin Botha, Human Sciences Research
   Council, Group for Social Dynamics, Private Bag x41, Pretoria
   0001, South Africa, tel.: 012/202-2308

SCHWEITZER   *LAMBARENE/THE LIGHT IN THE JUNGLE*
   Concorde, 1990, South African
SWEET 'N' SHORT   Toron-Koukos-Troika, 1991, South African
DIRTY GAMES   August Entertainment, 1993, South African
YANKEE ZULU   Distant Horizon/Toron Screen Corporation/Koukos
   Troika, 1994, South African
THERE'S A ZULU ON MY STOEP   Toron Koukus-Troika,
   1994, South African

JACK HOFSISS*

b. September 28, 1950 - Brooklyn, New York
Contact: Directors Guild of America - Los Angeles, 213/851-3671

I'M DANCING AS FAST AS I CAN   Paramount, 1982
FAMILY SECRETS (TF)   Katz-Gallin/Half-Pint Productions/Karoger
   Productions, 1984

P.J. HOGAN

(Paul J. Hogan)
Agent: William Morris Agency - Beverly Hills, 310/859-4000

MURIEL'S WEDDING   Miramax Films, 1994, Australian

HORANT H. HOHLFIELD

LEONARD BERNSTEIN: THE GIFT OF MUSIC (TD)   Amberson
   Productions/WNET-13/KERA/KQED/MPT/SCET/WTTW, 1993

ROD HOLCOMB*

Agent: Elliot Webb, Broder-Kurland-Webb-Uffner Agency -
   Beverly Hills, 310/281-3400

CAPTAIN AMERICA (TF)   Universal TV, 1979
MIDNIGHT OFFERINGS (TF)   Stephen J. Cannell
   Productions, 1981
THE GREATEST AMERICAN HERO (TF)   Stephen J. Cannell
   Productions, 1981
THE QUEST (TF)   Stephen J. Cannell Productions, 1982

MOONLIGHT (TF)   co-director with Jackie Cooper, both directed
   under pseudonym of Alan Smithee, Universal TV, 1982
THE A TEAM (TF)   Stephen J. Cannell Productions, 1983
THE RED-LIGHT STING (TF)   J.E. Productions/Universal TV, 1984
NO MAN'S LAND (TF)   Jadda Productions/Warner Bros. TV, 1984
THE CARTIER AFFAIR (TF)   Hill-Mandelker Productions, 1984
TWO FATHERS' JUSTICE (TF)   A. Shane Company, 1985
STARK (TF)   CBS Entertainment, 1985
STITCHES   directed under pseudonym of Alan Smithee,
   International Film Marketing, 1985
CHASE (TF)   CBS Entertainment, 1985
BLIND JUSTICE (TF)   CBS Entertainment, 1986
STILLWATCH (TF)   Zev Braun Pictures/Interscope Communications/
   Potomac Productions, 1987
THE LONG JOURNEY HOME (TF)   Andrea Baynes Productions/
   Grail Productions/Lorimar-Telepictures, 1987
WISEGUY (TF)   Stephen J. Cannell Productions, 1987
CHINA BEACH (TF)   Sacret Inc. Productions/Warner Bros. TV, 1988
WOLF (TF)   CBS Entertainment, 1989
CHAINS OF GOLD   New Line Cinema, 1991
FINDING THE WAY HOME (TF)   Peter K. Duchow Enterprises, 1991
ANGEL STREET (TF)   John Wells and Friends/Warner
   Bros. TV, 1992
A MESSAGE FROM HOLLY (TF)   Corapeake Productions/
   The Polson Company, 1992
DONATO AND DAUGHTER (TF)   Multimedia Motion Pictures, 1993
ROYCE (CTF)   Gerber-ITC Productions/Showtime, 1994
ER (TF)   Constant C Productions/Amblin TV Productions/
   Warner Bros. TV, 1994
CONVICT COWBOY (CTF)   Viacom/MGM TV/Showtime, 1995

AGNIESZKA HOLLAND*

b. November 28, 1948 - Warsaw, Poland
Agent: William Morris Agency - Beverly Hills, 310/859-4000

AN EVENING WITH ABDON   1975, Polish
SUNDAY'S CHILDREN (TF)   1976, Polish
PROVINCIAL ACTORS   New Yorker, 1979, Polish
FEVER   Film Polski, 1980, Polish
WOMAN ON HER OWN   1981, Polish
LE CARTES POSTALES DE PARIS (TF)   1982, French
ANGRY HARVEST   European Classics, 1985, West German
TO KILL A PRIEST   Columbia, 1988, U.S.-French
THE LION'S DEN   CCR/BR, 1989, West German
EUROPA EUROPA   Orion Classics, 1991, French-German-Polish
OLIVIER, OLIVIER   Sony Pictures Classics, 1992, French
THE SECRET GARDEN   Warner Bros., 1993, U.S.-British
TOTAL ECLIPSE   New Line Cinema, 1995, French-U.S.

RANDY HOLLAND

THE FIRE THIS TIME (FD)   Blacktop Films, 1994

SAVAGE STEVE HOLLAND*

Agent: CAA - Beverly Hills, 310/288-4545

BETTER OFF DEAD   Warner Bros., 1985
ONE CRAZY SUMMER   Warner Bros., 1986
HOW I GOT INTO COLLEGE   20th Century Fox, 1989

TODD HOLLAND*

Agent: CAA - Beverly Hills, 310/288-4545

THE WIZARD   Universal, 1989

TOM HOLLAND*

b. July 11 - Poughkeepsie, New York
Agent: Becsey/Wisdom/Kalajian - Los Angeles, 310/550-0535

FRIGHT NIGHT   Columbia, 1985
FATAL BEAUTY   MGM/UA, 1987
CHILD'S PLAY   MGM/UA, 1988
THE STRANGER WITHIN (TF)   Goodman-Rosen Productions/
   New World TV, 1990
THE TEMP   Paramount, 1993
STEPHEN KING'S THE LANGOLLIERS   *THE LANGOLLIERS* (TF)
   Laurel-King, 1994

ALAN HOLLEB
Agent: Peter Turner Agency - Los Angeles, 310/315-4772

CANDY STRIPE NURSES   New World, 1974
SCHOOL SPIRIT   Concorde/Cinema Group, 1985

GRAHAM HOLLOWAY
Contact: British Film Commission, 70 Baker Street, London
   W1M 1DJ, England, tel.: 171/224-5000

CHASING THE DEER   Cromwell Productions, 1994, Scottish

JAY HOLMAN
LIFE UNDER WATER (TF)   H.J. Holman Productions, 1989

CHRISTOPHER HOLMES
TAKEN ALIVE   Trident Releasing, 1994

FRED HOLMES
Agent: Epstein-Wyckoff-Lamanna & Associates - Beverly Hills,
   310/278-7222

DAKOTA   Miramax Films, 1988

JASON HOLT
TUESDAY NEVER COMES   3 Star Releasing, 1991
DEATH DANCERS   V.I.P., 1993

ROGER HOLZBERG
Personal Manager: Chris Black Management - 818/955-9540

MIDNIGHT CROSSING   Vestron, 1988

ALLAN HOLZMAN*
Agent: Premiere Artists Agency - Los Angeles, 310/271-1414

FORBIDDEN WORLD   New World, 1982
OUT OF CONTROL   New World, 1985
GRUNT! THE WRESTLING MOVIE   New World, 1985
PROGRAMMED TO KILL   co-director with Robert Short,
   Trans World Entertainment, 1987
INTIMATE STRANGER (CTF)   South Gate Entertainment, 1991,
   originally filmed for theatrical release

ELLIOTT HONG
KILL THE GOLDEN GOOSE   Lone Star, 1979
THEY CALL ME BRUCE?   *A FISTFUL OF CHOPSTICKS*
   Artists Releasing Corporation/Film VenturesInternational, 1982
HOT AND DEADLY   Saturn International, 1983

JAMES HONG
Business: Universe II Productions, Inc., 11684 Ventura Blvd. -
   Suite 948, Studio City, CA 91604, 818/763-2028

THE VINEYARD   co-director with Bill Rice, Northstar
   Entertainment, Inc., 1988

HARRY HOOK*
Address: 59 Sisters Avenue, Clapham, London SW11, England
Agent: CAA - Beverly Hills, 310/288-4545 or:
   Rochelle Stevens & Co. - London, tel.: 171/359-3900

SINS OF THE FATHERS   NFS, 1982, British
THE KITCHEN TOTO   Cannon, 1987, British-Kenyan
LORD OF THE FLIES   Columbia, 1990
THE LAST OF HIS TRIBE (CTF)   River City Productions, 1992

KEVIN HOOKS*
b. September 19, 1958 - Philadelphia, Pennsylvania
Agent: UTA - Beverly Hills, 310/273-6700

VIETNAM WAR STORY (CTF)   co-director with
   Georg Stanford Brown & Ray Danton, Nexus Productions, 1987
ROOTS: THE GIFT (TF)   Wolper Productions/Warner
   Bros. TV, 1988
HEATWAVE (CTF)   The Avnet-Kerner Company/Turner
   Network TV, 1990
STRICTLY BUSINESS   Warner Bros., 1991
MURDER WITHOUT MOTIVE: THE EDMUND PERRY STORY (TF)
   Leonard Hill Films, 1992
PASSENGER 57   Warner Bros., 1992
TO MY DAUGHTER WITH LOVE (TF)   Disney Family Classics/
   Steve White Productions, 1994

LANCE HOOL*
b. May 11, 1948 - Mexico City, Mexico
Business: Silver Lion Films, 715 Broadway - Suite 320,
   Santa Monica, CA 90401, 310/393-9177

MISSING IN ACTION 2: THE BEGINNING   Cannon, 1984
STEEL DAWN   Vestron, 1987

TOBE HOOPER*
b. 1943 - Austin, Texas
Agent: Major Clients Agency - Los Angeles, 310/284-6400

THE TEXAS CHAINSAW MASSACRE   Bryanston, 1974
EATEN ALIVE   Virgo International, 1977
SALEM'S LOT (TF)   Warner Bros. TV, 1979
THE FUNHOUSE   Universal, 1981
POLTERGEIST   MGM/UA, 1982
LIFEFORCE   TriStar, 1985, British
INVADERS FROM MARS   Cannon, 1986
THE TEXAS CHAINSAW MASSACRE 2   Cannon, 1986
SPONTANEOUS COMBUSTION   Taurus Entertainment, 1990
I'M DANGEROUS TONIGHT (CTF)   BBK Productions/MCA-TV
   Entertainment, 1990
NIGHTMARE   Cannon, 1993, U.S.-Israeli
THE MANGLER   Distant Horizon/Filmex (Pty) Ltd./Allied Film
   Productions, 1994, British-South African

CLAUDIA HOOVER
DOUBLE EXPOSURE   Falcon Arts & Entertainment, 1994

MARGOT HOPE
Business: Hope Productions, 3122 Arrowhead Drive, Hollywood,
   CA 90068, 213/469-5596

FEMME FONTAINE: KILLER BABE FOR THE C.I.A.   Troma, 1994

ANTHONY HOPKINS
b. December 31, 1937 - Port Talbot, Wales
Agent: ICM - Beverly Hills, 310/550-4000

DYLAN THOMAS - A RETURN JOURNEY (TF)   YOD Productions/
   Daniel TV/British Satellite Broadcasting, 1992, British-Welsh
AUGUST   Granada Film/Majestic Films, 1995, British-Welsh

JOHN HOPKINS
TORMENT   co-director with Samson Asianian, New World, 1986

STEPHEN HOPKINS*
b. Jamaica
Address: 7524 Mulholland Drive, Los Angeles, CA 90046,
   213/850-6698
Agent: ICM - Beverly Hills, 310/550-4000

DANGEROUS GAME   Four Seasons Entertainment,
   1987, Australian
A NIGHTMARE ON ELM STREET 5: THE DREAM CHILD
   New Line Cinema, 1989

PREDATOR 2   20th Century Fox, 1990
JUDGMENT NIGHT   Universal, 1993
BLOWN AWAY   MGM-UA, 1994

DENNIS HOPPER*
b. May 17, 1936 - Dodge City, Kansas
Agent: CAA - Beverly Hills, 310/288-4545
Business Manager: Larry Berkin, Berkin Accountancy,
   3205 Ocean Park Blvd., Santa Monica, CA 90405,
   310/450-1040

EASY RIDER   Columbia, 1969
THE LAST MOVIE   Universal, 1971
OUT OF THE BLUE   Discovery Films, 1982, Canadian
COLORS   Orion, 1988
THE HOT SPOT   Orion, 1990
BACKTRACK   *CATCHFIRE*   Vestron, 1991
CHASERS   Warner Bros., 1994

RICHARD HORIAN
STUDENT CONFIDENTIAL   Troma, 1987

REBECCA HORN
BUSTER'S BEDROOM   Metropolis Filmproduktion/Les Productions
   du Verseau/Prole Films/Limbo Film/Westdeutscher Rundfunk,
   1991, German-Canadian-Portuguese-Swiss

JEFFREY HORNADAY*
Agent: ICM - Beverly Hills, 310/550-4000

SHOUT   Universal, 1991

PETER HORTON*
Agent: UTA - Beverly Hills, 310/273-6700

AMAZON WOMEN ON THE MOON   co-director with Joe Dante,
   John Landis, Carl Gottlieb & Robert K. Weiss, Universal, 1987
EXTREME CLOSE-UP (TF)   Bedford Falls Productions/Robert
   Greenwald Productions, 1990
THE CURE   Universal, 1995

ALEKS HORVAT
Business: 310/449-4049

KISSING MIRANDA   Cinequanon Pictures International, 1995

BOB HOSKINS
b. December 26, 1942 - Bury St. Edmunds, Suffolk, England
Agent: Casarotto Comapny Ltd. - London, 171/287-4450

THE RAGGEDY RAWNEY   Four Seasons Entertainment,
   1988, British
RAINBOW   Winchester Pictures Ltd./Filmline International/
   United Film Partners/Ealing Studios/Screen Partners,
   1995, British-Canadian

DAN HOSKINS
CHOPPER CHICKS IN ZOMBIE TOWN   Troma, 1991

ROBERT HOSSEIN
(Robert Hosseinoff)
b. December 30, 1927 - Paris, France
Agent: M. Lenoir - Paris., tel.: 1/45-63-59-20
Contact: French Film Office, 745 Fifth Avenue, New York,
   NY 10151, 212/832-8860

THE WICKED GO TO HELL   *LES SALAUDS VONT EN ENFER*
   Fanfare, 1955, French
PARDONNEZ-NOUS NOS OFFENSES   1956, French
NUDE IN A WHITE CAR   *TOI LE VENIN*   Trans-Lux Distributing,
   1958, French
LA NUIT DES ESPIONS   1959, French
LES SCELERATS   1960, French

LE GOUT DE LA VIOLENCE   1961, French
LE JEU DE LA VERITE   1961, French
LA MORT D'UN TUEUR   1963, French
LES YEUX CERNES   1964, French
LE VAMPIRE DE DUSSELDORF   1964, French
RASPUTIN   *J'AI TUE RASPOUTINE*   Paramount,
   1967, French-Italian
UNE CORDE...UN COLT   1968, French
POINT DE CHUTE   1970, French
LES MISERABLES   1982, French
LE CAVIAR ROUGE   1985, French

HSIAO-HSIEN HOU
(See Hou HSIAO-HSIEN)

JOHN HOUGH*
b. November 21, 1941 - London, England
Business: The Grade Company, 8 Queen Street, Mayfair, London
   W1X 7PH, England, tel.: 171/409-1925
Agent: The Gersh Agency - Beverly Hills, 310/274-6611 or:
   AIM/John Redway Associates - London, tel.: 171/836-2001

WOLFHEAD   1970, British
SUDDEN TERROR   *EYEWITNESS*   National General,
   1971, British
THE PRACTICE   1971, British
TWINS OF EVIL   Universal, 1972, British
TREASURE ISLAND   National General, 1972,
   British-French-West German- Spanish
THE LEGEND OF HELL HOUSE   20th Century-Fox,
   1974, British
DIRTY MARY CRAZY LARRY   20th Century-Fox, 1974
ESCAPE TO WITCH MOUNTAIN   Buena Vista, 1975
BRASS TARGET   MGM/United Artists, 1978
THE WATCHER IN THE WOODS   Buena Vista, 1980
THE INCUBUS   Artists Releasing Corporation/Film Ventures
   International, 1982, Canadian
TRIUMPHS OF A MAN CALLED HORSE   Jensen Farley Pictures,
   1983, U.S.- Mexican
BLACK ARROW (CTF)   Harry Alan Towers Productions/Pan-Atlantic
   Pictures Productions, 1985, British
BIGGLES   Compact Yellowbill/Tambarle, 1986, British
AMERICAN GOTHIC   Vidmark, 1987, British
A HAZARD OF HEARTS (TF)   The Grade Company/Gainsborough
   Pictures, 1987, British
HOWLING IV...THE ORIGINAL NIGHTMARE   Allied Entertainment,
   1988, British
DANGEROUS LOVE (TF)   The Grade Company/Gainsborough
   Pictures, 1988, British
THE LADY AND THE HIGHWAYMAN (TF)   The Grade Company/
   Gainsborough Pictures, 1989, British
A GHOST IN MONTE CARLO (CTF)   The Grade Co./Gainsborough
   Pictures, 1990, British
DUEL OF HEARTS (CTF)   Turner Network TV/The Grade Company/
   Gainsborough Pictures, 1992, British-U.S.

ROBERT (BOBBY) HOUSTON
Agent: Jim Preminger Agency - Los Angeles, 310/475-9491

SHOGUN ASSASSIN   director of U.S. version, New World,
   1980, Japanese-U.S.
BAD MANNERS   *GROWING PAINS*   New World, 1984
TRUST ME   Cinecom, 1989
HOTEL OKLAHOMA   European American Entertainment, 1991

ELLEN HOVDE*
Home: 51 Franklin Street, Brooklyn, NY 11222, 718/349-3922

GREY GARDENS (FD)   co-director with Albert Maysles,
   David Maysles & Muffie Meyer, 1975
ENORMOUS CHANGES AT THE LAST MINUTE   co-director with
   Mirra Bank, TC Films International, 1985

ADAM COLEMAN HOWARD
Agent: William Morris Agency - Beverly Hills, 310/274-7451

DEAD GIRL   CineTel Pictures/Peacetime Entertainment, 1995

KARIN HOWARD*
Home: 3541 Landa Street, Los Angeles, CA 90039, 213/662-9411

THE TIGRESS   Cinevox/Defa Studio, 1992, German

RON HOWARD*
b. March 1, 1954 - Duncan, Oklahoma
Business: Imagine Entertainment, 1925 Century Park East -
  Suite 230, Los Angeles, CA 90067, 310/277-1665
Agent: CAA - Beverly Hills, 310/288-4545
Attorney: Peter Dekom, Bloom, Dekom & Hergott, 150 S. Rodeo
  Drive - Third Floor, Beverly Hills, CA 90212, 310/859-6800

GRAND THEFT AUTO   New World, 1977
COTTON CANDY (TF)   Major H Productions, 1978
SKYWARD (TF)   Major H-Anson Productions, 1980
THROUGH THE MAGIC PYRAMID (TF)   Major H Productions, 1981
NIGHT SHIFT   The Ladd Company/Warner Bros., 1982
SPLASH   Buena Vista, 1984
COCOON   20th Century Fox, 1985
GUNG HO   Paramount, 1986
WILLOW   MGM/UA, 1988
PARENTHOOD   Universal, 1989
BACKDRAFT   Universal, 1991
FAR AND AWAY   Universal, 1992
THE PAPER   Universal, 1994
APOLLO 13   Universal, 1995

JOHN HOWLEY
HAPPILY EVER AFTER (AF)   Kel-Air Entertainment, 1993

FRANK HOWSON
Contact: Australian Film Commission, 150 William Street,
  Woolloomooloo NSW 2011, Australia, tel.: 2/321-6444

BEYOND MY REACH   Boulevard Films, 1990, Australian
HUNTING   Skouras Pictures, 1992, Australian
MY FORGOTTEN MAN   Boulevard Films, 1993, Australian

HOU HSIAO-HSIEN
b. 1947 - Mei County, Kwantung, China
Contact: Department of Motion Picture Affairs, 2 Tientsin Street,
  Taipei, Taiwan, Republic of China, tel.: 2/351-6591

GREEN, GREEN GRASS OF HOME   1982, Taiwanese
GROWING UP   1982, Taiwanese
THE SANDWICH MAN   1983, Taiwanese
THE BOYS FROM FENGKUEI   1983, Taiwanese
A SUMMER AT GRANDPA'S   1985, Taiwanese
A TIME TO LIVE AND A TIME TO DIE   Central Motion Picture
  Corporation, 1985, Taiwanese
DUST IN THE WIND   International Film Circuit, 1987, Taiwanese
DAUGHTER OF THE NILE   PV Films, 1988, Taiwanese
A CITY OF SADNESS   ERA International Ltd./3-H Films, Ltd.,
  1989, Taiwanese
THE PUPPETMASTER   ERA International, 1993, Taiwanese
GOOD MAN, GOOD WOMAN   1995, Taiwanese

TALUN HSU
WITCHCRAFT 5
THE SILENCER   West Side Studios, 1994

V. V. HSU
PALE BLOOD   Noble Entertainment Group/Alpine
  Releasing Group, 1991

ANN HU
DREAM AND MEMORY   C&A Productions, 1994, U.S.-Chinese

KING HU
(Hu Chin Ch'uan)
b. April 29, 1931 - Peking, China
Business: King Hu Film Productions, 6363 Sunset Blvd. -
  Penthouse 930, Hollywood, CA 90028
Contact: Hong Kong Film Liaison, 10940 Wilshire Blvd. - Suite 1220,
  Los Angeles, CA 90024, 310/208-2678

ETERNAL LOVE   co-director, Shaw Brothers, 1963, Hong Kong
SONS OF THE GOOD EARTH   Shaw Brothers, 1964, Hong Kong
COME DRINK WITH ME   Union Film Company, 1966, Hong Kong
DRAGON GATE INN   Shaw Brothers, 1966, Hong Kong
A TOUCH OF ZEN   Union Film Company, 1968, Hong Kong
FOUR MOODS   co-director, 1970, Hong Kong
THE FATE OF LEE KHAN   King Hu Film Productions,
  1973, Hong Kong
THE VALIANT ONES   King Hu Film Productions,
  1974, Hong Kong
RAINING ON THE MOUNTAIN   King Hu Film Productions,
  1977, Hong Kong
LEGEND OF THE MOUNTAIN   King Hu Film Productions,
  1978, Hong Kong
THE REJUVENATOR   King Hu Film Productions,
  1981, Taiwanese
ALL THE KING'S MEN   Sunny Overseas Corporation/CMPC,
  1983, Hong Kong
THE WHEEL OF LIFE   co-director with Li Hsing & Pai Ching-Jui,
  1983, Taiwanese
THE BOILING SEA (AF)   1985, Hong Kong
SWORDSMAN   co-director with Tsui Hark, Ann Hui, Ching Siu Tung,
  Lee Wai Man & Kam Yeung Wah, Film Workshop Company,
  1990, Hong Kong
PAINTED SKIN   1993, Hong Kong

GEORGE HUANG
Agent: UTA - Beverly Hills, 310/273-6700

SWIMMING WITH SHARKS   THE BUDDY FACTOR
  Trimark Pictures, 1994

JIANXIN HUANG
(See Huang JIANXIN)

JEAN-LOUP HUBERT
b. October 4, 1949 - France
Agent: JFPM et Associes, 11 rue Chanez, 75781 Paris, France,
  tel.: 1/47-43-13-14

L'ANNER PROCHAINE SI TOUT VA BIEN   1981, French
LA SMALA   1984, French
THE GRAND HIGHWAY   Miramax Films, 1987, French
APRES LA GUERRE   AMLF, 1989, French
LA REINE BLANCHE   Camera One/TF1/CIBY 2000, 1991, French
CONTRE L'OUBLI   co-director, Les Films du Paradoxe/Amnesty
  International/PRV, 1992, French
A CAUSE D'ELLE   AMLF, 1993, French

TOM HUCKABEE
b. September 2, 1955 - Fort Worth, Texas

TAKING TIGER MOUNTAIN   co-director with Kent Smith,
  Horizon, 1983

JOHN W. HUCKERT
b. June 26, 1954 - Washington, D.C.
Address: P.O. Box 2270, Hollywood, CA 90028, 213/660-3549

ORANGE SUNSHINE: THE REINCARNATION OF LUDWIG VAN
  BEETHOVEN   Huckert Productions, 1972
ERNIE & ROSE   Huckert Productions, 1982
THE PASSING   Huckert Productions, 1983

REGINALD HUDLIN*
Business: Hudlin Brothers Productions, Inc., Tribeca Film Center,
    375 Greenwich Street, New York, NY 10013, 212/941-4004
Agent: ICM - Beverly Hills, 310/550-4000

HOUSE PARTY   New Line Cinema, 1990
BOOMERANG   Paramount, 1992
COSMIC SLOP (CTF)   Hudlin Brothers Productions/HBO, 1994

GARY HUDSON
Contact: Writers Guild of America, West - Los Angeles,
    310/550-1000

THUNDER RUN   Cannon, 1986

HUGH HUDSON*
b. 1936 - London, England
Address: 11, Queensgate Place Mews, London SW7 5BG,
    England, tel.: 171/581-3133
Agent: CAA - Beverly Hills, 310/288-4545

FANGIO (FD)   1976, British
CHARIOTS OF FIRE ★   The Ladd Company/Warner Bros.,
    1981, British
GREYSTOKE: THE LEGEND OF TARZAN, LORD OF THE APES
    Warner Bros., 1984, British-U.S.
REVOLUTION   Warner Bros., 1985, British-Norwegian
LOST ANGELS   Orion, 1989

ROLANDO HUDSON
GO BEVERLY   IMPix, Inc., 1991

ROY HUGGINS*
July 18, 1914 - Litelle, Washington
Business: Public Arts, Inc., 1928 Mandeville Canyon,
    Los Angeles, CA 90049, 310/476-7892

HANGMAN'S KNOT   Columbia, 1952
THE YOUNG COUNTRY (TF)   Universal TV, 1970

ALBERT HUGHES*
b. Detroit, Michigan
Agent: Writers & Artists Agency - Los Angeles, 310/824-6300

MENACE II SOCIETY   co-director with Allen Hughes,
    New Line Cinema, 1993
DEAD PRESIDENTS   co-director with Allen Hughes,
    Buena Vista, 1995

ALLEN HUGHES*
b. Detroit, Michigan
Agent: Writers & Artists Agency - Los Angeles, 310/824-6300

MENACE II SOCIETY   co-director with Albert Hughes,
    New Line Cinema, 1993
DEAD PRESIDENTS   co-director with Albert Hughes,
    Buena Vista, 1995

CAROL HUGHES
Contact: Writers Guild of America, West - Los Angeles,
    310/550-1000

MISSING LINK   co-director with David Hughes, Universal, 1988

DAVID HUGHES
Contact: Writers Guild of America, West - Los Angeles,
    310/550-1000

MISSING LINK   co-director with Carol Hughes, Universal, 1988

JOHN HUGHES*
b. February 18, 1950 - Lansing, Michigan
Agent: CAA - Beverly Hills, 310/288-4545
Attorney: Jake Bloom, Bloom, Dekom & Hergott, 150 S. Rodeo Drive -
    Third Floor, Beverly Hills, CA 90212, 310/859-6800

SIXTEEN CANDLES   Universal, 1984
THE BREAKFAST CLUB   Universal, 1985
WEIRD SCIENCE   Universal, 1985
FERRIS BUELLER'S DAY OFF   Paramount, 1986
PLANES, TRAINS AND AUTOMOBILES   Paramount, 1987
SHE'S HAVING A BABY   Paramount, 1988
UNCLE BUCK   Universal, 1989
CURLY SUE   Warner Bros., 1991

KENNETH (KEN) HUGHES
b. January 19, 1922 - Liverpool, England
Home: 2218 Beachwood Drive - Apt. 301, Los Angeles, CA 90068,
    213/469-7716

WIDE BOY   Realart, 1952, British
HEAT WAVE   *THE HOUSE ACROSS THE LAKE*   Lippert,
    1954, British
BLACK 13   Archway, 1954, British
THE BRAIN MACHINE   RKO Radio, 1955, British
THE CASE OF THE RED MONKEY   *LITTLE RED MONKEY*
    Allied Artists, 1955, British
THE DEADLIEST SIN   *CONFESSION*   Allied Artists, 1955, British
THE ATOMIC MAN   *TIMESLIP*   Allied Artists, 1955, British
JOE MACBETH   Columbia, 1956, British
WICKED AS THEY COME   Columbia, 1957, British
THE LONG HAUL   Columbia, 1957, British
JAZZ BOAT   Columbia, 1960, British
IN THE NICK   Columbia, 1960, British
THE TRIALS OF OSCAR WILDE   Kinglsey International,
    1960, British
PLAY IT COOLER   Columbia, 1961, British
THE SMALL WORLD OF SAMMY LEE   7 Arts, 1963, British
OF HUMAN BONDAGE   MGM, 1964, British
ARRIVEDERCI, BABY!   *DROP DEAD, DARLING*   Paramount,
    1966, British
CASINO ROYALE   co-director with Val Guest, John Huston,
    Joseph McGrath & Robert Parrish, Columbia, 1967, British
CHITTY CHITTY BANG BANG   United Artists, 1968, British
CROMWELL   Columbia, 1970, British
THE INTERNECINE PROJECT   Allied Artists, 1974, British
ALFIE DARLING   *OH! ALFIE*   1975, British
SEXTETTE   Crown International, 1978
NIGHT SCHOOL   *TERROR EYES*   Paramount, 1981

ROBERT C. HUGHES
Agent: Dennis Loonan, Shooting Stars Productions, 9 East 47th
    Street, New York, NY 10016, 212/888-8999

HUNTER'S BLOOD   Concorde, 1987
MEMORIAL VALLEY MASSACRE   Concorde, 1988
ZADAR! COW FROM HELL   Stone Peach Productions, 1989
DOWN THE DRAIN   RCA-Columbia Home Video/Trans World
    Entertainment/Epic Pictures, 1990
BACK TO BACK   Motion Picture Corporation of America, 1991

TERRY HUGHES*
Address: 4633 Arcola Avenue, Toluca Lake, CA 91602,
    818/508-7330
Agent: William Morris Agency - Beverly Hills, 310/859-4000
Business Manager: Burton Merrill, Individual Productions, Inc.,
    3000 Olympic Blvd. - Bldg. 4 Suite 2312, Santa Monica,
    CA 90404, 310/315-4725

MONTY PYTHON LIVE AT THE HOLLYWOOD BOWL (PF)
    Columbia, 1982, British
SUNSET LIMOUSINE (TF)   Witzend Productions/ITC, 1983
FOR LOVE OR MONEY (TF)   Robert Papazian Productions/
    Henerson-Hirsch Productions, 1984
THE BUTCHER'S WIFE   Paramount, 1991

ANN HUI
(Xu Anhua)
b. 1947 - Manchuria, China
Business: Shaw Brothers (HK) Ltd., Lot 220, Clear Water Bay Road,
   Kowloon, Hong Kong, tel.: 3/719-1551
Contact: Hong Kong Film Liaison, 10940 Wilshire Blvd. - Suite 1220,
   Los Angeles, CA 90024, 310/208-2678

THE SECRET   1979, Hong Kong
THE SPOOKY BUNCH   1980, Hong Kong
THE STORY OF WOO VIET   1981, Hong Kong
BOAT PEOPLE   Spectrafilm, 1983, Hong Kong
LOVE IN A FALLEN CITY   Shaw Brothers, 1984, Hong Kong
THE ROMANCE OF BOOK AND SWORD   Yeung Tse Ke Movie
   Enterprises/SIL-Metropole Organisation, 1987, Hong Kong
STARRY IS THE NIGHT   Shaw Bros., 1988, Hong Kong
SONG OF THE EXILE   Kino International, 1990,
   Hong Kong-Taiwanese
SWORDSMAN   co-directed with King Hu, Tsui Hark,
   Ching Siu Tung, Lee Wai Man & Kam Yeung Wah,
   Film Workshop Company, 1990, Hong Kong
THE ZODIAC KILLERS   Golden Harvest, 1991, Hong Kong
MY AMERICAN GRANDSON   Golden Film, 1992,
   Taiwanese-Chinese
SUMMER SNOW   Golden Harvest, 1995, Hong Kong

MICHAEL HUI
b. 1942 - Canton, China
Contact: Hong Kong Film Liaison, 10940 Wilshire Blvd. - Suite 1220,
   Los Angeles, CA 90024, 310/208-2678

GAMES GAMBLERS PLAY   1974, Hong Kong
THE LAST MESSAGE   1975, Hong Kong
THE PRIVATE EYES   MR. BOO   1977, Hong Kong
THE CONTRACT   1978, Hong Kong
SECURITY UNLIMITED   1981, Hong Kong
TEPPANYAKI   1983, Hong Kong
HAPPY DING DONG   1985, Hong Kong
INSPECTOR CHOCOLATE   1986, Hong Kong
THE MAGIC TOUCH   1992, Hong Kong

DANIELE HUILLET
Contact: French Film Office, 745 Fifth Avenue, New York,
   NY 10151, 212/832-8860

OTHON   co-director with Jean-Marie Straub, 1969, French
GESCHICHTSUNTERRICHT   co-director with Jean-Marie Straub,
   1972, West German
MOSES AND AARON   co-director with Jean-Marie Straub,
   New Yorker, 1975, West German
I CANI DEL SINAI   co-director with Jean-Marie Straub,
   1976, Italian
DELLA NUBE ALLA RESISTENZA   co-director with
   Jean-Marie Straub, 1979, Italian
CLASS RELATIONS   KLASSENVERHALF-NISSE   co-director with
   Jean-Marie Straub, New Yorker, 1984, West German-French
DER TOD DES EMPEDOKLES   co-director with Jean-Marie Straub,
   Janus/Les Films du Losange, 1986, West German-French

DONALD HULETTE
b. November 29, 1937 - Los Angeles, California
Home: 8835 Crescent Drive, Los Angeles, CA 90046, 213/654-9680

BREAKER BREAKER   American International, 1978
A GREAT RIDE   Manson International, 1978
TENNESSEE STALLION   Vestron, 1983
YOU'RE IT   Merlin Film Corporation, 1987

RON HULME
Contact: Directors Guild of Canada, 225 Richmond Street, Toronto,
   Ontario M5V 1W2, Canada, 416/351-8200

FEARLESS TIGER   Le Monde Entertainment, 1994, Canadian

EDWARD HUME
Agent: Broder-Kurland-Webb-Uffner Agency - Los Angeles,
   310/281-3400

STRANGER ON MY LAND (TF)   Edgar J. Scherick Associates/
   Taft Entertainment TV, 1988

SAMO HUNG
(Sammo Hung/Hung Jinbao)
b. January 7, 1952 - Hong Kong
Contact: Hong Kong Film Liaison, 10940 Wilshire Blvd. - Suite 1220,
   Los Angeles, CA 90024, 310/208-2678

THE MAGNIFICENT BUTCHER   1980, Hong Kong
ENCOUNTER OF THE SPOOKY KIND   1981, Hong Kong
PRODIGAL SON   1983, Hong Kong
WINNERS AND SINNERS   1984, Hong Kong
PROJECT A   1984, Hong Kong
WHEELS ON MEALS   1984, Hong Kong
TWINKLE, TWINKLE, LUCKY STARS   1985, Hong Kong
HEART OF THE DRAGON   1985, Hong Kong
EASTERN CONDORS   1987, Hong Kong
PANTYHOSE HERO   1991, Hong Kong
THE EAGLE SHOOTING HEROES: DONG CHENG XI JIU
   director of action sequences, Jet Tone Productions/
   Scholar Films, 1993, Hong Kong

TRAN ANH HUNG
b. 1962 - Vietnam
Contact: French Film Office, 745 Fifth Avenue, New York,
   NY 10151, 212/832-8860

THE SCENT OF GREEN PAPAYA   First Look Pictures, 1993,
   French-Vietnamese
CYCLO   Les Productions Lazennec/Lumiere, 1995, French-Vietnamese

JACKSON HUNSICKER
THE FROG PRINCE   Cannon, 1987, U.S.-Israeli
ODD BALL HALL   The Movie Group, 1989

MAURICE HUNT
THE PAGEMASTER   co-director with Joe Johnston,
   20th Century Fox, 1994

PETER HUNT*
b. March 11, 1928 - London, England
Address: 2337 Roscomare Road - Suite 2, Los Angeles, CA 90077
Agent: Shapiro-Lichtman Talent Agency - Los Angeles, 310/859-8777

ON HER MAJESTY'S SECRET SERVICE   United Artists,
   1969, British
GOLD   Allied Artists, 1974, British
SHOUT AT THE DEVIL   American International, 1976, British
GULLIVER'S TRAVELS   EMI, 1977, British-Belgian
THE BEASTS ARE ON THE STREETS (TF)   Hanna-Barbera
   Productions, 1978
DEATH HUNT   20th Century-Fox, 1981
PHILIP MARLOWE - PRIVATE EYE   CHANDLERTOWN (CMS)
   co-director with Bryan Forbes, Sidney Hayers & David Wickes,
   HBO/David Wickes Television Ltd./London Weekend Television,
   1983, British
THE LAST DAYS OF POMPEII (MS)   David Gerber Company/
   Columbia TV/Centerpoint Films/RAI, 1984, U.S.-British-Italian
WILD GEESE II   Universal, 1985, British
HYPER SAPIEN   Taliafilm II, 1986
ASSASSINATION   Cannon, 1987
EYES OF A WITNESS (TF)   RHI Entertainment Productions, 1991
P.S.I. LUV U (TF)   CBS Entertainment/Glen Larson
   Productions, 1991
RETURN OF THE H.M.S. BOUNTY   BIP/FAB International
   Productions, 1993, British-Italian
HART TO HART RETURNS (TF)   Papazian-Hirsch Entertainment/
   Robert Wagner Productions/Columbia TV, 1993

PETER H. HUNT*
b. December 19, 1938 - Pasadena, California
Agent: CAA - Beverly Hills, 310/288-4545

1776   Columbia, 1972
FLYING HIGH (TF)   Mark Carliner Productions, 1978
BULLY   Maturo Image, 1978
WHEN SHE WAS BAD... (TF)   Ladd Productions/Henry Jaffe
   Enterprises, 1979
RENDEZVOUS HOTEL (TF)   Mark Carliner Productions, 1979
LIFE ON THE MISSISSIPPI (TF)   The Great Amwell Company/
   Nebraska ETV Network/WNET-13/Taurus Films, 1980
THE PRIVATE HISTORY OF A CAMPAIGN THAT FAILED (TF)
   The Great Amwell Company/Nebraska ETV Network/
   WNET-13, 1981
THE MYSTERIOUS STRANGER (TF)   The Great Amwell
   Company/Nebraska ETV Network/WNET-13/MR Film/
   Taurus Films, 1982
SKEEZER (TF)   Margie-Lee Enterprises/The Blue Marble
   Company/Marble Arch Productions, 1982
MASQUERADE (TF)   Renee Valente Productions/Glen A.
   Larson Productions/20th Century-Fox TV, 1983
THE PARADE (TF)   Hill-Mandelker Productions, 1984
SINS OF THE PAST (TF)   Sinpast Entertainment Company
   Productions, 1984
IT CAME UPON THE MIDNIGHT CLEAR (TF)   Schenck-Cardea
   Productions/Columbia TV/LBS Communications, 1984
THE ADVENTURES OF HUCKLEBERRY FINN (TF)   The Great
   Amwell Company, 1986
CHARLEY HANNAH (TF)   A. Shane Company, 1986
DANIELLE STEEL'S SECRETS   SECRETS (TF)   The Cramer
   Company/NBC Productions, 1992
SWORN TO VENGEANCE (TF)   A. Shane Company/RHI Inc., 1993

TIM HUNTER*
Agent: William Morris Agency - Beverly Hills, 310/859-4000

TEX   Buena Vista, 1982
SYLVESTER   Columbia, 1985
RIVER'S EDGE   Hemdale, 1987
PAINT IT BLACK   Vestron, 1990
BEVERLY HILLS, 90210 (TF)   Propaganda Films/Turand
   Productions, 1990
LIES OF THE TWINS (CTF)   Ricochet Productions, 1991
THE SAINT OF FORT WASHINGTON   Warner Bros., 1993

CAROLINE HUPPERT
Agent: Voyez Mon Agent - Paris, France, tel.: 1/47-23-55-80
Contact: French Film Office, 745 Fifth Avenue, New York,
   NY 10151, 212/832-8860

SINCERELY CHARLOTTE   New Line Cinema, 1986, French

WILLIAM T. HURTZ
LITTLE NEMO: ADVENTURES IN SLUMBERLAND (AF)
   co-director with Masami Hata, Hemdale, 1992, Japanese

HARRY HURWITZ*
Business: 450 N. Rossmore Avenue, Los Angeles, CA 90004,
   213/466-5225

THE ETERNAL TRAMP   CHAPLINESQUE, MY LIFE AND
   HARD TIMES (FD)   Maglan Films, 1964
THE PROJECTIONIST   Maron Films Limited, 1971
THE COMEBACK TRAIL   Dynamite Entertainment/Rearguard
   Productions, 1971
RICHARD   co-director with Lorees Yerby, Billings, 1972
FAIRY TALES   directed under pseudonym of Harry Tampa, 1978
AUDITIONS   directed under pseudonym of Harry Tampa,
   Charles Band Productions, 1978
NOCTURNA   directed under pseudonym of Harry Tampa,
   Compass International, 1979
SAFARI 3000   United Artists, 1982
THE ROSEBUD BEACH HOTEL   Almi Pictures, 1985
THAT'S ADEQUATE   South Gate Entertainment, 1988
FLESHTONE   Prism Pictures, 1994

SAM HURWITZ
b. April 20, 1965 - Poughkeepsie, New York
Agent: Favored Artists Agency - Los Angeles, 310/247-1040

ON THE MAKE   Taurus Entertainment, 1989

WARIS HUSSEIN*
b. 1938 - Lucknow, India
Address: 1422 N. Sweetzer Avenue - Suite 307, Los Angeles,
   CA 90069
Agent: ICM - Beverly Hills, 310/550-4000

THANK YOU ALL VERY MUCH   A TOUCH OF LOVE   Columbia,
   1969, British
QUACKSER FORTUNE HAS A COUSIN IN THE BRONX   UMC,
   1970, British
MELODY   S.W.A.L.K.   Levitt-Pickman, 1971, British
THE POSSESSION OF JOEL DELANEY   Paramount, 1972
HENRY VIII AND HIS SIX WIVES   Levitt-Pickman, 1973, British
DIVORCE HIS/DIVORCE HERS (TF)   World Film Services, 1973
AND BABY MAKES SIX (TF)   Alan Landsburg Productions, 1979
DEATH PENALTY (TF)   Brockway Productions/NBC
   Productions, 1980
THE HENDERSON MONSTER (TF)   Titus Productions, 1980
BABY COMES HOME (TF)   Alan Landsburg Productions, 1980
CALLIE & SON (TF)   Rosilyn Heller Productions/Hemdale
   Presentations/City Films/Motown Productions, 1981
COMING OUT OF THE ICE (TF)   The Konigsberg Company, 1982
LITTLE GLORIA...HAPPY AT LAST (TF)   Edgar J. Scherick
   Associates/Metromedia Producers Corporation, 1982,
   U.S.-Canadian-British
PRINCESS DAISY (MS)   NBC Productions/Steve Krantz
   Productions, 1983
THE WINTER OF OUR DISCONTENT (TF)
   Lorimar Productions, 1983
SURVIVING (TF)   Telepictures Productions, 1985
ARCH OF TRIUMPH (TF)   Newland-Raynor Productions/HTV,
   1985, U.S.-British
COPACABANA (TF) ☆☆   Dick Clark Cinema Productions/
   Stiletto Ltd., 1985
WHEN THE BOUGH BREAKS (TF)   Taft Entertainment TV/
   TDF Productions, 1986
INTIMATE CONTACT (MS)   Zenith Productions/Central TV,
   1987, British
DOWNPAYMENT ON MURDER (TF)   Adam Productions/
   20th Century Fox TV, 1987
THE RICHEST MAN IN THE WORLD: THE ARISTOTLE ONASSIS
   STORY (TF)   The Konigsberg-Sanitsky Company, 1988
KILLER INSTINCT (TF)   Millar-Bromberg Productions/ITC, 1988
THOSE SHE LEFT BEHIND (TF)   NBC Productions, 1989
THE SHELL SEEKERS (TF)   Marian Rees Associates/Central
   Films Ltd., 1989, U.S.-British
FORBIDDEN NIGHTS (TF)   Tristine Rainer Productions/Warner
   Bros. TV, 1990
SWITCHED AT BIRTH (TF)   O'Hara-Horowitz Productions/
   Morrow-Heus Productions/Guber-Peters Entertainment Group/
   Columbia TV, 1991
SHE WOKE UP (TF)   Mandy Films/ABC Productions, 1991
CLOTHES IN THE WARDROBE   BBC Films/Screen 2/NFH Ltd.,
   1992, British
FOR THE LOVE OF MY CHILD: THE ANISSA AYALA STORY (TF)
   Viacom/Stonehenge Productions, 1993
MURDER BETWEEN FRIENDS (TF)   Gimbel-Adelson Productions/
   Multimedia TV Productions, 1994
THE SUMMER HOUSE   The Samuel Goldwyn Company,
   1993, British
FORTITUDE (TF)   Pascale Breugnot Productions/BSkyB/
   Rysher Productions/TF1/Reteitalia/Banco, 1994,
   French-British-U.S.-Italian

DANNY HUSTON*
Agent: ICM - Beverly Hills, 310/550-4000

BIGFOOT (TF)   Walt Disney TV, 1987
MR. NORTH   The Samuel Goldwyn Company, 1988
BECOMING COLETTE   Castle Hill Productions, 1992,
   U.S.-German-French
THE MADDENING   Trimark Pictures, 1995

JIMMY HUSTON
Agent: Writers & Artists Agency - Los Angeles, 310/820-2240

DEATH RIVER   Omni, 1977
DARK SUNDAY   Intercontinental, 1978
BUCKSTONE COUNTY PRISON   Film Ventures International, 1978
SEABO   E.O. Corporation, 1978
FINAL EXAM   MPM, 1981
THE SLEUTH SLAYER   Private Eye Productions, 1984
MY BEST FRIEND IS A VAMPIRE   Kings Road, 1988

BRIAN G. HUTTON*
b. 1935 - New York, New York
Contact: Directors Guild of America - Los Angeles, 213/851-3671

WILD SEED   Universal, 1965
THE PAD (...AND HOW TO USE IT)   Universal, 1966
SOL MADRID   MGM, 1968
WHERE EAGLES DARE   MGM, 1969, British
KELLY'S HEROES   MGM, 1970, U.S.-Yugoslavian
X Y & ZEE   ZEE & CO.   Columbia, 1972, British
NIGHT WATCH   Avco Embassy, 1973, British
THE FIRST DEADLY SIN   Filmways, 1980
HIGH ROAD TO CHINA   Warner Bros., 1983, U.S.-Yugoslavian

WILLARD HUYCK*
Agent: CAA - Beverly Hills, 310/288-4545

MESSIAH OF EVIL   International Cinefilm, 1975
FRENCH POSTCARDS   Paramount, 1979
BEST DEFENSE   Paramount, 1984
HOWARD THE DUCK   Universal, 1986

NESSA HYAMS*
Contact: Directors Guild of America - Los Angeles, 213/851-3671

LEADER OF THE BAND   New Century/Vista, 1987

PETER HYAMS*
b. July 26, 1943 - New York, New York
Agent: ICM - Beverly Hills, 310/550-4000

ROLLING MAN (TF)   ABC Circle Films, 1972
GOODNIGHT MY LOVE (TF)   ABC Circle Films, 1972
BUSTING   United Artists, 1974
OUR TIME   Warner Bros., 1974
PEEPER   20th Century-Fox, 1976
CAPRICORN ONE   20th Century-Fox, 1978
HANOVER STREET   Columbia, 1979
OUTLAND   The Ladd Company/Warner Bros., 1981
THE STAR CHAMBER   20th Century-Fox, 1983
2010   MGM/UA, 1984
RUNNING SCARED   MGM/UA, 1986
THE PRESIDIO   Paramount, 1988
NARROW MARGIN   TriStar, 1990
STAY TUNED   Warner Bros., 1992
TIMECOP   Universal, 1994
SUDDEN DEATH   Universal, 1995

NICHOLAS HYTNER
Agent: CAA - Beverly Hills, 310/288-4545

THE MADNESS OF KING GEORGE   The Samuel Goldwyn
   Company, 1994, British-U.S.

I

LEON ICHASO*
Address: 11915 Riverside Drive, North Hollywood, CA 91607,
   818/753-9545
Agent: CAA - Beverly Hills, 310/288-4545

EL SUPER   co-director with Orlando Jimenez-Leal, Columbia, 1979
CROSSOVER DREAMS   Miramax Films, 1985
TALES FROM THE HOLLYWOOD HILLS: A TABLE AT CIRO'S (TF)
   WNET/Zenith Productions/KCET, 1987
THE TAKE (CTF)   Cine-Nevada Inc./MCA-TV/USA Network, 1990
THE FEAR INSIDE (CTF)   Viacom Pictures, 1992
SUGAR HILL   20th Century Fox, 1993
A KISS TO DIE FOR (TF)   The Polone Company/Hearst
   Entertainment, 1993
ZOOMAN (CTF)   The Manheim Company/Logo Productions, 1995

KON ICHIKAWA
b. November 20, 1915 - Ise, Mie Prefecture, Japan
Contact: Nihon Eiga Kantoku Kyokai (Japan Film Directors
   Association), La Fontenu Building -4th Floor, 23-2 Maruyama-cho,
   Shibuya-ku, Tokyo, Japan, tel.: 3/3461-4411

A GIRL AT DOJO TEMPLE   J.O./oho, 1946, Japanese
1001 NIGHTS WITH TOHO   co-director, Shin Toho,
   1947, Japanese
A FLOWER BLOOMS   Shin Toho, 1948, Japanese
365 NIGHTS   Shin Toho, 1948, Japanese
HUMAN PATTERNS   Shin Toho, 1949, Japanese
PASSION WITHOUT END   Shin Toho, 1949, Japanese
SANSHIRO OF GINZA   Shin Toho, 1950, Japanese
HEAT AND MUD   Shin Toho, 1950, Japanese
PURSUIT AT DAWN   Tanaka Productions/Shin Toho,
   1950, Japanese
NIGHTSHADE FLOWER   Shoei Productions/Shin Toho,
   1951, Japanese
THE LOVER   Shin Toho, 1951, Japanese
THE MAN WITHOUT A NATIONALITY   Toyoka Eiga/Toei,
   1951, Japanese
STOLEN LOVE   Aoyagi Productions/Shin Toho, 1951, Japanese
RIVER SOLO FLOWS   Shin Toho, 1951, Japanese
WEDDING MARCH   Toho, 1951, Japanese
MR. LUCKY   Toho, 1952, Japanese
YOUNG PEOPLE   Toho, 1952, Japanese
THE WOMAN WHO TOUCHED LEGS   Toho, 1952, Japanese
THIS WAY - THAT WAY   Daiei, 1952, Japanese
MR. PU   Toho, 1953, Japanese
THE BLUE REVOLUTION   Toho, 1953, Japanese
THE YOUTH OF HEIJI ZENIGATA   Toho, 1953, Japanese
THE LOVER   Toho, 1953, Japanese
ALL OF MYSELF   Toho, 1954, Japanese
A BILLIONAIRE   Seinen Haiyu Club/Shin Toho, 1954, Japanese
TWELVE CHAPTERS ON WOMEN   Toho, 1954, Japanese
GHOST STORY OF YOUTH   Nikkatsu, 1955, Japanese
THE HEART   Nikkatsu, 1955, Japanese
THE BURMESE HARP   HARP OF BURMA   Nikkatsu,
   1956, Japanese
PUNISHMENT ROOM   Daiei, 1956, Japanese
NIHOMBASHI   Daiei, 1956, Japanese
THE CROWDED STREETCAR   Daiei, 1957, Japanese
THE MEN OF TOHOKU   Toho, 1957, Japanese
THE PIT   Daiei, 1957, Japanese
CONFLAGRATION   Daiei, 1958, Japanese
GOODBY, HELLO   Daiei, 1959, Japanese
ODD OBSESSION   Daiei, 1959, Japanese
FIRES ON THE PLAIN   Daiei, 1959, Japanese
A WOMAN'S TESTAMENT   co-director with Kozaburo Yoshimura &
   Yasuzo Masamura, Daiei, 1959, Japanese
BONCHI   Daiei, 1960, Japanese

HER BROTHER   Daiei, 1960, Japanese
TEN DARK WOMEN   Daiei, 1961, Japanese
THE BROKEN COMMANDMENT   *THE OUTCAST*   Daiei, 1962, Japanese
I AM TWO   *BEING TWO ISN'T EASY*   Daiei, 1962, Japanese
AN ACTOR'S REVENGE   *THE REVENGE OF UKENO-JO* Daiei, 1963, Japanese
ALONE ON THE PACIFIC   Ishihara Productions/Nikkatsu, 1963, Japanese
MONEY TALKS   *THE MONEY DANCE*   Daiei, 1964, Japanese
TOKYO OLYMPIAD (FD)   13th Olympic Organizing Committee, 1965, Japanese
TOPO GIGIO E SEI LADRI   Kon Ichikawa Productions/Perego, 1967, Italian- Japanese
YOUTH (FD)   Asahi Shimbunsha/Asahi Television News/Toho, 1968, Japanese
TO LOVE AGAIN   Toho, 1972, Japanese
THE WANDERERS   Kon Ichikawa Productions/ATG, 1973, Japanese
VISIONS OF EIGHT (FD)   co-director with Yuri Ozerov, Mai Zetterling, Arthur Penn, Michael Pfleghar, Milos Forman, Claude Lelouch & John Schlesinger, Cinema 5, 1973
I AM A CAT   Geiensha/Toho, 1975, Japanese
BETWEEN WOMEN AND WIVES   co-director with Shiro Toyoda, Geiensha/Toho, 1976, Japanese
THE INUGAMI FAMILY   Haruki Kadokawa Productions/Geiensha/ Toho, 1976, Japanese
THE DEVIL'S BOUNCING BALL SONG   Toho, 1977, Japanese
ISLAND OF HORRORS   Toho, 1977, Japanese
QUEEN BEE   Toho, 1978, Japanese
FIREBIRD   *HI NO TORI*   Hi no Tori Productions/Toho, 1978, Japanese
THE HOUSE OF THE HANGING ON HOSPITAL HILL Toho Eiga/Toho, 1979, Japanese
THE OLD CAPITAL   *KOTO*   Toho, 1980, Japanese
HAPPINESS   For Life-Toho Eiga/Toho, 1982, Japanese
THE MAKIOKA SISTERS   *SASEMEYUKI*   Toho, 1983, Japanese
OHAN   Toho, 1984, Japanese
THE HARP OF BURMA   Toho, 1985, Japanese
ROKUMEIKAN   Marugen Production Company, 1986, Japanese
FILM ACTRESS   Toho, 1987, Japanese
PRINCESS FROM THE MOON   Toho, 1987, Japanese
CRANE   Toho, 1988, Japanese
NOH MASK MURDERS   Toei, 1991, Japanese
THE RETURN OF MONJIRO KOGARASHI   Fuji TV/C.A.L., 1993, Japanese
47 RONIN   *47 KILLERS*   Toho/NTV/Suntory, 1994, Japanese

ERIC IDLE*
b. March 29, 1943 - South Shields, Durham, England
Business: Prominent Features Ltd., 68a Delancey Street, London NW1 7RY, England, tel.: 171/284-0242
Agent: ICM - Beverly Hills, 310/550-4000

ALL YOU NEED IS CASH   *THE RUTLES* (TF)   co-director with Gary Weis, Rutles Corps Productions, 1978, British

HASSAN ILDARI
Business: Golden Quill, 8439 Sunset Blvd. - Suite 107, Los Angeles, CA 90069, 213/656-7075
Agent: Mark Harris, I.R.S./Harris Management, 3520 Hayden Avenue, Culver City, CA 90232, 310/838-7800

FACE OF THE ENEMY   INI Entertainment Group, 1990

YURI ILLIENKO
b. Ukraine, Soviet Union
Address: Mykhaila Kotsiubynskogo str., 9/22, Kiev-30, Ukraine 252030, tel.: 9044/224-75-40

WELL FOR THE THIRSTY   1965, Soviet
THE EVE OF IVAN KUPALO   International Film Circuit, 1968, Soviet
TO DREAM AND TO LIVE   1973, Soviet
SWAN LAKE - THE ZONE   Kodza International/Cinephile Ltd., 1990, Soviet-U.S.

KWON-TAEK IM
(See Im KWON-TAEK)

SHOHEI IMAMURA
b. 1926 - Tokyo, Japan
Contact: Nihon Eiga Kantoku Kyokai (Japan Film Directors Association), La Fontenu Building -4th Floor, 23-2 Maruyama-cho, Shibuya-ku, Tokyo, Japan, tel.: 3/3461-4411

STOLEN DESIRE   Nikkatsu, 1958, Japanese
NISHI GINZA STATION   Nikkatsu, 1958, Japanese
ENDLESS DESIRE   Nikkatsu, 1958, Japanese
MY SECOND BROTHER   Nikkatsu, 1959, Japanese
PIGS AND BATTLESHIPS   Nikkatsu, 1961, Japanese
THE INSECT WOMAN   Nikkatsu, 1963, Japanese
INTENTIONS OF MURDER   *UNHOLY DESIRE*   Nikkatsu, 1964, Japanese
THE PORNOGRAPHERS: INTRODUCTION OF ANTHROPOLOGY   East West Classics, 1966, Japanese
A MAN VANISHES   Imamura Productions/Nihon Eiga Shinsha/ATG, 1967, Japanese
THE PROFOUND DESIRE OF THE GODS   *KURAGEJIMA: TALES FROM A SOUTHERN ISLAND*   /Imamura Productions Nikkatsu, 1968, Japanese
HISTORY OF POST-WAR JAPAN AS TOLD BY A BAR HOSTESS (FD)   Nihon Eiga Shinsha/Toho, 1970, Japanese
KARAYUKI-SAN, THE MAKING OF A PROSTITUTE (TD) Imamura Productions/Shibata Organization, 1975, Japanese
VENGEANCE IS MINE   Shochiku, 1979, Japanese
EIJANAIKA   Shochiku, 1981, Japanese
THE BALLAD OF NARAYAMA   Toei-Imamura Productions/Toei, 1983, Japanese
ZEGEN   Toei, 1987, Japanese
BLACK RAIN   Angelika Films, 1989, Japanese

SAMUEL (SHMUEL) IMBERMAN
Contact: Israel Film Centre, Ministry of Industry & Trade, 30 Agron Street, P.O. Box 299, 94190 Jerusalem, Israel, tel.: 972/210433 or 210297

I DON'T GIVE A DAMN   Trans World Entertainment, 1987, Israeli
TEL AVIV - LOS ANGELES   Galia Communic Ltd./Five-Five Productions, 1988, Israeli
OVERDOSE   Sunrise Films Ltd., 1993, Israeli

MARKUS IMHOOF
b. 1941 - Winterthur, Switzerland
Contact: Swiss Film Center, Muenstergasse 18, CH-8001 Zurich, Switzerland, tel.: 01/472-860

FLUCHTGEFAHR   1974, Swiss
TAUWETTER   1978, Swiss
ISEWIXER   1979, Swiss
THE BOAT IS FULL   Quartet, 1980, Swiss
DIE REISE   Regina Ziegler Filmproduktion/Limbo Film/WDR/SRG, 1986, West German-Swiss
DER BERG   Bernard Lang AG Zurich/Markus Imhoof/Ulrich Bar/Werner Merzbacher/SRG/ZDF/ORF, 1990, Swiss-German-Austrian

KEVIN INCH*
Agent: APA - Los Angeles, 310/273-0744

REMINGTON STEELE: THE STEELE THAT WOULDN'T DIE (TF) MTM Productions, 1987
CARLY'S WEB (TF)   MTM Enterprises, 1987

KEITH INGHAM
STARWATCHER (AF)   co-director with Moebius, Videosystem/ Percy Main Productions, 1993

OTAR IOSELLIANI

b. February 2, 1934 - Georgia, U.S.S.R.
Contact: French Film Office, 745 Fifth Avenue, New York,
NY 10151, 2I2/832-8860

APRIL *STORIES ABOUT THINGS* 1964, Soviet, unreleased
FALLING LEAVES 1966, Soviet
THERE WAS A SINGING BLACKBIRD 1972, Soviet
PASTORAL 1982, Soviet, filmed in 1976
LES FAVOURIS DE LA LUNE 1984, French
ET LA LUMIERE FUT Films du Triangle/La Sept/Direkt Film/RAI,
1989, French-West German-Italian
LA CHASSE AUX PAPILLONS Pierre Grise Productions/
Sodaperaga/France 3 Cinema/Metropolis Films/Best
International Films, 1992, French-German-Italian
SEULE, GEORGIE (TD) Arte TV, 1994, French

MATTHEW IRMAS

WHEN THE PARTY'S OVER August Entertainment, 1992

DANIEL IROM*

Home: 7077 Alvern Street - Apt. A325, Los Angeles, CA 90045,
310/641-5667

BUM RAP Millennium Productions, 1988

JOHN IRVIN*

b. May 7, 1940 - Newcastle, England
Home: 6 Lower Common South, London SW15, England,
tel.: 181/789-1514
Agent: ICM - Beverly Hills, 310/550-4000

TINKER, TAILOR, SOLDIER, SPY (TF) BBC/Paramount TV,
1979, British
THE DOGS OF WAR United Artists, 1981, U.S.-British
GHOST STORY Universal, 1981
CHAMPIONS Embassy, 1983, British
TURTLE SUMMER The Samuel Goldwyn Company,
1985, British
RAW DEAL DEG, 1986
HAMBURGER HILL Paramount, 1987
NEXT OF KIN Warner Bros., 1989
EMINENT DOMAIN Triumph Releasing Corporation, 1990,
Canadian-Israeli-French
ROBIN HOOD (TF) Working Title Films/20th Century Fox,
1991, U.S.-British
FREEFALL (CTF) Nu World Productions, 1994, South African
WIDOWS' PEAK Fine Line Features/New Line Cinema,
1994, British-Irish
A MONTH BY THE LAKE Miramax Films, 1995, British

SAM IRVIN

Agent: Innovative Artists - Los Angeles, 310/553-5200

GUILTY AS CHARGED I.R.S. Releasing, 1991
ACTING ON IMPULSE Spectator Films, 1993
OBLIVION R.S. Entertainment, 1994
MAGIC ISLAND (HVF) Moonbeam Ent./Paramount
Home Video, 1995
OUT THERE (CTF) I.R.S. Media/Showtime, 1995

DAVID IRVING

GOOD-BYE, CRUEL WORLD Sharp Features, 1982
RUMPELSTILTSKIN Cannon, 1987, U.S.-Israeli
SLEEPING BEAUTY Cannon, 1987, U.S.-Israeli
THE EMPEROR'S NEW CLOTHES Cannon, 1987, U.S.-Israeli
C.H.U.D. II MCEG, 1988
PERFUME OF THE CYCLONE The Movie Group, 1990

ALBERTO ISAAC

b. Colima, Mexico
Contact: IMCINE, Tepic #40, P.B. Colonia Roma Sur, Mexico City,
C.P. 06760, Mexico, tel.: 525/584-7283

EN ESTE PUEBLO NO HAY LADRONES Azteca Films,
1965, Mexican
LA OLIMPIADA EN MEXICO (FD) Azteca Films, 1968, Mexican
LAS VISITACIONES DEL DIABLO Azteca Films, 1971, Mexican
LOS DIAS DE AMOR Azteca Films, 1971, Mexican
EL RINCON DE LAS VIRGINES Azteca Films, 1972, Mexican
TIVOLI Azteca Films, 1974, Mexican
CUARTELAZO Azteca Films, 1976, Mexican
LAS NOCHES DE PALOMA Azteca Films, 1978, Mexican
TIEMPO DE LOBOS Azteca Films, 1982, Mexican
UN HOGAR MUY DECENTE Azteca Films, 1987, Mexican
LAS BATALLAS EN EL DESIERTO Conacine, 1987, Mexican
MARIANA, MARIANA Azteca Films, 1988, Mexican
NAVIDAD SANGRIENTE Conacine, 1989, Mexican
MATAN A CHINTO Conacine/Estudios Churubusco,
1990, Mexican
MUJERES INSUMISAS IMCINE, 1995, Mexican

JAMES ISAAC

THE HORROR SHOW MGM/UA, 1989

EVA ISAKSEN

b. Norway
Contact: Norwegian Film Institute, Grev Wedels Plass 1,
N-0105 Oslo 1, Norway, tel.: 2/42-87-40

DEATH AT OSLO CENTRAL Norsk Film, 1990, Norwegian
THE PERFECT MURDER Moviemakers/Norsk Film,
1992, Norwegian
STORK STARING MAD Moviemakers/Norsk Film,
1995, Norwegian

ROBERT ISCOVE*

b. Toronto, Ontario, Canada
Address: 16045 Royal Oak Road, Encino, CA 91436,
818/981-7836
Agent: CAA - Beverly Hills, 310/288-4545

CHAUTAUQUA GIRL (TF) CBC, 1983, Canadian
LOVE & LARCENY (TF) CBC, 1985, Canadian
THE PRODIGIOUS HICKEY (TF) Ronald J. Kahn Productions/
American Playhouse, 1987
MURDER IN BLACK AND WHITE (TF) Titus Productions, 1990
THE FLASH (TF) Pet Fly Productions/Warner Bros. TV, 1990
MISSION OF THE SHARK (TF) Richard Maynard Productions/
Fries Entertainment, 1991
BREAKING THE SILENCE (TF) Permut Presentations Inc./
Finnegan-Pinchuk Company, 1992
TERROR ON TRACK 9 (TF) Richard Crenna Productions/
Spelling Entertainment, 1992
MIRACLE ON I-880 (TF) Glen Oak Productions/
Columbia TV, 1993
DYING TO LOVE YOU (TF) Louis Rudolph Films/Fenton
Entertainment Group/Fries Entertainment, 1993
RIVER OF RAGE: THE TAKING OF MAGGIE KEENE (TF)
David C. Thomas Productions, 1993
THE FORGET ME NOT MURDERS (TF) Janek Productions/
Pendick Enterprises/Spelling TV, 1994
WITHOUT CONSENT (TF) Once Upon A Time Films Ltd./Blue
Puddle Productions, 1994
A SILENT BETRAYAL (TF) Pendick Enterprises/
Spelling TV, 1994

GERALD I. ISENBERG

b. May 13, 1940 - Cambridge, Massachusetts
Business: Hearst Entertainment, 1640 S. Sepulveda Blvd. - 4th Floor,
Los Angeles, CA 90025, 310/478-1700

SEIZURE: THE STORY OF KATHY MORRIS (TF) The Jozak
Company, 1980

SOGO ISHII

b. 1957 - Hakata, Fukuoka, Japan
Contact: Nihon Eiga Kantoku Kyokai (Japan Film Directors
    Association), La Fontenu Building -4th Floor, 23-2 Maruyama-cho,
    Shibuya-ku, Tokyo, Japan, tel.: 3/3461-4411

PANIC IN HIGH SCHOOL   Kyoeisha - Crazy Film Group,
    1977, Japanese
PANIC IN HIGH SCHOOL   Nikkatsu, 1978, Japanese
CRAZY THUNDER ROAD   Kyoeisha/Dynamite Productions,
    1980, Japanese
BURST CITY   Dynamite Productions, 1982, Japanese
THE CRAZY FAMILY   *THE BACK-JET FAMILY*   Directors
    Company/International Film/ATG, 1984, Japanese
ANGEL DUST   Twins Japan/Eurospace, 1994, Japanese

NEAL ISRAEL*

Agent: William Morris Agency - Beverly Hills, 310/859-4000

TUNNELVISION   co-director with Brad Swirnoff, World Wide, 1976
AMERICATHON   United Artists, 1979
BACHELOR PARTY   20th Century Fox, 1984
MOVING VIOLATIONS   20th Century Fox, 1985
COMBAT HIGH (TF)   Frank von Zerneck Productions/Lynch-Biller
    Productions, 1986
THE COVER GIRL AND THE COP (TF)   Barry-Enright Productions/
    Alexander Productions, 1988
BREAKING THE RULES   Miramax Films, 1992, filmed in 1989
SURF NINJAS   New Line Cinema, 1993

PETER ISRAELSON*

Business: Levinson, Israelson & Bell, 12-1/2 East 82nd Street,
    New York, NY 10028, 212/472-8888

SIDE OUT   TriStar, 1990

JUZO ITAMI

b. 1933 - Kyoto, Japan
Agent: ICM - Beverly Hills, 310/550-4000

THE FUNERAL   New Yorker, 1985, Japanese
TAMPOPO   New Yorker, 1986, Japanese
A TAXING WOMAN   Original Cinema, 1987, Japanese
A TAXING WOMAN RETURNS   New Yorker, 1988, Japanese
A-GE-MAN: TALES OF A GOLDEN GEISHA   Itami Films,
    1990, Japanese
MINBO - OR THE GENTLE ART OF JAPANESE EXTORTION
    MINBO NO ONNA   Northern Arts Entertainment,
    1992, Japanese
THE SERIOUSLY ILL   Toho, 1993, Japanese

JAMES IVORY*

b. June 7, 1928 - Berkeley, California
Business: Merchant-Ivory Productions, 400 East 52nd Street,
    New York, NY 10022, 212/759-3694
Agent: CAA - Beverly Hills, 310/288-4545 or:
    Peters Fraser & Dunlop - London, tel.: 171/344-1000

THE HOUSEHOLDER   Royal Films International, 1963, Indian-U.S.
SHAKESPEARE WALLAH   Continental, 1966, Indian
THE GURU   20th Century-Fox, 1969, British-Indian
BOMBAY TALKIE   Dia Films, 1970, Indian
SAVAGES   Angelika, 1972
THE WILD PARTY   American International, 1975
AUTOBIOGRAPHY OF A PRINCESS (TF)   Merchant Ivory
    Productions, 1975
SWEET SOUNDS   Merchant Ivory Productions, 1976
ROSELAND   Cinema Shares International, 1977
THE 5:48 (TF)   PBS, 1979
HULLABALOO OVER GEORGIA & BONNIE'S PICTURES
    Corinth, 1979
THE EUROPEANS   Levitt-Pickman, 1979, British
JANE AUSTEN IN MANHATTAN   Contemporary, 1980
QUARTET   New World, 1981, British-French
HEAT AND DUST   Universal Classics, 1983, British
THE BOSTONIANS   Almi Pictures, 1984

A ROOM WITH A VIEW ★   Cinecom, 1986, British
MAURICE   Cinecom, 1987, British
SLAVES OF NEW YORK   TriStar, 1989
MR. & MRS. BRIDGE   Miramax Films, 1990
HOWARDS END ★   Sony Pictures Classics, 1992, British
THE REMAINS OF THE DAY ★   Columbia, 1993, British
JEFFERSON IN PARIS   Buena Vista, 1995

KENCHI IWAMOTO

b. Japan
Contact: Nihon Eiga Kantoku Kyokai (Japan Film Directors
    Association), La Fontenu Building -4th Floor, 23-2 Maruyama-cho,
    Shibuya-ku, Tokyo, Japan, tel.: 3/3461-4411

KIKUCHI   Vortex Japan, 1991, Japanese
MONKEYS IN PARADISE   Vortex Japan, 1994, Japanese

J

DAVID JABLIN

Agent: The Gersh Agency - Beverly Hills, 3210/274-6611
Personal Manager: Brillstein/Grey Entertainment - Beverly Hills,
    310/275-6135

SEX, SHOCK AND CENSORSHIP IN THE '90S (CTF)
    Imagination Productions, 1993

DEL JACK

JAMES STEWART: HOMETOWN HERO (TD)   Millenial
    Entertainment/Archive Films/Arts & Entertainment Network, 1993

DAVID S. JACKSON*

Home: 344 E. Rustic Road, Santa Monica, CA 90402, 310/573-6264
Agent: William Morris Agency - Beverly Hills, 310/859-4000

ALISTAIR MACLEAN'S DEATH TRAIN   *DEATH TRAIN* (CTF)
    USA Network/British Lion Entertainment/Yorkshire TV/Jadran
    Film of Croatia, 1993, U.S.-British-Croatian

DONALD G. JACKSON

Home: 7007 Comanche Avenue, Canoga Park, CA 91306,
    818/716-9539

I LIKE TO HUNT PEOPLE   New World, 1985
ROLLERBLADE   New World, 1985
HELL COMES TO FROGTOWN   co-director with R.J. Kizer,
    New World, 1988
ROLLERBLADE WARRIORS   Golden Circle Productions, 1988
FROGTOWN II   York Pictures, 1991
THE ROLLERBLADE SEVEN   The Rebel Corporation, 1992
THE ROLLERBLADE SEVEN, PART 2   The Rebel
    Corporation, 1992
ONE SHOT SAM   One Shot Productions, 1992

DOUGLAS JACKSON

b. 1940 - Montreal, Quebec, Canada
Agent: The Barry Perelman Agency - Los Angeles, 310/274-5999

NORMAN JEWISON, FILMMAKER (TD)   1971, Canadian
THE HUNTSMAN   1972, Canadian
THE SLOANE AFFAIR (TF)   1973, Canadian
THE HEATWAVE LASTED FOUR DAYS (TF)   1974, Canadian
WHY MEN RAPE (TD)   1980, Canadian
THE ART OF EATING   1981, Canadian
DEAN KOONTZ'S WHISPERS   *WHISPERS*   ITC Entertainment
    Group/Cinepix, 1990, Canadian

THE PAPERBOY   Allegro Films/Blue Rider Pictures,
   1993, Canadian
DEADBOLT (TF)   Allegro Films/Image Organization,
   1993, Canadian
THE WRONG WOMAN   Allegro Films/Image Organization,
   1994, Canadian

GEORGE JACKSON
Agent: William Morris Agency - Beverly Hills, 310/859-4000

HOUSE PARTY 2   co-director with Doug McHenry,
   New Line Cinema, 1991

LEWIS JACKSON
Contact: Writers Guild of America, East - New York City,
   212/767-7800

YOU BETTER WATCH OUT   *CHRISTMAS EVIL*
   Edward R. Pressman Productions, 1980

MICK JACKSON*
Address: 1349 Berea Place, Pacific Palisades, CA 90272,
   310/459-2683
Agent: ICM - Beverly Hills, 310/550-4000

THREADS (TF)   Western-World TV/BBC/Nine Network,
   1984, British-American
YURI NOSENKO, KGB (CTF)   HBO Showcase/BBC/Premiere TV,
   1986, U.S.- British
DOUBLE HELIX   *LIFE STORY* (TF)   BBC, 1987, British
A VERY BRITISH COUP (TF)   Skreba Films/Channel 4,
   1988, British
CHATTAHOOCHIE   Hemdale, 1989
L.A. STORY   TriStar, 1991
THE BODYGUARD   Warner Bros., 1992
CLEAN SLATE   MGM, 1994
INDICTMENT: THE McMARTIN TRIAL (CTF)   Ixtlan/Abby Mann
   Productions/Breakheart Films, 1995

PETER JACKSON
b. 1961 - New Zealand
Agent: ICM - Beverly Hills, 310/550-4000

BAD TASTE   1987, New Zealand
MEET THE FEEBLES   Greycat Films, 1989, New Zealand
DEAD ALIVE   *BRAINDEAD*   Trimark Pictures,
   1992, New Zealand
HEAVENLY CREATURES   Miramax Films, 1993, New Zealand
THE FRIGHTENERS   Universal, 1995

PHILIP JACKSON
Contact: Directors Guild of Canada, 225 Richmond Street, Toronto,
   Ontario M5V 1W2, Canada, 416/351-8200

STRANGE HORIZONS   Lightscape Motion Pictures,
   1993, Canadian
REPLIKATOR   Prism Pictures, 1994, Canadian

SIMCHA JACOBOVICI
b. 1953 - Israel
Business: Associated Producers, 957 Broadview Avenue - Unit D,
   Toronto, Ontario M4K 2R5, Canada, 416/422-1270

FALASHA: EXILE OF THE BLACK JEWS (FD)   Matara Film
   Productions, 1983, Canadian
REVOLUTION AND THE CROSS (TD)   1984, Canadian
JOURNEY'S END: THE FORGOTTEN REFUGEES (TD)
   1985, Canadian
WINGS OF EAGLES (TD)   1986, Canadian
UNFINISHED EXODUS: ANATOMY OF AN AIRLIFT (TD)
   1986, Canadian
A QUESTION OF TIME (FD)   1988, Canadian
HEMOPHILIA: IN PERSPECTIVE (TD)   1989, Canadian
DEADLY CURRENTS (FD)   Telefilm Canada/Ontario Film
   Development Corporation/City-TV, 1991, Canadian

ALAN JACOBS
Agent: ICM - Beverly Hills, 310/550-4000

NINA TAKES A LOVER   Triumph Films, 1994

JERRY P. JACOBS
A DANGEROUS PLACE   PM Entertainment Group, 1994

JON JACOBS
THE GIRL WITH THE HUNGRY EYES   Kastenbaum Films/
   Smoking Gun, 1995

RON JACOBS*
(Ronald S. Jacobs)
Business: Jaguar Productions, 235 East 34th Street, New York,
   NY 10016, 212/889-9494

A NEED OF HELL   Jaguar Productions, 1994

LAWRENCE-HILTON JACOBS
Contact: Screen Actors Guild - Los Angeles, 213/954-1600

QUIET FIRE   *ANGELS OF THE CITY*   PM Entertainment
   Group, 1990

RICK JACOBSON
Agent: Cavaleri & Associates - Los Angeles, 213/583-1354

DRAGON FIRE   Concorde, 1993
LION STRIKE   PM Entertainment Group, 1994
BLOODFIST VI: GROUND ZERO   Concorde, 1994

JOSEPH JACOBY
b. September 22, 1942 - Brooklyn, New York
Contact: Writers Guild of America, East - New York City,
   212/767-7800
Business Manager: Royal E. Blakeman - New York, 212/421-4100

SHAME, SHAME, EVERYBODY KNOWS HER NAME   JER, 1970
HURRY UP OR I'LL BE THIRTY   Avco Embassy, 1973
THE GREAT BANK HOAX   *SHENANIGANS*   Warner Bros., 1979

GUALTIERO JACOPETTI
b. 1919 - Barga, Italy
Home: via Monte delle Gioie 9, Rome, Italy, tel.: 6/86211326

MONDO CANE (FD)   co-director with Paolo Cavara &
   Franco Prosperi, Times Film Corporation, 1962, Italian
WOMEN OF THE WORLD   *EVA SCONOSCIUTA* (FD)   co-director
   with Paolo Cavara & Franco Prosperi, Embassy, 1963, Italian
MONDO PAZZO   *MONDO CANE N. 2/CRAZY WORLD/
   MONDO INSANITY* (FD)   co-director with Franco Prosperi,
   Rizzoli Film, 1964, Italian
AFRICA ADDIO (FD)   co-director with Franco Prosperi, Rizzoli Film,
   1966, Italian
FAREWELL UNCLE TOM (FD)   co-director with Franco Prosperi,
   Euro International Film, 1972, Italian
MONDO CANDIDO (FD)   co-director with Franco Proisperi,
   Perugia Cinematografica, 1975, Italian

JUST JAECKIN*
b. 1940 - Vichy, France
Agent: JFPM et Associes, 11 Rue Chanez, Paris 75016, France,
   tel.: 1/47-43-13-14
Contact: French Film Office, 745 Fifth Avenue, New York,
   NY 10151, 212/832-8860

EMMANUELLE   Columbia, 1974, French
THE STORY OF O   Allied Artists, 1975, French
THE FRENCH WOMAN   *MADAME CLAUDE*   Monarch,
   1979, French
THE LAST ROMANTIC LOVER   New Line Cinema,
   1980, French

GIRLS   Caneuram Films, 1980, Canadian-French-Israeli
COLLECTIONS PRIVEES   co-director with Shuji Terayama &
   Walerian Borowczyk, Jeudi Films/Toei/French Movies,
   1979, French-Japanese
LADY CHATTERLEY'S LOVER   Cannon, 1982, French-British
THE PERILS OF GWENDOLINE   *GWENDOLINE*   The Samuel
   Goldwyn Company, 1984, French

RAY JAFELICE
THE CARE BEARS' ADVENTURE IN WONDERLAND (AF)
   Cineplex Odeon, 1987, Canadian

STANLEY JAFFE*
b. July 31, 1940 - New Rochelle, New York
Business Manager: Martin Eisman, Eisman & Company,
   2001 Palmer Avenue, Larchmont, NY 10538

WITHOUT A TRACE   20th Century-Fox, 1983

STEVEN CHARLES JAFFE*
Business: Pari Passu Productions, 5555 Melrose Avenue,
   Los Angeles, CA 90028, 213/956-4827
Attorney: Stan Coleman, Weissmann, Wolff, Bergman, Coleman &
   Silverman, 9665 Wilshire Blvd. - Suite 900, Beverly Hills,
   CA 90212, 310/858-7888

SCARAB   1982

HENRY JAGLOM*
b. January 26, 1943 - New York, New York
Business: International Rainbow Pictures, 9165 Sunset Blvd. -
   Penthouse, Los Angeles, CA 90069, 310/271-0202 or:
   888 Seventh Avenue - 34th Floor, New York, NY 10106,
   212/245-8300

A SAFE PLACE   Columbia, 1971
TRACKS   Castle Hill Productions, 1976
SITTING DUCKS   Speciality Films, 1980
NATIONAL LAMPOON'S MOVIE MADNESS   co-director with
   Bob Giraldi, United Artists, 1981
CAN SHE BAKE A CHERRY PIE?   Castle Hill Productions/
   Quartet Films, 1983
ALWAYS   The Samuel Goldwyn Company, 1985
SOMEONE TO LOVE   Rainbow/Castle Hill Productions, 1987
NEW YEAR'S DAY   International Rainbow Pictures, 1988
EATING   International Rainbow Pictures, 1989
VENICE/VENICE   Rainbow Releasing, 1992
BABYFEVER   The Rainbow Film Company, 1994

PATRICK JAMAIN
Home: 6, rue de la Basse Cour, 77560 Villiers-St-Georges,
   France, tel.: 1/64-01-97-49
Contact: French Film Office, 745 Fifth Avenue, New York,
   NY 10151, 212/832-8860

HONEYMOON   International Film Marketing,
   1985, Canadian-French
TWO FOR ADVENTURE (MS)   Raspail/TaurusFilm/Antenne-2/
   ORF/SAT 1, 1991, French-German-Austrian

PEDR JAMES
Contact: British Film Commission, 70 Baker Street, London
   W1M 1DJ, England, tel.: 171/224-5000

MARTIN CHUZZLEWIT (MS)   BBC Pebble Mill/WGBH-Boston,
   1995, British-U.S.

STEVE JAMES
Agent: William Morris Agency - Beverly Hills, 310/859-4000

HOOP DREAMS (FD)   Fine Line Features/New Line
   Cinema, 1994

JERRY JAMESON*
b. Hollywood, California
Contact: Directors Guild of America - Los Angeles, 213/851-3671

BRUTE CORPS   General Films, 1971
THE DIRT GANG   American International, 1972
THE BAT PEOPLE   American International, 1974
HEATWAVE! (TF)   Universal TV, 1974
THE ELEVATOR (TF)   Universal TV, 1974
HURRICANE (TF)   Metromedia Productions, 1974
TERROR ON THE 4TH FLOOR (TF)   Metromedia Productions, 1974
THE SECRET NIGHT CALLER (TF)   Charles Fries Productions/
   Penthouse Productions, 1975
THE DEADLY TOWER (TF)   MGM TV, 1975
THE LIVES OF JENNY DOLAN (TF)   Ross Hunter Productions/
   Paramount TV, 1975
THE CALL OF THE WILD (TF)   Charles Fries Productions, 1976
THE INVASION OF JOHNSON COUNTY (TF)   Roy Huggins
   Productions/Universal TV, 1976
AIRPORT '77   Universal, 1977
SUPERDOME (TF)   ABC Circle Films, 1978
A FIRE IN THE SKY (TF)   Bill Driskill Productions, 1978
RAISE THE TITANIC   AFD, 1980, British-U.S.
HIGH NOON - PART II: THE RETURN OF WILL KANE (TF)
   Charles Fries Productions, 1980
STAND BY YOUR MAN (TF)   Robert Papazian Productions/Peter
   Guber-Jon Peters Productions, 1981
KILLING AT HELL'S GATE (TF)   CBS Entertainment, 1981
HOTLINE (TF)   Wrather Entertainment International/Ron Samuels
   Productions, 1982
STARFLIGHT: THE PLANE THAT COULDN'T LAND (TF)
   Orgolini-Nelson Productions, 1983
COWBOY (TF)   Bercovici-St. Johns Productions/MGM TV, 1983
THIS GIRL FOR HIRE (TF)   Barney Rosenzweig Productions/
   Orion TV, 1983
LAST OF THE GREAT SURVIVORS (TF)   CBS Entertainment, 1984
THE COWBOY AND THE BALLERINA (TF)   Cowboy
   Productions, 1984
STORMIN' HOME (TF)   CBS Entertainment, 1985
ONE POLICE PLAZA (TF)   CBS Entertainment, 1986
THE RED SPIDER (TF)   CBS Entertainment, 1988
TERROR ON HIGHWAY 91 (TF)   Katy Film Productions, 1989
FIRE AND RAIN (CTF)   Wilshire Court Productions, 1989
GUNSMOKE: TO THE LAST MAN (TF)   CBS Entertainment, 1992
GUNSMOKE: THE LONG RIDE (TF)   CBS Entertainment, 1993
BONANZA: THE RETURN (TF)   Legend Entertainment/NBC
   Productions, 1993
GUNSMOKE: ONE MAN'S JUSTICE (TF)   CBS Entertainment, 1994

MIKLOS JANCSO
b. September 27, 1921 - Vac, Hungary
Contact: Hungarian Film Institute, Budakeszi u 51 B, 1012 Budapest,
   Hungary, tel.: 176-1018 or 176-1322

THE BELLS HAVE GONE TO ROME   Mafilm, 1958, Hungarian
THREE STARS   co-director, Mafilm, 1960, Hungarian
CANTATA   Studio Budapest, 1963, Hungarian
MY WAY HOME   Mafilm, 1964, Hungarian
THE ROUND-UP   Altura, 1965, Hungarian
THE RED AND THE WHITE   Brandon, 1967, Hungarian-Soviet
SILENCE AND CRY   Mafilm, 1967, Hungarian
THE CONFRONTATION   Mafilm, 1967, Hungarian
WINTER WIND   SIROKKO   Marquise Film/Mafilm,
   1969, French-Hungarian
LA PACIFISTA   Cinematografia Lombarda, 1970,
   Italian-French-West German
AGNUS DEI   Mafilm, 1971, Hungarian
LA TECNICA E IL RITO   RAI, 1971, Italian
RED PSALM   Mafilm, 1972, Hungarian
ROMA RIVUOLE CESARE   RAI, 1973, Italian
SZERELEM, ELEKTRA   Studio Hunnia, 1974, Hungarian
PRIVATE VICES - PUBLIC VIRTUE   1976, Italian-Yugoslavian
MASTERWORK   1977, Hungarian
HUNGARIAN RHAPSODY   Studio Dialog/Hungarofilm,
   1978, Hungarian
ALLEGRO BARBARO   Mafilm, 1979, Hungarian
HEART OF A TYRANT   Sacis, 1981, Italian-Hungarian
HUZSIKA (TD)   Magyar TV, 1984, Hungarian

OMEGA, OMEGA... (TD)   Dialog Studios/Mafilm/Magyar TV,
   1985, Hungarian
BUDAPEST (FD)   1985, Italian
DAWN   Odessa Films, 1986, French
SEASON OF MONSTERS   Dialog Studio/Mafilm,
   1987, Hungarian
JESUS CHRIST'S HOROSCOPE   Mafilm, 1989, Hungarian
GOD WALKS BACKWARDS   TPA/Filmex, 1991, Hungarian
BLUE DANUBE WALTZ   HR Productions/NEF/Filmex, 1992,
   Hungarian-French-U.S.

LEE JANG-HO
b. January 16, 1945 - Seoul, Korea
Contact: Korean Motion Pictures Promotion Corporation, 34-5,
   3KA Namsan-Dong, Chung-Ku, Seoul, South Korea,
   tel.: 755-9291

STARS' HOME   1974, South Korean
THE RAIN YESTERDAY   1974, South Korean
DEEP LOVE   1975, South Korean
FINE WINDY DAYS   1980, South Korean
THE SONS OF DARKNESS   1981, South Korean
COME UNTO DAWN   1981, South Korean
DANCE OF THE WIDOW   1983, South Korean
DECLARATION OF FOOLS   1983, South Korean
BETWEEN KNEE AND KNEE   1984, South Korean
THE ENTERTAINER ER WOO-DONG   1985, South Korean
ALIEN BASEBALL TEAM   1986, South Korean
A MAN WITH THREE COFFINS   1988, South Korean
MISS RHINOCEROS AND MR. KORANDO   Pan Film Company,
   1989, South Korean

CONRAD JANIS
b. February 11, 1928 - New York, New York
Contact: Screen Actors Guild - Los Angeles, 213/954-1600

THE FEMININE TOUCH   Marius Productions, 1994

ANNABEL JANKEL*
Address: c/o Hill Wooldridge, 107 Hindes Road, Harrow,
   Middlesex HA1 1RU, England, tel.: 181/427-1944
Agent: UTA - Beverly Hills, 310/273-6700

THE MAX HEADROOM STORY (TF)   co-director with
   Rocky Morton, 1985, British
D.O.A.   co-director with Rocky Morton, Buena Vista, 1988
SUPER MARIO BROS.   co-director with Rocky Morton,
   Buena Vista, 1993, U.S.-British

FREDERIC JARDIN
Contact: French Film Office, 745 Fifth Avenue, New York,
   NY 10151, 212/832-8860

LA FOLIE DOUCE   Sara Films/Investimage 4/Cofimage 5/Canal
   Plus/Procirep, 1994, French

JIM JARMUSCH
b. 1953 - Akron, Ohio
Business: Black Snake Productions, Inc., 24 Prince Street - Suite 7,
   New York, NY 10012, 212/226-1341

PERMANENT VACATION   Gray City, 1982
STRANGER THAN PARADISE   The Samuel Goldwyn
   Company, 1984
DOWN BY LAW   Island Pictures, 1986
MYSTERY TRAIN   Orion Classics, 1989, U.S.-Japanese
NIGHT ON EARTH   FineLine Features/New Line Cinema,
   1991, U.S.-Japanese-French-German-British
DEAD MAN   Twelve Gauge Productions, 1995

CHARLES JARROTT*
b. June 6, 1927 - London, England
Agent: The Chasin Agency - Los Angeles, 310/278-7505
Business Manager: Jess Morgan & Company, 5750 Wilshire Blvd. -
   Suite 590, Los Angeles, CA 90036, 213/937-1552

ANNE OF THE THOUSAND DAYS   Universal, 1969, British
MARY, QUEEN OF SCOTS   Universal, 1971, British
LOST HORIZON   Columbia, 1972
THE DOVE   Paramount, 1974
THE LITTLEST HORSE THIEVES   *ESCAPE FROM THE DARK*
   Buena Vista, 1977, U.S.-British
THE OTHER SIDE OF MIDNIGHT   20th Century-Fox, 1977
THE LAST FLIGHT OF NOAH'S ARK   Buena Vista, 1980
CONDORMAN   Buena Vista, 1981
THE AMATEUR   20th Century-Fox, 1981, Canadian
A MARRIED MAN (TF)   London Weekend TV Productions/Lionhead
   Productions, 1984, British
THE BOY IN BLUE   20th Century Fox, 1985, Canadian
POOR LITTLE RICH GIRL: THE BARBARA HUTTON STORY (MS)
   Lester Persky Productions/ITC Productions, 1987
THE WOMAN HE LOVED (TF)   The Larry Thompson Organization/
   HTV/New World TV, 1988, U.S.-British
JUDITH KRANTZ'S TILL WE MEET AGAIN   *TILL WE MEET
   AGAIN* (MS)   Steve Krantz Productions/Yorkshire TV,
   1989, U.S.-British
NIGHT OF THE FOX (MS)   ITC Entertainment/Tribune
   Entertainment/Dove Inc./TF1/Canal Plus/Societe
   Francaise de Production/Channel 60/Group Media TV,
   1990, U.S.-British-French-West German
LUCY & DESI: BEFORE THE LAUGHTER (TF)
   Larry Thompson Entertainment, 1991
DANIELLE STEEL'S 'CHANGES'   *CHANGES* (TF)
   The Cramer Company/NBC Productions, 1991
YES, VIRGINIA, THERE IS A SANTA CLAUS (TF)
   Andrew J. Fenady Productions/Paradigm Entertainment/
   Quinta Communications, 1991
JACKIE COLLINS' 'LADY BOSS'   *LADY BOSS* (TF)
   Puma Productions/ABC Video Productions/von
   Zerneck-Sertner Films, 1992
TRADEWINDS (TF)   The Cramer Company/NBC Productions, 1993
A STRANGER IN THE MIRROR (TF)   Sidney Sheldon
   Productions/Paragon Entertainment Corporation/Spelling TV,
   1993, U.S.-Canadian
TREACHEROUS BEAUTIES (TF)   Alliance Communications
   Corporation/CBS/CTV/UFA, 1994, Canadian-U.S.

LAURENCE JARVIK
b. October 30, 1956 - New York, New York
Business: The Jarvik-Strickland Company, 944 Berkeley Street,
   Santa Monica, CA 90403, 310/828-7794

WHO SHALL LIVE AND WHO SHALL DIE? (FD)
   Kino International, 1981

VADIM JEAN
Agent: Peters Fraser & Dunlop - London, tel.: 171/344-1000
Contact: British Film Commission, 70 Baker Street, London
   W1M 1DJ, England, tel.: 171/224-5000

LEON THE PIG FARMER   co-director with Gary Sinyor,
   Leon the Pig Farmer Productions, 1992, British
BEYOND BEDLAM   Metrodome Films, 1994, British

ROLAND JEFFERSON
PERFUME   NTN Productions/FEC Entertainment Group, 1989

LIONEL JEFFRIES
b. 1926 - London, England
Contact: British Film Commission, 70 Baker Street, London
   W1M 1DJ, England, tel.: 171/224-5000

THE RAILWAY CHILDREN   Universal, 1971, British
THE AMAZING MR. BLUNDEN   Goldstone, 1972, British
BAXTER!   National General, 1973, British

THE WATER BABIES   Pethurst International/Film Polski,
   1978, British-Polish
WOMBLING FREE   Satori, 1979, British

MICHAEL JENKINS
Agent: The Artists Agency - Los Angeles, 310/277-7779

RUSH (MS)   co-director with Frank Arnold & Rob Stewart,
   Australian Broadcasting Corporation/Scottish & Global/
   Antenne-2, 1976, Australian-French
FIVE MILE CREEK (MS)   co-director with Frank Arnold,
   George Miller & Di Drew, Valstar/The Disney Channel,
   1983, Australian-U.S.
REBEL   Vestron, 1985, Australian
SHARK'S PARADISE (TF)   McElroy & McElroy, 1986, Australian
THE DIRTWATER DYNASTY (MS)   co-director with John Power,
   Kennedy Miller Productions, 1988, Australian
EMERALD CITY   Limelight Productions, 1989, Australian
SWEET TALKER   Seven Arts/New Line Cinema, 1991, Australian
THE LEAVING OF LIVERPOOL (MS)   Australian Broadcasting
   Corporation, 1992, Australian
THE HEARTBREAK KID   Roadshow, 1993, Australian

ALAIN JESSUA
b. January 16, 1932 - Paris, France
Address: 70, avenue d'Iena, 75016 Paris, France, tel.: 1/47-23-02-48
Contact: French Film Office, 745 Fifth Avenue, New York,
   NY 10151, 212/832-8860

LA VIE A L'ENVERS   1964, French
JEU DE MASSACRE   1967, French
TRAITEMENT DE CHOC   1972, French
ARMAGUEDON   1977, French
LES CHIENS   1978, French
PARADIS POUR TOUS   1982, French
FRANKENSTEIN 90   1984, French
EN TOUTE INNOCENCE   Morris Projects Inc., 1988, French

JEAN-PIERRE JEUNET
Agent: ICM - Beverly Hills, 310/550-4000

DELICATESSEN   co-director with Marc Caro, Miramax Films,
   1991, French
THE CITY OF LOST CHILDREN   co-director with Marc Caro,
   Sony Pictures Classics, 1995, French

NORMAN JEWISON*
b. July 21, 1926 - Toronto, Canada
Business: Yorktown Productions Ltd., Lantana Center,
   3000 W. Olympic Blvd. - Suite 1314, Los Angeles, CA 90404,
   310/264-4155 or: Yorktown Productions Ltd., 18 Gloucester
   Street, Toronto, Ontario M4Y 1L5, Canada, 416/923-2787
Agent: ICM - Beverly Hills, 310/550-4000

40 POUNDS OF TROUBLE   Universal, 1962
THE THRILL OF IT ALL   Universal, 1963
SEND ME NO FLOWERS   Universal, 1964
THE ART OF LOVE   Universal, 1965
THE CINCINNATI KID   MGM, 1965
THE RUSSIANS ARE COMING THE RUSSIANS ARE COMING
   United Artists, 1966
IN THE HEAT OF THE NIGHT ★   United Artists, 1967
THE THOMAS CROWN AFFAIR   United Artists, 1968
GAILY, GAILY   United Artists, 1969
FIDDLER ON THE ROOF ★   United Artists, 1971
JESUS CHRIST SUPERSTAR   Universal, 1973
ROLLERBALL   United Artists, 1975
F.I.S.T.   United Artists, 1978
...AND JUSTICE FOR ALL   Columbia, 1979
BEST FRIENDS   Warner Bros., 1982
A SOLDIER'S STORY   Columbia, 1984
AGNES OF GOD   Columbia, 1985
MOONSTRUCK ★   MGM/UA, 1987
IN COUNTRY   Warner Bros., 1989
OTHER PEOPLE'S MONEY   Warner Bros., 1991
ONLY YOU   TriStar, 1994
WHOOPI GOLDBERG UNTITLED   Warner Bros., 1995

CHUNG JI-YOUNG
(See Ji-Young CHUNG)

WEN JIANG
(See Jiang WEN)

HE JIANJUN
Contact: China Film Import & Export Office, 2500 Wilshire Blvd. -
   Suite 1028, Los Angeles, CA 90057, 213/380-7520

RED BEADS   released under pseudonym of He Yi, 1993, Chinese
POSTMAN   Shu Kei Creative Workshop/Hubert Bals Fund/United
   Color of Benetton, 1995, Chinese

HUANG JIANXIN
b. 1952 - China
Contact: China Film Import & Export Office, 2500 Wilshire Blvd. -
   Suite 1028, Los Angeles, CA 90057, 213/380-7520

THE BLACK CANNON INCIDENT   China Film Import & Export,
   1985, Chinese
THE STAND-IN   China Film Import & Export, 1987, Chinese
SAMSARA   China Film Import & Export, 1989, Chinese
STAND UP, DON'T BEND OVER   Xi'an Film Studio, 1993, Chinese
THE WOODEN MAN'S BRIDE   Arrow Releasing, 1994, Taiwanese
BACK TO BACK, FACE TO FACE   Simpson Communication/China
   Film Coproduction Corporation/Xi'an Film Studio, 1994,
   Hong Kong-Chinese

NEAL JIMENEZ
Agent: Richland/Wunsch/Hohman Agency - Los Angeles,
   310/278-1955

THE WATERDANCE   co-director with Michael Steinberg,
   The Samuel Goldwyn Company, 1992

ORLANDO JIMENEZ-LEAL
b. Cuba
Contact: Sally Marr, Gueda Films, Inc., 155 Avenue of the Americas -
   Suite 1101, New York, NY 10013, 212/206-6312 or 310/659-8022

EL SUPER   co-director with Leon Ichaso, Columbia, 1979
EVERYDAY ONE DAY   TODOS LOS DIAS UN DIA
   Columbia, 1982
IMPROPER CONDUCT (FD)   co-director with Nestor Almendros,
   Cinevista/Promovision International, 1984, French
THE OTHER CUBA (FD)   Cinevista/Promovision International,
   1985, French
OCHO-A (FD)   P.M. Films/RAI, 1993, U.S.-Italian

XIE JIN
b. 1923 - Shaoxin, China
Contact: China Film Import & Export Office, 2500 Wilshire Blvd. -
   Suite 1028, Los Angeles, CA 90057, 213/380-7520

A CRISIS   China Film Import & Export, 1954, Chinese
A WAVE OF UNREST   China Film Import & Export, 1954, Chinese
RENDEZVOUS AT ORCHARD BRIDGE   China Film Import &
   Export, 1954, Chinese
WOMAN BASKETBALL PLAYER NUMBER 5   China Film Import &
   Export, 1957, Chinese
THE RED DETACHMENT OF WOMEN   China Film Import &
   Export, 1960, Chinese
BIG LI, YOUNG LI, AND OLD LI   China Film Import & Export,
   1962, Chinese
TWO STAGE SISTERS   China Film Import & Export,
   1964, Chinese
YOUTH   China Film Import & Export, 1977, Chinese
AH, CRADLE   China Film Import & Export, 1980, Chinese
THE LEGEND OF TIANYUAN MOUNTAIN   China Film Import &
   Export, 1981, Chinese
THE HERDSMAN   China Film Import & Export, 1982, Chinese
QIU JIN   China Film Import & Export, 1983, Chinese
REEDS AT THE FOOT OF THE MOUNTAIN   China Film Import &
   Export, 1984, Chinese

F
I
L
M

D
I
R
E
C
T
O
R
S

**F
I
L
M

D
I
R
E
C
T
O
R
S**

HIBISCUS TOWN   China Film Import & Export, 1986, Chinese
THE LAST ARISTOCRATS   China Film Import & Export,
    1989, Chinese
AN OLD MAN AND HIS DOG   China Film Import & Export,
    1994, Chinese

ROBERT JIRAS
Contact: Writers Guild of America, East - New York City,
    212/767-7800

I AM THE CHEESE   Libra Cinema 5, 1983

JAROMIL JIRES
b. December 10, 1935 - Bratislava, Czechoslovakia
Contact: Czech Film Institute, Narodni tr. 40, 110 00 Prague 1,
    Czech Republic, tel.: 02/26-00-87

THE FIRST CRY   1963, Czechoslovakian
PEARLS IN THE DEEP   co-director, 1965, Czechoslovakian
BITTER ALMONDS   1966, Czechoslovakian, unfinished
THE JOKE   1969, Czechoslovakian
VALERIE AND THE WEEK OF WONDERS   1970, Czechoslovakian
AND GIVE MY LOVE TO THE SWALLOWS
    1971, Czechoslovakian
THE SAFECRACKER   1973, Czechoslovakian
PEOPLE FROM THE METRO   1974, Czechoslovakian
THE ISLAND OF SILVER HERONS   1976, Czechoslovakian
FLYING SAUCERS OVER OUR TOWN   1977, Czechoslovakian
THE YOUNG MAN AND THE WHITE WHALE
    1978, Czechoslovakian
THE RABBIT CASE   1979, Czechoslovakian
ESCAPES HOME   1980, Czechoslovakian
PARTIAL ECLIPSE   1982, Czechoslovakian
LEV S. BILOU HRIVOU   1986, Czechoslovakian
HELIMADOE (TF)   Czech Television/KF a.s./Studio 1, 1994, Czech
TEACHER OF THE DANCE (TF)   Czech Television, 1994, Czech

MIKE JITTLOV
THE WIZARD OF SPEED AND TIME   Shapiro Glickenhaus
    Entertainment, 1988

PHIL JOANOU*
b. November 20, 1961
Agent: CAA - Beverly Hills, 310/288-4545

THREE O'CLOCK HIGH   Universal, 1987
U2 RATTLE AND HUM (FCD)   Paramount, 1988
STATE OF GRACE   Orion, 1990
FINAL ANALYSIS   Warner Bros., 1992
WILD PALMS (MS)   co-director with Peter Hewitt, Kathryn Bigelow &
    Keith Gordon, Ixtlan Corporation/Greengrass Productions, 1993
HEAVEN'S PRISONERS   Savoy Pictures, 1995

ALEJANDRO JODOROWSKY
(Alexandro Jodorowsky)
b. Bolivia

FANDO AND LIS   Cannon, 1970, Mexican
EL TOPO   ABKCO, 1971, Mexican
THE HOLY MOUNTAIN   ABKCO, 1974, Mexican
TUSK   Yank Films-Films 21, 1980, French
SANTA SANGRE   Expanded Entertainment, 1989, Italian
THE RAINBOW THIEF   Timothy Burrill Productions, 1990, British

STEVE JODRELL
Contact: Australian Film Commission, 8 West Street, North Sydney,
    NSW 2026, Australia, tel.: 2/925-7333

SHAME   Skouras Pictures, 1988, Australian

MICHAEL JOENS
MY LITTLE PONY - THE MOVIE (AF)   DEG, 1986

ARTHUR JOFFE
Agent: N. Cann, 4, rue du Gal de Castelnau, 75015 Paris, France,
    tel.: 1/45-67-33-03
Contact: French Film Office, 745 Fifth Avenue, New York,
    NY 10151, 212/832-8860

HAREM   Sara Films, 1985, French
LA COMEDIE D'UN JOUR   UGC, 1990, French
ALBERTO EXPRESS   MK2 Productions USA, 1990,
    Canadian-French

MARK JOFFE
Agent: UTA - Beverly Hills, 310/273-6700

THE GREAT BOOKIE ROBBERY (MS)   1985, Australian
THE LIFE IN A DAY OF BARRY HUMPHRIES (TD)
    1986, Australian
WATCH THE SHADOWS DANCE (TF)   1986, Australian
GRIEVOUS BODILY HARM   Fries Entertainment, 1987, Australian
SHADOW OF THE COBRA (MS)   1989, Australian
TOY SOLDIERS (TF)   Lea Films/Australian Children's Television
    Foundation, 1989, Australian
THE EFFICIENCY EXPERT   *SPOTSWOOD*   Miramax Films,
    1991, Australian
COSI   Miramax Films, 1995, Australian

ROLAND JOFFE*
b. November 17, 1945 - London, England
Business: Lightmotive, 662 N. Robertson Blvd., Los Angeles,
    CA 90069, 310/659-6200
Agent: ICM - Beverly Hills, 310/550-4000 or:
    Judy Daish Associates - London, tel.: 171/262-1101

THE LEGION HALL BOMBING (TF)   BBC, 1978, British
THE SPONGERS (TF)   BBC, 1978, British
NO, MAMA, NO (TF)   Thames TV, 1979, British
UNITED KINGDOM (TF)   BBC, 1981, British
THE KILLING FIELDS ★   Warner Bros., 1984, British
THE MISSION ★   Warner Bros., 1986, British
FAT MAN AND LITTLE BOY   Paramount, 1989
CITY OF JOY   TriStar, 1992, British-French
THE SCARLET LETTER   Buena Vista, 1995

KRISTIN JOHANNESDOTTIR
b. Iceland
Contact: Icelandic Film Fund, Laugavegur 24, 121 Reykjavik, Iceland,
    tel.: 1/623580

RAINBOW'S END   1983, Icelandic
AS IN HEAVEN   Tiu-Tiu Film Productions/Metronome/
    Norsk Film/Suomen Elokuvasaatio/Svenska Filminstitutet/
    Nordic Film & TV Fund/Icelandic Film Fund, 1992,
    Icelandic-Danish-Norwegian-Finnish-Swedish

ALAN JOHNSON*
Agent: Jim Lenny, 9454 Wilshire Blvd., Beverly Hills, CA 90212,
    310/271-2174

TO BE OR NOT TO BE   20th Century-Fox, 1983
SOLARBABIES   MGM/UA, 1986

CINDY LOU JOHNSON
Agent: William Morris Agency - Beverly Hills, 310/859-4000

TRUSTING BEATRICE   *CLAUDE*   Castle Hill Productions, 1991

DAVID JOHNSON
(David Clark Johnson)
Agent: Scott Yoselow, The Gersh Agency - New York City,
    212/997-1818

DROP SQUAD   Gramercy Pictures, 1994

JED JOHNSON
ANDY WARHOL'S BAD   New World, 1977

KENNETH JOHNSON*
b. October 26, 1942 - Pine Bluff, Arkansas
Business: Kenneth Johnson Productions, 4528 Colbath Avenue - Suite 8, Sherman Oaks, CA 91423, 818/905-5255
Agent: William Morris Agency - Beverly Hills, 310/859-4000

THE INCREDIBLE HULK (TF)   Universal TV, 1977
SENIOR TRIP (TF)   Kenneth Johnson Productions, 1981
V (TF)   Kenneth Johnson Productions/Warner Bros. TV, 1984
HOT PURSUIT (TF)   Kenneth Johnson Productions/NBC Productions, 1984
SHADOW CHASERS (TF)   Kenneth Johnson Productions/Brian Grazer Productions/Warner Bros. TV, 1985
THE LIBERATORS (TF)   Kenneth Johnson Productions/ Walt Disney TV, 1987
SHORT CIRCUIT 2   TriStar, 1988
ALIEN NATION (TF)   20th Television Corp., 1989
SHERLOCK HOLMES RETURNS (TF)   Paagon Entertainment Corporation/Kenneth Johnson Productions, 1993
ALIEN NATION: DARK HORIZON (TF)   Foxstar Productions/ Kenneth Johnson Productions, 1994

LAMONT JOHNSON*
b. September 20, 1922 - Stockton, California
Agent: Geoffrey Brandt, The Brandt Company - Sherman Oaks, 818/784-6012

THIN ICE   20th Century-Fox, 1961
A COVENANT WITH DEATH   Warner Bros., 1966
KONA COAST   Warner Bros., 1968
DEADLOCK (TF)   Universal TV, 1969
THE MACKENZIE BREAK   United Artists, 1970
MY SWEET CHARLIE (TF) ☆   Universal TV, 1970
A GUNFIGHT   Paramount, 1971
THE GROUNDSTAR CONSPIRACY   Universal, 1972, U.S.-Canadian
YOU'LL LIKE MY MOTHER   Universal, 1972
THAT CERTAIN SUMMER (TF) ☆   Universal TV, 1972
THE LAST AMERICAN HERO   20th Century-Fox, 1973
VISIT TO A CHIEF'S SON   United Artists, 1974
THE EXECUTION OF PRIVATE SLOVIK (TF) ☆   Universal TV, 1974
FEAR ON TRIAL (TF) ☆   Alan Landsburg Productions, 1975
LIPSTICK   Paramount, 1976
ONE ON ONE   Warner Bros., 1977
SOMEBODY KILLED HER HUSBAND   Columbia, 1978
PAUL'S CASE (TF)   Learning in Focus, 1979
OFF THE MINNESOTA STRIP (TF)   Cherokee Productions/ Universal TV, 1980
CATTLE ANNIE AND LITTLE BRITCHES   Universal, 1981
CRISIS AT CENTRAL HIGH (TF)   Time-Life Productions, 1981
ESCAPE FROM IRAN: THE CANADIAN CAPER (TF)   Canamedia Productions, 1981, Canadian
DANGEROUS COMPANY (TF)   The Dangerous Company/ Finnegan Associates, 1982
LIFE OF THE PARTY: THE STORY OF BEATRICE (TF)   Welch-Welch Productions/Columbia TV, 1982
SPACEHUNTER: ADVENTURES IN THE FORBIDDEN ZONE   Columbia, 1983, Canadian-U.S.
ERNIE KOVACS: BETWEEN THE LAUGHTER (TF) ☆   ABC Circle Films, 1984
WALLENBERG: A HERO'S STORY (TF) ☆☆   Dick Berg-Stonehenge Productions/Paramount TV, 1985
UNNATURAL CAUSES (TF) ☆   Blue Andre Productions/ITC Productions, 1986
GORE VIDAL'S LINCOLN (TF) ☆☆   Chris-Rose Productions/ Finnegan-Pinchuk Company, 1988
THE KENNEDYS OF MASSACHUSETTS (MS) ☆   Edgar J. Scherick Associates/Orion TV, 1990
VOICES WITHIN: THE LIVES OF TRUDDI CHASE (TF)   Itzbinzo Long Productions/P.A. Productions/New World TV, 1990
A THOUSAND HEROES (TF)   Dorothea G. Petrie Productions/ Helios Productions/Paradigm Entertainment/World International Network, 1991

CRASH LANDING: THE RESCUE OF FLIGHT 232 (TF) ☆   Dorothea G. Petrie Productions/Helios Productions/Bob Banner Associates/Gary L. Pudney Company/World International Network, 1992
THE BROKEN CHAIN (CTF)   von Zerneck-Sertner Films/ Turner Network TV, 1993

PATRICK READ JOHNSON*
Agent: William Morris Agency - Beverly Hills, 310/274-7451

SPACED INVADERS   Buena Vista, 1990
BABY'S DAY OUT   20th Century Fox, 1994
ANGUS   New Line Cinema, 1995

SANDY JOHNSON
b. November 13, 1953 - Glasgow, Scotland
Agent: Seifert Dench Associates - London, tel.: 171/437-4551

NEVER SAY DIE!   NFS, 1980, British
THE MAGNIFICENT ONE (TF)   C4, 1982, British
COAST TO COAST (TF)   BBC, 1986, British
LEAVING (TF)   BBC, 1987, British
DEFROSTING THE FRIDGE (TF)   BBC, 1988, British
THE GIFT (TF)   BBC, 1989, British
THE WRECK ON THE HIGHWAY (TF)   BBC, 1990, British

AARON KIM JOHNSTON
Contact: Directors Guild of Canada, 225 Richmond Street, Toronto, Ontario M5V 1W2, Canada, 416/351-8200

THE LAST WINTER   Brightstar, 1990, Canadian
FOR THE MOMENT   John Aaron Features II/Rogers Telefund/ Telefilm Canada/Manitoba Cultural Industries Development Office/ Canadian Broadcasting Corporation, 1993, Canadian

HEATHER JOHNSTON
SCENES FROM THE NEW WORLD   co-director with Gordon Eriksen, RKGM, 1994

JIM JOHNSTON*
Agent: Paul Kohner, Inc. - Los Angeles, 310/550-1060

BLUE DeVILLE (TF)   B & E Enterprises Ltd./NBC Productions, 1986

JOE JOHNSTON*
Home: 96 Hillside Avenue, San Anselmo, CA 94960, 415/258-9061
Agent: CAA - Beverly Hills, 310/288-4545

HONEY, I SHRUNK THE KIDS   Buena Vista, 1989
THE ROCKETEER   Buena Vista, 1991
THE PAGEMASTER   co-director with Maurice Hunt, 20th Century Fox, 1994
JUMANJI   TriStar, 1995

SCOTT JOHNSTON
Business: Walt Disney Animation, 500 S. Buena Vista Street, Burbank, CA 91521, 818/560-1000

FANTASIA CONTINUED (AF)   co-director with Hendel Butoy & George Scribner, Buena Vista, 1997

JYLL JOHNSTONE
MARTHA & ETHEL (FD)   Sony Pictures Classics, 1994

OSKAR JONASSON
Contact: The Icelandic Film Fund, Laugavegur 24, P.O. Box 320, 121 Reykjavik, Iceland, tel.: 1/623850

REMOTE CONTROL   Moli, 1993, Icelandic

AMY HOLDEN JONES
Agent: UTA - Beverly Hills, 310/273-6700

SLUMBER PARTY MASSACRE   Santa Fe, 1982
LOVE LETTERS   New World, 1983
MAID TO ORDER   New Century/Vista, 1987

CHARLES M. (CHUCK) JONES
b. September 1, 1912 - Spokane, Washington

THE PHANTOM TOLLBOOTH (AF)   MGM, 1970
GREAT AMERICAN BUGS BUNNY - ROAD RUNNER CHASE (AF)
   Warner Bros., 1979
DAFFY DUCK'S MOVIE: FANTASTIC ISLAND (AF)
   Warner Bros., 1983
PORKY PIG IN HOLLYWOOD (AF)   Warner Bros., 1986
DAFFY DUCK'S QUACKBUSTERS (AF)   co-director,
   Warner Bros., 1988
THE SHORT HAPPY LIVES OF BARNABY SCRATCH (AF)
   Impossible Productions/Industrial F/X Films, 1993

DAVID JONES*
b. February 19, 1934 - Poole, Dorset, England
Home: 227 Clinton Street, Brooklyn, NY 11201, 718/834-0810
Agent: William Morris Agency - Beverly Hills, 310/859-4000

BETRAYAL   20th Century-Fox International Classics, 1983, British
84 CHARING CROSS ROAD   Columbia, 1987, British
THE CHRISTMAS WIFE (CTF)   HBO Showcase, 1988
JACKNIFE   Cineplex Odeon, 1989
FIRE IN THE DARK (TF)   Kushner-Locke Company/Don
   Gregory-Bernie Kahn Productions, 1991
IN MY DEFENCE (TF)   Oyster Television Film Theatre/BBC,
   1992, British
THE TRIAL   Angelika Films, 1993, British
AND THEN THERE WAS ONE (TF)   Freyda Rothstein Productions/
   Hearst Entertainment, 1994
IS THERE LIFE OUT THERE? (TF)   Hallmark Entertainment, 1995

EUGENE S. JONES*
Home: 1963 Stradella Road, Los Angeles, CA 90077, 310/472-4314

A FACE OF WAR (FD)   Commonwealth, 1968
TWO MEN OF KARAMOJA   *THE WILD AND THE BRAVE* (FD)
   Tomorrow Entertainment, 1974
HIGH ICE (TF)   ESJ Productions, 1980

GARY JONES
MOSQUITO   Hemdale, 1994

JAMES CELLAN JONES
(See James CELLAN-JONES)

L.Q. JONES*
(Justice Ellis McQueen)
b. August 19, 1927 - Beaumont, Texas
Address: 2144 N. Cahuenga Blvd., Hollywood, CA 90068,
   213/463-4426

A BOY AND HIS DOG   Pacific Film Enterprises, 1975

MARK JONES
LEPRECHAUN   Trimark Pictures, 1993
RUMPELSTILTSKIN   Dino De Laurentiis Communications, 1994

ROBERT JONES
b. November 2, 1942 - Boston, Massachusetts
Business: Still River Films, 1834 Harvard Blvd., Hollywood, CA
   90027, 213/469-2846
Agent: Fred Amsel & Associates - Beverly Hills, 213/855-1200

CARRY IT ON (FD)   United Productions of America, 1970
MISSION HILL   Atlantic Releasing Corporation, 1983

TERRY JONES
b. February 1, 1942 - Colwyn Bay, Wales
Business: Prominent Features Ltd., 68A Delancey Street, London
   NW1 7RY, England, tel.: 171/284-0242
Agent: CAA - Beverly Hills, 310/288-4545 or:
   The Casarotto Company - London, tel.: 171/287-4450

MONTY PYTHON AND THE HOLY GRAIL   co-director with
   Terry Gilliam, Cinema 5, 1974, British
MONTY PYTHON'S LIFE OF BRIAN   Orion/Warner Bros.,
   1979, British
MONTY PYTHON'S THE MEANING OF LIFE   Universal,
   1983, British
PERSONAL SERVICES   Vestron, 1987, British
ERIK THE VIKING   Orion, 1989, British

TOMMY LEE JONES
b. September 15, 1946 - San Saba, Texas
Agent: ICM - Beverly Hills, 310/550-4000

THE GOOD OLD BOYS (CTF)   Turner Pictures/Edgar J. Scherick
   Associates/Firebrand Productions/The Javelina Film
   Company, 1995

GLENN JORDAN*
April 5, 1936 - San Antonio, Texas
Agent: CAA - Beverly Hills, 310/288-4545

FRANKENSTEIN (TF)   Dan Curtis Productions, 1973
THE PICTURE OF DORIAN GRAY (TF)   Dan Curtis
   Productions, 1973
SHELL GAME (TF)   Thoroughbred Productions, 1975
ONE OF MY WIVES IS MISSING (TF)   Spelling-Goldberg
   Productions, 1975
DELTA COUNTY, U.S.A. (TF)   Leonard Goldberg Productions/
   Paramount TV, 1977
SUNSHINE CHRISTMAS (TF)   Universal TV, 1977
IN THE MATTER OF KAREN ANN QUINLAN (TF)   Warren V. Bush
   Productions, 1977
THE DISPLACED PERSON (TF)   Learning in Focus, 1977
LES MISERABLES (TF) ☆   Norman Rosemont Productions/ITV
   Entertainment, 1978
SON RISE: A MIRACLE OF LOVE (TF)   Rothman-Wohl
   Productions/Filmways, 1979
THE FAMILY MAN (TF)   Time-Life Productions, 1979
THE WOMEN'S ROOM (TF)   Philip Mandelker Productions/Warner
   Bros. TV, 1980
NEIL SIMON'S ONLY WHEN I LAUGH   Columbia, 1981
THE PRINCESS AND THE CABBIE (TF)   Freyda Rothstein
   Productions/Time-Life Productions, 1981
LOIS GIBBS AND THE LOVE CANAL (TF)   Moonlight Productions/
   Filmways, 1982
THE BUDDY SYSTEM   20th Century Fox, 1984
HEARTSOUNDS (TF)   Embassy TV, 1984
MASS APPEAL   Universal, 1984
TOUGHLOVE (TF)   Fries Entertainment, 1985
DRESS GRAY (TF)   Frank von Zerneck Productions/Warner
   Bros. TV, 1986
PROMISE (TF) ☆☆   Garner-Duchow Productions/Warner
   Bros. TV, 1986
SOMETHING IN COMMON (TF)   New World TV/Freyda Rothstein
   Productions/Littke-Grossbart Productions, 1986
JOSEPH WAMBAUGH'S ECHOES IN THE DARKNESS
   ECHOES IN THE DARKNESS (MS) ☆   Litke-Grossbart
   Productions/New World TV, 1987
JESSE (TF)   Turman-Foster Company/Jordan Productions/
   Republic Pictures, 1988
HOME FIRES BURNING (TF)   Marian Rees Associates, 1989
CHALLENGER (TF)   The IndieProd Company/King Phoenix
   Entertainment/George Englund, Jr. Productions, 1990
SARAH, PLAIN AND TALL (TF) ☆   Self Help Productions/Trillium
   Productions, 1991
AFTERMATH: A TEST OF LOVE (TF)   Clandon Productions/
   Interscope Communications, 1991
THE BOYS (TF)   Willian Link Productions/Papazian-Hirsch
   Productions, 1991
O PIONEERS! (TF)   Craig Anderson Productions/Lorimar TV/Prairie
   Films, 1992

BARBARIANS AT THE GATE (CTF) ☆ Columbia TV/HBO, 1993
TO DANCE WITH THE WHITE DOG (TF) ☆ Patricia Clifford
 Productions/Signboard Hill Productions, 1993
JANE'S HOUSE (TF) Michael Phillips Productions/
 Spelling TV, 1994
MY BROTHER'S KEEPER (TF) Holiday Productions/RHI
 Entertainment, 1995

NEIL JORDAN*
(Neil Patrick Jordan)
b. February 25, 1950 - County Sligo, Ireland
Address: 6 Sorrento Terrace, Dalkey, County Dublin, Ireland,
 tel.: 353-1/285-7949
Agent: ICM - Beverly Hills, 310/550-4000 or:
 The Casarotto Company - London, tel.: 171/287-4450

DANNY BOY *ANGEL* Triumph/Columbia, 1983, Irish
THE COMPANY OF WOLVES Cannon, 1984, British
MONA LISA Island Pictures, 1986, British
HIGH SPIRITS TriStar, 1988, British
WE'RE NO ANGELS Paramount, 1989
THE MIRACLE Miramax Films, 1991, British-Irish
THE CRYING GAME ★ Miramax Films, 1992, British
INTERVIEW WITH THE VAMPIRE Geffen Pictures/Warner
 Bros., 1994

JON JOST
b. 1943 - Chicago, Illinois
Business: Complex Corp., 535 Stevenson Street, San Francisco,
 CA 94103, 415/864-8123

SPEAKING DIRECTLY: SOME AMERICAN NOTES
 Jon Jost Films, 1974
ANGEL CITY Jon Jost Films, 1977
LAST CHANTS FOR A SLOW DANCE Jon Jost Films, 1977
CHAMELEON Jon Jost Films, 1978
STAGE FRIGHT Jon Jost Films, 1981
SLOW MOVES Jon Jost Films, 1983
BELL DIAMOND Jon Jost Films, 1986
PLAIN TALK AND COMMON SENSE (uncommon senses) (FD)
 Jon Jost Films, 1987
LAUGHING REMBRANDT Jon Jost Films, 1988
ALL THE VERMEERS IN NEW YORK Strand Releasing, 1991
SURE FIRE Complex Corp. 1992
THE BED YOU SLEEP IN Complex Corp., 1993
FRAMEUP Complex Corp., 1993
UNO A TE, UNO A ME E UNO A RAFFAELE Alia Film/RAI-3,
 1994, Italian
ENGLISH LESSONS Independent Film Workshop, 1995, British

PAUL JOYCE
Business: Lucida Productions Ltd., 53 Greek Street, London
 W1V 3TA, England, tel.: 171/437-1140
Agent: Elizabeth Dench, Seifert Dench Associates - London,
 tel.: 171/437-4551

NOTHING AS IT SEEMS (TD) Channel 4, 1982, British
SUMMER LIGHTNING (TF) Channel 4, 1984, British
OUT OF THE BLUE & IN TO THE BLACK (TF) Channel 4,
 1985, British
EVERYONE A WINNER (TF) Channel 4, 1988, British
MOTION AND EMOTION: THE FILMS OF WIM WENDERS (TD)
 Channel 4, 1989, British
PICTURES OF EUROPE (TD) Channel 4, 1990, British
SAM PECKINPAH: MAN OF IRON (TD) BBC, 1991, British
MARLON BRANDO, WILD ONE (TD) Lucida Productions/
 Channel 4, 1994, British

C. COURTNEY JOYNER
TRANCERS III Full Moon Entertainment, 1992
LURKING FEAR Full Moon Entertainment, 1994

GERARD JUGNOT
Contact: French Film Office, 745 Fifth Avenue, New York,
 NY 10151, 212/832-8860

UNE EPOQUE FORMIDABLE CIBY 2000, 1991, French
CASQUE BLEU AMLF, 1994, French

ISAAC JULIEN
b. London, England
Agent: The Casarotto Company - London, tel.: 171/287-4450

YOUNG SOUL REBELS Prestige, 1991,
 British-French-German-Spanish
THE ATTENDANT (TF) BBC, 1992, British
DARKER SIDE OF BLACK (TD) Black Audio Film Collective/Normal
 Films/BBC-TV/Arts Council of Great Britain, 1994, British
TESTING THE LIMITS (TF) BBC, 1994, British

JAN JUNG
b. Denmark
Contact: Danish Film Institute, Store Sondervoldstraede 4, DK-1419
 Copenhagen K, Denmark, tel.: 31-57-65-00

THREE DAYS IN AUGUST Panorama Film International/Socrat
 Film/Scancar, 1992, U.S.-Soviet-Danish

NATHAN JURAN*
b. September 1, 1907 - Austria
Home: 623 Via Horquilla, Palos Verdes Estates, CA 90274

THE BLACK CASTLE Universal, 1952
GUNSMOKE Universal, 1953
LAW AND ORDER Universal, 1953
THE GOLDEN BLADE Universal, 1953
TUMBLEWEED Universal, 1953
HIGHWAY DRAGNET Allied Artists, 1954
DRUMS ACROSS THE RIVER Universal, 1954
THE CROOKED WEB Columbia, 1955
THE DEADLY MANTIS Universal, 1957
HELLCATS OF THE NAVY Columbia, 1957
TWENTY MILLION MILES TO EARTH Columbia, 1957
ATTACK OF THE 50 FOOT WOMAN Allied Artists, 1958
BRAIN FROM PLANET AROUS Howco International, 1958
THE 7TH VOYAGE OF SINBAD Columbia, 1958
GOOD DAY FOR A HANGING Columbia, 1959
FLIGHT OF THE LOST BALLOON Woolner Brothers, 1961
JACK THE GIANT KILLER United Artists, 1962
SIEGE OF THE SAXONS Columbia, 1963, British
FIRST MEN IN THE MOON Columbia, 1964, British
EAST OF SUDAN Columbia, 1964, British
LAND RAIDERS Columbia, 1970
THE BOY WHO CRIED WEREWOLF Universal, 1973

PAUL JUSTMAN
Contact: Writers Guild of America, East - New York City,
 212/767-7800

GIMME AN F 20th Century Fox, 1984

K

GASTON KABORÉ

b. 1951 - Bobo Dioulasso, Upper Volta (Burkina Faso)
Business: FEPACI (Pan-African Federation of Film-Makers), 01 B.P.
2524, Ouagadougou 01, Burkina Faso, tel.: 226/31-02-58

WEND KUUNI   National Cinema Centre, 1982, Burkina Faso
ZAN BOKO   1988, Burkina Faso
RABI   BBC/TVE/One World Group of Broadcasters/French Ministry
of Cooperation, 1993, Burkina Faso-British-Spanish-French
MADAME HADO (FD)   1993, Burkina Faso

KAREL KACHYNA

b. May 1, 1924 - Vyskov, Czechoslovakia
Contact: Czech Film Institute, Narodni tr. 40, 110 00 Prague 1,
Czech Republic, tel.: 02/260087

EVERYTHING ENDS TONIGHT   co-director with Vojtech Jasny,
1954, Czechoslovakian
THE LOST TRAIL   1956, Czechoslovakian
THAT CHRISTMAS   1958, Caechoslovakian
SMUGGLERS OF DEATH   1959, Czechoslovakian
THE SLINGER   1960, Czechoslovakian
FETTERS   1961, Caechoslovakian
TRIALS OF YOUTH   1961, Czechoslovakian
VERTIGO   1962, Czechoslovakian
HOPE   1963, Czechoslovakian
THE HIGH WALL   1964, Czechoslovakian
LONG LIVE THE REPUBLIC!   1965, Czechoslovakian
COACH TO VIENNA   1966, Czechoslovakian
THE NIGHT OF THE BRIDE   1967, Czechoslovakian
CHRISTMAS WITH ELIZABETH   1968, Czechoslovakian
OUR FOOLISH FAMILY   1969, Czechoslovakian
JUMPING OVER PUDDLES AGAIN   1971, Czechoslovakian
LOVE   1972, Czechoslovakian
THE LITTLE MERMAID   1977, Czechoslovakian
MEETING IN JULY   1978, Czechoslovakian
WAITING FOR THE RAIN   1978, Czechoslovakian
CARRIAGE TO VIENNA   1979, Czechoslovakian, unreleased
LOVE BETWEEN THE RAINDROPS   1979, Czechoslovakian
SUGAR HUT   1980, Czechoslovakian
VISIT   1981, Czechoslovakian
FANDY & FANDY   1982, Czechoslovakian
NURSING SISTERS   1983, Czechoslovakian
FORBIDDEN DREAMS   1987, Czechoslovakian
THE EAR   1990, Czechoslovakian, filmed in 1979
THE LAST BUTTERFLY   New Line Cinema,
1991, Czechoslovakian-French
THE COW (TF)   Czech Television, 1993, Czech
ST. NICHOLAS IS IN TOWN (TF)   Czech Television/Mirage,
1994, Czech
THE SWELL SEASON (MS)   Czech Television, 1995, Czech

GEORGE KACZENDER*

b. April 19, 1933 - Budapest, Hungary
Agent: Tom Chasin, The Chasin Agency - Los Angeles,
310/278-7505

DON'T LET THE ANGELS FALL   National Film Board of Canada,
1968, Canadian
THE GIRL IN BLUE   U-TURN   Cinerama Releasing Corporation,
1973, Canadian
IN PRAISE OF OLDER WOMEN   Avco Embassy, 1978, Canadian
AGENCY   Taft International, 1980, Canadian
YOUR TICKET IS NO LONGER VALID   RSL Productions/
Ambassador, 1981, Canadian
CHANEL SOLITAIRE   United Film Distribution,
1981, French-British

PRETTYKILL   Spectrafilm, 1987, Canadian
A SEDUCTION IN TRAVIS COUNTY (TF)   David Braun Productions/
Co-Star Entertainment/Zev Braun Pictures/New World TV, 1991
CHRISTMAS ON DIVISION STREET (TF)   Guber-Peters
Entertainment Company Productions/Morrow-Heus
Productions/WIC/Columbia TV, 1991
JONATHAN: THE BOY NOBODY WANTED (TF)   Gross-Weston
Productions/Cannell Entertainment, 1992
BETRAYAL OF TRUST (TF)   Cosgrove-Meurer Productions,
1994, U.S.-Canadian
WHERE ARE MY CHILDREN? (TF)   MDT Productions/Andrea
Baynes Productions/Warner Bros. TV, 1994
DANIELLE STEEL'S VANISHED   VANISHED (TF)   The Cramer
Company/NBC Productions, 1995

HARUKI KADOKAWA

b. 1942 - Toyama Prefecture, Japan
Business: Haruki Kadokawa Films, Inc., 5-24-5, Bunkyo-ku, Tokyo,
Japan, tel.: 3/817-8552

THE LAST HERO   Haruki Kadokawa Productions/Toei,
1982, Japanese
THE CURTAIN CALL   Haruki Kadokawa Productions,
1984, Japanese
CABARET   Haruki Kadokawa Productions, 1986, Japanese
HEAVEN & EARTH   Triton Pictures, 1990, Japanese
REX   Rex Production Group, 1993, Japanese

JEREMY PAUL KAGAN*

b. December 14, 1945 - Mt. Vernon, New York
Address: 2024 N. Curson Avenue, Los Angeles, CA 90046,
Agent: Becsey/Wisdom/Kalajian - Los Angeles, 310/550-0535

UNWED FATHER (TF)   Wolper Productions, 1974
JUDGE DEE AND THE MONASTERY MURDERS (TF)
ABC Circle Films, 1974
KATHERINE (TF)   The Jozak Company, 1975
HEROES   Universal, 1977
SCOTT JOPLIN   Universal, 1977
THE BIG FIX   Universal, 1978
THE CHOSEN   20th Century-Fox International Classics, 1982
THE STING II   Universal, 1983
THE JOURNEY OF NATTY GANN   Buena Vista, 1985
COURAGE (TF)   Highgate Pictures/New World TV, 1986
CONSPIRACY: TRIAL OF THE CHICAGO 8 (CTF)   Jeremy Kagan
Productions/Inter Planetary Productions, 1987
BIG MAN ON CAMPUS   Vestron, 1989
DESCENDING ANGEL (CTF)   HBO Pictures, 1990
BY THE SWORD   SVS Films, 1991
DR. QUINN, MEDICINE WOMAN (TF)   The Sullivan Company/CBS
Entertainment, 1993
ROSWELL (CTF)   Showtime Entertainment, 1994

JEFF KAHN

Agent: William Morris Agency - Beverly Hills, 310/859-4000

REVOLUTION!   Northern Arts Entertainment, 1991

CHEN KAIGE

b. August 12, 1952 - Beijing, China
Agent: William Morris Agency - Beverly Hills, 310/859-4000

YELLOW EARTH   China Film Import & Export, 1984, Chinese
FORCED TAKE-OFF (TF)   1985, Chinese
THE BIG PARADE   China Film Import & Export, 1986, Chinese
KING OF THE CHILDREN   Orion Classics, 1988, Chinese
LIFE ON A STRING   Kino International, 1991,
Chinese-British-German-Japanese
FAREWELL MY CONCUBINE   Miramax Films, 1992,
Hong Kong-Chinese
TEMPTRESS MOON   Tomson Films, 1995, Hong Kong-Chinese

CONSTANCE KAISERMAN

MY LITTLE GIRL   Hemdale, 1986
SECOND DAUGHTER   Black Swan Productions/Merchant Ivory
Productions, 1992

TOM KALIN
SWOON   Fine Line Features/New Line Cinema, 1992

SCOTT KALVERT
Agent: CAA - Beverly Hills, 310/288-4545

THE BASKETBALL DIARIES   New Line Cinema, 1995

JAY KAMEN
b. July 21, 1953 - New York, New York
Home: 3233 DeWitt Drive, Hollywood, CA 90068, 213/876-4173
Agent: David Warden, Warden-White & Associates - Los Angeles,
   213/852-1028

TRANSFORMATIONS   Empire Pictures, 1988

STUART KAMINSKY
Contact: Writers Guild of America, East - New York City,
   212/767-7800

HIDDEN FEARS   Prism Pictures, 1993

STEVEN KAMPMANN
Agent: ICM - Beverly Hills, 310/550-4000

STEALING HOME   co-director with Will Aldis, Warner Bros., 1988

SHUSUKE KANEKO
b. 1955 - Tokyo, Japan
Contact: Nihon Eiga Kantoku Kyokai (Japan Film Directors
   Association), La Fontenu Building -4th Floor, 23-2 Maruyama-cho,
   Shibuya-ku, Tokyo, Japan, tel.: 3/3461-4411

KOICHIRO UNO'S WET AND HIT   Nikkatsu, 1984, Japanese
O.L. LILLY FAMILY   New Century Producers, 1984, Japanese
I'LL GIVE YOU EVERYTHING   Nikkatsu, 1985, Japanese
SUMMER VACATION 1999   New Yorker, 1988, Japanese
YAMADA VILLAGE WALTZ   Temporary Center, 1988, Japanese
LAST CABARET   Nikkatsu/New Century Producers,
   1988, Japanese
WHICH DO YOU WANT?   Burning Productions/Sundance
   Company, 1989, Japanese
HONG KONG PARADISE   Toho/Sundance Company,
   1990, Japanese
I WANT TO BITE   Casutosu/MMI/Toho, 1991, Japanese
ALL QUIET ON THE JOB HUNT FRONT   Fuji TV,
   1991, Japanese
GRADUATE TRIP: I COME FROM JAPAN   Toho/Bandai Visual,
   1993, Japanese
H.P. LOVECRAFT'S NECRONOMICON   *NECRONOMICON*
   co-director with Christophe Gans & Brian Yuzna, Necronomicon
   Productions, 1993, U.S.-French-Japanese
EVERY DAY IS A SUMMER VACATION   Kuzui Enterprises,
   1994, Japanese
GAMERA: AIR BATTLE OF THE MONSTERS   Daiei,
   1995, Japanese

VITALI KANEVSKI
Contact: Confederation of Film-Makers Unions, Vasilyevskaya
   Street 13, 123 825 Moscow, Russia, tel.: 095/250-4114

FREEZE, DIE, COME TO LIFE!   1990, Soviet
AN INDEPENDENT LIFE   1992, Russian
NOUS, LES ENFANTS DU XXEME SICLE (FD)   Lapsus/La
   Sept-Arte/D.A.R. St. Petersburg/RAI-3/Danmarks Radio,
   1994, French-Russian-Italian-Danish

JEFF KANEW*
Agent: The Gersh Agency - Beverly Hills, 310/274-6611

BLACK RODEO (FD)   Cinerama Releasing Corporation, 1972
NATURAL ENEMIES   Cinema 5, 1979
EDDIE MACON'S RUN   Universal, 1983
REVENGE OF THE NERDS   20th Century Fox, 1984
GOTCHA!   Universal, 1985

TOUGH GUYS   Buena Vista, 1986
TROOP BEVERLY HILLS   Columbia/WEG, 1989
V. I. WARSHAWSKI   Buena Vista, 1991
ICE CREAM MAN   Capella International, 1995

WOO-SUK KANG
Contact: Korean Motion Picture Promotion Corp., 34-5, 3KA
   Namsan-Dong, Chung-Ku, Seoul, South Korea, tel.: 755-9291

TWO COPS   Morning Calm Cinema, 1994, South Korean
HOW TO TOP MY WIFE   Morning Calm Cinema,
   1995, South Korean

CHARLES T. KANGANIS
Agent: ICM - Beverly Hills, 310/550-4000

A TIME TO DIE   PM Entertainment Group, 1991
NO ESCAPE, NO RETURN   PM Entertainment Group, 1993
3 NINJAS KICK BACK   TriStar, 1994
RACE THE SUN   TriStar, 1995

MAREK KANIEVSKA*
b. London, England
Agent: ICM - Beverly Hills, 310/550-4000

ANOTHER COUNTRY   Orion Classics, 1984, British
LESS THAN ZERO   20th Century Fox, 1987

GARSON KANIN*
b. November 24, 1912 - Rochester, New York
Business: TFT Corporation, 200 West 57th Street - Suite 1203,
   New York, NY 10019, 212/586-7850

A MAN TO REMEMBER   RKO Radio, 1938
NEXT TIME I MARRY   RKO Radio, 1938
THE GREAT MAN VOTES   RKO Radio, 1939
BACHELOR MOTHER   RKO Radio, 1939
MY FAVORITE WIFE   RKO Radio, 1940
THEY KNEW WHAT THEY WANTED   Columbia, 1940
TOM, DICK AND HARRY   RKO Radio, 1941
THE TRUE GLORY   co-director with Carol Reed,
   Columbia, 1945
WHERE IT'S AT   United Artists, 1969
SOME KIND OF NUT   United Artists, 1969

ALEXIS KANNER
b. May 2, 1952 - Luchon, France
Contact: Screen Actors Guild - Los Angeles, 213/954-1600

HELLO THE UNIVERSAL   1982, British
KINGS AND DESPERATE MEN, a hostage incident
   1985, Canadian
DOWNTOWN FARMER   1988

HAL KANTER*
b. December 18, 1918 - Savannah, Georgia
Business Manager: James Harper, Harper & Associates,
   13063 Ventura Blvd., Studio City, CA 91604, 818/788-8683

LOVING YOU   Paramount, 1957
I MARRIED A WOMAN   Universal, 1958
ONCE UPON A HORSE   Universal, 1958
FOR THE LOVE OF IT (TF)   Charles Fries Productions/Neila
   Productions, 1980

BETTY KAPLAN
Agent: ICM - Beverly Hills, 310/550-4000

BOLIVAR (MS)   Venezuelan
CAMINOS QUE ANDAN (MS)   Venezuelan
OF LOVE AND SHADOWS   Betka Film Ltd., 1994,
   British-Spanish-Argentine

ED KAPLAN*
Agent: Innovative Artists - Los Angeles, 310/553-5200

WALKING ON AIR (TF)   WonderWorks, 1987
CHIPS, THE WAR DOG (CTF)   W.G. Productions, 1990
FOR THEIR OWN GOOD (TF)   Avnet-Kerner Company, 1993
TRICK OF THE EYE (TF)   Hallmark Entertainment/Craig Anderson
   Productions/Signboard Hill Productions, 1994

JONATHAN KAPLAN*
b. November 25, 1947 - Paris, France
Agent: CAA - Beverly Hills, 310/288-4545

THE STUDENT TEACHERS   New World, 1973
THE SLAMS   MGM, 1973
TRUCK TURNER   American International, 1974
NIGHT CALL NURSES   New World, 1974
WHITE LINE FEVER   Columbia, 1975
MR. BILLION   20th Century-Fox, 1976
OVER THE EDGE   Orion/Warner Bros., 1979
THE 11TH VICTIM (TF)   Marty Katz Productions/
   Paramount TV, 1979
THE HUSTLER OF MUSCLE BEACH (TF)   Furia-Oringer
   Productions, 1980
THE GENTLEMAN BANDIT (TF)   Highgate Pictures, 1981
HEART LIKE A WHEEL   20th Century-Fox, 1983
GIRLS OF THE WHITE ORCHID (TF)   Hill-Mandelker
   Films, 1983
PROJECT X   20th Century Fox, 1987
THE ACCUSED   Paramount, 1988
IMMEDIATE FAMILY   Columbia, 1989
LOVE FIELD   Orion, 1992
UNLAWFUL ENTRY   20th Century Fox, 1992
BAD GIRLS   20th Century Fox, 1994
REBEL HIGHWAY: REFORM SCHOOL GIRL   *REFORM SCHOOL
   GIRL* (CTF)   Drive-In Classics Cinema/Showtime, 1994

MIKE KAPLAN
LUCK, TRUST & KETCHUP: ROBERT ALTMAN IN CARVER
   COUNTRY (TD)   co-director with John Dorr, EZTV/Circle
   Associates, 1994

NELLY KAPLAN
b. 1931 - Buenos Aires, Argentina
Business: Cythere Films, 34, avenue Champs Elysees,
   Paris 75008, France, tel.: 1/42-89-07-67
Contact: French Film Office, 745 Fifth Avenue, New York,
   NY 10151, 212/832-8860

GUSTAVE MOREAU (FD)   Cythere Films, 1961, French
ABEL GANCE HIER ET DEMAIN (FD)   Cythere Films,
   1963, French
LE REGARD PICASSO (FD)   Cythere Films, 1966, French
A VERY CURIOUS GIRL   *LE FIANCEE DU PIRATE*   Regional,
   1970, French
PAPA LES PETITS BATEAUX   Cythere Films, 1971, French
NEA   *NEA - A YOUNG EMMANUELLE*   Libra, 1976, French
CHARLES ET LUCIE   Nu-Image, 1980, French
ABEL GANCE ET SON NAPOLEON (FD)   Cythere Films,
   1983, French
PATTES DE VELOURS (TF)   Antenne-2, 1986, French
PLAISIR D'AMOUR   Cythere Films/Boulogne/Pathe,
   1991, French

SHEKHAR KAPUR
Contact: National Film Development Corporation of India,
   Discovery of India Building, Nehru Centre, Dr Annie Besant
   Road, Worli, Bombay 400018, India, tel.: 4949856

BANDIT QUEEN   Arrow Releasing, 1994, British-Indian

WONG KAR-WAI
Contact: Hong Kong Film Liaison, 10940 Wilshire Blvd. - Suite 1220,
   Los Angeles, CA 90024, 310/208-2678

AS TEARS GO BY   1988, Hong Kong
DAYS OF BEING WILD   In-Gear Film Production, 1990, Hong Kong
CHUNG KING EXPRESS   Jet Tone Production Company,
   1994, Hong Kong
ASHES OF TIME   Scholar Films Company/Jet Tone Production
   Company/Tsui Siu-ming Production Company/Beijing Film
   Studio/Pony Canyon, 1994, Hong Kong-Chinese

MICHAEL KARBELNIKOFF*
Business: HKM Films, 1641 N. Ivar Avenue, Hollywood, CA 90028,
   213/465-9414
Agent: ICM - Beverly Hills, 310/550-4000

MOBSTERS   Universal, 1991
F.T.W.   Nu Image, 1994

JANICE KARMAN
THE CHIPMUNK ADVENTURE (AF)   The Samuel Goldwyn
   Company, 1986

ERIC KARSON*
Business: Karsonfilms, 11818 Riverside Drive - Suite 321,
   North Hollywood, CA 91607, 818/506-1517
Business: Imperial Entertainment, 4640 Lankershim Blvd. -
   Fourth Floor, North Hollywood, CA 91607, 818/762-0005

DIRT   co-director with Cal Naylor, American Cinema, 1979
THE OCTAGON   American Cinema, 1980
OPPOSING FORCE   *HELL CAMP*   Orion, 1986
BLACK EAGLE   Taurus Entertainment, 1988
ANGEL TOWN   Taurus Entertainment, 1990

LAWRENCE KASDAN*
b. January 14, 1949 - Miami Beach, Florida
Agent: UTA - Beverly Hills, 310/273-6700

BODY HEAT   The Ladd Company/Warner Bros., 1981
THE BIG CHILL   Columbia, 1983
SILVERADO   Columbia, 1985
THE ACCIDENTAL TOURIST   Warner Bros., 1988
I LOVE YOU TO DEATH   TriStar, 1990
GRAND CANYON   20th Century Fox, 1991
WYATT EARP   Warner Bros., 1994
FRENCH KISS   20th Century Fox, 1995

MATHIEU KASSOVITZ
Contact: French Film Office, 745 Fifth Avenue, New York,
   NY 10151, 212/832-8860

CAFE AU LAIT   *METISSE*   New Yorker, 1993, French
LA HAINE   Les Productions Lazennec, 1995, French

LEONARD KASTLE
THE HONEYMOON KILLERS   Cinerama Releasing
   Corporation, 1970

DAPHNA KASTNER
Business: c/o Cineville, 225 Santa Monica Blvd. - Seventh Floor,
   Santa Monica, CA 90401, 310/394-4699

FRENCH EXIT   Cineville III, 1995

ELLIOTT KASTNER*
b. January 7, 1933 - New York, New York
Business: Pinewood Studios, Iver Heath, Bucks SI0 0NH, England,
   tel.: 75/654171

LIKEWISE   co-director with Arthur Sherman, Cinema Group, 1988

MICHAEL KATLEMAN*
Agent: ICM - Beverly Hills, 310/550-4000

NO CHILD OF MINE (TF)   Bonnie Raskin Productions/
    Green-Epstein Productions/Warner Bros. TV, 1993
THE SPIDER AND THE FLY (CTF)   The Haft-Nasatir Company/
    Heartstar Productions/Wilshire Court Productions, 1994

MILTON KATSELAS*
b. December 22, 1933 - Pittsburgh, Pennsylvania
Business: Beverly Hills Playhouse, 254 S. Robertson Blvd.,
    Beverly Hills, CA 90211, 310/931-3895

BUTTERFLIES ARE FREE   Columbia, 1972
40 CARATS   Columbia, 1973
REPORT TO THE COMMISSIONER   United Artists, 1975
WHEN YOU COMIN' BACK, RED RYDER?   Columbia, 1979
STRANGERS: THE STORY OF A MOTHER AND A
    DAUGHTER (TF)   Chris-Rose Productions, 1979
THE RULES OF MARRIAGE (TF)   Entheos Unlimited Productions/
    Brownstone Productions/20th Century-Fox TV, 1982

DOUGLAS KATZ
LIFE IN THE FOOD CHAIN   Katzfilms, 1992

MICHAEL KATZ
CALIFORNIA MYTH   Filmo Inc., 1994

LEE H. KATZIN*
b. April 12, 1935 - Detroit, Michigan
Home: 13425 Java Drive, Beverly Hills, CA 90210, 310/278-7726
Agent: Shapiro-Lichtman Talent Agency - Los Angeles, 310/859-8877

HONDO AND THE APACHES   MGM, 1967
HEAVEN WITH A GUN   MGM, 1969
WHAT EVER HAPPENED TO AUNT ALICE?   Cinerama Releasing
    Corporation, 1969
THE PHYNX   Warner Bros., 1970
LE MANS   National General, 1970
ALONG CAME A SPIDER (TF)   20th Century-Fox TV, 1970
THE SALZBURG CONNECTION   20th Century-Fox, 1972
VISIONS... (TF)   CBS, Inc., 1972
THE VOYAGE OF THE YES (TF)   Bing Crosby Productions, 1973
THE STRANGER (TF)   Bing Crosby Productions, 1973
ORDEAL (TF)   20th Century-Fox TV, 1973
SAVAGES (TF)   Spelling-Goldberg Productions, 1974
STRANGE HOMECOMING (TF)   Alpine Productions/
    Worldvision, 1974
THE LAST SURVIVORS (TF)   Bob Banner Associates, 1975
SKY HEI$T (TF)   Warner Bros. TV, 1975
THE QUEST (TF)   David Gerber Company/Columbia TV, 1976
THE MAN FROM ATLANTIS (TF)   Solow Production
    Company, 1977
RELENTLESS (TF)   CBS, Inc., 1977
THE BASTARD (TF)   Universal TV, 1978
ZUMA BEACH (TF)   Edgar J. Scherick Associates/Warner
    Bros. TV, 1978
TERROR OUT OF THE SKY (TF)   Alan Landsburg
    Productions, 1978
REVENGE OF THE SAVAGE BEES (TF)   1979
SAMURAI (TF)   Danny Thomas Productions/Universal TV, 1979
DEATH RAY 2000 (TF)   Woodruff Productions/QM
    Productions, 1981
THE NEIGHBORHOOD (TF)   David Gerber Company/
    Columbia TV, 1982
AUTOMAN (TF)   Kushner-Locke Company/Glen A. Larson
    Productions/20th Century-Fox TV, 1983
SPENSER: FOR HIRE (TF)   John Wilder Productions/
    Warner Bros. TV, 1985
THE DIRTY DOZEN: THE DEADLY MISSION (TF)
    MGM-UA TV/Jadran Film, 1987, U.S.-Yugoslavian
WORLD GONE WILD   Lorimar, 1988
THE DIRTY DOZEN: THE FATAL MISSION (TF)
    MGM-UA TV, 1988
JAKE SPANNER, PRIVATE EYE (CTF)   Andrew J. Fenady
    Productions/Scotti-Vinnedge TV/USA Network, 1989
THE BREAK   Autumn Winds Productions, 1995

JONATHAN KAUFER*
b. March 14, 1955 - Los Angeles, California
Agent: Hilary Wayne Agency - Beverly Hills, 310/289-6186

SOUP FOR ONE   Warner Bros., 1982

CHARLES KAUFMAN
THE SECRET DREAMS OF MONA Q   Troma, 1977
MOTHER'S DAY   United Film Distribution, 1980
WHEN NATURE CALLS   Troma, 1985
JAKARTA   MCEG, 1989, Indonesian-U.S., filmed in 1986

JIM KAUFMAN
b. 1949 - Montreal, Quebec, Canada
Business: J.T.K. Productions, 241 Clarke Avenue, Montreal,
    Quebec H3Z 2E3, Canada, 514/931-7463
Agent: Charles Northcote, The Core Group, 489 College Street -
    Suite 501, Toronto, Ontario M6G 1A5, Canada, 416/944-0193

MAKE MINE CHARTREUSE   1986, U.S.-Canadian
SHADES OF LOVE   1987, Canadian-U.S.
FORGIVING HARRY (TF)   1987, Canadian
THE THRILLER (TF)   3 Themes, 1989, Canadian
BACK STAB   Allegro Films/Westwind, 1990, Canadian
A STAR FOR TWO   InterStar Releasing, 1992, French-Canadian
RED RAIN   Angelika Films, 1993, Australian

LLOYD KAUFMAN
b. November 30, 1945 - New York, New York
Business: Troma, Inc., 733 Ninth Avenue, New York, NY 10019,
    212/757-4555

SQUEEZE PLAY!   co-director with Michael Herz under pseudonym
    of Samuel Weil, Troma, 1980
WAITRESS!   co-director with Michael Herz under pseudonym
    of Samuel Weil, Troma, 1982
STUCK ON YOU!   co-director with Michael Herz under pseudonym
    of Samuel Weil, Troma, 1983
THE FIRST TURN-ON!   co-director with Michael Herz under
    pseudonym of Samuel Weil, Troma, 1984
THE TOXIC AVENGER   co-director with Michael Herz under
    pseudonym of Samuel Weil, Troma, 1984
NUKE 'EM HIGH   CLASS OF NUKE 'EM HIGH   co-director with
    Michael Herz under pseudonym of Samuel Weil, Troma, 1985
THE TOXIC AVENGER: PART II   co-director with Michael Herz
    under pseudonym of Samuel Weil, Troma, 1988
TROMA'S WAR   co-director with Michael Herz under pseudonym
    of Samuel Weil, Troma, 1988
THE TOXIC AVENGER, PART III: THE LAST TEMPTATION
    OF TOXIE   co-director with Michael Herz, Troma, 1989
SGT. KABUKIMAN NYPD   co-director with Michael Herz,
    Troma, 1991

PHILIP KAUFMAN*
b. October 23, 1936 - Chicago, Illinois
Agent: CAA - Beverly Hills, 310/288-4545

GOLDSTEIN   co-director with Benjamin Manaster, Altura, 1965
FEARLESS FRANK   American International, 1969
THE GREAT NORTHFIELD, MINNESOTA RAID   Universal, 1972
THE WHITE DAWN   Paramount, 1974
INVASION OF THE BODY SNATCHERS   United Artists, 1978
THE WANDERERS   Orion/Warner Bros., 1979
THE RIGHT STUFF   The Ladd Company/Warner Bros., 1983
THE UNBEARABLE LIGHTNESS OF BEING   Orion, 1988
HENRY & JUNE   Universal, 1990
RISING SUN   20th Century Fox, 1993

MANI KAUL
b. India
Contact: National Film Development Corporation of India,
    Discovery of India Building, Nehru Centre, Dr Annie Besant
    Road, Worli, Bombay 400018, India, tel.: 494856

A DAY'S BREAD   1969, Indian
A MONSOON DAY   1971, Indian
IN TWO MINDS   1973, Indian

RISING FROM THE SURFACE   1980, Indian
DHRUPAD (FD)   National Film Development Corporation of India,
   1983, Indian
SIDDHESHWARI   1990, Indian
NAZAR   National Film Development Corporation of India/
   Doordarshan, 1991, Indian
EROTIC TALES   co-director with Bob Rafelson, Susan Seidelman,
   Ken Russell, Melvin Van Peebles & Paul Cox, Regina Ziegler
   Filmproduktion/Tele-Munchen/Westdeutscher Rundfunk,
   1994, German

AKI KAURISMÄKI
b. April 4, 1957 - Helsinki, Finland
Business: Villealfa Filmproductions Oy, Vainamoisenkatu 19 A,
   SF-00100 Helsinki, Finland, tel.: 0/49-83-66

CRIME AND PUNISHMENT   Villealfa Filmproductions,
   1983, Finnish
CALAMARI UNION   Villealfa Filmproductions, 1985, Finnish
SHADOWS IN PARADISE   Villealfa Filmproductions, 1986, Finnish
HAMLET GOES BUSINESS   Villealfa Filmproductions,
   1987, Finnish
ARIEL   Kino International, 1989, Finnish
LENINGRAD COWBOYS GO AMERICA   Orion Classics,
   1989, Finnish-Swedish
I HIRED A CONTRACT KILLER   Villealfa Filmproductions/Swedish
   Film Institute/Finnkino/Esselte Video/Megemania/Pandora Film/
   Pyramide/Channel 4, 1990, Finnish-Swedish-French-British
THE MATCH FACTORY GIRL   Kino International, 1990,
   Finnish-Swedish
LA VIE DE BOHEME   Kino International, 1992,
   Finnish-French-Swedish
LENINGRAD COWBOYS MEET MOSES   Sputnik Oy/Pandora
   Film/Pyramide Productions, 1994, Finnish-German-French
TOTAL BALALAIKA SHOW (FD)   Sputnik Productions/YLE/TF-1/
   Eila Werning/Megamania, 1994, Finnish
TAKE CARE OF YOUR SCARF, TATIANA!   Sputnik Oy/Pandora
   Film, 1994, Finnish-German

MIKA KAURISMÄKI
b. September 21, 1955 - Orimattila, Finland
Business: Villealfafilmproductions Oy, Vaionamoisenkatu 19 A,
   SF-00100 Helsinki, Finland, tel.: 0/49-83-66

THE SAIMAA GESTURE   Villealfa Filmproductions, 1981, Finnish
THE LIAR   Mika Kaurismaki/Hochschule fur Fernsehen und Film,
   1981, Finnish-West German
THE WORTHLESS   Villealfa Filmproductions, 1982, Finnish
THE CLAN - THE TALE OF THE FROGS   Villealfa Filmproductions,
   1984, Finnish
ROSSO   Villealfa Filmproductions, 1985, Finnish
HELSINKI-NAPOLI: ALL NIGHT LONG   Villealfa Filmproductions,
   1987, Finnish
PAPER STAR   Villealfa Filmproductions/Swedish Film Institute,
   1989, Finnish-Swedish
AMAZON   Cabriolet Films, 1991, U.S.-Finnish-Swiss-French
ZOMBIE AND THE GHOST TRAIN   Marianna Films/Villealfa
   Filmproductions, 1992, Finnish-Brazilian
THE LAST BORDER   Last Border/Connexion Films/Sandrews/
   MC4, 1993, Finnish-German-Swedish
TIGRERO: A FILM THAT WAS NEVER MADE   Arrow Releasing,
   1994, Finnish-German-Brazilian
CONDITION RED   Beyond the Law Inc., 1995

ANWAR KAWADRI
b. January 17, 1953 - Damascus, Syria
Address: 115 Wendell Road, London W12 9SD, England,
   tel.: 171/740-1341
Contact: British Film Commission, 70 Baker Street, London
   W1M 1DJ, England, tel.: 171/224-5000

SEX WITH THE STARS   ITC, 1980, British
NUTCRACKER   Rank, 1983, British
CLAUDIA'S STORY (TF)   ITC, 1986, British
OUT OF TIME   Alexander's Treasure Projects/Tamido Film
   Productions, 1989, British-Egyptian-Greek

JERZY KAWALEROWICZ
b. January 15, 1922 - Gwozdziec, Poland
Contact: Film Polski, ul. Mazowiecka 6/8, 00048 Warsaw, Poland,
   tel.: 48-22/26-84-55 or 48-22/26-09-49

COMMUNE   co-director with Kazimierz Sumerski, 1950, Polish
CELLULOSE   1954, Polish
UNDER THE PHRYGIAN STAR   1954, Polish
THE SHADOW   1956, Polish
THE REAL END OF THE GREAT WAR   1957, Polish
NIGHT TRAIN   *BALTIC EXPRESS*   Curzon, 1959, Polish
JOAN OF THE ANGELS?   *MOTHER JOAN OF THE ANGELS?*
   Telepix Corporation, 1961, Polish
PHAROAH   1965, Polish
THE GAME   1969, Polish
MADDALENA   1971, Italian-Yugoslavian
DEATH OF THE PRESIDENT   1978, Polish
CHANCE MEETING ON THE ATLANTIC   1979, Polish
AUSTERIA   1982, Polish

GILBERT LEE KAY
b. June 28 - Chicago, Illinois
Home: 105 Barbara Street, Louisville, CO 80027

THREE BAD SISTERS   United Artists, 1956
NOW IT CAN BE TOLD   Toronto-Lisboa Productions, 1961
THE SECRET DOOR   Allied Artists, 1961, British
THE TOWER   1965, Spanish
A HARVEST OF EVIL   1966, Spanish
RAGAN   1967, Spanish
WHITE COMANCHE   RKO, 1968, Spanish
DEVIL MAY CARE   1969, Spanish
MAYBE SEPTEMBER   1970, Spanish

JONATHON KAY
Contact: 213/829-5070

WALKING AFTER MIDNIGHT (FD)   Kay's Film Productions,
   1988, Canadian
STARLIGHT   Angelika Films, 1991, Canadian

ROBERT KAYLOR*
Agent: Irv Schecter Company - Beverly Hills, 310/278-8070

DERBY (FD)   Cinerama Releasing Corporation, 1971
CARNY   United Artists, 1980
NOBODY'S PERFECT   Moviestore Entertainment, 1990

ELIA KAZAN*
(Elia Kazanjoglou)
b. September 7, 1909 - Constantinople, Turkey
Home: 174 East 95th Street, New York, NY 10128

A TREE GROWS IN BROOKLYN   20th Century-Fox, 1945
SEA OF GRASS   MGM, 1947
BOOMERANG!   20th Century-Fox, 1947
GENTLEMAN'S AGREEMENT ★★   20th Century-Fox, 1947
PINKY   20th Century-Fox, 1949
PANIC IN THE STREETS   20th Century-Fox, 1950
A STREETCAR NAMED DESIRE ★   Warner Bros., 1951
VIVA ZAPATA!   20th Century-Fox, 1952
MAN ON A TIGHTROPE   20th Century-Fox, 1953
ON THE WATERFRONT ★★   Columbia, 1954
EAST OF EDEN ★   Warner Bros., 1955
BABY DOLL   Warner Bros., 1956
A FACE IN THE CROWD   Warner Bros., 1957
WILD RIVER   20th Century-Fox, 1960
SPLENDOR IN THE GRASS   Warner Bros., 1961
AMERICA AMERICA ★   Warner Bros., 1963
THE ARRANGEMENT   Warner Bros., 1969
THE VISITORS   United Artists, 1972
THE LAST TYCOON   Paramount, 1975

NICHOLAS KAZAN*
Agent: Sanford-Gross & Associates - Los Angeles,
310/208-2100

DREAM LOVER   Gramercy Pictures, 1994

JAMES KEACH*
Agent: The Gersh Agency - Beverly Hills, 310/274-6611

THE FORGOTTEN (CTF)   Keach-Railsback Productions/Wilshire
   Court Productions, 1989
FALSE IDENTITY   RKO Pavilion/Prism Entertainment, 1990
SUNSTROKE (CTF)   Wilshire Court Productions, 1992
PRAYING MANTIS (CTF)   Fast Track Films/Wilshire Court
   Productions, 1993
A PASSION FOR JUSTICE: THE HAZEL BRANNON
   SMITH STORY (TF)   David Brooks Productions/Catfish
   Productions/Saban-Scherick Productions/Procter &
   Gamble Productions, 1994
THE STARS FELL ON HENRIETTA   Warner Bros., 1995

DIANE KEATON*
(Diane Hall)
b. January 5, 1949 - Santa Ana, California
Agent: William Morris Agency - Beverly Hills, 310/859-4000

HEAVEN (FD)   Island Pictures, 1987
WILDFLOWER (CTF)   Lifetime Productions/Freed-Laufer
   Productions/The Polone Company/Hearst
   Entertainment, 1991

BOB KEEN
PROTEUS   Trimark Pictures, 1995

NIETZCHKA KEENE
THE JUNIPER TREE   Keene-Moyroud Productions,
   1991, U.S.-Icelandic

DON KEESLAR
BOG   Marshall Films, 1978
THE CAPTURE OF GRIZZLY ADAMS (TF)   Sunn Classic
   Productions, 1982

DOUGLAS KEEVE
UNZIPPED (FD)   Miramax Films, 1995

MICHAEL KEHOE
DOMINION   Prism Pictures, 1995

PATRICK KEILLER
Contact: British Film Commission, 70 Baker Street, London
   W1M 1DJ, England, tel.: 171/224-5000

LONDON   Zeitgeist Films, 1994, British

P. JAMES KEITEL
BELOW 30/ABOVE 10,000   Damaged Californians, 1994

DAVID KEITH*
b. 1954 - Knoxville, Tennessee
Agent: William Morris Agency - Beverly Hills, 310/859-4000

THE CURSE   Trans World Entertainment, 1987
SACRIFICE   Trans World Entertainment, 1988
THE FURTHER ADVENTURES OF TENNESSEE BUCK
   Trans World Entertainment, 1988

HARVEY KEITH*
Address: 1541 N. Laurel - Suite 202, Los Angeles, CA 90046,
   213/859-5519
Agent: The Gersh Agency - Beverly Hills, 310/274-6611
Personal Manager: Carthay Circle Pictures and Management -
   Beverly Hills, 310/657-5454

MONDO NEW YORK   Fourth and Broadway Films/Island
   Pictures, 1988
JEZEBEL'S KISS   Shapiro Glickenhaus Entertainment, 1990

ASAAD KELADA*
Agent: Mitch Kaplan, The Kaplan-Stahler Agency - Beverly Hills,
   310/653-4483

THE FACTS OF LIFE GOES TO PARIS (TF)   Embassy TV, 1982

FREDERICK KING KELLER*
Home: 73 Richmond Avenue, Buffalo, NY 14222, 716/881-1058
Agent: Paul Kohner, Inc. - Los Angeles, 310/550-1060

TUCK EVERLASTING   1981
VAMPING   Atlantic Releasing Corporation, 1984
MY DARK LADY   Film Gallery/Artist Entertainment Group, 1987

HARRY KELLER
b. February 22, 1913 - Los Angeles, California

THE BLONDE BANDIT   1949
TARNISHED   Republic, 1950
FORT DODGE STAMPEDE   1951
DESERT OF LOST MEN   1951
ROSE OF CIMARRON   20th Century-Fox, 1952
LEADVILLE GUNSLINGER   1952
THUNDERING CARAVANS   1952
BLACK HILLS AMBUSH   1952
MARSHAL OF CEDAR ROCK   1953
BANDITS OF THE WEST   1953
SAVAGE FRONTIER   1953
EL PASO STAMPEDE   1953
RED RIVER SHORE   1954
PHANTOM STALLION   1954
THE UNGUARDED MOMENT   Universal, 1956
MAN AFRAID   Universal, 1957
QUANTEZ   Universal, 1957
THE FEMALE ANIMAL   Universal, 1958
DAY OF THE BADMAN   Universal, 1958
VOICE IN THE MIRROR   Universal, 1958
STEP DOWN TO TERROR   Universal, 1958
SEVEN WAYS FROM SUNDOWN   Universal, 1960
TAMMY TELL ME TRUE   Universal, 1961
SIX BLACK HORSES   Universal, 1962
TAMMY AND THE DOCTOR   Universal, 1963
THE BRASS BOTTLE   Universal, 1964
IN ENEMY COUNTRY   Universal, 1968

BARNET KELLMAN*
b. November 9, 1947 - New York, New York
Agent: CAA - Beverly Hills, 310/288-4545

KEY EXCHANGE   TLC Films/20th Century Fox, 1985
STRAIGHT TALK   Buena Vista, 1992

DAVID KELLOGG
COOL AS ICE   Universal, 1991

DIANE KELLY
UNSTRUNG HEROES   Buena Vista, 1995

GENE KELLY*
(Eugene Curran Kelly)
b. August 23, 1912 - Pittsburgh, Pennsylvania
Agent: ICM - Beverly Hills, 310/550-4000
Business Manager: Linda Judd, Bamberger Business
  Management - Los Angeles, 213/446-2783

ON THE TOWN   co-director with Stanley Donen, MGM, 1949
SINGIN' IN THE RAIN   co-director with Stanley Donen,
  MGM, 1952
IT'S ALWAYS FAIR WEATHER   co-director with Stanley Donen,
  MGM, 1955
INVITATION TO THE DANCE   MGM, 1956
THE HAPPY ROAD   co-director with Noel Howard, MGM, 1957
THE TUNNEL OF LOVE   MGM, 1958
GIGOT   20th Century-Fox, 1962
A GUIDE FOR THE MARRIED MAN   20th Century-Fox, 1967
HELLO, DOLLY!   20th Century-Fox, 1969
THE CHEYENNE SOCIAL CLUB   National General, 1970
THAT'S ENTERTAINMENT, PART 2 (FD)   co-director with
  Jack Haley, Jr., MGM/United Artists, 1976

JUDE KELLY
Contact: British Film Commission, 70 Baker Street, London
  W1M 1DJ, England, tel.: 171/224-5000

MIGHTY MOMENTS FROM WORLD HISTORY (TF)   Channel 4,
  1985, British

NANCY KELLY
b. March 1953 - North Adams, Massachusetts
Business: Mother Lode Productions, 397 Miller Avenue - Suite 1,
  Mill Valley, CA 94941, 415/381-3573
Agent: The Artists Agency - Los Angeles, 310/277-7779
Attorney: Peter S. Buchanan, 170 Columbus Avenue - 5th Floor,
  San Francisco, CA 94133

THOUSAND PIECES OF GOLD   Greycat Films, 1990

RORY KELLY
Agent: UTA - Beverly Hills, 310/273-6700

SLEEP WITH ME   MGM/UA, 1994

NICHOLAS KENDALL
Contact: Directors Guild of Canada, 225 Richmond Street, Toronto,
  Ontario M5V 1W2, Canada, 416/351-8200

CADILLAC GIRLS   Cineplex Odeon, 1993, Canadian

FRED KENNAMER
NOT AGAIN!   Privateer Pictures, 1994

BURT KENNEDY*
b. September 3, 1922 - Muskegon, Michigan
Business: Brigade Productions, 13138 Magnolia Blvd.,
  Sherman Oaks, CA 91403, 818/986-8759

THE CANADIANS   20th Century-Fox, 1961
MAIL ORDER BRIDE   MGM, 1963
THE ROUNDERS   MGM, 1965
THE MONEY TRAP   MGM, 1966
RETURN OF THE SEVEN   United Artists, 1966
WELCOME TO HARD TIMES   MGM, 1967
THE WAR WAGON   Universal, 1967
SUPPORT YOUR LOCAL SHERIFF   United Artists, 1969
YOUNG BILLY YOUNG   United Artists, 1969
THE GOOD GUYS AND THE BAD GUYS   Warner Bros., 1969
DIRTY DINGUS MAGEE   MGM, 1970
SUPPORT YOUR LOCAL GUNFIGHTER   United Artists, 1971
HANNIE CAULDER   Paramount, 1971, British
THE DESERTER   Paramount, 1971, Italian-Yugoslavian
THE TRAIN ROBBERS   Warner Bros., 1973
SHOOTOUT IN A ONE-DOG TOWN (TF)   Hanna-Barbera
  Productions, 1974

SIDEKICKS (TF)   Warner Bros. TV, 1974
ALL THE KIND STRANGERS (TF)   Cinemation TV, 1974
THE KILLER INSIDE ME   Warner Bros., 1976
HOW THE WEST WAS WON (MS)   co-director with Daniel Mann,
  MGM TV, 1977
THE RHINEMANN EXCHANGE (MS)   Universal TV, 1977
KATE BLISS & THE TICKER TAPE KID (TF)   Aaron Spelling
  Productions, 1978
THE WILD WILD WEST REVISITED (TF)
  CBS Entertainment, 1979
THE CONCRETE COWBOYS (TF)   Frankel Films, 1979
MORE WILD WILD WEST   CBS Entertainment, 1980
WOLF LAKE   *THE HONOR GUARD*   Filmcorp Distribution,
  1981, Canadian
THE ALAMO: 13 DAYS TO GLORY (TF)   Briggle, Hennessy,
  Carrothers Productions/The Finnegan Company/Fries
  Entertainment, 1987
DOWN THE LONG HILLS (TF)   The Finnegan Company/Walt
  Disney TV, 1987
THE TROUBLE WITH SPIES   DEG, 1987
ONCE UPON A TEXAS TRAIN (TF)   CBS Entertainment, 1988
WHERE THE HELL'S THAT GOLD?!! (TF)   Willie Nelson
  Productions/Brigade Productions/Konigsberg-Sanitsky
  Company, 1988
BIG BAD JOHN   Magnum Entertainment, 1990
SUBURBAN COMMANDO   New Line Cinema, 1992

CHRIS KENNEDY
Contact: Australian Film Commission, 150 William Street,
  Woolloomooloo NSW 2011, Australia, tel.: 2/321-6444

THIS WON'T HURT A BIT!   Dendy Films, 1993, Australian

MICHAEL KENNEDY
b. 1954 - Prince Edward Island, Canada
Home: 614 Sweetwater Place, Port Credit, Ontario L5H 3Y8,
  Canada, 416/278-5830
Agent: Great North Artists Management, 350 Dupont Street,
  Toronto, Ontario M5R 1V9, Canada, 416/925-2051

CARIBE   Miramax Films, 1988, Canadian
ERIK   Miramax Films, 1989, Canadian
IN SEARCH OF ALEXANDER   SC Entertainment, 1991, Canadian
TALONS OF THE EAGLE   Shapiro Glickenhaus Entertainment,
  1992, Canadian
RED SCORPION 2   Northwood Pictures, 1994, Canadian
THE POSSESSION OF MICHAEL D. (TF)   Atlantis Films/
  Flashner-Gernon Productions/CTV, 1995, Canadian

TOM KENNEDY*
Contact: Directors Guild of America - Los Angeles, 213/851-3671

TIME WALKER   New World, 1983

DONALD KENT
Contact: Directors Guild of Canada, 225 Richmond Street, Toronto,
  Ontario M5V 1W2, Canada, 416/351-8200

EDEN RIVER   Saban Pictures, 1993, Canadian

GARY KENT
RAINY DAY FRIENDS   Powerdance Films, 1985

LARRY KENT
Contact: Directors Guild of Canada, 225 Richmond Street, Toronto,
  Ontario M5V 1W2, Canada, 416/351-8200

SLAVERS   Astral Communications, 1992, Canadian
MOTHERS AND DAUGHTERS   Palama Films, 1992, Canadian

FRANK KERR
Telephone: 617/925-9555

TRUE BLOOD   Fries Entertainment, 1989

IRVIN KERSHNER*
b. April 29, 1923 - Philadelphia, Pennsylvania
Agent: Writers & Artists Agency - Los Angeles, 310/824-6300
Attorney: Diane Golden, Silverberg, Katz, Thompson, Leon & Braun,
    11766 Wilshire Blvd. - Suite 700, Los Angeles, CA 90025,
    310/445-5800

STAKEOUT ON DOPE STREET   Warner Bros., 1958
THE YOUNG CAPTIVES   Paramount, 1959
THE HOODLUM PRIEST   United Artists, 1961
A FACE IN THE RAIN   Embassy, 1963
THE LUCK OF GINGER COFFEY   Continental, 1964, Canadian
A FINE MADNESS   Warner Bros., 1966
THE FLIM-FLAM MAN   20th Century-Fox, 1967
LOVING   Columbia, 1970
UP THE SANDBOX   National General, 1972
S*P*Y*S   20th Century-Fox, 1974, British-U.S.
THE RETURN OF A MAN CALLED HORSE   United Artists, 1976
RAIN ON ENTEBBE (TF) ☆   Edgar J. Scherick Associates/20th
    Century-Fox TV, 1977
EYES OF LAURA MARS   Columbia, 1978
THE EMPIRE STRIKES BACK   20th Century-Fox, 1980
NEVER SAY NEVER AGAIN   Warner Bros., 1983
TRAVELING MAN (CTF) ☆   HBO Pictures, 1989
ROBOCOP 2   Orion, 1990
SEAQUEST DSV (TF)   Amblin TV/Universal TV, 1993

ALEK KESHISHIAN
b. Lebanon
Agent: CAA - Beverly Hills, 310/288-4545
Personal Manager: Brillstein/Grey Entertainment - Beverly Hills,
    310/275-6135

TRUTH OR DARE (FCD)   Miramax Films, 1991
WITH HONORS   Warner Bros., 1994

BRUCE KESSLER*
b. March 23, 1936 - California
Home: 4335 Marina City Drive - Apt. 740, Marina del Rey,
    CA 90292, 310/823-2394

ANGELS FROM HELL   American International, 1968
KILLERS THREE   American International, 1968
THE GAY DECEIVERS   Fanfare, 1969
SIMON, KING OF WITCHES   Fanfare, 1971
MURDER IN PEYTON PLACE (TF)   20th Century-Fox TV, 1977
THE TWO-FIVE (TF)   Universal TV, 1978
DEATH MOON (TF)   Roger Gimbel Productions/EMI TV, 1978
CRUISE INTO TERROR (TF)   Aaron Spelling Productions, 1978

MICHAEL KEUSCH
b. 1955 - Calgary, Alberta, Canada
Home: 2014 N. Hoover Street, Los Angeles, CA 90027,
    213/665-8443
Agent: Gray/Goodman - Beverly Hills, 310/276-7070

ROMANTIC MANEUVERS (TF)   1983, Canadian
HACKER JOHN (TF)   1986, Canadian
LENA'S HOLIDAY   Prism Entertainment, 1991
NIGHT CLUB   Crown International, 1991
JUST ONE OF THE GIRLS (TF)   Entertainment Securities Ltd./
    Saban Entertainment/Neal and Gary Productions, 1993
HUCK & THE KING OF HEARTS   Crystal Sky Communications/
    Prism Pictures, 1993

MUSTAPHA KHAN
IMAGINING AMERICA (TF)   co-director with Ralph Bakshi,
    Matt Mahurin & Ed Lachman, Vanguard Films, 1989

MICHEL KHLEIFI
b. Palestine
Address: Place Brugman 33, B-1060 Brussels, Belgium

LA MEMOIRE FERTILE (FD)   1980, Belgian
WEDDING IN GALILEE   Kino International, 1987,
    Belgian-French-West German

CANTIQUE DES PIERRES   1991, Belgian-German
L'ORDRE DU JOUR   Sourat Films/Filmedia/Samsa Films, 1992,
    Belgian-Luxembourgian-French

ABBAS KIAROSTAMI
b. 1940 - Teheran, Iran
Contact: Department of Photography and Film Production,
    Ministry of Culture and Islamic Guidance, Baharestan Square,
    Teheran, Iran, tel.: 391333

THE TRAVELLER   1974, Iranian
THE REPORT   1978, Iranian
FIRST GRADERS   1986, Iranian
WHERE IS THE FRIEND'S HOME?   1987, Iranian
HOMEWORK   1989, Iranian
AND LIFE GOES ON...   Institute for the Intellectual Development
    of Children and Young Adults, 1992, Iranian
THROUGH THE OLIVE TREES   Miramax Films, 1994, Iranian

MICHAEL KIDD*
b. August 12, 1919 - Brooklyn, New York
Agent: William Morris Agency - New York City, 212/586-5100

MERRY ANDREW   MGM, 1958

BEEBAN KIDRON*
Contact: Cling Film/Jerry Ward, 10474 Santa Monica Blvd.,
    Los Angeles, CA 90025, 310/474-8254
Agent: UTA - Beverly Hills, 310/372-6700

ORANGES ARE NOT THE ONLY FRUIT (TF)   1990, British
ANTONIA AND JANE   Miramax Films, 1991, British,
    originally made for television
USED PEOPLE   20th Century Fox, 1992
GREAT MOMENTS IN AVIATION   Miramax Films, 1994,
    British-U.S.
TO WONG FOO, THANKS FOR EVERYTHING, JULIE NEWMAR
    Universal, 1995

FRITZ KIERSCH*
b. July, 1951 - Alpine, Texas
Agent: David Gersh, The Gersh Agency - Beverly Hills, 310/274-6611

CHILDREN OF THE CORN   New World, 1984
TUFF TURF   New World, 1985
WINNERS TAKE ALL   Apollo Pictures, 1987
UNDER THE BOARDWALK   New World, 1989
INTO THE SUN   Trimark Pictures, 1992
FATAL CHARM (CTF)   directed under pseudonym of Allen Smithee,
    Jonathan D. Krane/Bruce Cohn Curtis Productions, 1992
SHATTERED IMAGE (CTF)   Rysher Productions, 1994

KRZYSZTOF KIESLOWSKI
b. June 27, 1941 - Warsaw, Poland
Agent: ICM - Beverly Hills, 310/550-4000

PICTURE   1969, Polish
WORKERS   1972, Polish
FIRST LOVE   1974, Polish
PERSONNEL   1975, Polish
BIOGRAPHY   1975, Polish
SCAR   1976, Polish
POLITICS   1976, Polish
HOSPITAL   1977, Polish
CALM   1977, Polish
SEEN BY THE NIGHT PORTER   1978, Polish
STATION   1978, Polish
CAMERA BUFF   1979, Polish
TALKING HEADS   1980, Polish
A SHORT DAY'S WORK   1982, Polish, banned
NO END   New Yorker, 1984, Polish
BLIND CHANCE   1987, Polish, filmed in 1982
DEKALOG (MS)   Poltel/Sender Freies Berlin, 1988,
    Polish-West German
A SHORT FILM ABOUT KILLING   1988, Polish-West German
A SHORT FILM ABOUT LOVE   1988, Polish-West German

CITY LIFE (FD)   co-director, Nederlands Film Museum/
   International Art Film, 1990, Dutch
THE DOUBLE LIFE OF VERONIQUE   Miramax Films, 1991,
   French-Polish-Danish
BLUE   *TROIS COULEURS: BLEU*   Miramax Films, 1993,
   Swiss-French-Polish
WHITE   *TROIS COULEURS: BLANC*   Miramax Films, 1993,
   French-Swiss-Polish
RED   *TROIS COULEURS: ROUGE* ★   Miramax Films, 1994,
   French-Swiss-Polish

GERARD KIKOINE
Contact: British Film Commission, 70 Baker Street, London
   W1M 1DJ, England, tel.: 171/224-5000

DRAGONARD   Cannon, 1987, British
MASTER OF DRAGONARD HILL   Cannon, 1988, British
EDGE OF SANITY   Millimeter Films, 1989, British-Hungarian
BURIED ALIVE   21st Century Distribution, 1990,
   British-South African

J. DOUGLAS KILGORE
THE TRUST   Quadrangle Films, 1993

BRUCE KIMMEL*
b. December 8, 1947 - Los Angeles, California
Business: Bay Cities, 9336 W. Washington Blvd., Culver City,
   CA 90230, 310/559-0346

THE FIRST NUDIE MUSICAL   co-director with Mark Haggard,
   Paramount, 1976
SPACESHIP   *THE CREATURE WASN'T NICE*
   Almi Cinema 5, 1982

JOHN KINCADE
Contact: Writers Guild of America, West - Los Angeles, 310/550-1000

TERMINAL ENTRY   United Film Distribution, 1987
BACK TO BACK   Concorde, 1990

TIM KINCAID
ESCAPE FROM BAD GIRLS DORMITORY   Films Around
   the World, 1985
BREEDERS   Empire Pictures, 1986
MUTANT HUNT   Tycin Entertainment, 1986
ROBOT HOLOCAUST   Tycin Entertainment, 1987
THE OCCULTIST   Urban Classics, 1989
SHE'S BACK   Vestron, 1989

ALLAN KING
b. 1930 - Vancouver, British Columbia, Canada
Business: Allan King Associates Ltd., 965 Bay Street - Suite 2209,
   Toronto, Ontario M5S 2A3, Canada, 416/964-7284
Agent: Great North Artists Management Inc., 350 Dupont Street,
   Toronto, Ontario M5R 1V9, Canada, 416/925-2051

PEMBERTON VALLEY (FD)   CBC, 1957, Canadian
A MATTER OF PRIDE (FD)   CBC, 1961, Canadian
COMING OF AGE IN IBIZA   *RUNNING AWAY BACKWARDS* (FD)
   CBC, 1964, Canadian
WARRENDALE (FD)   Grove Press, 1968, Canadian
A MARRIED COUPLE (FD)   Aquarius, 1970, Canadian
COME ON CHILDREN (FD)   Allan King Associates,
   1972, Canadian
WHO HAS SEEN THE WIND   Astral Bellevue, 1977, Canadian
MARIA (TF)   CBC, 1977, Canadian
ONE-NIGHT STAND   Janus, 1978, Canadian
SILENCE OF THE NORTH   Universal, 1981, Canadian
READY FOR SLAUGHTER (TF)   CBC, 1983, Canadian
THE LAST SEASON (TF)   1986, Canadian
TERMINI STATION   Northern Arts Entertainment, 1989, Canadian
KURT VONNEGUT'S MONKEY HOUSE   *MONKEY HOUSE* (CTF)
   co-director with Paul Shapiro & Gilbert Shilton, Atlantis Films
   Ltd./Crescent Entertainment/Canwest Broadcasting Ltd.,
   1991, Canadian
BY WAY OF THE STARS (MS)   Sullivan Films/Beta-Taurus,
   1992, Canadian-German

CHRISTOPHER LLOYD KING
Agent: Seifert Dench Associates - London, tel.: 171/437-4551

SHOOT-OUT   Worldmark Productions, 1990, British
HEAD OVER HEELS (TF)   Carnival Films/Carlton, 1992, British
ANNA LEE: DUPE (TF)   Carnival Films/Granada LWT Productions,
   1994, British
ANNA LEE: DIVERSION (TF)   Carnival Films/Granada LWT
   Productions, 1994, British

RICK KING*
Home: 1007 Cedar Street, Santa Monica, CA 90405,
   310/399-9219
Agent: Jim Preminger Agency - Los Angeles, 310/475-9491

HARD CHOICES   Lorimar, 1986
HOTSHOT   International Film Marketing, 1987
THE KILLING TIME   New World, 1987
FORCED MARCH   A-Pix, 1989
PRAYER OF THE ROLLERBOYS   Castle Hill Productions, 1991,
   U.S.-Japanese
KICKBOXER III: THE ART OF WAR   Kings Road
   Entertainment, 1993
QUICK   Academy Entertainment, 1993
A PASSION TO KILL   A-Pix Entertainment, 1994

ROBERT LEE KING
Contact: Writers Guild of America, West - Los Angeles,
   310/550-1000

BOYS LIFE   co-director with Brian Sloan & Raoul O'Connell,
   Strand Rrleasing, 1994

STEPHEN KING
b. 1947 - Maine
Agent: CAA - Beverly Hills, 310/288-4545

MAXIMUM OVERDRIVE   DEG, 1986

ZALMAN KING*
Agent: William Morris Agency - Beverly Hills, 310/859-4000

WILDFIRE   Zupnick Enterprises/Jody Ann Productions, 1987
TWO MOON JUNCTION   Lorimar, 1988
WILD ORCHID   Triumph Releasing Corporation, 1990
WILD ORCHID 2: TWO SHADES OF BLUE   Triumph Releasing
   Corporation, 1992
RED SHOE DIARIES (CTF)   Saunders-King Productions, 1992
DELTA OF VENUS   Venus Productions, 1995

ALAN KINGSBERG
Agent: Scott Yoselow, The Gersh Agency - New York City,
   212/997-1818

ALMOST PARTNERS (TF)   South Carolina Educational
   TV Network, 1987

MARGY KINMONTH
Agent: ICM - London, tel.: 171/636-6565

TO THE WESTERN WORLD (TF)   Channel 4, 1981, British
FANTASY ISLAND (TF)   BBC, 1989, British
THE SOUTH BANK SHOW: STEVEN BERKOFF (TD)   London
   Weekend TV, 1989, British
NAKED HOLLYWOOD (TD)   BBC, 1990, British
THE SOUTH BANK SHOW: DAWN FRENCH (TD)   London
   Weekend TV, 1993, British

RICHARD KINON*
Contact: Directors Guild of America - Los Angeles, 310/851-3671

THE LOVE BOAT (TF)   co-director with Alan Myerson,
   Douglas S. Cramer Productions, 1976
THE NEW LOVE BOAT (TF)   Douglas S. Cramer Productions, 1977
ALOHA PARADISE (TF)   Aaron Spelling Productions, 1981

KEISUKE KINOSHITA

b. December 1912 - Hamamatsu, Shizuoka Prefecture, Japan
Contact: Nihon Eiga Kantoku Kyokai (Japan Film Directors
    Association), La Fontenu Building -4th Floor, 23-2 Maruyama-cho,
    Shibuya-ku, Tokyo, Japan, tel.: 3/3461-4411

THE BLOSSOMING PORT   Shochiku, 1943, Japanese
THE LIVING MAGOROKU   Shochiku, 1943, Japanese
JUBILATION STREET   Shochiku, 1944, Japanese
ARMY   Shochiku, 1944, Japanese
MORNING FOR THE OSONE FAMILY   Shochiku,
    1946, Japanese
THE GIRL I LOVED   Shochiku, 1946, Japanese
MARRIAGE   Shochiku, 1947, Japanese
PHOENIX   Shochiku, 1947, Japanese
WOMAN   Shochiku, 1948, Japanese
THE PORTRAIT   Shochiku, 1948, Japanese
APOSTASY   Shochiku, 1948, Japanese
A TOAST TO THE YOUNG MISS   *HERE'S TO THE GIRLS*
    Shochiku, 1949, Japanese
THE YOTSUYA GHOST STORY, PART I   Shochiku,
    1949, Japanese
THE YOTSUYA GHOST STORY, PART II   Shochiku,
    1949, Japanese
BROKEN DRUM   Shochiku, 1949, Japanese
ENGAGEMENT RING   Shochiku, 1950, Japanese
THE GOOD FAIRY   Shochiku, 1951, Japanese
CARMEN COMES HOME   Shochiku, 1951, Japanese
A RECORD OF YOUTH   Shochiku, 1951, Japanese
FIREWORKS OVER THE SEA   Shochiku, 1951, Japanese
CARMEN'S PURE LOVE   Shochiku, 1952, Japanese
A JAPANESE TRAGEDY   Shochiku, 1953, Japanese
THE GARDEN OF WOMEN   Shochiku, 1954, Japanese
TWENTY-FOUR EYES   Shochiku, 1954, Japanese
DISTANT CLOUDS   Shochiku, 1955, Japanese
YOU WERE LIKE A WILD CHRYSANTHEMUM   Shochiku,
    1955, Japanese
CLOUDS AT TWILIGHT   Shochiku, 1956, JapaneseK O B A
THE ROSE ON HIS ARM   Shochiku, 1956, Japanese
TIMES OF JOY AND SORROW   *THE LIGHTHOUSE*   Shochiku,
    1957, Japanese
A CANDLE IN THE WIND   *DANGER STALKS NEAR*   Shochiku,
    1957, Japanese
THE BALLAD OF NARAYAMA   Shochiku, 1958, Japanese
THE ETERNAL RAINBOW   Shochiku, 1958, Japanese
SNOW FLURRY   Shochiku, 1959, Japanese
THE BIRD OF SPRINGS PAST   Shochiku, 1959, Japanese
THUS ANOTHER DAY   Shochiku, 1959, Japanese
SPRING DREAMS   Shochiku, 1960, Japanese
THE RIVER FUEFUKI   Shochiku, 1960, Japanese
THE BITTER SPIRIT   *IMMORTAL LOVE*   Shochiku,
    1961, Japanese
THIS YEAR'S LOVE   Shochiku, 1962, Japanese
THE SEASONS WE WALKED TOGETHER   Shochiku,
    1962, Japanese
SING, YOUNG PEOPLE!   Shochiku, 1963, Japanese
LEGEND OF A DUEL TO THE DEATH   *A LEGEND, OR WAS IT?*
    Shochiku, 1963, Japanese
THE SCENT OF INCENSE   Shochiku, 1964, Japanese
LOVELY FLUTE AND DRUM   Toho, 1967, Japanese
LOVE AND SEPARATION IN SRI LANKA   Toho,
    1976, Japanese
THE IMPULSE MURDER OF MY SON   Shochiku-Tokyo
    Broadcasting, 1979, Japanese
PARENTS, AWAKE!   Shochiku, 1980, Japanese
LEAVING THESE CHILDREN BEHIND   Shochiku-Hori Kikaku,
    1983, Japanese
TIMES OF JOY AND SORROW   Shochiku/Tokyo Hoso/Hakuhodo,
    1986, Japanese
FATHER   Shochiku, 1988, Japanese

ROBERT KIRK*

Address: 9016 Wilshire Blvd. - Suite 417, Beverly Hills, CA 90211,
    310/550-8687

DESTROYER   Moviestore Entertainment, 1988

EPHRAIM KISHON

Contact: Israel Film Centre, Ministry of Industry & Trade,
    30 Agron Street, P.O. Box 299, 94190 Jerusalem, Israel,
    tel.: 972/210433 or 210297

SALLAH   Palisades International, 1963, Israeli
THE BIG DIG   Canal, 1969, Israeli
THE POLICEMAN   Cinema 5, 1972, Israeli
ERVINKA   1974, Israeli
FOX IN THE CHICKEN COOP   Hashu'alim Ltd., 1978, Israeli
THE MARRIAGE CONTRACT (TF)   1983, West German

TAKESHI KITANO
(Beat Takeshi)

b. 1948 - Tokyo, Japan
Business: Office Kitano, Toredo Akasaka Building - 6th Floor,
    5-4-14 Akasaka, Minato-ku, Tokyo, Japan, tel.: 3/3588-8121

VIOLENT COP   *I WARN YOU THIS MAN IS REALLY VIOLENT*
    Shochiku, 1989, Japanese
3 - 4 X OCTOBER   Shochiku/Bandai Visual, 1990, Japanese
THE SILENT SEA IN THE SUMMER   Kitano Film Office/Totsu,
    1991, Japanese
SONATINE   Shochiku/Bandai Visual, 1993, Japanese
GETTING ANY?   Office Kitano/BandiaiVisual/Right Vision,
    1994, Japanese

R.J. KIZER

b. September 27, 1952 - Long Island City, New York
Home: P.O. Box 668, Hollywood, CA 90078, 213/469-3321

GODZILLA 1985   co-director with Kohji Yamamoto, New World,
    1985, Japanese-U.S.
HELL COMES TO FROGTOWN   co-director with Donald G. Jackson,
    New World, 1987
DEATH RING   Trans Atlantic Entertainment, 1992

ROBERT KLANE*

Agent: William Morris Agency - Beverly Hills, 310/859-4000

THANK GOD IT'S FRIDAY   Columbia, 1978
WEEKEND AT BERNIE'S II   TriStar, 1993
THE ODD COUPLE (TF)   Howard W. Koch Productions/Paramount
    Network TV, 1993

RICK KLASS

ELLIOT FAUMAN, Ph.D.   Taurus Entertainment, 1990

DAMIAN KLAUS

FUTURE KICK   Concorde, 1991

DENNIS KLEIN*

Agent: UTA - Beverly Hills, 310/273-6700

ONE MORE SATURDAY NIGHT   Columbia, 1986

JONATHAN KLEIN

Agent: ICM - Beverly Hills, 310/550-4000

BEFORE YOUR EYES: A HEART FOR OLIVIA   *A HEART FOR
    OLIVIA* (TD)   CBS News, 1995

KI

**FILM
DIRECTORS**
GUIDE

F
I
L
M

D
I
R
E
C
T
O
R
S

KI

**F
I
L
M

D
I
R
E
C
T
O
R
S**

WILLIAM KLEIN
b. 1926 - New York, New York
Address: 5, rue de Medicis, 75006 Paris, France, tel.: 1/43-26-93-76

QUI ETES-VOUS POLLY MAGGOO?   1966, French
FAR FROM VIETNAM (FD)   co-director with Jean-Luc Godard,
    Joris Ivens, Alain Resnais & Agnes Varda, New Yorker,
    1967, French
MISTER FREEDOM   1969, French
FLOAT LIKE A BUTTERFLY - STING LIKE A BEE (FD)
    Delpire Advico/Films Paris-New York, 1969, French
FESTIVAL PANAFRICAIN (FD)   1969, French
ELDRIDGE CLEAVER (FD)   1970, French
LE COUPLE TEMOIN   Planfilm, 1977, French
THE FRENCH (FD)   AAA, 1981, French
MODE IN FRANCE (FD)   KVIV Productions, 1985, French

RANDAL KLEISER*
b. July 20, 1946
Business: Randal Kleiser Productions, 3050 Runyon Canyon Road,
    Los Angeles, CA 90046, 213/851-5224
Agent: ICM - Beverly Hills, 310/550-4000

ALL TOGETHER NOW (TF)   RSO Films, 1975
DAWN: PORTRAIT OF A TEENAGE RUNAWAY (TF)
    Douglas S. Cramer Productions, 1976
THE BOY IN THE PLASTIC BUBBLE (TF)   Spelling-Goldberg
    Productions, 1976
THE GATHERING (TF) ☆   Hanna-Barbera Productions, 1977
GREASE   Paramount, 1978
THE BLUE LAGOON   Columbia, 1980
SUMMER LOVERS   Filmways, 1982
GRANDVIEW, U.S.A.   Warner Bros., 1984
FLIGHT OF THE NAVIGATOR   Buena Vista, 1986
BIG TOP PEE-WEE   Paramount, 1988
GETTING IT RIGHT   MCEG, 1989, U.S.-British
WHITE FANG   Buena Vista, 1991
HONEY, I BLEW UP THE KID   Buena Vista, 1992
IT'S MY PARTY   Opala Films, 1995

WALTER KLENHARD
Agent: Paradigm - Los Angeles, 310/277-4400

THE HAUNTING OF SEACLIFF INN (CTF)   May Day
    Productions/MTE, 1994

RICHARD KLETTER*
Contact: Directors Guild of America - Los Angeles, 213/851-3671

THE TOWER (TF)   Catalina Production Group/FNM Films, 1993
BIG DOGS   Chanticleer Films, 1994, Canadian

MAX J. KLEVEN*
Home: 2.2 Ranch, 33150 Barber Road, Agua Dulce, CA 91350,
    805/268-1681

RUCKUS   International Vision Productions, 1982
THE NIGHT STALKER   PSO, 1987
BORDER HEAT   MCEG, 1988
W.B., BLUE AND THE BEAN   The Movie Group, 1988

ELEM KLIMOV
b. 1933 - Volgograd, U.S.S.R.
Contact: Confederation of Film-Makers Unions, Vasilyevskaya
    Street 13, 123 825 Moscow, Russia, tel.: 095/250-4114

WELCOME, OR NO ENTRY FOR UNAUTHORIZED PERSONS
    1964, Soviet
ADVENTURES OF A DENTIST   1965, Soviet
SPORT, SPORT, SPORT   1971, Soviet
AND NONETHELESS I BELIEVE   co-director, 1974, Soviet
LARISSA (FD)   1980, Soviet
RASPUTIN   *AGONIYA*   International Film Exchange, 1982, Soviet
FAREWELL TO MATYORA   International Film Exchange,
    1982, Soviet
COME AND SEE   International Film Exchange, 1985, Soviet

HERBERT KLINE*
b. March 13, 1909 - Chicago, Illinois
Home: 128 S. Kilkea Drive, Los Angeles, CA 90046, 213/651-2289
    or: Nell Gwynn House, Sloane Avenue, London SW3 3AX,
    England, tel.: 171/581-2559

CRISIS (FD)   1938
LIGHTS OUT IN EUROPE (FD)   1939
THE FORGOTTEN VILLAGE (FD)   1941
MY FATHER'S HOUSE (FD)   Mayer-Burstyn, 1946
THE KID FROM CLEVELAND   Republic, 1949
THE FIGHTER   United Artists, 1951
JACK LONDON'S TALES OF ADVENTURE (TF)   1952
WALLS OF FIRE (FD)   Mentor Productions, 1974
THE CHALLENGE: A TRIBUTE TO MODERN ART (FD)
    New Line Cinema, 1975
ACTING: LEE STRASBERG AND THE ACTORS STUDIO (FD)
    Davada Enterprises, 1981
GREAT THEATRES OF THE WORLD (FD)   1987

STEVE KLOVES*
Agent: UTA - Beverly Hills, 310/273-6700

THE FABULOUS BAKER BOYS   20th Century Fox, 1989
FLESH AND BONE   Paramount, 1993

ALEXANDER KLUGE
b. 1932 - Halbertstadt, Harz, Germany
Address: Elisabethstrasse 38, 8000 Munich 40, Germany
Contact: Federal Union of Film and Television Directors in Germany,
    Adelheidstrasse 7, 8000 Munich 40, Germany, tel.: 089/271-6380

ABSCHIED VON GESTERN   1966, West German
DIE ARTISTEN IN DER ZIRKUSKUPPEL: RATLOS
    1968, West German
WILLI TOBLER UND DER UNTERGANG DER 6 FLOTTE
    1970, West German
DER GROSSE VERHAU   1971, West German
GELEGENHEITSARBEIT EINER SKLAVIN   1974, West German
IN GEFAHR GROSSTER NOT BRINGT DER MITTELWEG DEN TOD
    1975, West German
DER STARKE FERDINAND   1976, West German
DIE MENSCHEN, DIE STAUFAUER - AUSTELLUNG
    VORBEREITEN   1977, West German
ZU BOSER SCHLACHT SCHLEICH ICH HEUT NACHT SO BANG
    1977, West German
DEUTSCHLAND IM HERBST (FD)   co-director,
    1978, West German
DIE PATRIOTIN   1979, West German
DER KANDIDAT   1980, West German
KRIEG UND FRIEDEN   1982, West German
DIE MACHT DER GEFUHLE   1983, West German
DER ANGRIFF DER GEGENWART AUF DIE UBRIGE ZEIT
    1985, West German
VERMISCHTE NACHRICHTEN   1986, West German

ROBERT KNIGHTS
b. 1942
Address: 49 Whitehall Park, London N19 3YW, England
Agent: ICM - London, tel.: 171/636-6565

A BIT OF SINGING AND DANCING (TF)   Granada TV/
    WGBH-Boston, 1981, British-U.S.
THE EBONY TOWER (TF)   Granada TV, 1984, British
TENDER IS THE NIGHT (CMS)   Showtime/BBC/Seven Network,
    1985, U.S.- British-Australian
THE GLITTERING PRIZES (TF)   BBC, 1986, British
PORTERHOUSE BLUE (MS)   Picture Partnership Productions/
    Channel 4, 1987, British
THE OLD JEST (TF)   Lawson Productions/Television South,
    1988, British
THE DAWNING (TF)   TVS Entertainment/Vista Organization,
    1988, British
AND A NIGHTINGALE SANG (TF)   Portman Productions/Tyne
    Tees TV, 1988, British

DOUBLE VISION   Cameras Contentales/Steve Walsh Productions,
   1992, French-British
THE GOVERNOR   co-director with Alan Dossor & Bob Mahoney,
   La Plante Productions/Samson Films, 1995, British

MASAKI KOBAYASHI
b. February 14, 1916 - Otaru City, Hokkaido, Japan
Contact: Nihon Eiga Kantoku Kyokai (Japan Film Directors
   Association), La Fontenu Building -4th Floor, 23-2 Maruyama-cho,
   Shibuya-ku, Tokyo, Japan, tel.: 3/3461-4411

MY SONS' YOUTH   Shochiku, 1952, Japanese
SINCERITY   Shochiku, 1953, Japanese
THE THICK-WALLED ROOM   Shinei Productions/Shochiku,
   1953, Japanese
THREE LOVES   Shochiku, 1954, Japanese
SOMEWHERE UNDER THE BROAD SKY   Shochiku,
   1954, Japanese
BEAUTIFUL DAYS   Shochiku, 1955, Japanese
THE SPRING   Shochiku, 1956, Japanese
I'LL BUY YOU   Shochiku, 1956, Japanese
BLACK RIVER   Shochiku, 1957, Japanese
THE HUMAN CONDITION, PART I: NO GREATER LOVE
   Kabukiza/Ninjin Club/Shochiku, 1959, Japanese
THE HUMAN CONDITION, PART II: ROAD TO ETERNITY
   Ninjin Productions/Shochiku, 1959, Japanese
THE HUMAN CONDITION, PART III: A SOLDIER'S PRAYER
   Shochiku/Ninjin Club, 1961, Japanese
THE INHERITANCE THE ENTANGLEMENT   Bungei
   Productions/Ninjin ClubShochiku, 1962, Japanese
HARAKIRI SEPPUKU   Shochiku, 1962, Japanese
KWAIDAN   Ninjin Club/Toho, 1964, Japanese
REBELLION SAMURAI REBELLION   Mifune Productions/Toho,
   1967, Japanese
HYMN TO A TIRED MAN THE YOUTH OF JAPAN   Tokyo Eiga/
   Toho, 1968, Japanese
INN OF EVIL   Haiyuza Eiga Hoso/Toho, 1971, Japanese
KASEKI FOSSILS (MS)   Haiyuza Eiga Hoso/Yonki no Kai/Fuji TV,
   1975, Japanese
FIERY AUTUMN   Mitsukoshi-Toho/Toho, 1978, Japanese
THE TOKYO TRIALS (FD)   Kodansha Ltd.,/Toho-Towa,
   1983, Japanese
THE EMPTY TABLE   Marugen/Herald Ace, 1985, Japanese

HOWARD W. KOCH*
b. April 11, 1916 - New York, New York
Business: Aries Films, Inc., Paramount Pictures, 5555 Melrose
   Avenue, Los Angeles, CA 90038, 213/956-5000

SHIELD FOR MURDER   co-director with Edmond O'Brien,
   United Artists, 1954
BIG HOUSE, U.S.A.   United Artists, 1955
UNTAMED YOUTH   Warner Bros., 1957
BOP GIRL   United Artists, 1957
JUNGLE HEAT   United Artists, 1957
THE GIRL IN BLACK STOCKINGS   United Artists, 1957
FORT BOWIE   United Artists, 1958
VIOLENT ROAD   Warner Bros., 1958
FRANKENSTEIN - 1970   Allied Artists, 1958
ANDY HARDY COMES HOME   MGM, 1958
THE LAST MILE   United Artists, 1959
BORN RECKLESS   Warner Bros., 1959
BADGE 373   Paramount, 1973

PHILLIP KOCH
PINK NIGHTS   Koch-Marschall Productions, 1991, filmed in 1987

OJA KODAR
Attorney: Myron Meisel, 3264 Ellenda Avenue, Los Angeles,
   CA 90034, 310/474-5346

JADED   Olpal Productions, 1989
A TIME FOR...   RAI/Ellepi Film/Jadran Studios of Croatia,
   1993, Italian-Croatian

HANNAH KODICEK
Address: 9b The Orchard, London SE3 0QS, England,
   tel.: 181/318-1458
Agent: Janet Fillingham - London, tel.: 181/392-9818

A PIN FOR THE BUTTERFLY   Heureka Film Prague/Channel 4/
   Skreba Film, 1994, Czech-British

PANCHO KOHNER
b. January 7, 1939 - Los Angeles, California
Agent: Paul Kohner, Inc. - Los Angeles, 310/550-1060

THE BRIDGE IN THE JUNGLE   United Artists, 1971, Mexican
MR. SYCAMORE   Film Ventures International, 1975

WINRICH KOLBE*
Agent: Ronald Leif, Contemporary Artists - Santa Monica,
   310/395-1800

STAR TREK: THE NEXT GENERATION - ALL GOOD THINGS (TF)
   Paramount TV, 1994
STAR TREK: VOYAGER (TF)   Paramount Network TV, 1995

AMOS KOLLEK
b. Israel
Contact: Israel Film Centre, Ministry of Industry & Trade,
   30 Agron Street, P.O. Box 299, 94190 Jerusalem, Israel,
   tel.: 972/210433 or 210297

WORLDS APART   1980, Israeli
GOODBYE NEW YORK   Castle Hill Productions, 1985, U.S.-Israeli
FOREVER, LULU   TriStar, 1987
HIGH STAKES   Vidmark Entertainment, 1989
THREE WEEKS IN JERUSALEM   1991, Israeli
DOUBLE EDGE   Castle Hill Productions, 1992, U.S.-Israeli

XAVIER KOLLER*
Agent: ICM - Beverly Hills, 310/550-4000

JOURNEY OF HOPE   Miramax Films, 1990, Swiss-Italian-German
SQUANTO: A WARRIOR'S TALE   Buena Vista, 1994

JAMES KOMACK*
b. August 3, 1930 - New York, New York
Agent: Paradigm - Los Angeles, 310/277-4400
Business Manager: Marvin "Dusty" Snyder, J.P.M., 760 N. La Cienega
   Blvd., Los Angeles, CA 90069, 213/652-0222

PORKY'S REVENGE   20th Century Fox, 1985, U.S.-Canadian

ANDREI KONCHALOVSKY*
(Andrei Mikhalkov-Konchalovsky)
b. August 20, 1937 - U.S.S.R.
Agent: CAA - Beverly Hills, 310/288-4545
Business Manager: Oberman, Tivoli & Miller, 500 S. Sepulveda Blvd. -
   Suite 500, Los Angeles, CA 90049, 310/471-9338

A BOY AND A PIGEON   Mosfilm, 1960, Soviet
THE FIRST TEACHER   Mosfilm/Kirghizfilm, 1965, Soviet
ASYA'S HAPPINESS   Mosfilm, 1967, Soviet
A NEST OF GENTRY   Corinth, 1969, Soviet
UNCLE VANYA   Mosfilm, 1971, Soviet
A LOVER'S ROMANCE   Mosfilm, 1974, Soviet
SIBERIADE   IFEX Film, 1979, Soviet
MARIA'S LOVERS   Cannon, 1984
RUNAWAY TRAIN   Cannon, 1985
DUET FOR ONE   Cannon, 1986
SHY PEOPLE   Cannon, 1987
HOMER AND EDDIE   Skouras Pictures, 1989
TANGO & CASH   Warner Bros., 1989
THE INNER CIRCLE   Columbia, 1991, Italian-Soviet
RYABA, MY CHICKEN   Parimedia/Russian Roulette/Centre
   Nationale de la Cinematographie/Films Committee/Canal Plus,
   1994, Russian-French

Ko

F
I
L
M

D
I
R
E
C
T
O
R
S

JACKIE KONG
Business: TVF Inc. Production Office, 3021 Airport Avenue -
    Suite #101-D, Santa Monica, CA 90405, 310/390-0820
Attorney: Jay Kenoff, Esq. - Los Angeles, 310/552-0808

THE BEING   BFV Films, 1983
NIGHT PATROL   New World, 1984
BLOOD DINER   Vestron, 1987
THE UNDERACHIEVERS   Lightning Pictures, 1988

DAN KOONTZ
TERRORIST WITHOUT A CAUSE   KEG Films, 1994

BARBARA KOPPLE*
b. Scarsdale, New York
Business: Cabin Creek Films, 58 East 11th Street, New York,
    NY 10003, 212/533-7157
Agent: William Morris Agency - Beverly Hills, 310/859-4000

HARLAN COUNTY, U.S.A. (FD)   Cabin Creek Films, 1976
KEEPING ON   Many Mansions Institute, 1983
AMERICAN DREAM (FD)   Cabin Creek Films, 1992
A CENTURY OF WOMEN (MS)   co-director with Sylvia Morales,
    Turner Broadcasting System, 1994
WOODSTOCK '94 (FCD)   Polygram/Propaganda Films, 1995

JOHN KORTY*
b. July 22, 1936 - Lafayette, Indiana
Business: Korty Films, Inc., 1001 Bridgeway - Suite 247,
    Sausalito, CA 94965, 415/332-5246
Agent: Richland/Wunsch/Hohman Agency - Los Angeles,
    310/278-1955

CRAZY QUILT   Farallon, 1965
FUNNYMAN   New Yorker, 1967
RIVERRUN   Columbia, 1970
THE PEOPLE (TF)   Metromedia Productions/American
    Zoetrope, 1972
GO ASK ALICE (TF)   Metromedia Productions, 1973
CLASS OF '63 (TF)   Metromedia Productions/Stonehenge
    Productions, 1973
SILENCE   Cinema Financial of America, 1974
THE AUTOBIOGRAPHY OF MISS JANE PITTMAN (TF) ☆☆
    Tomorrow Entertainment, 1974
THE MUSIC SCHOOL (TF)   Learning in Focus, 1975
ALEX & THE GYPSY   20th Century-Fox, 1976
FAREWELL TO MANZANAR (TF)   Korty Films/Universal TV, 1976
WHO ARE THE DE BOLTS? ...AND WHERE DID THEY
    GET 19 KIDS? (FD)   Pyramid Films, 1977
FOREVER (TF)   Roger Gimbel Productions/EMI TV, 1978
OLIVER'S STORY   Paramount, 1979
A CHRISTMAS WITHOUT SNOW (TF)   Korty Films/The
    Konigsberg Company, 1980
TWICE UPON A TIME (AF)   co-director with Charles Swenson,
    The Ladd Company/Warner Bros., 1983
THE HAUNTING PASSION (TF)   BSR Productions/ITC, 1983
SECOND SIGHT: A LOVE STORY (TF)   Entheos Unlimited
    Productions/T.T.C. Enterprises, 1984
THE EWOK ADVENTURE (TF)   Lucasfilm Ltd./Korty Films, 1984
A DEADLY BUSINESS (TF)   Thebaut-Frey Productions/Taft
    Entertainment TV, 1986
RESTING PLACE (TF) ☆   Marian Rees Associates, 1986
BABY GIRL SCOTT (TF)   Polson Company Productions/The
    Finnegan-Pinchuk Company, 1987
EYE ON THE SPARROW (TF)   Sarabande Productions/
    Republic Pictures, 1987
WINNIE (TF)   All Girls Productions/NBC Productions, 1988
CAST THE FIRST STONE (TF)   Mench Productions/
    Columbia TV, 1989
A SON'S PROMISE (TF)   Marian Rees Associates, 1990
LINE OF FIRE: THE MORRIS DEES STORY (TF)   BoJames
    Entertainment/Papazian-Hirsch Productions, 1991
LONG ROAD HOME (TF)   Rosemont Productions, 1991
KEEPING SECRETS (TF)   Freyda Rothstein Productions/
    Hamel-Somers Productions/Finnegan-Pinchuk Productions, 1991
DEADLY MATRIMONY (TF)   Steve Krantz Productions/Multimedia
    TV Productions, 1992

THEY (CTF)   Bridget Terry Productions/Viacom Productions, 1993
GETTING OUT (TF)   Dorothea G. Petrie Productions/Signboard Hill
    Productions/RHI Entertainment, 1994
REDWOOD CURTAIN (TF)   Chris-Rose Productions, 1995

WALDEMAR KORZENIOWSKY
THE CHAIR   Angelika Films, 1987

PETER KOSMINSKY
Agent: ICM - Beverly Hills, 310/550-4000 or:
    Peters Fraser & Dunlop - London, tel.: 171/344-1000

EMILY BRONTE'S WUTHERING HEIGHTS   *WUTHERING HEIGHTS*
    Paramount, 1992, British

TOM KOTANI
THE LAST DINOSAUR (TF)   co-director with Alex Grasshoff,
    Rankin-Bass Productions, 1977, U.S.-Japanese
THE BERMUDA DEPTHS (TF)   Rankin-Bass Productions, 1978
THE IVORY APE (TF)   Rankin-Bass Productions, 1980,
    U.S.-Japanese
THE BUSHIDO BLADE   Aquarius, 1982, U.S.-Japanese

TED KOTCHEFF*
(William T. Kotcheff)
b. April 7, 1931 - Toronto, Ontario, Canada
Agent: ICM - Beverly Hills, 310/550-4000

TIARA TAHITI   Zenith International, 1962, British
LIFE AT THE TOP   Columbia, 1965, British
TWO GENTLEMEN SHARING   American International,
    1969, British
OUTBACK   *WAKE IN FRIGHT*   United Artists, 1971, Australian
BILLY TWO HATS   United Artists, 1972, British
THE APPRENTICESHIP OF DUDDY KRAVITZ   Paramount,
    1974, Canadian
FUN WITH DICK & JANE   Columbia, 1977
WHO IS KILLING THE GREAT CHEFS OF EUROPE?   Warner
    Bros., 1978
NORTH DALLAS FORTY   Paramount, 1979
SPLIT IMAGE   Orion, 1982
FIRST BLOOD   Orion, 1982, Canadian
UNCOMMON VALOR   Paramount, 1983
JOSHUA THEN AND NOW   20th Century Fox, 1985, Canadian
SWITCHING CHANNELS   Columbia, 1988
WINTER PEOPLE   Columbia, 1989
WEEKEND AT BERNIE'S   20th Century Fox, 1989
FOLKS!   20th Century Fox, 1992
THE SHOOTER   Adelson-Baumgarten Productions/Muraglia-Saldek
    Films/Newmarket Capitol Group, 1995, U.S.-Czech

YAPHET KOTTO
b. November 15, 1937 - New York, New York
Agent: Metropolitan Talent Agency - Beverly Hills, 213/857-4500

THE LIMIT   *TIME LIMIT/SPEED LIMIT 65*   Cannon, 1972
NIGHTMARES OF THE DEVIL   Edgewood Productions, 1988

JIM KOUF
Business: Kouf-Bigelow Productions, 500 S. Buena Vista Street -
    Animation Building 1A11, Burbank, CA 91521, 818/560-5103
Agent: ICM - Beverly Hills, 310/550-4000

MIRACLES   Orion, 1986
DISORGANIZED CRIME   Buena Vista, 1989

VICHIT KOUNAVUDHI
b. 1922 - Chachoengsao Province, Thailand
Contact: Thailand Film Promotion Center, 599 Bumrung Muang
    Road, Bangkok 10100, Thailand, tel.: 2/223-4690

PHALEESAU   1954, Thai
MUE JOAN   1960, Thai
MIA LUANG   Five Star Productions, 1979, Thai
MOUNTAIN PEOPLE   *KHON PHOO KHAO*   Five Star Productions,
    1979, Thai

SON OF THE NORTH-EAST *LOOK E-SARN* Five Star
   Productions, 1982, Thai
THE HOUSEBOAT *RUEN PAE* Five Star Productions,
   1989, Thai

STEVEN KOVACS
'68 New World, 1988

BERNARD L. KOWALSKI*
August 2, 1929 - Brownsville, Texas
Agent: Irv Schechter Company - Beverly Hills, 310/278-8070

HOT CAR GIRL Allied Artists, 1958
NIGHT OF THE BLOOD BEAST American International, 1958
THE GIANT LEECHES American International, 1959
BLOOD AND STEEL 20th Century-Fox, 1959
KRAKATOA, EAST OF JAVA Cinerama Releasing
   Corporation, 1969
STILETTO Avco Embassy, 1969
MACHO CALLAHAN Avco Embassy, 1970
HUNTERS ARE FOR KILLING (TF) Cinema Center, 1970
TERROR IN THE SKY (TF) Paramount TV, 1971
BLACK NOON (TF) Fenady Associates/Screen Gems, 1971
WOMEN IN CHAINS (TF) Paramount TV, 1972
TWO FOR THE MONEY (TF) Aaron Spelling Productions, 1972
THE WOMAN HUNTER (TF) Bing Crosby Productions, 1972
SHE CRIED MURDER (TF) 1973
Sssssss Universal, 1973
IN TANDEM (TF) D'Antoni Productions, 1974
FLIGHT TO HOLOCAUST (TF) Aycee Productions/
   First Artists, 1977
THE NATIVITY (TF) D'Angelo-Bullock-Allen Productions/
   20th Century-Fox TV, 1978
MARCIANO (TF) ABC Circle Films, 1979
B.A.D. CATS (TF) Aaron Spelling Productions, 1980
TURNOVER SMITH (TF) Wellington Productions, 1980
NIGHTSIDE (TF) Stephen J. Cannell Productions/Glen A. Larson
   Productions/Universal TV, 1980
MIRACLE AT BEEKMAN'S PLACE (TF) Em/BE Productions, 1988
NASHVILLE BEAT (CTF) Buck Productions/RDK Productions/
   NAC Productions, 1989

SOREN KRAGH-JACOBSEN
b. March 2, 1947 - Copenhagen, Denmark
Home: Overgaden Oven Vandet 22, DK-1415 Copenhagen K,
   Denmark, tel.: 31/952333
Contact: Danish Film Institute, Store Sondervoldsstraede 4,
   DK-1419 Copenhagen K, Denmark, tel.: 31-57-65-00

VIL DU SE MIN SMUKKE NAVLE *YOU WANNA SEE MY
   BEAUTIFUL NAVEL* Sten Herdel, 1978, Danish
FARVEL LULOU *FAREWELL LULOU* (TF) DR-TV, 1979, Danish
GUMMITARZAN *RUBBER TARZAN* Sten Herdel, 1980, Danish
ISFUGLE *THUNDERBIRDS* Metronome, 1983, Danish
LIVET ER EN GOD GRUND *LIFE IS A GOOD REASON* (TF)
   DR-TV, 1985, Danish
GULOREGN *A SHOWER OF GOLD* Metronome, 1986, Danish
SKYGGEN AF EMMA *EMMA'S SHADOW* Metronome,
   1987, Danish
DRENGENE FRA SANKT PETRI *THE BOYS FROM ST. PETRI*
   Metronome/Swedish Film Institute/Norwegian Film/Kinofinlandia/
   Kvikmyndasjodur/Danish Film Institute/DR-FI/Nordic Film & TV
   Foundation, 1991, Danish-Swedish-Norwegian-Finnish-Icelandic

JULIAN KRAININ*
b. January 24, 1941 - New York, New York
Home: 8 Century Road, Palisades, NY 10964, 914/359-0445

THE RELUCTANT REVOLUTION (TD) Westinghouse
   Television, 1968
THE OTHER AMERICANS (TD) Westinghouse Television, 1969
ART IS... (FD) Henry Strauss Associates, 1971
OCEANS, THE SILENT CRISIS (TD) ABC-TV, 1972
PRINCETON (FD) Krainin-Sage Productions, 1973
TO AMERICA (TF) CBS Entertainment, 1976
THE WORLD OF JAMES MICHENER: HAWAII (FD)
   Reader's Digest Films, 1977

THE WORLD OF JAMES MICHENER: THE END OF EDEN! (FD)
   Reader's Digest Films, 1978
DON'T TOUCH THAT DIAL! (TD) CBS-TV, 1983
CIVILIZATION AND THE JEWS (TD) co-director with
   Eugene Marner, PBS, 1984
VERDICT: THE WRONG MAN (CTD) HBO, 1986

JERRY KRAMER*
Address: 730 Arizona Avenue - 2nd Floor, Santa Monica, CA 90401,
   310/394-6852

MODERN GIRLS Atlantic Releasing Corporation, 1986
MOONWALKER (FCD) co-director with Colin Chilvers,
   Warner Bros., 1988
INFLUENCES: JAMES BROWN AND M.C. HAMMER (CTD)
   Delilah Music Pictures, 1991
VIVA VIETNAM: A WHITE TRASH ADVENTURE TOUR (CTD)
   Visualize Studio/Comedy Central, 1995

ROBERT KRAMER
b. June, 1939 - New York, New York
Agent: M.-Cl. de la Motte, 10, rue de Cheroy, 75017 Paris, France,
   tel.: 1/42-94-08-22
Contact: French Film Office, 745 Fifth Avenue, New York,
   NY 10151, 212/832-8860

FALN (FD) 1965
IN THE COUNTRY Newsreel, 1968
THE EDGE Film-Makers, 1968
PEOPLE'S WAR (FD) co-director, Newsreel, 1969
ICE New Yorker, 1970
MILESTONES co-director with John Douglas, Stone, 1975
SCENES FROM THE PORTUGUESE CLASS
   STRUGGLE (FD) 1977
GUNS S.N.D., 1980, French
BIRTH 1982, French
A TOUT ALLURE INA, 1982, French
UNSER NAZI Cannon International, 1984, West German-French
DIESEL Distributeurs Associes, 1985, French
ACROSS THE HEART Films du Passage/Garance, 1987, French
DOC'S KINGDOM Garance/Filmargem, 1988, French-Portuguese
CONTRE L'OUBLI co-director, Les Films du Paradoxe/Amnesty
   International/PRV, 1992, French
STARTING PLACES/POINT DE DEPART (FD) Film D'Ici/Ruben
   Korenfeld/Richard Copans Productions, 1993, French

STANLEY KRAMER*
b. September 29, 1913 - New York, New York
Contact: P.O. Box 4613, Valley Village, CA 91617, 818/760-3106

NOT AS A STRANGER United Artists, 1955
THE PRIDE AND THE PASSION United Artists, 1957
THE DEFIANT ONES ★ United Artists, 1958
ON THE BEACH United Artists, 1959
INHERIT THE WIND United Artists, 1960
JUDGMENT AT NUREMBERG ★ United Artists, 1961
IT'S A MAD, MAD, MAD, MAD WORLD United Artists, 1963
SHIP OF FOOLS Columbia, 1965
GUESS WHO'S COMING TO DINNER ★ Columbia, 1967
THE SECRET OF SANTA VITTORIA United Artists, 1969
R.P.M.* Columbia, 1970
BLESS THE BEASTS & CHILDREN Columbia, 1971
OKLAHOMA CRUDE Columbia, 1973
THE DOMINO PRINCIPLE Avco Embassy, 1977
THE RUNNER STUMBLES 20th Century-Fox, 1979

ALEXIS KRASILOVSKY
b. July 5, 1950 - Juneau, Alaska
Business: Rafael Film, P.O. Box 3091, Los Angeles, CA 90051,
   213/662-5746

END OF THE ART WORLD Rafael Film, 1971
BLOOD Rafael Film, 1975
CREATED AND CONSUMED BY LIGHT Rafael Film, 1976
CHILDBIRTH DREAM Rafael Film, 1978
BEALE STREET (TF) co-director, Real to Reel Productions, 1978
EXILE Rafael Film, 1984

**F
I
L
M

D
I
R
E
C
T
O
R
S**

PAUL KRASNY*
b. August 8, 1935 - Cleveland, Ohio
Business: Pako Films Ltd., 3620 Goodland Drive, Studio City,
   CA 91604, 818/506-4200
Agent: Barry Perelman Agency - Los Angeles, 310/274-5999

THE D.A.: CONSPIRACY TO KILL (TF)   Universal TV/
   Mark VII Ltd., 1971
THE ADVENTURES OF NICK CARTER (TF)   Universal TV, 1972
THE LETTERS (TF)   co-director with Gene Nelson,
   ABC Circle Films, 1973
CHRISTINA   International Amusements, 1974
BIG ROSE (TF)   20th Century-Fox TV, 1974
JOE PANTHER   Artists Creation & Associates, 1976
CENTENNIAL (MS)   co-director with Harry Falk,
   Bernard McEveety & Virgil Vogel, Universal TV, 1978
THE ISLANDER (TF)   Universal TV, 1978
WHEN HELL WAS IN SESSION (TF)   Aubrey-Hamner
   Productions, 1979
240-ROBERT (TF)   Rosner TV/Filmways TV Productions, 1979
ALCATRAZ: THE WHOLE SHOCKING STORY (TF)
   Pierre Cossette Productions, 1980
FUGITIVE FAMILY (TF)   Aubrey-Hamner Productions, 1980
TERROR AMONG US (TF)   David Gerber Company, 1981
FLY AWAY HOME (TF)   An Lac Productions/Warner Bros. TV, 1981
TIME BOMB (TF)   Barry Weitz Films/Universal TV, 1984
STILL CRAZY LIKE A FOX (TF)   Schenck-Cardea Productions/
   Columbia TV, 1987
KOJAK (TF)   Universal TV, 1989
BACK TO HANNIBAL: THE RETURN OF TOM SAWYER AND
   HUCKLEBERRY FINN (CTF)   Gay-Jay Productions/The Disney
   Channel/WonderWorks, 1990
DRUG WARS II: THE COCAINE CARTEL (TF)   ZZY 1, Inc., 1992
SEARCH AND RESCUE (TF)   Black Sheep Productions/NBC
   Productions, 1994

GERARD KRAWCZYK
b. May 17, 1953 - Paris, France
Address: 4 bis, rue Jules Vales, 750-11 Paris, France,
   tel.: 1/43-48-27-00
Contact: French Film Office, 745 Fifth Avenue, New York,
   NY 10151, 212/832-8860

MEME LES MOULES ONT DU VAGUE A L'AME   1982, French
I HATE ACTORS   Galaxy International, 1986, French
DOWNHILL SUMMER   *L'ETE EN PENTE DOUCE*
   Galaxy International, 1987, French

JOHN KRISH
Business: Sierra Productions Ltd., 8-8 Old Bond Street, London W1

THE SALVAGE GANG   Children's Film Foundation, 1958, British
THE WILD AFFAIR   Goldstone, 1963, British
THE UNEARTHLY STRANGER   American International,
   1964, British
DECLINE AND FALL OF A BIRD WATCHER   20th Century-Fox,
   1969, British
THE MAN WHO HAD POWER OVER WOMEN   Avco Embassy,
   1971, British
JESUS   co-director with Peter Sykes, Warner Bros., 1979, British
OUT OF THE DARKNESS   Children's Film & TV Foundation/Rank,
   1985, British

PRADIP KRISHEN
Contact: British Film Commission, 70 Baker Street, London
   W1M 1DJ, England, tel.: 171/224-5000

ELECTRIC MOON   Winstone Films, 1992, British-Indian

SRINIVAS KRISHNA
Agent: Daniel Ostroff, The Daniel Ostroff Agency - Los Angeles,
   310/278-2020

MASALA   Strand Releasing, 1991, Canadian
PROMISE OF HEAVEN   Divani Films, 1995, Canadian

SURI KRISHNAMMA
Agent: CAA - Beverly Hills, 310/288-4545 or:
   Peters Fraser & Dunlop - London, tel.: 171/344-1000
Contact: British Film Commission, 70 Baker Street, London
   W1M 1DJ, England, tel.: 171/224-5000

SOLDIER SOLDIER (TF)   Central TV, 1993, British
OH MARY THIS LONDON   The Samuel Goldwyn Company,
   1994, British
A MAN OF NO IMPORTANCE   Sony Pictures Classics,
   1994, British

VIACHESLAV KRISHTOFOVICH
Contact: Confederation of Film-Makers Unions, Vasilyevskaya
   Street 13, 123 825 Moscow, Russia, tel.: 095/250-4114

ADAM'S RIB   October Films, 1991, Soviet
A WOMAN IN THE SEA   Mosfilm, 1993, Russian

ALLEN KROEKER
b. 1951 - St. Boniface, Manitoba, Canada
Home: 633 Bay Street - Apt. 2701, Toronto, Ontario M5G 2G4,
   Canada, 416/593-5138
Agent: Sy Fischer Company - Los Angeles, 310/470-0917

HOW MUCH LAND DOES A MAN NEED (TF)   1979, Canadian
TRAMP AT THE DOOR (TF)   Can West, 1985, Canadian
FRONTIER (MS)   Primedia, 1986, Canadian
HEAVEN ON EARTH (TF)   Primedia-Opix/CBC/BBC Wales/Allied
   Entertainment/Telefilm Canada/Ontario Film Development
   Corporation, 1987, Canadian-Welsh
AGE-OLD FRIENDS (CTF)   Granger Productions/HBO Showcase,
   1989, U.S.-Canadian
KOOTENAI BROWN   Kootenai Productions/Crescent Productions/
   National Film Board of Canada, 1991, Canadian

BILL KROHN
Home: 1414 1/2 N. Sierra Bonita, Los Angeles, CA 90046,
   213/969-9074

IT'S ALL TRUE: BASED ON AN UNFINISHED FILM BY ORSON
   WELLES (FD)   co-director with Richard Wilson & Myron Meisel,
   Paramount, 1993, U.S.-French

ROMAN KROITER
Business: IMAX Corporation, 45 Charles Street East, Toronto,
   Ontario M4Y 1S2, Canada, 416/960-8509

AT THE MAX   *ROLLING STONES AT THE MAX* (FCD)
   co-director with Julien Temple, David Douglas & Noel Archambault,
   BCL Presentation/IMAX Corporation, 1991, U.S.-Canadian

WILLIAM KRONICK*
Business: William Kronick Productions, 950 N. Kings Road,
   Los Angeles, CA 90069, 213/650-1568
Agent: Ben Conway & Associates - 805/565-3508

THE 500-POUND JERK (TF)   Wolper Productions, 1973
TO THE ENDS OF THE EARTH (TD)   Armand Hammer
   Productions, 1984

JEREMY JOE KRONSBERG*
Business Manager: Leonard Grainger, 9903 Kip Drive, Beverly Hills,
   CA 90210, 310/858-1573

GOING APE!   Paramount, 1981

BILL KROYER
Business: Kroyer Films, 7521 Woodman Avenue, Van Nuys,
   CA 91405, 818/778-2366

FERNGULLY...THE LAST RAINFOREST (AF)
   20th Century Fox, 1992

STANLEY KUBRICK*

b. July 26, 1928 - Bronx, New York
Business: Warner Bros., Pinewood Studios, Iver Heath,
  Bucks SL0 0NH, England, tel.: 0753/651-700
Agent: CAA - Beverly Hills, 310/288-4545

FEAR AND DESIRE   Joseph Burstyn, Inc., 1954
KILLER'S KISS   United Artists, 1955
THE KILLING   United Artists, 1956
PATHS OF GLORY   United Artists, 1957
SPARTACUS   Universal, 1960
LOLITA   MGM, 1962, British
DR. STRANGELOVE OR: HOW I LEARNED TO STOP WORRYING
  AND LOVE THE BOMB ★   Columbia, 1964, British
2001: A SPACE ODYSSEY ★   MGM, 1968, British
A CLOCKWORK ORANGE ★   Warner Bros., 1971, British
BARRY LYNDON ★   Warner Bros., 1975, British
THE SHINING   Warner Bros., 1980, British
FULL METAL JACKET   Warner Bros., 1987, British

ANDREW J. KUEHN*

Business: Kaleidoscope Films Ltd., 844 N. Seward Street,
  Hollywood, CA 90038, 213/465-1151

TERROR IN THE AISLES (FD)   Universal, 1984
ROLLING IN THE AISLES (FD)   TriStar, 1987

BUZZ KULIK*

b. 1923 - New York, New York
Agent: William Morris Agency - Beverly Hills, 310/859-4000

THE EXPLOSIVE GENERATION   United Artists, 1961
THE YELLOW CANARY   20th Century-Fox, 1963
READY FOR THE PEOPLE   Warner Bros., 1964
WARNING SHOT   Paramount, 1968
SERGEANT RYKER   THE CASE AGAINST PAUL RYKER
  Universal, 1968, originally filmed for television in 1963
VILLA RIDES!   Paramount, 1968
RIOT   Paramount, 1969
VANISHED (TF)   Universal TV, 1971
OWEN MARSHALL, COUNSELOR AT LAW (TF)
  Universal TV, 1971
BRIAN'S SONG (TF) ☆   Screen Gems/Columbia TV, 1971
TO FIND A MAN   THE BOY NEXT DOOR/SEX AND
  THE TEENAGER   Columbia, 1972
INCIDENT ON A DARK STREET (TF)   20th Century-Fox TV, 1973
PIONEER WOMAN (TF)   Filmway, 1973
SHAMUS   Columbia, 1973
BAD RONALD (TF)   Lorimar Productions, 1974
REMEMBER WHEN (TF)   Danny Thomas Productions/
  The Raisin Company, 1974
CAGE WITHOUT A KEY (TF)   Columbia TV, 1975
MATT HELM (TF)   Columbia TV, 1975
BABE (TF) ☆   MGM TV, 1975
THE LINDBERGH KIDNAPPING CASE (TF)   Columbia TV, 1976
COREY: FOR THE PEOPLE (TF)   Columbia TV, 1977
KILL ME IF YOU CAN (TF)   Columbia TV, 1977
ZIEGFELD: THE MAN AND HIS WOMEN (TF)
  Frankovich Productions/Columbia TV, 1978
FROM HERE TO ETERNITY (MS)   Bennett-Katleman Productions/
  Columbia TV, 1979
THE HUNTER   Paramount, 1980
SIDNEY SHELDON'S RAGE OF ANGELS   RAGE OF ANGELS (TF)
  Furia-Oringer Productions/NBC Productions, 1983
GEORGE WASHINGTON (MS)   David Gerber Company/
  MGM-UA TV, 1984
KANE & ABEL (MS)   Schrekinger Communications/
  Embassy TV, 1985
WOMEN OF VALOR (TF)   Inter Planetary Productions/Jeni
  Productions, 1986
HER SECRET LIFE (TF)   Phoenix Entertainment Group, 1987
TOO YOUNG THE HERO (TF)   Rick-Dawn Productions/Pierre
  Cossette Productions/The Landsburg Company, 1988
AROUND THE WORLD IN 80 DAYS (MS)   Harmony Gold/
  ReteEuropa/Valente-Baerwald Productions, 1989
JACKIE COLLINS' LUCKY CHANCES   LUCKY CHANCES (MS)
  NBC Productions, 1990
MILES FROM NOWHERE (TF)   The Sokolow Company/
  New World TV, 1992

VICTOR KULLE

ILLUSIONS   Paul Entertainment/Prism Entertainment, 1991

KEI KUMAI

b. 1930 - Nagano Prefecture, Japan
Contact: Nihon Eiga Kantoku Kyokai (Japan Film Directors
  Association), La Fontenu Building -4th Floor, 23-2 Maruyama-cho,
  Shibuya-ku, Tokyo, Japan, tel.: 3/3461-4411

EMPIRE BANK INCIDENT - THE CONDEMNED CRIMINAL
  Nikkatsu, 1964, Japanese
JAPANESE ISLANDS   WHITE SHADOW   Nikkatsu,
  1965, Japanese
CHI NO MURE   Erufu Productions/ATG, 1970, Japanese
RIVER OF PATIENCE   Hayuza Eiga Hoso/Toho, 1972, Japanese
SONG OF THE RED SUNRISE   Hayuza Eiga Hoso/Toho,
  1973, Japanese
SANDANKAN 8   Toho/Hayuza Eiga Hoso, 1974, Japanese
WOLF OF THE NORTH   Toho/Hayuza Eiga Hoso, 1976, Japanese
OGIN   Takarazuka Eiga, 1978, Japanese
TEMPYO NO IRAKA   Tempyo No Iraka Productions,
  1980, Japanese
HOT DAYS IN JAPAN: PREMEDITATED MURDER, SHIMOYAMA
  INCIDENT   Hayuza Eiga Hoso, 1981, Japanese
SEA AND POISON   Sea and Poison Productions, 1986, Japanese
SEN NO RIKYU   DEATH OF THE TEA MASTER   Saison Group,
  1989, Japanese
THE STORY OF SHIKIBU   Seiyu, 1990, Japanese
HIKARIGOKEI   Nippon Herald, 1992, Japanese

HARRY KUMEL

b. 1940 - Antwerp, Belgium
Address: Sint Jozefsstraat 46, B-2000 Anvers, Belgium,
  tel.: 3/139-4127

DAUGHTERS OF DARKNESS   Maron Films Limited, 1971,
  Belgian-French-West German-Italian
MALPERTIUS   1973, Belgian
DE KOMST VAN JOACHIM STILLER   1976, Belgian
HET VERLOREN PARADIJS   1978, Belgian
THE SECRETS OF LOVE   1986, Belgian
ELINE VERE   Sigma Filmproductions/Silent Sunset Productions/
  Odessa Films, 1991, Dutch-Belgian-French

PETER W. KUNHARDT

LINCOLN (TD)   Kunhardt Productions, 1992

KOREYOSHI KURAHARA

b. 1927 - Borneo, Sarawak Kingdom (Malaysia)
Contact: Nihon Eiga Kantoku Kyokai (Japan Film Directors
  Association), La Fontenu Building - 4th Floor, 23-2 Maruyama-cho,
  Shibuya-ku, Tokyo, Japan, tel.: 3/3461-4411

RUN IN THE STORM   Nikkatsu, 1958, Japanese
MAN IN THE MIST   Nikkatsu, 1958, Japanese
WIND VELOCITY 40   Nikkatsu, 1959, Japanese
OUR GENERATION   Nikkatsu, 1959, Japanese
SEASON OF THE CRAZY HEAT   Nikkatsu, 1960, Japanese
JET PLANE ACROSS THE STORM   Nikkatsu, 1961, Japanese
GAMBLER OF THE SEA   Nikkatsu, 1961, Japanese
RECKLESSLY   Nikkatsu, 1961, Japanese
GLASS JOHNNY   Nikkatsu, 1962, Japanese
GINZA LOVE STORY   Nikkatsu, 1962, Japanese
GODDAMNIT, I HATE YOU   Nikkatsu, 1962, Japanese
A VAGABOND IN MEXICO   Nikkatsu, 1962, Japanese
IS THERE SOMETHING INTERESTING?   Nikkatsu,
  1963, Japanese
BLACK SUN   Nikkatsu, 1964, Japanese
SHUEN   Nikkatsu, 1964, Japanese
SONG OF THE SUNRISE   Nikkatsu, 1965, Japanese
DOCUMENT OF LOVE AND DEATH   Nikkatsu, 1966, Japanese
THIRSTY FOR LOVE   Nikkatsu, 1967, Japanese
1000 KILOMETRES TO SUCCESS   Ishihara Productions,
  1969, Japanese
BAD GIRL MAKO   Nikkatsu, 1971, Japanese
SUNRISE, SUNSET   Nikkatsu, 1973, Japanese

AMSTERDAM IN THE RAIN   Toho/Watanabe Kikaku,
    1975, Japanese
THE GLACIER FOX   Sanrio Film, 1978, Japanese
ELEPHANT STORY   Toho/Japan TV, 1980, Japanese
GATE OF THE YOUTH   Toei, 1981, Japanese
GATE OF THE YOUTH: CHAPTER OF INDEPENDENCE
    Toei, 1982, Japanese
ANTARCTICA   20th Century Fox, 1983, Japanese
BELL OF THE SPRING   Toho, 1985, Japanese
THE ROAD   Toei, 1986, Japanese
SEE YOU   Toho/New Century Producers, 1988, Japanese
STRAWBERRY ROAD   Tokyo Hoei TV/Fuji TV,
    1991, Japanese-U.S.

HANIF KUREISHI
b. 1954 - Bromley, Kent, England
Agent: The Artists Agency - Los Angeles, 310/277-7779

LONDON KILLS ME   Fine Line Features/New Line Cinema,
    1992, British

AKIRA KUROSAWA
b. March 23, 1910 - Tokyo, Japan
Business: Kurosawa Production Inc., 3-2-1, Kirigaoka, Midori-ku,
    Yokohama, Japan 227, tel.: 045/922-0850

SANSHIRO SUGATA   Toho, 1943, Japanese
THE MOST BEAUTIFUL   Toho, 1944, Japanese
SANSHIRO SUGATA, PART II   Toho, 1945, Japanese
THOSE WHO TREAD ON THE TIGER'S TAIL
    Toho, 1945, Japanese
THOSE WHO MAKE TOMORROW   co-director with
    Kajiro Yamamoto & Hideo Sekigawa, Toho, 1946, Japanese
NO REGRETS FOR OUR YOUTH   Toho, 1946, Japanese
ONE WONDERFUL SUNDAY   Toho, 1947, Japanese
DRUNKEN ANGEL   Toho, 1948, Japanese
THE QUIET DUEL   Daiei, 1949, Japanese
STRAY DOG   Shin Toho, 1949, Japanese
SCANDAL   Shochiku, 1959, Japanese
RASHOMON   Daiei, 1950, Japanese
THE IDIOT   Shochiku, 1951, Japanese
IKIRU (TO LIVE!)   Toho, 1952, Japanese
SEVEN SAMURAI   Toho, 1954, Japanese
I LIVE IN FEAR   *RECORD OF A LIVING BEING*   Toho,
    1955, Japanese
THRONE OF BLOOD   *THE CASTLE OF THE SPIDER'S WEB*
    Toho, 1957, Japanese
THE LOWER DEPTHS   Toho, 1957, Japanese
THE HIDDEN FORTRESS   *THREE BAD MEN IN A
    HIDDEN FORTRESS*   Toho, 1958, Japanese
THE BAD SLEEP WELL   Kurosawa Productions/Toho,
    1960, Japanese
YOJIMBO   Kurosawa Productions/Toho, 1961, Japanese
SANJURO   *TSUBAKI SANJURO*   Kurosawa Productions/Toho,
    1962, Japanese
HIGH AND LOW   Kurosawa Productions/Toho, 1963, Japanese
RED BEARD   Kurosawa Productions/Toho, 1965, Japanese
DODES'KA'DEN   Yonki no Kai/Toho, 1970, Japanese
DERSU UZALA   New World, 1975, Soviet-Japanese
KAGEMUSHA: THE SHADOW WARRIOR   20th Century-Fox,
    1980, Japanese
RAN ★   Orion Classics, 1985, French-Japanese
AKIRA KUROSAWA'S DREAMS   *DREAMS*   Warner Bros.,
    1990, Japanese-U.S.
RHAPSODY IN AUGUST   Orion Classics, 1991, Japanese
MADADAYO   Daiei Co., Ltd./Dentsu Inc./Kurosawa Productions
    Inc./Tokuma Shoten Publishing Co., 1993, Japanese

DIANE KURYS
b. December 3, 1948 - Lyons, France
Business: Alexandre Films, 14, rue de Marignan, 75008 Paris,
    France, tel.: 1/45-62-02-04
Agent: William Morris Agency - Beverly Hills, 310/859-4000

PEPPERMINT SODA   *DIABOLO MENTHE*   New Yorker,
    1977, French
COCKTAIL MOLOTOV   Putnam Square, 1980, French

ENTRE NOUS   *COUP DE FOUDRE*   United Artists Classics,
    1983, French
A MAN IN LOVE   Cinecom, 1987, French
C'EST LA VIE   *LE BAULE-LES PINS*   The Samuel Goldwyn
    Company, 1990, French
LOVE AFTER LOVE (APRES L'AMOUR)   Rainbow Releasing,
    1992, French
6 DAYS 6 NIGHTS   *A LA FOLIE*   Fine Line Features/New Line
    Cinema, 1994, French

EMIR KUSTURICA*
b. 1955 - Sarajevo, Yugoslavia
Agent: CAA - Beverly Hills, 310/288-4545

DO YOU REMEMBER DOLLY BELL?   International Home
    Cinema, 1981, Yugoslavian
WHEN FATHER WAS AWAY ON BUSINESS   Cannon,
    1985, Yugoslavian
TIME OF THE GYPSIES   Columbia, 1989, Yugoslavian
ARIZONA DREAM   UGC, 1993, French-U.S.
UNDERGROUND   Novofilm/CIBY 2000/Pandora Film, 1995,
    Hungarian-French-German
ONCE UPON A TIME THERE WAS A COUNTRY   1995, Serbian

FRAN RUBEL KUZUI
Business: Kuzui Enterprises, 7920 Sunset Blvd. - 4th Floor,
    Los Angeles, CA 90046, 213/851-9047 or:
    Kuzui Enterprises, Hill's Aoyama - 3rd Floor, 3-39-9 Jungumae,
    Shibuya-ku, Tokyo 150, Japan, tel.: 3/3497-1981
Agent: UTA - Beverly Hills, 310/273-6700

TOKYO POP   Spectrafilm, 1988, U.S.-Japanese
BUFFY THE VAMPIRE SLAYER   20th Century Fox, 1992

STANLEY KWAN
(Kwan Kam-Pang/Guan Jinpang)
b. October 9, 1957 - Hong Kong
Address: Pearl City Ltd., Room 303, Austin Tower, Austin Avenue,
    Kowloon, Hong Kong, tel.: 3/722-0240
Contact: Hong Kong Film Liaison, 10940 Wilshire Blvd. - Suite 1220,
    Los Angeles, CA 90024, 310/208-2678

LOVE UNTO WASTE   1986, Hong Kong
ROUGE   1988, Hong Kong
FULL MOON IN NEW YORK   Shiobu Film Co., 1990, Hong Kong
CENTER STAGE   *RUAN LING-YU*   Golden Way/Golden Harvest,
    1992, Hong Kong-Taiwanese
RED ROSE, WHITE ROSE   Golden Flare Films,
    1995, Hong Kong

KEN KWAPIS*
Agent: CAA - Beverly Hills, 310/288-4545

THE BENIKER GANG   1985
SESAME STREET PRESENTS: FOLLOW THAT BIRD
    Warner Bros., 1985
VIBES   Columbia, 1988
HE SAID, SHE SAID   co-director with Marisa Silver,
    Paramount, 1991
DUNSTON CHECKS IN   20th Century Fox, 1995

JEFF KWITNY
ICED   Mikon Releasing Corporation, 1988
THE TRAIN   International Movie Service, 1989, Italian
LIGHTNING IN A BOTTLE   Matovich Productions, 1994

IM KWON-TAEK
b. May 2, 1936 - Kwangju, Jonlanamdo, Korea
Contact: Korean Motion Pictures Promotion Corporation, 34-5,
    3KA Namsan-Dong, Chung-Ku, Seoul, South Korea,
    tel.: 755-9291

GOOD-BYE! DUMAN RIVER   1961, South Korean
THE GREAT LONG FOR HUSBAND   1963, South Korean
WAR AND WOMAN TEACHER   1966, South Korean
WEEDS   1973, South Korean

TESTIMONY   1973, South Korean
WANGSIBRI STREET   1976, South Korean
WAR! NAKDONG RIVER!   1976, South Korean
THE FAMILY TREE BOOK   1978, South Korean
THE HIDDEN HERO   1979, South Korean
MANDALA   1981, South Korean
VILLAGE IN THE MIST   1982, South Korean
GILSODOM   Hwa Chun Trading Company, 1985, South Korean
TICKET   1986, South Korean
SURROGATE WOMAN   1986, South Korean
COME, COME, COME UPWARD   Korean Motion Picture
   Promotion Corporation, 1989, South Korean
THE GENERAL'S SON   Korean Motion Picture Promotion
   Corporation, 1991, South Korean
THE CREATION   Korean Motion Picture Promotion Corporation,
   1992, South Korean
FLY HIGH RUN FAR - KAE BYOK   Chun Woo Film Company,
   1992, South Korean
THE GENERAL'S SON II   Korean Motion Picture Promotion
   Corporation, 1992, South Korean
SONPYONJE   Tae-Hung Production Company,
   1993, South Korean
THE GENERAL'S SON III   Korean Motion Picture Promotion
   Corporation, 1994, South Korean
THE TAEBAEK MOUNTAINS   Taehung Pictures,
   1995, South Korean

L

RICHARD LABRIE
THE OX AND THE EYE   The Ox and the Eye L.P., 1995

ED LACHMAN
b. 1948

IMAGINING AMERICA (TF)   co-director with Ralph Bakshi,
   Matt Mahurin & Mustapha Khan, Vanguard Films, 1989
SONGS FOR DRELLA (TCD)   Initial Film and Television/
   Channel 4/Sire Records, 1991, U.S.-British

MORT LACHMAN*
b. March 20, 1918 - Seattle, Washington
Agent: Paradigm - Los Angeles, 310/277-4400

THE GIRL WHO COULDN'T LOSE (TF) ☆☆   Filmways, 1975

DIANE LADD
(Rose Diane Ladner)
b. November 29, 1939 - Meridian, Minnesota
Agent: The Marion Rosenberg Office - Los Angeles, 213/653-7383

MRS. MUNCK (CTF)   Showtime, 1995

JOHN LAFIA*
Agent: CAA - Beverly Hills, 310/288-4545

THE BLUE IGUANA   Paramount, 1988
CHILD'S PLAY 2   Universal, 1990
MAN'S BEST FRIEND   New Line Cinema, 1993

RON LAGOMARSINO*
Agent: CAA - Beverly Hills, 310/288-4545

DINNER AT EIGHT (CTF)   Think Entertainment/Turner
   Network TV, 1989
HOMEFRONT (TF) ☆   Roundelay/Latham-Lechowick
   Productions/Lorimar TV, 1991

PICKET FENCES (TF)   Twentieth TV, 1992
THE COUNTERFEIT CONTESSA (TF)   Fox West Pictures/
   Sanford-Pillsbury Productions, 1994

HARVEY LAIDMAN*
b. February 22, 1942 - Cleveland, Ohio
Business Manager: Freedman, Broder & Angen, 2501 Colorado
   Avenue - Suite 350, Santa Monica, CA 90404, 310/449-6700

STEEL COWBOY (TF)   Roger Gimbel Productions/EMI TV, 1978
FLATBUSH (TF)   Lorimar Productions, 1979
THE BOY WHO LOVED TROLLS (TF)   Q Productions, 1984

JOHN LAING
b. February 9, 1948
Business: Meridian Film Productions, P.O. Box 6279, Te Aro,
   Wellington, New Zealand, tel.: 4/851-807
Contact: New Zealand Film Commission, P.O. Box 11-546,
   Wellington, New Zealand, tel.: 4/385-9754

BEYOND REASONABLE DOUBT   Endeavour Productions/New
   Zealand Film Commission, 1980, New Zealand
THE LOST TRIBE   Meridian Films/Film Investment Corporation of
   New Zealand/New Zealand Film Commission, 1983, New Zealand
OTHER HALVES   Finlayson Hill Productions, 1985, New Zealand
DANGEROUS ORPHANS   Cinepro/New Zealand Film Commission,
   1986, New Zealand
ABSENT WITHOUT LEAVE   Meridian Film Productions/New
   Zealand Film Commission/NZ on Air/Avalon-NFU Studios,
   1993, New Zealand

MARLENA LAIRD*
b. March 21, 1949 - London, England
Home: 6208 Mulholland Highway, Hollywood, CA 90068,
   213/465-6400
Agent: APA - Los Angeles, 310/273-0744

FRIENDSHIP, SECRETS AND LIES   co-director with
   Ann Zane Shanks, Wittman-Riche Productions/Warner
   Bros. TV, 1979

FRANK LALOGGIA
Agent: Becsey/Wisdom/Kalajian - Los Angeles, 310/550-0535

FEAR NO EVIL   Avco Embassy, 1981
LADY IN WHITE   New Century/Vista, 1987
THE MOTHER   Osmosis Productions, 1994
THE HAUNTED HEART   Kings Road Entertainment/SK Films, 1994

LORENZO LAMAS
b. January 20, 1958 - Los Angeles, California
Agent: David Shapira & Associates - Sherman Oaks, 818/906-0322

C.I.A. II: TARGET ALEXA   PM Entertainment Group, 1993

MARY LAMBERT*
b. Arkansas
Agent: ICM - Beverly Hills, 310/550-4000

SIESTA   Lorimar, 1987, British
PET SEMATARY   Paramount, 1989
GRAND ISLE   Kelly McGillis Productions/Turner Pictures, 1991
PET SEMATARY II   Paramount, 1992
REBEL HIGHWAY: DRAGSTRIP GIRL   DRAGSTRIP GIRL (CTF)
   Drive-In Classics Cinema/Showtime, 1994

MARY LAMPSON
UNDERGROUND (FD)   co-director with Emile de Antonio &
   Haskell Wexler, New Yorker, 1976
UNTIL SHE TALKS (TF)   Alaska Street Productions, 1983

JOHN LANDIS*
b. August 3, 1950 - Chicago, Illinois
Agent: CAA - Beverly Hills, 310/288-4545

SCHLOCK   Jack H. Harris Enterprises, 1973
THE KENTUCKY FRIED MOVIE   United Film Distribution, 1977
NATIONAL LAMPOON'S ANIMAL HOUSE   Universal, 1978
THE BLUES BROTHERS   Universal, 1980
AN AMERICAN WEREWOLF IN LONDON   Universal, 1981
TWILIGHT ZONE - THE MOVIE   co-director with Steven Spielberg,
    Joe Dante & George Miller, Warner Bros., 1983
TRADING PLACES   Paramount, 1983
COMING SOON (CTD)   Universal Pay TV, 1983
INTO THE NIGHT   Universal, 1985
SPIES LIKE US   Warner Bros., 1985
THREE AMIGOS   Orion, 1986
AMAZON WOMEN ON THE MOON   co-director with Joe Dante,
    Carl Gottlieb, Robert K. Weiss & Peter Horton, Universal, 1987
COMING TO AMERICA   Paramount, 1988
OSCAR   Buena Vista, 1991
DREAM ON: THE SECOND GREATEST STORY EVER TOLD (CTF)
    Kevin Bright Productions/MCA TV Entertainment, 1991
INNOCENT BLOOD   Warner Bros., 1992
DREAM ON: ORAL SEX, LIES, AND VIDEOTAPE (CTF)
    Kevin Bright Productions/St. Clare Entertainment/MCA TV
    Entertainment, 1993
BEVERLY HILLS COP III   Paramount, 1994

PAUL LANDRES*
b. August 21, 1912 - New York, New York
Home: 5343 Amestoy Avenue, Encino, CA 91316, 818/789-0927

GRAND CANYON   1949
SQUARE DANCE JUBILEE   1949
HOLLYWOOD VARIETIES   1950
A MODERN MARRIAGE   *FRIGID WIFE*   1950
NAVY BOUND   Monogram, 1951
RHYTHM INN   Monogram, 1951
ARMY BOUND   Monogram, 1952
EYES OF THE JUNGLE   1953
HELL CANYON OUTLAWS   Republic, 1957
LAST OF THE BADMEN   Allied Artists, 1957
THE VAMPIRE   United Artists, 1957
CHAIN OF EVIDENCE   Allied Artists, 1957
OREGON PASSAGE   Allied Artists, 1958
MAN FROM GOD'S COUNTRY   Allied Artists, 1958
JOHNNY ROCCO   Allied Artists, 1958
THE RETURN OF DRACULA   *THE CURSE OF DRACULA*
    United Artists, 1958
THE FLAME BARRIER   United Artists, 1958
FRONTIER GUN   20th Century-Fox, 1958
THE LONE TEXAN   20th Century-Fox, 1959
THE MIRACLE OF THE HILLS   20th Century-Fox, 1959
SON OF A GUNFIGHTER   MGM, 1966, Spanish-U.S.

ALAN LANDSBURG*
b. May 10, 1933 - New York, New York
Business: Alan Landsburg Productions, Inc., 11811 W. Olympic
    Blvd., Los Angeles, CA 90064, 310/478-7878

BLACK WATER GOLD (TF)   Metromedia Productions, 1970

ANDREW LANE
Business: Gibraltar Entertainment, Inc., 14101 Valleyheart Drive -
    Suite 205, Sherman Oaks, CA 91423, 818/501-2076
Agent: The Marion Rosenberg Office - Los Angeles, 213/653-7383

JAKE SPEED   New World, 1986
MORTAL PASSIONS   MGM/UA, 1990
LONELY HEARTS   LIVE Entertainment/Gibraltar Releasing, 1991
DISTANT COUSINS   New Line Cinema, 1993
THE SECRETARY   Republic Pictures, 1994
TRADE OFF (CTF)   Showtime Entertainment/Viacom
    Productions, 1995

CHARLES LANE
b. December 26, 1953 - New York, New York
Agent: Paradigm - Los Angeles, 310/277-4400

SIDEWALK STORIES   Island Pictures, 1989
TRUE IDENTITY   Buena Vista, 1991
HALLELUJAH (TF)   Rhinoceros Productions, 1993

ERIC LANEUVILLE*
Home: 5138 W. Slauson Avenue, Los Angeles, CA 90056,
    213/293-1277
Agent: Mitch Kaplan, The Kaplan-Stahler Agency - Beverly Hills,
    310/653-4483

THE GEORGE McKENNA STORY (TF)   Alan Landsburg
    Productions, 1986
MIGHTY PAWNS (TF)   WonderWorks/PBS, 1987
SECRET WITNESS (TF)   Just Greene Productions/CBS
    Entertainment, 1988
A BRAND NEW LIFE (TF)   NBC Productions, 1989
THE UNTOUCHABLES (TF)   Christopher Crowe Productions/
    Paramount Network TV, 1993
THE ERNEST GREEN STORY (CTF)   Emmalyn Enterprises/Walt
    Disney TV, 1993
STOLEN BABIES (CTF)   ABC Video Enterprises/Sander-Moses
    Productions, 1993
STAYING AFLOAT (TF)   The Ruddy Morgan Organization/
    TriStar TV, 1993
M.A.N.T.I.S. (TF)   Wilbur Force Productions/Renaissance Pictures/
    Universal TV, 1994
SOMEONE SHE KNOWS (TF)   Thomas Carter Company/Warner
    Bros. TV, 1994
IF SOMEONE HAD KNOWN (TF)   The Landsburg Company, 1995

KRZYSZTOF LANG
Contact: Film Polski, ul. Mazowiecka 6/8, 00 0048 Warsaw, Poland,
    tel.: 48-22/26-84-55 or 48-22/26-09-49

PAPER MARRIAGE   Mark Forstater Productions/Zodiak Film Studio,
    1993, British-Polish
PROVOCATEUR   Filmcontract/Balzer International/Mark Forstater
    Productions/Premiere Productions, 1995, Polish-Czech-British

PERRY LANG
Agent: ICM - Beverly Hills, 310/550-4000

LITTLE VEGAS   I.R.S. Releasing, 1990
MEN OF WAR   Dimension/Miramax Films, 1994

RICHARD LANG*
Agent: Stone Manners Agency - Los Angeles, 213/654-7575

FANTASY ISLAND (TF)   Spelling-Goldberg Productions, 1977
THE HUNTED LADY (TF)   QM Productions, 1977
NOWHERE TO RUN (TF)   MTM Enterprises, 1978
NIGHT CRIES (TF)   Charles Fries Productions, 1978
DR. SCORPION (TF)   Universal TV, 1978
VEGA$ (TF)   Aaron Spelling Productions, 1978
THE WORD (MS)   Charles Fries Productions/Stonehenge
    Productions, 1978
THE MOUNTAIN MEN   Columbia, 1980
A CHANGE OF SEASONS   20th Century-Fox, 1980
MATT HOUSTON (TF)   Largo Productions/Aaron Spelling
    Productions, 1982
DON'T GO TO SLEEP (TF)   Aaron Spelling Productions, 1982
SHOOTING STARS (TF)   Aaron Spelling Productions, 1983
DARK MIRROR (TF)   Aaron Spelling Productions, 1984
VELVET (TF)   Aaron Spelling Productions, 1984
OBSESSED WITH A MARRIED WOMAN (TF)   Sidaris-Camhe
    Productions/The Feldman-Meeker Company, 1985
IN LIKE FLYNN (TF)   Glen A. Larson Productions/20th Century
    Fox TV/Astral Film Productions, 1985, U.S.-Canadian
KUNG FU: THE MOVIE (TF)   Lou-Step Productions/Warner
    Bros. TV, 1985

HOUSTON KNIGHTS (TF)   co-director with Gary Nelson,
   Jay Bernstein Productions/Columbia TV, 1987
PERRY MASON: THE CASE OF THE SINISTER SPIRIT (TF)
   The Fred Silverman Company/Strathmore Productions/Viacom
   Productions, 1987
CHRISTMAS COMES TO WILLOW CREEK (TF)   Blue Andre
   Productions/ITC Productions, 1987
THE ROAD RAIDERS (TF)   New East Entertainment/
   Universal TV, 1989
JAMES A. MICHENER'S TEXAS   TEXAS (HVMS)
   Spelling Entertainment, 1994

ROCKY LANG*
Agent: Renaissance/H.N. Swanson - Los Angeles, 310/246-6000

ALL'S FAIR   Moviestore Entertainment, 1989
RACE FOR GLORY   New Century/Vista, 1989
NERVOUS TICKS   I.R.S. Releasing, 1993

MICHAEL LANGE*
Agent: Shapiro-Lichtman Talent Agency - Los Angeles,
   310/859-8877

PARADISE (TF)   co-director with Clifford Bole, CBS, 1989

TED LANGE*
Agent: William Morris Agency - Beverly Hills, 310/859-4000

OTHELLO   Uptown Films, 1989

MURRAY LANGSTON
Contact: Screen Actors Guild - Los Angeles, 213/954-1600

WISHFUL THINKING   Broadstar Entertainment, 1989

SIMON LANGTON*
b. November 5, 1941 - Amersham, England
Address: 26 Madrid Road, Barnes, London SW13 9PD, England,
   tel.: 181/748-4589
Agent: Peter Murphy, Curtis Brown - London, tel.: 171/872-0331

REBECCA (TF)   BBC, 1979, British
THERESE RAQUIN (TF)   BBC, 1980, British
SMILEY'S PEOPLE (MS) ☆   BBC/Paramount TV, 1982, British
THE LOST HONOR OF KATHRYN BECK (TF)   Open Road
   Productions, 1984
ANNA KARENINA (TF)   Rastar Productions/Colgems
   Productions, 1985
THE WHISTLE BLOWER   Hemdale, 1987
CASANOVA (TF)   Konigsberg-Sanitsky Company/Reteitalia,
   1987, U.S.-Italian
LAGUNA HEAT (CTF)   HBO Pictures/Jay Weston
   Productions, 1987
JEEVES AND WOOSTER II (TF)   Carnival Films, 1989, British
MOTHER LOVE (MS)   BBC/WGBH-Boston, 1990, British-U.S.
THE GOOD GUYS (MS)   co-director with Roy Ward Baker &
   Stuart Urban, Havahall Pictures/London Weekend TV,
   1991, British
HEADHUNTERS (TF)   BBC, 1992, British
THE CINDER PATH (TF)   World Wide Intl. TV/Festival
   Films TV, 1995

LAWRENCE LANOFF
Business: L.G.L. Productions, Inc., 2522 S. Centinela - Suite 7,
   Los Angeles, CA 90064, 310/477-3224

INDECENT BEHAVIOR   Promark Entertainment Group, 1993
PLAYING DANGEROUS   Promark Entertainment Group, 1993
TEMPTRESS   Motion Picture Corporation of America, 1994

CLAUDE LANZMANN
Business: Aleph Films, 18 rue Marbeuf, 75008 Paris, France,
   tel.: 04/723-5547
Contact: French Film Office, 745 Fifth Avenue, New York,
   NY 10151, 212/832-8860

PORQUOI ISRAEL? (FD)   New Yorker, 1973, French
SHOAH (FD)   New Yorker, 1985, French
THOU SHALT NOT SLAY (FD)   UGC, 1992, French
TSAHAL (FD)   Les Productions Dussart/Les Films Aleph/France 2
   Cinema/Bavaria Films, 1994, French-German

JAMES LAPINE*
Agent: ICM - New York City, 212/556-5600

IMPROMPTU   Hemdale, 1991
LIFE WITH MIKEY   Buena Vista, 1993

STEPHEN LA ROCQUE
Agent: APA - Los Angeles, 310/273-0744

SAMANTHA   Academy Entertainment, 1991

SHELDON LARRY*
b. October 3, 1949 - Toronto, Ontario, Canada
Contact: Directors Guild of America - Los Angeles, 213/851-3671

TERMINAL CHOICE   Almi, 1985, Canadian
FIRST STEPS (TF)   CBS Entertainment, 1985
BEHIND ENEMY LINES (TF)   TVS Productions/MTM Enterprises,
   1985, British-U.S.
HOME (TF)   Leonard Goldberg Productions, 1986
HOT PAINT (TF)   Catalina Production Group/MGM-UA TV, 1988
BURNING BRIDGES (TF)   Andrea Baynes Productions/
   Lorimar TV, 1990
THE FIRST CIRCLE (MS)   CBC/Primedia, 1991, Canadian-French
PANIC IN THE CITY (TF)   Sunrise Films, 1992, U.S.-Canadian
A FAMILY OF STRANGERS (TF)   Alliance Communications,
   1993, Canadian
LONG SHADOWS   NHK-Japan/KCET-Los Angeles/KCTS-Seattle,
   1994, U.S.-Japanese

GLEN A. LARSON*
Business: Glen Larson Productions, 10 Universal Plaza,
   Universal City, CA 91608, 818/505-7585
Agent: David Shapira & Associates - Sherman Oaks, 818/906-0322

CHAMELEONS (TF)   Glen A. Larson Productions/NBC
   Productions, 1989

JOHN LASSITER
TOY STORY (AF)   Buena Vista, 1995

STAN LATHAN*
b. July 8, 1945 - Philadelphia, Pennsylvania
Agent: CAA - Beverly Hills, 310/288-4545
Personal Manager: Brillstein/Grey Entertainment - Beverly Hills,
   310/275-6135

SAVE THE CHILDREN (FCD)   Paramount, 1973
AMAZING GRACE   United Artists, 1974
THE SKY IS GRAY (TF)   Learning in Focus, 1980
DENMARK VESEY'S REBELLION (TF)   WPBT-Miami, 1982
BEAT STREET   Orion, 1984
BOOKER (TF)   KQED-Frisco, 1984
GO TELL IT ON THE MOUNTAIN (TF)   Learning in Focus, 1984
UNCLE TOM'S CABIN (CTF)   Edgar J. Scherick Productions/Taft
   Entertainment TV, 1987
THE CHILD SAVER (TF)   Michael Filerman Productions/NBC
   Productions, 1988
AN EIGHT IS ENOUGH WEDDING (TF)   Lorimar TV, 1989

STEVE LATSHAW
BIOHAZARD 2   Curb Organization, 1994

ALBERTO LATTUADA

b. November 13, 1914 - Milan, Italy
Address: Via N. Paganini, 7 Rome, Italy, tel.: 06/855-2035

GIACOMO L'IDEALISTA 1942, Italian
LA FRECCIA NEL FIANCO 1943, Italian
LA NOSTRA GUERRA 1943, Italian
IL BANDITO Lux Film, 1946, Italian
IL DELITTO DI GIOVANNI EPISCOPO Lux Film, 1947, Italian
SENZA PIETA Lux Film, 1948, Italian
LUCI DEL PO 1949, Italian
VARIETY LIGHTS co-director with Federico Fellini, Pathe
   Contemporary, 1950, Italian
ANNA Italian Films Export, 1951, Italian
IL CAPPOTTO Faro Film, 1952, Italian
LA LUPA Republic, 1953, Italian
LOVE IN THE CITY co-director, Italian Films Export, 1953, Italian
LA SPIAGGIA Titanus, 1954, Italian
SCUOLA ELEMENTARE Titanus/Societe General de
   Cinematographie, 1954, Italian-French
GUENDALINA Carlo Ponti/Les Films Marceau,
   1957, Italian-French
TEMPEST Paramount, 1958, Italian-French-Yugoslavian
I DOLCI INGANNI Carlo Ponti/Titanus, 1960, Italian
LETTERA DI UNA NOVIZIA Champion/Euro International,
   1960, Italian
L'IMPREVISTO Documento Film/Orsay Film, 1961, Italian-French
MAFIOSO Zenith International, 1962, Italian
LA STEPPA Zebra Film/Aera Film, 1962, Italian
LA MANDRAGOLA Arco Film/Lux Compagnie Cinematographie,
   1965, Italian-French
MATCHLESS United Artists, 1966, Italian
DON GIOVANNI IN SICILIA Adelphia, 1967, Italian
FRAULEIN DOKTOR Paramount, 1969, Italian-Yugoslavian
L'AMICA Fair Film, 1969, Italian
VENGA A PRENDERE IL CAFFE' DA NOI Mass Film,
   1970, Italian
WHITE SISTER *BIANCO, ROSSOE...* Columbia, 1971,
   Italian-French-Spanish
SONO STATO IO Dear Film, 1973, Italian
LE FARO DA PADRE Clesi Cinematografica, 1974, Italian
LA BAMBINA 1974, Italian
CUORE DI CANE Italnoleggio, 1975, Italian
OH, SERAFINA Cineriz, 1976, Italian
COSI' COME SEI CEIAD, 1978, Italian-Spanish
LA CICALA PIC, 1979, Italian
CHRISTOPHER COLUMBUS (MS) RAI/Clesi Cinematografica/
   Antenne-2/Bavaria Atelier/Lorimar Productions, 1985,
   Italian-West German-U.S.-French
UNA SPINA DEL CUORE Titanus, 1985, Italian
FRATELLI (MS) Solaris Cinematografica/Reteitalia/Beta Film,
   1988, Italian-West German
AMORI (TF) co-director, Reteitalia, 1989, Italian

PATRICK LAU

Agent: Peters Fraser & Dunlop - London, tel.: 171/344-1000

DOCTOR FINLAY (MS) co-director with Aisling Walsh,
   Scottish TV Enterprises, 1993, Scottish
DOCTOR FINLAY (MS) co-director with Sarah Pia Anderson,
   Scottish TV Enterprises, 1994, Scottish

EREZ LAUFER

WOODSTOCK: THE LOST PERFORMANCES (CTCD)
   co-director with D.A. Pennebaker & Chris Hegedus,
   Showtime Entertainment Group/Gravity Unlimited/
   Pennebaker Associates, 1994

FRANK LAUGHLIN

Home: 415/931-8024
Business Manager: Ronald Dorfman, 15910 Ventura Blvd. -
   Suite 1501, Encino, CA 91436, 818/906-8555

THE TRIAL OF BILLY JACK Taylor-Laughlin, 1974
THE MASTER GUNFIGHTER Taylor-Laughlin, 1975

MICHAEL LAUGHLIN

STRANGE BEHAVIOR *DEAD KIDS* World Northal, 1981,
   New Zealand-Australian
STRANGE INVADERS Orion, 1983, Canadian
MESMERIZED RKO/Challenge Corporation Services, 1984,
   New Zealand-Australian-British

TOM LAUGHLIN*

b. 1938 - Minneapolis, Minnesota
Contact: Directors Guild of America - Los Angeles, 213/851-3671

THE PROPER TIME Lopert, 1960
THE YOUNG SINNER United Screen Arts, 1965
BORN LOSERS directed under pseudonym of T.C. Frank,
   American International, 1967
BILLY JACK directed under pseudonym of T.C. Frank,
   Warner Bros., 1973
BILLY JACK GOES TO WASHINGTON Taylor-Laughlin, 1978
THE RETURN OF BILLY JACK Billy Jack Productions,
   1986, unfinished

FRANK LAUNDER

b. 1907 - Hitchin, England
Contact: British Film Commission, 70 Baker Street, London
   W1M 1DJ, England, tel.: 171/224-5000

MILLIONS LIKE US co-director with Sidney Gilliat, 1943, British
TWO THOUSAND WOMEN Academy-Lux, 1944, British
THE ADVENTURESS *I SEE A DARK STRANGER* Eagle Lion,
   1947, British
CAPTAIN BOYCOTT Universal, 1947, British
THE BLUE LAGOON Universal, 1949, British
THE HAPPIEST DAYS OF YOUR LIFE London Films, 1950, British
LADY GODIVA RIDES AGAIN 1951, British
FOLLY TO BE WISE Fine Arts, 1952, British
THE BELLES OF ST. TRINIAN'S Continental, 1954, British
WEE GEORDIE *GEORDIE* George K. Arthur, 1955, British
BLUE MURDER AT ST. TRINIAN'S Continental, 1957, British
THE BRIDAL PATH Kingsley International, 1959, British
THE PURE HELL OF ST. TRINIAN'S Continental, 1960, British
JOEY BOY 1965, British
THE GREAT ST. TRINIAN'S TRAIN ROBBERY co-director with
   Sidney Gilliat, 1966, British
THE WILDCATS OF ST. TRINIAN'S 1980, British

DALE LAUNER*

Business: Anarchy Productions, Inc., 10201 W. Pico Blvd. - Building 1,
   Room 146, Los Angeles, CA 90035, 310/203-2081

LOVE POTION #9 20th Century Fox, 1992

GEORGES LAUTNER

b. January 24, 1926 - Nice, France
Address: 1, boulevard Richard Wallace, 92200 Neuilly, France,
   tel.: 1/47-43-09-50
Agent: ICM France - Paris, tel.: 1/723-7860
Contact: French Film Office, 745 Fifth Avenue, New York, NY 10151,
   212/832-8860

LA MOME AUX BOUTONS 1958, French
MARCHE OU CREVE 1960, French
WOMEN AND WAR *ARRETEZ LES TAMBOURS/WOMEN IN WAR*
   Parade, 1961, French
LE MONOCLE NOIR 1961, French
EN PLAIN CIRAGE 1961, French
LA SEPTIEME JURE 1961, French
L'OEIL DU MONOCLE 1962, French
LES TONTONS FLINGUEURS 1963, French
LE MONOCLE RIT JAUNE 1964, French
THE GREAT SPY CHASE *LES BARBOUZES* American
   International, 1964, French
GALIA *I, AND MY LOVERS/I AND MY LOVE* Zenith International,
   1966, French
SAUTERELLE 1967, French
FLEUR D'OSEILLE 1967, French
LE PACHA 1968, French

ROAD TO SALINA *SUR LA ROUTE DE SALINA* Avco Embassy,
    1969, French-Italian
LAISSE ALLER-C'EST UNE VALSE 1971, French
IL ETAIT UN FOIS UN FLIC 1972, French
LA VALISE 1973, French
QUELQUE MESSIEURS TROP TRANQUILLES 1973, French
LES SEINS DE GLACE 1974, French
ON AURA TOUT VA 1975, French
MORT D'UN POURRI 1977, French
IL SONT FOUS CES SORCIERS 1978, French
FLIC OU VOYOU 1979, French
LE GUIGNOLO 1980, French
LE PROFESSIONEL 1981, French
ATTENTION! UNE FEMME PEUT EN CACHER UNE AUTRE!
    1983, French
JOYEUSES PAQUES 1984, French
LE COWBOY 1985, French
LA CAGE AUX FOLLES III: THE WEDDING MGM-UA,
    1985, French

GERARD LAUZIER
Agent: ICM France - Paris, tel.: 4/723-7860
Contact: French Film Office, 745 Fifth Avenue, New York,
    NY 10151, 212/832-8860

TU EMPECHES TOUT LE MONDE DE DORMIR 1982, French
PETIT CON The Samuel Goldwyn Company, 1984, French
LA TETE DANS LE SAC Parafrance, 1984, French
MON PERE, CE HEROS AMLF, 1991, French

JEAN-CLAUDE LAUZON
b. 1953 - Montreal, Quebec, Canada
Agent: ICM - Beverly Hills, 310/550-4000

NIGHT ZOO *UN ZOO LA NUIT* FilmDallas, 1987, Canadian
LEOLO Fine Line Features/New Line Cinema, 1992,
    Canadian-French

ARNOLD LAVEN*
b. February 23, 1922 - Chicago, Illinois
Business: Levy-Gardner-Laven Productions, 9595 Wilshire Blvd. -
    Suite 610, Beverly Hills, CA 90212, 310/278-9820

WITHOUT WARNING United Artists, 1952
VICE SQUAD United Artists, 1953
DOWN THREE DARK STREETS United Artists, 1954
THE RACK MGM, 1956
THE MONSTER THAT CHALLENGED THE WORLD
    United Artists, 1957
SLAUGHTER ON TENTH AVENUE Universal, 1957
ANNA LUCASTA United Artists, 1958
GERONIMO United Artists, 1962
THE GLORY GUYS United Artists, 1965
ROUGH NIGHT IN JERICHO Universal, 1967
SAM WHISKEY United Artists, 1969

JULIANNA LAVIN
Agent: UTA - Beverly Hills, 310/273-6700

LIVE NUDE GIRLS Republic Pictures, 1995

MARTIN LAVUT
b. 1939 - Montreal, Quebec, Canada
Home: 367 Sackville Street, Toronto, Ontario M5A 3G5, Canada,
    416/929-9677
Agent: Charles Northcote, The Core Group, 489 College Street -
    Suite 501, Toronto, Ontario M6G 1A5, Canada, 416/944-0193

MARSHALL McLUHAN (TD) 1965, Canadian
LENI RIEFENSTAHL, HITLER'S CAMERA (TD) 1965, Canadian
AT HOME 1968, Canadian
THE LIFE GAME (TF) 1970, Canadian
WITHOUT A HOBBY, IT'S NO LIFE (TF) 1973, Canadian
ORILLIA: OUR TOWN (TF) 1974, Canadian
MIDDLE GAME (TF) 1974, Canadian
MELONY (TF) 1974, Canadian
TOGETHERNESS (TF) 1975, Canadian

SAM, GRACE, DOUG AND THE DOG (TF) 1976, Canadian
THIS WILL DO FOR TODAY (TF) 1977, Canadian
NORTHERN LIGHTS (TF) 1980, Canadian
WAR BRIDES (TF) 1980, Canadian
RUMOURS OF GLORY (TF) Rumours of Glory Productions/Extra
    Modern Productions Ltd., 1981, Canadian
MAGGIE AND PIERRE (TF) 1983, Canadian
CHARLIE GRANT'S WAR (TF) 1984, Canadian
RED RIVER (TF) 1985, Canadian
THE MARRIAGE BED (TF) 1986, Canadian
PALAIS ROYALE Spectrafilm, 1988, Canadian
INVENTORS AREN'T CRAZY (TF) 1991, Canadian

CLARA LAW
Contact: Hong Kong Film Liaison, 10940 Wilshire Blvd. - Suite 1220,
    Los Angeles, CA 90024, 310/208-2678

THE REINCARNATION OF GOLDEN LOTUS East-West Classics,
    1989, Hong Kong
FAREWELL CHINA Friends Cheers Ltd., 1990, Hong Kong
FRUIT PUNCH 1991, Hong Kong
AUTUMN MOON Right Staff Office/Eizo Tanteisha/Trix Films,
    1992, Hong Kong-Japanese
TEMPTATION OF A MONK Tedpoly Films, 1993,
    Hong Kong-Chinese
EROTIQUE co-director with Lizzie Borden & Monika Treut,
    Group 1/Trigon/Tedpoly Films, 1994, U.S.-Hong Kong-German

TOM LAW
TAX SEASON Prism Entertainment, 1990

JONATHAN (J.F.) LAWTON
(J.D. Athens)
Agent: UTA - Beverly Hills, 310/273-6700
Personal Manager: Gary W. Goldstein - Los Angeles, 310/659-9511

CANNIBAL WOMEN IN THE AVOCADO JUNGLE OF DEATH
    directed under pseudonym of J.D. Athens, Megalomania
    Productions, 1988
PIZZA MAN directed under pseudonym of J.D. Athens,
    Megalomania Productions, 1991
THE HUNTED Universal, 1995

RAY LAWRENCE
Agent: Becsey/Wisdom/Kalajian - Los Angeles, 310/550-0535

BLISS New World, 1985, Australian

DAVID LAYTON
DEMON HUNTERS Golden Harvest, 1989, Hong Kong

ASHLEY LAZARUS*
Address: 2000 Broadway - Apt. 7E, New York, NY 10023,
    212/877-1012

FOREVER YOUNG, FOREVER FREE *E'LOLLIPOP*
    Universal, 1976, British
GOLDEN RENDEZVOUS Rank, 1977, British

PAUL LEAF*
b. May 2, 1929 - New York, New York
Home: 2800 Neilson Way, Santa Monica, CA 90405, 310/392-5276
Business Manager: Alan U. Schwartz, Shea & Gould, 1800 Avenue
    of the Stars, Los Angeles, CA 90067, 310/277-1000

TOP SECRET (TF) Jemmin, Inc./Sheldon Leonard
    Productions, 1978
SERGEANT MATLOVICH VS. THE U.S. AIR FORCE (TF)
    Tomorrow Entertainment, 1978
GOD, SEX AND APPLE PIE Centaur Productions, 1995

LARRY LEAHY
13 O'CLOCK co-director with Frank Mazzola, Third Coast
    Entertainment, 1988
FALLEN ANGELS Paul International, 1991

ORLANDO JIMENEZ-LEAL
(See Orlando JIMENEZ-LEAL)

NORMAN LEAR*
b. July 27, 1922 - New Haven, Connecticut
Business Manager: Sandy Mills, Perry & Neidorf, 9720 Wilshire
Blvd. - 3rd Floor, Beverly Hills, CA 90212, 310/550-2039

COLD TURKEY   United Artists, 1971
THE POWERS THAT BE (TF)   Act III TV/Castle Rock
Entertainment/Columbia TV, 1992

MARIA C. LEASE
Agent: Shapiro-Lichtman Talent Agency - Los Angeles,
310/859-8877

DOLLY DEAREST   Trimark Pictures, 1992

PATRICE LECONTE
b. November 12, 1947 - Paris, France
Agent: APA - Los Angeles, 310/273-0744

MONSIEUR HIRE   Orion Classics, 1989, French
THE HAIRDRESSER'S HUSBAND   *LE MARI DE LA COIFFEUSE*
Triton Pictures, 1990, French
CONTRE L'OUBLI   co-director, Les Films du Paradoxe/Amnesty
International/PRV, 1992, French
TANGO   AMLF, 1993, French
LE PARFUM D'YVONNE   Lambart Productions/Zoulou Films/
Centre Europeen Cinematographique Rhone-Alpes/M6 Films/
Cofimage 5/Investimage 4/Sofiarp 2/Canal Plus/CNC,
1994, French

BRUCE LEDDY
Agent: Scott Yoselow, The Gersh Agency - New York City,
212/997-1818

BAD WITH NUMBERS   Savoy Pictures, 1995

MIMI LEDER*
Agent: ICM - Beverly Hills, 310/550-4000

NIGHTINGALES (TF)   Aaron Spelling Productions, 1988
WOMAN WITH A PAST (TF)   World International Network/
Greystone Communications/Art Harris Productions/Neal and
Gary Productions/von Zerneck-Sertner Films, 1992
A LITTLE PIECE OF HEAVEN (TF)   Grossbart-Barnett
Productions, 1991
THE SANDMAN (TF)   Finnegan-Pinchuk Company/NBC
Productions, 1993
THERE WAS A LITTLE BOY (TF)   Craig Anderson Productions/
Lorimar TV, 1993
RIO SHANNON (TF)   Sacret Inc./Warner Bros. TV, 1993
HOUSE OF SECRETS (TF)   Steve Krantz Productions/Multimedia
Motion Pictures, 1993
BABY BROKERS (TF)   Steinbardt Baer Pictures Company/BBK
Productions/Columbia TV, 1994
THE INNOCENT (TF)   Todman-Simon Productions/Grammnet
Productions/Warner Bros. TV, 1994

PAUL LEDER
Agent: Irv Schechter Company - Beverly Hills, 310/278-8070

FRAME-UP   Independent, 1990
GOIN' TO CHICAGO   Independent, 1991
EXILED   Curb/Esquire Films, 1992
FRAME UP II: THE COVER-UP   Promark Entertainment
Group, 1992
THE BABY DOLL MURDERS   Republic Pictures, 1993
MOLLY & GINA   Curb Entertainment, 1993

JACQUES LEDUC
Contact: Directors Guild of Canada, 225 Richmond Street, Toronto
M5V 1W2, Canada, 416/351-8200

TROIS POMMES A COTE DU SOMMEIL   Malofilm/National Film
Board of Canada, 1990, Canadian
MONTREAL VU PAR...   co-director with Patricia Rozema,
Michel Brault, Atom Egoyan, Lea Pool & Denys Arcand,
Cinema Plus Distribution, 1991, Canadian
LA VIE FANTOME   Max Films/National Film Board of Canada/
Telefilm Canada/La Societe de Radio-Television du Quebec/
Super Ecran, 1992, Canadian

PAUL LEDUC
b. March 11, 1942 - Mexico City, Mexico
Address: Calvario 4 Bis, Colonia Tlalpan, 1400 Mexico D.F.
Contact: IMCINE, Tepic #40, P.B. Colonia Roma Sur, Mexico City,
C.P. 06760, Mexico, tel.: 525/584-7283

REED: INSURGENT MEXICO   New Yorker, 1970, Mexican
ETNOCIDIA, NOTAS SOBRE MEZQUITAL (TD)   Azteca Films,
1976, Mexican-Canadian
ESTUDIOS PARA UN RETRATO (FD)   Azteca Films,
1978, Mexican
FRANCIS BACON (FD)   Azteca Films, 1978, Mexican
MONJAS CORONADAS (FD)   Azteca Films, 1978, Mexican
HISTORIAS PROHIBIDAS DE PULGARCITO   Azteca Films,
1980, Mexican
LA CABEZA DE LA HIDRA (TF)   Azteca Films, 1981, Mexican
FRIDA: NATURALEZA VIVA   Azteca Films, 1985, Mexican
HAMBRE COMO VES?   Azteca Films, 1986, Mexican
BARROCO   Television Espanola/Opulo Films/ICAIC/Quinto
Centenario, 1989, Spanish-Cuban
LATINO BAR   Opal Films/University of Los Andes/ICAIC/Channel 4/
TVE, 1990, Spanish-Venezuelan-Cuban-British
DOLLAR MAMBO   Programa Doble/Igeldo Zine Produkzioak,
1993, Mexican-Spanish

ANG LEE
Agent: CAA - Beverly Hills, 310/288-4545

PUSHING HANDS   Cinepix Film Properties, 1991, Taiwanese-U.S.
THE WEDDING BANQUET   The Samuel Goldwyn Company,
1993, U.S.-Taiwanese
EAT DRINK MAN WOMAN   The Samuel Goldwyn Company,
1994, Taiwanese
SENSE AND SENSABILITY   Columbia, 1995, Britsh

DOO-YONG LEE
(See Lee DOO-YONG)

JACK LEE
b. 1913 - Stroud, England
Contact: British Film Commission, 70 Baker Street, London
W1M 1DJ, England, tel.: 171/224-5000

THE PILOT IS SAFE (FD)   GPO Film Unit, 1941, British
ORDINARY PEOPLE (FD)   co-director with J.B. Holmes,
GPO Film Unit, 1942, British
CLOSE QUARTERS   *UNDERSEA RAIDER* (FD)   GPO Film Unit,
1943, British
BY SEA AND LAND (FD)   GPO Film Unit, 1944, British
THE EIGHTH PLAGUE (FD)   GPO Film Unit, 1945, British
CHILDREN ON TRIAL   1946, British
THE WOMAN IN THE HALL   1947, British
ONCE A JOLLY SWAGMAN   1948, British
THE WOODEN HORSE   British Lion, 1950, British
THE GOLDEN MASK   *SOUTH OF ALGIERS*   United Artists,
1953, British
TURN THE KEY SOFTLY   Rank, 1953, British
A TOWN LIKE ALICE   Lopert, 1956, British
ROBBERY UNDER ARMS   Rank, 1957, British
THE CAPTAIN'S TABLE   20th Century-Fox, 1959, British
CIRCLE OF DECEPTION   20th Century-Fox, 1960, British

JANG-HO LEE
(See Lee JANG-HO)

JOANNA LEE*
Address: 11415 Cashmere Street, Los Angeles, CA 90049,
310/476-2845
Agent: Irv Schechter Company - Beverly Hills, 310/278-8070

MIRROR, MIRROR (TF)   Christiana Productions, 1979
CHILDREN OF DIVORCE (TF)   Christiana Productions/Marble
Arch Productions, 1980

JOE LEE
Contact: Irish Film Institute, 6 Eustace Street, Dublin 2, Ireland,
tel.: 795744

THE COURIER   co-director with Frank Deasy, Vestron,
1988, Irish-British

SPIKE LEE
(Shelton Jackson Lee)
b. 1956 - Atlanta, Georgia
Business: 40 Acres & A Mule Productions, 124 DeKalb Avenue,
Brooklyn, NY 11217, 718/624-3703
Agent: ICM - Beverly Hills, 310/550-4000

JOE'S BED-STUY BARBERSHOP: WE CUT HEADS
First Run Features, 1983
SHE'S GOTTA HAVE IT   Island Pictures, 1986
SCHOOL DAZE   Columbia, 1988
DO THE RIGHT THING   Universal, 1989
MO' BETTER BLUES   Universal, 1990
JUNGLE FEVER   Universal, 1991
MALCOLM X   Warner Bros., 1992
CROOKLYN   Universal, 1994
CLOCKERS   Universal, 1995
GIRL 6   20th Century Fox, 1995

ROBERT LEEDS*
Contact: Directors Guild of America - Los Angeles, 213/851-3671

RETURN OF THE BEVERLY HILLBILLIES (TF)   CBS, 1981

DOUG LEFLER*
Agent: Stephanie Rogers & Associates - Los Angeles, 213/851-5155

HERCULES AND THE CIRCLE OF FIRE (TF)   Renaissance Films/
Universal TV, 1994

MICHEL LEGRAND
Contact: French Film Office, 745 Fifth Avenue, New York,
NY 10151, 212/832-8860

CINQ JOURS EN JUIN   Compagnie Francaise Cinematographique/
Productions Michel Legrand/Films A2, 1989, French

ERNEST LEHMAN
b. 1920 - New York, New York
Agent: The Gersh Agency - Beverly Hills, 310/274-6611
Business Manager: Henry J. Bamberger, 2049 Century Park East,
Los Angeles, CA 90067, 310/553-0581

PORTNOY'S COMPLAINT   Warner Bros., 1972

MICHAEL LEHMANN*
b. 1957 - San Francisco, California
Agent: CAA - Beverly Hills, 310/288-4545
Personal Manager: Brillstein/Grey Entertainment - Beverly Hills,
310/275-6135

HEATHERS   New World, 1989
MEET THE APPLEGATES   Triton Pictures, 1990
HUDSON HAWK   TriStar, 1991
AIRHEADS   20th Century Fox, 1994
THE TRUTH ABOUT CATS AND DOGS   20th Century Fox, 1995

PETER LEHNER
MEGAVILLE   Expanded Entertainment/Backstreet Films, 1990

ARNOLD LEIBOVIT
b. June 18, 1950 - Miami, Florida
Business: Talking Rings Entertainment, P.O. Box 2019, Beverly Hills,
CA 90213, 310/306-1909
Contact: John E. Mason, Attorney, 100 Wilshire Blvd., Santa Monica,
CA 90401, 310/319-0120 or 702/588-6963

THE FANTASY FILM WORLDS OF GEORGE PAL (FD)
Leibovit Productions, 1986
THE PUPPETOON MOVIE (FD)   Expanded Entertainment, 1987

NEIL LEIFER
YESTERDAY'S HERO   Elliott Kastner Productions, 1981, British
TRADING HEARTS   Cineworld, 1988

MIKE LEIGH
b. 1943 - Salford, England
Agent: William Morris Agency - Beverly Hills, 310/859-4000 or:
Peters Fraser & Dunlop - London, tel.: 171/344-1000

BLEAK MOMENTS   1971, British
HARD LABOUR (TF)   BBC, 1972, British
NUTS IN MAY (TF)   BBC, 1976, British
ABIGAIL'S PARTY (TF)   Hampstead/BBC, 1977, British
GROWN-UPS (TF)   BBC, 1980, British
MEANTIME (TF)   Channel 4/Mostpoint/Central Film, 1983
FOUR DAYS IN JULY (TF)   BBC, 1984, British
HIGH HOPES   Skouras Pictures, 1988, British
LIFE IS SWEET   October Films, 1990, British
NAKED   Fine Line Features/New Line Cinema, 1993, British

WARREN LEIGHT
Agent: William Morris Agency - Beverly Hills, 310/859-4000

THE NIGHT WE NEVER MET   Miramax Films, 1993

CHRISTOPHER LEITCH*
Agent: Innovative Artists - Los Angeles, 310/553-5200
Personal Manager: Carthay Circle Pictures and Management -
Beverly Hills, 310/657-5454

TEEN WOLF TOO   Atlantic Releasing Corporation, 1987
COURAGE MOUNTAIN   Triumph Releasing Corporation,
1989, U.S.-French

DAVID LEIVICK
Agent: Sam Schwartz, Gorfaine/Schwartz Agency - Los Angeles,
213/969-1011

GOSPEL (FD)   co-director with Frederick Ritzenberg,
20th Century-Fox, 1983

LARRY LEKER
Business: MGM Animation, 1545 26th Street, Santa Monica,
CA 90404, 310/449-3250

ALL DOGS GO TO HEAVEN II (AF)   co-director with Paul Sabella,
MGM-UA, 1995

DAVID LELAND
b. April 20, 1947 - Cambridge, England
Agent: CAA - Beverly Hills, 213/388-4545 or:
The Casarotto Company - London, tel.: 171/287-4450

WISH YOU WERE HERE   Atlantic Releasing Corporation,
1987, British
CHECKING OUT   Warner Bros., 1989, U.S.-British
CROSSING THE LINE   *THE BIG MAN*   Miramax Films,
1990, British

CLAUDE LELOUCH
b. October 30, 1937 - Paris, France
Business: Les Films 26, 15, avenue Hoche, 75008 Paris, France,
tel.: 1/42-25-00-89
Contact: French Film Office, 745 Fifth Avenue, New York,
NY 10151, 212/832-8860

LE PROPRE DE L'HOMME   1960, French
L'AMOUR AVEC DES SI   1963, French
LA FEMME SPECTACLE   1964, French
TO BE A CROOK   UNE FILLE ET DES FUSILS   Comet,
  1965, French
LES GRAND MOMENTS   1965, French
A MAN AND A WOMAN ★   Allied Artists, 1966, French
LIVE FOR LIFE   United Artists, 1967, French
FAR FROM VIETNAM (FD)   co-director with Jean-Luc Godard,
  Joris Ivens, William Klein, Alain Resnais & Agnes Varda,
  New Yorker, 1967, French
GRENOBLE (FD)   co-director with Francois Reichenbach,
  United Producers of America, 1968, French
LIFE LOVE DEATH   Lopert, 1969, French
LOVE IS A FUNNY THING   UN HOMME QUI ME PLAIT
  United Artists, 1970, French-Italian
THE CROOK   United Artists, 1971, French
SMIC, SMAC, SMOC   GSF, 1971, French
MONEY MONEY MONEY   L'AVENTURE C'EST L'AVENTURE
  GSF, 1972, French
HAPPY NEW YEAR   LA BONNE ANNEE   Avco Embassy,
  1973, French-Italian
VISIONS OF EIGHT (FD)   co-director with Yuri Ozerov,
  Mai Zetterling, Michael Pfleghar, Kon Ichikawa, Milos Forman &
  John Schlesinger, Cinema 5, 1973
AND NOW MY LOVE   TOUTE UNE VIE   Avco Embassy,
  1975, French-Italian
MARIAGE   1975, French
CAT AND MOUSE   Quartet, 1975, French
THE GOOD AND THE BAD   Paramount, 1976, French
SECOND CHANCE   SI C'ETAIT A REFAIRE   United Artists
  Classics, 1976, French
ANOTHER MAN, ANOTHER CHANCE   United Artists,
  1977, U.S.-French
ROBERT ET ROBERT   Quartet, 1978, French
A NOUS DEUX   AMLF, 1979, French-Canadian
BOLERO   LES UNS ET LES AUTRES/WITHIN MEMORY
  Double 13/Sharp Features, 1982, French
EDITH AND MARCEL   Miramax, 1983, French
VIVA LA VIE   UGC, 1984, French
PARTIR REVENIR   UGC, 1985, French
A MAN AND A WOMAN: 20 YEARS LATER   Warner Bros.,
  1986, French
BANDITS   ATTENTION BANDITS   Grange Communications/
  Jerry Winters, 1987, French
L'ITINERAIRE D'UN ENFANT GATE   Films 13/Cerito Films, 1988,
  French-West German
IL Y A DES JOURS...ET DES LUNES   Films 13/TF1/Sofica Valor,
  1990, French
LA BELLE HISTOIRE   AFMD, 1992, French
TOUR CA...POUR CA!   Bac Films, 1993, French
LES MISERABLES   Les Films 13/TF 1 Films/Canal Plus/
  Franche-Comte Region, 1995, French

JAMES LEMMO
Agent: Onorato/Guillod Entertainment - Burbank, 818/566-6607

HEART   New World, 1987
WE'RE TALKIN' SERIOUS MONEY   RS Entertainment, 1993
DREAM A LITTLE DREAM 2   CineTel Films, 1994
BODILY HARM   Rysher Entertainment, 1994

JACK LEMMON*
(John Uhler Lemmon III)
b. February 8, 1925 - Boston, Massachusetts
Agent: CAA - Beverly Hills, 310/288-4545
Business: Jalem Productions, Inc., 141 El Camino - Suite 201,
  Beverly Hills, CA 90212, 310/278-7750
Business Manager: Premier Business Management, 13400 Riverside
  Drive - Suite 107, Sherman Oaks, CA 91423, 818/382-3599

KOTCH   Cinerama Releasing Corporation, 1971

RUSTY LEMORANDE*
Business Manager: Craig Jacobson, Hansen, Jacobson & Teller,
  335 N. Maple Drive - Suite 270, Beverly Hills, CA 90210,
  310/271-8777

JOURNEY TO THE CENTER OF THE EARTH   Cannon, 1989
THE TURN OF THE SCREW   Electric Pictures/Michael White
  Productions, 1992, British-French

TERRY LENNON
DAFFY DUCK'S QUACKBUSTERS (AF)   co-director with Greg Ford,
  Warner Bros., 1988

MALCOLM LEO*
b. October 9, 1944 - New York, New York
Business: Malcolm Leo Productions, 6536 Sunset Blvd.,
  Los Angeles, CA 90028, 213/464-4448
Agent: APA - Los Angeles, 310/273-0744

HEROES OF ROCK AND ROLL (TD)   co-director with Andrew Solt,
  ABC, 1979
THIS IS ELVIS (FD)   co-director with Andrew Solt,
  Warner Bros., 1981
IT CAME FROM HOLLYWOOD (FD)   co-director with Andrew Solt,
  Paramount, 1982
SUPER NIGHT OF ROCK AND ROLL (TCD)   Malcolm Leo
  Productions, 1984
THE BEACH BOYS: AN AMERICAN BAND (FCD)   Vestron, 1985
WILL ROGERS - LOOK BACK IN LAUGHTER (CTD)   Malcolm Leo
  Productions, 1987
ROLLING STONE - TWENTY YEARS OF ROCK 'N ROLL (TD)
  Malcolm Leo Productions, 1987

BRETT LEONARD
Agent: CAA - Beverly Hills, 310/288-4545
Personal Manager: Steve Freedman - Studio City, 818/508-5115
Attorney: Dennis Cline, Behr and Robinson, 2049 Century Park East -
  Suite 2690, Los Angeles, CA 90067, 310/556-9210

THE LAWNMOWER MAN   New Line Cinema, 1992
HIDEAWAY   TriStar, 1995
VIRTUOSITY   Paramount, 1995

HERBERT B. LEONARD*
b. October 8, 1922 - New York, New York
Address: 4956 Los Feliz Blvd., Los Angeles, CA 90027,
  213/465-1148

THE PERILS OF PAULINE   Universal, 1967
GOING HOME   MGM, 1971

TERRY LEONARD*
Home: The Runnin' W Ranch, 11244 Darling Road, Agua Dulce,
  CA 91350, 213/462-2301

DEATH BEFORE DISHONOR   New World, 1987

JOHN LEONE*
Contact: Directors Guild of America - Los Angeles, 213/851-3671

THE GREAT SMOKEY ROADBLOCK   THE LAST OF THE
  COWBOYS   Dimension, 1978

PO-CHIH LEONG
(Liang Puzhl)
b. 1939 - London, England
Agent: Peters Fraser & Dunlop - London, tel.: 171/344-1000

JUMPING ASH   1976, Hong Kong
FOXBAT   1977, Hong Kong
ITCHY FINGERS   1977, Hong Kong
NO BIG DEAL   1979, Hong Kong
SUPER FOOL   1981, Hong Kong
HE LIVES BY NIGHT   1982, Hong Kong
BANANA COP   1984, Hong Kong

HONG KONG 1941   D&B/Bo Ho, 1985, Hong Kong
TIME TRAVELLER   1985, Hong Kong
THE ISLAND   1985, Hong Kong
PING PONG   The Samuel Goldwyn Company, 1985, British
CARRY ON DANCING   co-director with Kam Kwok-Leung,
   D&B Films, 1989, Hong Kong
SHANGHAI 1920   Fu Ngai Film Production Co., 1991, Hong Kong

SERGE LEPERON
Contact: French Film Office, 745 Fifth Avenue, New York,
   NY 10151, 212/832-8860

LAISSE BETON   Luna Films, 1984, French

DAN LERNER*
Home: 20706 Hillside Drive, Topanga, CA 90290
Agent: ICM - Beverly Hills, 310/550-4000

JUST LIFE (TF)   Victoria Principal Productions/Aaron Spelling
   Productions, 1990
SHAME (CTF)   Dalrymple Productions/Steinhardt Baer Pictures/
   Viacom, 1992
DESPERATE JOURNEY: THE ALLISON WILCOX STORY (TF)
   D'Antoni Productions/Viacom Productions, 1993

MURRAY LERNER*
Business: MLF Productions Inc., 630 Ninth Avenue, New York,
   NY 10036, 212/581-6772

FESTIVAL (FCD)   Original Cinema, 1967
JIMI HENDRIX AT THE ISLE OF WIGHT (FCD)
   Original Cinema, 1991

RICHARD LERNER
WHAT HAPPENED TO KEROUAC? (FD)   co-director with
   Lewis MacAdams, New Yorker, 1986

MICHAEL LESSAC*
Agent: UTA - Beverly Hills, 310/273-6700

HOUSE OF CARDS   Miramax Films, 1993

MARK L. LESTER*
(Mark Leslie Lester)
b. November 26, 1948 - Cleveland, Ohio
Business: American World Pictures, 11845 W. Olympic Blvd. -
   Suite 901, Los Angeles, CA 90064, 310/312-8010

TRICIA'S WEDDING   Lester Pictures, 1971
TWILIGHT OF THE MAYAS   Lester Pictures, 1972
STEEL ARENA   L-T, 1973
TRUCK STOP WOMEN   L-T, 1974
WHITE HOUSE MADNESS   Lester Pictures, 1975
BOBBI JO AND THE OUTLAW   American International, 1976
STUNTS   New Line Cinema, 1977
GOLD OF THE AMAZON WOMEN (TF)   Mi-Ka Productions, 1979
ROLLER BOOGIE   United Artists, 1979
CLASS OF 1984   United Film Distribution, 1982, Canadian
FIRESTARTER   Universal, 1984
COMMANDO   20th Century Fox, 1985
ARMED AND DANGEROUS   Columbia, 1986
CLASS OF 1999   Taurus Entertainment, 1990
SHOWDOWN IN LITTLE TOKYO   Warner Bros., 1991
EXTREME JUSTICE (CTF)   Trimark Pictures, 1993,
   originally filmed for theatrical distribution
NIGHT OF THE RUNNING MAN   Trimark Pictures, 1995

RICHARD LESTER*
b. January 19, 1932 - Philadelphia, Pennsylvania
Agent: CAA - Beverly Hills, 310/288-4545

RING-A-DING RHYTHM   IT'S TRAD, DAD   Columbia, 1962, British
THE MOUSE ON THE MOON   United Artists, 1963, British
A HARD DAY'S NIGHT   United Artists, 1964, British
THE KNACK...AND HOW TO GET IT   Lopert, 1965, British

HELP!   United Artists, 1965, British
A FUNNY THING HAPPENED ON THE WAY TO THE FORUM
   United Artists, 1966, British
TEENAGE REBELLION   MONDO TEENO   co-director with
   Norman Herbert, Trans-American, 1967, British-U.S.
HOW I WON THE WAR   United Artists, 1967, British
PETULIA   Warner Bros., 1968, U.S.-British
THE BED SITTING ROOM   United Artists, 1969, British
THE THREE MUSKETEERS (THE QUEEN'S DIAMONDS)
   20th Century-Fox, 1974, British
JUGGERNAUT   United Artists, 1974, British
THE FOUR MUSKETEERS (MILADY'S REVENGE)
   20th Century-Fox, 1975, British
ROYAL FLASH   20th Century-Fox, 1976, British
ROBIN AND MARIAN   Columbia, 1976, British
THE RITZ   Warner Bros., 1976
BUTCH AND SUNDANCE: THE EARLY DAYS
   20th Century-Fox, 1979
CUBA   United Artists, 1979
SUPERMAN II   Warner Bros., 1981, U.S.-British
SUPERMAN III   Warner Bros., 1983, U.S.-British
FINDERS KEEPERS   Warner Bros., 1984
RETURN OF THE MUSKETEERS   Universal, 1989,
   British-Spanish-French
PAUL McCARTNEY: GET BACK (CTD)   Allied Filmmakers/
   M.P.L./Front Page Films, 1991, British

SHELDON LETTICH*
Agent: APA - Los Angeles, 310/273-0744

LIONHEART   Universal, 1990
DOUBLE IMPACT   Columbia, 1991
ONLY THE STRONG   20th Century Fox, 1993

DON LETTS
THE PUNK ROCK MOVIE (FCD)   Cinematic, 1978

BRIAN LEVANT*
Business: Telvan Productgions, 9528 Dalegrove Drive, Beverly Hills,
   CA 90210, 310/275-9622
Agent: UTA - Beverly Hills, 310/273-6700

PROBLEM CHILD II   Universal, 1991
BEETHOVEN   Universal, 1992
THE FLINTSTONES   Universal, 1994

JEREMY LEVEN
b. Rye, New York
Agent: ICM - Beverly Hills, 310/550-4000

DON JUAN DeMARCO   New Line Cinema, 1995

JAY LEVEY*
Contact: Directors Guild of America - Los Angeles, 213/851-3671

U.H.F.   Orion, 1989

WILLIAM A. LEVEY*
b. March 31, 1943 - Stamford, Connecticut
Telephone: 310/273-3838
Business Manager: Leon R. Berro, 2001 S. Barrington Avenue -
   Suite 210, West Los Angeles, CA 90025, 310/478-3531

BLACKENSTEIN   LFG, 1973
TO BE A ROSE   Cinemation, 1974
WAM BAM THANK YOU SPACEMAN   Box Office
   International, 1975
SLUMBER PARTY '57   Cannon, 1977
THE HAPPY HOOKER GOES TO WASHINGTON   Cannon, 1977
SKATETOWN, U.S.A.   Columbia, 1979
LIGHTNING: THE WHITE STALLION   Cannon, 1986
HELLGATE   Ghost Town Film Management/Distant Horizon/Anant
   Singh Productions, 1989, Australian-British
COMMITTED   Trans World Entertainment, 1991, filmed in 1988
EROTIC ENCOUNTERS OF THE FOURTH KIND
   Valiant International Pictures, 1994

ALAN J. LEVI*
b. St. Louis, Missouri
Home: 3951 Longridge Avenue, Sherman Oaks, CA 91423, 818/981-3417
Agent: Irv Schechter Company - Beverly Hills, 310/278-8070

GEMINI MAN (TF)   Universal TV, 1976
THE RETURN OF THE INCREDIBLE HULK (TF)
    Universal TV, 1977
GO WEST, YOUNG GIRL (TF)   Bennett-Katleman Productions/
    Columbia TV, 1978
THE IMMIGRANTS (TF)   Universal TV, 1978
THE LEGEND OF THE GOLDEN GUN (TF)   Bennett-Katleman
    Productions/Columbia TV, 1979
SCRUPLES (TF)   Lou-Step Productions/Warner Bros. TV, 1980
THE LAST SONG (TF)   Ron Samuels Productions/Motown
    Pictures, 1980
THE STEPFORD CHILDREN (TF)   Edgar J. Scherick Productions/
    Taft Entertainment TV, 1987
ISLAND SONS (TF)   Universal TV, 1987
THE RETURN OF SAM McCLOUD (TF)   Michael Sloan
    Productions/Universal TV, 1989
THE BIONIC SHOWDOWN: THE SIX-MILLION DOLLAR MAN
    AND THE BIONIC WOMAN (TF)   Universal TV, 1989
KNIGHT RIDER 2000 (TF)   Desperado Films, 1991
COLUMBO AND THE MURDER OF A ROCK STAR (TF)
    Universal TV, 1991
NO TIME TO DIE (TF)   Universal TV, 1992
WITHOUT WARNING: TERROR IN THE TOWERS (TF)
    Melniker Productions/Wilshire Court Productions, 1993
DEADMAN'S REVENGE (CTF)   MTE Inc./Finnegan-Pinchuk
    Productions/USA Network, 1994

MARC LEVIN
BLOWBACK   Northern Arts Entertainment, 1991
MOB STORIES (CTD)   Blowback Productions/HBO, 1993
THE LAST PARTY (FD)   co-director with Mark Benjamin,
    Triton Pictures, 1993
GANG WAR: BANGIN' IN LITTLE ROCK (CTD)
    Blowback Productions/HBO, 1994

PETER LEVIN*
b. Trenton, New Jersey
Agent: William Morris Agency - Beverly Hills, 310/859-4000

HEART IN HIDING (TF)   Filmways, 1973
PALMERSTOWN, U.S.A. (TF)   Haley-TAT Productions, 1980
THE COMEBACK KID (TF)   ABC Circle Films, 1980
RAPE AND MARRIAGE: THE RIDEOUT CASE (TF)   Stonehenge
    Productions/Blue Greene Productions/Lorimar
    Productions, 1980
THE MARVA COLLINS STORY (TF)   NRW Features, 1981
WASHINGTON MISTRESS (TF)   Lorimar Productions, 1982
THE ROYAL ROMANCE OF CHARLES AND DIANA (TF)
    Chrysalis-Yellen Productions, 1982
A DOCTOR'S STORY (TF)   Embassy TV, 1984
A REASON TO LIVE (TF)   Rastar Productions/Robert Papazian
    Productions, 1985
CALL TO GLORY: JFK (TF)   Tisch-Avnet Productions/
    Paramount TV, 1985
BETWEEN THE DARKNESS AND THE DAWN (TF)   Doris Quinlan
    Productions/Warner Bros. TV, 1985
NORTHSTAR (TF)   Daniel Grodnik Productions/Clyde Phillips
    Productions/Warner Bros. TV, 1986
"POPEYE" DOYLE (TF)   December 3rd Productions/Robert Singer
    Productions/20th Century Fox TV, 1986
HOUSTON: THE LEGEND OF TEXAS (TF)   Taft Entertainment
    TV/J.D. Feigelson Productions, 1986
SWORN TO SILENCE (TF)   Daniel H. Blatt-Robert Singer
    Productions, 1987
HOSTAGE (TF)   CBS Entertainment, 1988
IN THE HEAT OF THE NIGHT (TF)   NBC, 1988
THE LITTLEST VICTIMS (TF)   CBS Entertainment, 1989
LADY IN A CORNER (TF)   Sagaponack Films/Pantheon Pictures/
    Allen Leicht Productions/Fries Entertainment, 1989

A KILLER AMONG US (TF)   Dave Bell Associates, 1990
MY SON JOHNNY (TF)   Capital Cities-ABC Video Productions/
    Citadel Entertainment/Carla Singer Productions, 1991
DELIVER THEM FROM EVIL: THE TAKING OF ALTA VIEW (TF)
    Citadel Entertainment, 1992
OVERKILL: THE AILEEN WUORNOS STORY (TF)
    Republic Pictures, 1992
THE MAN WITH THREE WIVES (TF)   CBS Entertainment
    Productions/Arnold Shapiro Productions, 1993
PRECIOUS VICTIMS (TF)   Laurel Entertainment, 1993
FIGHTING FOR MY DAUGHTER: THE ANNE DION STORY (TF)
    Longbow Productions/Mike Robe Productions, 1995
A STRANGER IN TOWN (TF)   Avenue Pictures/Hearst
    Entertainment, 1995

SIDNEY LEVIN*
Contact: Directors Guild of America - Los Angeles, 213/851-3671

LET THE GOOD TIMES ROLL (FCD)   co-director with
    Robert J. Abel, Columbia, 1973
THE GREAT BRAIN   Osmond Distribution Company, 1978

PAUL LEVINE
Contact: Writers Guild of America, West - Los Angeles, 310/550-1000
Agent: Camden-ITG - Los Angeles, 310/289-2700

NIGHTWATCH   Hess-Kallberg Associates, 1994

BARRY LEVINSON*
b. 1942 - Baltimore, Maryland
Business: Baltimore Pictures, 4000 Warner Blvd., Burbank,
    CA 91522, 818/954-2666
Agent: CAA - Beverly Hills, 310/288-4545

DINER   MGM/United Artists, 1982
THE NATURAL   TriStar, 1984
YOUNG SHERLOCK HOLMES   Paramount, 1985
TIN MEN   Buena Vista, 1987
GOOD MORNING, VIETNAM   Buena Vista, 1987
RAIN MAN ★★   MGM/UA, 1988
AVALON   TriStar, 1990
BUGSY ★   TriStar, 1991
TOYS   20th Century Fox, 1992
JIMMY HOLLYWOOD   Paramount, 1994
DISCLOSURE   Warner Bros., 1994

MARK A. LEVINSON
PRISONER OF TIME   Prize Productions, 1994

GENE LEVITT*
b. May 28, 1920 - New York, New York
Agent: Wile Enterprises, 2730 Wilshire Blvd., Santa Monica,
    CA 90403

ANY SECOND NOW (TF)   Universal TV, 1969
RUN A CROOKED MILE (TF)   Universal TV, 1969
ALIAS SMITH AND JONES (TF)   Universal TV, 1971
COOL MILLION (TF)   Universal TV, 1972
THE PHANTOM OF HOLLYWOOD   MGM TV, 1974
SHE'LL BE SWEET (MS)   Australian Broadcasting Commission/
    Trans-Atlantic Enterprises, 1979, Australian

EDMOND LEVY*
b. September 26, 1929 - Toronto, Ontario, Canada
Home: 135 Central Park West, New York, NY 10023, 212/595-7666

TROUBLE IN THE FAMILY (TF)   Harold Mayer Productions,
    1972, Canadian
MOM, THE WOLFMAN AND ME (TF)   Time-Life Productions, 1981
STRESS (TD)   Time-Life Productions, 1982

EUGENE LEVY*
b. December 17, 1946 - Toronto, Ontario, Canada
Agent: William Morris Agency - Beverly Hills, 310/859-4000

ONCE UPON A CRIME   MGM-Pathe Communications,
   1992, U.S.-Italian
PARTNERS 'N LOVE (CTF)   Atlantis Films/Barry Jossen
   Productions/The Family Channel, 1992, Canadian-U.S.
SODBUSTERS (CTF)   Atlantis Films/Bond Street Productions/
   Telefilm Canada/OFIP, 1994, Canadian-U.S.

JEFERY LEVY
Agent: UTA - Beverly Hills, 310/273-6700

DRIVE   MEI Releasing, 1991
INSIDE MONKEY ZETTERLAND   I.R.S. Releasing, 1993
S.F.W.   Gramercy Pictures, 1994

RALPH LEVY*
Home: 206 McKenzie Street, Santa Fe, NM 87501, 505/983-7545

BEDTIME STORY   Universal, 1964
DO NOT DISTURB   20th Century-Fox, 1965

SCOTT D. LEVY
Contact: Concorde Pictures, 11600 San Vicente Blvd., Los Angeles,
   CA 90049, 310/826-0978

OF UNKNOWN ORIGIN   Concorde, 1994
MIDNIGHT TEASE   Concorde, 1994

SHUKI LEVY
TWILIGHT BLUE   Vertigo Pictures, 1991
BLIND VISION   Saban Entertainment/Vertigo Productions, 1992

BEN LEWIN
b. August 6, 1946 - Poland
Home: 73 St. George's Road, Elsternwick 3185, Melbourne,
   Australia, tel.: 523-7979
Agent: Innovative Artists - Los Angeles, 310/553-5200

THE DUNERA BOYS (TF)   The Ten Network, 1985, Australian
MATTER OF CONVENIENCE (TF)   Australian Broadcasting
   Corporation/Revcom, 1987, Australian
GEORGIA   Hoyts, 1989, Australian
THE FAVOR, THE WATCH AND THE VERY BIG FISH
   THE FAVOUR, THE WATCH & THE VERY BIG FISH
   Trimark Pictures, 1991, French-British
LUCKY BREAK   The Samuel Goldwyn Company, 1994, Australian

AUDREY LEWIS
THE GIFTED   Lewco, 1994

CHRISTOPHER LEWIS
DAN TURNER, HOLLYWOOD DETECTIVE (TF)
   Fries Entertainment/LBS Communications, 1990

DAVID LEWIS
DANGEROUS CURVES   Lightning Pictures, 1988

EVERETT LEWIS
LAZARUS   1987
THE NATURAL HISTORY OF PARKING LOTS
   Strand Releasing, 1990
AN AMBUSH OF GHOSTS   Stress Fiesta Films, 1993

HERSCHELL GORDON LEWIS
LIVING VENUS   Creative Services, 1960
THE ADVENTURES OF LUCKY PIERRE   directed under the
   pseudonym of Lewis H. Gordon, 1961
DAUGHTER OF THE SUN   directed under the pseudonym of
   Lewis H. Gordon, 1962
NATURE'S PLAYMATES   directed under the pseudonym of
   Lewis H. Gordon, Dore Productions, 1962

BOIN-N-G   directed under the pseudonym of Lewis H. Gordon,
   Box Office Spectaculars, 1963
BLOOD FEAST   Box Office Spectaculars, 1963
GOLDILOCKS AND THE THREE BEARS   *GOLDILOCKS' THREE
   CHICKS* directed under the pseudonym of Lewis H. Gordon,
   Dore Productions, 1963
BELL, BARE AND BEAUTIFUL   directed under the pseudonym of
   Lewis H. Gordon, Griffith Productions, 1963
SCUM OF THE EARTH   *DEVIL'S CAMERA* directed under the
   pseudonym of Lewis H. Gordon, Box Office Spectaculars, 1963
2000 MANIACS   Box Office Spectaculars, 1964
MOONSHINE MOUNTAIN   Herschell Gordon Lewis
   Productions, 1964
COLOR ME BLOOD RED   Jacqueline Kay, Inc., 1965
MONSTER A GO-GO   *TERROR AT HALFDAY* directed under the
   pseudonym of Sheldon Seymour, 1965
SIN, SUFFER AND REPENT   director of additional scenes,
   1965, British-U.S.
JIMMY, THE BOY WONDER   Mayflower Pictures, 1966
ALLEY TRAMP   directed under the pseudonym of Armand Parys,
   United Picture Organization, 1966
AN EYE FOR AN EYE   Creative Film Enterprises, 1966
SANTA CLAUS VISITS THE LAND OF MOTHER GOOSE   1967
SUBURBAN ROULETTE   Argent Film Productions, 1967
SOMETHING WEIRD   Mayflower Pictures, 1967
A TASTE OF BLOOD   Creative Film Enterprises, 1967
THE GRUESOME TWOSOME   Mayflower Pictures, 1967
THE GIRL, THE BODY, AND THE PILL   Creative Film
   Enterprises, 1967
BLAST-OFF GIRLS   Creative Film Enterprises, 1967
THE ECSTASIES OF WOMEN   directed under the pseudonym of
   Mark Hansen, United Pictures Organization, 1969
LINDA AND ABILENE   directed under the pseudonym of
   Mark Hansen, United Pictures Organization, 1969
MISS NYMPHET'S ZAP-IN   directed under the pseudonym of
   Sheldon Seymour, Mayflower Pictures, 1970
THE WIZARD OF GORE   Mayflower Pictures, 1970
THIS STUFF'LL KILL YA!   Ultima Productions, 1971
YEAR OF THE YAHOO!   International Arts Corporation, 1972
BLACK LOVE   directed under the pseudonym of R.L. Smith,
   Lewis Motion Picture Enterprises, 1972
THE GORE-GORE GIRLS   Lewis Motion Picture Enterprises, 1972

JERRY LEWIS*
(Joseph Levitch)
b. March 16, 1926 - Newark, New Jersey
Business: 3160 W. Sahara Avenue - Suite C-16, Las Vegas, NV
   89102, 702/362-9730
Agent: William Morris Agency - Beverly Hills, 310/859-4000

THE BELLBOY   Paramount, 1960
THE LADIES' MAN   Paramount, 1961
THE ERRAND BOY   Paramount, 1962
THE NUTTY PROFESSOR   Paramount, 1963
THE PATSY   Paramount, 1964
THE FAMILY JEWELS   Paramount, 1965
THREE ON A COUCH   Columbia, 1966
THE BIG MOUTH   Columbia, 1967
ONE MORE TIME   United Artists, 1970, British
WHICH WAY TO THE FRONT?   Warner Bros., 1970
THE DAY THE CLOWN CRIED   Europa Film, 1972,
   French-Swedish, unfinished
HARDLY WORKING   20th Century-Fox, 1981
SMORGASBORD   Warner Bros., 1983

JOSEPH H. LEWIS*
b. April 6, 1900 - New York, New York
Home: 14069 Marquesas Way, Marina del Rey, CA 90292,
   310/823-3372

NAVY SPY   co-director with Crane Wilbur, 1937
COURAGE OF THE WEST   1937
SINGING OUTLAW   1937
THE SPY RING   *INTERNATIONAL SPY* 1938
BORDER WOLVES   1938
THE LAST STAND   1938
TWO-FISTED RANGERS   1940
BLAZING SIX-SHOOTERS   1940

TEXAS STAGECOACH   1940
THE MAN FROM TUMBLEWEEDS   1940
BOYS OF THE CITY   1940
THE RETURN OF WILD BILL   1940
THAT GANG OF MINE   Monogram, 1940
THE INVISIBLE GHOST   Monogram, 1941
PRIDE OF THE BOWERY   Monogram, 1941
CRIMINALS WITHIN   1941
ARIZONA CYCLONE   1941
BOMBS OVER BURMA   Producers Releasing Corporation, 1942
THE SILVER BULLET   1942
SECRETS OF A CO-ED   *SILENT WITNESS*   1942
THE BOSS OF HANGTOWN MESA   1942
THE MAD DOCTOR OF MARKET STREET   Universal, 1942
MINSTREL MAN   1944
THE FALCON IN SAN FRANCISCO   RKO Radio, 1945
MY NAME IS JULIA ROSS   Columbia, 1945
SO DARK THE NIGHT   Columbia, 1946
THE SWORDSMAN   Columbia, 1947
THE RETURN OF OCTOBER   Columbia, 1948
THE UNDERCOVER MAN   Columbia, 1949
GUN CRAZY   *DEADLY IS THE FEMALE*   United Artists, 1949
A LADY WITHOUT PASSPORT   MGM, 1950
RETREAT, HELL!   Warner Bros., 1952
DESPERATE SEARCH   MGM, 1953
CRY OF THE HUNTED   MGM, 1953
THE BIG COMBO   Allied Artists, 1955
A LAWLESS STREET   Columbia, 1955
THE 7TH CAVALRY   Columbia, 1956
THE HALLIDAY BRAND   United Artists, 1957
TERROR IN A TEXAS TOWN   United Artists, 1958

MARK LEWIS*

Agenbt: UTA - Beverly Hills, 310/273-6700

GORDY   Miramax Films, 1995

RICHARD J. LEWIS

Agent: The Gersh Agency - Beverly Hills, 3210/274-6611
Contact: Directors Guild of Canada, 225 Richmond Street, Toronto, Ontario M5V 1W2, Canada, 416/351-8200

WHALE MUSIC   Alliance Communications, 1994, Canadian

ROBERT M. LEWIS*

b. November 9, 1934 - New York, New York
Agent: Shapiro-Lichtman Talent Agency - Los Angeles, 310/859-8877

THE ASTRONAUT (TF)   Universal TV, 1972
THE ALPHA CAPER (TF)   Universal TV, 1973
MONEY TO BURN (TF)   Universal TV, 1973
MESSAGE TO MY DAUGHTER (TF)   Metromedia Productions, 1973
PRAY FOR THE WILDCATS (TF)   ABC Circle Films, 1974
THE DAY THE EARTH MOVED (TF)   ABC Circle Films, 1975
THE INVISIBLE MAN (TF)   Universal TV, 1975
GUILTY OR INNOCENT: THE SAM SHEPPARD MURDER CASE (TF)   Universal TV, 1975
NO ROOM TO RUN (TF)   Australian Broadcasting Commission/ Trans-Atlantic Enterprises, 1977, Australian
THE NIGHT THEY TOOK MISS BEAUTIFUL (TF)   Don Kirshner Productions, 1977
RING OF PASSION (TF)   20th Century-Fox TV, 1980
S*H*E (TF)   Martin Bregman Productions, 1980
IF THINGS WERE DIFFERENT (TF)   Bob Banner Associates, 1980
ESCAPE (TF)   Henry Jaffe Enterprises, 1980
A PRIVATE BATTLE (TF)   Procter & Gamble Productions/Robert Halmi, Inc., 1980
FALLEN ANGEL (TF)   Green-Epstein Productions/ Columbia TV, 1981
THE MIRACLE OF KATHY MILLER (TF)   Rothman-Wohl Productions/Universal TV, 1981
CHILD BRIDE OF SHORT CREEK (TF)   Lawrence Schiller-Paul Monash Productions, 1981

DESPERATE LIVES (TF)   Fellows-Keegan Company/Lorimar Productions, 1982
BETWEEN TWO BROTHERS (TF)   Turman-Foster Company/ Finnegan Associates, 1982
COMPUTERCIDE (TF)   Anthony Wilson Productions, 1982
SUMMER GIRL (TF)   Bruce Lansbury Productions/Roberta Haynes Productions/Finnegan Associates, 1983
AGATHA CHRISTIE'S 'A CARIBBEAN MYSTERY' (TF)   Stan Margulies Productions/Warner Bros. TV, 1983
AGATHA CHRISTIE'S 'SPARKLING CYANIDE' (TF)   Stan Margulies Productions/Warner Bros. TV, 1983
FLIGHT 90: DISASTER ON THE POTOMAC (TF)   Sheldon Pinchuk Productions/Finnegan Associates, 1984
CITY KILLER (TF)   Stan Shpetner Productions, 1984
A SUMMER TO REMEMBER (TF)   Inter Planetary Productions, 1985
EMBASSY (TF)   Stan Margulies Company/ABC Circle Films, 1985
LOST IN LONDON (TF)   Emmanuel Lewis Entertainment Enterprises/D'Angelo Productions/Group W. Productions, 1985
FIREFIGHTER (TF)   Forest Hills Productions/Embassy TV, 1986
A STRANGER WAITS (TF)   Bruce Lansbury Productions/Edgar Lansbury Productions/Lewisfilm Ltd./New Century TV Productions, 1987
DEEP DARK SECRETS (TF)   Gross-Weston Productions/Fries Entertainment, 1987
THE SECRET LIFE OF KATHY McCORMICK (TF)   Tamara Asseyev Productions/New World TV, 1988
LADYKILLERS (TF)   Barry Weitz Films/ABC Circle Films, 1988
DEAD RECKONING (CTF)   Houston Lady Productions, 1990
MEMORIES OF MURDER (CTF)   Houston Lady Company/Viacom Enterprises, 1990
DON'T TALK TO STRANGERS (CTF)   Pacific Motion Pictures/Barry Weitz Films/MTE, 1994
CIRCUMSTANCES UNKNOWN (CTF)   Shooting Star Entertainment/ Wilshire Court Productions, 1995

YIN LI

Contact: China Film Import & Export Office, 2500 Wilshire Blvd. - Suite 1028, Los Angeles, CA 90057, 213/380-7520

THE STORY OF XINGHUA   Arrow Releasing, 1994, Chinese

HOWARD LIBOV

Agent: Paradigm - Los Angeles, 310/277-4400

MIDNIGHT EDITION   Shapiro Glickenhaus Entertainment, 1993

JEFF LIEBERMAN*

Agent: Irv Schwartz, Renaissance/H.N. Swanson - Los Angeles, 310/246-6000

SQUIRM   American International, 1976
BLUE SUNSHINE   Cinema Shares International, 1979
DOCTOR FRANKEN (TF)   co-director with Marvin J. Chomsky, Titus Productions/Janus Productions, 1980
JUST BEFORE DAWN   Picturmedia Limited, 1981
REMOTE CONTROL   Vista Organization, 1988

ROBERT LIEBERMAN*

Business: Crystal Beach Entertainment, 2921 W. Alameda Avenue, Burbank, CA 91505, 818/846-6700
Agent: William Morris Agency - Beverly Hills, 310/859-4000

FIGHTING BACK (TF)   MTM Enterprises, 1980
WILL: G. GORDON LIDDY (TF)   A. Shane Company, 1982
TABLE FOR FIVE   Warner Bros., 1983
TO SAVE A CHILD (TF)   Konigsberg-Sanitsky Productions/Crystal Beach Entertainment/ABC Productions, 1991
ALL I WANT FOR CHRISTMAS   Paramount, 1991
FIRE IN THE SKY   Paramount, 1993
UNDER SUSPICION (TF)   Lakeside Productions/Warner Bros. TV, 1994

ROBERT H. LIEBERMAN
b. February 4, 1941
Business: Ithaca Filmworks, 400 Nelson Road, Ithaca,
   NY 14850, 607/273-8801
Attorney/Personal Manager: Jay Kramer, 135 East 55th Street,
   New York, NY 10022, 212/753-5420

HONG KONG AND ONWARD (FD)   Gamma Films, 1967
FACES IN A FAMINE (FD)   Ithaca Filmworks, 1986

JIMMY LIFTON
RAVEN DANCE   Orphan Eyes, 1993

RACHEL LIEBLING
HIGH LONESOME: THE STORY OF BLUEGRASS MUSIC (FD)
   Tara Releasing, 1993

PETER LILIENTHAL
Address: Stuttgarter Platz 22, 1000 Berlin, Germany,
   tel.: 030/323-9392
Contact: Federal Union of Film and Television Directors in
   Germany, Adelheidstrasse 7, 8000 Munich 40, Germany,
   tel.: 089/271-6380

LA VICTORIA (FD)   1973, West German
ER HERRSCHT RUHE IM LAND   Filmverlag Der Autoren,
   1976, West German
DAVID   Kino International, 1979, West German
THE UPRISING   Kino International, 1981, El Salvador
DEAR MR. WONDERFUL   Joachim von Vietinghoff Produktion/
   Westdeutscher Rundfunk/Sender Freis Berlin,
   1982, West German
THE AUTOGRAPH   Cine-International, 1984,
   West German-French
DAS SCHWEIGEN DES DICHTERS   Edgar Reitz Filmproduktion,
   1986, West German
FACING THE FOREST   Angelika Films, 1994, Israeli-German

ADAM LIMA
b. September 11, 1963 - Houston, Texas
Agent: Mike Guerra, Alum Associates - Los Angeles, 310/546-2762

SEVEN DAYS TO KILL   Westbound Productions, 1994
BEASTGIRL AND THUNDERHAWK (TF)   Fossilized
   Entertainment, 1994

KEVIN LIMA
Agent: UTA - Beverly Hills, 310/273-6700
Business: Walt Disney Animation, 500 S. Buena Vista Street,
   Burbank, CA, 818/956-1000

A GOOFY MOVIE (AF)   Buena Vista, 1994

DOUG LIMAN
STUDENT BODY   Ulysse Entertainment/Lindemann Entertainment
   Group/Foxboro Entertainment, 1994

ERIC STEVEN LINDEN
SLAVE MASTER   Mutual General Entertainment, 1991

VIVECA LINDFORS
(Elsa Viveca Torstensdotter Lindford)
b. December 29, 1920 - Uppsala, Sweden
Contact: Screen Actors Guild - Los Angeles, 213/954-1600

UNFINISHED BUSINESS...   American Film Institute, 1987

ELEANORE LINDO
CATWALK (TF)   Franklin-Waterman-Marvellous TV/Lewis B.
   Chesler Productions/King St. Entertainment, 1992

MICHAEL LINDSAY-HOGG*
b. May 5, 1940 - New York, New York
Agent: William Morris Agency - Beverly Hills, 310/859-4000

LET IT BE (FCD)   United Artists, 1970, British
NASTY HABITS   Brut Productions, 1977, British
BRIDESHEAD REVISITED (MS) ☆   co-director with
   Charles Sturridge, Granada TV/WNET-13/NDR Hamburg,
   1982, British-U.S.-West German
DOCTOR FISCHER OF GENEVA (TF)   Consolidated Productions/
   BBC, 1985, British
NAZI HUNTER: THE BEATE KLARSFELD STORY (TF)
   William Kayden Productions/Orion TV/Silver Chalice/Revcom/
   George Walker TV/TF1/SFP, 1986, U.S.-British-French
THE LITTLE MATCH GIRL (TF)   NBC Productions, 1987
MURDER BY MOONLIGHT (TF)   Tamara Asseyev Productions/
   London Weekend TV/Viacom, 1989, U.S.-British
THE STRANGE CASE OF DR. JEKYLL AND MR. HYDE (CTF)
   Think Entertainment, 1989
THE OBJECT OF BEAUTY   Avenue Pictures, 1991, British-U.S.
THE HABITATION OF DRAGONS (CTF)   Brandman Productions/
   Amblin Entertainment/Turner Pictures, 1992
RUNNING MATES (CTF)   HBO Pictures/Marvin Worth
   Productions, 1992
FRANKIE STARLIGHT   Fine Line Features/New Line Cinema,
   1995, Irish-British

RON LINK
ZOMBIE HIGH   Cinema Group, 1987

RICHARD LINKLATER
b. 1961 - Austin, Texas
Business: Detour, Inc., 2118 Guadalupe - Suite 133, Austin, TX
   78705, 512/322-0031
Agent: William Morris Agency - Beverly Hills, 310/859-4000

IT'S IMPOSSIBLE TO LEARN TO PLOW BY READING
   BOOKS   1987
SLACKER   Orion Classics, 1991
DAZED AND CONFUSED   Gramercy Pictures, 1993
BEFORE SUNRISE   Columbia, 1995

ART LINSON*
b. Chicago, Illinois
Business: Art Linson Productions, 4000 Warner Blvd., Burbank,
   CA 91522, 818/954-3386

WHERE THE BUFFALO ROAM   Universal, 1980
THE WILD LIFE   Universal, 1984

AARON LIPSTADT*
b. November 12, 1952 - Southington, Connecticut
Agent: UTA - Beverly Hills, 310/273-6700

ANDROID   Island Alive/New Realm, 1982
CITY LIMITS   Atlantic Releasing Corporation, 1985
POLICE STORY: MONSTER MANOR (TF)   Columbia TV, 1988
PAIR OF ACES (TF)   Pedernales Films/Once Upon A
   Time Films, 1990

STEVEN LISBERGER*
b. April 24, 1951 - Rye, New York
Agent: Tom Chasin, The Chasin Agency - Los Angeles, 310/278-7505

ANIMALYMPICS (AF)   Lisberger Studios, 1980
TRON   Buena Vista, 1982
HOT PURSUIT   Paramount, 1987
SLIPSTREAM   Entertainment Film Productions, 1989, British

DAVID LISTER
b. June 4, 1947 - Barberton, South Africa
Home: 87 Athol Street, Waverley, Johannesburg 2090, South Africa,
   tel.: 011/786-4096

RIDING HIGH (MS)   SABC-TV, 1983, South African
RIVER HORSE LAKE (MS)   SABC-TV, 1984, South African

MY FRIEND ANGELO (TF)   IFC, 1985, South African
JOHN ROSS, AN AFRICAN ADVENTURE (MS)   SABC-TV,
   1986, South African
THE SEA TIGER (MS)   IFC/Toron, 1987, South African
BARNEY BARNATO (MS)   IFC/Toron/Tele-Saar, 1988,
   South African-West German
THE RUTANGA TAPES   The Movie Group, 1989, Namibian
KWAGGA STRIKES BACK   Genesis Releasing,
   1991, South African
TRIGGER FAST   Vidmark Entertainment, 1993, South African

PETER MACKENZIE LITTEN
Contact: British Film Commission, 70 Baker Street, London
W1M 1DJ, England, tel.: 171/224-5000

TO DIE FOR   Victor Film Company, 1994, British

MIGUEL LITTIN
b. August 9, 1942 - Palmilla, Colchagua, Chile
Business: Cine Chile S.A., Huerfanos 878 - Suite 918, Santiago,
Chile, tel.: 633-3948

EL CHACAL DE NAHUELTORO   1970, Chilean
COMPANERO PRESIDENTE (FD)   1971, Chilean
LA TIERRA PROMETIDA   1972, Chilean
LETTERS FROM MARUSIA   Azteca Films, 1975, Mexican
EL RECURSO DEL METODO   Azteca Films, 1978,
   Mexican-French-Cuban
LA VIUDA DE MONTIEL   Azteca Films, 1980, Mexican
ALSINO AND THE CONDOR   1982, Cuban-Nicaraguan
ACTA GENERAL DE CHILE (FD)   Alfil Uno Cinematografica/TVE,
   1983, Cuban
SANDINO   RTVE/Miguel Littin Productions/TVE/
   Umanzor/Beta Film/Reteitalia/Granada TV, 1990,
   Spanish-Chilean-Nicaraguan-Italian-British-West German
LOS NAUFRAGOS   ACI Communicaciones/Productions
   D'Amerique Francaise/Arion Productions, 1994, Chilean-French

DWIGHT H. LITTLE*
Agent: CAA - Beverly Hills, 310/288-4545
Personal Manager: Friend Entertainment - Los Angeles,
   213/962-6090

KGB - THE SECRET WAR   LETHAL   Cinema Group, 1986
GETTING EVEN   American Distribution Group, 1986
HALLOWEEN 4   Galaxy International, 1988
BLOODSTONE   Omega Pictures, 1989
THE PHANTOM OF THE OPERA   21st Century Distribution, 1989
MARKED FOR DEATH   20th Century Fox, 1990
RAPID FIRE   20th Century Fox, 1992
FREE WILLY 2: THE ADVENTURE HOME   Warner Bros., 1995

LYNNE LITTMAN*
Home: 6620 Cahuenga Terrace, Los Angeles, CA 90068,
   213/467-6802
Agent: William Morris Agency - Beverly Hills, 310/859-4000

NUMBER OUR DAYS (FD)   1977
TESTAMENT   Paramount, 1983
IN HER OWN TIME (FD)   Direct Cinema Limited, 1985

STEVEN C.C. LIU
(Liu Chia-Ch'ang)
Contact: Department of Motion Picture Affairs, 2 Tientsin Street,
   Taipei, Taiwan, Republic of China, tel.: 2/351-6591

MAY JEAN   New Asian Horizons/Golden Entertainment Company,
   1994, Taiwanese

JENNIE LIVINGSTON
Agent: William Morris Agency - Beverly Hills, 310/859-4000

PARIS IS BURNING (FD)   Prestige, 1991

CARLO LIZZANI
b. April 3, 1917 - Rome, Italy
Home: Via F. Corridoni 7, Rome, Italy, tel.: 06/372-0185

ACHTUNG! BANDITI!   Cooperative Spettori Produti Cinematografici,
   1951, Italian
AL MARGINI DELLA METROPOLI   Elios Film, 1953, Italian
LOVE IN THE CITY   co-director, Italian Films Export, 1953
CRONACHE DI POVERI AMANTI   Cooperative Spettori Produtti
   Cinematografici, 1954, Italian
LO SVITATO   Galatea/ENIC, 1956, Italian
BEHIND THE GREAT WALL   LA MURAGLIA CINESE (FD)
   Continental, 1958, Italian
ESTERINA   Italia Prod. Film, 1959, Italian
IL GOBBO   Dino De Laurentiis Cinematografica, 1960, Italian
IL CARABINIERE A CAVALLO   Maxima Film, 1961, Italian
IL PROCESSO DI VERONA   Duilio Cinematografica/Dino De
   Laurentiis Cinematografica, 1963, Italian
LA VITA AGRA   Film Napoleon, 1964, Italian
AMORI PERICLOSI   co-director with Giulio Questi &
   Alfredo Giannetti, Zebra Film/Fulco Film/Aera Film,
   1964, Italian-French
LA CELESTINA P... R...   Aston Film, 1965, Italian
THE DIRTY GAME   GUERRE SECRETE   co-director with
   Terence Young, Christian-Jacque & Werner Klinger,
   American International, 1966, French-Italian-West German
THRILLING   co-director with Ettore Scola & Gian Luigi Polidori,
   Dino De Laurentiis Cinematografica, 1965, Italian
SVEGLIATI E UCCIDI   Sanson Film/Castoro Film, 1966, Italian
THE HILLS RUN RED   UN FIUME DI DOLLARI   directed under
   pseudonym of Lee W. Beaver, United Artists, 1966, Italian
REQUIESCANT   Castoro Film, 1967, Italian
THE VIOLENT FOUR   BANDITI A MILANO   Paramount,
   1968, Italian
L'AMANTE DI GRAMIGNA   Dino De Laurentiis Cinematografica,
   1969, Italian
AMORE E RABBIA   co-director with Bernardo Bertolucci,
   Pier Paolo Pasolini, Jean-Luc Godard & Marco Bellocchio,
   Castoro Film, 1969, Italian
BARBAGIA   Dino De Laurentiis Cinematografica, 1969, Italian
ROMA BENE   Castoro Film, 1971, Italian
TORINO NERA   Dino De Laurentiis Cinematografica,
   1972, Italian
CRAZY JOE   Columbia, 1974, Italian-U.S.
THE LAST FOUR DAYS   MUSSOLINI - ULTIMO ATTO
   Group 1, 1974, Italian
SAN BABILA ORE 20: UN DELITTO INUTILE   Agora,
   1976, Italian
KLEINHOFF HOTEL   Capitol, 1977, Italian
FONTAMARA   Sacis, 1980, Italian
LA CASA DEL TAPPETO GIALLO   Gaumont, 1983, Italian
ROME: THE IMAGE OF A CITY (FD)   Transworld Film,
   1983, Italian
NUCLEO ZERO   Diamant Film/RAI, 1984, Italian
MAMMA EBE   Clemi Cinematografica, 1985, Italian
UN' ISOLA (TF)   RAI, 1986, Italian
UNA MOGLIE (TF)   Regency Film/RAI, 1987, Italian
CARO GORBACIOV   UIP, 1988, Italian
THE MISSING FORMULA (MS)   Reteitalia/Titanus/Dean Film,
   1989, Italian
CATTIVA   PAC, 1991, Italian
IL CASO BIANCO   1993, Italian

LUIS 'LUCHO' LLOSA
b. Peru
Agent: CAA - Beverly Hills, 213-288-4545

HOUR OF THE ASSASSIN   Concorde, 1987, U.S.-Peruvian
CRIME ZONE   Concorde, 1989, U.S.-Peruvian
800 LEAGUES DOWN THE AMAZON   Concorde,
   1993, U.S.-Peruvian
SNIPER   TriStar, 1993
THE SPECIALIST   Warner Bros., 1994

KENNETH LOACH

b. June 17, 1936 - Nuneaton, Warwickshire, England
Address: 46 Charlotte Street, London W1, England
Agent: Judy Daish - London, tel.: 171/262-1101

DIARY OF A YOUNG MAN (TF)   1964, British
THREE CLEAR SUNDAYS (TF)   1965, British
THE END OF ARTHUR'S MARRIAGE (TF)   1965, British
UP THE JUNCTION (TF)   1965, British
COMING OUT PARTY (TF)   1965, British
CATHY COME HOME (TF)   1966, British
IN TWO MINDS (TF)   1966, British
THE GOLDEN VISION (TF)   1968, British
THE BIG FLAME (TF)   1968, British
POOR COW   National General, 1968, British
IN BLACK AND WHITE (TF)   1969, British
KES   United Artists, 1970, British
THE RANK AND FILE (TF)   1971, British
WEDNESDAY'S CHILD *FAMILY LIFE*   Cinema 5, 1972, British
BLACK JACK   Boyd's Company, 1979, British
THE GAMEKEEPER   ATV, 1980, British
AUDITIONS (TF)   ATV, 1980, British
LOOKS AND SMILES   Black Lion Films/Kestrel Films/MK2,
   1981, British- French
THE RED AND THE BLUE (TF)   1983, British
WHICH SIDE ARE YOU ON? (TD)   London Weekend TV, 1984
SINGING THE BLUES IN RED *FATHERLAND*   Angelika Films,
   1986, British-West German-French
HIDDEN AGENDA   Hemdale, 1990, British
RIFF-RAFF   Fine Line Features/New Line Cinema, 1991, British
RAINING STONES   Parallax Pictures/Channel 4, 1993, British
LADYBIRD LADYBIRD   The Samuel Goldwyn Company,
   1994, British
LAND AND FREEDOM   Parallax Pictures/Messidor Films/Road
   Movies/Television Espanola/British Screen, 1995,
   British-Spanish-German

TONY LO BIANCO*

b. New York, New York
Agent: David Shapira & Associates - Sherman Oaks, 818/906-0322
Business Manager: Unicorn Entertainment Inc., 327 Central
   Park West - Apt. 16B, New York, NY 10025, 212/222-7332

TOO SCARED TO SCREAM   The Movie Store, 1984

VICTOR LOBL*

Agent: Irv Schechter Company - Beverly Hills, 310/278-8070

BRAKER (TF)   Blatt-Singer Productions/Centerpoint Productions/
   MGM-UA TV, 1985
THE REVOLT OF MOTHER (TF)   Learning in Focus, 1988
BEAUTY AND THE BEAST (TF)   Witt-Thomas Productions/Ron
   Koslow Films/Republic Pictures Corporation, 1989
EDEN: FORBIDDEN INTERLUDES (CTF)   Pacific Rim Ltd., 1993

SONDRA LOCKE*

b. May 28, 1947 - Shelbyville, Tennessee
Agent: ICM - Beverly Hills, 310/550-4000

RATBOY   Warner Bros., 1986
IMPULSE   Warner Bros., 1990
DEATH IN SMALL DOSES (TF)   Robert Greenwald
   Productions, 1994

DOUG LODATO

Address: c/o Wilson, Sonsini, Goodrich & Rosati - San Francisco,
   415/493-9300

BEST SHOTS   Triax Entertainment Group, 1991

BRENT LOEFKE*

Telephone: 213/507-5772

GOLDILOCKS AND THE THREE BEARS   Santa Monica
   Pictures, 1995

BOB LOGAN

Agent: Elliot Wax & Associates, 9255 Sunset Blvd., Suite 612,
   Los Angeles, CA 90069, 310/273-8217; fax: 310/273-3551

UP YOUR ALLEY   LIVE Entertainment, 1989
REPOSSESSED   Seven Arts/New Line Cinema, 1990
MEATBALLS 4   Moviestore Entertainment, 1992

BRUCE LOGAN*

Home: 1803 N. Stanley Avenue, Los Angeles, CA 90046
Agent: Smith-Gosnell-Nicholson & Associates - Pacific Palisades,
   310/459-0307
Business Manager: John Mercedes, 3330 W. Cahuenga Blvd. -
   Suite 500, Los Angeles, CA 90068, 213/969-2821

VENDETTA   Concorde, 1986

DIMITRI LOGOTHETIS

PRETTY SMART   New World, 1987
SLAUGHTERHOUSE ROCK   Artists Entertainment Group, 1988
CHAMPIONS FOREVER (FD)   Ion Pictures, 1989
THE CLOSER   Ion Pictures, 1990
BODY SHOT   Eternity Pictures, 1993

LOUIS LOMBARDO*

Home: 5455 Longridge Avenue, Van Nuys, CA 91401, 818/902-0422

RUSSIAN ROULETTE   Avco Embassy, 1975, U.S.-Canadian
P.K. AND THE KID   Castle Hill Productions, 1987, filmed in 1982

ULLI LOMMEL

b. West Germany

TENDERNESS OF THE WOLVES   Monument, 1973, West German
DER MANN VON OBERZALZBERG - ADOLF UND MARLENE
   Albatros Produktion/Trio Film, 1976, West German
BLANK GENERATION   International Harmony, 1979, West German
COCAINE COWBOYS   International Harmony, 1979, West German
THE BOOGEY MAN   Jerry Gross Organization, 1980
A TASTE OF SIN   Ambassador, 1983
BRAINWAVES   MPM, 1983
THE DEVONSVILLE TERROR   MPM, 1983
STRANGERS IN PARADISE   New West, 1984
REVENGE OF THE STOLEN STARS   New West, 1985
DEFENSE PLAY   Kodiak Films, 1986
IFO   Kodiak Films, 1986
OVERKILL   United Independent Films, 1987
A YEAR AT LINCOLN PLAINS   Horizons Productions, 1987
WAR BIRDS   Vidmark Entertainment/Hess Kallberg Associates/
   Skyhawk Enterprises, 1989
COLD HEAT   Skyhawk Enterprises, 1989
DESTINATION UNKNOWN   Hess-Kallberg Associates, 1990
THE BIG SWEAT   Falcon Arts and Entertainment, 1991
NATURAL INSTINCT   Hatch Entertainment, 1991
A SMILE IN THE DARK   Hatch Entertainment, 1991

RICHARD LONCRAINE

b. October 20, 1946 - Cheltenham, England
Address: 86B Golborne Road, London W10 5PS, England,
   tel.: 181/968-8741
Agent: ICM - London, tel.: 171/636-6565

RADIO WONDERFUL   1972, British
FLAME   Goodtime Enterprises, 1975, British
THE HAUNTING OF JULIA *FULL CIRCLE*   Discovery Films,
   1977, British-Canadian
OY VAY MARIA (TF)   BBC, 1977, British
THE VANISHING ARMY (TF)   BBC, 1978, British
SECRET ORCHARDS (TF)   Granada TV, 1979, British
BLADE ON THE FEATHER (TF)   London Weekend TV,
   1980, British
BRIMSTONE AND TREACLE   United Artists Classics, 1982, British
THE MISSIONARY   Columbia, 1982, British
BELLMAN AND TRUE   Island Pictures, 1987, British
THE WEDDING GIFT   Miramax Films, 1994, British,
   originally filmed for television

FILM DIRECTORS

JERRY LONDON*
(Jerome R. London)
b. September 21, 1937 - Los Angeles, California
Contact: Directors Guild of America - Los Angeles, 213/851-3671

KILLDOZER (TF) Universal TV, 1974
McNAUGHTON'S DAUGHTER (TF) Universal TV, 1976
COVER GIRLS (TF) Columbia TV, 1977
ARTHUR HAILEY'S WHEELS (MS) Universal TV, 1978
EVENING IN BYZANTIUM (TF) Universal TV, 1978
WOMEN IN WHITE (MS) NBC, 1979
SWAN SONG (TF) Renee Valente Productions/Topanga Services
    Ltd./20th Century-Fox, 1980
SHOGUN (MS) ☆ Paramount TV/NBC Entertainment,
    1980, U.S.-Japanese
FATHER FIGURE (TF) Finnegan Associates/Time-Life
    Productions, 1980
THE CHICAGO STORY (TF) Eric Bercovici Productions/
    MGM TV, 1981
THE ORDEAL OF BILL CARNEY (TF) Belle Company/Comworld
    Productions, 1981
THE GIFT OF LIFE (TF) CBS Entertainment, 1982
THE SCARLET AND THE BLACK (TF) Bill McCutchen Productions/
    ITC/RAI, 1983, U.S.-Italian
ARTHUR HAILEY'S HOTEL *HOTEL* (TF) Aaron Spelling
    Productions, 1983
CHIEFS (MS) Highgate Pictures, 1983
ELLIS ISLAND (MS) Pantheon Pictures/Telepictures Productions,
    1984, U.S.-British
MacGRUDER AND LOUD (TF) Aaron Spelling Productions, 1985
HOLLYWOOD BEAT (TF) Aaron Spelling Productions, 1985
DARK MANSIONS (TF) Aaron Spelling Productions, 1986
IF TOMORROW COMES (MS) CBS Entertainment, 1986
MANHUNT FOR CLAUDE DALLAS (TF) London Films, Inc., 1986
HARRY'S HONG KONG (TF) Aaron Spelling Productions, 1987
RENT-A-COP Kings Road Productions, 1988
DADAH IS DEATH (TF) Steve Krantz Productions/Roadshow,
    Coote & Carroll Productions/Samuel Goldwyn TV,
    1988, U.S.-Australian
KISS SHOT (TF) Lonson Productions/Whoop Inc., 1989
THE HAUNTING OF SARAH HARDY (TF) USA Network, 1989
VESTIGE OF HONOR (TF) Desperado Pictures/Dan Wigutow
    Productions/Envoy Productions/Spanish TrailProductions, 1990
A SEASON OF GIANTS (CMS) Turner Network TV/RAI/Tiber
    Cinematografica, 1991, U.S.-Italian
VICTIM OF LOVE (TF) Nevermore Productions, 1991
GRASS ROOTS (TF) Team Cherokee Inc./JBS Productions, 1992
CALENDAR GIRL, COP KILLER?: THE BAMBI BEMBENEK
    STORY (TF) von Zerneck-Sertner Films, 1992
A TWIST OF THE KNIFE (TF) Dean Hargrove Productions/
    The Fred Silverman Company/Viacom, 1993
LABOR OF LOVE: THE ARLETTE SCHWEITZER STORY (TF)
    Lauren Film Productions/KLM Productions, 1993
THE COSBY MYSTERIES (TF) SAH Enterprises/Columbia TV/
    NBC Productions, 1994
I SPY RETURNS (TF) SAH Enterprises/Sheldon Leonard
    Enterprises/Citadel Entertainment, 1994
DR. QUINN, MEDICINE WOMAN (TF) The Sullivan Company/
    CBS Entertainment, 1994
DR. QUINN, MEDICINE WOMAN: LADIES NIGHT (TF)
    The Sullivan Company/CBS Entertainment, 1994
A MOTHER'S GIFT (TF) RHI Entertainment/TeleVest, 1995

ROBERT LONGO*
Agent: UTA - Beverly Hills, 310/273-6700
Fax: 212/925-8417

JOHNNY MNEMONIC TriStar, 1995, Canadian-U.S.

HARRY S. LONGSTREET*
Contact: Directors Guild of America - Los Angeles, 213/851-3671

SEX, LOVE, AND COLD HARD CASH (CTF) Citadel Pictures/
    MTE, 1993
A VOW TO KILL (CTF) Power Pictures Corporation/Wilshire
    Court Productions, 1995

TEMISTOCLES LOPEZ
b. Valencia, Venezuela

EXQUISITE CORPSES ASA Communications, 1989
CHAIN OF DESIRE Distant Horizon, 1992
BIRD OF PREY Sneak Preview Productions/BM 5 Film Productions,
    1995, U.S.-Bulgarian

JACK LORD
(John Joseph Ryan)
b. December 30, 1928 - New York, New York
Business: Lord & Lady Enterprises, Inc., 4999 Kahala Avenue,
    Honolulu, HI 96816, 808/735-5070
Business Manager: J. William Hayes, Executive Business
    Management, Inc., 132 S. Rodeo Drive, Beverly Hills, CA 90212,
    310/858-2013

M STATION: HAWAII (TF) Lord & Lady Enterprises, 1980

JEAN-CLAUDE LORD
b. 1943 - Montreal, Quebec, Canada
Address: 311 rue Notre-Dame, Saint-Lambert, Quebec J4P 2K2,
    Canada, 514/466-2602

DELIVREZ-NOUS DU MAL Cooperativo, 1965, Canadian
LES COLOMBES Les Films Jean-Claude Lord, 1972, Canadian
BINGO Les Films Mutuels, 1974, Canadian
PARLEZ-NOUS D'AMOUR Les Films Mutuels, 1977, Canadian
ECLAIR AU CHOCOLAT Les Films Mutuels, 1978, Canadian
VISITING HOURS 20th Century-Fox, 1982, Canadian
COVERGIRL New World, 1984, Canadian
THE VINDICATOR *FRANKENSTEIN '88* 20th Century Fox,
    1985, Canadian
TOBY McTEAGUE Filmline International Productions/Telefilm/
    Societe Generale du Cinema/CBS/Radio-Canada TV Network,
    1985, Canadian
HE SHOOTS, HE SCORES (MS) Communications Claude Heroux/
    CBC/Societe Radio-Canada/O'Keefe Breweries/TF-1/Telefilm
    Canada, 1986, Canadian-French
TADPOLE AND THE WHALE New World Mutual, 1988, Canadian
EDDIE AND THE CRUISERS II: EDDIE LIVES Scotti Bros.,
    1989, U.S.-Canadian
MINDFIELD Cinegem, 1990, Canadian
LANDSLIDE Northern Screen, 1992, British-Canadian

EMIL LOTEANU
b. November 6, 1936 - Bukovina, U.S.S.R.
Contact: Confederation of Film-Makers Unions, Vasilyevskaya
    Street 13, 123 825 Moscow, Russia, tel.: 095/250-4114

WAIT FOR US AT DAWN Moldovafilm, 1963, Soviet
RED MEADOWS Moldovafilm, 1966, Soviet
FRESCOS ON THE WHITE Moldovafilm, 1968, Soviet
THIS INSTANT Moldovafilm, 1969, Soviet
LAUTARY Moldovafilm, 1972, Soviet
MY WHITE CITY Moldovafilm, 1973, Soviet
INTO THE SUNSET Mosfilm, 1976, Soviet
THE SHOOTING PARTY Mosfilm, 1978, Soviet
ANNA PAVLOVA: A WOMAN FOR ALL TIME Cinema Development
    Corporation, 1985, Soviet-British-French

EB LOTTIMER
Agent: Premiere Artists Agency - Los Angeles, 310/271-1414

LOVE MATTERS (CTF) Chanticleer Films, 1993

PAVEL LOUNGUINE
b. Moscow, U.S.S.R.
Contact: Confederation of Film-Makers Unions, Vasilyevskaya
    Street 13, 123 825 Moscow, Russia, tel.: 250-4114

TAXI BLUES MK2 Productions USA, 1990, Soviet
LUNA PARK Northern Arts Entertainment, 1992, Russian-French

ERIC LOUZIL

LUST FOR FREEDOM   Troma, 1987
FORTRESS OF AMERIKKA   Troma, 1989
CLASS OF NUKE 'EM HIGH PART II: SUBHUMANOID
   MELTDOWN   Troma, 1991
WILDING   Action International, 1991
CASTING AGENCY   Mesa Films, 1991
LUKAS' CHILD   Triple-O-Seven Productions, 1991
THE COCO BAY BED RACE   Panther Films/Triple "O" Seven/JWP
   Productions, 1992
THE GOOD, THE BAD AND THE SUBHUMANOID   Troma, 1993
DYING FOR LOVE   H.O.D. Film Productions, 1994
MISCONCEPTION   Amethyst Films, 1995

TONY LOVE

TEENAGE MUTANT NINJA TURTLES (AF)   Fred Wolf Films, 1995

CHARLIE LOVENTHAL

Agent: APA - Los Angeles, 310/273-0744

THE FIRST TIME   New Line Cinema, 1983
MY DEMON LOVER   New Line Cinema, 1987
MR. WRITE   SGE, 1994

BERT LOVITT

Agent: Smith-Gosnell-Nicholson & Associates - Pacific Palisades,
   310/459-0307

PRINCE JACK   Castle Hill Productions, 1984

ROBERT LOVY

PLUGHEAD REQUIRED: CIRCUITRY MAN II   co-director with
   Steven Lovy, Trans Atlantic Entertainment/I.R.S. Media, 1994

STEVEN LOVY

CIRCUITRY MAN   I.R.S. Releasing, 1990
PLUGHEAD REQUIRED: CIRCUITRY MAN II   co-director with
   Robert Lovy, Trans Atlantic Entertainment/I.R.S. Media, 1994

RICHARD LOWENSTEIN

Agent: The Cameron Creswell Agency - Sydney, tel.: 02/358-6433

STRIKEBOUND   TRM Productions, 1985, Australian
WHITE CITY   1985, British
DOGS IN SPACE   Skouras Pictures, 1987, Australian
AUSTRALIAN MADE (FD)   Hoyts Distribution, 1987, Australian
SAY A LITTLE PRAYER   Flying Films/Australian Film Finance
   Corporation, 1993, Australian

DECLAN LOWNEY

Contact: British Film Commission, 70 Baker Street, London
   W1M 1DJ, England, tel.: 171/224-5000

TIME WILL TELL *BOB MARLEY - TIME WILL TELL* (TD)
   Island Visual Arts/Polygram Video International/Initial
   Film & TV, 1991, British

DICK LOWRY*

b. Bartlesville, Oklahoma
Agent: Elliot Webb, Broder-Kurland-Webb-Uffner Agency -
   Los Angeles, 213/281-3400

OHMS (TF)   Grant-Case-McGrath Enterprises, 1980
KENNY ROGERS AS THE GAMBLER (TF)   Kragen & Co., 1980
THE JAYNE MANSFIELD STORY (TF)   Alan Landsburg
   Productions, 1980
ANGEL DUSTED (TF)   NRW Features, 1981
COWARD OF THE COUNTY (TF)   Kraco Productions, 1981
A FEW DAYS IN WEASEL CREEK (TF)   Hummingbird Productions/
   Warner Bros., 1981
RASCALS AND ROBBERS: THE SECRET ADVENTURES
   OF TOM SAWYER AND HUCKLEBERRY FINN (TF)
   BS Entertainment, 1982
MISSING CHILDREN: A MOTHER'S STORY (TF)
   Kayden-Gleason Productions, 1982

LIVING PROOF: THE HANK WILLIAMS, JR. STORY (TF)
   Procter & Gamble Productions/Telecom Entertainment/
   Melpomene Productions, 1983
SMOKEY AND THE BANDIT PART 3   Universal, 1983
KENNY ROGERS AS THE GAMBLER - THE ADVENTURE
   CONTINUES (TF)   Lion Share Productions, 1983
OFF SIDES (TF)   Ten-Four Productions, 1984, filmed in 1980
WET GOLD (TF)   Telepictures Productions, 1984
THE TOUGHEST MAN IN THE WORLD (TF)   Guber-Peters
   Productions/Centerpoint Productions, 1984
AGATHA CHRISTIE'S 'MURDER WITH MIRRORS' (TF)
   Hajeno Productions/Warner Bros. TV, 1985
WILD HORSES (TF)   Wild Horses Productions/Telepictures
   Productions, 1985
DREAM WEST (MS)   Sunn Classic Pictures, 1986
AMERICAN HARVEST (TF)   Ruth-Stratton Productions/The
   Finnegan Company, 1987
KENNY ROGERS AS THE GAMBLER III: THE LEGEND
   CONTINUES (TF)   Lion Share Productions, 1987
CASE CLOSED (TF)   Houston Motion Picture Entertainment Inc./
   CBS Entertainment, 1988
IN THE LINE OF DUTY: THE FBI MURDERS (TF)   Telecom
   Entertainment/World International Network, 1988
UNCONQUERED (TF)   Alexandra Film Productions/Double Helix
   Films/Dick Lowry Productions, 1989
HOWARD BEACH: MAKING THE CASE FOR MURDER (TF)
   Patchett-Kaufman Entertainment Productions/WIN, 1989
MIRACLE LANDING (TF)   CBS Entertainment, 1990
ARCHIE: TO RIVERDALE AND BACK AGAIN (TF)   Patchett
   Kaufman Entertainment/DIC Enterprises, 1990
IN THE LINE OF DUTY: A COP FOR THE KILLING (TF)
   Patchett Kaufman Entertainment/Brittcadia Productions/World
   International Network, 1990
IN THE LINE OF DUTY: MANHUNT IN THE DAKOTAS (TF)
   Patchett Kaufman Entertainment/World International Network, 1991
THE GAMBLER RETURNS: THE LUCK OF THE DRAW (TF)
   Kenny Rogers Productions, 1991
A WOMAN SCORNED (TF)   Patchett Kaufman Entertainment, 1992
HER FINAL FURY: BETTY BRODERICK, THE LAST CHAPTER (TF)
   Patchett Kaufman Entertainment/Lowry-Rawls Productions, 1992
IN THE LINE OF DUTY: AMBUSH IN WACO (TF)   Patchett Kaufman
   Entertainment/World International Network, 1993
IN THE LINE OF DUTY: THE PRICE OF VENGEANCE (TF)
   Patchett Kaufman Entertainment, 1994
ONE MORE MOUNTAIN (TF)   Marian Rees Associates/Walt
   Disney TV, 1994
TEXAS JUSTICE (TF)   Patchett-Kaufman Entertainment/World
   International Network/Nancy Hardin Productions, 1995

NANNI LOY

b. October 23, 1925 - Cagliari, Sardinia, Italy
Home: via dei Greci 43, Rome, Italy, tel.: 06/679-4034

PAROLA DI LADRO   co-director with Gianni Puccini, Panal Film,
   1957, Italian
IL MARITO   co-director with Gianni Puccini, Fortuna Film/Chamartin,
   1957, Italian-Spanish
AUDACE COLPO DEI SOLITI IGNOTI   Titanus/Vides/SGC,
   1959, Italian
UN GIORNO DA LEONI   Lux Film/Vides/Galatea, 1961, Italian
THE FOUR DAYS OF NAPLES   MGM, 1962, Italian
MADE IN ITALY   Royal Films International, 1965, Italian-French
IL PADRE DI FAMIGLIA   Ultra/CFC/Marianne Productions,
   1967, Italian-French
ROSOLINO PATERNO' SOLDATO   Dino De Laurentiis
   Cinematografica, 1970, Italian
WHY *DETENUTO IN ATTESA DI GIUDIZIO*   Documento Film,
   1971, Italian
SISTEMO L'AMERICA E TORNO   Documento Film, 1973, Italian
SIGNORE E SIGNORI BUONANOTTE   co-director, Titanus,
   1976, Italian
CAFE EXPRESS   Summit Features, 1980, Italian
TESTA O CROCE   Filmauro, 1982, Italian
WHERE'S PICONE? *MI MANDA PICONE*   Italtoons, 1984, Italian
AMICI MIEI III   Filmauro, 1985, Italian
AMORI (TF)   co-director, Reteitalia, 1989, Italian
SCUGNIZZI   Titanus, 1989, Italian
PACCO, DOPPIO PACCO E CONTROPACCOTTO   CDI, 1993, Italian
HOW LONG TILL DAYLIGHT (TF)   Sacis, 1994, Italian

ARTHUR LUBIN†
b. July 25, 1901 - Los Angeles, California
d. 1995

A SUCCESSFUL FAILURE   Monogram, 1934
GREAT GOD GOLD   Monogram, 1935
HONEYMOON LIMITED   1935
TWO SINNERS   Republic, 1935
FRISCO WATERFRONT   Republic, 1935
THE HOUSE OF A THOUSAND CANDLES   Republic, 1936
YELLOWSTONE   Universal, 1936
MYSTERIOUS CROSSING   Universal, 1937
CALIFORNIA STRAIGHT AHEAD   Universal, 1937
I COVER THE WAR   Universal, 1937
IDOL OF THE CROWDS   Universal, 1937
ADVENTURE'S END   Universal, 1937
MIDNIGHT INTRUDER   Universal, 1938
THE BELOVED BRAT   Warner Bros., 1938
PRISON BREAK   Universal, 1938
SECRETS OF A NURSE   Universal, 1938
RISKY BUSINESS   Universal, 1939
BIG TOWN CZAR   Universal, 1939
MICKEY THE KID   Republic, 1939
CALL A MESSENGER   Universal, 1939
THE BIG GUY   Universal, 1940
BLACK FRIDAY   Universal, 1940
GANGS OF CHICAGO   Republic, 1940
I'M NOBODY'S SWEETHEART NOW   Universal, 1940
MEET THE WILDCAT   Universal, 1940
WHO KILLED AUNT MAGGIE?   Universal, 1940
SAN FRANCISCO DOCKS   Universal, 1941
WHERE DID YOU GET THAT GIRL?   Universal, 1941
BUCK PRIVATES   Universal, 1941
IN THE NAVY   Universal, 1941
HOLD THAT GHOST   Universal, 1941
KEEP 'EM FLYING   Universal, 1941
RIDE 'EM COWBOY   Universal, 1942
EAGLE SQUADRON   Universal, 1942
WHITE SAVAGE   Universal, 1943
THE PHANTOM OF THE OPERA   Universal, 1943
ALI BABA AND THE 40 THIEVES   Universal, 1944
DELIGHTFULLY DANGEROUS   United Artists, 1945
THE SPIDER WOMAN STRIKES BACK   Universal, 1946
NIGHT IN PARADISE   Universal, 1946
NEW ORLEANS   United Artists, 1947
IMPACT   United Artists, 1949
FRANCIS   Universal, 1950
QUEEN FOR A DAY   United Artists, 1951
FRANCIS GOES TO THE RACES   Universal, 1951
RHUBARB   Paramount, 1951
FRANCIS GOES TO WEST POINT   Universal, 1952
IT GROWS ON TREES   Universal, 1952
SOUTH SEA WOMAN   Warner Bros., 1953
FRANCIS COVERS THE BIG TOWN   Universal, 1953
FRANCIS JOINS THE WACS   Universal, 1954
FRANCIS IN THE NAVY   Universal, 1955
FOOTSTEPS IN THE FOG   Columbia, 1955
LADY GODIVA   Universal, 1955
STAR OF INDIA   United Artists, 1953, British-Italian
THE FIRST TRAVELING SALESLADY   RKO Radio, 1956
ESCAPADE IN JAPAN   Universal, 1957
THE THIEF OF BAGHDAD   MGM, 1961, Italian-French
THE INCREDIBLE MR. LIMPET   Universal, 1964
HOLD ON!   MGM, 1966
RAIN FOR A DUSTY SUMMER   Do'Bar, 1971, Spanish-U.S.

JACK LUCARELLI
A GIFT FROM HEAVEN   Hatchwell-Lucarelli Productions, 1994

GEORGE LUCAS
b. May 14, 1944 - Modesto, California
Business: Lucasfilm Ltd., P.O. Box 2459, San Rafael, CA 94912,
   415/662-1800

THX 1138   Warner Bros., 1971
AMERICAN GRAFFITI ★   Universal, 1973
STAR WARS ★   20th Century-Fox, 1977

PHIL LUCAS
THE NATIVE AMERICANS (CTD)   co-director with John Borden &
   George Burdeau, Turner Broadcasting, 1994

FRANCESCO LUCENTE
Contact: Directors Guild of Canada, 225 Richmond Street, Toronto,
   Ontario M5V 1W2, Canada, 416/351-8200

THE VIRGIN QUEEN OF ST. FRANCIS HIGH   Crown International,
   1987, Canadian

DANIELE LUCHETTI
b. July 25, 1960 - Rome, Italy
Home: viale Oceano Atlantico 31, Rome, Italy, tel.: 06/501-4889

JUKE BOX   co-director, Gaumont, 1983, Italian
DOMANI ACCADRA'   Sacher Film/RAI-1/So.Fin.A., 1987, Italian
LA SETTIMANA DELLA SFINGE   Erre Produzioni/Silvio Berlusconi
   Communications, 1990, Italian
IL PORTABORSE   Sacher Film/Banfilm/Pyramide Production/
   Eidoscope Productions/Canal Plus, 1991, Italian-French
ARRIVA LA BUFERA   Media Fiction, 1993, Italian
LA SCUOLA   CGG Tiger Cinematografica/Les Films Alain Sarde,
   1995, Italian-French

LAURENCE LUCKINBILL
b. November 21, 1934 - Fort Smith, Arkansas
Contact: Screen Actors Guild - Los Angeles, 213/954-1600

LUCY AND DESI: A HOME MOVIE (TD)   co-director with
   Lucie Arnaz, Arluck Entertainment, 1993

BAZ LUHRMANN
Business: c/o 20th Century Fox, P.O. Box 900, Beverly Hills,
   CA 90213, 310/203-3412
Agent: ICM - Beverly Hills, 310/550-4000

STRICTLY BALLROOM   Miramax Films, 1992, Australian

ERIC LUKE*
Contact: Directors Guild of America - Los Angeles, 213/851-3671

STILL NOT QUITE HUMAN (CTF)   Resnick-Margellos
   Productions, 1992

SIDNEY LUMET*
b. June 25, 1924 - Philadelphia, Pennsylvania
Agent: ICM - Beverly Hills, 310/550-4000

TWELVE ANGRY MEN ★   United Artists, 1957
STAGE STRUCK   RKO Radio, 1958
THAT KIND OF WOMAN   Paramount, 1959
THE FUGITIVE KIND   United Artists, 1960
A VIEW FROM THE BRIDGE   Allied Artists, 1961, French-Italian
LONG DAY'S JOURNEY INTO NIGHT   Embassy, 1962
FAIL SAFE   Columbia, 1964
THE PAWNBROKER   Landau/Allied Artists, 1965
THE HILL   MGM, 1965, British
THE GROUP   United Artists, 1965
THE DEADLY AFFAIR   Columbia, 1967, British
BYE BYE BRAVERMAN   Warner Bros., 1968
THE SEA GULL   Warner Bros., 1968, British
THE APPOINTMENT   MGM, 1969
LAST OF THE MOBILE HOT-SHOTS   Warner Bros., 1970
KING: A FILMED RECORD...MONTGOMERY TO MEMPHIS (FD)
   co-director with Joseph L. Mankiewicz, Maron Films Limited, 1970
THE ANDERSON TAPES   Columbia, 1971
CHILD'S PLAY   Paramount, 1972
THE OFFENSE   United Artists, 1973, British
SERPICO   Paramount, 1973
LOVIN' MOLLY   Columbia, 1974
MURDER ON THE ORIENT EXPRESS   Paramount, 1974, British
DOG DAY AFTERNOON ★   Warner Bros., 1975
NETWORK ★   MGM/United Artists, 1976
EQUUS   United Artists, 1977, British
THE WIZ   Universal, 1978

JUST TELL ME WHAT YOU WANT   Columbia, 1980
PRINCE OF THE CITY   Orion/Warner Bros., 1981
DEATHTRAP   Warner Bros., 1982
THE VERDICT ★   20th Century-Fox, 1982
DANIEL   Paramount, 1983
GARBO TALKS   MGM/UA, 1984
POWER   20th Century Fox, 1986
THE MORNING AFTER   20th Century Fox, 1986
RUNNING ON EMPTY   Warner Bros., 1988
FAMILY BUSINESS   TriStar, 1989
Q&A   TriStar, 1990
A STRANGER AMONG US   Buena Vista, 1992
GUILTY AS SIN   Buena Vista, 1993

BIGAS LUNA
(Juan Jose Bigas Luna)
Business: Lolafilms, Pintor Gimeno 12, 08022 Barcelona,
   Spain, tel.: 418-40-44

TATUAJE   1976, Spanish
BILBAO, UNA HISTORIA DEL AMOR   Figaro Films/Ona/Pepon
   Coromina, 1978, Spanish
CANICHE   Figaro Films, 1979, Spanish
REBORN   Diseno y Produccion de Films/Diamant/Laurel,
   1982, Spanish-Italian-U.S.
ANGUISH   Spectrafilm, 1987, Spanish
LULU   *LAS EDADES DE LULU*   Academy Entertainment,
   1990, Spanish
JAMON JAMON   Academy Entertainment, 1992, Spanish
HUEVOS DE ORO   Lolafilms/Ovideo TV/Filmauro/Hugo Films,
   1993, Spanish-Italian-French
LA TETA Y LA LUNA   Lolafilms/Cartel/Hugo Films,
   1994, Spanish-French

IDA LUPINO*
b. February 4, 1918 - London, England
Business Manager: Mary Ann Anderson, Personalized Business
   Management, 11666 Weddington Street, North Hollywood, CA
   91601, 818/761-0461

OUTRAGE   RKO Radio, 1950
HARD, FAST AND BEAUTIFUL   RKO Radio, 1951
THE HITCH-HIKER   RKO Radio, 1953
THE BIGAMIST   Filmmakers, 1953
THE TROUBLE WITH ANGELS   Columbia, 1966

TONY LURASCHI
THE OUTSIDER   Paramount, 1980, U.S.-Irish

DON LUSK
JONNY'S GOLDEST QUEST (ATF)   co-director with Paul Sommer,
   Hanna-Barbera Productions/USA Network/Fil-Cartoons, 1993,
   U.S.-Filipino

STEVEN LUSTGARDEN
b. August 1, 1951

AMERICAN TABOO   Motion Pictures International, 1983
AMERICAN HERO   Appaloosa Films, 1986
POWER SLIDE   Filmtown Entertainment Group, 1991

WILLIAM LUSTIG
b. February 1, 1955 - Bronx, New York
Home: 14960 Dickens Street - Suite 314, Sherman Oaks,
   CA 91403, 818/783-9336

MANIAC   Analysis Film Corp., 1981
VIGILANTE   Artists Releasing Corporation/Film Ventures
   International, 1983
MANIAC COP   Shapiro Glickenhaus Entertainment, 1987
HIT LIST   New Line Cinema/Warner Bros., 1988
RELENTLESS   New Line Cinema/Warner Bros., 1989
MANIAC COP 2   LIVE Home Video/The Movie House
   Sales Co. Ltd., 1990
BRUTE FORCE   Axis Films International, 1994

DAVID LYNCH*
b. January 20, 1946 - Missoula, Montana
Agent: CAA - Beverly Hills, 310/288-4545

ERASERHEAD   Libra, 1978, re-released by Miramax Films in 1991
THE ELEPHANT MAN ★   Paramount, 1980, British-U.S.
DUNE   Universal, 1984
BLUE VELVET ★   DEG, 1986
TWIN PEAKS (TF) ☆   Lynch-Frost Productions/Propaganda Films/
   World Vision Enterprises, 1990
WILD AT HEART   The Samuel Goldwyn Company, 1990
TWIN PEAKS (Second Season Premiere) (TF)   Lynch-Frost
   Productions/Propaganda Films/Spelling Entertainment, 1990
TWIN PEAKS: FIRE WALK WITH ME   New Line Cinema, 1992,
   U.S.-French
HOTEL ROOM (CTF)   co-director with James Signorelli,
   Propaganda Films/Assymetrical Productions, 1993
LES FRANCAIS VUS PAR...   co-director with Werner Herzog,
   Andrzej Wajda & Luigi Comencini, 1993, French

JENNIFER CHAMBERS LYNCH
Agent: CAA - Beverly Hills, 310/288-4545
Personal Manager: Atlas Entertainment - Los Angeles, 213/658-9100

BOXING HELENA   Orion Classics, 1993

PAUL LYNCH*
b. November 6, 1946
Agent: Scott Harris, Innovative Artists - Los Angeles, 310/535-5200
Business Manager: Stan Nugit, 1750 Ocean Park Avenue - Suite 204,
   Los Angeles, CA, 310/450-7020

THE HARD PART BEGINS   Cinepix, 1974, Canadian
BLOOD AND GUTS   Ambassador, 1978, Canadian
PROM NIGHT   Avco Embassy, 1980, Canadian
HUMONGOUS   Avco Embassy, 1982, Canadian
CROSS-COUNTRY   New World, 1983, Canadian
FLYING   Golden Harvest, 1985
BULLIES   Universal, 1986, Canadian
MANIA   co-director with John Sheppard & D.M. Robertson,
   Simcom Productions, 1986, Canadian
BLINDSIDE   Norstar Entertainment, 1987, Canadian
REALLY WEIRD TALES (CTF)   co-director, HBO/Atlantis Films,
   1987, U.S.-Canadian
GOING TO THE CHAPEL (TF)   The Furia Organization/
   Finnegan- Pinchuk Productions, 1988
SHE KNOWS TOO MUCH (TF)   The Fred Silverman Company/
   Finnegan-Pinchuk Productions/MGM TV, 1989
MURDER BY NIGHT (CTF)   USA Network, 1989
DOUBLE YOUR PLEASURE (TF)   Steve White Productions/
   Spectator Films, 1989
DROP DEAD GORGEOUS (CTF)   Power Pictures Corporation,
   1991, U.S.-Canadian
ROBOCOP: THE SERIES (TF)   Skyvision Entertainment
   Productions/RoboCop Productions Limited Partnership/Rysher
   Entertainment, 1994, Canadian-U.S.
NO CONTEST   Norstar Entertainment, 1994, Canadian

ADRIAN LYNE*
Agent: CAA - Beverly Hills, 310/288-4545

FOXES   United Artists, 1980
FLASHDANCE   Paramount, 1983
9-1/2 WEEKS   MGM/UA, 1986
FATAL ATTRACTION ★   Paramount, 1987
JACOB'S LADDER   TriStar, 1990
INDECENT PROPOSAL   Paramount, 1993

JONATHAN LYNN*
b. 1943 - Bath, England
Agent: ICM - Beverly Hills, 310/550-4000 or:
   Peters Fraser & Dunlop - London, tel.: 171/344-1000

CLUE   Paramount, 1985
NUNS ON THE RUN   20th Century Fox, 1990, British
MY COUSIN VINNY   20th Century Fox, 1992
THE DISTINGUISHED GENTLEMAN   Buena Vista, 1992
GREEDY   Universal, 1994
SGT. BILKO   Universal, 1995

F
I
L
M

D
I
R
E
C
T
O
R
S

M

DICK MAAS

Business: First Floor Features, P.O. Box 53221, 1007 RE
Amsterdam, Netherlands, tel.: 20/664-7471
Agent: William Morris Agency - Beverly Hills, 310/859-4000

RIGOR MORTIS   1981, Dutch
THE LIFT   Island Alive/Media Home Entertainment, 1983, Dutch
FLODDER   Concorde Films, 1986, Dutch
AMSTERDAMNED   Vestron, 1987, Dutch
FLODDER DOES MANHATTAN   First Floor Features, 1993, Dutch
FLODDER: THE FINAL STORY   First Floor Features, 1994, Dutch

LEWIS MacADAMS

Contact: Writers Guild of America, West - Los Angeles, 310/550-1000

WHAT HAPPENED TO KEROUAC? (FD)   co-director with
Richard Lerner, New Yorker, 1986

SYDNEY (SYD) MACARTNEY*

b. July 24, 1954 - Ballymena, Northern Ireland
Business: Rawi Macartney Ltd., 55-57 Great Marlborough Street,
London W1, England, tel.: 171/437-0868
Agent: Shapiro-Lichtman Talent Agency - Los Angeles, 310/859-8877
or: CCA Management - London, tel.: 171/730-8857

YELLOWTHREAD STREET (MS)   VTV, 1989, British-Hong Kong
THE BRIDGE   British Screen/Film Four International/Moonlight Film,
1991, British
THE YOUNG INDIANA JONES CHRONICLES: NEW
YORK 1920 (TF)   Lucasfilm Ltd./Paramount TV, 1992
THE WHIPPING BOY (CTF)   Gemini Films/Jones Entertainment
Group/The Disney Channel, 1994, British-French-German-U.S.

PETER MACDONALD*

Home: 23 Wensleydale Road, Hampton, Middlesex, England
TW122LP, tel. 171/979-5142
Agent: UTA - Beverly Hills, 310/273-6700

RAMBO III   TriStar, 1988
MO' MONEY   Columbia, 1992
THE NEVERENDING STORY III   CineVox Filmproduktion/Studio
Babelsberg/Dieter Geissler Filmproduktion/Videal/Bibo TV/
Media Investment Club, 1994, German

JOHN MACKENZIE*

b. 1932 - Edinburgh, Scotland
Home: 7 Clifton Hill Road, St. Johns Wood, London MW8 0RE,
England, tel.: 171/624-4233
Agent: ICM - Beverly Hills, 310/550-4000 or:
Peters Fraser & Dunlop - London, tel.: 171/344-1000

ONE BRIEF SUMMER   Cinevision, 1970, British
UNMAN, WITTERING & ZIGO   Paramount, 1971, British
THE CHEVIOT (TF)   1973, British
THE STAG AND THE BLACK (TF)   1973, British
BLACK OIL (TF)   1973, British
SHUTDOWN (TF)   1974, British
JUST ANOTHER SATURDAY (TF)   1975, British
MADE   International Co-productions, 1975, British
DOUBLE DARE (TF)   1976, British
PASSAGE TO ENGLAND (TF)   1976, British
RED SHIFT (TF)   1977, British
JUST A BOY'S GAME (TF)   BBC, 1979, British

A SENSE OF FREEDOM (TF)   J. Isaacs Productions/STV,
1979, British
THE LONG GOOD FRIDAY   Embassy, 1982, British
BEYOND THE LIMIT   THE HONORARY CONSUL   Paramount,
1983, British
THE INNOCENT   TVS Ltd./Tempest Films, 1985, British
ACT OF VENGEANCE (CTF)   HBO Premiere Films/Telepix
Canada Corporation, 1986, U.S.-Canadian
THE FOURTH PROTOCOL   Lorimar, 1987, British
THE LAST OF THE FINEST   Orion, 1990
RUBY   Triumph Releasing Corporation, 1992
VOYAGE (CTF)   Davis Entertainment/Quinta Communications/
USA Network, 1993
THE INFILTRATOR (CTF)   HBO Showcase/Francine LeFrak
Productions/Carnival Films, 1995

PETER M. MacKENZIE

Contact: Robert Zipser, 2121 Avenue of the Stars - Suite 1700,
Los Angeles, CA 90067, 310/203-8600 ext. 128

MISSION MANILA   Overseas Filmgroup, 1988
MERCHANTS OF WAR   Triax Entertainment, 1988

WILL MACKENZIE*

Agent: Elliot Webb, Broder-Kurland-Webb-Uffner Agency -
Los Angeles, 213/281-3400

FAMILY TIES VACATION (TF)   Paramount TV/Ubu Productions/
NBC Entertainment, 1985
A HOBO'S CHRISTMAS (TF)   Joe Byrnne-Falrose Productions/
Phoenix Entertainment, 1987
WORTH WINNING   20th Century Fox, 1989
PERFECT HARMONY (CTF)   Sea Breeze Productions/The Disney
Channel, 1991
STORMY WEATHERS (TF)   Haft-Nasatir Productions/River Siren
Productions/TriStar TV, 1992

GILLIES MACKINNON*

b. January 8, 1948 - Glasgow, Scotland
Agent: ICM - Beverly Hills, 310/550-4000

CONQUEST OF THE SOUTH POLE   1989, Scottish
NEEDLE (TF)   1990, Scottish
THE GRASS ARENA (TF)   BBC, 1990, British
THE PLAYBOYS   The Samuel Goldwyn Company, 1992, U.S.-Irish
A SIMPLE TWIST OF FATE   Buena Vista, 1994
EASTERHOUSE   Skyline Easterhouse Ltd./Worlds End Films/BBC
Scotland, 1995, Scottish

ALISON MACLEAN

Agent: William Morris Agency - Beverly Hills, 310/859-4000

CRUSH   Strand Releasing, 1992, New Zealand

STEPHEN MACLEAN

Agent: APA - Los Angeles, 310/273-0744

AROUND THE WORLD IN 80 WAYS   Alive Films, 1987, Australian

W. H. MACY

Agent: William Morris Agency - Beverly Hills, 310/859-4000

LIP SERVICE (CTF)   HBO Showcase/Cinehaus, 1988

DAVID MADDEN

Business: Interscope Communications, 10900 Wilshire Blvd. -
Suite 1400, Los Angeles, CA 90024, 310/208-8525

A PART OF THE FAMILY (CTF)   Interscope Communications,
1994, originally filmed for theatrical release
SEPARATE LIVES   Trimark Pictures, 1994

JOHN MADDEN*

Agent: William Morris Agency - Beverly Hills, 310/859-4000

AFTER THE WAR (MS)   Granada TV, 1989, British
THE WIDOW MAKER (TF)   Central Films/ITV, 1990, British
INSPECTOR MORSE - DEAD ON TIME (TF)   Zenith Productions/
   Central TV, 1991, British
THE DISAPPEARANCE OF LADY FRANCES CARAFAX (TF)
   Granada TV/WGBH-Boston, 1992, British-U.S.
ETHAN FROME   Miramax Films, 1993
GOLDEN GATE   The Samuel Goldwyn Company, 1994
PRIME SUSPECT: THE LOST CHILD (TF)   Granada TV,
   1995, British

LEE MADDEN

Home: 16918 Marquez Avenue, Pacific Palisades, CA 90272,
   310/454-6255

HELL'S ANGELS '69   American International, 1969
ANGEL UNCHAINED   American International, 1970
THE MANHANDLERS   Premiere, 1975
THE NIGHT GOD SCREAMED   Cinemation, 1973
OUT OF THE DARKNESS   *NIGHT CREATURES*
   Dimension, 1978
GHOST FEVER   released under pseudonym of Alan Smithee,
   Miramax, 1987

PAUL M. MADDEN

b. April 26, 1950 - Boston
Business: Madden Corporation, 12100 NE 16th Avenue - Suite 201,
   North Miami Beach, FL 33161, 303/895-6080
Agent: Richard Seres - Miami, 305/895-6080

SUMMER JOB   SVS Films, 1989
MEDIUM RARE   High Point Films & Television, 1990
TROPICAL TEASE   Jaguar Films, 1993
MIAMI MODELS   Madden Corporation, 1994
THE WET ONE   Madden Corporation, 1994

GUY MADDIN

Contact: Academy of Canadian Cinema and Television,
   753 Yonge Street - 2nd Floor, Toronto, Ontario M4Y 1Z9,
   Canada, 416/967-0315

TALES FROM THE GIMLI HOSPITAL   Circle Releasing/Cinephile
   USA, 1988, Canadian
ARCHANGEL   1991, Canadian
CAREFUL   Cinephile, 1992, Canadian

KENNETH MADSEN

b. Denmark
Business: Kenneth Madsen Filmproduktion, Guldbergsgade 29F,
   2200 Copenhagen, Denmark, tel.: 35-36-00-36
Attorney: Kenmad Inc., c/o Weisbarth, Alman & Michaelson,
   156 West 56th Street, New York, NY 10019

A DAY IN OCTOBER   Castle Hill Productions, 1991, U.S.-Danish

GUY MAGAR*

Home: 7185 Woodrow Wilson Drive, Los Angeles, CA 90068,
   213/461-9009
Agent: The Wallerstein Company - Los Angeles, 213/782-0225
Business: Magar Films, 3518 Cahuenga Blvd. West, Suite 307,
   Los Angeles, CA 90068, 213/436-0344

RETRIBUTION   United Film Distribution, 1987
DARK AVENGER (TF)   Columbia TV/A-L Productions, 1990
STEPFATHER III (CTF)   ITC Entertainment Group, 1992
LOOKIN' ITALIAN   Vision Quest Entertainment, 1994

MARIA MAGGENTI

THE INCREDIBLY TRUE ADVENTURE OF TWO GIRLS IN LOVE
   Fine Line Features/New Line Cinema, 1994

MARK MAGIDSON

TOWARD THE WITHIN (FCD)   Tara Releasing, 1994

ALBERT MAGNOLI*

Personal Manager: Carlyle Productions and Management, 639 N.
   Larchmont - Suite 207, Los Angeles, CA 90004, 213/469-3086

PURPLE RAIN   Warner Bros., 1984
AMERICAN ANTHEM   Columbia, 1986
STREET KNIGHT   Cannon, 1993
BORN TO RUN (TF)   Fox West Pictures, 1993

DEZSO MAGYAR*

Home: 864 Harvard Street, Santa Monica, CA 90403, 310/450-4247
Agent: William Morris Agency - Beverly Hills, 310/859-4000

THE AGITATORS   Hungarofilm, 1969, Hungarian
THREE GIRLS   Hungarian
PUNITIVE EXPEDITION   Hungarian
RAPPACINI'S DAUGHTER (TF)   Learning in Focus, 1980
SUMMER (TF)   Cinelit Productions/WNET-13, 1981
KING OF AMERICA (TF)   Center for Television in the
   Humanities, 1982
NO SECRETS   I.R.S. Releasing, 1992

REDGE MAHAFFEY

LIFE 101   Ramsway, 1994

ANTHONY MAHARAJ

RAGE   21st Century Distribution, 1992
INNOCENT ADULTERY   Chrissey Productions, 1993

BARRY MAHON

(Jackson B. Mahon)

Contact: Sinetron Corporation - North Hollywood, 818/762-5674

WHITE SLAVE RACKET   Independent, 1953
CUBAN REBEL GIRLS   Joseph Brenner Associates, 1957
GIRLS INC.   Independent, 1960
HOUSEWIVES INC.   Independent, 1960
SMORGASBROAD   Independent, 1960
PROSTITUTES PROTECTIVE SOCIETY   Independent, 1961
THE BEAST THAT KILLED WOMEN   Independent, 1962
FANNY HILL MEETS LADY CHATTERLEY   Independent, 1967
FANNY HILL MEETS THE RED BARON   Independent, 1967
FANNY HILL MEETS DR. EROTICO   Independent, 1967
THE WONDERFUL LAND OF OZ   Childhood Productions, 1968
SANTA'S CHRISTMAS ELF   Cineworld, 1969

BOB MAHONEY

Business: Bob Mahoney Associates, 41 Devonshire Close,
   London W1N 1LL, England, tel.: 171/636-3020
Agent: William Morris Agency - London, tel.: 171/434-2191

LINDA CLEAR   1984, British
OPERATION JULIE (TF)   Tyne Tees TV, 1985, British
MAY WE BORROW YOUR HUSBAND (TF)   Yorkshire TV,
   1986, British
A DAY IN SUMMER (TF)   Yorkshire TV, 1989, British
HEARTBEAT (TF)   Yorkshire TV, 1992, British
THE GOVERNOR   co-director with Alan Dossor & Robert Knights,
   La Plante Productions/Samson Films, 1995, British

MATT MAHURIN

IMAGINING AMERICA (TF)   co-director with Ralph Bakshi,
   Mustapha Khan & Ed Lachman, Vanguard Films, 1989

NORMAN MAILER*

b. January 31, 1923 - Long Beach, New Jersey
Telephone: 718/858-0892
Agent: ICM - Beverly Hills, 310/550-4000

WILD 90   Supreme Mix, 1968
BEYOND THE LAW   Grove Press, 1968
MAIDSTONE   Supreme Mix, 1971
TOUGH GUYS DON'T DANCE   Cannon, 1987

STEWART MAIN
Contact: New Zealand Film Commission, P.O. Box 11-546,
Wellington, New Zealand, tel.: 4/385-9754

DESPERATE REMEDIES   co-director with Peter Wells,
Miramax Films, 1993, New Zealand

LECH MAJEWSKI*
Telephone: 818/248-2368

THE FLIGHT OF THE SPRUCE GOOSE   Michael Hausman/
Filmhaus, 1986
PRISONER OF RIO   Multi Media AG/Samba Corporation,
1988, Swiss
DESERT LUNCH   Propaganda Films, 1993, U.S.-Polish

JOHNNY MAK
(Mai Dangxiong)
b. 1949 - Hong Kong
Business: Johnny Mak Productions Ltd., 8 Hammer Hill Road,
Kowloon, Hong Kong, tel:: 3/795-4901
Contact: Hong Kong Film Liaison, 10940 Wilshire Blvd. -
Suite 1220, Los Angeles, CA 90024, 310/208-2678

LONG ARM OF THE LAW   Johnny Mak Productions/Bo Ho Films,
1984, Hong Kong
RED GUARDS IN HONG KONG   Golden Communications,
1987, Hong Kong

MICHAEL MAK
Business: Johnny Mak Productions Ltd., 8 Hammer Hill Road,
Kowloon, Hong Kong, tel.: 3/795-4901
Contact: Hong Kong Film Liaison, 10940 Wilshire Blvd. -
Suite 1220, Los Angeles, CA 90024, 310/208-2678

SEX AND ZEN   Rim Film Distributors, 1991, Hong Kong

DUSAN MAKAVEJEV
b. October 13, 1932 - Belgrade, Yugoslavia
Address: 56, rue de Seine, 75006 Paris, France,
tel.: 1/46-34-20-71
Contact: Institut za Film, Cika Ljubina 15, 11000 Beograd, Serbia

MAN IS NOT A BIRD   Grove Press, 1965, Yugoslavian
LOVE AFFAIR; OR THE CASE OF THE MISSING SWITCHBOARD
OPERATOR   Brandon, 1966, Yugoslavian
INNOCENCE UNPROTECTED   Grove Press, 1968, Yugoslavian
WR - MYSTERIES OF THE ORGANISM   Cinema 5,
1971, Yugoslavian
SWEET MOVIE   Biograph, 1975,
French-Canadian-West German
MONTENEGRO   *MONTENEGRO, OR PIGS AND PEARLS*
Atlantic Releasing Corporation, 1981, Swedish
THE COCA COLA KID   Cinecom/Film Gallery, 1985, Australian
MANIFESTO   Cannon, 1988, U.S.-Yugoslavian
THE GORILLA BATHES AT NOON   Alert Film/Von Vietinghoff
Filmproduktion/Ekstaza Film Belgrade, 1992, German-Yugoslavian
A HOLE IN THE SOUL (TD)   Triangle Film/BBC Scotland, 1995,
Yugoslavian-Scottish

ALEKSI MAKELA
b. Finland
Contact: Finnish Film Foundation, Kanavakatu 12, SF-00160
Helsinki, Finland, tel.: 0/17-77-27

THE ROMANOV STONES   Spede/Tuotanto Oy, 1994, Finnish
SUNSET RIDERS   Harlin-Selin Productions/Finnish Film
Foundation, 1995, Finnish

KELLY MAKIN
Agent: William Morris Agency - Beverly Hills, 310/859-4000

TIGER CLAWS   Shapiro Glickenhaus Entertainment, 1992
NATIONAL LAMPOON'S SENIOR TRIP   New Line Cinema,
1995, Canadian

KAROLY MAKK
b. 1925 - Hungary
Contact: Hungarian Film Institute, Budakeszi u 51 B, 1012 Budapest,
Hungary, tel.: 176-1018 or 176-1322

LILOMFI   1954, Hungarian
WARD NO. 8   1955, Hungarian
THE HOUSE UNDER THE ROCKS   1958, Hungarian
THE FANATICS   1961, Hungarian
THE LOST PARADISE   1962, Hungarian
THE LAST BUT ONE   1963, Hungarian
A CLOUDLESS VACATION   1967, Hungarian
BEFORE GOD AND MAN   1967, Hungarian
LOVE   Ajay, 1971, Hungarian
CAT'S PLAY   1974, Hungarian
A VERY MORAL NIGHT   1978, Hungarian
BEHIND THE BRICK WALL   1980, Hungarian
ANOTHER WAY   1983, Hungarian
LILY IN LOVE   New Line Cinema, 1985, Hungarian-U.S.
THE LAST MANUSCRIPT   Mafilm/Studio Dialog,
1987, Hungarian
HUNGARIAN REQUIEM   Dialog Filmstudio/Clasart/Transatlantic
Media Associates, 1991, Hungarian

TERRENCE MALICK*
b. November 30, 1943 - Ottawa, Illinois
Business Manager: Henry Bamberger - Los Angeles, 310/446-2780

BADLANDS   Warner Bros., 1974
DAYS OF HEAVEN   Paramount, 1978

LOUIS MALLE*
b. October 30, 1932 - Thumeries, France
Agent: Sam Cohn, ICM - New York City, 212/556-5600

FONTAINE DE VAUCLUSE   1953, French
STATION 307   1955, French
THE SILENT WORLD (FD)   co-director with Jacques-Yves Cousteau,
Columbia, 1956, French
FRANTIC   *ASCENSEUR POUR L'ECHAFAUD*   Times,
1957, French
THE LOVERS   Zenith International, 1958, French
ZAZIE   *ZAZIE DANS LE METRO*   Astor, 1960, French
A VERY PRIVATE AFFAIR   MGM, 1962, French-Italian
THE FIRE WITHIN   Governor, 1963, French
VIVA MARIA!   United Artists, 1965, French-Italian
THE THIEF OF PARIS   *LE VOLEUR*   Lopert,
1967, French-Italian
SPIRITS OF THE DEAD   *HISTOIRES EXTRAORDINAIRES*
co-director with Federico Fellini & Roger Vadim,
American International, 1969, French-Italian
CALCUTTA (FD)   1969, French
PHANTOM INDIA (TD)   Olympic, 1969, French
MURMUR OF THE HEART   *LE SOUFFLE AU COEUR*
Palomar, 1971, French
HUMAIN, TROP HUMAIN (FD)   New Yorker, 1972, French
PLACE DE LA REPUBLIQUE (FD)   NEF Diffusion, 1974, French
LACOMBE LUCIEN   20th Century-Fox, 1974,
French-Italian-West German
BLACK MOON   20th Century-Fox, 1975, French
PRETTY BABY   Paramount, 1978
ATLANTIC CITY ★   Paramount, 1981, Canadian-French
MY DINNER WITH ANDRE   New Yorker, 1981
CRACKERS   Universal, 1984
ALAMO BAY   TriStar, 1985
AND THE PURSUIT OF HAPPINESS   *GOD'S COUNTRY* (FD)
Pretty Mouse Films, 1985
AU REVOIR LES ENFANTS (GOODBYE CHILDREN)
Orion Classics, 1987, French-West German
MAY FOOLS   *MILOU EN MAI*   Orion Classics, 1990, French
DAMAGE   New Line Cinema, 1992, French-British
VANYA ON 42ND STREET   Sony Pictures Classics, 1994

BRUCE MALMUTH*
b. February 4, 1934 - Brooklyn, New York
Business: Soularview Productions, Inc., 9981 Robbins Drive,
    Beverly Hills, CA 90212, 310/277-4555
Agent: Becsey/Wisdom/Kalajian - Los Angeles, 310/550-0535

FORE PLAY   co-director with John G. Avildsen & Robert McCarty,
    Cinema National, 1975
NIGHTHAWKS   Universal, 1981
THE MAN WHO WASN'T THERE   Paramount, 1983
WHERE ARE THE CHILDREN?   Columbia, 1986
HARD TO KILL   Warner Bros., 1990
PENTATHALON   LIVE Entertainment, 1994

MARK MALONE
Agent: ICM - Beverly Hills, 310/288-4545
Personal Manager: Addis-Wechsler & Associates - Los Angeles,
    213/954-9000

BULLETPROOF HEART   Keystone Pictures/Republic Pictures,
    1995, Canadian

NANCY MALONE*
Telephone: 818/506-5130 or 818/762-8641
Business Manager: Guild Management, 9911 W. Pico Blvd.,
    Los Angeles, CA 90035, 310/277-9711

THERE WERE TIMES, DEAR (TF)   Lilac Productions, 1987

WILLIAM MALONE*
Agent: APA - Los Angeles, 310/273-0744

SCARED TO DEATH   Lone Star, 1982
CREATURE   Cardinal Releasing, 1985

DJIBRIL DIOP MAMBETY
Contact: SIDEC, 12 rue Beranger Ferraud, B P 335, Dakar,
    Senegal, tel.: 21-45-76

TOUKI BOUKI   1973, Senegalese
HYENAS   Triton Pictures, 1992, Senegalese-French-Swiss

DAVID MAMET*
b. November 30, 1947 - Chicago, Illinois
Agent: Howard Rosenstone, Rosenstone/Wender -
    New York City, 212/832-8330

HOUSE OF GAMES   Orion, 1987
THINGS CHANGE   Columbia, 1988
HOMICIDE   Triumph Releasing Corporation, 1991
OLEANNA   The Samuel Goldwyn Company, 1994

YURI MAMIN
Contact: Confederation of Film-Makers Unions, Vasilyevskaya
    Street 13, 123 825 Moscow, Russia, tel.: 095/250-4114

THE FOUNTAIN   1988, Soviet
WINDOW TO PARIS   Sony Pictures Classics, 1994,
    Russian-French
RAINS IN THE OCEAN   co-director with Viktor Aristov,
    Lenfilm Studios, 1995, Russian

MILCHO MANCHEVSKI
b. Skopje, Macedonia, Yugoslavia
Agent: ICM - Beverly Hills, 310/550-4000 or London,
    tel.: 171/636-6565

BEFORE THE RAIN   Gramercy Pictures, 1994,
    British-French-Macedonian

ROBERT MANDEL*
Agent: ICM - Beverly Hills, 310/550-4000

INDEPENDENCE DAY   Warner Bros., 1983
TOUCH & GO   TriStar, 1986
F/X   Orion, 1986
BIG SHOTS   20th Century Fox, 1987
PERFECT WITNESS (CTF)   HBO Pictures/Granger
    Productions, 1989
THE HAUNTED (TF)   FNM Films, 1991
SCHOOL TIES   Paramount, 1992

LUIS MANDOKI*
Agent: CAA - Beverly Hills, 310/288-4545

MOTEL   1983, Mexican
GABY - A TRUE STORY   TriStar, 1987, U.S.-Mexican
WHITE PALACE   Universal, 1990
BORN YESTERDAY   Buena Vista, 1993
WHEN A MAN LOVES A WOMAN   Buena Vista, 1994

JOSEPH MANDUKE*
Telephone: 310/657-1311

JUMP   Cannon, 1971
CORNBREAD, EARL AND ME   American International, 1975
KID VENGEANCE   Irwin Yablans, 1977, U.S.-Israeli
BEATLEMANIA   American Cinema, 1981
OMEGA SYNDROME   New World, 1987
THE GUMSHOE KID   Skouras Pictures, 1989

JAMES MANGOLD
Agent: William Morris Agency - Beverly Hills, 310/859-4000

HEAVY   Available Light Inc., 1995

TOM MANKIEWICZ*
b. June 1, 1942 - Los Angeles, California
Agent: ICM - Beverly Hills, 310/550-4000

HART TO HART (TF)   Spelling-Goldberg Productions, 1979
DRAGNET   Universal, 1987
DELIRIOUS   MGM/Pathe Communications, 1991
TAKING THE HEAT   Viacom, 1993

ABBY MANN
(Abraham Goodman)
b. 1927 - Philadelphia, Pennsylvania
Agent: APA - Los Angeles, 310/273-0744

KING (MS) ☆   Abby Mann Productions/Filmways, 1978

DELBERT MANN*
b. January 30, 1920 - Lawrence, Kansas
Agent: William Morris Agency - Beverly Hills, 310/859-4000

MARTY ★★   United Artists, 1955
THE BACHELOR PARTY   United Artists, 1957
DESIRE UNDER THE ELMS   Paramount, 1958
SEPARATE TABLES   United Artists, 1958
MIDDLE OF THE NIGHT   Columbia, 1959
THE DARK AT THE TOP OF THE STAIRS   Warner Bros., 1960
THE OUTSIDER   Universal, 1961
LOVER, COME BACK   Universal, 1962
THAT TOUCH OF MINK   Universal, 1962
A GATHERING OF EAGLES   Universal, 1963
DEAR HEART   Warner Bros., 1964
QUICK BEFORE IT MELTS   MGM, 1965
MISTER BUDDWING   MGM, 1966
FITZWILLY   United Artists, 1967
HEIDI (TF)   Omnibus Productions, 1968
THE PINK JUNGLE   Universal, 1968
DAVID COPPERFIELD (TF)   Omnibus Productions/Sagittarius
    Productions, 1970, British-U.S.
KIDNAPPED   American International, 1971, British

JANE EYRE (TF)   Omnibus Productions/Sagittarius Productions, 1971, British-U.S.
SHE WAITS (TF)   Metromedia Productions, 1972
NO PLACE TO RUN (TF)   ABC Circle Films, 1972
THE MAN WITHOUT A COUNTRY (TF)   Norman Rosemont Productions, 1973
A GIRL NAMED SOONER (TF)   Frederick Brogger Associates/ 20th Century-Fox TV, 1975
BIRCH INTERVAL   Gamma III, 1976
FRANCIS GARY POWERS: THE TRUE STORY OF THE U-2 SPY INCIDENT (TF)   Charles Fries Productions, 1976
TELL ME MY NAME (TF)   Talent Associates, 1977
BREAKING UP (TF) ☆   Time-Life Productions, 1978
LOVE'S DARK RIDE (TF)   Mark VII Ltd./Worldvision, 1978
HOME TO STAY (TF)   Time-Life Productions, 1978
THOU SHALT NOT COMMIT ADULTERY (TF)   Edgar J. Scherick Associates, 1978
TORN BETWEEN TWO LOVERS (TF)   Alan Landsburg Productions, 1979
ALL QUIET ON THE WESTERN FRONT (TF) ☆   Norman Rosemont Productions/Marble Arch Productions, 1979
TO FIND MY SON (TF)   Green-Epstein Productions/ Columbia TV, 1980
NIGHT CROSSING   Buena Vista, 1982
BRONTE   Charlotte Ltd. Partnership/Radio Telefis Eireann, 1983, U.S-Irish
THE GIFT OF LOVE: A CHRISTMAS STORY (TF)   Telecom Entertainment/Amanda Productions, 1983
LOVE LEADS THE WAY (CTF)   Hawkins-Permut Productions, 1984
A DEATH IN CALIFORNIA (TF)   Mace Neufeld Productions/ Lorimar Productions, 1985
THE LAST DAYS OF PATTON (TF)   Entertainment Partners, 1986
THE TED KENNEDY, JR. STORY (TF)   Entertainment Partners, 1986
APRIL MORNING (TF)   Robert Halmi, Inc./Samuel Goldwyn TV, 1988
IRONCLADS (CTF)   Rosemont Productions, 1991
AGAINST HER WILL: AN INCIDENT IN BALTIMORE (TF)   RHI Entertainment, 1992
INCIDENT IN A SMALL TOWN (TF)   RHI Entertainment, 1994
LILY IN WINTER (CTF)   USA Pictures/Walter Mirisch Productions/MTE, 1994

FARHAD MANN*
Business: 5300 Melrose Avenue - Suite 8130, Hollywood, CA 90038, 213/960-4744
Agent: Broder-Kurland-Webb-Uffner Agency - Beverly Hills, 310/281-3400

NICK KNIGHT (TF)   Barry Weitz Films/Robirdle Pictures/ New World TV, 1989
FACE OF FEAR (TF)   Lee Rich Productions/Warner Bros. TV, 1990
A RETURN TO TWO MOON JUNCTION   Trimark Pictures, 1994
LAWNMOWER MAN II   New Line Cinema, 1995

MICHAEL MANN*
b. Chicago, Illinois
Business: ZZY Inc., 9200 Sunset Blvd. - Suite 1005, Los Angeles, CA 90069, 310/273-9802
Agent: CAA - Beverly Hills, 310/288-4545

THE JERICHO MILE (TF)   ABC Circle Films, 1979
THIEF   United Artists, 1981
THE KEEP   Paramount, 1983
MANHUNTER   DEG, 1986
L.A. TAKEDOWN (TF)   AJAR Inc./Movies Film Productions/ Cia Ibero de T.V. S.A./World International Network, 1989
THE LAST OF THE MOHICANS   20th Century Fox, 1992
HEAT   Warner Bros., 1995

RON MANN
b. 1958 - Toronto, Ontario, Canada
Business: Sphinx Productions, 24 Mercer Street, Toronto, Ontario M5V 1H3, Canada, 416/971-9131
Agent: The Colbert Agency, 303 Davenport Road, Toronto, Ontario M5R 1K5, 416/964-3302

DEPOT   co-director, 1978, Canadian
THE ONLY GAME IN TOWN   co-director, 1979, Canadian
FEELS SO GOOD   co-director, 1980, Canadian
SSHHH!   1980, Canadian
IMAGINE THE SOUND   Harmony Films, 1981, Canadian
POETRY IN MOTION (FD)   Sphinx Productions, 1981, Canadian
ECHOES WITHOUT SAYING (TD)   1983, Canadian
LISTEN TO THE CITY   Spectrafilm, 1984, Canadian
MARCIA RESNICK'S BAD BOYS (FD)   1985, Canadian
HOODS IN THE WOODS (FD)   1986, Canadian
COMIC BOOK CONFIDENTIAL (FD)   Cinecom, 1988, Canadian
SPECIAL OF THE DAY (TD)   1989, Canadian
TWIST (FD)   Triton Pictures, 1992, Canadian

KIM MANNERS*
Agent: Becsey/Wisdom/Kalajian - Los Angeles, 310/550-0535

21 JUMP STREET (TF)   Stephen J. Cannell Productions, 1987
K-9000 (TF)   De Souza Productions/Fries Entertainment, 1991
GREYHOUNDS (TF)   Stu Segall Productions/Cannell Entertainment, 1994

LESLEY MANNING
Agent: Rochelle Stevens & Co. - London, tel.: 171/354-5729

MY SISTER WIFE (TF)   BBC, British
GHOSTWATCH (TF)   BBC, British
MASSAGE (TF)   BBC, British
THREE MILES HIGH (TF)   BBC, 1994, British

MICHELLE MANNING*
Business: Paramount Pictures, 5555 Melrose Avenue, Hollywood, CA 90028, 213/956-5000
Business Manager: Alan Hergott, Bloom, Dekom & Hergott, 150 S. Rodeo Drive - Third Floor, Beverly Hills, CA 90212, 310/859-6800

BLUE CITY   Paramount, 1986

PETER MANOOGIAN
THE DUNGEONMASTER   co-director, Empire Pictures, 1985
ELIMINATORS   Empire Pictures, 1986
ENEMY TERRITORY   Empire Pictures, 1987
ARENA   Empire Pictures, 1991
YOUNG COMMANDOS   Cannon, 1991
DEMONIC TOYS   Full Moon Entertainment, 1992
SEEDPEOPLE   Full Moon Entertainment, 1992

MARK MANOS
b. Detroit, Michigan
Agent: Writers & Artists Agency - Los Angeles, 310/824-6300

LIQUID DREAMS   Fox-Elwes Corporation, 1991
SPIRIT OF THE NIGHT   Full Moon Entertainment, 1994

DAVID MANSON*
Business: Sarabande Productions, 530 Wilshire Blvd. - Suite 308, Santa Monica, CA 90401, 310/395-4842
Agent: ICM - Beverly Hills, 310/550-4000

THOSE SECRETS (TF)   Sarabande Productions/ MGM-UA TV, 1992

RENE MANZOR
Address: 5, rue du Temple, 95880 Enghien-les-Bains, France,
tel.: 1/34-12-10-82
Contact: French Film Office, 745 Fifth Avenue, New York,
NY 10151, 212/832-8860

ESPERANZA Trimark Pictures, 1994, Canadian

ROBERT MARCARELLI
ORIGINAL INTENT Skouras Pictures, 1992
I DON'T BUY KISSES ANYMORE Skouras Pictures, 1992

TERRY MARCEL*
(Terence G. Marcel)
b. 1942 - Oxford, England
Home: 4 Gaston Bell Close, Richmond, Surrey TW9 2DR, England,
tel.: 171/940-3310
Personal Manager: Friend Entertainment - Los Angeles,
213/962-6090 or: JLM Personal Management - London,
tel.: 181/747-8223

THERE GOES THE BRIDE Vanguard, 1980, British
HAWK THE SLAYER ITC, 1980, British
PRISONERS OF THE LOST UNIVERSE (CTF) Marcel-Robertson
Productions/Showtime, 1983, British
JANE AND THE LOST CITY Marcel-Robertson Productions/Glen
Films Productions, 1987, British
BEJEWELLED (CTF) TVS Productions/PWD Productions/
The Disney Channel, 1991, U.S.-British

DAVID MARCONI
Agent: William Morris Agency - Beverly Hills, 310/859-4000

THE HARVEST Curb Musifilm/Mike Curb & Lester Korn/Ron Stone
Productions/Morgan Mason-Jason Clark/RCA-Columbia TriStar
Home Video, 1994

ADAM MARCUS
JASON GOES TO HELL: THE FINAL FRIDAY
New Line Cinema, 1993

ANTONIO MARGHERITI
(See Anthony B. DAWSON)

STUART MARGOLIN*
b. January 31 - Davenport, Iowa
Agent: ICM - Los Angeles, 213/550-4000

SUDDENLY, LOVE (TF) Ross Hunter Productions, 1978
A SHINING SEASON (TF) Green-Epstein Productions/T-M
Productions/Columbia TV, 1979
BRET MAVERICK (TF) Comanche Productions/Warner
Bros. TV, 1981
THE LONG SUMMER OF GEORGE ADAMS (TF)
Warner Bros. TV, 1982
THE GLITTER DOME (CTF) HBO Premiere Films/Telepictures
Productions/Trincomali Productions, 1984, U.S.-Canadian
THE ROOM UPSTAIRS (TF) Marian Rees Associates/
The Alexander Group, 1987
THE FACTS OF LIFE DOWN UNDER (TF) Embassy TV/Crawford
Productions, 1987, U.S.-Australian
PARAMEDICS Vestron, 1988
VENDETTA: SECRETS OF A MAFIA BRIDE
DONNA D'ONORE (TF) Titanus/Reteitalia/Beta-Taurus/
Tribune Entertainment/Silvio Berlusconi Communications,
1991, Italian-German-U.S.
MEDICINE RIVER Medicine River Productions/CBC,
1993, Canadian
HOW THE WEST WAS FUN (TF) Dualstar Productions/
Green-Epstein Productions/Kicking Horse Productions/
Warner Bros. TV, 1994, U.S.-Canadian

JEFF MARGOLIS*
Agent: William Morris Agency - Beverly Hills, 310/859-4000

RICHARD PRYOR LIVE IN CONCERT (PF) Special Event
Entertainment, 1979
OSCAR'S GREATEST MOMENTS (HVD) Columbia TriStar Home
Video/Acaemy of Motion Picture Arts and Sciences, 1992

CHEECH MARIN*
(Richard Marin)
b. July 13, 1946 - Los Angeles, California
Agent: CAA - Beverly Hills, 310/288-4545

BORN IN EAST L.A. Universal, 1987

PETER MARIS
TERROR SQUAD 1987
VIPER Fries Distribution, 1988
MINISTRY OF VENGEANCE Concorde, 1989
HANGFIRE Motion Picture Corporation of America, 1991
FIREHEAD Pyramid Distribution, 1991
DIPLOMATIC IMMUNITY Fries Distribution, 1991
BLACK BELT UNDERCOVER Comet Entertainment, 1992

CHRIS MARKER
(Christian Francois Bouche-Villeneuve)
b. July 29, 1921 - Neuilly-sur-Seine, France
Contact: French Film Office, 745 Fifth Avenue, New York,
NY 10151, 212/832-8860

LES STATUES MEURENT AUSSI (FD) 1953, French
DESCRIPTION D'UN COMBAT (FD) 1960, French
CUBA SI! (FD) 1961, French
LE JOLI MAI 1963, French
LIBERTE (FD) 1963, French
LE MYSTERE KOUMIKO (FD) 1965, French
SI J'AVAIS QUATRE DROMADAIRES (FD) 1966, French
LE VOLCAN INTERDIT (FD) 1966, French
LES MOTS ONT UN SENS (FD) 1967, French
JOUR DE TOURNAGE (FD) 1969, French
LA BATAILLE DES DIX MILLIONS (FD) 1970, French
LA SOLITUDE DU CHANTEUR DE FOND (FD) 1974, French
LA SPIRALE (FD) 1975, French
LE FOND DE L'AIR EST ROUGE (FD) 1977, French
SANS SOLEIL 1982, French
A.K. (FD) Orion Classics, 1985, French
L'HERITAGE DE LA CHOUETTE (FD) 1989, French
LE TOMBEAU D'ALEXANDRE *THE LAST BOLSHEVIK* (FD)
Les Film de L'Astrophore/Mr. Kustow Productions/La Sept-Arte,
1993, French

ANTHONY MARKES
BIKINI ISLAND Curb-Esquire Films, 1991
LAST DANCE Curb-Esquire Films, 1991

DAVID MARKEY
DESPERATE TEENAGE LOVEDOLLS 1984
1991: THE YEAR PUNK BROKE (FD) Tara Releasing, 1992

CURT MARKHAM
b. June 5, 1973 - Rochester, New York
Personal Manager: Judy Adams, 3494 Brockport Road,
Spencerport, NY 14559, 716/352-0621

THE SEARCH FOR SILVERSPEAR (AF) 1987-89

MONTE MARKHAM*
b. June 21, 1938 - Manatee, Florida
Home: P.O. Box 607, Malibu, CA 90265
Agent: David Shapira & Associates - Sherman Oaks, 818/906-0322

DEFENSE PLAY Trans World Entertainment, 1988
NEON CITY Vidmark, 1991

PETER MARKLE*

b. September 24, 1946 - Danville, Pennsylvania
Business: Blueline Productions, 1680 N. Vine Street - Suite 502,
    Hollywood, CA 90028, 213/469-4538
Agent: CAA - Beverly Hills, 310/288-4545

THE PERSONALS   New World, 1982
HOT DOG...THE MOVIE   MGM/UA, 1984
YOUNGBLOOD   MGM/UA, 1986
DESPERATE (TF)   Toots Productions/Warner Bros. TV, 1987
BAT-21   TriStar, 1988
BREAKING POINT (CTF)   Avnet-Kerner Company, 1989
EL DIABLO (CTF)   HBO Pictures/Wizan-Black Films, 1990
IN THE LINE OF DUTY: MOB JUSTICE (TF)   Patchett Kaufman
    Entertainment/World International Network, 1991
DEAD AND ALIVE (TF)   Patchett-Kaufman Entertainment, 1991
THROUGH THE EYES OF A KILLER (TF)   Pacific Motion Pictures/
    Morgan Hill Films/Wilshire Court Productions, 1992
WAGONS EAST   TriStar, 1994
JAKE LASSITER: JUSTICE IN THE BAYOU (TF)   Stephen J.
    Cannell Productions/Big Productions/Spanish Trail
    Productions, 1995
WHITE DWARF (TF)   RHI Entertainment/American Zoetrope/
    Elemental Films Productions, 1995

ROBERT MARKOWITZ*

Business: Moon River Productions Ltd., 11521 Amanda Drive,
    Studio City, CA 91604
Agent: William Morris Agency - Beverly Hills, 310/859-4000

THE STORYTELLER (TF)   Universal TV, 1977
THE DEADLIEST SEASON (TF)   Titus Productions, 1977
VOICES   MGM/United Artists, 1979
THE WALL (TF)   Cinetex International/Time-Life Productions,
    1982, U.S-Polish
A LONG WAY HOME (TF)   Alan Landsburg Productions, 1981
PRAY TV (TF)   ABC Circle Films, 1982
PHANTOM OF THE OPERA (TF)   Robert Halmi Inc., 1983
MY MOTHER'S SECRET LIFE (TF)   Furia-Oringer Productions/
    ABC Circle Films, 1984
KOJAK: THE BELARUS FILE (TF)   Universal TV, 1985
CHILDREN OF THE NIGHT (TF)   Robert Guenette
    Productions, 1985
ALEX: THE LIFE OF A CHILD (TF)   Mandy Productions, 1986
ADAM: HIS SONG CONTINUES (TF)   Alan Landsburg
    Productions, 1986
A DANGEROUS LIFE (CTF)   HBO/McElroy & McElroy/Film
    Accord Corporation/Australian Broadcasting Corporation/
    Zenith Productions, 1988, U.S.-Australian
A CRY FOR HELP: THE TRACEY THURMAN STORY (TF)
    Dick Clark Productions, 1989
TOO YOUNG TO DIE? (TF)   von Zerneck-Sertner Films, 1990
DECORATION DAY (TF) ☆   Marian Rees Associates, 1990
LOVE, LIES AND MURDER (TF)   Republic Pictures, 1991
AFTERBURN (CTF)   Steve Tisch Company, 1992
OVEREXPOSED (TF)   LOMO Productions, 1992
MURDER IN THE HEARTLAND (TF)   O'Hara-Horowitz
    Productions, 1993
TWILIGHT ZONE: ROD SERLING'S LOST CLASSICS (TF)
    O'Hara-Horowitz Productions, 1994
BECAUSE MOMMY WORKS (TF)   Newport-Balboa Productions/
    Spring Creek Productions/Warner Bros. TV, 1994
THE TUSKEGEE AIRMEN (CTF)   HBO Pictures, 1995

ARTHUR MARKS*

b. August 2, 1927 - Los Angeles, California
Telephone: 818/887-1007
Attorney: Sam Pearlmutter, 5757 Wilshire Blvd. - Suite 636,
    Los Angeles, CA 90036, 213/931-1017

CLASS OF '74   co-director with Mack Bing, Crest, 1972
BONNIE'S KIDS   General Film Corporation, 1973
THE ROOM MATES   General Film Corporation, 1973
DETROIT 9000   General Film Corporation, 1973
A WOMAN FOR ALL MEN   General Film Corporation, 1975
BUCKTOWN   American International, 1975
FRIDAY FOSTER   American International, 1975
J.D.'S REVENGE   American International, 1976
THE MONKEY HUSTLE   American International, 1976

ROSS KAGAN MARKS

Agent: William Morris Agency - Beverly Hills, 310/859-4000

HOMAGE   Skyline Entertainment, 1995

BRAD MARLOWE

THE WEBBERS   Blue Ridge Filmtrust/DEN Films, 1993

JAMES MARLOWE

SENSEI   Shower Productions, 1991

MALCOLM MARMORSTEIN

Agent: Preferred Artists - Encino, 818/990-0305

DEAD MEN DON'T DIE   JGM Enterprises, 1991
THE RELUCTANT VAMPIRE   Waymar Productions, 1992

EUGENE MARNER*

Home: 141 Bergen Street, Brooklyn, NY 11217, 718/875-8205

CIVILIZATION AND THE JEWS (TD)   co-director with Julian Krainin,
    PBS, 1984
BEAUTY AND THE BEAST   Cannon, 1987, U.S.-Israeli
PUSS IN BOOTS   Cannon, 1987, U.S.-Israeli
CHILDHOOD (TD)   co-director with Erna Akuginow &
    Geoff Haines-Stiles, WNET-13/Childhood Project Inc./
    Channel 4/Antelope Films Ltd., 1991, U.S.-British

CHRISTIAN MARQUAND

b. March 15, 1927 - Marseille, France
Contact: French Film Office, 745 Fifth Avenue, New York,
    NY 10151, 212/832-8860

OF FLESH AND BLOOD   LES GRANDS CHEMINS   Times Film
    Corporation, 1963, French-Italian
CANDY   Cinerama Releasing Corporation, 1968,
    U.S.-French-Italian

LEON MARR

b. 1948 - Toronto, Ontario, Canada
Address: 19 Beech Avenue, Toronto, Ontario M4E 3H3, Canada,
    416/691-1215

CLARE'S WISH (TF)   1979, Canadian
FLOWERS IN THE SAND (TF)   1980, Canadian
DANCING IN THE DARK   New World, 1986, Canadian

FRANK MARSHALL*

b. September 13, 1946 - Los Angeles, California
Business: The Kennedy/Marshall Company, 650 N. Bronson Avenue -
    Clinton #100, Hollywood, CA 90004, 213/960-4900
Agent: CAA - Beverly Hills, 310/288-4545

ARACHNOPHOBIA   Buena Vista, 1990
ALIVE   Paramount/Buena Vista, 1993
CONGO   Paramount, 1995

GARRY MARSHALL*

(Garry Marscharelli)
b. November 13, 1934 - New York, New York
Agent: ICM - Beverly Hills, 310/550-4000
Business: Henderson Productions, 10067 Riverside Drive,
    North Hollywood, CA 91602, 818/985-6417

YOUNG DOCTORS IN LOVE   20th Century-Fox, 1982
THE FLAMINGO KID   20th Century Fox, 1984
NOTHING IN COMMON   TriStar, 1986
OVERBOARD   MGM/UA, 1987
BEACHES   Buena Vista, 1988
PRETTY WOMAN   Buena Vista, 1990
FRANKIE AND JOHNNY   Paramount, 1991
EXIT TO EDEN   Savoy Pictures, 1994

PENNY MARSHALL*
(Penny Marscharelli)
b. October 15, 1942 - New York, New York
Business: Parkway Productions, 10202 W. Washington Blvd.,
  Culver City, CA 90232, 310/280-4474
Agent: CAA - Beverly Hills, 310/288-4545

JUMPIN' JACK FLASH   20th Century Fox, 1986
BIG   20th Century Fox, 1988
AWAKENINGS   Columbia, 1990
A LEAGUE OF THEIR OWN   Columbia, 1992
RENAISSANCE MAN   *BY THE BOOK*   Buena Vista, 1994

DARNELL MARTIN
Agent: William Morris Agency - Beverly Hills, 310/859-4000

I LIKE IT LIKE THAT   Columbia, 1994

FRANK MARTIN
Home: 7415 Costello Avenue, Van Nuys, CA 91405,
  818/782-1028
Business: Man In The Moon Films, Inc., 11812 San Vicente Blvd. -
  Suite 210, Los Angeles, CA 90049, 310/826-1149

JOHN HUSTON: THE MAN, THE MOVIES, THE MAVERICK (CTD)
  Point Blank, 1988
MGM: WHEN THE LION ROARS (CTD)   Joni Levin Point Blank
  Productions, 1992
THE WONDERFUL WORLD OF DISNEY: 40 YEARS OF
  TELEVISION MAGIC (TD)   Walt Disney TV/ZM
  Productions, 1994

RICHARD MARTIN
Agent: The Kaplan-Stahler Agency - Beverly Hills, 213/653-4483

NORTH OF PITTSBURGH   Cinephile, 1992, Canadian

STEVEN M. MARTIN
THEREMIN: AN ELECTRONIC ODYSSEY (FD)   Kaga Bay
  Productions, 1993

WRYE MARTIN
THE UNEARTHLING   co-director with Barry Poltermann,
  Forefront Films, 1994

CHUCK MARTINEZ*
Telephone: 213/874-1586

SNACKS   New World, 1985
NICE GIRLS DON'T EXPLODE   New World, 1987

RICHARD MARTINI
Agent: The Gersh Agency - Beverly Hills, 310/274-6611

YOU CAN'T HURRY LOVE   MCEG, 1989
LIMIT UP   New Line Cinema, 1989
SHATTERED TRUST   The Jonathan Krane Group, 1995

RAYMOND MARTINO
DA VINCI'S WAY   Baby Dica Productions, 1992

LESLIE H. MARTINSON*
b. Boston, Massachusetts
Home: 2288 Coldwater Canyon Blvd., Beverly Hills, CA 90210,
  310/271-4127

THE ATOMIC KID   Republic, 1954
HOT ROD GIRL   American International, 1956
HOT ROD RUMBLE   Allied Artists, 1957
LAD: A DOG   co-director with Aram Avakian, Warner Bros., 1961
PT 109   Warner Bros., 1963
BLACK GOLD   Warner Bros., 1963
F.B.I. CODE 98   Warner Bros., 1964
FOR THOSE WHO THINK YOUNG   United Artists, 1964

BATMAN   20th Century-Fox, 1966
FATHOM   20th Century-Fox, 1967
THE CHALLENGERS (TF)   Universal TV, 1970
MRS. POLLIFAX - SPY   United Artists, 1971
HOW TO STEAL AN AIRPLANE (TF)   Universal TV, 1971
ESCAPE FROM ANGOLA   Doty-Dayton, 1976
CRUISE MISSILE   Eichberg Film/Cinelux-Romano Film/Mundial
  Film/Cine-Luce/Noble Productions/FPDC, 1978,
  West German-Spanish-U.S.-Iranian
RESCUE FROM GILLIGAN'S ISLAND (TF)   Sherwood Schwartz
  Productions, 1978
THE KID WITH THE BROKEN HALO (TF)   Satellite
  Productions, 1982
THE KID WITH THE 200 I.Q. (TF)   Guillaume-Margo Productions/
  Zephyr Productions, 1983
THE FANTASTIC WORLD OF D.C. COLLINS (TF)   Guillaume-Margo
  Productions/Zephyr Productions, 1984

MARIO MARTONE
b. 1959 - Naples, Italy
Contact: Teatri Uniti Cooperativa, Piazza dei Martiri 58, Naples,
  Italy, tel.: 081/402939

MORTE DI UN MATEMATICO NAPOLETANO   Teatri Uniti
  Cooperativa/Angio Films/RAI, 1992, Italian
RASOI   Teatri Uniti, 1994, Italian
L'AMORE MOLESTO   Lucky Red/Teatri Uniti/RAI-3, 1995, Italian

MICHAEL (MIKE) MARVIN
HAMBURGER...THE MOTION PICTURE   FM Entertainment, 1986
THE WRAITH   New Century/Vista, 1986
WISHMAN   Curb/Esquire Films, 1992

PAUL MASLANSKY*
b. November 23, 1933 - New York, New York
Business Manager: Henry J. Bamberger, 10866 Wilshire Blvd. -
  Suite 1000, Los Angeles, 310/446-2780

SUGAR HILL   American International, 1974

CLAUDE MASSOT
Contact: French Film Office, 745 Fifth Avenue, New York,
  NY 10151, 212/832-8860

NANOOK   *KABLOONAK*   Ima Films/Bloom Films/Christian
  Bourgeois Productions/France 3 Cinema/Telefilm Canada,
  1994, French-Canadian

QUENTIN MASTERS*
b. July 12, 1946 - Australia
Contact: Directors Guild of America - Los Angeles, 213/851-3671

THUMB TRIPPING   Avco Embassy, 1973
THE STUD   Trans-American, 1978, British
THE PSI FACTOR   1981, British
A DANGEROUS SUMMER   Filmco Ltd., 1982, Australian
MIDNITE SPARES   Filmco Australia, 1983, Australian

PETER MASTERSON*
(Carlos Bee Masterson)
b. June 1, 1934 - Houston, Texas
Business: Tejas Productions, 1165 Fifth Avenue - Apt. 15A,
  New York, NY 10029, 212/427-4055
Agent: ICM - Beverly Hills, 310/550-4000

THE TRIP TO BOUNTIFUL   Island Pictures/Film Dallas, 1985
FULL MOON IN BLUE WATER   Trans World Entertainment, 1988
NIGHT GAME   Trans World Entertainment, 1989
BLOOD RED   Hemdale, 1990
CONVICTS   MCEG, 1991
ARCTIC BLUE   Arctic Blue Productions, 1994

F
I
L
M

D
I
R
E
C
T
O
R
S

NICO MASTORAKIS

b. April 28, 1941 - Athens, Greece
Business: Omega Pictures, 8760 Shoreham Drive - Suite 501,
 Los Angeles, CA 90069, 213/855-0516

DEATH HAS BLUE EYES   Omega Pictures, 1974, British
ISLAND OF DEATH   Omega Pictures, 1975, British
THE NEXT ONE   *THE TIME TRAVELLER*   Allstar Productions,
 1982, British-Greek
BLIND DATE   New Line Cinema, 1984, British-Greek
SKYHIGH   Omega Pictures, 1985
THE ZERO BOYS   Omega Pictures, 1986
DOUBLE EXPOSURE   United Film Distribution, 1987
THE WIND   Omega Pictures, 1987
GLITCH!   Omega Pictures, 1988
NIGHTMARE AT NOON   Omega Pictures, 1990, filmed in 1987
HIRED TO KILL   co-director with Peter Rader,
 Omega Pictures, 1990
NINJA ACADEMY   Omega Pictures, 1990
IN THE COLD OF THE NIGHT   Omega Pictures, 1991
THE NAKED TRUTH   Omega Pictures, 1991
14 LENIN STREET   Omega Pictures/Slovo Studios,
 1992, U.S.-Russian

ARMAND MASTROIANNI*

b. Brooklyn, New York
Home: 248 Ridgecrest Avenue, Staten Island, NY 10312,
 718/948-1051
Agent: William Morris Agency - Beverly Hills, 310/859-4000

HE KNOWS YOU'RE ALONE   MGM/United Artists, 1980
THE CLAIRVOYANT   *THE KILLING HOUR*
 20th Century-Fox, 1983
THE SUPERNATURALS   Republic Entertainment/Sandy Howard
 Productions, 1985
DISTORTIONS   Cori Films, 1987
CAMERON'S CLOSET   SVS Films, 1989
DOUBLE REVENGE   Smart Egg Releasing, 1989
WHEN NO ONE WOULD LISTEN (TF)   Bruce Sallan Productions/
 Michele Lee Productions/Papazian-Hirsch Entertainment/
 Canal Plus, 1992
DEEP TROUBLE (CTF)   Papazian-Hirsch Entertainment/Ellipse
 Programme, 1993, U.S.-French
A MOTHER'S REVENGE (TF)   Carla Singer Productions, 1993
CRIES UNHEARD: THE DONNA YAKLICH STORY (TF)
 Carla Singer Productions, 1994
ONE OF HER OWN (TF)   Grossbart-Barnett Productions/
 ABC-TV, 1994
COME DIE WITH ME: A MICKEY SPILLANE'S MIKE
 HAMMER MYSTERY (TF)   Caroline Film Productions/
 CBS Entertainment, 1994
ROBIN COOK'S VIRUS   *VIRUS* (TF)   von Zerneck-Sertner
 Films, 1995

TOSHIO MASUDA

b. 1927 - Hyogo Prefecture, Japan
Contact: Nihon Eiga Kantoku Kyokai (Japan Film Directors
 Association), La Fontenu Building - 4th Floor, 23-2 Maruyama-cho,
 Shibuya-ku, Tokyo, Japan, tel.: 3/3461-4411

RED WHARF   Nikkatsu, 1958, Japanese
COMPLETED GAME   Nikkatsu, 1958, Japanese
RUSTY KNIFE   Nikkatsu, 1958, Japanese
MAN EXPLODES   Nikkatsu, 1959, Japanese
FORGET THE WOMAN   Nikkatsu, 1959, Japanese
LIVE FOR TODAY   Nikkatsu, 1959, Japanese
THE MAN WHO RAN IN HEAVEN AND EARTH   Nikkatsu,
 1959, Japanese
FIGHTING BOY   Nikkatsu, 1960, Japanese
THREE OF THE YOUNGER GENERATION   Nikkatsu,
 1960, Japanese
THE MAN WHO BET ON BULLFIGHTING   Nikkatsu,
 1960, Japanese
YAKUZA POET   Nikkatsu, 1960, Japanese
A QUIET MAN IN GANGLAND   Nikkatsu, 1961, Japanese
STRAY DOG STILL ALIVE   Nikkatsu, 1961, Japanese
WHEN THE SUN DIES IN THE SEA   Nikkatsu, 1961, Japanese
THE SUN IS GOING CRAZY   Nikkatsu, 1961, Japanese

BODYGUARD WORK   Nikkatsu, 1961, Japanese
LET'S WALK WITH OUR CHINS UP   Nikkatsu, 1962, Japanese
THE TOWN WHERE MEN ARE LIVING   Nikkatsu, 1962, Japanese
ZERO-SEN'S BLACK CLOUD FAMILY   Nikkatsu, 1962, Japanese
ESCAPE FROM THE SUN   Nikkatsu, 1962, Japanese
FLOWER AND DRAGON   Nikkatsu, 1962, Japanese
WE'RE THE ONLY ONES IN THE WORLD, BUT...   Nikkatsu,
 1962, Japanese
RED HANDKERCHIEF   Nikkatsu, 1964, Japanese
ERASE THE MURDER   Nikkatsu, 1964, Japanese
FIGHT OF RED VALLEY   Nikkatsu, 1965, Japanese
TAKE THE CASTLE   Nikkatsu, 1965, Japanese
WHAT IS THE SPRINGTIME OF LIFE?   Nikkatsu, 1965, Japanese
THE MAN WHO CAN MAKE A STORM   Nikkatsu, 1966, Japanese
CHALLENGE FOR SUCCESS   Nikkatsu, 1966, Japanese
ERASE THE ROSE OF THE NIGHT   Nikkatsu, 1966, Japanese
THE STORM CAME AND LEFT   Nikkatsu, 1967, Japanese
RED SHOOTING STAR   Nikkatsu, 1967, Japanese
BLOOD FIGHT   Nikkatsu, 1967, Japanese
CONFRONTATION   Nikkatsu, 1967, Japanese
DON'T GRIEVE, STAR - MEN OF VICTORY   Nikkatsu,
 1967, Japanese
HIMEYURI TOWER   Nikkatsu, 1968, Japanese
SHOWA LIFESPAN   Nikkatsu, 1968, Japanese
FROM BURAI TO BIG BOSS   Nikkatsu, 1968, Japanese
SONG OF MY LIFESPAN   Nikkatsu, 1968, Japanese
HEROES OF THE STORM   Nikkatsu, 1969, Japanese
HELL'S EXCOMMUNICATION LETTER   Nikkatsu, 1969, Japanese
BIG BOSS - STAKEOUT   Nikkatsu, 1969, Japanese
TORA! TORA! TORA!   co-director with Richard Fleischer &
 Kinji Fukasaku, 20th Century-Fox, 1970, U.S.-Japanese
GOODBYE TO LAW   Shochiku/Asai Productions, 1971, Japanese
PURSUIT   Shochiku, 1972, Japanese
SHADOW HUNT   Ishihara Productions, 1972, Japanese
SHADOW HUNT - FIRE CANNON   Ishihara Productions,
 1972, Japanese
SWORD AND FLOWER   Shochiku, 1972, Japanese
MY BLOOD IS THE OTHER PERSON'S BLOOD   Shochiku,
 1974, Japanese
NOSTRADAMUS' PROPHECY: CATASTROPHE 1999   Toho,
 1974, Japanese
203 KOCHI   *HILL 203*   Toei, 1980, Japanese
EMPIRE OF GREATER JAPAN   Toei, 1982, Japanese
HIGH TEEN BOOGIE   Toho, 1982, Japanese
LOVING   Toho/Johnny's Productions, 1983, Japanese
BATTLE OF THE SEA OF JAPAN   Toei, 1983, Japanese
ZERO   *ZERO-SEN BURNING*   Toho/Watanabe Productions,
 1984, Japanese
LOVE - JOURNEY BEGINS   Filmlink International, 1985, Japanese
THE ANGEL WITH ONE WING   Project A/Herald Ace,
 1986, Japanese
STORY OF THIS LOVE   Shochiku Fuji/Nippon TV, 1987, Japanese
DISAPPEARING CAPITOL   Kansai TV/Tokuma Shoten/Daiei,
 1987, Japanese
PUBLIC FUNERAL   Toei, 1989, Japanese
CHAOS IN EDO CASTLE   Fuji TV/Toei, 1991, Japanese
DOHTEN   Tohmen, 1991, Japanese
HISSATSU! 5 - GOLD'S BLOOD   Shochiku/Asah Hosoi/Kyoto Eiga,
 1991, Japanese
HEAVEN'S GREAT CRIME   Toei/TV Asahi, 1992, Japanese

VIVIAN MATALON*

b. October 11, 1929 - Manchester, England
Home: Box 24, Margaretville, NY 12455, 914/586-4530
Agent: APA - New York City, 212/582-1500

PRIVATE CONTENTMENT (TF)   WNET-13/South Carolina
 Educational TV, 1982

TED MATHER

DANCE TO WIN   MGM/UA, 1989, U.S.-Italian
FIRST FORCE   Studio Three Film Corporation, 1991

CHRIS MATHESON

Contact: Writers Guild of America, West - Los Angeles, 310/550-1000

MONKEYS   Fake Films, 1991

TIM MATHESON*
b. December 31, 1947 - Glendale, California
Agent: CAA - Beverly Hills, 310/288-4545

BREACH OF CONDUCT (CTF)   Finnegan-Pinchuk Productions/
   MTE, 1994

CHARLES MATTHAU*
b. December 10, 1964 - New York, New York
Business: The Matthau Company, 1999 Avenue of the Stars -
   Suite 2100, Los Angeles, CA 90067, 310/557-2727

DOIN' TIME ON PLANET EARTH   Cannon, 1988
MRS. LAMBERT REMEMBERS LOVE (TF)   RHI Entertainment,
   1991
THE GRASS HARP   New Line Cinema, 1995

WALTER MATTHAU
b. October 1, 1920 - New York, New York
Business: The Matthau Company, 1999 Avenue of the Stars -
   Suite 2100, Los Angeles, CA 90067, 310/557-2727
Agent: William Morris Agency - Beverly Hills, 310/859-4000

GANGSTER STORY   RCIP-States Rights, 1960

BURNY MATTINSON
THE GREAT MOUSE DETECTIVE (AF)   co-director with
   Ron Clements, Dave Michener & John Musker,
   Buena Vista, 1986

SALLY MATTISON
SLUMBER PARTY MASSACRE 3   Concorde, 1990

CHARLES MATTON
Contact: French Film Office, 745 Fifth Avenue, New York,
   NY 10151, 212/832-8860

L'ITALIEN DES ROSES   French
L'AMOUR EST UN FLEUVE EN RUSSIE   French
LA LUMIERE DES ETOILES MORTES   Les Acacias Cineaudience,
   1994, French-German

RICHARD MAURO
NICK AND JANE   Emeralde Productions, 1995

GODWIN MAWURU
Contact: Ministry of Information, Film Section, P.O. Box 8150,
   Causeway, Harare, Zimbabwe, tel.: 707210 or 703891

NERIA   co-director with John Riber, KJM3 Entertainment Group/
   Media for Development Trust, 1992, Zimbabwean
I AM THE FUTURE   Kubi Chaza-Indi Productions,
   1994, Zimbabwean

RONALD F. MAXWELL*
b. January 5, 1947 - Tripoli, Libya
Agent: William Morris Agency - Beverly Hills, 310/859-4000
Attorney: Weissman-Wolff, 9665 Wilshire Blvd., Beverly Hills,
   CA 90212, 310/858-7888
Business Manager: DeLoitte-Touche - Los Angeles, 310/277-3000

SEA MARKS (TF)   PBS, 1976
VERNA: USO GIRL (TF) ☆   PBS, 1978
LITTLE DARLINGS   Paramount, 1980
THE NIGHT THE LIGHTS WENT OUT IN GEORGIA
   Avco Embassy, 1981
KIDCO   20th Century-Fox, 1983
PARENT TRAP II (TF)   The Landsburg Company/Walt
   Disney TV, 1987
IN THE LAND OF POETS (FD)   Person to Person Films, 1989
GETTYSBURG   New Line Cinema, 1993
GETTYSBURG (MS)   Turner Pictures, 1994

BRADFORD MAY*
Home: 2949 Deep Canyon Drive, Beverly Hills, CA 90210,
   310/273-0125
Agent: William Morris Agency - Beverly Hills, 310/859-4000

THE LADY FORGETS (TF)   Leonard Hill Films, 1989
OVER MY DEAD BODY (TF)   Universal TV, 1990
FATAL FRIENDSHIP (TF)   Papazian-Hirsch Entertainment, 1991
DRIVE LIKE LIGHTNING (CTF)   Papazian-Hirsch Productions/
   Canal Plus, 1992
LEGACY OF LIES (CTF)   BAL Productions/MTE, 1992
MORTAL SINS (CTF)   Blake Edwards TV/Barry Weitz Films, 1992
AMY FISHER: MY STORY (TF)   KLM/Spectator Films/Michael
   Jaffe Films, 1992
IT'S NOTHING PERSONAL (TF)   The Lee Rich Company/Bruce
   Sallan Productions/Papazian-Hirsch Entertainment, 1993
MARILYN & BOBBY: HER FINAL AFFAIR (CTF)   Barry Weitz Films/
   The Auerbach Company/Reteitalia Productions, 1993
TROUBLE SHOOTERS: TRAPPED BENEATH THE EARTH (TF)
   Ginkgo Productions/Walter Mirisch Productions, 1993
MADONNA: INNOCENCE LOST (TF)   Jaffe-Braunstein Films/Fox
   Broadcasting Company, 1994
DARKMAN II: THE RETURN OF DURANT (HVF)   MCA Home
   Entertainment, 1995
THE RETURN OF HUNTER: EVERYONE WALKS IN L.A. (TF)
   Stephen J. Cannell Productions/NBC, 1995
GRAMPS (TF)   Initial Entertainment Group/Viacom, 1995

ELAINE MAY*
(Elaine Berlin)
b. April 21, 1932 - Philadelphia, Pennsylvania
Agent: CAA - Beverly Hills, 310/288-4545
Business Manager: Julian Schlossberg, Castle Hill Productions,
   1414 Avenue of the Americas, New York, NY 10019,
   212/888-0080

A NEW LEAF   Paramount, 1971
THE HEARTBREAK KID   20th Century-Fox, 1972
MIKEY AND NICKY   Paramount, 1977
ISHTAR   Columbia, 1987

RUSS MAYBERRY*
Agent: Shapiro-Lichtman Agency - Los Angeles, 310/859-8877

THE JESUS TRIP   EMCO, 1971
PROBE (TF)   Warner Bros. TV, 1972
A VERY MISSING PERSON (TF)   Universal TV, 1972
FER-DE-LANCE (TF)   Leslie Stevens Productions, 1974
SEVENTH AVENUE (MS)   co-director with Richard Irving,
   Universal TV, 1977
STONESTREET: WHO KILLED THE CENTERFOLD MODEL? (TF)
   Universal TV, 1977
THE 3,000 MILE CHASE (TF)   Universal TV, 1977
THE YOUNG RUNAWAYS (TF)   NBC, 1978
THE MILLION DOLLAR DIXIE DELIVERY (TF)   NBC, 1978
THE REBELS (MS)   Universal TV, 1979
UNIDENTIFIED FLYING ODDBALL   Buena Vista, 1979
THE $5.20 AN HOUR DREAM (TF)   Thompson-Sagal Productions/
   Big Deal Inc./Finnegan Associates, 1980
MARRIAGE IS ALIVE AND WELL (TF)   Lorimar Productions, 1980
REUNION (TF)   Barry Weitz Films, 1980
A MATTER OF LIFE AND DEATH (TF)   Big Deal Inc./Raven's Claw
   Productions/Lorimar Productions, 1981
SIDNEY SHORR (TF)   Hajeno Productions/Warner Bros. TV, 1981
THE FALL GUY (TF)   Glen A. Larson Productions/20th
   Century-Fox TV, 1981
SIDE BY SIDE: THE TRUE STORY OF THE OSMOND FAMILY (TF)
   Osmond Productions/Comworld Productions, 1982
ROOSTER (TF)   Glen A. Larson Productions/Tugboat Productions/
   20th Century- Fox TV, 1982
MANIMAL (TF)   Glen A. Larson Productions/20th
   Century-Fox TV, 1983
CHALLENGE OF A LIFETIME (TF)   Moonlight Productions, 1985
A PLACE TO CALL HOME (TF)   Big Deal Productions/Crawford
   Productions/Embassy TV, 1987, U.S.-Australian
DANGER DOWN UNDER (TF)   Weintraub Entertainment Goup/
   Hoyts Productions, Ltd., 1988, U.S.-Australian

PAUL MAYERSBERG
b. 1941

CAPTIVE *HEROINE*   CineTel Films, 1986, British-French
NIGHTFALL   Concorde, 1988
THE LAST SAMURAI   Goldenberg Films, 1990

LES MAYFIELD*
Business: ZM Productions, 100 Universal City Plaza - MT27,
   Universal City, CA 91608, 818/777-4664
Agent: CAA - Beverly Hills, 310/288-4545

ENCINO MAN   Buena Vista, 1992
MIRACLE ON 34TH STREET   20th Century Fox, 1994

TONY MAYLAM*
b. May 26, 1943 - London, England
Business: Filmplan Ltd., 4 Radley Mews, Kensington,
   London W8, England
Contact: British Film Commission, 70 Baker Street, London
   W1M 1DJ, England, tel.: 171/224-5000

WHITE ROCK (FD)   EMI, 1977, British
THE RIDDLE OF THE SANDS   Satori, 1979, British
THE BURNING   Orion, 1982
THE SINS OF DORIAN GRAY (TF)   Rankin-Bass
   Productions, 1983
SPLIT SECOND   InterStar Releasing, 1992, British

MELANIE MAYRON*
b. October 20, 1952 - Philadelphia, Pennsylvania
Agent: The Gersh Agency - Beverly Hills, 310/274-6611

FRAKY FRIDAY (TF)   ZM Productions/Walt Disney TV, 1995
BABY SITTERS CLUB   Columbia, 1995

ALBERT MAYSLES
b. November 26, 1926 - Brookline, Massachusetts
Business: Maysles Films, Inc., 250 West 54th Street, New York,
   NY 10019

PSYCHIATRY IN RUSSIA (FD)   1955
YOUTH IN POLAND (FD)   co-director with David Maysles, 1962
SHOWMAN (FD)   co-director with David Maysles, 1962
WHAT'S HAPPENING: THE BEATLES IN THE USA (FD)
   co-director with David Maysles, 1964
MEET MARLON BRANDO (FD)   co-director with
   David Maysles, 1965
WITH LOVE FROM TRUMAN (FD)   co-director with
   David Maysles, 1966
SALESMAN (FD)   co-director with David Maysles &
   Charlotte Zwerin, Maysles Film, 1969
GIMME SHELTER (FCD)   co-director with David Maysles &
   Charlotte Zwerin, Cinema 5, 1971
CHRISTO'S VALLEY CURTAIN (FD)   co-director with
   David Maysles & Ellen Giffard, 1972
GREY GARDENS (FD)   co-director with David Maysles,
   Ellen Hovde & Muffie Meyer, 1975
RUNNING FENCE (FD)   co-director with David Maysles &
   Charlotte Zwerin, 1977
VLADIMIR HOROWITZ: THE LAST ROMANTIC (TD) ☆
   co-director with David Maysles, Cami Video, 1985
ISLANDS (FD)   co-director with David Maysles & Charlotte Zwerin,
   Maysles Films, 1986
OZAWA (TD)   co-director with David Maysles, Deborah Dickson &
   Susan Froemke, Columbia Artists, 1986
HOROWITZ PLAYS MOZART (FCD)   co-director with
   Susan Froemke & Charlotte Zwerin, 1987
JESSYE NORMAN SINGS CARMEN (HVCD)   co-director with
   Susan Froemke & Charlotte Zwerin, Cami Video, 1989
SOLDIERS OF MUSIC (TD)   co-director with Susan Froemke,
   Peter Gelb & Bob Eisenhardt, Cami Video/Peter Gelb/Maysles
   Films-Froemke Productions, 1990
CHRISTO IN PARIS (FD)   co-director with David Maysles,
   Maysles Films, 1991

THE BEATLES: THE FIRST U.S. VISIT (HVCD)   MPI Video, 1991
ABORTION: DESPERATE CHOICES (FD)   co-director with
   Susan Froemke & Deborah Dickson, 1993
UMBRELLAS (FD)   co-director with Henry Corra &
   Graham Weinbren, Maysles Films, 1994, U.S.-Japanese

RENTARO MAYUZUMI
Contact: Nihon Eiga Kantoku Kyokai (Japan Film Directors
   Association), La Fontenu Building -4th Floor, 23-2 Maruyama-cho,
   Shibuya-ku, Tokyo, Japan, tel.: 3/3461-4411

RAMPO: MAYUZUMI VERSION   Shochiku, 1994, Japanese

MICHAEL MAZO
Business: North American Releasing, 808 Nelson Street, Vancouver,
   British Columbia V6Z 2H2, Canada, 604/681-2165

IN EXILE   North American Releasing, 1992, Canadian
CRACKERJACK   North American Releasing, 1994, Canadian

PAUL MAZURSKY*
(Irwin Mazursky)
b. April 25, 1930 - Brooklyn, New York
Agent: ICM - Beverly Hills, 310/550-4000

BOB & CAROL & TED & ALICE   Columbia, 1969
ALEX IN WONDERLAND   MGM, 1970
BLUME IN LOVE   Warner Bros., 1973
HARRY AND TONTO   20th Century-Fox, 1974
NEXT STOP, GREENWICH VILLAGE   20th Century-Fox, 1976
AN UNMARRIED WOMAN   20th Century-Fox, 1978
WILLIE AND PHIL   20th Century-Fox, 1980
TEMPEST   Columbia, 1982
MOSCOW ON THE HUDSON   Columbia, 1984
DOWN AND OUT IN BEVERLY HILLS   Buena Vista, 1986
MOON OVER PARADOR   Universal, 1988, U.S.-Brazilian
ENEMIES, A LOVE STORY   20th Century Fox, 1989
SCENES FROM A MALL   Buena Vista, 1991
THE PICKLE   Columbia, 1993
FAITHFUL   Savoy Pictures, 1995

CARLO MAZZACURATI
b. March 2, 1956 - Padua, Italy
Business: SACIS, via Tornacelli 139, 00186 Rome, Italy,
   tel.: 06/396841

NOTTE ITALIANA   Sacher Film/RAI/So.Fin.A., 1987, Italian
IL PRETE BELLO   Nickelodeon/Partner's Production/RAI,
   1989, Italian
UN'ALTRA VITA   Erre Produzioni/RAI, 1992, Italian
IL TORO   Cecchi Gori Group, 1994, Italian

THOMAS MAZZIOTTI
UNDERTOW   Capstone Films, 1991

FRANK MAZZOLA
13 O'CLOCK   co-director with Frank Leahy, Third Coast
   Entertainment, 1988

MASSIMO MAZZUCCO
Agent: Susan Grant, The Artists Group - Los Angeles, 310/552-1100

SUMMERTIME   1983, Italian
ROMANCE   MVM Films, 1986, Italian
HIDDEN LENS   Silvio Berlusconi Communications/Casanova
   Productions, 1992, Italian
SHADOW OF A KISS   France 2/Technisonor/CEP, 1993, Italian

ROGER GNOAN M'BALA
Contact: Ministry of Information, BP 138, Abidjan, Ivory Coast,
   tel.: 442585

AU NOM DU CHRIST   Les Films Abyssa/Amka Films Productions,
   1993, Ivory Coast-Swiss

DON McBREARTY

Address: 117 Niagara Street, Toronto, Ontario M5V 1C6, Canada, 416/365-1810
Agent: Pamela Paul, 1778 Bloor Street West - Suite 14, Toronto, Ontario M6P 3K4, Canada, 416/975-9334

THE RACE TO FREEDOM: THE UNDERGROUND RAILROAD (CTF) Atlantis Films/United Image Entertainment/The Family Channel/BET/CTV TV Network/Telefilm Canada/OFDC/Rogers Telefund, 1994, Canadian-U.S.

JIM McBRIDE*

b. September 16, 1941 - New York, New York
Agent: Daniel Ostroff, The Daniel Ostroff Agency - Los Angeles, 310/278-2020

DAVID HOLZMAN'S DIARY Grove Press, 1967
MY GIRLFRIEND'S WEDDING 1968
GLEN AND RANDA UMC, 1971
A HARD DAY FOR ARCHIE *HOT TIMES* 1973, re-released under title MY EROTIC FANTASIES in 1974 with additional footage by another director
BREATHLESS Orion, 1983
THE BIG EASY Columbia, 1987
GREAT BALLS OF FIRE Orion, 1989
BLOOD TIES (TF) Shapiro Entertainment, 1991
THE WRONG MAN (CTF) Viacom Pictures, 1993
UNCOVERED CIBY UK/Filmania, 1994, British-Spanish

ROD McCALL

Agent: Epstein-Wyckoff-Lamanna & Associates - Beverly Hills, 310/278-7222

CHEATIN' HEARTS *PAPER HEARTS* King/Moonstone, 1993

PETER McCARTHY

Agent: William Morris Agency - Beverly Hills, 310/859-4000

FLOUNDERING Front Films, 1994

TODD McCARTHY

Business: Daily Variety, 5700 Wilshire Blvd. - Suite 120, Los Angeles, CA 90036, 213/857-6600

VISIONS OF LIGHT: THE ART OF CINEMATOGRAPHY (FD) co-director with Arnold Glassman, Kino International, 1992, U.S.-Japanese

ROBERT McCARTY

Home: 222 West 83rd Street - Apt. 11-C, New York, NY 10024, 212/580-1034
Attorney: Franklin Weinrib, Ruddel & Vassallo, 950 Third Avenue, New York, NY 10022

LIGHT FANTASTIC Embassy, 1965
I COULD NEVER HAVE SEX WITH A MAN WHO HAS SO LITTLE REGARD FOR MY HUSBAND Cinema 5, 1973
FORE PLAY co-director with John G. Avildsen & Bruce Malmuth, Cinema National, 1975

J. MICHAEL McCLARY*

Home: 8941 Ashcroft Avenue, Los Angeles, CA 90048, 310/858-1426
Agent: ICM - Beverly Hills, 310/550-4000

CURSE OF THE STARVING CLASS (CTF) Trimark Pictures, 1994, originally filmed for theatrical release

DAN McCORMACK

MINOTAUR Headliner Entertainment Group, 1994

GEORGE McCOWAN

b. Winnipeg, Manitoba, Canada
Contact: Directors Guild of Canada, 225 Richmond Street, Toronto, Ontario M5V 1W2, Canada, 416/351-8200

THE MONK (TF) Thomas-Spelling Productions, 1969
THE BALLAD OF ANDY CROCKER (TF) Thomas-Spelling Productions, 1969
CARTER'S ARMY (TF) Thomas-Spelling Productions, 1970
THE LOVE WAR (TF) Thomas-Spelling Productions, 1970
THE OVER-THE-HILL GANG RIDES AGAIN (TF) Thomas-Spelling Productions, 1970
RUN, SIMON, RUN (TF) Aaron Spelling Productions, 1970
LOVE, HATE, LOVE (TF) Aaron Spelling Productions, 1971
CANNON (TF) QM Productions, 1971
THE FACE OF FEAR (TF) QM Productions, 1971
IF TOMORROW COMES (TF) Aaron Spelling Productions, 1971
WELCOME HOME, JOHNNY BRISTOL (TF) Cinema Center, 1972
THE MAGNIFICENT SEVEN RIDE! United Artists, 1972
FROGS American International, 1972
MURDER ON FLIGHT 502 (TF) Spelling-Goldberg Productions, 1975
SHADOW OF THE HAWK Columbia, 1976, Canadian
SEPARATION (TF) CFTO-TV, 1978, Canadian
RETURN TO FANTASY ISLAND (TF) Spelling-Goldberg Productions, 1978
THE RETURN OF THE MOD SQUAD (TF) Thomas-Spelling Productions, 1979
THE SHAPE OF THINGS TO COME Film Ventures International, 1979, Canadian
SANITY CLAUSE (TF) co-director with David Barlow, Canadian Broadcasting Corporation, 1990, Canadian

JIM McCULLOUGH, SR.

MOUNTAINTOP MOTEL MASSACRE New World, 1985
THE AURORA ENCOUNTER New World, 1986
WHERE THE RED FERN GROWS PART TWO August Entertainment, 1992

BRUCE McDONALD

b. 1959
Contact: Directors Guild of Canada, 225 Richmond Street, Toronto, Ontario M5V 1W2, Canada, 416/351-8200
Contact: Credentials - Canada, 416/926-1507

ROADKILL (TF) 1989, Canadian
HIGHWAY 61 Skouras Pictures, 1991, Canadian-British
DANCE ME OUTSIDE Rez Films Ltd., 1994, Canadian

LeROY McDONALD*

Contact: Directors Guild of America - Los Angeles, 213/851-3671

TUSKEGEE SUBJECT #626 Quiet Majesty Productions, 1993

MICHAEL JAMES McDONALD

HOW MUCH ARE THOSE CHILDREN IN THE WINDOW? Concorde, 1994

RODNEY (ROD) McDONALD

Business: Oujaba Productions, 8734 Holloway Drive - Suite B, Los Angeles, CA 90069, 310/652-8713
Agent: Beth Bohn, Paul Kohner Agency - Beverly Hills, 310/550-1060

NIGHT EYES II Prism Entertainment, 1991
ULTIMATE DESIRE Westwind Productions, 1994

DON McDOUGALL

Home: 1269 Shadybrook Drive, Beverly Hills, CA 90210, 310/265-4578

ESCAPE TO MINDANAO (TF) Universal TV, 1968
WILD WOMEN (TF) Aaron Spelling Productions, 1970
THE AQUARIANS (TF) Ivan Tors Productions, 1975
THE HEIST (TF) Paramount TV, 1972
THE MARK OF ZORRO (TF) 20th Century-Fox, 1974
THE MISSING ARE DEADLY (TF) Lawrence Gordon Productions, 1975

RODDY McDOWALL
b. September 17, 1928 - London, England
Business: Foxboro Entertainment, 8222 Melrose Avenue - Suite 301,
    Los Angeles, CA 90046, 213/966-4371

TAM LIN *THE DEVIL'S WIDOW* American International, 1971

ROSS McELWEE
SHERMAN'S MARCH (FD) First Run Features, 1988
SOMETHING TO DO WITH THE WALL (FD) co-director with
    Marilyn Levine, First Run Features, 1991
TIME INDEFINITE (FD) First Run Features, 1993

BERNARD McEVEETY*
Contact: Directors Guild of America - Los Angeles, 213/851-3671

RIDE BEYOND VENGEANCE Columbia, 1966
A STEP OUT OF LINE (TF) Cinema Center, 1971
THE BROTHERHOOD OF SATAN Columbia, 1971
KILLER BY NIGHT (TF) Cinema Center, 1972
NAPOLEON AND SAMANTHA Buena Vista, 1972
ONE LITTLE INDIAN Buena Vista, 1973
THE BEARS AND I Buena Vista, 1974
THE MACAHANS (TF) Albert S. Ruddy Productions/
    MGM TV, 1976
THE HOSTAGE HEART (TF) Andrew J. Fenady Associates/
    MGM TV, 1977
DONOVAN'S KID (TF) NBC, 1979
CENTENNIAL (MS) co-director with Harry Falk, Paul Krasny &
    Virgil Vogel, Universal TV, 1979
ROUGHNECKS (TF) Douglas Netter Productions/Metromedia
    Producers Corporations, 1980

VINCENT McEVEETY*
Agent: Shapiro-Lichtman Talent Agency - Los Angeles,
    310/859-8877

THIS SAVAGE LAND (TF) 1968
FIRECREEK Warner Bros., 1968
CUTTER'S TRAIL (TF) CBS Studio Center, 1970
THE MILLION DOLLAR DUCK Buena Vista, 1971
THE BISCUIT EATER Buena Vista, 1972
CHARLEY AND THE ANGEL Buena Vista, 1972
WONDER WOMAN (TF) Warner Bros. TV, 1974
SUPERDAD Buena Vista, 1972
THE CASTAWAY COWBOY Buena Vista, 1974
THE STRONGEST MAN IN THE WORLD Buena Vista, 1975
THE LAST DAY (TF) Paramount TV, 1975
THE TREASURE OF MATECUMBE Buena Vista, 1976
GUS Buena Vista, 1976
HERBIE GOES TO MONTE CARLO Buena Vista, 1976
THE APPLE DUMPLING GANG RIDES AGAIN Buena Vista, 1979
HERBIE GOES BANANAS Buena Vista, 1980
AMY Buena Vista, 1981
MCCLAIN'S LAW (TF) Eric Bercovici Productions/
    Epipsychidion Inc., 1982
BLOOD SPORT (TF) Spelling-Goldberg Productions/
    Columbia TV, 1986
GUNSMOKE: RETURN TO DODGE (TF)
    CBS Entertainment, 1987
STRANGER AT MY DOOR (TF) Dry Canyon One, 1991
DEAD RUN (TF) World International Network, 1991
COLUMBO: DEATH HITS THE JACKPOT (TF)
    Universal TV, 1991
COLUMBO: A BIRD IN THE HAND (TF) Universal TV, 1992
COLUMBO: IT'S ALL IN THE GAME (TF) Universal TV, 1993
COLUMBO: UNDERCOVER (TF) Universal TV, 1994
COLUMBO: STRANGE BEDFELLOWS (TF) Universal TV, 1995

DARREN McGAVIN*
b. May 7, 1922 - Spokane, Washington
Address: P.O. Box 2939, Beverly Hills, CA 90213, 310/550-5917
Agent: Phil Gersh, The Gersh Agency - Beverly Hills, 310/274-6611

HAPPY MOTHER'S DAY - LOVE, GEORGE Cinema 5, 1973

SCOTT McGEHEE
Agent: William Morris Agency - Beverly Hills, 310/859-4000

SUTURE co-director with David Siegel, The Samuel Goldwyn
    Company, 1993

SCOTT McGINNIS
CAROLINE AT MIDNIGHT Concorde, 1993

DON McGLYNN
Home: 314 S. Alexandria Avenue - Apt. 405, Los Angeles,
    CA 90020, 213/389-0173

ART PEPPER: NOTES FROM A JAZZ SURVIVOR (FD)
    Winter Moon Productions, 1982
JAZZ PROFILES: JOE WILLIAMS (FD) Productions in
    Tempo, 1985
THE SOUNDIES (FD) Euphoria Productions, 1986
THE MILLS BROTHERS STORY (FD) Storyville Films/Winter
    Moon Productions, 1986
TV'S FIRST MUSIC VIDEOS (FD) Storyville Films/Winter Moon
    Productions, 1988
THE SPIKE JONES STORY (FD) Storyville Films/Winter Moon
    Productions, 1988
HOLLYWOOD MAVERICKS (TD) American Film Institute/NHK
    Enterprises, 1990, U.S.-Japanese

PATRICK McGOOHAN*
b. May 19, 1928 - New York, New York
Agent: ICM - Beverly Hills, 310/859-4000

CATCH MY SOUL Cinerama Releasing Corporation, 1974
COLUMBO: AGENDA FOR MURDER (TF) Universal TV, 1990

JOSEPH McGRATH
Contact: British Film Commission, 70 Baker Street, London
    W1M 1DJ, England, tel.: 71/224-5000

CASINO ROYALE co-director with Val Guest, Ken Hughes,
    John Huston & Robert Parrish, Columbia, 1967, British
30 IS A DANGEROUS AGE, CYNTHIA Columbia, 1968, British
THE BLISS OF MRS. BLOSSOM Paramount, 1969, British
NER IST WER? 1970, West German
THE MAGIC CHRISTIAN Commonwealth United, 1970, British
DIGBY, THE BIGGEST DOG IN THE WORLD Cinerama Releasing
    Corporation, 1974, British
THE GREAT McGONAGALL Scotia American, 1975, British
I'M NOT FEELING MYSELF TONIGHT New Realm, 1976, British
THE STRANGE CASE OF THE END OF CIVILISATION AS
    WE KNOW IT (TF) Shearwater Films/London Weekend TV,
    1978, British
RISING DAMP ITC, 1980, British
NIGHT TRAIN TO MURDER (TF) Thames TV, 1983, British
WHAT THE DICKENS? (TF) HTV, 1984, British
JUST DESSERTS (TF) 1986, British
STARLETS 1987, British

THOMAS McGUANE
Home: Hoffman Route, Livingston, Montana 59047
Agent: ICM - Beverly Hills, 310/550-4000

92 IN THE SHADE United Artists, 1975

MARY McGUCKIAN
Contact: Irish Film Centre, 6 Eustace Street, Dublin 2, Ireland,
    tel.: 679-5744

WORDS UPON THE WINDOW PANE Pembridge Productions Ltd./
    Calypso Film/Delux Productions/Northpro/British Screen/Irish Film
    Board/NRW/WFF, 1994, Irish-German-Luxembourgian-British

DOUG McHENRY
Agent: William Morris Agency - Beverly Hills, 310/859-4000

HOUSE PARTY 2 co-director with George Jackson,
New Line Cinema, 1991
JASON'S LYRIC Gramercy Pictures, 1994

GEORGE McINDOE
b. May 17, 1949 - Montrose, Scotland
Home: P.O. Box 66, Santa Monica, CA 90406, 310/276-7554
Agent: Marc Sullivan, DOC Management, 14 St. Georges Drive,
London WC1, England, tel.: 171/834-9226

STAGE SCHOOL (TF) Speake Films, 1971, British
THE ROLLER SKATING GROUPIE Rainbow Film Productions,
1971, British
THE STUDIO KIDS (TF) co-director with Sean Barry, BMPC,
1973, British
LAZY DAYS (TF) co-director with Sean Barry, Sean Barry
Productions, 1973, British
HYDE PARK POP (FD) co-director, Unit Two Film Productions,
1973, British

LAURIE McINNES
Contact: Australian Film Commission, 150 William Street,
Woolloomooloo NSW 2011, Australia, tel.: 2/321-6444

BROKEN HIGHWAY Black Ray Films/Australian Film Commission/
Queensland Film Development Corporation, 1993, Australian

CHRIS McINTYRE
DEAD WRONG Prism Pictures, 1993
BACKSTREET JUSTICE Prism Pictures, 1993

DUNCAN McLACHLAN
DOUBLE O KID Prism Entertainment, 1992

ANDREW V. McLAGLEN*
b. July 28, 1920 - London, England
Home: 3110 San Juan Valley Road, P.O. Box 1056, Friday Harbor,
WA 98250, 206/378-4990
Agent: BDP & Associates, 10637 Burbank Blvd., North Hollywood,
CA 91601, 818/506-7615

GUN THE MAN DOWN United Artists, 1956
MAN IN THE VAULT Universal, 1956
THE ABDUCTORS 20th Century-Fox, 1957
FRECKLES 20th Century-Fox, 1960
THE LITTLE SHEPHERD OF KINGDOM COME
20th Century-Fox, 1961
McLINTOCK! United Artists, 1963
SHENANDOAH Universal, 1965
THE RARE BREED Universal, 1966
MONKEYS, GO HOME! Buena Vista, 1967
THE WAY WEST United Artists, 1967
THE BALLAD OF JOSIE Universal, 1968
THE DEVIL'S BRIGADE United Artists, 1968
BANDOLERO! 20th Century-Fox, 1968
HELLFIGHTERS Universal, 1969
THE UNDEFEATED 20th Century-Fox, 1969
CHISUM Warner Bros., 1970
ONE MORE TRAIN TO ROB Universal, 1971
FOOLS' PARADE Columbia, 1971
SOMETHING BIG National General, 1971
CAHILL, U.S. MARSHAL Warner Bros., 1973
MITCHELL Allied Artists, 1975
THE LOG OF THE BLACK PEARL (TF) Universal TV/
Mark VII Ltd., 1975
STOWAWAY TO THE MOON (TF) 20th Century-Fox TV, 1975
BANJO HACKETT: ROAMIN' FREE (TF) Bruce Lansbury
Productions/Columbia TV, 1976
THE LAST HARD MEN 20th Century-Fox, 1976
MURDER AT THE WORLD SERIES (TF) ABC Circle Films, 1977
THE FANTASTIC JOURNEY (TF) Bruce Lansbury Productions/
Columbia TV, 1977

BREAKTHROUGH *SERGEANT STEINER* Maverick Pictures
International, 1978, West German
THE WILD GEESE Allied Artists, 1979, British
ffolkes *NORTH SEA HIJACK* Universal, 1980, British
THE SEA WOLVES Paramount, 1981, British
THE SHADOW RIDERS (TF) The Pegasus Group Ltd./
Columbia TV, 1982
THE BLUE AND THE GRAY (MS) Larry White-Lou Reda
Productions/Columbia TV, 1982
TRAVIS McGEE (TF) Hajeno Productions/Warner Bros. TV, 1983
SAHARA MGM/UA/Cannon, 1984
THE DIRTY DOZEN: THE NEXT MISSION (TF) MGM-UA TV, 1985
ON WINGS OF EAGLES (MS) Edgar J. Scherick Productions/Taft
Entertainment TV, 1986
RETURN FROM THE RIVER KWAI Screenlife Establishment/
Leisure Time Productions, 1989, British
EYE OF THE WIDOW InterStar Releasing, 1990, British-French

STEVE McLEAN
POSTCARDS FROM AMERICA Islet/Channel 4 Films/Normal,
1994, U.S.-British

DON McLENNAN
b. January 7, 1950 - Leeton, Australia
Agent: Susan Smith & Associates - Beverly Hills, 213/852-4777

HARD KNOCKS Andromeda Films, 1980, Australian
VALLEY OF GIANTS (TF) Barron Films, 1984, Australian
SLATE, WYN & ME Hemdale, 1987, Australian
MULL Hemdale, 1989, Australian
BREAKAWAY Smart Egg Pictures, 1990, Australian

TOM McLOUGHLIN*
Agent: CAA - Beverly Hills, 310/288-4545

ONE DARK NIGHT Comworld, 1983
FRIDAY THE 13TH, PART VI: JASON LIVES Paramount, 1986
DATE WITH AN ANGEL DEG, 1987
FRIDAY THE 13TH - THE PROPHECIES (TF) Triumphant
Entertainment Corporation of Canada/Hometown Films,
1989, Canadian-U.S.
STEPHEN KING'S SOMETIMES THEY COME BACK *SOMETIMES
THEY COME BACK* (TF) Come Back Productions, 1991
IN A CHILD'S NAME (TF) New World TV, 1991
SOMETHING TO LIVE FOR: THE ALISON GERTZ STORY (TF)
Grossbart-Barnett Productions, 1992
THE FIRE NEXT TIME (TF) RHI Entertainment/KirchGroup,
1993, U.S.-German
MURDER OF INNOCENCE (TF) The Samuels Film Company/The
Polone Company/Hearst Entertainment, 1993
THE YARN PRINCESS (TF) Konigsberg-Sanitsky Company, 1994
LEAVE OF ABSENCE (TF) Grossbart-Barnett Productions/NBC
Productions, 1994
TAKE ME HOME AGAIN (TF) von Zerneck-Sertner Films, 1994

KEN McMULLEN
b. 1948 - Manchester, England
Contact: British Film Commission, 70 Baker Street, London
W1M 1DJ, England, tel.: 171/224-5000

RESISTANCE 1976, British
GHOST DANCE 1983, British
BEING AND DOING 1984, British
ZINA 1985, British
PARTITION 1988, British
1871 Norstar/Film Four International/La Sept, 1990, British-French

MARY McMURRAY
b. March 31, 1949 - Manchester, England
Contact: British Film Commission, 70 Baker Street, London
W1M 1DJ, England, tel.: 171/224-5000

THE ASSAM GARDEN The Moving Picture Company, 1985, British
TO HAVE AND TO HOLD (TF) London Weekend TV, 1986, British
BORN IN THE R.S.A. (TF) Channel 4, 1986, British
MISS MARPLE: AT BERTRAM'S HOTEL (TF) BBC, 1987, British

THE VEILED ONE (TF)   TVS, 1989, British
FAMILY (TF)   Channel 4, 1989, British
FROM DOON WITH DEATH (TF)   TVS, 1991, British
KISSING THE GUNNER'S DAUGHTER (TF)   TVS,
   1992, British
HARRY (MS)   co-director with Robert Walker & Martin Stellman,
   Union Pictures/BBC, 1993, British

JOHN McNAUGHTON*
Address: 1370 N. Milwaukee Avenue, Chicago, IL 60622,
   312/384-6306
Agent: ICM - Beverly Hills, 310/550-4000

HENRY...PORTRAIT OF A SERIAL KILLER
   Greycat Films, 1989
THE BORROWER   Cannon, 1991, filmed in 1988
SEX, DRUGS, ROCK & ROLL (PF)   Avenue Pictures, 1991
MAD DOG AND GLORY   Universal, 1993
REBEL HIGHWAY: GIRLS IN PRISON   GIRLS IN PRISON (CTF)
   Drive-In Classics Cinema/Showtime, 1994
NEVERLAND   McNaughton/Jones Motion Pictures Ltd., 1995

JOHN McPHERSON*
Agent: The Maggie Field Agency - Studio City, 818/980-2001

STRAYS (CTF)   Niki Marvin Productions/MTE
   Entertainment, 1991
DIRTY WORK (CTF)   Wilshire Court Productions/Pacific Motion
   Pictures, 1992
FADE TO BLACK (CTF)   Francine LeFrak Productions/Wilshire
   Court Productions, 1993
SIMON & SIMON: PRECIOUS CARGO (TF)   Windy City
   Productions, 1995

GERALD McRANEY*
Business: Spanish Trail Productions, 100 Universal City Plaza -
   Building 426 Suite E, Universal City, CA 91608, 818/777-2745

LOVE AND CURSES...AND ALL THAT JAZZ (TF)
   Delmac Entertainment Productions/CBS-TV, 1991

JOHN McTIERNAN*
b. January 8, 1951 - Albany, New York
Agent: CAA - Beverly Hills, 310/288-4545

NOMADS   Atlantic Releasing Corporation, 1985
PREDATOR   20th Century Fox, 1987
DIE HARD   20th Century Fox, 1988
THE HUNT FOR RED OCTOBER   Paramount, 1990
MEDICINE MAN   Buena Vista, 1992
LAST ACTION HERO   Columbia, 1993
DIE HARD WITH A VENGEANCE   20th Century Fox, 1995

NICK MEAD
Agent: ICM - London, tel.: 171/636-6565

BANK ROBBER   I.R.S. Releasing, 1993

NANCY MECKLER
Agent: The Casarotto Company - London, tel.: 171/287-4450

SISTER MY SISTER   Seventh Art Releasing, 1994, British

PETER MEDAK*
b. Budapest, Hungary
Home: 1712 N. Stanley, Los Angeles, CA 90046
Agent: CAA - Beverly Hills, 310/288-4545
Personal Manager: Addis-Wechsler & Associates - Los Angeles,
   213/954-9000

NEGATIVES   Continental, 1968, British
A DAY IN THE DEATH OF JOE EGG   Columbia, 1972, British
THE RULING CLASS   Avco Embassy, 1972, British

THE THIRD GIRL FROM THE LEFT (TF)   Playboy
   Productions, 1973
GHOST IN THE NOONDAY SUN   Columbia, 1974, British
THE ODD JOB   Columbia, 1978, British
THE CHANGELING   AFD, 1980, Canadian
THE BABYSITTER (TF)   Moonlight Productions/Filmways, 1980
ZORRO, THE GAY BLADE   20th Century-Fox, 1981
MISTRESS OF PARADISE (TF)   Lorimar Productions, 1981
CRY FOR THE STRANGERS (TF)   David Gerber Company/
   MGM TV, 1982
THE MEN'S CLUB   Atlantic Releasing Corporation, 1986
LA VOIX HUMAINE   Erato Films, 1990, French
THE KRAYS   Miramax Films, 1990, British
LET HIM HAVE IT   Fine Line Features/New Line Cinema, 1991,
   British-French-Dutch
ROMEO IS BLEEDING   Gramercy Pictures, 1993, U.S.-British
PONTIAC MOON   Paramount, 1994

DON MEDFORD*
Home: 13900 Panay Way - Apt. R-216, Marina Del Rey, CA 90292,
   310/827-3519
Agent: Contemporary Artists - Santa Monica, 310/395-1800

TO TRAP A SPY   MGM, 1966
THE HUNTING PARTY   United Artists, 1970
INCIDENT IN SAN FRANCISCO (TF)   QM Productions, 1971
THE ORGANIZATION   United Artists, 1971
THE NOVEMBER PLAN   1976
THE CLONE MASTER (TF)   Mel Ferber Productions/
   Paramount TV, 1978
COACH OF THE YEAR (TF)   A. Shane Company, 1980
SIZZLE (TF)   Aaron Spelling Productions, 1981
HELL TOWN (TF)   Breezy Productions, 1985

CARY MEDOWAY*
b. May 16, 1949 - Philadelphia, Pennsylvania
Agent: Shapiro/Lichtman - Los Angeles, 310/859-8877

PARADISE MOTEL   Saturn International, 1985
THE HEAVENLY KID   Orion, 1985

LESLIE MEGAHEY
Agent: Peters Fraser & Dunlop - London, tel.: 171/344-1000

THE ADVOCATE   THE HOUR OF THE PIG   Miramax Films,
   1993, British-French

FRANCIS MEGAHY
Business: Bedford Productions, Canalot Studios, 222 Kensal Road,
   London W10, England
Agent: ICM - London, tel.: 171/636-6565

FREELANCE   1970, British
ONLY TAKES TWO   1978, British
SEWERS OF GOLD   1981, British
MINDER ON THE ORIENT EXPRESS (TF)   1986, British
TAFFIN   MGM/UA, 1988, U.S.-Irish
MINDER VI (MS)   co-director with Roy Ward Baker, Terry Green &
   Bill Brayne, Euston Films, 1988, British
LA REDDITION   Le Sept, 1990, French
LOVEJOY (TF)   BBC/Arts & Entertainment Network,
   1992, British-U.S.
HIGHLAND FLING (TF)   BBC/Arts & Entertainment Network,
   1992, British-U.S.
RED SUN RISING   RSR Productions, 1993
THE DISAPPEARANCE OF KEVIN JOHNSON   Makani Kai
   Productions/Wobblyscope, 1995

DARIUSH MEHRJUI

b. 1940 - Teheran, Iran
Contact: Department of Photography and Film Production, Ministry of Culture and Islamic Guidance, Baharestan Square, Teheran, Iran, tel. 391333

DIAMOND 33 1967, Iranian
THE COW 1967, Iranian
MR. SIMPLETON 1971, Iranian
THE POSTMAN 1973, Iranian
MINA'S CYCLE *THE CYCLE* 1976, Iranian
THE SCHOOL WE WENT TO 1981, Iranian
JOURNEY TO THE LAND OF RIMBAUD 1984, French
LODGERS *THE TENANTS* 1987, Iranian
SHIRAK 1989, Iranian
HAMOON 1990, Iranian
BANOO 1992, Iranian
SARA Hashem Seifi/Dariush Mehrjui, 1993, Iranian

DEEPA MEHTA

(Deepa Mehta Saltzman)
b. 1949 - Amritsar, India
Business: Sunrise Films Limited, 160 Perth Avenue, Toronto, Ontario M6P 3X5, Canada, 416/535-2900
Agent: UTA - Beverly Hills, 310/273-6700

AT 99: A PORTRAIT OF LOUISE TANDY MURCH (TD) 1974, Canadian-U.S.
WHAT'S THE WEATHER LIKE UP THERE (TD) 1977, Canadian
K.Y.T.E.S. HOW WE DREAM OURSELVES (TD) 1985, Canadian
TRAVELLING LIGHT: THE PHOTOJOURNALISM OF DILIP MEHTA (TD) 1986, Canadian
MARTHA, RUTH & EDIE co-director with Daniele J. Suissa, 1987, Canadian
SAM & ME Sunrise Films Ltd./Deepa Mehta Film/Film Four International/ITC Distribution/Astral Film Enterprises, 1991, Canadian-British
CAMILLA Miramax Films, 1994, British-Canadian

KETAN MEHTA

b. July 21, 1952 - Gujarat, India
Contact: National Film Development Corporation, Discovery of India Building, Nehru Centre, Dr Annie Besant Road, Worli, Bombay 400018, India, tel.: 4949856

A FOLK TALE 1980, Indian
FIRE FESTIVAL 1984, Indian
SPICES Upfront Films/Cinema Four, 1986, Indian
HILLALAL 1989, Indian
SARDAR PATEL The Foundation for Films on India's War of Independence, 1991, Indian
MAYA MEMSAAB National Film Development Board of India/Channel 4/Video Cinema 13 Productions/Film Four International, 1993, Indian-British
OH DARLING, THIS IS INDIA Ketan Mehta Films, 1993, Indian

MYRON MEISEL

Address: 3264 Ellenda Avenue, Los Angeles, CA 90034, 310/474-5346

IT'S ALL TRUE: BASED ON AN UNFINISHED FILM BY ORSON WELLES (FD) co-director with Richard Wilson & Bill Krohn, Paramount, 1993, U.S.-French

ADOLFAS MEKAS

b. 1925 - Lithuania

HALLELUJAH THE HILLS New York Cinema Company, 1963
WINDFLOWERS 1968

JONAS MEKAS

b. December 24, 1922 - Semeniskiai, Lithuania

GRAND STREET 1953
SILENT JOURNEY 1955
GUNS OF THE TREES 1961

THE SECRET PASSIONS OF SALVADOR DALI 1961
FILM MAGAZINE OF THE ARTS 1963
THE BRIG 1964
THE MILLBROOK REPORT 1966
HARE KRISHNA 1966
DIARIES NOTES AND SKETCHES 1969
REMINISCENCES OF A JOURNEY TO LITHUANIA 1972
LOST LOST LOST 1976
IN BETWEEN 1978
PARADISE NOT YET LOST 1980
NOTES FOR JEROME 1981

ANDRE MELANCON

b. 1942 - Rouyn, Quebec, Canada
Home: Ruisseau-Nord, St-Ours sur le Richelieu, Quebec JOG 1PO, Canada, 514/785-5586

DES ARMES ET LES HOMMES (TF) 1972, Canadian
LES OREILLES MENE L'ENQUETTE (TF) 1973, Canadian
LES TACOTS (TF) 1973, Canadian
LE VIOLON DE GASTON (TF) 1974, Canadian
LES VRAIS PERDANTS (TF) 1977, Canadian
COMME LES SIX DOIGTS DE LA MAIN (TF) 1978, Canadian
LA PAROLE AUX ENFANTS (TF) 1979, Canadian
L'ESPACE D'UN ETE (TF) 1980, Canadian
ZIG ZAGS (TF) 1982, Canadian
THE DOG WHO STOPPED THE WAR New World, 1984, Canadian
CECI EST MON CORPS (TF) 1986, Canadian
BACH ET BOTTINE Cinema Plus, 1987, Canadian
SUMMER OF THE COLT Productions La Fete/GEA Cinematografia, 1989, Canadian-Argentine
RAFALES Aska Films/National Film Board of Canada/Telefilm Canada, 1990, Canadian

IB MELCHIOR*

b. September 17, 1917 - Copenhagen, Denmark
Home: 8228 Marmont Lane, Los Angeles, CA 90069, 213/654-6679

THE ANGRY RED PLANET American International, 1960
THE TIME TRAVELERS American International, 1964

ARTHUR N. MELE*

Business: Shining Horizon Productions, P.O. Box 626, Santa Margarita, CA 93453, 805/430-3013

SOLDIER'S FORTUNE Republic Pictures, 1992

BILL MELENDEZ

Business: Bill Melendez Productions, 439 N. Larchmont Blvd., Los Angeles, CA 90004, 213/463-4101

A BOY NAMED CHARLIE BROWN (AF) National General, 1968
SNOOPY, COME HOME (AF) National General, 1972
DICK DEADEYE, OR DUTY DONE (AF) Intercontinental, 1976, British
RACE FOR YOUR LIFE, CHARLIE BROWN (AF) Paramount, 1978
BON VOYAGE, CHARLIE BROWN (AND DON'T COME BACK!) (AF) Paramount, 1980
HAPPILY EVER AFTER (ATF) JZM Productions, 1985
THIS IS AMERICA, CHARLIE BROWN (AMS) co-director with Everett Brown & Sam Jaimes, Lee Mendelson-Bill Melendez Productions/Charles Schulz Creative Associates/United Media, 1988-89
TWO DADDIES? (ATF) co-director with Dick Horn & Eddie Raddage, JZM Productions/Bill Melendez Productions/WonderWorks, 1989

JAMES MELKONIAN

THE STONED AGE Trimark Pictures, 1994
THE JERKY BOYS Buena Vista, 1995

JOHN MELLENCAMP

FALLING FROM GRACE Columbia, 1992

JEFFREY MELMAN*
Agent: ICM - Beverly Hills, 310/550-4000

A FAMILY FOR JOE (TF)   Grosso-Jacobson Productions/NBC
    Productions, 1990
SAVED BY THE BELL (TF)   Peter Engel Productions/NBC
    Productions, 1994

CHRISTOPHER MENAUL*
Address: 62 Narbonne Avenue, Clapham, London SW4 9JT,
    England, tel.: 181/673-0361
Agent: CAA - Beverly Hills, 310/288-4545 or:
    Peterrs Fraser & Dunlop - London, tel.: 171/344-1000

BIG DEAL (TF)   BBC, 1985, British
WORLDS BEYOND (TF)   PKP/Walker TV, 1986, British
PRECIOUS BANE (TF)   BBC, 1988, British
PRIME SUSPECT (MS)   Granada TV, 1991, British
A DANGEROUS MAN - LAWRENCE AFTER ARABIA (TF)
    Enigma TV Productions/Anglia Films/Sands Films/
    WNET-New York, 1992, British-U.S.
FATHERLAND (CTF)   HBO Pictures, 1994
THE FEAST OF JULY   Buena Vista, 1995, British

GEORGE MENDELUK*
b. March 20, 1948 - Augsburg, West Germany
Business: World Classic Pictures, 6263 Tapia Drive, Malibu,
    CA 90265, 310/457-9911
Agent: David Shapira & Associates - Sherman Oaks, 818/906-0322
Business Manager: Stan Kamens, K&K Entertainment,
    260 S. Beverly Drive - Suite 210, Beverly Hills, CA 90212,
    310/288-4500

STONE COLD DEAD   Dimension, 1979, Canadian
THE KIDNAPPING OF THE PRESIDENT   Crown International,
    1980, Canadian
DOIN' TIME   The Ladd Company/Warner Bros., 1984
MEATBALLS III   *SUMMER JOB*   TMS Pictures, 1986, Canadian
BY THE RIVERS OF BABYLON (TF)   Universal TV, 1989
BOLT   Multipix Productions, 1994, Canadian

RAMON MENENDEZ*
Agent: UTA - Beverly Hills, 310/273-6700

STAND AND DELIVER   Warner Bros., 1988
MONEY FOR NOTHING   Buena Vista, 1993

CHRIS MENGES*
b. September 15, 1940 - Kingston, England
Agent: UTA - Beverly Hills, 310/273-6700 or:
    The Casarotto Company - London, tel.: 171/287-4450

A WORLD APART   Atlantic Releasing Corporation, 1988, British
CRISSCROSS   MGM-Pathe Communications, 1992
SECOND BEST   Warner Bros., 1994, British

VLADIMIR MENSHOV
Contact: Confederation of Film-Makers Unions, Vasilyevskaya
    Street 13, 123 825 Moscow, Russia, tel.: 095/250-4114

MOSCOW DOES NOT BELIEVE IN TEARS   IFEX Film,
    1980, Soviet
LOVE AND DOVES   Mosfilm, 1985, Soviet
SHIRLI-MYRLI   Mosfilm, 1994, Russian
WHAT A MESS...   Mosfilm/Genre Studios Roskomkino/Tepeobank,
    1995, Russian

JIRI MENZEL
b. February 23, 1938 - Prague, Czechoslovakia
Agent: Peters Fraser & Dunlop - London, tel.: 171/344-1000

PEARLS OF THE DEEP   co-director, 1965, Czechoslovakian
CRIME AT A GIRL'S SCHOOL   co-director, 1965, Czechoslovakian
CLOSELY WATCHED TRAINS   Sigma III, 1966, Czechoslovakian
CAPRICIOUS SUMMER   Sigma III, 1968, Czechoslovakian
CRIME IN A NIGHT CLUB   1968, Czechoslovakian
LARKS ON A STRING   IFEX Film, 1969, Czechoslovakian
WHO LOOKS FOR GOLD?   1974, Czechosloviakian
SECLUSION NEAR A FOREST   1976, Czechoslovakian
THOSE WONDERFUL MEN WITH A CRANK
    1978, Czechoslovakian
MAGICIANS OF THE SILVER SCREEN   1979, Czechoslovakian
SHORT CUT   1980, Czechoslovakian
A HIGH-SPIRITED BLONDE   1980, Czechoslovakian
THE SNOWDROP FESTIVAL   1983, Czechoslovakian
PRAGUE (FD)   1985, Czechoslovakian
MY SWEET LITTLE VILLAGE   Circle Releasing,
    1986, Czechoslovakian
THE END OF OLD TIMES   IFEX Film, 1989, Czechoslovakian
THE BEGGAR'S OPERA   Barrandov Film Studios,
    1991, Czechoslovakian
THE ENGINEER OF HUMAN SOULS   KF Ltd./PVS Films, 1992,
    Czechoslovakian-Canadian
THE LIFE AND EXTRAORDINARY ADVENTURES OF PRIVATE
    IVAN CHONKIN   Portobello Pictures/MK2/Fandango/
    La Sept Cinema/Canal Plus/Centre National de la
    Cinematographie/Channel 4/European Co-Production
    Fund/Cable Plus/KF/EFA/Studio 89/Studio Trite, 1994,
    British-French-Czech-Russian-Italian

ISMAIL MERCHANT
b. December 25, 1936 - Bombay, India
Business: Merchant-Ivory Productions, 400 East 52nd Street,
    New York, NY 10022, 212/759-3694

COURTESANS OF BOMBAY (TD)   Merchant-Ivory Productions,
    1982, British-Indian
IN CUSTODY   Merchant-Ivory Productions/Channel 4 Films,
    1993, British-Indian

JAMES MERENDINO
Contact: William Morris Agency - Beverly Hills, 310/859-4000

THE UPSTAIRS NEIGHBOR   Brandon Foley/Matt Devlin, 1994
TOUGHGUY   Green Tea Pictures/Net City Filmgroup, 1994

JALAL MERHI
TC 2000   Shapiro Glickenhaus Entertainment, 1993
OPERATION GOLDEN PHOENIX   Le Monde Entertainment,
    1994, Canadian

JOSEPH MERHI
Business: PM Entertainment Group, Inc., 9450 Chivers Avenue,
    Sun Valley, CA 91352, 818/504-6332

THE LAST RIDERS   PM Entertainment Group, 1991
THE KILLER'S EDGE   PM Entertainment Group, 1991
MAXIMUM FORCE   PM Entertainment Group, 1992
C.I.A.: CODE NAME ALEXA   PM Entertainment Group, 1993
TO BE THE BEST   PM Entertainment Group, 1993
NINJA DRAGONS   PM Entertainment Group, 1993
DIRECT HIT   PM Entertainment Group, 1993
ICE   PM Entertainment Group, 1993
ZERO TOLERANCE   PM Entertainment Group, 1994
LAST MAN STANDING   PM Entertainment Group, 1995

ELIAS MERHIGE
BEGOTTEN   Complex Corp., 1994

KIETH MERRILL*
b. May 22, 1940 - Utah
Home: 25355 La Loma Drive, Los Altos Hills, CA 94022,
    415/941-8720

THE GREAT AMERICAN COWBOY (FD)   Sun International, 1974
THREE WARRIORS   United Artists, 1978
TAKE DOWN   Buena Vista, 1979
WINDWALKER   Pacific International, 1980
MR. KRUEGER'S CHRISTMAS (TF)   Bonneville
    Productions, 1980

HARRY'S WAR   Taft International, 1981
THE CHEROKEE TRAIL (TF)   Walt Disney Productions, 1981
THE WILD WEST (TD)   Rattlesnake Productions/Tele-Pictures
    Productions, 1993

ROLAND MESA*
Agent: William Morris Agency - Beverly Hills, 310/859-4000

REVENGE OF THE NERDS III: THE NEXT GENERATION (TF)
    FNM Films/Zacharias and Buhai Productions, 1992

WILLIAM MESA
TERMINAL FORCE   Interlight Pictures, 1994

MATTHEW MESHEKOFF*
Address: 170 Fifth Avenue, New York, NY 10010, 212/243-4369
Agent: ICM - Beverly Hills, 310/550-4000
Personal Manager: 3 Arts Entertainment - Beverly Hills,
    310/888-3200

THE OPPOSITE SEX AND HOW TO LIVE WITH THEM
    Miramax Films, 1993

PHILIP F. MESSINA*
Home: 358 S. Citrus Avenue, Los Angeles, CA 90036,
    213/938-7433
Agent: Paul Kohner, Inc. - Los Angeles, 310/550-1060

SPY (CTF)   Deadly Productions/Wilshire Court Productions, 1989

MARTA MESZAROS
b. September 19, 1931 - Budapest, Hungary
Contact: Hungarian Film Institute, Budakeszi u 51 B, 1012
    Budapest, Hungary, tel.: 176-1018 or 176-1322

THE GIRL   Mafilm Studio, 1968, Hungarian
BINDING SENTIMENTS   Mafilm Studio, 1969, Hungarian
DON'T CRY, PRETTY GIRLS   Mafilm Studio, 1970, Hungarian
RIDDANCE   Studio Hunnia, 1973, Hungarian
ADOPTION   Studio Hunnia, 1975, Hungarian
NINE MONTHS   Studio Hunnia, 1976, Hungarian
THE TWO OF THEM   Studio Dialog, 1977, Hungarian
JUST LIKE AT HOME   Studio Hunnia, 1978, Hungarian
EN COURS DE ROUTE   1979, French
THE HEIRESSES   1980, Hungarian
MOTHER AND DAUGHTER   1981, Hungarian-French
DIARY FOR MY CHILDREN   Budapest Studio, 1982, Hungarian
THE LAND OF MIRAGES   1983, Hungarian
DIARY FOR MY LOVES   Jasmine Tea Films, 1987, Hungarian
BYE BYE RED RIDING HOOD   Productions La Fete/Budapest
    Studio, 1989, Canadian-Hungarian
DIARY FOR MY FATHER AND MOTHER   Budapest Studio/
    Mafilm, 1990, Hungarian
FOETUS   Budapest Film Studio/Magyar TV/Telewizja Polska,
    1994, Hungarian-Polish
THE SEVENTH ROOM   Studio Tor, 1995, Polish

TIM METCALFE
Agent: William Morris Agency - Beverly Hills, 310/859-4000

KILLER: A JOURNAL OF MURDER   Ixtlan/Spelling Films
    International/Breakheart Films, 1995

ALAN METTER*
Agent: APA - Los Angeles, 310/273-0744

GIRLS JUST WANT TO HAVE FUN   New World, 1985
BACK TO SCHOOL   Orion, 1986
MOVING   Warner Bros., 1988
COLD DOG SOUP   HandMade Films, 1990
WORKING TRASH (TF)   Westgate Productions/Aurora
    Development Fund/FNM Company, 1990
POLICE ACADEMY: MISSION TO MOSCOW   Warner Bros., 1994
SUMMERTIME SWITCH (TF)   Louis Rudolph Family Films/
    Victor TV Productions, 1994

ALAN METZGER*
Home: 145 West 86th Street, New York, NY 10024, 212/586-8418
Agent: William Morris Agency - Beverly Hills, 310/859-4000

KOJAK: THE PRICE OF JUSTICE (TF)   MCA/Universal TV, 1987
TOP OF THE HILL (TF)   Stephen J. Cannell Productions, 1989
THE CHINA LAKE MURDERS (CTF)   Papazian-Hirsch
    Entertainment, 1990
FATAL EXPOSURE (CTF)   GC Group/Wilshire Court
    Productions, 1991
RED WIND (CTF)   MCA TV, 1991
EXCLUSIVE (TF)   Hamel-Somers Productions/Freyda Rothstein
    Productions/Hearst Entertainment, 1992
FROM THE FILES OF JOSEPH WAMBAUGH: A JURY OF ONE (TF)
    Grossbart-Barnett Productions/TriStar TV, 1992
BLACK WIDOW MURDERS: THE BLANCHE TAYLOR MOORE
    STORY (TF)   Andrea Baynes Productions/Finnegan-Pinchuk
    Company/Lorimar TV, 1993
ROOMMATES (TF)   Pacific Motion Picture Productions/Michael
    Filerman Productions, 1994
DEADLY VOWS (TF)   Carla Singer Productions/World International
    Network, 1994
A DANGEROUS AFFAIR (TF)   Stalking Productions/Greengrass
    Productions, 1995
NEW EDEN (CTF)   Davis Entertainment/MTE, 1995

RADLEY METZGER
b. 1930

DARK ODYSSEY   co-director with William Kyriaksys, ERA, 1961
DICTIONARY OF SEX   1964
THE DIRTY GIRLS   1965
THE ALLEY CATS   1966
CARMEN, BABY   Audubon, 1967, U.S.-Yugoslavian-West German
THERESE AND ISABELLE   Audubon, 1968, West German-U.S.
CAMILLE 2000   Audubon, 1969, Italian
THE LICKERISH QUARTET   Audubon, 1970,
    U.S.-Italian-West German
LITTLE MOTHER   Audubon, 1972
SCORE   Audubon, 1973
NAKED CAME THE STRANGER   directed under pseudonym
    of Henry Paris, Catalyst, 1975
THE PRIVATE AFTERNOONS OF PAMELA MANN   directed under
    pseudonym of Henry Paris, Hudson Valley, 1975
ESOTIKA, EROTIKA, PSICOTIKA FAB   1975, Italian-Monocan
THE PUNISHMENT OF ANNE   1975
THE IMAGE   Audubon, 1976
THE OPENING OF MISTY BEETHOVEN   directed under pseudonym
    of Henry Paris, Catalyst, 1976
BARBARA BROADCAST   directed under pseudonym of Henry Paris,
    Crescent, 1977
MARASCHINO CHERRY   directed under pseudonym of
    Henry Paris, 1978
THE CAT AND THE CANARY   Quartet, 1978, British
THE TALE OF TIFFANY LUST   directed under pseudonym of
    Henry Paris, Entertainment Ventures, 1981
THE PRINCESS AND THE CALL GIRL   Highbridge Film
    Productions, 1984

KEVIN MEYER
b. April 17, 1959 - Greeley, Colorado
Business: Rocky Mountain Pictures, 9200 Sunset Blvd.,
    Penthouse 22, Los Angeles, CA 90069, 310/858-2200

DIVIDED WE FALL   co-director, Conquest Entertainment/Pegasus
    Productions, 1982
ACROSS FIVE APRILS (TF)   Advanced American Communications/
    New World Entertainment, 1989
INVASION OF PRIVACY (CTF)   Amitraj Entertainment/Promark
    Entertainment Group/ Prism Entertainment, 1992
UNDER INVESTIGATION   New Line Cinema, 1993
PERFECT ALIBI   Rysher Entertainment, 1994

NICHOLAS MEYER*

b. December 24, 1945 - New York, New York
Agent: CAA - Beverly Hills, 310/288-4545

TIME AFTER TIME   Orion/Warner Bros., 1979
STAR TREK II: THE WRATH OF KHAN   Paramount, 1982
THE DAY AFTER (TF) ☆   ABC Circle Films, 1983
VOLUNTEERS   TriStar, 1985
THE DECEIVERS   Cinecom, 1988
COMPANY BUSINESS   MGM-Pathe Communications, 1991
STAR TREK VI: THE UNDISCOVERED COUNTRY
   Paramount, 1991

RUSS MEYER*

b. March 21, 1922 - Oakland, California
Home: 3121 Arrowhead Drive, Hollywood, CA 90068, 213/466-7791

THE IMMORAL MR. TEAS   Pad-Ram, 1959
EVE AND THE HANDYMAN   Eve, 1961
EROTICA   Pad-Ram, 1961
WILD GALS OF THE NAKED WEST   THE IMMORAL WEST AND
   HOW IT WAS LOST   Films Pacifica, Inc., 1961
EUROPE IN THE RAW   Eve, 1963
HEAVENLY BODIES   Eve, 1963
LORNA   Eve, 1964
FANNY HILL: MEMOIRS OF A WOMAN OF PLEASURE
   Famous Players Corporation/CCC Filmkunst GMBH,
   1964, U.S.-West German
MUDHONEY   ROPE OF FLESH   Eve, 1965
MOTORPSYCHO!   Eve, 1965
FASTER, PUSSYCAT! KILL! KILL!   Eve, 1966
MONDO TOPLESS   Eve, 1966
COMMON-LAW CABIN   HOW MUCH LOVING DOES A NORMAL
   COUPLE NEED?   Eve, 1967
GOOD MORNING...AND GOODBYE   Eve, 1967
FINDERS KEEPERS, LOVERS WEEPERS   Eve, 1968
RUSS MEYER'S VIXEN   Eve, 1968
CHERRY, HARRY AND RAQUEL   Eve, 1969
BEYOND THE VALLEY OF THE DOLLS   20th Century-Fox, 1970
THE SEVEN MINUTES   20th Century-Fox, 1971
BLACKSNAKE!   SWEET SUZY   Signal 166, 1973
SUPERVIXENS   RM Films, 1975
RUSS MEYER'S UP!   RM Films, 1976
BENEATH THE VALLEY OF THE ULTRAVIXENS
   RM Films, 1979
THE BREAST OF RUSS MEYER   RM Films, 1979

TURI MEYER

SLEEPSTALKER   Prism Pictures, 1994

ERIC MEZA*

Business Manager: Turner Irvine, 6500 Wilshire Blvd. - Suite 2040,
   Los Angeles, CA 90048, 213/243-5399
Agent: The Gersh Agency - Beverly Hills, 310/274-6611

HOUSE PARTY 3   New Line Cinema, 1994

MIKE MICHAELS

b. December 15, 1946 - Ohio
Business: Studio M Productions, 8715 Waikiki Station, Honolulu, HI
   96815, 808/734-3345

THE WORLD OF TRAVEL: SRI LANKA (TD)   Studio M
   Productions, 1981
THE WORLD OF TRAVEL: BANGKOK (FD)   Studio M
   Productions, 1982
THE WORLD OF TRAVEL: LAS VEGAS (FD)   Studio M
   Productions, 1984
THE WORLD OF TRAVEL: KOREA (TD)   Studio M
   Productions, 1984
THE WORLD OF TRAVEL: NEW ZEALAND (TD)   Studio M
   Productions, 1985
THE WORLD OF TRAVEL: ROME (TD)   Studio M
   Productions, 1985

THE WORLD OF TRAVEL: MALAYSIA (TD)   Studio M
   Productions, 1986
THE WORLD OF TRAVEL: SINGAPORE (TD)   Studio M
   Productions, 1986
THE WORLD OF TRAVEL: OSAKA (FD)   Studio M
   Productions, 1987

RICHARD MICHAELS*

b. February 15, 1936
Agent: David Gersh, The Gersh Agency - Beverly Hills,
   310/274-6611

HOW COME NOBODY'S ON OUR SIDE?   American
   Films Ltd., 1975
DEATH IS NOT THE END   Libert Films International, 1976
ONCE AN EAGLE (MS)   co-director with E.W. Swackhamer,
   Universal TV, 1976
CHARLIE COBB: NICE NIGHT FOR HANGING (TF)
   Universal TV, 1977
HAVING BABIES II (TF)   The Jozak Company, 1977
LEAVE YESTERDAY BEHIND (TF)   ABC Circle Films, 1978
MY HUSBAND IS MISSING (TF)   Bob Banner Associates, 1978
...AND YOUR NAME IS JONAH (TF)   Charles Fries
   Productions, 1979
ONCE UPON A FAMILY (TF)   Universal TV, 1980
THE PLUTONIUM INCIDENT (TF)   Time-Life Productions, 1980
HOMEWARD BOUND (TF)   Tisch-Avnet Productions, 1990
SCARED STRAIGHT! ANOTHER STORY (TF)
   Golden West TV, 1980
BERLIN TUNNEL 21 (TF)   Cypress Point Productions/
   Filmways, 1981
THE CHILDREN NOBODY WANTED (TF)   Blatt-Singer
   Productions, 1981
BLUE SKIES AGAIN   Warner Bros., 1983
ONE COOKS, THE OTHER DOESN'T (TF)   Kaleidoscope Films
   Ltd./Lorimar Productions, 1983
SADAT (TF)   Blatt-Singer Productions/Columbia TV, 1983
JESSIE (TF)   Lindsay Wagner Productions/MGM-UA TV, 1984
SILENCE OF THE HEART (TF)   David A. Simons Productions/
   Tisch-Avnet Productions, 1984
HEART OF A CHAMPION: THE RAY MANCINI STORY (TF)
   Rare Titles Productions/Robert Papazian Productions, 1985
ROCKABYE (TF)   Roger Gimbel Productions/Peregrine
   Entertainment/Bertinelli Productions, 1986
I'LL TAKE MANHATTAN (MS)   co-director with Douglas Hickox,
   Steve Krantz Productions, 1987
RED RIVER (TF)   Catalina Production Group/MGM-UA TV, 1988
INDISCREET (TF)   Karen Mack Productions/HTV/Republic
   Pictures, 1988, U.S.-British
LOVE AND BETRAYAL (TF)   Gross-Weston Productions/ITC
   Entertainment Group, 1989
HER WICKED WAYS (TF)   Lois Luger Productions/Freyda
   Rothstein Productions/Bar-Gene Productions/ITC
   Entertainment, 1990
LEONA HELMSLEY: THE QUEEN OF MEAN (TF)
   Fries Entertainment/Golman-Taylor Entertainment, 1990
A TRIUMPH OF THE HEART: THE RICKY BELL STORY (TF)
   Procter & Gamble Productions/The Landsburg Company, 1991
BACKFIELD IN MOTION (TF)   Think Entertainment/The
   Avnet-Kerner Company, 1991
MISS AMERICA: BEHIND THE CROWN (TF)   Katz-Rush
   Entertainment, 1992
FATHER AND SCOUT (TF)   New Line Productions, 1994

ROGER MICHELL

Agent: ICM - London, tel.: 171/636-6565

THE BUDDHA OF SUBURBIA (MS)   BBC, 1994, British

SCOTT MICHELL

Contact: British Film Commission, 70 Baker Street, London
   W1M 1DJ, England, tel.: 171/224-5000

THE INNOCENT SLEEP   Timedial Films, 1995, British

DAVE MICHENER

THE GREAT MOUSE DETECTIVE (AF)   co-director with
    Dave Clements, Burny Mattinson & John Musker,
    Buena Vista, 1986
ONCE UPON A FOREST (AF)   co-director with Charles Grosvenor,
    20th Century Fox, 1993

GEORGE MIHALKA

b. 1952 - Budapest, Hungary
Home: 2030 Lambert Closse - Suite 4, Montreal, Quebec H3H 1Z8,
    Canada, 514/937-4740

MY BLOODY VALENTINE   Paramount, 1981, Canadian
PICK-UP SUMMER   *PINBALL SUMMER*   Film Ventures
    International, 1981, Canadian
SCANDALE   Vivafilm/Cine 360, 1982, Canadian
ETERNAL EVIL   Seymour Borde & Associates, 1987,
    Canadian-U.S.
OFFICE PARTY   Miramax Films, 1988, Canadian
LE CHEMIN DE DAMES (TF)   Cinema Plus/Les Producteurs
    TV-Films Associes/National Film Board for Radio-Quebec,
    1988, Canadian
STRAIGHT LINE (TF)   1988, Canadian-U.S.
PSYCHIC (CTF)   Trimark Pictures 1991, Canadian-U.S.
LA FLORIDA   Alliance Communications/Les Films Vision 4/Les
    Productions Pierre Sarrazin, 1993, Canadian
THE CHILD   Westwind/Norstar, 1994, Canadian
EDGE OF DECEPTION   Ed Productions Ltd., 1994, Canadian
RELATIVE FEAR   Norstar Entertainment/Allegro/Westwind,
    1994, Canadian
BULLET TO BEIJING   Harry Alan Towers Productions,
    1995, British

TED V. MIKELS

STRIKE ME DEADLY   1963
THE DOCTORS   1963
ONE SHOCKING MOMENT   *SUBURBAN AFFAIR*   1964
THE BLACK KLANSMAN   *I CROSSED THE COLOR LINE*
    SGS Productions, 1965
THE UNDERTAKER AND HIS PALS   1966
THE ASTRO-ZOMBIES   Gemini Films, 1967
UP YOUR TEDDY BEAR   1968
THE GIRL IN GOLD BOOTS   1968
THE CORPSE GRINDERS   1972
BLOOD ORGY OF THE SHE-DEVILS   Gemini Films, 1973
THE DOLL SQUAD   *SEDUCE AND DESTROY*   1974
THE WORM EATERS   New American, 1975
ALEX JOSEPH AND HIS WIVES   *THE REBEL BREED*   1978
DEVIL'S GAMBIT   1982
OPERATION OVERKILL   1982
TEN VIOLENT WOMEN   1982
SPACE ANGELS   1985
ANGEL OF VENGEANCE   Majestic, 1987

NIKITA MIKHALKOV

(Nikita Sergeyevich Mikhalkov-Konchalovsky)
b. October 21, 1945 - Moscow, U.S.S.R.
Agent: ICM - Beverly Hills, 310/550-4000

AT HOME AMONG STRANGERS   1974, Soviet
A SLAVE OF LOVE   Cinema 5, 1976, Soviet
AN UNFINISHED PIECE FOR PLAYER PIANO
    Corinth, 1977, Soviet
FIVE EVENINGS   IFEX Film, 1979, Soviet
OBLOMOV   IFEX Film, 1981, Soviet
FAMILY RELATIONS   Mosfilm, 1983, Soviet
WITHOUT WITNESS   IFEX Film, 1984, Soviet
DARK EYES   Island Pictures, 1987, Italian-French
CLOSE TO EDEN   *URGA*   Miramax Films, 1991, French-Soviet
ANNA: 6-18 (FD)   Studio Tri T/Camera One, 1994, Russian-French
BURNT BY THE SUN   Sony Pictures Classics,
    1994, Russian-French

ANDREI
MIKHALKOV-KONCHALOVSKY

(See Andrei KONCHALOVSKY)

RENTARO MIKUNI

b. 1923 - Guma Prefecture, Japan
Contact: Nihon Eiga Kantoku Kyokai (Japan Film Directors
    Association), La Fontenu Building -4th Floor, 23-2 Maruyama-cho,
    Shibuya-ku, Tokyo, Japan, tel.: 3/3461-4411

SHINRAN - THE PATH TO PURITY   Shochiku, 1987, Japanese

KATHY MILANI

b. November 25, 1963 - New Haven, Connecticut
Business: Generic Films, Inc., P.O. Box 2715, Waterbury, CT 06723,
    203/756-3017

B-MOVIE   Generic Films, 1988

CHRISTOPHER MILES

b. April 19, 1939 - London, England
Business: Milesian Film Productions Ltd., 10 Selwood Place, London
    SW7 3QQ, England, tel.: 171/373-8858

UP JUMPED A SWAGMAN   Anglo-Amalgamated/Warner-Pathe,
    1966, British
THE VIRGIN AND THE GYPSY   Chevron, 1970, British
TIME FOR LOVING   Hemdale, 1972, British
ZINOTCHKA (TF)   BBC, 1973, British
THE MAIDS   American Film Theatre, 1975, British-Canadian
THAT LUCKY TOUCH   Allied Artists, 1975, British
ALTERNATIVE 3 (TF)   1976, British
NECK (TF)   ITV/Anglia, 1978, British
PRIEST OF LOVE   Filmways, 1981, British
DALEY'S DECATHLON (TF)   BBC/Milesian Films, 1982, British
THE MARATHON (TF)   Channel 4, 1983, British
APHRODISIAC (TF)   1984, British
LORD ELGIN AND SOME STONES OF NO VALUE (TF)
    Milesian Films/Channel 4/ERT-TV, 1985, British-Greek

JOHN MILIUS*

b. April 11, 1944 - St. Louis, Missouri
Business: Sony Studios, 10202 W. Washington Blvd. - Clark Gable
    Building, Suite 105, Culver City, CA 90232, 310/280-3036
Agent: ICM - Beverly Hills, 310/550-4000

DILLINGER   American International, 1973
THE WIND AND THE LION   MGM/United Artists, 1975
BIG WEDNESDAY   Warner Bros., 1978
CONAN THE BARBARIAN   Universal, 1982
RED DAWN   MGM/UA, 1984
FAREWELL TO THE KING   Orion, 1989
FLIGHT OF THE INTRUDER   Paramount, 1991
REBEL HIGHWAY: MOTORCYCLE GANG   *MOTORCYCLE
    GANG* (CTF)   Drive-In Classics Cinema/Showtime, 1994

CATHERINE MILLAR

Contact: Australian Film Commission, 150 William Street,
    Woolloomooloo NSW 2011, Australia, tel.: 2/321-6444

DARLINGS OF THE GODS (MS)   Simpson Le Mesurier Films/
    Australian Broadcasting Corporation/Thames TV/Film Victoria,
    1989, Australian-British

GAVIN MILLAR

b. January 11, 1938 - Clydebank, Scotland
Agent: ICM - London, tel.: 171/636-6565

THE GOLDWYN TOUCH (TD)   BBC, 1973, British
AN IMAGINATIVE WOMAN (TF)   BBC, 1973, British
BUSBY BERKELEY - THE YEARS AT WARNERS (TD)
    BBC, 1974, British
GOODBYE (TF)   BBC, 1975, British
TRAVELS WITH A DONKEY (TF)   BBC, 1978, British
CREAM IN MY COFFEE (TF)   London Weekend TV,
    1981, British
INTENSIVE CARE (TF)   BBC, 1982, British
STAN'S LAST GAME (TF)   BBC, 1983, British
SECRETS   The Samuel Goldwyn Company, 1983, British

THE WEATHER IN THE STREETS (TF)   Rediffusion Films/BBC/
   Britannia TV, 1983, British
UNFAIR EXCHANGES (TF)   BBC, 1984, British
THE RUSSIAN SOLDIER (TF)   BBC, 1985, British
MR. & MRS. EDGEHILL (TF)   BBC, 1985, British
DREAMCHILD   Universal, 1985, British
SCOOP (TF)   London Weekend TV, 1987, British
TIDY ENDINGS (CTF)   HBO Showcase/Sandollar
   Productions, 1988
THE MOST DANGEROUS MAN IN THE WORLD (TF)
   BBC/Iberoamericana/Celtic Films, 1988, British
DANNY, THE CHAMPION OF THE WORLD   Portobello
   Productions/British Screen/Thames TV/The Disney Channel/
   WonderWorks/Children's Film & Television Foundation,
   1989, British-U.S.
A MURDER OF QUALITY (TF)   Portobello Productions/
   Thames TV, 1990, British
MY FRIEND WALTER (TF)   Portobello Productions/Thames TV/
   WonderWorks/The Children's Film and Television Foundation,
   1992, British
LOOK AT IT THIS WAY (TF)   BBC, 1992, British
THE DWELLING PLACE (TF)   World Wide/Festival Films/Tyne
   Tees TV, 1993, British
PAT AND MARGARET (TF)   BBC, 1995, British

STUART MILLAR*
b. 1929 - New York, New York
Home: 300 Central Park East - Suite 15G, New York,
   NY 10024, 212/873-5515

WHEN THE LEGENDS DIE   20th Century-Fox, 1972
ROOSTER COGBURN   Universal, 1975
VITAL SIGNS (TF)   CBS Entertainment, 1986
THE O'CONNORS (TF)   CBS Entertainment, 1989

CLAUDE MILLER
Agent: ICM France - Paris, tel.: 1/723-7860
Contact: French Film Office, 745 Fifth Avenue, New York,
   NY 10151, 212/832-8860

THE BEST WAY   LA MEILLEURE FACON DE MARCHER
   1976, French
THE SWEET SICKNESS   DITES LUI QUE JE L'AIME
   1977, French
GARDE A VUE   1981, French
MARTELLE RANEE   1983, French
CHARLOTTE AND LULU   L'EFFRONTEE   New Yorker,
   1985, French
THE LITTLE THIEF   Miramax Films, 1989, French
THE ACCOMPANIST   Sony Pictures Classics, 1992, French
LA SOURIRE   AMLF, 1994, French

DAVID LEE MILLER
Agent: The Gersh Agency - Beverly Hills, 310/274-6611

BREAKFAST OF ALIENS   Hemdale, 1993, filmed in 1989

GEORGE MILLER*
b. March 3, 1945 - Cinchilla, Queensland, Australia
Business: Kennedy Miller Productions, 30 Orwell Street,
   Kings Cross, Sydney 2011, Australia
Agent: ICM - Beverly Hills, 310/550-4000
Business Manager: Arnold Burk, Gang, Tyre & Brown, Inc.,
   6400 Sunset Blvd., Los Angeles, CA 90028, 213/463-4863

MAD MAX   American International, 1979, Australian
THE ROAD WARRIOR   MAD MAX II   Warner Bros.,
   1982, Australian
THE DISMISSAL (MS)   co-director with Phillip Noyce,
   George Ogilvie, Carl Schultz & John Power, 1983, Australian
TWILIGHT ZONE - THE MOVIE   co-director with John Landis,
   Steven Spielberg & Joe Dante, Warner Bros., 1983
MAD MAX BEYOND THUNDERDOME   co-director with
   George Ogilvie, Warner Bros., 1985, Australian

THE WITCHES OF EASTWICK   Warner Bros., 1987
LORENZO'S OIL   Universal, 1992

GEORGE TRUMBULL MILLER*
Agent: Writers & Artists Agency - Los Angeles, 310/824-6300
Business Manager: Jenni Tosi, 4 Keyes Street, Ashburton,
   Victoria 3147, Australia, tel.: 03/885-8003

CASH & CO. (MS)   co-director with Russell Hagg, Homestead
   Films/Network Seven, 1975, Australian
AGAINST THE WIND (MS)   co-director with Simon Wincer,
   Pegasus Productions, 1978, Australian
THE LAST OUTLAW (MS)   co-director with Kevin Dobson,
   Network Seven/Pegasus Productions, 1980, Australian
THE MAN FROM SNOWY RIVER   20th Century-Fox,
   1982, Australian
FILE MILE CREEK (MS)   co-director with Frank Arnold,
   Michael Jenkins & Di Drew, Valstar/The Disney Channel,
   1983, Australian-U.S.
ALL THE RIVERS RUN (CMS)   co-director with Pino Amenta,
   Crawford Productions/Nine Network, 1984, Australian
THE AVIATOR   MGM/UA, 1985
ANZACS: THE WAR DOWN UNDER   ANZACS (MS)   co-director
   with Pino Amenta & John Dixon, Burrowes Dixon Productions,
   1985, Australian
COOL CHANGE   Hoyts, 1986, Australian
LES PATTERSON SAVES THE WORLD   Hoyts Distribution,
   1987, Australian
THE FAR COUNTRY (MS)   Crawford Productions,
   1987, Australian
THE CHRISTMAS VISITOR   BUSHFIRE MOON (CTF)
   Entertainment Media/The Disney Channel/WonderWorks,
   1987, Australian-U.S.
THE NEVERENDING STORY II THE NEXT CHAPTER
   Warner Bros., 1990, West German
IN THE NICK OF TIME (TF)   Spectator Films/Walt Disney TV, 1991
OVER THE HILL   Greater Union Distributors, 1992, Australian
FROZEN ASSETS   RKO Pictures Distribution, 1992
GROSS MISCONDUCT   PRO Film/David Hannah Productions/
   Underworld Productions/Australian Film Finance Corporation,
   1993, Australian
ANDRE   Paramount, 1994
ROBINSON CRUSOE   co-director with Rod Hardy,
   Miramax Films, 1995
THE GREAT ELEPHANT ESCAPE (TF)   Signboard Hill
   Productions, 1995

HARVEY MILLER*
b. June 15, 1935 - New York, New York
Home: 5538 Calhoun Avenue, Van Nuys, CA 91401, 818/997-6760
Agent: ICM - Beverly Hills, 310/550-4000
Business Manager: Jess Morgan, Jess Morgan & Company,
   6420 Wilshire Blvd. - 19th Floor, Los Angeles, CA 90048,
   213/651-1601

BAD MEDICINE   20th Century Fox, 1985
GETTING AWAY WITH MURDER   Savoy Pictures, 1995

JASON MILLER*
b. April 22, 1939 - New York, New York
Agent: Mickey Freiberg, The Artists Agency - Los Angeles,
   310/277-7779

THAT CHAMPIONSHIP SEASON   Cannon, 1982

JONATHAN MILLER
b. July 21, 1934 - London, England
Business: BBC Television Center, Wood Lane, London
   W12, England
Contact: British Film Commission, 70 Baker Street, London
   W1M 1DJ, England, tel.: 171/224-5000

TAKE A GIRL LIKE YOU   Columbia, 1970, British

MICHAEL MILLER*
Agent: David Gersh, The Gersh Agency - Beverly Hills,
310/274-6611

STREET GIRLS   New World, 1975
JACKSON COUNTY JAIL   New World, 1976
OUTSIDE CHANCE (TF)   New World Productions/Miller-Begun
Productions, 1978
SILENT RAGE   Columbia, 1982
NATIONAL LAMPOON'S CLASS REUNION
20th Century-Fox, 1983
SILENT WITNESS (TF)   Robert Greenwald Productions, 1985
CRIME OF INNOCENCE (TF)   Ohlmeyer Communications
Company, 1985
A CASE OF DEADLY FORCE (TF)   Telecom Entertainment, 1986
CAN YOU FEEL ME DANCING? (TF)   Robert Greenwald
Productions, 1986
ROSES ARE FOR THE RICH (TF)   Phoenix Entertainment
Group, 1987
NECESSITY (TF)   Barry-Enright Productions/Alexander
Productions, 1988
DANGEROUS PASSION (TF)   Stormy Weathers/Davis
Entertainment TV, 1990
ALWAYS REMEMBER I LOVE YOU (TF)   Gross-Weston
Productions/Stephen J. Cannell Productions, 1990
DANIELLE STEEL'S PALOMINO *PALOMINO* (TF)   The Cramer
Company/NBC Productions, 1991
DANIELLE STEEL'S DADDY *DADDY* (TF)   The Cramer
Company/NBC Productions, 1991
CRIMINAL BEHAVIOR (TF)   Preston Stephen Fischer Company/
Tolivar Productions/World International Network, 1992
DANIELLE STEEL'S HEARTBEAT *HEARTBEAT* (TF)
The Cramer Company/NBC Productions, 1993
JUDITH KRANTZ'S TORCH SONG *TORCH SONG* (TF)
Steve Krantz Productions/Multimedia Motion Pictures, 1993
DANIELLE STEEL'S STAR *STAR* (TF)   Schoolfield
Productions, 1993
DANIELLE STEEL'S ONCE IN A LIFETIME *ONCE IN A
LIFETIME* (TF)   The Cramer Company/NBC Productions, 1994
DANIELLE STEEL'S A PERFECT STRANGER *A PERFECT
STRANGER* (TF)   The Cramer Company/NBC
Productions, 1994

MOLLIE MILLER*
Home: 2190 Moreno Drive, Los Angeles, CA 90039, 213/664-0807
Agent: CAA - Beverly Hills, 310/288-4545

THE B.R.A.T. PATROL (TF)   Mark H. Ovitz Productions/
Walt Disney Productions, 1986
STUDENT EXCHANGE (TF)   Walt Disney TV, 1987
TALES FROM THE HOLLYWOOD HILLS: THE CLOSED SET (TF)
WNET-NY/Zenith Productions, 1988
PARENT TRAP: HAWAIIAN HONEYMOON (TF)
Walt Disney TV, 1989

NEAL MILLER
b. Chicago, Illinois
Business: Rubicon Film Productions, 505 Chicago Avenue,
Evanston, IL 60202

UNDER THE BILTMORE CLOCK (TF)   Rubicon Film Productions/
KTCA/American Playhouse, 1985

RANDALL MILLER*
Agent: CAA - Beverly Hills, 310/288-4545

CLASS ACT   Warner Bros., 1992
HOUSEGUEST   Buena Vista, 1995

REBECCA MILLER
ANGELA   Tree Farm Pictures, 1995

ROBERT ELLIS MILLER*
b. July 18, 1932 - New York, New York
Agent: Innovative Artists - Los Angeles, 310/553-5200
Business Manager: McGuire Management, 1901 Avenue of the Stars,
Los Angeles, CA 90067, 310/277-5902

ANY WEDNESDAY   Warner Bros., 1966
SWEET NOVEMBER   Warner Bros., 1967
THE HEART IS A LONELY HUNTER   Warner Bros., 1968
THE BUTTERCUP CHAIN   Warner Bros., 1970, British
BIG TRUCK AND POOR CLARE   Kastner-Ladd-Winkler/
Pashanel-Topol-Gottesman, 1972, U.S-Israel
THE GIRL FROM PETROVKA   Universal, 1974
JUST AN OLD SWEET SONG (TF)   MTM Enterprises, 1976
ISHI: THE LAST OF HIS TRIBE (TF)   Edward & Mildred Lewis
Productions, 1978
THE BALTIMORE BULLET   Avco Embassy, 1980
MADAME X (TF)   Levenback-Riche Productions/
Universal TV, 1981
REUBEN, REUBEN   20th Century-Fox International Classics, 1983
HER LIFE AS A MAN (TF)   LS Entertainment, 1984
THE OTHER LOVER (TF)   Larry Thompson Productions/
Columbia TV, 1985
INTIMATE STRANGERS (TF)   Nederlander TV & Film Productions/
Telepictures Productions, 1986
HAWKS   Skouras Pictures, 1989, British
BRENDA STARR   Triumph Releasing Corporation, 1992,
filmed in 1987
BED AND BREAKFAST   Hemdale, 1992
KILLER RULES (TF)   Lee Rich Company/Warner Bros. TV, 1993
A WALTON WEDDING (T)   Lee Rich Co./Amanda Prods./
Warner Bros., 1995

SHARRON MILLER*
b. Enid, Oklahoma
Agent: David Shapira & Associates - Sherman Oaks, 818/906-0322

PLEASURES (TF)   Catalina Production Group/Columbia TV, 1986
PIGEON FEATHERS (TF)   Learning in Focus, 1988
LITTLE GIRL LOST (TF)   Marian Rees Associates, 1988
THE OUTSIDERS (TF)   co-director with Alan Shapiro, Zoetrope
Studios/Papazian-Hirsch Productions, 1990
SECOND CHANCES (TF)   Latham-Lechowick Productions, 1993

TONY MILLER
MUSTANG: THE HIDDEN KINGDOM (CTD)   Intrepid Films Ltd./
The Discovery Channel, 1994

WALTER C. MILLER*
Home: 2401 Crest View Drive, Los Angeles, CA 90046,
213/656-2819

THE BORROWERS (TF)   Walt DeFaria Productions/20th
Century-Fox TV, 1973
CAN I SAVE MY CHILDREN? (TF) ☆   Stanley L. Colbert
Co-Production Associates/20th Century-Fox TV, 1974

WILLIAM P. (BILL) MILLING
Agent: Solomon Weingarten & Associates - Los Angeles,
310/474-8703

WOLFPACK   JER, 1986
LAUDERDALE   Omega Pictures, 1988
CAGED FURY   21st Century Film Corp., 1989
JOKER'S WILD   Omega Pictures, 1991

REGINALD MILLS
Contact: British Film Commission, 70 Baker Street, London
W1M 1DJ, England, tel.: 171/224-5000

PETER RABBIT & TALES OF BEATRIX POTTER
MGM, 1971, British

F
I
L
M

D
I
R
E
C
T
O
R
S

Mi

**F
I
L
M

D
I
R
E
C
T
O
R
S**

MICHAEL MINER
Agent: UTA - Beverly Hills, 310/273-6700

DEADLY WEAPON   Empire Pictures, 1989

STEVE MINER*
b. June 18, 1951 - Chicago, Illinois
Agent: David Gersh, The Gersh Agency - Beverly Hills,
   310/274-6611

FRIDAY THE 13TH PART 2   Paramount, 1981
FRIDAY THE 13TH PART 3   Paramount, 1982
HOUSE   New World, 1986
SOUL MAN   New World, 1986
WARLOCK   Trimark Pictures, 1989
WILD HEARTS CAN'T BE BROKEN   Buena Vista, 1991
FOREVER YOUNG   Warner Bros., 1992
MY FATHER, THE HERO   Buena Vista, 1994
BIG BULLY   Warner Bros., 1995

TSAI MING-LIANG
Contact: Department of Motion Picture Affairs, 2 Tientsin Street,
   Taipei, Taiwan, Republic of China, tel.: 2/351-6591

REBELS OF THE NEON GOD   1993, Taiwanese
VIVE L'AMOUR   Sunny Overseas Corporation/Shiung Fa
   Corporation/Central Motion Picture Corporation,
   1994, Taiwanese

DAVID MINGAY
Contact: British Film Commission, 70 Baker Street, London
   W1M 1DJ, England, tel.: 171/224-5000

RUDE BOY   co-director with Jack Hazan, Atlantic Releasing
   Corporation, 1980, British
SOPHISTICATED LADY (FD)   co-director with David Robinson,
   1990, British

ANTHONY MINGHELLA*
Agent: William Morris Agency - Beverly Hills, 310/859-4000

TRULY, MADLY, DEEPLY   *CELLO*   The Samuel Goldwyn
   Company, 1991, British
MR. WONDERFUL   Warner Bros., 1993

HO QUANG MINH
b. 1949 - Hanoi, Vietnam
Contact: Swiss Film Center, Munstergasse 18, 8001 Zurich,
   Switzerland, tel.: 01/472860

KARMA   1985, Vietnamese
THE PEASANT   1990, Vietnamese
PAGE BLANCHE   MHK Films, 1991, Swiss-Cambodian

TRINH T. MINH-HA
b. 1953 - Vietnam
Business: Moon Gift Film,1614 Sixth Street, Berkeley, CA 94710,
   510/527-2584

NAKED SPACES - LIVING IS ROUND   Moon Gift Film, 1985
SURNAME VIET GIVEN NAME NAM   Moon Gift Film, 1989
SHOOT FOR THE CONTENTS   Moon Gift Film, 1991

JOSEPH MINION
Agent: William Morris Agency - Beverly Hills, 310/859-4000

DADDY'S BOYS   Concorde, 1988

CECILIA MINIUCCHI
CLUCK   Cinema Paradiso Inc., 1995

ROB MINKOFF
Agent: CAA - Beverly Hills, 310/288-4545

THE LION KING (AF)   co-director with Roger Allers,
   Buena Vista, 1994

MURRAY MINTZ*
Address: P.O. Box 3911, Beverly Hills, CA 90212, 310/396-2759
Attorney: Stuart Berton, Berton & Feigen, 9777 Wilshire Blvd. -
   Suite 715, Beverly Hills, CA 90212, 310/271-5123

CARDIAC ARREST   Film Ventures International, 1980

SORAYA MIRE
b. Somalia

FIRE EYES (FD)   Persistent Productions, 1994

DAN MIRVISH
Agent: UTA - Beverly Hills, 310/273-6700

OMAHA (THE MOVIE)   Dana Altman/Bugeater Films Ltd., 1995

BOB MISIOROWSKI
Contact: Writers Guild of America, West - Los Angeles, 310/550-1000

SPANISH ROSE   Nu Image, 1993
ANGEL OF DEATH   Nu Image, 1994, U.S.-Polish

MERATA MITA
Contact: New Zealand Film Commission, P.O. Box 11-546,
   Wellington, New Zealand, tel.: 4/385-9754

PATUI (FD)   Awatea Films, 1983, New Zealand
MAURI   Awatea Films, 1988, New Zealand
MANA WAKA (FD)   Te Puea Estate/Turangawaewae Marae
   Productions, 1990, New Zealand

DAVID MITCHELL
Contact: Directors Guild of Canada, 225 Richmond Street, Toronto,
   Ontario M5V 1W2, Canada, 416/351-8200

THE KILLING MACHINE   C/FP Distribution, 1994, Canadian
MASK OF DEATH   Mask of Death Productions, 1995, Canadian

SOLLACE MITCHELL
Agent: CAA - Beverly Hills, 310/288-4545

CALL ME   Vestron, 1988

ALEXANDER MITTA
(Aleksandr Naumovich Mitta)
b. 1933 - Moscow, U.S.S.R.
Contact: Confederation of Film-Makers Unions, Vasilyevskaya
   Street 13, 123 825 Moscow, Russia, tel.: 095/250-4114

MY FRIEND, KOLKAI   co-director with Alexey Saltykov, Mosfilm,
   1961, Soviet
SUN, AIR AND WATER   Mosfilm, 1961, Soviet
WITHOUT FEAR AND REPROACH   Mosfilm, 1963, Soviet
THE BIG MATCH   Mosfilm, 1964, Soviet
SOMEONE'S RINGING, OPEN THE DOOR   Mosfilm, 1966, Soviet
SHINE BRIGHT, MY STAR   Mosfilm, 1969, Soviet
DOT, DOT, COMMA   Mosfilm, 1972, Soviet
MOSCOW, MY LOVE   co-director with Kenji Yoshida, 1974,
   Soviet-Japanese
THE TALE OF HOW TSAR PETER MARRIED OFF HIS
   BLACKMOOR   Mosfilm, 1976, Soviet
THE CREW   Mosfilm, 1980, Soviet
A TALE OF WANDERINGS   Mosfilm/Filmove Studio Barrandov/
   Romania Film Bucuresti, 1983, Soviet-Czechoslovakian-Romanian
LOST IN SIBERIA   Spectator International, 1991, British-Soviet

HAYAO MIYAZAKI

b. 1941 - Tokyo, Japan
Business: Studio Ghibli, 1-18-21 1 Hibiya Building - 8th Floor,
    Shinbashi, Minato-ku, Tokyo 105, Japan, tel.: 3/35084912
Contact: Yoshio Tsuboike, Tokuma Shoten Publishing Co., Ltd.,
    10900 NE 4th - Suite 1150, Bellevue, WA 98004, 206/646-8340

THE CASTLE OF CAGLIOSTRO LUPIN THE THIRD: CASTLE
    OF CAGLIOSTRO (AF) Streamline, 1979, Japanese
NAUSICAA OF THE VALLEY OF THE WIND (AF)
    Tokuma Shoten/Hakuhodo, 1984, Japanese
LAPUTA - THE CASTLE IN THE SKY (AF) Tokuma Shoten,
    1986, Japanese
MY NEIGHBOR TOTORO (AF) Studio Ghibli, 1988, Japanese
KIKI'S DELIVERY SERVICE (AF) Studio Ghibli, 1989, Japanese
PORCO ROSSO THE CRIMSON PIG (AF) Studio Ghibli,
    1993, Japanese

MOSHE MIZRAHI

b. 1931 - Egypt
Business: Rosa Productions, 5 rue D'Artois, 75008 Paris,
    France, tel.: 04/359-4704
Agent: The Gersh Agency - Beverly Hills, 310/274-6611 or:
    M. Lenoir - Paris, tel.: 1/45-63-59-20

LES STANCES A SOPHIE Prodis, 1971, French
I LOVE YOU ROSA Leisure Media, 1973, Israeli
THE HOUSE ON CHELOUCHE STREET Productions Unlimited,
    1974, Israeli
DAUGHTERS! DAUGHTERS! Steinmann-Baxter, 1975, Israeli
RACHEL'S MAN Allied Artists, 1976, Israeli
MADAME ROSA LA VIE DEVANT SOI Atlantic Releasing
    Corporation, 1978, French
I SENT A LETTER TO MY LOVE CHERE INCONNUE
    Atlantic Releasing Corporation, 1980, French
LA VIE CONTINUE Triumph/Columbia, 1982, French
UNE JEUNESSE 1983, French
WAR AND LOVE Cannon, 1985
EVERY TIME WE SAY GOODBYE TriStar, 1987, Israeli
MANGECLOUS AAA, 1988, French
A MAN OF INFLUENCE (MS) Mod Film/TF1/Reteitalia, 1990,
    French-Italian-Canadian

SERGE MOATI

Contact: French Film Office, 745 Fifth Avenue, New York,
    NY 10151, 212/832-8860

DES FEUX MAL ETEINTS Pan-Europeene, 1994, French

BEN MODEL

THE PUERTO RICAN MAMBO (NOT A MUSICAL) Cabriolet, 1991

MOEBIUS

(Jean Giraud)
Agent: The Starwatcher Agency - San Fernando Valley,
    818/343-9922

STARWATCHER (AF) co-director with Keith Ingham,
    Videosystem/Percy Main Productions, 1994
MOEBIUS' AIRTIGHT GARAGE (AF) Starwatcher Graphics/
    Kurosawa Enterprises USA, 1994, U.S.-Japanese-French

DAVID MOESSINGER*

Home: 3861 Kingswood Road, Sherman Oaks, CA 91403

MOBILE TWO (TF) Universal TV/Mark VII Ltd., 1975

JOHN MOFFITT*

Business: Moffitt-Lee Productions, 1438 N. Gower Street,
    Los Angeles, CA 90028, 213/463-6646
Agent: ICM - Beverly Hills, 310/550-4000
Personal Manager: Brillstein/Grey Entertainment - Beverly Hills,
    310/275-6135

LOVE AT STAKE BURNIN' LOVE TriStar, 1988

EDOUARD MOLINARO

b. May 13, 1928 - Bordeaux, France
Agent: ICM France - Paris, tel.: 1/723-7860
Contact: French Film Office, 745 Fifth Avenue, New York,
    NY 10151, 212/832-8860

BACK TO THE WALL Ellis, 1958, French
DES FEMMES DISPARAISSENT 1959, French
UNE FILLE POUR L'ETE 1960, French
THE PASSION OF SLOW FIRE LA MORT DE BELLE
    Trans-Lux, 1961, French
SEVEN CAPITAL SINS co-director with Jean-Luc Godard,
    Roger Vadim, Sylvaine Dhomme, Philippe De Broca, Claude
    Chabrol, Jacques Demy, Marie-Jose Nat, Dominique Paturel,
    Jean-Marc Tennberg & Perrette Pradier, Embassy,
    1962, French-Italian
LES ENNEMIS 1962, French
ARSENE LUPIN CONTRE ARSENE LUPIN 1962, French
UNE RAVISSANTE IDIOTE 1964, French
MALE HUNT Pathe Contemporary, 1965, French-Italian
QUAND PASSENT LES FAISANS 1965, French
TO COMMIT A MURDER PEAU D'ESPION Cinerama Releasing
    Corporation, 1967, French-Italian-West German
OSCAR 1968, French
HIBERNATUS 1969, French
MON ONCLE BENJAMIN 1969, French
LA LIBERTEEN CROUPE 1970, French
LES AVEUX LES PLUS DOUX MGM, 1971, French
LA MANDARINE Prodis, 1972, French-Italian
A PAIN IN THE A— L'EMMERDEUR Corwin-Mahler,
    1973, French
LE GANG DES OTAGES Gaumont, 1973, French
L'IRONIE DU SORT CFDC, 1974, French
THE PINK TELEPHONE SJ International, 1975, French
DRACULA PERE ET FILS Gaumont, 1976, French
L'HOMME PRESSE AMLF, 1977, French
LA CAGE AUX FOLLES ★ United Artists, 1979, French-Italian
LA PITIE DANGEREUSE (TF) Christine Gouze-Renal Progefi/
    Antenne-2, 1979, French
CAUSE TOUJOURS...TU M'INTERESSES Albina Productions,
    1979, French
SUNDAY LOVERS co-director with Bryan Forbes, Dino Risi &
    Gene Wilder, MGM/United Artists, 1981,
    U.S.-British-Italian-French
LA CAGE AUX FOLLES II United Artists, 1981, French-Italian
POUR 100 BRIQUES, T'AS PLUS RIENI UGC, 1982, French
JUST THE WAY YOU ARE MGM/UA, 1984
L'AMOUR EN DOUCE European Classics, 1985, French
PALACE Parafrance, 1985, French-West German
ENCHANTE Renn Productions, 1988, French
A GAUCHE EN SORTANT DE L'ACENSEUR AMLF,
    1988, French
L'AMOUR MAUDIT (TF) Progefi/FR3/KirchGroup, 1992,
    French-Italian-German
LE SOUPER Trinacra/Parma Films/France 2 Cinema/Canal Plus/
    Soficas/Investimage 4/Cofimage 4/Procirep, 1993, French
CE QUE SAVAIT MAISIE (TF) TF1, 1995, French

RAUNI MOLLBERG

b. 1929 - Hameenlinna, Finland
Contact: Finnish Film Foundation, Kanavakatu 12, SF-00160
    Helsinki, Finland, tel.: 0/17-77-27

THE EARTH IS A SINFUL SONG Seaberg, 1973, Finnish
PRETTY GOOD FOR A HUMAN BEING 1977, Finnish
MILKA 1980, Finnish
THE UNKNOWN SOLDIER 1985, Finnish
FRIENDS, COMRADES Filmi-Molle Oy/Swedish Film Institute/
    Norsk Film, 1990, Finnish-Swedish-Norwegian

SARAH MONDALE

MARCEL PROUST: A WRITER'S LIFE (TD) Wolfe-Carter
    Productions/Stone Lantern Films, 1993

PAUL MONES
Agent: ICM - Beverly Hills, 310/550-4000
Personal Manager: Addis-Wechsler & Associates - Los Angeles,
 213/954-9000

THE BEAT   Vestron, 1987
FATHERS AND SONS   Pacific Pictures, 1992
SAINTS AND SINNERS   Signature/The Farm, 1995

MARIO MONICELLI
b. May 16, 1915 - Viareggio, Italy
Address: Via del Babuino, 135 Rome, Italy, tel.: 06/6566126

I RAGAZZI DELLA VIA PAAL   co-director with Alberto Mondadori,
 1935, Italian
PIOGGIA D'ESTATE   Zacconi, 1937, Italian
AL DIAVOLO LA CELEBRITA   co-director with Steno,
 Produttori Associati, 1949, Italian
TOTO' CERCA CASA   co-director with Steno, ATA, 1949, Italian
VITA DA CANI   co-director with Steno, ATA, 1950, Italian
E ARRIVATO IL CAVALIERE   co-director with Steno, ATA/
 Excelsa Film, 1950, Italian
GUARDIE E LADRI   co-director with Steno, Carlo Ponti/Dino
 De Laurentiis Cinematografica/Golden Film, 1951, Italian
TOTO' E I RE DI ROMA   co-director with Steno, Golden Film/
 Humanitas Film, 1952, Italian
TOTO' E LE DONNE   co-director with Steno, Rosa Film,
 1952, Italian
THE UNFAITHFULS   co-director with Steno, Allied Artists,
 1953, Italian
PROIBITO   Documento Film/UGC/Cormoran Film, 1954, Italian
TOTO' E CAROLINA   Rosa, 1955, Italian
UN EROE DEI NOSTRI TEMPI   Titanus/Vides, 1955, Italian
DONATELLA   Sud Film, 1956, Italian
THE TAILOR'S MAID   *PADRI E FIGLI*   Trans-Lux, 1957, Italian
IL MEDICO E LO STREGONE   Royal Film/Francinex,
 1957, Italian-French
BIG DEAL ON MADONNA STREET   *I SOLITI IGNOTI*
 United Motion Picture Organization, 1958, Italian
THE GREAT WAR   United Artists, 1959, Italian
THE PASSIONATE THIEF   Embassy, 1960, Italian
BOCCACCIO '70   co-director with Federico Fellini, Vittorio De Sica &
 Luchino Visconti, Embassy, 1962, Italian
THE ORGANIZER   *I COMPAGNI*   Continental,
 1963, Italian-French-Yugoslavian
HIGH INFIDELITY   co-director with Franco Rossi, Elio Petri &
 Luciano Salce, Magna, 1964, Italian-French
CASANOVA '70   Embassy, 1965, Italian-French
L'ARMATA BRANCALEONE   Fair Film, 1966, Italian
THE QUEENS   *LE FATE*   co-director with Luciano Salce,
 Mauro Bolognini & Antonio Pietrangeli, Royal Films International,
 1966, Italian-French
RAGAZZA CON LA PISTOLA   Documento Film, 1968, Italian
CAPRICCIO ALL'ITALIANA   co-director with Steno,
 Mauro Bolognini & Pier Paolo Pasolini, Dino De Laurentiis
 Cinematografica, 1968, Italian
TO'E MORTA LA NONNA   Vides, 1969, Italian
LE COPPIE   co-director with Alberto Sordi & Vittorio De Sica,
 Documento Film, 1970, Italian
BRANCALEONE ALLE CROCIATE   Fair Film, 1970, Italian
LADY LIBERTY   *MORTADELLA*   United Artists, 1971, Italian
VOGLIAMO I COLONNELLI   Dean Film, 1973, Italian
ROMANZO POPOLARE   Capitolina, 1975, Italian
MY FRIENDS   Allied Artists, 1975, Italian
CARO MICHELE   Cineriz, 1976, Italian
SIGNORE E SIGNORI BUONANOTTE   co-director, Titanus,
 1976, Italian
UN BORGHESE PICCOLO PICCOLO   Cineriz, 1977, Italian
VIVA ITALIA!   *I NUOVI MOSTRI*   co-director with Dino Risi &
 Ettore Scola, Cinema 5, 1978, Italian
LOVERS AND LIARS   *TRAVELS WITH ANITA*   Levitt-Pickman,
 1979, Italian-French
HURRICANE ROSY   United Artists, 1979,
 Italian-French-West German
CAMERA D'ALBERGO   Filmauro/Nouvelle Cinevog,
 1980, Italian-French
LE COPPIE   co-director with Alberto Sordi, Documento Film,
 1980, Italian

IL MARCHESE DEL GRILLO   Opera/RAI, 1981, Italian-French
AMICI MIEI II   Sacis, 1982, Italian
BERTOLDO BERTOLDINO E...CACASENNO   Gaumont,
 1984, Italian
LE DUE VITE DI MATTIA PASCAL   Sacis, 1985,
 Italian-French-West German
SPERIAMO CHE SIA FEMMINA   Clemi Cinematografica/
 Producteurs Associes, 1986, Italian-French
I PICARI   Clemi Cinematografica, 1987, Italian
IL MALE OSCURO   Clemi Cinematografica, 1989, Italian
ROSSINI! ROSSINI!   Enrico Roseo Film/RAI/Istituto Luce/Velarde
 Film/Carthago Film/Beta Taurus Film, 1991,
 Italian-Spanish-French-German
PARENTI SERPENTI   Clemi Cinematografica, 1992, Italian
CARI FOTTUSTISSIMI AMICI   Cecchi Gori Group Tiger
 Cinematografica, 1994, Italian

CHRISTOPHER MONGER
b. November 9, 1950 - Wales
Home: 115 S. Catalina, Los Angeles, CA 90004, 310/388-4788
Agent: The Artists Agency - Los Angeles, 310/277-7779

ENOUGH CUTS FOR A MURDER   1979, British
REPEATER   WAC Films, 1980, British
VOICE OVER   WAC Films, 1981, British
THE MABINOGI (TD)   S4C/Channel 4, 1984, Welsh-British
CRIME PAYS   *MAE'N TALU WITHE*   Thread Cross Films/
 Channel 4, 1986, British
WAITING FOR THE LIGHT   Triumph Releasing Corporation, 1990
JUST LIKE A WOMAN   Zenith Productions/Rank Film Distributors/
 London Weekend TV/British Screen, 1992, British
THE ENGLISHMAN WHO WENT UP A HILL BUT CAME DOWN
 A MOUNTAIN   Miramax Films, 1995, British-U.S.

MEREDITH MONK
BOOK OF DAYS   Tatge-Lasseur Productions/Foundation for the Arts/
 La Sept/Alive From Off Center, 1988

PHILIPPE MONNIER
Home: 24, rue Las Cases, 75007 Paris, France, tel.: 1/45-55-02-64
Contact: French Film Office, 745 Fifth Avenue, New York,
 NY 10151, 212/832-8860

A TALE OF TWO CITIES (TF)   Granada TV/Dune of France/
 Antenne-2, 1989, British-French

CAROL MONPERE*
Agent: William Morris Agency - Beverly Hills, 310/859-4000

PINK LIGHTNING (TF)   FNM Films, 1991

GIULIANO MONTALDO
b. February 22, 1930 - Genua, Italy
Home: Via Paolo Emilio 32, Rome, Italy, tel.: 06/324-2080
Agent: Carol Levi, via G. Carducci 10, Rome, Italy 00187,
 tel.: 06/486961

TIRO AL PICCIONE   Ajace Cinematografica, 1961, Italian
EXTRACONIUGALE   co-director, D.S. Produzione, 1965, Italian
UNA BELLA GRINTA   Ager Film/Clodio Cinematografica,
 1965, Italian
GRAND SLAM   *AD OGNI COSTO*   Paramount, 1968,
 Italian-Spanish-West German
GOTT MIT UNS   Clesi Cinematografica/Jadran, 1969,
 Italian-Yugoslavian
MACHINE GUN McCAIN   *GLI INTOCCABILI*   1969,
 Italian-Yugoslavian
SACCO AND VANZETTI   UMC, 1971, Italian
GIORDANO BRUNO   Champion/Les Films Concordia,
 1973, Italian-French
L'AGNESE VA A MORIRE   Indipendenti Regionali, 1976, Italian
CIRCUITO CHIUSO   Filmalpha/RAI, 1978, Italian
IL GIOCATTOLO   Titanus, 1978, Italian
MARCO POLO (MS)   RAI/Franco Cristaldi Productions/Vincenzo
 Labella Productions, 1982, Italian

CONTROL (CTF)   HBO Showcase/Alliance Entertainment
    Corporation/Cristaldifilm/Les Films Ariane, 1987,
    Italian-Canadian-French
THE GOLD-RIMMED GLASSES   European Classics, 1987,
    Italian-French-Yugoslavian
TEMPO DI UCCIDERE   Titanus, 1989, Italian-French

EDUARDO MONTES
MIRROR IMAGE   Mirror Image Inc., 1991

JORGE MONTESI*
b. 1950 - Valparaiso, Chile
Address: 50 Quebec Avenue - Suite 1601, Toronto, Ontario,
    Canada M6P 3B4, 416/259-7684
Agent: APA - Los Angeles, 310/273-0744

BIRDS OF PREY (TF)   1984, Canadian
SENTIMENTAL REASONS (TF)   1985, Canadian
OMEN IV: THE AWAKENING (TF)   co-director with
    Dominique Othenin-Girard, FNM Films, 1991, U.S.-Canadian
STEALTH FORCE   G.E.L. Productions, 1993
LIAR, LIAR (TF)   CBC Productions, 1993, Canadian
MOMENT OF TRUTH: A CHILD TOO MANY (TF)   O'Hara-Horowitz
    Productions, 1993, U.S.-Canadian
HUSH LITTLE BABY (CTF)   Power Pictures/Hearst Entertainment/
    USA Pictures, 1994
ISLAND CITY (TF)   Lee Rich Company/MDT Productions/Prime
    Time Entertainment Network, 1994
MOMENT OF TRUTH: BROKEN PLEDGES (TF)   O'Hara-Horowitz
    Productions, 1994, U.S.-Canadian
SOFT DECEIT   Le Monde Entertainment, 1994, Canadian
FALLING FROM THE SKY! FLIGHT 174 (TF)   Pacific Motion
    Pictures/Hill-Fields Ent., 1995, U.S.-Canadian

MONTY MONTGOMERY
Business: Propaganda Films, 940 N. Mansfield Avenue,
    Los Angeles, CA 90038, 213/462-6400

THE LOVELESS   co-director with Kathryn Bigelow,
    Atlantic Releasing Corporation, 1981

PATRICK MONTGOMERY
b. September 13, 1949 - Cincinnati, Ohio
Contact: Archive Film Productions, Inc., 530 West 25th Street,
    New York, NY 10001, 212/620-3955

THE COMPLEAT BEATLES (FD)   TeleCulture, 1984,
    originally released by MGM/UA Home Video in 1982
ROCK & ROLL: THE EARLY DAYS (HVD)   co-director with
    Pamela Page, RCA/Columbia Home Video/Fox-Lorber/
    Archive Film Productions, 1984
BRITISH ROCK: THE FIRST WAVE (HVD)   co-director with
    Pamela Page, RCA/Columbia Home Video/Archive Film
    Productions, 1985

CHARLES PHILLIP MOORE
DANCE WITH DEATH   Concorde, 1991
BLACKBELT   Concorde, 1992
ANGEL OF DESTRUCTION   Concorde, 1994

D. MICHAEL (MICKY) MOORE*
b. Victoria, British Columbia, Canada
Home: 26706 Latigo Shore Drive, Malibu, CA 90265,
    310/457-2618

PARADISE - HAWAIIAN STYLE   Paramount, 1966
AN EYE FOR AN EYE   Embassy, 1966
THE FASTEST GUITAR ALIVE   MGM, 1967
TO KILL A DRAGON   Embassy, 1968
BUCKSKIN   Paramount, 1968

MICHAEL MOORE
b. 1954 - Davison, Michigan
Business: Center for Alternative Media, 2025 Pennsylvania Avenue -
    Suite 918, Washington, D.C. 20006, 202/287-4974
Agent: CAA - Beverly Hills, 310/288-4545

ROGER & ME (FD)   Warner Bros., 1989
CANADIAN BACON   Gramercy Pictures, 1995, U.S.-Canadian

RICHARD MOORE*
b. October 4, 1925 - Jacksonville, Illinois
Home: 21618 Oak Orchard Road, Santa Clarita, CA 91321,
    805/254-0147

CIRCLE OF IRON   Avco Embassy, 1979

RONALD W. MOORE
FUTURE-KILL   International Film Marketing, 1985

SIMON MOORE
Agent: Sanford-Gross & Associates - Los Angeles, 310/208-2100 or:
    Rochelle Stevens & Co. - London, tel.: 171/359-3900

UNDER SUSPICION   Columbia, 1991, British

STEVE MOORE
BETTY BOOP (AF)   MGM-UA, 1995

TOM MOORE*
Agent: Broder-Kurland-Webb-Uffner Agency - Beverly Hills,
    310/281-3400
Personal Manager: Jon Brown, The Brown Group - Beverly Hills,
    310/247-2755

'NIGHT, MOTHER   Universal, 1986
MAYBE BABY (TF)   Perry Lafferty Productions/von
    Zerneck- Samuels Productions, 1988
DANIELLE STEEL'S FINE THINGS   FINE THINGS
    The Cramer Co./NBC Productions, 1990

JOCELYN MOORHOUSE
Agent: CAA - Beverly Hills, 310/288-4545

PROOF   Fine Line Features/New Line Cinema, 1991, Australian
HOW TO MAKE AN AMERICAN QUILT   Universal, 1995

PHILIPPE MORA*
Business Manager: Fred Altman, Fred Altman & Company,
    9255 Sunset Blvd. - Suite 901, Los Angeles, CA 90046,
    310/278-4201

TROUBLE IN MOLOPOLIS   Mora Productions, 1969, British
SWASTIKA (FD)   Cinema 5, 1974, British
BROTHER, CAN YOU SPARE A DIME? (FD)   Dimension,
    1975, Canadian
MAD DOG   MAD DOG MORGAN   Cinema Shares International,
    1976, Australian
THE BEAST WITHIN   United Artists, 1982
THE RETURN OF CAPTAIN INVINCIBLE   LEGEND IN LEOTARDS
    New World, 1983, Australian
A BREED APART   Orion, 1983
HOWLING II...YOUR SISTER IS A WEREWOLF   Thorn-EMI,
    1985, British
DEATH OF A SOLDIER   Scotti Brothers, 1986, Australian
HOWLING III   THE MARSUPIALS: THE HOWLING III
    Square Pictures, 1987, Australian
COMMUNION   New Line Cinema, 1989
PTERODACTYL WOMAN FROM BEVERLY HILLS
    Experimental Pictures, 1994
ART DECO DETECTIVE   Trident Releasing, 1994

ANDY MORAHAN*
(Andrew Douglas Morahan)
Address: 18 Court Lane Gardens, Dulwich, London SE21 7DZ,
England, tel.: 181/299-4391
Agent: Renaissance/H.N. Swanson - Los Angeles, 310/246-6000

HIGHLANDER - THE FINAL DIMENSION *HIGHLANDER III:
THE SORCERER* Dimension/Miramax Films 1994,
Canadian-French-British

CHRISTOPHER MORAHAN
b. July 9, 1929 - London, England
Agent: UTA - Beverly Hills, 310/273-6700 or:
Michael Whitehall Ltd. - London, tel.: 171/244-8466

TALKING TO A STRANGER (TF) BBC, 1966, British
THE GORGE (TF) BBC, 1968, British
DIAMONDS FOR BREAKFAST Paramount, 1968, British
ALL NEAT IN BLACK STOCKINGS National General,
1969, British
THE JEWEL IN THE CROWN (MS) ☆ co-director with Jim O'Brien,
Granada TV, 1984, British
IN THE SECRET STATE Greenpoint Films, 1985, British
CLOCKWISE Universal, 1986, British
AFTER PILKINGTON (TF) BBC, 1987, British
TROUBLES (TF) Little Bird Productions/London Weekend TV,
1988, British
THE HEAT OF THE DAY (TF) Granada TV, 1989, British
PAPER MASK FFI/British Screen, 1990, British
OLD FLAMES (TF) 1990, British
CAN YOU HEAR ME THINKING? (TF) 1990, British
ASHENDEN (CTF) Kelso Films/BBC-TV/A&E Network/BBC
Enterprises, 1991, British-U.S.
COMMON PURSUIT *UNNATURAL PURSUITS* (TF)
BBC/WNET-13, 1992, British-U.S.
THE BULLION BOYS (TF) BBC/Mentorn, 1993, British

JACOBO MORALES
b. Puerto Rico
Contact: Puerto Rico Film Commission, Commonwealth of
Puerto Rico, Economic Development Administration, P.O. Box
362350, San Juan, Puerto Rico 00936-2350, 809/758-4747

DIOS LOS CRIAS 1980, Puerto Rican
NICOLAS Y LOS DEMAS Puerto Rican
LO QUE LE PASO A SANTIAGO Dios los Crias Producciones/
Pedro Muniz Producciones, 1989, Puerto Rican
LINDA SARA Banco Popular, 1994, Puerto Rican

SYLVIA MORALES*
Address: P.O. Box 341410, Los Angeles, CA 90034,
310/391-0070
Agent: Sheri Mann Agency - Los Angeles, 310/285-9999

CHICANA (FD) 1979
LOS LOBOS...AND A TIME TO DANCE (TD) PBS, 2984
VAYAN CON DIOS (TD) PBS, 1985
ESPERANZA 1985
SIDA IS AIDS (TD) PBS/Univision, 1988
A CENTURY OF WOMEN (MS) co-director with Barbara Kopple,
VU Productions, 1994

RICK MORANIS
b. Toronto, Ontario, Canada
Agent: William Morris Agency - Beverly Hills, 310/859-4000

STRANGE BREW co-director with Dave Thomas, MGM/UA,
1983, Canadian

GERARD MORDILLAT
Agent: Voyez Mon Agent - Paris, tel.: 1/47-23-55-80
Contact: French Film Office, 745 Fifth Avenue, New York,
NY 10151, 212/832-8860

EN COMPAGNIE D'ANTONIN ARTAUD Archipal 33/Laura
Productions/La Sept-Arte/France 2, 1994, French
LA VERITABLE HISTOIRE D'ARTAUD LE MOMO (FD) co-director
with Jerome Prieur, Laura Productions/Les Films D'Ici/La
Sept-Arte/Arcanal/Centre Georges Pompidou, 1994, French

JEANNE MOREAU
b. January 23, 1928 - Paris, France
Address: 193, rue de l''universite, 75007 Paris, France
Contact: French Film Office, 745 Fifth Avenue, New York,
NY 10151, 212/832-8860

LUMIERE New World, 1976, French
L'ADOLESCENTE Landmark Releasing, 1979,
French-West German

NANNI MORETTI
b. August 19, 1953 - Brunico, Bolzano, Italy
Home: via Piramide Cestia 1, Rome, Italy, tel.: 06/574-5353

IO SONO UN AUTARCHICO Nanni Moretti, 1976, Italian
ECCE BOMBO Filmalpha/Alphabeta, 1978, Italian
SOGNI D'ORO Operafilm/RAI, 1981, Italian
BIANCA Faso Film/Reteitalia, 1984, Italian
LA MESSA E' FINITA Faso Film, 1985, Italian
PALOMBELLA ROSSA Titanus, 1989, Italian-French
CARO DIARIO (DEAR DIARY) Fine Line Features/New Line
Cinema, 1993, Italian-French

W.T. MORGAN
Home: 733 Levering Avenue, Los Angeles, CA 90024, 310/208-4198

THE UNHEARD MUSIC (FCD) Skouras Pictures, 1985
A MATTER OF DEGREES Backbeat Productions/New Front Films/
Linus Associates/George Gund/Fujisankei Communications, 1990

ROBERT MORIN
Contact: Directors Guild of Canada, 225 Richmond Street, Toronto,
Ontario M5V 1W2, Canada, 416/351-8200

REQUIEM POUR UN BEAU SANS-COEUR 1992, Canadian
WINDIGO Allegro Films, 1994, Canadian

YOSHIMITSU MORITA
b. 1950 - Kyoto, Japan
Contact: Nihon Eiga Kantoku Kyokai (Japan Film Directors
Association), La Fontenu Building -4th Floor, 23-2 Maruyama-cho,
Shibuya-ku, Tokyo, Japan, tel.: 3/3461-4411

LIVE IN CHIGASAKI Independent, 1978, Japanese
SOMETHING LIKE THAT N.E.W.S. Corporation, 1981, Japanese
BOYS AND GIRLS Premiere International/Johnny's Production,
1982, Japanese
TRENDY STRIPPER Nikkatsu, 1982, Japanese
THE FAMILY GAME New Yorker, 1983, Japanese
TOKIMEKI NISHISU New Century Producers, 1984, Japanese
MAIN THEME Haruki Kadokawa Productions, 1984, Japanese
SOREKARA (AND THEN) New Yorker, 1985, Japanese
SOROBANZUKU *THE MERCENARIES* Fuji TV/Nippon Hoso/
A to Z, 1986, Japanese
THE COLOR OF SADNESS Toei/Sundance Company,
1988, Japanese
HEISEI ERA WOMANIZER Kowa International, 1989, Japanese
KITCHEN Kowa International, 1989, Japanese
LUCKY MARRIAGE Toho/Sundance Company, 1991, Japanese
LAST CHRISTMAS - MEMORY OF THE FUTURE Kowa
International/Fujiko F Fujiyo Productions, 1992, Japanese

JON MORITSUGU
MOD FUCK EXPLOSION Apathy Productions/Complex Corp., 1994

LOUIS MORNEAU

Agent: Innovative Artists - Los Angeles, 310/553-5200

CRACKDOWN   Concorde, 1991
UNCAGED   *ANGEL IN RED*   director of additional scenes,
   Califilm, 1991
FINAL JUDGMENT   Concorde, 1992
QUAKE   Concorde, 1993
CARNOSAUR II   Concorde, 1994

BOB MORONES

WHO WILL SING THE SONGS?   Universal, 1991
DOUBLE CROSS   Frank Cinelli Productions, 1991

DAVID BURTON MORRIS*

b. Kansas Cuty, Missouri
Home: 3640 Dixie Canyon Place, Sherman Oaks, CA 91423,
   818/906-0239
Agent: Paradigm - Los Angeles, 310/277-4400

LOOSE ENDS   Twyman Films, 1975
PURPLE HAZE   Triumph/Columbia, 1983
PATTI ROCKS   FilmDallas, 1987
HOME TOWN BOY MAKES GOOD (CTF)   HBO, 1990
VIETNAM WAR STORY: THE LAST DAYS (CTF)   co-director with
   Luis Soto & Sandy Smolan, HBO, 1989
JERSEY GIRL   Triumph Releasing Corporation, 1992
THE GETBACKS   Aurora Productions, 1995

ERROL MORRIS*

b. 1948 - Hewlett, New York
Business: Fourth Floor Productions, Inc., 678 Massachusetts
   Avenue, Cambridge, MA 02139, 617/876-4499
Agent: ICM - Beverly Hills, 310/550-4000

GATES OF HEAVEN (FD)   1978
VERNON, FLORIDA (FD)   1981
THE THIN BLUE LINE   Miramax Films, 1988
THE DARK WIND   Seven Arts/New Line Cinema, 1991
A BRIEF HISTORY OF TIME   Triton Pictures, 1992,
   U.S.-British-Japanese

GRAHAM MORRIS

THE LAND BEFORE TIME II: THE GREAT VALLEY
   ADVENTURE (AHVF)   Universal Home Video, 1995

HOWARD MORRIS*

b. September 4, 1919 - New York, New York
Agent: Broder-Kurland-Webb-Uffner Agency - Beverly Hills,
   310/281-3400

WHO'S MINDING THE MINT?   Columbia, 1967
WITH SIX YOU GET EGGROLL   National General, 1968
DON'T DRINK THE WATER   Avco Embassy, 1969
OH! BABY, BABY, BABY... (TF)   Alan Landsburg Productions, 1974
GOIN' COCONUTS   Osmond Distribution, 1978

JUDY MORRIS

Contact: Australian Film Commission, 150 William Street,
   Woolloomooloo NSW 2011, Australia, tel.: 2/321-6444

LUIGI'S LADIES   Hoyts Distribution, 1989, Australian

LEN MORRIS*

(Leonard M. Morris)
Business: Galen Film & Video, Harness Shop Square, Box 4219,
   Vineyard Harbor, MA 02568, 508/693-0752

AD ROME OF THE EMPERORS (TD)   NBC, 1984
MUSSOLINI: THE WOLF OR ROME (TD)   NBC, 1985
TASTE LADIES (FD)   1989
THE REPUBLIC PICTURES STORY (CTD)   Republic Pictures, 1990
AFRICA ON THE MOVE (FD)   Global Hunger Project, 1991
ROY ROGERS: KING OF THE COWBOYS (CTD)
   Republic Pictures, 1993
GENE AUTRY: MELODY OF THE WEST (CTD)   Galen Films, 1994

BRUCE MORRISON

b. New Zealand
Address: P.O. Box 46-090, Herne Bay, Auckland, New Zealand

CONSTANCE   Mirage Films/New Zealand Film Commission,
   1984, New Zealand
SHAKER RUN   Challenge Film Corporation, 1985, New Zealand
TEARAWAY   *QUEEN CITY ROCKER*   Spectrafilm,
   1987, New Zealand

PAUL MORRISSEY

b. 1939 - New York, New York

FLESH   Warhol, 1968
TRASH   Warhol, 1970
ANDY WARHOL'S WOMEN   Warhol, 1971
HEAT   Warhol, 1972
L'AMOUR   co-director with Andy Warhol, Altura, 1973
ANDY WARHOL'S FRANKENSTEIN   *FLESH FOR FRANKENSTEIN*
   Bryanston, 1974, Italian-French
ANDY WARHOL'S DRACULA   *BLOOD FOR DRACULA*   Bryanston,
   1974, Italian-French
THE HOUND OF THE BASKERVILLES   Atlantic Releasing
   Corporation, 1979, British
MADAME WANG'S   1981
FORTY-DEUCE   Island Alive, 1982
MIXED BLOOD   Sara Films, 1984, U.S.-French
BEETHOVEN'S NEPHEW   FilmDallas, 1985,
   French-West German-Austrian
SPIKE OF BENSONHURST   FilmDallas, 1988

JEFF MORTON

DOUBLE JEOPARDY (CTF)   Boxleitner-Bernstein Productions/CBS
   Entertainment, 1992

ROCKY MORTON

Address: c/o Hill Woolridge, 107 Hindes Road, Harrow, Middlesex
   HA1 1RU, England, tel.: 171/794-6871
Agent: UTA - Beverly Hills, 310/273-6700

THE MAX HEADROOM STORY (TF)   co-director with
   Annabel Jankel, 1985, British
D.O.A.   co-director with Annabel Jankel, Buena Vista, 1988
SUPER MARIO BROS.   co-director with Annabel Jankel,
   Buena Vista, 1993, U.S.-British

BEN MOSES*

Contact: Directors Guild of America - Los Angeles, 213/851-3671

NICKEL & DIME   August Entertainment, 1992

GILBERT MOSES†

b. August 20, 1942 - Cleveland, Ohio
d. 1995

WILLIE DYNAMITE   Universal, 1974
ROOTS (MS) ☆   co-director with Marvin J. Chomsky, John Erman &
   David Greene, Wolper Productions, 1977
THE GREATEST THING THAT ALMOST HAPPENED (TF)
   Charles Fries Productions, 1977
THE FISH THAT SAVED PITTSBURGH   United Artists, 1979
A FIGHT FOR JENNY (FT)   Robert Greenwald Productions, 1986
RUNAWAY (TF)   WonderWorks Inc., 1989

HARRY MOSES*

Home: 103 East 84th Street, New York, NY 10028, 212/535-2699
Business: The Mosaic Group, 145 East 49th Street - Suite 5A,
   New York, NY 10017, 212/371-6161

THORNWELL (TF)   MTM Enterprises, 1981
THE TRIAL OF BERNHARD GOETZ (TF)   Litchfield Films, 1988
ASSAULT AT WEST POINT (CTF)   Ultra Entertainment/The Mosaic
   Group, 1994

GREGORY MOSHER*
Agent: CAA - Beverly Hills, 310/288-4545

A LIFE IN THE THEATRE (CTF)   Turner Pictures/Beacon
   Communications/Bay Kinescope/Jalem Productions, 1993

ELIJAH MOSHINSKY
Contact: British Film Commission, 70 Baker Street, London
   W1M 1DJ, England, tel.: 171/224-5000

THE GREEN MAN (CTF)   BBC-TV/Arts & Entertainment Network,
   1991, British-U.S.
GENGHIS COHN (TF)   BBC/Arts & Entertainment Network,
   1993, British-U.S.

ROGER E. MOSLEY
Contact: Screen Actors Guild - Los Angeles, 213/954-1600

THE FIELD OF COTTON   Cottonfield Productions, 1995

JONATHAN MOSTOW
Agent: CAA - Beverly Hills, 310/288-4545

FLIGHT OF BLACK ANGEL   BLACK ANGEL (CTF)
   Hess-Kallberg Productions, 1991

CAROLINE AHLFORS MOURIS
BEGINNER'S LUCK   co-director with Frank Mouris,
   New World, 1986

FRANK MOURIS
BEGINNER'S LUCK   co-director with Caroline Ahlfors Mouris,
   New World, 1986

MALCOLM MOWBRAY*
Home: 20 Denton Road, London N8 9NS, England, tel.: 181/340-6983
Agent: The Gersh Agency - Beverly Hills, 310/274-6611 or:
   Peters Fraser & Dunlop - London, tel.: 171/344-1000

A PRIVATE FUNCTION   Island Alive, 1984, British
OUT COLD   Hemdale, 1989
DON'T TELL HER IT'S ME   Hemdale, 1990

JOHN LLEWELLYN MOXEY*
b. 1925 - Hurlingham, Argentina
Contact: Directors Guild of America - Los Angeles, 213/851-3671

HORROR HOTEL   CITY OF THE DEAD   Trans-World,
   1960, British
FOXHOLE IN CAIRO   Paramount, 1961, British
DEATH TRAP   Anglo-Amalgamated, 1962, British
THE 20,000 POUND KISS   Anglo-Amalgamated, 1963, British
RICOCHET   Warner-Pathe, 1963, British
DOWNFALL   Embassy, 1964, British
FACE OF A STRANGER   Warner-Pathe, 1964, British
STRANGLER'S WEB   Embassy, 1965, British
PSYCHO-CIRCUS   CIRCUS OF FEAR   American International,
   1967, British
THE TORMENTOR   ITC, 1967, British
SAN FRANCISCO INTERNATIONAL AIRPORT (TF)
   Universal TV, 1970
THE HOUSE THAT WOULD NOT DIE (TF)   Aaron Spelling
   Productions, 1970
ESCAPE (TF)   Paramount TV, 1971
THE LAST CHILD (TF)   Aaron Spelling Productions, 1971
A TASTE OF EVIL (TF)   Aaron Spelling Productions, 1971
THE DEATH OF ME YET! (TF)   Aaron Spelling Productions, 1971
THE NIGHT STALKER (TF)   ABC, Inc., 1972
HARDCASE (TF)   Hanna-Barbera Productions, 1972
THE BOUNTY MAN (TF)   ABC Circle Films, 1972
HOME FOR THE HOLIDAYS (TF)   ABC Circle Films, 1972
GENESIS II (TF)   Warner Bros. TV, 1973
THE STRANGE AND DEADLY OCCURENCE (TF)   Metromedia
   Productions, 1974

WHERE HAVE ALL THE PEOPLE GONE? (TF)   Metromedia
   Productions, 1974
FOSTER AND LAURIE (TF)   Charles Fries Productions, 1975
CHARLIE'S ANGELS (TF)   Spelling-Goldberg Productions, 1976
CONSPIRACY OF TERROR (TF)   Lorimar Productions, 1976
NIGHTMARE IN BADHAM COUNTY (TF)   ABC Circle Films, 1976
SMASH-UP ON INTERSTATE 5 (TF)   Filmways, 1976
PANIC IN ECHO PARK (TF)   Edgar J. Scherick Associates, 1977
INTIMATE STRANGERS (TF)   Charles Fries Productions, 1977
THE PRESIDENT'S MISTRESS (TF)   Stephen Friedman/Kings
   Road Productions, 1978
THE COURAGE AND THE PASSION (TF)   David Gerber Company/
   Columbia TV, 1978
SANCTUARY OF FEAR (TF)   Marble Arch Productions, 1979
THE POWER WITHIN (TF)   Aaron Spelling Productions, 1979
THE SOLITARY MAN (TF)   Universal TV, 1979
EBONY, IVORY AND JADE (TF)   Frankel Films, 1979
THE CHILDREN OF AN LAC (TF)   Charles Fries Productions, 1980
THE MATING SEASON (TF)   Highgate Pictures, 1980
NO PLACE TO HIDE (TF)   Metromedia Producers Corporation, 1981
THE VIOLATION OF SARAH McDAVID (TF)
   CBS Entertainment, 1981
KILLJOY (TF)   Lorimar Productions, 1981
I, DESIRE (TF)   Green-Epstein Productions/Columbia TV, 1982
THE CRADLE WILL FALL (TF)   Cates Films Inc./Procter & Gamble
   Productions, 1983
THROUGH NAKED EYES (TF)   Charles Fries Productions, 1983
WHEN DREAMS COME TRUE (TF)   I & C Productions, 1985
BLACKE'S MAGIC (TF)   Universal TV, 1986
SADIE AND SON (TF)   Norton Wright Productions/Kenny Rogers
   Organization/ITC Productions, 1987
LADY MOBSTER (TF)   Danjul Films/Frank von Zerneck
   Productions, 1988
OUTBACK BOUND (TF)   Andrew Gottlieb Productions/CBS
   Entertainment, 1988

ALLAN MOYLE*
Agent: William Morris Agency - Beverly Hills, 310/859-4000
Personal Manager: Jan McCormack, JSO Management, 11342 Dona
   Lisa Drive, Studio City, CA 97604, 213/650-3801
Business Manager: Robert E. Fromson, Fromson & Scissors,
   2020 Avenue of the Stars - Suite 290, Los Angeles, CA 90067,
   310/557-2540

MONTREAL MAIN   co-director with Frank Vitale &
   Maxine McGillivray, President Films/Canadian Film
   Development Corporation, 1978, Canadian
THE RUBBER GUN   Schuman-Katzka, 1978, Canadian
TIMES SQUARE   AFD, 1980
PUMP UP THE VOLUME   New Line Cinema, 1990, U.S.-Canadian
THE GUN IN BETTY LOU'S HANDBAG   Buena Vista, 1992
EMPIRE   Warner Bros., 1995

ERIC MUELLER
WORLD AND TIME ENOUGH   1 in 10 Films, 1994

KATHY MUELLER
Contact: Australian Film Commission, 150 William Street,
   Woolloomooloo NSW 2011, Australia, tel.: 2/321-6444

DAYDREAM BELIEVER   THE GIRL WHO CAME LATE
   Beyond Films, 1991, Australian

ROBERT MUGGE
b. May 8, 1950 - Chicago, Illinois
Business: Mug-Shot Productions, 1271 Nicole Lane, Secane,
   PA 19018, 610/583-3133

GEORGE CRUMB: VOICE OF THE WHALE (FD)   Mug-Shot
   Productions, 1973
AMATEUR NIGHT AT CITY HALL (FD)   Mug-Shot
   Productions, 1978
SUN RA: A JOYFUL NOISE (FD)   Mug-Shot Productions, 1980
BLACK WAX (FD)   Mug-Shot Productions, 1982
COOL RUNNINGS: THE REGGAE MOVIE (FCD)   Mug-Shot
   Productions, 1983

GOSPEL ACCORDING TO AL GREEN (FD)   Mug-Shot
   Productions, 1984
THE RETURN OF RUBEN BLADES (FD)   Mug-Shot
   Productions, 1985
SAXOPHONE COLOSSUS (FD)   Mug-Shot Productions, 1986
HAWAIIN RAINBOW (FD)   Mug-Shot Productions, 1987
ENTERTAINING THE TROOPS (FD)   Mug-Shot Productions, 1988
KUMU HULA: KEEPERS OF A CULTURE (FD)   Mug-Shot
   Productions, 1989
DEEP BLUES (FD)   Radio Active Films/Oil Factory Ltd., 1991
PRIDE & JOY: THE STORY OF ALLIGATOR RECORDS (FD)
   Mug-Shot Productions, 1992
GATHER AT THE RIVER: A BLUEGRASS CELEBRATION (FD)
   Mug-Shot Productions, 1994
GREAT MOMENTS IN BLUEGRASS (CTD)   Mug-Shot
   Productions/The Nashville Network, 1994
THE KINGDOM OF ZYDECO (FD)   Mug-Shot Productions, 1994
TRUE BELIEVERS: THE MUSICAL FAMILY OF ROUNDER
   RECORDS (FD)   Mug-Shot Productions, 1994

RUSSELL MULCAHY*

b. 1953 - Melbourne, Australia
Business: Le Bad Inc., 1900 Avenue of the Stars - 22nd Floor,
   Los Angeles, CA 90067, 310/277-1900 or:
   Le Bad Pty. Ltd., Suite 1202, 8-12 Bridge Street, Sydney,
   N.S.W. 2000, Australia, tel.: 2/247-7766 or:
   Le Bad Ltd., 67 Oakley Square, London NW1 1NJ,
   England, tel.: 171/388-0823
Agent: William Morris Agency - Beverly Hills, 310/859-4000

ELTON JOHN - THE FOX VIDEO ALBUM (HVCD)
   Rocket Records Productions, 1980, British
THE TUBES - COMPLETION BACKWARDS (HVCD)
   Capitol Records, 1981
DEREK AND CLIVE GET THE HORN (PF)   Peter Cook
   Productions, 1981, British
DURAN DURAN VIDEO ALBUM (HVCD)   DD Productions,
   1982, British
RAZORBACK   Warner Bros., 1984, Australian
DURAN DURAN - ARENA - AN ABSURD NOTION (HVCD)
   DD Productions, 1985, British
HIGHLANDER   20th Century Fox, 1986, British-U.S.
HIGHLANDER 2 - THE QUICKENING   InterStar Releasing, 1991
RICOCHET   Warner Bros., 1991
BLUE ICE   M&M Productions/HBO Pictures, 1992, British-U.S.
THE REAL McCOY   Universal, 1993
THE SHADOW   Universal, 1994

MARILYN MULFORD

FREEDOM ON MY MIND (FD)   co-director with Connie Field,
   Clarity Film Productions, 1994

RAY MULLER

Contact: Federal Union of Film and Television Directors in
   Germany, Adelheidstrasse 7, 8000 Munich 40, Germany,
   tel.: 089/271-6380

THE WONDERFUL HORRIBLE LIFE OF LENI RIEFENSTAHL
   DIE MACHT DER BILER: LENI RIEFENSTAHL (FD)
   Kino International, 1993, German

ROBERT MULLIGAN*

b. August 23, 1925 - Bronx, New York
Business: Boardwalk Productions, 5150 Wilshire Blvd. - Suite 505,
   Los Angeles, CA 90036, 213/938-0109
Agent: UTA - Beverly Hills, 310/273-6700

FEAR STRIKES OUT   Paramount, 1957
THE RAT RACE   Paramount, 1960
THE GREAT IMPOSTER   Universal, 1961
COME SEPTEMBER   Universal, 1961
THE SPIRAL ROAD   Universal, 1962
TO KILL A MOCKINGBIRD ★★   Universal, 1962
LOVE WITH THE PROPER STRANGER   Paramount, 1964
BABY, THE RAIN MUST FALL   Columbia, 1965
INSIDE DAISY CLOVER   Warner Bros., 1966
UP THE DOWN STAIRCASE   Warner Bros., 1967

THE STALKING MOON   National General, 1969
THE PURSUIT OF HAPPINESS   Columbia, 1971
SUMMER OF '42   Warner Bros., 1971
THE OTHER   20th Century-Fox, 1972
THE NICKEL RIDE   20th Century-Fox, 1975
BLOODBROTHERS   Warner Bros., 1979
SAME TIME, NEXT YEAR   Universal, 1979
KISS ME GOODBYE   20th Century-Fox, 1982
CLARA'S HEART   Warner Bros., 1988
THE MAN IN THE MOON   MGM-Pathe Communications, 1991

MARK MULLIN

Agent: Lynn Pleshette, The Pleshette and Green Literary Agency -
   Hollywood, 213/465-0428

COOL BLUE   co-director with Richard Shepard, Cinema
   Corporation of America, 1989

RON MULVIHILL

Business: Gris-Gris Films, 17962 Valley Vista Blvd., Encino, CA
   91316, 818/881-8725

MAANGAMIZU - THE ANCIENT ONE   Gris-Gris Films/Martin
   Mhando, 1995, U.S.-Tanzanian

CHRISTOPHER MUNCH

Agent: William Morris Agency - Beverly Hills, 310/859-4000

THE HOURS AND TIMES   Antarctic Pictures, 1992, British
COLOR OF A BRISK AND LEAPING DAY   1995, British

RICHARD W. MUNCHKIN

Business: Century Film Partners, 5731 Bonsall Drive, Malibu,
   CA 90265, 310/457-5895

DEADLY BET   PM Entertainment Group, 1992
RING OF FIRE II   PM Entertainment Group, 1992
GUARDIAN ANGEL   PM Entertainment Group, 1993
TEXAS PAYBACK   Century Film Partners, 1995

JAG MUNDHRA

(Jag Mohan Mundhra)
b. October 29, 1948 - India
Business: 1642 20th Street, Santa Monica, CA 90404, 310/828-8434

SURAAG   1982, Indian
KAMLA   1985, Indian
OPEN HOUSE   I.R.C./Prism Entertainment, 1986
HALLOWEEN NIGHT   Legacy Entertainment/Spencer Films, 1987
THE JIGSAW MURDERS   1988
EYEWITNESS TO MURDER   1989
NIGHT EYES   Trimark Pictures, 1990
LAST CALL   Prism Entertainment, 1990
LEGAL TENDER   Prism Entertainment, 1991
THE OTHER WOMAN   Axis Films International, 1992
L.A. GODDESS   Mark 1 Funding, 1992
SEXUAL MALICE   Axis Films International, 1993
IMPROPER CONDUCT   Everest Pictures, 1994
TAINTED LOVE   Everest Pictures, 1994
IRRESISTABLE IMPULSE   Everest Pictures, 1995

IAN MUNE

b. August 9, 1941 - Auckland, New Zealand
Address: Stony Creek Road, RD1, Kaukapakapa, New Zealand
Agent: Susan Smith & Associates - Beverly Hills, 213/852-4777

WINNERS AND LOSERS (TF)   co-director, 1975, New Zealand
DEREK (TF)   co-director, 1975, New Zealand
THE SILENT ONE   1984, New Zealand
CAME A HOT FRIDAY   Mirage Films, 1984, New Zealand
BRIDGE TO NOWHERE   Mirage Films, 1985, New Zealand
THE GRASSCUTTER (TF)   1988, New Zealand
THE END OF THE GOLDEN WEATHER   South Pacific Pictures,
   1991, New Zealand

JIMMY T. MURAKAMI
BATTLE BEYOND THE STARS   New World, 1979
WHEN THE WIND BLOWS (AF)   Kings Road, 1988, British

RYU MURAKAMI
b. 1952 - Nagasaki Prefecture, Japan
Contact: Nihon Eiga Kantoku Kyokai (Japan Film Directors
   Association), La Fontenu Building -4th Floor, 23-2 Maruyama-cho,
   Shibuya-ku, Tokyo, Japan, tel.: 3/3461-4411

ALMOST TRANSPARENT BLUE   Kitty Film/Toho, 1979, Japanese
DAIJOBU, MY FRIEND   Kitty Film, 1983, Japanese
RAFFLES HOTEL   Shochiku, 1989, Japanese
TOKYO DECADENCE *TOPAZ*   Melsato, 1992, Japanese

WALTER MURCH*
b. New York, New York
Agent: William Morris Agency - Beverly Hills, 310/859-4000

RETURN TO OZ   Buena Vista, 1985

FREDI M. MURER
Contact: Swiss Film Center, Munstergasse 18, 8001 Zurich,
   Switzerland, tel.: 01/472-860

ALPINE FIRE   Vestron, 1986, Swiss
DER GRUNE BERG (FD)   Fredi M. Murer/Pio Corradi, 1990, Swiss

JOHN MURLOWSKI
AMITYVILLE: A NEW GENERATION   Republic Pictures, 1993
AUTOMATIC   AK Productions, 1994

JAMES MURO
Agent: Wendy Schneider - Studio City, 818/990-7307

STREET TRASH   Lightning Pictures, 1987

DEAN MURPHY
Contact: Australian Film Commission, 150 William Street,
   Woolloomooloo NSW 2011, Australia, tel.: 2/321-6444

LEX AND RORY   Colorim International Releasing Corporation,
   1994, Australian

DON MURPHY
b. April 28, 1962 - Brooklyn, New York
Attorney: Karl Austen - Los Angeles, 310/557-8819

CLASS OF FEAR *MONDAY MORNING*   Fox-Lorber
   Home Video, 1990

EDDIE MURPHY*
b. April 3, 1961 - Hempstead, New York
Business: Eddie Murphy Productions, Carnegie Hall Tower,
   152 West 57th Street - 47th Floor, New York, NY 10019,
   212/399-9900 or:
   5555 Melrose Avenue - DeMille Building, Hollywood,
   CA 90038, 213/956-4545
Agent: CAA - Beverly Hills, 310/288-4545

HARLEM NIGHTS   Paramount, 1989

EDWARD MURPHY
RAW FORCE   American Panorama, 1982
HEATED VENGEANCE   Media Home Entertainment/Jungle
   Production Corporation, 1985

GEOFF MURPHY*
b. October 10, 1938 - Wellington, New Zealand
Agent: ICM - Beverly Hills, 310/550-4000

WILDMAN   1976, New Zealand
GOODBYE PORK PIE   The Samuel Goldwyn Company,
   1980, New Zealand

UTU   Pickman Films, 1983, New Zealand
THE QUIET EARTH   Skouras Pictures, 1985, New Zealand
NEVER SAY DIE   Everard Films, 1988, New Zealand
RED KING, WHITE KNIGHT (CTF)   HBO Pictures/Zenith
   Productions/John Kemeny Productions/Citadel
   Entertainment, 1989, U.S.-British-Canadian
YOUNG GUNS II   20th Century Fox, 1990
FREEJACK   Warner Bros., 1992
BLIND SIDE (CTF)   Chestnut Hill Productions/HBO Pictures, 1993
THE LAST OUTLAW (CTF)   Davis Entertainment/HBO
   Pictures, 1993
UNDER SIEGE II: DARK TERRITORY   Warner Bros., 1995

MAURICE MURPHY
Contact: Australian Film Commission, 8 West Street, North Sydney,
   NSW 2026, Australia, tel.: 2/925-7333

EXCHANGE LIFEGUARDS   Avalon Films, 1993, Australian

TAB MURPHY
Agent: Peter Turner Agency - Santa Monica, 310/315-4772

LAST OF THE DOGMEN   Savoy Pictures, 1995

BILL MURRAY*
b. September 21, 1950 - Chicago, Illinois
Agent: CAA - Beverly Hills, 310/288-4545

QUICK CHANGE   co-director with Howard Franklin,
   Warner Bros., 1990

DON MURRAY
b. July 29, 1929 - Hollywood, California
Agent: F.A.M.E. - Los Angeles, 213/656-7590

THE CROSS AND THE SWITCHBLADE   Dick Ross, 1970

ROBIN P. MURRAY
SEASON OF CHANGE   Jaguar Pictures, 1994
BOLERO (man and woman)   White Hawk Pictures Corp., 1995

PAUL MURTON
Agent: Kerry Gardner Management - London, tel.: 171/937-4478

TIN FISH (TF)   MFTS, 1990, British
THE END OF THE PARTY (TF)   Berwick Universal/Channel 4,
   1992, British
THE BLUE BOY (TF)   BBC-Scotland/WGBH-Boston,
   1994, Scottish-U.S.

JOHN MUSKER
Business: Walt Disney Animation, 500 S. Buena Vista Street,
   Burbank, CA 91521, 818/560-1000

THE GREAT MOUSE DETECTIVE (AF)   co-director with
   Ron Clements, Burny Mattinson & Dave Michener,
   Buena Vista, 1986
THE LITTLE MERMAID (AF)   co-director with Ron Clements,
   Buena Vista, 1989
ALADDIN (AF)   co-director with Ron Clements, Buena Vista, 1992

FLOYD MUTRUX*
(Charles Floyd Mutrux)
Agent: ICM - Beverly Hills, 310/550-4000

DUSTY AND SWEETS McGEE   Warner Bros., 1971
ALOHA, BOBBY AND ROSE   Columbia, 1975
AMERICAN HOT WAX   Paramount, 1978
THE HOLLYWOOD KNIGHTS   Columbia, 1980
THERE GOES MY BABY   Orion, 1994, filmed in 1992

ALAN MYERSON*
Agent: Abrams Artists & Associates - Los Angeles, 310/859-0625
Personal Manager: George Shapiro, Shapiro-West, 141 El Camino
    Drive, Beverly Hills, CA 90212, 310/278-8896

STEELYARD BLUES   Warner Bros., 1973
THE LOVE BOAT (TF)   co-director with Richard Kinon,
    Douglas S. Cramer Productions, 1976
PRIVATE LESSONS   Jensen Farley Pictures, 1981
POLICE ACADEMY 5: ASSIGNMENT MIAMI BEACH
    Warner Bros., 1988
HI HONEY, I'M DEAD (TF)   FNM Films, 1991
BAD ATTITUDES (TF)   FNM Films, 1991

MARVA NABILI
NIGHTSONGS (TF)   FN Films/American Playhouse, 1984

AMIR NADERI
b. 1945 - Abadan, Iran

GOODBYE MY FRIEND   1970, Iranian
TANGSIR   1973, Iranian
THE IMPASSE   1973, Iranian
HARMONICA   1973, Iranian
AN ELEGY   1975, Iranian
MADE IN IRAN, MADE IN USA   1975, Iranian
THE WINNER   1979, Iranian, unfinished
THE SEARCH (FD)   1981, Iranian
THE SEARCH II (FD)   1982, Iranian
DAVANDEH   1984, Iranian
THE RUNNER   Institute for the Intellectual Development of
    Children and Young Adults, 1985, Iranian
WATER, WIND, DUST   Islamic Republic of Iran Broadcasting,
    1989, Iranian
MANHATTAN BY NUMBERS   Rising Star Productions/Pardis/
    International Film & Video Center, 1993

IVAN NAGY*
b. January 23, 1938 - Budapest, Hungary
Contact: Directors Guild of America - Los Angeles, 213/851-3671

BAD CHARLESTON CHARLIE   International Cinema, 1973
MONEY, MARBLES AND CHALK   American International, 1973
FIVE MINUTES OF FREEDOM   Cannon, 1973
DEADLY HERO   Avco Embassy, 1976
MIND OVER MURDER (TF)   Paramount TV, 1979
ONCE UPON A SPY (TF)   David Gerber Company/
    Columbia TV, 1980
MIDNIGHT LACE (TF)   Four R Productions/Universal TV, 1981
A GUN IN THE HOUSE (TF)   Channing-Debin-Locke
    Company, 1981
JANE DOE (TF)   ITC, 1983
A TOUCH OF SCANDAL (TF)   Doris M. Keating Productions/
    Columbia TV, 1984
PLAYING WITH FIRE (TF)   Zephyr Productions, 1985
ENCOUNTERS (TF)   Larry A. Thompson Productions/Donna
    Mills Productions/Columbia TV, 1986

ROBERT KENT NAGY
ROCKIN' THE JOINT: THE LIFE AND TIMES OF BILL HALEY AND
    THE COMETS   co-director with Joe Graeff, Kent-Graeff
    Productions, 1993

MIRA NAIR
b. 1957 - Bhubaneswar, Orissa, India
Business: Mirabai Films, 6 Rivington Street, New York, NY 10002,
    212/254-7826
Agent: Sam Cohn, ICM - New York City, 212/556-5600

JAMA MASJID STREET JOURNAL (FD)   Mirabai Films, 1979
SO FAR FROM INDIA (FD)   Mirabai Films, 1982
INDIA CABARET (FD)   Mirabai Films, 1985
CHILDREN OF A DESIRED SEX (FD)   Mirabai Films, 1987
SALAAM BOMBAY!   Cinecom, 1988, Indian-British-French
MISSISSIPPI MASALA   The Samuel Goldwyn Company,
    1991, U.S.-British
THE PEREZ FAMILY   The Samuel Goldwyn Company, 1995

DESMOND NAKANO
Contact: Writers Guild of America - Los Angeles, 310/550-1000

WHITE MAN'S BURDEN   Rysher Entertainment, 1995

MICHAEL NANKIN*
b. December 26, 1955 - Los Angeles, California
Agent: Broder-Kurland-Webb-Uffner Agency - Beverly Hills,
    310/281-3400

MIDNIGHT MADNESS   co-director with David Wechter,
    Buena Vista, 1981

JOE NAPOLITANO*
Contact: Directors Guild of America - Los Angeles, 213/851-3671

EARTH ANGEL (TF)   Ron Gilbert Productions/Leonard
    Hill Films, 1991

YOKO NARAHASHI
Contact: Nihon Eiga Kantoku Kyokai (Japan Film Directors
    Association), La Fontenu Building - 4th Floor, 23-2 Maruyama-cho,
    Shibuya-ku, Tokyo, Japan, tel.: 3/3461-4411

WINDS OF GOD   Sachie Oayama Productions, 1993, Japanese

LEON NARBEY
b. August 2, 1947 - New Zealand
Business: Leon Narbey Ltd., P.O. Box 67-045, Auckland,
    New Zealand, tel.: 9/605-316
Contact: New Zealand Film Commission, P.O. Box 11-546,
    Wellington, New Zealand, tel.: 4/385-9754

ILLUSTRIOUS ENERGY   Challenge Film Corporation/Cinepro
    Productions/New Zealand Film Commission,
    1987, New Zealand
THE FOOTSTEP MAN   John Maynard Productions/New Zealand
    Film Commission/Avalon-NFU Studios/NZ on Air, 1992,
    New Zealand

SILVIO NARIZZANO*
b. February 8, 1928 - Montreal, Quebec, Canada
Home: 3 Bernard Shaw Court, St. Pancras Way, London NW1 9NG,
    England, tel.: 171/482-1135
Agent: The Strick Agency - Beverly Hills, 310/285-1560 or:
    Elspeth Cochrane Agency - London, tel.: 171/622-0314

DIE! DIE! MY DARLING! *FANATIC* Columbia, 1965, British
GEORGY GIRL   Columbia, 1967, British
BLUE   Paramount, 1968, British
LOOT   Cinevision, 1972, British
REDNECK   International Amusements, 1975, British-Italian
THE SKY IS FALLING   1976, Canadian
WHY SHOOT THE TEACHER   Quartet, 1977, Canadian
COME BACK, LITTLE SHEBA (TF)   Granada TV, 1977, British
THE CLASS OF MISS MacMICHAEL   Brut Productions,
    1979, British
STAYING ON (TF)   Granada TV, 1980, British

CHOICES   1981, Canadian
THE ALLEYN MYSTERIES: THE NURSING HOME MURDER (TF)
   BBC, 1991, British
ARTISTS IN CRIME (TF)   BBC/WGBH-Boston, 1991, British-U.S.

YOUSRY NASRALLAH

Contact: National Film Centre, City of Arts, Al Ahram Avenue,
   Giza, Cairo, Egypt, tel.: 854807

VOLS D'ETE   Egyptian-French
MARCIDES   Misr International Films/Paris Classics Productions/
   La Sept, 1993, Egyptian-French

GREGORY NAVA

b. April 10, 1949 - San Diego, California
Agent: ICM - Beverly Hills, 310/550-4000

THE CONFESSIONS OF AMANS   Independent Productions, 1976
EL NORTE   Cinecom/Island Alive, 1984
A TIME OF DESTINY   Columbia, 1988
MY FAMILY, MI FAMILIA   New Line Cinema, 1995

CAL NAYLOR*

Home: 17606 Posetano Road, Pacific Palisades, CA 90272,
   310/454-7229

DIRT   co-director with Eric Karson, American Cinema, 1979

RONALD NEAME*

b. April 23, 1911 - London, England
Business: Kimridge Corporation, 2317 Kimridge Road, Beverly Hills,
   CA 90210, 310/271-2970
Agent: The Gersh Agency - Beverly Hills, 310/274-6611

TAKE MY LIFE   Eagle Lion, 1947, British
THE GOLDEN SALAMANDER   Eagle Lion, 1950, British
THE PROMOTER   *THE CARD*   Universal, 1952, British
MAN WITH A MILLION   *THE MILLION POUND NOTE*
   United Artists, 1954, British
THE MAN WHO NEVER WAS   20th Century-Fox, 1956, British
THE SEVENTH SIN   MGM, 1957
WINDOM'S WAY   Rank, 1958, British
THE HORSE'S MOUTH   United Artists, 1959, British
TUNES OF GLORY   Lopert, 1960, British
ESCAPE FROM ZAHRAIN   Paramount, 1962
I COULD GO ON SINGING   United Artists, 1963, British
THE CHALK GARDEN   Universal, 1964, British
MISTER MOSES   United Artists, 1965, British
A MAN COULD GET KILLED   co-directed with Cliff Owen,
   Universal, 1966
GAMBIT   Universal, 1966
THE PRIME OF MISS JEAN BRODIE   20th Century-Fox,
   1969, British
SCROOGE   National General, 1970, British
THE POSEIDON ADVENTURE   20th Century-Fox, 1972
THE ODESSA FILE   Columbia, 1974, British-West German
METEOR   American International, 1979
HOPSCOTCH   Avco Embassy, 1980
FIRST MONDAY IN OCTOBER   Paramount, 1981
FOREIGN BODY   Orion, 1986, British

HAL NEEDHAM*

b. March 6, 1931 - Memphis, Tennessee
Agent: Camden-ITG - Los Angeles, 310/289-2700
Business Manager: Laura Lizer, Laura Lizer & Associates,
   12711 Ventura Blvd. - Suite 440, Studio City, CA 91604,
   818/508-3440

SMOKEY AND THE BANDIT   Universal, 1977
HOOPER   Warner Bros., 1978
THE VILLAIN   Columbia, 1979
DEATH CAR ON THE FREEWAY (TF)   Shpetner
   Productions, 1979
STUNTS UNLIMITED (TF)   Lawrence Gordon Productions/
   Paramount TV, 1980
SMOKEY AND THE BANDIT, PART II   Universal, 1980

THE CANNONBALL RUN   20th Century-Fox, 1981
MEGAFORCE   20th Century-Fox, 1982
STROKER ACE   Universal, 1983
CANNONBALL RUN II   Warner Bros., 1984
RAD   TriStar, 1986
BODY SLAM   DEG, 1987
B.L. STRYKER (TF)   Blue Period Productions/TWS Productions/
   Universal TV, 1989
BANDIT: BEAUTY AND THE BANDIT (TF)   Yahi Productions/IPS
   Productions/Universal TV, 1994
BANDIT BANDIT (TF)   Yahi Productions/PS Productions/
   Universal TV, 1994
BANDIT GOES COUNTRY (TF)   Yahi Productions/PS Productions/
   Universal TV, 1994

THOMAS L. NEFF

Business: Wild Wolf Productions, Inc., 10401 Venice Blvd. -
   Suite 200, Los Angeles, CA 90034, 310/280-6800

RUNNING MATES   New World, 1985
FREDERIC REMINGTON: 'THE TRUTH OF OTHER DAYS' (FD)
   Wild Wolf Productions, 1991
BEATRICE WOOD: MAMA OF DADA (TD)   Wild Wolf
   Productions, 1993

ALBERTO NEGRIN

Home: via Compagnano 56, Rome, Italy, tel.: 06/331-3717

MUSSOLINI: THE DECLINE AND FALL OF IL DUCE (CTF)
   HBO Premiere Films/RAI/Antenne-2/Beta Film/TVE/RTSI,
   1985, U.S.-Italian-French-West German
IL SECRETO DEL SAHARA (MS)   RAI/TF1/TVE/Beta Film/Racing
   Pictures, 1987, Italian-French-West German-Spanish
VOYAGE OF TERROR: THE ACHILLE LAURO AFFAIR (TF)
   RAI/Tribune Entertainment/TF1/Taurusfilm/ORF/HR/Filmalpha,
   1990, Italian-U.S.-French-West German
ENVOY (TF)   Sacis, 1994, Italian

DAN NEIRA

RESORT TO KILL   Blue Ridge Entertainment, 1994

DAVID NELSON*

b. October 24, 1936 - New York, New York
Address: 8544 Sunset Blvd., Los Angeles, CA 90069, 310/659-2067

DEATH SCREAMS   ABA Productions, 1981
LAST PLANE OUT   New World, 1983
A RARE BREED   New World, 1984

GARY NELSON*

Agent: Martin Hurwitz Associates - Beverly Hills, 310/274-0240
Attorney: Armstrong & Hirsch, 1888 Century Park East, Los Angeles,
   CA 90067, 310/553-0305

MOLLY AND LAWLESS JOHN   Producers Distribution
   Corporation, 1972,
SANTEE   Crown International, 1973
THE GIRL ON THE LATE, LATE SHOW (TF)   Screen Gems/
   Columbia TV, 1974
MEDICAL STORY (TF)   David Gerber Company/Columbia TV, 1975
PANACHE (TF)   Warner Bros. TV, 1976
WASHINGTON: BEHIND CLOSED DOORS (MS) ☆
   Paramount TV, 1977
FREAKY FRIDAY   Buena Vista, 1977
TO KILL A COP (TF)   David Gerber Company/Columbia TV, 1978
THE BLACK HOLE   Buena Vista, 1979
THE PRIDE OF JESSE HALLAM (TF)   The Konigsberg Company
SEVEN BRIDES FOR SEVEN BROTHERS (TF)   David Gerber
   Company/MGM-UA TV, 1982
JIMMY THE KID   New World, 1983
MURDER IN COWETA COUNTY (TF)   Telecom Entertainment/
   The International Picture Show Co., 1983
MICKEY SPILLANE'S 'MURDER ME, MURDER YOU' (TF)
   Jay Bernstein Productions/Columbia TV, 1983
FOR LOVE AND HONOR (TF)   David Gerber Company/
   MGM-UA TV, 1983

THE BARON AND THE KID (TF)   Telecom Entertainment, 1984
LADY BLUE (TF)   David Gerber Productions/MGM-UA TV, 1985
AGATHA CHRISTIE'S 'MURDER IN THREE ACTS' (TF)
   Warner Bros. TV, 1986
ALLAN QUATERMAIN AND THE LOST CITY OF GOLD
   Cannon, 1987
HOUSTON KNIGHTS (TF)   co-director with Richard Lang,
   Jay Bernstein Productions/Columbia TV, 1987
JAMES CLAVELL'S NOBLE HOUSE   *NOBLE HOUSE* (MS)
   Noble House Productions Ltd./De Laurentiis Entertainment
   Group, 1988
SHOOTER (TF)   UBU Productions/Paramount TV, 1988
GET SMART, AGAIN! (TF)   Phoenix Entertainment Group/
   IndieProd Co., 1989
THE LOOKALIKE (CTF)   Gallo Entertainment, 1990
THE HIT MAN (TF) . Schenck-Cardea Productions/Christopher
   Morgan Company/ABC Circle Films, 1991
SIDNEY SHELDON'S MEMORIES OF MIDNIGHT   *MEMORIES
OF MIDNIGHT* (TF)   Dove Audio/World International Network/
   Tribune Entertainment, 1991
REVOLVER (TF)   Victoria Productions/Noel Films/Catalunya
   Productions/Columbia TV, 1992
SIDNEY SHELDON'S 'THE SANDS OF TIME'   *THE SANDS
OF TIME* (TF)   Dove Audio Inc./Jadran Films/Tribune
   Entertainment, 1992
FUGITIVE NIGHTS: DANGER IN THE DESERT (TF)
   TriStar TV, 1993
RAY ALEXANDER: A TASTE FOR JUSTICE (TF)   Dean Hargrove
   Productions/Logo Productions/Viacom Productions, 1994

GENE NELSON*
(Gene Berg)
b. March 24, 1920 - Seattle, Washington
Home: 835 Catamaran Street - Apt. 1, Foster City, CA 94404,
   415/345-7489 or 415/322-7362

HAND OF DEATH   20th Century-Fox, 1962
HOOTENANNY HOOT   MGM, 1962
KISSIN' COUSINS   MGM, 1964
YOUR CHEATIN' HEART   MGM, 1964
HARUM SCARUM   MGM, 1965
THE COOL ONES   Warner Bros., 1967
WAKE ME WHEN THE WAR IS OVER (TF)   Thomas-Spelling
   Productions, 1969
THE LETTERS (TF)   co-director with Paul Krasny, ABC Circle
   Films, 1973
THE BARON AND THE KID (TF)   Telecom Entertainment, 1984
THE RETURN OF IRONSIDE (TF)   Riven Rocks Productions/
   Windy City Productions, 1993

JESSIE NELSON
Agent: UTA - Beverly Hills, 310/273-6700

CORRINA, CORRINA   New Line Cinema, 1994

JAN NEMEC
b. July 2, 1936 - Prague, Czechoslovakia
Contact: Czech Film Institute, Narodni tr. 40, 110 00 Prague 1,
   Czech Republic, tel.: 422/26-00-87

DIAMONDS OF THE NIGHT   Impact, 1964, Czechoslovakian
PEARLS OF THE DEEP   co-director, 1965, Czechoslovakian
MARTYRS OF LOVE   1966, Czechoslovakian
A REPORT ON THE PARTY AND THE GUESTS   Sigma III,
   1966, Czechoslovakian
IN THE LIGHT OF THE KING'S LOVE   Barrandov Film Studio,
   1991, Czechoslovakian

PENGAU NENGO
b. Morobe, Papua New Guinea

TINPIS RUN   JBA Productions/Tinpis/La Sept/RTBF/Femmis/
   Skul Bilong Wokim Piksa/Channel 4, 1991,
   Papua New Guinean-French-Belgian-British

GREG NERI
b. September 6, 1963 - Pasadena, California
Business: Rabbit in the Moon Films, 516 5th Street,
   Manhattan Beach, CA 90266, 310/379-5505

A PICASSO ON THE BEACH   Rabbit in the Moon Films, 1988
A WEEKEND WITH BARBARA UND INGRID   Rabbit in the
   Moon Films, 1992

AVI NESHER*
Agent: David Gersh, The Gersh Agency - Beverly Hills, 310/273-0744

THE TROUPE   *HALAHAKA*   Eastways Productions, 1978, Israeli
DIZENGOFF 99   Shapira Films, 1979, Israeli
SHE   American National Enterprises, 1983, Italian
RAGE AND GLORY   Interpictures, 1985, Israeli
SMASH   Zygmunt P. Barwaz Productions, 1986, Israeli
TIMEBOMB   *NAMELESS*   MGM-Pathe Communications, 1991
DOPPELGANGER   Planet Productions, 1993
SAVAGE   Mahagonny Pictures, 1995

CATHE NEUKUM
THE UNTOLD WEST (TD)   Modern Times Film Company/TBS
   Productions, 1993

CHRIS NEWBY
Agent: Peters Fraser & Dunlop - London, tel.: 171/344-1000

ANCHORESS   British Film Institute/Corsan Productions/Ministry of
   the Flemish Community/BRTN/ASLF-CGER/National Loterij/CR TV,
   1993, British-Belgian
MADAGASCAR SKIN   1995, British

MIKE NEWELL*
b. 1942 - England
Home: 55 St. George's Avenue, London N7 0AJ, England,
   tel.: 171/607-9523
Agent: ICM - London, tel.: 171/636-6565

THE MAN IN THE IRON MASK (TF)   Norman Rosemont
   Productions/ITC, 1977, U.S.-British
THE AWAKENING   Orion/Warner Bros., 1980
BLOOD FEUD (TF)   20th Century-Fox TV/Glickman-Selznick
   Productions, 1983
BAD BLOOD   Southern Pictures/New Zealand Film Commission,
   1983, New Zealand
DANCE WITH A STRANGER   The Samuel Goldwyn Company,
   1985, British
THE GOOD FATHER   Skouras Pictures, 1986, British
AMAZING GRACE AND CHUCK   TriStar, 1987
SOURSWEET   First Film Company/Zenith Productions,
   1988, British
COMMON GROUND (TF)   Daniel H. Blatt Productions/
   Lorimar TV, 1990
ENCHANTED APRIL   Miramax Films, 1991, British
INTO THE WEST   Miramax Films, 1992, British-Irish-Japanese
FOUR WEDDINGS AND A FUNERAL   Gramercy Pictures,
   1994, British
AN AWFULLY BIG ADVENTURE   Fine Line Features/New Line
   Cinema, 1995, British

JOHN NEWLAND*
b. November 23, 1917 - Cincinnati, Ohio
Contact: Directors Guild of America - Los Angeles, 213/851-3671

THAT NIGHT   Universal, 1957
THE VIOLATORS   Universal, 1957
THE SPY WITH MY FACE   MGM, 1966
MY LOVER, MY SON   MGM, 1970, British
THE DEADLY HUNT (TF)   Four Star International, 1971
CRAWLSPACE (TF)   Titus Productions, 1972
DON'T BE AFRAID OF THE DARK (TF)   Lorimar Productions, 1972
WHO FEARS THE DEVIL   *THE LEGEND OF HILLBILLY JOHN*
   Jack H. Harris Enterprises, 1974

A SENSITIVE, PASSIONATE MAN (TF)   Factor-Newland
    Production Corporation, 1977
OVERBOARD (TF)   Factor-Newland Production Corporation, 1978
THE SUICIDE'S WIFE (TF)   Factor-Newland Production
    Corporation, 1979

ANTHONY NEWLEY
b. September 24, 1931 - London, England
Contact: British Film Commission, 70 Baker Street, London
    W1M 1DJ, England, tel.: 171/224-5000

CAN HIERONYMOUS MERKIN EVER FORGET MERCY HUMPPE
    AND FIND TRUE HAPPINESS?   Regional, 1969, British
SUMMERTREE   Columbia, 1971

JOSEPH M. NEWMAN*
b. August 7, 1909 - Logan, Utah
Contact: Directors Guild of America - Los Angeles, 213/851-3671

NORTHWEST RANGERS   MGM, 1942
DIARY OF A SERGEANT (FD)   1945
JUNGLE PATROL   20th Century-Fox, 1948
THE GREAT DAN PATCH   United Artists, 1949
ABANDONED   Universal, 1949
711 OCEAN DRIVE   Columbia, 1950
LUCKY NICK CAIN   I'LL GET YOU FOR THIS
    20th Century-Fox, 1951
THE GUY WHO CAME BACK   20th Century-Fox, 1951
LOVE NEST   20th Century-Fox, 1951
RED SKIES OF MONTANA   SMOKE JUMPERS
    20th Century-Fox, 1952
PONY SOLDIER   20th Century-Fox, 1952
THE OUTCASTS OF POKER FLAT   20th Century-Fox, 1952
DANGEROUS CROSSING   20th Century-Fox, 1953
THE HUMAN JUNGLE   Allied Artists, 1954
THIS ISLAND EARTH   Universal, 1955
KISS OF FIRE   Universal, 1955
FLIGHT TO HONG KONG   United Artists, 1956
DEATH IN SMALL DOSES   Allied Artists, 1957
FORT MASSACRE   United Artists, 1958
THE GUNFIGHT AT DODGE CITY   United Artists, 1959
THE BIG CIRCUS   Allied Artists, 1959
TARZAN, THE APE MAN   MGM, 1959
KING OF THE ROARING TWENTIES - THE STORY OF
    ARNOLD ROTHSTEIN   Allied Artists, 1961
A THUNDER OF DRUMS   MGM, 1961
TWENTY PLUS TWO   Allied Artists, 1961
THE GEORGE RAFT STORY   Allied Artists, 1961

PAUL NEWMAN*
b. January 26, 1925 - Cleveland, Ohio
Agent: CAA - Beverly Hills, 310/288-4545

RACHEL, RACHEL   Warner Bros., 1968
SOMETIMES A GREAT NOTION   NEVER GIVE AN INCH
    Universal, 1971
THE EFFECT OF GAMMA RAYS ON MAN-IN-THE-MOON
    MARIGOLDS   20th Century-Fox, 1973
THE SHADOW BOX (TF) ☆   The Shadow Box Film Company, 1980
HARRY & SON   Orion, 1984
THE GLASS MENAGERIE   Cineplex Odeon, 1987

TED NEWSOM
ED WOOD: LOOK BACK IN ANGORA (HVD)
    Rhino Home Video, 1994

PHIL NIBBELINK
AN AMERICAN TAIL: FIEVEL GOES WEST (AF)   co-director with
    Simon Wells, Universal, 1991
WE'RE BACK! A DINOSAUR'S STORY (AF)   co-director with
    Dick Zondag, Ralph Zondag & Simon Wells, Universal, 1993

MAURIZIO NICHETTI
b. 1948 - Milan, Italy
Home: via E. De Marchi 3, Milan, Italy, tel.: 02/66985217
Agent: William Morris Agency - Beverly Hills, 310/859-4000

RATATAPLAN   Vides, 1979, Italian
HO FATTO SPLASH   Vides, 1980, Italian
DOMANI SI BALA   Vides, 1982, Italian
IL BI E IL BA   San Francisco/New Team, 1985, Italian
THE ICICLE THIEF   Aries Film, 1989, Italian
VOLERE VOLARE   co-director with Guido Manuli, Fine Line
    Features/New Line Cinema, 1991, Italian
STEFANO QUANTESTORIE   Penta Distribuzione, 1993, Italian
SNOWBALL   1995, Italian

PAUL NICHOLAS*
(Lutz Schaarwaechter)
Business: Monarex Hollywood Corporation, 9421 1/2 W. Pico Blvd.,
    Los Angeles, CA 90035, 310/552-1069

BAD BLOOD   JULIE DARLING   Twin Continental, 1982,
    Canadian-West German
CHAINED HEAT   Jensen Farley Pictures, 1983
THE NAKED CAGE   Cannon, 1986
NIGHT OF THE ARCHER   Trident Releasing, 1994

ALLAN NICHOLLS*
b. April 8, 1945 - Montreal, Quebec, Canada
Home: 225 West 14th Street - Apt. 5E, New York, NY 10011,
    212/924-6323

DEAD RINGER   Feature Films, 1982

MIKE NICHOLS*
(Michael Igor Peschkowsky)
b. November 6, 1931 - Berlin, Germany
Agent: CAA - Beverly Hills, 310/288-4545
Attorney: Marvin B. Meyer, Rosenfeld, Meyer & Susman -
    Beverly Hills, 310/858-7700

WHO'S AFRAID OF VIRGINIA WOOLF? ★   Warner Bros., 1966
THE GRADUATE ★★   Avco Embassy, 1967
CATCH-22   Paramount, 1970
CARNAL KNOWLEDGE   Avco Embassy, 1971
THE DAY OF THE DOLPHIN   Avco Embassy, 1973
THE FORTUNE   Columbia, 1975
GILDA LIVE (PF)   Warner Bros., 1980
SILKWOOD ★   20th Century-Fox, 1983
HEARTBURN   Paramount, 1986
BILOXI BLUES   Universal, 1988
WORKING GIRL ★   20th Century Fox, 1988
POSTCARDS FROM THE EDGE   Columbia, 1990
REGARDING HENRY   Paramount, 1991
WOLF   Columbia, 1994
BIRDS OF A FEATHER   MGM-UA, 1995

JACK NICHOLSON*
b. April 22, 1937 - Neptune, New Jersey
Agent: Sandy Bresler, Bresler-Kelly-Kipperman -Encino,
    818/905-1155

DRIVE, HE SAID   Columbia, 1971
GOIN' SOUTH   Paramount, 1979
THE TWO JAKES   Paramount, 1990

MARTIN NICHOLSON*
Agent: Sanford-Gross & Associates - Los Angeles, 310/208-2100

THE NIGHT MY PARENTS RAN AWAY (TF)   Fox West Pictures/
    New Line TV/Chanticleer Films, 1993

MICHAEL NICKLES
DESERT WINDS   Desert Winds Productions, 1995

TED NICOLAOU
THE DUNGEONMASTER   co-director, Empire Pictures, 1985
TERRORVISION   Empire Pictures, 1986
SUBSPECIES   Full Moon Entertainment, 1991
BAD CHANNELS   Full Moon Entertainment, 1992
DRAGON WORLD   Full Moon Entertainment, 1993, U.S.-British
BLOODLUST: SUBSPECIES III   Full Moon Entertainment, 1993

JOHN NICOLELLA*
Agent: Joel Gotler, Renaissance/H.N. Swanson - Los Angeles,
   310/246-6000

FINISH LINE (CTF)   Guber-Peters Entertainment Productions/
   Phoenix Entertainment Group, 1989
MICKEY SPILLANE'S MIKE HAMMER: MURDER TAKES ALL (TF)
   Jay Bernstein Productions/Columbia TV, 1989
ROCK HUDSON (TF)   The Konigsberg-Sanitsky Company, 1990
RUNAWAY FATHER (TF)   Polone Company/Bonaparte
   Productions/Lee Levinson Productions, 1991
MIDNIGHT HEAT   New Line Cinema, 1992
VANISHING SON (TF)   Universal-MCA TV, 1994
VANISHING SON II (TF)   Universal-MCA TV, 1994
VANISHING SON III (TF)   Universal-MCA TV, 1994

WU NIEN-JEN
Contact: Department of Motion Picture Affairs, 2 Tientsin Street,
   Taipei, Taiwan, Republic of China, tel.: 2/351-6591

A BORROWED LIFE   DUO-SANG   Chang Su A&V Company/
   Long Shong Films, 1994, Taiwanese

GEORGE T. NIERENBERG
b. Roslyn Heights, New York
Business: GTN Productions, 341 Madison Avenue - 20th Floor,
   New York, NY 10017, 212/599-3032

NO MAPS ON MY TAPS (FD)   Direct Cinema, 1979
SAY AMEN, SOMEBODY (FD)   United Artists Classics, 1983
THAT RHYTHM, THOSE BLUES (FD)   Tap Productions, 1988

ROB NILSSON
Business: Snowball Pictures, 415/567-4404

NORTHERN LIGHTS   co-director with John Hanson,
   Cine-Manifest, 1979
ON THE EDGE   Skouras Pictures, 1986
SIGNAL 7   Myron-Taylor Productions, 1986
HEAT AND SUNLIGHT   New Front Alliance/Snowball
   Productions, 1987
CHALK   Tenderloin Action Group, 1993

LEONARD NIMOY*
b. March 26, 1931 - Boston, Massachusetts
Agent: The Gersh Agency - Beverly Hills, 310/274-6611
Business Manager: Carol Oster, Francis & Freedman,
   501 S. Beverly Drive - Third Floor, Beverly Hills,
   CA 90212, 310/277-7351

STAR TREK III: THE SEARCH FOR SPOCK   Paramount, 1984
STAR TREK IV: THE VOYAGE HOME   Paramount, 1986
THREE MEN AND A BABY   Buena Vista, 1987
THE GOOD MOTHER   Buena Vista, 1988
FUNNY ABOUT LOVE   Paramount, 1990
HOLY MATRIMONY   Buena Vista, 1994

MICHELE NOBLE
RUNAWAY DREAMS   Cinema Spectrum/Swanyard Films, 1990

NIGEL NOBLE*
Home: 816 Accabonac Road, East Hampton, NY 11937,
   516/329-3787

VOICES OF 'SARAFINA!' (FD)   New Yorker, 1988

CHRIS NOONAN
Contact: Australian Film Commission, 150 William Street,
   Woolloomooloo NSW 2011, Australia, tel.: 2/321-6444

BABE, THE GALLANT SHEEP PIG   Universal, 1995, Australian

TOM NOONAN
Agent: David Guc, The Gersh Agency - New York City, 212/997-1818

WHAT HAPPENED WAS   The Samuel Goldwyn Company, 1994
THE WIFE   CIBY 2000/Genre Film, 1995, U.S.-French

LESLIE NORMAN
b. 1911 - London, England
Contact: British Film Commission, 70 Baker Street, London
   W1M 1DJ, England, tel.: 171/224-5000

DANGEROUS TO LIVE   co-director, 1939, British
THE NIGHT MY NUMBER CAME UP   Continental, 1955, British
X THE UNKNOWN   Warner Bros., 1956, British
THE SHIRALEE   1957, British
DUNKIRK   MGM, 1958, British
SEASON OF PASSION   SUMMER OF THE SEVENTEENTH DOLL
   United Artists, 1959, Australian-British
THE LONG AND THE SHORT AND THE TALL   JUNGLE FIGHTERS
   Continental, 1961, British
SPARE THE ROD   Embassy, 1961, British
MIX ME A PERSON   British Lion, 1962, British

RON NORMAN
b. November 2, 1953 - New York, New York
Business: Horizons Productions, 1134 N. Ogden Drive, Los Angeles,
   CA 90046, 213/654-6911

A DEATH   Venice Pictures, 1979
VT   Marshfield Productions, 1980
RENNIE   Horizons Productions, 1982
HORIZONS   Horizons Productions, 1983

ZACK NORMAN
Contact: Screen Actors Guild - Los Angeles, 213/954-1600

RICH BOYS   CHIEF ZABU   co-director with Neil Cohen under
   pseudonym of Howard Zuker, International Film Marketing, 1988

AARON NORRIS*
Business: Tamglewood, 4560 Sherman Oaks Avenue,
   Sherman Oaks, CA 91403, 818/783-4430
Agent: The Gersh Agency - Beverly Hills, 310/274-6611
Attorney: Henry Holmes, Cooper, Epstein & Hurewitz, 345 N. Maple
   Drive - Suite 200, Beverly Hills, CA 90210, 310/205-8320

BRADDOCK: MISSING IN ACTION III   Cannon, 1988
PLATOON LEADER   Cannon, 1988
DELTA FORCE 2: THE COLOMBIAN CONNECTION
   Cannon, 1990
THE HIT MAN   Cannon, 1991
SIDEKICKS   Triumph Releasing Corporation, 1993
HELLBOUND   Cannon, 1993
TOP DOG   MGM-UA, 1995

BILL L. NORTON*
(William Lloyd Norton)
b. August 13, 1943 - California
Agent: CAA - Beverly Hills, 310/288-4545

CISCO PIKE   Columbia, 1971
GARGOYLES (TF)   Tomorrow Entertainment, 1972
MORE AMERICAN GRAFFITI   Universal, 1979
BABY - SECRET OF THE LOST LEGEND   Buena Vista, 1985
THREE FOR THE ROAD   New Century/Vista, 1987
TOUR OF DUTY (TF)   Zev Braun Productions/New World TV, 1987
GRAND SLAM (TF)   Bill L. Norton Productions/New World TV, 1990
ANGEL OF DEATH (TF)   Once Upon A Time Films, 1990

FALSE ARREST (TF)   Ron Gilbert Associates/Leonard
   Hill Films, 1991
HERCULES AND THE AMAZON WOMEN (TF)   Renaissance
   Pictures/Universal TV, 1994
HERCULES IN THE UNDERWORLD (TF)   Renaissance Pictures/
   Universal TV, 1994
THE WOMEN OF SPRING BREAK (TF)   Ron Gilbert Associates/
   Hill-Fields Entertainment, 1995
DEADLY WHISPERS (TF)   Hill-Fields Entertainment/ACI, 1995

NOEL NOSSECK*
Agent: APA - Los Angeles, 310/273-0744

BEST FRIENDS   Crown International, 1973
LAS VEGAS LADY   Crown International, 1976
YOUNGBLOOD   American International, 1978
DREAMER   20th Century-Fox, 1979
KING OF THE MOUNTAIN   Universal, 1981
RETURN OF THE REBELS (TF)   Moonlight Productions/
   Filmways, 1981
THE FIRST TIME (TF)   Moonlight Productions, 1982
NIGHT PARTNERS (TF)   Moonlight Productions II, 1983
SUMMER FANTASIES (TF)   Moonlight Productions II, 1984
STARK: MIRROR IMAGE (TF)   CBS Entertainment, 1986
A DIFFERENT AFFAIR (TF)   Rogers-Samuels Productions, 1987
ROMAN HOLIDAY (TF)   Jerry Ludwig Enterprises/
   Paramount TV, 1987
AARON'S WAY: THE HARVEST (TF)   Blinn-Thorpe Productions/
   Lorimar Telepictures, 1988
FULL EXPOSURE: THE SEX TAPES SCANDAL (TF)
   Von Zerneck- Sertner Films, 1989
FOLLOW YOUR HEART (TF)   Force Ten Productions/
   Danson-Fauci Productions/NBC Productions, 1990
OPPOSITES ATTRACT (TF)   Bar-Gene Productions/Rastar
   Productions/von Zerneck-Sertner Films, 1990
A MOTHER'S JUSTICE (TF)   Green-Epstein Productions/
   Longbow Productions/Lorimar TV, 1991
WITHOUT A KISS GOODBYE (TF)   Green-Epstein
   Productions, 1993
BORN TOO SOON (TF)   Adam Productions/Republic
   Pictures, 1993
FRENCH SILK (TF)   Lee Rich Company/von Zerneck-Sertner
   Films, 1994

JONATHAN NOSSITER
RESIDENT ALIEN   Greycat Films, 1991

GEOFFREY NOTTAGE*
Telephone: Sydney, Australia, 2/8171804
Contact: Directors Guild of America - Los Angeles, 213/851-3671

WOMEN OF THE SUN (MS)   co-director with David Stevens,
   Stephen Wallace & James Ricketson, Generation Films,
   1983, Australian
WHITE MAN'S LEGEND (TF)   1983, Australian
DISPLACED PERSONS (TF)   1984, Australian
JOE WILSON (MS)   1986, Australian
THE LIZARD KING (TF)   1987, Australian

THIERRY NOTZ*
b. Switzerland
Agent: UTA - Beverly Hills, 310/273-6700

THE TERROR WITHIN   Concorde, 1989
WATCHERS II   Concorde, 1990
FORTUNES OF WAR   New Moon Productions, 1993

RACHID NOUGMANOV
Contact: Confederation of Film-Makers Unions, Vasilyevskaya
   Street 13, 123 825 Moscow, Russia, tel.: 095/250-4114

THE NEEDLE   Kazakhfilm, 1988, Soviet
THE WILD EAST: OR THE LAST SOVIET FILM   Mourat/Studio
   Kino, 1993, Kazakh

BLAINE NOVAK
Agent: Innovative Artists - Los Angeles, 310/553-5200

GOOD TO GO   Island Pictures, 1986
BLUE CHAMPAGNE   Independent, 1992

MARIA NOVARO
b. September 11, 1951 - Mexico City, Mexico
Contact: IMCINE, Tepic #40, P.B. Colonia Roma Sur, Mexico City,
   C.P. 06760, Mexico, tel.: 525/584-7283

AZUL CELESTE   DIAC/UNAM, 1990, Mexican
LOLA   Macondo Cine-Video/Conacite II/Cooperative Jose
   Revueltas/Television Espanola, 1990, Mexican
DANZON   Sony Pictures Classics, 1991, Mexican
EL JARDIN DE EDEN   Macondo Cine Video/IMCINE/Verseau
   International, 1994, Mexican

AMRAM NOWAK*
Contact: Directors Guild of America - New York City, 212/581-0370

THE CAFETERIA (TF)   Amram Nowak Associates, 1984
ISAAC IN AMERICA: A JOURNEY WITH ISAAC BASHEVIS
   SINGER (FD)   Amram Nowak Associates, 1986
NEIL SIMON: NOT JUST FOR LAUGHS (TD)   American Masters/
   WNET-TV/Amram Nowak Association for the Arts, 1989

CYRUS NOWRASTEH*
b. 1956 - U.S.A.
Agent: Caa - Beverly Hills, 310/288-4545

VEILED THREAT   *THREAT*   Comet Entertainment, 1989

PHILLIP NOYCE*
b. 1950 - Griffith, New South Wales, Australia
Agent: ICM - Los Angeles, 310/550-4000 or:
   The Cameron Creswell Agency - Sydney, tel.: 02/358-6433

BACKROADS   Cinema Ventures, 1978, Australian
NEWSFRONT   New Yorker, 1979, Australian
THE DISMISSAL (MS)   co-director with George Miller,
   George Ogilvie, Carl Schultz & John Power, 1983, Australian
HEATWAVE   New Line Cinema, 1982, Australian
THE COWRA BREAKOUT (MS)   co-director with Chris Noonan,
   Kennedy-Miller Productions, 1985, Australian
PROMISES TO KEEP   Laughing Kookaburra Productions,
   1986, Australian
ECHOES OF PARADISE   *SHADOWS OF THE PEACOCK*
   Castle Hill Productions/Quartet Films, 1987, Australian
DEAD CALM   Warner Bros., 1989, Australian
BLIND FURY   TriStar, 1989
PATRIOT GAMES   Paramount, 1992
SLIVER   Paramount, 1993
CLEAR AND PRESENT DANGER   Paramount, 1994

SIMON NUCHTERN
b. Belgium
Agent: Jack Tantleff, The Tantleff Office, 360 West 20th Street -
   Suite 4F, New York, NY 10011, 212/627-2105
Business: August Films, 321 West 44th Street, New York,
   NY 10036, 212/582-7025

GIRL GRABBERS   RAF Distribution, 1968
TO HEX WITH SEX   RAF Industries, 1969
THE COWARDS   Jaylo, 1970
WHAT DO I TELL THE BOYS AT THE STATION?   August, 1972
THE BROAD COALITION   August, 1972
THE BODYGUARD   Aquarius, 1976
SILENT MADNESS   Almi Pictures, 1984
NEW YORK NIGHTS   International Talent Marketing, 1984
SAVAGE DAWN   MAG Enterprises/Gregory Earls
   Productions, 1985

VICTOR NUÑEZ

Home: 227 Westminster Drive, Tallahassee, FL 32304,
   904/575-2696 or 904/618-3662
Agent: Paul Kohner, Inc. - Los Angeles, 310/550-1060

GAL YOUNG UN   Nuñez Films, 1979
A FLASH OF GREEN   Spectrafilm, 1984
RUBY IN PARADISE   October Films, 1993

WILLIAM NUNEZ

THE GAME   Shapiro Glickenhaus Entertainment, 1991

TREVOR NUNN

b. January 14, 1940 - Ipswich, Suffolk, England
Agent: ICM - London, tel.: 171/636-6565
Business: Homevale Ltd., Gloucester Mansions, Cambridge Circus,
   London WC2H 8HD, England, tel.: 171/240-5435

HEDDA   Brut Productions, 1975, British
LADY JANE   Paramount, 1986, British
PORGY AND BESS (TPF)   Primetime/BBC/Homevale/Greg Smith
   Productions/American Playhouse Great Performances/
   WNET-13/EMI Classics/ZDF/Arte/FR3/RTP/RM Associates,
   1993, U.S.-British-French-German

FRANCESCO NUTI

b. May 17, 1955 - Prato, Italy
Home: via G. Nicotera 29, Rome, Italy, tel.: 06/322-3394

CASABLANCA CASABLANCA   Union P.N./C.G. Silver Film,
   1985, Italian
STREGATI   Union P.N./C.G. Silver Film, 1986, Italian
CARUSO PASCOSKI DI PADRE POLACCO   Union P.N./Cecchi
   Gori Group/Tiger Cinematografica, 1988, Italian
WILLY SIGNORI E VENGO DA LONTANO   Warner Bros. Italia,
   1990, Italian
DONNE CON LE GONNE   Piccioli Film/Filmone/Filmauro,
   1991, Italian
OCCHIOPINOCCHIO   Cecchi Gori Group Tiger Cinematografica,
   1994, Italian

COLIN NUTLEY

b. England
Contact: Swedish Film Institute, P.O. Box 27126, 102 52 Stockholm,
   Sweden, tel.: 08/665-1100

THE NINTH BATALLION   Svensk Filmindustri, 1988, Swedish
BLACK JACK   Svensk Filmindustri, 1990, Swedish
HOUSE OF ANGELS   Sony Pictures Classics, 1992,
   Swedish-Danish-Norwegian
THE LAST DANCE   Sandrew Film/SVT-2/Metronome Productions/
   Schibstedt FilmEurimages/Nordisk Film & TV Fund/Swedish
   Film Institute, 1993, Swedish-Danish-Norwegian
HOUSE OF ANGELS: THE SECOND SUMMER   Sweetwater
   Productions/Svensk Filmindustri/SVT-2 Goteborg/Swedish
   Film Institute, 1994, Swedish

DAVID NUTTER*

Agent: Shapiro-Lichtman Talent Agency - Los Angeles, 310/859-8877

CEASE FIRE   Cineworld, 1985
TRANCERS 4: JACK OF SWORDS   Full Moon Entertainment, 1994

BRUNO NUYTTEN

b. August 28, 1945 - Paris, France
Home: 49, rue Monsieur le Prince, 75005 Paris, France,
   tel.: 1/43-26-73-60
Contact: French Film Office, 745 Fifth Avenue, New York,
   NY 10151, 212/832-8860

CAMILLE CLAUDEL   Orion Classics, 1988, French
ALBERT SOUFFRE   AMLF, 1992, French

CHRISTIAN I. NYBY II*

b. June 1, 1941 - Glendale, California
Agent: Irv Schechter Company - Beverly Hills, 310/278-8070

THE RANGERS (TF)   Universal TV/Mark VII Ltd., 1974
PINE CANYON IS BURNING (TF)   Universal TV, 1977
RIPTIDE (TF)   Stephen J. Cannell Productions, 1984
WACO & RINEHART (TF)   Touchstone Films TV, 1987
PERRY MASON: THE CASE OF THE SCANDALOUS
   SCOUNDREL (TF)   The Fred Silverman Company/
   Strathmore Productions/Viacom, 1987
PERRY MASON: THE CASE OF THE AVENGING ACE (TF)
   The Fred Silverman Company/Strathmore Productions/
   Viacom, 1988
A WHISPER KILLS (TF)   Sandy Hook Productions/Steve Tisch
   Company/Phoenix Entertainment Group, 1988
TOO GOOD TO BE TRUE (TF)   Newland-Raynor Productions, 1988
PERRY MASON: THE CASE OF THE LETHAL LESSON (TF)
   The Fred Silverman Company/Dean Hargrove Productions/
   Viacom, 1989
PERRY MASON: THE CASE OF THE MUSICAL MURDER (TF)
   The Fred Silverman Company/Dean Hargrove Productions/
   Viacom, 1989
PERRY MASON: THE CASE OF THE ALL-STAR ASSASSIN (TF)
   The Fred Silverman Company/Dean Hargrove Productions/
   Viacom, 1989
PERRY MASON: THE CASE OF THE PARISIAN PARADOX (TF)
   The Fred Silverman Company/Dean Hargrove Productions/
   Viacom, 1990
PERRY MASON: THE CASE OF THE POISONED PEN (TF)
   The Fred Silverman Company/Dean Hargrove Productions/
   Viacom, 1990
PERRY MASON: THE CASE OF THE DESPERATE
   DECEPTION (TF)   The Fred Silverman Company/Dean
   Hargrove Productions/Viacom, 1990
PERRY MASON: THE CASE OF THE DEFIANT DAUGHTER (TF)
   The Fred Silverman Company/Dean Hargrove Productions/
   Viacom, 1990
PERRY MASON: THE CASE OF THE RUTHLESS REPORTER (TF)
   The Fred Silverman Company/Dean Hargrove Productions/
   Viacom, 1991
PERRY MASON: THE CASE OF THE GLASS COFFIN (TF)
   The Fred Silverman Company/Dean Hargrove Productions/
   Viacom, 1991
PERRY MASON: THE CASE OF THE FATAL FASHION (TF)
   Dean Hargrove Productions/The Fred Silverman Company/
   Viacom, 1991
PERRY MASON: THE CASE OF THE FATAL FRAMING (TF)
   Dean Hargrove Productions/The Fred Silverman Company/
   Viacom, 1992
THE HOUSE ON SYCAMORE STREET (TF)   The Fred Silverman
   Company/Dean Hargrove Productions/Viacom, 1992
PERRY MASON: THE CASE OF THE RECKLESS ROMEO (TF)
   The Fred Silverman Company/Dean Hargrove Productions/
   Viacom, 1992
PERRY MASON: THE CASE OF THE HEARTBROKEN BRIDE (TF)
   Dean Hargrove Productions/The Fred Silverman Company/
   Viacom, 1992
PERRY MASON: THE CASE OF THE SKIN-DEEP SCANDAL (TF)
   The Fred Silverman Company/Dean Hargrove Productions/
   Viacom, 1993
PERRY MASON: THE CASE OF THE KILLER KISS (TF)
   Dean Hargrove Productions/The Fred Silverman Company/
   Viacom, 1993
A PERRY MASON MYSTERY: THE CASE OF THE WICKED
   WIVES (TF)   The Fred Silverman Company/Dean Hargrove
   Productions/Viacom, 1993

PETER NYDRLE

b. November 16, 1954 - Prague, Czechoslovakia
Business: Peter Nydrle Productions, P.O. Box 582, Beverly Hills,
   CA 90213, 310/659-6967

EUGENE AMONG US   F.A.M.U., 1981, Czechoslovakian

ROGER NYGARD

HIGH STRUNG   Greycat, 1993

**F
I
L
M

D
I
R
E
C
T
O
R
S**

SVEN NYKVIST
b. December 3, 1922 - Moheda, Sweden
Agent: Smith-Gosnell-Nicholson & Associates - Pacific Palisades,
310/459-0307

THE VINE BRIDGE 1964, Swedish
EN OCH EN 1978, Swedish
MARMELADUPPRORET 1980, Swedish
THE OX Castle Hill Productions, 1991, Swedish-Danish

RON NYSWANER
Agent: Sanford-Gross & Associates - Los Angeles, 310/208-2100

THE PRINCE OF PENNSYLVANIA New Line Cinema, 1988

O

VERN OAKLEY
MR. 247 In Pictures, 1994

DAN O'BANNON
b. 1946 - St. Louis, Missouri
Agent: APA - Los Angeles, 310/273-0744

THE RETURN OF THE LIVING DEAD Orion, 1985
THE RESURRECTED Scotti Bros., 1992

ROCKNE S. O'BANNON
Agent: CAA - Beverly Hills, 310/288-4545

FEAR (CTF) Vestron, 1990
DEADLY INVASION: THE KILLER BEE NIGHTMARE (TF)
St. Francis of Assisi Pictures/World International Network/von
Zerneck-Sertner Films, 1995

JIM O'BRIEN
b. February 15, 1947 - Dundee, Scotland
Agent: ICM - London, tel.: 171/636-6565

SHADOWS ON OUR SKIN (TF) BBC, 1980, British
JAKE'S END (TF) BBC, 1981, British
THE JEWEL IN THE CROWN (MS) ☆ co-director with
Christopher Morahan, Granada TV, 1984, British
THE MONOCLED MUTINEER (TF) BBC, 1986, British
THE DRESSMAKER Euro-American, 1988, British
THE YOUNG INDIANA JONES CHRONICLES: YOUNG INDIANA
JONES AND THE CURSE OF THE JACKAL (TF) co-director
with Carl Schultz, Lucasfilm Ltd./Paramount TV, 1992
FOREIGN AFFAIRS (CTF) Stagescreen Productions/Interscope
Communications, 1993

JOHN O'BRIEN
THE BIG DIS co-director with Gordon Eriksen, First Run
Features, 1989
VERMONT IS FOR LOVERS Zeitgeist Films, 1992

JEFFREY OBROW
THE DORM THAT DRIPPED BLOOD PRANKS co-director with
Stephen Carpenter, New Image Releasing, 1982
THE POWER co-director with Stephen Carpenter, Artists
Releasing Corporation/Film Ventures International, 1984
THE KINDRED co-director with Stephen Carpenter,
FM Entertainment, 1987
DEAN R. KOONTZ'S SERVANTS OF TWILIGHT SERVANTS OF
TWILIGHT (CTF) Trimark Pictures/Gibraltar Entertainment, 1991

MAURICE O'CALLAGHAN
Contact: Irish Film Institute, 6 Eustace Street, Dublin 2, Ireland,
tel.: 795744

BROKEN HARVEST Destiny Films, 1994, Irish

MIKE OCKRENT
Address: 124 West 60th Street - Apt. 45C, New York, NY 10023,
212/765-6627
Agent: The Lantz Office - New York City, 212/586-0200 or:
Saraband Associates - London, tel.: 171/609-5313

MRS. CAPPER'S BIRTHDAY (TF) BBC, 1985, British
DANCIN' THRU THE DARK Palace Pictures/British Screen/
BBC Films/Formost Films, 1990, British

JACK O'CONNELL
GREENWICH VILLAGE STORY Lion International, 1963
REVOLUTION (FD) Lopert, 1968
SWEDISH FLY GIRLS CHRISTA American International,
1971, U.S.-Danish

RAOUL O'CONNELL
BOYS LIFE co-director with Brian Sloan & Robert Lee King,
Strand Releasing, 1994

JAMES O'CONNOLLY
Address: 61 Edith Grove, London SW10, England, tel.: 171/352-1242

THE HI-JACKERS Butcher, 1964, British
SMOKESCREEN Butcher, 1964, British
THE LITTLE ONES Columbia, 1965, British
BERSERK! Columbia, 1968, British
THE VALLEY OF GWANGI Warner Bros., 1969, British
SOPHIE'S PLACE CROOKS AND CORONETS Warner Bros.,
1969, British
HORROR ON SNAPE ISLAND BEYOND THE FOG
Fanfare, 1972, British
MISTRESS PAMELA Fanfare, 1974, British

PAT O'CONNOR*
b. 1943 - Ardmore, Ireland
Agent: UTA - Beverly Hills, 310/273-6700 or
ICM - London, tel.: 171/636-6565

CAL Warner Bros., 1984, Irish
A MONTH IN THE COUNTRY Orion Classics, 1987, British
STARS AND BARS Columbia, 1988
THE JANUARY MAN MGM/UA, 1989
FOOLS OF FORTUNE New Line Cinema, 1990, British
FORCE OF DUTY BBC Northern Ireland/RTE Dublin, 1992,
Northern Irish-Irish
ZELDA (CTF) Turner Pictures/ZDF Enterprises/ORF/SRG,
1993, U.S.-German
CIRCLE OF FRIENDS Savoy Pictures, 1995, British-Irish

DAVID ODELL
Agent: The Peter Turner Agency - Los Angeles, 310/315-4772

MARTIANS GO HOME Taurus Entertainment, 1990

KEITH O'DEREK
STRAIGHT FROM THE STREETS (FD) co-director with
Robert Corsini, Upfront Productions, 1994

STEVE OEDEKERK
ACE VENTURA II: WHEN NATURE CALLS Warner Bros., 1995

PETER O'FALLON*
Agent: William Morris Agency - Beverly Hills, 310/859-4000

DEAD SILENCE (TF) FNM Films, 1991

TAKAO OGAWARA

Contact: Nihon Eiga Kantoku Kyokai (Japan Film Directors
Association), La Fontenu Building - 4th Floor, 23-2 Maruyama-cho,
Shibuya-ku, Tokyo, Japan, tel.: 3/3461-4411

GODZILLA VS. MOTHRA   Toho, 1992, Japanese
GODZILLA VS. MECHA-GODZILLA   Toho, 1993, Japanese
YAMATO TAKERU   Toho, 1994, Japanese

GEORGE OGILVIE

Agent: Hilary Linstead and Associates, 223 Commonwealth Street,
Surry Hills, NSW 2010, Australia
Contact: Australian Film Commission, 150 William Street,
Woolloomooloo NSW 2011, Australia, tel.: 2/321-6444

THE DISMISSAL (MS)   co-director with George Miller,
Phillip Noyce, Carl Schultz & John Power, 1983, Australian
BODYLINE (MS)   co-director with Carl Schultz, Denny Lawrence &
Lex Marinos, 1984, Australian
MAD MAX BEYOND THUNDERDOME   co-director with
George Miller, Warner Bros., 1985, Australian
SHORT CHANGED   Greater Union, 1985, Australian
THE PLACE AT THE COAST   Daedalus Films, 1986, Australian
THE SHIRALEE (MS)   SAFC Productions, 1988, Australian
PRINCESS KATE (TF)   Australian Children's TV Foundation/
Australian Broadcasting Corporation/Revcom, 1990, Australian
THE CROSSING   South Gate Entertainment, 1990, Australian
THE BATTLERS (MS)   South Australian Film Corporation/Australian
Film Finance Corporation, 1994, Australian

KOHEI OGURI

b. 1945 - Guma Prefecture, Japan
Contact: Nihon Eiga Kantoku Kyokai (Japan Film Directors
Association), La Fontenu Building -4th Floor, 23-2 Maruyama-cho,
Shibuya-ku, Tokyo, Japan, tel.: 3/3461-4411

MUDDY RIVER   Kimura Productions, 1981, Japanese
FOR KAYAKO   Theatre Group Himawari, 1984, Japanese
THE STING OF DEATH   Shochiku, 1990, Japanese

GERRY O'HARA

b. 1924 - Boston, Lincolnshire, England
Address: Flat K, 51 Elm Park Gardens, London SW10 9PA,
England, tel.: 171/352-6153

MODELS, INC. *THAT KIND OF GIRL*   Mutual, 1963, British
A GAME FOR THREE LOSERS   Embassy, 1963, British
THE PLEASURE GIRLS   Times, 1965, British
MAROC 7   Paramount, 1966, British
AMSTERDAM AFFAIR   Lippert, 1968, British
FIDELIA   1970, British
ALL THE RIGHT NOISES   20th Century-Fox, 1971, British
THE BRUTE   Rank, 1976, British
LEOPARD IN THE SNOW   New World, 1978, Canadian-British
THE BITCH   Brent Walker Productions, 1979, British
FANNY HILL   Playboy Enterprises, 1983, British
STRICTLY FOR CASH   Harry Alan Towers Productions,
1984, British
THE MUMMY LIVES   Cannon, 1993, British-Israeli

TERRENCE O'HARA*

Agent: The Maggie Field Agency - Studio City, 818/980-2001

THE PERFECT BRIDE (CTF)   Perfect Bride Inc./Westwind
Productions, 1991, Canadian

MICHAEL O'HERLIHY*

b. April 1, 1928 - Dublin, Ireland
Home: Rockfort House, Innishannon, County Cork, Ireland,
tel.: 201/775385

THE FIGHTING PRINCE OF DONEGAL   Buena Vista,
1966, British-U.S.
THE ONE AND ONLY GENUINE, ORIGINAL FAMILY BAND
Buena Vista, 1968
SMITH!   Buena Vista, 1969

DEADLY HARVEST (TF)   CBS, Inc., 1972
YOUNG PIONEERS (TF)   ABC Circle Films, 1976
KISS ME, KILL ME (TF)   Columbia TV, 1976
YOUNG PIONEERS' CHRISTMAS (TF)   ABC Circle Films, 1976
PETER LUNDY AND THE MEDICINE HAT STALLION (TF)
Ed Friendly Productions, 1977
BACKSTAIRS AT THE WHITE HOUSE (MS)   Ed Friendly
Productions, 1979
THE FLAME IS LOVE (TF)   Ed Friendly Productions/
Friendly-O'Herlihy Ltd., 1979
DALLAS COWBOYS CHEERLEADERS II (TF)   Aubrey-Hamner
Productions, 1980
DETOUR TO TERROR (TF)   Orenthal Productions/Playboy
Productions/Columbia TV, 1980
THE GREAT CASH GIVEAWAY GETAWAY (TF)
Penthouse Productions/Cine Guarantors, Inc., 1980
CRY OF THE INNOCENT (TF)   Tara Productions, 1980
DESPERATE VOYAGE (TF)   Barry Weitz Films/Joe Wizan TV
Productions, 1980
A TIME FOR MIRACLES (TF)   ABC Circle Films, 1980
THE MILLION DOLLAR FACE (TF)   Nephi-Hamner
Productions, 1981
I MARRIED WYATT EARP (TF)   Osmond TV Productions, 1983
TWO BY FORSYTH (TF)   Tara Productions/Mobil Corporation,
1984, U.S.-Irish
HOOVER VS. THE KENNEDYS: THE SECOND CIVIL WAR (TF)
Sunrise Films/Selznick-Glickman Productions, 1987, Canadian

TOM O'HORGAN*

Address: 840 Broadway, New York, NY 10003
Business Manager: Carl Goldstein, 250 West 57th Street - Suite 2332,
New York, NY 10107, 212/581-3780

FUTZ   Commonwealth United, 1969
RHINOCEROS   American Film Theatre, 1974

KIHACHI OKAMOTO

b. 1924 - Totori Prefecture, Japan
Contact: Nihon Eiga Kantoku Kyokai (Japan Film Directors
Association), La Fontenu Building -4th Floor, 23-2 Maruyama-cho,
Shibuya-ku, Tokyo, Japan, tel.: 3/3461-4411

EVERYTHING ABOUT MARRIAGE   Toho, 1958, Japanese
YOUNG GIRLS   Toho, 1958, Japanese
ONE DAY WE ARE...   Toho, 1959, Japanese
GANGLAND BOSS   Toho, 1959, Japanese
INDEPENDENT GANG   Toho, 1959, Japanese
BANDITS IN THE UNIVERSITY   Toho, 1960, Japanese
INDEPENDENT GANG GO TO THE WEST   Toho, 1960, Japanese
BULLET MARK OF GANGLAND   Toho, 1961, Japanese
THE BOSS DIED FOR THE SUNRISE   Toho, 1961, Japanese
HELL PARTY   Tokyo Eiga, 1961, Japanese
PAY ROBBER   Toho, 1962, Japanese
OPERATION GUTTER RAT   Toho, 1962, Japanese
MANSHI EBURI'S GLAMOROUS LIFE   Toho, 1963, Japanese
SAMURAI ASSASSIN   Toho, 1963, Japanese
OH BOMB   Toho, 1964, Japanese
SAMURAI   Mifune Productions/Toho, 1965, Japanese
BLOOD AND DOOM   Toho/Mifune Productions, 1965, Japanese
THE SWORD OF DOOM *DAIBOSATSU PASS*   Toho/Takarazuka
Eiga, 1966, Japanese
THE KILLING GENERATION   Toho, 1967, Japanese
THE EMPEROR AND THE GENERAL *THE LONGEST DAY
IN JAPAN*   Toho, 1967, Japanese
KILL!   Toho, 1968, Japanese
THE HUMAN BULLET   ATG/Human Bullet Association,
1968, Japanese
RED LION   Mifune Productions, 1969, Japanese
ZATOICHI MEETS YOJIMBO   Toei, 1970, Japanese
SHOWA ERA AGITATION - OKINAWA DECISIVE BATTLE
Toho, 1971, Japanese
JAPANESE THREE MUSKETEERS: GOODBYE TOKYO
Tokyo Eiga, 1972, Japanese
JAPANESE THREE MUSKETEERS: HAKATA   Tokyo Eiga,
1973, Japanese
THICK GREENERY   Toho, 1974, Japanese
TOKKAN   Kihachi Productions/ATG, 1975, Japanese
SANSHIRO SUGATA   Toho, 1977, Japanese

DYNAMITE DONDON   Toei/Daiei, 1978, Japanese
BLUE CHRISTMAS   Toho, 1978, Japanese
CHEERING SONG OF THE SPIRITS OF THE WAR DEAD
   Tokyo Channel 12, 1979, Japanese
RECENTLY, I FEEL CHARLESTON   Kihachi Production/ATG,
   1981, Japanese
DIXIELAND DAIMYO   Daiei, 1986, Japanese
RAINBOW KIDS: THE BIG KIDNAPPING   Kihachi Productions/
   Nichimen/Fuji 8, 1991, Japanese
EAST MEETS WEST   Shochiku, 1995, Japanese

STEVEN OKAZAKI
b. March 12, 1952 - Los Angeles, California

UNFINISHED BUSINESS (FD)   Mouchette Films, 1986
LIVING ON TOKYO TIME   Skouras Pictures, 1987
TROUBLED PARADISE (FD)   Farallon Films, 1992
THE LISA THEORY   Farallon Films/Colossal Pictures, 1994

KAZUYOSHI OKUYAMA
Business: Shochiku Co., Ltd., 13-5, Tsukiji 1-Chome, Chuo-ku,
   Tokyo 104, Japan, tel.: 3/3542-5551

THE MYSTERY OF RAMPO   *RAMPO*   The Samuel Goldwyn
   Company, 1994, Japanese

RONAN O'LEARY
Contact: Irish Film Centre, 6 Eustace Street, Dublin 2, Ireland,
   tel.: 795744

DRIFTWOOD   Mary-Breen Farrelly Productions, 1995, Irish

CHRISTOPHER OLGIATI
SOUTHERN JUSTICE: THE MURDER OF MEDGAR EVERS (CTD)
   HBO/BBC, 1994, U.S.-British

JOEL OLIANSKY*
b. October 11, 1935 - New York, New York
Agent: CAA - Beverly Hills, 310/288-4545

THE COMPETITION   Columbia, 1980
ALFRED HITCHCOCK PRESENTS (TF)   co-director with
   Steve DeJarnatt, Randa Haines & Fred Walton,
   Universal TV, 1985
THE SILENCE AT BETHANY   Keener Productions/American
   Playhouse Theatrical Films, 1988
IN DEFENSE OF A MARRIED MAN (TF)   The Landsburg
   Company, 1990

KEN OLIN*
Agent: UTA - Beverly Hills, 310/273-6700

DOING TIME ON MAPLE DRIVE (TF)   FNM Films, 1992
WHITE FANG 2: MYTH OF THE WHITE WOLF   Buena Vista, 1994
IN PURSUIT OF HONOR (CTF)   Marian Rees Associates/Village
   Roadshow Pictures/HBO Pictures, 1995, U.S.-Australian

DAVID OLIVER
CAVEGIRL   Crown International, 1985

MICHAEL OLIVER
THE DRAGON GATE   Century Group Ltd., 1994

RON OLIVER
Agent: Gray/Goodman - Beverly Hills, 310/276-7070 or:
   Lesley Harrison, MGA, 10 St. Mary Street - Suite 510,
   Toronto, Ontario, M4Y 1P9, Canada, 416/964-3302

THE LAST KISS - PROM NIGHT III   co-director, 1989, Canadian
DELUSIONS   Norstar Entertainment, 1991, Canadian
LIAR'S EDGE (CTF)   Showtime/New Line Cinema/Norstar
   Entertainment, 1992, Canadian

RUBY L. OLIVER
LOVE YOUR MAMA   Hemdale, 1993

HECTOR OLIVERA
b. April 5, 1931 - Olivos, Argentina
Contact: Aries International, S.A., Lavalle 1860, 1051 Buenos Aires,
   Argentina, tel.: 46-9249

PSEXOANALISIS   Aries Films, 1967, Argentine
LAS VENGANZAS DE BETO SANCHEZ   Aries Films,
   1972, Argentine
LA PATAGONIA REBELDE   Aries Films, 1974, Argentine
EL MUERTO   Aries Films, 1975, Argentine
LA NONA   Aries Films, 1978, Argentine
LOS VIERNES DE LA ETERNIDAD   Aries Films, 1981, Argentine
BUENOS AIRES ROCK 82 (FD)   Aries Films, 1983, Argentine
A FUNNY DIRTY LITTLE WAR   *NO HABRA MAS PENAS
   NI OLVIDO*   Cinevista, 1984, Argentine
WIZARDS OF THE LOST KINGDOM   Concorde/Cinema Group,
   1985, U.S.-Argentine
BARBARIAN QUEEN   Concorde/Cinema Group,
   1985, U.S.-Argentine
COCAINE WARS   Concorde, 1986, U.S.-Argentine
NIGHT OF THE PENCILS   Marquis Pictures, 1986, Argentine
TWO TO TANGO   Concorde, 1989, U.S.-Argentine
PLAY MURDER FOR ME   Concorde, 1991, U.S.-Argentine
THE GOSPEL ACCORDING TO MARCUS   Ibero-Americana Films/
   Aries Cinematografica, 1991, Spanish-Argentine
CUENTOS DE BORGES I   co-director with Gerardo Vera,
   Iberoamericana/TVE/Sociedad Estatal Quinto Centenario,
   1991, Spanish
EL CASO MARIA SOLEDAD   Aries Cinematografica,
   1993, Argentine
UNA SOMBRA YA PRONTO SERAS   Hector Olivera/Tercer Milenio/
   Instituto Nacional de Cinematografia, 1994, Argentine

MARTY OLLSTEIN
DANGEROUS LOVE   Concorde, 1988

ERMANNO OLMI
b. July 24, 1931 - Bergamo, Italy
Home: via Rigoni di Sotto 36, Asiago, Italy, tel.: 0424/63220

IL TEMPO SI E FERMATO   Sezione Cinema Edison Volta,
   1959, Italian
THE SOUND OF TRUMPETS   Janus, 1961, Italian
THE FIANCES   Janus, 1963, Italian
AND THERE CAME A MAN   Brandon, 1965, Italian
UN CERTO GIORNO   Cinema Spa/Italnoleggio, 1968, Italian
I RECUPERANTI (TF)   RAI/Produzione Palumbo, 1969, Italian
DURANTE L'ESTATE (TF)   RAI, 1971, Italian
LA CIRCOSTANZA (TF)   RAI/Italnoleggio, 1974, Italian
THE TREE OF WOODEN CLOGS   New Yorker, 1979, Italian,
   originally made for televison
CAMMINACAMMINA   Grange Communications, 1983, Italian
MILANO '83 (FD)   1983, Italian
LONG LIVE THE LADY   International Film Exchange, 1987, Italian
LA LEGGENDA DEL SANTO BEVITORE   Columbia Italia,
   1988, Italian
LUNGO IL FIUME (TD)   RAI/Cinemaundici, 1992, Italian
IL SEGRETO DEL BOSH VECCHIO   Pentafilm, 1993, Italian
THE BIBLE: GENESIS (TF)   LUBE Productions/Lux/Betafilm/
   Raiuno/France-2/ORF/Antena-3/BSkyB/NCRV, 1994,
   Italian-German-French

EDWARD JAMES OLMOS*
b. February 24, 1947 - Los Angeles, California
Agent: The Artists Agency - Los Angeles, 310/277-7779

AMERICAN ME   Universal, 1992

WILLIAM OLSEN
b. December 17, 1950 - North Carolina

THE HAUNTED PALACE (TF)   Poe Society, 1978
GETTING IT ON   Comworld, 1983

ROCKIN' ROAD TRIP   Troma, 1985
AFTER SCHOOL   Moviestore Entertainment, 1989
RETURN TO EDEN   Quest Entertainment, 1989

STELLAN OLSSON
Contact: Swedish Film Institute, P.O. Box 27-126, S-102-52
   Stockholm, Sweden, tel.: 08/665-1100

GOOD NIGHT, IRENE   Triangelfilm/Kedjan/Moviemakers/SVT2/
   Danmarks Radio/Kenneth Madsen Filmproduktion/Nordic
   Film & TV Fund, 1994, Swedish-Danish

DAVID O'MALLEY
b. June 14, 1944 - Woonsocket, Rhode Island
Agent: The Daniel Ostroff Agency - Los Angeles, 310/278-2020

MOUNTAIN MAN   Taft Entertainment, 1978
THE CHAMPION (TF)   Ammi Productions, 1982
AWESOME LOTUS   Double "O" Associates, 1983
KID COLTER   TMS Pictures, 1985
EASY WHEELS   Fries Distribution, 1989

EMIKO OMORI
HOT SUMMER WINDS (TF)   KCET-TV/One Pass Inc., 1991

KAZUKI OMORI
b. 1952 - Osaka Prefecture, Japan
Contact: Nihon Eiga Kantoku Kyokai (Japan Film Directors
   Association), La Fontenu Building -4th Floor, 23-2 Maruyama-cho,
   Shibuya-ku, Tokyo, Japan, tel.: 3/3461-4411

I CAN'T WAIT UNTIL DARK   Momoiroyugi, 1975, Japanese
ORANGE ROAD EXPRESS   Shochiku/Omori Productions,
   1978, Japanese
HIPPOCRATES   Cinema Hauto/ATG, 1980, Japanese
LISTEN TO THE WINDSONG   Cinema Hauto, 1981, Japanese
SUKAMPIN WALK   Watanabe Productions/Cinema Hauto/New
   Century Producers, 1984, Japanese
YOU'VE GOT THE CHANCE   Watanabe Productions/New Century
   Producers/Cinema Hauto, 1985, Japanese
WOMEN IN LOVE   Toho, 1986, Japanese
TAKE IT EASY: MODERN TIMES   Watanabe Productions/New
   Century Producers, 1986, Japanese
WOMEN OF SAYONARA   Toho, 1987, Japanese
TOTTO-CHANNEL   Toho, 1987, Japanese
GODZILLA VS. BIOLLANTE   Toho, 1989, Japanese
THE AFTERNOON FLOWER IS FALLING   Haruki Kadokawa
   Productions, 1989, Japanese
THE REASON WHY I GOT SICK   Cinema Hauto/Suntory,
   1990, Japanese
GODZILLA VS. KING GHIDORAH   Toho, 1991, Japanese
MR. MOONLIGHT   Shochiku, 1991, Japanese
PASSING THE CUP   Toei, 1992, Japanese
DAI-SHITSUREN   Toei, 1995, Japanese

RON O'NEAL
b. September 1, 1937 - Utica, New York
Agent: Los Angeles, 213/857-1234

SUPERFLY T.N.T.   Paramount, 1973
UP AGAINST THE WALL   African American Images, 1991

ROBERT VINCENT O'NEIL*
Contact: Directors Guild of America - Los Angeles, 213/851-3671

THE LOVING TOUCH   Medford, 1970
BLOOD MANIA   Crown International, 1971
WONDER WOMEN   1973
PACO   Cinema National, 1975
ANGEL   New World, 1984
AVENGING ANGEL   New World, 1985
THE SET-UP   Riverwalk Films, 1993
CHAMPION   Peacock, 1995

MARCEL OPHULS
b. November 1, 1927 - Frankfurt-am-Main, Germany
Address: 10, rue Ernest Deloison, 9220 Neuilly, France,
   tel.: 1/46-24-89-78
Contact: French Film Office, 745 Fifth Avenue, New York,
   NY 10151, 212/832-8860

LOVE AT TWENTY   co-director with Francois Truffaut,
   Andrzej Wajda, Renzo Rossellini & Shintaro Ishihara,
   Embassy, 1962, French-Italian-Japanese-Polish-West German
BANANA PEEL   Pathe Contemporary, 1965, French-Italian
FEU A VOLONTE   1965, French-Italian
MUNICH, OU LA PRIX POUR CENT ANS (TD)   1967, French
CLAVIGO (TF)   1970, French
THE HARVEST OF MY LAI (TD)   1970, French
AMERICA REVISITED (TD)   1971, French
ZWEI GANZE TAGE (TF)   1971, West German
THE SORROW AND THE PITY (FD)   Cinema 5, 1972,
   French-Swiss-West German
A SENSE OF LOSS (FD)   Cinema 5, 1972, U.S.-Swiss
THE MEMORY OF JUSTICE (FD)   Paramount, 1976,
   British-West German
KORTNER GESCHICHTE (TD)   1980, West German
YORKTOWN, LE SANS D'UNE BETAILLE (TD)   1982, French
HOTEL TERMINUS: THE LIFE AND TIMES OF KLAUS BARBIE (FD)
   The Samuel Goldwyn Company, 1988, French
NOVEMBER DAYS (TD)   BBC/Regina Ziegler Productions/Arthur
   Cohn Productions, 1992, British-German
VEILLES D'ARMES: LE JOURNALISME EN TEMPS DE GUERRE
   (1ER ET 2EME VOYAGES) (FD)   Little Bear Productions/
   Premiere/Canal Plus/BBC, 1994, French-German-British

PEER J. OPPENHEIMER
Business: Peer Oppenheimer Productions, Inc., 3971 Royal
   Oak Place, Encino, CA 91436, 818/995-0234

TERROR IN PARADISE   Concorde, 1991, U.S.-Filipino

MARIO ORFINI
Contact: Ministero del Turismo e dello Spettacolo, Via Della
   Ferratella in Laterano, 45, 00184 Rome, Italy, tel.: 779309

CYBEREDEN   Eidoscope/Canal Plus, 1993, Italian-French

DOMINIC ORLANDO
KNIGHTS OF THE CITY   New World, 1986

STUART ORME*
Address: 40 Weston Park, Thames Ditton, Surrey KT7 0HL,
   England, tel.: 181/398-6839
Agent: UTA - Beverly Hills, 310/273-6700 or
   ICM - London, tel.: 171/636-6565

THE FEAR (MS)   Euston Films, 1987, British
THE HEIST (CTF)   HBO Pictures/Chris-Rose Productions/
   Paramount TV, 1989
THE WOLVES OF WILLOUGHBY CHASE   Zenith Productions,
   1990, British
HANDS OF A MURDERER (TF)   Storke-Fuisz Productions/
   Yorkshire TV, 1990, British-U.S.
SHRINKS (TF)   Euston Films, 1991, British
JUTE CITY (TF)   BBC, 1991, British
THE BLACKHEATH POISONINGS (TF)   Central Independent TV/
   WGBH-Boston, 1992, British-U.S.
ROBERT A. HEINLEIN'S THE PUPPET MASTERS   THE PUPPET
   MASTERS   Buena Vista, 1994

PETER ORMROD
Contact: Irish Film Institute, 6 Eustace Street, Dublin 2, Ireland,
   tel.: 679-5744

EAT THE PEACH   Skouras Pictures, 1986, Irish

EMMERICH OROSS
b. September 20, 1940 - Hungary
Home: P.O. Box 46163, Denver, CO 80201, 303/733-3265

FORM OF LIFE (TD)   1966, Hungarian
DESIGN FOR AUTOMOBILES (TD)   1966, Hungarian
TESTAMENTUM HUNGARORUM (TD)   1967, Hungarian
SOUTH AMERICAN PHOTOGRAPHS (TF)   1969, Hungarian
THE WITCH DOCTORS OF THE ORINOCO (TD)   1969, Hungarian
AGAIN   1969, Hungarian
THE PIAROA INDIANS (TD)   1970, Hungarian
KODALY'S METHODS (FD)   1970, Hungarian
THE PRINCESS (TF)   1970, Hungarian
PHOTOMEDITATION (TF)   1971, Hungarian
MADAMA BUTTERFLY (TF)   Racana Company, 1984
LAST CALL   Vu Jade Productions, 1985
COLORADO INDIAN MARKET (TD)   Diva Productions, 1988
KIRKLAND'S VISUAL LANGUAGE (TD)   KRMA-Denver, 1993

DENNIS O'ROURKE
b. 1945 - Brisbane, Australia
Contact: Australian Film Commission, 150 William Street,
   Woolloomooloo NSW 2011, Australia, tel.: 2/321-6444

YUMI YET (FD)   Dennis O'Rourke & Associates, 1976, Australian
ILEKSEN (FD)   Dennis O'Rourke & Associates, 1978, Australian
YAP...HOW DID THEY KNOW WE'D LIKE TV? (FD)   Dennis
   O'Rourke & Associates, 1980, Australian
THE SHARKCALLERS OF KONTU (FD)   Dennis O'Rourke &
   Associates, 1982, Australian
THE HUMAN FACE OF THE PACIFIC (FD)   Dennis O'Rourke &
   Associates, 1984, Australian
...COULDN'T BE FAIRER (FD)   Dennis O'Rourke & Associates,
   1984, Australian
HALF LIFE: A PARABLE FOR THE NUCLEAR AGE (FD)
   Kino International, 1985, Australian
"CANNIBAL TOURS" (FD)   Dennis O'Rourke & Associates,
   1988, Australian
THE GOOD WOMAN OF BANGKOK (FD)   Roxie Releasing,
   1991, Australian

JAMES ORR*
Agent: CAA - Beverly Hills, 310/288-4545

BREAKING ALL THE RULES   New World, 1985, Canadian
YOUNG HARRY HOUDINI (TF)   Walt Disney TV, 1987
MR. DESTINY   Buena Vista, 1990
MAN OF THE HOUSE   Buena Vista, 1995

JAMES R. ORR
THEY STILL CALL ME BRUCE   co-director with Johnny Yune,
   Shapiro Entertainment, 1987

KENNY ORTEGA*
b. Palo Alto, California
Address: 5309 Fulton Avenue, Van Nuys, CA 91401
Agent: CAA - Beverly Hills, 310/288-4545

NEWSIES   Buena Vista, 1992
HOCUS POCUS   Buena Vista, 1993

NAGISA OSHIMA
b. March 31, 1932 - Kyoto, Japan
Contact: Nihon Eiga Kantoku Kyokai (Japan Film Directors
   Association), La Fontenu Building -4th Floor, 23-2 Maruyama-cho,
   Shibuya-ku, Tokyo, Japan, tel.: 3/3461-4411

A TOWN OF LOVE AND HOPE   Shochiku, 1959, Japanese
CRUEL STORY OF YOUTH   NAKED YOUTH, A STORY
   OF CRUELTY   Shochiku, 1960, Japanese
THE SUN'S BURIAL   Shochiku, 1960, Japanese
NIGHT AND FOG IN JAPAN   Shochiku, 1960, Japanese
THE CATCH   Palace Productions/Taiho, 1961, Japanese
SHIRO TOKISADA FROM AMAKUSA   THE REVOLUTIONARY
   Toei, 1962, Japanese
A SMALL CHILD'S FIRST ADVENTURE   Nissei Insurance
   Company, 1964, Japanese

IT'S ME HERE, BELLETT   Society of Japanese Film Directors,
   1964, Japanese
THE PLEASURES OF THE FLESH   Sozosha/Shochiku,
   1965, Japanese
THE DIARY OF YUNBOGI (FD)   Sozosha/Shibata Organization,
   1965, Japanese
VIOLENCE AT NOON   Sozosha/Shochiku, 1966, Japanese
BAND OF NINJA   Sozosha/ATG, 1967, Japanese
A TREATISE ON JAPANESE BAWDY SONGS   SING A SONG
   OF SEX   Sozosha/Shochiku, 1967, Japanese
JAPANESE SUMMER: DOUBLE SUICIDE   Sozosha/Shochiku,
   1967, Japanese
DEATH BY HANGING   Grove Press, 1968, Japanese
THREE RESURRECTED DRUNKARDS   Sozosha/Shochiku,
   1968, Japanese
DIARY OF A SHINJUKU THIEF   Grove Press, 1968, Japanese
BOY   Grove Press, 1969, Japanese
THE MAN WHO LEFT HIS WILL ON FILM   Sozosha/ATG,
   1970, Japanese
THE CEREMONY   New Yorker, 1971, Japanese
DEAR SUMMER SISTER   New Yorker, 1973, Japanese
IN THE REALM OF THE SENSES   Surrogate Releasing, 1976,
   Japanese-French
EMPIRE OF PASSION   CORRIDA OF LOVE   Barbary Coast,
   1980, Japanese
MERRY CHRISTMAS, MR. LAWRENCE   Universal,
   1983, British-Japanese
MAX MON AMOUR   Greenwich Films/Films A2, 1986, French

AZIZ M. OSMAN
b. Malaysia
Contact: FINAS (The National Film Development Corporation
   Malaysia), Studio Merdeka Complex, Lot 1662, Hulu Klang,
   68000 Ampang, Selangor, Malaysia, tel.: 03/408-5722

MAWAS (TF)   Malaysian
UBI (TF)   Malaysian
KAKI MONYET (TF)   Malaysian
TIME BOMB (TF)   Malaysian
ALINA (TF)   Malaysian
PRIMADONA (MS)   Malaysian
FENOMENA   Teletrade Sdn. Bhd., 1990, Malaysian
FANTASIA   Teletrade Sdn. Bhd., 1991, Malaysian
XX RAY   Nizarman Productions, 1992, Malaysian
XX RAY 2   Nizarman Productions/TV 3, 1994, Malaysian

CLIFF OSMOND
b. February 26, 1937
Contact: Screen Actors Guild - Los Angeles, 213/954-1600

THE PENITENT   Cineworld, 1988

SAM O'STEEN*
b. November 6, 1923
Contact: Morgan & Martindale, 10780 Santa Monica Blvd. -
   Suite 280, Los Angeles, CA 90025, 310/474-0810

A BRAND NEW LIFE (TF)   Tomorrow Entertainment, 1973
I LOVE YOU, GOODBYE (TF)   Tomorrow Entertainment, 1974
QUEEN OF THE STARDUST BALLROOM (TF) ☆
   Tomorrow Entertainment, 1975
HIGH RISK (TF)   Danny Thomas Productions/MGM TV, 1976
SPARKLE   Warner Bros., 1976
LOOK WHAT'S HAPPENED TO ROSEMARY'S BABY (TF)
   Paramount TV, 1976
THE BEST LITTLE GIRL IN THE WORLD (TF)   Aaron Spelling
   Productions, 1981
KIDS DON'T TELL (TF)   Chris-Rose Productions/Viacom
   Productions, 1985

SUZANNE OSTEN
Contact: Swedish Film Institute, P.O. Box 27-126, S-102-52
   Stockholm, Sweden, tel.: 08/665-1100

SPEAK UP! IT'S SO DARK   Swedish
JUST YOU & ME   Mekano Pictures/Swedish Film Institute/
   FilmTeknik/Getfilm/Per Holst Filmproduktion/Nordic Film &
   TV Fund, 1994, Swedish-Danish

MARTIN OSTROW
Business: Fine Cut Productions - Boston, 617/787-4141

AMERICA AND THE HOLOCAUST: DECEIT AND
    INDIFFERENCE (TD) PBS/The American Experience, 1994

THADDEUS O'SULLIVAN
Agent: Peters Fraser & Dunlop - London, tel.: 171/344-1000

DECEMBER BRIDE   M.D. WaxProds./Courier Films,
    1990, Irish-British
ALL OUR FAULT   Little Bird/Film Four Intl./British Screen/Irsh
    Film Board, 1995, Irish-British

DOMINIQUE OTHENIN-GIRARD
Agent: The Apelian Agency - Bel Air, 310/476-4732

HALLOWEEN 5   Galaxy, 1989
NIGHT ANGEL   Fries Distribution, 1990
OMEN IV: THE AWAKENING (TF)   co-director with Jorge Montesi,
    FNM Films, 1991
PRIVATE LESSONS II   Nu Image, 1994
BEYOND DESIRE   1994

KATSUHIRO OTOMO
Contact: Nihon Eiga Kantoku Kyokai (Japan Film Directors
    Association), La Fontenu Building -4th Floor, 23-2 Maruyama-cho,
    Shibuya-ku, Tokyo, Japan, tel.: 3/3461-4411

AKIRA (AF)   Streamline Pictures, 1989, Japanese
WORLD APARTMENT HORROR   Embodiment Films,
    1991, Japanese

LINDA OTTO*
Business: Linda Otto & Associates, 11811 W. Olympic Blvd.,
    Los Angeles, CA 90064, 310/996-7740
Agent: The Gersh Agency - Beverly Hills, 310/274-6611

UNSPEAKABLE ACTS (TF)   The Landsburg Company, 1990
PRISONERS OF WEDLOCK (CTD)   The Landsburg
    Company, 1991
A MOTHER'S RIGHT: THE ELIZABETH MORGAN STORY (TF)
    The Landsburg Company, 1992
GREGORY K (TF)   Spectator Films/Michael Jaffe Films, 1993
NOT IN MY FAMILY (TF)   Robert Greenwald Films, 1993

FILIPPO OTTONI
Home: via Famagosta 8, Rome, Italy, tel.: 06/325-3089

QUESTO SI' CHE E'AMORE   Creative Films Century, 1977, Italian
DETECTIVE SCHOOL DROPOUTS   Cannon, 1986, U.S.-Italian
STRAY DAYS   Cannon, 1987, Italian
L'ASSASSINO E' QUELLO CON LE SCARPE GIALLE   Sacis,
    1995, Italian

IDRISSA OUEDRAOGO
b. 1952 - Banfora, Upper Volta (Burkina Faso)
Business: Les Films de la Plaine, 148 Rue du Fauborg Saint
    Denis, 75010 Paris, France, tel.: 42-09-18-19
Contact: FEPACI (Pan-African Federation of Film-Makers), 01 B.P.
    2524, Ouagadougou 01, Burkina Faso, tel.: 226/31-02-58

YAM DAABO   1987, Burkina Faso-French
YAABA   New Yorker, 1989, Burkina Faso-French-Swiss
TILAI   Les Films de l'Avenir/Waka Film/Rhea Film, 1990,
    Burkina Faso-French-Swiss
A KARIM NA SALA   Arcadia Films, 1991, Burkina Faso-German
SAMBA TRAORE   Les Films de L'Avenir/Les Films de la Plaine/
    Waka Films, 1992, Burkina Faso-French-Swiss
THE THREE FRIENDS   Les Films de la Plaine/Canal Plus/BBC/
    Vega Films/Cinafric, 1993, Burkina Faso-French-British-Swiss
LA CRI DU COEUR   Les Films de la Plaine/Les Films de L'Avenir/
    Centre Europeen Cinematographique Rhone-Alpes, 1994, French
AFRIQUE, MON AFRIQUE...   Noe Productions/La Sept/Plan Intl.,
    1995, Burkina Faso-French

GERARD OURY
(Max-Gerard Houry Tannenbaum)
b. April 29, 1919 - Paris, France
Agent: ICM France - Paris, tel.: 1/723-7860
Contact: French Film Office, 745 Fifth Avenue, New York,
    NY 10151, 212/832-8860

LA MAIN CHAUDE   Films de France, 1960, French
THE MENACE   Warner Bros., 1961, French
CRIME DOES NOT PAY   Embassy, 1962, French-Italian
THE SUCKER   Royal Films International, 1966, French-Italian
DON'T LOOK NOW...WE'RE BEING SHOT AT   LA GRANDE
    VADROVILLE   Cinepix, 1966, French-British
THE BRAIN   Paramount, 1969, French-Italian
DELUSIONS OF GRANDEUR   Joseph Green Pictures,
    1971, French
THE MAD ADVENTURES OF 'RABBI' JACOB
    20th Century-Fox, 1974, French-Italian
LA CARAPATE   Gaumont, 1978, French
LE COUP DU PARAPLUIE   Gaumont, 1980, French
L'AS DES AS   Gaumont/Cerito Rene Chateau, 1982,
    French-West German
LA VENGEANCE DU SERPENT A PLUMES   AMLF, 1984, French
LEVY AND GOLIATH   LEVI ET GOLIATH   Kino International,
    1986, French
VANILLE FRAISE   Ariane Films/Cristaldi Film, 1989, French-Italian
LA SOIF DE L'OR   Gaumont, 1993, French

HORACE OVE
Business: Anancy Films, 3 Kelly Street, London NW1 8PG,
    England, tel.: 171/482-3332

PRESSURE   British Film Institute, 1974, British
A HOLE IN BABYLON (TF)   BBC, 1979, British
THE PROFESSIONALS (MS)   London Weekend TV, 1980, British
THE GARLAND (TF)   BBC, 1981, British
WHO SHALL WE TELL? (TF)   Channel 4, 1985, British
DABBAWALLAHS (TF)   Channel 4, 1985, British
PLAYING AWAY (TF)   Channel 4, 1986, British

CLIFF OWEN
b. April 22, 1919 - London, England
Address: 20 Marlborough Place, London NW8, England

OFFBEAT   1961, British
A PRIZE OF ARMS   British Lion, 1961, British
THE WRONG ARM OF THE LAW   Continental, 1963, British
A MAN COULD GET KILLED   co-director with Ronald Neame,
    Universal, 1966
THAT RIVIERA TOUCH   Continental, 1966, British
WHAT HAPPENED AT CAMPO GRANDE?   THE MAGNIFICENT
    TWO   Alan Enterprises, 1967, British
THE VENGEANCE OF SHE   20th Century-Fox, 1968, British
STEPTOE AND SON   MGM-EMI, 1972, British
OOH...YOU ARE AWFUL   Lion International, 1973, British
NO SEX PLEASE - WE'RE BRITISH   Columbia-Warner,
    1973, British
THE BAWDY ADVENTURES OF TOM JONES   Universal,
    1975, British
GET CHARLIE TULLY   TBS Distributing Corporation, 1976, British

DON OWEN
b. 1935 - Toronto, Ontario, Canada
Home: Glenstreams, RR#1, Locust Hill, Ontario LOH 1JO, Canada,
    416/294-5163
Business: Zebra Films, 55 Charles Street East - Suite 303, Toronto,
    Ontario M4Y 1S9, Canada, 416/926-8086

NOBODY WAVED GOODBYE   Cinema 5, 1964, Canadian
HIGH STEEL   1965, Canadian
THE ERNIE GAME   CBC/National Film Board of Canada,
    1967, Canadian
RICHLER OF ST. URBAIN (TD)   1971, Canadian
COUGHTRY IN IBIZA (TD)   1977, Canadian
COWBOY AND INDIAN (FD)   1972, Canadian
THE ST. LAWRENCE (TD)   1973, Canadian

NOT FAR FROM HOME (TD)   1973, Canadian
PARTNERS   Astral Films, 1976, Canadian
HOLSTEIN   1977, Canadian
TANYA'S MOSCOW PUPPETS (TD)   1981, Canadian
UNFINISHED BUSINESS   Zebra Films/National Film Board of
   Canada/CBC, 1984, Canadian
TURNABOUT   Zebra Films, 1988, Canadian

JAN OXENBERG

THANK YOU AND GOOD NIGHT! (FD)   Aries Film Releasing, 1992

FRANK OZ*
(Frank Oznowicz)
b. May 25, 1944 - Hereford, England
Agent: CAA - Beverly Hills, 310/288-4545

THE DARK CRYSTAL   co-director with Jim Henson,
   Universal/AFD, 1982, British
THE MUPPETS TAKE MANHATTAN   TriStar, 1984
LITTLE SHOP OF HORRORS   The Geffen Company/
   Warner Bros., 1986
DIRTY ROTTEN SCOUNDRELS   Orion, 1988
WHAT ABOUT BOB?   Burna Vista, 1991
HOUSESITTER   Universal, 1992
THE INDIAN IN THE CUPBOARD   Paramount/Columbia, 1995

P

ANTHONY PAGE*
b. September 21, 1935 - Bangalore, India
Agent: ICM - Beverly Hills, 310/550-4000

INADMISSABLE EVIDENCE   Paramount, 1968, British
ALPHA BETA   Cine III, 1976, British
F. SCOTT FITZGERALD IN HOLLYWOOD (TF)
   Titus Productions, 1976
I NEVER PROMISED YOU A ROSE GARDEN   New World, 1977
ABSOLUTION   Trans World Entertainment, 1979, British
THE LADY VANISHES   Rank, 1979, British
THE PATRICIA NEAL STORY (TF)   co-director with
   Anthony Harvey, Lawrence Schiller Productions, 1981
BILL (TF)   Alan Landsburg Productions, 1981
JOHNNY BELINDA (TF)   Dick Berg-Stonehenge Productions/
   Lorimar Productions, 1982
GRACE KELLY (TF)   The Kota Company/Embassy TV, 1983
BILL: ON HIS OWN (TF)   Alan Landsburg Productions, 1983
FORBIDDEN (CTF)   HBO Premiere Films/Mark Forstater
   Productions/Clasart/Anthea Productions, 1985,
   U.S.-British-West German
MURDER: BY REASON OF INSANITY (TF)
   LS Entertainment, 1985
SECOND SERVE (TF)   Linda Yellen Productions/Lorimar-
   Telepictures, 1986
MONTE CARLO (TF)   New World TV/Phoenix Entertainment
   Group/Collins-Holm Productions/Highgate Pictures, 1986
PACK OF LIES (TF)   Robert Halmi, Inc., 1987
SCANDAL IN A SMALL TOWN (TF)   Carliner-Rappoport
   Productions, 1988
THE NIGHTMARE YEARS (CMS)   Consolidated Productions, 1989
CHERNOBYL: THE FINAL WARNING (CTF)   Carolco TV
   Productions/Gimbel Productions/USSR Film Service
   Corporation, 1991, U.S.-Soviet
SILENT CRIES (TF)   Sokolow Entertainment Productions/
   Yorkshire TV/TriStar TV, 1993, U.S.-British
MIDDLEMARCH (MS)   BBC/WGBH-Boston, 1994, British-U.S.

PAMELA PAGE
ROCK & ROLL: THE EARLY DAYS (HVD)   co-director with
   Patrick Montgomery, RCA/Columbia Home Video/Fox-Lorber/
   Archive Film Productions, 1984
BRITISH ROCK: THE FIRST WAVE (HVD)   co-director with
   Patrick Montgomery, RCA/Columbia Home Video/Archive Film
   Productions, 1985

CHALONG PAKDEEVICHIT
(P. Chalong)
b. Thailand
Contact: Thailand Film Promotion Center, 599 Bumrung Muang
   Road, Bangkok 10100, Thailand, tel.: 2/223-4690

IN GOLD WE TRUST   AIP, 1990, Thai

ALAN J. PAKULA*
b. April 7, 1928 - New York, New York
Business: The Pakula Company, 330 West 58th Street - Suite 5H,
   New York, NY 10019, 212/664-0640
Agent: ICM - New York City, 212/556-5600

THE STERILE CUCKOO   Paramount, 1969
KLUTE   Warner Bros., 1971
LOVE AND PAIN AND THE WHOLE DAMNED THING
   Columbia, 1973, British-U.S.
THE PARALLAX VIEW   Paramount, 1974
ALL THE PRESIDENT'S MEN ★   Warner Bros., 1976
COMES A HORSEMAN   United Artists, 1978
STARTING OVER   Paramount, 1979
ROLLOVER   Orion/Warner Bros., 1981
SOPHIE'S CHOICE   Universal/AFD, 1982
DREAM LOVER   MGM/UA, 1986
ORPHANS   Lorimar, 1987
SEE YOU IN THE MORNING   Warner Bros., 1989
PRESUMED INNOCENT   Warner Bros., 1990
CONSENTING ADULTS   Buena Vista, 1992
THE PELICAN BRIEF   Warner Bros., 1993

LASZLO PAL
b. May 14, 1937 - Fuzesabony, Hungary
Business: Pal Productions, Inc., 17409 Beach Drive N.E., Seattle,
   WA 98155, 800/965-8777

EVEREST NORTH WALL (TD)   Pal Productions, Inc., 1983
WINDS OF EVEREST (TD)   Pal Productions, Inc., 1985
ALASKA'S GREAT RACE (TD)   Pal Productions, Inc., 1989
THREE FLAGS OVER EVEREST (TD)   Pal Productions, Inc., 1991
BLUE WATER HUNTERS (TD)   Pal Productions, Inc., 1992
JOURNEY TO SPIRIT ISLAND ☆☆ (CTF)   The Disney
   Channel, 1992

ERAN PALATNIK
b. January 12, 1960 - Tel Aviv, Israel
Business: Ecco Films, Inc., 98 Third Avenue - Suite 3, New York,
   NY 10003, 212/353-0740

THE ROOK   Ecco Films, 1994

EUZHAN PALCY
b. 1957 - Martinique
Agent: William Morris Agency - Beverly Hills, 310/859-4000

SUGAR CANE ALLEY   Orion, 1983, French
A DRY WHITE SEASON   MGM-UA, 1989
SIMEON   AMLF, 1993, Martinique-French

ROSPO PALLENBERG*
Home: 9021 Burroughs Road, Los Angeles, CA 90046,
   213/654-0380
Agent: David Gersh, The Gersh Agency - Beverly Hills,
   310/274-6611

CUTTING CLASS   Republic Pictures, 1989

THOMAS PALMER, JR.
FOREVER Triax Entertainment Group/DDM Films, 1993
PIZZA GIRLS Jackelyn Giroux Productions, 1994, Canadian

TONY PALMER
Business: Ladbroke Films Ltd., 4 Kensington Park Gardens,
 London W11, England, tel.: 171/727-3541

FAREWELL CREAM (FCD) 1968, British
200 MOTELS co-director with Frank Zappa, United Artists,
 1971, British
BIRD ON A WIRE (FCD) EMI, 1974, British
A TIME THERE WAS *A PROFILE OF BENJAMIN BRITTEN* (TD)
 London Weekend TV, 1980, British
THE SPACE MOVIE (FD) International Harmony, 1980, British
WAGNER (MS) London Trust Productions/Richard Wagner
 Productions/Ladbroke Productions/Hungarofilm, 1983,
 British-Hungarian-Austrian
GEORGE FREDERIC HANDEL (1685-1759) Arts International,
 1985, British
TESTIMONY (TF) European Classics, 1987, British
MARIA CALLAS: AN OPERATIC BIOGRAPHY (TD) Isolde Films/
 London Trust Productions, 1988, British
RICHARD BURTON: IN FROM THE COLD (TD) Isolde Films/
 Thames TV, 1989
THE CHILDREN Coyote Releasing/Hemdale, 1990,
 British-West German
MENUHIN: A FAMILY PORTRAIT (TD) Isolde Films/RM Arts/
 Channel 4/RTE TV2/WNET, 1991, British-Danish-U.S.

CONRAD E. PALMISANO*
Business Manager: Lawrence Lerner, 20300 Ventura Blvd. -
 Suite 360, Woodland Hills, CA 91364, 818/719-6541

SPACE RAGE Vestron, 1985
BUSTED UP Shapiro Entertainment, 1987, Canadian

BRUCE PALTROW*
b. November 26, 1943 - New York, New York
Agent: CAA - Beverly Hills, 310/288-4545

A LITTLE SEX Universal, 1982
ED McBAIN'S 87TH PRECINCT *87TH PRECINCT* (TF)
 Diana Kerew Productions/Hearst Entertainment, 1995

NORMAN PANAMA*
b. April 21, 1914 - Chicago, Illinois
Agent: Mitchell Kaplan, The Kaplan-Stahler Agenbcy - Beverly Hills,
 213/653-4483

THE REFORMER AND THE REDHEAD co-director with
 Melvin Frank, MGM, 1950
STRICTLY DISHONORABLE co-director with Melvin Frank,
 MGM, 1951
CALLAWAY WENT THATAWAY co-director with Melvin Frank,
 MGM, 1951
ABOVE AND BEYOND co-director with Melvin Frank, MGM, 1952
KNOCK ON WOOD co-director with Melvin Frank,
 Paramount, 1954
THE COURT JESTER co-director with Melvin Frank,
 Paramount, 1956
THAT CERTAIN FEELING co-director with Melvin Frank,
 Paramount, 1956
THE TRAP Paramount, 1959
THE ROAD TO HONG KONG United Artists, 1962
NOT WITH MY WIFE, YOU DON'T! Warner Bros., 1966
HOW TO COMMIT MARRIAGE Cinerama Releasing
 Corporation, 1969
THE MALTESE BIPPY MGM, 1969
COFFEE, TEA OR ME? (TF) CBS, Inc., 1973
I WILL, I WILL...FOR NOW 20th Century-Fox, 1976
BARNABY AND ME Trans-Atlantic Enterprises, 1978

GLEB PANFILOV
b. May 21, 1937 - Magnitogorsk, U.S.S.R.
Contact: Confederation of Film-Makers Unions, Vasilyevskaya
 Street 13, 123 825 Moscow, Russia, tel.: 095/250-4114

ACROSS THE STREAM AND FIRE Lenfilm, 1968, Soviet
THE DEBUT Lenfilm, 1970, Soviet
MAY I HAVE THE FLOOR? Lenfilm, 1975, Soviet
VALENTINA, VALENTINA 1981, Soviet
VASSA 1983, Soviet
THEME International Film Exchange, 1984, Soviet
THE MOTHER Cinefin/Mosfilm/RAI, 1990, Italian-Soviet

RITHY PANH
b. Cambodia
Contact: French Film Office, 745 Fifth Avenue, New York, NY 10151,
 212/832-8860

RICE PEOPLE JBA Production/Thelma Film/La Sept Cinema/
 ZDF/TSR/Canal Plus/Channel 4/ARP/Direction du Cinema du
 Cambodge/CNC/French Ministries of Foreign Affairs &
 Culture/EDI-DEH/Ecrans du Sud, 1994,
 Cambodian-French-Swiss-German-British

PHEDON PAPAMICHAEL
Personal Manager: Jon Brown, The Brown Group - Beverly Hills,
 310/247-2755

SKETCH ARTIST (CTF) Motion Picture Corporation of
 America, 1992
DARK SIDE OF GENIUS Pacific Shore Pictures, 1994

JOHN PARAGON
Agent: William Morris Agency - Beverly Hills, 310/859-4000

DOUBLE TROUBLE Motion Picture Corporation of America, 1992
TWIN SITTERS Guts & Glory Productions, 1994
RING OF THE MUSKETEERS Motion Picture Corporation of
 America, 1994

PAUL PARCO
PUCKER UP AND BARK LIKE A DOG Paragon Arts
 International, 1989
HEARTFELT Heartfelt Productions/Flora Films, 1992

PEKKA PARIKKA
b. May 2, 1939 - Helsinki, Finland
Personal Manager: Jon Brown, The Brown Group - Beverly Hills,
 310/247-2755

POHJANMAA Finnkino, 1988, Finnish
THE WINTER WAR *TALVISOTA* Finnkino, 1989, Finnish

DOMONIC PARIS
b. September 28, 1950

DRACULA'S LAST RITES Cannon, 1980
SPLITZ Film Ventures International, 1984
AMAZING MASTERS Vestron, 1986
FILMHOUSE FEVER Lightning Video, 1986

HENRY PARIS
(See Radley METZGER)

DEAN PARISOT*
Agent: UTA - Beverly Hills, 310/273-6700
Personal Manager: 3 Arts Entertainment - Beverly Hills, 213/888-3200

FRAMED (CTF) HBO Pictures, 1990

CHOI-SU PARK
(See Park CHOI-SU)

F
I
L
M

D
I
R
E
C
T
O
R
S

ALAN PARKER*
b. February 14, 1944 - Islington, England
Agent: CAA - Beverly Hills, 310/288-4545

THE EVACUEES (TF)   BBC, 1975, British
BUGSY MALONE   Paramount, 1976, British
MIDNIGHT EXPRESS ★   Columbia, 1978, British
FAME   MGM/United Artists, 1980
SHOOT THE MOON   MGM/United Artists, 1982
PINK FLOYD - THE WALL   MGM/UA, 1982, British
BIRDY   TriStar, 1984
A TURNIP HEAD'S GUIDE TO THE BRITISH CINEMA (TD)
    Thames TV, 1985, British
ANGEL HEART   TriStar, 1987
MISSISSIPPI BURNING ★   Orion, 1988
COME SEE THE PARADISE   20th Century Fox, 1990
THE COMMITMENTS   20th Century Fox, 1991, U.S.-British-Irish
THE ROAD TO WELLVILLE   Columbia, 1994

BILL PARKER
Contact: Jamaica Film and Entertainment Office, 35 Trafalgar Road -
    3rd Floor, Kingston, 10 Jamaica, tel.: 809/929-9450

KLA$H   Kingston Productions/Hawk's Nest Pictures,
    1995, U.S.-Jamaican

CARY PARKER
b. Atlanta, Georgia

THE GIRL IN THE PICTURE   The Samuel Goldwyn Company,
    1986, British

DAVID PARKER
Contact: Australian Film Commission, 150 William Street,
    Woolloomooloo NSW 2011, Australia, tel.: 2/321-6444

HERCULES RETURNS   Roadshow, 1993, Australian

FRANCINE PARKER*
Home: 874 N. Alexandria Avenue, Los Angeles, CA 90029,
    213/662-1341

F.T.A. (PF)   American International, 1972

WALTER F. PARKES
Business: Amblin Entertainment, 100 Universal City Plaza -
    Bungalow 477, Universal City, CA 91608, 818/777-4600
Agent: CAA - Beverly Hills, 310/288-4545

THE CALIFORNIA REICH (FD)   co-director with Keith F. Critchlow,
    Paramount Home Video, 1977

ERIC PARKINSON
FUTURE SHOCK   Hemdale, 1993

GORDON PARKS*
b. November 30, 1912 - Fort Scott, Kansas
Home: 860 U.N. Plaza, New York, NY 10017

THE LEARNING TREE   Warner Bros., 1969
SHAFT   MGM, 1971
SHAFT'S BIG SCORE!   MGM, 1972
THE SUPER COPS   MGM, 1974
LEADBELLY   Paramount, 1976
SUPER COPS (TF)   MGM TV, 1976
SOLOMON NORTHUP'S ODYSSEY (TF)   Past America, Inc., 1985

MICHAEL PARKS
b. April 4, 1938 - Corona, California
Contact: Screen Actors Guild - Los Angeles, 213/954-1600

THE RETURN OF JOSEY WALES   Reel Movies International, 1986

EDWARD PARONE
Telephone: 505/455-3605

PROMISE HIM ANYTHING... (TF)   ABC Circle Films, 1975
LETTERS FROM FRANK (TF)   The Jozak Company/Cypress Point
    Productions, 1979

LARRY PARR
Contact: New Zealand Film Commission, P.O. Box 11-546,
    Wellington, New Zealand, tel.: 4/385-9754

A SOLDIER'S TALE   Atlantic Releasing Corporation, 1988,
    New Zealand-U.S.

JAMES D. PARRIOTT*
Agent: CAA - Beverly Hills, 310/288-4545

MISFITS OF SCIENCE (TF)   James D. Parriott Productions/
    Universal TV, 1985
HEART CONDITION   New Line Cinema, 1990

ROBERT PARRISH*
b. January 4, 1916 - Columbus, Georgia
Business Manager: Jess S. Morgan & Co., 5750 Wilshire Blvd. -
    Suite 590, Los Angeles, CA 90036, 213/937-1552

CRY DANGER   RKO Radio, 1951
THE MOB   Columbia, 1951
THE SAN FRANCISCO STORY   Warner Bros., 1952
ASSIGNMENT - PARIS   Columbia, 1952
MY PAL GUS   20th Century-Fox, 1952
SHOOT FIRST   *ROUGH SHOOT*   United Artists, 1953, British
THE PURPLE PLAIN   United Artists, 1954, British
LUCY GALLANT   Paramount, 1955
FIRE DOWN BELOW   Columbia, 1957
SADDLE THE WIND   MGM, 1957
THE WONDERFUL COUNTRY   United Artists, 1959
IN THE FRENCH STYLE   Columbia, 1963, French-U.S.
UP FROM THE BEACH   20th Century-Fox, 1965
CASINO ROYALE   co-director with Val Guest, Ken Hughes,
    John Huston & Joseph McGrath, Columbia, 1967, Columbia
THE BOBO   Warner Bros., 1967, British
DUFFY   Columbia, 1968, British
JOURNEY TO THE FAR SIDE OF THE SUN   *DOPPELGANGER*
    Universal, 1969, British
A TOWN CALLED BASTARD   *A TOWN CALLED HELL*
    Scotia International, 1971, British-Spanish
THE DESTRUCTORS   *THE MARSEILLES CONTRACT*
    American International, 1974, British-French
MISSISSIPPI BLUES (FD)   co-director with Bertrand Tavernier,
    Little Bear Productions/Odessa Films, 1984, French

MICHAEL PART
b. March 29, 1949 - Sheboygan, Wisconsin
Home: Wicked Scherzo Productions, 14248 Dickens Street -
    Apt. 115, Sherman Oaks, CA 91423, 818/906-8566

STARBIRDS (ATF)   3B Productions Ltd., 1982, Japanese
REVENGE OF THE DEFENDERS (ATF)   3B Productions Ltd.,
    1982, Japanese
SHADOW WORLD (ATF)   3B Productions Ltd., 1983, Japanese
THE RAFT ADVENTURES OF HUCK AND JIM (ATF)
    3B Productions Ltd., 1984, Japanese

MICHEL PASCAL
Contact: French Film Office, 745 Fifth Avenue, New York, NY 10151,
    212/832-8860

FRANCOIS TRUFFAUT: STOLEN PORTRAITS (FD)   co-director
    with Serge Toubiana, Myriad Pictures, 1993, French

MICHAEL PASEORNEK
Contact: Writers Guild of America, East - New York City,
    212/767-7800

VIBRATIONS   Cinepix Inc./Tanglewood Films, 1994

GORAN PASKALJEVIC

THE BEACH GUARD IN WINTER   Center FRZ,
   1976, Yugoslavian
THE DOG THAT LIKED TRAINS   Yugoslav Film Releasing,
   1978, Yugoslavian
THE DAYS ARE PASSING   Yugoslav Film Releasing,
   1980, Yugoslavian
SPECIAL TREATMENT   International Home Cinema,
   1982, Yugoslavian
TWILIGHT TIME   MGM/UA, 1983, U.S.-Yugoslavian
THE ILLUSORY SUMMER OF '68   1984, Yugoslavian
GUARDIAN ANGEL   Jugoart-Singidunum/Morava Film,
   1987, Yugoslavian
TIME OF MIRACLES   Singidunum Film Productions/Televizija
   Belgrade/Channel 4/Metropolitan Pictures, 1990,
   Yugoslavian-British
TANGO ARGENTINO   Singidunum Film Productions/
   Beograd-Vans/TV Beograd/Jugoexport Avala Film
   International, 1992, Yugoslavian
SOMEONE ELSE'S AMERICA   MACT Productions,
   1994, French-U.S.

JOHN PASQUIN*

Agent: CAA - Beverly Hills, 310/288-4545

OUT ON THE EDGE (TF)   Rick Dawn Enterprises/The Steve Tisch
   Company/King Phoenix Entertainment, 1989
DON'T TOUCH MY DAUGHTER (TF)   Patchett Kaufman
   Entertainment/Victoria Principal Productions, 1991
THE SANTA CLAUSE   Buena Vista, 1994

IVAN PASSER*

b. July 10, 1933 - Prague, Czechoslovakia
Business: Creative Road Corporation, 8170 Beverly Blvd. -
   Suite 106, Los Angeles, CA 90048, 213/658-7224
Agent: The Agency - Los Angeles, 310/551-3000

A BORING AFTERNOON   1965, Czech
INTIMATE LIGHTING   Altura, 1965, Czech
BORN TO WIN   United Artists, 1971
LAW AND DISORDER   Columbia, 1974
CRIME AND PASSION   American International, 1976
SILVER BEARS   Columbia, 1978
CUTTER'S WAY   CUTTER AND BONE   United Artists
   Classics, 1981
CREATOR   Universal, 1985
HAUNTED SUMMER   Cannon, 1988
FOURTH STORY (CTF)   Konigsberg-Sanitsky Productions/
   Viacom, 1991
PRETTY HATTIE'S BABY   Cacti Films, 1992
STALIN (CTF)   Mark Carliner Productions/Hungarian
   TV-Channel 1, 1992, U.S.-Hungarian

MICHAEL PATE

b. 1920 - Sydney, Australia
Business: Pisces Productions, 21 Bundarra Road, Bellevue Hill,
   NSW, 2023, Australia, tel.: 02/30-4208

TIM   Satori, 1979, Australian

RAJU SHARAD PATEL

b. India
Business: Vision International, 3330 W. Cahuenga Blvd.,
   Los Angeles, CA 90068, 213/969-2900

AMIN: THE RISE AND FALL   THE RISE AND FALL OF IDI AMIN
   Twin Continental, 1983, British-Kenyan
IN THE SHADOW OF KILIMANJARO   Scotti Brothers,
   1986, Kenyan

VINCENT PATERSON

IN SEARCH OF DR. SEUSS (CTF)   Point Blank
   Productions, 1994

MATTHEW PATRICK*

Agent: The Gersh Agency - Beverly Hills, 310/274-6611

HIDER IN THE HOUSE   Vestron, 1989
TAINTED BLOOD (CTF)   Fast Track Films/Wilshire Court
   Productions, 1993
NIGHT OWL (CTF)   Morgan Hill Films/Hearst Entertainment, 1993

JOHN PATTERSON*

Agent: William Morris Agency - Beverly Hills, 310/859-4000

INDEPENDENCE (TF)   Sunn Classic Pictures, 1987
GIDEON OLIVER: SLEEP WELL, PROFESSOR OLIVER (TF)
   Wolf Films/Crescendo Productions/Logo Productions/
   Universal TV, 1989
A DEADLY SILENCE (TF)   Robert Greenwald Productions, 1989
TAKEN AWAY (TF)   Hart, Thomas & Berlin Productions, 1989
A MOTHER'S COURAGE: THE MARY THOMAS STORY (TF)
   Interscope Communications/Chet Walker Enterprises/
   Walt Disney TV, 1989
SINS OF THE MOTHER (TF)   Corapeake Productions/The
   Polson Company, 1991
MARILYN & ME (TF)   World International Network/Samuels
   Film Company, 1991
GRAVE SECRETS: THE LEGACY OF HILLTOP DRIVE (TF)
   Freyda Rothstein Productions/Hearst Entertainment, 1992
RELENTLESS: MIND OF A KILLER (TF)   Universal TV, 1993
DARKNESS BEFORE DAWN (TF)   Diana Kerew Productions/
   The Polone Company/Hearst Entertainment, 1993
LOVE, HONOR & OBEY: THE LAST MAFIA MARRIAGE (TF)
   CBS Entertainment, 1993
ROBIN COOK'S HARMFUL INTENT   HARMFUL INTENT (TF)
   Rosemont Productions, 1993
SEE JANE RUN (TF)   Avenue Pictures/Hearst Entertainment, 1995

RAY PATTERSON

GOBOTS: BATTLE OF THE ROCK LORDS (AF)   Clubhouse/Atlantic
   Releasing Corporation, 1986
THE JETSONS MEET THE FLINTSTONES (ATF)   Hanna-Barbera
   Productions, 1987
ROCKIN' WITH JUDY JETSON (ATF)   Hanna-Barbera
   Productions, 1988
I YABBA DABBA DO! (ATF)   co-director with William Hanna,
   Joanna Romersa & Gordon Hunt, Hanna-Barbera
   Productions, 1993

WILLI PATTERSON*
(William Patterson)

Business: Propaganda Films, 940 N. Mansfield Avenue,
   Hollywood, CA 90036, 213/462-6400
Agent: Susan Smith & Associates - Beverly Hills, 213/852-4777 or:
   Linda Seifert, Seifert Dench Associates - London,
   tel.: 171/437-4551

TIMESLIP (TF)   Yorkshire TV, 1984, British
DREAMS LOST, DREAMS FOUND (CTF)   Atlantic Video Ventures
   Productions/Yorkshire TV, 1987, British
OUT OF THE SHADOWS (CTF)   Showtime/Yorkshire TV/Atlantic
   Videoventures Productions, 1988, British
SARACEN (TF)   Central TV, 1989, British

MICHAEL PATTINSON

Agent: ICM - Beverly Hills, 310/550-4000

MOVING OUT   Pattinson Ballantine Pictures, 1982, Australian
GROUND ZERO   Avenue Pictures, 1987, Australian
WENDY CRACKED A WALNUT   Australian Broadcasting
   Corporation/Australian Classic Films, 1990, Australian
SECRETS   Victorian International Pictures/Avalon-NFU Studios/
   Australian Film Finance Corporation/Film Victoria, 1992,
   Australian-New Zealand

STEVEN PAUL
b. May 16, 1958 - New York, New York
Business: Paul International, 1800 Century Park East - 6th Floor,
    Los Angeles, CA 90067, 310/843-0223

FALLING IN LOVE AGAIN   International Picture Show
    Company, 1980
SLAPSTICK OF ANOTHER KIND *SLAPSTICK* Entertainment
    Releasing Corporation/International Film Marketing, 1983
FATE   Paul Entertainment, 1990

STUART PAUL
Business: Paul International, 1800 Century Park East - 6th Floor,
    Los Angeles, CA 90067, 310/843-0223

EMANON   Paul Releasing, 1987

DAVID PAULSEN*
Telephone: 818/789-3013

SAVAGE WEEKEND *THE UPSTATE MURDERS* Cannon, 1976
SCHIZOID   Cannon, 1980

GEORGE PAVLOU
b. November 5, 1953
Contact: British Film Commission, 70 Baker Street, London
    W1M 1DJ, England, tel.: 171/224-5000

UNDERWORLD   Empire Pictures, 1985, British
RAWHEAD REX   Empire Pictures, 1987, British

MICHAEL PEARCE
JAMES JOYCE'S WOMEN   Universal, 1985
INITIATION   International Film Management/Goldfarb Distributors,
    1987, Australian

RICHARD PEARCE*
b. San Diego, California
Agent: UTA - Beverly Hills, 310/273-6700

THE GARDENER'S SON (TF)   RIP/Filmhaus, 1977
SIEGE (TF)   Titus Productions, 1978
NO OTHER LOVE (TF)   Tisch-Avnet Productions, 1979
HEARTLAND   Levitt-Pickman, 1979
THRESHOLD   20th Century-Fox International Classics,
    1983, Canadian
SESSIONS (TF)   Roger Gimbel Productions/EMI TV/Sarabande
    Productions, 1983
COUNTRY   Buena Vista, 1984
NO MERCY   TriStar, 1987
DEAD MAN OUT (CTF)   HBO Showcase/Citadel Entertainment
    Productions/Granada TV, 1989, U.S.-Canadian-British
THE FINAL DAYS (TF) ☆   The Samuels Film Company, 1989
THE LONG WALK HOME   Miramax Films, 1990
LEAP OF FAITH   Paramount, 1993

BRIAN PECK
THE WILLIES   Prism Entertainment, 1991

RON PECK
Contact: British Film Commission, 70 Baker Street, London
    W1M 1DJ, England, tel.: 171/224-5000

NIGHTHAWKS   1978, British
EMPIRE STATE   Virgin/Miracle, 1987, British
STRIP JACK NAKED (NIGHTHAWKS II)   Frameline, 1991, British

STEPHEN J. PECK*
Home: 1617 N. Courtney Avenue, Los Angeles, CA 90046,
    213/850-5231

HEART OF THE WARRIOR (FD)   The Video Project, 1990
FAR FROM HOME (FD)   Far From Home Foundation, 1992

LARRY PEERCE*
b. Bronx, New York
Address: 225 West 34th Street - Suite 1012, New York, NY 10125,
    212/564-6656
Agent: Geoffrey Brandt, The Brandt Company - Sherman Oaks,
    818/783-7747

ONE POTATO, TWO POTATO   Cinema 5, 1964
THE BIG T.N.T. SHOW (FD)   American International, 1966
THE INCIDENT   20th Century-Fox, 1967
GOODBYE, COLUMBUS   Paramount, 1969
THE SPORTING CLUB   Avco Embassy, 1971
A SEPARATE PEACE   Paramount, 1972
ASH WEDNESDAY   Paramount, 1973
THE STRANGER WHO LOOKS LIKE ME (TF)   Filmways, 1974
THE OTHER SIDE OF THE MOUNTAIN   Universal, 1975
TWO-MINUTE WARNING   Universal, 1976
THE OTHER SIDE OF THE MOUNTAIN - PART 2   Universal, 1978
THE BELL JAR   Avco Embassy, 1979
WHY WOULD I LIE?   MGM/United Artists, 1980
LOVE CHILD   The Ladd Company/Warner Bros., 1982
I TAKE THESE MEN (TF)   Lillian Gallo Productions/United
    Artists TV, 1983
HARD TO HOLD   Universal, 1984
LOVE LIVES ON (TF)   Script-Song Productions/ABC Circle
    Films, 1985
THE FIFTH MISSILE (TF)   Bercovici-St. Johns Productions/
    MGM-UA TV, 1986
PRISON FOR CHILDREN (TF)   Knopf-Simons Productions/Viacom
    Productions, 1987
QUEENIE (MS)   von Zerneck-Samuels Productions/Highgate
    Pictures, 1987
ELVIS AND ME (TF)   Navarone Productions/New World TV, 1988
WIRED   Taurus Entertainment, 1989
THE NEON EMPIRE (CMS)   Richard Maynard Productions/Fries
    Entertainment, 1989
THE COURT-MARTIAL OF JACKIE ROBINSON (CTF)
    von Zerneck-Sertner Films/Turner Network TV, 1990
MURDER AT THE PTA LUNCHEON (TF)   Patricia K. Meyer
    Productions/von Zerneck-Sertner Films, 1990
A WOMAN NAMED JACKIE (TF)   Lester Persky Productions/World
    International Network, 1991
CHILD OF RAGE (TF)   Gilliam Productions/C.M. Two Productions/
    Republic Pictures, 1992
POISONED BY LOVE: THE KERN COUNTY MURDERS (TF)
    Morgan Hill Films/Hearst Entertainment Productions, 1993
JOHN JAKES' HEAVEN AND HELL: NORTH AND SOUTH
    PART 3 (TF)   The Wolper Organization/Warner Bros. TV, 1994
A BURNING PASSION: THE MARGARET MITCHELL STORY (TF)
    Renee Valente Productions/NBC Productions, 1994

MELISSA JO PELTIER*
Business: M.J. Pictures - Sherman Oaks, 818/784-3329
Agent: Leslie Parness, The Parness Agency, 1424 4th Street -
    Suite 404, Santa Monica, CA 90401, 310/319-1664

TITANIC: DEATH OF A DREAM (CTD)   Greystone Communications/
    A&E TV Network, 1994

ARTHUR PENN*
b. September 27, 1922 - Philadelphia, Pennsylvania
Agent: William Morris Agency - Beverly Hills, 310/859-4000

THE LEFT-HANDED GUN   Warner Bros., 1958
THE MIRACLE WORKER ★   United Artists, 1962
MICKEY ONE   Columbia, 1965
THE CHASE   Columbia, 1966
BONNIE AND CLYDE ★   Warner Bros., 1967
ALICE'S RESTAURANT ★   United Artists, 1969
LITTLE BIG MAN   National General, 1970
NIGHT MOVES   Warner Bros., 1975
THE MISSOURI BREAKS   United Artists, 1976
FOUR FRIENDS   Filmways, 1981
TARGET   Warner Bros., 1985
DEAD OF WINTER   MGM/UA, 1987
PENN & TELLER GET KILLED   Warner Bros., 1989
THE PORTRAIT (CTF)   Robert Greenwald Productions/Atticus
    Corporation/urner Network TV, 1993

LEO PENN*

Contact: Directors Guild of America - Los Angeles, 213/851-3671

A MAN CALLED ADAM Embassy, 1966
QUARANTINED (TF) Paramount TV, 1970
TESTIMONY OF TWO MEN (MS) co-director with Larry Yust,
    Universal TV, 1977
THE DARK SECRET OF HARVEST HOME (TF)
    Universal TV, 1978
MURDER IN MUSIC CITY (TF) Frankel Films, 1979
HELLINGER'S LAW (TF) Universal TV, 1981
JUDGMENT IN BERLIN New Line Cinema, 1988
COLUMBO GOES TO THE GUILLOTINE (TF) Universal TV, 1989

SEAN PENN

b. August 17, 1960 - Burbank, California
Agent: William Morris Agency - Beverly Hills, 310/859-4000

THE INDIAN RUNNER MGM-Pathe Communications, 1991
THE CROSSING GUARD Miramax Films, 1995

D.A. PENNEBAKER

(Donn Alan Pennebaker)
b. 1930 - Evanston, Illinois
Business: Pennebaker Associates, 21 West 86th Street, New York,
    NY 10024, 212/496-9199

DON'T LOOK BACK (FCD) Leacock-Pennebaker, 1967
MONTEREY POP (FCD) Leacock-Pennebaker, 1967
SWEET TORONTO *KEEP ON ROCKIN'* (FCD) Pennebaker
    Associates, 1972
THE ENERGY WAR (TD) Pennebaker Associates/Corporation for
    Public Broadcasting, 1979
ELLIOTT CARTER (FD) Pennebaker Associates, 1980
TOWN BLOODY HALL (FD) co-director with Chris Hegedus,
    Pennebaker Associates, 1980
DeLOREAN (TD) Pennebaker Associates, 1981
ROCKABY (TD) co-director with Chris Hegedus, Pennebaker
    Associates, 1983
ZIGGY STARDUST AND THE SPIDERS FROM MARS (FCD)
    20th Century-Fox International Classics/Miramax Films,
    1983, filmed in 1973
DANCE BLACK AMERICA (FD) co-director with Chris Hegedus,
    Pennebaker Associates, 1985
ROCKY X (FD) co-director with Chris Hegedus, Pennebaker
    Associates, 1986
JIMI (FCD) Pennebaker Associates, 1986
DEPECHE MODE 101 (FD) co-director with Chris Hegedus &
    David Dawkins, Westwood One Radio, 1989
ORIGINAL CAST ALBUM: COMPANY (FD) Pennebaker
    Associates, 1992, filmed in 1970
THE MUSIC TELLS YOU (FD) co-director with Chris Hegedus,
    Pennebaker Associates, 1992
THE WAR ROOM (FD) co-director with Chris Hegedus,
    October Films, 1993
WOODSTOCK: THE LOST PERFORMANCES (CTCD)
    co-director with Chris Hegedus & Erez Laufer, Showtime
    Entertainment Group/Gravity Unlimited/Pennebaker
    Associates, 1994

EAGLE PENNELL

b. Texas
Contact: Tom Garvin, Ervin, Cohen & Jessup, 9401 Wilshire Blvd.,
    Beverly Hills, CA 90212, 310/273-6333

THE WHOLE SHOOTIN' MATCH First Run Features, 1979
LAST NIGHT AT THE ALAMO Cinecom, 1983
CITY LIFE City Life Foundation, 1988
ICE HOUSE Upfront Films, 1989
CITY LIFE (FD) co-director, Nederlands Film Museum/
    International Art Film, 1990, Dutch
A HEART FULL OF SOUL Original Cinema, 1991
DOC'S FULL SERVICE Brazos Films, 1994

DAVID WEBB PEOPLES

b. 1940
Contact: Shapiro-Lichtman Talent Agency - Los Angeles,
    310/859-8877

THE BLOOD OF HEROES *THE SALUTE OF THE JUGGER*
    New Line Cinema, 1989, U.S.-Australian

RICHARD PEPIN

Business: PM Entertainment Group, Inc., 9450 Chivers Avenue,
    Sun Valley, CA 91352, 818/504-6332

FINAL IMPACT PM Entertainment Group, 1992
FIST OF HONOR PM Entertainment Group, 1993
FIREPOWER PM Entertainment Group, 1993
CYBER-TRACKER PM Entertainment Group, 1994
T-FORCE PM Entertainment Group, 1994
HOLOGRAM MAN PM Entertainment Group, 1995

CLARE PEPLOE

Agent: ICM - London, tel.: 171/636-6565

COUPLES & ROBBERS 1981, British
HIGH SEASON Hemdale, 1987, British
ROUGH MAGIC Savoy Pictures, 1995, British-French

MARK PEPLOE

b. Kenya
Agent: ICM - Beverly Hills, 310/550-4000 or: Peters Fraser &
    Dunlop - London, tel.: 171/344-1000

AFRAID OF THE DARK Fine Line Features/New Line Cinema,
    1992, British-French
VICTORY Miramax Films, 1995, British-French

HOPE PERELLO

HOWLING VI - THE FREAKS Allied/Lane-Pringle Productions, 1991

SEVERO PEREZ

...and the earth did not swallow him American Playhouse Theatrical
    Films/KPBS/Severo Perez, 1994

ETIENNE PERIER

Home: 52, rue de Bourgogne, 75007 Paris, France,
    tel.: 1/45-51-31-07
Contact: French Film Office, 745 Fifth Avenue, New York,
    NY 10151, 212/832-8860

BOBOSSE 1959, Belgian
MEURTRE EN 45 TOURS 1960, Belgian
BRIDGE TO THE SUN MGM, 1961, U.S.-French
SWORDSMAN OF SIENA MGM, 1962, Italian-French
DIS-MOI QUI TUER 1965, Belgian
DES GARCONS ET DES FILLES 1968, French
RUBLO DE LOS CARAS 1969, Spanish
WHEN EIGHT BELLS TOLL Cinerama Releasing Corporation,
    1971, British
ZEPPELIN Warner Bros., 1971, British
A MURDER IS A MURDER...IS A MURDER Levitt-Pickman,
    1972, French
LA MAIN A COUPER Planfilm, 1974, French-Italian
THE INVESTIGATION *UN SI JOLI VILLAGE* Quartet/Films Inc.,
    1978, French
LA PART DU FEU Planfilm, 1978, French
LA CONFUSION DES SENTIMENTS (TF) Christine Gouze-Renel
    Progefi/FR3, 1979, French
VENEZIA ROSSO SANGUE Scena/Reteitalia/Clea Productions/
    President Film, 1989, Italian-French

ZORAN PERISIC

b. March 16, 1940 - Yugoslavia
Business: Zoptic Special Effects, 100 Universal City Plaza -
  Building 480/3, Universal City, CA 91608, 818/777-7420
Agent: L'Epine Smith and Carney Associates - London,
  tel.: 171/724-0739

SKY BANDITS   Galaxy International, 1986, British
THE PHOENIX AND THE MAGIC CARPET   Smart Egg Pictures,
  1994, British

FRANK PERRY*

b. 1930 - New York, New York
Home: 130 Mt. Laurel Drive, Aspen, CO 81611, 303/920-1060

DAVID AND LISA ★   Continental, 1962
LADYBUG, LADYBUG   United Artists, 1963
THE SWIMMER   Columbia, 1968
LAST SUMMER   Allied Artists, 1969
TRILOGY   Allied Artists, 1969
DIARY OF A MAD HOUSEWIFE   Universal, 1970
DOC   United Artists, 1971
PLAY IT AS IT LAYS   Universal, 1972
MAN ON A SWING   Paramount, 1974
RANCHO DeLUXE   United Artists, 1975
DUMMY (TF)   The Konigsberg Company/Warner Bros. TV, 1979
SKAG (TF) ☆   NBC, 1980
MOMMIE DEAREST   Paramount, 1981
MONSIGNOR   20th Century-Fox, 1982
COMPROMISING POSITIONS   Paramount, 1985
HELLO AGAIN   Buena Vista, 1987
ON THE BRIDGE (FD)   Blackhawk Enterprises, 1992

HART PERRY

RHYTHM, COUNTRY & BLUES (TD)   WNET-13/Perry Films/MCA
  Music Entertainment Group, 1994
THE PAPAL CONCERT TO COMMEMORATE THE
  HOLOCAUST (TPF)   Delilah Music Pictures/Perry Films, 1994

STEVE PERRY*

Business: Steve Perry Productions, c/o Fromson & Scissors,
  1900 Avenue of the Stars - Suite 290, Los Angeles, CA 90067

PARKER KANE (TF)   Parker Kane Productions/Silver Pictures TV/
  Orion TV, 1990

BILL PERSKY*

b. 1931 - New Haven Connecticut
Agent: CAA - Beverly Hills, 310/288-4545

ROLL, FREDDY, ROLL! (TF)   ABC Circle Films, 1974
HOW TO PICK UP GIRLS! (TF)   King-Hitzig Productions, 1978
SERIAL   Paramount, 1980
WAIT TILL YOUR MOTHER GETS HOME (TF)   Blue-Greene
  Productions/NBC Productions, 1983
TRACKDOWN: FINDING THE GOODBAR KILLER (TF)
  Grosso-Jacobson Productions, 1983
FOUND MONEY (TF)   Cypress Point Productions/Warner
  Bros. TV, 1983

P.J. PESCE

Agent: UTA - Beverly Hills, 310/273-6700

BODY WAVES   Concorde, 1991
THE DESPERATE TRAIL   Motion Picture Corporation of America/
  Turner Entertainment, 1994

CHRIS PESCHKEN

THE COVENANT   Bel Air Entertainment/Covenant
  Productions, 1991

BARBARA PETERS

(Barbara Peeters)
Address: 1118 Magnolia Blvd., North Hollywood, CA 91601,
  818/980-1660

THE DARK SIDE OF TOMORROW   co-director with
  Jacque Beerson, Able, 1970
BURY ME AN ANGEL   New World, 1972
SUMMER SCHOOL TEACHERS   New World, 1975
JUST THE TWO OF US   Boxoffice International, 1975
STARHOPS   First American, 1978
HUMANOIDS FROM THE DEEP   New World, 1980

CHARLIE PETERS*

Contact: Directors Guild of America - Los Angeles, 213/851-3671

PASSED AWAY   Buena Vista, 1992

WOLFGANG PETERSEN*

b. March 14, 1941 - Emden, Germany
Agent: CAA - Beverly Hills, 310/288-4545

EINER VON UNS BEIDEN   1973, West German
VIER GEGEN DIE BLANK   1976, West German
REIFEZEUGNIS   1976, West German
PLANUBUNG   1977, West German
THE CONSEQUENCE   Libra, 1977, West German
BLACK AND WHITE LIKE DAY AND NIGHT   New Yorker,
  1978, West German
DAS BOOT (THE BOAT) ★   Triumph/Columbia,
  1981, West German
THE NEVERENDING STORY   Warner Bros., 1984, West German
ENEMY MINE   20th Century Fox, 1985
SHATTERED   MGM-Pathe Communications, 1991, U.S.-German
IN THE LINE OF FIRE   Columbia, 1993
OUTBREAK   Warner Bros., 1995

KRISTINE PETERSON

Agent: William Morris Agency - Beverly Hills, 310/859-4000
Personal Manager: Creative Alliance Management - Los Angeles,
  213/962-6090

DEADLY DREAMS   Concorde, 1988
BODY CHEMISTRY   Concorde, 1990
CRITTERS 3   New Line Cinema, 1992
THE HARD TRUTH   Promark Entertainment Group/Spectator
  Films, 1994

CHRIS PETIT

b. 1949 - England
Address: 7 Barnsway, Kings Langley, Hertfordshire WD4 9PW,
  England, tel.: 0923/269599
Business: Pace Productions, 12 The Green, Newport Pagnell,
  Buckinghamshire MK16 0JW, England, tel.: 0908/618767

RADIO ON   British Film Institute/Road Movies, 1979,
  British-West German
AN UNSUITABLE JOB FOR A WOMAN   Boyd's Co., 1982, British
FLYING FISH OVER HOLLYWOOD (FD)   1983, British
FLIGHT TO BERLIN   Road Movies/British Film Institute/Channel 4,
  1984, West German-British
CHINESE BOXES   Chris Sievernich Productions/Palace
  Productions, 1984, West German-British

ANN PETRIE*

Home: 225 West 106th Street - Penthouse K, New York, NY 10025,
  212/866-8676

MOTHER TERESA (FD)   co-director with Jeanette Petrie,
  Petrie Productions, 1986

DANIEL PETRIE*

b. November 26, 1920 - Glace Bay, Nova Scotia, Canada
Address: 13201 Haney Place, Los Angeles, CA 90049,
310/451-9157
Agent: CAA - Beverly Hills, 310/288-4545

THE BRAMBLE BUSH   Warner Bros., 1960
A RAISIN IN THE SUN   Columbia, 1961
THE MAIN ATTRACTION   MGM, 1962
STOLEN HOURS   United Artists, 1963
THE IDOL   Embassy, 1966, British
THE SPY WITH A COLD NOSE   Embassy, 1966, British
SILENT NIGHT, LONELY NIGHT (TF)   Universal TV, 1969
THE CITY (TF)   Universal TV, 1971
A HOWLING IN THE WOODS (TF)   Universal TV, 1971
MOON OF THE WOLF (TF)   Filmways, 1972
HEC RAMSEY (TF)   Universal TV/Mark VII Ltd., 1972
TROUBLE COMES TO TOWN (TF)   ABC Circle Films, 1973
THE NEPTUNE FACTOR   20th Century-Fox, 1973, Canadian
MOUSEY (TF)   Universal TV/Associated British Films,
1974, U.S.-British
THE GUN AND THE PULPIT (TF)   Danny Thomas
Productions, 1974
BUSTER AND BILLIE   Columbia, 1974
RETURNING HOME (TF)   Lorimar Productions/Samuel Goldwyn
Productions, 1975
ELEANOR AND FRANKLIN (TF) ☆☆   Talent Associates, 1976
SYBIL (TF)   Lorimar Productions, 1976
LIFEGUARD   Paramount, 1976
ELEANOR AND FRANKLIN: THE WHITE HOUSE YEARS (TF) ☆☆
Talent Associates, 1977
THE QUINNS (TF)   Daniel Wilson Productions, 1977
THE BETSY   Allied Artists, 1978
RESURRECTION   Universal, 1980
FORT APACHE, THE BRONX   20th Century-Fox, 1981
SIX PACK   20th Century-Fox, 1982
THE DOLLMAKER (TF)   Finnegan Associates/IPC Films, Inc./
Dollmaker Productions, 1984
THE BAY BOY   Orion, 1984, Canadian-French
HALF A LIFETIME (CTF)   HBO Showcase/Astral Film Enterprises/
Martin Bregman Productions, 1986, U.S.-Canadian
SQUARE DANCE   Island Pictures, 1986
ROCKET GIBRALTAR   Columbia, 1988
COCOON: THE RETURN   20th Century Fox, 1988
MY NAME IS BILL W. (TF) ☆   Garner-Duchow Productions, 1989
MARK TWAIN AND ME (CTF) ☆   Chilmark Productions/The
Disney Channel, 1991
A TOWN TORN APART (TF) ☆   Paragon Entertainment
Corporation/World International Network/David W. Rintels
Productions, 1992
LASSIE   Paramount, 1994

DANIEL PETRIE, JR.*

Business: Dan Petrie, Jr. & Co., 500 S. Buena Vista Street -
Animation 2B5, Burbank, CA 91521, 818/560-6450
Agent: Robert Wunsch, Richland/Wunsch/Hohman Agency -
Los Angeles, 310/278-1955

TOY SOLDIERS   TriStar, 1991
IN THE ARMY NOW   Buena Vista, 1994

DONALD PETRIE*

Agent: UTA - Beverly Hills, 310/273-6700

MYSTIC PIZZA   The Samuel Goldwyn Company, 1988
OPPORTUNITY KNOCKS   Universal, 1990
GRUMPY OLD MEN   Warner Bros., 1993
THE FAVOR   Orion, 1994, filmed in 1991
RICHIE RICH   Warner Bros., 1994

JEANETTE PETRIE

MOTHER TERESA (FD)   co-director with Ann Petrie,
Petrie Productions, 1986

ALEXANDER PETROVIC

b. 1929 - Yugoslavia

WHERE LOVE HAS GONE   1961, Yugoslavian
THE DAYS   1963, Yugoslavian
THREE   1965, Yugoslavian
I EVEN MET HAPPY GYPSIES   Prominent Films,
1967, Yugoslavian
IT RAINS IN MY VILLAGE   1969, Yugoslavian
IL MAESTRO E MARGHERITA   1972, Italian-Yugoslavian
GRUPPENBILD MIT DAME   1977, West German-French
THE MOST GLORIOUS WAR   1989, Yugoslavian

JOSEPH PEVNEY*

b. 1920 - New York, New York
Business Manager: T.J. Smith, 17826 Chatsworth Street,
Granada Hills, CA 91344, 818/366-1144

SHAKEDOWN   Universal, 1950
UNDERCOVER GIRL   Universal, 1950
AIR CADET   Universal, 1951
IRON MAN   Universal, 1951
THE LADY FROM TEXAS   Universal, 1951
THE STRANGE DOOR   Universal, 1951
MEET DANNY WILSON   Universal, 1952
FLESH AND FURY   Universal, 1952
JUST ACROSS THE STREET   Universal, 1952
BECAUSE OF YOU   Universal, 1952
DESERT LEGION   Universal, 1953
IT HAPPENS EVERY THURSDAY   Universal, 1953
BACK TO GOD'S COUNTRY   Universal, 1953
YANKEE PASHA   Universal, 1954
PLAYGIRL   Universal, 1954
THREE RING CIRCUS   Paramount, 1954
SIX BRIDGES TO CROSS   Universal, 1955
FOXFIRE   Universal, 1955
FEMALE ON THE BEACH   Universal, 1955
AWAY ALL BOATS   Universal, 1956
CONGO CROSSING   Universal, 1956
ISTANBUL   Universal, 1956
TAMMY AND THE BACHELOR   Universal, 1957
THE MIDNIGHT STORY   Universal, 1957
MAN OF A THOUSAND FACES   Universal, 1957
TWILIGHT FOR THE GODS   Universal, 1958
TORPEDO RUN   MGM, 1958
CASH McCALL   Warner Bros., 1960
THE PLUNDERERS   Allied Artists, 1960
THE CROWDED SKY   Warner Bros., 1960
PORTRAIT OF A MOBSTER   Warner Bros., 1961
THE NIGHT OF THE GRIZZLY   Paramount, 1966
MY DARLING DAUGHTERS' ANNIVERSARY (TF)
Universal TV, 1973
WHO IS THE BLACK DAHLIA? (TF)   Douglas S. Cramer
Productions, 1975
MYSTERIOUS ISLAND OF BEAUTIFUL WOMEN (TF)
Alan Landsburg Productions, 1977
PRISONERS OF THE SEA   McLane Enterprises, 1985

JOHN PEYSER*

b. August 10, 1916 - New York, New York
Home: 19721 Redwing Street, Woodland Hills, CA 91364,
818/884-7730

UNDERSEA GIRL   Allied Artists, 1958
THE MURDER MEN   MGM, 1964
THE YOUNG WARRIORS   Universal, 1967
HONEYMOON WITH A STRANGER (TF)
20th Century-Fox TV, 1969
MASSACRE HARBOR   United Artists, 1970
CENTER FOLD GIRLS   Dimension, 1974
STUNT SEVEN (TF)   Martin Poll Productions, 1979

WILLIAM PHELPS*

Home: 9019 Elevado Street, Los Angeles, CA 90069, 310/271-9466
Agent: Barry Perelman Agency - Los Angeles, 310/274-5999

WAVE WARRIORS (FD)   1986
THE NORTH SHORE   Universal, 1987

Ph

F I L M   D I R E C T O R S

WIN PHELPS*
Agent: Mitchell Kaplan, The Kaplan-Stahler Agency - Beverly Hills, 213/653-4483

APPEARANCES (TF)   Echo Coves Productions/
Touchstone TV, 1990

NICHOLAS PHILIBERT
Contact: French Film Office, 745 Fifth Avenue, New York, NY 10151, 212/832-8860

IN THE LAND OF THE DEAF (FD)   International Film Circuit, 1993, French

LEE PHILIPS*
b. Brooklyn, New York
Home: 11939 Gorham Avenue - Suite 104, Los Angeles, CA 90049, 310/820-7464
Agent: Shapiro-Lichtman Talent Agency - Los Angeles, 310/859-8877

GETTING AWAY FROM IT ALL (TF)   Palomar Pictures
International, 1972
THE GIRL MOST LIKELY TO... (TF)   ABC Circle Films, 1973
THE STRANGER WITHIN (TF)   Lorimar Productions, 1974
THE RED BADGE OF COURAGE (TF)   20th Century-Fox TV, 1974
SWEET HOSTAGE (TF)   Brut Productions, 1975
LOUIS ARMSTRONG - CHICAGO STYLE (TF)   Charles Fries
Productions, 1975
JAMES A. MICHENER'S DYNASTY (TF)   David Paradine TV, 1976
WANTED: THE SUNDANCE WOMAN (TF)
20th Century-Fox TV, 1976
THE SPELL (TF)   Charles Fries Productions, 1977
THE WAR BETWEEN THE TATES (TF)   Talent Associates, 1977
SPECIAL OLYMPICS (TF)   Roger Gimbel Productions/
EMI TV, 1978
THE COMEDY COMPANY (TF)   Merrit Malloy-Jerry Adler
Productions, 1978
SALVAGE (TF)   Bennett-Katleman Productions/Columbia TV, 1979
VALENTINE (TF)   Malloy-Philips Productions/Edward S. Feldman
Company, 1979
HARDHAT AND LEGS (TF)   Syzygy Productions, 1980
CRAZY TIMES (TF)   Kayden-Gleason Productions/George Reeves
Productions/Warner Bros. TV, 1981
ON THE RIGHT TRACK   20th Century-Fox, 1981
A WEDDING ON WALTON'S MOUNTAIN (TF)   Lorimar
Productions/Amanda Productions, 1982
MAE WEST (TF) ☆   Hill-Mandelker Films, 1982
GAMES MOTHER NEVER TAUGHT YOU (TF)
CBS Entertainment, 1982
LOTTERY! (TF)   Rosner TV Productions/Orion TV, 1983
HAPPY (TF)   Bacchus Films Inc., 1983
SAMSON AND DELILAH (TF)   Catalina Production Group/
Comworld Productions, 1984
SPACE (MS)   co-director with Joseph Sargent, Stonehenge
Productions/Paramount TV, 1985
AMERICAN GEISHA (TF)   Interscope Communications/Stonehenge
Productions, 1986
THE BLUE LIGHTNING (TF)   Alan Sloan Productions/The Seven
Network/Coote-Carroll Australia/Roadshow, 1986, U.S.-Australian
BARNUM (TF)   Robert Halmi, Inc./Filmline International,
1986, U.S.-Canadian
SIDNEY SHELDON'S WINDMILLS OF THE GODS   WINDMILLS
OF THE GODS (TF)   Dove Productions/ITC Productions, 1988
KING OF THE OLYMPICS (TF)   Harmony Gold/ReteEuropa/SFP
Productions, 1988, U.S.-Italian
MONEY, POWER, MURDER (TF)   Skids Productions/CBS
Entertainment, 1989
BLIND VENGEANCE (CTF)   Spanish Trail Productions/MCA-TV
Entertainment, 1990
SILENT MOTIVE (CTF)   Farrell-Minoff Productions/Viacom, 1991

BILL PHILLIPS
Agent: The Gersh Agency - Beverly Hills, 310/274-6611

THERE GOES THE NEIGHBORHOOD   Paramount, 1992

LOU DIAMOND PHILLIPS
b. February 17, 1962 - Philippines
Agent: Innovative Artists - Los Angeles, 310/553-5200

DANGEROUS TOUCH   Trimark Pictures, 1994
SIOUX CITY   I.R.S. Releasing, 1994

MAURICE PHILLIPS*
Address: 419 N. Larchmont - Suite 95, Los Angeles, CA 90004, 213/957-5775
Agent: Paradigm - Los Angeles, 310/277-4400 or:
Rochelle Stevens & Co. - London, tel.: 171/359-3900

RIDERS OF THE STORM   THE AMERICAN WAY   Miramax Films,
1986, British
OVER HER DEAD BODY   ENID IS SLEEPING   Vestron, 1990
ANOTHER YOU   TriStar, 1991
SIGNS AND WONDERS (MS)   BBC, 1994, British

MAURICE PIALAT
b. August 21, 1925 - Puy-de-Dome, France
Home: 80, res. Sainte-Claire, 78170 La Celle-St-Cloud, France,
tel.: 1/39/69-82-46
Contact: French Film Office, 745 Fifth Avenue, New York,
NY 10151, 212/832-8860

ME   L'ENFANCE NUE   Altura Films Limited, 1968, French
NOUS NE VIEILLIRONS PAS ENSEMBLE   Corona,
1972, French
LA GUEULE OUVERTE   Lido Films La Boetie, 1974, French
GRADUATE FIRST   PASSE TON BAC D'ABORD   New Yorker,
1979, French
LOULOU   Gaumont, 1979, French
A NOS AMOURS   Les Films du Livradois/Gaumont/FR3,
1983, French
POLICE   New Yorker, 1985, French
UNDER THE SUN OF SATAN   Alive Films, 1987, French
VAN GOGH   Sony Pictures Classics, 1991, French
LE GARCU   1995, French

FRANCO PIAVOLI
b. June 21, 1933 - Pozzolengo (Brescia), Italy
Home: Pozzolengo (Brescia), tel.: 030/918104

IL PIANETA AZZURRO   11 Marzo Cinematografica,
1981, Italian
NOSTOS - IL RITORNO   Zefiro Film/Immaginazione,
1989, Italian

VASILY PICHUL
Contact: Confederation of Film-Makers Unions, Vasilyevskaya
Street 13, 123 825 Moscow, Russia, tel.: 095/250-4114

LITTLE VERA   International Film Exchange, 1988, Soviet
DARK IS THE NIGHT ON THE BLACK SEA   Podaro/Sacis/Silvia
D'Amico/RAI, 1990, Soviet-Italian

REX PICKETT
Agent: William Morris Agency - Beverly Hills, 310/859-4000

FROM HOLLYWOOD TO DEADWOOD   Island Pictures, 1988

ANDREW PIDDINGTON
Agent: ICM - London, tel.: 171/636-6565

SHUTTLECOCK   KM Films/Les Productions Belles Rives/Channel 4,
1991, British-French

CHARLES B. PIERCE
THE LEGEND OF BOGGY CREEK   Howco International, 1973
BOOTLEGGERS   Howco International, 1974
WINTERHAWK   Howco International, 1975
THE WINDS OF AUTUMN   Howco International, 1976

THE TOWN THAT DREADED SUNDOWN   American
   International, 1977
GREYEAGLE   American International, 1977
THE NORSEMEN   American International, 1978
THE EVICTORS   American International, 1979
SACRED GROUND   Pacific International, 1983
BOGGY CREEK II   Howco International, 1985
HAWKEN'S BREED   Vidmark, 1989
LEGEND OF THE JERSEY DEVIL   Paragon Pictures, 1990

HAL PIERCE
THE LOWER DEPTHS   Eternity Pictures, 1994

FRANK PIERSON*
b. May 12, 1925 - New York, New York
Agent: UTA - Beverly Hills, 310/273-6700
Home: 1223 N. Amalfi Drive, Pacific Palisades, CA 90272,
   310/454-8944

THE LOOKING GLASS WAR   Columbia, 1970, British
THE NEON CEILING (TF)   Universal TV, 1971
A STAR IS BORN   Warner Bros., 1976
KING OF THE GYPSIES   Paramount, 1978
SOMEBODY HAS TO SHOOT THE PICTURE (CTF)   Alan Barnette
   Productions/Frank Pierson Films/MCA-TV Entertainment/
   Scholastic Productions, 1990
CITIZEN COHN (CTF) ☆   Spring Creek Productions/Breakheart
   Films/Viacom Productions, 1992
LAKOTA WOMAN: SIEGE AT WOUNDED KNEE (CTF)
   Turner Pictures/Fonda Films, 1994
TRUMAN (CTF)   HBO Pictures, 1995

SAM PILLSBURY*
(Samuel Wallace Pillsbury)
Agent: Paradigm - Los Angeles, 310/277-4400

THE SCARECROW   Rob Whitehouse Productions,
   1982, New Zealand
HEART OF THE HIGH COUNTRY (MS)   Phillips/Whitehouse,
   1985, New Zealand-British
STARLIGHT HOTEL   Republic Pictures, 1987, New Zealand
ZANDALEE   Electric Pictures/ITC Entertainment Group, 1991
INTO THE BADLANDS (CTF)   Ogiens-Kane Productions, 1991
THE PRESIDENT'S CHILD (TF)   Lauren Film Productions, 1992
EYES OF TERROR (TF)   Bar-Gene Productions/Freyda Rothstein
   Productions/Hearst Entertainment, 1994
SEARCH FOR GRACE (TF)   CBS Entertainment
   Productions, 1994
SHADOWS OF DESIRE (TF)   The Konigsberg Company, 1994
BETWEEN LOVE AND HONOR (TF)   Grossbart-Barnett
   Prods., 1995

HE PING
Contact: China Film Import & Export Office, 2500 Wilshire Blvd. -
   Suite 1028, Los Angeles, CA 90057, 213/380-7520

RED FIRECRACKER, GREEN FIRECRACKER   October Films,
   1994, Chinese

SETH PINSKER*
Agent: Amsel, Eisenstadt & Frazier - Los Angeles, 310/939-1188
Manager: Somers Teitelbaum David - Beverly Hills, 310/203-8000

THE HIDDEN 2 - THE SPAWNING   New Line Cinema, 1994

HAROLD PINTER
b. October 10, 1930 - Hackney, East London, England
Agent: Judy Daish Associates - London, tel.: 171/262-1101

BUTLEY   American Film Theatre, 1974, British
THE REAR COLUMN (TF)   1980, British
THE HOTHOUSE (TF)   1982, British

LUCIAN PINTILIE
Contact: French Film Office, 745 Fifth Avenue, New York, NY 10151,
   212/832-8860

THE OAK   1992, French
UN ETE INOUBLIABLE   MK2 Productions/La Sept Cinema/Le Studio
   de Creation Cinematographique de Ministere de la Culture de
   Roumanie/Canal Plus/CNC/Filmex, 1994, French-Romanian

ERNEST PINTOFF*
b. December 15, 1931 - Watertown, Connecticut
Agent: Ronald Leif, Contemporary Artists - Beverly Hills,
   310/395-1800

HARVEY MIDDLEMAN, FIREMAN   Columbia, 1965
WHO KILLED MARY WHAT'S'ERNAME   Cannon, 1971
DYNAMITE CHICKEN   EYR, 1972
HUMAN FEELINGS (TF)   Crestview Productions/Worldvision, 1978
JAGUAR LIVES   American International, 1979
LUNCH WAGON   LUNCH WAGON GIRLS   Seymour Borde
   Associates, 1981
ST. HELENS   Davis-Panzer Productions, 1981

MARIE-FRANCE PISIER
b. May 1944 - Dalat, French Indochina
Contact: French Film Office, 745 Fifth Avenue, New York,
   NY 10151, 212/832-8860

LE BAL DU GOUVERNEUR   Cinea-FR3 Productions, 1990, French

PETER PISTOR
THE FENCE   Showcase Entertainment, 1994

GLEN PITRE
b. 1955 - Louisiana

BELIZAIRE THE CAJUN   Skouras Pictures, 1986

BRUCE PITTMAN
b. 1950 - Toronto, Ontario, Canada
Agent: The Gersh Agency - Beverly Hills, 310/274-6611
Business: Worthwhile Movies Inc., 191 Logan Avenue, Toronto,
   Ontario M4M 2N2, Canada, 416/469-0459

FOUR TO FOUR (TF)   1982, Canadian
THE CHORUS OF XMAS (TF)   1985, Canadian
THE MARK OF CAIN   Brightstar Films, 1985, Canadian
CONFIDENTIAL   Cineplex Odeon, 1986, Canadian
HELLO MARY LOU: PROM NIGHT II   THE HAUNTING OF
   HAMILTON HIGH   The Samuel Goldwyn Company,
   1987, Canadian
CHASING RAINBOWS (MS)   co-director with William Fruet,
   Mark Blandford & Susan Martin, CBC, 1988, Canadian
WHERE THE SPIRIT LIVES (TF)   Amazing Spirit Productions/
   CBC/Mid-Canada TV/TV Ontario, 1989, Canadian
SILENT WITNESS: WHAT A CHILD SAW (CTF)
   USA Pictures, 1994
HARRISON BERGERON (CTF)   Atlantis Films/Cypress Films/
   OFIP/Rogers Telefilm, 1995, U.S.-Canadian

MICHELE PLACIDO
b. 1946 - Ascoli Satriano, Italy
Contact: Studio Antonangeli, via Lutezia 5, Rome, Italy,
   tel.: 06/841-7436

PUMMARO'   Numero Uno/Cineuropa '92, 1990, Italian
LE AMICHE DEL CUORE   Clemi Cinematografica/Pladi
   Audiovisivi/RAI, 1992, Italian
UN EROE BORGHESE   Istituto Luce/Taodue Film/Mact
   Productions/Corsan Productions/Mediaset/Canal Plus,
   1995, Italian-French

ROGER PLANCHON
Contact: French Film Office, 745 Fifth Avenue, New York,
NY 10151, 212/832-8860

LOUIS, ENFANT ROI   Les Films du Losange/Le Centre Europeen
Cinematographique/TSF Productions/Telema/La Sept/France 2,
1993, French

LUCAS PLATT
GIRL IN THE CADILLAC   Steinhardt Baer Pictures Co., 1995

ALLEN PLONE*
Home: 319 N. Orange Drive, Los Angeles, CA 90036
Business Manager: Michael Donaldson - Los Angeles, 310/557-0417

NIGHT SCREAMS
PHANTOM OF THE RITZ
SWEET JUSTICE   Double Helix Films, 1992

BILL PLYMPTON
THE TUNE (AF)   October Films, 1992

LEONG PO-CHIH
(See Po-Chih LEONG)

JEREMY PODESWA
Business: Rebelfilms Inc., 345 Adelaide Street West - Suite 606,
Toronto, Ontario M5V 1R5, Canada, 416/593-1616
Home: 494 Euclid Avenue - Apt. 3, Toronto, Ontario M6G 2S9,
Canada, 416/963-8692

ECLIPSE   Malofilm Distribution, 1994, Canadian-German

AMOS POE
b. 1950 - Tel Aviv, Israel
Business: Poe Productions, 611 Broadway - Suite 812, New York,
NY 10012, 212/529-3662
Agent: William Morris Agency - Beverly Hills, 310/859-4000

THE FOREIGNER   Amos Poe Visions, 1978
SUBWAY RIDERS   Hep Pictures, 1981
ALPHABET CITY   Atlantic Releasing Corporation, 1984
TRIPLE BOGEY ON A PAR 5 HOLE   Poe Productions/Meridien
Theatrical, 1991

S. LEE POGOSTIN*
Contact: Directors Guild of America - Los Angeles, 213/851-3671

HARD CONTRACT   20th Century-Fox, 1969

WILLIAM POHLAD
OLD EXPLORERS   Taurus Entertainment, 1990

JEAN-MARIE POIRE
Agent: ICM France - Paris, tel.: 1/723-7860
Contact: French Film Office, 745 Fifth Avenue, New York,
NY 10151, 212/832-8860

LES VISITEURS   Miramax Films, 1993, French
LES ANGES GARDIENS   Gaumont, 1994, French

SIDNEY POITIER*
b. February 20, 1924 - Miami, Florida
Agent: CAA - Beverly Hills, 310/288-4545

BUCK AND THE PREACHER   Columbia, 1972
A WARM DECEMBER   National General, 1973
UPTOWN SATURDAY NIGHT   Warner Bros., 1974
LET'S DO IT AGAIN   Warner Bros., 1975
A PIECE OF THE ACTION   Warner Bros., 1977
STIR CRAZY   Columbia, 1980
HANKY PANKY   Columbia, 1982
FAST FORWARD   Columbia, 1985
GHOST DAD   Universal, 1990

ROMAN POLANSKI
b. August 18, 1933 - Paris, France
Agent: ICM - Beverly Hills, 310/550-4000 or:
Georges Beaume, Agents Associes - Paris, tel.: 1/42-56-21-22

KNIFE IN THE WATER   Kanawha, 1963, Polish
THE BEAUTIFUL SWINDLERS   *LES PLUS BELLES
ESCROQUERIES DU MONDE*, co-director with Ugo Grigoretti,
Claude Chabrol & Hiromichi Horikawa, Jack Ellis Films, 1964,
French-Italian-Japanese-Dutch
REPULSION   Royal Films International, 1965, British
CUL-DE-SAC   Sigma III, 1966, British
THE FEARLESS VAMPIRE KILLERS, OR PARDON ME BUT YOUR
TEETH ARE IN MY NECK   *DANCE OF THE VAMPIRES*
MGM, 1967, British
ROSEMARY'S BABY   Paramount, 1968
MACBETH   Columbia, 1971, British
WHAT?   Avco Embassy, 1973, Italian-French-West German
CHINATOWN ★   Paramount, 1974
THE TENANT   Paramount, 1976, French-U.S.
TESS ★   Columbia, 1980, French-British
PIRATES   Cannon, 1986, French-Tunisian
FRANTIC   Warner Bros., 1988
BITTER MOON   Fine Line Features/New Line Cinema,
1992, French-British
DEATH AND THE MAIDEN   Fine Line Features/New Line Cinema,
1994, U.S.-French-British

STEPHEN POLIAKOFF
Contact: British Film Commission, 70 Baker Street, London
W1M 1DJ, England, tel.: 171/224-5000

HIDDEN CITY   Hidden City Films/Channel 4, 1987, British
CLOSE MY EYES   Castle Hill Productions, 1991, British
CENTURY   I.R.S. Releasing, 1993, British

BARRY POLLACK
COOL BREEZE   MGM, 1972
THIS IS A HIJACK   Fanfare, 1973

JEFF POLLACK*
Contact: Directors Guild of America - Los Angeles, 213/851-3671

ABOVE THE RIM   New Line Cinema, 1994

SYDNEY POLLACK*
b. July 1, 1934 - Lafayette, Indiana
Business: Mirage Enterprises, 100 Universal City Plaza - Suite 414,
Universal City, CA 91608, 818/777-2000
Agent: CAA - Beverly Hills, 310/288-4545

THE SLENDER THREAD   Paramount, 1965
THIS PROPERTY IS CONDEMNED   Paramount, 1966
THE SCALPHUNTERS   United Artists, 1968
CASTLE KEEP   Columbia, 1969
THEY SHOOT HORSES, DON'T THEY? ★   Cinerama Releasing
Corporation, 1969
JEREMIAH JOHNSON   Warner Bros., 1972
THE WAY WE WERE   Columbia, 1973
THE YAKUZA   Warner Bros., 1975
3 DAYS OF THE CONDOR   Paramount, 1975
BOBBY DEERFIELD   Columbia, 1977
THE ELECTRIC HORSEMAN   Columbia, 1979
ABSENCE OF MALICE   Columbia, 1981
TOOTSIE ★   Columbia, 1982
OUT OF AFRICA ★★   Universal, 1985
HAVANA   Universal, 1990
THE FIRM   Paramount, 1993
SABRINA   Paramount, 1995

ABRAHAM POLONSKY*
b. December 5, 1910 - New York, New York
Agent: Phil Gersh, The Gersh Agency - Beverly Hills, 310/274-6611

FORCE OF EVIL   MGM, 1948
TELL THEM WILLIE BOY IS HERE   Universal, 1969
ROMANCE OF A HORSETHIEF   Allied Artists, 1971

BARRY POLTERMANN
ASWANG   Young American Films/Purple Onion Productions, 1994
THE UNEARTHLING   co-director with Wrye Martin,
   Forefront Films, 1994

GILLO PONTECORVO
(Gilberto Pontecorvo)
b. November 19, 1919 - Pisa, Italy
Home: via Paolo Frisi 18, Rome, Italy, tel.: 06/808-6514

DIE WINDROSE   co-director, 1956, East German
LA GRANDE STRADA AZZURRA   Ge-Si Malenotti/Play Art/
   Eichberg/Triglav Film, 1957, Italian-Yugoslavian
KAPO'   Vides/Zebra Film/Cineriz, 1960, Italian
BATTLE OF ALGIERS ★   Rizzoli, 1967, Italian-Algerian
BURN! *QUEIMADA!*   United Artists, 1970, Italian-French
OPERATION OGRO   CIDIF, 1979, Italian-Spanish-French

MAURIZIO PONZI
b. May 8, 1939 - Rome
Home: Vicolo del Bologna 51, Rome, Italy, tel.: 06/588-2877

I VISIONARI   21 Marzo Cinematografica, 1969, Italian
EQUINOZIO   San Diego, 1971, Italian
IL CASO RAOUL   Iskra Cinematografica, 1975, Italian
MADONNA CHE SILENZIO C'E' STASERA   Hera International
   Film/Mirage Film, 1982, Italian
SON CONTENTO   Hera International Film, 1983
THE POOL HUSTLERS   *IO CHIARA E LO SCURO*
   Orion Classics, 1983, Italian
AURORA (TF)   Roger Gimbel Productions/The Peregrine
   Producers Group/Sacis, 1984, U.S.-Italian
IL TENENTE DEI CARABINIERI   Columbia, 1986, Italian
NOI UOMINI DURI   CDI, 1987, Italian
IL VOLPONE   Maura Film/Cecchi Gori/Tiger Cinematografica,
   1988, Italian
VOLEVO I PANTOLINI   Penta Distribuzione, 1990, Italian
NERO COME IL CUORE   CEP, 1991, Italian
VIETATO AI MINORI   1992, Italian
ANCHE I COMMERCIALISTI HANNO UN'ANIMA   Erre
   Cinematografica/Alto Verbano/Reteitalia, 1994, Italian

LEA POOL
b. Soglio, Switzerland
Address: 5964, rue Hutchison, Outremont, Quebec H2V 4C1,
   Canada, 514/273-9351

LA FEMME DE L'HOTEL   1984, Canadian
ANNE TRISTER   1985, Canadian
A CORPS PERDU   1988, Canadian
HOTEL CHRONICLES (FD)   National Film Board of Canada,
   1991, Canadian
LA DEMOISELLE SAUVAGE   Cinemaginaire/Limbo Film/Telefilm
   Canada, 1991, Canadian-Swiss
MONTREAL VU PAR...   co-director with Patricia Rozema,
   Jacques Leduc, Michel Brault, Atom Egoyan & Denys Arcand,
   Cinema Plus Distribution, 1991, Canadian
MOUVEMENTS DU DESIR   Cinemaginaire Inc./National Film
   Board of Canada/Catpics Co-Productions Ltee./Telefilm
   Canada/SOGIC, 1994, Canadian-Swiss

ANGELA POPE
Agent: UTA - Beverly Hills, 310/273-6700 or:
   The Casarotto Company - London, tel.: 171/287-4450

SHIFTWORK (TF)   BBC, 1987, British
SWEET AS YOU ARE (TF)   BBC, 1988, British
DREAM BABY (TF)   BBC, 1989, British
CHILDREN CROSSING (TF)   BBC, 1990, British
MR. WAKEFIELD'S CRUSADE (MS)   BBC, 1992, British
A MAN YOU DON'T MEET EVERY DAY (TF)   Channel 4,
   1994, British
CAPTIVES   Miramax Films, 1994, British
THE HOLLOW REED   Scala Productions/Senator Film/
   Iberoamericana, 1995, British-German-Spanish

PETRU POPESCU
b. Romania
Agent: APA - Los Angeles, 310/273-0744

DEATH OF AN ANGEL   20th Century Fox, 1985

TED POST*
b. March 31, 1918 - Brooklyn, New York
Business Manager: Norman Blumenthal, 11030 Santa Monica Blvd.,
   Los Angeles, CA 90025, 310/479-8469

THE PEACEMAKER   United Artists, 1956
THE LEGEND OF TOM DOOLEY   Columbia, 1959
HANG 'EM HIGH   United Artists, 1968
BENEATH THE PLANET OF THE APES   20th Century-Fox, 1970
NIGHT SLAVES (TF)   Bing Crosby Productions, 1970
DR. COOK'S GARDEN (TF)   Paramount TV, 1970
YUMA (TF)   Aaron Spelling Productions, 1971
FIVE DESPERATE WOMEN (TF)   Aaron Spelling
   Productions, 1971
DO NOT FOLD, SPINDLE OR MUTILATE (TF)   Lee Rich
   Productions, 1971
THE BRAVOS (TF)   Universal TV, 1972
SANDCASTLES (TF)   Metromedia Productions, 1972
THE BABY   Scotia International, 1973, British
THE HARRAD EXPERIMENT   Cinerama Releasing
   Corporation, 1973
MAGNUM FORCE   Warner Bros., 1973
WHIFFS   20th Century-Fox, 1975
GOOD GUYS WEAR BLACK   American Cinema, 1978
GO TELL THE SPARTANS   Avco Embassy, 1978
DIARY OF A TEENAGE HITCHHIKER (TF)   The Shpetner
   Company, 1979
THE GIRLS IN THE OFFICE (TF)   ABC Circle Films, 1979
NIGHTKILL (TF)   Cine Artists, 1980
CAGNEY & LACEY (TF)   Mace Neufeld Productions/
   Filmways, 1981
STAGECOACH (TF)   Raymond Katz Productions/Heritage
   Entertainment, 1986
THE HUMAN SHIELD   Cannon, 1992

SALLY POTTER
b. England
Agent: Alexandra Cann Representation, 337 Fulham Road, London
   SW10 9TW, England, tel.: 171/352-6266

THE GOLD DIGGERS   British Film Institute/Channel 4,
   1984, British
TEARS, LAUGHTER, FEARS AND RAGE (TD)   1987, British
ORLANDO   Sony Pictures Classics, 1992,
   British-Russian-Italian-French-Dutch

GERALD POTTERTON
b. 1931 - London, England
Home: R.R. #3, Brome Lake, Cowansville, Quebec J2K 3G8,
   Canada, 514/263-3282
Business: Crayon Animation Inc., 4030 St-Ambroise - Suite 333,
   Montreal, Quebec H4C 2C8, Canada, 514/933-6396

HEAVY METAL (AF)   Columbia, 1981, Canadian

MICHEL POULETTE
Contact: Directors Guild of Canada, 225 Richmond Street, Toronto,
   Ontario M5V 1W2, Canada, 416/351-8200

LOUIS 19, LE ROI DES ONDES   Malofilm Distribution, 1994,
   Canadian-French

GERRY POULSON*
Agent: London Management - London, tel.: 171/287-9000

BLACK BEAUTY (TF)   London Weekend TV, 1979, British
DICK TURPIN (TF)   London Weekend TV, 1980, British
THE LEGENDARY STORY OF DICK TURPIN   London Weekend
   TV/RKO, 1981, British

PULASKI (TF)   BBC, 1988, British
LONDON'S BURNING (TF)   London Weekend TV, 1989, British

TRISTRAM POWELL
b. April 1940 - Oxford, England
Agent: The Casarotto Company - London, tel.: 171/287-4450

THE GHOST WRITER (TF)   WGBH-Boston/Malone-Gill
   Productions/BBC, 1984, U.S.-British
SOLDIERING ON (TF)   BBC, 1988, British
THE TEMPTATION OF EILEEN HUGHES (TF)   BBC, 1988, British
NUMBER 27 (TF)   BBC, 1989, British
THE KREMLIN FAREWELL (TF)   BBC, 1990, British
AMERICAN FRIENDS   Prominent Features, 1991, British
THE OLD DEVILS (TF)   BBC Wales, 1992, Welsh
THE LONG ROADS (TF)   BBC, 1992, British
SELECTED EXITS (TF)   BBC, 1993, British
TEARS BEFORE BEDTIME (TF)   BBC, 1994, British

JOHN POWER*
(John Beresford Power)
Agent: Becsey/Wisdom/Kalajian - Los Angeles, 310/550-0535

THE PICTURE SHOW MAN   Australian
THE DISMISSAL   Australian
THE GREAT GOLD SWINDLE   Australian
A SINGLE LIFE   Australian
ALICE TO NOWHERE   Australian
SKYTRACKERS   Australian
THE DIRTWATER DYNASTY (MS)   co-director with
   Michael Jenkins, Kennedy Miller Productions, 1988, Australian
TANAMERA: LION OF SINGAPORE (MS)   co-director with
   James Dobson, Reg Grundy Productions/Central
   Independent Television, 1989, Australian-British
CHARLES AND DIANA: UNHAPPILY EVER AFTER (TF)
   Konigsberg-Sanitsky Productions, 1992
STEPHEN KING'S THE TOMMYKNOCKERS
   THE TOMMYKNOCKERS (TF)   Konigsberg-Sanitsky
   Company, 1993
BETRAYED BY LOVE (TF)   Greengrass Productions/Edgar
   Scherick & Associates, 1994
FATAL VOWS: THE ALEXANDRA O'HARA STORY (TF)
   Roaring Fork Productions/Karen Danaher-Dorr Productions/
   Republic Pictures/Spelling Entertainment, 1994
SOMEONE ELSE'S CHILD (TF)   Greengrass Productions/de Passe
   Entertainment, 1994

PASQUALE POZZESSERE
b. 1957 - Lizzano, Italy
Contact: S.I.A.E., Sezione Cinema, viale della Letterature 30,
   Rome, Italy, tel.: 6/59901

VERSO SUD   Demian Film/Regione Puglia, 1992, Italian
PADRE E FIGLIO   Erre Cinematografica/Reteitalia/Flach Film/K2
   Two/Reteitalia, 1994, Italian-French

UDAYAN PRASAD
Agent: The Casarotto Company - London, tel.: 171/287-4450

102 BOULEVARD HAUSSMANN (TF)   BBC/La Sept,
   1990, British-French
THEY NEVER SLEPT (TF)   BBC, 1990, British
RUNNING LATE (TF)   BBC, 1992, British
FEMME FATALE (TF)   BBC/Screen TV, 1993, British

MICHAEL PREECE*
b. September 15, 1936 - Los Angeles, California
Home: 6930 Dume Drive, Malibu, CA 90265
Agent: Contemporary Artists - Beverly Hills, 310/395-1800

THE PRIZE FIGHTER   New World, 1979
PARADISE CONNECTION (TF)   Woodruff Productions/QM
   Productions, 1979
DALLAS: PHANTOM OF THE OIL RIG (TF)   co-director with
   Irving J. Moore, Lorimar TV, 1989

BERETTA'S ISLAND   Weaks-Durney Productions/Franco Columbu
   Productions, 1993
WALKER, TEXAS RANGER: THE REUNION (TF)   Top Kick
   Productions/Columbia Pictures TV/Ruddy & Greif Productions/
   CBS Entertainment, 1994

MICHAEL PRESSMAN*
b. July 1, 1950 - New York, New York
Agent: William Morris Agency - Beverly Hills, 310/859-4000

THE GREAT TEXAS DYNAMITE CHASE   New World, 1976
THE BAD NEWS BEARS IN BREAKING TRAINING
   Paramount, 1977
LIKE MOM, LIKE ME (TF)   CBS Entertainment, 1978
BOULEVARD NIGHTS   Warner Bros., 1979
THOSE LIPS, THOSE EYES   United Artists, 1980
SOME KIND OF HERO   Paramount, 1982
DOCTOR DETROIT   Universal, 1983
THE IMPOSTER (TF)   Gloria Monty Productions/Comworld
   Productions, 1984
AND THE CHILDREN SHALL LEAD (TF)   Rainbow TV
   Workshop, 1985
PRIVATE SESSIONS (TF)   The Belle Company/Seltzer-Gimbel
   Productions/Raven's Claw Productions/Comworld
   Productions, 1985
FINAL JEOPARDY (TF)   Frank von Zerneck Productions, 1985
THE CHRISTMAS GIFT (TF)   Rosemont Productions/Sunn Classic
   Pictures, 1986
HAUNTED BY HER PAST (TF)   Norton Wright Productions/ITC
   Productions, 1987
TO HEAL A NATION (TF)   Lionel Chetwynd Productions/Orion TV/
   von Zerneck-Samuels Productions, 1988
SHOOTDOWN (TF)   Leonard Hill Films, 1988
INCIDENT AT DARK RIVER (CTF)   Farrell-Minoff Productions/
   Turner Network TV, 1989
MAN AGAINST THE MOB: THE CHINATOWN MURDERS (TF)
   von Zerneck-Sertner Productions, 1989
JOSHUA'S HEART (TF)   Spectator Productions, 1990
TEENAGE MUTANT NINJA TURTLES II: THE SECRET OF
   THE OOZE   New Line Cinema, 1991
QUICKSAND: NO ESCAPE (CTF)   Finnegan-Pinchuk
   Productions/MCA-TV Entertainment, 1992
MIRACLE CHILD (TF)   Steve White Productions, 1993

GAYLENE PRESTON
b. June 1, 1947 - Greymouth, New Zealand
Contact: New Zealand Film Commission, P.O. Box 11-546,
   Wellington, New Zealand, tel.: 4/385-9754

ALL THE WAY UP THERE (FD)   1978, New Zealand
LEARNING FAST (FD)   1981, New Zealand
MAKING UTU (FD)   1982, New Zealand
DARK OF THE NIGHT   *MR. WRONG*   Quartet, 1985, New Zealand
RUBY AND RATA   Preston Laing Productions/New Zealand Film
   Commission, 1990, New Zealand
BREAD & ROSES   Preston Laing Productions, 1993, New Zealand
WAR STORIES   New Zealand Film Commission,
   1995, New Zealand

RUBEN PREUSS*
Contact: Directors Guild of America - Los Angeles, 213/851-3671

IN DANGEROUS COMPANY   Manson International, 1988
DECEPTIONS   Alpha Entertainment, 1989
BLACKMAIL (CTF)   Pacific Motion Picture Corporation/Barry Weitz
   Films/Wilshire Court Productions, 1991
DECEPTIONS 2   Saban Pictures, 1993
RESURRECTION   Delta Entertainment, 1993
DEAD ON SIGHT   MCEG Sterling Entertainment, 1994

DAVID F. PRICE
Business: Summerwind Productions, Inc., 2241 So. Malcolm Avenue,
   Los Angeles, CA 90064, 310475-2456

SON OF DARKNESS: TO DIE FOR II   Trimark Pictures, 1991
CHILDREN OF THE CORN II: THE FINAL SACRIFICE
   Dimension, 1993
DR. JEKYLL AND MS. HYDE   Savoy Pictures, 1995

JEROME PRIEUR
Contact: French Film Office, 745 Fifth Avenue, New York,
NY 10151, 212/832-8860

LA VERITABLE HISTOIRE D'ARTAUD LE MOMO (FD)   co-director
with Gerard Mordillat, Laura Productions/Les Films D'Ici/La
Sept-Arte/Arcanal/Centre Georges Pompidou, 1994, French

BARRY PRIMUS*
b. New York, New York - February 16, 1938
Home: 2735 Creston Drive, Los Angeles, CA 90068, 213/962-3007
Agent: Innovative Artists - Los Angeles, 310/553-5200

MISTRESS   Rainbow Releasing/Tribeca Releasing, 1992

PRINCE
(Rogers Nelson/The Artist Formerly Known as Prince)
b. Minneapolis, Minnesota
Agent: CAA - Beverly Hills, 310/288-4545

UNDER THE CHERRY MOON   Warner Bros., 1986
SIGN 'O' THE TIMES   Cineplex Odeon, 1987
GRAFFITI BRIDGE   Warner Bros., 1990

HAROLD PRINCE
b. January 30, 1928
Business: 1270 Avenue of the Americas, New York,
NY, 212/399-0960

SOMETHING FOR EVERYONE   National General, 1970, British
A LITTLE NIGHT MUSIC   New World, 1978, Austrian-U.S.

JONATHAN PRINCE*
Agent: UTA - Beverly Hills, 310/273-6700
Telephone: 310/556-8322 or 213/462-7893

CAMP NOWHERE   Buena Vista, 1994

DAVID A. PRIOR
Business: West Side Studios, 10726 McCune Avenue, Los Angeles,
CA 90034, 213/559-8805

CHASE   AIP, 1987
DEADLY PREY   AIP, 1987
MANKILLERS   AIP, 1987
NIGHTWARS   AIP, 1987
BATTLEGROUND   AIP, 1989
C.O.P.S.   AIP, 1989
JUNGLE ASSAULT   AIP, 1989
THE LOST PLATOON   AIP, 1989
BACK TO THE PAST   American-Independent, 1990
FUTURE ZONE   AIP, 1990
THE FINAL SANCTION   American-Independent, 1990
OPERATION WARZONE   AIP, 1990
THAT'S ACTION (HVD)   AIP, 1990
RAW NERVE   Pyramid Distribution, 1991
LOCK N' LOAD   AIP, 1991
WHITE FURY   AIP, 1991
CENTER OF THE WEB   Pyramid Distribution, 1992
DOUBLE THREAT   AIP, 1992
NIGHT TRAP   *MARDI GRAS FOR THE DEVIL*   West Side
Studios, 1993
GOOD COP, BAD COP   West Side Studios, 1993
BIOFORCE 1   Southern Star Studios, 1995

VINCE PRIVITERA
WITCHFIRE   Shapiro Glickenhaus Entertainment, 1986

ANDREW PROWSE
DEMONSTONE   *HEARTSTONE*   Fries Entertainment, 1990

ALEX PROYAS*
Agent: CAA - Beverly Hills, 310/288-4545

THE CROW   Dimension Films/Miramax, 1994

CRAIG PRYCE
Contact: Directors Guild of Canada, 225 Richmond Street,
Toronto, Ontario M5V 1W2, Canada, 416/351-8200

REVENGE OF THE RADIO ACTIVE REPORTER   Astral Film,
1991, Canadian
THE DARK   Norstar Entertainment, 1993, Canadian

RICHARD PRYOR*
b. December 1, 1940 - Peoria, Illinois
Business: 16030 Ventura Blvd. - Suite 380, Encino, CA 91436,
818/905-9500
Agent: Irvin Arthur Associates - Beverly Hills, 310/278-5934

RICHARD PRYOR HERE AND NOW (PF)   Columbia, 1983
JO JO DANCER, YOUR LIFE IS CALLING   Columbia, 1986

LUIS PUENZO*
b. February 24, 1940- Buenos Aires, Argentina
Agent: William Morris Agency - Beverly Hills, 310/859-4000

LUCES EN MI ZAPATOS   Cinemania Corporation, 1974, Argentine
THE OFFICIAL STORY   Historias Cinematograficas,
1985, Argentina
OLD GRINGO   Columbia, 1989
THE PLAGUE   Cyril de Rouvre/The Pepper-Prince Company/Oscar
Kramer SA/Cinemania/Canal Plus, 1992, French-Argentine

ABRAHAM PULIDO
b. March 18, 1953 - Caracas, Venezuela
Business: Esteban Films, Inc., 250 West 57th Street - Suite 606-7,
New York, NY 10107, 212/489-1491

LILY   Creacolor, 1983, Venezuelan

LOU PUOPOLO*
Home: 1204-1/2 Larrabee Street, West Hollywood, CA 90069,
310/652-5779
Business: Puopolo Productions Inc., 61 Lloyd Road, Montclair,
NJ 07042, 201/783-0110

HOME FIRES BURNING   White Deer/Puopolo Productions, 1992

EVELYN PURCELL*
Agent: William Morris Agency - Beverly Hills, 310/859-4000

NOBODY'S FOOL   Island Pictures, 1986
THE LAND OF LITTLE RAIN   Denver Center for the Performing
Arts/Mayport Productions/Brockman Seawell, 1988

JOSEPH PURCELL*
Home: 13627 Morrison Street, Sherman Oaks, CA 91423,
818/789-9294

THE DELOS ADVENTURE   American Cine Marketing, 1987

JON PURDY
Business: Concorde Pictures, 11600 San Vicente Blvd., Los Angeles,
CA 90049, 310/826-0978

REFLECTIONS ON A CRIME   Concorde, 1995
DILLINGER AND CAPONE   Concorde, 1995

DOROTHY ANN PUZO*
Home: 12050 Valleyheart Drive - Apt. 303, Studio City, CA
Agent: Harold Greene, 8455 Beverly Blvd. - Suite 309,
Los Angeles, CA 90048, 213/852-4959

COLD STEEL   CineTel, 1987

JOE PYTKA*
Business Manager: Suellen Wagner, 916 Main Street, Venice,
CA 90291, 310/392-9571

LET IT RIDE   Paramount, 1989

ALBERT PYUN*
Agent: ICM - Beverly Hills, 310/550-4000

THE SWORD AND THE SORCERER   Group 1, 1982
RADIOACTIVE DREAMS   DEG, 1986
DANGEROUSLY CLOSE   Cannon, 1986
VICIOUS LIPS   Empire Pictures, 1987
DOWN TWISTED   Cannon, 1987
ALIEN FROM L.A.   Cannon, 1988
CYBORG   Cannon, 1989
DECEIT   21st Century Distribution, 1989
BLOODMATCH   Power Pictures, 1990
KICKBOXER 2   Trimark Pictures, 1991
ARCADE   Full Moon Entertainment, 1991
DOLLMAN   Full Moon Entertainment, 1991
CAPTAIN AMERICA   21st Century Distribution, 1992
NEMESIS   Imperial Entertainment, 1993
KNIGHTS   Moonstone Entertainment, 1993
BRAIN SMASHER...A LOVE STORY   Kings Road
    Entertainment, 1993
RAVEN HAWK   Raven Hawk Productions, 1993
KICKBOXER 4: THE AGGRESSOR   Kings Road
    Entertainment, 1994
HEATSEEKER   Trimark Pictures, 1994
HONG KONG '97   Trimark Pictures, 1994

Q

JOHN QUESTED
Business: Goldcrest Films and Television Ltd., 65-66 Dean Street,
    London W1V 6PL, England, tel.: 171/437-8696

PHILADELPHIA, HERE I COME   Irish
HERE ARE LADIES   Arthur Cantor Films, 1971, Irish
LOOPHOLE   MGM/United Artists, 1981, British

FOLCO QUILICI
b. April 9, 1930 - Ferrara, Italy
Home: viale H. Cesare 47, Rome, Italy, tel.: 06/321-6730

SESTO CONTINENTE   Delphinus, 1954, Italian
TAM TAM MAYUMBE   co-director with Gian Gaspare Napolitano,
    Documento Film/Franco London Film, 1955, Italian-French
L'ULTIMO PARADISO   Paneuropa, 1957, Italian
DAGLI APPENNINI ALLE ANDE   David Film/Mondial Cine/
    Argentina Sono Film, 1959, Italian-Argentinian
TI - KOJO E IL SUO PESCECANE   Titanus, 1963, Italian
LE SCHIAVE ESISTONO ANCORA   co-director with Roberto
    Malenotti & Piero Nelli, Ge.Si. Cinematografica, 1964, Italian
UNA SPIAGGIA LONTANA (TF)   RAI, 1970, Italian
OCEANO   P.E.A., 1971, Italian
IL DIO SOTTO LA PELLE   co-director with Carlo Alberto Pinelli,
    Unidis, 1974, Italian
FRATELLO MARE   Shansa, 1975, Italian
L'ITALIA VISTA DAL CIELO (TF)   RAI, 1978, Italian
CACCIATORI DI NAVI   C.E.P./RAI, 1990, Italian
ONLY ONE SURVIVED (TF)   CBS Entertainment/RAI,
    1990, U.S.-Italian

ANTHONY QUINN
b. April 21, 1915 - Chihuahua, Mexico
Agent: Metropolitan Talent Agency - Los Angeles, 213/857-4500 -
    Beverly Hills, 310/247-5500

THE BUCCANEER   Paramount, 1958

JAMES QUINN*
Agent: William Morris Agency - Beverly Hills, 310/859-4000

BLIND MAN'S BLUFF (CTF)   Wilshire Court Productions/Pacific
    Motion Pictures, 1992

JOHN QUINN
GOLDY III: THE MAGIC OF THE GOLDEN BEAR
    LIVE Entertainment, 1994

GENE QUINTANO*
(Eugene Francis Quintano)
Agent: ICM - Beverly Hills, 310/550-4000

HONEYMOON ACADEMY   Triumph Releasing Corporation, 1990
WHY ME?   Triumph Releasing Corporation, 1990
NATIONAL LAMPOON'S LOADED WEAPON 1
    New Line Cinema, 1993

CARLO U. QUINTERIO*
Home: 20522 Pacific Coast Highway, Malibu, CA 90265,
    310/456-2849

NIGHT TRAIN TO VENICE   Take Munich Filmproduktion,
    1993, German

JOSE QUINTERO
b. October 15, 1924 - Panama City, Panama

THE ROMAN SPRING OF MRS. STONE   Warner Bros., 1961

R

DENIS RABAGLIA
Contact: French Film Office, 745 Fifth Avenue, New York,
    NY 10151, 212/832-8860

GROSSESSE NERVEUSE   Bloody Mary Productions/France 2/
    Crittin & Thiebaud/TSR/Afitec Valais, 1994, French-Swiss

FONS RADEMAKERS
b. September 5, 1920 - Rosendaal, Brabant, Netherlands
Business: Fons Rademakers Productie B.V., Prinsengracht 685,
    1017 JT Amsterdam, Netherlands, tel.: 20/221298
Agent: Paul Kohner, Inc. - Los Angeles, 310/550-1060

VILLAGE ON THE RIVER   1958, Dutch
THAT JOYOUS EVE   1960, Dutch
THE KNIFE   1961, Dutch
THE SPITTING IMAGE   1963, Dutch
THE DANCE OF THE HERON   1966, Dutch
MIRA   1971, Dutch
BECAUSE OF THE CATS   1973, Dutch
MAX HAVELAAR   1976, Dutch
MY FRIEND   1979, Dutch
THE ASSAULT   Cannon, 1987, Dutch
THE ROSE GARDEN   Cannon, 1989, West German

PETER RADER*

Agent: CAA - Beverly Hills, 310/288-4545

GRANDMOTHER'S HOUSE Omega Pictures, 1989
HIRED TO KILL co-director with Nico Mastorakis, Omega
Pictures, 1990

MICHAEL RADFORD

b. November 14, 1950 - New Delhi, India
Agent: Sanford-Gross & Associates - Los Angeles, 310/208-2100 or:
Voyez Mon Agent - Paris, tel.: 1/47-23-55-80

VAN MORRISON IN IRELAND (FCD) Caledonia-Angle Films,
1981, British
THE WHITE BIRD PASSES (TF) BBC, 1981, British
ANOTHER TIME, ANOTHER PLACE The Samuel Goldwyn
Company, 1983, British
1984 Atlantic Releasing Corporation, 1984, British
WHITE MISCHIEF Columbia, 1987, British
IL POSTINO Pentafilm/Esterno Mediterraneo Film/Blue Dahlia
Productions/K2T, 1994, Italian-French-Belgian

ROBERT RADLER

Agent: The Gersh Agency - Beverly Hills, 310/274-6611

BEST OF THE BEST Taurus Entertainment/SVS Films, 1989
BEST OF THE BEST II 20th Century Fox, 1993
FULL CONTACT Tilford Productions, 1993

ERIC RADOMSKI

BATMAN: MASK OF THE PHANTASM (AF) co-director with
Bruce W. Timm, Warner Bros., 1993

MICHAEL RAE

LASERBLAST Irwin Yablans, 1978

MICHAEL RAEBURN

b. January 22, 1943 - Cairo, Egypt
Business: Signfour Films Ltd., 10 Spencer Park, London SW18,
England, tel.: 171/874-0205

KILLING HEAT THE GRASS IS SINGING Satori, 1983,
British-Swedish-Zambian
SOWETO General Entertainment/S&S Productions/Nigerian TV,
1987, British-Finnish-Nigerian
JIT Northern Arts Entertainment, 1990, Zimbabwean

BOB RAFELSON*

b. 1935 - New York, New York
Agent: ICM - Beverly Hills, 310/550-4000
Business: Marmont Productions, Inc., 1022 Palm Avenue, Suite #3,
Los Angeles, CA 90069, 310/659-0768

HEAD Columbia, 1968
FIVE EASY PIECES Columbia, 1970
THE KING OF MARVIN GARDENS Columbia, 1972
STAY HUNGRY United Artists, 1976
THE POSTMAN ALWAYS RINGS TWICE Paramount, 1981
BLACK WIDOW 20th Century Fox, 1987
MOUNTAINS OF THE MOON TriStar, 1990
MAN TROUBLE 20th Century Fox, 1992
EROTIC TALES co-director with Susan Seidelman, Ken Russell,
Melvin Van Peebles, Paul Cox & Mani Kaul, Regina Ziegler
Filmproduktion/Tele-Munchen/Westdeutscher Rundfunk,
1994, German

KEVIN RAFFERTY

THE ATOMIC CAFE (FD) co-director, 1982
HURRY TOMORROW (FD) 1982
BLOOD IN THE FACE (FD) co-director with James Ridgeway &
Anne Bohlen, Right Thinking Productions, 1991
FEED (FD) co-director with James Ridgeway, Original
Cinema, 1992

STEWART RAFFILL*

b. 1942 - Kettering, England
Home: P.O. Box 117, Tarzana, CA 91356, 818/991-8987
Agent: Preferred Artists - Encino, 818/990-0305

THE TENDER WARRIOR Safari, 1971
THE ADVENTURES OF THE WILDERNESS FAMILY
Pacific International, 1975
ACROSS THE GREAT DIVIDE Pacific International, 1976
THE SEA GYPSIES Warner Bros., 1978
HIGH RISK American Cinema, 1981
THE ICE PIRATES MGM/UA, 1983
THE PHILADELPHIA EXPERIMENT New World, 1984
MAC AND ME Orion, 1988
MANNEQUIN TWO ON THE MOVE 20th Century Fox, 1991
LOST IN AFRICA Hotspur Productions/Creative Visions/Archview
Films, 1994, British
TAMMY AND THE T. REX (HVF) Image Ent., 1995

ALAN RAFKIN*

b. July 23, 1938 - New York, New York
Personal Manager: Brillstein/Grey Entertainment - Beverly Hills,
310/275-6135
Business Manager: Gelfand, Rennert & Feldman, 1880 Century
Park East - Suite 900, Los Angeles, CA 90067, 310/556-6652

SKI PARTY American International, 1965
THE GHOST AND MR. CHICKEN Universal, 1966
THE RIDE TO HANGMAN'S TREE Universal, 1967
NOBODY'S PERFECT Universal, 1968
THE SHAKIEST GUN IN THE WEST Universal, 1968
ANGEL IN MY POCKET Universal, 1969
HOW TO FRAME A FIGG Universal, 1971
LET'S SWITCH (TF) Universal TV, 1975

SLAMET RAHARDJO

(See Slamet Rahardjo DJAROT)

STEVE RAILSBACK

b. 1948 - Dallas, Texas
Contact: Screen Actors Guild - Los Angeles, 213/954-1600

THE SPY WITHIN Concorde, 1994

SAM RAIMI*

b. 1960 - Detroit, Michigan
Business: Renaissance Pictures, 6381 Hollywood Blvd. -
Suite 680, Hollywood, CA 90028, 213/463-9965
Agent: ICM - Beverly Hills, 310/550-4000

THE EVIL DEAD New Line Cinema, 1983
CRIMEWAVE BROKEN HEARTS AND NOSES Columbia, 1985
EVIL DEAD 2 Rosebud Releasing Corporation, 1987
DARKMAN Universal, 1990
ARMY OF DARKNESS Universal, 1992
THE QUICK AND THE DEAD TriStar, 1995

FRANK RAINONE

ME AND THE MOB Arrow Releasing, 1994

ALVIN RAKOFF

b. 1937 - Toronto, Canada
Home: 1 The Orchard, Chiswick, London W4 1JZ, England,
tel.: 181/994-1269
Agent: Paul Kohner, Inc. - Los Angeles, 310/550-1060 or:
Nigel Britten Management - London, tel.: 171/379-0349

HOT MONEY GIRL THE TREASURE OF SAN TERESA
United Producers Releasing Organization, 1959, British
ROOM 43 PASSPORT TO SHAME British Lion, 1959, British
ON FRIDAY AT ELEVEN British Lion, 1961, West German-British
WORLD IN MY POCKET MGM, 1962, West German-French-Italian
THE COMEDY MAN Continental, 1964, British
CROSSPLOT United Artists, 1969, British
HOFFMAN Levitt-Pickman, 1971, British

SAY HELLO TO YESTERDAY   Cinerama Releasing Corporation,
1971, British
THE ADVENTURES OF DON QUIXOTE (TF)   Universal TV/BBC,
1973, U.S.-British
KING SOLOMON'S TREASURE   Filmco Limited, 1978, Canadian
CITY ON FIRE!   Avco Embassy, 1979, Canadian
DEATH SHIP   Avco Embassy, 1980, Canadian
DIRTY TRICKS   Avco Embassy, 1981, Canadian
A VOYAGE ROUND MY FATHER (TF)   Thames TV/D.L.
Taffner Ltd., 1983, British
THE FIRST OLYMPICS—ATHENS 1896 (MS)   Larry White-Gary
Allison Productions/Columbia TV, 1984
PARADISE POSTPONED (MS)   Euston Films, 1985, British
GAS & CANDLES (TF)   1990, British
THE BEST OF FRIENDS (TF)   London Film Productions/Table
Top Productions/Limehouse Productions, 1991, British
SAM SATURDAY (TF)   1992, British
MOLLY (TF)   Carlton, 1993, British

ALEXANDER RAMATI
SANDS OF BEERSHEBA   *REBELS AGAINST THE LIGHT*
Landau-Unger, 1964, U.S.-Israeli
THE ASSISI UNDERGROUND   Cannon, 1985, Italian-British
AND THE VIOLINS STOPPED PLAYING   David Films/Film Polski,
1989, Polish-U.S.

VICTOR J. RAMBALDI
Address: 5116 Allentown Place, Woodland Hills, CA 91364
Contact: Dave Gilmoure, C.R.P. Associates - 818/701-5868 or
818/347-7004

PRIMAL RAGE   Columbia/TriStar, 1989, U.S.-Italian
LEONARDO'S POLYHEDRON   Artstudio/Planet Image Productions,
1990, Italian-U.S.
DECOY   Prism Pictures, 1994, U.S.-Canadian

HAROLD RAMIS*
b. November 21, 1944 - Chicago, Illinois
Business: Ocean Pictures, 10202 W. Washington Blvd., Capra
Building - Suite 103, Culver City, CA 90232, 310/280-4644
Agent: CAA - Beverly Hills, 310/288-4545

CADDYSHACK   Orion/Warner Bros., 1980
NATIONAL LAMPOON'S VACATION   Warner Bros., 1983
CLUB PARADISE   Warner Bros., 1986
GROUNDHOG DAY   Columbia, 1993
STUART SAVES HIS FAMILY   Paramount, 1995

PATRICK RAND
Agent: William Morris Agency - Beverly Hills, 310/859-4000

MOM   RCA/Columbia Home Video, 1991

JOHN RANDALL
b. January 22, 1929 - Oakland, California
Business: Cinetex, P.O. Box 3584, Chula Vista, CA 92011,
619/420-2053

DEADLY REEF   Cinetex, 1978
J. J. GARCIA   Filmrand, 1984

TONY RANDEL
HELLBOUND: HELLRAISER II   New World, 1988, British-U.S.
CHILDREN OF THE NIGHT   Fangoria Films, 1992
AMITYVILLE 1992: IT'S ABOUT TIME   Republic Pictures, 1992
TICKS   First Look Pictures, 1993
FIST OF THE NORTHSTAR   First Look Pictures, 1995

ARTHUR RANKIN, JR.
Business: Rankin-Bass Productions, Inc., 24 West 55th Street,
New York, NY 10019, 212/582-4017

WILLY McBEAN AND HIS MAGIC MACHINE (AF)   1967
THE HOBBIT (ATF)   co-director with Jules Bass, Rankin-Bass
Productions, 1979

THE RETURN OF THE KING (ATF)   co-director with Jules Bass,
Rankin-Bass Productions, 1979
THE LAST UNICORN (AF)   co-director with Jules Bass,
Jensen Farley Pictures, 1982
THE FLIGHT OF DRAGONS (ATF)   co-director with Jules Bass,
Rankin-Bass Productions, 1986
THE WIND IN THE WILLOWS (ATF)   co-director with Jules Bass,
Rankin-Bass Productions, 1987, filmed in 1985

MORT RANSEN
Business: Ranfilm Productions Inc., P.O. Box 411, Ganges, British
Columbia V0S 1C0, 604/653-9100
Agent: Great North Management, 350 Dupont Street, Toronto,
Ontario M5R 1V9, Canada, 416/925-2051

FALLING OVER BACKWARDS   Ranfilm Productions//CBC,
1991, Canadian
THE GLACE BAY MINER'S MUSEUM   Glace Bay Pictures, 1995,
Canadian-British

WHITNEY RANSICK
Agent: William Morris Agency - Beverly Hills, 310/859-4000

HANDGUN   Workin' Man Films/Odessa Films/Shooting
Gallery, 1994

FREDERIC RAPHAEL
b. 1931 - Chicago, Illinois
Contact: British Film Commission, 70 Baker Street, London
W1M 1DJ, England, tel.: 71/224-5000

SOMETHING'S WRONG (TF)   BBC, 1978, British
HE'LL SEE YOU NOW (TF)   BBC, 1984, British
WOMEN & MEN: STORIES OF SEDUCTION (CTF)
co-director with Tony Richardson & Ken Russell,
HBO Showcase/David Brown Productions, 1990

I. C. RAPOPORT*
Home: 559 Muskingum Avenue, Pacific Palisades, CA 90272,
310/454-3120
Agent: Broder-Kurland-Webb-Uffner Agency - Beverly Hills,
310/281-3400

THOU SHALT NOT KILL (TF)   Edgar J. Scherick Associates/
Warner Bros. TV, 1982

JEAN-PAUL RAPPANEAU
b. April 8, 1932 - Auxerre, France
Agent: William Morris Agency - Beverly Hills, 310/859-4000 or:
ICM France - Paris, tel.: 1/723-7860

LA VIE DE CHATEAU   1965, French
LES MARIES DE L'AN   1970, French
LE SAUVAGE   1975, French
TOUT FEU TOUT FLAMME   1982, French
CYRANO DE BERGERAC   Orion Classics, 1990, French
REAP THE WHIRLWIND (MS)   1992, South African-French
LE HUSSARD SUR LE TOIT   Miramax Films, 1995, French

IRVING RAPPER*
b. 1898 - London, England
Home: 515 East 72nd Street - Apt. 27J, New York, NY 10021,
212/249-1156

SHINING VICTORY   Warner Bros., 1941
ONE FOOT IN HEAVEN   Warner Bros., 1941
THE GAY SISTERS   Warner Bros., 1942
NOW, VOYAGER   Warner Bros., 1942
THE ADVENTURES OF MARK TWAIN   Warner Bros., 1944
THE CORN IS GREEN   Warner Bros., 1945
RHAPSODY IN BLUE   Warner Bros., 1945
DECEPTION   Warner Bros., 1946
THE VOICE OF THE TURTLE   Warner Bros., 1947
ANNA LUCASTA   Columbia, 1949
THE GLASS MENAGERIE   Warner Bros., 1950
ANOTHER MAN'S POISON   United Artists, 1952, British

BAD FOR EACH OTHER Columbia, 1954
FOREVER FEMALE Paramount, 1954
STRANGE INTRUDER Allied Artists, 1956
THE BRAVE ONE Universal, 1956
MARJORIE MORNINGSTAR Warner Bros., 1958
THE MIRACLE Warner Bros., 1959
THE STORY OF JOSEPH AND HIS BRETHREN *GIUSEPPE VENDUTO DAI FRATELLI* co-director with Luciano Ricci, Colorama, 1960, Italian
PONTIUS PILATE US Films, 1962, Italian-French
THE CHRISTINE JORGENSEN STORY United Artists, 1970
BORN AGAIN Avco Embassy, 1978

STEVE RASH*
Agent: Broder-Kurland-Webb-Uffner Agency - Beverly Hills, 310/281-3400

THE BUDDY HOLLY STORY Columbia, 1978
UNDER THE RAINBOW Orion/Warner Bros., 1981
VANISHING AMERICA (CTF) Showtime, 1985
CAN'T BUY ME LOVE Buena Vista, 1987
QUEENS LOGIC Seven Arts/New Line Cinema, 1991
SON-IN-LAW Buena Vista, 1993

DANIEL RASKOV*
Business: Exposition Park Pictures, The Raleigh Studios, 650 N. Bronson Avenue - Suite B122, Hollywood, CA 90004

WEDDING BAND I.R.S. Releasing, 1990
MASTERS OF MENACE New Line Cinema, 1990
A KISS GOODNIGHT Exposition Park Pictures, 1994

HARRY RASKY*
b. 1928 - Toronto, Ontario, Canada
Business: CBC, P.O. Box 500, Terminal A, Toronto, Ontario 4W 2X7, Canada, 416/205-6867

PANAMA: DANGER ZONE (TD) 1960
THE LION AND THE CROSS (TD) 1961
MAHATMA: THE GREAT SOUL (TD) 1962
ELEANOR ROOSEVELT: FIRST LADY OF THE WORLD (TD) 1963
THE NOBEL PRIZE (TD) 1964
CUBA AND CASTRO TODAY (TD) 1965
HALL OF KINGS (TD) 1967
ZOOS OF THE WORLD (TD) 1968
THE LEGEND OF SILENT NIGHT (TD) 1969
UPON THIS ROCK (FD) Levitt-Pickman, 1971
THE WIT AND WORLD OF G. BERNARD SHAW (TD) 1972, Canadian-British
AN INVITATION TO THE ROYAL WEDDING (TD) 1973, Canadian-U.S.
TENNESSEE WILLIAMS' SOUTH (TD) 1973, Canadian
NEXT YEAR IN JERUSALEM (TD) 1973, Canadian
HOMAGE TO CHAGALL: THE COLORS OF LOVE (FD) CBC/Maragall Productions, 1975
TRAVELS THROUGH LIFE WITH LEACOCK (TD) 1976, Canadian
ARTHUR MILLER ON HOME GROUND (FD) 1979, Canadian
THE SONG OF LEONARD COHEN (TD) 1979, Canadian
THE MAN WHO HID ANNE FRANK (TD) 1980, Canadian
THE SPIES WHO NEVER WERE (TD) 1981, Canadian
BEING DIFFERENT (TD) Astral Films, 1981, Canadian
STRATASPHERE (TD) 1982, Canadian
RAYMOND MASSEY: ACTOR OF THE CENTURY (TD) 1982, Canadian
THE MYSTERY OF HENRY MOORE (TD) 1984, Canadian
KARSH, THE SEARCHING EYE (TD) 1986, Canadian
TO MEND THE WORLD (TD) Canadian Broadcasting Corporation, 1987, Canadian
DEGAS (TD) l988, Canadian
NORTHROP FRYE (TD) 1989, Canadian
THE MAGIC SEASON OF ROBERTSON DAVIES (TD) Canadian Broadcasting Corporation, 1990, Canadian
THE WAR AGAINST THE INDIANS (TD) Canadian Broadcasting Corporation, 1992, Canadian
PROPHECY (FD) 1994, Canadian

TINA RATHBORNE*
Home: 18 Craigie Street, Cambridge, MA 02138, 617/491-2991
Agent: Metropolitan Talent Agency - Los Angeles, 213/857-4500
Attorney: Harold Brown, Gang, Tyre, Ramer & Brown, 6400 Sunset Blvd., Los Angeles, CA 90028, 213/463-4863

THE JOY THAT KILLS (TF) Cypress Point Productions, 1985
ZELLY & ME Columbia, 1988

DAVID RATHOD
b. July 15, 1952 - Chicago, Illinois
Business: P.O. Box 536, Fairfax, CA 94930, 415/457-3500

WEST IS WEST Rathod Productions, 1989

OUSAMA RAWI*
b. May 3, 1939 - Baghdad, Iraq
Address: 62 Walker Avenue, Toronto, Ontario M4V 1G2, Canada, 416/929-3854

THE HOUSEKEEPER *A JUDGEMENT IN STONE* Castle Hill Productions, 1986, Canadian

CHRISTOPHER RAWLENCE
Contact: British Film Commission, 70 Baker Street, London W1M 1DJ, England, tel.: 171/224-5000

THE MISSING REEL (CTF) Zed Ltd./Channel 4/La Sept, 1990, British-French

JOHN RAWLINS*
b. June 9, 1902 - Long Beach, California
Contact: Directors Guild of America - Los Angeles, 213/851-3671

STATE POLICE 1938
YOUNG FUGITIVES 1938
THE MISSING GUEST 1938
AIR DEVILS 1938
THE GREEN HORNET STRIKES AGAIN (S) co-director with Ford Beebe, Universal, 1940
JUNIOR G-MEN (S) co-director with Ford Beebe, Universal, 1940
THE LEATHER PUSHERS Universal, 1940
SEA RAIDERS (S) co-director with Ford Beebe, Universal, 1941
SIX LESSONS FROM MADAME LA ZONGA Universal, 1941
A DANGEROUS GAME Universal, 1941
MR. DYNAMITE Universal, 1941
MUTINY IN THE ARCTIC Universal, 1941
MEN OF THE TIMBERLAND Universal, 1941
RAIDERS OF THE DESERT Universal, 1941
OVERLAND MAIL (S) co-director with Ford Beebe, Universal, 1942
BOMBAY CLIPPER Universal, 1942
UNSEEN ENEMY Universal, 1942
MISSISSIPPI GAMBLER Universal, 1942
HALF WAY TO SHANGHAI Universal, 1942
SHERLOCK HOLMES AND THE VOICE OF TERROR Universal, 1942
THE GREAT IMPERSONATION Universal, 1942
ARABIAN NIGHTS Universal, 1942
WE'VE NEVER BEEN LICKED Universal, 1943
LADIES COURAGEOUS Universal, 1944
SUDAN Universal, 1945
STRANGE CONQUEST Universal, 1946
HER ADVENTUROUS NIGHT Universal, 1946
DICK TRACY'S DILEMMA RKO Radio, 1947
DICK TRACY MEETS GRUESOME RKO Radio, 1947
THE ARIZONA RANGER 1948
MICHAEL O'HALLORAN 1948
MASSACRE RIVER Allied Artists, 1949
BOY FROM INDIANA Eagle Lion, 1950
ROGUE RIVER Eagle Lion, 1950
FORT DEFIANCE United Artists, 1951
SHARK RIVER United Artists, 1953
LOST LAGOON United Artists, 1958

FRED OLEN RAY
b. September 10, 1954 - Wellston, Ohio

THE ALIEN DEAD *IT FELL FROM THE SKY* 1981, filmed in 1978
SCALPS 21st Century Distribution, 1984
THE TOMB Trans World Entertainment, 1985
COMMANDO SQUAD Trans World Entertainment, 1986
ARMED RESPONSE CineTel, 1986
CYCLONE CineTel, 1987
PRISON SHIP: THE ADVENTURES OF TAURA, PART I
STAR SLAMMER Worldwide Entertainment, 1987
DEMENTED DEATH FARM MASSACRE co-director with
Donn Davison, Troma, 1987
DEEP SPACE Trans World Entertainment, 1987
HOLLYWOOD CHAINSAW HOOKERS Camp Motion Pictures/
American-Independent , 1988
THE PHANTOM EMPIRE American-Independent, 1989,
filmed in 1986
BEVERLY HILLS VAMP American-Independent, 1989
WARLORDS American-Independent, 1989
ALIENATOR American-Independent, 1989
HAUNTING FEAR Troma, 1990
MOB BOSS Trimark Pictures, 1990
TERMINAL FORCE American-Independent, 1990, filmed in 1987
SPIRITS Cinema Group Productions, 1990
BAD GIRLS FROM MARS Vidmark, 1991
INNER SANCTUM Vision International, 1991
EVIL TOONS American-Independent, 1991
LITTLE DEVILS American-Independent, 1991
WIZARDS OF THE DEMON SWORD Troma, 1991
MIND TWISTER Smart Egg Pictures, 1993
INNER SANCTUM 2 MDP Worldwide, 1994
POSSESSED BY THE NIGHT MDP Worldwide, 1994
BIKINI DRIVE-IN Showcase Entertainment, 1994

SANDIP RAY
Contact: National Film Development Corporation of India,
Discovery of India Building, Nehru Centre, Dr Annie Besant
Road, Worli, Bombay 400018, India, tel.: 4949856

THE BROKEN JOURNEY National Film Development
Corporation of India/Doordarshan, 1994, Indian
TARGET OEG Worldwide, 1995, Indian

SPIRO RAZATOS*
Home: 7657 East Bridgewood Drive, Anaheim Hills, CA 92808,
714/280-0344

FAST GETAWAY New Line Cinema, 1991
CLASS OF 1999 PART II: THE SUBSTITUTE CineTel Films, 1994

ERIC RED*
Agent: ICM - Beverly Hills, 310/550-4000

COHEN & TATE Hemdale, 1988
BODY PARTS Paramount, 1991
UNDERTOW Tarnview Ltd., 1995

ROBERT REDFORD*
(Charles Robert Redford)
b. August 18, 1937 - Santa Monica, California
Business: Wildwood Productions, 1101 Montana Avenue - Suite E,
Santa Monica, CA 90403, 310/395-5155
Agent: CAA - Beverly Hills, 310/288-4545

ORDINARY PEOPLE ★★ Paramount, 1980
THE MILAGRO BEANFIELD WAR Universal, 1988
A RIVER RUNS THROUGH IT Columbia, 1992
QUIZ SHOW ★ Buena Vista, 1994

LEE REDMOND
THE FINAL MISSION Trimark Pictures, 1993

ALAN L. REED
AS LONG AS YOU'RE ALIVE Satori Films, 1992

JERRY REED
b. March 20, 1937
Address: 116 Wilson Peak - Suite 210, Brentwood, TN 37027,
615/377-3038

WHAT COMES AROUND W.O. Associates, 1986

PEYTON REED*
Contact: Directors Guild of America - Los Angeles, 213/851-3671

THE COMPUTER WORE TENNIS SHOES (TF) ZM Productions/
Walt Disney TV, 1995

CLIVE REES
Address: 11 Portland Mews, London W1V 3FJ, England,
tel.: 171/439-1555

THE BLOCKHOUSE 1973, British
WHEN THE WHALES CAME 20th Century Fox, 1989, British

JERRY REES*
Agent: UTA - Beverly Hills, 310/273-6700

THE BRAVE LITTLE TOASTER (AF) Hyperion-Kushner-Locke
Productions, 1987
THE MARRYING MAN Buena Vista, 1991

GEOFFREY REEVE
b. October 28, 1932 - Tring, Hertfordshire, England
Business: GRO Ltd., 10 Grafton Street, London
W1X 3LA, England

PUPPET ON A CHAIN co-director with Don Sharp, Cinerama
Releasing Corporation, 1972, British
CARAVAN TO VACCARES Bryanston, 1976, British-French
SOUVENIR (CTF) Fancyfree Productions Ltd., 1988, British
RED EAGLE (MS) 1993, French-Luxembourgian
THE WAY TO DUSTY DEATH (TF) Delux Productions,
1994, Luxembourgian

PATRICK REGAN*
b. January 23, 1939 - Los Angeles, California
Address: P.O. Box 3680, Santa Monica, CA 90403, 310/281-7070

KISS DADDY GOODBYE Pendragon Film Ltd./Wrightwood
Entertainment, 1981

GODFREY REGGIO
b. New Orleans, Louisiana

KOYAANISQATSI Island Alive/New Cinema, 1983
POWAQQATSI Cannon, 1988

KELLY REICHARDT
RIVER OF GRASS Plan B Pictures, 1994

JULIA REICHERT
SEEING RED (FD) co-director
UNION MAIDS (FD) co-director
EMMA AND ELVIS Northern Arts Entertainment, 1992

MARK REICHERT
UNION CITY Kinesis, 1980

ALASTAIR REID*
b. July 21, 1939 - Edinburgh, Scotland
Address: The Old Stores, Curload Stoke, St. Gregory, Taunton,
  Somerset, TA3 6JE England, tel.: 0182/369-8645
Agent: Innovative Artists - Los Angeles, 310/553-5200 or:
  Peters Fraser & Dunlop - London, tel.: 171/344-1000

BABY LOVE   Avco Embassy, 1969, British
THE NIGHT DIGGER   MGM, 1971, British
SOMETHING TO HIDE   1971, British
SIX FACES (TF)   1972, British
A BURNT-OUT CASE (TF)   1973, British
THE FILE ON JILL HATCH (TF)   WNET-13/BBC, 1983, U.S.-British
MAN ON THE SCREEN (TF)   1983, British
THE SECRET SERVANT (TF)   BBC/Channel 7,
  1984, British-Australian
THE DEAD OF JERICHO (TF)   Zenith Productions, 1986, British
THE STORY OF A RECLUSE (TF)   BBC, 1987, British
THE WOLVERCOTE TONGUE (TF)   Zenith Productions,
  1987, British
TRAFFIK (MS)   Picture Partnership Productions/Channel 4,
  1989, British
SELLING HITLER (MS)   Euston Films/Warner Sisters/Thames TV,
  1991, British
TEAMSTER BOSS: THE JACKIE PRESSER STORY (CTF)
  HBO Pictures/Abby Mann Productions, 1992
ARMISTEAD MAUPIN'S TALES OF THE CITY   TALES OF THE
  CITY (MS)   Working Title/Propaganda Films/Channel 4/
  American Playhouse/KQED-San Francisco, 1993, British-U.S.
NOSTROMO (MS)   Pixit Productions/BBC/RAI/TVE/WGBH-Boston,
  1995, British-Italian-Spanish-U.S.

JOHN REID
b. October 21, 1946
Business: Plumb Productions Ltd., P.O. Box 2070, Wellington,
  New Zealand, tel.: 4/851-283

MIDDLE AGE SPREAD   Endeavour Productions/New Zealand
  Film Commission, 1979, New Zealand
CARRY ME BACK   Kiwi Films/New Zealand Film Commission,
  1982, New Zealand
LEAVE ALL FAIR   Pacific Films, 1985, New Zealand
THE LAST TATTOO   Plumb Productions/Capella International/
  New Zealand Film Commission/Avalon CFU/NZ On Air, 1994,
  New Zealand

MAX REID
b. November 19, 1944 - Berkeley, California
Contact: Writers Guild of America, West - Los Angeles, 310/550-1000

WILD THING   Atlantic Releasing Corporation, 1987, U.S.-Canadian
TEEN ANGEL (CTF)   The Disney Channel, 1989
MATCH POINT (CTF)   The Disney Channel, 1989
IN THE EYE OF THE SNAKE   Primwest/Jaques Sandoz Film
  Production/Television Suisse Romande, 1991, Swiss

TIM REID
b. December 19, 1944 - Norfolk, Virginia
Contact: Screen Actors Guild - Los Angeles, 213/954-1600

ONCE UPON A TIME...WHEN WE WERE COLORED
  BET Films, 1994

DONALD REIKER*
Agent: William Morris Agency - Beverly Hills, 310/859-4000

MONA MUST DIE   Jones & Reiker/Rhino Films/MMD
  Productions/VCL-Carolco Communications/Jugendfilm
  Verleih/Bernd Gaumer, 1994, U.S.-German

WILLIAM REILLY
Agent: William Morris Agency - Beverly Hills, 310/859-4000

MEN OF RESPECT   Columbia, 1990

CARL REINER*
b. March 20, 1922 - Bronx, New York
Agent: CAA - Beverly Hills, 310/288-4545
Personal Manager: George Shapiro, Shapiro-West, 141 El Camino
  Drive, Beverly Hills, CA 90212, 310/278-8896

ENTER LAUGHING   Columbia, 1967
THE COMIC   Columbia, 1969
WHERE'S POPPA?   United Artists, 1970
THE ONE AND ONLY   Paramount, 1978
OH, GOD!   Warner Bros., 1978
THE JERK   Universal, 1979
DEAD MEN DON'T WEAR PLAID   Universal, 1979
THE MAN WITH TWO BRAINS   Warner Bros., 1983
ALL OF ME   Universal, 1984
SUMMER RENTAL   Paramount, 1985
SUMMER SCHOOL   Paramount, 1987
BERT RIGBY, YOU'RE A FOOL   Warner Bros., 1989
SIBLING RIVALRY   Columbia, 1991
FATAL INSTINCT   MGM, 1993

JEFFREY REINER
b. 1960

BLOOD AND CONCRETE, A LOVE STORY   I.R.S. Releasing, 1991
TROUBLE BOUND   ITC Entertainment Group, 1993

LUCAS REINER
Agent: ICM - Beverly Hills, 310/550-4000

THE SPIRIT OF '76   Columbia, 1990

ROB REINER*
b. March 6, 1945 - Beverly Hills, California
Agent: CAA - Beverly Hills, 310/288-4545
Business: Castle Rock Entertainment, 335 N. Maple Drive - Suite 135,
  Beverly Hills, CA 90210, 310/285-2300

THIS IS SPINAL TAP   Embassy, 1984
THE SURE THING   Embassy, 1985
STAND BY ME   Columbia, 1986
THE PRINCESS BRIDE   20th Century Fox, 1987
WHEN HARRY MET SALLY...   Columbia, 1989
MISERY   Columbia, 1990
A FEW GOOD MEN   Columbia, 1992
NORTH   Columbia, 1994
THE AMERICAN PRESIDENT   Columbia, 1995

AL REINERT
Business: Apollo Associates, 1815 Norfolk Street, Houston, TX 77098

FOR ALL MANKIND (FD)   Apollo Associates, 1989

DEBORAH REINISCH*
Agent: ICM - Beverly Hills, 310/550-4000

ASK ME AGAIN (TF)   DBR Films Ltd./American Playhouse, 1989
ANDRE'S MOTHER (TF)   DBR Films, 1990
CAUGHT IN THE ACT (CTF)   Davis Entertainment TV/
  Meltzer-Viviano Productions/MTE Productions, 1993

BRUCE REISMAN
THE HIGHER GROUND   Premiere Productions, 1993
BLADE BOXER   Glider Entertainment, 1995

ALLEN REISNER*
b. New York, New York
Business: Clarmax Productions, Inc., 9165 Cordell Drive,
  Los Angeles, CA 90069, 213/274-2844
Agent: The Coppage Company - 818/980-1106

ST. LOUIS BLUES   Paramount, 1958
ALL MINE TO GIVE   THE DAY THEY GAVE BABIES AWAY
  Universal, 1958
TO DIE IN PARIS (TF)   co-director with Charles Dubin,
  Universal TV, 1968

YOUR MONEY OR YOUR WIFE (TF)   Brentwood Productions, 1972
CAPTAINS AND THE KINGS (MS)   co-director with Douglas Heyes,
    Universal TV, 1976
MARY JANE HARPER CRIED LAST NIGHT (TF)
    Paramount TV, 1977
COPS AND ROBIN (TF)   Paramount TV, 1978
THE LOVE TAPES (TF)   Christiana Productions/MGM TV, 1980

KAREL REISZ*
b. July 21, 1926 - Ostrava, Czechoslovakia
Address: 11 Chalcot Gardens, Englands Lane, London
    NW3 4YB, England
Agent: Sam Cohn, ICM - New York City, 212/556-5600 or:
    Judy Daish Associates - London, tel.: 171/262-1101

WE ARE THE LAMBETH BOYS   Rank, 1958, British
SATURDAY NIGHT AND SUNDAY MORNING   Continental,
    1961, British
NIGHT MUST FALL   Embassy, 1964, British
MORGAN! *MORGAN: A SUITABLE CASE FOR TREATMENT*
    Cinema 5, 1966, British
ISADORA *THE LOVES OF ISADORA*   Universal, 1969, British
THE GAMBLER   Paramount, 1974
WHO'LL STOP THE RAIN   United Artists, 1978
THE FRENCH LIEUTENANT'S WOMAN   United Artists,
    1981, British
SWEET DREAMS   TriStar, 1985
EVERYBODY WINS   Orion, 1990, British-U.S.

IVAN REITMAN*
b. October 26, 1946 - Komano, Czechoslovakia
Business: Northern Lights Entertainment, 100 Universal City Plaza -
    Building 489, Universal City, CA 91608, 818/777-8080
Agent: CAA - Beverly Hills, 310/288-4545

COLUMBUS OF SEX   New Cinema Canada, 1970, Canadian
FOXY LADY   Cinepix of Canada, 1971, Canadian
CANNIBAL GIRLS   American International, 1973, Canadian
MEATBALLS   Paramount, 1979, Canadian
STRIPES   Columbia, 1981
GHOSTBUSTERS   Columbia, 1984
LEGAL EAGLES   Universal, 1986
TWINS   Universal, 1988
GHOSTBUSTERS II   Columbia, 1989
KINDERGARTEN COP   Universal, 1990
DAVE   Warner Bros., 1993
JUNIOR   Universal, 1994

EDGAR REITZ
b. 1932 - Hunsruck, Germany
Contact: Federal Union of Film and Television Directors in Germany,
    Adelheidstrasse 7, 8000 Munich 40, Germany, tel.: 089/271-6380

MAHLZEITEN   1966, West German
FUSSNOTEN   1967, West German
UXMAL   1968, West German
CARDILLAC   1969, West German
DER SCHNEIDER VON ULM   1981, West German
HEIMAT (MS)   Edgar Reitz Filmproduktion/WDR/SFB,
    1980-84, West German
DIE ZWEITE HEIMAT (MS)   WDR/BR/HR/NDR/SFB/SWF/
    BBC/TVE/TV-1/YLE/DR/NRK/ORF, 1992, German-British-
    Spanish-Swedish-Finnish-Danish-Norwegian-Austrian
DIE NACHT DER REGISSEURE (FD)   ERF-Edgar Reitz
    Filmproduktions/Arte/ZDF/Premiere/British Film Institute TV,
    1995, German-British

NORMAN RENE*
Agent: Spyros Skouras, The Skouras Agency - Santa Monica,
    310/395-9550

LONGTIME COMPANION   The Samuel Goldwyn Company, 1990
PRELUDE TO A KISS   20th Century Fox, 1992
RECKLESS   The Samuel Goldwyn Company, 1995

BARBARA RENNIE
Agent: Peters Fraser & Dunlop - London, tel.: 171/344-1000

SACRED HEARTS (TF)   Channel 4, 1985, British
ECHOES   Working Title Productions/Channel 4, 1988, British

ALAIN RESNAIS
b. June 3, 1922 - Vannes, France
Agent: ICM France - Paris, tel.: 1/723-7860
Contact: French Film Office, 745 Fifth Avenue, New York,
    NY 10151, 212/832-8860

HIROSHIMA, MON AMOUR   Zenith, 1959, French
LAST YEAR AT MARIENBAD   Astor, 1961, French-Italian
MURIEL   Lopert, 1963, French-Italian
LA GUERRE EST FINIE   Brandon, 1966, French-Swedish
FAR FROM VIETNAM (FD)   co-director with Jean-Luc Godard,
    William Klein, Claude Lelouch, Agnes Varda & Joris Ivens,
    New Yorker, 1967, French
JE T'AIME, JE T'AIME   New Yorker, 1968, French-Spanish
STAVISKY   Cinemation, 1974, French
PROVIDENCE   Cinema 5, 1977, French-Swiss
MON ONCLE D'AMERIQUE   New World, 1980, French
LIFE IS A BED OF ROSES *LA VIE EST UN ROMAN*
    Spectrafilm, 1983, French
L'AMOUR A MORT   Roissy Film, 1984, French
MELO   European Classics, 1986, French
I WANT TO GO HOME   MK2/Films A2/La Sept, 1989, French
CONTRE L'OUBLI   co-director, Les Films du Paradoxe/Amnesty
    International/PRV, 1992, French
SMOKING   October Films, 1993, French-Italian-Swiss
NO SMOKING   October Films, 1993, French-Italian-Swiss

ADAM RESNICK*
Agent: UTA - Beverly Hills, 310/273-6700

CABIN BOY   Buena Vista, 1994

ROBERT RESNIKOFF
Agent: Innovative Artists - Los Angeles, 310/553-5200

THE FIRST POWER   Orion, 1990

GABRIEL RETES
Contact: IMCINE, Tepic #40, P.B. Colonia Roma Sur, Mexico City,
    C.P. 06760, Mexico, tel.: 525/584-7283

BIENVENIDO/WELCOME   Rio Mixcoac/Universidad de Guadalajara/
    Cooperative Conexion/Eduardo de la Barcena/IMCINE/Gabriel
    Beristain, 1995, Mexican

DIANE REYNA
SURVIVING COLUMBUS (TD)   KNME-TV/Institute of American
    Indian Arts, 1992

BURT REYNOLDS*
b. February 11, 1936 - Waycross, Georgia
Business: 4024 Radford Avenue - Building 5, Suite 202, Studio City,
    CA 91604, 818/760-5034; fax: 818/760-5629
Agent: ICM - New York, 212/556-5614

GATOR   United Artists, 1976
THE END   United Artists, 1978
SHARKY'S MACHINE   Orion/Warner Bros., 1982
STICK   Universal, 1985
THE MAN FROM LEFT FIELD (TF)   Burt Reynolds
    Productions, 1993

GENE REYNOLDS*

b. April 4, 1925 - Cleveland, Ohio
Agent: CAA - Beverly Hills, 310/288-4545

IN DEFENSE OF KIDS (TF)   MTM Enterprises, 1983
DOING LIFE (TF)   Castilian Productions/Phoenix Entertainment
   Group, 1986
TALES FROM THE HOLLYWOOD HILLS: GOLDEN LAND (TF)
   WNET-NY/Zenith Productions, 1988
THE WHEREABOUTS OF JENNY (TF)   Katie Face Productions/
   Columbia TV, 1991

KEVIN REYNOLDS*

b. January 17, 1952 - San Antonio, Texas
Agent: William Morris Agency - Beverly Hills, 310/859-4000

FANDANGO   Warner Bros., 1985
THE BEAST   Columbia, 1988
ROBIN HOOD: PRINCE OF THIEVES   Warner Bros.,
   1991, U.S.-British
RAPA NUI   Warner Bros., 1994
WATERWORLD   Universal, 1995

MARK REZYKA

b. 1949 - Breslau, Poland

SOUTH OF RENO   Open Road Productions/Pendulum
   Productions, 1987

PHILLIP RHEE

Contact: Screen Actors Guild - Los Angeles, 213/954-1600

BEST OF THE BEST 3: NO TURNING BACK
   Dimension/Miramax Films, 1995

MICHAEL RAY RHODES*

Home: 640 Via de la Paz, Pacific Palisades, CA 90272,
   310/459-0901
Agent: Shapiro-Lichtman Talent Agency - Los Angeles,
   310/859-8877

MATTERS OF THE HEART (CTF)   Tahse-Bergman Productions/
   MCA-TV Entertainment, 1990
THE KILLING MIND (CTF)   Hearst Entertainment Productions, 1991
REASON FOR LIVING: THE JILL IRELAND STORY (TF)
   Bonny Dore Productions/Ten-Four Productions, 1991
IN THE BEST INTEREST OF THE CHILDREN (TF)
   NBC Productions, 1992
SEDUCTION: THREE TALES FROM THE INNER SANCTUM (TF)
   Carroll Newman Productions/Victoria Principal Productions/The
   Polone Company/Hearst Entertainment, 1992
HEIDI (CTF)   William McCutchen Productions/Silvio Berlusconi
   Communications/Harmony Gold/The Disney Channel,
   1993, U.S.-Italian
VISIONS OF MURDER (TF)   Bar-Gene Productions/Freyda
   Rothstein Productions/Hearst Entertainment, 1993
CHRISTY (TF)   Family Productions/The Rosenzweig Company/
   MTM Enterprises, 1994
NOT OUR SON (TF)   Multimedia Motion Pictures, 1995
DOROTHY DAY   Paulist Pictures, 1995

JOHN RIBER

Contact: Ministry of Information, Film Section, P.O. Box 8150,
   Causeway, Harare, Zimbabwe, tel.: 707210 or 703891

NERIA   co-director with Godwin Mawuru, KJM3 Entertainment
   Group/Media for Development Trust, 1992, Zimbabwean

DAVID LOWELL RICH*

b. August 31, 1920 - New York, New York
Business: B&B Entertainment, 260 So. Beverly Drive - Suite 210,
   Beverly Hills, CA 90212, 310/288-4500
Agent: Shapiro-Lichtman Talent Agency - Los Angeles,
   310/859-8877

NO TIME TO BE YOUNG   Columbia, 1957
SENIOR PROM   Columbia, 1958

HEY BOY! HEY GIRL!   Columbia, 1959
HAVE ROCKET, WILL TRAVEL   Columbia, 1959
SEE HOW THEY RUN (TF)   Universal TV, 1964
MADAME X   Universal, 1966
THE PLAINSMAN   Universal, 1966
ROSIE!   Universal, 1967
WINGS OF FIRE (TF)   Universal TV, 1967
THE BORGIA STICK (TF)   Universal TV, 1967
A LOVELY WAY TO DIE   Universal, 1968
THREE GUNS FOR TEXAS   co-director with Paul Stanley &
   Earl Bellamy, Universal, 1968
MARCUS WELBY, M.D. (TF)   Universal TV, 1969
EYE OF THE CAT   Universal, 1969
THE MASK OF SHEBA (TF)   MGM TV, 1970
BERLIN AFFAIR (TF)   Universal TV, 1970
THE SHERIFF (TF)   Screen Gems/Columbia TV, 1971
ASSIGNMENT: MUNICH (TF)   MGM TV, 1972
LIEUTENANT SCHUSTER'S WIFE (TF)   Universal TV, 1972
ALL MY DARLING DAUGHTERS (TF)   Universal TV, 1972
THAT MAN BOLT   co-director with Henry Levin, Universal, 1972
THE JUDGE AND JAKE WYLER (TF)   Universal TV, 1972
SET THIS TOWN ON FIRE (TF)   Universal TV, 1973
THE HORROR AT 37,000 FEET (TF)   CBS, Inc., 1973
BROCK'S LAST CASE (TF)   Talent Associates/Universal TV, 1973
CRIME CLUB (TF)   CBS, Inc., 1973
BEG, BORROW...OR STEAL (TF)   Universal TV, 1973
SATAN'S SCHOOL FOR GIRLS (TF)   Spelling-Goldberg
   Productions, 1973
RUNAWAY! (TF)   Universal TV, 1973
DEATH RACE (TF)   Universal TV, 1973
THE CHADWICK FAMILY (TF)   Universal TV, 1974
THE SEX SYMBOL (TF)   Screen Gems/Columbia, 1974
ALOHA MEANS GOODBYE (TF)   Universal TV, 1974
THE DAUGHTERS OF JOSHUA CABE RETURN (TF)
   Spelling-Goldberg Productions, 1975
ADVENTURES OF THE QUEEN (TF)   20th Century-Fox TV, 1975
YOU LIE SO DEEP, MY LOVE (TF)   Universal TV, 1975
BRIDGER (TF)   Universal TV, 1976
THE SECRET LIFE OF JOHN CHAPMAN (TF)
   The Jozak Company, 1976
THE STORY OF DAVID (TF)   co-director with Alex Segal,
   Mildred Freed Alberg Productions/Columbia TV, 1976
SST - DEATH FLIGHT (TF)   ABC Circle Films, 1977
RANSOM FOR ALICE! (TF)   Universal TV, 1977
TELETHON (TF)   ABC Circle Films, 1977
THE DEFECTION OF SIMAS KUDIRKA (TF) ☆☆   The Jozak
   Company/Paramount TV, 1978
A FAMILY UPSIDE DOWN (TF)   Ross Hunter-Jacques Mapes
   Film/Paramount TV, 1978
LITTLE WOMEN (TF)   Universal TV, 1978
THE CONCORDE - AIRPORT '79   Universal, 1979
NURSE (TF)   Robert Halmi, Inc., 1980
ENOLA GAY (TF)   The Production Company/Viacom, 1980
CHU CHU AND THE PHILLY FLASH   20th Century-Fox, 1981
THURSDAY'S CHILD (TF)   The Catalina Production Group/
   Viacom, 1983
THE FIGHTER (TF)   Martin Manulis Productions/The Catalina
   Production Group, 1983
I WANT TO LIVE (TF)   United Artists Corporation, 1983
THE SKY'S THE LIMIT (TF)   Palance-Levy Productions, 1984
HIS MISTRESS (TF)   David L. Wolper Productions/Warner
   Bros. TV, 1984
THE HEARST AND DAVIES AFFAIR (TF)   ABC Circle Films, 1985
SCANDAL SHEET (TF)   Fair Dinkum Productions, 1985
THE DEFIANT ONES (TF)   MGM-UA TV, 1986
CHOICES (TF)   Robert Halmi, Inc., 1986
CONVICTED (TF)   Larry A. Thompson Productions, 1986
INFIDELITY (TF)   Mark-Jett Productions/ABC Circle Films, 1987

JOHN RICH*

b. July 6, 1925 - Rockaway Beach, New York
Agent: Major Clients Agency - Los Angeles, 310/205-5000

WIVES AND LOVERS   Paramount, 1963
THE NEW INTERNS   Columbia, 1964
ROUSTABOUT   Paramount, 1964
BOEING BOEING   Paramount, 1965
EASY COME, EASY GO   Paramount, 1967

MATTY RICH*
(Matthew Satterfield Richardson)
b. 1971 - Brooklyn, New York
Business: Blacks 'n Progress, 671 Vanderbilt, Brooklyn, NY 11238, 718/230-0010
Agent: The Gersh Agency - Beverly Hills, 310/274-6611

STRAIGHT OUT OF BROOKLYN   The Samuel Goldwyn
   Company, 1991
THE INKWELL   Buena Vista, 1994

RICHARD RICH
Business: Rich Animation Studios, 333 N. Glenoaks Blvd. -
   3rd Floor, Burbank, CA 91502, 818/846-0166

THE FOX AND THE HOUND (AF)   co-director with Art Stevens &
   Ted Berman, Buena Vista, 1981
THE BLACK CAULDRON (AF)   co-director with Ted Berman,
   Buena Vista, 1985
ANIMATED STORIES FROM THE NEW TESTAMENT (AHV)
   Family Entertainment Network, 1987
THE SWAN PRINCESS (AF)   New Line Cinema, 1994
FEATHERTOP (AF)   Rich Animation Studios/Nest
   Entertainment, 1995

DICK RICHARDS*
b. 1936
Address: P.O. Box 491238, Los Angeles, CA 90049

THE CULPEPPER CATTLE CO.   20th Century-Fox, 1972
RAFFERTY AND THE GOLD DUST TWINS   Warner Bros., 1975
FAREWELL, MY LOVELY   Avco Embassy, 1975
MARCH OR DIE   Columbia, 1977, British
DEATH VALLEY   Universal, 1981
MAN, WOMAN AND CHILD   Paramount, 1983
HEAT   New Century/Vista, 1987

H. CLIVE RICHARDS
b. Jamaica
Contact: Lee Collver, Oakwood Station, 265 S. Western Avenue -
   #74343, Los Angeles, CA 90004, 213/664-6622

JAMMIN'   1989

LLOYD RICHARDS*
Business: O'Neill Theater Center, 234 West 44th Street - 9th Floor,
   New York, NY 10036
Business Manager: DaSilva & DaSilva, 502 Park Avenue,
   New York, NY 10022, 212/752-9323

ROOTS: THE NEXT GENERATIONS (MS)   co-director with
   John Erman, Charles S. Dubin & Georg Stanford Brown,
   Wolper Productions, 1979
THE PIANO LESSON (TF)   Signboard Hill Prods./
   Hallmark Ent., 1995

RON RICHARDS*
Home: 13950 Northwest Passage - Apt. 307, Marina del Rey,
   CA 90292, 310/578-2074

THE MINX   Cambist, 1970
RELATIONS   Cambist, 1972
KISS OF VENUS   1987, unfinished

MARK RICHARDSON
Agent: Scott Yoselow, The Gersh Agency - New York City,
   212/997-1818

GOLDDIGGER   Long Island Expressway Productions, 1990

PETER RICHARDSON
Agent: ICM - London, tel.: 171/636-6565

THE SUPERGRASS   Hemdale, 1985, British
EAT THE RICH   New Line Cinema, 1987, British
THE COMIC STRIP PRESENTS...THE STRIKE (TF)   co-director with
   Pete Richens, Channel 4, 1988, British
THE POPE MUST DIE   *THE POPE MUST DIET*   Miramax Films,
   1991, British

WILLIAM RICHERT*
Agent: The Marion Rosenberg Office - Los Angeles, 213/653-7383

FIRST POSITION (FD)   Roninfilm, 1973
WINTER KILLS   Avco Embassy, 1979
THE AMERICAN SUCCESS CO.   *SUCCESS*   Columbia, 1979,
   West German-U.S.
A NIGHT IN THE LIFE OF JIMMY REARDON
   20th Century Fox, 1988
THE MAN IN THE IRON MASK   Ethos Films, 1995

ANTHONY RICHMOND*
b. July 7, 1942 - London, England
Agent: Smith-Gosnell-Nicholson & Associates - Pacific Palisades,
   310/459-0307
Business Manager: Harry Schaffer, Guild Management,
   9911 W. Pico Blvd., Los Angeles, CA 90035, 310/277-9711

DEJA VU   Cannon, 1985, British

W.D. RICHTER*
b. December 7, 1945 - New Britain, Connecticut
Agent: Shapiro-Lichtman Talent Agency - Los Angeles, 310/859-8877

THE ADVENTURES OF BUCKAROO BANZAI: ACROSS THE
   8TH DIMENSION   20th Century Fox, 1984
LATE FOR DINNER   Columbia, 1991

TOM RICKMAN*
(James Thomas Rickman)
Home: 14265 Greenleaf Street, Sherman Oaks, CA 91423,
   818/501-8537
Agent: CAA - Beverly Hills, 310/288-4545

THE RIVER RAT   Paramount, 1984

JAMES RIDGEWAY
BLOOD IN THE FACE (FD)   co-director with Anne Bohlen & Kevin
   Rafferty, Right Thinking Productions, 1991
FEED (FD)   co-director with Kevin Rafferty, Original Cinema, 1992

PHILIP RIDLEY
Agent: A.P. Watt Ltd., 20 John Street, London WC1N 2DR, England,
   tel.: 171/405-6774, fax: 171/831-2154

THE REFLECTING SKIN   Miramax Films, 1990, British-Canadian
THE PASSION OF DARKLY NOON   Entertainment Film Distributors/
   Fugitive Features/Hauskunst/Keytsman, 1994, British-German

WILLIAM RIEAD
SCORPION   Crown International, 1986

LENI RIEFENSTAHL
(Helene Bertha Amalie Riefenstahl)
b. August 22, 1902 - Berlin, Germany
Contact: Federal Union of Film and Television Directors in Germany,
   Adelheidstrasse 7, 8000 Munich 40, Germany, tel.: 089/271-6380

THE BLUE LIGHT   Du World, 1932, German
SIEG DES GLAUBENS   1933, German
TRIUMPH OF THE WILL (FD)   Contemporary, 1935, German
TAG DER FREIHEIT - UNSERE WEHRMACHT (FD)
   1935, German

OLYMPIAD, PART I: FESTIVAL OF THE NATIONS (FD)
    Contemporary, 1938, German
OLYMPIAD, PART II: FESTIVAL OF BEAUTY (FD)
    Contemporary, 1938, German
TIEFLAND   1954, West German

DANIEL RIESENFELD
IN DARKEST HOLLYWOOD: CINEMA & APARTHEID (FD)
    co-director with Peter Davis, Nightingale Productions/
    McKinnon Associates, 1994, U.S.-Canadian

JED RIFFE
ISHI, THE LAST YAHI (FD)   co-director with Pamela Roberts,
    Rattlesnake Productions, 1993

ADAM RIFKIN
(Rif Coogan)
Agent: William Morris Agency - Beverly Hills, 310/859-4000

NEVER ON TUESDAY   Cinema Group, 1988
TALE OF TWO SISTERS   Vista Street Entertainment, 1989
THE DARK BACKWARD   Greycat Films, 1991
PSYCHO COP II: PSYCHO COP RETURNS   directed under
    pseudonym of Rif Coogan, Film Nouveau, 1992
THE NUTTY NUT   Connexion American Media, 1992
THE CHASE   20th Century Fox, 1994

ERAN RIKLIS
Contact: Israel Film Centre, Ministry of Industry & Trade,
    P.O. Box 299, 941 90 Jerusalem, Israel,
    tel.: 972-2-750433 or 750297

CUP FINAL   Local Productions, 1991, Israeli
ZOHAR: MEDITERRANEAN BLUES   New Films, 1993, Israeli

WOLF RILLA
Home: Moulin de la Camandoule, Chemin N-D des Cypre,
    83440, France

VILLAGE OF THE DAMNED   MGM, 1960, British
THE WORLD TEN TIMES OVER   1962, British
PAX?   Mexican Olympic Committee, 1968, Mexican
THE GREATER GOOD (TF)   BBC, 1972, British
ROSIE   1975, British
TRAINING SALESMEN (FD)   1980, British

ALFREDO RINGEL
UN-BECOMING AGE   co-director with Deborah Taper Ringel,
    Castle Hill Productions, 1993
THE MAGIC BUBBLE   co-director with Deborah Taper Ringel,
    Amazing Movies, 1994

DEBORAH TAPER RINGEL
UN-BECOMING AGE   co-director with Alfredo Ringel,
    Castle Hill Productions, 1993
THE MAGIC BUBBLE   co-director with Alfredo Ringel,
    Amazing Movies, 1994

ARTURO RIPSTEIN
b. 1943 - Mexico City, Mexico
Contact: IMCINE, Tepic #40, P.B. Colonia Roma Sur, Mexico City,
    C.P. 06760, Mexico, tel.: 525/584-7283

TIEMPO DE MORIR   Azteca Films, 1965, Mexican
H.O.   Azteca Films, 1966, Mexican
LOS RECUERDOS DEL PORVENIR   Azteca Films, 1968, Mexican
LA HORA DE LOS NINOS   Azteca Films, 1969, Mexican
EL CASTILLO DE LA PUREZA   Azteca Films, 1972, Mexican
EL SANTO OFICIO   Azteca Films, 1974, Mexican
FOXTROT   New World, 1975, Mexican-Swiss
LECUMBERRI   Azteca Films, 1976, Mexican
EL LUGAR SIN LIMITES   Azteca Films, 1977, Mexican
CADENA PERPETUA   Azteca Films, 1978, Mexican
LA TIA ALEXANDRA   Azteca Films, 1980, Mexican

LA SEDUCCION   Azteca Films, 1983, Mexican
RASTRO DE LA MUERTE   Azteca Films, 1983, Mexican
EL OTRO   Azteca Films, 1984, Mexican
EL IMPERIO DE LA FORTUNA   Conacine, 1986, Mexican
MENTIRAS PIADOSOS   Filmicas Internacionales/Fondo de Apoyo,
    1989, Mexican
LA MUJER DEL PUERTO   Chariot 7/Doc Producciones, 1991,
    Mexican-U.S.
PRINCIPIO Y FIN   IMCINE/Fondo de Fomento a la Calidad
    Cinematografica/Alameda Films, 1994, Mexican
LA REINA DE LA NOCHE   Ultra Films/IMCINE/Film Works/Les
    Films du Nopal, 1994, Mexican-U.S.-French

LEIDULV RISAN
Contact: Norwegian Film Institute, Grev Wedels Plass 1, N-0105 Oslo,
    Norway, tel.: 2/42-87-40

THE SUNSET BOYS   Norsk Film/Yellow Cottage/Schibsted Film/
    TAG-Traum Filmproduktion/Crone Film Produktion/Norwegian
    Film Institute/Filmstiftung Nordrhein-Westfalen/Eurimages/
    Danish Film Institute, 1995, Norwegian-Danish-German

DINO RISI
b. December 23, 1917 - Milan, Italy
Home: Residence Aldrovandi, via Aldrovandi, Rome, Italy,
    tel.: 06/322-1429

VACANZE COL GANGSTER   Mambretti Film, 1952, Italian
VIALE DELLA SPERANZA   Mambretti Film/ENIC, 1953, Italian
LOVE IN THE CITY   co-director with Michelangelo Antonioni,
    Federico Fellini, Alberto Lattuada, Carlo Lizzani &
    Francesco Maselli, Italian Films Export, 1953, Italian
IL SEGNO DI VENERE   Titanus, 1955, Italian
SCANDAL IN SORRENTO   *PANE, AMORE E...*   DCA, 1955, Italian
POOR BUT BEAUTIFUL   Trans-Lux, 1956, Italian-French
LA NONNA SABELLA   Titanus/Franco-London Films,
    1957, Italian-French
BELLE MA POVERE   Titanus, 1957, Italian
VENEZIA, LA LUNA E TU   Titanus/Societe Generale de
    Cinematographie, 1958, Italian-French
POVERI MILIONARI   Titanus, 1958, Italian
IL VEDOVO   Paneuropa/Cino Del Duca, 1959, Italian
LOVE AND LARCENY   *IL MATTATORE*   Major Film,
    1960, Italian-French
UN AMORE A ROMA   CEI Incom/Fair Film/Laetitia Film/Les Films
    Cocinor/Alpha Film, 1960, Italian-French-West German
A PORTE CHIUSE   Fair Film/Cinematografica Rire/Societe
    Generale de Cinematographie/Ultra Film/Lyre Film/Roxy Film,
    1960, Italian-French-West German
UNA VITA DIFFICILE   Dino De Laurentiis Cinematographica,
    1961, Italian
LA MARCIA SU ROMA   Fair Film/Orsay Films, 1962, Italian-French
THE EASY LIFE   *IL SORPASSO*   Embassy, 1962, Italian
IL GIOVEDI   Dino De Laurentiis Cinematografica/Center Film,
    1963, Italian
15 FROM ROME   *I MOSTRI*   McAbee, 1963, Italian-French
IL GAUCHO   Fair Film/Clemente Lococo, 1964, Italian-Argentinian
BAMBOLE!   co-director with Luigi Comencini, Franco Rossi &
    Mauro Bolognini, Royal Films International, 1965, Italian
I COMPLESSI   co-director with Franco Rossi & Luigi Filippo D'Amico,
    Documento Film/SPCE, 1965, Italian-French
WEEKEND, ITALIAN STYLE   *L'OMBRELLONE*   Marvin Films,
    1965, Italian- French-Spanish
I NOSTRI MARITI   co-director with Luigi Filippo D'Amico &
    Luigi Zampa, Documento Film, 1966, Italian
TREASURE OF SAN GENNARO   *OPERAZIONE SAN GENNARO*
    Paramount, 1966, Italian-French-West German
THE TIGER AND THE PUSSYCAT   *IL TIGRE*   Embassy,
    1967, Italian-U.S.
THE PROPHET   Joseph Green Pictures, 1967, Italian
STRAZIAMI DA MI BACI SAZIAMI   FIDA Cinematografica/
    Productions Jacques Roitfeld, 1968, Italian-French
VEDO NUDO   Dean Film/Jupiter Generale Cinematografica,
    1969, Italian
IL GIOVANE NORMALE   Dean Film/Italnoleggio, 1969, Italian
THE PRIEST'S WIFE   Warner Bros., 1970, Italian-French

NOI DONNE SIAMO FATTE COSI' Apollo International Film,
   1971, Italian
IN NOME DEL POPOLO ITALIANO Apollo International Film,
   1972, Italian
MORDI E FUGGI C.C. Champion/Les Films Concordia,
   1973, Italian-French
HOW FUNNY CAN SEX BE? *SESSOMATTO* In-Frame,
   1973, Italian
TELEFONI BIANCHI Dean Film, 1975, Italian
SCENT OF A WOMAN 20th Century-Fox, 1976, Italian
ANIMA PERSA Dean Film/Les Productions Fox Europe,
   1977, Italian-French
LA STANZA DEL VESCOVO Merope Film/Carlton Film Export/
   Societe Nouvelle Prodis, 1977, Italian-French
VIVA ITALIA! *I NUOVI MOSTRI* co-director with Mario Monicelli &
   Ettore Scola, Cinema 6, 1978, Italian
PRIMO AMORE Dean Film, 1978, Italian
CARO PAPA' Dean Film/AMLF/Prospect Film, 1979,
   Italian-French-Canadian
SUNDAY LOVERS co-director with Bryan Forbes,
   Edouard Molinaro & Gene Wilder, MGM/United Artists,
   1980, U.S.-British-Italian-French
SONO FOTOGENICO Dean Film/Marceau Cocinor,
   1980, Italian-French
GHOST OF LOVE Dean Film/AMLF/Roxy Film, 1981,
   Italian-French-West German
SESSO E VOLENTIERI Dean Film, 1982, Italian
LA VITA CONTINUA (MS) RAI, 1984, Italian
LE BON ROI DAGOBERT Gaumount, 1984, French-Italian
SCEMO DI GUERRA Titanus, 1985, Italian-French
IL COMMISSARIO LO GATTO Dean Film/Reteitalia,
   1987, Italian
TERESA Dean Film/Reteitalia, 1987, Italian
TWO WOMEN (TF) Reteitalia, 1989, Italian
AMORI (TF) co-director, Reteitalia, 1989, Italian
TOLGO IL DISTURBO International Dean Film/Starlet
   International/Flore, 1990, Italian-French
VITA COI FIGLI (MS) Reteitalia/Polyphon, 1991, Italian
MISSIONE D'AMORE (MS) CEP, 1993, Italian

MARCO RISI
b. June 4, 1951 - Milan, Italy
Home: via Misurina 78, Rome, Italy, tel.: 06/327-9692

APPUNTI SU HOLLYWOOD (TD) Rail, 1978, Italian
VADO A VIVERE DA SOLO Numero Uno Cinematografica,
   1981, Italian
UN RAGAZZO, UNA RAGAZZA Numero Uno Cinematografica,
   1983, Italian
COLPO DI FULMINE Numero Uno Cinematografica, 1984, Italian
SOLDATI. 365 ALL' ALBA Numero Uno Cinematografica/
   Reteitalia, 1987, Italian
FOREVER MARY Cinevista, 1989, Italian
RAGAZZI FUORI Numero Uno Cinematografica, 1990, Italian
IL MURO DI GOMMA Pentafilm/Trio Cinema e Televisione,
   1991, Italian
NEI CONTINENTE NERO Penta Distribuzione, 1993, Italian
IL BRANCO Cecchi Gori Group Tiger Cinematografica,
   1994, Italian

MICHAEL RITCHIE*
b. 1938 - Waukesha, Wisconsin
Agent: ICM - Beverly Hills, 310/550-4000

THE OUTSIDER (TF) Universal TV, 1967
THE SOUND OF ANGER (TF) Universal TV, 1968
DOWNHILL RACER Paramount, 1969
PRIME CUT National General, 1972
THE CANDIDATE Warner Bros., 1972
SMILE United Artists, 1975
THE BAD NEWS BEARS Paramount, 1976
SEMI-TOUGH United Artists, 1978
AN ALMOST PERFECT AFFAIR Paramount, 1979
THE ISLAND Universal, 1980
DIVINE MADNESS (FD) The Ladd Company/Warner Bros., 1980
THE SURVIVORS Columbia, 1983
FLETCH Universal, 1985
WILDCATS Warner Bros., 1986

THE GOLDEN CHILD Paramount, 1986
THE COUCH TRIP Orion, 1988
FLETCH LIVES Universal, 1989
DIGGSTOWN MGM-UA, 1992
THE POSITIVELY TRUE ADVENTURES OF THE ALLEGED TEXAS
   CHEERLEADER-MURDERING MOM (CTF) ☆ Frederick S.
   Pierce Company/Sudden Entertainment Productions, 1993
COPS & ROBBERSONS TriStar, 1994
THE SCOUT 20th Century Fox, 1994
THE FANTASTICKS MGM-UA, 1995

JOE RITTER
BEACH BALLS Concorde, 1988
THE NEW GLADIATORS Concorde, 1989

FREDERICK RITZENBERG
GOSPEL (FD) co-director with David Leivick,
   20th Century-Fox, 1983

DANIEL RIVERA
JIMI Joy Productions, 1994

JOAN RIVERS*
b. June 8, 1933 - New York, New York
Personal Manager: DTM Management, 15237 Sunset Blvd. -
   Suite 69, Pacific Palisades, CA 90272, 310/933-3764

RABBIT TEST Avco Embassy, 1978

JACQUES RIVETTE
b. March 1, 1978 - Rouen, France
Address: 20, boulevard de la Bastille, 75012 Paris, France,
   tel.: 1/46-28-85-14
Agent: Voyez Mon Agent - Paris, tel.: 1/47-23-55-80

AUX QUATRE COINS 1950, French
LE QUADRILLE 1950, French
LE DIVERTISSEMENT 1952, French
LE COUP DE BERGER 1956, French
PARIS BELONGS TO US 1961, French
THE NUN Altura, 1966, French
JEAN RENOIR, LE PATRON (FD) 1966, French
L'AMOUR FOU 1968, French
OUT 1: SPECTRE Sunchild Productions, 1974, French
CELINE AND JULIE GO BOATING 1974, French
DUELLE Valoria, 1976, French
NOROIT Sunchild Productions, 1976, French
MERRY-GO-ROUND 1979, French
LE PONT DU NORD Gerik Distribution, 1981, French
PARIS S'EN VA 1981, French
LOVE ON THE GROUND Spectrafilm, 1984, French
HURLEVENT *WUTHERING HEIGHTS* AMLF, 1985, French
LA BANDE DES QUARTRE 1989, French-Swiss
LA BELLE NOISEUSE MK2 Productions USA, 1991, French-Swiss
JEANNE LA PUCELLE I: LES BATAILLES Pierre Grise Production/
   La Sept Cinema/France 3 Cinema/Canal Plus/CNC, 1994, French
JEANNE LA PUCELLE II: LES PRISONS Pierre Grise Production/La
   Sept Cinema/France 3 Cinema/Canal Plus/CNC, 1994, French
HAUT BAS FRAGILE 1995, French

ADAM ROARKE
TRESPASSES co-director with Loren Bivens, Shapiro
   Entertainment, 1987

ALAIN ROBBE-GRILLET
b. August 18, 1922 - Brest, France
Home: 18, Boulevard Maillot, 92200 Neuilly, France,
   tel.: 1/47-22-31-22

L'IMMORTELLE Grove Press, 1963, French
TRANS-EUROP-EXPRESS Trans-American, 1967, French
THE MAN WHO LIES Grove Press, 1968, French-Czech
L'EDEN ET APRES Como Films, 1971, French-Czech-Tunisian
GLISSMENTS PROGRESSIFS DU PLAISIR SNETC,
   1974, French

LE JEU AVEC LE FEU   Arcadie Productions, 1975, Italian-French
LA BELLE CAPTIVE   Argos Films, 1983, French
UN BRUIT QUI REND FOU   co-director with Dimitri De Clercq,
   Nomad FilmsEuripide Productions/La Sept Cinema/CAB
   Productions/RTBF/Canal Plus/Investimage 4/CNC,
   1995, French-Swiss-Belgian

SEYMOUR ROBBIE*
Home: 9980 Liebe Drive, Beverly Hills, CA 90210, 310/274-6713

C.C. AND COMPANY   Avco Embassy, 1970
MARCO   Cinerama Releasing Corporation, 1974

BRIAN ROBBINS
Business: Tollin/Robbins Productions, 6156 Simpson Avenue,
   North Hollywood, CA 91606, 818/766-5004

THE SHOW   Rysher Entertainment, 1995

JEROME ROBBINS*
(Jerome Rabinowitz)
b. October 11, 1918 - Weehawken, New Jersey
Contact: Directors Guild of America - Los Angeles, 213/851-3671

WEST SIDE STORY ★★   co-director with Robert Wise,
   United Artists, 1961

MATTHEW ROBBINS*
b. New York
Agent: ICM - Beverly Hills, 310/550-4000

CORVETTE SUMMER   MGM/United Artists, 1978
DRAGONSLAYER   Paramount, 1981, U.S.-British
THE LEGEND OF BILLIE JEAN   TriStar, 1985
*batteries not included   Universal, 1987
MOTHERS, DAUGHTERS & LOVERS (TF)   Katz-Huyck Film
   Productions/NBC Productions, 1989
BINGO   TriStar, 1991

TIM ROBBINS
b. October 16, 1958 - West Covina, California
Agent: ICM - Beverly Hills, 310/550-4000

BOB ROBERTS   Paramount/Miramax Films, 1992
DEAD MAN WALKING   Gramercy Pictures, 1995

MIKE ROBE*
Agent: CAA - Beverly Hills, 310/288-4545

WITH INTENT TO KILL (TF)   London Productions, 1984
NEWS AT ELEVEN (TF)   Turman-Foster Productions/Finnegan
   Associates, 1986
MURDER ORDAINED (TF)   Zev Braun Productions/Interscope
   Communications, 1987
GO TOWARD THE LIGHT (TF)   Corapeak Productions/The Polson
   Company, 1988
GUTS & GLORY: THE RISE AND FALL OF OLIVER NORTH (TF)
   Mike Robe Productions/Papazian-Hirsch Entertainment, 1989
CHILD IN THE NIGHT (TF)   Mike Robe Productions, 1990
SON OF THE MORNING STAR (TF)   The Mount Company/Preston
   Stephen Fischer Company/Republic Pictures TV, 1991
THE BURDEN OF PROOF (TF)   Mike Robe Productions/Capital
   Cities-ABC Video Productions, 1992
RETURN TO LONESOME DOVE (MS)   RHI Entertainment/
   de Passe Entertainment/Nightwatch Productions, 1993

JAMES ROBERSON*
Home: P.O. Box 2803, Arnold, CA 95223, 209/795-7237

THE GIANT OF THUNDER MOUNTAIN   Castle Hill
   Productions, 1991

GENEVIEVE ROBERT
Agent: CAA - Beverly Hills, 310/288-4545

CASUAL SEX?   Universal, 1988

VINCENT ROBERT
b. 1958 - Montreal, Quebec, Canada
Business: Sudden Light Productions, 322 S. Westminster Avenue,
   Los Angeles, CA 90020, 213/931-0730
Agent: Media Artists Group - Los Angeles, 213/463-5610 or
   Writers & Artists Agency - Los Angeles, 310/824-6300

THE FEAR   Devin International, 1995

YVES ROBERT
b. June 19, 1920 - Saumur, France
Business: La Gueville Productions, 16, rue de Marignan, 75008 Paris,
   France, tel.: 1/43-59-28-02
Contact: French Film Office, 745 Fifth Avenue, New York, NY 10151,
   212/832-8860

LES HOMMES NE PENSENT QU'A ÇA   1954, French
SIGNE ARSENE LUPIN   1959, French
LA FAMILLE FENOUILLARD   1961, French
LA GUERRE DES BOUTONS   LGE, 1962, French
BEBERT ET L'OMNIBUS   1963, French
LES COPAINS   1964, French
MONNAIRE DE SINGE   1965, French
VERY HAPPY ALEXANDER   ALEXANDER   Cinema 5,
   1968, French
CLERAMBARD   1969, French
THE TALL BLOND MAN WITH ONE BLACK SHOE   Cinema 5,
   1972, French
SALUT L'ARTISTE   Exxel, 1973, French
RETURN OF THE TALL BLOND MAN WITH ONE BLACK SHOE
   Lanir Releasing, 1974, French
PARDON MON AFFAIRE   AN ELEPHANT CA TROMPE
   ENORMEMENT   First Artists, 1976, French
PARDON MON AFFAIRE, TOO!   NOUS IRONS TOUS AU PARADIS
   First Artists, 1977, French
COURAGE FUYONS   Gaumont, 1979, French
LE JUMEAU   AAA, 1984, French
MY FATHER'S GLORY   Orion Classics, 1990, French
MY MOTHER'S CASTLE   Orion Classics, 1990, French
LE BAL DES CASSE-PIEDS   Gaumont, 1992, French
MONTPARNASSE-PONTDICHERY   Gaumont Buena Vista
   International, 1994, French

ALAN ROBERTS
Contact: Writers Guild of America, West - Los Angeles, 310/550-1000

THE ZODIAC COUPLES   co-director with Bob Stein, SAE, 1970
PANORAMA BLUE   Ellman Film Enterprises, 1974
YOUNG LADY CHATTERLEY   PRO International, 1977
THE HAPPY HOOKER GOES HOLLYWOOD   Cannon, 1980
FLASHDANCE FEVER   Shapiro Entertainment, 1983
PRIVATE PROPERTY   Park Lane Productions, 1985
OMEGA COP II: THE CHALLENGE   Romarc, 1991
DON'T MESS WITH THE U.S.   Action International, 1991
ROUND TRIP TO HEAVEN   Vertigo Pictures, 1992
SAVE ME   Vision International, 1993

DARRYL ROBERTS
Agent: Writers & Artists Agency - Los Angeles, 310/824-6300
Contact: Avant Garde Productions, 312/488-4787

HOW U LIKE ME NOW   SGE Entertainment, 1993

DEBORAH ROBERTS
FRANKENSTEIN GENERAL HOSPITAL   New Star
   Entertainment, 1988

JOHN ROBERTS
Agent: CAA - Beverly Hills, 310/288-4545

WAR OF THE BUTTONS   Warner Bros., 1994, British-French

PAMELA ROBERTS
ISHI, THE LAST YAHI (FD)   co-director with Jed Riffe,
   Rattlesnake Productions, 1993

CLIFF ROBERTSON*
b. September 9, 1925 - La Jolla, California
Business: P.O. Box 55049, Sherman Oaks, CA 91403, 818/988-1130
Agent: ICM - Beverly Hills, 310/550-4000

J.W. COOP   Columbia, 1972
THE PILOT   Summit Features, 1981

MICHAEL ROBERTSON
b. Drummovne, Australia
Business: Michael Robertson Film Productions, 666 N. Robertson
Blvd., Los Angeles, CA 90069, 310/659-0175
Attorney: Peter Martin Nelson, Nelson, Guggenheim & Felker,
12424 Wilshire Blvd., Los Angeles, CA 90025, 310/207-8337

THE BEST OF FRIENDS   Friendly Film Co., 1981, Australian
GOING SANE   Sea-Change Films, 1985, Australian
BACK OF BEYOND   Beyond Films, 1995, Australian

TOM G. ROBERTSON
GOOD OLD BOY (TF)   Multimedia Entertainment/The Disney
Channel/WonderWorks, 1989

JOHN ROBINS
Home: 6637 Zumirez Drive, Malibu, CA 90265, 310/457-9966
Business Manager: Stanley Margolis, Financial Management Inc.,
6404 Wilshire Blvd. - Suite 1230, Los Angeles, CA 90048,
213/651-4141

HOT RESORT   Cannon, 1985

BRUCE ROBINSON*
b. May 2, 1946 - London, England
Agent: CAA - Beverly Hills, 310/288-4545

WITHNAIL AND I   Cineplex Odeon, 1987, British
HOW TO GET AHEAD IN ADVERTISING   Warner Bros.,
1989, British
JENNIFER EIGHT   Paramount, 1992

JOHN MARK ROBINSON
b. 1949 - Toronto, Ontario, Canada
Business: Modern Productions, 4112 Del Rey Avenue, Venice,
CA, 310/578-1112
Personal Manager: Creative Alliance Management - Los Angeles,
213/962-6090

ROADHOUSE 66   Atlantic Releasing Corporation, 1984
KID   Tapestry Films, 1991
ALL TIED UP   Moonstone Entertainment, 1993

PHIL ALDEN ROBINSON*
Agent: CAA - Beverly Hills, 310/288-4545 or
Peter Turner Agency - Santa Monica, 310/315-4772

IN THE MOOD   THE WOO WOO KID   Lorimar, 1987
FIELD OF DREAMS   Universal, 1989
SNEAKERS   Universal, 1992

MARC ROCCO*
Agent: CAA - Beverly Hills, 310/288-4545
Business: 3815 W. Olive, Suite 201, Burbank, CA 91505,
818/954-0780

SCENES FROM THE GOLDMINE   Hemdale, 1988
DREAM A LITTLE DREAM   Vestron, 1989
WHERE THE DAY TAKES YOU   New Line Cinema, 1992
MURDER IN THE FIRST   Warner Bros., 1995

ERIC ROCHANT
b. February 24, 1961 - Paris, France
Contact: French Film Office, 745 Fifth Avenue, New York,
NY 10151, 212/832-8860

TOUGH LIFE   Les Productions Lazennec, 1989, French

LOVE WITHOUT PITY   UN MONDE SANS PITIE   Orion Classics,
1991, French
AUX YEUX DU MONDE   UGC, 1991, French
LES PATRIOTES   Gaumont Buena Vista International,
1994, French

ALEXANDRE ROCKWELL
Agent: UTA - Beverly Hills, 310/273-6700

SONS   Pacific Pictures, 1989
IN THE SOUP   Triton Pictures, 1992,
U.S.-Japanese-German-French-Spanish-Italian
SOMEBODY TO LOVE   Lumiere Pictures, 1994
FOUR ROOMS   co-director with Quentin Tarantino, Allison Anders &
Robert Rodriguez, Mirmax Films, 1995

FRANC RODDAM*
(Francis George Roddam)
b. April 29, 1946 - Stockton, England
Business: Union Pictures, 36 Marshall Street, London W1, England,
tel.: 171/287-5110
Agent: ICM - London, tel.: 171/636-6565 or Beverly Hills,
310/550-4000

MINI (TF)   BBC, 1975, British
DUMMY (TF)   ATV Network, 1977, British
QUADROPHENIA   World Northal, 1979, British
THE LORDS OF DISCIPLINE   Paramount, 1983
THE BRIDE   Columbia, 1985, British
ARIA   co-director, Miramax Films, 1987, British
WAR PARTY   Hemdale, 1988
K2   Paramount, 1991, British

PAUL RODRIGUEZ
Agent: William Morris Agency - Beverly Hills, 310/859-4000

A MILLION TO JUAN   The Samuel Goldwyn Company, 1994

ROBERT RODRIGUEZ*
b. Austin, Texas
Agent: ICM - Beverly Hills, 310/550-4000

EL MARIACHI   Columbia, 1992
REBEL HIGHWAY: ROADRACERS   ROADRACERS (CTF)
Drive-In Classics Cinema/Showtime, 1994
DESPERADO   Columbia, 1995
FOUR ROOMS   co-director with Quentin Tarantino, Allison Anders &
Alexandre Rockwell, Miramax Films, 1995

NICOLAS ROEG*
b. August 15, 1928 - London, England
Agent: ICM - London, tel.: 171/636-6565
Contact: London, fax: 171/727-5659 or
Los Angeles, fax: 310/859-9665

PERFORMANCE   co-director with Donald Cammell, Warner Bros.,
1970, British
WALKABOUT   20th Century-Fox, 1971, British-Australian
DON'T LOOK NOW   Paramount, 1974, British-Italian
THE MAN WHO FELL TO EARTH   Cinema 5, 1976, British
BAD TIMING/A SENSUAL OBSESSION   World Northal,
1980, British
EUREKA   MGM/UA Classics, 1984, British
INSIGNIFICANCE   Island Alive, 1985, British
CASTAWAY   Cannon, 1986, British
ARIA   co-director, Miramax Films, 1987, British
TRACK 29   Island Pictures, 1988
TENNESSEE WILLIAMS' SWEET BIRD OF YOUTH   SWEET BIRD
OF YOUTH (TF)   Atlantic/Kushner-Locke Productions, 1989
THE WITCHES   Warner Bros., 1990, British
COLD HEAVEN   Hemdale, 1992
HEART OF DARKNESS (CTF)   Chris-Rose Productions/Turner
Pictures, 1994
TWO DEATHS   BBC Films/British Screen, 1995

MICHAEL ROEMER

b. January 1, 1928 - Berlin, Germany
Contact: Yale School of Art, Box 1605A, Yale Station,
New Haven, CT 06520, 203/432-2600

A TOUCH OF THE TIMES   1949
THE INFERNO   *CORTILE CASCINO, ITALY* (FD)   co-director with
Robert M. Young, Robert M. Young Productions, 1962
NOTHING BUT A MAN   co-director with Robert M. Young,
Cinema 5, 1965
FACES OF ISRAEL (FD)   1967
THE PLOT AGAINST HARRY   New Yorker, 1969-1989
DYING (TD)   WGBH-Boston, 1976
PILGRIM, FAREWELL   Post Mills Productions, 1980
HAUNTED (TF)   Post Mills Productions/WGBH-Boston, 1984

DOUG ROGERS*

Agent: William Morris Agency - New York City, 212/586-5100

DENNIS THE MENACE (TF)   DIC Enterprises Productions, 1987

LIONEL ROGOSIN

b. 1924 - New York, New York

ON THE BOWERY (FD)   Film Representations, 1957
COME BACK, AFRICA (FD)   Rogosin, 1959
GOOD TIMES, WONDERFUL TIMES (FD)   Rogosin, 1966
BLACK ROOTS (FD)   Rogosin, 1970
BLACK FANTASY (FD)   Impact, 1972
WOODCUTTERS OF THE DEEP SOUTH (FD)   Rogosin, 1973

ERIC ROHMER

(Jean-Marie Maurice Scherer)
b. April 4, 1920 - Nancy, France
Business: Les Films du Losange, 20, avenue Pierre-ler-de-Serbie,
75016, Paris, France, tel.: 1/47-20-54-12
Contact: French Film Office, 745 Fifth Avenue, New York,
NY 10151, 212/832-8860

LE SIGNE DU LION   1959, French
LA CARRIERE DE SUZANNE   Films du Losange, 1963, French
PARIS VU PAR...   co-director, New Yorker, 1965, French
LA COLLECTIONNEUSE   Pathe Contemporary, 1967, French
MY NIGHT AT MAUD'S   Pathe Contemporary, 1970, French
CLAIRE'S KNEE   *L'AMOUR, L'APRES-MIDI*   Columbia,
1971, French
CHLOE IN THE AFTERNOON   Columbia, 1972, French
THE MARQUISE OF O...   New Line Cinema, 1976,
French-West German
PERCEVAL   *PERCEVAL LE GALLOIS*   New Yorker, 1978, French
THE AVIATOR'S WIFE   New Yorker, 1981, French
LE BEAU MARIAGE   United Artists Classics, 1982, French
PAULINE AT THE BEACH   Orion Classics, 1983, French
FULL MOON IN PARIS   *LES NUITS DE LA PLEINE LUNE*
Orion Classics, 1984, French
SUMMER   *LE RAYON VERT*   Orion Classics, 1985, French
FOUR ADVENTURES OF REINETTE AND MIRABELLE
New Yorker, 1987, French
BOYFRIENDS AND GIRLFRIENDS   *L'AMI DE MON AMIE*
Orion Classics, 1987, French
TALE OF SPRINGTIME   Orion Classics, 1990, French
A TALE OF WINTER   MK2 Productions USA, 1992, French
L'ARBRE, LE MAIRE ET LA MEDIATHEQUE   Les Films du
Losange, 1993, French
LES RENDEZ-VOUS DE PARIS   Les Films du Losange,
1995, French

SUSAN ROHRER

Business: NorthStar Entertainment Group, 1000 Centerville
Turnpike, Virginia Beach, VA 23463, 804/523-7180
Agent: Irv Schechter Company - Beverly Hills, 310/278-8070

NEVER SAY GOODBYE (TF)   NorthStar Entertainment Group, 1988
TERRIBLE THINGS MY MOTHER TOLD ME (TF)   NorthStar
Entertainment Group, 1988
FOR JENNY WITH LOVE (CTF)   NorthStar Entertainment
Group, 1989

MOTHER'S DAY (CTF)   NorthStar Entertainment Group, 1990
THE EMANCIPATION OF LIZZIE STERN (TF) ☆   NorthStar
Entertainment Group, 1991
SEXUAL CONSIDERATIONS (TF)   NorthStar Entertainment
Group, 1992

SUTTON ROLEY*

b. Belle Vernon, Pennsylvania
Home: 777 Arden Road, Pasadena, CA 91106, 818/449-2491

HOW TO STEAL THE WORLD   MGM, 1966
SWEET, SWEET RACHEL (TF)   ABC, Inc., 1971
THE LONERS   Fanfare, 1972
SNATCHED (TF)   ABC Circle Films, 1973
SATAN'S TRIANGLE (TF)   Danny Thomas Productions, 1975
CHOSEN SURVIVORS   Columbia, 1974

PHIL ROMAN

Business: Film Roman, 12020 Chandler Blvd. - Suite 200,
North Hollywood, CA 91607, 818/761-2544

TOM AND JERRY - THE MOVIE (AF)   Miramax Films, 1993

TONY ROMAN

Business: Outpost Entertainment Group, 270 N. Canon Drive,
Beverly Hills, CA 90210, 310/281-7575

BREAKING NEW YORK STYLE   Rene Malo Film, 1986, Canadian

MARK ROMANEK

b. Chicago, Illinois
Agent: UTA - Beverly Hills, 310/273-6700

STATIC   Cinecom, 1985

EDDIE ROMERO

b. July 7, 1924 - Negros Oriental, Philippines
Contact: Film Commission, National Commission for Culture and Arts,
Intramuros, Manila, Philippines

THE DAY OF THE TRUMPET   1957, U.S.-Filipino
LOST BATALLION   American International, 1962, Filipino-U.S.
THE RAIDERS OF LEYTE GULF   Hemisphere, 1963, Filipino-U.S.
MORO WITCH DOCTOR   20th Century-Fox, 1964, Filipino-U.S.
THE KIDNAPPERS   *MAN ON THE RUN*   1964
THE WALLS OF HELL   co-director with Gerardo De Leon,
Hemisphere, 1964, U.S.-Filipino
THE RAVAGERS   Hemisphere, 1965, U.S.-Filipino
MANILA OPEN CITY   1967, Filipino
BEAST OF THE YELLOW NIGHT   New World, 1970, Filipino
TWILIGHT PEOPLE   Dimension, 1972, U.S.-Filipino
BEAST OF BLOOD   Marvin Films, 1971, U.S.-Filipino
BLACK MAMA, WHITE MAMA   American International,
1973, U.S.-Filipino
BEYOND ATLANTIS   Dimension, 1973, U.S.-Filipino
SAVAGE SISTERS   American International, 1974, U.S.-Filipino
THE WOMAN HUNT   New World, 1975, U.S.-Filipino
GANITO KAMI NOON, PAANO KAYO NGAYON?   1976, Filipino
SUDDEN DEATH   Topar, 1977, U.S.-Filipino
SINO'NG KAPILING, SINO'NG KASIPING?   1977, Filipino
AGUILA   Bancom Audiovision Corporation, 1980, Filipino
DESIRE   Hemisphere, 1983, Filipino
HARI SA HARI, LAHI SA LAHI   co-director with Hsiao Lang &
Chao Lili, Cultural Center of the Philippines/Beijing Film
Studios, 1987, Filipino-Chinese
WHITEFORCE   Eastern Film Management/FGH Corporation,
1989, Australian-Filipino

GEORGE A. ROMERO*

b. February 4, 1940 - New York, New York
Agent: David Gersh, The Gersh Agency - Beverly Hills, 310/274-6611

NIGHT OF THE LIVING DEAD   Continental, 1968
THERE'S ALWAYS VANILLA   Cambist, 1972
THE CRAZIES   *CODE NAME: TRIXIE*   Cambist, 1972
HUNGRY WIVES   Jack H. Harris Enterprises, 1973

F
I
L
M

D
I
R
E
C
T
O
R
S

MARTIN   Libra, 1978
DAWN OF THE DEAD   United Film Distribution, 1979
KNIGHTRIDERS   United Film Distribution, 1981
CREEPSHOW   Warner Bros., 1982
DAY OF THE DEAD   United Film Distribution, 1985
MONKEY SHINES   Orion, 1988
TWO EVIL EYES   co-director with Dario Argento,
   Taurus Entertainment, 1990, Italian
THE DARK HALF   Orion, 1992

MIKHAIL ROMM
b. January 24, 1901 - Zaigrayevo, Siberia, Russia
Contact: Confederation of Film-Makers Unions, Vasilyevskaya
   Street 13, 123 825 Moscow, Russia, tel.: 095/250-4114

PYSHKA   1934, Soviet
TGHE THIRTEEN   1937, Soviet
LENIN IN OCTOBER   1937, Soviet
LENIN IN 1918   1939, Soviet
DREAM   1943, Soviet
GIRL NO. 217   1944, Soviet
THE RUSSIAN QUESTION   1948, Soviet
VLADIMIR ILYICH LENIN   1948, Soviet
SECRET MISSION   1950, Soviet
ADMIRAL USHAKOV   1953, Soviet
ADMIRAL USHAKOV, PART II: ATTACK FROM THE SEA
   1953, Soviet
MURDER ON DANTE STREET   1956, Soviet
NINE DAYS OF ONE YEAR   1962, Soviet
ORDINARY FASCISM (FD)   1964, Soviet
A NIGHT OF THOUGHT   1966, Soviet

DARRELL JAMES ROODT*
Agent: ICM - Beverly Hills, 310/550-4000

PLACE OF WEEPING   New World, 1986, South African
CITY OF BLOOD   Distant Horizon International,
   1987, South African
TENTH OF A SECOND   Distant Horizon International,
   1987, South African
THE STICK   New World, 1987, South African
JOBMAN   Gibraltar Releasing, 1990, South African
SARAFINA!   Buena Vista/Miramax Films, 1992,
   South African-British-French
FATHER HOOD   Buena Vista, 1993
CRY, THE BELOVED COUNTRY   Distant Horizon/Alpine Films,
   1995, South African

CONRAD ROOKS
CHAPPAQUA   Regional, 1968
SIDDHARTHA   Columbia, 1973

BETHANY ROONEY*
Home: 4459 Kraft Avenue, North Hollywood, CA 91602,
   818/761-1100
Agent: Bruce Brown, 1033 Gayley Avenue - Suite 207,
   Los Angeles, CA 90024, 310/208-1835

LOCKED UP: A MOTHER'S RAGE (TF)   Steve White
   Productions, 1991
MOMENT OF TRUTH: THE OTHER MOTHER (TF)
   O'Hara-Horowitz Productions, 1995

TOM ROPELEWSKI*
Agent: Linne Radmin, The Radmin Company, 260 S. Beverly Drive,
   Beverly Hills, CA 90212, 310/274-9515

MADHOUSE   Orion, 1990
LOOK WHO'S TALKING NOW   TriStar, 1993

MARK ROPER
Contact Information: Dr. Martin Botha, Human Sciences Research
   Council, Group for Social Dynamics, Private Bag x41,
   Pretoria 0001, South Africa, tel.: 012/202-2308

HUMAN TIME BOMB   Nu Image, 1995, South African

BERNARD ROSE
Agent: CAA - Beverly Hills, 310/288-4545 or:
   The Casarotto Company - London, tel.: 171/287-4450
Contact: British Film Commission, 70 Baker Street, London
   W1M 1DJ, England, tel.: 171/224-5000

PAPERHOUSE   Vestron, 1988, British
CHICAGO JOE & THE SHOWGIRL   New Line Cinema,
   1990, British
CANDYMAN   TriStar, 1992
IMMORTAL BELOVED   Columbia, 1994, U.S.-British

LES ROSE
Agent: Jeanine Edwards/Fifi Oscard - New York City, 212/764-1100

THREE CARD MONTE   Arista, 1977, Canadian
TITLE SHOT   Arista, 1979, Canadian
HOG WILD   Avco Embassy, 1980, Canadian
GAS   Paramount, 1981, Canadian
GORDON PINSENT AND THE LIFE AND TIMES OF EDWIN
   ALONZO BOYD (TF)   Poundmaker Productions, 1982, Canadian
ISAAC LITTLEFEATHERS   Lauron Productions, 1985, Canadian
COVERT ACTION   Spooks Productions/CBC, 1987, Canadian

MICKEY ROSE
Agent: Larry Grossman & Associates - Beverly Hills, 310/508127

STUDENT BODIES   Paramount, 1981

MARTIN ROSEN
Address: 305 San Anselmo Avenue, San Anselmo, CA 94960,
   415/456-1414

WATERSHIP DOWN (AF)   Avco Embassy, 1978, British
THE PLAGUE DOGS (AF)   Nepenthe Productions, 1982, British
STACKING   Spectrafilm, 1987

ROBERT L. ROSEN*
b. January 7, 1937 - Palm Springs, California
Attorney: Marty Weiss, Weiss, Block & Associates, 12301 Wilshire
   Blvd. - Suite 203, Los Angeles, CA 90025, 310/820-8872

COURAGE   New World, 1984

ANITA ROSENBERG
Attorney: Linda Lichter, Lichter, Grossman & Nichols, 9200 Sunset
   Blvd. - Suite 530, Los Angeles, CA 90069, 310/205-6999

ASSAULT OF THE KILLER BIMBOS   Empire Pictures, 1988

STUART ROSENBERG*
b. 1928 - New York, New York
Agent: William Morris Agency - Beverly Hills, 310/859-4000

MURDER, INC.   co-director with Burt Balaban,
   20th Century-Fox, 1960
QUESTION 7   De Rochemont, 1961, U.S.-West German
FAME IS THE NAME OF THE GAME (TF)   Universal TV, 1966
ASYLUM FOR A SPY (TF)   Universal TV, 1967
COOL HAND LUKE   Warner Bros., 1967
THE APRIL FOOLS   National General, 1969
MOVE   20th Century-Fox, 1970
WUSA   Paramount, 1970
POCKET MONEY   National General, 1972
THE LAUGHING POLICEMAN   20th Century-Fox, 1973
THE DROWNING POOL   Warner Bros., 1975
VOYAGE OF THE DAMNED   Avco Embassy, 1977, British
LOVE AND BULLETS   AFD, 1979
THE AMITYVILLE HORROR   American International, 1979
BRUBAKER   20th Century-Fox, 1980
THE POPE OF GREENWICH VILLAGE   MGM/UA, 1984
LET'S GET HARRY   released under pseudonym of Alan Smithee,
   TriStar, 1986
MY HEROES HAVE ALWAYS BEEN COWBOYS   The Samuel
   Goldwyn Company, 1991

RALPH ROSENBLUM*
b. October 13, 1925 - New York, New York
Home: 165 West 91st Street, New York, NY 10024, 212/595-7975

THE GREATEST MAN IN THE WORLD (TF)   Learning in
Focus, 1979
ANY FRIEND OF NICHOLAS NICKLEBY IS A FRIEND
OF MINE (TF)   Rubicon Productions, 1982
STIFFS   Serious Productions, 1986

KEVA ROSENFELD*
Agent: Peter Turner Agency - Santa Monica, 310/315-4772

ALL AMERICAN HIGH (FD)
TWENTY BUCKS   Triton Pictures, 1993

SCOTT ROSENFELT*
Agent: Innovative Artists - Los Angeles, 310/553-5200
Attorney: Peter Grossman, 9200 Sunset Blvd. - Suite 530,
Los Angeles, CA 90069, 310/205-6999

FAMILY PRAYERS   Arrow Entertainment, 1993

MARK ROSENTHAL
Agent: CAA - Beverly Hills, 310/288-4545

THE IN CROWD   Orion, 1988

RICK ROSENTHAL*
b. June 15, 1949 - New York, New York
Agent: The Gersh Agency - Beverly Hills, 310/274-6611

HALLOWEEN II   Universal, 1981
BAD BOYS   Universal/AFD, 1983
AMERICAN DREAMER   Warner Bros., 1984
CODE OF VENGEANCE (TF)   Universal TV, 1985
HARD COPY (TF)   Universal TV, 1987
RUSSKIES   New Century/Vista, 1987
DISTANT THUNDER   Paramount, 1988
NASTY BOYS (TF)   Wolf Films/Universal TV, 1989
DEVLIN (CTF)   Viacom Pictures, 1992
THE BIRDS II: LAND'S END (CTF)   released under pseudonym of
Alan Smithee, Rosemont Productions/MTE-Universal, 1994

ROBERT J. ROSENTHAL
Contact: Gunther Schiff - Los Angeles, 310/557-9081
Business: Apple-Rose Productions, 3961 Landmark Street,
Culver City, CA 90232, 310/204-1000

MALIBU BEACH   Crown International, 1978
ZAPPED!   Embassy, 1982

FRANCESCO ROSI
b. November 15, 1922 - Naples, Italy
Home: via Gregoriana 36, Rome, Italy, tel.: 06/6791742

LA SFIDA   Lux/Vices/Suevia Film, 1958, Italian-Spanish
I MAGLIARI   Vides/Titanus, 1959, Italian
SALVATORE GIULIANO   CCM Films, 1962, Italian-French
LE MANI SULLA CITTA'   Galatea Film, 1963, Italian
THE MOMENT OF TRUTH   Rizzoli, 1965, Italian-Spanish
MORE THAN A MIRACLE   C'ERA UNA VOLTA   MGM,
1967, Italian-French
UOMINI CONTRO   Prima Cinematografica/Jadran Film,
1970, Italian-Yugoslavian
THE MATTEI AFFAIR   Paramount, 1973, Italian
LUCKY LUCIANO   Avco Embassy, 1974, Italian
CADAVERI ECCELENTI   United Artists, 1976, Italian-French
EBOLI   CHRIST STOPPED AT EBOLI   Franklin Media, 1980,
Italian-French
THREE BROTHERS   New World, 1981, Italian
BIZET'S CARMEN   CARMEN   Triumph/Columbia,
1984, Italian-French
CHRONICLE OF A DEATH FORETOLD   Mediactuel/Italmedia/
Soprofilms/Focine, 1986, Italian-French-Colombian

THE PALERMO CONNECTION   DIMENTICARE PALERMO
Mario & Vittorio Cecchi Gori/Pentafilm/Reteitalia, 1990, Italian
DIARIO NAPOLETANO (TD)   RAI, 1992, Italian
LA TREGUA   1993, Italian

MARK ROSMAN
Agent: APA - Los Angeles, 310/273-0744

THE HOUSE ON SORORITY ROW   Artists Releasing Corporation/
Film Ventures International, 1983
TIME FLYER (TF)   Three Blind Mice Productions, 1986
SPOT MARKS THE X (CTF)   Catalina Production Group, 1986
THE FORCE   Republic Pictures, 1994
EVOLVER   Trimark Pictures, 1994

MARK ROSNER*
Address: 6305 Yucca Street - Suite 400, Los Angeles, CA 90028,
213/463-1166
Agent: UTA - Beverly Hills, 310/273-6700

DREAM STREET (TF)   The Bedford Falls Company/
Finnegan- Pinchuk Productions/MGM-UA TV, 1989

BENJAMIN ROSS
Contact: British Film Commission, 70 Baker Street, London
W1M 1DJ, England, tel.: 171/224-5000

THE YOUNG POISONER'S HANDBOOK   Mass-Sam Taylor
Productions/Kinowelt/Haut et Court/Bavarian Film Fund/British
Screen/Eurimages/Pandora, 1995, British-German

COURTNEY SALE ROSS
IN SEARCH OF ROTHKO (FD)   Atlantic Richfield Company, 1979

HERBERT ROSS*
b. May 13, 1927 - New York, New York
Agent: ICM - Beverly Hills, 310/550-4000
Attorney: Ken Ziffren, Ziffren, Brittenham & Branca, 2121 Avenue
of the Stars, Los Angeles, CA 90067, 310/552-3388

GOODBYE, MR. CHIPS   MGM, 1969, British
THE OWL AND THE PUSSYCAT   Columbia, 1970
T.R. BASKIN   Paramount, 1971
PLAY IT AGAIN, SAM   Paramount, 1972
THE LAST OF SHEILA   Warner Bros., 1973
FUNNY LADY   Columbia, 1975
THE SUNSHINE BOYS   MGM/United Artists, 1975
THE SEVEN-PER-CENT SOLUTION   Universal, 1976, British
THE TURNING POINT ★   20th Century-Fox, 1977
THE GOODBYE GIRL   Warner Bros., 1977
CALIFORNIA SUITE   Columbia, 1978
NIJINSKY   Paramount, 1980
PENNIES FROM HEAVEN   MGM/United Artists, 1981
I OUGHT TO BE IN PICTURES   20th Century-Fox, 1982
MAX DUGAN RETURNS   20th Century-Fox, 1983
FOOTLOOSE   Paramount, 1984
PROTOCOL   Warner Bros., 1984
THE SECRET OF MY SUCCESS   Universal, 1987
DANCERS   Cannon, 1987
STEEL MAGNOLIAS   TriStar, 1989
MY BLUE HEAVEN   Warner Bros., 1990
TRUE COLORS   Paramount, 1991
UNDERCOVER BLUES   MGM, 1993
BOYS ON THE SIDE   Warner Bros., 1995

KASPAR ROSTRUP
Contact: Danish Film Institute, Store Sondervoldsstraede 4, DK-1419
Copenhagen K, Denmark, tel.: 31-57-65-00

JEPPE PA BJERGET   Nordisk Film, 1980, Danish
MEMORIES OF A MARRIAGE   WALTZING REGITZE
City Cinemas, 1989, Danish

**F
I
L
M

D
I
R
E
C
T
O
R
S**

DANA ROTBERG
Contact: IMCINE, Tepic #40, P.B. Colonia Roma Sur, Mexico City,
C.P. 06760, Mexico, tel.: 525/584-7283

INTIMIDAD   Producciones Metropolis, 1990, Mexican
ANGEL DE FUEGO   IMCINE/Producciones Metropolis/Fondo de
Fomento a la Calidad Cinematografica/Otra Productoria Mas,
1992, Mexican

BOBBY ROTH*
(Robert J. Roth)
Agent: The Marion Rosenberg Office - Los Angeles, 213/653-7383

INDEPENDENCE DAY   Unifilm, 1977
THE BOSS' SON   Circle Associates, 1980
CIRCLE OF POWER   *MYSTIQUE/BRAINWASH/
THE NAKED WEEKEND*   Televicine, 1983
HEARTBREAKERS   Orion, 1984
TONIGHT'S THE NIGHT (TF)   Indieprod Productions/Phoenix
Entertainment Group, 1987
THE MAN WHO FELL TO EARTH (TF)   David Gerber Productions/
MGM TV, 1987
BAJA OKLAHOMA (CTF)   HBO Pictures/Rastar Productions, 1988
DEAD SOLID PERFECT (CTF)   HBO Pictures/David Merrick
Productions, 1988
THE MAN INSIDE   New Line Cinema, 1990, French-U.S.
RAINBOW DRIVE (CTF)   Dove Inc./ITC Entertainment/Viacom
Pictures, 1990
KEEPER OF THE CITY (CTF)   Viacom Pictures, 1992
THE SWITCH (TF)   The Avnet-Kerner Company/Companionway
Films, 1993
JUDGMENT DAY: THE JOHN LIST STORY (TF)
Republic Pictures, 1993
RIDE WITH THE WIND (TF)   Family Tree Productions/Peter
Frankovich Productions/Hearst Entertainment, 1994
NOWHERE TO HIDE (TF)   Stan Rogow Productions/Paramount
Network TV, 1994
IN THE LINE OF DUTY: KIDNAPPED (TF)   Patchett Kaufman
Entertainment/World International Network, 1995
NAOMI & WYNONNA: LOVE CAN BUILD A BRIDGE (TF)
Avnet-Kerner Company, 1995

JOE ROTH*
b. June 13, 1948 - New York, New York
Business: Walt Disney Company, 500 S. Buena Vista Street,
Burbank, CA 91521, 818/560-1000

STREETS OF GOLD   20th Century Fox, 1986
REVENGE OF THE NERDS II: NERDS IN PARADISE
20th Century Fox, 1987
COUPE DE VILLE   Universal, 1990

PHILLIP J. ROTH
APEX   Republic Pictures, 1994
DIGITAL MAN   Sci-Fi Productions, 1994
PROTOTYPE   Green Communication, 1994

MARKUS ROTHCRANZ
THE JUNGLE BOOK   Indiana Communications, 1995

STEPHANIE ROTHMAN
b. November 9, 1936 - Paterson, New Jersey
Contact: Writers Guild of America, West - Los Angeles, 310/550-1000

BLOOD BATH   co-director with Jack Hill, American
International, 1966
IT'S A BIKINI WORLD   American International, 1967
THE STUDENT NURSES   New World, 1970
THE VELVET VAMPIRE   New World, 1971
GROUP MARRIAGE   Dimension, 1972
TERMINAL ISLAND   Dimension, 1973
THE WORKING GIRLS   Dimension, 1974

RICHARD ROTHSTEIN*
Agent: Martin Hurwitz Associates - Beverly Hills, 310-274-0240

BATES MOTEL (TF)   Universal TV, 1987

BRIGITTE ROUAN
Contact: French Film Office, 745 Fifth Avenue, New York,
NY 10151, 212/832-8860

OVERSEAS   Aries Film Releasing, 1991, French

GEORGE ROWE
b. December 9, 1938 - Manila, Philippines
Business: Intercontinent Cinema Corporation, 69-48 136th Street,
Kew Garden Hills, NY 11367, 718/793-0763 or: Coastal Studios,
Inc., 500 Memorial Avenue, Walterboro, SC 29488, 803/538-5000
Agent: Susan Crawford, Crawford Literary Agency, 198 Evans Road,
Barnstead, NH 03218, 603/269-5851
Business Manager: Max Crevani, 325 West 87th Street, New York,
NY 10024, 212/595-7511
Attorney: Alan J. Azzara - New York, 516/741-8521

SHIP OF SAND   Jowell Films, 1973, Hong Kong
SAIGON STREETS   Golden Harvest, 1975, Hong Kong
BLACKBELT   Jowell Films, 1977, Hong Kong
GOLDEN TRIANGLE   Shaw Bros., 1978, Hong Kong
LOVE GAMES   Jowell Films, 1980, Hong Kong
RUN TO ANOTHER WORLD   Golden Harvest, 1981, Hong Kong
SHINTO   Toho, 1982, Japanese
WITCHCRAFT   Shaw Bros., 1984, Hong Kong
FORTRESS IN THE SUN   Jowell Films, 1986, Hong Kong
CHAIN REACTION   Golden Harvest, 1987, Hong Kong
ENEMY   Gaga Communications, 1989, Japanese
FATAL MISSION   Media Home Entertainment, 1990

PETER ROWE
b. July 23, 1947 - Winnipeg, Manitoba, Canada
Business: 435 The Thicket, Port Credit, Ontario, Canada L5G 4P6,
416/271-5757
Agent: Charles Northcote, The Core Group, 489 College Street -
Suite 501, Toronto, Ontario M6G 1A5, Canada, 416/944-0193

THE NEON PALACE   Acme Idea & Sale, 1971, Canadian
FINAL EDITION (TF)   CBC, 1980, Canadian
TAKEOVER (TF)   CBC, 1981, Canadian
LOST!   Rosebud Films, 1985, Canadian
ARCHITECTS OF FEAR   Palette Productions, 1986, Canadian
TAKE TWO   TBJ Films, 1988
PERSONAL EXEMPTIONS   Curb/Esquite Films, 1989

PATRICIA ROZEMA
b. 1958 - Ontario, Canada
Business: Vos Productions Inc., 209 Adelaide Street East - Suite 300,
Toronto, Ontario M5A 2MB, Canada, 416/777-1890

I'VE HEARD THE MERMAIDS SINGING   Miramax Films,
1987, Canadian
WHITE ROOM   Alliance Releasing, 1990, Canadian
MONTREAL VU PAR...   co-director with Jacques Leduc,
Michel Brault, Atom Egoyan, Lea Pool & Denys Arcand,
Cinema Plus Distribution, 1991, Canadian
WHEN NIGHT IS FALLING   Alliance Communications Corp./
Crucial Pictures/Telefilm Canada/Ontario Film Development
Corp., 1994, Canadian

JOHN RUANE
Agent: ICM - London, tel.: 171/636-6565

DEATH IN BRUNSWICK   Meridian Films, 1991, Australian
THAT EYE, THE SKY   Entertainment Media/Working Title Films,
1994, Australian-British

MICHAEL RUBBO
b. 1938 - Melbourne, Australia
Home: 719 de l'Epee, Montreal, Quebec H2V 3V1, Canada,
514/274-3148

SAD SONG OF YELLOW SKIN (TD)   1969, Canadian
WET EARTH AND WARM PEOPLE (TD)   1971, Canadian
WAITING FOR FIDEL (TD)   1973, Canadian
SOLZHENITSYN'S CHILDREN...ARE MAKING A LOT OF NOISE
IN PARIS (FD)   Le Cinema Parallele, 1979, Canadian

DAISY: STORY OF A FACELIFT (TD) 1980, Canadian
THE PEANUT BUTTER SOLUTION New World, 1985, Canadian
TOMMY TRICKER AND THE STAMP TRAVELER Les Productions
La Fete, 1988, Canadian
VINCENT AND ME Les Productions La Fete, 1990, Canadian
THE RETURN OF TOMMY TRICKER Les Productions La Fete/
Telefilm Canada/Sogic Quebec/Government of Quebec/The
Movie Network/Super Ecran/Canada Post Corporation/La
Societe Radio-Canada/CFCF /Television Inc./Radio-Quebec/
Endeavour Tucker Ltd., 1994, Canadian

JOSEPH RUBEN*

b. 1951 - Briarcliff, New York
Business: Joseph Ruben Productions, 221 West 82nd Street,
New York, NY 10024
Agent: UTA - Beverly Hills, 310/273-6700

THE SISTER-IN-LAW Crown International, 1975
THE POM-POM GIRLS Crown International, 1976
JOYRIDE American International, 1977
OUR WINNING SEASON American International, 1978
GORP American International, 1980
DREAMSCAPE 20th Century Fox, 1984
THE STEPFATHER New Century/Vista, 1987
TRUE BELIEVER Columbia, 1989
SLEEPING WITH THE ENEMY 20th Century Fox, 1991
THE GOOD SON 20th Century Fox, 1993
THE MONEY TRAIN Columbia, 1995

KATT SHEA RUBEN

(See Katt SHEA)

PERCIVAL RUBENS

Contact Information: Dr. Martin Botha, Human Sciences Research
Council, Group for Social Dynamics, Private Bag x41,
Pretoria 0001, South Africa, tel.: 012/202-2308

THE FOSTER GANG 1964, South African-British
THREE DAYS OF FIRE 1967, Italian
STRANGERS AT SUNRISE 1969, South African
MISTER KINGSTREETS WAR 1970, South African
SABOTEURS 1974, South African-West German-British
THE MIDNIGHT CALLER 1980, South African
SURVIVAL ZONE 1981, South African
RAW TERROR 1985, South African
WILD COUNTRY 1988, South African
OKAVANGO Transworld Entertainment, 1989, South African
SWEET MURDER Trans Atlantic Pictures/Moviworld,
1990, South African

BRUCE JOEL RUBIN*

Agent: Sanford-Gross & Associates - Los Angeles, 310/208-2100

MY LIFE Columbia, 1993

RICK RUBIN

TOUGHER THAN LEATHER New Line Cinema, 1988

SERGIO RUBINI

Contact: S.I.A.E., Sezione Cinema, viale della Letteratura 30,
Rome, Italy, tel.: 6/59901

THE STATION Aries Film Releasing, 1991, Italian
PRESTAZIONE STRAORDINARIA Mario & Vittorio Cecchi
Gori/Pentafilm/Cecchi Gori Group Tiger Cinematografica/
Videomaura, 1994, Italian
LA BIONDA Fandango, 1994, Italian

ALAN RUDOLPH*

b. December 18, 1943 - Los Angeles, California
Agent: William Morris Agency - Beverly Hills, 310/859-4000

PREMONITION TransVue, 1972
TERROR CIRCUS *BARN OF THE NAKED DEAD* 1973
WELCOME TO L.A. United Artists/Lions Gate, 1977
REMEMBER MY NAME Columbia/Lagoon Associates, 1979

ROADIE United Artists, 1980
ENDANGERED SPECIES MGM/UA, 1982
RETURN ENGAGEMENT (FD) Island Alive, 1983
CHOOSE ME Island Alive/New Cinema, 1984
SONGWRITER TriStar, 1984
TROUBLE IN MIND Alive Films, 1985
MADE IN HEAVEN Lorimar, 1987
THE MODERNS Alive Films, 1988
LOVE AT LARGE Orion, 1990
MORTAL THOUGHTS Columbia, 1991
EQUINOX I.R.S. Releasing, 1993
MRS. PARKER AND THE VICIOUS CIRCLE Fine Line Features/
New Line Cinema, 1994

LOUIS RUDOLPH*

Business: Louis Rudolph Productions, 6922 Hollywood Blvd.,
Los Angeles, CA 90028, 213/468-8330

DOUBLE STANDARD (TF) Louis Rudolph Productions/Fenton
Entertainment Group/Fries Entertainment, 1988

RAUL RUIZ

b. July 25, 1941 - Puerto Montt, Chile
Contact: French Film Office, 745 Fifth Avenue, New York,
NY 10151, 212/832-8860

TRES TRISTES TIGRES 1968, Chilean
QUE HACER? 1970, Chilean
LA COLONIA PENAL 1971, Chilean
NADIE DIJO NADA 1971, Chilean
LA EXPROPRIACION 1972, Chilean
EL REALISMO SOCIALISTA 1973, Chilean
PALOMILLA BRAVA (FD) 1973, Chilean
PALOMITA BLANCA Brochitel Uno S.A. Film1973, Chilean
DIALOGO DE EXILADOS 1974, French
MENSCH VERSTREUT UND WELT VERKEHRT
1975, West German
LA VOCATION SUSPENDUE 1977, French
THE HYPOTHESIS OF THE STOLEN PAINTING Coralie Films
International, 1979, French
DE GRAND EVENEMENT ET DES GENS ORDINAIRES
1979, French
IMAGES DU DEBAT 1979, French
JEUX 1979, French
LA VILLE NOUVELLE 1980, French
L'OR GRIS 1980, French
PAGES D'UN CATALOGUE 1980, French
FAHSTROM 1980, West German
LE BORGNE 1981, French
THE TERRITORY 1981, Portuguese
HET DAK VAN DE WALVIS 1982, Dutch
LES TROIS COURONNES DU MATELOT 1982, French
BERENICE 1983, French
LA PRESENCE REELLE 1983, French
LA VILLE DES PIRATES Les Films du Passage/Metro Films,
1983, French-Portuguese
POINT DE FUITE 1983, French-Portuguese
VOYAGE AUTOUR D'UNE MAIN 1983, French
ADVENTURES A L'ILE DE MADERE 1984, French
L'EVEILE DU PONT DE L'ALMA Les Films du Passage,
1983, French
LES DESTINS DE MANOEL 1985, French
REGIME SANS PAIN Lasa Films, 1986, French
MAMMAME Maison de la Culture du Havre, 1986, French
LA CHOUETTE AVEUGLE La Sept/Night Productions/Radio
Television Suisse Romande, 1987, French-Swiss
MEMOIRE DES APPARENCES: LA VIE EST UN SONGE
INA/Maison de la Culture du Havre/La Sept/Ministere des
Affaires Etrangeres/CNC/Ministere de PPT, 1987, French
THE GOLDEN BOAT Strand Releasing, 1990
TREASURE ISLAND Anatole Dauman/Les Films du Passage/
Cannon International, 1991, French-U.S., filmed in 1986
BASTA LA PALABRA 1991, Chilean
L'OEIL QUI MENT Sideral/Animatografo/Canal Plus, 1992,
French-Portuguese
IL VIAGGIO CLANDESTINO: VITE DI SANTI E PECCATORI
Fiumara d'Arte, 1994, Italian
FADO MAJEUR ET MINEUR Gemini Films/Madragoa Filmes,
1994, French-Portuguese

RICHARD RUSH*

b. 1930 - New York, New York
Agent: William Morris Agency - Beverly Hills, 310/859-4000

TOO SOON TO LOVE   Universal, 1960
OF LOVE AND DESIRE   20th Century-Fox, 1963
FICKLE FINGER OF FATE   Pro International, 1967
THUNDER ALLEY   American International, 1967
HELL'S ANGELS ON WHEELS   American International, 1967
A MAN CALLED DAGGER   MGM, 1968
PSYCH-OUT   American International, 1968
THE SAVAGE SEVEN   American International, 1968
GETTING STRAIGHT   Columbia, 1970
FREEBIE AND THE BEAN   Warner Bros., 1974
THE STUNT MAN ★   20th Century-Fox, 1980
COLOR OF NIGHT   Buena Vista, 1994

CHARLES (CHUCK) RUSSELL

Agent: UTA - Beverly Hills, 310/273-6700

A NIGHTMARE ON ELM STREET, PART 3: DREAM WARRIORS
   New Line Cinema, 1987
THE BLOB   TriStar, 1988
THE MASK   New Line Cinema, 1994

DAVID O. RUSSELL

Agent: UTA - Beverly Hills, 310/273-6700

SPANKING THE MONKEY   Fine Line Features/New Line
   Cinema, 1994
FLIRTING WITH DISASTER   Miramax Films, 1995

JAY RUSSELL

Business Manager: Michael Adler, Mitchell, Silberberg, Knupp,
   11377 W. Olympic Blvd., Los Angeles, CA 90064

END OF THE LINE   Orion Classics, 1988

KEN RUSSELL*

(Henry Kenneth Alfred Russell)
b. July 3, 1927 - Southampton, England
Address: 16 Salisbury Place, London W1H 1FH, England
Agent: Renaissance/H.N. Swanson - Los Angeles, 310/246-6000 or:
   Conway van Gelder Ltd. - London, tel.: 171/287-0077

FRENCH DRESSING   Warner-Pathe, 1963, British
THE DEBUSSY FILM (TF)   BBC, 1965, British
ISADORA DUNCAN, THE BIGGEST DANCER IN THE WORLD (TF)
   BBC, 1966, British
BILLION DOLLAR BRAIN   United Artists, 1967, British
DANTE'S INFERNO (TF)   BBC, 1967, British
SONG OF SUMMER (TF)   BBC, 1968, British
THE DANCE OF THE SEVEN VEILS (TF)   BBC, 1970, British
WOMEN IN LOVE ★   United Artists, 1970, British
THE MUSIC LOVERS   United Artists, 1971, British
THE DEVILS   Warner Bros., 1971, British
THE BOY FRIEND   MGM, 1971, British
SAVAGE MESSIAH   MGM, 1972, British
MAHLER   Mayfair, 1974, British
TOMMY   Columbia, 1975, British
LISZTOMANIA   Warner Bros., 1975, British
VALENTINO   United Artists, 1977, British
CLOUDS OF GLORY: WILLIAM AND DOROTHY (TF)
   Granada TV, 1978, British
CLOUDS OF GLORY: THE RIME OF THE ANCIENT
   MARINER (TF)   Granada TV, 1978, British
ALTERED STATES   Warner Bros., 1980
CRIMES OF PASSION   New World, 1984
GOTHIC   Vestron, 1987, British
ARIA   co-director, Miramax Films, 1987, British
SALOME'S FIRST NIGHT   Vestron, 1988, British
THE LAIR OF THE WHITE WORM   Vestron, 1988, British
THE RAINBOW   Vestron, 1989, British
WOMEN & MEN: STORIES OF SEDUCTION (CTF)
   co-director with Frederic Raphael & Tony Richardson,
   HBO Showcase/David Brown Productions, 1990

WHORE   Trimark Pictures, 1991
PRISONER OF HONOR (CTF)   HBO Pictures/Etude
   Productions, 1991
LADY CHATTERLEY   Global Arts/London Films/BBC, 1993, British
THE SOUTH BANK SHOW: THE SECRET LIFE OF ARNOLD BAX
   THE SECRET LIFE OF ARNOLD BAX (TF)   London Weekend TV,
   1994, British
EROTIC TALES   co-director with Bob Rafelson, Susan Seidelman,
   Melvin Van Peebles, Paul Cox & Mani Kaul, Regina Ziegler
   Filmproduktion/Tele-Munchen/Westdeutscher Rundfunk,
   1994, German

AARON RUSSO*

Address: 12 East 82nd Street, New York, NY 10028

RUDE AWAKENING   co-director with David Greenwalt, Orion, 1989

MARK RUTLAND

PRIME SUSPECT   Premiere Pictures, 1988

ELDAR RYAZANOV

Contact: Confederation of Film-Makers Unions, Vasilyevskaya
   Street 13, 123 825 Moscow, Russia, tel.: 095/250-4114

A FORGOTTEN TUNE FOR THE FLUTE   Fries Entertainment,
   1988, Soviet

MARK RYDELL*

b. March 23, 1934 - New York, New York
Agent: UTA - Beverly Hills, 310/273-6700

THE FOX   Claridge, 1968
THE REIVERS   National General, 1969
THE COWBOYS   Warner Bros., 1972
CINDERELLA LIBERTY   20th Century-Fox, 1974
HARRY AND WALTER GO TO NEW YORK   Columbia, 1976
THE ROSE   20th Century-Fox, 1979
ON GOLDEN POND ★   Universal/AFD, 1981
THE RIVER   Universal, 1984
FOR THE BOYS   20th Century Fox, 1991
INTERSECTION   Paramount, 1994

RENNY RYE

Agent: William Morris Agency - Beverly Hills, 310/859-4000 or:
   Scott Marshall - London, tel.: 181/749-7962

THE BOX OF DELIGHTS (TF)   BBC, 1984, British
THE DECEMBER ROSE (TF)   BBC, 1985, British
CASUALTY (TF)   BBC, 1986, British
PARADISE CLUB (TF)   Zenith Productions/BBC, 1990, British
THE OTHER SIDE OF PARADISE (TF)   Central Films, 1991, British
LIPSTICK ON YOUR COLLAR (TF)   Channel 4, 1992, British
MIDNIGHT MOVIE   BBC Films/Whistling Gypsy Productions,
   1994, British

NICK RYLE

Contact: British Film Commission, 70 Baker Street, London
   W1M 1DJ, England, tel.: 171/224-5000

THE WHO: THIRTY YEARS OF MAXIMUM R&B (TD)   Trinifold
   Management Ltd./Thirteen-WNET, 1994, British-U.S.

JOHN RYMAN

b. Mineral Wells, Texas

GALAXIES ARE COLLIDING   Covert Productions,
   1992, U.S.-Canadian

S

RANDA CHAHAL SABBAG
b. Libya
Contact: French Film Office, 745 Fifth Avenue, New York,
NY 10151, 212/832-8860

ECRANS DE SABLE   Carthago Films/Leil Productions/La Sept/
Apec/Radio Television Tunisien/French Ministry of Culture/French
Foreign Ministry/Canal Plus/RAI, 1991, French-Tunisian-Italian

PAUL SABELLA
Business: MGM Animation, 1545 26th Street, Santa Monica,
CA 90404, 310/449-3250

ALL DOGS GO TO HEAVEN II   co-director with Larry Leker,
MGM-UA, 1995

WILLIAM SACHS*
Business: Hollywood Independent Pictures, 3739 Montuso Place,
Encino, CA 91436, 818/907-5667

SECRETS OF THE GODS   Film Ventures International, 1976
THERE IS NO THIRTEEN   Film Ventures International, 1977
THE INCREDIBLE MELTING MAN   American International, 1977
VAN NUYS BLVD.   Crown International, 1979
GALAXINA   Crown International, 1980
HOT CHILI   Cannon, 1985
JUDGMENT   Juvie Productions, 1989

DANIEL SACKHEIM*
Agent: William Morris Agency - Beverly Hills, 310/859-4000

MIDNIGHT RUN FOR YOUR LIFE (TF)   Toto Productions/
Universal TV, 1994
IN THE SHADOW OF EVIL (TF)   D.W. Productions/
CBS Entertainment, 1995

ALAN SACKS
Agent: Annette Van Duren Agency - Los Angeles, 213/650-3643

DU BEAT-E-O   H-Z-H Presentation, 1984

JAMES STEVEN SADWITH*
b. October 20, 1952 - Plainfield, New Jersey
Agent: UTA - Beverly Hills, 310/273-6700

BLUFFING IT (TF)   Ohlmeyer Communications, 1987
BABY M (TF)   ABC Circle Films, 1988
DEADLY INTENTIONS...AGAIN? (TF)   Green-Epstein
Productions/Lorimar TV, 1991
IN BROAD DAYLIGHT (TF)   Force Ten Productions/New
World TV, 1991
SINATRA (TF) ☆☆   TS Productions/Warner Bros. TV, 1992

HENRI SAFRAN
b. October 7, 1932 - Paris, France
Contact: Mitch Consultancy, 98 Bay Road, Waverton, NSW,
2060, Australia, tel.: 02/922-6566

TROUBLE SHOOTER (MS)   1975, Australian
SOFTLY SOFTLY (MS)   1975, Australian
ELEPHANT BOY   1975, Australian
LOVE STORY (MS)   1976, Australian
STORM BOY   South Australian Film Corporation, 1976, Australian
NORMAN LOVES ROSE   Atlantic Releasing Corporation,
1981, Australian

THE WILD DUCK   RKR Releasing, 1983, Australian
PRINCE AND THE GREAT RACE   BUSH CHRISTMAS
Quartet/Films Inc., 1983, Australian
A FORTUNATE LIFE (MS)   co-director with Marcus Cole,
PBL Productions, 1986, Australian
THE LANCASTER MILLER AFFAIR (MS)   Lancaster Miller
Productions, 1986, Australian
THE RED CRESCENT   Somerset Films, 1987, Australian
JACK SIMPSON (TF)   Transmedia Productions/Roadshow/
Coote & Carroll/Film Australia, 1988, Australian
BONY (TF)   Reg Grundy Organization/Seven Network/Beta/Taurus,
1990, Australian-West German

YOICHI SAI
b. 1949 - Nagano Prefecture, Japan
Contact: Nihon Eiga Kantoku Kyokai (Japan Film Directors
Association), La Fontenu Building -4th Floor, 23-2 Maruyama-cho,
Shibuya-ku, Tokyo, Japan, tel.: 3/3461-4411

SOMEDAY SOMEBODY WAS MURDERED   Haruki Kadokawa
Productions, 1983, Japanese
MOSQUITO OF THE TENTH FLOOR   New Century Producers,
1983, Japanese
DEAR FRIENDS, SLEEP WITH SILENCE   Haruki Kadokawa
Productions, 1985, Japanese
WOMEN OF THE BLACK DRESS   Haruki Kadokawa Productions,
1987, Japanese
HANANO ASKAGUMII   Haruki Kadokawa Productions,
1988, Japanese
A-SIGN DAYS   Daiei, 1989, Japanese
ALL UNDER THE MOON   WHICH WAY TO THE MOON
Cine Qua Non, 1993, Japanese
MARKS MOUNTAIN   Shochiku, 1995, Japanese
TOKYO DELUXE   Toho, 1995, Japanese

JUNJI SAKAMOTO
b. 1958 - Osaka, Japan
Contact: Nihon Eiga Kantoku Kyokai (Japan Film Directors
Association), La Fontenu Building -4th Floor, 23-2 Maruyama-cho,
Shibuya-ku, Tokyo, Japan, tel.: 3/3461-4411

DOTSUITARUNEM   Arado Genjiro Productions, 1989, Japanese
FIST   Arado Genjiro Productions, 1990, Japanese
CHECKMATE   Arado Genjiro Productions/Apollon/Mainichi Hoso,
1991, Japanese
TOKAREV   Japan Foundation Film Library/Herald/Argo Pictures/
Suntory Bandai Visual Company, 1994, Japanese

GENE SAKS*
b. November 8, 1921 - New York, New York
Agent: Sam Cohn, ICM - New York City, 212/556-5600

BAREFOOT IN THE PARK   Paramount, 1967
THE ODD COUPLE   Paramount, 1968
CACTUS FLOWER   Columbia, 1969
LAST OF THE RED HOT LOVERS   Paramount, 1972
MAME   Warner Bros., 1974
BRIGHTON BEACH MEMOIRS   Universal, 1986
A FINE ROMANCE   TCHIN-TCHIN   Castle Hill Productions,
1991, Italian

SIDNEY SALKOW*
b. June 16, 1909 - New York, New York
Address: 12336 Addison Street, North Hollywood, CA 91607,
818/985-6691

FOUR DAYS' WONDER   1937
GIRL OVERBOARD   1937
BEHIND THE MIKE   1937
THAT'S MY STORY   1938
THE NIGHT HAWK   1938
STORM OVER BENGAL   1938
FIGHTING THOROUGHBREDS   1939
WOMAN DOCTOR   1939
STREET OF MISSING MEN   1939
ZERO HOUR   1939
SHE MARRIED A COP   1939

FLIGHT AT MIDNIGHT   1939
CAFE HOSTESS   *STREET OF MISSING WOMEN*   1940
THE LONE WOLF STRIKES   Columbia, 1940
THE WOLF WOLF MEETS A LADY   Columbia, 1940
GIRL FROM GOD'S COUNTRY   Columbia, 1940
THE LONE WOLF KEEPS A DATE   Columbia, 1941
THE LONE WOLF TAKES A CHANCE   Columbia, 1941
TIME OUT FOR RHYTHM   Columbia, 1941
TILLIE THE TOILER   Columbia, 1941
THE ADVENTURES OF MARTIN EDEN   *MARTIN EDEN*
    Columbia, 1942
FLIGHT LIEUTENANT   Columbia, 1942
CITY WITHOUT MEN   Columbia, 1943
THE BOY FROM STALINGRAD   Columbia, 1943
FAITHFUL IN MY FASHION   MGM, 1946
MILLIE'S DAUGHTER   Columbia, 1947
BULLDOG DRUMMOND AT BAY   Columbia, 1947
SWORD OF THE AVENGER   1948
LA STRADA BUIA   co-director with Marino Girolami,
    1949, Italian
LA RIVALE DELL'IMPERATRICE   co-director with
    Jacopo Comin, 1949, Italian
SHADOW OF THE EAGLE   1950, British
SCARLET ANGEL   Universal, 1952
THE GOLDEN HAWK   Columbia, 1952
THE PATHFINDER   Columbia, 1953
THE PRINCE OF PIRATES   Columbia, 1953
JACK McCALL, DESPERADO   Columbia, 1953
RAIDERS OF THE SEVEN SEAS   United Artists, 1953
SITTING BULL   United Artists, 1954, U.S.-Mexican
ROBBER'S ROOST   United Artists, 1955
LAS VEGAS SHAKEDOWN   Allied Artists, 1955
THE TOUGHEST MAN ALIVE   Allied Artists, 1955
GUN BROTHERS   United Artists, 1956
THE LONG RIFLE AND THE TOMAHAWK (TF)   co-director with
    Sam Newfield, ITC, 1956
THE IRON SHERIFF   United Artists, 1957
GUN DUEL IN DURANGO   United Artists, 1957
CHICAGO CONFIDENTIAL   United Artists, 1957
THE BIG NIGHT   Paramount, 1960
TWICE-TOLD TALES   United Artists, 1963
THE QUICK GUN   Columbia, 1964
THE LAST MAN ON EARTH   American International,
    1964, Italian-U.S.
BLOOD ON THE ARROW   Allied Artists, 1964
THE GREAT SIOUX MASSACRE   Columbia, 1965
THE MURDER GAME   1966

DAVID SALLE

SEARCH & DESTROY   October Films, 1995

WALTER SALLES, JR.

Contact: National Cinema Council (CONCINE), Rua Mayrink
    Veiga 28, Rio de Janeiro, Brazil, tel.: 2/233-8329

EXPOSURE   Miramax Films, 1991, Brazilian

MIKAEL SALOMON*

b. 1945 - Copenhagen, Denmark
Agent: ICM - Beverly Hills, 310/550-4000

A FAR OFF PLACE   Buena Vista, 1993

JAMES SALTER

Agent: Peter Matson, Sterling Lord Literistic, 1 Madison Avenue,
    New York, NY 10010, 212/696-2800

THREE   United Artists, 1969, British

DEEPA MEHTA SALTZMAN
(See Deepa MEHTA)

PAUL SALTZMAN

b. 1943 - Toronto, Ontario, Canada
Business: Sunrise Films Ltd., 160 Perth Avenue, Toronto, Ontario
    M6P 3X5, Canada, 416/535-2900

INDIA (FD)   1973, Canadian
INDIRA GANDHI: THE STATE OF INDIA (TD)   1975,
    Canadian-U.S.-British
TO BE A CLOWN (TD)   1976, Canadian
DOLPHI GEORGE DANCES (TD)   1977, Canadian
WHEN WE FIRST MET (CTF)   Learning Corporation of
    America, 1984
VALENTINE'S REVENGE (TF)   Learning Corporation of America/
    Family Communications/Sunrise Films, Ltd., 1986

VICTOR SALVA

Agent: The Gersh Agency - Beverly Hills, 310/274-6611

NATURE OF THE BEAST   New Line Cinema, 1994
POWDER   Caravan Pictures, 1995

GABRIELE SALVATORES

b. July 20, 1950 - Naples, Italy
Home: via Pergine 3, Milan, Italy, tel.: 02/439-2973

SOGNO DI UNA NOTTE DI MEZZA ESTATE   Politecne
    Cinematografica/RAI, 1983, Italian
KAMIKAZEN - ULTIMA NOTTE A MILANO   Colorado Film/Reteitalia,
    1987, Italian
MARRAKECH EXPRESS   Cecchi Gori Group Tiger Cinematografica/
    A.M.A. Film/Reteitalia, 1989, Italian
TURNE'   Cecchi Gori Group Tiger/ CinematograficaA.M.A. Film/
    Reteitalia, 1989, Italian
MEDITERRANEO   Miramax Films, 1991, Italian
PUERTO ESCONDIDO   Penta Distribuzione, 1993, Italian
SUD   Pentafilm, 1993, Italian

COKE SAMS*

Business: Studio Productions, 4610 Charlotte Avenue, Nashville,
    TN 37209, 615/298-5818

ERNEST GOES TO SCHOOL (HVF)   Emshell Home Video, 1994

HAROLD (HAL) SALWEN

Agent: Scott Yoselow, The Gersh Agency - New York City,
    212/997-1818

DENISE CALLS UP   Off the Hook Productions, 1995

GLEN SALZMAN

b. 1951 - Montreal, Quebec, Canada
Business: Cineflix Inc., 238 Davenport Road - Suite 190, Toronto,
    Ontario M5R 1J6, Canada, 416/531-2612

HOME FREE (TF)   co-director with Rebecca Yates, 1976, Canadian
ANOTHER KIND OF MUSIC (TF)   co-director with Rebecca Yates,
    1977, Canadian
NIKKOLINA (TF)   co-director with Rebecca Yates, 1978, Canadian
CORLETTO & SON (TF)   co-director with Rebecca Yates,
    1980, Canadian
REACHING OUT (TF)   co-director with Rebecca Yates,
    1980, Canadian
INTRODUCING...JANET (TF)   co-director with Rebecca Yates,
    1981, Canadian
JEN'S PLACE (TF)   co-director with Rebecca Yates,
    1982, Canadian
MILK AND HONEY   co-director with Rebecca Yates, Castle Hill
    Productions, 1987, Canadian-British

BARRY SAMSON

Agent: The Agency - Los Angeles, 310/551-3000

THE ICE RUNNER   Trident Releasing, 1992, U.S.-Russian

IAN SANDER*

Agent: CAA - Beverly Hills, 310/288-4545

I'LL FLY AWAY - THEN AND NOW (TF)   Brand-Falsey
   Productions/Lorimar TV, 1993

AKE SANDGREN

Contact: Swedish Film Institute, P.O. BOX 27-126, S-102-52
   Stockholm, Sweden, tel.: 08/665-1100

THE MIRACLE IN VALBY   1989, Swedish
THE SLINGSHOT   Sony Pictures Classics, 1993, Swedish
BIG MEN, LITTLE MEN   Svensk Filmindustri/SVT-1/Nordisk Film,
   1994, Swedish

JAY SANDRICH*

b. February 24, 1932 - Los Angeles, California
Agent: CAA - Beverly Hills, 310/288-4545

THE CROOKED HEARTS (TF)   Lorimar Productions, 1972
WHAT ARE BEST FRIENDS FOR? (TF)   ABC Circle Films, 1973
NEIL SIMON'S SEEMS LIKE OLD TIMES   SEEMS LIKE OLD TIMES
   Columbia, 1980
THE LONELY HEARTS (TF)   Lorimar Productions, 1984
FOR RICHER, FOR POORER (CTF)   Citadel Entertainment
   Productions, 1992

ARLENE SANFORD*

Agent: Irv Schechter Company - Beverly Hills, 310/278-8070

BABYMAKER: THE CECIL JACOBSON STORY (TF)
   Jaffe-Braunstein Films/Heartstar Productions, 1994

JONATHAN SANGER*

Agent: The Gersh Agency - Beverly Hills, 310/274-6611
Business Manager: Judy Pollack, 136 El Camino Road - Suite 201,
   Beverly Hills, CA 90212, 310/276-8811

CODE NAME: EMERALD   MGM/UA, 1985
CHILDREN OF THE BRIDE (TF)   Leonard Hill Films, 1990
CHANCE OF A LIFETIME (TF)   Lynn Roth Productions/Fries
   Entertainment, 1991
OBSESSED (TF)   Peter K. Duchow Enterprises/World International
   Network, 1992
JUST MY IMAGINATION (TF)   Andrea Baynes Productions/
   Lorimar TV, 1992
THE SECRETS OF LAKE SUCCESS (TF)   co-director with
   Arthur Allan Seidelman, The Cramer Company/NBC
   Productions, 1993

JERRY SANGIULIANO

BRAIN TWISTERS   Crown International, 1991

JIMMY SANGSTER*

b. December 2, 1927 - England
Business Manager: Francis & Freedman, 328 S. Beverly Drive -
   Suite A, Beverly Hills, CA 90212, 310/277-7351

THE HORROR OF FRANKENSTEIN   Levitt-Pickman, 1970, British
LUST FOR A VAMPIRE   American Continental, 1971, British
FEAR IN THE NIGHT   International Co-Productions, 1972, British

JORGE SANJINES

b. 1936 - La Paz, Bolivia
Contact: Consejo Nacional del Cine, Casilla 9933, La Paz,
   Bolivia, tel.: 325346

UKAMAU   1966, Bolivian
YAWAR MALLKU   1969, Bolivian
EL CORAJE DEL PUEBLO   1971, Bolivian
FUERA DE AQUI   1974, Bolivian
EL ENEMIGO PRINCIPAL   1977, Bolivian
LAS BANDERAS DEL AMANECER   1983, Bolivian
LA NACION CLANDESTINA   1989, Bolivian

CIRIO H. SANTIAGO

b. January 18, 1936 - Manila, Philippines
Business: Premiere Films International, Builders Centre Building,
   170 Salcedo Street, Legaspi Vill., Makati, Metro Mla., Philippines,
   tel.: 816-1839 or 815-3594
U.S. Address: 1907-A Farrell Avenue, Redondo Beach, CA 90278,
   310/379-4413

WOMEN IN CAGES   New World, 1972, U.S.-Filipino
BAMBOO GODS AND IRON MEN   American International,
   1974, U.S.-Filipino
FLY ME   New World, 1974, U.S.-Filipino
TNT JACKSON   New World, 1975, U.S.-Filipino
COVER GIRL MODELS   New World, 1975, U.S.-Filipino
SAVAGE   New World, 1975, U.S.-Filipino
THE MUTHERS   Dimension, 1976, U.S.-Filipino
EBONY, IVORY AND JADE   Dimension, 1976, U.S.-Filipino
VAMPIRE HOOKERS   Capricorn Three, 1978, U.S.-Filipino
DEATH FORCE   Capricorn Three, 1978, U.S.-Filipino
FIRECRACKER   New World, 1981, U.S.-Filipino
STRYKER   New World, 1982, U.S.-Filipino
CAGED FURY   Saturn International, 1984, U.S.-Filipino
DESERT WARRIOR   Concorde, 1985, U.S.-Filipino
THE DESTROYERS   Concorde/Cinema Group, 1985, U.S.-Filipino
NAKED VENGEANCE   Concorde/Cinema Group, 1986
SILK   Concorde/Cinema Group, 1986, U.S.-Filipino
EYE OF THE EAGLE   Premiere International, 1986, Filipino
FINAL MISSION   Westbrook-M.P. Films/D.S. Pictures,
   1986, Filipino-U.S.
THE DEVASTATOR   Concorde, 1986
DEMON OF PARADISE   Concorde, 1987
KILLER INSTINCT   Eastern Film Management Corporation,
   1987, Filipino
EQUALIZER 2000   Concorde, 1987, U.S.-Filipino
FAST GUN   Juno Media/Premiere International, 1987, Filipino
THE SISTERHOOD   Concorde, 1988, U.S.-Filipino
THE EXPENDABLES   Concorde, 1988, U.S.-Filipino
FUTURE HUNTERS   Lightning Pictures, 1989, U.S.-Filipino
NAM ANGELS   Concorde, 1989, U.S.-Filipino
LAST STAND AT LANG VEI   Concorde, 1990, U.S.-Filipino
FULL BATTLE GEAR   Concorde, 1990, U.S.-Filipino
BEHIND ENEMY LINES   Concorde, 1990, U.S.-Filipino
DUNE WARRIORS   Califilm, 1991, U.S.-Filipino
BEYOND THE CALL OF DUTY   Concorde, 1991, U.S.-Filipino
SILK 2   Concorde, 1991, U.S.-Filipino
ANGELFIST   Concorde, 1991, U.S.-Filipino
RAIDERS OF THE SUN   Concorde, 1991, U.S.-Filipino
FIREHAWK   Concorde, 1992, U.S.-Filipino
LIVE BY THE FIST   Concorde, 1992, U.S.-Filipino
KILL ZONE   Concorde, 1993, U.S.-Filipino
CAGED HEAT 2   Concorde, 1994, U.S.-Filipino
ONE MAN ARMY   Concorde, 1994, U.S.-Filipino
STRANGLEHOLD   Concorde, 1994, U.S.-Filipino

DAMON SANTOSTEFANO

Agent: William Morris Agency - Beverly Hills, 310/859-4000

SEVERED TIES   Fangoria Films, 1992

DAVID SAPERSTEIN*

b. Brooklyn, New York
Address: P.O. Box 42, Wykagyl Station, New Rochelle, NY 10804,
   914/636-1281
Agent: Sara Margoshes, Amsel, Eisenstadt & Frazier,
   6310 San Vicente Blvd. - Suite 407, Los Angeles, CA 90048,
   213/939-1188

A KILLING AFFAIR   Hemdale, 1986
BEYOND THE STARS   PERSONAL CHOICE   Moviestore
   Entertainment, 1989

DERAN SARAFIAN*

Agent: William Morris Agency - Beverly Hills, 310/859-4000

ALIEN PREDATOR   Trans World Entertainment, 1987
INTERZONE   Trans World Entertainment, 1987
TO DIE FOR   Skouras Pictures, 1989

DEATH WARRANT   MGM/UA, 1991
BACK IN THE U.S.S.R.   20th Century Fox, 1992, U.S.-Soviet
GUNMEN   Dimension Films/Miramax, 1994
ROADFLOWER   Miramax Films, 1994
TERMINAL VELOCITY   Buena Vista, 1994

RICHARD C. SARAFIAN*
b. April 28, 1932 - New York, New York
Business Manager: Weiss, Block & Associates, 12100 Wilshire Blvd. -
   Suite 200, Los Angeles, CA 90025, 310/820-8872

TERROR AT BLACK FALLS   Beckman, 1962
ANDY   Universal, 1965
SHADOW ON THE LAND (TF)   Screen Gems/Columbia TV, 1968
RUN WILD, RUN FREE   Columbia, 1969, British
FRAGMENT OF FEAR   Columbia, 1971, British
MAN IN THE WILDERNESS   Warner Bros., 1971
VANISHING POINT   20th Century-Fox, 1971
LOLLY-MADONNA XXX   MGM, 1973
THE MAN WHO LOVED CAT DANCING   MGM, 1973
ONE OF OUR OWN (TF)   Universal TV, 1975
THE NEXT MAN   Allied Artists, 1976
A KILLING AFFAIR (TF)   Columbia TV, 1977
SUNBURN   Paramount, 1979, U.S.-British
DISASTER ON THE COASTLINER (TF)   Moonlight Productions/
   Filmways, 1979
THE GOLDEN MOMENT: AN OLYMPIC LOVE STORY (TF)
   Don Ohlmeyer Productions/Telepictures Corporation, 1980
THE GANGSTER CHRONICLES (TF)   Universal TV, 1981
SPLENDOR IN THE GRASS (TF)   Katz-Gallin Productions/Half-Pint
   Productions/Warner Bros. TV, 1981
THE BEAR   Embassy, 1984
LIBERTY (TF)   Robert Greenwald Productions, 1986
EYE OF THE TIGER   Scotti Bros., 1986
STREET JUSTICE   Lorimar/Sandy Howard Productions, 1989
SOLAR CRISIS   Japan America Picture Co., 1990, Japanese-U.S.

JOSEPH SARGENT*
(Giuseppe Danielle Sorgente)
b. July 25, 1925 - Jersey City, New Jersey
Agent: Shapiro-Lichtman Talent Agency - Los Angeles,
   310/859-8877

ONE SPY TOO MANY   MGM, 1966
THE HELL WITH HEROES   Universal, 1968
THE SUNSHINE PATRIOT (TF)   Universal TV, 1968
THE IMMORTAL (TF)   Paramount TV, 1969
COLOSSUS: THE FORBIN PROJECT   Universal, 1970
TRIBES (TF) ☆   20th Century-Fox, 1970
MAYBE I'LL COME HOME IN THE SPRING (TF)
   Metromedia Productions, 1971
LONGSTREET (TF)   Paramount TV, 1971
MAN ON A STRING (TF)   Screen Gems/Columbia TV, 1972
THE MAN   Paramount, 1972
THE MARCUS-NELSON MURDERS (TF) ☆☆   Universal TV, 1973
THE MAN WHO DIED TWICE (TF)   Cinema Center, 1973
SUNSHINE (TF)   Universal TV, 1973
WHITE LIGHTNING   United Artists, 1973
THE TAKING OF PELHAM 1-2-3   United Artists, 1974
HUSTLING (TF)   Filmways, 1975
FRIENDLY PERSUASION (TF)   International TV Productions/
   Allied Artists, 1975
THE NIGHT THAT PANICKED AMERICA (TF)
   Paramount TV, 1975
MacARTHUR   Universal, 1977
GOLDENGIRL   Avco Embassy, 1979
AMBER WAVES (TF) ☆   Time-Life Productions, 1980
COAST TO COAST   Paramount, 1980
FREEDOM (TF)   Hill-Mandelker Films, 1981
THE MANIONS OF AMERICA (MS)   co-director with
   Charles S. Dubin, Roger Gimbel Productions/EMI TV/
   Argonaut Films Ltd., 1981
TOMORROW'S CHILD (TF)   20th Century-Fox TV, 1982
NIGHTMARES   Universal, 1983
CHOICES OF THE HEART (TF)   Katz-Gallin/Half-Pint
   Productions, 1983
MEMORIAL DAY (TF)   Charles Fries Productions, 1983
TERRIBLE JOE MORAN (TF)   Robert Halmi, Inc., 1984

SPACE (MS)   co-director with Lee Philips, Stonehenge Productions/
   Paramount TV, 1985
LOVE IS NEVER SILENT (TF) ☆☆   Marian Rees Associates, 1985
PASSION FLOWER (TF)   Doris Keating Productions/
   Columbia TV, 1986
THERE MUST BE A PONY (TF)   R.J. Productions/
   Columbia TV, 1986
OF PURE BLOOD (TF)   K-M Productions/Joseph Sargent
   Productions/Warner Bros. TV, 1986
JAWS THE REVENGE   Universal, 1987
DAY ONE (TF)   Aaron Spelling Productions/Paragon Motion
   Pictures, David W. Rintels Productions, 1989
THE KAREN CARPENTER STORY (TF)   Weintraub Entertainment
   Group, 1989
CAROLINE? (TF) ☆   Barry & Enright Productions, 1990
THE INCIDENT (TF)   Qintex Entertainment, 1990
THE LAST ELEPHANT (CTF)   RHI Entertainment/Qintex
   Entertainment, 1990
THE LOVE SHE SOUGHT (TF)   Orion TV/Andrew J. Fenady
   Productions, 1990
A GREEN JOURNEY (TF)   Orion TV, 1990
NEVER FORGET (CTF)   Turner Network TV, 1991
MISS ROSE WHITE (TF) ☆☆   Marian Rees Associates/
   Lorimar TV, 1992
SOMEBODY'S DAUGHTER (TF)   Karen Danaher-Dorr Productions/
   Republic Pictures TV, 1992
SKYLARK (TF)   Self Productions/Trillium Productions, 1993
THE BIBLE: ABRAHAM *ABRAHAM* (TF)   LUBE Productions//Lux/
   Betafilm Italiano/Raiuno/Turner Pictures/ORF/BSkyB, 1994,
   Italian-German-U.S.
WORLD WAR II; WHEN LIONS ROARED (TF)   WWH Co. Inc./
   Gideon Productions, 1994, filmed in HDTV
MY ANTONIA (CTF)   Wilshire Court Productions/USA Network, 1995
STREETS OF LAREDO (MS)   de Passe Entertainment/Larry
   Levinson Productions/RHI Entertainment, 1995

MARINA SARGENTI*
Contact: Directors Guild of America - Los Angeles, 213/851-3671

MIRROR, MIRROR   Shapiro Glickenhaus Entertainment, 1990
CHILD OF DARKNESS, CHILD OF LIGHT (CTF)   Wilshire Court
   Productions/G.C. Group Ltd., 1991

VIC SARIN
b. 1941 - Srinigar, Kashmir, India
Address: 84 Hillsdale Avenue East, Toronto, Ontario M4S 1T5,
   Canada, 416/484-8415

ISLAND LOVE SONG (TF)   1986, Canadian
SO MANY MIRACLES (TF)   1987, Canadian
FAMILY REUNION (TF)   1987, Canadian
COLD COMFORT   1988, Canadian
SOLITARY JOURNEY (TF)   1989, Canadian
MILLENNIUM (TD)   co-director, Biniman Productions Ltd./Adrian
   Malone Productions Ltd./KCET-TV/BBC/The Global TV Network/
   Rogers Telefund/Telefilm Canada, 1991, Canadian-British
SPENSER: PALE KINGS AND PRINCES (TF)   Norstar
   Entertainment/Boardwalk Entertainment/Ultra Entertainment/
   ABC Video Enterprises, 1994, Canadian-U.S.
TRIAL AT FORTITUDE BAY (TF)   Atlantis Films/Imagex/Magic
   Nance Productions/Credo Group/Telefilm Canada/CIDO/BC Film/
   Government of the North West Territories, 1994, Canadian

VALERIA SARMIENTO
b. Chile

AMELIA LOPES O'NEILL   Arion Productions/Ariane Films/
   Thelma Film, 1991, Spanish-French

MICHAEL SARNE
b. August 6, 1939 - London, England
Business: Leo Films, 61 Campden Hill Towers, London W11 3QP,
   England, tel.: 171/727-8047
Agent: Eric L'Epine Smith - London, tel.: 171/724-0739

LA ROUTE DE ST. TROPEZ   1966, French
JOANNA   20th Century-Fox, 1968, British

MYRA BRECKINRIDGE   20th Century-Fox, 1970
INTIMIDADE   *VERA VERAO*   Relevo Productions,
   1972, Brazilian
TROUBLE WITH A BATTERY   Luna Films, 1986, Spanish
THE PUNK   Videodrome, 1993, British

P E T E R   S A S D Y *
b. Budapest, Hungary
Address: 11911 Magnolia Blvd. - Suite 38, North Hollywood, CA
   91607, 818/753-1747
Agent: Shapiro-Lichtman Talent Agency - Los Angeles,
   310/859-8877 or: Jean Diamond, London Management -
   London, tel.: 171/287-9000

TASTE THE BLOOD OF DRACULA   Warner Bros.,
   1970, British
COUNTESS DRACULA   20th Century-Fox, 1972, British
HANDS OF THE RIPPER   Universal, 1972, British
DOOMWATCH   Avco Embassy, 1972, British
THE STONE TAPE (TF)   1973, British
NOTHING BUT THE NIGHT   Cinema Systems, 1975, British
THE DEVIL WITHIN HER   *I DON'T WANT TO BE BORN*
   20th Century-Fox, 1976, British
WELCOME TO BLOOD CITY   EMI, 1977, British
IF WINTER COMES (TF)   1981, British
THE LONELY LADY   Universal, 1983
THE SECRET DIARY OF ADRIAN MOLE (MS)   Thames TV,
   1985, British
THE GROWING PAINS OF ADRIAN MOLE (TF)   Thames TV,
   1987, British
IMAGINARY FRIENDS (TF)   Thames TV, 1987, British
ENDING UP (TF)   Thames TV, 1989, British
MAKING NEWS (MS)   Thames TV, 1990, British
SHERLOCK HOLMES AND THE LEADING LADY (MS)   1990
WITCHCRAFT (TF)   BBC, 1991, British
ALEXANDER KORDA (TD)   BBC, 1993, British
JOSH KIRBY: TIME WARRIOR   co-director with Ernest Farino &
   Frank Arnold, Full Moon Entertainment, 1994

O L E Y   S A S S O N E *
(Francis Sassone)
Agent: APA - Los Angeles, 310/273-0744

BLOODFIST III: FORCED TO FIGHT   Concorde, 1991
FANTASTIC FOUR   Concorde, 1993
FAST GETAWAY II   CineTel Films, 1994

R O N   S A T L O F *
Agent: Barry Perelman Agency - Los Angeles, 310/274-5999

BENNY & BARNEY: LAS VEGAS UNDERCOVER (TF)
   Universal TV, 1977
WAIKIKI (TF)   Aaron Spelling Productions, 1980
THE MURDER THAT WOULDN'T DIE (TF)   Universal TV, 1980
HUNTER (TF)   Stephen J. Cannell Productions, 1984
J.O.E. AND THE COLONEL (TF)   Mad Dog Productions/
   Universal TV, 1985
PERRY MASON RETURNS (TF)   Intermedia Productions/
   Strathmore Productions/Viacom Productions, 1985
PERRY MASON: THE CASE OF THE NOTORIOUS NUN (TF)
   Intermedia Productions/Strathmore Productions/Viacom
   Productions, 1986
PERRY MASON: THE CASE OF THE SHOOTING STAR (TF)
   Intermedia Entertainment Company/Strathmore Productions/
   Viacom Productions, 1986
PERRY MASON: THE CASE OF THE LOST LOVE (TF)
   The Fred Silverman Company/Strathmore Productions/
   Viacom Productions, 1987
PERRY MASON: THE CASE OF THE MURDERED MADAM (TF)
   The Fred Silverman Company/Strathmore Productions/
   Viacom, 1987
JAKE AND THE FATMAN (TF)   The Fred Silverman Company/
   Strathmore Productions/Viacom, 1987
PERRY MASON: THE CASE OF THE LADY IN THE LAKE (TF)
   The Fred Silverman Company/Strathmore Productions/
   Viacom, 1988
ORIGINAL SIN (TF)   Larry A. Thompson Organization/
   New World TV, 1989

THE LOVE BOAT: A VALENTINE VOYAGE (TF)   Aaron Spelling
   Productions/Douglas C. Cramer Company, 1990
PERRY MASON: THE CASE OF THE MALIGNED MOBSTER (TF)
   The Fred Silverman Company/Dean Hargrove Productions/
   Viacom, 1991

J U N Y A   S A T O
b. 1932 - Tokyo, Japan
Contact: Nihon Eiga Kantoku Kyokai (Japan Film Directors
   Association), La Fontenu Building -4th Floor, 23-2 Maruyama-cho,
   Shibuya-ku, Tokyo, Japan, tel.: 3/3461-4411

KURUWA SODACHI   Toei, 1964, Japanese
DESIRE FOR LOVE   Toei, 1966, Japanese
SOSHIKI BOHRUOKU   Toei, 1967, Japanese
SOSHIKI BOHRUOKU 2   Toei, 1967, Japanese
OUTLAW IN THE OUTBACK   Toei, 1968, Japanese-Australian
THE GANG THAT TOOK A TRIP   Toei, 1969, Japanese
SOSHIKI BOHRUOKU 3   Toei, 1969, Japanese
THE LAST KAMIKAZE   Toei, 1970, Japanese
GANG ATTACK FORCE   Toei, 1971, Japanese
YAKUZA READY TO FIGHT AGAIN   Toei, 1971, Japanese
GANG VS. GANG   Toei, 1972, Japanese
YAKUZA DUEL   Toei, 1972, Japanese
GOGO 13   Toei, 1973, Japanese
DOCUMENTARY: ANDOGUMI   Toei, 1973, Japanese
DOCUMENTARY: PRIVATE GINZA POLICE DEPARTMENT
   Toei, 1973, Japanese
BULLET TRAIN EXPLOSION   Toei, 1975, Japanese
PASSING THROUGH THE RIVER OF ANGER   Nagata Productions/
   Daiei, 1976, Japanese
HUMAN IMPROVEMENT   Haruki Kadokawa Productions,
   1977, Japanese
WILD IMPROVEMENT   Haruki Kadokawa Productions,
   1978, Japanese
RUNWAY FAR AWAY   Shochiku, 1980, Japanese
THE GO MASTERS   Mikan No Taikyuku Production Group/Toko
   Tokuma/China Beijing Film, 1982, Japanese-Chinese
KUHKAI   Toei/Shingon Religion Movie Producing Group,
   1984, Japanese
UNDER THE AURORA   *THE NAOMI UEMURA STORY*
   Dentsu-Mainichi Broadcasting System, 1986, Japanese
THE SILK ROAD   *DUN-HUANG/TONKO*   Trimark Pictures
   1988, Japanese-Chinese
KODAYU   *DREAM OF RUSSIA*   Daiei/Dentsu Inc./Toyo Suisan
   Kaisha/Toppan Printing Co., Ltd./Tokuma Shoten Publishing Co.,
   Ltd./Daiei Eizo Film, Inc./Lenfilm Studio, 1991, Japanese-Soviet
PLEASE HUG ME AND KISS ME   Toei, 1992, Japanese
PSYCHOKINESIS: JOURNEY OF ENCOUNTER   Toei,
   1994, Japanese

S H I M A K O   S A T O
Contact: Nihon Eiga Kantoku Kyokai (Japan Film Directors
   Association), La Fontenu Building - 4th Floor, 23-2 Maruyama-cho,
   Shibuya-ku, Tokyo, Japan, tel.: 3/3461-4411

TALE OF A VAMPIRE   Tsuburaya/State Screen Productions,
   1992, Japanese-British
WIZARD OF DARKNESS   Gaga Communications, 1995, Japanese

B R A D D   S A U N D E R S
THE LOUNGE PEOPLE   Blue Ridge/Filmtrust, 1991

S C O T T   S A U N D E R S
THE LOST WORDS   Film Crash, 1994

C A R L O S   S A U R A
b. January 4,1932 - Huesca, Aragon, Spain
Business: Iberoamericana Films, Velazquez 12, Madrid 28001,
   Spain, tel.: 1/431-4246
Contact: Spanish Film Institute, San Marcos 40, Madrid 28004,
   Spain, tel.: 1/532-5089

CUENCA   1959, Spanish
LOS GOLFOS   1960, Spanish
LLANTO POR UN BANDITO   1964, Spanish
THE HUNT   Trans-Lux, 1966, Spanish

PEPPERMINT FRAPPE   Elias Querejeta Productions,
   1967, Spanish
STRESS ES TRES TRES   Elias Querejeta Productions,
   1968, Spanish
HONEYCOMB *LA MADRIGUERA*   CineGlobe, 1969, Spanish
THE GARDEN OF DELIGHTS   Perry/Fleetwood, 1970, Spanish
ANA Y LOS LOBOS   1973, Spanish
COUSIN ANGELICA   New Yorker, 1974, Spanish
CRIA! *CRIA CUERVOS*   Jason Allen, 1976, Spanish
ELISA, VIDA MIA   Elias Querejeta Productions, 1977, Spanish
LOS OJOS VENDADOS   Elias Querejeta Productions,
   1978, Spanish
MAMA CUMPLE CIEN ANOS   Elias Querejeta Productions/Films
   Moliere/Pierson Productions, 1979, Spanish-French
DEPRISA, DEPRISA   Films Moliere, 1981, Spanish-French
BLOOD WEDDING   New Yorker, 1981, Spanish
SWEET HOURS   New Yorker, 1982, Spanish
ANTONIETA   Gaumont/Conacine/Nuevo Cine,
   1982, French-Mexican
CARMEN   Orion Classics, 1983, Spanish
LOS ZANCOS   Emiliano Piedra Productions, 1984, Spanish
EL AMOR BRUJO (LOVE, THE MAGICIAN)   Orion Classics,
   1986, Spanish
EL DORADO   Iberoamericana/Chrysalide Film/Canal Plus/FR3/
   TVE/RAI/Sacis, 1988, Spanish-French-Italian
LA NOCHE OSCURA   Iberoamericana/La Generale D'Images/
   TVE, 1989, Spanish-French
AY, CARMELA!   Prestige, 1990, Spanish-Italian
EL SUR (TF)   Iberoamericana/Quinto Centenario/Television
   Espanola, 1992, Spanish
DISPARA!   Arco Films/Metrofilms, 1993, Spanish-Italian
MARATHON (FD)   Iberoamericana, 1993, Spanish

CLAUDE SAUTET
b. February 23, 1924 - Montrouge, France
Agent: ICM France - Paris, tel.: 1/723-7860
Contact: French Film Office, 745 Fifth Avenue, New York,
   NY 10151, 212/832-8860

BONJOUR SOURIRE   Vox, 1955, French
THE BIG RISK   United Artists, 1960, French-Italian
L'ARME A GAUCHE   1965, French
THE THINGS OF LIFE   Columbia, 1970, French
MAX ET LES FERRAILLEURS   CFDC, 1971, French
CESAR AND ROSALIE   Cinema 5, 1972,
   French-Italian-West German
VINCENT, FRANÇOIS, PAUL AND THE OTHERS   Joseph Green
   Pictures, 1974, French-Italian
MADO   Joseph Green Pictures, 1976, French
A SIMPLE STORY   Quartet, 1979, French
UN MAUVAIS FIL   Sara Films/Antenne-2, 1980, French
GARCON   Sara Film/Renn Productions, 1983, French
A FEW DAYS WITH ME   Galaxy International, 1988, French
UN COEUR EN HIVER   October Films, 1992, French
NELLY ET MR ARNAUD   Canal Plus, 1994, French

PIERRE SAUVAGE
b. Le Cambon-Sur-Ligny, France
Address: Friends of Le Chambon, 8033 Sunset Blvd. - Suite 784,
   Los Angeles, CA 90046, 213/650-1774

WEAPONS OF THE SPIRIT (FD)   First Run Features, 1989

PHILIP SAVILLE*
b. London, England
Agent: The Casarotto Company - London, tel.: 171/287-4450

STOP THE WORLD - I WANT TO GET OFF   Warner Bros.,
   1966, British
OEDIPUS THE KING   Regional, 1968, British
THE BEST HOUSE IN LONDON   MGM, 1969, British
THE RAINBIRDS (TF)   BBC, 1970, British
SECRETS   Lone Star, 1971, British
GANGSTERS (TF)   BBC, 1975, British
COUNT DRACULA (TF)   1977, British
THE JOURNAL OF BRIDGET HITLER (TF)   BBC, 1981, British
BOYS FROM THE BLACKSTUFF (TF)   BBC, 1982, British

THOSE GLORY, GLORY DAYS   Cinecom, 1983, British,
   originally made for television
SHADEY   Skouras Pictures, 1986, British
MANDELA (CTF)   Titus Productions/Polymuse Inc./TVS Ltd.,
   1987, U.S.-British
WONDERLAND *THE FRUIT MACHINE*   Vestron, 1988, British
FIRST BORN (TF)   BBC/Australian Broadcasting Corporation/TV
   New Zealand, 1989, British-Australian-New Zealand
MAX AND HELEN (CTF)   Citadel Entertainment, 1990
FELLOW TRAVELLER (CTF)   British Film Institute/BBC Films/HBO
   Showcase, 1990, British-U.S.
CRASH: THE MYSTERY OF FLIGHT 1501 (TF)   Schaepfer-Karpf
   Productions/Citadel Entertainment/ConsolidatedProductions, 1990
THE CLONING OF JOANNA MAY (TF)   Granada TV/A&E Network,
   1991, British-U.S.
FAMILY PICTURES (TF)   Alexander, Enright & Associates/Hearst
   Entertainment, 1993
WALL OF SILENCE (TF)   BBC, 1993, British
THE BUCCANEERS (TF)   BBC, 1994, British

TOM SAVINI*
Address: 311 Taylor Street, Pittsburgh, PA 15224, 412/681-8325

NIGHT OF THE LIVING DEAD   Columbia, 1990

NANCY SAVOCA
Agent: UTA - Beverly Hills, 310/273-6700
Business: Forward Films, 2445 Herring Avenue, Bronx, NY 10469

TRUE LOVE   MGM/UA, 1989
DOGFIGHT   Warner Bros., 1991
HOUSEHOLD SAINTS   Fine Line Features/New Line Cinema, 1993

GEOFFREY SAX
Agent: ICM - London, tel.: 171/636-6565

THE DISPUTATION (TF)   Electric Rainbow/Channel 4, 1985, British
CREDITORS (TF)   Strongbow Films, 1986, British
SLEEPERS (MS)   Cinema Verity Productions/BBC, 1991, British
THE PRAGUE SUN (TF)   BBC/Barrandov Studios,
   1992, British-Czech
FRAMED (MS)   Anglia Films/A&E Entertainment/Tesauro
   Productions, 1993, British-Spanish-U.S.
CIRCLE OF DECEIT (TF)   Yorkshire TV, 1993, British

JOHN SAXON
(Carmine Orrico)
b. August 5, 1936 - New York, New York
Contact: Screen Actors Guild - Los Angeles, 213/954-1600

DEATH HOUSE   Nick Marino Presents, 1988

DAOUD ABDEL SAYED
b. Egypt
Contact: National Film Centre, City of Arts, Al Ahram Avenue,
   Giza, Cairo, Egypt, tel.: 854-807

THE VAGABONDS   1985, Egyptian
THE SEARCH FOR SAYED MARZOUK   Video 2000,
   1991, Egyptian
KIT KAT   El Alamia for TV and Cinema, 1991, Egyptian

JOHN SAYLES
b. September 28, 1950 - Schenectady, New York
Agent: Paradigm - Los Angeles, 310/277-4400

RETURN OF THE SECAUCUS SEVEN   Libra/Specialty Films, 1980
LIANNA   United Artists Classics, 1983
BABY IT'S YOU   Paramount, 1983
THE BROTHER FROM ANOTHER PLANET   Cinecom, 1984
MATEWAN   Cinecom, 1987
EIGHT MEN OUT   Orion, 1988
CITY OF HOPE   The Samuel Goldwyn Company, 1991
PASSION FISH   Miramax Films, 1992
THE SECRET OF ROAN INISH   First Look Pictures,
   1994, U.S.-Irish
LONE STAR   Columbia, 1995

LAWRENCE J. SCHILLER*

b. December 28, 1936 - New York, New York
Business: Polaris Communications, P.O. Box 56056, Sherman Oaks, CA 91413, 818/906-0926
Agent: The Chasin Agency - Los Angeles, 310/278-7505

THE LEXINGTON EXPERIENCE (FD) Corda, 1971
THE AMERICAN DREAMER (FD) co-director with L.M. Kit Carson, EYR, 1971
HEY, I'M ALIVE! (TF) Charles Fries Productions/Worldvision, 1975
MARILYN: THE UNTOLD STORY (TF) co-director with Jack Arnold & John Flynn, Lawrence Schiller Productions, 1980
THE EXECUTIONER'S SONG (TF) Film Communications Inc., 1982
PETER THE GREAT (MS) co-director with Marvin J. Chomsky, PTG Productions/NBC Productions, 1986
MARGARET BOURKE-WHITE (CTF) Turner Network TV/Project VII/Central TV Enterprises, 1989
THE PLOT TO KILL HITLER (TF) Wolper Productions/Bernard Sofronski Productions/Warner Bros. TV, 1990

TOM SCHILLER*

Home: 260 West 22nd Street, New York, NY 10011
Attorney: Marc Chamlin, Loeb & Loeb, 230 Park Avenue, New York, NY 10169, 212/692-4855

NOTHING LASTS FOREVER MGM/UA Classics, 1984

THOMAS SCHLAMME*

Agent: UTA - Beverly Hills, 310/273-6700

MISS FIRECRACKER Corsair Pictures, 1989
CRAZY FROM THE HEART (CTF) Papazian-Hirsch Entertainment/DeMann Entertainment, 1991
MAMBO MOUTH (CPF) HBO/Island Visual Arts/Martin Bregman Productions, 1991
SO I MARRIED AN AXE MURDERER TriStar, 1993
MARTIN LAWRENCE YOU SO CRAZY YOU SO CRAZY (PF) The Samuel Goldwyn Company, 1994
KINGFISH: A STORY OF HUEY P. LONG (CTF) Turner Pictures/Chris-Rose Prods., 1995

GEORGE SCHLATTER*

b. December 31, 1932
Agent: Nathan Golden, 5757 Wilshire Blvd. - Suite 249, Los Angeles, CA 90036, 213/965-0044

NORMAN...IS THAT YOU? MGM/United Artists, 1976

JOHN SCHLESINGER*

b. February 16, 1926 - London, England
Home: 10 Victoria Road, London W8 5RD, England, tel.: 171/937-3983
Agent: UTA - Beverly Hills, 310/273-6700

A KIND OF LOVING Continental, 1962, British
BILLY LIAR Continental, 1963, British
DARLING ★ Embassy, 1965, British
FAR FROM THE MADDING CROWD MGM, 1967, British
MIDNIGHT COWBOY ★★ United Artists, 1969
SUNDAY BLOODY SUNDAY ★ United Artists, 1970, British
VISIONS OF EIGHT (FD) co-director with Yuri Ozerov, Mai Zetterling, Arthur Penn, Michael Pfleghar, Kon Ichikawa, Milos Forman & Claude Lelouch, Cinema 5, 1973
THE DAY OF THE LOCUST Paramount, 1975
MARATHON MAN Paramount, 1976
YANKS Universal, 1979, British
HONKY TONK FREEWAY Universal/AFD, 1981
AN ENGLISHMAN ABROAD (TF) BBC, 1983, British
THE FALCON AND THE SNOWMAN Orion, 1985
THE BELIEVERS Orion, 1987
MADAME SOUSATZKA Universal, 1988, British
PACIFIC HEIGHTS 20th Century Fox, 1990
A QUESTION OF ATTRIBUTION (TF) BBC/WGBH-Boston, 1992, British-U.S.

THE INNOCENT Miramax Films, 1993, British-German
COLD COMFORT FARM (TF) BBC, 1994, British
EYE FOR AN EYE Paramount, 1995

VOLKER SCHLONDORFF*

b. March 31, 1939 - Wiesbaden, Germany
Agent: Sam Cohn, ICM - New York City, 212/556-5600

YOUNG TORLESS Kanawha, 1966, West German-French
A DEGREE OF MURDER Universal, 1967, West German
MICHAEL KOHLHAAS Columbia, 1969, West German
THE SUDDEN WEALTH OF THE POOR PEOPLE OF KOMBACK New Yorker, 1970, West German
BAAL (TF) Hessischer Rundfunk/Bayerischer Rundfunk/Hallelujah Film, 1970, West German
DIE MORAL DER RUTH HALBFASS Hallelujah Film/Hessischer Rundfunk, 1971, West German
A FREE WOMAN STROHFEUER New Yorker, 1971, West German
UBERNACHTUNG IN TIROL (TF) Hessischer Rundfunk, 1974, West German
GEORGINAS GRUNDE (TF) West Deutscher Rundfunk/ORTF, 1975, West German-Austrian
THE LOST HONOR OF KATHARINA BLUM co-director with Margaretha Von Trotta, New World, 1975, West German
COUP DE GRACE Cinema 5, 1976, West German
NUR ZUM SPASS - NUR ZUM SPIEL (TD) Kaleidoskop Valeska Gert/Bioskop Film, 1977
DEUTSCHLAND IM HERBST (FD) co-director, Filmverlag der Autoren/Hallelujah Film/Kairos Film, 1978, West German
THE TIN DRUM New World, 1980, West German
CIRCLE OF DECEIT DIE FALSCHUNG United Artists Classics, 1982, West German-French
KRIEG UND FRIEDEN (FD) co-director with Heinrich Boll, Alexander Kluge, Stefan Aust & Axel Engstfeld, TeleCulture, 1983, West German
SWANN IN LOVE Orion Classics, 1984, French-West German
DEATH OF A SALESMAN (TF) ☆ Roxbury and Punch Productions, 1985
A GATHERING OF OLD MEN (TF) Consolidated Productions/Jennie & Company/Zenith Productions, 1987
THE HANDMAID'S TAIL Cinecom, 1990
VOYAGER PASSAGIER FABER Castle Hill Productions, 1991, German-French-Greek

JULIAN SCHLOSSBERG

Business: Castle Hill Productions, 1414 Avenue of the Americas, New York, NY 10019, 212/888-0080

NO NUKES (FCD) co-director with Danny Goldberg & Anthony Potenza, Warner Bros., 1980
GOING HOLLYWOOD - THE 30'S (FD) Castle Hill Productions, 1984
GOING HOLLYWOOD - THE WAR YEARS (FD) Castle Hill Productions, 1988

OLIVER SCHMITZ

Contact Information: Dr. Martin Botha, Human Sciences Research Council, Group for Social Synamics, Private Bag x41, Pretoria 0001, South Africa, tel.: 012/202-2308

MAPANTSULA Ray Wave Productions, 1988, South African-Australian-British

DAVID SCHMOELLER

Business: The Schmoeller Corporation, 2244 Stanley Hills Drive, Los Angeles, CA 90046, 213/654-0748
Agent: Shapiro-Lichtman Talent Agency - Los Angeles, 310/859-8877

TOURIST TRAP Compass International, 1979
THE SEDUCTION Avco Embassy, 1981
CRAWLSPACE Empire Pictures, 1986
CATACOMBS Empire Pictures, 1988
PUPPET MASTER Full Moon Entertainment, 1989
THE ARRIVAL Del Mar Entertainment, 1990
WHISPERS AND SHADOWS Full Moon Entertainment, 1991
NETHERWORLD Full Moon Entertainment, 1991

ROBERT SCHEERER*
b. Santa Barbara, California
Agent: The Cooper Agency - Los Angeles, 310/277-8422

HANS BRINKER (TF)   NBC, 1969
ADAM AT SIX A.M.   National General, 1970
THE WORLD'S GREATEST ATHLETE   Buena Vista, 1973
POOR DEVIL (TF)   Paramount TV, 1973
TARGET RISK (TF)   Universal TV, 1975
IT HAPPENED AT LAKEWOOD MANOR (TF)   Alan Landsburg
   Productions, 1977
HAPPILY EVER AFTER (TF)   Tri-Media II, Inc./Hamel-Somers
   Entertainment, 1978
HOW TO BEAT THE HIGH COST OF LIVING
   American International, 1980
MATLOCK: THE HUNTING PARTY (TF)   The Fred Silverman
   Company/Dean Hargrove Productions/Viacom, 1989

ANDREW SCHEINMAN*
Contact: Directors Guild of America - Los Angeles, 213/851-3671

LITTLE BIG LEAGUE   Castle Rock Entertainment, 1994

MAXIMILIAN SCHELL
b. December 8, 1930 - Vienna, Austria
Agent: Camden-ITG - Los Angeles, 310/289-2700

FIRST LOVE   UMC, 1970, Swiss-West German
THE PEDESTRIAN   Cinerama Releasing Corporation, 1974,
   West German-Swiss-Israeli
END OF THE GAME   20th Century-Fox, 1976, West German-Italian
TALES FROM THE VIENNA WOODS   Cinema 5, 1979,
   Austrian-West German
MARLENE (FD)   Alive Films, 1984, West German
AN AMERICAN PLACE   OKO/B.A., 1989, West German-U.S.
CANDLES IN THE DARK (CTF)   Taska Films/Kushner-Locke
   Company/Family Productions, 1993

HENNING SCHELLERUP
Home: 11247 La Maida Street - Apt. 205, North Hollywood, CA
   91601, 818/505-8862

THE BLACK BUNCH   Entertainment Pyramid, 1973
SWEET JESUS, PREACHER MAN   MGM, 1973
THE BLACK ALLEYCATS   Entertainment Pyramid, 1974
THE TIME MACHINE (TF)   Sunn Classic Productions, 1978
IN SEARCH OF HISTORIC JESUS   Sunn Classic, 1979
BEYOND DEATH'S DOOR   Sunn Classic, 1979
THE LEGEND OF SLEEPY HOLLOW   Sunn Classic, 1979
THE ADVENTURES OF NELLIE BLY (TF)   Sunn Classic, 1981
CAMP-FIRE GIRLS   Rainbow Spectrum Film Co., 1984
BERSERKER   Shapiro Entertainment, 1987
ANCIENT SECRETS OF THE BIBLE (TD)   Sun International
   Pictures/Charles E. Sellier Productions/PKO TV, 1992

CARL SCHENKEL*
b. Switzerland
Agent: CAA - Beverly Hills, 310/288-4545

OUT OF ORDER   Sandstar Releasing Corporation,
   1984, West German
BAY COVEN (TF)   Guber-Peters Company/Phoenix Entertainment
   Group, 1987
THE MIGHTY QUINN   MGM/UA, 1989
SILENCE LIKE GLASS   Moviestore Entertainment,
   1989, West German
SILHOUETTE (CTF)   Dutch Productions/MCA-TV
   Entertainment, 1990
KOAN   Royal/ZDF, 1991, German
KNIGHT MOVES   Lamb Bear Entertainment/Ink Slinger
   Productions/El Khoury-Defait Productions, 1992, U.S.-German
EXQUISITE TENDERNESS   Capella International, 1994, Canadian
BEYOND BETRAYAL (TF)   Daniel H. Blatt Productions/
   Warner Bros. TV, 1994

RICHARD SCHENCKMAN*
Home: 101 West 12th Street - Apt. 21A, New York, NY 10011,
   212/691-7296 or: 7250 Franklin Avenue - Apt. 616, Hollywood,
   CA 90046, 213/874-2398

THE POMPATUS OF LOVE   Counterproductions Inc., 1995

FRED SCHEPISI*
(Frederici Alan Schepisi)
b. December 26, 1939 - Melbourne, Australia
Agent: ICM - Beverly Hills, 310/550-4000

LIBIDO   co-director with John B. Murray, Tim Burstall &
   David Baker, Producers & Directors Guild of Australia,
   1973, Australian
THE DEVIL'S PLAYGROUND   Entertainment Marketing,
   1976, Australian
THE CHANT OF JIMMIE BLACKSMITH   New Yorker,
   1978, Australian
BARBAROSA   Universal/AFD, 1982, West German
ICEMAN   Universal, 1984
PLENTY   20th Century-Fox, 1985, British
ROXANNE   Columbia, 1987
A CRY IN THE DARK   *EVIL ANGELS*   Warner Bros.,
   1988, Australian
THE RUSSIA HOUSE   MGM-Pathe Communications, 1990
MR. BASEBALL   Universal, 1992, U.S.-Japanese
SIX DEGREES OF SEPARATION   MGM, 1993
I.Q.   Paramount, 1994

JEFFREY NOYES SCHER
Business: Northwinds Entertainment, 3 Sheridan Square - Apt. 8A,
   New York, NY 10014

PRISONERS OF INERTIA   Northwinds Entertainment, 1989

PAUL SCHIBLI
THE NUTCRACKER PRINCE (AF)   Warner Bros., 1990, Canadian
HOLLYROCK-A-BYE BABY (ATF)   co-director with William Hanna,
   Gordon Hunt, Kris Zimmerman, Steven McCallum & Glenn Chaika,
   Hanna-Barbera Productions Animation/Wang Film Production
   Company Ltd. Taiwan, 1993, U.S.-Taiwanese

RICHARD SCHICKEL*
Home: 9051 Dicks Street, Los Angeles, CA 90069, 213/286-7234

THE MEN WHO MADE THE MOVIES (TD)   PBS, 1972
INTO THE MORNING: WILLA CATHER'S AMERICA (TD)
   PBS, 1978
FUNNY BUSINESS (TD)   CBS, 1978
THE HORROR SHOW (TD)   CBS, 1979
JAMES CAGNEY, THAT YANKEE DOODLE DANDY (TD)
   PBS, 1981
MINNELLI ON MINNELLI: LIZA REMEMBERS VINCENTE (TD)
   PBS, 1987
GARY COOPER: AMERICAN LIFE, AMERICAN LEGEND (CTD)
   LORAC Productions, 1988
MYRNA LOY: SO NICE TO COME HOME TO (CTD)
   LORAC Productions, 1990
BARBARA STANWYCK: FIRE AND DESIRE (CTD)
   LORAC Productions, 1991
HOLLYWOOD ON HOLLYWOOD (CTD)
   LORAC Productions, 1993

SUZANNE SCHIFFMAN
Contact: French Film Office, 745 Fifth Avenue, New York,
   NY 10151, 212/832-8860

SORCERESS   *LA MOINE ET LA SORCIERE*   European Classics,
   1987, French-U.S.
FEMME DE PAPIER   Pierre Grise Productions/La Sept/La Cine/
   Canal Plus, 1989, French

JOSEPH L. SCANLAN*

Contact: Directors Guild of America - Los Angeles, 213/851-3671

OUR MAN FLINT: DEAD ON TARGET (TF)
  20th Century-Fox TV, 1976
STARTING OVER (TF) 1979, Australian
SPRING FEVER Comworld, 1983, Canadian
NIGHTSTICK Production Distribution Company, 1987, Canadian
THE RETURN OF BEN CASEY (TF) Cooper Canadian Films, Inc.,
  1988, Canadian
I STILL DREAM OF JEANNIE (TF) Jeannie Entertainment/Carla
  Singer Productions/Bar-Gene Productions, 1991
SPENSER: THE JUDAS GOAT (CTF) Norstar Entertainment/
  Boardwalk Entertainment/Ultra Entertainment/ABC Video
  Enterprises, 1994, U.S.-Canadian

DON SCARDINO*

Agent: William Morris Agency - Beverly Hills, 310/274-7451

ME AND VERONICA True Pictures, 1992
TRACEY ULLMAN TAKES ON NEW YORK (CTPF) ☆
  Witzend Productions/Select TV PLC, 1993

ALLEN SCHAAF

b. December 6, 1942 - San Francisco, California
Business: Tenth Street Production Group, Inc., 147 10th Street,
  San Francisco, CA 94103, 415/621-3395

DRACULA'S DISCIPLE Tenth Street Production Group, 1984

STEVEN SCHACHTER*

Home: 570 N. Rossmore - Apt. 503, Los Angeles, CA, 213/462-6336
Agent: Paradigm - Los Angeles, 310/277-4400

GETTING UP AND GOING HOME (CTF) Carroll Newman
  Productions/The Polone Company/Hearst Entertainment
  Productions, 1992
THE WATER ENGINE (CTF) Turner Pictures/Brandman
  Productions/Amblin TV, 1992
THE RHINEHART THEORY Repentino Productions/Rysher
  Entertainment, 1995
LADY KILLER (TF) Kushner-Locke Company/CBS
  Entertainment, 1995

GEORGE SCHAEFER*

b. December 16, 1920 - Wallingford, Connecticut
Address: 1040 Woodland Drive, Beverly Hills, CA 90210,
  310/274-6017
Agent: CAA - Beverly Hills, 310/288-4545

MACBETH British Lion, 1961, British
PENDULUM Columbia, 1969
GENERATION Avco Embassy, 1969
DOCTORS' WIVES Columbia, 1971
A WAR OF CHILDREN (TF) ☆ Tomorrow Entertainment, 1972
F. SCOTT FITZGERALD AND "THE LAST OF THE BELLES" (TF)
  Titus Productions, 1974
ONCE UPON A SCOUNDREL Image International,
  1974, U.S.-Mexican
IN THIS HOUSE OF BREDE (TF) Tomorrow Entertainment, 1975
AMELIA EARHART (TF) Universal TV, 1976
THE GIRL CALLED HATTER FOX (TF) Roger Gimbel
  Productions/EMI TV, 1978
FIRST YOU CRY (TF) MTM Enterprises, 1978
AN ENEMY OF THE PEOPLE Warner Bros., 1978
WHO'LL SAVE OUR CHILDREN? (TF) Time-Life Productions, 1978
BLIND AMBITION (TF) Time-Life Productions, 1979
MAYFLOWER: THE PILGRIMS' ADVENTURE (TF)
  Syzygy Productions, 1979
THE BUNKER (TF) Time-Life Productions/SFP France/Antenne-2,
  1981, U.S.-French
A PIANO FOR MRS. CIMINO (TF) Roger Gimbel Productions/
  EMI TV, 1982
RIGHT OF WAY (CTF) HBO Premiere Films, Schaefer-Karpf
  Productions/Post-Newsweek Video, 1983

CHILDREN IN THE CROSSFIRE (TF) Schaefer-Karpf Productions/
  Prendergast-Brittcadia Productions/Gaylord Production
  Company, 1984
STONE PILLOW (TF) Schaefer-Karpf Productions/Gaylord
  Productions, 1985
MRS. DELAFIELD WANTS TO MARRY (TF) Schaefer-Karpf
  Productions/Gaylord Production Company, 1986
LAURA LANSING SLEPT HERE (TF) Schaefer-Karpf-Eckstein
  Productions/Gaylord Production Company, 1988
THE MAN UPSTAIRS (TF) Burt Reynolds Productions, 1992

ERIC SCHAEFFER

Agent: CAA - Beverly Hills, 310/288-4545

MY LIFE'S IN TURNAROUND co-director with Daniel Lardner Ward,
  Arrow Releasing, 1993
IF LUCY FELL Motion Picture Corporation of America, 1995

FRANCIS (FRANKY) SCHAEFFER

Agent: Epstein-Wyckoff-Lamanna & Associates - Beverly Hills,
  310/278-7222

WIRED TO KILL American Distribution Group, 1986
RISING STORM Gibraltar Releasing, 1989
HEAD HUNTER Academy Entertainment/Gibraltar Releasing, 1990
BABY ON BOARD World Entertainment-Business Network/
  Rose & Ruby Productions, 1992, Canadian

JERRY SCHAFER*

Home: 3661 S. Maryland Parkway - Apt. 35-47, Las Vegas,
  NV 89109, 702/796-1934
Agent: Sanford International Entertainment, P.O. Box 25202,
  Las Vegas, NV 89114, 702/737-1100

FISTS OF STEEL FoS Productions, 1989

DON SCHAIN*

Home: 1865 N. Fuller Avenue - Apt. 203, Los Angeles, CA 90046,
  213/851-8455

GINGER Joseph Brenner Associates, 1971
THE ABDUCTORS Joseph Brenner Associates, 1972
A PLACE CALLED TODAY Avco Embassy, 1972
GIRLS ARE FOR LOVING Continental, 1973
TOO HOT TO HANDLE Derio Productions, 1978

JERRY SCHATZBERG*

b. June 26, 1927 - New York, New York
Agent: ICM - Beverly Hills, 310/550-4000

PUZZLE OF A DOWNFALL CHILD Universal, 1970
PANIC IN NEEDLE PARK 20th Century-Fox, 1971
SCARECROW Warner Bros., 1973
SWEET REVENGE DANDY, THE ALL-AMERICAN GIRL
  MGM/United Artists, 1976
THE SEDUCTION OF JOE TYNAN Universal, 1979
HONEYSUCKLE ROSE Warner Bros., 1980
MISUNDERSTOOD MGM/UA, 1984
NO SMALL AFFAIR Columbia, 1984
STREET SMART Cannon, 1987
CLINTON AND NADINE (CTF) HBO Pictures/ITC, 1988
REUNION Castle Hill Productions, 1989, French-German-British

DANNY SCHECHTER

COUNTDOWN TO FREEDOM: 10 DAYS THAT CHANGED SOUTH
  AFRICA (FD) Videovision Enterprises/Globalvision/Distant
  Horizon/SCY Productions, 1994, South African

HANS SCHEEPMAKER

Contact: NBF, Jan Luykenstraat 2, 1071 CM Amsterdam,
  Netherlands, tel.: 31 20/6646588

FIELD OF HONOR Cannon, 1986, U.S.-Dutch

PAUL SCHNEIDER*

Agent: Elliot Webb, Broder-Kurland-Webb-Uffner Agency - Beverly Hills, 310/281-3400

SOMETHING SPECIAL *WILLY MILLY/I WAS A TEENAGE BOY* Cinema Group, 1986
THE LEFTOVERS (TF)   Walt Disney TV, 1986
DANIEL AND THE TOWERS (TF)   Mark Taper Forum, 1987
14 GOING ON 30 (TF)   Walt Disney TV, 1988
DANCE 'TIL DAWN (TF)   Konigsberg-Sanitsky Productions, 1989
BABYCAKES (TF)   Konigsberg-Sanitsky Productions, 1989
MY BOYFRIEND'S BACK (TF)   Interscope Communications, 1989
HOW TO MURDER A MILLIONAIRE (TF)   Robert Greenwald Productions, 1990
GUESS WHO'S COMING FOR CHRISTMAS? (TF)   Corapeake Productions/Fox Unicorn/The Polson Company, 1990
MAID FOR EACH OTHER (TF)   Alexander-Enright & Associates/ Hearst Entertainment, 1992
A HOUSE OF SECRETS AND LIES (TF)   Elliot Friedgen & Co./ Chris-Rose Productions, 1992
WITH HOSTILE INTENT (TF)   CBS Entertainment Productions, 1993
EMPTY CRADLE (TF)   Bein-Mills Productions/Papazian-Hirsch Entertainment, 1993
HONOR THY FATHER AND MOTHER: THE TRUE STORY OF THE MENENDEZ MURDERS (TF)   Saban Entertainment, 1994
FOR THE LOVE OF NANCY (TF)   Vin Di Bona Productions/ ABC TV Network, 1994
ROSEANNE: AN UNAUTHORIZED BIOGRAPHY (TF) DDF Films, 1994

SASCHA SCHNEIDER*

Home: 1927 Benecia Avenue, Los Angeles, CA 90025, 310/556-7746
Agent: Irv Schechter Company - Beverly Hills, 310/278-8070

CHUPPA: THE WEDDING CANOPY (FD)   co-director with Laurie Zemelman, GEO Film, 1994

ROBERT A. SCHNITZER

Business: Movicorp, 9887 Santa Monica Blvd., Beverly Hills, CA 90212, 310/553-4300

NO PLACE TO HIDE   American Films Ltd., 1975
THE PREMONITION   Avco Embassy, 1976
KANDYLAND   New World, 1988

PIERRE SCHOENDOERFFER

Home: 13, villa Dupont, 75116 Paris, France
Contact: French Film Office, 745 Fifth Avenue, New York, NY 10151, 212/832-8860

THE ANDERSON PLATOON   French
LA 317EME SECTION   Rome Paris Films/Productions Georges de Beauregard/Benito Perojo, 1965, French-Spanish
LE CRABE TAMBOUR   Bela Productions/Lira Productions/Renn Productions, 1977, French
DIEN BIEN PHU   AMLF, 1992, French

RENEN SCHORR

Contact: Israel Film Centre, Ministry of Industry & Trade, 30 Agron Street, P.O. Box 299, 94190 Jerusalem, Israel, tel.: 972/210433 or 210297

LATE SUMMER BLUES   Kino International, 1988, Israeli

DALE SCHOTT

CARE BEARS MOVIE II: A NEW GENERATION (AF) Columbia, 1986, Canadian

LEONARD SCHRADER

Agent: Writers & Artists Agency - Los Angeles, 310/824-6300
Business Manager: Cooper, Epstein, Hurewitz - Beverly Hills, 310/278-1111

NAKED TANGO   New Line Cinema, 1990, U.S.-Argentine-Japanese

PAUL SCHRADER*

b. July 22, 1946 - Grand Rapids, Michigan
Agent: ICM - Beverly Hills, 310/550-4000

BLUE COLLAR   Universal, 1978
HARDCORE   Columbia, 1979
AMERICAN GIGOLO   Paramount, 1980
CAT PEOPLE   Universal, 1982
MISHIMA: A LIFE IN FOUR CHAPTERS   Warner Bros., 1985, Japanese-U.S.
LIGHT OF DAY   TriStar, 1987
PATTY HEARST   Atlantic Releasing Corporation, 1988
THE COMFORT OF STRANGERS   Skouras Pictures, 1990, Italian-U.S.
LIGHT SLEEPER   Fine Line Features/New Line Cinema, 1992
WITCH HUNT (CTF)   Pacific Western Productions/ HBO Pictures, 1994

MYRL A. SCHREIBMAN*

Home: 7721 Atron Avenue, West Hills, CA 91304, 818/348-9107
Business: 310/206-6879

THE ITALIAN   Caracosta Films, 1979
ANGEL OF H.E.A.T.   Summa Vista, 1982
LIBERTY & BASH   Chariot 7 Productions/Chippewa Productions, 1990

WILLIAM SCHREINER

Contact: Writers Guild of America, West - Los Angeles, 310/550-1000

A SINFUL LIFE   New Line Cinema, 1989

BARBET SCHROEDER*

b. August 26, 1941 - Teheran, Iran
Address: 26, avenue Pierre 1er de Serbie, 75116 Paris, France, tel.: 1/47-20-54-12
Business: 10125 W. Washington Blvd. - Suite 212, Culver City, CA 90230, 310/280-5459
Agent: CAA - Beverly Hills, 310/288-4545

MORE   Cinema 5, 1969, Luxembourg
THE VALLEY obscured by clouds   Lagoon Associates, 1972, French
IDI AMIN DADA   *GENERAL IDI AMIN DADA* (FD) Tinc, 1974, French
MAITRESSE   Tinc, 1976, French
KOKO, A TALKING GORILLA (FD)   New Yorker, 1978, French
TRICHEURS   Gaumont, 1983, French-West German
BARFLY   Cannon, 1987
REVERSAL OF FORTUNE ★   Warner Bros., 1990
SINGLE WHITE FEMALE   Columbia, 1992
KISS OF DEATH   20th Century Fox, 1995
BEFORE AND AFTER   Buena Vista, 1995

FRANK C. SCHROEDER

THE PISTOL: THE BIRTH OF A LEGEND   Premiere Pictures, 1991

MICHAEL SCHROEDER

b. November 12, 1952 - Klamath Falls, Oregon
Agent: APA - Los Angeles, 310/273-0744

MORTUARY ACADEMY   Landmark Releasing, 1987
OUT OF THE DARK   New Line Cinema, 1989
DAMNED RIVER   MGM-UA, 1989
DEAD ON: RELENTLESS II   New Line Cinema, 1991
CYBORG 2   Trimark Pictures, 1993
CYBORG 3   Trimark Pictures, 1994

WERNER SCHROETER

b. April 7, 1945 - Georgenthal, Thurinigia, Germany
Contact: Federal Union of Film and Television Directors in Germany, Adelheidstrasse 7, 8000 Munich 40, Germany, tel.: 089/271-6380

EIKA KATAPPA   1969, West German
DER BOMBERPILOT   1970, West German
SALOME (TF)   1971, West German

MACBETH (TF)   1971, West German
DER TOD DER MARIA MALIBRAN   1972, West German
WILLOW SPRINGS   1973, West German
DER SCHWARZE ENGEL   1974, West German
JOHANES TRAUM   1975, West German
NEAPOLITANISCHE GESCHWISTER   1978, West German
PALERMO ODER WOLFSBURG   1980, West German
WEISSE REISE   1980, West German
DIE GENERALPROBE   1980, West German
DER TAG DER IDICTEN   1982, West German
LOVERS' COUNCIL   1982, West German
DER LACHENDE STERN   1983, West German
ZUM BEISPIEL ARGENTINIEN (FD)   1985, West German
DER ROSENKONIG   1985, West German
MALINA   1991, West German

CARL SCHULTZ*
b. September 19, 1939 - Budapest, Hungary
Agent: ICM - Los Angeles, 310/550-4000 or:
   Cameron Creswell Agency - Sydney, 2/358-6433

THE TICHBORNE AFFAIR (TF)   Australian Broadcasting
   Commission, 1977, Australian
BLUE FIN   Roadshow Distributors, 1978, Australian
RIDE ON STRANGER (TF)   Australian Broadcasting Commission,
   1979, Australian
GOODBYE PARADISE   New South Wales Film Corporation,
   1982, Australian
CAREFUL HE MIGHT HEAR YOU   TLC Films/20th Century Fox,
   1983, Australian
THE DISMISSAL (MS)   co-director with George Miller, Phillip Noyce,
   George Ogilvie & John Power, 1983, Australian
BODYLINE (MS)   co-director with George Ogilvie,
   Denny Lawrence & Lex Marinos, 1984, Australian
TOP KID (TF)   Australian Children's Television Foundation/
   Australian Film Commission/Film Victoria/New South
   Wales Film Corporation, 1985, Australian
BULLSEYE   Cinema Group, 1986, Australian
TRAVELLING NORTH   Cineplex Odeon, 1987, Australian
THE SEVENTH SIGN   TriStar, 1988
CASSIDY (MS)   Five Arrow Films/Australian Broadcasting
   Corporation/Archive Film, 1989, Australian
WHICH WAY HOME (CTF)   McElroy and McElroy/Television
   New Zealand, 1991, Australian-New Zealand
THE YOUNG INDIANA JONES CHRONICLES: YOUNG INDIANA
   JONES AND THE CURSE OF THE JACKAL (TF)   co-director
   with Jim O'Brien, Lucasfilm Ltd./Paramount TV, 1992
THE YOUNG INDIANA JONES CHRONICLES: INDIANA JONES
   AND THE MYSTERY OF THE BLUES (TF)   Lucasfilm Ltd./
   Paramount TV, 1993
CURACAO (CTF)   Jones Programming Partners/Circling
   Curacao N. V. Productions, 1993
YOUNG INDIANA JONES AND THE TREASURE OF THE
   PEACOCK'S EYE (CTF)   Amblin Entertainment/Lucasfilm
   Ltd./Paramount TV, 1995

MICHAEL SCHULTZ*
b. November 10, 1938 - Milwaukee, Wisconsin
Address: P.O. Box 1940, Santa Monica, CA 90406, 310/457-2560
Agent: Major Clients Agency - Los Angeles, 310/284-6400

TOGETHER FOR DAYS   Olas, 1973
HONEYBABY, HONEYBABY   Kelly-Jordan, 1974
COOLEY HIGH   American International, 1975
CAR WASH   Universal, 1976
GREASED LIGHTNING   Warner Bros., 1977
WHICH WAY IS UP?   Universal, 1978
SGT. PEPPER'S LONELY HEARTS CLUB BAND   Universal, 1978
SCAVENGER HUNT   20th Century-Fox, 1979
CARBON COPY   Avco Embassy, 1981
BENNY'S PLACE (TF)   Titus Productions, 1982
FOR US, THE LIVING (TF)   Charles Fries Productions, 1983
THE JERK, TOO (TF)   40 Share Productions/Universal TV, 1984
BERRY GORDY'S THE LAST DRAGON   *THE LAST DRAGON*
   TriStar, 1985
KRUSH GROOVE   Warner Bros., 1985
TIMESTALKERS (TF)   Fries Entertainment/Newland-Raynor
   Productions, 1987
DISORDERLIES   Warner Bros., 1987

THE SPIRIT (TF)   von Zerneck-Samuels Productions/Warner
   Bros. TV, 1987
ROCK 'N' ROLL MOM (TF)   Walt Disney TV, 1988
TARZAN IN MANHATTAN (TF)   American First Run
   Studios, 1989
JURY DUTY: THE COMEDY (TF)   Steve White Productions/
   Spectator Films, 1990
LIVIN' LARGE   The Samuel Goldwyn Company, 1991
DAYO (TF)   Steve White Productions, 1992
YOUNG INDIANA JONES AND THE HOLLYWOOD FOLLIES (CTF)
   Lucasfilm/Amblin Entertainment/Paramount TV, 1994

JOEL SCHUMACHER*
b. New York, New York
Business: Joel Schumacher Productions, 4000 Warner Blvd.,
   Producers Building 1 - Suite 209, Burbank, CA 91522,
   818/954-4837
Agent: CAA - Beverly Hills, 310/288-4545

THE VIRGINIA HILL STORY (TF)   RSO Films, 1974
AMATEUR NIGHT AT THE DIXIE BAR & GRILL (TF)
   Motown/Universal TV, 1979
THE INCREDIBLE SHRINKING WOMAN   Universal, 1981
D.C. CAB   Universal, 1983
ST. ELMO'S FIRE   Columbia, 1985
THE LOST BOYS   Warner Bros., 1987
COUSINS   Paramount, 1989
FLATLINERS   Columbia, 1990
DYING YOUNG   20th Century Fox, 1991
2000 MALIBU ROAD (TF)   Spelling TV/Fisher Entertainment/
   CGD Productions, 1992
FALLING DOWN   Warner Bros., 1993
THE CLIENT   Warner Bros., 1994
BATMAN FOREVER   Warner Bros., 1995

DOUGLAS SCHWARTZ*
Contact: Directors Guild of America - Los Angeles, 213/851-3671

THUNDER IN PARADISE (TF)   Berk-Schwartz-Bonann Productions/
   Rysher Entertainment/Trimark Pictures, 1994

STEFAN SCHWARTZ
Agent: ICM - London, tel.: 171/636-6565

SOFT TOP HARD SHOULDER   Mayfair Entertainment,
   1993, British

ARNOLD SCHWARTZMAN
Business: Moriah Films, c/o Simon Wiesenthal Center, 9760 W.
   Pico Blvd., Los Angeles, CA 90035, 310/553-9036 ext. 237

GENOCIDE (FD)   Simon Wiesenthal Center, 1982
ECHOES THAT REMAIN (FD)   Simon Wiesenthal Center, 1990
LIBERATION (FD)   Moriah Films, 1994

ARNOLD SCHWARZENEGGER*
b. July 30, 1947 - Graz, Austria
Agent: ICM - Beverly Hills, 310/550-4000

CHRISTMAS IN CONNECTICUT (CTF)   Once Upon A
   Time Films, 1992

ETTORE SCOLA
b. May 10, 1931 - Trevico, Italy
Home: via Bertoloni 1/E, Rome, Italy, tel.: 06/875-174

LET'S TALK ABOUT WOMEN   *SE PERMETTETE, PARLIAMO
   DI DONNE*   Embassy, 1964, Italian-French
LA CONGIUNTURA   Fair Film/Les Films Concordia,
   1965, Italian-French
THRILLING   co-director, 1966, Italian
THE DEVIL IN LOVE   *L'ARCIDIAVOLO*   Warner Bros., 1966, Italian
RIUSCIRANNO I NOSTRI EROI A TROVARE L'AMICO
   MISTERIOSAMENTE SCOMPARSO IN AFRICA?
   Documento Film, 1968, Italian
IL COMMISSARIO PEPE   Dean Film, 1969, Italian

339

THE PIZZA TRIANGLE   *DRAMMA DELLA GELOSIA - TUTTI I PARTICOLARI IN CRONACA*   Warner Bros., 1970, Italian-Spanish
MY NAME IS ROCCO PAPALEO   Rumson, 1971, Italian
LA PIU BELLA SERATA DELLA MIA VITA   Dino De Laurentiis Cinematografica, 1972, Italian
TREVICO-TORINO...VIAGGIO NEL FIAT NAM   1973, Italian
WE ALL LOVED EACH OTHER SO MUCH   Cinema 5, 1975, Italian
DOWN AND DIRTY   *BRUTTI, SPORCHI E CATTIVI*   New Line Cinema, 1976, Italian
SIGNORE E SIGNORI BUONANOTTE   co-director, Titanus, 1976, Italian
A SPECIAL DAY   Cinema 5, 1977, Italian
VIVA ITALIA!   *I NUOVI MOSTRI*   co-director with Mario Monicelli & Dino Risi, Cinema 5, 1978, Italian
LA TERRAZZA   United Artists, 1980, Italian-French
PASSIONE D'AMORE   Putnam Square, 1982, Italian-French
LA NUIT DE VARENNES   Triumph/Columbia, 1982, French-Italian
LE BAL   Almi Classics, 1983, French-Italian-Algerian
MACARONI   Paramount, 1985, Italian
THE FAMILY   Vestron, 1987, Italian
SPLENDOR   RAI/Studio EL, 1988, Italian
CHE ORA E'?   RAI/Studio EL, 1989, Italian
IL VIAGGIO DI CAPITAN FRACASSA   Tiger Cinematografica/ Gaumont, 1990, Italian-French
MARIO, MARIA E MARIO   Massfilm/Studio El/Matopigia/Sacis/ Les Films Alain Sarde/Filmtel, 1994, Italian-French
STORY OF A POOR YOUNG MAN   1995, Italian

MARTIN SCORSESE*

b. November 17, 1942 - Flushing, New York
Business: Cappa Productions, 445 Park Avenue, New York, NY 10022, 212/906-8800
Agent: CAA - Beverly Hills, 310/288-4545
Business Manager: Barbara Moskowitz, Yohalem Gillman & Co., 477 Madison Avenue - 9th Floor, New York, NY 10022, 212/371-2100

WHO'S THAT KNOCKING AT MY DOOR?   Joseph Brenner Associates, 1968
BOXCAR BERTHA   American International, 1972
MEAN STREETS   Warner Bros., 1973
ALICE DOESN'T LIVE HERE ANYMORE   Warner Bros., 1975
ITALIANAMERICAN (FD)   Scorsese Productions, 1974
TAXI DRIVER   Columbia, 1976
NEW YORK, NEW YORK   United Artists, 1977
AMERICAN BOY (FD)   Scorsese Productions, 1978
THE LAST WALTZ (FCD)   United Artists, 1978
RAGING BULL ★   United Artists, 1980
THE KING OF COMEDY   20th Century-Fox, 1983
AFTER HOURS   The Geffen Company/Warner Bros., 1985
THE COLOR OF MONEY   Buena Vista, 1986
THE LAST TEMPTATION OF CHRIST ★   Universal, 1988
NEW YORK STORIES   co-director with Woody Allen & Francis Ford Coppola, Buena Vista, 1989
GOODFELLAS ★   Warner Bros., 1990
CAPE FEAR   Universal, 1991
THE AGE OF INNOCENCE   Columbia, 1993
CASINO   Universal, 1995

ART SCOTT

THE MIGHTY KONG (AF)   Hemdale, 1995, U.S.-Japanese

CAMPBELL SCOTT

b. July 19, 1961 - New York, New York
Agent: Paradigm - Los Angeles, 310/277-4400

BIG NIGHT   co-director with Stanley Tucci, Rysher Entertainment, 1996

CYNTHIA SCOTT

b. 1939 - Winnipeg, Manitoba, Canada
Address: 225 Clarke, Montreal, Quebec H3Z 2E3, Canada
Agent: Becsey/Wisdom/Kalajian - Los Angeles, 310/550-0535

GALA   co-director, 1981, Canadian
FIRST WINTER   1981, Canadian
FOR THE LOVE OF DANCE (TD)   1981, Canadian
FLAMENCO AT 5:15 (FD)   1983, Canadian
STRANGERS IN GOOD COMPANY   First Run Features/Castle Hill Productions/Bedford Entertainment, 1991, Canadian

GEORGE C. SCOTT*

b. October 18, 1927 - Wise, Virginia
Business Manager: Becker, London & Kossow, 1841 Broadway - Suite 600, New York, NY 10023, 212/541-7070

RAGE   Warner Bros., 1972
THE SAVAGE IS LOOSE   Campbell Devon, 1974

JAMES SCOTT*

b. July 9, 1941 - Wells, England
Agent: Richard Hatton Ltd. - London, tel.: 181/876-6699
Address: P.O. Box 1003, Santa Monica, CA 90410, 213/462-6066

EVERY PICTURE TELLS A STORY   Channel 4, 1984, British
STRIKE IT RICH   Millimeter Films, 1990, British-U.S.

MICHAEL SCOTT*

b. 1942 - Winnipeg, Manitoba, Canada
Address: 38 Spruce Hill Road, Toronto, Ontario M4E 3G3, Canada, 416/973-3013
Agent: ICM - Beverly Hills, 310/550-4000

STATION 10 (TF)   1973, Canadian
WHISTLING SMITH (TF)   1975, Canadian
FOR GENTLEMEN ONLY (TF)   1976, Canadian
RED DRESS (TF)   1977, Canadian
CAGES (TF)   1984, Canadian
LOST IN THE BARRENS (CTF)   Atlantis Films/Muddy River Films/ CBC/CanWest Broadcasting, 1991, Canadian
CURSE OF THE VIKING GRAVE (CTF)   Muddy River Films/ Atlantis Films/South Pacific Pictures Ltd./CanWest Broadcasting, 1992, Canadian-New Zealand
LADYKILLER (CTF)   MTE, 1992
HARVEST (TF)   Atlantis Films/Credo Group/NBC Productions/ CIDO/Feature Films for Families/Rogers Telefund, 1994, Canadian-U.S.
FROM THE FILES OF "UNSOLVED MYSTERIES": ESCAPE FROM TERROR   THE TERESA STAMPER STORY   *ESCAPE FROM TERROR: THE TERESA STAMPER STORY* (TF) Cosgrove-Meurer Productions, 1995

OZ SCOTT*

Home: 15027 Valley Vista Blvd.., Sherman Oaks, CA 91403, 818/789-2099
Business Manager: Larry Rogers, Jorgensen & Rogers, 10100 Santa Monica Blvd., Los Angeles, CA 90067, 310/203-3940

BUSTIN' LOOSE   Universal, 1981
DREAMLAND   co-director with Nancy Baker & Joel Schulman, First Run Features, 1983
BRIDE OF BOOGEDY (TF)   Walt Disney TV, 1987
CRASH COURSE (TF)   Fries Entertainment, 1988
CLASS CRUISE (TF)   Portoangelo Productions, 1989
TEARS AND LAUGHTER: THE JOAN AND MELISSA RIVERS STORY (TF)   Davis Entertainment, 1994

RIDLEY SCOTT*

b. 1939 - South Shields, Northumberland, England
Business: Percy Main Productions, Paramount Pictures, Chevalier Building - Suite 117, 555 Melrose Avenue, Hollywood, CA 90038, 213/654-4417
Agent: CAA - Beverly Hills, 310/288-4545

THE DUELLISTS   Paramount, 1978, British
ALIEN   20th Century-Fox, 1979, U.S.-British
BLADE RUNNER   The Ladd Company/Warner Bros., 1982, U.S.-British
LEGEND   Universal, 1986, British
SOMEONE TO WATCH OVER ME   Columbia, 1987
BLACK RAIN   Paramount, 1989
THELMA & LOUISE ★   MGM-Pathe Communications, 1991
BLADE RUNNER: THE DIRECTOR'S CUT   Warner Bros., 1992, U.S.-British
1492: CONQUEST OF PARADISE   Paramount, 1992, British-Spanish-French
WHITE SQUALL   Buena Vista, 1995

TONY SCOTT*

b. Newcastle, England
Business: Totem Productions, 8009 Santa Monica Blvd.,
    Los Angeles, CA 90046, 213/650-4994
Agent: CAA - Beverly Hills, 310/288-4545

THE HUNGER   MGM/UA, 1983, British
TOP GUN   Paramount, 1986
BEVERLY HILLS COP II   Paramount, 1987
REVENGE   Columbia, 1990
DAYS OF THUNDER   Paramount, 1990
THE LAST BOY SCOUT   Geffen Pictures/Warner Bros., 1991
TRUE ROMANCE   Warner Bros., 1993
CRIMSON TIDE   Buena Vista, 1995

GEORGE SCRIBNER

Business: Walt Disney Animation, 500 S. Buena Vista Street,
    Burbank, CA 91521, 818/560-1000

OLIVER AND COMPANY (AF)   Buena Vista, 1988
FANTASIA CONTINUED (AF)   co-director with Hendel Butoy &
    Scott Johnston, Buena Vista, 1997

SANDRA SEACAT

IN THE SPIRIT   Castle Hill Productions, 1990

STEVEN SEAGAL*

b. April 10, 1952 - Lansing, Michigan
Business: Steamroller Productions, 1041 N. Formosa Avenue,
    West Hollywood, CA 90046, 213/850-2940

ON DEADLY GROUND   Warner Bros., 1994

JOHN SEALE

b. 1942 - Warwick, Queensland, Australia
Agent: Smith-Gosnell-Nicholson & Associates - Pacific Palisades,
    310/459-0307

TILL THERE WAS YOU   Ayer Productions/Five Arrow Films/
    Australian Film Finance Corporation, 1991, Australian

MIKE SEDAN

GAMES PEOPLE PLAY   Miklen Entertainment, 1993
MARRIED PEOPLE SINGLE SEX   Sunset Films International, 1993
NIGHTFIRE   Sunset Films International, 1994
MARRIED PEOPLE SINGLE SEX PART II   Sunset Films
    International, 1994

JAKOV SEDLAR

Contact: Jadran Film, Oporovecka 12, 41000 Zagreb, Croatia,
    tel.: 41/251-222

GOSPA   Wayne Films/Marianfilm/Jadran Film, 1994,
    U.S.-Canadian-Croatian

PAUL SEED

b. September 18, 1947 - Devon, England
Address: Birches, Macrae Road, Yateley Green, Yateley, Surrey
    GU17 7NQ, England, tel.: 0252/872178
Agent: Peters Fraser & Dunlop - London, tel.: 171/344-1000

ACROSS THE WATER (TF)   BBC, 1982, British
WYNNE & PENKOVSKY   MAN FROM MOSCOW (TF)
    BBC, 1984, British
INAPPROPRIATE BEHAVIOUR (TF)   BBC, 1986, British
EVERY BREATH YOU TAKE (TF)   Granada TV, 1987, British
THE PICNIC (TF)   BBC, 1987, British
CAPITAL CITY (MS)   co-director with Sarah Hellings & Mike Vardy,
    Euston Films/Thames TV, 1989, British
HOUSE OF CARDS (MS)   BBC, 1990, British
EX (TF)   Talkback Productions/BBC Screen One, 1991, British
DEAD AHEAD: THE EXXON VALDEZ DISASTER (CTF)
    BBC/HBO Showcase, 1992, British-U.S.
TO PLAY THE KING (MS)   BBC, 1993, British

BOB SEELEY

ROVER DANGERFIELD (AF)   co-director with Jim George,
    Warner Bros., 1991

PETER SEGAL*

Home: 5227 Alta Canada Road, La Canada, CA 91011,
    818/957-5301
Agent: William Morris Agency - Beverly Hills, 310/859-4000

NAKED GUN 33-1/3: THE FINAL INSULT   Paramount, 1994
TOMMY BOY   Paramount, 1995

ARTHUR ALLAN SEIDELMAN*

b. New York, New York
Business: Entpro, Inc., 1015 Gayley Avenue - Suite 1149,
    Los Angeles, CA 90024, 310/473-5711
Agent: Becsey/Wisdom/Kalajian - Los Angeles, 310/550-0535
Personal Manager: Creative Alliance Management - Los Angeles,
    213/962-6090

HERCULES IN NEW YORK   HERCULES GOES BANANAS/
    HERCULES   Filmpartners, 1970
CEREMONY OF INNOCENCE (TF)   PBS, 1971
CHILDREN OF RAGE   LSF, 1975, U.S.-Israeli
MACBETH (CTF)   Shakespeare Video Society/Cinemax, 1981
ECHOES   Entertainment Professionals, 1983
SIN OF INNOCENCE (TF)   Renee Valente Productions/Jeremac
    Productions/20th Century Fox TV, 1986
KATE'S SECRET (TF)   Andrea Baynes Productions/
    Columbia TV, 1986
GLORY YEARS (CTF)   HBO, 1986
THE CALLER   Empire Pictures, 1987
POKER ALICE (TF)   New World TV, 1987
STRANGE VOICES (TF)   The Landsburg Company, 1987
A PLACE AT THE TABLE (TF)   The Landsburg Company, 1987
AN ENEMY AMONG US (TF)   Helios Productions, 1987
STRANGE VOICES (TF)   Forrest Hills Productions/Dacks-Geller
    Productions/TLC, 1987
ADDICTED TO HIS LOVE (TF)   Green-Epstein Productions/
    Columbia TV, 1988
A FRIENDSHIP IN VIENNA (CTF)   Finnegan-Pinchuk
    Productions, 1988
THE PEOPLE ACROSS THE LAKE (TF)   Bill McCutchen
    Productions/Columbia TV, 1988
FALSE WITNESS (TF)   Valente-Kritzer-EPI Productions/
    New World TV, 1989
THE KID WHO LOVED CHRISTMAS (TF)   Eddie Murphy TV/
    Paramount Domestic TV, 1990
BODY LANGUAGE (CTF)   Wilshire Court Productions, 1992
RESCUE ME   Cannon, 1993
DYING TO REMEMBER (CTF)   Pacific Motion Pictures/Wilshire
    Court Productions, 1993
THE SECRETS OF LAKE SUCCESS (TF)   co-director with
    Jonathan Sanger, The Cramer Company/NBC Productions, 1993
TRAPPED IN SPACE (CTF)   CNM Entertainment/Village Roadshow
    Pictures/Wilshire Court Productions, 1995, U.S.-Australian

SUSAN SEIDELMAN*

b. December 11, 1952 - Philadelphia, Pennsylvania
Agent: William Morris Agency - Beverly Hills, 310/859-4000
Business Manager: Michael Shedler, 225 West 34th Street -
    Suite 1012, New York, NY 10122, 212/564-6656

SMITHEREENS   New Line Cinema, 1982
DESPERATELY SEEKING SUSAN   Orion, 1985
MAKING MR. RIGHT   Orion, 1987
COOKIE   Warner Bros., 1989
SHE-DEVIL   Orion, 1990
EROTIC TALES   co-director with Bob Rafelson, Ken Russell,
    Melvin Van Peebles, Paul Cox & Mani Kaul, Regina Ziegler
    Filmproduktion/Tele-Munchen/Westdeutscher Rundfunk,
    1994, German

MICHAEL SEITZMAN

FARMER AND CHASE   Red Sky Films, 1995

HENRY SELICK

Business: Skellington Productions, 375 7th Street, San Francisco,
CA 94103, 415/864-2846
Agent: CAA - Beverly Hills, 310/288-4545

TIM BURTON'S THE NIGHTMARE BEFORE CHRISTMAS
THE NIGHTMARE BEFORE CHRISTMAS (AF)
Buena Vista, 1993
JAMES AND THE GIANT PEACH   Buena Vista, 1995

ARNAUD SELIGNAC

b. February 2, 1957 - France
Contact: French Film Office, 745 Fifth Avenue, New York,
NY 10151, 212/832-8860

DREAM ONE   Columbia, 1984, British-French
SUEURS FROIDES (MS)   co-director, 1988, French
GAWIN   Loco Corto International/Soprofilms/TF1, 1991, French

JACK M. SELL*

b. September 15, 1954 - Albany, Georgia
Business: Sell Pictures, Inc., 9454 Wilshire Blvd. - Suite 600,
Beverly Hills, CA 90212, 310/874-5402

THE PSYCHOTRONIC MAN   International Harmony, 1980
OUTTAKES (FD)   Marketechnics, 1987
DEADLY SPYGAMES   Sell Entertainment/Double Helix, 1989
BANNER   Sell Entertainment, 1991
REVENGE OF THE PSYCHOTRONIC MAN
Sell Entertainment, 1991
MORE OUTTAKES (FD)   Sell Entertainment, 1991

IAN SELLAR

Agent: The Artists Agency - Los Angeles, 310/277-7779 or:
Peters Fraser & Dunlop - London, tel.: 171/344-1000

OVER GERMANY   1987, British-West German
ALBERT'S MEMORIAL   1988, British
VENUS PETER   Miramax Films, 1989, British
PRAGUE   British Screen/BBC Films/UGC/Scottish Film Production
Fund/Christopher Young Films/Constellation Productions/
Hachette Premiere, 1992, British-Scottish-French

PETER SELLARS

Agent: CAA - Beverly Hills, 310/288-4545

THE CABINET OF DR. RAMIREZ   Mediascope/Mod
Films/Paladin Films/Canal Plus/Laurenfilm/Hamon
Investment/WNET/BBC/WDR, 1991,
U.S.-French-Spanish-British-German-Hong Kong

CHARLES E. SELLIER, JR.

Agent: Major Clients Agency - Los Angeles, 310/284-6400

THE CAPTURE OF GRIZZLY ADAMS (TF)
NBC Entertainment, 1981
IN SEARCH OF A GOLDEN SKY   Comworld, 1983
SMOOTH MOVES   *SNOW BALLING*   Comworld, 1984
SILENT NIGHT, DEADLY NIGHT   TriStar, 1984
THE ANNIHILATORS   New World, 1986

DAVID SELTZER*

Business: David Seltzer Productions, 1350 Avenue of the Americas -
25th Floor, New York, NY 10019, 212/708-0356
Agent: CAA - Beverly Hills, 310/288-4545

LUCAS   20th Century Fox, 1986
PUNCHLINE   Columbia, 1988
SHINING THROUGH   20th Century Fox, 1992

ARNA SELZNICK

b. 1948 - Toronto, Ontario, Canada
Address: 387 Kingswood Road, Toronto, Ontario M4E 2P2,
Canada, 416/690-4242

THE CARE BEARS MOVIE (AF)   The Samuel Goldwyn Company,
1985, Canadian

OUSMANE SEMBENE

b. January 1, 1923 - Ziguenchor, Casamance, Senegal
Contact: SIDEC, 12 rue Beranger Ferraud, B P 335, Dakar,
Senegal, tel.: 21-45-76

BLACK GIRL   *LA NOIRE DE...*   New Yorker, 1966, Senegalese
MANDABI   Grove Press, 1968, Senegalese
EMITAI   New Yorker, 1974, Senegalese
XALA   New Yorker, 1974, Senegalese
CEDDO   New Yorker, 1977, Senegalese
CAMP DE THIAROYE   co-director with Thierno Faty Sow,
New Yorker, 1988, Senegalese-Algerian-Tunisian-Italian
GUELWAAR   *GUELWAAR: LEGENDE AFRICAINE DE L'AFRIQUE
DU XXIe SIECLE*   New Yorker, 1992,
Senegalese-French-British-German

MRINAL SEN

b. May 4, 1923 - East Bengal, India
Address: 14 Belatola Road, Calcutta 26, India
Contact: National Film Development Corporation of India, Discovery
of India Building, Nehru Centre, Dr Annie Besant Road, Worli,
Bombay 400018, India, tel.: 4949856

THE DAWN   1956, Indian
UNDER THE BLUE SKY   1959, Indian
THE WEDDING DAY   1960, Indian
OVER AGAIN   1961, Indian
AND AT LAST   1962, Indian
THE REPRESENTATIVE   1964, Indian
UP IN THE CLOUDS   1965, Indian
TWO BROTHERS   1967, Indian
MOVING PERSPECTIVES (FD)   1967, Indian
MR. SHOME   1969, Indian
THE WISH-FULFILLMENT   1970, Indian
INTERVIEW   1971, Indian
CALCUTTA 71   1972, Indian
AN UNFINISHED STORY   1972, Indian
THE GUERILLA FIGHTER   1973, Indian
CHORUS   1974, Indian
THE ROYAL HUNT   1976, Indian
THE OUTSIDERS   1977, Indian
THE MAN WITH THE AXE   1978, Indian
AND QUIET ROLLS THE DAWN   1979, Indian
IN SEARCH OF FAMINE   1980, Indian
THE KALEIDOSCOPE   1981, Indian
THE CASE IS CLOSED   1981, Indian
PORTRAIT OF A NEW MAN   1984, Indian
THE RUINS   Jagadish/Pushpa Chowkhani, 1984, Indian
GENESIS   Scarabee/French Ministry of Culture/Films de la Dreve/
Cactus Film/Mrinal Sen Productions, 1986,
French-Belgian-Swiss-Indian
SUDDENLY, ONE DAY   National Film Development Corporation
of India/Doordarshan, 1989, Indian
CITY LIFE (FD)   co-director, Nederlands Film Museum/International
Art Film, 1990, Dutch
WORLD WITHIN, WORLD WITHOUT   G.G. Films, 1991, Indian
MAHAPRITHIVI   GG Films, 1992, Indian
THE CONFINED   *ANTAREEN*   National Film Development
Corporation of India/Doordarshan, 1994, Indian

DOMINIC SENA

Agent: ICM - Beverly Hills, 310/550-4000

KALIFORNIA   Gramercy Pictures, 1993

RALPH SENENSKY*
b. May 1, 1923 - Mason City, Iowa
Agent: Gerald K. Smith Associates, P.O. Box 7430, Burbank,
   CA 91510, 213/849-5388

A DREAM FOR CHRISTMAS (TF) Lorimar Productions, 1973
THE FAMILY KOVACK (TF) Playboy Productions, 1974
DEATH CRUISE (TF) Spelling-Goldberg Productions, 1974
THE FAMILY NOBODY WANTED (TF) Universal TV, 1975
THE NEW ADVENTURES OF HEIDI (TF) Pierre Cossette
   Enterprises, 1978
DYNASTY (TF) Aaron Spelling Productions/Fox-Cat
   Productions, 1981

RON SENKOWSKI
b. October 7, 1963 - Livonia, Michigan
Business: Lighten Up Films, 333 N. Screenland Drive - Suite 326,
   Burbank, CA 91505, 818/954-8685

LET'S KILL ALL THE LAWYERS Barrister Films, 1994

EVA SERENY
FOREIGN STUDENT Gramercy Pictures, 1994,
   French-Italian-British-Dutch-U.S.

MICHAEL SERESIN*
Contact: Directors Guild of America - Los Angeles, 213/851-3671

HOMEBOY Redbury Ltd./Elliott Kastner Productions, 1988

YAHOO SERIOUS
(Greg Pead)
Contact: Australian Film Commission, 150 William Street,
   Woolloomooloo NSW 2011, Australia, tel.: 2/321-6444

YOUNG EINSTEIN Warner Bros., 1988, Australian
RECKLESS KELLY Warner Bros., 1993, Australian

COLINE SERREAU*
b. 1947 - France
Agent: William Morris Agency - Beverly Hills, 310/859-4000

MAIS QU'EST-CE QU'ELLES VEULENT? (FD) 1977, French
PORQUOI PAS! 1979, French
QU'EST-CE QU'ON ATTEND POUR ETRE HEUREUX!
   1982, French
3 MEN AND A CRADLE The Samuel Goldwyn Company,
   1985, French
MAMA, THERE'S A MAN IN YOUR BED ROMAULD ET JULIETTE
   Miramax Films, 1988, French
CONTRE L'OUBLI co-director, Les Films du Paradoxe/Amnesty
   International/PRV, 1992, French
LA CRISE AMLF, 1992, French
L'EMMERDEUSE Canal Plus, 1994, French
LA BELLE VERTE Canal Plus, 1995, French

ALEX SESSA
b. 1944 - Buenos Aires, Argentina
Business: Aries International, S.A., Lavalle 1860, 1051 Buenos
   Aires, Argentina, tel.: 40-3430

AMAZONS Concorde, 1987, U.S.-Argentine
STORMQUEST Aries Film/Benlux Investment, 1988, Argentine
THE EYE OF THE HURRICANE Aries Film/Bouchard Productions,
   1988, Argentine

PHILIP SETBON
Agent: ICM - Beverly Hills, 310/550-4000

MR. FROST Triumph Releasing Corporation,
   1990, French-British

VERNON SEWELL
b. 1903 - London, England
Contact: British Film Commission, 70 Baker Street, London
   W1M 1DJ, England, tel.: 171/224-5000

THE MEDIUM 1934, British
THE SILVER FLEET 1942, British
LATIN QUARTER FRENZY 1945, British
GHOSTS OF BERKELEY SQUARE NTA Pictures, 1947, British
JACK OF DIAMONDS 1949, British
BLACK WIDOW 1951, British
GHOST SHIP Lippert, 1952, British
COUNTERSPY 1953, British
DANGEROUS VOYAGE 1954, British
SOHO INCIDENT 1955, British
BATTLE OF THE V-1 1956, British
WRONG NUMBER Anglo Amalgamated, 1959, British
URGE TO KILL Anglo Amalgamated, 1960, British
HOUSE OF MYSTERY Anglo Amalgamated, 1961, British
STRONGROOM Union Film Distributors, 1962, British
MATTER OF CHOICE 1963, British
SOME MAY LIVE Showcorporation, 1967, British
THE VAMPIRE BEAST CRAVES BLOOD THE BLOOD BEAST
   TERROR Pacemaker Pictures, 1968, British
THE CRIMSON CULT CURSE OF THE CRIMSON ALTAR
   American International, 1968, British
BURKE AND HARE 1971, British

JEFF SEYMOUR
RAVE REVIEW Curb Entertainment, 1994

JOHN SEXTON
Contact: Australian Film Commission, 150 William Street,
   Woolloomooloo NSW 2011, Australia, tel.: 2/321-6444

WRANGLER OUTBACK Hemdale, 1990, Australian

NICHOLAS SGARRO*
Contact: Directors Guild of America - Los Angeles, 213/851-3671

THE HAPPY HOOKER Cannon, 1975
THE MAN WITH THE POWER (TF) Universal TV, 1977
BERRENGER'S (TF) co-director with Larry Elikann, Roundelay
   Productions/Lorimar Productions, 1985
FORTUNE DANE (TF) Stormy Weathers Productions/The Movie
   Company Enterprises/The Rosenzweig Company, 1986

SHABBA-DOO
(Adolfo Quinones)
Agent: Writers & Artists Agency - Los Angeles, 310/824-6300

RAVE - DANCING TO A DIFFERENT BEAT Smart Egg
   Pictures, 1993

MICHAEL SHACKLETON
Address: 43 Klea Avenue, Clapham, London SW4 9HG,
   England, tel.: 181/673-2801 or:
   H.I.M., 14-15 D'Arblay Street, London W1V 3FP,
   England, tel.: 181/439-1651

SURVIVOR (HVF) Vestron Video/Omega Entertainment/Matrix
   Motion Pictures, 1988

SUSAN SHADBURNE
Business: Millenium Pictures, Inc., 2580 N.W. Upshur, Portland,
   OR 97210, 503/227-7041

SHADOW PLAY New World, 1986
GRANDPA'S MUSICAL TOYS (HVF) Price Stern Sloan/Wee Sing
   Productions, 1988

THOMAS (TOM) SHADYAC*
Agent: UTA - Beverly Hills, 310/273-6700

FRANKENSTEIN: THE COLLEGE YEARS (TF)
   Spirit Productions/FNM Films, 1991
ACE VENTURA: PET DETECTIVE   Warner Bros., 1994
THE NUTTY PROFESSOR   Universal, 1995

KRISHNA SHAH*
b. May 10, 1938 - India
Business: 7135 Hollywood Blvd. - Suite 104, Los Angeles,
   CA 90046, 213/876-9236
Agent: Sheri Mann, The Sheri Mann Agency - Los Angeles,
   213/850-1777

RIVALS   *SINGLE PARENT*   Avco Embassy, 1972
THE RIVER NIGER   Cine Artists, 1976
SHALIMAR   *THE DEADLY THIEF*   Judson Productions/Laxmi
   Productions, 1978, U.S.-Indian
CINEMA-CINEMA (FD)   Shahab Ahmed Productions, 1980, Indian
HARD ROCK ZOMBIES   Cannon, 1985
AMERICAN DRIVE-IN   Cinevest, 1985

STEVEN SHAINBERG
ICE CREAM DIMENSION   The Ice Cream Dimension, 1995

PETE SHANER
LOVER'S KNOT   Two Pauls Entertainment, 1994

LINA SHANKLIN*
Business: Films That Make A Difference, Inc., 408 Linnie Canal
   Court, Venice, CA 90291, 310/827-4472

SUMMERSPELL   Summerspell Productions, 1983

ANN SHANKS*
b. New York, New York
Address: 160 East 65th Street, New York, NY 10021, 212/861-8282
Business Manager: Ferlito Management, 119 West 57th Street,
   New York, NY 10002, 212/262-3176

FRIENDSHIPS, SECRETS AND LIES (TF)   co-director with
   Marlena Laird, Wittman-Riche Productions/Warner
   Bros. TV, 1979

JOHN PATRICK SHANLEY*
b. October 13, 1950 - New York, New York
Agent: William Morris Agency - Beverly Hills, 310/859-4000

JOE VERSUS THE VOLCANO   Warner Bros., 1990

ALAN SHAPIRO*
Agent: William Morris Agency - Beverly Hills, 310/859-4000

TIGER TOWN (CTF)   Thompson Street Pictures, 1983
THE CHRISTMAS STAR (TF)   Lake Walloon Productions/Catalina
   Production Group/Walt Disney TV, 1986
THE OUTSIDERS (TF)   co-director with Sharron Miller,
   Zoetrope Studios/Papazian-Hirsch Productions, 1990
THE CRUSH   Warner Bros., 1993

KEN SHAPIRO
b. 1943 - New Jersey
Contact: 20115 Observation Drive, Topanga, CA 90290,
   310/455-1222

THE GROOVE TUBE   Levitt-Pickman, 1974
MODERN PROBLEMS   20th Century-Fox, 1981

MELVIN SHAPIRO*
Contact: Directors Guild of America - Los Angeles, 213/851-3671

SAMMY STOPS THE WORLD (FCD)   Elkins, 1979

PAUL SHAPIRO*
b. 1955 - Regina, Saskatchewan, Canada
Business: Decal Film, Inc., 41 Shanly Street - Suite 10, Toronto,
   Ontario M6H 1S2, Canada, 416/461-3614

THE UNDERSTUDY (TF)   1975, Canadian
CLOWN WHITE (TF)   Martin-Paul Productions, 1980, Canadian
R.W. (TF)   Atlantis Films, 1982, Canadian
HOCKEY NIGHT (TF)   Martin-Paul Productions/CBS,
   1984, Canadian
MIRACLE AT MOREAUX (TF)   Atlantis Films, 1985, Canadian
THE TRUTH ABOUT ALEX (CTF)   Scholastic Productions/Insight
   Productions, 1987, Canadian
ROAD TO AVONLEA (CMS)   Sullivan Films/The Disney Channel/
   CBC, 1990, Canadian-U.S.
ROOKIES (TF)   Atlantis Films/Martin-Paul Productions/CBC,
   1990, Canadian
KURT VONNEGUT'S MONKEY HOUSE   *MONKEY HOUSE* (CTF)
   co-director with Gilbert Shilton & Allan King, Atlantis Films Ltd./
   Crescent Entertainment/Canwest Broadcasting Ltd.,
   1991, Canadian
THE LOTUS EATERS   Malofilm Distribution, 1993, Canadian
HEADS (CTF)   Showtime Entertainment/Atlantis Films/Credo
   Group/Sojourn Pictures/Tudor-Evenmore Entertainment/Davis
   Entertainment TV/CIDO, 1994, Canadian-U.S.
AVALANCHE (TF)   Atlantis Films/Propaganda Films/CTV TV
   Net Ltd., 1994, Canadian-U.S.
CHOICES OF THE HEART: THE MARGARET SANGER
   STORY (CTF)   Power Pictures/Morgan Hill Films/Hearst
   Entertainment, 1995

JIM SHARMAN
Contact: M & L Casting Consultants, 49 Darlinghurst Road,
   Kings Cross, NSW, 2100, Australia, tel.: 02/358-3111

SHIRLEY THOMPSON VERSUS THE ALIENS   Kolossal Piktures,
   1972, Australian
SUMMER OF SECRETS   Greater Union Film Distribution,
   1976, Australian
THE ROCKY HORROR PICTURE SHOW   20th Century-Fox,
   1976, British
THE NIGHT THE PROWLER   International Harmony,
   1978, Australian
SHOCK TREATMENT   20th Century-Fox, 1981, British

ALAN SHARP*
Agent: CAA - Beverly Hills, 310/288-4545

LITTLE TREASURE   TriStar, 1985

DON SHARP
b. April, 1922 - Hobart, Tasmania
Agent: ICM - London, tel.: 171/629-8080

THE GOLDEN AIRLINER   British Lion/Children's Film Foundation,
   1955, British
THE ADVENTURES OF HAL 5   Children's Film Foundation,
   1958, British
THE IN-BETWEEN AGE   *THE GOLDEN DISC*   Allied Artists,
   1958, British
THE PROFESSIONALS   American International, 1960, British
LINDA   British Lion, 1961, British
IT'S ALL HAPPENING   *THE DREAM MAKER*   Universal,
   1963, British
KISS OF THE VAMPIRE   Universal, 1963, British
THE DEVIL-SHIP PIRATES   Columbia, 1964, British
WITCHCRAFT   20th Century-Fox, 1964, British
THE FACE OF FU MANCHU   7 Arts, 1965, British
CURSE OF THE FLY   20th Century-Fox, 1965, British
RASPUTIN - THE MAD MONK   *I KILLED RASPUTIN*
   20th Century-Fox, 1966, British-French-Italian
BANG, BANG, YOU'RE DEAD!   *OUR MAN IN MARRAKESH*
   American International, 1966, British
THE BRIDES OF FU MANCHU   7 Arts, 1966, British
THOSE FANTASTIC FLYING FOOLS   *BLAST OFF/*
   JULES VERNE'S ROCKET TO THE MOON
   American International, 1967, British

TASTE OF EXCITEMENT   Crispin, 1968, British
THE VIOLENT ENEMY   1969, British
PUPPET ON A CHAIN   co-director with Geoffrey Reeve,
   Cinerama Releasing Corporation, 1972, British
THE DEATH WHEELERS *PSYCHOMANIA* Scotia International,
   1973, British
DARK PLACES   Cinerama Releasing Corporation, 1974, British
HENNESSY   American International, 1975, British
CALLAN   Cinema National, 1975, British
THE FOUR FEATHERS (TF)   Norman Rosemont Productions/
   Trident Films Ltd., 1978, U.S.-British
THE 39 STEPS   International Picture Show Company, 1978, British
BEAR ISLAND   Taft International, 1980, Canadian-British
Q.E.D. (TF)   1982, British
WHAT WAITS BELOW   Blossom Pictures, 1984
A WOMAN OF SUBSTANCE (MS)   Artemis Portman Productions,
   1984, British
TUSITALA (MS)   Australian Broadcasting Corporation/Portman
   Productions/Channel 4, 1986, Australian-British
HOLD THE DREAM (TF)   Robert Bradford Productions/Taft
   Entertainment TV, 1986, U.S.-British
TEARS IN THE RAIN (CTF)   British Lion/Yorkshire TV/Atlantic
   Videoventures, 1988, British
ACT OF WILL (TF)   1989, British

IAN SHARP
b. November 13, 1946 - Clitheroe, Lancashire, England
Address: c/o Great Guns, 28-32 Shelton Street, London WC2,
   England, tel.: 171/379-3338
Agent: ICM - London, tel.: 171/636-6565

THE MUSIC MACHINE   Norfolk International Pictures/Target
   International Pictures, 1979, British
THE FINAL OPTION *WHO DARES WINS* MGM/UA,
   1983, British
ROBIN OF SHERWOOD (TF)   HTV/Goldcrest Films & Television,
   1983, British
THE CORSICAN BROTHERS (TF)   Rosemont Productions,
   1985, British-U.S.
C.A.T.S. EYES (TF)   TVS, 1985, British
YESTERDAY'S DREAMS (MS)   Central TV, 1987, British
CODENAME: KYRIL (TF)   HTV/Incito Productions, 1988, British
TWIST OF FATE (TF)   Henry Plitt-Larry White Productions/HTV/
   Columbia TV, 1989, British-U.S.
PRIDE AND EXTREME PREJUDICE (CTF)   F.F.S. Productions/
   Taurusfilm/Blair Communications, 1990,
   British-West German-U.S.
SECRET WEAPON (CTF)   Griffin-Elysian Productions/
   TVS/ABC-Australia, 1990, U.S.-British-Australian
SPLIT SECOND   director of additional sequences,
   InterStar Releasing, 1992, British

PETER SHATALOW
b. Brussels, Belgium
Address: 1438 Queen Street East, Toronto, Ontario M4L 1E1,
   Canada, 416/461-3614

BLACK ICE (TD)   1980, Canadian
CHALLENGE: THE CANADIAN ROCKIES (FD)   1981, Canadian
HEART OF AN ARTIST (TD)   1983, Canadian
THE MAKING OF LA CAGE (TD)   1985, Canadian
BLUE CITY SLAMMERS   Cineplex Odeon, 1988, Canadian

WILLIAM SHATNER*
b. March 22, 1931 - Montreal, Quebec, Canada
Agent: William Morris Agency - Beverly Hills, 310/274-7451

STAR TREK V: THE FINAL FRONTIER   Paramount, 1989
TEKWAR (TF)   Atlantis Films Ltd./Western International
   Communications/Lemli Productions/Universal City Studios,
   1994, U.S.-Canadian

MELVILLE SHAVELSON*
b. April 1, 1917 - Brooklyn, New York
Agent: Don Kopaloff, The Agency - Los Angeles, 310/551-3000

THE SEVEN LITTLE FOYS   Paramount, 1955
BEAU JAMES   Paramount, 1957
HOUSEBOAT   Paramount, 1958
THE FIVE PENNIES   Paramount, 1959
IT STARTED IN NAPLES   Paramount, 1960
ON THE DOUBLE   Paramount, 1961
THE PIGEON THAT TOOK ROME   Paramount, 1962
A NEW KIND OF LOVE   Paramount, 1963
CAST A GIANT SHADOW   United Artists, 1966
YOURS, MINE AND OURS   United Artists, 1968
THE WAR BETWEEN MEN AND WOMEN   National General, 1972
MIXED COMPANY   United Artists, 1974
THE LEGEND OF VALENTINO (TF)   Spelling-Goldberg
   Productions, 1975
THE GREAT HOUDINIS (TF)   ABC Circle Films, 1976
IKE (MS)   co-director with Boris Sagal, ABC Circle Films, 1979
THE OTHER WOMAN (TF)   CBS Entertainment, 1983
DECEPTIONS (TF)   co-director with Robert Chenault,
   Louis Rudolph Productions/Consolidated Productions/
   Columbia TV, 1985, U.S.-British

ANTHONY SHAW*
Agent: William Morris Agency - Beverly Hills, 310/859-4000
Business Manager: Cohen-Pivo and Company, 9171 Wilshire Blvd. -
   Suite 530, Beverly Hills, CA 90210, 213/274-5847

MRS. 'ARRIS GOES TO PARIS (TF)   Accent Films/Novo Films/
   Corymore Productions, 1992, U.S.-British-French

CHRIS SHAW
SPLIT   Starker Films, 1991, filmed in 1988

LARRY SHAW*
Agent: CAA - Beverly Hills, 310/288-4545

POLICE STORY: COP KILLER (TF)   Columbia TV, 1988
FEAR STALK (TF)   Donald March Productions/ITC Entertainment
   Group/CBS Entertainment, 1989
DONOR (TF)   CBS Entertainment/Peter Frankovich-Daniel A.
   Sherkow Productions, 1990
TO MY DAUGHTER (TF)   Zacs Productions/Nugget Entertainment/
   Warner Bros. TV, 1990
LIVING A LIE (TF)   Bernhardt-Freistat Productions/Stephen J.
   Cannell Productions, 1991
NURSES ON THE LINE: THE CRASH OF FLIGHT 7 (TF)
   Cosgrove-Meurer Productions/World International Network, 1993
TONYA & NANCY: THE INSIDE STORY (TF)   Brian Pike
   Productions/NBC Productions, 1994
ROBIN COOK'S MORTAL FEAR *MORTAL FEAR* (TF)
   von Zerneck-Sertner Films, 1994

SCOTT SHAW
Business: Buddha Rose International, P.O. Box 548, Hermosa Beach,
   CA 90254, 310/543-9673

GUANGDONG PROVINCE, CHINA: POVERTY AND PROMISE (FD)
   Asian Studies Ltd. Film Production Division, 1990
LOVE IS A SHADOW   Fiji Films, 1990
ATOMIC SAMURAI   No Mercy Productions, 1992
SURF SAMURAIS FROM ATLANTIS   No Mercy Productions, 1993
SAMURAI VAMPIRE BIKERS FROM HELL   No Mercy
   Productions, 1993
ALL THE WAY DEAD   No Mercy Productions, 1994

STEVEN SHAW
WHEN THE EAGLE CRIES   Primm Spring Pictures, 1994

ROBERT SHAYE

Business: New Line Cinema, 116 N. Robertson Blvd. - Suite 200,
Los Angeles, CA 90048, 310/854-5811

BOOK OF LOVE   New Line Cinema, 1991

LINDA SHAYNE

Agent: Abrams Artists & Associates - Los Angeles, 310/859-0625

PURPLE PEOPLE EATER   Concorde, 1988
HOW I SAVED THE PRESIDENT   Leucadia Films, 1995

BASHAR SHBIB

Business: Oneira Pictures International, 5437 Park Avenue,
Montreal, Quebec H2V 4G9, Canada, 514/277-4246

JULIA HAS TWO LOVERS   South Gate Entertainment, 1990
CRACK ME UP   Shbib Productions, 1991
LANA IN LOVE   Oneira Pictures 1991, Canadian
LOVE $ GREED   Oneira Pictures International, 1992
CRACK ME UP   Oneira Pictures International, 1993
DRAGULA   Oneira Pictures International, 1994, Canadian

JACK SHEA*

b. August 1, 1928 - New York, New York
Agent: Bob Broder, Broder-Kurland-Webb-Uffner Agency -
Beverly Hills, 310/281-3400

DAYTON'S DEVILS   Commonwealth United, 1968
THE MONITORS   Commonwealth United, 1969

KATT SHEA

Agent: ICM - Beverly Hills, 310/550-4000

STRIPPED TO KILL   Concorde, 1987
DANCE OF THE DAMNED   Concorde, 1989
STRIPPED TO KILL II   Concorde, 1989
STREETS   Concorde, 1990
POISON IVY   New Line Cinema, 1992

DONALD SHEBIB

b. 1938 - Toronto, Canada
Business: Evdon Films Ltd., 312 Wright Avenue, Toronto, Ontario
M6R 1L9, Canada, 416/536-8969

GOIN' DOWN THE ROAD   Chevron, 1970, Canadian
RIP-OFF   Alliance, 1971, Canadian
BETWEEN FRIENDS   Eudon Productions, 1973, Canadian
SECOND WIND   Health and Entertainment Corporation of
America, 1976, Canadian
FISH HAWK   Avco Embassy, 1981, Canadian
HEARTACHES   MPM, 1982, Canadian
RUNNING BRAVE   directed under pseudonym of D.S. Everett,
Buena Vista, 1983, Canadian
THE CLIMB   CineTel Films, 1987, Canadian
THE LITTLE KIDNAPPERS (CTF)   Jones 21st Century
Entertainment/The Disney Channel/CBC/Resnick-Margellos
Productions, 1990, U.S.-Canadian
CHANGE OF HEART   Desca, 1993, Canadian
THE ASCENT   RHI Entertainment/Cabin Fever Entertainment,
1994, Canadian

MARTIN SHEEN*

(Ramon Estevez)
b. August 3, 1940 - Dayton, Ohio
Personal Manager: Glennis Liberty, The Liberty Agency -
Los Angeles, 310/824-7937

CADENCE   New Line Cinema, 1990

SIMON S. SHEEN

3 NINJAS KNUCKLE UP   TriStar, 1995, filmed in 1992

STANLEY SHEFF

LOBSTER MAN FROM MARS   Electric Pictures, 1989

RIKI SHELACH

Public Relations: Chen Sedan Public Relations, 11 Rabina Street,
Tel Aviv 69395, Israel, tel.: 3/412669
Contact: Israel Film Centre, Ministry of Industry & Trade,
30 Agron Street, P.O. Box 299, Jerusalem 94190, Israel,
tel.: 02/210297

THE LAST WINTER   Triumph/Columbia, 1983, Israeli
MERCENARY FIGHTERS   Cannon, 1988

JAMES SHELDON*

(James Schleifer)
b. November 12 - New York, New York
Agent: Ronald Leif, Contemporary Artists - Beverly Hills,
310/395-1800

GIDGET GROWS UP (TF)   Screen Gems/Columbia TV, 1969
WITH THIS RING (TF)   The Jozak Company/
Paramount TV, 1978
THE GOSSIP COLUMNIST (TF)   Universal TV, 1980

SIDNEY SHELDON*

b. February 11, 1917 - Chicago, Illinois
Agent: ICM - Beverly Hills, 310/550-4000

DREAM WIFE   MGM, 1953
THE BUSTER KEATON STORY   Paramount, 1957

RON SHELTON*

b. September 15, 1945 - Whittier, California
Business: Raleigh Studios, 650 N. Bronson, Los Angeles,
CA 90004, 213/462-5095
Agent: Geoffrey Sanford, Sanford-Gross & Associates -
Los Angeles, 310/208-2100

BULL DURHAM   Orion, 1988
BLAZE   Buena Vista, 1989
WHITE MEN CAN'T JUMP   20th Century Fox, 1992
COBB   Warner Bros., 1994

TOBY SHELTON

Business: Walt Disney Animation, 500 S. Buena Vista Street,
Burbank, CA 91521, 818/956-1000

THE RETURN OF JAFAR (AHVF)   co-director with Tad Stones &
Alan Zaslove, Walt Disney Television Animation, 1994

RICHARD SHEPARD

Agent: The Marion Rosenberg Office - Los Angeles,
213/653-7383
Personal Manager: Carthay Circle Pictures and Management -
Beverly Hills, 310/657-5454

COOL BLUE   co-director with Mark Mullin, Cinema Corporation
of America, 1989
THE LINGUINI INCIDENT   Academy Entertainment, 1992
MERCY   Injosho Films/Elevator Pictures, 1995

SAM SHEPARD

(Samuel Shepard Rogers)
b. November 5, 1943 - Fort Sheridan, Illinois
Agent: ICM - Beverly Hills, 310/550-4000

FAR NORTH   Alive Films, 1988
SILENT TONGUE   Trimark Pictures, 1993, U.S.-French

BILL SHEPHERD

FOR PARENTS ONLY   Nova Plus, 1993

JOHN SHEPPARD
b. 1956 - Toronto, Ontario, Canada
Business: 923 12th Street - Suite 4, Santa Monica, CA 90403,
Fax: 310/395-7773
Attorney: Linda Lechter, Lechter, Grossman & Nichols,
9200 Sunset Blvd. - Suite 530, Los Angeles, CA 90069

MANIA   co-director with Paul Lynch & D.M. Robertson,
Simcom Productions, 1986, Canadian
HIGHER EDUCATION   Norstar Releasing, 1987, Canadian

JOHN SHEPPHIRD
TEENAGE BONNIE AND KLEPTO CLYDE   Trimark Pictures, 1993

ADRIAN SHERGOLD
Home: Mill Cottage, Sculthorpe, Nr. Fakenham, Norfolk NR21 9QG,
England, tel.: 03288/55972
Agent: Peters Fraser & Dunlop - London, tel.: 171/344-1000

CHRISTABEL (MS)   BBC, 1988, British
MORSE (TF)   Zenith Productions/Central TV, 1990, British
INSPECTOR MORSE: HAPPY FAMILIES (TF)
Zenith Productions/Central TV, 1991, British
GOODBYE CRUEL WORLD (TF)   BBC, 1992, British

JIM SHERIDAN
b. 1949 - Dublin, Ireland
Agent: CAA - Beverly Hills, 310/288-4545

MY LEFT FOOT ★   Miramax Films, 1989, Irish-British
THE FIELD   Avenue Pictures, 1990, Irish-British
IN THE NAME OF THE FATHER ★   Universal, 1993,
Irish-British-U.S.

MICHAEL J. SHERIDAN*
Contact: Directors Guild of America - Los Angeles, 213/851-3671

THAT'S ENTERTAINMENT! III (FD)   co-director with Bud Friedgen,
MGM, 1994

EDWIN (ED) SHERIN*
b. January 15, 1930 - Harrisburg, Pennsylvania
Home: Gordon Road, R.D. 2, Carmel, NY 10512, 914/225-4544
Agent: William Morris Agency - Beverly Hills, 310/859-4000

VALDEZ IS COMING   United Artists, 1971
MY OLD MAN'S PLACE   GLORY BOY   Cinerama Releasing
Corporation, 1972
THE FATHER CLEMENTS STORY (TF)   Zev Braun Productions/
Interscope Communications, 1987
LENA: MY 100 CHILDREN (TF)   Robert Greenwald
Productions, 1987
SETTLE THE SCORE (TF)   Steve Sohmer Inc. Productions/ITC
Entertainment Group, 1989
DAUGHTER OF THE STREETS (TF)   Adam Productions/
20th Century Fox TV, 1990

ARTHUR SHERMAN*
Agent: The Lantz Office - New York City, 212/586-0200
Personal Manager: Creative Alliance Management -
Los Angeles, 213/962-6090

LIKEWISE   co-director with Elliott Kastner, Cinema Group, 1989

GARY A. SHERMAN*
Agent: William Morris Agency - Beverly Hills, 310/859-4000

RAW MEAT   DEATH LINE   American International, 1973
DEAD AND BURIED   Avco Embassy, 1981
VICE SQUAD   Avco Embassy, 1982
MYSTERIOUS TWO (TF)   Alan Landsburg Productions, 1982
WANTED DEAD OR ALIVE   New World, 1986
POLTERGEIST III   MGM/UA, 1988
LISA   MGM/UA, 1990

MURDEROUS VISION (CTF)   Gary Sherman Productions/Wilshire
Court Productions, 1991
AFTER THE SHOCK (CTF)   USA Network, 1991
MISSING PERSONS (TF)   Stephen J. Cannell Productions, 1993

VINCENT SHERMAN*
b. July 16, 1906 - Vienna, Georgia
Home: 6355 Sycamore Meadows Drive, Malibu, CA 90265,
310/457-2229

THE RETURN OF DOCTOR X   Warner Bros., 1939
SATURDAY'S CHILDREN   Warner Bros., 1940
THE MAN WHO TALKED TOO MUCH   Warner Bros., 1940
FLIGHT FROM DESTINY   Warner Bros., 1942
UNDERGROUND   Warner Bros., 1941
ALL THROUGH THE NIGHT   Warner Bros., 1942
THE HARD WAY   Warner Bros., 1942
OLD ACQUAINTANCE   Warner Bros., 1942
IN OUR TIME   Warner Bros., 1944
MR. SKEFFINGTON   Warner Bros., 1945
PILLOW TO POST   Warner Bros., 1945
NORA PRENTISS   Warner Bros., 1947
THE UNFAITHFUL   Warner Bros., 1947
THE ADVENTURES OF DON JUAN   Warner Bros., 1949
THE HASTY HEART   Warner Bros., 1949
BACKFIRE   Warner Bros., 1950
THE DAMNED DON'T CRY   Warner Bros., 1950
HARRIET CRAIG   Columbia, 1950
GOODBYE, MY FANCY   Warner Bros., 1951
LONE STAR   MGM, 1952
AFFAIR IN TRINIDAD   Columbia, 1952
DIFENDO IL MIO AMORE   1956, Italian
THE GARMENT JUNGLE   Columbia, 1957
THE NAKED EARTH   20th Century-Fox, 1959
THE YOUNG PHILADELPHIANS   Warner Bros., 1959
ICE PALACE   Warner Bros., 1960
A FEVER IN THE BLOOD   Warner Bros., 1961
THE SECOND TIME AROUND   20th Century-Fox, 1961
THE YOUNG REBEL   CERVANTES   American International,
1968, Italian-Spanish-French
THE LAST HURRAH (TF)   O'Connor-Becker Productions/
Columbia TV, 1977
LADY OF THE HOUSE (TF)   co-director with Ralph Nelson,
Metromedia Productions, 1978
WOMEN AT WEST POINT (TF)   Green-Epstein Productions/Alan
Sacks Productions, 1979
BOGIE: THE LAST HERO (TF)   Charles Fries Productions, 1980
THE DREAM MERCHANTS (TF)   Columbia TV, 1980
TROUBLE IN HIGH TIMBER COUNTRY (TF)   Witt-Thomas
Productions/Warner Bros. TV, 1980

FRANK SHIELDS
NO CAUSE FOR ALARM   International Film Management/
Jadran Film, 1990, U.S.-Yugoslavian

PETER SHILLINGFORD
b. London, England
Home: Shillingford & Company, 231 S. Orange Drive, Los Angeles,
CA 90036, 213/939-2881

TODAY MEXICO - TOMORROW THE WORLD   Shillingford &
Company/Rank, 1970, British
THE MAKING OF 'STAR WARS' (TD)   co-director, Lucasfilm/
20th Century-Fox TV, 1977
THE ENGLISH GIRL ABROAD   Border Films, 1979, British

BARRY SHILS
Agent: Preferred Artists - Encino, 818/990-0305

MOTORAMA   Two Moon Releasing, 1991
WIGSTOCK: THE MOVIE (FD)   The Samuel Goldwyn
Company, 1995

**F
I
L
M

D
I
R
E
C
T
O
R
S**

GILBERT SHILTON*

b. 1945
Agent: Shapiro-Lichtman Talent Agency - Los Angeles,
310/859-8877

SPEARFIELD'S DAUGHTER (MS)   Robert Halmi, Inc./Channel
Seven, 1986, U.S.-Australian
KURT VONNEGUT'S MONKEY HOUSE   *MONKEY HOUSE* (CTF)
co-director with Paul Shapiro & Allan King, Atlantis Films Ltd./
Crescene Entertainment/Canwest Broadcasting Ltd.,
1991, Canadian

NELSON SHIN

THE TRANSFORMERS - THE MOVIE (AF)   DEG, 1986

STEPHEN SHIN

Contact: Hong Kong Film Liaison, 10940 Wilshire Blvd. - Suite 1220,
Los Angeles, CA 90024, 310/208-2678

HEART TO HEARTS   1989, Hong Kong
HEART INTO HEARTS   1990, Hong Kong
HAPPY TOGETHER   1990, Hong Kong
BLACK CAT   1991, Hong Kong
THE GREAT CONQUEROR'S CONCUBINE   Great Dragon
Films Co., 1994, Hong Kong

KANETO SHINDO

b. April 22, 1912 - Hiroshima Prefecture, Japan
Contact: Nihon Eiga Kantoku Kyokai (Japan Film Directors
Association), La Fontenu Building -4th Floor, 23-2 Maruyama-cho,
Shibuya-ku, Tokyo, Japan, tel.: 3/3461-4411

STORY OF MY LOVING WIFE   Daiei, 1951, Japanese
CHILDREN OF THE ATOM BOMB   Kindai Eiga Kyokai,
1952, Japanese
A WOMAN'S LIFE   Kindai Eiga Kyokai, 1953, Japanese
EPITOME OF LIFE   Kindai Eiga Kyokai, 1953, Japanese
BEFORE THE SUNRISE   Kindai Eiga Kyokai, 1953, Japanese
GUTTER   Kindai Eiga Kyokai, 1954, Japanese
WOLVES   Kindai Eiga Kyokai, 1955, Japanese
AN ACTRESS   Kindai Eiga Kyokai, 1956, Japanese
GUYS OF THE SEA   Nikkatsu, 1957, Japanese
SORROW IS ONLY FOR WOMEN   Daiei, 1958, Japanese
DAI GO FUKURYU-MARU   Kindai Eiga Kyokai/Shinseki Eiga,
1959, Japanese
THE ISLAND   *NAKED ISLAND*   Kindai Eiga Kyokai,
1960, Japanese
HUMAN BEING   Kindai Eiga Kyokai, 1962, Japanese
MOTHER   Kindai Eiga Kyokai, 1963, Japanese
ONIBABA   Kindai Eiga Kyokai/Tokyo Eiga, 1964, Japanese
A SCOUNDREL   Tokyo Eiga/Kindai Eiga Kyokai,
1965, Japanese
INSTINCT   Kindai Eiga Kyokai, 1966, Japanese
KURONEKO   *BLACK CAT IN THE BUSHES*   Kindai Eiga Kyokai/
Nippon Eiga Shinsha, 1968, Japanese
HEAT HAZE   Kindai Eiga Kyokai, 1969, Japanese
NAKED 19-YEAR-OLD   Kindai Eiga Kyokai, 1970, Japanese
A PAEAN   Kinda Eiga Kyokai/ATG, 1972, Japanese
KOKORO   Kindai Eiga Kyokai/ATG, 1973, Japanese
MY WAY   Wagamichi Production Company/Kindai Eiga Kyokai,
1974, Japanese
LIFE OF A FILM DIRECTOR: RECORD OF KENJI
MIZOGUCHI (FD)   Kindai Eiga Kyokai, 1975, Japanese
CHIKUZAN: TRAVELS BY MYSELF   Kindai Eiga Kyokai/Janjan,
1977, Japanese
DEATH BY HANGING   Kindai Eiga Kyokai/ATG,
1979, Japanese
HOKUSAI MANGA   Shochiku, 1981, Japanese
THE HORIZON   Marugen, 1984, Japanese
BLACKBOARD   Chiki Bunka Suishin No Kai, 1986, Japanese
A DECIDUOUS TREE   Kindai Eiga Kyokai, 1986, Japanese
SAKUR TAI 8-6 (FD)   Kindai Eiga Kyokai, 1988, Japanese
BOKUTOYKITAN   Kindai Eiga Kyokai/ATG, 1992, Japanese
THE STRANGE STORY OF OYUKI   Toho, 1993, Japanese

MASAHIRO SHINODA

b. March 9, 1931 - Gifu Prefecture, Japan
Address: 1-11-16 Kita-Senzoku, Ota-ku, Tokyo 145, Japan,
tel.: 03/723-4060
Business Manager: Herald Ace Inc., No. 1 Ekimae Building, 2-20-15,
Shimbashi, Minato-ku, Tokyo 105, Japan, tel.: 03/573-1150
Contact: Nihon Eiga Kantoku Kyokai (Japan Film Directors
Association), La Fontenu Building -4th Floor, 23-2 Maruyama-cho,
Shibuya-ku, Tokyo, Japan, tel.: 3/3461-4411

ONE WAY TICKET FOR LOVE   Shochiku, 1960, Japanese
DRY LAKE   *YOUTH IN FURY*   Shochiku, 1960, Japanese
MY FACE RED IN THE SUNSET   *KILLERS ON PARADE*
Shochiku, 1961, Japanese
EPITAPH TO MY LOVE   Shochiku, 1961, Japanese
SHAMISEN AND MOTORCYCLE   *LOVE OLD AND NEW*
Shochiku, 1961, Japanese
OUR MARRIAGE   Shochiku, 1962, Japanese
GLORY ON THE SUMMIT: BURNING YOUTH   Shochiku,
1962, Japanese
TEARS ON THE LION'S MANE   Shochiku, 1962, Japanese
PALE FLOWER   Shochiku, 1963, Japanese
ASSASSINATION   Shochiku, 1964, Japanese
WITH BEAUTY AND SORROW   Shochiku, 1965, Japanese
SAMURAI SPY   Shochiku, 1965, Japanese
PUNISHMENT ISLAND   Nissei Productions/Daiei, 1966, Japanese
CLOUDS AT SUNSET   Hyogensha/Shochiku, 1967, Japanese
DOUBLE SUICIDE   Hyogensha/ATG, 1969, Japanese
THE SCANDALOUS ADVENTURES OF BURAIKAN   Ninjin Club/
Toho, 1970, Japanese
SILENCE   Hyogensha/Mako International/Toho, 1971, Japanese
SAPPORO WINTER OLYMPIC GAMES (FD)   News Eiga
Seisakusha Remmei/Toho, 1972, Japanese
THE PETRIFIED FOREST   Hyogensha/Toho, 1973, Japanese
HIMIKO   Hyogensha/ATG, 1974, Japanese
UNDER THE CHERRY BLOSSOMS   Geiensha/Toho,
1975, Japanese
NIHON-MARU SHIP (FD)   1976, Japanese
THE BALLAD OF ORIN   Hyogensha/Toho, 1977, Japanese
DEMON POND   Shochiku, 1979, Japanese
ISLAND OF THE EVIL SPIRIT   Haruki Kadokawa Office/Toei-Nippon
Herald, 1981, Japanese
MacARTHUR'S CHILDREN   *THE INLAND SEA BOYS'
BASEBALL TEAM*   Orion Classics, 1984, Japanese
GONZA THE SPEARMAN   Shochiku/Hyogensha, 1986, Japanese
DIE TANZERIN   Manfred Durniok Productions/Herald Ace, 1990,
West German-Japanese
SHONEN JIDAI   Fujiko Fujio Productions, 1990, Japanese
SHARAKU   Herald Ace, 1995, Japanese

TALIA SHIRE
(Talia Coppola)
b. 1947 - Lake Success, New York
Contact: Screen Actors Guild - Los Angeles, 213/954-1600

ONE NIGHT STAND   Concorde, 1993
BEFORE THE NIGHT   New Line Cinema, 1994

JACK SHOLDER*

b. June 8, 1945 - Philadelphia, Pennsylvania
Agent: ICM - Beverly Hills, 310/550-4000

ALONE IN THE DARK   New Line Cinema, 1982
A NIGHTMARE ON ELM STREET, PART 2: FREDDY'S REVENGE
New Line Cinema, 1985
THE HIDDEN   New Line Cinema, 1987
RENEGADES   Universal, 1989
GRAND TOUR (CTF)   HBO Pictures, 1989
BY DAWN'S EARLY LIGHT (CTF)   HBO Pictures/Paravision
International, 1990
12:01 (TF)   Fox West Pictures/New Line TV/Chanticleer Films, 1993
DARK REFLECTION (TF)   Stillwater Productions/World International
Network/Fox West Pictures, 1993
SKETCH ARTIST II: HANDS THAT SEE (CTF)   Motion Picture
Corporation of America, 1995

SIG SHORE*
(Samuel R. Shore)
Contact: Directors Guild of America - Los Angeles, 213/851-3671

THAT'S THE WAY OF THE WORLD *SHINING STAR*
    United Artists, 1975
THE ACT   Artists Releasing Corporation/Film Ventures
    International, 1984
SUDDEN DEATH   Marvin Films, 1985
THE SURVIVALIST   Skouras Pictures, 1987
THE RETURN OF SUPERFLY   Triton Pictures, 1990

JOHN SHORNEY
SECOND COUSIN, ONCE REMOVED   Intrepid Ventures
    Group, 1994

KEN SHORT
IN SEARCH OF ANGELS (TD)   Perennial Productions, 1994

ROBERT SHORT*
b. December 22, 1950 - Santa Monica, California
Business: Robert Short Productions, 4228 Glencoe Avenue,
    Marina del Rey, CA 90292, 310/306-6842

PROGRAMMED TO KILL   co-director with Allan Holzman,
    Trans World Entertainment, 1987

MINA SHUM
Agent: Becsey/Wisdom/Kalajian - Los Angeles, 310/550-0535

DOUBLE HAPPINESS   Fine Line Features/New Line Cinema,
    1994, Canadian

M. NIGHT SHYAMALAN
b. India
Agent: ICM - Beverly Hills, 310/550-4000

PRAYING WITH ANGER   Northern Arts Entertainment/Unipix
    Corporation, 1992

CHARLES SHYER*
b. October 11, 1941 - Los Angeles, California
Agent: ICM - Beverly Hills, 310/550-4000

IRRECONCILABLE DIFFERENCES   Warner Bros., 1984
BABY BOOM   MGM/UA, 1987
FATHER OF THE BRIDE   Buena Vista, 1991
I LOVE TROUBLE   Buena Vista, 1994
FATHER OF THE BRIDE 2   Buena Vista, 1995

MUSSEF SIBAY
b. Homs, Syria
Business: Apsicon Productions Inc., 9600 Kirkside Road,
    Los Angeles, CA 90035, 310/558-0531

A WOMAN, HER MEN AND HER FUTON   Republic Pictures, 1992

ANDY SIDARIS
b. February 20, 1933 - Chicago, Illinois
Business: The Sidaris Company/Malibu Bay Films, 9229 Sunset
    Blvd. - Suite 208, Los Angeles, CA 90069, 310/278-5056

THE RACING SCENE (FD)   Filmways, 1970
STACEY   New World, 1973
SEVEN   American International, 1979
MALIBU EXPRESS   Malibu Bay Films, 1984
HARD TICKET TO HAWAII   Malibu Bay Films, 1987
PICASSO TRIGGER   Malibu Bay Films, 1988
SAVAGE BEACH   Malibu Bay Films, 1989
GUNS   Malibu Bay Films, 1990
DO OR DIE   Malibu Bay Films, 1991
HARD HUNTED   Malibu Bay Films, 1992
FIT TO KILL   Malibu Bay Films, 1993

ADI SIDEMAN
CHICKEN HAWK: MEN WHO LOVE BOYS (FD)   Stranger Than
    Fiction Films, 1994

GEORGE SIDNEY*
b. October 4, 1916 - Long Island City, New York
Home: 910 N. Rexford Drive, Beverly Hills, CA 90210

FREE AND EASY   MGM, 1941
PACIFIC RENDEZVOUS   MGM, 1942
PILOT NO. 5   MGM, 1943
THOUSANDS CHEER   MGM, 1943
BATHING BEAUTY   MGM, 1944
ANCHORS AWEIGH   MGM, 1945
THE HARVEY GIRLS   MGM, 1946
HOLIDAY IN MEXICO   MGM, 1946
CASS TIMBERLANE   MGM, 1947
THE THREE MUSKETEERS   MGM, 1948
THE RED DANUBE   MGM, 1949
KEY TO THE CITY   MGM, 1950
ANNIE GET YOUR GUN   MGM, 1950
SHOW BOAT   MGM, 1951
SCARAMOUCHE   MGM, 1952
YOUNG BESS   MGM, 1953
KISS ME KATE   MGM, 1953
JUPITER'S DARLING   MGM, 1955
THE EDDY DUCHIN STORY   Columbia, 1956
JEANNE EAGELS   Columbia, 1957
PAL JOEY   Columbia, 1957
WHO WAS THAT LADY?   Columbia, 1960
PEPE   Columbia, 1960
BYE BYE BIRDIE   Columbia, 1963
A TICKLISH AFFAIR   MGM, 1963
VIVA LAS VEGAS   MGM, 1964
THE SWINGER   Paramount, 1966
HALF A SIXPENCE   Paramount, 1968, British

DAVID SIEGEL
Agent: William Morris Agency - Beverly Hills, 310/859-4000

SUTURE   co-director with Scott McGehee, Samuel Goldwyn
    Pictures, 1993

ROBERT J. SIEGEL*
Contact: Directors Guild of America - Los Angeles, 213/851-3671

PARADES   Cinerama Releasing Corporation, 1972

JAMES SIGNORELLI*
Agent: Martin Hurwitz Associates - Beverly Hills, 310/274-0240

EASY MONEY   Orion, 1983
ELVIRA, MISTRESS OF THE DARK   New World, 1988
HOTEL ROOM (CTF)   co-director with David Lynch, Propaganda
    Films/Assymetrical Productions, 1993

SLOBODAN SIJAN
Address: 14 Decembra 61, 11000 Belgrade, Serbia

WHO'S SINGING OVER THERE?   Centar Film, 1982, Yugoslavian
THE MARATHON FAMILY   Centar Film, 1984, Yugoslavian
HOW I WAS SYSTEMATICALLY DESTROYED BY AN IDIOT
    Paris-Union Film, 1984, Yugoslavian
STRANGLER VS. STRANGLER   Centar Film, 1986, Yugoslavian
SECRET INGREDIENT   Hemdale, 1988, U.S.-Yugoslavian

JOEL SILBERG*
(Yoel Zilberg)
Agent: David Gersh, The Gersh Agency - Beverly Hills, 310/274-6611

GET ZORKIN   1968, Israeli
GAMLIEL   1972, Israeli
THE RABBI AND THE SHIKSE   Roll Films, 1976, Israeli
MILLIONAIRE IN TROUBLE   Shapira Films, 1978, Israeli
MARRIAGE, TEL AVIV STYLE   Noah Films, 1979, Israeli
MY MOTHER THE GENERAL   Noah Films, 1981, Israeli

BREAKDANCIN' MGM/UA/Cannon, 1984
RAPPIN' Cannon, 1985
BAD GUYS Interpictures, 1986
CATCH THE HEAT *FEEL THE HEAT* Trans World
 Entertainment, 1987
LAMBADA Warner Bros., 1990
PRISON HEAT Global Pictures, 1992, Israeli

BRAD SILBERLING*
Agent: CAA - Beverly Hills, 310/288-4545

CASPER Universal, 1995

ANDREW SILVER
Business: Silver Productions, 260 Beacon Street, Boston,
 MA 02116, 617/266-6482 or:
 24 Central Park South, New York, NY 10019, 212/355-5291

RETURN Silver Productions, 1985

DIANE SILVER
IT'S NOT MY FAULT Diane Silver Productions, 1991

JOAN MICKLIN SILVER*
b. May 24, 1935 - Omaha, Nebraska
Business: Midwest Film Productions, 600 Madison Avenue,
 New York, NY 10022, 212/355-0282
Agent: William Morris Agency - Beverly Hills, 310/859-4000

HESTER STREET Midwest Film Productions, 1975
BETWEEN THE LINES Midwest Film Productions, 1977
HEAD OVER HEELS *CHILLY SCENES OF WINTER*
 United Artists, 1979
HOW TO BE A PERFECT PERSON IN JUST THREE DAYS (TF)
 Mark Gordon Productions/WonderWorks, 1984
FINNEGAN BEGIN AGAIN (CTF) HBO Premiere Films/Zenith
 Productions/Jennie & Co. Film Productions, 1985, U.S.-British
CROSSING DELANCEY Warner Bros., 1988
LOVERBOY TriStar, 1989
BIG GIRLS DON'T CRY...THEY GET EVEN New Line
 Cinema, 1992
A PRIVATE MATTER (CTF) HBO Pictures/Longbow Productions/
 Mirage Enterprises 1992

MARISA SILVER*
b. April 23, 1960 - Cleveland, Ohio
Agent: Richland/Wunsch/Hohman Agency - Los Angeles,
 310/278-1955

OLD ENOUGH Orion Classics, 1984
PERMANENT RECORD Paramount, 1988
VITAL SIGNS 20th Century Fox, 1990
HE SAID, SHE SAID co-director with Ken Kwapis, Paramount, 1991
INDECENCY (CTF) Point of View Productions/MTE, 1992

RAPHAEL D. SILVER*
Business: Midwest Film Productions, 600 Madison Avenue,
 New York, NY 10022, 212/355-0200

ON THE YARD Midwest Film Productions, 1979
A WALK ON THE MOON Skouras Pictures, 1987

RON SILVER*
b. July 2, 1946 - New York, New York
Agent: ICM - Beverly Hills, 310/550-4000

LIFEPOD (TF) RHI Entertainment Group/Trilogy
 Entertainment Group, 1993

MARC SILVERMAN
Business: 62 West Productions, 62 West 70th Street, New York,
 NY 10023, 212/595-5464

LE FILM NOIR Worthwhile Pictures, 1983
RUMSEY STATUES (FD) Dubin/Rumsey Foundation, 1986

ELLIOT SILVERSTEIN*
b. 1927 - Boston, Massachusetts
Agent: Phil Gersh, The Gersh Agency - Beverly Hills, 310/274-6611

BELLE SOMMARS Columbia, 1962
CAT BALLOU Columbia, 1965
THE HAPPENING Columbia, 1967
A MAN CALLED HORSE National General, 1970
DEADLY HONEYMOON *NIGHTMARE HONEYMOON* MGM, 1974
THE CAR Universal, 1977
BETRAYED BY INNOCENCE (TF) Inter Planetary Pictures/CBS
 Entertainment, 1986
NIGHT OF COURAGE (TF) Titus Productions/The Eugene O'Neill
 Memorial Theater Center, 1987
FIGHT FOR LIFE (TF) Fries Entertainment, 1987
RICH MEN, SINGLE WOMEN (TF) Aaron Spelling
 Productions, 1990
FLASHFIRE Silver Lion Films/Avondale Pictures, 1994

LAWRENCE L. SIMEONE
EYES OF THE BEHOLDER Eyes of the Beholder
 Productions, 1992
BLINDFOLD: ACTS OF OBSESSION (CTF) Saban Pictures/Libra
 Pictures 1994, originally filmed for theatrical release

ANTHONY SIMMONS
Business: West One Film Productions, c/o Cooper Murray,
 Mappin House, Winsley Street, London W1N 7AR, England
Agent: Richard Hatton Ltd. - London, tel.: 181/876-6699

YOUR MONEY OR YOUR WIFE Rank, 1960, British
FOUR IN THE MORNING West One, 1965, British
THE OPTIMISTS *THE OPTIMISTS OF NINE ELMS* Paramount,
 1973, British
BLACK JOY Hemdale, 1977, British
ON GIANT'S SHOULDERS (TF) BBC, 1979, British
SUPERGRAN (TF) Newcastle, 1984, British
DAY AFTER THE FAIR (TF) BBC/Bill Kenwright Films Ltd./Arts &
 Entertainment Network, 1987, British
LITTLE SWEETHEART Columbia, 1988, U.S.-British

ADAM SIMON
Agent: ICM - Beverly Hills, 310/550-4000

BRAIN DEAD Concorde, 1990
BODY CHEMISTRY II: THE VOICE OF A STRANGER
 Concorde, 1992
CARNOSAUR Concorde, 1993

FRANCIS SIMON
THE CHICKEN CHRONICLES Avco Embassy, 1977

ROGER L. SIMON*
Contact: Directors Guild of America - Los Angeles, 213/851-3671

MY MAN ADAM TriStar, 1985

YVES SIMONEAU*
Agent: William Morris Agency - Beverly Hills, 310/859-4000

LES CELEBRATIONS Le Loup Blanc, 1979, Canadian
LES YEUX ROUGES OU LES VERITES ACCIDENTELLES
 Les Films du Crepuscule, 1982, Canadian
POURQUOI L'ETRANGE MONSIEUR ZOLOCK S'INTERESSAIT-IL
 TANT A LA BANDE DESSINEE? Salon International du Livre
 du Quebec, 1983, Canadian
POUVOIR INTIME Cinema Group, 1986, Canadian
LES FOUS DE BASSAN 1987, Canadian
DAN LE VENTRE DU DRAGON Quebec-Amerique/Lenox
 Productions, 1989, Canadian
PERFECTLY NORMAL Four Seasons Entertainment,
 1990, Canadian
MEMPHIS (CTF) Propaganda Films, 1992
TILL DEATH DO US PART (TF) Saban-Scherick
 Productions, 1992

CRUEL DOUBT (TF)   Susan Baerwald Productions/NBC
   Productions, 1992
MOTHER'S BOYS   Miramax Films, 1994
AMELIA EARHART: THE FINAL FLIGHT (CTF)   Avenue
   Pictures/TBS Productions, 1994, U.S.-Canadian

JANE SIMPSON
NUMBER ONE FAN   MCEG Sterling Entertainment, 1994

MICHAEL A. SIMPSON
Business: Double Helix Films, Inc., 303 West 76th Street - Suite B,
   New York, NY 10023

IMPURE THOUGHTS   ASA Communications, 1986
FUNLAND   Vestron, 1987
SLEEPAWAY CAMP II: UNHAPPY CAMPERS   Double Helix, 1988
SLEEPAWAY CAMP III: TEENAGE WASTELAND
   Double Helix, 1988
FAST FOOD   Fries Distribution, 1989
HARD EVIDENCE   Falcon Arts and Entertainment, 1994

FRANK SINATRA*
(Francis Albert Sinatra)
b. December 12, 1915 - Hoboken, New Jersey
Business Manager: Nathan Golden, Golden-Goldberg Accounting
   Corporation, 5757 Wilshire Blvd., Los Angeles, CA 90046,
   213/965-0044

NONE BUT THE BRAVE   Warner Bros., 1964, U.S.-Japanese

ANDREW SINCLAIR
Contact: British Film Commission, 70 Baker Street, London
   W1M 1DJ, England, tel.: 171/224-5000

THE BREAKING OF BUMBO   Timon/ABPC, 1971, British
UNDER MILD WOOD   Altura, 1973, British
BLUE BLOOD   Mallard Productions, 1975, British

GERALD SETH SINDELL
b. April 15, 1944 - Cleveland, Ohio
Home: 9655 Yoakum Drive, Beverly Hills, CA 90210, 310/275-3353

DOUBLE-STOP   World Entertainment, 1967
HARPY (TF)   Cinema Center 100, 1970
TEENAGER   National Cinema, 1974
H.O.T.S.   Derio Productions, 1979

ALEXANDER SINGER*
b. 1932 - New York, New York
Agent: Michael Rosen, Harry Gold Associates, 3500 W. Olive
   Avenue - Suite 1400, Burbank, CA 91505, 818/972-4300

A COLD WIND IN AUGUST   Lopert, 1961
PSYCHE 59   Royal Films International, 1964, British
LOVE HAS MANY FACES   Columbia, 1965
CAPTAIN APACHE   Scotia International, 1971, British
GLASS HOUSES   Columbia, 1972
THE FIRST 36 HOURS OF DR. DURANT (TF)   Columbia TV, 1975
TIME TRAVELERS (TF)   Irwin Allen Productions/20th
   Century-Fox TV, 1976
THE MILLION DOLLAR RIP-OFF (TF)   Charles Fries
   Productions, 1976
HUNTERS OF THE REEF (TF)   Writers Company Productions/
   Paramount TV, 1978
THE RETURN OF MARCUS WELBY, M.D. (TF)   Marstar
   Productions/Universal TV, 1984

BRYAN SINGER
Agent: Becsey/Wisdom/Kalajian - Los Angeles, 310/550-0535

PUBLIC ACCESS   Cinemabeam, 1993
THE USUAL SUSPECTS   Gramercy Pictures, 1995

GAIL SINGER
b. 1943 - Winnipeg, Manitoba, Canada
Address: 82 Willcocks Street, Toronto, Ontario M5S 1C8, Canada,
   416/923-4245

RIVERAIN: GIFT OF PASSAGE (FD)   1976, Canadian
TIME OF THE CREE (FD)   1976, Canadian
FIDDLERS OF JAMES BAY (FD)   1979, Canadian
LOVED, HONOURED AND BRUISED (FD)   1980, Canadian
PORTRAIT OF THE ARTIST AS AN OLD LADY (FD)
   1982, Canadian
A MOVEABLE FEAST: A FILM ABOUT BREASTFEEDING (FD)
   1982, Canadian
THE WRITER AND HUMAN RIGHTS (TD)   1982, Canadian
ABORTIONS: STORIES FROM NORTH AND SOUTH (FD)
   1984, Canadian
TRADE SECRETS (TD)   1985, Canadian
NEIGHBOURHOODS (TD)   1985, Canadian
PROFILE OF BARTON MYERS (TD)   1986, Canadian
HAILEY'S HOME MOVIE (TD)   1987, Canadian
IS EVERYONE CRAZY? (TF)   1988, Canadian
CHRIS (TF)   1990, Canadian
WISECRACKS (FD)   Alliance Films, 1991, Canadian
TRUE CONFECTIONS   Manon Films, 1992, Canadian

JOHN SINGLETON*
b. 1967 - Los Angeles, California
Business: New Deal Productions, 10202 W. Washington Blvd. -
   Capra Building, Room 203, Culver City, CA 90232, 310/280-4504
Agent: CAA - Beverly Hills, 310/288-4545

BOYZ N THE HOOD ★   Columbia, 1991
POETIC JUSTICE   Columbia, 1993
HIGHER LEARNING   Columbia, 1995

RALPH S. SINGLETON*
Business: Lone Eagle Publishing, 2337 Roscomare Road - Suite 9,
   Los Angeles, CA 90077, 310/471-8066
Business Manager: Perry & Neidorf, 9720 Wilshire Blvd. - Third Floor,
   Beverly Hills, CA 90212, 310/550-1254
Agent: The Mirisch Agency - Los Angeles, 310/282-9940

STEPHEN KING'S GRAVEYARD SHIFT   *GRAVEYARD SHIFT*
   Paramount, 1990

GARY SINISE*
b. 1955 - Chicago, Illinois
Agent: CAA - Beverly Hills, 310/288-4545
Personal Manager: Brillstein/Grey Entertainment - Beverly Hills,
   310/275-6135
Business Manager: Marty Licker, Nugit & Livcker, 11999 San Vicente
   Blvd. - Suite 400, Los Angeles, CA 90049, 310/472-8900

MILES FROM HOME   Cinecom, 1988
OF MICE AND MEN   MGM-UA, 1992

BERNHARD SINKEL
Contact: Federal Union of Film and Television Directors in Germany,
   Adelheidstrasse 7, 8000 Munich 40, Germany, tel.: 089/271-6380

SINS OF THE FATHERS   *FATHERS AND SONS* (MS)
   Bavaria Atelier/WDR/Taurus Film/FR3/ORF/RAI, 1987,
   West German-French-Italian
HEMINGWAY (MS)   Alcor Films/Daniel Wilson Productions/
   DWP/Cine Alliance/Channel 4/RAI/TFI/ZDF, 1988,
   West German-U.S.-French-British-Italian
DER KINOERZAEHLER   Allianz Filmproduktion/ABS Film/Roxy
   Film/Bioskop Film/ZDF, 1993, German

GARY SINYOR
Agent: William Morris Agency - Beverly Hills, 310/859-4000

LEON THE PIG FARMER   co-director with Vadim Jean,
   Leon the Pig Productions, 1992, British
SOLITAIRE FOR 2   Trident Releasing, 1995, British

CURT SIODMAK*
b. August 10, 1902 - Dresden, Germany
Home: Old South Fork Ranch, 43422 So. Fork Drive, Three Rivers,
   CA 93271, 209/561-4350

BRIDE OF THE GORILLA   Realart, 1951
THE MAGNETIC MONSTER   United Artists, 1953
CURUCU - BEAST OF THE AMAZON   Universal, 1956
LOVE SLAVES OF THE AMAZON   Universal, 1957
SKI FEVER   *LIEBESSPIELE IM SCHNEE*   1967,
   Austrian-Czechoslovakian-U.S.

ANDREW SIPES*
Agent: Shapiro-Lichtman Talent Agency - Los Angeles, 310/859-8877

FAIR GAME   Warner Bros., 1995

HAL SITOWITZ*
Agent: William Morris Agency - Beverly Hills, 310/274-7451

A LAST CRY FOR HELP (TF)   Myrt-Hal Productions/Viacom, 1979

VILGOT SJOMAN
(David Harald Vilgot Sjoman)
b. December 2, 1924 - Stockholm, Sweden
Contact: Swedish Film Institute, P.O. Box 27126, 102 52 Stockholm,
   Sweden, tel.: 08/665-1100

THE SWEDISH MISTRESS   1962, Swedish
491   Peppercorn-Wormser, 1964, Swedish
THE DRESS   1964, Swedish
STIMULANTIA   co-director, 1965, Swedish
MY SISTER, MY LOVE   *SYSKONBADD 1782*   Sigma III,
   1966, Swedish
I AM CURIOUS (YELLOW)   Grove Press, 1967, Swedish
I AM CURIOUS (BLUE)   Grove Press, 1968, Swedish
YOU'RE LYING   Grove Press, 1969, Swedish
BLUSHING CHARLIE   1970, Swedish
TILL SEX DO US PART   *TROLL*   Astro, 1971, Swedish
THE KARLSSON BROTHERS   1972, Swedish
A HANDFUL OF LOVE   1974, Swedish
GARAGET   1975, Swedish
TABU   Svensk Filminstitut, 1977, Swedish
LINUS ELLER TEGELHUSETS HEMLIGHET   Svensk Filmindustri,
   1979, Swedish
JAG RODNAR   1982, Swedish
MALACCA   Filmstallet/TV-2/Swedish Film Institute/Vilgot Sjoman
   Film, 1986, Swedish
FALLGROPEN   Facta & Fiction/Swedish TV/Swedish Film Institute/
   Sandrews, 1989, Swedish
ALFRED   Sandrew Film/Volvo AB/SVT-1/Metronome Film,
   1995, Swedish-Danish

CALVIN SKAGGS
THE FIG TREE (TF)   KERA/Lumiere Productions/
   WonderWorks, 1987

JERZY SKOLIMOWSKI
b. May 5, 1938 - Warsaw, Poland
Home: 514 Alta Avenue, Santa Monica, CA, 310/451-1010
Agent: ICM - Beverly Hills, 310/550-4000

IDENTIFICATION MARKS: NONE   New Yorker, 1964, Polish
WALKOVER   New Yorker, 1965, Polish
BARRIER   Film Polski, 1966, Polish
LE DEPART   Pathé Contemporary, 1967, Belgian
HANDS UP!   1967, Polish
DIALOGUE   co-director, 1968, Czech
THE ADVENTURES OF GIRARD   United Artists,
   1969, British-Swiss
DEEP END   Paramount, 1971, British-West German
KING, QUEEN, KNAVE   Avco Embassy, 1972,
   West German-British
THE SHOUT   Films Inc., 1979, British

MOONLIGHTING   Universal Classics, 1982, British
SUCCESS IS THE BEST REVENGE   Triumph/Columbia,
   1984, British
THE LIGHTSHIP   Castle Hill Productions, 1985, U.S.-West German
TORRENTS OF SPRING   Millimeter Films, 1989, Italian-French
THIRTY DOOR KEY FERDYDURKE   Million Frames/Cinea Sarl,
   1993, Polish-French

BOB SKOTAK
Agent: The Gersh Agency - Beverly Hills, 310/274-6611

INVASION EARTH: THE ALIENS ARE HERE   New World, 1987

LANE SLATE
CLAY PIGEON   co-director with Tom Stern, MGM, 1971
DEADLY GAME (TF)   MGM TV, 1977

AVIVA SLESIN*
b. February 5, 1946 - Shaulen, Lithuania
Address: 155 East 77th Street - Apt. 5A, New York, NY 10021,
   212/734-1940

DIRECTED BY WILLIAM WYLER (FD)   Topgallant Productions/
   Tatge Productions, 1986
THE TEN YEAR LUNCH: THE WIT AND LEGEND OF THE
   ALGONQUIN ROUND TABLE (FD)   Aviva Films, 1987

BRIAN SLOAN
BOYS LIFE   co-director with Raoul O'Connell & Robert Lee King,
   Strand Releasing, 1994

HOLLY GOLDBERG SLOAN
Agent: Sanford-Gross & Associates - Los Angeles, 310/208-2100

THE BIG GREEN   Buena Vista, 1995

JAMES SLOCUM
Address: 962 N. Madison, Pasadena, CA 91104, 818/398-0930

AN AMERICAN SUMMER   Boss Entertainment Group, 1990

GEORGE SLUIZER*
b. Netherlands
Business: MGS Film Amsterdam, b.v., Singel 64, 1015 AC
   Amsterdam, The Netherlands, tel.: 20/23-15-93
Agent: CAA - Beverly Hills, 310/288-4545 or:
   The Casarotto Company - London, tel.: 171/287-4450

THE VANISHING   Tara Releasing, 1988, Dutch
UTZ   First Run Features/Castle Hill Productions, 1992,
   British-Dutch-Italian-German
THE VANISHING   20th Century Fox, 1992
DARK BLOOD   Fine Line Features/New Line Cinema,
   1993, unfinished

JON SMALL
THE TEDDY BEAR HABIT   Advocate Productions, 1990

JOHN SMALLCOMBE
Contact: British Film Commission, 70 Baker Street, London
   W1M 1DJ, England, tel.: 171/224-5000

AN AFRICAN DREAM   Hemdale, 1988, British

ROBERT J. SMAWLEY*
Home: 39785 Verona Lane, Palmdale, CA 93551, 805/947-7557

MURPHY'S FAULT   Triax Entertainment Group, 1989, British
AMERICAN EAGLE   Triax Entertainment Group, 1990
RIVER OF DIAMONDS   Karat Film/IMV, 1990,
   South African-West German

JACK SMIGHT*
b. March 9, 1926 - Minneapolis, Minnesota
Business Manager: Eric Weissman, Weissman-Wolff, 966 Wilshire
    Blvd. - Suite 900, Beverly Hills, CA 90212, 310/858-7888

I'D RATHER BE RICH   Universal, 1964
THE THIRD DAY   Warner Bros., 1965
HARPER   Warner Bros., 1966
KALEIDOSCOPE   Warner Bros., 1966, British
THE SECRET WAR OF HARRY FRIGG   Universal, 1968
NO WAY TO TREAT A LADY   Paramount, 1968
STRATEGY OF TERROR   *IN DARKNESS WAITING*   Universal,
    1969, originally made for television
THE ILLUSTRATED MAN   Warner Bros., 1969
RABBIT, RUN   Warner Bros., 1970
THE TRAVELING EXECUTIONER   MGM, 1970
THE SCREAMING WOMAN (TF)   Universal TV, 1972
BANACEK: DETOUR TO NOWHERE (TF)   Universal TV, 1972
THE LONGEST NIGHT (TF)   Universal TV, 1972
PARTNERS IN CRIME (TF)   Universal TV, 1973
DOUBLE INDEMNITY (TF)   Universal TV, 1973
LINDA (TF)   Universal TV, 1973
FRANKENSTEIN: THE TRUE STORY (TF)   Universal TV, 1973
AIRPORT 1975   Universal, 1974
MIDWAY   Universal, 1976
DAMNATION ALLEY   20th Century-Fox, 1977
ROLL OF THUNDER, HEAR MY CRY (TF)   Tomorrow
    Entertainment, 1978
FAST BREAK   Columbia, 1979
LOVING COUPLES   20th Century-Fox, 1980
REMEMBRANCE OF LOVE (TF)   Doris Quinlan Productions/
    Comworld Productions, 1982
NUMBER ONE WITH A BULLET   Cannon, 1987
THE FAVORITE   Ascona Films, 1989, Swiss

BRUCE SMITH
BEBE'S KIDS (AF)   Paramount, 1992
HAPPILY EVER AFTER: FAIRY TALES FOR EVERY CHILD (ACTF)
    Two Oceans Entertainment Group/Confetti Entertainment
    Company/Hyperion Studio Entertainment/Wang Film
    Productions Co. Ltd., 1995

BUD SMITH*
b. Tulsa, Oklahoma
Address: 9696 Culver Blvd. - Suite 203, Culver City, CA 90232,
    310/558-8110
Agent: UTA - Beverly Hills, 310/273-6700

JOHNNY BE GOOD   Orion, 1988

CHARLES MARTIN SMITH*
b. October 30, 1953 - Van Nuys, California
Agent: APA - Los Angeles, 310/273-0744

TRICK OR TREAT   DEG, 1986
FIFTY/FIFTY   Cannon, 1991
BORIS & NATASHA   MCEG, 1992, filmed in 1989

CLIVE A. SMITH
b. England
Business: Nelvana Productions, 32 Atlantic Avenue, Toronto,
    Ontario M6K 1X8, Canada, 416/588-5588

ROCK & RULE   *RING OF POWER* (AF)   MGM/UA,
    1983, Canadian

HOWARD SMITH
MARJOE (FD)   co-director with Sarah Kernochan, Cinema 5, 1972
GIZMO! (FD)   New Line Cinema, 1977

JOHN N. SMITH
b. 1943 - Montreal, Quebec, Canada
Telephone: 514/933-4885

THE MASCULINE MYSTIQUE   co-director, 1983, Canadian
A GIFT FOR KATE (TF)   1985, Canadian

THE REBELLION OF YOUNG DAVID (TF)   1985, Canadian
FIRST STOP CHINA (TD)   1985, Canadian
SITTING IN LIMBO   1985, Canadian
TRAIN OF DREAMS   1986, Canadian
THE BOYS OF ST. VINCENT (TF)   Les Productions Tele-Action/
    National Film Board of Canada/CBC/Telefilm Canada,
    1993, Canadian
DIEPPE (TF)   CBC, 1994, Canadian
DANGEROUS MINDS   Buena Vista, 1995

KEVIN SMITH
Agent: CAA - Beverly Hills, 310/288-4545

CLERKS   Miramax Films, 1994
MALL RATS   Gramercy Pictures, 1995

KENT SMITH
TAKING TIGER MOUNTAIN   co-director with Tom Huckabee,
    Horizon, 1983

MEL SMITH*
(Melvyn Kenneth Smith)
b. 1952 - London, England
Agent: UTA - Beverly Hills, 310/273-6700 or:
    Peters Fraser & Dunlop - London, tel.: 171/344-1000

THE TALL GUY   Miramax Films, 1989, British
RADIOLAND MURDERS   Universal, 1994

NOELLA SMITH
Agent: Peters Fraser & Dunlop - London, tel.: 171/344-1000

THE HUMMINGBIRD TREE   BBC Films/BBC Enterprises,
    1992, British

PETER SMITH
Agent: Peters Fraser & Dunlop - London, tel.: 171/344-1000

CHILDREN OF THE DRAGON (MS)   Southern Star Xanadu/Zenith
    Productions, 1992, Australian-British

TONY SMITH
Agent: Peters Fraser & Dunlop - London, tel.: 171/344-1000

HANCOCK (TF)   BBC, 1991, British
GRUSHKO (TF)   Mark Forstater Productions/BBC/Europool,
    1993, British-Russian

ALAN SMITHEE*
(Allen Smithee)
b. 1969 - Los Angeles, California
Contact: Directors Guild of America - Los Angeles, 213/851-3671

DEATH OF A GUNFIGHTER   (Don Siegel/Robert Totten)
    Universal, 1969
FADE IN   (Jud Taylor)   Paramount, 1968
THE CHALLENGE (TF)   20th Century-Fox TV, 1970
CITY IN FEAR   (Jud Taylor) (TF)   Trans World International, 1980
FUN AND GAMES   (Paul Bogart) (TF)   Kanin-Gallo Productions/
    Warner Bros. TV, 1980
MOONLIGHT   (Jackie Cooper/Rod Holcomb) (TF)
    Universal TV, 1982
STITCHES   (Rod Holcomb)   International Film Marketing, 1985
LET'S GET HARRY   (Stuart Rosenberg)   TriStar, 1986
DALTON: CODE OF VENGEANCE II   1986
MORGAN STEWART'S COMING HOME   (Terry Winsor/Paul Aaron)
    New Century/Vista, 1987
RIVIERA (TF)   MTM Productions, 1987
GHOST FEVER   (Lee Madden)   Miramax, 1987
I LOVE N.Y.   (Gianni Bozzacchi)   Manhattan Films, 1988
THE SHRIMP ON THE BARBIE   Vestron,
    1990, U.S.-New Zealand
STARFIRE   (Richard C. Sarafian)   re-edited version of SOLAR
    CRISIS, Japan-American Film Co., 1990, Japanese-U.S.

FATAL CHARM (CTF)   (Fritz Kiersch)   Jonathan D. Krane/Bruce
   Kohn Curtis Productions, 1992
THE CALL OF THE WILD (TF)   RHI Entertainment/Silvio Berlusconi
   Communications, 1993, U.S.-Italian
THE BIRDS II: LAND'S END (CTF)   (Rick Rosenthal)
   Rosemont Productions/MTE-Universal, 1994
THE O.J. SIMPSON STORY (TF)   (Jerrold Freedman)
   National Studios, 1995

*Note: Alan Smithee is the pseudonym designated by the Directors
Guild of America for those members who wish to remove their
names from the screen and advertising credits of a particular film.
This is usually the result of studio and/or network interference with
their intended cut of a film, and therefore a loss of creative control.*
                                                              — M.S.

SANDY SMOLAN*
Agent: Richland/Wunsch/Hohman Agency - Los Angeles,
   310/278-1955

RACHEL RIVER   Taurus Entertainment, 1987
VIETNAM WAR STORY: THE LAST DAYS (CTF)   co-director with
   David Burton Morris & Luis Soto, HBO, 1989
MIDDLE AGES (TF)   Stan Rogow Productions/
   Paramount TV, 1992
A PLACE TO BE LOVED (TF)   The Polson Company/Corapeake
   Productions/Procter & Gamble Productions, 1993

JONATHAN SMYTHE
THE WHOLE TRUTH   co-director with Dan Cohen,
   Cinevista, 1993

ROBERTO SNEIDER
Contact: IMCINE, Tepic #40, P.B. Colonia Roma Sur, Mexico City,
   C.P. 06760, Mexico, tel.: 525/584-7283

DOS CRIMENES   IMCINE/Fondo de Fomento a la Calidad/
   Cuevano Films, 1994, Mexican

SHERRY SNELLER
ROBINSON CRUSOE   PSM Entertainment, 1987

SKOTT SNIDER*
Telephone: 310/457-1042

MIRACLE BEACH   Motion Picture Corporation of America, 1992

MICHELE SOAVI
b. July 3, 1957 - Milan, Italy
Home: via Appia Antica 91, Rome, Italy, tel.: 6/514-1989

WORLD OF HORROR - IL MEGLIO DI DARIO ARGENTO (FD)
   1986, Italian
DELIRIA   Filmirage, 1987, Italian
LA CHIESA   Tiger Cinematografica, 1989, Italian
LA SETTA   ADC, 1990, Italian
DELLAMORTE DELLAMORE   Audifilm/Urania Film/KG
   Productions/Bibofilm & TV/Silvio Berlusconi Communications,
   1994, Italian-French-German

MARK S. SOBEL*
b. June 10, 1956 - Toronto, Ontario, Canada
Business: Cinecan Film Productions, P.O. Box 8601,
   Universal City, CA 91608
Agent: Becsey/Wisdom/Kalajian - Los Angeles, 310/550-0535

ACCESS CODE   Intercontinental Releasing, 1984
SWEET REVENGE   Concorde, 1987
little secrets   Cinecam Films, 1991
ORDEAL IN THE ARCTIC (TF)   Citadel Pictures/Alliance
   Communications, 1993, U.S.-Canadian
TRIAL AND ERROR (CTF)   Alliance Communications/USA Network,
   1993, Canadian-U.S.
BERMUDA GRACE (TF)   Catalyst Productions, 1994

STEVEN SODERBERGH
b. January 14, 1963 - Atlanta, Georgia
Agent: William Morris Agency - Beverly Hills, 310/273-7451

sex, lies, and videotape   Miramax Films, 1989
KAFKA   Miramax Films, 1991, U.S.-French
KING OF THE HILL   Gramercy Pictures, 1993
THE UNDERNEATH   Gramercy Pictures, 1995

RAINER SOEHNLEIN
b. May 6, 1941 - Coburg, Germany

MARIANNE AND SOFIE   Jugendfilm, 1984, West German

IAIAN SOFTLEY
Agent: ICM - Beverly Hills, 310/550-4000 or:
   The Casarotto Company - London, tel.: 171/287-4450

BACKBEAT   Gramercy Pictures, 1994, British
HACKERS   MGM-UA, 1995

FERNANDO E. SOLANAS
(Fernando Ezequiel Solanas)
b. February 16, 1936 - Olivos, Argentina
Home: 29, boulevard Sebastopol, 75001 Paris, France,
   tel.: 1/42-33-36-27
Contact: French Film Office, 745 Fifth Avenue, New York,
   NY 10151, 212/832-8860

LA HORA DE LOS HORNOS (FD)   co-director with Octavio Getino,
   Grupo Cine Liberacion, 1968, Argentine
ACTUALIZACION POLITICA Y DOCTRINARIA PARA LA TOMA
   DEL PODER (FD)   co-director with Octavio Getino, Grupo Cine
   Liberacion, 1971, Argentine
LA REVOLUCION JUSTICIALISTA (FD)   co-director with
   Octavio Getino, Grupo Cine Liberacion, 1971, Argentine
LOS HIJOS DE FIERRO   1977, Argentine
THE LOOK OF OTHERS (FD)   1979, French
TANGOS: THE EXILE OF GARDEL   New Yorker,
   1986, French-Argentine
SUR   Pacific Productions/Cinesur/Instituto de Cinematografica,
   1988, Argentine-French
EL VIAJE   CineSur/Les Films du Sud/Films A2/Television
   Espanola/Sociedad Estatal Quinto Centenario/Channel 4/
   IMCINE/Ministry of French Culture/Canal Plus/Antenne-2/
   Telemunchen/BIM Distribuzione/Herald Ace/Malo Films/
   Istituto Nacional de Cinematografica, 1992,
   Argentine-French-Spanish-British-Mexican-German-Japanese

ABBIE C. SOLAREZ
A CHILD'S CRY FOR HELP (TF)   AMI-TV Entertainment, 1991

RUSSELL SOLBERG
FORCED TO KILL   PM Entertainment, 1993

SILVIO SOLDINI
b. August 11, 1958 - Milan, Italy
Contact: Monogatari SRL, via Orti 16, Milan, Italy, tel.: 02/545-6579

PAESAGGIO CON FIGURE   Bilicofilm/Iceberg Film, 1983, Italian
GIULIA IN OTTOBRE   Bilicofilm, 1984, Italian
L'ARIA SERENA DELL'OVEST   Monogatari/Pic Film/SSR-RTSI,
   Italian-Swiss
UN'ANIMA DIVISA IN DUE   DARC, 1993, Italian-French-Swiss

ALFRED SOLE*
b. July 2, 1943 - Paterson, New Jersey
Contact: Directors Guild of America - Los Angeles, 213/851-3671

ALICE, SWEET ALICE   COMMUNION/HOLY TERROR
   Allied Artists, 1977
TANYA'S ISLAND   International Film Exchange/Fred Baker Films,
   1981, Canadian
PANDEMONIUM   MGM/UA, 1982

TODD SOLONDZ

Contact: Frankfurt, Garbus, Klein & Selz - New York, 212/980-0120

FEAR, ANXIETY AND DEPRESSION   The Samuel Goldwyn
   Company, 1989

ANDREW SOLT*

b. December 13, 1947 - London, England
Business: Andrew Solt Productions, 9121 Sunset Blvd.,
   Los Angeles, CA 90069, 310/276-9522
Agent: William Morris Agency - Beverly Hills, 310/859-4000

HEROES OF ROCK AND ROLL (TD)   co-director with
   Malcolm Leo, ABC, 1979
THIS IS ELVIS (FD)   co-director with Malcolm Leo,
   Warner Bros., 1981
IT CAME FROM HOLLYWOOD (FD)   co-director with Malcolm Leo,
   Paramount, 1982
IMAGINE: JOHN LENNON (FD)   Warner Bros., 1988
ELVIS: THE GREAT PERFORMANCES (HVCD)   Buena Vista
   Home Video, 1990
ELVIS: CENTER STAGE (CCD)   Andrew Solt Productions, 1991
THE VERY BEST OF THE ED SULLIVAN SHOW (TD)
   Andrew Solt Productions, 1991
THE VERY BEST OF THE ED SULLIVAN SHOW 2 (TD)
   Andrew Solt Productions/Sofa Entertainment, 1991
THE HISTORY OF ROCK 'N' ROLL (TD)   co-director,
   Andrew Solt Productions/QDE/Telepictures Productions/
   Time-Life Video & Television/Warner Bros. TV Distribution
   Prime Time Entertainment Network, 1995

OLA SOLUM

b. 1943 - Norway
Address: Nils Huusgt. 18, 0482 Oslo 4, Norway, tel.: 2/57-90-64
Contact: Norwegian Film Institute, Grev Wedels Plass 1,
   N-0105 Oslo 1, Norway, tel.: 2/42-87-40

ORION'S BELT   New World, 1985, Norwegian
DEADLY ILLUSION   Cinema Group, 1987, British-Norwegian
WANDERERS   Norsk Film, 1989, Norwegian
THE POLAR BEAR KING   Connexion Film/Moviemakers/
   Northern Lights Film & TV Production Company, 1991,
   Norwegian-German-British-Swedish
SECOND SIGHT   Northern Lights Productions/Moviemakers,
   1995, Norwegian

PAUL SOMMER

JONNY'S GOLDEST QUEST (ATF)   co-director with Don Lusk,
   Hanna-Barbera Productions/USA Network/Fil-Cartoons,
   1993, U.S.-Filipino

STEPHEN SOMMERS*

Agent: William Morris Agency - Beverly Hills, 310/859-4000

CATCH ME IF YOU CAN   MCEG, 1989
THE ADVENTURES OF HUCK FINN   Buena Vista, 1993
RUDYARD KIPLING'S THE JUNGLE BOOK   *THE JUNGLE BOOK*
   Buena Vista, 1994

CHERD SONGSRI

b. Thailand
Business: Cherdchai Productions, 523-5 Suttisarn Road,
   Huikwang, Bangkok, Thailand
Contact: Thailand Film Promotion Center, 599 Bumnrung
   Muang Road, Bangkok 10100, Thailand, tel.: 2/223-4690

NOH-SAH   1966, Thai
MEKALA   1967, Thai
OK-TORANEE   1968, Thai
PAYASOKE   1969, Thai
LAMPOO   1970, Thai
KHAN-CHAI-BOD   1970, Thai
POH-PLA-LAI   1971, Thai
THE LOVE   Cherdchai Productions, 1973, Thai
POH-KAI-CHAE   Cherdchai Productions, 1976, Thai

THE SCAR   Cherdchai Productions, 1979, Thai
THE BLOOD OF SUPAN   Cherdchai Productions, 1980, Thai
POH-PLA-LAI   Cherdchai Productions, 1981, Thai
PUEN PAENG   Cherdchai Productions, 1983, Thai
TAWIPOP   Cherdchai Productions, 1990, Thai
THE TREE OF LIFE   Cherdchai Productions, 1993, Thai
SOUTHERN WINDS   co-director with Shoji Kogami,
   Slamet Rahardjo Djarot & Mike De Leon, NHK Enterprises,
   1993, Japanese-Indonesian-Filipino-Thai
MUEN AND RID   Five Stars Production Company/Cherdchai
   Productions, 1994, Thai

BARRY SONNENFELD*

b. 1953 - New York, New York
Agent: UTA - Beverly Hills, 310/273-6700

THE ADDAMS FAMILY   Paramount, 1991
FOR LOVE OR MONEY   Universal, 1993
ADDAMS FAMILY VALUES   Paramount, 1993
GET SHORTY   MGM-UA, 1995

SUSAN SONTAG

DUET FOR CANNIBALS   Grove Press, 1969, Swedish
BROTHER CARL   New Yorker, 1972, Swedish
PROMISED LANDS (FD)   New Yorker, 1974, French

ALBERTO SORDI

b. June 15, 1920 - Rome, Italy
Home: via Druso 45, Rome, Italy, tel.: 06/484896

FUMO DI LONDRA   Fono Roma, 1966, Italian
SCUSI, LEI E' FAVOREVOLE O CONTRARIO?   Fono Roma,
   1966, Italian
UN ITALIANO IN AMERICA   Euro International Film, 1967, Italian
AMORE MIO AIUTAMI   Documento Film, 1969, Italian
LE COPPIE   co-director, Documento Film, 1970, Italian
POLVERE DI STELLE   Capitolina Produzioni Cinematografiche,
   1973, Italian
FINCHE' C'E' GUERRA C'E' SPERANZA   Rizzoli Film,
   1974, Italian
IL COMUNE SENSO DEL PUDORE   Rizzoli Film, 1976, Italian
DOVE VAI IN VACANZA?   co-director, Rizzoli Film, 1978, Italian
IO E CATERINA   Italian International Films/Cathago Film,
   1980, Italian-French
IO SO CHE TU SAI CHE IO SO   Scena Film, 1982, Italian
IN VIAGGIO CON PAPA'   Scena Film, 1982, Italian
STORIA DI UN ITALIANO (MS)   RAI, 1982, Italian
IL TASSINARO   Italian International Films, 1982, Italian
TUTTI DENTRO   Scena Film, 1984, Italian
UN TASSINARO A NEW YORK   Italian International Films,
   1987, Italian
MISTERIOSA GILDA   Mito Film, 1991, Italian
ASSOLTO PER AVER COMMESSO IL FATTO   Filmauro
   Distribuzione, 1992, Italian
NESTORE - L'ULTIMA CORSA   Aurelia Cinematografica/Silvio
   Berlusconi Communications/Florida Movies,
   1994, Italian-French

DROR SOREF

Agent: Premiere Artists Agency - Los Angeles, 310/271-1414

THE SEVENTH COIN   Hemdale, 1993, U.S.-Israeli

CARLOS SORIN

b. October 21, 1944 - Buenos Aires, Argentina
Contact: Instituto Nacional de Cinematografia, Lima 319, 1073
   Buenos Aires, Argentina, tel.: 37-9091

LA PELICULA DEL REY   1985, Argentine
EVERSMILE, NEW JERSEY   J&M Entertainment,
   1989, Argentine-British

DIMITRI SOTIRAKIS*
(Jim Sotos)
b. September 17, 1935 - New York, New York
Business: DK Productions, Inc., 3135 Industrial - Suite 219,
  Las Vegas, NV 89109, 702/735-6600

THE LAST VICTIM   Howard Mahler Films, 1975
FORCED ENTRY   Century International, 1980
SWEET SIXTEEN   Century International, 1981
HOT MOVES   Cardinal Releasing, 1984
BEVERLY HILLS BRATS   Taurus Entertainment, 1989

LUIS SOTO*
Business: Cool Moss, Inc., 7559 Kimdale Lane, Los Angeles,
  CA 90046, 213/969-9905
Agent: The Agency - Los Angeles, 310/551-3000

THE HOUSE OF RAMON IGLESIA (TF)   LFS Productions, 1986
VIETNAM WAR STORY: THE LAST DAYS (CTF)   co-director with
  David Burton Morris & Sandy Smolan, HBO, 1989

JIM SOTOS
(See Dimitri SOTIRAKIS)

THIERNO FATY SOW
b. 1941 - Thies, Senegal
Contact: SIDEC, 12 rue Berenger Ferraud, B P 335, Dakar,
  Senegal, tel.: 21-45-76

L'OPTION   1974, Senegalese
L'OEIL   1979, Senegalese
CAMP DE THIAROYE   co-director with Ousmane Sembene,
  New Yorker, 1988, Senegalese-Algerian-Tunisian-Italian

KEVEN SPACEY
ALBINO ALLIGATOR   Motion Picture Corp. of America, 1996

LARRY G. SPANGLER
THE SOUL OF NIGGER CHARLEY   Paramount, 1973
A KNIFE FOR THE LADIES   Bryanston, 1974
THE LIFE AND TIMES OF XAVIERA HOLLANDER   Mature, 1974
JOSHUA   Lone Star, 1976
SILENT SENTENCE   Intercontinental, 1983

TERESA SPARKS
b. June 27, 1952 - Kentucky
Agent: J. Michael Bloom, Ltd. - Los Angeles, 310/275-6800

OVER THE SUMMER   Shine Productions, 1984

AARON SPEISER
TALKING ABOUT SEX   Pegasus Productions, 1994

MICHAEL SPENCE
EDGE OF HONOR   Wind River, 1991

RICHARD SPENCE*
Agent: Peters Fraser & Dunlop - London, tel.: 171/344-1000

NIGHT VOICE (TF)   1990, British
THACKER (TF)   1991, British
YOU, ME & MARLEY (TF)   BBC North, 1992, British-Northern Irish
SKALLAGRIGG (TF)   BBC, 1994, British
BLIND JUSTICE (CTF)   Heyman-Moritz Productions/
  HBO Pictures, 1994

ALAN SPENCER*
Business: Alan Spencer Film Company, 3/4 Bywell Place,
  Wells Street, London W1, England, tel.: 171/637-7503
Agent: UTA - Beverly Hills, 310/273-6700
Personal Manager: 3 Arts Entertainment - Beverly Hills,
  310/888-3200

HEXED   Columbia, 1992

BRENTON SPENCER
Contact: Directors Guild of Canada, 225 Richmond Street, Toronto,
  Ontario M5V 1W2, Canada, 416/351-8200

BLOWN AWAY   Norstar Entertainment, 1992, Canadian
THE CLUB   Norstar Entertainment, 1993, Canadian

JANE SPENCER
LITTLE NOISES   Monument Pictures, 1991

PENELOPE SPHEERIS*
b. 1945 - New Orleans, Louisiana
Agent: David Gersh, The Gersh Agency - Beverly Hills, 310/274-6611

THE DECLINE OF WESTERN CIVILIZATION (FD)
  Spheeris Films Inc., 1981
SUBURBIA   *THE WILD SIDE*   New World, 1984
THE BOYS NEXT DOOR   New World, 1985
HOLLYWOOD VICE SQUAD   Concorde/Cinema Group, 1986
DUDES   Cineworld, 1987
THE DECLINE OF WESTERN CIVILIZATION II: THE METAL
  YEARS (FCD)   New Line Cinema, 1988
WAYNE'S WORLD   Paramount, 1992
THE BEVERLY HILLBILLIES   20th Century Fox, 1993
THE LITTLE RASCALS   Universal, 1994

BRYAN SPICER*
Personal Manager: Robert Stein Management - Los Angeles,
  310/207-5705

THE ADVENTURES OF BRISCO COUNTY, JR. (TF)
  Boam-Cuse Productions/Warner Bros. TV, 1993
SEAQUEST DSV: SECOND SEASON PREMIERE (TF)
  Amblin TV/Universal TV, 1994
MIGHTY MORPHIN POWER RANGERS - THE MOVIE
  20th Century Fox, 1995

SCOTT SPIEGEL
Agent: APA - Los Angeles, 310/273-0744

INTRUDER   Phantom Productions, 1989

STEVEN SPIELBERG*
b. December 18, 1947 - Cincinnati, Ohio
Business: Amblin Entertainment, 100 Universal City Plaza -
  Bungalow 477, Universal City, CA 91608, 818/777-4600
Agent: CAA - Beverly Hills, 310/288-4545

NIGHT GALLERY (TF)   co-director with Boris Sagal & Barry Shear,
  Universal TV, 1969
DUEL (TF)   Universal TV, 1971
SOMETHING EVIL (TF)   Belford Productions/CBS
  International, 1972
SAVAGE (TF)   Universal TV, 1973
THE SUGARLAND EXPRESS   Universal, 1974
JAWS   Universal, 1975
CLOSE ENCOUNTERS OF THE THIRD KIND ★   Columbia, 1977
1941   Universal/Columbia, 1979
RAIDERS OF THE LOST ARK ★   Paramount, 1981
E.T. THE EXTRA-TERRESTRIAL ★   Universal, 1982
TWILIGHT ZONE - THE MOVIE   co-director with John Landis,
  Joe Dante & George Miller, Warner Bros., 1983
INDIANA JONES AND THE TEMPLE OF DOOM   Paramount, 1984
THE COLOR PURPLE   Warner Bros., 1985
EMPIRE OF THE SUN   Warner Bros., 1987
INDIANA JONES AND THE LAST CRUSADE   Paramount, 1989
ALWAYS   Universal, 1989
HOOK   TriStar, 1991
JURASSIC PARK   Universal, 1993
SCHINDLER'S LIST ★★   Universal, 1993

TONY SPIRADAKIS
Agent: UTA - Beverly Hills, 310/273-6700

THE LAST WORD   Nu Image, 1995

ROGER SPOTTISWOODE*
b. England
Agent: William Morris Agency - Beverly Hills, 310/859-4000

TERROR TRAIN 20th Century-Fox, 1980, Canadian
THE PURSUIT OF D.B. COOPER Universal, 1982
THE RENEGADES (TF) Lawrence Gordon Productions/
   Paramount TV, 1982
UNDER FIRE Orion, 1983
THE BEST OF TIMES Universal, 1986
THE LAST INNOCENT MAN (CTF) HBO Pictures/Maurice Singer
   Productions, 1987
SHOOT TO KILL Buena Vista, 1988
THIRD DEGREE BURN (CTF) HBO Pictures/MTM Entertainment/
   Paramount TV, 1989
TIME FLIES WHEN YOU'RE ALIVE (CTF) HBO Showcase/Kings
   Road Entertainment, 1989
TURNER & HOOCH Buena Vista, 1989
AIR AMERICA TriStar, 1990
STOP! OR MY MOM WILL SHOOT Universal, 1992
AND THE BAND PLAYED ON (CTF) ☆ HBO Pictures/Spelling
   Entertainment, 1993
MESMER Levergreen Ltd./Accent Entertainment/Defa/Studio
   Babelsberg, 1994, Canadian-British-German

G. D. SPRADLIN
Contact: Screen Actors Guild - Los Angeles, 213/954-1600

THE ONLY WAY HOME Regional, 1972

TIM SPRING
Business: SCY Productions, Hiross House, 7 Geneva Road,
   Blairgowrie 2194, P.O. Box 2980, Randburg 2125, South Africa,
   tel.: 27-11/789-1353

DOUBLE BLAST Davian Productions, 1993
NO HERO SCY Productions, 1993, South African
RAW TARGET The Michael Company, 1994

ROBIN SPRY*
b. October 25, 1939 - Toronto, Canada
Address: 3340 Glencoe, Montreal, Quebec H3R 2C6, Canada,
   514/738-2525
Business: Telescene Film Group Inc., 5510 Ferrier Street,
   Montreal, Quebec H4P 1M2, Canada, 514/737-5512

FLOWERS ON A ONE WAY STREET (FD) 1968, Canadian
PROLOGUE Vaudeo, 1969, Canadian
ACTION: THE OCTOBER CRISIS OF 1970 (FD) National Film
   Board of Canada, 1974
ONE MAN National Film Board of Canada, 1977, Canadian
DRYING UP THE STREETS CBC, 1978, Canadian
DON'T FORGET - JE ME SOUVIENS (TF) CBC, 1979, Canadian
HIT AND RUN Agora Productions, 1981, Canadian
SUZANNE 20th Century-Fox, 1982, Canadian
KEEPING TRACK Shapiro Entertainment, 1987, Canadian
OBSESSED *HITTING HOME* New Star Entertainment,
   1988, Canadian
A CRY IN THE NIGHT Telescene Film Group, 1993, Canadian

CHRISTOPHER ST. JOHN
TOP OF THE HEAP Fanfare, 1972

STEVE STAFFORD*
(Steven Thomas Stafford)
Contact: Directors Guild of America - Los Angeles, 213/851-3671

THE COLOR OF EVENING Christrara Pictures, 1991
POSING: INSPIRED BY THREE REAL STORIES (TF)
   Alta Loma Productions/Republic Pictures, 1991
DOUBLE EDGE (TF) Konigsberg-Sanitsky Company, 1992
BIONIC EVER AFTER (TF) Michael Sloan Productions/Gallant
   Entertainment/MTE, 1994

ERIC STEVEN STAHL
Agent: Circle Talent Associates - Beverly Hills, 310/285-1585

FINAL APPROACH Trimark Pictures, 1991

SYLVESTER STALLONE*
b. July 6, 1946 - New York, New York
Agent: CAA - Beverly Hills, 310/288-4545

PARADISE ALLEY Universal, 1978
ROCKY II United Artists, 1979
ROCKY III MGM/UA, 1982
STAYING ALIVE Paramount, 1983
ROCKY IV MGM/UA, 1985

TERENCE STAMP
b. July 23, 1939 - Stepney, East London, England
Contact: Screen Actors Guild - Los Angeles, 213/954-1600

STRANGER IN THE HOUSE Multifilm Productions, 1991

JEREMY STANFORD
Contact: Concorde Pictures, 11600 San Vicente Blvd.,
   Los Angeles, CA 90049, 310/826-0978

STEPMONSTER Concorde, 1993
WATCHERS III Concorde, 1994

PAUL STANLEY*
Business: Worldstar International Corporation, Airport Station -
   Box 460-304, San Antonio, TX 78246, 512/222-2880

CRY TOUGH United Artists, 1959
THREE GUNS FOR TEXAS co-director with David Lowell Rich &
   Earl Bellamy, Universal, 1968
SOLE SURVIVOR (TF) Cinema Center, 1969
RIVER OF MYSTERY (TF) Universal TV, 1971
NICKY'S WORLD (TF) Tomorrow Entertainment, 1974
CRISIS IN SUN VALLEY (TF) Columbia TV, 1978
THE ULTIMATE IMPOSTER (TF) Universal TV, 1979

RICHARD STANLEY
b. South Africa
Agent: CAA - Beverly Hills, 310/288-4545

HARDWARE Miramax Films, 1990, British-U.S.
DUST DEVIL Miramax Films, 1992, British

JEFF STANZLER
Agent: UTA - Beverly Hills, 310/273-6700

JUMPIN AT THE BONEYARD 20th Century Fox, 1991

RINGO STARR
(Richard Starkey)
b. July 7, 1940 - Liverpool, England
Contact: British Film Commission, 70 Baker Street, London
   W1M 1DJ, England, tel.: 171/224-5000

BORN TO BOOGIE (FCD) MGM-EMI, 1972, British

STEVEN STARR
Agent: William Morris Agency - Beverly Hills, 310/859-4000

JOEY BREAKER Skouras Pictures, 1993

RAY DENNIS STECKLER
DRIVERS IN HELL *WILD ONES ON WHEELS* 1961
WILD GUITAR Fairway International, 1962
THE INCREDIBLY STRANGE CREATURES WHO STOPPED
   LIVING AND BECAME MIXED-UP ZOMBIES
   Fairway International, 1962
THE THRILL KILLERS 1964
RAT PFINK A-BOO-BOO 1964

SCREAM OF THE BUTTERFLY   1965
LEMON GROVE KIDS MEET THE MONSTERS   1966
SINTHIA, THE DEVIL'S DOLL   1968
SUPER COOL   *BODY FEVER/THE LAST ORIGINAL
B-MOVIE*   1969
THE CHOOPER   *BLOOD SHACK*   1971
BLOODY JACK THE RIPPER   1972, unreleased
THE HOLLYWOOD STRANGLER MEETS THE SKID ROW
SLASHER   1979

JEFF STEIN
Address: 680 So. Avenue 21, Los Angeles, CA 90031,
213/221-2003

THE KIDS ARE ALRIGHT (FCD)   New World, 1979, British

KEN STEIN
PRIMARY TARGET   Concorde, 1990
RAIN OF DEATH   Concorde, 1990
MAD DOG COLL   co-director with Greydon Clark, 21st Century
Distribution, 1992, U.S.-Russian

DAVID STEINBERG*
b. August 9, 1942 - Winnipeg, Canada
Business: c/o Highlight Commercials, 1049 N. Las Palmas,
Los Angeles, CA 90038, 213/871-8488
Agent: CAA - Beverly Hills, 310/288-4545

PATERNITY   Paramount, 1981
GOING BERSERK   Universal, 1983, Canadian

MICHAEL STEINBERG
Agent: UTA - Beverly Hills, 310/273-6700

THE WATERDANCE   co-director with Neal Jimenez,
The Samuel Goldwyn Company, 1992
BODIES, REST & MOTION   Fine Line Features/New Line
Cinema, 1993

SUSAN STEINBERG*
Home: 101 Central Park West, New York, NY 10023,
212/787-4836

PAUL SIMON: BORN AT THE RIGHT TIME (TD)   WNET-13, 1993
THE HISTORY OF ROCK 'N' ROLL (TD)   co-director,
Andrew Solt Productions/QDE/Telepictures Productions/
Time-Life Video & Television/Warner Bros. TV Distribution
Prime Time Entertainment Network, 1995

ZIGGY STEINBERG
Attorney: Ted Steinberg, Esq. - Los Angeles, 213/553-4070

THE BOSS'S WIFE   TriStar, 1987

DANIEL STEINMANN
SAVAGE STREETS   Entermark Corporation, 1985
FRIDAY THE 13TH PART V - A NEW BEGINNING
Paramount, 1985
SUBTERRANEANS   Empire Pictures, 1988

MARTIN STELLMAN
Agent: ICM - London, tel.: 171/636-6565

FOR QUEEN AND COUNTRY   Zenith Productions, 1968, British
HARRY (MS)   co-director with Mary McMurray & Robert Walker,
Union Pictures/BBC, 1993, British

DANIEL STERN*
b. August 28, 1957 - Bethesda, Maryland
Agent: CAA - Beverly Hills, 310/288-4545

ROOKIE OF THE YEAR   20th Century Fox, 1993

LEONARD B. STERN*
b. December 23, 1923 - New York, New York
Business: 11150 Olympic Blvd. - Sujite 650, Los Angeles, CA 90064,
310/657-6100 ext. 133
Agent: Sy Fischer, The Sy Fischer Company - Los Angeles,
310/470-0917

ONCE UPON A DEAD MAN (TF)   Universal TV, 1971
THE SNOOP SISTERS (TF)   Universal TV, 1972
JUST YOU AND ME, KID   Columbia, 1979
MISSING PIECES   Orion, 1992

NOAH STERN
Agent: William Morris Agency - Beverly Hills, 310/859-4000

PYRATES   Seven Arts/New Line Cinema, 1991

SANDOR STERN*
b. July 13, 1936 - Timmins, Ontario, Canada
Address: 521 N. Camden Drive, Beverly Hills, CA 90210,
310/275-0180
Agent: Elliot Webb, Broder-Kurland-Webb-Uffner Agency -
Beverly Hills, 310/281-3400

THE SEEDING OF SARAH BURNS (TF)   Michael Klein
Productions, 1979
MUGGABLE MARY: STREET COP (TF)   CBS Entertainment, 1982
MEMORIES NEVER DIE (TF)   Groverton Productions/Scholastic
Productions/Universal TV, 1982
PASSIONS (TF)   Carson Production Group/Wizan TV
Enterprises, 1984
JOHN & YOKO - A LOVE STORY (TF)   Carson Production
Group, 1985
ASSASSIN (TF)   Sankan Productions, 1986
EASY PREY (TF)   New World TV/Rene Malo Productions,
1987, U.S.-Canadian
PROBE (TF)   MCA Television, Ltd., 1988
SHATTERED INNOCENCE (TF)   Green-Epstein Productions/
Lorimar TV, 1988
GLITZ (TF)   Robert Cooper Films, 1988
PIN   New World, 1989, Canadian
WITHOUT HER CONSENT (TF)   Raymond Katz Enterprises/Half
Pint Productions/Carla Singer Productions, 1990
AMITYVILLE: THE EVIL ESCAPES (TF)   Steve White Productions/
Spectator Films, 1990
WEB OF DECEIT (CTF)   SanKan Productions/Wilshire Court
Productions, 1990
DECEPTION: A MOTHER'S SECRET (TF)   SanKan
Productions, 1991
DUPLICATES (CTF)   Sankan Productions/Wilshire Court
Productions, 1992
WOMAN ON THE RUN: THE LAWRENCIA BEMBENEK STORY (TF)
Alliance Communications Corporation/CanWest Global TV
Network/NBC Productions, 1993, U.S.-Canadian
JERICHO FEVER (CTF)   Sankan Productions/Wilshire Court
Productions, 1993
HEART OF A CHILD (TF)   O'Hara-Horowitz Productions, 1994
A CHILD'S CRY FOR HELP (TF)   Longbow Productions/RHI
Entertainment/Ronald J. Kahn Productions, 1994

STEVEN HILLIARD STERN*
b. November 1, 1937 - Timmins, Ontario, Canada
Home: 4321 Clear Valley Drive, Encino, CA 91436, 818/788-3607
Agent: The Brandt Company - Sherman Oaks, 818/783-7747

B.S. I LOVE YOU   20th Century-Fox, 1971
NEITHER BY DAY NOR BY NIGHT   Motion Pictures International,
1972, U.S.-Israeli
THE HARRAD SUMMER   Cinerama Releasing Corporation, 1974
ESCAPE FROM BOGEN COUNTY (TF)   Paramount TV, 1977
THE GHOST OF FLIGHT 401 (TF)   Paramount TV, 1978
DOCTORS' PRIVATE LIVES (TF)   David Gerber Company/
Columbia TV, 1978
GETTING MARRIED (TF)   Paramount TV, 1978
FAST FRIENDS (TF)   Columbia TV, 1979
ANATOMY OF A SEDUCTION (TF)   Moonlight Productions/
Filmways, 1979

YOUNG LOVE, FIRST LOVE (TF)   Lorimar Productions, 1979
RUNNING   Columbia, 1979, Canadian-U.S.
PORTRAIT OF AN ESCORT (TF)   Moonlight Productions/
   Filmways, 1980
THE DEVIL AND MAX DEVLIN   Buena Vista, 1981
MIRACLE ON ICE (TF)   Moonlight Productions/Filmways, 1981
A SMALL KILLING (TF)   Orgolini-Nelson Productions/Motown
   Productions, 1982
THE AMBUSH MURDERS (TF)   David Goldsmith Productions/
   Charles Fries Productions, 1982
PORTRAIT OF A SHOWGIRL (TF)   Hamner Productions, 1982
NOT JUST ANOTHER AFFAIR (TF)   Ten-Four Productions, 1982
FORBIDDEN LOVE (TF)   Gross-Weston Productions, 1982
RONA JAFFE'S MAZES AND MONSTERS   McDermott
   Productions/Procter & Gamble Productions, 1982
BABY SISTER (TF)   Moonlight Productions II, 1983
STILL THE BEAVER (TF)   Bud Austin Productions/
   Universal TV, 1983
AN UNCOMMON LOVE (TF)   Beechwood Productions/Lorimar
   Productions, 1983
GETTING PHYSICAL (TF)   CBS Entertainment, 1984
DRAW! (CTF)   HBO Premiere Films/Astral Film Productions/Bryna
   Company, 1984, U.S.-Canadian
OBSESSIVE LOVE (TF)   Onza Inc./Moonlight Productions, 1984
THE PARK IS MINE (CTF)   HBO Premiere Films/Astral Film
   Productions/ICC, 1985, U.S.-Canadian
MURDER IN SPACE (CTF)   Robert Cooper Productions/Zenith
   Productions/CTV Network, 1985, Canadian-British
THE UNDERGRADS (CTF)   Sharmhill Productions/The Disney
   Channel, 1985, U.S.-Canadian
HOSTAGE FLIGHT (TF)   Frank von Zerneck Films, 1985
YOUNG AGAIN (TF)   Sharmhill Productions/Walt Disney
   Productions, 1986, U.S.-Canadian
MANY HAPPY RETURNS (TF)   Alan M. Levin & Steven H. Stern
   Films, 1986, U.S.-Canadian
ROLLING VENGEANCE   Apollo Pictures, 1987, U.S.-Canadian
NOT QUITE HUMAN (TF)   Sharmhill Productions/Walt
   Disney TV, 1987
WEEKEND WAR (TF)   Pompian-Atamvan Productions/
   Columbia TV, 1988
CROSSING THE MOB (TF)   Bateman Company Productions/
   Interscope Communications, 1988
LOVE AND MURDER   Southpaw Releasing, 1990, Canadian
PERSONALS (CTF)   Sharmhill Productions/Wilshire Court
   Productions, 1990, Canadian-U.S.
MONEY   Andre Djaoui Productions/Cinemax/Telemax/Antenne-2/
   Films A2/Pat Inc./Malofilm Production/Canal/Coficine Credit
   Lyonnais Rotterdam/Centre National de la Cinematographie,
   1991, French-Canadian-Italian-Dutch
THE WOMEN OF WINDSOR (TF)   Sharmhill Productions/Samuels
   Film Company/World International Network, 1992
MORNING GLORY   Academy Entertainment, 1993, Canadian
TO SAVE THE CHILDREN (TF)   Children's Films/Westcom
   Entertainment Group/Kushner-Locke Productions, 1994

TOM STERN
Agent: ICM - Beverly Hills, 310/550-4000

FREAKED   co-director with Alex Winter, 20th Century Fox, 1993

JEAN-FRANÇOIS STEVENIN
b. 1943 - France
Address: 31, avenue de la Republique, 75011 Paris, France,
   tel.: 1/48-06-86-01
Contact: French Film Office, 745 Fifth Avenue, New York,
   NY 10151, 212/832-8860

PASSE MONTAGNE   1979, French
DOUBLE MESSIEURS   Sagamore Cinema/Mallia Films/FR3,
   1986, French

ANDREW STEVENS*
b. June 10, 1955 - Memphis, Tennessee
Business: Sunset Films International, 8285 Sunset Blvd. - Suite 2,
   Los Angeles, CA 90046, 213/848-7031

THE TERROR WITHIN II   Concorde, 1992
NIGHT EYES III: ON GUARD   Prism Pictures, 1993

A HARD BARGAIN   Prism/Moonstone Entertainment, 1994
ILLICIT DREAMS   Nu Image, 1994
THE SKATEBOARD KID II   Sunset Films International, 1994

ART STEVENS
THE FOX AND THE HOUND (AF)   co-director with Ted Berman &
   Richard Rich, Buena Vista, 1981

DAVID STEVENS
Contact: Writers Guild of America, West - Los Angeles, 310/550-1000
Agent: Renaissance-H.N. Swanson - Los Angeles, 310/246-6000

NUMBER 96 (MS)   1974, Australian
THE SULLIVANS (MS)   co-director with Simon Wincer,
   1976, Australian
THE JOHN SULLIVAN STORY (TF)   Crawford Productions/Nine
   Network/Australian Film Commission, 1979, Australian
A TOWN LIKE ALICE (MS)   Seven Network/Victorian Film
   Corporation, 1981, Australian
THE CLINIC   Film House/Generation Films, 1982, Australian
UNDERCOVER   Filmco, 1983, Australian
WOMEN OF THE SUN (MS)   co-director with Stephen Wallace,
   James Ricketson & Geoffrey Nottage, Generation Films,
   1983, Australian
A THOUSAND SKIES (MS)   Dimsey Ginn Ltd., 1985, Australian
ALWAYS AFTERNOON (MS)   The Special Broadcasting
   Service/Norddeutsche Rundfunk/Multimedia/Primetime TV,
   1987, Australian-West German- British
KANSAS   Trans World Entertainment, 1988

GEORGE STEVENS, JR.*
b. April 3, 1932 - Los Angeles, California
Business: The Kennedy Center - 3rd Floor, Washington, D.C. 20566,
   202/416-7960

AMERICA AT THE MOVIES (FD)   American Film Institute, 1976
GEORGE STEVENS: A FILMMAKER'S JOURNEY (FD)
   Castle Hill Productions, 1984
SEPARATE BUT EQUAL (TF)   New Lib erty Productions/Republic
   Pictures, 1991

LESLIE STEVENS*
b. February 3, 1924 - Washington, D.C.
Agent: CAA - Beverly Hills, 310/288-4545

PRIVATE PROPERTY   Citation, 1960
INCUBUS   1961
HERO'S ISLAND   United Artists, 1962
DELLA   Four Star, 1964
FANFARE FOR A DEATH SCENE   Four Star, 1967
I LOVE A MYSTERY (TF)   Universal TV, 1973
THREE KINDS OF HEAT   Cannon, 1987

STELLA STEVENS
(Estelle Egglestone)
b. October 1, 1938 - Yazoo City, Mississippi
Contact: Screen Actors Guild - Los Angeles, 213/954-1600

THE RANCH   Sky Nest Productions, 1989, Canadian

RICK STEVENSON
Agent: William Morris Agency - Beverly Hills, 310/859-4000

MAGIC IN THE WATER   TriStar/Triumph Films,
   1995, U.S.-Canadian

ALAN STEWART
GHETTO BLASTERS   CHVP Inc., 1989

DOUGLAS DAY STEWART*
Home: 6384 Rodgerton Drive, Los Angeles, CA 90068, 213/465-1965
Agent: William Morris Agency - Beverly Hills, 310/859-4000

THIEF OF HEARTS   Paramount, 1984
LISTEN TO ME   WEG/Columbia, 1989

JOHN STEWART
CLICK: THE CALENDAR GIRL KILLER   co-director with
   Ross Hagen, Crown International, 1989
CARTEL   Cobra Entertainment Group, 1989
THUNDER AND LIGHTNING   Red Rock Productions, 1990
HIDDEN OBSESSION   Broadstar Entertainment Corporation, 1992

LARRY STEWART*
Agent: Arthur Kennard Associates, 6894 Parsons Trail, Tujunga,
   CA 91042, 818/352-0001

THE INITIATION   New World, 1984

BEN STILLER*
Agent: CAA - Beverly Hills, 310/288-4545

REALITY BITES   Universal, 1994

WHIT STILLMAN
Agent: William Morris Agency - Beverly Hills, 310/859-4000

METROPOLITAN   New Line Cinema, 1990
BARCELONA   New Line Cinema, 1994

JOHN STIX
b. November 14, 1920 - St. Louis, Missouri

THE GREAT ST. LOUIS BANK ROBBERY   co-director with
   Charles Guggenheim, United Artists, 1959
FAMILY BUSINESS (TF)   Screenscope Inc./South Carolina
   Educational TV Network, 1983

JOHN STOCKWELL*
Agent: UTA - Beverly Hills, 310/273-6700

UNDER COVER   Cannon, 1987
JUPITER BROWN   Jupiter Productions, 1995

JERRY STOEFFHAAS
Telephone: 716/244-6041

CHEAP SHOTS   co-director with Jeff Ureles, Hemdale, 1988

BRYAN MICHAEL STOLLER
Business: B.M. Stoller Film Fun Ltd., 11850 Riverside Drive -
   Suite 118, Valley Village, CA 91607
Agent: Cindy Turtle/Beth Bohn, The Turtle Agency - Studio City,
   CA 91604, 818/506-6898

APPLE & EVE   Garden of Eden Productions, 1993
THE RANDOM FACTOR   B.M. Stoller Film Fun Ltd., 1993
TURN OF THE BLADE   Showcase Entertainment, 1994

ANDREW L. STONE*
b. July 16, 1902 - Oakland, California
Home: 10478 Wyton Drive, Los Angeles, CA 90024, 310/279-2427

SOMBRAS DE GLORIA   Sono Arts, 1930
HELL'S HEADQUARTERS   Capitol, 1932
THE GIRL SAID NO   Grand National, 1937
STOLEN HEAVEN   Paramount, 1938
SAY IT IN FRENCH   Paramount, 1938
THE GREAT VICTOR HERBERT   Paramount, 1939
THERE'S MAGIC IN MUSIC   Paramount, 1941
STORMY WEATHER   20th Century-Fox, 1943
HI DIDDLE DIDDLE   RKO Radio, 1943
SENSATIONS OF 1945   United Artists, 1944
BEDSIDE MANNER   United Artists, 1945
THE BACHELOR'S DAUGHTER   United Artists, 1946
FUN ON A WEEKEND   United Artists, 1947
HIGHWAY 301   Warner Bros., 1950
CONFIDENCE GIRL   United Artists, 1951
THE STEEL TRAP   20th Century-Fox, 1952
A BLUEPRINT FOR MURDER   20th Century-Fox, 1953
THE NIGHT HOLDS TERROR   Columbia, 1955

JULIE   MGM, 1956
CRY TERRORI   MGM, 1958
THE DECKS RAN RED   MGM, 1958
THE LAST VOYAGE   MGM, 1960
RING OF FIRE   MGM, 1961
THE PASSWORD IS COURAGE   MGM, 1963, British
NEVER PUT IT IN WRITING   Allied Artists, 1964, British
THE SECRET OF MY SUCCESS   MGM, 1965, British
SONG OF NORWAY   Cinerama Releasing Corporation, 1970
THE GREAT WALTZ   MGM, 1972

NORMAN STONE
Contact: British Film Commission, 70 Baker Street, London
   W1M 1DJ, England, tel.: 171/224-5000

SHADOWLANDS (TF)   BBC Wales/Gateway Films/The Episcopal
   Radio-TV Foundation/Lella Productions/E.O. TV, 1985,
   British-Welsh
CROSSING TO FREEDOM (TF)   Procter & Gamble Productions/
   Stan Margulies Productions/Granada TV, 1990, U.S.-British
THE BLACK VELVET GOWN (TF)   World Wide International TV
   Productions/Tyne Tees TV/Portman Entertainment, 1991, British

OLIVER STONE*
b. September 15, 1946 - New York, New York
Business: Ixtlan, 201 Santa Monica Blvd. - Suite 610, Santa Monica,
   CA 90401, 310/395-0525
Agent: CAA - Beverly Hills, 310/288-4545

SEIZURE   Cinerama Releasing Corporation, 1974, Canadian
THE HAND   Orion/Warner Bros., 1981
SALVADOR   Hemdale, 1986
PLATOON ★★   Orion, 1986
WALL STREET   20th Century Fox, 1987
TALK RADIO   Universal, 1988
BORN ON THE FOURTH OF JULY ★★   Universal, 1989
THE DOORS   TriStar, 1991
JFK ★   Warner Bros., 1991
HEAVEN AND EARTH   Warner Bros., 1993
NATURAL BORN KILLERS   Warner Bros., 1994
NIXON   Buena Vista, 1995

TAD STONES
Business: Walt Disney Animation, 500 S. Buena Vista Street,
   Burbank, CA 91521, 818/560-1000

THE RETURN OF JAFAR (AHVF)   co-director with Toby Shelton &
   Alan Zaslove, Walt Disney Television Animation, 1994

TOM STOPPARD
(Tomas Straussler)
b. July 3, 1937 - Zlin, Czechoslovakia
Agent: Peters Fraser & Dunlop - London, tel.: 171/344-1000

ROSENCRANTZ AND GUILDENSTERN ARE DEAD
   Cinecom, 1990

ESBEN STORM
b. Denmark
Business: MoirStorm Productions, 72 Queen Street, Woollahra,
   NSW 2025, Australia, tel.: 2/362-3923

27A   1974, Australian
IN SEARCH OF ANNA   1979, Australian
WITH PREJUDICE   1983, Australian
STANLEY   1984, Australian
DEVIL'S HILL   1988, Australian
DEADLY   Hoyts, 1991, Australian

HOWARD STORM*
b. New York, New York
Agent: The Artists Agency - Los Angeles, 310/277-7779

ONCE BITTEN   The Samuel Goldwyn Company, 1985

MARK STORY*
Business: Crossroads Films, 136 West 21st Street - 5th Floor,
    New York, NY 10011, 212/647-1300

ODD JOBS   TriStar, 1986

MARK STOUFFER*
Address: 365 Hot Springs Road, Montecito, CA 93108,
    805/969-6482

MAN OUTSIDE   Stouffer Enterprise Film Partners, 1987
NATIONAL GEOGRAPHIC: BRAVING ALASKA (TD)   National
    Geographic/WETA-Washington, D.C., 1992
NATIONAL GEOGRAPHIC: SKELETON COAST AFRICA (TD)
    National Geographic/WETA-Washington, D.C., 1993
NATIONAL GEOGRAPHIC: GIANT PANDAS OF CHINA (TD)
    National Geographic/WETA-Washington, D.C., 1994

JEAN-MARIE STRAUB
b. January 8, 1933 - Metz, Germany
Contact: French Film Office, 745 Fifth Avenue, New York,
    NY 10151, 212/832-8860

NICHT VERSOHNT ODER, ES HILFT NUR GEWALT, WO
    GEWALT HERRSCHT   1965, West German
THE CHRONICLE OF ANNA MAGDALENA BACH   New Yorker,
    1968, West German
OTHON   co-director with Daniele Huillet, 1969, French
GESCHICHTSUNTERRICHT   co-director with Daniele Huillet,
    1972, West German
MOSES AND AARON   co-director with Daniele Huillet,
    New Yorker, 1975, West German
I CANI DEL SINAI   co-director with Daniele Huillet, 1976, Italian
DELLA NUBE ALLA RESISTENZA   co-director with Daniele Huillet,
    1979, Italian
CLASS RELATIONS   KLASSENVERHALF-NISSE   co-director with
    Daniele Huillet, New Yorker, 1984, West German-French
DER TOD DES EMPEDOKLES   co-director with Daniele Huillet,
    Janus Film/Les Films du Losange, 1987, West German-French
ANTIGONE   Antigone Film/Projektdurchfuhrungs, 1991, German

BARBRA STREISAND*
(Barbara Joan Streisand)
b. April 24, 1942 - New York, New York
Business: Barwood Films, 330 West 58th Street - Suite 301,
    New York, NY 10019, 212/765-7191
Agent: CAA - Beverly Hills, 310/288-4545

YENTL   MGM/UA, 1983
THE PRINCE OF TIDES   Columbia, 1991

JOSEPH STRICK
b. July 6, 1923 - Braddock, Pennsylvania
Home: 266 River Road, Grandview, NY 10960, 914/359-9527 or:
    29 rue de Tournon, Paris 75006, France, tel.: 331/4354-2712

THE SAVAGE EYE   co-director with Ben Maddow &
    Sidney Meyers, Trans-Lux, 1959
THE BALCONY   Continental, 1963
THE HECKLERS (TF)   1966, British
ULYSSES   Continental, 1967
TROPIC OF CANCER   Paramount, 1970
ROAD MOVIE   Grove Press, 1974
A PORTRAIT OF THE ARTIST AS A YOUNG MAN
    Howard Mahler Films, 1979
UNDERWORLD   Angelika Films, 1991
CRIMINALS (FD)   Reality Productions, 1995

WESLEY STRICK
Agent: CAA - Beverly Hills, 310/288-4545

THE TIE THAT BINDS   Tied Up Productions, 1995

JOHN STRICKLAND
Agent: ICM - London, tel.: 171/636-6565

THE LAST HAIRCUT (TF)   BBC, 1989, British
JUNE (TF)   BBC, 1990, British
PRIME SUSPECT 2 (MS)   Granada TV/WGBH-Boston,
    1993, British-U.S.
FAITH (TF)   Central TV, 1993, British

HERBERT L. STROCK*
Home: 1630 Hilts Avenue - Suite 205, Los Angeles, CA 90024,
    310/474-7240
Business: Herbert L. Strock Productions, 6311 Romaine Street -
    Suite 7113, Hollywood, CA 90038, 213/461-1298

STORM OVER TIBET   Columbia, 1952
GOG   United Artists, 1954
BATTLE TAXI   United Artists, 1955
I WAS A TEENAGE FRANKENSTEIN   American
    International, 1957
BLOOD OF DRACULA   American International, 1957
THE DEVIL'S MESSENGER   Herts-Lion International,
    1961, U.S.-Swedish
RIDERS ON A DEAD HORSE   Allied Artists, 1962
THE CRAWLING HAND   Medallion, 1963

JOHN STRYSIK
SAM AND SARAH   Full Circle Films, 1991

BRIAN STUART
SORCERESS   New World, 1982

MEL STUART*
b. September 2, 1928
Address: 1551 S. Robertson Blvd., Los Angeles, CA 90035,
    310/785-9080
Agent: Shapiro-Lichtman Talent Agency - Los Angeles,
    310/859-8877

THE MAKING OF THE PRESIDENT (TD)   David Wolper
    roductions, 1960
THE MAKING OF THE PRESIDENT (TD)   David Wolper
    Productions, 1964
FOUR DAYS IN NOVEMBER (FD)   United Artists, 1965
CHINA: ROOTS OF MADNESS (TD)   David Wolper
    Productions, 1967
RISE AND FALL OF THE THIRD REICH (TD)   David Wolper
    Productions, 1968
THE MAKING OF THE PRESIDENT (TD)   David Wolper
    Productions, 1968
IF IT'S TUESDAY, THIS MUST BE BELGIUM
    United Artists, 1969
I LOVE MY WIFE   Universal, 1970
WILLY WONKA AND THE CHOCOLATE FACTORY   Paramount,
    1971, British
ONE IS A LONELY NUMBER   MGM, 1972
WATTSTAX (FCD)   Columbia, 1973
BRENDA STARR (TF)   Wolper Productions, 1976
LIFE GOES TO THE MOVIES (TD)   David Wolper
    Productions, 1976
OSCAR GOES TO WAR (TD)   David Wolper Productions, 1977
MEAN DOG BLUES   American International, 1978
RUBY AND OSWALD (TF)   Alan Landsburg Productions, 1978
THE TRIANGLE FACTORY FIRE SCANDAL (TF)   Alan Landsburg
    Productions/Don Kirshner Productions, 1979
THE CHISHOLMS (MS)   Alan Landsburg Productions, 1979
THE WHITE LIONS   Alan Landsburg Productions, 1979
SOPHIA LOREN: HER OWN STORY (TF)   Roger Gimbel
    Productions/EMI TV, 1980
WITH PETER BEARD IN AFRICA (TD)   co-director with
    Robert H. Nixon, NDEFU Productions, 1988

CHARLES STURRIDGE

b. June 24, 1951 - London, England
Agent: UTA - Beverly Hills, 310/172-6700 or:
   Peters Fraser & Dunlop - London, tel.: 171/344-1000

BRIDESHEAD REVISITED (MS) ☆ co-director with
   Michael Lindsay-Hogg, Granada TV/WNET-13/NDR
   Hamburg, 1982, British-U.S.-West German
SOFT TARGETS (TF) BBC, 1982, British
RUNNERS Goldcrest Films & TV, 1983, British
ARIA co-director, Miramax Films, 1987, British
A HANDFUL OF DUST New Line Cinema, 1988, British
WHERE ANGELS FEAR TO TREAD Fine Line Features/
   New Line Cinema, 1992, British
A FOREIGN FIELD Fingertip Film Productions, 1993, British
GULLIVER'S TRAVELS (TF) RHI Entertainment/Channel 4/Jim
   Henson Productions, 1995, British-U.S.

ELISEO SUBIELA

b. December 27, 1944 - Buenos Aires, Argentina
Agent: ICM - Beverly Hills, 310/550-4000

LA CONQUISTA DEL PARAISO 1981, Argentine
MAN FACING SOUTHEAST FilmDallas, 1987, Argentine
ULTIMAS IMAGENES DEL NAUFRAGIO Films Cinequanon/
   Enrique Marti/Virrey Olaguer 7 Feliu, 1989, Argentine-Spanish
EL LADO OSCURO DEL CORAZON Max Films International/
   Telefilm Canada/L'Instituto Nacional de Cinematografia de la
   Republica Argentina, 1992, Argentine-Canadian

RICHARD RAINER SUDBOROUGH

b. November 28, 1953 - Seattle, Washington
Business: Sudborough Productions, 8548 Minuet Place,
   Panorama City, CA 91402, 818/893-8811

L.A. GUITAR MURDERS Sudborough Productions, 1994

ANDREW SUGERMAN

Business: Greenwich Films, 7655 Sunset Blvd., Los Angeles,
   CA 90046, 213/969-9900

BASIC TRAINING The Movie Store, 1985

DANIELE J. SUISSA

b. 1940 - Casablanca, Morocco
Home: 3 Westmount Square - Apt. 1712, Westmount,
   Quebec H3Z 2S5, Canada, 514/937-7171

KATE MORRIS: VICE-PRESIDENT (TF) 1983, Canadian
DIVINE SARAH (TF) 1983, Canadian
EVANGELINE THE SECOND (TF) 1983, Canadian
THE ROSE CAFE (TF) 1986, Canadian
GARNET PRINCESS (TF) 1986, Canadian
MORNING MAN 1985, Canadian
MARTHA, RUTH & EDIE co-director with Deepa Mehta,
   1988, Canadian
THE SECRET OF NANDY (TF) 1989, Canadian

FRED G. SULLIVAN

COLD RIVER 1978
THE BEER DRINKER'S GUIDE TO FITNESS AND FILMMAKING
   SULLIVAN'S PAVILLION Adirondack Alliance Film
   Corporation, 1987

KEVIN SULLIVAN

b. May 28, 1955 - Toronto, Ontario, Canada
Business: Sullivan Films, 16 Clarence Square, Toronto, Ontario
   M5V 1H1, Canada, 416/597-0029
Agent: William Morris Agency - Beverly Hills, 310/859-4000

KRIEGHOFF (TF) Sullivan Films, Inc., 1981, Canadian
THE WILD PONY (TF) Sullivan Films, Inc., 1982, Canadian
ANNE OF GREEN GABLES (MS) Anne of Green Gables
   Productions/PBS WonderWorks/CBS/60 Film Productions/ZDF/
   City TV/Telefilm Canada, 1985, Canadian-U.S.-West German

ANNE OF AVONLEA: THE CONTINUING STORY OF ANNE OF
   GREEN GABLES (MS) Sullivan Films/CBC/The Disney Channel/
   PBS WonderWorks/Teleflim Canada, 1987, Canadian-U.S.
LOOKING FOR MIRACLES (CTF) Sullivan Films/CBC/The Disney
   Channel/Telefilm Canada, 1989, Canadian-U.S.
LANTERN HILL (TF) Lantern Hill Motion Pictures/The Disney
   Channel/CBC/WonderWorks/Corporation for Public Broadcasting/
   Teleflim Canada, 1991, Canadian-U.S.

TIM SULLIVAN

Agent: UTA - Beverly Hills, 310/273-6700 or:
   Peters Fraser & Dunlop - London, tel.: 171/344-1000

SHERLOCK HOLMES: THE LAST VAMPYRE (TF) Granada TV/
   WGBH-Boston, 1994, British-U.S.
JACK AND SARAH Granada Film, 1994, British

JEREMY SUMMERS

Agent: Michael Ladkin Personal Management - London,
   tel.: 171/402-6644

DEPTH CHARGE British Lion, 1960, British
CROOKS IN CLOISTERS Warner-Pathe, 1964, British
FERRY CROSS THE MERSEY United Artists, 1965, British
SAN FERRY ANN British Lion, 1966, British
DATELINE DIAMONDS Rank, 1966, British
HOUSE OF 1,000 DOLLS American International, 1967, British
FIVE GOLDEN DRAGONS Warner-Pathe, 1968, British
THE VENGEANCE OF FU MANCHU Warner Bros.,
   1968, British
FALLEN HERO (TF) Granada TV, 1979, British
TOURIST (TF) Castle Combe Productions/Paramount TV, 1980
A KIND OF LOVING (TF) Granada TV, 1981, British
THE BILL (TF) Thames TV, 1988, British
HOWARDS WAY (TF) BBC, 1989, British

SHIRLEY SUN

Business: Sun Productions, 110 Greene Street - Suite 12G,
   New York, NY 10012

IRON & SILK Prestige, 1991, U.S.-Chinese

CEDRIC SUNDSTRÖM

Agent: Jerry Davidson, 20th Century Artists Inc. - Sherman Oaks,
   818/788-5516
Address: 5 Stanton Road, Barnes, SW 13, London, England

THE MOUNTAIN (TF) CMS Film Productions, 1984, British
FAIR TRADE The Movie Group, 1988
THE SHADOWED MIND Have Beam X, 1988, British-Austrian
AMERICAN NINJA 3: BLOOD HUNT Cannon, 1989
THE REVENGER American-Independent, 1990
AMERICAN NINJA 4: THE ANNIHILATION Cannon, 1991

STEPHEN SURJIK*

b. 1958
Agent: Scott Yoselow, The Gersh Agency - New York City,
   212/997-1818

WAYNE'S WORLD 2 Paramount, 1993
MARY SILLIMAN'S WAR (CTF) Heritage Films/Citadel Films, 1994

HAL SUTHERLAND

JOURNEY BACK TO OZ (AF) EBA Film Distributors, 1973,
   filmed in 1964
PINOCCHIO AND THE EMPEROR OF THE NIGHT (AF)
   New World, 1987

KIEFER SUTHERLAND

b. December 18, 1966 - London, England
Agent: CAA - Beverly Hills, 310/288-4545

LAST LIGHT (CTF) Stillwater Productions, 1993

SEIJUN SUZUKI

(Seitaro Suzuki)
b. 1923 - Tokyo Prefecture, Japan
Contact: Nihon Eiga Kantoku Kyokai (Japan Film Directors
Association), La Fontenu Building - 4th Floor, 23-2 Maruyama-cho,
Shibuya-ku, Tokyo, Japan, tel.: 3/3461-4411

DEVIL'S TOWN   Nikkatsu, 1956, Japanese
SAIL ROPE SINGING   Nikkatsu, 1956, Japanese
TOAST OF THE SEAPORT   Nikkatsu, 1956, Japanese
DUCKWEED INN   Nikkatsu, 1957, Japanese
FEAR OF EIGHT HOURS   Nikkatsu, 1957, Japanese
NAKED WOMAN AND GUN   Nikkatsu, 1957, Japanese
BLUE BREAST   Nikkatsu, 1958, Japanese
BEAUTIFUL WOMEN IN GANGLAND   Nikkatsu, 1958, Japanese
THE VOICE WITHOUT SHADOW   Nikkatsu, 1958, Japanese
TRIP INTO SPRING   Nikkatsu, 1958, Japanese
PASSPORT OF DARKNESS   Nikkatsu, 1959, Japanese
NAKED AGE   Nikkatsu, 1959, Japanese
LOVE LETTER   Nikkatsu, 1959, Japanese
GODDAMN DELINQUENT ARMY   Nikkatsu, 1960, Japanese
SLEEP OF THE ANIMAL   Nikkatsu, 1960, Japanese
FROM TURNOUT 13   Nikkatsu, 1960, Japanese
EVERYTHING IS CRAZY   Nikkatsu, 1960, Japanese
STOWAWAY ZERO LINE   Nikkatsu, 1960, Japanese
A STREET DYED WITH BLOOD   Nikkatsu, 1961, Japanese
MEN OF THE SHOTGUN   Nikkatsu, 1961, Japanese
TOKYO KNIGHTS   Nikkatsu, 1961, Japanese
YOUNG WIND BLEW BY THE PASS   Nikkatsu, 1961, Japanese
TURN OUT 100 MILLION DOLLARS   Nikkatsu, 1961, Japanese
RECKLESS MASTER   Nikkatsu, 1961, Japanese
THE GUYS WHO BET ON ME   Nikkatsu, 1962, Japanese
HIGH TEEN YAKUZA   Nikkatsu, 1962, Japanese
AKUTARO   Nikkatsu, 1963, Japanese
KANTO WANDERER   Nikkatsu, 1963, Japanese
DETECTIVE BUREAU 23: DOWN WITH THE WICKED
Nikkatsu, 1963, Japanese
YOUTH OF THE WILD BEAST   Nikkatsu, 1963, Japanese
OUR BLOOD IS NEVER FORGIVEN   Nikkatsu, 1964, Japanese
FLOWER AND ANGRY WAVES   Nikkatsu, 1964, Japanese
GATE OF FLESH   Nikkatsu, 1964, Japanese
AKUTARO LEGEND   Nikkatsu, 1965, Japanese
ONE GENERATION OF TATTOOS   Nikkatsu, 1965, Japanese
STORY OF A PROSTITUTE   Nikkatsu, 1965, Japanese
KAWACHI KARUMEN   Nikkatsu, 1966, Japanese
ELEGY TO VIOLENCE   Nikkatsu, 1966, Japanese
TOKYO DRIFTER   Nikkatsu, 1966, Japanese
BRANDED TO KILL   Nikkatsu, 1967, Japanese
STORY OF SADNESS   Shochiku/Sankyo Eiga, 1977, Japanese
ZIGEUNERWEISEN   Cinema Plaset, 1980, Japanese
HEAT SHIMMER THEATRE   *KAGEROZA*   Cinema Plaset,
1981, Japanese
CAPONE CRIES A LOT   Kei Enterprises/System Japan/Nihon
Columbia, 1985, Japanese
YUMEJI   Genjiro Arado Productions, 1991, Japanese
MARRIAGE   Cecille, 1993, Japanese

JAN SVANKMAJER

Contact: Czech Film Institute, Narodni tr. 40, 110 00 Prague 1,
Czech Republic, tel.: 02/26-00-87

FAUST (AF)   Heart of Europe/Lumen Films/BBC Bristol/Koninck/
Pandora Film/Althanor/CNC/Czech Ministry of Culture, 1994,
Czech-French-British-German

PETER SVATEK

Contact: Directors Guild of Canada, 225 Richmond Street,
Toronto, Ontario M5V 1W2, Canada, 416/351-8200

WITCHBOARD III   Telescene Communications, 1995, Canadian

JAN SVERAK

Contact: Czech Film Institute, Narodni tr. 40, 110 00 Prague 1,
Czech Republic, tel.: 02/26-00-87

ELEMENTARY SCHOOL   1992, Czechoslovakian
AKUMULATOR 1   Heureka Film, 1994, Czech
THE RIDE   Luxor, 1995, Czech

BOB SWAIM*

b. November 2, 1943 - Evanston, Illinois
Agent: ICM - Beverly Hills, 310/550-4000

LA NUIT DE SAINT-GERMAIN-DES-PRES   Filmologies,
1977, French
LA BALANCE   Spectrafilm, 1982, French
HALF MOON STREET   20th Century Fox, 1986, British
MASQUERADE   MGM/UA, 1988
L'ATLANTIDE   RCS Production/Aura Film/RAI/CFC/Canal Plus,
1992, French-Italian
TARGET OF SUSPICION (CTF)   USA Pictures/Ellipse
Programme/Barry Weitz Films, 1994, U.S.-French

STEPHEN SWARTZ

NEVER LEAVE NEVADA   Cabriolet Films, 1991

CHARLES SWENSON

DIRTY DUCK (AF)   New World, 1977
THE MOUSE AND HIS CHILD (AF)   co-director with Fred Wolf,
Sanrio, 1977
TWICE UPON A TIME (AF)   co-director with John Korty,
The Ladd Company/Warner Bros., 1983

LARRY SWERDLOVE

THE SKATEBOARD KID   Concorde, 1992

JO SWERLING, JR.*

b. June 18, 1931 - Los Angeles, California
Business: The Cannell Studios, 7083 Hollywood Blvd., Hollywood,
CA 90028, 213/465-5800

THE LAST CONVERTIBLE (MS)   co-director with Sidney Hayers &
Gus Trikonis, Roy Huggins Productions/Universal TV, 1979

DAVID SWIFT*

b. 1929 - Minneapolis, Minnesota
Business: Thalia Films Ltd., 12831 Hanover Street,
West Los Angeles, CA 90049

POLLYANNA   Buena Vista, 1960
THE PARENT TRAP   Buena Vista, 1961
THE INTERNS   Columbia, 1962
LOVE IS A BALL   United Artists, 1962
UNDER THE YUM YUM TREE   Columbia, 1963
GOOD NEIGHBOR SAM   Columbia, 1964
HOW TO SUCCEED IN BUSINESS WITHOUT REALLY TRYING
United Artists, 1967

SAUL SWIMMER

FORCE OF IMPULSE   Sutton, 1961
MRS. BROWN, YOU'VE GOT A LOVELY DAUGHTER
MGM, 1968, British
COMETOGETHER   Allied Artists, 1971, U.S.-Italian
THE CONCERT FOR BANGLADESH (FCD)
20th Century-Fox, 1972
THE BLACK PEARL   Diamond, 1977
WE WILL ROCK YOU (FCD)   Mobilevision/Yellowbill,
1983, Canadian

BRAD SWIRNOFF

TUNNELVISION   co-director with Neil Israel, World Wide, 1976
AMERICAN RASPBERRY   Cannon, 1980

MICHAEL SWITZER*

Agent: CAA - Beverly Hills, 310/288-4545

RAGS TO RICHES (TF)   Leonard Hill Films, 1987
FRANK NITTI: THE ENFORCER (TF)   Leonard Hill Films, 1988
POLICE STORY: THE FAR TURN (TF)   Columbia TV, 1989
HEROES AND VILLAINS (TF)   Leonard Hill Films, 1990
THE STORY OF THE BEACH BOYS: SUMMER DREAMS (TF)
Leonard Hill Films, 1990
REVEALING EVIDENCE (TF)   T.W.S. Productions/
Universal TV, 1990

LIGHTNING FIELD (CTF)   Mark Gordon Company/Christopher
     Meledandri Productions/Wilshire Court Productions, 1991
THE WOMAN WHO SINNED (TF)   World International
     Network/Samuels Film Company, 1991
WITH A VENGEANCE (TF)   Citadel Pictures, 1992
FERGIE & ANDREW: BEHIND THE PALACE DOORS (TF)
     Rosemont Productions, 1992, U.S.-British
I CAN MAKE YOU LOVE ME: THE STALKING OF LAURA
     BLACK (TF)   Joel Fields Productions/Frank Abetemarco
     Productions/Leonard Hill Films, 1993
FINAL JUSTICE (TF)   NBC, 1993
CHILDREN OF THE DARK (TF)   Steve Krantz Productions/
     Multimedia Motion Pictures, 1994
PAST THE BLEACHERS (TF)   Hallmark Entertainment, 1994
CRIES FROM THE HEART (TF)   WildRice Productions/
     Gross-Barnett-Iezman Entertainment, 1994

HANS-JURGEN SYBERBERG

b. December 8, 1935 - Nossendorf, Germany
Contact: Federal Union of Film and Television Directors in
     Germany, Adelheidstrasse 7, 8000 Munich 40, Germany,
     tel.: 089/271-6380

FUNFTER AKT, SIEBTE SZENE. FRITZ KORTNER PROBT
     KABALE UND LIEBE (FD)   1965, West German
ROMY. ANATOMIE EINES GESICHT (FD)   1965, West German
FRITZ KORTNER SPRICHT MONOLOGE FUR EINE
     SCHALLPLATTE (FD)   1966
DIE GRAFFEN POCCI - EINIGE KAPITEL ZUR GESCHICHTE
     EINER FAMILIE (FD)   1967, West German
SCARABEA - WIENVIEL ERDE BRAUCHT DER MENSCH?
     1968, West German
SEX-BUSINESS - MADE IN PASSING (FD)   1969, West German
SAN DOMINGO   co-director with Christian Blackwood,
     1970, West German
NACH MEINEM LETZEN UMZUG   1970, West German
THEODOR HIERNEIS ODER: WIE MAN EHEM. HOFKOCH WIRD
     1972, West German
LUDWIG: REQUIEM FOR A VIRGIN KING   Zoetrope,
     1972, West German
KARL MAY   7MS Film Gesellschaft, 1974, West German
WINIFRED WAGNER (FD)   *WINIFRED WAGNER UND DIE
     GESCHICHTE DES HAUSES WAHNFRIED VON 1914-1975*
     Bauer International, 1978, West German
HITLER: A FILM FROM GERMANY   Zoetrope,
     1980, West German
PARSIFAL   Triumph/Columbia, 1981, French-West German
DIE NACHT   TMS Film, 1985, West German

PETER SYKES

b. June 17, 1939 - Melbourne, Australia
Address: 66 Highgate Hill - No. 6, London NW19, England,
     tel.: 171/272-1664
Agent: Jonathan Clowes, 22 Prince Albert Street,
     London NW1, England

THE COMMITTEE   Planet, 1968, British
DEMONS OF THE MIND   MGM-EMI, 1972, British
THE HOUSE IN NIGHTMARE PARK   MGM-EMI, 1973, British
STEPTOE AND SON RIDE AGAIN   MGM-EMi, 1973, British
LEGEND OF SPIDER FOREST   *VENOM*   New Line Cinema,
     1974, British
TO THE DEVIL A DAUGHTER   EMI, 1976, British
CRAZY HOUSE   Constellation, 1977, British
JESUS   co-director with John Krish, Warner Bros., 1979, British
THE SEARCH FOR ALEXANDER THE GREAT (MS)   Time-Life
     Productions/Video Arts TV Productions, 1981, U.S.-British

PAUL SYLBERT*

Home: 724 Winding Road, Jenkintown, PA 19046, 215/884-9849

THE STEAGLE   Avco Embassy, 1971

ISTVAN SZABO

b. February 18, 1938 - Budapest, Hungary
Agent: Paul Kohner, Inc. - Los Angeles, 310/550-1060
Contact: Hungarian Film Institute, Budakeszi u 51 B, 1012 Budapest,
     Hungary, tel.: 176-1018 or 176-1322

AGE OF ILLUSIONS   Brandon, 1964, Hungarian
FATHER   Continental, 1966, Hungarian
LOVE FILM   Mafilm, 1970, Hungarian
25, FIREMAN'S STREET   Unifilm, 1970, Hungarian
PREMIERE (TF)   Hungarian TV, 1974, Hungarian
BUDAPEST TALES   Hunnia Studios, 1976, Hungarian
CONFIDENCE   Mafilm, 1979, Hungarian
THE GREEN BIRD   Teleculture, 1979, West German
MEPHISTO   Analysis, 1980, Hungarian-West German
COLONEL REDL   Orion Classics, 1985,
     West German-Austrian-Hungarian
HANUSSEN   Studio Objektiv/CCC Filmkunst/Hungarofilm/MOKEP,
     1988, Hungarian-West German
MEETING VENUS   Warner Bros., 1991, British
SWEET EMMA, DEAR BOBE — SKETCHES, NUDES   Objektiv
     Filmstudio/Manfred Durniok Filmproduktion, 1992, Hungarian

JEANNOT SZWARC*

b. November 21, 1937 - Paris, France
Contact: Coleen Olds, P.O. Box 8639, Calabasas, CA 91372,
     818/883-8016
Agent: APA - Los Angeles, 310/273-0744

NIGHT OF TERROR (TF)   Paramount TV, 1972
THE WEEKEND SUN (TF)   Paramount TV, 1972
THE DEVIL'S DAUGHTER (TF)   Paramount TV, 1973
YOU'LL NEVER SEE ME AGAIN (TF)   Universal TV, 1973
LISA, BRIGHT AND DARK (TF)   Bob Banner Associates, 1973
A SUMMER WITHOUT BOYS (TF)   Playboy Productions, 1973
THE SMALL MIRACLE (TF)   FCB Productions/Alan Landsburg
     Productions, 1973
EXTREME CLOSE-UP   National General, 1973
CRIME CLUB (TF)   Universal TV, 1975
BUG   Paramount, 1975
CODE NAME: DIAMOND HEAD (TF)   QM Productions, 1977
JAWS 2   Universal, 1978
SOMEWHERE IN TIME   Universal, 1980
ENIGMA   Embassy, 1982, British-French
SUPERGIRL   Warner Bros., 1984, British
SANTA CLAUS: THE MOVIE   TriStar, 1985, U.S.-British
THE MURDERS IN THE RUE MORGUE (TF)   Robert Halmi, Inc./
     International Film Productions, 1986
GRAND LARCENY (TF)   Robert Halmi, Inc., 1988
MAXIMUM EXPOSURE (MS)   co-director with Vittorio Sindoni,
     Reteitalia/Falcon S.A./TV3 Televisio de Catalunya, Italian-Spanish
HONOR BOUND   MGM-Pathe Communications,
     1991, U.S.-French
THE BURNING SHORE (MS)   Titanus/Tricom Productions/
     Betafilm/Silvio Berlusconi Communications/TF1,
     1991, French-Italian
LA VENGEANCE D'UNE BLONDE   Les Films de la Colline/TF1/
     Lumiere/Canal Plus/Cofimage 4/Investimage 4, 1993, French

T

MICHAEL TAAV
Agent: ICM - Beverly Hills, 310/550-4000

THE PAINT JOB   Second Son Entertainment Company, 1992

SYLVIO TABET
Business: Films 21, 10845 Sunset Blvd., Los Angeles, CA 90077

BEASTMASTER 2: THROUGH THE PORTAL OF TIME
New Line Cinema, 1991

JUAN CARLOS TABIO
Contact: Instituto Cubano del Arte e Industria Cinematograficas
(ICAIC), Calle 23, No. 1155, Vedado, Havana, Cuba,
tel.: 53-7/30-5041

STRAWBERRY AND CHOCOLATE   co-director with
Tomas Gutierrez Alea, Miramax Films, 1994,
Cuban-Spanish-Mexican
GUANTANAMERA   co-director with Tomas Gutierrez Alea,
Tornasol Films/Alta Films/Prime Films/Television Espanola/
ICAA/Canal Plus Espana, 1995, Cuban-Spanish

JEAN-CHARLES TACCHELLA
b. September 23, 1925 - Cherbourg, France
Agent: Voyez Mon Agent - Paris, tel.: 1/47-23-55-80

VOYAGE TO GRAND TARTARIE   New Line Cinema,
1973, French
COUSIN COUSINE   Libra, 1975, French
THE BLUE COUNTRY   Quartet, 1977, French
IT'S A LONG TIME THAT I'VE LOVED YOU   SOUPCON
Durham/Pike, 1979, French
CROQUE LA VIE   Prodis, 1981, French
ESCALIER C   AMLF, 1985, French
L'HEURE SIMENON (TF)   TF1, 1986, French
TRAVELLING AVANT   Erato Film/La Sept, 1987, French
LES DAMES GALANTES   Gaumont, 1991,
French-Canadian-Italian
L'HOMME DE MA VIE   Optima Productions/Cine Cinq/Prodeve/
Cineroux Films/Sofica Valor 2/Canal Plus/CNC/Telefilm
Canada, 1992, French-Canadian
SEVEN SUNDAYS   Erato Films/Filmtre/TF1 Films/ICE Films/JCT
Productions, 1994, French-Italian

ROBERT TAICHER
INSIDE OUT   Hemdale, 1986

RENEE TAJIMA
WHO KILLED VINCENT CHIN? (FD)   co-director with
Christine Choy, 1988
THE BEST HOTEL ON SKID ROW (CTD)   co-director with
Christine Choy, HBO, 1990

REA TAJIRI
YURI KOCHIYAMA: PASSION FOR JUSTICE (FD)
co-director with Pat Saunders, 1993
STRAWBERRY FIELDS   Strawberry Fields/AMIC, 1995

TIBOR TAKACS*
b. 1954 - Budapest, Hungary
Business: Image Pictures, 104 Richview Avenue, Toronto, Ontario
M5P 3E9, Canada, 416/483-7301
Agent: APA - Los Angeles, 213/273-0744

METAL MESSIAH   Mega Media Communications Corporation,
1977, Canadian
THE TOMORROW MAN   PRISONER 984 (TF)   Mega Media
Communications Corporation, 1979, Canadian
THE GREAT AMERICAN TRAGEDY   Gilmark Picture Corporation,
1984, Canadian
THE GATE   New Century/Vista, 1987, Canadian
I, MADMAN   Trans World Entertainment, 1989
EARTH CREATURE   First Look Pictures, 1991
GATE II   Triumph Releasing Corporation, 1992, Canadian
PAST TENSE   Past Tense Productions, 1994

ISAO TAKAHATA
b. 1935 - Mie Prefecture, Japan
Business: c/o Studio Ghibli, 1-18-21 1 Hibiya Building - 8th Floor,
Shinbashi, Minato-ku, Tokyo 105, Japan, tel.: 3/35084912
Contact: Yoshio Tsuboike, Tokuma Shoten Publishing Co., Ltd.,
10900 NE 4th - Suite 1150, Bellevue, WA 98004, 206/646-8340

PRINCE OF THE SUN: HORUSU'S GREAT ADVENTURE (AF)
Toei, 1968, Japanese
GOSHU THE CELLIST (AF)   Oh Productions, 1982, Japanese
GRAVE OF THE FIREFLIES (AF)   Central Park Media,
1988, Japanese
ONLY YESTERDAY   OMOHIDE PORO PORO/MEMORIES FALL
LIKE TEARDROPS (AF)   Studio Ghibli, 1991, Japanese
HEISEI TANUKI GASSEN POM POKO   POM POKO: THE GREAT
RACCOON WAR/POM POKO (AF)   Hatake Office-Tokuma
Shoten/NTV/Hakuhodo/Studio Ghibli, 1994, Japanese

BEAT TAKESHI
(See Takeshi KITANO)

YOJIRO TAKITA
b. 1955 - Toyama Prefecture, Japan
Contact: Nihon Eiga Kantoku Kyokai (Japan Film Directors
Association), La Fontenu Building -4th Floor, 23-2 Maruyama-cho,
Shibuya-ku, Tokyo, Japan, tel.: 3/3461-4411

COMIC MAGAZINE   M&R Films/Cinecom, 1985, Japanese
MY DEAR HALF-MOON   Nikkatsu/New Century Producers,
1987, Japanese
THE YEN FAMILY   PEOPLE OF KIMURA FAMILY   Herald Ace/
Nippon Herald Films, 1988, Japanese
LET'S GO TO THE HOSPITAL   Fuji TV, 1990, Japanese
LET'S GO TO THE HOSPITAL 2: SICKNESS COMES FROM
FEELINGS   Fuji TV/Meriesu, 1992, Japanese
THE TOWN THAT NEVER SLEEPS - SHINJUKU SHACK
Fuji TV, 1993, Japanese
WE ALL HAVE TO LIVE   Shochiku, 1993, Japanese
THE TROPICAL PEOPLE   NETTAI RAKUEN CLUB
Shochiku, 1994, Japanese

RACHEL TALALAY*
Agent: ICM - Beverly Hills, 310/550-4000

FREDDY'S DEAD: THE FINAL NIGHTMARE
New Line Cinema, 1991
GHOST IN THE MACHINE   20th Century Fox, 1993
TANK GIRL   MGM-UA, 1995

LEN TALAN
HANSEL AND GRETEL   Cannon, 1987, U.S.-Israeli

C.M. TALKINGTON
LOVE & A .45   Trimark Pictures, 1994

F
I
L
M

D
I
R
E
C
T
O
R
S

LEE TAMAHORI
b. Tawa, New Zealand
Contact: New Zealand Film Commission, P.O. Box 11-546,
　Wellington, New Zealand, tel.: 4/385-9754

ONCE WERE WARRIORS　Fine Line Features/New Line Cinema,
　1994, New Zealand
MULHOLLAND FALLS　MGM-UA, 1995

AUGUSTO TAMAYO
WELCOME TO OBLIVION　Concorde, 1990, U.S.-Peruvian

HARRY TAMPA
(See Harry HURWITZ)

GINO TANASESCU*
Agent: Shapiro-Lichtman Talent Agency - Los Angeles, 310/859-8877

THANKSGIVING DAY (TF)　Zacharias-Buhai Productions/NBC
　Productions, 1990

BILL TANNEBRING
b. March 9, 1937 - Bermuda
Business: Tannebring Rose Associates, 10300 N. Central
　Expressway, Dallas, TX 75231, 214/363-3464

VOYEUR　Crystal Productions, 1984

TERREL TANNEN
Agent: CAA - Beverly Hills, 310/288-4545

SHADOWS IN THE STORM　Vidmark, 1990

WILLIAM TANNEN*
Agent: Becsey/Wisdom/Kalajian - Los Angeles, 310/550-0535

FLASHPOINT　TriStar, 1984
DEADLY ILLUSION　co-director with Larry Cohen,
　CineTel Films, 1987
HERO AND THE TERROR　Cannon, 1988
DEADLY ICE　One World Films, 1993, U.S.-Mexican, unfinished

ALAIN TANNER
b. December 6, 1929 - Geneva, Switzerland
Contact: Swiss Film Center, Munstergasse 18, 8001 Zurich,
　Switzerland, tel.: 01/472860

LES APPRENTIS (FD)　1964, Swiss
UNE VILLE A CHANDIGARH　1966, Swiss
CHARLES, DEAD OR ALIVE　New Yorker, 1969, Swiss-French
LA SALAMANDRE　New Yorker, 1971, Swiss
LA RETOUR D'AFRIQUE　Alain Tanner/Groupe 5, 1973, Swiss
THE MIDDLE OF THE WORLD　New Yorker, 1974, Swiss
JONAH WHO WILL BE 25 IN THE YEAR 2000　New Yorker,
　1976, Swiss
MESSIDOR　New Yorker, 1979, Swiss-French
LIGHT YEARS AWAY　New Yorker, 1981, Swiss-French
IN THE WHITE CITY　Gray City, 1983, Swiss
NO MAN'S LAND　New Yorker, 1985, French-Swiss
LA VALLEE FANTOME　MK2, 1987, French-Swiss
A FLAME IN MY HEART　Roxie Releasing, 1987, Swiss
LA FEMME DE ROSE HILL　Filmograph, 1989,
　Swiss-French-West German
L'HOMME QUI A PERDUE SON OMBRE　Tornasol Films/
　Filmograph/Gemini Films, 1991, Swiss-Spanish-French
LE JOURNAL DE LADY M.　Filmograph/Nomad Film/
　Messidor Films/Les Productions Lanzennec, 1993,
　Swiss-Belgian-Spanish-French

DANIEL TAPLITZ
Agent: CAA - Beverly Hills, 310/288-4545

NIGHTLIFE (CTF)　Cine Enterprises Mexico/MTE,
　1989, U.S.-Mexican

DANIEL TARADASH*
b. January 29, 1913 - Louisville, Kentucky
Contact: Directors Guild of America - Los Angeles, 213/851-3671

STORM CENTER　Columbia, 1956

QUENTIN TARANTINO
b. 1963 - Knoxville, Tennessee
Agent: William Morris Agency - Beverly Hills, 310/859-4000

RESERVOIR DOGS　Miramax Films, 1992
PULP FICTION ★　Miramax Films, 1994
FOUR ROOMS　co-director with Allison Anders,
　Alexandre Rockwell & Robert Rodriguez, Miramax Films, 1995

MAX TASH*
Agent: Shapiro-Lichtman Talent Agency - Los Angeles, 310/859-8877

THE RUNNIN' KIND　MGM/UA, 1989
HUMAN TARGET (TF)　co-director with Danny Bilson, Pet Fly
　Productions/Warner Bros. TV, 1992
A PERRY MASON MYSTERY: THE CASE OF THE GRIMACING
　GOVERNOR (TF)　The Fred Silverman Company/Dean
　Hargrove Productions/Viacom, 1994

NADIA TASS*
Business: Cascade Films, 117 Rouse Street, Port Melbourne 3027,
　Australia, tel.: 613/646-4022
Agent: The Gersh Agency - Beverly Hills, 310/274-6611

MALCOLM　Vestron, 1986, Australian
RIKKY AND PETE　MGM/UA, 1988, Australian
THE BIG STEAL　Hoyts Distribution, 1990, Australian
OVER THE HILL　Glasshouse Pictures/Village Roadshow,
　1990, Australian
PURE LUCK　Universal, 1991
STARK (TF)　Cascade Ash Productions/Australian Broadcasting
　Corporation/BBC, 1993, Australian-British

PAUL TASSIE*
Contact: Directors Guild of America - Los Angeles, 213/851-3671

UNTITLED SUMMER CAMP MOVIE　Gramercy Pictures, 1994

CATHERINE TATGE*
MARTHA GRAHAM: THE DANCER REVEALED (TD)
　Thirteen-WNET/Cameras Continentales, 1994

ANNA MARIA TATO
THE NIGHT AND THE MOMENT　Miramax Films, 1994,
　British-French-Italian

DAVID TAUSIK
KILLER INSTINCT　Concorde, 1992
SYMPHONY　Concorde, 1993, U.S.-Russian

JOHN TATOULIS
Contact: Australian Film Commission, 150 William Street,
　Woolloomooloo NSW 2011, Australia, tel.: 2/321-6444

THE SILVER STALLION: KING OF THE WILD BRUMBIES
　THE SILVER BRUMBY　Skouras Pictures, 1993, Australian

BERTRAND TAVERNIER
b. April 25, 1941 - Lyons, France
Business: Little Bear Productions, 5, rue Arthur Groussier, 75010
　Paris, France, tel.: 1/42-38-06-55
Agent: ICM - Beverly Hills, 310/550-4000

LES BAISERS　co-director, 1963, French
LA CHANCE ET L'AMOUR　co-director, 1964, French
THE CLOCKMAKER OF ST. PAUL　Joseph Green Pictures,
　1974, French

LET JOY REIGN SUPREME *QUE LA FETE COMMENCE...*
   SJ International, 1975, French
THE JUDGE AND THE ASSASSIN Libra, 1976, French
SPOILED CHILDREN Corinth, 1977, French
FEMMES FATALES 1979, French
DEATH WATCH Quartet, 1980, French-West German
A WEEK'S VACATION *UNE SEMAINE DE VACANCES*
   Biograph, 1982, French
COUP DE TORCHON *CLEAN SLATE* Biograph/Quartet/Films
   Inc./The Frank Moreno Company, 1982, French
MISSISSIPPI BLUES (FD) co-director with Robert Parrish,
   Little Bear Productions/Odessa Films, 1984, French
A SUNDAY IN THE COUNTRY MGM/UA Classics, 1984, French
ROUND MIDNIGHT Warner Bros., 1986, U.S.-French
BEATRICE *LA PASSION BEATRICE* The Samuel Goldwyn
   Company, 1987, French
LIFE AND NOTHING BUT... Orion Classics, 1989, French-Italian
DADDY NOSTALGIA Avenue Pictures, 1990, French
LA GUERRE SANS NOM (FD) Canal Plus/GMT Productions/
   Little Bear Productions, 1992, French
CONTRE L'OUBLI co-director, Les Films du Paradoxe/Amnesty
   International/PRV, 1992, French
L.627 Kino International, 1992, French
LA FILLE DE D'ARTAGNAN Miramax Films, 1994, French
L'APPAT Hachette Premiere, 1995, French
CAPITAINE CUNAN Canal Plus, 1995, French

PAOLO TAVIANI
b. November 8, 1931 - San Miniato, Italy
Home: via dell'Ongaro 41, Rome, Italy, tel.: 06/5817231

UN UOMO DA BRUCIARE co-director with Vittorio Taviani &
   Valentino Orsini, Moira Film/Ager Film/Sancro Film,
   1963, Italian
I FUORILEGGE DEL METRIMONIO co-director with
   Vittorio Taviani & Valentino Orsini, Ager Film/Filmcoop/
   D'errico Film, 1963, Italian
SOVVERSIVI co-director with Vittorio Taviani, Ager Film,
   1967, Italian
SOTTO IL SEGNO DELLO SCORPIONE co-director with
   Vittorio Taviani, Ager Film, 1969, Italian
SAN MICHELE AVEVA UN GALLO (TF) co-director with
   Vittorio Taviani, Igor Film/RAI, 1971, Italian
ALLONSANFAN co-director with Vittorio Taviani, Italtoons/
   Wonder Movies, 1974, Italian
PADRE PADRONE co-director with Vittorio Taviani, New Yorker,
   1977, Italian originally made for television
THE MEADOW co-director with Vittorio Taviani, New Yorker,
   1979, Italian-French
THE NIGHT OF THE SHOOTING STARS *LA NOTTE DI SAN
   LORENZO* co-director with Vittorio Taviani, United Artists
   Classics, 1981, Italian
KAOS co-director with Vittorio Taviani, MGM/UA Classics,
   1985, Italian
GOOD MORNING, BABYLON co-director with Vittorio Taviani,
   Vestron, 1987, Italian-French-U.S.
IL SOLE ANCHE DI NOTTE co-director with Vittorio Taviani,
   Film 3, 1989, Italian
FIORILE co-director with Vittorio Taviani, Fine Line Features/
   New Line Cinema, 1993, Italian
AFFINITA' ELETTIVE co-director with Vittorio Taviani, Sacis,
   1995, Italian

VITTORIO TAVIANI
b. September 20, 1929 - San Miniato, Italy
Home: via Orti D'Alibert 4, Rome, Italy, tel.: 06/6541834

UN UOMO DA BRUCIARE co-director with Paolo Taviani &
   Valentino Orsini, Moira Film/Ager Film/Sancro Film,
   1963, Italian
I FUORILEGGE DEL METRIMONIO co-director with
   Paolo Taviani & Valentino Orsini, Ager Film/Filmcoop/
   D'errico Film, 1963, Italian
SOVVERSIVI co-director with Paolo Taviani, Ager Film,
   1967, Italian
SOTTO IL SEGNO DELLO SCORPIONE co-director with
   Paolo Taviani, Ager Film, 1969, Italian

SAN MICHELE AVEVA UN GALLO (TF) co-director with
   Paolo Taviani, Igor Film/RAI, 1971, Italian
ALLONSANFAN co-director with Paolo Taviani, Italtoons/Wonder
   Movies, 1974, Italian
PADRE PADRONE co-director with Paolo Taviani, New Yorker,
   1977, Italian, originally made for television
THE MEADOW co-director with Paolo Taviani, New Yorker, 1979,
   Italian-French
THE NIGHT OF THE SHOOTING STARS *LA NOTTE DI SAN
   LORENZO* co-director with Paolo Taviani, United Artists
   Classics, 1981, Italian
KAOS co-director with Paolo Taviani, MGM/UA Classics,
   1985, Italian
GOOD MORNING, BABYLON co-director with Paolo Taviani,
   Vestron, 1987, Italian-French-U.S.
IL SOLE ANCHE DI NOTTE co-director with Paolo Taviani,
   Film 3, 1989, Italian
FIORILE co-director with Paolo Taviani, Fine Line Features/
   New Line Cinema, 1993, Italian
AFFINITA' ELETTIVE co-director with Paolo Taviani, Sacis,
   1995, Italian

ALEX TAYLOR
PALOOKAVILLE The Samuel Goldwyn Company, 1995

BAZ TAYLOR
Address: 17 Alexander Street, London W2 5NT, England,
   tel.: 171/727-1191
Agent: ICM - London, tel.: 171/636-6565

TALENT (TF) Granada TV, 1982, British
AUF WIEDERSEHN PET (TF) Central TV, 1983, British
LOVEJOY (TF) BBC, 1985, British
DEMPSEY & MAKEPEACE - THE MOVIE 1986, British
WHERE THERE'S A WILL (TF) 1987, British
THE YOUNG CHARLIE CHAPLIN (TF) Thames TV,
   1989, British
NEAR MISSES Chrysalide Films/Canal Plus/The Movie Group,
   1992, U.S.-French
SHOOTING ELIZABETH The Movie Group, 1992, French
KISS AND TELL The Movie Group, 1992, U.S.-French
ALL IN THE GAME (MS) Central Films/TVC/Sunset & Vine,
   1993, British

DON TAYLOR*
b. December 13, 1920 - Freeport, Pennsylvania
Agent: Phil Gersh, The Gersh Agency - Beverly Hills, 310/274-6611

EVERTHING'S DUCKY Columbia, 1961
RIDE THE WILD SURF Columbia, 1964
JACK OF DIAMONDS MGM, 1967, U.S.-West German
SOMETHING FOR A LONELY MAN (TF) Universal TV, 1968
THE FIVE MAN ARMY MGM, 1970, Italian
WILD WOMEN (TF) Aaron Spelling Productions, 1970
ESCAPE FROM THE PLANET OF THE APES
   20th Century-Fox, 1971
HEAT OF ANGER (TF) Metromedia Productions, 1972
TOM SAWYER United Artists, 1973
NIGHT GAMES (TF) Paramount TV, 1974
HONKY TONK (TF) MGM TV, 1974
ECHOES OF A SUMMER Cine Artists, 1976, U.S.-Canadian
THE MAN-HUNTER (TF) Universal TV, 1976
THE GREAT SCOUT AND CATHOUSE THURSDAY
   American International, 1976
A CIRCLE OF CHILDREN (TF) Edgar J. Scherick Associates/
   20th Century-Fox TV, 1977
THE ISLAND OF DR. MOREAU American International, 1977
DAMIEN - OMEN II 20th Century-Fox, 1978
THE GIFT (TF) The Jozak Company/Cypress Point Productions/
   Paramount TV, 1979
THE FINAL COUNTDOWN United Artists, 1980
THE PROMISE OF LOVE (TF) Pierre Cossette Productions, 1980
BROKEN PROMISE (TF) 1981
RED FLAG: THE ULTIMATE GAME (TF) Marble Arch
   Productions, 1981
DROP-OUT FATHER (TF) CBS Entertainment, 1982
LISTEN TO YOUR HEART (TF) CBS Entertainment, 1983

SEPTEMBER GUN (TF)   QM Productions/Taft Entertainment/
   Brademan-Self Productions, 1983
HE'S NOT YOUR SON (TF)   CBS Entertainment, 1984
MY WICKED, WICKED WAYS: THE LEGEND OF
   ERROL FLYNN (TF)   CBS Entertainment, 1985
SECRET WEAPONS (TF)   Goodman-Rosen Productions/ITC
   Productions, 1985
GOING FOR THE GOLD: THE BILL JOHNSON STORY (TF)
   ITC Productions/Sullivan-Carter Interests/Goodman-Rosen
   Productions, 1985
CLASSIFIED LOVE (TF)   CBS Entertainment, 1986
GHOST OF A CHANCE (TF)   Stuart-Phoenix Productions/Thunder
   Bird Road Productions/Lorimar-Telepictures Productions, 1987
THE DIAMOND TRAP (TF)   Jay Bernstein Productions/
   Columbia TV, 1988

JUD TAYLOR*
b. February 25, 1940
Agent: The Brandt Company - Sherman Oaks, 818/783-7747

FADE-IN   directed under pseudonym of Allen Smithee,
   Paramount, 1968
WEEKEND OF TERROR (TF)   Paramount TV, 1970
SUDDENLY SINGLE (TF)   Chris-Rose Productions, 1971
REVENGE (TF)   Mark Carliner Productions, 1972
THE ROOKIES (TF)   Aaron Spelling Productions, 1972
SAY GOODBYE, MAGGIE COLE (TF)   Spelling-Goldberg
   Productions, 1972
HAWKINS ON MURDER (TF)   Arena-Leda Productions/
   MGM TV, 1973
WINTER KILL (TF)   Andy Griffith Enterprises/MGM TV, 1974
THE DISAPPEARANCE OF FLIGHT 412 (TF)   Cinemobile
   Productions, 1975
SEARCH FOR THE GODS (TF)   Warner Bros. TV, 1975
FUTURE COP (TF)   Paramount TV, 1976
RETURN TO EARTH (TF)   King-Hitzig Productions, 1976
WOMAN OF THE YEAR (TF)   MGM TV, 1976
TAIL GUNNER JOE (TF) ☆   Universal TV, 1977
MARY WHITE (TF)   Radnitz/Mattel Productions, 1977
CHRISTMAS MIRACLE IN CAUFIELD, U.S.A. (TF)
   20th Century-Fox TV, 1977
THE LAST TENANT (TF)   Titus Productions, 1978
LOVEY: A CIRCLE OF CHILDREN, PART II (TF)
   Time-Life Productions, 1978
FLESH AND BLOOD (TF)   The Jozak Company/Cypress Point
   Productions/Paramount TV, 1979
CITY IN FEAR (TF)   directed under pseudonym of Alan Smithee,
   Trans World International, 1980
ACT OF LOVE (TF)   Cypress Point Productions/
   Paramount TV, 1980
MURDER AT CRESTRIDGE (TF)   Jaffe-Taylor Productions, 1981
A QUESTION OF HONOR (TF)   Roger Gimbel Productions/
   EMI TV/Sonny Grosso Productions, 1982
PACKIN' IT IN (TF)   Roger Gimbel Productions/Thorn EMI TV/
   Jones-Reiker Ink Corporation, 1983
LICENSE TO KILL (TF)   Marian Rees Associates/D. Petrie
   Productions, 1984
OUT OF THE DARKNESS (TF)   Grosso-Jacobson Productions/
   Centerpoint Productions, 1985
DOUBLETAKE (TF)   Titus Productions, 1985
BROKEN VOWS (TF)   Brademan-Self Productions/Robert
   Halmi, Inc., 1987
FOXFIRE (TF)   Marian Rees Associates, 1987
THE GREAT ESCAPE II: THE UNTOLD STORY (TF)
   director of part 2, Spectator Films/Michael Jaffe Films, 1988
THE OLD MAN AND THE SEA (TF)   Storke Enterprises/Green
   Pond Productions/Yorkshire TV, 1990
END RUN (TF)   Titus Productions, 1990
MURDER TIMES SEVEN (TF)   Titus Productions, 1990
DANIELLE STEEL'S KALEIDOSCOPE (TF)   *KALEIDOSCOPE*
   The Cramer Company/NBC Productions, 1990
IN MY DAUGHTER'S NAME (TF)   Cates-Doty Productions, 1992
KUNG FU: THE LEGEND CONTINUES (TF)   Warner Bros. TV/
   Warner Bros. Distributing Canada Ltd., 1993, U.S.-Canadian
PROPHET OF EVIL: THE ERVIL LeBARON STORY (TF)
   Dream City Films/Hearst Entertainment, 1993

RENEE TAYLOR*
b. March 19, 1945
Business: Taylor/Bologna Productions, Inc., 613 N. Arden Drive,
   Beverly Hills, CA 90210, 310/274-8965
Business Manager: Larry Kantor, Zipperstein & Kantor,
   16830 Ventura Blvd. - Suite 326, Encino, CA 91436,
   818/986-4640

IT HAD TO BE YOU   co-director with Joseph Bologna,
   Limelite Studios, 1989
OH NO, NOT HER!   co-director with Joseph Bologna,
   Cinema Seven Productions, 1995

ROBERT TAYLOR
THE NINE LIVES OF FRITZ THE CAT (AF)
   American International, 1974
HEIDI'S SONG (AF)   Paramount, 1982

RODERICK TAYLOR*
Agent: Martin Hurwitz Associates - Beverly Hills, 310/274-0240

INSTANT KARMA   MGM/UA, 1990

LEWIS TEAGUE*
b. 1941
Agent: David Gersh, The Gersh Agency - Beverly Hills, 310/274-6611

DIRTY O'NEIL   co-director with Howard Freen,
   American International, 1974
THE LADY IN RED   New World, 1979
ALLIGATOR   Group 1, 1980
FIGHTING BACK   Paramount, 1982
CUJO   Warner Bros., 1983
STEPHEN KING'S CAT'S EYE   *CAT'S EYE*   MGM/UA, 1985
THE JEWEL OF THE NILE   20th Century-Fox, 1985
SHANNON'S DEAL (TF)   Stan Rogow Productions/NBC
   Productions, 1989
COLLISION COURSE   DEG, 1990, filmed in 1988
NAVY SEALS   Orion, 1990
WEDLOCK (CTF)   HBO Pictures/The Frederick S. Pierce
   Company/Spectator Films, 1991
T BONE N WEASEL (CTF)   Turner Network TV, 1992
TIME TRAX (TF)   Gary Nardino Productions/Lorimar TV, 1993
TOM CLANCY'S OP CENTER   *OP CENTER* (TF)   Jack Ryan
   Limited Partnership/Steve Pieczenik Productions/Steve Sohmer
   Inc./Moving Target Productions, 1995

ANDRE TECHINE
b. 1943 - France
Agent: ICM France - Paris, tel.: 1/723-7860
Contact: French Film Office, 745 Fifth Avenue, New York,
   NY 10151, 212/832-8860

SOUVENIRS D'EN FRANCE   1975, French
BAROCCO   1977, French
LES SOEURS BRONTE   1978, French
HOTEL DES AMERIQUES   1982, French
RENDEZVOUS   1985, French
LE LIEU DU CRIME   1986, French
LES INNOCENTS   1987, French
J'EMBRASSE PAS   BAC, 1991, French
MA SAISON PREFEREE   AMLF, 1993, French
WILD REEDS   Strand Releasing, 1994, French
L'ENFANT DE LA NUIT   Canal Plus, 1995, French

JULIEN TEMPLE
b. November 26, 1953 - London, England
Business: Nitrate Films Ltd., 47 Dean Street, London W1,
   England, tel.: 171/734-0386
Agent: ICM - Beverly Hills, 310/550-4000
Personal Manager: Brillstein/Grey Entertainment - Beverly Hills,
   310/275-6135

THE GREAT ROCK 'N' ROLL SWINDLE (FCD)   Kendon Films/
   Matrix Best/Virgin Records, 1980, British
THE SECRET POLICEMAN'S OTHER BALL (PF)   Miramax,
   1981, British

IT'S ALL TRUE (FCD)   Island Pictures/BBC, 1983, British
RUNNING OUT OF LUCK (FCD)   Nitrate Film Ltd./Julien Temple
    Production Company, 1985, British
ABSOLUTE BEGINNERS   Orion, 1986, British
ARIA   co-director, Miramax Films, 1987, British
EARTH GIRLS ARE EASY   Vestron, 1989
AT THE MAX   ROLLING STONES AT THE MAX   (FCD)
    co-director with Roman Kroitor, David Douglas &
    Noel Archambault, BCL Presentation/IMAX
    Corporation, 1991, U.S.-Canadian
BULLET   Village Roadshow Pictures/Bullet Productions, 1995

CONNY TEMPLEMAN
Contact: British Film Commission, 70 Baker Street, London
    W1M 1DJ, England, tel.: 171/224-5000

NANOU   Umbrella-Caulfield Films Ltd./National Film Finance
    Corporation/Curzon Film Distributors Ltd./French Ministry of
    Culture, 1986, British-French

ANDREW (ANDY) TENNANT*
Agent: Broder-Kurland-Webb-Uffner Agency - Beverly Hills,
    310/281-3400

KEEP THE CHANGE (CTF)   Steve Tisch Company/High
    Horse Films, 1992
DESPERATE CHOICES: TO SAVE MY CHILD (TF)
    Andrew Adelson Productions/ABC Productions, 1992
BEYOND CONTROL: THE AMY FISHER STORY (TF)
    Andrew Adelson Productions/ABC Productions, 1993
SOUTH OF SUNSET: SATYRICON (TF)   Stan Rogow Productions/
    Byrum Power & Light/Paramount Network TV, 1993
SLIDERS (TF)   Cinevu Films/St. Clare Entertainment/MCA TV/
    Fox Broadcasting, 1995, U.S.-Canadian
ME AND MY SHADOW   Warner Bros., 1995, U.S.-Canadian

KEVIN S. TENNEY
WITCHBOARD   Cinema Group, 1986
NIGHT OF THE DEMONS   International Film Marketing, 1988
WITCHTRAP   Cinema Plus/GCO Pictures/Mentone
    Pictures, 1989
PEACEMAKER   Fries Entertainment, 1990
WITCHBOARD 2: THE DEVIL'S GAME   Republic Pictures, 1993

RINKEN TERUYA
b. Koza (Okinawa City), Okinawa Prefecture, Japan
Contact: c/o Pisa Wave Soft Jigyobu, 6-2-27 Roppongi, Minato-ku,
    Tokyo 106, Japan

TINK TINK (FCD)   Eurospace, 1994, Japanese (Okinawan)

HIROSHI TESHIGAHARA
b. 1927 - Tokyo, Japan
Contact: Nihon Eiga Kantoku Kyokai (Japan Film Directors
    Association), La Fontenu Building - 4th Floor, 23-2 Maruyama-cho,
    Shibuya-ku, Tokyo, Japan, tel.: 3/3461-4411

THE PITFALL   Teshigahara Productions, 1962, Japanese
THAT TENDER AGE   co-director, 1964,
    Canadian-French-Italian-Japanese
WOMAN IN THE DUNES   Teshigahara Productions,
    1964, Japanese
THE FACE OF ANOTHER   Tokyo Movie/Teshigahara Productions,
    1966, Japanese
MAN WITHOUT A MAP   Katsu Productions, 1968, Japanese
SUMMER SOLDIERS   Teshigahara Productions,
    1972, Japanese
OUT OF WORK FOR YEARS   Teshigahara Productions,
    1975, Japanese
ANTONIO GAUDI (FD)   Teshigahara Productions,
    1984, Japanese
RIKYU   Teshigahara Productions/Shochiku/Ito Tadashi Shoji/
    Hakuhoudo, 1989, Japanese
BASARA, THE PRINCESS GOH   Shochiku, 1992, Japanese

TED TETZLAFF*
b. June 3, 1903 - Los Angeles, California
Contact: Directors Guild of America - Los Angeles, 213/851-3671

WORLD PREMIERE   Paramount, 1941
RIFF-RAFF   RKO Radio, 1947
FIGHTING FATHER DUNNE   RKO Radio, 1948
JOHNNY ALLEGRO   Columbia, 1949
THE WINDOW   RKO Radio, 1949
A DANGEROUS PROFESSION   RKO Radio, 1949
THE WHITE TOWER   RKO Radio, 1950
UNDER THE GUN   Universal, 1951
GAMBLING HOUSE   RKO Radio, 1951
THE TREASURE OF LOST CANYON   Universal, 1952
TERROR ON A TRAIN   TIME BOMB   MGM, 1953, British-U.S.
SON OF SINBAD   A NIGHT IN A HAREM   RKO Radio, 1955
SEVEN WONDERS OF THE WORLD (FD)   co-director,
    Stanley Warner Cinema Corporation, 1956
THE YOUNG LAND   Columbia, 1959

JOAN TEWKESBURY*
b. 1937 - Redlands, California
Agent: CAA - Beverly Hills, 310/288-4545

OLD BOYFRIENDS   Avco Embassy, 1979
THE TENTH MONTH (TF)   Joe Hamilton Productions, 1979
THE ACORN PEOPLE (TF)   Rollins-Joffe-Morra-Brezner
    Productions, 1980
COLD SASSY TREE (CTF)   Faye Dunaway Productions/Ohlmeyer
    Communications/Turner Network TV, 1989
WILD TEXAS WIND (TF)   Sandollar Productions, 1991
THE STRANGER (CTF)   co-director with Daniel Vigne &
    Wayne Wang, HBO Pictures, 1992
ON PROMISED LAND (CTF)   Anasazi Productions/Walt Disney
    Company, 1994

PETER TEWKSBURY
b. 1924

SUNDAY IN NEW YORK   MGM, 1964
EMIL AND THE DETECTIVES   Buena Vista, 1964
DOCTOR, YOU'VE GOT TO BE KIDDING   MGM, 1967
STAY AWAY, JOE   MGM, 1968
THE TROUBLE WITH GIRLS   MGM, 1969
SECOND CHANCE (TF)   Metromedia Productions, 1972

TIANA THI THANH NGA
(Tiana Alexandra)
Business: Indochina Film Arts Foundation, 245 W. 55th Street -
    Suite 1101, New York, NY 10019, 212/735-3970

FROM HOLLYWOOD TO HANOI (FD)   Friendship Bridge
    Productions, 1992

ANNA THOMAS
b. July 12, 1948 - Stuttgart, West Germany
Agent: ICM - Beverly Hills, 310/550-4000

THE HAUNTING OF M   Independent Productions, 1981

ANTONY THOMAS
Address: 77 Masbro Road, London W14 0LR, England,
    tel.: 171/602-5820
Agent: Jonathan Altaras Associates, 2 Goodwin's Court, London
    WC2N 4LL, England, tel.: 171/497-8878

THE JAPANESE EXPERIENCE (TD)   1974, British
THE ARAB EXPERIENCE (TD)   1975, British
THE GOOD, THE BAD AND THE INDIFFERENT (TF)   1976, British
THE SOUTH AFRICAN EXPERIENCE (TD)   1977, British
DEATH OF A PRINCESS (TF)   1980, British-U.S.
FRANK TERPIL: PORTRAIT OF A DANGEROUS MAN (TF)
    1982, British-U.S.
THY KINGDOM COME...THY WILL BE DONE (TF)
    1987, British-U.S.

S.P.O.O.K.S.   Vestron, 1991
NEVER SAY DIE: THE PURSUIT OF ETERNAL YOUTH (CTD)
   HBO/Central Independent TV, 1992, U.S.-British
IN SATAN'S NAME (TD)   1993, British-U.S.

BETTY THOMAS*
Agent: ICM - Los Angeles, 310/550-4000

ONLY YOU   Highlight Communications/Live America/Pro Filmworks/
   Rank Film Distributors/Dayjob Films, 1992, British-U.S.
DREAM ON: SILENT NIGHT, HOLY COW (CTF)   Kevin Bright
   Productions/St. Clare Entertainment/MCA TV Entertainment, 1993
MY BREAST (TF) ☆   Diana Kerew Productions/The Polone
   Company/Hearst Entertainment, 1994
THE BRADY BUNCH MOVIE   Paramount, 1995

DAVE THOMAS*
b. St. Catharines, Ontario, Canada
Address: 1640 5th Street - Suite 114, Santa Monica, CA 90401,
   310/458-8163
Agent: CAA - Beverly Hills, 310/288-4545
Personal Manager: Brillstein/Grey Entertainment - Beverly Hills,
   310/275-6135

STRANGE BREW   co-director with Rick Moranis, MGM/UA,
   1983, Canadian
THE EXPERTS   Paramount, 1989
GHOST MOM (TF)   A Power Pictures/Richard Crystal Company/
   Hearst Entertainment, 1993, U.S.-Canadian

JOHN G. THOMAS
Agent: Irv Schechter Company - Beverly Hills, 310/278-8070

TIN MAN   1984
BANZAI RUNNER   Montage Films, 1987
ARIZONA HEAT   Republic Pictures/Spectrum Entertainment, 1988
HEALER   1994

PASCAL THOMAS
b. April 2, 1945 - Montargis, France
Contact: French Film Office, 745 Fifth Avenue, New York,
   NY 10151, 212/832-8860

LES ZOZOS   1972
DON'T CRY WITH YOUR MOUTH FULL   PLEURE PAS LA
   BOUCHE PLEINE   1973, French
LE CHAUD LAPIN   1974, French
NONO NENESSE   co-director with Jacques Rozier,
   1975, unreleased
LA SURPRISE DU CHEF   1976, French
UN OURSIN DANS LA POCHE   1977, French
CONFIDENCES POUR CONFIDENCES   1979, French
CELLES QU'ON N'A PAS EUES   1981, French
LES MARIS, LES FEMMES, LES AMANTS   1989, French
PAGAILLE   1991, French

RALPH THOMAS
b. August 10, 1915 - Hull, England
Contact: British Film Commission, 70 Baker Street, London
   W1M 1DJ, England, tel.: 171/224-5000

HELTER SKELTER   General Film Distributors, 1949, British
ONCE UPON A DREAM   General Film Distributors, 1949, British
TRAVELLER'S JOY   General Film Distributors, 1949, British
THE CLOUDED YELLOW   General Film Distributors, 1950, British
ISLAND RESCUE   APPOINTMENT WITH VENUS   Universal,
   1951, British
THE ASSASSIN   THE VENETIAN BIRD   United Artists,
   1952, British
THE DOG AND THE DIAMONDS   Associated British Film
   Distributors/Children's Film Foundation, 1953, British
A DAY TO REMEMBER   Republic, 1953, British
DOCTOR IN THE HOUSE   Republic, 1954, British
MAD ABOUT MEN   General Film Distributors, 1954, British
DOCTOR AT SEA   Republic, 1955, British

ABOVE US THE WAVES   Republic, 1955, British
THE IRON PETTICOAT   MGM, 1956, British
CHECKPOINT   Rank, 1956, British
DOCTOR AT LARGE   Universal, 1957, British
CAMPBELL'S KINGDOM   Rank, 1957, British
A TALE OF TWO CITIES   Rank, 1958, British
THE WIND CANNOT READ   20th Century-Fox, 1959, British
THE 39 STEPS   20th Century-Fox, 1959, British
UPSTAIRS AND DOWNSTAIRS   20th Century-Fox, 1959, British
CONSPIRACY OF HEARTS   Paramount, 1960, British
DOCTOR IN LOVE   Governor, 1960, British
NO LOVE FOR JOHNNIE   Embassy, 1961, British
NO, MY DARLING DAUGHTER   Zenith, 1961, British
A PAIR OF BRIEFS   Rank, 1962, British
YOUNG AND WILLING   THE WILD AND THE WILLING
   Universal, 1962, British
DOCTOR IN DISTRESS   Governor, 1963, British
AGENT 8 3/4   HOT ENOUGH FOR JUNE   Continental,
   1963, British
McGUIRE, GO HOME!   THE HIGH BRIGHT SUN
   Continental, 1964, British
CARNABY, M.D.   DOCTOR IN CLOVER   Continental, 1965, British
DEADLIER THAN THE MALE   Universal, 1966, British
SOME GIRLS DO   United Artists, 1968, British
THE HIGH COMMISSIONER   NOBODY RUNS FOREVER
   Cinerama Releasing Corporation, 1968, British
DOCTOR IN TROUBLE   Rank, 1970, British
PERCY   MGM, 1971, British
QUEST FOR LOVE   Rank, 1971, British
IT'S A 2'6" ABOVE THE GROUND WORLD   British Lion,
   1972, British
THE LOVE BAN   1973, British
IT'S NOT THE SIZE THAT COUNTS   PERCY'S PROGRESS
   Joseph Brenner Associates, 1974, British
A NIGHTINGALE SANG IN BERKELEY SQUARE   S. Benjamin Fisz
   Productions/Nightingale Productions, 1980, British

RALPH L. THOMAS*
b. Sao Luiz, Maranhao, Brazil
Agent: David Wardlow, Camden-ITG - Los Angeles, 310/289-2700

TYLER (TF)   CBC, 1977, Canadian
CEMENTHEAD (TF)   CBC, 1978, Canadian
A PAID VACATION (TF)   CBC, 1979, Canadian
AMBUSH AT IROQUOIS POINT (TF)   CBC, 1979, Canadian
TICKET TO HEAVEN   United Artists Classics, 1981, Canadian
THE TERRY FOX STORY (CTF)   HBO Premiere Films/Robert
   Cooper Films II, 1983, Canadian
APPRENTICE TO MURDER   New World, 1987, Canadian
THE FIRST SEASON   Orange Productions, 1989, Canadian
VENDETTA II: THE NEW MAFIA (TF)   Titanus/Silvio Berlusconi
   Communications/Tribune Entertainment, 1993, Italian-U.S.

THEODORE THOMAS
FRANK AND OLLIE (FD)   Walt Disney Pictures, 1995

BARNABY THOMPSON*
b. March 29, 1961 - London, England
Business: Broadway Pictures, 5555 Melrose Avenue, Hollywood,
   CA 90038, 213/956-5655

REFUGEES OF FAITH (TD)   co-director with George Case,
   Malone Gill Productions, 1984, British
A SENSE OF WONDER (TD)   co-director with George Case,
   Mark Forstater Productions, 1986, British
SINGING FOR YOUR SUPPER (TD)   co-director with
   Tom McGuinness, World's End Productions, 1988, British
JIMI HENDRIX (TD)   co-director with Tom McGuinness,
   World's End Productions, 1989, British

BRETT THOMPSON
Agent: APA - Los Angeles, 310/273-0744

DINOSAURS   Smart Egg Pictures, 1991

CAROLINE THOMPSON*
Agent: William Morris Agency - Beverly Hills, 310/859-4000

BLACK BEAUTY   Warner Bros., 1994, British-U.S.

ERNEST THOMPSON
b. 1950
Agent: CAA - Beverly Hills, 310/288-4545

1969   Atlantic Releasing Corporation, 1988

HARRY THOMPSON
Agent: MLR Representation - London, tel.: 171/351-5442

THE PASSAGE   Spectrum Films, 1988

J. LEE THOMPSON*
(John Lee Thompson)
b. 1914 - Bristol, England
Home: 9595 Lime Orchard Road, Beverly Hills, CA 90210,
   310/858-3958
Business Manager: Dick deBlois, 9171 Wilshire Blvd., Beverly Hills,
   CA 90210, 310/273-7769

MURDER WITHOUT CRIME   Associated British Picture
   Corporation, 1950, British
THE YELLOW BALLOON   Allied Artists, 1952, British
THE WEAK AND THE WICKED   Allied Artists, 1954, British
COCKTAILS IN THE KITCHEN   *FOR BETTER OR WORSE*
   Associated British Picture Corporation, 1954, British
AS LONG AS THEY'RE HAPPY   Rank, 1955, British
AN ALLIGATOR NAMED DAISY   Rank, 1955, British
BLONDE SINNER   *YIELD TO THE NIGHT*   Allied Artists,
   1956, British
THE GOOD COMPANIONS   Rank, 1957, British
WOMAN IN A DRESSING GOWN   Warner Bros., 1957, British
DESERT ATTACK   *ICE COLD IN ALEX*   20th Century-Fox,
   1958, British
NO TREES IN THE STREET   Associated British Picture
   Corporation, 1959, British
TIGER BAY   Continental, 1959, British
FLAME OVER INDIA   *NORTH WEST FRONTIER*
   20th Century-Fox, 1959, British
I AIM AT THE STARS   Columbia, 1960, U.S.-West German
THE GUNS OF NAVARONE ★   Columbia, 1961, U.S.-British
CAPE FEAR   Universal, 1962
TARAS BULBA   United Artists, 1962
KINGS OF THE SUN   United Artists, 1963
WHAT A WAY TO GO!   20th Century-Fox, 1964
JOHN GOLDFARB, PLEASE COME HOME
   20th Century-Fox, 1965
RETURN FROM THE ASHES   United Artists, 1965, British-U.S.
EYE OF THE DEVIL   MGM, 1967, British
BEFORE WINTER COMES   Columbia, 1969, British
THE CHAIRMAN   20th Century-Fox, 1969, British
MACKENNA'S GOLD   Columbia, 1969
BROTHERLY LOVE   *COUNTRY DANCE*   MGM, 1970, British
CONQUEST OF THE PLANET OF THE APES
   20th Century-Fox, 1972
A GREAT AMERICAN TRAGEDY (TF)   Metromedia
   Productions, 1972
BATTLE FOR THE PLANET OF THE APES
   20th Century-Fox, 1973
HUCKLEBERRY FINN   United Artists, 1974
THE BLUE KNIGHT (TF)   Lorimar Productions, 1975
THE REINCARNATION OF PETER PROUD   American
   International, 1975
ST. IVES   Warner Bros., 1976
WIDOW (TF)   Lorimar Productions, 1976
THE WHITE BUFFALO   United Artists, 1977
THE GREEK TYCOON   Universal, 1978
THE PASSAGE   United Artists, 1979, British
CABOBLANCO   Avco Embassy, 1981
HAPPY BIRTHDAY TO ME   Columbia, 1981, Canadian
CODE RED (TF)   Irwin Allen Productions/Columbia TV, 1981
10 TO MIDNIGHT   Cannon, 1983
THE EVIL THAT MEN DO   TriStar, 1984

THE AMBASSADOR   MGM/UA/Cannon, 1984
KING SOLOMON'S MINES   Cannon, 1985
MURPHY'S LAW   Cannon, 1986
FIREWALKER   Cannon, 1986
DEATH WISH 4: THE CRACKDOWN   Cannon, 1988
MESSENGER OF DEATH   Cannon, 1988
KINJITE (FORBIDDEN SUBJECTS)   Cannon, 1989

RANDY THOMPSON
MONTANA RUN   Greycat Films, 1992

ROB THOMPSON*
Home: 1302 N. Sweetzer Avenue - Apt. 401, Los Angeles, CA 90069,
   213/650-2070
Agent: Elliot Webb, Broder-Kurland-Webb-Uffner Agency -
   Beverly Hills, 310/281-3400

TALES FROM THE HOLLYWOOD HILLS: PAT HOBBY TEAMED
   WITH GENIUS (TF)   WNET/Zenith Productions, 1987
TAD (CTF)   Chris-Rose Prods./Family Prods., 1995

ROBERT C. THOMPSON*
b. May 31, 1937 - Palmyra, New York
Business Manager: Group Three Management, 13914 Addison Street,
   Sherman Oaks, CA 92423, 818/501-3714

BUD AND LOU (TF)   Bob Banner Associates, 1978

CHRIS THOMSON*
Agent: Shapiro-Lichtman Talent Agency - Los Angeles, 310/859-8877

MOVING TARGET (TF)   Lewis B. Chesler Productions/
   Bateman Company Productions/Finnegan-Pinchuk
   Company/MGM-UA TV, 1988
STRINGER (TF)   co-director with Ken Cameron & Kathy Mueller,
   Australian Broadcasting Corporation/Televenture Film
   Productions, 1988, Australian-British
THE RAINBOW WARRIOR CONSPIRACY (TF)   Golden Dolphin
   Productions/ATNT/Television New Zealand, 1989,
   Australian-New Zealand
SHE WAS MARKED FOR MURDER (TF)   Jack Grossbart
   Productions, 1988
SWIMSUIT (TF)   Musifilm Productions/American First Run
   Studios, 1989
THE DELINQUENTS   Warner Bros. International, 1989, Australian
STOP AT NOTHING (CTF)   Empty Chair Productions/ABC
   Productions, 1991
WOMAN ON THE LEDGE (TF)   Louis Rudolph Films/Fenton
   Entertainment Group/Fries Entertainment, 1993
THE FLOOD: WHO WILL SAVE OUR CHILDREN? (TF)
   The Wolper Organization/Warner Bros. TV, 1993

JERRY THORPE*
b. 1930
Agent: Metropolitan Talent Agency - Los Angeles, 213/857-4500

THE VENETIAN AFFAIR   MGM, 1968
DAY OF THE EVIL GUN   MGM, 1968
DIAL HOT LINE (TF)   Universal TV, 1970
LOCK, STOCK AND BARREL (TF)   Universal TV, 1971
THE CABLE CAR MURDER (TF)   Warner Bros. TV, 1971
KUNG FU (TF)   Warner Bros. TV, 1972
COMPANY OF KILLERS   *THE PROTECTORS*   Universal, 1972
SMILE JENNY, YOU'RE DEAD (TF)   Warner Bros. TV, 1974
THE DARK SIDE OF INNOCENCE (TF)   Warner Bros. TV, 1976
I WANT TO KEEP MY BABY (TF)   CBS, Inc., 1976
THE POSSESSED (TF)   Warner Bros. TV, 1977
STICKIN' TOGETHER (TF)   Blinn-Thorpe Productions/Viacom, 1978
A QUESTION OF LOVE (TF)   Viacom, 1978
THE LAZARUS SYNDROME (TF)   Blinn-Thorpe Productions/
   Viacom, 1979
ALL GOD'S CHILDREN (TF)   Blinn-Thorpe Productions/
   Viacom, 1980
HAPPY ENDINGS (TF)   Blinn-Thorpe Productions, 1983
BLOOD AND ORCHIDS (TF)   Lorimar Productions, 1986

F I L M   D I R E C T O R S

KAREN THORSEN
Contact: Writers Guild of America, East - New York City,
212/767-7800

JAMES BALDWIN: THE PRICE OF THE TICKET (TD)
Nobody Knows Productions/Maysles Films/WNET-TV/
American Masters, 1989

ZHUANGZHUANG TIAN
(See Tian ZHUANGZHUANG)

TIANA
(See Tiana Thi THANG-NGA)

WU TIANMING
b. October 1939 - Shaanxi Province, China
Contact: China Film Import & Export Office, 2500 Wilshire Blvd. -
Suite 1028, Los Angeles, CA 90057, 213/380-7520

A RIVER WITHOUT BUOYS   China Film Import & Export,
1982, Chinese
LIFE   China Film Import & Export, 1985, Chinese
THE OLD WELL   China Film Import & Export, 1987, Chinese

ANTONIO TIBALDI
Agent: UTA - Beverly Hills, 310/273-6700 or:
Artists Agency - New York, 212/245-6960

ON MY OWN   Alliance Communications Corporation/Ellepi Film/
Rosa Colosimo Pty. Ltd./Australian Film Finance Corporation/
Telefilm Canada/Ontario Film Development Corporation/RAI/Arbo
Film/Maran Film, 1992, Canadian-Italian-Australian-German

ROBERT TIFFE
SWORD OF HONOR   PM Entertainment Group, 1994

ERIC TILL*
b. 1929- London, England
Business: Coquihala Films, 62 Chaplin Crescent, Toronto,
Ontario M5P 1A3, Canada, 416/488-4068
Agent: Preferred Artists - Encino, 818/990-0305

A GREAT BIG THING   Argofilms, 1967, British
HOT MILLIONS   MGM, 1968, British
THE WALKING STICK   MGM, 1970, British
TALKING TO A STRANGER (TF)   1971, Canadian
FOLLOW THE NORTH STAR (TF)   1972, Canadian
A FAN'S NOTES   Warner Bros., 1972, Canadian
ALL THINGS BRIGHT AND BEAUTIFUL   *IT SHOULDN'T HAPPEN
TO A VET*   World Northal, 1978, British
WILD HORSE HANK   Film Consortium of Canada, 1979, Canadian
AN AMERICAN CHRISTMAS CAROL (TF)   ABC, 1979
MARY AND JOSEPH: A STORY OF FAITH (TF)   Lorimar
Productions/CIP-Europaische Treuhand AG,
1979, U.S.-West German
MAD SHADOWS (TF)   1979, Canadian
EYE OF THE BEHOLDER (TF)   1980, Canadian
IMPROPER CHANNELS   Crown International, 1981, Canadian
IF YOU COULD SEE WHAT I HEAR   Jensen Farley Pictures,
1982, Canadian
SHOCKTRAUMA (TF)   1983, Canadian
GENTLE SINNERS (TF)   CBC, 1983, Canadian
BRIDGE TO TERABITHIA (TF)   Twenty Minute Productions/
Kicking Horse Productions, 1985, Canadian
THE CUCKOO BIRD (TF)   CBC, 1985, Canadian
TURNING TO STONE (TF)   CBC, 1985, Canadian
GLENN GOULD: A PORTRAIT (TD)   co-director, 1985, Canadian
THE CHALLENGERS (TF)   CBC/Lauron Productions,
1989, Canadian
GETTING MARRIED IN BUFFALO JUMP (TF)   CBC,
1990, Canadian
GLORY ENOUGH FOR ALL (TF)   Gemstone/Primedia,
1990, Canadian

CLARENCE (CTF)   Atlantis Films/South Pacific Pictures, Ltd./
North Star Entertainment Group/The Family Channel/Television
New Zealand, 1991, Canadian-U.S.-New Zealand
COMFORT CREEK   Norstar Entertainment, 1992, Canadian
OH, WHAT A NIGHT   Norstar Entertainment/Telefilm Canada/
The Ontario Film Development Corporation, 1992, Canadian
TO CATCH A KILLER (TF)   Schreckinger-Kinberg Productions/
Creative Entertainment Group/Tribune Entertainment/Saban
International, 1992, U.S.-Canadian
LIFELINE TO VICTORY   Primedia/Cochran, 1993, Canadian
LYING IN WAIT   Republic Pictures, 1993, U.S.-Canadian
FINAL APPEAL (TF)   Republic Pictures Productions,
1993, U.S.-Canadian
VOICES FROM WITHIN (TF)   Vin Di Bona Productions/World
International Network, 1994
FALLING FOR YOU (TF)   Falling For You Productions/BBC
Prods., 1995, Canadian-British

BRUCE W. TIMM
Business: Warner Bros. Animation, 4000 Warner Blvd., Burbank,
CA 91522, 818/954-6000

BATMAN: MASK OF THE PHANTASM (AF)   co-director with
Eric Radomski, Warner Bros., 1993

MARK TINKER*
Agent: CAA - Beverly Hills, 310/288-4545

PRIVATE EYE (TF)   Yerkovich Productions/Universal TV, 1987
CAPITAL NEWS (TF)   MTM Enterprises, 1990
N.Y.P.D. MOUNTED (TF)   Patrick Hasburgh Productions/
Orion TV, 1991
BABE RUTH (TF)   A Lyttle Production Company/Warner
Bros. TV, 1991
BONANZA: UNDER ATTACK (TF)   NBC, 1995

DOUGLAS TIROLA
A REASON TO BELIEVE   Pioneer Pictures, 1994

STACY TITLE
Agent: Susan Smith & Associates - Beverly Hills, 213/852-4777
Contact: Armstrong & Hirsch - Los Angeles, 310/553-0305

THE LAST SUPPER   The Vault Inc., 1995

MOUFIDA TLATLI
THE SILENCES OF THE PALACE   1994, Tunisian

JAMES TOBACK*
b. November 23, 1944 - New York, New York
Home: 11 East 87th Street, New York, NY 10028, 212/427-5606
Agent: ICM - Beverly Hills, 310/550-4000
Business Manager: David Kaufman, Kaufman & Nachbar,
100 Merrick Road, Rockville Centre, NY, 516/536-5760

FINGERS   Brut Productions, 1978
LOVE AND MONEY   Paramount, 1982
EXPOSED   MGM/UA, 1983
THE PICK-UP ARTIST   20th Century-Fox, 1987
THE BIG BANG (FD)   Triton Pictures, 1989

STEPHEN TOBOLOWSKY
b. May 30, 1951 - Dallas, Texas
Contact: Screen Actors Guild - Los Angeles, 213/954-1600
Agent: William Morris Agency - Beverly Hills, 310/274-7451

TWO IDIOTS IN HOLLYWOOD   FilmDallas, 1989

VALERI TODOROVSKI
Contact: Confederation of Film-Makers Unions, Vasilyevskaya
Street 13, 123 825 Moscow, Russia, tel.: 095/250-4114

KATIA ISMAILOVA   Films du Rivage/Studio TTL/Lumiere/CNC/
Russian Cinema Committee/Russian Television/Dekar/Image
Ltd./Gorki Studios, 1994, French-Russian

SUSAN TODD

CHILDREN OF FATE: LIFE AND DEATH IN A SICILIAN
   FAMILY (FD)   co-director with Andrew Young,
   Young-Friedson/Archipelago Films, 1993
LIVES IN HAZARD (FD)   co-director with Andrew Young,
   Olmos Productions/Archipelago Films, 1993

RICKY TOGNAZZI

b. May 1, 1955 - Milan, Italy
Agent: Carol Levi, via Carducci 10, Rome, Italy, tel.: 06/486961

FERNANDA (TF)   Mass Film/RAI, 1987, Italian
PICCOLI EQUIVOCI   Mass Film, 1989, Italian
ULTRA'   Uno Cinematografica/RAI, 1990, Italian
LA SCORTA   First Look Pictures, 1993, Italian

SERGIO TOLEDO

b. 1956
Contact: National Cinema Council (CONCINE), Rua Mayrink
   Veiga 28, Rio de Janeiro, Brazil, tel.: 2/233-8329

VERA   1986, Brazilian
ONE MAN'S WAR (CTF)   HBO Showcase/Film Four International/
   TVS/Skreba, 1991, U.S.-British

MICHAEL TOLKIN*

b. 1950 - New York, New York
Agent: CAA - Beverly Hills, 310/288-4545
Personal Manager: Addis-Wechsler & Associates - Los Angeles,
   213/954-9000

THE RAPTURE   Fine Line Features/New Line Cinema, 1991
THE NEW AGE   Warner Bros., 1994

STEPHEN TOLKIN

Agent: Richland/Wunsch/Hohman Agency - Los Angeles,
   310/278-1955

DAYBREAK (CTF)   Foundation Entertainment Productions/
   HBO Showcase, 1993

RO TOMONO

Contact: Nihon Eiga Kantoku Kyokai (Japan Film Directors
   Association), La Fontenu Building -4th Floor, 23-2 Maruyama-cho,
   Shibuya-ku, Tokyo, Japan, tel.: 3/3461-4411

THE SETTING SUN   Nikkatsu, 1992, Japanese

STANLEY TONG

Contact: Hong Kong Film Liaison, 10940 Wilshire Blvd. - Suite 1220,
   Los Angeles, CA 90024, 310/208-2678

RUMBLE IN THE BRONX   New Line Cinema, 1994,
   Canadian-Hong Kong

TOM TOPOR*

Contact: Howard Rosenstone, 3 East 48th Street, New York,
   NY 10017, 212/832-8330

JUDGMENT (CTF)   Tisch-Wigutow-Hershman
   Productions, 1990

RALPH TOPOROFF*

Contact: Directors Guild of America - Los Angeles,
   213/851-3671

AMERICAN BLUE NOTE   Panorama Entertainment, 1989

BURT TOPPER*

b. July 31, 1928 - New York, New York
Address: P.O. Box 10488, Marina del Rey, CA 90292, 310/823-6434

HELL SQUAD   American International, 1958
TANK COMMANDOS   American International, 1959
THE DIARY OF A HIGH SCHOOL BRIDE   American
   International, 1959
WAR IS HELL   Allied Artists, 1964
THE STRANGLER   Allied Artists, 1964
THE DEVIL'S 8   American International, 1968
THE HARD RIDE   American International, 1971
THE DAY THE LORD GOT BUSTED   American, 1976

RIP TORN*

(Elmore Rual Torn, Jr.)
b. February 6, 1931 - Temple, Texas
Agent: The Gersh Agency - Beverly Hills, 310/274-6611

THE TELEPHONE   New World, 1988

GIUSEPPE TORNATORE

b. May 27, 1956 - Bagheria, Palermo, Italy
Home: via Santamaura 7, Rome, Italy, tel.: 06/374-2106

IL CAMORRISTA   Aria Cinematografica/Titanus/Reteitalia,
   1986, Italian
CINEMA PARADISO   *NUOVO CINEMA PARADISO*
   Miramax Films, 1989, Italian-French
EVERYBODY'S FINE   Miramax Films, 1990, Italian
LA DOMENICA SPECIALMENTE   co-director with
   Marco Tullio Giordana, Giuseppe Bertolucci & Francesco Barilli,
   Titanus Distribuzione, 1991, Italian-French-Belgian
A SIMPLE FORMALITY   Sony Pictures Classics,
   1994, Italian-French
THE STAR MAN   Miramax Films, 1995, Italian

JOE TORNATORE

GROTESQUE   Concorde, 1988
DEMON KEEPER   Concorde, 1993

GABE TORRES

Contact: Writers Guild of America, West - Los Angeles, 310/550-1000
Agent: Innovative Artists - Los Angeles, 310/553-5200

DECEMBER   I.R.S. Releasing, 1991

CINZIA TH TORRINI

b. 1954 - Florence, Italy
Home: via Costantino Morin 25, Rome, Italy, tel.: 06/325-1962

GIOCARE D'AZZARDO   Cassiopea/Grokenberger, 1982, Italian
HOTEL COLONIAL   Hemdale, 1987, U.S.-Italian
PLAGIO   co-director with Silvia Napolitano, RAI/WDR/Tangram/
   The Senate of West Berlin, 1990, Italian-West German
FROM NIGHT TO DAWN (MS)   RAI, 1992, Italian
WDR NIGHT SHADOW (TF)   RAI-1, 1993, Italian

SERGE TOUBIANA

Contact: French Film Office, 745 Fifth Avenue, New York,
   NY 10151, 212/832-8860

FRANCOIS TRUFFAUT, STOLEN PORTRAITS (FD)
   co-director with Michel Pascal, AAA, 1993, French

MOUSSA TOURE

b. Senegal
Contact: Bureau du Cinema, Ministere de la Culture et de la
   Communication, B.P. 4027, Dakar, Senegal

TOUBAB-BI   Valprod, 1992, French-Senegalese
LA MEMOIRE OUBLIEE   *THE SENEGALESE INFANTRYMAN* (TF)
   FR3/GMT Productions, 1993, French

ROBERT TOWNE*
b. 1936
Agent: CAA - Beverly Hills, 310/288-4545

PERSONAL BEST   The Geffen Company/Warner Bros., 1982
TEQUILA SUNRISE   Warner Bros., 1988

BUD TOWNSEND
Home: 5917 Blairstone Drive, Culver City, CA 90230,
   310/870-1559

NIGHTMARE IN WAX   Crown International, 1969
THE FOLKS AT RED WOLF INN   *TERROR HOUSE*
   Scope III, 1972
ALICE IN WONDERLAND   General National Enterprises, 1976
COACH   Crown International, 1978
LOVE SCENES   Playboy Enterprises, 1984

PAT TOWNSEND
Business: Crown International Pictures, 292 S. La Cienega Blvd.,
   Beverly Hills, CA 90211, 213/657-6700

THE BEACH GIRLS   Crown International, 1982

ROBERT TOWNSEND*
b. February 6, 1957 - Chicago, Illinois
Business: Tinsel Townsend, 8033 Sunset Blvd. - Suite 890,
   Los Angeles, CA 90046, 213/962-2240
Agent: CAA - Beverly Hills, 310/288-4545

HOLLYWOOD SHUFFLE   The Samuel Goldwyn Company, 1987
EDDIE MURPHY RAW (PF)   Paramount, 1987
THE FIVE HEARTBEATS   20th Century Fox, 1991
THE METEOR MAN   MGM, 1993

IAN TOYNTON
Business: Turning Point Productions, Pinewood Studios,
   Iver Heath, Buckinghamshire, England, tel.: 0753/630666
Agent: Peters Fraser & Dunlop - London, tel.: 171/344-1000

WIDOWS (TF)   Euston Films, 1983, British
THE FOURTH FLOOR (TF)   1985, British
THE CONTRACT (TF)   Yorkshire TV, 1987, British
THE SAINT: THE BRAZILIAN CONNECTION (TF)
   Saint Productions/London Weekend TV/CD & MG/Toro
   GMBH/Taffner Ramsay Productions, 1989, British
PIECE OF CAKE (MS)   Holmes Associates Productions/London
   Weekend TV, 1990, British
THE MAID   Chrysalide Film/Canal Plus/The Movie Group,
   1991, French-U.S.
RED FOX (TF)   Fitzroy Films Ltd./London Weekend TV,
   1992, British
SHE'S OUT   Cinema Verity/La Plante Productions, 1994, British

JEAN-CLAUDE TRAMONT*
b. May 5, 1934 - Brussels, Belgium
Agent: ICM - New York City, 212/556-5600

LE POINT DE MIRE   Warner-Columbia, 1977, French
ALL NIGHT LONG   Universal, 1981
AS SUMMERS DIE (CTF)   HBO Premiere Films/Chris-Rose
   Productions/Baldwin/Aldrich Productions/Lorimar-Telepictures
   Productions, 1986

JOHN TRAVERS
DEEP DOWN   Deep Down Productions, 1993

MARK W. TRAVIS*
Business: The Travis Group, 12229 Ventura Blvd. - Suite 204,
   Studio City, CA 91604, 818/508-4600

GOING UNDER   Warner Bros., 1991

JOEY TRAVOLTA
Contact: Screen Actors Guild - Los Angeles, 213/954-1600

VEGAS VICE   Blue Ridge Entertainment/Raejoe Productions/Good
   Doctor Productions, 1994

TOM TRBOVICH*
Home: 20140 Pacific Coast Highway, Malibu, CA 90265,
   310/456-9417
Agent: Larry Grossman & Associates - Beverly Hills, 310/550-8127

FREE RIDE   Galaxy International, 1986

BRIAN TRENCHARD-SMITH
b. 1946
Business: Trenchard Productions, 26 Maranta Street, Hornsby,
   Sydney, Australia, tel.: 477-6913
Agent: The Wallerstein Company - Los Angeles, 213/782-0225

THE WORLD OF KUNG FU (TF)   1974, Australian
THE KUNG FU KILLERS (TF)   1974, Australian
THE LOVE EPIDEMIC   Hexagon Production, 1975, Australian
THE MAN FROM HONG KONG   The Movie Company/
   Golden Harvest, 1975, Australian-Hong Kong
DEATHCHEATERS   Trenchard Productions/D.L. Taffner,
   1976, Australian
STUNT ROCK   1978, British
THE DAY OF THE ASSASSIN   1981, Mexican
TURKEY SHOOT   Second FGH Film Consortium, 1982, Australian
BMX BANDITS   Nilsen Premiere, 1985, Australian
JENNY KISSED ME   Nilsen Premiere, 1985, Australian
THE QUEST   Miramax, 1986, Australian
DEAD END DRIVE-IN   New World, 1986, Australian
THE DAY OF THE PANTHER   International Film Marketing,
   1987, Australian
OUT OF THE BODY   David Hannay Productions, 1988, Australian
STRIKE OF THE PANTHER   Virgo Productions/TVM Studios/
   Mandemar Group, 1988, Australian
THE SIEGE OF FIREBASE GLORIA   Fries Entertainment,
   1989, U.S.-Filipino-Australian
DELTA FORCE - THE KILLING GAME   Global Pictures, 1990
OFFICIAL DENIAL (CTF)   Wilshire Court Productions, 1993
NIGHT OF THE DEMONS 2   Blue Rider Pictures/Republic
   Pictures, 1994

BARBARA TRENT
Business: Empowerment Project, 1653 18th Street - Suite 3,
   Santa Monica, CA 90404, 310/828-8807

COVERUP: BEHIND THE IRAN-CONTRA AFFAIR (FD)
   Empowerment Project, 1988
THE PANAMA DECEPTION (FD)   Empowerment Project/
   Channel 4, 1992, U.S.-British

BLAIR TREU
JUST LIKE DAD   Leucadia Film Corporation, 1995

DALE TREVILLION
ONE MAN FORCE   Shapiro Glickenhaus Entertainment, 1989

JESUS SALVADOR TREVINO*
Home: 1854 Phillips Way, Los Angeles, CA 90042, 213/258-0802
Agent: Scott Schwartz, Dytman & Schwartz, 9200 Sunset Blvd. -
   Suite 809, Los Angeles, CA 90069, 310/204-3341

RAICES DE SANGRE   Conacine, 1977, Mexican
MARIPOSA (TF)   Rainbow Productions, 1979
SEGUIN (TF)   KCET, 1982
YO SOY (TD)   co-director with Jose Luis Ruiz,
   WNET/KCET/KAET, 1985

GUS TRIKONIS*

b. New York, New York
Contact: Directors Guild of America - Los Angeles, 213/851-3671

FIVE THE HARD WAY   Fantascope, 1969
THE SWINGING BARMAIDS   Premiere, 1975
SUPERCOCK   Hagen-Wayne, 1975
NASHVILLE GIRL   New World, 1976
MOONSHINE COUNTY EXPRESS   New World, 1977
NEW GIRL IN TOWN   New World, 1977
THE EVIL   New World, 1978
THE DARKER SIDE OF TERROR (TF)   Shaner-Ramrus
   Productions/Bob Banner Associates, 1979
SHE'S DRESSED TO KILL (TF)   Grant-Case-McGrath
   Enterprises/Barry Weitz Films, 1979
THE LAST CONVERTIBLE (MS)   co-director with Sidney Hayers &
   Jo Swerling, Jr., Roy Huggins Productions/Universal TV, 1979
FLAMINGO ROAD (TF)   MF Productions/Lorimar Productions, 1980
TOUCHED BY LOVE   Columbia, 1980
ELVIS AND THE BEAUTY QUEEN (TF)   David Gerber Company/
   Columbia TV, 1981
TAKE THIS JOB AND SHOVE IT   Avco Embassy, 1981
TWIRL (TF)   Charles Fries Productions, 1981
MISS ALL-AMERICAN BEAUTY (TF)   Marian Rees
   Associates, 1982
DEMPSEY (TF)   Charles Fries Productions, 1983
DANCE OF THE DWARFS   Dove, Inc., 1983
FIRST AFFAIR (TF)   CBS Entertainment, 1983
MALICE IN WONDERLAND (TF)   ITC Productions, 1985
MIDAS VALLEY (TF)   Edward S. Feldman Company/Warner
   Bros. TV, 1985
LOVE ON THE RUN (TF)   NBC Productions, 1985
OPEN ADMISSIONS (TF)   The Mount Company/Viacom
   Productions, 1988
THE GREAT PRETENDER (TF)   Stephen J. Cannell
   Productions, 1991

NADINE TRINTIGNANT

(Nadine Marquand)
b. November 11, 1934 - Nice, France
Agent: ICM France - Paris, tel.: 1/723-7860
Contact: French Film Office, 745 Fifth Avenue, New York,
   NY 10151, 212/832-8860

MON AMOUR, MON AMOUR   1967, French
LE VOLEUR DE CRIMES   1969, French
IT ONLY HAPPENS TO OTHERS   GSF Productions,
   1971, French-Italian
DEFENSE DE SAVOIR   1973, French
LE VOYAGE DE NOCES   1976, French
PREMIER VOYAGE   1979, French
L'ETE PROCHAIN   1984, French
LA MAISON DE JADE   1988, French
CONTRE L'OUBLI   co-director, Les Films du Paradoxe/Amnesty
   International/PRV, 1992, French
UN FILLE GALANTE   Canal Plus, 1995, French

ROSE TROCHE

Agent: The Gersh Agency - Beverly Hills, 310/274-6611

GO FISH   The Samuel Goldwyn Company, 1994

JAN TROELL

b. July 23, 1931 - Limhamn, Skane, Sweden
Contact: Swedish Film Institute, P.O. Box 27126, 102 52 Stockholm,
   Sweden, tel.: 08/665-1100

4 X 4   co-director, 1965, Swedish-Finnish-Norwegian-Danish
HERE'S YOUR LIFE   Brandon, 1966, Swedish
EENY, MEENY, MINY, MO   *WHO SAW HIM DIE?*
   Svensk Filmindustri, 1968, Swedish
THE EMIGRANTS   *UTVANDRARNA* ★   Warner Bros.,
   1972, Swedish
THE NEW LAND   *NYBYGGARNA*   Warner Bros., 1973, Swedish
ZANDY'S BRIDE   Warner Bros., 1974
BANG!   Svensk Filminstitut, 1977, Swedish
HURRICANE   Paramount, 1979

THE FLIGHT OF THE EAGLE   Summit Features, 1982,
   Swedish-West German-Norwegian
SAGOLANDET (FD)   Swedish Film Institute, 1988, Swedish
IL CAPITANO   PanfilmAB/Film Teknik/Four Seasons/Bold
   Productions/Villealfa Productions/Polyphon Film UndTV,
   1991, Swedish-Finnish-German
HAMSUN   Nordisk Film, 1995, Norwegian-Danish

MARC C. TROPIA

Business: Vantage Point Entertainment, P.O. Box 60171,
   San Diego, CA 92106, 619/225-9206
Agent: Harry S. Hamlin, Motion Picture Production Institute,
   5410 SW 127 Place, Miami, FL 33175, 305/553-8256

MIAMI BEACH BUG POLICE   co-director with Tano Tropia,
   Cinemaworld Pictures, 1986
FRIARS ROAD   Vantage Point Entertainment, 1986
NATURAL CAUSES   Moving Pictures Entertainment/MPPI/Fujimoto
   Partners, 1994

TANO TROPIA

Business: Vantage Point Entertainment, P.O. Box 60171,
   San Diego, CA 92106, 619/225-9206
Agent: Harry S. Hamlin, Motion Picture Production Institute,
   5410 SW 127 Place, Miami, FL 33175, 305/553-8256

MIAMI BEACH BUG POLICE   co-director with Marc C. Tropia,
   Cinemaworld Pictures, 1986

GARY TROUSDALE

Business: Walt Disney Animation, 500 S. Buena Vista Street,
   Burbank, CA 91521, 818/560-1000

BEAUTY AND THE BEAST (AF)   co-director with Kirk Wise,
   Buena Vista, 1991
THE HUNCHBACK OF NOTRE DAME (AF)   co-director with
   Kirk Wise, Buena Vista, 1996

FERNANDO TRUEBA

b. January 18, 1955 - Madrid, Spain
Business: Fernando Trueba PC, Antonio Cavera 37, Madrid 28043,
   Spain, tel.: 34-1-759-6264
Agent: CAA - Beverly Hills, 310/288-4545

OPERA PRIMA   New Yorker, 1980, Spanish-French
MIENTRAS EL CUERPO AGUANTE   Opera Films, 1982, Spanish
SAL GORDA   Opera Films, 1983, Spanish
SE INFIEL Y NO MIRES CON QUIEN   Iberoamericana,
   1985, Spanish
EL ANO DE LAS LUCES   Iberoamericana, 1986, Spanish
TWISTED OBSESSION   *THE MAD MONKEY*   IVE,
   1989, Spanish-French
BELLE EPOQUE (THE AGE OF BEAUTY)   Sony Pictures Classics,
   1993, Spanish-Portuguese-French
TWO MUCH   Fernando Trueba PC/Iberoamericana Film Productions,
   1995, Spanish-U.S.

DOUGLAS TRUMBULL*

b. 1942 - Los Angeles, California
Business: The Trumbull Company, Inc., P.O. Box 847, Riverview
   Road, Lenox, MA 01240, 413/637-0500
Agent: The Gersh Agency - Beverly Hills, 310/274-6611
Attorney: Kenneth Kleinberg, Kleinberg & Lange, 1880 Century
   Park East - Suite 1150, Los Angeles, CA 90067

SILENT RUNNING   Universal, 1972
BRAINSTORM   MGM/UA, 1983

MING-LIANG TSAI

(See Tsai MING-LIANG)

TALAN TSU

THE SILENCER   West Side Studios, 1994

HARK TSUI

(See Tsui HARK)

SHINYA TSUKAMOTO
b. Japan
Contact: Nihon Eiga Kantoku Kyokai (Japan Film Directors Association), La Fontenu Building - 4th Floor, 23-2 Maruyama-cho,
Shibuya-ku, Tokyo, Japan, tel.: 3/3461-4411

TETSUO: THE IRON MAN   Kaijyu Theatre, 1991, Japanese
TETSUO II: BODY HAMMER   Toshiba EMI/Kaijyu Theatre,
1992, Japanese

SLAVA TSUKERMAN
b. Moscow, U.S.S.R.
Telephone: New York - 212/620-0110

LIQUID SKY   Cinevista, 1983

STANLEY TUCCI
b. 1960 - New York, New York
Agent: William Morris Agency - Beverly Hills, 310/859-4000

BIG NIGHT   co-director with Campbell Scott,
Rysher Entertainment, 1996

MICHAEL TUCHNER*
b. June 24, 1934 - Berlin, Germany
Home: 15377 Longbow Drive, Sherman Oaks, CA 91403,
818/995-6700
Agent: CAA - Beverly Hills, 310/288-4545

VILLAIN   MGM, 1971, British
FEAR IS THE KEY   Paramount, 1973, British
MR. QUILP   Avco Embassy, 1975, British
BAR MITZVAH BOY (TF)   BBC, 1976, British
THE LIKELY LADS   EMI, 1976, British
THE ONE AND ONLY PHYLLIS DIXEY (TF)   Thames TV,
1979, British
SUMMER OF MY GERMAN SOLDIER (TF)
Highgate Productions, 1978
HAYWIRE (TF)   Pando Productions/Warner Bros. TV, 1980
THE HUNCHBACK OF NOTRE DAME (TF)   Norman Rosemont
Productions/Columbia TV, 1982, U.S.-British
PAROLE (TF)   RSO Films, 1982
TRENCHCOAT   Buena Vista, 1983
ADAM (TF)   Alan Landsburg Productions, 1983
NOT MY KID (TF)   Beth Polson Productions/Finnegan
Associates, 1985
GENERATION (TF)   Embassy TV, 1985
AMOS (TF)   The Bryna Company/Vincent Pictures, 1985
TRAPPED IN SILENCE (TF)   Reader's Digest Productions, 1986
AT MOTHER'S REQUEST (TF)   Vista Organization Ltd., 1987
MISTRESS (TF)   Jaffe-Lansing Productions/Republic Pictures, 1987
INTERNAL AFFAIRS (TF)   Titus Productions, 1988
DESPERATE FOR LOVE (TF)   Vishudda Productions/Andrew
Adelson Productions/Lorimar Telepictures, 1989
THE MISADVENTURES OF MR. WILT   WILT   The Samuel
Goldwyn Company, 1990, British
WHEN WILL I BE LOVED? (TF)   Nederlander Television &
Film Productions, 1990
THE SUMMER MY FATHER GREW UP (TF)   Robert Shapiro
Productions, 1991
CAPTIVE (TF)   Capital Cities/ABC Video Enterprises/Bonny Dore
Productions/Ten-Four Productions, 1991
WITH MURDER IN MIND (TF)   Helios Productions/Bob Banner
Associates, 1992
FIRESTORM: 72 HOURS IN OAKLAND (TF)   Gross-Weston
Productions/Capital Cities-ABC Video Productions/Cannell
Entertainment, 1993
THE CONVICTION OF KITTY DODDS (TF)   Republic Pictures
Productions, 1993
GOOD KING WENCESLAS (CTF)   Griffin Productions/Family
Productions, 1994, U.S.-British

ANAND TUCKER
Contact: British Film Commission, 70 Baker Street, London
W1M 1DJ, England, tel.: 171/224-5000

ANNE RICE: BIRTH OF A VAMPIRE (TD)   Oxford Television
Company/BBC, 1994, British

DAVID TUCKER
Agent: ICM - London, tel.: 171/636-6565

MISS MARPLE: NEMESIS (TF)   BBC, 1986, British
TICKET TO RIDE (TF)   ITV, 1988, British
BEHAVING BADLY (MS)   Channel 4, 1988, British
THE GRAVY TRAIN (MS)   Channel 4, 1989, British
STANLEY AND THE WOMEN (MS)   ITV, 1991, British
A VERY POLISH PRACTICE (TF)   BBC Screenb One, 1992, British
A YEAR IN PROVENCE (MS)   BBC/Arts & Entertainment Network,
1993, British-U.S.
UNDER THE HAMMER (MS)   co-director with Robert Tronson,
New Pennt Productions/Meridian Broadcasting, 1993, British

RICHARD TUGGLE*
b. August 8, 1948 - Coral Gables, Florida
Agent: UTA - Beverly Hills, 310/273-6700
Attorney: Wayne Alexander, Alexander, Halloran & Nau,
2029 Century Park East - Suite 1690, Los Angeles, CA 90067,
310/552-0035

TIGHTROPE   Warner Bros., 1984
OUT OF BOUNDS   Columbia, 1986

MONTGOMERY TULLY
b. May 6, 1904 - Dublin, Ireland
Contact: British Film Commission, 70 Baker Street, London
W1M 1DJ, England, tel.: 171/224-5000

MURDER IN REVERSE   Four Continents, 1945, British
SPRING SONG   1946, British
MRS. FITZHERBERT   1947, British
BOYS IN BROWN   1950, British
A TALE OF FIVE CITIES   co-director, 1951,
British-French-Italian-West German
SMALL TOWN STORY   1953, British
THE DIAMOND WIZARD   *THE DIAMOND*   United Artists,
1954, British
36 HOURS   1954, British
THE WAY OUT   *DIAL 999*   RKO Radio, 1955, British
THE GLASS TOMB   *THE GLASS CAGE*   Lippert, 1955, British
THE COUNTERFEIT PLAN   Warner Bros., 1957, British
THE HYPNOTIST   1957, British
MAN IN THE SHADOW   *PAY THE DEVIL*   Universal, 1957, British
THE ELECTRONIC MONSTER   *ESCAPEMENT*   Columbia,
1958, British
STRANGE AWAKENING   Anglo Amalgamated, 1958, British
THE LONG KNIFE   1958, British
MAN WITH A GUN   1958, British
DIPLOMATIC CORPSE   Rank, 1958, British
MAN ACCUSED   1959, British
JACKPOT   Grand National, 1960, British
THE PRICE OF SILENCE   Allied Artists, 1960, British
DEAD LUCKY   1960, British
THE THIRD ALIBI   Modern Sound Films, 1961, British
OUT OF THE FOG   1962, British
MASTER SPY   Allied Artists, 1963, British
ESCAPE BY NIGHT   *CLASH BY NIGHT*   Allied Artists,
1964, British
THE TERRORNAUTS   Embassy, 1967, British
BATTLE BENEATH THE EARTH   MGM, 1968, British
THE HAWKS   1969, British

SANDY TUNG*
Home: 8377 Gregory Way, Beverly Hills, CA 90211, 310/852-4941
Agent: The Gersh Agency - Beverly Hills, 310/274-6611
Attorney: Shelley Surpin, Surpin, Mayersohn & Edelstone,
1880 Century Park East - Suite 618, Los Angeles,
CA 90067, 310/852-1808

BROKEN PROMISE   *A MARRIAGE*   Cinecom, 1983
ACROSS THE TRACKS   Desert Productions, 1990

SOPHIA TURKIEWICZ
b. Poland
Agent: Anthony Williams Management, 55 Victoria Street, Potts Point,
    Sydney, NSW 2027, Australia
Contact: Australian Film Commission, 150 William Street,
    Woolloomooloo NSW 2011, Australia, tel.: 2/321-6444

TIME'S RAGING (TF)   1984, Australian
SILVER CITY   The Samuel Goldwyn Company, 1984, Australian

ROSE-MARIE TURKO
b. April 14, 1951 - Orleans, France

SCARRED *STREET LOVE*   Seymour Borde & Associates, 1983
THE DUNGEONMASTER   co-director, Empire Pictures, 1985

LAWRENCE TURMAN*
b. November 28, 1926 - Los Angeles, California
Address: P.O. Box 2416, Beverly Hills, CA 90213

MARRIAGE OF A YOUNG STOCKBROKER   20th Century-Fox, 1971
SECOND THOUGHTS   Universal, 1983

ANN TURNER
b. Adelaide, Australia
Agent: ICM - London, tel.: 171/636-6565

CELIA   Kim Lewis Marketing, 1988, Australian
HAMMERS OVER THE ANVIL   South Australian Film Corporation/
    Harvest Productions/Film Finance Corporation Film Fund,
    1993, Australian
DALLAS DOLL   Dallas Doll Productions/Australian Film Finance
    Corporation/Australian Broadcasting Corporation/BBC Films,
    1994, Australian-British

CLIVE TURNER
Contact: British Film Commission, 70 Baker Street, London
    W1M 1DJ, England, tel.: 171/224-5000

HOWLING V   Allied Vision, 1989, British

PAUL TURNER
Address: 118 Valley Road, London SW16 2XR, England,
    tel.: 181/769-9750
Agent: Shaun Redmayne, Tigermain - London, tel.: 171/373-4105

HEDD WYN   Miramax Films, 1993, Welsh
WILD JUSTICE *DIAL*   Pendefig/S4C (Wales), 1994, Welsh

ROB TURNER
b. 1951 - Vancouver, British Columbia, Canada
Business: Circle Productions Limited, 1700 Cypress Street,
    Vancouver, British Columbia V6J 4W2, Canada, 604/733-5727

DIGGER   Western International Communications/Circle
    Northwood, 1993, Canadian

JON TURTELTAUB*
Agent: ICM - Beverly Hills, 310/550-4000

THINK BIG   Motion Picture Corporation of America, 1990
DRIVING ME CRAZY *TRABBI GOES TO HOLLYWOOD*
    Motion Picture Corporation of America, 1991
3 NINJAS   Buena Vista, 1992
COOL RUNNINGS   Buena Vista, 1993
WHILE YOU WERE SLEEPING   Buena Vista, 1995

JOHN TURTURRO
b. February 28, 1957 - Brooklyn, New York
Agent: ICM - Beverly Hills, 310/550-4000

MAC   The Samuel Goldwyn Company, 1992

DAVID N. TWOHY
Agent: William Morris Agency - Beverly Hills, 310/859-4000

DISASTER IN TIME (CTF)   Wildstreet Pictures, 1992,
    originally filmed for theatrical distribution

TRACY TYNAN
b. London, England
Attorney: Frank Gruber, 9601 Wilshire Blvd., Beverly Hills,
    CA 90210, 310/274-5638

A GREAT BUNCH OF GIRLS (FD)   co-director with
    Mary Ann Braubach, Cowgirl Productions, 1978

LIV ULLMANN
b. December 16, 1939 - Tokyo, Japan
Contact: Norwegian Film Institute, Grev Wedels Plass 1, N-0105
    Oslo 1, Norway, tel.: 2/42-87-40
Agent: The Lantz Office - New York, 212/586-0200

LOVE   co-director with Annette Cohen, Nancy Dowd & Mai Zetterling,
    Velvet Films, 1982, Canadian
SOFIE   Arrow Releasing, 1992, Danish-Norwegian-Swedish
KRISTIN LAVRANSDATTER   Lavransdatter Productions/Norsk
    Film/Movies Entertainment Ltd./Northern Light Productions/
    Tonefilm, 1995, Norwegian

RON UNDERWOOD*
b. November 6, 1953 - Glendale, California
Personal Manager: Nancy Roberts, The Roberts Company -
    Los Angeles, 310/552-7800
Agent: UTA - Beverly Hills, 310/273-6700

TREMORS   Universal, 1990
CITY SLICKERS   Columbia, 1991
HEART AND SOULS   Universal, 1993
SPEECHLESS   MGM-UA, 1994

MICHAEL TOSHIYUKI UNO*
Agent: ICM - Beverly Hills, 310/550-4000

HOME FIRES (CMS)   Edgar J. Scherick Productions, 1987
THE WASH   Skouras Pictures, 1988
WITHOUT WARNING: THE JAMES BRADY STORY (CTF)
    Enigma TV Productions, 1991
FUGITIVE AMONG US (TF)   ABC Productions, 1991
IN THE EYES OF A STRANGER (TF)   Power Pictures/Avenue
    Entertainment, 1992
BLIND SPOT (TF)   Signboard Hill Productions/RHI
    Entertainment, 1993
LIES OF THE HEART: THE STORY OF LAURIE KELLOGG (TF)
    MDT Productions/Daniel H. Blatt Productions/Warner
    Bros. TV, 1994
A TIME TO HEAL (TF)   Susan Baerwald Productions/NBC
    Productions, 1994
DANGEROUS INTENTIONS (TF)   The Kaufman Company/Wild
    Rice Productions/The Kushner Locke Company, 1995

STUART URBAN
Agent: Linda Seifert, Seifert Dench Associates - London,
    tel.: 171/437-4551

POCKETFUL OF DREAMS (TF)   BBC, 1982, British
THE LIVING BODY (TD)   Goldcrest Productions, 1984-85, British
OFF TO THE WARS (TF)   Channel 4, 1986, British
AN UNGENTLEMANLY ACT (TF)   London Films/Union Pictures/
    BBC, 1992, British

Ur

F
I
L
M

D
I
R
E
C
T
O
R
S

JEFF URELES
Contact: Writers Guild of America, East - New York City,
  212/767-7800
Agent: The Artists Agency - Los Angeles, 310/277-7779

CHEAP SHOTS   co-director with Jerry Stoeffhaas, Hemdale, 1988

PETER USTINOV*
b. April 16, 1921 - London, England
Home: Rue de Silly, 91200 Boulogne, France, tel.: 1/603-8753

SCHOOL FOR SECRETS   General Film Distributors, 1946, British
VICE VERSA   General Film Distributors, 1948, British
PRIVATE ANGELO   co-director with Michael Anderson,
  Associated British Picture Corporation, 1949, British
ROMANOFF AND JULIET   Universal, 1961
BILLY BUDD   Allied Artists, 1962, British
LADY L   MGM, 1966, U.S.-Italian-French
HAMMERSMITH IS OUT   Cinerama Releasing Corporation, 1972
MEMED, MY HAWK   Filmworld Distributors, 1984,
  British-Yugoslavian

JAMIE UYS
(Jacobus Johannes Uys)
b. 1921 - Boksburg, South Africa
Contact Information: Dr. Martin Botha, Human Sciences Research
  Council, Group for Social Dynamics, Private Bag x41,
  Pretoria 0001, South Africa, tel.: 012/202-2308

DINGAKA   Embassy, 1965, South African
AFTER YOU, COMRADE   Continental, 1967, South African
LOST IN THE DESERT   Columbia-Warner, 1971, South African
ANIMALS ARE BEAUTIFUL PEOPLE (FD)   *BEAUTIFUL PEOPLE*
  Warner Bros., 1974, South African
THE GODS MUST BE CRAZY   TLC Films/20th Century-Fox,
  1979, Botswana
BEAUTIFUL PEOPLE II (FD)   1983, South African
THE GODS MUST BE CRAZY 2   WEG/Columbia, 1989, Botswana

UZO
CUL-DE-SAC   Cold Grey Entertainment Corporation, 1995

ROGER VADIM*
(Roger Vadim Plemiannikov)
b. January 26, 1928 - Paris, France
Contact: Directors Guild of America - Los Angeles, 213/851-3671

AND GOD CREATED WOMAN   Kingsley International,
  1956, French
NO SUN IN VENICE   *SAIT-ON JAMAIS?*   Kingsley International,
  1957, French-Italian
THE NIGHT HEAVEN FELL   *LES BIJOUTIERS DU CLAIR
  DE LUNES*   Kingsley International, 1957, French-Italian
LES LIAISONS DANGEREUSES   *DANGEROUS LIAISONS 1960*
  Astor, 1959, French-Italian, re-released in 1989 by Interama
BLOOD AND ROSES   *ET MOURIR DE PLAISIR*   Paramount,
  1960, Italian
PLEASE, NOT NOW!   *LA BRIDE SUR LE COU*
  20th Century-Fox, 1961, French
SEVEN CAPITAL SINS   co-director with Jean-Luc Godard, Sylvaine
  Dhomme, Edouard Molinaro, Philippe De Broca, Claude Chabrol,
  Jacques Demy, Marie-Jose Nat, Dominique Paturel, Jean-Marc
  Tennberg & Perrette Pradier, Embassy, 1962, French-Italian
LOVE ON A PILLOW   *LE REPOS DU GUERRIER*   Royal Films
  International, 1962, French-Italian
OF FLESH AND BLOOD   *LES GRANDS CHEMINS*
  Times, 1963, French-Italian

VICE AND VIRTUE   MGM, 1963, French
NUTTY, NAUGHTY CHATEAU   *CHATEAU EN SUEDE*
  Lopert, 1963, French-Italian
CIRCLE OF LOVE   *LA RONDE*   Continental, 1964, French
THE GAME IS OVER   *LA CUREE*   Royal Films International,
  1966, French-Italian
SPIRITS OF THE DEAD   *HISTOIRES EXTRAORDINAIRES*
  co-director with Federico Fellini & Louis Malle, American
  International, 1968, Italian-French
BARBARELLA   Paramount, 1968, Italian-French
PRETTY MAIDS ALL IN A ROW   MGM, 1971
HELLE   Cocinor, 1972, French
MS. DON JUAN   *DON JUAN ETAIT UNE FEMME*   Scotia American,
  1973, French
CHARLOTTE   *LA JEUNE FILLE ASSASSINEE*   Gamma III,
  1974, French
UNE FEMME FIDELE   FFCM, 1976, French
NIGHT GAMES   Avco Embassy, 1980, French
THE HOT TOUCH   Astral Bellevue, 1981, Canadian
SURPRISE PARTY   Uranium Films, 1982, French
COME BACK   Comeci, 1983, French
AND GOD CREATED WOMAN   Vestron, 1988
LE FOU AMOUREAUX   Anabase Productions/Gemka Productions,
  1991, French

JOHN VALADEZ
PASSIN' IT ON (TD)   Nosotros Moving Pictures, 1994

LUIS VALDEZ*
b. June 26, 1940 - Delano, California
Home: P.O. Box 1009, San Juan Bautista, CA 95045, 408/623-4895
Agent: Writers & Artists Agency - Los Angeles, 310/820-6300

ZOOT SUIT   Universal, 1981
LA BAMBA   Columbia, 1987
LA PASTORELA (TF)   El Teatro Campesino/Richard Soto
  Productions/WNET-13/Channel 4/TVE, 1991,
  U.S.-British-Spanish
THE CISCO KID (CTF)   Esparza-Katz Productions/Goodman-Rosen
  Productions/Turner Pictures, 1994

MIKE VALERIO
KING B: A LIFE IN THE MOVIES   Bennett King Pictures
  Productions, 1993

NICK VALLELONGA
A BRILLIANT DISGUISE   Prism Pictures, 1994
IN THE KINGDOM OF THE BLIND THE MAN WITH ONE
  EYE IS KING   Larry Estes Productions, 1995

JEAN-CLAUDE VAN DAMME
b. Belgium
Agent: ICM - Beverly Hills, 310/550-4000

THE QUEST   Universal, 1995

JACO VAN DORMAEL
b. February 9, 1957 - Ixelles, Belgium
Home: rue Potapere 150, B-1030 Brussels, Belgium, tel.: 2/217-7320
Agent: CAA - Beverly Hills, 310/288-4545

TOTO THE HERO   Triton Pictures, 1991, Belgian-French-German
EIGHTH DAY   1995, French

BRUCE VAN DUSEN*
Contact: Directors Guild of America - Los Angeles, 213/851-3671

COLD FEET   Cinecom, 1984

BUDDY VAN HORN*
Home: 4409 Ponca Avenue, Toluca Lake, CA 91602, 213/462-2301
Agent: The Sy Fischer Company - Los Angeles, 310/470-0917

ANY WHICH WAY YOU CAN   Warner Bros., 1980
THE DEAD POOL   Warner Bros., 1988
PINK CADILLAC   Warner Bros., 1989

KEES VAN OOSTRUM*

b. July 5, 1954 - Amsterdam, Netherlands
Attorney: Peter Nichols, Weissmann, Wolff, Bergman, Coleman &
Silverman, 9665 Wilshire Blvd. - Suite 900, Beverly Hills,
CA 90212, 310/858-7888

MISSING PERSONS: FOUR TRUE STORIES (CTD)
Dave Bell Associates, 1984
HET BITTERE KRUID   Verenigde Nederlandsche Filmcompagnie,
1985, Dutch

MARIO VAN PEEBLES*

Agent: ICM - Beverly Hills, 310/550-4000
Personal Manager: Tobie Haggerty - New Jersey, 201/746-8351

NEW JACK CITY   Warner Bros., 1991
POSSE   Gramercy Pictures, 1993, U.S.-British
PANTHER   Gramercy Pictures, 1995

MELVIN VAN PEEBLES

(Melvin Peebles)
b. August 21, 1932 - Chicago, Illinois
Business: 353 West 56th Street - Apt. 10F, New York, NY 10019,
212/489-6570

THE STORY OF A THREE-DAY PASS   LA PERMISSION
Sigma III, 1968, French
WATERMELON MAN   Columbia, 1970
SWEET SWEETBACK'S BAADASSSSSS SONG   Cinemation, 1971
DON'T PLAY US CHEAP   Movin On Distribution, 1973
IDENTITY CRISIS   Block & Chip Productions, 1989
EROTIC TALES   co-director with Bob Rafelson, Susan Seidelman,
Ken Russell, Paul Cox & Mani Kaul, Regina Ziegler
Filmproduktion/Tele-Munchen/Westdeutscher Rundfunk,
1994, German

WILLIAM VANDERKLOOT

Business: Double Helix Films, Inc., 303 West 76th Street -
Suite B, New York, NY 10023

MACE   Film Ventures International, 1987

NORMAN THADDEUS VANE

Business: American New Wave Films, 7441 Sunset Blvd. -
Suite 201-202, Hollywood, CA 90046, 213/851-1987

THE BLACK ROOM   co-director with Elly Kenner, CH Films, 1984
FRIGHTMARE   Saturn International, 1983
KING OF THE CITY   CLUB LIFE   M.P.R./V.T.C./Prism
Entertainment, 1986
MIDNIGHT   SVS Films, 1989
TAXI DANCER   Trident Releasing, 1993

GUS VAN SANT, JR.

b. 1952 - Louisville, Kentucky
Agent: William Morris Agency - Beverly Hills, 310/859-4000

MALA NOCHE   Northern Film Company, 1985
DRUGSTORE COWBOY   Avenue Pictures, 1989
MY OWN PRIVATE IDAHO   Fine Line Features/New Line
Cinema, 1991
EVEN COWGIRLS GET THE BLUES   Fine Line Features/
New Line Cinema, 1993
TO DIE FOR   Columbia, 1995

STERLING VANWAGENEN

ALAN AND NAOMI   Triton Pictures, 1992

CARLO VANZINA

b. 1952 - Florence, Italy
Home: via Pezzana 9, Rome, Italy, tel.: 06/807-7319

LUNA DI MIELE IN TRE   Irrigazione Cinematografica, 1976, Italian
FIGLIO DELLE STELLE   San Francisco, 1979, Italian
ARRIVANO I GATTI   Adap/Mondial/Laser, 1979, Italian

I FICHISSIMI   Dean International, 1981, Italian
ECCEZZIUNALE VERAMENTE   Cinemedia, 1982, Italian
VIUUULENTEMENTE...MIA   Horizont Produzioni, 1982, Italian
SAPORE DI MARE   Dean International, 1982, Italian
IL RAS DEL QUARTIERE   Ypsilon Cinematografica/Italian
International Films, 1983, Italian
MYSTERE   Tris Film, 1983, Italian
VACANZE DI NATALE   Filmauro, 1983, Italian
AMARSI UN PO'   C.G. Silver Film, 1984, Italian
VACANZE IN AMERICA   C.G. Silver Film, 1984, Italian
SOTTO IL VESTITO NIENTE   Faso Film, 1985, Italian
YUPPIES, I GIOVANI DI SUCCESSO   Filmauro, 1986, Italian
VIA MONTENAPOLEONE   Reteitalia/C.G. Silver Film/Video 80,
1987, Italian
I MIEI PRIMI QUARANT' ANNI   Columbia, 1987, Italian
MONTECARLO GRAN CASINO'   Filmauro, 1988, Italian
LA PARTITA   Mario & Vittorio Cecchi Gori/C.G. Silver, 1989, Italian
LA FINTE BIONDE   Reteitalia, 1989, Italian
TRE COLONNE IN CRONACA   Pixit/Pentafilm, 1990, Italian
MILIARDI   Cecchi Gori Group Tiger Cinematografica/International
Video 80/Pentafilm, 1991, Italian
PIEDIPIATTI   Pentafilm, 1991, Italian
SOGNANDO LA CALIFORNIA   Filmauro, 1993, Italian
PICCOLO GRANDE AMORE   Video 80/Reteitalia, 1993, Italian
I MITICI - COLPO GOBBO A MILANO   Video 80/Dean Film,
1994, Italian
S.P.Q.R. 2,000 E 1/2 ANNI FA   Filmauro Distribuzione, 1995, Italian

AGNES VARDA

b. May 30, 1928 - Brussels, Belgium
Business: Cine-Tamaris, 88, rue Daguerre, 75014 Paris, France,
tel.: 1/43-22-66-00
Contact: French Film Office, 745 Fifth Avenue, New York,
NY 10151, 212/832-8860

LA POINTE COURTE   1954, French
CLEO FROM 5 TO 7   Zenith, 1962, French
LE BONHEUR   Clover, 1965, French
LES CREATURES   New Yorker, 1966, French-Swedish
FAR FROM VIETNAM (FD)   co-director with Jean-Luc Godard,
Claude Lelouch, Alain Resnais, William Klein & Joris Ivens,
New Yorker, 1967, French
LIONS LOVE   Raab, 1969
NAUSICAA (TF)   1970, French
DAGUERREOTYPES (FD)   1975, French
ONE SINGS, THE OTHER DOESN'T   Cinema 5, 1977, French
MUR MURS (FD)   Cine-Tamaris, 1981, French
DOCUMENTEUR: AN EMOTION PICTURE   Cine-Tamaris,
1981, French
VAGABOND   SANS TOIT NI LOI   Grange Communications/IFEX
Film, 1985, French
JANE B. PAR AGNES V. (FD)   Cine-Tamaris/La Sept, 1987, French
KUNG FU MASTER   Heritage Entertainment, 1988, French
JACQUOT   JACQUOT DE NANTES   Sony Pictures Classics,
1991, French
LES DEMOISELLES ONT EU 25 ANS (FD)   Cine-Tamaris/CNC/
Procirep TV Commission/France 2, 1993, French
LES CENT ET UNE NUITS   Cine-Tamaris, 1995, French

JOSEPH B. VASQUEZ

b. New York, New York
Agent: William Morris Agency - Beverly Hills, 310/859-4000

STREET STORY
THE BRONX WAR   Northern Arts Entertainment, 1989
HANGIN' WITH THE HOMEBOYS   New Line Cinema, 1991

FRANCIS VEBER*

b. July 28, 1937 - Neuilly-sur-Seine, France
Agent: CAA - Beverly Hills, 310/288-4545

THE TOY   Show Biz Company, 1976, French
LE CHEVRE   European International, 1981, French
LES COMPERES   European International, 1983, French
LES FUGITIFS   Gaumont, 1986, French
THREE FUGITIVES   Buena Vista, 1989
OUT ON A LIMB   Universal, 1992

ISELA VEGA

b. Sonora, Mexico
Contact: Isela Vega Video, 1076 El Centro Avenue, Hollywood,
 CA 90038, 213/465-5438
Contact: IMCINE, Tepic #40, P.B. Colonia Roma Sur, Mexico City,
 C.P. 06760, Mexico, tel.: 525/584-7283

LAS AMANTES DEL SENOR DE LA NOCHE   Fenix
 Cinematografica S.A./Avpasa, S.A., 1983, Mexican

MIKE VEJAR*
(Lawrence Mike Vejar)
Home: 2239 Penmar Avenue, Venice, CA 90271, 310/398-8704
Agent: Stone Manners Agency - Los Angeles, 213/654-7575

HAWAIIAN HEAT (TF)   James D. Parriott Productions/
 Universal TV, 1984
DOUBLE AGENT (TF)   Walt Disney TV, 1987
MacGYVER: LOST TREASURE OF ATLANTIS (TF)   Gekko Film
 Corporation/Henry Winkler-John Rich Productions, 1994

ADRIAN VELICESCU
THE SECRET LIFE OF HOUSES   Tainbreaker Films, 1994

MICHAEL VENTURA
Contact: Writers Guild of America, West - Los Angeles,
 310/550-1000

"I'M ALMOST NOT CRAZY..." JOHN CASSAVETES: THE MAN
 AND HIS WORK (FD)   Cannon, 1984

GERALDO VERA
Contavt: Spanish Film Institute, San Marcos 40, Madrid 28004,
 Spain, tel.: 1/532-5089

CUENTOS DE BORGES I   co-director with Hector Olivera,
 Iberoamericana/TVE/Sociedad Estatal Quinto Centenario,
 1991, Spanish
UNA MUJER BAJO LA LLUVIA   Atrium Productions/
 Iberoamericana/Sogetel/Sogepaq, 1992, Spanish

BEN VERBONG
b. 1949 - Tegelen, Limburg, Netherlands
Contact: NBF, Jan Luykenstraat 2, 1071 CM Amsterdam,
 Netherlands, tel.: 31 10/6646588

THE SEDUCTION (TF)   1979, Dutch
THE GIRL WITH THE RED HAIR   1981, Dutch
DE SCHORPIOEN   1984, Dutch
SALTIMBANK (TF)   1989, Dutch
LILY WAS HERE   1989, Dutch
THIS PROPERTY IS CONDEMNED (TF)   1990, Dutch
DE ONFATOENLIJKE VROUW   Lenox Holdings, 1991, Dutch
HITTE   Movies Film Productions, 1993, Dutch
HOUSE CALL DE FLAT   Polygram, 1994, Dutch
CHARLOTTE SOPHIE BENTINCK (TF)   1994, Dutch

CARLO VERDONE
b. 1950 - Rome, Italy
Home: via dei Banchi Vecchi, 61, Rome, Italy, tel.: 06/656-8902
Agent: International Artists, via dei Banchi Vecchi 61, Rome,
 Italy, tel.: 06/686-8902

UN SACCO BELLO   Medusa Distribuzione, 1980, Italian
BIANCO, ROSSO E VERDONE   Medusa Distribuzione,
 1981, Italian
BOROTALCO   Intercapital, 1981, Italian
ACQUA E SAPONE   Intercapital, 1983, Italian
I DUE CARABINIERI   C.G. Silver Film, 1984, Italian
TROPPO FORTE   Scena Film Produzioni, 1985, Italian
IO E MIA SORELLA   C.G. Silver, 1988, Italian
COMPAGNI DI SCUOLA   Mario & Vittorio Cecchi Gori, 1989, Italian
IL BAMBINO E IL POLIZIOTTO   Pentafilm, 1990, Italian
STASERA A CASA DI ALICE   Cecchi Gori Group Tiger
 Cinematografica/Pentafilm, 1990, Italian

MALEDETTO IL GIORNO CHE T'HO INCONTRATO
 Penta Distribuzione, 1992, Italian
AL LUPO AL LUPO   Penta Distribuzione, 1993, Italian
PERDIAMOCI DI VISA   Penta Distribuzione, 1994, Italian

PAT VERDUCCI
b. January 4, 1960 - Colorado Springs, Colorado
Agent: William Morris Agency - Beverly Hills, 310/859-4000

TRUE CRIME   Trimark Pictures, 1994

MICHAEL VERHOEVEN
b. 1938 - Berlin, Germany
Contact: Federal Union of Film and Television Directors in
 Germany, Adelheidstrasse 7, 8000 Munich 40, Germany,
 tel.: 089/271-6380

PAARUNGEN   Sentana Films, 1968, West German
o.k.   Sentana Films, 1970, West German
WER IM GLASHAUS LIEBT...   Sentana Films,
 1970, West German
MITGIFT   Sentana Films, 1975, West German
GEFUNDENES FRESSEN   Sentana Films, 1976, West German
DAS MANNERSQUARTETT   Sentana Films,
 1977, West German
GUTENBACH   Sentana Films, 1978, West German
SONNTAGSKINDER   Sentana Films, 1980, West German
THE WHITE ROSE   Sentana Films, 1982, West German
THE NASTY GIRL   Miramax Films, 1990, West German
NEW GERMANY   co-director with Reinhard Hauff & Bernhard Wicki,
 WDR/ZDF/BR/Futura/Sentana, 1990, German
EINE UNHEILIGE LIEBE   Sentana, 1993, German
MOTHER'S COURAGE   Santana, 1995, German

PAUL VERHOEVEN*
b. 1938 - Amsterdam, Netherlands
Business Manager: Ronald Brenner, Brenner & Glassberg,
 2049 Century Park East - Suite 950, Los Angeles, CA 90067,
 310/277-0933

WAT ZIEN IK   Rob Houwer Film, 1971, Dutch
TURKISH DELIGHT   Cinemation, 1973, Dutch
KEETJE TIPPEL   Cinema National, 1975, Dutch
SOLDIER OF ORANGE   The Samuel Goldwyn Company,
 1977, Dutch
SPETTERS   The Samuel Goldwyn Company, 1980, Dutch
THE 4TH MAN   Spectrafilm, 1983, Dutch
FLESH + BLOOD   Orion, 1985, U.S.-Dutch
ROBOCOP   Orion, 1987
TOTAL RECALL   TriStar, 1990
BASIC INSTINCT   TriStar, 1992
SHOWGIRLS   MGM-UA, 1995, U.S.-French

HENRI VERNEUIL
(Achod Malakian)
b. October 15, 1920 - Rodosto, Turkey
Agent: ICM France - Paris, tel.: 1/723-7860
Contact: French Film Office, 745 Fifth Avenue, New York,
 NY 10151, 212/832-8860

LA TABLE AUX CREVES   1951, French
BRELAN D'AS   1952, French
FORBIDDEN FRUIT   Films Around the World, 1952, French
LE BOULANGER DE VALORGUE   1953, French
CARNAVAL   1953, French
THE MOST WANTED MAN IN THE WORLD ENNEMI PUBLIC NO. 1
 Astor, 1953, French-Italian
THE SHEEP HAS FIVE LEGS   United Motion Picture Organization,
 1954, French
LES AMANTS DU TAGE   1955, French
DES GENS SANS IMPORTANCE   1955, French
PARIS-PALACE-HOTEL   1956, French
WHAT PRICE MURDER UNE MANCHE ET LA BELLE
 United Motion Picture Organization, 1957, French
MAXIME   Interworld, 1958, French
THE BIG CHIEF   Continental, 1959, French-Italian

THE COW AND I *LA VACHE ET LE PRISONNIER* Zenith,
1959, French-West German
L'AFFAIRE D'UNE NUIT 1960, French
LA FRANCAISE ET L'AMOUR co-director, Auerbach Film
Enterprises/Kingsley International, 1960, French
LE PRESIDENT 1961, French-Italian
THE LIONS ARE LOOSE Franco-London, 1961, French-Italian
A MONKEY IN WINTER MGM, 1962, French
ANY NUMBER CAN WIN *MELODIE EN SOUS-SOL*
MGM, 1963, French
GREED IN THE SUN MGM, 1964, French
WEEKEND AT DUNKIRK *WEEKEND A ZUYDCOOTE*
20th Century-Fox, 1965, French-Italian
THE 25TH HOUR MGM, 1967, French-Italian-Yugoslavian
GUNS FOR SAN SEBASTIAN *LA BATAILLE DE SAN
SEBASTIAN* MGM, 1968, French-Italian-Mexican
THE SICILIAN CLAN 20th Century-Fox, 1970, French
THE BURGLARS Columbia, 1972, French-Italian
THE SERPENT *NIGHT FLIGHT TO MOSCOW* Avco Embassy,
1973, French-Italian-West German
THE NIGHT CALLER *PEUR SUR LA VILLE* Columbia,
1975, French-Italian
LE CORPS DE MON ENNEMI AMLF, 1976, French
I...COMME ICARE V Films/SFP/Antenne-2, 1979, French
MILLE MILLIARDS DE DOLLARS V Films/Films A2,
1982, French
LES MORFALOUS AAA, 1984, French
MAYRIG AMLF, 1991, French
588 RUE PARADIS AMLF, 1992, French

STEPHEN F. VERONA*
b. September 11, 1940 - Illinois
Home: 1251 Stone Canyon Road, Bel Air, CA 90024, 310/476-7387
Agent: Mark Harris, Metropolitan Talent Agency - Los Angeles,
310/857-4500

THE LORDS OF FLATBUSH co-director with Martin Davidson,
Columbia, 1974
PIPE DREAMS Avco Embassy, 1976
BOARDWALK Atlantic Releasing Corporation, 1979
TALKING WALLS Drummond Productions, 1987
STEPHEN VERONA: SELF PORTRAIT
August Entertainment, 1992

DANIEL VIGNE
b. 1942 - France
Agent: Voyez Mon Agent - Paris, tel.: 1/47-23-55-80
Contact: French Film Office, 745 Fifth Avenue, New York,
NY 10151, 212/832-8860

LES HOMMES Cocinor, 1973, French-Italian
THE RETURN OF MARTIN GUERRE European International,
1983, French
ONE WOMAN OR TWO Orion Classics, 1985, French
COMEDIE D'ETE Partners Productions, 1989, French
THE STRANGER (CTF) co-director with Joan Tewkesbury &
Wayne Wang, HBO Pictures, 1992
3000 SCENARIOS CONTRE UN VIRUS co-director, CRIPS/
Medecine du Monde/APS/AESSA/Blue Films/Bernard Verley
Films/Frouma Films International/Les Productions de 3eme
Etage/CNC/Procirep/AFLS/TF1/France 2/France 3/Canal
Plus/Arte/M6/Agfa, 1994, French

CAMILO VILA
b. December 14, 1947 - Havana, Cuba

A LITTLE RAIN Three C Productions, 1976
LOS GUSANOS South American Shorts, 1977
THE UNHOLY Vestron, 1988
OPTIONS Vestron, 1989

REYNALDO VILLALOBOS
LOUIS L'AMOUR'S CONAGHER *CONAGHER* (CTF)
Imagine TV, 1991

TERESA VILLAVERDE
Contact: Instituto Portugues de Cinema, Rua San Pedrode
Alcantara 45, 1200 Lisbon, Portugal, tel.: 3511/346-7395

TRES IRMAOS Grupo de Estudos & Realizacoes/Arion Productions/
ZDF/CNC/RTP/IPACA/European Script Fund, 1994,
Portuguese-French-German

JOSEPH VILSMAIER
b. 1939 - Munich, Germany
Contact: Federal Union of Film and Television Directors in Germany,
Adelheidstrasse 7, 8000 Munich 40, Germany, tel.: 089/271-6380

AUTUMN MILK Peraton Film, 1989, West German
STALINGRAD Senator, 1992, German
CHARLIE & LOUISE Bavaria Film, 1994, German
SCHLAFES BRUDER Perathon, 1995, German

CHRISTIAN VINCENT
Contact: French Film Office, 745 Fifth Avenue, New York,
NY 10151, 212/832-8860

LA DISCRETE MK2 Productions USA, 1991, French
BEAU FIXE Pan-Europeenne, 1992, French
LA SEPARATION AMLF, 1994, French

JESSE VINT
Contact: Screen Actors Guild - Los Angeles, 213/954-1600

ANOTHER CHANCE Moviestore Entertainment, 1988

WILL VINTON
Business: Will Vinton Productions, Inc., 1400 NW 22nd Street,
Portland, OR 97210, 503/225-1130 or:
Will Vinton Entertainment, 28014 Dorothy Drive, Agoura Hills,
CA 91301, 818/706-9812
Agent: UTA - Beverly Hills, 310/273-6700

THE ADVENTURES OF MARK TWAIN (AF) Atlantic Releasing
Corporation, 1985
THE FROG PRINCE (AF) Will Vinton Productions, 1994

MARCELA FERNANDEZ VIOLANTE
(See Marcela FERNANDEZ VIOLANTE)

VIRGIL W. VOGEL*
b. Peoria, Illinois
Business Manager: Lester Stine, 10350 Santa Monica Blvd. -
Suite 350, Los Angeles, CA 90025, 310/556-2235
Agent: David Shapira & Associates - Sherman Oaks, 818/906-0322

THE MOLE PEOPLE Universal, 1956
THE KETTLES ON OLD McDONALD'S FARM Universal, 1957
THE LAND UNKNOWN Universal, 1957
INVASION OF THE ANIMAL PEOPLE co-director with Jerry Warren,
ADP, 1962
THE SWORD OF ALI BABA Universal, 1965
THE RETURN OF JOE FORRESTER (TF) Columbia TV, 1975
THE DEPUTIES (TF) 1976
LAW OF THE LAND (TF) QM Productions, 1976
CENTENNIAL (MS) co-director with Paul Krasny, Harry Falk &
Bernard McEveety, Universal TV, 1978
POWER (TF) co-director with Barry Shear, David Gerber
Company/Columbia TV, 1980
PORTRAIT OF A REBEL: MARGARET SANGER (TF)
Marvin Minoff Productions/David Paradine TV, 1980
BEULAH LAND (MS) co-director with Harry Falk, David Gerber
Company/Columbia TV, 1980
TODAY'S FBI (TF) David Gerber Company, 1981
STREET HAWK (TF) Limekiln and Templar Productions/
Universal TV, 1985
CONDOR (TF) Jaygee Productions/Orion TV, 1986
DESPERADO (TF) Walter Mirisch Productions/Charles E. Sellier
Productions/Universal TV, 1987
LONGARM (TF) Universal TV, 1988
WALKER, TEXAS RANGER: ONE RIOT, ONE RANGER (TF)
Cannon TV, 1993

F
I
L
M

D
I
R
E
C
T
O
R
S

**F
I
L
M
D
I
R
E
C
T
O
R
S**

JON VOIGHT
b. December 29, 1938 - Yonkers, New York
Agent: CAA - Beverly Hills, 310/288-4545
Contact: Screen Actors Guild - Los Angeles, 213/954-1600

THE TIN SOLDIER (CTF)   co-director with Gregory Gieras,
    Crystal Sky Communications/Showtime, 1995

PAUL G. VOLK
STEEL FRONTIER   co-director with Jacobsen Hart,
    PM Entertainment Group, 1994

GABE VON DETTRE
Contact: Hungarian Film Institute, Budakeszi u 51 B, 1012 Budapest,
    Hungary, tel.: 176-1018 or 176-1322

THE DIARY OF THE HURDY-GURDY MAN   Timnberlake
    Productions/Mafilm, 1992, U.S.-Hungarian
THE ACTRESS AND THE DEATH   MIT Studio, 1994, Hungarian

KATJA VON GARNIER
Agent: CAA - Beverly Hills, 310/288-4545

MAKING UP   1993, German

ROSA VON PRAUNHEIM
(Holger Mischwitzki)
b. November 25, 1942 - Riga, Latvia, U.S.S.R.
Contact: Federal Union of Film and Television Directors in Germany,
    Adelheidstrasse 7, 8000 Munich 40, Germany, tel.: 089/271-6380

BERLINER BETTWURST   1973, West German
ICH BIN EIN ANTISTAR...   1973, West German
UNDERGROUND AND EMIGRANTS   1976, West German
ARMEE DER LIEBENDEN ODER AUFSTAND DER PERVERSEN
    1978, West German
TALLY BROWN, N.Y.   1979, West German
STADT DER VERLORENEN SEELEN   1983, West German
EIN VIRUS KENNT KEINE MORAL   1986, West German
ANITA - TANZE DER LASTERS   1987, West German
DOLLY, LOTTE UND MARIA   1988, West German
POSITIV   1989, West German
SILENCE = DEATH   First Run Features, 1990, West German
UBERLEBEN IN NEW YORK   1990, West German
AFFENGEIL   First Run Features, 1992, German
I AM MY OWN WOMAN (FD)   Cinevista, 1992, German

DAISY von SCHERLER MAYER
PARTY GIRL   First Look Pictures, 1995

MAX VON SYDOW
(Carl Adolf von Sydow)
b. April 10, 1929 - Lund, Sweden
Contact: Swedish Film Institute, P.O. Box 27126, 102 52 Stockholm,
    Sweden, tel.: 08/665-1100
Contact: British Film Commission, 70 Baker Street, London
    W1M 1DJ, England, tel.: 171/224-5000

KATINKA   Nordiskfilm/Svensk Filmindustri/Danish Film Institute/
    British Film Institute/Film Four International, 1988,
    Danish-Swedish-British

LARS von TRIER
b. 1956 - Denmark
Contact: Danish Film Institute, Store Sondervoldsstraede 4,
    DK-1419 Copenhagen K, Denmark, tel.: 31-57-65-00

NOCTURNE   1981, Danish
PICTURES OF A LIBERATION   1982, Danish
THE ELEMENT OF CRIME   Per Holst Filmproduktion, 1984, Danish
EPIDEMIC   1987, Danish
MEDEA   1988, Danish
ZENTROPA   *EUROPA*   Prestige, 1991, Danish-French-German
THE KINGDOM (MS)   October Films, 1994,
    Danish-Swedish-German-French

MARGARETHE von TROTTA
b. February 21, 1942 - Berlin, Germany
Contact: Federal Union of Film and Television Directors in Germany,
    Adelheidstrasse 7, 8000 Munich 40, Germany, tel.: 089/271-6380

THE LOST HONOR OF KATHARINA BLUM   co-director with
    Volker Schlondorff, New World, 1975, West German
THE SECOND AWAKENING OF CHRISTA KLAGES   Bioskop Film/
    WDR/First City Films/Cinema of Women, 1977, West German
SCHWESTERN ODER DIE BALANCE DES GLUCKS   Bioskop Film/
    First City Films/Blue Dolphin Films, 1979, West German
MARIANNE AND JULIANNE   *DIE BLEIRNE ZEIT*
    1981, West German
SHEER MADNESS   RS/58, 1983, West German
ROSA LUXEMBOURG   New Yorker, 1986, West German
PAURA E AMORE   Erre Productions/Reteitalia/Bioskop Film/
    Cinemax Generale D'Images, 1988, Italian-French-West German
L'AFRICANA   Artisti Associati, 1990, Italian-West German-French
IL LUNGO SILENZIO   UIP, 1993, Italian-French-German
THE PROMISE   Fine Line Features/New Line Cinema/Bioskop-Film,
    1995, German-French-Swiss

FRANK von ZERNECK, JR.
GOD'S LONELY MAN   St. Francis of Assisi Pictures, 1994

KURT VOSS
Agent: Innovative Artists - Los Angeles, 310/553-5200

BORDER RADIO   co-director with Allison Anders & Dean Lent,
    International Film Marketing, 1988
HORSEPLAYER   Greycat Films, 1989
GENUINE RISK   I.R.S. Releasing, 1990

ORIN WACHSBERG
STARLIGHT   Starlight Ltd. Partnership, 1986

DANIEL WACHSMANN
Contact: Israel Film Centre, Ministry of Industry & Trade,
    30 Agron Street, P.O. Box 299, 94190 Jerusalem, Israel,
    tel.: 9722/210433 or 210297

TRANSIT   Jacob Goldwasser Productions, 1979, Israeli
HOT WIND   *HAMSIN*   Hemdale, 1982, Israeli
THE APPOINTED   21st Century Distribution, 1990, Israeli

JONATHAN WACKS*
b. 1948
Agent: UTA - Beverly Hills, 310/273-6700

POWWOW HIGHWAY   Warner Bros., 1989, U.S.-British
MYSTERY DATE   Orion, 1991
ED AND HIS DEAD MOTHER   ITC Entertainment Group, 1993

MICHAEL WADLEIGH*
Contact: Directors Guild of America - Los Angeles, 213/851-3671

WOODSTOCK (FCD)   Warner Bros., 1970
WOLFEN   Orion/Warner Bros., 1981
WOODSTOCK: 3 DAYS OF PEACE & MUSIC - THE
    DIRECTOR'S CUT (FCD)   Warner Bros., 1994,
    re-edited version of WOODSTOCK

JANE WAGNER
b. February 2, 1935 - Morristown, Tennessee
Agent: William Morris Agency - Beverly Hills, 310/859-4000

MOMENT BY MOMENT   Universal, 1978

PAUL WAGNER
OUT OF IRELAND (FD)   American Focus, 1994

RUPERT WAINWRIGHT*
Agent: UTA - Beverly Hills, 310/273-6700

DILLINGER (TF)   Wolper Productions/Bernard Sofronski
   Productions, 1991
BLANK CHECK   Buena Vista, 1994

RALPH WAITE*
b. June 22, 1928 - White Plains, New York
Business Manager: Global Business Management, 15250 Ventura
   Blvd. - Suite 710, Sherman Oaks, CA 90069

ON THE NICKEL   Rose's Park, 1980

ANDRZEJ WAJDA
b. March 6, 1926 - Suwalki, Poland
Agent: Georges Beaume, Artists Associes - Paris, tel.: 42-56-21-22
Contact: Film Polski, ul. Mazowiecka 6/8, 00-048 Warsaw,
   Poland, tel.: 48-22/26-84-55 or 48-22/26-09-49 or:
   French Film Office, 745 Fifth Avenue, New York,
   NY 10151, 212/832-8860

A GENERATION   WFF Wroclaw, 1954, Polish
JE VAIS VERS LE SOLEIL   WFD Warsaw, 1955, French-Polish
KANAL   Frankel, 1957, Polish
ASHES AND DIAMONDS   Janus, 1958, Polish
LOTNA   KADR Unit, 1959, Polish
INNOCENT SORCERERS   KADR Unit, 1960, Polish
SAMSON   Droga-KADR Unit, 1961, Polish
SIBERIAN LADY MACBETH   Avala Film, 1961, Polish
LOVE AT TWENTY   co-director with Francois Truffaut,
   Renzo Rossellini, Shintaro Ishihara & Marcel Ophuls, Embassy,
   1962, French-Italian-Japanese-Polish-West German
ASHES   1965, Polish
GATES TO PARADISE   1967, British
EVERYTHING FOR SALE   New Yorker, 1968, Polish
HUNTING FLIES   1969, Polish
LANDSCAPE AFTER BATTLE   New Yorker, 1970, Polish
THE BIRCH-WOOD   1971, Polish
PILATUS UND ANDERE (TF)   1972, West German
THE WEDDING   Film Polski, 1972, Polish
THE PROMISED LAND   Film Polski, 1974, Polish
SHADOW LINE   1976, Polish
MAN OF MARBLE   New Yorker, 1977, Polish
WITHOUT ANESTHETIC   New Yorker, 1979, Polish
THE GIRLS FROM WILKO   1979, Polish-French
THE CONDUCTOR   Film Polski, 1980, Polish
ROUGH TREATMENT   Film Polski, 1980, Polish
MAN OF IRON   United Artists Classics, 1981, Polish
DANTON   Triumph/Columbia, 1983, French-Polish
A LOVE IN GERMANY   Triumph/Columbia,
   1983, West German-French
CHRONICLE OF LOVE AFFAIRS   Film Polski/Film Group
   Perspektyva, 1985, Polish
LES POSSEDES   Gaumont, 1988, French-Japanese
KORCZAK   DR. KORCZAK   New Yorker, 1990,
   German-French-Polish
THE RING WITH A CROWNED EAGLE   Film Group Perspektyva/
   Heritage Films/Erato Film/Cine Electra/Regina Ziegler
   Productions, 1993, Polish-French-British-German
LES FRANCAIS VUS PAR...   Erato Films/Socpresse/Socpresse/
   Figaro Magazine/Antenne-2/Centre National de la
   Cinematographie, 1993, French
NASTAZJA   HIT/Say-To Workshop Inc./Television Tokyo
   Channel 12 Ltd., 1994, Polish-Japanese

CHRIS WALAS*
b. Chicago, Illinois
Agent: William Morris Agency - Beverly Hills, 310/859-4000
Business: 415/479-5040

THE FLY II   20th Century Fox, 1989, U.S.-Canadian
THE VAGRANT   MGM, 1992

GRANT AUSTIN WALDMAN
THE CHANNELER   Magnum Entertainment, 1991

DORIAN WALKER*
(Charles Dorian Walker)
Contact: Directors Guild of America - Los Angeles, 213/851-3671

MAKING THE GRADE   MGM/UA/Cannon, 1984
TEEN WITCH   Trans World Entertainment, 1989

GILES WALKER
b. 1946 - Dundee, Scotland
Address: 4039 Grand Avenue, Montreal, Quebec H4B 2X4,
   Canada, 514/483-3270
Agent: Becsey/Wisdom/Kalajian - Los Angeles, 310/550-0535

DESCENT   1975, Canadian
I WASN'T SCARED (TF)   1977, Canadian
BRAVERY IN THE FIELD (TF)   1978, Canadian
TWICE UPON A TIME   1979, Canadian
THE MASCULINE MYSTIQUE (FD)   co-director with John Smith,
   1985, Canadian
90 DAYS   Cinecom, 1985, Canadian
THE LAST STRAW   National Film Board of Canada,
   1987, Canadian
CADDIE WOODLAWN (CTF)   Churchill Entertainment/
   WonderWorks/The Disney Channel, 1989, Canadian-U.S.
PRINCES IN EXILE   Cinepix/National Film Board of Canada,
   1990, Canadian
GANESH   The Film Works, 1993, Canadian

PETER WALKER
Address: 23 Bentick Street, London W1, England

I LIKE BIRDS   1966, British
GIRLS FOR MEN ONLY   1967, British
SCHOOL FOR SEX   1968, British
STRIP POKER   Miracle, 1969, British
COOL IT CAROL!   Miracle, 1970, British
MAN OF VIOLENCE   Miracle, 1971, British
DIE SCREAMING, MARIANNE   1971, British
THE FLESH AND BLOOD SHOW   Tigon, 1972, British
THE FOUR DIMENSIONS OF GRETA   Hemdale, 1972, British
TIFFANY JONES   Hemdale, 1973, British
HOUSE OF WHIPCORD   Miracle, 1974, British
FRIGHTMARE   Miracle, 1975, British
HOUSE OF MORTAL SIN   Miracle, 1976, British
SCHIZO   Warner Bros., 1976, British
THE COMEBACK   Enterprise, 1978, British
HOME BEFORE MIDNIGHT   Heritage/EMI, 1979, British
HOUSE OF THE LONG SHADOWS   MGM/UA/Cannon,
   1983, British
BLIND SHOT   Agincourt Ventures Ltd., 1988, British

ROBERT WALKER
Agent: ICM - London, tel.: 171/636-6565

DEADHEAD (TF)   BBC, British
BLIND JUSTICE (TF)   BBC, British
WILDTHINGS (TF)   BBC, British
DIE KINDER (TF)   BBC, British
FLASHPOINT (MS)   co-director with Gero Erhardt & Philippe Tribolt,
   Tele-Terra/BetaFilm/Falcon Productions/ZDF/La Cinq/Reteitalia/
   TVE/SRG/ORF, German-French-Italian-British-Austrian
HARRY (MS)   co-director with Mary McMurray & Martin Stellman,
   Union Pictures/BBC, 1993, British

SUSAN F. WALKER*
Telephone: 818/985-3691

THE ONE, THE ONLY GROUCHO (CTD)
THE DIVINE GARBO (CTD)
KNOCKOUT - HOLLYWOOD'S LOVE AFFAIR WITH BOXING (CTD)
STARRING NATALIE WOOD (CTD)
TALL, DARK AND HANDSOME: ROCK HUDSON (CTD)
ALL ABOUT BETTE (CTD)   Turner Pictures, 1994

GARY WALKOW*
Contact: Frank Gruber, Gruber, Wender & Levine - Beverly Hills,
    310/553-6900

THE TROUBLE WITH DICK   Fever Dream Production
    Company, 1987
NOTES FROM UNDERGROUND   NFU Productions, 1995

RICK WALLACE*
Agent: William Morris Agency - Beverly Hills, 310/859-4000

CALIFORNIA GIRLS (TF)   ABC Circle Films, 1985
A TIME TO LIVE (TF)   Blue Andre Productions/ITC
    Productions, 1985
ACCEPTABLE RISKS (TF)   ABC Circle Films, 1986
A FATHER'S HOMECOMING (TF)   NBC Productions, 1988

STEPHEN WALLACE
Contact: Australian Film Commission, 150 William Street,
    Woolloomooloo NSW 2011, Australia, tel.: 2/321-6444

WOMEN OF THE SUN (MS)   co-director with David Stevens,
    James Ricketson & Geoffrey Nottage, Generation Films,
    1983, Australian
PRISONERS OF THE SUN *BLOOD OATH*   Skouras Pictures,
    1990, Australian
TURTLE BEACH   Warner Bros., 1992, Australian,
    filmed in 1989

TOMMY LEE WALLACE*
Agent: Innovative Artists - Los Angeles, 310/553-5200

HALLOWEEN III: SEASON OF THE WITCH   Universal, 1982
ALOHA SUMMER *HANAUMA BAY*   Spectrafilm, 1988
FRIGHT NIGHT PART 2   New Century/Vista, 1989
IT (TF)   Konigsberg-Sanitsky Productions/Green-Epstein
    Productions/Lorimar TV, 1990
AND THE SEA WILL TELL (TF)   Green-Epstein Productions/
    Columbia TV, 1991
THE COMRADES OF SUMMER (CTF)   HBO Pictures/
    Grossbart-Barnett Productions, 1992
DANGER ISLAND (TF)   von Zerneck-Sertner Films/NBC
    Productions, 1992
WITNESS TO THE EXECUTION (TF)   Frederick S. Pierce
    Company, 1994
GREEN DOLPHIN BEAT (TF)   Robert Ward Productions/
    Spelling TV, 1994

ANTHONY WALLER
Agent: UTA - Beverly Hills, 310/273-6700
Contact: British Film Commission, 70 Baker Street, London
    W1M 1DJ, England, tel.: 171/224-5000

MUTE WITNESS   Sony Pictures Classics, 1995, British

AISLING WALSH
Agent: Peters Fraser & Dunlop - London, tel.: 171/344-1000

DOCTOR FINLAY (MS)   co-director with Patrick Lau, Scottish TV
    Enterprises, 1993, Scottish

FRED WALTON*
(Frederick R. Walton)
Personal Manager: Jon Brown, The Brown Group - Beverly Hills,
    310/247-2755

WHEN A STRANGER CALLS   Columbia, 1979
HADLEY'S REBELLION   American Film Distributors, 1984
ALFRED HITCHCOCK PRESENTS (TF)   co-director with
    Steve DeJarnatt, Randa Haines & Joel Oliansky,
    Universal TV, 1985
APRIL FOOL'S DAY   Paramount, 1986
THE ROSARY MURDERS   New Line Cinema, 1987
I SAW WHAT YOU DID (TF)   Universal TV, 1988
TRAPPED (CTF)   Cine Enterprises, 1989
MURDER IN PARADISE (TF)   Bill McCutchen Productions/
    Columbia TV, 1990
THE PRICE SHE PAID (TF)   Producers Entertainment Group/
    Sandy Hook Productions/World International Network, 1992
WHEN A STRANGER CALLS BACK (CTF)   Krost-Chapin
    Productions/The Producers Entertainment Group/MTE, 1993
DEAD AIR (CTF)   Alan Barnette Productions/MTE
    Entertainment, 1994
THE COURTYARD (CTF)   Nasatir-Haft Productions/Showtime, 1995

PETER WANG
(Wang Zhengfang)
b. Beijing, China
Business: Peter Wang Films, Inc., 594 Broadway - Suite 906,
    New York, NY 10012

A GREAT WALL   Orion Classics, 1986, U.S.-Chinese
THE LASER MAN   Original Cinema, 1988
FIRST DATE   Peter Wang Films, 1989, Taiwanese

STEVE WANG
Business: Biomorph Inc., 7700 Gloria Avenue, Van Nuys, CA 91406,
    818/786-8286

THE GUYVER   co-director with Screaming Mad George, Imperial
    Entertainment, 1991, U.S.-Japanese-Taiwanese-South Korean
GUYVER: DARK HERO (HVF)   New Line Home Video, 1994
THE DAUGHTER IN LAW   1995, Taiwanese

WAYNE WANG
b. January 12, 1949 - Hong Kong
Agent: William Morris Agency - Beverly Hills, 310/859-4000
Business: C.I.M. Productions, 665 Bush Street, San Francisco,
    CA 94108, 415/433-2342

A MAN, A WOMAN, AND A KILLER   co-director with
    Rick Schmidt, 1975
CHAN IS MISSING   New Yorker, 1982
DIM SUM: A LITTLE BIT OF HEART   Orion Classics, 1985
SLAMDANCE   Island Pictures, 1987
EAT A BOWL OF TEA   Columbia, 1989
LIFE IS CHEAP...BUT TOILET PAPER IS EXPENSIVE *LIFE IS*
    CHEAP Silverlight Entertainment, 1989, U.S.-Hong Kong
THE STRANGER (CTF)   co-director with Joan Tewkesbury &
    Daniel Vigne, HBO Pictures, 1992
THE JOY LUCK CLUB   Buena Vista, 1993
SMOKE   Miramax Films, 1995
BLUE IN THE FACE   co-director with Paul Auster,
    Miramax Films, 1995

DANIEL LARDNER WARD
Agent: CAA - Beverly Hills, 310/288-4545

MY LIFE'S IN TURNAROUND   co-director with Eric Schaeffer,
    Arrow Releasing, 1993

DAVID S. WARD*
b. October 25, 1945
Agent: CAA - Beverly Hills, 310/288-4545

CANNERY ROW   MGM/United Artists, 1981
MAJOR LEAGUE   Paramount, 1989

KING RALPH   Universal, 1991
THE PROGRAM   Buena Vista, 1993
MAJOR LEAGUE II   Warner Bros., 1994
DOWN PERISCOPE   20th Century Fox, 1995

NICK WARD
b. 1962 - Geelong, Australia
Contact: British Film Commission, 70 Baker Street, London
    W1M 1DJ, England, tel.: 171/224-5000

DAKOTA ROAD   Film Four International/British Screen/
    Working Title, 1991, British
LOOK ME IN THE EYE   Skreba-Creon Films/BBC Films,
    1994, British

VINCENT WARD
b. 1956 - Greytown, New Zealand
Address: P.O. Box 423, Kings Cross, NSW 2011, Australia
Agent: CAA - Beverly Hills, 310/288-4545

VIGIL   John Maynard Productions/Film Investment Corporation of
    New Zealand/New Zealand Film Commission,
    1984, New Zealand
THE NAVIGATOR: AN ODYSSEY ACROSS TIME
    THE NAVIGATOR - A MEDIEVAL ODYSSEY   Circle Releasing,
    1988, Australian-New Zealand
MAP OF THE HUMAN HEART   Miramax Films, 1992,
    British-Australian-French-New Zealand-Canadian-Japanese

CLYDE WARE*
b. December 22, 1936 - West Virginia
Home: 1252 N. Laurel Avenue, Los Angeles, CA 90046,
    213/650-8205

NO DRUMS, NO BUGLES   Cinerama Releasing Corporation, 1971
THE STORY OF PRETTY BOY FLOYD (TF)   Universal TV, 1974
THE HATFIELDS AND THE McCOYS (TF)   Charles Fries
    Productions, 1975
THREE HUNDRED MILES FOR STEPHANIE (TF)   Edward S.
    Feldman Company/Yellow Ribbon Productions/PKO, 1981
WHEN THE LINE GETS THROUGH   Lorimar, 1985
HUMAN ERROR   Wouk-Ware Productions, 1989
ANOTHER TIME, ANOTHER PLACE   Transcontinental
    Pictures Industries, 1989
BAD JIM   21st Century Distribution, 1990

REGIS WARGNIER
Agent: ICM - Beverly Hills, 310/550-4000 or:
    Voyez Mon Agent - Paris, tel.: 1/47-23-55-80

INDOCHINE   Sony Pictures Classics, 1992, French
UNE FEMME FRANCAISE   UGC Images/TFI Films Production/
    D.A. Films/Recorded Pictures Company/Studio Babelsberg/
    Fonds Eurimages du Conseil De L'europe/British Screen/
    Filmforderung Berlin/Canal Plus/Soficas Sofinergie 3,
    1995, French-British-German

PAUL WARNER
Agent: UTA - Beverly Hills, 310/273-6700

FALL TIME   Capitol Film Ltd., 1995

CATHERINE WARNOW
PAUL BOWLES: THE COMPLETE OUTSIDER (FD)
    co-director with Regina Weinreich, First Run Features, 1994

DERYN WARREN
BLACK MAGIC WOMAN   Trimark Pictures, 1991

JENNIFER WARREN
b. August 12 - New York, New York
Contact: Screen Actors Guild - Los Angeles, 213/954-1600

THE BEANS OF EGYPT, MAINE   I.R.S Releasing, 1994

MARK WARREN*
b. September 24, 1938
Agent: Barry Perelman Agency - Los Angeles, 310/274-5999
Business Manager: Ben Hill, 6605 Gerald Avenue, Van Nuys,
    CA 91406, 818/787-3755

COME BACK CHARLESTON BLUE   Warner Bros., 1972
TULIPS   co-director with Rex Bromfield & Al Waxman, all directed
    under pseudonym of Stan Ferris, Avco Embassy, 1981, Canadian
THE KINKY COACHES AND THE POM-POM PUSSYCATS
    CRUNCH   Summa Vista, 1981, Canadian

DON WAS
I JUST WASN'T MADE FOR THESE TIMES (FD)
    Palomar Pictures/Cro-Magnon Films, 1995

JOHN WATERS*
b. April 22, 1946 - Baltimore, Maryland
Agent: ICM - Beverly Hills, 310/550-4000

MONDO TRASHO   Film-Makers, 1970
PINK FLAMINGOS   Saliva Films, 1974
FEMALE TROUBLE   New Line Cinema, 1975
DESPERATE LIVING   New Line Cinema, 1977
POLYESTER   New Line Cinema, 1981
HAIRSPRAY   New Line Cinema, 1988
CRY-BABY   Universal, 1990
SERIAL MOM   Savoy Pictures, 1994

PETER WATKINS
b. October 29, 1935 - Norbiton, Surrey, England
Contact: Swedish Film Institute, Film House, Box 27126, 102 52
    Stockholm, Sweden, tel.: 08/665-1100

CULLODEN (TF)   BBC, 1964, British
THE WAR GAME   Pathe Contemporary, 1966, British
PRIVILEGE   Universal, 1967, British
GLADIATORS   1969, Swedish
PUNISHMENT PARK   Sherplx, 1971, British
EDVARD MUNCH   New Yorker, 1974, Swedish-Norwegian
70-TALETS   Manniskor, 1975, Swedish
FALLEN   1975, Swedish
EVENING LAND   Panorama-ASA, 1977, Danish
THE JOURNEY (FD)   Swedish Peace and Arbitration Society/
    Peter Watkins Productions/Cinergy Films/Sky Works
    Charitable Foundation, 1987, Swedish-Canadian

JOHN WATSON*
b. 1947 - England
Business: Trilogy Entertainment Group, 2401 Colorado Blvd. -
    Suite 100, Santa Monica, CA 90404, 310/449-3095
Agent: ICM - Beverly Hills, 310/550-4000

THE ZOO GANG   co-director with Pen Densham, New World, 1985

JOHN WATSON
DEATHSTALKER   New World, 1983, U.S.-Argentine

PAUL WATSON
b. February 17, 1942 - London, England
Address: 103 Grandison Road, London SW11, England
Agent: ICM - London, tel.: 171/636-6565

THE ROTHKO CONSPIRACY (TF)   BBC/Lionheart TV,
    1983, British
REVELATIONS (TD)   BBC, 1988, British

ROY WATTS
HAMBONE AND HILLIE   New World, 1984

AL WAXMAN*

b. 1935 - Toronto, Ontario, Canada
Home: 87 Forest Hill Road, Toronto, Ontario, Canada, 416/483-7400
Agent: Stone Manners Agency - Los Angeles, 213/654-7575

THE CROWD INSIDE   National General, 1971, Canadian
MY PLEASURE IS MY BUSINESS   Brian Distributing Corporation,
   1975, Canadian-West German
TULIPS   co-director with Rex Bromfield & Mark Warren,
   all released under pseudonym of Stan Ferris, Avco Embassy,
   1981, Canadian
WHITE LIGHT   Brightstar Films, 1991, Canadian
THE DIAMOND FLEECE (CTF)   Alan Landsburg Productions/
   Astral Film Enterprises/Moving Image Productions,
   1992, U.S.-Canadian

KEONI WAXMAN

Agent: The Agency - Los Angeles, 310/551-3000

ALMOST BLUE   Curb/Esquire Films, 1992
I SHOT A MAN IN RENO   Reno Productions, 1994

KEENEN IVORY WAYANS*

b. June 8, 1958 - New York, New York
Business: Ivory Way Productions, 5746 Sunset Blvd., Hollywood,
   CA 90028, 213/856-1190
Agent: CAA - Beverly Hills, 310/288-4545

I'M GONNA GIT YOU SUCKA   MGM/UA, 1989
A LOW DOWN DIRTY SHAME   Buena Vista, 1994

PETER WEBB

Address: 1 Park Village East, London NW1, England,
   tel.: 171/387-8077
Agent: Seifert Dench Associates - London, tel.: 171/437-4551

GIVE MY REGARDS TO BROAD STREET   20th Century Fox,
   1984, British

WILLIAM WEBB*

Contact: Directors Guild of America - Los Angeles, 213/851-3671

DIRTY LAUNDRY   Seymour Borde & Associates, 1987
DISCOVERY BAY   Big Guy Productions, 1987
PARTY LINE   SVS Films, 1988
THE BANKER   Westwind Productions, 1989
THE HIT LIST (CTF)   Westwind Productions, 1993

BILLY WEBER*

(William M. Weber)
Agent: CAA - Beverly Hills, 310/288-4545

JOSH AND S.A.M.   Columbia, 1993

BRUCE WEBER*

Business: Little Bear Films, Inc., 135 Watts Street, New York,
   NY 10012, 212/226-0814

BROKEN NOSES (FD)   Little Bear Films, 1987
LET'S GET LOST (FD)   Zeitgeist Films, 1988

NICHOLAS WEBSTER*

b. July 24, 1922 - Spokane, Washington
Home: 1040 Monument Stret, Pacific Palisades, CA 90272,
   310/573-1936

DEAD TO THE WORLD   United Artists, 1961
GONE ARE THE DAYS! PURLIE VICTORIOUS   Trans-Lux, 1963
SANTA CLAUS CONQUERS THE MARTIANS   Embassy, 1964
MISSION MARS   Allied Artists, 1968
NO LONGER ALONE   World Wide, 1978, British
MANBEAST (TF)   Alan Landsburg Productions, 1981

DAVID WECHTER*

b. June 27, 1956 - Los Angeles, California
Agent: William Morris Agency - Beverly Hills, 310/859-4000

MIDNIGHT MADNESS   co-director with Michael Nankin,
   Buena Vista, 1980
THE BIKINI SHOP   THE MALIBU BIKINI SHOP   International Film
   Marketing, 1986

STEPHEN WEEKS

b. 1948
Address: Penhow Castle, Nr. Newport, Gwent., Penhow WP6 3AD,
   England, tel.: 0633/400800

GAWAIN AND THE GREEN KNIGHT   United Artists, 1972, British
I, MONSTER   Cannon, 1974, British
CLASH OF THE SWORDS   Cannon, 1984, British

JOHN WEIDNER

PRIVATE WARS   PM Entertainment, 1993
MIDNIGHT MAN   A.N.A. Productions, 1994

SAMUEL WEIL

(See Lloyd KAUFMAN)

PAUL WEILAND*

Address: 14 Newburgh Street, London W1V 1LF, England,
   tel.: 171/287-6900
Agent: ICM - Beverly Hills, 310/550-4000 or:
   The Casarotto Company - London, tel.: 171/287-4450

LEONARD PART 6   Columbia, 1987
CITY SLICKERS II: THE LEGEND OF CURLY'S GOLD
   Columbia, 1994

CLAUDIA WEILL*

b. 1947 - New York, New York
Home: 2800 Seattle Drive, Los Angeles, CA 90046, 213/850-1772
Agent: UTA - Beverly Hills, 310/273-6700

THE OTHER HALF OF THE SKY: A CHINA MEMOIR (FD)
   co-director with Shirley MacLaine, 1975
GIRLFRIENDS   Warner Bros., 1978
IT'S MY TURN   Columbia, 1980
JOHNNY BULL (TF)   Titus Productions/Eugene O'Neill Memorial
   Theatre Center, 1986
FACE OF A STRANGER (TF)   Linda Gottlieb Productions/Viacom
   Productions, 1991
A CHILD LOST FOREVER (TF)   ERB Productions/
   TriStar TV, 1992

YOSSI WEIN

NEVER SAY DIE   Nu Image, 1994
CYBORG COP 3   Nu Image, 1995, U.S.-South African

HAL WEINER

THE IMAGEMAKER   Castle Hill Productions, 1986

REGINA WEINREICH

PAUL BOWLES: THE COMPLETE OUTSIDER (FD)   co-director with
   Catherine Warnow, First Run Features, 1994

BOB WEINSTEIN*

Business: Miramax Films, Tribeca Film Center, 375 Greenwich Street,
   New York, NY 10013, 212/941-3800

PLAYING FOR KEEPS   co-director with Harvey Weinstein,
   Universal, 1986

HARVEY WEINSTEIN*
Business: Miramax Films, Tribeca Film Center, 375 Greenwich
Street, New York, NY 10013, 212/941-3800

PLAYING FOR KEEPS   co-director with Bob Weinstein,
Universal, 1986

SANDRA WEINTRAUB
Business: Fred Weintraub Productions, 1900 Avenue of the Stars -
Suite 1500, Los Angeles, CA 90067, 310/788-9380

THE WOMEN'S CLUB   Weintraub-Cloverleaf/Scorsese
Productions, 1987
THE BEST OF THE MARTIAL ARTS FILMS (FD)
Miramax Films, 1991

PETER WEIR*
b. August 8, 1944 - Sydney, Australia
Agent: CAA - Beverly Hills, 310/288-4545

THREE TO GO   co-director with Brian Hannant & Oliver Howes,
Commonwealth Film Unit Production, 1971, Australian
THE CARS THAT EAT PEOPLE   THE CARS THAT ATE PARIS
New Line Cinema, 1974, Australian
PICNIC AT HANGING ROCK   Atlantic Releasing Corporation,
1975, Australian
THE PLUMBER   Barbary Coast, 1978, Australian,
originally made for television
THE LAST WAVE   World Northal, 1978, Australian
GALLIPOLI   Paramount, 1981, Australian
THE YEAR OF LIVING DANGEROUSLY   MGM/UA,
1983, Australian
WITNESS ★   Paramount, 1985
THE MOSQUITO COAST   Warner Bros., 1986
DEAD POETS SOCIETY ★   Buena Vista, 1989
GREEN CARD   Buena Vista, 1990, Australian-French-U.S.
FEARLESS   Warner Bros., 1993

DON WEIS*
b. May 13, 1922 - Milwaukee, Wisconsin
Business Manager: A. Morgan Maree Jr. & Associates,
6363 Wilshire Blvd. - Suite 600, Los Angeles, CA 90048,
213/653-7330

BANNERLINE   MGM, 1951
IT'S A BIG COUNTRY   co-director with Charles Vidor,
Richard Thorpe, John Sturges, Don Hartman,
Clarence Brown & William Wellman, MGM, 1951
JUST THIS ONCE   MGM, 1952
YOU FOR ME   MGM, 1952
I LOVE MELVIN   MGM, 1953
REMAINS TO BE SEEN   MGM, 1953
A SLIGHT CASE OF LARCENY   MGM, 1953
THE AFFAIRS OF DOBIE GILLIS   MGM, 1953
HALF A HERO   MGM, 1953
THE ADVENTURES OF HAJJI BABA   20th Century-Fox, 1954
RIDE THE HIGH IRON   Columbia, 1957
MR. PHAROAH AND HIS CLEOPATRA   1959
THE GENE KRUPA STORY   Columbia, 1960
CRITIC'S CHOICE   Warner Bros., 1963
LOOKING FOR LOVE   MGM, 1964
PAJAMA PARTY   American International, 1964
BILLIE   United Artists, 1965
THE GHOST IN THE INVISIBLE BIKINI   American
International, 1966
THE KING'S PIRATE   Universal, 1967
THE LONGEST 100 MILES (TF)   Universal TV, 1967
NOW YOU SEE IT, NOW YOU DON'T (TF)   Universal TV, 1968
DID YOU HEAR THE ONE ABOUT THE TRAVELING
SALESLADY?   Universal, 1968
DEADLOCK (TF)   Universal TV, 1969
THE MILLIONAIRE (TF)   Don Fedderson Productions, 1978
ZERO TO SIXTY   First Artists, 1978
THE MUNSTERS' REVENGE (TF)   Universal TV, 1981

GARY WEIS*
Business Manager: Goodfriend & Associates, 1299 Ocean Avenue -
Suite 620, Santa Monica, CA 90401, 310/451-0744

JIMI HENDRIX (FCD)   co-director with Joe Boyd & John Head,
Warner Bros., 1973
ALL YOU NEED IS CASH (TF)   THE RUTLES   co-director with
Eric Idle, Rutles Corps Productions, 1978, British
80 BLOCKS FROM TIFFANY'S (FD)   Above Average
Productions, 1980
WHOLLY MOSES   Columbia, 1980
YOUNG LUST   RSO Films, 1982
MARLEY (FCD)   Island Alive, 1985

ROGER WEISBERG
ROAD SCHOLAR (FD)   The Samuel Goldwyn Company, 1993

SAM WEISMAN*
Agent: CAA - Beverly Hills, 310/288-4545

SUNSET BEAT (TF)   Patrick Hasburgh Productions, 1990
D2: THE MIGHTY DUCKS   Buena Vista, 1994
BYE BYE, LOVE   20th Century Fox, 1995

ROB WEISS
Agent: UTA - Beverly Hills, 310/273-6700

AMONGST FRIENDS   Fine Line Features/New Line Cinema, 1993

ROBERT K. WEISS*
Business: St. Clare Entertainment, Universal Studios, 100 Universal
City Plaza, Universal City, CA 91608, 818/777-6759

THE COMPLEAT AL (CTF)   Showtime/CBS-Fox, 1985
AMAZON WOMEN ON THE MOON   co-director with Joe Dante,
Carl Gottlieb, Peter Horton & John Landis, Universal, 1987

ELLEN WEISSBROD
LISTEN UP: THE LIVES OF QUINCY JONES (FD)
Warner Bros., 1990

DAVID WELLINGTON
Agent: Scott Yoselow, The Gersh Agency - New York City,
212/997-1818

A MAN IN UNIFORM   I LOVE A MAN IN UNIFORM
Miracle Pictures, 1993, Canadian

PETER WELLS
Contact: New Zealand Film Commission, P.O. Box 11-546,
Wellington, New Zealand, tel.: 4/385-9754

DESPERATE REMEDIES   co-director with Stewart Main,
Miramax Films, 1993, New Zealand

SIMON WELLS
AN AMERICAN TAIL: FIEVEL GOES WEST (AF)   co-director with
Phil Nibbelink, Universal, 1991
WE'RE BACK! A DINOSAUR'S STORY (AF)   co-director with
Dick Zondag, Ralph Zondag & Phil Nibbelink, Universal, 1993
BALTO (AF)   Universal, 1995

JIANG WEN
Contact: China Film Import & Export Office, 2500 Wilshire Blvd. -
Suite 1028, Los Angeles, CA 90057, 213/380-7520

IN THE HEAT OF THE SUN   DAYS OF BRILLIANT SUNLIGHT
King's Video/Star City Film & TV Development/Dragon Film
International/China Film Co-Production Corporation, 1994,
Hong Kong-Taiwanese-Chinese

WIM WENDERS

b. August 14, 1945 - Dusseldorf, Germany
Business: Gray City Inc., 853 Broadway, New York, NY 10007,
212/473-3600

SUMMER IN THE CITY (DEDICATED TO THE KINKS)
1970, West German
THE GOALIE'S ANXIETY AT THE PENALTY KICK
Bauer International, 1972, West German
THE SCARLET LETTER   Bauer International,
1973, West German-Spanish
ALICE IN THE CITIES   New Yorker, 1974, West German
THE WRONG MOVE   New Yorker, 1975, West German
KINGS OF THE ROAD   Bauer International, 1976, West German
THE AMERICAN FRIEND   New Yorker, 1977,
West German-French
LIGHTNING OVER WATER   *NICK'S MOVIE*   co-director with
Nicholas Ray, Pari Films, 1980, West German-Swiss-U.S.
THE STATE OF THINGS   Gray City, 1982,
U.S.-West German-Portuguese
HAMMETT   Orion/Warner Bros., 1982
PARIS, TEXAS   TLC Films/20th Century Fox, 1984,
West German-French
TOKYO-GA (FD)   Wim Wenders Produktion/Gray City/Chris
Sievernich Produktion, 1985, West German-U.S.
WINGS OF DESIRE   *DER HIMMEL UBER BERLIN*   Orion Classics,
1987, West German-French
AUFZEICHNUNGEN ZU KLEIDERN UND STADTEN (FD)
Road Movies, 1989, West German
UNTIL THE END OF THE WORLD   Warner Bros.,
1991, German-French-Australian
FARAWAY, SO CLOSE!   Sony Pictures Classics, 1993, German
BEYOND THE CLOUDS   co-director with Michelangelo Antonioni,
Cecchi Gori Group/Road Movies/Stephan Tchalgadjeff/Philippe
Carcasson, 1995, Italian-French-German
LISBON STORY   Road Movies Filmproduktion, 1995, German

PAUL WENDKOS*

b. September 20, 1922 - Philadelphia, Pennsylvania
Contact: Directors Guild of America - Los Angeles, 213/851-3671

THE BURGLAR   Columbia, 1957
THE CASE AGAINST BROOKLYN   Columbia, 1958
TARAWA BEACHHEAD   Columbia, 1958
GIDGET   Columbia, 1959
FACE OF A FUGITIVE   Columbia, 1959
BATTLE OF THE CORAL SEA   Columbia, 1959
BECAUSE THEY'RE YOUNG   Columbia, 1960
GIDGET GOES HAWAIIAN   Columbia, 1961
ANGEL BABY   Allied Artists, 1961
TEMPLE OF THE SWINGING DOLL   20th Century-Fox, 1961
GIDGET GOES TO ROME   Columbia, 1963
RECOIL   Lion, 1963
JOHNNY TIGER   Universal, 1966
ATTACK ON THE IRON COAST   United Artists, 1968, U.S.-British
HAWAII FIVE-O (TF)   Leonard Freeman Productions, 1968
GUNS OF THE MAGNIFICENT SEVEN   United Artists, 1969
FEAR NO EVIL (TF)   Universal TV, 1969
CANNON FOR CORDOBA   United Artists, 1970
THE BROTHERHOOD OF THE BELL (TF)   Cinema Center, 1970
THE MEPHISTO WALTZ   20th Century-Fox, 1971
TRAVIS LOGAN, D.A. (TF)   QM Productions, 1971
A TATTERED WEB (TF)   Metromedia Productions, 1971
A LITTLE GAME (TF)   Universal TV, 1971
A DEATH OF INNOCENCE (TF)   Mark Carliner Productions, 1971
THE DELPHI BUREAU (TF)   Warner Bros. TV, 1972
THE FAMILY RICO (TF)   CBS, Inc., 1972
HAUNTS OF THE VERY RICH (TF)   ABC Circle Films, 1972
FOOTSTEPS (TF)   Metromedia Productions, 1972
THE STRANGERS IN 7A (TF)   Palomar Pictures International, 1972
HONOR THY FATHER (TF)   Metromedia Productions, 1973
TERROR ON THE BEACH (TF)   20th Century-Fox TV, 1973
THE UNDERGROUND MAN (TF)   Paramount TV, 1974
THE LEGEND OF LIZZIE BORDEN (TF)   Paramount TV, 1975
DEATH AMONG FRIENDS (TF)   Douglas S. Cramer Productions/
Warner Bros. TV, 1975
SPECIAL DELIVERY   American International, 1976
THE DEATH OF RICHIE (TF)   Henry Jaffe Enterprises, 1977

SECRETS (TF)   The Jozak Company, 1977
GOOD AGAINST EVIL (TF)   Frankel-Bolen Productions/20th
Century-Fox TV, 1977
HAROLD ROBBINS' 79 PARK AVENUE   *79 PARK AVENUE* (MS)
Universal TV, 1978
BETRAYAL (TF)   Roger Gimbel Productions/EMI TV, 1978
A WOMAN CALLED MOSES (TF)   Henry Jaffe Enterprises, 1978
THE ORDEAL OF PATTY HEARST (TF)   Finnegan Associates/
David Paradine TV, 1979
ACT OF VIOLENCE (TF)   Emmett G. Lavery, Jr. Productions/
Paramount TV, 1979
THE ORDEAL OF DR. MUDD (TF)   BSR Productions/Marble Arch
Productions, 1980
A CRY FOR LOVE (TF)   Charles Fries Productions/Alan Sacks
Productions, 1980
THE FIVE OF ME (TF)   Jack Farren Productions/Factor-Newland
Production Corporation, 1981
GOLDEN GATE (TF)   Lin Bolen Productions/Warner Bros. TV, 1981
FARRELL FOR THE PEOPLE (TF)   InterMedia Entertainment/TAL
Productions/MGM-UA TV, 1982
COCAINE: ONE MAN'S SEDUCTION (TF)   Charles Fries
Productions/David Goldsmith Productions, 1983
INTIMATE AGONY (TF)   Henerson-Hirsch Productions/Robert
Papazian Productions, 1983
BOONE (TF)   Lorimar Productions, 1983
CELEBRITY (MS)   NBC Productions, 1984
SCORNED AND SWINDLED (TF)   Cypress Point Productions, 1984
THE EXECUTION (TF)   Newland-Raynor Productions/Comworld
Productions, 1985
THE BAD SEED (TF)   Hajeno Productions/Warner Bros. TV, 1985
PICKING UP THE PIECES (TF)   CBS Entertainment, 1985
SISTER MARGARET AND THE SATURDAY NIGHT LADIES (TF)
Poolhouse Productions, 1986
RAGE OF ANGELS: THE STORY CONTINUES (MS)
NBC Productions, 1986
BLOOD VOWS: THE STORY OF A MAFIA WIFE (TF)
Louis Rudolph Films/Fries Entertainment, 1987
SIX AGAINST THE ROCK (TF)   Schaefer-Karpf-Epstein
Productions/Gaylord Production Company, 1987
RIGHT TO DIE (TF)   Ohlmeyer Communications, 1987
THE TAKING OF FLIGHT 847: THE ULI DERICKSON
STORY (TF) ☆   Columbia TV, 1988
THE GREAT ESCAPE II: THE UNTOLD STORY (TF)
director of part 1, Spectator Films/Michael Jaffe Films, 1988
FROM THE DEAD OF NIGHT (TF)   Shadowplay Films/Phoenix
Entertainment Group, 1989
CROSS OF FIRE (TF)   Leonard Hill Films, 1989
BLIND FAITH (TF)   NBC Productions, 1990
GOOD COPS, BAD COPS (TF)   Kushner-Locke Company/
Commonwealth Films, 1990
THE CHASE (TF)   Steve White Productions/Spectator Films, 1991
WHITE HOT: THE MYSTERIOUS MURDER OF THELMA TODD (TF)
Sandy Hook Productions/Neufeld-Keating Productions/
von Zerneck-Sertner Films, 1991
GUILTY UNTIL PROVEN INNOCENT (TF)   Cosgrove-Meurer
Productions, 1991
TRIAL: THE PRICE OF PASSION (TF)   The Sokolow Company/
TriStar TV, 1992
BLOODLINES: MURDER IN THE FAMILY (TF)   Stonehenge
Productions/Lorimar TV, 1993
DANIELLE STEEL'S MESSGE FROM NAM   *MESSAGE FROM
NAM* (TF)   The Cramer Company/NBC Productions, 1993

RICHARD WENK

Agent: The Gersh Agency - Beverly Hills, 310/274-6611

VAMP   New World, 1986
NATIONAL LAMPOON'S ATTACK OF THE 5 FT. 2 WOMEN (CTF)
co-director with Julie Brown, Showtime/National Lampoon/
Imagination Productions, 1994

JEFF WERNER*

Home: 4211 Kester Avenue, Studio City, CA 91403, 818/981-8651

CHEERLEADERS' WILD WEEKEND   Dimension, 1979
DIE LAUGHING   Orion/Warner Bros., 1980
THE GODFATHER FAMILY: A LOOK INSIDE (TD)
Zoetrope Studios, 1991

PETER WERNER*

b. January 17, 1947 - New York, New York
Business: A Joyful Noise Unlimited, 196 Granville Avenue,
  Los Angeles, CA 90049, 310/440-2696
Agent: William Morris Agency - Beverly Hills, 310/859-4000

FINDHORD (FD)   Moving Pictures, 1976
BATTERED (TF)   Henry Jaffe Enterprises, 1978
AUNT MARY (TF)   Henry Jaffe Enterprises, 1979
DON'T CRY, IT'S ONLY THUNDER   Sanrio, 1981, U.S.-Japanese
HARD KNOX (TF)   A. Shane Company, 1984
I MARRIED A CENTERFOLD (TF)   Moonlight II Productions, 1984
PRISONERS   20th Century Fox, 1984, New Zealand
WOMEN IN SONG (TD)   KCET/Marc Robertson Productions, 1985
SINS OF THE FATHER (TF)   Fries Entertainment, 1985
OUTLAWS (TF)   Mad Dog Productions/Universal TV, 1986
LBJ: THE EARLY YEARS (TF)   Louis Rudolph Films/Fries
  Entertainment, 1987
NO MAN'S LAND   Orion, 1987
THE IMAGE (CTF)   HBO Pictures/Citadel Entertainment, 1990
HIROSHIMA: OUT OF THE ASHES (TF)   Robert Greenwald
  Productions, 1990
NED BLESSING (TF)   Hearst Entertainment, 1991
THE SUBSTITUTE WIFE (TF)   The Frederick S. Pierce
  Company, 1994

LINA WERTMULLER

*(Arcangela Felice Assunta Wertmuller von Elgg Spanol
von Brauelch)*
b. August 14, 1928 - Rome, Italy
Home: Piazza Coltilde 5, Rome, Italy, tel.: 06/360-7501

I BALISCHI   22 Dicembre/Galatea, 1963, Italian
LET'S TALK ABOUT MEN   *QUESTA VOLTA PARLIAMO
  DI UOMINI*   Allied Artists, 1965, Italian
RITA LA ZANZARA   Mondial, 1966, Italian
NON STUZZICATE LA ZANZARA   Mondial, 1967, Italian
THE SEDUCTION OF MIMI   *MIMI METALLURGICO FERITO
  NELL'ONORE*   New Line Cinema, 1972, Italian
LOVE AND ANARCHY   *FILM D'AMORE E D'ANARCHIA*
  Peppercorn-Wormser, 1973, Italian
ALL SCREWED UP   *TUTTO A POSTE E NIENTE IN ORDINE*
  New Line Cinema, 1974, Italian
SWEPT AWAY BY AN UNUSUAL DESTINY IN THE BLUE SEA
  OF AUGUST   Cinema 5, 1974, Italian
SEVEN BEAUTIES   *PASQUALINO SETTEBELLEZZE* ★
  Cinema 5, 1976, Italian
THE END OF THE WORLD IN OUR USUAL BED IN A NIGHT
  FULL OF RAIN   Warner Bros., 1978, Italian-U.S.
BLOOD FEUD   *FATTO DI SANGUE FRA DUE UOMINI
  PER CAUSA DI UNA VEDOVA (SI SOSPETTANO
  MOVENTI POLITICI)*   AFD, 1980, Italian
A JOKE OF DESTINY lying in wait around the corner like a street
  bandit, The Samuel Goldwyn Company, 1983, Italian
SOTTO, SOTTO   Triumph/Columbia, 1984, Italian
CAMORRA   *UN COMPLICATO INTRIGO DI DONNE, VICOLI E
  DELITTI*   Cannon, 1986, Italian
SUMMER NIGHT WITH GREEK PROFILE, ALMOND EYES AND
  SCENT OF BASIL   New Line Cinema, 1986, Italian
IL DECIMO CLANDESTINO (TF)   Reteitalia, 1989, Italian
ON A MOONLIT NIGHT   *IN UNA NOTTE DI CHIARO DI LUNA*
  Motion Picture Corporation of America, 1989, Italian
SABATO DOMENICA LUNEDI   Silvio Berlusconi Communications/
  Reteitalia/Carlo Ponti Productions, 1990, Italian
CIAO, PROFESSORE!   *IO SPERIAMO CHE ME LA CAVO*
  Miramax Films, 1993, Italian

ERIC WESTON*

Agent: ICM - Beverly Hills, 310/550-4000

THEY WENT THAT-A-WAY AND THAT-A-WAY   International
  Picture Show Company, 1979
EVILSPEAK   The Frank Moreno Company, 1982
MARVIN AND TIGE   *LIKE FATHER AND SON*   20th Century-Fox
  International Classics, 1983
THE IRON TRIANGLE   Scotti Bros., 1989
TO PROTECT AND TO SERVE   Apsicon Productions/Capital
  Entertainment, 1992

HASKELL WEXLER*

b. February 6, 1926 - Chicago, Illinois
Business: 1341 Ocean Avenue - Suite 111, Santa Monica, CA 90401,
  310/395-0090
Agent: The Skouras Agency - Santa Monica, 310/295-9550

THE BUS (FD)   1965
MEDIUM COOL   Paramount, 1969
BRAZIL: A REPORT ON TORTURE (FD)   co-director with
  Saul Landau, 1971
INTRODUCTION TO THE ENEMY (FD)   co-director, 1974
UNDERGROUND (FD)   co-director with Emile De Antonio &
  Mary Lampson, New Yorker, 1976
BUS II (FD)   co-director with Bonnie Bass Parker &
  Tom Tyson, 1983
LATINO   Cinecom, 1985

HOWARD WEXLER

Business: Check Entertainment, 7906 Santa Monica Blvd. - Suite 217,
  Los Angeles, CA 90046, 213/650-7227

LOVING LULU   MBG/Starlight Film, 1992

GEORGE WHALEY

Contact: Australian Film Commission, 150 William Street,
  Woolloomooloo NSW 2011, Australia, tel.: 2/321-6444

ON OUR SELECTION   Icon Productions/Anthony Buckley
  Productions, 1995, Australian

TONY WHARMBY*

Contact: Directors Guild of America - Los Angeles, 213/851-3671

DEMPSEY AND MAKEPEACE (TF)   London Weekend TV,
  1985, British
SORRY, WRONG NUMBER (CTF)   USA Network, 1989
VOICE OF THE HEART (TF)   Robert Bradford Productions,
  1990, British-U.S.
THE KISSING PLACE (TF)   Cynthia Cherbak Productions/Wilshire
  Court Productions, 1990
DEADLY CROSSING (CTF)   Wilshire Court Productions, 1991
TO BE THE BEST (TF)   Gemmy Productions, 1992, U.S.-British
WILD JUSTICE (TF)   Reteitalia Productions/Tribune Entertainment/
  Taurus Film, 1993, Italian-U.S.-British
SEDUCED BY EVIL (CTF)   CNM Entertainment/Cinestage
  Productions/Wilshire Court Productions, 1994

CLAUDE WHATHAM

Address: Camp House, Camp, Miserden, Stroud,
  Gloucestershire, England

CIDER WITH ROSIE (TF)   1972, British
THAT'LL BE THE DAY   EMI, 1974, British
ALL CREATURES GREAT AND SMALL (TF)   Talent Associates/
  EMI TV, 1975, British
SWALLOWS AND AMAZONS   LDS, 1977, British
SWEET WILLIAM   Kendon Films, 1980, British
HOODWINK   CB Films, 1982, Australian
MURDER IS EASY (TF)   David L. Wolper-Stan Margulies
  Productions/Warner Bros., 1982
MURDER ELITE (TF)   Tyburn Productions, 1985, British
JUMPING THE QUEUE (TF)   BBC, 1987, British
BUDDY'S SONG   Castle Premier, 1991, British

JIM WHEAT

Agent: The Gersh Agency - Beverly Hills, 310/274-6611

LIES   co-director with Ken Wheat, International Film
  Marketing, 1983
EWOKS: THE BATTLE FOR ENDOR (TF)   co-director with
  Ken Wheat, Lucasfilm Ltd., 1985
AFTER MIDNIGHT   co-director with Ken Wheat, MGM/UA, 1989

KEN WHEAT
Agent: The Gersh Agency - Beverly Hills, 310/274-6611

LIES   co-director with Jim Wheat, International Film
   Marketing, 1983
EWOKS: THE BATTLE FOR ENDOR (TF)   co-director with
   Jim Wheat, Lucasfilm Ltd., 1985
AFTER MIDNIGHT   co-director with Jim Wheat,
   MGM/UA, 1989

DAVID WHEATLEY
Agent: UTA - Beverly Hills, 310/273-6700

THE MAGIC TOYSHOP   Roxie Releasing, 1986, British
THE MARCH (TF)   BBC/One World Consortium, 1991, British
HOSTAGES (CTF)   HBO Showcase/Granada TV,
   1993, British-U.S.
NOBODY'S CHILDREN (CTF)   Winkler-Daniel Productions/Quinta
   Communications/USA Pictures, 1994, U.S.-French

ANNE WHEELER
b. September 23, 1946 - Edmonton, Alberta, Canada
Business: Wheeler Hendren Enterprises Ltd., R.R. 1,
   212 Sunset Drive, Ganges, British Columbia V0S 1E0,
   Canada, 604/537-9916
Agent: Writers & Artists Agency - Los Angeles, 310/820-6300

A WAR STORY   National Film Board of Canada,
   1981, Canadian
LOYALTIES   Cinema Group, 1986, Canadian-British
COWBOYS DON'T CRY   Cineplex Odeon, 1988, Canadian
BYE BYE BLUES   Circle Releasing, 1989, Canadian
ANGEL SQUARE   Rendezvous Films/National Film Board
   of Canada, 1990, Canadian
THE DIVINERS (TF)   Atlantis Films/Credo Group/CBC,
   1993, Canadian
OTHER WOMEN'S CHILDREN (CTF)   Crescent Entertainment/
   Western International Communications/Lifetime TV,
   1993, Canadian
HAKUJIN (TF)   Atlantis Films/Troika Films/Telefilm Canada/BC
   Film/Rogers Telefund, 1995, Canadian

FOREST WHITAKER*
b. 1961 - Longview, Texas
Agent: ICM - Beverly Hills, 310/550-4000
Contact: Directors Guild of America - Los Angeles, 213/851-3671

STRAPPED (CTF)   Osiris Films/HBO Showcase, 1993
WAITING TO EXHALE   20th Century Fox, 1995

JOHN WHITESELL*
Agent: UTA - Beverly Hills, 310/273-6700
Personal Manager: 3 Arts Entertainment - Beverly Hills,
   310/888-3200

CALENDAR GIRL   Columbia, 1993

HELEN WHITNEY*
Address: 168 East 98th Street, New York, NY 10128, 212/831-1388
Agent: ICM - Beverly Hills, 310/550-4000

LETHAL INNOCENCE (TF)   The Entertainment Group/Turtleback
   Productions, 1991

JAMES WHITMORE, JR.*
Agent: Paradigm - Los Angeles, 310/277-4400

QUANTUM LEAP: THE OSWALD CONSPIRACY (TF)
   Belisarius Productions/Universal TV, 1992
THE ROCKFORD FILES: I LOVE L.A. (TF)   MGB Productions/
   Universal TV, 1994

PRESTON A. WHITMORE, II
Agent: William Morris Agency - Beverly Hills, 310/859-4000

THE WALKING DEAD   Savoy Pictures, 1995

STEPHEN WHITTAKER
Agent: Becsey/Wisdom/Kalajian - Los Angeles, 310/550-0535

PORTRAIT OF A MARRIAGE (MS)   BBC/WGBH-Boston/TV
   New Zealand, 1991, British-U.S.-New Zealand
CLOSING NUMBERS (TF)   Arden Films/Channel 4,
   1994, British

ROB WHITTLESEY
APOLLO 13: TO THE EDGE AND BACK (TD)   WGBH-Boston/TV
   Asahi/Central TV, 1994, U.S.-Japanese-British

MICHAEL WHYTE
Agent: ICM - London, tel.: 171/636-6565

CREGGAN (TD)   Thames TV, 1980, British
CHINA ACROBATS (TD)   Thames TV, 1981, British
THE GOURMET (TF)   Channel 4, 1985, British
ON THE PALM (TF)   BBC, 1986, British
CATHERINE (TF)   Thames TV, 1988, British
THE RAILWAY STATION MAN   Turner Pictures/BBC Films/First
   Film/Sands Productions, 1992, British
THE MAN WHO CRIED (MS)   Tyne Tees TV, 1992, British

DAVID WICKES
Agent: William Morris Agency - Beverly Hills, 310/859-4000

SWEENEY   EMI, 1977, British
SILVER DREAM RACER   Almi Cinema 5, 1980, British
PHILIP MARLOWE - PRIVATE EYE   CHANDLERTOWN
   co-director with Sidney Hayers, Bryan Forbes & Peter Hunt,
   HBO/David Wickes Television, Ltd./London Weekend Television,
   1983, British
JACK THE RIPPER (TF)   Euston Films/Thames TV/Hill-O'Connor
   Entertainment/Lorimar TV, 1988, British-U.S.
JEKYLL & HYDE (TF)   King-Phoenix Entertainment/London
   Weekend TV, 1990, U.S.-British
FRANKENSTEIN (CTF)   Turner Pictures/David Wickes
   Television, Ltd./Thames TV, 1993, British-U.S.

BERNHARD WICKI*
b. October 28, 1919 - St. Polten, Austria
Home: Restelbergstrasse 60, 8 Zurich, Switzerland,
   tel.: 041/361-3745
Agent: Alexander Agency, William Morris Organization,
   Lamontstrasse 9, 8 Munich 80, Germany, tel.: 089-47-60-81

WARUM SIND SIE GEGEN UNS?   1958, West German
THE BRIDGE   Allied Artists, 1959, West German
DAS WUNDER DES MALACHIAS   1961, West German
THE LONGEST DAY   co-director with Ken Annakin &
   Andrew Marton, 20th Century-Fox, 1962
THE VISIT   20th Century-Fox, 1964,
   West German-Italian-French-U.S.
MORITURI   THE SABOTEUR, CODE NAME "MORITURI"
   20th Century-Fox, 1965
TRANSIT   1966, West German
QUADRIGA   co-director, 1967, West German
DAS FALSCHE GEWICHT   1971, West German
DIE EROBERUNG DER ZITADELLE   Scorpion Film,
   1977, West German
DIE GRUNSTEIN-VARIANTE   Futura Film, 1985, West German
DAS SPINNENNETZ   Beta/Kirch Group/Provobis/ZDF/ORF/
   RAI/TVE, 1989, West German
NEW GERMANY   co-director with Michael Verhoeven &
   Reinhard Hauff, WDR/ZDF/BR/Futura/Sentana,
   1990, West German

GREGORY C. WIDEN
Agent: Writers & Artists Agency - Los Angeles, 310/824-6300

GOD'S ARMY   Miramax Films, 1995

BO WIDERBERG
b. June 8, 1930 - Malmo, Sweden
Contact: Swedish Film Institute, P.O. Box 27126, 102 52 Stockholm,
   Sweden, tel.: 08/665-1100

THE BABY CARRIAGE   Europa Film, 1962, Swedish
RAVEN'S END   New Yorker, 1963, Swedish
LOVE 65   Europa Film, 1965, Swedish
THIRTY TIMES YOUR MONEY   Europa Film, 1965, Swedish
ELVIRA MADIGAN   Cinema 5, 1967, Swedish
THE WHITE GAME   co-director, 1968, Swedish
ADALEN '31   Paramount, 1971, Swedish-U.S.
JOE HILL   Paramount, 1971, Swedish-U.S.
FIMPEN   1974, Swedish
MAN ON THE ROOF   Cinema 5, 1977, Swedish
VICTORIA   1979, Swedish-West German
GRISFESTEN   Nordiskfilm/Svensk Filmindustri/TV2/Drakfilm/
   Svenska Filminstitut, 1983, Swedish-Danish
MANNEN FRAN MALLORCA   Swedish Film Institute/Drakfilm/
   Svensk Filmindustri/SVT2/Filmhuset KB/Crone Film Sales,
   1985, Swedish-Danish
THE SERPENT'S WAY UP THE NAKED ROCK   European
   Classics, 1987, Swedish
JOY AND ALL THINGS FAIR   Per Holst Productions/TV2/Egmont
   Film/Von Viddinghoff Film, 1994, Danish-Swedish

KEN WIEDERHORN*
Agent: The Marion Rosenberg Office - Los Angeles, 213/653-7383

SHOCK WAVES   Joseph Brenner Associates, 1977
KING FRAT   Mad Makers, 1979
EYES OF A STRANGER   Warner Bros., 1981
MEATBALLS PART II   TriStar, 1984
RETURN OF THE LIVING DEAD PART II   Lorimar, 1988
A HOUSE IN THE HILLS   LIVE Entertainment/Delux Productions,
   1993, U.S.-Luxembourgian

ROBERT WIEMER*
b. January 30, 1938 - Detroit, Michigan
Business: Golden Tiger Pictures, 205 S. Beverly Drive - Suite 200,
   Beverly Hills, CA 90212, 310/271-5213
Agent: Cindy Turtle/Beth Bohn, The Turtle Agency - Studio City,
   818/506-6898

MY SEVENTEENTH SUMMER (TF)   BMC, Inc., 1980
WITCH'S SISTER (TF)   BMC, Inc., 1981
DO ME A FAVOR (TF)   BMC, Inc., 1982
ANNA TO THE INFINITE POWER (TF)   Tigerfilm, 1983
SOMEWHERE, TOMORROW   Comworld, 1984
THE NIGHT TRAIN TO KATHMANDU   Paramount, 1988

ANDREW WILD
Contact: Directors Guild of Canada, 225 Richmond Street, Toronto
   5V 1W2, Canada, 416/351-8200

SPENSER: CEREMONY (CTF)   Norstar Entertainment/Boardwalk
   Entertainment/Ultra Entertainment/ABC Video Enterprises,
   1993, U.S.-Canadian

DAVID WILD*
Address: Box 240, Onekama, MI 49675

BETWEEN THE TEETH (PF)   co-director with David Byrne,
   Playdate/Theatre, 1994

BILLY WILDER*
(Samuel Wilder)
b. June 22, 1906 - Vienna, Austria
Agent: Paul Kohner, Inc. - Los Angeles, 310/550-1060

MAUVAISE GRAINE   co-director with Alexander Esway,
   1933, German
THE MAJOR AND THE MINOR   Paramount, 1942
FIVE GRAVES TO CAIRO   Paramount, 1943
DOUBLE INDEMNITY ★   Paramount, 1944
THE LOST WEEKEND ★★   Paramount, 1945
THE EMPEROR WALTZ   Paramount, 1948
A FOREIGN AFFAIR   Paramount, 1948
SUNSET BOULEVARD ★   Paramount, 1950
THE BIG CARNIVAL   *ACE IN THE HOLE*   Paramount, 1951
STALAG 17 ★   Paramount, 1953
SABRINA ★   Paramount, 1954
THE SEVEN YEAR ITCH   20th Century-Fox, 1955
THE SPIRIT OF ST. LOUIS   Warner Bros., 1957
LOVE IN THE AFTERNOON   Allied Artists, 1957
WITNESS FOR THE PROSECUTION ★   United Artists, 1957
SOME LIKE IT HOT ★   United Artists, 1959
THE APARTMENT ★★   United Artists, 1960
ONE, TWO, THREE   United Artists, 1961
IRMA LA DOUCE   United Artists, 1963
KISS ME, STUPID   Lopert, 1964
THE FORTUNE COOKIE   United Artists, 1966
THE PRIVATE LIFE OF SHERLOCK HOLMES   United Artists,
   1970, U.S.-British
AVANTI!   United Artists, 1972, U.S.-Italian
THE FRONT PAGE   Universal, 1974
FEDORA   United Artists, 1979, West German-French
BUDDY BUDDY   MGM/United Artists, 1981

GENE WILDER*
(Jerry Silberman)
b. June 11, 1935 - Milwaukee, Wisconsin
Agent: CAA - Beverly Hills, 310/288-4545

THE ADVENTURE OF SHERLOCK HOLMES' SMARTER BROTHER
   20th Century-Fox, 1975
THE WORLD'S GREATEST LOVER   20th Century-Fox, 1977
SUNDAY LOVERS   co-director with Bryan Forbes,
   Edouard Molinaro & Dino Risi, MGM/United Artists,
   1981, U.S.-British-French-Italian
THE WOMAN IN RED   Orion, 1984
HAUNTED HONEYMOON   Orion, 1986

JOHN WILDER*
Agent: CAA - Beverly Hills, 310/288-4545

NORMAN ROCKWELL'S 'BREAKING HOME TIES'
   BREAKING HOME TIES (TF)   ABC, 1987

GORDON WILES
Home: 24 Delphinus, Irvine, CA 92715, 714/854-4484

GINGER IN THE MORNING   National Film, 1974

ETHAN WILEY
Contact: Writers Guild of America, West - Los Angeles,
   310/550-1000
Agent: Above The Line - West Hollywood, 310/859-6115

HOUSE II: THE SECOND STORY   New World, 1987

JENNY WILKES
Agent: Rochelle Stevens & Co. - London, tel.: 171/359-3900

SITTING TARGETS (TF)   BBC, British

ANTHONY WILKINSON*

Address: 38 Trewince Road, London 8W20 8RD, England,
tel.: 181/946-5078
Agent: Richard Hatton Ltd. - London, tel.: 181/876-6699

THE KING OF LOVE (TF)   Sarabande Productions/
MGM-UA TV, 1987

CHARLES WILKINSON

b. 1952 - Calgary, Alberta, Canada
Business: Apple Pie Pictures, 617 Beachview Drive, Deep Cove,
North Vancouver, British Columbia V7G 1P8, Canada,
604/929-8280

BLOOD CLAN   1990, Canadian
MAX   Astral Films, 1994, Canadian
CRASH   Bad Boy Films for Keystone Films, 1995, Canadian

ANSON WILLIAMS*

b. Los Angeles, California
Agent: Tim Stone, Stone Manners Agency - Los Angeles,
213/654-7575

THE LONE STAR KID (TF)   Major H/Anson Productions, 1986
YOUR MOTHER WEARS COMBAT BOOTS (TF)   Kushner-Locke
Productions, 1989
DREAM DATE (TF)   Frederic Golchan-Robert Kosberg
Productions/Gary Hoffman-Neal Israel Productions/
Saban International, 1989
LITTLE WHITE LIES (TF)   Larry A. Thompson Organization/
New World TV, 1989
A QUIET LITTLE NEIGHBORHOOD, A PERFECT LITTLE
MURDER (TF)   Neal & Gary Productions/Saban
International, 1990
ALL AMERICAN MURDER   Trimark Pictures, 1992

ELMO WILLIAMS*

(James Elmo Williams)
Contact: Directors Guild of America - Los Angeles, 213/851-3671

THE TALL TEXAN   Lippert, 1953
THE COWBOY (FD)   Lippert, 1954
APACHE WARRIOR   20th Century-Fox, 1957
HELL SHIP MUTINY   co-director with Lee Sholem, Republic, 1957

OSCAR WILLIAMS*

b. May 20, 1944 - St. Croix, Virgin Islands
Home: 3657 Lowry Road, Los Angeles, CA 90027, 213/661-7700
Agent: David Dworski & Associates - Los Angeles, 310/273-6173

THE FINAL COMEDOWN   New World, 1972
FIVE ON THE BLACK HAND SIDE   United Artists, 1973
HOT POTATO   Warner Bros., 1976
ANGER IN THE DARK   Oscar Williams and Associates, 1992

PAUL WILLIAMS

b. November 12, 1943 - New York, New York
Home: 990 Hanley Avenue, Los Angeles, CA 90049,
310/471-0669

OUT OF IT   United Artists, 1969
THE REVOLUTIONARY   United Artists, 1970
DEALING: OR THE BERKELEY-TO-BOSTON FORTY-BRICK
LOST-BAG BLUES   Warner Bros., 1972
NUNZIO   Universal, 1978
MISS RIGHT   IAP, 1981, Italian
A LIGHT IN THE AFTERNOON   Starfighter Productions, 1986
MIRROR, MIRROR II   Orphan Eyes Productions, 1992
THE NOVEMBER MEN   Arrow Releasing, 1993
MIRAGE   Roadhouse/Tiogertail Flicks/Shonderosa, 1995

RICHARD WILLIAMS

b. March 19, 1933 - Toronto, Canada
Business: Richard Williams Animation Ltd., The Forum, 74-80
Camden Street, London NW1 0EG, England, tel.: 171/383-3831

RAGGEDY ANN AND ANDY (AF)   20th Century-Fox, 1977
ARABIAN KNIGHT   *THE THIEF AND THE COBBLER* (AF)
Miramax Films, 1995, British

WADE WILLIAMS

DETOUR   1992

FRED WILLIAMSON

b. March 5, 1938 - Gary, Indiana
Business: Po' Boy Productions, 5907 W. Pico Blvd.,
West Los Angeles, CA 90035, 310/855-1285

ADIOS AMIGO   Atlas, 1976
MEAN JOHNNY BARROWS   Atlas, 1976
DEATH JOURNEY   Atlas, 1976
NO WAY BACK   Atlas, 1976
MR. MEAN   Lone Star/Po' Boy, 1977, Italian-U.S.
ONE DOWN TWO TO GO   Almi Films, 1982
THE LAST FIGHT   Marvin Films, 1983
THE BIG SCORE   Almi Distribution, 1983
FOXTRAP   Snizzlefritz Distribution, 1986, Italian-U.S.
THE MESSENGER   Snizzlefritz Distribution, 1987, U.S.-Italian
JUSTICE DONE   Arista, 1990
CRITICAL ACTION   21st Century Distribution, 1990
THE KILL REFLEX   Po'Boy Productions, 1991
THREE DAYS TO A KILL   21st Century Distribution, 1992
THE NIGHT CALLER   Double Helix Films, 1992
SOUTH BEACH   Prism Entertainment, 1992

GORDON WILLIS*

Agent: ICM - Beverly Hills, 310/550-4000
Business Manager: Ron Taft - New York City, 212/586-8844

WINDOWS   United Artists, 1979

BRUCE WILSON

b. February 3, 1942 - Burlington, Wisconsin
Agent: Solomon Weingarten & Associates - Santa Monica,
310/394-8866

DOUBLES   Shaprio Entertainment, 1978
BOMBS AWAY   TMS Pictures, 1985

HUGH WILSON*

b. August 21, 1943 - Miami, Florida
Agent: William Morris Agency - Beverly Hills, 310/859-4000

POLICE ACADEMY   The Ladd Company/Warner Bros., 1984
RUSTLERS' RHAPSODY   Paramount, 1985
BURGLAR   Warner Bros., 1987
GUARDING TESS   TriStar, 1994

JIM WILSON

Business: Tig Productions, 4000 Warner Blvd., Burbank, CA 91522,
818/954-6000
Agent: CAA - Beverly Hills, 310/288-4545

HOLLYWOOD DREAMING   American Twist/Boulevard
Productions, 1986

SANDRA (SANDY) WILSON

b. 1947 - Penticton, British Columbia, Canada
Address: 2576 West 6th Avenue, Vancouver, British Columbia
V6K 1W5, Canada, 604/734-4688

MY AMERICAN COUSIN   Spectrafilm, 1985, Canadian
MAMA'S GOING TO BUY YOU A MOCKINGBIRD (TF)   CBC,
1988, Canadian

AMERICAN BOYFRIENDS   Alliance Entertainment,
   1989, Canadian
HARMONY CATS   Alan Morinis-Richard Davis Productions/BC
   Film/National Film Board of Canada/CBC, 1993, Canadian

KURT WIMMER
NORTH'S WAR   LIVE Entertainment, 1995

SCOTT WINANT*
Agent: CAA - Beverly Hills, 310/288-4545

EARTH 2 (TF)   Amblin TV/Universal TV, 1994

SIMON WINCER*
b. Sydney, Australia
Agent: CAA - Beverly Hills, 310/288-4545

TANDARRA (MS)   1976, Australian
THE SULLIVANS (MS)   co-director with David Stevens,
   1976, Australian
AGAINST THE WIND (MS)   co-director with George Miller,
   Pegasus Productions, 1978, Australian
THE DAY AFTER HALLOWEEN *SNAPSHOT* Group 1,
   1979, Australian
HARLEQUIN   New Image, 1980, Australian
PHAR LAP   20th Century-Fox, 1983, Australian
D.A.R.Y.L.   Paramount, 1985
THE GIRL WHO SPELLED FREEDOM (TF)   Knopf-Simons
   Productions/ITC Productions/Walt Disney Productions, 1986
THE LAST FRONTIER (TF)   McElroy & McElroy Productions,
   1986, Australian
THE LIGHTHORSEMEN   Cinecom, 1987, Australian
BLUEGRASS (TF)   The Landsburg Company, 1988
LONESOME DOVE (MS) ☆☆   Motown Productions/Pangaea/
   Qintex Entertainment Inc., 1989
QUIGLEY DOWN UNDER   MGM/Pathe Communications,
   1990, U.S.-Australian
HARLEY DAVIDSON AND THE MARLBORO MAN
   MGM-Pathe Communications, 1991
THE YOUNG INDIANA JONES CHRONICLES: CONGO, 1917 (TF)
   Lucasfilm Ltd./Paramount TV, 1992
THE YOUNG INDIANA JONES CHRONICLES: SOMME, 1916 (TF)
   Lucasfilm Ltd./Paramount TV, 1992
FREE WILLY   Warner Bros., 1993
LIGHTNING JACK   Savoy Pictures, 1994, Australian-U.S.
OPERATION DUMBO DROP   Buena Vista, 1995

HARRY WINER*
b. May 4, 1947 - Detroit, Michigan
Agent: CAA - Beverly Hills, 310/288-4545

ONE OF A KIND (TF)   ABC, 1982
PAPER DOLLS (TF)   Mandy Productions/MGM-UA TV, 1984
SINGLE BARS, SINGLE WOMEN (TF)   Carsey-Werner
   Productions/Sunn Classic Pictures, 1984
MIRRORS (TF)   Leonard Hill Films, 1985
SPACECAMP   20th Century Fox, 1986
HEARTBEAT (TF)   Aaron Spelling Productions, 1988
I LOVE YOU PERFECT (TF)   Gross-Weston Productions/Susan
   Dey Productions/Stephen J. Cannell Productions, 1989
WHEN YOU REMEMBER ME (TF)   Wolper Productions/Bernard
   Sofronski Productions/Warner Bros. TV, 1990
UNDER COVER (TF)   Sacret Inc./Paint Rock Productions/
   Warner Bros. TV, 1991
TAKING BACK MY LIFE (TF)   Elliot Fredgen & Co./Lyttle-Heshty
   Productions/Warner Bros. TV, 1992
STAY THE NIGHT (TF)   Stan Margulies Company/New
   World TV, 1992
MEN DON'T TELL (TF)   Daniel H. Blatt Productions/Nancy Bein
   Productions/Lorimar TV, 1993
JFK: RECKLESS YOUTH (TF)   The Polone Company/Hearst
   Entertainment, 1993
HOUSE ARREST   Rysher Entertainment, 1995

JONATHAN ALLEN WINFREY
RED TARGET: THE PLOT TO OVERTHROW THE U.S.S.R.
   Concorde, 1992
NEW CRIME CITY: LOS ANGELES 1010   Concorde, 1993
MANHUNT: BLOODFIST VII   Concorde, 1995

GARY WINICK
OUT OF THE RAIN   The Acme Company, 1991
SWEET NOTHING   The Acme Company, 1994

CHARLES WINKLER*
Business: Winkler Films, Inc., 211 S. Beverly Drive - Suite 200,
   Beverly Hills, CA 90212, 310/858-5780
Agent: Shapiro-Lichtman Talent Agency - Los Angeles, 310/859-8877

YOU TALKIN' TO ME   MGM/UA, 1987
DISTURBED   LIVE Entertainment/Odyssey Distributors, 1990
RED RIBBON BLUES   Red Ribbon Productions, 1995

HENRY WINKLER*
b. October 30, 1946 - New York, New York
Address: P.O. Box 1764, Studio City, CA 91604, 213/956-5700
Contact: Disney Studios, 500 South Buena Vista Street,
   Animation 2F5, Burbank, CA 91521, 818/560-4640
Agent: ICM - Beverly Hills, 310/550-4000

A SMOKEY MOUNTAIN CHRISTMAS   Sandollar Productions, 1986
MEMORIES OF ME   MGM/UA, 1988
COP AND A HALF   Universal, 1993

IRWIN WINKLER*
b. May 28, 1931 - New York, New York
Business: Irwin Winkler Films, Inc., 211 S. Beverly Drive - Suite 200,
   Beverly Hills, CA 90212, 310/858-5780
Agent: CAA - Beverly Hills, 310/288-4545

GUILTY BY SUSPICION   Warner Bros., 1991
NIGHT AND THE CITY   20th Century Fox, 1992
THE NET   Columbia, 1995

TERENCE H. WINKLESS
Agent: Peter Turner Agency - Santa Monica, 310/315-4772

THE NEST   Concorde, 1988
BLOODFIST   Concorde, 1989
CORPORATE AFFAIRS   Concorde, 1990
THE BERLIN CONSPIRACY   Concorde, 1991
RAGE AND HONOR   I.R.S. Releasing, 1992

MICHAEL WINNER*
b. October 30, 1935 - London, England
Address: 31 Melbury Road, London W14 8AB, England,
   tel.: 171/602-3725
Agent: ICM - London, tel.: 171/636-6565

CLIMB UP THE WALL   New Realm, 1960, British
SHOOT TO KILL   New Realm, 1960, British
OLD MAC   Carlyle, 1961, British
SOME LIKE IT COOL   Carlyle, 1961, British
MURDER ON THE CAMPUS *OUT OF THE SHADOW*
   New Realm, 1961, British
PLAY IT COOL   Allied Artists, 1962, British
THE COOL MIKADO   United Artists, 1962, British
WEST 11   Warner-Pathe, 1963, British
THE GIRL GETTERS *THE SYSTEM* American International,
   1964, British
YOU MUST BE JOKING!   Columbia, 1965, British
THE JOKERS   Universal, 1967, British
I'LL NEVER FORGET WHAT'S 'IS NAME   Regional, 1968, British
HANNIBAL BROOKS   United Artists, 1969, British
THE GAMES   20th Century-Fox, 1970, British
LAWMAN   United Artists, 1971
CHATO'S LAND   United Artists, 1972
THE NIGHTCOMERS   Avco Embassy, 1972, British

F
I
L
M

D
I
R
E
C
T
O
R
S

THE MECHANIC   United Artists, 1972
SCORPIO   United Artists, 1973
THE STONE KILLER   Columbia, 1973
DEATH WISH   Paramount, 1974
WON TON TON, THE DOG WHO SAVED HOLLYWOOD
   Paramount, 1976
THE SENTINEL   Universal, 1977
THE BIG SLEEP   United Artists, 1978, British
FIREPOWER   AFD, 1979, British
DEATH WISH II   Filmways, 1982
THE WICKED LADY   MGM/UA/Cannon, 1983, British
SCREAM FOR HELP   Lorimar Distribution International, 1984
DEATH WISH 3   Cannon, 1985
APPOINTMENT WITH DEATH   Cannon, 1988, U.S.-British
A CHORUS OF DISAPPROVAL   South Gate Entertainment,
   1989, British
BULLSEYE!   21st Century Distribution, 1990, U.S.-British
DIRTY WEEKEND   UIP, 1993, British

DAVID WINNING

b. 1961 - Calgary, Alberta, Canada
Business: Groundstar Entertainment Group, 918 16th Avenue NW -
   Suite 4001, Calgary, Alberta T2M 0K3, Canada, 403/284-2889

STORM   Groundstar Entertainment, 1985, Canadian
KILLER IMAGE   Image Organization, 1991, Canadian

TERRY WINSOR

PARTY PARTY   A&M Pictures, 1983, British
MORGAN STEWART'S COMING HOME   co-director with
   Paul Aaron, both directed under pseudonym of Alan Smithee,
   New Century/Vista, 1987

STAN WINSTON*

Business: 7032 Valjean Avenue, Van Nuys, CA 91406,
   818/782-0870
Agent: The Gersh Agency - Beverly Hills, 310/274-6611

PUMPKINHEAD   MGM/UA, 1988
A GNOME NAMED GNORM   Carolco, 1992

ALEX WINTER

Agent: ICM - Beverly Hills, 310/550-4000

FREAKED   co-director with Tom Stern, 20th Century Fox, 1993

DONOVAN WINTER

Business: Donwin Productions Ltd., 7 St. James House, Kensington
   Square, London W8 5HD, England, tel.: 171/937-4491

THE TRUNK   Columbia, 1960, British
WORLD WITHOUT SHAME   Donwin Productions, 1961, British
A PENNY FOR YOUR THOUGHTS   Donwin Productions,
   1964, British
PROMENADE   Donwin Productions, 1965, British
COME BACK, PETER   Donwin Productions, 1969, British
SUNDAY IN THE PARK   Donwin Productions, 1970, British
ESCORT GIRLS   Donwin Productions, 1973, British
THE DEADLY FEMALES   Donwin Productions, 1976, British
GIVE US TOMORROW   Donwin Productions, 1978, British

MICHAEL WINTERBOTTOM

Agent: CAA - Beverly Hills, 310/288-4545

FORGET ABOUT ME (TF)   British
UNDER THE SUN (TF)   British
CRACKER: THE MAD WOMAN IN THE ATTIC (TF)   British
FAMILY   BBC Films, 1994, British
BUTTERFLY KISS   British Screen/Merseyside Film, 1995, British

DAVID WINTERS*
(David Weizer)

b. April 5, 1939 - London, England
Business: West Side Studios, 10726 McCune Avenue, Los Angeles,
   CA 90034, 213/559-8805

WELCOME TO MY NIGHTMARE (FCD)   Warner Bros., 1976
RACQUET   Cal-Am Artists, 1979
JAYNE MANSFIELD - AN AMERICAN TRAGEDY   1981
THE LAST HORROR FILM   FANATIC   Twin Continental, 1982
MISSION KILL   Media Home Entertainment, 1985
THRASHIN'   Fries Entertainment, 1986
RAGE TO KILL   AIP, 1989
SPACE MUTINY   AIP, 1989
CODE NAME VENGEANCE   AIP, 1989

FRANZ PETER WIRTH

Contact: Filmforderungsantalt des Offentlichenrechts, Budapester
   Strasse 41, P.O. Box 301/87, 1000 Berlin 31, Germany,
   tel.: 49 30/261-6006

ARMS AND THE MAN   HELDEN   Casino, 1958, West German
INSEL DER ROSEN (TF)   Suddeutscher Rundfunk,
   1976, West German
BUDDENBROOKS (MS)   Taurus Film/Hessisher Rundfunk/
   TF-1/Film Polski, 1984, West German-French-Polish
A SQUARE OF SKY (MS)   1986, West German

FOREST WISE

I AM THE ELEPHANT AND YOU ARE THE MOUSE
   Freaky Pig Productions, 1993

HERBERT WISE*
(Herbert Weisz)

b. August 31, 1924 - Vienna, Austria
Home: 13 Despard Road, London N19 5NP, England,
   tel.: 171/272-5047
Agent: Peters Fraser & Dunlop - London, tel.: 171/344-1000

ALONE AGAINST ROME   Medallion, 1962, Italian
TO HAVE AND TO HOLD   Warner-Pathe, 1963, British
THE LOVERS!   British Lion, 1973, British
THE GATHERING STORM (TF)   BBC/Clarion Productions/Levien
   Productions, 1974, British
SKOKIE (TF) ☆   Titus Productions, 1981
DEATH OF AN EXPERT WITNESS (MS)   Anglia TV,
   1982, British
LYTTON'S DIARY (TF)   1984, British
POPE JOHN PAUL II (TF)   Alvin Cooperman-Judith DePaul
   Productions/Taft Entertainment Company, 1984
REUNION AT FAIRBOROUGH (CTF)   HBO Premiere Films/Alan
   Wagner Productions/Alan King Productions/Columbia TV, 1985
THE CHRISTMAS TREE (TF)   1986, British
WELCOME HOME, BOBBY (TF)   Titus Productions, 1986
STRANGE INTERLUDE (TF)   Fries Entertainment, 1987
INSPECTOR MORSE III: THE GHOST IN THE MACHINE (TF)
   Zenith Productions, 1988, British
THE WOMAN IN BLACK (TF)   1989, British
A NEW LEASE OF DEATH (TF)   1991, British
THE SPEAKER OF MANDARIN (TF)   1992, British
MORSE - THE FINAL CASE: TWILIGHT OF THE GODS (TF)
   1993, British
THE STRAWBERRY TREE (TF)   1994, British

KIRK WISE

Business: Walt Disney Animation, 500 S. Buena Vista Street,
   Burbank, CA 91521, 818/560-1000

BEAUTY AND THE BEAST (AF)   co-director with Gary Trousdale,
   Buena Vista, 1991
THE HUNCHBACK OF NOTRE DAME (AF)   co-director with
   Gary Trousdale, Buena Vista, 1996

ROBERT WISE*

b. September 10, 1914 - Winchester, Indiana
Business: Robert Wise Productions, 315 S. Beverly Drive -
   Suite 214, Beverly Hills, CA 90212, 310/284-7932
Agent: Phil Gersh, The Gersh Agency - Beverly Hills, 310/274-6611

THE CURSE OF THE CAT PEOPLE co-director with
   Gunther von Fritsch, RKO Radio, 1944
MADEMOISELLE FIFI RKO Radio, 1944
THE BODY SNATCHER RKO Radio, 1945
A GAME OF DEATH RKO Radio, 1945
CRIMINAL COURT RKO Radio, 1946
BORN TO KILL RKO Radio, 1947
MYSTERY IN MEXICO RKO Radio, 1948
BLOOD ON THE MOON RKO Radio, 1948
THE SET-UP RKO Radio, 1949
TWO FLAGS WEST 20th Century-Fox, 1950
THREE SECRETS Warner Bros., 1950
THE HOUSE ON TELEGRAPH HILL 20th Century-Fox, 1951
THE DAY THE EARTH STOOD STILL 20th Century-Fox, 1951
THE CAPTIVE CITY United Artists, 1952
SOMETHING FOR THE BIRDS MGM, 1952
THE DESERT RATS 20th Century-Fox, 1953
DESTINATION GOBI 20th Century-Fox, 1953
SO BIG Warner Bros., 1953
EXECUTIVE SUITE MGM, 1954
HELEN OF TROY Warner Bros., 1955, Italian-French
TRIBUTE TO A BAD MAN MGM, 1956
SOMEBODY UP THERE LIKES ME MGM, 1957
THIS COULD BE THE NIGHT MGM, 1957
UNTIL THEY SAIL MGM, 1957
RUN SILENT, RUN DEEP United Artists, 1958
I WANT TO LIVE! ★ United Artists, 1958
ODDS AGAINST TOMORROW United Artists, 1959
WEST SIDE STORY ★★ co-director with Jerome Robbins,
   United Artists, 1961
TWO FOR THE SEESAW United Artists, 1962
THE HAUNTING MGM, 1963, British-U.S.
THE SOUND OF MUSIC ★★ 20th Century-Fox, 1965
THE SAND PEBBLES 20th Century-Fox, 1966
STAR! *THOSE WERE THE HAPPY TIMES*
   20th Century-Fox, 1968
THE ANDROMEDA STRAIN Universal, 1971
TWO PEOPLE Universal, 1973
THE HINDENBURG Universal, 1975
AUDREY ROSE United Artists, 1977
STAR TREK - THE MOTION PICTURE Paramount, 1979
ROOFTOPS New Century/Vista, 1989

CAROL WISEMAN

Address: 53 Cleveland Square, London W2 6DB, England,
   tel.: 171/229-3253
Agent: ICM - London, tel.: 171/636-6565

BIG DEAL (MS) BBC, 1985, British
A LITTLE PRINCESS (MS) London Weekend TV, 1987, British
CITY TAILS (TF) Thames TV, 1988, British
SOMEWHERE TO RUN (TF) Thames TV, 1989, British
MAY WINE Canal Plus/The Movie Group/Chrysalide Films,
   1990, French-U.S.
THE FINDING (TF) Thames TV, 1990, British
DOES THIS MEAN WE'RE MARRIED The Movie Group,
   1991, French
LOVE HURTS (MS) co-director with Guy Slater & Roger Bamford,
   Alomo Productions/BBC, 1992, British
FACE THE MUSIC The Movie Group, 1992, French
GOGGLE-EYES (TF) BBC, 1993, British

FREDERICK WISEMAN

b. January 1, 1930 - Boston, Massachusetts
Home/Business: Zipporah Films, Inc., 1 Richdale Avenue - Suite 4,
   Cambridge, MA 02140, 617/576-3603

TITICUT FOLLIES (FD) Zipporah Films, 1967
HIGH SCHOOL (FD) Zipporah Films, 1968
LAW AND ORDER (FD) Zipporah Films, 1969
HOSPITAL (FD) ☆☆ Zipporah Films, 1970
BASIC TRAINING (FD) Zipporah Films, 1971

ESSENE (FD) Zipporah Films, 1972
JUVENILE COURT (FD) Zipporah Films, 1973
PRIMATE (FD) Zipporah Films, 1974
WELFARE (FD) Zipporah Films, 1975
MEAT (FD) Zipporah Films, 1976
CANAL ZONE (FD) Zipporah Films, 1977
SINAI FIELD MISSION (FD) Zipporah Films, 1978
MANOEUVRE (FD) Zipporah Films, 1979
MODEL (FD) Zipporah Films, 1980
SERAPHITA'S DIARY Zipporah Films, 1982
THE STORE (FD) Zipporah Films, 1983
RACETRACK (FD) Zipporah Films, 1985
DEAF (FD) Zipporah Films, 1986
BLIND (FD) Zipporah Films, 1986
MULTI-HANDICAPPED (FD) Zipporah Films, 1986
ADJUSTMENT AND WORK (FD) Zipporah Films, 1986
MISSLE (FD) Zipporah Films, 1988
NEAR DEATH (FD) Zipporah Films, 1989
CENTRAL PARK (TD) Zipporah Films, 1990
ASPEN (TD) Zipporah Films, 1991
ZOO (FD) Zipporah Films/Channel 4, 1993
HIGH SCHOOL II (FD) Zipporah Films, 1994
BALLET (FD) Zipporah Films, 1995

STEPHEN WITHROW

FRIENDS, LOVERS AND LUNATICS *CRAZY HORSE/SHE DRIVES
   ME CRAZY* Fries Entertainment, 1989, Canadian

WILLIAM WITNEY*

b. May 15, 1910 - Lawton, Oklahoma
Contact: Directors Guild of America - Los Angeles, 213/851-3671

S.O.S. COAST GUARD (S) Republic, 1937
ZORRO RIDES AGAIN (S) co-director with John English,
   Republic, 1937
THE TRIGGER TRIO Republic, 1937
DICK TRACY RETURNS (S) co-director with John English,
   Republic, 1938
HAWK OF THE WILDERNESS (S) co-director with John English,
   Republic, 1938
THE LONE RANGER (S) co-director with John English,
   Republic, 1938
DICK TRACY'S G-MEN (S) co-director with John English,
   Republic, 1939
ZORRO'S FIGHTING LEGION (S) co-director with John English,
   Republic, 1939
ADVENTURES OF RED RYDER (S) co-director with John English,
   Republic, 1940
DRUMS OF FU MANCHU (S) co-director with John English,
   Republic, 1940
KING OF THE ROYAL MOUNTED (S) co-director with John English,
   Republic, 1940
MYSTERIOUS DR. SATAN (S) co-director with John English,
   Republic, 1940
HI-YO SILVER co-director with John English, Republic, 1940
HEROES OF THE SADDLE Republic, 1940
DICK TRACY VS. CRIME INC. (S) co-director with John English,
   Republic, 1941
ADVENTURES OF CAPTAIN MARVEL (S) co-director with
   John English, Republic, 1941
JUNGLE GIRL (S) co-director with John English, Republic, 1941
KING OF THE TEXAS RANGERS (S) co-director with John English,
   Republic, 1941
KING OF THE MOUNTIES (S) Republic, 1942
SPY SMASHER (S) Republic, 1942
OUTLAWS OF PINE RIDGE Republic, 1942
THE YUKON PATROL co-director with John English,
   Republic, 1942
G-MEN VS. THE BLACK DRAGON (S) Republic, 1943
HELLDORADO Republic, 1946
APACHE ROSE Republic, 1947
BELLS OF SAN ANGELO Republic, 1947
SPRINGTIME IN THE SIERRAS Republic, 1947
ON THE SPANISH TRAIL Republic, 1947
THE GAY RANCHERO Republic, 1948
UNDER CALIFORNIA SKIES Republic, 1948
EYES OF TEXAS Republic, 1948
THE FAR FRONTIER Republic, 1949

THE LAST MUSKETEER   Republic, 1952
THE OUTCAST   Republic, 1954
HEADLINE HUNTERS   Republic, 1955
CITY OF SHADOWS   Republic, 1955
A STRANGE ADVENTURE   Republic, 1956
PANAMA SAL   Republic, 1957
YOUNG AND WILD   Republic, 1958
JUVENILE JUNGLE   Republic, 1958
THE COOL AND THE CRAZY   American International, 1958
THE BONNIE PARKER STORY   American International, 1958
PARATROOP COMMAND   American International, 1959
SECRET OF THE PURPLE REEF   20th Century-Fox, 1960
MASTER OF THE WORLD   American International, 1961
THE LONG ROPE   20th Century-Fox, 1961
APACHE RIFLES   20th Century-Fox, 1964
THE GIRLS ON THE BEACH   Paramount, 1965
ARIZONA RAIDERS   Columbia, 1965
FORTY GUNS TO APACHE PASS   Columbia, 1967
I ESCAPED FROM DEVIL'S ISLAND   United Artists, 1973
DARKTOWN STRUTTERS   *GET DOWN AND BOOGIE*
    New World, 1975

WILLIAM D. (BILL) WITTLIFF*
Business: 510 Baylor, Austin, TX 78703, 512/476-6821
Agent: CAA - Beverly Hills, 310/288-4545

RED HEADED STRANGER   Alive Films, 1987

PETER WITTMAN
PLAY DEAD   Troma, 1981
ELLIE   Shapiro Entertainment, 1984

IRA WOHL
BEST BOY (FD)   International Film Exchange, 1980

ANNETT WOLF
Address: L'Ermitage, 9291 Burton Way, Beverly Hills, CA 90210,
    213/278-3344
Agent: La Rocca Talent Group - Burbank, 818/841-8000
Attorney: Robert Myman, Shagin & Myman, 11777 San Vicente
    Blvd. - Suite 600, Los Angeles, CA 90049, 213/820-7717

CHARLES CHAPLIN: "THE MAN, THE DIRECTOR AND
    THE CLOWN" (TD)   1965, Danish
A TWIST OF LEMON (TD)   Danish TV, 1976, Danish
ELVIS IN CONCERT (TCD)   Smith-Hemion Productions, 1977
THE WORLD OF INGMAR BERGMAN (TD)   1983

ART WOLFF*
Business: Petunia Productions, Inc., 3138 Oakshire Drive,
    Los Angeles, CA 90068, 213/851-1547
Agent: William Morris Agency - Beverly Hills, 310/859-4000

BATTLING FOR BABY (TF)   von Zerneck-Sertner Films, 1992

KIRK WOLFINGER
MOON SHOT (CTD)   Varied Directions International/TBS
    Productions, 1994

ANDREW R. (ANDY) WOLK*
Home: 251 West 76th Street - Apt. 3A, New York, NY 10023,
    212/873-2216
Agent: CAA - Beverly Hills, 310/288-4545

CRIMINAL JUSTICE (CTF)   Elysian Films/HBO Showcase, 1990
TRACES OF RED   The Samuel Goldwyn Company, 1992

PETER WOLLEN
Contact: British Film Commission, 70 Baker Street, London
    W1M 1DJ, England, tel.: 171/224-5000

RIDDLES OF THE SPHINX   1976, British
AMY!   1980, British
CRYSTAL GAZING   1982, British
FRIENDSHIP'S DEATH   1987, British

DAN WOLMAN
b. October 28, 1941 - Jerusalem, Israel
Contact: Israel Film Centre, Ministry of Industry & Trade,
    30 Agron Street, P.O. Box 299, 94190 Jerusalem, Israel,
    tel.: 297/210433 or 210297

THE MORNING BEFORE SLEEP   Toda Films, 1969, Israeli
THE DREAMER   Cannon, 1979, Israeli
FLOCH   Aldan Films/Floch Ltd., 1972, Israeli
MY MICHAEL   Alfred Plaine, 1976, Israeli
HIDE AND SEEK   1980, Israeli
NANA   MGM/UA/Cannon, 1983, Italian-U.S.
BABY LOVE (LEMON POPSICLE V)   Noah Films, 1983, Israeli
SOLDIER OF THE NIGHT   Cannon, 1983, Israeli
ANCHORS AWEIGH (LEMON POPSICLE VI)   Noah Films,
    1985, Israeli
CONTRACT FOR LOVE   Dan Wolman Productions, 1986, Israeli
THE GREAT DAYS, SMALL STORIES (FD)   1989, Israeli
THE DISTANCE   Lonely Spy Ltd., 1994, Israeli

WALLACE WOLODARSKY
Agent: UTA - Beverly Hills, 310/273-6700

COLDBLOODED   Polygram Filmed Entertainment/Propaganda
    Films/Motion Picture Corporation of America, 1995

RON WOLOTZKY*
Home: 839 N. Stanley Avenue, Los Angeles, CA 90046,
    213/655-2438
Agent: UTA - Beverly Hills, 310/273-6700

DREAM ON: THE TAKING OF PABLUM 1-2-3 (CTF)
    St. Clare Entertainment/MTE, 1994

KAR-WAI WONG
(See Wong KAR-WAI)

KIRK WONG
(Wong Che-Keung)
b. 1949 - Hong Kong
Business: Sky Point Film Investment Co. Ltd., Highgrade Building,
    #402, 117 Chatham Road, Kowloon, Hong Kong,
    tel.: 852/2377-2592, fax: 852/2377-1645
Contact: Hong Kong Film Liaison, 10940 Wilshire Blvd. - Suite 1220,
    Los Angeles, CA 90024, 310/208-2678

THE CLUB   1981, Hong Kong
HEALTH WARNING   1983, Hong Kong
LIFELINE EXPRESS   1984, Hong Kong
TRUE COLOURS   1986, Hong Kong
GUNMEN   1989, Hong Kong
TAKING MANHATTAN   1991, Hong Kong
CRIME STORY   1993, Hong Kong
ORGANIZED CRIME & TRIAD BUREAU   Sky Point Film Investment,
    1994, Hong Kong
ROCK N' ROLL COP   Sky Point Film Investment, 1994, Hong Kong
HOTLINE - THE ICAC FILES   Sky Point Film Investment,
    1995, Hong Kong

LENNY WONG*
Contact: Directors Guild of America - Los Angeles, 213/851-3671

COMEDY'S DIRTIEST DOZEN (FD)   Fourth & Broadway Films/
    Island Pictures, 1989

JOHN WOO*
(Ng Yu-Sum/Woo Yu-sen)
b. 1946 - Guangzhou (Canton), China
Business: Metropolis Entertainment, P.O. Box 900, Beverly Hills,
    CA 90213, 310/277-2211
Agent: William Morris Agency - Beverly Hills, 310/859-4000

YOUNG DRAGON   Golden Harvest, 1973, Hong Kong
THE DRAGON TAMERS   Golden Harvest, 1974, Hong Kong
PRINCESS CHEUNG PING   Golden Harvest, 1975, Hong Kong
HAND OF DEATH   *COUNTDOWN IN KUNG FU*   Golden Harvest,
    1975, Hong Kong

MONEY CRAZY   Golden Harvest, 1977, Hong Kong
FOLLOW THE STAR   Golden Harvest, 1977, Hong Kong
LAST HURRAH FOR CHIVALRY   Golden Harvest,
   1978, Hong Kong
FROM RAGS TO RICHES   Golden Harvest, 1979, Hong Kong
TO HELL WITH THE DEVIL   Golden Harvest, 1981, Hong Kong
LAUGHING TIMES   Cinema City, 1981, Hong Kong
PLAIN JANE TO THE RESCUE   Golden Harvest, 1982, Hong Kong
SUNSET WARRIOR   *HEROES SHED NO TEARS*
   Golden Harvest, 1983, Hong Kong, released in 1986
THE TIME YOU NEED A FRIEND   Cinema City, 1984, Hong Kong
RUN, TIGER, RUN   Cinema City, 1985, Hong Kong
A BETTER TOMORROW   Film Workshop/Cinema City,
   1986, Hong Kong
A BETTER TOMORROW PART 2   Film Workshop/Cinema City,
   1987, Hong Kong
THE KILLER   Film Workshop/Golden Princess, 1989, Hong Kong
JUST HEROES   co-director, Magnum, 1990, Hong Kong
BULLET IN THE HEAD   John Woo Productions/Golden Princess,
   1990, Hong Kong
ONCE A THIEF   Milestone/Golden Princess, 1991, Hong Kong
HARD-BOILED   Milestone/Golden Princess, 1992, Hong Kong
HARD TARGET   Universal, 1993
BROKEN ARROW   20th Century Fox, 1995

KANG WOO-SUK
(See Woo-Suk KANG)

LESLIE WOODHEAD
Agent: The Casarotto Company - London, tel.: 171/287-4450

INVASION (TF)   Granada TV, British
THE TRAGEDY OF FLIGHT 103: THE INSIDE STORY (CTF)
   HBO Showcase/Granada TV, 1990, U.S.-British
THE LAST SOVIET CITIZEN (TF)   BBC, British
COMRADE ROCK STAR (TF)   BBC, British

DAN WOODRUFF
Business: Dan Woodruff Productions, P.O. Box 487, Beverly Hills,
   CA 90213, 310/878-2291

CINEMA BIZARRE   Dan Woodruff Productions, 1992

MEL WOODS
Contact: British Film Commission, 70 Baker Street, London
   W1M 1DJ, England, tel.: 171/224-5000

NTIMATE WITH A STRANGER   Independent International Pictures,
   1994, British-U.S.

JOANNE WOODWARD*
b. February 27, 1930 - Thomasville, Georgia
Agent: ICM - New York City, 212/556-5600

COME ALONG WITH ME (TF)   Rubicon Productions, 1982

ABBE WOOL
Agent: Stephanie Mann & Associates - Los Angeles, 213/653-7130

ROADSIDE PROPHETS   Fine Line Features/New Line Cinema, 1991

JEFF WOOLNOUGH
Contact: Directors Guild of Canada, 225 Richmond Street, Toronto,
   Ontario M5V 1W2, Canada, 416/351-8200

FIRST DEGREE   Norstar Ent./OTC Ent. Group/Westcom Ent.
   Group, 1995, Canadian

CHUCK WORKMAN*
(Carl Workman)
Address: 195 S. Beverly Drive, Beverly Hills, CA 90212,
   310/271-0964
Agent: William Morris Agency - Beverly Hills, 310/859-4000

THE MONEY   Coliseum, 1977
STOOGEMANIA   Atlantic Releasing Corporation, 1985

SUPERSTAR: THE LIFE AND TIMES OF ANDY WARHOL (FD)
   Aries Releasing, 1990
THE FIRST 100 YEARS (TD)   HBO, 1995
THE SOURCE (FD)   Hiro Yamagata Productions, 1995

AARON WORTH
9 1/2 NINJAS (HVF)   Republic Pictures Home Video, 1991

DAVID WORTH
Agent: Gray/Goodman - Beverly Hills, 310/276-7070

WARRIOR OF THE LOST WORLD   Visto International, 1985, Italian
KICKBOXER   co-director with Mark DiSalle, Cannon, 1989
LADY DRAGON   Rapi Films, 1992, Indonesian
WHITE SUN   G.G. Israel Studios, 1993, Israeli

SOENKE WORTMANN
Contact: Federal Union of Film and Television Directors in Germany,
   Adelheidstrasse 7, 8000 Munich 4, Germany, tel.: 089/271-6380

ALLEIN UNTER FRAUEN   1991, West German
KLEINE HAIE   1992, West German
MR. BLUESMAN   1993, German
DER BEWEGTE MANN   Neue Constantin, 1994, German

CASPER WREDE
Contact: British Film Commission, 70 Baker Street, London
   W1M 1DJ, England, tel.: 171/224-5000

PRIVATE POTTER   MGM, 1964, British
ONE DAY IN THE LIFE OF IVAN DENISOVICH   Cinerama Releasing
   Corporation, 1971, British-Norwegian
THE TERRORISTS   *RANSOM*   20th Century-Fox, 1975, British

GEOFFREY WRIGHT
Contact: Australian Film Commission, 150 William Street,
   Woolloomooloo NSW 2011, Australia, tel.: 2/321-6444

ROMPER STOMPER   Academy Entertainment, 1992, Australian
METAL SKIN   Daniel Scharf Productions, 1994, Australian

PATRICK WRIGHT
b. November 28, 1939 - San Francisco, California
Business: The People People, Inc., 8776 Sunset Blvd., Los Angeles,
   CA 90069, 310/652-9320 or 213/256-5552

HOLLYWOOD HIGH   Lone Star, 1976

RICHARD "DUB" WRIGHT*
Home: 17728 Revello Drive, Pacific Palisades, CA 90272,
   310/454-3578

MONASTERY   Barrandov Studio/Boucek-Wright-Zboril Productions,
   1995, Czech-U.S.

THOMAS J. WRIGHT*
Agent: Premiere Artists Agency - Los Angeles, 310/271-1414

TORCHLIGHT   International Film Marketing, 1984, U.S.-Mexican
NO HOLDS BARRED   New Line Cinema, 1989
THE OPERATION (TF)   Moress, Nanas, Golden Entertainment/
   Viacom, 1990
OVER THE EDGE (CTF)   USA Network, 1990
SNOW KILL (CTF)   Wilshire Court Productions, 1990
THE FATAL IMAGE (TF)   Ellipse Programme/Hearst Entertainment
   Productions, 1990, U.S.-British
HELL HATH NO FURY (TF)   Bar-Gene Productions/The
   Finnegan-Pinchuk Company, 1991
DEADLY GAME (CTF)   Osiris Productions/Wilshire Court
   Productions, 1991
CHROME SOLDIERS (CTF)   Wilshire Court Productions, 1992

THOMAS LEE WRIGHT
EIGHT-TRAY GANGSTER: THE MAKING OF A CRIP (FD)
   ETG-Saramatt, 1993

DONALD WRYE*
Agent: William Morris Agency - Beverly Hills, 310/859-4000

THE MAN WHO COULD TALK TO KIDS (TF)
   Tomorrow Entertainment, 1973
BORN INNOCENT (TF)   Tomorrow Entertainment, 1974
DEATH BE NOT PROUD (TF)   Good Housekeeping Productions/
   Westfall Productions, 1975
THE ENTERTAINER (TF)   RSO Films, 1976
IT HAPPENED ONE CHRISTMAS (TF)   Universal TV, 1977
ICE CASTLES   Columbia, 1979
THE HOUSE OF GOD   *H.O.G.*   United Artists, 1981
FIRE ON THE MOUNTAIN (TF)   Bonnard Productions, 1982
DIVORCE WARS: A LOVE STORY (TF)   Wrye-Konigsberg Films/
   Warner Bros. TV, 1982
THE FACE OF RAGE (TF)   Hal Sitowitz Productions/Viacom, 1983
HEART OF STEEL (TF)   Beowulf Productions, 1983
AMERIKA (MS)   ABC Circle Films, 1987
83 HOURS 'TIL DAWN (TF)   Consolidated Productions, 1990
LUCKY DAY (TF)   Hearst Entertainment Productions/Polongo
   Productions, 1991
STRANGER IN THE FAMILY (TF)   Polongo Pictures/Hearst
   Entertainment Productions, 1991
BROKEN PROMISES: TAKING EMILY BACK (TF)   Larry Thompson
   Entertainment/RHI Entertainment, 1993
ULTIMATE BETRAYAL (TF)   Polonga Productions/Hearst
   Entertainment, 1994
SEPARATED BY MURDER (TF)   Larry Thompson Entertainment/
   CBS Entertainment, 1994
A FAMILY DIVIDED (TF)   Citadel Entertainment, 1995

NIEN-JEN WU
(See Wu NIEN-JEN)

TIANMING WU
(See Wu TIANMING)

ROBERT WUHL
Agent: The Gersh Agency - Beverly Hills, 310/274-6611
Contact: Screen Actors Guild - Los Angeles, 213/954-1600

OPEN SEASON   Frozen Rope Productions, 1995

RUDOLPH (RUDY) WURLITZER
Business: Together Brothers Productions, 9405 W. Washington
   Blvd., Culver City, CA 90230, 310/841-2301

CANDY MOUNTAIN   co-director with Robert Frank,
   Metropolis Film, 1987, Swiss-French-Canadian

DAVID WYLES
Contact: Directors Guild of Canada, 225 Richmond Street, Toronto,
   Ontario M5V 1W2, Canada, 416/351-8200

MAN WITH A GUN   October Films, 1996, Canadian

TRACY KEENAN WYNN*
b. February 28, 1945 - Los Angeles, California
Contact: Directors Guild of America - Los Angeles, 213/851-3671
Agent: Renaissance-H.N. Swanson - Los Angeles, 310/246-6000

HIT LADY (TF)   Spelling-Goldberg Productions, 1974

JIM WYNORSKI
b. August 14, 1950 - Long Island, New York

THE LOST EMPIRE   JGM Enterprises, 1984
CHOPPING MALL   Concorde/Cinema Group, 1986
DEATHSTALKER II   Concorde, 1986, U.S.-Argentine
BIG BAD MAMA II   Concorde, 1987
NOT OF THIS EARTH   Concorde, 1988
THE RETURN OF SWAMP THING   Lightyear Entertainment, 1989
TRANSYLVANIA TWIST   Concorde, 1989
THE HAUNTING OF MORELLA   Concorde, 1990
HORRORSCOPE   Seven Arts/New Line Cinema, 1991

NIGHTIE NIGHTMARE   Concorde, 1991
976-EVIL II: THE ASTRAL FACTOR   CineTel Films, 1991
MUNCHIES II   Concorde, 1992
HARD TO DIE   Concorde, 1993
TOUGH COOKIES   Concorde, 1993
VICTIM OF DESIRE   Victim's Desire Inc., 1994
MUNCHIE STRIKES BACK   Concorde, 1994
DINOSAUR ISLAND   Concorde, 1994
IMPLICATED   MCEG Sterling Entertainment, 1994
TEMPTRESS OF THE DARK   Sunset Films International, 1994
BODY CHEMISTRY III: POINT OF SEDUCTION   Sunset Films
   International, 1994
BODY CHEMISTRY IV: FULL EXPOSURE   Sunset Films
   International, 1994
HARD BOUNTY   Sunset Films International, 1994

X

JIN XIE
(See Xie JIN)

ZHOU XIAOWEN
Contact: China Film Import & Export Office, 2500 Wilshire Blvd. -
   Suite 1028, Los Angeles, CA 90057, 213/380-7520

IN THEIR PRIME   Xi'an Film Studio, 1987, Chinese
THE BLACK MOUNTAIN   China Film Import & Export,
   1990, Chinese
THE LIE DETECTOR   China Film Import & Export, 1993, Chinese
ERMO   Arrow Releasing, 1994, Chinese

Y

GREG YAITANES
HARD JUSTICE   Nu Image, 1994

BOAZ YAKIN
Agent: UTA - Beverly Hills, 310/273-6700

FRESH   Miramax Films, 1994, U.S.-French

YOJI YAMADA
b. 1931 - Japan
Business: Shochiku Co., Ltd., 13-5, Tsukiji 1-Chome, Chuo-ku,
   Tokyo 104, Japan, tel.: 1/35542-5551

THE STRANGERS UPSTAIRS   Shochiku, 1961, Japanese
THE SUNSHINE GIRL   Shochiku, 1963, Japanese
HONEST FOOL   Shochiku, 1964, Japanese
HONEST FOOL - SEQUEL   Shochiku, 1964, Japanese
THE DONKEY COMES ON A TANK   Shochiku,
   1964, Japanese
THE TRAP   Shochiku, 1965, Japanese
GAMBLER'S LUCK   Shochiku, 1966, Japanese
THE LOVABLE TRAMP   Shochiku, 1966, Japanese
LET'S HAVE A DREAM   Shochiku, 1967, Japanese
SONG OF LOVE   Shochiku, 1967, Japanese
THE GREATEST CHALLENGE OF ALL   Shochiku, 1967, Japanese

THE MILLION DOLLAR PURSUIT Shochiku, 1968, Japanese
THE SHY DECEIVER Shochiku, 1968, Japanese
VAGABOND SCHEMER Shochiku, 1969, Japanese
TORA-SAN, OUR LOVABLE TRAMP Shochiku, 1969, Japanese
TORA-SAN'S CHERISHED MOTHER Shochiku, 1969, Japanese
TORA-SAN'S RUNAWAY Shochiku, 1970, Japanese
WHERE SPRING COMES LATE Shochiku, 1970, Japanese
TORA-SAN'S SHATTERED ROMANCE Shochiku,
   1971, Japanese
TORA-SAN: THE GOOD SAMARITAN Shochiku,
   1971, Japanese
TORA-SAN'S LOVE CALL Shochiku, 1971, Japanese
TORA-SAN'S DEAR OLD HOME Shochiku, 1972, Japanese
HOME FROM THE SEA Shochiku, 1972, Japanese
TORA-SAN'S DREAM COME TRUE Shochiku, 1972, Japanese
TORA-SAN'S FORGET-ME-NOT Shochiku, 1973, Japanese
TORA-SAN LOVES AN ARTIST Shochiku, 1973, Japanese
TORA-SAN'S LOVESICK Shochiku, 1974, Japanese
TORA-SAN'S LULLABY Shochiku, 1974, Japanese
TORA-SAN MEETS THE SONGSTRESS AGAIN Shochiku,
   1975, Japanese
THE VILLAGE Shochiku, 1975, Japanese
TORA-SAN, THE INTELLECTUAL Shochiku, 1975, Japanese
TORA-SAN'S SUNRISE, SUNSET Shochiku, 1976, Japanese
TORA-SAN'S HEART OF GOLD Shochiku, 1976, Japanese
TORA-SAN MEETS HIS LORDSHIP Shochiku, 1977, Japanese
THE YELLOW HANDKERCHIEF Shochiku, 1977, Japanese
TORA-SAN PLAYS CUPID Shochiku, 1977, Japanese
STAGE-STRUCK TORA-SAN Shochiku, 1978, Japanese
TALK-OF-THE-TOWN TORA-SAN Shochiku, 1978, Japanese
TORA-SAN, THE MATCHMAKER Shochiku, 1979, Japanese
TORA-SAN'S DREAM OF SPRING Shochku, 1979, Japanese
A DISTANT CRY FROM SPRING Shochiku, 1980, Japanese
TORA-SAN'S TROPICAL FEVER Shochiku, 1980, Japanese
FOSTER DADDY TORA-SAN Shochiku, 1981, Japanese
TORA-SAN'S MANY-SPLINTERED LOVE Shochiku,
   1981, Japanese
TORA-SAN'S PROMISE Shochiku, 1981, Japanese
HEARTS AND FLOWERS FOR TORA-SAN Shochiku,
   1982, Japanese
TORA-SAN, THE EXPERT Shochiku, 1982, Japanese
TORA-SAN'S SONG OF LOVE Shochiku, 1983, Japanese
TORA-SAN GOES RELIGIOUS? Shochiku, 1983, Japanese
MARRIAGE COUNSELOR TORA-SAN Shochiku,
   1984, Japanese
TORA-SAN'S FORBIDDEN LOVE Shochiku, 1984, Japanese
TORA-SAN, THE GO-BETWEEN Shochiku, 1985, Japanese
TORA-SAN'S ISLAND ENCOUNTER Shochiku, 1985, Japanese
FINAL TAKE Shochiku, 1986, Japanese
TORA-SAN'S BLUEBIRD FANTASY Shochiku, 1986, Japanese
TORA-SAN GOES NORTH Shochiku, 1987, Japanese
TORA-SAN PLAYS DADDY Shochiku, 1987, Japanese
HOPE AND PAIN Shochiku, 1988, Japanese
TORA-SAN'S SALAD DATE MEMORIAL Shochiku,
   1989, Japanese
TORA-SAN GOES TO VIENNA Kino International/Shochiku,
   1989, Japanese
TORA-SAN, MY UNCLE Shochiku, 1989, Japanese
TORA-SAN TAKES A VACATION Shochiku, 1990, Japanese
TORA-SAN CONFESSES Shochiku, 1991, Japanese
MY SONS Shochiku, 1992, Japanese
TORA-SAN MAKES EXCUSES Shochiku, 1992, Japanese
A CLASS TO REMEMBER GAKKO/SCHOOL Shochiku,/Nippon
   TV/Sumitomo Corporation 1993, Japanese
TORA-SAN'S MARRIAGE PROPOSAL Shochiku,
   1993, Japanese
DEAR MR. TORAJIRO-SAMA Shochiku, 1994, Japanese

TAKAYA YAMAZAKI
b. Japan

I'M NOT COOKING TONIGHT Cinema Island, 1994

MITSUO YANAGIMACHI
b. 1945 - Ibaraki Prefecture, Japan
Contact: Nihon Eiga Kantoku Kyokai (Japan Film Directors
   Association), La Fontenu Building -4th Floor, 23-2 Maruyama-cho,
   Shibuya-ku, Tokyo, Japan, tel.: 3/3461-4411

GOD SPEED YOU! BLACK EMPEROR (FD) Toei,
   1976, Japanese
A 19-YEAR-OLD'S PLAN Production Gunjo, 1979, Japanese
FAREWELL TO THE LAND Auteur Duncan, 1982, Japanese
HIMATSURI (FIRE FESTIVAL) Kino International,
   1985, Japanese
SHADOW OF CHINA New Line Cinema, 1991, Japanese-U.S.
ABOUT LOVE, TOKYO About-Love-Tokyo Production Committee,
   1992, Japanese

EDWARD YANG
(Yang Dechang)
b. 1947 - Shanghai, China
Business: Yang and His Gang, 12 Lane 350, Guang Fu South Road,
   Taipei, Taiwan, Republic of China, tel.: 773-7557
Contact: Department of Motion Picture Affairs, 2 Tientsin Street,
   Taipei, Taiwan, Republic of China, tel.: 2/351-6591

IN OUR TIME co-director, 1982, Taiwanese
THAT DAY ON THE BEACH Central Motion Picture Corporation,
   1983, Taiwanese
TAIPEI STORY Evergreen Film Production Company,
   1985, Taiwanese
THE TERRORIZERS Central Motion Picture Corporation,
   1986, Taiwanese
A BRIGHTER SUMMER DAY Jane Balfour Films/Yang and
   His Gang Filmmakers, 1991, Taiwanese
A CONFUCIAN CONFUSION Atom Films & Theatre,
   1994, Taiwanese

LOUIS YANSEN
b. Poland
Agent: Paul Kohner, Inc. - Los Angeles, 310/550-1060

MISPLACED Subway Films, 1991

BOB YARI
MIND GAMES MGM/UA, 1989

PETER YATES*
b. July 24, 1929 - Ewshott, Surrey, England
Agent: UTA - Beverly Hills, 310/273-6700

SUMMER HOLIDAY American International, 1963, British
ONE WAY PENDULUM Lopert, 1964, British
ROBBERY Avco Embassy, 1967, British
BULLITT Warner Bros., 1968
JOHN AND MARY 20th Century-Fox, 1969
MURPHY'S WAR Paramount, 1971, British
THE HOT ROCK 20th Century-Fox, 1972
THE FRIENDS OF EDDIE COYLE Paramount, 1973
FOR PETE'S SAKE Columbia, 1974
MOTHER, JUGS AND SPEED 20th Century-Fox, 1976
THE DEEP Columbia, 1977
BREAKING AWAY ★ 20th Century-Fox, 1979
EYEWITNESS 20th Century-Fox, 1981
KRULL Columbia, 1983, U.S.-British
THE DRESSER ★ Columbia, 1983, British
ELENI Warner Bros., 1985
SUSPECT TriStar, 1987
THE HOUSE ON CARROLL STREET Orion, 1988
AN INNOCENT MAN Buena Vista, 1989
YEAR OF THE COMET Columbia, 1992
ROOMMATES Buena Vista, 1995
THE RUN OF THE COUNTRY Columbia, 1995, U.S.-British-Irish

F
I
L
M

D
I
R
E
C
T
O
R
S

REBECCA YATES
b. 1950 - London, England
Business: Cineflix Inc., 238 Davenport Road - Suite 190, Toronto, Ontario M5R 1J6, Canada, 416/531-2612

HOME FREE (TF)   co-director with Glen Salzman, 1976, Canadian
ANOTHER KIND OF MUSIC (TF)   co-director with Glen Salzman, 1977, Canadian
NIKKOLINA (TF)   co-director with Glen Salzman, 1978, Canadian
CORLETTO & SON (TF)   co-director with Glen Salzman, 1980, Canadian
REACHING OUT (TF)   co-director with Glen Salzman, 1980, Canadian
INTRODUCING...JANET (TF)   co-director with Glen Salzman, 1981, Canadian
JEN'S PLACE (TF)   co-director with Glen Salzman, 1982, Canadian
MILK AND HONEY   co-director with Glen Salzman, Castle Hill Productions, 1987, Canadian

LINDA YELLEN*
b. Queens, New York
Agent: William Morris Agency - Beverly Hills, 310/859-4400
Business Manager: Krost/Chapin Management, 9150 Wilshire Blvd. - Suite 205, Beverly Hills, CA 90212

COME OUT, COME OUT   Beacon Productions, 1969
LOOKING UP   Levitt-Pickman, 1977
JACOBO TIMERMAN: PRISONER WITHOUT A NAME, CELL WITHOUT A NUMBER (TF)   Chrysalis-Yellen Productions, 1983
CHANTILLY LACE (CTF)   Showtime Entertainment Group, 1993
PARALLEL LIVES   Showtime Entertainment, 1994

YEVGENY YEVTUSHENKO
Contact: Confederation of Film-Makers Unions, Vasilyevskaya Street 13, 123 825 Moscow, Russia, tel.: 095/250-4114

THE KINDERGARTEN   IFEX Film, 1984, Soviet
STALIN'S FUNERAL   Mosfilm, 1991, Soviet

LI YIN
(See Yin LI)

HO YIM
(See Yim HO)

ZHANG YIMOU
b. 1950 - Xi'an, Shaanxi Province, China
Contact: China Film Import & Export Office, 2500 Wilshire Blvd. - Suite 1028, Los Angeles, CA 90057, 213/380-7520

RED SORGHUM   New Yorker, 1988, Chinese
CODE NAME "COU GAR"   Xi'An Film Studio/Xi'an Modern Science & Technology Cultural Development Board, 1989, Chinese
JU DOU   co-director with Yang Fengliang, Miramax Films, 1990, Chinese-Japanese
RAISE THE RED LANTERN   Orion Classics, 1991, Chinese-Hong Kong-Taiwanese
THE STORY OF QIU JU   Sony Pictures Classics, 1992, Hong Kong-Chinese
TO LIVE   The Samuel Goldwyn Company, 1994, Hong Kong-Chinese
LA PEINTRE   Golden Tripod/Shanghai Film Studio, 1994, Taiwanese-Chinese, supervising director
SHANGHAI TRIAD   *ROW, ROW, ROW TO GRANDMA'S BRIDGE* Shanghai Film Studio, 1995, Chinese

BAE YONG-KYUN
Contact: Korean Motion Pictures Promotion Corporation, 34-5, 3KA Namsan-Dong, Chung-Ku, Seoul, South Korea, tel.: 755-9291

WHY HAS BODHI-DARMA LEFT FOR THE EAST?   Milestone Film, 1993, South Korean

JEFF YONIS
BLOODFIST V - HUMAN TARGET   New Horizons, 1993

BUD YORKIN*
(Alan David Yorkin)
b. February 22, 1926 - Washington, Pennsylvania
Business: Bud Yorkin Productions, 345 N. Maple Drive - Suite 206, Beverly Hills, CA 90210, 310/274-8111
Agent: APA - Los Angeles, 310/273-0744

COME BLOW YOUR HORN   Paramount, 1963
NEVER TOO LATE   Warner Bros., 1965
DIVORCE AMERICAN STYLE   Columbia, 1967
INSPECTOR CLOUSEAU   United Artists, 1968, British
START THE REVOLUTION WITHOUT ME   Warner Bros., 1970, British
THE THIEF WHO CAME TO DINNER   Warner Bros., 1972
TWICE IN A LIFETIME   The Yorkin Company, 1985
ARTHUR 2 ON THE ROCKS   Warner Bros., 1988
LOVE HURTS   Vestron, 1990

YAKY YOSHA
Business: Yaky Yosha Ltd., 29 Lilienblum Street, Tel Aviv 65133, Israel, tel.: 03/659108

SHALOM   Yaky Yosha Ltd., 1973, Israeli
ROCKINGHORSE   Sus-Etz, 1978, Israeli
THE VULTURE   New Yorker, 1981, Israeli
DEAD END STREET   Lelo Motza Ltd., 1982, Israeli
SUNSTROKE   Shapira Films, 1984, Israeli
SEXUAL RESPONSE   Vision International, 1992

HIROAKI YOSHIDA
Contact: Nihon Eiga Kantoku Kyokai (Japan Film Directors Association), La Fontenu Building -4th Floor, 23-2 Maruyama-cho, Shibuya-ku, Tokyo, Japan, tel.: 3/3461-4411

TWILIGHT OF THE COCKROACHES (AF)   Streamline, 1987, Japanese
IRON MAZE   Castle Hill Productions, 1991, U.S.-Japanese

ANDREW YOUNG
CHILDREN OF FATE: LIFE AND DEATH IN A SICILIAN FAMILY (FD)   co-director with Susan Todd, Young-Friedson/Archipelago Films, 1993
LIVES IN HAZARD (FD)   co-director with Susan Todd, Olmos Productions/Archipelago Films, 1993

FREDDIE YOUNG
(Frederick A. Young)
b. 1902 - England
Address: 3 Roehampton Close, London SW15, England
Agent: London Management - London, tel.: 171/287-9000

ARTHUR'S HALLOWED GROUND   Cinecom, 1983, British, originally made for television

JEFFREY YOUNG*
Home: 9422 Readcrest Dr., Beverly Hills, CA 90210, 310/205-8961

BEEN DOWN SO LONG IT LOOKS LIKE UP TO ME   Paramount, 1971

JOHN G. YOUNG
PARALLEL SONS   Black Brook Films, 1995

ROBERT M. YOUNG*

(Robert Milton Young)
b. November 22, 1924 - New York, New York
Agent: CAA - Beverly Hills, 310/288-4545

THE INFERNO *CORTILE CASCINO, ITALY* (FD)
co-director with Michael Roemer, Robert M. Young
Film Productions, 1962
NOTHING BUT A MAN co-director with Michael Roemer,
Cinema 5, 1965
ALAMBRISTA! Bobwin/Films Haus, 1977
SHORT EYES The Film League, 1978
RICH KIDS United Artists, 1979
ONE-TRICK PONY Warner Bros., 1980
THE BALLAD OF GREGORIO CORTEZ Embassy, 1983
SAVING GRACE Columbia, 1986
EXTREMITIES Atlantic Releasing Corporation, 1986
WE ARE THE CHILDREN (TF) Paulist Pictures/Dan Fauci-Ted
Danson Productions/The Furia Organization, 1987
DOMINICK AND EUGENE Orion, 1988
TRIUMPH OF THE SPIRIT Triumph Releasing Corporation,
1989, U.S.-Israeli
TALENT FOR THE GAME Paramount, 1991
ROOSTERS I.R.S. Releasing, 1993
SOLOMON + SHEBA (CTF) Dino DeLaurentiis
Communications, 1995

ROBERT WILLIAM YOUNG

Address: 28 Kew Green, Kew, Surrey TW9 3BH, England,
tel.: 181/948-2310
Agent: ICM - London, tel.: 171/636-6565

VAMPIRE CIRCUS Rank, 1972, British
THE WORLD IS FULL OF MARRIED MEN New Realm,
1979, British
THE MAD DEATH (TF) BBC Scotland, 1981, Scottish
ROBIN OF SHERWOOD (MS) HTV, 1985-86, British
WORST WITCH (TF) Central TV, 1986, British
HARRY'S KINGDOM (TF) BBC, 1987, British
BLUE BLOOD (TF) Tele-Munchen, 1987, West German
THREE WISHES FOR JAMIE (TF) Hill-St. Johns Films/HTV Ltd./
Columbia TV, 1987, British-U.S.
ONE WAY OUT (TF) BBC, 1988, British
BLORE MP (TF) BBC, 1989, British
GBH (MS) GBH Films/Channel 4, 1990, British
ALIVE AND KICKING (TF) BBC, 1991, British
HOSTAGE Pinnacle Pictures/Tyne Tees TV/ Portman
Entertainment/Independent Image/Jorge Estrada Mora
Producciones, 1992, British-Argentine
SPLITTING HEIRS Universal, 1993, British-U.S.
DOOMSDAY GUN (CTF) Griffin Production/HBO Showcase,
1994, British-U.S.
FIERCE CREATURES Universal, 1995, British-U.S.

ROGER YOUNG*

b. May 13, 1942 - Champaign, Illinois
Agent: CAA - Beverly Hills, 310/288-4545

BITTER HARVEST (TF) ☆ Charles Fries Productions, 1981
AN INNOCENT LOVE (TF) Steve Binder Productions, 1982
DREAMS DON'T DIE (TF) Hill-Mandelker Films, 1982
TWO OF A KIND (TF) Lorimar Productions, 1982
HARDCASTLE AND McCORMICK (TF) Stephen J. Cannell
Productions, 1983
LASSITER Warner Bros., 1984
GULAG (CTF) Lorimar Productions/HBO Premiere Films, 1985
INTO THIN AIR (TF) Tony Ganz Productions/Major H
Productions, 1985
UNDER SIEGE (TF) Ohlmeyer Communications
Company/Telepictures Productions, 1986
LOVE AMONG THIEVES (TF) Robert A. Papazian
Productions, 1987
THE SQUEEZE TriStar, 1987
THE BOURNE IDENTITY (TF) Alan Shayne Productions/Warner
Bros. TV, 1988

MURDER IN MISSISSIPPI (TF) Wolper Productions/Bernard
Sofronski Productions/Warner Bros. TV, 1990
LOVE AND LIES (TF) Freyda Rothstein Productions/ITC
Entertainment Group, 1990
HEARTS ARE WILD (TF) CBS, 1991
HELD HOSTAGE: THE SIS AND JERRY LEVIN STORY (TF)
Paragon Entertainment Corp./Carol Polakoff Productions, 1991
DEATH OF INNOCENCE (TF) CBS, 1991
DOUBLECROSSED (CTF) Green-Epstein Productions/
Lorimar TV, 1991
NIGHTMARE IN COLUMBIA COUNTY (TF) The Landsburg
Company, 1991
SHENANDOAH (TF) CBS, 1992
DANIELLE STEEL'S 'JEWELS' *JEWELS* (MS) List-Estrin
Productions/RCS Video/NBC Productions, 1992
FOR LOVE AND GLORY (TF) The Gerber Company/CBS
Entertainment, 1993
GERONIMO (CTF) Yorktown Productions/von Zerneck-Sertner
Films/Turner Network TV, 1993
MERCY MISSION: THE RESCUE OF FLIGHT 771 (TF)
RHI Entertainment/Anasazi Productions, 1993, U.S.-Australian
GETTING GOTTI (TF) Kushner-Locke Company, 1994
JOSEPH (CTF) LUBE/RAI/Turner Network TV,
1994, U.S.-German-Italian

RONNY YU

Agent: Richard Arlock, The Gersh Agency - Beverly Hills,
310/274-6611

THE SERVANTS 1979, Hong Kong
CHINA WHITE Fu Ngai Film Productions, 1990, Hong Kong
THE BRIDE WITH WHITE HAIR *JIANG-HU: BETWEEN LOVE &
GLORY* Rim Film Distributors, 1993, Hong Kong
SLAYER - THE DEVIL'S ASSASSIN Freestone Pictures/
Davis Films, 1995

ZHANG YUAN

Contact: China Film Import & Export Office, 2500 Wilshire Blvd. -
Suite 1028, Los Angeles, CA 90057, 213/380-7520

MAMA Chinese
BEIJING BASTARDS Beijing Bastards Group/Hubert Bals Fund,
1993, Chinese-Hong Kong-French
THE SQUARE (FD) co-director with Duan Jingchuan,
1995, Chinese

COREY YUEN

(Cory Yuen)
Contact: Hong Kong Film Liaison, 10940 Wilshire Blvd. - Suite 1220,
Los Angeles, CA 90024, 310/208-2678

NO RETREAT NO SURRENDER New World, 1986, Hong Kong
NO RETREAT, NO SURRENDER II Shapiro Glickenhaus
Entertainment, 1989, Hong Kong
SAVIOUR OF THE SOUL co-director with David Lai, Team Work
Production House, 1992, Hong Kong
FONG SAI-YUK Golden Harvest, 1993, Hong Kong
FONG SAI-YUK II Golden Harvest, 1993, Hong Kong
THE BODYGUARD FROM BEIJING Golden Communications,
1994, Hong Kong

ROBERT YUHAS

THE INFAMOUS DOROTHY PARKER: WOULD YOU KINDLY
DIRECT ME TO HELL? (CTD) Robert Yuhas Productions/A&E
Network, 1994

JAMES YUKICH*

Personal Manager: Brillstein/Grey Entertainment - Beverly Hills,
310/275-6135

DOUBLE DRAGON Gramercy Pictures, 1994

PRINCE CHATRI YUKOL
(Than Mul)
b. Thailand
Contact: Thailand Film Promotion Center, 599 Bumrung Muang
   Road, Bangkok 10100, Thailand, tel.: 2/223-4690

CENTRE OF THE NATION (FD)   1990, Thai
THE ELEPHANT KEEPER   Prommitri Productions/Manfred Durniok
   Productions, 1990, Thai-West German
SONG FOR CHAO PHYA   Prommitri Productions, 1991, Thai
SALWEEN   1993, Thai

PAUL YULE
Address: 42 De Beauvoir Crescent, London N1 5SN, England,
   tel.: 171/923-1998

MARTIN CHAMBI AND THE HEIRS OF THE INCAS (TD)
   BBC, 1986, British
OUR GOD THE CONDOR (TD)   BBC, 1987, British
THE NOVELIST WHO WOULD BE PRESIDENT (TD)
   BBC, 1990, British
TRAINS THAT PASSED IN THE NIGHT (TD)   Channel 4,
   1990, British
DAMNED IN THE USA (TD)   Channel 4, 1991, British
AS AMERICAN AS APPLE PIE (TD)   Channel 4, 1992, British
GOOD MORNING MR HITLER! (TD)   Channel 4, 1993, British
RETURN TO THE SACRED ICE (TD)   BBC, 1993, British

JOHNNY YUNE
THEY STILL CALL ME BRUCE   co-director with James R. Orr,
   Shapiro Entertainment, 1987

LARRY YUST*
Address: 500 S. Rossmore Avenue, Los Angeles, CA 90020,
   213/934-4706
Agent: ICM - Beverly Hills, 310/550-4000

TRICK BABY   Universal, 1973
HOMEBODIES   Avco Embassy, 1974
TESTIMONY OF TWO MEN (TF)   co-director with Leo Penn,
   Universal TV, 1977
"SAY YES"   Cinetel, 1986

PETER YUVAL
Business: Go Pictures/Triad Entertainment, 8318 Ridpath Drive -
   Suite 100, Los Angeles, CA 90046, 213/650-2988

DEAD END CITY   AIP, 1989
TIME BURST - THE FINAL ALLIANCE   AIP, 1989
THE SHOOTERS   AIP, 1990
FIREHEAD   Pyramid Distribution, 1991

BRIAN YUZNA
SOCIETY   Wild Street Pictures, 1989
SILENT NIGHT, DEADLY NIGHT PART IV: THE INITIATION
   Silent Films/Richard N. Gladstein Productions, 1990
BRIDE OF RE-ANIMATOR   50th Street Films, 1991
H.P. LOVECRAFT'S NECRONOMICON   co-director with
   Christophe Gans & Shusuke Kaneko, Necronomicon
   Productions, 1993, U.S.-French-Japanese
RETURN OF THE LIVING DEAD 3   Trimark Pictures, 1993

MAURIZIO ZACCARO
b. May 8, 1952 - Milan, Italy
Contact: 02/39310375

IN CODA ALLA CODA (TF)   Ipotesi Cinema/RAI, 1988, Italian
WHERE THE NIGHT BEGINS   Due A/Filmauro/RAI, 1991, Italian
LA VALLE DI PIETRA KALKSTEIN   Pentafilm/Aura Film/Produzioni
   Sire, 1992, Italian
L'ARTICOLO 2   Bambu Cinema & TV/Produzione SI.RE.,
   1994, Italian

STEVE ZACHARIAS
Agent: UTA - Beverly Hills, 310/273-6700

REVENGE OF THE NERDS IV: NERDS IN LOVE (TF)
   Zacharias-Buhai Productgions/Fox West Pictures, 1994

STEVEN ZAILLIAN*
Agent: Harold R. Greene, Inc. - Marina del Rey, 310/823-5393

SEARCHING FOR BOBBY FISCHER   Paramount, 1993

NANCY ZALA
ROUND NUMBERS   Filumthropix, 1992

ALAIN ZALOUM
Contact: French Film Office, 745 Fifth Avenue, New York,
   NY 10151, 212/832-8860

CANVAS   Optima Productions/ABC Distribution, 1992, French

LILI FINI ZANUCK*
Business: The Zanuck Company, 202 N. Canon Drive, Beverly Hills,
   CA 90210, 310/274-0209
Agent: ICM - Beverly Hills, 310/550-4000

RUSH   MGM-Pathe Communications, 1991

KRZYSZTOF ZANUSSI
b. July 17, 1939 - Warsaw, Poland
Contact: Film Polski, ul. Mazowiecka 6/8, 00 0048 Warsaw, Poland,
   tel.: 48-22/26-84-55 or: 26-09-49

THE STRUCTURE OF CRYSTALS   1969, Polish
MOUNTAINS AT DUSK (TF)   1970, Polish
DIE ROLLE (TF)   1971, West German
FAMILY LIFE   1971, Polish
BEHIND THE WALL   1971, Polish
HYPOTHESIS (TF)   1972, Polish
ILLUMINATION   1973, Polish
THE CATAMOUNT KILLING   1974
NIGHT DUTY (TF)   1975, Polish
A WOMAN'S DECISION   Tinc, 1975, Polish
CAMOUFLAGE   Libra, 1977, Polish
THE SPIRAL   1978, Polish
WAYS IN THE NIGHT   TeleCulture, 1980, West German
THE CONSTANT FACTOR   New Yorker, 1980, Polish
CONTRACT   New Yorker, 1981, Polish
FROM A FAR COUNTRY (POPE JOHN PAUL II) (TF)   Trans World
   Film/ITC/RAI/Film Polski, 1981, British-Italian-Polish
IMPERATIV (TF)   TeleCulture, 1982, West German
THE UNAPPROACHABLE   TeleCulture, 1982, West German
BLAUBART (TF)   Westdeutscher Rundfunk/DRS,
   1984, West German-Swiss
A YEAR OF THE QUIET SUN   Sandstar Releasing Company,
   1984, Polish-West German-U.S.

LE POUVOIR DU MAL   Films Moliere, 1985, French-Italian
WHEREVER YOU ARE   Mark Forstater Productions/Gerhard
   Schmidt Filmproduktion/Film Polski, 1988,
   British-West German-Polish
INVENTORY   Polish Film Unit TOR/Polish TV/Regina Ziegler
   Filmproduktion, 1989, Polish-West German
INTERROGATION   Circle Releasing, 1990, Polish-West German
A LIFE FOR A LIFE   Regina Ziegler Filmproduktion,
   1991, Polish-German
A LONG CONVERSATION WITH A BIRD   Regina Ziegler
   Filmpruktion, 1991, Polish-German
RUSSIA TODAY (FD)   Polish Film Unit TOR, 1991, Polish
THE SILENT TOUCH   Mark Forstater Productions/Polish Film Unit
   TOR/Metronome Productions/British Screen/The European
   Co-Production Fund, 1992, British-Polish-Danish-British

JOHN ZARITSKY
b. 1943 - St-Catherines, Ontario, Canada
Business: K.A. Productions, 49 Cavell Avenue, Toronto,
   Ontario M4J 1H5, Canada, 416/466-8202

THE MAKING OF A MARTYR (TD)   1976, Canadian
STEELTOWN STAR (TD)   1976, Canadian
GORD S. (TD)   1976, Canadian
I DID NOT KILL BOB (TD)   1977, Canadian
BETSY'S LAST CHANCE (TD)   1978, Canadian
CARING FOR CHRYSLER (TD)   1978, Canadian
CHARITY BEGINS AT HOME (TD)   1979, Canadian
THE LOSER'S GAM (TD)   1980, Canadian
JUST ANOTHER MISSING KID (TD)   1981, Canadian
BJORN BORG (TD)   1983, Canadian
I'LL GET THERE SOMEHOW (TD)   1984, Canadian
THE BOYS NEXT DOOR (TD)   1984, Canadian
RAPISTS: CAN THEY BE STOPPED? (TD)
   1985, U.S.-Canadian
TEARS ARE NOT ENOUGH (FD)   Pan-Canadian Film
   Distributors, 1985, Canadian
THE REAL STUFF (TD)   K.A. Productions/Jack of Hearts
   Productions/CBC, 1987, Canadian
BROKEN PROMISES (TD)   1988, Canadian
MY HUSBAND IS GOING TO KILL ME (TD)   PBS, 1988
THALIDOMIDE (TD)   1988, Canadian
EXTRAORDINARY PEOPLE (TD)   PBS, 1989
BORN IN AFRICA (TD)   K.A. Productions/WGBH-Boston/CBC,
   1990, Canadian-U.S.
MY DOCTOR, MY LOVER (TD)   K.A. Productions/WGBH-Boston/
   CBC, 1991, U.S.-Canadian

ALAN ZASLOVE
Business: Walt Disney Animation, 500 S. Buena Vista Street,
   Burbank, CA 91521, 818/560-1000

THE RETURN OF JAFAR (AHVF)   co-director with Toby Shelton &
   Tad Stones, Walt Disney Television Animation, 1994

YOLANDE ZAUBERMAN
Contact: French Film Office, 745 Fifth Avenue, New York,
   NY 10151, 212/832-8860

IVAN AND ABRAHAM   *MOI IVAN, TOI ABRAHAM*
   New Yorker, 1993, French

KRISTI ZEA*
b. October 24, 1948 - New York, New York
Agent: ICM - New York City, 212/556-5600

WOMEN & MEN 2: IN LOVE THERE ARE NO RULES (CTF)
   co-director with Walter Bernstein & Mike Figgis,
   David Brown Productions/HBO Showcase, 1991

FRANCO ZEFFIRELLI*
b. February 12, 1923 - Florence, Italy
Home: via Lucio Volumnio 37, Rome, Italy, tel.: 06/718-4442
Agent: ICM - Beverly Hills, 310/550-4000

CAMPING   1957, Italian
LA BOHEME   Warner Bros., 1965, Swiss

FLORENCE - DAYS OF DESTRUCTION (FD)   1966, Italian
THE TAMING OF THE SHREW   Columbia, 1967, Italian-British
ROMEO AND JULIET ★   Paramount, 1968, Italian-British
BROTHER SUN SISTER MOON   Paramount, 1973, Italian-British
JESUS OF NAZARETH (MS)   Sir Lew Grade Productions/ITC,
   1978, British-Italian
THE CHAMP   MGM/United Artists, 1979
ENDLESS LOVE   Universal, 1981
I PAGLIACCI (TPF)   1981, Italian
LA TRAVIATA   Universal Classics, 1982, Italian
CAVALLERIA RUSTICANA (TPF) ☆   1986, Italian
OTELLO   Cannon, 1986, Italian
YOUNG TOSCANINI   Motion Picture Corporation of America,
   1988, Italian-French
HAMLET   Warner Bros., 1990, British
SPARROW   Mario & Vittorio Cecchi Gori/Nippon Film
   Development & Finance Inc./Officine Cinematografica/
   Tiger Film, 1993, Italian-Japanese
JANE EYRE   Miramax Films, 1995, British

PAUL ZEHRER
BLESSING   Starr Valley Films, 1994

JIMMY ZEILINGER
Agent: Renaissance/H.N. Swanson - Los Angeles, 310/246-6000

LITTLE SISTER   InterStar Releasing, 1992

YURI ZELTSER
Agent: Innovative Artists - Los Angeles, 310/553-5200

EYE OF THE STORM   Senator Films/Eurofilm/Odyssey Distributors,
   1992, U.S.-German
PLAYMAKER   Orion, 1994

ROBERT ZEMECKIS*
b. 1952 - Chicago, Illinois
Business: South Side Amusement, 100 Universal City Plaza -
   Bungalow 127, Universal City, CA 91608, 818/777-8313
Agent: CAA - Beverly Hills, 310/288-4545
Business Manager: Gelfand, Rennert & Feldman, 1880 Century
   Park East - Suite 900, Los Angeles, CA 90067, 310/556-6652

I WANNA HOLD YOUR HAND   Universal, 1978
USED CARS   Columbia, 1980
ROMANCING THE STONE   20th Century Fox, 1984
BACK TO THE FUTURE   Universal, 1985
WHO FRAMED ROGER RABBIT   Buena Vista, 1988
BACK TO THE FUTURE PART II   Universal, 1989
BACK TO THE FUTURE PART III   Universal, 1990
DEATH BECOMES HER   Universal, 1992
FORREST GUMP ★★   Universal, 1994

LAURIE ZEMELMAN
CHUPPA: THE WEDDING CANOPY (FD)   co-director with
   Sascha Schneider, GEO Film, 1994

YIMOU ZHANG
(See Zhang YIMOU)

XIAOWEN ZHOU
(See Zhou XIAOWEN)

TIAN ZHUANGZHUANG
b. 1952 - Beijing, China
Contact: China Film Import & Export Office, 2500 Wilshire Blvd. -
   Suite 1028, Los Angeles, CA 90057, 213/380-7520

THE SUMMER EXPERIENCE (TF)   1983, Chinese
RED ELEPHANT   co-director with Zhang Jianya & Xie Xiaojing,
   1983, Chinese
SEPTEMBER   Kunming Studio, 1984, Chinese
ON THE HUNTING GROUND   China Film Import & Export,
   1985, Chinese
HORSE THIEF   China Film Import & Export, 1986, Chinese

ROCK KIDS   China Film Import & Export, 1988, Chinese
THE IMPERIAL EUNUCH   China Film Import & Export,
   1991, Chinese
THE BLUE KITE   Kino International, 1993, Chinese

CLAUDE ZIDI
b. July 25, 1934 - Paris, France
Agent: ICM France - Paris, tel.: 1/723-7860
Contact: French Film Office, 745 Fifth Avenue, New York,
   NY 10151, 212/832-8860

LES BIDASSES EN FOLIE   1972, French
LES FOUS DU STADE   1972
LE GRAND BAZAR   1973, French
LA MOUTARDE ME MONTE AU NEZ   1974, French
LES BISSADES S'EN VONT EN GUERRE   1974, French
LA COURSE A L'ECHALOTTE   1975, French
L'AILE OU LA CUISSE   1976, French
L'ANIMAL   1977, French
LA ZIZANIE   1978, French
DUMB BUT DISCIPLINED   1979, French
MY NEW PARTNER   LES RIPOUX   1984, French
LA TOTALE   1992, French
PROFIL BAS   AMLF, 1993, French

HOWARD ZIEFF*
b. 1943 - Los Angeles, California
Agent: CAA - Beverly Hills, 310/288-4545

SLITHER   MGM, 1973
HEARTS OF THE WEST   MGM/United Artists, 1975
HOUSE CALLS   Universal, 1978
THE MAIN EVENT   Warner Bros., 1979
PRIVATE BENJAMIN   Warner Bros., 1980
UNFAITHFULLY YOURS   20th Century Fox, 1984
THE DREAM TEAM   Universal, 1989
MY GIRL   Columbia, 1991
MY GIRL 2   Columbia, 1994

HOWARD ZIEHM
FLESH GORDON   Mammoth Films, 1974
FLESH GORDON MEETS THE COSMIC CHEERLEADERS
   Filmvest International, 1991

RAFAL ZIELINSKI
b. 1959 - Warsaw, Poland
Agent: APA - Los Angeles, 310/273-0744

HEY BABE!   Rafal Productions/Canadian Film Development
   Corporation/L'Institut Quebecois du Cinema/Famous
   Players Ltd., 1980, Canadian
SCREWBALLS   New World, 1983, Canadian
LOOSE SCREWS   Concorde, 1985, Canadian
RECRUITS   Concorde, 1986, Canadian
VALET GIRLS   Empire Pictures, 1986
SPELLCASTER   Empire Pictures, 1987
STATE PARK   ITC, 1987, Canadian
SCREWBALL HOTEL   Universal, 1989, U.S.-British
GINGERALE AFTERNOON   Skouras Pictures, 1989
NIGHT OF THE WARRIOR   Trimark Pictures, 1991
UNDER SURVEILLANCE   Fries Entertainment, 1992
STREETWISE   Skouras Pictures, 1993
NATIONAL LAMPOON'S LAST RESORT   Trimark Pictures, 1994
FUN   Neo Modern Entertainment, 1994

PAUL ZILLER
DIE TRYING   Concorde, 1992
DOUBLE SUSPICION   Trimark Pictures, 1993
PROBABLE CAUSE (CTF)   Wilmont Productions/Showtime
   Entertainment, 1994, Canadian-U.S.

VERNON ZIMMERMAN*
Agent: Renaissance/H.N. Swanson - Los Angeles, 310/246-6000

DEADHEAD MILES   Paramount, 1971
UNHOLY ROLLERS   American International, 1972
FADE TO BLACK   American Cinema, 1980

MICHAEL ZINBERG*
Agent: Bob Broder, Broder-Kurland-Webb-Uffner Agency -
   Beverly Hills, 310/281-3400

FOR THE VERY FIRST TIME (TF)   American Flyer Productions/
   Lorimar TV, 1991

ZOE ZINMAN
CITY NEWS   co-director with David Fishelson, Cinecom, 1983

FRED ZINNEMANN*
b. April 29, 1907 - Vienna, Austria
Business: 98 Mount Street, London W1Y 5HF, England
Agent: William Morris Agency - Beverly Hills, 310/859-4000

THE WAVE (FD)   co-director with Emilio Gomez Muriel,
   Strand, 1935, Mexican
KID GLOVE KILLER   MGM, 1942
EYES IN THE NIGHT   MGM, 1942
THE SEVENTH CROSS   MGM, 1944
LITTLE MR. JIM   MGM, 1946
MY BROTHER TALKS TO HORSES   MGM, 1947
THE SEARCH ★   MGM, 1948, U.S.-Swiss
ACT OF VIOLENCE   MGM, 1949
THE MEN   Columbia, 1950
TERESA   MGM, 1951
HIGH NOON ★   United Artists, 1952
THE MEMBER OF THE WEDDING   Columbia, 1952
FROM HERE TO ETERNITY ★★   Columbia, 1953
OKLAHOMA!   Magna, 1955
A HATFUL OF RAIN   20th Century-Fox, 1957
THE NUN'S STORY ★   Warner Bros., 1959
THE SUNDOWNERS ★   Warner Bros., 1960
BEHOLD A PALE HORSE   Columbia, 1964
A MAN FOR ALL SEASONS ★★   Columbia, 1966, British
THE DAY OF THE JACKAL   Universal, 1973, British-French
JULIA ★   20th Century-Fox, 1977
FIVE DAYS ONE SUMMER   The Ladd Company/Warner Bros.,
   1982, British

PETER ZINNER
b. July 24, 1919 - Vienna, Austria

THE SALAMANDER   ITC, 1981, British-Italian-U.S.

RANDALL ZISK*
Agent: ICM - Beverly Hills, 310/550-4000

MOMENT OF TRUTH: TO WALK AGAIN (TF)   O'Hara-Horowitz
   Productions, 1994

JOSEPH ZITO*
b. May 14, 1946 - New York, New York
Agent: ICM - Beverly Hills, 310/550-4000

ABDUCTION   United Film Distribution, 1981
THE PROWLER   Sandhurst Corporation, 1982
FRIDAY THE 13TH - THE FINAL CHAPTER   Paramount, 1984
MISSING IN ACTION   Cannon, 1984
INVASION U.S.A.   Cannon, 1985
RED SCORPION   Shapiro Glickenhaus Entertainment, 1989

MILAN ZIVKOVICH
THE ART OF MURDER   Concorde, 1990
CONCEALED WEAPON   co-director with David Payne,
   Concorde, 1995

LEE DAVID ZLOTOFF*
Home: 1628 Alta Avenue, Santa Monica, CA 90402, 310/451-0430
Agent: Norman Kurland, Broder-Kurland-Webb-Uffner Agency -
   Beverly Hills, 310/281-3400

PLYMOUTH (TF)   Touchstone TV/RAI/Zlotoff Inc.,
   1991, U.S.-Italian
THE SPITFIRE GRILL   Mendocino Corp., 1995

DICK ZONDAG
WE'RE BACK! A DINOSAUR'S STORY (AF)   co-director with
   Ralph Zondag, Phil Nibbelink & Simon Wells, Universal, 1993

RALPH ZONDAG
WE'RE BACK! A DINOSAUR'S STORY (AF)   co-director with
   Dick Zondag, Phil Nibbelink & Simon Wells, Universal, 1993

VILMOS ZSIGMOND*
b. June 16, 1930 - Czeged, Hungary
Agent: Smith-Gosnell-Nicholson & Associates - Pacific Palisades,
   310/459-0307

THE LONG SHADOW   Israfilm/Prolitera/Novo Film,
   1992, Israeli-Hungarian-U.S.

DAVID ZUCKER*
b. October 16, 1947 - Milwaukee, Wisconsin
Business: Zucker Brothers Productions, 10202 W. Washington Blvd. -
   Lean Building, Suite 119, Culver City, CA 90232, 310/280-4433
Agent: CAA - Beverly Hills, 310/288-4545
Business Manager: Tony Peyser, Peyser & Alexander
   Management, 500 Fifth Avenue - Suite 2800, New York,
   NY 10110, 212/764-6455

AIRPLANE!   co-director with Jim Abrahams & Jerry Zucker,
   Paramount, 1980
TOP SECRET!   co-director with Jim Abrahams & Jerry Zucker,
   Paramount, 1984
RUTHLESS PEOPLE   co-director with Jim Abrahams &
   Jerry Zucker, Buena Vista, 1986
THE NAKED GUN: FROM THE FILES OF POLICE SQUAD!
   Paramount, 1988
THE NAKED GUN 2-1/2: THE SMELL OF FEAR   Paramount, 1991

JERRY ZUCKER*
b. March 11, 1950 - Milwaukee, Wisconsin
Business: Zucker Brothers Productions, 10202 W. Washington Blvd. -
   Lean Building, Suite 119, Culver City, CA 90232, 310/280-4433
Agent: CAA - Beverly Hills, 310/288-4545
Business Manager: David Alexander, Peyser & Alexander
   Management, 500 Fifth Avenue - Suite 2800, New York,
   NY 10110, 212/764-6455

AIRPLANE!   co-director with Jim Abrahams & David Zucker,
   Paramount, 1980
TOP SECRET!   co-director with Jim Abrahams & David Zucker,
   Paramount, 1984
RUTHLESS PEOPLE   co-director with Jim Abrahams &
   David Zucker, Buena Vista, 1986
GHOST   Paramount, 1990
FIRST KNIGHT   Columbia, 1995, U.S.-British

ALBERT ZUGSMITH
b. April 24, 1910 - Atlantic City, New Jersey
Address: 23388 Mulholland Drive, Woodland Hills, CA 91364

COLLEGE CONFIDENTIAL   Universal, 1960
SEX KITTENS GO TO COLLEGE   Allied Artists, 1960
THE PRIVATE LIVES OF ADAM AND EVE   Universal, 1960
DONDI   Allied Artists, 1961
CONFESSIONS OF AN OPIUM EATER   *EVILS OF CHINATOWN*
   Allied Artists, 1962
THE INCREDIBLE SEX REVOLUTION   1965
MOVIE STAR AMERICAN STYLE OR LSD - I HATE YOU   1966
ON HER BED OF ROSES   Famous Players International, 1966
THE VERY FRIENDLY NEIGHBORS   1969
TWO ROSES AND A GOLDEN ROD   1969

HOWARD ZUKER
(See Zack NORMAN)

FRANK ZUNIGA
(Francisco Zuniga)
b. March 20, 1936 - Gallup, New Mexico
Business: Pisces Productions, 948 N. Cahuenga Blvd. - Suite 212,
   Los Angeles, CA 90038, 213/461-6800

FURTHER ADVENTURES OF THE WILDERNESS FAMILY - PART 2
   Pacific International, 1978
HEARTBREAKER   Monarex/Emerson Film Enterprises, 1983
THE GOLDEN SEAL   The Samuel Goldwyn Company, 1983
WHAT COLOR IS THE WIND   Pisces Productions, 1984
STRANGE COMPANIONS (TF)   Walt Disney TV, 1987
FISTFIGHTER   Taurus Entertainment, 1989

MARCOS ZURINAGA
Business: Zaga Films, Edificio Ballester, Paseo Covadonga 104,
   Puerta de Tierra, San Juan, Puerto Rico 00901, 809/721-6930

STEP AWAY   1979, Puerto Rican
LA GRAN FIESTA   Jack R. Crosby/The Frank Moreno Company,
   1986, Puerto Rican
TANGO BAR   Beco Films/Zaga Films, 1988,
   Puerto Rican-Argentine
A FLOR DE PIEL (TF)   Comision Para los Asuntos de la Mujer/
   Zaga Films, 1990, Puerto Rican

CHARLOTTE ZWERIN*
Home: 43 Morton Street, New York, NY 10014, 212/645-1284

SALESMAN (FD)   co-director with Albert Maysles & David Maysles,
   Maysles Films, 1969
GIMME SHELTER (FCD)   co-director with Albert Maysles &
   David Maysles, Cinema 5, 1971
RUNNING FENCE (FD)   co-director with Albert Maysles &
   David Maysles, 1977
ARSHILE GORKY (FD)   1982
DEKOONING ON DEKOONING (FD)   1983
ISLANDS (FD)   co-director with Albert Maysles & David Maysles,
   Maysles Films, 1986
HOROWITZ PLAYS MOZART (PF)   co-director with Albert Maysles &
   Susan Froemke, 1987
THELONIOUS MONK: STRAIGHT, NO CHASER (FD)
   Warner Bros., 1989
JESSYE NORMAN SINGS CARMEN (HVCD)   co-director with
   Albert Maysles & Susan Froemke, Cami Video, 1989
THE FLANAGAN TOUCH (FD)   Charlotte Zwerin Productions, 1990
MUSIC FOR THE MOVIES: TORU TAKEMITSU (FD)
   Alternate Current/Les Films D'Ici/La Sept-Arte/NHK,
   1994, U.S.-French-Japanese

EDWARD ZWICK*
b. October 8, 1952 - Winnetka, Illinois
Agent: ICM - Beverly Hills, 310/550-4000

PAPER DOLLS (TF)   Leonard Goldberg Productions, 1982
HAVING IT ALL (TF)   Hill-Mandelker Films, 1982
ABOUT LAST NIGHT...   TriStar, 1986
GLORY   TriStar, 1989
LEAVING NORMAL   Universal, 1992
LEGENDS OF THE FALL   TriStar, 1994

JOEL ZWICK*
Home: 18588 Linnet Street, Tarzana, CA 91356, 818/881-8392
Agent: Irv Schechter Company - Beverly Hills, 310/278-8070

SECOND SIGHT   Warner Bros., 1989

TERRY ZWIGOFF
CRUMB (FD)   Sony Pictures Classics, 1994

NOTABLE DIRECTORS
OF THE PAST

IN MEMORIAM

GEORGE ABBOTT (U.S.)

TENGIZ ABULADZE (Georgia)

IGOR ALEINIKOV (Russia)

VERA ALEINIKOV (Russia)

RENE ALLIO (French)

LINDSAY ANDERSON (Great Britain)

EMILE ARDOLINO (U.S.)

MAROUN BAGDADI (France)

HALL BARTLETT (U.S.)

RICHARD BARTLETT (U.S.)

ROBERT BECKER (U.S.)

MARIA LUISA BEMBERG (Argentina)

BILL BIXBY (U.S.)

ROBERT BOLT (Great Britain)

SERGEI BONDARCHUK (Russia)

PHILLIP BORSOS (Canada)

JOHN CANDY (Canada/U.S.)

CHRISTIAN-JAQUE (France)

JAMES CLAVELL (Great Britain/Australia)

JACK CALYTON (Great Britain/U.S.)

WILLIAM CONRAD (U.S.)

ALAN COOKE (Great Britain/U.S.)

AXEL CORTI (Austria)

MANMOHAN DESAI (India)

GORDON DOUGLAS (U.S.)

ARTHUR DREIFUSS (U.S.)

CY ENDFIELD (U.S.)

ZOLTAN FABRI (Hungary)

WILLIAM C. FAURE (South Africa)

FEDERICO FELLINI (Italy)

NIGEL FINCH (Great Britain)

CHRISTOPHER FRANK (France)

GEORGE FREEDLAND (France)

DUNCAN GIBBINS (U.S.)

SIDNEY GILLIAT (Great Britain)

AMOS GUTMAN (Israel)

JACK HANNAH (U.S.)

JAMES HILL (Great Britain)

JOE HOLLAND (U.S.)

HARRY HORNER (U.S.)

DEREK JARMAN (Great Britain)

TOM JOSLIN (U.S.)

PATRICK KELLY (U.S.)

ELMAR KLOS (Czechoslovakia)

CHARLES LAMONT (U.S.)

BURT LANCASTER (U.S.)

WALTER LANTZ (U.S.)

JOE LAYTON (U.S.)

ARTHUR LUBIN (U.S.)

ALEXANDER MACKENDRICK (Great Britain/U.S.)

MASAHIRO MAKINO (Japan)

IRVING J. MOORE (U.S.)

GILBERT MOSES (U.S.)

RAPHAEL NUSSBAUM (U.S.)

CHRISTIAN NYBY (U.S.)

MICHAEL O'DONOGHUE (U.S.)

GEORGE PEPPARD (U.S.)

DENNIS POTTER (Great Britain)

YULI RAIZMAN (Russia)

PETER REED (U.S.)

GOTTFRIED REINHARDT (U.S.)

MARLON T. RIGGS (U.S.)

TELLY SAVALAS (U.S.)

E.W. SWACKHAMER (U.S.)

DUCCIO TESSARI (Italy)

GERALD THOMAS (Great Britain)

ROBERT TOTTEN (U.S.)

MANIE von RENSBURG (South Africa)

SAM WANAMAKER (U.S./Great Britain)

TERENCE YOUNG (Great Britain)

FRANK ZAPPA (U.S.)

MAI ZETTERLING (Sweden)

Note: As we were going to press Rene Allio, Maria Luisa Bemberg, Cy Endfield, Arthur Lubin and Gilbert Moses passed away. Their list of credits can still be found in the main listing section.

INDEX OF NOTABLE FILM DIRECTORS

Note: This is not an index of every director, only those listed in this directory. As we were going to press Rene Allio, Maria Luisa Bemberg, Cy Endfield, Arthur Lubin and Gilbert Moses passed away. Their list of credits can still be found in the main listing section.

† = denotes deceased

A

George Abbott†
Tengiz Abuladze†
Luis Alcoriza†
Robert Aldrich†
Grigori Alexandrov†
Marc Allegret†
Yves Allegret†
Irwin Allen†
Rene Allio†
Robert Alton†
Lindsay Anderson†
Joseph Anthony†
Roscoe "Fatty" Arbuckle†
Emile Ardolino†
Leslie Arliss†
Jack Arnold†
Dorothy Arzner†
Hal Ashby†
Anthony Asquith†
John H. Auer†
Aram Avakian†

B

Lloyd Bacon†
Lionel Barrymore†
Hall Bartlett†
Charles T. Barton†
Mario Bava†
William Beaudine†
Harry Beaumont†
Ford Beebe†
Maria Luisa Bemberg†
Laslo Benedek†
Richard (Dick) Benner†
Spencer Gordon Bennett†
Compton Bennett†
Busby Berkeley†
Curtis Bernhardt†
Herbert J. Biberman†
Bill Bixby†
J. Stuart Blackton†
Christian Blackwood†
Alessandro Blasetti†
Richard Boleslawski†
Robert Bolt†
Sergei Bondarchuk†
Phillip Borsos†
Frank Borzage†

John Boulting†
Jean Boyer†
Charles J. Brabin†
John Brahm†
Herbert Brenon†
James Bridges†
Lino Brocka†
Richard Brooks†
Clarence Brown†
Tod Browning†
Franco Brusati†
Luis Buñuel†
David Butler†
Edward (Eddie) Buzzell†

C

Christy Cabanne†
Edward L. Cahn†
Mario Camerini†
Pasquale Festa Campanile†
Carlo Campogalliani†
Marcel Camus†
Frank Capra†
John Cassavetes†
Renato Castellani†
William Castle†
Alberto Cavalcanti†
Andre Cayatte†
Don Chaffey†
Charles (Charlie) Chaplin†
Charley Chase†
Benjamin Christensen†
Christian-Jaque†
Alan Clarke†
James Clavell†
Jack Clayton†
Edward F. (Eddie) Cline†
Henri-Georges Clouzot†
Jean Cocteau†
Lance Comfort†
Jack Conway†
Alan Cooke†
Merian C. Cooper†
Sergio Corbucci†
Henry Cornelius†
Axel Corti†
John Cromwell†
Alan Crosland†
James Cruze†
George Cukor†
Irving Cummings†
Michael Curtiz†
Paul Czinner†

D

Morton Da Costa†
Delmer Daves†
J. Searle Dawley†
Emile De Antonio†
Basil Dearden†
Eduardo De Filippo†
Fernando De Fuentes†
Roy Del Ruth†
Cecil B. De Mille†
Jacques Demy†
Vittorio De Sica†
Thorold Dickinson†
William Dieterle†
Jack Donohue†
Bill Douglas†
Gordon Douglas†
Alexander Petrovich Dovzhenko†
Michel Drach†
Arthur Dreifuss†
Carl Theodor Dreyer†
George Dunning†
E. A. Dupont†
Julien Duvivier†
Allan Dwan†

E

B. Reeves Eason†
Sergei Eisenstein†
Maurice Elvey†
Cy Endfield†
John English†
Ray Enright†
Chester Erskine†
Jean Eustache†

F

Zoltan Fabri†
Arnold Fanck†
John Farrow†
Rainer Werner Fassbinder†
Felix E. Feist†
Federico Fellini†
Leslie Fenton†
Emilio (El Indio) Fernandez†

Jose Ferrer†
Jacques Feyder†
Terence Fisher†
George Fitzmaurice†
Robert J. Flaherty†
Victor Fleming†
Robert Florey†
Aleksander Ford†
Francis Ford†
John Ford†
Carl Foreman†
Bob Fosse†
Lewis R. Foster†
Norman Foster†
Georges Franju†
Melvin Frank†
Sidney Franklin†
Thornton Freeland†
Hugo Fregonese†
Harold French†
Charles Frend†
Karl Freund†

G

Pal Gabor†
Carlo Gallone†
Abel Gance†
Tay Garnett†
Louis J. Gasnier†
Roberto Gavaldon†
Sergei Gerasimov†
Pietro Germi†
Steven Gethers†
Alan Gibson†
Sidney Gilliat†
John Gilling†
Michael Gordon†
Hideo Gosha†
Edmund Goulding†
Alfred E. Green†
Tom Gries†
D. W. Griffith†
Yilmaz Guney†
Alice Guy-Blache†

H

Hugo Haas†
Alexander Hall†
Robert Hamer†

Don Siegel†
S. Sylvan Simon†
Robert Siodmak†
Douglas Sirk†
Alf Sjoberg†
Victor Sjostrom†
Phillips Smalley†
Mrs. Phillips Smalley†
George Albert Smith†
R. G. (Bud) Springsteen†
John M. Stahl†
Jack Starrett†
Steno†
George Stevens†
Robert Stevenson†
Mauritz Stiller†
John Sturges†
Preston Sturges†
Edward Sutherland†
E.W. Swackhamer†

T

Andrei Tarkovsky†
Frank Tashlin†
Jacques Tati†
Norman Taurog†
Ray Taylor†
William Desmond Taylor†
Gerald Thomas†
Richard Thorpe†
Leopoldo Torre Nilsson†
Robert Totten†
Victor Tourjansky†
Jacques Tourneur†
Maurice Tourneur†
Shiro Toyoda†
John Trent†
Jiri Trnka†
François Truffaut†
Dalton Trumbo†

U

Edgar G. Ulmer†

V

W. S. ("Woody") Van Dyke†
Stefano Vanzina†
Dziga Vertov†
Charles Vidor†
King Vidor†
Jean Vigo†
Luchino Visconti†
Josef Von Sternberg†
Erich Von Stroheim†

W

George Waggner†
Hal Walker†
Stuart Walker†
Richard Wallace†
Raoul Walsh†
Charles Walters†
Sam Wanamaker†
Andy Warhol†
Charles Marquis Warren†
John Wayne†
Jack Webb†
Robert D. Webb†
Lois Weber†
Paul Wegener†
Orson Welles†
William A. Wellman†
Alfred L. Werker†
James Whale†
Tim Whelan†
Richard Whorf†
Robert Wiene†
Herbert Wilcox†
Cornel Wilde†
Richard Wilson†
Bretaigne Windust†
Edward D. Wood, Jr.†
Sam Wood†
William Wyler†

Y

Kajiro Yamamoto†
Satsuo Yamamoto†
Jean Yarbrough†
Harold Young†
Terence Young†
Sergei Yutkevich†

Z

Luigi Zampa†
Karel Zeman†
Mai Zetterling†
Valerio Zurlini†

★ ★ ★

A

GEORGE ABBOTT
b. June 25, 1887 - Forestville, New York
d. 1995

WHY BRING THAT UP?   Paramount, 1929
HALF-WAY TO HEAVEN   Paramount, 1929
MANSLAUGHTER   Paramount, 1930
THE SEA GOD   Paramount, 1930
STOLEN HEAVEN   Paramount, 1931
SECRETS OF A SECRETARY
   Paramount, 1931
MY SIN   Paramount, 1931
THE CHEAT   Paramount, 1931
TOO MANY GIRLS   RKO Radio, 1940
THE PAJAMA GAME   co-director with
   Stanley Donen, Warner Bros., 1957
DAMN YANKEES   co-director with
   Stanley Donen, Warner Bros., 1958

TENGIZ ABULADZE
b. January 31, 1924 - Kutaisi, Georgia, U.S.S.R.
d. 1994

MAGDAN'S DONKEY   Gruziafilm,
   1955, Soviet
SOMEONE ELSE'S CHILDREN   Gruziafilm,
   1958, Soviet
ME, GRANDMA, ILIKO AND HILLARION
   Gruziafilm, 1963, Soviet
THE ENTREATY   Gruziafilm, 1969, Soviet
A NECKLACE FOR MY BELOVED
   Gruziafilm, 1972, Soviet
THE MIRACLE TREE   Gruziafilm,
   1977, Soviet
REPENTANCE   Cannon, 1984, Soviet,
   originally made for television
HADJI MURAT   1989, Soviet

LUIS ALCORIZA
b. 1920 - Badajoz, Spain
d. 1992

LOS JOVENES   Azteca Films,
   1960, Mexican
TLAYUCAN   Azteca Films, 1961, Mexican
TIBURONEROS   Azteca Films,
   1962, Mexican
AMOR Y SEXO   SAFO 63   Filmex,
   1963, Mexican
TARAHUMARA   Azteca Films,
   1964, Mexican
EL GANGSTER   S.T.P.C., 1964, Mexican
JUEGO PELIGROSO   co-director, Cesar
   Santos Galindo/Nacional Cinematografica
   Brasil, 1966, Mexican-Brazilian
LA PUERTA Y LA MUJER DEL CARNICERO
   co-director, Peliculas Rodriguez,
   1968, Mexican
EL OFICIO MAS ANTIGUO DEL MUNDO
   Cima Films, 1968, Mexican
PARAISO   Cinematografica Morte,
   1969, Mexican
EL MURO DEL SILENCIO   Escorpion/Estudios
   Churubusco Azteca, 1971, Mexican
MECANICA NACIONAL   Azteca Films,
   1971, Mexican

FE, ESPERANZA & CARIDAD   co-director,
   Azteca Films, 1973, Mexican
PRESAGIO   Azteca Films, 1974, Mexican
LAS FUERZAS VIVAS   Conacine/Unifilms,
   1975, Mexican
A PASO DE COJO   1980, Mexican
VIACRUCIS NACIONAL   SEMANA SANTA EN
   ACAPULCO   1980, Mexican
TAC-TAC   HAN VIOLADO A UNA MUJER
   Peliculas Trio/Alcion Films, 1981,
   Spanish-Mexican
EL AMOR ES UN JUEGO EXTRANO
   1983, Mexican
TERROR Y ENCAJES NEGROS   Conacite II,
   1986, Mexican
LO QUE IMPORTA ES VIVIR   Peliculas
   Mexicanas, 1989, Mexican
DIA DE DIFUNTOS   Televicine,
   1989, Mexican
CUATRO POSTES   Rosa Garcia PC,
   1990, Spanish

ROBERT ALDRICH
b. August 9, 1918 - Cranston, Rhode Island
d. 1983

THE BIG LEAGUER   MGM, 1953
WORLD FOR RANSOM   Allied Artists, 1954
APACHE   United Artists, 1954
VERA CRUZ   United Artists, 1954
KISS ME DEADLY   United Artists, 1955
THE BIG KNIFE   United Artists, 1955
AUTUMN LEAVES   Columbia, 1956
ATTACK!   United Artists, 1956
THE ANGRY HILLS   MGM, 1959
TEN SECONDS TO HELL   United Artists,
   1959, British
THE LAST SUNSET   Universal, 1961
SODOM AND GOMORRAH   20th Century-Fox,
   1961, Italian-French-U.S.
WHAT EVER HAPPENED TO BABY JANE?
   Warner Bros., 1962
4 FOR TEXAS   Warner Bros., 1963
HUSH...HUSH, SWEET CHARLOTTE
   20th Century-Fox, 1964
THE FLIGHT OF THE PHOENIX
   20th Century-Fox, 1965
THE DIRTY DOZEN   MGM, 1967
THE LEGEND OF LYLAH CLARE
   MGM, 1968
THE KILLING OF SISTER GEORGE
   Cinerama Releasing Corporation, 1968
WHAT EVER HAPPENED TO AUNT ALICE?
   Cinerama Releasing Corporation, 1968
TOO LATE THE HERO   Cinerama Releasing
   Corporation, 1970
THE GRISSOM GANG   Cinerama Releasing
   Corporation, 1971
ULZANA'S RAID   Universal, 1972
EMPEROR OF THE NORTH POLE
   EMPEROR OF THE NORTH
   20th Century-Fox, 1973
THE LONGEST YARD   Paramount, 1974
HUSTLE   Paramount, 1975
TWILIGHT'S LAST GLEAMING   Allied Artists,
   1977, U.S.-West German
THE CHOIRBOYS   Universal, 1977
THE FRISCO KID   Warner Bros., 1979
...ALL THE MARBLES   MGM/United
   Artists, 1981

GRIGORI ALEXANDROV
(Grigori Mormonenko)
b. February 23, 1903 - Yekaterinburg, Russia
d. ?

OCTOBER   co-director with Sergei Eisenstein,
   Amkino, 1928, Soviet
THE GENERAL LINE   OLD AND NEW
   co-director with Sergei Eisenstein,
   1929, Soviet
MEETING ON THE ELBE   1949, Soviet
GLINKA   1952, Soviet

MARC ALLEGRET
b. December 22, 1900 - Basle, Switzerland
d. 1973

LES AMANTS DE MINUIT   co-director with
   Augusto Genina, 1931, French
MAM'ZELLE NITOUCHE   1931, French
LA PETITE CHOCOLATIERE   1932, French
FANNY   Pathe Contemporary, 1932, French
LAC AUX DAMES   1934, French
L'HOTEL DU LIBRE-ECHANGE   1934, French
ZOU-ZOU   1934, French
SANS FAMILLE   1934, French
LES BEAUX JOURS   1935, French
SOUS LES YEUX D'OCCIDENT
   1936, French
LES AMANTS TERRIBLES   1936, French
AVENTURE A PARIS   1936, French
GRIBOUILLE   1937, French
LA DAME DE MALACCA   1937, French
ORAGE   1938, French
ENTREE DE ARTISTES   1938, French
LE CORSAIRE   1939, French
PARADE EN SEPT NUITS   1941, French
L'ARLESIENNE   1942, French
FELICIE NANTEUIL   1943, French
LES PETITES DU QUAI AUX FLEURS
   1944, French
LA BELLE AVENTURE   1945, French
LUNEGARDE   1946, French
PETRUS   1946, French
BLANCHE FURY   Eagle Lion, 1948, British
THE NAKED HEART   MARIA CHAPDELAINE
   Associated Artists, 1950,
   British-French-Canadian
BLACKMAILED   Bell Pictures, 1951, British
AVEC ANDRE GIDE (FD)   1952, French
LA DEMOISELLE ET SON REVENANT
   1952, French
JULIETTA   Kingsley International,
   1953, French
LOVE OF THREE QUEENS   L'AMANTE DI
   PARIDE   Robert Patrick Productions,
   1954, Italian
FUTURES VEDETTES   1955, French
LADY CHATTERLEY'S LOVER   Kingsley
   International, 1955, French
PLEASE, MR. BALZAC   EN EFFEUILLANT LA
   MARGUERITE   DCA, 1956, French
L'AMOUR EST EN JEU   1957, French
BE BEAUTIFUL, BUT SHUT UP   SOIS BELLE
   ET TAIS-TOI   1957, French
UN DROLE DE DIMANCHE   1958, French
LES AFFREUX   1959, French
LES DEMONS DE MINUIT   co-director with
   Charles Gerard, 1961, French
TALES OF PARIS   LES PARISIENNES   Times
   Film Corporation, 1962, French-Italian
L'ABOMINABLE HOMME DES DOUANES
   1963, French
LE BAL DU COMTE D'ORGEL   1970, French

YVES ALLEGRET
b. October 13, 1907 - Paris, France
d. 1987

TOBIE EST UN ANGE   1941,
   French, unreleased
LES DEUX TIMIDES   1942, French
LA BOITE AUX REVES   1945, French
LES DEMONS DE L'AUBE   1946, French
DEDEE D'ANVERS   1948, French
UNE SI JOLIE PETITE PLAGE   1949, French
MANEGES   1950, French
LES MIRACLES N'ONT LIEU QU'UNE FOIS
   1951, French
SEVEN DEADLY SINS   co-director,
   Arian Pictures, 1952, French
NEZ DE CUIR   1952, French
LA JEUNE FOLLE   1952, French
THE PROUD AND THE BEAUTIFUL
   LES ORGUEILLEUX   Kingsley International,
   1953, French
MAM'ZELLE NITOUCHE   1954, French
OASIS   20th Century-Fox, 1954,
   French-West German
LA MEILLEURE PART   1956, French
QUAND LA FEMME S'EN MELE
   1957, French
YOUNG GIRLS BEWARE   United Motion
   Picture Organization, 1957, French
LA FILLE DE HAMBOURG   1958, French
L'AMBITIEUSE   1959, French
LA CHIEN DE PIQUE   1961, French
KONGA YO (FD)   1962, French
GERMINAL   1963, French-Hungarian
JOHNNY BANCO   Ben Barry and Associates,
   1967, West German-French-Italian
L'INVASION   1970, French
ORZOWEI   1975, French
MORDS PAS - ON T'AIME   1976, French

IRWIN ALLEN
b. June 12, 1916 - New York, New York
d. 1991

THE SEA AROUND US (FD)
   RKO Radio, 1951
THE ANIMAL WORLD (FD)
   Warner Bros., 1956
THE STORY OF MANKIND
   Warner Bros., 1957
THE LOST WORLD   20th Century-Fox, 1960
VOYAGE TO THE BOTTOM OF THE SEA
   20th Century-Fox, 1961
FIVE WEEKS IN A BALLOON
   20th Century-Fox, 1962
CITY BENEATH THE SEA (TF)
   20th Century-Fox TV/Motion Pictures
   International, 1971
THE TOWERING INFERNO
   20th Century-Fox, 1974,
   action sequences only
THE SWARM   Warner Bros., 1978
BEYOND THE POSEIDON ADVENTURE
   Warner Bros., 1979

ROBERT ALTON
(Robert Alton Hart)
b. January 28, 1903 - Bennington, Vermont
d. 1957

MERTON OF THE MOVIES   MGM, 1947
PAGAN LOVE SONG   MGM, 1950

LINDSAY ANDERSON
b. April 17, 1923 - Bangalore, India
d. 1994

THIS SPORTING LIFE   Continental,
   1962, British
IF...   Paramount, 1969, British
O LUCKY MAN!   Warner Bros., 1973, British
IN CELEBRATION   American Film Theatre,
   1975, British-Canadian
BRITTANIA HOSPITAL   United Artists
   Classics, 1982, British
WISH YOU WERE THERE   FOREIGN
   SKIES (FCD) 1985, British
THE WHALES OF AUGUST   Alive Films, 1987
GLORY! GLORY! (CTF)   HBO Pictures/
   Atlantis Films Ltd./Orion TV/Stan Daniels
   Productions/Greif-Dore Company, 1989

JOSEPH ANTHONY
b. May 24, 1912 - Milwaukee, Wisconsin
d. 1993

THE RAINMAKER   Paramount, 1956
THE MATCHMAKER   Paramount, 1958
CAREER   Paramount, 1959
ALL IN A NIGHT'S WORK   Paramount, 1961
CONQUERED CITY   American International,
   1966, Italian
TOMORROW   Filmgroup, 1972

ROSCOE "FATTY" ARBUCKLE
(Roscoe Conkling Arbuckle/
   William B. Goodrich)
b. March 24, 1887 - Smith Center, Kansas
d. 1933

THE ALARM   co-director with
   Eddie Dillon, 1914
THE SKY PIRATE   co-director with
   Eddie Dillon, 1914
FATTY AND THE HEIRESS   co-director with
   Eddie Dillon, 1914
FATTY'S GIFT   co-director with
   Eddie Dillon, 1914
A BRAND NEW HERO   co-director with
   Eddie Dillon, 1914
FATTY'S DEBUT   co-director with
   Eddie Dillon, 1914
FATTY AGAIN   1914
LEADING LIZZIE ASTRAY   co-director with
   Eddie Dillon, 1914
FATTY'S JONAH DAY   co-director with
   Eddie Dillon, 1914
FATTY'S MAGIC PANTS   co-director with
   Eddie Dillon, 1914
FATTY'S WINE PARTY   co-director with
   Eddie Dillon, 1914
FATTY AND MINNIE HE-HAW   co-director
   with Eddie Dillon, 1915
FATTY'S FAITHFUL FIDO   co-director with
   Eddie Dillon, 1915
THAT LITTLE BAND OF GOLD   1915
WHEN LOVE TOOK WINGS   1915
FATTY'S NEW ROLE   co-director with
   Eddie Dillon, 1915
FICKLE FATTY'S FALL   1915
FATTY AND THE BROADWAY STARS
   co-director with Eddie Dillon, 1915
THE VILLAGE SCANDAL   1915
FATTY AND MABEL ADRIFT   1916
HE DID AND HE DIDN'T
   LOVE AND LOBSTERS   1916
BRIGHT LIGHTS
   THE LURE OF BROADWAY   1916
HIS WIFE'S MISTAKE   1916
THE OTHER MAN   1916

THE WAITER'S BALL   1916
HIS ALIBI   1916
A CREAM PUFF ROMANCE
   A RECKLESS ROMEO   1916
THE MOONSHINERS   1916
THE BUTCHER BOY   1917
THE ROUGH HOUSE   1917
HIS WEDDING NIGHT   1917
OH DOCTOR!   1917
FATT AT CONEY ISLAND   1917
A COUNTRY HERO   1917
OUT WEST   1918
THE BELL BOY   1918
MOONSHINE   1918
GOOD NIGHT NURSE   1918
THE COOK   1918
LOVE   1919
A DESERT HERO   1919
BACK STAGE   1919
THE HAYSEED   1919
THE GARAGE   1920
THE MOVIES   1925, directed under
   pseudonym of William B. Goodrich
THE TOURIST   1925, directed under
   pseudonym of William B. Goodrich
THE FIGHTING DUDE   1925, directed under
   pseudonym of William B. Goodrich
CLEANING UP   1926, directed under
   pseudonym of William B. Goodrich
MY STARS   1926, directed under pseudonym
   of William B. Goodrich
FOOL'S LUCK   1926, directed under
   pseudonym of William B. Goodrich
HIS PRIVATE LIFE   1926, directed under
   pseudonym of William B. Goodrich
THE RED MILL   1927, directed under
   pseudonym of William B. Goodrich
SPECIAL DELIVERY   1927, directed under
   pseudonym of William B. Goodrich
WON BY A NECK   1930, directed under
   pseudonym of William B. Goodrich
UP A TREE   1930, directed under pseudonym
   of William B. Goodrich
SMART WORK   1931, directed under
   pseudonym of William B. Goodrich
THE TAMALE VENDOR   1931, directed under
   pseudonym of William B. Goodrich
THE LURE OF HOLLYWOOD   1931, directed
   under pseudonym of William B. Goodrich
HONEYMOON TRIO   1931, directed under
   pseudonym of William B. Goodrich
UP POPS THE DUKE   1931, directed under
   pseudonym of William B. Goodrich
THE BACK PAGE   1931, directed under
   pseudonym of William B. Goodrich
MARRIAGE ROWS   1931, directed under
   pseudonym of William B. Goodrich
BEACH PAJAMAS   1931, directed under
   pseudonym of William B. Goodrich
BRIDGE WIVES   1932, directed under
   pseudonym of William B. Goodrich
IT'S A CINCH   1932, directed under
   pseudonym of William B. Goodrich
KEEP LAUGHING   1932, directed under
   pseudonym of William B. Goodrich
MOONLIGHT AND CACTUS   1932, directed
   under pseudonym of William B. Goodrich
NIAGARA FALLS   1932, directed under
   pseudonym of William B. Goodrich
GIGOLETTES   1932, directed under
   pseudonym of William B. Goodrich
HOLLYWOOD LUCK   1932, directed under
   pseudonym of William B. Goodrich
ANYBODY'S GOAT   1932, directed under
   pseudonym of William B. Goodrich

EMILE ARDOLINO
b. Queens, New York
d. 1993

HE MAKES ME FEEL LIKE DANCIN' (FD)
NBC, 1983
DIRTY DANCING   Vestron, 1987
CHANCES ARE   TriStar, 1989
THREE MEN AND A LITTLE LADY
Buena Vista, 1990
SISTER ACT   Buena Vista, 1992
GEORGE BALANCHINE'S THE
NUTCRACKER *THE NUTCRACKER* (PF)
Warner Bros., 1993
GYPSY (TF) ☆ RHI Entertainment 1993

LESLIE ARLISS
(Leslie Andrews)
b. 1901 - London, England
d. 1988

THE FARMER'S WIFE   co-director with
Norman Lee, 1941, British
THE NIGHT HAS EYES   1942, British
THE MAN IN GREY   Universal, 1943, British
A LADY SURRENDERS *LOVE STORY*
Universal, 1944, British
THE WICKED LADY   Universal, 1945, British
A MAN ABOUT THE HOUSE
20th Century-Fox, 1947, British
IDOL OF PARIS   1948, British
SAINTS AND SINNERS   Lopert, 1949, British
THE WOMAN'S ANGLE   1952, British
SEE HOW THEY RUN   1955, British
MISS TULIP STAYS THE NIGHT   1955, British

JACK ARNOLD
b. October 14, 1916 - New Haven, Connecticut
d. 1992

GIRLS IN THE NIGHT   Universal, 1953
IT CAME FROM OUTER SPACE
Universal, 1953
THE GLASS WEB   Universal, 1953
THE CREATURE FROM THE BLACK
LAGOON   Universal, 1954
REVENGE OF THE CREATURE
Universal, 1955
THE MAN FROM BITTER RIDGE
Universal, 1955
TARANTULA   Universal, 1955
OUTSIDE THE LAW   Universal, 1956
RED SUNDOWN   Universal, 1956
THE INCREDIBLE SHRINKING MAN
Universal, 1957
THE TATTERED DRESS   Universal, 1957
MAN IN THE SHADOW   Universal, 1958
THE LADY TAKES A FLYER   Universal, 1958
THE SPACE CHILDREN   Paramount, 1958
MONSTER ON THE CAMPUS   Universal, 1958
THE MOUSE THAT ROARED   Columbia,
1959, British
NO NAME ON THE BULLET   Universal, 1959
BACHELOR IN PARADISE   MGM, 1961
THE LIVELY SET   Universal, 1964
A GLOBAL AFFAIR   MGM, 1964
HELLO DOWN THERE   Paramount, 1969
BLACK EYE   Warner Bros., 1974
THE GAMES GIRLS PLAY
General Films, 1975
BOSS NIGGER   Dimension, 1975
THE SWISS CONSPIRACY
SJ International, 1977
SEX AND THE MARRIED WOMAN (TF)
Universal TV, 1977
MARILYN: THE UNTOLD STORY (TF)
co-director with John Flynn & Lawrence
Schiller, Lawrence Schiller Productions, 1980

DOROTHY ARZNER
b. January 3, 1900 - San Francisco, California
d. 1979

FASHIONS FOR WOMEN   Paramount, 1927
TEN MODERN COMMANDMENTS
Paramount, 1927
GET YOUR MAN   Paramount, 1927
MANHATTAN COCKTAIL   Paramount, 1928
THE WILD PARTY   Paramount, 1928
SARAH AND SON   Paramount, 1930
PARAMOUNT ON PARADE   co-director,
Paramount, 1930
ANYBODY'S WOMAN   Paramount, 1930
HONOR AMONG LOVERS   Paramount, 1931
WORKING GIRLS   Paramount, 1931
MERRILY WE GO TO HELL   Paramount, 1932
CHRISTOPHER STRONG   RKO Radio, 1933
NANA   United Artists, 1934
CRAIG'S WIFE   Columbia, 1936
THE BRIDE WORE RED   MGM, 1937
DANCE, GIRL, DANCE   RKO Radio, 1940
FIRST COMES COURAGE   Columbia, 1943

HAL ASHBY
b. 1936 - Ogden, Utah
d. 1988

THE LANDLORD   United Artists, 1970
HAROLD AND MAUDE   Paramount, 1971
THE LAST DETAIL   Columbia, 1973
SHAMPOO   Columbia, 1975
BOUND FOR GLORY   United Artists, 1976
COMING HOME ★   United Artists, 1978
BEING THERE   United Artists, 1979
SECOND HAND HEARTS   Paramount, 1981
LOOKIN' TO GET OUT   Paramount, 1982
LET'S SPEND THE NIGHT TOGETHER (FCD)
Embassy, 1983
THE SLUGGER'S WIFE   Columbia, 1985
8 MILLION WAYS TO DIE   TriStar, 1986

ANTHONY ASQUITH
b. November 9, 1902 - London, England
d. 1968

SHOOTING STARS   New Era, 1928
UNDERGROUND   Pro Patria, 1928, British
THE RUNAWAY PRINCESS   VMG,
1929, German
A COTTAGE ON DARTMOOR
ESCAPED FROM DARTMOOR
Pro Patria, 1930, British
TELL ENGLAND *THE BATTLE OF
GALLIPOLI*   co-director with
Geoffrey Barkas, Wardour, 1931, British
DANCE PRETTY LADY   Wardour,
1932, British
LUCKY NUMBER   Ideal, 1933, British
THE UNFINISHED SYMPHONY
co-director with Will Forst, Gaumont, 1934,
British-German
I STAND CONDEMNED *MOSCOW NIGHTS*
United Artists, 1935, British
PYGMALION   co-director with Leslie Howard,
MGM, 1938, British
FRENCH WITHOUT TEARS   Paramount,
1940, British
A VOICE IN THE NIGHT *FREEDOM RADIO*
Columbia, 1941, British
QUIET WEDDING   Universal, 1941, British
COTTAGE TO LET *BOMBSIGHT STOLEN*
Rank, 1941, British
UNCENSORED   General Film Distributors,
1942, British
THE DEMI-PARADISE *ADVENTURE
FOR TWO*   General Film Distributors,
1943, British

WE DIVE AT DAWN   General Film Distributors,
1943, British
WELCOME TO BRITAIN (FD)   co-director with
Burgess Meredith, 1943, British
MAN OF EVIL *FANNY BY GASLIGHT*
United Artists, 1944, British
THE WAY TO THE STARS *JOHNNY IN THE
CLOUDS*   United Artists, 1945, British
WHILE THE SUN SHINES   Pathé,
1947, British
THE WINSLOW BOY   British Lion Film
Corporation, 1948, British
THE WOMAN IN QUESTION *FIVE ANGLES
ON MURDER*   Columbia, 1950, British
THE BROWNING VERSION   Universal,
1951, British
THE IMPORTANCE OF BEING EARNEST
Universal, 1952, British
PROJECT M-7 *THE NET*   Universal,
1953, British
CHANCE MEETING *THE YOUNG LOVERS*
Pacemaker Pictures, 1954, British
COURT MARTIAL *CARRINGTON, V.C.*
Kingsley International, 1955, British
ORDERS TO KILL   United Motion Picture
Organization, 1958, British
THE DOCTOR'S DILEMMA   MGM,
1958, British
LIBEL   MGM, 1959, British
THE MILLIONAIRESS   20th Century-Fox,
1960, British
TWO LIVING, ONE DEAD   Emerson Films,
1961, British-Swedish
GUNS OF DARKNESS   Warner Bros.,
1962, British
THE V.I.P.'S   MGM, 1963, British-U.S.
AN EVENING WITH THE ROYAL BALLET (PF)
co-director with Anthony Havelock-Allan,
Sigma III, 1964, British
THE YELLOW ROLLS-ROYCE   MGM,
1965, British

JOHN H. AUER
b. August 3, 1906 - Budapest, Austria-Hungary
d. 1975

UNA VIDA PER OTRA   1933, Mexican
SU ULTIMA CANCION   1934, Mexican
THE PERVERT   1934, Mexican
REST IN PEACE   1934, Mexican
FRANKIE AND JOHNNIE   Republic, 1935
THE CRIME OF DR. CRESPI   Republic, 1935
A MAN BETRAYED   Republic, 1937
CIRCUS GIRL   Republic, 1937
RHYTHM IN THE CLOUDS   Republic, 1937
OUTSIDE OF PARADISE   Republic, 1938
INVISIBLE ENEMY   Republic, 1938
A DESPERATE ADVENTURE   Republic, 1938
I STAND ACCUSED   Republic, 1938
ORPHANS OF THE STREET   Republic, 1938
FORGED PASSPORT   Republic, 1939
S.O.S. TIDAL WAVE   Republic, 1939
SMUGGLED CARGO   Republic, 1939
CALLING ALL MARINES   Republic, 1939
THOU SHALT NOT KILL   Republic, 1940
WOMEN IN WAR   Republic, 1940
THE HIT PARADE OF 1941   Republic, 1940
A MAN BETRAYED *WHEEL OF FORTUNE*
Republic, 1941
THE DEVIL PAYS OFF   Republic, 1941
PARDON MY STRIPES   Republic, 1942
MOONLIGHT MASQUERADE   Republic, 1942
JOHNNY DOUGHBOY   Republic, 1942
TAHITI HONEY   Republic, 1943
GANGWAY FOR TOMORROW
RKO Radio, 1943
SEVEN DAYS ASHORE   RKO Radio, 1944
MUSIC IN MANHATTAN   RKO Radio, 1944

PAN-AMERICANA   RKO Radio, 1945
BEAT THE BAND   RKO Radio, 1947
THE FLAME   Republic, 1947
I, JANE DOE   Republic, 1948
ANGEL ON THE AMAZON   Republic, 1948
THE AVENGERS   Republic, 1950
THE HIT PARADE OF 1951   Republic, 1950
THUNDERBIRDS   Republic, 1952
THE CITY THAT NEVER SLEEPS
   Republic, 1953
HELL'S HALF ACRE   Republic, 1954
THE ETERNAL SEA   Republic, 1955
JOHNNY TROUBLE   Warner Bros., 1957

ARAM AVAKIAN
b. 1926 - New York, New York
d. 1987

LAD: A DOG   co-director with
   Leslie H. Martinson, Warner Bros., 1961
END OF THE ROAD   Allied Artists, 1970
COPS AND ROBBERS   United Artists, 1973
11 HARROWHOUSE   20th Century-Fox,
   1974, British

B

LLOYD BACON
b. January 16, 1890 - San Jose, California
d. 1955

BROKEN HEARTS OF HOLLYWOOD
   Warner Bros., 1926
PRIVATE IZZY MURPHY   Warner Bros., 1926
FINGER PRINTS   Warner Bros., 1927
WHITE FLANNELS   Warner Bros., 1927
THE HEART OF MARYLAND
   Warner Bros., 1927
A SAILOR'S SWEETHEART
   Warner Bros., 1927
BRASS KNUCKLES   Warner Bros., 1927
PAY AS YOU ENTER   Warner Bros., 1928
THE LION AND THE MOUSE
   Warner Bros., 1928
WOMEN THEY TALK ABOUT
   Warner Bros., 1928
THE SINGING FOOL   Warner Bros., 1928
STARK MAD   Warner Bros., 1929
NO DEFENSE   Warner Bros., 1929
HONKY TONK   Warner Bros., 1929
SAY IT WITH SONGS   Warner Bros., 1929
SO LONG LETTY   Warner Bros., 1929
THE OTHER TOMORROW
   First National, 1930
SHE COULDN'T SAY NO   Warner Bros., 1930
A NOTORIOUS AFFAIR   First National, 1930
MOBY DICK   Warner Bros., 1930
THE OFFICE WIFE   Warner Bros., 1930
SIT TIGHT   Warner Bros., 1931
KEPT HUSBANDS   RKO, 1931
FIFTY MILLION FRENCHMEN
   Warner Bros., 1931
GOLD DUST GERTIE   Warner Bros., 1931
HONOR OF THE FAMILY   First National, 1931
MANHATTAN PARADE   Warner Bros., 1932
FIREMAN SAVE MY CHILD
   First National, 1932
THE FAMOUS FERGUSON CASE
   First National, 1932

ALIAS THE DOCTOR   co-director with
   Michael Curtiz, Warner Bros., 1932
MISS PINKERTON   First National, 1932
CROONER   First National, 1932
YOU SAID A MOUTHFUL   First National, 1932
42ND STREET   Warner Bros., 1933
PICTURE SNATCHER   Warner Bros., 1933
MARY STEVENS, M.D.   Warner Bros., 1933
FOOTLIGHT PARADE   Warner Bros., 1933
SON OF A SAILOR   First National, 1933
WONDER BAR   First National, 1934
A VERY HONORABLE GUY
   First National, 1934
HE WAS HER MAN   Warner Bros., 1934
HERE COMES THE NAVY
   Warner Bros., 1934
SIX-DAY BIKE RIDER   Warner Bros., 1934
DEVIL DOGS OF THE AIR
   Warner Bros., 1935
IN CALIENTE   First National, 1935
BROADWAY GONDOLIER
   Warner Bros., 1935
THE IRISH IN US   Warner Bros., 1935
FRISCO KID   Warner Bros., 1935
SONS O'GUNS   Warner Bros., 1936
CAIN AND MABEL   Warner Bros., 1936
GOLD DIGGERS OF 1937
   Warner Bros., 1936
MARKED WOMAN   Warner Bros., 1937
EVER SINCE EVE   Warner Bros., 1937
SAN QUENTIN   Warner Bros., 1937
SUBMARINE D-1   First National, 1937
A SLIGHT CASE OF MURDER
   Warner Bros., 1938
COWBOY FROM BROOKLYN
   Warner Bros., 1938
RACKET BUSTERS   Warner Bros., 1938
BOY MEETS GIRL   Warner Bros., 1938
WINGS OF THE NAVY   Warner Bros., 1939
THE OKLAHOMA KID   Warner Bros., 1939
INDIANAPOLIS SPEEDWAY
   Warner Bros., 1939
ESPIONAGE AGENT   Warner Bros., 1939
A CHILD IS BORN   Warner Bros., 1940
INVISIBLE STRIPES   Warner Bros., 1940
THREE CHEERS FOR THE IRISH
   Warner Bros., 1940
BROTHER ORCHID   Warner Bros., 1940
KNUTE ROCKNE - ALL AMERICAN
   Warner Bros., 1940
HONEYMOON FOR THREE
   Warner Bros., 1941
FOOTSTEPS IN THE DARK
   Warner Bros., 1941
AFFECTIONATELY YOURS
   Warner Bros., 1941
NAVY BLUES   Warner Bros., 1941
LARCENY INC.   Warner Bros., 1941
WINGS FOR THE EAGLE
   Warner Bros., 1941
SILVER QUEEN   Warner Bros., 1942
ACTION IN THE NORTH ATLANTIC
   Warner Bros., 1943
THE SULLIVANS   20th Century-Fox, 1944
SUNDAY DINNER FOR A SOLDIER
   20th Century-Fox, 1944
CAPTAIN EDDIE   20th Century-Fox, 1945
HOME SWEET HOMICIDE
   20th Century-Fox, 1946
WAKE UP AND DREAM
   20th Century-Fox, 1946
I WONDER WHO'S KISSING HER NOW
   20th Century-Fox, 1947
YOU WERE MEANT FOR ME
   20th Century-Fox, 1948
GIVE MY REGARDS TO BROADWAY
   20th Century-Fox, 1948

DON'T TRUST YOUR HUSBAND   AN
   INNOCENT AFFAIR   United Artists, 1948
MOTHER IS A FRESHMAN
   20th Century-Fox, 1949
IT HAPPENS EVERY SPRING
   20th Century-Fox, 1949
MISS GRANT TAKES RICHMOND
   Columbia, 1949
KILL THE UMPIRE   Columbia, 1950
THE GOOD HUMOR MAN   Columbia, 1950
THE FULLER BRUSH GIRL   Columbia, 1950
CALL ME MISTER   20th Century-Fox, 1951
THE FROGMEN   20th Century-Fox, 1951
GOLDEN GIRL   20th Century-Fox, 1951
THE I DON'T CARE GIRL
   20th Century-Fox, 1953
THE GREAT SIOUX UPRISING
   Universal, 1953
WALKING MY BABY BACK HOME
   Universal, 1953
THE FRENCH LINE   RKO Radio, 1953
SHE COULDN'T SAY NO   RKO Radio, 1953

LIONEL BARRYMORE
(Lionel Blythe)
b. April 29, 1878 - Philadelphia, Pennsylvania
d. 1954

LIFE'S WHIRLPOOL   1917
MADAME X ★   MGM, 1929
HIS GLORIOUS NIGHT   MGM, 1929
THE UNHOLY NIGHT   MGM, 1929
THE ROGUE SONG   MGM, 1930
TEN CENTS A DANCE   MGM, 1931

HALL BARTLETT
b. November 27, 1922 - Kansas City, Missouri
d. 1993

NAVAJO   Lippert, 1952
CRAZYLEGS   Republic, 1954
UNCHAINED   Warner Bros., 1955
DURANGO   co-director with Jules Bricken,
   United Artists, 1957
ZERO HOUR   Paramount, 1957
ALL THE YOUNG MEN   Columbia, 1960
THE CARETAKERS   United Artists, 1963
CHANGES   Cinerama Releasing
   Corporation, 1969
THE WILD PACK   THE SANDPIT GENERALS/
   THE DEFIANT   American
   International, 1972
JONATHAN LIVINGSTON SEAGULL
   Paramount, 1973
THE CHILDREN OF SANCHEZ   Lone Star,
   1978, U.S.-Mexican
LOVE IS FOREVER (TF)   Michael Landon-
   Hall Bartlett Films/NBC-TV/20th
   Century-Fox TV, 1983
LEAVING HOME   Hall Bartlett Films, 1986

CHARLES T. BARTON
b. May 25, 1902 - San Francisco, California
d. 1981

WAGON WHEELS   Paramount, 1934
CAR 99   Paramount, 1935
ROCKY MOUNTAIN MYSTERY
   Paramount, 1935
THE LAST OUTPOST   co-director with
   Louis J. Gasnier, Paramount, 1935
TIMOTHY'S QUEST   Paramount, 1936
NEVADA   Paramount, 1936
AND SUDDEN DEATH   Paramount, 1936
ROSE BOWL   1936
MURDER WITH PICTURES   1936
THE CRIME NOBODY SAW   1937

FORLORN RIVER 1937
THUNDER TRAIL 1937
BORN TO THE WEST 1938
TITANS OF THE DEEP 1938
BEHIND PRISON GATES 1939
FIVE LITTLE PEPPERS AND HOW THEY
    GREW Columbia, 1939
MY SON IS GUILTY Columbia, 1940
FIVE LITTLE PEPPERS AT HOME
    Columbia, 1940
ISLAND OF DOOMED MEN Columbia, 1940
BABIES FOR SALE Columbia, 1940
OUT WEST WITH THE PEPPERS
    Columbia, 1940
FIVE LITTLE PEPPERS IN TROUBLE
    Columbia, 1940
NOBODY'S CHILDREN Columbia, 1940
THE PHANTOM SUBMARINE
    Columbia, 1941
THE BIG BOSS Columbia, 1941
RICHEST MAN IN TOWN Columbia, 1941
TWO LATINS FROM MANHATTAN
    Columbia, 1941
HARMON OF MICHIGAN Columbia, 1941
SING FOR YOUR SUPPER Columbia, 1941
HONOLULU LU Columbia, 1941
SHUT MY BIG MOUTH Columbia, 1942
TRAMP, TRAMP, TRAMP Columbia, 1942
HELLO, ANNAPOLIS Columbia, 1942
SWEETHEART OF THE FLEET
    Columbia, 1942
PARACHUTE NURSE Columbia, 1942
A MAN'S WORLD Columbia, 1942
LUCKY LEGS Columbia, 1942
SPIRIT OF STANFORD Columbia, 1942
LAUGH YOUR BLUES AWAY
    Columbia, 1942
REVEILLE WITH BEVERLY Columbia, 1943
LET'S HAVE FUN Columbia, 1943
SHE HAS WHAT IT TAKES Columbia, 1943
WHAT'S BUZZIN', COUSIN?
    Columbia, 1943
IS EVERYBODY HAPPY? Columbia, 1943
BEAUTIFUL BUT BROKE Columbia, 1944
HEY, ROOKIE Columbia, 1944
JAM SESSION Columbia, 1944
LOUISIANA HAYRIDE Columbia, 1944
THE BEAUTIFUL CHEAT Universal, 1945
MEN IN HER DIARY Universal, 1945
SMOOTH AS SILK Universal, 1946
WHITE TIE AND TAILS Universal, 1946
THE TIME OF THEIR LIVES THE GHOST
    STEPS OUT Universal, 1946
BUCK PRIVATES COME HOME
    Universal, 1947
THE WISTFUL WIDOW OF WAGON GAP
    Universal, 1947
THE NOOSE HANGS HIGH Universal, 1948
ABBOTT AND COSTELLO MEET
    FRANKENSTEIN Universal, 1948
MEXICAN HAYRIDE Universal, 1948
AFRICA SCREAMS Universal, 1949
ABBOTT AND COSTELLO MEET THE KILLER
    BORIS KARLOFF Universal, 1949
FREE FOR ALL Universal, 1949
THE MILKMAN Universal, 1950
DOUBLE CROSSBONES Universal, 1951
MA & PA KETTLE AT THE FAIR
    Universal, 1952
DANCE WITH ME, HENRY
    United Artists, 1956
THE SHAGGY DOG Buena Vista, 1959
TOBY TYLER Buena Vista, 1960
SWINGIN' ALONG 20th Century-Fox, 1962

MARIO BAVA
b. July 31, 1914 - San Remo, Italy
d. 1980

BLACK SUNDAY LA MASCHERA DEL
    DEMONIO American International,
    1960, Italian
ERIK THE CONQUEROR GLI INVASORI/
    FURY OF THE VIKINGS American
    International, 1961, Italian-French
HERCULES IN THE HAUNTED WORLD
    ERCOLE AL CENTRO DELLA TERRA
    Woolner Brothers, 1961, Italian
EVIL EYE LA RAGAZZA CHE SAPEVE
    TROPPO American International,
    1963, Italian
WHAT! LA FRUSTA E IL CORPO Futuramic
    Releasing Organization, 1963,
    Italian-French-British
BLACK SABBATH I TRE VOLTI DELLA
    PAURA American International, 1963,
    U.S.-French-Italian
BLOOD AND BLACK LACE SEI DONNE PER
    L'ASSASSINO Allied Artists, 1964,
    Italian-French-Monocan
LA STRADA PER FORT ALAMO 1965, Italian
RAFFICA DI COLTELLI 1965 Italian
PLANET OF THE VAMPIRES PLANET
    OF BLOOD/TERRORE NELLO SPAZIO
    American International, 1965,
    Italian-Spanish-U.S.
KILL BABY KILL OPERAZIONE PAURA
    Europix-Consolidated, 1966, Italian
DR. GOLDFOOT AND THE GIRL BOMBS
    LE SPIEVENGONO DAL SEMIFREDDO
    American International, 1966, U.S.-Italian
KNIVES OF THE AVENGER 1967, Italian
DANGER: DIABOLIK Paramount, 1967,
    Italian-French
CINQUE BAMBOLE PER LA LUNA
    DI AGOSTO 1967, Italian
ROY COLT E WINCHESTER JACK
    1970, Italian
HATCHET FOR THE HONEYMOON
    IL ROSSOSEGNO DELLA FOLLIA/
    UN'ACCETTAPER LA LUNA DI MIELE
    GGP, 1970, Italian-Spanish
ECOLOGIA DEL DELITTO 1970, Italian
ANTEFATTO 1971, Italian
BARON BLOOD GLI ORRORI DEL
    CASTELLO DE NORIMBERGA American
    International, 1972, Italian-West German
REAZIONE A CATENA 1973, Italian
QUANTE VOLTE...QUELLA NOTTE
    1973, Italian
IL DIAVOLO E IL MORTO 1974, Italian
SHOCK 1977, Italian
BABY KONG 1977, Italian
LA VENERE DELL'ILLE 1979, Italian

WILLIAM BEAUDINE
b. January 15, 1892 - New York, New York
d. 1970

ALMOST A KING 1915
A BAD LITTLE GOOD MAN 1917
WATCH YOUR STEP Goldwyn, 1922
CATCH MY SMOKE 1922
HEROES OF THE STREET
    Warner Bros., 1922
HER FATAL MILLIONS Metro, 1923
PENROD AND SAM First National, 1923
THE PRINTER'S DEVIL 1923
THE COUNTRY KID Warner Bros., 1923
BOY OF MINE First National, 1923
DARING YOUTH Principal, 1924
DAUGHTERS OF PLEASURE Principal, 1924

WANDERING HUSBANDS Producers
    Distributing Corporation, 1924
A SELF-MADE FAILURE First National, 1924
CORNERED Warner Bros., 1924
LOVER'S LANE Warner Bros., 1924
THE NARROW STREET Warner Bros., 1924
A BROADWAY BUTTERFLY
    Warner Bros., 1925
LITTLE ANNIE ROONEY United Artists, 1925
THAT'S MY BABY Paramount, 1926
THE SOCIAL HIGHWAYMAN
    Pearless-World, 1926
SPARROWS United Artists, 1926
THE CANADIAN Paramount, 1926
FRISCO SALLY LEVY MGM, 1927
THE LIFE OF RILEY First National, 1927
THE IRRESISTABLE LOVER Universal, 1927
THE COHENS AND THE KELLYS IN PARIS
    Universal, 1928
HEART TO HEART First National, 1928
HOME JAMES Universal, 1928
DO YOUR DUTY First National, 1928
GIVE AND TAKE Universal, 1928
FUGITIVES Fox, 1929
TWO WEEKS OFF First National, 1929
THE GIRL FROM WOOLWORTH'S
    First National, 1929
WEDDING RINGS First National, 1929
THOSE WHO DANCE Warner Bros., 1930
THE ROAD TO PARADISE
    Warner Bros., 1930
FATHER'S SON Warner Bros., 1931
THE LADY WHO DARED Warner Bros., 1931
THE MAD PARADE Paramount, 1931
PENROD AND SAM Warner Bros., 1931
MISBEHAVING LADIES Warner Bros., 1931
THE MEN IN HER LIFE Columbia, 1931
THREE WISE GIRLS Columbia, 1932
MAKE ME A STAR Paramount, 1932
CRIME OF THE CENTURY Paramount, 1933
HER BODYGUARD Paramount, 1933
THE OLD FASHIONED WAY
    Paramount, 1934
DANDY DICK BIP, 1934, British
TWO HEARTS IN HARMONY Wardour,
    1935, British
BOYS WILL BE BOYS First National,
    1935, British
MR. COHEN TAKES A WIFE Warner Bros.,
    1935, British
IT'S IN THE BAG Warner Bros., 1936, British
WHERE THERE'S A WILL First National,
    1936, British
WINDBAG THE SAILOR Gaumont-British,
    1936, British
EDUCATED EVANS First National, 1936
SAID O'REILLY TO McNAB SEZ O'REILLY
    TO McNAB Gaumont-British, 1937, British
TAKE IT FROM ME First National,
    1937, British
FEATHER YOUR NEST Associated British
    Film Distributors, 1937, British
TORCHY GETS HER MAN
    Warner Bros., 1938
TORCHY BLANE IN CHINATOWN
    Warner Bros., 1939
MISBEHAVING HUSBANDS PRC, 1940
FEDERAL FUGITIVES PRC, 1941
EMERGENCY LANDING PRC, 1941
DESPERATE CARGO PRC, 1941
DUKE OF THE NAVY PRC, 1942
THE BROADWAY BIG SHOT
    Monogram, 1942
THE PANTHER'S CLAW PRC, 1942
THE MIRACLE KID PRC, 1942
MEN OF SAN QUENTIN PRC, 1942
GALLANT LADY PRC, 1942
ONE THRILLING NIGHT Monogram, 1942

THE PHANTOM KILLER   Monogram, 1942
FOREIGN AGENT   Monogram, 1942
THE LIVING GHOST   Monogram, 1942
CLANCY STREET BOYS   Monogram, 1943
THE APE MAN   Monogram, 1943
SPOTLIGHT SCANDALS   Monogram, 1943
HERE COMES KELLY   Monogram, 1943
THE MYSTERY OF THE 13TH GUEST
   Monogram, 1943
WHAT A MAN!   Monogram, 1944
VOODOO MAN   Monogram, 1944
HOT RHYTHM   Monogram, 1944
DETECTIVE KITTY O'DAY   Monogram, 1944
FOLLOW THE LEADER   Monogram, 1944
LEAVE IT TO THE IRISH   Monogram, 1944
OH, WHAT A NIGHT!   Monogram, 1944
SHADOW OF SUSPICION   Monogram, 1944
BOWERY CHAMPS   Monogram, 1944
CRAZY KNIGHTS   Monogram, 1944
FASHION MODEL   Monogram, 1945
COME OUT FIGHTING   Monogram, 1945
BLONDE RANSOM   Universal, 1945
SWINGIN' ON A RAINBOW   Republic, 1945
BLACK MARKET BABIES   Monogram, 1945
THE SHADOW RETURNS   1946
THE FACE OF MARBLE   Monogram, 1946
DON'T GAMBLE WITH STRANGERS
   Monogram, 1946
SPOOK BUSTERS   Monogram, 1946
BELOW THE DEADLINE   Monogram, 1946
MR. HEX   Monogram, 1946
PHILO VANCE RETURNS   PRC, 1947
HARD-BOILED MAHONEY   Monogram, 1947
TOO MANY WINNERS   PRC, 1947
KILLER AT LARGE   PRC, 1947
NEWS HOUNDS   Monogram, 1947
GAS HOUSE KIDS GO WEST   PRC, 1947
BOWERY BUCKAROOS   Monogram, 1947
THE CHINESE RING   THE RED HORNET
   Monogram, 1947
ANGEL'S ALLEY   Monogram, 1948
JINX MONEY   Monogram, 1948
JIGGS AND MAGGIE IN COURT   co-director
   with Edward F. Cline, Monogram, 1948
THE SHANGHAI CHEST   Monogram, 1948
THE GOLDEN EYE   Monogram, 1948
KIDNAPPED   Monogram, 1948
SMUGGLERS' COVE   Monogram, 1948
THE FEATHERED SERPENT
   Monogram, 1948
INCIDENT   Monogram, 1948
TUNA CLIPPER   Monogram, 1949
FORGOTTEN WOMEN   Monogram, 1949
TRAIL OF THE YUKON   1949
TOUGH ASSIGNMENT   Lippert, 1949
BLUE GRASS OF KENTUCKY
   Monogram, 1950
JUGGS AND MAGGIE OUT WEST
   Monogram, 1950
COUNTY FAIR   Monogram, 1950
THE PRINCE OF PEACE   THE LAWTON
   STORY   co-director with Harold Daniels,
   Hallmark Productions, 1951
BOWERY BATALLION   Monogram, 1951
CUBAN FIREBALL   Republic, 1951
GHOST CHASERS   Monogram, 1951
LET'S GO NAVY!   Monogram, 1951
HAVANA ROSE   Republic, 1951
RODEO   Monogram, 1952
JET JOB   Monogram, 1952
HERE COME THE MARINES!
   Monogram, 1952
THE ROSE BOWL STORY   Monogram, 1952
YUKON GOLD   Allied Artists, 1953
JALOPY   Allied Artists, 1952
ROAR OF THE CROWD   Allied Artists, 1953
MURDER WITHOUT TEARS
   Allied Artists, 1953

YUKON VENGEANCE   Allied Artists, 1954
PARIS PLAYBOYS   Allied Artists, 1954
PRIDE OF THE BLUE GRASS
   Allied Artists, 1954
HIGH SOCIETY   Allied Artists, 1955
JAIL BUSTERS   Allied Artists, 1955
MOM AND DAD   Hygienic Productions,
   1957, filmed in 1944
IN THE MONEY   Allied Artists, 1957
WESTWARD HO THE WAGONS!
   Buena Vista, 1957
TEN WHO DARED   Buena Vista, 1960
LASSIE'S GREATEST ADVENTURE
   20th Century-Fox, 1963,
   originally filmed for television
BILLY THE KID VS. DRACULA
   Embassy, 1966
JESSE JAMES MEETS FRANKENSTEIN'S
   DAUGHTER   Embassy, 1966

HARRY BEAUMONT
b. February 10, 1888 - Abilene, Kansas
d. 1966

THE CALL OF THE CITY   Essanay, 1915
TRUANT SOULS   Essanay, 1917
SKINNER'S DRESS SUIT   Essanay, 1917
SKINNER'S BUBBLE   Essanay, 1917
SKINNER'S BABY   Essanay, 1917
BURNING THE CANDLE   Essanay, 1917
FILLING HIS OWN SHOES   Essanay, 1917
BROWN OF HARVARD   Essanay, 1918
THIRTY A WEEK   Goldwyn, 1918
LITLE ROWDY   Triangle, 1919
WILD GOOSE CHASE   Triangle, 1919
A MAN AND HIS MONEY   Goldwyn, 1919
GO WEST YOUNG MAN   Goldwyn, 1919
ONE OF THE FINEST   Goldwyn, 1919
THE CITY OF COMRADES   Goldwyn, 1919
HEARTSEASE   Goldwyn, 1919
LORD AND LADY ALGY   Goldwyn, 1919
TOBY'S BOW   Goldwyn, 1919
THE GAY LORD QUEX   Goldwyn, 1919
THE GREAT ACCIDENT   Goldwyn, 1920
DOLLARS AND SENSE   Goldwyn, 1920
GOING SOME   Goldwyn, 1920
STOP THIEF!   Goldwyn, 1920
OFFICER 666   Goldwyn, 1920
THE FOURTEENTH LOVER   Metro, 1922
GLASS HOUSES   Metro, 1922
THE RAGGED HEIRESS   Fox, 1922
VERY TRULY YOURS   Fox, 1922
SEEING'S BELIEVING   Metro, 1922
THE FIVE DOLLAR BABY   Metro, 1922
LIGHTS OF THE DESERT   Fox, 1922
THEY LIKE 'EM ROUGH   Metro, 1922
JUNE MADNESS   Metro, 1922
LOVE IN THE DARK   Metro, 1922
CRINOLINE AND ROMANCE   Metro, 1923
A NOISE IN NEWBORO   Metro, 1923
MAIN STREET   Warner Bros., 1923
THE GOLD DIGGERS   Warner Bros., 1923
BEAU BRUMMEL   Warner Bros., 1924
DON'T DOUBT YOUR HUSBAND
   MGM, 1924
BABBITT   Warner Bros., 1924
THE LOVER OF CAMILLE
   Warner Bros., 1924
A LOST LADY   Warner Bros., 1924
RECOMPENSE   Warner Bros., 1925
HIS MAJESTY BUNKER BEAN
   Warner Bros., 1925
ROSE OF THE WORLD   Warner Bros., 1925
SANDY   Fox, 1926
WOMANPOWER   Fox, 1926
ONE INCREASING PURPOSE   Fox, 1927
FORBIDDEN HOURS   MGM, 1928
OUR DANCING DAUGHTERS   MGM, 1928

A SINGLE MAN   MGM, 1929
THE BROADWAY MELODY ★   MGM, 1929
SPEEDWAY   MGM, 1929
LORD BYRON OF BROADWAY   co-director
   with William Nigh, MGM, 1930
CHILDREN OF PLEASURE   MGM, 1930
THE FLORADORA GIRL   MGM, 1930
OUR BLUSHING BRIDES   MGM, 1930
THOSE THREE FRENCH GIRLS   MGM, 1930
DANCE FOOLS DANCE   MGM, 1931
LAUGHING SINNERS   MGM, 1931
THE GREAT LOVER   MGM, 1931
WEST OF BROADWAY   MGM, 1931
ARE YOU LISTENING?   MGM, 1932
UNASHAMED   MGM, 1932
FAITHLESS   MGM, 1932
MADE ON BROADWAY   MGM, 1933
WHEN LADIES MEET   MGM, 1933
SHOULD LADIES BEHAVE?   MGM, 1933
MURDER IN THE PRIVATE CAR   MGM, 1934
ENCHANTED APRIL   RKO, 1935
THE GIRL ON THE FRONT PAGE
   Universal, 1936
WHEN'S YOUR BIRTHDAY?   RKO, 1937
MAISIE GOES TO RENO   MGM, 1944
TWICE BLESSED   MGM, 1945
UP GOES MAISIE   MGM, 1946
THE SHOW-OFF   MGM, 1946
UNDERCOVER MAISIE   MGM, 1947
ALIAS A GENTLEMAN   MGM, 1948

FORD BEEBE
b. November 26, 1888 - Grand Rapids, Michigan
d. ?

THE HONOR OF THE RANGE (S)
   co-director with Leo Maloney, 1920
THE LAST OF THE MOHICANS (S)
   co-director with B. Reeves Eason, 1932
THE SHADOW OF THE EAGLE (S)   1932
THE PRIDE OF THE LEGION
   THE BIG PAY-OFF   1932
LAUGHING AT LIFE   1933
THE ADVENTURES OF REX AND RINTY (S)
   co-director with B. Reeves Eason, 1935
LAW BEYOND THE RANGE   1935
THE MAN FROM GUNTOWN   1935
ACE DRUMMOND (S)   co-director with
   Cliff Smith, 1936
STAMPEDE   1936
JUNGLE JIM (S)   co-director with Cliff Smith,
   Columbia, 1937
RADIO PATROL (S)   co-director with
   Cliff Smith, Columbia, 1937
SECRET AGENT X-9 (S)   co-director with
   Cliff Smith, Columbia, 1937
TIM TYLER'S LUCK (S)   1937
WILD WEST DAYS (S)   co-director with
   Cliff Smith, Columbia, 1937
WESTBOUND LIMITED   1937
TROUBLE AT MIDNIGHT   1937
FLASH GORDON'S TRIP TO MARS (S)
   co-director with Robert Hill, Universal, 1938
THE DEADLY RAY FROM MARS   MARS
   ATTACKS THE WORLD   co-director with
   Robert Hill, Universal, 1938
RED BARRY (S)   co-director with Alan James,
   Universal, 1938
BUCK ROGERS (S)   co-director with
   Saul Goodkind, Universal, 1939
DESTINATION SATURN   co-director with
   Saul Goodkind, Universal, 1939
THE PHANTOM CREEPS (S)   co-director with
   Saul Goodkind, Universal, 1939
THE OREGON TRAIL (S)   Universal, 1939
OKLAHOMA FRONTIER   Universal, 1939
THE GREEN HORNET (S)   co-director with
   Ray Taylor, Universal, 1940

THE GREEN HORNET STRIKES AGAIN (S)
co-director with John Rawlins,
Universal, 1940
FLASH GORDON CONQUERS THE
UNIVERSE   co-director with Ray Taylor,
Universal, 1940
JUNIOR G-MEN (S)   co-director with
John Rawlins, Universal, 1940
WINNERS OF THE WEST (S)   co-director
with Ray Taylor, Universal, 1940
SON OF ROARING DAN   Universal, 1940
RIDERS OF DEATH VALLEY (S)   co-director
with Ray Taylor, Universal, 1941
SEA RAIDERS (S)   co-director with
John Rawlins, Universal, 1941
SKY RAIDERS (S)   co-director with Ray Taylor,
Universal, 1941
DON WINSLOW OF THE NAVY (S)
co-director with Ray Taylor, Universal, 1942
OVERLAND MAIL (S)   co-director with
John Rawlins, Universal, 1942
NIGHT MONSTER   Universal, 1942
FRONTIER BADMEN   Universal, 1943
THE INVISIBLE MAN'S REVENGE
Universal, 1943
ENTER ARSENE LUPIN   Universal, 1944
EASY TO LOOK AT   Universal, 1945
MY DOG SHEP   Monogram, 1946
SIX GUN SERENADE   Monogram, 1947
COURTIN' TROUBLE   Monogram, 1948
SHEP COMES HOME   Monogram, 1948
BOMBA, THE JUNGLE BOY
Monogram, 1949
THE DALTON GANG   Monogram, 1949
SATAN'S CRADLE   Monogram, 1949
RED DESERT   Monogram, 1949
BOMBA ON PANTHER ISLAND
Monogram, 1949
THE LOST VOLCANO   Monogram, 1950
BOMBA AND THE HIDDEN CITY
Monogram, 1950
THE LION HUNTERS   Monogram, 1951
ELEPHANT STAMPEDE   Monogram, 1951
AFRICAN TREASURE   Monogram, 1952
WAGONS WEST   Monogram, 1952
BOMBA AND THE JUNGLE GIRL
Monogram, 1952
SAFARI DRUMS   Allied Artists, 1953
THE GOLDEN IDOL   Allied Artists, 1954
KILLER LEOPARD   Allied Artists, 1954
LORD OF THE JUNGLE   Allied Artists, 1956

LASLO BENEDEK
(Laszlo Benedek)
b. March 5, 1907 - Budapest, Hungary
d. 1992

THE KISSING BANDIT   MGM, 1948
PORT OF NEW YORK   Eagle-Lion, 1949
DEATH OF A SALESMAN   Columbia, 1951
THE WILD ONE   Columbia, 1954
BENGAL BRIGADE   Columbia, 1954
KINDER, MUTTER UND EIN GENERAL
1955, West German
AFFAIR IN HAVANA   Allied Artists, 1957
MALAGA   *MOMENT OF DANGER*
Warner Bros., 1959, British
RECOURSE EN GRACE   1960, French
NAMU, THE KILLER WHALE
United Artists, 1966
DARING GAME   Paramount, 1968
THE NIGHT VISITOR   UMC, 1971
ASSAULT ON AGATHON
Nine Network, 1976

RICHARD (DICK) BENNER
b. 1946 - Sterling, Illinois
d. 1990

LONDON DRAG   1969
OUTRAGEOUS!   Cinema 5, 1977, Canadian
HAPPY BIRTHDAY GEMINI   United Artists,
1980, U.S.-Canadian
TOO OUTRAGEOUS!   Spectrafilm, 1987,
Canadian-U.S.

SPENCER GORDON BENNET
(Spencer Gordon Bennett)
b. January 5, 1893 - Brooklyn, New York
d. 1987

BEHOLD THE MAN   co-director, 1921
PLAY BALL (S)   1925
THE GREEN ARCHER (S)   1925
THE FIGHTING MARINE (S)   1926
THE FIGHTING MARINE   1926
THE HOUSE WITHOUT A KEY (S)   1926
HAWK OF THE HILLS (S)   1927
THE MAN WITHOUT A FACE (S)   1928
THE TERRIBLE PEOPLE (S)   1928
THE YELLOW CAMEO (S)   1928
THE TIGER'S SHADOW (S)   1928
THE BLACK BOOK (S)   co-director with
Thomas Storey, 1929
ROGUE OF THE RIO GRANDE   1930
THE LAST FRONTIER (S)   1932
MIDNIGHT WARNING   1933
NIGHT ALARM   1934
CALLING ALL CARS   1935
RESCUE SQUAD   1935
WESTERN COURAGE   1935
LAWLESS RIDERS   1935
HEROES OF THE RANGE   1936
THE CATTLE THIEF   1936
THE UNKNOWN RANGER   1936
THE FUGITIVE SHERIFF   1936
THE MYSTERIOUS PILOT (S)   1937
THE RANGERS STEP IN   1937
RIO GRANDE   1938
ACROSS THE PLAINS   1939
COWBOY FROM SUNDOWN   1940
ARIZONA BOUND   1941
THE SECRET CODE (S)   1942
THEY RAID BY NIGHT   1942
SECRET SERVICE IN DARKEST
AFRICA (S)   1943
THE MASKED MARVEL (S)   1943
CALLING WILD BILL ELLIOTT   1943
CANYON CITY   1943
THE TIGER WOMAN (S)   1944
BENEATH WESTERN SKIES (S)   1944
THE PURPLE MONSTER STRIKES (S)
co-director with Fred Brannon, 1945
LONE TEXAS RANGER   1945
KING OF THE FOREST RANGERS (S)
co-director with Fred Brannon, 1946
THE PHANTOM RIDER (S)   co-director with
Fred Brannon, 1946
THE BLACK WIDOW (S)   co-director with
Fred Brannon, 1947
BRICK BRADFORD (S)   1947
SON OF ZORRO (S)   co-director with
Fred Brannon, 1947
SUPERMAN (S)   co-director with Thomas Carr,
Columbia, 1948
CONGO BILL (S)   co-director with
Thomas Carr, Columbia, 1948
ADVENTURES OF SIR GALAHAD (S)
Columbia, 1949
BATMAN AND ROBIN (S)   Columbia, 1949
CODY OF THE PONY EXPRESS (S)
Columbia, 1950

ATOM MAN VS. SUPERMAN (S)
Columbia, 1950
CAPTAIN VIDEO (S)   co-director with
Wallace Grissell, Columbia, 1951
MYSTERIOUS ISLAND (S)   Columbia, 1951
BLACKHAWK (S)   Columbia, 1952
KING OF THE CONGO (S)   co-director with
Wallace Grissell, Columbia, 1952
SON OF GERONOMO (S)   Columbia, 1952
BRAVE WARRIOR   Columbia, 1952
VOODOO TIGER   Columbia, 1952
THE LOST PLANET (S)   Columbia, 1953
SAVAGE MUTINY   Columbia, 1953
KILLER APE   Columbia, 1953
RIDING WITH BUFFALO BILL (S)
Columbia, 1954
ADVENTURES OF CAPTAIN AFRICA (S)
Columbia, 1956
DEVIL GODDESS   Columbia, 1956
PERILS OF THE WILDERNESS (S)   1956
SUBMARINE SEAHAWK   American
International, 1959
THE ATOMIC SUBMARINE
Allied Artists, 1960
THE BOUNTY KILLER   Embassy, 1965
REQUIEM FOR A GUNFIGHTER
Embassy, 1965

COMPTON BENNETT
(Robert Compton-Bennett)
b. January 15, 1900 - Tunbridge Wells, England
d. 1974

FIND, FIX AND STRIKE (FD)   1942, British
MEN OF ROCHDALE (FD)   1944, British
THE SEVENTH VEIL   Universal, 1945, British
THE YEARS BETWEEN   Universal,
1946, British
DAYBREAK   Rank, 1947, British
MY OWN TRUE LOVE   Paramount, 1949
THAT FORSYTE WOMAN   MGM, 1949
KING SOLOMON'S MINES   co-director with
Andrew Marton, MGM, 1950
IT STARTED IN PARADISE   Astor,
1952, British
SO LITTLE TIME   MacDonald, 1952, British
DESPERATE MOMENT   Universal,
1953, British
GLORY AT SEA   *THE GIFT HORSE*
M&A Alexander, 1952, British
AFTER THE BALL   Romulus Films,
1957, British
CITY AFTER MIDNIGHT   *THAT WOMAN
OPPOSITE*   RKO Radio, 1957, British
MAILBAG ROBBERY   *THE FLYING SCOT*
Tudor Pictures, 1957, British
BEYOND THE CURTAIN   Rank, 1960, British
HOW TO UNDRESS IN PUBLIC WITHOUT
UNDUE EMBARRASSMENT   1965, British

BUSBY BERKELEY
(William Berkeley Enos)
b. November 29, 1895 - Los Angeles, California
d. 1976

SHE HAD TO SAY YES   co-director with
George Amy, First National, 1933
GOLD DIGGERS OF 1935
First National, 1935
BRIGHT LIGHTS   First National, 1935
I LIVE FOR LOVE   First National, 1935
STAGE STRUCK   First National, 1936
THE GO-GETTER   Warner Bros., 1937
HOLLYWOOD HOTEL   Warner Bros., 1937
MEN ARE SUCH FOOLS   Warner Bros., 1938
GARDEN OF THE MOON
Warner Bros., 1938

COMET OVER BROADWAY
   Warner Bros., 1938
THEY MADE ME A CRIMINAL
   Warner Bros., 1939
BABES IN ARMS   MGM, 1939
FAST AND FURIOUS   MGM, 1939
STRIKE UP THE BAND   MGM, 1940
FORTY LITTLE MOTHERS   MGM, 1940
BLONDE INSPIRATION   MGM, 1941
BABES ON BROADWAY   MGM, 1941
FOR ME AND MY GAL   MGM, 1942
THE GANG'S ALL HERE
   20th Century-Fox, 1943
CINDERELLA JONES   Warner Bros., 1946
TAKE ME OUT TO THE BALL GAME
   MGM, 1949

CURTIS BERNHARDT

(Kurt Bernhardt)
b. April 15, 1899 - Worms, Germany
d. 1981

QUALEN DER NACHT   1926, German
DIE WAISE VON LOWOOD   1926, German
KINDERSEELEN KLAGEN AN   1927, German
DAS MADCHEN MIT DEN FUNF NULLEN
   1927, German
SCHINDERHANNES *THE PRINCE OF
   ROGUES*   1927, German
DAS LETZTE FORT   1928, German
DIE FRAU NACH DER MANN SICH SEHNT
   THREE LOVES   1929, German
DIE LEZTE KOMPANIE *13 MEN AND A GIRL*
   1930, German
DER MANN DER DEN MORD BEGING
   1931, German
DER REBELL   co-director with Luis Trenker,
   1932, German
DER GROSSE RAUSCH   1932, German
DER TUNNEL   1933, German
L'OR DANS LA RUE   1934, French
THE BELOVED VAGABOND   1934, British
CARREFOUR   1938, French
NUIT DE DECEMBRE   1939, French
MY LOVE CAME BACK   Warner Bros., 1940
LADY WITH RED HAIR   Warner Bros., 1940
MILLION DOLLAR BABY   Warner Bros., 1941
JUKE GIRL   Warner Bros., 1942
HAPPY GO LUCKY   Paramount, 1943
CONFLICT   Warner Bros., 1945
MY REPUTATION   Warner Bros., 1946
DEVOTION   Warner Bros., 1946
A STOLEN LIFE   Warner Bros., 1946
POSSESSED   Warner Bros., 1947
HIGH WALL   MGM, 1948
THE DOCTOR AND THE GIRL   MGM, 1949
PAYMENT ON DEMAND   RKO Radio, 1951
SIROCCO   Columbia, 1951
THE BLUE VEIL   RKO Radio, 1951
THE MERRY WIDOW   MGM, 1952
MISS SADIE THOMPSON   Columbia, 1954
BEAU BRUMMEL   MGM, 1954
INTERRUPTED MELODY   MGM, 1955
GABY   MGM, 1956
STEPHANIE IN RIO   Casino,
   1960, West German
DAMON AND PYTHIAS *IL TIRANO DI
   SIRACUSA*   MGM, 1962, Italian-U.S.
KISSES FOR MY PRESIDENT
   Warner Bros., 1964

HERBERT J. BIBERMAN

d. March 4, 1900 - Philadelphia, Pennsylvania
d. 1971

ONE-WAY TICKET   Columbia, 1935
MEET NERO WOLFE   Columbia, 1936

KING OF CHINATOWN   Paramount, 1939
THE MASTER RACE   RKO Radio, 1944
SALT OF THE EARTH   Independent
   Productions, 1954
SLAVES   Continental, 1969

BILL BIXBY

b. January 22, 1934 - San Francisco, California
d. 1993

THE BARBARY COAST (TF)
   Paramount TV, 1975
THREE ON A DATE (TF)   ABC Circle
   Films, 1978
THE INCREDIBLE HULK RETURNS (TF)
   B&B Productions/New World TV, 1988
THE TRIAL OF THE INCREDIBLE HULK (TF)
   Bixby-Brandon Productions/New
   World TV, 1989
THE DEATH OF THE INCREDIBLE HULK (TF)
   Bixby-Brandon Productions/New
   World TV, 1990
ANOTHER PAIR OF ACES: THREE OF
   A KIND (TF)   Pedernales Films/Once
   Upon A Time Films Ltd., 1991
BABY OF THE BRIDE (TF)   Baby Productions/
   Leonard Hill Films, 1991
THE WOMAN WHO LOVED ELVIS (TF)
   Wapello County Productions/Grossbart-
   Barnett Productions, 1993

J. STUART BLACKTON

(James Stuart Blackton)
b. January 5, 1875 - Sheffield, England
d. 1941

THE BURGLAR ON THE ROOF
   Vitagraph, 1898
TEARING DOWN THE SPANISH FLAG
   co-director with Albert E. Smith,
   Vitagraph, 1898
SPOT FILMING OF WINDSOR HOTEL FIRE
   IN NEW YORK   Vitagraph, 1899
A GENTLEMAN OF FRANCE
   Vitagraph, 1903
RAFFLES THE AMATEUR CRACKSMAN
   Vitagraph, 1903
A MODERN OLIVER TWIST   Vitagraph, 1906
THE SAN FRANCISCO EARTHQUAKE
   Vitagraph, 1906
HUMOROUS PHASES OF A FUNNY FACE
   Vitagraph, 1906
THE HAUNTED HOTEL   Vitagraph, 1906
THE MAGIC FOUNTAIN PEN
   Vitagraph, 1907
A CURIOUS DREAM   Vitagraph, 1907
MACBETH   Vitagraph, 1908
ROMEO AND JULIET   Vitagraph, 1908
SALOME   Vitagraph, 1908
THE MERCHANT OF VENICE
   Vitagraph, 1908
BARBARA FRIETCHIE   Vitagraph, 1908
THE VIKING'S DAUGHTER   Vitagraph, 1908
NAPOLEON - THE MAN OF DESTINY
   Vitagraph, 1909
PRINCESS NICOTINE OR THE SMOKE
   FAIRY   co-director, Vitagraph, 1909
SAUL AND DAVID   Vitagraph, 1909
OLIVER TWIST   Vitagraph, 1909
LES MISERABLES   Vitagraph, 1909
THE LIFE OF MOSES   Vitagraph, 1909-10
ELEKTRA   Vitagraph, 1910
UNCLE TOM'S CABIN   Vitagraph, 1910
A MODERN CINDERELLA   Vitagraph, 1910
LINCOLN'S GETTYSBURG ADDRESS
   co-director with James Young,
   Vitagraph, 1912

THE TWO PORTRAITS   Vitagraph, 1912
CARDINAL WOLSEY   co-director with
   Lawrence Trimble, Vitagraph, 1912
THE LADY OF THE LAKE   Vitagraph, 1912
AS YOU LIKE IT   co-director with
   James Young, Vitagraph, 1912
WOMANHOOD   1917
THE GLORY OF A NATION   co-director with
   William Earle, 1917
THE MESSAGE OF THE MOUSE   1917
THE JUDGMENT HOUSE   1917
THE WORLD FOR SALE   1918
LIFE'S GREATEST PROBLEM   1919
THE COMMON CAUSE   1919
A HOUSE DIVIDED   1919
THE MOONSHINE TRAIL   1919
MY HUSBAND'S OTHER WIFE   1920
RESPECTABLE BY PROXY   1920
THE BLOOD BARRIER   1920
PASSERS-BY   1920
MAN AND HIS WOMAN   1920
THE HOUSE OF THE TOLLING BELL   1920
FORBIDDEN VALLEY   1920
THE GLORIOUS ADVENTURE
   1922, U.S.-British
A GYPSY CAVALIER   1922, British
THE VIRGIN QUEEN   1923, British
ON THE BANKS OF THE WABASH   1923
LET NOT MAN PUT ASUNDER   1924
BETWEEN FRIENDS   1924
THE CLEAN HEART   1924
THE BELOVED BRUTE   1924
BEHOLD THIS WOMAN   1924
THE REDEEMING SIN   1925
TIDES OF PASSION   1925
THE HAPPY WARRIOR   1925
BRIDE OF THE STORM   1926
THE GILDED HIGHWAY   1926
HELL-BENT FOR HEAVEN   1926
THE PASSIONATE QUEST   1926

CHRISTIAN BLACKWOOD

d. 1992

SPOLETO: FESTIVAL OF TWO WORLDS (FD)
   Christian Blackwood Productions, 1967
HARLEM THEATER (FD)   Christian Blackwood
   Productions, 1968
SUMMER IN THE CITY (FD)   Christian
   Blackwood Productions, 1968
SAN DOMINGO   co-director with Hans-Jurgen
   Syberberg, 1970, West German
ELIOT FELD: ARTISTIC DIRECTOR (FD)
   Christian Blackwood Productions, 1970
JUILLIARD (FD)   Christian Blackwood
   Productions, 1971
KENTUCKY KITH AND KIN (FD)   Christian
   Blackwood Productions, 1972
BLACK HARVEST   Christian Blackwood
   Productions, 1973
YESTERDAY'S WITNESS: A TRIBUTE TO
   THE AMERICAN NEWSREEL (FD)
   Christian Blackwood Productions, 1974
LIVING WITH FEAR (FD)   Christian
   Blackwood Productions, 1974
TO BE A MAN (FD)   Christian Blackwood
   Productions, 1977
ROGER CORMAN: HOLLYWOOD'S WILD
   ANGEL (FD)   Christian Blackwood
   Productions, 1978
COUSINS (FD)   Christian Blackwood
   Productions, 1979
TAPDANCIN' (FD)   Christian Blackwood
   Productions, 1980
ALL BY MYSELF (FD)   Christian Blackwood
   Productions, 1982

CHARLES AZNAVOUR: BREAKING
AMERICA (FD)   Christian Blackwood
Productions, 1983
OBSERVATIONS UNDER THE VOLCANO (FD)
Christian Blackwood Productions, 1984
MY LIFE FOR ZARAH LEANDER (FD)
Christian Blackwood Productions, 1985
PRIVATE CONVERSATIONS (FD)   Christian
Blackwood Productions, 1985
NIK AND MURRAY (FD)   Christian Blackwood
Productions, 1986
SIGNED: LINO BROCKA (FD)   Christian
Blackwood Productions, 1987
TWO HOTELS IN OUR TROUBLED MIDDLE
EAST (FD)   Christian Blackwood
Productions, 1988
MOTEL (FD)   Christian Blackwood
Productions, 1989

ALESSANDRO BLASETTI

b. July 3, 1900 - Rome, Italy
d. 1987

SOLE   Augustus, 1929, Italian
NERONE   Cines, 1930, Italian
RESURRECTIO   Cines, 1931, Italian
TERRA MADRE   Cines, 1931, Italian
PALIO   Cines, 1932, Italian
LA TAVOLA DEI POVERI   Cines, 1932, Italian
IL CASO HALLER   Cines, 1933, Italian
1860   Cines, 1934
L'IMPIEGATA DI PAPA' SAPF, 1933, Italian
VECCHIA GUARDIA   Fauno Film,
1934, Italian
ALDEBARAN   Manenti Film, 1935, Italian
LA CONTESSA DI PARMA   ICI, 1937, Italian
ETTORE FIERAMOSCA   Nembo Film,
1938, Italian
RETROSCENA   Continentalcine, 1939, Italian
UN'AVVENTURA DI SALVATOR ROSA
Stella Film, 1940, Italian
LA CORONA DI FERRO   ENIC Lux,
1941, Italian
LA CENA DELLE BEFFE   Cines, 1941, Italian
QUATTRO PASSI FRA LE NUVOLE   Cines,
1942, Italian
NESSUNO TORNA INDIETRO   Artisti
Associati/Quarta Film, 1943, Italian
UN GIORNO NELLA VITA   Orbis Film,
1946, Italian
FABIOLA   20th Century-Fox, 1948, Italian
FATHER'S DILEMMA   PRIMA COMUNIONE
Davis Distribution Company, 1950, Italian
TIMES GONE BY   Italian Films Export,
1952, Italian
LA FIAMMATA   Cines, 1953, Italian
THE ANATOMY OF LOVE   TEMPI NOSTRI
Kassler Films, 1953, Italian-French
TOO BAD SHE'S BAD   PECCATO CHE SIA
UNA CANAGLIA   Getz-Kingsley,
1955, Italian
LUCKY TO BE A WOMAN   Films Around
the World, 1955, Italian-French
AMORE E CHIACCHIERE   Electra
Compagnia Cinematografica/Societe
Francaise de Cinematographie/Ariel Film,
1957, Italian-French-Spanish
EUROPA DI NOTTE   Avers Production/Avers
Film, 1959, Italian-French
IO AMO, TU AMI   Dino De Laurentiis/Orsay
Film, 1961, Italian-French
THREE FABLES OF LOVE   LES QUATRES
VERITES   co-director, Janus Films, 1963,
French-Italian-Spanish
LIOLA'   Film Napoleon/Federiz/Cinecitta/France
Cinema/Francinex, 1963 Italian-French
IO, IO, IO...E GLI ALTRI   Cineluxor/Rizzoli
Film, 1966, Italian

LA RAGAZZA DEL BERSAGLIERE   Rizzoli
Film, 1967, Italian
SIMON BOLIVAR   Jupiter Generale
Cinematografica/Finarco Productores
Exhibidores Films/S.A. Pefsa,
1969, Italian-Spanish

RICHARD BOLESLAWSKI

(Ryszard Srzednicki Boleslawsky)

b. February 4, 1889 - Warsaw, Poland
d. 1937

TRI VSTRECHI   1915, Russian
BREAD   co-director with Boris Suskevich,
1918, Soviet
THE MIRACLE OF THE VISTULA
1921, Polish
THE LAST OF THE LONE WOLF
Columbia, 1930
THE GAY DIPLOMAT   RKO, 1931
WOMAN PURSUED   RKO, 1931
RASPUTIN AND THE EMPRESS   MGM, 1933
STORM AT DAYBREAK   MGM, 1933
BEAUTY FOR SALE   MGM, 1933
FUGITIVE LOVERS   MGM, 1934
MEN IN WHITE   MGM, 1934
OPERATOR 13   MGM, 1934
THE PAINTED VEIL   MGM, 1934
CLIVE OF INDIA   20th Century-Fox, 1935
LES MISERABLES   20th Century-Fox, 1935
O'SHAUGHNESSY'S BOY   MGM, 1935
METROPOLITAN   20th Century-Fox, 1935
THREE GODFATHERS   MGM, 1936
THEODORA GOES WILD   Columbia, 1936
THE GARDEN OF ALLAH
United Artists, 1936
THE LAST OF MRS. CHEYNEY   co-director
with George Fitzmaurice, MGM, 1937

ROBERT BOLT

b. August 15, 1924 - Sayles, Manchester,
England
d. 1995

LADY CAROLINE LAMB   United Artists,
1973, British

SERGEI BONDARCHUK

b. September 25, 1920 - Belozersk, Ukraine,
U.S.S.R.
d. 1994

FATE OF A MAN   Lopert, 1961, Soviet
WAR AND PEACE, PART I: ANDREI
BOLKONSKY   Mosfilm, 1965, Soviet
WAR AND PEACE, PART II: NATASHA
ROSTOV   Mosfilm, 1965, Soviet
WAR AND PEACE, PART III: 1812   Mosfilm,
1967, Soviet
WAR AND PEACE, PART IV: PIERRE
BEZUKHOV   Mosfilm, 1967, Soviet
WAR AND PEACE   Continental, 1968, Soviet,
edited from four part original version
WATERLOO   Paramount, 1971, Italian-Soviet
THEY FOUGHT FOR THEIR MOTHERLAND
Mosfilm, 1974, Soviet
THE STEPPE   IFEX Film/Sovexport film,
1977, Soviet
RED BELLS: MEXICO IN FLAMES   Mosfilm/
Conacite-2/RAI/Vides International/Cinefin,
1982, Soviet-Mexican-Italian
RED BELLS: I'VE SEEN THE BIRTH OF THE
NEW WORLD   Mosfilm/Conacite-2/Vides
International, 1983, Soviet-Mexican-Italian
BORIS GODOUNOV   Sovfilm/Barrandov
Studio, 1986, Soviet-Czechoslovakian
AND QUIET FLOWS THE DON (MS)   Mosfilm,
1994, Russian-Italian

PHILLIP BORSOS

b. 1953 - Tasmania, Australia
d. 1995

THE GREY FOX   United Artists Classics,
1983, Canadian
THE MEAN SEASON   Orion, 1985
ONE MAGIC CHRISTMAS   Buena Vista,
1985, U.S.-Canadian
DR. BETHUNE   BETHUNE: THE MAKING
OF A HERO   Tara Releasing, 1990,
Canadian-Chinese-French
FAR FROM HOME: THE ADVENTURES OF
YELLOW DOG   20th Century Fox, 1995,
U.S.-Canadian

FRANK BORZAGE

b. April 23, 1893 - Salt Lake City, Utah
d. 1962

THAT GAL OF BURKE'S   1916
MAMMY'S ROSE   co-director with
James Douglass, 1916
LIFE'S HARMONY   co-director with
Lorimer Johnson, 1916
THE SILKEN SPIDER   1916
THE CODE OF HONOR   1916
NELL DALE'S MEN FOLKS   1916
THE FORGOTTEN PRAYER   1916
THE COURTIN' OF CALLIOPE CLEW   1916
NUGGET JIM'S PARDNER   1916
THE DEMON OF FEAR   1916
LAND O' LIZARDS   SILENT SHELBY
Mutual, 1916
IMMEDIATE LEE   HAIR TRIGGER CASEY
Mutual, 1916
ENCHANTMENT   1916
THE PRIDE AND THE MAN   1916
DOLLARS OF DROSS   1916
WEE LADY BETTY   co-director with
Charles Miller, 1917
FLYING COLORS   Triangle, 1917
UNTIL THEY GET ME   Triangle, 1917
THE ATOM   1918
THE GUN WOMAN   Triangle, 1918
THE SHOES THAT DANCED   Triangle, 1918
INNOCENT'S PROGRESS   Triangle, 1918
AN HONEST MAN   Triangle, 1918
SOCIETY FOR SALE   Triangle, 1918
WHO IS TO BLAME?   Triangle, 1918
THE GHOST FLOWER   Triangle, 1918
THE CURSE OF IKU   Essanay, 1918
TOTON   Triangle, 1919
PRUDENCE OF BROADWAY   Triangle, 1919
WHOM THE GODS DESTROY
First National, 1919
ASHES OF DESIRE   1919
HUMORESQUE   Paramount, 1920
THE DUKE OF CHIMNEY BUTTE
Federated, 1921
GET-RICH-QUICK WALLINGFORD
Paramount, 1921
BACK PAY   Paramount, 1922
BILLY JIM   Film Booking Offices, 1922
THE GOOD PROVIDER   Paramount, 1922
THE VALLEY OF SILENT MEN
Paramount, 1922
THE PRIDE OF PALOMAR   Paramount, 1922
THE NTH COMMANDMENT
Paramount, 1923
CHILDREN OF THE DUST   Associated First
National, 1923
AGE OF DESIRE   Associated First
National, 1923
SECRETS   First National, 1924
THE LADY   First National, 1925
DADDY'S GONE A-HUNTING
Metro-Goldwyn, 1925

LAZYBONES   Fox, 1925
WAGES FOR WIVES   Fox, 1925
THE CIRCLE   Metro-Goldwyn, 1925
THE FIRST YEAR   Fox, 1926
THE DIXIE MERCHANT   Fox, 1926
EARLY TO WED   Fox, 1926
MARRIAGE LICENSE?   Fox, 1926
SEVENTH HEAVEN ★★   Fox, 1927
STREET ANGEL   Fox, 1928
THE RIVER   Fox, 1929
LUCKY STAR   Fox, 1929
THEY HAD TO SEE PARIS   Fox, 1929
SONG O' MY HEART   Fox, 1930
LILIOM   Fox, 1930
DOCTORS' WIVES   Fox, 1930
YOUNG AS YOU FEEL   Fox, 1931
BAD GIRL ★★   Fox, 1931
AFTER TOMORROW   Fox, 1932
YOUNG AMERICA   Fox, 1932
A FAREWELL TO ARMS   Paramount, 1932
SECRETS   United Artists, 1933
A MAN'S CASTLE   Columbia, 1933
NO GREATER GLORY   Columbia, 1934
LITTLE MAN, WHAT NOW?
   Universal, 1934
FLIRTATION WALK   First National, 1934
LIVING ON VELVET   First National, 1935
STRANDED   Warner Bros., 1935
SHIPMATES FOREVER
   First National, 1935
DESIRE   Paramount, 1936
HEARTS DIVIDED   First National, 1936
GREEN LIGHT   Warner Bros., 1937
HISTORY IS MADE AT NIGHT
   United Artists, 1937
BIG CITY   MGM, 1937
MANNEQUIN   MGM, 1937
THREE COMRADES   MGM, 1938
THE SHINING HOUR   MGM, 1938
DISPUTED PASSAGE   Paramount, 1939
STRANGE CARGO   MGM, 1940
THE MORTAL STORM   MGM, 1940
FLIGHT COMMAND   MGM, 1940
SMILIN' THROUGH   MGM, 1941
THE VANISHING VIRGINIAN   MGM, 1942
SEVEN SWEETHEARTS   MGM, 1942
STAGE DOOR CANTEEN
   United Artists, 1943
HIS BUTLER'S SISTER   Universal, 1943
TILL WE MEET AGAIN   Paramount, 1944
THE SPANISH MAIN   RKO Radio, 1945
I'VE ALWAYS LOVED YOU   Republic, 1946
THE MAGNIFICENT DOLL   Universal, 1946
THAT'S MY MAN   Republic, 1947
MOONRISE   Republic, 1948
CHINA DOLL   United Artists, 1958
THE BIG FISHERMAN   Buena Vista, 1959

JOHN BOULTING

b. November 21, 1913 - Bray, Buckinghamshire,
   England
d. 1985

JOURNEY TOGETHER   RKO Radio,
   1945, British
YOUNG SCARFACE   BRIGHTON ROCK
   Mayer-Kingsley, 1947, British
SEVEN DAYS TO NOON   Mayer-Kingsley,
   1950, British
THE MAGIC BOX   Rank, 1952, British
CREST OF THE WAVE   SEAGULLS OVER
   SORRENTO   co-director with Roy Boulting,
   MGM, 1954, British
PRIVATE'S PROGRESS   DCA, 1956, British
LUCKY JIM   Kingsley International,
   1957, British
I'M ALL RIGHT, JACK   Columbia,
   1960, British

THE RISK   SUSPECT   co-director with
   Roy Boulting, Kingsley International,
   1961, British
HEAVENS ABOVE!   Janus, 1963, British
ROTTEN TO THE CORE   Cinema 5,
   1965, British

JEAN BOYER

b. January 26, 1901 - Paris, France
d. 1965

MONSIEUR, MADAME ET BIBI   1932, French
UN MAUVAIS GARCON   1936, French
PRENDS LA ROUTE   1937, French
LA CHALEUR DU SEIN   1938, French
MA SOEUR DE LAI   1938, French
NOIX DE COCO   1939, French
CIRCONSTANCES ATTENUATES
   1939, French
MIQUETTE ET SA MERE   1940, French
SERENADE   1940, French
L'ACROBATE   1941, French
ROMANCE DE PARIS   1941, French
LE PRINCE CHARMANT   1942, French
BOLERO   1942, French
LA BONNE ETOILE   1943, French
LA FEMME FATALE   1945, French
LES AVENTURES DE CASANOVA
   1947, French
MADEMOISELLE S'AMUSE   1948, French
TOUS LES CHEMINS MENENT A ROME
   1949, French
NOUIS IRONS A PARIS   1950, French
LA VALSE BRILLANTE   1950, French
LE ROSIER DE MADAME HUSSON
   1950, French
MR. PEEK-A-BOO   LA PASSE-MURAILLE
   Eagle Lion, 1951, French
MONTE CARLO BABY   NOUS IRONS A
   MONTE CARLO   Monogram, 1951, French
CRAZY FOR LOVE   LE TOUR NORMAND
   Ellis Films, 1951, French
COIFFEUR POUR DAMES   1952, French
FEMMES DE PARIS   1953, French
MY SEVEN LITTLE SINS   J'AVAIS SEPT
   FILLES   Kingsley International, 1956,
   French-Italian
LA MADELON   1955, French
FERNANDEL THE DRESSMAKER
   LES COUTURIER DE CES DAMES
   Union Films, 1956, French
SENECHAL THE MAGNIFICENT   DCA,
   1957, French
LE CHOMEUR DE CLOCHEMERLE
   1957, French
NINA   1958, French
LES VIGNES DU SEIGNEUR   1958, French
LE CONFIDENT DE CES DAMES
   1959, French
COUP DE BAMBOO   1962, French
RELAXE-TOI CHERIE   1964, French

CHARLES J. BRABIN

b. April 17, 1883 - Liverpool, England
d. 1957

THE AWAKENING OF JOHN BOND   1911
THE MAN WHO DISAPPEARED
   Edison, 1914
THE MIDNIGHT RIDE OF PAUL
   REVERE   1914
HOUSE OF THE LOST COURT   Edison, 1915
THE RAVEN   Essanay, 1915
THE PRICE OF FAME   Vitagraph, 1916
MARY JANE'S PA   Vitagraph, 1917
THE SIXTEENTH WIFE   Vitagraph, 1917
THE SECRET KINGDOM   co-director with
   Theodore Marston, Vitagraph, 1917

BABETTE   Vitagraph, 1917
PERSUASIVE PEGGY   Mayfair
   Shallenberger & Priest, 1917
THE ADOPTED SON   Metro, 1917
RED, WHITE AND BLUE BLOOD
   Metro, 1917
BREAKERS AHEAD   Metro, 1918
SOCIAL QUICKSANDS   Metro, 1918
A PAIR OF CUPIDS   Metro, 1918
THE POOR RICH MAN   Metro, 1918
BUCHANAN'S WIFE   Fox, 1918
HIS BONDED WIFE   Metro, 1918
THOU SHALT NOT   Fox, 1919
KATHLEEN MAVOURNEEN   Fox, 1919
LA BELLE RUSSE   Fox, 1919
WHILE NEW YOUK SLEEPS   Fox, 1920
BLIND WIFES   Fox, 1920
FOOTFALLS   Fox, 1921
THE BROADWAY PEACOCK   Fox, 1922
THE LIGHTS OF NEW YORK   Fox, 1922
DRIVEN   Universal, 1923
SIX DAYS   Goldwyn, 1923
SO BIG   First National, 1925
STELLA MARIS   Universal, 1925
MISMATES   First National, 1926
TWINKLETOES   First National, 1926
FRAMED   First National, 1927
HARD-BOILED HAGGERTY
   First National, 1927
THE VALLEY OF THE GIANTS
   First National, 1927
BURNING DAYLIGHT   First National, 1928
THE WHIP   First National, 1928
THE BRIDGE OF SAN LUIS REY   MGM, 1929
THE SHIP FROM SHANGHAI   MGM, 1930
CALL OF THE FLESH   MGM, 1930
THE GREAT MEADOW   MGM, 1931
SPORTING BLOOD   MGM, 1931
THE BEAST OF THE CITY   MGM, 1932
NEW MORALS FOR OLD   MGM, 1932
THE WASHINGTON MASQUERADE
   MGM, 1932
THE MASK OF FU MANCHU   MGM, 1932
THE SECRET OF MADAME BLANCHE
   MGM, 1932
STAGE MOTHER   MGM, 1933
DAY OF RECKONING   MGM, 1932
A WICKED WOMAN   MGM, 1932

JOHN BRAHM
(Hans Brahm)
b. August 17, 1893 - Hamburg, Germany
d. 1982

BROKEN BLOSSOMS   Twickenham,
   1936, British
COUNSEL FOR CRIME   Columbia, 1937
PENITENTIARY   Columbia, 1938
GIRL'S SCHOOL   Columbia, 1938
LET US LIVE   Columbia, 1939
RIO   Universal, 1939
ESCAPE TO GLORY   SUBMARINE ZONE
   Columbia, 1940
WILD GEESE CALLING
   20th Century-Fox, 1941
THE UNDYING MONSTER
   20th Century-Fox, 1942
TONIGHT WE RAID CALAIS
   20th Century-Fox, 1943
WINTERTIME   20th Century-Fox, 1943
THE LODGER   20th Century-Fox, 1944
GUEST IN THE HOUSE   United Artist, 1944
HANGOVER SQUARE
   20th Century-Fox, 1945
THE LOCKET   RKO RADIO, 1946
THE BRASHER DOUBLOON
   20th Century-Fox, 1947
SINGAPORE   Universal, 1947

THE THIEF OF VENICE   1950, Italian
THE MIRACLE OF OUR LADY OF FATIMA
  Warner Bros., 1952
FACE TO FACE   co-director with
  Bretaigne Windust, RKO Radio, 1952
THE DIAMOND QUEEN   Warner Bros., 1953
THE MAD MAGICIAN   Columbia, 1952
DIE GOLDENE PEST   1952, West German
SPECIAL DELIVERY   VON HIMMEL
  GEFALLEN   Columbia, 1955,
  West German-U.S.
BENGAZI   RKO Radio, 1955
HOT RODS TO HELL   MGM, 1967

HERBERT BRENON
b. January 13, 1880 - Dublin, Ireland
d. 1958

ALL FOR HER   1912
THE CLOWN'S TRIUMPH   1912
LEAH THE FORSAKEN   1912
KATHLEEN MAVOURNEEN   1913
THE ANGEL OF DEATH   1913
IVANHOE   1913, British
THE ANARCHIST   1913
ABSINTHE   1914, French
ACROSS THE ATLANTIC   1914, British
NEPTUNE'S DAUGHTER   co-director with
  Otis Turner, 1914
THE KREUTZER SONATA   1915
THE CLMENCEAU CASE   1915
THE TWO ORPHANS   1915
SIN   1915
THE SOUL OF BROADWAY   1915
WHOM THE GODS DESTROY   1916
A DAUGHTER OF THE GODS   1916
WAR BRIDES   1916
MARBLE HEART   1916
THE RULING PASSION   1916
THE ETERNAL SIN   1917
THE LONE WOLF   1917
THE FALL OF THE ROMANOFFS   1917
EMPTY POCKETS   1917
VICTORY AND PEACE   1918, British
THE PASSING OF THE THIRD
  FLOOR BACK   1918
PRINCIPESSA MISTERIOSA   1919, Italian
TWELVE: TEN   1919, British
A SINLESS SINNER   1919, British
CHAINS OF EVIDENCE   1920
THE PASSION FLOWER   1921
THE SIGN ON THE DOOR   1921
THE WONDERFUL THING   1921
ANY WIFE   1922
A STAGE ROMANCE   1922
SHACKLES OF GOLD   1922
MOONSHINE VALLEY   1922
THE CUSTARD CUP   1923
THE RUSTLE OF SILK   1923
SISTER AGAINST SISTER   1923
THE WOMAN WITH FOUR FACES   1923
THE SPANISH DANCER   1923
SHADOWS OF PARIS   1924
THE BREAKING POINT   1924
THE SIDE SHOW OF LIFE   1924
THE ALASKAN   1924
PETER PAN   1924
THE LITTLE FRENCH GIRL   1925
THE STREET OF FORGOTTEN MEN   1925
THE SONG AND DANCE MAN   1926
DANCING MOTHERS   1926
BEAU GESTE   Paramount, 1926
THE GREAT GATSBY   Paramount, 1926
GOD GAVE ME TWENTY CENTS   1926
A KISS FOR CINDERELLA   1926
THE TELEPHONE GIRL   1927
SORRELL AND SON ★   United Artists, 1927
LAUGH CLOWN LAUGH   1928

THE RESCUE   1929
LUMMOX   1930
THE CASE OF SERGEANT GRISHA   1930
BEAU IDEAL   1931
TRANSGRESSION   1931
GIRL OF THE RIO   1932
WINE, WOMEN AND SONG   1933
ROYAL CAVALCADE (FD)   1935, British
HONORS EASY   1935, British
LIVING DANGEROUSLY   1936, British
SOMEONE AT THE DOOR   1936, British
THE DOMINANT SEX   1937, British
SPRING HANDICAP   1937, British
THE LIVE WIRE   1937, British
HOUSEMASTER   1938, British
YELLOW SANDS   1938, Briitsh
BLACK EYES   1939, British
THE FLYING SQUAD   1940, British

JAMES BRIDGES
b. February 3, 1936 - Paris, Arkansas
d. 1993

THE BABY MAKER   National General, 1970
THE PAPER CHASE   20th Century-Fox, 1973
9/30/55   SEPTEMBER 30, 1955
  Universal, 1977
THE CHINA SYNDROME   Columbia, 1979
URBAN COWBOY   Paramount, 1980
MIKE'S MURDER   The Ladd Company/
  Warner Bros., 1984
PERFECT!   Columbia, 1985
BRIGHT LIGHTS, BIG CITY   MGM/UA, 1988

LINO BROCKA
b. 1940 - San Jose, Nuevo Ecija, Philippines
d. 1991

WANTED: PERFECT MOTHER
  1970, Filipino
SANTIAGO   1970, Filipino
TUBOG SA GINTO   1970, Filipino
NOW   1971, Filipino
LUMUHA PATI MGA ANGHEL   1971, Filipino
CADENA DE AMOR   1971, Filipino
STARDOOM   1971, Filipino
CHERRY BLOSSOMS   1972, Filipino
VILLA MIRANDA   1972, Filipino
YOU ARE WEIGHED IN THE BALANCE BUT
  ARE FOUND LACKING   1974, Filipino
TATLO, DALAWA, ISA   1974, Filipino
DUNG-AW   1975, Filipino
MANILA IN THE CLAWS OF LIGHT
  1975, Filipino
LUNES, MARTES, MYERKOLES...
  1976, Filipino
INSIANG   1976, Filipino
TAHAN NA EMPOY, TAHAN   1977, Filipino
INAY   1977, Filipino
LAHING PILIPINO   1977, Filipino
GUMISING KA, MARUJA   1978, Filipino
HAYOP SA HAYOP   1978, Filipino
INIT   1978, Filipino
RUBIA SERVIOS   1978, Filipino
INA, KAPATID, ANAK   1979, Filipino
INA KA NG ANAK MO   1979, Filipino
JAGUAR   1979, Filipino
BONA   1980, Filipino
NAKAW NA PAG-IBIG   1980, Filipino
ANGELA MARKADO   1980, Filipino
BORGIS   1981, Filipino
HELLO, YOUNG LOVERS   1981, Filipino
BINATA SI MISTER, BALAGA SI MISIS
  1981, Filipino
LAMENTATIONS (TF)   1981, Filipino
CAIN AT ABEL   1982, Filipino
P.X.   1982, Filipino

KONTROBERSYAL   1982, Filipino
IN THIS CORNER   1982, Filipino
CAUGHT IN THE ACT   1982, Filipino
PALIPAT-LIPAT, PAPALIT-PALIT   1982, Filipino
MOTHER DEAR   1982, Filipino
EXPERIENCE   1983, Filipino
STRANGERS IN PARADISE   1983, Filipino
HOT PROPERTY   1984, Filipino
MY COUNTRY: IN DESPERATE STRAITS
  BAYAN-KO   1984, Filipino
MISQUELITO   1984, Filipino
ANO ANG KULAY NG MUKHA NG DIYOS?
  LEA Productions, 1985, Filipino
HINUGOT SA LANGIT   1986, Filipino
MACHO DANCER   Special People
  Productions, 1988, Filipino
I CARRY THE WORLD   1988, Filipino
FIGHT FOR US   Cannon, 1989,
  French-Filipino
DIRTY AFFAIR   Viva Films, 1990, Filipino

RICHARD BROOKS
b. May 18, 1912 - Philadelphia, Pennsylvania
d. 1992

CRISIS   MGM, 1950
THE LIGHT TOUCH   MGM, 1951
DEADLINE - U.S.A.   MGM, 1952
BATTLE CIRCUS   MGM, 1953
TAKE THE HIGH GROUND   MGM, 1953
FLAME AND THE FLESH   MGM, 1954
THE LAST TIME I SAW PARIS   MGM, 1954
THE BLACKBOARD JUNGLE   MGM, 1955
THE LAST HUNT   MGM, 1956
THE CATERED AFFAIR   MGM, 1956
SOMETHING OF VALUE   MGM, 1957
CAT ON A HOT TIN ROOF ★   MGM, 1958
THE BROTHERS KARAMAZOV   MGM, 1958
ELMER GANTRY   United Artists, 1960
SWEET BIRD OF YOUTH   MGM, 1962
LORD JIM   Columbia, 1964
THE PROFESSIONALS ★   Columbia, 1966
IN COLD BLOOD ★   Columbia, 1967
THE HAPPY ENDING   United Artists, 1969
$ DOLLARS   Columbia, 1971
BITE THE BULLET   Columbia, 1975
LOOKING FOR MR. GOODBAR
  Paramount, 1977
WRONG IS RIGHT   Columbia, 1982
FEVER PITCH   MGM/UA, 1985

CLARENCE BROWN
b. May 10, 1890 - Clinton, Massachusetts
d. 1987

THE GREAT REDEEMER   co-director with
  Maurice Tourneur, Metro, 1920
THE LAST OF THE MOHICANS   co-director
  with Maurice Tourneur, 1920
THE FOOLISH MATRONS   co-director with
  Maurice Tourneur, 1921
THE LIGHT IN THE DARK   Associated First
  National, 1922
DON'T MARRY FOR MONEY   Webster, 1923
THE ACQUITTAL   Universal, 1923
THE SIGNAL TOWER   Universal, 1924
BUTTERFLY   Universal, 1924
SMOULDERING FIRES   Universal, 1925
THE EAGLE   Universal, 1925
THE GOOSE WOMAN   Universal, 1925
KIKI   MGM, 1926
FLESH AND THE DEVIL   MGM, 1927
THE TRAIL OF '98   MGM, 1928
A WOMAN OF AFFAIRS   MGM, 1928
THE WONDER OF WOMEN   MGM, 1929
NAVY BLUES   MGM, 1929
ANNA CHRISTIE ★   MGM, 1930

ROMANCE ★ MGM, 1930
INSPIRATION MGM, 1931
A FREE SOUL ★ MGM, 1931
POSSESSED MGM, 1931
EMMA MGM, 1932
LETTY LYNTON MGM, 1932
THE SON-DAUGHTER MGM, 1932
LOOKING FORWARD MGM, 1933
NIGHT FLIGHT MGM, 1933
SADIE MCKEE MGM, 1934
CHAINED MGM, 1934
ANNA KARENINA MGM, 1935
AH WILDERNESS! MGM, 1935
WIFE VERSUS SECRETARY MGM, 1936
THE GORGEOUS HUSSY MGM, 1936
CONQUEST *MARIA WALEWSKA*
MGM, 1937
OF HUMAN HEARTS MGM, 1938
IDIOT'S DELIGHT MGM, 1939
THE RAINS CAME MGM, 1939
EDISON THE MAN MGM, 1940
COME LIVE WITH ME MGM, 1941
THEY MET IN BOMBAY MGM, 1941
THE HUMAN COMEDY ★ MGM, 1943
THE WHITE CLIFFS OF DOVER MGM, 1944
NATIONAL VELVET ★ MGM, 1945
THE YEARLING ★ MGM, 1947
SONG OF LOVE MGM, 1947
INTRUDER IN THE DUST MGM, 1950
TO PLEASE A LADY MGM, 1950
ANGELS IN THE OUTFIELD MGM, 1951
IT'S A BIG COUNTRY co-director with
CharlesVidor, Richard Thorpe, John Sturges,
Don Hartman, Don Weis & William Wellman,
MGM, 1952
WHEN IN ROME MGM, 1952
PLYMOUTH ADVENTURE MGM, 1952

TOD BROWNING

b. July 12, 1882 - Louisville, Kentucky
d. 1962

JIM BLUDSO co-director with Wilfred Lucas,
Fine Arts-Triangle, 1917
A LOVE SUBLIME co-director with
Wilfred Lucas, Fine Arts-Triangle, 1917
HANDS UP co-director with Wilfred Lucas,
Fine Arts-Triangle, 1917
PEGGY THE WILL-0'-THE-WISP Metro, 1917
THE JURY OF FATE Metro, 1917
THE EYES OF MYSTERY Metro, 1918
WHICH WOMAN Bluebird-Universal, 1918
THE DECIDING KISS
Bluebird-Universal, 1918
REVENGE Metro, 1918
THE LEGION OF DEATH Metro, 1918
THE BRAZEN BEAUTY Universal, 1918
SET FREE Bluebird-Universal, 1918
THE UNPAINTED WOMAN Universal, 1919
THE WICKED DARLING Universal, 1919
THE EXQUISITE THIEF Universal, 1919
A PETAL ON THE CURRENT
Universal, 1919
BONNIE BONNIE LASSIE Universal, 1919
THE VIRGIN OF STAMBOUL Universal, 1920
OUTSIDE THE LAW Universal, 1921
NO WOMAN KNOWS Universal, 1921
THE WISE KID Universal, 1922
MAN UNDER COVER Universal, 1922
UNDER TWO FLAGS Universal, 1922
DRIFTING Universal, 1923
WHITE TIGER Universal, 1923
THE DAY OF FAITH Goldwyn, 1923
THE DANGEROUS FLIRT Film Booking
Office, 1924
SILK STOCKING SAL Film Booking
Office, 1924
THE UNHOLY THREE MGM, 1925

THE MYSTIC MGM, 1925
DOLLAR DOWN Truart, 1925
THE BLACK BIRD MGM, 1926
THE ROAD TO MANDALAY MGM, 1926
THE SHOW MGM, 1927
THE UNKNOWN MGM, 1927
LONDON AFTER MIDNIGHT MGM, 1927
THE BIG CITY MGM, 1928
WEST OF ZANZIBAR MGM, 1928
WHERE EAST IS EAST MGM, 1929
THE THIRTEENTH CHAIR MGM, 1929
OUTSIDE THE LAW Universal, 1930
DRACULA Universal, 1931
THE IRON MAN Universal, 1931
FREAKS MGM, 1932
FAST WORKERS MGM, 1933
MARK OF THE VAMPIRE MGM, 1935
THE DEVIL DOLL MGM, 1936
MIRACLES FOR SALE MGM, 1939

FRANCO BRUSATI

b. August 4, 1922 - Milan, Italy
d. 1993

IL PADRONE SONO ME Rizzoli Film,
1956, Italian
IL DISORDINE Titanus/Societe Nouvelle
Pathe, 1962, Italian-French
TENDERLY Italnoleggio, 1968, Italian
I TULIPANI DI HAARLEM Ultra Film,
1970, Italian
BREAD AND CHOCOLATE World Northal,
1978, Italian
TO FORGET VENICE Quartet, 1980,
Italian-French
THE GOOD SOLDIER Gaumont,
1982, Italian
THE SLEAZY UNCLE Castle Hill Productions/
Quartet Films, 1989, Italian

LUIS BUÑUEL

b. February 22, 1900 - Calanda, Spain
d. 1983

UN CHIEN ANDALOU co-director with
Salvador Dali, 1928, French
L'AGE D'OR 1930, French
LAS HURDES 1932, Spanish
GRAN CASINO Azteca Films, 1947, Mexican
EL GRAN CALAVERA Azteca Films,
1949, Mexican
LOS OLVIDADOS *THE YOUNG AND THE
DAMNED* Mayer-Kingsley, 1950, Mexican
SUSANA *DEMONIO Y CARNE* Azteca Films,
1951, Mexican
LA HIJA DEL ENGANO Azteca Films,
1951, Mexican
UNA MUJER SIN AMOR Azteca Films,
1951, Mexican
SUBIDA AL CIELO *MEXICAN BUS RIDE*
Azteca Films, 1951, Mexican
EL BRUTO Azteca Films, 1952, Mexican
THE ADVENTURES OF ROBINSON CRUSOE
United Artists, 1952, Mexican
EL *THIS STRANGE PASSION* Azteca Films,
1952, Mexican
ABISMOS DE PASION *CUMBRES
BORRASCOSAS/WUTHERING HEIGHTS*
Azteca Films, 1953, Mexican
LA ILUSION VIAJA EN TRANVIA
Azteca Films, 1953, Mexican
EL RIO Y LA MUERTE Azteca Films,
1954, Mexican
THE CRIMINAL LIFE OF ARCHIBALDO DE
LA CRUZ Azteca Films, 1955, Mexican
CELA S'APPELLE L'AURORE 1956,
French-Italian

DEATH IN THE GARDEN Bauer International,
1956, French-Mexican
NAZARIN Altura Films Limited,
1959, Mexican
LA FIEVRE MONTE A EL PAO *REPUBLIC
OF SIN* 1960, French-Mexican
THE YOUNG ONE Vitalite, 1961, Mexican
VIRIDIANA Kingsley International, 1961,
Spanish-Mexican
THE EXTERMINATING ANGEL Altura Films
Limited, 1962, Mexican
DIARY OF A CHAMBERMAID International
Classics, 1964, French-Italian
SIMON OF THE DESERT Altura Films
Limited, 1965, Mexican
BELLE DE JOUR Allied Artists, 1967,
French-Italian
THE MILKY WAY United Artists, 1967,
French-Italian
TRISTANA Maron Films Limited, 1970,
Spanish-French-Italian
THE DISCREET CHARM OF THE
BOURGEOISIE 20th Century-Fox,
1972, French
THE PHANTOM OF LIBERTE
20th Century-Fox, 1974, French
THAT OBSCURE OBJECT OF DESIRE
First Artists, 1977, French

DAVID BUTLER

b. December 17, 1894 - San Francisco,
California
d. 1979

HIGH SCHOOL HERO Fox, 1927
THE NEWS PARADE Fox, 1928
WIN THAT GIRL Fox, 1928
PREP AND PEP Fox, 1928
MASKED EMOTIONS co-director with
Kenneth Hawks, Fox, 1929
FOX MOVIETONE FOLLIES OF 1929
Fox, 1929
CHASING THROUGH EUROPE co-director
with Alfred Werker, Fox, 1929
SUNNY SIDE UP Fox, 1929
HIGH SOCIETY BLUES Fox, 1930
JUST IMAGINE Fox, 1930
A CONNECTICUT YANKEE Fox, 1931
DELICIOUS Fox, 1931
BUSINESS AND PLEASURE Fox, 1932
DOWN TO EARTH Fox, 1932
HANDLE WITH CARE Fox, 1932
HOLD ME TIGHT Fox, 1933
MY WEAKNESS Fox, 1933
BOTTOMS UP Fox, 1934
HANDY ANDY Fox, 1934
HAVE A HEART Fox, 1934
BRIGHT EYES Fox, 1934
THE LITTLE COLONEL
20th Century-Fox, 1935
DOUBTING THOMAS
20th Century-Fox, 1935
THE LITTLEST REBEL
20th Century-Fox, 1935
CAPTAIN JANUARY 20th Century-Fox, 1936
WHITE FANG 20th Century-Fox, 1936
PIGSKIN PARADE 20th Century-Fox, 1936
ALI BABA GOES TO TOWN
20th Century-Fox, 1937
YOU'RE A SWEETHEART Universal, 1937
KENTUCKY MOONSHINE
20th Century-Fox, 1938
STRAIGHT PLACE AND SHOW
20th Century-Fox, 1938
KENTUCKY 20th Century-Fox, 1938
EAST SIDE OF HEAVEN Universal, 1939
THAT'S RIGHT, YOU'RE WRONG
RKO Radio, 1939

IF I HAD MY WAY   Universal, 1940
YOU'LL FIND OUT   RKO Radio, 1940
CAUGHT IN THE DRAFT   Paramount, 1941
PLAYMATES   RKO Radio, 1941
THE ROAD TO MOROCCO   Paramount, 1942
THEY GOT ME COVERED   RKO Radio, 1943
THANK YOUR LUCKY STARS
   Warner Bros., 1943
SHINE ON HARVEST MOON
   Warner Bros., 1944
THE PRINCESS AND THE PIRATE
   RKO Radio, 1944
SAN ANTONIO   Warner Bros., 1945
TWO GUYS FROM MILWAUKEE
   Warner Bros., 1946
THE TIME, THE PLACE AND THE GIRL
   Warner Bros., 1946
MY WILD IRISH ROSE   Warner Bros., 1947
TWO GUYS FROM TEXAS
   Warner Bros., 1948
JOHN LOVES MARY   Warner Bros., 1949
LOOK FOR THE SILVER LINING
   Warner Bros., 1949
IT'S A GREAT FEELING   Warner Bros., 1949
THE STORY OF SEABISCUIT
   Warner Bros., 1949
THE DAUGHTER OF ROSIE O'GRADY
   Warner Bros., 1950
TEA FOR TWO   Warner Bros., 1950
THE LULLABY OF BROADWAY
   Warner Bros., 1951
PAINTING THE CLOUDS WITH SUNSHINE
   Warner Bros., 1951
WHERE'S CHARLEY?   Warner Bros., 1952
APRIL IN PARIS   Warner Bros., 1952
BY THE LIGHT OF THE SILVERY MOON
   Warner Bros., 1953
CALAMITY JANE   Warner Bros., 1953
THE COMMAND   Warner Bros., 1954
KING RICHARD AND THE CRUSADERS
   Warner Bros., 1954
JUMP INTO HELL   Warner Bros., 1955
GLORY   RKO Radio, 1956
THE GIRL HE LEFT BEHIND
   Warner Bros., 1956
THE RIGHT APPROACH
   20th Century-Fox, 1961
C'MON, LET'S LIVE A LITTLE
   Paramount, 1967

EDWARD (EDDIE) BUZZELL
b. November 13, 1897 - Brooklyn, New York
d. 1985

THE BIG TIMER   Columbia, 1932
HOLLYWOOD SPEAKS   Columbia, 1932
VIRTUE   Columbia, 1932
CHILD OF MANHATTAN   Columbia, 1933
ANN CARVER'S PROFESSION
   Columbia, 1933
LOVE, HONOR AND OH BABY!
   Universal, 1933
CROSS COUNTRY CRUISE   Universal, 1934
THE HUMAN SIDE   Universal, 1934
TRANSIENT LADY   Universal, 1935
THE GIRL FRIEND   Columbia, 1935
THREE MARRIED MEN   Paramount, 1936
THE LUCKIEST GIRL IN THE WORLD
   Universal, 1936
AS GOOD AS MARRIED   Universal, 1937
PARADISE FOR THREE   MGM, 1938
FAST COMPANY   MGM, 1938
HONOLULU   MGM, 1939
AT THE CIRCUS   MGM, 1939
GO WEST   MGM, 1940
THE GET-AWAY   MGM, 1941
MARRIED BACHELOR   MGM, 1941
SHIP AHOY   MGM, 1942

THE OMAHA TRAIL   MGM, 1942
THE YOUNGEST PROFESSION   MGM, 1943
BEST FOOT FORWARD   MGM, 1943
KEEP YOUR POWDER DRY   MGM, 1945
EASY TO WED   MGM, 1946
THREE WISE FOOLS   MGM, 1946
SONG OF THE THIN MAN   MGM, 1947
NEPTUNE'S DAUGHTER   MGM, 1949
A WOMAN OF DISTINCTION
   Columbia, 1950
EMERGENCY WEDDING   Columbia, 1950
CONFIDENTIALLY CONNIE   MGM, 1953
AIN'T MISBEHAVIN'   Universal, 1955
MARY HAD A LITTLE...   1961, British

C

CHRISTY CABANNE
(William Christy Cabanne)
b. April 16, 1888 - St. Louis Missouri
d. 1950

THE ADOPTED BROTHER   1913
THE BLUE OR THE GRAY   1913
THE CONSCIENCE OF HASSAN BEY   1913
THE SUFFRAGETTE MINSTRELS   1913
THE VENGEANCE OF GALORA   1913
THE GREAT LEAP   1914
THE DISHONORED MEDAL   1914
THE LIFE OF GENERAL VILLA   co-director
   with Raoul Walsh, Biograph, 1914
THE SMUGGLERS OF SLIGO   1914
FOR THOSE UNBORN   1914
HER AWAKENING   1914
THE ODALISQUE   1914
ARMS AND THE GRINGO   1914
THE BETTER WAY   1914
THE GANGSTERS OF NEW YORK
   Biograph, 1914
GRANNY   1914
THE REBELLION OF KITTY BELLE   1914
THE SISTERS   1914
THE LOST HOUSE   1915
ENOCH ARDEN   *THE FATAL*
   MARRIAGE   1915
THE MARTYRS OF THE ALAMO
   Triangle Film Corporation, 1915
THE ABSENTEE   co-director with
   Frank E. Woods, 1915
THE FAILURE   1915
THE LAMB   1915
DOUBLE TROUBLE   1915
SOLD FOR MARRIAGE   1916
THE FLYING TORPEDO   1916
DIANE OF THE FOLLIES   1916
REGGIE MIXES IN   1916
DAPHNE AND THE PIRATE   1916
FLIRTING WITH FATE   1916
THE GREAT SECRET (S)   1917
ONE OF MANY   1917
MISS ROBINSON CRUSOE   1917
THE SLACKER   1917
DRAFT 258   1918
CYCLONE OF HIGGINS D.D.   1918
GOD'S OUTLAW   1919
FIGHTING THROUGH   1919
THE PEST   1919
A REGULAR FELLOW   1919
THE MAYOR OF FILBERT   1919

THE BELOVED CHEATER   1919
THE TRIFLERS   1920
BURNT WINGS   1920
THE NOTORIOUS MRS. SANDS   1920
LIFE'S TWIST   1920
WHAT'S A WIFE WORTH?   1921
LIVE AND LET LIVE   1921
THE BARRICADE   1921
AT THE STAGE DOOR   1921
BEYOND THE RAINBOW   1922
TILL WE MEET AGAIN   1922
THE AVERAGE WOMAN   1924
THE SPITFIRE   1924
THE SIXTH COMMANDMENT   1924
LEND ME YOUR HUSBAND   1924
YOUTH FOR SALE   1924
IS LOVE EVERYTHING?   1924
THE MIDSHIPMAN   1925
THE MASKED BRIDE   co-director with
   Josef Von Sternberg, MGM, 1925
MONTE CARLO   1926
ALTARS OF DESIRE   1927
NAMELESS MEN   1928
DRIFTWOOD   1928
ANNAPOLIS   1928
RESTLESS YOUTH   1928
CONSPIRACY   1930
THE DAWN TRAIL   1930
CARNE DE CABARET   1931
SKYRAIDERS   1931
CONVICTED   1931
GRAFT   1931
HOTEL CONTINENTAL   1932
THE MIDNIGHT PATROL   1932
HEARTS OF HUMANITY   1932
THE WESTERN LIMITED   1932
RED-HAIRED ALIBI   1932
THE UNWRITTEN LAW   1932
THE ELEVENTH COMMANDMENT   1933
DARING DAUGHTERS   1933
THE WORLD GONE MAD   1933
MIDSHIPMAN JACK   1933
MONEY MEANS NOTHING   1934
JANE EYRE   Monogram, 1934
A GIRL OF THE LIMBERLOST   1934
WHEN STRANGERS MEET   1934
BEHIND THE GREEN LIGHTS   1935
RENDEZVOUS AT MIDNIGHT   1935
ONE FRIGHTENED NIGHT   1935
THE KEEPER OF THE BEES   1935
STORM OVER THE ANDES   1935
ANOTHER FACE   1935
THE LAST OUTLAW   1936
WE WHO ARE ABOUT TO DIE   1937
CRIMINAL LAWYER   1937
DON'T TELL THE WIFE   1937
THE OUTCASTS OF POKER FLAT   1937
YOU CAN'T BEAT LOVE   1937
ANNAPOLIS SALUTE   1937
THE WESTLAND CASE   1937
EVERYBODY'S DOING IT   1938
NIGHT SPOT   1938
THIS MARRIAGE BUSINESS   1938
SMASHING THE SPY RING   1938
MUTINY ON THE BLACKHAWK
   Universal, 1939
TROPIC FURY   1939
LEGION OF LOST FLYERS   1939
MAN FROM MONTREAL   1940
DANGER ON WHEELS   1940
ALIAS THE DEACON   1940
HOT STEEL   1940
BLACK DIAMONDS   1940
THE MUMMY'S HAND   Universal, 1940
THE DEVIL'S PIPELINE   1940
SCATTERGOOD BAINES   1941
SCATTERGOOD PULLS THE STRING   1941
SCATTERGOOD MEETS BROADWAY   1941

SCATTERGOOD RIDES HIGH   1942
DRUMS OF THE CONGO   1942
TIMBER   1942
TOP SERGEANT   1942
SCATTERGOOD SURVIVES A
   MURDER   1942
KEEP 'EM SLUGGING   1943
DIXIE JAMBOREE   1944
THE MAN WHO WALKED ALONE   1945
SENSATION HUNTERS   1946
ROBIN HOOD OF MONTEREY   1947
KING OF THE BANDITS   1947
SCARED TO DEATH   1947
BLACK TRAIL   1948
SILVER TRAILS   1948

EDWARD L. CAHN
b. February 12, 1899 - Brooklyn, New York
d. 1963

HOMICIDE SQUAD   co-director with
   George Melford, Universal, 1931
LAW AND ORDER   Universal, 1932
RADIO PATROL   Universal, 1932
AFRAID TO TALK   Universal, 1932
LAUGHTER IN HELL   Universal, 1933
EMERGENCY CALL   Universal, 1933
CONFIDENTIAL   1935
BAD GUY   1937
REDHEAD   1941
MAIN STREET AFTER DARK   1945
DANGEROUS PARTNERS   1945
BORN TO SPEED   1947
GAS HOUSE KIDS IN HOLLYWOOD   1947
THE CHECKERED COAT   1948
BUNGALOW 13   1948
I CHEATED THE LAW   1949
PREJUDICE   1949
THE GREAT PLANE ROBBERY   1950
DESTINATION MURDER   1950
EXPERIMENT ALCATRAZ   1950
TWO DOLLAR BETTOR   1951
THE CREATURE WITH THE ATOM BRAIN
   Columbia, 1955
BETRAYED WOMEN   Allied Artists, 1955
GIRLS IN PRISON   American
   International, 1956
THE SHE-CREATURE   American
   International, 1956
FLESH AND THE SPUR   1956
RUNAWAY DAUGHTERS   American
   International, 1956
SHAKE, RATTLE AND ROCK!   American
   International, 1956
VOODOO WOMAN   American
   International, 1957
ZOMBIES OF MORA-TAU   Columbia, 1957
DRAGSTRIP GIRL   American
   International, 1957
INVASION OF THE SAUCER MEN   American
   International, 1957
MOTORCYCLE GANG   American
   International, 1957
JET ATTACK   American International, 1958
SUICIDE BATALLION   American
   International, 1958
IT! - THE TERROR FROM BEYOND SPACE
   United Artists, 1958
THE CURSE OF THE FACELESS MAN
   United Artists, 1958
HONG KONG CONFIDENTIAL
   United Artists, 1958
GUNS, GIRLS AND GANGSTERS
   United Artists, 1959
RIOT IN JUVENILE PRISON
   United Artists, 1959
INVISIBLE INVADERS   United Artists, 1959

THE FOUR SKULLS OF JONATHAN DRAKE
   United Artists, 1959
PIER 5 - HAVANA   United Artists, 1959
INSIDE THE MAFIA   United Artists, 1959
VICE RAID   United Artists, 1960
GUNFIGHTERS OF ABILENE
   United Artists, 1960
A DOG'S BEST FRIEND   United Artists, 1960
OKLAHOMA TERRITORY
   United Artists, 1960
THREE CAME TO KILL   United Artists, 1960
TWELVE HOURS TO KILL
   20th Century-Fox, 1960
NOOSE FOR A GUNMAN
   United Artists, 1960
THE MUSIC BOX KID   United Artists, 1960
CAGE OF EVIL   United Artists, 1960
THE WALKING TARGET   United Artists, 1960
THE POLICE DOG STORY
   United Artists, 1961
FRONTIER UPRISING   United Artists, 1961
OPERATION BOTTLENECK
   United Artists, 1961
FIVE GUNS TO TOMBSTONE
   United Artists, 1961
THE GAMBLER WORE A GUN
   United Artists, 1961
WHEN THE CLOCK STRIKES
   United Artists, 1961
YOU HAVE TO RUN FAST
   United Artists, 1961
SECRET OF DEEP HARBOR
   United Artists, 1961
THE BOY WHO CAUGHT A CROOK
   United Artists, 1961
GUN FIGHT   United Artists, 1961
GUN STREET   United Artists, 1961
THE CLOWN AND THE KID
   United Artists, 1961
INCIDENT IN AN ALLEY   United Artists, 1962
BEAUTY AND THE BEAST
   United Artists, 1963

MARIO CAMERINI
b. February 6, 1895 - Rome, Italy
d. 1981

JOLLY - CLOWN DA CIRCO   DDAA,
   1923, Italian
LA CASA DEI PULCINI   Fert, 1924, Italian
SAETTA - PRINCIPE PER UN GIORNO
   Fert, 1924, Italian
VOGLIO TRADIRE MIO MARITO!
   Fert, 1925, Italian
MACISTE CONTRO LO SCEICCO   Fert, 1926
KIFF TEBBI   ADIA, 1928, Italian
ROTAIE SACIA   Nero Film, 1929,
   Italian-German
LA RIVA DEI BRUTI   Paramount Joinville,
   1930, Italian-French
FIGARO E LA SUA GRAN GIORNATA
   Cines, 1931, Italian
L'ULTIMA AVVENTURA   Cines, 1932, Italian
GLI UOMINI, CHE MASCALZONI!   Cines,
   1932, Italian
T'AMERO' SEMPRE   Cines, 1933, Italian
CENTO DI QUESTI GIORNI   1933, Italian
GIALLO   Cines, 1933, Italian
IL CAPPELLO A TRE PUNTE   Lido Film,
   1934, Italian
COME LE FOGLIE   ICI, 1934, Italian
DARO' UN MILIONE   Novella Film,
   1935, Italian
IL GRANDE APPELLO   Artisti Associati,
   1936, Italian
MA NON E UNA COSA SERIA   1936, Italian
IL SIGNOR MAX   Astra Film, 1937, Italian
BATTICUORE   1938, Italian

DER MANN, DER NICHT NEIN SAGEN KANN
   Itala Film/Max Huske, 1938, German-Italian
BATTICUORE   Era Film, 1939, Italian
IL DOCUMENTO   Secret/Scalera,
   1939, Italian
CENTOMILA DOLLARI   Astra Film,
   1940, Italian
UNA ROMANTICA AVVENTURA   ENIC,
   1940, Italian
I PROMESSI SPOSI   Lux Film, 1941, Italian
UNA STORIA D'AMORE   Lux Film,
   1942, Italian
T'AMERO' SEMPRE   Cines, 1943, Italian
DUE LETTERE ANONIME   Ninfa/Lux Film,
   1945, Italian
L'ANGELO E IL DIAVOLO   Lore Film,
   1946, Italian
LA FIGLIA DEL CAPITANO   Lux Film/RDL,
   1947, Italian
MOLTI SOGNI PER LE STRADE   Lux Film,
   1948, Italian
DUE MOGLI SONO TROPPE
   HONEYMOON DEFERRED   Cines/Vic Film,
   1950, Italian-British
IL GRIGANTE MUSOLINO   Ponti/De
   Laurentiis, 1950, Italian
MOGLIE PER UNNA NOTTE   Rizzoli & Cie,
   1952, Italian-French
GLI EROI DELLA DOMENICA   Rizzoli & Cie,
   1952, Italian-French
ULYSSES   Paramount, 1954, Italian-French
THE MILLER'S BEAUTIFUL WIFE   *LA BELLA
   MUGNAIA*   DCA, 1955, Italian
THE AWAKENING   *SUOR LETIZIA*
   Kingsley International, 1956, Italian
VACANZE A ISCHIA   Rizzoli Film/Francinex/
   Bavaria Filmkunst, 1957,
   Italian-French-West German
PRIMO AMORE   CIRAC, 1958, Italian
VIA MARGUTTA   Documento Film,
   1960, Italian
...AND SUDDENLY IT'S MURDER!
   CRIMEN   Royal Films International, 1960,
   Italian-French
I BRIGANTI ITALIANI   Fairfilm/Orsay Film,
   1961, Italian-French
KALI YUG - LA DEA DELLA VENDETTA
   Serena Film/Criterion Film/Eichberg Film,
   1963, Italian-French-West German
IL MISTERO DEL TEMPIO INDIANO   Serena
   Film/Criterion Film/Eichberg Film, 1963,
   Italian-French-West German
DELITTO QUASI PERFETTO   Rizzoli Film/
   Franco London Film, 1966, Italian-French
IO NON VEDO TU NON PARLI LUI NON
   SENTE   De Laurentiis IMC, 1971, Italian
DON CAMILLO E I GIOVANI D'OGGI
   Rizzoli Film/Francoriz Production, 1972,
   Italian-French

PASQUALE FESTA CAMPANILE
b. July 28, 1927 - Melfi, Italy
d. 1986

UN TENTATIVE SENTIMENTALE   co-director
   with Massimo Franciosa, 1963, Italian
WHITE VOICES   co-director with Massimo
   Franciosa, Rizzoli, 1964, Italian-French
LA COSTANZA DELLA REGIONE
   1964, Italian
A MAIDEN FOR A PRINCE   Royal Films
   International, 1965, Italian-French
ADULTERIO ALL' ITALIANA   1966, Italian
THE GIRL AND THE GENERAL   MGM, 1967,
   Italian-French
ON MY WAY TO THE CRUSADES, I MET A
   GIRL WHO...   *THE CHASTITY BELT*
   Warner Bros., 1969, Italian-U.S.

IL MARITO E MIO E L'AMAZZO QUANDO
 MI PARE 1968, Italian
THE LIBERTINE Audubon, 1968, Italian
DOVE VAI TUTTA NUDA? 1969, Italian
SCACCO ALLA REGINA 1970, Italian
CON QUALE AMORE CON QUANTO AMORE
 1970, Italian
WHEN WOMEN HAD TAILS Film Ventures
 International, 1970, Italian
IL MERLO MASCHIO 1971, Italian
JUS PRIMA NOCTIS 1972, Italian
LA CALANDRIA 1972, Italian
WHEN WOMEN LOST THEIR TAILS
 Film Ventures International, 1972,
 Italian-West German
L'EMIGRANTE 1973, Italian
RUGANTINO 1973, Italian
LA SCULACCIATA 1974, Italian
SOLDIER OF FORTUNE 1975, Italian
HUMUNQUS HECTOR 1976, Italian
CARA SPOSA 1977, Italian
AUTOSTOP 1977, Italian
PARLAMI D'AMORE MARIA 1977, Italian
IL RITORNO DI CASANOVA (TF)
 1978, Italian
CORNE PERDERE UNA MOGLIE E TROVARE
 UN' AMANTE 1978, Italian
BELLOW MA DANNATO 1979, Italian
GEGE BELLAVITA 1979, Italian

CARLO CAMPOGALLIANI

b. October 10, 1885 - Concordia, Italy
d. 1974

TRENO REALE 1915, Italian
QUANDO SI AMA 1915, Italian
L'AMAZONE MACABRA 1916, Italian
L'ISOLA TENEBROSA 1916, Italian
LA SERATA D'HONORE DI BUFFALO
 1916, Italian
L'AERONAVE IN FIAMME 1918, Italian
L'OMBRA CHE PARLA 1918, Italian
IL MARCHI ROSSO 1918, Italian
MACISTE I 1919, Italian
LA CASA DELLA PAURA 1919, Italian
MACISTE CONTRO LA MORTE 1919, Italian
SCACCO MATTO 1919, Italian
UN SIMPATICO MASCALZONE 1919, Italian
IL TESCHIO D'ORO 1921, Italian
BRESAGLIO UMANO 1922, Italian
L'ANTENATO 1922, Italian
LA VUELTA DEL TORO 1924, Argentine
CORTILE Cines, 1930, Italian
MEDICO PER FORZA Cines, 1931, Italian
LA LANTERNA DEL DIAVOLO Cines,
 1931, Italian
STADIO Ardita Societa Anonima, 1934, Italian
I QUATTRO MOSCHETTIERI Miniatura Film,
 1936, Italian
MONTEVERGINE LA GRANDE LUCE
 Diana Film, 1938, Italian
LA NOTTE DELLE BEFFE Iris Film,
 1940, Italian
CUORI NELLA TORMENTA Atesia,
 1941, Italian
IL CAVALIERE DI KRUJA Capitani Film,
 1940, Italian
IL BRAVO DI VENEZIA Scalera Film,
 1941, Italian
PERIDIZIONE Scalera Film, 1942, Italian
MUSICA PROIBITA Elica Film/APPIA,
 1943, Italian
L'INNOCENTE CASIMIRIO Ars Societa
 Produzioni Cinematografiche, 1945, Italian
LA GONDOLA DEL DIAVOLO Scalera Film,
 1947, Italian
LA MANO DELLA MORTA Icet, 1949, Italian

BELLEZZE IN BICICLETTA Edic,
 1951, Italian
BELLEZZE IN MOTOSCOOTER
 Safa Palatino, 1952, Italian
L'ORFANA DEL GHETTO Ambra Film,
 1954, Italian
FOGLIO DI VIA Ambra Film, 1954, Italian
TORNA, PICCINA MIA! Glomer Film,
 1955, Italian
LA CANZONE DEL CUORE Jonia Film,
 1955, Italian
L'ANGELO DELLA ALPI Prora Film,
 1957, Italian
SERENATELLA SCIUE' SCIUE' CINEF,
 1958, Italian
CAPITAN FUOCO Transfilm Importazione
 Distribuzione, 1959, Italian
GOLIATH AND THE BARBARIANS
 IL TERRORE DEI BARBARI American
 International, 1959, Italian
FONTANA DI TREVI Cineproduzioni
 Associete/Tiber Film/AIT/Cineprodex,
 1960, Italian-French-Yugoslavian
SON OF SAMSON MACISTE NELLA VALLE
 DEI RE Medallion, 1960,
 Italian-French-Yugoslavian
MIGHTY URSUS URSUS United Artists,
 1961, Italian-Spanish
SWORD OF THE CONQUEROR ROSMUNDA
 E ALBOINO United Artists, 1961, Italian

MARCEL CAMUS

b. April 21, 1912 - Chappes, France
d. 1982

FUGITIVE IN SAIGON MORT EN FRAUDE
 Rank, 1957, French
BLACK ORPHEUS Lopert, 1959,
 Brazilian-French
OS BANDEIRANTES 1960, Brazilian-French
L'OISEAU DE PARADIS 1962, French
LE CHANT DU MONDE 1965, French
L'HOMME DE NEW YORK 1967, French
VIVRE LA NUIT 1968, French
LE MUR DE L'ATLANTIQUE 1970, French
UN ETE SAUVAGE 1970, French
OS PASTORIS DA NOITE 1977,
 Brazilian-French

FRANK CAPRA

b. May 18, 1897 - Bisaquino, Sicily, Italy
d. 1991

THE STRONG MAN First National, 1926
LONG PANTS First National, 1927
FOR THE LOVE OF MIKE
 First National, 1927
THAT CERTAIN THING Columbia, 1928
SO THIS IS LOVE Columbia, 1928
THE MATINEE IDOL Columbia, 1928
THE WAY OF THE STRONG Columbia, 1928
SAY IT WITH SABLES Columbia, 1928
SUBMARINE Columbia, 1928
THE POWER OF THE PRESS
 Columbia, 1928
THE YOUNGER GENERATION
 Columbia, 1929
THE DONOVAN AFFAIR Columbia, 1929
FLIGHT Columbia, 1929
LADIES OF LEISURE Columbia, 1930
RAIN OR SHINE Columbia, 1930
DIRIGIBLE Columbia, 1931
THE MIRACLE WOMAN Columbia, 1931
PLATINUM BLONDE Columbia, 1931
FORBIDDEN Columbia, 1932
AMERICAN MADNESS Columbia, 1932
THE BITTER TEA OF GENERAL YEN
 Columbia, 1933

LADY FOR A DAY ★ Columbia, 1933
IT HAPPENED ONE NIGHT ★★
 Columbia, 1934
BROADWAY BILL Columbia, 1934
MR. DEEDS GOES TO TOWN ★★
 Columbia, 1936
LOST HORIZON Columbia, 1937
YOU CAN'T TAKE IT WITH YOU ★★
 Columbia, 1938
MR. SMITH GOES TO WASHINGTON ★
 Columbia, 1939
MEET JOHN DOE Warner Bros., 1941
PRELUDE TO WAR (FD) U.S. Army, 1942
THE NAZIS STRIKE (FD) co-director with
 Anatole Litvak, U.S. Army, 1942
DIVIDE AND CONQUER (FD) co-director
 with Anatole Litvak, U.S. Army, 1943
BATTLE OF BRITAIN (FD) co-director,
 U.S. Army, 1943
BATTLE OF CHINA (FD) co-director with
 Anatole Litvak, U.S. Army, 1943
THE NEGRO SOLDIER (FD) U.S. Army, 1944
TUNISIAN VICTORY (FD) co-director with
 Roy Boulting, Army Film Unit, 1944, British
ARSENIC AND OLD LACE
 Warner Bros., 1944
KNOW YOUR ENEMY: JAPAN (FD)
 co-director with Joris Ivens, 1945
TWO DOWN AND ONE TO GO (FD) 1945
IT'S A WONDERFUL LIFE ★
 RKO Radio, 1946
STATE OF THE UNION MGM, 1948
RIDING HIGH Paramount, 1950
HERE COMES THE GROOM
 Paramount, 1951
A HOLE IN THE HEAD United Artists, 1959
POCKETFUL OF MIRACLES
 United Artists, 1961

JOHN CASSAVETES

b. December 9, 1929 - New York, New York
d. 1989

SHADOWS Lion International, 1961
TOO LATE BLUES Paramount, 1962
A CHILD IS WAITING United Artists, 1963
FACES Continental, 1968
HUSBANDS Columbia, 1970
MINNIE AND MOSKOWITZ Universal, 1971
A WOMAN UNDER THE INFLUENCE ★
 Faces International, 1974
THE KILLING OF A CHINESE BOOKIE
 Faces International, 1976
OPENING NIGHT Faces International, 1979
GLORIA Columbia, 1980
LOVE STREAMS Cannon, 1984
BIG TROUBLE Columbia, 1986

RENATO CASTELLANI

b. September 4, 1913 - Finale Ligure, Italy
d. 1985

UN COLPO DI PISTOLA Lux Film,
 1941, Italian
ZAZA' Lux Film, 1942, Italian
LA DONNA DELLA MONTAGNA Lux Film,
 1943, Italian
MIO FIGLIO PROFESSORE Lux Film,
 1946, Italian
SOTTO IL SOLE DI ROMA
 Universalcine, 1948, Italian
E' PRIMAVERA Universalcine, 1949, Italian
TWO CENTS WORTH OF HOPE Times Film
 Corporation, 1952, Italian
ROMEO AND JULIET United Artists,
 1954, British
I SOGNI NEL CASSETTO Rizzoli Film/
 Francinex, 1956, Italian

...AND THE WILD, WILD WOMEN
  NELLA CITTA L'INFERNO Rima Films,
  1958, Italian
IL BRIGANTE Cineriz, 1961, Italian
MARE MATTO Lux/Vides Film/Ariane/
  Filmsonor, 1962, Italian-Italian
TRE NOTTI D'AMORE co-director, Jolly Film/
  Cormoran Films, 1964, Italian-French
CONTROSESSO co-director, Champion/Les
  Films Concordia, 1964, Italian-French
GHOSTS - ITALIAN STYLE *QUESTI
  FANTASMI* MGM, 1967, Italian-French
UNA BREVA STAGIONE Dino De Laurentiis,
  1969, Italian
VITA DI LEONARDO (TF) RAI/ORTF/TVE/
  Istituto Luce, 1973, Italian-French-Spanish
IL FURTO DELLA GIOCONDA (TF)
  RAI, 1977, Italian
GIUSEPPE VERDI (TF) RAI/Antenne 2/
  Bavaria/BBC/SVT 2/TSS, 1982,
  Italian-French-West German-British-Swiss

WILLIAM CASTLE

b. April 24, 1914 - New York, New York
d. 1977

THE CHANCE OF A LIFETIME
  Columbia, 1943
KLONDIKE KATE Columbia, 1943
THE WHISTLER Columbia, 1944
SHE'S A SOLDIER TOO Columbia, 1944
THE MARK OF THE WHISTLER
  Columbia, 1944
WHEN STRANGERS MARRY
  Columbia, 1944
VOICE OF THE WHISTLER Columbia, 1944
THE CRIME DOCTOR'S WARNING
  Columbia, 1945
JUST BEFORE DAWN Columbia, 1946
THE MYSTERIOUS INTRUDER
  Columbia, 1946
THE RETURN OF RUSTY Columbia, 1946
THE CRIME DOCTOR'S MAN HUNT
  Columbia, 1946
THE CRIME DOCTOR'S GAMBLE
  Columbia, 1947
TEXAS, BROOKLYN AND HEAVEN
  United Artists, 1948
THE GENTLEMAN FROM NOWHERE 1948
JOHNNY STOOL PIGEON Universal, 1949
UNDERTOW Universal, 1949
IT'S A SMALL WORLD Universal, 1950
THE FAT MAN Universal, 1951
HOLLYWOOD STORY Universal, 1951
CAVE OF OUTLAWS Universal, 1951
SERPENT OF THE NILE Columbia, 1953
FORT TI Columbia, 1953
CONQUEST OF COCHISE Columbia, 1953
SLAVES OF BABYLON Columbia, 1953
DRUMS OF TAHITI Columbia, 1954
CHARGE OF THE LANCERS
  Columbia, 1954
BATTLE OF ROGUE RIVER Columbia, 1954
JESSE JAMES VS. THE DALTONS
  Columbia, 1954
THE IRON GLOVE Columbia, 1954
THE LAW VS. BILLY THE KID
  Columbia, 1954
MASTERSON OF KANSAS Columbia, 1954
THE AMERICANO Columbia, 1954
NEW ORLEANS UNCENSORED
  Columbia, 1954
THE GUN THAT WON THE WEST
  Columbia, 1955
DUEL ON THE MISSISSIPPI Columbia, 1955
THE HOUSTON STORY Columbia, 1956
URANIUM BOOM Columbia, 1956

MACABRE Allied Artists, 1958
HOUSE ON HAUNTED HILL
  Allied Artists, 1959
THE TINGLER Columbia, 1959
13 GHOSTS Columbia, 1960
HOMICIDAL Columbia, 1961
MR. SARDONICUS Columbia, 1961
ZOTZ! Columbia, 1962
13 FRIGHTENED GIRLS Columbia, 1963
THE OLD DARK HOUSE Columbia, 1963,
  British-U.S.
STRAIT-JACKET Columbia, 1964
THE NIGHT WALKER Universal, 1965
I SAW WHAT YOU DID Universal, 1965
LET'S KILL UNCLE Universal, 1966
THE BUSY BODY Paramount, 1967
THE SPIRIT IS WILLING Paramount, 1967
PROJECT X Paramount, 1968
SHANKS Paramount, 1974

ALBERTO CAVALCANTI
(Alberto de Almeida-Cavalcanti)

b. February 6, 1897 - Rio de Janeiro, Brazil
d. 1982

RIEN QUE LES HEURES (FD) 1926, French
LA P'TITE LILIE, YVETTE 1927, French
EN RADE 1927, French
LE TRAIN SANS YEUX 1928, French,
  filmed in 1926
LE CAPITAINE FRACASSE 1929, French
LA JALOUSIE DE BARBOUILLE
  1929, French
LE PETIT CHAPERON ROUGE
  1929, French
VOUS VERREZ LA SEMAINE PROCHAINE
  1929, French
TOUTE SA VIE 1930, French
A CANCAO DO BERCO 1930, Portuguese
DANS UNE ILE PERDUE 1931, French
A MI-CHEMIN DU CIEL 1931, French
LES VACANCES DU DIABLE 1931, French
TOUR DE CHANT (FD) 1932, French
EN LISANT LE JOURNAL 1932, French
LE JOUR DU FROTTEUR 1932, French
REVUE MONTMARTROISE 1932, French
NOUS NE FERONS JAMAIS LE CINEMA (FD)
  1932, French
LE MARI GARCON 1934, French
PLAISIRS DEFENDU 1933, French
SOS RADIO SERVICE (FD) 1934, French
CORALIE & CIE 1934, French
NEW RATES 1934, British
COAL FACE (FD) GPO Film Unit,
  1935, British
MESSAGE FROM GENEVA (FD)
  GPO Film Unit, 1936, British
WE LIVE IN TWO WORLDS (FD)
  GPO Film Unit, 1937, British
THE LINE TO TCHERVA HUT (FD)
  GPO Film Unit, 1937, British
WHO WRITES TO SWITZERLAND (FD)
  GPO Film Unit, 1937, British
FOUR BARRIERS (FD) GPO Film Unit,
  1938, British
MEN OF THE ALPS (FD) Crown Film Unit,
  1939, British
MIDSUMMER DAY'S WORK (FD)
  Crown Film Unit, 1939, British
THE YELLOW CAESAR (FD)
  Crown Film Unit, 1941, British
FILM AND REALITY (FD) British Film Institute,
  1942, British
WENT THE DAY WELL? *48 HOURS*
  United Artists, 1942, British
GREEK TESTAMENT (FD) 1942, British
WATERTIGHT Ealing, 1943, British

CHAMPAGNE CHARLIE Ealing, 1944, British
DEAD OF NIGHT co-director with
  Basil Dearden, Robert Hamer &
  Charles Crichton, Universal, 1946, British
NICHOLAS NICKLEBY Universal,
  1947, British
I BECAME A CRIMINAL *THEY MADE ME A
  FUGITIVE* Warner Bros., 1947, British
THE FIRST GENTLEMAN 1948, British
FOR THEM THAT TRESPASS 1949, British
SIMAO O CAOLHO Vera Cruz Production
  Group, 1952, Brazilian
O CANTO DO MAR Vera Cruz Production
  Group, 1953, Brazilian
MULHER DE VERDADE Vera Cruz
  Production Group, 1954, Brazilian
HERR PUNTILE UND SEIN KNECHT MATTI
  1955, Austrian
CASTLE IN THE CARPATHIANS
  1957, Romanian
LA PRIMA NOTTE 1958, Italian
THE STORY OF ISRAEL *THUS SPAKE
  THEODOR HERZL* (FD) 1967, Israeli

ANDRE CAYATTE

b. February 3, 1909 - Carcassonne, France
d. 1989

LA FAUSSE MAITRESSE 1942, French
AU BONHEUR DES DAMES 1943, French
PIERRE ET JEAN 1943, French
LE DERNIER SOU 1945, French
SERENADE AUX NUAGES 1945, French
ROGER-LA-HONTE 1945, French
LA REVANCHE DE ROGER-LA-HONTE
  1946, French
LA CHANTEUR INCONNU 1947, French
LES DESSOUS DES CARTES 1948, French
LES AMANTS DE VERONE 1949, French
RETOUR A LA VIE co-director, 1949, French
JUSTICE IS DONE Joseph Burstyn,
  1950, French
WE ARE ALL MURDERERS Kingsley
  International, 1952, French
AVANT LE DELUGE 1954, French
LE DOSSIER NOIR 1955, French
AN EYE FOR AN EYE Ajay Films,
  1957, French
THE MIRROR HAS TWO FACES Continental,
  1958, French
TOMORROW IS MY TURN *LE PASSAGE
  DU RHIN* Showcorporation, 1960,
  French-Italian-West German
TWO WE GUILTY *LA GLAIVE ET LA
  BALANCE* MGM, 1962, French-Italian
ANATOMY OF A MARRIAGE: MY DAYS WITH
  JEAN-MARC *LA VIE CONJUGAL:
  JEAN-MARC* Janus, 1963, French-Italian
ANATOMY OF A MARRIAGE: MY NIGHTS
  WITH FRANCOISE *LA VIE CONJUGAL:
  FRANCOISE* Janus, 1963, French-Italian
PIEGE POUR CENDRILLON 1965, French
LES RISQUES DU METIER 1967, French
LES CHEMINS DE KATMANDOU
  1969, French
TO DIE OF LOVE MGM, 1970, French-Italian
IL N'Y A PAS DE FUMEE SANS FEU
  1973, French
LE TESTAMENT 1975, French
A CHACUN SON ENFER 1977, French
LA RAISON D'ETAT 1978, French
JUSTICES 1978, French
L'AMOUR EN QUESTION 1978, French

DON CHAFFEY
b. August 5, 1917 - England
d. 1990

THE MYSTERIOUS POACHER   General Film
   Distributors, 1954, British
THE CASE OF THE MISSING SCENE
   General Film Distributors, 1951, British
SKID KIDS   Associated British Film
   Distributors/Children's Film Foundation,
   1953, British
TIME IS MY ENEMY   Independent Film
   Distributors, 1954, British
THE SECRET TENT   British Lion,
   1956, British
THE GIRL IN THE PICTURE   Eros,
   1957, British
THE FLESH IS WEAK   DCA, 1957, British
A QUESTION OF ADULTERY   Eros,
   1958, British
THE MAN UPSTAIRS   Kingsley International,
   1958, British
DANGER WITHIN   British Lion, 1959, British
DENTIST IN THE CHAIR   Ajay, 1960, British
LIES MY FATHER TOLD ME   Eire,
   1960, British
NEARLY A NASTY ACCIDENT   Universal,
   1961, British
GREYFRIARS BOBBY   Buena Vista, 1961,
   U.S.-British
A MATTER OF WHO   Herts Lion,
   1962, British
THE PRINCE AND THE PAUPER
   Buena Vista, 1962, U.S.-British
THE WEBSTER BOY   RFI, 1963, British
THE HORSE WITHOUT A HEAD   Buena Vista,
   1963, British
JASON AND THE ARGONAUTS   Columbia,
   1963, British
THEY ALL DIED LAUGHING   *A JOLLY BAD*
   FELLOW   Continental, 1963, British
THE THREE LIVES OF THOMASINA
   Buena Vista, 1963, British-U.S.
THE CROOKED ROAD   7 Arts, 1965,
   British-Yugoslavian
ONE MILLION YEARS B.C.   20th Century-Fox,
   1967, British
THE VIKING QUEEN   American International,
   1967, British
A TWIST OF SAND   United Artists,
   1968, British
CREATURES THE WORLD FORGOT
   Columbia, 1971, British
CLINIC XCLUSIVE   Doverton, 1972, British
CHARLEY-ONE-EYE   Paramount,
   1973, British
THE TERROR OF SHEBA   *PERSECUTION*
   Blueberry Hill, 1974, British
THE FOURTH WISH   South Australian Film
   Corporation, 1975, Australian
BEN HALL (MS)   co-director with
   Frank Arnold, BBC/Australian Broadcasting
   Corporation/20th Century-Fox, 1975,
   British-Australian
HARNESS FEVER   Walt Disney Productions,
   1976, Australian
RIDE A WILD PONY   *BORN TO RUN*
   Buena Vista, 1976, U.S.-Australian
SURF   Trans-Atlantic Enterprises, 1977
PETE'S DRAGON   Buena Vista, 1977
SHIMMERING LIGHT (TF)   Australian
   Broadcasting Commission/Trans-Atlantic
   Enterprises, 1978, Australian
THE MAGIC OF LASSIE   International
   Picture Show, 1978
THE GIFT OF LOVE (TF)   Osmond
   Productions, 1978
C.H.O.M.P.S.   American International, 1979

CASINO (TF)   Trellis Productions/Aaron
   Spelling Productions, 1980
INTERNATIONAL AIRPORT (TF)   co-director
   with Charles S. Dubin, Aaron Spelling
   Productions, 1985
MISSION IMPOSSIBLE (TF) - THE GOLDEN
   SERPENT (TF)   Paramount TV, 1989

CHARLES (CHARLIE) CHAPLIN
b. April 16, 1889 - London, England
d. 1977

CAUGHT IN A CABARET   co-director with
   Mabel Normand, Keystone, 1914
CAUGHT IN THE RAIN   Keystone, 1914
A BUSY DAY   Keystone, 1914
THE FATAL MALLET   Keystone, 1914
HER FRIEND THE BANDIT   co-director with
   Mabel Normand, Keystone, 1914
MABEL'S BUSY DAY   co-director with
   Mabel Normand, Keystone, 1914
MABEL'S MARRIED LIFE   co-director with
   Mabel Normand, Keystone, 1914
LAUGHING GAS   Keystone, 1914
THE PROPERTY MAN   Keystone, 1914
THE FACE ON THE BARROOM FLOOR
   Keystone, 1914
RECREATION   Keystone, 1914
THE MASQUERADER   Keystone, 1914
HIS NEW PROFESSION   Keystone, 1914
THE ROUNDERS   Keystone, 1914
THE NEW JANITOR   Keystone, 1914
THOSE LOVE PANGS   Keystone, 1914
DOUGH AND DYNAMITE   Keystone, 1914
GENTLEMEN OF NERVE   Keystone, 1914
HIS MUSICAL CAREER   Keystone, 1914
HIS TRYSTING PLACE   Keystone, 1914
GETTING ACQUAINTED   Keystone, 1914
HIS PREHISTORIC PAST   Keystone, 1914
HIS NEW JOB   Essanay, 1915
A NIGHT OUT   Essanay, 1915
THE CHAMPION   Essanay, 1915
IN THE PARK   Essanay, 1915
A JITNEY ELOPEMENT   Essanay, 1915
THE TRAMP   Essanay, 1915
BY THE SEA   Essanay, 1915
WORK   Essanay, 1915
A WOMAN   Essanay, 1915
THE BANK   Essanay, 1915
SHANGHAIED   Essanay, 1915
A NIGHT IN THE SHOW   Essanay, 1915
CARMEN   Essanay, 1916
POLICE   Essanay, 1916
THE FLOORWALKER   Mutual, 1916
THE FIREMAN   Mutual, 1916
THE VAGABOND   Mutual, 1916
ONE A.M.   Mutual, 1916
THE COUNT   Mutual, 1916
THE PAWNSHOP   Mutual, 1916
BEHIND THE SCREEN   Mutual, 1916
THE RINK   Mutual, 1916
EASY STREET   Mutual, 1917
THE CURE   Mutual, 1917
THE IMMIGRANT   Mutual, 1917
THE ADVENTURER   Mutual, 1917
A DOG'S LIFE   First National, 1918
TRIPLE TROUBLE   Essanay, 1918
THE BOND   First National, 1918
SHOULDER ARMS   First National, 1918
SUNNYSIDE   First National, 1919
A DAY'S PLEASURE   First National, 1919
THE NUT   First National, 1921
THE KID   First National, 1921
THE IDLE CLASS   First National, 1921
PAY DAY   First National, 1922
THE PILGRIM   First National, 1923
A WOMAN OF PARIS   United Artists, 1923
THE GOLD RUSH   United Artists, 1925

THE CIRCUS ★   United Artists, 1928
CITY LIGHTS   United Artists, 1931
MODERN TIMES   United Artists, 1936
THE GREAT DICTATOR   United Artists, 1940
MONSIEUR VERDOUX   United Artists, 1947
LIMELIGHT   United Artists, 1952
A KING IN NEW YORK   Archway,
   1957, British
A COUNTESS FROM HONG KONG
   Universal, 1967, British

CHARLEY CHASE
(Charles Parrott)
b. October 20, 1893 - Baltimore, Maryland
d. 1940

THE ANGLERS   1914
DO-RE-MI-PA   1915
A DASH OF COURAGE   1916
CHASED INTO LOVE   1917
HELLO TROUBLE   1918
SHIP AHOY!   1919
KIDS IS KIDS   1920
SHERMAN SAID IT   1933
MIDSUMMER MUSH   1933
LUNCHEON AT TWELVE   1933
THE CRACKED ICEMAN   co-director with
   Eddie Dunn, 1934
FOUR PARTS   co-director with
   Eddie Dunn, 1934
I'LL TAKE VANILLA   co-director with
   Eddie Dunn, 1934
ANOTHER WILD IDEA   co-director with
   Eddie Dunn, 1934
IT HAPPENED ONE DAY   co-director with
   Eddie Dunn, 1934
SOMETHING SIMPLE   co-director with
   Walter Weems, 1934
YOU SAID A HATEFUL!   1934
FATE'S FATHEAD   1934
THE CHASES OF PIMPLE STREET   1934
OKAY TOOTS!   co-director with
   William Terhune, 1936
POKER AT EIGHT   1936
SOUTHERN EXPOSURE   1936
THE FOUR-STAR BOARDER   1936
NURSE TO YOU   co-director with
   Jefferson Moffitt, 1936
MANHATTAN MONKEY BUSINESS
   co-director with Harold Law, 1936
PUBLIC GHOST NO. 1   co-director with
   Harold Law, 1936
LIFE HESITATES AT 40   co-director with
   Harold Law, 1936
THE COUNT TAKES THE COUNT   co-director
   with Harold Law, 1936
VAMP TILL READY   co-director with
   Harold Law, 1936
ON THE WRONG TREK   co-director with
   Harold Law, 1936
NEIGHBORHOOD HOUSE   co-director with
   Harold Law, 1936

BENJAMIN CHRISTENSEN
(Benjamin Christiansen)
b. September 28, 1879 - Viborg, Denmark
d. 1959

THE MYSTERIOUS X   1913, Danish
NIGHT OF VENGEANCE   1915, Danish
WITCHCRAFT THROUGH THE AGES
   HAXAN   1922, Swedish
UNTER JUDEN   UFA, 1923, German
SEINE FRAU DIE UNBEKKANTE   UFA,
   1923, German
DIE FRAU MIT DEM SCHLECHTEN RUF
   UFA, 1925, German

THE DEVIL'S CIRCUS   1926
MOCKERY   1927
THE HAWK'S NEST   1928
THE HAUNTED HOUSE   1928
SEVEN FOOTPRINTS TO SATAN   1929
THE HOUSE OF HORROR   1929
CHILDREN OF DIVORCE   1939, Danish
THE CHILD   1940, Danish
COME HOME WITH ME   1941, Danish
THE LADY WITH THE LIGHT GLOVES
   1943, Danish

CHRISTIAN-JAQUE
(Christian Maudet)
b. September 4, 1904 - Paris, France
d. 1994

LE BIDON D'OR   1932, French
ADHEMAR LAMPIOT   1933, French
LE TENDRON D'ACHILLE   1933, French
CA COLLE   1933, French
LA BOEUF SUR LA LANGUE   1933, French
L'HOTEL DU LIBRE-ECHANGE   1934, French
COMPARTIMNENT DES DAMES SEULES
   1935, French
LE PERE LAMPION   1935, French
SOUS LA GRIFFE   1935, French
LA SONNETTE D'ALARME   1935, French
LA FAMILLE PONT-BIQUET   1935, French
SACRE LEONCE   1935, French
VOYAGE D'AGREMENT   1935, French
MONSIEUR PERSONNE   1936, French
UN DE LA LEGION   1936, French
L'ECOLE DES JOURNALISTES   1936, French
RIGOLBOCHE   1936, French
JOSETTE   1936, French
ON NE ROULE PAS ANTOINETTE
   1936, French
LA MAISON D'EN FACE   1937, French
A VENISE UNE NUIT   1937, French
LES PERLES DE LA COURONNE
   co-director with Sacha Guitry, 1937, French
FRANCIS 1ER   1937, French
LES DEGOURDIS DE LA ONZIEME
   1937, French
LES PIRATES DU RAIL   1938, French
ERNEST LE REBELLE   1938, French
LES DISPARUS DE SAINT-AGIL
   1938, French
RAPHAEL LE TATOUE   1939, French
C'ETAIT MOI   1939, French
L'ENFER DES ANGES   1939, French
LE GRAND ELAN   1940, French
L'ASSASSINAT DU PERE NOEL
   1941, French
PREMIER BAL   1941, French
LA SYMPHONIE FANTASTIQUE
   1942, French
VOYAGE SANS ESPOIT   1943, French
CARMEN   1945, Italian-French,
   filmed in 1942
SORTILEGES   1945, French
BOULE DE SUIF   1945, French
UN REVENANT   1946, French
LA CHARTREUSE DE PARME   1948,
   French-Italian
D'HOMME A HOMMES   1948, French-Swiss
SINGOALLA   1950, Swiss-French
SOUVENIRS PERDUS   1950, French
BARBE-BLEUE   1951, French
FANFAN THE TULIP   United Artists,
   1952, French
ADORABLE CREATURES   Continental,
   1952, French
LUCRECE BORGIA   1953, French-Italian
DAUGHTERS OF DESTINY   *DESTINEES*
   co-director, Arlan Pictures, 1954,
   French-Italian

MADAME DU BARRY   1954, French
NANA   Times Film Corporation, 1955,
   French-Italian
IF ALL THE GUYS IN THE WORLD...
   Buena Vista, 1956, French
THE FOXIEST GIRL IN PARIS   *NATHALIE*
   Times Film Corporation, 1957, French
THE LAW IS THE LAW   Continental, 1957,
   French-Italian
BABETTE GOES TO WAR   Columbia,
   1959, French
LOVE AND THE FRENCHWOMAN
   co-director, Kingsley International,
   1960, French
MADAME   *MADAME SANS-GENE*   Embassy,
   1962, French-Italian-Spanish
DON'T TEMPT THE DEVIL   *LES BONNES
   CAUSES*   United Motion Picture
   Organization, 1963, French-Italian
LA TULIPE NOIRE   1964, French
LE REPAS DES FAUVES   1964, French
MAN FROM COCODY   American International,
   1965, French-Italian
THE DIRTY GAME   co-director with
   Terence Young, Carlo Lizzani &
   Werner Klingler, American International,
   1965, French-Italian-West German
LA SECONDE VERITE   1966, French
LE SAINT PREND L'AFFUT   1966, French
DEUX BILLETS POUR MEXICO   1967,
   French-Italian-West German
LES AMOURS DE LADY HAMILTON   1968,
   French-Italian-West German
THE LEGEND OF FRENCHIE KING
   LES PETROLEUSES   K-Tel, 1971,
   French-Spanish-Italian-British
DR. JUSTICE   1975, French
LA VIE PARISIENNE   1978, French

ALAN CLARKE
b. October 28, 1935 - Liverpool, England
d. 1990

SCUM   Berwick Street Films, 1979, British,
   originally made for television
CONTACT (TF)   BBC, 1985, British
MADE IN BRITAIN (TF)   1985, British
BILLY THE KID AND THE GREEN BAIZE
   VAMPIRE   Zenith Productions/ITC,
   1985, British
RITA, SUE AND BOB, TOO   Orion Classics,
   1987, British

JAMES CLAVELL
(Charles Edmund DuMaresq de Clavelle)
b. October 10, 1924 - Sydney, Australia
d. 1994

FIVE GATES TO HELL
   20th Century-Fox, 1959
WALK LIKE A DRAGON   Paramount, 1960
TO SIR, WITH LOVE   Columbia, 1967, British
THE SWEET AND THE BITTER   Monarch,
   1968, British
WHERE'S JACK?   Paramount, 1969, British
THE LAST VALLEY   Cinerama Releasing
   Corporation, 1971, British

JACK CLAYTON
b. March 1, 1921 - Brighton, Sussex, England
d. 1995

ROOM AT THE TOP ★   Continental,
   1959, British
THE INNOCENTS   20th Century-Fox,
   1962, British
THE PUMPKIN EATER   Royal International,
   1964, British

OUR MOTHER'S HOUSE   MGM,
   1967, British
THE GREAT GATSBY   Paramount, 1974
SOMETHING WICKED THIS WAY COMES
   Buena Vista, 1983
THE LONELY PASSION OF JUDITH HEARNE
   Island Films, 1987, British
MEMENTO MORI (TF)   BBC TV/WGBH-
   Boston/BBC Enterprises, 1992, British-U.S.

EDWARD F. (EDDIE) CLINE
b. November 7, 1892 - Kenosha, Wisconsin
d. 1961

THE WINNING PUNCH   Keystone, 1916
HIS BUSTED TRUST   Keystone, 1916
SUNSHINE   Keystone, 1916
THE DOG CATCHER'S LOVE
   Keystone, 1917
THE PAWNBROKER'S HEART
   Keystone, 1917
A BEDROOM BLUNDER   Keystone, 1917
THAT NIGHT   Keystone, 1917
THE KITCHEN LADY   Keystone, 1918
THOSE ATHLETIC GIRLS   Keystone, 1918
HIS SMOTHERED LOVE   Keystone, 1918
THE SUMMER GIRLS   Keystone, 1918
WHOSE LITTLE WIFE ARE YOU?
   Keystone, 1918
HIDE AND SEEK DETECTIVES
   Keystone, 1918
CUPID'S DAY OFF   1919
EAST LYNNE WITH VARIATIONS   1919
WHEN LOVE IS BLIND   1919
HEARTS AND FLOWERS   1919
ONE WEEK   co-director with
   Buster Keaton, 1920
CONVICT 13   co-director with
   Buster Keaton, 1920
THE SCARECROW   co-director with
   Buster Keaton, 1920
NEIGHBORS   co-director with
   Buster Keaton, 1920
THE HAUNTED HOUSE   co-director with
   Buster Keaton, 1921
HARD LUCK   co-director with
   Buster Keaton, 1921
THE HIGH SIGN   co-director with
   Buster Keaton, 1921
THE PLAYHOUSE   co-director with
   Buster Keaton, 1921
THE BOAT   co-director with
   Buster Keaton, 1921
THE PALEFACE   co-director with
   Buster Keaton, 1922
COPS   co-director with Buster Keaton, 1922
MY WIFE'S RELATIONS   co-director with
   Buster Keaton, 1922
THE FROZEN NORTH   co-director with
   Buster Keaton, 1922
THE ELECTRIC HOUSE   co-director with
   Buster Keaton, 1922
DAY DREAMS   co-director with
   Buster Keaton, 1922
THE BALLOONATIC   co-director with
   Buster Keaton, 1923
THE LOVE NEST   co-director with
   Buster Keaton, 1923
THE THREE AGES   co-director with
   Buster Keaton, 1923
CIRCUS DAYS   First National, 1923
THE MEANEST MAN IN THE WORLD
   First National, 1923
WHEN A MAN'S A MAN   First National, 1924
THE PLUMBER   1924
LITTLE ROBINSON CRUSOE   MGM, 1924
GOOD BAD BOY   Principal, 1924
CAPTAIN JANUARY   Principal, 1924

ALONG CAME RUTH   MGM, 1924
BASHFUL JIM   1925
TEE FOR TWO   1925
COLD TURKEY   1925
LOVE AND KISSES   1925
DANGEROUS CURVES BEHIND   1925
THE RAG MAN   MGM, 1925
OLD CLOTHES   MGM, 1925
THE GOSH-DARN MORTGAGE   1926
SPANKING BREEZES   1926
A LOVE SUNDAE   1926
THE GHOST OF FOLLY   1926
PUPPY LOVETIME   1926
SMITH'S BABY   1926
WHEN A MAN'S A PRINCE   1926
FLIRTY FOUR-FLUSHERS   1926
GOOSELAND   1926
A HAREM KNIGHT   1926
A BLONDE'S REVENGE   1926
THE JOLLY JILTER   1927
LET IT RAIN   Paramount, 1927
SOFT CUSHIONS   1927
THE GIRL FROM EVERYWHERE   1927
THE BULLFIGHTERS   1927
HOLD THAT POSE   1928
LOVE AT FIRST SIGHT   1928
LADIES' NIGHT IN A TURKISH BATH   1928
VAMPING VENUS   First National, 1928
MAN CRAZY   1928
THE HEAD MAN   First National, 1928
THE CRASH   First National, 1928
BROADWAY FEVER   Tiffany Star, 1929
HIS LUCKY DAY   Universal, 1929
THE FORWARD PASS   First National, 1929
IN THE NEXT ROOM   First National, 1930
SWEET MAMA   First National, 1930
LEATHERNECKING   RKO, 1930
THE WIDOW FROM CHICAGO
   First National, 1930
HOOK, LINE AND SINKER   1930
CRACKED NUTS   1931
THE NAUGHTY FLIRT   First National, 1931
THE GIRL HABIT   Paramount, 1931
MILLION DOLLAR LEGS   Paramount, 1932
SO THIS IS AFRICA   Columbia, 1933
PAROLE GIRL   1933
THE DUDE RANGER   Fox, 1934
PECK'S BAD BOY   Fox, 1934
WHEN A MAN'S A MAN   British Lion, 1935
THE COWBOY MILLIONAIRE   Fox, 1935
IT'S A GREAT LIFE   Paramount, 1936
F-MAN   Paramount, 1936
ON AGAIN, OFF AGAIN   RKO, 1937
FORTY NAUGHTY GIRLS   RKO, 1937
HIGH FLYERS   RKO, 1937
HAWAII CALLS   RKO, 1938
GO CHASE YOURSELF   RKO, 1938
BREAKING THE ICE   RKO, 1938
PECK'S BAD BOY WITH THE CIRCUS
   FOX, 1938
MY LITTLE CHICKADEE   Universal, 1940
THE VILLAIN STILL PURSUED HER
   RKO Radio, 1940
THE BANK DICK   Universal, 1940
MEET THE CHUMP   Universal, 1941
HELLO SUCKER   Universal, 1941
NEVER GIVE A SUCKER AN EVEN BREAK
   Universal, 1941
SNUFFY SMITH THE YARD BIRD
   Monogram, 1942
WHAT'S COOKIN'?   Universal, 1942
PRIVATE BUCKAROO   Universal, 1942
GIVE OUT SISTERS   Universal, 1942
BEHIND THE EIGHT BALL   Universal, 1942
HE'S MY GUY   Universal, 1943
CRAZY HOUSE   Universal, 1943
SWINGTIME JOHNNY   Universal, 1944
GHOST CATCHERS   Universal, 1944

MOONLIGHT AND CACTUS   Universal, 1944
NIGHT CLUB GIRL   Universal, 1944
SLIGHTLY TERRIFIC   Universal, 1944
SEE MY LAWYER   Universal, 1945
PENTHOUSE RHYTHM   Universal, 1945
BRINGING UP FATHER   Monogram, 1946
JIGGS AND MAGGIE IN SOCIETY
   Monogram, 1948
JIGGS AND MAGGIE IN COURT   co-director
   with William Beaudine, Monogram, 1948

HENRI-GEORGES CLOUZOT
b. November 20, 1907 - Niort, France
d. 1977

L'ASSASSIN HABITE AU 21   1941, French
LE CORBEAU   1934, French
QUAI DES ORFEVRES   1947, French
MANON   1949, French
RETOUR A LA VIE   co-director, 1949, French
MIQUETTE ET SA MERE   1950, French
THE WAGES OF FEAR   DCA, 1953, French,
   re-released in 1991 by Kino International
DIABOLIQUE   United Motion Picture
   Organization, 1955, French
THE MYSTERY OF PICASSO (FD)   Samuel
   Goldwyn Company, 1956, French
LES ESPIONS   1957, French
THE TRUTH   Kingsley International, 1960,
   French-Italian
LA PRISONNIERE   Avco Embassy, 1968,
   French-Italian
MESSA DA REQUIEM   1969,
   Swiss-West German

JEAN COCTEAU
b. July 5, 1889 - Maisons-Lafitte, France
d. 1963

THE BLOOD OF A POET   Brandon,
   1930, French
BEAUTY AND THE BEAST   Lopert,
   1946, French
L'AIGLE A DEUX TETES   1948, French
LES PARENTS TERRIBLES   1948, French
ORPHEUS   Discina International,
   1950, French
LE TESTAMENT D'ORPHEE   1960, French

LANCE COMFORT
b. 1908 - Harrow, England
d. 1967

HATTER'S CASTLE   Paramount,
   1941, British
COURAGEOUS MR. PENN   PENN OF
   PENNSYLVANIA   Hoffberg, 1941, British
THOSE KIDS FROM TOWN   1942, British
SQUADRON LEADER X   1942, British
ESCAPE TO DANGER   1943, British
OLD MOTHER RILEY - DETECTIVE
   1943, British
WHEN WE ARE MARRIED   1943, British
HOTEL RESERVE   RKO Radio, 1944, British
GREAT DAY   RKO Radio, 1945, British
BEDELIA   Eagle Lion, 1946, British
TEMPTATION HARBOR   1947, British
DAUGHTERS OF DARKNESS   1948, British
SILENT DUST   1949, British
PORTRAIT OF CLARE   Stratford Pictures,
   1950, British
THE GIRL ON THE PIER   1953, British
GAME OF DANGER   BANG! YOU'RE DEAD
   Associated Artists, 1954, British
EIGHT O'CLOCK WALK   Associated Artists,
   1954, British

THE MAN IN THE ROAD   Republic,
   1956, British
AT THE STROKE OF NINE   Grand National,
   1957, British
THUNDER OVER TANGIER   THE MAN
   FROM TANGIER   Republic, 1957, British
MENACE IN THE NIGHT   FACE IN
   THE NIGHT   United Artists, 1958, British
MAKE MINE A MILLION   1959, British
THE UGLY DUCKLING   1959, British
THE BREAKING POINT   1961, British
RAG DOLL   1961, British
PIT OF DARKNESS   1961, British
THE PAINTED SMILE   1962, British
TOUCH OF DEATH   Planet, 1962, British
THE BREAK   British Lion, 1963, British
TOMORROW AT TEN   Governor,
   1963, British
SING AND SWING   LIVE IT UP   Universal,
   1963, British
MAN IN THE DARK   BLIND CORNER
   Universal, 1964, British
DEVILS OF DARKNESS   20th Century-Fox,
   1965, British
BE MY GUEST   Columbia, 1965, British

JACK CONWAY
b. July 17, 1887 - Graceville, Minnesota
d. 1952

THE OLD ARMCHAIR   1913
CAPTAIN McLEAN   1914
THE PENITENTS   Triangle, 1915
THE BECKONING TRAIL   Red Films, 1916
SOCIAL BUCCANEERS   Bluebird, 1916
THE MEASURE OF A MAN   Bluebird, 1916
THE MAINSPRING   Red Films, 1916
THE SILENT BATTLE   Bluebird, 1916
POLLY'S REDHEAD   POLLY REDHEAD
   Bluebird, 1917
JEWEL IN PAWN   A JEWEL IN THE PAWN
   Bluebird, 1917
THE LITTLE ORPHAN   Pathé, 1917
HER SOUL'S INSPIRATION   Bluebird, 1917
COME THROUGH   Universal, 1917
THE CHARMER   Bluebird, 1917
THE BOND OF FEAR   Triangle, 1917
BECAUSE OF A WOMAN   Triangle, 1917
LITTLE RED DECIDES   Triangle, 1918
HER DECISION   Triangle, 1918
YOU CAN'T BELIEVE EVERYTHING
   Triangle, 1918
DOING THEIR BIT   1918
DIPLOMATIC MISSION   Vitagraph, 1918
DESERT LAW   Triangle, 1918
RESTLESS SOULS   Triangle, 1919
LOMBARDI LTD.   Metro, 1919
RIDERS OF THE DAWN   DESERT OF WHEAT
   W.W. Hodkinson, 1920
THE SERVANT IN THE HOUSE   FBO, 1920
THE DWELLING PLACE OF LIGHT
   W.W. Hodkinson, 1920
THE MONEY CHANGERS   Pathé, 1920
THE U.P. TRAIL   W.W. Hodkinson, 1920
THE SPENDERS   W. W. Hodkinson, 1921
THE KISS   Universal, 1921
A DAUGHTER OF THE LAW   Universal, 1921
THE KILLER   1921
THE LURE OF THE ORIENT   1921
THE RAGE OF PARIS   Universal, 1921
THE MILLIONAIRE   Universal, 1921
STEP ON IT!   Universal, 1922
ACROSS THE DEADLINE   Universal, 1922
ANOTHER MAN'S SHOES   Universal, 1922
DON'T SHOOT   Universal, 1922
THE LONG CHANCE   Universal, 1922
THE PRISONER   Universal, 1923
SAWDUST   Universal, 1923

WHAT WIVES WANT   Universal, 1923
QUICKSANDS   Selznick, 1923
TRIMMED IN SCARLET   Universal, 1923
LUCRETIA LOMBARD   Warner Bros., 1923
THE TROUBLE SHOOTER   Fox, 1924
THE HEART BUSTER   Fox, 1924
THE ROUGHNECK   Fox, 1924
THE HUNTED WOMAN   Fox, 1925
THE ONLY THING   MGM, 1925
SOUL MATES   MGM, 1926
BROWN OF HARVARD   MGM, 1926
THE UNDERSTANDING HEART   MGM, 1927
TWELVE MILES OUT   MGM, 1927
THE SMART SET   MGM, 1928
WHILE THE CITY SLEEPS   MGM, 1928
BRINGING UP FATHER   MGM, 1928
ALIAS JIMMY VALENTINE   MGM, 1928
OUR MODERN MAIDENS   MGM, 1929
UNTAMED   MGM, 1929
THEY LEARNED ABOUT WOMEN
  co-director with Sam Wood, MGM, 1930
THE UNHOLY THREE   MGM, 1930
NEW MOON   MGM, 1931
THE EASIEST WAY   MGM, 1931
JUST A GIGOLO   MGM, 1931
ARSENE LUPIN   MGM, 1932
BUT THE FLESH IS WEAK   MGM, 1932
RED-HEADED WOMAN   MGM, 1932
HELL BELOW   MGM, 1933
THE NUISANCE   MGM, 1933
THE SOLITAIRE MAN   MGM, 1933
VIVA VILLA!   MGM, 1934
THE GIRL FROM MISSOURI   MGM, 1934
THE GAY BRIDE   MGM, 1934
ONE NEW YORK NIGHT   MGM, 1935
A TALE OF TWO CITIES   MGM, 1935
LIBELED LADY   MGM, 1936
SARATOGA   MGM, 1937
A YANK AT OXFORD   MGM, 1938
TOO YOUNG TO HANDLE   MGM, 1938
LET FREEDOM RING   MGM, 1939
LADY OF THE TROPICS   MGM, 1939
BOOM TOWN   MGM, 1940
LOVE CRAZY   MGM, 1941
HONKY-TONK   MGM, 1941
CROSSROADS   MGM, 1942
ASSIGNMENT IN BRITTANY   MGM, 1943
DRAGON SEED   co-director with
  Harold S. Bucquet, MGM, 1944
HIGH BARBAREE   MGM, 1947
THE HUCKSTERS   MGM, 1947
JULIA MISBEHAVES   MGM, 1948

ALAN COOKE

b. April 29, 1935 - London, England
d. 1994

FLAT TWO   Anglo-Amalgamated,
  1962, British
THE MIND OF MR. SOAMES   Columbia,
  1970, British
THE RIGHT PROSPECTUS (TF)   BBC-TV,
  1972, British
BLODWYN HOME FROM RACHEL'S
  MARRIAGE (TF)   BBC-TV, 1972, British
A PICTURE OF KATHERINE MANSFIELD (MS)
  BBC, 1973, British
SHADES OF GREENE (MS)   Thames TV,
  1976, British
THE HUNCHBACK OF NOTRE DAME (TF)
  BBC-TV, 1978, British
RENOIR, MY FATHER (TF)   BBC-TV,
  1979, British
COVER (MS)   ITC, 1980, British
NADIA (TF)   Dave Bell Productions/Tribune
  Entertainment Company/Jadran Film,
  1984, U.S.-Yugoslavian

MERIAN C. COOPER

b. October 24, 1893 - Jacksonville, Florida
d. 1973

GRASS   GRASS: A NATION'S BATTLE
  FOR LIFE/GRASS: THE EPIC OF A
  LOST TRIBE (FD)   co-director with
  Ernest B. Schoedsack, Paramount, 1925
CHANG (FD)   co-director with Ernest B.
  Schoedsack, Paramount, 1927
THE FOUR FEATHERS   co-director with
  Ernest B. Schoedsack & Lothar Mendes,
  United Artists, 1933
KING KONG   co-director with Ernest B.
  Schoedsack, RKO Radio, 1933

SERGIO CORBUCCI

b. December 6, 1927 - Rome, Italy
d. 1990

SALVATE MIA FIGLIA   Lauro, 1951, Italian
LA PECCATRICE DELL'ISOLA   Audax Film,
  1953, Italian
TWO COLONELS   Comet, 1961, Italian
DUEL OF THE TITANS   ROMOLO E REMO
  Paramount, 1961, Italian
GOLIATH AND THE VAMPIRES   MACISTE
  CONTROL IL VAMPIRO   co-director with
  Giacomo Gentilomo, American International,
  1961, Italian
THE SLAVE   IL FIGLIO DI SPARTACUS
  MGM, 1962, Italian
IL GIORNO PIU' CORTO   Titanus,
  1963, Italian
MINNESOTA CLAY   Harlequin International,
  1965, Italian-Spanish-French
DJANGO   BRC, 1966, Italian
NAVAJO JOE   UN DOLLARO A TESTA
  United Artists, 1966, Italian-Spanish
JOHNNY ORO   Sanson, 1966, Italian
THE HELLBENDERS   Embassy, 1966,
  Italian-Spanish
BERSAGLIO MOBILE   Rizzoli Film,
  1967, Italian
IL GRANDE SILENZIO   Adelphia
  Cinematografica, 1967, Italian
THE MERCENARY   United Artists, 1969,
  Italian-Spanish
GLI SPECIALISTI   Adelphia Cinematografica,
  1969, Italian
COMPAÑEROS   VAMOS A MATAR
  COMPAÑEROS   Cinerama
  Releasing Corporation, 1971,
  Spanish-Italian-West German
VIVA LA MUERTE...TUA!   Tritone Filmind,
  1971, Italian
CHE C'ENTRIAMO NOI CON LA
  RIVOLUZIONE?   Fair Film, 1972, Italian
LA BANDA J & S - CRONACA CRIMINALE
  DEL FAR-WEST   Roberto Loyola
  Cinematografica/Orfeo/Terra Film Kunst,
  1973, Italian-Spanish-Monacan
IL BESTIONE   C.C. Champion, Inc., 1974,
  Italian-French
BLUFF - STORIE DI TRUFFE E DI
  IMBRAGLIONE   Cineriz, 1975, Italian
UN GENIO, DUE COMPARI, UN POLLO
  Titanus, 1975, Italian-French-West German
DI CHE SEGNO SEI?   PIC, 1976, Italian
IL SIGNOR ROBINSON - MOSTRUOSA
  STORIA D'AMORE E D'AVVENTURE
  United Artists, 1976, Italian
TRE TIGRI CONTRO TRE TIGRI
  co-director with Steno, Primex/Italian
  International Film, 1977, Italian
ECCO NOI PER ESEMPIO   CIDIF,
  1977, Italian

LA MAZZETTA   United Artists, 1978, Italian
GIALLO NAPOLETANO   CIDIF, 1979, Italian
PARI E DISPARI   CIDIF, 1979, Italian
I DON'T UNDERSTAND YOU ANYMORE
  Capital, 1980, Italian
I'M GETTING MYSELF A YACHT   Capital,
  1981, Italian
CHI TROVO UN AMICO, TROVA UN TESORO
  CEIAD, 1981, Italian
SUPER FUZZ   Avco Embassy, 1981, Italian
MY DARLING, MY DEAREST   PLM Film,
  1982, Italian
THREE WISE KINGS   PLM Film, 1982, Italian
COUNT TACCHIA   DAC/Adige, 1982, Italian
SING SING   Columbia, 1983, Italian
QUESTO E QUELLO   CIDIF, 1983, Italian
A TU PER TU   DAC, 1984, Italian
SONO UN FENOMENO PARANORMALE
  Columbia, 1986, Italian
RIMINI RIMINI   Medusa, 1987, Italian
ROBA DA RICCHI   Scena Film, 1987, Italian
I GIORNI DEL COMMISSARIO AMBROSIO
  Numero Uno International/Reteitalia,
  1988, Italian
NIGHT CLUB   Reteitalia, 1989, Italian
DONNE ARMATE (TF)   Italian International
  Film/RAI/Taurus Film/Pathe Italia, 1990,
  Italian-German

HENRY CORNELIUS

b. August 18, 1913 - South Africa
d. 1958

PASSPORT TO PIMLICO   Eagle Lion,
  1948, British
THE GALLOPING MAJOR   Souvaine
  Selective, 1950, British
GENEVIEVE   Universal, 1953, British
I AM A CAMERA   DCA, 1955, British
NEXT TO NO TIME   Showcorporation,
  1958, British

AXEL CORTI

b. 1933 - Paris, France
d. 1993

KAISER JOSEF UND DIE
  BAHNWARTERSTOCHTER
  1962, Austrian
DER FALL JAGERSTATTER   1971, Austrian
DER VERWEIGERUNG   1972, Austrian
TOTSTELLEN   1975, Austrian
A WOMAN'S PALE BLUE
  HANDKERCHIEF (TF)   ORF/RAI,
  1984, Austrian-Italian
GOD DOES NOT BELIEVE IN US ANYMORE
  Roxie Releasing, 1981,
  Austrian-West German-Swiss
SANTA FE   Roxie Releasing, 1985, Austrian
WELCOME IN VIENNA   Roxie Releasing,
  1986, Austrian
THE KING'S WHORE   Cinema & Cinema/
  AFC France, 1990, French-Italian
RADETZKYMARSCH   co-director with Gernot
  Roll, Satel/ORF/Progefi/Taurus Film/BR,
  1994, Austrian-French-German

JOHN CROMWELL

b. December 23, 1888 - Toledo, Ohio
d. 1979

CLOSE HARMONY   co-director with
  Edward Sutherland, Paramount, 1929
THE DANCE OF LIFE   co-director with
  Edward Sutherland, Paramount, 1929
THE MIGHTY   Paramount, 1929
STREET OF CHANCE   Paramount, 1930

THE TEXAN   Paramount, 1930
FOR THE DEFENSE   Paramount, 1930
TOM SAWYER   Paramount, 1930
SCANDAL SHEET   Paramount, 1931
UNFAITHFUL   Paramount, 1931
THE VICE SQUAD   Paramount, 1931
RICH MAN'S FOLLY   Paramount, 1931
THE WORLD AND THE FLESH
   Paramount, 1932
SWEEPINGS   RKO, 1933
THE SILVER CORD   RKO, 1933
DOUBLE HARNESS   RKO, 1933
ANN VICKERS   RKO, 1933
SPITFIRE   RKO Radio, 1934
THIS MAN IS MINE   RKO Radio, 1934
OF HUMAN BONDAGE   RKO Radio, 1934
THE FOUNTAIN   RKO Radio, 1934
VILLAGE TALE   RKO Radio, 1935
JALNA   RKO Radio, 1935
I DREAM TOO MUCH   RKO Radio, 1935
LITTLE LORD FAUNTLEROY
   United Artists, 1936
TO MARY - WITH LOVE
   20th Century-Fox, 1936
BANJO ON MY KNEE
   20th Century-Fox, 1936
THE PRISONER OF ZENDA
   United Artists, 1937
ALGIERS   United Artists, 1938
MADE FOR EACH OTHER
   United Artists, 1939
IN NAME ONLY   RKO Radio, 1939
ABE LINCOLN IN ILLINOIS   RKO Radio, 1940
VICTORY   Paramount, 1940
SO ENDS OUR NIGHT   United Artists, 1941
SON OF FURY   20th Century-Fox, 1942
SINCE YOU WENT AWAY
   United Artists, 1944
THE ENCHANTED COTTAGE
   RKO Radio, 1945
ANNA AND THE KING OF SIAM
   20th Century-Fox, 1946
DEAD RECKONING   Columbia, 1947
NIGHT SONG   RKO Radio, 1947
CAGED   Warner Bros., 1950
THE COMPANY SHE KEEPS
   RKO Radio, 1951
THE RACKET   RKO Radio, 1951
THE GODDESS   Columbia, 1958
THE SCAVENGERS   Paramount, 1959
A MATTER OF MORALS   United Artists,
   1960, U.S.-Swedish

ALAN CROSLAND

b. August 10, 1894 - New York, New York
d. 1936

THE LIGHT IN DARKNESS   Edison, 1917
KIDNAPPED   Forum, 1917
THE APPLE TREE GIRL
   Edison Perfection, 1917
THE WHIRLPOOL   Select, 1918
THE UNBELIEVER   Edison-Kleine, 1918
THE COUNTRY COUSIN   Select, 1919
THE FLAPPER   Select, 1920
YOUTHFUL FOLLY   Select, 1920
BROADWAY AND HOME   Select, 1920
GREATER THAN FLAME   Select, 1920
POINT OF VIEW   Select, 1920
WORLDS APART   Select, 1921
IS LIFE WORTH LIVING?   Select, 1921
ROOM AND BOARD   Paramount, 1921
SLIM SHOULDERS   W.W. Hodkinson, 1922
WHY ANNOUNCE YOUR MARRIAGE?
   Select, 1922
THE PROPHET'S PARADISE   Select, 1922
SHADOWS OF THE SEA   Select, 1922

THE SNITCHING HOUR   Clark-Cornelius
   Corp., 1922
THE FACE IN THE FOG   Paramount, 1922
THE ENEMIES OF WOMEN   Goldwyn, 1923
UNDER THE RED ROBE   Goldwyn, 1923
THREE WEEKS   Goldwyn, 1924
MIAMI   W.W. Hodkinson, 1924
UNGUARDED WOMEN   Paramount, 1924
SINNERS IN HEAVEN   Paramount, 1924
CONTRABAND   Paramount, 1925
COMPROMISE   Warner Bros., 1925
BOBBED HAIR   Warner Bros., 1925
DON JUAN   Warner Bros., 1926
WHEN A MAN LOVES   Warner Bros., 1927
THE BELOVED ROGUE   United Artists, 1927
OLD SAN FRANCISCO   Warner Bros., 1927
THE JAZZ SINGER   Warner Bros., 1927
GLORIOUS BETSY   Warner Bros., 1928
THE SCARLET LADY   Columbia, 1928
ON WITH THE SHOW   Warner Bros., 1929
GENERAL CRACK   Warner Bros., 1929
THE FURIES   First National, 1930
SONG OF THE FLAME   First National, 1930
BIG BOY   Warner Bros., 1930
VIENNESE NIGHTS   Warner Bros., 1930
CAPTAIN THUNDER   Warner Bros., 1930
CHILDREN OF DREAMS   Warner Bros., 1931
THE SILVER LINING   United Artists, 1932
WEEK-ENDS ONLY   Fox, 1932
HELLO, SISTER   Fox, 19333
MASSACRE   First National, 1934
MIDNIGHT ALIBI   First National, 1934
THE PERSONALITY KID   Warner Bros., 1934
THE CASE OF THE HOWLING DOG
   Warner Bros., 1934
THE WHITE COCKATOO   Warner Bros., 1935
IT HAPPENED IN NEW YORK
   Universal, 1935
MR. DYNAMITE   Universal, 1935
LADY TUBBS   Universal, 1935
KING SOLOMON OF BROADWAY
   Universal, 1935
THE GREAT IMPERSONATION
   United Artists, 1935

JAMES CRUZE
(Jens Cruz Bosen)
b. March 27, 1884 - Ogden, Utah
d. 1942

TOO MANY MILLIONS   Paramount, 1918
THE DUB   Paramount, 1919
ALIAS MIKE MORAN   Paramount, 1919
THE ROARING ROADS   Paramount, 1919
YOU'RE FIRED   Paramount, 1919
THE LOVE BURGLAR   Paramount, 1919
VALLEY OF THE GIANTS   1919
AN ADVENTURE IN HEARTS
   Paramount, 1919
HAWTHORNE OF THE U.S.A.
   Paramount, 1919
THE LOTTERY MAN   Paramount, 1919
MRS. TEMPLE'S TELEGRAM
   Paramount, 1920
TERROR ISLAND   Paramount, 1920
A FULL HOUSE   Paramount, 1920
THE SINS OF ST. ANTHONY
   Paramount, 1920
WHAT HAPPENED TO JONES?
   Paramount, 1920
ALWAYS AUDACIOUS   Paramount, 1920
THE CHARM SCHOOL   Paramount, 1921
THE DOLLAR-A-YEAR MAN
   Paramount, 1921
FOOD FOR SCANDAL   Realart, 1921
LEAP YEAR   SKIRT SHY   Paramount, 1921
THE FAST FREIGHT   Paramount, 1921
GASOLINE GUS   Paramount, 1921

CRAZY TO MARRY   Paramount, 1921
ONE GLORIOUS DAY   Paramount, 1922
IS MATRIMONY A FAILURE?
   Paramount, 1922
THE DICTATOR   Paramount, 1922
THE OLD HOMESTEAD   Paramount, 1922
THIRTY DAYS   Paramount, 1922
THE COVERED WAGON   Paramount, 1923
HOLLYWOOD   Paramount, 1923
RUGGLES OF RED GAP   Paramount, 1923
TO THE LADIES   Paramount, 1923
MERTON OF THE MOVIES   Paramount, 1924
THE FIGHTING COWARD   Paramount, 1924
THE GARDEN OF WEEDS   Paramount, 1924
THE CITY THAT NEVER SLEEPS
   Paramount, 1924
THE ENEMY SEX   Paramount, 1924
THE PONY EXPRESS   Paramount, 1925
BEGGAR ON HORSEBACK
   Paramount, 1925
THE GOOSE HANGS HIGH
   Paramount, 1925
MARRY ME   Paramount, 1925
WELCOME HOME   Paramount, 1925
WAKING UP THE TOWN   United Artists, 1925
MANNEQUIN   Paramount, 1926
THE WAITER FROM THE RITZ   1926
OLD IRONSIDES   Paramount, 1926
WE'RE ALL GAMBLERS   Paramount, 1927
THE CITY GONE WILD   Paramount, 1927
ON TO RENO   Pathé, 1928
THE RED MARK   Pathé, 1928
EXCESS BAGGAGE   MGM, 1928
THE MATING CALL   Paramount, 1928
THE DUKE STEPS OUT   MGM, 1929
A MAN'S MAN   MGM, 1929
THE GREAT GABBO
   Sono Art-World Wide, 1929
ONCE A GENTLEMAN
   Sono Art-World Wide, 1930
SHE GOT WHAT SHE WANTED
   Tiffany, 1930
SALVATION NELL   Tiffany, 1931
IF I HAD A MILLION   co-director,
   Paramount, 1932
WASHINGTON MERRY-GO-ROUND   1932
RACETRACK   World Wide, 1933
SAILOR BE GOOD   RKO, 1933
I COVER THE WATERFRONT
   United Artists, 1933
MR. SKITCH   Fox, 1933
DAVID HARUM   Fox, 1934
THEIR BIG MOMENT   RKO, 1934
HELLDORADO   Fox, 1935
TWO-FISTED   Paramount, 1935
SUTTER'S GOLD   Universal, 1936
THE WRONG ROAD   Republic, 1937
PRISON NURSE   Republic, 1938
THE GANGS OF NEW YORK   Republic, 1938
COME ON LEATHERNECKS!   Republic, 1938

GEORGE CUKOR

b. July 7, 1899 - New York, New York
d. 1983

GRUMPY   co-director with Cyril Gardner,
   Paramount, 1930
THE VIRTUOUS SIN   co-director with
   Louis Gasnier, Paramount, 1930
THE ROYAL FAMILY OF BROADWAY
   co-director with Cyril Gardner,
   Paramount, 1930
TARNISHED LADY   Paramount, 1931
GIRLS ABOUT TOWN   Paramount, 1931
WHAT PRICE HOLLYWOOD?
   RKO Radio, 1932
A BILL OF DIVORCEMENT   RKO Radio, 1932
ROCKABYE   RKO Radio, 1932

OUR BETTERS RKO Radio, 1933
DINNER AT EIGHT MGM, 1933
LITTLE WOMEN ★ RKO Radio, 1933
DAVID COPPERFIELD MGM, 1935
SYLVIA SCARLETT RKO Radio, 1935
ROMEO AND JULIET MGM, 1936
CAMILLE MGM, 1937
HOLIDAY Columbia, 1938
ZAZA Paramount, 1939
THE WOMEN MGM, 1939
THE PHILADELPHIA STORY ★ MGM, 1940
SUSAN AND GOD MGM, 1940
A WOMAN'S FACE MGM, 1941
TWO-FACED WOMAN MGM, 1941
HER CARDBOARD LOVER MGM, 1942
KEEPER OF THE FLAME MGM, 1943
RESISTANCE AND OHM'S LAW (FD)
  Army Signal Corps, 1944
GASLIGHT MGM, 1944
WINGED VICTORY 20th Century-Fox, 1944
A DOUBLE LIFE ★ Universal, 1947
EDWARD, MY SON MGM, 1949
ADAM'S RIB MGM, 1949
A LIFE OF HER OWN MGM, 1950
BORN YESTERDAY ★ Columbia, 1950
THE MODEL AND THE MARRIAGE BROKER
  20th Century-Fox, 1951
THE MARRYING KIND Columbia, 1952
PAT AND MIKE MGM, 1952
THE ACTRESS MGM, 1953
A STAR IS BORN Warner Bros., 1954
IT SHOULD HAPPEN TO YOU
  Columbia, 1954
BHOWANI JUNCTION MGM, 1956
LES GIRLS MGM, 1957
WILD IS THE WIND Paramount, 1957
HELLER IN PINK TIGHTS Paramount, 1960
SONG WITHOUT END co-director with
  Charles Vidor, Columbia, 1960
LET'S MAKE LOVE 20th Century-Fox, 1960
THE CHAPMAN REPORT
  Warner Bros., 1962
SOMETHING'S GOT TO GIVE
  20th Century-Fox, 1962, incomplete
MY FAIR LADY ★★ Warner Bros., 1964,
  re-released in 1994 by 20th Century Fox
JUSTINE 20th Century-Fox, 1969
TRAVELS WITH MY AUNT MGM,
  1972, British
LOVE AMONG THE RUINS (TF) ☆☆
  ABC Circle Films, 1975
THE BLUE BIRD 20th Century-Fox, 1976,
  U.S.-Soviet
THE CORN IS GREEN (TF)
  Warner Bros. TV, 1979
RICH AND FAMOUS
  MGM/United Artists, 1981

IRVING CUMMINGS

b. Ocotober 9, 1888 - New York, New York
d. 1959

THE MAN FROM HELL'S RIVER
  Western, 1922
FLESH AND BLOOD Western, 1922
PAID BACK Universal, 1922
BROAD DAYLIGHT Universal, 1922
THE JILT Universal, 1922
ENVIRONMENT Principal, 1922
THE DRUG TRAFFICE Western, 1923
EAST SIDE - WEST SIDE Principal, 1923
BROKEN HEARTS OF BROADWAY
  Western, 1923
STOLEN SECRETS Universal, 1924
FOOLS' HIGHWAY Universal, 1924
THE DANCING CHEAT Universal, 1924
RIDERS UP Universal, 1924

IN EVERY WOMAN'S LIFE
  First National, 1924
THE ROSE OF PARIS Universal, 1924
AS MAN DESIRES First National, 1925
ONE YEAR TO LIVE First National, 1925
THE DESERT FLOWER First National, 1925
JUST A WOMAN First National, 1925
INFATUATION First National 1925
THE JOHNSTOWN FLOOD Fox, 1926
RUSTLING FOR CUPID Fox, 1926
THE MIDNIGHT KISS Fox, 1926
THE COUNTRY BEYOND Fox, 1926
BERTHA THE SEWING MACHINE GIRL
  Fox, 1926
THE BRUTE Warner Bros., 1927
THE PORT OF MISSING GIRLS
  Brenda, 1928
DRESSED TO KILL Fox, 1928
ROMANCE OF THE UNDERWORLD
  ROMANCE AND BRIGHT LIGHTS
  Fox, 1928
IN OLD ARIZONA ★ co-director with
  Raoul Walsh, Fox, 1929
NOT QUITE DECENT Fox, 1929
BEHIND THAT CURTAIN Fox, 1929
CAMEO KIRBY Fox, 1930
ON THE LEVEL Fox, 1930
A DEVIL WITH WOMEN Fox, 1930
A HOLY TERROR Fox, 1932
THE CISCO KID Fox, 1932
ATTORNEY FOR THE DEFENSE
  Columbia, 1932
THE NIGHT CLUB LADY Columbia, 1932
MAN AGAINST WOMAN Columbia, 1932
MAN HUNT RKO, 1933
THE WOMAN I STOLE Columbia, 1933
THE MAD GAME Fox, 1933
I BELIEVED IN YOU Fox, 1934
GRAND CANARY Fox, 1934
THE WHITE PARADE Fox, 1934
IT'S A SMALL WORLD Fox, 1935
CURLY TOP Fox, 1935
NOBODY'S FOOL Universal, 1936
THE POOR LITTLE RICH GIRL
  20th Century-Fox, 1936
GIRLS' DORMITORY 20th Century-Fox, 1936
WHITE HUNTER 20th Century-Fox, 1936
VOGUES OF 1938 United Artists, 1937
MERRY-GO-ROUND OF 1938
  Universal, 1937
LITTLE MISS BROADWAY
  20th Century-Fox, 1938
JUST AROUND THE CORNER
  20th Century-Fox, 1938
THE STORY OF ALEXANDER GRAHAM BELL
  20th Century-Fox, 1939
HOLLYWOOD CAVALCADE
  20th Century-Fox, 1939
EVERYTHING HAPPENS AT NIGHT
  20th Century-Fox, 1939
LILILIAN RUSSELL 20th Century-Fox, 1940
DOWN ARGENTINE WAY
  20th Century-Fox, 1940
THAT NIGHT IN RIO 20th Century-Fox, 1941
BELLE STARR 20th Century-Fox, 1941
LOUISIANA PURCHASE Paramount, 1941
MY GAL SAL 20th Century-Fox, 1942
SPRINGTIME IN THE ROCKIES
  20th Century-Fox, 1942
SWEET ROSIE O'GRADY
  20th Century-Fox, 1943
WHAT A WOMAN! Columbia, 1943
THE IMPATIENT YEARS Columbia, 1944
THE DOLLY SISTERS
  20th Century-Fox, 1945
DOUBLE DYNAMITE RKO, 1951

MICHAEL CURTIZ
(MIhaly Kertesz)

b. December 24, 1888 - Budapest, Hungary
d. 1962

AZ UTOLSO BOHÉM 1912, Hungarian
MA ES HOLNAP 1912, Hungarian
RABELEK 1913, Hungarian
HAZASOKIK AZ URAM 1913, Hungarian
AS EJSZAKA RABJA 1914, Hungarian
A TOLONE 1914, Hungarian
A KOLESONKERT CSECSEMOK
  1914, Hungarian
A HERCEGNO PONGYOLABAN
  1914, Hungarian
BANK BAN 1914, Hungarian
AKIT KETTEN SZERETNEK 1915, Hungarian
A MEDIKUS 1916, Hungarian
A KARTHAUZI 1916, Hungarian
A FEKETE SZIVARVANY 1916, Hungarian
DOKTOR UR 1916, Hungarian
A FARKAS 1916, Hungarian
MAKKHETES 1916, Hungarian
A MAGYAR FOLD EREJE 1916, Hungarian
AZ EZREDES 1917, Hungarian
ZOARD MESTER 1917, Hungarian
A VOROS SAMSON 1917, Hungarian
A FOLD EMBERE 1917, Hungarian
TATARJARAS 1917, Hungarian
LILIOM 1918, Hungarian
JUDAS 1918, Hungarian
LULU 1918, Hungarian
ALRAUNE 1918, Hungarian
DIE DAME MIT DEM SCHWARZEN
  HANDSCHUH 1919, German
DIE GOTTESGEISSEL 1919, German
DER STERN VON DAMASKUS
  1920, German
DIE DAME MIT DEN SONNENBLUMEN
  1920, German
HERZOGIN SATANELLA 1920, German
BOCCACCIO 1920, German
CHERCHEZ LA FEMME 1921, German
FRAU DOROTHY'S BEKENNTNIS
  1921, German
WEGE DES SCHRECKENS LABYRINTH
  DESGRAUENS 1921, German
SODOM UND GOMORRAH LEGENDE VON
  SUNDEUND STAFE/THE QUEEN OF SIN
  AND THESPECTACLE OF SODOM AND
  GOMORRAH 1922-23, German
DIE LAWINE AVALANCHE 1923, German
DER JUNGE MEDARDUS 1923, German
NAMENLOS 1923, German
EIN SPIEL UNS LEBEN 1924, German
HARUN AL RASCHID 1924, German
DIE SKLAVENKONIGIN MOON OF ISRAEL
  1924, German
CELIMENE - LA POUPEE DE MONTMARTRE
  1925, French-Austrian-German
DER GOLDENE SCHMETTERLING
  THE ROAD TO HAPPINESS 1926,
  Austrian-German-Danish
FLAKER NR. 13 1926, German
THE THIRD DEGREE Warner Bros., 1927
A MILLION BID Warner Bros., 1927
THE DESIRED WOMAN Warner Bros., 1927
GOOD TIME CHARLEY Warner Bros., 1927
TENDERLOIN Warner Bros., 1928
NOAH'S ARK Warner Bros., 1929
THE GLAD RAG DOLL Warner Bros., 1929
THE MADONNA OF AVENUE A
  Warner Bros., 1929
THE GAMBLERS Warner Bros., 1929
HEARTS IN EXILE Warner Bros., 1929
MAMMY Warner Bros., 1930
UNDER A TEXAS MOON Warner Bros., 1930
THE MATRIMONIAL BED Warner Bros., 1930

D

BRIGHT LIGHTS   Warner Bros., 1930
A SOLDIER'S PLAYTHING
   Warner Bros., 1930
RIVER'S END   Warner Bros., 1930
GOD'S GIFT TO WOMEN
   Warner Bros., 1931
THE MAD GENIUS   Warner Bros., 1931
THE WOMAN FROM MONTE CARLO
   Warner Bros., 1932
ALIAS THE DOCTOR   co-director with
   Lloyd Bacon, Warner Bros., 1932
THE STRANGE LOVE OF MOLLY LOUVAIN
   Warner Bros., 1932
DOCTOR X   Warner Bros., 1932
CABIN IN THE COTTON   Warner Bros., 1932
20,000 YEARS IN SING SING
   Warner Bros., 1933
THE MYSTERY OF THE WAX MUSEUM
   Warner Bros.,1933
THE KEYHOLE   Warner Bros., 1933
PRIVATE DETECTIVE 62   Warner Bros., 1933
GOODBYE AGAIN   Warner Bros., 1933
THE KENNEL MURDER CASE
   Warner Bros., 1933
FEMALE   Warner Bros., 1933
MANDALAY   Warner Bros., 1934
JIMMY THE GENT   Warner Bros., 1934
THE KEY   HIGH PERIL   Warner Bros., 1934
BRITISH AGENT   Warner Bros., 1934
BLACK FURY   Warner Bros., 1935
THE CASE OF THE CURIOUS BRIDE
   Warner Bros., 1935
FRONT PAGE WOMAN   Warner Bros., 1935
LITTLE BIG SHOT   Warner Bros., 1935
CAPTAIN BLOOD   Warner Bros., 1935
THE WALKING DEAD   Warner Bros., 1936
THE CHARGE OF THE LIGHT BRIGADE
   Warner Bros.,1936
STOLEN HOLIDAY   Warner Bros., 1937
MOUNTAIN JUSTICE   Warner Bros., 1937
KID GALAHAD   THE BATTLING BELLHOP
   Warner Bros., 1937
THE PERFECT SPECIMEN
   Warner Bros., 1937
GOLD IS WHERE YOU FIND IT
   Warner Bros., 1938
THE ADVENTURES OF ROBIN HOOD
   co-director with William Keighley,
   Warner Bros., 1938
FOUR'S A CROWD   Warner Bros., 1938
FOUR DAUGHTERS ★   Warner Bros., 1938
ANGELS WITH DIRTY FACES ★
   Warner Bros., 1938
DODGE CITY   Warner Bros., 1939
DAUGHTERS COURAGEOUS
   Warner Bros., 1939
THE PRIVATE LIVES OF ELIZABETH
   AND ESSEX   ELIZABETH THE QUEEN
   Warner Bros., 1939
FOUR WIVES   Warner Bros., 1939
VIRGINIA CITY   Warner Bros., 1940
THE SEA HAWK   Warner Bros., 1940
SANTA FE TRAIL   Warner Bros., 1940
THE SEA WOLF   Warner Bros., 1941
DIVE BOMBER   Warner Bros., 1941
CAPTAINS OF THE CLOUDS
   Warner Bros., 1942
YANKEE DOODLE DANDY ★
   Warner Bros., 1942
CASABLANCA ★★   Warner Bros., 1943
MISSION TO MOSCOW   Warner Bros., 1943
THIS IS THE ARMY   Warner Bros., 1943
PASSAGE TO MARSEILLE
   Warner Bros., 1944
JANIE   Warner Bros., 1944
ROUGHLY SPEAKING   Warner Bros., 1945
MILDRED PIERCE   Warner Bros., 1945
NIGHT AND DAY   Warner Bros., 1946

LIFE WITH FATHER   Warner Bros., 1947
THE UNSUSPECTED   Warner Bros., 1947
ROMANCE ON THE HIGH SEAS
   Warner Bros., 1948
MY DREAM IS YOURS   Warner Bros., 1949
FLAMINGO ROAD   Warner Bros., 1949
THE LADY TAKES A SAILOR
   Warner Bros., 1949
BRIGHT LEAF   Warner Bros., 1950
YOUNG MAN WITH A HORN
   Warner Bros., 1950
THE BREAKING POINT   Warner Bros., 1950
FORCE OF ARMS   Warner Bros., 1951
JIM THORPE - ALL AMERICAN
   Warner Bros., 1951
I'LL SEE YOU IN MY DREAMS
   Warner Bros., 1951
THE STORY OF WILL ROGERS
   Warner Bros., 1952
THE JAZZ SINGER   Warner Bros., 1953
TROUBLE ALONG THE WAY
   Warner Bros., 1953
THE BOY FROM OKLAHOMA
   Warner Bros., 1954
THE EGYPTIAN   20th Century-Fox, 1954
WHITE CHRISTMAS   Paramount, 1954
WE'RE NO ANGELS   Paramount, 1955
THE VAGABOND KING   Paramount, 1956
THE SCARLET HOUR   Paramount, 1956
THE BEST THINGS IN LIFE ARE FREE
   20th Century-Fox, 1956
THE HELEN MORGAN STORY
   Warner Bros., 1957
KING CREOLE   Paramount, 1958
THE PROUD REBEL   Buena Vista, 1958
THE HANGMAN   Paramount, 1959
THE MAN IN THE NET   United Artists, 1959
THE ADVENTURES OF HUCKLEBERRY FINN
   MGM, 1960
A BREATH OF SCANDAL   Paramount, 1960
FRANCIS OF ASSISI   20th Century-Fox, 1961
THE COMANCHEROS
   20th Century-Fox, 1961

PAUL CZINNER
b. 1890 - Budapest, Hungary
d. 1972

HOMO IMMANIS   DER UNMENSCH
   1919, Austrian
INFERNO   1923, Austrian
NJU   1924, German
DER GEIGER VON FLORENZ   1926, German
LIEBE   1926, German
DONA JUANA   1927, German
FRAULEIN ELSE   1929, German
THE WOMAN HE SCORNED   THE WAY OF
   LOST SOULS   Warner Bros., 1930, British
ARIANE   THE LOVES OF ARIANE
   1931, German
DER TRAUMENDE MUND   1932, German
CATHERINE THE GREAT   United Artist,
   1934, British
ESCAPE ME NEVER   United Artists,
   1935, British
AS YOU LIKE IT   co-director with Dallas
   Bower, 20th Century-Fox, 1936, British
DREAMING LIPS   co-director with
   Lee Garmes, United Artists, 1937, British
MELO   1938, French
STOLEN LIFE   Paramount, 1939, British
DON GIOVANNI   co-director with
   Maxwell Travers, 1955, British
THE BOLSHOI BALLET (PF)   RFD,
   1960, British
DER ROSENKAVALIER   RFD, 1962, British
ROMEO AND JULIET   RFD, 1966, British

MORTON DA COSTA
(Morton Tecosky)
b. March 7, 1914 - Philadelphia, Pennsylvania
d.1989

AUNTIE MAME   Warner Bros., 1958
THE MUSIC MAN   Warner Bros., 1962
ISLAND OF LOVE   Warner Bros., 1963

DELMER DAVES
b. July 24, 1904 - San Francisco, California
d. 1977

DESTINATION TOKYO   Warner Bros., 1943
THE VERY THOUGHT OF YOU
   Warner Bros., 1944
HOLLYWOOD CANTEEN   Warner Bros., 1944
PRIDE OF THE MARINES
   Warner Bros., 1945
THE RED HOUSE   Warner Bros., 1947
DARK PASSAGE   Warner Bros., 1947
TO THE VICTOR   Warner Bros., 1948
A KISS IN THE DARK   Warner Bros., 1949
TASK FORCE   Warner Bros., 1949
BROKEN ARROW   20th Century-Fox, 1950
BIRD OF PARADISE   20th Century-Fox, 1951
RETURN OF THE TEXAN
   20th Century-Fox, 1952
TREASURE OF THE GOLDEN CONDOR
   20th Century-Fox, 1953
NEVER LET ME GO   MGM,
   1953, British-U.S.
DEMETRIUS AND THE GLADIATORS
   20th Century-Fox, 1954
DRUM BEAT   Warner Bros., 1954
JUBAL   Columbia, 1956
THE LAST WAGON   20th Century-Fox, 1956
3:10 TO YUMA   Columbia, 1957
COWBOY   Columbia, 1958
KINGS GO FORTH   United Artists, 1958
THE BADLANDERS   MGM, 1958
THE HANGING TREE   Warner Bros., 1959
A SUMMER PLACE   Warner Bros., 1959
PARRISH   Warner Bros., 1961
SUSAN SLADE   Warner Bros., 1961
ROME ADVENTURE   Warner Bros., 1962
SPENCER'S MOUNTAIN   Warner Bros., 1963
YOUNGBLOOD HAWKE   Warner Bros., 1964
THE BATTLE OF THE VILLA FIORITA
   Warner Bros., 1965, British-U.S.

J. SEARLE DAWLEY
b. Del Norte, Colorado
d. 1950

RESCUED FROM AN EAGLE'S NEST
   co-director with Edwin S. Porter,
   Edison, 1907
THE PRINCE AND THE PAUPER
   Edison, 1909
HANSEL AND GRETEL   Edison, 1909
FAUST   Edison, 1909
BLUEBEARD   Edison, 1909
MICHAEL STROGOFF   Edison, 1910
FRANKENSTEIN   Edison, 1910
A CHRISTMAS CAROL   Edison, 1910
AIDA   co-director with Oscar Apfel, 1911

435

THE DOCTOR   1911
VAN BIBBER'S EXPERIMENT   1911
THE BATTLE OF BUNKER HILL   1911
UNDER THE TROPICAL SUN   1911
THE BATTLE OF TRAFALGAR   1911
TREASURE ISLAND   1912
THE CHARGE OF THE LIGHT
   BRIGADE   1912
PARTNERS FOR LIFE   1912
ALLADDIN UP-TO-DATE   1912
TESS OF THE D'URBERVILLES   co-director
   with Edwin S. Porter, Paramount, 1913
IN THE BISHOP'S CARRIAGE   co-director
   with Edwin S. Porter, Famous Players, 1913
CAPRICE   1913
AN HOUR BEFORE DAWN   1913
MARY STUART   1913
THE DIAMOND CROWN   1913
A GOOD LITTLE DEVIL   co-director with
   Edwin S. Porter, Famous Players, 1913
A DAUGHTER OF THE HILLS   1913
THE PORT OF DOOM   1913
AN AMERICAN CITIZEN   1914
THE OATH OF A VIKING   1914
MARTA OF THE LOWLANDS   1914
ONE OF MILLIONS   1914
IN THE NAME OF THE PRINCE OF
   PEACE   1914
ALWAYS IN THE WAY   1915
A DAUGHTER OF THE PEOPLE   1915
FOUR FEATHERS   1915
MICE AND MEN   1916
SNOW WHITE   1916
THE VALENTINE GIRL   1917
THE MYSTERIOUS MISS TERRY   1917
BAB'S MATINEE IDOL   1917
UNCLE TOM'S CABIN   1918
THE SEVEN SWANS   1918
THE LIE   1918
RICH MAN POOR MAN   1918
THE DEATH DANCE   1918
THE PHANTOM HONEY MOON   1919
EVERYBODY'S BUSINESS   1919
TWILIGHT   1919
HARVEST MOON   1920
A VIRGIN PARADISE   1921
BEYOND PRICE   1921
WHO ARE MY PARENTS?   1922
AS A MAN LIVES   1923
HAS THE WORLD GONE MAD?   1923
BROADWAY BROKE   1923

EMILE DE ANTONIO
b. 1920 - Scranton, Pennsylvania
d. 1989

POINT OF ORDER (FD)   Point, 1963
RUSH TO JUDGMENT (FD)   Impact, 1967
AMERICA IS HARD TO SEE (FD)   1968
IN THE YEAR OF THE PIG (FD)
   Pathe Contemporary, 1969
MILLHOUSE: A WHITE COMEDY
   New Yorker, 1971
PAINTERS PAINTING (FD)
   New Yorker, 1973
UNDERGROUND (FD)   co-director with
   Mary Lampson & Haskell Wexler,
   New Yorker, 1976
IN THE KING OF PRUSSIA   Turin Film
   Corporation, 1983
MR. HOOVER AND I (FD)   Turin Film
   Corporation, 1990

BASIL DEARDEN
b. January 1, 1911 - Westcliffe, England
d. 1971

THE BLACK SHEEP OF WHITEHALL
   co-director with Will Hay, United Artists, 1941
THE GOOSE STEPS OUT   co-director with
   Will Hay, United Artists, 1942, British
MY LEARNED FRIEND   co-director with
   Will Hay, Ealing, 1943, British
THE BELLS GO DOWN   United Artists,
   1943, British
HALFWAY HOUSE   Ealing, 1944, British
THEY CAME TO A CITY   Ealing, 1944, British
DEAD OF NIGHT   co-director with
   Alberto Cavalcanti, Robert Hamer &
   Charles Crichton, Universal, 1946, British
THE CAPTIVE HEART   Universal,
   1946, British
FRIEDA   Universal, 1947, British
SARABAND   SARABAND FOR DEAD
   LOVERS   Eagle Lion, 1948, British
TRAIN OF EVENTS   co-director with
   Sidney Cole & Charles Crichton,
   Rank, 1949, British
THE BLUE LAMP   Eagle Lion, 1950, British
CAGE OF GOLD   Ellis Films, 1950, British
POOL OF LONDON   Universal, 1951, British
I BELIEVE IN YOU   co-director with
   Michael Relph, Universal, 1952, British
THE GENTLE GUNMAN   Universal, 1952
THE SQUARE RING   co-director with
   Michael Relph, Republic, 1953, British
THE RAINBOW JACKET   Rank, 1954, British
OUT OF THE CLOUDS   co-director with
   Michael Relph, Rank, 1954, British
THE SHIP THAT DIED OF SHAME
   Continental, 1955, British
WHO DONE IT?   RFD, 1956, British
THE SMALLEST SHOW ON EARTH
   Times Film Corporation, 1957, British
VIOLENT PLAYGROUND   Lopert,
   1958, British
SAPPHIRE   Universal, 1959, British
THE LEAGUE OF GENTLEMEN
   Kingsley International, 1960, British
MAN IN THE MOON   Trans-Lux, 1960, British
THE SECRET PARTNER   MGM, 1961, British
VICTIM   Pathé-America, 1961, British
ALL NIGHT LONG   Continental, 1961, British
WALK IN THE SHADOW   LIFE FOR RUTH
   Continental, 1962, British
THE MIND BENDERS   American International,
   1963, British
A PLACE TO GO   Continental, 1964, British
WOMAN OF STRAW   United Artists,
   1964, British
MASQUERADE   United Artists, 1965, British
KHARTOUM   United Artists, 1966, British
ONLY WHEN I LARF   Paramount,
   1968, British
THE ASSASSINATION BUREAU   Paramount,
   1969, British
THE MAN WHO HAUNTED HIMSELF
   Levitt-Pickman, 1970, British

EDUARDO DE FILIPPO
(Eduardo Passarelli)
b. May 24, 1900 - Naples, Italy
d. 1984

IN CAMPAGNA E' CADUTA UNA STELLA
   Defilm S.A., 1940, Italian
TI CONOSCO, MASCHERINA!
   Cines/Juventus, 1943, Italian
NAPOLI MILIONARIA   Teatri della Farnesina,
   1950, Italian

FILUMENA MARTURANO   Arco Film,
   1951, Italian
SEVEN CAPITAL SINS   co-director,
   Arlan Pictures, 1952, French-Italian
MARITO E MOGLIE   Film Costellazione,
   1952, Italian
RAGAZZE DA MARITO   Forges Davanzati,
   1952, Italian
NAPOLETANI A MILANO   Virtus Film/
   Produzione Volonteri, 1953, Italian
QUESTI FANTASMI   San Ferdinando Film,
   1954, Italian
FORTUNELLA   Dino De Laurentiis/Les
   Films Marceau, 1958, Italian-French
SOGNI DI UNA NOTTE DI MEZZA SBORNIA
   Titanus, 1959, Italian
KISS THE OTHER SHEIK   OGGI, DOMANI E
   DOPODOMANI   MGM, 1965, Italian-French
SHOOT LOUD...LOUDER...I DON'T
   UNDERSTAND   Embassy, 1966, Italian

FERNANDO DE FUENTES
b. December 13, 1895 - Vera Cruz, Mexico
d. 1952

EL ANONIMO   Azteca Films, 1932, Mexican
EL PRISONERO 13   Azteca Films,
   1933, Mexican
LA CALANDRIA   Azteca Films,
   1933, Mexican
EL COMPADRE MENDOZA   Azteca Films,
   1934, Mexican
CRUZ DIABLO   Azteca Films, 1934, Mexican
VAMONOS CON PANCHO VILLA
   Azteca Films, 1935, Mexican
LA FAMILIA DRESSEL   Azteca Films,
   1935, Mexican
ALLA EN EL RANCHO GRANDE
   Azteca Films, 1936, Mexican
BAJO EL CIELO DE MEXICAO   Azteca Films,
   1937, Mexican
LA ZANDUNGA   Azteca Films, 1937, Mexican
LA CASA DEL OGRO   Azteca Films,
   1937, Mexican
SU GRAN AVENTURA   Azteca Films,
   1938, Mexican
PAPACITO LINDO   Azteca Films,
   1938, Mexican
ALLA EN EL TROPICO   Azteca Films,
   1940, Mexican
CREO EN DIOS   Azteca Films,
   1941, Mexican
ASI SE QUIERE EN JALISCO   Azteca Films,
   1942, Mexican
DONA BARBARA   Azteca Films,
   1942, Mexican
LA SELVA DEL FUEGO   Azteca Films,
   1945, Mexican
LA DEVORADOR   Azteca Films,
   1946, Mexican
CANCION DE CUNA   Azteca Film,
   1952, Mexican

ROY DEL RUTH
b. October 18, 1895 - Philadelphia,
   Pennsylvania
d. 1961

EVE'S LOVER   Warner Bros., 1925
HOGAN'S ALLEY   Warner Bros., 1925
THREE WEEKS IN PARIS
   Warner Bros., 1926
THE MAN UPSTAIRS   Warner Bros., 1926
THE LITTLE IRISH GIRL   Warner Bros., 1926
FOOTLOOSE WIDOWS   Warner Bros., 1926
ACROSS THE PACIFIC   Warner Bros., 1926
WOLF'S CLOTHING   Warner Bros., 1927

THE FIRST AUTO   Warner Bros., 1927
HAM AND EGGS AT THE FRONT
   Warner Bros., 1927
IF I WERE SINGLE   Warner Bros., 1928
FIVE AND TEN CENT ANNIE
   Warner Bros., 1928
POWDER MY BACK   Warner Bros., 1928
THE TERROR   Warner Bros., 1928
BEWARE OF BACHELORS
   Warner Bros., 1928
CONQUEST   Warner Bros., 1929
THE DESERT SONG   Warner Bros., 1929
THE HOTTENTOT   Warner Bros., 1929
THE GOLD DIGGERS OF BROADWAY
   Warner Bros., 1929
THE AVIATOR   Warner Bros., 1930
HOLD EVERYTHING   Warner Bros., 1930
THE SECOND FLOOR MYSTERY
   Warner Bros., 1930
THREE FACES EAST   Warner Bros., 1930
THE LIFE OF THE PARTY
   Warner Bros., 1930
DIVORCE AMONG FRIENDS
   Warner Bros., 1930
MY PAST   Warner Bros., 1931
THE MALTESE FALCON   Warner Bros., 1931
SIDE SHOW   Warner Bros., 1931
BLONDE CRAZY   *LARCENY LANE*
   Warner Bros., 1931
TAXI   Warner Bros., 1932
BEAUTY AND THE BOSS
   Warner Bros., 1932
WINNER TAKE ALL   Warner Bros., 1932
BLESSED EVENT   Warner Bros., 1932
EMPLOYEES' ENTRANCE
   Warner Bros., 1933
THE MIND READER   Warner Bros., 1933
THE LITTLE GIANT   Warner Bros., 1933
BUREAU OF MISSING PERSONS
   Warner Bros., 1933
CAPTURED   Warner Bros., 1933
LADY KILLER   Warner Bros., 1933
BULLDOG DRUMMOND STRIKES BACK
   United Artists, 1934
UPPER WORLD   Warner Bros., 1934
KID MILLIONS   United Artists, 1934
BROADWAY MELODY OF 1936   MGM, 1935
FOLIES-BERGERE   United Artists, 1935
THANKS A MILLION   20th Century-Fox, 1935
IT HAD TO HAPPEN   20th Century-Fox, 1936
PRIVATE NUMBER   20th Century-Fox, 1936
BORN TO DANCE   MGM, 1936
ON THE AVENUE   20th Century-Fox, 1937
BROADWAY MELODY OF 1938   MGM, 1937
HAPPY LANDING   20th Century-Fox, 1938
MY LUCKY STAR   20th Century-Fox, 1938
TAIL SPIN   20th Century-Fox, 1939
THE STAR MAKER   Paramount, 1939
HERE I AM A STRANGER
   20th Century-Fox, 1939
HE MARRIED HIS WIFE
   20th Century-Fox, 1940
TOPPER RETURNS   United Artists, 1941
THE CHOCOLATE SOLDIER   MGM, 1941
MAISIE GETS HER MAN   MGM, 1942
DU BARRY WAS A LADY   MGM, 1943
BROADWAY RHYTHM   MGM, 1944
BARBARY COAST GENT   MGM, 1944
IT HAPPENED ON FIFTH AVENUE
   Allied Artists, 1947
THE BABE RUTH STORY   Allied Artists, 1948
RED LIGHT   United Artists, 1949
ALWAYS LEAVE THEM LAUGHING
   Warner Bros., 1949
THE WEST POINT STORY
   Warner Bros., 1948
ON MOONLIGHT BAY   Warner Bros., 1951
STARLIFT   Warner Bros., 1951

ABOUT FACE   Warner Bros., 1952
STOP, YOU'RE KILLING ME
   Warner Bros., 1953
THREE SAILORS AND A GIRL
   Warner Bros., 1953
PHANTOM OF THE RUE MORGUE
   Warner Bros., 1954
THE ALLIGATOR PEOPLE
   20th Century-Fox, 1959
WHY MUST I DIE?   American
   International, 1960

CECIL B. DE MILLE
b. August 12, 1881 - Ashfield, Massachusetts
d. 1959

THE SQUAW MAN   co-director with
   Oscar Apfel, Jesse L. Lasky Feature
   Play Co., 1914
BREWSTER'S MILLIONS   co-director with
   Oscar Apfel, Jesse L. Lasky Feature
   Play Co., 1914
THE CALL OF THE NORTH   Jesse L. Lasky
   Feature Play Co., 1914
THE MAN ON THE BOX   co-director with
   Oscar Apfel & Wilfred Buckland,
   Jesse L. Lasky Feature Play Co., 1914
THE VIRGINIAN   Jesse L. Lasky Feature
   Play Co., 1914
WHAT'S HIS NAME   Jesse L. Lasky Feature
   Play Co., 1914
THE MAN FROM HOME   Jesse L. Lasky
   Feature Play Co., 1914
ROSE OF THE RANCHO   Jesse L. Lasky
   Feature Play Co., 1914
THE GIRL OF THE GOLDEN WEST
   Paramount, 1915
THE WARRENS OF VIRGINIA
   Paramount, 1915
THE UNAFRAID   Paramount, 1915
THE CAPTIVE   Paramount, 1915
THE WILD GOOSE CHASE   Paramount, 1915
THE ARAB   Paramount, 1915
CHIMMIE FADDEN   Paramount, 1915
KINDLING   Paramount, 1915
CARMEN   Paramount, 1915
CHIMMIE FADDEN OUT WEST
   Paramount, 1915
THE CHEAT   Paramount, 1915
THE GOLDEN CHANCE   Paramount, 1915
TEMPTATION   Paramount, 1916
THE TRAIL OF THE LONESOME PINE
   Paramount, 1916
THE HEART OF NORA FLYNN
   Paramount, 1916
MARIA ROSA   Paramount, 1916
THE DREAM GIRL   Paramount, 1916
JOAN THE WOMAN   Paramount, 1917
ROMANCE OF THE REDWOODS
   Paramount, 1971
THE LITTLE AMERICAN   Paramount, 1917
THE WOMAN GOD FORGOT
   Paramount, 1917
THE DEVIL STONE   Paramount, 1917
THE WHISPERING CHORUS
   Paramount, 1918
OLD WIVES FOR NEW   Paramount, 1918
YOU CAN'T HAVE EVERYTHING
   Paramount, 1918
TILL I COME BACK TO YOU
   Paramount, 1918
THE SQUAW MAN   Paramount, 1918
DON'T CHANGE YOUR HUSBAND
   Paramount, 1919
FOR BETTER OR WORSE   Paramount, 1919
MALE AND FEMALE   Paramount, 1919
WHY CHANGE YOUR WIFE?
   Paramount, 1920

SOMETHING TO THINK ABOUT
   Paramount, 1920
FORBIDDEN FRUIT   Paramount, 1921
THE AFFAIRS OF ANATOL   Paramount, 1921
FOOL'S PARADISE   Paramount, 1921
SATURDAY NIGHT   Paramount, 1922
MANSLAUGHTER   Paramount, 1922
ADAM'S RIB   Paramount, 1923
THE TEN COMMANDMENTS
   Paramount, 1923
TRIUMPH   Paramount, 1924
FEET OF CLAY   Paramount, 1924
THE GOLDEN BED   Paramount, 1925
THE ROAD TO YESTERDAY   Producers
   Distributing Corp., 1925
THE VOLGA BOATMAN   Producers
   Distributing Corp., 1926
THE KING OF KINGS   Pathé, 1927
THE GODLESS GIRL   Pathé, 1929
DYNAMITE   MGM, 1929
MADAME SATAN   MGM, 1930
THE SQUAW MAN   Paramount, 1931
THE SIGN OF THE CROSS   Paramount, 1932
THIS DAY AND AGE   Paramount, 1933
FOUR FRIGHTENED PEOPLE
   Paramount, 1934
CLEOPATRA   Paramount, 1934
THE CRUSADES   Paramount, 1935
THE PLAINSMAN   Paramount, 1937
THE BUCCANEER   Paramount, 1938
UNION PACIFIC   Paramount, 1939
NORTH WEST MOUNTED POLICE
   Paramount, 1940
REAP THE WILD WIND   Paramount, 1942
THE STORY OF DR. WASSELL
   Paramount, 1944
UNCONQUERED   Paramount, 1947
SAMSON AND DELILAH   Paramount, 1949
THE GREATEST SHOW ON EARTH ★
   Paramount, 1952
THE TEN COMMANDMENTS
   Paramount, 1956

JACQUES DEMY
b. June 5, 1931 - Pont-Chateau, France
d. 1990

LOLA   Films Around the World, 1961, French
SEVEN CAPITAL SINS   co-director with
   Jean-Luc Godard, Roger Vadim,
   Sylvaine Dhomme, Edouard Molinaro,
   Philippe de Broca, Claude Chabrol,
   Marie-Jose Nat, Dominique Paturel,
   Jean-Marc Tennberg & Perrette Pradier,
   Embassy, 1962, French-Italian
BAY OF THE ANGELS   Pathe Contemporary,
   1964, French
THE UMBRELLAS OF CHERBOURG
   Landau, 1964, French-West German
THE YOUNG GIRLS OF ROCHEFORT
   Warner Bros., 1968, French
MODEL SHOP   Columbia, 1969
DONKEY SKIN   Janus, 1971, French
THE PIED PIPER   Paramount, 1972,
   British-West German
L'EVENEMENT LE PLUS IMPORTANT DEPUIS
   QUE L'HOMME A MARCHE SUR LA LUNE
   Lira Films/Roas Production, 1973,
   French-Italian
A SLIGHTLY PREGNANT MAN
   SJ International, 1977, French
LADY OSCAR   Toho, 1978, Japanese-French
UN CHAMBRE EN VILLE   UGC,
   1982, French
PARKING   A.M. Films, 1985, French
LA TABLE TOURNANTE   Films Paul Grimault,
   1987, French
TROIS PLACES POUR LE 26   AMLF,
   1988, French

VITTORIO DE SICA
b. July 7, 1902 - Sora, Italy
d. 1974

ROSE SCARLATTE 1940, Italian
MADDALENA ZERO IN CONDOTTA
  1941, Italian
TERESA VENERDI 1941, Italian
UN GARIBALDINO AL CONVENTO
  1941, Italian
I BAMBINI CI GUARDANO THE CHILDREN
  ARE WATCHING US 1943, Italian
LA PORTA DEL CIELO 1946, Italian
SHOESHINE Lopert, 1946, Italian
THE BICYCLE THIEF Mayer-Burstyn,
  1949, Italian
MIRACLE IN MILAN Joseph Burstyn,
  1951, Italian
UMBERTO D Harrison Pictures, 1952, Italian
INDISCRETION OF AN AMERICAN WIFE
  STAZIONE TERMINI Columbia, 1953,
  U.S.-Italian
GOLD OF NAPLES DCA, 1955, Italian
THE ROOF Trans-Lux, 1956, Italian
TWO WOMEN LA CIOCIARA Embassy,
  1960, Italian-French
IL GIUDIZIO UNIVERSALE 1961, Italian
BOCCACCIO '70 co-director with Federico
  Fellini & Luchino Visconti, Embassy, 1962,
  Italian-French
THE CONDEMNED OF ALTONA
  20th Century-Fox, 1963, Italian-French
IL BOOM Italian, 1963
YESTERDAY, TODAY AND TOMORROW
  Embassy, 1963, Italian-French
MARRIAGE ITALIAN STYLE Embassy, 1964,
  Italian-French
UN MONDE NOUVEAU 1966, French-Italian
AFTER THE FOX United Artists, 1966,
  Italian-U.S.-British
THE WITCHES co-director, Lopert, 1967,
  Italian-French
WOMAN TIMES SEVEN Avco Embassy,
  1967, French-Italian-U.S.
A PLACE FOR LOVERS AMANTI MGM,
  1968, Italian-French
SUNFLOWER Avco Embassy, 1969,
  Italian-French
THE GARDEN OF THE FINZI-CONTINIS
  Cinema 5, 1971, Italian-West German
LE COPPIE co-director, 1971, Italian
LO CHIAMEREMO ANDREA 1972, Italian
A BRIEF VACATION Allied Artists,
  1973, Italian
THE VOYAGE United Artists, 1974, Italian

THOROLD DICKINSON
b. November 16, 1903 - Bristol, England
d. 1984

THE HIGH COMMAND 1937, British
SPANISH ABC (FD) 1938, British
THE ARSENAL STADIUM MYSTERY
  1939, British
ANGEL STREET GASLIGHT
  Anglo-American, 1940, British
THE PRIME MINISTER Warner Bros.,
  1941, British
NEXT OF KIN Universal, 1942, British
MEN OF TWO WORLDS KISENGA - MAN
  OF AFRICA/WITCH DOCTOR Universal,
  1946, British
THE QUEEN OF SPADES Stratford Pictures,
  1949, British
THE SECRET PEOPLE Lippert, 1952, British
HILL 24 DOESN'T ANSWER Continental,
  1955, Israeli-British

WILLIAM DIETERLE
(Wilhelm Dieterle)
b. July 15, 1893 - Ludwigshafen, Germany
d. 1972

DER MENSCH AM WEGE 1923, German
DER MANN DER NICHT LIEBEN DARK
  DASGEHEIMNIS DES ABBE X
  1927, German
GESCHLECHT IN FESSELN 1928, German
DER HEILIGE UND IHR NARR
  1928, German
FRUHLINGSRAUSCHEN 1929, German
ICH LEBE FUR DICH 1929, German
LUDWIG DER ZWEITE - KONIG VON BAYERN
  1929, German
DAS SCHWEIGEN IM WALDE 1929, German
EINE STUNDE GLUCK 1929, German
DEI TANZ GEHT WEITER
  First National, 1930
DIE MASKE FALLT First National, 1930
KISMET First National, 1931, German
THE LAST FLIGHT Warner Bros., 1931
HER MAJESTY LOVE Warner Bros., 1932
MAN WANTED Warner Bros., 1932
JEWEL ROBBERY Warner Bros., 1932
THE CRASH Warner Bros., 1932
SIX HOURS TO LIVE Warner Bros., 1932
SCARLET DAWN Warner Bros., 1932
LAWYER MAN Warner Bros., 1932
GRAND SLAM Warner Bros., 1933
ADORABLE Warner Bros., 1933
THE DEVIL'S IN LOVE Warner Bros., 1933
FEMALE Warner Bros., 1933
FROM HEADQUARTERS
  Warner Bros., 1933
FASHIONS OF 1934 Warner Bros., 1934
FOG OVER FRISCO Warner Bros., 1934
MADAME DU BARRY Warner Bros., 1934
THE FIREBIRD Warner Bros., 1934
THE SECRET BRIDE Warner Bros., 1935
A MIDSUMMER NIGHT'S DREAM co-director
  with Max Reinhardt, Warner Bros., 1935
DR. SOCRATES Warner Bros., 1935
THE STORY OF LOUIS PASTUER
  Warner Bros., 1936
THE WHITE ANGEL Warner Bros., 1936
SATAN MET A LADY Warner Bros., 1936
THE GREAT O'MALLEY Warner Bros., 1937
ANOTHER DAWN Warner Bros., 1937
THE LIFE OF EMILE ZOLA ★
  Warner Bros., 1937
BLOCKADE Warner Bros., 1938
JUAREZ Warner Bros., 1939
THE HUNCHBACK OF NOTRE DAME
  RKO Radio, 1939
DR. EHRLICH'S MAGIC BULLET
  Warner Bros., 1940
A DISPATCH FROM REUTERS
  Warner Bros., 1940
THE DEVIL AND DANIEL WEBSTER
  ALL THAT MONEY CAN BUY
  RKO Radio, 1941
SYNCOPATION RKO Radio, 1942
TENNESSEE JOHNSON MGM, 1942
KISMET MGM, 1944
I'LL BE SEEING YOU United Artists, 1944
LOVE LETTERS Paramount, 1945
THIS LOVE OF OURS Universal, 1945
THE SEARCHING WIND Paramount, 1946
THE ACCUSED Paramount, 1948
PORTRAIT OF JENNIE Selznick, 1948
ROPE OF SAND Paramount, 1949
VOLCANO United Artists, 1950, Italian-U.S.
PAID IN FULL Paramount, 1950
DARK CITY Paramount, 1950
SEPTEMBER AFFAIR Paramount, 1951
PEKING EXPRESS Paramount, 1951

RED MOUNTAIN Paramount, 1951
THE TURNING POINT Paramount, 1952
BOOTS MALONE Columbia, 1952
SALOME Columbia, 1953
ELEPHANT WALK Paramount, 1954
MAGIC FIRE Republic, 1956
OMAR KHAYYAM Paramount, 1957
IL VENDICATORE 1959, Italian-Yugoslavian
DIE FASTNACHTSBEICHTE 1960,
  West German
HERRIN DER WELT 1960, West German
THE CONFESSION Golden Eagle, 1965

JACK DONOHUE
(John Francis Donohue)
b. November 3, 1908 - New York, New York
d. 1984

CLOSE-UP Eagle Lion, 1948
THE YELLOW CAB MAN MGM, 1950
WATCH THE BRIDE MGM, 1951
LICKY ME Warner Bros., 1954
BABES IN TOYLAND Buena Vista, 1961
MARRIAGE ON THE ROCKS
  Warner Bros., 1965
ASSAULT ON A QUEEN Paramount, 1965

BILL DOUGLAS
b. 1934 - Scotland
d. 1991

MY CHILDHOOD British Film Institute,
  1972, British
MY AIN FOLK British Film Institute,
  1973, British
MY WAY HOME British Film Institute,
  1978, British
COMRADES British Film Institute, 1986,
  British-Australian

GORDON DOUGLAS
b. December 5, 1909 - New York, New York
d. 1993

GENERAL SPANKY co-director with
  Fred Newmayer, MGM, 1936
ZENOBIA United Artists, 1939
SAPS AT SEA United Artists, 1940
ROAD SHOW co-director with Hal Roach &
  Hal Roach, Jr., United Artists, 1941
BROADWAY LIMITED United Artists, 1941
NIAGARA FALLS United Artists, 1941
THE DEVIL WITH HITLER RKO Radio, 1942
THE GREAT GILDERSLEEVE
  RKO Radio, 1942
GILDERSLEEVE'S BAD DAY
  RKO Radio, 1943
GILDERSLEEVE ON BROADWAY
  RKO Radio, 1943
GILDERSLEEVE'S GHOST RKO Radio, 1944
A NIGHT OF ADVENTURE RKO Radio, 1944
GIRL RUSH RKO Radio, 1944
THE FALCON IN HOLLYWOOD
  RKO Radio, 1944
ZOMBIES ON BROADWAY RKO Radio, 1945
FIRST YANK INTO TOKYO RKO Radio, 1945
DICK TRACY VS. CUEBALL
  RKO Radio, 1946
SAN QUENTIN RKO Radio, 1946
IF YOU KNEW SUSIE RKO Radio, 1948
THE BLACK ARROW Columbia, 1948
WALK A CROOKED MILE Columbia, 1948
MR. SOFT TOUCH co-director with
  Henry Levin, Columbia, 1949
THE DOOLINS OF OKLAHOMA
  Columbia, 1949
THE NEVADAN Columbia, 1950

FORTUNES OF CAPTAIN BLOOD
Columbia, 1950
ROGUES OF SHERWOOD FOREST
Columbia, 1950
KISS TOMORROW GOODBYE
United Artists, 1950
BETWEEN MIDNIGHT AND DAWN
Columbia, 1950
THE GREAT MISSOURI RAID
Paramount, 1951
ONLY THE VALIANT   Warner Bros., 1951
I WAS A COMMUNIST FOR THE FBI
Warner Bros., 1951
COME FILL THE CUP   Warner Bros., 1951
MARU MARU   Warner Bros., 1952
THE IRON MISTRESS   Warner Bros., 1952
SHE'S BACK ON BROADWAY
Warner Bros., 1953
THE CHARGE AT FEATHER CREEK
Warner Bros., 1953
SO THIS IS LOVE   Warner Bros., 1953
THEM   Warner Bros., 1954
YOUNG AT HEART   Warner Bros., 1954
THE McCONNELL STORY
Warner Bros., 1955
SINCERELY YOURS   Warner Bros., 1955
SANTIAGO   Warner Bros., 1956
THE BIG LAND   Warner Bros., 1957
BOMBERS B-52   Warner Bros., 1957
FORT DOBBS   Warner Bros., 1958
THE FIEND WHO WALKED THE WEST
20th Century-Fox, 1958
UP PERISCOPE   Warner Bros., 1959
YELLOWSTONE KELLY   Warner Bros., 1959
GOLD OF THE SEVEN SAINTS
Warner Bros., 1961
THE SINS OF RACHEL CADE
Warner Bros., 1961
CLAUDELLE INGLISH   Warner Bros., 1961
FOLLOW THAT DREAM   United Artists, 1962
CALL ME BWANA   United Artists, 1963
ROBIN AND THE SEVEN HOODS
Warner Bros., 1964
RIO CONCHOS   20th Century-Fox, 1964
SYLVIA   Paramount, 1965
HARLOW   Paramount, 1965
STAGECOACH   20th Century-Fox, 1966
WAY...WAY OUT!   20th Century-Fox, 1966
IN LIKE FLINT   20th Century-Fox, 1967
CHUKA   Paramount, 1967
TONY ROME   20th Century-Fox, 1967
THE DETECTIVE   20th Century-Fox, 1968
LADY IN CEMENT   20th Century-Fox, 1968
SKULLDUGGERY   Universal, 1970
BARQUERO   United Artists, 1970
THEY CALL ME MISTER TIBBS!
United Artists, 1970
SLAUGHTER'S BIG RIP-OFF   American
International, 1973
NEVADA SMITH (TF)   Rackin-Hayes
Productions/Paramount TV, 1975
VIVA KNIEVEL!   Warner Bros., 1978

ALEXANDER PETROVICH DOVZHENKO

b. September 12, 1894 - Sosnitsa, Ukraine,
Russia
d. 1956

VASYA THE REFORMER   co-director with
F. Lokatinsi & Yosef Rona, 1926, Soviet
THE DIPLOMATIC POUCH   1927, Soviet
ZVENIGORA   1928, Soviet
ARSENAL   1929, Soviet
EARTH   Vufku, 1930, Soviet
IVAN   1932, Soviet
AEROGARD   1935, Soviet

SHCHORS   1939, Soviet
VICTORY IN THE UKRAINE AND THE
EXPULSION OF THE GERMANS FROM
THE BOUNDARIES OF THE UKRAINIAN
SOVIET EARTH   *VICTORY IN THE
UKRAINE* (FD)   co-director, 1945, Soviet
LIFE IN BLOOM   1949, Soviet

MICHEL DRACH

b. October 19, 1930 - Paris, France
d. 1990

ON N'ENTERRE PAS LE DIMANCHE
1959, French
AMELIE OU LE TEMPS D'AIMER
1961, French
LES BELLES CONDUITES   *LA BONNE
OCCASE*   1964, French
SAFARI DIAMANTS   1965, French
ELISE OU LA VRAIE VIE   1970, French
LES VIOLONS DU BAL   Levitt-Pickman,
1974, French
PARLEZ MOI D'AMOUR   1975, French
REPLAY   *LE PASSE SIMPLE*   1977, French
LE PULL-OVER ROUGE   1979, French
GUY DE MAUPASSANT   1982, French
IL EST GENIAL PAPY   1987, French

ARTHUR DREIFUSS

b. March 25, 1908 - Frankfurt am Main,
Germany
d. 1993

DOUBLE DEAL   International Road
Shows, 1939
MYSTERY IN SWING   International Road
Shows, 1940
MURDER ON LENOX AVENUE   International
Road Shows, 1941
SUNDAY SINNERS   International Road
Shows, 1941
REG'LAR FELLERS   Producers Releasing
Corporation, 1941
BABY FACE MORGAN   Producers Releasing
Corporation, 1942
THE BOSS OF BIG TOWN   Producers
Releasing Corporation, 1942
THE PAY-OFF   Producers Releasing
Corporation, 1942
SARONG GIRL   Monogram, 1943
MELODY PARADE   Monogram, 1943
CAMPUS RHYTHM   Monogram, 1943
NEARLY EIGHTEEN   Monogram, 1943
THE SULTAN'S DAUGHTER
Monogram, 1944
EVER SINCE VENUS   Columbia, 1944
EDDIE WAS A LADY   Columbia, 1945
BOSTON BLACKIE BOOKED ON SUSPICION
Columbia, 1945
BOSTON BLACKIE'S RENDEZVOUS
Columbia, 1945
THE GAY SENORITA   Columbia, 1945
PRISON SHIP   Columbia, 1945
JUNIOR PROM   Monogram, 1946
FREDDIE STEPS OUT   Monogram, 1946
HIGH SCHOOL HERO   Monogram, 1946
VACATION DAYS   Monogram, 1947
BETTY CO-ED   Columbia, 1947
LITTLE MISS BROADWAY   Columbia, 1947
TWO BLONDES AND A REDHEAD
Columbia, 1947
SWEET GENEVIEVE   Columbia, 1947
GLAMOUR GIRL   Columbia, 1948
MARY LOU   Columbia, 1948
I SURRENDER DEAR   Columbia, 1948
AN OLD-FASHIONED GIRL   Eagle Lion, 1948
MANHATTAN ANGEL   Columbia, 1948

ALL AMERICAN PRO   Columbia, 1948
SHAMROCK HILL   Eagle Lion, 1949
THERE'S A GIRL IN MY HEART
Allied Artists, 1949
SECRET FILE   Triangle, 1955, British-Dutch
ASSIGNMENT ABROAD   Triangle,
1956, British-Dutch
LIFE BEGINS AT 17   Columbia, 1958
THE LAST BLITZKRIEG   Columbia, 1959
JUKE BOX RHYTHM   Columbia, 1959
THE QUARE FELLOW   Astor, 1962,
Irish-British
RIOT ON SUNSET STRIP   American
International, 1967
THE LOVE-INS   Columbia, 1967
FOR SINGLES ONLY   Columbia, 1968
A TIME TO SING   MGM, 1968
THE YOUNG RUNAWAYS   MGM, 1968

CARL THEODOR DREYER

b. February 3, 1889 - Copenhagen, Denmark
d. 1968

THE PRESIDENT   1919, Danish
LEAVES FROM SATAN'S BOOK
1920, Danish
THE PARSON'S WIDOW   *THE WITCH
WOMAN/THE FOURTH MARRIAGE OF
DAME MARGARET*   1920, Danish
LOVE ONE ANOTHER   1922, Danish
ONCE UPON A TIME   1922, Danish
MIKAEL   1924, German
MASTER OF THE HOUSE   1925, Danish
THE BRIDE OF GLOMDAL   1925, Danish
THE PASSION OF JOAN OF ARC
M.J. Gourland, 1928, French
VAMPYR   *VAMPYR OU L'ETRANGE
AVENTURE DE DAVID GRAY*   1932,
French-German
DAY OF WRATH   George Schaefer,
1943, Danish
TWO PEOPLE   1945, Swedish
ORDET   Kingsley International, 1955, Danish
GERTRUD   Pathé Contemporary,
1964, Danish

GEORGE DUNNING

b. 1920 - Toronto, Ontario, Canada
d. 1979

YELLOW SUBMARINE (AF)   United Artists,
1968, British

E. A. DUPONT
(Ewald Andre Dupont)
b. December 25, 1891 - Leitz, Germany
d. 1956

DIE JANANERIN   1917, German
DAS GEHEIMNIS   *DES AMERIKA-DOCKA*
1918, German
EUROPA POSTLAGERND   1918, German
DER LEBENDE SCHATTEN   1918, German
ES WERDE LICHT   co-director with
Richard Oswald, 1918
DER AMM AUS NEAPEL   1918, German
DIE SCHWARZE SCHACHDAME
1918, German
DER TEUFEL   1918, German
DIE APACHEN   1919, German
DAS GRAND HOTEL BABYLON
1919, German
MORD OHNE TATER   1920, German
DER WEISSE PFAU   1920, German
DIE GEIERWALLY   1921, German
WHITECHAPEL   1921, German
KINDER DER FINSTERNIS   1922, German

SIE UND DIE DREI 1922, German
DAS ALTE GESETZ 1923, German
DIE GRUNE MANUELA 1923, German
DER DEMUTIGE UND DIE SANGERIN
   1925, German
LVARIETY Paramount, 1925, German
LOVE ME AND THE WORLD IS MINE
   1928, British
MOULIN ROUGE BIP, 1928, British
PICCADILLY BIP, 1929, British
ATLANTIC BIP, 1929, British
TWO WORLDS BIP, 1930, British
CAPE FORLORN *LOVE STORM* BIP,
   1931, British
SALTO MORTALE *TRAPEZE* 1931, German
PETER VOSS DER MILLIONENDIEB
   1932, German
DER LAUFER VON MARATHON
   1933, German
LADIES MUST LOVE Universal, 1933
THE BISHOP MISBEHAVES MGM, 1935
A SON COMES HOME Paramount, 1936
FORGOTTEN FACES Paramount, 1936
A NIGHT OF MYSTERY Paramount, 1937
ON SUCH A NIGHT Paramount, 1937
LOVE ON TOAST Paramount, 1937
HELL'S KITCHEN co-director with
   Lewis Seiler, Warner Bros., 1939
THE SCARF United Artists, 1951
PROBLEM GIRLS Columbia, 1953
THE NEANDERTHAL MAN
   United Artists, 1953
THE STEEL LADY United Artists, 1953
RETURN TO TREASURE ISLAND
   United Artists, 1954

JULIEN DUVIVIER
b. October 8, 1896 - Lille, France
d. 1967

HACELDMA *LE PRIX DU SANG*
   1919, French
LA REINCARNATION DE SERGE
   RENAUDIER 1920, French
L'AGONIE DES AIGLES 1921, French
LES ROQUEVILLARD 1922, French
L'OURAGAN SUR LA MONTAGNE
   1922, French
DER UNHEIMLICHE GAST 1922, German
LE REFLET DE CLAUDE MERCOEUR
   1923, French
CREDO OU LA TRAGEDIE DE LOURDES
   1924, French
COEURS FAROUCHES 1924, French
LA MACHINE A REFAIRE LA VIE (FD)
   co-director, 1924, French
L'OEUVRE IMMORTELLE 1924, Belgian
L'ABBE CONSTANTIN 1925, French
POIL DE CAROTTE 1925, French
L'AGONIE DE JERUSALEM 1926, French
L'HOMME A L'HISPANO 1926, French
LE MARIAGE DE MADEMOISELLE
   BEULEMANS 1927, French
LE MYSTERE DE LA TOUR EIFFEL
   1927, French
LE TOURBILLON DE PARIS 1928, French
LA VIE MIRACULEUSE DE THERESE
   MARTIN 1929, French
LA DIVINE CROISIERE 1929, French
MAMAN COLIBRI 1929, French
AU BONHEUR DES DAMES 1930, French
DAVID GOLDER 1930, French
LES CINQ GENTLEMEN MAUDITS *SOUS
   LA LUNE DU MAROC* 1932, French
ALLO BERLIN? ICI PARISI 1932, French
POIL DE CAROTTE 1932, French
LA VENUS DU COLLEGE 1932, French
LA TETE D'UN HOMME 1933, French

LA MACHINE A REFAIRE LA VIE
   1933, French
LE PETIT ROI 1933, French
LA PAQUEBOT "TENACITY" 1934, French
MARIA CHAPDELAINE 1934, French
GOLGOTHA 1935, French
LA BANDERA 1935, French
THE GOLEM *THE LEGEND OF PRAGUE*
   United Artists, 1936,
   French-Czechoslovakian
L'HOMME DU JOUR 1936, French
LA BELLE EQUIPE 1936, French
PEPE LE MOKO Paris Film, 1936, French
UN CARNET DE BAL *CHRISTINE*
   1937, French
THE GREAT WALTZ MGM, 1938
LA FIN DU JOUR 1939, French
LA CHARRETTE FANTOME 1939, French
UNTEL, PERE ET FILS *HEART OF A NATION*
   1940, French
LYDIA United Artists, 1941
TALES OF MANHATTAN RKO, 1942
FLESH AND FANTASY Universal, 1943
THE IMPOSTOR Universal, 1944
PANIC Tricolore, 1946, French
ANNA KARENINA 20th Century-Fox,
   1947, British
AU ROYAUME DES CIEUX *WOMAN HUNT*
   1949, French
CAPTAIN BLACK JACK United Artists, 1950,
   French-British-Spanish
UNDER THE PARIS SKY Discina
   International, 1951, French
THE LITTLE WORLD OF DON CAMILLO
   Italian Films Export, 1951, French
ON TRIAL *L'AFFAIRE MAURIZIUS*
   New Realm, 1953, French-Italian
THE RETURN OF DON CAMILLO 1953,
   French-Italian
LA FETE A HENRIETTE *HOLIDAY FOR
   HENRIETTE* 1953, French
MARIANNE OF MY YOUTH United Motion
   Picture Organization, 1955, French
DEADLIER THAN THE MALE *VOICI LE
   TEMPS DES ASSASSINS* Continental,
   1955, French
THE MAN IN THE RAINCOAT Kingsley
   International, 1956, French-Italian
POT BOUILLE *THE HOUSE OF LOVERS*
   Continental, 1957, French
A WOMAN LIKE SATAN *THE FEMALE/LA
   FEMMEET LA PANTIN* Lopert, 1958,
   French-Italian
MARIE OCTOBRE 1958, French
LA GRANDE VIE 1960, French-West German
BOULEVARD 1960, French
LA CHAMBRE ARDENTE *THE CURSE
   AND THE COFFIN* 1962,
   French-Italian-West German
THE DEVIL AND THE TEN COMMANDMENTS
   Union Films, 1962, French-Italian
CHAIR DE POULE *HIGHWAY PICKUP*
   1963, French-Italian
DIABOLIQUEMENT VOTRE 1967,
   French-Italian-West German

ALLAN DWAN
(Joseph Aloysius Dwan)
b. April 3, 1885 - Toronto, Ontario, Canada
d. 1981

BRANDISHING A BAD MAN 1911
RATTLESNAKES AND GUNPOWDER 1911
THE ANGEL OF PARADISE RANCH 1911
THE YIDDISHER COWBOY 1911
THE POISONED FLUME 1911
THREE MILLION DOLLARS 1911
THE GUNMAN 1911

THE GOLD LUST 1911
THE LOCKET 1912
THE MORMON 1912
FIDELITY 1912
THE COWARD 1912
THE HATERS 1912
THE GREEN EYED MONSTER 1912
THE MARAUDERS 1912
THE ANIMAL WITHIN 1912
THE BATTLEGROUND 1912
THE FEAR 1912
CALAMITY ANNE'S WARD 1912
THE POWER OF LOVE 1912
THE FUGITIVE 1913
CALAMITY ANN, DETECTIVE 1913
ANGEL OF THE CANYONS 1913
THE ANIMAL 1913
ANOTHER MAN'S LIFE 1913
ASHES OF THREE 1913
WHEN LUCK CHANGES 1913
CUPID THROWS A BRICK 1913
THE SPIRIT OF THE FLAG 1913
THE CALL TO ARMS 1913
CRIMINALS 1913
BACK TO LIFE 1913
THE MENACE 1913
THE LIE 1914
DISCORD AND HARMONY 1914
THE EMBEZZLER 1914
TRAGEDY OF WHISPERING CREEK 1914
THE FORBIDDEN ROOM 1914
RICHILIEU Universal, 1914
WILDFLOWER Paramount, 1914
THE COUNTY CHAIRMAN
   Paramount, 1914
THE STRAIGHT ROAD Paramount, 1914
THE UNWELCOME MRS. HATCH
   Paramount, 1914
HONOR OF THE MOUNTED 1914
THE HOPES OF BLIND ALLEY 1914
THE CONSPIRACY Paramount, 1914
THE DANCING GIRL Paramount, 1915
DAVID HARUM Paramount, 1915
THE LOVE ROUTE Paramount, 1915
THE COMMANDING OFFICER
   Paramount, 1915
MAY BLOSSOM Pathé, 1915
THE PRETTY SISTER OF JOSE
   Paramount, 1915
A GIRL OF YESTERDAY Paramount, 1915
THE FOUNDLING Paramount, 1915
JORDAN IS A HARD ROAD
   Fine Arts-Triangle, 1915
BETTY OF GREYSTONE
   Fine Arts-Triangle, 1916
THE HABIT OF HAPPINESS
   Fine Arts-Triangle, 1916
THE GOOD BAD MAN
   Fine Arts-Triangle, 1916
AN INNOCENT MAGDALENE
   Fine Arts-Triangle, 1916
THE HALF-BREED Fine Arts-Triangle, 1916
MANHATTAN MADNESS
   Fine Arts-Triangle, 1916
FIFTY-FIFTY Fine Arts-Triangle, 1916
PANTHEA Selznick, 1917
THE FIGHTING ODDS Goldwyn, 1917
A MODERN MUSKETEER Artcraft, 1917
MR. FIX-IT Artcraft, 1918
BOUND IN MOROCCO Artcraft, 1918
HE COMES UP SMILING Artcraft, 1918
CHEATING CHEATERS Select, 1919
GETTING MARY MARRIED Select, 1919
THE DARK STAR Artcraft, 1919
SOLDIERS OF FORTUNE Realart, 1919
THE LUCK OF THE IRISH Realart, 1920
THE FORBIDDEN THING Associated
   Producers, 1920

E

A PERFECT CRIME   Associated
  Producers, 1921
A BROKEN DOLL   Associated
  Producers, 1921
THE SCOFFER   Realart, 1921
THE SINS OF MARTHA QUEED   Associated
  Exibitors, 1921
IN THE HEART OF A FOOL   Associated First
  National, 1921
THE HIDDEN WOMAN   Nanuet Amusement/
  American Releasing, 1922
SUPERSTITION   Artlee, 1922
ROBIN HOOD   United Artists, 1922
THE GLIMPSES OF THE MOON
  Paramount, 1923
LAWFUL LARCENY   Paramount, 1923
ZAZA   Paramount, 1923
BIG BROTHER   Paramount, 1923
A SOCIETY SCANDAL   Paramount, 1924
MANHANDLED   Paramount, 1924
HER LOVE STORY   Paramount, 1924
WAGES OF VIRTUE   Paramount, 1924
ARGENTINE LOVE   Paramount, 1924
NIGHT LIFE OF NEW YORK
  Paramount, 1925
COAST OF FOLLY   Paramount, 1925
STAGE STRUCK   Paramount, 1925
SEA HORSES   Paramount, 1926
PADLOCKED   Paramount, 1926
TIN GODS   Paramount, 1926
SUMMER BACHELORS   Fox, 1926
THE MUSIC MASTER   Fox, 1927
WEST POINT (FD)   1927
THE JOY GIRL   1927
EAST SIDE, WEST SIDE   Fox, 1927
FRENCH DRESSING   First National, 1927
THE BIG NOISE   First National, 1928
THE IRON MASK   United Artists, 1929
TIDE OF EMPIRE   MGM, 1929
THE FAR CALL   Fox, 1929
FROZEN JUSTICE   Fox, 1929
SOUTH SEA ROSE   Fox, 1929
WHAT A WIDOW!   United Artists, 1930
MAN TO MAN   First National, 1930
CHANCES   First National, 1931
WICKED   Fox, 1931
WHILE PARIS SLEEPS   Fox, 1932
HER FIRST AFFAIR   Associated British,
  1933, British
COUNSEL'S OPINION   London
  Films-Paramount, 1933, British
I SPY   THE MORNING AFTER
  Wardour-Majestic, 1934
BLACK SHEEP   Fox, 1935
NAVY WIFE   20th Century-Fox, 1935
THE SONG AND DANCE MAN
  20th Century-Fox, 1936
HUMAN CARGO   20th Century-Fox, 1936
HIGH TENSION   20th Century-Fox, 1936
15 MAIDEN LANE   20th Century-Fox, 1936
WOMAN-WISE   20th Century-Fox, 1937
THAT I MAY LIVE   20th Century-Fox, 1937
ONE MILE FROM HEAVEN
  20th Century-Fox, 1937
HEIDI   20th Century-Fox, 1937
REBECCA OF SUNNYBROOK FARM
  20th Century-Fox, 1938
JOSETTE   20th Century-Fox, 1938
SUEZ   20th Century-Fox, 1938
THE THREE MUSKETEERS
  20th Century-Fox, 1939
THE GORILLA   20th Century-Fox, 1939
FRONTIER MARSHAL
  20th Century-Fox, 1939
SAILOR'S LADY   20th Century-Fox, 1940
YOUNG PEOPLE   20th Century-Fox, 1940
TRAIL OF THE VIGILANTES
  Universal, 1940

LOOK WHO'S LAUGHING   RKO Radio, 1941
RISE AND SHINE   20th Century-Fox, 1941
FRIENDLY ENEMIES   United Artists, 1942
HERE WE GO AGAIN   RKO Radio, 1942
AROUND THE WORLD   RKO Radio, 1943
UP IN MABEL'S ROOM   United Artists, 1944
ABROAD WITH TWO YANKS
  United Artists, 1944
BREWSTER'S MILLIONS
  United Artists, 1945
GETTING GERTIE'S GARTER
  United Artists, 1945
RENDEZVOUS WITH ANNIE
  Republic, 1946
CALENDAR GIRL   Republic, 1947
NORTHWEST OUTPOST   Republic, 1947
DRIFTWOOD   Republic, 1947
THE INSIDE STORY   Republic, 1948
ANGEL IN EXILE   co-director with Philip Ford,
  Republic, 1948
SANDS OF IWO JIMA   Republic, 1949
SURRENDER   Republic, 1950
BELLE LE GRANDE   Republic, 1951
THE WILD BLUE YONDER   Republic, 1951
I DREAM OF JEANIE   Republic, 1952
MONTANA BELLE   RKO Radio, 1952
THE WOMAN THEY ALMOST LYNCHED
  Republic, 1953
SWEETHEARTS ON PARADE
  Republic, 1953
FLIGHT NURSE   Republic, 1954
SILVER LODE   RKO Radio, 1954
PASSION   RKO Radio, 1954
CATTLE QUEEN OF MONTANA
  RKO Radio, 1954
ESCAPE TO BURMA   RKO Radio, 1955
PEARL OF THE SOUTH PACIFIC
  RKO Radio, 1955
TENNESSEE'S PARTNER
  RKO Radio, 1955
SLIGHTLY SCARLET   RKO Radio, 1956
HOLD BACK THE NIGHT
  Allied Artists, 1956
THE RIVER'S EDGE
  20th Century-Fox, 1957
THE RESTLESS BREED
  20th Century-Fox, 1957
ENCHANTED ISLAND   Warner Bros., 1958
MOST DANGEROUS MAN ALIVE
  Columbia, 1961

B. REEVES EASON
("Breezy" Eason)
b. 1886 - Friar Point, Missouri
d. 1956

THE DAY OF RECKONING   1915
THE ASSAYER OF LONE GAP   1915
THE SPIRIT OF ADVENTURE   1915
NINE-TENTHS OF THE LAW   1918
THE MOON RIDERS (S)   1920
HUMAN STUFF   1920
BLUE STREAK McCXOY   1920
PINK TIGHTS   1920
TWO KINDS OF LOVE   1920
THE BIG ADVENTURE   1921
COLORADO   1921
RED COURAGE   1921
THE FIRE EATER   1921
PARDON MY NERVE!   1922
WHEN EAST COMES WEST   1922
ROUGH SHOD   1922
THE LONE HAND   1922
AROUND THE WORLD (S)   1923
HIS LAST RACE   1923
TRIGGER FINGER   1924
WOMEN FIRST   1924
FLASHING SPURS   1924
FIGHTING THE FLAMES   1925
BORDER JUSTICE   1925
FIGHTING YOUTH   1925
THE SHADOW ON THE WALL   1925
THE SIGN OF THE CLAW   1926
THE TEST OF DONALD NORTON   1926
THE DENVER DUDE   1927
THE PRAIRIE KING   1927
PAINTED PONY   1927
A TRICK OF HEARTS   1928
THE FLYIN' COWBOY   1928
RIDING FOR FAME   1928
THE LARIAT KID   1929
THE WINGED HORSEMAN   co-director with
  Arthur Rosson, 1929
TROOPERS THREE   co-director with
  Norman Taurog, Tiffany, 1930
THE ROARING RANCH   1930
TRIGGER TRICKS   1930
SPURS   1930
THE GALLOPING GHOST (S)   1931
THE VANISHING LEGION (S)   1931
THE LAST OF THE MOHICANS (S)
  co-director with Ford Beebe, 1932
THE SUNSET TRAIL   1932
HONOR OF THE PRESS   1932
THE HEART PUNCH   1932
CORNERED   1933
BEHIND JURY DOORS   1933
ALIMONY MADNESS   1933
REVENGE AT MONTE CARLO   1933
HER RESALE VALUE   1933
DANCE HALL HOSTESS   1933
LAW OF THE WILD (S)   co-director with
  Armond L. Schaefer, 1934
THE PHANTOM EMPIRE (S)   co-director with
  Ottol Brower, 1935
THE ADVENTURES OF REX AND RINTY (S)
  co-director with Ford Beebe, 1935
THE FIGHTING MARINES (S)   co-director with
  Joseph Kane, Republic, 1935

DARKEST AFRICA (S) co-director with
  Joseph Kane, Republic, 1936
THE UNDERSEA KINGDOM (S) co-director
  with Joseph Kane, Republic, 1936
RED RIVER VALLEY 1936
EMPTY HOLSTERS 1937
PRAIRIE THUNDER 1937
SERGEANT MURPHY 1938
THE KID COMES BACK 1938
BLUE MONTANA SKIES 1939
MOUNTAIN RHYTHM 1939
MEN WITH STEEL FACES co-director with
  Ottol Brower, 1940
MURDER IN THE BIG HOUSE
  Warner Bros., 1942
SPY SHIP Warner Bros., 1942
THE PHANTOM (S) 1943
TRUCK BUSTERS Warner Bros., 1943
BLACK ARROW (S) 1944
THE DESERT HAWK (S) 1944
RIMFIRE 1949

SERGEI EISENSTEIN

(Sergei Mikhailovich Eisenstein)
b. January 23, 1898 - Riga, Latvia, Russia
d. 1948

STRIKE Brandon, 1925, Soviet
THE BATTLESHIP POTEMKIN *POTEMKIN*
  Amkino, 1925, Soviet
OCTOBER *TEN DAYS THAT SHOOK THE
  WORLD* co-director with Grigori Alexandrov,
  Amkino, 1928, Soviet
THE GENERAL LINE *OLD AND NEW*
  co-director with Grigori Alexandrov,
  1929, Soviet
STURM UBER LA SARRAZ co-director
  with Hans Richter & Ivor Montagu,
  1929, Swiss
ROMANCE SENTIMENTALE co-director
  with Grigori Alexandrov, 1930, French
QUE VIVA MEXICO! (FD) 1931-32,
  Soviet, unfinished
BEZHIN MEADOW 1935-37,
  Soviet, unfinished
ALEXANDER NEVSKY Amkino,
  1938, Soviet
THE FERGANA CANAL 1939,
  Soviet, unfinished
IVAN THE TERRIBLE, PART I Artkino,
  1945, Soviet
IVAN THE TERRIBLE, PART II Artkino,.
  1946, Soviet
IVAN THE TERRIBLE, PART III 1947,
  Soviet, unfinished

MAURICE ELVEY

(William Seward Folkard)
b. November 11, 1887 - Darlington, England
d. 1967

THE GREAT GOLD ROBBERY 1913, British
MARIA MARTEN 1913, British
THE SUICIDE CLUB 1914, British
THE CUP FINAL MYSTERY 1914, British
FLORENCE NIGHTINGALE 1915, British
VICE VERSA 1916, British
WHEN KNIGHTS WERE BOLD
  1916, British
THE KING'S DAUGHTER 1916, British
THE GRIT OF A JEW 1917, British
FLAMES 1917, British
JUSTICE 1917, British
THE GAY LORD QUEX 1917, British
HINDLE WAKES 1918, British
ADAM BEDE 1918, British
BLEAK HOUSE 1919, British

COMRADESHIP *COMRADES IN ARMS*
  1919, British
MR. WA 1919, British
THE ELUSIVE PIMPERNEL 1920, British
THE AMATEUR GENTLEMAN 1920, British
AT THE VILLA ROSA 1920, British
THE HOUND OF THE BASKERVILLES
  1921, British
THE ADVENTURES OF SHERLOCK
  HOLMES (S) 1921, British
THE PASSIONATE FRIENDS 1922, British
THE SIGN OF FOUR 1923, British
THE WANDERING JEW 1923, British
DON QUIXOTE 1923, British
SALLY BISHOP 1923, British
MY HUSBAND'S WIVES 1924
CURLY TOP 1925
THE FOLLY OF VANITY 1925
SHE WOLVES 1925
EVERY MAN'S WIFE 1925
THE FLAG LIEUTENANT 1926, British
THE WOMAN TEMPTED 1926, British
MADEMOISELLE FROM ARMENTIERES
  1926, British
HINDLE WAKES *FANNY HAWTHORN*
  1927, British
ROSES OF PICARDY 1927, British
THE FLIGHT COMMANDER 1927, British
PALAIS DE DANSE 1928, British
YOU KNOW WHAT SAILORS ARE
  1928, British
HIGH TREASON 1929, British
BALACLAVA *JAWS OF HELL* co-director
  with Milton Rosmer, 1930, British
SCHOOL FOR SCANDAL 1930, British
SALLY IN OUR ALLEY 1931, British
IN A MONASTERY GARDEN 1932, British
THE LODGER *PHANTOM FIEND*
  1932, British
DIAMOND CUT DIAMOND *BLAME THE
  WOMAN* 1932, British
SOLDIERS OF THE KING *THE WOMAN IN
  COMMAND* 1933, British
THE WANDERING JEW 1933, British
PRINCESS CHARMING 1934, British
LILY OF KILLARNEY *THE BRIDE OF
  THE LAKE* 1934, British
MY SONG FOR YOU 1934, British
TRANSATLANTIC TUNNEL *THE TUNNEL*
  Gaumont-British, 1935, British
THE CLAIRVOYANT 1935, British
SPY OF NAPOLEON 1936, British
THE MAN IN THE MIRROR 1936, British
A ROMANCE IN FLANDERS 1937, British
THE SPIDER 1939, British
SONS OF THE SEA 1939, British
UNDER YOUR HAT 1940, British
THE GENTLE SEX co-director with Leslie
  Howard, Two Cities, 1943, British
THE LAMP STILL BURNS General Film,
  1943, British
MEDAL FOR THE GENERAL *THE GAY
  INTRUDERS* 1944, British
BEWARE OF PITY Two Cities, 1946, British
OBSESSED *THE LATE EDWINA BLACK*
  United Artists, 1951, British
HOUSE OF BLACKMAIL 1953, British
WHAT EVERY WOMAN WANTS
  United Artists, 1954, British
YOU LUCKY PEOPLE 1955, British
STARS IN YOUR EYES 1956, British
SECOND FIDDLE 1957, British

JOHN ENGLISH

b. 1903 - Cumberland, England
d. 1969

HIS FIGHTING BLOOD Republic, 1935
ARIZONA DAYS Republic, 1937
ZORRO RIDES AGAIN (S) co-director with
  William Witney, Republic, 1937
DICK TRACY RETURNS (S) co-director with
  William Witney, Republic, 1938
HAWK OF THE WILDERNESS (S) co-director
  with William Witney, 1938
THE LONE RANGER (S) co-director with
  William Witney, Republic, 1938
CALL OF THE MESQUITEERS Republic, 1938
DICK TRACY'S G-MEN (S) co-director with
  William Witney, Republic, 1939
ZORRO'S FIGHTING LEGION (S) co-director
  with William Witney, Republic, 1939
ADVENTURES OF RED RYDER (S)
  co-director with William Witney,
  Republic, 1940
DRUMS OF FU MANCHU (S) co-director with
  William Witney, Republic, 1940
KING OF THE ROYAL MOUNTED (S)
  co-director with William Witney,
  Republic, 1940
MYSTERIOUS DR. SATAN (S) co-director
  with William Witney, Republic, 1940
HI-YO SILVER co-director with William Witney,
  Republic, 1940
ADVENTURES OF CAPTAIN MARVEL (S)
  co-director with William Witney,
  Republic, 1941
DICK TRACY VS. CRIME INC. (S) co-director
  with William Witney, Republic, 1941
JUNGLE GIRL (S) co-director with
  William Witney, Republic, 1941
KING OF THE TEXAS RANGERS (S)
  co-director with William Witney,
  Republic, 1941
THE YUKON PATROL co-director with
  William Witney, Republic, 1942
WESTWARD HO! Republic, 1943
THE PHANTOM PLAINSMEN Republic, 1943
DAREDEVILS OF THE WEST (S)
  Republic, 1943
OVERLAND MAIL ROBBERY Republic, 1943
CAPTAIN AMERICA (S) co-director with
  Elmer Clifton, Republic, 1944
SAN FERNANDO VALLEY Republic, 1944
FACES IN THE FOG Republic, 1944
UTAH Republic, 1945
DON'T FENCE ME IN Republic, 1945
THE PHANTOM SPEAKS Republic, 1945
MURDER IN THE MUSIC HALL
  Republic, 1945
THE LAST ROUND-UP Republic, 1947
LOADED PISTOLS Republic, 1948
RIDERS IN THE SKY Republic, 1949
MULE TRAIN Republic, 1950
BLAZING SUN Republic, 1950
SILVER CANYON Republic, 1951
VALLEY OF FIRE Republic, 1951

RAY ENRIGHT

(Raymond E. Enright)
b. March 25, 1896 - Anderson, Indiana
d. 1965

TRACKER BY THE POLICE
  Warner Bros., 1927
JAWS OF STEEL Warner Bros., 1927
THE GIRL FROM CHICAGO
  Warner Bros., 1927
DOMESTIC TROUBLES Warner Bros., 1928
LAND OF THE SILVER FOX
  Warner Bros., 1928

THE LITTLE WILDCAT   Warner Bros., 1929
STOLEN KISSES   Warner Bros., 1929
KID GLOVES   Warner Bros., 1929
SKIN DEEP   Warner Bros., 1929
SONG OF THE WEST   Warner Bros., 1930
GOLDEN DAWN   Warner Bros., 1930
DANCING SWEETIES   Warner Bros., 1930
SCARLET PAGES   Warner Bros., 1930
PLAY GIRL   Warner Bros., 1932
THE TENDERFOOT   First National, 1932
BLONDIE JOHNSON   First National, 1933
THE SILK EXPRESS   Warner Bros., 1933
TOMORROW AT SEVEN   RKO, 1933
HAVANA WIDOWS   First National, 1933
I'VE GOT YOUR NUMBER
   Warner Bros., 1934
20 MILLION SWEETHEARTS
   First National, 1934
THE CIRCUS CLOWN   First National, 1934
DAMES   Warner Bros., 1934
THE ST. LOUIS KID   Warner Bros., 1934
WHILE THE PATIENT SLEPT
   First National, 1935
TRAVELING SALESLADY
   First National, 1935
ALIBI IKE   First National, 1935
WE'RE IN THE MONEY   Warner Bros., 1935
MISS PACIFIC FLEET   Warner Bros., 1935
SNOWED UNDER   First National, 1936
EARTHWORM TRACTORS
   First National, 1936
CHINA CLIPPER   First National, 1936
SING ME A LOVE SONG   First National, 1937
READY, WILLING AND ABLE
   Warner Bros., 1937
SLIM   Warner Bros., 1937
THE SINGING MARINE   Warner Bros., 1937
BACK IN CIRCULATION   Warner Bros., 1937
SWING YOUR LADY   Warner Bros., 1938
GOLD DIGGERS IN PARIS
   Warner Bros., 1938
HARD TO GET   Warner Bros., 1938
GOING PLACES   Warner Bros., 1938
NAUGHTY BUT NICE   Warner Bros., 1939
ANGELS WASH THEIR FACES
   Warner Bros., 1939
ON YOUR TOES   Warner Bros., 1939
BROTHER RAT AND A BABY
   Warner Bros., 1940
AN ANGEL FROM TEXAS
   Warner Bros., 1940
RIVER'S END   Warner Bros., 1940
THE WAGONS ROLL AT NIGHT
   Warner Bros., 1941
THIEVES FALL OUT   Warner Bros., 1941
BAD MEN OF MISSOURI   Warner Bros., 1941
LAW OF THE TROPICS   Warner Bros., 1941
WILD BILL HICKOK RIDES
   Warner Bros., 1942
THE SPOILERS   Universal, 1942
MEN OF TEXAS   Universal, 1942
SIN TOWN   Universal, 1942
GOOD LUCK, MR. YATES   Columbia, 1943
THE IRON MAJOR   RKO Radio, 1943
GUNG HO!   Universal, 1943
CHINA SKY   RKO Radio, 1945
MAN ALIVE   RKO Radio, 1945
ONE WAY TO LOVE   Columbia, 1946
TRAIL STREE   RKO Radio, 1947
ALBUQUERQUE   Paramount, 1948
RETURN OF THE BAD MEN
   RKO Radio, 1948
CORONER CREEK   Columbia, 1948
SOUTH OF ST. LOUIS   Warner Bros., 1949
MONTANA   Warner Bros., 1950
THE KANSAS RAIDERS   Universal, 1950
FLAMING FEATHER   Paramount, 1952
THE MAN FROM CAIRO   Lippert, 1953

CHESTER ERSKINE

b. November 29, 1905 - Vienna, Austria
d. 1986

MIDNIGHT   Universal, 1934
FRANKIE AND JOHNNY   Republic, 1935
THE EGG AND I   Universal, 1947
TAKE ONE FALSE STEP   Universal, 1949
A GIRL IN EVERY PORT   RKO Radio, 1952
ANDROCLES AND THE LION
   RKO Radio, 1953

JEAN EUSTACHE

b. 1938 - Pessac, France
d. 1981

LES MAUVAISES FREQUENTATIONS
   1963, French
LE PERE NOEL A LES YEUX BLEUS
   Anouchka Films, 1966, French
LA ROSIERE DE PESSAC (I)   Jean Eustache
   Film, 1968, French
LE COCHON   Luc Moullet/Francoise Lebrun,
   1970, French
NUMERO ZERO   Jean Eustache Film,
   1971, French
THE MOTHER AND THE WHORE
   New Yorker, 1973, French
MES PETITES AMOUREUSES   New Yorker,
   1974, French
UNE SALE HISTOIRE   Les Films du Losange,
   1977, French
LA ROSIERE DE PESSAC (II)   INA/ZDF/
   Mediane Films, 1979, French-West German
LE JARDIN DES DELICES DE JEROME
   BOSCHINA   1979, French
LES PHOTOS D'ALIX   Mediane Films,
   1980, French
OFFRE D'EMPLOI   INA, 1980, French

F

ZOLTAN FABRI

b. 1917 - Budapest, Hungary
d. 1994

THE STORM   1952, Hungarian
FOURTEEN LIVES   1954, Hungarian
MERRY-GO-ROUND   1955, Hungarian
PROFESSOR HANNIBAL   1956, Hungarian
SUMMER CLOUDS   1957, Hungarian
ANNA   1958, Hungarian
THE BRUTE   1959, Hungarian
THE LAST GOAL   1961, Hungarian
DARKNESS IN DAYTIME   1963, Hungarian
TWENTY HOURS   1964, Hungarian
LATE SEASON   1967, Hungarian
THE BOYS OF PAUL STREET
   20th Century-Fox, 1969, Hungarian
THE TOTH FAMILY   1970, Hungarian
ONE DAY MORE ONE DAY LESS
   1973, Hungarian
141 MINUTES FROM THE UNFINISHED
   SENTENCE   1975, Hungarian
THE FIFTH SEAL   1977, Hungarian
THE HUNGARIANS   1978, Hungarian
BALINT FABIAN MEETS GOD
   1980, Hungarian
REQUIEM   1982, Hungarian

ARNOLD FANCK

b. March 6, 1889 - Frankenthal, Germany
d. 1974

DAS WUNDER DES SCHNEESCHUHS
   1921, German
POMPERLY'S KAMPF MIT DEM
   SCHNEESCHUH   1922, German
IM KAMPF MIT DEM BERGE   1922, German
DER BERG DES SCHICKSALS
   1924, German
DER HEILIGE BERG   1926, German
DER GROSSE SPRUNG   1927, German
DIE WEISSE HOLLE VOM PIZ PALU
   co-director with G.W. Pabst, 1929, German
STURME UBER DEM MONTBLANC
   1930, German
DER WEISSE RAUSCH   1931, German
S.O.S. ICEBERG   co-director with Tay Garnett,
   Universal, 1933, U.S.-German
DER WEIGE TRAUM   1934, German
DIE TOCHTER DES SAMURAI   1937,
   German-Japanese
EIN ROBINSON   1940, German-Chilean

JOHN FARROW
(John Villiers Farrow)

b. February 10, 1904 - Sydney, Australia
d. 1963

WARLORD   Warner Bros., 1937
MEN IN EXILE   Warner Bros., 1937
WEST OF SHANGHAI   Warner Bros., 1937
SHE LOVED A FIREMAN   Warner Bros., 1938
THE INVISIBLE MENACE
   Warner Bros., 1938
LITTLE MISS THOROUGHBRED
   Warner Bros., 1938
MY BILL   Warner Bros., 1938
BROADWAY MUSKETEERS
   Warner Bros., 1938
WOMEN IN THE WIND   Warner Bros., 1939
THE SAINT STRIKES BACK
   RKO Radio, 1939
SORORITY HOUSE   RKO Radio, 1939
FIVE CAME BACK   RKO Radio, 1939
FULL CONFESSION   RKO Radio, 1939
RENO   RKO Radio, 1939
MARRIED AND IN LOVE   1940
A BILL OF DIVORCEMENT   RKO Radio, 1940
WAKE ISLAND ★   Paramount, 1942
THE COMMANDOS STRIKE AT DAWN
   Columbia, 1943
CHINA   Paramount, 1943
THE HITLER GANG   Paramount, 1944
YOU CAME ALONG   Paramount, 1945
TWO YEARS BEFORE THE MAST
   Paramount, 1946
CALIFORNIA   Paramount, 1946
EASY COME, EASY GO   Paramount, 1947
BLAZE OF NOON   Paramount, 1947
CALCUTTA   Paramount, 1947
THE BIG CLOCK   Paramount, 1948
BEYOND GLORY   Paramount, 1948
THE NIGHT HAS A THOUSAND EYES
   Paramount, 1948
ALIAS NICK BEAL   Paramount, 1949
RED, HOT AND BLUE   Paramount, 1949
WHERE DANGER LIVES   RKO Radio, 1950
COPPER CANYON   Paramount, 1950
HIS KIND OF WOMAN   RKO Radio, 1951
SUBMARINE COMMAND   Paramount, 1951
RIDE, VAQUERO   MGM, 1953
PLUNDER OF THE SUN   Warner Bros., 1953
BOTANY BAY   Paramount, 1953
HONDO   Warner Bros., 1953
A BULLET IS WAITING   Columbia, 1954

THE SEA CHASE   Warner Bros., 1955
BACK FROM ETERNITY   RKO Radio, 1956
THE UNHOLY WIFE   Universal, 1957
JOHN PAUL JONES   Warner Bros., 1959

RAINER WERNER FASSBINDER
b. May 31, 1946 - Bad Worishofen, Bavaria,
   West Germany
d. 1982

LIEBE IST KALTER ALS DER TOD   1969,
   West German
KATZELMACHER   1969, West German
GOTTER DER PEST   1970, West German
WHY DOES HERR R. RUN AMOK?
   co-director with Michael Fengler,
   New Yorker, 1970, West German
THE AMERICAN SOLDIER   New Yorker,
   1970, West German
DIE NIKLASHAUSER FAHRT   co-director with
   Michael Fengler, 1970, West German
RIO DAS MORTE   1971, West German
PIONIERE IN INGOLSTADT   1971,
   West German
WHITY   1971, West German
BEWARE THE HOLY WHORE   New Yorker,
   1971, West German
THE MERCHANT OF FOUR SEASONS
   New Yorker, 1972, West German
THE BITTER TEARS OF PETRA VON KANT
   New Yorker, 1972, West German
ACHT STUNDEN SIND KEIN TAG (MS)
   1972, West German
WILDWECHSEL (TF)   1973, West German
WELT AM DRAHT (TF)   1973, West German
ALI: FEAR EATS THE SOUL   New Yorker,
   1974, West German
MARTHA   1974, West German
EFFI BRIEST   New Yorker, 1974,
   West German
FOX AND HIS FRIENDS   *FAUSTRECHT
   DER FREIHEIT*   New Yorker, 1975,
   West German
MOTHER KUSTERS GOES TO HEAVEN
   New Yorker, 1975, West German
FEAR OF FEAR   1976, West German
CHINESE ROULETTE   New Yorker, 1976,
   West German
SATAN'S BREW   New Yorker, 1976,
   West German
DEUTSCHLAND IM HERBST (FD)
   co-director, Filmverlag der Autoren/Hallelujah
   Film/Kairos Film, 1978, West German
IN A YEAR OF 13 MONTHS   New Yorker,
   1978, West German
DESPAIR   New Line Cinema, 1978,
   West German
BERLIN ALEXANDERPLATZ (MS)   1979,
   West German
THE MARRIAGE OF MARIA BRAUN
   New Yorker, 1979, West German
DIE DRITTE GENERATION   1979,
   West German
QUERELLE   Triumph/Columbia, 1983,
   West German

FELIX E. FEIST
b. February 28, 1906 - New York, New York
d. 1965

THE DELUGE   RKO Radio, 1933
ALL BY MYSELF   Universal, 1943
YOU'RE A LUCKY FELLOW   Universal, 1943
MR. SMITH   Universal, 1943
THIS IS THE LIFE   Universal, 1944
PARDON MY RHYTHM   Universal, 1944
THE RECKLESS AGE   Universal, 1944

GEORGE WHITE'S SCANDALS
   RKO Radio, 1945
THE DEVIL THUMBS A RIDE
   RKO Radio, 1947
THE WINNER'S CIRCLE   RKO Radio, 1948
THE THREAT   RKO Radio, 1949
GUILTY OF TREASON   Eagle Lion, 1950
THE GOLDEN GLOVES STORY
   Eagle Lion, 1950
THE MAN WHO CHEATED HIMSELF
   20th Century-Fox, 1951
TOMORROW IS ANOTHER DAY
   Warner Bros., 1951
THE BASKETBALL FIX   Realart, 1951
THE BIG TREES   Warner Bros., 1952
THIS WOMAN IS DANGEROUS
   Warner Bros., 1952
THE MAN BEHIND THE GUN
   Warner Bros., 1953
DONOVAN'S BRAIN   United Artists, 1953
PIRATES OF TRIPOLI   Columbia, 1955

FEDERICO FELLINI
b. January 20, 1920 - Rimini, Italy
d. 1993

VARIETY LIGHTS   co-director with
   Alberto Lattuada, Pathe Contemporary, 1950,
   Italian
THE WHITE SHEIK   Pathe Contemporary,
   1952, Italian
I VITELLONI   API Productions, 1953, Italian
LOVE IN THE CITY   co-director with
   Michelangelo Antonioni, Alberto Lattuada,
   Carlo Lizzani, Francesco Maselli & Dino Risi,
   Italian Films Export, 1953, Italian
LA STRADA   Trans-Lux, 1954, Italian
IL BIDONE   Astor, 1955, Italian
NIGHTS OF CABIRIA   Lopert, 1957, Italian
LA DOLCE VITA ★   Astor, 1960, Italian
BOCCACCIO '70   co-director with
   Luchino Visconti & Vittorio De Sica, Embassy,
   1962, Italian
8-1/2 ★   Embassy, 1963, Italian
JULIET OF THE SPIRITS   Rizzoli, 1965,
   Italian-French-West German
SPIRITS OF THE DEAD   *HISTOIRES
   EXTRAORDINAIRES*   co-director with Roger
   Vadim & Louis Malle, American International,
   1969, French-Italian
FELLINI SATYRICON ★   United Artists, 1970,
   Italian-French
THE CLOWNS   Levitt-Pickman, 1971,
   Italian-French-West German,
   originally made for television
FELLINI'S ROMA   United Artists, 1972,
   Italian-French
AMARCORD ★   New World, 1974, Italian
CASANOVA   *IL CASANOVA DI FEDERICO
   FELLINI*   Universal, 1977, Italian
ORCHESTRA REHEARSAL   New Yorker,
   1979, Italian-West German,
   originally made for television
CITY OF WOMEN   New Yorker, 1981,
   Italian-French
AND THE SHIP SAILS ON   Triumph/Columbia,
   1983, Italian-French
GINGER AND FRED   MGM/UA, 1986,
   Italian-French-West German
INTERVISTA   Castle Hill Productions,
   1987, Italian
LA VOCE DELLA LUNA   Penta Distribuzione,
   1990, Italian-French

LESLIE FENTON
b. March 12, 1902 - Liverpool, England
d. 1978

TELL NO TALES   1939
STRONGER THAN DESIRE   1939
THE MAN FROM DAKOTA   MGM, 1940
THE GOLDEN FLEECING   1940
THE SAINT'S VACATION   RKO Radio,
   1941, British-U.S.
THERE'S A FUTURE IN IT   1943, British
TOMORROW THE WORLD
   United Artists, 1944
PARDON MY PAST   Columbia, 1945
ON OUR MERRY WAY   *A MIRACLE CAN
   HAPPEN*   co-director with King Vidor,
   United Artists, 1948
SAIGON   Paramount, 1948
LULU BELLE   Columbia, 1948
WHISPERING SMITH   Paramount, 1949
STREETS OF LAREDO   Paramount, 1949
THE REDHEAD AND THE COWBOY
   Paramount, 1951

EMILIO (EL INDIO) FERNANDEZ
b. March 26, 1904 - El Hondo, Mexico
d. 1986

LA ISLA DE LA PASION   Azteca Films,
   1941, Mexican
SOY PURO MEXICANO   Azteca Films,
   1942, Mexican
FLOR SILVESTRE   Azteca Films,
   1943, Mexican
MARIA CANDELARIA   Azteca Films,
   1943, Mexican
LAS ABANDONADAS   Azteca Films,
   1944, Mexican
BUGAMBILLIA   Azteca Films, 1945, Mexican
PEPITA JIMENEZ   Azteca Films,
   1945, Mexican
THE PEARL   Azteca Films, 1946, Mexican
ENAMORADA   Azteca Films, 1947, Mexican
RIO ESCONDIDO   Azteca Films,
   1947, Mexican
MACLOVIA   Azteca Films, 1948, Mexican
SALON MEXICO   Azteca Films,
   1948, Mexican
PUEBLERINA   Azteca Films, 1949, Mexican
LA MALQUERIDA   Azteca Films,
   1949, Mexican
DUELO EN LAS MONTANAS   Azteca Films,
   1949, Mexican
THE TORCH   Eagle Lion, 1950, U.S.-Mexican
UN DIA DE VIDA   Azteca Films,
   1950, Mexican
VICTIMAS DEL PECADO   Azteca Films,
   1951, Mexican
LA BIENAMADA   Azteca Films,
   1951, Mexican
ACAPULCO   Azteca Films, 1951, Mexican
ISLAS MARIAS   Azteca Films, 1951, Mexican
SUAVE PATRIA   Azteca Films, 1951, Mexican
SIEMPRE TUYA   Azteca Films,
   1951, Mexican
TU Y EL MAR   Azteca Films, 1952, Mexican
CUANDO LEVANTA LA NIEBLA   Azteca Films,
   1952, Mexican
LA RED   Azteca Films, 1953, Mexican
EL REPORTAJE   Azteca Films,
   1953, Mexican
EL RAPTO   Azteca Films, 1953, Mexican
LA ROSA BLANCA   Azteca Films,
   1954, Mexican
LA REBELION DE LOS COLGADOS   Azteca
   Films, 1954, Mexican
NOSOTROS DOS   1954, Spanish

LA TIERRA DEL FUEGO SE APAGA
1955, Argentine
UNA CITA DE AMOR   Azteca Films,
1956, Mexican
EL IMPOSTOR   Azteca Films, 1957, Mexican
PUEBLITO, O EL AMOR   Azteca Films,
1962, Mexican
UN DORADO DE PANCHO VILLA
Azteca Films, 1966, Mexican
AQUEL MEXICO LINDO   Azteca Films,
1968, Mexican
LA CHOCA   Azteca Films, 1973, Mexican
MEXICO NORTE   Azteca Films,
1974, Mexican
ZONA ROJA   Azteca Films, 1976, Mexican
EROTICA   Azteca Films, 1978, Mexican

JOSE FERRER
*(Jose Vincente Ferrer de Otero y
Cintron)*
b. January 8, 1912 - Santurce, Puerto Rico
d. 1992

THE SHRIKE   Universal, 1955
THE COCKLESHELL HEROES   Columbia,
1956, British
THE GREAT MAN   Universal, 1956
I ACCUSE!   MGM, 1958
THE HIGH COST OF LOVING   MGM, 1958
RETURN TO PEYTON PLACE
20th Century-Fox, 1961
STATE FAIR   20th Century-Fox, 1962

JACQUES FEYDER
(Jacques Frederix)
b. July 21, 1885 - Ixelles, Belgium
d. 1948

M. PINSON - POLICIER   co-director with
Gaston Ravel, 1916, French
TETES DE FEMMES - FEMMES DE TETE
1916, French
LE PIED QUI ETREINT   1916, French
LE BLUFF   1916, French
UN CONSEIL D'AMI   1916, French
L'HOMME DE CONPAGNIE   1916, French
TIENS VOUS ETES A POITIERS?
1916, French
LA FRERE DE LAIT   1916, French
L'INSTINCT EST MAITRE   1917, French
LE BILLARD CASSE   1917, French
ABREGEONS LES FORMALITES!
1917, French
LA TROUVAILLE DE BUCHU   1917, French
LE PARDESSUS DE DEMI-SAISON
1917, French
LES VIEILLES FEMMES DE L'HOSPICE
1917, French
LE RAVIN SANS FOND   co-director with
Raymond Bernard, 1917, French
LA FAUTE D'ORTHOGRAPHE   1919, French
L'ATLANTIDE   *MISSING HUSBANDS*
1921, French
CRAINQUEBILLE   1922, French
VISAGES D'ENFANTS   1925, Swiss
L'IMAGE   1925, French
GRIBICHE   1925, French
CARMEN   co-director with Francoise Rosay,
1926, French
AU PAYS DU ROI LEPREUX   1927, French
THERESE RAQUIN   *SHADOWS OF FEAR*
1928, French
LES NOUVEAUX MESSIEURS   1928, French
THE KISS   MGM, 1929
DAYBREAK   MGM, 1931
SON OF INDIA   MGM, 1931
LE GRAND JEU   1934, French

PENSION MIMOSAS   1935, French
CARNIVAL IN FLANDERS   *LA KERMESSE
HEROIQUE*   American Tobis, 1935, French
LES GENS DU VOYAGE   1937, French
KNIGHT WITHOUT ARMOR   United Artists,
1937, British
FAHRENDES VOLK   1938, German
LA LOI DU NORD   1942, French-Norwegian
UNE FEMME DISPARAIT   1942, Swiss
MACADAM   1946, French

TERENCE FISHER
b. February 23, 1904 - London, England
d. 1980

COLONEL BOGEY   GFD, 1948, British
TO THE PUBLIC DANGER   GFD,
1948, British
PORTRAIT FROM LIFE   *THE GIRL IN THE
PAINTING*   Universal, 1948, British
SONG OF TOMORROW   GFD, 1948, British
MARRY ME!   GFD, 1949, British
THE ASTONISHED HEART   co-director with
Anthony Darnborough, GFD, 1950, British
SO LONG AT THE FAIR   co-director with
Anthony Darnborough, GFD, 1950, British
HOME TO DANGER   Eros, 1951, British
A DISTANT TRUMPET   Apex, 1952, British
MAN BAIT   *THE LAST PAGE*   Exclusive
Films, 1952, British
STOLEN FACE   Exclusive Films, 1952,
U.S.-British
WINGS OF DANGER   *DEAD ON COURSE*
Exclusive Films, 1952, British
FOUR-SIDED TRIANGLE   Exclusive Films,
1953, British
WOMAN IN HIDING   *MANTRAP*
United Artists, 1953, British
SPACEWAYS   Exclusive Films, 1953, British
BLOOD ORANGE   Exclusive Films,
1953, British
FINAL APPOINTMENT   Monarch,
1954, British
MASK OF DUST   *RACE FOR LIFE*
Exclusive Films, 1954, British
THE BLACK GLOVE   *FACE THE MUSIC*
Exclusive Films, 1954, British
CHILDREN GALORE   GFD, 1954, British
THE UNHOLY FOUR   *THE STRANGER CAME
HOME*   Exclusive Films, 1954, British
BLACKOUT   *MURDER BY PROXY*
Exclusive Films, 1954, British
STOLEN ASSIGNMENT   1955, British
THE FLAW   Renown, 1955, British
THE LAST MAN TO HANG?   Columbia,
1956, British
THE CURSE OF FRANKENSTEIN
Warner Bros., 1957, British
KILL ME TOMORROW   Tudor Pictures,
1957, British
HORROR OF DRACULA   *DRACULA*
Universal, 1958, British
THE REVENGE OF FRANKENSTEIN
Columbia, 1958, British
THE HOUND OF THE BASKERVILLES
United Artists, 1959, British
THE MUMMY   Universal, 1959, British
THE MAN WHO COULD CHEAT DEATH
Paramount, 1959, British
THE STRANGLERS OF BOMBAY   Columbia,
1959, British
THE BRIDES OF DRACULA   Universal,
1960, British
THE SWORD OF SHERWOOD FOREST
Columbia, 1960, British
HOUSE OF FRIGHT   *THE TWO FACES
OF DR. JEKYLL*   American International,
1960, British

THE CURSE OF THE WEREWOLF   Universal,
1961, British
THE PHANTOM OF THE OPERA   Universal,
1962, British
SHERLOCK HOLMES AND THE DEADLY
NECKLACE   Screen Gems, 1962,
West German-British
SHERLOCK HOLMES   1963, British
THE HORROR OF IT ALL   20th Century-Fox,
1964, British
THE EARTH DIES SCREAMING
20th Century-Fox, 1965, British
THE GORGON   Columbia, 1964, British
DRACULA - PRINCE OF DARKNESS
20th Century-Fox, 1965, British
ISLAND OF TERROR   Universal,
1966, British
FRANKENSTEIN CREATED WOMAN
20th Century-Fox, 1967, British
NIGHT OF THE BIG HEAT   Planet,
1967, British
THE DEVIL'S BRIDE   *THE DEVIL RIDES OUT*
20th Century-Fox, 1968, British
FRANKENSTEIN MUST BE DESTROYED!
Warner Bros., 1970, British
FRANKENSTEIN AND THE MONSTER
FROM HELL   Paramount, 1974, British

GEORGE FITZMAURICE
b. February 13, 1885 - Paris, France
d. 1940

THE QUEST OF THE SACRED GEM
Pathé, 1914
THE BOMB BOY   1914
STOP THIEF!   Kleine, 1915
WHO'S WHO IN SOCIETY   Kleine, 1915
THE COMMUTERS   Kleine, 1915
THE MONEY MASTER   Kleine, 1915
VIA WIRELESS   Pathé, 1915
AT BAY   Pathé, 1915
NEW YORK   Pathé, 1916
BIG JIM GARRITY   Pathé, 1916
ARMS AND THE WOMAN   Pathé, 1916
THE TEST   Astra, 1916
THE ROMANTIC JOURNEY   Pathé, 1916
THE HUNTING OF THE HAWK   Pathé, 1917
BLIND MAN'S LUCK   Pathé, 1917
THE RECOIL   Pathé, 1917
THE IRON HEART   Pathé, 1917
THE MARK OF CAIN   Pathé, 1917
SYLVIA OF THE SECRET SERVICE
Pathé, 1917
INNOCENCE   Pathé, 1918
THE NAULAHKA   Pathé, 1918
THE HILLCREST MYSTERY   Pathé, 1918
THE NARROW PATH   Pathé, 1918
THE JAPANESE NIGHTINGALE   Pathé, 1918
COMMON CLAY   Pathé, 1919
THE WITNESS FOR THE DEFENSE
Paramount, 1919
THE CRY OF THE WEAK   Pathé, 1919
OUR BETTER SELVES   Pathé, 1919
PROFITEER   Pathé, 1919
THE AVALANCHE   Artclass-Paramount, 1919
A SOCIETY EXILE   Paramount, 1919
COUNTERFEIT   Paramount, 1919
ON WITH THE DANCE   Paramount, 1920
THE RIGHT TO LOVE   Paramount, 1920
IDOLS OF CLAY   Paramount, 1920
PAYING THE PIPER   Paramount, 1921
EXPERIENCE   Paramount, 1921
PETER IBBETSON   1921
FOREVER   Paramount, 1921
THREE LIVE GHOSTS   Paramount, 1922
THE MAN FROM HOME   Paramount, 1922
TO HAVE AND TO HOLD   Paramount, 1922
KICK IN   Paramount, 1922

BELLA DONNA   Paramount, 1923
THE CHEAT   Paramount, 1923
THE ETERNAL CITY   Associated First
   National, 1923
CYTHEREA   Associated First National, 1924
TARNISH   Associated First National, 1924
A THIEF IN PARADISE   First National, 1925
HIS SUPREME MOMENT
   First National, 1925
THE DARK ANGEL   First National, 1925
THE SON OF THE SHEIK
   United Artists, 1926
THE NIGHT OF LOVE   United Artists, 1927
THE TENDER HOUR   First National, 1927
ROSE OF THE GOLDEN WEST
   First National, 1927
THE LOVE MART   First National, 1927
LILAC TIME   First National, 1928
THE BARKER   First National, 1928
HIS CAPTIVE WOMAN   First National, 1929
THE MAN AND THE MOMENT
   First National, 1929
THE LOCKED DOOR   United Artists, 1929
TIGER ROSE   Warner Bros., 1929
THE BAD ONE   United Artists, 1930
RAFFLES   co-director with Harry D'Abbadie
   D'Arrast, United Artists, 1930
THE DEVIL TO PAY   United Artists, 1931
ONE HEAVENLY NIGHT   United Artists, 1931
STRANGERS MAY KISS   MGM, 1931
THE UNHOLY GARDEN   United Artists, 1931
MATA HARI   MGM, 1932
AS YOU DESIRE ME   MGM, 1932
ALL MEN ARE ENEMIES   MGM, 1934
PETTICOAT FEVER   MGM, 1936
SUZY   MGM, 1936
THE EMPEROR'S CANDLESTICKS
   MGM, 1937
LIVE, LOVE AND LEARN   MGM, 1937
ARSENE LUPIN RETURNS   MGM, 1938
VACATION FROM LOVE   MGM, 1938
ADVENTURE IN LOVE   *ADVENTURE IN
   DIAMONDS*   Paramount, 1940

ROBERT J. FLAHERTY

b. February 16, 1884 - Iron Mountain, Michigan
d. 1951

NANOOK OF THE NORTH (FD)   Pathé, 1922
THE POTTERY-MAKER (FD)   1925
MOANA (FD)   Paramount, 1926
THE TWENTY-FOUR DOLLAR
   ISLAND (FD)   1927
WHITE SHADOWS OF THE SOUTH SEAS
   co-director with W. S. Van Dyke, MGM, 1928
ACOMA, THE SKY CITY   Fox,
   1928, unreleased
TABU   co-director with F.W. Murnau,
   Paramount, 1931
INDUSTRIAL BRITAIN (FD)   1933, British
MAN OF ARAN (FD)   Gaumont-British,
   1934, British
ELEPHANT BOY   co-director with
   Zoltan Korda, United Artists, 1937, British
THE LAND (FD)   Department of
   Agriculture, 1942
LOUISIANA STORY (FD)   Lopert, 1948

VICTOR FLEMING

b. February 23, 1883 - Pasadena, California
d. 1949

WHEN THE CLOUDS ROLL BY   co-director
   with Ted Reed, United Artists, 1919
THE MOLLYCODDLE   United Artists, 1920
WOMAN'S PLACE   First National, 1921
MAMMA'S AFFAIR   Associated First
   National, 1921

THE LANE THAT HAD NO TURNING
   Paramount, 1922
RED HOT ROMANCE   First National, 1922
ANNA ASCENDS   Paramount, 1922
DARK SECRETS   Paramount, 1923
LAW OF THE LAWLESS   Paramount, 1923
TO THE LAST MAN   Paramount, 1923
THE CALL OF THE CANYON
   Paramount, 1923
EMPTY HANDS   Paramount, 1924
CODE OF THE SEA   Paramount, 1924
THE DEVIL'S CARGO   Paramount, 1925
ADVENTURE   Paramount, 1925
A SON OF HIS FATHER   Paramount, 1925
LORD JIM   Paramount, 1925
BLIND GODDESS   Paramount, 1926
MANTRAP   Paramount, 1926
THE ROUGH RIDERS   Paramount, 1927
THE WAY OF ALL FLESH   Paramount, 1927
HULA   Paramount, 1927
ABIE'S IRISH ROSE   Paramount, 1928
THE AWAKENING   Paramount, 1928
WOLF SONG   Paramount, 1929
THE VIRGINIAN   Paramount, 1929
COMMON CLAY   Fox, 1930
RENEGADES   Fox, 1930
AROUND THE WORLD IN 80 MINUTES
   co-director with Douglas Fairbanks,
   United Artists, 1931
THE WET PARADE   MGM, 1932
RED DUST   MGM, 1932
THE WHITE SISTER   MGM, 1933
BOMBSHELL   MGM, 1933
TREASURE ISLAND   MGM, 1934
RECKLESS   MGM, 1935
THE FARMER TAKES A WIFE   Fox, 1935
CAPTAINS COURAGEOUS   MGM, 1937
TEST PILOT   MGM, 1938
THE WIZARD OF OZ   MGM, 1939
GONE WITH THE WIND ★★   MGM, 1939
DR. JEKYLL AND MR. HYDE   MGM, 1941
TORTILLA FLAT   MGM, 1942
A GUY NAMED JOE   MGM, 1943
ADVENTURE   MGM, 1946
JOAN OF ARC   RKO Radio, 1948

ROBERT FLOREY

b. September 14, 1900 - Paris, France
d. 1979

ONE HOUR OF LOVE   Tiffany, 1927
THE ROMANTIC AGE   Columbia, 1927
FACE VALUE   Sterling, 1927
FIGHT CLUB   Paramount, 1928
THE HOLE IN THE WALL   Paramount, 1929
THE COCOANUTS   co-director with
   Joseph Santley, Paramount, 1929
THE BATTLE OF PARIS   Paramount, 1929
LA ROUTE EST BELLE   Paramount,
   1930, French
L'AMOUR CHATTE   1930, French
LE BLANC ET LE NOIR   co-director with
   Marc Allegret, 1930, French
MURDERS IN THE RUE MORGUE
   Universal, 1932
THE MAN CALLED BACK   World Wide, 1932
THOSE WE LOVE   World Wide, 1932
GIRL MISSING   Warner Bros., 1933
EX-LADY   Warner Bros., 1933
THE HOUSE ON 56TH STREET
   Warner Bros., 1933
BEDSIDE   First National, 1934
SMARTY   Warner Bros., 1934
REGISTERED NURSE   First National, 1934
I SELL ANYTHING   First National, 1934
I AM A THIEF   Warner Bros., 1935
THE WOMAN IN RED   First National, 1935

THE FLORENTINE DAGGER
   Warner Bros., 1935
DON'T BET ON BLONDES
   Warner Bros., 1935
GOING HIGHBROW   Warner Bros., 1935
THE PAY-OFF   Warner Bros., 1935
SHIP CAFE   Paramount, 1935
THE PREVIEW MURDER MYSTERY
   Paramount, 1936
TILL WE MEET AGAIN   Paramount, 1936
HOLLYWOOD BOULEVARD
   Paramount, 1936
OUTCAST   Paramount, 1937
KING OF GAMBLERS   Paramount, 1936
MOUNTAIN MUSIC   Paramount, 1937
THIS WAY PLEASE   Paramount, 1937
DAUGHTER OF SHANGHAI
   Paramount, 1937
DANGEROUS TO KNOW   Paramount, 1938
KING OF ALCATRAZ   Paramount, 1938
DISBARRED   Paramount, 1939
HOTEL IMPERIAL   Paramount, 1939
THE MAGNIFICENT FRAUD
   Paramount, 1939
DEATH OF A CHAMPION   Paramount, 1939
PAROLE FIXER   Paramount, 1940
WOMEN WITHOUT NAMES
   Paramount, 1940
THE FACE BEHIND THE MASK
   Columbia, 1941
MEET BOSTON BLACKIE   Columbia, 1941
TWO IN A TAXI   Columbia, 1941
DANGEROUSLY THEY LIVE
   Warner Bros., 1942
LADY GANGSTER   directed under pseudonym
   of Florian Roberts, Warner Bros., 1942
THE DESERT SONG   Warner Bros., 1944
MAN FROM FRISCO   Republic, 1944
ROGER TOUHY - GANGSTER
   20th Century-Fox, 1944
GOD IS MY CO-PILOT   Warner Bros., 1945
DANGER SIGNAL   Warner Bros., 1945
THE BEAST WITH FIVE FINGERS
   Warner Bros., 1946
TARZAN AND THE MERMAIDS
   RKO Rado, 1948
ROGUES' REGIMENT   Universal, 1948
OUTPOST IN MOROCCO
   United Artists, 1949
THE CROOKED WAY   United Artists, 1949
THE VICIOUS YEARS   Film Classics, 1950
JOHNNY ONE-EYE   United Artists, 1950

ALEKSANDER FORD

(Alexander Ford)
b. November 24, 1908 - Lodz, Poland
d. 1980

THE MASCOT   1930, Polish
LEGION OF THE STREETS   1932, Polish
SABRA   *CHALUTZIM*   1934, Palestinian
AWAKENING   1934, Polish
FORWARD COOPERATION (FD)
   1935, Polish
ROAD OF YOUTH   *STREET OF THE YOUNG/
   CHILDREN MUST LAUGH*   1936, Polish
PEOPLE OF THE VISTULA   co-director,
   1937, Polish
BORDER STREET   1948, Polish
YOUNG CHOPIN   1952, Polish
FIVE FROM BARSKA STREET   1953, Polish
THE EIGHTH DAY OF THE WEEK
   1958, Polish
KNIGHTS OF THE BLACK CROSS
   *KRZYZACY/THE KNIGHTS OF THE
   TEUTONIC ORDER*   Telewide Systems,
   1960, Polish
THE FIRST DAY OF FREEDOM   1964, Polish

DER ARZT STELLT FEST *ANGEKLAGT NACH PARAGRAPH 218* (FD) 1966, Swiss-West German
GOOD MORNING POLAND (FD) 1970, Polish
THE FIRST CIRCLE Paramount, 1972, Danish-West German-U.S.
DER MARTYRER *SIE SIND FREI DOKTOR KORCZAK* 1975, West German-Israeli

FRANCIS FORD
(Francis O'Feeney/Francis O'Fearna)
b. August 15, 1882 - Portland, Maine
d. 1953

THE INVADERS co-director with Thomas H. Ince, 1912
THE ARMY SURGEON 1912
WHEN LINCOLN PAID 1913
THE FAVORITE SON 1913
WYNONA'S VENGEANCE 1913
WASHINGTON AT VALLEY FORGE 1914
THE PHANTOM VIOLIN 1914
LUCILLE LOVE - THE GIRL OF MYSTERY (S) 1914
THE MYSTERIOUS ROSE 1914
THREE BAD MEN AND A GIRL 1915
THE HIDDEN CITY 1915
AND THEY CALLED HIM HERS 1915
THE DOORWAY OF DESTRUCTION 1915
THE BROKEN COIN (S) 1915
THE CAMPBELLS ARE COMING 1915
THE LUMBER YARD GANG 1916
CHICKEN-HEARTED JIM 1916
AND THEY CALLED HIM HERO 1916
THE ADVENTURES OF PEG O' THE RING (S) co-director with Jacques Jaccard, 1916
THE BANDIT'S WAGER 1916
THE PURPLE MASK (S) 1916-17
THE TRAIL OF HATE 1917
JOHN ERMINE OF YELLOWSTONE 1917
WHO WAS THE OTHER MAN? 1917
THE AVENGING TRAIL 1918
BERLIN VIA AMERICA 1918
THE CRAVING 1918
THE SILENT MYSTERY (S) 1918-19
THE MYSTERY OF 13 (S) 1919
THE CRIMSON SHOALS 1919
THE MAN FROM NOWHERE 1920
CYCLONE BLISS 1921
THE STAMPEDE 1921
I AM THE WOMAN 1921
SO THIS IS ARIZONA 1922
ANGEL CITIZENS 1922
TRAIL'S END 1922
THUNDERING HOOFS 1922
THEY'RE OFF 1922
STORM GIRL 1922
THE HEART OF LINCOLN 1922
GOLD GRABBERS 1922
CUPID'S RUSTLER 1925
A RODEO MIXUP 1925
WESTERN YESTERDAYS 1925
RANGE BLOOD 1925
LASH OF THE WHIP 1925
MIDNIGHT SHADOWS 1925
THE COWBOY PRINCE 1925
THE DIAMOND BANDIT 1925
LASH OF PINTO PETE 1925
WESTERN FEUDS 1925
THE WINKING IDOL (S) 1926
HER OWN STORY 1926
THE GHETTO SHAMROCK 1926
FALSE FRIENDS 1926
WOLVES OF THE AIR 1927
WOLF'S TRAIL 1927
CALL OF THE HEART 1928

JOHN FORD
(Sean Aloyslus O'Feeney/Sean Aloyslus O'Fearna/Jack Ford)
b. February 1, 1895 - Cape Elizabeth, Maine
d. 1973

THE TORNADO Universal, 1917
THE TRAIL OF HATE Universal, 1917
THE SCRAPPER Universal, 1917
THE SOUL HERDER Universal, 1917
CHEYENNE'S PAL Universal, 1917
STRAIGHT SHOOTING Universal, 1917
THE SECRET MAN Universal, 1917
A MARKED MAN Universal, 1917
BUCKING BROADWAY Universal, 1917
THE PHANTOM RIDERS Universal, 1918
WILD WOMEN Universal, 1918
THIEVES' GOLD Universal, 1918
THE SCARLET DROP Universal, 1918
HELL BENT Universal, 1918
A WOMAN'S FOOL Universal, 1918
THREE MOUNTED MEN Universal, 1918
THE CRAVING co-director with Francis Ford, Universal, 1919
ROPED Universal, 1919
THE FIGHTING BROTHERS Universal, 1919
A FIGHT FOR LOVE Universal, 1919
BY INDIAN POST Universal, 1919
THE RUSTLERS Universal, 1919
BARE FISTS Universal, 1919
GUN LAW Universal, 1919
THE GUN PACKER Universal, 1919
RIDERS OF VENGEANCE Universal, 1919
THE LAST OUTLAW Universal, 1919
THE OUTCASTS OF POKER FLAT Universal, 1919
THE AGE OF THE SADDLE Universal, 1919
THE RIDER OF THE LAW Universal, 1919
A GUN FIGHTIN' GENTLEMAN Universal, 1919
MARKED MEN Universal, 1919
THE PRINCE OF AVENUE A Universal, 1920
THE GIRL IN NO. 29 Universal, 1920
HITCHIN' POSTS Universal, 1920
JUST PALS 20th Century Brand, 1920
THE BIG PUNCH 20th Century Brand, 1921
THE FREEZE OUT Universal, 1921
THE WALLOP Universal, 1921
DESPERATE TRAILS Universal, 1921
ACTION Universal, 1921
SURE FIRE Universal, 1921
JACKIE William Fox, 1921
LITTLE MISS SMILES William Fox, 1922
SILVER WINGS co-director with Edwin Carewe, William Fox, 1922
THE VILLAGE BLACKSMITH William Fox, 1922
THE FACE ON THE BARROOM FLOOR William Fox, 1923
THREE JUMPS AHEAD William Fox, 1923
CAMEO KIRBY William Fox, 1923
NORTH OF HUDSON BAY William Fox, 1923
HOODMAN BLIND William Fox, 1923
THE IRON HORSE William Fox, 1924
HEARTS OF OAK William Fox, 1924
LIGHTNIN' William Fox, 1925
KENTUCKY PRIDE William Fox, 1925
THE FIGHTING HEART William Fox, 1925
THANK YOU William Fox, 1925
3 BAD MEN William Fox, 1926
THE BLUE EAGLE William Fox, 1926
UPSTREAM William Fox, 1927
MOTHER MACHREE William Fox, 1928
FOUR SONS William Fox, 1928
HANGMAN'S HOUSE William Fox, 1928
RILEY THE COP William Fox, 1928
STRONG BOY William Fox, 1929
THE BLACK WATCH William Fox, 1929

SALUTE William Fox, 1929
MEN WITHOUT WOMEN William Fox, 1930
BORN RECKLESS William Fox, 1930
UP THE RIVER William Fox, 1930
SEAS BENEATH William Fox, 1931
THE BRAT Fox Film Corporation, 1931
ARROWSMITH United Artists, 1931
AIR MAIL Universal, 1932
FLESH MGM, 1932
PILGRIMAGE Fox Film Corporation, 1933
DOCTOR BULL Fox Film Corporation, 1933
THE LOST PATROL RKO Radio, 1934
THE WORLD MOVES ON Fox Film Corporation, 1934
JUDGE PRIEST Fox Film Corporation, 1934
THE WHOLE TOWN'S TALKING Columbia, 1935
THE INFORMER ★★ RKO Radio, 1935
STEAMBOAT ROUND THE BEND 20th Century-Fox, 1935
THE PRISONER OF SHARK ISLAND 20th Century-Fox, 1936
MARY OF SCOTLAND RKO Radio, 1936
THE PLOUGH AND THE STARS RKO Radio, 1936
WEE WILLIE WINKIE 20th Century-Fox, 1937
THE HURRICANE United Artists, 1937
FOUR MEN AND A PRAYER 20th Century-Fox, 1938
SUBMARINE PATROL 20th Century-Fox, 1938
STAGECOACH ★ United Artists, 1939
YOUNG MR. LINCOLN 20th Century-Fox, 1939
DRUMS ALONG THE MOHAWK 20th Century-Fox, 1939
THE GRAPES OF WRATH ★★ 20th Century-Fox, 1940
THE LONG VOYAGE HOME United Artists, 1940
TOBACCO ROAD 20th Century-Fox, 1941
HOW GREEN WAS MY VALLEY ★★ 20th Century-Fox, 1941
DECEMBER 7TH co-director with Gregg Toland, War and Navy Department, 1943
THEY WERE EXPENDABLE MGM, 1945
MY DARLING CLEMENTINE 20th Century-Fox, 1946
THE FUGITIVE RKO Radio, 1947
FORT APACHE RKO Radio, 1948
THREE GODFATHERS MGM, 1948
SHE WORE A YELLOW RIBBON RKO Radio, 1949
WHEN WILLIE COMES MARCHING HOME 20th Century-Fox, 1950
WAGON MASTER RKO Radio, 1950
RIO GRANDE Republic, 1950
THE QUIET MAN ★★ Republic, 1952
WHAT PRICE GLORY 20th Century-Fox, 1952
THE SUN SHINES BRIGHT Republic, 1953
MOGAMBO MGM, 1953
THE LONG GRAY LINE Columbia, 1955
MISTER ROBERTS co-director with Mervyn LeRoy, Warner Bros., 1955
THE SEARCHERS Warner Bros., 1956
THE RISING OF THE MOON Warner Bros., 1957
THE WINGS OF EAGLES MGM, 1957
GIDEON OF SCOTLAND YARD *GIDEON'S DAY* Columbia, 1958, British
THE LAST HURRAH Columbia, 1958
THE HORSE SOLDIERS United Artists, 1959
SERGEANT RUTLEDGE Warner Bros., 1960
TWO RODE TOGETHER Columbia, 1961
THE MAN WHO SHOT LIBERTY VALANCE Paramount, 1962

HOW THE WEST WAS WON   co-director with
George Marshall & Henry Hathaway,
MGM/Cinerama, 1962
DONOVAN'S REEF   Paramount, 1963
CHEYENNE AUTUMN   Warner Bros., 1964
7 WOMEN   MGM, 1965

CARL FOREMAN

b. July 23, 1914 - Chicago, Illinois
d. 1984

THE VICTORS   Columbia, 1963

BOB FOSSE

b. June 23, 1927 - Chicago, Illinois
d. 1987

SWEET CHARITY   Universal, 1969
CABARET ★★   Allied Artists, 1972
LENNY ★   United Artists, 1974
ALL THAT JAZZ ★   20th Century-Fox, 1979
STAR 80   The Ladd Company/Warner
Bros., 1983

LEWIS R. FOSTER

b. August 5, 1900 - Brookfield, Missouri
d. 1974

LOVE LETTERS OF A STAR   co-director with
Milton Carruth, Universal, 1936
SHE'S DANGEROUS   co-director with
Milton Carruth, Universal, 1937
ARMORED CAR   Universal, 1937
THE MAN WHO CRIED WOLF
Universal, 1937
THE LUCKY STIFF   United Artists, 1949
EL PASO   Paramount, 1949
MANHANDLED   Paramount, 1949
CAPTAIN CHINA   Paramount, 1950
THE EAGLE AND THE HAWK
Paramount, 1950
THE LAST OUTPOST   Paramount, 1951
PASSAGE WEST   Paramount, 1951
CROSSWINDS   Paramount, 1951
HONG KONG   Paramount, 1951
TROPIC ZONE   Paramount, 1953
JAMAICA RUN   Paramount, 1953
THOSE REDHEADS FROM SEATTLE
Paramount, 1953
CRASHOUT   Filmmakers, 1955
TOP THE WORLD   United Artists, 1955
THE BOLD AND THE BRAVE
RKO Radio, 1956
DAKOTA INCIDENT   Republic, 1956
TONKA   Buena Vista, 1958
THE SIGN OF ZORRO   co-director with
Norman Foster, Buena Vista, 1960

NORMAN FOSTER
(Norman Hoeffer)
b. December 13, 1900 - Richmond, Indiana
d. 1976

I COVER CHINATOWN
20th Century-Fox, 1936
FAIR WARNING   20th Century-Fox, 1937
THINK FAST, MR. MOTO
20th Century-Fox, 1937
THANK YOU, MR. MOTO
20th Century-Fox, 1937
WALKING DOWN BROADWAY
20th Century-Fox, 1938
MR. MOTO TAKES A CHANCE
20th Century-Fox, 1938
MYSTERIOUS MR. MOTO
20th Century-Fox, 1938

MR. MOTO'S LAST WARNING
20th Century-Fox, 1939
CHARLIE CHAN IN RENO
20th Century-Fox, 1939
MR. MOTO TAKES A VACATION
20th Century-Fox, 1939
CHARLIE CHAN AT TREASURE ISLAND
20th Century-Fox, 1939
CHARLIE CHAN IN PANAMA
20th Century-Fox, 1940
VIVA CISCO KID   20th Century-Fox, 1940
RIDE, KELLY, RIDE   20th Century-Fox, 1941
SCOTLAND YARD   20th Century-Fox, 1941
JOURNEY INTO FEAR   RKO Radio, 1942
IT'S ALL TRUE   co-director with Orson Welles,
RKO Radio, 1942, unfinished
SANTA   1943, Mexican
HORA DE LA VERDAD   1945, Mexican
RACHEL AND THE STRANGER
RKO Radio, 1948
KISS THE BLOOD OFF MY HANDS
Universal, 1948
TELL IT TO THE JUDGE   Columbia, 1949
FATHER IS A BACHELOR   co-director with
Abby Berlin, Columbia, 1950
WOMAN ON THE RUN   Universal, 1950
NAVAJO   Lippert, 1952
SKY FULL OF MOON   MGM, 1952
SOMBRERO   MGM, 1953
DAVY CROCKETT, KING OF THE WILD
FRONTIER   Buena Vista, 1955
DAVY CROCKETT AND THE RIVER PIRATES
Buena Vista, 1956
THE NINE LIVES OF ELFEGO
BACA (TF)   1959
THE SIGN OF ZORRO   co-director with
Lewis R. Foster, Buena Vista, 1960
HANS BRINKER   *THE SILVER SKATES*
Buena Vista, 1962
VON DRAKE IN SPAIN   Buena Vista, 1962
INDIAN PAINT   Crown International, 1966
BRIGHTY OF GRAND CANYON
Feature Film Corporation, 1967
DEATHBED   Wargay, 1973

GEORGES FRANJU

b. April 12, 1912 - Fougeres, France
d. 1987

LA TETE CONTRE LES MURS   1959, French
THE HORROR CHAMBER OF DR. FAUSTUS
LES YEUX SANS VISAGE   Lopert,
1960, French-Italian
PLEINS FEUX SUR L'ASSASSIN
1961, French
THERESE DESQUEYROUX   1962, French
JUDEX   1964, French
THOMAS L'IMPOSTEUR   1965, French
LA FAUTE DE L'ABBE MOURET
1970, French
L'HOMME SANS VISAGE   1974, French

MELVIN FRANK

b. August 13, 1913 - Chicago, Illinois
d. 1988

THE REFORMER AND THE REDHEAD
co-director with Norman Panama,
MGM, 1950
CALLAWAY WENT THATAWAY   co-director
with Norman Panama, MGM, 1951
STRICTLY DISHONORABLE   co-director with
Norman Panama, MGM, 1951
ABOVE AND BEYOND   co-director with
Norman Panama, MGM, 1952
KNOCK ON WOOD   co-director with
Norman Panama, Paramount, 1954

THE COURT JESTER   co-director with
Norman Panama, Paramount, 1956
THAT CERTAIN FEELING   co-director with
Norman Panama, Paramount, 1956
THE JAYHAWKERS   Paramount, 1959
LI'L ABNER   Paramount, 1959
THE FACTS OF LIFE   United Artists, 1960
STRANGE BEDFELLOWS   Universal, 1965
BUONA SERA, MRS. CAMPBELL
United Artists, 1968
A TOUCH OF CLASS   Avco Embassy,
1973, British
THE PRISONER OF SECOND AVENUE
Warner Bros., 1975
THE DUCHESS AND THE DIRTWATER FOX
20th Century-Fox, 1976
LOST AND FOUND   Columbia, 1979
WALK LIKE A MAN   MGM/UA, 1987

SIDNEY FRANKLIN

b. March 21, 1893 - San Francisco, California
d. 1972

LET KATY DO IT   co-director with
Chester Franklin, Triangle, 1915
MARTHA'S VINDICATION   co-director with
Chester Franklin, Triangle, 1915
THE CHILDREN IN THE HOUSE
co-director with Chester Franklin,
Fine Arts-Triangle, 1916
GOING STRAIGHT   co-director with
Chester Franklin, Fine Arts-Triangle, 1916
THE LITTLE SCHOOL MA'AM   co-director with
Chester Franklin, Fine Arts-Triangle, 1916
GRETCHEN THE GREENHORN
co-director with Chester Franklin,
Fine Arts-Triangle, 1916
SISTER OF SIX   co-director with
Chester Franklin, Fine Arts-Triangle, 1916
JACK AND THE BEANSTALK   co-director with
Chester Franklin, Fox, 1917
ALADDIN AND THE WONDERFUL LAMP
co-director with Chester Franklin, Fox, 1917
BABES IN THE WOODS   co-director with
Chester Franklin, Fox, 1917
FAN FAN   co-director with Chester Franklin,
Fox, 1918
TREASURE ISLAND   co-director with
Chester Franklin, Fox, 1918
ALI BABA AND THE FORTY THIEVES
co-director with Chester Franklin, Fox, 1918
SIX SHOOTER ANDY   Fox, 1918
CONFESSION   Fox, 1918
THE BRIDE OF FEAR   Fox, 1918
THE SAFETY CURTAIN   Select, 1918
THE FORBIDDEN CITY   Select, 1918
HER ONLY WAY   Select, 1918
THE HEART OF WETONA   Select, 1918
PROBATION WIFE   Select, 1919
THE HOODLUM   First National, 1919
HEART O' THE HILLS   First National, 1919
TWO WEEKS   First National, 1920
UNSEEN FORCES   First National, 1920
NOT GUILTY   Associated First National, 1921
COURAGE   Associated First National, 1921
SMILIN' THROUGH   Associated First
National, 1922
THE PRIMITIVE LOVER   Associated First
National, 1922
EAST IS WEST   Associated First
National, 1922
BRASS   Warner Bros., 1923
DULCY   Associated First National, 1923
TIGER ROSE   Warner Bros., 1923
HER NIGHT OF ROMANCE
First National, 1924
LEARNING TO LOVE   First National, 1924

HER SISTER FROM PARIS
First National, 1925
BEVERLY OF GRAUSTARK MGM, 1926
THE DUCHESS OF BUFFALO MGM, 1926
QUALITY STREET MGM, 1927
THE ACTRESS MGM, 1928
WILD ORCHIDS MGM, 1928
THE LAST OF MRS. CHEYNEY MGM, 1929
DEVIL MAY CARE MGM, 1930
THE LADY OF SCANDAL MGM, 1930
A LADY'S MORALS MGM, 1930
THE GUARDSMAN MGM, 1931
PRIVATE LIVES MGM, 1931
SMILIN' THROUGH MGM, 1932
REUNION IN VIENNA MGM, 1933
THE BARRETTS OF WIMPOLE STREET
MGM, 1934
THE DARK ANGEL MGM, 1935
THE GOOD EARTH ★ MGM, 1937
THE BARRETTS OF WIMPOLE STREET
MGM, 1957

THORNTON FREELAND

b. February 10, 1898 - Hope, North Dakota
d. ?

THREE LIVE GHOSTS 1929
BE YOURSELF 1930
WHOOPEE! United Artists, 1930
SIX CYLINDER LOVE 1931
TERROR BY NIGHT 1931
THE SECRET WITNESS 1931
THE UNEXPECTED FATHER 1932
LOVE AFFAIR 1932
WEEK-END MARRIAGE First National, 1932
THEY CALL IT SIN First National, 1932
FLYING DOWN TO RIO RKO Radio, 1933
GEORGE WHITE'S SCANDALS
RKO Radio, 1934
BREWSTER'S MILLIONS 1935, British
SKYLARKS 1936, British
THE AMATEUR GENTLEMAN 1936, British
ACCUSED 1936
PARADISE FOR TWO THE GAIETY GIRLS
1937, British
JERICHO DARK SANDS 1937, British
HOLD MY HAND 1938, British
OVER THE MOON United Artists,
1940, British
SO THIS IS LONDON 1939, British
THE AMAZING MR. FORREST THE GANG'S
ALL HERE PRC, 1939, British
TOO MANY BLONDES 1941
MARRY THE BOSS' DAUGHTER
20th Century-Fox, 1941
MEET ME AT DAWN 1946, British
LUCKY MASCOT THE BRASS MONKEY
1947, British
DEAR MR. PROHACK Rank, 1949, British

HUGO FREGONESE

b. April 18, 1908 - Buenos Aires, Argentina
d. 1987

PAMPA BARBARA co-director with
Lucas Demare, 1943, Argentine
DONDE MUEREN LAS PALABRAS
1946, Argentine
APENAS UN DELINCUENTE 1947, Argentine
DE HOMBRE A HOMBRE 1949, Argentine
ONE WAY STREET Universal, 1950
SADDLE TRAMP Universal, 1950
APACHE DRUMS Universal, 1951
MARK OF THE RENEGADE Universal, 1951
MY SIX CONVICTS Universal, 1952
UNTAMED FRONTIER Universal, 1952
BLOWING WILD Warner Bros., 1953
DECAMERON NIGHTS RKO Radio,
1953, British-U.S.

MAN IN THE ATTIC 20th Century-Fox, 1953
THE RAID 20th Century-Fox, 1954
BLACK TUESDAY United Artists, 1955
I GIROVAGHI 1956, Italian
BEAST OF MARSEILLES THE SEVEN
THUNDERS Lopert, 1957, British
HARRY BLACK AND THE TIGER
20th Century-Fox, 1958, British
MARCO POLO co-director with Piero Pierotti,
American International, 1961, Italian-French
OLD SHATTERHAND
SHATTERHAND Constantin, 1964,
West German-French-Italian-Yugoslavian
THE TESTAMENT OF DR. MABUSE Thunder,
1964, West German-Italian-French
SAVAGE PAMPAS Comet, 1966,
Spanish-Argentine-U.S.
OPERAZIONE BALLABREK co-director with
Giuliano Cannimro, 1965, Italian
LA MALA VIDA 1973, Argentine
MAS ALLA DEL SOL 1975, Argentine

HAROLD FRENCH

b. April 23, 1897 - London, England
d. ?

CAVALIER OF THE STREETS 1937, British
DEAD MEN ARE DANGEROUS 1939, British
THE HOUSE OF THE ARROW 1940, British
JEANNIE English Films, 1941, British
SECRET MISSION English Films,
1942, British
UNPUBLISHED STORY 1942, British
THE DAY WILL DAWN THE AVENGERS
1942, British
DEAR OCTOPUS RANDOLPH FAMILY
1943, British
HER MAN GILBEY ENGLISH WITHOUT
TEARS Universal, 1944, British
QUIET WEEKEND 1946, British
HIGH FURY WHITE CRADLE INN
United Artists, 1948, British
BLIND GODDESS Universal, 1949, British
QUARTET co-director with Ken Annakin,
Ralph Smart & Arthur Crabtree, Eagle Lion,
1948, British
MY BROTHER JONATHAN 1948, British
ADAM AND EVELYN ADAM AND EVELYNE
Universal, 1949, British
TRIO co-director with Ken Annakin,
Paramount, 1950, British
THE DANCING YEARS 1950, British
ENCORE co-director with Pat Jackson,
Paramount, 1951, British
THE PARIS EXPRESS THE MAN WHO
WATCHED THE TRAINS GO BY
George Schaefer, 1953, British
THE HOUR OF 13 MGM, 1952, British
ISN'T LIFE WONDERFUL 1953, British
ROB ROY, THE HIGHLAND ROGUE
RKO Radio, 1953, British-U.S.
FORBIDDEN CARGO Fine Arts, 1954, British
THE MAN WHO LOVED REDHEADS
United Artists, 1955, British

CHARLES FREND

b. November 21, 1909 - Pulborough, England
d. 1977

THE BIG BLOCKADE 1941, British
THE FOREMAN WENT TO FRANCE
United Artists, 1942, British
SAN DEMETRIO, LONDON
20th Century-Fox, 1943, British
JOHNNY FRENCHMAN 1945, British
RETURN OF THE VIKINGS (FD)
1945, British
THE LOVES OF JOANNA GODDEN
Associated British-Pathe, 1947, British

SCOTT OF THE ANTARCTIC Eagle Lion,
1948, British
A RUN FOR YOUR MONEY Universal,
1949, British
THE MAGNET Universal, 1951, British
THE CRUEL SEA Universal, 1952, British
LEASE OF LIFE Italisn Films Export,
1954, British
THE THIRD KEY THE LONG ARM Rank,
1956, British
ALL AT SEA BARNACLE BILL MGM,
1958, British
TROUBLE IN THE SKY CONE OF SILENCE
Universal, 1960, British
GIRL ON APPROVAL Continental,
1962, British
TORPEDO BAY FINCHE DURA LA
TEMPESTA American International,
1963, Italian-French
THE SKY BIKE 1967, British

KARL FREUND

b. January 16, 1890 - Koniginhof, Bohemia
d. 1969

THE MUMMY Universal, 1932
MOONLIGHT AND PRETZELS Universal, 1933
MADAME SPY Universal, 1934
THE COUNTESS OF MONTE CRISTO
Universal, 1934
UNCERTAIN LADY Universal, 1934
I GIVE MY LOVE Universal, 1934
GIFT OF GAB Universal, 1934
MAD LOVE MGM, 1935

G

PAL GABOR

b. 1932 - Budapest, Hungary
d. 1987

FORBIDDEN GROUND 1968, Hungarian
JOURNEY WITH JACOB 1973, Hungarian
EPIDEMIC 1978, Hungarian
ANGI VERA New Yorker, 1979, Hungarian
WASTED LIVES Budapest Studio,
1982, Hungarian
BRADY'S ESCAPE THE LONG RUN
Satori, 1984, U.S.-Hungarian
LA SPOSA ERA BELLISSIMA Titanus, 1986,
Italian-Hungarian

CARLO GALLONE

b. September 18, 1886 - Taggia, Italy
d. 1973

IL BACIO DI CIRANO 1913, Italian
LA DONNA NUDA 1914, Italian
AVATAR 1915, Italian
MALOMBRA 1916, Italian
LA FALENA 1916, Italian
STORIA DEI TREDICI 1917, Italian
LA FIGLIE DEL MARE 1919, Italian
AMLETO E IL SUO CLOWN 1920, Italian
NEMESIS 1921, Italian
MARCELLA 1922, Italian
LA FIGLIA DELLA TEMPESTA 1922, Italian
IL COLONNELLO CHABERT 1922, Italian
IL CORSARO 1923, Italian

AMORE   1923, Italian
LA CAVALCATA ARDENTE   1923, Italian
TORMENTA   1923, Italian
LA FIAMMATA   1924, Italian
GLI ULTIMI GIRONI DI POMPEI   1926, Italian
CELLE QUI DOMINE   1927, French
LIEBESHOLLE   1928, German-Polish
DAS LAND OHNE FRAUEN   1929, German
DIE SINGENDE STADT   1930, German
LE CHANT DU MARIN   1931, German
THE CITY OF SONG   *FAREWELL TO LOVE*
   1931, British
UN SOIR DE RAFLE   1931, French
UN FILS D'AMERIQUE   1932, French
LE ROI DES PALACES   1932, French
MA COUSINE DE VARSOVIE   1932, French
MEIN HERZ RUFT NACH DIR   1934, German
MON COEUR T'APPELLE   1934, French
MY HEART IS CALLING   1934, British
CASTA DIVA   Alleanza Cinematografica
   Italiana, 1935, Italian
IM SONNENSCHEIN   1936, Austrian
SCIPIO AFRICANUS   Telewide Systems,
   1937, Italian
SOLO PER TE   Itala Film, 1938, Italian
MARIONETTE   Itala Film, 1938, Italian
GIUSEPPE VERDI   Grandi Film Storici,
   1938, Italian
IL SOGNO DI BUTTERFLY   Grandi Film
   Storici, 1939, Italian
MANON LESCAUT   Grandi Film Storici,
   1939, Italian
OLTRE L'AMORE   Grandi Film Storici,
   1940, Italian
MELODIE ETERNE   ENIC, 1940, Italian
LA REGINA DI NAVARRA   Juventus Film,
   1941, Italian
PRIMO AMORE   Grandi Film Storici,
   1941, Italian
LA DUE ORFANELLE   Grandi Film Storici/
   SAFIC, 1942, Italian
ODESSA IN FIAMME   Grandi Film Storici,
   1942, Italian
TRISTI AMORI   Cines/Juventus Film,
   1943, Italian
IL CANTO DELLA VITA   Excelsa Film,
   1945, Italian
DAVANTI A LUI TREMAVA TUTTA ROMA
   Excelsa Film, 1946, Italian
BIRAGHIN   Excelsa Film, 1946, Italian
RIGOLETTO   Excelsa Film, 1946, Italian
LA SIGNORA DELLE CAMELIE   Cineopera/
   Grandi Film Storici, 1947, Italian
ADDIO MIMI'!   Cineopera, 1947, Italian
THE LOST ONE   *IL TROVATORE*   Columbia,
   1948, Italian
FAUST AND THE DEVIL   *LA LEGGENDA DI*
   FAUST   Columbia, 1948, Italian
LA FORZA DEL DESTINO   Produzioni
   Gallone/Union Film, 1949, Italian
TAXI DI NOTTE   Produzioni Gallone,
   1950, Italian
AFFAIRS OF MESSALINA   *MESSALINA*
   Columbia, 1952, Italian
SENZA VELI   Rizzoli Film/Produzioni Gallone/
   Alfram, 1953, Italian-West German
PUCCINI   Rizzoli Film, 1953, Italian
FATAL DESIRE   *CAVALLERIA RUSTICANA*
   Ultra Pictures Corporation, 1953, Italian
HOUSE OF RICORDI   Manson,
   1954, Italian-French
CASTA DIVA   Documento Film/ICS/
   Cormoran Film, 1954, Italian-French
MADAME BUTTERFLY   Italian Films Export,
   1955, Italian-Japanese
DON CAMILLO E L'ONOREVOLE PEPPONE
   Rizzoli Film, 1955, Italian
TOSCA   Casolaro-Giglio/Sol Hurok,
   1956, Italian

MICHAEL STROGOFF   Continental, 1956,
   Italian-French-West German
POLIKUSKA   Produzioni Gallone/Criterion
   Film/CCC Filmkunst, 1958,
   Italian-French-West German
CARTHAGE IN FLAMES   Columbia, 1959,
   Italian-French
DON CAMILLO MONSIGNORE MA NON
   TROPPO   Cineriz, 1961, Italian
LA MONACA DI MONZA   Globe International
   Film/Produzioni Gallone/Paris Elysee Film,
   1962, Italian-French
CARMEN DI TRASTEVERE   Globe
   International Film/Produzioni Gallone/Les
   Films Marceau Cocinor, 1962, Italian-French

ABEL GANCE

b. October 25, 1889 - Paris, France
d. 1981

LA DIGUE   1911, French
LE NEGRE BLANC   co-director with
   Jean Joulout, 1912, French
IL Y A DES PIEDS AU PLAFOND
   1912, French
LE MASQUE D'HORREUR   1912, French
UN DRAME AU CHATEAU D'ACRE
   1915, French
LA FOLIE DU DOCTEUR TUBE   1915, French
L'ENIGME DE DIX HEURES   1915, French
LA FLEUR DES RUINES   1915, French
L'HEROISME DE PADDY   1915, French
STRASS ET COMPAGNIE   1915, French
FIORITURES   1916, French
LE FOU DE LA FALAISE   1916, French
CE QUE LES FLOTS RACONTENT
   1916, French
LE PERISCOPE   1916, French
LES GAZ MORTELS   1916, French
LE DROIT A LA VIE   1916, French
BARBEROUSSE   1917, French
LA ZONE DE LA MORT   1917, French
MATER DOLOROSA   1917, French
LA DIXIEME SYMPHONIE   1918, French
J'ACCUSE   1919, French
LA ROUE   1923, French
AU SECOURS!   1923, French
NAPOLEON   Zoetrope, 1927, French
MARINES   1928, French
CRISTAUX   1928, French
LA FIN DU MONDE   1931, French
MATER DOLOROSA   1932, French
LE MAITRE DE FORGES   1933, French
POLICHE   1934, French
LA DAME AUX CAMELIAS   co-director with
   Fernand Rivers, 1934, French
LE ROMAN D'UN JEUNE HOMME PAUVRE
   1935, French
LUCRECE BORGIA   1935, French
JEROME PERREAU   *JEROME PERREAU,*
   HEROSDES BARRICADES   1936, French
UN GRAND AMOUR DE BEETHOVEN
   1936, French
LE VOLEUR DE FEMMES   1936, French
J'ACCUSE   1938, French
LOUISE   1939, French
LE PARADIS PERDU   1939, French
LA VENUS AVEUGLE   1941, French
LE CAPITAINE FRACASSE   1943, French
QUATORZE JULIET   1953, French
LA TOUR DE NESLES   *THE TOWER*
   OF LUST   1955, French
MAGIRAMA   1956, French
THE BATTLE OF AUSTERLITZ   *AUSTERLITZ*
   20th Century-Fox, 1960, French
CYRANO ET D'ARTAGNAN   1963,
   French-Italian-Spanish

TAY GARNETT
(William Taylor Garnett)
b. June 13, 1894 - Los Angeles, California
d. 1977

CELEBRITY   Pathé, 1928
THE SPIELER   Pathé, 1928
THE FLYING FOOL   Pathé, 1929
OH YEAH!   Pathé, 1929
OFFICER O'BRIEN   Pathé, 1930
HER MAN   Pathé, 1930
BAD COMPANY   Pathé, 1931
PRESTIGE   RKO, 1932
OKAY AMERICA   Universal, 1932
ONE WAY PASSAGE   Warner Bros., 1932
DESTINATION UNKNOWN   Universal, 1933
S.O.S. ICEBERG   co-director with
   Arnold Fanck, Universal, 1933,
   U.S.-German
CHINA SEAS   MGM, 1935
SHE COULDN'T TAKE IT   Columbia, 1935
PROFESSIONAL SOLDIER
   20th Century-Fox, 1936
LOVE IS NEWS   20th Century-Fox, 1937
SLAVE SHIP   20th Century-Fox, 1937
STAND-IN   Warner Bros., 1937
JOY OF LIVING   RKO Radio, 1938
TRADE WINDS   United Artists, 1939
ETERNALLY YOURS   United Artists, 1939
SLIGHTLY HONORABLE   United Artists, 1940
SEVEN SINNERS   Universal, 1940
CHEERS FOR MISS BISHOP
   United Artists, 1941
MY FAVORITE SPY   RKO Radio, 1942
BATAAN   MGM, 1943
THE CROSS OF LORRAINE   MGM, 1943
MRS. PARKINGTON   MGM, 1944
THE VALLEY OF DECISION   MGM, 1945
THE POSTMAN ALWAYS RINGS TWICE
   MGM, 1946
WILD HARVEST   Paramount, 1947
A CONNECTICUT YANKEE IN KING
   ARTHUR'S COURT   Paramount, 1949
THE FIREBALL   20th Century-Fox, 1950
CAUSE FOR ALARM   MGM, 1951
SOLDIERS THREE   MGM, 1951
ONE MINUTE TO ZERO   RKO Radio, 1952
MAIN STREET TO BROADWAY
   MGM, 1953
THE BLACK KNIGHT   Columbia,
   1954, British
SEVEN WONDERS OF THE WORLD (FD)
   co-director, Stanley Warner Cinema
   Corporation, 1956
THE NIGHT FIGHTERS   *A TERRIBLE*
   BEAUTY   United Artists, 1960, British
CATTLE KING   MGM, 1963
THE DELTA FACTOR   American
   International, 1971
THE MAD TRAPPER   Alaska Pictures, 1972
TIMBER TRAMP   Alaska Pictures, 1973

LOUIS J. GASNIER
b. September 15, 1878 - Paris, France
d. 1963

LA PREMIERE SORTIE D'UN COLEGIEN
   Pathe, 1905, French
LE PENDU   Pathe, 1906, French
LA MORT D'UN TOREADOR   Pathe,
   1907, French
TIREZ S'IL VOUS PLAIT·   Pathe,
   1908, French
MAX FAIT DU SKI   Pathe, 1910, French
THE PERILS OF PAULINE (S)
   co-director with Donald Mackenzie,
   Pathe, 1914

DETECTIVE SWIFT   co-director with
  Donald Mackenzie, Pathe, 1914
THE STOLEN BIRTHRIGHT   Pathe, 1914
THE EXPLOITS OF ELAINE (S)   co-director
  with George B. Seitz, Pathe, 1914
THE SHIELDING SHADOW (S)   co-director
  with Donald Mackenzie, Pathe, 1916
ANNABEL'S ROMANCE   Pathe, 1916
HAZEL KIRKE   Pathe, 1916
THE MYSTERY OF THE DOUBLE
  CROSS (S)   1917
THE SEVEN PEARLS (S)   1918
HANDS UP! (S)   1918
THE TIGER'S TAIL (S)   1919
THE BELOVED CHEATER   1919
THE CORSICAN BROTHERS   1920
THE BUTTERFLY MAN   1920
KISMET   1920
GOOD WOMEN   1921
A WIFE'S AWAKENING   1921
SILENT YEARS   1921
THE CALL OF HOME   1922
RICH MEN'S WIVES   1922
THORNS AND ORANGE BLOSSOMS   1922
THE HERO   1923
POOR MEN'S WIVES   1923
DAUGHTERS OF THE RICH   1923
MOTHERS-IN-LAW   1923
MAYTIME   1923
POISONED PARADISE: THE FORBIDDEN
  STORY OF MONTE CARLO   1924
THE BREATH OF SCANDAL   1924
WINE   1924
WHITE MAN   1924
THE TRIFLERS   1924
THE PARASITE   1925
THE BOOMERANG   1925
PARISIAN LOVE   1925
FAINT PERFUME   1925
PLEASURES OF THE RICH   1926
OUT OF THE STORM   1926
SIN CARGO   1926
THE MODEL FROM PARIS   1926
LOST AT SEA   1926
THE BEAUTY SHOPPERS   1927
STREETS OF SHANGHAI   1928
FASHION MADNESS   1928
DARKENED ROOMS   1929
SLIGHTLY SCARLET   co-director with
  Edwin H. Knopf, 1930
THE SHADOW OF THE LAW   1930
THE VIRTUOUS SIN   co-director with
  George Cukor, Paramount, 1930
THE LAWYER'S SECRET   co-director with
  Max Marcin, 1930
SILENCE   co-director with
  Max Marcin, 1931
THE STRANGE CASE OF CLARA DEANE
  co-director with Max Marcin, 1931
FORGOTTEN COMMANDMENTS
  co-director with William Schorr, 1932
GAMBLING SHIP   co-director with
  Max Marcin, 1933
ESPERAME   1933, Spanish
MELODIA DE ARRABAL   1933, Spanish
IRIS PERDUE ET RETROUVEE
  1933, French
TOPAZE   RKO Radio, 1933
FEDORA   1934, French
CUESTA ABAJO   1934, Spanish
EL TANGO EN BROADWAY   1934, Spanish
THE LAST OUTPOST   co-director with
  Charles Barton, 1935
THE GOLD RACKET   1937
BANK ALARM   1937
LA IMMACULADA   1939, Spanish
MURDER ON THE YUKON   1940

REEFER MADNESS   *THE BURNING
  QUESTION/TELL YOUR CHILDREN/DOPE
  ADDICT/DOPED YOUTH/LOVE MADNESS*
  Dwain Esper Productions, 1939
STOLEN PARADISE   1941
FIGHT ON MARINES!   1942

ROBERTO GAVALDON
b. June 7, 1909 - Jimenez, Mexico
d. 1990

EL CONDE DE MONTE CRISTO   Azteca
  Films, 1941, Mexican
LA BARRACA   Azteca Films, 1944, Mexican
EL SOCIO   Azteca Films, 1945, Mexican
LA VIDA INTIMA DE MARCO-ANTONIO Y
  CLEOPATRA   Azteca Films,
  1946, Mexican
LA OTRA   Azteca Films, 1946, Mexican
ADVENTURES OF CASANOVA
  Eagle Lion, 1948
LA CASA CHICA   Azteca Films,
  1949, Mexican
DESEADA   Azteca Films, 1950, Mexican
EL REBOZO DE SOLEDAD   Azteca Films,
  1953, Mexican
CAMELIA   Azteca Films, 1953, Mexican
THE LITTLEST OUTLAW
  Buena Vista, 1955
LA ESCONDIDA   Azteca Films,
  1956, Mexican
FLOR DE MAYO   Azteca Films,
  1957, Mexican
MACARIO   CLASA Films Mundiales,
  1959, Mexican
LA ROSA BLANCA   CLASA Films Mundiales,
  1972, Mexican, filmed in 1961
EL HOMBRE DE LOS HONGOS   Azteca
  Films, 1976, Mexican
LA PLAYA VACIA   Azteca Films,
  1979, Mexican

SERGEI GERASIMOV
b. May 21, 1906 - Zlatoust, Urals, Russia
d. 1985

22 MISFORTUNES   co-director with
  D. Bartenev, 1930, Soviet
THE FOREST   1931, Soviet
THE HEART OF SOLOMON   co-director with
  M. Kressin, 1932, Soviet
DO I LIOVE YOU?   1934, Soviet
THE BOLD SEVEN   1936, Soviet
CITY OF YOUTH   1938, Soviet
THE TEACHER   1939, Soviet
FIGHTING FILM ALBUM #1 (FD)   co-director,
  1941, Soviet
MASQUERADE   1941, Soviet
THE OLD GUARD   1941, Soviet
INVINCIBLE   co-director with
  Mikhail Kalatozov, 1943, Soviet
MOSCOW MUSIC HALL (PF)   co-director
  with Efim Dzigan & Mikhail Kalatozov,
  1943, Soviet
THE BIG LAND   1944, Soviet
YOUNG GUARD   1947-48, Soviet
LIBERATED CHINA (FD)   co-director,
  1950, Soviet
THE COUNTRY DOCTOR   1952, Soviet
NADEZHDA   1955, Soviet
AND QUIET FLOWS THE DON
  United Artists, 1957-58, Soviet
SPUTNIK SPEAKING   co-director,
  1959, Soviet
MEN AND BEASTS   1962,
  Soviet-East German
THE JOURNALIST   1967, Soviet

BY THE LAKE   1970, Soviet
FOR THE LOVE OF MAN   1972, Soviet
MOTHERS AND DAUGHTERS   1974, Soviet
THE RED AND THE BLACK (MS)
  1976, Soviet
PETER THE GREAT, PART I: THE YOUTH
  OF PETER   1981, Soviet
PETER THE GREAT, PART II: AT THE
  BEGINNING OF GLORIOUS DEEDS
  1981, Soviet
LEO TOLSTOY   1984, Soviet

PIETRO GERMI
b. September 14, 1914 - Colombo, Liguaria, Italy
d. 1974

IL TESTIMONE   1945, Italian
GIOVENTU PERDUTA   *LOST YOUTH*
  1947, Italian
IL NOME DELLA LEGGE   1949, Italian
IL CAMINO DELLA SPERANZA   1950, Italian
LA CITTA SI DIFENDE   *FOUR WAYS OUT*
  1951, Italian
LA PRESIDENTESSA   1952, Italian
IL BRIGANTE DI TACCA DEL LUPO
  1952, Italian
GELOSIA   1953, Italian
AMORI DI MEZZO SECOLO   co-director,
  1954, Italian
THE RAILROAD MAN   *IL FERROVIERE*
  Continental, 1956, Italian
L'UOMO DI PAGLIA   1957, Italian
THE FACTS OF MURDER
  UN MALADETTOIMBROGLIO
  Seven Arts, 1959, Italian
DIVORCE ITALIAN STYLE ★   Embassy,
  1961, Italian
SEDUCED AND ABANDONED   Continental,
  1964, Italian-French
THE BIRDS, THE BEES AND THE ITALIANS
  SIGNORE E SIGNORI   Claridge,
  1966, Italian
THE CLIMAX   *L'IMMORALE*   Lopert, 1967,
  Italian-French
SERAFINO   Royal Films International, 1968,
  Italian-French
TILL DIVORCE DO YOU PART   *LE
  CASTAGNE SONO BUONE*   1971, Italian
ALFREDO, ALFREDO   Paramount,
  1973, Italian

STEVEN GETHERS
b. June 8, 1922
d. 1989

BILLY: PORTRAIT OF A STREET KID (TF)
  Mark Carliner Productions, 1977
DAMIEN...THE LEPER PRIEST (TF)
  Tomorrow Entertainment, 1980
JACQUELINE BOUVIER KENNEDY (TF)
  ABC Circle Films, 1981
CONFESSIONS OF A MARRIED MAN (TF)
  Gloria Monty Productions/Comworld
  Productions, 1983
JENNY'S WAR (TF)   Louis Rudolph
  Productions/HTV/Columbia TV,
  1985, U.S.-British
MERCY OR MURDER? (TF)
  John J. McMahon Productions/
  MGM-UA TV, 1987
MARCUS WELBY, M.D.: A HOLIDAY
  AFFAIR (TF)   Marstar Ltd./Condor
  Productions, 1988
TWO OF A KIND: THE CASE OF THE
  HILLSIDE STRANGLER (TF)   ABC, 1989

ALAN GIBSON

b. April 28, 1938 - Canada
d. 1987

GOODBYE GEMINI   Cinerama Releasing
  Corporation, 1970, British
CRESCENDO   Warner Bros., 1972, British
DRACULA TODAY   *DRACULA A.D. 1972*
  Warner Bros., 1972, British
THE PLAYBOY OF THE WESTERN
  WORLD (TF)   BBC, 1975, British
COUNT DRACULA AND HIS VAMPIRE BRIDE
  SATANIC RITES OF DRACULA   Dynamite
  Entertainment, 1978, British
CHECKERED FLAG OR CRASH
  Universal, 1978
CHURCHILL AND THE GENERALS (TF)
  BBC/Le Vien International, 1979, British
A WOMAN CALLED GOLDA (TF)   Harve
  Bennett Productions/Paramount TV, 1982
WITNESS FOR THE PROSECUTION (TF)
  Norman Rosemont Productions/United
  Artists Productions, 1982, U.S.-British
HELEN KELLER - THE MIRACLE
  CONTINUES (TF)   Castle Combe
  Productions/20th Century-Fox TV,
  1984, U.S.-British
MARTIN'S DAY   MGM/UA, 1985, British

SIDNEY GILLIAT

b. February 15, 1908 - Edgeley, England
d. 1994

MILLIONS LIKE US   co-director with
  Frank Launder, 1943, British
WATERLOO ROAD   Eagle Lion, 1944, British
NOTORIOUS GENTLEMAN   *THE RAKE'S
  PROGRESS*   Universal, 1945, British
GREEN FOR DANGER   Eagle Lion,
  1947, British
DULCIMBER STREET   *LONDON BELONGS
  TO ME*   Universal, 1948, British
STATE SECRET   Columbia, 1950, British
GILBERT AND SULLIVAN   *THE STORY OF
  GILBERT AND SULLIVAN /THE GREAT
  GILBERT AND SULLIVAN*   United Artists,
  1953, British
THE CONSTANT HUSBAND
  Showcorporation, 1955, British
SHE PLAYED WITH FIRE   *FORTUNE IS A
  WOMAN*   Columbia, 1957, British
LEFT, RIGHT AND CENTRE   BCG Films,
  1959, British
ONLY TWO CAN PLAY   Columbia,
  1961, British
THE GREAT ST. TRINIAN'S TRAIN ROBBERY
  co-director with Frank Launder, 1966, British
ENDLESS NIGHT   British Lion, 1972, British

JOHN GILLING

b. May 29, 1910 - England
d. 1984

ESCAPE FROM BROADMOOR   1948, British
A MATTER OF MURDER   1949, British
NO TRACE   1950, British
BLACKOUT   Lippert, 1950, British
THE QUIET WOMAN   Eros Films,
  1951, British
THE FRIGHTENED MAN   1952, British
MY SON, THE VAMPIRE   *OLD MOTHER
  RILEY MEETS THE VAMPIRE/VAMPIRE
  OVER LONDON/KING ROBOT/MOTHER
  RILEY RUNS RIOT/MOTHER RILEY IN
  DRACULA'S DESIRE*   Blue Chip,
  1952, British

MURDER WILL OUT   *THE VOICE OF
  MERRILL*   Kramer Hyams, 1952, British
RECOIL   1953, British
WHITE FIRE   *THREE STEPS TO THE
  GALLOWS*   Lippert, 1953, British
ESCAPE BY NIGHT   Eros Films, 1953, British
THE DEADLY NIGHTSHADE   1953, British
DOUBLE EXPOSURE   Rank, 1954, British
THE EMBEZZLER   Rank, 1954, British
CROSS UP   *TIGER BY THE TAIL*
  United Artists, 1955, British
THE GILDED CAGE   1955, British
THE GAMMA PEOPLE   Columbia,
  1956, British
ODONGO   Columbia, 1956, British
HIGH FLIGHT   Columbia, 1957, British
PICKUP ALLEY   *INTERPOL*   Columbia,
  1957, British
THE MAN INSIDE   Columbia, 1958, British
THE BANDIT OF ZHOBE   Columbia,
  1959, British
IDLE ON PARADE   1959, Columbia
MANIA   *THE FLESH AND THE FIENDS/THE
  FIENDISH GHOULS*   Valiant, 1960, British
IT TAKES A THIEF   *THE CHALLENGE*
  Valiant, 1960, British
FURY AT SMUGGLER'S BAY   Embassy,
  1961, British
SHADOW OF THE CAT   Universal,
  1961, British
THE PIRATES OF BLOOD RIVER   Columbia,
  1962, British
THE CRIMSON BLADE   *THE SCARLET
  BLADE*   Columbia, 1963, British
PANIC   Columbia, 1965, British
THE BRIGAND OF KANDAHAR   Columbia,
  1965, British
THE PLAGUE OF THE ZOMBIES
  20th Century-Fox, 1966, British
THE REPTILE   20th Century-Fox,
  1966, British
WHERE THE BULLETS FLY   Embassy,
  1966, British
BLOOD BEAST FROM OUTER SPACE
  THE NIGHT CALLER   World Entertainment,
  1966, British
THE MUMMY'S SHROUD   20th Century-Fox,
  1967, British
LA CRUZ DEL DIABLO   1974, Spanish

MICHAEL GORDON

b. September 6, 1909 - Baltimore, Maryland
d. 1993

BOSTON BLACKIE GOES HOLLYWOOD
  Columbia, 1942
UNDERGROUND AGENT   Columbia, 1942
ONE DANGEROUS NIGHT   Columbia, 1943
CRIME DOCTOR   Columbia, 1943
THE WEB   Universal, 1947
ANOTHER PART OF THE FOREST
  Universal, 1948
AN ACT OF MURDER   Universal, 1948
THE LADY GAMBLES   Universal, 1949
WOMAN IN HIDING   Universal, 1950
CYRANO DE BERGERAC
  United Artists, 1950
I CAN GET IT FOR YOU WHOLESALE
  20th Century-Fox, 1951
THE SECRET OF CONVICT LAKE
  20th Century-Fox, 1951
WHEREVER SHE GOES   Mayer-Kingsley,
  1953, Australian
PILLOW TALK   Universal, 1959
PORTRAIT IN BLACK   Universal, 1960
BOYS' NIGHT OUT   MGM, 1962
FOR LOVE OR MONEY   Universal, 1963

MOVE OVER, DARLING
  20th Century-Fox, 1963
A VERY SPECIAL FAVOR   Universal, 1965
TEXAS ACROSS THE RIVER
  Universal, 1966
THE IMPOSSIBLE YEARS   MGM, 1968
HOW DO I LOVE THEE?   Cinerama Releasing
  Corporation, 1970

HIDEO GOSHA

b. 1929 - Tokyo, Japan
d. 1992

THREE OUTLAW SAMURAIS   Shochiku/
  Samurai Productions, 1964, Japanese
SWORD OF THE BEAST   Hayuza,
  1965, Japanese
SAZEN TANGE   Toei, 1966, Japanese
GOYOKIN   Fuji TV/Tokyo Eiga,
  1969, Japanese
KILLING PEOPLE   Fuji TV/Katsu Productions,
  1969, Japanese
THE WOLVES   Tokyo Eiga, 1971, Japanese
VIOLENT CITY   Toei, 1974, Japanese
NIZAIMON KUMOKIRI   Shochiku/Hayuza
  Eiga Hoso, 1978, Japanese
HUNTER IN THE DARK   Shochiku/Hayuza
  Eiga Hoso, 1979, Japanese
ONIMASA   *THE LIFE OF HANAKO KIRYUIN*
  Toei/Hayuza Eiga Hoso, 1982, Japanese
YOKIRO   Toei/Hayuza Eiga Hoso,
  1983, Japanese
FIREFLIES OF THE NORTH   Toei/Hayuza
  Eiga Hoso, 1984, Japanese
USUGESHO   Shochiku/Gosha Productions/
  Eizo Kyoto, 1985, Japanese
ROW   Toei, 1985, Japanese
YAKUZA WIVES   Toei, 1986, Japanese
JUTEMAI   Shochiku/Gosha Productions/
  Eizo Kyoto, 1986, Japanese
YOSHIWARA IN FLAMES   *TOKYO
  BORDELLO*   Toei, 1987, Japanese
THE GATES OF FLESH   Toei,
  1988, Japanese
THE FOUR DAYS OF SNOW AND BLOOD
  226   Future Film Enterprise,
  1989, Japanese
KAGERO   Shochiku/Daichi Kogyo/Bandai,
  1991, Japanese
THE OIL-HELL MURDER   Shochiku/Fuji TV/
  Kyoto Eiga, 1992, Japanese

EDMUND GOULDING

b. March 20, 1891 - London, England
d. 1959

SUN-UP   MGM, 1925
SALLY, IRENE AND MARY   MGM, 1925
PARIS   MGM, 1926
WOMEN LOVE DIAMONDS   MGM, 1927
LOVE   MGM, 1927
THE TRESPASSER   United Artists, 1929
PARAMOUNT ON PARADE   co-director,
  Paramount, 1930
THE DEVIL'S HOLIDAY   Paramount, 1930
REACHING FOR THE MOON
  United Artists, 1931
THE NIGHT ANGEL   Paramount, 1931
GRAND HOTEL   MGM, 1932
BLONDIE OF THE FOLLIES   MGM, 1932
RIPTIDE   MGM, 1934
THE FLAME WITHIN   MGM, 1935
THAT CERTAIN WOMAN   Warner Bros., 1937
WHITE BANNERS   Warner Bros., 1938
THE DAWN PATROL   Warner Bros., 1938
DARK VICTORY   Warner Bros., 1939
THE OLD MAID   Warner Bros., 1939

WE ARE NOT ALONE   Warner Bros., 1939
'TIL WE MEET AGAIN   Warner Bros., 1940
THE GREAT LIE   Warner Bros., 1941
FOREVER AND A DAY   co-director,
  RKO Radio, 1943
THE CONSTANT NYMPH
  Warner Bros., 1943
CLAUDIA   20th Century-Fox, 1943
OF HUMAN BONDAGE   Warner Bros., 1946
THE RAZOR'S EDGE
  20th Century-Fox, 1946
NIGHTMARE ALLEY   20th Century-Fox, 1947
EVERYBODY DOES IT
  20th Century-Fox, 1949
MISTER 880   20th Century-Fox, 1950
WE'RE NOT MARRIED!
  20th Century-Fox, 1952
DOWN AMONG THE SHELTERING PALMS
  20th Century-Fox, 1953
TEENAGE REBEL   20th Century-Fox, 1956
MARDI GRAS   20th Century-Fox, 1958

ALFRED E. GREEN
b. 1889 - Ferris, California
d. 1960

LOST AND FOUND   Selig, 1917
THE PRINCESS OF PATCHES   Selig, 1917
LITTLE LOST SISTER   Selig, 1917
THE LAD AND THE LION   Selig, 1917
THE WEB OF CHANCE   Fox, 1919
THE DOUBLE-DYED DECEIVER
  Goldwyn, 1920
SILK HUSBANDS AND CALICO WIVES
  Equity, 1920
JUST OUT OF COLLEGE   Goldwyn, 1921
THE MAN WHO HAD EVERYTHING
  Goldwyn, 1921
THROUGH THE BACK DOOR   co-director
  with Jack Pickford, United Artists, 1921
LITTLE LORD FAUNTLEROY   co-director
  with Jack Pickford, United Artists, 1921
COME ON OVER   Goldwyn, 1922
OUR LEADING CITIZEN   Paramount, 1922
THE BACHELOR DADDY   Paramount, 1922
THE GHOST BREAKER   Paramount, 1922
THE MAN WHO SAW TOMORROW
  Paramount, 1922
BACK HOME AND BROKE   Paramount, 1922
THE NE'ER-DO-WELL   Paramount, 1923
WOMAN PROOF   Paramount, 1923
PIED PIPER MALONE   Paramount, 1924
IN HOLLYWOOD WITH POTASH AND
  PERLMUTTER   First National, 1924
INEZ FROM HOLLYWOOD   First
  National, 1924
SALLY   First National, 1925
THE TALKER   1925
THE MAN WHO FOUND HIMSELF
  Paramount, 1925
IRENE   First National, 1926
ELLA CINDERS   First National, 1926
IT MUST BE LOVE   First National, 1926
LADIES AT PLAY   First National, 1926
THE GIRL FROM MONTMARTRE
  First National, 1926
IS ZAT SO?   Fox, 1927
THE AUCTIONEER   Fox, 1927
TWO GIRLS WANTED   Fox, 1927
COME TO MY HOUSE   Fox, 1927
HONOR BOUND   Fox, 1928
MAKING THE GRADE   Fox, 1929
DISRAELI   Warner Bros., 1929
THE GREEN GODDESS   Warner Bros., 1930
THE MAN FROM BLANKLEY'S
  Warner Bros., 1930
OLD ENGLISH   Warner Bros., 1930

SWEET KITTY BELLAIRS
  Warner Bros., 1930
SMART MONEY   Warner Bros., 1931
MEN OF THE SKY   Warner Bros., 1931
THE ROAD TO SINGAPORE
  Warner Bros., 1931
UNION DEPOT   Warner Bros., 1932
IT'S TOUGH TO BE FAMOUS
  Warner Bros., 1932
THE RICH ARE ALWAYS WITH US
  Warner Bros., 1932
THE DARK HORSE   Warner Bros., 1932
SILVER DOLLAR   Warner Bros., 1932
PARACHUTE JUMPER   Warner Bros., 1933
BABY FACE   Warner Bros., 1933
THE NARROW CORNER   Warner Bros., 1933
I LOVED A WOMAN   Warner Bros., 1933
DARK HAZARD   Warner Bros., 1934
AS THE EARTH TURNS   Warner Bros., 1934
THE MERRY FRINKS   Warner Bros., 1934
HOUSEWIFE   Warner Bros., 1934
SIDE STREETS   Warner Bros., 1934
A LOST LADY   Warner Bros., 1934
GENTLEMAN ARE BORN
  Warner Bros., 1934
SWEET MUSIC   Warner Bros., 1935
THE GIRL FROM 10TH AVENUE
  Warner Bros., 1935
THE GOOSE AND THE GANDER
  Warner Bros., 1935
HERE'S TO ROMANCE   Warner Bros., 1935
DANGEROUS   Warner Bros., 1935
COLLEEN   Warner Bros., 1936
THE GOLDEN ARROW   First National, 1936
THEY MET IN A TAXI   Columbia, 1936
TWO IN A CROWD   Universal, 1936
MORE THAN A SECRETARY   Columbia, 1936
LET'S GET MARRIED   Columbia, 1937
THE LEAGUE OF FRIGHTENED MEN
  Columbia, 1937
MR. DODD TAKES THE AIR
  Warner Bros., 1937
THOROUGHBREDS DON'T CRY
  MGM, 1937
THE DUKE OF WEST POINT
  United Artists, 1938
RIDE A CROOKED MILE   Paramount, 1938
KING OF THE TURF   United Artists, 1939
THE GRACIE ALLEN MURDER CASE
  Paramount, 1939
20,000 MEN A YEAR   1939
SHOOTING HIGH   20th Century-Fox, 1940
SOUTH OF PAGO-PAGO   United Artists, 1940
FLOWING GOLD   Warner Bros., 1940
EAST OF THE RIVER   Warner Bros., 1940
ADVENTURE IN WASHINGTON
  Columbia, 1941
BADLANDS OF DAKOTA   Universal, 1941
THE MAYOR OF 44TH STREET
  RKO Radio, 1942
MEET THE STEWARTS   Columbia, 1942
APPOINTMENT IN BERLIN   Columbia, 1943
THERE'S SOMETHING ABOUT A SOLDIER
  Columbia, 1943
MR. WINKLE GOES TO WAR
  Columbia, 1944
STRANGE AFFAIR   Columbia, 1944
A THOUSAND AND ONE NIGHTS
  Columbia, 1945
TARS AND SPARS   Columbia, 1946
THE JOLSON STORY   Columbia, 1946
THE FABULOUS DORSEYS
  United Artists, 1947
COPACABANA   United Artists, 1947
FOUR FACES WEST   United Artists, 1948
THE GIRL FROM MANHATTAN
  United Artists, 1948
COVER-UP   United Artists, 1949

THE JACKIE ROBINSON STORY
  Eagle Lion, 1950
SIERRA   Universal, 1950
TWO GALS AND A GUY   United Artists, 1951
INVASION, U.S.A.   Columbia, 1953
PARIS MODEL   Columbia, 1953
THE EDDIE CANTOR STORY
  Warner Bros., 1954
TOP BANANA   United Artists, 1954

TOM GRIES
(Thomas S. Gries)
b. December 20, 1922 - Chicago, Illinois
d. 1977

WILL PENNY   Paramount, 1968
100 RIFLES   20th Century-Fox, 1969
NUMBER ONE   United Artists, 1969
THE HAWAIIANS   United Artists, 1970
FOOLS   Cinerama Releasing
  Corporation, 1970
EARTH II (TF)   MGM TV, 1971
JOURNEY THROUGH ROSEBUD   GSF, 1972
TRUMAN CAPOTE'S THE GLASS HOUSE
  THE GLASS HOUSE (TF) ☆☆   Tomorrow
  Entertainment, 1972
LADY ICE   National General, 1973
A CALL TO DANGER (TF)
  Paramount TV, 1973
THE CONNECTION (TF)   D'Antoni
  Productions, 1973
THE MIGRANTS (TF) ☆   CBS, Inc., 1974
QB VII (MS) ☆   Screen Gems/Columbia TV/
  The Douglas Cramer Company, 1974
THE HEALERS (TF)   Warner Bros. TV, 1974
BREAKOUT   Columbia, 1975
BREAKHEART PASS   United Artists, 1976
HELTER SKELTER (TF) ☆   Lorimar
  Productions, 1976
THE GREATEST   Columbia, 1977

D. W. GRIFFITH
(David (Lewelyn) Wark Griffith)
b. January 22, 1875 - La Grange, Kentucky
d. 1948

THE ADVENTURES OF DOLLIE
  Biograph, 1908
THE FIGHT FOR FREEDOM   Biograph, 1908
THE REDMAN AND THE CHILD
  Biograph, 1908
THE BANDIT'S WATERLOO   Biograph, 1908
A CALAMITOUS ELEPHANT   Biograph, 1908
THE GREASER'S GAUNTLET
  Biograph, 1908
THE FATAL HOUR   Biograph, 1908
FOR LOVE OF GOLD   Biograph, 1908
BALKED AT THE ALTAR   Biograph, 1908
FOR A WIFE'S HONOR   Biograph, 1908
BETRAYED BY A HANDPRINT
  Biograph, 1908
THE GIRL AND THE OUTLAW
  Biograph, 1908
BEHIND THE SCENES: WHERE ALL IS NOT
  GOLD THAT GLITTERS   Biograph, 1908
THE RED GIRL   Biograph, 1908
THE HEART OF O YAMA   Biograph, 1908
WHERE THE BREAKERS ROAR
  Biograph, 1908
A SMOKED HUSBAND   Biograph, 1908
THE STOLEN JEWELS   Biograph, 1908
THE DEVIL   Biograph, 1908
THE ZULU'S HEART   Biograph, 1908
FATHER GETS IN THE GAME
  Biograph, 1908
THE BARBARIAN INGOMAR   Biograph, 1908
THE VAQUERO'S VOW   Biograph, 1908

D. W. GRIFFITH (continued)

THE PLANTER'S WIFE   Biograph, 1908
THE ROMANCE OF A JEWESS
   Biograph, 1908
THE CALL OF THE WILD   Biograph, 1908
CONCEALING A BURGLAR   Biograph, 1908
AFTER MANY YEARS   Biograph, 1908
THE PIRATE'S GOLD   Biograph, 1908
THE TAMING OF THE SHREW
   Biograph, 1908
THE GUERILLA   Biograph, 1908
THE SONG OF THE SHIRT   Biograph, 1908
THE INGRATE   Biograph, 1908
A WOMAN'S WAY   Biograph, 1908
THE CLUBMAN AND THE TRAMP
   Biograph, 1908
THE VALET'S WIFE   Biograph, 1908
MONEY MAD   Biograph, 1908
THE FEUD AND THE TURKEY
   Biograph, 1908
THE RECKONING   Biograph, 1908
THE TEST OF FRIENDSHIP   Biograph, 1908
AN AWFUL MOMENT   Biograph, 1908
THE CHRISTMAS BURGLARS
   Biograph, 1908
MR. JONES AT THE BALL   Biograph, 1908
THE HELPING HAND   Biograph, 1908
ONE TOUCH OF NATURE   Biograph, 1909
THE MANIAC COOK   Biograph, 1909
MRS. JONES ENTERTAINS   Biograph, 1909
THE HONOR OF THIEVES   Biograph, 1909
LOVE FINDS A WAY   Biograph, 1909
A RURAL ELOPEMENT   Biograph, 1909
THE SACRIFICE   Biograph, 1909
THE CRIMINAL HYPNOTIST   Biograph, 1909
THOSE BOYS!   Biograph, 1909
MR. JONES HAS A CARD PARTY
   Biograph, 1909
THE FASCINATING MRS. FRANCIS
   Biograph, 1909
THE WELCOME BURGLAR   Biograph, 1909
THOSE AWFUL HATS   Biograph, 1909
THE CORD OF LIFE   Biograph, 1909
THE GIRLS AND DADDY   Biograph, 1909
THE BRAHMA DIAMOND   Biograph, 1909
A WREATH IN TIME   Biograph, 1909
EDGAR ALLAN POE   Biograph, 1909
TRAGIC LOVE   Biograph, 1909
THE CURTAIN POLE   Biograph, 1909
HIS WARD'S LOVE   Biograph, 1909
THE HINDOO DAGGER   Biograph, 1909
THE JONESES HAVE AMATEUR
   THEATRICALS   Biograph, 1909
THE POLITICIAN'S LOVE STORY
   Biograph, 1909
THE GOLDEN LOUIS   Biograph, 1909
AT THE ALTAR   Biograph, 1909
HIS WIFE'S MOTHER   Biograph, 1909
THE PRUSSIAN SPY   Biograph, 1909
A FOOL'S REVENGE   Biograph, 1909
THE ROUE'S HEART   Biograph, 1909
THE WOODEN LEG   Biograph, 1909
THE SALVATION ARMY LASS
   Biograph, 1909
THE LURE OF THE GOWN   Biograph, 1909
I DID IT MAMA   Biograph, 1909
THE VOICE OF THE VIOLIN   Biograph, 1909
THE DECEPTION   Biograph, 1909
AND A LITTLE CHILD SHALL LEAD THEM
   Biograph, 1909
A BURGLAR'S MISTAKE   Biograph, 1909
THE MEDICINE BOTTLE   Biograph, 1909
JONES AND HIS NEW NEIGHBORS
   Biograph, 1909
A DRUNKARD'S REFORMATION
   Biograph, 1909
THE ROAD TO THE HEART   Biograph, 1909

TRYING TO GET ARRESTED   Biograph, 1909
A RUDE HOSTESS   Biograph, 1909
SCHNEIDER'S ANTI-NOISE CRUSADE
   Biograph, 1909
THE WINNING COAT   Biograph, 1909
A SOUND SLEEPER   Biograph, 1909
CONFIDENCE   Biograph, 1909
LADY HELEN'S ESCAPADE   Biograph, 1909
A TROUBLESOME SATCHEL
   Biograph, 1909
THE DRIVE FOR A LIFE   Biograph, 1909
LUCKY JIM   Biograph, 1909
TWIN BROTHERS   Biograph, 1909
'TIS AN ILL WIND THAT BLOWS NO GOOD
   Biograph, 1909
THE EAVESDROPPER   Biograph, 1909
THE SUICIDE CLUB   Biograph, 1909
THE NOTE IN THE SHOE   Biograph, 1909
ONE BUSY HOUR   Biograph, 1909
JONES AND THE LADY BOOK AGENT
   Biograph, 1909
THE FRENCH DUEL   Biograph, 1909
A BABY'S SHOE   Biograph, 1909
THE JILT   Biograph, 1909
RESURRECTION   Biograph, 1909
ELOPING WITH AUNTY   Biograph, 1909
TWO MEMORIES   Biograph, 1909
THE CRICKET ON THE HEARTH
   Biograph, 1909
ERADICATING AUNTY   Biograph, 1909
HIS DUTY   co-director with Frank Powell,
   Biograph, 1909
WHAT DRINK DID   Biograph, 1909
THE VIOLIN MAKER OF CREMONA
   Biograph, 1909
THE LONELY VILLA   Biograph, 1909
A NEW TRICK   Biograph, 1909
THE SON'S RETURN   Biograph, 1909
HER FIRST BISCUITS   Biograph, 1909
THE FADED LILIES   Biograph, 1909
WAS JUSTICE SERVED?   Biograph, 1909
THE PEACHBASKET HAT   Biograph, 1909
THE MEXICAN SWEETHEARTS
   Biograph, 1909
THE WAY OF MAN   Biograph, 1909
THE NECKLACE   Biograph, 1909
THE MESSAGE   Biograph, 1909
THE COUNTRY DOCTOR   Biograph, 1909
THE CARDINAL'S CONSPIRACY   co-director
   with Frank Powell, Biograph, 1909
THE FRIEND OF THE FAMILY
   Biograph, 1909
TENDER HEARTS   Biograph, 1909
THE RENUNCIATION   Biograph, 1909
SWEET AND TWENTY   Biograph, 1909
JEALOUSY AND THE MAN   Biograph, 1909
A CONVICT'S SACRIFICE   Biograph, 1909
THE SLAVE   Biograph, 1909
A STRANGE MEETING   Biograph, 1909
THE MENDED LUTE   Biograph, 1909
THEY WOULD ELOPE   Biograph, 1909
JONES' BURGLAR   Biograph, 1909
THE BETTER WAY   Biograph, 1909
WITH HER CARD   Biograph, 1909
HIS WIFE'S VISITOR   Biograph, 1909
MRS. JONES' LOVER   *I WANT MY HAT*
   Biograph, 1909
THE INDIAN RUNNER'S ROMANCE
   Biograph, 1909
OH UNCLE!   Biograph, 1909
THE SEVENTH DAY   Biograph, 1909
THE MILLS OF THE GODS   Biograph, 1909
THE LITTLE DARLING   Biograph, 1909
THE SEALED ROOM   Biograph, 1909
1776   *THE HESSIAN RENEGADES*
   Biograph, 1909
COMATA THE SIOUX   Biograph, 1909
THE CHILDREN'S FRIEND   Biograph, 1909

GETTING EVEN   Biograph, 1909
THE BROKEN LOCKET   Biograph, 1909
IN OLD KENTUCKY   Biograph, 1909
A FAIR EXCHANGE   Biograph, 1909
LEATHER STOCKING   Biograph, 1909
THE AWAKENING   Biograph, 1909
WANTED - A CHILD   Biograph, 1909
PIPPA PASSES   *THE SONG OF
   CONSCIENCE*   Biograph, 1909
FOOLS OF FATE   Biograph, 1909
THE LITTLE TEACHER   Biograph, 1909
A CHANGE OF HEART   Biograph, 1909
HIS LOST LOVE   Biograph, 1909
THE EXPIATION   Biograph, 1909
IN THE WATCHES OF THE NIGHT
   Biograph, 1909
LINES OF WHITE ON A SULLEN SEA
   Biograph, 1909
THE GIBSON GODDESS   Biograph, 1909
WHAT'S YOUR HURRY?   Biograph, 1909
NURSING A VIPER   Biograph, 1909
THE RESTORATION   Biograph, 1909
THE LIGHT THAT CAME   Biograph, 1909
TWO WOMEN AND A MAN   Biograph, 1909
A MIDNIGHT ADVENTURE   Biograph, 1909
SWEET REVENGE   Biograph, 1909
THE OPEN GATE   Biograph, 1909
THE MOUNTAINEER'S HONOR
   Biograph, 1909
THE TRICK THAT FAILED   Biograph, 1909
IN THE WINDOW RECESS   Biograph, 1909
THE DEATH DISC   Biograph, 1909
THROUGH THE BREAKERS   Biograph, 1909
THE REDMAN'S VIEW   Biograph, 1909
A CORNER IN WHEAT   Biograph, 1909
IN A HEMPEN BAG   Biograph, 1909
THE TEST   Biograph, 1909
A TRAP FOR SANTA CLAUS   Biograph, 1909
IN LITTLE ITALY   Biograph, 1909
TO SAVE HER SOUL   Biograph, 1909
CHOOSING HER HUSBAND   Biograph, 1909
THE ROCKY ROAD   Biograph, 1910
THE DANCING GIRL OF BUTTE
   Biograph, 1910
HER TERRIBLE ORDEAL   Biograph, 1910
ON THE REEF   Biograph, 1910
THE CALL   Biograph, 1910
THE HONOR OF HIS FAMILY   Biograph, 1910
THE LAST DEAL   Biograph, 1910
THE CLOISTER'S TOUCH   Biograph, 1910
THE WOMAN FROM MELLON'S
   Biograph, 1910
THE COURSE OF TRUE LOVE
   Biograph, 1910
THE DUKE'S PLAN   Biograph, 1910
ONE NIGHT AND THEN   Biograph, 1910
THE ENGLISHMAN AND THE GIRL
   Biograph, 1910
HIS LAST BURGLARY   Biograph, 1910
TAMING A HUSBAND   Biograph, 1910
THE FINAL SETTLEMENT   Biograph, 1910
THE NEWLYWEDS   Biograph, 1910
THE THREAD OF DESTINY   Biograph, 1910
IN OLD CALIFORNIA   Biograph, 1910
THE CONVERTS   Biograph, 1910
THE MAN   Biograph, 1910
FAITHFUL   Biograph, 1910
THE TWISTED TRAIL   Biograph, 1910
GOLD IS NOT ALL   Biograph, 1910
AS IT IS IN LIFE   Biograph, 1910
A RICH REVENGE   Biograph, 1910
A ROMANCE OF THE WESTERN HILLS
   Biograph, 1910
THOU SHALT NOT   Biograph, 1910
THE WAY OF THE WORLD   Biograph, 1910
THE GOLD-SEEKERS   Biograph, 1910
THE UNCHANGING SEA   Biograph, 1910
LOVE AMONG THE ROSES   Biograph, 1910

OVER SILENT PATHS   Biograph, 1910
AN AFFAIR OF HEARTS   Biograph, 1910
RAMONA   Biograph, 1910
THE IMPALEMENT   Biograph, 1910
IN THE SEASON OF BUDS   Biograph, 1910
A CHILD OF THE GHETTO   Biograph, 1910
A VICTIM OF JEALOUSY   Biograph, 1910
IN THE BORDER STATES   Biograph, 1910
THE FACE AT THE WINDOW   Biograph, 1910
THE MARKED TIME-TABLE   Biograph, 1910
A CHILD'S IMPULSE   Biograph, 1910
MUGGSY'S FIRST SWEETHEART
   Biograph, 1910
THE PURGATION   Biograph, 1910
A MIDNIGHT CUPID   Biograph, 1910
WHAT THE DAISY SAID   Biograph, 1910
A CHILD'S FAITH   Biograph, 1910
A FLASH OF LIGHT   Biograph, 1910
AS THE BELLS RANG OUT   Biograph, 1910
SERIOUS SIXTEEN   Biograph, 1910
THE CALL TO ARMS   Biograph, 1910
UNEXPECTED HELP   Biograph, 1910
AN ARCADIAN MAID   Biograph, 1910
HER FATHER'S PRIDE   Biograph, 1910
THE HOUSE WITH CLOSED SHUTTERS
   Biograph, 1910
A SALUTARY LESSON   Biograph, 1910
THE USURER   Biograph, 1910
THE SORROWS OF THE UNFAITHFUL
   Biograph, 1910
WILFUL PEGGY   Biograph, 1910
THE MODERN PRODIGAL   Biograph, 1910
A SUMMER IDYLL   Biograph, 1910
LITTLE ANGELS OF LUCK   Biograph, 1910
A MOHAWK'S WAY   Biograph, 1910
IN LIFE'S CYCLE   Biograph, 1910
THE OATH AND THE MAN   Biograph, 1910
ROSE O'SALEM-TOWN   Biograph, 1910
EXAMINATION DAY AT SCHOOL
   Biograph, 1910
THE ICONOCLAST   Biograph, 1910
THE CHINK AT GOLDEN GULCH
   Biograph, 1910
THE BROKEN DOLL   Biograph, 1910
THE MESSAGE OF THE VIOLIN
   Biograph, 1910
TWO LITTLE WAIFS: A MODERN
   FAIRY TALE   Biograph, 1910
WAITER NO. 5   Biograph, 1910
THE FUGITIVE   Biograph, 1910
SIMPLE CHARITY   Biograph, 1910
THE SONG OF THE WILDWOOD FLUTE
   Biograph, 1910
A PLAIN SONG   Biograph, 1910
EFFECTING A CURE   Biograph, 1910
A CHILD'S STRATEGEM   Biograph, 1910
THE GOLDEN SUPPER   Biograph, 1910
THE LESSON   Biograph, 1910
WINNING BACK HIS LOVE   Biograph, 1910
THE TWO PATHS   Biograph, 1911
WHEN A MAN LOVES   Biograph, 1911
THE ITALIAN BARBER   Biograph, 1911
HIS TRUST   Biograph, 1911
HIS TRUST FULFILLED   Biograph, 1911
FATE'S TURNING   Biograph, 1911
THREE SISTERS   Biograph, 1911
HEART BEATS OF LONG AGO
   Biograph, 1911
WHAT SHALL WE DO WITH OUR OLD
   Biograph, 1911
FISHER FOLKS   Biograph, 1911
THE DIAMOND STAR   Biograph, 1911
HIS DAUGHTER   Biograph, 1911
THE LILY OF THE TENEMENTS
   Biograph, 1911
THE HEART OF A SAVAGE   Biograph, 1911
A DECREE OF DESTINY   Biograph, 1911
CONSCIENCE   Biograph, 1911
WAS HE A COWARD?   Biograph, 1911

THE LONEDALE OPERATOR   Biograph, 1911
THE SPANISH GYPSY   Biograph, 1911
THE BROKEN CROSS   Biograph, 1911
THE CHIEF'S DAUGHTER   Biograph, 1911
MADAME REX   Biograph, 1911
A KNIGHT OF THE ROAD   Biograph, 1911
HIS MOTHER'S SCARF   Biograph, 1911
HOW SHE TRIUMPHED   Biograph, 1911
THE TWO SIDES   Biograph, 1911
IN THE DAYS OF '49   Biograph, 1911
THE NEW DRESS   Biograph, 1911
THE WHITE ROSE OF THE WILDS
   Biograph, 1911
A ROMANY TRAGEDY   Biograph, 1911
A SMILE OF A CHILD   Biograph, 1911
ENOCH ARDEN PART I   Biograph, 1911
ENOCH ARDEN PART II   Biograph, 1911
THE PRIMAL CALL   Biograph, 1911
FIGHTING BLOOD   Biograph, 1911
THE THIEF AND THE GIRL   Biograph, 1911
BOBBY THE COWARD   Biograph, 1911
THE INDIAN BROTHERS   Biograph, 1911
THE LAST DROP OF WATER
   Biograph, 1911
OUT FROM THE SHADOW   Biograph, 1911
THE RULING PASSION   Biograph, 1911
THE SORROWFUL EXAMPLE
   Biograph, 1911
THE BLIND PRINCESS AND THE POET
   Biograph, 1911
THE ROSE OF KENTUCKY   Biograph, 1911
SWORDS AND HEARTS   Biograph, 1911
THE SQUAW'S LOVE   Biograph, 1911
DAN THE DANDY   Biograph, 1911
THE REVENUE MAN AND THE GIRL
   Biograph, 1911
HER AWAKENING   Biograph, 1911
THE MAKING OF A MAN   Biograph, 1911
ITALIAN BLOOD   Biograph, 1911
THE UNVEILING   Biograph, 1911
THE ADVENTURES OF BILLY
   Biograph, 1911
THE LONG ROAD   Biograph, 1911
LOVE IN THE HILLS   Biograph, 1911
THE BATTLE   Biograph, 1911
THE TRAIL OF BOOKS   Biograph, 1911
THROUGH DARKENED VALES
   Biograph, 1911
THE MISER'S HEART   Biograph, 1911
SUNSHINE THROUGH THE DARK
   Biograph, 1911
A WOMAN SCORNED   Biograph, 1911
THE FAILURE   Biograph, 1911
SAVED FROM HIMSELF   Biograph, 1911
AS IN A LOOKING GLASS   Biograph, 1911
A TERRIBLE DISCOVERY   Biograph, 1911
THE VOICE OF A CHILD   Biograph, 1911
A TALE OF THE WILDERNESS
   Biograph, 1912
THE ETERNAL MOTHER   Biograph, 1912
THE OLD BOOKKEEPER   Biograph, 1912
FOR HIS SON   Biograph, 1912
A BLOT IN THE 'SCUTCHEON
   Biograph, 1912
THE TRANSFORMATION OF MIKE
   Biograph, 1912
BILLY'S STRATAGEM   Biograph, 1912
THE MENDER OF NETS   Biograph, 1912
UNDER BURNING SKIES   Biograph, 1912
THE SUNBEAM   Biograph, 1912
A SIREN OF IMPULSE   Biograph, 1912
A STRING OF PEARLS   Biograph, 1912
IOLA'S PROMISE   Biograph, 1912
THE ROOT OF EVIL   Biograph, 1912
THE GODDESS OF SAGEBRUSH GULCH
   Biograph, 1912
THE GIRL AND HER TRUST   Biograph, 1912
THE PUNISHMENT   Biograph, 1912
FATE'S INTERCEPTION   Biograph, 1912

THE FEMALE OF THE SPECIES
   Biograph, 1912
JUST LIKE A WOMAN   Biograph, 1912
ONE IS BUSINESS, THE OTHER CRIME
   Biograph, 1912
THE LESSER EVIL   Biograph, 1912
THE OLD ACTOR   Biograph, 1912
A LODGING FOR THE NIGHT
   Biograph, 1912
HIS LESSON   Biograph, 1912
WHEN KINGS WERE THE LAW
   Biograph, 1912
A BEAST AT BAY   Biograph, 1912
AN OUTCAST AMONG THE OUTCASTS
   Biograph, 1912
HOME FOLKS   Biograph, 1912
A TEMPORARY TRUCE   Biograph, 1912
LENA AND THE GEESE   Biograph, 1912
THE SPIRIT AWAKENED   Biograph, 1912
THE SCHOOL TEACHER AND THE WAIF
   Biograph, 1912
MAN'S LUST FOR GOLD   Biograph, 1912
A MAN'S GENESIS   Biograph, 1912
THE SANDS OF DEE   Biograph, 1912
THE BLACK SHEEP   Biograph, 1912
THE NARROW ROAD   Biograph, 1912
A CHILD'S REMORSE   Biograph, 1912
THE INNER CIRCLE   Biograph, 1912
A CHANGE OF SPIRIT   Biograph, 1912
A PUEBLO LEGEND   Biograph, 1912
AN UNSEEN ENEMY   Biograph, 1912
TWO DAUGHTERS OF EVE   Biograph, 1912
FRIENDS   Biograph, 1912
SO NEAR, YET SO FAR   Biograph, 1912
A FEUD IN THE KENTUCKY HILLS
   Biograph, 1912
IN THE AISLES OF THE WILD
   Biograph, 1912
THE ONE SHE LOVED   Biograph, 1912
THE PAINTED LADY   Biograph, 1912
THE MUSKETEERS OF PIG ALLEY
   Biograph, 1912
HEREDITY   Biograph, 1912
THE INFORMER   Biograph, 1912
BRUTALITY   Biograph, 1912
THE NEW YORK HAT   Biograph, 1912
THE BURGLAR'S DILEMMA   Biograph, 1912
A CRY FOR HELP   Biograph, 1912
THE GOD WITHIN   Biograph, 1912
THREE FRIENDS   Biograph, 1913
THE TELEPHONE GIRL AND THE LADY
   Biograph, 1913
AN ADVENTURE IN THE AUTUMN WOODS
   Biograph, 1913
OIL AND WATER   Biograph, 1913
BROKEN WAYS   Biograph, 1913
THE UNWELCOME GUEST   Biograph, 1913
FATE   co-director with Frank Powell,
   Biograph, 1913
THE SHERIFF'S BABY   Biograph, 1913
THE LITTLE TEASE   Biograph, 1913
A MISUNDERSTOOD BOY   Biograph, 1913
THE LADY AND THE MOUSE
   Biograph, 1913
THE YAQUI CUR   Biograph, 1913
JUST GOLD   Biograph, 1913
HIS MOTHER'S SON   Biograph, 1913
DEATH'S MARATHON   Biograph, 1913
THE MOTHERING HEART   Biograph, 1913
THE MISTAKE   Biograph, 1913
THE REFORMERS OR THE LOST ART OF
   MINDING ONE'S BUSINESS
   Biograph, 1913
TWO MEN OF THE DESERT   Biograph, 1913
THE MASSACRE   Biograph, 1914
THE BATTLE AT ELDERBUSH GULCH
   Biograph, 1914
JUDITH OF BETHULIA   Artcraft, 1914
BRUTE FORCE   Reliance-Majestic, 1914

D. W. GRIFFITH (continued)

THE BATTLE OF THE SEXES *THE SINGLE STANDARD* Mutual, 1914
THE ESCAPE Mutual, 1914
HOME, SWEET, HOME Mutual, 1914
THE AVENGING CONSCIENCE Mutual, 1914
THE BIRTH OF A NATION Mutual, 1915
INTOLERANCE Triangle, 1916
HEARTS OF THE WORLD Artcraft, 1918
THE GREAT LOVE Artcraft, 1918
THE GREATEST THING IN LIFE
   Artcraft, 1918
A ROMANCE OF HAPPY VALLEY
   Artcraft, 1919
THE GIRL WHO STAYED AT HOME
   Artcraft, 1919
BROKEN BLOSSOMS United Artists, 1919
TRUE HEART SUSIE Artcraft, 1919
SCARLET DAYS Artcraft, 1919
THE GREATEST QUESTION
   First National, 1919
THE IDOL DANCER First National, 1920
THE LOVE FLOWER First National, 1920
WAY DOWN EAST United Artists, 1920
DREAM STREET United Artists, 1921
ORPHANS OF THE STORM
   United Artists, 1922
ONE EXCITING NIGHT United Artists, 1922
THE WHITE ROSE United Artists, 1923
AMERICA United Artists, 1924
ISN'T LIFE WONDERFUL
   United Artists, 1924
SALLY OF THE SAWDUST Paramount, 1925
THAT ROYLE GIRL Paramount, 1926
THE SORROWS OF SATAN
   Paramount, 1926
DRUMS OF LOVE United Artists, 1928
THE BATTLE OF THE SEXES
   United Artists, 1928
LADY OF THE PAVEMENTS
   United Artists, 1929
ABRAHAM LINCOLN United Artists, 1930
THE STRUGGLE United Artists, 1931

YILMAZ GUNEY

b. 1937 - Adana, Turkey
d. 1984

MY NAME IS KERIM Sahinler Film,
   1967, Turkish
NURI THE FLEA co-director with Serif Gedik,
   Guney Film, 1968, Turkish
BRIDE OF THE EARTH Erman Film,
   1968, Turkish
THE HUNGRY WOLVES Iale Film,
   1969, Turkish
AN UGLY MAN Guney Film, 1969, Turkish
HOPE Guney Film, 1970, Turkish
THE FUGITIVES Alfan Film, 1971, Turkish
THE WRONGDOERS Guney Film,
   1971, Turkish
TOMORROW IS THE FINAL DAY Irfan Film,
   1971, Turkish
THE HOPELESS ONES Akin Film,
   1971, Turkish
PAIN Azleyis Film, 1971, Turkish
ELEGY Guney Film, 1971, Turkish
THE FATHER Akun Film, 1971, Turkish
THE FRIEND Guney Film, 1974, Turkish
ANXIETY co-director with Serif Goren,
   Guney Film, 1974, Turkish
THE POOR ONES co-director with Atif Yilmaz,
   Guney Film, 1975, Turkish
YOL directed by Serif Goren, supervised by
   Yilmaz Guney, Triumph/Columbia, 1982,
   Turkish-Swiss-West German
THE WALL MK2/TF1, 1983, French

ALICE GUY-BLACHE
(Alice Guy/Alice Blache)
b. July 1, 1873 - Saint-Monde, France
d. 1968

LA FEE AUX CHOUX Gaumont,
   1896, French
LES DANGERS DE L'ALCOOLISME
   Gaumont, 1899, French
LA DANSE DES SAISONS Gaumont,
   1900, French
AU BAL DE FLORE Gaumont, 1900, French
HUSSARDS ET GRISETTES Gaumont,
   1901, French
LE POMMIER Gaumont, 1902, French
LE VOLEUR SACRILEGE Gaumont,
   1903, French
PARIS LA NUIT Gaumont, 1904, French
LE COURRIER DE LYON Gaumont,
   1904, French
LE CRIME DE LA RUE DU TEMPLE
   Gaumont, 1904, French
LA ESMERALDA Gaumont, 1905, French
REHABILITATION Gaumont, 1905, French
LA VIE DU CHRIST Gaumont, 1906, French
LA FEE PRINTEMPS Gaumont,
   1906, French
FANFAN LA TULIPE Gaumont, 1907, French
ROSE OF THE CIRCUS Solax, 1911
THE DOLL Solax, 1911
THE VIOLIN MAKER OF NUREMBERG
   Solax, 1911
THE FACE AT THE WINDOW Solax, 1912
MIGNON Solax, 1912
FALLING LEAVES Solax, 1912
IN THE YEAR 2000 Solax, 1912
FRA DIAVOLO Solax, 1912
THE BLOOD STAIN Solax, 1912
PLAYING TRUMPS Solax, 1912
PHANTOM PARADISE Solax, 1912
DICK WHITTINGTON AND HIS CAT
   Solax, 1913
THE PIT AND THE PENDULUM Solax, 1913
A TERRIBLE NIGHT Solax, 1913
THE LITTLE HUNCHBACK Solax, 1913
ROGUES OF PARIS Solax, 1913
THE STAR OF INDIA Solax, 1913
BENEATH THE CZAR Solax, 1914
SHADOWS OF THE MOULIN ROUGE
   Solax, 1914
THE MONSTER AND THE GIRL Solax, 1914
THE DREAM WOMAN Solax, 1914
THE WOMAN OF MYSTERY Solax, 1914
THE LURE Solax, 1914
THE HEART OF A PAINTED WOMAN
   Solax, 1915
MY DONNA Solax, 1915
THE VAMPIRE Solax, 1915
WHAT WILL PEOPLE SAY? Solax, 1916
THE WAIF Solax, 1916
THE ADVENTURER Solax, 1917
THE EMPRESS Solax, 1917
A MAN AND THE WOMAN Solax, 1917
HOUSE OF CARDS Solax, 1917
WHEN YOU AND I WERE YOUNG
   Solax, 1917
BEHIND THE MASK Solax, 1917
THE GREAT ADVENTURE 1918
TARNISHED REPUTATIONS
   A SOUL ADRIFT 1920

HUGO HAAS

b. February 19, 1901 - Brno, Czechoslovakia
d. 1968

A CAMEL THROUGH A NEEDLE'S EYE
   co-director, 1936, Czechoslovakian
GIRL, DEFEND YOURSELF! co-director,
   1937, Czechoslovakian
THE WHITE PLAGUE 1937, Czechoslovakian
WHAT IS WHISPERED 1938,
   Czechoslovakian
PICKUP Columbia, 1951
THE GIRL ON THE BRIDGE
   20th Century-Fox, 1951
STRANGE FASCINATION Columbia, 1952
ONE GIRL'S CONFESSION Columbia, 1953
THY NEIGHBOR'S WIFE
   20th Century-Fox, 1953
BAIT Columbia, 1954
THE OTHER WOMAN
   20th Century-Fox, 1954
HOLD BACK TOMORROW Universal, 1955
EDGE OF HELL Universal, 1956
HIT AND RUN United Artists, 1957
LIZZIE MGM, 1957
NIGHT OF THE QUARTER MOON
   MGM, 1959
BORN TO BE LOVED Universal, 1959
PARADISE ALLEY Pathe-American, 1961

ALEXANDER HALL

b. 1894 - Boston, Massachusetts
d. 1968

SINNERS IN THE SUN Paramount, 1932
MADAME RACKETEER co-director with
   Harry Wagstaff Gribble, Paramount, 1932
THE GIRL IN 419 co-director with
   George Somnes, Paramount, 1933
MIDNIGHT CLUB co-director with
   George Somnes, Paramount, 1933
TORCH SINGER co-director with
   George Somnes, Paramount, 1933
MISS FANE'S BABY IS STOLEN
   Paramount, 1934
LITTLE MISS MARKER Paramount, 1934
THE PURSUIT OF HAPPINESS
   Paramount, 1934
LIMEHOUSE BLUES Paramount, 1934
GOIN' TO TOWN Paramount, 1935
ANNAPOLIS FAREWELL Paramount, 1935
GIVE US THIS NIGHT Paramount, 1936
YOURS FOR THE ASKING Paramount, 1936
EXCLUSIVE Paramount, 1937
THERE'S ALWAYS A WOMAN
   Columbia, 1938
I AM THE LAW Columbia, 1938
THERE'S THAT WOMAN AGAIN
   Columbia, 1938
THE LADY'S FROM KENTUCKY
   Paramount, 1939
GOOD GIRLS GO TO PARIS Columbia, 1939
THE AMAZING MR. WILLIAMS
   Columbia, 1939
THE DOCTOR TAKES A WIFE
   Columbia, 1940
HE STAYED FOR BREAKFAST
   Columbia, 1940

THIS THING CALLED LOVE   Columbia, 1941
HERE COMES MR. JORDAN ★
   Columbia, 1941
BEDTIME STORY   Columbia, 1941
THEY ALL KISSED THE BRIDE
   Columbia, 1942
MY SISTER EILEEN   Columbia, 1942
THE HEAVENLY BODY   MGM, 1943
ONCE UPON A TIME   Columbia, 1944
SHE WOULDN'T SAY YES   Columbia, 1945
DOWN TO EARTH   Columbia, 1947
THE GREAT LOVER   Paramount, 1949
LOVE THAT BRUTE   20th Century-Fox, 1950
LOUISA   Universal, 1950
UP FRONT   Universal, 1951
BECAUSE YOU'RE MINE   MGM, 1952
LET'S DO IT AGAIN   Columbia, 1953
FOREVER DARLING   MGM, 1956

ROBERT HAMER

b. March 31, 1911 - Kidderminster, England
d. 1963

DEAD OF NIGHT   co-director with
   Alberto Cavalcanti, Basil Dearden &
   Charles Crichton, Universal, 1945, British
PINK STRING AND SEALING WAX
   Eagle Lion, 1945, British
IT ALWAYS RAINS ON SUNDAY   General
   Film Distributors, 1947, British
KIND HEARTS AND CORONETS   General
   Film Distributors, 1949, British
THE SPIDER AND THE FLY   General Film
   Distributors, 1949, British
HIS EXCELLENCY   General Film Distributors,
   1952, British
THE LONG MEMORY   General Film
   Distributors, 1952, British
THE DETECTIVE   *FATHER BROWN*
   Columbia, 1954, British
TO PARIS, WITH LOVE   General Film
   Distributors, 1955, British
THE SCAPEGOAT   MGM, 1959, British
SCHOOL FOR SCOUNDRELS
   Warner Bros., 1960, British

HARVEY HART

b. March 19, 1928 - Toronto, Canada
d. 1989

BUS RILEY'S BACK IN TOWN
   Universal, 1965
DARK INTRUDER   Universal, 1965
SULLIVAN'S EMPIRE   co-director with
   Thomas Carr, Universal, 1967
THE SWEET RIDE   20th Century-Fox, 1968
THE YOUNG LAWYERS (TF)
   Paramount TV, 1969
FORTUNE AND MEN'S EYES   MGM,
   1971, Canadian
MAHONEY'S ESTATE (TF)   Topaz
   Productions, 1972, Canadian
THE PYX   Cinerama Releasing Corporation,
   1973, Canadian
CAN ELLEN BE SAVED? (TF)   ABC Circle
   Films, 1974
MURDER OR MERCY (TF)
   QM Productions, 1974
PANIC ON THE 5:22 (TF)
   QM Productions, 1974
SHOOT   Avco Embassy, 1976, Canadian
STREET KILLING (TF)   ABC Circle
   Films, 1976
THE CITY (TF)   QM Productions, 1977
GOLDENROD (TF)   Talent Associates/
   Film Funding Ltd. of Canada, 1977,
   U.S.-Canadian

THE PRINCE OF CENTRAL PARK (TF)
   Lorimar Productions, 1977
CAPTAINS COURAGEOUS (TF)   Norman
   Rosemont Productions, 1977
STANDING TALL (TF)   QM Productions, 1978
W.E.B. (TF)   NBC, 1978
LIKE NORMAL PEOPLE (TF)   Christiana
   Productions/20th Century-Fox TV, 1979
THE ALIENS ARE COMING (TF)   Woodruff
   Productions/QM Productions, 1980
JOHN STEINBECK'S EAST OF EDEN
   EAST OF EDEN (MS)   Mace Neufeld
   Productions, 1981
THE HIGH COUNTRY   Crown International,
   1981, Canadian
MASSARATI AND THE BRAIN (TF)
   Aaron Spelling Productions, 1982
BORN BEAUTIFUL (TF)   Procter &
   Gamble Productions/Telecom
   Entertainment Inc., 1982
GETTING EVEN   New World,
   1983, Canadian
MASTER OF THE GAME (MS)   co-director
   with Kevin Connor, Rosemont
   Productions, 1984
RECKLESS DISREGARD (CTF)
   Telecom Entertainment/Polar Film
   Corporation/Fremantle of Canada Ltd.,
   1985, U.S.-Canadian
BEVERLY HILLS MADAM (TF)
   NLS Productions/Orion TV, 1986
STONE FOX (TF)   Hanna-Barbera
   Productions/Allarcom Ltd./Taft
   Entertainment TV, 1987, U.S.-Canadian
MURDER SEES THE LIGHT (TF)   CBC,
   1987, Canadian
PASSION AND PARADISE (TF)   Picturebase
   International/Primedia Productions/Leonard
   Hill Films, 1989, U.S.-Canadian
BLOOD SPORT   Comedia Entertainment/
   Radio Telefis Eirrean, 1989, Canadian-Irish

WILLIAM S. HART

b. December 6, 1865 - Newburgh, New York
d. 1946

THE PASSING OF TWO-GUN HICKS
   TAMING THE FOUR-FLUSHER   1915
IN THE SAGE BRUSH COUNTRY
   MR. NOBODY   1915
THE SCOURGE OF THE DESERT   1915
MR. SILENT HASKINS   1915
THE SHERIFF'S STREAK OF
   YELLOW   1915
THE GRUDGE   1915
THE ROUGHNECK   *THE GENTLEMAN
   FROM BLUE GULCH*   1915
THE TAKING OF LUKE McVANE
   THE FUGITIVE   1915
THE MAN FROM NOWHERE
   THE SILENT STRANGER   1915
THE BAD BUCK OF SANTA YNEZ
   *THE BAD MAN/REVOLVER BILL/
   A DESPERATE CHANCE*   1915
THE DARKENING TRAIL   *HELL HOUND
   OF ALASKA*   1915
THE CONVERSION OF FROSTY BLAKE
   THE CONVERT/STAKING HIS LIFE   1915
TOOLS OF PROVIDENCE   *DAKOTA DAN/
   EVERY INCH A MAN/THE STRUGGLE IN
   THE STEEPLE*   1915
THE RUSE   *SQUARE DEAL MAN/
   A SQUARE DEAL*   1915
CASH PARRISH'S PAL   *DOUBLE
   CROSSED*   1915
PINTO BEN   *HORNS AND HOOFS*   1915
A KNIGHT OF THE TRAILS   *PROWLERS OF
   THE PLAINS*   1915

KENO BATES - LIAR THE
   LAST CARD   1915
THE DISCIPLE   1915
BETWEEN MEN   1916
HELL'S HINGES   co-director with
   Charles Swickard, 1916
THE ARYAN   1916
THE PRIMAL LURE   1916
THE APOSTLE OF VENGEANCE   1916
THE DAWN MAKER   1916
THE RETURN OF DRAW EGAN   1916
THE PATRIOT   1916
THE DEVIL'S DOUBLE   1916
TRUTHFUL TULLIVER   1916
THE GUN FIGHTER   1917
THE SQUARE DEAL MAN   1917
THE DESERT MAN   1917
WOLF LOWRY   1917
THE COLD DECK   1917
THE SILENT MAN   1917
WOLVES OF THE RAIL   1918
BLUE BLAZES RAWDEN   1918
THE TIGER MAN   1918
SELFISH YATES   1918
SHARK MONROE   1918
RIDDLE GAWNE   1918
THE BORDER WIRELESS   1918
BRANDING BROADWAY   1918
THE POPPY GIRL'S HUSBAND   1919
THE MONEY CORRAL   1919
SQUARE DEAL SANDERSON   co-director
   with Lambert Hillyer, 1919

BYRON HASKIN

b. 1899 - Portland, Oregon
d. 1984

MATINEE LADIES   1927
IRISH HEARTS   1927
GINSBERG THE GREAT   Warner Bros., 1927
THE SIREN   Columbia, 1928
I WALK ALONE   Paramount, 1947
MAN-EATER OF KUMAON   Universal, 1948
TOO LATE FOR TEARS   United Artists, 1949
TREASURE ISLAND   RKO Radio,
   1950, U.S.-British
TARZAN'S PERIL   RKO Radio, 1951
WARPATH   Paramount, 1951
SILVER CITY   Paramount, 1951
THE DENVER AND RIO GRANDE
   Paramount, 1952
THE WAR OF THE WORLDS
   Paramount, 1953
HIS MAJESTY O'KEEFE   Warner Bros., 1954
THE NAKED JUNGLE   Paramount, 1954
LONG JOHN SILVER   New Trends Associates,
   1955, Australian
CONQUEST OF SPACE   Paramount, 1955
THE FIRST TEXAN   Allied Artists, 1956
THE BOSS   United Artists, 1956
FROM THE EARTH TO THE MOON
   Warner Bros., 1958
THE LITTLE SAVAGE
   20th Century-Fox, 1959
JET OVER THE ATLANTIC
   Intercontinental, 1959
SEPTEMBER STORM
   20th Century-Fox, 1960
ARMORED COMMAND   Allied Artists, 1961
CAPTAIN SINDBAD   MGM, 1963
ROBINSON CRUSOE ON MARS
   Paramount, 1964
THE POWER   MGM, 1968

HENRY HATHAWAY
(Henri Leopold de Fiennes)
b. March 13, 1898 - Sacramento, California
d. 1985

HERITAGE OF THE DESERT   1932
WILD HORSE MESA   1932
UNDER THE TONTO RIM   1933
SUNSET PASS   1933
MAN OF THE FOREST   1933
TO THE LAST MAN   1933
THE THUNDERING HERD   1933
THE LAST ROUND-UP   1934
COME ON MARINES!   1934
THE WITCHING HOUR   Paramount, 1934
NOW AND FOREVER   Paramount, 1934
THE LIVES OF A BENGAL LANCER ★
   Paramount, 1935
PETER IBBETSON   Paramount, 1935
THE TRAIL OF THE LONESOME PINE
   Paramount, 1936
GO WEST, YOUNG MAN   Paramount, 1936
SOULS AT SEA   Paramount, 1937
SPAWN OF THE NORTH   Paramount, 1938
THE REAL GLORY   United Artists, 1939
JOHNNY APOLLO   20th Century-Fox, 1940
BRIGHAM YOUNG, FRONTIERSMAN
   20th Century-Fox, 1940
THE SHEPHERD OF THE HILLS
   Paramount, 1941
SUNDOWN   United Artists, 1941
TEN GENTLEMEN FROM WEST POINT
   20th Century-Fox, 1942
CHINA GIRL   20th Century-Fox, 1942
HOME IN INDIANA   20th Century-Fox, 1944
WING AND A PRAYER
   20th Century-Fox, 1944
NOB HILL   20th Century-Fox, 1945
THE HOUSE ON 92ND STREET
   20th Century-Fox, 1945
THE DARK CORNER
   20th Century-Fox, 1946
13 RUE MADELEINE
   20th Century-Fox, 1947
KISS OF DEATH   20th Century-Fox, 1947
CALL NORTHSIDE 777
   20th Century-Fox, 1948
DOWN TO THE SEA IN SHIPS
   20th Century-Fox, 1949
THE BLACK ROSE   20th Century-Fox, 1950,
   British-U.S.
YOU'RE IN THE NAVY NOW
   20th Century-Fox, 1951
FOURTEEN HOURS   20th Century-Fox, 1951
RAWHIDE   20th Century-Fox, 1951
THE DESERT FOX   20th Century-Fox, 1951
DIPLOMATIC COURIER
   20th Century-Fox, 1952
O. HENRY'S FULL HOUSE   co-director with
   Howard Hawks, Henry King, Henry Koster &
   Jean Negulesco, 20th Century-Fox, 1952
NIAGARA   20th Century-Fox, 1953
WHITE WITCH DOCTOR
   20th Century-Fox, 1953
PRINCE VALIANT   20th Century-Fox, 1954
GARDEN OF EVIL   20th Century-Fox, 1954
THE RACERS   20th Century-Fox, 1955
THE BOTTOM OF THE BOTTLE
   20th Century-Fox, 1956
23 PACES TO BAKER STREET
   20th Century-Fox, 1956, British-U.S.
LEGEND OF THE LOST   United Artists, 1957
FROM HELL TO TEXAS
   20th Century-Fox, 1958
WOMAN OBSESSED
   20th Century-Fox, 1959
SEVEN THIEVES   20th Century-Fox, 1960

NORTH TO ALASKA   20th Century-Fox, 1960
HOW THE WEST WAS WON   co-director
   with John Ford & George Marshall,
   MGM/Cinerama, 1962
CIRCUS WORLD   Paramount, 1964
THE SONS OF KATIE ELDER
   Paramount, 1965
NEVADA SMITH   Paramount, 1966
THE LAST SAFARI   Paramount,
   1967, British
5 CARD STUD   Paramount, 1968
TRUE GRIT   Paramount, 1969
RAIN ON ROMMEL   Universal, 1971
SHOOT-OUT   Universal, 1971
HANGUP   *SUPER DUDE*   Universal, 1974

HOWARD HAWKS
b. May 30, 1896 - Goshen, Indiana
d. 1977

THE ROAD TO GLORY   Fox, 1926
FIG LEAVES   Fox, 1926
THE CRADLE SNATCHERS   Fox, 1927
PAID TO LOVE   Fox, 1927
A GIRL IN EVERY PORT   Fox, 1928
FAZIL   Fox, 1928
THE AIR CIRCUS   co-director with
   Lewis Seiler, Fox, 1928
TRENT'S LAST CASE   Fox, 1929
THE DAWN PATROL   First National, 1930
THE CRIMINAL CODE   Columbia, 1931
THE CROWD ROARS   Warner Bros., 1932
SCARFACE   *SCARFACE: SHAME OF
A NATION*   United Artists, 1932
TIGER SHARK   First National, 1932
TODAY WE LIVE   MGM, 1933
TWENTIETH CENTURY   Columbia, 1934
BARBARY COAST   United Artists, 1935
CEILING ZERO   Warner Bros., 1935
THE ROAD TO GLORY
   20th Century-Fox, 1936
COME AND GET IT   co-director with
   William Wyler, United Artists, 1936
BRINGING UP BABY   RKO Radio, 1938
ONLY ANGELS HAVE WINGS
   Columbia, 1939
HIS GIRL FRIDAY   Columbia, 1940
SERGEANT YORK ★   Warner Bros., 1941
BALL OF FIRE   RKO Radio, 1941
AIR FORCE   Warner Bros., 1943
TO HAVE AND HAVE NOT
   Warner Bros., 1944
THE BIG SLEEP   Warner Bros., 1946
RED RIVER   United Artists, 1948
A SONG IS BORN   RKO Radio, 1948
I WAS A MALE WAR BRIDE
   20th Century-Fox, 1949
THE BIG SKY   RKO Radio, 1952
O. HENRY'S FULL HOUSE   co-director with
   Henry Hathaway, Henry King, Henry Koster &
   Jean Negulesco, 20th Century-Fox, 1952
MONKEY BUSINESS
   20th Century-Fox, 1952
GENTLEMEN PREFER BLONDES
   20th Century-Fox, 1953
LAND OF THE PHAROAHS
   Warner Bros., 1955
RIO BRAVO   Warner Bros., 1959
HATARI!   Paramount, 1962
MAN'S FAVORITE SPORT?   Universal, 1964
RED LINE 7000   Paramount, 1965
EL DORADO   Paramount, 1967
RIO LOBO   National General, 1970

BEN HECHT
b. February 28, 1893 - New York, New York
d. 1964

CRIME WITHOUT PASSION   co-director with
   Charles MacArthur, Paramount, 1934
THE SCOUNDREL   co-director with
   Charles MacArthur, Paramount, 1935
ONCE IN A BLUE MOON   co-director with
   Charles MacArthur, Paramount, 1936
SOAK THE RICH   co-director with
   Charles MacArthur, Paramount, 1936
ANGELS OVER BROADWAY   co-director with
   Lee Garmes, Columbia, 1940
SPECTER OF THE ROSE   Republic, 1946
ACTORS AND SIN   United Artists, 1952

STUART HEISLER
b. 1894 - Los Angeles, California
d. 1979

STRAIGHT FROM THE SHOULDER
   Paramount, 1936
THE BISCUIT EATER   Paramount, 1940
THE MONSTER AND THE GIRL
   Paramount, 1941
AMONG THE LIVING   Paramount, 1941
THE REMARKABLE ANDREW
   Paramount, 1942
THE GLASS KEY   Paramount, 1942
THE NEGRO SOLDIER (FD)
   United States Army, 1944
ALONG CAME JONES   RKO Radio, 1945
BLUE SKIES   Paramount, 1946
SMASH-UP   *SMASH-UP - THE STORY OF
A WOMAN*   Universal, 1947
THE STORY OF A WOMAN   1947
TULSA   Eagle Lion, 1949
TOKYO JOE   Columbia, 1949
CHAIN LIGHTNING   Warner Bros., 1950
DALLAS   Warner Bros., 1950
STORM WARNING   Warner Bros., 1951
JOURNEY INTO LIGHT
   20th Century-Fox, 1951
ISLAND OF DESIRE   *SATURDAY ISLAND*
   United Artists, 1952
THE STAR   20th Century-Fox, 1952
BEACHHEAD   United Artists, 1954
THIS IS MY LOVE   RKO Radio, 1954
I DIED A THOUSAND TIMES
   Warner Bros., 1955
THE LONE RANGER   Warner Bros., 1956
THE BURNING HILLS   Warner Bros., 1956
HITLER   Allied Artists, 1962

PAUL HENREID
(Paul George Julius von Henreid)
b. January 10, 1908 - Trieste, Italy
d. 1992

FOR MEN ONLY   Lippert, 1952
A WOMAN'S DEVOTION   Republic, 1956
GIRLS ON THE LOOSE   Universal, 1958
LIVE FAST, DIE YOUNG   Universal, 1958
DEAD RINGER   Warner Bros., 1964
BLUES FOR LOVERS   *BALLAD IN BLUE*
   1965, British

JIM HENSON
b. September 24, 1936 - Greenville,
   North Carolina
d. 1990

THE GREAT MUPPET CAPER
   Universal/AFD, 1981, British
THE DARK CRYSTAL   co-director with
   Frank Oz, Universal/AFD, 1982, British
LABYRINTH   TriStar, 1986, British

DOUGLAS HEYES
d. 1993

KITTEN WITH A WHIP   Universal, 1964
BEAU GESTE   Universal, 1966
THE LONELY PROFESSION (TF)
   Universal TV, 1969
POWDERKEG (TF)   Filmways/Rodphi, 1969
DRIVE HARD, DRIVE FAST (TF)
   Universal TV, 1973
CAPTAINS AND THE KINGS (MS)   co-director
   with Allen Reisner, Universal TV, 1976
ASPEN (MS)   Universal TV, 1977
THE FRENCH ATLANTIC AFFAIR (TF)   Aaron
   Spelling Productions/MGM TV, 1979
THE HIGHWAYMAN (TF)   Glen A. Larson
   Productions/20th Century Fox TV, 1987

JESSE HIBBS
b. January 11, 1906 - Normal, Illinois
d. 1985

THE ALL-AMERICAN   Universal, 1953
RIDE CLEAR OF DIABLO   Universal, 1954
BLACK HORSE CANYON   Universal, 1954
RAILS INTO LARAMIE   Un iversal, 1954
THE YELLOW MOUNTAIN   Universal, 1954
TO HELL AND BACK   Universal, 1955
THE SPOILERS   Universal, 1955
WORLD IN MY CORNER   Universal, 1956
WALK THE PROUD LAND   Universal, 1956
JOE BUTTERFLY   Universal, 1957
RIDE A CROOKED TRAIL   Universal, 1958

DOUGLAS HICKOX
b. January 10, 1929 - London, England
d. 1988

IT'S ALL OVER TOWN   British Lion,
   1963, British
DISK-O-TEK HOLIDAY   JUST FOR YOU
   Columbia, 1963, British
ENTERTAINING MR. SLOANE   Continental,
   1970, British
SITTING TARGET   MGM, 1972, British
THEATRE OF BLOOD   United Artists,
   1973, British
BRANNIGAN   United Artists, 1975, British
SKY RIDERS   20th Century-Fox, 1976
ZULU DAWN   American Cinema,
   1979, British
THE PHOENIX (TF)   Mark Carliner
   Productions, 1981
THE HOUND OF THE BASKERVILLES
   Mapleton Films Ltd., 1983, British
THE MASTER OF BALLANTRAE (TF)
   Larry White-Hugh Benson Productions/
   HTV/Columbia TV, 1984, U.S.-British
MISTRAL'S DAUGHTER (MS)   co-director
   with Kevin Connor, Steve Krantz
   Productions/R.T.L. Productions/Antenne-2,
   1984, U.S.-French
BLACKOUT (CTF)   HBO Premiere Films/
   Roger Gimbel Productions/Peregrine
   Entertainment Ltd./Lee Buck Industries/
   Alexander Smith & Parks, 1985,
   U.S.-Canadian
SINS (MS)   New World TV/The Greif-Dore
   Company/Collins-Holm Productions, 1986
I'LL TAKE MANHATTAN (MS)   co-director
   with Richard Michaels, Steve Krantz
   Productions, 1987

COLIN HIGGINS
b. July 28, 1941 - Noumea, New Caledonia
d. 1988

FOUL PLAY   Paramount, 1978
NINE TO FIVE   20th Century-Fox, 1980
THE BEST LITTLE WHOREHOUSE IN TEXAS
   Universal, 1982

JAMES HILL
b. 1919 - England
d. 1994

THE STOLEN PLANS   Associated British
   Film Distributors/Children's Film Foundation,
   1952, British
THE CLUE OF THE MISSING APE
   Associated British Film Distributors/
   Children's Film Foundation, 1953, British
PERIL FOR THE GUY   British Lion/Children's
   Film Foundation, 1956, British
MYSTERY IN THE MINE   Children's Film
   Foundation, 1959, British
THE KITCHEN   British Lion, 1961, British
THE DOCK BRIEF   MGM, 1962, British
LUNCH HOUR   Bryanston, 1962, British
SEASIDE SWINGERS   EVERY DAY'S A
   HOLIDAY   Embassy, 1964, British
A STUDY IN TERROR   Columbia,
   1966, British
BORN FREE   Columbia, 1966, British
THE CORRUPT ONES   THE PEKING
   MEDALLION   Warner Bros., 1967,
   West German-French-Italian
CAPTAIN NEMO AND THE UNDERWATER
   CITY   MGM, 1970, British
AN ELEPHANT CALLED SLOWLY   American
   Continental, 1971, British
BLACK BEAUTY   Paramount, 1971,
   British-West German-Spanish
THE BELSTONE FOX   FREE SPIRIT
   Cine III, 1973, British
CHRISTIAN THE LION   THE LION AT
   WORLD'S END   co-director with
   Bill Travers, Scotia American, 1974, British
WORZEL GUMMIDGE (TF)   1978, British
THE WILD AND THE FREE (TF)   BSR
   Productions/Marble Arch Productions, 1980
YOU KNOW WHAT I MEAN (TF)   1982, British
THE FETCHIT (TF)   1983, British
OWAIN GLYNDWR - PRINCE OF WALES (TF)
   OPIX/S4C, 1983, British
THE YOUNG VISITERS (TF)   Channel 4,
   1984, British
THE ALASKA KID (MS)   CCC Television,
   1991, German

ALFRED HITCHCOCK
b. August 13, 1899 - London, England
d. 1980

NUMBER THIRTEEN   1922,
   British, unfinished
ALWAYS TELL YOUR WIFE   co-director with
   Seymour Hicks, 1922, British
THE PLEASURE GARDEN
   Gainsborough-Emelka, 1925,
   British-German
THE MOUNTAIN EAGLE   FEAR O' GOD
   Gainsborough-Emelka, 1926, British-German
THE LODGER   Gainsborough, 1926, British
DOWNHILL   WHEN BOYS LEAVE HOME
   Gainsborough, 1927, British
EASY VIRTUE   Gainsborough, 1927, British
THE RING   British International Pictures,
   1927, British

THE FARMER'S WIFE   British International
   Pictures, 1928, British
CHAMPAGNE   British International Pictures,
   1928, British
HARMONY HEAVEN   co-director with
   Eddie Pola & Edward Brandt, 1929, British
THE MANXMAN   British International Pictures,
   1929, British
BLACKMAIL   British International Pictures,
   1929, British
ELSTREE CALLING   co-director with
   Andre Charlot, Jack Hulbert & Paul Murray,
   British International Pictures, 1930, British
JUNO AND THE PAYCOCK   THE SHAME OF
   MARY BOYLE   British International Pictures,
   1930, British
MURDER   British International Pictures,
   1930, British
THE SKIN GAME   British International
   Pictures, 1931, British
RICH AND STRANGE   EAST OF SHANGHAI
   British International Pictures, 1932, British
NUMBER SEVENTEEN   British International
   Pictures, 1932, British
WALTZES FROM VIENNA   STRAUSS'S
   GREAT WALTZ   Gaumont-British,
   1933, British
THE MAN WHO KNEW TOO MUCH
   Gaumont-British, 1934, British
THE THIRTY-NINE STEPS   Gaumont-British,
   1935, British
THE SECRET AGENT   Gaumont-British,
   1936, British
SABOTAGE   A WOMAN ALONE
   Gaumont-British, 1936, British
YOUNG AND INNOCENT   THE GIRL WAS
   YOUNG   Gaumont-British, 1937, British
THE LADY VANISHES   United Artists,
   1938, British
JAMAICA INN   Paramount, 1939, British
REBECCA ★   United Artists, 1940
FOREIGN CORRESPONDENT
   United Artists, 1940
MR. AND MRS. SMITH   RKO Radio, 1941
SUSPICION   RKO Radio, 1941
SABOTEUR   Universal, 1942
SHADOW OF A DOUBT   Universal, 1943
LIFEBOAT ★   20th Century-Fox, 1944
BON VOYAGE (FD)   British Ministry of
   Information, 1944, British
SPELLBOUND ★   United Artists, 1945
NOTORIOUS   RKO Radio, 1946
THE PARADINE CASE   Selznick
   Releasing, 1947
ROPE   Warner Bros., 1948, U.S.-British
UNDER CAPRICORN   Warner Bros.,
   1949, British-U.S.
STAGE FRIGHT   Warner Bros., 1950
STRANGERS ON A TRAIN
   Warner Bros., 1951
I CONFESS   Warner Bros., 1953
DIAL M FOR MURDER   Warner Bros., 1954
REAR WINDOW ★   Paramount, 1954
TO CATCH A THIEF   Paramount, 1955
THE TROUBLE WITH HARRY
   Paramount, 1955
THE MAN WHO KNEW TOO MUCH
   Paramount, 1956
THE WRONG MAN   Warner Bros., 1957
VERTIGO   Paramount, 1958
NORTH BY NORTHWEST   MGM, 1959
PSYCHO ★   Paramount, 1960
THE BIRDS   Universal, 1963
MARNIE   Universal, 1964
TORN CURTAIN   Universal, 1966
TOPAZ   Universal, 1969
FRENZY   Universal, 1972, British
FAMILY PLOT   Universal, 1976

SETH HOLT
b. 1923 - Palestine
d. 1971

NOWHERE TO GO   MGM, 1958, British
SCREAM OF FEAR   *TASTE OF FEAR*
  Columbia, 1961, British
STATION SIX - SAHARA   Allied Artists, 1963,
  British-West German
THE NANNY   20th Century-Fox, 1965, British
DANGER ROUTE   United Artists,
  1968, British
BLOOD FROM THE MUMMY'S TOMB
  co-director with Michael Carreras,
  American International, 1971, British

INOSHIRO (ISHIRO) HONDA
b. 1911 - Yamagata Prefecture, Japan
d. 1993

EAGLE OF THE PACIFIC   Toho,
  1953, Japanese
GODZILLA   Toho, 1954, Japanese
LOVE COSMETIC   Toho, 1955, Japanese
HALF HUMAN   DCA, 1955, Japanese
GODZILLA, KING OF THE MONSTERS
  co-director with Terry Morse, Embassy,
  1966, Japanese-U.S., re-edited version
  of GODZILLA
RODAN   *RADON, GREAT MONSTER
  OF THE SKY*   DCA, 1956, Japanese
THE MYSTERIANS   *THE EARTH DEFENSE
  FORCE*   Columbia, 1957, Japanese
VARAN THE UNBELIEVABLE   Crown
  International, 1958, Japanese-U.S.
THE H-MAN   *THE BEAUTIFUL LADY
  AND THE LIQUID HUMAN*   Columbia,
  1959, Japanese
BATTLE IN OUTER SPACE   Columbia,
  1959, Japanese
GAS HUMAN NUMBER ONE   Toho,
  1960, Japanese
MOTHRA   Columbia, 1961, Japanese
KING KONG VS. GODZILLA   Universal,
  1962, Japanese
ATRAGON   *BATTLESHIP UNDER THE SEA*
  American International, 1963, Japanese
ATTACK OF THE MUSHROOM PEOPLE
  MATANGO   American International,
  1963, Japanese
DAGORA, THE SPACE MONSTER   Toho,
  1964, Japanese
GODZILLA VS. THE THING   *GODZILLA VS.
  MOTHRA*   American International,
  1964, Japanese
GHIDRAH, THE THREE-HEADED MONSTER
  *THREE BIG MONSTERS - THE BIGGEST
  FIGHT ON EARTH*   Continental,
  1964, Japanese
GORATH   Brenco, 1964, Japanese
BIG MONSTER WAR   Toho, 1965, Japanese
FRANKENSTEIN CONQUERS THE WORLD
  *FRANKENSTEIN VS. MONSTER FROM
  BENEATH THE EARTH*   American
  International, 1965, Japanese
COME BE MY WIFE   Toho, 1966, Japanese
WAR OF THE GARGANTUAS   *THUNDER
  OF THE FRANKENSTEIN MONSTER
  VS. GAILAH*   Toho/Benedict Productions,
  1966, Japanese-U.S.
KING KONG ESCAPES   *KING KONG'S
  REVENGE*   Universal, 1967 Japanese
DESTROY ALL MONSTERS   American
  International, 1968, Japanese
LATITUDE ZERO   National General,
  1969, Japanese

GODZILLA'S REVENGE   *ALL MONSTERS
  MUST BE DESTROYED*   UPA,
  1969, Japanese
YOG - MONSTER FROM SPACE   *GREAT
  MONSTER OF THE SOUTH SEA - GEZORA,
  GANIME, KAMEBA*   American International,
  1970, Japanese
REVENGE OF MECHA-GODZILLA
  Toho, 1975, Japanese

JERRY HOPPER
b. July 29, 1907 - Guthrie, Oklahoma
d. 1988

THE ATOMIC CITY   Paramount, 1952
HURRICANE SMITH   Paramount, 1952
PONY EXPRESS   Paramount, 1953
ALASKA SEAS   Paramount, 1954
SECRET OF THE INCAS   Paramount, 1954
NAKED ALIBI   Universal, 1955
SMOKE SIGNAL   Universal, 1955
THE PRIVATE WAR OF MAJOR BENSON
  Universal, 1955
ONE DESIRE   Universal, 1955
THE SQUARE JUNGLE   Universal, 1956
NEVER SAY GOODBYE   Universal, 1956
TOY TIGER   Universal, 1956
THE MISSOURI TRAVELER
  Buena Vista, 1958
BLUEPRINT FOR MURDER
  Paramount, 1961
MADRON   Four Star-Excelsior,
  1970, U.S.-Israeli

JAMES W. HORNE
b. December 14, 1880 - San Francisco,
  California
d. 1942

THE ACCOMPLICE   1915
THE BARNSTORMERS   1915
THE PITFALL   1915
STINGAREE (S)   1915-16
MYSTERY OF THE GRAND HOTEL   1916
SOCIAL PIRATES   1916
BULL'S EYE (S)   1918
HANDS UP (S)   1918
THE MIDNIGHT MAN (S)   1919
THE THIRD EYE (S)   1920
OCCASIONALLY YOURS   1920
THE BRONZE BELL   1921
DANGEROUS PASTIME   1921
DON'T DOUBT YOUR WIFE   1922
THE FORGOTTEN LAW   1922
THE HOTTENTOT   1922
CAN A WOMAN LOVE TWICE?   1923
THE SUNSHINE TRIAL   1923
A MAN OF ACTION   1923
ITCHING PALMS   1923
BLOW YOUR OWN HORN   1923
ALIMONY   1924
THE YANKEE CONSUL   1924
AMERICAN MANNERS   1924
HAIL THE HERO   1924
IN FAST COMPANY   1924
STEPPING LIVELY   1924
LAUGHING AT DANGER   1924
YOUTH AND ADVENTURE   1925
KOSHER KITTY KELLY   1926
THE CRUISE OF THE JASPER B   1926
COLLEGE   United Artists, 1927
THE BIG HOP   1928
BLACK BUTTERFLIES   1928
BONNIE SCOTLAND   MGM, 1935
THE BOHEMIAN GIRL   co-director with
  Charles Rogers, MGM, 1936
WAY OUT WEST   MGM, 1936

ALL OVER TOWN   1937
THE SPIDER'S WEB (S)   co-director with
  Ray Taylor, 1938
FLYING G-MEN (S)   co-director with
  Ray Taylor, 1939
DEADWOOD DICK (S)   1940
THE GREEN ARCHER (S)   1940
THE SHADOW (S)   1940
TERRY AND THE PIRATES (S)   1940
HOLT OF THE SECRET SERVICE (S)   1941
THE IRON CLAW (S)   1941
THE SPIDER RETURNS (S)   1941
WHITE EAGLE (S)   1941
CAPTAIN MIDNIGHT (S)   1942
PERILS OF THE ROYAL MOUNTED (S)   1942

LESLIE HOWARD
(Leslie Stainer)
b. April 24, 1893 - London, England
d. 1943

PYGMALION   co-director with Anthony Asquith,
  MGM, 1938, British
PIMPERNEL SMITH   *MISTER V*
  Anglo-American, 1941, British
SPITFIRE   *THE FIRST OF THE FEW*
  RKO Radio, 1942, British
THE GENTLE SEX   co-director with
  Maurice Elvey, Two Cities, 1943, British

NOEL HOWARD
b. December 25, 1920
d. 1987

THE HAPPY ROAD   co-director with
  Gene Kelly, MGM, 1957
MARCO THE MAGNIFICENT   co-director with
  Denys de la Patelliere & Christian-Jaque,
  MGM, 1966, French-Afghanistani-
  Egyptian-Italian-Yugoslavian
D'OU VIENS TO JOHNNY   Hoche
  Productions, French
DON'T YOU HEAR THE DOGS BARK? (FD)
  co-director with Francois Reichenbach,
  1975, Mexican-French

WILLIAM K. HOWARD
b. June 16, 1889 - St. Mary's, Ohio
d. 1954

GET YOUR MAN   co-director with
  George W. Hill, 1921
PLAY SQUARE   1921
WHAT LOVE WILL DO   1921
DESERTED AT THE ALTAR   co-director with
  Al Kelley, 1922
EXTRA! EXTRA!   1922
LUCKY DAN   1922
CAPTAIN FLY-BY-NIGHT   1922
THE FOURTH MUSKETEER   1923
DANGER AHEAD   1923
LET'S GO   1923
THE BORDER LEGION   1924
EAST OF BROADWAY   1924
THE THUNDERING HERD   1925
CODE OF THE WEST   1925
THE LIGHT OF WESTERN STARS   1925
RED DICE   1926
BACHELOR BRIDES   1926
VOLCANO   1926
GIGOLO   1926
WHITE GOLD   1927
THE MAIN EVENT   1927
A SHIP COMES IN   1928
THE RIVER PIRATE   1928
THE VALIANT   1929

LOVE, LIVE AND LAUGH   1929
CHRISTINA   1929
GOOD INTENTIONS   1930
SCOTLAND YARD   1930
DON'T BET ON WOMEN   1931
TRANSATLANTIC   Fox, 1931
SURRENDER   Fox, 1931
THE TRIAL OF VIVIENNE WARE   Fox, 1932
THE FIRST YEAR   Fox, 1932
SHERLOCK HOLMES   Fox, 1932
THE POWER AND THE GLORY   Fox, 1933
THIS SIDE OF HEAVEN   MGM, 1934
THE CAT AND THE FIDDLE   MGM, 1934
EVELYN PRENTICE   MGM, 1934
VANESSA, HER LOVE STORY   MGM, 1935
RENDEZVOUS   MGM, 1935
MARY BURNS, FUGITIVE   Paramount, 1935
THE PRINCESS COMES ACROSS
   Paramount, 1936
MURDER ON DIAMOND ROW   *THE
   SQUEAKER*   United Artists, 1937, British
FIRE OVER ENGLAND   United Artists, 1937
BACK DOOR TO HEAVEN
   Paramount, 1939
MONEY AND THE WOMAN
   Warner Bros., 1940
BULLETS FOR O'HARA   1941
KLONDIKE FURY   1942
JOHNNY COME LATELY   United Artists, 1943
WHEN THE LIGHTS GO ON AGAIN   1944
A GUY COULD CHANGE   1946

HOWARD HUGHES
b. December 24, 1905 - Houston, Texas
d. 1976

HELL'S ANGELS   United Artists, 1930
THE OUTLAW   RKO Radio, 1943

H. BRUCE (LUCKY) HUMBERSTONE
b. November 18, 1903 - Buffalo, New York
d. 1984

STRANGERS OF THE EVENING
   Tiffany, 1932
THE CROOKED CIRCLE
   Sono Art-World Wide, 1932
IF I HAD A MILLION   co-director,
   Paramount, 1932
KING OF THE JUNGLE   co-director with
   Max Marcin, Paramount, 1933
GOODBYE LOVE   RKO, 1933
THE MERRY WIVES OF RENO
   Warner Bros., 1934
THE DRAGON MURDER CASE
   First National, 1934
SILK HAT KID   Fox, 1935
LADIES LOVE DANGER   Fox, 1935
THREE LIVE GHOSTS   MGM, 1936
CHARLIE CHAN AT THE RACE TRACK
   20th Century-Fox, 1936
CHARLIE CHAN AT THE OPERA
   20th Century-Fox, 1936
CHARLIE CHAN AT THE OLYMPICS
   20th Century-Fox, 1937
CHECKERS   20th Century-Fox, 1938
RASCALS   20th Century-Fox, 1938
TIME OUT FOR MURDER
   20th Century-Fox, 1938
WHILE NEW YORK SLEEPS
   20th Century-Fox, 1938
CHARLIE CHAN IN HONOLULU
   20th Century-Fox, 1938
PACK UP YOUR TROUBLES
   20th Century-Fox, 1939
LUCKY CISCO KID   20th Century-Fox, 1940

THE QUARTERBACK   Paramount, 1940
TALL, DARK AND HANDSOME
   20th Century-Fox, 1941
SUN VALLEY SERENADE
   20th Century-Fox, 1941
I WAKE UP SCREAMING
   20th Century-Fox, 1941
TO THE SHORES OF TRIPOLI
   20th Century-Fox, 1942
ICELAND   20th Century-Fox, 1942
HELLO, FRISCO, HELLO
   20th Century-Fox, 1943
PIN-UP GIRL   20th Century-Fox, 1944
WONDER MAN   RKO Radio, 1945
WITHIN THESE WALLS
   20th Century-Fox, 1946
THREE LITTLE GIRLS IN BLUE
   20th Century-Fox, 1946
THE HOMESTRETCH
   20th Century-Fox, 1947
FURY AT FURNACE CREEK
   20th Century-Fox, 1948
SOUTH SEA SINNER   Universal, 1950
HAPPY GO LOVELY   RKO Radio,
   1951, British
SHE'S WORKING HER WAY THROUGH
   COLLEGE   Warner Bros., 1952
THE DESERT SONG   Warner Bros., 1953
THE PURPLE MASK   Universal, 1955
TEN WANTED MEN   Columbia, 1955
TARZAN AND THE LOST SAFARI   MGM,
   1957, British-U.S.
TARZAN'S FIGHT FOR LIFE   MGM, 1958
TARZAN AND THE TRAPPERS (TF)
   Warner Bros. TV, 1958
MADISON AVENUE   20th Century-Fox, 1962

BRIAN DESMOND HURST
b. February 12, 1900 - Castle Reagh, Ireland
d. 1986

THE TELL-TALE HEART   *BUCKET OF
   BLOOD*   Fox British, 1934, British
IRISH HEARTS   *NORAH O'NEALE*   MGM,
   1934, Irish
RIDERS TO THE SEA   MGM, 1935, British
OURSELVES ALONE   *RIVER OF UNREST*
   co-director with Walter Summers, Wardour,
   1936, British
THE TENTH MAN   Wardour, 1936, British
SENSATION   Associated British Picture
   Corp., 1937, British
GLAMOROUS NIGHT   Associated British
   Picture Corp., 1937, British
PRISON WITHOUT BARS   United Artists,
   1938, British
THE LION HAS WINGS   co-director with
   Michael Powell & Adrian Brunel,
   United Artists, 1939, British
ON THE NIGHT OF THE FIRE
   THE FUGITIVE   General Film
   Distributors, 1939, British
SUICIDE SQUADRON   *DANGEROUS
   MOONLIGHT*   RKO Radio, 1941, British
ALIBI   British Lion, 1942, British
THE HUNDRED POUND WINDOW
   Warner Bros.-First National, 1944, British
HUNGRY HILL   Universal, 1947, British
MARK OF CAIN   Rank, 1948, British
THE GAY LADY   *TROTTIE TRUE*
   Eagle Lion, 1949, British
A CHRISTMAS CAROL   *SCROOGE*
   United Artists, 1951, British
THE MALTA STORY   Universal,
   1953, British
SIMBA   Lippert, 1955, British
THE BLACK TENT   Rank, 1956, British

DANGEROUS EXILE   Rank, 1957, British
BEHIND THE MASK   Showcorporation,
   1958, British
HIS AND HERS   Eros, 1961, British
THE PLAYBOY OF THE WESTERN WORLD
   Janus, 1962, Irish

JOHN HUSTON
b. August 5, 1906 - Nevada, Montana
d. 1987

THE MALTESE FALCON   Warner Bros., 1941
IN THIS OUR LIFE   Warner Bros., 1942
ACROSS THE PACIFIC   Warner Bros., 1942
THE TREASURE OF THE SIERRA MADRE ★★
   Warner Bros., 1948
KEY LARGO   Warner Bros., 1948
WE WERE STRANGERS   Columbia, 1949
THE ASPHALT JUNGLE ★   MGM, 1950
THE RED BADGE OF COURAGE
   MGM, 1951
THE AFRICAN QUEEN ★
   United Artists, 1951
MOULIN ROUGE ★   United Artists,
   1952, British
BEAT THE DEVIL   United Artists,
   1954, British
MOBY DICK   Warner Bros., 1956, British
HEAVEN KNOWS, MR. ALLISON
   20th Century-Fox, 1957
THE BARBARIAN AND THE GEISHA
   20th Century-Fox, 1958
THE ROOTS OF HEAVEN
   20th Century-Fox, 1958
THE UNFORGIVEN   United Artists, 1960
THE MISFITS   United Artists, 1961
FREUD   Universal, 1963
THE LIST OF ADRIAN MESSENGER
   Universal, 1963
NIGHT OF THE IGUANA   MGM, 1964
THE BIBLE...IN THE BEGINNING
   20th Century-Fox, 1966, Italian
REFLECTIONS IN A GOLDEN EYE
   Warner Bros., 1967
CASINO ROYALE   co-director with
   Val Guest, Ken Hughes, Joseph McGrath &
   Robert Parrish, Columbia, 1967, British
A WALK WITH LOVE AND DEATH
   20th Century-Fox, 1969, British
SINFUL DAVEY   United Artists, 1969, British
THE KREMLIN LETTER
   20th Century-Fox, 1970
FAT CITY   Columbia, 1972
THE LIFE AND TIMES OF JUDGE ROY BEAN
   National General, 1973
THE MACKINTOSH MAN   Warner Bros.,
   1973, U.S.-British
THE MAN WHO WOULD BE KING
   Allied Artists, 1975, British
WISE BLOOD   New Line Cinema, 1979
PHOBIA   Paramount, 1981, Canadian
VICTORY   Paramount, 1981
ANNIE   Columbia, 1982
UNDER THE VOLCANO   Universal, 1984
PRIZZI'S HONOR ★   20th Century Fox, 1985
THE DEAD   Vestron, 1987

I

TADASHI IMAI

b. January 8, 1912 - Tokyo, Japan
d. 1992

THE NUMAZU MILITARY ACADEMY
Toho, 1939, Japanese
OUR INSTRUCTOR   Toho, 1939, Japanese
THE VILLAGE OF TAJINKO   Toho,
1940, Japanese
WOMEN'S TOWN   Toho, 1940, Japanese
THE GENERAL   Toho, 1940, Japanese
MARRIED LIFE   Toho, 1941, Japanese
THE SUICIDE TROOPS OF THE WATCH
TOWER   Toho, 1943, Japanese
THE ANGRY SEA   Toho, 1944, Japanese
AN ENEMY OF THE PEOPLE   Toho,
1946, Japanese
LIFE IS LIKE A SOMERSAULT   Toho,
1946, Japanese
24 HOURS OF A SECRET LIFE   co-director,
Toho, 1947, Japanese
BLUE MOUNTAINS   Fujimoto Productions/
Toho, 1949, Japanese
A WOMAN'S FACE   Toho, 1949, Japanese
TILL WE MEET AGAIN   Toho, 1950, Japanese
AND YET WE LIVE   Shinsei Eiga/Gekidan
Zenshinza, 1951, Japanese
PICTURES OF THE ATOM BOMB (FD)
1952, Japanese
ECHO SCHOOL   Yagi Productions/Japan
Teacher's Association, 1952, Japanese
MUDDY WATER   Bunkaguza/Shinseiki Eiga,
1953, Japanese
THE TOWER OF LILIES   Toei,
1953, Japanese
BECAUSE I LOVE   co-director,
1955, Japanese
HERE IS A SPRING   Chuo Eiga/Shochiku,
1955, Japanese
YUKIKO   1955, Japanese
DARKNESS AT NOON   Gendai Productions,
1956, Japanese
RICE   Toei, 1957, Japanese
A STORY OF PURE LOVE   Toei,
1957, Japanese
NIGHT DRUM   THE ADULTERESS
1958, Japanese
KIKU AND ISAMU   Daito Movie,
1959, Japanese
THE CLIFF   1960, Japanese
THE LIGHT OF THE WHARF   Toei,
1961, Japanese
THE OLD WOMEN'S PARADISE
MII Productions/Shochiku, 1962, Japanese
BUSHIDO: SAMURAI AND SALARYMAN
SAGA   Toei, 1963, Japanese
REVENGE   Toei, 1964, Japanese
A STORY FROM ECHIGO   Toei, 1964
WHEN THE COOKIE CRUMBLES
1967, Japanese
THE TIME OF RECKONING   Toei,
1968, Japanese
RIVER WITHOUT A BRIDGE PART I
Horupu Eiga, 1969, Japanese
RIVER WITHOUT A BRIDGE PART II
Horupu Eiga, 1970, Japanese
A WOMAN CALLED "EN"   Horupu Eiga,
1971, Japanese

THE NAVY AND ARMY SPECIAL CADETS
Toho, 1972, Japanese
TAKIJI KOBAYASHI   THE LIFE OF A
COMMUNIST WRITER   1974, Japanese
BROTHER AND SISTER   MON AND INO/
HIS YOUNGER SISTER   Toho,
1976, Japanese
YOBA   Nagata Productions/Daiei,
1976, Japanese
KOSODATE GOKO   Hayuza Eiga Hoso,
1979, Japanese
THE TOWER OF LILIES   Geiensha,
1982, Japanese
WAR AND YOUTH   Shochiku,
1991, Japanese

HIROSHI INAGAKI

b. December 30, 1905 - Tokyo, Japan
d. 1980

PEACE ON EARTH   1928, Japanese
THE WANDERING GAMBLER   Chiezo
Productions, 1928, Japanese
ELEGY OF HELL   1929, Japanese
A SAMURAI'S CAREER   Chiezo Productions,
1929, Japanese
THE IMAGE OF A MOTHER   1931, Japanese
A SWORD AND THE SUMO RING
1931, Japanese
TRAVELS UNDER THE BLUE SKY   Chiezo
Productions, 1932, Japanese
CHUJI KUNISHADA   1933, Japanese
BAD LUCK PART   1934, Japanese
WHITE SNOWS OF FUJI   1935, Japanese
THE WHITE HOOD   1935, Japanese
JOURNEY OF A THOUSAND AND ONE
NIGHTS   1936, Japanese
SPIRIT OF THE WILDERNESS
1937, Japanese
A GREAT WORLD POWER RISING   Nikkatsu,
1938, Japanese
SHADOWS OF DARKNESS   Nikkatsu,
1938, Japanese
MAZO   Nikkatsu, 1939, Japanese
THE LADY DAYS OF EDO   Nikkatsu,
1941, Japanese
ONE-EYED DRAGON   Daiei,
1942, Japanese
MUSASHI MIYAMOTO   Nikkatsu,
1942, Japanese
THE LIFE OF MATSU THE UNTAMED
Daiei, 1943, Japanese
SIGNAL FIRES OF SHANGHAI   Daiei,
1945, Japanese
THE LAST ABDICATION   Daiei,
1945, Japanese
CHILDREN HAND IN HAND   Daiei,
1947, Japanese
FORGOTTEN CHILDREN   Inagaki
Productions/Shin Toho, 1949, Japanese
KOJIRO SASAKI   Toho/Morita Productions,
1950, Japanese
INAZUMA ZOSHI   Shochiku,
1951, Japanese
KOJIRO SASAKI, PART II   Toho/Morita
Productions, 1951, Japanese
KOJIRO SASAKI, PART III: BATTLE OF
GANRYU ISLAND   Toho, 1951, Japanese
SWORD FOR HIRE   Toho, 1952, Japanese
OMATSURI HANJIRO   Toho,
1953, Japanese
SAMURAI, PART I: THE LEGEND OF
MUSASHI   MUSASHI MIYAMOTO
Toho, 1954, Japanese
SAMURAI, PART II: DUEL AT ICHIJOJI
TEMPLE   MUSASHI MIYAMOTO:
BATTLE OF ICHOJOJI TEMPLE
Toho, 1955, Japanese

THE STORM   Toho, 1956, Japanese
SAMURAI, PART III: DUEL AT GANRYU
ISLAND   MUSASHI MIYAMOTO : THE
BATTLE OF GANRYU ISLAND   Toho,
1956, Japanese
A GEISHA IN THE OLD CITY   FOR DAYU-SAN
Takarazuka Eiga, 1957, Japanese
SECRET SCROLLS, PART I   YAGYU SECRET
SCROLLS   Toho, 1957, Japanese
NEZUMI KOZO   Toho, 1958, Japanese
THE RICKSHAW MAN   THE RIKISHA MAN/
MATSUGORO, THE RIKISHA MAN/
THE LIFE OF MATSU THE UNTAMED
Toho, 1958, Japanese
SECRET SCROLLS, PART II   YAGYU SECRET
SCROLLS, PART II   Toho, 1958, Japanese
SAMURAI SAGA   Toho, 1959, Japanese
BIRTH OF JAPAN   Toho, 1959, Japanese
LIFE OF A COUNTRY DOCTOR   Toho,
1960, Japanese
DAREDEVIL IN THE CASTLE   OSAKA
CASTLE STORY   Toho, 1961, Japanese
GEN AND FUDOMYOU   THE YOUTH AND
HIS AMULET   Toho, 1961, Japanese
BANDITS ON THE WIND   Toho,
1961, Japanese
CHUSHINGURA   THE 47 RONIN   Toho,
1962, Japanese
SECRET SWORD   Toho, 1963, Japanese
GOUEMON THE TROUBLEMAKER   Toho,
1966, Japanese
KOJIRO SASAKI   Toho, 1967, Japanese
SAMURAI BANNERS   UNDER THE BANNER
OF SAMURAI/WIND, FOREST, FIRE,
MOUNTAIN   Toho/Mifune Productions,
1969, Japanese
MACHIBUSE   THE AMBUSH   Mifune
Productions/Toho, 1970, Japanese

THOMAS H. INCE

b. November 6, 1882 - Newport, Rhode Island
d. 1924

LITTLE NELL'S TOBACCO   1910
THEIR FIRST MISUNDERSTANDING
co-director with George Loane Tucker, 1911
THE DREAM   co-director with
George Loane Tucker, 1911
ARTFUL KATE   1911
BEHIND THE STOCKADE   co-director with
George Loane Tucker, 1911
HER DARKEST HOUR   1911
A MANLY MAN   1911
IN OLD MADRID   1911
SWEET MEMORIES   1911
THE AGGRESSOR   co-director with
George Loane Tucker, 1911
THE INDIAN MASSACRE   1912
THE DESERTER   1912
THE WAR ON THE PLAINS   1912
THE CRISIS   1912
THE HIDDEN TRAIL   1912
ON THE FIRING LINE   1912
CUSTER'S LAST RAID   1912
THE COLONEL'S WARD   1912
THE BATTLE OF THE RED MEN   1912
WHEN LEE SURRENDERS   1912
THE INVADERS   co-director with
Francis Ford, 1912
THE LAW OF THE WEST   1912
A DOUBLE REWARD   1912
A SHADOW OF THE PAST   1913
THE MOSAIC LAW   1913
WITH LEE IN VIRGINIA   1913
BREAD CAST UPON THE WATERS   1913
THE DRUMMER OF THE EIGHTH   1913
THE BOOMERANG   1913
THE SEAL OF SILENCE   1913

DAYS OF '49   1913
THE BATTLE OF GETTYSBURG   co-director
   with Charles Giblyn & Raymond B. West,
   Ince, 1914
LOVE'S SACRIFICE   co-director with
   William Clifford, 1914
A RELIC OF OLD JAPAN   1914
THE GOLDEN GOOSE   co-director with
   William Clifford, 1914
ONE OF THE DISCARD   co-director with
   C. Gardner Sullivan, 1914
THE LAST OF THE LINE   1915
THE DEVIL   1915
THE ALIEN   1915
CIVILIZATION   co-director with
   Raymond B. West, Reginald Barker,
   Scott Sidney & J. Parker Read, Jr.,
   Ince, 1916

REX INGRAM

(Reginald Ingram Montgomery
Hitchcock)
b. January 15, 1892 - Dublin, Ireland
d. 1950

THE GREAT PROBLEM   Universal, 1916
BROKEN FETTERS   Universal, 1916
THE CHALICE OF SORROWS
   Universal, 1916
BLACK ORCHIDS   Universal, 1917
THE REWARD OF THE FAITHLESS
   Universal, 1917
THE PULSE OF LIFE   Universal, 1917
THE FLOWER OF DOOM   Universal, 1917
THE LITTLE TERROR   Universal, 1917
HIS ROBE OF HONOR   Universal, 1918
HUMDRUM BROWN   Universal, 1918
THE DAY SHE PAID   Universal, 1919
UNDER CRIMSON SKIES   MGM, 1920
SHORE ACRES   MGM, 1920
HEARTS ARE TRUMPS   MGM, 1920
THE FOUR HORSEMEN OF THE
   APOCALYPSE   MGM, 1921
THE CONQUERING POWER   MGM, 1921
TURN TO THE RIGHT   MGM, 1922
THE PRISONER OF ZENDA   MGM, 1922
TRIFLING WOMEN   MGM, 1922
WHERE THE PAVEMENT ENDS   MGM, 1923
SCARAMOUCHE   MGM, 1923
THE ARAB   MGM, 1924
MARE NOSTRUM   MGM, 1926
THE MAGICIAN   MGM, 1926
THE GARDEN OF ALLAH   MGM, 1927
THE THREE PASSIONS   MGM, 1929
BAROUD   *LOVE IN MOROCCO*   MGM, 1933

RICHARD IRVING

b. February 13, 1917 - New York, New York
d. 1990

ISTANBUL EXPRESS (TF)
   Universal TV, 1968
PRESCRIPTION: MURDER (TF)
   Universal TV, 1968
BREAKOUT (TF)   Universal TV, 1970
RANSOM FOR A DEAD MAN (TF)
   Universal TV, 1971
CUTTER (TF)   Universal TV, 1972
THE SIX-MILLION DOLLAR MAN (TF)
   Universal TV, 1973
THE ART OF CRIME (TF)   Universal TV, 1975
EXO-MAN (TF)   Universal TV, 1977
SEVENTH AVENUE (MS)   co-director with
   Russ Mayberry, Universal TV, 1977
CLASS OF '65 (TF)   Universal TV, 1978
THE JESSE OWENS STORY (TF)   Harve
   Bennett Productions/Paramount TV, 1984

JORIS IVENS

(Georg Henrl Anton Ivens)
b. November 18, 1898 - Nijmegen, Holland
d. 1989

FLAMING ARROW   1911, Dutch
ZEEDIJK FILM STUDY (FD)   1927, Dutch
ETUDES DES MOUVEMENTS   1928, French
THE BRIDGE (FD)   1928, Dutch
BREAKERS   co-director, 1929, Dutch
RAIN   1929, Dutch
SKATING   1929, Dutch, unfinished
'I' FILM   1929, Dutch, unfinished
WE ARE BUILDING (FD)   1929, Dutch
PILE DRIVING (FD)   1929, Dutch
NEW ARCHITECTURE (FD)   1929, Dutch
CAISSONBOUW ROTTERDAM (FD)
   1929, Dutch
SOUTH LIMBUYRG (FD)   1929, Dutch
NVV CONGRESS (FD)   1929, Dutch
POOR DRENTHE (FD)   1929, Dutch
ZUIDERSEE (FD)   1930, Dutch
THE TRIBUNE FILM (FD)   1930, Dutch
BREAK AND BUILD (FD)   1930, Dutch
NEWS FROM THE SOVIET UNION (FD)
   1930, Dutch
DEMONSTRATION OF PROLETARIAN
   SOLIDARITY (FD)   1930, Dutch
PHILIPS RADIO   *INDUSTRIAL*
   SYMPHONY (FD)   1931, Dutch
CREOSOTE (FD)   1931, Dutch
SONG OF HEROES   *KOMSOMOL* (FD)
   1932, Soviet
MISERE AU BORINAGE   *BORINAGE* (FD)
   co-director, 1934, Belgian
NEW EARTH (FD)   1934, Dutch
THE SPANISH EARTH (FD)   1937
THE 400 MILLION (FD)   1938
THE POWER AND THE LAND (FD)   U.S.
   Department of Agriculture, 1940
OUR RUSSIAN FRONT (FD)   co-director with
   Lewis Milestone & Harry Rathner, 1941
OIL FOR ALADDIN'S LAMP (FD)   1942
ACTION STATIONS! (FD)   1943, Canadian
INDONESIA CALLING! (FD)   1946, Australian
THE FIRST YEARS (FD)   1949,
   Czechoslovakian-Bulgarian-Polish
PEACE WILL WIN (FD)   co-director,
   1951, Polish
FRENDSHIP TRIUMPHS (FD)   co-director with
   Gerard Philipe, 1952, Soviet-East German
PEACE TOUR (FD)   1952,
   Polish-East German
LIED DER STROME (FD)   1954, East German
LES AVENTURES DE TILL L'ESPIEGLE
   co-director, 1956, French-East German
LA SEINE A RECONTRE PARIS (FD)
   1957, French
EARLY SPRING (FD)   1958, Chinese
600 MILLION PEOPLE ARE WITH YOU (FD)
   1958, Chinese
L'ITALIA NON E UN PAESE POVERE (FD)
   1960, Italian
DEMAIN A NANGUILA (FD)   1960, Malian
CARNET DE VIAJE (FD)   1961, Cuban
CUBA, PUEBLO ARMADO (FD)   1961, Cuban
A VALPARAISO (FD)   1963, Chilean-French
LE PETIT CHAPITEAU (FD)   1963,
   Chilean-French
LE CIEL LA TERRE (FD)   1965,
   North Vietnamese-French
POUR LE MISTRAL   *MISTRAL* (FD)
   1966, French
ROTTERDAM-EUROPORT (FD)   1966, Dutch
FAR FROM VIETNAM (FD)   co-director
   with Jean-Luc Godard, Alain Resnais,
   William Klein, Agnes Varda & Claude Lelouch,
   New Yorker, 1967, French

LE 17E PARALLELE: LE VIETNAM EN
   GUERRE (FD)   co-director, 1968, French
LE PEUPLE ET SES FUSILS (FD)   co-director,
   1970, French
RECONTRE AVEC LE PRESIDENT HO
   CHI MINH (FD)   co-director, 1970,
   North Vietnamese
COMMENT YUKONG DEPLACE LES
   MONTAGNES (FD)   co-director,
   1976, French
LES KAZAKS - MINORITE NATIONALE -
   SINKIANO (FD)   co-director, 1977, French
LES QUIGOURS - MINORITE NATIONALE -
   SINKIANO (FD)   co-director, 1977, French
LE VENT (FD)   co-director, 1988, French

J

DEREK JARMAN

b. 1942 - England
d. 1994

SEBASTIANE   co-director with Paul Humfress,
   Discopat, 1977, British
JUBILEE   Libra, 1979, British
THE TEMPEST   World Northal, 1980, British
IN THE SHADOW OF THE SUN   ICA,
   1981, British
ANGELIC CONVERSATIONS   British Film
   Institute, 1985, British
CARAVAGGIO   British Film Institute,
   1986, British
ARIA   co-director, RCA VP/Virgin Vision,
   1987, British
THE LAST OF ENGLAND   International Film
   Circuit, 1987, British
WAR REQUIEM   Movie Visions, 1988, British
THE GARDEN   Bazilisk Productions/
   Channel 4/British Screen/ZDF/Uplink,
   1990, British-West German
EDWARD II   Fine Line Features/New Line
   Cinema, 1991, British
WITTGENSTEIN   British Film Institute,
   1993, British-Japanese
BLUE   Channel 4/Arts Council of Great Britain/
   Opal/BBC Radio 3/Baselisk Communications/
   Uplink Productions, 1993, British
GLITTERBUG   Basilisk Communications/BBC/
   Opal/Dangerous to Know, 1994, British

NUNNALLY JOHNSON

b. December 5, 1897 - Columbus, Georgia
d. 1977

NIGHT PEOPLE   20th Century-Fox, 1954
BLACK WIDOW   20th Century-Fox, 1954
HOW TO BE VERY, VERY POPULAR
   20th Century-Fox, 1955
THE MAN IN THE GRAY FLANNEL SUIT
   20th Century-Fox, 1956
OH MEN! OH WOMEN!
   20th Century-Fox, 1957
THE THREE FACES OF EVE
   20th Century-Fox, 1957
THE MAN WHO UNDERSTOOD WOMEN
   20th Century-Fox, 1959
THE ANGEL WORE RED   MGM, 1960,
   Italian-U.S.

HARMON JONES
b. June 3, 1911 - Canada
d. 1972

AS YOUNG AS YOU FEEL
  20th Century-Fox, 1952
THE PRIDE OF ST. LOUIS
  20th Century-Fox, 1952
BLOODHOUNDS OF BROADWAY
  20th Century-Fox, 1952
THE SILVER WHIP 20th Century-Fox, 1953
CITY OF BAD MEN 20th Century-Fox, 1953
THE KID FROM LEFT FIELD
  20th Century-Fox, 1953
GORILLA AT LARGE 20th Century-Fox, 1954
PRINCESS OF THE NILE
  20th Century-Fox, 1954
TARGET ZERO Warner Bros., 1955
A DAY OF FURY Universal, 1956
CANYON RIVER Allied Artists, 1956
THE BEAST OF BUDAPEST
  Allied Artists, 1958
BULLWHIP Allied Artists, 1958
WOLF LARSEN Allied Artists, 1958
DON'T WORRY, WE'LL THINK OF A TITLE
  United Artists, 1966

RUPERT JULIAN
b. January 25, 1889 - Auckland, New Zealand
d. 1943

JEWEL Universal, 1915
THE WATER CLUE 1915
THE TURN OF THE WHEEL Universal, 1916
NAKED HEARTS Universal, 1916
BETTINA LOVED A SOLDIER
  Universal, 1916
THE BUGLER OF ALGIERS Universal, 1916
THE EVIL WOMEN DO Universal, 1916
THE RIGHT TO BE HAPPY Universal, 1916
WE FRENCH Universal, 1916
THE GIFT GIRL Universal, 1917
THE CIRCUS OF LIFE Universal, 1917
THE MYSTERIOUS MR. TILLER
  Bluebird, 1917
THE DESIRE OF THE MOTH Bluebird, 1917
A KENTUCKY CINDERELLA Universal, 1917
MOTHER O'MINE Universal, 1917
THE DOOR BETWEEN Bluebird, 1917
THE SAVAGE Bluebird, 1917
THE KAISER - THE BEAST OF BERLIN
  Universal, 1918
HUNGRY EYES Bluebird, 1918
HANDS DOWN Bluebird, 1918
MIDNIGHT MADNESS Bluebird, 1918
CREAKING STAIRS Universal, 1919
THE SLEEPING LION Universal, 1919
THE FIRE FLINGERS Universal, 1919
MILLIONAIRE PIRATE Bluebird, 1919
THE HONEY BEE Pathé, 1920
THE GIRL WHO RAN WILD Universal, 1922
MERRY-GO-ROUND co-director with
  Erich Von Stroheim, Universal-Jewel, 1923
LOVE AND GLORY Universal-Jewel, 1924
HELL'S HIGHROAD Producers Distributing
  Corp., 1925
THE PHANTOM OF THE OPERA
  Universal-Jewel, 1925
THREE FACES EAST Producers Distributing
  Corp., 1926
SILENCE Producers Distributing Corp., 1926
THE YANKEE CLIPPER Producers
  Distributing Corp., 1927
THE COUNTRY DOCTOR Pathé, 1927
THE LEOPARD LADY Pathé, 1928
WALKING BACK Pathé, 1928
LOVE COMES ALONG RKO, 1930
THE CAT CREEPS Universal, 1930

CLAUDE JUTRA
b. March 11, 1930 - Montreal, Quebec, Canada
d. 1987

LES MAINS NETTES NFB, 1958, Canadian
LE NIGER - JEUNE REPUBLIQUE (FD)
  NFB, 1961, Canadian
A TOUT PRENDE Lopert, 1963, Canadian
COMMENT SAVOIR NFB, 1966, Canadian
WOW! NFB, 1969, Canadian
MON ONCLE ANTOINE NFB/Gendon
  Films Ltd., 1970, Canadian
KAMOURASKA New Line Cinema,
  1974, Canadian
POUR LE MEILLEUR ET POUR LE PIRE
  1975, Canadian
DREAMSPEAKER (TF) CBC,
  1977, Canadian
ADA (TF) CBC, 1977, Canadian
SURFACING Arista, 1981, Canadian
BY DESIGN Atlantic Releasing Corporation,
  1982, Canadian
LA DAME EN COULEURS Les Productions
  Pierre Lamy/NFB, 1985, Canadian
MY FATHER, MY RIVAL (CTF) Scholastic
  Productions/Insight Productions, 1985

K

JAN KADAR
(Janos Kadar)
b. April 1, 1918 - Budapest, Hungary
d. 1979

KATYA 1950, Czechoslovakian
KIDNAPPED co-director with Elmar Klos,
  1952, Czechoslovakian
MUSIC FROM MARS co-director with
  Elmar Klos, 1954, Czechoslovakian
YOUNG DAYS co-director with Elmar Klos,
  1956, Czechoslovakian
THE HOUSE AT THE TERMINUS co-director
  with Elmar Klos, 1957, Czechoslovakian
THREE WISHES co-director with Elmar Klos,
  1958, Czechoslovakian
YOUTH (FD) co-director with Elmar Klos,
  1960, Czechoslovakian
THE SPARTAKIADE (FD) co-director with
  Elmar Klos, 1960, Czechoslovakian
DEATH IS CALLED ENGELCHEN co-director
  with Elmar Klos, 1963, Czechoslovakian
THE DEFENDANT co-director with
  Elmar Klos, 1964, Czechoslovakian
THE SHOP ON MAIN STREET co-director
  with Elmar Klos, Prominent Films,
  1965, Czechoslovakian
ADRIFT MPO Films, 1970,
  Czechoslovakian-U.S.
THE ANGEL LEVINE United Artists, 1970
LIES MY FATHER TOLD ME Columbia,
  1975, Canadian
THE OTHER SIDE OF HELL (TF)
  Aubrey-Lyon Productions, 1978
FREEDOM ROAD (TF) Zev Braun
  Productions/Freedom Road Films, 1979

MIKHAIL KALATOZOV
(Mikhail Kalatozishvili)
b. December 23, 1903 - Tiflis, Georgia, Russia
d. 1973

BLIND 1930, Soviet
SALT FOR SVANETIA 1930, Soviet
A NAIL IN THE BOOT 1932, Soviet
MANHOOD 1939, Soviet
VALERI CHKALOV 1941, Soviet
INVINCIBLE co-director with
  Sergei Gerasimov, 1943, Soviet
MOSCOW MUSIC-HALL 1945, Soviet
CONSPIRACY OF THE DOOMED
  1950, Soviet
TRUE FRIENDS 1954, Soviet
THE FIRST ECHELON 1956, Soviet
THE HOSTILE WIND 1956, Soviet
WOMAN FROM WARSAW 1956, Soviet
THE CRANES ARE FLYING Artkino,
  1958, Soviet
THE LETTER THAT WAS NEVER SENT
  1960, Soviet
I AM CUBA! (FD) ICAIC/Mosfilm, 1964,
  Soviet-Cuban
THE RED TENT Paramount, 1971,
  Italian-Soviet

JOSEPH (JOE) KANE
b. March 19, 1897 - San Diego, California
d. 1975

FIGHTING MARINES (S) co-director with
  B. Reeves Eason, Republic, 1935
TUMBLING TUMBLEWEEDS Republic, 1935
MELODY TRAIL Republic, 1935
DARKEST AFRICA (S) co-director with
  B. Reeves Eason, Republic, 1936
THE UNDERSEA KINGDOM (S) co-director
  with B. Reeves Eason, Republic, 1936
THE LAWLESS NINETIES Republic, 1936
THE LONELY TRAIL Republic, 1936
GUNS AND GUITARS Republic, 1936
OH SUSANNAH! Republic, 1936
PARADISE EXPRESS Republic, 1937
COME ON COWBOYS! Republic, 1937
BOOTS AND SADDLES Republic, 1937
SPRINGTIME IN THE ROCKIES
  Republic, 1937
BORN TO BE WILD Republic, 1938
ARSON RACKET SQUAD Republic, 1938
UNDER WESTERN STARS Republic, 1938
MAN FROM MUSIC MOUNTAIN
  Republic, 1938
BILLY THE KID RETURNS Republic, 1938
SHINE ON HARVEST MOON Republic, 1938
SOUTHWARD HO! Republic, 1939
IN OLD MONTEREY Republic, 1939
WALL STREET COWBOY Republic, 1939
THE ARIZONA KID Republic, 1939
DAYS OF JESSE JAMES Republic, 1939
SAGA OF DEATH VALLEY Republic, 1939
YOUNG BUFFALO BILL Republic, 1940
THE RANGER AND THE LADY
  Republic, 1940
COLORADO Republic, 1940
THE BORDER LEGION Republic, 1940
ROBIN HOOD OF THE PECOS
  Republic, 1941
SHERIFF OF TOMBSTONE Republic, 1941
THE GREAT TRAIN ROBBERY
  Republic, 1941
NEVADA CITY Republic, 1941
RAGS TO RICHES Republic, 1941
RED RIVER VALLEY Republic, 1941
SUNSET ON THE DESERT Republic, 1942
ROMANCE OF THE RANGE Republic, 1942
SONS OF THE PIONEERS Republic, 1942

HEART OF THE GOLDEN WEST
  Republic, 1942
IDAHO Republic, 1943
KING OF THE COWBOYS Republic, 1943
SONG OF TEXAS Republic, 1943
HANDS ACROSS THE BORDER
  Republic, 1943
THE COWBOY AND THE SENORITA
  Republic, 1944
THE YELLOW ROSE OF TEXAS
  Republic, 1944
SONG OF NEVADA Republic, 1944
FLAME OF THE BARBARY COAST
  Republic, 1945
THE CHEATERS Republic, 1945
DAKOTA Republic, 1945
IN OLD SACRAMENTO Republic, 1946
THE PLAINSMAN AND THE LADY
  Republic, 1946
WYOMING Republic, 1947
OLD LOS ANGELES Republic, 1948
THE GALLANT LEGION Republic, 1948
THE PLUNDERERS Republic, 1948
THE LAST BANDIT Republic, 1949
BRIMSTONE Republic, 1949
ROCK ISLAND TRAIL Republic, 1950
THE SAVAGE HORDE Republic, 1950
CALIFORNIA PASSAGE Republic, 1950
OH SUSANNAH! Republic, 1951
FIGHTING COAST GUARD Republic, 1951
THE SEA HORNET Republic, 1951
HOODLUM EMPIRE Republic, 1952
WOMAN OF THE NORTH COUNTRY
  Republic, 1952
RIDE THE MAN DOWN Republic, 1953
SAN ANTONE Republic, 1953
FAIR WIND TO JAVA Republic, 1953
SEA OF LOST SHIPS Republic, 1954
JUBILEE TRAIL Republic, 1954
HELL'S OUTPOST Republic, 1955
TIMBERJACK Republic, 1955
THE ROAD TO DENVER Republic, 1955
THE VANISHING AMERICAN Republic, 1955
THE MAVERICK QUEEN Republic, 1956
THUNDER OVER ARIZONA Republic, 1956
ACCUSED OF MURDER Republic, 1956
DUEL AT APACHE WELLS Republic, 1957
SPOILERS OF THE FOREST Republic, 1957
LAST STAGECOACH WEST Republic, 1957
THE CROOKED CIRCLE Republic, 1957
GUNFIRE AT INDIAN GAP Republic, 1958
THE NOTORIOUS MR. MONKS
  Republic, 1958
THE LAWLESS EIGHTIES Republic, 1958
THE MAN WHO DIED TWICE Republic, 1958
COUNTRY BOY *HERE COMES THAT
  NASHVILLE SOUND* 1966

PHIL KARLSON
(Philip Karlstein)
b. July 2, 1908 - Chicago, Illinois
d. 1986

A WAVE, A WAC AND A MARINE
  Monogram, 1944
THERE GOES KELLY Monogram, 1945
G.I. HONEYMOON Monogram, 1945
THE SHANGHAI COBRA Monogram, 1945
DARK ALIBI Monogram, 1946
LIVE WIRES Monogram, 1946
THE MISSING LADY Monogram, 1946
SWING PARADE OF 1946 Monogram, 1946
BEHIND THE MASK Monogram, 1946
BOWERY BOMBSHELL Monogram, 1946
WIFE WANTED Monogram, 1946
BLACK GOLD Allied Artists, 1947
KILROY WAS HERE Monogram, 1947
LOUISIANA Monogram, 1947

ADVENTURES IN SILVERADO
  Columbia, 1948
ROCKY Monogram, 1948
THUNDERHOOF Columbia, 1948
THE LADIES OF THE CHORUS
  Columbia, 1948
DOWN MEMORY LANE Eagle Lion, 1949
THE BIG CAT Eagle Lion, 1949
THE IROQUOIS TRAIL United Artists, 1950
LORNA DOONE Columbia, 1951
THE TEXAS RANGERS Columbia, 1951
MASK OF THE AVENGER Columbia, 1951
SCANDAL SHEET Columbia, 1952
KANSAS CITY CONFIDENTIAL
  United Artists, 1952
THE BRIGAND Columbia, 1952
99 RIVER STREET United Artists, 1953
THEY RODE WEST Columbia, 1954
HELL'S ISLAND Paramount, 1955
TIGHT SPOT Columbia, 1955
FIVE AGAINST THE HOUSE Columbia, 1955
THE PHENIX CITY STORY
  Allied Artists, 1955
THE BROTHERS RICO Columbia, 1957
GUNMAN'S WALK Columbia, 1958
HELL TO ETERNITY Allied Artists, 1960
KEY WITNESS MGM, 1960
THE SECRET WAYS Universal, 1961
THE YOUNG DOCTORS United Artists, 1961
THE SCARFACE MOB Desilu, 1962
KID GALAHAD United Artists, 1962
RAMPAGE Warner Bros., 1963
THE SILENCERS Columbia, 1966
A TIME FOR KILLING Columbia, 1967
THE WRECKING CREW Columbia, 1968
HORNET'S NEST United Artists, 1970
BEN Cinerama Releasing Corporation, 1972
WALKING TALL Cinerama Releasing
  Corporation, 1973
FRAMED Paramount, 1974

BUSTER KEATON
(Joseph Francis Keaton)
b. October 4, 1895 - Piqua, Kansas
d. 1966

ONE WEEK co-director with
  Eddie Cline, 1920
CONVICT 13 co-director with
  Eddie Cline, 1920
THE SCARECROW co-director with
  Eddie Cline, 1920
NEIGHBORS co-director with
  Eddie Cline, 1920
THE HAUNTED HOUSE co-director with
  Eddie Cline, 1921
HARD LUCK co-director with
  Eddie Cline, 1921
THE HIGH SIGN co-director with
  Eddie Cline, 1921
THE GOAT co-director with
  Mal St. Clair, 1921
THE PLAYHOUSE co-director with
  Eddie Cline, 1921
THE BOAT co-director with Eddie Cline, 1921
THE PALEFACE co-director with
  Eddie Cline, 1921
COPS co-director with Eddie Cline, 1922
MY WIFE'S RELATIONS co-director with
  Eddie Cline, 1922
THE BLACKSMITH co-director with
  Mal St. Clair, 1922
THE FROZEN NORTH co-director with
  Eddie Cline, 1922
DAY DREAMS co-director with
  Eddie Cline, 1922
THE ELECTRIC HOUSE co-director with
  Eddie Cline, 1922

THE BALLOONATIC co-director with
  Eddie Cline, 1923
THE LOVE NEST 1923
THE THREE AGES co-director with
  Eddie Cline, Metro, 1923
OUR HOSPITALITY co-director with
  John G. Blystone, Metro, 1923
SHERLOCK, JR. Metro, 1923
THE NAVIGATOR co-director with
  Donald Crisp, Metro, 1924
SEVEN CHANCES Metro, 1925
GO WEST Metro, 1925
BATTLING BUTLER Metro, 1925
THE GENERAL co-director with
  Clyde Bruckman, United Artists, 1927
LIFE IN SOMETOWN, USA 1938
HOLLYWOOD HANDICAP 1938
STREAMLINED SWING 1938

WILLIAM KEIGHLEY
b. August 4, 1889 - Philadelphia, Pennsylvania
d. 1986

THE MATCH KING co-director with
  Howard Bretherton, Warner Bros., 1933
LADIES THEY TALK ABOUT co-director with
  Howard Bretherton, Warner Bros., 1933
EASY TO LOVE Warner Bros., 1934
JOURNAL OF A CRIME Warner Bros., 1934
DR. MONICA Warner Bros., 1934
KANSAS CITY PRINCESS
  Warner Bros., 1934
BIG HEARTED HERBERT
  Warner Bros., 1934
BABBITT Warner Bros., 1934
THE RIGHT TO LIVE Warner Bros., 1935
G-MEN Warner Bros., 1935
SPECIAL AGENT Warner Bros., 1935
STARS OVER BROADWAY
  Warner Bros., 1935
MARY JANE'S PA Warner Bros., 1935
THE SINGING KID Warner Bros., 1936
BULLETS OR BALLOTS Warner Bros., 1936
THE GREEN PASTURES co-director with
  Marc Connelly, Warner Bros., 1936
GOD'S COUNTRY AND THE WOMAN
  Warner Bros., 1937
THE PRINCE AND THE PAUPER
  Warner Bros., 1937
VARSITY SHOW Warner Bros., 1937
THE ADVENTURES OF ROBIN HOOD
  co-director with Michael Curtiz,
  Warner Bros., 1938
VALLEY OF THE GIANTS
  Warner Bros., 1938
SECRETS OF AN ACTRESS
  Warner Bros., 1938
BROTHER RAT Warner Bros., 1938
YES, MY DARLING DAUGHTER
  Warner Bros., 1939
EACH DAWN I DIE Warner Bros., 1939
THE FIGHTING 69TH Warner Bros., 1940
TORRID ZONE Warner Bros., 1940
NO TIME FOR COMEDY Warner Bros., 1940
FOUR MOTHERS Warner Bros., 1941
THE BRIDE CAME C.O.D.
  Warner Bros., 1941
THE MAN WHO CAME TO DINNER
  Warner Bros., 1942
GEORGE WASHINGTON SLEPT HERE
  Warner Bros., 1942
HONEYMOON RKO Radio, 1947
THE STREET WITH NO NAME
  20th Century-Fox, 1948
ROCKY MOUNTAIN Warner Bros., 1950
CLOSE TO MY HEART Warner Bros., 1951
THE MASTER OF BALLANTRAE
  Warner Bros., 1953, British

CHARLES KENT

b. 1852
d. 1923

ANTONY AND CLEOPATRA   Vitagraph, 1908
A MIDSUMMER NIGHT'S DREAM
 Vitagraph, 1909
TWELFTH NIGHT   Vitagraph, 1910
BARNABY RUDGE   Vitagraph, 1911
A CHRISTMAS CAROL   Vitagraph, 1911
VANITY FAIR   Vitagraph, 1911
FORTUNES OF A COMPOSER
 Vitagraph, 1912
RIP VAN WINKLE   Vitagraph, 1913
THE TABLES TURNED   V itagraph, 1913

ERLE C. KENTON

b. August 1, 1896 - Norboro, Montana
d. 1980

DOWN ON THE FARM   1920
MARRIED LIFE   1920
LOVE, HONOR AND BEHAVE   co-director
 with Richard Jones, 1920
A SMALL TOWN IDOL   1921
TEA WITH A KICK   1923
THE DANGER SIGNAL   1925
A FOOL AND HIS MONEY   1925
RED HOT TIRES   1925
THE PALM BEACH GIRL   1926
THE SAP   1926
LOVE TOY   1926
OTHER WOMEN'S HUSBANDS   1926
THE GIRL IN THE PULLMAN   1927
WEDDING BILL$ 1927
THE REJUVENATION OF AUNT MARY   1927
BARE KNEES   1928
THE COMPANIONATE MARRIAGE   1928
GOLF WIDOWS   1928
NAME THE WOMAN   1928
NOTHING TO WEAR   1928
THE SIDE SHOW   1928
THE SPORTING AGE   1928
THE STREET OF ILLUSION   1928
FATHER AND SON   1929
TRIAL MARRIAGE   1929
THE SONG OF LOVE   1929
MEXICALI ROSE   1929
A ROYAL ROMANCE   1930
THE LAST PARADE   1931
LOVER COME BACK   1931
LEFTOVER LADIES   1931
X MARKS THE SPOT   1931
STRANGER IN TOWN   1932
GUILTY AS HELL   1932
ISLAND OF LOST SOULS   Paramount, 1933
FROM HELL TO HEAVEN   1933
DISGRACED   1933
BIG EXECUTIVE   1933
SEARCH FOR BEAUTY   1934
YOU'RE TELLING ME   1934
BEST MAN WINS   1935
PARTY WIRE   1935
THE PUBLIC MENACE   1935
GRAND EXIT   1935
DEVIL'S SQUADRON   1936
COUNTERFEIT   1936
END OF THE TRAIL   1936
DEVIL'S PLAYGROUND   Columbia, 1937
RACKETEERS IN EXILE   1937
SHE ASKED FOR IT   1937
THE LADY OBJECTS   1938
LITTLE TOUGH GUYS IN SOCIETY   1938
EVERYTHING'S ON ICE   1939
ESCAPE TO PARADISE   1939
REMEDY FOR RICHES   RKO Radio, 1940
PETTICOAT POLITICS   RKO Radio, 1941

MELODY FOR THREE   RKO Radio, 1941
NAVAL ACADEMY   1941
THEY MEET AGAIN   1941
FLYING CADETS   Universal, 1941
FRISCO LIL   Universal, 1942
NORTH TO THE KLONDIKE   Universal, 1942
THE GHOST OF FRANKENSTEIN
 Universal, 1942
PARDON MY SARONG   Universal, 1942
WHO DONE IT?   Universal, 1942
HOW'S ABOUT IT?   Universal, 1943
IT AIN'T HAY   Universal, 1943
ALWAYS A BRIDESMAID   Universal, 1943
HOUSE OF FRANKENSTEIN   Universal, 1945
SHE GETS HER MAN   Universal, 1945
HOUSE OF DRACULA   Universal, 1945
THE CAT CREEPS   Universal, 1946
LITTLE MISS BIG   Universal, 1946
BOB AND SALLY   1948
ONE TOO MANY   1950

ANTHONY KIMMINS

b. November 10, 1901 - Harrow, England
d. 1963

KEEP FIT   1937, British
I SEE ICE   1938, British
IT'S IN THE AIR   1938, British
COME ON GEORGE   1939, British
TROUBLE BREWING   1939, British
MINE OWN EXECUTIONER
 20th Century-Fox, 1947, British
BONNIE PRINCE CHARLIE   British Lion,
 1948, British
FLESH AND BLOOD   Showcorporation,
 1949, British
MR. DENNING DRIVES NORTH
 Carroll Pictures, 1951, British
THE PASSIONATE SENTRY   WHO GOES
 THERE!   Fine Arts, 1952, British
THE CAPTAIN'S PARADISE
 United Artists, 1953, British
AUNT CLARA   Showcorporation,
 1954, British
SMILEY   20th Century-Fox, 1956,
 British-Australian
SMILEY GETS A GUN   20th Century-Fox,
 1958, British-Australian
THE AMOROUS MR. PRAWN
 THE AMOROUS PRAWN
 Union Films, 1962, British

HENRY KING

b. June 24, 1888 - Christiansburg, Virginia
d. 1982

WHO PAYS?   Pathé, 1915
THE BRAND OF MAN   1915
JOY AND THE DRAGON   Pathé, 1916
PAY DIRT   Pathé, 1916
THE STAINED PEARL   Pathé, 1916
LITTLE MARY SUNSHINE   Pathé, 1916
ONCE UPON A TIME   Pathé, 1916
THE CHILD OF M'SIEU   Triangle, 1916
TWIN KIDDIES   Pathé, 1917
THE CLIMBER   1917
TOLD AT TWILIGHT   Pathé, 1917
SUNSHINE AND GOLD   Pathé, 1917
SOULS IN PAWN   American Mutual, 1917
THE BRIDE'S SILENCE
 American Mutual, 1917
THE UNAFRAID   1917
THE UPPER CRUST   1917
SCEPTER OF SUSPICION   THE SPECTOR
 OF SUSPICION   Mutual, 1917
THE MAINSPRING   Mutual, 1917
SOUTHERN PRIDE   Mutual, 1917

A GAME OF WITS   American Mutual, 1917
THE MATE OF SALLY ANN
 American Mutual, 1917
KING SOCIAL BRIARS   1918
THE GHOST OF ROSY TAYLOR   1918
BEAUTY AND THE ROGUE
 American Mutual, 1918
POWERS THAT PREY
 American Mutual, 1918
THE LOCKED HEART   General, 1918
HEARTS AND DIAMONDS   HEARTS OR
 DIAMONDS?   Mutual, 1918
UP ROMANCE ROAD   1918
ALL THE WORLD TO NOTHING   Pathé, 1918
HOBBS IN A HURRY   Pathé, 1918
WHEN A MAN RIDES ALONE   Pathé, 1918
CUPID BY PROXY   Pathé, 1918
WHERE THE WEST BEGINS   Pathé, 1919
BRASS BUTTONS   Pathé, 1919
SOME LIAR   Pathé, 1919
A SPORTING CHANCE   Pathé, 1919
THIS HERO STUFF   Pathé, 1919
SIX FEET FOUR   Pathé, 1919
231/2 HOURS LEAVE   F.P.L., 1919
A FUGITIVE FROM MATRIMONY
 Robertson-Cole, 1919
HAUNTING SHADOWS
 Robertson-Cole, 1919
THE WHITE DOVE   Robertson-Cole, 1920
UNCHARTED CHANNELS
 Robertson-Cole, 1920
ONE HOUR BEFORE DAWN   Pathé, 1920
DICE OF DESTINY   Pathé, 1920
HELP WANTED - MALE   Pathé, 1920
WHEN WE WERE 21   Pathé, 1921
THE MISTRESS OF SHENSTONE
 Robertson-Cole, 1921
SALVAGE   Robertson-Cole, 1921
THE STING OF THE LASH
 Robertson-Cole, 1921
TOL'ABLE DAVID   First National, 1921
THE SEVENTH DAY   First National, 1922
SONNY   First National, 1922
THE BOND BOY   First National, 1922
FURY   First National, 1923
THE WHITE SISTER   Metro, 1923
ROMOLA   Metro-Goldwyn, 1924
SACKCLOTH AND SCARLET
 Paramount, 1925
ANY WOMAN   Paramount, 1925
STELLA DALLAS   United Artists, 1925
PARTNERS AGAIN   United Artists, 1926
THE WINNING OF BARBARA WORTH
 United Artists, 1926
THE MAGIC FLAME   United Artists, 1927
THE WOMAN DISPUTED   co-director with
 Sam Taylor, United Artists, 1928
SHE GOES TO WAR   United Artists, 1929
HELL HARBOR   United Artists, 1930
THE EYES OF THE WORLD   Fox, 1930
LIGHTNIN'   Fox, 1930
MERELY MARY ANN   Fox, 1931
OVER THE HILL   Fox, 1931
THE WOMAN IN ROOM 13   Fox, 1932
STATE FAIR   Fox, 1933
I LOVED YOU WEDNESDAY   co-director with
 William Cameron Menzies, Fox, 1933
CAROLINA   Fox, 1934
MARIE GALANTE   Fox, 1934
ONE MORE SPRING   20th Century-Fox, 1935
WAY DOWN EAST   20th Century-Fox, 1935
THE COUNTRY DOCTOR
 20th Century-Fox, 1936
RAMONA   20th Century-Fox, 1936
LLOYDS OF LONDON
 20th Century-Fox, 1936
SEVENTH HEAVEN   20th Century-Fox, 1937
IN OLD CHICAGO   20th Century-Fox, 1938

ALEXANDER'S RAGTIME BAND
  20th Century-Fox, 1938
JESSE JAMES 20th Century-Fox, 1939
STANLEY AND LIVINGSTONE
  20th Century-Fox, 1939
LITTLE OLD NEW YORK
  20th Century-Fox, 1940
MARYLAND 20th Century-Fox, 1940
CHAD HANNA 20th Century-Fox, 1940
A YANK IN THE R.A.F.
  20th Century-Fox, 1941
REMEMBER THE DAY
  20th Century-Fox, 1942
THE BLACK SWAN 20th Century-Fox, 1942
THE SONG OF BERNADETTE ★
  20th Century-Fox, 1943
WILSON ★ 20th Century-Fox, 1944
A BELL FOR ADANO 20th Century-Fox, 1945
MARGIE 20th Century-Fox, 1946
CAPTAIN FROM CASTILE
  20th Century-Fox, 1947
DEEP WATERS 20th Century-Fox, 1948
PRINCE OF FOXES 20th Century-Fox, 1949
TWELVE O'CLOCK HIGH
  20th Century-Fox, 1949
THE GUNFIGHTER 20th Century-Fox, 1950
I'D CLIMB THE HIGHEST MOUNTAIN
  20th Century-Fox, 1951
WAIT 'TILL THE SUN SHINES, NELLIE
  20th Century-Fox, 1952
THE SNOWS OF KILIMANJARO
  20th Century-Fox, 1952
DAVID AND BATHSHEBA
  20th Century-Fox, 1952
O. HENRY'S FULL HOUSE co-director with
  Henry Hathaway, Howard Hawks,
  Henry Koster & Jean Negulesco,
  20th Century-Fox, 1952
KING OF THE KHYBER RIFLES
  20th Century-Fox, 1953
UNTAMED 20th Century-Fox, 1955
LOVE IS A MANY-SPLENDORED THING
  20th Century-Fox, 1955
CAROUSEL 20th Century-Fox, 1956
THE SUN ALSO RISES
  20th Century-Fox, 1957
THE BRAVADOS 20th Century-Fox, 1958
THIS EARTH IS MINE
  20th Century-Fox, 1959
BELOVED INFIDEL 20th Century-Fox, 1959
TENDER IS THE NIGHT
  20th Century-Fox, 1962

LOUIS KING

b. June 28, 1898 - Christiansburg, Virginia
d. 1962

IS YOUR DAUGHTER SAFE? FBO,
  co-director with Leon Lee, 1927
THE BOY RIDER FBO, 1927
THE SLINGSHOT KID FBO, 1927
THE LITTLE BUCKAROO FBO, 1928
THE PINTO KID FBO, 1928
THE FIGHTIN' REDHEAD FBO, 1928
THE BANTAM COWBOY FBO, 1928
TERROR FBO, 1928
YOUNG WHIRLWIND FBO, 1928
ROUGH RIDIN' RED FBO, 1928
ORPHAN OF THE SAGE FBO, 1928
THE VAGABOND CUB Columbia, 1929
THE FRECKLED RASCAL Columbia, 1929
THE LITTLE SAVAGE Columbia, 1929
PALS OF THE PRAIRIE Columbia, 1929
THE LONE RIDER 1930
SHADOW RANCH 1930
MEN WITHOUT LAW 1930
DESERT VENGEANCE 1931
THE FIGHTING SHERIFF 1931

BORDER LAW 1931
THE DECEIVER 1931
POLICE COURT 1932
THE COUNTY FAIR 1932
FAME STREET 1932
ARM OF THE LAW 1932
DRIFTING SOULS 1932
ROBBERS' ROOST 1933
LIFE IN THE RAW 1933
LA CIUDAD DE CARTON 1934
MURDER IN TRINIDAD 1934
PURSUED 1934
BACHELOR OF ARTS 1934
JULIETA COMPRA EN HIJO 1935
CHARLIE CHAN IN EGYPT
  20th Century-Fox, 1935
ANGELITA 1935
ROAD GANG 1936
SPECIAL INVESTIGATOR 1936
SONG OF THE SADDLE 1936
BENGAL TIGER 1936
THAT MAN'S HERE AGAIN 1937
MELODY FOR TWO 1937
DRAGGERMAN COURAGE 1937
WILD MONEY 1937
BULLDOG DRUMMOND COMES BACK
  Paramount, 1937
WINE, WOMEN AND HORSES 1937
BULLDOG DRUMMOND'S REVENGE
  Paramount, 1937
TIP-OFF GIRLS Paramount, 1938
HUNTED MEN Paramount, 1938
PRISON FARM Paramount, 1938
BULLDOG DRUMMOND IN AFRICA
  Paramount, 1938
ILLEGAL TRAFFIC Paramount, 1938
TOM SAWYER, DETECTIVE
  Paramount, 1938
PERSONS IN HIDING Paramount, 1939
UNDERCOVER DOCTOR Paramount, 1939
SEVENTEEN Paramount, 1940
TYPHOON Paramount, 1940
THE WAY OF ALL FLESH Paramount, 1940
MOON OVER BURMA Paramount, 1940
YOUNG AMERICA 1942
CHETNIKS! 20th Century-Fox, 1943
LADIES OF WASHINGTON
  20th Century-Fox, 1944
THUNDERHEAD, SON OF FLICKA
  20th Century-Fox, 1945
SMOKY 20th Century-Fox, 1946
THUNDER IN THE VALLEY
  20th Century-Fox, 1947
GREEN GRASS OF WYOMING
  20th Century-Fox, 1948
SAND 20th Century-Fox, 1949
MRS. MIKE United Artists, 1949
FRENCHIE Universal, 1950
THE LION AND THE HORSE
  Warner Bros., 1952
POWDER RIVER 20th Century-Fox, 1953
SABRE JET United Artists, 1953
DANGEROUS MISSION RKO Radio, 1954
MASSACRE 20th Century-Fox, 1956

TEINOSUKE KINUGASA

b. January 1, 1896 - Mie Prefecture, Japan
d. 1982

TWO LITTLE BIRDS 1922, Japanese
THE GOLDEN DEMON 1923, Japanese
BEYOND DECAY 1923, Japanese
SHE HAS LIVED HER OWN DESTINY
  1924, Japanese
SECRET OF A LIFE 1924, Japanese
LOVE, FOG AND RAIN 1924, Japanese
LOVE AND THE WARRIOR 1925, Japanese
THE SUN 1925, Japanese

A CRAZY PAGE *A PAGE OF MADNESS*
  Shin Kankaku Ha Eiga Remmei,
  1926, Japanese
EPOCH OF LOYALTY 1927, Japanese
MOONLIGHT MADNESS 1927, Japanese
JUJIRO *CROSSROADS/CROSSWAYS/*
  THE SHADOWS OF THE YOSHIWARA
  Kinugasa Eiga Remmei/Shochiku Kinema,
  1928, Japanese
THE GAY MASQUERADE 1928, Japanese
TALES FROM A COUNTRY BY THE SEA
  1928, Japanese
BEFORE DAWN 1931, Japanese
THE LOYAL FORTY-SEVEN RONIN
  1932, Japanese
TWO STONE LANTERNS 1933, Japanese
THE SWORD AND THE SUMO RING
  1934, Japanese
YUKINOJO'S DISGUISE, PART I Shochiku,
  1935, Japanese
YUKINOJO'S DISGUISE, PART II Shochiku,
  1935, Japanese
YUKINOJO'S DISGUISE, PART III Shochiku,
  1936, Japanese
HITOHADA KANO Shochiku,
  1937, Japanese
THE SUMMER BATTLE OF OSAKA
  1937, Japanese
MISS SNAKE PRINCESS, PART I
  1940, Japanese
MISS SNAKE PRINCESS, PART II
  1940, Japanese
THE BATTLE OF KAWANAKAJIMA Toho,
  1941, Japanese
GO INDEPENDENT FLAG Toho,
  1943, Japanese
ROSE OF THE SEA Toho, 1945, Japanese
LORD FOR A NIGHT Toho, 1946, Japanese
FOUR LOVE STORIES co-director
  with Mikio Naruse, Shiro Toyoda &
  Kajiro Yamamoto, Toho, 1947, Japanese
ACTRESS Toho, 1947, Japanese
KOBANZAME Shin Engiza Productions,
  1948, Japanese
KOGA MANSION Shin Engiza Productions,
  1949, Japanese
RED BAT *THE FACE OF A MURDERER*
  Toei, 1950, Japanese
PASSAGE BIRD OF THE MOON Daiei,
  1951, Japanese
THE SECRET OF SHURA CASTLE Daiei,
  1952, Japanese
SAGA OF THE GREAT BUDDHA
  DEDICATION OF THE GREAT BUDDHA
  Daiei, 1952, Japanese
GATE OF HELL Daiei, 1953, Japanese
DUEL OF A SNOWY NIGHT Daiei,
  1954, Japanese
IT HAPPENED IN TOKYO Daiei,
  1955, Japanese
THE ROMANCE OF YUSHIMA Daiei,
  1955, Japanese
SHIN HEIKE MONOGATARI: YOSHINAKA AND
  THREE WOMEN *NEW TALES OF THE*
  TAIRA CLAN Daiei, 1956, Japanese
HAMPEITA TSUKIGATA Daiei,
  1956, Japanese
TALE OF GENJI Daiei, 1957, Japanese
A FANTASTIC TALE OF NARUTO Daiei,
  1957, Japanese
A WOMAN OF OSAKA Daiei,
  1958, Japanese
THE WHITE HERON Daiei, 1958, Japanese
TORMENTED FLAME Daiei, 1959, Japanese
SONG OF THE LANTERN Daiei,
  1960, Japanese
OKOTO AND SASUKE Daiei,
  1961, Japanese

TOUSLED HAIR   Daiei, 1961, Japanese
THE SORCERER   Daiei, 1963, Japanese
THE LITTLE RUNAWAY   co-director with
   Edouard Bocharov, Gorky Studio/Daiei,
   1966, Soviet-Japanese

SIR ALEXANDER KORDA
(Sandor Laszlo Korda)
b. September 16, 1893 - Pusztaturpaszto,
   Hungary
d. 1956

A BECSAPOT UJSAGIRO   co-director with
   Gyula Zilahi, 1914, Hungarian
A TISZTI KARDBOJT   1915, Hungarian
TUTYU ES TOTYO   co-director with
   Gyula Zilahi, 1915, Hungarian
LYON LEA   co-director with
   Miklos M. Pasztory, 1915, Hungarian
FEHER EJSZAKAK   FEDORA
   1916, Hungarian
CIKLAMEN   1916, Hungarian
THE OFFICER'S SWORD   1916, Hungarian
WHITE NIGHTS   1916, Hungarian
BATTLING HEARTS   1916, Hungarian
GRANDMOTHER   1916, Hungarian
A TYPEWRITER'S TALE   1916, Hungarian
A MILLION POUND NOTE   1916, Hungarian
MISKA THE GREAT   1917, Hungarian
A DOUBLE-HEARTED MAN   1917, Hungarian
THE ST. PETER'S UMBRELLA
   1917, Hungarian
THE STORK CALIPH   1917, Hungarian
MAGIC   1917, Hungarian
THE FAUN   1917, Hungarian
HARRISON AND HARRISON
   1917, Hungarian
THE WOMAN WITH TWO SOULS
   1917, Hungarian
GOLDEN MAN   1918, Hungarian
MARY ANN   1918, Hungarian
NEITHER AT HOME NOR ABROAD
   1918, Hungarian
AVE CAESARI   1919, Hungarian
WHITE ROSES   1919, Hungarian
THE 111TH   1919, Hungarian
YAMATA   1919, Hungarian
SEINE MAJESTAT DES BETTLEKIND
   THE PRINCE AND THE PAUPER
   1920, Austrian
DIETRO LA MASCHERA   Italian, 1921
HERRIN DER MEERE   1922, Austrian
EINE VERSUNKENE WELT   1922, Austrian
SAMSON UND DALILA   1922, Austrian
DAS UNBEKANNTE MORGEN
   1923, German
TRAGODIE IN HAUSE HAPSBURG
   1924, German
JEDERMANNS FRAU   1924, German
DER TANZER MEINE FRAU   DANCE FEVER
   1925, German
EINE DUBARRY VON HEUTE   A MODERN
   DUBARRY   1926, German
MADAME WUNSCHT KEINE KINDER
   MADAME WANTS NO CHILDREN
   1926, German
THE STOLEN BRIDE   First National, 1927
THE PRIVATE LIFE OF HELEN OF TROY
   First National, 1927
THE YELLOW LILY   First National, 1928
THE NIGHT WATCH   First National, 1928
LOVE AND THE DEVIL   First National, 1929
THE SQUALL   First National, 1929
HER PRIVATE LIFE   First National, 1929
LILIES OF THE FIELD   First National, 1930
WOMEN EVERYWHERE   Fox, 1930
THE PRINCESS AND THE PLUMBER
   Fox, 1930

RIVE GAUCHE   Paramount, 1931, French
DIE MANNER UM LUCIE   Paramount,
   1931, German
MARIUS   1931, French
ZUM GOLDENEN AUKER   Paramount,
   1931, German
RESERVED FOR LADIES   SERVICE FOR
   LADIES   Paramount, 1932, British
WEDDING REHEARSAL   Ideal, 1932, British
LA DAME CHEZ MAXIM'S   1932, French
THE GIRL FROM MAXIM'S   1933, British
THE PRIVATE LIFE OF HENRY VIII
   United Artists, 1933, British
THE PRIVATE LIFE OF DON JUAN
   United Artists, 1934, British
REMBRANDT   United Artists, 1936, British
THAT HAMILTON WOMAN   LADY HAMILTON
   United Artists, 1941, British
VACATION FROM MARRIAGE   PERFECT
   STRANGERS   MGM, 1945, British
AN IDEAL HUSBAND   20th Century-Fox,
   1947, British

ZOLTAN KORDA
b. May 3, 1895 - Pusztaturpaszto, Hungary
d. 1961

DIE ELF TEUFEL   1927, German
CASH   1933, British
SANDERS OF THE RIVER   1935, British
FORGET ME NOT   1936, British
CONQUEST OF THE AIR (FD)   United Artists,
   1936, British
ELEPHANT BOY   co-director with
   Robert J. Flaherty, United Artists,
   1937, British
THE DRUM   United Artists, 1938, British
THE FOUR FEATHERS   United Artists,
   1939, British
THE JUNGLE BOOK   United Artists, 1942
SAHARA   Columbia, 1943
COUNTER-ATTACK   Columbia, 1945
THE MACOMBER AFFAIR
   United Artists, 1947
A WOMAN'S VENGEANCE   Universal, 1948
CRY, THE BELOVED COUNTRY
   United Artists, 1951, British
STORM OVER THE NILE   co-director with
   Terence Young, Columbia, 1955, British

HENRY KOSTER
(Hermann Kosterlitz)
b. May 1, 1905 - Berlin, Germany
d. 1988

DAS ABENTEUER DER THEA ROLAND
   1932, German
DAS HASSLICHE MADCHEN   1933, German
PETER   1934, Austrian-Hungarian
KLEINE MUTTI   1934, Austrian-Hungarian
KATHARINA DIE LETZTE   1935, Austrian
DAS TAGEBUCH DER GELIEBTEN
   1936, Austrian-Italian
THREE SMART GIRLS   Universal, 1936
100 MEN AND A GIRL   Universal, 1937
THE RAGE OF PARIS   Universal, 1938
THREE SMART GIRLS GROW UP
   Universal, 1939
FIRST LOVE   Universal, 1939
SPRING PARADE   Universal, 1940
IT STARTED WITH EVE   Universal, 1941
BETWEEN US GIRLS   Universal, 1942
MUSIC FOR MILLIONS   MGM, 1944
TWO SISTERS FROM BOSTON   MGM, 1946
THE UNFINISHED DANCE   MGM, 1947
THE BISHOP'S WIFE ★   RKO Radio, 1947
THE LUCK OF THE IRISH
   20th Century-Fox, 1948

COME TO THE STABLE
   20th Century-Fox, 1949
THE INSPECTOR GENERAL
   Warner Bros., 1949
WABASH AVENUE   20th Century-Fox, 1950
MY BLUE HEAVEN   20th Century-Fox, 1950
HARVEY   Universal, 1950
NO HIGHWAY IN THE SKY   NO HIGHWAY
   20th Century-Fox, 1951, British
MR. BELVEDERE RINGS THE BELL
   20th Century-Fox, 1951
ELOPEMENT   20th Century-Fox, 1951
O. HENRY'S FULL HOUSE   co-director with
   Henry Hathaway, Howard Hawks,
   Henry King & Jean Negulesco,
   20th Century-Fox, 1952
STARS AND STRIPES FOREVER
   20th Century-Fox, 1953
MY COUSIN RACHEL
   20th Century-Fox, 1952
THE ROBE   20th Century-Fox, 1953
DESIREE   20th Century-Fox, 1954
A MAN CALLED PETER
   20th Century-Fox, 1955
THE VIRGIN QUEEN   20th Century-Fox, 1955
GOOD MORNING, MISS DOVE
   20th Century-Fox, 1955
D-DAY, THE SIXTH OF JUNE
   20th Century-Fox, 1956
THE POWER AND THE PRIZE   MGM, 1956
MY MAN GODFREY   Universal, 1957
FRAULEIN   20th Century-Fox, 1958
THE NAKED MAJA   United Artists, 1959
THE STORY OF RUTH
   20th Century-Fox, 1960
FLOWER DRUM SONG   Universal, 1961
MR. HOBBS TAKES A VACATION
   20th Century-Fox, 1962
TAKE HER, SHE'S MINE
   20th Century-Fox, 1963
DEAR BRIGITTE   20th Century-Fox, 1965
THE SINGING NUN   MGM, 1966

GRIGORI KOZINTSEV
(Grigorii Mikhailowich Kozintsev)
b. March 22, 1905 - Kiev, Russia
d. 1973

THE ADVENTURES OF OKTYABRINA
   co-director with Leonid Trauberg,
   1924, Soviet
MISHKA VERSUS YUDENICH   co-director
   with Leonid Trauberg, 1925, Soviet
THE DEVIL'S WHEEL   co-director with
   Leonid Trauberg, 1925, Soviet
THE OVERCOAT   co-director with
   Leonid Trauberg, 1926, Soviet
BRATISHK   co-director with Leonid Trauberg,
   1926, Soviet
THE CLUB OF THE BIG DEED   co-director
   with Leonid Trauberg, 1927, Soviet
THE NEW BABYLON   co-director with
   Leonid Trauberg, 1929, Soviet
ALONE   co-director with Leonid Trauberg,
   1931, Soviet
THE YOUTH OF MAXIM   co-director with
   Leonid Trauberg, 1935
THE RETURN OF MAXIM   co-director with
   Leonid Trauberg, 1937, Soviet
THE VYBORG SIDE   co-director with
   Loenid Trauberg, 1939, Soviet
PLAIN PEOPLE   co-director with
   Leonid Trauberg, 1956, Soviet
PIROGOV   1947, Soviet
BELINSKI   1953, Soviet
DON QUIXOTE   MGM, 1957, Soviet
HAMLET   United Artists, 1964, Soviet
KING LEAR   Artkino, 1971, Soviet

LEV KULESHOV

b. January 14, 1899 - Tambov, Russia
d. 1970

THE PROJECT OF ENGINEER PRITE
  1918, Soviet
THE UNFINISHED LOVE SONG   co-director
  with Vitold Polonsky, 1919, Soviet
ON THE RED FRONT   1920, Soviet
THE EXTRAORDINARY ADVENTURES OF
  MR. WEST IN THE LAND OF THE
  BOLSHEVIKS   1924, Soviet
THE DEATH RAY   1925, Soviet
DURA LEX   BY THE LAW   1926, Soviet
YOUR ACQUAINTANCE   1927, Soviet
THE GAY CANARY   1929, Soviet
TWO-BULDI-TWO   co-director with
  Nina Agadzhanova-Shutko, 1930, Soviet
FORTY HEARTS   1931, Soviet
HORIZON/HORIZON - THE WANDERING
  JEW   1933, Soviet
THE GREAT CONSOLER   1933, Soviet
THE SIBERIANS   1940, Soviet
INCIDENT IN A VOLCANO   co-director,
  1941, Soviet
TIMUR'S OATH   1942, Soviet
WE ARE FROM THE URALS   1944, Soviet

GREGORY LA CAVA

b. March 10, 1892 - Towanda, Pennsylvania
d. 1952

HIS NIBS   Exceptional Pictures, 1921
RESTLESS WIVES   C.C. Burr, 1924
THE NEW SCHOOL TEACHER
  C.C. Burr, 1924
WOMANHANDLED   Paramount, 1925
LET'S GET MARRIED   Paramount, 1926
SO'S YOUR OLD MAN   Paramount, 1926
SAY IT AGAIN   Paramount, 1926
PARADISE FOR TWO   Paramount, 1927
RUNNING WILD   Paramount, 1927
TELL IT TO SWEENEY   Paramount, 1927
THE GAY DEFENDER   Paramount, 1927
FEEL MY PULSE   Paramount, 1928
HALF A BRIDE   Paramount, 1928
SATURDAY'S CHILDREN
  First National, 1929
BIG NEWS   Pathé, 1929
HIS FIRST COMMAND   Pathé, 1930
LAUGH AND GET RICH   RKO, 1931
SMART WOMAN   RKO, 1931
SYMPHONY OF SIX MILLION
  RKO Radio, 1932
THE AGE OF CONSENT   RKO, 1932
THE HALF-NAKED TRUTH   RKO, 1932
GABRIEL OVER THE WHITE HOUSE
  MGM, 1933
BED OF ROSES   RKO, 1933
GALLANT LADY   United Artists, 1934
THE AFFAIRS OF CELLINI
  United Artists, 1934
WHAT EVERY WOMAN KNOWS   MGM, 1934
PRIVATE WORLDS   Paramount, 1935
SHE MARRIED HER BOSS   Columbia, 1935
MY MAN GODFREY ★   Universal, 1936
STAGE DOOR ★   RKO Radio, 1937

FIFTH AVENUE GIRL   RKO Radio, 1939
THE PRIMROSE PATH   RKO Radio, 1940
UNFINISHED BUSINESS   Universal, 1941
LADY IN A JAM   Universal, 1942
LIVING IN A BIG WAY   MGM, 1947

CHARLES LAMONT

b. May 5, 1898 - San Francisco, California
d. 1993

THE CURTAIN FALLS   Universal, 1934
TOMORROW'S YOUTH   Universal, 1935
THE WORLD ACCUSES   Universal, 1935
SON OF STEEL   Universal, 1935
FALSE PRETENSES   Universal, 1935
GIGOLETTE   Universal, 1935
A SHOT IN THE DARK   Universal, 1935
CIRCUMSTANTIAL EVIDENCE
  Universal, 1935
THE GIRL WHO CAME BACK
  Universal, 1935
HAPPINESS C.O.D.   Universal, 1935
THE LADY IN SCARLET   Universal, 1935
RING AROUND THE MOON   Universal, 1936
LITTLE RED SCHOOL HOUSE
  Universal, 1936
BELOW THE DEADLINE   Universal, 1936
AUGUST WEEK-END   Universal, 1936
THE DARK HOUR   Universal, 1936
LADY LUCK   Universal, 1936
BULLDOG EDITION   Universal, 1936
WALLABY JIM OF THE ISLANDS
  Universal, 1937
INTERNATIONAL CRIME   Universal, 1938
SHADOWS OVER SHANGHAI
  Universal, 1938
SLANDER HOUSE   Universal, 1938
CIPHER BUREAU   Universal, 1938
THE LONG SHOT   Universal, 1939
VERBENA TRAGICA   Universal, 1939
PRIDE OF THE NAVY   Universal, 1939
PANAMA PATROL   Universal, 1939
INSIDE INFORMATION   Universal, 1939
UNEXPECTED FATHER   Universal, 1939
LITTLE ACCIDENT   Universal, 1939
OH JOHNNY, HOW YOU CAN LOVE!
  Universal, 1940
SANDY IS A LADY   Universal, 1940
LOVE, HONOR AND OH BABY!
  Universal, 1940
GIVE US WINGS   Universal, 1940
SAN ANTONIO ROSE   Universal, 1941
SING ANOTHER CHORUS   Universal, 1941
MOONLIGHT IN HAWAII   Universal, 1941
MELODY LANE   Universal, 1941
ROAD AGENT   Universal, 1941
DON'T GET PERSONAL   Universal, 1942
YOU'RE TELLING ME!   Universal, 1942
ALMOST MARRIED   Universal, 1942
HI NEIGHBOR!   Universal, 1942
GET HEP TO LOVE   Universal, 1942
WHEN JOHNNY COMES MARCHING HOME
  Universal, 1943
IT COMES UP LOVE   Universal, 1943
MR. BIG   Universal, 1943
HIT THE ICE   Universal, 1943
FIRED WIFE   Universal, 1943
TOP MAN   Universal, 1943
CHIP OFF THE OLD BLOCK   Universal, 1944
HER PRIMITIVE MAN   Universal, 1944
THE MERRY MONAHANS   Universal, 1944
BOWERY TO BROADWAY   Universal, 1944
SALOME, WHERE SHE DANCED
  Universal, 1945
THAT'S THE SPIRIT   Universal, 1945
FRONTIER GAL   Universal, 1945
THE RUNAROUND   Universal, 1946
SLAVE GIRL   Universal, 1946

THE UNTAMED BREED   Universal, 1948
MA & PA KETTLE   Universal, 1949
BAGDAD   Universal, 1949
MA & PA KETTLE GO TO TOWN
  Universal, 1950
I WAS A SHOPLIFTER   Universal, 1950
ABBOTT & COSTELLO IN THE FOREIGN
  LEGION   Universal, 1950
CURTAIN CALL AT CACTUS CREEK
  Universal, 1950
ABBOTT & COSTELLO MEET THE INVISIBLE
  MAN   Universal, 1951
COMIN' ROUND THE MOUNTAIN
  Universal, 1951
FLAME OF ARABY   Universal, 1951
ABBOTT & COSTELLO MEET CAPTAIN KIDD
  Universal, 1952
ABBOTT & COSTELLO GO TO MARS
  Universal, 1953
MA & PA KETTLE ON VACATION
  Universal, 1953
ABBOTT & COSTELLO MEET DR. JEKYLL
  AND MR. HYDE   Universal, 1953
MA & PA KETTLE AT HOME   Universal, 1954
UNTAMED HEIRESS   Universal, 1954
RICOCHET ROMANCE   Universal, 1954
CAROLINE CANNONBALL   Universal, 1955
ABBOTT & COSTELLO MEET THE
  KEYSTONE KOPS   Universal, 1955
ABBOTT & COSTELLO MEET THE MUMMY
  Universal, 1955
LAY THAT RIFLE DOWN   Universal, 1955
THE KETTLES IN THE OZARKS
  Universal, 1956
FRANCIS IN THE HAUNTED HOUSE
  Universal, 1956

ALBERT LAMORISSE

b. January 13, 1922 - Paris, France
d. 1970

DJERBA   1947, French
BIM   1949, French
WHITE MANE   William Snyder, 1953, French
THE RED BALLOON   Lopert, 1956
STOWAWAY IN THE SKY   LE VOYAGE EN
  BALLON   Lopert, 1960, French
FIFI LA PLUME   1965, French
VERSAILLES (FD)   1967, French
PARIS JAMAIS VE (FD)   1968, French
THE LOVERS' WIND (FD)   1968, French

BURT LANCASTER

b. November 2, 1913 - New York, New York
d. 1994

THE KENTUCKIAN   United Artists, 1955
THE MIDNIGHT MAN   co-director with
  Roland Kibbee, Universal, 1974

LEW LANDERS

(Louis Friedlander)
b. January 2, 1901 - New York, New York
d. 1962

THE RED RIDER   Universal, 1934
TAILSPIN TOMMY   Universal, 1934
THE VANISHING SHADOW   Universal, 1934
THE CALL OF THE SAVAGE   Universal, 1935
RUSTLERS OF RED DOG   Universal, 1935
THE RAVEN   Universal, 1935
STORMY   Universal, 1935
PAROLE!   Universal, 1936
WITHOUT ORDERS   RKO, 1936
NIGHT WAITRESS   RKO Radio 1936
THEY WANTED TO MARRY
  RKO Radio, 1937

THE MAN WHO FOUND HIMSELF
  RKO Radio, 1937
YOU CAN'T BUY LUCK   RKO RADIO, 1937
BORDER CAFE   RKO RADIO, 1937
FLIGHT FROM GLORY   RKO Radio, 1937
LIVING ON LOVE   RKO Radio, 1937
DANGER PATROL   RKO Radio, 1937
CRASHING HOLLYWOOD   RKO Radio, 1938
DOUBLE DANGER   RKO Radio, 1938
CONDEMNED WOMEN   RKO Radio, 1938
LAW OF THE UNDERWORLD
  RKO Radio, 1938
BLIND ALIBI   RKO Radio, 1938
SKY GIANT   RKO Radio, 1938
SMASHING THE RACKETS
  RKO Radio, 1938
ANNABEL TAKES A TOUR   RKO Radio, 1938
PACIFIC LINER   RKO Radio, 1939
TWELVE CROWDED HOURS
  RKO Radio, 1939
FIXER DUGAN   RKO Radio, 1939
THE GIRL AND THE GAMBLER
  RKO Radio, 1939
BAD LANDS   RKO Radio, 1939
CONSIPRACY   RKO Radio, 1939
HONEYMOON DEFERRED   Universal, 1940
ENEMY AGENT   Universal, 1940
SKI PATROL   Universal, 1940
LA CONGA NIGHTS   Universal, 1940
WAGONS WESTWARD   Republic, 1940
SING DANCE - PLENTY HOT   Republic, 1940
GIRL FROM HA\'ANA   Republic, 1940
SLIGHTLY TEMPTED   Republic, 1940
RIDIN' ON A RAINBOW   Republic, 1941
LUCKY DEVILS   Universal, 1941
BACK IN THE SADDLE   1941
THE SINGING HILL   Republic, 1941
I WAS A PRISONER ON DEVIL'S ISLAND
  Columbia, 1941
MYSTERY SHIP   Columbia, 1941
THE STORK PAYS OFF   Columbia, 1941
THE MAN WHO RETURNED TO LIFE
  Columbia, 1942
ALIAS BOSTON BLACKIE   Columbia, 1942
CANAL ZONE   Columbia, 1942
HARVARD, HERE I COME   Columbia, 1942
NOT A LADIES' MAN   Columbia, 1942
SUBMARINE RAIDERS   Columbia, 1942
CADETS ON PARADE   Columbia, 1942
ATLANTIC CONVOY   Columbia, 1942
SABOTAGE SQUAD   Columbia, 1942
THE BOOGIE MAN WILL GET YOU
  Columbia, 1942
SMITH OF MINNESOTA   Columbia, 1942
STAND BY ALL NETWORKS   Columbia, 1942
JUNIOR ARMY   Columbia, 1942
AFTER MIDNIGHT WITH BOSTON BLACKIE
  Columbia, 1942
REDHEAD FROM MANHATTAN
  Columbia, 1943
MURDER IN TIMES SQUARE
  Columbia, 1943
POWER OF THE PRESS   Columbia, 1943
DOUGHBOYS IN IRELAND   Columbia, 1943
THE DEERSLAYER   Columbia, 1943
THE RETURN OF THE VAMPIRE
  Columbia, 1944
COWBOY CANTEEN   Columbia, 1944
THE GHOST THAT WALKS ALONE
  Columbia, 1944
TWO-MAN SUBMARINE   Columbia, 1944
STARS ON PARADE   Columbia, 1944
THE BLACK PARACHUTE   Columbia, 1944
U-BOAT PRISONER   Columbia, 1944
SWING IN THE SADDLE   Columbia, 1944
I'M FROM ARKANSAS   Columbia, 1944
CRIME, INC.   Columbia/Producers
  Releasing Corp., 1945

THE POWER OF THE WHISTLER
  Columbia, 1945
TROUBLE CHASERS   1945
FOLLOW THAT WOMAN   Paramount, 1945
ARSON SQUAD   Producers Releasing
  Corp., 1945
SHADOW OF TERROR   Producers
  Releasing Corp., 1945
THE ENCHANTED FOREST   Producers
  Releasing Corp., 1945
TOKYO ROSE   Paramount, 1945
THE MASK OF DIJON   Producers
  Releasing Corp., 1946
A CLOSE CALL FOR BOSTON BLACKIE
  Columbia, 1946
THE TRUTH ABOUT MURDER
  RKO Radio, 1946
HOT CARGO   Paramount, 1946
SECRETS OF A SORORITY GIRL   Producers
  Releasing Corp., 1946
DEATH VALLEY   Screen Guild, 1947
DANGER STREET   RKO RADIO, 1947
SEVEN KEYS TO BALDPATE
  RKO Radio, 1947
UNDER THE TONTO RIM   RKO RADIO, 1947
THUNDER MOUNTAIN   RKO RADIO, 1947
THE SON OF RUSTY   Columbia, 1947
DEVIL SHIP   Columbia, 1947
MY DOG RUSTY   Columbia, 1948
ADVENTURES OF GALLANT BESS
  Eagle Lion, 1948
INNER SANCTUM   Film Classics, 1948
STAGECOACH KID   RKO RADIO, 1949
LAW OF THE BARBARY COAST
  Columbia, 1949
AIR HOSTESS   Columbia, 1949
BARBARY PIRATE   Columbia, 1949
DAVY CROCKETT, INDIAN SCOUT
  United Artists, 1950
GIRLS' SCHOOL   Columbia, 1950
DYNAMITE PASS   Columbia, 1950
TYRANT OF THE SEA   Columbia, 1950
STATE PENITENTIARY   Columbia, 1950
BEAUTY ON PARADE   Columbia, 1950
CHAIN GANG   Columbia, 1950
LAST OF THE BUCCANEERS
  Columbia, 1950
REVENUE AGENT   Columbia, 1950
BLUE BLOOD   Monogram, 1951
A YANK IN KOREA   Columbia, 1951
WHEN THE REDSKINS RODE
  Columbia, 1951
THE BIG GUSHER   Columbia, 1951
HURRICANE ISLAND   Columbia, 1951
THE MAGIC CARPET   Columbia, 1951
JUNGLE MANHUNT   Columbia, 1951
ALADDIN AND HIS LAMP   Monogram, 1952
JUNGLE JIM IN THE FORBIDDEN LAND
  Columbia, 1952
CALIFORNIA CONQUEST   Columbia, 1952
ARCTIC FLIGHT   Monogram, 1952
RIDERS OF CAPISTRANO
  Revue-Exclusive, 1952
BAD MEN OF MARYSVILLE
  Revue-Exclusive, 1952
THE RANGE MASTERS
  Revue-Exclusive, 1952
THE NEON TORNADO
  Revue-Exclusive, 1953
THE RETURN OF TRIGGER JOHNSON
  Revue-Exclusive, 1953
ROARING CHALLENGE
  Revue-Exclusive, 1953
TORPEDO ALLEY   Allied Artists, 1953
TANGIER INCIDENT   co-director with
  Paul Landres, Allied Artists, 1953
MAN IN THE DARK   Columbia, 1953
RUN FOR THE HILLS   Broder, 1953

CAPTAIN JOHN SMITH AND POCAHONTAS
  United Artists, 1953
CAPTAIN KIDD AND THE SLAVE GIRL
  United Artists, 1954
THE CRUEL TOWER   Allied Artists, 1956
HOT ROD GANG   American
  International, 1958
THE CHALLENGE OF RIN-TIN-TIN
  Columbia, 1958
TERRIFIED!   Crown International, 1963

MICHAEL LANDON
(Eugene Orowitz)
b. October 31, 1937 - Forest Hills, New York
d. 1991

IT'S GOOD TO BE ALIVE (TF)   Metromedia
  Productions, 1974
LITTLE HOUSE ON THE PRAIRIE (TF)
  NBC Productions, 1974
THE LONELIEST RUNNER (TF)
  NBC Productions, 1976
KILLING STONE (TF)   Universal TV, 1978
FATHER MURPHY (TF)
  NBC Productions, 1981
LITTLE HOUSE: THE LAST FAREWELL (TF)
  NBC Productions/Ed Friendly
  Productions, 1984
SAM'S SON   Invictus Entertainment
  Corporation, 1984
HIGHWAY TO HEAVEN (TF)   Michael
  Landon Productions, 1984
WHERE PIGEONS GO TO DIE (TF)   Michael
  Landon Productions/World International
  Network, 1990
US (TF)   Michael Landon Productions/
  Columbia TV, 1991

SIDNEY LANFIELD
b. April 20, 1898 - Chicago, Illinois
d. 1972

CHEER UP AND SMILE   Fox, 1930
THREE GIRLS LOST   Fox, 1931
HUSH MONEY   Fox, 1931
DANCE TEAM   Fox, 1931
SOCIETY GIRL   Fox, 1931
HAT CHECK GIRL   Fox, 1932
BROADWAY BAD   Fox, 1933
MOULIN ROUGE   Fox, 1934
THE LAST GENTLEMAN   Fox, 1934
HOLD 'EM YALE   20th Century-Fox, 1935
RED SALUTE   20th Century-Fox, 1936
KING OF BURLESQUE
  20th Century-Fox, 1936
HALF ANGEL   20th Century-Fox, 1936
SING, BABY SING   20th Century-Fox, 1936
ONE IN A MILLION   20th Century-Fox, 1937
WAKE UP AND LIVE   20th Century-Fox, 1937
THIN ICE   20th Century-Fox, 1937
LOVE AND HISSES   20th Century-Fox, 1937
ALWAYS GOODBYE   20th Century-Fox, 1938
THE HOUND OF THE BASKERVILLES
  20th Century-Fox, 1939
SECOND FIDDLE   20th Century-Fox, 1939
SWANEE RIVER   20th Century-Fox, 1939
YOU'LL NEVER GET RICH   Columbia, 1941
THE LADY HAS PLANS   Paramount, 1942
MY FAVORITE BLONDE   Paramount, 1942
THE MEANEST MAN IN THE WORLD
  20th Century-Fox, 1943
LET'S FACE IT   Paramount, 1943
STANDING ROOM ONLY   Paramount, 1944
BRING ON THE GIRLS   Paramount, 1945
THE WELL-GROOMED BRIDE
  Paramount, 1946

THE TROUBLE WITH WOMEN
  Paramount, 1947
WHERE THERE'S LIFE   Paramount, 1947
STATION WEST   RKO Radio, 1948
SORROWFUL JONES   Paramount, 1949
THE LEMON DROP KID   Paramount, 1951
FOLLOW THE SUN   20th Century-Fox, 1951
SKIRTS AHOY!   MGM, 1952

FRITZ LANG

b. December 5, 1890 - Vienna, Austria
d. 1976

HALBBLUT   1919, German
DER HERR DER LIEBE   1919, German
DIE SPINNEN: DER GOLDENE SEE
  1919, German
HARAKIRI   1919, German
DER SPINNEN: DAS BRILLANTENSCHIFF
  1920, German
DAS WANDERNDE BILD   1920, German
VIER UM DIE FRAU   1920, German
DER MUDE TOD   1921, German
DR. MABUSE DER SPIELER: SPIELER
  AUSLEIDENSCHAFT   1922, German
DR. MABUSE DER SPIELER: INFERNO
  DESVERBRECHENS   1922, German
DIE NIBELUNGEN: SIEGFRIEDS TOD
  UFA, 1924, German
DIE NIBELUNGEN: KRIEMHILDS RACHE
  UFA, 1924, German
METROPOLIS   UFA, 1927, German
SPIES   MGM, 1928, German
BY ROCKET TO THE MOON   DIE FRAU IM
  MOND   1929, German
M   Paramount, 1930, German
THE TESTAMENT OF DR. MABUSE   Janus,
  1933, German
LILIOM   Fox-Europa, 1934, French
FURY   MGM, 1936
YOU ONLY LIVE ONCE   United Artists, 1937
YOU AND ME   Paramount, 1938
THE RETURN OF FRANK JAMES
  20th Century-Fox, 1940
WESTERN UNION   20th Century-Fox, 1941
MAN HUNT   20th Century-Fox, 1941
HANGMEN ALSO DIE   United Artists, 1943
WOMAN IN THE WINDOW   RKO Radio, 1944
MINISTRY OF FEAR   Paramount, 1944
SCARLET STREET   Universal, 1945
CLOAK AND DAGGER   Warner Bros., 1945
SECRET BEYOND THE DOOR
  Universal, 1948
HOUSE BY THE RIVER   Republic, 1950
AMERICAN GUERILLA IN THE PHILIPPINES
  20th Century-Fox, 1950
RANCHO NOTORIOUS   RKO Radio, 1952
CLASH BY NIGHT   RKO Radio, 1952
THE BLUE GARDENIA   Warner Bros., 1953
THE BIG HEAT   Columbia, 1953
HUMAN DESIRE   Columbia, 1954
MOONFLEET   MGM, 1955
WHILE THE CITY SLEEPS
  RKO Radio, 1956
BEYOND A REASONABLE DOUBT
  RKO Radio, 1956
DER TIGER VON ESCHNAPUR   JOURNEY
  TO THE LOST CITY   American International,
  1959, West German-French-Italian
DAS INDISCHE GRABMAL   JOURNEY TO
  THE LOST CITY   American International,
  1959, West German-French-Italian
THE 1000 EYES OF DR. MABUSE   Ajay
  Films, 1960, West German-French-Italian

WALTER LANG

b. August 10, 1898 - Memphis, Tennessee
d. 1972

RED KIMONO   Vital Exchange, 1925
THE CARNIVAL GIRL   Vitagraph, 1926
THE EARTH WOMAN   Associated
  Exhibitors, 1926
THE GOLDEN WEB   Lumas, 1926
MONEY TO BURN   Lumas, 1926
THE LADYBIRD   Chadwick, 1927
THE SATIN WOMAN   Lumas, 1927
SALLY IN OUR ALLEY   Columbia, 1927
BY WHOSE HAND?   Columbia, 1927
THE COLLEGE HERO   Columbia, 1927
THE NIGHT FLYER   Pathé, 1928
SHADOWS OF THE PAST   1928
THE DESERT BRIDE   Columbia, 1928
THE SPIRIT OF YOUTH   Tiffany, 1929
HELLO SISTER   World Wide, 1930
COCK O' THE WALK   co-director with
  Roy William Neill, World Wide, 1930
THE BIG FIGHT   World Wide, 1930
THE COSTELLO CASE   World Wide, 1930
BROTHERS   Columbia, 1930
COMMAND PERFORMANCE   1931
HELL BOUND   Tiffany, 1931
WOMEN GO ON FOREVER   1931
NO MORE ORCHIDS   Columbia, 1932
THE WARRIOR'S HUSBAND   Fox, 1933
MEET THE BARON   1933
THE PARTY'S OVER   1934
WHOM THE GODS DESTROY   1934
THE MIGHTY BARNUM   United Artists, 1934
CARNIVAL   Columbia, 1935
HOORAY FOR LOVE   1935
LOVE BEFORE BREAKFAST   Universal, 1936
WIFE, DOCTOR AND NURSE
  20th Century-Fox, 1937
SECOND HONEYMOON
  20th Century-Fox, 1937
THE BARONESS AND THE BUTLER
  20th Century-Fox, 1938
I'LL GIVE A MILLION   20th Century-Fox, 1938
THE LITTLE PRINCESS
  20th Century-Fox, 1939
THE BLUE BIRD   20th Century-Fox, 1940
STAR DUST   20th Century-Fox, 1940
THE GREAT PROFILE
  20th Century-Fox, 1940
TIN PAN ALLEY   20th Century-Fox, 1940
MOON OVER MIAMI   20th Century-Fox, 1941
WEEK-END IN HAVANA
  20th Century-Fox, 1941
SONG OF THE ISLANDS
  20th Century-Fox, 1942
THE MAGNIFICENT DOPE
  20th Century-Fox, 1942
CONEY ISLAND   20th Century-Fox, 1943
GREENWICH VILLAGE
  20th Century-Fox, 1944
STATE FAIR   20th Century-Fox, 1945
SENTIMENTAL JOURNEY
  20th Century-Fox, 1946
CLAUDIA AND DAVID
  20th Century-Fox, 1946
MOTHER WORE TIGHTS
  20th Century-Fox, 1947
SITTING PRETTY   20th Century-Fox, 1947
WHEN MY BABY SMILES AT ME
  20th Century-Fox, 1948
YOU'RE MY EVERYTHING
  20th Century-Fox, 1949
CHEAPER BY THE DOZEN
  20th Century-Fox, 1950
THE JACKPOT   20th Century-Fox, 1950
ON THE RIVIERA   20th Century-Fox, 1951

WITH A SONG IN MY HEART
  20th Century-Fox, 1952
CALL ME MADAM   20th Century-Fox, 1953
THERE'S NO BUSINESS LIKE SHOW
  BUSINESS   20th Century-Fox, 1954
THE KING AND I ★   20th Century-Fox, 1956
THE DESK SET   20th Century-Fox, 1957
BUT NOT FOR ME   20th Century-Fox, 1959
CAN-CAN   20th Century-Fox, 1960
THE MARRIAGE-GO-ROUND
  20th Century-Fox, 1961
SNOW WHITE AND THE THREE STOOGES
  20th Century-Fox, 1961

CHARLES LAUGHTON

b. July 1, 1899 - Scarborough, England
d. 1962

THE NIGHT OF THE HUNTER
  United Artists, 1955

PHILIP LEACOCK

b. October 8, 1917 - London, England
d. 1990

RIDERS OF THE NEW FOREST   Crown,
  1946, British
THE BRAVE DON'T CRY   Mayer-Kingsley,
  1952, British
APPOINTMENT IN LONDON   Associated
  Artists, 1953, British
THE LITTLE KIDNAPPERS
  THE KIDNAPPERS   United Artists,
  1954, British
ESCAPADE   DCA, 1955, British
THE SPANISH GARDENER   Rank,
  1956, British
HIGH TIDE AT NOON   Rank, 1957, British
INNOCENT SINNERS   Rank, 1958, British
THE RABBIT TRAP   United Artists, 1959
LET NO MAN WRITE MY EPITAPH
  Columbia, 1960
TAKE A GIANT STEP   United Artists, 1960
HAND IN HAND   Columbia, 1961, British
REACH FOR GLORY   Royal Films
  International, 1962, British
13 WEST STREET   Columbia, 1962
THE WAR LOVER   Columbia, 1962, British
TAMAHINE   MGM, 1964, British
ADAM'S WOMAN   Warner Bros.,
  1970, Australian
THE BIRDMEN (TF)   Universal TV, 1971
WHEN MICHAEL CALLS (TF)   Palomar
  International, 1972
THE DAUGHTERS OF JOSHUA CABE (TF)
  Spelling-Goldberg Productions, 1972
BAFFLED! (TF)   Arena Productions/ITC, 1973
THE GREAT MAN'S WHISKERS (TF)
  Universal TV, 1973
DYING ROOM ONLY (TF)   Lorimar
  Productions, 1973
KEY WEST (TF)   Warner Bros. TV, 1973
KILLER ON BOARD (TF)   Lorimar
  Productions, 1977
WILD AND WOOLY (TF)   Aaron Spelling
  Productions, 1978
THE CURSE OF KING TUT'S TOMB (TF)
  Stromberg-Kerby Productions/Columbia TV/
  HTV West, 1980
ANGEL CITY (TF)   Factor-Newland
  Productions, 1980
THE TWO LIVES OF CAROL LETNER (TF)
  Penthouse One Presentations, 1981
THE WILD WOMEN OF CHASTITY
  GULCH (TF)   Aaron Spelling
  Productions, 1982
THREE SOVEREIGNS FOR SARAH (TF)
  Night Owl Productions, 1985

DAVID LEAN
b. March 25, 1908 - Croydon, England
d. 1991

IN WHICH WE SERVE   co-director with
   Noel Coward, Universal, 1942, British
THIS HAPPY BREED   Universal,
   1944, British
BLITHE SPIRIT   United Artists, 1945, British
BRIEF ENCOUNTER   Universal, 1946, British
GREAT EXPECTATIONS ★   Universal,
   1947, British
OLIVER TWIST   United Artists, 1948, British
ONE WOMAN'S STORY *THE PASSIONATE
   FRIENDS*   Universal, 1949, British
MADELEINE   Universal, 1950, British
BREAKING THE SOUND BARRIER
   THE SOUND BARRIER   United Artists,
   1952, British
HOBSON'S CHOICE   United Artists,
   1954, British
SUMMERTIME *SUMMER MADNESS* ★
   United Artists, 1955, British
THE BRIDGE ON THE RIVER KWAI ★★
   Columbia, 1957, British
LAWRENCE OF ARABIA ★★   Columbia,
   1962, British
DOCTOR ZHIVAGO ★   MGM, 1965, British
RYAN'S DAUGHTER   MGM, 1970, British
A PASSAGE TO INDIA ★   Columbia,
   1984, British

REGINALD LE BORG
b. December 11, 1902 - Vienna, Austria
d. 1989

SHE'S FOR ME   Universal, 1943
CALLING DR. DEATH   Universal, 1943
ADVENTURE IN MUSIC   co-director, 1944
WEIRD WOMAN   Universal, 1944
THE MUMMY'S GHOST   Universal, 1944
JUNGLE WOMAN   Universal, 1944
SAN DIEGO - I LOVE YOU   Universal, 1944
DEAD MAN'S EYES   Universal, 1944
DESTINY   Universal, 1944
HONEYMOON AHEAD   Universal, 1945
JOE PALOOKA - CHAMP   Monogram, 1946
LITTLE IODINE   United Artists, 1946
SUSIE STEPS OUT   United Artists, 1946
FALL GUY   Monogram, 1947
THE ADVENTURES OF DON COYOTE
   United Artists, 1947
PHILO VANCE'S SECRET MISSION
   Eagle-Lion, 1947
JOE PALOOKA IN THE KNOCKOUT
   Monogram, 1947
PORT SAID   Columbia, 1948
JOE PALOOKA IN WINNER TAKE ALL
   Monogram, 1948
FIGHTING MAD   Monogram, 1948
TROUBLE MAKERS   Monogram, 1948
FIGHTING FOOLS   Monogram, 1949
HOLD THAT BABY   Monogram, 1949
JOE PALOOKA IN THE COUNTERPUNCH
   Monogram, 1949
YOUNG DANIEL BOONE   Monogram, 1950
WYOMING MAIL   Universal, 1950
JOE PALOOKA IN THE SQUARED CIRCLE
   Monogram, 1950
G.I. JANE   Lippert, 1950
JOE PALOOKA IN TRIPLE CROSS
   Monogram, 1950
MODELS, INC.   Mutual Pictures, 1951
BAD BLONDE *THE FLANAGAN BOY*
   Lippert, 1951, British
THE GREAT JESSE JAMES RAID
   Lippert, 1953

SINS OF JEZEBEL   Lippert, 1953
THE WHITE ORCHID   United Artists, 1954
THE BLACK SHEEP   United Artists, 1956
VOODOO ISLAND   United Artists, 1957
THE DALTON GIRLS   United Artists, 1957
THE FLIGHT THAT DISAPPEARED
   United Artists, 1961
DEADLY DUO   United Artists, 1962
DIARY OF A MADMAN   United Artists, 1963
THE EYES OF ANNIE JONES
   20th Century-Fox, 1964, U.S.-British
SO EVIL MY SISTER   Zenith
   International, 1973

ROWLAND V. LEE
b. September 6, 1891 - Findlay, Ohio
d. 1975

THE CUP OF LIFE   Associated
   Producers, 1921
BLIND HEARTS   Associated Producers, 1921
CUPID'S BRAND   Arrow, 1921
THE SEA LION   Associated Producers, 1921
THE DUST FLOWER   Goldwyn, 1922
HIS BACK AGAINST THE WALL
   Goldwyn, 1922
THE MEN OF ZANZIBAR   Fox, 1922
MIXED FACES   Fox, 1922
MONEY TO BURN   Fox, 1922
A SELF-MADE MAN   Fox, 1922
SHIRLEY OF THE CIRCUS   Fox, 1922
WHIMS OF THE GODS   Goldwyn, 1922
ALICE ADAMS   co-director with King Vidor,
   Associated Exhibitors, 1923
DESIRE   Metro, 1923
YOU CAN'T GET AWAY WITH IT   Fox, 1923
GENTLE JULIA   Fox, 1923
IN LOVE WITH LOVE   Fox, 1924
THE MAN WITHOUT A COUNTRY   Fox, 1925
HAVOC   Fox, 1925
THE OUTSIDER   Fox, 1926
THE SILVER TREASURE   Fox, 1926
THE WHIRLWIND OF YOUTH   Fox, 1927
BARBED WIRE   1927
THE SECRET HOUR   Paramount, 1928
DOOMSDAY   Paramount, 1928
THREE SINNERS   Paramount, 1928
THE FIRST KISS   Paramount, 1928
LOVES OF AN ACTRESS   Paramount, 1928
THE WOLF OF WALL STREET
   Paramount, 1929
A DANGEROUS WOMAN   Paramount, 1929
THE MYSTERIOUS DR. FU MANCHU
   Paramount, 1929
PARAMOUNT ON PARADE   co-director,
   Paramount, 1930
THE RETURN OF DR. FU MANCHU
   Paramount, 1930
LADIES LOVE BRUTES   Paramount, 1930
A MAN FROM WYOMING   Paramount, 1930
DERELICT   Paramount, 1930
UPPER UNDERWORLD   First National, 1931
THE RULING VOICE   First National, 1931
THE GUILTY GENERATION
   Paramount, 1931
THAT NIGHT IN LONDON *OVER NIGHT*
   Paramount, 1932, British
ZOO IN BUDAPEST   Fox, 1933
I AM SUZANNE   Fox, 1934
THE COUNT OF MONTE CRISTO
   Universal, 1934
GAMBLING   Fox, 1934
CARDINAL RICHILIEU   United Artists, 1935
THE THREE MUSKETEERS
   RKO Radio, 1935
ONE RAINY AFTERNOON
   United Artists, 1936

LOVE FROM A STRANGER   United Artists,
   1937, British
THE TOAST OF NEW YORK
   RKO Radio, 1937
MOTHER CAREY'S CHICKENS
   RKO Radio, 1938
SERVICE DE LUXE   Universal, 1938
THE SON OF FRANKENSTEIN
   Universal, 1939
THE SUN NEVER SETS   Paramount, 1939
TOWER OF LONDON   Universal, 1939
THE SON OF MONTE CRISTO
   United Artists, 1940
POWDER TOWN   RKO Radio, 1942
THE BRIDGE OF SAN LUIS REY
   United Artists, 1944
CAPTAIN KIDD   United Artists, 1945

MITCHELL LEISEN
b. October 6, 1898 - Menominee, Michigan
d. 1972

CRADLE SONG   Paramount, 1933
DEATH TAKES A HOLIDAY   Paramount, 1934
MURDER AT THE VANITIES
   Paramount, 1934
BEHOLD MY WIFE   Paramount, 1935
FOUR HOURS TO KILL   Paramount, 1935
HANDS ACROSS THE TABLE
   Paramount, 1935
13 HOURS BY AIR   Paramount, 1936
THE BIG BROADCAST OF 1937
   Paramount, 1936
SWING, HIGH, SWING LOW
   Paramount, 1937
EASY LIVING   Paramount, 1937
THE BIG BROADCAST OF 1938
   Paramount, 1938
ARTISTS AND MODELS ABROAD
   Paramount, 1938
MIDNIGHT   Paramount, 1939
REMEMBER THE NIGHT   Paramount, 1940
ARISE, MY LOVE   Paramount, 1940
I WANTED WINGS   Paramount, 1941
HOLD BACK THE DAWN   Paramount, 1941
THE LADY IS WILLING   Columbia, 1942
TAKE A LETTER, DARLING
   Paramount, 1942
NO TIME FOR LOVE   Paramount, 1943
LADY IN THE DARK   Paramount, 1944
FRENCHMAN'S CREEK   Paramount, 1944
PRACTICALLY YOURS   Paramount, 1944
KITTY   Paramount, 1945
MASQUERADE IN MEXICO
   Paramount, 1945
TO EACH HIS OWN   Paramount, 1946
SUDDENLY IT'S SPRING   Paramount, 1947
GOLDEN EARRINGS   Paramount, 1947
DREAM GIRL   Paramount, 1948
BRIDE OF VENGEANCE   Paramount, 1949
SONG OF SURRENDER   Paramount, 1949
CAPTAIN CAREY, USA   Paramount, 1950
NO MAN OF HER OWN   Paramount, 1950
THE MATING SEASON   Paramount, 1951
DARLING, HOW COULD YOU!
   Paramount, 1951
YOUNG MAN WITH IDEAS   MGM, 1952
TONIGHT WE SING   20th Century-Fox, 1953
BEDEVILLED   MGM, 1955
THE GIRL MOST LIKELY   Universal, 1958
SPREE (FD)   co-director with Walon Green,
   United Producers, 1967

PAUL LENI

b. July 8, 1885 - Stuttgart, Germany
d. 1929

DAS TAGEBUCH DES DR. HART
1916, German
DORNROSCHEN 1917, German
DIE PLATONISCHE EHE 1919, German
PRINZ KUCKUCK 1919, German
PATIENCE 1920, German
FIESCO DIE VERSCHWORUNG ZU GENUA
1921, German
DAS GESPENSTERSCHIFF 1921, German
HINTERTREPPE co-director with
Leopold Jessner, 1924, German
KOMODIE DER LEIDENSCHAFTEN
1921, German
DAS WACHSFIGURENKABINETT
1924, German
THE CAT AND THE CANARY Universal, 1927
THE CHINESE PARROT Universal, 1927
THE MAN WHO LAUGHS Universal, 1928
THE LAST WARNING Universal, 1929

ROBERT Z. LEONARD

(Robert Zigler Leonard)
b. October 7, 1889 - Chicago, Illinois
d. 1968

THE MASTER KEY Universal, 1914
HERITAGE Universal, 1915
THE SILENT COMMAND Universal, 1915
JUDGE NOT THE WOMAN OF MONA
DIGGINS Universal, 1915
THE LOVE GIRL Universal, 1916
THE CRIPPLED HAND co-director with
David Kirkland, 1916, Universal
THE PLOW GIRL Paramount, 1916
THE EAGLE'S WINGS Universal, 1916
LITTLE EVA EGERTON Universal, 1916
SECRET LOVE Universal, 1916
THE LITTLE ORPHAN Universal, 1917
AT FIRST SIGHT Universal, 1917
THE PRIMROSE RING Paramount, 1917
A MORMON MAID Paramount, 1917
PRINCESS VIRTUE Bluebird, 1917
FACE VALUE Bluebird, 1917
THE BRIDE'S AWAKENING Universal, 1918
HER BODY IN BOND Murray, 1918
DANGER - GO SLOW Universal, 1918
MODERN LOVE Universal, 1918
THE DELICIOUS LITTLE DEVIL
Universal, 1919
THE BIG LITTLE PERSON Universal, 1919
WHAT AM I BID? Universal, 1919
THE SCARLET SHADOW Universal, 1919
THE WAY OF A WOMAN Selznick, 1919
MIRACLE OF LOVE Paramount, 1919
APRIL FOLLY Paramount, 1920
THE RESTLESS SEX Paramount, 1920
THE GILDED LILY Paramount, 1921
HEEDLESS MOTHS Equity, 1921
PEACOCK ALLEY Metro, 1921
FASCINATION Metro, 1922
BROADWAY ROSE Metro, 1922
JAZZMANIA Metro, 1923
THE FRENCH DOLL Metro, 1923
FASHION ROW Metro, 1923
MADEMOISELLE MIDNIGHT
Metro-Goldwyn, 1924
CIRCE THE ENCHANTRESS Metro, 1924
LOVE'S WILDERNESS First National, 1924
CHEAPER TO MARRY Metro-Goldwyn, 1925
BRIGHT LIGHTS Metro-Goldwyn, 1925
TIME THE COMEDIAN Metro-Goldwyn, 1925
DANCE MADNESS MGM, 1926
MADEMOISELLE MODISTE MGM, 1926

THE WANING SEX MGM, 1926
A LITTLE JOURNEY MGM, 1927
THE DEMI-BRIDE MGM, 1927
ADAM AND EVIL MGM, 1927
TEA FOR THREE MGM, 1927
BABY MINE MGM, 1928
THE CARDBOARD LOVER MGM, 1928
A LADY OF CHANCE MGM, 1928
MARIANNE MGM, 1929
THE DIVORCEE ★ MGM, 1930
IN GAY MADRID MGM, 1930
LET US BE GAY MGM, 1930
THE BACHELOR FATHER MGM, 1931
IT'S A WISE CHILD MGM, 1931
FIVE AND TEN MGM, 1931
SUSAN LENNOX: HER FALL AND RISE
MGM, 1931
LOVERS COURAGEOUS MGM, 1932
STRANGE INTERLUDE MGM, 1932
PEG O' MY HEART MGM, 1933
DANCING LADY MGM, 1933
OUTCAST LADY MGM, 1934
AFTER OFFICE HOURS MGM, 1935
ESCAPADE MGM, 1935
THE GREAT ZIEGFELD ★ MGM, 1936
PICCADILLY JIM MGM, 1936
MAYTIME MGM, 1937
THE FIREFLY MGM, 1937
THE GIRL OF THE GOLDEN WEST
MGM, 1938
BROADWAY SERENADE MGM, 1939
NEW MOON MGM, 1940
PRIDE AND PREJUDICE MGM, 1940
THIRD FINGER, LEFT HAND MGM, 1940
ZIEGFELD GIRL MGM, 1941
WHEN LADIES MEET MGM, 1941
WE WERE DANCING MGM, 1942
STAND BY FOR ACTION MGM, 1942
THE MAN FROM DOWN UNDER
MGM, 1943
MARRIAGE IS A PRIVATE AFFAIR
MGM, 1944
WEEK-END AT THE WALDORF MGM, 1945
THE SECRET HEART MGM, 1946
CYNTHIA MGM, 1947
B.F.'S DAUGHTER MGM, 1948
THE BRIBE MGM, 1949
IN THE GOOD OLD SUMMERTIME
MGM, 1949
NANCY GOES TO RIO MGM, 1950
DUCHESS OF IDAHO MGM, 1950
GROUNDS FOR MARRIAGE MGM, 1950
TOO YOUNG TO KISS MGM, 1951
EVERYTHING I HAVE IS YOURS
MGM, 1952
THE CLOWN MGM, 1953
THE GREAT DIAMOND ROBBERY
MGM, 1953
HER TWELVE MEN MGM, 1954
THE KING'S THIEF MGM, 1955
BEAUTIFUL BUT DANGEROUS
LA DONNA PIUBELLA DEL MONDO
20th Century-Fox, 1955, Italian
KELLY AND ME Universal, 1957

SERGIO LEONE

b. January 3, 1929 - Rome, Italy
d. 1990

THE COLOSSUS OF RHODES MGM, 1960,
Italian-French-Spanish
A FISTFUL OF DOLLARS United Artists,
1964, Italian-Spanish-West German
FOR A FEW DOLLARS MORE United Artists,
1966, Italian-Spanish-West German
THE GOOD, THE BAD AND THE UGLY
United Artists, 1966, Italian

ONCE UPON A TIME IN THE WEST
Paramount, 1969, Italian-U.S.
DUCK! YOU SUCKER FISTFUL OF
DYNAMITE United Artists, 1971,
Italian-U.S.
ONCE UPON A TIME IN AMERICA
The Ladd Company/Warner Bros., 1984,
U.S.-Italian-Canadian

IRVING LERNER

b. March 7, 1909 - New York, New York
d. 1976

C-MAN Four Continents, 1949
SUICIDE ATTACK 1951
MAN CRAZY 20th Century-Fox, 1953
EDGE OF FURY co-director with
Robert Gurney, Jr., United Artists, 1958
MURDER BY CONTRACT Columbia, 1958
CITY OF FEAR Columbia, 1959
STUDS LONIGAN United Artists, 1960
CRY OF BATTLE Allied Artists, 1963
THE ROYAL HUNT OF THE SUN
National General, 1969

MERVYN LEROY

b. October 15, 1900 - San Francisco, California
d. 1987

NO PLACE TO GO First National, 1927
FLYING ROMEOS First National, 1928
HAROLD TEEN First National, 1928
OH KAY! First National, 1928
NAUGHTY BABY First National, 1929
HOT STUFF First National, 1929
BROADWAY BABIES First National, 1929
LITTLE JOHNNY JONES First National, 1929
PLAYING AROUND First National, 1929
SHOWGIRL IN HOLLYWOOD
First National, 1930
NUMBERED MEN First National, 1930
TOP SPEED First National, 1930
LITTLE CAESAR First National, 1931
GENTLEMAN'S FATE First National, 1931
TOO YOUNG TO MARRY
First National, 1931
BROAD MINDED First National, 1931
FIVE STAR FINAL First National, 1931
LOCAL BOY MAKES GOOD
First National, 1931
TONIGHT OR NEVER United Artists, 1931
HIGH PRESSURE Warner Bros., 1932
TWO SECONDS First National, 1932
BIG CITY BLUES Warner Bros., 1932
THREE ON A MATCH First National, 1932
I AM A FUGITIVE FROM A CHAIN GANG
Warner Bros., 1932
HARD TO HANDLE Warner Bros., 1933
ELMER THE GREAT First National, 1933
GOLD DIGGERS OF 1933
Warner Bros., 1933
TUGBOAT ANNIE MGM, 1933
THE WORLD CHANGES First National, 1933
HI, NELLIE! Warner Bros., 1934
HEAT LIGHTNING Warner Bros., 1934
HAPPINESS AHEAD First National, 1934
SWEET ADELINE Warner Bros., 1935
OIL FOR THE LAMPS OF CHINA
Warner Bros., 1935
PAGE MISS GLORY Warner Bros., 1935
I FOUND STELLA PARISH
First National, 1935
ANTHONY ADVERSE Warner Bros., 1936
THREE MEN ON A HORSE
First National, 1936
THE KING AND THE CHORUS GIRL
Warner Bros., 1937

473

THEY WON'T FORGET   Warner Bros., 1937
FOOLS FOR SCANDAL   Warner Bros., 1938
WATERLOO BRIDGE   MGM, 1940
ESCAPE   MGM, 1940
BLOSSOMS IN THE DUST   MGM, 1941
UNHOLY PARTNERS   MGM, 1941
JOHNNY EAGER   MGM, 1941
RANDOM HARVEST ★   MGM, 1942
MADAME CURIE   MGM, 1943
THIRTY SECONDS OVER TOKYO
   MGM, 1944
WITHOUT RESERVATIONS
   RKO Radio, 1946
HOMECOMING   MGM, 1948
LITTLE WOMEN   MGM, 1949
ANY NUMBER CAN PLAY   MGM, 1949
EAST SIDE, WEST SIDE   MGM, 1950
QUO VADIS   MGM, 1951
LOVELY TO LOOK AT   MGM, 1952
MILLION DOLLAR MERMAID   MGM, 1952
LATIN LOVERS   MGM, 1953
ROSE MARIE   MGM, 1954
STRANGE LADY IN TOWN
   Warner Bros., 1955
MISTER ROBERTS   co-director with
   John Ford, Warner Bros., 1955
THE BAD SEED   Warner Bros., 1956
TOWARD THE UNKNOWN
   Warner Bros., 1956
NO TIME FOR SERGEANTS
   Warner Bros., 1958
HOME BEFORE DARK   Warner Bros., 1958
THE FBI STORY   Warner Bros., 1959
WAKE ME WHEN IT'S OVER
   20th Century-Fox, 1960
THE DEVIL AT 4 O'CLOCK   Columbia, 1961
A MAJORITY OF ONE   Warner Bros., 1962
GYPSY   Warner Bros., 1962
MARY, MARY   Warner Bros., 1963
MOMENT TO MOMENT   Universal, 1966

HENRY LEVIN
b. June 5, 1909 - Trenton, New Jersey
d. 1980

THE CRY OF THE WEREWOLF
   Columbia, 1944
SERGEANT MIKE   Columbia, 1944
DANCING IN MANHATTAN   Columbia, 1944
I LOVE A MYSTERY   Columbia, 1945
THE FIGHTING GUARDSMAN
   Columbia, 1945
THE BANDIT OF SHERWOOD FOREST
   co-director with George Sherman,
   Columbia, 1946
NIGHT EDITOR   Columbia, 1946
THE UNKNOWN   Columbia, 1946
THE DEVIL'S MASK   Columbia, 1946
THE RETURN OF MONTE CRISTO
   Columbia, 1946
THE GUILT OF JANET AMES
   Columbia, 1948
THE CORPSE CAME C.O.D.   Columbia, 1948
THE MATING OF MILLIE   Columbia, 1948
GALLANT BLADE   Columbia, 1948
THE MAN FROM COLORADO
   Columbia, 1948
MR. SOFT TOUCH   co-director with
   Gordon Douglas, Columbia, 1949
JOLSON SINGS AGAIN   Columbia, 1949
AND BABY MAKES THREE   Columbia, 1949
CONVICTED   Columbia, 1950
THE PETTY GIRL   Columbia, 1950
THE FLYING MISSILE   Columbia, 1951
TWO OF A KIND   Columbia, 1951
THE FAMILY SECRET   Columbia, 1951
BELLES ON THEIR TOES
   20th Century-Fox, 1952

THE PRESIDENT'S LADY
   20th Century-Fox, 1953
THE FARMER TAKES A WIFE
   20th Century-Fox, 1953
MR. SCOUTMASTER
   20th Century-Fox, 1953
THREE YOUNG TEXANS
   20th Century-Fox, 1954
THE GAMBLER FROM NATCHEZ
   20th Century-Fox, 1954
THE WARRIORS   Allied Artists, 1955
THE LONELY MAN   Paramount, 1957
LET'S BE HAPPY   Allied Artists, 1957, British
BERNADINE   20th Century-Fox, 1957
APRIL LOVE   20th Century-Fox, 1957
A NICE LITTLE BANK THAT SHOULD BE
   ROBBED   20th Century-Fox, 1958
THE REMARKABLE MR. PENNYPACKER
   20th Century-Fox, 1958
HOLIDAY FOR LOVERS
   20th Century-Fox, 1959
JOURNEY TO THE CENTER OF THE EARTH
   20th Century-Fox, 1959
WHERE THE BOYS ARE   MGM, 1960
THE WONDERS OF ALADDIN   MGM, 1961,
   Italian-U.S.
THE WONDERFUL WORLD OF THE
   BROTHERS GRIMM   co-director with
   George Pal, MGM/Cinerama, 1962
IF A MAN ANSWERS   Universal, 1962
COME FLY WITH ME   MGM, 1963
HONEYMOON HOTEL   MGM, 1964
GENGHIS KHAN   Columbia, 1965,
   U.S.-British-West German-Yugoslavian
MURDERERS' ROW   Columbia, 1966
KISS THE GIRLS AND MAKE THEM DIE
   SE TUTTE LE DONNE DEL MONDO/
   OPERAZIONE PARADISO   co-director with
   Dino Maiuri, Columbia, 1967, Italian-U.S.
THE AMBUSHERS   Columbia, 1967
THE DESPERADOS   Columbia, 1969
THAT MAN BOLT   co-director with
   David Lowell Rich, Universal, 1973
RUN FOR THE ROSES
   THE THOROUGHBREDS
   Kodiak Films, 1978
SCOUT'S HONOR (TF)   Zephyr
   Productions, 1980

ALBERT LEWIN
b. September 23, 1894 - Newark, New Jersey
d. 1968

THE MOON AND SIXPENCE
   United Artists, 1942
THE PICTURE OF DORIAN GRAY
   MGM, 1945
THE PRIVATE AFFAIRS OF BEL AMI
   United Artists, 1947
PANDORA AND THE FLYING DUTCHMAN
   MGM, 1951, British
SAADIA   MGM, 1954
THE LIVING IDOL   MGM, 1957

MAX LINDER
(Gabriel-Maximilien Leuvielle)
b. December 16, 1883 - Caverne, France
d. 1925

MAX DANS SA FAMILLE   1911, French
MAX ET LES FEMMES   1912, French
LE MAL DE MER   1912, French
MAX ASTHMATIQUE   1913, French
MAX VIRTUOSE   1913, French
MAX DANS LES AIRES   1914, French
MAX ET L'ESPION   1915, French
MAX COMES ACROSS   Essanay, 1917

MAX WANTS A DIVORCE   Essanay, 1917
MAX IN A TAXI   Essanay, 1917
LE PETIT CAFE   1919, French
BE MY WIFE   United Artists, 1921
SEVEN YEARS BAD LUCK
   United Artists, 1921
THE THREE MUST-GET-THERES
   United Artists, 1922
DER ZIRKUSKONIG   co-director with
   E.E. Violet, 1924, Austrian

OLDRICH LIPSKY
b. 1924 - Czechoslovakia
d. 1986

THE SHOW IS ON   1954, Czechoslovakian
THE CIRCUS IS COMING   1960,
   Czechoslovakian
THE MAN FROM THE FIRST CENTURY
   1961, Czechoslovakian
LEMONADE JOE   Allied Artists, 1964,
   Czechoslovakian
HAPPY END   Continental, 1967,
   Czechoslovakian
I KILLED EINSTEIN   1969, Czechoslovakian
SIX BEARS AND A CLOWN   1976,
   Czechoslovakian, filmed in 1972
ADELE HASN'T HAD HER SUPPER YET
   1978, Czechoslovakian
NICK CARTER IN PRAGUE   1978,
   Czechoslovakian
LONG LIVE GHOSTS!   1979,
   Czechoslovakian
MYSTERIOUS CASTLE IN THE CARPATHIANS
   1981, Czechoslovakian

ANATOLE LITVAK
(Michael Anatol Litwak)
b. May 10, 1902 - Kiev, Russia
d. 1974

TATIANA   1925, Russian
DOLLY MACHT KARRIERE   1930, German
NIE WIEDER LIEBE   1931, German
DAS LIED EINER NACHT   1932, German
COEUR DE LILAS   1932, French
LA CHANSON D'UNE NUIT   1932, German
TELL ME TONIGHT   BE MINE TONIGHT
   1932, German
SLEEPING CAR   Gaumont-British,
   1933, British
CETTE VIEILLE CANAILLE   1933, French
L'EQUIPAGE   FLIGHT INTO DARKNESS
   1935, French
MADEMOISELLE DOCTEUR   co-director with
   G.W. Pabst, 1935, French
MAYERLING   1936, French
THE WOMAN I LOVE   RKO Radio, 1937
TOVARICH   Warner Bros., 1937
THE AMAZING DR. CLITTERHOUSE
   Warner Bros., 1938
THE SISTERS   Warner Bros., 1938
CONFESSIONS OF A NAZI SPY
   Warner Bros., 1939
CASTLE ON THE HUDSON
   Warner Bros., 1940
ALL THIS AND HEAVEN TOO
   Warner Bros., 1940
CITY FOR CONQUEST   Warner Bros., 1940
OUT OF THE FOG   Warner Bros., 1941
BLUES IN THE NIGHT   Warner Bros., 1941
THIS ABOVE ALL   20th Century-Fox, 1942
THE NAZIS STRIKE (FD)   co-director with
   Frank Capra, U.S. Army, 1942
DIVIDE AND CONQUER (FD)   co-director with
   Frank Capra, U.S. Army, 1943
OPERATION TITANIC (FD)   U.S. Army, 1943

THE BATTLE OF RUSSIA (FD)
U.S. Army, 1943
THE BATTLE OF CHINA (FD) co-director with
Frank Capra, U.S. Army, 1944
WAR COMES TO AMERICA (FD)
U.S. Army, 1945
THE LONG NIGHT RKO Radio, 1947
SORRY, WRONG NUMBER
Paramount, 1948
THE SNAKE PIT ★ 20th Century-Fox, 1949
DECISION BEFORE DAWN
20th Century-Fox, 1949
ACT OF LOVE United Artists, 1953,
French-U.S.
THE DEEP, BLUE SEA 20th Century-Fox,
1955, British
ANASTASIA 20th Century-Fox, 1956
THE JOURNEY MGM, 1959
GOODBYE AGAIN *AIMEZ-VOUS BRAHMS?*
United Artists, 1961, French-U.S.
FIVE MILES TO MIDNIGHT United Artists,
1963, U.S.-French-Italian
THE NIGHT OF THE GENERALS Columbia,
1967, British-French
THE LADY IN THE CAR WITH GLASSES AND
A GUN Columbia, 1970, French-U.S.

FRANK LLOYD

b. February 2, 1888 - Glasgow, Scotland
d. 1960

JANE Paramount, 1915
THE REFORM CANDIDATE
Paramount, 1915
FOR HIS SUPERIOR'S HONOR 1915
BILLIE'S BABY 1915
ELEVEN TO ONE 1915
FATE'S ALIBI 1915
FROM THE SHADOWS 1915
THE BAY OF SEVEN ISLANDS 1915
DR. MASON'S TEMPTATION 1915
A DOUBLE DEAL IN PORK 1915
AN ARRANGEMENT WITH FATE 1915
LITTLE MR. FIXER 1915
IN THE GRASP OF THE LAW 1915
HIS LAST TRICK 1915
THE LITTLE GIRL OF THE ATTIC 1915
THE PINCH 1915
THE PROPHET OF THE HILLS 1915
MARTIN LOWE - FIXER 1915
PATERNAL LOVE 1915
THEIR GOLDEN WEDDING 1915
10,000 DOLLARS 1915
THE TOLL OF YOUTH 1915
TRICKERY 1915
TO REDEEM AN OATH 1915
THE SOURCE OF HAPPINESS 1915
TO REDEEM A VALUE 1915
THE GENTLEMAN FROM INDIANA
Paramount, 1915
THE CALL OF THE CUMBERLANDS
Paramount, 1915
THE INTRIGUE Paramount, 1915
THE TONGUES OF MEN Paramount, 1916
MADAME PRESIDENT Paramount, 1916
AN INTERNATIONAL MARRIAGE
Paramount, 1916
THE CODE OF MARCIA GRAY
Paramount, 1916
THE INTRIGUE Paramount, 1915
THE MAKING OF MADDALENA
Paramount, 1916
SINS OF HER PARENTS Fox, 1916
THE STRONGER LOVE Paramount, 1916
DAVID GARRICK Paramount, 1916
THE PRICE OF SILENCE Fox, 1917
THE HEART OF A LION Fox, 1917
AMERICAN METHODS Fox, 1917

A TALE OF TWO CITIES Fox, 1917
WHEN A MAN SEES RED Fox, 1917
THE PLUNDERER Fox, 1918
THE KINGDOM OF LOVE Fox, 1919
LES MISERABLES Fox, 1919
THE BLINDNESS OF DIVORCE Fox, 1919
TRUE BLUE Fox, 1919
FOR FREEDOM Fox, 1919
THE RAINBOW TRAIL Fox, 1919
THE RIDERS OF THE PURPLE SAGA
Fox, 1919
THE MAN HUNTER Fox, 1919
PITFALLS OF A BIG CITY Fox, 1919
THE WORLD AND ITS WOMEN
Goldwyn, 1919
THE LOVERS OF LETTY Fox, 1920
THE SILVER HORDE Goldwyn, 1920
THE WOMAN IN ROOM 13 Goldwyn, 1920
MADAME X Goldwyn, 1920
THE GREAT LOVER Goldwyn, 1920
A TALE OF TWO WORLDS Goldwyn, 1921
ROADS TO DESTINY *ROADS OF DESTINY*
Goldwyn, 1921
A VOICE IN THE DARK Goldwyn, 1921
THE INVISIBLE POWER Goldwyn, 1921
THE MAN FROM LOST RIVER
Goldwyn, 1921
THE SIN FLOOD Goldwyn, 1921
THE GRIM COMEDIAN Goldwyn, 1922
THE ETERNAL FLAME Associated First
National, 1922
OLIVER TWIST Associated First
National, 1922
THE VOICE FROM THE MINARET
Associated First National, 1923
WITHIN THE LAW Associated First
National, 1923
ASHES OF VENGEANCE Associated First
National, 1923
BLACK OXEN First National, 1924
THE SEA HAWK First National, 1924
THE SILENT WATCHER First National, 1924
WINDS OF CHANCE First National, 1925
HER HUSBAND'S SECRET
First National, 1925
THE SPLENDID ROAD First National, 1925
THE WISE GUY First National, 1926
THE EAGLE OF THE SEA Paramount, 1926
CHILDREN OF DIVORCE Paramount, 1927
ADORATION First National, 1928
WEARY RIVER ★★ First National, 1929
THE DIVINE LADY ★★ First National, 1929
DRAG ★★ First National, 1929
DARK STREETS First National, 1929
YOUNG NOWHERES First National, 1929
SON OF THE GODS First National, 1930
THE WAY OF ALL MEN First National, 1930
THE LASH First National, 1930
EAST LYNNE Fox, 1931
THE RIGHT OF WAY First National, 1931
THE AGE FOR LOVE United Artists, 1931
A PASSPORT TO HELL Fox, 1932
CAVALCADE ★★ Fox, 1933
BERKELEY SQUARE Fox, 1933
HOOPLA Fox, 1933
SERVANTS' ENTRANCE Fox, 1934
MUTINY ON THE BOUNTY ★ MGM, 1935
UNDER TWO FLAGS
20th Century-Fox, 1936
MAID OF SALEM Paramount, 1937
WELLS FARGO Paramount, 1937
IF I WERE KING co-director,
Paramount, 1938
RULERS OF THE SEA Paramount, 1939
THE HOWARDS OF VIRGINIA
Columbia, 1940
THE LADY FROM CHEYENNE
Universal, 1941

THIS WOMAN IS MINE Universal, 1941
FOREVER AND A DAY co-director,
RKO Radio, 1943
BLOOD ON THE SUN United Artists, 1945
THE SHANGHAI STORY Republic, 1954
THE LAST COMMAND Republic, 1955

JOSHUA LOGAN

b. October 5, 1908 - Texarkana, Texas
d. 1988

I MET MY LOVE AGAIN co-director with
Arthur Ripley, United Artists, 1938
PICNIC ★ Columbia, 1955
BUS STOP 20th Century-Fox, 1956
SAYONARA ★ Warner Bros., 1957
SOUTH PACIFIC Magna, 1958
TALL STORY Warner Bros., 1960
FANNY Warner Bros., 1961
ENSIGN PULVER Warner Bros., 1964
CAMELOT Warner Bros., 1967
PAINT YOUR WAGON Paramount, 1969

PARE LORENTZ

b. December 11, 1905 - Clarksburg,
West Virginia
d. 1992

THE PLOW THAT BROKE THE PLAINS (FD)
U.S. Resettlement Administration, 1936
THE RIVER (FD) U.S. Resettlement
Administration, 1937
THE FIGHT FOR LIFE (FD) U.S. Film
Service, 1940

JOSEPH LOSEY

b. January 14, 1909 - La Crosse, Wisconsin
d. 1984

THE BOY WITH GREEN HAIR
RKO Radio, 1948
THE LAWLESS Paramount, 1950
M Columbia, 1951
THE PROWLER United Artists, 1951
THE BIG NIGHT United Artists, 1951
STRANGER ON THE PROWL directed under
pseudonym of Andrea Forzano, United
Artists, 1952, U.S.-Italian
THE SLEEPING TIGER directed under
pseudonym of Victor Hanbury, Astor,
1954, British
FINGER OF GUILT *THE INTIMATE
STRANGER* directed under pseudonym of
Joseph Walton, RKO Radio, 1955, British
TIME WITHOUT PITY Astor, 1956, British
THE GYPSY AND THE GENTLEMAN Rank,
1958, British
CHANCE MEETING *BLIND DATE*
Paramount, 1959, British
THE CONCRETE JUNGLE *THE CRIMINAL*
Fanfare, 1960, British
THESE ARE THE DAMNED *THE DAMNED*
Columbia, 1961, British
EVA Times, 1962, French-Italian
THE SERVANT Landau, 1964, British
KING AND COUNTRY Allied Artists,
1965, British
MODESTY BLAISE 20th Century-Fox,
1966, British
ACCIDENT Cinema 5, 1967, British
SECRET CEREMONY Universal, 1968,
British-U.S.
BOOM! Universal, 1968, British-U.S.
FIGURES IN A LANDSCAPE National
General, 1971, British
THE GO-BETWEEN Columbia, 1971, British

THE ASSASSINATION OF TROTSKY
Cinerama Releasing Corporation, 1972,
French-Italian-British
A DOLL'S HOUSE Tomorrow Entertainment,
1973, British-French
GALILEO American Film Theatre, 1975,
British-Canadian
THE ROMANTIC ENGLISHWOMAN
New World, 1975, British
MR. KLEIN Quartet, 1977, French-Italian
LES ROUTES DU SUD Parafrance,
1978, French
DON GIOVANNI Gaumont/New Yorker,
1980, French
STEAMING New World, 1984, British

EUGENE LOURIE
b. 1908 - France
d. 1991

THE BEAST FROM 20,000 FATHOMS
Warner Bros., 1953
THE COLOSSUS OF NEW YORK
Paramount, 1958
THE GIANT BEHEMOTH Allied Artists,
1959, British
GORGO MGM, 1961, British

ERNST LUBITSCH
b. January 28, 1892 - Berlin, Germany
d. 1947

FRAULEIN SEIFENSCHAUM 1914, German
BLINDE KUH 1915, German
AUF EIS GEFUHRT 1915, German
DAS SCHONSTE GESCHENK
1916, German
ZUCKER UND ZIMT co-director with
Ernst Matray, 1915, German
LEUTNANT AUF BEFEHL 1916, German
WO IST MEIN SCHATZ? 1916, German
DER SCHWARZE MORITZ 1916, German
SCHUHPALAST PINKUS 1916, French
DER GEMISCHTE FRAUENCHOR
1916, German
DER G.M.B.H. TENOR 1916, German
DER ERSTE PATIENT 1916, German
DER KRAFTMEYER 1916, German
OSSIS TAGEBUCH 1917, German
DER BLUSEKONIG 1917, German
WENN VIER DASSELBE TUN
1917, German
EIN FIDELES GEFANGNIS 1917, German
DER LETZTE ANZUG 1917, German
PRINZ SAMI 1918, German
DER RODELKAVALIER 1918, German
DER FALL ROSENTOPF 1918, German
FUHRMANN HENSCHEL 1918, German
DAS MODEL VON BALLETT 1918, German
MARIONETTEN 1918, German
MEYER AUS BERLIN 1919, German
ICH MACHTE KEIN MANN SEIN
1919, German
DAS SCHWABENMADLE 1919, German
ROMEO UND JULIA IM SCHNEE
1916, German
ALS ICH TOT WAR 1916, German
DIE AUGEN DER MUMMIE MA
1918, German
CARMEN GYPSY BLOOD 1918, German
MEINE FRAU DIE FILMSCHAUSPIELERIN
1919, German
DIE AUSTERNPRINZESSIN 1919, German
RAUSCH 1919, German
MADAME DUBARRY PASSION
1919, German
DIE PUPPE 1919, German

KOHLHIESELS TOCHTER 1920, German
SUMURUN ONE ARABIAN NIGHT
1920, German
ANNA BOLEYN DECEPTION
1920, German
DIE BERGKATZE 1921, German
DAS WEIB DER PHARAO THE LOVES OF
PHARAO 1922, German
DIE FLAMME MONTMARTRE
1923, German
ROSITA United Artists, 1923
THE MARRIAGE CIRCLE
Warner Bros., 1924
THREE WOMEN Warner Bros., 1924
FORBIDDEN PARADISE Paramount, 1924
KISS ME AGAIN Warner Bros., 1925
LADY WINDERMERE'S FAN
Warner Bros., 1925
SO THIS IS PARIS Warner Bros., 1926
THE STUDENT PRINCE MGM, 1927
THE PATRIOT ★ Paramount, 1928
ETERNAL LOVE United Artists, 1929
THE LOVE PARADE ★ Paramount, 1929
PARAMOUNT ON PARADE co-director,
Paramount, 1930
MONTE CARLO Paramount, 1930
THE SMILING LIEUTENANT
Paramount, 1931
BROKEN LULLABY THE MAN I KILLED
Paramount, 1932
ONE HOUR WITH YOU Paramount, 1932
TROUBLE IN PARADISE Paramount, 1932
IF I HAD A MILLION co-director,
Paramount, 1932
DESIGN FOR LIVING Paramount, 1933
THE MERRY WIDOW Paramount, 1933
ANGEL Paramount, 1937
BLUEBEARD'S EIGHTH WIFE
Paramount, 1938
NINOTCHKA MGM, 1939
THE SHOP AROUND THE CORNER
MGM, 1940
THAT UNCERTAIN FEELING
United Artists, 1941
TO BE OR NOT TO BE United Artists, 1942
HEAVEN CAN WAIT ★
20th Century-Fox, 1943
CLUNY BROWN 20th Century-Fox, 1946
THAT LADY IN ERMINE co-director with
Otto Preminger, 20th Century-Fox, 1948

EDWARD LUDWIG
b. 1899 - Russia
d. 1982

STEADY COMPANY 1932
THEY JUST HAD TO GET MARRIED 1933
A WOMAN'S MAN 1934
LET'S BE RITZY 1934
FRIENDS OF MR. SWEENEY 1934
THE MAN WHO RECLAIMED HIS HEAD
Universal, 1934
AGE OF INDISCRETION 1935
OLD MAN RHYTHM 1935
THREE KIDS AND A QUEEN 1935
FATAL LADY 1936
ADVENTURE IN MANHATTAN
Columbia, 1936
HER HUSBAND LIES 1937
THE BARRIER 1937
THE LAST GANGSTER MGM, 1937
THAT CERTAIN AGE Universal, 1938
COAST GUARD 1939
SWISS FAMILY ROBINSON
RKO Radio, 1940
THE MAN WHO LOST HIMSELF 1941
BORN TO SING MGM, 1942

THEY CAME TO BLOW UP AMERICA
20th Century-Fox, 1943
THE FIGHTING SEABEES Republic, 1944
THREE IS A FAMILY United Artists, 1944
THE FABULOUS TEXAN Republic, 1947
WAKE OF THE RED WITCH Republic, 1948
THE BIG WHEEL United Artists, 1949
SMUGGLER'S ISLAND Universal, 1951
CARIBBEAN Paramount, 1952
BIG JIM McLAIN Warner Bros., 1952
THE BLAZING FOREST Paramount, 1952
THE VANQUISHED Paramount, 1953
SANGAREE Paramount, 1953
JIVARO Paramount, 1954
FLAME OF THE ISLANDS Republic, 1955
THE BLACK SCORPION Warner Bros., 1957
THE GUN HAWK Allied Artists, 1963

CHARLES MacARTHUR
b. May 5, 1895 - Scranton, Pennsylvania
d. 1956

CRIME WITHOUT PASSION co-director with
Ben Hecht, Paramount, 1934
ONCE IN A BLUE MOON co-director with
Ben Hecht, Paramount, 1936
THE SCOUNDREL co-director with
Ben Hecht, Paramount, 1935
SOAK THE RICH co-director with Ben Hecht,
Paramount, 1936

DAVID MacDONALD
b. May 9, 1904 - Helensburgh, Scotland
d. 1983

DOUBLE ALIBI 1940, British
THE LAST CURTAIN 1937, British
RIDING HIGH 1937, British
DEAD MEN TELL NO TALES 1938, British
THIS MAN IS NEWS 1939, British
SPIES OF THE AIR 1939, British
LAW AND DISORDER RKO Radio,
1940, British
THIS ENGLAND 1941, British
THE BROTHERS Universal, 1947, British
GOOD TIME GIRL Film Classics,
1948, British
SNOWBOUND Universal, 1948, British
CHRISTOPHER COLUMBUS Universal,
1949, British
THE BAD LORD BYRON Rank, 1949, British
CAIRO ROAD Continental, 1950, British
THE GREAT ADVENTURE
THE ADVENTURERS Rank, 1951, British
THE BIG FRAME THE LOST HOURS
RKO Radio, 1952, British
DEVIL GIRL FROM MARS DCA,
1955, British
SMALL HOTEL 1957, British
THE MOONRAKER Associated British-Pathe,
1958, British
PETTICOAT PIRATES 1961, British
THE GOLDEN RABBIT 1962, British

RANALD MacDOUGALL
b. March 10, 1915 - Schenectady, New York
d. 1973

QUEEN BEE   Columbia, 1955
MAN ON FIRE   MGM, 1957
THE WORLD, THE FLESH AND THE DEVIL
   MGM, 1959
THE SUBTERRANEANS   MGM, 1960
GO NAKED IN THE WORLD   MGM, 1961

ALEXANDER MACKENDRICK
b. 1912 - Boston, Massachusetts
d. 1993

TIGHT LITTLE ISLAND   *WHISKEY GALORE!*
   Rank, 1949, British
THE MAN IN THE WHITE SUIT   Rank,
   1951, British
CRASH OF SILENCE   *MANDY*   Universal,
   1952, British
HIGH AND DRY   *THE MAGGIE*   Universal,
   1954, British
THE LADYKILLERS   Continental,
   1956, British
SWEET SMELL OF SUCCESS
   United Artists, 1957
A BOY TEN FEET TALL   *SAMMY GOING
   SOUTH*   Paramount, 1963, British
A HIGH WIND IN JAMAICA   20th Century-Fox,
   1965, British
DON'T MAKE WAVES   MGM, 1967

NORMAN Z. MacLEOD
(Norman Zenos MacLeod)
b. September 20, 1898 - Grayling, Michigan
d. 1964

TAKING A CHANCE   Fox, 1928
ALONG CAME YOUTH   co-director with
   Lloyd Corrigan, Paramount, 1930
FINN AND HATTIE   co-director with
   Norman Taurog, Paramount, 1931
MONKEY BUSINESS   Paramount, 1931
TOUCHDOWN   Paramount, 1931
THE MIRACLE MAN   Paramount, 1932
HORSE FEATHERS   Paramount, 1932
IF I HAD A MILLION   co-director,
   Paramount, 1932
A LADY'S PROFESSION   Paramount, 1933
MAMA LOVES PAPA   Paramount, 1933
ALICE IN WONDERLAND   Paramount, 1933
MELODY IN SPRING   Paramount, 1934
MANY HAPPY RETURNS
   Paramount, 1934
IT'S A GIFT   Paramount, 1934
REDHEADS ON PARADE
   Paramount, 1935
HERE COMES COOKIE   Paramount, 1935
CORONADO   Paramount, 1936
EARLY TO BED   Paramount, 1936
PENNIES FROM HEAVEN   Columbia, 1936
MIND YOUR OWN BUSINESS
   Paramount, 1937
TOPPER   MGM, 1937
MERRILY WE LIVE   MGM, 1938
THERE GOES MY HEART
   United Artists, 1938
TOPPER TAKES A TRIP   MGM, 1939
REMEMBER?   MGM, 1939
LITTLE MEN   RKO Radio, 1940
THE TRIAL OF MARY DUGAN   1941
LADY BE GOOD   MGM, 1941
JACKASS MAIL   MGM, 1942
PANAMA HATTIE   MGM, 1942
THE POWERS GIRL   United Artists, 1943

SWING SHIFT MAISIE   MGM, 1943
THE KID FROM BROOKLYN
   RKO Radio, 1946
THE SECRET LIFE OF WALTER MITTY
   RKO Radio, 1947
THE ROAD TO RIO   Paramount, 1947
ISN'T IT ROMANTIC?   Paramount, 1948
THE PALEFACE   Paramount, 1948
LET'S DANCE   Paramount, 1950
MY FAVORITE SPY   Paramount, 1951
NEVER WAVE AT A WAC   RKO Radio, 1953
CASANOVA'S BIG NIGHT   Paramount, 1954
PUBLIC PIGEON NO. 1   Universal, 1957
ALIAS JESSE JAMES   United Artists, 1959

ROUBEN MAMOULIAN
b. October 8, 1897 - Tiflis, Georgia, Russia
d. 1987

APPLAUSE   Paramount, 1929
CITY STREETS   Paramount, 1931
DR. JEKYLL AND MR. HYDE
   Paramount, 1932
LOVE ME TONIGHT   Paramount, 1932
SONG OF SONGS   Paramount, 1933
QUEEN CHRISTINA   MGM, 1933
WE LIVE AGAIN   United Artists, 1934
BECKY SHARP   RKO Radio, 1935
THE GAY DESPERADO   United Artists, 1936
HIGH, WIDE, AND HANDSOME
   Paramount, 1937
GOLDEN BOY   Columbia, 1939
THE MARK OF ZORRO
   20th Century-Fox, 1940
BLOOD AND SAND   20th Century-Fox, 1941
RINGS ON HER FINGERS
   20th Century-Fox, 1942
SUMMER HOLIDAY   MGM, 1948
SILK STOCKINGS   MGM, 1957

FRANCIS MANKIEWICZ
b. 1944 - Shanghai, China
d. 1993

VALENTIN (TF)   1973,
   Canadian-Chinese-French
LE TEMPS D'UNE CHASSE   Cinepix,
   1973, Canadian
PROCES CRIMINEL   *ORIENTATION/
   CAUSE CIVILE* (FD)   1974, Canadian
EXPROPRIATION (TF)   1975, Canadian
POINTE PELEE   1976, Canadian
UNE AMIE D'ENFANCE   1977, Canadian
A MATTER OF CHOICE (TD)
   1977, Canadian
I WAS DYING AWAY (FD)   1977, Canadian
LES BONS DEBARRAS—GOOD RIDDANCE
   International Film Exchange,
   1978, Canadian
LES BEAUX SOUVENIRS   National Film
   Board of Canada, 1980, Canadian
AND THEN YOU DIE (TF)   CBC,
   1987, Canadian
LES PORTES TOURNANTES   Malofilm
   Group/UGC/Canal Plus/ACPAV, 1988,
   Canadian-French
LOVE AND HATE: A MARRIAGE MADE IN
   HELL   *LOVE AND HATE: THE STORY OF
   COLIN AND JOANNE THATCHER* (MS)
   CBC, 1989, Canadian
CONSPIRACY OF SILENCE (MS)
   CBC, 1991, Canadian

JOSEPH L. MANKIEWICZ
b. February 11, 1909 - Wilkes-Barre,
   Pennsylvania
d. 1993

DRAGONWYCK   20th Century-Fox, 1946
SOMEWHERE IN THE NIGHT
   20th Century-Fox, 1946
THE LATE GEORGE APLEY
   20th Century-Fox, 1947
THE GHOST AND MRS. MUIR
   20th Century-Fox, 1947
ESCAPE   20th Century-Fox, 1948
A LETTER TO THREE WIVES ★★
   20th Century-Fox, 1949
HOUSE OF STRANGERS
   20th Century-Fox, 1949
NO WAY OUT   20th Century-Fox, 1950
ALL ABOUT EVE ★★   20th Century-Fox, 1950
PEOPLE WILL TALK   20th Century-Fox, 1951
FIVE FINGERS ★   20th Century-Fox, 1952
JULIUS CAESAR   MGM, 1953
THE BAREFOOT CONTESSA   United Artists,
   1954, U.S.-Italian
GUYS AND DOLLS   MGM, 1955
THE QUIET AMERICAN   United Artists, 1958
SUDDENLY LAST SUMMER   Columbia, 1959
CLEOPATRA   20th Century-Fox, 1963
THE HONEY POT   United Artists, 1967,
   British-U.S.-Italian
THERE WAS A CROOKED MAN
   Warner Bros., 1970
KING: A FILMED RECORD...MONTGOMERY
   TO MEMPHIS (FD)   co-director with
   Sidney Lumet, Maron Films Limited, 1970
SLEUTH ★   20th Century-Fox, 1972, British

ANTHONY MANN
(Emil Anton Bundmann)
b. June 30, 1906 - San Diego, California
d. 1967

DR. BROADWAY   Paramount, 1942
MOONLIGHT IN HAVANA   Universal, 1942
NOBODY'S DARLING   Republic, 1943
MY BEST GAL   Republic, 1944
STRANGERS IN THE NIGHT   Republic, 1944
THE GREAT FLAMARION   Republic, 1945
TWO O'CLOCK COURAGE
   RKO RADIO, 1945
SING YOUR WAY HOME   RKO Radio, 1945
STRANGE IMPERSONATION   Republic, 1946
THE BAMBOO BLONDE   RKO RADIO, 1946
DESPERATE   RKO Radio, 1947
RAILROADED   Eagle Lion, 1947
T-MEN   Eagle Lion, 1947
RAW DEAL   Eagle Lion, 1948
REIGN OF TERROR   *THE BLACK BOOK*
   Eagle Lion, 1949
BORDER INCIDENT   MGM, 1949
SIDE STREET   MGM, 1950
WINCHESTER '73   Universal, 1950
THE FURIES   Paramount, 1950
DEVIL'S DOORWAY   MGM, 1950
THE TALL TARGET   MGM, 1951
BEND OF THE RIVER   Universal, 1952
THE NAKED SPUR   MGM, 1953
THUNDER BAY   Universal, 1953
THE GLENN MILLER STORY
   Universal, 1954
THE FAR COUNTRY   Universal, 1954
STRATEGIC AIR COMMAND
   Paramount, 1955
THE MAN FROM LARAMIE   Columbia, 1955
THE LAST FRONTIER   Columbia, 1956
SERENADE   Warner Bros., 1956
MEN IN WAR   United Artists, 1957

THE TIN STAR   Paramount, 1957
GOD'S LITTLE ACRE   United Artists, 1958
MAN OF THE WEST   United Artists, 1958
CIMARRON   MGM, 1960
EL CID   Allied Artists, 1961, re-released in
   1993 by Miramax Films
THE FALL OF THE ROMAN EMPIRE
   Paramount, 1964
THE HEROES OF TELEMARK   Columbia,
   1965, British
A DANDY IN ASPIC   Columbia, 1968, British

DANIEL MANN
(Daniel Chugerman)
b. August 8, 1912 - Brooklyn, New York
d. 1991

COME BACK, LITTLE SHEBA
   Paramount, 1952
ABOUT MRS. LESLIE   Paramount, 1954
THE ROSE TATTOO   Paramount, 1955
I'LL CRY TOMORROW   MGM, 1955
TEAHOUSE OF THE AUGUST MOON
   MGM, 1956
HOT SPELL   Paramount, 1958
THE LAST ANGRY MAN   Columbia, 1959
THE MOUNTAIN ROAD   Columbia, 1960
BUTTERFIELD 8   MGM, 1960
ADA   MGM, 1961
FIVE FINGER EXERCISE   Columbia, 1962
WHO'S GOT THE ACTION?
   Paramount, 1962
WHO'S BEEN SLEEPING IN MY BED?
   Paramount, 1963
JUDITH   Paramount, 1965, U.S.-British-Israeli
OUR MAN FLINT   20th Century-Fox, 1966
FOR LOVE OF IVY   Cinerama Releasing
   Corporation, 1968
A DREAM OF KINGS   National General, 1969
WILLARD   Cinerama Releasing
   Corporation, 1971
THE REVENGERS   National General, 1972,
   U.S.-Mexican
INTERVAL   Avco Embassy, 1973,
   U.S.-Mexican
MAURIE   *BIG MO*   National General, 1973
LOST IN THE STARS   American Film
   Theatre, 1974
JOURNEY INTO FEAR   Stirling Gold,
   1976, Canadian
HOW THE WEST WAS WON (MS)
   co-director with Burt Kennedy,
   MGM TV, 1977
MATILDA   American International, 1978
PLAYING FOR TIME (TF)   Syzygy
   Productions, 1980
THE DAY THE LOVING STOPPED (TF)
   Monash-Zeitman Productions, 1981
THE MAN WHO BROKE 1,000 CHAINS (CTF)
   HBO Pictures/Journey Entertainment, 1987

EDWIN L. MARIN
b. February 21, 1899 - Jersey City, New Jersey
d. 1951

THE DEATH KISS   World Wide, 1933
A STUDY IN SCARLET   World Wide, 1933
THE AVENGER   Monogram Pictures
   Corp., 1933
THE SWEETHEART OF SIGMA CHI
   Monogram, 1933
BOMBAY MAIL   Universal, 1934
THE CROSBY CASE   Universal, 1934
AFFAIRS OF A GENTLEMAN
   Universal, 1934
PARIS INTERLUDE   MGM, 1934

THE CASINO MURDER CASE   MGM, 1935
PURSUIT   MGM, 1935
MOONLIGHT MURDER   MGM, 1935
THE GARDEN MURDER CASE   MGM, 1936
SPEED   MGM, 1936
I'D GIVE MY LIFE   MGM, 1936
SWORN ENEMY   MGM, 1936
ALL AMERICAN CHUMP   MGM, 1936
MAN OF THE PEOPLE   MGM, 1937
MARRIED BEFORE BREAKFAST
   MGM, 1937
EVERYBODY SING   MGM, 1938
HOLD THAT KISS   MGM, 1938
THE CHASER   MGM, 1938
LISTEN, DARLING   MGM, 1938
A CHRISTMAS CAROL   MGM, 1938
FAST AND LOOSE   MGM, 1939
SOCIETY LAWYER   MGM, 1939
MAISIE   MGM, 1939
HENRY GOES ARIZONA   MGM, 1939
FLORIAN   MGM, 1940
GOLD RUSH MAISIE   MGM, 1940
HULLABALOO   MGM, 1940
MAISIE WAS A LADY   MGM, 1941
RINGSIDE MAISIE   MGM, 1941
PARIS CALLING   Universal, 1942
A GENTLEMAN AFTER DARK
   United Artists, 1942
MISS ANNIE ROONEY   United Artists, 1942
INVISIBLE AGENT   Universal, 1942
TWO TICKETS TO LONDON
   Universal, 1943
SHOW BUSINESS   RKO Radio, 1944
TALL IN THE SADDLE   RKO Radio, 1944
JOHNNY ANGEL   RKO Radio, 1945
ABILENE TOWN   United Artists, 1946
YOUNG WIDOW   United Artists, 1946
MR. ACE   United Artists, 1946
LADY LUCK   RKO Radio, 1946
NOCTURNE   RKO Radio, 1946
CHRISTMAS EVE   United Artists, 1947
INTRIGUE   United Artists, 1947
RACE STREET   RKO Radio, 1948
CANADIAN PACIFIC
   20th Century-Fox, 1949
THE YOUNGER BROTHERS
   Warner Bros., 1949
FIGHTING MAN OF THE PLAINS
   20th Century-Fox, 1949
COLT .45   Warner Bros., 1950
THE CARIBOO TRAIL
   20th Century-Fox, 1950
SUGARFOOT   Warner Bros., 1951
RATON PASS   Warner Bros., 1951
FORT WORTH   Warner Bros., 1951

RICHARD MARQUAND
b. September 22, 1937 - Cardiff, Wales
d. 1987

THE SEARCH FOR THE NILE (MS)
   BBC/Time-Life Productions, 1972, British
THE LEGACY   Universal, 1979
BIRTH OF THE BEATLES (TF)   Dick Clark
   Productions, 1979, British-U.S.
EYE OF THE NEEDLE   United Artists,
   1981, U.S.-British
RETURN OF THE JEDI
   20th Century-Fox, 1983
UNTIL SEPTEMBER   MGM/UA, 1984
JAGGED EDGE   Columbia, 1985
HEARTS OF FIRE   Lorimar, 1987,
   U.S.-British

GEORGE MARSHALL
b. December 29, 1891 - Chicago, Illinois
d. 1975

LOVE'S LARIAT   Bluebird, 1916
THE MAN FROM MONTANA   Butterfly, 1917
THE EMBARRASSMENT OF RICHES
   W. W. Hodkinson, 1918
THE ADVENTURES OF RUTH   Pathé, 1919
RUTH OF THE ROCKIES   Pathé, 1920
PRAIRIE TRAILS   Fox, 1920
WHY TRUST YOUR HUSBAND?   Fox, 1921
HANDS OFF   Fox, 1921
A RIDIN' ROMEO   Fox, 1921
AFTER YOUR OWN HEART   Fox, 1921
THE LADY FROM LONGACRE   Fox, 1921
THE JOLT   1921
SMILES ARE TRUMPS   Fox, 1922
HAUNTED VALLEY   Pathé, 1923
DON QUICKSHOT OF THE RIO GRANDE
   Universal, 1923
MEN IN THE RAW   Universal, 1923
A TRIP TO CHINATOWN   Fox, 1926
THE GAY RETREAT   Fox, 1927
THE ADVENTURES OF RUTH   Pathé, 1929
PACK UP YOUR TROUBLES   co-director with
   Raymond McCarey, MGM, 1932
THEIR FIRST MISTAKE   1932
TOWED IN A HOLE   1932
EVER SINCE EVE   Warner Bros., 1934
WILD GOLD   Fox, 1934
SHE LEARNED ABOUT SAILORS   Fox, 1934
365 NIGHTS IN HOLLYWOOD   Fox, 1934
LIFE BEGINS AT 40   20th Century-Fox, 1935
TEN DOLLAR RAISE   20th Century-Fox, 1935
IN OLD KENTUCKY   20th Century-Fox, 1935
MUSIC IS MAGIC   20th Century-Fox, 1935
SHOW THEM NO MERCY
   20th Century-Fox, 1935
A MESSAGE TO GARCIA
   20th Century-Fox, 1936
THE CRIME OF DR. FORBES
   20th Century-Fox, 1936
CAN THIS BE DIXIE?
   20th Century-Fox, 1936
NANCY STEELE IS MISSING!
   20th Century-Fox, 1937
LOVE UNDER FIRE   20th Century-Fox, 1937
THE GOLDWYN FOLLIES
   United Artists, 1938
BATTLE OF BROADWAY   1938
HOLD THAT CO-ED   20th Century-Fox, 1938
YOU CAN'T CHEAT AN HONEST MAN
   Universal, 1939
DESTRY RIDES AGAIN   Universal, 1939
THE GHOST BREAKERS   Paramount, 1940
WHEN THE DALTONS RODE
   Universal, 1940
POT O'GOLD   United Artists, 1941
TEXAS   Columbia, 1941
VALLEY OF THE SUN   RKO Radio, 1942
THE FOREST RANGERS   Paramount, 1942
STAR SPANGLED RHYTHM
   Paramount, 1942
TRUE TO LIFE   Paramount, 1943
RIDING HIGH   Paramount, 1943
AND THE ANGELS SING   Paramount, 1944
MURDER, HE SAYS   Paramount, 1945
INCENDIARY BLONDE   Paramount, 1945
HOLD THAT BLONDE   Paramount, 1945
THE BLUE DAHLIA   Paramount, 1946
MONSIEUR BEAUCAIRE   Paramount, 1946
THE PERILS OF PAULINE   Paramount, 1947
VARIETY GIRL   Paramount, 1947
HAZARD   Paramount, 1948
TAP ROOTS   Paramount, 1948
MY FRIEND IRMA   Paramount, 1949

FANCY PANTS   Paramount, 1950
NEVER A DULL MOMENT   RKO Radio, 1950
A MILLIONAIRE FOR CHRISTY
   20th Century-Fox, 1951
THE SAVAGE   Paramount, 1952
OFF LIMITS   Paramount, 1953
SCARED STIFF   Paramount, 1953
HOUDINI   Paramount, 1953
MONEY FROM HOME   Paramount, 1954
RED GARTERS   Paramount, 1954
DUEL IN THE JUNGLE   Warner Bros., 1954
DESTRY   Universal, 1955
THE SECOND GREATEST SEX
   Universal, 1955
PILLARS OF THE SKY   Universal, 1956
THE GUNS OF FORT PETTICOAT
   Columbia, 1957
BEYOND MOMBASA   Columbia, 1956
THE SAD SACK   Paramount, 1957
THE SHEEPMAN   MGM, 1958
IMITATION GENERAL   MGM, 1958
THE MATING GAME   MGM, 1959
IT STARTED WITH A KISS   MGM, 1959
THE GAZEBO   MGM, 1960
CRY FOR HAPPY   Columbia, 1961
THE HAPPY THIEVES   United Artists, 1962
HOW THE WEST WAS WON   co-director with
   Henry Hathaway & John Ford,
   MGM/Cinerama, 1962
PAPA'S DELICATE CONDITION
   Paramount, 1963
DARK PURPOSE   L'INTRIGO   Universal,
   1964, Italian-French-U.S.
ADVANCE TO THE REAR   MGM, 1964
BOY, DID I GET A WRONG NUMBER!
   United Artists, 1966
EIGHT ON THE LAM   United Artists, 1967
THE WICKED DREAMS OF PAULA SCHULTZ
   United Artists, 1968
HOOK, LINE AND SINKER   Columbia, 1969

ANDREW MARTON
(Endre Marton)
b. January 26, 1904 - Budapest, Hungary
d. 1992

TWO O'CLOCK IN THE MORNING   1929
DIE NACHT OHNE PAUSE   co-director with
   Franz Wenzler, 1931, German
NORDPOL-AHOI!   1933, German
DER DAMON DER BERGE   1934, Swiss
MISS PRESIDENT   1935, Hungarian
THE SECRET OF STAMBOUL   THE SPY
   IN WHITE   1936, British
WOLF'S CLOTHING   1936, British
SCHOOL FOR HUSBANDS   1937, British
A LITTLE BIT OF HEAVEN   Universal, 1940
GENTLE ANNIE   MGM, 1944
GALLANT BESS   MGM, 1946
KING SOLOMON'S MINES   co-director with
   Compton Bennett, MGM, 1950
THE WILD NORTH   MGM, 1952
STORM OVER TIBET   Columbia, 1952
MASK OF THE HIMALAYAS   1952
THE DEVIL MAKES THREE   MGM, 1952
MEN OF THE FIGHTING LADY   1954
GYPSY COLT   MGM, 1954
PRISONER OF WAR   MGM, 1954
MEN OF THE FIGHTING LADY   MGM, 1954
GREEN FIRE   MGM, 1955
SEVEN WONDERS OF THE WORLD
   co-director, Stanley Warner Cinema
   Corporation, 1956
UNDERWATER WARRIOR   MGM, 1958
THE LONGEST DAY   co-director with
   Ken Annakin & Bernhard Wicki,
   20th Century-Fox, 1962

IT HAPPENED IN ATHENS
   20th Century-Fox, 1962
THE THIN RED LINE   Allied Artists, 1964
CRACK IN THE WORLD   Paramount,
   1965, British
CLARENCE, THE CROSS-EYED LION
   MGM, 1965
AROUND THE WORLD UNDER THE SEA
   MGM, 1966
BIRDS DO IT   Columbia, 1966
AFRICA - TEXAS STYLE!   Paramount,
   1967, British-U.S.

RUDOLPH MATE
(Rudolf Matheh)
b. January 21, 1898 - Cracow, Poland
d. 1964

IT HAD TO BE YOU   co-director with
   Don Hartman, Columbia, 1947
THE DARK PAST   Columbia, 1949
NO SAD SONGS FOR ME   Columbia, 1950
D.O.A.   United Artists, 1950
UNION STATION   Paramount, 1950
BRANDED   Paramount, 1951
THE PRINCE WHO WAS A THIEF
   Universal, 1951
WHEN WORLDS COLLIDE   Paramount, 1951
THE GREEN GLOVE   United Artists, 1952
PAULA   Columbia, 1952
SALLY AND ST. ANNE   Universal, 1952
THE MISSISSIPPI GAMBLER
   Universal, 1953
SECOND CHANCE   RKO Radio, 1953
FORBIDDEN   Universal, 1954
THE SIEGE AT RED RIVER
   20th Century-Fox, 1954
THE BLACK SHIELD OF FALWORTH
   Universal, 1954
THE VIOLENT MEN   Columbia, 1955
THE FAR HORIZONS   Paramount, 1955
MIRACLE IN THE RAIN   Warner Bros., 1956
THE RAWHIDE YEARS   Universal, 1956
PORT AFRIQUE   Columbia, 1956, British
THREE VIOLENT PEOPLE   Paramount, 1957
SERANADE EINER GROSSEN LIEBE
   German, 1958
THE DEEP SIX   Warner Bros., 1958
FOR THE FIRST TIME   MGM, 1959,
   U.S.-West German-Italian
REVAK - LO SCHIAVO DI CARTAGINE
   1960, Italian
THE IMMACULATE ROAD
   20th Century-Fox, 1960
THE 300 SPARTANS   20th Century-Fox, 1962
SEVEN SEAS TO CALAIS   IL DOMINATORE
   DEI SETTE MARI   MGM, 1962, Italian
ALIKI   Funos-Aquarius, 1963,
   West German-U.S.

JOE MAY
(Joseph Mandel)
b. November 7, 1880 - Vienna, Austria
d. 1954

IN DER TIEFE DES SCHACHTS
   1912, German
HEIMAT UND FREMDE   1913, German
DIE GEHEIMNISVOLLE VILLA   1914, German
DIE PAGODE   1914, German
DER SCHUSS IM TRAUM   1915, German
DAS GESETZ DER MINE   1916, German
NEBEL UND SONNE   1916, German
DIE SUNDE DER HELGA ARNDT
   1916, German
WIE ICH DETEKTIV WURDE   1916, German

HILDE WARREN UND DER TOD
   1917, German
DIE HOCHZEIT IM EXENTRICCLUB
   1917, German
DIE SILHOUETTE DES TEUFELS
   1917, German
DER ONYXKNOPF   1917, German
DER SCHWARZE CHAUFFEUR
   1917, German
DIE LIEBE DER HETTY RAYMOND
   1917, German
SEIN BESTER FREUND   1918, German
OPFER   1918, German
IHR GROSSES GEHEIMNIS   1918, German
VERITAS VINCIT   1918, German
DIE GRAFIN VON MONTE CHRISTO
   1919, German
DIE WAHRE LIEBE   1919, German
DIE HEILIGE SIMPLIZIA   1920, German
DIE HERRIN DER WELT   1920, German
SODOM UND GOMORRA   1920, German
DAS INDISCHE GRABMAL   1921, German
TRAGODIE DER LIEBE   1923, German
DER FARMER AUS TEXAS   1925, German
DAGFIN   1926, German
HEIMKEHR   1928, German
ASPHALT   1929, German
IHRE MAJESTAT DIE LIEBE   1931, German
UND DAS IST DIE HAUPTSACHE
   1931, German
PARIS - MEDITERRANEE   ON DEMANDE
   UN COMPAGNON   1932, French
LE CHEMIN DE BONHEUR   1932, French
VOYAGES DES NOCES   1933, French
TOUT POUR L'AMOUR   1933, French
EIN LIED FUR DICH   1933, French
MUSIC IN THE AIR   Fox, 1934
CONFESSION   Warner Bros., 1937
SOCIETY SMUGGLERS   Universal, 1939
HOUSE OF FEAR   Universal, 1939
THE INVISIBLE MAN RETURNS
   Universal, 1940
THE HOUSE OF THE SEVEN GABLES
   Universal, 1940
YOU'RE NOT SO TOUGH   Universal, 1940
HIT THE ROAD   Universal, 1941
JOHNNY DOESN'T LIVE HERE ANYMORE
   Monogram, 1944

ARCHIE MAYO
(Archibald L. Mayo)
b. 1891 - New York, New York
d. 1968

MONEY TALKS   MGM, 1926
UNKNOWN TREASURES   Sterling, 1926
CHRISTINE OF THE BIG TOPS
   Sterling, 1926
JOHNNY, GET YOUR HAIR CUT   co-director
   with B. Reaves Easton, MGM, 1927
QUARANTINED RIVALS   Lumas, 1927
DEARIE   Warner Bros., 1927
SLIGHTLY USED   Warner Bros., 1927
THE COLLEGE WIDOW   Warner Bros., 1927
BEWARE OF MARRIED MEN
   Warner Bros., 1928
THE CRIMSON CITY   Warner Bros., 1928
STATE STREET SADIE   Warner Bros., 1928
ON TRIAL   Warner Bros., 1928
MY MAN   Warner Bros., 1928
SONNY BOY   Warner Bros., 1929
THE SAP   Warner Bros., 1929
IS EVERYBODY HAPPY?
   Warner Bros., 1929
THE SACRED FLAME   Warner Bros., 1929
VENGEANCE   Columbia, 1930
WIDE OPEN   Warner Bros., 1930

COURAGE   Warner Bros., 1930
OH SAILOR, BEHAVE!   Warner Bros., 1930
THE DOORWAY TO HELL
   Warner Bros., 1930
ILLICIT   Warner Bros., 1931
SVENGALI   Warner Bros., 1931
BOUGHT   Warner Bros., 1931
UNDER EIGHTEEN   Warner Bros., 1932
THE EXPERT   Warner Bros., 1932
STREET OF WOMEN   Warner Bros., 1932
TWO AGAINST THE WORLD
   Warner Bros., 1932
NIGHT AFTER NIGHT   Warner Bros., 1932
THE LIFE OF JIMMY DOLAN
   Warner Bros., 1933
THE MAYOR OF HELL   Warner Bros., 1933
EVER IN MY HEART   Warner Bros., 1933
CONVENTION CITY   Warner Bros., 1933
GAMBLING LADY   Warner Bros., 1934
THE MAN WITH TWO FACES
   Warner Bros., 1934
DESIRABLE   Warner Bros., 1934
BORDERTOWN   Warner Bros., 1935
GO INTO YOUR DANCE   Warner Bros., 1935
THE CASE OF THE LUCKY LEGS
   Warner Bros., 1935
THE PETRIFIED FOREST
   Warner Bros., 1936
I MARRIED A DOCTOR   Warner Bros., 1936
GIVE ME YOUR HEART   Warner Bros., 1936
BLACK LEGION   Warner Bros., 1937
CALL IT A DAY   Warner Bros., 1937
IT'S LOVE I'M AFTER   Warner Bros., 1937
THE ADVENTURES OF MARCO POLO
   United Artists, 1938
YOUTH TAKES A FLING   Universal, 1938
THEY SHALL HAVE MUSIC
   United Artists, 1939
THE HOUSE ACROSS THE BAY
   United Artists, 1940
FOUR SONS   20th Century-Fox, 1940
THE GREAT AMERICAN BROADCAST
   20th Century-Fox, 1941
CHARLEY'S AUNT   20th Century-Fox, 1941
CONFIRM OR DENY   20th Century-Fox, 1941
MOONTIDE   20th Century-Fox, 1942
ORCHESTRA WIVES
   20th Century-Fox, 1942
CRASH DIVE   20th Century-Fox, 1943
SWEET AND LOW-DOWN
   20th Century-Fox, 1944
A NIGHT IN CASABLANCA
   United Artists, 1946
ANGEL ON MY SHOULDER
   United Artists, 1946

DAVID MAYSLES
b. January 10, 1932 - Brookline, Massachusetts
d. 1987

YOUTH IN POLAND (FD)   co-director with
   Albert Maysles, 1957
SHOWMAN (FD)   co-director with
   Albert Maysles, 1962
WHAT'S HAPPENING: THE BEATLES IN
   THE USA (FD)   co-director with
   Albert Maysles, 1964
MEET MARLON BRANDO (FD)   co-director
   with Albert Maysles, 1965
WITH LOVE FROM TRUMAN (FD)   co-director
   with Albert Maysles, 1966
SALESMAN (FD)   co-director with
   Albert Maysles & Charlotte Zwerin,
   Maysles Film, 1969
GIMME SHELTER (FD)   co-director with
   Albert Maysles & Charlotte Zwerin,
   Cinema 5, 1971

CHRISTO'S VALLEY CURTAIN (FD)
   co-director with Albert Maysles &
   Ellen Giffard, 1972
GREY GARDENS (FD)   co-director with
   Albert Maysles, Ellen Hovde &
   Muffie Meyer, 1975
RUNNING FENCE (FD)   co-director with
   Albert Maysles & Charlotte Zwerin, 1977
VLADIMIR HOROWITZ: THE LAST
   ROMANTIC (TD) ☆   co-director with
   Albert Maysles, Cami Video, 1985
ISLANDS (FD)   co-director with
   Albert Maysles & Charlotte Zwerin,
   Maysles Film, 1986
OZAWA (TD)   co-director with Albert Maysles,
   Deborah Dickson & Susan Froemke,
   Columbia Artists, 1986
CHRISTO IN PARIS (FD)   co-director with
   Albert Maysles, Maysles Films, 1991

LEO McCAREY
b. October 3, 1898 - Los Angeles, California
d. 1969

ALL WET   1924
BAD BOY   1925
INNOCENT HUSBANDS   1926
WE FAW DOWN   1928
LIBERTY   1929
WRONG AGAIN   1929
SOCIETY SECRETS   Universal, 1921
THE SOPHOMORE   Pathé, 1929
RED HOT RHYTHM   Pathé, 1929
WILD COMPANY   Fox, 1930
LET'S GO NATIVE   Paramount, 1930
PART TIME WIFE   Fox, 1930
INDISCREET   United Artists, 1931
THE KID FROM SPAIN   United Artists, 1932
DUCK SOUP   Paramount, 1933
SIX OF A KIND   Paramount, 1934
BELLE OF THE NINETIES   Paramount, 1934
RUGGLES OF RED GAP   Paramount, 1935
THE MILKY WAY   Paramount, 1936
MAKE WAY FOR TOMORROW
   Paramount, 1937
THE AWFUL TRUTH ★★   Columbia, 1937
LOVE AFFAIR   RKO Radio, 1939
ONCE UPON A HONEYMOON
   RKO Radio, 1942
GOING MY WAY ★★   Paramount, 1944
THE BELLS OF ST. MARY'S ★
   Paramount, 1945
GOOD SAM   RKO Radio, 1948
MY SON JOHN   Paramount, 1952
AN AFFAIR TO REMEMBER
   20th Century-Fox, 1957
RALLY ROUND THE FLAG, BOYS!
   20th Century-Fox, 1958
SATAN NEVER SLEEPS   20th Century-Fox,
   1962, U.S.-British

WINSOR McCAY
b. September 26, 1871 - Spring Lake, Michigan
d. 1934

LITTLE NEMO (AF)   1909
HOW A MOSQUITO OPERATES   THE STORY
   OF A MOSQUITO (AF)   1912
GERTIE THE DINOSAUR   GERTIE THE
   TRAINED DINOSAUR (AF)   1914
THE SINKING OF THE LUSITANIA (AF)   1918
THE CENTAURS (AF)   1919
DREAMS OF A RAREBIT FIEND (AF)   1921

GEORGES MELIES
b. December 8, 1861 - Paris, France
d. 1938

UNE PARTIE DE CARTES   Star Film,
   1896, French
SEANCE DE PRESTIDIGITATION   Star Film,
   1896, French
UN BON PETIT DIABLE   Star Film,
   1896, French
LES CHEVAUX DU BOIS   Star Film,
   1896, French
L'ARROSEUR   Star Film, 1896, French
ARRIVEE D'UN TRAIN GARE DE VINCENNES
   Star Film, 1896, French
PLACE DE L'OPERA   Star Film, 1896, French
BATEAU-MOUCHE SUR LA SEINE   Star Film,
   1896, French
UNE NUIT TERRIBLE   Star Film,
   1896, French
TRIBULATIONS D'UN CONCIERGE
   Star Film, 1896, French
ENFANTS JOUANT SUR LA PLAGE
   Star Film, 1896, French
DANSE SERPENTINE   Star Film,
   1896, French
CORTEGE DU TSAR ALLANT A VERSAILLES
   Star Film, 1896, French
GRANDES MANOEUVRES   Star Film,
   1896, French
ESCAMOTAGE D'UNE DAME CHEZ
   ROBERT-HOUDIN   Star Film, 1896, French
LE FAKIR - MYSTERE INDIEN   Star Film,
   1896, French
L'HOTEL EMPOISONNE   Star Film,
   1896, French
CHICOT DENTISTE AMERICAIN   Star Film,
   1897, French
COQUIN DE PRINTEMPS   Star Film,
   1897, French
LE MALADE IMAGINAIRE   Star Film,
   1897, French
L'HALLUCINATION DE L'ALCHIMESTE
   Star Films, 1897, French
LE CHATEAU HANTE   Star Film,
   1897, French
EPISODE DE GUERRE   Star Film,
   1897, French
EXECUTION D'UN ESPION   Star Film,
   1897, French
MASSACRES DE CRETE   Star Film,
   1897, French
GUGUSSE ET L'AUTOMATE   Star Film,
   1897, French
LA CIGALE ET LA FOURMI   Star Film,
   1897, French
LE CABINET DE MEPHISTOPHELES
   Star Film, 1897, French
FIGARO ET L'AUVERGNANT   Star Film,
   1897, French
ARLEQUIN ET CHARBONNIER   Star Film,
   1897, French
APRES LE BAL   Star Film, 1897, French
VENTE D'ESCLAVES AU HAREM   Star Film,
   1897, French
FAUST ET MARGUERITE   Star Film,
   1897, French
CARREFOUR DE L'OPERA   Star Film,
   1898, French
MAGIE DIABOLIQUE   Star Film,
   1898, French
LES RAYONS X   Star Film, 1898, French
VISITE DE L'EPAVE DU MAINE   Star Film,
   1898, French
LE MAGICIEN   Star Film, 1898, French
ILLUSIONS FANTASMAGORIQUES
   Star Film, 1898, French

PYGMALION ET GALATHEE   Star Film,
1898, French
DAMNATION DE FAUST   Star Film,
1898, French
GUILLAUME TELL ET LE CLOWN   Star Film,
1898, French
LA LUNE A UN METRE   Star Film,
1898, French
LA CAVERNE MAUDITE   Star Film,
1898, French
REVE D'ARTISTE   Star Film, 1898, French
L'HOMME DE TETES   Star Film,
1898, French
DEDOUBLEMENT CABALISTIQUE
Star Film, 1898, French
CREATIONS SPONTANEES   Star Film,
1898, French
CLEOPATRE   Star Film, 1899, French
RICHESSE ET MISERIE   Star Film,
1899, French
LE SPECTRE   Star Film, 1899, French
LE DIABLE AU COUVENT   Star Film,
1899, French
LA DANSE DU DEU   Star Film, 1899, French
LE PORTRAIT MYSTERIEUX   Star Film,
1899, French
LE MIROIR DE CAGLIOSTRO   Star Film,
1899, French
NEPTUNE ET AMPHITRITE   Star Film,
1899, French
LE CHRIST MARCHANT SUR LES FLOTS
Star Films, 1899, French
EVOCATION SPIRITE   Star Film,
1899, French
L'AFFAIRE DREYFUS   Star Film,
1899, French
L'ILE DU DIABLE   Star Film, 1899, French
CENDRILLON   Star Film, 1899, French
LE CHEVALIER MYSTERE   Star Film,
1899, French
TOM WHISKY OU L'ILLUSTRIONISTE TOQUE
Star Film, 1899, French
LES MIRACLES DU BRAHMINE   Star Film,
1899, French
EXPOSITION DE 1900   Star Film,
1900, French
L'HOMME-ORCHESTRE   Star Film,
1900, French
JEANNE D'ARC   Star Film, 1900, French
LES SEPT PECHES CAPITAUX   Star Film,
1900, French
LE REVE DU RADJAH   Star Film,
1900, French
LE FOU ASSASSIN   Star Film, 1900, French
LE LIVRE MAGIQUE   Star Film, 1900, French
SPIRITISME ABRACADABRANT   Star Film,
1900, French
L'ILLUSIONISTE DOUBLE ET LA TETE
VIVANTE   Star Film, 1900, French
LE REVE DE NOEL   Star Film, 1900, French
COPPELIA   Star Film, 1900, French
GENS QUI PLEURENT ET GENS QUI RIENT
Star Film, 1900, French
LE DESHABILLAGE IMPOSSIBLE   Star Film,
1900, French
L'HOMME AUX CENT TRUCS   Star Film,
1900, French
LA MAISON TRANQUILLE   Star Film,
1900, French
MESAVENTURES D'UN AERONAUTE
Star Film, 1900, French
LA TOUR MAUDITE   Star Film, 1900, French
BOUQUET D'ILLUSIONS   Star Film,
1900, French
LE PETIT CHAPERON ROUGE   Star Film,
1901, French
CHEZ LA SORCIERE   Star Film,
1901, French

LE TEMPLE DE LA MAGIE   Star Film,
1901, French
LE CHARLATAN   Star Film, 1901, French
EXCELSIOR!   Star Film, 1901, French
LA FONTAINE SACREE   Star Film,
1901, French
BARBE-BLEUE   Star Film, 1901, French
LE PHRENOLOGIE BURLESQUE   Star Film,
1901, French
L'ECOLE INFERNALE   Star Film,
1901, French
LE REVE DU PARIA   Star Film, 1901, French
LE BATAILLON ELASTIQUE   Star Film,
1901, French
L'HOMME A LA TETE EN CAOUTCHOUC
Star Film, 1901, French
LE DIABLE GEANT   Star Film, 1901, French
L'OEUF DU SORCIER   Star Film,
1901, French
LA DANSEUSE MICROSCOPIQUE   Star Film,
1901, French
ERUPTION VOLCANIQUE A LA MARTINIQUE
Star Film, 1902, French
A TRIP TO THE MOON   Star Film,
1902, French
LA CLOWNESSE FANTOME   Star Film,
1902, French
LE SACRE D'EDOUARD VII   Star Film,
1902, French
LES TRESORS DE SATAN   Star Film,
1902, French
L'HOMME-MOUCHE   Star Film, 1902, French
LA FEMME VOLANTE   Star Film,
1902, French
L'EQUILIBRE IMPOSSIBLE   Star Film,
1902, French
LE POCHARD ET L'INVENTEUR   Star Film,
1902, French
LE VOYAGE DE GULLIVER A LILLIPUT ET
CHEZLES GEANTS   Star Film,
1902, French
LES AVENTURES DE ROBINSON CRUSOE
Star Film, 1902, French
LES FILLES DU DIABLE   Star Film,
1903, French
LE CAKE-WALK INFERNAL   Star Film,
1903, French
LES MOUSQUETAIRES DE LA REINE
Star Film, 1903, French
LA STATUE ANIMEE   Star Film, 1903, French
LA FLAMME MERVEUILLEUSE   Star Film,
1903, French
LE SORCIER   Star Film, 1903, French
L'ORACLE DE DELPHES   Star Film,
1903, French
LE MELOMANE   Star Film, 1903, French
LE MONSTRE   Star Film, 1903, French
LE ROYAUME DES FEES   Star Film,
1903, French
LE REVENANT   Star Film, 1903, French
LE TONNERRE DE JUPITER   Star Film,
1903, French
LA PARAPLUIE FANTASTIQUE   Star Film,
1903, French
TOM TIGHT ET DUM DUM   Star Film,
1903, French
LA LANTERNE MAGIQUE   Star Film,
1903, French
LE REVE DU MAITRE DE BALLET   Star Film,
1903, French
FAUST AUX ENFERS   Star Film,
1903, French
LES APACHES   Star Film, 1904, French
AU CLAIR DE LA LUNE   Star Film,
1904, French
LE COFFRE ENCHANTE   Star Film,
1904, French

LES APPARITIONS FUGITIVES   Star Film,
1904, French
LE ROI DU MAQUILLAGE   Star Film,
1904, French
LE REVE D'HORLOGER   Star Film,
1904, French
LES TRANSMUTATIONS IMPERCEPTIBLES
Star Film, 1904, French
UN MIRACLE SOUS L'INQUISITION
Star Film, 1904, French
BENVENUTO CELLINI   Star Film,
1904, French
DAMNATION DU DOCTEUR FAUST
Star Film, 1904, French
LE MERVEILLEUX EVENTAIL VIVANT
Star Film, 1904, French
LA SIRENE   Star Film, 1904, French
LE BARBIER DE SEVILLE   Star Film,
1904, French
LES COSTUMES ANIMES   Star Film,
1904, French
LA DAME FANTOME   Star Film,
1904, French
VOYAGE A TRAVERS L'IMPOSSIBLE
Star Film, 1904, French
LE JUIF ERRANT   Star Film, 1905, French
A PRESIDENT-ELECT ROOSEVELT
Star Film, 1905, French
LE CARTES VIVANTES   Star Film,
1905, French
LE DIABLE NOIR   Star Film, 1905, French
LE PHENIX   Star Film, 1905, French
LE BAQUET DE MESMER   Star Film,
1905, French
TABLEAU DIABOLIQUE   Star Film,
1905, French
LE MIROIR DE VENISE   Star Film,
1905, French
UNE MESAVENTURE DE SHYLOCK
Star Film, 1905, French
LES CHEVALIERS DU CHLOROFORME
Star Film, 1905, French
LE PALAIS DES MILLE ET UNE NUITS
Star Film, 1905, French
LA TOUT DE LONDRES   Star Film,
1905, French
LA LEGENDE DE RIP VAN WINKLE
Star Film, 1905, French
LE DIRIGEABLE FANTASTIQUE   Star Film,
1906, French
JACK LE RAMONEUR   Star Film,
1906, French
LA MAGIE A TRAVERS LES AGES   Star Film,
1906, French
LES INCENDIAIRES   Star Film, 1906, French
L'ANARCHIE CHEZ GUIGNOL   Star Film,
1906, French
LE FANTOME D'ALGER   Star Film,
1906, French
LES QUATRE CENT FARCES DU DIABLE
Star Film, 1906, French
L'ALCHIMESTE PARAFARAGARAMUS
Star Film, 1906, French
LE FEE CARABOSSE   Star Film,
1906, French
LE CARTON FANTASTIQUE   Star Film,
1906, French
LA DOUCE D'EAU BOUILLANTE   Star Film,
1907, French
VINGT MILLE LIEUES SOUS LES MERS
Star Films, 1907, French
LE TUNNEL SOUS LA MANCHE   Star Film,
1907, French
LE DELIRIUM TREMENS   Star Film,
1907, French
L'ECLIPSE DE SOLEIL EN PLEIN LUNE
Star Film, 1907, French

GEORGES MELIES (continued)

LA MARCHE FUNEBRE DE CHOPIN
  Star Film, 1907, French
HAMLET   Star Film, 1907, French
LA MORT DE JULES CESAR   Star Film,
  1907, French
SATAN EN PRISON   Star Film, 1907, French
LA CUISINE DE L'OGRE   Star Film,
  1908, French
LA CIVILISATION A TRAVERS LES AGES
  Star Film, 1908, French
TORCHES HUMAINES   Star Film,
  French
LE REVE D'UN FUMEUR D'OPIUM   Star Film,
  1908, French
NUIT DE CARNAVAL   Star Film,
  1908, French
LA PHOTOGRAPHIE ELECTRIQUE A
  DISTANCE   Star Film, 1908, French
LA PROPHETESSE DE THEBES   Star Film,
  1908, French
MARIAGE DE RAISON ET MARIAGE
  D'AMOUR   Star Film, 1908, French
L'AVARE   Star Film, 1908, French
LE SERPENT DE LA RUE DE LA LUNE
  Star Film, 1908, French
TARTARIN DE TARASCON   Star Film,
  1908, French
LE RAID PARIS - NEW YORK EN
  AUTOMOBILE   Star Film, 1908, French
AU PAYS DES JOUETS   Star Film,
  1908, French
HALLUCINATION PHARMACEUTIQUE
  Star Film, 1908, French
LA POUPEE VIVANTE   Star Film,
  1908, French
LE FAKIR DE SINGAPOUR   Star Film,
  1908, French
HYDROTHERAPIE FANTASTIQUE   Star Film,
  1909, French
LES ILLUSIONS FANTAISISTES   Star Film,
  1909, French
LA GIGUE MERVEILLEUSE   Star Film,
  1909, French
LE PAPILLON FANTASTIQUE   Star Film,
  1910, French
SI J'ETAIS ROI   Star Film, 1910, French
L'HOMME AUX MILLE INVENTIONS
  Star Film, 1910, French
LE SECRET DU MEDECIN   Star Film,
  1910, French
LES HALLUCINATIONS DU BARON DE
  MUNCHHAUSEN   Pathé, 1911, French
A LA CONQUETE DU POLE   Pathé,
  1912, French
CENDRILLON   Pathé, 1912, French
LE CHEVALIER DES NEIGES   Pathé,
  1913, French
LE VOYAGE DE LA FAMILLE BOURRICHON
  Pathé, 1913, French

JEAN-PIERRE MELVILLE
(Jean-Pierre Grumbach)
b. October 20, 1917 - Paris, France
d. 1973

LE SILENCE DE LA MER   1949, French
LES ENFANTS TERRIBLES   THE STRANGE
  ONES   Mayer-Kingsley, 1949, French
QUAND TU LIRAS CETTE LETTRE
  1953, French
BOB LE FLAMBEUR   Samuel Goldwyn
  Company, 1955, French
DEUX HOMMES DANS MANHATTAN
  1959, French
LEON MORIN, PRETRE   1961,
  French-Italian

LE DOULOS   1962, French-Italian
L'AINE DES FERCHAUX   1962,
  French-Italian
LE DEUXIEME SOUFFLE   SECOND BREATH
  1966, French
LE SAMOURAI   1967, French-Italian
L'ARMEE DES OMBRES   1969, French-Italian
LE CERCLE ROUGE   1970, French-Italian
UN FLIC   DIRTY MONEY   1972, French

LOTHAR MENDES
b. May 19, 1894 - Berlin, Germany
d. 1974

DER ABENTEUER   1921, German
DEPORTIERT   1922, German
SOS - DIE INSEL DER TRANEN
  1923, German
LIEBE MACHT BLIND   1925, German
DIE DREI KUCKUCKSUHREN   1926, German
THE PRINCE OF TEMPTERS   1926
A NIGHT OF MYSTERY   1928
INTERFERENCE   co-director with
  Roy J. Pomeroy, 1929
THE FOUR FEATHERS   co-director with
  Merian C. Cooper & Ernest B. Schoedsack,
  United Artists, 1929
ILLUSION   1929
THE MARRIAGE PLAYGROUND   1929
DANGEROUS CURVES   1929
PARAMOUNT ON PARADE   co-director,
  Paramount, 1930
LADIES' MAN   Paramount, 1931
PERSONAL MAID   co-director with Monta Bell,
  Paramount, 1931
STRANGERS IN LOVE   Paramount, 1932
PAYMENT DEFERRED   MGM, 1932
LUXURY LINER   MGM, 1933
JEW SUSS   POWER   Gaumont-British,
  1934, British
THE MAN WHO COULD WORK MIRACLES
  United Artists, 1937, British
MOONLIGHT SONATA   1937, British
INTERNATIONAL SQUADRON
  Warner Bros., 1941
FLIGHT FOR FREEDOM   RKO Radio, 1943
TAMPICO   20th Century-Fox, 1944
THE WALLS CAME TUMBLING DOWN
  Columbia, 1946

WILLIAM CAMERON MENZIES
b. July 29, 1896 - New Haven, Connecticut
d. 1957

THE SPIDER   co-director with
  Kenneth McKenna, Fox, 1931
ALWAYS GOODBYE   co-director with
  Kenneth McKenna, Fox, 1931
CHANDU THE MAGICIAN   co-director with
  Marcel Varnel, Fox, 1932
I LOVED YOU WEDNESDAY   co-director with
  Henry King, Fox, 1933
THE WHARF ANGEL   co-director with
  George Somnes, Paramount, 1934
THINGS TO COME   United Artists,
  1936, British
THE GREEN COCKATOO   FOUR DARK
  HOURS   1937, British
ADDRESS UNKNOWN   Columbia, 1944
DRUMS IN THE DEEP SOUTH
  RKO Radio, 1951
THE WHIP HAND   RKO RADIO, 1951
INVADERS FROM MARS
  20th Century-Fox, 1953
THE MAZE   Allied Artists, 1953

OSCAR MICHEAUX
b. 1884 - Metropolis, Illinois
d. 1951

THE HOMESTEADER   Micheaux, 1919
WITHIN OUR GATES   Micheaux, 1920
THE BRUTE   Micheaux, 1921
THE SHADOW   Micheaux, 1921
THE GUNSAULUS MYSTERY
  Micheaux, 1921
THE HYPOCRITE   Micheaux, 1921
THE WAGES OF SIN   Micheaux, 1921
UNCLE JASPER'S WILL   Micheaux, 1922
THE DUNGEON   Micheaux, 1922
THE HOUSE BEHIND THE CEDARS
  Micheaux, 1923
DECEIT   Micheaux, 1923
A SON OF SATAN   Micheaux, 1924
BIRTHRIGHT   Micheaux, 1924
BODY AND SOUL   Micheaux, 1925
THE COMJURE WOMAN   Micheaux, 1926
THE DEVIL'S DISCIPLE   Micheaux, 1926
THE SPIDER'S WEB   Micheaux, 1927
THE MILLIONAIRE   Micheaux, 1927
THE GIRL FROM CHICAGO   Micheaux, 1927
THE BROKEN VIOLIN   Micheaux, 1927
THIRTY YEARS LATER   Micheaux, 1928
WHEN MEN BETRAY   Micheaux, 1928
A DAUGHTER OF THE CONGO
  Micheaux, 1930
EASY STREET   Micheaux, 1930
THE EXILE   Micheaux, 1931
THE VEILED ARISTOCRATS   Micheaux, 1932
TEN MINUTES TO LIVE   Micheaux, 1932
HARLEM AFTER MIDNIGHT   Micheaux, 1935
LEM HAWKINS' CONFESSION   THE BRAND
  OF CAIN   Micheaux, 1935
SWING   Micheaux, 1936
TEMPTATION   Micheaux, 1936
UNDERWORLD   Micheaux, 1936
GOD'S STEPCHILDREN   Micheaux, 1938
BIRTHRIGHT   Micheaux, 1939
THE NOTORIOUS ELINOR LEE
  Micheaux, 1940
LYING LIPS   Micheaux, 1940
THE BETRAYAL   Micheaux, 1948

LEWIS MILESTONE
b. September 30, 1895 - Chisinau, Russia
d. 1980

SEVEN SINNERS   Warner Bros., 1925
THE CAVEMAN   Warner Bros., 1926
THE NEW KLONDIKE   Paramount, 1926
TWO ARABIAN KNIGHTS ★★
  United Artists, 1927
THE GARDEN OF EDEN   United Artists, 1928
THE RACKET   Paramount, 1928
BETRAYAL   Paramount, 1929
NEW YORK NIGHTS   United Artists, 1929
ALL QUIET ON THE WESTERN FRONT ★★
  Universal, 1930
THE FRONT PAGE ★   United Artists, 1931
RAIN   United Artists, 1932
HALLELUJAH, I'M A BUM!
  United Artists, 1933
THE CAPTAIN HATES THE SEA
  Columbia, 1934
PARIS IN SPRING   Paramount, 1935
ANYTHING GOES   TOPS IS THE LIMIT
  Paramount, 1936
THE GENERAL DIED AT DAWN
  Paramount, 1936
THE NIGHT OF NIGHTS   American
  Releasing, 1939
OF MICE AND MEN   United Artists, 1940
LUCKY PARTNERS   RKO Radio, 1940

MY LIFE WITH CAROLINE   RKO Radio, 1941
OUR RUSSIAN FRONT (FD)   co-director with
  Joris Ivens & Harry Rathner, 1942
EDGE OF DARKNESS   Warner Bros., 1943
THE NORTH STAR   *ARMORED ATTACK*
  RKO Radio, 1943
THE PURPLE HEART
  20th Century-Fox, 1944
A WALK IN THE SUN   20th Century-Fox, 1946
THE STRANGE LOVE OF MARTHA IVERS
  Paramount, 1946
THE ARCH OF TRIUMPH
  United Artists, 1948
NO MINOR VICES   MGM, 1948
THE RED PONY   Republic, 1949
THE HALLS OF MONTEZUMA
  20th Century-Fox, 1951
KANGAROO   20th Century-Fox, 1952
LES MISERABLES   20th Century-Fox, 1952
MELBA   United Artists, 1953, British
THEY WHO DARE   Allied Artists, 1953
THE WIDOW   DCA, 1955, Italian-French
PORK CHOP HILL   United Artists, 1959
OCEAN'S 11   Warner Bros., 1960
MUTINY ON THE BOUNTY   MGM, 1962

RAY MILLAND

(Reginald Truscott-Jones)
b. January 3, 1905 - Neath, Wales
d. 1986

A MAN ALONE   Republic, 1955
LISBON   Republic, 1956
THE SAFECRACKER   MGM, 1958, British
PANIC IN YEAR ZERO!   American
  International, 1962
HOSTILE WITNESS   1967, British

DAVID MILLER

b. November 28, 1909 - Paterson, New Jersey
d. 1992

BILLY THE KID   MGM, 1941
SUNDAY PUNCH   MGM, 1942
FLYING TIGERS   Republic, 1942
TOP O' THE MORNING   Paramount, 1948
LOVE HAPPY   United Artists, 1949
OUR VERY OWN   RKO Radio, 1950
SATURDAY'S HERO   Columbia, 1951
SUDDEN FEAR   RKO Radio, 1952
TWIST OF FATE   *THE BEAUTIFUL*
  STRANGER   United Artists, 1954, British
DIANE   MGM, 1956
THE OPPOSITE SEX   MGM, 1956
THE STORY OF ESTHER COSTELLO
  Columbia, 1957
HAPPY ANNIVERSARY   United Artists, 1959
MIDNIGHT LACE   Universal, 1961
BACK STREET   Universal, 1961
LONELY ARE THE BRAVE   Universal, 1962
CAPTAIN NEWMAN, M.D.   Universal, 1964
HAMMERHEAD   Columbia, 1968, British
HAIL, HERO!   National General, 1969
EXECUTIVE ACTION
  National General, 1973
BITTERSWEET LOVE   Avco Embassy, 1976
LOVE FOR RENT (TF)   Warren V. Bush
  Productions, 1979
THE BEST PLACE TO BE (TF)   Ross Hunter
  Productions, 1979
GOLDIE AND THE BOXER (TF)   Orenthal
  Productions/Columbia TV, 1979
GOLDIE AND THE BOXER GO TO
  HOLLYWOOD (TF)   Orenthal Productions/
  Columbia TV, 1981

VINCENTE MINNELLI

b. February 28, 1910 - Chicago, Illinois
d. 1986

CABIN IN THE SKY   MGM, 1943
I DOOD IT   MGM, 1943
MEET ME IN ST. LOUIS   MGM, 1944
YOLANDA AND THE THIEF   MGM, 1945
THE CLOCK   MGM, 1945
ZIEGFELD FOLLIES   MGM, 1946
TILL THE CLOUDS ROLL BY   co-director with
  Richard Whorf, MGM, 1946
UNDERCURRENT   MGM, 1946
THE PIRATE   MGM, 1948
MADAME BOVARY   MGM, 1949
FATHER OF THE BRIDE   MGM, 1950
AN AMERICAN IN PARIS ★   MGM, 1951
FATHER'S LITTLE DIVIDEND   MGM, 1951
THE BAD AND THE BEAUTIFUL   MGM, 1952
THE STORY OF THREE LOVES   co-director
  with Gottfried Reinhardt, MGM, 1953
THE BAND WAGON   MGM, 1953
THE LONG, LONG TRAILER   MGM, 1954
BRIGADOON   MGM, 1954
THE COBWEB   MGM, 1955
KISMET   MGM, 1955
LUST FOR LIFE   MGM, 1956
TEA AND SYMPATHY   MGM, 1956
DESIGNING WOMAN   MGM, 1957
GIGI ★   MGM, 1958
THE RELUCTANT DEBUTANTE   MGM, 1958
SOME CAME RUNNING   MGM, 1958
HOME FROM THE HILL   MGM, 1960
BELLS ARE RINGING   MGM, 1960
THE FOUR HORSEMEN OF THE
  APOCALYPSE   MGM, 1962
TWO WEEKS IN ANOTHER TOWN
  MGM, 1962
THE COURTSHIP OF EDDIE'S FATHER
  MGM, 1963
GOODBYE, CHARLIE
  20th Century-Fox, 1964
THE SANDPIPER   MGM, 1965
ON A CLEAR DAY YOU CAN SEE FOREVER
  Paramount, 1970
A MATTER OF TIME   American International,
  1976, U.S.-Italian

KENJI MISUMI

b. 1921 - Kyoto Prefecture, Japan
d. 1975

SAZEN TANGE: MONKEY'S POT   Toei,
  1954, Japanese
ASATARO THE CROW   Daiei,
  1956, Japanese
MOMOTARO THE SAMURAI   Daiei,
  1957, Japanese
CURSE OF THE CAT'S GHOST   Daiei,
  1958, Japanese
YOTSUYA KAIDAN   Daiei, 1959, Japanese
KOMAKO SHIRAKOMA   Daiei,
  1960, Japanese
PRINCESS SEN'S CASTLE   Daiei,
  1960, Japanese
DAIBOSATSU PASS   Daiei, 1960, Japanese
DAIBOSATSU PASS: THE DRAGON GOD
  Daiei, 1960, Japanese
SHAKA   Daiei, 1961, Japanese
HEIJI ZENIGATA'S REPORT: BEAUTIFUL
  SHARK   Daiei, 1961, Japanese
GHOST OF AOBA CASTLE   Daiei,
  1962, Japanese
KILL!   Daiei, 1962, Japanese
STORY OF ZATOICHI   *THE LIFE & OPINION*
  OF MASSEUR ICHI   Daiei, 1962, Japanese

SHINSEN GUMI SHIMATSUKI   Daiei,
  1963, Japanese
SWORD   Daiei, 1964, Japanese
FIGHT, ZATOICHI, FIGHT!   Daiei,
  1964, Japanese
NEMURI KYOSHIRO SHOBU   Daiei,
  1964, Japanese
VAGABOND   Daiei, 1964, Japanese
DEVIL OF THE SWORD   Daiei,
  1965, Japanese
ZATOICHI AND THE CHESS EXPERT   Daiei,
  1965, Japanese
NEZUMI KOZO JIROKICHI   Daiei,
  1965, Japanese
NEMURI KYOSHIRO ENJO KEN   Daiei,
  1965, Japanese
THE LIFE OF MATSU THE UNTAMED   Daiei,
  1965, Japanese
DAIMAJIN GETS ANGRY   *RETURN OF GIANT*
  MAJIN   Daiei, 1966, Japanese
NEMURI KYOSHIRO BURAIKEN   Daiei,
  1966, Japanese
DRUNKEN DOCTOR   Daiei, 1966, Japanese
SISTERS IN KYOTO   Daiei, 1967, Japanese
ZATOICHI CHALLENGED!   Daiei,
  1967, Japanese
TEARS RIVER   Daiei, 1967, Japanese
THE CREST OF THE SNOW   Daiei,
  1967, Japanese
ZATOICHI: THE BLIND SWORDSMAN
  SAMARITAN   *ZATOICHI FIGHTING DRUM*
  Daiei, 1968, Japanese
TOMURAI SHI TACHI   Daiei, 1968, Japanese
THE HOUSE WHERE DEMONS LIVE
  Daiei, 1969, Japanese
SHIRIKURAE MAGOICHI   Daiei,
  1969, Japanese
KYOJO NAGARE DOSU   Daiei,
  1970, Japanese
ZATOICHI'S WILD FIRE FESTIVAL   Daiei,
  1970, Japanese
THE BABY THE FOX GAVE ME   Daiei,
  1971, Japanese
LONE WOLF: I CAN RENT MY CHILD, I CAN
  RENT MY ARM   Katsu Productions,
  1972, Japanese
LONE WOLF: BABY CART OF SANZU RIVER
  Katsu Productions, 1972, Japanese
LONE WOLF: THE BABY CART WHICH GOES
  TO WIND AND DEATH   Katsu Productions,
  1972, Japanese
GOYOKIBA   Katsu Productions,
  1972, Japanese
LONE WOLF: THE ROAD OF DEMONS
  Katsu Productions, 1973, Japanese
SPARE CREST OF CHERRY BLOSSOMS
  Katsu Productions, 1973, Japanese
WOLF! CUT THE SUNSET   Shochiku,
  1974, Japanese

KENJI MIZOGUCHI

b. May 16, 1898 - Tokyo, Japan
d. 1956

THE RESURRECTION OF LOVE   Nikkatsu,
  1923, Japanese
HOMETOWN   Nikkatsu, 1923, Japanese
THE DREAM PATH OF YOUTH   Nikkatsu,
  1923, Japanese
CITY OF DESIRE   Nikkatsu, 1923, Japanese
813: THE ADVENTURES OF ARSENE LUPIN
  Nikkatsu, 1923, Japanese
FOGGY HARBOR   Nikkatsu, 1923, Japanese
BLOOD AND SOUL   Nikkatsu,
  1923, Japanese
THE NIGHT   Nikkatsu, 1923, Japanese
IN THE RUINS   Nikkatsu, 1923, Japanese

THE SONG OF THE MOUNTAIN PASS
Nikkatsu, 1924, Japanese
THE SAD IDIOT Nikkatsu, 1924, Japanese
THE QUEEN OF MODERN TIMES Nikkatsu,
1924, Japanese
WOMEN ARE STRONG Nikkatsu,
1924, Japanese
THIS DUSTY WORLD Nikkatsu,
1924, Japanese
TURKEYS IN A ROW Nikkatsu,
1924, Japanese
A CHRONICLE OF MAY RAIN Nikkatsu,
1924, Japanese
NO MONEY, NO FIGHT Nikkatsu,
1924, Japanese
A WOMAN OF PLEASURE Nikkatsu,
1924, Japanese
DEATH AT DAWN Nikkatsu,
1924, Japanese
QUEEN OF THE CIRCUS Nikkatsu,
1925, Japanese
OUT OF COLLEGE Nikkatsu,
1925, Japanese
THE WHITE LILY LAMENTS Nikkatsu,
1925, Japanese
THE EARTH SMILES Nikkatsu,
1925, Japanese
SHINING IN THE RED SUNSET Nikkatsu,
1925, Japanese
THE SONG OF HOME Nikkatsu,
1925, Japanese
THE HUMAN BEING Nikkatsu,
1925, Japanese
STREET SKETCHES Nikkatsu,
1925, Japanese
GENERAL NOGI AND KUMA-SAN Nikkatsu,
1926, Japanese
THE COPPER COIN KING Nikkatsu,
1926, Japanese
A PAPER DOLL'S WHISPER OF SPRING
Nikkatsu, 1926, Japanese
MY FAULT, NEW VERSION Nikkatsu,
1926, Japanese
THE PASSION OF A WOMAN TEACHER
Nikkatsu, 1926, Japanese
THE BOY OF THE SEA Nikkatsu,
1926, Japanese
MONEY Nikkatsu, 1926, Japanese
THE IMPERIAL GRACE Nikkatsu,
1927, Japanese
THE CUCKOO Nikkatsu, 1927, Japanese
A MAN'S LIFE Nikkatsu, 1928, Japanese
NIHOMBASHI Nikkatsu, 1929, Japanese
TOKYO MARCH Nikkatsu, 1929, Japanese
THE MORNING SUN SHINES Nikkatsu,
1929, Japanese
METROPOLITAN SYMPHONY Nikkatsu,
1929, Japanese
HOME TOWN Nikkatsu, 1930, Japanese
MISTRESS OF A FOREIGNER Nikkatsu,
1930, Japanese
AND YET THEY GO Nikkatsu,
1931, Japanese
THE MAN OF THE MOMENT Nikkatsu,
1932, Japanese
THE DAWN OF MANCHUKUO AND
MONGOLIA Irie Productions/Nakano
Productions/Shinko, 1932, Japanese
TAKI NO SHIRAITO, THE WATER MAGICIAN
Irie Productions, 1933, Japanese
GION FESTIVAL Shinko, 1933, Japanese
THE JIMPU GROUP Irie Productions/Shinko,
1933, Japanese
THE MOUNTAIN PASS OF LOVE AND HATE
Nikkatsu, 1934, Japanese
THE DOWNFALL OF OSEN Daiichi Eiga,
1934, Japanese

OYUKI THE MADONNA Daiichi Eiga,
1935, Japanese
POPPY Daiichi Eiga, 1935, Japanese
OSAKA ELEGY Daiichi Eiga,
1936, Japanese
SISTERS OF THE GION Daiichi Eiga,
1936, Japanese
THE STRAITS OF LOVE AND HATE Shinko,
1937, Japanese
AH, MY HOME TOWN Shinko,
1938, Japanese
THE SONG OF THE CAMP Shinko,
1938, Japanese
THE STORY OF THE LAST
CHRYSANTHEMUM Shochiku,
1939, Japanese
THE WOMAN OF OSAKA Shochiku,
1940, Japanese
THE LIFE OF AN ACTOR Shochiku,
1941, Japanese
THE LOYAL 47 RONIN, PART I Shochiku
Koa Eiga, 1941, Japanese
THE LOYAL 47 RONIN, PART II Shochiku
Koa Eiga, 1941, Japanese
THREE GENERATIONS OF DANJURO
Shochiku, 1944, Japanese
MUSASHI MIYAMOTO Shochiku,
1944, Japanese
THE FAMOUS SWORD BIJOMARU
Shochiku, 1945, Japanese
VICTORY SONG co-director with
Masahiro Makino & Hiroshi Shimizu,
Shochiku, 1945, Japanese
THE VICTORY OF WOMEN Shochiku,
1946, Japanese
UTAMARO AND HIS FIVE WOMEN Shochiku,
1946, Japanese
THE LOVE OF SUMAKO THE ACTRESS
Shochiku, 1947, Japanese
WOMEN OF THE NIGHT Shochiku,
1948, Japanese
MY LOVE BURNS Shochiku,
1949, Japanese
A PICTURE OF MADAME YUKI Takimura
Productions/Shin Toho, 1950, Japanese
MISS OYU Daiei, 1951, Japanese
LADY MUSASHINO Toho, 1951, Japanese
THE LIFE OF OHARU Shin Toho,
1952, Japanese
UGETSU Daiei, 1953, Japanese
GION FESTIVAL MUSIC Daiei,
1953, Japanese
SANSHO THE BAILIFF Daiei,
1954, Japanese
THE WOMAN OF THE RUMOR Daiei,
1954, Japanese
A STORY FROM CHIKAMATSU CRUCIFIED
LOVERS Daiei, 1954, Japanese
THE PRINCESS YANG KWEI-FEI Shaw
Bros./Daiei, 1955, Hong Kong-Japanese
NEW TALES OF THE TAIRA CLAN Daiei,
1955, Japanese
STREET OF SHAME Daiei, 1956, Japanese

ROBERT MONTGOMERY
(Henry Montgomery, Jr.)
b. May 21, 1904 - Beacon, New York
d. 1981

LADY IN THE LAKE MGM, 1946
RIDE THE PINK HORSE Universal, 1947
ONCE MORE, MY DARLING Universal, 1949
EYE WITNESS YOUR WITNESS
Eagle Lion, 1950, British
THE GALLANT HOURS United Artists, 1960

ROBERT MOORE
b. August 17, 1927 - Detroit, Michigan
d. 1984

THURSDAY'S GAME (TF) ABC Circle
Films, 1974
MURDER BY DEATH Columbia, 1976
THE CHEAP DETECTIVE Columbia, 1978
CHAPTER TWO Columbia, 1980

ANDRZEJ MUNK
b. October 16, 1921 - Cracow, Poland
d. 1961

ART OF YOUTH (FD) 1949, Polish
IT BEGAN IN SPAIN (FD) 1950, Polish
SCIENCE CLOSER TO LIFE (FD)
1951, Polish
DIRECTION: NOWA HUTA (FD) 1951, Polish
THE TALE OF URSUS (FD) 1952, Polish
DIARIES OF THE PEASANTS (FD)
1952, Polish
A RAILWAYMAN'S WORD (FD) 1953, Polish
THE STARS MUST SHINE (FD) co-director,
1954, Polish
SUNDAY MORNING (FD) 1955, Polish
MEN OF THE BLUE CROSS (FD)
1955, Polish
A WALK IN THE OLD CITY OF WARSAW (FD)
1959, Polish
MAN ON THE TRACK 1956, Polish
EROICA 1958, Polish
BAD LUCK 1960, Polish
THE PASSENGER Altura Films Limited,
1963, Polish

F. W. MURNAU
(Friedrich Wilhelm Plumpe)
b. December 28, 1888 - Bielefeld, Germany
d. 1931

DER KNABE IN BLAU DER
TODESSMARAGD 1919, German
SATANAS 1920, German
SEHNSUCHT BAJAZZO 1920, German
DER BUCKLIGE UND DIE TANZERIN
1920, German
DER JANUSKOPF SCHRECKEN
1920, German
ABEND...NACHT...MORGEN 1920, German
DER GANG IN DIE NACHT 1920, German
SCHLOSS VOGELOD 1921, German
MARIZZA - GENNANT DIE SCHMUGGLER
MADONNA 1922, German
NOSFERATU THE VAMPIRE
NOSFERATU - EINE SYMPHONIE DES
GRAUENS Film Arts Guild, 1922, German
DER BRENNENDE ACKER 1922, German
PHANTOM 1922, German
DIE AUSTREIBUNG 1923, German
DIE FINANZEN DES GROSSHERZOGS
1924, German
THE LAST LAUGH DER LETZE MANN
Universal, 1924, German
TARTUFF 1926, German
FAUST 1926, German
SUNRISE - A STORY OF TWO HUMANS
Fox, 1927
FOUR DEVILS Fox, 1928
OUR DAILY BREAD CITY GIRL Fox, 1930
TABU co-director with Robert Flaherty,
Paramount, 1931

N

MIKIO NARUSE

b. August 20, 1905 - Tokyo, Japan
d. 1969

MR. AND MRS. SWORDPLAY   Shochiku,
   1930, Japanese
PURE LOVE   Shochiku, 1930, Japanese
HARD TIMES   Shochiku, 1930, Japanese
LOVE IS STRENGTH   Shochiku,
   1930, Japanese
A RECORD OF SHAMELESS NEWLYWEDS
   Shochiku, 1930, Japanese
NOW DON'T GET EXCITED   Shochiku,
   1931, Japanese
SCREAMS FROM THE SECOND FLOOR
   Shochiku, 1931, Japanese
FLUNKY, WORK HARD!   Shochiku,
   1931, Japanese
FICKLENESS GETS ON THE TRAIN
   Shochiku, 1931, Japanese
THE STRENGTH OF A MOUSTACHE
   Shochiku, 1931, Japanese
UNDER THE NEIGHBORS' ROOF   Shochiku,
   1931, Japanese
LADIES, BE CAREFUL OF YOUR SLEEVES
   Shochiku, 1932, Japanese
CRYING TO THE BLUE SKY   Shochiku,
   1932, Japanese
BE GREAT!   Shochiku, 1932, Japanese
MOTHEATEN SPRING   Shochiku,
   1932, Japanese
CHOCOLATE GIRL   Shochiku,
   1932, Japanese
NOT BLOOD RELATIONS   Shochiku,
   1932, Japanese
APART FROM YOU   Shochiku,
   1932, Japanese
EVERY NIGHT DREAMS   Shochiku,
   1933, Japanese
A MAN WITH A MARRIED WOMAN'S HAIRDO
   Shochiku, 1933, Japanese
TWO EYES   Shochiku, 1933, Japanese
STREET WITHOUT END   Shochiku,
   1934, Japanese
THREE SISTERS WITH MAIDEN HEARTS
   PCL, 1935, Japanese
THE ACTRESS AND THE POET   PCL,
   1935, Japanese
WIFE! BE LIKE A ROSE!   KIMIKO   PCL,
   1935, Japanese
FIVE MEN IN THE CIRCUS   PCL,
   1935, Japanese
THE GIRL IN THE RUMOR   PCL,
   1935, Japanese
KUMOEMON TOCHUKEN   PCL,
   1936, Japanese
THE ROAD I TRAVEL WITH ME   PCL, 1936,
   Japanese
MORNING'S TREE-LINED STREET   PCL,
   1936, Japanese
A WOMAN'S SORROWS   PCL,
   1937, Japanese
AVALANCHE   PCL, 1937, Japanese
LEARN FROM EXPERIENCE, PART I
   Toho Tokyo, 1937, Japanese
LEARN FROM EXPERIENCE, PART II
   Toho Tokyo, 1937, Japanese

TSURUHACHI AND TSURUJIRO   Toho Tokyo,
   1938, Japanese
THE WHOLE FAMILY WORKS   Toho,
   1939, Japanese
SINCERITY   Toho, 1939, Japanese
TRAVELING ACTORS   Toho, 1940, Japanese
A FACE FROM THE PAST   Toho,
   1941, Japanese
SHANGHAI MOON   Toho, 1941, Japanese
HIDEKO THE BUS CONDUCTOR   Nanyo,
   1941, Japanese
MOTHER NEVER DIES   Toho,
   1942, Japanese
THE SONG LANTERN   Toho,
   1943, Japanese
THIS HAPPY LIFE   Toho, 1944, Japanese
THE WAY OF DRAMA   Toho, 1944, Japanese
UNTIL VICTORY DAY   Toho, 1945, Japanese
A TALE OF ARCHERY AT THE
   SANJUSANGENDO   Toho,
   1945, Japanese
THE DESCENDENTS OF TARO URASHIMA
   Toho, 1946, Japanese
BOTH YOU AND I   Toho, 1946, Japanese
FOUR LOVE STORIES   co-director with
   Shiro Toyoda, Kajiro Yamamoto &
   Teinosuke Kinugasa, Toho, 1947, Japanese
SPRING AWAKENS   Toho, 1947, Japanese
DELINQUENT GIRL   Toyoko Eiga,
   1949, Japanese
CONDUCT REPORT ON PROFESSOR
   ISHINAKA   Shin Toho, 1950, Japanese
THE ANGRY STREET   Toho, 1950, Japanese
WHITE BEAST   Toho, 1950, Japanese
THE BATTLE OF ROSES   Eiga Geijutsu
   Kyokai/Shochiku, 1950, Japanese
GINZA COSMETICS   Shin Toho,
   1951, Japanese
DANCING GIRL   Toho, 1951, Japanese
REPAST   Toho, 1951, Japanese
OKUNI AND GOHEI   Toho, 1952, Japanese
MOTHER   Shin Toho, 1952, Japanese
LIGHTNING   Daiei, 1952, Japanese
HUSBAND AND WIFE   Toho, 1953, Japanese
WIFE   Toho, 1953, Japanese
OLDER BROTHER, YOUNGER SISTER
   Daiei, 1953, Japanese
SOUND OF THE MOUNTAIN   Toho,
   1954, Japanese
LATE CHRYSANTHEMUMS   Toho,
   1954, Japanese
FLOATING CLOUDS   Toho, 1955, Japanese
THE KISS   co-director with Hideo Suzuki &
   Masanori Kakei, Toho, 1955, Japanese
SUDDEN RAIN   Toho, 1956, Japanese
A WIFE'S HEART   Toho, 1956, Japanese
FLOWING   Toho, 1956, Japanese
UNTAMED   Toho, 1957, Japanese
ANZUKKO   Toho, 1958, Japanese
HERRINGBONE CLOUDS   Toho,
   1958, Japanese
WHISTLING IN KOTAN   A WHISTLE IN
   MY HEART   Toho, 1959, Japanese
WHEN A WOMAN ASCENDS THE STAIRS
   Toho, 1960, Japanese
DAUGHTERS, WIVES AND MOTHERS
   Toho, 1960, Japanese
EVENING STREAM   co-director with
   Yuzo Kawashima, Toho, 1960, Japanese
THE APPROACH OF AUTUMN   Toho,
   1960, Japanese
AS A WIFE, AS A WOMAN   THE OTHER
   WOMAN   Toho, 1961, Japanese
WOMAN'S STATUS   Toho, 1962, Japanese
A WANDERER'S NOTEBOOK   LONELY LANE
   Takarazuka Eiga/Toho, 1962, Japanese
A WOMAN'S STORY   Toho, 1963, Japanese
YEARNING   Toho, 1964, Japanese

THE STRANGER WITHIN A WOMAN
   THE THIN LINE   Toho, 1966, Japanese
HIT AND RUN   MOMENT OF TERROR
   Toho, 1966, Japanese
SCATTERED CLOUDS   TWO IN THE
   SHADOW   Toho, 1967, Japanese

JEAN NEGULESCO

b. February 29, 1900 - Craiova, Romania
d. 1993

SINGAPORE WOMAN   Warner Bros., 1941
THE MASK OF DIMITRIOS
   Warner Bros., 1944
THE CONSPIRATORS   Warner Bros., 1944
THREE STRANGERS   Warner Bros., 1946
NOBODY LIVES FOREVER
   Warner Bros., 1946
HUMORESQUE   Warner Bros., 1947
DEEP VALLEY   Warner Bros., 1947
JOHNNY BELINDA ★   Warner Bros., 1948
ROAD HOUSE   20th Century Fox, 1948
THE FORBIDDEN STREET   BRITANNIA
   MEWS   20th Century-Fox, 1949
UNDER MY SKIN   20th Century-Fox, 1950
THREE CAME HOME
   20th Century-Fox, 1950
THE MUDLARK   20th Century-Fox, 1950
TAKE CARE OF MY LITTLE GIRL
   20th Century-Fox, 1951
PHONE CALL FROM A STRANGER
   20th Century-Fox, 1952
LYDIA BAILEY   20th Century-Fox, 1952
LURE OF THE WILDERNESS
   20th Century-Fox, 1952
O. HENRY'S FULL HOUSE   co-director with
   Howard Hawks, Henry King & Henry Koster,
   20th Century-Fox, 1952
TITANIC   20th Century-Fox, 1953
HOW TO MARRY A MILLIONAIRE
   20th Century-Fox, 1953
SCANDAL AT SCOURIE   MGM, 1953
THREE COINS IN THE FOUNTAIN
   20th Century-Fox, 1954
A WOMAN'S WORLD
   20th Century-Fox, 1954
DADDY LONG LEGS   20th Century-Fox, 1955

MARSHALL (MICKEY) NEILAN

b. April 11, 1891 - San Bernardino, California
d. 1958

THE AMERICAN PRINCESS   American Film
   Company, 1913
HAM THE PIANO MOVER   Kalem, 1914
HAM THE LINEMAN   Kalem, 1914
THE CYCLE OF FATE   1916
THE PRINCE CHAP   1916
THE COUNTRY GOD FORGOT   1916
THOSE WITHOUT SIN   1917
THE BOTTLE IMP   1917
THE TIDES OF BARNEGAT   1917
THE GIRL AT HOME   1917
THE SILENT PARTNER   1917
FRECKLES   1917
THE JAGUAR'S CLAWS   1917
REBECCA OF SUNNYBROOK FARM   1917
THE LITTLE PRINCESS   1917
STELLA MARIS   1918
AMARILLY OF CLOTHESLINE ALLEY   1918
M'LISS   1918
HIT-THE-TRAIL HOLLIDAY   1918
HEART OF THE WILDS   1918
OUT OF A CLEAR SKY   1918
THREE MEN AND A GIRL   1919
DADDY LONG LEGS   1919
THE UNPARDONABLE SIN   1919

HER KINGDOM OF DREAMS 1919
IN OLD KENTUCKY 1920
THE RIVER'S END 1920
DON'T EVER MARRY co-director with
  Victor Heerman, 1920
GO AND GET IT 1920
DINTY 1920
BOB HAMPTON OF PLACER 1921
BITS OF LIFE 1921
THE LOTUS EATER 1921
PENROD 1922
FOOLS FIRST 1922
MINNIE co-director with Frank Urson, 1922
THE STRANGER'S BANQUET 1922
THE ETERNAL THREE co-director with
  Frank Urson, 1923
THE RENDEZVOUS 1923
DOROTHY VERNON OF HADDON
  HALL 1924
TESS OF THE D'URBERVILLES 1924
THE SPORTING VENUS 1925
THE GREAT LOVE 1925
MIKE 1926
THE SKYROCKET 1926
WILD OATS LANE 1926
DIPLOMACY 1926
EVERYBODY'S ACTING 1926
VENUS OF VENICE 1927
HER WILD OAT 1927
THREE-RING MARRIAGE 1928
TAKE ME HOME 1928
TAXI 13 1928
HIS LAST HAUL 1928
BLACK WATERS 1929, British
THE AWFUL TRUTH 1929
TANNED LEGS 1929
THE VAGABOND LOVER 1929
SWEETHEARTS ON PARADE 1930
CHLOE 1935
SOCIAL REGISTER 1935
THE LEMON DROP KID 1935
THIS IS THE LIFE 1935
SING WHILE YOU'RE ABLE 1937
THANKS FOR LISTENING 1937
SWING IT, PROFESSOR 1937

ROY WILLIAM NEILL
(Roland de Gostrie)
b. 1886 - Ireland
d. 1946

THE GIRL GLORY 1917
THE MOTHER INSTINCT 1917
THEY'RE OFF 1917
THE PRICE MARK 1917
LOVE LETTERS 1917
FLARE-UP SAL 1918
LOVE ME 1918
FREE AND EQUAL 1918
TYRANT FEAR 1918
THE MATING OF MARCELLA 1918
THE KAISER'S SHADOW *THE TRIPLE
  CROSS* 1918
GREEN EYES 1918
VIVE LA FRANCE! 1918
PUPPY LOVE 1919
CHARGE IT TO ME 1919
TRIXIE FROM BROADWAY 1919
THE CAREER OF KATHERINE BUSH 1919
THE BANDBOX 1919
THE INNER VOICE 1920
THE WOMAN GIVES 1920
YES OR NO 1920
GOOD REFERENCES 1920
DANGEROUS BUSINESS 1920
SOMETHING DIFFERENT 1921
THE IDOL OF THE NORTH 1921

THE CONQUEST OF CANAAN 1921
THE IRON TRAIL 1921
WHAT'S WRONG WITH THE WOMEN? 1922
RADIO-MANIA 1923
TOILERS OF THE SEA 1923
BY DIVINE RIGHT
  THE WAY MEN LOVE 1924
VANITY'S PRICE 1924
BROKEN LAWS 1924
THE KISS BARRIER 1925
MARRIAGE IN TRANSIT 1925
GREATER THAN A CROWN 1925
PERCY 1925
THE CITY 1926
BLACK PARADISE 1926
THE COWBOY AND THE COUNTESS 1926
THE FIGHTING BUCKAROO 1926
A MAN FOUR-SQUARE 1926
MARRIAGE 1926
THE ARIZONA WILDCAT 1927
SAN FRANCISCO NIGHTS 1928
LADY RAFFLES 1928
THE OLYMPIC HERO
  THE ALL AMERICAN 1928
THE VIKING 1928
BEHIND CLOSED DOORS 1929
WALL STREET 1929
THE MELODY MAN 1930
COCK O' THE WALK co-director with
  Walter Lang, World Wide, 1930
JUST LIKE HEAVEN 1930
THE AVENGER 1931
THE GOOD BAD GIRL 1931
FIFTY FATHOMS DEEP 1931
THE MENACE 1932
THAT'S MY BOY 1932
THE CIRCUS QUEEN MURDER 1933
AS THE DEVIL COMMANDS 1933
ABOVE THE CLOUDS 1933
FURY OF THE JUNGLE 1934
THE NINTH GUEST 1934
WHIRLPOOL 1934
BLACK MOON 1934
BLIND DATE 1934
I'LL FIX IT 1934
JEALOUSY 1934
MILLS OF THE GODS 1935
EIGHT BELLS 1935
THE BACK ROOM 1935
THE LONE WOLF RETURNS
  Columbia, 1936
DR. SYN Gaumont-British, 1937, British
THANK EVANS 1938, British
THE VIPER 1938, British
SIMPLY TERRIFIC 1938, British
EVERYTHING HAPPENS TO ME
  1938, British
MANY TANKS, MR. ATKINS 1938, British
THE GOOD OLD DAYS 1939, British
MURDER WILL OUT 1939, British
HOOTS MAN 1939, British
MADAME SPY Universal, 1942
EYES OF THE UNDERWORLD
  Universal, 1943
SHERLOCK HOLMES AND THE SECRET
  WEAPON Universal, 1943
FRANKENSTEIN MEETS THE WOLF MAN
  Universal, 1943
RHTYHM OF THE ISLANDS
  Universal, 1943
SHERLOCK HOLMES IN WASHINGTON
  Universal, 1943
SHERLOCK HOLMES FACES DEATH
  Universal, 1943
SHERLOCK HOLMES AND THE SPIDER
  WOMAN *THE SPIDER WOMAN*
  Universal, 1944

THE SCARLET CLAW *SHERLOCK HOLMES
  AND THE SCARLET CLAW*
  Universal, 1944
PEARL OF DEATH *SHERLOCK HOLMES
  AND THE PEARL OF DEATH*
  Universal, 1944
GYPSY WILDCAT Universal, 1944
THE HOUSE OF FEAR Universal, 1945
THE WOMAN IN GREEN *SHERLOCK
  HOLMES AND THE WOMAN IN GREEN*
  Universal, 1945
PURSUIT TO ALGIERS *SHERLOCK HOLMES
  IN PURSUIT TO ALGIERS* Universal, 1945
TERROR BY NIGHT *SHERLOCK HOLMES
  IN TERROR BY NIGHT* Universal, 1946
DRESSED TO KILL Universal, 1946
BLACK ANGEL Universal, 1946

JAMES NEILSON
b. 1910
d. 1979

NIGHT PASSAGE Universal, 1957
THE COUNTRY HUSBAND 1958
MOON PILOT Buena Vista, 1962
BON VOYAGE! Buena Vista, 1962
DR. SYN, ALIAS THE SCARECROW
  Buena Vista, 1964, British-U.S.
SUMMER MAGIC Buena Vista, 1963
THE MOON-SPINNERS Buena Vista,
  1964, U.S.-British
THE ADVENTURES OF BULLWHIP GRIFFIN
  Buena Vista, 1967
GENTLE GIANT Paramount, 1967
WHERE ANGELS GO...TROUBLE FOLLOWS!
  Columbia, 1968
THE FIRST TIME United Artists, 1969
FLAREUP MGM, 1969

RALPH NELSON
b. August 12, 1916 - New York, New York
d. 1987

REQUIEM FOR A HEAVYWEIGHT
  Columbia, 1962
LILIES OF THE FIELD United Artists, 1963
SOLDIER IN THE RAIN Allied Artists, 1963
FATE IS THE HUNTER
  20th Century-Fox, 1964
FATHER GOOSE Universal, 1964
ONCE A THIEF MGM, 1965
DUEL AT DIABLO United Artists, 1966
COUNTERPOINT Universal, 1968
CHARLY Cinerama Releasing
  Corporation, 1968
...tick...tick...tick MGM, 1970
SOLDIER BLUE Avco Embassy, 1970
FLIGHT OF THE DOVES Columbia,
  1971, British
THE WRATH OF GOD MGM, 1972
THE WILBY CONSPIRACY United Artists,
  1975, British
EMBRYO Cine Artists, 1976
A HERO AIN'T NOTHIN' BUT A SANDWICH
  New World, 1977
LADY OF THE HOUSE (TF) co-director
  with Vincent Sherman, Metromedia
  Productions, 1978
BECAUSE HE'S MY FRIEND (TF) Australian
  Broadcasting Commission/Trans-Atlantic
  Enterprises, 1979, Australian
CHRISTMAS LILIES OF THE FIELD (TF)
  Rainbow Productions/Osmond
  Productions, 1979
YOU CAN'T GO HOME AGAIN (TF)
  CBS Entertainment, 1979

KURT NEUMANN

b. April 5, 1906 - Nuremberg, Germany
d. 1958

THE KING OF JAZZ   Universal, 1930
FAST COMPANIONS   Universal, 1932
INFORMATION KID   Universal, 1932
MY PAL, THE KING   Universal, 1932
THE BIG CAGE   Universal, 1933
SECRETS OF THE BLUE ROOM
   Universal, 1933
KING FOR A NIGHT   Universal, 1933
LET'S TALK IT OVER   Universal, 1934
HALF A SINNER   Universal, 1934
WAKE UP AND DREAM   1934
ALIAS MARY DOW   Universal, 1935
THE AFFAIR OF SUSAN   Universal, 1935
LET'S SING AGAIN   RKO RADIO, 1936
RAINBOW ON THE RIVER
   RKO RADIO, 1936
ESPIONAGE   MGM, 1937
MAKE A WISH   RKO RADIO, 1937
HOLD 'EM NAVY   Paramount, 1937
WIDE OPEN FACES   Columbia, 1938
TOUCHDOWN ARMY   Paramount, 1938
AMBUSH   Paramount, 1939
UNMARRIED   Paramount, 1939
ISLAND OF LOST MEN   Paramount, 1939
ALL WOMEN HAVE SECRETS
   Paramount, 1940
ELLERY QUEEN - MASTER DETECTIVE
   Columbia, 1940
A NIGHT AT EARL CARROLL'S
   Paramount, 1940
BROOKLYN ORCHID   United Artists, 1942
ABOUT FACE   United Artists, 1942
THE McGUERINS FROM BROOKLYN
   United Artists, 1942
FALL IN   United Artists, 1943
TAXI MISTER   United Artists, 1943
YANKS AHOY!   United Artists, 1943
THE UNKNOWN GUEST   Monogram, 1943
THE RETURN OF THE VAMPIRE   co-director
   with Lew Landers, Columbia, 1943
TARZAN AND THE AMAZONS
   RKO Radio, 1945
TARZAN AND THE LEOPARD WOMAN
   RKO Radio, 1946
TARZAN AND THE HUNTRESS
   RKO Radio, 1947
THE DUDE GOES WEST   Allied Artists, 1948
BAD MEN OF TOMBSTONE
   Allied Artists, 1949
BAD BOY   Allied Artists, 1949
THE KID FROM TEXAS   Universal, 1950
ROCKETSHIP X-M   Lippert, 1950
CATTLE DRIVE   Universal, 1951
REUNION IN RENO   Universal, 1951
SON OF ALI BABA   Universal, 1952
THE RING   United Artists, 1952
HIAWATHA   Allied Artists, 1952
TARZAN AND THE SHE-DEVIL
   RKO Radio, 1953
CARNIVAL STORY   RKO Radio, 1954
THEY WERE SO YOUNG   Lippert, 1955,
   U.S.-West German
MOHAWK   20th Century-Fox, 1956
THE DESPERADOES ARE IN TOWN
   20th Century-Fox, 1956
KRONOS   20th Century-Fox, 1957
THE SHE-DEVIL   20th Century-Fox, 1957
THE DEERSLAYER   20th Century-Fox, 1957
THE FLY   20th Century-Fox, 1958
CIRCUS OF LOVE   DCA, 1958, German
MACHETE   United Artists, 1958
WATUSI   MGM, 1959
COUNTERPLOT   United Artists, 1959

FRED NIBLO

(Federico Nobile)
b. January 6, 1874 - York, Nebraska
d. 1948

A DESERT WOOING   Paramount, 1918
THE MARRIAGE RING   Paramount, 1918
WHEN DO WE EAT?   Paramount, 1918
FUSS AND FEATHERS   Paramount, 1918
HAPPY THOUGH MARRIED
   Paramount, 1919
THE HAUNTED BEDROOM
   Paramount, 1919
THE LAW OF MEN   Paramount, 1919
PARTNERS THREE   Paramount, 1919
THE VIRTUOUS THIEF   Paramount, 1919
STEPPING OUT   Paramount, 1919
WHAT EVERY WOMAN LEARNS
   Paramount, 1919
THE WOMAN IN THE SUITCASE
   Paramount, 1920
DANGEROUS HOURS   Paramount, 1920
SEX   W.W. Hodkinson, 1920
THE FALSE ROAD   Paramount, 1920
HAIRPINS   Paramount, 1920
HER HUSBAND'S FRIEND   Paramount, 1920
THE MARK OF ZORRO   United Artists, 1920
SILK HOSIERY   Paramount, 1921
MOTHER O' MINE   Associated
   Producers, 1921
GREATER THAN LOVE   Associated
   Producers, 1921
THE THREE MUSKETEERS
   United Artists, 1921
THE WOMAN HE MARRIED
   First National, 1922
ROSE O' THE SEA   First National, 1922
BLOOD AND SAND   Paramount, 1922
THE FAMOUS MRS. FAIR   Metro, 1923
STRANGERS OF THE NIGHT   Metro, 1923
THY NAME IS WOMAN   Metro-Goldwyn, 1924
THE RED LILY   Metro-Goldwyn, 1924
BEN-HUR   MGM, 1926
THE TEMPTRESS   MGM, 1926
CAMILLE   First National, 1927
THE DEVIL DANCER   United Artists, 1927
THE ENEMY   MGM, 1928
TWO LOVERS   United Artists, 1928
THE MYSTERIOUS LADY   MGM, 1928
DREAM OF LOVE   MGM, 1928
REDEMPTION   MGM, 1930
WAY OUT WEST   MGM, 1930
YOUNG DONOVAN'S KID   MGM, 1931
THE BIG GAMBLE   Pathé, 1931
TWO WHITE ARMS   1932, British
DIAMOND CUT DIAMOND   co-director with
   Maurice Elvey, 1932, British
BLAME THE WOMAN   1932

MAX NOSSECK

b. September 19, 1902 - Nakel, Poland
d. 1972

UM DIE WELT OHNE GELD   1927, Austrian
DER TANZ INS GLUCK   1930, German
DER SCHLEMIEL   1930, German
EINMAL MOCHT' ICH KEINE SORGEN
   HABEN   1932, German
GADO BRAVO   1933, Portuguese
ALEGRE VOY!   1934, Spanish
UNA SEMANA DE FELICIDAD   1934, Spanish
PONDEROSO CABALLERO   1934, Spanish
LE ROI DES CHAMPS ELYSEES
   1934, French
OVERTURE TO GLORY   1940
GIRLS UNDER 21   1940
GAMBLING DAUGHTERS   1941

DILLINGER   Monogram, 1945
THE BRIGHTON STRANGLER
   RKO Radio, 1945
BLACK BEAUTY   20th Century-Fox, 1946
THE RETURN OF RIN TIN TIN   1947
KILL OR BE KILLED   Eagle Lion, 1950
THE HOODLUM   United Artists, 1951
KOREA PATROL   1951
BODY BEAUTIFUL   1953
DER HAUPTMANN UND SEIN   1955,
   West German
SINGING IN THE DARK   Budsam Distribution
   Company, 1956
THE GARDEN OF EDEN   1957
GESCH-MINKTE JUGEND   1960,
   West German

ELLIOTT NUGENT

b. September 20, 1899 - Dover, Ohio
d. 1980

THE MOUTHPIECE   co-director with
   James Flood, Warner Bros., 1932
LIFE BEGINS   co-director with James Flood,
   Warner Bros., 1932
WHISTLING IN THE DARK   MGM, 1933
THREE-CORNERED MOON
   Paramount, 1933
IF I WERE FREE   Paramount, 1933
TWO ALONE   Paramount, 1934
STRICTLY DYNAMITE   Paramount, 1934
SHE LOVES ME NOT   Paramount, 1934
ENTER MADAME   Paramount, 1935
LOVE IN BLOOM   Paramount, 1935
COLLEGE SCANDAL   Paramount, 1935
SPLENDOR   United Artists, 1935
AND SO THEY WERE MARRIED
   Columbia, 1936
WIVES NEVER KNOW   Paramount, 1936
IT'S ALL YOURS   Columbia, 1937
PROFESSOR BEWARE   Paramount, 1938
GIVE ME A SAILOR   Paramount, 1938
NEVER SAY DIE   Paramount, 1939
THE CAT AND THE CANARY
   Paramount, 1939
NOTHING BUT THE TRUTH
   Paramount, 1941
THE MALE ANIMAL   Warner Bros., 1942
THE CRYSTAL BALL   United Artists, 1943
UP IN ARMS   RKO Radio, 1944
MY FAVORITE BRUNETTE   Paramount, 1947
WELCOME STRANGER   Paramount, 1947
MY GIRL TISA   United Artists, 1948
MR. BELVEDERE GOES TO COLLEGE
   20th Century-Fox, 1949
THE GREAT GATSBY   Paramount, 1949
THE SKIPPER SURPRISED HIS WIFE
   MGM, 1950
MY OUTLAW BROTHER   Eagle Lion, 1951
JUST FOR YOU   Paramount, 1952

CHRISTIAN NYBY

b. September 9, 1913 - Los Angeles, California
d. 1994

THE THING (FROM ANOTHER WORLD)
   THE THING   RKO Radio, 1951
HELL ON DEVIL'S ISLAND
   20th Century-Fox, 1957
YOUNG FURY   1965
OPERATION C.I.A.   Allied Artists, 1965
FIRST TO FIGHT   Warner Bros., 1967

ARCH OBOLER

b. December 7, 1909 - Chicago, Illinois
d. 1987

BEWITCHED   MGM, 1945
STRANGE HOLIDAY   PRC, 1946
THE ARNELO AFFAIR   MGM, 1947
FIVE   Columbia, 1951
BWANA DEVIL   United Artists, 1952
THE TWONKY   United Artists, 1953
ONE PLUS ONE: EXPLORING THE KINSEY
   REPORTS   Selected Films, 1961,
   U.S.-Canadian
THE BUBBLE   Oboler Films, 1967
THE STEWARDESSES   directed under
   pseudonym of Alf Silliman, Sherpix, 1969
DOMO ARIGATO (FD)   Oboler Films, 1972

SIDNEY OLCOTT

(John S. Alcott)

b. September 20, 1873 - Toronto, Canada
d. 1949

BEN-HUR   co-director with
   Frank Oakes Rose, 1907
THE SLEIGH BELLS   1907
A FLORIDA FEUD   1909
ESCAPE FROM ANDERSONVILLE   1909
THE LAD FROM OLD IRELAND   1909
THE CONSPIRATORS   1909
THE DEACON'S DAUGHTER   1910
THE MISER'S CHILD   1910
THE FURTHER ADVENTURES OF
   A GIRL SPY   1910
AN INDIAN SCOUT'S VENGEANCE   1910
SETH'S TEMPTATION   1910
THE GIRL SPY BEFORE VICKSBURG   1910
ARRAH-NA-POGUE   1911
THE COLLEEN BAWN   1911
THE FISHERMAN OF BALLYDAVID   1911
RORY O'MORE   1911
THE SHAUGHRAUN   1912
THE KERRY GOW   1912
IRELAND THE OPPRESSED   1913
FROM MANGER TO THE CROSS
   Kalem, 1913
DAUGHTER OF THE CONFEDERACY
   co-director with George Melford, 1913
THE PERILS OF THE SEA   co-director with
   George Melford, 1913
IN THE CLUTCHES OF THE KLU
   KLUX KLAN   1913
THE VAMPIRE   co-director with
   Thomas Hayes Hunter, 1913
THE OCTOROON   1913
A PASSOVER MIRACLE   1914
ALL FOR IRELAND   Lubin, 1915
BOLD EMMETT - IRELAND'S MARTYR   1915
NAN OF THE BACKWOODS   1915
MADAME BUTTERFLY   1915
THE SEVEN SISTERS   Paramount, 1915
THE MOTH AND THE FLAME
   Paramount, 1916
MY LADY INCOGNITO   Paramount, 1916
POOR LITTLE PEPPINA   Paramount, 1916
DIPLOMACY   Paramount, 1916
THE INNOCENT LIE   Paramount, 1916
THE SMUGGLERS   Paramount, 1916

THE DAUGHTER OF MacGREGOR
   Paramount, 1916
LESS THAN THE DUST   1916
THE BELGIAN   World, 1917
MARRIAGE FOR CONVENIENCE
   Sherry, 1919
MOTHERS OF MEN   1920
SCRATCH MY BACK   Goldwyn, 1920
THE RIGHT WAY   Producers Security
   Corp., 1921
PARDON MY FRENCH   Goldwyn, 1921
GOD'S COUNTRY AND THE LAW
   Arrow, 1921
TIMOTHY'S QUEST   American
   Releasing, 1922
THE GREEN GODDESS   Goldwyn, 1923
LITTLE OLD NEW YORK   Goldwyn, 1923
THE HUMMING BIRD   Paramount, 1924
MONSIEUR BEAUCAIRE   Paramount, 1924
THE ONLY WOMAN   First National, 1924
SALOME OF THE TENEMENTS
   Paramount, 1925
THE CHARMER   Paramount, 1925
NOT SO LONG AGO   Paramount, 1925
THE BEST PEOPLE   Paramount, 1925
RANSON'S FOLLY   First National, 1926
THE AMATEUR GENTLEMAN
   First National, 1926
THE WHITE BLACK SHEEP
   First National, 1926
THE CLAW   Universal-Jewel, 1927

LAURENCE OLIVIER

b. May 22, 1907 - Dorking, England
d. 1989

HENRY V   Rank, 1945, British
HAMLET ★   Universal, 1948, British
RICHARD III   Lopert, 1956, British
THE PRINCE AND THE SHOWGIRL
   Warner Bros., 1957, U.S.-British
THREE SISTERS   American Film Theatre,
   1970, British

MAX OPHULS

(Max Oppenheimer)

b. May 6, 1902 - Saarbrucken, Germany
d. 1957

DAS SCHON LIEBER LEBERTRAN
   1930, German
DIE VERLIEBTE FIRMA   1932, German
DIE VERKAUFTE BRAUT   1932, German
DIE LACHENDE ERBEN   1933, German
LIEBELEI   1933, German
UNE HISTOIRE D'AMOUR   1933, French
ON A VOLE UN HOMME   1934, French
LA SIGNORA DI TUTTI   1934, Italian
DIVINE   1935, French
KOMEDIE OM GELD   1936, Dutch
AVE MARIA   1936, French
LA VALSE BRILLANTE   1936, French
LA TENDRE ENNEMIE   1936, French
YOSHIWARA   1937, French
LE ROMAN DE WERTHER   1938, French
SANS LENDEMAIN   1940, French
DE MAYERLING A SARAJEVO
   1940, French
L'ECOLE DES FEMMES   1940,
   French, unfinished
THE EXILE   Universal, 1947
LETTER FROM AN UNKNOWN WOMAN
   Universal, 1948
CAUGHT   MGM, 1949
THE RECKLESS MOMENT   Columbia, 1949
LA RONDE   Commercial Pictures,
   1950, French

LE PLAISIR   1952, French
THE EARRINGS OF MADAME DE...
   MADAME DE   Arian Pictures,
   1953, French
LOLA MONTES   THE SINS OF LOLA
   MONTES   Brandon, 1955,
   French-West German

GERD OSWALD

b. June 9, 1916 - Berlin, Germany
d. 1989

A KISS BEFORE DYING
   United Artists, 1956
THE BRASS LEGEND   United Artists, 1956
CRIME OF PASSION   United Artists, 1957
FURY AT SHOWDOWN
   United Artists, 1957
VALERIE   United Artists, 1957
PARIS HOLIDAY   United Artists, 1958
SCREAMING MIMI   Columbia, 1958
AM TAG ALS DER REGEN KAM   1959,
   West German
BRAINWASHED   Allied Artists, 1960,
   West German
TEMPESTA SU CEYLON   co-director with
   Giovanni Roccardi, FICIT/Rapid Film, 1963,
   Italian-French
AGENT FOR H.A.R.M.   Universal, 1966
80 STEPS TO JONAH   Warner Bros., 1969
BUNNY O'HARE   American
   International, 1971
BIS ZUR BITTEREN NEIGE   1975,
   West German-Australian

YASUJIRO OZU

b. December 15, 1903 - Tokyo, Japan
d. 1963

SWORD OF PENITENCE   Shochiku,
   1927, Japanese
THE DREAMS OF YOUTH   Shochiku,
   1928, Japanese
WIFE LOST   Shochiku, 1928, Japanese
PUMPKIN   Shochiku, 1928, Japanese
A COUPLE ON THE MOVE   Shochiku,
   1928, Japanese
BODY BEAUTIFUL   Shochiku,
   1928, Japanese
TREASURE MOUNTAIN   Shochiku,
   1929, Japanese
DAYS OF YOUTH   Shochiku,
   1929, Japanese
FIGHTING FRIENDS   Shochiku,
   1929, Japanese
I GRADUATED, BUT...   Shochiku,
   1929, Japanese
THE LIFE OF AN OFFICE WORKER
   Shochiku, 1929, Japanese
A STRAIGHTFORWARD BOY   Shochiku,
   1929, Japanese
AN INTRODUCTION TO MARRIAGE
   Shochiku, 1930, Japanese
WALK CHEERFULLY   Shochiku,
   1930, Japanese
I FLUNKED, BUT...   Shochiku,
   1930, Japanese
THAT NIGHT'S WIFE   Shochiku,
   1930, Japanese
THE REVENGEFUL SPIRIT OF EROS
   Shochiki, 1930, Japanese
LOST LUCK   Shochiku, 1930, Japanese
YOUNG MISS   Shochiku, 1930, Japanese
THE LADY AND THE BEARD   Shochiku,
   1931, Japanese
BEAUTY'S SORROWS   Shochiku,
   1931, Japanese

TOKYO CHORUS   Shochiku,
   1931, Japanese
SPRING COMES FROM THE LADIES
   Shochiku, 1932, Japanese
I WAS BORN, BUT...   Shochiku,
   1932, Japanese
WHERE NOW ARE THE DREAMS OF YOUTH?
   Shochiku, 1932, Japanese
UNTIL THE DAY WE MEET AGAIN   Shochiku,
   1932, Japanese
A TOKYO WOMAN   Shochiku,
   1933, Japanese
DRAGNET GIRL   Shochiku, 1933, Japanese
PASSING FANCY   Shochiku,
   1933, Japanese
A MOTHER SHOULD BE LOVED   Shochiku,
   1934, Japanese
A STORY OF FLOATING WEEDS   Shochiku,
   1934, Japanese
AN INNOCENT MAID   Shochiku,
   1935, Japanese
AN INN IN TOKYO   Shochiku,
   1935, Japanese
COLLEGE IS A NICE PLACE   Shochiku,
   1936, Japanese
THE ONLY SON   Shochiku, 1936, Japanese
WHAT DID THE LADY FORGET?   Shochiku,
   1937, Japanese
THE BROTHERS AND SISTERS OF THE
   TODA FAMILY   Shochiku, 1941, Japanese
THERE WAS A FATHER   Shochiku,
   1942, Japanese
THE RECORD OF A TENEMENT GENTLEMAN
   Shochiku, 1947, Japanese
A HEN IN THE WIND   Shochiku,
   1948, Japanese
LATE SPRING   Shochiku, 1949, Japanese
THE MUNEKATA SISTERS   Shin Toho,
   1950, Japanese
EARLY SUMMER   Shochiku,
   1951, Japanese
THE FLAVOR OF GREEN TEA OVER RICE
   Shochiku, 1952, Japanese
TOKYO STORY   Shochiku, 1953, Japanese
EARLY SPRING   Shochiku, 1956, Japanese
TWILIGHT IN TOKYO   Shochiku,
   1957, Japanese
EQUINOX FLOWER   Shochiku,
   1958, Japanese
OHAYO   Shochiku, 1959, Japanese
FLOATING WEEDS   Daiei, 1959, Japanese
LATE AUTUMN   Shochiku, 1960, Japanese
THE END OF SUMMER   Toho,
   1961, Japanese
AN AUTUMN AFTERNOON   Shochiku,
   1962, Japanese

G. W. PABST
(Georg Wilhelm Pabst)
b. August 27, 1885 - Raudnitz, Bohemia,
   Germany
d. 1967

DER SCHATZ   1923, German
GRAFIN DONELLI   1924, German
DIE FREUDLOSE GASSE   1925, German
GEHEIMNISSE EINER SEELE
   1926, German
MAN SPIELT NICHT MIT DER LIEBE
   1926, German
DIE LIEBE DER JEANNE NEY
   1927, German
ABWEGE   1928, German
DIE BUCHSE DER PANDORA
   1929, German
DIE WEISSE HOLLE VOM PIZ PALU
   co-director with Arnold Fanck,
   1929, German
DAS TAGEBUCH EINER VERLORENEN
   1929, German
WESTFRONT 1918   1930, German
SKANDAL UM EVA   1930, German
THE THREEPENNY OPERA   Brandon,
   1931, German
L'OPERA DE QUAT'SOUS   1931,
   German-French
KAMERADSCHAFT   1931, German
DIE HERRIN VON ATLANTIS
   1932, German
LA TRAGÉDIE DE LA MINE   1932,
   German-French
L'ATLANTIDE   German, 1932
DON QUIXOTE   1933, British
DON QUICHOTTE   1933, French
DU HAUT EN BAS   1933, French
A MODERN HERO   Warner Bros., 1934
MADEMOISELLE DOCTEUR   *SALONIQUE
   SHANGHAI*   1937, French
LE DRAME DE SHANGHAI   1938, French
JEUNES FILLES EN DETRESSE
   1939, French
FEUERTAUFE   1940, German
KOMODIANTEN   1941, German
PARACELSUS   1943, German
MEINE VIER JUNGENS   1944, German
DER FALL MOLANDER   1945, German
DER PROZESS   1948, Austrian
GEHEIMNISVOLLE TIEFEN   1949, Austrian
LA VOCE DEL SILENZIO   1952, Italian
COSE DA PAZZI   1953, Italian
DAS BEKENNTNIS DER INA KAHR   1954,
   West German
THE LAST TEN DAYS   Columbia, 1955,
   West German
ES GESCHAH AM 20   1955, West German
JULI   1955, West German
BALLERINA   *ROSEN FUR BETTINA*
   Sam Baker Associates, 1956, West German
DURCH DIE WALDER, DURCH DIE AUEN
   1956, West German

MARCEL PAGNOL
b. February 28, 1895 - Aubagne, France
d. 1974

DIRECT AU COEUR   co-director with
   Roger Lion, 1933, French
LA GENDRE DE MONSIEUR POIRIER
   1933, French
LEOPOLD LE BIEN-AIME   1933, French
WAYS OF LOVE   *JOFROI*   1934, French
ANGELE   1934, French
LE VOYAGE DE MONSIEUR PERRICHON
   1934, French
L'ARTICLE 330   1934, French
MERLUSSE   1935, French
CIGALON   1935, French
CESAR   1936, French
TOPAZE   1936, French
REGAIN   1937, French
LE SCHPOUNTZ   1938, French
THE BAKER'S WIFE   The Baker's Wife Inc.,
   1938, French
THE WELLDIGGER'S DAUGHTER   Siritzky
   International, 1941, French
NAIS   French, 1946
LA BELLE MEUNIERE   1948, French
TOPAZE   1952, French
MANON DES SOURCES   French, 1952
LETTERS FROM MY WINDMILL   Tohan,
   1954, French

GEORGE PAL
b. February 1, 1908 - Cegled, Hungary
d. 1980

tom thumb   MGM, 1958
THE TIME MACHINE   MGM, 1960, British
ATLANTIS, THE LOST CONTINENT
   MGM, 1961
THE WONDERFUL WORLD OF THE
   BROTHERS GRIMM   co-director with
   Henry Levin, MGM/Cinerama, 1962
THE SEVEN FACES OF DR. LAO
   MGM, 1964

SERGEI PARADJANOV
(Sergej Iosifovich Paradzhanov)
b. March 18, 1924 - Georgia, U.S.S.R.
d. 1990

ANDRIESH   1954, Soviet
THE FIRST LAD   1958, Soviet
UKRAINIAN RHAPSODY   1961, Soviet
FLOWER ON THE STONE   1963, Soviet
THE BALLAD   1964, Soviet
SHADOWS OF OUR FORGOTTEN
   ANCESTORS   1964, Soviet
SAYAT NOVAR   1968, Soviet
THE LEGEND OF SURAM FORTRESS
   co-director with David Abachidze,
   International Film Exchange, 1985, Soviet
ASHIK KERIB   co-director with
   David Abachidze, International Film
   Exchange, 1988, Soviet
THE GENTLE ONE   Gruziafilm, 1990, Soviet

JERRY PARIS
b. July 25, 1925 - San Francisco, California
d. 1986

DON'T RAISE THE BRIDGE - LOWER
   THE RIVER   Columbia, 1968, British
NEVER A DULL MOMENT   Buena Vista, 1968
HOW SWEET IT IS!   Buena Vista, 1968
VIVA MAX!   Commonwealth United, 1969
THE GRASSHOPPER   National
   General, 1969

BUT I DON'T WANT TO GET MARRIED! (TF)
Aaron Spelling Productions, 1970
THE FEMINIST AND THE FUZZ (TF)
Screen Gems/Columbia TV, 1970
TWO ON A BENCH (TF)   Universal TV, 1971
WHAT'S A NICE GIRL LIKE YOU...?
Universal TV, 1971
STAR SPANGLED GIRL   Paramount, 1971
CALL HER MOM (TF)   Screen Gems/
Columbia TV, 1972
EVIL ROY SLADE (TF)   Universal TV, 1972
THE COUPLE TAKES A WIFE (TF)
Universal TV, 1972
EVERY MAN NEEDS ONE (TF)   ABC Circle
Films, 1972
ONLY WITH MARRIED MEN (TF)
Spelling-Goldberg Productions, 1974
HOW TO BREAK UP A HAPPY DIVORCE (TF)
Charles Fries Productions, 1976
MAKE ME AN OFFER (TF)   ABC Circle
Films, 1980
LEO AND LOREE   United Artists, 1980
POLICE ACADEMY 2: THEIR FIRST
ASSIGNMENT   Warner Bros., 1985
POLICE ACADEMY 3: BACK IN TRAINING
Warner Bros., 1986

GABRIEL PASCAL

b. June 4, 1894 - Arad, Transylvania
d. 1954

MAJOR BARBARA   United Artists,
1941, British
CAESAR AND CLEOPATRA   United Artists,
1945, British

PIER PAOLO PASOLINI

b. March 5, 1922 - Bologna, Italy
d. 1975

ACCATONE!   Brandon, 1961, Italian
MAMMA ROMA   Milestone Film, 1962, Italian
ROGOPAG   co-director, 1962, Italian
LA RABBIA   co-director, 1963, Italian
SOPRALUOGHI IN PALESTINA PER IL FILM
'VANGELO SECONDO MATTEO' (FD)
1964, Italian
THE GOSPEL ACCORDING TO ST. MATTHEW
Continental, 1964, Italian
COMIZI D'AMORE (FD)   1964, Italian
THE HAWKS AND THE SPARROWS
Brandon, 1966, Italian
THE WITCHES   co-director, Lopert,
1967, Italian-French
OEDIPUS REX   Europix International,
1967, Italian
CAPRICCIO ALL'ITALIANA   co-director,
1968, Italian
TEOREMA   Continental, 1968, Italian
AMORE E RABBIA   co-director, 1969, Italian
PIGPEN   New Line Cinema, 1969,
Italian-French
MEDEA   New Line Cinema, 1970,
Italian-French-West German
THE DECAMERON   United Artists, 1971,
Italian-French-West German
THE CANTERBURY TALES   United Artists,
1972, Italian
THE ARABIAN NIGHTS   IL FIORE DELL
MILLE EUNA NOTTE   United Artists,
1974, Italian-French
SALO: THE LAST 120 DAYS OF SODOM
Zebra, 1975, Italian
ORESTIADE AFRICANO   1976, Italian
LA RICOTTA   1976, Italian

SAM PECKINPAH

b. February 21, 1925 - Fresno, California
d. 1984

THE DEADLY COMPANIONS
Pathé-American, 1961
RIDE THE HIGH COUNTRY   MGM, 1962
MAJOR DUNDEE   Columbia, 1965
THE WILD BUNCH   Warner Bros., 1969
THE BALLAD OF CABLE HOGUE
Warner Bros., 1970
STRAW DOGS   Cinerama Releasing
Corporation, 1972, British
THE GETAWAY   National General, 1972
JUNIOR BONNER   Cinerama Releasing
Corporation, 1973
PAT GARRETT & BILLY THE KID   MGM, 1973
BRING ME THE HEAD OF ALFREDO GARCIA
United Artists, 1974
THE KILLER ELITE   United Artists, 1975
CROSS OF IRON   Avco Embassy, 1977,
British-West German
CONVOY   United Artists, 1978
THE OSTERMAN WEEKEND
20th Century-Fox, 1983

ELIO PETRI

b. January 29, 1929 - Rome, Italy
d. 1982

THE ASSASSIN   THE LADY KILLER OF
ROME   Manson, 1961, Italian-French
I GIORNI CONTATI   1962, Italian
IL MAESTRO DI VIGEVANO   1963, Italian
HIGH INFIDELITY   co-director, Magna,
1964, Italian-French
THE TENTH VICTIM   Embassy, 1965, Italian
WE STILL KILL THE OLD WAY   A CIASCUNO
IL SUO   Lopert, 1967, Italian
A QUIET PLACE IN THE COUNTRY
United Artists, 1968, Italian-French
INVESTIGATION OF A CITIZEN ABOVE
SUSPICION   Columbia, 1970, Italian
LA CLASSE OPERAIA VA IN PARADISO
1971, Italian
LA PROPRIETA NON E PIU UN FURTO
1973, Italian
TODO MODO   1976, Italian

VLADIMIR PETROV

b. 1896 - St. Petersburg, Russia
d. 1966

GOLDEN HONEY   co-director, 1929, Soviet
DZHOI AND HIS FRIENDS   co-director,
1928, Soviet
ADDRESS BY LENIN   1929, Soviet
FRITZ BAUER   1930, Soviet
CHILDREN OF THE NEW DAY   1930, Soviet
THE COLD FEAST   1930, Soviet
THE FUGITIVE   1932, Soviet
THE CARPENTER   1932, Soviet
THUNDERSTORM   1934, Soviet
PETER THE FIRST   1937, Soviet
THE CONQUESTS OF PETER THE GREAT
1939, Soviet
CHAPAYEV IS WITH US   1941, Soviet
THE ELUSIVE JAN   co-director, 1943, Soviet
KUTUZOV   1812   1944, Soviet
JUBILEE   1944, Soviet
GUILTY THOUGH INNOCENT   1945, Soviet
BATTLE OF STALINGRAD, PART I: THE
FIRST FRONT   1949, Soviet
BATTLE OF STALINGRAD, PART II: THE
VICTORS AND THE VANQUISHED
1950, Soviet
SPORTING HONOR   1951, Soviet

THE INSPECTOR GENERAL   1952, Soviet
300 YEARS AGO   1956, Soviet
THE DUEL   1957, Soviet
PARVI UROK   1959, Bulgarian-Soviet
ON THE EVE   1959, Soviet
THE RUSSIAN FOREST   1963, Soviet

IRVING PICHEL

b. June 25, 1891 - Pittsburgh, Pennsylvania
d. 1954

THE MOST DANGEROUS GAME
co-director with Ernest B. Schoedsack,
RKO Radio, 1932
BEFORE DAWN   RKO RADIO, 1933
SHE   co-director with Lansing C. Holden,
RKO Radio, 1935
THE GENTLEMAN FROM LOUISIANA
Republic, 1936
BEWARE OF LADIES   LADIES BEWARE
Republic, 1936
LARCENY ON THE AIR   Republic, 1937
THE SHEIK STEPS OUT   Republic, 1937
THE DUKE COMES BACK   Republic, 1937
EARTHBOUND   20th Century-Fox, 1940
THE MAN I MARRIED
20th Century-Fox, 1940
HUDSON'S BAY   20th Century-Fox, 1941
DANCE HALL   20th Century-Fox, 1941
THE GREAT COMMANDMENT
20th Century-Fox, 1941
SECRET AGENT OF JAPAN
20th Century-Fox, 1942
THE PIED PIPER   20th Century-Fox, 1942
LIFE BEGINS AT 8:30
20th Century-Fox, 1942
THE MOON IS DOWN
20th Century-Fox, 1943
THE HAPPY LAND   20th Century-Fox, 1943
AND NOW TOMORROW   Paramount, 1944
A MEDAL FOR BENNY   Paramount, 1945
COLONEL EFFINGHAM'S RAID
20th Century-Fox, 1945
TOMORROW IS FOREVER
RKO Radio, 1946
O.S.S.   Paramount, 1946
THE BRIDE WORE BOOTS   Paramount, 1946
TEMPTATION   Universal, 1946
THEY WON'T BELIEVE ME
RKO Radio, 1947
SOMETHING IN THE WIND   Universal, 1947
THE MIRACLE OF THE BELLS
RKO Radio, 1948
MR. PEABODY AND THE MERMAID
Universal, 1948
WITHOUT HONOR   United Artists, 1949
THE GREAT RUPERT   Eagle Lion, 1950
QUICKSAND   United Artists, 1950
DESTINATION MOON   Eagle Lion, 1950
SANTA FE   Columbia, 1951
MARTIN LUTHER   De Rochemont, 1953
DAY OF TRIUMPH   co-director with
John T. Coyle & George J. Schaefer, 1954

EDWIN S. PORTER
(Edwin Stanton Porter)

b. April 21, 1869 - Cannellsville, Pennsylvania
d. 1941

THE AMERICA'S CUP RACE   Edison, 1899
WHY MRS. JONES GOT A DIVORCE
Edison, 1900
ANIMATED LUNCHEON   Edison, 1900
AN ARTIST'S DREAM   Edison, 1900
THE MYSTIC SWING   Edison, 1900
CHING LIN FOO OUTDONE   Edison, 1900
FAUST AND MARGUERITE   Edison, 1900

THE CLOWN AND THE ALCHEMIST
Edison, 1900
A WRINGING GOOD JOKE   Edison, 1900
THE ENCHANTED DRAWING   Edison, 1900
TERRIBLE TEDDY THE GRIZZLY KING
Edison, 1901
LOVE IN A HAMMOCK   Edison, 1901
A DAY AT THE CIRCUS   Edison, 1901
WHAT DEMORALIZED THE BARBER SHOP
Edison, 1901
THE FINISH OF BRIDGET McKEEN
Edison, 1901
HAPPY HOOLIGAN SURPRISED
Edison, 1901
MARTYRED PRESIDENTS   Edison, 1901
LOVE BY THE LIGHT OF THE MOON
Edison, 1901
CIRCULAR PANORAMA OF THE ELECTRIC
TOWER   Edison, 1901
PANORAMA OF THE ESPLANADE BY NIGHT
Edison, 1901
THE MYSTERIOUS CAFE   Edison, 1901
UNCLE JOSH AT THE MOVING PICTURE
SHOW   Edison, 1902
CHARLESTON CHAIN GANG   Edison, 1902
BURLESQUE SUICIDE   Edison, 1902
ROCK OF AGES   Edison, 1902
JACK AND THE BEANSTALK   Edison, 1902
THE LIFE OF AN AMERICAN FIREMAN
Edison, 1903
THE STILL ALARM   Edison, 1903
ARABIAN JEWISH DANCE   Edison, 1903
RAZZLE DAZZLE   Edison, 1903
SEASHORE FROLICS   Edison, 1903
SCENES IN AN ORPHAN'S ASYLUM
Edison, 1903
THE GAY SHOE CLERK   Edison, 1903
THE BABY REVIEW   Edison, 1903
THE ANIMATED POSTER   Edison, 1903
THE OFFICE BOY'S REVENGE
Edison, 1903
UNCLE TOM'S CABIN   Edison, 1903
THE GREAT TRAIN ROBBERY   Edison, 1903
THE EX-CONVICT   Edison, 1904
COHEN'S ADVERTISING SCHEME
Edison, 1904
EUROPEAN REST CURE   Edison, 1904
PARSIFAL   Edison, 1904
THE KLEPTOMANIAC   Edison, 1905
STOLEN BY GYPSIES   Edison, 1905
HOW JONES LOST HIS ROLL   Edison, 1905
THE LITTLE TRAIN ROBBERY   Edison, 1905
THE WHITE CAPS   Edison, 1905
SEVEN AGES   Edison, 1905
THE LIFE OF A COWBOY   Edison, 1906
THREE AMERICAN BEAUTIES   Edison, 1906
KATHLEEN MAVOURNEEN   Edison, 1906
DANIEL BOONE   Edison, 1907
LOST IN THE ALPS   Edison, 1907
THE MIDNIGHT RIDE OF PAUL REVERE
Edison, 1907
LAUGHING GAS   Edison, 1907
RESCUED FROM AN EAGLE'S NEST
Edison, 1907
THE TEDDY BEARS   Edison, 1907
NERO AND THE BURNING OF ROME
Edison, 1908
THE PAINTER'S REVENGE   Edison, 1908
THE MERRY WIDOW WALTZ CRAZE
Edison, 1908
THE GENTLEMAN BURGLAR   Edison, 1908
HONESTY IS THE BEST POLICY
Edison, 1908
LOVE WILL FIND A WAY   Edison, 1908
SKINNY'S FINISH   Edison, 1908
THE FACE ON THE BARROOM FLOOR
Edison, 1908
THE BOSTON TEA PARTY   Edison, 1908

ROMANCE OF A WAR NURSE   Edison, 1908
A VOICE FROM THE DEAD   Edison, 1908
SAVED BY LOVE   Edison, 1908
SHE   Edison, 1908
LORD FEATHERTOP   Edison, 1908
THE ANGEL CHILD   Edison, 1908
MISS SHERLOCK HOLMES   Edison, 1908
AN UNEXPECTED SANTA CLAUS
Edison, 1908
THE ADVENTURES OF AN OLD FLIRT
Edison, 1909
A MIDNIGHT SUPPER   Edison, 1909
LOVE IS BLIND   Edison, 1909
A CRY FROM THE WILDERNESS
Edison, 1909
HARD TO BEAT   Edison, 1909
ON THE WESTERN FRONTIER
Edison, 1909
FUSS AND FEATHERS   Edison, 1909
PONY EXPRESS   Edison, 1909
ALL ON ACCOUNT OF A LAUNDRY MARK
Defender Pictures, 1910
RUSSIA - THE LAND OF OPPRESSION
Defender Pictures, 1910
TOO MANY GIRLS   Defender Pictures, 1910
ALMOST A HERO   Defender Pictures, 1910
THE TOYMAKER, THE DOLL AND THE DEVIL
Defender Pictures, 1910
BY THE LIGHT OF THE MOON   Rex Film
Company, 1911
ON THE BRINK   Rex Film Company, 1911
THE WHITE RED MAN   Rex Film
Company, 1911
SHERLOCK HOLMES, JR.   Rex Film
Company, 1911
LOST ILLUSIONS   Rex Film Company, 1911
A SANE ASYLUM   Famous Players, 1912
EYES THAT SEE NOT   Famous Players, 1912
THE FINAL PARDON   Famous Players, 1912
TAMING MRS. SHREW   Famous
Players, 1912
TESS OF THE D'URBERVILLES   co-director
with J. Searle Dawley, Paramount, 1913
THE PRISONER OF ZENDA   co-director with
Hugh Ford, Famous Players, 1913
HIS NEIGHBOR'S WIFE   Famous
Players, 1913
THE COUNT OF MONTE CRISTO   co-director
with Joseph Golden, Famous Players, 1913
IN THE BISHOP'S CARRIAGE   co-director
with J. Searle Dawley, Famous Players, 1913
A GOOD LITTLE DEVIL   co-director with
J. Searle Dawley, Famous Players, 1913
HEARTS ADRIFT   Paramount,
Famous Players, 1914
TESS OF THE STORM COUNTRY
Famous Players, 1914
SUCH A LITTLE QUEEN   co-director with
Hugh Ford, Famous Players, 1914
THE ETERNAL CITY   co-director with
Hugh Ford, Famous Players, 1914
THE SCALES OF JUSTICE   Paramount, 1914
A WOMAN'S TRIUMPH   Paramount, 1914
THE CRUCIBLE   Paramount, 1914
THE DICTATOR   Paramount, 1915
SOLD   Paramount, 1915
THE WHITE PEARL   Paramount, 1915
JIRM THE PENMAN   Paramount, 1915
ZAZA   co-director with Hugh Ford, Famous
Players, 1915
SOLD   co-director with Hugh Ford, Famous
Players, 1915
THE PRINCE AND THE PAUPER   co-director
with Hugh Ford, Famous Players, 1915
BELLA DONNA   co-director with Hugh Ford,
Famous Players, 1915
LYDIA GILMORE   co-director with Hugh Ford,
Famous Players, 1916

H. C. (HANK) POTTER
(Henry Codman Potter)
b. November 13, 1904 - New York, New York
d. 1977

BELOVED ENEMY   United Artists, 1936
WINGS OVER HONOLULU   Universal, 1937
ROMANCE IN THE DARK   Paramount, 1938
THE COWBOY AND THE LADY
United Artists, 1938
THE SHOPWORN ANGEL   MGM, 1938
THE STORY OF VERNON AND IRENE
CASTLE   RKO Radio, 1939
BLACKMAIL   MGM, 1939
CONGO MAISIE   MGM, 1940
SECOND CHORUS   Paramount, 1940
HELLZAPOPPIN!   Universal, 1941
VICTORY THROUGH AIR POWER (FD)   1943
MR. LUCKY   RKO Radio, 1943
THE FARMER'S DAUGHTER
RKO Radio, 1947
A LIKELY STORY   RKO Radio, 1947
MR. BLANDINGS BUILDS HIS DREAM HOUSE
RKO Radio, 1948
THE TIME OF YOUR LIFE
United Artists, 1948
YOU GOTTA STAY HAPPY   Universal, 1948
THE MINIVER STORY   MGM, 1950
THREE FOR THE SHOW   Columbia, 1955
TOP SECRET AFFAIR   Warner Bros., 1957

DICK POWELL
(Richard E. Powell)
b. November 14, 1904 - Mountain View,
Arkansas
d. 1963

SPLIT SECOND   RKO Radio, 1953
THE CONQUEROR   RKO Radio, 1956
YOU CAN'T RUN AWAY FROM IT
Columbia, 1956
THE ENEMY BELOW
20th Century-Fox, 1957
THE HUNTERS   20th Century-Fox, 1958

MICHAEL POWELL
b. September 30, 1905 - Canterbury, England
d. 1990

TWO CROWDED HOURS   Fox, 1931, British
MY FRIEND THE KING   Fox, 1931, British
RYNOX   Ideal, 1931, British
THE RASP   Fox, 1931, British
THE STAR REPORTER   Fox, 1931, British
HOTEL SPLENDIDE   Ideal, 1932, British
BORN LUCKY   MGM, 1932, British
C.O.D.   United Artists, 1932, British
HIS LORDSHIP   United Artists, 1932, British
THE FIRE RAISERS   Woolf & Freedman,
1933, British
THE NIGHT OF THE PARTY   Gaumont,
1934, British
RED ENSIGN   Gaumont, 1934, British
SOMETHING ALWAYS HAPPENS
Warner Bros., 1934, British
THE GIRL IN THE CROWD   First National,
1934, British
THE LOVE TEST   Fox British, 1935, British
LAZYBONES   Radio, 1935, British
SOME DAY   Warner Bros., 1935, British
HER LAST AFFAIRE   Producers Distributing
Corporation, 1935, British
THE PRICE OF A SONG   Fox British,
1935, British
THE PHANTOM LIGHT   Gaumont,
1935, British

THE BROWN WALLET   First National,
   1936, British
CROWN VS. STEVENS   Warner Bros.,
   1936, British
THE MAN BEHIND THE MASK   MGM,
   1936, British
THE EDGE OF THE WORLD   British
   Independent Exhibitors' Distributors,
   1937, British
U-BOAT 29   *THE SPY IN BLACK*   Columbia,
   1939, British
THE LION HAS WINGS   co-director with
   Brian Desmond Hurst & Adrian Brunel,
   United Artists, 1939, British
THE THIEF OF BAGDAD   co-director with
   Ludwig Berger & Tim Whelan, United Artists,
   1940, British
CONTRABAND   *BLACKOUT*
   Anglo-American, 1940, British
THE FORTY-NINTH PARALLEL   *THE
   INVADERS* Columbia, 1941, British
ONE OF OUR AIRCRAFT IS MISSING
   co-director with Emeric Pressburger,
   United Artists, 1942, British
THE VOLUNTEER   co-director with
   Emeric Pressburger, Anglo, 1943, British
COLONEL BLIMP   *THE LIFE AND DEATH
   OF COLONEL BLIMP*   co-director with
   Emeric Pressburger, GFO, 1943, British
A CANTERBURY TALE   co-director with
   Emeric Pressburger, Eagle-Lion,
   1944, British
I KNOW WHERE I'M GOING   co-director
   with Emeric Pressburger, Universal,
   1945, British
STAIRWAY TO HEAVEN   *A MATTER OF
   LIFE AND DEATH*   co-director with
   Emeric Pressburger, Universal,
   1946, British
BLACK NARCISSUS   co-director with
   Emeric Pressburger, Universal,
   1947, British
THE RED SHOES   co-director with
   Emeric Pressburger, Eagle-Lion,
   1948, British
THE SMALL BACK ROOM   *HOUR OF GLORY*
   co-director with Emeric Pressburger,
   Snader Productions, 1948, British
THE WILD HEART   *GONE TO EARTH*
   co-director with Emeric Pressburger,
   RKO Radio, 1950, British
THE ELUSIVE PIMPERNEL   co-director
   with Emeric Pressburger, British Lion,
   1950, British
THE TALES OF HOFFMAN   co-director with
   Emeric Pressburger, Lopert, 1951, British
OH ROSALINDA!   co-director with
   Emeric Pressburger, Associated British
   Picture Corporation, 1955, British
PURSUIT OF THE GRAF SPEE   *THE BATTLE
   OF THE RIVER PLATE*   co-director with
   Emeric Pressburger, Rank, 1956, British
NIGHT AMBUSH   *ILL MET BY MOONLIGHT*
   co-director with Emeric Pressburger,
   Rank, 1957, British
HONEYMOON   *LUNA DE MIEL*   RKO Radio,
   1958, Spanish
PEEPING TOM   Astor, 1960, British
THE QUEEN'S GUARDS   20th Century-Fox,
   1961, British
THEY'RE A WEIRD MOB   Williamson/Powell,
   1966, Australian
AGE OF CONSENT   Columbia,
   1970, Australian
THE TEMPEST   1974, Greek-British

OTTO PREMINGER

b. December 5, 1906 - Vienna, Austria
d. 1986

DIE GROSSE LIEBE   1931, Austrian-German
UNDER YOUR SPELL
   20th Century-Fox, 1936
DANGER - LOVE AT WORK
   20th Century-Fox, 1937
MARGIN FOR ERROR
   20th Century-Fox, 1943
IN THE MEANTIME, DARLING
   20th Century-Fox, 1944
LAURA ★   20th Century-Fox, 1944
A ROYAL SCANDAL   20th Century-Fox, 1945
FALLEN ANGEL   20th Century-Fox, 1945
CENTENNIAL SUMMER
   20th Century-Fox, 1946
FOREVER AMBER   20th Century-Fox, 1947
DAISY KENYON   20th Century-Fox, 1947
THE FAN   20th Century-Fox, 1949
WHIRLPOOL   20th Century-Fox, 1950
WHERE THE SIDEWALK ENDS
   20th Century-Fox, 1950
THE 13TH LETTER   20th Century-Fox, 1951
ANGEL FACE   RKO Radio, 1953
THE MOON IS BLUE   United Artists, 1953
RIVER OF NO RETURN
   20th Century-Fox, 1954
CARMEN JONES   20th Century-Fox, 1954
THE MAN WITH THE GOLDEN ARM
   United Artists, 1955
THE COURT-MARTIAL OF BILLY MITCHELL
   Warner Bros., 1955
SAINT JOAN   United Artists, 1957
BONJOUR TRISTESSE   Columbia, 1958
PORGY AND BESS   Columbia, 1959
ANATOMY OF A MURDER   Columbia, 1959
EXODUS   United Artists, 1960
ADVISE AND CONSENT   Columbia, 1962
THE CARDINAL ★   Columbia, 1963
IN HARM'S WAY   Paramount, 1964
BUNNY LAKE IS MISSING   Columbia,
   1965, British
HURRY SUNDOWN   Paramount, 1967
SKIDOO   Paramount, 1968
TELL ME THAT YOU LOVE ME, JUNIE MOON
   Paramount, 1970
SUCH GOOD FRIENDS   Paramount, 1971
ROSEBUD   United Artists, 1975
THE HUMAN FACTOR   United Artists,
   1979, British

EMERIC PRESSBURGER

b. December 5, 1902 - Miskolc, Hungary
d. 1988

ONE OF OUR AIRCRAFT IS MISSING
   co-director with Michael Powell,
   United Artists, 1942, British
THE VOLUNTEER   co-director with
   Michael Powell, Anglo, 1943, British
COLONEL BLIMP   *THE LIFE AND DEATH
   OF COLONEL BLIMP*   co-director with
   Michael Powell, GFO, 1943, British
A CANTERBURY TALE   co-director with
   Michael Powell, Eagle-Lion, 1944, British
I KNOW WHERE I'M GOING   co-director with
   Michael Powell, Universal, 1945, British
STAIRWAY TO HEAVEN   *A MATTER OF
   LIFE AND DEATH*   co-director with
   Michael Powell, Universal, 1946, British
BLACK NARCISSUS   co-director with
   Michael Powell, Universal, 1947, British
THE RED SHOES   co-director with
   Michael Powell, Eagle-Lion, 1948, British

THE SMALL BACK ROOM   *HOUR OF GLORY*
   co-director with Michael Powell,
   Snader Productions, 1948, British
THE WILD HEART   *GONE TO EARTH*   co-
   director with Michael Powell, RKO Radio,
   1950, British
THE ELUSIVE PIMPERNEL   co-director with
   Michael Powell, British Lion, 1950, British
THE TALES OF HOFFMANN   co-director with
   Michael Powell, Lopert, 1951, British
TWICE UPON A TIME   1953, British
OH ROSALINDA!   co-director with
   Michael Powell, Associated British
   Picture Corporation, 1955, British
PURSUIT OF THE GRAF SPEE   *THE BATTLE
   OF THE RIVER PLATE*   co-director with
   Michael Powell, Rank, 1956, British
NIGHT AMBUSH   *ILL MET BY MOONLIGHT*
   co-director with Michael Powell, Rank,
   1957, British

ALEXANDER PTUSHKO

b. April 6, 1900 - Lugansk, Ukraine, Russia
d. 1973

THE NEW GULLIVER   1935, Soviet
THE GOLDEN KEY   1939, Soviet
THE STONE FLOWER   1946, Soviet
THREE ENCOUNTERS   co-director with
   Sergei Yutkevich & Vsevelod Pudovkin,
   1948, Soviet
THE MAGIC VOYAGE OF SINBAD   *SADKO*
   Filmgroup, 1953, Sovieet
THE SWORD AND THE DAGON   *ILYA
   MOUROMETZ*   Valiant, 1956, Soviet
CRIMSON SAILS   1961, Soviet
TALES OF LOST TIME   1964, Soviet
THE TALE OF CZAR SALTAN   1966, Soviet

VSEVELOD PUDOVKIN

b. February 6, 1893 - Penza, Russia
d. 1953

HUNGER - HUNGER - HUNGER
   1921, Russian
CHESS FEVER   co-director, 1925, Soviet
MOTHER   Amkino, 1926, Soviet
MECHANICS OF THE BRAIN (FD)
   1926, Soviet
THE END OF ST. PETERSBURG
   1927, Soviet
STORM OVER ASIA   *THE HEIR TO
   GENGHIS KHAN*   1928, Soviet
A SIMPLE CASE   *LIFE IS BEAUTIFUL*
   1932, Soviet
DESERTER   1933, Soviet
VICTORY   *MOTHERS AND SONS*
   co-director with Mikhail Doller, 1938, Soviet
MININ AND POZHARSKY   co-director with
   Mikhail Doller, 1939, Soviet
TWENTY YEARS OF CINEMA (FD)
   co-director with Esther Shub, 1940, Soviet
SUVOROV   co-director with Mikhail Doller,
   1941, Soviet
FEAST AT ZHIRMUNKA (FD)   co-director,
   1941, Soviet
THE MURDERERS ARE COMING   co-director,
   1942, Soviet
IN THE NAME OF THE FATHERLAND
   co-director with Dimitri Vasiliev, 1943, Soviet
ADMIRAL NAKHIMOV   1946, Soviet
THREE ENCOUNTERS   co-director with
   Sergei Yutkevich & Alexander Ptushko,
   1948, Soviet
ZHUKOVSKY   co-director with Dimitri Vasiliev,
   1951, Soviet
VASILI'S RETURN   1953, Soviet

IVAN PYRIEV
b. 1901 - Kamen, Russia
d. 1968

STRANGE WOMAN   1929, Soviet
THE FUNCTIONARY   1930, Soviet
CONVEYOR OF DEATH   1933, Soviet
THE PARTY CARD   1936, Soviet
THE RICH BRIDE   1938, Soviet
TRACTOR DRIVERS   1939, Soviet
THE LOVED ONE   1940, Soviet
SWINEHERD AND SHEPHERD   1941, Soviet
SECRETARY OF THE DISTRICT COMMITTEE
   1942, Soviet
AT 6 P.M. AFTER THE WAR   1944, Soviet
TALES OF THE SIBERIAN LAND
   1947, Soviet
COSSACKS OF THE KUBAN   1949, Soviet
WE ARE ALL FOR PEACE (FD)   co-director
   with Joris Ivens, 1952, Soviet-East German
TEST OF FIDELITY   1954, Soviet
THE IDIOT   Artkino, 1958, Soviet
WHITE NIGHTS   1960, Soviet
OUR MUTUAL FRIEND   1961, Soviet
LIGHT OF A DISTANT STAR   1965, Soviet
THE BROTHERS KARAMAZOV   1968, Soviet

Q

RICHARD QUINE
b. November 12, 1920 - Detroit, Michigan
d. 1989

LEATHER GLOVES   co-director with
   William Asher, Columbia, 1948
SUNNY SIDE OF THE STREET
   Columbia, 1951
PURPLE HEART DIARY   Columbia, 1951
SOUND OFF   Columbia, 1952
RAINBOW 'ROUND MY SHOULDER
   Columbia, 1952
ALL ASHORE   Columbia, 1953
SIREN OF BAGDAD   Columbia, 1953
CRUISIN' DOWN THE RIVER
   Columbia, 1953
DRIVE A CROOKED ROAD   Columbia, 1954
PUSHOVER   Columbia, 1954
SO THIS IS PARIS   Universal, 1955
MY SISTER EILEEN   Universal, 1955
THE SOLID GOLD CADILLAC
   Columbia, 1956
FULL OF LIFE   Columbia, 1957
OPERATION MAD BALL   Columbia, 1957
BELL, BOOK AND CANDLE   Columbia, 1958
IT HAPPENED TO JANE   Columbia, 1959
STRANGERS WHEN WE MEET
   Columbia, 1960
THE WORLD OF SUZIE WONG
   Paramount, 1960
THE NOTORIOUS LANDLADY   Columbia, 1962
PARIS WHEN IT SIZZLES   Paramount, 1964
SEX AND THE SINGLE GIRL
   Warner Bros., 1965
HOW TO MURDER YOUR WIFE
   United Artists, 1965
SYNANON   Columbia, 1965
OH DAD, POOR DAD, MOMMA'S HUNG YOU
   IN THE CLOSET AND I'M FEELING SO SAD
   Paramount, 1967

HOTEL   Warner Bros., 1967
A TALENT FOR LOVING   1969
THE MOONSHINE WAR   MGM, 1970
"W"   Cinerama Releasing Corporation,
   1974, British
THE SPECIALISTS (TF)   Mark VII Ltd./
   Universal TV, 1975
THE PRISONER OF ZENDA   Universal, 1979

R

YULI RAIZMAN
(Yuli Raisman)
b. December 15, 1903 - Moscow, Russia
d. 1994

THE CIRCLE   THE RING/DUTY AND LOVE
   co-director with A. Gavronsky, Gosvoyenkino,
   1927, Soviet
FORCED LABOR   Gosvoyenkino,
   1928, Soviet
THE EARTH THIRSTS   Vostok Studios,
   1930, Soviet
AVIATORS   Mosfilm, 1935, Soviet
THE LAST NIGHT   Mosfilm, 1937, Soviet
VIRGIN SOIL UPTURNED   Mosfilm,
   1940, Soviet
MASHENKA   Mosfilm, 1942, Soviet
ABOUT THE TRUTH WITH FINLAND (FD)
   Mosfilm, 1944, Soviet
MOSCOW SKY   Mosfilm, 1944, Soviet
BERLIN   THE FALL OF BERLIN (FD)
   Mosfilm, 1945, Soviet
THE TRAIN GOES EAST   Mosfilm,
   1948, Soviet
RAINIS   Mosfilm, 1949, Soviet
CAVALIER OF THE GOLDEN STAR   DREAM
   OF A COSSACK   Mosfilm, 1951, Soviet
A LESSON IN LIFE   CONFLICT   Mosfilm,
   1955, Soviet
THE COMMUNIST   Mosfilm, 1958, Soviet
IF THIS BE LOVE   Mosfilm, 1961, Soviet
YOUR CONTEMPORARY   Mosfilm,
   1967, Soviet
A COURTESY CALL   Mosfilm, 1973, Soviet
A STRANGE WOMAN   Mosfilm, 1977, Soviet
PRIVATE LIFE   Mosfilm, 1982, Soviet
A TALE OF WISHES   Mosfilm, 1984, Soviet

GREGORY RATOFF
b. April 20, 1897 - St. Petersburg, Russia
d. 1960

SINS OF MAN   co-director with Otto Brower,
   20th Century-Fox, 1936
THE LANCER SPY   20th Century-Fox, 1937
WIFE, HUSBAND AND FRIEND
   20th Century-Fox, 1939
ROSE OF WASHINGTON SQUARE
   20th Century-Fox, 1939
HOTEL FOR WOMEN
   20th Century-Fox, 1939
INTERMEZZO   United Artists, 1939
DAYTIME WIFE   20th Century-Fox, 1939
BARRICADE   20th Century-Fox, 1939
I WAS AN ADVENTURESS
   20th Century-Fox, 1940
PUBLIC DEB NO. 1   20th Century-Fox, 1940

ADAM HAD FOUR SONS   Columbia, 1941
THE MEN IN HER LIFE   Columbia, 1941
THE CORSICAN BROTHERS
   United Artists, 1941
TWO YANKS IN TRINIDAD   Columbia, 1942
FOOTLIGHT SERENADE
   20th Century-Fox, 1942
SOMETHING TO SHOUT ABOUT
   Columbia, 1943
THE HEAT'S ON   Columbia, 1943
SONG OF RUSSIA   MGM, 1943
IRISH EYES ARE SMILING
   20th Century-Fox, 1944
WHERE DO WE GO FROM HERE?
   20th Century-Fox, 1945
PARIS UNDERGROUND   United Artists, 1945
DO YOU LOVE ME?   20th Century-Fox, 1946
CARNIVAL IN COSTA RICA
   20th Century-Fox, 1947
MOSS ROSE   20th Century-Fox, 1947
BLACK MAGIC   United Artists, 1949
IF THIS BE SIN   THAT DANGEROUS AGE
   United Artists, 1950, British
OPERATION X   MY DAUGHTER JOY
   Columbia, 1950
TAXI   20th Century-Fox, 1953
ABDULLAH'S HAREM   20th Century-Fox,
   1956, Egyptian
OSCAR WILDE   Films Around the World,
   1960, British

MAN RAY
(Emmanuel Rudnitsky)
b. August 17, 1890 - Philadelphia, Pennsylvania
d. 1976

LE RETOUR A LA RAISON   1923, French
EMAK BAKIA   1927, French
L'ETOILE DE MER   1928, French
LES MYSTERES DU CHATEAU DU DE
   1929, French
DREAMS THAT MONEY CAN BUY   1946

NICHOLAS RAY
(Raymond Nicholas Kienzle)
b. August 7, 1911 - La Crosse, Wisconsin
d. 1979

THEY LIVE BY NIGHT   THE TWISTED ROAD
   RKO Radio, 1949
A WOMAN'S SECRET   RKO Radio, 1949
KNOCK ON ANY DOOR   Columbia, 1949
IN A LONELY PLACE   Columbia, 1950
BORN TO BE BAD   RKO Radio, 1950
FLYING LEATHERNECKS   RKO Radio, 1951
ON DANGEROUS GROUND
   RKO Radio, 1952
THE LUSTY MEN   RKO Radio, 1952
JOHNNY GUITAR   Republic, 1954
RUN FOR COVER   Paramount, 1955
REBEL WITHOUT A CAUSE
   Warner Bros., 1955
HOT BLOOD   Columbia, 1956
BIGGER THAN LIFE   20th Century-Fox, 1956
THE TRUE STORY OF JESSE JAMES
   20th Century-Fox, 1957
BITTER VICTORY   Columbia, 1957,
   U.S.-French
WIND ACROSS THE EVERGLADES
   Warner Bros., 1958
PARTY GIRL   MGM, 1958
THE SAVAGE INNOCENTS   Paramount,
   1960, Italian-French-British-U.S.
KING OF KINGS   MGM, 1961
55 DAYS AT PEKING   Allied Artists, 1963
YOU CAN'T GO HOME AGAIN   1976

SATYAJIT RAY
b. May 2, 1921 - Calcutta, India
d. 1992

PATHER PANCHALI   Harrison, 1955, Indian
APARAJITO   Harrison, 1956, Indian
PARAS PATHAR   1957, Indian
THE MUSIC ROOM   Harrison, 1958, Indian
THE WORLD OF APU   Harrison, 1959, Indian
DEVI   Harrison, 1960, Indian
RABINDRANATH TAGORE   1961, Indian
TWO DAUGHTERS   Janus, 1961, Indian
KANCHENJUNGHA   Harrison, 1962, Indian
ABHIJAN   1962, Indian
MAHANAGAR   1963, Indian
CHARULATA   *THE LONELY WIFE*
   Trans-World, 1964, Indian
KAPURUSH-O-MAHAPURUSH   1966, Indian
NAYAK   1966, Indian
CHIRIAKHANA   1967, Indian
GOOPY GYNE BAGHA BYNE   Purnima
   Pictures, 1968, Indian
DAYS AND NIGHTS IN THE FOREST
   Pathe Contemporary, 1970, Indian
THE ADVERSARY   Audio Brandon,
   1971, Indian
SIKKIM   1971, Indian
THE INNER EYE   1972, Indian
SIMABADDHA   1972, Indian
DISTANT THUNDER   Cinema 5, 1973, Indian
SONAR KELLA   1974, Indian
BALA   1976, Indian
THE MIDDLEMAN   Bauer International,
   1976, Indian
THE CHESS PLAYERS   Creative,
   1977, Indian
JOI BABA FELUNATH   1978, Indian
HEERAK RAJAR DESHE   1979, Indian
THE ELEPHANT GOD   R.D. Bansal &
   Company, 1979, Indian
THE KINGDOM OF DIAMONDS (TF)
   GOVWB, 1980, Indian
SADGATI   1982, Indian
THE HOME AND THE WORLD   European
   Classics, 1984, Indian
GANASHATRU   National Film Development
   Corporation of India, 1989, Indian
SHAKHA PROSHAKHA   Satyajit Ray
   Productions/Erato Films-DD Productions/
   Distri Films/Sopro Films, 1990, Indian-French
AGANTUK   National Film Development
   Corporation of India, 1991, Indian

SIR CAROL REED
b. December 30, 1906 - London, England
d. 1976

IT HAPPENED IN PARIS   co-director with
   Robert Wyler, Associated British Film
   Distributors, 1935, British
MIDSHIPMAN EASY   *MEN OF THE SEA*
   Associated British Film Distributors,
   1935, British
LABURNUM GROVE   Associated British
   Film Distributors, 1936, British
TALK OF THE DEVIL   United Artists,
   1937, British
WHO'S YOUR LADY FRIEND?   Associated
   British Film Distributors, 1937, British
THREE ON A WEEK-END   *BANK HOLIDAY*
   Gaumont-British, 1938, British
PENNY PARADISE   Associated British Film
   Distributors, 1938, British
CLIMBING HIGH   MGM, 1939, British
A GIRL MUST LIVE   20th Century-Fox,
   1939, British
THE STARS LOOK DOWN   MGM,
   1939, British

NIGHT TRAIN   *NIGHT TRAIN TO MUNICH*
   MGM, 1940, British
THE GIRL IN THE NEWS   MGM,
   1940, British
THE REMARKABLE MR. KIPPS   *KIPPS*
   20th Century-Fox, 1941, British
THE YOUNG MR. PITT   20th Century-Fox,
   1942, British
THE NEW LOT   Army Kinematograph Unit,
   1943, British
THE WAY AHEAD   *THE IMMORTAL
   BATTALION*   20th Century-Fox,
   1944, British
THE TRUE GLORY (FD)   co-director with
   Garson Kanin, Columbia, 1945, British
ODD MAN OUT   General Film Distributors,
   1947, British
THE FALLEN IDOL ★   Selznick Releasing,
   1948, British
THE THIRD MAN ★   Selznick Releasing,
   1949, British
OUTCAST OF THE ISLANDS   United Artists,
   1951, British
THE MAN BETWEEN   United Artists,
   1953, British
A KID FOR TWO FARTHINGS   Lopert,
   1955, British
TRAPEZE   United Artists, 1956
THE KEY   Columbia, 1958, British
OUR MAN IN HAVANA   Columbia,
   1959, British
THE RUNNING MAN   Columbia, 1963, British
THE AGONY AND THE ECSTASY
   20th Century-Fox, 1965
OLIVER! ★★   Columbia, 1968, British
FLAP   *THE LAST WARRIOR*
   Warner Bros., 1970
FOLLOW ME!   Rank Film Distributors, 1971
THE PUBLIC EYE   Universal, 1972

MICHAEL REEVES
b. 1944 - London, England
d. 1969

THE REVENGE OF THE BLOOD BEAST
   THE SHE BEAST   1966,
   British-Italian-Yugoslavian
THE SORCERERS   Allied Artists,
   1967, British
THE CONQUEROR WORM   *WITCHFINDER
   GENERAL*   American International,
   1968, British

FRANÇOIS REICHENBACH
b. July 3, 1922 - Paris, France
d. 1993

L'AMERIQUE INSOLITE (FD)   1960, French
UN COEUR GROS COMME CA (FD)
   1961, French
LES AMOUREAUX DU "FRANCE" (FD)
   co-director with Pierre Grimblat,
   1963, French
GRENOBLE (FD)   co-director with Claude
   Lelouch, United Producers of America,
   1968, French
MEXICO MEXICO (FD)   1969, French
ARTHUR RUBINSTEIN: LOVE OF LIFE (FD)
   co-director with Gerard Patris, New Yorker,
   1970, French
L'INDISCRETE (FD)   1970, French
MEDICINE BALL CARAVAN (FCD)
   Warner Bros., 1971, French-U.S.
YEHUDI MENUHIN - CHEMIN DE
   LUMIERE (FD)   co-director with
   Bernard Gavoty, 1971, French
LA RAISON DU PLUS FOU   Gaumont,
   1973, French

JOHNNY HALLYDAY (FD)   Prodis,
   1972, French
LE HOLD-UP AU CRAYON (FD)
   Films du Prisme, 1973, French
DON'T YOU HEAR THE DOGS BARK?
   co-director with Noel Howard, 1975,
   Mexican-French
SEX O'CLOCK USA (FD)   1976
ANOTHER WAY TO LIVE (FD)   1976
PELE (FD)   Televisa, 1977, French-Mexican
HOUSTON, TEXAS (FD)   Camera One/TFI/
   Prisme Films, 1980, French
FRANÇOIS REICHENBACH'S JAPAN (FD)
   CIDIF, 1983, French
VISAGES SUISSES (FD)   co-director,
   Video Films, 1991, Swiss

GOTTFRIED REINHARDT
b. 1911 - Berlin, Germany
d. 1994

INVITATION   MGM, 1952
THE STORY OF THREE LOVES   co-director
   with Vincente Minnelli, MGM, 1953
BETRAYED   MGM, 1954
VOR SONNENUNTERGANG   1956,
   West German
MENSCHEN IM HOTEL   1959,
   West German-French
REBEL FLIGHT TO CUBA   *ABSCHIED
   DER GOTTER*   Telewide Systems,
   1961, West German
TOWN WITHOUT PITY   United Artists, 1960,
   U.S.-West German-Swiss
ELF JAHRE UND EIN TAG   1963,
   West German
SITUATION HOPELESS - BUT NOT SERIOUS
   Paramount, 1965

MAX REINHARDT
(Maximilian Goldman)
b. September 8, 1873 - Baden, Austria
d. 1943

SUMURUN   1908, German
DAS MIRAKEL   1912, German
INSEL DER SELIGEN   1913, German
VENIZIANISCHE NACHT   1914, German
A MIDSUMMER NIGHT'S DREAM   co-director
   with William Dieterle, Warner Bros., 1935

IRVING REIS
b. May 7, 1906 - New York, New York
d. 1953

ONE CROWDED NIGHT   RKO Radio, 1940
I'M STILL ALIVE   RKO Radio, 1940
FOOTLIGHT FEVER   RKO Radio, 1941
THE GAY FALCON   RKO Radio, 1941
WEEKEND FOR THREE   RKO Radio, 1941
A DATE WITH THE FALCON
   RKO Radio, 1941
THE FALCON TAKES OVER
   RKO Radio, 1942
THE BIG STREET   RKO Radio, 1942
CRACK-UP   20th Century-Fox, 1946
THE BACHELOR AND THE BOBBY-SOXER
   RKO Radio, 1947
ALL MY SONS   Universal, 1948
ENCHANTMENT   RKO Radio, 1948
ROSEANNA McCOY   RKO Radio, 1949
DANCING IN THE DARK
   20th Century-Fox, 1949
THREE HUSBANDS   United Artists, 1950
OF MEN AND MUSIC (FD)   co-director with
   Alex Hammid, 20th Century-Fox, 1951
NEW MEXICO   United Artists, 1951
THE FOUR POSTER   Columbia, 1953

WOLFGANG REITHERMAN
b. 1909
d. 1985

101 DALMATIANS (AF) co-director with
  Hamilton S. Luske & Clyde Geronimi,
  Buena Vista, 1961
THE SWORD IN THE STONE (AF)
  Buena Vista, 1963
THE JUNGLE BOOK (AF) Buena Vista, 1967
THE ARISTOCATS (AF) Buena Vista, 1970
ROBIN HOOD (AF) Buena Vista, 1973
THE RESCUERS (AF) Buena Vista, 1977

JEAN RENOIR
b. September 15, 1894 - Paris, France
d. 1979

LA FILLE DE L'EAU 1925, French
NANA 1926, French
CHARLESTON 1927, French
MARQUITTA 1927, French
LE PETITE MARCHANDE D'ALLUMETTES
  co-director with Jean Tedesco, 1928, French
TIRE-AU-FLANC 1929, French
LE TOURNOI 1928, French
LE BLED 1929, French
ON PURGE BEBE 1931, French
LA CHIENNE 1931, French
LA NUIT DE CAREFOUR 1932, French
BOUDOU SAVED FROM DROWNING
  Pathé Contemporary, 1932, French
CHOTARD ET COMPAGNIE 1933, French
MADAME BOVARY 1934, French
TONI 1935, French
THE CRIME OF MONSIEUR LANGE
  Brandon, 1936, French
LA VIE EST A NOUS 1936, French
A DAY IN THE COUNTRY UNE PARTIE
  DE CAMPAGNE 1936, French
LES BAS-FONDS 1936, French
GRAND ILLUSION World Pictures,
  1937, French
LA MARSEILLAISE 1938, French
LA BETE HUMAINE 1938, French
THE RULES OF THE GAME Janus,
  1983, French
LA TOSCA co-director, 1940, Italian-French
SWAMP WATER 20th Century-Fox, 1941
THIS LAND IS MINE RKO Radio, 1943
SALUTE TO FRANCE (FD) co-director, 1944
THE SOUTHERNER ★ United Artists, 1945
THE DIARY OF A CHAMBERMAID
  United Artists, 1946
THE WOMAN ON THE BEACH
  RKO Radio, 1947
THE RIVER United Artists, 1951, U.S.-Indian
THE GOLDEN COACH Italian Films Export,
  1952, Italian-French
FRENCH-CANCAN ONLY THE FRENCH CAN
  United Motion Picture Organization,
  1954, French
PARIS DOES STRANGE THINGS ELENA ET
  LES HOMMES Warner Bros., 1957, French
PICNIC ON THE GRASS Kingsley-Union,
  1959, French
LE TESTAMENT DU DR. CORDELIER (TF)
  1961, French
THE ELUSIVE CORPORAL LE CAPORAL
  EPINGLE Pathé Contemporary,
  1962, French
LA DIRECTION D'ACTEUR PAR JEAN
  RENOIR 1968, French
THE LITTLE THEATRE OF JEAN
  RENOIR (TF) Phoenix Films, 1969,
  French-Italian-West German

TONY RICHARDSON
(Cecil Antonio Richardson)
b. June 5, 1928 - Shipley, England
d. 1991

LOOK BACK IN ANGER Warner Bros.,
  1958, British
THE ENTERTAINER Continental,
  1960, British
SANCTUARY 20th Century-Fox, 1961
A TASTE OF HONEY Continental,
  1962, British
THE LONELINESS OF THE LONG DISTANCE
  RUNNER Continental, 1962, British
TOM JONES ★★ Lopert, 1963, British,
  re-released by The Samuel Goldwyn
  Company in 1989
THE LOVED ONE MGM, 1965
MADEMOISELLE Lopert, 1966,
  French-British
THE SAILOR FROM GIBRALTER Lopert,
  1967, British
THE CHARGE OF THE LIGHT BRIGADE
  United Artists, 1968, British
LAUGHTER IN THE DARK Lopert, 1969,
  British-French
HAMLET Columbia, 1969, British
NED KELLY United Artists, 1970, British
A DELICATE BALANCE American Film
  Theatre, 1973
DEAD CERT United Artists, 1973, British
JOSEPH ANDREWS Paramount,
  1977, British
A DEATH IN CANAAN (TF) Chris-Rose
  Productions/Warner Bros. TV, 1978
THE BORDER Universal, 1982
THE HOTEL NEW HAMPSHIRE Orion, 1984
PENALTY PHASE (TF) Tamara Asseyev
  Productions/New World TV, 1986
BERYL MARKHAM: A SHADOW ON
  THE SUN (TF) Tamara Asseyev
  Productions/New World TV, 1988
THE PHANTOM OF THE OPERA (TF)
  Saban-Scherick Productions, 1990
WOMEN & MEN: STORIES OF
  SEDUCTION (CTF) co-director with
  Ken Russell & Frederic Raphael, HBO
  Showcase/David Brown Productions, 1990
BLUE SKY Orion, 1994, filmed in 1991

MARTIN RITT
b. March 2, 1913 - New York, New York
d. 1990

EDGE OF THE CITY MGM, 1957
NO DOWN PAYMENT
  20th Century-Fox, 1957
THE LONG HOT SUMMER MGM, 1958
THE BLACK ORCHID Paramount, 1959
THE SOUND AND THE FURY
  20th Century-Fox, 1959
FIVE BRANDED WOMEN Paramount, 1960,
  Italian-Yugoslavian-U.S.
PARIS BLUES United Artists, 1961
HEMINGWAY'S ADVENTURES OF A
  YOUNG MAN 20th Century-Fox, 1962
HUD ★ Paramount, 1963
THE OUTRAGE MGM, 1964
THE SPY WHO CAME IN FROM THE COLD
  Paramount, 1965, British
HOMBRE 20th Century-Fox, 1967
THE BROTHERHOOD Paramount, 1968
THE MOLLY MAGUIRES Paramount, 1970
THE GREAT WHITE HOPE
  20th Century-Fox, 1970
SOUNDER 20th Century-Fox, 1972
PETE N' TILLIE Universal, 1972

CONRACK 20th Century-Fox, 1974
THE FRONT Columbia, 1976
CASEY'S SHADOW Columbia, 1978
NORMA RAE 20th Century-Fox, 1979
BACK ROADS Warner Bros., 1981
CROSS CREEK Universal/AFD, 1983
MURPHY'S ROMANCE Columbia, 1985
NUTS Universal, 1987
STANLEY & IRIS MGM/UA, 1990

JOHN S. ROBERTSON
b. June 14, 1878 - London, Ontario, Canada
d. 1964

BABY MINE Goldwyn, 1917
INTRIGUE Vitagraph, 1917
THE BOTTOM OF THE WELL
  Vitagraph, 1917
THE MONEY MILL Vitagraph, 1917
THE MENACE Vitagraph, 1918
GIRL OF TODAY Vitagraph, 1918
THE MAKE-BELIEVE WIFE
  Paramount, 1918
HERE COMES THE BRIDE Paramount, 1919
COME OUT OF THE KITCHEN
  Paramount, 1919
THE MISLEADING WIDOW
  Paramount, 1919
LITTLE MISS HOOVER Paramount, 1919
THE TEST OF HONOR Paramount, 1919
LET'S ELOPE Paramount, 1919
ERSTWHILE SUSAN Realart, 1919
SADIE LOVE Paramount, 1919
THE BETTER HALF Select, 1919
DR. JEKYLL AND MR. HYDE
  Paramount, 1920
AWAY GOES PRUDENCE Paramount, 1920
A DARK LANTERN Realart, 1920
39 EAST Realart, 1920
THE MAGIC CUP Realart, 1921
SENTIMENTAL TOMMY Paramount, 1921
FOOTLIGHTS Paramount, 1921
LOVE'S BOOMERANG Paramount, 1922
THE SPANISH JADE Paramount, 1922
TESS OF THE STORM COUNTRY
  United Artists, 1922
THE BRIGHT SHAWL Associated First
  National, 1923
THE FIGHTING BLADE Associated First
  National, 1923
TWENTY-ONE Associated First
  National, 1923
THE ENCHANTED COTTAGE
  First National, 1924
CLASSMATES First National, 1924
NEW TOYS First National, 1925
SOUL-FIRE First National, 1925
SHORE LEAVE First National, 1925
ANNIE LAURIE First National, 1927
CAPTAIN SALVATION MGM, 1927
THE ROAD TO ROMANCE MGM, 1927
THE SINGLE STANDARD MGM, 1929
SHANGHAI LADY Universal, 1929
NIGHT RIDE Universal, 1930
CAPTAIN OF THE GUARD co-director with
  Paul Fejos, 1930, Universal
MADONNA OF THE STREETS
  Columbia, 1930
ONE MAN'S JOURNEY RKO RADIO, 1933
THE CRIME DOCTOR RKO RADIO, 1934
HIS GREATEST GAMBLE RKO RADIO, 1934
WEDNESDAY'S CHILD RKO RADIO, 1934
CAPTAIN HURRICANE RKO RADIO, 1935
GRAND OLD GIRL RKO RADIO, 1935
OUR LITTLE GIRL Fox, 1935

MARK ROBSON

b. December 4, 1913 - Montreal, Canada
d. 1978

THE SEVENTH VICTIM   RKO Radio, 1943
THE GHOST SHIP   RKO Radio, 1943
YOUTH RUNS WILD   RKO Radio, 1944
ISLE OF THE DEAD   RKO Radio, 1945
BEDLAM   RKO Radio, 1946
CHAMPION   United Artists, 1949
HOME OF THE BRAVE   United Artists, 1949
ROUGHSHOD   RKO Radio, 1949
MY FOOLISH HEART   RKO Radio, 1949
EDGE OF DOOM   RKO Radio, 1950
BRIGHT VICTORY   Universal, 1951
I WANT YOU   RKO Radio, 1952
RETURN TO PARADISE   United Artists, 1953
HELL BELOW ZERO   MGM, 1954, British
PHFFFT   Columbia, 1954
THE BRIDGES AT TOKO-RI
   Paramount, 1955
A PRIZE OF GOLD   Columbia, 1954
TRIAL   MGM, 1955
THE HARDER THEY FALL   Columbia, 1956
THE LITTLE HUT   MGM, 1957
PEYTON PLACE ★   20th Century-Fox, 1957
THE INN OF THE SIXTH HAPPINESS ★
   20th Century-Fox, 1958, British
FROM THE TERRACE
   20th Century-Fox, 1960
LISA   THE INSPECTOR   20th Century-Fox,
   1962, British-U.S.
NINE HOURS TO RAMA   20th Century-Fox,
   1963, British-U.S.
THE PRIZE   MGM, 1963
VON RYAN'S EXPRESS
   20th Century-Fox, 1965
LOST COMMAND   Columbia, 1966
VALLEY OF THE DOLLS
   20th Century-Fox, 1967
DADDY'S GONE A-HUNTING   National
   General, 1969
HAPPY BIRTHDAY, WANDA JUNE
   Columbia, 1971
LIMBO   Universal, 1972
EARTHQUAKE   Universal, 1974
AVALANCHE EXPRESS
   20th Century-Fox, 1979

GLAUBER ROCHA

b. March 14, 1938 - Victoria da Conquista,
   Bahia, Brazil
d. 1981

BARRAVENTO   New Yorker, 1961, Brazilian
BLACK GOD - WHITE DEVIL   DEUS E O
   DIABO NA TERRA DEL SOL
   1964, Brazilian
TERRA EM TRANSE   1967, Brazilian
ANTONIO DAS MORTES   O DRAGAO DA
   MALADECONTRA O SANTO GUERREIRO
   1969, Brazilian
THE LION HAS SEVEN HEADS   1970, African
CABEZAS CORTADAS   1970, African
CLARO   1975, Italian

ROBERTO ROSSELLINI

b. May 8, 1906 - Rome, Italy
d. 1977

LA NAVE BIANCA   1941, Italian
UNA PILOTA RITORNA   1942, Italian
I TRE AGUILLOTTI   co-director with
   Mario Mattoli, 1942, Italian
L'UOMO DELLA CROCE   1943, Italian
DESIDERIO   co-director with
   Marcello Pagliero, 1943, Italian

OPEN CITY   ROMA, CITTA APERTA
   Mayer-Burstyn, 1945, Italian
PAISAN   Mayer-Burstyn, 1946, Italian
GERMANY YEAR ZERO   Superfilm, 1947,
   West German-French
L'AMORE   1948, Italian
LA MACCHINA AMMAZZACATTIVI
   1948, Italian
STROMBOLI   RKO Radio, 1949, Italian
FRANCESCO - GIULLARE DI DIO
   FLOWERS OF ST. FRANCIS   1950, Italian
THE SEVEN DEADLY SINS   co-director,
   Arian Pictures, 1952, French-Italian
THE GREATEST LOVE   EUROPA '51
   Italian Films Export, 1952, Italian
DOV'E LA LIBERTA?   1953, Italian
STRANGERS   VIAGGIO IN ITALIA   Fine Arts,
   1954, Italian
SIAMO DONNE   co-director, 1953, Italian
AMORI DI MEZZO SECOLO   co-director,
   1954, Italian
GIOVANNA D'ARCO AL ROGO   1954, Italian
FEAR   LA PAURA   Astor, 1955,
   West German-Italian
LE PSYCHODRAME   1957, Italian
L'INDIA VISITA DA ROSSELLINI (TD)
   1958, Italian
IL GENERALE DELLA ROVERE   Continental,
   1959, Italian-French
ERA NOTTE A ROMA   1960, Italian
VIVA L'ITALIA   1960, Italian
VANINA VANINI   THE BETRAYER
   1961, Italian
TORINO NEI CENTI'ANNI (TD)
   1961, Italian T.V.
ANIMA NERA   1962, Italian
ROGOPAG   co-director, 1962, Italian
L'ETA DEL FERRO (TF)   1964, Italian T.V.
THE RISE OF LOUIS XIV   Brandon, 1966,
   French, originally made for television
IDEA DI UN'ISOLA (TD)   1967
GLI ATTI DEGLI APOSTOLI (TF)
   1968, Italian
SOCRATES   New Yorker, 1969, Italian,
   originally made for television
LA LOTTA DELL'VORRO PER LE SOPRA
   VIVENZ (TF)   1970, Italian T.V.
AGOSTINO DI IPPONA   1972, Italian
PASCAL (TF)   1972, Italian T.V.
L'AMORA VANTI ANNI   1972, Italian-French
L'ETA DI COSIMO (TF)   1973, Italian T.V.
THE AGE OF THE MEDICIS (TF)
   1973, Italian T.V.
CARTESIO (TF)   1974, Italian T.V.
ANNI CALDI (TF)   1974, Italian
BLAISE PASCAL (TF)   1975, Italian
ANNO UNO   1975, Italian
THE MESSIAH   1978, Italian

ROBERT ROSSEN

(Robert Rosen)
b. March 16, 1908 - New York, New York
d. 1966

JOHNNY O'CLOCK   Columbia, 1947
BODY AND SOUL   United Artists, 1947
ALL THE KING'S MEN ★   Columbia, 1949
THE BRAVE BULLS   Columbia, 1951
MAMBO   Paramount, 1954, U.S.-Italian
ALEXANDER THE GREAT
   United Artists, 1956
ISLAND IN THE SUN   20th Century-Fox, 1957
THEY CAME TO CORDURA   Columbia, 1959
THE HUSTLER ★   20th Century-Fox, 1961
LILITH   Columbia, 1964

FREDERIC ROSSIF

b. August 14, 1922 - Cetinje, Montenegro,
   Yugoslavia
d. 1990

THE WITNESSES   LE TEMPS DU
   GHETTO (FD)   Altura Films Limited,
   1961, French
TO DIE IN MADRID (FD)   Altura Films
   Limited, 1963, French
THE ANIMALS (FD)   Four Star,
   1963, French
LE REVOLUTION D'OCTOBRE (FD)
   1963, French
A WALL IN JERUSALEM (FD)   co-director with
   Albert Knobler, Eyr Campus Programs,
   1968, French
POURQUOI L'AMERIQUE (FD)
   1969, French
AUSSI LOIN QUE L'AMOUR (FD)
   1971, French
LA FETE SAUVAGE (FD)   1976, French
PABLO PICASSO (FD)   1982, French
BREL (FD)   1982, French
SAUVAGE ET BEAU (FD)   1984, French
LE COEUR MUSICIEN (FD)   1987, French

PAUL ROTHA

(Paul Thompson)
b. June 3, 1907 - London, England
d. 1984

CONTACT (FD)   1933, British
THE RISING TIDE   GREAT CARGOES (FD)
   1933, British
SHIPYARD   1934, British
THE FACE OF BRITAIN (FD)   1935, British
DEATH ON THE ROAD (FD)   1935, British
THE FUTURE'S IN THE AIR (FD)
   1936, British
COVER TO COVER (FD)   1936, British
THE WAY TO THE SEA (FD)   1936, British
PEACE OF BRITAIN (FD)   1936, British
STATUE P (FD)   1937, British
TODAY WE LIVE (FD)   1937, British
HERE IS THE LAND (FD)   1937, British
NEW WORLDS FOR OLD (FD)   1939, British
ROADS ACROSS BRITAIN (FD)   co-director
   with Sidney Cole, 1939, British
THE FOURTH ESTATE (FD)   1940, British
MR. BORLAND THINS AGAIN (FD)
   1940, British
WORLD OF PLENTY (FD)   1943, British
SOVIET VILLAGE (FD)   1944, British
LAND OF PROMISE (FD)   1945, British
TOTAL WAR IN BRITAIN (FD)   1945, British
A CITY SPEAKS (FD)   1946, British
THE WORLD IS RICH (FD)   1947, British
NO RESTING PLACE   Classics Pictures,
   1951, British
WORLD WITHOUT END (FD)   co-director with
   Basil Wright, 1953, British
HOPE FOR THE HUNGRY (FD)
   1954, British
THE WAITING PEOPLE (FD)   1954, British
NO OTHER WAY (FD)   1955, British
THE WEALTH OF WATERS (FD)
   1955, British
THE VIRUS STORY (FD)   1955, British
CAT AND MOUSE   Eros Films, 1958, British
CRADLE OF GENIUS (FD)   1959, British
THE LIFE OF ADOLF HITLER (FD)   1961,
   British-West German
DE OVERVAL   1962, Dutch

RUSSELL ROUSE
b. April 3, 1915 - New York, New York
d. 1987

THE WELL   co-director with Leo Popkins,
   United Artists, 1951
THE THIEF   United Artists, 1952
WICKED WOMAN   United Artists, 1954
NEW YORK CONFIDENTIAL
   Warner Bros., 1955
THE FASTEST GUN ALIVE   MGM, 1956
HOUSE OF NUMBERS   Columbia, 1957
THUNDER IN THE SUN   Paramount, 1959
A HOUSE IS NOT A HOME   Embassy, 1964
THE OSCAR   Embassy, 1966
THE CAPER OF THE GOLDEN BULLS
   Embassy, 1967

WESLEY RUGGLES
b. June 11, 1889 - Los Angeles, California
d. 1972

FOR FRANCE   Vitagraph, 1917
THE BLIND ADVENTURE   Vitagraph, 1918
THE WINCHESTER WOMAN
   Vitagraph, 1919
PICCADILLY JIM   Select, 1920
SOONER OR LATER   1920
THE DESPERATE HERO   Selznick, 1920
THE LEOPARD WOMAN   Associated
   Producers, 1920
LOVE   Associated Producers, 1920
THE GREATER CLAIM   Metro, 1921
UNCHARTED SEAS   Metro, 1921
OVER THE WIRE   Metro, 1921
WILD HONEY   Universal, 1922
IF I WERE QUEEN   Film Booking
   Offices, 1922
SLIPPERY McGEE   First National, 1922
MR. BILLINGS SPENDS HIS DIME
   Paramount, 1923
THE REMITTANCE WOMAN   Film Booking
   Offices, 1923
THE HEART RAIDER   Paramount, 1923
THE AGE OF INNOCENCE
   Warner Bros., 1924
THE PLASTIC AGE   B.P. Schulberg, 1925
BROADWAY LADY   Film Booking
   Offices, 1925
THE KICK-OFF   Excellent, 1926
A MAN OF QUALITY   Excellent, 1926
BEWARE OF WIDOWS   Universal, 1927
SILK STOCKINGS   Universal, 1927
THE FOURFLUSHER   Universal, 1928
FINDERS KEEPERS   Universal, 1928
STREET GIRL   RKO RADIO, 1929
SCANDAL   Universal, 1929
CONDEMNED   United Artists, 1929
GIRL OVERBOARD   Universal, 1929
HONEY   Paramount, 1930
THE SEA BAT   MGM, 1930
CIMARRON ★   RKO Radio, 1931
ARE THESE OUR CHILDREN?
   RKO RADIO, 1931
ROAR OF THE DRAGON   RKO RADIO, 1932
NO MAN OF HER OWN   Parmaount, 1932
THE MONKEY'S PAW   RKO RADIO, 1933
COLLEGE HUMOR   Paramount, 1933
I'M NO ANGEL   Paramount, 1933
BOLERO   Paramount, 1934
SHOOT THE WORKS   Paramount, 1934
THE GILDED LILY   Paramount, 1935
ACCENT ON YOUTH   Paramount, 1935
THE BRIDE COMES HOME
   Paramount, 1935
VALIANT IS THE WORD FOR CARRIE
   Paramount, 1936

I MET HIM IN PARIS   Paramount, 1937
TRUE CONFESSION   Paramount, 1937
SING YOU SINNERS   Paramount, 1938
INVITATION TO HAPPINESS
   Paramount, 1939
TOO MANY HUSBANDS   Columbia, 1940
ARIZONA   Columbia, 1940
YOU BELONG TO ME   Columbia, 1941
SOMEWHERE I'LL FIND YOU   MGM, 1942
SLIGHTLY DANGEROUS   MGM, 1943
SEE HERE, PRIVATE HARGROVE
   MGM, 1944
LONDON TOWN   *MY HEART GOES CRAZY*
   Continental, 1946, British

S

BORIS SAGAL
b. 1923 - Dnepropettrovsk, Soviet Union
d. 1981

THE CRIMEBUSTER   MGM, 1961
DIME WITH A HALO   MGM, 1963
TWILIGHT OF HONOR   MGM, 1963
GIRL HAPPY   MGM, 1965
MADE IN PARIS   MGM, 1966
THE HELICOPTER SPIES   MGM, 1968
THE 1,000 PLANE RAID   United Artists, 1969
U.M.C.   *OPERATION HEARTBEAT* (TF)
   MGM TV, 1969
DESTINY OF A SPY (TF)   Universal TV, 1969
NIGHT GALLERY (TF)   co-director with
   Barry Shear & Steven Spielberg,
   Universal TV, 1969
THE D.A.: MURDER ONE (TF)   Mark VII Ltd./
   Universal TV/Jack Webb Productions, 1969
MOSQUITO SQUADRON   United Artists, 1970
THE MOVIE MURDERER (TF)
   Universal TV, 1970
HAUSER'S MEMORY (TF)
   Universal TV, 1970
THE OMEGA MAN   Warner Bros., 1971
THE HARNESS (TF)   Universal TV, 1971
THE FAILING OF RAYMOND (TF)
   Universal TV, 1971
HITCHED (TF)   Universal TV, 1973
DELIVER US FROM EVIL (TF)   Playboy
   Productions, 1973
INDICT AND CONVICT (TF)
   Universal TV, 1974
A CASE OF RAPE (TF) ☆   Universal TV, 1974
THE GREATEST GIFT (TF)
   Universal TV, 1974
THE DREAM MAKERS (TF)   MGM-TV, 1975
THE RUNAWAY BARGE (TF)
   Lorimar Productions, 1975
MAN ON THE OUTSIDE (TF)
   Universal TV, 1975
OREGON TRAIL (TF)   Universal TV, 1976
RICH MAN, POOR MAN (MS) ☆   co-director
   with David Greene, Universal TV, 1976
MALLORY: CIRCUMSTANTIAL
   EVIDENCE (TF)   Universal TV/Crescendo
   Productions/R.B. Productions, 1976
SHERLOCK HOLMES IN NEW YORK (TF)
   20th Century-Fox TV, 1976
ARTHUR HAILEY'S "THE MONEYCHANGERS"
   THE MONEYCHANGERS (MS)   Ross
   Hunter Productions/Paramount TV, 1976

ANGELA   1978, Canadian
THE AWAKENING LAND (MS)
   Bensen-Kuhn-Sagal Productions/
   Warner Bros. TV, 1978
IKE (MS)   co-director with Melville Shavelson,
   ABC Circle Films, 1979
THE DIARY OF ANNE FRANK (TF)
   Katz-Gallin/Half-Pint Productions/
   20th Century-Fox TV, 1980
WHEN THE CIRCUS CAME TO TOWN (TF)
   Entheos Unlimited Productions/Meteor
   Films, 1981
MASADA (MS) ☆   Arnon Milchan
   Productions/Universal TV, 1981
DIAL M FOR MURDER (TF)   Freyda Rothstein
   Productions/Time Life TV, 1981

LUCIANO SALCE
b. September 22, 1922 - Italy
d. 1989

LE PILLOLE D'ERCOLE   Maxima Film/Dino De
   Laurentiis Cinematografica, 1960, Italian
IL FEDERALE   Dino De Laurentiis
   Cinematografica, 1961, Italian
CRAZY DESIRE   LA VOGLIA MATTA
   Embassy, 1962, Italian
LA CUCCAGNA   CIRAC/Agliani
   Cinematografica, 1962, Italian
THE HOURS OF LOVE   Cinema 5,
   1963, Italian
THE LITTLE NUNS   Embassy, 1963, Italian
HIGH INFIDELITY   co-director with
   Mario Monicelli, Franco Rossi & Elio Petri,
   Magna, 1964, Italian-French
KISS THE OTHER SHEIK   *OGGI, DOMANI E
   DOPODOMANI*   co-director with
   Marco Ferreri & Eduardo de Filippo, MGM,
   1965, Italian-French
SLALOM   Fair Film/Cocinor/Copro Film, 1965,
   Italian-French-British
EL GRECO   20th Century-Fox, 1966,
   Italian-French
THE QUEENS   *LE FATE*   co-director with
   Mario Monicelli, Mauro Bolognini &
   Antonio Pietrangeli, Royal Films
   International, 1966, Italian-French
TI HO SPOSATO PER ALLEGRIA   Fair Film,
   1967, Italian
LA PECORA NERA   Fair Film, 1969, Italian
COLPO DI STATO   Vides, 1969, Italian
IL PROF. DR. GUIDO TERSILLI, PRIMARIO
   DELLA CLINICA VILLA CELESTE,
   CONVENZIONATA CON LE MUTUE
   San Marco, 1969, Italian
BASTA GUARDARLA   Fair Film, 1971, Italian
IL PROVINCIALE   Fair Film, 1971, Italian
IO E LUI   Dino De Laurentiis Cinematografica,
   1973, Italian
FANTOZZI   Cineriz, 1975, Italian
IL SECONDO TRAGICO FANTOZZI
   Cineriz, 1976, Italian
LA PRESIDENTESSA   Gold Film,
   1976, Italian
L'ANATRA ALL'ARANCIA   Cineriz,
   1976, Italian
IL...BELPAESE   77 Cinematografica,
   1977, Italian
DOVE VAI IN VACANZA?   co-director with
   Mauro Bolognini & Alberto Sordi, Cineriz,
   1978, Italian
PROFESSOR KRANZ TEDESCO DI
   GERMANIA   Gold Film, 1979,
   Italian-Brazilian
RIAVANTI...MARSCH!   PAC, 1980, Italian
RAG. ARTURO DE FANTI BANCARIO
   PRECARIO   PAC, 1980, Italian

THE INNOCENTS ABROAD (TF)   Nebraska
ETV Network/The Great Amwell Company/
WNET-13, 1983
VEDIAMOCI CHIARO   Adige Film 76,
1984, Italian
QUELLI DELL CASCO   Filmauro,
1988, Italian

MARK SANDRICH

b. August 26, 1900 - New York, New York
d. 1945

RUNAWAY GIRLS   Columbia, 1928
THE TALK OF HOLLYWOOD
Sono Art-World Wide, 1930
MELODY CRUISE   RKO RADIO, 1933
AGGIE APPLEBY - MAKER OF MEN
RKO RADIO, 1933
HIPS HIPS HOORAY   RKO RADIO, 1934
COCKEYED CAVALIERS   RKO RADIO, 1934
THE GAY DIVORCEE   RKO Radio, 1934
TOP HAT   RKO Radio, 1935
FOLLOW THE FLEET   RKO Radio, 1936
A WOMAN REBELS   RKO Radio, 1936
SHALL WE DANCE?   RKO Radio, 1937
CAREFREE   RKO Radio, 1938
MAN ABOUT TOWN   Paramount, 1939
BUCK BENNY RIDES AGAIN
Paramount, 1940
LOVE THY NEIGHBOR   Paramount, 1940
SKYLARK   Paramount, 1941
HOLIDAY INN   Paramount, 1941
SO PROUDLY WE HAIL!   Paramount, 1943
HERE COME THE WAVES   Paramount, 1944
I LOVE A SOLDIER   Paramount, 1944

ALFRED SANTELL

b. September 14, 1895 - San Francisco,
California
d. 1981

MY VALET   1915
OUT OF THE BAG   1917
HOME JAMES   1918
VAMPING THE VAMP   1918
IT MIGHT HAPPEN TO YOU   1920
WILDCAT JORDAN   Phil Goldstone, 1922
LIGHTS OUT   Film Booking Offices, 1923
FOOLS IN THE DARK   FBO, 1924
EMPTY HEARTS   Banner, 1924
THE MAN WHO PLAYED SQUARE
Fox, 1924
THE MARRIAGE WHIRL   First National, 1925
PARISIAN NIGHTS   FBO, 1925
CLASSIFIED   First National, 1925
BLUEBEARD'S SEVEN WIVES
First National, 1926
THE DANCER OF PARIS   First National, 1926
SWEET DADDIES   First National, 1926
SUBWAY SADIE   First National, 1926
JUST ANOTHER BLONDE
First National, 1926
ORCHIDS AND ERMINE   First National, 1927
THE PATENT LEATHER KID
First National, 1927
THE GORILLA   First National, 1927
THE LITTLE SHEPHERD OF KINGDOM COME
First National, 1928
WHEEL OF CHANCE   First National, 1928
SHOW GIRL   First National, 1928
THIS IS HEAVEN   United Artists, 1929
TWIN BEDS   First National, 1929
ROMANCE OF THE RIO GRANDE   Fox, 1929
THE ARIZONA KID   Fox, 1930
THE SEA WOLF   Fox, 1930
BODY AND SOUL   Fox, 1931
DADDY LONG LEGS   Fox, 1931

SOB SISTER   Fox, 1931
POLLY OF THE CIRCUS   Fox, 1932
REBECCA OF SUNNYBROOK FARM
Fox, 1932
TESS OF THE STORM COUNTRY   Fox, 1932
BONDAGE   Fox, 1933
THE RIGHT TO ROMANCE
RKO RADIO, 1933
THE LIFE OF VERGIE WINTERS
RKO RADIO, 1934
PEOPLE WILL TALK   Paramount, 1935
A FEATHER IN HER HAT   Columbia, 1935
WINTERSET   RKO RADIO, 1936
INTERNES CAN'T TAKE MONEY
Paramount, 1937
BREAKFAST FOR TWO   RKO Radio, 1937
COCONUT GROVE   Paramount, 1938
HAVING A WONDERFUL TIME
RKO Radio, 1938
THE ARKANSAS TRAVELER
Paramount, 1938
OUR LEADING CITIZEN   Paramount, 1939
ALOMA OF THE SOUTH SEAS
Paramount, 1941
BEYOND THE BLUE HORIZON
Paramount, 1942
JACK LONDON   United Artists, 1943
THE HAIRY APE   United Artists, 1944
MEXICANA   Republic, 1945
THAT BRENNAN GIRL   Republic, 1946

JOSEPH SANTLEY
(Joseph Mansfield)
b. January 10, 1889 - Salt Lake City, Utah
d. 1971

THE COCOANUTS   co-director with
Robert Florey, Paramount, 1929
SWING HIGH   1930
THE LOUDSPEAKER   1934
YOUNG AND BEAUTIFUL   1934
MILLION DOLLAR BABY   1935
HARMONY LANE   1935
WATERFRONT LADY   1935
DANCING FEET   1936
LAUGHING IRISH EYES   1936
HER MASTER'S VOICE   1936
THE HARVESTER   1936
WE WENT TO COLLEGE   1936
WALKING ON AIR   1936
THE SMARTEST GIRL IN TOWN   1936
MEET THE MISSUS   1937
THERE GOES THE GROOM   1937
SHE'S GOT EVERYTHING   1938
BLONDE CHEAT   1938
ALWAYS IN TROUBLE   1938
SWING, SISTER, SWING   1938
SPIRIT OF CULVER   Universal, 1939
THE FAMILY NEXT DOOR   1939
TWO BRIGHT BOYS   1939
MUSIC IN MY HEART   Columbia, 1940
MELODY AND MOONLIGHT   1940
MELODY RANCH   1940
BEHIND THE NEWS   1940
DANCING ON A DIME   Paramount, 1941
SIS HOPKINS   Republic, 1941
ROOKIES ON PARADE   Republic, 1941
PUDDIN'HEAD   Republic, 1941
ICE-CAPADES   Republic, 1941
DOWN MEXICO WAY   Republic, 1941
A TRAGEDY AT MIDNIGHT   Republic, 1942
YOKEL BOY   Republic, 1942
REMEMBER PEARL HARBOR
Republic, 1942
JOAN OF OZARK   Republic, 1942
CALL OF THE CANYON   Republic, 1942
CHATTERBOX   Republic, 1943
SHANTYTOWN   Republic, 1943

THUMBS UP   Republic, 1943
SLEEPY LAGOON   Republic, 1943
HERE COMES ELMER   Republic, 1943
ROSIE THE RIVETER   Republic, 1944
JAMBOREE   Republic, 1944
GOODNIGHT SWEETHEART   Republic, 1944
THREE LITTLE SISTERS   Republic, 1944
BRAZIL   Republic, 1944
EARL CARROLL VANITIES   Republic, 1945
HITCHHIKE TO HAPPINESS   Republic, 1945
SHADOW OF A WOMAN   Warner Bros., 1946
MAKE BELIEVE BALLROOM   Columbia, 1949
WHEN YOU'RE SMILING   Columbia, 1950

VICTOR SAVILLE

b. September 25 - Birmingham, England
d. 1979

CONQUEST OF OIL (FD)   1921, British
THE ARCADIANS   Gaumont-British,
1927, British
A WOMAN IN PAWN   co-director with
Edwin Greenwood, 1927, British
THE GLAD EYE   co-director with
Maurice Elvey, Gaumont-British,
1927, British
TESHA   British International, 1928, British
KITTY   British International, 1929, British
WOMAN TO WOMAN   Gainsborough,
1929, British
THE W PLAN   Gaumont-British, 1930, British
A WARM CORNER   Gaumont-British,
1930, British
THE SPORT OF KINGS   Gaumont-British,
1931, British
THE CALENDAR   co-director with
T. Hayes Hunter, 1931, British
SUNSHINE SUSIE   Gaumont-British,
1931, British
MICHAEL AND MARY   Gaumont-British,
1931, British
HINDLE WAKES   Gaumont-British,
1932, British
THE FAITHFUL HEART   Gaumont-British,
1932, British
LOVE ON WHEELS   Gaumont-British,
1932, British
THE GOOD COMPANIONS   Gaumont-British,
1933, British
I WAS A SPY   Gaumont-British, 1933, British
FRIDAY THE 13TH   Gaumont-British,
1933, British
EVENSONG   Gaumont-British, 1934, British
EVERGREEN   Gaumont-British, 1934, British
THE IRON DUKE   Gaumont-British,
1934, British
THE DICTATOR   *THE LOVE AFFAIR OF A
DICTATOR/LOVES OF A DICTATOR*
1935, British
ME AND MARLBOROUGH   Gaumont-British,
1935, British
FIRST A GIRL   Gaumont-British, 1935, British
IT'S LOVE AGAIN   Gaumont-British,
1936, British
DARK JOURNEY   1937, British
STORM IN A TEACUP   co-director with
Ian Dalrymple, 1937, British
ACTION FOR SLANDER   co-director with
Tim Whelan, 1937, British
SOUTH RIDING   1938, British
FOREVER AND A DAY   co-director,
RKO Radio, 1943
TONIGHT AND EVERY NIGHT
Columbia, 1945
THE GREEN YEARS   MGM, 1946
GREEN DOLPHIN STREET   MGM, 1947
IF WINTER COMES   MGM, 1948
CONSPIRATOR   MGM, 1949, British

KIM   MGM, 1950
CALLING BULLDOG DRUMMOND   MGM,
  1951, British
AFFAIR IN MONTE CARLO   *24 HOURS IN A*
  WOMAN'S LIFE   Allied Artists, 1952, British
THE LONG WAIT   United Artists, 1954
THE SILVER CHALICE   Warner Bros., 1955

FRANKLIN J. SCHAFFNER

b. May 30, 1920 - Tokyo, Japan
d. 1989

THE STRIPPER   20th Century-Fox, 1962
THE BEST MAN   United Artists, 1964
THE WAR LORD   Universal, 1965
THE DOUBLE MAN   Warner Bros.,
  1968, British
PLANET OF THE APES
  20th Century-Fox, 1968
PATTON ★★   20th Century-Fox, 1970
NICHOLAS AND ALEXANDRA   Columbia,
  1971, British
PAPILLON   Allied Artists, 1973
ISLANDS IN THE STREAM   Paramount, 1977
THE BOYS FROM BRAZIL
  20th Century-Fox, 1978
SPHINX   Orion/Warner Bros., 1981
YES, GIORGIO   MGM/UA, 1982
LIONHEART   Orion, 1987
WELCOME HOME   Columbia, 1989

DORE SCHARY

b. August 31, 1905 - Newark, New Jersey
d. 1980

ACT ONE   Warner Bros., 1963

VICTOR SCHERTZINGER

b. April 8, 1880 - Mahanoy City, Pennsylvania
d. 1941

THE CLODHOPPER   Triangle, 1917
THE MILLIONAIRE VAGRANT   Triangle, 1917
THE PINCH HITTER   Triangle, 1917
SUDDEN JIM   Triangle, 1917
THE SON OF HIS FATHER   Paramount, 1917
HIS MOTHER'S BOY   Paramount, 1918
THE HIRED MAN   Paramount, 1918
THE FAMILY SKELETON   Ince-Triangle, 1918
PLAYING THE GAME   Paramount, 1918
HIS OWN HOME TOWN   Paramount, 1918
THE CLAWS OF THE HUN   Paramount, 1918
A NINE O'CLOCK TOWN   Ince-Triangle, 1918
STRING BEANS   Paramount, 1918
THE HOMEBREAKER   Paramount, 1919
HARD BOILED   Paramount, 1919
THE LADY OF RED BUTTE   Paramount, 1919
OTHER MEN'S WIVES   Paramount, 1919
THE SHERIFF'S SON   Paramount, 1919
QUICKSAND   Paramount, 1919
UPSTAIRS   Goldwyn, 1919
THE PEACE OF ROARING RIVER
  Goldwyn, 1919
WHEN DOCTORS DISAGREE
  Goldwyn, 1919
THE JINX   Goldwyn, 1919
PINTO   Goldwyn, 1920
THE BLOOMING ANGEL   Goldwyn, 1920
THE SLIM PRINCESS   Goldwyn, 1920
MADE IN HEAVEN   Goldwyn, 1921
THE CONCERT   Goldwyn, 1921
WHAT HAPPENED TO ROSA?
  Goldwyn, 1921
BEATING THE GAME   Goldwyn, 1921
MR. BARNES OF NEW YORK
  Goldwyn, 1921

HEAD OVER HEELS   Goldwyn, 1921
THE BOOTLEGGER'S DAUGHTER
  Associated Exhibitors, 1921
THE KINGDOM WITHIN
  WW. Hodkinson, 1921
SCANDALOUS TONGUES   Associated
  Exhibitors, 1921
THE LONELY ROAD   First National, 1922
THE SCARLET LILY   First National, 1922
REFUGE   First National, 1923
DOLLAR DEVILS   W.W. Hodkinson, 1923
THE MAN NEXT DOOR   Vitagraph, 1923
LONG LIVE THE KING   Metro, 1923
THE MAN LIFE PASSED BY   Metro, 1923
CHASTITY   First National, 1923
A BOY OF FLANDERS   Metro-Goldwyn, 1924
BREAD   Metro-Goldwyn, 1924
FRIVOLOUS SAL   First National, 1925
MAN AND MAID   Metro-Goldwyn, 1925
THE WHEEL   Fox, 1925
THUNDER MOUNTAIN   Fox, 1925
THE GOLDEN STRAIN   First National, 1925
SIBERIA   Fox, 1926
THE LILY   Fox, 1926
THE RETURN OF PETER GRIMM   Fox, 1926
STAGE MADNESS   Fox, 1927
THE HEART OF SALOME   Fox, 1927
THE SECRET STUDIO   Fox, 1927
THE SHOWDOWN   Paramount, 1928
FORGOTTEN FACES   Paramount, 1928
MANHATTAN COCKTAIL   Paramount, 1928
REDSKIN   Paramount, 1929
FASHIONS IN LOVE   Paramount, 1929
THE WHEEL OF LIFE   Paramount, 1929
NOTHING BUT THE TRUTH
  Paramount, 1929
THE LAUGHING LADY   Paramount, 1929
PARAMOUNT ON PARADE   co-director,
  Paramount, 1930
SAFETY IN NUMBERS   Paramount, 1930
HEADS UP   Paramount, 1930
THE WOMAN BETWEEN   RKO RADIO, 1931
FRIENDS AND LOVERS   RKO RADIO, 1931
STRANGE JUSTICE   RKO RADIO, 1932
UPTOWN NEW YORK   Sono Art-World
  Wide, 1932
COCKTAIL HOUR   Columbia, 1933
THE CONSTANT WOMAN   World Wide, 1933
MY WOMAN   Columbia, 1933
BELOVED   Universal, 1934
ONE NIGHT OF LOVE ★   Columbia, 1934
LET'S LIVE TONIGHT   Columbia, 1935
LOVE ME FOREVER   Columbia, 1935
THE MUSIC GOES 'ROUND   Columbia, 1936
FOLLOW YOUR HEART   1936
SOMETHING TO SING ABOUT
  Grand National, 1937
THE MIKADO   Universal, 1939, British
ROAD TO SINGAPORE   Paramount, 1940
RHYTHM ON THE RIVER   Paramount, 1940
ROAD TO ZANZIBAR   Paramount, 1941
KISS THE BOYS GOODBYE
  Paramount, 1941
BIRTH OF THE BLUES   Paramount, 1941
THE FLEET'S IN   Paramount, 1942

ERNEST B. SCHOEDSACK
(Ernest Beaumont Schoedsack)
b. June 8, 1893 - Council Bluffs, Iowa
d. 1979

GRASS: A NATION'S BATTLE FOR LIFE
  GRASS: THE EPIC OF A LOST TRIBE (FD)
  co-director with Merian C. Cooper,
  Paramount, 1926
CHANG   co-director with Merian C. Cooper,
  Paramount, 1927

THE FOUR FEATHERS   co-director with
  Merian C.Cooper & Lothar Mendes,
  United Artists, 1929
RANGE (FD)   Paramount, 1931
THE MOST DANGEROUS GAME   co-director
  with Irving Pichel, RKO Radio, 1932
KING KONG   co-director with
  Merian C. Cooper, RKO Radio, 1933
THE SON OF KONG   RKO Radio, 1933
BLIND ADVENTURE   RKO Radio, 1933
LONG LOST FATHER   RKO Radio, 1934
THE LAST DAYS OF POMPEII
  RKO Radio, 1935
TROUBLE IN MOROCCO   Columbia, 1937
OUTLAWS OF THE ORIENT   Columbia, 1937
DR. CYCLOPS   Paramount, 1940
MIGHTY JOE YOUNG   RKO Radio, 1949

HAROLD SCHUSTER

b. August 1, 1902 - Cherokee, Iowa
d. 1986

WINGS OF THE MORNING   20th Century-Fox,
  1937, British
DINNER AT THE RITZ
  20th Century-Fox, 1937
STRANGE CARGO   MGM, 1940
ZANZIBAR   Universal, 1940
SMALL TOWN DEB   20th Century-Fox, 1941
A VERY YOUNG LADY
  20th Century-Fox, 1941
GIRL TROUBLE   20th Century-Fox, 1942
BOMBER'S MOON   20th-Century Fox, 1943
MY FRIEND FLICKA   20th Century-Fox, 1943
MARINE RAIDERS   RKO Radio, 1944
BLACK BEAUTY   20th Century-Fox, 1946
BREAKFAST IN HOLLYWOOD
  United Artists, 1946
FRAMED   Columbia, 1947
SO DEAR TO MY HEART   RKO Radio, 1948
THE TENDER YEARS
  20th Century-Fox, 1948
JACK SLADE   Allied Artists, 1953
LOOPHOLE   Allied Artists, 1954
SECURITY RISK   Allied Artists, 1954
PORT OF HELL   Allied Artists, 1954
TARZAN'S HIDDEN JUNGLE
  RKO Radio, 1955
FINGER MAN   Allied Artists, 1955
THE RETURN OF JACK SLADE
  Allied Artists, 1955
PORTLAND EXPOSE   Allied Artists, 1957
DRAGOON WELLS MASSACRE
  Allied Artists, 1957

FRED F. SEARS

b. July 7, 1913 - Boston, Massachusetts
d. 1957

DESERT VIGILANTE   Columbia, 1949
HORSEMEN OF THE SIERRA
  Columbia, 1949
ACROSS THE BADLANDS   Columbia, 1950
RAIDERS OF TOMAHAWK CREEK
  Columbia, 1950
LIGHTNING GUNS   Columbia, 1950
PRAIRIE ROUNDUP   Columbia, 1951
RIDIN' THE OUTLAW TRAIL   Columbia, 1951
SNAKE RIVER DESPERADOES
  Columbia, 1951
BONANZA TOWN   Columbia, 1951
PECOS RIVER   Columbia, 1951
SMOKY CANYON   Columbia, 1952
THE HAWK OF WILD RIVER   Columbia, 1952
THE KID FROM BROKEN GUN
  Columbia, 1952

LAST TRAIN FROM BOMBAY
  Columbia, 1952
TARGET - HONG KONG   Columbia, 1953
AMBUSH AT TOMAHAWK GAP
  Columbia, 1953
THE 49TH MAN   Columbia, 1953
MISSION OVER KOREA   Columbia, 1953
SKY COMMANDO   Columbia, 1953
THE NEBRASKAN   Columbia, 1953
EL ALAMEIN   Columbia, 1954
OVERLAND PACIFIC   Columbia, 1954
THE MIAMI STORY   Columbia, 1954
MASSACRE CANYON   Columbia, 1954
THE OUTLAW STALLION   Columbia, 1954
WYOMING RENEGADES   Columbia, 1955
CELL 2455 - DEATH ROW   Columbia, 1955
CHICAGO SYNDICATE   Columbia, 1955
APACHE AMBUSH   Columbia, 1955
TEEN-AGE CRIME WAVE   Columbia, 1955
INSIDE DETROIT   Columbia, 1956
FURY AT GUNSIGHT PASS   Columbia, 1956
ROCK AROUND THE CLOCK
  Columbia, 1956
EARTH VS. THE FLYING SAUCERS
  Columbia, 1956
THE WEREWOLF   Columbia, 1956
MIAMI EXPOSE   Columbia, 1956
CHA-CHA-CHA BOOM!   Columbia, 1956
RUMBLE ON THE DOCKS   Columbia, 1956
DON'T KNOCK THE ROCK   Columbia, 1957
UTAH BLAINE   Columbia, 1957
CALYPSO HEAT WAVE   Columbia, 1957
THE NIGHT THE WORLD EXPLODED
  Columbia, 1957
THE GIANT CLAW   Columbia, 1957
ESCAPE FROM SAN QUENTIN
  Columbia, 1957
THE WORLD WAS HIS JURY
  Columbia, 1958
GOING STEADY   Columbia, 1958
CRASH LANDING   Columbia, 1958
BADMAN'S COUNTRY   Columbia, 1958
GHOST OF THE CHINA SEAS
  Columbia, 1958

VICTOR SEASTROM
(See Victor SJOSTROM)

GEORGE SEATON
b. April 17, 1911 - South Bend, Indiana
d. 1979

BILLY ROSE'S DIAMOND HORSESHOE
  20th Century-Fox, 1945
JUNIOR MISS   20th Century-Fox, 1945
THE SHOCKING MISS PILGRIM
  20th Century-Fox, 1947
MIRACLE ON 34TH STREET
  20th Century-Fox, 1947
APARTMENT FOR PEGGY
  20th Century-Fox, 1948
CHICKEN EVERY SUNDAY
  20th Century-Fox, 1949
THE BIG LIFT   20th Century-Fox, 1950
FOR HEAVEN'S SAKE
  20th Century-Fox, 1950
ANYTHING CAN HAPPEN   Paramount, 1952
LITTLE BOY LOST   Paramount, 1953
THE COUNTRY GIRL ★   Paramount, 1954
THE PROUD AND THE PROFANE
  Paramount, 1956
WILLIAMSBURG: THE STORY OF
  A PATRIOT (FD)   1957
TEACHER'S PET   Paramount, 1958
THE PLEASURE OF HIS COMPANY
  Paramount, 1961

THE COUNTERFEIT TRAITOR
  Paramount, 1962
THE HOOK   MGM, 1963
36 HOURS   MGM, 1966
WHAT'S SO BAD ABOUT FEELING GOOD?
  Universal, 1968
AIRPORT   Universal, 1970
SHOWDOWN   Universal, 1973

LEWIS SEILER
b. 1891 - New York, New York
d. 1963

DARWIN WAS RIGHT   1924
NO MAN'S GOLD   1926
THE GREAT K&A TRAIN ROBBERY   1926
THE LAST TRAIL   1927
TUMBLING RIVER   1927
OUTLAWS OF RED RIVER   1927
WOLF FANGS   1927
SQUARE CROOKS   1928
THE AIR CIRCUS   co-director with
  Howard Hawks, Fox, 1928
THE GHOST WALKS   1929
GIRLS GONE WILD   1929
A SONG OF KENTUCKY   1929
NO GREATER LOVE   1932
DECEPTION   1932
FRONTIER MARSHAL   1934
ASEGURE A SU MUJER   1935
CHARLIE CHAN IN PARIS
  20th Century-Fox, 1935
GINGER   1935
PADDY O'DAY   1935
HERE COMES TROUBLE   1936
THE FIRST BABY   1936
STAR FOR A NIGHT   1936
CAREER WOMAN   1936
TURN OFF THE MOON   Paramount, 1937
HE COULDN'T SAY NO   1938
CRIME SCHOOL   Warner Bros., 1938
PENROD'S DOUBLE TROUBLE
  Warner Bros., 1938
HEART OF THE NORTH   Warner Bros., 1938
KING OF THE UNDERWORLD
  Warner Bros., 1939
YOU CAN'T GET AWAY WITH MURDER
  Warner Bros., 1939
THE KID FROM KOKOMO
  Warner Bros., 1939
HELL'S KITCHEN   co-director with
  E.A. Dupont, Warner Bros., 1939
DUST BE MY DESTINY   Warner Bros., 1939
IT ALL CAME TRUE   Warner Bros., 1940
FLIGHT ANGELS   Warner Bros., 1940
MURDER IN THE AIR   Warner Bros., 1940
TUGBOAT ANNIE SAILS AGAIN
  Warner Bros., 1940
SOUTH OF SUEZ   Warner Bros., 1940
KISSES FOR BREAKFAST
  Warner Bros., 1941
THE SMILING GHOST   Warner Bros., 1941
YOU'RE IN THE ARMY NOW
  Warner Bros., 1941
THE BIG SHOT   Warner Bros., 1942
PITTSBURGH   Universal, 1942
GUADALCANAL DIARY
  20th Century-Fox, 1943
SOMETHING FOR THE BOYS
  20th Century-Fox, 1944
DOLL FACE   20th Century-Fox, 1945
MOLLY AND ME   20th Century-Fox, 1945
IF I'M LUCKY   20th Century-Fox, 1946
WHIPLASH   Warner Bros., 1949
BREAKTHROUGH   Warner Bros., 1950
THE TANKS ARE COMING
  Warner Bros., 1951
THE WINNING TEAM   Warner Bros., 1952

OPERATION SECRET   Warner Bros., 1952
THE SYSTEM   Warner Bros., 1953
THE BAMBOO PRISON   Columbia, 1955
WOMEN'S PRISON   Columbia, 1955
BATTLE STATIONS   Columbia, 1956

WILLIAM A. SEITER
b. June 10, 1892 - New York, New York
d. 1964

TANGLED THREADS   1919
THE KENTUCKY COLONEL
  W.W. Hodkinson, 1920
HEARTS AND MASKS   Film Booking
  Offices, 1921
PASSING THROUGH   Paramount, 1921
THE FOOLISH AGE   Robertson-Cole, 1921
EDEN AND RETURN   Robertson-Cole, 1921
BOY CRAZY   Robertson-Cole, 1922
GAY AND DEVILISH   Robertson-Cole, 1922
THE UNDERSTUDY   FBO, 1922
UP AND AT 'EM   FBO, 1922
WHEN LOVE COMES   FBO, 1922
THE BEAUTIFUL AND THE DAMNED
  Warner Bros., 1922
BELL BOY 13   Associated First National, 1923
LITTLE CHURCH AROUND THE CORNER
  Warner Bros., 1923
DADDIES   Warner Bros., 1924
THE WHITE SIN   FBO, 1924
HIS FORGOTTEN WIFE   FBO, 1924
LISTEN LESTER   Principal, 1924
HELEN'S BABIES   Principal, 1924
THE FAMILY SECRET   Universal-Jewel, 1924
THE FAST WORKER   Universal-Jewel, 1924
THE MAD WHIRL   Universal-Jewel, 1925
DANGEROUS INNOCENCE
  Universal-Jewel, 1925
THE TEASER   Universal-Jewel, 1925
WHERE WAS I?   Universal-Jewel, 1925
WHAT HAPPENED TO JONES
  Universal-Jewel, 1926
SKINNER'S DRESS SUIT
  Universal-Jewel, 1926
ROLLING HOME   Universal, 1926
TAKE IT FROM ME   Universal-Jewel, 1926
THE CHEERFUL FRAUD   Universal, 1927
THE SMALL BACHELOR
  Universal-Jewel, 1927
OUT ALL NIGHT   Universal-Jewel, 1927
THANKS FOR THE BUGGY RIDE
  Universal-Jewel, 1928
GOOD MORNING JUDGE
  Universal-Jewel, 1928
HAPPINESS AHEAD   First National, 1928
WATERFRONT   First National, 1928
OUTCAST   First National, 1928
SYNTHETIC WIFE   *SYNTHETIC SON*
  First National, 1929
WHY BE GOOD?   First National, 1929
PRISONERS   First National, 1929
SMILING IRISH EYES   First National, 1929
FOOTLIGHTS AND FOOLS
  First National, 1929
THE LOVE RACKET   First National, 1929
STRICTLY MODERN   First National, 1930
BACK PAY   First National, 1930
THE FLIRTING WIDOW   First National, 1930
THE TRUTH ABOUT YOUTH
  First National, 1930
GOING WILD   First National, 1930
SUNNY   First National, 1930
KISS ME AGAIN   First National, 1931
BIG BUSINESS GIRL   First National, 1931
TOO MANY CROOKS   RKO RADIO, 1931
FULL OF NOTIONS   RKO RADIO, 1931
CAUGHT PLASTERED   RKO RADIO, 1931
PEACH O'RENO   RKO RADIO, 1931

WAY BACK HOME   RKO RADIO, 1932
GIRL CRAZY   RKO RADIO, 1932
YOUNG BRIDE   *LOVE STARVED*
   RKO RADIO, 1932
IS MY FACE RED?   RKO RADIO, 1932
HOT SATURDAY   Paramount, 1932
IF I HAD A MILLION   co-director,
   Paramount, 1932
HELLO EVERYBODY!   Paramount, 1933
DIPLOMANIACS   RKO RADIO, 1933
PROFESSIONAL SWEETHEART   RKO
   RADIO, 1933
CHANCE AT HEAVEN   RKO RADIO, 1933
SONS OF THE DESERT   MGM, 1934
RAFTER ROMANCE   RKO RADIO, 1934
SING AND LIKE IT   RKO RADIO, 1934
LOVE BIRDS   Universal, 1934
WE'RE RICH AGAIN   RKO RADIO, 1934
THE RICHEST GIRL IN THE WORLD
   RKO RADIO, 1934
ROBERTA   RKO Radio, 1935
THE DARING YOUNG MAN   Fox, 1935
ORCHIDS TO YOU   Fox, 1935
IN PERSON   RKO RADIO, 1935
IF YOU COULD ONLY COOK
   Columbia, 1935
THE MOON'S OUR HOME
   Paramount, 1936
THE CASE AGAINST MRS. AMES
   Paramount, 1936
DIMPLES   20th Century-Fox, 1936
STOWAWAY   20th Century-Fox, 1936
THIS IS MY AFFAIR   20th Century-Fox, 1937
THE LIFE OF THE PARTY
   20th Century-Fox, 1937
LIFE BEGINS IN COLLEGE
   20th Century-Fox, 1937
SALLY, IRENE AND MARY
   20th Century-Fox, 1938
THREE BLIND MICE
   20th Century-Fox, 1938
ROOM SERVICE   RKO Radio, 1938
THANKS FOR EVERYTHING
   20th Century-Fox, 1938
SUSANNAH OF THE MOUNTIES
   20th Century-Fox, 1939
ALLEGHENY UPRISING   RKO Radio, 1940
IT'S A DATE   Universal, 1940
HIRED WIFE   Universal, 1940
NICE GIRL?   Universal, 1941
APPOINTMENT FOR LOVE   Universal, 1941
BROADWAY   Universal, 1942
YOU WERE NEVER LOVELIER
   Columbia, 1942
DESTROYER   Columbia, 1943
A LADY TAKES A CHANCE
   RKO Radio, 1943
FOUR JILLS IN A JEEP
   20th Century-Fox, 1944
BELLE OF THE YUKON   RKO Radio, 1944
IT'S A PLEASURE   RKO Radio, 1945
THE AFFAIRS OF SUSAN   Paramount, 1945
THAT NIGHT WITH YOU   Universal, 1945
LITTLE GIANT   Universal, 1946
LOVER COME BACK   Universal, 1946
I'LL BE YOURS   Universal, 1947
UP IN CENTRAL PARK   Universal, 1948
ONE TOUCH OF VENUS   Universal, 1948
BORDERLINE   Universal, 1950
DEAR BRAT   Paramount, 1951
THE LADY WANTS MINK   Republic, 1953
CHAMP FOR A DAY   Republic, 1953
MAKE HASTE TO LIVE   Republic, 1954

GEORGE B. SEITZ
(George Brackett Seltz)
b. January 3, 1888 - Boston, Massachusetts
d. 1944

THE EXPLOITS OF ELAINE (S)   co-director
   with Louis Gasnier, Pathé, 1914
THE NEW EXPLOITS OF ELAINE (S)
   Pathé, 1915
THE ROMANCE OF ELAINE (S)   Pathé, 1915
THE IRON CLAW (S)   co-director with
   Edward Jose, 1916
THE KING'S GAME   1916
THE LAST OF THE CARNABYS   Pathé, 1917
THE HUNTING OF THE HAWK   Pathé, 1917
NEW YORK NIGHTS   Pathé, 1917
THE FATAL RING (S)   Pathé, 1917
GETAWAY KATE   Pathé, 1918
THE HONEST THIEF   Pathé, 1918
THE HOUSE OF HATE (S)   Pathé, 1918,
THE LIGHTNING RAIDER (S)   Pathé, 1918
THE BLACK SECRET (S)   Pathé, 1919
BOUND AND GAGGED (S)   Pathé, 1919
PIRATE GOLD (S)   Pathé, 1920
VELVET FINGERS (S)   1920
ROGUES AND ROMANCE   Pathé, 1920
THE SKY RANGER (S)   Pathé, 1921
HURRICANE HUTCH (S)   Pathé, 1922
SPEED (S)   Pathé, 1922
PLUNDER   Pathé, 1923, serial
THE WAY OF A MAN (S)   Pathé, 1924
LEATHERSTOCKING (S)   Pathé, 1924
THE 40TH DOOR (S)   Pathé, 1924
GALLOPING HOOFS (S)   Pathé, 1924
INTO THE NET   Pathé, 1924, serial
SUNKEN SILVER (S)   *SUNKEN SAILOR*
   Pathé, 1925
WILD HORSE MESA   Paramount, 1925
THE VANISHING AMERICAN
   Paramount, 1925
DESERT GOLD   Paramount, 1926
PALS IN PARADISE   Producers Distributing
   Corporation, 1926
THE ICE FLOOD   Universal, 1926
THE LAST FRONTIER   Producers Distributing
   Corporation, 1926
JIM THE CONQUEROR   Producers
   Distributing Corporation, 1927
THE GREAT MAIL ROBBERY   FBO, 1927
THE BLOOD SHIP   Columbia, 1927
THE TIGRESS   Columbia, 1927
THE ISLE OF FORGOTTEN WOMEN
   Columbia, 1927
THE WARNING   Columbia, 1927
RANSOM   Columbia, 1928
BEWARE OF BLONDES   Columbia, 1928
COURT-MARTIAL   Columbia, 1928
THE CIRCUS KID   Columbia, 1928
BLOCKADE   RKO RADIO, 1928
HEY RUBE!   FBO, 1928
BLACK MAGIC   Fox, 1929
MURDER ON THE ROOF   Columbia, 1930
GUILTY?   Columbia, 1930
MIDNIGHT MYSTERY   RKO RADIO, 1930
DANGER LIGHTS   RKO RADIO, 1930
THE DRUMS OF JEOPARDY   Tiffany, 1931
THE LION AND THE LAMB   Columbia, 1931
ARIZONA   *MEN ARE LIKE THAT*
   Columbia, 1931
SHANGHAIED LOVE   Columbia, 1931
NIGHT BEAT   Action, 1931
SALLY OF THE SUBWAY   Mayfair, 1932
DOCKS OF SAN FRANCISCO   Mayfair, 1932
SIN'S PAY DAY   Mayfair, 1932
PASSPORT TO PARADISE   Mayfair, 1932
THE WIDOW IN SCARLET   Mayfair, 1932
TREASON   Columbia, 1933
THE THRILL HUNTER   Columbia, 1933

THE WOMAN IN HIS LIFE   MGM, 1933
LAZY RIVER   MGM, 1934
THE FIGHTING RANGER   Columbia, 1934
ONLY EIGHT HOURS   MGM, 1935
SOCIETY DOCTOR   1935
SHADOW OF DOUBT   MGM, 1935
TIMES SQUARE LADY   MGM, 1935
CALM YOURSELF   MGM, 1935
WOMAN WANTED   MGM, 1935
KIND LADY   MGM, 1935
EXCLUSIVE STORY   MGM, 1936
ABSOLUTE QUIET   1936
THE THREE WISE GUYS   MGM, 1936
THE LAST OF THE MOHICANS
   United Artists, 1936
MAD HOLIDAY   MGM, 1936
UNDER COVER OF NIGHT   MGM, 1937
A FAMILY AFFAIR   MGM, 1937
THE 13TH CHAIR   MGM, 1937
MAMA STEPS OUT   MGM, 1937
BETWEEN TWO WOMEN   MGM, 1937
MY DEAR MISS ALDRICH   MGM, 1937
YOU'RE ONLY YOUNG ONCE   MGM, 1938
JUDGE HARDY'S CHILDREN   MGM, 1938
YELLOW JACK   MGM, 1938
LOVE FINDS ANDY HARDY   MGM, 1938
OUT WEST WITH THE HARDYS   MGM, 1938
THE HARDYS RIDE HIGH   MGM, 1939
SIX THOUSAND ENEMIES   MGM, 1939
THUNDER AFLOAT   MGM, 1939
JUDGE HARDY AND SON   MGM, 1939
ANDY HARDY MEETS DEBUTANTE
   MGM, 1940
KIT CARSON   United Artists, 1940
SKY MURDER   MGM, 1940
GALLANT SONS   MGM, 1940
ANDY HARDY'S PRIVATE SECRETARY
   MGM, 1941
LIFE BEGINS FOR ANDY HARDY
   MGM, 1941
A YANK ON THE BURMA ROAD   MGM, 1942
THE COURTSHIP OF ANDY HARDY
   MGM, 1942
PIERRE OF THE PLAINS   MGM, 1942
ANDY HARDY'S DOUBLE LIFE   MGM, 1942
ANDY HARDY'S BLONDE TROUBLE
   MGM, 1944

STEVE SEKELY
(Istvan Szekely)
b. February 25, 1899 - Budapest, Hungary
d. 1979

RHAPSODIE DER LIEBE   1929, Austrian
DIE GROSSE SEHNSUCHT   1930, German
SEITENSPRUNGE   1930, German
ER UND SEIN DIENER   1931, German
EIN STEINREICHER MANN   1932, German
PIRI MINDONT TUD   1932, Hungarian
SCANDAL IN BUDAPEST   co-director with
   Geza von Bolvary, 1933, German-Hungarian
RAKOCZI MARSCH   1933,
   German-Hungarian
IDA REGENYE   1934, Hungarian
LILA AKAC   1934, Hungarian
BALL IM SAVOY   1934, Austrian-Hungarian
EMMY   1934, Hungarian
CAFE MOSZKVA   1936, Hungarian
SZENSACIO   co-director with Ladislao Vajda,
   1936, Hungarian
AN AFFAIR OF HONOR   1936
TWO PRISONERS   1937, Hungarian
BEAUTY OF THE PUSZTA   1937, Hungarian
I MARRIED FOR LOVE   1937, Hungarian
HEART TO HEART   1938, Hungarian
A MIRACLE ON MAIN STREET
   Columbia, 1940

BEHIND PRISON WALLS   PRC, 1941
REVENGE OF THE ZOMBIES
   Monogram, 1943
WOMEN IN BONDAGE   Monogram, 1944
LADY IN THE DEATH HOUSE   PRC, 1944
WATERFRONT   PRC, 1944
MY BUDDY   Republic, 1944
LAKE PLACID SERENADE   Republic, 1944
THE FABULOUS SUZANNE   Republic, 1946
BLONDE SAVAGE   Eagle Lion, 1947
HOLLOW TRIUMPH   *THE SCAR*
   Eagle Lion, 1948
AMAZON QUEST   Film Classics, 1949
STRONGHOLD   Lippert, 1952
L'AVVENTURE DI CARTOUCHE   co-director
   with Gianni Vernuccio, 1954, Italian
THE DAY OF THE TRIFFIDS   Allied Artists,
   1963, British
KENNER   MGM, 1969
THE GIRL WHO LIKED PURPLE FLOWERS
   1973, Hungarian

LESLEY SELANDER
b. May 26, 1900 - Los Angeles, California
d. 1979

RIDE 'EM COWBOY   Universal, 1936
EMPTY SADDLES   Universal, 1936
THE BOSS RIDER OF GUN CREEK
   Universal, 1936
SMOKE TREE RANGE   Universal, 1937
SANDFLOW   Universal, 1937
LEFT-HANDED LAW   Universal, 1937
THE BARRIER   Paramount, 1937
HOPALONG RIDES AGAIN   Paramount, 1937
BLACK ACES   1937
PARTNERS OF THE PLAINS
   Paramount, 1938
BAR 20 JUSTICE   Paramount, 1938
HEART OF ARIZONA   Paramount, 1938
PRIDE OF THE WEST   Paramount, 1938
THE MYSTERIOUS RIDER   Paramount, 1938
SUNSET TRAIL   Paramount, 1938
THE FRONTIERSMAN   Paramount, 1938
SILVER ON THE SAGE   Paramount, 1939
THE RENEGADE TRAIL   Paramount, 1939
HERITAGE OF THE DESERT
   Paramount, 1939
RANGE WAR   Paramount, 1939
SANTA FE MARSHAL   Paramount, 1939
THREE MEN FROM TEXAS
   Paramount, 1940
KNIGHTS OF THE RANGE   Paramount, 1940
HIDDEN GOLD   Paramount, 1940
STAGECOACH WAR   Paramount, 1940
THE LIGHT OF THE WESTERN STARS
   Mayer-Burstyn, 1940
CHEROKEE STRIP   Paramount, 1940
WIDE OPEN TOWN   Paramount, 1941
RIDERS OF THE TIMBERLINE
   Paramount, 1941
STICK TO YOUR GUNS   Paramount, 1941
THE ROUNDUP   Paramount, 1941
DOOMED CARAVAN   Paramount, 1941
PIRATES ON HORSEBACK
   Paramount, 1941
THUNDERING HOOFS   RKO RADIO, 1941
BANDIT RANGER   RKO RADIO, 1942
THE UNDERCOVER MAN
   United Artists, 1942
LOST CANYON   United Artists, 1942
BAR 20   United Artists, 1943
RIDERS OF THE DEADLINE
   United Artists, 1943
COMRADES   United Artists, 1943
BUCKSKIN FRONTIER   United Artists, 1943
BORDER PATROL   United Artists, 1943

COLT COMRADES   United Artists, 1943
RIDERS OF THE DEADLINE   Republic, 1944
BORDERLINE TRAIL   Republic, 1944
STAGECOACH TO MONTEREY
   Republic, 1944
CHEYENNE WILDCAT   Republic, 1944
FIREBRANDS OF ARIZONA   Republic, 1944
SHERIFF OF LAS VEGAS   Republic, 1944
SHERIFF OF SUNDOWN   Republic, 1944
LUMBERJACK   United Artists, 1944
CALL OF THE ROCKIES   Republic, 1944
FORTY THIEVES   United Artists, 1944
THE GREAT STAGECOACH ROBBERY
   Republic, 1945
PHANTOM OF THE PLAINS   Republic, 1945
JUNGLE RAIDERS (S)   Columbia, 1945
THE TRAIL OF KIT CARSON   Republic, 1945
THE VAMPIRE'S GHOST   Republic, 1945
THE LAST FRONTIER UPRISING
   Republic, 1946
THE CATMAN OF PARIS   Republic, 1946
PASSKEY TO DANGER   Republic, 1946
TRAFFIC IN CRIME   Republic, 1946
NIGHT TRAIN TO MEMPHIS   Republic, 1946
OUT CALIFORNIA WAY   Republic, 1946
SADDLE PALS   Republic, 1947
THE PILGRIM LADY   Republic, 1947
ROBIN HOOD OF TEXAS   Republic, 1947
BLACKMAIL   Republic, 1947
THE RED STALLION   Eagle Lion, 1947
STRIKE IT RICH   Allied Artists, 1948
PANHANDLE   Allied Artists, 1948
GUNS OF HATE   RKO Radio, 1948
BELLE STARR'S DAUGHTER
   20th Century-Fox, 1948
INDIAN AGENT   RKO Radio, 1948
RUSTLERS   RKO RADIO, 1949
BROTHERS IN THE SADDLE
   RKO Radio, 1949
RIDERS OF THE RANGE   RKO Radio, 1949
RIDER FROM TUCSON   RKO Radio, 1950
RIO GRANDE PATROL   RKO Radio, 1950
SHORT GRASS   Allied Artists, 1950
STAMPEDE   Monogram, 1949
SKY DRAGON   Monogram, 1949
MASKED RAIDERS   RKO Radio, 1949
THE MYSTERIOUS DESPERADO
   RKO Radio, 1949
DAKOTA LIL   20th Century-Fox, 1950
STORM OVER WYOMING   RKO Radio, 1950
THE KANGAROO KID   Eagle Lion, 1950
LAW OF THE BADLANDS   RKO Radio, 1950
CAVALRY SCOUT   Monogram, 1951
I WAS AN AMERICAN SPY
   Allied Artists, 1951
THE HIGHWAYMAN   Allied Artists, 1951
SADDLE LEGION   RKO RADIO, 1951
GUNPLAY   RKO RADIO, 1951
FLIGHT TO MARS   Monogram, 1951
PISTOL HARVEST   RKO Radio, 1951
OVERLAND TELEGRAPH   RKO Radio, 1951
TRAIL GUIDE   RKO Radio, 1952
FORT OSAGE   Monogram, 1952
THE RIDING KID   United Artists, 1952
ROAD AGENT   RKO Radio, 1952
DESERT PASSAGE   RKO Radio, 1952
THE RAIDERS   Universal, 1952
BATTLE ZONE   Allied Artists, 1952
FLAT TOP   Allied Artists, 1952
COW COUNTRY   Allied Artists, 1953
FORT VENGEANCE   Allied Artists, 1953
WAR PAINT   United Artists, 1953
FORT ALGIERS   United Artists, 1953
THE ROYAL AFRICAN RIFLES
   Allied Artists, 1953
FIGHTER ATTACK   Allied Artists, 1953
ARROW IN THE DUST   Allied Artists, 1954
RETURN FROM THE SEA   Allied Artists, 1954

THE YELLOW TOMAHAWK
   United Artists, 1954
DRAGONFLY SQUADRON
   Allied Artists, 1954
SHOTGUN   Allied Artists, 1955
TALL MAN RIDING   Warner Bros., 1955
DESERT SANDS   United Artists, 1955
FORT YUMA   United Artists, 1955
QUINCANNON, FRONTIER SCOUT
   United Artists, 1956
THE BROKEN STAR   United Artists, 1956
TAMING SUTTON'S GAL   Republic, 1957
THE WAYWARD GIRL   Republic, 1957
TOMAHAWK TRAIL   United Artists, 1957
REVOLT AT FORT LARAMIE
   United Artists, 1957
OUTLAW'S SON   United Artists, 1957
THE LONE RANGER AND THE LOST CITY
   OF GOLD   United Artists, 1958
FORT COURAGEOUS
   20th Century-Fox, 1965
WAR PARTY   20th Century-Fox, 1965
CONVICT STAGE   20th Century-Fox, 1965
TOWN TAMER   Paramount, 1965
THE TEXICAN   Columbia, 1966
FORT UTAH   Paramount, 1967
ARIZONA BUSHWHACKERS
   Paramount, 1968

LARRY SEMON
b. July 6, 1889 - West Point, Mississippi
d. 1928

THE MAN FROM EGYPT   Vitagraph, 1916
A VILLAINOUS VILLAIN   Vitagraph, 1916
LOVE AND LOOT   Vitagraph, 1916
FOOTLIGHTS AND FAKERS   Vitagraph, 1917
ROUGH TOUGHS AND ROOF TOPS
   Vitagraph, 1917
BOASTS AND BOLDNESS   Vitagraph, 1917
SPOOKS AND SPASMS   Vitagraph, 1917
BABES AND BOOBS   Vitagraph, 1918
SPIES AND SPILLS   Vitagraph, 1918
PASSING THE BUCK   Vitagraph, 1919
THE SIMPLE LIFE   Vitagraph, 1919
THE STAGEHAND   co-director,
   Vitagraph, 1920
THE SUITOR   co-director, Vitagraph, 1920
THE SPORTSMAN   co-director,
   Vitagraph, 1921
THE FALL GUY   co-director, Vitagraph, 1921
THE SAWMILL   co-director, Vitagraph, 1922
THE SHOW   co-director, Vitagraph, 1922
THE SLEUTH   co-director, Vitagraph, 1922
NO WEDDING BELLS   1923
MIDNIGHT CABARET   1923
THE GIRL IN THE LIMOUSINE   1924
THE WIZARD OF OZ   1925
STOP, LOOK AND LISTEN   1926
SPUDS   1927

MACK SENNETT
(Mikall Sinnott)
b. January 17, 1880 - Danville, Quebec, Canada
d. 1960

THE LUCKY TOOTHACHE   Biograph, 1910
THE MASHER   Biograph, 1910
COMRADES   Biograph, 1911
CUPID'S JOKE   Biograph, 1911
THE COUNTRY LOVERS   Biograph, 1911
THE MANICURE LADY   Biograph, 1911
A DUTCH GOLD MINE   Biograph, 1911
THE WONDERFUL EYE   Biograph, 1911
THE GHOST   Biograph, 1911
THE BEAUTIFUL VOICE   Biograph, 1911
THE VILLAGE HERO   Biograph, 1911

TOO MANY BURGLARS   Biograph, 1911
THE INVENTOR'S SECRET   Biograph, 1911
THEIR FIRST DIVORCE   Biograph, 1911
RESOURCEFUL LOVERS   Biograph, 1911
CAUGHT WITH THE GOODS   Biograph, 1911
THE JOKE ON THE JOKER   Biograph, 1912
BRAVE AND BOLD   Biograph, 1912
PANTS AND PANSIES   Biograph, 1912
THE FATAL CHOCOLATE   Biograph, 1912
A SPANISH DILEMMA   Biograph, 1912
HOT STUFF   Biograph, 1912
OH THOSE EYES!   Biograph, 1912
THOSE HICKSVILLE BOYS   Biograph, 1912
THE LEADING MAN   Biograph , 1912
WHEN THE FIRE BELLS RANG
   Biograph, 1912
NEIGHBORS   Biograph, 1912
THE NEW BABY   Biograph, 1912
ONE-ROUND O'BRIEN   Biograph, 1912
THE SPEED DEMON   Biograph, 1912
WILLIE BECOMES AN ARTIST
   Biograph, 1912
THE TOURISTS   Biograph, 1912
COHEN COLLECTS A DEBT   Keystone, 1912
THE WATER NYMPH   Keystone, 1912
THE NEW NEIGHBOR   Keystone, 1912
PEDRO'S DILEMMA   Keystone, 1912
STOLEN GLORY   Keystone, 1912
THE AMBITIOUS BUTLER   Keystone, 1912
AT CONEY ISLAND   Keystone, 1912
MABEL'S LOVERS   Keystone, 1912
THE RIVALS   Keystone, 1912
MR. FIXIT   Keystone, 1912
BROWN'S SEANCE   Keystone, 1912
THE DRUMMER'S VACATION
   Keystone, 1912
THE DUEL   Keystone, 1912
A DOUBLE WEDDING   Keystone, 1913
THE MISTAKEN MASHER   Keystone, 1913
THE ELITE BALL   Keystone, 1913
THE BATTLE OF WHO RUN   Keystone, 1913
A RED HOT ROMANCE   Keystone, 1913
THE SLEUTH'S LAST STAND
   Keystone, 1913
A STRONG REVENGE   Keystone, 1913
AT TWELVE O'CLOCK   Keystone, 1913
HER NEW BEAU   Keystone, 1913
THOSE GOOD OLD DAYS   Keystone, 1913
A GAME OF POKER   Keystone, 1913
A LIFE IN THE BALANCE   Keystone, 1913
A FISHY AFFAIR   Keystone, 1913
THE BANGVILLE POLICE   Keystone, 1913
THE NEW CONDUCTOR   Keystone, 1913
THAT RAGTIME BAND   Keystone, 1913
ALGY ON THE FORCE   Keystone, 1913
HIS UPS AND DOWNS   Keystone, 1913
MABEL'S AWFUL MISTAKE   Keystone, 1913
THE FOREMAN OF THE JURY
   Keystone, 1913
THE GANGSTERS   Keystone, 1913
BARNEY OLDFIELD'S RACE FOR A LIFE
   Keystone, 1913
THE HANSOM DRIVER   Keystone, 1913
THE SPEED QUEEN   Keystone, 1913
THE WAITERS' PICNIC   Keystone, 1913
THE TALE OF A BLACK EYE   Keystone, 1913
SAFE IN JAIL   Keystone, 1913
THE TELLTALE LIGHT   Keystone, 1913
A NOISE FROM THE DEEP   Keystone, 1913
COHEN'S OUTING   Keystone, 1913
THE FIREBUGS   Keystone, 1913
MABEL'S NEW HERO   Keystone, 1913
THE GYPSY QUEEN   Keystone, 1913
THE FAITHFUL TAXICAB   Keystone, 1913
SCHNITZ THE TAILOR   Keystone, 1913
A HEALTHY NEIGHBORHOOD
   Keystone, 1913
TWO OLD TARS   Keystone, 1913

A QUIET LITTLE WEDDING   Keystone, 1913
THE SPEED KINGS   Keystone, 1913
LOVE SICKNESS AT SEA   Keystone, 1913
COHEN SAVES THE FLAG   Keystone, 1913
ZUZU THE BAND LEADER   Keystone, 1913
THE GUSHER   Keystone, 1913
A BAD GAME   Keystone, 1913
SOME NERVE   Keystone, 1913
LOVE AND DYNAMITE   Keystone, 1914
IN THE CLUTCHES OF THE GANG
   co-director with George Nicholls,
   Keystone, 1914
TOO MANY BRIDES   Keystone, 1914
MABEL'S STRANGE PREDICAMENT
   co-director with Henry "Pathé" Lehrman,
   Keystone, 1914
TANGO TANGLES   Keystone, 1914
MACK IT AGAIN   Keystone, 1914
A BATHING BEAUTY   Keystone, 1914
MABEL AT THE WHEEL   co-director with
   Mabel Normand, Keystone, 1914
TWENTY MINUTES OF LOVE
   Keystone, 1914
THE FATAL FLIRTATION   Keystone, 1914
THE KNOCKOUT   Keystone, 1914
MABEL'S LATEST PRANK   Keystone, 1914
HE LOVED THE LADIES   Keystone, 1914
THE HIGH SPOTS ON BROADWAY
   Keystone, 1914
STOUT HEART BUT WEAK KNEES
   Keystone, 1914
TILLIE'S PUNCTURED ROMANCE
   Keystone, 1914
A COLORED GIRL'S LOVE   Keystone, 1914
FOR BETTER - BUT WORSE   Triangle Film
   Corporation, 1915
THOSE COLLEGE GIRLS   Triangle Film
   Corporation, 1915
THE LITTLE TEACHER   Triangle Film
   Corporation, 1915
MY VALET   Triangle Film Corporation, 1915
A FAVORITE FOOL   Triangle Film
   Corporation, 1915
STOLEN MAGIC   Triangle Film
   Corporation, 1915
HOME TALENT   co-director with
   James E. Abbe, Mack Sennett
   Comedies, 1921
OH MABEL, BEHAVE   co-director with
   Ford Sterling, Mack Sennett
   Comedies, 1922
A FINISHED ACTOR   Pathé, 1928
THE LION'S ROAR   Pathé, 1928
THE BRIDE'S RELATIONS   Educational, 1929
WHIRLS AND GIRLS   Educational, 1929
THE BIG PALOOKA   Educational, 1929
GIRL CRAZY   Educational, 1929
JAZZ MAMAS   Educational, 1929
THE GOLFERS   Educational, 1929
A HOLLYWOOD STAR   Educational, 1929
CLANCY AT THE BAT   Educational, 1929
SCOTCH   Educational, 1930
SUGAR PLUM PAPA   Educational, 1930
BULLS AND BEARS   Educational, 1930
HONEYMOON ZEPPELIN   Educational, 1930
FAT WIVES FOR THIN   Educational, 1930
CAMPUS CRUSHERS   Educational, 1930
THE CHUMPS   Educational, 1930
GOODBYE LEGS   Educational, 1930
MIDNIGHT DADDIES   Educational, 1930
DIVORCED SWEETHEARTS
   Educational, 1930
RACKET CHEERS   Educational, 1930
A POOR FISH   Educational, 1931
DANCE HALL MARGE   Educational, 1931
GHOST PARADE   Educational, 1931
MONKEY BUSINESS IN AFRICA
   Educational, 1931

MOVIE TOWN   Educational, 1931
FAINTING LOVER   Educational, 1931
I SURRENDER DEAR   Educational, 1931
SPEED   Educational, 1931
ONE MORE CHANCE   Educational, 1931
HYPNOTIZED   Paramount, 1932
YE OLD SAW MILL   Educational, 1935
FLICKER FEVER   Educational, 1935
JUST ANOTHER MURDER
   Educational, 1935
THE TIMID YOUNG MAN   Educational, 1935
WAY UP THAR   Educational, 1935

BARRY SHEAR
b. 1923 - New York, New York
d. 1979

WILD IN THE STREETS   American
   International, 1968
NIGHT GALLERY (TF)   co-director with
   Boris Sagal & Steven Spielberg,
   Universal TV, 1969
THE TODD KILLINGS   National General, 1971
ELLERY QUEEN: YOU DON'T LOOK BEHIND
   YOU (TF)   Universal TV, 1971
ACROSS 110TH STREET
   United Artists, 1972
SHORT WALK TO DAYLIGHT (TF)
   Universal TV, 1972
THE DEADLY TRACKERS
   Warner Bros., 1973
JARRETT (TF)   Screen Gems/
   Columbia TV, 1973
PUNCH AND JODY (TF)   Metromedia
   Producers Corporation/Stonehenge
   Productions, 1974
STRIKE FORCE (TF)   D'Antoni-Weitz
   Television Productions, 1975
STARSKY AND HUTCH (TF)
   Spelling-Goldberg Productions, 1975
THE SAN PEDRO BEACH BUMS (TF)
   Aaron Spelling Productions, 1977
KEEFER (TF)   David Gerber Productions/
   Columbia TV, 1978
CRASH (TF)   Charles Fries Productions, 1978
THE BILLION DOLLAR THREAT (TF)   David
   Gerber Productions/Columbia TV, 1979
UNDERCOVER WITH THE KKK (TF)
   Columbia TV,1979
POWER (TF)   co-director with Virgil Vogel,
   David Gerber Company/Columbia TV, 1980

LARISSA SHEPITKO
b. 1939 - Armtervosk, Eastern Ukraine, U.S.S.R.
d. 1979

HEAT   1963, Soviet
WINGS   1966, Soviet
THE BEGINNING OF AN UNKNOWN
   CENTURY   1968, Soviet
THE ASCENT   1977, Soviet

JACK SHER
b. March 16, 1913 - Minneapolis, Minnesota
d. 1988

FOUR GIRLS IN TOWN   Universal, 1957
KATHY O'   Universal, 1958
THE WILD AND THE INNOCENT
   Universal, 1959
THE THREE WORLDS OF GULLIVER
   Columbia, 1960, British
LOVE IN A GOLDFISH BOWL
   Paramount, 1961

GEORGE SHERMAN
b. July 14, 1908 - New York, New York
d. 1991

WILD HORSE RODEO   Republic, 1938
THE PURPLE VIGILANTES   Republic, 1938
OUTLAWS OF SONORA   Republic, 1938
RIDERS OF THE BLACK HILLS
  Republic, 1938
PALS OF THE SADDLE   Republic, 1938
OVERLAND STAGE RAIDERS
  Republic, 1938
RHYTHM OF THE SADDLE   Republic, 1938
SANTA FE STAMPEDE   Republic, 1938
RED RIVER RANGE   Republic, 1938
MEXICALI ROSE   Republic, 1939
THE NIGHT RIDERS   Republic, 1939
THREE TEXAS STEERS   Republic, 1939
WYOMING OUTLAW   Republic, 1939
COLORADO SUNSET   Republic, 1939
NEW FRONTIER   Republic, 1939
COWBOYS FROM TEXAS   Republic, 1939
THE KANSAS TERRORS   Republic, 1939
ROVIN' TUMBLEWEEDS   Republic, 1939
SOUTH OF THE BORDER   Republic, 1939
GHOST VALLEY RAIDERS   Republic, 1940
ONE MAN'S LAW   Republic, 1940
THE TULSA KID   Republic, 1940
TEXAS TERRORS   Republic, 1940
COVERED WAGON DAYS   Republic, 1940
ROCKY MOUNTAIN RANGERS
  Republic, 1940
UNDER TEXAS SKIES   Republic, 1940
THE TRAIL BLAZERS   Republic, 1940
LONE STAR RAIDERS   Republic, 1940
FRONTIER VENGEANCE   Republic, 1940
WYOMING WILDCAT   Republic, 1941
THE PHANTOM COWBOY   Republic, 1941
TWO GUN SHERIFF   Republic, 1941
DESERT BANDIT   Republic, 1941
KANSAS CYCLONE   Republic, 1941
DEATH VALLEY OUTLAWS   Republic, 1941
A MISSOURI OUTLAW   Republic, 1941
CITADEL OF CRIME   Republic, 1941
THE APACHE KID   Republic, 1941
ARIZONA TERRORS   Republic, 1942
STAGECOACH EXPRESS   Republic, 1942
JESSE JAMES JR.   Republic, 1942
THE CYCLONE KID   Republic, 1942
THE SOMBRERO KID   Republic, 1942
X MARKS THE SPOT   Republic, 1942
LONDON BLACKOUT MURDERS
  Republic, 1942
THE PURPLE V   Republic, 1943
THE MANTRAP   Republic, 1943
THE WEST SIDE KID   Republic, 1943
MYSTERY BROADCAST   Republic, 1943
THE LADY AND THE MONSTER
  Republic, 1944
STORM OVER LISBON   Republic, 1944
THE CRIME DOCTOR'S COURAGE
  Columbia, 1945
THE GENTLEMAN MISBEHAVES
  Columbia, 1946
RENEGADES   Columbia, 1946
TALK ABOUT A LADY   Columbia, 1946
THE BANDIT OF SHERWOOD FOREST
  co-director with Henry Levin,
  Columbia, 1946
PERSONALITY KID   Columbia, 1947
SECRETS OF THE WHISTLER
  Columbia, 1947
LAST OF THE REDMEN   Columbia, 1947
RELENTLESS   Columbia, 1948
BLACK BART   Universal, 1948
RIVER LADY   Universal, 1948
LARCENY   Universal, 1948

RED CANYON   Universal, 1949
CALAMITY JANE AND SAM BASS
  Universal, 1949
YES SIR, THAT'S MY BABY   Universal, 1949
SWORD IN THE DESERT   Universal, 1949
SPY HUNT   Universal, 1950
THE SLEEPING CITY   Universal, 1950
FEUDIN', FUSSIN' AND A-FIGHTIN'
  Universal, 1950
COMANCHE TERRITORY   Universal, 1950
TOMAHAWK   Universal, 1951
TARGET UNKNOWN   Universal, 1951
THE RAGING TIDE   Universal, 1951
THE GOLDEN HORDE   Universal, 1951
STEEL TOWN   Universal, 1952
AGAINST ALL FLAGS   Universal, 1952
THE BATTLE AT APACHE PASS
  Universal, 1952
BACK AT THE FRONT   Universal, 1952
THE LONE HAND   Universal, 1953
WAR ARROW   Universal, 1953
VEILS OF BAGDAD   Universal, 1953
BORDER RIVER   Universal, 1954
DAWN AT SOCORRO   Universal, 1954
CHIEF CRAZY HORSE   Universal, 1955
COUNT THREE AND PRAY   Universal, 1955
THE TREASURE OF PANCHO VILLA
  Universal, 1955
COMANCHE   Universal, 1956
REPRISAL!   Columbia, 1956
THE HARD MAN   Columbia, 1957
THE LAST OF THE FAST GUNS
  Universal, 1958
TEN DAYS TO TULARA   United Artists, 1958
THE SON OF ROBIN HOOD
  20th Century-Fox, 1959
THE FLYING FONTAINES   Columbia, 1959
HELL BENT FOR LEATHER   Universal, 1960
FOR THE LOVE OF MIKE
  20th Century-Fox, 1960
THE ENEMY GENERAL   Columbia, 1960
THE WIZARD OF BAGHDAD
  20th Century-Fox, 1960
THE FIERCEST HEART
  20th Century-Fox, 1961
PANIC BUTTON   Gorton, 1964
MURIETA   Warner Bros., 1965, Spanish
SMOKY   20th Century-Fox, 1966
BIG JAKE   National General, 1971

ESTHER SHUB
b. March 3, 1894 - Chernigovsky District,
  Ukraine, Russia
d. 1959

THE FALL OF THE ROMANOV DYNASTY (FD)
  1927, Soviet
THE GREAT ROAD (FD)   1927, Soviet
THE RUSSIA OF NICHOLAS II AND LEO
  TOLSTOY (FD)   1928, Soviet
TODAY   CANNONS OR TRACTORS (FD)
  1930, Soviet
KSE   KOMSOMOL (FD)   1932, Soviet
MOSCOW BUILDS THE METRO (FD)
  1934, Soviet
LAND OF THE SOVIETS (FD)   1937, Soviet
SPAIN (FD)   1939, Soviet
TWENTY YEARS OF CINEMA (FD)
  co-director with Vsevelod Pudovkin,
  1940, Soviet
FASCISM WILL BE DESTROYED   THE FACE
  OF THE ENEMY   1941, Soviet
NATIVE COUNTRY (FD)   1942, Soviet
ACROSS THE ARAKS (FD)   1947, Soviet

VASILY SHUKSHIN
b. July 5, 1929 - Strotsky, Siberia, U.S.S.R.
d. 1974

REPORT FROM LEBIAZHE   1960, Soviet
THERE WAS A LAD   1964, Soviet
YOUR SON AND BROTHER   1966, Soviet
STRANGE PEOPLE   1970, Soviet
THAT'S THE WAY IT IS   HAPPY GO LUCKY
  1972, Soviet, unreleased
THE RED SNOWBALL TREE   1974, Soviet

HERMAN SHUMLIN
b. December 6, 1898 - Atwood, Colorado
d. 1979

WATCH ON THE RHINE   Warner Bros., 1943
CONFIDENTIAL AGENT   Warner Bros., 1945

DON SIEGEL
b. October 26, 1912 - Chicago, Illinois
d. 1991

THE VERDICT   Warner Bros., 1946
NIGHT UNTO NIGHT   Warner Bros., 1949
THE BIG STEAL   RKO Radio, 1949
DUEL AT SILVER CREEK   Universal, 1952
NO TIME FOR FLOWERS   RKO Radio, 1952
COUNT THE HOURS   RKO Radio, 1953
CHINA VENTURE   Columbia, 1953
RIOT IN CELL BLOCK 11   Allied Artists, 1954
PRIVATE HELL 36   Filmmakers, 1954
AN ANNAPOLIS STORY   Allied Artists, 1955
INVASION OF THE BODY SNATCHERS
  Allied Artists, 1956
CRIME IN THE STREETS   Allied Artists, 1956
BABY FACE NELSON   Allied Artists, 1957
SPANISH AFFAIR   Paramount, 1958, Spanish
THE LINEUP   Columbia, 1958
THE GUN RUNNERS   United Artists, 1958
HOUND DOG MAN   20th Century-Fox, 1959
EDGE OF ETERNITY   Columbia, 1959
FLAMING STAR   20th Century-Fox, 1960
HELL IS FOR HEROES   Paramount, 1962
THE KILLERS   Universal, 1964
THE HANGED MAN (TF)   Universal TV, 1964
STRANGER ON THE RUN (TF)
  Universal TV, 1967
MADIGAN   Universal, 1968
COOGAN'S BLUFF   Universal, 1968
DEATH OF A GUNFIGHTER   co-director with
  Robert Totten, both directed under
  pseudonym of Allen Smithee,
  Universal, 1969
TWO MULES FOR SISTER SARA   Universal,
  1970, U.S.-Mexican
THE BEGUILED   Universal, 1971
DIRTY HARRY   Warner Bros., 1972
CHARLEY VARRICK   Universal, 1973
THE BLACK WINDMILL   Universal,
  1974, British
THE SHOOTIST   Paramount, 1976
TELEFON   MGM/United Artists, 1977
ESCAPE FROM ALCATRAZ
  Paramount, 1979
ROUGH CUT   Paramount, 1980
JINXED   MGM/UA, 1982

S. SYLVAN SIMON
b. March 9, 1910 - Chicago, Illinois
d. 1951

A GIRL WITH IDEAS   Universal, 1937
PRESCRIPTION FOR ROMANCE
  Universal, 1937
THE CRIME OF DR. HALLET   Universal, 1938
NURSE FROM BROOKLYN   Universal, 1938

THE ROAD TO RENO   Universal, 1938
SPRING MADNESS   Universal, 1938
FOUR GIRLS IN WHITE   Universal, 1939
THE KID FROM TEXAS   Universal, 1939
THESE GLAMOUR GIRLS   MGM, 1939
DANCING CO-ED   MGM, 1939
TWO GIRLS ON BROADWAY   MGM, 1940
SPORTING BLOOD   MGM, 1940
DULCY   MGM, 1940
KEEPING COMPANY   MGM, 1940
WASHINGTON MELODRAMA   MGM, 1941
WHISTLING IN THE DARK   MGM, 1941
THE BUGLE SOUNDS   MGM, 1941
RIO RITA   MGM, 1942
GRAND CENTRAL MURDER   MGM, 1942
TISH   MGM, 1942
WHISTLING IN DIXIE   MGM, 1942
SALUTE TO THE MARINES   MGM, 1943
WHISTLING IN BROOKLYN   MGM, 1943
SONG OF THE OPEN ROAD
   United Artists, 1944
SON OF LASSIE   MGM, 1945
ABBOTT & COSTELLO IN HOLLYWOOD
   MGM, 1945
BAD BASCOMB   MGM, 1946
THE THRILL OF BRAZIL   Columbia, 1946
THE COCKEYED MIRACLE   MGM, 1946
HER HUSBAND'S AFFAIRS   Columbia, 1947
I LOVE TROUBLE   Columbia, 1947
THE FULLER BRUSH MAN   Columbia, 1948
LUST FOR GOLD   Columbia, 1949

ROBERT SIODMAK
b. August 8, 1900 - Memphis, Tennessee
d. 1973

MENSCHEN AM SONNTAG (FD)   co-director
   with Edgar G. Ulmer, 1929, German
ABSCHIED   SO SIND DIE MENSCHEN
   1930, German
DER MANN DER SEINEN MORDER SUCHT
   1931, German
VORUNTERSUCHUNG   1931, German
STURME DER LEIDENSCHAFT   TEMPEST
   1932, German
QUICK - KONIG DER CLOWNS
   1932, German
BRENNENDES GEHEIMNIS   THE BURNING
   SECRET   1933, German
LE SEXE FAIBLE   1933, French
LA CRISE EST FINIE   THE SLUMP IS OVER
   1934, French
LA VIE PARISIENNE   1936, French
MISTER FLOW   COMPLIMENTS OF MISTER
   FLOW   1936, French
CARGAISON BLANCHE   WOMAN RACKET
   1937, French
MOLLENARD   HATRED   1938, French
ULTIMATUM   co-director with Robert Wiene,
   1938, French
PIEGES   PERSONAL COLUMN
   1939, French
WEST POINT WIDOW   Paramount, 1941
FLY BY NIGHT   Paramount, 1942
THE NIGHT BEFORE THE DIVORCE
   20th Century-Fox, 1942
MY HEART BELONGS TO DADDY
   Paramount, 1942
SOMEONE TO REMEMBER   Republic, 1943
SON OF DRACULA   Universal, 1943
PHANTOM LADY   Universal, 1944
COBRA WOMAN   Universal, 1944
CHRISTMAS HOLIDAY   Universal, 1944
THE SUSPECT   Universal, 1945
CONFLICT   Warner Bros., 1945
UNCLE HARRY   THE STRANGE AFFAIR OF
   UNCLE HARRY   Universal, 1945
THE SPIRAL STAIRCASE   RKO Radio, 1946

THE KILLERS ★   Universal, 1946
THE DARK MIRROR   Universal, 1946
TIME OUT OF MIND   Universal, 1947
CRY OF THE CITY   20th Century-Fox, 1948
CRISS CROSS   Universal, 1949
THE GREAT SINNER   MGM, 1949
THE FILE ON THELMA JORDAN
   Paramount, 1949
DEPORTED   Universal, 1950
THE WHISTLE AT EATON FALLS
   Columbia, 1951
THE CRIMSON PIRATE   Warner Bros., 1952,
   U.S.-British
FLESH AND THE WOMAN   LE GRAND JEU
   Dominant Pictures, 1954, French-Italian
DIE RATTEN   1955, West German
MEIN VATER DER SCHAUSPIELER   1956,
   West German
THE DEVIL STRIKES AT NIGHT
   NACHTS, WENN DERTEUFEL KAM
   Zenith International, 1957, West German
DOROTHEA ANGERMANN   1959,
   West German
PORTRAIT OF A SINNER   THE ROUGH AND
   THE SMOOTH   American International,
   1959, British
MAGNIFICENT SINNER   UNE JEUNE FILLE,
   UN SEULAMOUR/KATYA   Film-Mart,
   1959, French
MEIN SCHULFREUND   1960, West German
L'AFFAIRE NINA B   1962,
   French-West German
ESCAPE FROM EAST BERLIN   MGM, 1962,
   West German-U.S.
DER SCHUT   1964, West German
DER SCHATZ DER AZTEKEN   1965,
   West German-Italian-Spanish
DIE PYRAMIDE DES SONNENGOTTES
   1965, West German-Italian-Spanish
CUSTER OF THE WEST   Cinerama Releasing
   Corporation, 1968, U.S.-Spanish
DER KAMPF UM ROM   1969,
   West German-Italian

DOUGLAS SIRK
(Detlef Sierck/Claus Detlev Sierk)
b. April 26, 1900 - Skagen, Denmark
d. 1987

APRIL APRIL   1935, German
STUTZEN DER GESELLSCHAFT
   1935, German
DAS MADCHEN VON MOORHOF
   1935, German
DAS HOFKONZERT   1936, German
SCHLUSSAKKORD   1936, German
LA HABANERA   1937, German
LIEBLING DER MATROSEN   1937, German
ZU NEUEN UFERN   1937, German
DIE HEIMAT RUFT   1937, German
WILTON'S ZOO   1938, South African
HITLER'S MADMAN   MGM, 1943
SUMMER DREAM   United Artists, 1944
A SCANDAL IN PARIS   United Artists, 1946
LURED   Universal, 1947
SLEEP MY LOVE   United Artists, 1948
SLIGHTLY FRENCH   Columbia, 1949
SHOCKPROOF   Columbia, 1949
MYSTERY SUBMARINE   Universal, 1950
THE FIRST LEGION   United Artists, 1951
THUNDER ON THE HILL   Universal, 1951
THE LADY PAYS OFF   Universal, 1951
WEEKEND WITH FATHER   1951
NO ROOM FOR THE GROOM
   Universal, 1952
HAS ANYBODY SEEN MY GAL?
   Universal, 1952

MEET ME AT THE FAIR   Universal, 1953
TAKE ME TO TOWN   Universal, 1953
ALL I DESIRE   Universal, 1953
TAZA, SON OF COCHISE   Universal, 1954
MAGNIFICENT OBSESSION   Universal, 1954
SIGN OF THE PAGAN   Universal, 1954
CAPTAIN LIGHTFOOT   Universal, 1955
THERE'S ALWAYS TOMORROW
   Universal, 1956
ALL THAT HEAVEN ALLOWS
   Universal, 1956
WRITTEN ON THE WIND   Universal, 1956
BATTLE HYMN   Universal, 1957
INTERLUDE   Universal, 1957
THE TARNISHED ANGELS   Universal, 1958
A TIME TO LOVE AND A TIME TO DIE
   Universal, 1958
IMITATION OF LIFE   Universal, 1959

ALF SJOBERG
b. June 21, 1903 - Stockholm, Sweden
d. 1980

THE STRONGEST   1929, Swedish
THEY STAKED THEIR LIVES   1940, Swedish
BLOSSOM TIME   1940, Swedish
HOME FROM BABYLON   1941, Swedish
HIMLASPELET   1942, Swedish
TORMENT   Oxford Films, 1944, Swedish
THE ROYAL HUNT   1944, Swedish
JOURNEY OUT   1945, Swedish
IRIS AND THE LIEUTENANT   1946, Swedish
ONLY A MOTHER   1949, Swedish
MISS JULIE   Trans-Global Pictures,
   1951, Swedish
BARABBAS   1953, Swedish
KARIN, DAUGHTER OF MAN   1954, Swedish
WILD BIRDS   1955, Swedish
LAST PAIR OUT   1956, Swedish
THE JUDGE   1960, Swedish
THE ISLAND   1966, Swedish
THE FATHER   1969, Swedish

VICTOR SJOSTROM
(Victor Seastrom)
b. September 20, 1879 - Silbodal, Sweden
d. 1960

THE GARDENER   1912, Swedish
A SECRET MARRIAGE   1912, Swedish
A SUMMER TALE   1912,
   Swedish, unreleased
THE MARRIAGE BUREAU   1913, Swedish
SMILES AND TEARS   1913, Swedish
LADY MARION'S SUMMER FLIRTATION
   1913, Swedish
THE VOICE OF BLOOD   1913, Swedish
INGEBORG HOLM   1913, Swedish
LIFE'S CONFLICTS   1913, Swedish
THE CLERGYMAN   1914, Swedish
LOVE STRONGER THAN HATE
   1914, Swedish
HALF-BREED   1914, Swedish
THE MIRACLE   1914, Swedish
DO NOT JUDGE   1914, Swedish
A GOOD GIRL SHOULD SOLVE HER OWN
   PROBLEMS   1914, Swedish
CHILDREN OF THE STREET   1914, Swedish
DAUGHTER OF THE HIGH MOUNTAIN
   1914, Swedish
HEARTS THAT MEET   1914, Swedish
THE STRIKE   1915, Swedish
ONE OUT OF MANY   1915, Swedish
EXPIATED GUILT   1915, Swedish
IT WAS IN MAY   1915, Swedish
KEEP TO YOUR TRADE   1915, Swedish
JUDAS MONEY   1915, Swedish

THE GOVERNOR'S DAUGHTERS
1916, Swedish
SEA VULTURES 1916, Swedish
AT THE MOMENT OF TRIAL 1916, Swedish
SHIPS THAT MEET 1916, Swedish
SHE WAS VICTORIOUS 1916, Swedish
THERESE 1916, Swedish
THE KISS OF DEATH 1917, Swedish
A MAN THERE WAS 1917, Swedish
THE OUTLAW AND HIS WIFE 1918, Swedish
THE SONS OF INGMAR, PART I
1919, Swedish
THE SONS OF INGMAR, PART II
1919, Swedish
A GIRL FROM THE MARSH CROFT
1919, Swedish
HIS GRACE'S WILL 1919, Swedish
THE MONASTERY OF SENDOMIR
1920, Swedish
KARIN, DAUGHTER OF INGMAR
1920, Swedish
THE EXECUTIONER 1920, Swedish
THE PHANTOM CARRIAGE 1921, Swedish
LOVE'S CRUCIBLE 1922, Swedish
THE SURROUNDED HOUSE 1922, Swedish
FIRE ON BOARD 1922, Swedish
NAME THE MAN MGM, 1924
HE WHO GETS SLAPPED MGM, 1924
CONFESSIONS OF A QUEEN MGM, 1925
THE TOWER OF LIES MGM, 1925
THE SCARLET LETTER MGM, 1926
THE DIVINE WOMAN MGM, 1928
THE WIND MGM, 1928
MARKS OF THE DEVIL MGM, 1928
A LADY TO LOVE MGM, 1930
MARKURELLS I WADKOPING
1931, Swedish
UNDER THE RED ROBE 20th Century-Fox,
1937, British

PHILLIPS SMALLEY
(Wendell Phillips Smalley)
b. August 7, 1875 - Brooklyn, New York
d. 1939

BELLA'S BEAU 1912
THE CHORUS GIRL 1912
THE MIND CURE 1912
HEROIC HAROLD 1913
THAT OTHER GIRL 1913
ACCIDENT INSURANCE 1913
PEARL'S ADMIRERS 1913
WHERE CHARITY BEGINS 1913
THE GIRL REPORTER 1913
THE BROKEN SPELL 1913
WILLIE'S GREAT SCHEME 1913
THE JEW'S CHRISTMAS co-director with
Lois Weber, 1913
THE RING 1914
LIZZIE AND THE ICEMAN 1914
THE SPIDER AND HER WEB 1914
BEHIND THE VEIL co-director with
Lois Weber, 1914
THE MERCHANT OF VENICE co-director
with Lois Weber, Universal, 1914
SHADOWED 1914
WILLIE'S DISGUISE 1914
FALSE COLORS co-director with Lois Weber,
Paramount, 1914
SUNSHINE MOLLY co-director with
Lois Weber, Paramount, 1915
SCANDAL co-director with Lois Weber,
Universal, 1915
THE YANKEE GIRL 1915
A CIGARETTE - THAT'S ALL 1915
HOP - THE DEVIL'S BREW co-director with
Lois Weber, Universal, 1916

THE DUMB GIRL OF PORTICI co-director
with Lois Weber, Universal, 1916
WHERE ARE MY CHILDREN? co-director
with Lois Weber, Universal, 1916
THE FLIRT co-director with Lois Weber,
Universal, 1916

MRS. PHILLIPS SMALLEY
(See Lois WEBER)

GEORGE ALBERT SMITH
b. 1864 - Brighton, England
d. 1959

THE HAUNTED CASTLE 1897, British
THE CORSICAN BROTHERS 1897, British
WAVES AND SPRAY 1898, British
THE MILLER AND THE SWEEP 1898, British
CINDERELLA 1898, British
FAUST AND MEPHISTOPHELES
1898, British
THE LEGACY 1899, British
ALADDIN AND THE WONDERFUL LAMP
1899, British
THE HOUSE THAT JACK BUILT 1900, British
GRANDMA'S READING GLASS 1900, British
MOTHER GOOSE NURSERY RHYMES
1902, British
DOROTHY'S DREAM 1903, British
KINEMACOLOR PUZZLE 1909, British

R. G. (BUD) SPRINGSTEEN
b. September 8, 1904 - Tacoma, Washington
d. 1989

MARSHAL OF LAREDO Republic, 1945
WAGON WHEELS WESTWARD
Republic, 1945
CALIFORNIA GOLD RUSH Republic, 1946
HOME ON THE RANGE Republic, 1946
CONQUEST OF CHEYENNE Republic, 1946
SANTA FE UPRISING Republic, 1946
STAGECOACH TO DENVER Republic, 1946
MARSHAL OF CRIPPLE CREEK
Republic, 1947
ALONG THE OREGON TRAIL
Republic, 1947
UNDER COLORADO SKIES Republic, 1947
THE MAIN STREET KID Republic, 1948
HEART OF VIRGINIA Republic, 1948
SECRET SERVICE INVESTIGATOR
Republic, 1948
OUT OF THE STORM Republic, 1948
DEATH VALLEY GUNFIGHTERS
Republic, 1949
HELLFIRE Republic, 1949
THE RED MENACE Republic, 1949
FLAME OF YOUTH Republic, 1949
SINGING GUNS Republic, 1950
HARBOR OF MISSING MEN Republic, 1950
THE ARIZONA COWBOY Republic, 1950
HILLS OF OKLAHOMA Republic, 1950
MILLION DOLLAR PURSUIT Republic, 1951
HONEYCHILE Republic, 1951
STREET BANDITS Republic, 1951
THE FABULOUS SENORITA Republic, 1952
OKLAHOMA ANNIE Republic, 1952
GOBS AND GALS Republic, 1952
TROPICAL HEAT WAVE Republic, 1952
A PERILOUS JOURNEY Republic, 1953
GERALDINE Republic, 1954
I COVER THE UNDERWORLD
Republic, 1955
DOUBLE JEOPARDY Republic, 1955
TRACK THE MAN DOWN Republic,
1955, British
COME NEXT SPRING Republic, 1956

WHEN GANGLAND STRIKES Republic, 1956
AFFAIR IN RENO Republic, 1957
COLE YOUNGER - GUNFIGHTER
Allied Artists, 1958
REVOLT IN THE BIG HOUSE
Allied Artists, 1958
BATTLE FLAME Allied Artists, 1959
KING OF THE WILD STALLIONS
Allied Artists, 1959
OPERATION EICHMANN Allied Artists, 1961
SHOWDOWN Universal, 1963
HE RIDES TALL Universal, 1964
BULLET FOR A BADMAN Universal, 1964
TAGGART Universal, 1965
BLACK SPURS Paramount, 1965
APACHE UPRISING Paramount, 1966
JOHNNY RENO Paramount, 1966
WACO Paramount, 1966
RED TOMAHAWK Paramount, 1967
HOSTILE GUNS Paramount, 1967
TIGER BY THE TAIL 1970

JOHN M. STAHL
b. January 21, 1886 - New York, New York
d. 1950

WIVES OF MEN Pioneer, 1918
SUSPICION H.H. Hoffman, 1918
HER CODE OF HONOR
Tribune-United, 1919
A WOMAN UNDER OATH
Tribune-United, 1919
GREATER THAN LOVE American Cinema
Association, 1919
WOMEN MEN FORGET
United Pictures, 1920
THE WOMAN IN HIS HOUSE Associated
First National, 1920
THE CHILD THOU GAVEST ME Associated
First National, 1921
SOWING THE WIND Associated First
National, 1921
SUSPICIOUS WIVES State Rights, 1921
THE SONG OF LIFE Associated First
National, 1922
ONE CLEAR CALL Associated First
National, 1922
THE DANGEROUS AGE Associated First
National, 1923
WHY MEN LEAVE HOME
First National, 1924
HUSBANDS AND LOVERS
First National, 1924
FINE CLOTHES First National, 1925
MEMORY LANE First National, 1926
THE GAY DECEIVER MGM, 1926
LOVERS? MGM, 1927
IN OLD KENTUCKY MGM, 1927
A LADY SURRENDERS Universal, 1930
SEED Universal, 1931
STRICTLY DISHONORABLE Universal, 1931
BACK STREET Universal, 1932
ONLY YESTERDAY Universal, 1933
IMITATION OF LIFE Universal, 1934
MAGNIFICENT OBSESSION Universal, 1935
PARNELL MGM, 1937
LETTER OF INTRODUCTION
Universal, 1938
WHEN TOMORROW COMES
Universal, 1939
OUR WIFE Columbia, 1941
THE IMMORTAL SERGEANT
20th Century-Fox, 1943
HOLY MATRIMONY 20th Century-Fox, 1943
THE EVE OF ST. MARK
20th Century-Fox, 1944
THE KEYS OF THE KINGDOM
20th Century-Fox, 1944

LEAVE HER TO HEAVEN
  20th Century-Fox, 1945
THE FOXES OF HARROW
  20th Century-Fox, 1947
THE WALLS OF JERICHO
  20th Century-Fox, 1948
FATHER WAS A FULLBACK
  20th Century-Fox, 1949
OH, YOU BEAUTIFUL DOLL
  20th Century-Fox, 1949

JACK STARRETT

b. November 2, 1936 - Refugio, Texas
d. 1989

RUN, ANGEL, RUN! Fanfare, 1969
THE LOSERS Fanfare, 1970
CRY BLOOD, APACHE Golden Eagle
  International, 1970
NIGHT CHASE (TF) Cinema Center, 1970
THE STRANGE VENGEANCE OF ROSALIE
  20th Century-Fox, 1972
SLAUGHTER American International, 1972
CLEOPATRA JONES Warner Bros., 1973
GRAVY TRAIN *THE DION BROTHERS*
  Columbia, 1974
RACE WITH THE DEVIL
  20th Century-Fox, 1975
A SMALL TOWN IN TEXAS American
  International, 1976
FINAL CHAPTER - WALKING TALL
  American International, 1977
ROGER & HARRY: THE MITERA
  TARGET (TF) Bruce Lansbury
  Productions/Columbia TV, 1977
NOWHERE TO HIDE (TF) Mark Carliner
  Productions/Viacom, 1977
THADDEUS ROSE AND EDDIE (TF)
  CBS, Inc., 1978
BIG BOB JOHNSON AND HIS FANTASTIC
  SPEED CIRCUS (TF) Playboy
  Productions/Paramount TV, 1978
MR. HORN (TF) Lorimar Productions, 1979
SURVIVAL OF DANA (TF) EMI TV, 1979
KISS MY GRITS *A TEXAS LEGEND/
  SUMMER HEAT* Ambassador, 1982

STENO

(Stefano Vanzina)
b. January 19, 1915 - Rome, Italy
d. 1988

AL DIAVOLO LA CELEBRITA co-director with
  Mario Monicelli, Produttori Associati,
  1949, Italian
TOTO' CERCA CASA co-director with
  Mario Monicelli, ATA, 1949, Italian
VITA DA CANI co-director with
  Mario Monicelli, ATA, 1950, Italian
E ARRIVATO IL CAVALIERE co-director with
  Mario Monicelli, ATA/Excelsa Film,
  1950, Italian
GUARDIE E LADRI co-director with
  Mario Monicelli, Carlo Ponti/Dino De
  Laurentiis Cinematografica/Golden Film,
  1951, Italian
TOTO' E I RE DI ROMA co-director with
  Mario Monicelli, Golden Film/Humanitas
  Film, 1952, Italian
THE UNFAITHFULS co-director with
  Mario Monicelli, Allied Artists, 1952, Italian
TOTO' E LE DONNE co-director with
  Mario Monicelli, Rosa Film, 1952, Italian
TOTO' A COLORI Ponti De Laurentiis/Golden
  Film, 1952, Italian
L'UOMO, LA BESTIA, LA VIRTU' Rosa Film,
  1953, Italian

CINEMA D'ALTRI TEMPI Jolly Film/Cormoran
  Film, 1953, Italian-French
UN GIORNO IN PRETURA Documento
  Film/Excelsa, 1953, Italian
SINS OF CASANOVA *L'AVVENTURE DI
  GIACOMO CASANOVA* Times Film
  Corporation, 1954, Italian
UN AMERICANO A ROMA Ponti De
  Laurentiis, 1954, Italian
PICCOLA POSTA Incom, 1955, Italian
NERO'S MISTRESS *MIO FIGLIO NERONE*
  Manhattan Films, 1956, Italian-French
FEMMINE TRE VOLTE Carlo Ponti/Jesus
  Saiz, 1957, Italian-Spanish
SUSANNA TUTTA PANNA Carlo Ponti/
  Maxima Film/Jesus Saiz, 1957,
  Italian-Spanish
MIA NONNA POLIZZIOTO 1958, Italian
GUARDIA, LADRO E CAMERIERA
  Dino De Laurentiis, 1958, Italian
MIA NONNA POLIZIOTTO Jonia Film,
  1958, Italian
TOTO' NELLA LUNA Maxima Film/Montfluor
  Film/Variety Film, 1958, Italian
I TARTASSATI Maxima Film, 1959, Italian
TOTO', EVA I EL PENNELLO PROIBITO
  Jolly Film/Cormoran Film/Hesperia Film,
  1959, Italian-French-Spanish
UN MILITARE E MEZZO Titanus,
  1959, Italian
LETTO A TRE PIAZZE Cineriz, 1960, Italian
A NOI PIACE FREDDO Flora Film/Tai Film/
  Variety Film, 1960, Italian
PSYCOSISSIMO Flora Film/Variety Film,
  1961, Italian
I MOSCHETTIERI DEL MARE Morino Film/
  France Cinema Productions, 1961, Italian
LA RAGAZZA DI MILLE MESI Amato Film,
  1961, Italian
TOTO' DIABOLICUS Titanus, 1962, Italian
COPACABANA PALACE Ital Victoria Film/
  France Cinema Productions/Consorcio
  Paulista de Coproducao, 1962,
  Italian-French-Brazilian
TWO COLONELS Comet, 1962, Italian
TOTO' CONTRO I QUATTRO Titanus,
  1963, Italian
GLI EROI DEL WEST Emo Bistolfi/Fenix Film,
  1964, Italian-Spanish
I GEMELLI DEL TEXAS Emo Bistolfi/Fenix
  Film, 1964, Italian-Spanish
LETTI SBAGLIATI Adelphia, 1964, Italian
ROSE ROSSE PER ANGELICA Flora Film/
  West Film/Llama Film/Cineurop, 1966,
  Italian-Spanish-French
AMORE ALL'ITALIANA *I SUPERDIABOLICI*
  European Incorporation, 1966, Italian
ARRIVA DORELLIK Inter Jet Film/Mega Film,
  1967, Italian
LA FELDMARESCIALLA Frida, 1967, Italian
CAPRICCIO ALL'ITALIANA co-director,
  Dino De Laurentiis, 1968, Italian
IL TRAPIANTO Rizzoli Film/DIA, 1969,
  Italian-Spanish
COSE DI COSA NOSTRA Roberto Amoroso,
  1971, Italian
IL VICHINGO VENUTO DAL SUD IFC,
  1971, Italian
LA POLIZIA RINGRAZIA Primex Italiana,
  1972, Italian
L'UCCELLO MIGRATORE Medusa,
  1972, Italian
IL TERRONE CON GLI OCCHI STORTI
  Dino De Laurentiis, 1972, Italian
ANASTASIA MIO FRATELLO Documento
  Film, 1973, Italian
PIEDONE LO SBIRRO Mondial TEFI,
  1973, Italian

LA POLIZLOTTA CC Champion, 1974, Italian
PIEDONE A HONG KONG Mondial TEFI,
  1975, Italian
IL PADRONE E L'OPERAIO CC Champion,
  1975, Italian
L'ITALIA S'E' ROTTA Splendid Pictures,
  1976, Italian
FEBBRE DA CAVALLO Primex,
  1976, Italian
TRE TIGRI CONTRO TRE TIGRI co-director
  with Sergio Corbucci, Primex/Italian
  International Film, 1977, Italian
DOPPIO DELITTO Primex, 1977, Italian
PIEDONE L'AFRICANO Laser Film/Rialto,
  1978, Italian-West German
AMORI MIEI Vides, 1978, Italian
DOTTOR JEKYLL E GENTILE SIGNORA
  IL DOTTOR JEKYLL JR. 1979, Italian
LA PATATA BOLLENTE Irrigazione
  Cinematografica, 1979, Italian
FICO D'INDIA Intercontinental Film,
  1980, Italian
PIEDONE D'EGITTO Merope Film,
  1980, Italian
QUANDO LA COPPIA SCOPPIA Italian
  International Film, 1981, Italian
TANGO DELLA GELOSIA Laser Film/Ypsilon
  Film, 1981, Italian
DIO LI FA POI LI ACCOPPIA International
  Dean Film, 1982, Italian
BANANA JOE Derby Cinematografica/Lisa
  Film, 1982, Italian
SBALLATO, GASATO, COMPLETAMENTE
  FUSO International Dean Film,
  1982, Italian
BONNIE E CLYDE ALL'ITALIANA Faso Film,
  1983, Italian
MANI DI FATA Faso Film, 1983, Italian
MI FACCIA CAUSA Italian International Film,
  1984, Italian
CUORI DI PIETRA (TF) RAI, 1985, Italian
L'OMBRA NERA DEL VESUVIO (TF)
  RAI, 1986, Italian
ANIMALI METROPOLITANI International
  Dean Film, 1987, Italian
BIG MAN (MS) RAI, 1987, Italian

GEORGE STEVENS

b. December 18, 1904 - Oakland, California
d. 1975

THE COHENS AND KELLYS IN TROUBLE
  RKO Radio, 1933
BACHELOR BAIT RKO Radio, 1934
KENTUCKY KERNELS RKO Radio, 1934
LADDIE RKO Radio, 1935
THE NITWITS RKO Radio, 1935
ALICE ADAMS RKO Radio, 1935
ANNIE OAKLEY RKO Radio, 1935
SWING TIME RKO Radio, 1936
QUALITY STREET RKO Radio, 1937
A DAMSEL IN DISTRESS RKO Radio, 1937
VIVACIOUS LADY RKO Radio, 1938
GUNGA DIN RKO Radio, 1939
VIGIL IN THE NIGHT RKO Radio, 1940
PENNY SERENADE Columbia, 1941
WOMAN OF THE YEAR MGM, 1942
THE TALK OF THE TOWN Columbia, 1942
THE MORE THE MERRIER ★
  Columbia, 1943
I REMEMBER MAMA RKO Radio, 1948
A PLACE IN THE SUN ★★
  Paramount, 1951
SOMETHING TO LIVE FOR
  Paramount, 1952
SHANE ★ Paramount, 1953
GIANT ★★ Warner Bros., 1956

THE DIARY OF ANNE FRANK ★
20th Century-Fox, 1959
THE GREATEST STORY EVER TOLD
United Artists, 1965
THE ONLY GAME IN TOWN
20th Century-Fox, 1970

ROBERT STEVENSON

b. May 31, 1905 - London, England
d. 1986

HAPPILY EVER AFTER   Gaumont,
1932, British
FALLING FOR YOU   Woolf & Freedman,
1933, British
JACK OF ALL TRADES   Gaumont,
1936, British
NINE DAYS A QUEEN   TUDOR ROSE
Gaumont, 1936, British
THE MAN WHO LIVED AGAIN   THE MAN
WHO CHANGED HIS MIND
Gaumont, 1936, British
KING SOLOMON'S MINES   Gaumont,
1937, British
NON-STOP NEW YORK   General Film
Distributors, 1937, British
TO THE VICTOR   OWD BOB   Gaumont,
1938, British
THE WARE CASE   Associated British Film
Distributors, 1939, British
A YOUNG MAN'S FANCY   Associated British
Film Distributors, 1939, British
RETURN TO YESTERDAY   Associated British
Film Distributors, 1939, British
TOM BROWN'S SCHOOLDAYS
RKO Radio, 1940
BACK STREET   Universal, 1941
JOAN OF PARIS   RKO Radio, 1942
FOREVER AND A DAY   co-director with
Rene Clair, Edmund Goulding,
Cedric Hardwicke, Frank Lloyd,
Victor Saville & Herbert Wilcox,
RKO Radio, 1943
JANE EYRE   RKO Radio, 1944
DISHONORED LADY   United Artists, 1947
TO THE ENDS OF THE EARTH
RKO Radio, 1948
THE WOMAN ON PIER 13   I MARRIED A
COMMUNIST   RKO Radio, 1949
WALK SOFTLY, STRANGER   RKO Radio, 1950
MY FORBIDDEN PAST   RKO Radio, 1951
THE LAS VEGAS STORY   RKO Radio, 1952
JOHNNY TREMAIN   Buena Vista, 1957
OLD YELLER   Buena Vista, 1957
DARBY O'GILL AND THE LITTLE PEOPLE
Buena Vista, 1959
KIDNAPPED   Buena Vista, 1960, British-U.S.
THE ABSENT-MINDED PROFESSOR
Buena Vista, 1960
IN SEARCH OF THE CASTAWAYS
Buena Vista, 1962, British-U.S.
SON OF FLUBBER   Buena Vista, 1963
THE MISADVENTURES OF MERLIN JONES
Buena Vista, 1964
MARY POPPINS ★   Buena Vista, 1964
THE MONKEY'S UNCLE   Buena Vista, 1965
THAT DARN CAT   Buena Vista, 1965
THE GNOME-MOBILE   Buena Vista, 1967
BLACKBEARD'S GHOST   Buena Vista, 1968
THE LOVE BUG   Buena Vista, 1969
BEDKNOBS AND BROOMSTICKS
Buena Vista, 1971
HERBIE RIDES AGAIN   Buena Vista, 1974
THE ISLAND AT THE TOP OF THE WORLD
Buena Vista, 1974
ONE OF OUR DINOSAURS IS MISSING
Buena Vista, 1975, U.S.-British
THE SHAGGY D.A.   Buena Vista, 1976

MAURITZ STILLER

(Moshe Stiller)
b. July 17, 1883 - Helsinki, Finland
d. 1928

MOTHER AND DAUGHTER   1912, Swedish
THE BLACK MASKS   1912, Swedish
THE TYRANNICAL FIANCEE
1912, Swedish
THE VAMPIRE   1913, Swedish
WHEN LOVE KILLS   1913, Swedish
WHEN THE ALARM BELL RINGS
1913, Swedish
THE CHILD   1913, Swedish
THE UNKNOWN WOMAN   1913, Swedish
ON THE FATEFUL ROADS OF LIFE
1913, Swedish
THE MODERN SUFFRAGETTE
1913, Swedish
THE MODEL   1913, Swedish, unreleased
WHEN THE MOTHER-IN-LAW REIGNS
1914, Swedish
BROTHERS   1914, Swedish
PEOPLE OF THE BORDER   1914, Swedish
BECAUSE OF HER LOVE   1914, Swedish
THE CHAMBERLAIN   1914, Swedish
STORMY PETREL   1914, Swedish
THE SHOT   1914, Swedish
THE RED TOWER   1914, Swedish
WHEN ARTISTS LOVE   1915, Swedish
PLAYMATES   1915, Swedish
HIS WIFE'S PAST   1915, Swedish
ACE OF THIEVES   1915, Swedish
THE DAGGER   1915, Swedish
MADAME DE THEBES   1915, Swedish
THE AVENGER   1916, Swedish
THE MINE PILOT   1916, Swedish
HIS WEDDING NIGHT   1916, Swedish
THE LUCKY BROOCH   1916, Swedish
LOVE AND JOURNALISM   1916, Swedish
THE WINGS   1916, Swedish
THE FIGHT FOR HIS HEART
1916, Swedish
THE BALLET PRIMADONNA   1916, Swedish
THOMAS GRAAL'S BEST FILM
1917, Swedish
ALEXANDER THE GREAT   1917, Swedish
THOMAS GRAAL'S FIRST CHILD
1918, Swedish
SONG OF THE SCARLET FLOWER
1918, Swedish
SIR ARNE'S TREASURE   THE THREE WHO
WERE DOOMED   1919, Swedish
THE FISHING VILLAGE   1920, Swedish
EROTIKON   1920, Swedish
JOHAN   co-director with Arthur Nordeen,
1921, Swedish
THE EXILES   1921, Swedish
GUNNAR HEDE'S SAGA   1923, Swedish
THE STORY OF GOSTA BERLING
1924, Swedish
HOTEL IMPERIAL   Paramount, 1927
THE WOMAN ON TRIAL   Paramount, 1927
THE STREET OF SIN   Paramount, 1928

JOHN STURGES

b. January 3, 1911 - Oak Park, Illinois
d. 1992

THUNDERBOLT   co-director with
William Wyler, Monogram, 1945
THE MAN WHO DARED   Columbia, 1946
SHADOWED   Columbia, 1946
ALIAS MR. TWILIGHT   Columbia, 1946
FOR THE LOVE OF RUSTY   Columbia, 1947
KEEPER OF THE BEES   Columbia, 1947
BEST MAN WINS   Columbia, 1948

THE SIGN OF THE RAM   Columbia, 1948
THE WALKING HILLS   Columbia, 1949
THE CAPTURE   RKO Radio, 1950
MYSTERY STREET   MGM, 1950
RIGHT CROSS   MGM, 1950
THE MAGNIFICENT YANKEE   MGM, 1950
KIND LADY   MGM, 1951
THE PEOPLE AGAINST O'HARA
MGM, 1951
IT'S A BIG COUNTRY   co-director with
Charles Vidor, Richard Thorpe, Don Hartman,
Don Weis, Clarence Brown &
William Wellman, MGM, 1952
THE GIRL IN WHITE   MGM, 1952
JEOPARDY   MGM, 1953
FAST COMPANY   MGM, 1953
ESCAPE FROM FORT BRAVO   MGM, 1953
BAD DAY AT BLACK ROCK ★   MGM, 1955
UNDERWATER!   RKO Radio, 1955
THE SCARLET COAT   MGM, 1955
BACKLASH   MGM, 1956
GUNFIGHT AT THE O.K. CORRAL
Paramount, 1957
THE LAW AND JAKE WADE   MGM, 1958
THE OLD MAN AND THE SEA
Warner Bros., 1958
LAST TRAIN FROM GUN HILL
Paramount, 1959
NEVER SO FEW   MGM, 1959
THE MAGNIFICENT SEVEN
United Artists, 1960
BY LOVE POSSESSED
United Artists, 1961
SERGEANTS 3   United Artists, 1962
A GIRL NAMED TAMIKO   Paramount, 1963
THE GREAT ESCAPE   United Artists, 1963
THE SATAN BUG   United Artists, 1965
THE HALLELUJAH TRAIL
United Artists, 1965
HOUR OF THE GUN   United Artists, 1967
ICE STATION ZEBRA   MGM, 1968
MAROONED   Columbia, 1969
JOE KIDD   Universal, 1972
CHINO   THE VALDEZ HORSES
Intercontinental, 1973,
Italian-Spanish-French
McQ   Warner Bros., 1974
THE EAGLE HAS LANDED   Columbia,
1977, British

PRESTON STURGES

(Edmund P. Biden)
b. August 29, 1898 - Chicago, Illinois
d. 1959

THE GREAT McGINTY   Paramount, 1940
CHRISTMAS IN JULY   Paramount, 1940
THE LADY EVE   Paramount, 1941
SULLIVAN'S TRAVELS   Paramount, 1941
THE PALM BEACH STORY
Paramount, 1942
THE MIRACLE OF MORGAN'S CREEK
Paramount, 1944
HAIL THE CONQUERING HERO
Paramount, 1944
THE GREAT MOMENT   Paramount, 1944
MAD WEDNESDAY   THE SIN OF HAROLD
DIDDLEBOCK   RKO Radio, 1947
UNFAITHFULLY YOURS
20th Century-Fox, 1948
THE BEAUTIFUL BLONDE FROM BASHFUL
BEND   20th Century-Fox, 1949
THE FRENCH THEY ARE A FUNNY RACE
LES CARNETS DU MAJOR THOMPSON
Continental, 1957, French

EDWARD SUTHERLAND

b. January 5, 1895 - London, England
d. 1974

COMING THROUGH   Paramount, 1925
WILD WILD SUSAN   Paramount, 1925
A REGULAR FELLOW   Paramount, 1925
BEHIND THE FRONT   Paramount, 1926
IT'S THE OLD ARMY GAME
  Paramount, 1926
WE'RE IN THE NAVY NOW
  Paramount, 1926
LOVE'S GREATEST MISTAKE
  Paramount, 1927
FIREMAN SAVE MY CHILD   Paramount, 1927
FIGURES DON'T LIE   Paramount, 1927
TILLIE'S PUNCTURED ROMANCE
  Paramount, 1928
THE BABY CYCLONE   Paramount, 1928
WHAT A NIGHT!   Paramount, 1928
CLOSE HARMONY   co-director with
  John Cromwell, Paramount, 1929
THE DANCE OF LIFE   co-director with
  John Cromwell, Paramount, 1929
FAST COMPANY   Paramount, 1929
THE SATURDAY NIGHT KID
  Paramount, 1929
POINTED HEELS   Paramount, 1929
PARAMOUNT ON PARADE   co-director,
  Paramount, 1930
BURNING UP   Paramount, 1930
THE SOCIAL LION   Paramount, 1930
THE SAP FROM SYRACUSE
  Paramount, 1930
THE GANG BUSTER   Paramount, 1931
JUNE MOON   Paramount, 1931
UP POPS THE DEVIL   Paramount, 1931
PALMY DAYS   United Artists, 1931
SKY DEVILS   United Artists, 1932
MR. ROBINSON CRUSOE
  United Artists, 1932
SECRETS OF THE FRENCH POLICE
  RKO RADIO, 1932
MURDERS IN THE ZOO   Paramount, 1933
INTERNATIONAL HOUSE   Paramount, 1933
TOO MUCH HARMONY   Paramount, 1933
MISSISSIPPI   Paramount, 1935
DIAMOND JIM   Universal, 1935
POPPY   Paramount, 1936
CHAMPAGNE WALTZ   Paramount, 1937
EVERY DAY'S A HOLIDAY   Paramount, 1937
THE FLYING DEUCES   RKO Radio, 1939
THE BOYS FROM SYRACUSE
  Universal, 1940
BEYOND TOMORROW   RKO Radio, 1940
ONE NIGHT IN THE TROPICS
  Universal, 1940
THE INVISIBLE WOMAN   Universal, 1941
NINE LIVES ARE NOT ENOUGH
  Warner Bros., 1941
STEEL AGAINST THE SKY
  Warner Bros., 1941
SING YOUR WORRIES AWAY
  RKO Radio, 1942
ARMY SURGEON   RKO Radio, 1942
THE NAVY COME THROUGH
  RKO Radio, 1942
DIXIE   Paramount, 1943
FOLLOW THE BOYS   Universal, 1944
SECRET COMMAND   Columbia, 1944
HAVING A WONDERFUL CRIME
  RKO Radio, 1945
ABIE'S IRISH ROSE   United Artists, 1946
BERMUDA AFFAIR   Columbia, 1956

E.W. SWACKHAMER

d. 1994

IN NAME ONLY (TF)   Screen Gems/
  Columbia TV, 1969
MAN AND BOY   Levitt-Pickman, 1972
GIDGET GETS MARRIED (TF)   Screen
  Gems/Columbia TV, 1972
DEATH SENTENCE (TF)   Spelling-Goldberg
  Productions, 1974
DEATH AT LOVE HOUSE (TF)
  Spelling-Goldberg Productions, 1976
ONCE AN EAGLE (MS)   co-director with
  Richard Michaels, Universal, 1976
QUINCY, M.E. (TF)   Glen A. Larson
  Productions/Universal TV, 1976
NIGHT TERROR (TF)   Charles Fries
  Productions, 1977
SPIDER-MAN (TF)   Charles Fries
  Productions, 1977
THE DAIN CURSE (MS) ☆   Martin Poll
  Productions, 1978
THE WINDS OF KITTY HAWK (TF)
  Charles Fries Productions, 1978
VAMPIRE (TF)   MTM Enterprises, 1979
THE DEATH OF OCEAN VIEW PARK (TF)
  Furia-Oringer Productions/Playboy
  Productions, 1979
REWARD (TF)   Jerry Adler Productions/Espirit
  Enterprises/Lorimar Productions, 1980
TENSPEED AND BROWNSHOE (TF)
  Stephen J. Cannell Productions, 1980
THE OKLAHOMA CITY DOLLS (TF)
  IKE Productions/Columbia TV, 1981
LONGSHOT   GG Productions, 1981
COCAINE AND BLUE EYES (TF)   Orenthal
  Productions/Columbia TV, 1983
MALIBU (TF)   Hamner Productions/
  Columbia TV, 1983
CARPOOL (TF)   Charles Fries Productions/
  Cherryhill Productions, 1983
THE ROUSTERS (TF)   Stephen J. Cannell
  Productions, 1983
BROTHERS-IN-LAW (TF)   Stephen J. Cannell
  Productions, 1985
COMMAND 5 (TF)   Paramount TV, 1985
BRIDGE ACROSS TIME (TF)
  Fries Entertainment, 1985
THE RETURN OF DESPERADO (TF)   Walter
  Mirisch Productions/Charles E. Sellier, Jr.
  Productions/Universal TV, 1988
DESPERADO: THE OUTLAW WARS (TF)
  Walter Mirisch Productions/Charles E. Sellier,
  Jr. Productions/Universal TV, 1989
CHRISTINE CROMWELL: THINGS THAT GO
  BUMP IN THE NIGHT (TF)   Wolf Film
  Productions/Universal TV, 1989
COLUMBO GOES TO COLLEGE (TF)
  Universal TV, 1990
ARE YOU LONESOME TONIGHT? (CTF)
  OTML Productions/The Mahoney Company/
  Wilshire Court Productions, 1992
THE SECRET PASSION OF ROBERT
  CLAYTON (CTF)   Producers Entertainment
  Group Productions/Wilshire Court
  Productions, 1992
MacSHAYNE: WINNER TAKES ALL (TF)
  Larry Levinson Productions/Kenny Rogers
  Productions, 1994

T

ANDREI TARKOVSKY

b. April 4, 1932 - Zavrazhe, U.S.S.R.
d. 1986

THE ROLLER AND THE VIOLIN   Mosfilm,
  1906, Soviet
MY NAME IS IVAN   Shore International,
  1962, Soviet
ANDREI RUBLEV   Columbia, 1968, Soviet,
  re-released in 1992 by Kino International
SOLARIS   Mosfilm, 1972, Soviet
THE MIRROR   Mosfilm, 1974, Soviet
STALKER   New Yorker/Media Transactions
  Corporation, 1979, Soviet
NOSTALGHIA   Grange Communications,
  1983, Italian-Soviet
THE SACRIFICE   Orion Classics, 1986,
  Swedish-French

FRANK TASHLIN

b. February 19, 1913
d. 1972

THE FIRST TIME   Columbia, 1952
SON OF PALEFACE   Paramount, 1952
MARRY ME AGAIN   RKO Radio, 1954
SUSAN SLEPT HERE   RKO Radio, 1954
ARTISTS AND MODELS   Paramount, 1955
THE LIEUTENANT WORE SKIRTS
  20th Century-Fox, 1956
HOLLYWOOD OR BUST   Paramount, 1956
THE GIRL CAN'T HELP IT
  20th Century-Fox, 1956
WILL SUCCESS SPOIL ROCK HUNTER?
  20th Century-Fox, 1957
ROCK-A-BYE BABY   Paramount, 1958
THE GEISHA BOY   Paramount, 1958
SAY ONE FOR ME   20th Century-Fox, 1959
CINDERFELLA   Paramount, 1960
BACHELOR FLAT   20th Century-Fox, 1962
IT'S ONLY MONEY   Paramount, 1962
THE MAN FROM THE DINER'S CLUB
  Columbia, 1963
WHO'S MINDING THE STORE?
  Paramount, 1963
THE DISORDERLY ORDERLY
  Paramount, 1964
THE ALPHABET MURDERS   *THE A.B.C.
  MURDERS*   MGM, 1966, British
THE GLASS BOTTOM BOAT   MGM, 1966
CAPRICE   20th Century-Fox, 1967
THE PRIVATE NAVY OF SGT. O'FARRELL
  United Artists, 1968

JACQUES TATI
(Jacques Tatischeff)
b. October 9, 1908 - Le Pecq, France
d. 1982

L'ECOLE DES FACTEURS   1947, French
JOUR DE FETE   Mayer-Kingsley,
  1949, French
MR. HULOT'S HOLIDAY   G-B-D International,
  1953, French
MY UNCLE, MR. HULOT   *MON ONCLE*
  Continental, 1956, French

PLAYTIME Continental, 1968, French
TRAFFIC Columbia, 1971, French
PARADE (TF) 1974, French

NORMAN TAUROG

b. February 23, 1899 - Chicago, Illinois
d. 1981

THE FARMER'S DAUGHTER Fox, 1928
LUCKY BOY co-director with s
  Charles C. Wilson, Tiffany, 1929
TROOPERS THREE co-director with
  Reeves Eason, Tiffany, 1930
SUNNY SKIES Tiffany, 1930
HOT CURVES Tiffany, 1930
FOLLOW THE LEADER Paramount, 1930
FINN AND HATTIE co-director with
  Norman Z. MacLeod, Paramount, 1931
SKIPPY ★★ Paramount, 1931
NEWLY RICH Paramount, 1931
HUCKLEBERRY FINN Paramount, 1931
SOOKY Paramount, 1931
HOLD 'EM JAIL! Paramount, 1932
THE PHANTOM PRESIDENT
  Paramount, 1932
IF I HAD A MILLION co-director,
  Paramount, 1932
A BEDTIME STORY Paramount, 1933
THE WAY TO LOVE Paramount, 1933
WE'RE NOT DRESSING Paramount, 1934
MRS. WIGGS OF THE CABBAGE PATCH
  Paramount, 1934
COLLEGE RHYTHM Paramount, 1934
THE BIG BROADCAST OF 1936
  Paramount, 1936
STRIKE ME PINK United Artists, 1936
RHYTHM ON THE RANGE Paramount, 1936
REUNION 20th Century-Fox, 1936
FIFTY ROADS TO TOWN
  20th Century-Fox, 1937
YOU CAN'T HAVE EVERYTHING
  20th Century-Fox, 1937
THE ADVENTURES OF TOM SAWYER
  United Artists, 1938
MAD ABOUT MUSIC Universal, 1938
BOYS TOWN ★ MGM, 1938
THE GIRL DOWNSTAIRS MGM, 1938
LUCKY NIGHT MGM, 1939
YOUNG TOM EDISON MGM, 1940
BROADWAY MELODY OF 1940 MGM, 1940
LITTLE NELLIE KELLY MGM, 1940
MEN OF BOYS TOWN MGM, 1941
DESIGN FOR SCANDAL MGM, 1941
ARE HUSBANDS NECESSARY?
  Paramount, 1942
A YANK AT ETON MGM, 1942
PRESENTING LILY MARS MGM, 1943
GIRL CRAZY MGM, 1943
THE HOODLUM SAINT MGM, 1946
THE BEGINNING OR THE END MGM, 1947
BIG CITY MGM, 1948
THE BRIDE GOES WILD MGM, 1948
WORDS AND MUSIC MGM, 1948
THAT MIDNIGHT KISS MGM, 1949
PLEASE BELIEVE ME MGM, 1950
THE TOAST OF NEW ORLEANS
  MGM, 1950
MRS. O'MALLEY AND MR. MALONE
  MGM, 1950
RICH, YOUNG AND PRETTY MGM, 1951
ROOM FOR ONE MORE Warner Bros., 1952
JUMPING JACKS Paramount, 1952
THE STOOGE Paramount, 1953
THE STARS ARE SINGING Paramount, 1953
THE CADDY Paramount, 1953
LIVING IT UP Paramount, 1954
YOU'RE NEVER TOO YOUNG
  Paramount, 1955

THE BIRDS AND THE BEES
  Paramount, 1956
PARDNERS Paramount, 1956
BUNDLE OF JOY RKO Radio, 1956
THE FUZZY PINK NIGHTGOWN
  United Artists, 1957
ONIONHEAD Warner Bros., 1958
DON'T GIVE UP THE SHIP
  Paramount, 1959
VISIT TO A SMALL PLANET
  Paramount, 1960
G.I. BLUES Paramount, 1960
ALL HANDS ON DECK
  20th Century-Fox, 1961
BLUE HAWAII Paramount, 1961
GIRLS! GIRLS! GIRLS! Paramount, 1962
IT HAPPENED AT THE WORLD'S FAIR
  MGM, 1963
PALM SPRINGS WEEKEND
  Warner Bros., 1963
TICKLE ME Allied Artists, 1965
SERGEANT DEADHEAD American
  International, 1965
DR. GOLDFOOT AND THE BIKINI MACHINE
  American International, 1966
SPINOUT MGM, 1966
DOUBLE TROUBLE MGM, 1967
SPEEDWAY MGM, 1968
C'MON, LET'S LIVE A LITTLE
  Paramount, 1968
LIVE A LITTLE, LOVE A LITTLE   MGM, 1968

RAY TAYLOR

b. December 1, 1888 - Perham, Minnesota
d. 1952

FIGHTING WITH BUFFALO BILL (S)
  Universal, 1926
WHISPERING SMITH RIDES (S)
  Universal, 1927
THE VANISHING RIDER (S) Universal, 1928
THE AVENGING OF SHADOW
  Universal, 1928
BEAUTY AND BULLETS Universal, 1928
QUICK TRIGGERS Universal, 1928
THE ACE OF SCOTLAND YARD (S)
  Universal, 1929
EYES OF THE UNDERWORLD (S)
  co-director with Leigh Jason,
  Universal, 1929
COME ACROSS Universal, 1929
THE JADE BOX (S) Universal, 1930
DANGER ISLAND (S) Universal, 1931
THE AIRMAIL MYSTERY (S) Universal, 1932
CLANCY OF THE MOUNTED (S)
  Universal, 1933
GORDON OF GHOST CITY (S)
  Universal, 1933
THE RETURN OF CHANDU (S)
  Universal, 1934
THE RETURN OF CHANDU
  Universal, 1935
THE ROARING WEST (S) Universal, 1935
OUTLAWED GUNS Universal, 1935
CALL OF THE SAVAGE Universal, 1935
THE PHANTOM RIDER (S) Universal, 1936
THE THREE MESQUITEERS
  Universal, 1936
DICK TRACY (S) co-director with Alan James,
  Universal, 1937
DRUMS OF DESTINY Universal, 1937
THE SPIDER'S WEB (S) co-director with
  James W. Horne, Universl, 1938
RAWHIDE Universal, 1938
FLASH GORDON CONQUERS THE
  UNIVERSE (S) co-director with Ford Beebe,
  Universal, 1940

THE GREEN HORNET (S) co-director with
  Ford Beebe, Universal, 1940
WEST OF CARSON CITY Universal, 1940
RIDERS OF DEATH VALLEY (S) co-director
  with Ford Beebe, Universal, 1941
GANG BUSTERS (S) co-director with
  Ford Beebe, Universal, 1942
DESTINATION UNKNOWN Universal, 1942
MYSTERY OF THE RIVER BOAT (S)
  co-director with Lewis D. Collins,
  Universal, 1944
JUNGLE QUEEN (S) co-director with
  Lewis D. Collins, Universal, 1945
THE DALTONS RIDE AGAIN Universal, 1945
LOST CITY OF THE JUNGLE (S)
  co-director with Lewis D. Collins,
  Universal, 1946
THE VIGILANTES RETURN Universal, 1947
MARK OF THE LASH Universal, 1948
SON OF BILLY THE KID Universal, 1949

WILLIAM DESMOND TAYLOR
(William Cunningham Deane-Turner)

b. April 26, 1877 - Ireland
d. 1922

THE BEGGAR CHILD 1914
THE DIAMOND FROM THE SKY (S)
  co-director with Jacques Jaccard,
  American, 1915
THE LAST CHAPTER Reliance, 1915
THE HIGH HAND Reliance, 1915
THE AMERICAN BEAUTY Paramount, 1916
DAVY CROCKETT Paramount, 1916
HE FELL IN LOVE WITH HIS WIFE
  Paramount, 1916
BEN BLAIR Paramount, 1916
HER FATHER'S SON Paramount, 1916
THE HOUSE OF LIES Paramount, 1916
PASQUALE Paramount, 1916
THE PARSON OF PANAMINT
  Paramount, 1916
THE REDEEMING LOVE Paramount, 1917
THE HAPPINESS OF THREE WOMEN
  Paramount, 1917
THE VARMINT Paramount, 1917
THE WORLD APART Paramount, 1917
TOM SAWYER Paramount, 1917
JACK AND JILL Paramount, 1917
THE SPIRIT OF '17 Paramount, 1918
HUCK AND TOM Paramount, 1918
UP THE ROAD WITH SALLY Selznick, 1918
HIS MAJESTY BUNKER BEAN
  Paramount, 1918
MILE-A-MINUTE KENDALL Paramount, 1918
HOW COULD YOU, JEAN? Artclass, 1918
JOHANNA ENLISTS Artclass, 1918
CAPTAIN KIDD, JR. Artclass, 1919
ANNE OF GREEN GABLES Realart, 1919
JUDY OF ROGUE'S HARBOR Realart, 1920
NURSE MARJORIE Realart, 1920
JENNY BE GOOD Realart, 1920
HUCKLEBERRY FINN Paramount, 1920
THE SOUL OF YOUTH Paramount, 1920
THE WITCHING HOUR Paramount, 1921
SACRED AND PROFANE LOVE
  Paramount, 1921
BEYOND Paramount, 1921
WEALTH Paramount, 1921
MORALS Paramount, 1921
THE GREEN TEMPTATION
  Paramount, 1922
THE TOP OF NEW YORK Paramount, 1922

GERALD THOMAS

b. December 10, 1920 - Hull, England
d. 1993

CIRCUS FRIENDS   British Lion/Children's
  Film Foundation, 1956, British
TIMELOCK   DCA, 1957, British
THE CIRCLE   *THE VICIOUS CIRCLE*
  Kassler, 1957, British
THE DUKE WORE JEANS
  Anglo-Amalgamated, 1958, British
CHAIN OF EVENTS   British Lion,
  1958, British
CARRY ON SERGEANT   Governor,
  1958, British
CARRY ON NURSE   Governor, 1959, British
PLEASE TURN OVER   Columbia,
  1959, British
WATCH YOUR STERN   Magna, 1960, British
BEWARE OF CHILDREN   *NO KIDDING*
  American International, 1960, British
CARRY ON CONSTABLE   Governor,
  1960, British
ROOMMATES   *RAISING THE WIND*
  Herts-Lion International, 1961, British
CARRY ON REGARDLESS
  Anglo-Amalgamated, 1961, British
A SOLITARY CHILD   British Lion,
  1961, British
TWICE ROUND THE DAFFODILS
  Anglo-Amalgamated, 1962, British
CARRY ON CRUISING   Governor,
  1962, British
THE SWINGIN' MAIDEN   *THE IRON MAIDEN*
  Columbia, 1962, British
NURSE ON WHEELS   Janus, 1963, British
CARRY ON CABBY   Anglo-Amalgamated/
  Warner-Pathé, 1963, British
CARRY ON JACK   Anglo-Amalgamated/
  Warner-Pathé, 1964, British
CARRY ON SPYING   Governor, 1964, British
CARRY ON CLEO   Governor, 1964, British
THE BIG JOB   Anglo-Amalgamated/
  Warner-Pathé, 1966, British
CARRY ON COWBOY   Anglo-Amalgamated/
  Warner-Pathé, 1966, British
CARRY ON SCREAMING
  Anglo-Amalgamated/Warner-Pathé,
  1966, British
FOLLOW THAT CAMEL   Schoenfeld Film
  Distributing, 1967, British
CARRY ON DOCTOR   Rank, 1968, British
CARRY ON...UP THE KHYBER   Rank,
  1969, British
CARRY ON CAMPING   Rank, 1969, British
CARRY ON UP THE JUNGLE   Rank,
  1970, British
CARRY ON AGAIN, DOCTOR   Rank,
  1970, British
CARRY ON AT YOUR CONVENIENCE
  Rank, 1971, British
CARRY ON HENRY   Rank, 1971, British
CARRY ON LOVING   Rank, 1971, British
CARRY ON ABROAD   Rank, 1972, British
CARRY ON MATRON   Rank, 1972, British
BLESS THIS HOUSE   Rank, 1973, British
CARRY ON BEHIND   Rank, 1976, British
CARRY ON ENGLAND   Rank, 1976, British
CARRY ON EMMANUELLE   Rank,
  1978, British
THAT'S CARRY ON   Rank, 1978, British
CARRY ON COMEDY CLASSICS (TF)
  Thames TV, 1983, British
THE SECOND VICTORY   Filmworld
  Distributors, 1987, Australian-British
CARRY ON COLUMBUS   UIP, 1992, British

RICHARD THORPE

(Rollo Smolt Thorpe)

b. February 24, 1896 - Hutchinson, Kansas
d. 1991

BRINGING HOME THE BACON
  Artclass, 1924
ROUGH RIDIN'   Artclass, 1924
FAST AND FEARLESS   Action, 1924
HARD HITTIN' HAMILTON   Action, 1924
RARIN' TO GO   Action, 1924
RIP ROARIN' ROBERTS   Artclass, 1924
THUNDERING ROMANCE   Artclass, 1924
WALLOPING WALLACE   Artclass, 1924
THE DESERT DEMON   Artclass, 1925
SADDLE CYCLONE   Artclass, 1925
FULL SPEED   Artclass, 1925
DOUBLE ACTION DANIELS   Artclass, 1925
FAST FIGHTIN'   Artclass, 1925
GALLOPING ON   Artclass, 1925
GOLD AND GRIT   Artclass, 1925
ON THE GO   Artclass, 1925
QUICKER 'N LIGHTNIN'   Artclass, 1925
A STREAK OF LUCK   Artclass, 1925
TEARIN' LOOSE   Artclass, 1925
THE BANDIT BUSTER   Associated
  Exhibitors, 1926
COLLEGE DAYS   Tiffany, 1926
DOUBLE DEALING   Artclass, 1926
THE FIGHTING CHEAT   Artclass, 1926
RAWHIDE   Associated Exhibitors, 1926
TWIN TRIGGERS   Artclass, 1926
THE BONANZA BUCKAROO   Associated
  Exhibitors, 1926
COMING AN' GOING   Artclass, 1926
THE DANGEROUS DUB   Associated
  Exhibitors, 1926
DEUCE HIGH   Artclass, 1926
EASY GOING   Artclass, 1926
RIDING RIVALS   Artclass, 1926
ROARING RIDER   Artclass, 1926
SPEEDY SPURS   Artclass, 1926
TRUMPIN' TROUBLE   Artclass, 1926
TWISTED TRIGGERS   Associated
  Exhibitors, 1926
BETWEEN DANGERS   Pathé, 1927
THE CYCLONE COWBOY   Pathé, 1927
THE FIRST NIGHT   Tiffany, 1927
THE GALLOPING GOBS   Pathé, 1927
THE INTERFERIN' GENT   Pathé, 1927
THE MEDDLIN' STRANGER   Pathé, 1927
PALS IN PERIL   Pathé, 1927
RIDE 'EM HIGH   Pathé, 1927
THE RIDIN' ROWDY   Pathé, 1927
ROARIN' BRONCS   Pathé, 1927
SKEDADDLE GOLD   Pathé, 1927
THE OBLIGIN' BUCKAROO   Pathé, 1927
TEARIN' INTO TROUBLE   Pathé, 1927
THE DESERT OF THE LOST   Pathé, 1927
SODA WATER COWBOY   Pathé, 1927
WHITE PEBBLES   Pathé, 1927
THE VANISHING WEST (S)   Mascot, 1928
VULTURES OF THE SEA (S)   Mascot, 1928
THE COWBOY CAVALIER   Pathé, 1928
DESPERATE COURAGE   Pathé, 1928
THE VALLEY OF HUNTED MEN   Pathé, 1928
BALLYHOO BUSTER   Pathé, 1928
THE FLYING BUCKAROO   Pathé, 1928
SADDLE MATES   Pathé, 1928
THE FATAL WARNING (S)   Mascot, 1929
KING OF THE KONGO (S)   Mascot, 1929
THE BACHELOR GIRL   Columbia, 1929
THE LONE DEFENDER (S)   Mascot, 1930
BORDER ROMANCE   Tiffany, 1930
THE DUDE WRANGLER   Sono-Art World
  Wide, 1930
WINGS OF ADVENTURE   Tiffany, 1930
UNDER MONTANA SKIES   Tiffany, 1930

THE UTAH KID   Tiffany, 1930
THE THOROUGHBRED   Tiffany, 1930
KING OF THE WILD (S)   Mascot, 1931
THE LAWLESS WOMAN   Chesterfield, 1931
THE LADY FROM NOWHERE
  Chesterfield, 1931
WILD HORSES   co-director with Sidney Algier,
  M.H. Hoffman, 1931
SKY SPIDER   Action, 1931
GRIEF STREET   Chesterfield, 1931
NECK AND NECK   Sono-Art World
  Wide, 1931
THE DEVIL PLAYS   Chesterfield, 1931
CROSS EXAMINATION   Artclass, 1932
MURDER AT DAWN   Big Four, 1932
FORGOTTEN WOMEN   Monogram, 1932
PROBATION   Chesterfield, 1932
MIDNIGHT LADY   Chesterfield, 1932
ESCAPADE   Invincible, 1932
FORBIDDEN COMPANY   Invincible, 1932
BEAUTY PARLOR   Chesterfield, 1932
THE KING MURDER   Chesterfield, 1932
THE THRILL OF YOUTH   Invincible, 1932
SLIGHTLY MARRIED   Chesterfield, 1932
WOMEN WON'T TELL   Chesterfield, 1933
THE SECRETS OF WU SIN
  Chesterfield, 1933
LOVE IS DANGEROUS   Chesterfield, 1933
FORGOTTEN   Invincible, 1933
STRANGE PEOPLE   Chesterfield, 1933
I HAVE LIVED   Chesterfield, 1933
NOTORIOUS BUT NICE   Chesterfield, 1933
MAN OF SENTIMENT   Chesterfield, 1933
RAINBOW OVER BROADWAY
  Chesterfield, 1933
MURDER ON THE CAMPUS
  Chesterfield, 1934
THE QUITTER   Chesterfield, 1934
CITY PARK   Chesterfield, 1934
STOLEN SWEETS   Chesterfield, 1934
GREEN EYES   Chesterfield, 1934
CHEATING CHEATERS   Universal, 1934
SECRET OF THE CHATEAU   Universal, 1935
STRANGE WIVES   Universal, 1935
LAST OF THE PAGANS   MGM, 1935
THE VOICE OF BUGLE ANN   MGM, 1936
TARZAN ESCAPES   MGM, 1936
DANGEROUS NUMBER   MGM, 1937
NIGHT MUST FALL   MGM, 1937
DOUBLE WEDDING   MGM, 1937
MAN-PROOF   MGM, 1938
LOVE IS A HEADACHE   MGM, 1938
THE FIRST 100 YEARS   MGM, 1938
THE TOY WIFE   MGM, 1938
THE CROWD ROARS   MGM, 1938
THREE LOVES HAS NANCY   MGM, 1938
THE ADVENTURES OF HUCKLEBERRY FINN
  MGM, 1939
TARZAN FINDS A SON   MGM, 1939
THE EARL OF CHICAGO   MGM, 1940
TWENTY-MULE TEAM   MGM, 1940
WYOMING   MGM, 1940
THE BAD MAN   MGM, 1941
BARNACLE BILL   MGM, 1941
TARZAN'S SECRET TREASURE   MGM, 1941
JOE SMITH, AMERICAN   MGM, 1942
TARZAN'S NEW YORK ADVENTURE
  MGM, 1942
APACHE TRAIL   MGM, 1942
WHITE CARGO   MGM, 1942
THREE HEARTS FOR JULIA   MGM, 1943
ABOVE SUSPICION   MGM, 1943
CRY HAVOC   MGM, 1943
TWO GIRLS AND A SAILOR   MGM, 1944
THE THIN MAN GOES HOME   MGM, 1945
THRILL OF A ROMANCE   MGM, 1945
HER HIGHNESS AND THE BELLBOY
  MGM, 1945

WHAT NEXT, CORPORAL HARGROVE?
  MGM, 1945
FIESTA   MGM, 1947
THIS TIME FOR KEEPS   MGM, 1947
ON AN ISLAND WITH YOU   MGM, 1948
A DATE WITH JUDY   MGM, 1948
THE SUN COMES UP   MGM, 1949
BIG JACK   MGM, 1950
CHALLENGE TO LASSIE   MGM, 1949
MALAYA   MGM, 1950
THE BLACK HAND   MGM, 1950
THREE LITTLE WORDS   MGM, 1950
VENGEANCE VALLEY   MGM, 1951
THE GREAT CARUSO   MGM, 1951
THE UNKNOWN MAN   MGM, 1951
IT'S A BIG COUNTRY   co-director with
  Charles Vidor, John Sturges, Don Hartman,
  Clarence Brown, William Wellman &
  Don Weis, MGM, 1952
CARBINE WILLIAMS   MGM, 1952
IVANHOE   MGM, 1952
THE PRISONER OF ZENDA   MGM, 1952
THE GIRL WHO HAD EVERYTHING
  MGM, 1953
ALL THE BROTHERS WERE VALIANT
  MGM, 1953
KNIGHTS OF THE ROUND TABLE
  MGM, 1954
THE FLAME AND THE FLESH   MGM, 1954
THE STUDENT PRINCE   MGM, 1954
ATHENA   MGM, 1954
THE PRODIGAL   MGM, 1955
QUENTIN DURWARD   MGM, 1955
TEN THOUSAND BEDROOMS   MGM, 1957
TIP ON A DEAD JOCKEY   MGM, 1957
JAILHOUSE ROCK   MGM, 1957
THE HOUSE OF THE SEVEN HAWKS
  MGM, 1959, British
KILLERS OF KILIMANJARO   Columbia,
  1959, British
THE TARTARS   MGM, 1961,
  Italian-Yugoslavian
THE HONEYMOON MACHINE   MGM, 1961
THE HORIZONTAL LIEUTENANT
  MGM, 1962
FOLLOW THE BOYS   MGM, 1963
FUN IN ACAPULCO   Paramount, 1963
THE GOLDEN HEAD   Cinerama, 1965,
  Hungarian-U.S.
THE TRUTH ABOUT SPRING   Universal,
  1965, British-U.S.
THAT FUNNY FEELING   Universal, 1965
THE SCORPIO LETTERS (TF)
  MGM TV, 1967
THE LAST CHALLENGE   MGM, 1967

LEOPOLDO TORRE NILSSON
b. May 5, 1924 - Buenos Aires, Argentina
d. 1978

EL CRIMEN DE ORIBE   co-director with
  Leopoldo Torres-Rios, 1950, Argentine
EL HIJO DEL CRACK   co-director with
  Leopoldo Torres-Rios, 1950, Argentine
DIAS DE ODIO   1954, Argentine
LA TIGRA   1954, Argentine
PARA VESTIR SANTOS   1955, Argentine
GRACIELA   1956, Argentine
EL PROTEGIDO   1956, Argentine
LA CASA DEL ANGEL   1957, Argentine
EL SECUESTRADOR   1958, Argentine
LA CAIDA   1959, Argentine
FIN DE FIESTA   1960, Argentine
UN GUAPO DEL 900   1960, Argentine
LA MANO EN LA TRAMPA   1961, Argentine
SUMMERSKIN   Angel Productions,
  1961, Argentine

THE FEMALE   *SETENTA VECES SIETE*
  Cambist, 1962, Argentine
HOMENAJE A LA HORA DE LA SIESTA
  1962, Argentine
LA TERRAZA   1963, Argentine
EL OJO DE LA CERRADURA
  1964, Argentine
CAVAR UN FOSO   1966, Argentine
LA CHICA DEL LUNES   1966, Puerto Rican
LOS TRAIDORES DE SAN ANGEL
  1967, Puerto Rican
MARTIN FIERRO   1968, Argentine
EL SANTO DE LA ESPADA   1970, Argentine
LA MAFFIA   1972, Argentine
GUEMES - LA TIERRA EN ARMAS
  1972, Argentine
LOS SIETE LOCOS   1973, Argentine
BOQUITAS PINTADAS   1974, Argentine
DIARIO DE LA GUERRA DEL CERDO
  1975, Argentine
EL PIBE CABEZA   1976, Argentine
PIEDRA LIBRE   1976, Argentine

ROBERT TOTTEN
b. February 5, 1937 - Los Angeles, California
d. 1995

THE QUICK AND THE DEAD   Beckman, 1963
DEATH OF A GUNFIGHTER   co-director with
  Don Siegel, both directed under pseudonym
  of Allen Smithee, Universal, 1967
THE WILD COUNTRY   Buena Vista, 1971
THE RED PONY (TF)   Universal TV/Omnibus
  Productions, 1973
HUCKLEBERRY FINN (TF)   ABC Circle
  Films, 1975
PONY EXPRESS RIDER   Doty-Dayton, 1976
THE SACKETTS (TF)   Douglas Netter
  Enterprises/M.B. Scott Productions/Shalako
  Enterprises, 1979
DARK BEFORE DAWN
  PSM Entertainment, 1988

VICTOR TOURJANSKY
(Vyacheslav Turzhansky)
b. 1891 - Kiev, Russia

SYMPHONY OF LOVE AND DEATH
  1914, Russian
THE BROTHERS KARAMAZOV
  1915, Russian
WANDERER BEYOND THE GRAVE
  1915, Russian
ISLE OF OBLIVION   1917, Russian
PARADISE WITHOUT ADAM   1918, Soviet
L'ORDONNANCE   1921, French
LES CONTES DES MILLE ET UNE NUITS
  1921, French
LE 15e PRELUDE DE CHOPIN   1922, French
LE NUIT DU CARNAVAL   1922, French
LE CHANT DE L'AMOUR TRIOMPHANT
  1923, French
CE COCHON DE MORIN   1924, French
LA DAME MASQUEE   1924, French
LE PRINCE CHARMANT   1925, French
MICHEL STROGOFF   1926, French
THE ADVENTURER   1928
WOLGA-WOLGA   1928, German
MANOLESCU   1929, German
DER HERZOG VON REICHSTADT
  1931, German
L'AIGLON   1931, French
LE CHANTEUR INCONNU   1931, French
HOTEL DES ETUDIANTS   1932, French
L'ORDONNANCE   1933, French
VOLGA EN FLAMMES   1934, French
YEUX NOIRS   1935, French

DIE GANZE WELT DREHT SICH UM LIEBE
  1935, German
STADT ANATOL   1936, German
VERTIGE D'UN SOIR   1936, French
LE MENSONGE DE NINA PETROVNA
  1937, French
NOSTALGIE   1937, French
DER BLAUFUCHS   1938, German
VERKLUNGENE MELODIE   1938, German
EINE FRAU WIE DU   1939, German
DER GOUVERNEUR   1939, German
FEINDE   1940, German
ILLUSION   1941, German
LIEBESGESCHICHTEN   1943, German
TONELLI   1943, German
ORIENT-EXPRESS   1944, German
DREIMAL KOMODIE   1945, German
DER BLAUE STROHUT   1949, West German
VOM TEUFEL GEJAGT   1950, West German
EHE FUR EINE NACHT   1952, West German
SALTO MORTALE   1953, West German
MORGENGRAUEN   1954, West German
DIE TOTENINSEL   1955, West German
KONIGSWALZER   1955, West German
HERZ OHNE GNADE   1958, West German
LA VENERE DI CHERONEA   co-director with
  Fernando Cerchio, 1958, Italian-French
PRISONER OF THE VOLGA   *I BATELLIERI
  DEL VOLGA*   Paramount, 1958,
  Italian-French
HEROD THE GREAT   Allied Artists, 1959,
  Italian-French
THE COSSACKS   co-director with
  Giorgio Rivalta, Universal, 1959,
  Italian-French
TRIUMPH OF MICHAEL STROGOFF
  Columbia, 1964, French-Italian
UNA REGINA PER CESARE   co-director with
  Piero Pierotti, 1962, Italian-French

JACQUES TOURNEUR
b. November 12, 1904 - Paris, France
d. 1977

UN VIEUX GARCON   1931, French
TOUT CA NE VAUT PAS L'AMOUR
  1931, French
LA FUSEE   1933, French
TOTO   1933, French
POUR ETRE AIMEE   1933, French
LES FILLES DE LA CONCIERGE
  1934, French
THEY ALL CAME OUT   MGM, 1939
NICK CARTER - MASTER DETECTIVE
  MGM, 1939
PHANTOM RAIDERS   MGM, 1940
DOCTORS DON'T TELL   MGM, 1941
CAT PEOPLE   RKO Radio, 1942
I WALKED WITH A ZOMBIE
  RKO Radio, 1943
THE LEOPARD MAN   RKO Radio, 1943
DAYS OF GLORY   RKO Radio, 1944
EXPERIMENT PERILOUS   RKO Radio, 1944
CANYON PASSAGE   Universal, 1946
OUT OF THE PAST   RKO Radio, 1947
BERLIN EXPRESS   RKO Radio, 1948
EASY LIVING   RKO Radio, 1949
THE FLAME AND THE ARROW
  Warner Bros., 1950
STARS IN MY CROWN   MGM, 1950
CIRCLE OF DANGER   Eagle Lion,
  1951, British
ANNE OF THE INDIES
  20th Century-Fox, 1951
WAY OF A GAUCHO   20th Century-Fox, 1952
APPOINTMENT IN HONDURAS
  RKO Radio, 1953

STRANGER ON HORSEBACK
United Artists, 1955
WICHITA   Allied Artists, 1955
GREAT DAY IN THE MORNING
RKO Radio, 1956
NIGHTFALL   Columbia, 1957
CURSE OF THE DEMON   NIGHT OF THE
DEMON   Columbia, 1957, British
THE FEARMAKERS   United Artists, 1958
MISSION OF DANGER   co-director with
George Waggner, MGM, 1959
TIMBUKTU   United Artists, 1959
FRONTIER RANGERS (TF)   co-director with
George Waggner, MGM, 1959
FURY RIVER   co-director with
George Waggner, MGM, 1959
SAVAGE FRONTIER   MGM, 1960
THE GIANT OF MARATHON   LA BATTAGLIA
DIMARATONA   MGM, 1960, Italian
THE COMEDY OF TERRORS   American
International, 1963
WAR-GODS OF THE DEEP   THE CITY
UNDER THE SEA   American International,
1965, British-U.S.

MAURICE TOURNEUR
(Maurice Thomas)
b. February 2, 1876 - Paris, France
d. 1961

LE FRIQUET   1912, French
JEAN LA POUDRE   1912, French
LE SYSTEME DU DOCTEUR GOUDRON ET
DU PROFESSEUR PLUME   1912, French
FIGURES DE CIRE   1912, French
LE DERNIER PARDON   1913, French
LE PUITS MITOYEN   1913, French
LE CAMEE   1913, French
SOEURETTE   1913, French
LE CORSO ROUGE   1913, French
MADEMOISELLE 100 MILLIONS
1913, French
LES GAITES DE L'ESCADRON   1913, French
LA DAME DE MONTSOREAU   1913, French
MONSIEUR LECOCQ   1914, French
ROULETABILLE: LE MYSTERE DE LA
CHAMBRE JAUNE   1914, French
ROULETABILLE: LA DERNIERE INCARNA-
TION DE LARSAN   1914, French
THE MAN OF THE HOUR   World, 1914
MOTHER   World, 1914
THE WISHING RING   World, 1914
THE PIT   World, 1914
ALIAS JIMMY VALENTINE   World, 1915
THE CUB   World, 1915
THE IVORY SNUFF BOX   World, 1915
THE IRISH SNUFF BOX   World, 1915
TRILBY   World, 1915
THE BUTTERFLY ON THE WHEEL
World, 1915
HUMAN DRIFTWOOD   co-director with
Emile Chautard, 1916
THE PAWN OF FATE   World, 1916
THE HAND OF PERIL
Peerless-Brady-World, 1916
THE CLOSED ROAD   World, 1916
THE RAIL RIDER
Peerless-Brady-World, 1916
THE VELVET PAW
Peerless-Brady-World, 1916
A GIRL'S FOLLY   Peerless-Brady-World, 1917
THE WHIP   Paragon, 1917
THE UNDYING FLAME   Paramount, 1917
EXILE   Paramount, 1917
THE LAW OF THE LAND   Paramount, 1917
THE PRIDE OF THE CLAN   Artcraft, 1917
THE POOR LITTLE RICH GIRL   Artcraft, 1917

BARBARY SHEEP   Artcraft, 1917
THE RISE OF JENNY CUSHING
Artcraft, 1917
THE ROSE OF THE WORLD   Artcraft, 1918
A DOLL'S HOUSE   Artcraft, 1918
THE BLUE BIRD   Artcraft, 1918
PRUNELLA   Paramount, 1918
SPORTING LIFE   Hiller & Wilk, 1918
WOMAN   Hiller & Wilk, 1918
THE WHITE HEATHER   Hiller & Wilk, 1919
THE LIFE LINE   Paramount, 1919
THE BROKEN BUTTERFLY
Robertson-Cole, 1919
VICTORY   Paramount, 1919
THE COUNTY FAIR   co-director with
Edward J. Mortimer, 1920
MY LADY'S GARTER   Paramount, 1920
TREASURE ISLAND   Paramount, 1920
THE GREAT REDEEMER   co-director with
Clarence Brown, Metro, 1920
THE WHITE CIRCLE   Paramount, 1920
DEEP WATERS   Paramount, 1920
THE LAST OF THE MOHICANS   co-director
with Clarence Brown, Associated
Producers, 1920
THE BAIT   Paramount, 1921
THE FOOLISH MATRONS   co-director with
Clarence Brown, Associated Producers, 1921
LORNA DOONE   Associated First
National, 1922
WHILE PARIS SLEEPS   THE GLORY
OF LOVE   W.W. Hodkinson, 1923
THE CHRISTIAN   Goldwyn, 1923
THE ISLE OF LOST SHIPS   Associated First
National, 1923
THE BRASS BOTTLE   Associated First
National, 1923
JEALOUS HUSBANDS   Associated First
National, 1923
TORMENT   First National, 1924
THE WHITE MOTH   First National, 1924
SPORTING LIFE   Universal, 1925
NEVER THE TWAIN SHALL MEET
Metro-Goldwyn, 1925
CLOTHES MAKE THE PIRATE
First National, 1925
OLD LOVES AND NEW   First National, 1926
ALOMA OF THE SOUTH SEAS
Paramount, 1926
L'EQUIPAGE   1927, French
DAS SCHIFF DER VERLORENE MENSCHEN
1929, German
ACCUSEE - LEVEZ-VOUZ!   1930, French
MAISON DE DANSES   1931, French
PARTIR   1931, French
AU NOM DE LA LOI   1932, French
LES GAITES DE L'ESCADRON   1932, French
LIDOIRE   1932, French
LES DEUX ORPHELINES   1933, French
L'HOMME MYSTERIEUX   1933, French
LE VOLEUR   1934, French
JUSTIN DE MARSEILLES   1935, French
KOENIGSMARK   1936, French
SAMSON   1936, French
AVEC LE SOURIRE   1936, French
CRIMSON DYNASTY   1936, French
LE PATRIOTE   1938, French
KATIA   1938, French
VOLPONE   1941, French
PECHES DE JEUNESSE   1941, French
MAM'ZELLE BONAPARTE   1941, French
LA VAL D'ENFER   1943, French
LA MAIN DU DIABLE   1943, French
CECILE EST MORTE   1944, French
APRES L'AMOUR   1948, French
L'IMPASSE DES DEUX ANGES   1948, French

SHIRO TOYODA
b. January 3, 1906 - Kyoto, Japan
d. 1977

PAINTED LIPS   Shochiku, 1929, Japanese
THREE WOMEN   Shochiku, 1935, Japanese
YOUNG PEOPLE   Tokyo Hassei,
1937, Japanese
NIGHTINGALE   Tokyo Hassei,
1938, Japanese
NAKIMUSHI KOZO   Tokyo Hassei,
1938, Japanese
OHINATA VILLAGE   Tokyo Hassei,
1940, Japanese
SPRING ON LEPERS' ISLAND   Tokyo Hassei,
1940, Japanese
MEMORIAL OF MY LOVE   Tokyo Hassei,
1941, Japanese
YOUNG FIGURE   Chosen Eiga,
1943, Japanese
FOUR LOVE STORIES   co-director with
Mikio Naruse, Kajiro Yamamoto &
Teinosuke Kinogasa, Toho, 1947, Japanese
THE FOUR SEASONS OF WOMAN   Toho,
1950, Japanese
WHISPER OF SPRING   1952, Japanese
THE MISTRESS   WILD GEESE   Daiei,
1953, Japanese
SOME WOMEN   Daiei, 1954, Japanese
GRASS WHISTLE   1955, Japanese
MARITAL RELATIONS   Toho,
1955, Japanese
CAT AND SHOZO AND TWO WOMEN
Tokyo Eiga, 1956, Japanese
MRS. WHITESNAKE'S LOVE   Toho,
1956, Japanese
SNOW COUNTRY   Toho, 1957, Japanese
EVENING CALM   Toho, 1957, Japanese
STATION INN   Tokyo Eiga/Eiga,
1958, Japanese
PILGRIMAGE AT NIGHT   Tokyo Eiga,
1959, Japanese
THE CURIOSITY SHOP MASTER   Tokyo Eiga,
1960, Japanese
THE TWILIGHT STORY   Tokyo Eiga,
1960, Japanese
THE DIPLOMAT'S MANSION   Tokyo Eiga,
1961, Japanese
TILL TOMORROW COMES   Tokyo Eiga,
1962, Japanese
MADAME AKI   Tokyo Eiga, 1963, Japanese
NEW MARITAL RELATIONS   Tokyo Eiga,
1953, Japanese
SWEET SWEAT   Tokyo Eiga, 1964, Japanese
THE CHEERFUL WIDOW   Tokyo Eiga,
1964, Japanese
WAVE SHADOW   Tokyo Eiga,
1965, Japanese
ILLUSION OF BLOOD   YOTSUYA KAIDAN
Tokyo Eiga, 1965, Japanese
IN FRONT OF THE STATION: ONE HUNDRED
YEARS   Tokyo Eiga, 1967, Japanese
RIVER OF FOREVER   Tokyo Eiga,
1967, Japanese
IN FRONT OF THE STATION: GOOD LUCK
Tokyo Eiga, 1968, Japanese
PORTRAIT OF HELL   REVOLUTION OF HELL
Tokyo Eiga, 1969, Japanese
KOUKOTSU NO HITO   Geiensha,
1973, Japanese
BETWEEN WOMEN AND WIVES   co-director
with Kon Ichikawa, Geiensha/Toho,
1976, Japanese

JOHN TRENT
b. 1935
d. 1983

THE BUSHBABY   MGM, 1970, British
HOMER   National General, 1970, Canadian
THE MAN WHO WANTED TO LIVE
   FOREVER (TF)   Palomar Pictures
   International, 1970
JALNA (TF)   CBC/Thames TV, 1972,
   Canadian-British
SUNDAY IN THE COUNTRY   American
   International, 1973, British
IT SEEMED LIKE A GOOD IDEA AT THE TIME
   Selective Cinema, 1974, Canadian
FIND THE LADY   Danton, 1975, Canadian
RIEL (TF)   CBC, 1977, Canadian
CROSSBAR (TF)   CBC, 1978, Canadian
MIDDLE AGE CRAZY   20th Century-Fox,
   1980, Canadian-U.S.
BEST REVENGE   Lorimar Distribution
   International, 1983, Canadian

JIRI TRNKA
b. February 24, 1912 - Pl'zen, Czechoslovakia
d. 1969

GRANDPA PLANTED A BEET (AF)
   1945, Czechsolovakian
THE GIFT (AF)   1946, Czechoslovakian
THE ANIMALS AND THE BRIGANDS (AF)
   1946, Czechoslovakian
THE CZECH YEAR (AF)   1947,
   Czechoslovakian
THE EMPEROR'S NIGHTINGALE (AF)
   1948, Czechoslovakian
SONG OF THE PRAIRIE (AF)   1949,
   Czechoslovakian
PRINCE BAYAYA (AF)   1950,
   Czechoslovakian
THE GOLDEN FISH (AF)   1951,
   Czechoslovakian
OLD CZECH LEGENDS (AF)   1953,
   Czechoslovakian
THE GOOD SOLDIER SCHWEIK (AF)
   1954, Czechoslovakian
A MIDSUMMER NIGHT'S DREAM (AF)
   Showcorporation, 1959, Czechoslovakian
OBSESSION (AF)   1961, Czechoslovakian
CYBERNETIC GRANDMA (AF)
   1962, Czechoslovakian
THE ARCHANGEL GABRIEL AND MRS.
   GOOSE (AF)   1965, Czechoslovakian
THE HAND (AF)   1965, Czechoslovakian

FRANÇOIS TRUFFAUT
b. February 6, 1932 - Paris, France
d. 1984

THE 400 BLOWS   Zenith, 1959, French
SHOOT THE PIANO PLAYER   Astor,
   1960, French
JULES AND JIM   Janus, 1961, French
LOVE AT TWENTY   co-director with
   Renzo Rosselini, Shintaro Ishihara,
   Marcel Ophuls & Andrzej Wajda,
   Embassy, 1962, French-Italian-
   Japanese-Polish-West German
THE SOFT SKIN   Cinema 5, 1964, French
FAHRENHEIT 451   Universal, 1967, British
THE BRIDE WORE BLACK   Lopert, 1968,
   French-Italian
STOLEN KISSES   Lopert, 1969, French
MISSISSIPPI MERMAID   United Artists,
   1970, French-Italian
THE WILD CHILD   United Artists, 1970,
   French-Italian

BED AND BOARD   *DOMICILE CONJUGAL*
   Columbia, 1971, French
TWO ENGLISH GIRLS   *LES DEUX
ANGLAISES ET LE CONTINENT*
   Janus, 1972, French
SUCH A GORGEOUS KID LIKE ME
   Columbia, 1973, French
DAY FOR NIGHT   *LA NUIT AMERICAINE* ★
   Warner Bros., 1973, French-Italian
THE STORY OF ADELE H.   New World,
   1975, French
SMALL CHANGE   *L'ARGENT DE POCHE*
   New World, 1976, French
THE MAN WHO LOVED WOMEN   Cinema 5,
   1977, French
THE GREEN ROOM   New World,
   1978, French
LOVE ON THE RUN   New World,
   1979, French
THE LAST METRO   United Artists Classics,
   1980, French
THE WOMAN NEXT DOOR   United Artists
   Classics, 1981, French
VIVEMENT DIMANCHE   Spectrafilm,
   1983, French

DALTON TRUMBO
(James Dalton Trumbo)
b. December 9, 1905 - Montrose, Colorado
d. 1976

JOHNNY GOT HIS GUN   Cinemation, 1971

U

EDGAR G. ULMER
b. September 17, 1904 - Vienna, Austria
d. 1972

MENSCHEN AM SONNTAG (FD)   co-director
   with Robert Siodmak, 1929, German
DAMAGED LIVES   Weidon, 1933
MR. BROADWAY   Broadway-Hollywood, 1933
THE BLACK CAT   Universal, 1934
THUNDER OVER TEXAS   directed under
   pseudonym of John Warner, 1934
FROM NINE TO NINE   directed under
   pseudonym of John Warner, 1935
NATALKA POLTAVKA   1937
GREEN FIELDS   co-director with
   Jacob Ben-Ami, Collective, 1937
THE SINGING BLACKSMITH
   Collective, 1938
COSSACKS IN EXILE
   Avramenko Films, 1939
THE LIGHT AHEAD   1939
FISHKE THE LAME   *FISHKE DER DRUME*
   1939, German
MOON OVER HARLEM   Meteor, 1939
AMERIKANER SHADCHEN   *AMERICAN
   MATCHMAKER*   Fame Films, 1940
TOMORROW WE LIVE   Producers
   Releasing Corp., 1942
MY SON THE HERO   Producers
   Releasing Corp., 1943
GIRLS IN CHAINS   Producers
   Releasing Corp., 1943
ISLE OF FORGOTTEN SINS   *MONSOON*
   Producers Releasing Corp., 1943

JIVE JUNCTION   Producers Releasing
   Corp., 1943
BLUEBEARD   Producers Releasing
   Corp., 1944
STRANGE ILLUSION   *OUT OF THE NIGHT*
   Producers Releasing Corp., 1945
CLUB HAVANA   Producers Releasing
   Corp., 1945
DETOUR   Producers Releasing Corp., 1946
THE WIFE OF MONTE CRISTO   Producers
   Releasing Corp., 1946
HER SISTER'S SECRET   Producers
   Releasing Corp., 1946
THE STRANGE WOMAN   United Artists, 1946
CARNEGIE HALL   United Artists, 1947
RUTHLESS   Eagle Lion, 1948
THE PIRATES OF CAPRI   *CAPTAIN SIROCCO*
   Film Classics, 1949, Italian
ST. BENNY THE DIP   United Artists, 1951
THE MAN FROM PLANET X
   United Artists, 1951
BABES IN BAGDAD   United Artists, 1952
MURDER IS MY BEAT   Allied Artists, 1955
THE NAKED DAWN   Universal, 1955
THE DAUGHTER OF DR. JEKYLL
   Allied Artists, 1957
HANNIBAL   Warner Bros., 1960, Italian
THE AMAZING TRANSPARENT MAN
   American International, 1960
BEYOND THE TIME BARRIER   American
   International, 1960
JOURNEY BENEATH THE DESERT
   *ANTINEA, L'AMANTE DELLA CITTA
   SEPOLTA*   co-director with Giuseppe Masini,
   Embassy, 1961, Italian-French
THE CAVERN   *SETTE CONTRO LA MORTE*
   20th Century-Fox, 1965,
   Italian-West German

V

W. S. ("WOODY") VAN DYKE
(Woodbridge Strong Van Dyke II)
b. 1889 - Seattle, Washington
d. 1943

THE LAND OF LONG SHADOWS
   Essanay, 1917
THE RANGE BOSS   Essanay, 1917
OPEN PLACES   Essanay, 1917
MEN OF THE DESERT   Essanay, 1917
GIFT O'GAB   Essanay, 1917
THE LADY OF THE DUGOUT
   Jennings-Shipman, 1918
THE HAWK'S TRAIL (S)   Burston, 1918
DAREDEVIL JACK (S)   Pathé, 1920
DOUBLE ADVENTURE (S)   Pathé, 1921
THE AVENGING ARROW (S)   co-director with
   William J. Bowman, Pathé, 1921
WHITE EAGLE (S)   Pathé, 1922
ACCORDING TO HOYLE   Western, 1922
THE BOSS OF CAMP 4   Fox, 1922
FORGET-ME-NOT   Metro, 1922
THE LITTLE GIRL NEXT DOOR
   Blair-Coan, 1923
YOU ARE IN DANGER   Blair-Coan, 1923
THE DESTROYING ANGEL   Associated
   Exhibitors, 1923
THE MIRACLE MAKERS   Associated
   Exhibitors, 1923

LOVING LIES   Allied Producers &
   Distributors, 1924
THE BEAUTIFUL SINNER   Perfection, 1924
HALF-A-DOLLAR BILL   Metro, 1924
WINNER TAKE ALL   Fox, 1924
THE BATTLING FOOL   C.B.C., 1924
GOLD HEELS   Fox, 1924
BARRIERS BURNED AWAY   Associated
   Exhibitors, 1925
HEARTS AND SPURS   Fox, 1925
THE TRAIL RIDER   Fox, 1925
RANGER OF THE BIG PINES   Fox, 1925
THE TIMBER WOLF   Fox, 1925
THE DESERT'S PRICE   Fox, 1925
THE GENTLE CYCLONE   Fox, 1926
WAR PAINT   MGM, 1926
WINNERS OF THE WILDERNESS
   MGM, 1927
CALIFORNIA   Arrow, 1927
THE HEART OF THE YUKON   Pathé, 1927
EYES OF THE TOTEM   Pathé, 1927
SPOILERS OF THE WEST   MGM, 1927
FOREIGN DEVILS   MGM, 1927
WYOMING   MGM, 1928
UNDER THE BLACK EAGLE   MGM, 1928
WHITE SHADOWS OF THE SOUTH SEAS
   co-director with Robert J. Flaherty,
   MGM, 1928
THE PAGAN   MGM, 1929
TRADER HORN   MGM, 1931
NEVER THE TWAIN SHALL MEET
   MGM, 1931
GUILTY HANDS   MGM, 1931
THE CUBAN LOVE SONG   MGM, 1931
TARZAN, THE APE MAN   MGM, 1932
NIGHT COURT   MGM, 1932
PENTHOUSE   MGM, 1933
THE PRIZEFIGHTER AND THE LADY
   MGM, 1933
ESKIMO   MGM, 1933
LAUGHING BOY   MGM, 1934
MANHATTAN MELODRAMA   MGM, 1934
THE THIN MAN ★   MGM, 1934
HIDE-OUT   MGM, 1934
FORSAKING ALL OTHERS   MGM, 1934
NAUGHTY MARIETTA   MGM, 1935
I LIFE MY LIFE   MGM, 1935
ROSE-MARIE   MGM, 1936
SAN FRANCISCO ★   MGM, 1936
HIS BROTHER'S WIFE   MGM, 1936
THE DEVIL IS A SISSY   MGM, 1936
LOVE ON THE RUN   MGM, 1936
AFTER THE THIN MAN   MGM, 1936
PERSONAL PROPERTY   MGM, 1937
THEY GAVE HIM A GUN   MGM, 1937
ROSALIE   MGM, 1937
MARIE ANTOINETTE   MGM, 1938
SWEETHEARTS   MGM, 1938
STAND UP AND FIGHT   MGM, 1939
IT'S A WONDERFUL WORLD   MGM, 1939
ANDY HARDY GETS SPRING FEVER
   MGM, 1939
ANOTHER THIN MAN   MGM, 1939
I TAKE THIS WOMAN   MGM, 1940
I LOVE YOU AGAIN   MGM, 1940
BITTER SWEET   MGM, 1940
RAGE IN HEAVEN   MGM, 1941
SHADOW OF THE THIN MAN   MGM, 1941
THE FEMININE TOUCH   MGM, 1941
DR. KILDARE'S VICTORY   MGM, 1942
I MARRIED AN ANGEL   MGM, 1942
CAIRO   MGM, 1942
JOURNEY FOR MARGARET   MGM, 1942

STEFANO VANZINA
(See STENO)

DZIGA VERTOV
(Denis Arkadievitch Kaufman)
b. January 2, 1896 - Bialystok, Russia
d. 1954

ANNIVERSARY OF THE REVOLUTION (FD)
   1919, Russian
THE BATTLE OF TSARITSYN (FD)
   1920, Russian
KALININ - THE ELDER STATESMAN OF
   ALL RUSSIANS (FD)   1920, Russian
THE EXHUMATION OF THE REMAINS OF
   SERGEI RADONEZHSKY (FD)
   1920, Russian
THE MIRONOV TRIAL (FD)   1920, Russian
TRAIN OF THE CENTRAL COMMITTEE (FD)
   1921, Russian
HISTORY OF THE CIVIL WAR (FD)
   1922, Soviet
THE EZEROV TRIAL (FD)   1922, Soviet
UNIVERMAG (FD)   1922, Soviet
OCTOBER CINEMA TRUTH (FD)
   1923, Soviet
FIVE YEARS OF STRUGGLE AND
   VICTORY (FD)   1923, Soviet
TODAY (AF)   1924, Soviet
SOVIET PLAYTHINGS (AF)   1924, Soviet
KINO-GLAZ (FD)   1924, Soviet
STRIDE SOVIET! (FD)   1926, Soviet
A SIXTH OF THE WORLD (FD)   1926, Soviet
THE ELEVENTH YEAR (FD)   1928, Soviet
MAN WITH A MOVIE CAMERA (FD)
   1929, Soviet
ENTHUSIASM (FD)   1931, Soviet
THREE SONGS ABOUT LENIN (FD)
   1934, Soviet
LULLABY   1937, Soviet
SERGEI ORDZHONIKIDZE   1937, Soviet
THREE HEROINES   1938, Soviet
ELEVATION A   1941, Soviet
BLOOD FOR BLOOD - LIFE FOR LIFE
   1941, Soviet
CAMERA REPORTERS ON THE LINE
   OF FIRE (FD)   1941, Soviet
ON TO THE FRONT! (FD)   1943, Soviet
ON THE MOUNTAINS OF ALA-TAU (FD)
   1944, Soviet
THE OATH OF YOUTH   1947, Soviet

CHARLES VIDOR
b. July 27, 1900 - Budapest, Hungary
d. 1959

SENSATION HUNTERS   Monogram, 1934
DOUBLE DOOR   Paramount, 1934
STRANGERS ALL   RKO RADIO, 1935
THE ARIZONIAN   RKO RADIO, 1935
HIS FAMILY TREE   RKO RADIO, 1935
MUSS 'EM UP   RKO Radio, 1936
A DOCTOR'S DIARY   Paramount, 1937
THE GREAT GAMBINI   Paramount, 1937
SHE'S NO LADY   Paramount, 1937
ROMANCE OF THE REDWOODS
   Columbia, 1939
BLIND ALLEY   Columbia, 1939
THOSE HIGH GREY WALLS   Columbia, 1939
MY SON, MY SON   Columbia, 1940
THE LADY IN QUESTION   Columbia, 1940
LADIES IN RETIREMENT   Columbia, 1941
NEW YORK TOWN   Paramount, 1941
THE TUTTLES OF TAHITI   RKO Radio, 1942
THE DESPERADOES   Columbia, 1942
COVER GIRL   Columbia, 1944
TOGETHER AGAIN   Columbia, 1944
A SONG TO REMEMBER   Columbia, 1945
OVER 21   Columbia, 1945
GILDA   Columbia, 1946

THE LOVES OF CARMEN   Columbia, 1948
IT'S A BIG COUNTRY   co-director,
   MGM, 1952
HANS CHRISTIAN ANDERSEN
   RKO Radio, 1952
THUNDER IN THE EAST   Paramount, 1953
RHAPSODY   MGM, 1954
LOVE ME OR LEAVE ME   MGM, 1955
THE SWAN   MGM, 1956
THE JOKER IS WILD   *ALL THE WAY*
   Paramount, 1957
A FAREWELL TO ARMS
   20th Century-Fox, 1957
SONG WITHOUT END   co-director with
   George Cukor, Columbia, 1960

KING VIDOR
b. February 9, 1894 - Galveston, Texas
d. 1982

THE TURN IN THE ROAD
   Robertson-Cole, 1919
BETTER TIMES   Brentwood-Mutual, 1919
THE OTHER HALF   Exclusive
   International, 1919
POOR RELATIONS   Robertson-Cole, 1919
THE FAMILY HONOR   Associated First
   National, 1920
THE JACK-KNIFE MAN   Associated First
   National, 1920
THE SKY PILOT   Associated First
   National, 1921
LOVE NEVER DIES   Associated First
   National, 1921
THE REAL ADVENTURE   Associated
   Exhibitors, 1922
DUSK TO DAWN   Associated Exhibitors, 1922
CONQUERING THE WOMAN   Associated
   Exhibitors, 1922
WILD ORANGES   Goldwyn, 1922
WOMAN, WAKE UP   Associated
   Exhibitors, 1922
ALICE ADAMS   co-director with
   Rowland V. Lee, Associated Exhibitors, 1923
PEG O' MY HEART   Metro, 1923
THE WOMAN OF BRONZE   Metro, 1923
THREE WISE FOOLS   Goldwyn, 1923
HAPPINESS   Metro, 1924
WINE OF YOUTH   Metro-Goldwyn, 1924
HIS HOUR   Metro-Goldwyn, 1924
WIFE OF THE CENTAUR
   Metro-Goldwyn, 1924
PROUD FLESH   MGM, 1925
THE BIG PARADE   MGM, 1925
LA BOHEME   MGM, 1926
BARDELYS THE MAGNIFICENT   MGM, 1926
THE CROWD ★   MGM, 1927
THE PATSY   MGM, 1928
SHOW PEOPLE   MGM, 1928
HALLELUJAH! ★   MGM, 1929
NOT SO DUMB   MGM, 1930
BILLY THE KID   MGM, 1930
STREET SCENE   United Artists, 1931
THE CHAMP ★   MGM, 1931
BIRD OF PARADISE   RKO Radio, 1932
CYNARA   United Artists, 1932
THE STRANGER'S RETURN   MGM, 1933
OUR DAILY BREAD   United Artists, 1934
THE WEDDING NIGHT   United Artists, 1935
SO RED THE ROSE   Paramount, 1935
THE TEXAS RANGERS   Paramount, 1936
STELLA DALLAS   United Artists, 1937
THE CITADEL ★   MGM, 1938
NORTHWEST PASSAGE   MGM, 1940
COMRADE X   MGM, 1940
H.M. PULHAM, ESQ.   MGM, 1941
AN AMERICAN ROMANCE   MGM, 1944
DUEL IN THE SUN   Selznick Releasing, 1946

ON OUR MERRY WAY *A MIRACLE CAN HAPPEN* United Artists, 1948
THE FOUNTAINHEAD Warner Bros., 1949
BEYOND THE FOREST Warner Bros., 1949
LIGHTNING STRIKES TWICE
  Warner Bros., 1951
JAPANESE WAR BRIDE
  20th Century-Fox, 1952
RUBY GENTRY 20th Century-Fox, 1953
MAN WITHOUT A STAR Universal, 1955
WAR AND PEACE ★ Paramount,
  1956, Italian
SOLOMON AND SHEBA United Artists, 1959

JEAN VIGO

b. April 26, 1905 - Paris, France
d. 1934

A PROPOS DE NICE (FD) 1930, French
TARIS CHAMPION DE NATATION
  1931, French
ZERO FOR CONDUCT Brandon,
  1933, French
L'ATALANTE 1934, French

LUCHINO VISCONTI

(Count Don Luchino Visconti di Modrone)

b. November 2, 1906 - Milan, Italy
d. 1976

OSSESSIONE Brandon, 1942, Italian
GIORNI DI GLORIA (FD) co-director,
  1945, Italian
LA TERRA TREMA Fleetwood Films,
  1948, Italian
APPUNTI SU UN FATTO DI CRONACA (SD)
  1951, Italian
BELLISSIMA Italian Films Export,
  1951, Italian
OF LIFE AND LOVE *SIAMO DONNE*
  co-director, DCA, 1953, Italian
SENSO *THE WANTON CONTESSA*
  Fleetwood Films, 1955, Italian
WHITE NIGHTS *LE NOTTI BIANCHE*
  United Motion Picture Organization,
  1957, Italian-French
ROCCO AND HIS BROTHERS Astor, 1960,
  Italian-French, re-released in 1992
  by Milestone Films
BOCCACCIO '70 co-director with
  Federico Fellini & Vittorio De Sica,
  Embassy, 1962, Italian
THE LEOPARD 20th Century-Fox, 1963,
  Italian-French
VAGHE STELLE DELL'ORSA *SANDRA*
  1965, Italian
THE WITCHES co-director, Lopert, 1967,
  Italian-French
THE STRANGER Paramount, 1967,
  Italian-French-Algerian
THE DAMNED *LA CADUTA DEGLI DEI/ GOTTERDAMERUNG* Warner Bros.,
  1969, Italian-West German
DEATH IN VENICE Warner Bros., 1971,
  Italian-French
LUDWIG MGM, 1972,
  Italian-French-West German,
CONVERSATION PIECE *GRUPPO DI FAMIGLIAIN UNO INTERNO* New Line
  Cinema, 1975, Italian-French
THE INNOCENT 1976, Italian

JOSEF VON STERNBERG

(Josef Sternberg)

b. May 29, 1894 - Vienna, Austria
d. 1969

THE SALVATION HUNTERS
  United Artists, 1925
THE MASKED BRIDE co-director with
  Christy Cabanne, MGM, 1925
THE EXQUISITE SINNER co-director with
  Phil Rosen, MGM, 1926
A WOMAN OF THE SEA *THE SEA GULL*
  United Artists, 1926
UNDERWORLD Paramount, 1927
THE LAST COMMAND Paramount, 1928
THE DRAGNET Paramount, 1928
THE DOCKS OF NEW ORLEANS
  Paramount, 1928
THE CASE OF LENA SMITH
  Paramount, 1929
THUNDERBOLT Paramount, 1929
THE BLUE ANGEL UFA, 1930, German
MOROCCO ★ Paramount, 1930
DISHONORED Paramount, 1931
AN AMERICAN TRAGEDY Paramount, 1931
SHANGHAI EXPRESS ★ Paramount, 1932
BLONDE VENUS Paramount, 1932
THE SCARLET EMPRESS Paramount, 1934
THE DEVIL IS A WOMAN Paramount, 1935
CRIME AND PUNISHMENT Columbia, 1935
THE KING STEPS OUT Columbia, 1936
I, CLAUDIUS 1937, unfinished
SERGEANT MADDEN MGM, 1939
THE SHANGHAI GESTURE
  United Artists, 1941
MACAO RKO Radio, 1952
THE SAGA OF ANATAHAN *ANA-TA-HAN*
  1953, Japanese
JET PILOT Universal, 1957

ERICH VON STROHEIM

(Erich Oswald Stroheim)

b. September 22, 1885 - Vienna, Austria
d. 1957

BLIND HUSBANDS Universal, 1919
THE DEVIL'S PASS KEY Universal, 1920
FOOLISH WIVES Universal, 1922
MERRY-GO-ROUND co-director with
  Rupert Julian, Universal, 1923
GREED MGM, 1925
THE MERRY WIDOW MGM, 1925
THE WEDDING MARCH Paramount, 1928
QUEEN KELLY Paramount, 1928, unfinished
WALKING DOWN BROADWAY Paramount,
  1932, unfinished

GEORGE WAGGNER

(George Waggoner)

b. September 7, 1894 - New York, New York
d. 1984

WESTERN TRAILS 1938
OUTLAW EXPRESS 1938
GUILTY TRAILS 1938
PRAIRIE JUSTICE 1938
BLACK BANDIT 1938
GHOST TOWN RIDERS 1938
HONOR OF THE WEST 1939
MYSTERY PLANE 1939
WOLF CALL 1939
STUNT PILOT 1939
THE PHANTOM STAGE 1939
DRUMS OF THE DESERT 1940
MAN-MADE MONSTER Universal, 1941
HORROR ISLAND Universal, 1941
SOUTH OF TAHITI Universal, 1941
SEALED LIPS Universal, 1941
THE WOLF MAN Universal, 1941
THE CLIMAX Universal, 1944
FRISCO SAL Universal, 1945
SHADY LADY Universal, 1945
TANGIER Universal, 1946
GUNFIGHTERS Columbia, 1947
THE FIGHTING KENTUCKIAN
  Republic, 1949
OPERATION PACIFIC Warner Bros., 1951
PAWNEE Republic, 1957
DESTINATION 60,000 Allied Artists, 1957
FURY RIVER co-director with
  Jacques Tourneur, MGM, 1959
FRONTIER RANGERS (TF) co-director with
  Jacques Tourneur, MGM, 1959

HAL WALKER

b. March 20, 1896 - Ottumwa, Iowa
d. 1972

OUT OF THIS WORLD Paramount, 1945
DUFFY'S TAVERN Paramount, 1945
ROAD TO UTOPIA Paramount, 1946
MY FRIEND IRMA GOES WEST
  Paramount, 1950
AT WAR WITH THE ARMY
  Paramount, 1951
THAT'S MY BOY Paramount, 1951
SAILOR BEWARE Paramount, 1952
ROAD TO BALI Paramount, 1953

STUART WALKER

b. 1887 - Augusta, Kentucky
d. 1941

THE SECRET CALL Paramount, 1931
THE FALSE MADONNA Paramount, 1931
THE MISLEADING LADY Paramount, 1932
EVENINGS FOR SALE Paramount, 1932
TONIGHT IS OURS Paramount, 1933
THE EAGLE AND THE HAWK
  Paramount, 1933
WHITE WOMAN Paramount, 1933
ROMANCE IN THE RAIN Universal, 1934
GREAT EXPECTATIONS Universal, 1934

THE MYSTERY OF EDWIN DROOD
   Universal, 1935
THE WEREWOLF OF LONDON
   Universal, 1935
MANHATTAN MOON   Universal, 1935

RICHARD WALLACE
b. August 26, 1894
d. 1951

SYNCOPATING SUE   1926
McFADDEN'S FLATS   1927
POOR NAT   1927
AMERICAN BEAUTY   1927
TEXAS STEER   1927
LADY BE GOOD   1928
THE BUTTER AND EGG MAN   1928
THE SHOPWORN ANGEL   1929
INNOCENTS OF PARIS   1929
RIVER OF ROMANCE   1929
SEVEN DAYS LEAVE   1930
ANYBODY'S WAR   1930
THE RIGHT TO LOVE   1930
MAN OF THE WORLD   1931
KICK IN   1931
THE ROAD TO RENO   1931
TOMORROW AND TOMORROW   1932
THUNDER BELOW   Paramount, 1932
THE MASQUERADER   United Artists, 1933
EIGHT GIRLS IN A BOAT   1934
THE LITTLE MINISTER   RKO Radio, 1934
WEDDING PRESENT   1936
JOHN MEADE'S WOMAN   Paramount, 1937
BLOSSOMS ON BROADWAY   1937
THE YOUNG IN HEART   United Artists, 1938
THE UNDER-PUP   1939
CAPTAIN CAUTION   United Artists, 1940
A GIRL, A GUY AND A GOB
   RKO Radio, 1941
SHE KNEW ALL THE ANSWERS
   RKO Radio, 1941
OBLIGING YOUNG LADY   RKO Radio, 1941
THE WIFE TAKES A FLYER   Columbia, 1942
A NIGHT TO REMEMBER
   United Artists, 1942
BOMBARDIER   RKO Radio, 1943
THE FALLEN SPARROW   RKO Radio, 1943
MY KINGDOM FOR A COOK
   RKO Radio, 1943
BRIDE BY MISTAKE   RKO Radio, 1944
IT'S IN THE BAG   United Artists, 1945
KISS AND TELL   Columbia, 1945
BECAUSE OF HIM   Universal, 1946
SINBAD THE SAILOR   RKO Radio, 1947
FRAMED   Columbia, 1947
TYCOON   RKO Radio, 1947
LET'S LIVE A LITTLE   20th Century-Fox, 1948
ADVENTURE IN BALTIMORE
   RKO Radio, 1949
A KISS FOR CORLISS   United Artists, 1949

RAOUL WALSH
b. March 11, 1887 - New York, New York
d. 1980

THE LIFE OF GENERAL VILLA   co-director
   with Christy Cabanne, Biograph, 1914
THE DOUBLE KNOT   1914
THE MYSTERY OF THE HINDU IMAGE   1914
THE FINAL VERDICT   1914
HIS RETURN   1915
THE GREASER   1915
THE FENCING MASTER   1915
A MAN FOR ALL THAT   1915
ELEVEN-THIRTY P.M.   1915
THE BURIED HAND   1915
THE CELESTIAL CODE   1915

A BAD MAN AND OTHERS   1915
THE REGENERATION   Fox, 1915
CARMEN   Fox, 1915
PILLARS OF SOCIETY   1916
THE SERPENT   Fox, 1916
BLUE BLOOD AND RED   Fox, 1916
THE HONOR SYSTEM   Fox, 1916
THE CONQUEROR   Fox, 1917
BETRAYED   Fox, 1917
THIS IS THE LIFE   Fox, 1917
THE PRIDE OF NEW YORK   Fox, 1917
THE SILENT LIE   Fox, 1917
THE INNOCENT SINNER   Fox, 1917
THE WOMAN AND THE LAW   Fox, 1918
THE PRUSSIAN CUR   Fox, 1918
ON THE JUMP   Fox, 1918
EVERY MOTHER'S SON   Fox, 1918
I'LL SAY SO   Fox, 1918
EVANGELINE   Fox, 1919
THE STRONGEST   Fox, 1919
SHOULD A HUSBAND FORGIVE?   Fox, 1919
FROM NOW ON   Fox, 1920
THE DEEP PURPLE   Realart, 1920
THE OATH   Mayflower, 1921
SERENADE   Associated First National, 1921
KINDRED OF THE DUST   Associated First
   National, 1922
LOST AND FOUND ON A SOUTH SEA ISLAND
   Goldwyn, 1923
THE THIEF OF BAGDAD   United Artists, 1924
EAST OF SUEZ   Paramount, 1925
THE SPANIARD   Paramount, 1925
THE WANDERER   Paramount, 1925
THE LUCKY LADY   Paramount, 1926
THE LADY OF THE HAREM
   Paramount, 1926
WHAT PRICE GLORY   Fox, 1927
THE MONEY TALKS   Fox, 1927
THE LOVES OF CARMEN   Fox, 1927
SADIE THOMPSON   United Artists, 1928
THE RED DANCE   Fox, 1928
ME GANGSTER   Fox, 1928
IN OLD ARIZONA   co-director with
   Irving Cummings, Fox, 1929
THE COCK-EYED WORLD   Fox, 1929
HOT FOR PARIS   Fox, 1929
THE BIG TRAIL   Fox, 1930
THE MAN WHO CAME BACK   Fox, 1931
WOMEN OF ALL NATIONS   Fox, 1931
THE YELLOW TICKET   Fox, 1931
WILD GIRL   Fox, 1932
ME AND MY GAL   *PIER 13*   Fox, 1932
SAILOR'S LUCK   Fox, 1933
THE BOWERY   United Artists, 1933
GOING HOLLYWOOD   MGM, 1933
UNDER PRESSURE   Fox, 1935
BABY-FACE HARRINGTON   MGM, 1935
EVERY NIGHT AT EIGHT   Paramount, 1935
KLONDIKE ANNIE   Paramount, 1936
BIG BROWN EYES   Paramount, 1936
SPENDTHRIFT   Paramount, 1936
O.H.M.S.   *YOU'RE IN THE ARMY NOW*
   Gaumont-British, 1937, British
JUMP FOR GLORY   *WHEN THIEF
   MEETS THIEF*   Criterion, 1937, British
ARTISTS AND MODELS   Paramount, 1937
HITTING A NEW HIGH   RKO Radio, 1937
COLLEGE SWING   Paramount, 1938
ST. LOUIS BLUES   Paramount, 1939
THE ROARING TWENTIES
   Warner Bros., 1939
DARK COMMAND   Republic, 1940
THEY DRIVE BY NIGHT   Warner Bros., 1940
HIGH SIERRA   Warner Bros., 1941
THE STRAWBERRY BLONDE
   Warner Bros., 1941
MANPOWER   Warner Bros., 1941

THEY DIED WITH THEIR BOOTS ON
   Warner Bros., 1941
DESPERATE JOURNEY   Warner Bros., 1942
GENTLEMAN JIM   Warner Bros., 1942
BACKGROUND TO DANGER
   Warner Bros., 1943
NORTHERN PURSUIT   Warner Bros., 1943
UNCERTAIN GLORY   Warner Bros., 1944
OBJECTIVE, BURMA!   Warner Bros., 1945
THE HORN BLOWS AT MIDNIGHT
   Warner Bros., 1945
SALTY O'ROURKE   Paramount, 1945
THE MAN I LOVE   Warner Bros., 1947
PURSUED   Warner Bros., 1947
CHEYENNE   *THE WYOMING KID*
   Warner Bros., 1947
SILVER RIVER   Warner Bros., 1948
FIGHTER SQUADRON   Warner Bros., 1948
ONE SUNDAY AFTERNOON
   Warner Bros., 1948
COLORADO TERRITORY
   Warner Bros., 1949
WHITE HEAT   Warner Bros., 1949
ALONG THE GREAT DIVIDE
   Warner Bros., 1951
CAPTAIN HORATIO HORNBLOWER
   Warner Bros., 1951
DISTANT DRUMS   Warner Bros., 1951
GLORY ALLEY   MGM, 1952
THE WORLD IN HIS ARMS   Universal, 1952
BLACKBEARD THE PIRATE
   RKO Radio, 1952
THE LAWLESS BREED   Universal, 1953
SEA DEVILS   RKO Radio, 1953
A LION IS IN THE STREETS
   Warner Bros., 1953
GUN FURY   Columbia, 1953
SASKATCHEWAN   Universal, 1954
BATTLE CRY   Warner Bros., 1955
THE TALL MEN   20th Century-Fox, 1955
THE REVOLT OF MAMIE STOVER
   20th Century-Fox, 1956
THE KING AND FOUR QUEENS
   United Artists, 1956
BAND OF ANGELS   Warner Bros., 1957
THE NAKED AND THE DEAD
   Warner Bros., 1958
THE SHERIFF OF FRACTURED JAW
   20th Century-Fox, 1958, British
A PRIVATE'S AFFAIR
   20th Century-Fox, 1959
ESTHER AND THE KING   20th Century-Fox,
   1960, Italian-U.S.
MARINES, LET'S GO!
   20th Century-Fox, 1961
A DISTANT TRUMPET   Warner Bros., 1964

CHARLES WALTERS
b. November 17, 1911 - Brooklyn, New York
d. 1982

GOOD NEWS   MGM, 1947
EASTER PARADE   MGM, 1948
THE BARKLEYS OF BROADWAY
   MGM, 1949
SUMMER STOCK   MGM, 1950
THREE GUYS NAMED MIKE   MGM, 1951
TEXAS CARNIVAL   MGM, 1951
THE BELLE OF NEW YORK   MGM, 1952
LILI ★   MGM, 1953
DANGEROUS WHEN WET   MGM, 1953
TORCH SONG   MGM, 1953
EASY TO LOVE   MGM, 1953
THE GLASS SLIPPER   MGM, 1955
THE TENDER TRAP   MGM, 1955
HIGH SOCIETY   MGM, 1956
DON'T GO NEAR THE WATER   MGM, 1957
ASK ANY GIRL   MGM, 1959

PLEASE DON'T EAT THE DAISIES
MGM, 1960
TWO LOVES   MGM, 1961
JUMBO   BILLY ROSE'S JUMBO   MGM, 1962
THE UNSINKABLE MOLLY BROWN
MGM, 1964
WALK, DON'T RUN   Columbia, 1966

SAM WANAMAKER
b. June 14, 1919 - Chicago, Illinois
d. 1993

THE FILE ON THE GOLDEN GOOSE
United Artists, 1969, British
THE EXECUTIONER   Columbia, 1970, British
CATLOW   MGM, 1971, U.S.-Spanish
SINBAD AND THE EYE OF THE TIGER
Columbia, 1977, British
MY KIDNAPPER, MY LOVE (TF)
Roger Gimbel Productions/EMI TV, 1980
THE KILLING OF RANDY WEBSTER (TF)
Roger Gimbel Productions/EMI TV, 1981

ANDY WARHOL
(Andrew Warhola)
b. August 8, 1927 - Cleveland, Ohio
d. 1987

KISS   Film-Makers, 1963
EAT   Film-Makers, 1963
SLEEP   Film-Makers, 1963
HAIRCUT   Film-Makers, 1963
TARZAN AND JANE REGAINED...SORT OF
co-director, Film-Makers, 1964
DANCE MOVIE   Film-Makers, 1964
BLOW JOB   Film-Makers, 1964
BATMAN DRACULA   Film-Makers, 1964
SALOME AND DELILAH   Film-Makers, 1964
SOAP OPERA   co-director,
Film-Makers, 1964
COUCH   Film-Makers, 1964
13 MOST BEAUTIFUL WOMEN
Film-Makers, 1964
HARLOT   Film-Makers, 1964
THE LIFE OF JUANITA CASTRO
Film-Makers, 1965
EMPIRE   Film-Makers, 1965
POOR LITTLE RICH GIRL   Film-Makers, 1965
SCREEN TEST   Film-Makers, 1965
VINYL   Film-Makers, 1965
BEAUTY #2   Film-Makers, 1965
BITCH   Film-Makers, 1965
PRISON   Film-Makers, 1965
SPACE   Film-Makers, 1965
THE CLOSET   Film-Makers, 1965
HENRY GELDZAHLER   Film-Makers, 1965
TAYLOR MEAD'S ASS   Film-Makers, 1965
FACE   Film-Makers, 1965
MY HUSTLER   Film-Makers, 1965
CAMP   Film-Makers, 1965
SUICIDE   Film-Makers, 1965
DRUNK   Film-Makers, 1965
OUTER AND INNER SPACE
Film-Makers, 1966
HEDY   HEDY THE SHOPLIFTER
Film-Makers, 1966
PAUL SWAN   Film-Makers, 1966
MORE MILK, EVETTE   LANA TURNER
Film-Makers, 1965
THE VELVET UNDERGROUND AND NICO
Film-Makers, 1966
KITCHEN   Film-Makers, 1966
LUPE   Film-Makers, 1966
EATING TOO FAST   Film-Makers, 1966
THE CHELSEA GIRLS   Film-Makers, 1966
I, A MAN   Film-Makers, 1967
BIKE BOY   Film-Makers, 1967

NUDE RESTAURANT   Film-Makers, 1967
FOUR STARS   24-HOUR MOVIE
Film-Makers, 1967
IMITATION OF CHRIST   Film-Makers, 1967
THE LOVES OF ONDINE   Warhol, 1968
LONESOME COWBOYS   Sherpix, 1968
BLUE MOVIE   FUCK   Factory, 1969
WOMEN IN REVOLT   Warhol, 1972
L'AMOUR   co-director with Paul Morrissey,
Altura, 1973

CHARLES MARQUIS WARREN
b. December 16, 1917 - Baltimore, Maryland
d. 1990

LITTLE BIG HORN   Lippert, 1951
HELLGATE   Lippert, 1952
ARROWHEAD   Paramount, 1953
FLIGHT TO TANGIER   Paramount, 1953
SEVEN ANGRY MEN   Allied Artists, 1955
TENSION AT TABLE ROCK   Universal, 1956
THE BLACK WHIP   20th Century-Fox, 1956
TROOPER HOOK   United Artists, 1957
BACK FROM THE DEAD
20th Century-Fox, 1957
THE UNKNOWN TERROR
20th Century-Fox, 1957
COPPER SKY   20th Century-Fox, 1957
RIDE A VIOLENT MILE
20th Century-Fox, 1957
DESERT HELL   20th Century-Fox, 1958
CATTLE EMPIRE   20th Century-Fox, 1958
BLOOD ARROW   20th Century-Fox, 1958
CHARRO!   National General, 1969

JOHN WAYNE
(Marion Michael Morrison)
b. May 26, 1907 - Winterset, Iowa
d. 1979

THE ALAMO   United Artists, 1960
THE GREEN BERETS   co-director with
Ray Kellogg, Warner Bros., 1968

JACK WEBB
b. April 2, 1920 - Santa Monica, California
d. 1982

DRAGNET   Warner Bros., 1954
PETE KELLY'S BLUES   Warner Bros., 1955
THE D.I.   Warner Bros., 1957
-30-   Warner Bros., 1959
THE LAST TIME I SAW ARCHIE
United Artists, 1961
DRAGNET (TF)   Mark VII Ltd./
Universal TV, 1969
O'HARA, UNITED STATES TREASURY:
OPERATION COBRA (TF)
Mark VII Ltd./Universal TV, 1971
EMERGENCY! (TF)   Mark VII Ltd./
Universal TV, 1972
CHASE (TF)   Mark VII Ltd./Universal TV, 1973

ROBERT D. WEBB
b. January 3, 1903
d. 1990

THE CARIBBEAN MYSTERY
20th Century-Fox, 1945
THE SPIDER   20th Century-Fox, 1945
THE GLORY BRIGADE
20th Century-Fox, 1953
BENEATH THE 12-MILE REEF
20th Century-Fox, 1953
WHITE FEATHER   20th Century-Fox, 1955
SEVEN CITIES OF GOLD
20th Century-Fox, 1955

ON THE THRESHOLD OF SPACE
20th Century-Fox, 1956
THE PROUD ONES   20th Century-Fox, 1956
LOVE ME TENDER   20th Century-Fox, 1956
THE WAY TO THE GOLD
20th Century-Fox, 1957
GUNS OF THE TIMBERLAND
Warner Bros., 1960
PIRATES OF TORTUGA
20th Century-Fox, 1961
SEVEN WOMEN FROM HELL
20th Century-Fox, 1961
THE CAPETOWN AFFAIR   1967,
South African

LOIS WEBER
(Mrs. Phillips Smalley)
b. 1882 - Allegheny, Pennsylvania
d. 1939

THE TROUBADOUR'S TRIUMPH   1912
THE JEW'S CHRISTMAS   co-director with
Phillips Smalley, 1913
THE FEMALE OF THE SPECIES   1913
THE MERCHANT OF VENICE   co-director
with Phillips Smalley, Universal, 1914
A FOOL AND HIS MONEY   Universal, 1914
BEHIND THE VEIL   co-director with
Phillips Smalley, 1914
FALSE COLORS   co-director with
Phillips Smalley, Paramount, 1914
SUNSHINE MOLLY   co-director with
Phillips Smalley, Paramount, 1915
SCANDAL   co-director with Phillips Smalley,
Universal, 1915
HYPOCRITES   co-director with
Phillips Smalley, Bosworth, 1915
IT'S NO LAUGHING MATTER
Universal, 1915
A CIGARETTE, THAT'S ALL   Universal, 1915
HOP - THE DEVIL'S BREW   co-director with
Phillips Smalley, Universal, 1915
THE DUMB GIRL OF PORTICI   co-director
with Phillips Smalley, Universal, 1916
SAVING THE FAMILY NAME   Universal, 1916
THE PEOPLE VS. JOHN DOE
Universal, 1916
IDLE WIVES   Universal, 1916
WHERE ARE MY CHILDREN?   co-director
with Phillips Smalley, Universal, 1916
THE FLIRT   co-director with Phillips Smalley,
Universal, 1916
THE HAND THAT ROCKS THE CRADLE
Universal, 1917
EVEN AS YOU AND I   Peerless, 1917
THE PRICE OF A GOOD TIME
Universal-Jewel, 1917
THE MYSTERIOUS MRS. M
THE MYSTERIOUS MRS. MUSSELWHITE
Universal, 1917
FOR HUSBANDS ONLY   Weber-North, 1918
THE DOCTOR AND THE WOMAN
Universal, 1918
BORROWED CLOTHES   Universal, 1918
MARY REGAN   Associated First
National, 1919
A MIDNIGHT ROMANCE   Associated First
National, 1919
WHEN A GIRL LOVES   Universal, 1919
HOME   Universal, 1919
FORBIDDEN   Universal, 1920
TO PLEASE ONE WOMAN   Paramount, 1920
WHAT'S WORTH WHILE?   Paramount, 1921
TOO WISE WIVES   Paramount, 1921
THE BLOT   F.B. Warren, 1921
WHAT DO MEN WANT?   Wid Gunning, 1921
A CHAPTER IN HER LIFE
Universal-Jewel, 1923

THE MARRIAGE CLAUSE
  Universal-Jewel, 1926
SENSATION SEEKERS
  Universal-Jewel, 1927
THE ANGEL OF BROADWAY   Pathé, 1927
WHITE HEAT   Pinnacle, 1934

PAUL WEGENER
b. December 11, 1874 - Bischdorf, East Prussia
d. 1948

DIE AUGEN DES OLE BRANDIS
  1914, German
DER GOLEM   co-director, 1914, German
RUBEZAHLS HOCHZEIT   co-director,
  1916, German
DER RATTENFANGER VON HAMELIN
  co-director, 1916, German
DER YOGHI   co-director, 1916, German
HANS TRUTZ IN SCHLARAFFENLAND
  1917, German
DER GOLEM UND DIE TANZERIN
  co-director, 1917, German
DER FREMDE FURST   co-director,
  1918, German
WELT OHNE WAFFEN (FD)   1918, German
DER GOLEM - WIE ER IN DIE WELT KAM
  co-director, 1920, German
DER VERLORENE SCHATTEN   co-director,
  1921, German
HERZOG FERRANTES ENDE   co-director,
  1922, German
LEBENDE BUDDHAS   1924, German
EIN MANN WILL NACH DEUTSCHLAND
  1934, German
DIE FREUNDIN EINES GROSSEN MANNES
  1934, German
AUGUST DER STARKE   1936, German
MOSKAU-SHANGHAI   1936, German
DIE STUNDE DER VESUCHUNG
  1936, German
UNTER AUSSCHLUSS DER
  OEFFENTLICHKEIT   1937, German
KRACH UND GLUCK UM KUNNEMANN
  1937, German

ORSON WELLES
(George Orson Welles)
b. May 6, 1915 - Kenosha, Wisconsin
d. 1985

THE HEARTS OF AGE   co-director with
  William Vance, 1934
TOO MUCH JOHNSON   1938
CITIZEN KANE ★   RKO Radio, 1941
THE MAGNIFICENT AMBERSONS
  RKO Radio, 1942
IT'S ALL TRUE   co-director with
  Norman Foster, RKO Radio,
  1942, unfinished
THE STRANGER   RKO Radio, 1946
THE LADY FROM SHANGHAI
  Columbia, 1948
MACBETH   Republic, 1948
OTHELLO   United Artists, 1952,
  U.S.-Italian, re-released in 1992
  by Castle Hill Productions
MR. ARKADIN   *CONFIDENTIAL REPORT*
  Warner Bros., 1955, Spanish-Swiss
DON QUIXOTE   1955, Spanish, unfinished
TOUCH OF EVIL   Universal, 1958
THE TRIAL   Astor, 1962,
  French-Italian-West German
CHIMES AT MIDNIGHT   *FALSTAFF*
  Peppercorn-Wormser, 1966,
  Spanish-Swiss

THE IMMORTAL STORY   Fleetwood Films,
  1968, French, originally made for television
THE DEEP   1969, unfinished
THE OTHER SIDE OF THE WIND   1972,
  unfinished
F FOR FAKE   Specialty Films, 1974,
  French-Iranian-West German

WILLIAM A. WELLMAN
(William Augustus Wellman)
b. February 29, 1896 - Brookline,
  Massachusetts
d. 1975

THE MAN WHO WON   Fox, 1923
SECOND HAND LOVE   Fox, 1923
BIG DAN   Fox, 1923
CUPID'S FIREMAN   Fox, 1923
THE VAGABOND TRAIL   Fox, 1924
NOT A DRUM WAS HEARD   Fox, 1924
THE CIRCUS COWBOY   Fox, 1924
WHEN HUSBANDS FLIRT   Columbia, 1925
THE BOOB   MGM, 1926
THE CAT'S PAJAMAS   Paramount, 1926
YOU NEVER KNOW WOMEN
  Paramount, 1926
WINGS   Paramount, 1929
THE LEGION OF THE CONDEMNED
  Paramount, 1928
LADIES OF THE MOB   Paramount, 1928
BEGGARS OF LIFE   Paramount, 1928
CHINATOWN NIGHTS   Paramount, 1929
THE MAN I LOVE   Paramount, 1929
WOMAN TRAP   Paramount, 1929
DANGEROUS PARADISE   Paramount, 1930
YOUNG EAGLES   Paramount, 1930
MAYBE IT'S LOVE   Warner Bros., 1930
OTHER MEN'S WOMEN   *THE STEEL
  HIGHWAY*   Warner Bros., 1931
THE PUBLIC ENEMY   Warner Bros., 1931
NIGHT NURSE   Warner Bros., 1931
THE STAR WITNESS   Warner Bros., 1931
SAFE IN HELL   First National, 1931
THE HATCHET MAN   First National, 1932
SO BIG   Warner Bros., 1932
LOVE IS A RACKET   First National, 1932
THE PURCHASE PRICE   Warner Bros., 1932
THE CONQUERORS   RKO RADIO, 1932
FRISCO JENNY   First National, 1933
CENTRAL AIRPORT   First National, 1933
LILLY TURNER   First National, 1933
MIDNIGHT MARY   MGM, 1933
HEROES FOR SALE   First National, 1933
WILD BOYS OF THE ROAD
  First National, 1933
COLLEGE COACH   Warner Bros., 1933
LOOKING FOR TROUBLE
  United Artists, 1934
STINGAREE   RKO Radio, 1934
THE PRESIDENT VANISHES
  Paramount, 1935
CALL OF THE WILD   United Artists, 1935
THE ROBIN HOOD OF EL DORADO
  MGM, 1936
SMALL TOWN GIRL   MGM, 1936
A STAR IS BORN ★   United Artists, 1937
NOTHING SACRED   United Artists, 1937
MEN WITH WINGS   Paramount, 1938
BEAU GESTE   Paramount, 1939
THE LIGHT THAT FAILED   Paramount, 1939
REACHING FOR THE SUN   Paramount, 1941
ROXIE HART   20th Century-Fox, 1942
THE GREAT MAN'S LADY   Paramount, 1942
THUNDER BIRDS   20th Century-Fox, 1942
THE OX-BOW INCIDENT
  20th Century-Fox, 1943
LADY OF BURLESQUE   United Artists, 1943

BUFFALO BILL   20th Century-Fox, 1944
THIS MAN'S NAVY   MGM, 1945
THE STORY OF G.I. JOE   United Artists, 1945
GALLANT JOURNEY   Columbia, 1946
MAGIC TOWN   RKO Radio, 1947
THE IRON CURTAIN   20th Century-Fox, 1948
YELLOW SKY   20th Century-Fox, 1948
BATTLEGROUND ★   MGM, 1949
THE HAPPY YEARS   MGM, 1950
THE NEXT VOICE YOU HEAR   MGM, 1950
ACROSS THE WIDE MISSOURI   MGM, 1951
IT'S A BIG COUNTRY   co-director,
  MGM, 1952
WESTWARD THE WOMEN   MGM, 1952
MY MAN AND I   MGM, 1952
ISLAND IN THE SKY   Warner Bros., 1953
THE HIGH AND THE MIGHTY ★
  Warner Bros., 1954
TRACK OF THE CAT   Warner Bros., 1954
BLOOD ALLEY   Warner Bros., 1955
GOODBYE, MY LADY   Warner Bros., 1956
DARBY'S RANGERS   Warner Bros., 1958
LAFAYETTE ESCADRILLE
  Warner Bros., 1958

ALFRED L. WERKER
b. December 2, 1896 - Deadwood,
  South Dakota

RIDIN' THE WIND   co-director with
  Del Andrews, 1925
THE PIONEER SCOUT   co-director with
  Lloyd Ingraham, 1928
THE SUNSET LEGION   co-director with
  Lloyd Ingraham, 1928
KIT CARSON   1928
BLUE SKIES   1929
CHASING THROUGH EUROPE   co-director
  with David Butler, Fox, 1929
DOUBLE CROSS ROADS   Fox, 1930
LAST OF THE DUANES   Fox, 1930
FAIR WARNING   Fox, 1931
ANNABELLE'S AFFAIRS   Fox, 1931
HEARTBREAK   Fox, 1931
THE GAY CABALLERO   Fox, 1932
BACHELOR'S AFFAIRS   Fox, 1932
RACKETY RAX   Fox, 1932
IT'S GREAT TO BE ALIVE   Fox, 1933
HELLO, SISTER!   Fox, 1933
ADVICE TO THE FORLORN   Fox, 1933
THE HOUSE OF ROTHSCHILD
  United Artists, 1934
YOU BELONG TO ME   1934
STOLEN HARMONY   1935
LOVE IN EXILE   1936, British
WE HAVE OUR MOMENTS   1937
WILD AND WOOLLY   1937
BIG TOWN GIRL   1937
CITY GIRL   1938
KIDNAPPED   20th Century-Fox, 1938
UP THE RIVER   20th Century-Fox, 1938
IT COULD HAPPEN TO YOU
  20th Century-Fox, 1939
NEWS IS MADE AT NIGHT
  20th Century-Fox, 1939
THE ADVENTURES OF SHERLOCK HOLMES
  20th Century-Fox, 1939
THE RELUCTANT DRAGON (AF)
  RKO Radio, 1941
MOON OVER HER SHOULDER
  20th Century-Fox, 1941
WHISPERING GHOSTS
  20th Century-Fox, 1942
A-HAUNTING WE WILL GO
  20th Century-Fox, 1942
THE MAD MARTINDALES
  20th Century-Fox, 1942

MY PAL WOLF   RKO Radio, 1944
SHOCK   20th Century-Fox, 1946
REPEAT PERFORMANCE   Eagle Lion, 1947
PIRATES OF MONTEREY   Universal, 1947
HE WALKED BY NIGHT   Eagle Lion, 1948
LOST BOUNDARIES   Four Continents, 1949
SEALED CARGO   RKO Radio, 1951
WALK EAST ON BEACON   Columbia, 1952
THE LAST POSSE   Columbia, 1953
DEVIL'S CANYON   RKO Radio, 1953
THREE HOURS TO KILL   Columbia, 1954
CANYON CROSSROADS
   United Artists, 1955
AT GUNPOINT   Allied Artists, 1955
REBEL IN TOWN   United Artists, 1956
THE YOUNG DON'T CRY   Columbia, 1957

JAMES WHALE
b. July 22, 1896 - Dudley, England
d. 1957

JOURNEY'S END   Tiffany Productions, 1930
WATERLOO BRIDGE   Universal, 1931
FRANKENSTEIN   Universal, 1931
THE IMPATIENT MAIDEN   Universal, 1932
THE OLD DARK HOUSE   Universal, 1932
THE KISS BEFORE THE MIRROR
   Universal, 1933
THE INVISIBLE MAN   Universal, 1933
BY CANDLELIGHT   Universal, 1933
ONE MORE RIVER   Universal, 1934
THE BRIDE OF FRANKENSTEIN
   Universal, 1935
REMEMBER LAST NIGHT?   Universal, 1935
SHOW BOAT   Universal, 1936
THE ROAD BACK   Universal, 1937
THE GREAT GARRICK   Warner Bros., 1937
SINNERS IN PARADISE   Universal, 1938
WIVES   UNDER SUSPICION
   Universal, 1938
PORT OF SEVEN SEAS   MGM, 1938
THE MAN IN THE IRON MASK
   United Artists, 1939
GREEN HELL   Universal, 1940
THEY DARE NOT LOVE   Columbia, 1941

TIM WHELAN
b. November 2, 1893 - Indiana
d. 1957

ADAM'S APPLE   1928, British
WHEN KNIGHTS WERE BOLD   1929, British
IT'S A BOY   1929, British
AUNT SALLY   ALONG CAME SALLY
   1933, British
THE CAMELS ARE COMING   1934, British
MURDER MAN   MGM, 1935
THE PERFECT GENTLEMAN   1935
TWO'S COMPANY   1936, British
LARCENY STREET   SMASH AND GRAB
   1937, British
THE MILL ON THE FLOSS   1937, British
FAREWELL AGAIN   TROOPSHIP
   United Artists, 1937, British
ACTION FOR SLANDER   United Artists,
   1937, British
THE DIVORCE OF LADY X   United Artists,
   1938, British
SIDEWALKS OF LONDON   ST. MARTIN'S
   LANE   Paramount, 1938, British
CLOUDS OVER EUROPE   Q PLANES
   Columbia, 1939, British
TEN DAYS IN PARIS   MISSING TEN DAYS
   1939, British
THE THIEF OF BAGDAD   co-director with
   Michael Powell & Ludwig Berger,
   United Artists, 1940, British

THE MAD DOCTOR   Paramount, 1941
INTERNATIONAL LADY   United Artists, 1941
TWIN BEDS   United Artists, 1942
NIGHTMARE   Universal, 1942
SEVEN DAYS' LEAVE   RKO Radio, 1942
HIGHER AND HIGHER   RKO Radio, 1943
SWING FEVER   MGM, 1944
STEP LIVELY   RKO Radio, 1944
BADMAN'S TERRITORY   RKO Radio, 1946
THIS WAS A WOMAN   20th Century-Fox,
   1948, British
RAGE AT DAWN   RKO Radio, 1955
TEXAS LADY   RKO Radio, 1955

RICHARD WHORF
b. June 4, 1906 - Winthrop, Massachusetts
d. 1966

BLONDE FEVER   MGM, 1944
THE HIDDEN EYE   MGM, 1945
THE SAILOR TAKES A WIFE   MGM, 1946
TILL THE CLOUDS ROLL BY   MGM, 1946
IT HAPPENED IN BROOKLYN   MGM, 1947
LOVE FROM A STRANGER   Eagle Lion, 1947
LUXURY LINER   MGM, 1948
CHAMPAGNE FOR CAESAR   Universal, 1950
THE GROOM WORE SPURS
   Universal, 1951

ROBERT WIENE
b. 1881 - Sasku, Germany
d. 1938

ARME EVA   co-director with W.A. Berger,
   1914, German
ER RECHTS SIE LINKS   1915, German
DIE KONSERVENBRAUT   1915, German
ER RECHTS, SIE LINKS   1915, German
DER SEKRETAR DER KONIGIN
   1916, German
DIE LIEBESBRIEF DER KONIGIN
   1916, German
DER SEKRETAR DER KONIGIN
   1916, German
DER MANN IM SPIEGEL   1916, German
DIE RAUBERBRAUT   1916, German
DAS WANDERNDE LICHT   1916, German
THE CABINET OF DR. CALIGARI
   Samuel Goldwyn, 1919, German
DIE DREI TANZE DER MARY WILFORD
   1920, German
GENUINE   1920, German
DIE NACHT DER KONIGIN ISABEAU
   1920, German
DIE RAUCHE EINER FRAU   1920, German
HOLLISCHE NACHT   1921, German
DAS SPIEGEL MIT DEM FEUER   co-director
   with George Kroll, 1921, German
SALOME   1922, German
TRAGIKOMODIE   1922, German
I.N.R.I.   1923, German
DER PUPPENMACHER VON KIANG-NING
   1923, German
RASKOLNIKOFF   CRIME AND PUNISHMENT
   1923, German
ORLACS HANDE   1925, Austrian
PENSION GROONEN   1925, German
DER GARDEOFFIZIER   1926, German
DIE KONIGIN VOM MOULIN-ROUGE
   1926, German
DER ROSENKAVALIER   1926, German
DIE BERUHMTE FRAU   1927, German
DIE GELIEBTE   1927, German
DIE FRAU AUF DER FOLTER   1928, German
DIE GROSSE ABENTEURERIN
   1928, German
LEONTINES EHEMANNER   1928, German

UNFUG DER LIEBE   1928, German
DER ANDERE   1930, German
PANIK IN CHIKAGO   1931, German
DER LIEBESEXPRESS   ACHT TAGE GLUCK
   1931, German
POLIZEIAKTE 909   1934, German
EINE NACHT IN VENEDIG   1934, German
ULTIMATUM   co-director with Robert Siodmak,
   1938, French

HERBERT WILCOX
b. April 19, 1892 - Cork, Ireland
d. 1977

CHU CHIN CHOW   Graham-Wilcox,
   1923, British
SOUTHERN LOVE   A WOMAN'S SECRET
   Graham-Wilcox, 1924, British
DECAMERON NIGHTS
   Graham-Wilcox-Decla, 1924, British
THE ONLY WAY   First National, 1925, British
NELL GWYN   First National, 1926, British
LONDON   LIMEHOUSE   Paramount,
   1926, British
TIPTOES   TIP TOES   Paramount,
   1927, British
MADAME POMPADOUR   1927, British
MUMSIE   W&F, 1927, British
DAWN   W&F, 1928, British
THE BONDMAN   W&F, 1928, British
THE WOMAN IN WHITE   W&F, 1929, British
THE LOVES OF ROBERT BURNS
   W&F, 1930, British
CHANCE OF A NIGHT-TIME   co-director with
   Ralph Lynn, W&F, 1931, British
CARNIVAL   VENETIAN NIGHTS   W&F,
   1931, British
THE BLUE DANUBE   W&F, 1932, British
GOODNIGHT VIENNA   MAGIC NIGHT
   W&F, 1932, British
YES, MR. BROWN   co-director with
   Jack Buchanan, W&F, 1933, British
THE KING'S CUP   co-director with
   Robert J. Cullen, Alan Cobham &
   Donald Macardie, W&F, 1933, British
BITTER SWEET   United Artists, 1933, British
THE LITTLE DAMOZEL   W&F, 1933, British
THE QUEEN'S AFFAIR   RUNAWAY QUEEN
   United Artists, 1934, British
NELL GWYNN   United Artists, 1934, British
PEG OF OLD DRURY   United Artists,
   1935, British
LIMELIGHT   BACKSTAGE   GFD,
   1936, British
THE THREE MAXIMS   THE SHOW GOES ON
   GFD, 1936, British
THIS'LL MAKE YOU WHISTLE   GFD,
   1936, British
LONDON MELODY   GIRLS IN THE STREET
   GFD, 1937, British
OUR FIGHTING NAVY   TORPEDOED
   1937, British
VICTORIA THE GREAT   RKO Radio,
   1937, British
SIXTY GLORIOUS YEARS   QUEEN OF
   DESTINY   RKO Radio, 1938, British
NURSE EDITH CAVELL   RKO Radio, 1939
IRENE   RKO Radio, 1940
NO, NO, NANETTE   RKO Radio, 1940
SUNNY   RKO Radio, 1941
WINGS AND THE WOMAN   THEY FLEW
   ALONE   RKO Radio, 1942, British
FOREVER AND A DAY   co-director,
   RKO Radio, 1943
YELLOW CANARY   RKO Radio, 1943, British
A YANK IN LONDON   I LIVE IN GROSVENOR
   SQUARE   Pathé, 1945, British
PICCADILLY INCIDENT   Pathé, 1946, British

THE COURTNEY AFFAIR *THE COURTNEYS OF CURZON STREET* British Lion, 1947, British
SPRING IN PARK LANE British Lion, 1948, British
ELIZABETH OF LADYMEAD British Lion, 1948, British
MAYTIME IN MAYFAIR British Lion, 1949, British
ODETTE British Lion, 1950, British
INTO THE BLUE *THE MAN IN THE DINGHY* British Lion, 1951, British
THE LADY WITH A LAMP British Lion, 1951, British
DERBY DAY *FOUR AGAINST FATE* Continental, 1952, British
TRENT'S LAST CASE British Lion, 1952, British
LAUGHING ANNE Republic, 1953, British
TROUBLE IN THE GLEN Republic, 1953, British
LET'S MAKE UP *LILACS IN THE SPRING* Republic, 1954, British
KING'S RHAPSODY British Lion, 1955, British
TEENAGE BAD GIRL *MY TEENAGE DAUGHTER* British Lion, 1956, British
DANGEROUS YOUTH *THESE DANGEROUS YEARS* Warner Bros., 1957, British
THE MAN WHO WOULDN'T TALK British Lion, 1958, British
WONDERFUL THINGS! ABP, 1958, British
THE LADY IS A SQUARE ABP, 1959, British
THE HEART OF A MAN RFD, 1959, British

CORNEL WILDE
b. October 13, 1915 - New York, New York
d. 1989

STORM FEAR United Artists, 1956
THE DEVIL'S HAIRPIN Paramount, 1957
MARACAIBO Paramount, 1958
THE SWORD OF LANCELOT *LANCELOT AND GUINEVERE* Universal, 1963, British
THE NAKED PREY Paramount, 1966, U.S.-South African
BEACH RED United Artists, 1967
NO BLADE OF GRASS MGM, 1970, British
SHARK'S TREASURE United Artists, 1975

RICHARD WILSON
b. December 25, 1915 - McKeesport, Pennsylvania
d. 1991

MAN WITH THE GUN United Artists, 1955
THE BIG BOODLE United Artists, 1957
RAW WIND IN EDEN Universal, 1958
AL CAPONE Allied Artists, 1959
PAY OR DIE Allied Artists, 1960
WALL OF NOISE Warner Bros., 1963
INVITATION TO A GUNFIGHTER United Artists, 1964
THREE IN THE ATTIC American International, 1968
IT'S ALL TRUE: BASED ON AN UNFINISHED FILM BY ORSON WELLES (FD) co-director with Bill Krohn & Myron Meisel, Paramount, 1993, U.S.-French

BRETAIGNE WINDUST
b. January 20, 1906 - Paris, France
d. 1960

WINTER MEETING Warner Bros., 1948
JUNE BRIDE Warner Bros., 1948
PERFECT STRANGERS Warner Bros., 1950

PRETTY BABY Warner Bros., 1950
THE ENFORCER Warner Bros., 1951
FACE TO FACE co-director with John Brahm, RKO Radio, 1952
THE PIED PIPER OF HAMELIN NTA Pictures, 1957, originally filmed for television

EDWARD D. WOOD, JR.
b. 1924 - Poughkeepsie, New York
d. 1978

GLEN OR GLENDA *I CHANGED MY SEX/ I LED TWO LIVES* Screen Classics, 1953
JAILBAIT Howco, 1955
BRIDE OF THE MONSTER *BRIDE OF THE ATOM* Banner, 1956
PLAN NINE FROM OUTER SPACE *GRAVE ROBBERS FROM OUTER SPACE* DCA, 1959
THE SINISTER URGE Headliner, 1961
NIGHT OF THE GHOULS *REVENGE OF THE DEAD* 1981, filmed in 1959

SAM WOOD
(Samuel Grosvenor Wood)
b. July 18, 1883 - Philadelphia, Pennsylvania
d. 1949

DOUBLE SPEED Paramount, 1920
EXCUSE MY DUST Paramount, 1920
THE DANCIN' FOOL Paramount, 1920
SICK ABED *SICK-A-BED* Paramount, 1920
WHAT'S YOUR HURRY? Paramount, 1920
THE CITY SPARROW Paramount, 1920
HER BELOVED VILLAIN Realart, 1920
HER FIRST ELOPEMENT Realart, 1920
THE SNOB Realart, 1921
PECK'S BAD BOY First National, 1921
THE GREAT MOMENT Paramount, 1921
UNDER THE LASH Paramount, 1921
DON'T TELL EVERYTHING Paramount, 1921
HER HUSBAND'S TRADEMARK Paramount, 1922
BEYOND THE ROCKS Paramount, 1922
HER GILDED CAGE Paramount, 1922
THE IMPOSSIBLE MRS. BELLEW Paramount, 1922
MY AMERICAN WIFE Paramount, 1923
PRODIGAL DAUGHTERS Paramount, 1923
BLUEBEARD'S EIGHTH WIFE Paramount, 1923
HIS CHILDREN'S CHILDREN Paramount, 1923
THE NEXT CORNER Paramount, 1924
BLUFF Paramount, 1924
THE FEMALE First National, 1924
THE MINE WITH THE IRON DOOR Principal, 1924
THE RE-CREATION OF BRIAN KENT Principal, 1925
FASCINATING YOUTH Paramount, 1926
ONE MINUTE TO PLAY FBO, 1926
ROOKIES MGM, 1927
A RACING ROMEO FBO, 1927
THE FAIR CO-ED MGM, 1927
THE LATEST FROM PARIS MGM, 1928
TELLING THE WORLD MGM, 1928
SO THIS IS COLLEGE MGM, 1929
IT'S A GREAT LIFE MGM, 1929
THEY LEARNED ABOUT WOMEN co-director with Jack Conway, MGM, 1930
THE GIRL SAID NO MGM, 1930
SINS OF THE CHILDREN MGM, 1930
WAY FOR A SAILOR MGM, 1930
PAID MGM, 1930
A TAILOR-MADE MAN MGM, 1931
THE MAN IN POSSESSION MGM, 1931

GET-RICH-QUICK WALLINGFORD *NEW ADVENTURES OF GET-RICH-QUICK WALLINGFORD* MGM, 1931
HUDDLE MGM, 1932
PROSPERITY MGM, 1932
THE BARBARIAN MGM, 1933
HOLD YOUR MAN MGM, 1933
CHRISTOPHER BEAN MGM, 1933
STAMBOUL QUEST MGM, 1934
LET 'EM HAVE IT United Artists, 1935
A NIGHT AT THE OPERA MGM, 1935
WHIPSAW MGM, 1935
THE UNGUARDED HOUR MGM, 1936
A DAY AT THE RACES MGM, 1937
NAVY, BLUE AND GOLD MGM, 1937
MADAME X MGM, 1937
LORD JEFF MGM, 1938
STABLEMATES MGM, 1938
GOODBYE, MR. CHIPS ★ MGM, 1939
RAFFLES United Artists, 1939
OUR TOWN United Artists, 1940
RANGERS OF FORTUNE Paramount, 1940
KITTY FOYLE ★ RKO Radio, 1940
THE DEVIL AND MISS JONES RKO Radio, 1941
KINGS ROW ★ Warner Bros., 1942
THE PRIDE OF THE YANKEES RKO Radio, 1942
FOR WHOM THE BELL TOLLS Paramount, 1943
CASANOVA BROWN RKO Radio, 1944
SARATOGA TRUNK Warner Bros., 1945
GUEST WIFE United Artists, 1945
HEARTBEAT RKO Radio, 1946
IVY Universal, 1947
COMMAND DECISION MGM, 1948
THE STRATTON STORY MGM, 1949
AMBUSH MGM, 1950

WILLIAM WYLER
b. July 1, 1902 - Mulhouse, Alsace, Germany
d. 1981

CROOK BUSTERS 1925
LAZY LIGHTNING Universal, 1926
THE STOLEN RANCH Universal, 1926
BLAZING DAYS Universal, 1927
HARD FISTS Universal, 1927
STRAIGHT SHOOTIN' *SHOOTING STRAIGHT/RANGE RIDERS* Independent, 1927
THE BORDER CAVALIER Universal, 1927
DESERT DUST 1927
THUNDER RIDERS Universal, 1928
ANYBODY HERE SEEN KELLY? Universal, 1928
THE SHAKEDOWN Universal, 1929
THE LOVE TRAP Universal, 1929
HELL'S HEROES Universal, 1930
THE STORM Universal, 1930
A HOUSE DIVIDED Universal, 1932
TOM BROWN OF CULVER Universal, 1932
HER FIRST MATE Universal, 1933
COUNSELLOR-AT-LAW Universal, 1933
GLAMOUR Universal, 1934
THE GOOD FAIRY Universal, 1935
THE GAY DECEPTION 20th Century-Fox, 1935
THESE THREE United Artists, 1936
DODSWORTH ★ United Artists, 1936
COME AND GET IT co-director with Howard Hawks, United Artists, 1936
DEAD END United Artists, 1937
JEZEBEL Warner Bros., 1938
WUTHERING HEIGHTS ★ United Artists, 1939
THE WESTERNER United Artists, 1940
THE LETTER ★ Warner Bros., 1940

THE LITTLE FOXES ★   RKO Radio, 1941
MRS. MINIVER ★★   MGM, 1942
THE MEMPHIS BELLE (FD)
   Paramount, 1944
THE FIGHTING LADY (FD)
   20th Century-Fox, 1944
THUNDERBOLT (FD)   co-director with
   John Sturges, Monogram, 1945
THE BEST YEARS OF OUR LIVES ★★
   RKO Radio, 1946
THE HEIRESS ★   Paramount, 1949
DETECTIVE STORY ★   Paramount, 1951
CARRIE   Paramount, 1952
ROMAN HOLIDAY ★   Paramount, 1953
THE DESPERATE HOURS   Paramount, 1955
FRIENDLY PERSUASION ★
   Allied Artists, 1956
THE BIG COUNTRY   United Artists, 1958
BEN-HUR ★★   MGM, 1959
THE CHILDREN'S HOUR   United Artists, 1961
THE COLLECTOR ★   Columbia, 1965,
   U.S.-British
HOW TO STEAL A MILLION   Columbia, 1966
FUNNY GIRL   Columbia, 1968
THE LIBERATION OF L.B. JONES
   Columbia, 1970

KAJIRO YAMAMOTO

b. March 15, 1902 - Tokyo, Japan
d. 1974

DANUN   Nikkatsu, 1924, Japanese
BOMB HOUR   Nikkatsu, 1925, Japanese
ORDEAL   Nikkatsu, 1932, Japanese
LOVE CRISIS   Nikkatsu, 1933, Japanese
ENOKEN NO ISAMI KONDO   PCL,
   1935, Japanese
BO-CHAN   PCL, 1935, Japanese
ENOKEN NO DONGURI TOMBE   PCL,
   1935, Japanese
I AM A CAT   1936, Japanese
ENOKEN NO CHAKIRI KINTA   PCL,
   1937, Japanese
A HUSBAND'S CHASTITY   PCL,
   1937, Japanese
THE SPELLING CLASS   Toho,
   1938, Japanese
THE LOVES OF TOJIRO   *THE LOVES OF A
   KABUKI ACTOR*   Toho, 1938, Japanese
EASY ALLEY   Toho, 1939, Japanese
THE LOYAL 47 RONIN   Toho,
   1939, Japanese
DEAR MONKEY   Toho, 1940, Japanese
HORSE   Toho, 1941, Japanese
BATTLE OF HAWAII MARE BEACH   Toho,
   1942, Japanese
THE HOPE OF YOUTH   Toho,
   1942, Japanese
KATO HAYABUSA SENTOTAI   Toho,
   1944, Japanese
RAIGEKITAI SHUTSUDO   Toho,
   1944, Japanese
MISFORTUNES OF LOVE   Toho,
   1945, Japanese
THOSE WHO MAKE TOMORROW
   co-director with Akira Kurosawa &
   Hideo Sekigawa, Toho, 1946, Japanese

FOUR LOVE STORIES   co-director with
   Mikio Naruse, Shiro Toyoda &
   Teinosuke Kinugasa, Toho, 1947, Japanese
WIND OF HONOR   Toho, 1949, Japanese
SPRING FLIRTATION   Toho, 1949, Japanese
ELEGY   Toho, 1951, Japanese
GIRLS AMONG THE FLOWERS   Toho,
   1953, Japanese
MR. VALIANT   Toho, 1954, Japanese
SATURDAY ANGEL   Toho, 1954, Japanese
A MAN AMONG MEN   Toho, 1955, Japanese
THE HISTORY OF LOVE   Toho,
   1955, Japanese
THE UNDERWORLD   Toho, 1956, Japanese
AN ELEPHANT   Toho, 1957, Japanese
THE RISE AND FALL OF A JAZZ GIRL
   Toho, 1958, Japanese
HOLIDAY IN TOKYO   Toho, 1958, Japanese
GINZA TOMBOY   Toho, 1960, Japanese
STORY OF A GENIUS CONMAN   Toho,
   1964, Japanese
IRRESPONSIBLE OF GREAT EDO   Toho,
   1964, Japanese
SAMURAI JOKER   1965, Japanese
THIEF ON THE RUN   1965, Japanese
SWINDLER MEETS SWINDLER
   1967, Japanese

SATSUO YAMAMOTO

b. July 15, 1910 - Kagoshima Prefecture, Japan
d. 1983

YOUNG MISS   Toho, 1937, Japanese
LA SYMPHONIE PASTORALE   Toho,
   1938, Japanese
FAMILY DIARY   Toho, 1938, Japanese
THE STREET   Toho, 1939, Japanese
END OF ENGAGEMENT   Toho,
   1940, Japanese
HOT WIND   Toho, 1943, Japanese
WAR AND PEACE   co-director with
   Fumio Kamei, Toho, 1947, Japanese
THE STREET OF VIOLENCE   Nihon Eiga
   Engeki Rodokumiai, 1950, Japanese
VACUUM ZONE   Shinsei Eiga,
   1952, Japanese
STORM CLOUDS OVER MOUNT HAKONE
   Zenshinza/Shinsei Eiga, 1952, Japanese
THE STREET WITHOUT SUN   Shinsei Eiga/
   Dokuritsu Eiga, 1954, Japanese
END OF THE DAY   Yagi Productions,
   1954, Japanese
UMAGORO ICHIKAWA   Yamamoto
   Productions/Hayuza, 1955, Japanese
TYPHOON   Yamamoto Productions/Madoka
   Group, 1956, Japanese
RED JINBAORI   Kabukiza Eiga,
   1958, Japanese
THE SONG OF THE CART   Zenkoku Nouson
   Eiga Kyokai, 1959, Japanese
THE HUMAN WALL   Yamamoto Productions,
   1959, Japanese
BATTLE WITHOUT ARMS   Daito Eiga,
   1960, Japanese
A BAND OF ASSASSINS   Daiei,
   1962, Japanese
THE YOUNG LADIES WHO HOLD THEIR
   BREASTS   Zenkosu Nouson Eiga Kyokai/
   Daiei, 1962, Japanese
RED WATER   Daiei, 1963, Japanese
A BAND OF ASSASSINS, PART II   Daiei,
   1963, Japanese
THE MOUNTAIN AND RIVER WHICH HAVE
   A LOT OF SCARS   *TYCOON*   Daiei,
   1964, Japanese
THE WITNESS CHAIR   Yamamoto
   Productions, 1965, Japanese

THE BURGLAR STORY   Toei,
   1965, Japanese
THE GREAT WHITE TOWER   Daiei,
   1966, Japanese
FREEZING POINT   Daiei, 1966, Japanese
ZATOICHI JAILBREAK   Daiei,
   1967, Japanese
FAKE DETECTIVE   Daiei, 1967, Japanese
BOTAN LANTERN   *THE BRIDE FROM
   HADES*   Daiei, 1968, Japanese
TENGU   Daiei, 1969, Japanese
WAR AND HUMAN, PART I   Nikkatsu,
   1970, Japanese
WAR AND HUMAN, PART II   Nikkatsu,
   1971, Japanese
WAR AND HUMAN, PART III   Nikkatsu,
   1973, Japanese
SPLENDID FAMILY   Geiensha,
   1974, Japanese
ANNULAR ECLIPSE   Daiei, 1975, Japanese
THE STORY OF YUGAKU OHARA   Zenkosu
   Nouson Eiga Kyokai/Daiei, 1976, Japanese
THE BARREN GROUND   Geiensha,
   1976, Japanese
AUGUST WITHOUT THE EMPEROR
   Shochiku, 1978, Japanese
NOMUGI PASS   Shin Nihon Eiga,
   1979, Japanese
NOMUGI PASS: CHAPTER OF NEW
   GREEN ERY   Toho, 1982, Japanese

JEAN YARBROUGH

b. August 22, 1900 - Marianna, Arkansas
d. ?

REBELLIOUS DAUGHTERS   1938
DEVIL BAT   PRC, 1940
CAUGHT IN THE ACT   1941
SOUTH OF PANAMA   1941
KING OF THE ZOMBIES   Monogram, 1941
THE GANG'S ALL HERE   Monogram, 1941
FATHER STEPS OUT   1941
LET'S GO COLLEGIATE   1941
TO SERGEANT MULLIGAN   1941
FRECKLES COMES HOME   1942
MAN FROM HEADQUARTERS   1942
LAW OF THE JUNGLE   1942
SO'S YOUR AUNT EMMA!
   MEET THE MOB   1942
SHE'S IN THE ARMY   1942
POLICE BULLETS   1942
CRIMINAL INVESTIGATOR   1942
LURE OF THE ISLANDS   1942
SILENT WITNESS   1942
FOLLOW THE BAND   1943
GOOD MORNING JUDGE   1943
GET GOING   1943
HI' YA SAILOR   1943
SO'S YOUR UNCLE   1943
WEEKEND PASS   1944
MOON OVER LAS VEGAS   1944
SOUTH OF DIXIE   1944
IN SOCIETY   1944
TWILIGHT ON THE PRAIRIE   1944
UNDER WESTERN SKIES   Universal, 1945
HERE COME THE CO-EDS   Universal, 1945
THE NAUGHTY NINETIES   Universal, 1945
ON STAGE EVERYBODY   Universal, 1945
HOUSE OF HORRORS   Universal, 1946
SHE-WOLF OF LONDON   Universal, 1946
INSIDE JOB   Universal, 1946
CUBAN PETE   1946
THE BRUTE MAN   PRC, 1947
THE CHALLENGE   20th Century-Fox, 1948
SHED NO TEARS   20th Century-Fox, 1948
THE CREEPER   20th Century-Fox, 1948
TRIPLE THREAT   1948
HENRY THE RAINMAKER   Monogram, 1949

THE MUTINEERS Columbia, 1949
LEAVE IT TO HENRY Monogram, 1949
ANGELS IN DISGUISE Monogram, 1949
HOLIDAY IN HAVANA Columbia, 1949
MASTER MINDS Monogram, 1949
JOE PALOOKA MEETS HUMPHREY
  Monogram, 1950
SQUARE DANCE KATY Monogram, 1950
FATHER MAKES GOOD Monogram, 1950
JOE PALOOKA IN HUMPHREY TAKES
  A CHANCE Monogram, 1950
SIDESHOW Monogram, 1950
TRIPLE TROUBLE Monogram, 1950
BIG TIMBER Monogram, 1950
CASA MANANA Monogram, 1951
ACCORDING TO MRS. HOYLE
  Monogram, 1951
JACK AND THE BEANSTALK
  Warner Bros., 1952
LOST IN ALASKA Universal, 1952
NIGHT FREIGHT Allied Artists, 1955
CRASHING LAS VEGAS
  Allied Artists, 1956
YAQUI DRUMS Allied Artists, 1956
THE WOMEN OF PITCAIRN ISLAND
  20th Century-Fox, 1956
HOT SHOTS Allied Artists, 1956
FOOTSTEPS IN THE NIGHT
  Allied Artists, 1957
SAINTLY SINNERS United Artists, 1962
HILLBILLIES IN A HAUNTED HOUSE 1967

HAROLD YOUNG

b. November 13, 1897 - Portland, Oregon
d. 1970

TOO MANY MILLIONS 1934, British
THE SCARLET PIMPERNEL United Artists,
  1935, British
WITHOUT REGRET 1935
WOMAN TRAP 1936
MY AMERICAN WIFE 1936
LET THEM LIVE 1937
52ND STREET 1937
LITTLE TOUGH GUY 1938
THE STORM Universal, 1938
NEWSBOYS' HOME Universal, 1939
CODE OF THE STREETS Universal, 1939
THE FORGOTTEN WOMAN
  Universal, 1939
SABOTAGE Universal, 1939
HERO FOR A DAY Universal, 1939
DREAMING OUT LOUD Universal, 1940
BACHELOR DADDY Universal, 1941
JUKE BOX JENNY Universal, 1942
RUBBER RACKETEERS Universal, 1942
THE MUMMY'S TOMB Universal, 1942
THERE'S ONE BORN EVERY MINUTE
  Universal, 1942
HI, BUDDY Universal, 1943
HI' YA CHUM Universal, 1943
I ESCAPED FROM THE GESTAPO
  Monogram, 1943
SPY TRAIN 1943
MACHINE GUN MAMA 1944
JUNGLE CAPTIVE Universal, 1945
THE FROZEN GHOST Universal, 1945
I REMEMBER APRIL Universal, 1945
SONG OF THE SARONG Universal, 1945
CITIZEN SAINT 1947
ROOGIE'S BUMP 1954

TERENCE YOUNG

b. June 20, 1915 - Shanghai, China
d. 1994

MEN OF ARNHEM (FD) co-director with
  Brian Desmond Hurst, Army Film Unit,
  1944, British
CORRIDOR OF MIRRORS Universal,
  1948, British
ONE NIGHT WITH YOU Universal,
  1948, British
WOMAN HATER Universal, 1948, British
THEY WERE NOT DIVIDED General Film
  Distributors, 1950, British
VALLEY OF THE EAGLES Lippert,
  1951, British
THE FRIGHTENED BRIDE *THE TALL
  HEADLINES* Beverly, 1952, British
PARATROOPER *THE RED BERET*
  Columbia, 1953, British
THAT LADY 20th Century-Fox, 1954, British
STORM OVER THE NILE co-director with
  Zoltan Korda, Columbia, 1955, British
SAFARI Columbia, 1956, British
ZARAK Columbia, 1956, British
ACTION OF THE TIGER MGM,
  1957, British
TANK FORCE *NO TIME TO DIE* Columbia,
  1958, British
SERIOUS CHARGE Eros, 1959, British
BLACK TIGHTS Magna, 1960, French
PLAYGIRL AFTER DARK *TOO HOT TO
  HANDLE* Topaz, 1960, British
DUEL OF CHAMPIONS co-director with
  Ferdinando Baldi, Medallion, 1961,
  Italian-Spanish
DR. NO United Artists, 1962, British
FROM RUSSIA WITH LOVE United Artists,
  1963, British
THE AMOROUS ADVENTURES OF MOLL
  FLANDERS Paramount, 1965, British
THUNDERBALL United Artists, 1965, British
THE DIRTY GAME *GUERRE SECRETE*
  co-director with Christian-Jaque,
  Carlo Lizzani & Werner Klinger,
  American International, 1966,
  French-Italian-West German
TRIPLE CROSS Warner Bros., 1966,
  British-French
THE POPPY IS ALSO A FLOWER Comet,
  1966, European
WAIT UNTIL DARK Warner Bros., 1967
THE ROVER *L'AVVENTURIERO* Cinerama
  Releasing Corporation, 1967, Italian
MAYERLING MGM, 1969, British-French
THE CHRISTMAS TREE Continental, 1969,
  French-Italian
COLD SWEAT *DE LA PART DES COPAINS*
  Emerson, 1970, French
RED SUN National General, 1972,
  French-Italian-Spanish
THE VALACHI PAPERS *JOE VALACHI:
  I SEGRETI DI COSA NOSTRA* Columbia,
  1972, Italian-French
WAR GODDESS *LE GUERRIERE DEL SNO
  NUDA* American International, 1973, Italian
THE KLANSMAN Paramount, 1974
SIDNEY SHELDON'S BLOODLINE
  BLOODLINE Paramount, 1979
INCHON! MGM/UA, 1982, South Korean
THE JIGSAW MAN United Film Distribution,
  1984, British
L'ARBRE METALLIQUE Fontana Films,
  1993, French

SERGEI YUTKEVICH

b. September 15, 1904 - St. Petersburg, Russia
d. 1985

GIVE US RADIO! co-director with
  S. Greenberg, 1925, Soviet
LACE 1928, Soviet
THE BLACK SAIL 1929, Soviet
GOLDEN MOUNTAINS 1931, Soviet
COUNTERPLAN co-director with
  Friedrich Ermler, 1932, Soviet
ANKARA - HEART OF TURKEY (FD)
  co-director with Lev Arnshtam, 1934, Soviet
THE MINERS 1937, Soviet
THE MAN WITH THE GUN 1938, Soviet
YAKOV SVERDLOV 1940, Soviet
THE NEW ADVENTURES OF SCHWEIK
  1943, Russian
DIMITRI DONSKOI (FD) 1944, Soviet
FRANCE LIBERATED (FD) 1946, Soviet
HELLO MOSCOW! (FD) 1946, Soviet
OUR COUNTRY'S YOUTH (FD) 1946, Soviet
LIGHT OVER RUSSIA 1947,
  Soviet, unreleased
THREE ENCOUNTERS co-director with
  Vsevolod Pudovkin & Alexander Ptushko,
  1948, Russian
PRZHEVALSKY 1951, Soviet
SKANDERBEG 1954, Soviet-Albanian
OTHELLO Universal, 1956, Soviet
STORIES ABOUT LENIN 1958, Soviet
ENCOUNTER WITH FRANCE (FD)
  1960, Soviet
THE BATH HOUSE co-director with
  Anatoly Karanovich, 1962, Soviet
LENIN IN POLAND *PORTRAIT OF LENIN*
  1966, Russian-Polish
THEME FOR A SHORT STORY 1969,
  Soviet-French
MAYAKOVSKY LAUGHS co-director with
  Anatoly Karanovich, 1976, Soviet

Z

LUIGI ZAMPA

b. January 2, 1905 - Rome, Italy
d. 1991

L'ATTORE SCOMPARSO Imperial Film,
  1941, Italian
FRA' DIAVOLO Fotovox, 1941, Italian
SIGNORINETTE Ata/Imperial, 1942, Italian
C'E' SEMPRE UN MA! Consorzio Italiano
  Film, 1942, Italian
L'ABITO NERO DA SPOSA Vi.Va. Film,
  1942, Italian
UN AMERICANO IN VACANZA Lux Film/
  Castrignano, 1945, Italian
TO LIVE IN PEACE Times Film Corporation,
  1946, Italian
L'ONOREVOLE ANGELINA Ora Film/Lux
  Film, 1947, Italian
ANNI DIFFICILI Briguglio Film, 1948, Italian
CAMPANE A MARTELLO Lux Film,
  1949, Italian
CUORI SENZA FRONTIERE Lux Film,
  1950, Italian
E' PIU' \FACILE CHE UN CAMMELLO...
  Cines/Les Films Pathe, 1950, Italian-French

SIGNORI, IN CARROZZA! DFD,
 1951, Italian
PROCESSO ALLA CITTA' Film Costellazione,
 1952, Italian
ANNI FACILI 1953, Italian
ISA MIRANDA co-director, Titanus/Film
 Costellazione, 1953, Italian
LA PATENTE co-director, Fortunia Film,
 1954, Italian
WOMAN OF ROME DCA, 1954,
 Italian-French
RAGAZZE D'OGGI Ponti De Laurentiis/
 Excelsa Film/Les Films du Centaure/Omnium
 International, 1955, Italian-French
THE LOVE SPECIALIST *LA RAGAZZA DEL
 PALIO* Medallion, 1958, Italian
LADRO LUI, LADRA LEI Maxima Film/
 Montfluor Film, 1958, Italian
IL MAGISTRATO Titanus/Hispamer Film,
 1959, Italian-Spanish
IL VIGILE Royal Film, 1960, Italian
ANNI RUGGENTI Spa Cinematografica/
 Incei Film, 1962, Italian
FRENESIA DELL'ESTATE Ge. Si.
 Cinematografica/Federiz/CISA/Les
 Films Agimon, 1963, Italian-French
UNA QUESTIONE D'ONORE Mega Film/
 Orphee Production, 1965, Italian-French
I NOSTRI MARITI co-director, Documento
 Film/Les Films Corona, 1966, Italian-French
ANYONE CAN PLAY *LE DOLCI SIGNORE*
 Paramount, 1967, Italian
IL MEDICO DELLA MUTUA
 Euro International Film/Explorer
 Film '58, 1968, Italian
CONTESTAZIONE GENERALE Ultra Film,
 1969, Italian
BELLO, ONESTO, EMIGRATO AUSTRALIA,
 SPOSEREBBE COMPAESANA ILLIBATA
 Documento Film, 1971, Italian
BISTURI LA MAFIA BIANCA Roberto Loyola,
 1973, Italian
GENTE DI RISPETTO CC Champion,
 1975, Italian
IL MOSTRO Rizzoli, 1977, Italian
LETTI SELVAGGI Zodiac Film/Corona Film,
 1979, Italian-Spanish

KAREL ZEMAN
b. November 1910 - Moravia, Czechoslovakia
d. 1989

THE TREASURE OF BIRD ISLAND 1952,
 Czechoslovakian
JOURNEY TO THE BEGINNING OF TIME
 1955, Czechoslovakian
THE FABULOUS WORLD OF JULES VERNE
 AN INVENTION OF DESTRUCTION
 Warner Bros., 1958, Czechoslovakian
THE FABULOUS BARON MUNCHAUSEN
 BARON PRASIL/BARON MUNCHAUSEN
 Teleworld, 1961, Czechoslovakian
THE JESTER'S TALE 1964,
 Czechoslovakian
THE STOLEN AIRSHIP 1964,
 Czechoslovakian
MR. SVERDAC'S ARK 1968,
 Czechoslovakian

MAI ZETTERLING
b. May 24, 1925 - Vasteras, Sweden
d. 1994

LOVING COUPLES Prominent,
 1964, Swedish
NIGHT GAMES Mondial, 1966, Swedish
DOCTOR GLAS 20th Century-Fox,
 1968, Danish
THE GIRLS New Line Cinema,
 1969, Swedish
VINCENT THE DUTCHMAN 1972, Swedish
VISIONS OF EIGHT (FD) co-director with
 Yuri Ozerov, Arthur Penn, Michael Pfleghar,
 Kon Ichikawa, Milos Forman,
 Claude Lelouch & John Schlesinger,
 Cinema 5, 1973
WE HAVE MANY NAMES 1976, Swedish
STOCKHOLM (TD) 1977, Canadian
LOVE co-director with Annette Cohen,
 Nancy Dowd & Liv Ullmann, Velvet Films,
 1982, Canadian
SCRUBBERS Orion Classics, 1983, British
AMAROSA Sandrews/Swedish Film Institute,
 1986, Swedish

VALERIO ZURLINI
b. March 19, 1926 - Bologna, Italy
d. 1982

LE RAGAZZE DI SAN FREDIANO Lux Film,
 1954, Italian
VIOLENT SUMMER Films Around the World,
 1959, Italian-French
THE GIRL WITH A SUITCASE Ellis Films,
 1961, Italian-French
FAMILY DIARY MGM, 1962, Italian
LE SOLDATESSE Zebra Film/Debora
 Film/Franco London Film/Avala Film/
 Omnia Deutsch Film, 1965,
 Italian-French-Yugoslavian-West German
BLACK JESUS *SEDUTO ALLA SUA DESTRA*
 Plaza Pictures, 1968, Italian
LA PRIMA NOTTE DI QUIETE Mondial Te.
 Fi./Adel Productions, 1972, Italian-French
IL DESERTO DEI TARTARI Cinema Due/
 Reggane Films/Fidel Fildebroc/Films de
 l'Astrophore/FR3/Corona Filmproduktion,
 1976, Italian-French-West German-Iranian

★ ★ ★

INDEX BY FILM TITLE

Note: This is not an index of every film ever made,
only those listed in this directory.
† = denotes a deceased director.

INDEX OF FILM TITLES

ALADDIN (AF) ... John Musker
ALADDIN (AF) ... Ron Clements
ALADDIN AND HIS LAMP ... Lew Landers†
ALADDIN AND THE WONDERFUL LAMP ... George Albert Smith†
ALADDIN AND THE WONDERFUL LAMP ... Sidney Franklin†
ALAMBRISTA! ... Robert M. Young
ALAMO, THE ... John Wayne†
ALAMO BAY ... Louis Malle
ALAMO: 13 DAYS TO GLORY, THE ... Burt Kennedy
ALAN AND NAOMI ... Sterling VanWagenen
ALAN BENNETT'S TALKING HEADS (TF) ... Stuart Burge
ALARM, THE ... Roscoe "Fatty" Arbuckle†
ALASKA KID, THE (MS) ... James Hill†
ALASKA PASSAGE ... Edward Bernds
ALASKA SEAS ... Jerry Hopper†
ALASKA'S GREAT RACE (TD) ... Laszlo Pal
ALASKAN, THE ... Herbert Brenon†
ALBERT R.N. ... Lewis Gilbert
ALBERT SOUFFRE ... Bruno Nuytten
ALBERT'S MEMORIAL ... Ian Sellar
ALBERTO EXPRESS ... Arthur Joffe
ALBINO ALLIGATOR ... Keven Spacey
ALBUQUERQUE ... Ray Enright†
ALCATRAZ: THE WHOLE SHOCKING STORY (TF) ... Paul Krasny
ALDEBARAN ... Alessandro Blasetti†
ALEGRE VOY! ... Max Nosseck†
ALEX & THE GYPSY ... John Korty
ALEX FALLS IN LOVE ... Boaz Davidson
ALEX IN WONDERLAND ... Paul Mazursky
ALEX JOSEPH AND HIS WIVES ... Ted V. Mikels
ALEX: THE LIFE OF A CHILD (TF) ... Robert Markowitz
ALEXANDER ... Yves Robert
ALEXANDER BELL - THE SOUND AND THE SILENCE (MS) ... John Kent Harrison
ALEXANDER NEVSKY ... Sergei Eisenstein†
ALEXANDER THE GREAT ... Mauritz Stiller†
ALEXANDER THE GREAT ... Robert Rossen†
ALEXANDER: THE OTHER SIDE OF DAWN (TF) ... John Erman
ALEXANDER'S RAGTIME BAND ... Henry King†
ALEXANDRIA AGAIN AND FOREVER ... Youssef Chahine
ALEXANDRIA...WHY? ... Youssef Chahine
ALFIE ... Lewis Gilbert
ALFIE DARLING ... Kenneth (Ken) Hughes
ALFRED ... Vilgot Sjoman
ALFRED HITCHCOCK PRESENTS (TF) ... Fred Walton
ALFRED HITCHCOCK PRESENTS (TF) ... Joel Oliansky
ALFRED HITCHCOCK PRESENTS (TF) ... Randa Haines
ALFRED HITCHCOCK PRESENTS (TF) ... Steve Dejarnatt
ALFRED THE GREAT ... Clive Donner
ALFREDO, ALFREDO ... Pietro Germi†
ALGIERS ... John Cromwell†
ALGY ON THE FORCE ... Mack Sennett†
ALI BABA AND THE 40 THIEVES ... Arthur Lubin†
ALI BABA AND THE FORTY THIEVES ... Sidney Franklin†
ALI BABA GOES TO TOWN ... David Butler†
ALI: FEAR EATS THE SOUL ... Rainer Werner Fassbinder†
ALIAS A GENTLEMAN ... Harry Beaumont†
ALIAS BOSTON BLACKIE ... Lew Landers†
ALIAS JESSE JAMES ... Norman Z. MacLeod†
ALIAS JIMMY VALENTINE ... Jack Conway†
ALIAS JIMMY VALENTINE ... Maurice Tourneur†
ALIAS MARY DOW ... Kurt Neumann†
ALIAS MIKE MORAN ... James Cruze†
ALIAS MR. TWILIGHT ... John Sturges†
ALIAS NICK BEAL ... John Farrow†
ALIAS SMITH AND JONES (TF) ... Gene Levitt
ALIAS THE DEACON ... Christy Cabanne†
ALIAS THE DOCTOR ... Michael Curtiz†
ALIBI ... Brian Desmond Hurst†
ALIBI IKE ... Ray Enright†
ALICE ... Woody Allen
ALICE ADAMS ... George Stevens†
ALICE ADAMS ... King Vidor†
ALICE ADAMS ... Rowland V. Lee†
ALICE DOESN'T LIVE HERE ANYMORE ... Martin Scorsese
ALICE IN THE CITIES ... Wim Wenders
ALICE IN WONDERLAND (TF) ... Harry Harris
ALICE IN WONDERLAND ... Bud Townsend
ALICE IN WONDERLAND ... Norman Z. MacLeod†
ALICE OU LA DERNIERE FUGUE ... Claude Chabrol
ALICE, SWEET ALICE ... Alfred Sole
ALICE TO NOWHERE ... John Power
ALICE'S RESTAURANT ... ★ Arthur Penn
ALIEN ... Ridley Scott
ALIEN 3 ... David Fincher
ALIEN, THE ... Thomas H. Ince†
ALIEN CONTAMINATION ... Lewis Coates
ALIEN FROM L.A. ... Albert Pyun
ALIEN INTRUDER ... Ricardo Jacques Gale
ALIEN NATION (1988) ... Graham Baker
ALIEN NATION (TF - 1989) ... Kenneth Johnson
ALIEN NATION: DARK HORIZON (TF) ... Kenneth Johnson
ALIEN PREDATOR ... Deran Sarafian
ALIEN YEARS, THE (MS) ... Donald Crombie
ALIENATOR ... Fred Olen Ray
ALIENS ... James Cameron
ALIENS ARE COMING, THE (TF) ... Harvey Hart†
ALIKI ... Rudolph Mate†
ALIMONY ... James W. Horne†
ALIMONY MADNESS ... B. Reeves Eason†
ALINA (TF) ... Aziz M. Osman
ALISE AND CHLOÉ ... René Gainville
ALISTAIR MACLEAN'S DEATH TRAIN (CTF) ... David S. Jackson
ALIVE ... Frank Marshall
ALIVE AND KICKING ... Cyril Frankel
ALIVE AND KICKING (TF) ... Robert William Young
ALL ABOARD ... Charley Chase†
ALL ABOUT BETTE (CTD) ... Susan F. Walker
ALL ABOUT EVE ... ★★ Joseph L. Mankiewicz†
ALL AMERICAN, THE ... Roy William Neill†
ALL AMERICAN CHUMP ... Edwin L. Marin†
ALL AMERICAN HIGH (FD) ... Keva Rosenfeld
ALL AMERICAN MURDER ... Anson Williams
ALL AMERICAN PRO ... Arthur Dreifuss†
ALL ASHORE ... Richard Quine†
ALL AT SEA ... Charles Frend†
ALL AT SEA (TF) ... Igor Auzins
ALL BY MYSELF (FD) ... Christian Blackwood†
ALL BY MYSELF ... Felix E. Feist†
ALL CREATURES GREAT AND SMALL (TF) ... Claude Whatham
ALL DOGS GO TO HEAVEN (AF) ... Don Bluth
ALL DOGS GO TO HEAVEN II ... Paul Sabella
ALL DOGS GO TO HEAVEN II (AF) ... Larry Leker
ALL FALL DOWN ... John Frankenheimer
ALL FOR HER ... Herbert Brenon†
ALL FOR IRELAND ... Sidney Olcott†
ALL FOR LOVE: LETTING THE BIRDS GO FREE (TF) ... Moira Armstrong
ALL GOD'S CHILDREN (TF) ... Jerry Thorpe
ALL HANDS ON DECK ... Norman Taurog†
ALL I DESIRE ... Douglas Sirk†
ALL I WANT FOR CHRISTMAS ... Robert Lieberman
ALL IN A NIGHT'S WORK ... Joseph Anthony†
ALL IN THE GAME (MS) ... Baz Taylor
ALL MEN ARE ENEMIES ... George Fitzmaurice†
ALL MEN ARE MORTAL ... Ate De Jong
ALL MINE TO GIVE ... Allen Reisner
ALL MONSTERS MUST BE DESTROYED ... Inoshiro (Ishiro) Honda†
ALL MY DARLING DAUGHTERS (TF) ... David Lowell Rich
ALL MY HUSBANDS ... Andre Farwagi
ALL MY SONS ... Irving Reis†
ALL NEAT IN BLACK STOCKING ... Christopher Morahan
ALL NIGHT LONG ... Basil Dearden†
ALL NIGHT LONG ... Jean-Claude Tramont
ALL OF ME ... Carl Reiner
ALL OF MYSELF ... Kon Ichikawa
ALL ON ACCOUNT OF A LAUNDRY MARK ... Edwin S. Porter†
ALL OR NOTHING AT ALL (TF) ... Andrew Grieve
ALL OUR FAULT ... Thaddeus O'Sullivan
ALL OVER TOWN ... James W. Horne†
ALL QUIET ON THE JOB HUNT FRONT ... Shusuke Kaneko
ALL QUIET ON THE WESTERN FRONT (1930) ... ★★ Lewis Milestone†
ALL QUIET ON THE WESTERN FRONT (TF - 1979) ... ☆ Delbert Mann
ALL SCREWED UP ... Lina Wertmuller
ALL THAT HEAVEN ALLOWS ... Douglas Sirk†
ALL THAT I HAVE ... William F. Claxton
ALL THAT JAZZ ... ★ Bob Fosse†
ALL THAT MONEY CAN BUY ... William Dieterle†
ALL THE BROTHERS WERE VALIANT ... Richard Thorpe†
ALL THE FINE YOUNG CANNIBALS ... Michael Anderson
ALL THE KIND STRANGERS (TF) ... Burt Kennedy
ALL THE KING'S MEN ... ★ Robert Rossen†
ALL THE KING'S MEN ... King Hu
ALL THE LOVING COUPLES ... Mack Bing
...ALL THE MARBLES ... Robert Aldrich†
ALL THE MORNINGS OF THE WORLD ... Alain Corneau
ALL THE PRESIDENT'S MEN ... ★ Alan J. Pakula
ALL THE RIGHT MOVES ... Michael Chapman
ALL THE RIGHT NOISES ... Gerry O'Hara
ALL THE RIVERS RUN (CMS) ... George Trumbull Miller
ALL THE VERMEERS IN NEW YORK ... Jon Jost
ALL THE WAY ... Charles Vidor†
ALL THE WAY DEAD ... Scott Shaw
ALL THE WAY UP THERE (FD) ... Gaylene Preston
ALL THE WORLD TO NOTHING ... Henry King†
ALL THE WRONG CLUES ... Tsui Hark
ALL THE YOUNG MEN ... Hall Bartlett†
ALL THESE WOMEN ... Ingmar Bergman
ALL THINGS BRIGHT AND BEAUTIFUL ... Barry Devlin
ALL THINGS BRIGHT AND BEAUTIFUL ... Eric Till
ALL THIS AND HEAVEN TOO ... Anatole Litvak†
ALL THROUGH THE NIGHT ... Vincent Sherman
ALL TIED UP ... John Mark Robinson
ALL TOGETHER NOW (TF) ... Randal Kleiser
ALL UNDER THE MOON ... Yoichi Sai
ALL WET ... Leo McCarey†
ALL WOMEN HAVE SECRETS ... Kurt Neumann†
ALL YOU NEED IS CASH (TF) ... Eric Idle
ALL YOU NEED IS CASH (TF) ... Gary Weis
ALL'ONOREVOLE PIACCIONO LE DONNE ... Lucio Fulci
ALL'S FAIR ... Rocky Lang
ALL-AMERICAN, THE ... Jesse Hibbs†
ALL-AMERICAN BOY, THE ... Charles Eastman
ALLA EN EL RANCHO GRANDE ... Fernando De Fuentes†
ALLA EN EL TROPICO ... Fernando De Fuentes†
ALLADDIN UP-TO-DATE ... J. Searle Dawley†
ALLAN QUATERMAIN AND THE LOST CITY OF GOLD ... Gary Nelson
ALLEGHENY UPRISING ... William A. Seiter†
ALLEGRO BARBARO ... Miklos Jancso
ALLEIN UNTER FRAUEN ... Soenke Wortmann
ALLEY CATS, THE ... Radley Metzger
ALLEY TRAMP ... Herschell Gordon Lewis
ALLEYN MYSTERIES, THE (TF) ... Silvio Narizzano
ALLIGATOR ... Lewis Teague
ALLIGATOR II: THE MUTATION ... Jon Hess
ALLIGATOR EYES ... John Feldman
ALLIGATOR NAMED DAISY, AN ... J. Lee Thompson
ALLIGATOR PEOPLE, THE ... Roy Del Ruth†
ALLIGATOR SHOES ... Clay Borris
ALLNIGHTER, THE ... Tamar Simon Hoffs
ALLO BERLIN? ICI PARIS! ... Julien Duvivier†
ALLOMS Z'ENFANATS ... Yves Boisset
ALLONSANFAN ... Paolo Taviani
ALLONSANFAN ... Vittorio Taviani
ALMA'S RAINBOW ... Ayoka Chenzira
ALMOST A HERO ... Edwin S. Porter†
ALMOST A KING ... William Beaudine†
ALMOST AN ANGEL ... John Cornell
ALMOST BLUE ... Keoni Waxman
ALMOST GROWN (TF) ... David Chase
ALMOST MARRIED ... Charles Lamont†
ALMOST PARTNERS (TF) ... Alan Kingsberg
ALMOST PERFECT AFFAIR, AN ... Michael Ritchie
ALMOST SUMMER ... Martin Davidson
ALMOST TRANSPARENT BLUE ... Ryu Murakami
ALMOST YOU ... Adam Brooks
ALOHA, BOBBY AND ROSE ... Floyd Mutrux
ALOHA MEANS GOODBYE (TF) ... David Lowell Rich
ALOHA PARADISE (TF) ... Richard Kinon
ALOHA SUMMER ... Tommy Lee Wallace
ALOMA OF THE SOUTH SEAS ... Alfred Santell†
ALOMA OF THE SOUTH SEAS ... Maurice Tourneur†
ALONE ... Grigori Kozintsev†
ALONE AGAINST ROME ... Herbert Wise
ALONE IN THE DARK ... Jack Sholder
ALONE IN THE NEON JUNGLE (TF) ... Georg Stanford Brown
ALONE ON THE PACIFIC ... Kon Ichikawa
ALONG CAME A SPIDER (TF) ... Lee H. Katzin
ALONG CAME JONES ... Stuart Heisler†
ALONG CAME RUTH ... Edward F. (Eddie) Cline†
ALONG CAME SALLY ... Tim Whelan†

I
N
D
E
X

O
F

F
I
L
M

T
I
T
L
E
S

C

I
N
D
E
X

O
F

F
I
L
M

T
I
T
L
E
S

D

D2: THE MIGHTY DUCKS ... San Weisman
D'EST ... Chantal Akerman
D'HOMME A HOMMES ... Christian-Jaque†
D'OU VIENS TO JOHNNY ... Noel Howard†
D-DAY REMEMBERED (FD) ... Charles Guggenheim
D-DAY, THE SIXTH OF JUNE ... Henry Koster†
D.A.: CONSPIRACY TO KILL, THE (TF) ... Paul Krasny
D.A.: MURDER ONE, THE (TF) ... Boris Sagal†
D.A.R.Y.L. ... Simon Wincer
D.C. CAB ... Joel Schumacher
D.I., THE ... Jack Webb†
D.O.A. ... Annabel Jankel
D.O.A. ... Rocky Morton
D.O.A. ... Rudolph Mate†
DA ... Matt Clark
DA GRANDE ... Franco Amurri
DA QUI ALL'ERIDITA' ... Riccardo Freda
DA VINCI'S WAY ... Raymond Martino
DABBAWALLAHS (TF) ... Horace Ove
DAD ... Gary David Goldberg
DADAH IS DEATH (TF) ... Jerry London
DADDIES ... William A. Seiter†
DADDY (TF) ... John Herzfeld
DADDY (TF) ... Michael Miller
DADDY LONG LEGS ... Alfred Santell†
DADDY LONG LEGS ... Jean Negulesco†
DADDY LONG LEGS ... Marshall (Mickey) Neilan†
DADDY NOSTALGIA ... Bertrand Tavernier
DADDY'S BOYS ... Joseph Minion
DADDY'S DYIN'...WHO'S GOT THE WILL? ... Jack Fisk
DADDY'S GONE A-HUNTING ... Frank Borzage†
DADDY'S GONE A-HUNTING ... Mark Robson†
DADDY, I DON'T LIKE IT LIKE THIS (TF) ... Adell Aldrich
DAFFY DUCK'S MOVIE: FANTASTIC ISLAND (AF) ... Charles M. (Chuck) Jones
DAFFY DUCK'S QUACKBUSTERS (AF) ... Charles M. (Chuck) Jones
DAFFY DUCK'S QUACKBUSTERS (AF) ... Greg Ford
DAFFY DUCK'S QUACKBUSTERS (AF) ... Terry Lennon
DAGFIN ... Joe May†
DAGGER, THE ... Mauritz Stiller†
DAGGER, THE ... Robert Stevenson†
DAGLI APPENNINI ALLE ANDE ... Folco Quilici
DAGORA, THE SPACE MONSTER ... Inoshiro Honda†
DAGUERREOTYPES (FD) ... Agnes Varda
DAI GO FUKURYU-MARU ... Kaneto Shindo
DAI-SHITSUREN ... Kazuki Omori
DAIBOSATSU PASS ... Kenji Misumi†
DAIBOSATSU PASS ... Kihachi Okamoto
DAIBOSATSU PASS: THE DRAGON GOD ... Kenji Misumi†
DAIJOBU, MY FRIEND ... Ryu Murakami
DAIMAJIN GETS ANGRY ... Kenji Misumi†
DAIN CURSE, THE (MS) ... ☆ E.W. Swackhamer†
DAISIES ... Vera Chytilova
DAISY (TF) ... Peter John Duffell
DAISY ET MONA ... Claude D'Anna
DAISY KENYON ... Otto Preminger†
DAISY MILLER ... Peter Bogdanovich
DAISY: STORY OF A FACELIFT (TD) ... Michael Rubbo
DAKOTA ... Fred Holmes
DAKOTA ... Joseph (Joe) Kane†
DAKOTA DAN ... William S. Hart†
DAKOTA INCIDENT ... Lewis R. Foster†
DAKOTA LIL ... Lesley Selander†
DAKOTA ROAD ... Nick Ward
DALEKS - INVASION EARTH 2150 A.D. ... Gordon Flemyng
DALEY'S DECATHLON (TF) ... Christopher Miles
DALLAS ... Stuart Heisler†
DALLAS COWBOYS CHEERLEADERS (TF) ... Bruce Bilson
DALLAS COWBOYS CHEERLEADERS II (TF) ... Michael O'Herlihy
DALLAS DOLL ... Ann Turner
DALLAS: PHANTOM OF THE OIL RIG (TF) ... Irving J. Moore†
DALLAS: PHANTOM OF THE OIL RIG (TF) ... Michael Preece
DALLAS: THE EARLY YEARS (TF) ... Larry Elikann
DALTON GIRLS, THE ... Reginald Le Borg†
DALTONS RIDE AGAIN, THE ... Ray Taylor†
DAM BUSTERS, THE ... Michael Anderson
DAMAGE ... Louis Malle
DAMAGED LIVES ... Edgar G. Ulmer†
DAMES ... Ray Enright†
DAMIEN - OMEN II ... Don Taylor
DAMIEN...THE LEPER PRIEST (TF) ... Steven Gethers†
DAMN THE DEFIANT! ... Lewis Gilbert
DAMN YANKEES ... George Abbott†
DAMN YANKEES ... Stanley Donen
DAMNATION ALLEY ... Jack Smight
DAMNATION DE FAUST ... Georges Melies†
DAMNATION DU DOCTEUR FAUST ... Georges Melies†
DAMNED, THE ... Joseph Losey†
DAMNED, THE ... Luchino Visconti†
DAMNED DON'T CRY, THE ... Vincent Sherman
DAMNED IN THE USA (TD) ... Paul Yule
DAMON AND PYTHIAS ... Curtis Bernhardt†
DAMSEL IN DISTRESS, A ... George Stevens†
DAN LE VENTRE DU DRAGON ... Yves Simoneau
DAN THE DANDY ... D.W. Griffith†
DAN TURNER, HOLLYWOOD DETECTIVE (TF) ... Christopher Lewis
DANCE 'TIL DAWN (TF) ... Paul Schneider
DANCE BLACK AMERICA (FD) ... Chris Hegedus
DANCE BLACK AMERICA (FD) ... D.A. Pennebaker
DANCE FEVER ... Sir Alexander Korda†
DANCE FOOLS DANCE ... Harry Beaumont†
DANCE, GIRL, DANCE ... Dorothy Arzner†
DANCE GOES ON, THE ... Paul Almond
DANCE HALL ... Charles Crichton
DANCE HALL ... Irving Pichel†
DANCE HALL HOSTESS ... B. Reeves Eason†
DANCE HALL MARGE ... Mack Sennett†
DANCE IN THE SUN ... Shirley Clarke
DANCE LITTLE LADY ... Val Guest
DANCE MADNESS ... Robert Z. Leonard†
DANCE ME OUTSIDE ... Bruce McDonald
DANCE MOVIE ... Andy Warhol†
DANCE OF LIFE, THE ... Edward Sutherland†
DANCE OF LIFE, THE ... John Cromwell†
DANCE OF THE DAMNED ... Katt Shea
DANCE OF THE DWARFS ... Gus Trikonis
DANCE OF THE HERON, THE ... Fons Rademakers
DANCE OF THE SEVEN VEILS, THE (TF) ... Ken Russell
DANCE OF THE VAMPIRES ... Roman Polanski
DANCE OF THE WIDOW ... Lee Jang-Ho
DANCE PRETTY LADY ... Anthony Asquith†
DANCE TEAM ... Sidney Lanfield†
DANCE TO WIN ... Ted Mather
DANCE WITH A STRANGER ... Mike Newell
DANCE WITH ME, HENRY ... Charles T. Barton†
DANCER, THE ... Masahiro Shinoda
DANCER, THE ... Mikio Naruse†
DANCER OF PARIS, THE ... Alfred Santell†
DANCERS ... Herbert Ross
DANCES WITH WOLVES ... ★★ Kevin Costner
DANCIN' FOOL, THE ... Sam Wood†
DANCIN' THRU THE DARK ... Mike Ockrent
DANCING (TD) ... Geoff Dunlop
DANCING BULL ... Allen Fong
DANCING CHEAT, THE ... Irving Cummings†
DANCING CO-ED ... S. Sylvan Simon†
DANCING FEET ... Joseph Santley†
DANCING GIRL ... Mikio Naruse†
DANCING GIRL, THE ... Allan Dwan†
DANCING GIRL OF BUTTE, THE ... D.W. Griffith†
DANCING IN MANHATTAN ... Henry Levin†
DANCING IN THE DARK ... Irving Reis†
DANCING IN THE DARK ... Leon Marr
DANCING LADY ... Robert Z. Leonard†
DANCING MOTHERS ... Herbert Brenon†
DANCING ON A DIME ... Joseph Santley†
DANCING ON WATER ... Jovan Acin
DANCING PARADISE (TF) ... Pupi Avati
DANCING SWEETINES ... Ray Enright†
DANCING WITH DANGER (CTF) ... Stuart Cooper
DANCING YEARS, THE ... Harold French†
DANDELION DEAD (TF) ... Mike Hodges
DANDY DICK ... William Beaudine†
DANDY IN ASPIC, A ... Anthony Mann†
DANDY, THE ALL-AMERICAN GIRL ... Jerry Schatzberg
DANGER AHEAD ... William K. Howard†
DANGER: DIABOLIK ... Mario Bava†
DANGER DOWN UNDER (TF) ... Russ Mayberry
DANGER - GO SLOW ... Robert Z. Leonard†
DANGER IN PARADISE (TF) ... Marvin J. Chomsky
DANGER ISLAND (S) ... Ray Taylor†
DANGER ISLAND (TF) ... Tommy Lee Wallace
DANGER LIGHTS ... George B. Seitz†
DANGER - LOVE AT WORK ... Otto Preminger†
DANGER OF LOVE, THE (TF) ... Joyce Chopra
DANGER ON WHEELS ... Christy Cabanne†
DANGER PATROL ... Lew Landers†
DANGER ROUTE ... Seth Holt†
DANGER SIGNAL ... Robert Florey†
DANGER SIGNAL, THE ... Erle C. Kenton†
DANGER STALKS NEAR ... Keisuke Kinoshita
DANGER STREET ... Lew Landers†
DANGER UXB (MS) ... Ferdinand Fairfax
DANGER WITHIN ... Don Chaffey†
DANGER ZONE ... Allan Eastman
DANGEROUS ... Alfred E. Green†
DANGEROUS, THE ... Rod Hewitt
DANGEROUS AFFAIR, A (TF) ... Alan Metzger
DANGEROUS AFFECTION ... Larry Elikann
DANGEROUS AGE, A ... Sidney J. Furie
DANGEROUS AGE, THE ... John M. Stahl†
DANGEROUS BUSINESS ... Roy William Neill†
DANGEROUS COMPANY (TF) ... Lamont Johnson
DANGEROUS CROSSING ... Joseph M. Newman
DANGEROUS CURVES ... David Lewis
DANGEROUS CURVES ... Lothar Mendes†
DANGEROUS CURVES BEHIND ... Edward F. (Eddie) Cline†
DANGEROUS DAVIES - THE LAST DETECTIVE ... Val Guest
DANGEROUS DAYS OF KIOWA JONES, THE (TF) ... Alex March†
DANGEROUS DUB, THE ... Richard Thorpe†
DANGEROUS ENCOUNTER - FIRST KIND ... Tsui Hark
DANGEROUS EXILE ... Brian Desmond Hurst†
DANGEROUS FLIRT, THE ... Tod Browning†
DANGEROUS GAME ... Abel Ferrara
DANGEROUS GAME, A ... John Rawlins
DANGEROUS GAME, A ... Stephen Hopkins
DANGEROUS GAMES ... Mario Di Fiore
DANGEROUS GAMES ... Pierre Chenal
DANGEROUS HOURS ... Fred Niblo†
DANGEROUS INNOCENCE ... William A. Seiter†
DANGEROUS INTENTIONS (TF) ... Michael Toshiyuki Uno
DANGEROUS LIAISONS ... Stephen Frears
DANGEROUS LIAISONS (1960) ... Roger Vadim
DANGEROUS LIFE, A (CTF) ... Robert Markowitz
DANGEROUS LOVE ... Marty Ollstein
DANGEROUS LOVE (TF) ... John Hough
DANGEROUS MAN - LAWRENCE AFTER ARABIA, A (TF) ... Christopher Menaul
DANGEROUS MINDS ... John N. Smith
DANGEROUS MISSION ... Louis King†
DANGEROUS MOONLIGHT ... Brian Desmond Hurst†
DANGEROUS MOVES ... Richard Dembo
DANGEROUS NUMBER ... Richard Thorpe†
DANGEROUS OBSESSION ... Lucio Fulci
DANGEROUS ORPHANS ... John Laing
DANGEROUS PARADISE ... William A. Wellman†
DANGEROUS PARTNERS ... Edward L. Cahn†
DANGEROUS PASSION (TF) ... Michael Miller
DANGEROUS PASTIME ... James W. Horne†
DANGEROUS PLACE, A ... Jerry P. Jacobs
DANGEROUS PROFESSION, A ... Ted Tetzlaff
DANGEROUS SUMMER, A ... Quentin Masters
DANGEROUS TO KNOW ... Robert Florey†
DANGEROUS TO LIVE ... Leslie Norman
DANGEROUS TOUCH ... Lou Diamond Phillips
DANGEROUS VOYAGE ... Vernon Sewell
DANGEROUS WHEN WET ... Charles Walters†
DANGEROUS WOMAN, A ... Rowland V. Lee†
DANGEROUS YOUTH ... Herbert Wilcox†
DANGEROUSLY CLOSE ... Albert Pyun
DANGEROUSLY THEY LIVE ... Robert Florey†
DANIEL ... Sidney Lumet
DANIEL AND THE TOWERS (TF) ... Paul Schneider
DANIEL BOONE ... Edwin S. Porter†
DANIELLE STEEL'S A PERFECT STRANGER (TF) ... Michael Miller
DANIELLE STEEL'S 'CHANGES' (TF) ... Charles Jarrott
DANIELLE STEEL'S DADDY (TF) ... Michael Miller
DANIELLE STEEL'S FAMILY ALBUM (TF) ... Jack Bender
DANIELLE STEEL'S FINE THINGS ... Tom Moore
DANIELLE STEEL'S HEARTBEAT (TF) ... Michael Miller
DANIELLE STEEL'S 'JEWELS' (MS) ... Roger Young
DANIELLE STEEL'S KALEIDOSCOPE (TF) ... Jud Taylor
DANIELLE STEEL'S MESSGE FROM NAM (TF) ... Paul Wendkos
DANIELLE STEEL'S ONCE IN A LIFETIME (TF) ... Michael Miller
DANIELLE STEEL'S PALOMINO (TF) ... Michael Miller
DANIELLE STEEL'S SECRETS (TF) ... Peter H. Hunt

F-Fa
FILM DIRECTORS GUIDE

F

F FOR FAKE ... Orson Welles†
F.B.I. CODE 98 ... Leslie H. Martinson
F.I.S.T. ... Norman Jewison
FABIOLA ... Alessandro Blasetti†
FABULA DE LA BELA PALOMERA ... Ruy Guerra
FABULOUS BAKER BOYS, THE ... Steve Kloves
FABULOUS BARON MUNCHAUSEN, THE ... Karel Zeman†
FABULOUS DORSEYS, THE ... Alfred E. Green†
FABULOUS SENORITA, THE ... R.G. (Bud) Springsteen†
FABULOUS SUZANNE, THE ... Steve Sekely†
FABULOUS TEXAN, THE ... Edward Ludwig†
FABULOUS WORLD OF JULES VERNE, THE ... Karel Zeman†
FACCIA DI SPIA ... Giuseppe Ferrara
FACE ... Andy Warhol†
FACE AT THE WINDOW, THE ... Alice Guy-Blache†
FACE AT THE WINDOW, THE ... D.W. Griffith†
FACE BEHIND THE MASK, THE ... Robert Florey†
FACE FROM THE PAST, A ... Mikio Naruse†
FACE IN THE CROWD, A ... Elia Kazan
FACE IN THE FOG, THE ... Alan Crosland†
FACE IN THE NIGHT ... Lance Comfort†
FACE IN THE RAIN, A ... Irvin Kershner
FACE OF A FUGITIVE ... Paul Wendkos
FACE OF A MURDERER, THE ... Teinosuke Kinugasa†
FACE OF A STRANGER ... John Llewellyn Moxey
FACE OF A STRANGER (TF) ... Claudia Weill
FACE OF ANOTHER, THE ... Hiroshi Teshigahara
FACE OF BRITAIN, THE (FD) ... Paul Rotha†
FACE OF FEAR (TF) ... Farhad Mann
FACE OF FEAR, THE (TF) ... George McCowan
FACE OF FIRE ... Albert Band
FACE OF FU MANCHU, THE ... Don Sharp
FACE OF MARBLE, THE ... William Beaudine†
FACE OF RAGE, THE (TF) ... Donald Wrye
FACE OF THE EARTH (TF) ... Kevin Billington
FACE OF THE ENEMY ... Hassan Ildari
FACE OF THE ENEMY, THE ... Esther Shub†
FACE OF WAR, A (FD) ... Eugene S. Jones
FACE ON THE BARROOM FLOOR, THE ... Charles (Charlie) Chaplin†
FACE ON THE BARROOM FLOOR, THE ... Edwin S. Porter†
FACE ON THE BARROOM FLOOR, THE ... John Ford†
FACE THE MUSIC ... Carol Wiseman
FACE THE MUSIC ... Terence Fisher†
FACE TO FACE ... Bretaigne Windust†
FACE TO FACE ... ★ Ingmar Bergman
FACE TO FACE ... John Brahm†
FACE TO FACE (TF) ... Lou Antonio
FACE VALUE ... Robert Florey†
FACE VALUE ... Robert Z. Leonard†
FACES ... John Cassavetes†
FACES IN A FAMINE (FD) ... Robert H. Lieberman
FACES IN THE FOG ... John English†
FACES OF ISRAEL (FD) ... Michael Roemer
FACES OF THE ENEMY (TD) ... Jeffrey Friedman
FACES OF WOMEN ... Desire Ecaré
FACING THE FOREST ... Peter Lilienthal
FACTS OF LIFE, THE ... Melvin Frank†
FACTS OF LIFE DOWN UNDER, THE (TF) ... Stuart Margolin
FACTS OF LIFE GOES TO PARIS, THE (TF) ... Asaad Kelada
FACTS OF MURDER, THE ... Pietro Germi†
FADE TO BLACK ... Vernon Zimmerman
FADE TO BLACK (CTF) ... John McPherson
FADE-IN ... Alan Smithee
FADE-IN ... Jud Taylor
FADED LILIES, THE ... D.W. Griffith†
FADO MAJEUR ET MINEUR ... Raul Ruiz
FAHRENDES VOLK ... Jacques Feyder†
FAHRENHEIT 451 ... Francois Truffaut†
FAHSTROM ... Raul Ruiz
FAIL SAFE ... Sidney Lumet
FAILING OF RAYMOND, THE (TF) ... Boris Sagal†
FAILURE, THE ... Christy Cabanne†
FAILURE, THE ... D.W. Griffith†
FAINT PERFUME ... Louis J. Gasnier†
FAINTING LOVER ... Mack Sennett†
FAIR CO-ED, THE ... Sam Wood†
FAIR EXCHANGE, A ... D.W. Griffith†
FAIR GAME ... Andrew Sipes
FAIR GAME (TF) ... Alan Dossor
FAIR STOOD THE WIND FOR FRANCE (MS) ... Martyn Friend
FAIR TRADE ... Cedric Sundstrom
FAIR WARNING ... Norman Foster†
FAIR WIND TO JAVA ... Joseph (Joe) Kane†
FAIRLY SECRET ARMY II (MS) ... Roy Ward Baker
FAIRY TALES ... Harry Hurwitz
FAITH (TF) ... John Strickland
FAITHFUL ... D.W. Griffith†
FAITHFUL ... Paul Mazursky
FAITHFUL HEART, THE ... Victor Saville†
FAITHFUL IN MY FASHION ... Sidney Salkow
FAITHFUL TAXICAB, THE ... Mack Sennett†
FAITHLESS ... Harry Beaumont†
FAKE DETECTIVE ... Satsuo Yamamoto†
FAKE OUT ... Matt Cimber
FAKERS, THE ... Al Adamson
FALASHA: AGONY OF THE BLACK JEWS (TD) ... Simcha Jacobovici
FALASHA: EXILE OF THE BLACK JEWS (FD) ... Simcha Jacobovici
FALCON AND THE CO-EDS, THE ... William B. Clemens
FALCON AND THE SNOWMAN, THE ... John Schlesinger
FALCON IN DANGER, THE ... William B. Clemens
FALCON IN HOLLYWOOD, THE ... Gordon Douglas†
FALCON IN SAN FRANCISCO, THE ... Joseph H. Lewis
FALCON OUT WEST, THE ... William B. Clemens
FALCON STRIKES BACK, THE ... Edward Dmytryk
FALCON TAKES OVER, THE ... Irving Reis†
FALCON'S MALTESTER ... Stephen Bayly
FALL FROM GRACE (TF) ... Karen Arthur
FALL GUY ... Reginald Le Borg†
FALL GUY, THE ... Kinji Fukasaku
FALL GUY, THE ... Larry Semon†
FALL GUY, THE (TF) ... Russ Mayberry
FALL IN ... Kurt Neumann†
FALL OF THE HOUSE OF USHER, THE ... Alan Birkinshaw
FALL OF THE HOUSE OF USHER, THE ... James L. Conway
FALL OF THE LEAVES, THE ... Otar Ioselliani
FALL OF THE ROMAN EMPIRE, THE ... Anthony Mann†
FALL OF THE ROMANOFFS, THE ... Herbert Brenon†
FALL OF THE ROMANOV DYNASTY, THE (FD) ... Esther Shub†
FALL TIME ... Paul Warner
FALLEN ... Peter Watkins
FALLEN ANGEL ... Otto Preminger†
FALLEN ANGEL (TF) ... Robert M. Lewis
FALLEN ANGELS ... Larry Leahy
FALLEN HERO (TF) ... Jeremy Summers
FALLEN IDOL, THE ... ★ Sir Carol Reed
FALLEN SPARROW, THE ... Richard Wallace†
FALLGROPEN ... Vilgot Sjoman
FALLING DOWN ... Joel Schumacher
FALLING FOR YOU ... Robert Stevenson†
FALLING FOR YOU (TF) ... Eric Till
FALLING FROM GRACE ... John Mellencamp
FALLING FROM THE SKY! FLIGHT 174 (TF) ... Jorge Montesi
FALLING IN LOVE ... Ulu Grosbard
FALLING IN LOVE AGAIN ... Steven Paul
FALLING LEAVES ... Alice Guy-Blache†
FALLING OVER BACKWARDS ... Mort Ransen
FALLS, THE ... Peter Greenaway
FALN (FD) ... Robert Kramer
FALSE ARREST (TF) ... Bill L. Norton
FALSE COLORS ... Lois Weber†
FALSE COLORS ... Phillips Smalley†
FALSE FRIENDS ... Francis Ford†
FALSE IDENTITY ... James Keach
FALSE MADONNA, THE ... Stuart Walker†
FALSE PRETENSES ... Charles Lamont†
FALSE ROAD, THE ... Fred Niblo†
FALSE WITNESS (TF) ... Arthur Allan Seidelman
FALSTAFF ... Orson Welles†
FAME ... Alan Parker
FAME IS THE NAME OF THE GAME (TF) ... Stuart Rosenberg
FAME IS THE SPUR ... Roy Boulting
FAME STREET ... Louis King†
FAMILIARIDADES ... Felipe Cazals
FAMILICAO ... Manoel De Oliveira
FAMILIEN GYLDENKAAL ... Gabriel Axel
FAMILY ... Michael Winterbottom
FAMILY (TF) ... Mary McMurray
FAMILY, THE ... Ettore Scola
FAMILY AFFAIR, A ... George B. Seitz†
FAMILY ALBUM (TF) ... Jack Bender
FAMILY BUSINESS (TF) ... John Stix
FAMILY BUSINESS ... Sidney Lumet
FAMILY DIARY ... Satsuo Yamamoto†
FAMILY DIARY ... Valerio Zurlini†
FAMILY DIVIDED, A (TF) ... Donald Wrye
FAMILY FLIGHT (TF) ... Marvin J. Chomsky
FAMILY FOR JOE, A (TF) ... Jeffrey Melman
FAMILY GAME, THE ... Yoshimitsu Morita
FAMILY HONOR,THE ... King Vidor†
FAMILY JEWELS, THE ... Jerry Lewis
FAMILY KOVACK, THE (TF) ... Ralph Senensky
FAMILY LIFE ... Kenneth Loach
FAMILY LIFE ... Krzysztof Zanussi
FAMILY MAN, THE (TF) ... Glenn Jordan
FAMILY NEXT DOOR, THE ... Joseph Santley†
FAMILY NOBODY WANTED, THE (TF) ... Ralph Senensky
FAMILY OF SPIES (MS) ... Stephen Gyllenhaal
FAMILY OF STRANGERS, A (TF) ... Sheldon Larry
FAMILY PICTURES (TF) ... Philip Saville
FAMILY PLOT ... Alfred Hitchcock†
FAMILY PRAYERS ... Scott Rosenfelt
FAMILY RELATIONS ... Nikita Mikhalkov
FAMILY REUNION (TF) ... Fielder Cook
FAMILY REUNION (TF) ... Vic Sarin
FAMILY RICO, THE (TF) ... Paul Wendkos
FAMILY SECRET, THE ... Henry Levin†
FAMILY SECRET, THE ... William A. Seiter†
FAMILY SECRETS (TF) ... Jack Hofsiss
FAMILY SKELETON, THE ... Victor Schertzinger†
FAMILY TIES VACATION (TF) ... Will Mackenzie
FAMILY TORN APART, A (TF) ... Craig R. Baxley
FAMILY TREE BOOK, THE ... Im Kwon-Taek
FAMILY UPSIDE DOWN, A (TF) ... David Lowell Rich
FAMILY VIEWING ... Atom Egoyan
FAMILY WAY, THE ... Roy Boulting
FAMOUS FERGUSON CASE, THE ... Lloyd Bacon†
FAMOUS MRS. FAIR, THE ... Fred Niblo†
FAN, THE ... Edward Bianchi
FAN, THE ... Otto Preminger†
FAN FAN ... Sidney Franklin†
FAN'S NOTES, A ... Eric Till
FANATIC ... David Winters
FANATIC ... Silvio Narizzano
FANATICS, THE ... Karoly Makk
FANCY PANTS ... George Marshall†
FANDANGO ... Kevin Reynolds
FANDO AND LIS ... Alejandro Jodorowsky
FANDY & FANDY ... Karel Kachyna
FANFAN LA TULIPE ... Alice Guy-Blache†
FANFAN THE TULIP ... Christian-Jaque†
FANFARE FOR A DEATH SCENE ... Leslie Stevens
FANG OF THE GANGLAND ... Jun Fukuda
FANNY ... Joshua Logan†
FANNY ... Marc Allegret†
FANNY AND ALEXANDER ... ★ Ingmar Bergman
FANNY BY GASLIGHT ... Anthony Asquith†
FANNY HAWTHORN ... Maurice Elvey†
FANNY HILL ... Gerry O'Hara
FANNY HILL MEETS DR. EROTICO ... Barry Mahon
FANNY HILL MEETS LADY CHATTERLEY ... Barry Mahon
FANNY HILL MEETS THE RED BARON ... Barry Mahon
FANNY HILL: MEMOIRS OF A WOMAN OF PLEASURE ... Russ Meyer
FANNY PELOPAJA ... Vicente Aranda
FANTASIA ... Aziz M. Osman
FANTASIA CONTINUED (AF) ... George Scribner
FANTASIA CONTINUED (AF) ... Hendel Butoy
FANTASIA CONTINUED (AF) ... Scott Johnston
FANTASIES ... John Derek
FANTASIST, THE ... Robin Hardy
FANTASM ... Richard Franklin
FANTASTIC FOUR ... Oley Sassone
FANTASTIC JOURNEY, THE (TF) ... Andrew V. McLaglen
FANTASTIC TALE OF NARUTO, A ... Teinosuke Kinugasa†
FANTASTIC VOYAGE ... Richard Fleischer
FANTASTIC WORLD OF D.C. COLLINS, THE (TF) ... Leslie H. Martinson
FANTASTICA ... Gilles Carle
FANTASTICKS, THE ... Michael Ritchie
FANTASY FILM WORLDS OF GEORGE PAL, THE (FD) ... Arnold Leibovit
FANTASY ISLAND (TF) ... Margy Kinmouth
FANTASY ISLAND (TF) ... Richard Lang
FANTOMAS (TF) ... Claude Chabrol
FAR AND AWAY ... Ron Howard

INDEX OF FILM TITLES

Fe-Fi

FILM
DIRECTORS
GUIDE

INDEX OF FILM TITLES

573

G

GOODBYE AGAIN .... Michael Curtiz†
GOODBYE AND AMEN .... Damiano Damiani
GOODBYE, CHARLIE .... Vincente Minnelli†
GOODBYE CHILDREN .... Louis Malle
GOODBYE, COLUMBUS .... Larry Peerce
GOODBYE CRUEL WORLD (TF) .... Adrian Shergold
GOOD-BYE! DUMAN RIVER .... Im Kwon-Taek
GOODBYE GEMINI .... Alan Gibson†
GOODBYE GIRL, THE .... Herbert Ross
GOODBYE - GOOD DAY .... Kon Ichikawa
GOODBYE LEGS .... Mack Sennett†
GOODBYE LOVE .... H. Bruce (Lucky) Humberstone†
GOODBYE, MR. CHIPS .... ★ Sam Wood†
GOODBYE, MR. CHIPS .... Herbert Ross
GOODBYE, MY FANCY .... Vincent Sherman
GOODBYE MY FRIEND .... Amir Naderi
GOODBYE, MY LADY .... William A. Wellman†
GOODBYE MY LOVE .... Masato Harada
GOODBYE NEW YORK .... Amos Kollek
GOODBYE NORMA JEAN .... Larry Buchanan
GOODBYE PARADISE .... Carl Schultz
GOODBYE PEOPLE, THE .... Herb Gardner
GOODBYE PORK PIE .... Geoff Murphy
GOODBYE, RAGGEDY ANN (TF) .... Fielder Cook
GOODBYE TO LAW .... Toshio Masuda
GOODFELLAS .... Martin Scorsese
GOODNIGHT MY LOVE (TF) .... Peter Hyams
GOODNIGHT SWEETHEART .... Joseph Santley†
GOODNIGHT VIENNA .... Herbert Wilcox†
GOOFY MOVIE, A (AF) .... Kevin Lima
GOONIES, THE .... Richard Donner
GOOPY GYNE BAGHA BYNE .... Satyajit Ray†
GOOSE AND THE GANDER, THE .... Alfred E. Green†
GOOSE HANGS HIGH, THE .... James Cruze†
GOOSE STEPS OUT, THE .... Basil Dearden†
GOOSE WOMAN, THE .... Clarence Brown†
GOOSELAND .... Edward F. (Eddie) Cline†
GORATH .... Inoshiro Honda†
GORD S. (TD) .... John Zaritsky
GORDON OF GHOST CITY (S) .... Ray Taylor†
GORDON PINSENT AND THE LIFE AND TIMES OF EDWIN ALONZO BOYD (TF) .... Les Rose
GORDON'S WAR .... Ossie Davis
GORDY .... Mark Lewis
GORE VIDAL'S BILLY THE KID (CTF) .... William A. Graham
GORE VIDAL'S LINCOLN (TF) .... ☆☆ Lamont Johnson
GORE-GORE GIRLS, THE .... Herschell Gordon Lewis
GORGE, THE (TF) .... Christopher Morahan
GORGEOUS HUSSY, THE .... Clarence Brown†
GORGO .... Eugene Lourie†
GORGON, THE .... Terence Fisher†
GORILLA, THE .... Alfred Santell†
GORILLA, THE .... Allan Dwan†
GORILLA AT LARGE .... Harmon Jones†
GORILLA BATHES AT NOON, THE .... Dusan Makavejev
GORILLAS IN THE MIST .... Michael Apted
GORKY PARK .... Michael Apted
GORP .... Joseph Ruben
GOSH-DARN MORTGAGE, THE .... Edward F. (Eddie) Cline†
GOSHU THE CELLIST (AF) .... Isao Takahata
GOSPA .... Jakoy Sedlar
GOSPEL (FD) .... David Leivick
GOSPEL (FD) .... Frederick Ritzenberg
GOSPEL ACCORDING TO AL GREEN (FD) .... Robert Mugge
GOSPEL ACCORDING TO MARCUS, THE .... Hector Olivera
GOSPEL ACCORDING TO ST. MATTHEW, THE .... Pier Paolo Pasolini†
GOSPEL ACCORDING TO VIC .... Charles Gormley
GOSPEL ROAD, THE .... Robert Elfstrom
GOSSIP COLUMNIST, THE (TF) .... James Sheldon
GOT IT MADE .... James Kenelm Clarke
GOTCHA! .... Jeff Kanew
GOTHAM (CTF) .... Lloyd Fonvielle
GOTHIC .... Ken Russell
GOTO, L'ILE D'AMOUR .... Walerian Borowczyk
GOTT MIT UNS .... Giuliano Montaldo
GOTTER DER PEST .... Rainer Werner Fassbinder†
GOUEMON THE TROUBLEMAKER .... Hiroshi Inagaki†
GOUPI MAINS ROUGES (TF) .... Claude Goretta
GOURMET, THE (TF) .... Michael Whyte
GOVAN GHOST STORY (TF) .... David Hayman
GOVERNOR, THE .... Alan Dossor
GOVERNOR, THE .... Bob Mahoney
GOVERNOR, THE .... Robert Knights
GOVERNOR'S DAUGHTERS, THE .... Victor Sjostrom†
GOYOKIBA .... Kenji Misumi†
GOYOKIN .... Hideo Gosha†
GRACE KELLY (TF) .... Anthony Page
GRACE OF MY HEART .... Allison Anders
GRACE QUIGLEY .... Anthony Harvey
GRACIE ALLEN MURDER CASE, THE .... Alfred E. Green†
GRACIELA .... Leopoldo Torre Nilsson†
GRADUATE, THE .... ★★ Mike Nichols
GRADUATE FIRST .... Maurice Pialat
GRADUATE TRIP: I COME FROM JAPAN .... Shusuke Kaneko
GRADUATION DAY .... Herb Freed
GRAFFITI BRIDGE .... Prince
GRAFIN DONELLI .... G.W. Pabst†
GRAFT .... Christy Cabanne†
GRAMBLING'S WHITE TIGER (TF) .... Georg Stanford Brown
GRAMPS (TF) .... Bradford May
GRAN BOLLITO .... Mauro Bolognini
GRAN CASINO .... Luis Buñuel†
GRAND CANARY .... Irving Cummings†
GRAND CANYON .... Lawrence Kasdan
GRAND CANYON .... Paul Landres
GRAND CENTRAL MURDER .... S. Sylvan Simon†
GRAND EXIT .... Erle C. Kenton†
GRAND HIGHWAY, THE .... Jean-Loup Hubert
GRAND HOTEL .... Edmund Goulding†
GRAND ILLUSION .... Jean Renoir†
GRAND ISLE .... Mary Lambert
GRAND JURY .... Christopher Cain
GRAND LARCENY (TF) .... Jeannot Szwarc
GRAND OLD GIRL .... John S. Robertson†
GRAND PRIX .... John Frankenheimer
GRAND SLAM .... Giuliano Montaldo
GRAND SLAM .... William Dieterle†
GRAND SLAM (TF) .... Bill L. Norton
GRAND STREET .... Jonas Mekas
GRAND THEFT AUTO .... Ron Howard
GRAND TOUR (CTF) .... Jack Sholder
GRANDES MANOEUVRES .... Georges Melies†
GRANDEUR ET DECADENCE D'UN PETIT COMMERCE DE CINEMA (TF) .... Jean-Luc Godard
GRANDMA'S READING GLASS .... George Albert Smith†
GRANDMOTHER .... Sir Alexander Korda†
GRANDMOTHER'S HOUSE .... Peter Rader
GRANDPA PLANTED A BEET (AF) .... Jiri Trnka†
GRANDPA'S MUSICAL TOYS (HVF) .... Susan Shadburne
GRANDVIEW, U.S.A. .... Randal Kleiser
GRANNY .... Christy Cabanne†
GRAPES OF WRATH, THE .... ★★ John Ford†
GRASS (FD) .... Merian C. Cooper†
GRASS: A NATION'S BATTLE FOR LIFE (FD) .... Merian C. Cooper†
GRASS ARENA, THE (TF) .... Gillies Mackinnon
GRASS HARP, THE .... Charles Matthau
GRASS IS ALWAYS GREENER OVER THE SEPTIC TANK, THE (TF) .... Robert Day
GRASS IS GREENER, THE .... Stanley Donen
GRASS IS SINGING, THE .... Michael Raeburn
GRASS ROOTS (TF) .... Jerry London
GRASS: THE EPIC OF A LOST TRIBE (FD) .... Merian C. Cooper†
GRASS WHISTLE .... Shiro Toyoda†
GRASSCUTTER, THE (TF) .... Ian Mune
GRASSHOPPER, THE .... Jerry Paris†
GRAVE OF THE FIREFLIES (AF) .... Isao Takahata
GRAVE ROBBERS FROM OUTER SPACE .... Edward D. Wood, Jr.†
GRAVE SECRETS: THE LEGACY OF HILLTOP DRIVE (TF) .... John Patterson
GRAVEYARD SHIFT .... Gerard Ciccoritti
GRAVEYARD SHIFT .... Ralph S. Singleton
GRAVEYARD SHIFT II .... Gerard Ciccoritti
GRAVITY OF STARS, THE .... H. Gordon Boos
GRAVY TRAIN .... Jack Starrett†
GRAVY TRAIN, THE (MS) .... David Tucker
GRAY LADY DOWN .... David Greene
GREASE .... Randal Kleiser
GREASE 2 .... Patricia Birch
GREASED LIGHTNING .... Michael Schultz
GREASER, THE .... Raoul Walsh†
GREASER'S GAUNTLET, THE .... D.W. Griffith†
GREASER'S PALACE .... Robert Downey
GREAT ACCIDENT, THE .... Harry Beaumont†
GREAT ADVENTURE, THE .... Alice Guy-Blache†
GREAT ADVENTURE, THE .... David MacDonald†
GREAT AIR RACE, THE (TF) .... Marcus Cole
GREAT AMERICAN BEAUTY CONTEST, THE (TF) .... Robert Day
GREAT AMERICAN BROADCAST, THE .... Archie Mayo†
GREAT AMERICAN BUGS BUNNY - ROAD RUNNER CHASE (AF) .... Charles M. (Chuck) Jones
GREAT AMERICAN COWBOY, THE (FD) .... Kieth Merrill
GREAT AMERICAN TRAFFIC JAM, THE (TF) .... James Frawley
GREAT AMERICAN TRAGEDY, THE .... Tibor Takacs
GREAT AMERICAN TRAGEDY, A (TF) .... J. Lee Thompson
GREAT BALLS OF FIRE .... Jim McBride
GREAT BANK HOAX, THE .... Joseph Jacoby
GREAT BANK ROBERRY, THE .... Hy Averback
GREAT BIG THING, A .... Eric Till
GREAT BOOKIE ROBBERY, THE (MS) .... Marcus Cole
GREAT BOOKIE ROBBERY, THE (MS) .... Mark Joffe
GREAT BRAIN, THE .... Sidney Levin
GREAT BUNCH OF GIRLS, A (FD) .... Mary Ann Braubach
GREAT BUNCH OF GIRLS, A (FD) .... Tracy Tynan
GREAT CARGOES (FD) .... Paul Rotha†
GREAT CARUSO, THE .... Richard Thorpe†
GREAT CASH GIVEAWAY GETAWAY, THE (TF) .... Michael O'Herlihy
GREAT CATHERINE .... Gordon Flemyng
GREAT CHESS MOVIE, THE (FD) .... Gilles Carle
GREAT CHICAGO CONSPIRACY CIRCUS, THE .... Kerry Feltham
GREAT CLOWN, THE .... Youssef Chahine
GREAT COMMANDMENT, THE .... Irving Pichel†
GREAT CONQUEROR'S CONCUBINE, THE .... Stephen Shin
GREAT CONSOLER, THE .... Lev Kuleshov†
GREAT COUPS OF HISTORY .... Jack Darcus
GREAT DAN PATCH, THE .... Joseph M. Newman
GREAT DAY .... Lance Comfort†
GREAT DAY FOR BONZO, A (TF) .... Michael Apted
GREAT DAY IN HARLEM, A (FD) .... Jean Bach
GREAT DAY IN THE MORNING .... Jacques Tourneur†
GREAT DAYS, SMALL STORIES, THE (FD) .... Dan Wolman
GREAT DIAMOND ROBBERY, THE .... Robert Z. Leonard†
GREAT DICTATOR, THE .... Charles (Charlie) Chaplin†
GREAT ELEPHANT ESCAPE (TF) .... George Trumbull Miller
GREAT ESCAPE, THE .... John Sturges†
GREAT ESCAPE II: THE UNTOLD STORY, THE (TF) .... Jud Taylor
GREAT ESCAPE II: THE UNTOLD STORY, THE (TF) .... Paul Wendkos
GREAT EXPECTATIONS .... ★ David Lean†
GREAT EXPECTATIONS .... Stuart Walker†
GREAT EXPECTATIONS (CTF) .... Kevin Connor
GREAT EXPECTATIONS (TF) .... Joseph Hardy
GREAT EXPECTATIONS - THE UNTOLD STORY .... Tim Burstall
GREAT FLAMARION, THE .... Anthony Mann†
GREAT GABBO, THE .... James Cruze†
GREAT GAMBINI, THE .... Charles Vidor†
GREAT GARRICK, THE .... James Whale†
GREAT GATSBY, THE .... Elliott Nugent†
GREAT GATSBY, THE .... Herbert Brenon†
GREAT GATSBY, THE .... Jack Clayton†
GREAT GILBERT AND SULLIVAN, THE .... Sidney Gilliat†
GREAT GILDERSLEEVE, THE .... Gordon Douglas†
GREAT GOD GOLD .... Arthur Lubin†
GREAT GOLD ROBBERY, THE .... Maurice Elvey†
GREAT GOLD SWINDLE, THE .... John Power
GREAT HOUDINIS, THE (TF) .... Melville Shavelson
GREAT ICE RIP-OFF, THE (TF) .... Dan Curtis
GREAT IMPERSONATION, THE .... Alan Crosland†
GREAT IMPERSONATION, THE .... John Rawlins
GREAT IMPOSTER, THE .... Robert Mulligan
GREAT JAPAN PICKPOCKET GROUP .... Jun Fukuda
GREAT JESSE JAMES RAID, THE .... Reginald Le Borg†
GREAT K & A TRAIN ROBBERY, THE .... Lewis Seiler†
GREAT LEAP, THE .... Christy Cabanne†
GREAT LIE, THE .... Edmund Goulding†
GREAT LONG FOR HUSBAND, THE .... Im Kwon-Taek
GREAT LOVE, THE .... D.W. Griffith†
GREAT LOVE, THE .... Marshall (Mickey) Neilan†
GREAT LOVER, THE .... Alexander Hall†
GREAT LOVER, THE .... Frank Lloyd†
GREAT LOVER, THE .... Harry Beaumont†
GREAT MAIL ROBBERY, THE .... George B. Seitz†
GREAT MAN VOTES, THE .... Garson Kanin
GREAT MAN'S LADY, THE .... William A. Wellman†

H

I
N
D
E
X

O
F

F
I
L
M

T
I
T
L
E
S

Ho-Ho

FILM
DIRECTORS
GUIDE

INDEX OF FILM TITLES

591

I

INDEX OF FILM TITLES

INDEX OF FILM TITLES

K

Ma-Ma

FILM
DIRECTORS
GUIDE

INDEX OF FILM TITLES

619

I N D E X   O F   F I L M   T I T L E S

Ma-Me

FILM
DIRECTORS
GUIDE

I N D E X

O F

F I L M

T I T L E S

Mu-My

FILM
DIRECTORS
GUIDE

INDEX OF FILM TITLES

629

N

P

I
N
D
E
X

O
F

F
I
L
M

T
I
T
L
E
S

R

Sh-Sh

FILM
DIRECTORS
GUIDE

I N D E X   O F   F I L M   T I T L E S

659

INDEX OF FILM TITLES

T

To-To

FILM
DIRECTORS
GUIDE

INDEX OF FILM TITLES

677

Un-Ve

FILM
DIRECTORS
GUIDE

I N D E X   O F   F I L M   T I T L E S

683

INDEX OF FILM TITLES

INDEX OF FILM TITLES

I N D E X   O F   F I L M   T I T L E S

X

Y

★ ★ ★

INDICES

INDEX OF FOREIGN-BASED DIRECTORS
by Director

A

Veikko Aaltonen .... Finland
Sene Absa .... Senegal
Jovan Acin .... Yugoslavia
Jon Acevski .... England
David Acomba .... Canada/U.S.
Percy Adlon .... Germany/U.S.
Phil Agland .... England
Chantal Akerman .... Belgium/France
Mike Alexander .... Scotland
Don Allan .... Canada
Rene Allio .... France
Nestor Almendros .... U.S./Spain/France
Pedro Almodovar .... Spain
Paul Almond .... Canada/U.S.
Denis Amar .... France
Suzana Amaral .... Brazil
Gianni Amelio .... Italy
Jon Amiel .... England/U.S.
Franco Amurri .... U.S./Italy
Torgny Anderberg .... Sweden
Michael Anderson .... England/Canada/U.S.
Paul Anderson .... England/U.S.
Sarah Pia Anderson .... England
Mario Andreacchio .... Australia
Yves Angelo .... France
Theo Angelopoulos .... Greece
Ken Annakin .... England/U.S.
Jean-Jacques Annaud .... France/U.S.
Michelangelo Antonioni .... Italy
Michael Apted .... U.S./England
Vicente Aranda .... Spain
Alfonso Arau .... Mexico/U.S.
Denys Arcand .... Canada
Alexandre Arcady .... France
Francesca Archibugi .... Italy
Dario Argento .... Italy
Adolfo Aristarain .... Argentina
Gillian Armstrong .... Australia/U.S.
Michael Armstrong .... U.S./England
Moira Armstrong .... England
Vic Armstrong .... England
Frank Arnold .... Australia
Isaac Artenstein .... U.S./Mexico
Olivier Assayas .... France
Dimitri Astrakhan .... Russia
Francisco Athle .... Mexico
Richard Attenborough .... England/U.S.
David Attwood .... England
Bille August .... Denmark/Sweden
Michael Austin .... England
Claude Autant-Lara .... France
Igor Auzins .... Australia
Pupi Avati .... Italy
Gabriel Axel .... Denmark/France
Iradj Azimi .... France
Mario Azzopardi .... Canada

B

Bassek Ba Kobhio .... Cameroon
Hector Babenco .... Brazil/U.S.
Norma Bailey .... Canada
Robert S. Baker .... England
Roy Ward Baker .... England
Ferdinando Baldi .... Italy
Murray Ball .... New Zealand
John Banas .... Australia
Tamasaburo Bando .... Japan
Uri Barbash .... Israel
Eric Barbier .... France
Barry Barclay .... New Zealand
Georges Bardawil .... France
Juan Antonio Bardem .... Spain
Clive Barker .... England/U.S.
Bruno Barreto .... Brazil/U.S.
Lezli-An Barrett .... England
Steve Barron .... U.S./England
Zelda Barron .... U.S./England
Ian Barry .... Australia
Sean Barry .... England
Jahnu Barua .... India
Paolo Barzman .... France
Giulio Base .... Italy
Michal Bat-Adam .... Israel
Roy Battersby .... England
Giacomo Battiato .... Italy
Lamberto Bava .... Italy
Stephen Bayly .... England/Wales
Michael Beckham .... England
Terry Bedford .... England/U.S.
Ridha Behi .... Tunisia/France
Jean-Jacques Beineix .... France
Jean-Pierre Bekolo .... Cameroon
Mikhail Belikov .... Russia
Marco Bellocchio .... Italy
Vera Belmont .... France
Remy Belvaux .... Belgium
Maria Luisa Bemberg .... Argentina
Shyam Benegal .... India
Roberto Benigni .... Italy
Bill Bennett .... Australia/U.S.
Rodney Bennett .... England
Jacques W. Benoit .... Canada
Alain Berberian .... France
Bruce Beresford .... Australia/U.S.
Daniel Bergman .... Sweden
Ingmar Bergman .... Sweden
Steven Berkoff .... England
Chris Bernard .... England
Claude Berri .... France
John Berry .... France/U.S.
Tom Berry .... Canada
Attila Bertalan .... Canada
Bernardo Bertolucci .... Italy
Giuseppe Bertolucci .... Italy
Jean-Louis Bertucelli .... France
Luc Besson .... France/U.S.
Robert Bierman .... England/U.S.
Jean-Claude Biette .... France
Kevin Billington .... England
Antonia Bird .... England/U.S.
Andrew Birkin .... England
Alan Birkinshaw .... England

Jon Blair .... England
Les Blair .... England
Lorne Blair .... England/Indonesia
Michael Blakemore .... Australia/England/U.S.
Michel Blanc .... France
Bertrand Blier .... France
George Bloomfield .... Canada
Rex Bloomstein .... England
David Blyth .... New Zealand
Sergei Bodrov .... Russia
Yves Boisset .... France
Jerome Boivin .... France
Mauro Bolognini .... Italy
Ben Bolt .... England/U.S.
Robert Bolt .... England
Timothy Bond .... Canada
Rene Bonniere .... Canada
John Boorman .... England/U.S.
José Luis Borau .... U.S./Spain
Walerian Borowczyk .... France
Clay Borris .... U.S./Canada
Dave Borthwick .... England
Rachid Bouchareb .... Algeria/France
Patrick Bouchitey .... France
Roy Boulting .... England
Serge Bourguignon .... France
Anthony J. Bowman .... Australia
Muriel Box .... England
Don Boyd .... England
Danny Boyle .... England/Scotland
John Bradshaw .... Canada
Randy Bradshaw .... Canada
Kenneth Branagh .... England/U.S.
Klaus Maria Brandauer .... Germany/Austria
Charlotte Brandstrom .... France/U.S.
Patrick Braoude .... France
Tinto Brass .... Italy
Michel Brault .... Canada
Anja Breien .... Norway
Catherine Breillat .... France
Mario Brenta .... Italy
Robert Bresson .... France
Alan Bridges .... England
Hugh Brody .... England
Rex Bromfield .... Canada
Peter Brook .... France/England
Bob Brooks .... England
Nicholas (Nick) Broomfield .... England
Philip Brophy .... Australia
Kevin Brownlow .... England
Bill Bryden .... England
Colin Bucksey .... England/U.S.
Jan Bucquoy .... Belgium
Colin Budd .... Australia
Robin Budd .... Australia
Richard Bugajski .... Canada/Poland
Penelope Buitenhuis .... Canada
Alan Bunce .... Canada
Juan Buñuel .... France
Alexander Buravsky .... Russia
Derek Burbidge .... England
Stuart Burge .... England
Martyn Burke .... Canada
Geoff Burrowes .... Australia/U.S.
Tim Burstall .... Australia
Geoff Burton .... Australia

C

Sergio Cabrera .... Colombia
Michael Cacoyannis .... Greece
Simon Callow .... England
Ken Cameron .... Australia
Donald Cammell .... England/France
Graeme Campbell .... Canada
Martin Campbell .... England/U.S./Australia
Nicholas Campbell .... Canada
Norman Campbell .... Canada
Anna Campion .... New Zealand/Australia
Jane Campion .... New Zealand/Australia
Mario Camus .... Spain
Danny Cannon .... England/U.S.
Bernt Capra .... Switzerland
Leos Carax .... France
Jack Cardiff .... England
Gilles Carle .... Canada
Carlo Carlei .... Italy/U.S.
Henning Carlsen .... Denmark/U.S.
Marcel Carne .... France
Marc Caro .... France
Fabio Carpi .... Italy
Michael Carreras .... England
Michael Caton-Jones .... England/U.S.
Alain Cavalier .... France
Liliana Cavani .... Italy
Felipe Cazals .... Mexico
James Cellan-Jones .... England
Claude Chabrol .... France
Gurinder Chadha .... England
Youssef Chahine .... Egypt
Georges Chamchoum .... U.S./Lebanon
Jackie Chan .... Hong Kong
Pauline Chan .... Australia
Bae Chang-Ho .... South Korea
Mehdi Charef .... France
Etienne Chatiliez .... France
Peter Chelsom .... England
Pierre Chenal .... France
Patrice Chereau .... France
Jacob C.L. Cheung .... Hong Kong
Colin Chilvers .... Canada/U.S./U.S.
Mel Chionglo .... Philippines
Park Choi-Su .... South Korea
Mohamed Chouikh .... Algeria
Elie Chouraqui .... France
Roger Christian .... England
Grigori Chukhrai .... Russia
Ji-Young Chung .... South Korea
Vera Chytilova .... Czech Republic
Gerard Ciccoritti .... Canada
Souleymane Cissé .... Mali
Richard Ciupka .... Canada
Lawrence Gordon Clark .... England
Frank Clarke .... England
James Kenelm Clarke .... England/U.S.
Malcolm Clarke .... England
Jack Clayton .... England/U.S.
Tom Clegg .... England
Dick Clement .... England/U.S.
René Clément .... France
Graeme Clifford .... U.S./Australia
Peter Clifton .... England
Martin Clunes .... England
Lewis Coates .... Italy
Annette Cohen .... Canada
David Cohen .... England
Eli Cohen .... Israel/U.S./England
Harvey Cokliss .... U.S./England
Henry Cole .... England
Marcus Cole .... Australia/U.S.
Luigi Comencini .... Italy
Joe Comerford .... Ireland
Kevin Connor .... England/U.S.
Gerard Corbiau .... Belgium

Rafael Corkidi .... Mexico
Alain Corneau .... France
John Cornell .... Australia
Ian Corson .... Canada
Vittorio Cottafavi .... Italy
Jacques-Yves Cousteau .... France
Raoul Coutard .... France
Alex Cox .... U.S./England
Paul Cox .... Australia
Peter Crane .... U.S./England
Lol Creme .... England
Charles Crichton .... England
Donald Crombie .... Australia
David Cronenberg .... Canada
Harvey Crossland .... Canada
Alfonso Cuaron .... Mexico/U.S.

D

Renee Daalder .... U.S./Netherlands
Cetin (Sezerel) Daglar .... Turkey
Heinrich Dahms .... South Africa
Alessandro D'Alatri .... Italy
Zale Dalen .... Canada
Damiano Damiani .... Italy
Lawrence Dane .... Canada
Claude D'Anna .... France
Jack Darcus .... Canada
Jules Dassin .... U.S./Greece
Boaz Davidson .... U.S./Israel
Howard Davies .... England
John Davies .... England
John T. Davies .... England
Ray Davies .... England
Terence Davies .... England
Desmond Davis .... England
Anthony M. Dawson .... Italy
Ernest Day .... England
John Day .... New Zealand
Josee Dayan .... France
Nissim Dayan .... Israel
James Dearden .... England/U.S.
Frank Deasy .... Ireland
Gianfranco de Bosio .... Italy
Philippe de Broca .... France
Christian De Chalonge .... France
Dimitri De Clercq .... France
Rolf De Heer .... Australia
Jamil Dehlavi .... England/Pakistan
Ate De Jong .... Netherlands/U.S.
Alex De La Iglesia .... Spain
Jean Delannoy .... France
Mike de Leon .... Philippines
Peter Del Monte .... Italy
Nathalie Delon .... France
Guillermo Del Toro .... Mexico
Richard Dembo .... Switzerland
Claire Denis .... France
Jean-Pierre Denis .... France
Ruggero Deodato .... Italy
Manoel De Oliveira .... Portugal
Jacques Deray .... France
Dominique Deruddere .... Belgium/U.S.
Giuseppe De Santis .... Italy
Ross Devenish .... England/South Africa
Michel Deville .... France
Barry Devlin .... England
Patrick Dewolf .... France
Carlos Diegues .... Brazil
Helmut Dietl .... Germany
John Dingwall .... Australia
Eros Djarot .... Indonesia
Slamet Rahardjo Djarot .... Indonesia
Kevin James Dobson .... Australia/U.S.
Jacques Doillon .... France
Jerzy Domaradzki .... Poland

Roger Donaldson .... U.S./New Zealand
Clive Donner .... England/U.S.
Jörn Donner .... Finland/Sweden
Paul Donovan .... Canada
Lee Doo-Yong .... South Korea
Robert Dornhelm .... U.S./Austria
Doris Dorrie .... Germany/U.S.
Nelson Pereira Dos Santos .... Brazil
Alan Dossor .... England
Shimon Dotan .... Israel/U.S.
Kevin Dowling .... Australia
Di Drew .... Australia
Sara Driver .... U.S./Germany
David Drury .... England
Daniele Dubroux .... France
Remy Duchemin .... France
Peter John Duffell .... England
Christian Duguay .... Canada
John Duigan .... Australia
Daryl Duke .... Canada/U.S.
Francois Dupeyron .... France
Marguerite Duras .... France

E

Allan Eastman .... Canada
Andrew Eaton .... England
Desire Ecare .... Ivory Coast
Nicolas Echevarria .... Mexico
Uli Edel .... Germany/U.S.
Peter Edwards .... South Africa
Christine Edzard .... England
Atom Egoyan .... Canada
Stephan Elliott .... Australia
Arthur Ellis .... England
Bob Ellis .... Australia
Peter Ellis .... England
Ian Emes .... England
Roland Emmerich .... U.S./Germany
Robert Enders .... England
Andi Engel .... England
Robert Enrico .... France
Ildiko Enyedi .... Hungary
Victor Erice .... Spain
Nuria Espert .... England
Luis Estrada .... Mexico
Marc Evans .... England
Marianne Eyde .... Peru
Richard Eyre .... England
Mark Ezra .... England

F

Ottavio Fabbri .... Italy
Roberto Faenza .... Italy
Peter Faiman .... Australia/U.S.
Ferdinand Fairfax .... England
Jacques Fansten .... France
Claude Faraldo .... France
Andre Farwagi .... Canada
Neill Fearnley .... Canada
Christian Fechner .... France
Michael Ferguson .... England
Marcela Fernandez Violante .... Mexico
Giorgio Ferrara .... Italy
Giuseppe Ferrara .... Italy
Marco Ferreri .... Italy
Mike Figgis .... England/U.S.
Charles Finch .... England/U.S.
Albert Finney .... England
Sam Firstenberg .... U.S./Israel
Michael Firth .... New Zealand
Max Fischer .... Canada
Bernd Fischerauer .... Germany

Peter Fleischmann	Germany
Gordon Flemyng	England
Mandie Fletcher	England
Clive Fleury	England
Kim Flitcroft	England
Allen Fong	Hong Kong
Kathleen Fonmarty	France
Bryan Forbes	England
Timothy Forder	England
Milos Forman	U.S./Czech Repblic
Bill Forsyth	Scotland/U.S.
Giles Foster	England
Freddie Francis	England
Karl Francis	Wales/England
Robert Frank	Switzerland/U.S.
Cyril Frankel	England
Richard Franklin	U.S./Australia
Stephen Frears	U.S./England
Riccardo Freda	Italy
Fridrik Thor Fridriksson	Iceland
Martyn Friend	England
William Fruet	Canada
Benjamin Fry	England
Robert Fuest	England
Athol Fugard	South Africa/England
Kinji Fukasaku	Japan
Jun Fukuda	Japan
Lucio Fulci	Italy
Sidney J. Furie	U.S./Canada
Tim Fywell	England

G

Claude Gagnon	Canada
Rene Gainville	France/U.S.
Christophe Gans	Canada
Gianna Maria Garbelli	Italy
Jose Luis Garci	Spain
Carlos Garcia Agraz	Mexico
Jose Luis Garcia Agraz	Mexico
Luis Garcia Berlanga	Spain
Patrick Garland	England
Tony Garnett	England
Tony Gatlif	France
Nils Gaup	Norway
Victor Manuel Gaviria	Colombia
Costa-Gavras	France/U.S.
Gyula Gazdag	U.S./Hungary
Jozsef Gemes	Hungary
Nicolas Gessner	Switzerland/France/U.S.
Tulshi Ghimiray	Nepal
Constantine Giannaris	England
Rodney Gibbons	Canada
Brian Gibson	England/U.S.
Mel Gibson	U.S./Australia
Maria Giese	England
Brian Gilbert	England/U.S.
Lewis Gilbert	England
Stuart Gillard	Canada/U.S.
Terry Gilliam	England/U.S.
Francois Girard	Canada
Francis Girod	France
Amos Gitai	Israel
David Gladwell	England
John Glen	England
John Glenister	England
Pierre William Glenn	France
Peter Glenville	England
Kurt Gloor	Switzerland
Vadim Glowna	Germany
Jean-Luc Godard	France/Switzerland
Jim Goddard	England
Menahem Golan	U.S./Israel
Jack Gold	England
Paul Golding	England/U.S.
John Goldschmidt	England

Allan Goldstein	Canada/U.S.
Jacob Goldwasser	Israel
Servando Gonzalez	Mexico
Claude Goretta	Switzerland
Jean-Pierre Gorin	France
Charles Gormley	England
Peter Gothar	Hungary
Steven Gough	England
Brian Grant	U.S./England
Michael Grant	Canada/U.S.
Kjell Grede	Sweden
David Green	England/U.S.
Guy Green	England/U.S.
Terry Green	England
Peter Greenaway	England
David Greene	U.S./England
Paul Greengrass	England
Colin Gregg	England
Ezio Greggio	Italy
John Greyson	Canada
Andrew Grieve	England
Aurelio Grimaldi	Italy
Alan Grint	England
Yoram Gross	Australia
Ruy Guerra	Brazil
Val Guest	England
John Guillerman	U.S./England
Paul Gunczler	Germany
Sturla Gunnarsson	Canada
Hrafn Gunnlaugsson	Iceland
Erik Gustavson	Norway
Tomás Gutierrez Alea	Cuba
Manuel Gutierrez Aragon	Spain
Nathaniel Gutman	Germany/U.S.

H

Herve Hachuel	Spain
Russell Hagg	Australia
Piers Haggard	England/U.S.
Zafar Hai	India/England
Peter Hall	England
Gudny Halldorsdottir	Iceland
Lasse Hallstrom	Sweden/U.S.
David Hamilton	England/France
Guy Hamilton	England
John Hamilton	Canada
Peter Hammond	England
Christopher Hampton	England
Susumu Hani	Japan
Brian Hannant	Australia
Marion Hansel	Belgium
Kazuo Hara	Japan
Masato Harada	Japan
Justin Hardy	England
Robin Hardy	England
Rod Hardy	U.S./Australia
David Hare	England
Tsui Hark	Hong Kong
Paul Harmon	Australia
Damian Harris	U.S./England
Richard Harris	England
John Kent Harrison	Canada
Derek Hart	England
Anthony Harvey	England/U.S.
Gail Harvey	Canada
Masami Hata	Japan
Masanori Hata	Japan
Kayo Hatta	U.S./Japan
Maurice Hatton	England
Kaizo Hayashi	Japan
Sidney Hayers	England/U.S.
David Hayman	England
Jack Hazan	England
Simon Heath	Australia
Lynn Hegarty	Australia

Sarah Hellings	England
Gunnar Hellstrom	Sweden/U.S.
Henri Helman	France
David Hemmings	England/U.S.
John Henderson	England
Perry Henzell	Jamaica
Mark Herman	England
Jaime Humberto Hermosillo	Mexico
Denis Heroux	Canada
Gerardo Herrero	Spain/Puerto Rico
Werner Herzog	Germany
Gordon Hessler	U.S./England
Jochen Hick	Germany
Yim Ho	Hong Kong
Lyndall Hobbs	U.S./Australia
Mike Hodges	England/U.S.
Michael Hoffman	U.S./England
Gray Hofmeyr	South Africa
P.J. Hogan	Australia
Graham Holloway	Scotland
Harry Hook	England/U.S.
Anthony Hopkins	England/Wales/U.S.
Bob Hoskins	England
Robert Hossein	France
John Hough	England
Karin Howard	U.S./Germany
Frank Howson	Australia
Hou Hsiao-Hsien	Taiwan
King Hu	Hong Kong/Taiwan/U.S.
Jean-Loup Hubert	France
Hugh Hudson	England/U.S.
Kenneth (Ken) Hughes	England/U.S.
Ann Hui	Hong Kong
Michael Hui	Hong Kong
Daniele Huillet	France
Ron Hulme	Canada
Samo Hung	Hong Kong
Tran Anh Hung	France/Vietnam
Peter Hunt	England/U.S.
Caroline Huppert	France
Waris Hussein	U.S./England
Nicholas Hytner	England/U.S.

I

Kon Ichikawa	Japan
Eric Idle	England
Yuri Illienko	Ukraine
Shohei Imamura	Japan
Samuel (Shmuel) Imberman	Israel
Markus Imhoof	Switzerland
Otar Ioselliani	France/Georgia
John Irvin	England/U.S.
Alberto Isaac	Mexico
Eva Isaksen	Norway
Rob Iscove	U.S./Canada
Sogo Ishii	Japan
Juzo Itami	Japan/U.S.
James Ivory	U.S./England
Kenchi Iwamoto	Japan

J

Douglas Jackson	Canada
Peter Jackson	New Zealand
Philip Jackson	Canada
Simcha Jacobovici	Canada
Gualtiero Jacopetti	Italy
Just Jaeckin	France
Ray Jafelice	Canada
Patrick Jamain	France
Pedr James	England
Miklos Jancso	Hungary
Lee Jang-Ho	South Korea

Annabel Jankel	England/U.S.
Frederic Jardin	France
Charles Jarrott	U.S./England
Vadim Jean	England
Lionel Jeffries	England
Michael Jenkins	Australia
Alain Jessua	France
Jean-Pierre Jeunet	France
Norman Jewison	U.S./Canada
He Jianjun	China
Huang Jianxin	China
Xie Jin	China
Jaromil Jires	Czech Republic
Steve Jodrell	Australia
Arthur Joffe	France
Mark Joffe	Australia
Roland Joffé	U.S./England
Kristin Johannesdottir	Iceland
Sandy Johnson	England
Aaron Kim Johnston	Canada
Oskar Jonasson	Iceland
David Jones	U.S./England
Terry Jones	England
Neil Jordan	U.S./Ireland/England
Paul Joyce	England
Gerard Jugnot	France
Isaac Julien	England
Jan Jung	Denmark

K

Gaston Kabore	Burkina Faso
Karel Kachyna	Czech Republic
George Kaczender	U.S./Canada
Haruki Kadokawa	Japan/U.S.
Chen Kaige	China
Shusuke Kaneko	Japan
Vitali Kanevski	Russia
Woo-Suk Kang	South Korea
Marek Kanievska	England/U.S.
Betty Kaplan	Venezuela
Nelly Kaplan	France
Shekhar Kapur	India
Wong Kar-Wai	Hong Kong
Mathieu Kassovitz	France
Elliott Kastner	U.S./England
Jim Kaufman	Canada
Mani Kaul	India
Aki Kaurismäki	Finland
Mika Kaurismäki	Finland
Anwar Kawadri	England
Jerzy Kawalerowicz	Poland
Gilbert Lee Kay	U.S./Spain
Jonathon Kay	Canada
Patrick Keiller	England
Jude Kelly	England
Nicholas Kendall	Canada
Chris Kennedy	Australia
Michael Kennedy	Canada
Donald Kent	Canada
Larry Kent	Canada
Irvin Kershner	U.S./England
Michael Keusch	U.S./Canada
Michel Khleifi	Belgium
Abbas Kiarostami	Iran
Beeban Kidron	England/U.S.
Krzysztof Kieslowski	Poland/France
Gerard Kikoine	England
Allan King	Canada
Christopher Lloyd King	England
Margy Kinmouth	England
Keisuke Kinoshita	Japan
Ephraim Kishon	Israel
Takeshi Kitano	Japan
William Klein	France/U.S.
Elem Klimov	Russia
Herbert Kline	U.S./England
Alexander Kluge	Germany
Robert Knights	England
Masaki Kobayashi	Japan
Hannah Kodicek	Czech Republic
Amos Kollek	Israel/U.S.
Xavier Koller	Switzerland/U.S.
Andrei Konchalovsky	U.S./Russia
Peter Kosminsky	England
Ted Kotcheff	Canada/U.S.
Vichit Kounavudhi	Thailand
Soren Kragh-Jacobsen	Denmark
Robert Kramer	France/U.S.
Gerard Krawczyk	France
John Krish	England
Pradip Krishen	England/India
Srinivas Krishna	Canada
Suri Krishnamma	England
Viacheslav Krishtofovich	Russia
Allen Kroeker	Canada
Stanley Kubrick	England/U.S.
Kei Kumai	Japan
Harry Kumel	Belgium
Koreyoshi Kurahara	Japan
Hanif Kureishi	England
Akira Kurosawa	Japan
Diane Kurys	France
Emir Kusturica	Yugoslavia/U.S.
Fran Rubel Kuzui	U.S./Japan
Stanley Kwan	Hong Kong
Im Kwon-Taek	South Korea

L

John Laing	New Zealand
Krzysztof Lang	Poland/England
Simon Langton	England
Claude Lanzmann	France
Sheldon Larry	Canada/U.S.
Alberto Lattuada	Italy
Patrick Lau	Scotland
Michael Laughlin	New Zealand
Frank Launder	England
Georges Lautner	France
Gerard Lauzier	France
Jean-Claude Lauzon	Canada
Martin Lavut	Canada
Clara Law	Hong Kong
Ray Lawrence	Australia
Ashley Lazarus	England
Patrice Leconte	France
Jacques Leduc	Canada
Paul Leduc	Mexico
Ang Lee	Taiwan/U.S.
Jack Lee	England
Joe Lee	Ireland
Michel Legrand	France
Mike Leigh	England
David Leland	England
Claude Lelouch	France
Sergio Leone	Italy
Po-Chih Leong	Hong Kong
Serge LePeron	France
Richard Lester	England/U.S.
Ben Lewin	Australia
Richard J. Lewis	Canada
Yin Li	China
Peter Lilienthal	Germany
Michael Lindsay-Hogg	England/U.S.
David Lister	South Africa
Peter Mackenzie Litten	England
Miguel Littin	Mexico/Cuba/Chile
Steven C.C. Liu	Taiwan
Carlo Lizzani	Italy
Luis "Lucho" Llosa	U.S./Peru
Kenneth Loach	England
Ulli Lommel	U.S./Germany
Richard Loncraine	England
Jean-Claude Lord	Canada
Emil Loteanu	Russia
Pavel Lounguine	Russia
Richard Lowenstein	Australia
Declan Lowney	England
Nanni Loy	Italy
Francesco Lucente	Canada
Daniele Luchetti	Italy
Baz Luhrmann	Australia
Bigas Luna	Spain
Paul Lynch	Canada/U.S.
Adrian Lyne	U.S./England
Jonathan Lynn	U.S./England

M

Dick Maas	Netherlands
Sydney (Syd) Macartney	England/U.S.
Peter Macdonald	England/U.S.
John Mackenzie	U.S./England
Gillies Mackinnon	England
Alison Maclean	New Zealand
Stephen Maclean	Australia
John Madden	England/U.S.
Guy Maddin	Canada
Kenneth Madsen	Denmark
Bob Mahoney	England
Stewart Main	New Zealand
Johnny Mak	Hong Kong
Michael Mak	Hong Kong
Dusan Makavejev	Yugoslavia
Aleksi Makela	Finland
Karoly Makk	Hungary
Louis Malle	France/U.S
Djibril Diop Mambety	Senegal
Yuri Mamin	Russia
Milcho Manchevski	England/Macedonia
Luis Mandoki	U.S./Mexico
Ron Mann	Canada
Lesley Manning	England
Rene Manzor	France/U.S./Canada
Terry Marcel	England
Chris Marker	France
Christian Marquand	France
Leon Marr	Canada
Richard Martin	Canada
Mario Martone	Italy
Claude Massot	France
Quentin Masters	Australia
Nico Mastorakis	U.S./Greece
Toshio Masuda	Japan
Charles Matton	France
Godwin Mawuru	Zimbabwe
Paul Mayersberg	England/U.S.
Tony Maylam	England
Rentaro Mayuzumi	Japan
Michael Mazo	Canada
Carlo Mazzacurati	Italy
Massimo Mazzucco	Italy
Roger Gnoan M'Bala	Ivory Coast
Don McBrearty	Canada
George McCowan	Canada/U.S.
Bruce McDonald	Canada
Joseph McGrath	England
Mary McGuckian	Ireland
George McIndoe	U.S./England
Laurie McInnes	Australia
Don McLennan	Australia
Ken McMullen	England
Mary McMurray	England
Nancy Meckler	England
Peter Medak	U.S./England
Leslie Megahey	England
Francis Megahy	England/U.S.

N

P

O

R

Denis Rabaglia	France
Fons Rademakers	Netherlands
Michael Radford	England
Michael Raeburn	England/Africa
Alvin Rakoff	Canada/England
Alexander Ramati	Poland/Israel/Italy
Mort Ransen	Canada
Frederic Raphael	England
Jean-Paul Rappaneau	France
Harry Rasky	Canada
Ousama Rawi	Canada
Christopher Rawlence	England
Sandip Ray	India
Clive Rees	England
Geoffrey Reeve	England
Alastair Reid	England
John Reid	New Zealand
Karel Reisz	U.S./England
Edgar Reitz	Germany
Barbara Rennie	England
Alain Resnais	France
Gabriel Retes	Mexico
John Riber	Zimbabwe
Peter Richardson	England
Anthony Richmond	England/U.S.
Philip Ridley	England
Leni Riefenstahl	Germany
Eran Riklis	Israel
Wolf Rilla	England/France
Arturo Ripstein	Mexico
Leidulv Risan	Norway
Dino Risi	Italy
Marco Risi	Italy
Jacques Rivette	France
Alain Robbe-Grillet	France
Yves Robert	France
John Roberts	England
Michael Robertson	Australia
Bruce Robinson	England/U.S.
Eric Rochant	France
Franc Roddam	England/U.S.
Nicolas Roeg	England/U.S.
Eric Rohmer	France
Eddie Romero	Philippines
Mikhail Romm	Russia
Darrell James Roodt	South Africa/U.S.
Mark Roper	South Africa
Bernard Rose	England
Les Rose	Canada
Martin Rosen	U.S./England
Francesco Rosi	Italy
Benjamin Ross	England
Kaspar Rostrup	Denmark
Dana Rotberg	Mexico
Brigitte Rouan	France
George Rowe	U.S./Hong Kong/Japan
Peter Rowe	Canada
Patricia Rozema	Canada
John Ruane	Australia
Michael Rubbo	Canada
Percival Rubens	South Africa
Sergio Rubini	Italy
Raul Ruíz	France/Chile/Portugal/U.S.
Ken Russell	England/U.S.
Eldar Ryazanov	Russia
Renny Rye	England
Nick Ryle	England

S

Randa Chahal Sabbag	France
Henri Safran	Australia
Yoichi Sai	Japan
Junji Sakamoto	Japan
Walter Salles, Jr.	Brazil
Paul Saltzman	Canada/U.S.
Gabriele Salvatores	Italy
Glen Salzman	Canada
Ake Sandgren	Sweden
Jimmy Sangster	England
Jorge Sanjines	Bolivia
Cirio H. Santiago	Philippines
Vic Sarin	Canada
Valeria Sarmiento	Spain/Chile
Michael Sarne	England
Peter Sasdy	England
Junya Sato	Japan
Shimako Sato	Japan
Carlos Saura	Spain
Claude Sautet	France
Philip Saville	England/U.S.
Geoffrey Sax	England
Daoud Abdel Sayed	Egypt
Joseph L. Scanlan	U.S./Canada
Hans Scheepmaker	Netherlands
Maximilian Schell	Austria/Germany/U.S.
Carl Schenkel	U.S./Germany/Switzerland
Fred Schepisi	U.S./Australia
Paul Schibli	Canada
Suzanne Schiffman	France
John Schlesinger	England/U.S.
Volker Schlondorff	Germany/U.S.
Oliver Schmitz	South Africa
Pierre Schoendorffer	France
Renen Schorr	Israel
Dale Schott	Canada
Barbet Schroeder	France/U.S.
Werner Schroeter	Germany
Carl Schultz	Australia/U.S.
Stefan Schwartz	England
Ettore Scola	Italy
Cynthia Scott	Canada
James Scott	England
Michael Scott	Canada
Ridley Scott	England/U.S.
Tony Scott	England/U.S.
John Seale	Australia
Jakov Sedlar	Croatia
Paul Seed	England
Arnaud Selignac	France
Ian Sellar	England
Arna Selznick	Canada
Ousmane Sembene	Senegal
Dean Semler	Australia
Mrinal Sen	India
Michael Seresin	England/U.S.
Yahoo Serious	Australia
Coline Serreau	France/U.S.
Alex Sessa	Argentina
Philip Setbon	France
Vernon Sewell	England
John Sexton	Australia
Michael Shackleton	England
Krishna Shah	U.S./India
Paul Shapiro	Canada
Jim Sharman	Australia/England
Don Sharp	England
Ian Sharp	England
Peter Shatalow	Canada
Bashar Shbib	Canada
Donald Shebib	Canada
Riki Shelach	Israel
John Sheppard	Canada/U.S.
Adrian Shergold	England
Jim Sheridan	Ireland

Peter Shillingford	England/U.S.
Stephen Shin	Hong Kong
Kaneto Shindo	Japan
Masahiro Shinoda	Japan
Mina Shum	Canada
Slobodan Sijan	Serbia
Joel Silberg	Israel/U.S.
Anthony Simmons	England
Yves Simoneau	Canada/U.S.
Andrew Sinclair	England
Gail Singer	Canada
Bernard Sinkel	Germany
Gary Sinyor	England
Vilgot Sjoman	Sweden
Jerzy Skolimowski	U.S./Poland/England
John Smallcombe	England
Clive A. Smith	Canada
John N. Smith	Canada/U.S.
Mel Smith	England
Noella Smith	England
Peter Smith	Australia
Tony Smith	England
Roberto Sneider	Mexico
Michele Soavi	Italy
Rainer Soehnlein	Germany
Iaian Softley	England
Fernando E. Solanas	Argentina
Silvio Soldini	Italy
Ola Solum	Norway
Cherd Songsri	Thailand
Alberto Sordi	Italy
Carlos Sorin	Argentina
Thierno Faty Sow	Senegal
Richard Spence	England
Alan Spencer	England/U.S.
Brenton Spencer	Canada
Tim Spring	South Africa/U.S.
Robin Spry	Canada
Terence Stamp	U.S./England
Richard Stanley	England/South Africa
Ringo Starr	England
David Steinberg	Canada/U.S.
Martin Stellman	England
Sandor Stern	U.S./Canada
Steven Hilliard Stern	U.S./Canada
Jean-François Stevenin	France
David Stevens	Australia/U.S.
Norman Stone	England
Tom Stoppard	England
Esben Storm	Australia
Jean-Marie Straub	France/Germany
Charles Sturridge	England
Eliseo Subiela	Argentina
Daniele J. Suissa	Canada
Kevin Sullivan	Canada
Jeremy Summers	England
Shirley Sun	U.S./China
Cedric Sundstrom	England/U.S.
Seijun Suzuki	Japan
Jan Svankmajer	Czech Republic
Peter Svatek	Canada
Jan Sverak	Czech Republic
Bob Swaim	U.S./France
Hans-Jurgen Syberberg	Germany
Peter Sykes	England
Istvan Szabo	Hungary
Jeannot Szwarc	U.S./France

T

Juan Carlos Tabio	Cuba
Jean-Charles Tacchella	France
Tibor Takacs	Canada/U.S.
Isao Takahata	Japan
Yojiro Takita	Japan
Len Talan	Israel
Lee Tamahori	New Zealand

Augusto Tamayo .... Peru
Alain Tanner .... Switzerland
Nadia Tass .... Australia
John Tatoulis .... Australia
Bertrand Tavernier .... France
Paolo Taviani .... Italy
Vittorio Taviani .... Italy
Baz Taylor .... England
Andre Techine .... France
Julien Temple .... England/U.S.
Conny Templeman .... England
Rinken Teruya .... Okinawan
Hiroshi Teshigahara .... Japan
Tiana Thi Thanh Nga .... U.S./Vietnam
Antony Thomas .... England
Dave Thomas .... Canada/U.S.
Pascal Thomas .... France
Ralph Thomas .... England
Ralph L. Thomas .... Canada
Barnaby Thompson .... England/U.S.
J. Lee Thompson .... U.S./England
Chris Thomson .... Australia/U.S.
Wu Tianming .... China
Eric Till .... Canada
Moufida Tlatli .... Tunisia
Valeri Todorovski .... Russia
Ricky Tognazzi .... Italy
Sergio Toledo .... Brazil
Ro Tomono .... Japan
Stanley Tong .... Hong Kong
Giuseppe Tornatore .... Italy
Cinzia TH Torrini .... Italy
Serge Toubiana .... France
Moussa Toure .... Senegal
Ian Toynton .... England
Jean-Claude Tramont .... France/U.S.
Brian Trenchard -Smith .... Australia
Nadine Trintignant .... France
Jan Troell .... Sweden
Massimo Troisi .... Italy
Fernando Trueba .... Spain
Anand Tucker .... England
Michael Tuchner .... U.S./England
David Tucker .... England
Montgomery Tully .... England
Sophia Turkiewicz .... Australia
Ann Turner .... Australia
Clive Turner .... England
Paul Turner .... Wales
Rob Turner .... Canada

U

Liv Ullmann .... Norway/U.S./Sweden/Denmark
Stuart Urban .... England
Peter Ustinov .... England/U.S.
Jamie Uys .... South Africa

V

Roger Vadim .... U.S./France
Jaco Van Dormael .... Belgium
Kees Van Oostrum .... U.S./Netherlands
Carlo Vanzina .... Italy
Agnes Varda .... France
Francis Veber .... France/U.S.
Isela Vega .... Mexico
Geraldo Vera .... Spain
Ben Verbong .... Netherlands
Carlo Verdone .... Italy
Michael Verhoeven .... Germany
Paul Verhoeven .... U.S./Netherlands
Henri Verneuil .... France
Daniel Vigne .... France/U.S.

Teresa Villaverde .... Portugal
Joseph Vilsmaier .... Germany
Christian Vincent .... France
Katja Von Garnier .... Germany
Rosa Von Praunheim .... Germany
Max Von Sydow .... Sweden
Lars von Trier .... Denmark
Margarethe von Trotta .... Germany

W

Daniel Wachsmann .... Israel
Andrzej Wajda .... Poland
Giles Walker .... Canada
Peter Walker .... England
Robert Walker .... England
Stephen Wallace .... Australia
Anthony Waller .... England
Aisling Walsh .... Scotland
Peter Wang .... U.S./China/Taiwan
Wayne Wang .... U.S./Hong Kong
Nick Ward .... England
Vincent Ward .... New Zealand/Australia
Regis Wargnier .... France
Peter Watkins .... England/Sweden
Paul Watson .... England
Al Waxman .... Canada/U.S.
Peter Webb .... England
Stephen Weeks .... England
Paul Weiland .... England/U.S.
Peter Weir .... Australia/U.S.
David Wellington .... Canada
Peter Wells .... New Zealand
Jiang Wen .... China
Wim Wenders .... Germany
Lina Wertmuller .... Italy
Tony Wharmby .... England/U.S.
Claude Whatham .... England
David Wheatley .... England
Anne Wheeler .... Canada
Stephen Whittaker .... England
Michael Whyte .... England
David Wickes .... England
Bernhard Wicki .... Germany
Bo Widerberg .... Sweden
Andrew Wild .... Canada
Jane Wilkes .... England
Charles Wilkinson .... Canada
Richard Williams .... England/U.S.
Sandra (Sandy) Wilson .... Canada
Simon Wincer .... Australia/U.S.
Michael Winner .... England/U.S.
David Winning .... Canada
Terry Winsor .... England/U.S.
Donovan Winter .... England/U.S.
Michael Winterbottom .... England
Franz Peter Wirth .... Germany
Herbert Wise .... England/U.S.
Carol Wiseman .... England
Stephen Withrow .... Canada
Peter Wollen .... England
Dan Wolman .... Israel
Kirk Wong .... Hong Kong
John Woo .... Hong Kong/U.S.
Leslie Woodhead .... England
Jeff Woolnough .... Canada
Soenke Wortmann .... Germany
Casper Wrede .... England
Geoffrey Wright .... Australia
David Wyles .... Canada

X

Zhou Xiaowen .... China

Y

Yoji Yamada .... Japan
Mitsuo Yanagimachi .... Japan
Edward Yang .... Taiwan
Peter Yates .... U.S./England
Rebecca Yates .... Canada
Yegeny Yevtushenko .... Russia/Ukraine
Zhang Yimou .... China
Bae Yong-Kyun .... South Korea
Yaky Yosha .... Israel
Hiroaki Yoshida .... Japan/U.S.
Freddie Young .... England
Robert William Young .... England
Ronny Yu .... Hong Kong/U.S.
Zhang Yuan .... China
Corey Yuen .... Hong Kong
Prince Chatri Yukol .... Thailand
Paul Yule .... England

Z

Maurizio Zaccaro .... Italy
Krzysztof Zanussi .... Poland/Germany/
France/England
John Zaritsky .... Canada
Yolande Zauberman .... France
Franco Zeffirelli .... Italy
Tian Zhuangzhuang .... China
Claude Zidi .... France
Rafal Zielinski .... U.S./Canada
Fred Zinnemann .... England/U.S.
Vilmos Zsigmond .... U.S./Hungary
Marcos Zurinaga .... Puerto Rico

★ ★ ★

INDEX OF FOREIGN-BASED DIRECTORS
by Country

Al-Ca

FILM
DIRECTORS
GUIDE

* = also works in the United States

ALGERIA
Mohamed Chouikh

ALGERIA/FRANCE
Rachid Bouchareb

ARGENTINA
Adolfo Aristarain
Maria Luisa Bemberg
Hector Olivera
Luis Puenzo*
Alex Sessa
Fernando E. Solanas
Carlos Sorin
Eliseo Subiela

AUSTRALIA
Mario Andreacchio
Gillian Armstrong*
Moira Armstrong
Frank Arnold
Igor Auzins
John Banas
Ian Barry
Bill Bennett
Bruce Beresford*
Anthony J. Bowman
Philip Brophy
Geoff Burrowes*
Colin Budd
Robin Budd
Tim Burstall
Geoff Burton
Ken Cameron
Pauline Chan
Graeme Clifford*
Marcus Cole*
John Cornell
Paul Cox
Donald Crombie
Rolf De Heer
Kevin James Dobson*
Kevin Dowling
Di Drew
John Duigan
Stephan Elliott
Bob Ellis
Peter Faiman*
Richard Franklin*
Mel Gibson*
Yoram Gross
Russell Hagg
Brian Hannant
Rod Hardy*
Paul Harmon
Simon Heath
Lynn Hegarty
P.J. Hogan
Frank Howson

Michael Jenkins
Steve Jodrell
Mark Joffe
Chris Kennedy
Ray Lawrence
Richard Lowenstein
Baz Luhrmann
Stephen Maclean
Quentin Masters
Laurie McInnes
Don McLennan
George Miller*
George Miller*
Jocelyn Moorhouse
Philippe Mora*
Judy Morris
Kathy Mueller
Dean Murphy
Chris Noonan
Geoffrey Nottage
Phillip Noyce*
George Ogilvie
Dennis O'Rourke
Michael Pate
Michael Pattinson
Michael Pearce
John Power*
Michael Robertson
Henri Safran
Fred Schepisi*
Carl Schultz*
John Seale
Yahoo Serious
John Sexton
Peter Smith
David Stevens*
Esben Storm
Nadia Tass
John Tatoulis
Chris Thomson*
Brian Trenchard-Smith
Sophia Turkiewicz
Ann Turner
Stephen Wallace
Peter Weir*
Simon Wincer*
Geoffrey Wright

AUSTRALIA/ENGLAND
Ben Lewin
Russell Mulcahy*
Jim Sharman

AUSTRIA
Robert Dornhelm*

AUSTRIA/GERMANY
Maximilian Schell*

BELGIUM
Chantal Akerman
Remy Belvaux
Jan Bucquoy
Gerard Corbiau
Dominique Deruddere*
Marion Hansel
Michel Khleifi
Harry Kumel
Jaco Van Dormael

BOLIVIA
Jorge Sanjines

BRAZIL
Suzana Amaral
Hector Babenco*
Bruno Barreto*
Carlos Diegues
Nelson Pereira Dos Santos
Ruy Guerra
Walter Salles, Jr.
Sergio Toledo

BURKINA FASO
Gaston Kabore
Idrissa Ouedraogo

CAMBODIA/FRANCE
Rithy Panh

CAMEROON
Jean-Pierre Bekolo
Bassek Ba Kobhio

CANADA
David Acomba*
Don Allan
Paul Almond*
Denys Arcand
Mario Azzopardi
Norma Bailey
Jacques W. Benoit
Tom Berry
Attila Bertalan
George Bloomfield
Timothy Bond
Rene Bonniere
Clay Borris*
John Bradshaw
Randy Bradshaw
Michel Brault
Rex Bromfield
Alan Bunce
Martyn Burke
Graeme Campbell
Norman Campbell
Gilles Carle

705

**F
O
R
E
I
G
N

B
A
S
E
D

D
I
R
E
C
T
O
R
S**

Colin Chilvers
Gerard Ciccoritti
Richard Ciupka
Annette Cohen
Ian Corson
David Cronenberg
Harvey Crossland
Zale Dalen
Lawrence Dane
Jack Darcus
Paul Donovan
Christian Duguay
Daryl Duke*
Allan Eastman
Atom Egoyan
Neill Fearnley
Max Fischer
William Fruet
Sidney J. Furie*
Claude Gagnon
Christophe Gans
Rodney Gibbons
Stuart Gillard
Francois Girard
Allan Goldstein*
Michael Grant*
John Greyson
Sturla Gunnarsson
John Kent Harrison
Denis Heroux
Ron Hulme
Rob Iscove*
Douglas Jackson
Philip Jackson
Simcha Jacobovici
Ray Jafelice
Norman Jewison*
Aaron Kim Johnston
George Kaczender*
Jim Kaufman
Jonathon Kay
Nicholas Kendall
Michael Kennedy
Donald Kent
Larry Kent
Michael Keusch*
Allan King
Ted Kotcheff*
Srinivas Krishna
Allen Kroeker
Sheldon Larry*
Jean-Claude Lauzon
Martin Lavut
Jacques Leduc
Richard J. Lewis
Jean-Claude Lord
Francesco Lucente
Paul Lynch*
Guy Maddin
Ron Mann
Leon Marr
Richard Martin
Michael Mazo
Don McBrearty
George McCowan*
Deepa Mehta
Andre Melancon
George Mendeluk*
George Mihalka

Jorge Montesi
Rick Moranis*
Robert Morin
Allan Moyle*
Silvio Narizzano
Terrence O'Hara
Ron Oliver
Don Owen
Daniel Petrie*
Bruce Pittman
Jeremy Podeswa
Lea Pool
Gerald Potterton
Michel Poulette
Craig Pryce
Mort Ransen
Harry Rasky
Ousama Rawi
Les Rose
Peter Rowe
Patricia Rozema
Michael Rubbo
Glen Salzman
Paul Saltzman*
Vic Sarin
Joseph L. Scanlan*
Paul Schibli
Dale Schott
Cynthia Scott
Michael Scott
Arna Selznick
Paul Shapiro
Peter Shatalow
Bashar Shbib
Donald Shebib
John Sheppard
Mina Shum
Yves Simoneau
Gail Singer
Clive A. Smith
John N. Smith*
Brenton Spencer
Robin Spry
David Steinberg*
Sandor Stern*
Steven Hilliard Stern*
Daniele J. Suissa
Kevin Sullivan
Peter Svatek
Tibor Takacs*
Dave Thomas*
Ralph L. Thomas
Eric Till
Rob Turner
Giles Walker
Al Waxman*
David Wellington
Anne Wheeler
Andrew Wild
Charles Wilkinson
David Winning
Stephen Withrow
Rebecca Yates
Jeff Woolnough
David Wyles
John Zaritsky
Rafal Zielinski*

CANADA/ENGLAND
Alvin Rakoff

CANADA/POLAND
Richard Bugajski

CHINA
He Jianjun
Huang Jianxin
Xie Jin
Chen Kaige
Yin Li
He Ping
Shirley Sun*
Wu Tianming
Jiang Wen
Zhang Yimou
Zhang Yuan
Zhou Xiaowen
Tian Zhuangzhuang

CHINA/TAIWAN
Peter Wang*

COLOMBIA
Sergio Cabrera
Victor Manuel Gaviria

CROATIA
Jakov Sedlar

CUBA
Tomás Gutierrez Alea
Juan Carlos Tabio

CZECH REPUBLIC
Vera Chytilova
Milos Forman*
Karel Kachyna
Hannah Kodicek
Jiri Menzel
Jan Nemec
Peter Nydrle*
Ivan Passer*
Jan Svankmajer
Jan Sverak

DENMARK
Bille August
Henning Carlsen*
Jan Jung
Soren Kragh-Jacobsen
Kenneth Madsen*
Kaspar Rostrup
Lars von Trier

DENMARK/FRANCE
Gabriel Axel

EGYPT
Youssef Chahine
Yousry Nasrallah
Daoud Abdel Sayed

ENGLAND

Jon Acevski
Phil Agland
Jon Amiel
Paul Anderson*
Sarah Pia Anderson
Ken Annakin*
Michael Apted*
Michael Armstrong*
Vic Armstrong
Richard Attenborough*
Michael Austin
Robert S. Baker
Roy Ward Baker
Clive Barker
Lezli-An Barrett
Steve Barron*
Zelda Barron*
Sean Barry
Roy Battersby
Terry Bedford*
Michael Beckham
Rodney Bennett
Steven Berkoff
Chris Bernard
Robert Bierman*
Kevin Billington
Antonia Bird*
Andrew Birkin
Alan Birkinshaw
Les Blair
Michael Blakemore
Ben Bolt*
John Boorman*
Dave Borthwick
Roy Boulting
Don Boyd
Kenneth Branagh*
Alan Bridges
Hugh Brody
Bob Brooks
Nicholas (Nick) Broomfield
Kevin Brownlow
Bill Bryden
Colin Bucksey*
Derek Burbidge
Stuart Burge
John Byrne
Muriel Box
Simon Callow
Martin Campbell
Danny Cannon*
Jack Cardiff
Michael Carreras
Michael Caton-Jones*
James Cellan-Jones
Gurinder Chadha
Peter Chelsom
Roger Christian
Lawrence Gordon Clark
Frank Clarke
James Kenelm Clarke*
Malcolm Clarke
Tom Clegg
Dick Clement*
Peter Clifton
Martin Clunes
Harvey Cokliss*
David Cohen

Henry Cole
Kevin Connor*
Alex Cox*
Peter Crane*
Lol Creme
Charles Crichton
John Davies
John T. Davies
Ray Davies
Terence Davies
Desmond Davis
Ernest Day
James Dearden*
Barry Devlin
Clive Donner*
Alan Dossor
David Drury
Peter John Duffell
Andrew Eaton
Christine Edzard
Arthur Ellis
Peter Ellis
Ian Emes
Robert Enders
Andi Engel
Nuria Espert
Marc Evans
Richard Eyre
Mark Ezra
Ferdinand Fairfax
Michael Ferguson
Mike Figgis*
Charles Finch
Albert Finney
Clive Fleury
Gordon Flemyng
Mandie Fletcher
Kim Flitcroft
Bryan Forbes
Timothy Forder
Giles Foster
Freddie Francis
Cyril Frankel
Stephen Frears*
Benjamin Fry
Robert Fuest
Tim Fywell
Patrick Garland
Tony Garnett
Constantine Giannaris
Brian Gibson*
Maria Giese
Brian Gilbert*
Lewis Gilbert
Terry Gilliam*
David Gladwell
John Glen
John Glenister
Peter Glenville
Jim Goddard
Jack Gold
Paul Golding*
John Goldschmidt
Steven Gough
Brian Grant*
David Green*
Guy Green*
Terry Green
Peter Greenaway

David Greene*
Paul Greengrass
Colin Gregg
Andrew Grieve
Alan Grint
Val Guest
John Guillerman*
Piers Haggard*
Peter Hall
Guy Hamilton
Peter Hammond
Christopher Hampton
Justin Hardy
Robin Hardy
David Hare
Damian Harris*
Richard Harris
Derek Hart
Anthony Harvey*
Maurice Hatton
Sidney Hayers*
David Hayman
Jack Hazan
Sarah Hellings
David Hemmings*
John Henderson
Mark Herman
Gordon Hessler*
Mike Hodges*
Michael Hoffman*
Harry Hook*
Bob Hoskins
John Hough
Hugh Hudson*
Kenneth (Ken) Hughes*
Peter Hunt*
Waris Hussein*
Nicholas Hytner*
Eric Idle
John Irvin*
James Ivory*
Mick Jackson*
Pedr James
Annabel Jankel*
Charles Jarrott*
Vadim Jean
Lionel Jeffries
Roland Joffé*
Sandy Johnson
David Jones*
Terry Jones
Paul Joyce
Isaac Julien
Marek Kanievska*
Elliott Kastner*
Anwar Kawadri
Patrick Keiller
Jude Kelly
Irvin Kershner*
Beeban Kidron*
Gerard Kikoine
Christopher Lloyd King
Herbert Kline*
Margy Kinmouth
Robert Knights
Peter Kosminsky
John Krish
Suri Krishnamma
Stanley Kubrick*

F O R E I G N B A S E D D I R E C T O R S

Simon Langton
Frank Launder
Ashley Lazarus
Jack Lee
Mike Leigh
David Leland
Richard Lester*
Michael Lindsay-Hogg
Peter Mackenzie Litten
Kenneth Loach
Richard Loncraine
Declan Lowney
Adrian Lyne*
Jonathan Lynn*
Sydney (Syd) Macartney*
Peter Macdonald*
John Mackenzie*
Gillies Mackinnon
John Madden
Bob Mahoney
Lesley Manning
Terry Marcel
Paul Mayersberg*
Tony Maylam
Joseph McGrath
George McIndoe*
Ken McMullen
Mary McMurray
Nancy Meckler
Peter Medak*
Francis Megahy*
Christopher Menaul
Chris Menges*
Roger Michell
Scott Michell
Christopher Miles
Catherine Millar
Gavin Millar
Jonathan Miller
Reginald Mills
David Mingay
Anthony Minghella
Simon Moore
Christopher Morahan
Rocky Morton*
Elijah Moshinsky
Malcolm Mowbray*
John Llewellyn Moxey*
Paul Murton
Ronald Neame*
Chris Newby
Mike Newell*
Anthony Newley*
Leslie Norman
Trevor Nunn
Jim O'Brien
Mike Ockrent
James O'Connolly
Gerry O'Hara
Stuart Orme
Horace Ove
Cliff Owen
Anthony Page*
Tony Palmer
Alan Parker*
Cary Parker
Willi Patterson
George Pavlou

Ron Peck
Clare Peploe
Mark Peploe
Zoran Perisic*
Chris Petit
Maurice Phillips*
Andrew Piddington
Harold Pinter
Stephen Poliakoff
Angela Pope
Sally Potter
Tristram Powell
Udayan Prasad
John Quested
Michael Radford
Frederic Raphael
Christopher Rawlence
Clive Rees
Geoffrey Reeve
Alastair Reid
Karel Reisz*
Barbara Rennie
Peter Richardson
Anthony Richmond*
Philip Ridley
John Roberts
Bruce Robinson*
Franc Roddam*
Nicolas Roeg*
Bernard Rose
Martin Rosen*
Benjamin Ross
Ken Russell*
Renny Rye
Nick Ryle
Jimmy Sangster
Michael Sarne
Peter Sasdy
Philip Saville*
Geoffrey Sax
John Schlesinger*
Stefan Schwartz
James Scott
Ridley Scott*
Tony Scott*
Paul Seed
Ian Sellar
Michael Seresin*
Vernon Sewell
Stefan Schwartz
Michael Shackleton
Don Sharp
Ian Sharp
Adrian Shergold
Peter Shillingford*
Anthony Simmons
Andrew Sinclair
John Smallcombe
Mel Smith
Noella Smith
Tony Smith
Iaian Softley
Richard Spence
Terence Stamp*
Richard Stanley
Ringo Starr
Martin Stellman
Norman Stone

Tom Stoppard
Charles Sturridge
Jeremy Summers
Cedric Sundstrom*
Peter Sykes
Baz Taylor
Julien Temple*
Conny Templeman
Antony Thomas
Ralph Thomas
Barnaby Thompson*
J. Lee Thompson*
Ian Toynton
Michael Tuchner*
Anand Tucker
David Tucker
Montgomery Tully
Clive Turner
Stuart Urban
Peter Ustinov*
Peter Walker
Robert Walker
Anthony Waller
Nick Ward
Paul Watson
Peter Webb
Stephen Weeks
Paul Weiland*
Tony Wharmby*
Claude Whatham
David Wheatley
Stephen Whittaker
Michael Whyte
David Wickes
Jane Wilkes
Richard Williams*
Michael Winner*
Terry Winsor*
Donovan Winter*
Herbert Wise*
Carol Wiseman
Peter Wollen
Leslie Woodhead
Casper Wrede
Freddie Young
Robert William Young
Peter Yates*
Paul Yule
Fred Zinnemann*

ENGLAND/AFRICA
Michael Raeburn

ENGLAND/CANADA
Michael Anderson

ENGLAND/FRANCE
Peter Brook
Donald Cammell
David Hamilton
Wolf Rilla

ENGLAND/INDIA
Pradip Krishen

ENGLAND/INDONESIA
Lorne Blair

ENGLAND/MACEDONIA
Milcho Manchevski

ENGLAND/PAKISTAN
Jamil Dehlavi

ENGLAND/SCOTLAND
Danny Boyle

ENGLAND/SOUTH AFRICA
Ross Devenish

ENGLAND/SWEDEN
Peter Watkins
Colin Nutley

ENGLAND/WALES
Stephen Bayly
Karl Francis
Anthony Hopkins*
Christopher Monger*

FINLAND
Veikko Aaltonen
Aki Kaurismäki
Mika Kaurismäki
Aleksi Makela
Rauni Mollberg
Pekka Parikka

FINLAND/SWEDEN
Jörn Donner

FRANCE
Rene Allio
Denis Amar
Yves Angelo
Jean-Jacques Annaud
Alexandre Arcady
Olivier Assayas
Claude Autant-Lara
Iradj Azimi
Eric Barbier
Paolo Barzman
Jean-Jacques Beineix
Vera Belmont
Alain Berberian
Claude Berri
John Berry*
Jean-Louis Bertucelli
Luc Besson*
Jean-Claude Biette
Michel Blanc
Bertrand Blier
Jerome Boivin
Walerian Borowczyk
Patrick Bouchitey
Serge Bourguignon
Charlotte Brandstrom*
Patrick Braoude
Catherine Breillat
Robert Bresson
Juan Buñuel
Leos Carax
Marc Caro
Marcel Carne
Alain Cavalier

Claude Chabrol
Mehdi Charef
Etienne Chatiliez
Pierre Chenal
Elie Chouraqui
René Clément
Alain Corneau
Jacques-Yves Cousteau
Raoul Coutard
Claude D'Anna
Josee Dayan
Philippe de Broca
Christian De Chalonge
Dimitri De Clercq
Jean Delannoy
Nathalie Delon
Claire Denis
Jean-Pierre Denis
Jacques Deray
Michel Deville
Patrick Dewolf
Jacques Doillon
Jacques Dorfman
Daniele Dubroux
Remy Duchemin
Francois Dupeyron
Marguerite Duras
Robert Enrico
Jacques Fansten
Claude Faraldo
Andre Farwagi
Christian Fechner
Kathleen Fonmarty
Rene Gainville*
Tony Gatlif
Francis Girod
Pierre William Glenn
Jean-Pierre Gorin
Costa-Gavras*
Henri Helman
Robert Hossein
Jean-Loup Hubert
Daniele Huillet
Caroline Huppert
Just Jaeckin
Patrick Jamain
Frederic Jardin
Alain Jessua
Jean-Pierre Jeunet
Arthur Joffe
Gerard Jugnot
Nelly Kaplan
Mathieu Kassovitz
William Klein*
Robert Kramer*
Gerard Krawczyk
Diane Kurys
Claude Lanzmann
Georges Lautner
Gerard Lauzier
Patrice Leconte
Michel Legrand
Claude Lelouch
Serge LePeron
Louis Malle*
Chris Marker
Christian Marquand
Claude Massot

Charles Matton
Moebius
Edouard Molinaro
Philippe Monnier
Gerard Mordillat
Jeanne Moreau
Bruno Nuytten
Marcel Ophuls
Gerard Oury
Michel Pascal
Étienne Perier
Nicholas Philibert
Maurice Pialat
Lucian Pintilie
Marie-France Pisier
Roger Planchon
Jean-Marie Poire
Jerome Prieur
Denis Rabaglia
Jean-Paul Rappaneau
François Reichenbach
Alain Resnais
Jacques Rivette
Alain Robbe-Grillet
Yves Robert
Eric Rochant
Eric Rohmer
Brigitte Rouan
Randa Chahal Sabbag
Claude Sautet
Suzanne Schiffman
Pierre Schoendorffer
Barbet Schroeder*
Arnaud Selignac
Coline Serreau
Philip Setbon
Jean-François Stevenin
Bob Swaim*
Jeannot Szwarc*
Jean-Charles Tacchella
Bertrand Tavernier
Andre Techine
Serge Toubiana
Jean-Claude Tramont*
Nadine Trintignant
Roger Vadim*
Agnes Varda
Francis Veber*
Henri Verneuil
Daniel Vigne*
Christian Vincent
Regis Wargnier
Yolande Zauberman
Claude Zidi

FRANCE/BELGIUM
Jacques Fansten

FRANCE/CANADA
Rene Manzor*

FRANCE/CHILE/PORTUGAL
Raul Ruíz*

FRANCE/GEORGIA
Otar Ioselliani

**F
O
R
E
I
G
N

B
A
S
E
D

D
I
R
E
C
T
O
R
S**

FRANCE/GERMANY
Jean-Marie Straub

FRANCE/SWITZERLAND
Jean-Luc Godard

FRANCE/POLAND
Roman Polanski*

FRANCE/SWITZERLAND
Nicolas Gessner*

GERMANY
Percy Adlon*
Doris Dorrie*
Uli Edel*
Roland Emmerich*
Bernd Fischerauer
Peter Fleischmann
Vadim Glowna
Paul Gunczler
Nathaniel Gutman*
Werner Herzog
Jochen Hick
Karin Howard*
Alexander Kluge
Peter Lilienthal
Ulli Lommel*
Ray Muller
Paul Nicolas*
Edgar Reitz
Wolfgang Petersen*
Leni Riefenstahl
Volker Schlondorff*
Werner Schroeter
Bernard Sinkel
Rainer Soehnlein
Hans-Jurgen Syberberg
Michael Verhoeven
Katja Von Garnier
Rosa Von Praunheim
Margarethe von Trotta
Wim Wenders
Bernhard Wicki
Franz Peter Wirth
Soenke Wortmann

GERMANY/AUSTRIA
Klaus Maria Brandauer

GERMANY/SWITZERLAND
Carl Schenkel*

GREECE
Theo Angelopoulos
Michael Cacoyannis
Jules Dassin*
Nico Mastorakis*

HONG KONG
Jackie Chan
Jacob C.L. Cheung
Allen Fong
Tsui Hark
Yim Ho
Ann Hui
Michael Hui

Samo Hung
Wong Kar-Wai
Stanley Kwan
Clara Law
Po-Chih Leong
Johnny Mak
Michael Mak
Stephen Shin
Wayne Wang*
Kirk Wong
John Woo
Ronny Yu*
Corey Yuen

HONG KONG/JAPAN
George Rowe*

HONG KONG/TAIWAN
King Hu*

HUNGARY
Ildiko Enyedi
Gyula Gazdag*
Jozsef Gemes
Peter Gothar
Miklos Jancso
Karoly Makk
Marta Meszaros
Istvan Szabo
Vilmos Zsigmond*

ICELAND
Fridrik Thor Fridriksson
Hrafn Gunnlaugsson
Gudny Halldorsdottir
Kristin Johannesdottir
Oskar Jonasson

INDIA
Jahnu Barua
Shyam Benegal
Shekhar Kapur
Mani Kaul
Ketan Mehta
Jag Mundhra*
Mira Nair*
Sandip Ray
Satyajit Ray
Mrinal Sen
Krishna Shah*

INDIA/ENGLAND
Zafar Hai

INDONESIA
Eros Djarot
Slamet Rahardjo Djarot

IRAN
Dariush Mehrjui
Abbas Kiarostami
Amir Naderi*

IRELAND
Don Bluth*
Joe Comerford
Frank Deasy

Joe Lee
Mary McGuckian
Maurice O'Callaghan
Ronan O'Leary
Peter Ormrod
Thaddeus O'Sullivan
Jim Sheridan

IRELAND/ENGLAND
Pat O'Connor*
Neil Jordan*

ISRAEL
Uri Barbash
Michal Bat-Adam
Eli Cohen
Nissim Dayan
Shimon Dotan*
Sam Firstenberg*
Amos Gitai
Menahem Golan*
Jacob Goldwasser
Samuel (Shmuel) Imberman
Ephraim Kishon
Amos Kollek*
Avi Nesher*
Eran Riklis
Renen Schorr
Riki Shelach
Joel Silberg*
Yves Simoneau*
Len Talan
Daniel Wachsmann
Dan Wolman
Yaky Yosha
Boaz Davidson*

ISRAEL/CANADA
Eli Cohen*

ISRAEL/FRANCE
Moshe Mizrahi

ITALY
Franco Amurri*
Michelangelo Antonioni
Francesca Archibugi
Dario Argento
Pupi Avati
Ferdinando Baldi
Giulio Base
Giacomo Battiato
Lamberto Bava
Marco Bellocchio
Roberto Benigni
Bernardo Bertolucci
Giuseppe Bertolucci
Mauro Bolognini
Tinto Brass
Mario Brenta
Franco Brusati
Carlo Carlei*
Fabio Carpi
Liliana Cavani
Lewis Coates
Luigi Comencini
Vittorio Cottafavi

Alessandro D'Alatri
Damiano Damiani
Anthony M. Dawson
Gianfranco de Bosio
Peter Del Monte
Ruggero Deodato
Giuseppe De Santis
Gualtiero Jacopetti
Ottavio Fabbri
Roberto Faenza
Giorgio Ferrara
Giuseppe Ferrara
Marco Ferreri
Riccardo Freda
Lucio Fulci
Gianna Maria Garbelli
Ezio Greggio
Aurelio Grimaldi
Alberto Lattuada
Sergio Leone
Carlo Lizzani
Nanni Loy
Daniele Luchetti
Mario Martone
Carlo Mazzacurati
Mario Monicelli
Giuilano Montaldo
Nanni Moretti
Alberto Negrin
Maurizio Nichetti
Francesco Nuti
Ermanno Olmi
Mario Orfini
Filippo Ottoni
Franco Piavoli
Michele Placido
Gillo Pontecorvo
Maurizio Ponzi
Pasquale Pozzessere
Folco Quilici
Dino Risi
Marco Risi
Francesco Rosi
Sergio Rubini
Gabriele Salvatores
Ettore Scola
Silvio Soldini
Alberto Sordi
Paolo Taviani
Vittorio Taviani
Antonio Tibaldi
Ricky Tognazzi
Giuseppe Tornatore
Cinzia Th Torrini
Massimo Troisi
Carlo Vanzina
Carlo Verdone
Lina Wertmuller
Maurizio Zaccaro
Franco Zeffirelli

IVORY COAST
Desire Ecare
Roger Gnoan M'Bala

JAMAICA
Perry Henzell

JAPAN
Tamasaburo Bando
Kinji Fukasaku
Jun Fukuda
Hideo Gosha
Susumu Hani
Kazuo Hara
Masato Harada*
Masami Hata
Masanori Hata
Kayo Hatta*
Kaizo Hayashi
Inoshiro (Ishiro) Honda
Kon Ichikawa
Shohei Imamura
Sogo Ishii
Juzo Itami*
Kenchi Iwamoto
Seigi Izumi
Haruki Kadokawa*
Shusuke Kaneko
Keisuke Kinoshita
Takeshi Kitano
Masaki Kobayashi
Kei Kumai
Akira Kurosawa
Fran Rubel Kuzui*
Toshio Masuda
Rentaro Mayuzumi
Rentaro Mikuni
Hayao Miyazaki
Yoshimitsu Morita
Ryu Murakami
Yoko Narahashi
Takao Ogawara
Kohei Oguri
Kihachi Okamoto
Kazuyoshi Okuyama
Kazuki Omori
Nagisa Oshima
Katsuhiro Otomo
Yoichi Sai
Junji Sakamoto
Junya Sato
Shimako Sato
Kaneto Shindo
Masahiro Shinoda
Seijun Suzuki
Isao Takahata
Yojiro Takita
Hiroshi Teshigahara
Ro Tomono
Yoji Yamada
Mitsuo Yanagimachi
Hiroaki Yoshida*

KAZAKHSTAN
Rachid Nougmanov

KENYA
Raju Sharad Patel

LEBANON
Georges Chamchoum*

MALAYSIA
Aziz M. Osman

MALI
Souleymane Cissé

MARTINIQUE
Euzhan Palcy*

MEXICO
Luis Alcoriza
Alfonso Arau*
Isaac Artenstein*
Francisco Athle
Felipe Cazals
Rafael Corkidi
Alfonso Cuaron*
Guillermo Del Toro
Nicolas Echevarria
Luis Estrada
Marcela Fernandez Violante
Carlos Garcia Agraz
José Luis Garcia Agraz
Servando Gonzalez
Jaime Humberto Hermosillo
Alberto Isaac
Paul Leduc
Luis Mandoki*
Maria Novaro
Gabriel Retes
Arturo Ripstein
Dana Rotberg
Roberto Sneider
Isela Vega

MEXICO/CUBA/CHILE
Miguel Littin

NEPAL
Tulshi Ghimiray

NETHERLANDS
Renee Daalder*
Ate De Jong*
Dick Maas
Fons Rademakers
Hans Scheepmaker
Kees Van Oostrum*
Ben Verbong
Paul Verhoeven*

NEW ZEALAND
Murray Ball
Barry Barclay
David Blyth
John Day
Roger Donaldson*
Michael Firth
Peter Jackson
John Laing
Michael Laughlin
Alison Maclean
Stewart Main
Merata Mita
Bruce Morrison
Ian Mune
Geoff Murphy*
Leon Narbey
Larry Parr
Sam Pillsbury*

**F
O
R
E
I
G
N

B
A
S
E
D

D
I
R
E
C
T
O
R
S**

Gaylene Preston
John Reid
Lee Tamahori
Vincent Ward
Peter Wells

NEW ZEALAND/AUSTRALIA
Anna Campion
Jane Campion

NORWAY
Anja Breien
Nils Gaup
Erik Gustavson
Leidulv Risan
Ola Solum

NORWAY/SWEDEN/DENMARK
Liv Ullmann*

OKINAWA
Rinken Teruya

PAPUA NEW GUINEA
Pengau Nengo

PERU
Marianne Eyde
Luis "Lucho" Llosa*
Augusto Tamayo

PHILIPPINES
Mel Chionglo
Mike de Leon
Eddie Romero
Cirio H. Santiago

POLAND
Jerzy Domaradzki
Jerzy Kawalerowicz
Krzysztof Kieslowski
Krzysztof Lang
Andrzej Wajda

POLAND/ENGLAND
Jerzy Skolimowski*

POLAND/GERMANY
Agnieszka Holland

POLAND/GERMANY/FRANCE/ENGLAND
Krzysztof Zanussi

POLAND/ISRAEL/ITALY
Alexander Ramati

PORTUGAL
Manoel De Oliveira
Teresa Villaverde

PUERTO RICO
Jacobo Morales
Marcos Zurinaga

RUSSIA
Dimitri Astrakhan
Mikhail Belikov
Alexander Buravsky
Grigori Chukhrai
Elem Klimov
Andrei Konchalovsky*
Viacheslav Krishtofovich
Emil Loteanu
Pavel Lounguine
Yuri Mamin
Vladimir Menshov
Nikita Mikhalkov
Alexander Mitta
Gleb Panfilov
Vasily Pichul
Mikhail Romm
Eldar Ryazanov
Valeri Todorovski

SCOTLAND
Mike Alexander
Bill Forsyth*
Charles Gormley
Graham Holloway
Patrick Lau
Aisling Walsh

SENEGAL
Sene Absa
Djibril Diop Mambety
Ousmane Sembene
Thierno Faty Sow
Moussa Toure

SERBIA
Slobodan Sijan

SOMALIA
Soraya Mire*

SOUTH AFRICA
Heinrich Dahms
Athol Fugard
Gray Hofmeyr
David Lister
Darrell Roodt
Mark Roper
Percival Rubens
Oliver Schmitz
Tim Spring*
Jamie Uys

SOUTH KOREA
Bae Chang-Ho
Park Choi-Su
Ji-Young Chung
Lee Doo-Yong
Lee Jang-Ho
Woo-Suk Kang
Im Kwon-Taek
Bae Yong-Kyun

SPAIN
Pedro Almodovar
Vicente Aranda
Juan Antonio Bardem

Luis Garcia Berlanga
José Luis Borau*
Mario Camus
Alex De La Iglesia
Victor Erice
Jose Luis Garci
Manuel Gutierrez Aragon
Herve Hachuel
Gilbert Lee Kay*
Bigas Luna
Carlos Saura
Fernando Trueba
Gerardo Vera

SPAIN/CHILE
Valeria Sarmiento

SPAIN/FRANCE
Nestor Almendros*

SPAIN/PUERTO RICO
Gerardo Herrero

SWEDEN
Torgny Anderberg
Daniel Bergman
Ingmar Bergman
Kjell Grede
Lasse Hallstrom*
Gunnar Hellstrom*
Sven Nykvist
Stellan Olsson
Suzanne Osten
Ake Sandgren
Vilgot Sjoman
Jan Troell
Max Von Sydow
Bo Widerberg

SWITZERLAND
Bernt Capra
Richard Dembo
Robert Frank*
Kurt Gloor
Claude Goretta
Markus Imhoof
Xavier Koller
Fredi M. Murer
Alain Tanner

TAIWAN
Hou Hsiao-Hsien
Ang Lee*
Steven C.C. Liu
Tsai Ming-Liang
Edward Yang

THAILAND
Vichit Kounavudhi
Chalong Pakdeevichit
Cherd Songsri
Prince Chatri Yukol

TUNISIA
Moufida Tlatli

TUNISIA/FRANCE
Ridha Behi

TURKEY
Cetin (Sezerel) Daglar

UKRAINE
Yuri Illienko
Yevgeny Yevtushenko

VENEZUELA
Betty Kaplan
Abraham Pulido*

VIETNAM
Ho Quang Minh
Trinh T. Minh-Ha*
Tiana Thi Thanh Nga*

WALES
Paul Turner

YUGOSLAVIA
Jovan Acin
Emir Kusturica*
Dusan Makavejev
Goran Paskaljevic
Alexander Petrovic
Slobodan Sijan

ZIMBABWE
Godwin Mawuru
John Riber

**F
O
R
E
I
G
N

B
A
S
E
D

D
I
R
E
C
T
O
R
S**

GUILDS

USA

DIRECTORS GUILD OF AMERICA—West

7920 Sunset Blvd.
Los Angeles, CA 90046
310/289-2000
FAX 213/289-3671
213/851-3671 (Agency Information)

DIRECTORS GUILD OF AMERICA—East

110 West 57th Street
New York, NY 10019
212/581-0370
FAX 212/581-1441

DIRECTORS GUILD OF AMERICA—Midwest

400 North Michigan Avenue, Suite 307
Chicago, IL 60611
312/644-5050
FAX 312/644-5776

AUSTRALIA

**AUSTRALIAN SCREEN DIRECTORS
ASSOCIATION**

Box 22
Trades Hall Four
Goulbern Street
Sydney, NSW 2000
Australia
02/264-9986

GREAT BRITAIN (UK)

DIRECTORS GUILD OF GREAT BRITAIN

Suffolk House
1-8 Whitfield Place
London W1P 5SF, England
171/383-3858

CANADA

DIRECTORS GUILD OF CANADA

225 Richmond Street West, Suite 300
Toronto, Ontario M5V 1W2
Canada
416/351-8200
FAX 416/351-8205

DIRECTORS GUILD OF CANADA

524 11th Street S.W.
Calgery, Alberta T2R 0X8
Canada
403/237-0689

DIRECTORS GUILD OF CANADA

163 West Hastings Street, Suite 339
Vancouver, British Columbia V6B 1H5
Canada
604/688-2976

DIRECTORS GUILD OF CANADA

2250 Guy Street, Suite 506
Montreal, Quebec H3H 2M3
Canada
514/989-1714

WRITERS GUILD OF AMERICA-WEST, INC.
8955 Beverly Blvd.
Los Angeles, CA 90048
310/550-1000
310/205-2502 (Agency Information)

WRITERS GUILD OF AMERICA-EAST, INC.
555 West 57th St.
New York, NY 10019
212/245-6180

WRITERS GUILD OF GREAT BRITAIN
430 Edgeware Road
London W21 EH, England
011/071/723-8074

SCREEN ACTORS GUILD
5757 Wilshire Blvd.
Los Angeles, CA 90036
213/954-1600
213/549-6737 (Agency Information)

AGENTS AND MANAGERS

* = management company

A

ABRAMS ARTISTS & ASSOCIATES
9200 Sunset Blvd. , Suite 625
Los Angeles, CA 90069
310/859-0625

420 Madison Ave.
Suite 1400
New York, NY 10017
212/935-8980

Harry Abrams

ADDIS-WECHSLER & ASSOCIATES*
(In Association with the
Robert Littman Co.)
955 S. Carrillo Drive, 3rd Floor
Los Angeles, CA 90048
310/954-9000
FAX 310/954-9009

Keith Addis
Nick Wechsler

THE AGENCY
10351 Santa Monica Blvd., Suite 211
Los Angeles, CA 90025
310/551-3000

AGENCY FOR THE PERFORMING ARTS, INC. (APA)
9000 Sunset Blvd., Suite 1200
Los Angeles, CA 90069
310/273-0744
FAX 310/275-9401

888 Seventh Avenue
New York, NY 10106
212/582-1500
FAX 212/245-1647

AGENTS ASSOCIES
5, rue de Ponthieu
75008 Paris, France
1/42-56-21-22

Georges Beaume

AIM/JOHN REDWAY ASSOCIATES
5 Denmark Street
Lomdon WC2H 8LP England
71/836-2001
FAX 71/379-0848

Derek Webster

ALIDAN ASSOCIATES
1888 Century Park East, Suite 1900
Los Angeles, CA 9067
310/284-6800

ALL-STAR TALENT AGENCY
7834 Alabama Avenue
Canoga Park, CA 91304
818/346-4313

Robert Brad Allred

AMSEL, EISENSTADT & FRAZIER, INC.
6310 San Vicente Blvd., Suite 407
Los Angeles, CA 90048
310/939-1188
FAX 310/939-0630

THE APELIAN AGENCY
327 Church Lane
Bel Air, CA 90049
310/476-4732

ARTMEDIA
10 Avenue Georges V
75008 Paris, France
04/723-7860

THE ARTISTS AGENCY
10000 Santa Monica Blvd., Suite 305
Los Angeles, CA 90067
310/277-7779
FAX 310/785-9338

THE ARTISTS GROUP, LTD.
1930 Century Park West, Suite 403
Los Angeles, CA 90067
310/552-1100
FAX 310/277-9513

ASSOCIATED TALENT AGENCY
9744 Wilshire Blvd., Suite 312
Beverly Hills, CA 90212
310/271-4662

ATLAS ENTERTAINMENT
7471 Melrose Avenue, #11/12
Los Angeles, CA 90046
213/658-9100
FAX 213/658-8115

Cynthia Campos-Greenberg
Christopher E. Henze

B

BDP & Associates
10637 Burbank Blvd.
North Hollywood, CA 91601
818/506-7615
FAX 818/506-4983

GEORGES BEAUME
3 Quai Malaquais
Paris, 75006, France
1/42-56-21-22

BECSEY/WISDOM/KALAJIAN
9229 Sunset Blvd., Suite 710
Los Angeles, CA 90069
310/550-0535
FAX 310/246-4424

Larry Becsey
Victoria Wisdom
Jerry Kalajian

THE BENNETT AGENCY
150 S. Barrington Ave., Suite 1
Los Angeles, CA 90049
310/471-2251

Carole Bennett

BERZON TALENT AGENCY
1614 Victory Blvd., Suite 120
Glendale, CA 91201
818/548-1560

336 E. 17th St.
Costa Mesa, CA 92627
714/631-5936

Mike Ricciardi

J. MICHAEL BLOOM, LTD.
233 Park Avenue South, 10th Floor
New York, NY 10003
212/529-6500

9200 Sunset Blvd.
Suite 710
Los Angeles, CA 90069
310/275-6800

GEORGES BORCHARDT LITERARY AGENCY
136 East 57th Street
New York, NY 10022
212/753-5785

BORINSTEIN, ORECK, BOGART AGENCY
8271 Melrose Ave., Suite 110
Los Angeles, CA 90046
213/658-7500

Mark Borinstein
Mary Oreck
Bari Bogart

PAUL BRANDON & ASSOCIATES*
200 North Robertson Blvd., Suite 223
Beverly Hills, CA 90211
310/273-6173

THE BRANDT COMPANY
15250 Ventura Blvd., Suite 720
Sherman Oaks, CA 91403
818/783-7747
FAX 818/784-6012

Geoff Brandt

BRESLER-KELLY-KIPPERMAN*
15760 Ventura Blvd., Suite 1730
Encino, CA 91436
818/905-1155

111 West 57th St.
Suite 1409
New York, NY 10019
212/265-1980

Sandy Bresler
John S. Kelly
Perri Kipperman (NY)

BRILLSTEIN-GREY*
9200 Sunset Blvd., Suite 428
Los Angeles, CA 90069
310/275-6135

Bernie Brillstein
Brad Grey

NIGEL BRITTEN MANAGEMENT
Garden Studios
11-15 Betterton Street
London WC2H 9BP, England
71/379-0344
FAX 71/379-7027

THE BRODER-KURLAND-WEBB-UFFNER AGENCY
9242 Bevery Blvd., Suite 200
Beverly Hills, CA 90210
310/281-3400
FAX 310/276-3207

Bob Broder
Norman Kurland
Elliot Webb
Beth Uffner

THE BROWN GROUP*
9300 Wilshire Blvd., Suite 508
Beverly Hills, CA 90212
Burbank, CA 91505
310/247-2755
FAX 310/247-2758

Jon Brown

BRUCE BROWN AGENCY
1033 Gayley Ave., Suite 207
Los Angeles, CA 90024
310/208-1835

CURTIS BROWN, LTD.
10 Astor Place
New York, NY 10003
212/473-5400

162-168 Regent Street
London W1R 5TB, England
71/437-9700
FAX 71/872-0332

NED BROWN ASSOCIATES
10780 Santa Monica Blvd., Suite 28
Los Angeles, CA 90025
310/474-0528

THE BRUSTEIN CO.
2644 30th Street
Santa Monica, CA 90405
310/452-3330

Richard Brustein

C

LISA CALLAMARO AGENCY
427 N. Canon Drive
Beverly Hills, CA 90210
310/274-6783
FAX 310/274-6536

CAMDEN-ITG
(In Association with Candace Lake Agency)
822 S. Robertson Blvd., Suite 200
Los Angeles, CA 90035
310/289-2700
FAX 310/289-2718

729 Seventh Ave.
16th Floor
New York, NY 10019
212/221-7878

ROGER CAREY MANAGEMENT
64 Thornton Avenue
London W4 1QQ, England
81/995-4477
FAX 81/995-2382

WILLIAM CARROLL AGENCY
120 South Victory Blvd.
Burbank, CA 91502
818/845-3791

CARLYLE MANAGEMENT*
639 N. Larchmont, 2nd Floor
Los Angeles, CA 90038
213/469-3086

Phyllis Carlyle

CASAROTTO COMPANY LTD.
National House
60-66 Wardour Street
London W1V 3HP, England
71/287-4450
FAX 71/287-9128

Jenne Casarotto

CCA MANAGEMENT*
4 Court Lodge
48 Sloane Square
London SW1 W8AT, England
71/730-8857
FAX 71/730-6971

Flic McKinney

CENTURY ARTISTS, LTD.
9744 Wilshire Blvd., Suite 308
Beverly Hills, CA 90212
310/273-4366
FAX 310/273-1423

THE CHASIN AGENCY
8899 Beverly Blvd., Suite 713
Los Angeles, CA 90048
310/278-7505
FAX 310/275-6685

Tom Chasin

CHATTO & LINNIT
Prince of Wales Theatre
Coventry Street
London W1V 7FG, England
71/930-6677
FAX 71/930-0091

CINEMA TALENT INTERNATIONAL
8033 Sunset Blvd., Suite 808
West Hollywood, CA 90046
213/656-1937

CIRCLE TALENT ASSOCIATES
433 N. Camden Dr., Suite 400
Beverly Hills, CA 90210
310/285-1585
FAX 310/285-1580

CNA & ASSOCIATES
1801 Avenue of the Stars, Suite 1250
Los Angeles, CA 90067
310/556-4343
FAX 310/556-4633

CONTEMPORARY ARTISTS, LTD.
1427 3rd Street Promenade, Suite 205
Santa Monica, CA 90401
310/395-1800

CONWAY van GELDER LTD.
18-21 Jermyn Street
London SW1Y 6HP, England
71/287-0077
FAX 71/287-1940

THE COOPER AGENCY
10100 Santa Monica Blvd., Suite 310
Los Angeles, CA 90067
310/277-8422
FAX 310/277-8433

Frank Cooper
Jeff Cooper

THE COPPAGE COMPANY
11501 Chandler Blvd.
North Hollywood, CA 91601
818/980-1106

Judy Coppage

**CREATIVE ALLIANCE
MANAGEMENT***
1680 N. Vine Street, Suite 1117
Los Angeles, CA 90028
213/962-6090
FAX 213/962-2065

Jeffrey Thal
Judy Friend

CREATIVE ARTISTS AGENCY (CAA)
9830 Wilshire Blvd.
Beverly Hills, CA 90212
310/288-4545
FAX 310/288-4800

**THE CAMERON CRESWELL
AGENCY PTY LTD.**
163 Brougham Street
Woolloomooloo
Sydney 2011, Australia
2/358-6433
FAX 2/358-6433

**CARTHAY CIRCLE PICTURES AND
MANAGEMENT***
213 South Stanley Drive
Beverly Hills, CA 90211
310/657-5454
FAX 310/657-8783

PETER CROUCH & ASSOCIATES
59 Frith Street
London W1, England
71/734-2167

HARRIET CRUICKSHANK
97 Old South Lambeth Road
London SW8 1XU, England
71/735-2933
FAX 71/820-1081

CURTIS BROWN
162-168 Regent Street
London W1R 5TB, England
71/437-9700
FAX 71/872-0332

D

DADE, SCHULTZ ASSOCIATES
11846 Ventura Blvd., Suite 201
Studio City, CA 91604
818/760-3100

Ernie Dade
Kathleen Schultz

JUDY DAISH ASSOCIATES
83 Eastbourne Mews
London W2 61Q, England
71/262-1101
FAX 71/706-1027

DISKANT & ASSOCIATES
1033 Gayley Avenue, Suite 202
Los Angeles, CA 90024
310/824-3773

George Diskant

DOUROUX & CO.
445 S. Beverly Drive, Suite 310
Beverly Hills, CA 90210
310/557-0700

Michael Douroux

DYTMAN & SCHWARTZ
9200 Sunset Blvd., Suite 809
Los Angeles, CA 90069
310/274-8844

Jack Dytman
Scott Schwartz

E

ROBERT EISENBACH AGENCY
1010 S. Bedford Street, Suite 303
Los Angeles, CA 90035
310/657-9427

THE ANTHONY ELLIOT COMPANY
1888 Century Park East, Suite 1900
Los Angeles, CA 90067
310/284-6804

**L'EPINE SIMTH AND CARNEY
ASSOCIATES**
10 Wyndham Place
London W1H 1AS, England
71/724-0739
FAX 71/724-3725

**EPSTEIN-WYCKOFF-LAMANNA &
ASSOCIATES**
280 S. Beverly Drive, Suite 400
Beverly Hills, CA 90212
310/278-7222
FAX 310/278-4640

311 W. 43rd Street, Suite 1401
New York, NY 10036
212/586-9110
FAX 212/586-8019

F

FAVORED ARTISTS AGENCY
122 S. Robertson Blvd., Suite 202
Los Angeles, CA 90048
310/247-1040
FAX 310/247-1048

230 West 55th St., Suite 29D
New York, NY 10019
212/245-6960
FAX 212/333-7420

MAGGIE FIELD AGENCY
12725 Ventura Blvd., Suite D
Studio City, CA 91604
818/980-2001
FAX 818/980-0754

FILM ARTISTS ASSOCIATES
7080 Hollywood Blvd., Suite 704
Hollywood, CA 90028
213/463-1010

THE SY FISHER COMPANY
10590 Wilshire Blvd., Suite 1602
Los Angeles, CA 90024
310/470-0917

FRIEND ENTERTAINMENT*
1680 North Vine Street, Suite 117
Los Angeles, CA 90028
213/962-6090
FAX 213/962-2065

Judy Friend

A
G
E
N
T
S

&

M
A
N
A
G
E
R
S

G

THE GAGE GROUP INC.
9255 Sunset Blvd., Suite 515
Los Angeles, CA 90069
310/859-8777
FAX 310/859-8166

315 W. 57th St., Suite 4H
New York, NY 10019
212/541-5250
FAX 212/956-7466

Martin Gage

HELEN GARRETT AGENCY
P.O. Box 889
Hollywood, CA 90028
213/871-8707

GELFAND, RENNERT & FELDMAN
1880 Century Park East, Suite 900
Los Angeles, CA 90067
310/553-1707

THE GERSH AGENCY
232 N. Cañon Drive
Beverly Hills, CA 90210
310/274-6611

130 West 42nd St., Suite 2400
New York, NY 10036
212/997-1818

Bob Gersh
Dave Gersh
Phil Gersh

GOLD/MARSHAK ASSOCIATES
3500 West Olive Ave.
Burbank, CA 91505
818/972-4300
FAX 818/955-6411

Harry Gold
Darryl Marshak

THE GOLDSTEIN COMPANY*
864 S. Robertson Blvd., Suite 304
Los Angeles, CA 90035
310/659-9511

Gary W. Goldstein

THE GORFAINE/SCHWARTZ AGENCY
3301 Barham Blvd., Suite 201
Los Angeles, CA 90068
213/969-1011
FAX 213/969-1022

GRAY/GOODMAN, INC.
211 South Beverly Drive, Suite 100
Beverly Hills, CA 90212
310/276-7070
FAX 310/276-6049

Stefan Gray
Mark Goodman

ARTHUR B. GREENE
101 Park Avenue, 43rd Floor
New York, NY 10178
212/661-8200

HAROLD R. GREENE, INC.
13900 Marquesas Way, Bldg. C, #83
Marina del Rey, CA 90292
310/823-5393

LARRY GROSSMAN & ASSOCIATES
211 S. Beverly Drive, Suite 206
Beverly Hills, CA 90212
310/550-8127

H

REECE HALSEY AGENCY
8733 Sunset Blvd., Suite 101
Los Angeles, CA 90069
213/652-2409

THE MITCHELL J. HAMILBURG AGENCY
292 S. La Cienega Blvd., Suite 312
Los Angeles, CA 90211
310/657-1501

SUE HAMMER
Otterbourne House, Chobham Road
Ottershaw, Chertsey
Surrey KY16 0QF England
0932 874111
FAX 0932 872922

RICK HASHAGEN & ASSOCIATES
157 West 57th Street
New York, NY 10019
212/315-3130

RICHARD HATTON LTD.
29 Roehampton Gate
London SW15 5JR, England
81/876-6699
FAX 81/876-8278

HATTON & BAKER
18 Jermyn Street
London W1, England
71/439-2971

HEACOCK LITERARY & TALENT AGENCY
1523 Sixth Street, Suite 14
Los Angeles, CA 90401
310/393-6227
FAX 310/451-8524

HENDERSON/HOGAN AGENCY, INC.
247 S. Beverly Drive, Suite 102
Beverly Hills, CA 90212
310/274-7815

405 W. 44th Street
New York, NY 10036
212/765-5190

Margaret Henderson
Jerry Hogan (NY)

RICHARD HERMAN AGENCY
124 S. Lasky Drive
Beverly Hills, CA 90212
310/550-8913

MARTIN HURWITZ ASSOCIATES
427 N. Cañon Drive, Suite 215
Beverly Hills, CA 90210
310/274-0240

I

MICHAEL IMISON PLAYWRIGHTS
71/354-3274 (London)
212/874-2671 (New York)

INTERNATIONAL CREATIVE MANAGEMENT (ICM)
8942 Wilshire Blvd.
Beverly Hills, CA 90211
310/550-4000
FAX 310/550-4108

40 West 57th Street
New York, NY 10019
212/556-5600

Oxford House
76 Oxford House
London W1R 1RB, England
71/636-6565
FAX 71/323-0101

(TNA, The New Agency)
Viale Paroli, 41
Rome, Italy 00197
011/396-87.87.98

ICM France
10, avenue Georges V
75008 Paris, France
1/723-7860

INNOVATIVE ARTISTS
1999 Avenue of the Stars, Suite 2850
Los Angeles, CA 90067
310/553-5200
FAX 310/557-2211

130 W. 57th St., Suite 5B
New York, NY 10019-3316
212/315-4455
FAX 212/315-4688

J

JANKLOW & ASSOCIATES
5743 Corsa Ave., Suite 201
Westlake Village, CA 91362
310/785-9550

JANKLOW & NESBIT
598 Madison Avenue
New York, NY 10022
212/421-1700

Morton Janklow
Lynn Nesbit

JLM PERSONAL MANAGEMENT
242 Acton Lane
Chiswick
London W4 5DL, England
081/747-8223
FAX 081/747-8286

K

THE LESLIE KALLEN AGENCY
5323 Worster Avenue
Sherman Oaks, CA 91604
818/906-2785
FAX 818/906-8931

THE KAPLAN-STAHLER AGENCY
8383 Wilshire Blvd.
Beverly Hills, CA 90211
213/653-4483
FAX 213/653-4506

Mitch Kaplan
Elliot Stahler

PATRICIA KARLAN AGENCY
3575 Cahuenga Blvd. West, Suite 210
Los Angeles, CA 90068
818/752-4800

WILLIAM KERWIN AGENCY
1605 N. Cahuenga Blvd., Suite 202
Los Angeles, CA 90028
213/469-5155

PAUL KOHNER, INC.
9300 Wilshire Blvd., Suite 555
Beverly Hills, CA 90212
310/550-1060

KOPALOFF COMPANY
1930 Century Park West, Suite 403
Los Angeles, CA 90067
310/203-8430
FAX 310/277-9513

Don Kopaloff

LUCY KROLL AGENCY
390 West End Avenue
New York, NY 10024
212/877-0627
FAX 212/769-2832

L

THE CANDACE LAKE AGENCY
(In Association with Camden-ITG)
822 S. Robertson Blvd., Suite 200
Los Angeles, CA 90035
310/289-0600
FAX 310/289-0619

LANTZ-HARRIS
888 Seventh Avenue, 25th Floor
New York, NY 10106
212/586-0200
FAX 212/262-6659

Robert Lantz
Joy Harris

IRVING PAUL LAZAR AGENCY
120 El Camino Drive, Suite 108
Beverly Hills, CA 90212
310/275-6153
FAX 310/275-8668

One East 66th Street
New York, NY 10021
212/355-1177

LEMON UNNA & DURBRIDGE LTD.
24 Pottery Lane
Holland Park
London W11 4LZ, England
71/727-1346
FAX 71/727-9037

Stephen Durbridge
Sheila Lemon
Girsha Reid
Wendy Gresser
Bethan Evans
Hilary Delamere

LENHOFF/ROBINSTON TALENT
1728 S. La Cienega Blvd.
Los Angeles, CA 90035
310/558-4700

S. Charles Lenhoff
Lloyd Robinson

**L'EPINE SMITH AND CAREY
ASSOCIATES**
10 Wyndham Place
London W1H 1AS, England
71/724-0739
FAX 71/724-3725

THE ROBERT LITTMAN COMPANY
*(In Association with Addis-Wechsler &
Associates)*
409 N. Camden Dr.
Beverly Hills, CA 90210
310/278-1572

LONDON MANAGEMENT
2-4 Noel Street
London W1V 3RB, England
71/287-9000
FAX 71/287-3036

STERLING LORD LITERISTIC
One Madison Avenue
New York, NY 10010
212/696-2800
FAX 212/686-6976

LOVETT MANAGEMENT*
918 6th Street, Suite 5
Santa Monica, CA 90403
310/451-2536
FAX 310/451-0899

M

MAJOR CLIENTS AGENCY
2121 Avenue of the Stars, Suite 2450
Los Angeles, CA 90067
310/284-6400
FAX 310/284-6499

STEPHANIE MANN AGENCY
8323 Blackburn Avenue, Suite 5
Los Angeles, CA 90048
213/653-7130

**ELAINE MARKSON LITERARY
AGENCY**
44 Greenwich Village
New York, NY 10011
212/243-8480
FAX 212/691-9014

HAROLD MATSON COMPANY, INC.
276 Fifth Avenue
New York, NY 10001
212/679-4490

MEDIA ARTISTS GROUP
8383 Wilshire Blvd., Suite 954
Beverly Hills, CA 90211
213/658-5050

HELEN MERRILL
435 West 23rd Street, Suite 1-A
New York, NY 10011
212/691-5326

METROPOLITAN TALENT AGENCY
4526 Wilshire Blvd.
Los Angeles, CA 90010
213/857-4500
FAX 213/857-4560

A
G
E
N
T
S

&

M
A
N
A
G
E
R
S

THE MIRISCH AGENCY
10100 Santa Monica Blvd., Suite 700
Los Angeles, CA 90067
310/282-9940

Lawrence Mirisch

THE MISHKIN AGENCY
2355 Benedict Canyon
Beverly Hills, CA 90210
310/274-5261

MLR REPRESENTATION
(Mcnaughton Lowe Representation)
200 Fulham Road
London SW10 9PN, England
71/351-5442
FAX 71/351-4560

THE MONTEIRO ROSE AGENCY
17514 Ventura Blvd., Suite 205
Encino, CA 91316
818/501-1177
FAX 818/501-1194

Candy Monteiro
Fredda Rose

MORRA, BREZNER & STEINBERG*
801 Westmount Drive
Los Angeles, CA 90069
213/657-5384

WILLIAM MORRIS AGENCY
151 El Camino Drive
Beverly Hills, CA 90212
310/274-7451
FAX 310/859-4462

1350 Avenue of the Americas
New York, NY 10019
212/586-5100

2325 Crestmoore Road
Nashville, TN 37215
615/385-0310

31-32 Soho Square
London W12 5DG, England
71/434-2191
FAX 71/437-0238

Via Giosue Carducci, 10
00187 Rome, Italy
48-6961

Lamonstrasse 9
Munich 80, West Germany
011/47/608-1234

THE MORTON AGENCY
1650 Westwood Blvd., Suite 201
Los Angeles, CA 90024
310/824-4089

N

CNA & ASSOCIATES
1801 Avenue of the Stars, Suite 1250
Los Angeles, CA 90067
310/556-4343
FAX 310/556-4633

19 West 44th St., Suite 812
New York, NY 10036
212/840-7330
FAX 212/840-7527

Christopher Nassif

O

OMNI ARTISTS
9107 Wilshire Blvd., Suite 602
Beverly Hills, CA 90210
310/858-0085

**ONORATO/GUILLOD
ENTERTAINMENT**
217 E. Alameda Avenue, Suite 203
Burbank, CA 91502
818/566-6607

ORIGINAL ARTISTS
Santa Monica, CA
310/394-1067

Jordan Bayer

FIFI OSCARD AGENCY
24 West 40th Street, 17th Floor
New York, NY 10018
212/764-1100

THE DANIEL OSTROFF AGENCY
9200 Sunset Blvd., Suite 402
Los Angeles, CA 90069
310/278-2020

P

PARADIGM
10100 Santa Monica Blvd., 25th Floor
Los Angeles, CA 90067
310/277-4400
FAX 310/277-7820

200 West 57th Street, Suite 900
New York, NY 10019
212/246-1030
FAX 212/246-1521

PARAMUSE ARTISTS ASSOCIATION
1414 Avenue of the Americas
New York, NY 10019
212/758-5055

THE PARKS AGENCY
138 East 16th St., Suite 5B
New York, NY 10003
212/254-9067

Richard Parks

THE PARNESS AGENCY
1424 4th Street, Suite 404
Santa Monica, CA 90401
310/319-1664
FAX 310/319-3743

Leslie Parness

THE PARTOS COMPANY
3630 Barham Blvd., Suite 2108
Los Angeles, CA 90068
213/876-5500

Walter Partos

BARRY PERELMAN AGENCY
9200 Sunset Blvd., Suite 531
Los Angeles, CA 90069
310/274-5999

PETERS FRASER & DUNLOP
The Chambers, Chelsea Harbour
Lots Road, 5th Floor
London, SW10 OXF, England
71/376-7676
FAX 71/352-7356

PHOENIX LITERARY AGENCY
315 South F Street
Livingston, Montana 59047
406/222-2848

PLESHETTE & GREEN AGENCY
2700 North Beachwood Drive
Los Angeles, CA 90068
213/465-0428
FAX 213/465-6073

Lynn Pleshette
Richard Green

BARRY POLLACK
9255 Sunset Blvd., Suite 404
Los Angeles, CA 90069
310/550-4525

PREFERRED ARTISTS
16633 Ventura Blvd., Suite 1421
Encino, CA 91436
818/990-0305

PREMIERE ARTISTS AGENCY
8899 Beverly Blvd., Suite 102
Los Angeles, CA 90048
310/271-1414
FAX 310/205-3981

Susan Sussman

JIM PREMINGER AGENCY
1650 Westwood Blvd., Suite 201
Los Angeles, CA 90024
310/475-9491

PRO MANAGEMENT*
11849 Olympic Blvd., Suite 200
Los Angeles, CA 90068
310/478-5159
FAX 310/479-0617

Jonathan Baruch

**PRODUCTION VALUES
MANAGEMENT***
606 N. Larchmont, Suite 307
Los Angeles, CA 90004
213/461-0148

PTA
Bugle House
21a Noel Street
London W1V 3PD, England
71/434-9513

R

THE RADMIN COMPANY*
260 South Beverly Drive - 2nd Floor
Beverly Hills, CA 90212
310/274-9515

Linne Radmin

DOUGLAS RAE MANAGEMENT
28 Charing Cross Road
London, WC2, England
71/836-3903

MARGARET RAMSAY LTD.
London, England
71/240/240-0691

RENAISSANCE
152 N. La Peer
Los Angeles, CA 90048
310/246-6000
FAX 310/246-1633

Joel Gotler
Irv Schwartz
Mark Jacobson
Alan Nevins

**THE RICHLAND/WUNSCH/HOHMAN
AGENCY**
9220 Sunset Blvd., Suite 311
Los Angeles, CA 90069
310/278-1955
FAX 310/278-1156

Daniel A. Richland
Joseph Richland
Robert J. Wunsch
Robert Hohman

RKS ENTERTAINMENT GROUP*
4283 Murietta Avenue, Suite 7
Sherman Oaks, CA 91423
818/788-3616

Randall K. Skolnik

THE ROBERTS COMPANY
10345 W. Olympic Blvd., Penthouse
Los Angeles, CA 90064
310/552-7800
FAX 310/552-9324

Nancy Roberts

FLORA ROBERTS, INC.
157 West 57th Street
New York, NY 10019
212/355-4165

ROGERS & ASSOCIATES
3855 Lankershim Blvd.
North Hollywood, CA 91604
818/509-1010

Stephanie Rogers

ROLLINS & JOFFE INC.
130 West 57th Street, Suite 11-D
New York, NY 10019
212/582-1940

MICHAEL ROSEN CO.
818/990-9020

THE MARION ROSENBERG OFFICE
8428 Melrose Place, Suite C
Los Angeles, CA 90069
213/653-7383

ROSENSTONE/WENDER
Three East 48th Street
New York, NY 10017
212/832-8330

Howard Rosenstone
Phyllis Wender

THE ROTHMAN AGENCY
9401 Wilshire Blvd., Suite 830
Beverly Hills, CA 90212
310/247-9898
FAX 310/247-9888

Rob Rothman

S

SAMSEL-FORT
717 S. Cochran Ave., Suite 9
Los Angeles, CA 90036
213/935-7600

Jon Samsel
Clancy Fort

SANFORD-GROSS & ASSOCIATES
1015 Gayley Avenue, 3rd Floor
Los Angeles, CA 90024
310/208-2100
FAX 310/208-6704

Geoffrey Sanford
Brad Gross

SARABAND ASSOCIATES
265 Liverpool Road
London N1 1LX, England
71/609-5313
FAX 71/609-2370

THE SARNOFF COMPANY, INC.
12001 Ventura Place, Suite 300
Studio City, CA 91604
818/761-4495

Jim Sarnoff

JACK SCAGNETTI AGENCY
5330 Lankershim Blvd., Suite 210
North Hollywood, CA 91601
818/762-3871

THE IRV SCHECHTER COMPANY
9300 Wilshire Blvd., Suite 400
Beverly Hills, CA 90212
310/278-8070
FAX 310/278-6058

SCHIOWITZ/CLAY/ROSE, INC.
8228 Sunset Blvd., Suite 212
Los Angeles, CA 90046
213/650-7300

Sheri Mann

**SUSAN SCHULMAN LITERARY
AGENCY, INC.**
454 West 44th Street
New York, NY 10036
212/713-1633
FAX 212/581-8830

THE HAROLD SCHWARTZ CO.
935 N. Croft Ave.
Los Angeles, CA 90069
213/650-8006

SEIFERT DENCH ASSOCIATES
24 D'Arblay Street
London W1V 3FH, England
71/437-4551
FAX 71/439-1355

SELECT ARTISTS
337 West 43rd St., Suite1B
New York, NY 10036
212/586-4300

DAVID SHAPIRA & ASSOCIATES
15301 Ventura Blvd., Suite 345
Sherman Oaks, CA 91403
818/906-0322
FAX 818/783-2562

**SHAPIRO-LICHTMAN TALENT
AGENCY**
8827 Beverly Blvd.
Los Angeles, CA 90048
310/859-8877
FAX 310/859-7153

Martin Shapiro
Bob Shapiro
Mark Lichtman

A
G
E
N
T
S

&

M
A
N
A
G
E
R
S

SHAPIRO/WEST & ASSOCIATES*
141 El Camino Drive, Suite 205
Beverly Hills, CA 90212
310/278-8896

KEN SHERMAN & ASSOCIATES
9507 Santa Monica Blvd., Suite 211
Beverly Hills, CA 90210
310/273-8840

LINDA SIEFERT & ASSOCIATES
8A Brunswick Gardens
London W8 4AJ, England
71/229-5163

JEROME SIEGEL ASSOCIATES
7551 Sunset Blvd., Suite 203
Los Angeles, CA 90046
213/850-1275

MICHAEL SIEGEL & ASSOCIATES, INC.
8929 Rosewood Avenue
Los Angeles, CA 90048
310/274-5222
FAX 310/274-4987

Michael Siegel
Andrew Reich
Judy Clain (NY)

THE SKOURAS AGENCY
725 Arizona Avenue, Suite 406
Santa Monica, CA 90401
310/395-9550
FAX 310/395-4295

Spyros Skouras
Julia Kole
Lara Polivka

SUSAN SMITH & ASSOCIATES
121 N. San Vicente Blvd.
Beverly Hills, CA 90211
213/852-4777
FAX 213/658-7170

192 Lexington Ave.
New York, NY 10016
212/545-0500
FAX 212/545-7143

SMITH/GOSNELL/NICHOLSON & ASSOCIATES
P.O. Box 1166
1294 Calle de Sevilla
Pacific Palisades, CA 90272
310/459-0307

Creighton Smith
Ray Gosnell
Skip Nicholson

ELAINE STEEL
110 Gloucetser Avenue
London NW3 8JA, England
71/348-0918
71/483-2601
FAX 71/483-4541

STEVENS & ASSOCIATES
9454 Wilshire Blvd.
Beverly Hills, CA 90212
310/275-7541
FAX 310/275-5929

Neal Stevens

ROCHELLE STEVENS & CO.
2 Terretts Place
Upper Street
London N1 1QZ, England
71/359-3900
FAX 71/354-5729

STONE MANNERS TALENT AGENTS
8091 Selma Ave.
Los Angeles, CA 90046
213/654-7575
FAX 213/654-7676

Tim Stone
Scott Manners

THE STRICK AGENCY
433 Camden Drive, 4th Floor
Beverly Hills, CA 90210
310/285-1560

H. N. SWANSON, INC.
8523 Sunset Blvd.
Los Angeles, CA 90069
310/652-5385
FAX 310/652-3690

T

THE TANTLEFF OFFICE
375 Greenwich St., Suite 700
New York, NY 10013
212/941-3939
FAX 212/941-3997

Jack Tantleff

ROSLYN TARG LITERARY AGENCY, INC.
105 West 13th St.
New York, NY 10011
212/206-9390

3 ARTS ENTERTAINMENT*
9460 Wilshire Blvd., 7th Floor
Beverly Hills, CA 90212
310/888-3200
FAX 310/888-3210

830 Eighth Avenue, Suite 31
New York, NY 10019
212/262-6565
FAX 212/246-1522

PETER TURNER AGENCY
3000 Olympic Blvd., Suite 1438
Santa Monica, CA 90404
310/315-4772

THE TURTLE AGENCY
12456 Ventura Blvd., Suite 1
Studio City, CA 91604
818/506-6898
FAX 818/506-1723

Cindy Turtle
Beth Bohn

TWENTIETH CENTURY ARTISTS
14724 Ventura Blvd., Suite 401
Sherman Oaks, CA 91403
818/788-5516
FAX 818/788-2070

U

UNITED TALENT AGENCY
9560 Wilshire Blvd., 5th Floor
Beverly Hills, CA 90212
310/273-6700
FAX 310/247-1111

V

VOYEZ MON AGENT
40, rue Francois 1er
75008 Paris
1/47-23-55-80

W

THE WALLERSTEIN COMPANY
213/782-0225

WARDEN, WHITE & KANE, INC.
8444 Wilshire Blvd., 4th Floor
Beverly Hills, CA 90211
213/852-1028
FAX 213/852-0843

David Warden
Steve N. White
Michael Kane

SANDRA WATT & ASSOCIATES
8033 Sunset Blvd., Suite 4053
Los Angeles, CA 90046
213/653-2339

HILARY WAYNE AGENCY
8670 Wilshire Blvd., Suite 233
Beverly Hills, CA 90211
310/289-6186
FAX 310/855-0562

SOLOMON WEINGARTEN & ASSOCIATES
921 10th Street, Suite 203
Santa Monica, CA 90403
310/394-8866
FAX 310/394-7178

MICHAEL WHITEHALL LTD.
125 Gloucester Road
London SW7 4TE, England
71/244-8466
FAX 71/244-9060

Michael Whitehall
Louise Hillman
Stephen Scutt

WILE ENTERPRISES
2730 Wilshire Blvd., Suite 500
Santa Monica, CA 90403
213/828-9768

Shelly Wile

THE WILHITE AGENCY
15237 Sunset Blvd., Suite 131
Pacific Palisades, CA 90272
310/459-0627

Patricia Wilhite

**WRIGHT CONCEPT TALENT
AGENCY**
1811 West Burbank Blvd., Suite 201
Burbank, CA 91506
818/954-8943

Marcie Wright

WRITERS & ARTISTS AGENCY
924 Westwood Blvd., Suite 900
Los Angeles, CA 90024
310/824-6300
FAX 310/824-6343

70 West 36th St.
Suite 501
New York, NY 10018
212/947-8765

ACADEMY AWARDS—DIRECTORS
1927-1994

★★ = winner in category

1927-1928

Comedy
TWO ARABIAN KNIGHTS .... Lewis Milestone ★★
SPEEDY ....Ted Wilde

Dramatic
7TH HEAVEN .... Frank Borzage ★★
SORRELL AND SON .... Herbert Brenon
THE CROWD .... King Vidor

1928-1929

THE DIVINE LADY .... Frank Lloyd ★★
MADAME X .... Lionel Barrymore
THE BROADWAY MELODY .... Harry Beaumont
IN OLD ARIZONA .... Irving Cummings
WEARY RIVER .... Frank Lloyd
THE PATRIOT .... Ernst Lubitsch

1929-1930

ALL QUIET ON THE
    WESTERN FRONT .... Lewis Milestone ★★
ANNA CHRISTIE .... Clarence Brown
THE DIVORCEE .... Robert Leonard
THE LOVE PARADE .... Ernst Lubitsch
HALLELUJAH .... King Vidor

1930-1931

SKIPPY .... Norman Taurog ★★
A FREE SOUL .... Clarence Brown
THE FRONT PAGE .... Lewis Milestone
CIMARRON .... Wesley Ruggles
MOROCCO .... Josef Von Sternberg

1931-1932

BAD GIRL .... Frank Borzage ★★
THE CHAMP .... King Vidor
SHANGHAI EXPRESS .... Josef Von Sternberg

1932-1933

CAVALCADE .... Frank Lloyd ★★
LADY FOR A DAY .... Frank Capra
LITTLE WOMEN .... George Cukor

1934

IT HAPPENED ONE NIGHT .... Frank Capra ★★
ONE NIGHT OF LOVE .... Victor Schertzinger
THE THIN MAN .... W.S. Van Dyke

1935

THE INFORMER .... John Ford ★★
LIVES OF A BENGAL LANCER .... Henry Hathaway
MUTINY ON THE BOUNTY .... Frank Lloyd

1936

MR. DEEDS GOES TO TOWN .... Frank Capra ★★
MY MAN GODFREY .... Gregory LaCava
THE GREAT ZIEGFELD .... Robert Z. Leonard
SAN FRANCISCO .... W.S. Van Dyke
DODSWORTH .... William Wyler

1937

THE AWFUL TRUTH .... Leo McCarey ★★
THE LIFE OF EMILE ZOLA .... William Dieterle
THE GOOD EARTH .... Sidney Franklin
STAGE DOOR .... Gregory LaCava
A STAR IS BORN .... William Wellman

1938

YOU CAN'T TAKE IT WITH YOU .... Frank Capra ★★
ANGELS WITH DIRTY FACES .... Michael Curtiz
FOUR DAUGHTERS .... Michael Curtiz
BOYS TOWN .... Norman Taurog
THE CITADEL .... King Vidor

1939

GONE WITH THE WIND .... Victor Fleming ★★
MR. SMITH GOES TO WASHINGTON .... Frank Capra
STAGECOACH .... John Ford
GOODBYE, MR. CHIPS .... Sam Wood
WUTHERING HEIGHTS .... William Wyler

1940

THE GRAPES OF WRATH .... John Ford ★★
THE PHILADELPHIA STORY .... George Cukor
REBECCA .... Alfred Hitchcock
KITTY FOYLE .... Sam Wood
THE LETTER .... William Wyler

1941

HOW GREEN WAS MY VALLEY .... John Ford ★★
HERE COMES MR. JORDAN .... Alexander Hall
SERGEANT YORK .... Howard Hawks
CITIZEN KANE .... Orson Welles
THE LITTLE FOXES .... William Wyler

1942

MRS. MINIVER .... William Wyler ★★
YANKEE DOODLE DANDY .... Michael Curtiz
WAKE ISLAND .... John Farrow
RANDOM HARVEST .... Mervyn LeRoy
KINGS ROW .... Sam Wood

1943

CASABLANCA .... Michael Curtiz ★★
THE HUMAN COMEDY .... Clarence Brown
THE SONG OF BERNADETTE .... Henry King
HEAVEN CAN WAIT .... Ernst Lubitsch
THE MORE THE MERRIER .... George Stevens

A
C
A
D
E
M
Y

A
W
A
R
D
S

1944
GOING MY WAY .... Leo McCarey ★★
LIFEBOAT .... Alfred Hitchcock
WILSON .... Henry King
LAURA .... Otto Preminger
DOUBLE INDEMITY .... Billy Wilder

1945
THE LOST WEEKEND .... Billy Wilder ★★
NATIONAL VELVET .... Clarence Brown
SPELLBOUND .... Alfred Hitchcock
THE BELLS OF ST. MARY'S .... Leo McCarey
THE SOUTHERNER .... Jean Renoir

1946
THE BEST YEARS OF OUR LIVES .... William Wyler ★★
THE YEARLING .... Clarence Brown
IT'S A WONDERFUL LIFE .... Frank Capra
BRIEF ENCOUNTER .... David Lean
THE KILLERS .... Robert Siodmak

1947
GENTLEMAN'S AGREEMENT .... Elia Kazan ★★
A DOUBLE LIFE .... George Cukor
CROSSFIRE .... Edward Dmytryk
THE BISHOP'S WIFE .... Henry Koster
GREAT EXPECTATIONS .... David Lean

1948
THE TREASURE OF SIERRA MADRE .... John Huston ★★
THE SNAKE PIT .... Anatole Litvak
JOHNNY BELINDA .... Jean Negulesco
HAMLET .... Laurence Olivier
THE SEARCH .... Fred Zinnemann

1949
A LETTER TO THREE WIVES ...... Joseph L. Mankiewicz ★★
THE FALLEN IDOL .... Carol Reed
ALL THE KING'S MEN .... Robert Rossen
BATTLEGROUND .... William A. Wellman
THE HEIRESS .... William Wyler

1950
ALL ABOUT EVE .... Joseph L. Mankiewicz ★★
BORN YESTERDAY .... George Cukor
THE ASPHALT JUNGLE .... John Huston
THE THIRD MAN .... Carol Reed
SUNSET BOULEVARD .... Billy Wilder

1951
A PLACE IN THE SUN .... George Stevens ★★
THE AFRICAN QUEEN .... John Huston
A STREETCAR NAMED DESIRE .... Elia Kazan
AN AMERICAN IN PARIS .... Vincente Minnelli
DETECTIVE STORY .... William Wyler

1952
THE QUIET MAN .... John Ford ★★
THE GREATEST SHOW ON EARTH .... Cecil B. DeMille
MOULIN ROUGE .... John Huston
FIVE FINGERS .... Joseph L. Mankiewicz
HIGH NOON .... Fred Zinnemann

1953
FROM HERE TO ETERNITY .... Fred Zinnemann ★★
SHANE .... George Stevens
LILI .... Charles Walters
STALAG 17 .... Billy Wilder
ROMAN HOLIDAY .... William Wyler

1954
ON THE WATERFRONT .... Elia Kazan ★★
REAR WINDOW .... Alfred Hitchcock
THE COUNTRY GIRL .... George Seaton
THE HIGH AND THE MIGHTY .... William Wellman
SABRINA .... Billy Wilder

1955
MARTY .... Delbert Mann ★★
EAST OF EDEN .... Elia Kazan
SUMMERTIME .... David Lean
PICNIC .... Joshua Logan
BAD DAY AT BLACK ROCK .... John Sturges

1956
GIANT .... George Stevens ★★
AROUND THE WORLD IN 80 DAYS .... Michael Anderson
THE KING AND I .... Walter Lang
WAR AND PEACE .... King Vidor
FRIENDLY PERSUASION .... William Wyler

1957
THE BRIDGE ON THE RIVER KWAI .... David Lean ★★
SAYONARA .... Joshua Logan
12 ANGRY MEN .... Sidney Lumet
PEYTON PLACE .... Mark Robson
WITNESS FOR THE PROSECUTION .... Billy Wilder

1958
GIGI .... Vicente Minnelli ★★
CAT ON A HOT TIN ROOF .... Richard Brooks
THE DEFIANT ONES .... Stanley Kramer
THE INN OF THE SIXTH HAPPINESS .... Mark Robson
I WANT TO LIVE! .... Robert Wise

1959
BEN-HUR .... William Wyler ★★
ROOM AT THE TOP .... Jack Clayton
THE DIARY OF ANNE FRANK .... George Stevens
SOME LIKE IT HOT .... Billy Wilder
THE NUN'S STORY .... Fred Zinnemann

1960
THE APARTMENT .... Billy Wilder ★★
SONS AND LOVERS .... Jack Cardiff
NEVER ON SUNDAY .... Jules Dassin
PSYCHO .... Alfred Hitchcock
THE SUNDOWNERS .... Fred Zinnemann

1961
WEST SIDE STORY .... Robert Wise & Jerome Robbins ★★
LA DOLCE VITA .... Frederico Fellini
JUDGEMENT AT NUREMBERG .... Stanley Kramer
THE HUSTLER .... Robert Rossen
THE GUNS OF NAVARONE .... J. Lee Thompson

1962

LAWRENCE OF ARABIA .... David Lean ★★
DIVORCE—ITALIAN STYLE .... Pietro Germi
TO KILL A MOCKINGBIRD .... Robert Mulligan
THE MIRACLE WORKER .... Arthur Penn
DAVID AND LISA .... Frank Perry

1963

TOM JONES .... Tony Richardson ★★
FREDERICO FELLINI'S 8 1/2 .... Frederico Fellini
AMERICA AMERICA .... Elia Kazan
THE CARDINAL .... Otto Preminger
HUD .... Martin Ritt

1964

MY FAIR LADY .... George Cukor ★★
ZORBA THE GREEK........................ Michael Cacoyannis
BECKET .... Peter Glenville
DR. STANGELOVE, OR: HOW I LEARNED TO STOP
    WORRYING AND LOVE THE BOMB .... Stanley Kubrick
MARY POPPINS .... Robert Stevenson

1965

THE SOUND OF MUSIC .... Robert Wise ★★
DOCTOR ZHIVAGO .... David Lean
DARLING .... John Schlesinger
WOMAN IN THE DUNES .... Hiroshi Teshigahara
THE COLLECTOR .... William Wyler

1966

A MAN FOR ALL SEASONS .... Fred Zinnemann ★★
BLOW-UP .... Michelangelo Antonioni
THE PROFESSIONALS .... Richard Brooks
A MAN AND A WOMAN .... Claude Lelouch
WHO'S AFRAID OF VIRGINIA WOOLF? .... Mike Nichols

1967

THE GRADUATE .... Mike Nichols ★★
IN COLD BLOOD.. Richard Brooks
IN THE HEAT OF THE NIGHT .... Norman Jewison
GUESS WHO'S COMING TO DINNER .... Stanley Kramer
BONNIE AND CLYDE .... Arthur Penn

1968

OLIVER! .... Carol Reed ★★
THE LION IN WINTER .... Anthony Harvey
2001: A SPACE ODYSSEY .... Stanley Kubrick
THE BATTLE OF ALGIERS .... Gillo Pontecorvo
ROMEO AND JULIET .... Franco Zeffirelli

1969

MIDNIGHT COWBOY .... John Schlesinger ★★
Z .... Costa-Gavras
BUTCH CASSIDY AND THE
    SUNDANCE KID .... George Roy Hill
ALICE'S RESTAURANT .... Arthur Penn
THEY SHOOT HORSES DON'T THEY? .... Sydney Pollack

1970

PATTON .... Franklin J. Schaffner ★★
M*A*S*H .... Robert Altman
FELLINI SATYRICON .... Frederico Fellini
LOVE STORY .... Arthur Hiller
WOMEN IN LOVE .... Ken Russell

1971

THE FRENCH CONNECTION .... William Friedkin ★★
THE LAST PICTURE SHOW .... Peter Bogdanovich
FIDDLER ON THE ROOF .... Norman Jewison
A CLOCKWORK ORANGE .... Stanley Kubrick
SUNDAY BLOODY SUNDAY .... John Schlesinger

1972

CABARET .... Bob Fosse ★★
DELIVERANCE .... John Boorman
THE GODFATHER .... Francis Ford Coppola
SLEUTH .... Joseph L. Mankiewicz
THE EMIGRANTS .... Jan Troell

1973

THE STING .... George Roy Hill ★★
CRIES AND WHISPERS .... Ingmar Bergman
LAST TANGO IN PARIS .... Bernardo Bertolucci
THE EXORCIST .... William Friedkin
AMERICAN GRAFFITI .... George Lucas

1974

THE GODFATHER PART II .... Francis Ford Coppola ★★
A WOMAN UNDER THE INFLUENCE .... John Cassavetes
LENNY.. Bob Fosse
CHINATOWN .... Roman Polanski
DAY FOR NIGHT .... Francois Truffaut

1975

ONE FLEW OVER THE
    CUCKOO'S NEST .... Milos Forman ★★
NASHVILLE .... Robert Altman
AMARCORD .... Frederico Fellini
BARRY LYNDON .... Stanley Kubrick
DOG DAY AFTERNOON .... Sidney Lumet

1976

ROCKY .... John G. Avildsen ★★
ALL THE PRESIDENT'S MEN .... Alan J. Pakula
FACE TO FACE .... Ingmar Bergman
NETWORK .... Sidney Lumet
SEVEN BEAUTIES .... Lina Wertmuller

1977

ANNIE HALL .... Woody Allen ★★
CLOSE ENCOUNTERS OF
    THE THIRD KIND .... Steven Spielberg
JULIA .... Fred Zinnemann
STAR WARS .... George Lucas
THE TURNING POINT .... Herbert Ross

1978

THE DEER HUNTER .... Michael Cimino ★★
COMING HOME .... Hal Ashby
HEAVEN CAN WAIT .... Warren Beatty and Buck Henry
INTERIORS .... Woody Allen
MIDNIGHT EXPRESS .... Alan Parker

1979

KRAMER VS. KRAMER .... Robert Benton ★★
ALL THAT JAZZ.. Bob Fosse
APOCALYPSE NOW .... Francis Coppola
BREAKING AWAY...................................... Peter Yates
LA CAGE AUX FOLLES .... Edouard Molinaro

1980

ORDINARY PEOPLE .... Robert Redford ★★
THE ELEPHANT MAN .... David Lynch
RAGING BULL .... Martin Scorsese
THE STUNT MAN .... Richard Rush
TESS .... Roman Polanski

1981

REDS .... Warren Beatty ★★
ATLANTIC CITY .... Louis Malle
CHARIOTS OF FIRE .... Hugh Hudson
ON GOLDEN POND .... Mark Rydell
RAIDERS OF THE LOST ARK .... Steven Spielberg

1982

GANDHI .... Richard Attenborough ★★
DAS BOOT .... Wolfgang Petersen
E.T. THE EXTRA-TERRESTRIAL .... Steven Spielberg
TOOTSIE .... Sydney Pollack
THE VERDICT .... Sidney Lumet

1983

TERMS OF ENDEARMENT .... James L. Brooks ★★
THE DRESSER .... Peter Yates
FANNY & ALEXANDER .... Ingmar Bergman
SILKWOOD .... Mike Nichols
TENDER MERCIES .... Bruce Beresford

1984

AMADEUS .... Milos Forman ★★
BROADWAY DANNY ROSE .... Woody Allen
THE KILLING FIELDS .... Roland Joffe
A PASSAGE TO INDIA .... David Lean
PLACES IN THE HEART .... Robert Benton

1985

OUT OF AFRICA .... Sydney Pollack ★★
KISS OF THE SPIDER WOMAN .... Hector Babenco
PRIZZI'S HONOR .... John Huston
RAN .... Akira Kurosawa
WITNESS .... Peter Weir

1986

PLATOON .... Oliver Stone ★★
BLUE VELVET .... David Lynch
HANNAH AND HER SISTERS .... Woody Allen
THE MISSION .... Roland Joffe
A ROOM WITH A VIEW .... James Ivory

1987

THE LAST EMPEROR .... Bernardo Bertolucci ★★
FATAL ATTRACTION .... Adrian Lyne
HOPE AND GLORY .... John Boorman
MOONSTRUCK .... Norman Jewison
MY LIFE AS A DOG .... Lasse Hallstrom

1988

RAIN MAN .... Barry Levinson ★★
A FISH CALLED WANDA .... Charles Crichton
THE LAST TEMPTATION
  OF CHRIST .... Martin Scorsese
MISSISSIPPI BURNING .... Alan Parker
WORKING GIRL .... Mike Nichols

1989

BORN ON THE FOURTH OF JULY .... Oliver Stone ★★
CRIMES AND MISDEMEANORS .... Woody Allen
DEAD POETS SOCIETY .... Peter Weir
HENRY V .... Kenneth Branagh
MY LEFT FOOT .... Jim Sheridan

1990

DANCES WITH WOLVES .... Kevin Costner ★★
THE GODFATHER, PART III .... Francis Ford Coppola
GOODFELLAS .... Martin Scorsese
THE GRIFTERS .... Stephen Frears
REVERSAL OF FORTUNE .... Barbet Schroeder

1991

THE SILENCE OF THE LAMBS .... Jonathan Demme ★★
BOYZ N THE HOOD .... John Singleton
BUGSY .... Barry Levinson
JFK .... Oliver Stone
THELMA & LOUISE .... Ridley Scott

1992

UNFORGIVEN .... Clint Eastwood ★★
THE CRYING GAME .... Neil Jordan
HOWARDS END .... James Ivory
SCENT OF A WOMAN .... Martin Brest
THE PLAYER .... Robert Altman

1993

SCHINDLER'S LIST .... Steven Spielberg ★★
THE PIANO .... Jane Campion
THE REMAINS OF THE DAY .... James Ivory
IN THE NAME OF THE FATHER .... Jim Sheridan
SHORT CUTS .... Robert Altman

1994

FORREST GUMP .... Robert Zemeckis ★★
QUIZ SHOW .... Robert Redford
BULLETS OVER BROADWAY .... Woody Allen
PULP FICTION .... Quentin Tarantino
RED .... Krzysztof Kieslowski

★ ★ ★

CALLING ALL CREDITS!

The **Twelfth Edition of Michael Singer's FILM DIRECTORS: A Complete Guide** is now in preparation. It will be published in the spring of 1996. We update our records continuously. If you qualify to be listed (please read HOW TO USE THIS BOOK for qualifications), then send us your listing information **ASAP**. All listings are free. **Photocopy the form on the next page.**

Our editorial deadline is January 15, 1996
(Please do not wait until then.)

Send all listing information to:

Michael Singer's FILM DIRECTORS: A Complete Guide
Twelfth International Edition
2337 Roscomare Road, Suite Nine
Los Angeles, CA 90077

If you are a television director, a writer (*film or television*), film actor or actress, film composer, cinematographer, production designer, costume designer, editor, film producer, agent, casting director, studio personnel, special effects person or stunt coordinator and want to find out about getting listed in our other directories, call **310/471-8066** or write to:

LONE EAGLE PUBLISHING COMPANY
2337 Roscomare Road, Suite Nine
Los Angeles, CA 90077-1851
310/471-8066 • 310/471-4969 (FAX)

• ALL LISTINGS ARE FREE •

The TWELFTH EDITION of

Michael Singer's FILM DIRECTORS:
A Complete Guide
ALL LISTINGS ARE FREE.

DON'T BE LEFT OUT!!! Include your *FREE* listing (read *How To Use This Book* for qualifications) by filling out and returning this form to us *IMMEDIATELY.* *(Photocopy as many times as necessary).*

PLEASE PRINT OR TYPE

PERSONAL INFORMATION

Name (as you prefer to be listed)

Company

Address

City/State/Zip

Area Code/Telephone

Birth Date & Place
❏ Home   ❏ Business
❏ Please list my home address and phone number in your directory.

REPRESENTATIVE'S INFORMATION
Agent ❏   Personal Manager ❏   Attorney ❏
Business Manager ❏   Other ❏
(List as many representatives as you would like. Continue listing on reverse, if necessary.)

Name (as you prefer to be listed)

Company

Address

City/State/Zip

Area Code/Telephone

DGA MEMEBER?	❏ YES	❏ NO

CREDITS *(Attach a separate sheet, if necessary)*
List your credits as follows, noting title, type of work, distribution company, year of release, co-directors, alternate titles in parentheses, Academy and Emmy nominations/awards for your work, and country of origin.

UNFORGIVEN ★★   Warner Bros., 1992
FINAL CRY (SISTA SKRIGET) (TF)   SVT-1, 1994, Swedish
NEW YORK STORIES   co-director with Francis Ford Coppola & Martin Scorsese, Buena Vista, 1989

MAIL form IMMEDIATELY to
Michael Singer's FILM DIRECTORS: A Complete Guide
Twelfth International Edition
2337 Roscomare Road, Suite Nine
Los Angeles, CA 90077
310/471-8066 or 310/471-4969 (FAX)

Deadline:
January 1, 1994

Questions ???
Problems ???
Call 310/471-8066

ESSENTIAL PRODUCTION BOOKS FROM LONE EAGLE PUBLISHING CO.

FILM SCHEDULING
OR, HOW LONG WILL IT TAKE TO SHOOT YOUR MOVIE?
SECOND EDITION

Ralph S. Singleton
$19.95
ISBN 0-943728-39-8, 240 pages, full-color fold-out production board

"Detailing step-by-step how one creates a production board, shot-by-shot, day-by-day, set-by-set to turn a shooting schedule into a workable production schedule... For every film production student and most professionals."
—Los Angeles Times

The highly respected and best-selling book by Emmy award-winning producer Ralph Singleton. FILM SCHEDULING contains a new section on computerized film scheduling. This section not only analyzes and compares the various computer programs which are currently on the market but also instructs the reader on how to maintain personal control over the schedule while taking advantage of the incredible speed a computer offers. The definitive work on film scheduling.

FILM BUDGETING
OR, HOW MUCH WILL IT COST TO SHOOT YOUR MOVIE?
by Ralph S. Singleton
$22.95
ISBN 0-943728-65-7, approx. 300 pp, illustrated, Includes full theatrical feature budget.

"Read Film Budgeting if you want to know how budgets are done in Hollywood. Singleton is a pro who has written a common-sense, nuts-and-bolts book complete with detailed explanations and illustrations."
—Michael Hill, VP Production, Paramount Pictures

The companion book to the best-selling *Film Scheduling* and its workbook (*The Film Scheduling/Film Budgeting Workbook*), FILM BUDGETING takes the reader through the steps of converting a professional motion picture schedule to a professional motion picture budget. Using Francis Coppola's Academy Award nominated screenplay, *The Conversation,* as the basis for the examples, author Singleton explains the philosophy behind motion picture budgeting as well as the mechanics. Readers do not have to be computer-literate to use this text, although computer budgeting is discussed.

Included are a complete motion picture budget to *The Conversation* , as well as footnotes, glossary and index. When used in conjunction with its companion workbook *The Film Scheduling/Film Budgeting Workbook, Film Budgeting* can comprise a do-it-yourself course on motion picture budgeting.

FILM SCHEDULING/
FILM BUDGETING
WORKBOOK

Ralph S. Singleton
DO-IT-YOURSELF GUIDE
$19.95
ISBN 0-943728-07-X, 9 x 11, 296 pp

ALL SHEETS PERFORATED

Complete DO-IT-YOURSELF workbook companion to *Film Scheduling* and *Film Budgeting*.) Contains the entire screenplay to Francis Coppola's Academy Award nominated screenplay, THE CONVERSATION, as well as sample production and budget forms to be completed by the reader.

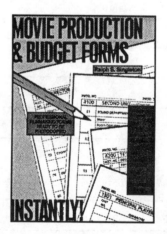

MOVIE PRODUCTION
AND
BUDGET
FORMS...INSTANTLY!

Ralph S. Singleton
$19.95
ISBN 0-943728-14-2, 9 x 12, 132 pp

PROFESSIONAL FORMS
ALL SHEETS PERFORATED

INCLUDES
Call Sheet • Production Report • Breakdown Sheets • Deal Memos 84-page Feature Budget Form, and more.

This book plus one photocopy machine equals every production and budget form needed to make a full-length feature or telefilm. Completely re-designed and integrated forms that are 8.5" x 11" format, ready to tear out and use over and over again.

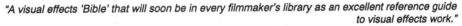

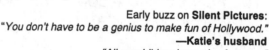

ESSENTIAL PRODUCTION BOOKS FROM LONE EAGLE PUBLISHING CO.

ANNUAL REFERENCE DIRECTORIES

1. FILM DIRECTORS: A COMPLETE GUIDE
2. FILM WRITERS GUIDE
3. FILM PRODUCERS, STUDIOS, AGENTS & CASTING DIRECTORS GUIDE
4. CINEMATOGRAPHERS, PRODUCTION DESIGNERS, COSTUME DESIGNERS & EDITORS GUIDE
5. SPECIAL EFFECTS & STUNTS GUIDE
6. FILM COMPOSERS GUIDE
7. FILM ACTORS GUIDE
8. TELEVISION WRITERS GUIDE
9. TELEVISION DIRECTORS GUIDE
10. FILM DISTRIBUTION GUIDE   NEW DIRECTORY
    (INCLUDES BOXOFFICE, MPAA RATINGS, GENRE CODES, RELEASING INFORMATION, AND MORE, FOR OVER 2,000 FILMS FROM 1986-1992)

These credit and contact directories feature:
- Working professionals of the film and television industry
- Contact information
- Credits
- Releasing information (date/studio or date/network)
- Academy & Emmy Awards & nominations
- Index of Names
- Index of Film (Television) Titles, cross-referenced
- Index of Agents & Managers
- Interviews (selected volumes)
- and more

CALL 1-800 FILMBKS
FOR CURRENT EDITIONS AND PRICES.

HOW TO ORDER

1.　**CALL 1-800-FILMBKS**. Have your credit card ready (Visa, MC or American Express.) Your order will be taken and your books shipped to you ASAP. We usually ship by UPS Ground, but other arrangements can be made.

2.　**MAIL** us your request with a check, money order or credit card information. California residents add in 8.25% sales tax. All orders should add in shipping charges: $4.00 for first book, $1.50 each additional book; $6.00 for first directory, $3.00 each additional directory. Do not forget to put expiration date and sign the request. Include your phone number.　Our mailing address is:

> **Lone Eagle Publishing Co.**
> **Dept. FD**
> **2337 Roscomare Road #9**
> **Los Angeles, CA 90077-1851**
> **310/471-8066**

3.　**FAX** us your request with all the information listed above. Our fax is **310/471-4969**.

INDEX OF ADVERTISERS

A special thanks to our advertisers whose support makes it possible to bring you the eleventh internation edition of **Michael Singer's FILM DIRECTORS: A Complete Guide.**

A
B
O
U
T

T
H
E

E
D
I
T
O
R

ABOUT THE EDITOR

MICHAEL SINGER has worked in motion pictures for nearly 25 years in various capacities, currently as a unit (production) publicist and author.

In edition to the eleven annual editions of *Michael Singer's Film Directors: A Complete Guide*, Singer has also authored *The Making of Oliver Stone's 'Heaven and Earth'*; *Batman Returns: The Official Movie Book*; and *Batman Forever: The Official Movie Book*. As a freelance journalist, he has contributed articles to such publications as *Film Comment*, *American Cinematographer* and *Film in Review*.

When not on location, Singer resides in Los Angeles with his wife, Yuko, and their baby daughter Miyako.